Washington Information Directory

2003–2004

Washington

Information Directory

2003–2004

CQ Press

A DIVISION OF CONGRESSIONAL QUARTERLY INC.
WASHINGTON, D.C.

Washington Information Directory, 2003–2004
Editor: Gwenda Larsen
Production Editor: Daphne Levitas
Researchers: Joan Gossett, Rosalie Ruane
Cover: Joan Stephens
Subject Index: Joan Stout
Electronic Composition: Jessica Forman

The Library of Congress cataloged the first edition of this
   title as follows:
Washington information directory. 1975/76—
Washington. Congressional Quarterly Inc.
   1. Washington, D.C.—Directories. 2. Washington metropolitan area—Directories. 3. United States—Executive
   departments—Directories. I. Congressional Quarterly
   Inc.
F192.3.W33   975.3'0025   75-646321

ISBN 1-56802-501-7
ISSN 0887-8064

CQ Press
1255 22nd Street N.W., Suite 400
Washington, D.C. 20037

(202) 729-1900
Toll-free, 1-866-4CQ-PRESS (1-866-427-7737)

www.cqpress.com

Contents

Boxes and Illustrations

Preface

Every year for more than a quarter century, the *Washington Information Directory* has been a trusted and indispensable guide to the key players and organizations in the national capital region. With so many structural changes occurring around Washington, it can take more than a quick trip to a Web site or a single phone call to find needed resources or personnel. This edition, which helps to navigate the unprecedented organizational transformations that have been under way since the events of September 11, 2001, is now, more than ever, an essential resource for finding the information you need in and around Washington.

In creating a new edition of the *Washington Information Directory* we research and update each existing entry in the book to bring you current addresses; phone, fax, and TTY numbers; e-mail and Internet addresses; and mission descriptions. We also add to each chapter relevant new government offices and nonprofit groups that have appeared in the last twelve months. This year in particular we focused a great deal of energy on researching and developing content to cover the most far-reaching government organization since 1947: the consolidation of more than twenty federal agencies into the newly created Homeland Security Department, which is expected to become the third-largest cabinet-level department in the federal government and the employer of some 170,000 people.

In the expanded "National and Homeland Security" chapter and elsewhere in the volume, we provide contact information and descriptions for selected offices within the Homeland Security Department; cover homeland security–related changes in other agencies that have created new branches or reconfigured the responsibilities of current personnel to address security challenges; capture organizational changes on Capitol Hill, where new committees and subcommittees have been formed and existing committees and subcommittees have shifted focus and jurisdiction to include homeland security; and add dozens of new volunteer and nonprofit organizations that have missions linked to protecting the nation from terrorist attacks.

The fully updated chapters are supplemented by a helpful appendix, which includes a guide to the members and committees of the 108th Congress, a directory of government Web addresses, a list of governors and other state officials, and a section on foreign embassies, U.S. ambassadors, and country desk offices at the State Department. Extensive name and subject indexes complete the volume.

Our goal is to make the *Washington Information Directory* the most valuable, comprehensive, and authoritative reference of its kind. We are pleased to offer this handy directory, which gives you fast and direct access to the people, agencies, committees, and nonprofit groups that interest you.

Feedback from our readers has always been helpful to us in making this book more useful. If you have comments, or suggestions for next year's edition, we invite you to share them by sending e-mail to wideditor@cqpress.com.

Gwenda Larsen, Editor

How to Use This Directory

The *Washington Information Directory* is designed to make your search for information fast and easy.

Each chapter covers a broad topic; within the chapters, information is grouped in more specific subject areas. This subject arrangement allows you to find in one place the departments and agencies of the federal government, congressional committees, and nonprofit organizations that have the information you need.

The directory divides information sources into three main categories: (1) agencies, (2) Congress, and (3) nonprofit organizations. Each entry includes the name, address, and telephone number of the organization; the name and title of the director or the best person to contact for information; fax and press numbers, hotlines, and Internet addresses whenever available; and a description of the work performed by the organization.

How Information Is Presented

Here are examples of the three main categories of entries, and of the other resources the directory provides. They are drawn from Parks and Recreation Areas, a subsection in chapter 9, Environment and Natural Resources.

AGENCIES

One main entry—the National Park Service—is a federal agency. It is listed in bold type under its commonly known name, with its government parent, the Interior Dept., shown in parentheses.

National Park Service (NPS), (Interior Dept.), *1849 C St. N.W., #3312 20240; (202) 208-4621. Fax, (202) 208-7889. Fran P. Mainella, Director. Press, (202) 208-6843. Washington area activities, (202) 619-7275 (recording).*
Web, www.nps.gov

Administers national parks, monuments, historic sites, and recreation areas. Oversees coordination, planning, and financing of public outdoor recreation programs at all levels of government. Conducts recreation research surveys; administers financial assistance program to states for planning and devel-opment of outdoor recreation programs. (Some lands designated as national recreation areas are not under NPS jurisdiction.)

CONGRESS

Entries under the Congress heading are usually Senate or House committees. (Also included here are agencies under congressional jurisdiction, such as the General Accounting Office and Library of Congress.) Committee entries include the chair and a key staff member. The descriptions give the committee's jurisdiction or its activities relating to the particular subject. Here is the entry for the Senate committee with jurisdiction over the national park system:

Senate Energy and Natural Resources Committee, *Subcommittee on National Parks, SD-364 20510; (202) 224-4971. Fax, (202) 228-6163. Sen. Craig Thomas, R-Wyo., Chair; Tom Lillie, Professional Staff Member.*
General e-mail, parks@energy.senate.gov
Web, energy.senate.gov

Jurisdiction over legislation on national parks, recreation areas, wilderness areas, trails, wild and scenic rivers, historic sites, and military parks and battlefields.

NONPROFIT

Thousands of nonprofit private and special-interest groups have headquarters or legislative offices in or near Washington. Their staffs are often excellent information sources, and these organizations frequently maintain special libraries or information centers. Here is an example of a group with an interest in parks and recreation areas:

Rails-to-Trails Conservancy, *1100 17th St. N.W., 10th Floor 20036; (202) 331-9696. Fax, (202) 331-9680. Keith Laughlin, President.*
General e-mail, railtrails@transact.org
Web, www.railtrails.org

Promotes the conversion of abandoned railroad corridors into hiking and biking trails for public use. Provides public education programs and technical and legal assistance. Publishes trail guides. Monitors legislation and regulations.

BOXES AND CHARTS

The directory includes organization charts to make the hierarchy of federal agencies easy to grasp, as well as boxes that provide essential agency contacts and other quick reference information. On the topic of parks, for example, you can locate the National Park Service within the Interior Dept. (see chart on p. 318) or consult a list of contacts at National Park Service Sites in the Capital Region (see box on p. 174). A general organization chart for the federal government appears on p. 892.

Reference Resources

TABLES OF CONTENTS

The summary table of contents (p. v) lists the directory's chapters and their major subheadings. A list of information boxes and organization charts within the chapters is given on p. viii. At the beginning of each chapter you will find a detailed table of contents that breaks the chapter into general and specific sections; for convenience, here again we list the boxes and charts that appear in the chapter.

CONGRESSIONAL INFORMATION

A special section on the 108th Congress, beginning on p. 777, provides extensive information about members and committees:

State Delegations. Here (p. 779) you can look up senators, representatives, and delegates by state (or territory) and congressional district.

Members' Offices. For both the House (p. 803) and Senate (p. 869), we provide each member's Capitol Hill office address, telephone and fax, Internet address, key professional aide, committee assignments, and district offices.

Committees. These sections provide the jurisdiction and membership for committees and subcommittees of the House (p. 784) and Senate (p. 858), as well as the joint committees of Congress (p. 856). Also included here are partisan committees and party leadership of the House (p. 801) and Senate (p. 867).

READY REFERENCE

A special section of reference lists, beginning on p. 887, gives information on the following subjects:

Government Information on the Internet. Organized by branch of government, this section (p. 888) lists Web addresses for locating information on the White House, cabinet departments, Congress, and the judiciary.

State Government. The list of state officials (p. 893) provides the name, address, and telephone number for each governor, lieutenant governor, secretary of state, attorney general, and state treasurer.

Diplomats. The foreign embassies section (p. 902) gives the names, official addresses, and telephone numbers of foreign diplomats in Washington; the names of the ranking U.S. diplomatic officials abroad; and the phone numbers for State Dept. country desk offices.

Federal Laws on Information. In this section you will find discussion of the Freedom of Information Act (p. 917) and privacy legislation (p. 919).

INDEXES

Use the name index (p. 921) to look up any person mentioned in the directory.

Use the subject index (p. 965) to look up a subject area or a specific organization or agency. If you need information on a particular topic but do not know a specific source, the index has subject entries to help you find where that topic is covered. For example, on the subject of equal employment for women, you can find index entries under both Women and Equal Employment Opportunity.

Reaching Your Information Source

PHONING AND FAXING

Call the information or toll-free number first. Often you can get the answer you need without going further. If not, a quick explanation of your query should put you in touch with the person

Map of Capitol Hill

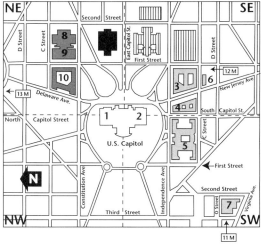

U.S. Capitol, Washington, D.C. 20510 or 20515*
1. Senate Wing
2. House Wing

House Office Buildings, Washington, D.C. 20515
3. Cannon
4. Longworth
5. Rayburn
6. O'Neill
7. Ford

Senate Office Buildings, Washington, D.C. 20510
8. Hart
9. Dirksen
10. Russell

Supreme Court, Washington, D.C. 20543

Library of Congress, Washington, D.C. 20540

M Subway System
11. Federal Center SW
12. Capitol South
13. Union Station

* Mail sent to the U.S. Capitol should bear the ZIP code of the chamber to which it is addressed.

Note: Dashed lines indicate the city's quadrants, which are noted in the corners of the map.

Remember that publications and documents are often available from a special office (for federal agencies, see p. 130) or, increasingly, by Web sites or special fax-on-demand services. Ask whether there is a faster way than by mail to receive the information you need.

Keep in mind the agency or organization, not the name of the director. Personnel changes are common, but for most inquiries you will want to stay with the organization you call, rather than track down a person who may have moved on to a new job.

With congressional questions, contact your own member of Congress first: your representative has staff people assigned to answer questions from constituents. Contact a committee only if you have a technical question that cannot be answered elsewhere.

WRITING

Address letters to the director of an office or organization—the contact person listed here. Your letter will be directed to the person who can answer your question. Be prepared to follow up by phone.

USING THE INTERNET

Most agencies and nonprofits have sites on the World Wide Web (for federal agencies, see p. 136), as well as e-mail addresses for general inquiries. Information available from these sources is expanding rapidly and is usually free once you are online. If you have Internet access, try the Web site, but bear in mind that this approach is not always faster or better than a phone call: connections can be slow, menus can be complex or confusing, information can be incomplete or out-of-date.

As with faxing, reserve e-mail for inquiries that may be too complex for a phone call, but phone first to establish that someone is ready to help.

Addresses and Area Codes

Listings in the directory include full contact information, including telephone area code and, when available, room or suite number and nine-digit ZIP code. If an office has a mailing address that is different from the physical location, we provide both. Note that a few listings are not a local call from Washington—the Social Security

who can answer your question. Rarely will you need to talk to the top administrator.

Offer to fax your query if it is difficult to explain over the phone, but make sure that the person helping you knows to expect your fax. Faxing promptly and limiting your transmission to a single page should bring the best results.

Administration headquarters in Baltimore and a small number of nonprofits in outlying suburbs. Other special cases to take note of:

WASHINGTON, D.C., ADDRESSES

For brevity, entries for agencies, organizations, and congressional offices in the District of Columbia (area code 202) do not include the city and state as part of the address. Here is the beginning of a typical Washington entry:

Equal Employment Opportunity Commission (EEOC), *1801 L St. N.W. # 10006 20507; (202) 663-4001.*

To complete the mailing address, add "Washington, D.C." before the zip code.

BUILDING ADDRESSES

Departments and agencies generally have their own ZIP codes; however, updates to our directory reflect the increasing use of street addresses by the federal government. Federal offices that we list by building name or abbreviation are at the following locations:

The White House. Located at 1600 Pennsylvania Ave. N.W. 20500.

Dwight D. Eisenhower Executive Office Building. Located at 17th St. and Pennsylvania Ave. N.W. 20500.

New Executive Office Building. Located at 725 17th St. N.W. 20505.

Main State Building. Located at 2201 C St. N.W. 20520.

The Pentagon. Located in Arlington, VA, but has a Washington mailing address and special ZIP codes for each branch of the military.

Navy Annex. Located at Columbia Pike and Southgate Rd., Arlington, VA 20370, but most offices use a Washington mailing address.

U.S. Capitol. Abbreviated as CAP; the letters *H* and *S* before the room number indicate the House or Senate side of the building. ZIP codes are 20510 for the Senate, 20515 for the House.

Senate Office Buildings. The ZIP code is 20510. Abbreviations, building names, and street addresses:

SD	Dirksen Senate Office Bldg., Constitution Ave. between 1st and 2nd Sts. N.E.
SR	Russell Senate Office Bldg., Constitution Ave. between Delaware Ave. and 1st St. N.E.
SH	Hart Senate Office Bldg., 2nd St. and Constitution Ave. N.E.

House Office Buildings. The ZIP code is 20515. Abbreviations, building names, and street addresses:

CHOB	Cannon House Office Bldg., Independence Ave. between New Jersey Ave. and 1st St. S.E.
FHOB	Ford House Office Bldg., 2nd and D Sts. S.W.
LHOB	Longworth House Office Bldg., Independence Ave. between S. Capitol St. and New Jersey Ave. S.E.
OHOB	O'Neill House Office Bldg., 300 New Jersey Ave. S.E.
RHOB	Rayburn House Office Bldg., Independence Ave. between S. Capitol and 1st Sts. S.W.

Washington Information Directory

2003–2004

1

Advocacy and Public Service

⚖️ CIVIL RIGHTS

AGENCIES

Commission on Civil Rights, *624 9th St. N.W., #700 20425; (202) 376-7700. Fax, (202) 376-7672. Mary Frances Berry, Chair; Cruz Reynoso, Vice Chair. Library, (202) 376-8110. Press, (202) 376-8312. TTY, (202) 376-8116. Locator, (202) 376-8177. Complaints, (800) 552-6843; in Washington, (202) 376-8582.*
Web, www.usccr.gov

Assesses federal laws and policies of government agencies and studies legal developments to determine the nature and extent of denial of equal protection under the law on the basis of race, color, religion, sex, national origin, age, or disability in many areas, including employment, voting rights, education, administration of justice, and housing. Reports and makes recommendations to the president and Congress; serves as national clearinghouse for civil rights information. Conducts studies relating to discrimination against certain groups, including women, African Americans, Hispanics, Asians, native Americans, and Pacific Island Americans. Issues public service announcements to discourage discrimination or denials of equal protection of the laws. Library open to the public.

Equal Employment Opportunity Commission (EEOC), *1801 L St. N.W., #10006 20507; (202) 663-4001. Fax, (202) 663-4110. Cari M. Dominguez, Chair. Information, (202) 663-4900. Library, (202) 663-4630. TTY, (202) 663-4494.*
Web, www.eeoc.gov

Works to end job discrimination by private and government employers based on race, color, religion, sex, national origin, disability, or age. Works to protect employees against reprisal for protest of employment practices alleged to be unlawful in hiring, promotion, firing, wages, and other terms and conditions of employment. Enforces Title VII of the Civil Rights Act of 1964, as amended, which includes the Pregnancy Discrimination Act; Americans with Disabilities Act; Age Discrimination in Employment Act; Equal Pay Act; and, in the federal sector, rehabilitation laws. Receives charges of discrimination; attempts conciliation or settlement; can bring court action to force compliance; has review and appeals responsibility in the federal sector.

Executive Office of the President, *Public Liaison, Dwight D. Eisenhower Executive Office Bldg., #186 20502; (202) 456-2380. Fax, (202) 456-2130. Lezlee Westine, Director.*
Web, www.whitehouse.gov

Serves as liaison between the administration and the public on issues of domestic and international concern, including women, minorities, and the elderly.

Health and Human Services Dept. (HHS), *Civil Rights, 200 Independence Ave. S.W., #522A 20201; (202) 619-0403. Fax, (202) 619-3437. Richard M. Campanelli, Director. TTY, (800) 537-7697. Toll-free hotline, (800) 368-1019.*
Web, www.hhs.gov/ocr

Administers and enforces laws prohibiting discrimination on the basis of race, color, sex, national origin, religion, age, or disability in programs receiving federal funds from the department; authorized to discontinue funding. Responsible for health information privacy under Health Insurance Portability and Accountability Act.

Justice Dept. (DOJ), *Civil Rights, 950 Pennsylvania Ave. N.W., #3623 20530; (202) 514-2151. Fax, (202) 514-0293. Ralph F. Boyd Jr., Assistant Attorney General. Library, (202) 514-3010. Press, (202) 514-2007. TTY, (202) 514-0716.*
Web, www.usdoj.gov/crt

Enforces federal civil rights laws prohibiting discrimination on the basis of race, color, religion, sex, disability, age, or national origin in voting, education, employment, credit, housing, public accommodations and facilities, and federally assisted programs.

CONGRESS

House Government Reform Committee, *Subcommittee on Criminal Justice, Drug Policy, and Human Resources, B373 RHOB 20515; (202) 225-2577. Fax, (202) 225-1154. Rep. Mark Souder, R-Ind., Chair; Christopher Donesa, Staff Director.*
Web, www.house.gov/reform

Oversees operations of the Equal Employment Opportunity Commission and the Commission on Civil Rights.

House Judiciary Committee, *Subcommittee on the Constitution, 362 FHOB 20515; (202) 226-7680. Fax, (202) 225-3746. Rep. Steve Chabot, R-Ohio, Chair; Crystal Roberts, Chief Counsel.*
General e-mail, Judiciary@mail.house.gov
Web, www.house.gov/judiciary

Jurisdiction over constitutional rights and civil rights legislation. Oversees the U.S. Commission on Civil Rights and the Justice Dept.'s Civil Rights Division.

Senate Health, Education, Labor, and Pensions Committee, *SD-428 20510; (202) 224-5375. Fax, (202)*

228-5044. Sen. Judd Gregg, R-N.H., Chair; Sharon Soder-strom, Staff Director.
Web, health.senate.gov

Oversees operations of the Equal Employment Opportunity Commission.

Senate Judiciary Committee, *Subcommittee on the Constitution, Civil Rights, and Property Rights,* SD-524 20510; (202) 224-4135. Fax, (202) 228-0463. Sen. John Cornyn, R-Texas, Chair; James Ho, Chief Counsel.
Web, Judiciary.senate.gov

Jurisdiction over civil and constitutional rights legislation; oversees operations of the Commission on Civil Rights.

NONPROFIT

Citizens' Commission on Civil Rights, 2000 M St. N.W., #400 20036-3307; (202) 659-5565. Fax, (202) 223-5302. Dianne M. Piché, Director.
General e-mail, citizens@cccr.org
Web, www.cccr.org

Bipartisan commission of former federal officials. Monitors compliance of federal agencies and judicial bodies with civil rights laws and education laws; conducts social science research and provides technical and legal assistance to other civil rights and public interest groups; interests include low- and moderate-income housing, voting rights, employment, school desegregation, and education of the disadvantaged.

Leadership Conference on Civil Rights, 1629 K St. N.W., #1000 20006; (202) 466-3311. Fax, (202) 466-3435. Wade Henderson, Executive Director.
Web, www.civilrights.org

Coalition of national organizations representing minorities, women, labor, older Americans, people with disabilities, and religious groups. Works for enactment and enforcement of civil rights, human rights, and social welfare legislation; acts as clearinghouse for information on civil rights legislation and regulations.

NAACP Legal Defense and Educational Fund, *Washington Office,* 1444 Eye St. N.W., 10th Floor 20005; (202) 682-1300. Fax, (202) 682-1312. Leslie M. Proll, Senior Attorney.

Civil rights litigation group that provides legal information on civil rights issues, including employment, housing, and educational discrimination; monitors federal enforcement of civil rights laws. Not affiliated with the National Assn. for the Advancement of Colored People (NAACP). (Headquarters in New York.)

National Center for Neighborhood Enterprise, 1424 16th St. N.W., #300 20036; (202) 518-6500. Fax, (202) 588-0314. Robert L. Woodson Sr., President.
General e-mail, info@ncne.com
Web, www.ncne.com

Provides community and faith-based organizations with training and technical assistance and links them to sources of support. Addresses issues such as youth violence, substance abuse, teen pregnancy, homelessness, joblessness, poor education, and deteriorating neighborhoods.

Poverty and Race Research Action Council, 3000 Connecticut Ave. N.W., #200 20008; (202) 387-9887. Fax, (202) 387-0764. Chester W. Hartman, Executive Director.
General e-mail, info@prrac.org
Web, www.prrac.org

Facilitates cooperative links between researchers and activists who work on race and poverty issues. Provides nonprofit organizations with funding for research on race and poverty.

African Americans

NONPROFIT

Blacks in Government, 3005 Georgia Ave. N.W. 20001-5015; (202) 667-3280. Fax, (202) 667-3705. Greg Reeves, President.
Web, www.bignet.org

Advocacy organization for public employees. Promotes equal opportunity and career advancement for African American government employees; provides career development information; seeks to eliminate racism in the federal workforce; sponsors programs, business meetings, and social gatherings; represents interests of African American government workers to Congress and the executive branch; promotes voter education and registration.

Congressional Black Caucus Foundation, 1004 Pennsylvania Ave. S.E. 20003; (202) 675-6730. Fax, (202) 547-3806. Weldon J. Rougeau, President.
Web, www.cbcfinc.org

Conducts research and programs on public policy issues of concern to African Americans. Sponsors fellowship programs in which professionals and academic candidates work on congressional committees and subcommittees. Holds issue forums and leadership seminars. Provides elected officials, organizations, and researchers with statistical, demographic, public policy, and political information. Sponsors internship and scholarship programs.

Joint Center for Political and Economic Studies, *1090 Vermont Ave. N.W., #1100 20005-4928; (202) 789-3500. Fax, (202) 789-6390. Eddie N. Williams, President. Web, www.jointcenter.org*

Documents and analyzes the political and economic status of African Americans and other minority populations, focusing on economic advancement, social policy, political participation, and international affairs. Publishes an annual profile of African American elected officials in federal, state, and local government; disseminates information through forums, conferences, publications, and the Internet.

Lincoln Institute for Research and Education, *1001 Connecticut Ave. N.W., #1135 20036; (202) 223-5112. J. A. Parker, President.*

Public policy research group that studies issues of interest to middle-class African Americans, including business, economics, employment, education, national defense, health, and culture. Sponsors seminars.

National Assn. for the Advancement of Colored People (NAACP), *Washington Office, 1025 Vermont Ave. N.W., #1120 20005; (202) 638-2269. Fax, (202) 638-5936. Hilary O. Shelton, Director. Web, www.naacp.org*

Membership: persons interested in civil rights for all minorities. Works for the political, educational, social, and economic equality and empowerment of minorities through legal, legislative, and direct action. (Headquarters in Baltimore, Md.)

National Assn. of Colored Women's Clubs, *1601 R St. N.W. 20009; (202) 667-4080. Fax, (202) 667-4113. Margaret J. Cooper, President.*

Seeks to promote education; protect and enforce civil rights; raise the standard of family living; promote interracial understanding; and enhance leadership development. Awards scholarships; conducts programs in education, social service, and philanthropy.

National Black Caucus of Local Elected Officials, *c/o National League of Cities, 1301 Pennsylvania Ave. N.W., #550 20004; (202) 626-3191. Fax, (202) 626-3043. E. W. Cromartie II. Press, (202) 626-3000. Web, www.nbc-leo.org*

Membership: elected officials at the local level and other interested individuals. Concerned with issues affecting African Americans, including housing, economics, the family, and human rights.

National Black Caucus of State Legislators, *444 N. Capitol St. N.W., #622 20001; (202) 624-5457. Fax, (202) 508-3826. Khalil Abdulah, Executive Director.*

General e-mail, staff@nbcsl.com Web, www.nbcsl.com

Membership: African American state legislators. Promotes effective leadership among African American state legislators; serves as an information network and clearinghouse for members.

National Council of Negro Women, *633 Pennsylvania Ave. N.W. 20004; (202) 737-0120. Fax, (202) 737-0476. Dorothy Height, President. Web, www.ncnw.org*

Coalition of domestic and international organizations and individuals interested in issues that affect African American women. Encourages the development of African American women; sponsors programs on family health care, career development, child care, juvenile offenders, housing discrimination against women, teenage pregnancy, and literacy improvement among female heads of households; promotes social and economic well-being of African American women through its Development Projects training program.

National Urban League, *Washington Office, 3501 14th Street N.W. 20010; (202) 265-8200. Fax, (202) 265-6122. Maudine R. Cooper, President. Web, www.gwul.org*

Social service organization concerned with the social welfare of African Americans and other minorities. Seeks elimination of racial segregation and discrimination; monitors legislation, policies, and regulations to determine impact on minorities; interests include employment, health, welfare, education, housing, and community development. (Headquarters in New York.)

Project 21, *777 N. Capitol St. N.E., #803 20002; (202) 371-1400. Fax, (202) 408-7773. David W. Almasi, Director. Web, www.nationalcenter.org*

Emphasizes spirit of entrepreneurship, sense of family, and traditional values among African Americans. (Initiative of the National Center for Public Policy Research.)

Hispanics

NONPROFIT

Congressional Hispanic Caucus Institute, *504 C St. N.E. 20002; (202) 543-1771. Fax, (202) 546-2143. Rep. Ciro D. Rodriguez, D-Texas, Chair; Ingrid Duran, President. Toll-free college scholarship information, (800) 392-3532.*

Develops educational and leadership programs to familiarize Hispanic students with policy-related careers and to encourage their professional development. Aids in the developing of future Latino leaders. Provides scholarship, internship, and fellowship opportunities.

League of United Latin American Citizens, *2000 L St. N.W., #610 20036; (202) 833-6130. Fax, (202) 833-6135. Brent Wilkes, Executive Director.*
Web, www.lulac.org

Seeks full social, political, economic, and educational rights for Hispanics in the United States. Programs include housing projects for the poor, employment and training for youth and women, and political advocacy on issues affecting Hispanics, including immigration. Operates National Educational Service Centers (NESCs) and awards scholarships. Holds exposition open to the public.

Mexican American Legal Defense and Educational Fund, *Washington Office, 1717 K St. N.W., #311 20036; (202) 293-2828. Fax, (202) 293-2849. Marisa Demeo, Regional Counsel.*
Web, www.maldef.org

Gives legal assistance to Mexican Americans and other Hispanics in such areas as equal employment, voting rights, bilingual education, and immigration. Monitors legislation and regulations. (Headquarters in Los Angeles, Calif.)

National Council of La Raza, *1111 19th St. N.W., #1000 20036; (202) 785-1670. Fax, (202) 776-1792. Raul Yzaguirre, President.*
General e-mail, info@nclr.org
Web, www.nclr.org

Offers technical assistance to Hispanic community organizations; operates policy analysis center with interests in education, employment and training, immigration, language issues, civil rights, and housing and community development. Special projects focus on the Hispanic elderly, teenage pregnancy, health, and AIDS. Monitors legislation and regulations.

National Puerto Rican Coalition, *1901 L St. N.W., #802 20036; (202) 223-3915. Fax, (202) 429-2223. Manuel Mirabal, President.*
General e-mail, nprc@nprcinc.org
Web, www.bateylink.org

Membership: Puerto Rican organizations and individuals. Analyzes and advocates for public policy that benefits Puerto Ricans; offers training and technical assistance to Puerto Rican organizations and individuals; develops national communication network for Puerto Rican community-based organizations and individuals.

U.S. Conference of Catholic Bishops (USCCB), *Secretariat for Hispanic Affairs, 3211 4th St. N.E., 4th Floor 20017-1194; (202) 541-3150. Fax, (202) 722-8717. Ronaldo M. Cruz, Director.*
General e-mail, hispanicaffairs@usccb.org
Web, www.usccb.org

Acts as an information clearinghouse on communications and pastoral and liturgical activities; serves as liaison for other church institutions, and government and private agencies concerned with Hispanics; provides information on legislation; acts as advocate for Hispanics within the National Conference of Catholic Bishops.

Lesbians and Gays

NONPROFIT

Dignity USA, *1500 Massachusetts Ave. N.W., #11 20005; (202) 861-0017. Fax, (202) 429-9808. Mary Louise Cervone, President. Information, (800) 877-8797.*
General e-mail, dignity@aol.com
Web, www.dignityusa.org

Membership: gay, lesbian, bisexual, and transgender Catholics, their families, and friends. Works to promote spiritual development, social interaction, educational outreach, and feminist issues.

Gay and Lesbian Activists Alliance (GLAA), *P.O. Box 75265 20013-5265; (202) 667-5139. Kevin Davis, President.*
General e-mail, equal@glaa.org
Web, www.glaa.org

Advances the rights of gays and lesbians within the Washington community. (Affiliated with International Lesbian and Gay Assn., Brussels, Belgium.)

Gay and Lesbian Victory Fund, *1705 DeSales St. N.W., #500 20036; (202) 842-8679. Fax, (202) 289-3863. Chuck Wolfe, Executive Director.*
General e-mail, victory@victoryfund.org
Web, www.victoryfund.org

Supports the candidacy of openly gay and lesbian individuals in federal, state, and local elections.

Human Rights Campaign (HRC), *919 18th St. N.W., #800 20006; (202) 628-4160. Fax, (202) 347-5323. Elizabeth Birch, Executive Director.*
General e-mail, hrc@hrc.org
Web, www.hrc.org

Provides campaign support and educates the public to ensure the rights of lesbians and gays at home, work, school, and in the community. Works to prohibit workplace discrimination based on sexual orientation, combat hate crimes, fund AIDS research, care, and prevention, and to repeal the policy on gays and lesbians in the military.

Log Cabin Republicans, *1607 17th St. N.W. 20009; (202) 347-5306. Fax, (202) 347-5224. Patrick Gueriero, Executive Director.*
General e-mail, info@lcr.org
Web, www.lcr.org

Membership: lesbian and gay Republicans. Educates conservative politicians and voters on gay and lesbian issues; disseminates information; conducts seminars for members. Raises campaign funds. Monitors legislation and regulations.

National Gay and Lesbian Task Force and Policy Institute (NGLTF), *1325 Massachusetts Ave., #600 20005; (202) 393-5177. Fax, (202) 393-2241. Lorri Jean, Executive Director.*
General e-mail, ngltf@ngltf.org
Web, www.ngltf.org

Educates the media and the public on issues affecting the lesbian and gay community. Interests include grassroots organizations, civil rights, antigay violence, sodomy law reform, and gays on campus. Monitors legislation.

National Lesbian and Gay Journalists Assn., *1420 K St. N.W., #910 20005; (202) 588-9888. Fax, (202) 588-1818. Steven Petrow, President.*
General e-mail, info@nlgja.org
Web, www.nlgja.org

Fosters fair and accurate coverage of lesbian and gay issues. Provides professional development support and networking services; sponsors conferences, seminars, and workshops.

National Organization for Women (NOW), *733 15th St. N.W., 2nd Floor 20005; (202) 628-8669. Fax, (202) 785-8576. Kim Gandy, President. TTY, (202) 331-9002.*
General e-mail, now@now.org
Web, www.now.org

Membership: women and men interested in feminist civil rights. Works to end discrimination against lesbians and gays. Promotes the development and enforcement of legislation prohibiting discrimination on the basis of sexual orientation.

Parents, Families, and Friends of Lesbians and Gays (PFLAG), *1726 M St. N.W., #400 20036; (202) 467-8180. Fax, (202) 467-8194. David Tseng, Executive Director.*
General e-mail, info@pflag.org
Web, www.pflag.org

Promotes the health and well-being of gay, lesbian, transgender, and bisexual persons, their families, and their friends through support, education, and advocacy. Works to change public policies and attitudes toward gay, lesbian, transgender, and bisexual persons. Monitors legislation and regulations.

Servicemembers Legal Defense Network (SLDN), *P.O. Box 65301 20035-5301; (202) 328-3244. Fax, (202) 797-1635. C. Dixon Osburn, Executive Director.*
General e-mail, sldn@sldn.org
Web, www.sldn.org

Provides legal assistance to individuals affected by the military's policy on gays and lesbians. Monitors legislation and regulations.

Sexual Minority Youth Assistance League (SMYAL), *410 7th St. S.E. 20003-2707; (202) 546-5940. Fax, (202) 544-1306. Arthur Padilla, Executive Director.*
General e-mail, smyal@smyal.org
Web, www.smyal.org

Provides support to youth who are lesbian, gay, bisexual, transgender, intersex, or who may be questioning their sexuality. Facilitates youth center and support groups; promotes HIV/AIDS awareness; coordinates public education programs about homophobia.

Native Americans

AGENCIES

Administration for Native Americans *(Health and Human Services Dept.), 370 L'Enfant Promenade S.W., M.S. Aerospace Center, 8th Floor, West 20447-0002; (202) 690-7776. Fax, (202) 690-7441. Quanah Crossland Stamps, Commissioner.*
Web, www.acf.hhs.gov/programs/ana

Awards grants for locally determined social and economic development strategies; promotes native American economic and social self-sufficiency; funds tribes and native American and native Hawaiian organizations. Commissioner chairs the Intradepartmental Council on Indian Affairs, which coordinates native American-related programs.

Bureau of Indian Affairs (BIA), *(Interior Dept.), 1849 C St. N.W., #4160, MS 4140 20240; (202) 208-7163. Fax, (202) 208-5320. Aurene M. Martin, Assistant Secretary (Acting). Information, (202) 208-3710. Press, (202) 219-4152.*
Web, www.doi.gov/bureau-indian-affairs.html

Works with federally recognized Indian tribal governments and Alaska native communities in a government-to-government relationship. Encourages and supports tribes' efforts to govern themselves and to provide needed programs and services on the reservations. Manages land held in trust for Indian tribes and individuals. Funds educational benefits, road construction and maintenance, social services, police protection, economic development efforts, and special assistance to develop governmental and administrative skills.

CONGRESS

House Resources Committee, *1324 LHOB 20515; (202) 225-2761. Fax, (202) 225-5929. Rep. Richard W. Pombo, R-Calif., Chair; Steve Ding, Chief of Staff.*
General e-mail, resources.committee@mail.house.gov
Web, resourcescommittee.house.gov

Jurisdiction over all matters regarding relations with and welfare of native Americans, including land management and trust responsibilities, education, health, special services, loan programs, and claims against the United States.

Senate Indian Affairs Committee, *SH-838 20510; (202) 224-2251. Fax, (202) 228-2589. Sen. Ben Nighthorse Campbell, R-Colo., Chair; Paul Moorehead, Staff Director.*
Web, indian.senate.gov

Jurisdiction over legislation on native Americans; oversight of all programs that affect native Americans.

JUDICIARY

U.S. Court of Federal Claims, *717 Madison Pl. N.W. 20005; (202) 219-9657. Fax, (202) 219-9593. Edward J. Damich, Chief Judge; Margaret Ernest, Clerk.*

Deals with native American tribal claims against the government that are founded upon the Constitution, congressional acts, government regulations, and contracts. Examples include congressional reference cases; patent cases; claims for land, water, and mineral rights; and the accounting of funds held for native Americans under various treaties.

NONPROFIT

National Congress of American Indians, *1301 Connecticut Ave. N.W., #200 20036; (202) 466-7767. Fax, (202) 466-7797. Jacqueline Johnson, Executive Director; Tex G. Hall, President; Joel A. Garcia, First Vice President; Alma Ransom, Treasurer; Colleen F. Cawston, Recording Secretary.*
Web, www.ncai.org

Membership: native American and Alaska native governments and individuals. Provides information and serves as general advocate for tribes. Monitors legislative and regulatory activities affecting native American affairs.

Native American Rights Fund, *Washington Office, 1712 N St. N.W. 20036; (202) 785-4166. Fax, (202) 822-0068. Tracy Lavin, Managing Attorney.*
Web, www.narf.org

Provides native Americans and Alaskan natives with legal assistance in land claims, water rights, hunting, and other areas. (Headquarters in Boulder, Colo.)

Navajo Nation, *Washington Office, 1101 17th St. N.W., #250 20036; (202) 775-0393. Fax, (202) 775-8075. G. Michelle Brown-Yazzie, Executive Director.*
General e-mail, panderson@nnwo.org
Web, www.nnwo.org

Monitors legislation and regulations affecting the Navajo people; serves as an information clearinghouse on the Navajo Nation. (Headquarters in Window Rock, Ariz.)

Senior Citizens

AGENCIES

Administration on Aging (AoA), *(Health and Human Services Dept.), 330 Independence Ave. S.W., #4716 20201; (202) 619-0724. Fax, (202) 357-3555. Josefina Carbonell, Assistant Secretary. Press, (202) 401-4541.*
General e-mail, AoAInfo@aoa.gov
Web, www.aoa.gov

Advocacy agency for older Americans and their concerns. Collaborates with state and area agencies on aging, tribal organizations, and local community and national organizations to implement grant programs and services designed to improve the quality of life for older Americans, such as information and referral, adult day care, elder abuse prevention, home delivered meals, in-home care, transportation and services for caregivers.

CONGRESS

House Education and the Workforce Committee, *Subcommittee on Select Education, 2181 RHOB 20515; (202) 225-4527. Fax, (202) 225-9571. Rep. Peter Hoekstra, R-Mich., Chair; Paula Nowakowski, Staff Director.*
Web, edworkforce.house.gov

Jurisdiction over legislation on all matters dealing with programs and services for the elderly, including health and nutrition programs and the Older Americans Act.

Senate Special Committee on Aging, *SD-G31 20510; (202) 224-5364. Fax, (202) 224-8660. Sen. Larry E. Craig, R-Idaho, Chair; Lupe Wissel, Staff Director.*
Web, aging.senate.gov

Oversight of all matters affecting older Americans. Studies and reviews public and private policies and programs that affect the elderly, including retirement income and maintenance, housing, health, welfare, employment, education, recreation, and participation in family and community life; provides other Senate committees with information. Cannot report legislation.

NONPROFIT

AARP, *601 E St. N.W. 20049; (202) 434-2277. Fax, (202) 434-2320. William D. Novelli, Chief Executive Officer. Library, (202) 434-6240. Press, (202) 434-2560. TTY, (202) 434-6561.*
Web, www.aarp.org

Membership organization for persons aged fifty and older. Provides members with training, employment information, and volunteer programs; offers financial services, including insurance, investment programs, and consumer discounts; makes grants through AARP Andrus Foundation for research on aging. Monitors legislation and regulations and disseminates information on issues affecting older Americans, including age discrimination, Social Security, Medicaid and Medicare, pensions and retirement, and consumer protection. Formerly the American Assn. of Retired Persons.

Alliance for Retired Americans, *888 16th St. N.W., #520 20006; (202) 974-8222. Fax, (202) 974-8256. George J. Kourpias, President. Information, (888) 373-6497.*
Web, www.retiredamericans.org

Alliance of retired members of unions affiliated with the AFL-CIO, senior citizen clubs, associations, councils, and other groups. Seeks to nationalize health care services and to strengthen benefits to the elderly, including improved Social Security payments, increased employment, and education and health programs. Offers prescription drug program and Medicare supplement. (Affiliate of the AFL-CIO.)

Gray Panthers Project Fund, *733 15th St. N.W., #437 20005; (202) 737-6637. Fax, (202) 737-1160. Tim Fuller, Executive Director. Information, (800) 280-5362.*
General e-mail, info@graypanthers.org
Web, www.graypanthers.org

Educational and advocacy organization that promotes national health care and economic and social justice for people of all ages; seeks the preservation of Social Security, affordable housing, access to education, and jobs for all with a living wage.

National Caucus and Center on Black Aged, *1220 L St. N.W., #800 20005-2407; (202) 637-8400. Fax, (202) 347-0895. Samuel J. Simmons, President.*
General e-mail, info@ncba-aged.org
Web, www.ncba-blackaged.org

Concerned with issues that affect elderly African Americans. Sponsors employment and housing programs for the elderly and education and training for professionals in gerontology. Monitors legislation and regulations.

National Council on the Aging, *300 D St. S.W., #801 20024; (202) 479-1200. Fax, (202) 479-0735. James P. Firman, President. Information, (202) 479-6653. Press, (202) 479-6975.*
General e-mail, info@ncoa.org
Web, www.ncoa.org

Serves as an information clearinghouse on training, technical assistance, advocacy, and research on every aspect of aging. Provides information on social services for older persons. Monitors legislation and regulations.

National Hispanic Council on Aging, *2713 Ontario Rd. N.W. 20009; (202) 265-1288. Fax, (202) 745-2522. Marta Sotomayor, President.*
General e-mail, nhcoa@nhcoa.org
Web, www.nhcoa.org

Membership: senior citizens, health care workers, professionals in the field of aging, and others in the United States and Puerto Rico who are interested in topics related to Hispanics and aging. Provides research training, policy analysis, consulting, and technical assistance; sponsors seminars, workshops, and management internships.

National Senior Citizens Law Center, *1101 14th St. N.W., #400 20005; (202) 289-6976. Fax, (202) 289-7224. Edward C. King, Executive Director.*
General e-mail, nsclc@nsclc.org
Web, www.nsclc.org

Organization funded by the Legal Services Corp. Litigates on behalf of legal services programs and elderly poor clients and client groups. Represents clients before Congress and federal departments and agencies. Interests include Social Security, Medicare, Medicaid, nursing home residents' rights, home health care, pensions, and protective services.

Seniors Coalition, *9001 Braddock Rd., #200, Springfield, VA 22151; (703) 239-1960. Fax, (703) 239-1985. Mary M. Martin, Executive Director.*
General e-mail, tsc@senior.org
Web, www.senior.org

Seeks to protect the quality of life and economic well-being of older Americans. Interests include health care, social security, taxes, pharmaceutical issues, and Medicare. Conducts seminars and monitors legislation and regulations.

60 Plus, *1600 Wilson Blvd., #960, Arlington, VA 22209; (703) 807-2070. Fax, (703) 807-2073. James L. Martin, President.*

General e-mail, info@60plus.org

Web, www.60plus.org

Advocates rights of senior citizens. Interests include free enterprise, less government regulation, and tax reform. Works to eliminate the estate tax. Publishes rating system of members of Congress. Monitors legislation and regulations.

United Seniors Assn., *3900 Jermantown Rd., #450, Fairfax, VA 22030; (703) 359-6500. Fax, (703) 359-6510. Charlie W. Jarvis, President. Information, (800) 887-2872.*

General e-mail, usa@unitedseniors.org

Web, www.unitedseniors.org

Advocates the rights of older Americans. Works to lower taxes, reduce wasteful government spending, and preserve the rights and benefits of senior citizens.

Women

NONPROFIT

Assn. for Women in Science, *1200 New York Ave. N.W., #650 20005; (202) 326-8940. Fax, (202) 326-8960. Catherine J. Didion, Executive Director.*

General e-mail, awis@awis.org

Web, www.awis.org

Promotes equal opportunity for women in scientific professions; provides career and funding information. Interests include international development.

Center for Women Policy Studies, *1211 Connecticut Ave. N.W., #312 20036; (202) 872-1770. Fax, (202) 296-8962. Leslie R. Wolfe, President.*

General e-mail, cwpsx@centerwomenpolicy.org

Web, www.centerwomenpolicy.org

Policy and advocacy organization concerned with women's issues, including educational and employment equity for women, women and AIDS, violence against women, economic opportunity for low-income women, women's health, and reproductive laws.

Church Women United, *Washington Office,* *100 Maryland Ave. N.E., #100 20002; (202) 544-8747. Fax, (202) 544-9133. Vacant, Legislative Director. Information, (800) CWU-5551.*

General e-mail, cwu-dc@churchwomen.org

Web, www.churchwomen.org

Ecumenical women's organization dedicated to spirituality and faith-based advocacy. Interests include defense policy, employment, family stability, health, human rights, justice, world peace, and hunger and poverty issues, especially as they affect women and children. (Headquarters in New York.)

Independent Women's Forum (IWF), *P.O. Box 3058, Arlington, VA 22203-0058; (703) 558-4991. Fax, (703) 558-4994. Nancy M. Pfotenhauer, Executive Director. Information, (800) 224-6000.*

General e-mail, info@iwf.org

Web, www.iwf.org

Membership: women and men interested in promoting individual responsibility, strong families, freedom, and opportunity. Conducts litigation; publishes periodical and media directory; maintains speakers bureau. Interests include maintaining single-sex schools and eliminating affirmative action programs. Monitors legislation and regulations.

Jewish Women International, *1828 L St. N.W., #250 20036; (202) 857-1300. Fax, (202) 857-1380. Lori Weinstein, Executive Director.*

General e-mail, jwi@jwi.org

Web, www.jewishwomen.org

Organization of Jewish women in the United States. Interests include emotional health of children and youth; family issues such as choice, family violence, and women's health care; civil and constitutional rights; community services; and anti-Semitism.

National Organization for Women (NOW), *733 15th St. N.W., 2nd Floor 20005; (202) 628-8669. Fax, (202) 785-8576. Kim Gandy, President. TTY, (202) 331-9002.*

General e-mail, now@now.org

Web, www.now.org

Membership: women and men interested in feminist civil rights. Uses traditional and nontraditional forms of political activism, including nonviolent civil disobedience, to improve the status of all women regardless of age, income, sexual orientation, or race. Maintains liaisons with counterpart organizations worldwide.

National Partnership for Women and Families, *1875 Connecticut Ave. N.W., #650 20009-5731; (202) 986-2600. Fax, (202) 986-2539. Judith L. Lichtman, President.*

General e-mail, info@nationalpartnership.org

Web, www.nationalpartnership.org

Advocacy organization that promotes fairness in the workplace, quality health care, and policies that help women and men meet the demands of work and family. Publishes and disseminates information in print and on the Web to heighten awareness of work and family issues. Monitors legislative activity and argues on behalf of family issues before Congress and in the courts.

National Women's Law Center, *11 Dupont Circle N.W., #800 20036; (202) 588-5180. Fax, (202) 588-5185. Nancy Duff Campbell, Co-President; Marcia D. Greenberger, Co-President.*
General e-mail, info@nwlc.org
Web, www.nwlc.org

Works to expand and protect women's legal rights through advocacy and public education. Interests include reproductive rights, health, education, employment, income security, and family support.

Older Women's League, *666 11th St. N.W., #700 20001; (202) 783-6686. Fax, (202) 638-2356. Laurie Young, Executive Director. Information, (800) 825-3695.*
General e-mail, owlinfo@owl-national.org
Web, www.owl-national.org

Grassroots organization concerned with the social and economic problems of middle-aged and older women. Interests include health care, Social Security, pension rights, housing, employment, women as caregivers, effects of budget cuts, and issues relating to death and dying.

Quota International, *1420 21st St. N.W. 20036; (202) 331-9694. Fax, (202) 331-4395. Kathleen Treiber, Executive Director.*
General e-mail, staff@quota.org
Web, www.quota.org

International service organization that links members in fourteen countries in a worldwide network of service and friendship. Interests include deaf, hard-of-hearing, and speech-impaired individuals and disadvantaged women and children.

The Woman Activist, *2310 Barbour Rd., Falls Church, VA 22043; (703) 573-8716. Flora Crater, President.*

Advocacy group that conducts research on individuals and groups in elective and appointive office, especially those who make decisions affecting women and minorities. Publishes the *Almanac of Virginia Politics.*

Women's Action for New Directions, *Washington Office, 322 4th St. N.E. 20002; (202) 543-8505. Fax, (202) 675-6469. Darcy Scott Martin, Director.*
General e-mail, wand@wand.org
Web, www.wand.org

Monitors legislation affecting women. Interests include the redirection of military spending toward domestic priorities. (Headquarters in Arlington, Mass.)

Women's Research and Education Institute, *1750 New York Ave. N.W., #350 20006; (202) 628-0444. Fax, (202) 628-0458. Susan Scanlan, President.*

General e-mail, wrei@wrei.org
Web, www.wrei.org

Analyzes policy-relevant information on women's issues. Sponsors fellowships in congressional offices; promotes public education through reports, conferences, and briefings; serves as an information clearinghouse. Interests include women's employment and economic status generally; women in nontraditional occupations; military women; employment opportunities for women veterans; older women; and women's health issues.

Other Minority Groups

NONPROFIT

American-Arab Anti-Discrimination Committee, *4201 Connecticut Ave. N.W., #300 20008-1158; (202) 244-2990. Fax, (202) 244-3196. Ziad Asali, President.*
General e-mail, adc@adc.org
Web, www.adc.org

Nonsectarian organization that seeks to protect the rights and heritage of Americans of Arab descent. Works to combat discrimination against Arab Americans in employment, education, and political life and to prevent stereotyping of Arabs in the media.

American Muslim Council, *721-R 2nd St. N.E., #200 20002; (202) 543-0075. Fax, (202) 543-0095. Yahya Mossa Basha, Chair.*
General e-mail, amc@amconline.org
Web, www.amconline.org

Promotes equal rights and political empowerment for Muslims in the United States. Opposes discrimination against Muslims; fosters cultural understanding and cooperation among organizations. (Plans to merge with the American Muslim Alliance in summer 2003 to form the National American Muslim Federation.)

Anti-Defamation League, *Washington Office, 1100 Connecticut Ave. N.W., #1020 20036; (202) 452-8310. Fax, (202) 296-2371. David Friedman, Regional Director.*
General e-mail, washington-dc@adl.org
Web, www.adl.org

Jewish organization interested in civil rights and liberties. Seeks to combat anti-Semitism and other forms of bigotry. Interests include discrimination in employment, housing, and education; U.S. foreign policy in the Middle East; and the treatment of Jews worldwide. Monitors legislation and regulations affecting Jewish interests and civil rights of all Americans. (Headquarters in New York.)

Japanese American Citizens League, *Washington Office, 1001 Connecticut Ave. N.W., #730 20036; (202) 223-1240. Fax, (202) 296-8082. Kristine Minami, Washington Representative.*

General e-mail, dc@jacl.org

Web, www.jacl.org

Monitors legislative and regulatory activities affecting the rights of Japanese Americans. Supports civil rights of all Americans, with a focus on Asian and Asian-Pacific Americans. (Headquarters in San Francisco, Calif.)

Organization of Chinese American Women, *4641 Montgomery Ave., #208, Bethesda, MD 20814; (301) 907-3898. Fax, (301) 907-3899. Pauline W. Tsui, Executive Director (Acting).*

General e-mail, ocawwomen@aol.com

Web, www.ocawwomen.org

Seeks to overcome racial and sexual discrimination and to ensure equal education and employment opportunities in professional and nonprofessional fields; provides members with leadership, skills, and employment training; assists newly arrived immigrants.

Organization of Chinese Americans, *1001 Connecticut Ave. N.W., #601 20036; (202) 223-5500. Fax, (202) 296-0540. Christine Chen, Executive Director.*

General e-mail, oca@ocanatl.org

Web, www.ocanatl.org

Advocacy group seeking equal opportunities for Chinese Americans and other Asian Americans. Interests include cultural heritage, education, voter registration, hate crimes, immigration, and civil rights issues; opposes adoption of English as official U.S. language.

CONSUMER PROTECTION

AGENCIES

Consumer Product Safety Commission (CPSC), *4330 East-West Hwy., #519, Bethesda, MD 20814 (mailing address: Washington, DC 20207-0001); (301) 504-6816. Fax, (301) 504-0124. Hal Stratton, Chair; Thomas W. Murr, Executive Director. Information, (301) 504-7908. Library, (301) 504-0000. TTY, (800) 638-8270. Locator, (301) 504-6816. Product safety hotline, (800) 638-2772.*

General e-mail, info@cpsc.gov

Web, www.cpsc.gov

Establishes and enforces product safety standards; collects data; studies the causes and prevention of product-related injuries; identifies hazardous products, including imports, and recalls them from the marketplace. Library open to the public.

Federal Trade Commission (FTC), *Consumer Protection, 600 Pennsylvania Ave. N.W., #466 20580; (202) 326-*

3665. Fax, (202) 326-3799. J. Howard Beales III, Director. Identity fraud report line, (877) IDTHEFT.

Web, www.ftc.gov

Enforces regulations dealing with unfair or deceptive business practices in advertising, credit, marketing, and service industries; educates consumers and business about these regulations; conducts investigations and litigation.

General Services Administration (GSA), *Consumer Information Center, 1800 F St. N.W., #G142 20405; (202) 501-1794. Fax, (202) 501-4281. Teresa N. Nasif, Director.*

Web, www.pueblo.gsa.gov

Publishes quarterly consumer information catalog that lists free and low-cost federal publications. Copies may be obtained from the Consumer Information Centers, Pueblo, CO 81009. Copies also available at Federal Information Centers.

AGENCY AND DEPARTMENT CONSUMER CONTACTS

Agriculture Dept. (USDA), *Communications and Governmental Affairs, 3101 Park Center Dr., #926, Alexandria, VA 22302; (703) 305-2281. Fax, (703) 305-2312. Scott Mexic, Deputy Administrator.*

Web, www.fns.usda.gov/cga

Commission on Civil Rights, *Public Affairs, 624 9th St. N.W., #730 20425; (202) 376-8312. Fax, (202) 376-8315. Terri Dickerson, Chief (Acting). TTY, (202) 376-8116.*

Web, www.usccr.gov

Consumer Product Safety Commission (CPSC), *Information and Public Affairs, 4330 East-West Hwy., #519, Bethesda, MD 20814 (mailing address: Washington, DC 20207-0001); (301) 504-7908. Fax, (301) 504-0862. Becky Bailey, Director. TTY, (800) 638-8270. Product safety hotline, (800) 638-2772.*

General e-mail, info@cpsc.gov

Web, www.cpsc.gov

Education Dept., *Intergovernmental and Interagency Affairs, 400 Maryland Ave. S.W., #5E317 20202-3500; (202) 401-0404. Fax, (202) 401-8607. Laurie M. Rich, Assistant Secretary. Press, (202) 401-1576. TTY, (800) 437-0833. Information, (800) USA-LEARN.*

Web, www.ed.gov/offices/OIIA

Energy Dept. (DOE), *Intergovernmental and External Affairs, 1000 Independence Ave. S.W., CI-10, #8G048*

CONSUMER PRODUCT SAFETY COMMISSION

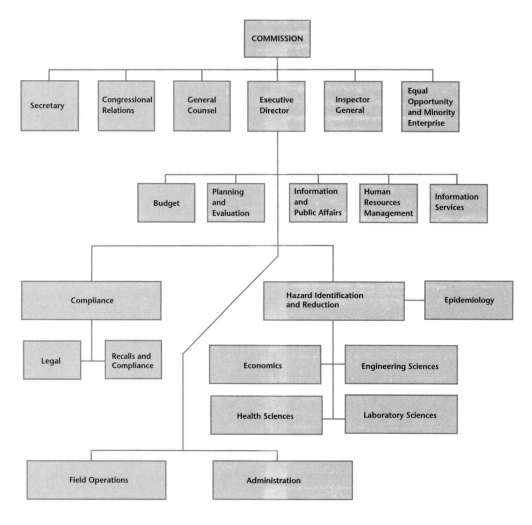

20585; (202) 586-5373. Fax, (202) 586-0539. Betty Nolan, Director.

Web, www.energy.gov

Environmental Protection Agency (EPA), *Headquarters Library,* 1200 Pennsylvania Ave. N.W. 20460; (202) 566-0556. Fax, (202) 566-0562. Lucy Park, Head Librarian.

General e-mail, library-hq@epa.gov

Web, www.epa.gov

Federal Communications Commission (FCC), *Consumer and Governmental Affairs Bureau,* 445 12th St. S.W., #7C485 20554; (888) 225-5322. Fax, (202) 418-

0232. K. Dane Snowden, Chief. TTY, (888) 835-5322. Fax-on-demand, (202) 418-2830.

General e-mail, fccinfo@fcc.gov

Web, www.fcc.gov/cgb

Federal Deposit Insurance Corp. (FDIC), *Compliance and Consumer Affairs,* 550 17th St. N.W. 20429-9990; (202) 942-3100. Fax, (202) 942-3427. Donna J. Gambrell, Deputy Director. Information, (877) ASK-FDIC. TTY, (800) 925-4618.

General e-mail, consumer@fdic.gov

Web, www.fdic.gov

Federal Maritime Commission, *Consumer Complaints,* 800 N. Capitol St. N.W., #970 20573; (202) 523-5807. Fax, (202) 275-0059. Joseph Farrell, Director.
Web, www.fmc.gov

Federal Reserve System, *Consumer and Community Affairs,* 20th and C Sts. N.W., Stop 802 20551-0001; (202) 452-2631. Fax, (202) 872-4995. Dolores S. Smith, Director. Complaints, (202) 452-3693.
Web, www.federalreserve.gov

Food and Drug Administration (FDA), *(Health and Human Services Dept.), Consumer Affairs,* 5600 Fishers Lane, Rockville, MD 20857-0001; (301) 827-4422. Fax, (301) 443-9767. Patricia Kuntze, Associate Director (Acting). Consumer inquiries, (888) 463-6332.
Web, www.fda.gov/oca/oca.htm

General Services Administration (GSA), *Consumer Information Center,* 1800 F St. N.W., #G142 20405; (202) 501-1794. Fax, (202) 501-4281. Teresa N. Nasif, Director.
Web, www.pueblo.gsa.gov

Interior Dept. (DOI), *Communications,* 1849 C St. N.W., #6013 20240; (202) 208-6416. Fax, (202) 208-5133. Eric Ruff, Director. TTY, (202) 208-4817.
Web, www.doi.gov

Justice Dept. (DOJ), *Civil Division: Consumer Litigation,* 1331 Pennsylvania Ave. N.W., #950N 20004; (202) 307-0066. Fax, (202) 514-8742. Eugene M. Thirolf, Director.
Web, www.usdoj.gov

Merit Systems Protection Board, 1615 M St. N.W., 5th Floor 20419; (202) 653-7200. Fax, (202) 653-7130. Bentley M. Roberts Jr., Clerk of the Board. TTY, (800) 877-8339.
Web, www.mspb.gov

National Institute of Standards and Technology (NIST), *(Commerce Dept.), Inquiries,* 100 Bureau Dr., Stop 3460, Gaithersburg, MD 20899-3460; (301) 975-6478. Fax, (301) 926-1630. Sharon Shaffer, Head.
General e-mail, inquiries@nist.gov
Web, www.nist.gov

Nuclear Regulatory Commission, *Public Affairs,* 11555 Rockville Pike, Rockville, MD 20852-2738 (mailing address: Washington, DC 20555); (301) 415-8200. Fax, (301) 415-3716. William M. Beecher, Director.
General e-mail, nrc@nrc.gov
Web, www.nrc.gov/opa

Postal Rate Commission, *Consumer Advocate,* 1333 H St. N.W., #300 20268-0001; (202) 789-6830. Fax, (202) 789-6819. Shelly S. Dreifuss, Director.
Web, www.prc.gov

Securities and Exchange Commission, *Filings and Information Services,* 6432 General Greenway, #0-18, Alexandria, VA 22312; (202) 942-8938. Fax, (703) 914-1005. Kenneth Fogash, Director.

Small Business Administration (SBA), *Capital Access,* 409 3rd St. S.W., #8200 20416; (202) 205-6657. Fax, (202) 205-7230. Ronald Bew, Associate Deputy Administrator.
Web, www.sba.gov

State Dept., *Commercial and Business Affairs,* 2201 C St. N.W., #2318 20520-5820; (202) 647-1625. Fax, (202) 647-3953. J. Frank Mermoud, Special Representative for Business Affairs.
General e-mail, cbaweb@state.gov
Web, www.state.gov/e/eb/cba

Transportation Dept. (DOT), *Aviation Consumer Protection,* 400 7th St. S.W., #4107 20590 (mailing address: Transportation Dept., C75, #4107 20590); (202) 366-2220. Fax, (202) 366-5944. Norman Strickman, Assistant Director.
General e-mail, airconsumer@ost.dot.gov
Web, www.dot.gov/airconsumer

Treasury Dept., *Public Affairs,* 1500 Pennsylvania Ave. N.W., #2321 20220; (202) 622-2960. Fax, (202) 622-1999. Rob Nichols, Assistant Secretary (Acting).
Web, www.ustreas.gov

U.S. Postal Service (USPS), *Office of Consumer Advocate,* 475 L'Enfant Plaza S.W., #5821 20260-2200; (202) 268-2284. Fax, (202) 268-2304. Francia G. Smith, Vice President and Consumer Advocate. TTY, (877) 877-7833. Inquiries, (800) ASK-USPS or (800) 275-8777.
Web, www.usps.gov

Veterans Affairs Dept. (VA), *Consumer Affairs,* 810 Vermont Ave. N.W., #915 20420; (202) 273-5770. Fax, (202) 273-5716. Clayton Cochran, Program Analyst; Shirley Mathis, Program Analyst.
Web, www.va.gov

CONGRESS

House Appropriations Committee, *Subcommittee on Commerce, Justice, State, and the Judiciary,* H309 CAP 20515; (202) 225-3351. Rep. Frank R. Wolf, R-Va., Chair; Mike Ringler, Staff Director.

CONSUMER AND EMERGENCY HOTLINES

DEPARTMENTS

Agriculture
Fraud, waste, and abuse hotline, (800) 424-9121

Meat and poultry safety inquiries, (800) 535-4555

Commerce
Export enforcement hotline, (800) 424-2980

Fraud, waste, and abuse hotline, (800) 424-5197

Trade Information Center, (800) 872-8723

Defense
Army espionage hotline, (800) 225-5779

Fraud, waste, and abuse hotline, (800) 424-9098

Education
Fraud, waste, and abuse hotline, (800) 647-8733

Student financial aid info., (800) 433-3243

Energy
Energy Efficiency and Renewable Energy Clearinghouse, (800) 363-3732

Fraud and abuse hotline, (800) 541-1625

Health and Human Services
AIDS info., (800) 342-2437; 332-2437 in Washington; TTY, (800) 243-7889. Spanish speaking, (800) 344-7432; (202) 328-0697 in Washington

Civil rights info., (800) 368-1019

Fraud hotline, (800) 447-8477

General health info., (800) 336-4797

Medicare hotline, (800) 633-4227

National Adoption Center, (800) 862-3678

National Cancer Institute cancer info., (800) 422-6237

National Runaway Switchboard, (800) 621-4000

Housing and Urban Development
Housing discrimination hotline, (800) 669-9777

Justice
Americans With Disabilities Act info., (800) 514-0301; TTY, (800) 514-0383

Arson hotline, (888) 283-3473

Criminal Justice Reference Service, (800) 638-8736

Illegal firearms activity hotline, (800) 283-4867

National Institute for Corrections Information Center, (800) 877-1461

Unfair employment hotline (immigration related), (800) 255-7688

Transportation
Auto safety hotline, (800) 424-9393; (202) 366-0123 in Washington

Aviation safety hotline, (800) 255-1111

Federal Aviation Administration consumer hotline, (800) 322-7873

Hazardous material, chemical, and oil spills, (800) 424-8802

Treasury
Comptroller of the Currency customer assistance hotline, (800) 613-6743

Fraud, waste, mismanagement, and abuse hotline (IRS programs), (800) 366-4484

Tax form requests, (800) 829-3676

Tax refund info., (800) 829-4477

Taxpayer Advocate Service, (877) 777-4778

Taxpayer assistance, (800) 829-1040

Veterans Affairs
Benefits hotline, (800) 827-1000

Debt Management Center, (800) 827-0648

Web, www.house.gov/appropriations

Jurisdiction over legislation to appropriate funds for the Federal Trade Commission.

House Appropriations Committee, *Subcommittee on VA, HUD, and Independent Agencies,* H143 CAP 20515; (202) 225-3241. Rep. James T. Walsh, R-N.Y., Chair; Tim Peterson, Staff Director.

Web, www.house.gov/appropriations

Jurisdiction over legislation to appropriate funds for the Consumer Information Center of the General Services Administration, the Consumer Product Safety Commission, and the U.S. Office of Consumer Affairs of the Health and Human Services Dept.

House Energy and Commerce Committee, *Subcommittee on Commerce, Trade, and Consumer Protection,* 2125 RHOB 20515; (202) 225-2927. Fax, (202) 225-1919. Rep. Cliff Stearns, R-Fla., Chair.

General e-mail, commerce@mail.house.gov

Web, energycommerce.house.gov/108/subcommittees/ Commerce_Trade_and_Consumer_Protection.htm

Jurisdiction over product liability and consumer protection legislation, the Consumer Product Safety Commission, the Federal Trade Commission, and interstate and foreign commerce, including general trade matters within the jurisdiction of the full committee.

CONSUMER AND EMERGENCY HOTLINES (continued)

Fraud, waste, and mismanagement hotline, (800) 488-8244

Insurance policy info., (800) 669-8477

Persian Gulf hotline, (800) 749-8387

AGENCIES

Consumer Product Safety Commission

Product safety info., (800) 638-2772

Environmental Protection Agency

Asbestos ombudsman, (800) 368-5888

Endangered species hotline, (800) 447-3813

National Lead Information Center, (800) 532-3394

National radon hotline, (800) 767-7236

Ozone information hotline, (800) 296-1996

Pesticides and related medical info., (800) 858-7378

Safe drinking water hotline, (800) 426-4791

Superfund hotline, (800) 424-9346; (703) 412-9810 in Washington

Wetlands information hotline, (800) 832-7828

Export-Import Bank

Export finance hotline, (800) 565-3946; (202) 565-3946 in Washington

Federal Deposit Insurance Corporation

Banking complaints and inquiries, (800) 934-3342

Federal Election Commission

Fund-raising laws info., (800) 424-9530; (202) 694-1100 in Washington

Federal Emergency Management Agency

Emergency management and training info., (800) 238-3358

Flood insurance service, (800) 638-6620

General Services Administration

Federal Information Center, (800) 688-9889

Nuclear Regulatory Commission

Nuclear power info., (800) 368-5642

Office of Special Counsel

Prohibited personnel practices info., (800) 872-9855; (202) 653-7188 in Washington

Small Business Administration

Fraud, waste, and abuse hotline, (800) 767-0385

Small business assistance, (800) 827-5722

Social Security Administration

Fraud and abuse hotline, (800) 269-0271

Social Security benefits (including Medicare) info., (800) 772-1213

PRIVATE ORGANIZATIONS

GED Hotline on Adult Education, (800) 626-9433

National Center for Missing and Exploited Children, (800) 843-5678

National Insurance Consumer Helpline, (800) 942-4242

National Literacy Hotline, (800) 228-8813

National Organization for Victim Assistance, (800) 879-6682; (202) 232-6682 in Washington

Project Vote Smart, (800) 622-7627

United Network for Organ Sharing, (888) 894-6361

House Energy and Commerce Committee, *Subcommittee on Health,* 2125 RHOB 20515; (202) 225-2927. *Fax, (202) 225-1919. Rep. Michael Bilirakis, R-Fla., Chair; David V. Marventano, Staff Director.*
General e-mail, commerce@mail.house.gov
Web, energycommerce.house.gov/108/subcommittees/Health.htm

Jurisdiction over legislation on vaccines; food and drugs; labeling and packaging, including tobacco products and alcohol beverages; and the use of vitamins. Oversight of the Food and Drug Administration.

House Financial Services Committee, *Subcommittee on Financial Institutions and Consumer Credit, 2129*

RHOB 20515; (202) 225-7502. Rep. Spencer Bachus, R-Ala., Chair; Bob Foster, Staff Director.
Web, www.house.gov/financialservices/finin108.htm

Jurisdiction over legislation on consumer protection, including fair lending and regulatory issues.

House Government Reform Committee, *Subcommittee on Energy Policy, Natural Resources, and Regulatory Affairs, B377 RHOB 20515; (202) 225-4407. Fax, (202) 225-2441. Rep. Doug Ose, R-Calif., Chair; Dan Skopec, Staff Director.*
Web, www.house.gov/reform

Oversight of the Federal Trade Commission and the Consumer Product Safety Commission.

House Science Committee, *Subcommittee on Research,* B374 RHOB 20515; (202) 225-7858. Fax, (202) 225-7815. Rep. Nick Smith, R-Mich., Chair; Peter Rooney, Staff Director.
General e-mail, science@mail.house.gov
Web, www.house.gov/science/committeeinfo/members/research/index.htm

Jurisdiction over legislation related to the U.S. Fire Administration and Building and Fire Research Laboratory of the National Institute of Standards and Technology; oversight of federal fire prevention and the Earthquake Hazards Reduction Act. Jurisdiction over research and development involving government nutritional programs.

Senate Appropriations Committee, *Subcommittee on Commerce, Justice, State, and the Judiciary,* S-206 CAP 20510; (202) 224-7277. Fax, (202) 228-0587. Sen. Judd Gregg, R-N.H., Chair; James Morhard, Clerk.
Web, appropriations.senate.gov

Jurisdiction over legislation to appropriate funds for the Commerce Dept., the Securities and Exchange Commission, the Small Business Administration, the Competitiveness Policy Council, the Federal Trade Commission, the International Trade Commission, and the Office of the U.S. Trade Representative.

Senate Appropriations Committee, *Subcommittee on VA, HUD, and Independent Agencies,* SD-130 20510; (202) 224-8252. Fax, (202) 228-1624. Sen. Christopher S. Bond, R-Mo., Chair; Jon Kamarck, Clerk.
Web, appropriations.senate.gov

Jurisdiction over legislation to appropriate funds for the Consumer Information Center of the General Services Administration, the Consumer Product Safety Commission, and the U.S. Office of Consumer Affairs.

Senate Banking, Housing, and Urban Affairs Committee, SD-534 20510; (202) 224-7391. Fax, (202) 224-5137. Sen. Richard C. Shelby, R-Ala., Chair; Kathy Casey, Staff Director.
Web, banking.senate.gov

Jurisdiction over legislation on consumer protection, including the Community Reinvestment Act and the Fair Credit Reporting Act, and regulatory oversight issues.

Senate Commerce, Science, and Transportation Committee, SD-508 20510; (202) 224-5115. Fax, (202) 224-1459. Sen. John McCain, R-Ariz., Chair; Jeanne Bumpus, Staff Director.
Web, commerce.senate.gov

Jurisdiction over regulation of consumer products and services, including testing related to toxic substances.

Jurisdiction over legislation related to the U.S. Fire Administration and the Building and Fire Research Laboratory of the National Institute of Standards and Technology; oversight of federal fire prevention and the Earthquake Hazards Reduction Act.

Senate Commerce, Science, and Transportation Committee, *Subcommittee on Consumer Affairs and Product Safety,* SH-428 20510; (202) 224-5183. Fax, (202) 228-0326. Sen. Peter G. Fitzgerald, R-Ill., Chair; Carlos Fierro, Senior Counsel.
Web, commerce.senate.gov

Jurisdiction over legislation on the Consumer Product Safety Commission. Jurisdiction over consumer law; product safety and liability; flammable products; insurance; and labeling and packaging legislation, including advertising and packaging of tobacco products and alcohol beverages.

Senate Health, Education, Labor, and Pensions Committee, SD-428 20510; (202) 224-5375. Fax, (202) 228-5044. Sen. Judd Gregg, R-N.H., Chair; Sharon Soderstrom, Staff Director.
Web, health.senate.gov

Jurisdiction over legislation on vaccines, drug labeling and packaging, and the use of vitamins.

NONPROFIT

Automotive Consumer Action Program, 8400 Westpark Dr., MS 2, McLean, VA 22102; (703) 821-7411. Fax, (703) 821-7075. Seena Faqiri, Director. Public Affairs, (703) 827-7407.
General e-mail, nadapublicaffairs@nada.org
Web, www.nada.org

Third-party mediation program that promotes national standards and procedures in resolving auto dealer/manufacturer and consumer disputes.

Center for Auto Safety, 1825 Connecticut Ave. N.W., #330 20009; (202) 328-7700. Fax, (202) 387-0140. Clarence M. Ditlow III, Executive Director.
Web, www.autosafety.org

Public interest organization that receives written consumer complaints against auto manufacturers; monitors federal agencies responsible for regulating and enforcing auto and highway safety rules.

Consumer Alert, 1001 Connecticut Ave. N.W., #1128 20036; (202) 467-5809. Fax, (202) 467-5814. Frances B. Smith, Executive Director.
General e-mail, info@consumeralert.org
Web, www.consumeralert.org

Membership: individual consumers. Promotes consumer choice and economic competition to advance consumers' interests.

Consumer Federation of America, *1424 16th St. N.W., #604 20036; (202) 387-6121. Fax, (202) 265-7989. Stephen Brobeck, Executive Director.*
Web, www.consumerfed.org

Federation of national, regional, state, and local pro-consumer organizations. Promotes consumer interests in banking, credit, and insurance; telecommunications; housing; food, drugs, and medical care; safety; energy and natural resources development; and indoor air quality.

Consumer Federation of America's Insurance Group, *1424 16th St. N.W., #604 20036; (202) 387-6121. Fax, (202) 265-7989. J. Robert Hunter, Director.*
Web, www.consumerfed.org

Public interest organization that conducts research and provides consumers with information on buying insurance. Interests include auto, homeowner, renter, and life insurance. Monitors legislation and regulations.

Consumers Union of the United States, *Washington Office, 1666 Connecticut Ave. N.W., #310 20009; (202) 462-6262. Fax, (202) 265-9548. Gene Kimmelman, Director.*
Web, www.consumersunion.org

Consumer advocacy group that represents consumer interests before Congress and regulatory agencies and litigates consumer affairs cases involving the government. Interests include consumer impact of world trade. Publishes *Consumer Reports* magazine. (Headquarters in Yonkers, N.Y.)

Council of Better Business Bureaus, *4200 Wilson Blvd., #800, Arlington, VA 22203-1838; (703) 276-0100. Fax, (703) 525-8277. Kenneth Hunter, President.*
Web, www.bbb.org

Membership: businesses and Better Business Bureaus in the United States and Canada. Promotes ethical business practices and truth in national advertising; mediates disputes between consumers and businesses.

National Assn. of Consumer Agency Administrators, *1010 Vermont Ave. N.W., #514 20005; (202) 347-7395. Fax, (202) 347-2563. Nancy Sabella, Executive Director.*
General e-mail, nacaa@erols.com
Web, www.nacaanet.org

Membership: federal, state, and local government consumer affairs professionals. Seeks to enhance consumer services available to the public. Acts as a clearing-house for consumer information and legislation. Serves as liaison with federal agencies and Congress. Offers training programs, seminars, and conferences.

National Consumers League, *1701 K St. N.W., #1200 20006; (202) 835-3323. Fax, (202) 835-0747. Linda F. Golodner, President.*
Web, www.nclnet.org

Advocacy group that engages in research and educational activities related to consumer and worker issues. Interests include health care; child labor; food, drug, and product safety; environment; telecommunications; and financial services. Web resources include fraud.org and lifesmarts.org.

National SAFE KIDS Campaign, *1301 Pennsylvania Ave. N.W., #1000 20004; (202) 662-0600. Fax, (202) 393-2072. Heather Paul, Executive Director.*
Web, www.safekids.org

Promotes awareness among adults that unintentional injury is the leading cause of death among children ages fourteen and under. Conducts educational programs on childhood injury prevention; sponsors National SAFE KIDS Week.

Public Citizen, *1600 20th St. N.W. 20009; (202) 588-1000. Fax, (202) 588-7798. Joan Claybrook, President.*
Web, www.citizen.org

Public interest consumer advocacy organization comprising the following projects: Buyers Up, Congress Watch, Critical Mass Energy Project, Health Research Group, Litigation Group, and Global Trade Watch.

Trial Lawyers for Public Justice, *1717 Massachusetts Ave. N.W., #800 20036; (202) 797-8600. Fax, (202) 232-7203. Arthur H. Bryant, Executive Director.*
General e-mail, tlpj@tlpj.org
Web, www.tlpj.org

Membership: consumer activists, trial lawyers, and public interest lawyers. Litigates to influence corporate and government decisions about products or activities adversely affecting health or safety. Interests include toxic torts, environmental protection, civil rights and civil liberties, workers' safety, consumer protection, and the preservation of the civil justice system.

U.S. Chamber of Commerce, *Congressional and Public Affairs, 1615 H St. N.W. 20062-2000; (202) 463-5600. Fax, (202) 887-3430. Rolf T. Lundberg, Senior Vice President.*
Web, www.uschamber.com

Monitors legislation and regulations regarding business and consumer issues, including legislation and policies affecting the Federal Trade Commission, the Consumer Product Safety Commission, and other agencies.

U.S. Public Interest Research Group (USPIRG),
218 D St. S.E. 20003; (202) 546-9707. Fax, (202) 546-2461. Gene Karpinski, Executive Director.
General e-mail, uspirg@pirg.org
Web, www.uspirg.org

Conducts research and advocacy on consumer and environmental issues, including telephone rates, banking practices, insurance, campaign finance reform, product safety, toxic and solid waste, safe drinking water, and energy; monitors private and governmental actions affecting consumers; supports efforts to challenge consumer fraud and illegal business practices. Serves as national office for state groups.

Credit Practices

AGENCIES

Comptroller of the Currency *(Treasury Dept.), Compliance Operations and Policy,* *250 E St. S.W. 20219-0001; (202) 874-4428. Fax, (202) 874-5221. Dave Hammaker, Deputy Comptroller.*
Web, www.occ.treas.gov

Develops policy for enforcing consumer laws and regulations that affect national banks, including the Truth-in-Lending, Community Reinvestment, and Equal Credit Opportunity acts.

Comptroller of the Currency *(Treasury Dept.), Law Dept.,* *250 E St. S.W., 8th Floor 20219; (202) 874-5200. Fax, (202) 874-5374. Julie L. Williams, First Senior Deputy Comptroller and Chief Counsel. Library, (202) 874-4720.*
Web, www.occ.treas.gov

Enforces and oversees compliance by nationally chartered banks with laws prohibiting discrimination in credit transactions on the basis of sex or marital status. Enforces regulations concerning bank advertising; may issue cease-and-desist orders.

Comptroller of the Currency *(Treasury Dept.), Public Affairs,* *250 E St. S.W. 20219; (202) 874-4880. Fax, (202) 874-5678. Mark Nishan, Senior Deputy Comptroller (Acting).*
Web, www.occ.treas.gov

Advises the comptroller on relations with the media, the banking industry, Congress, and consumer and community development groups.

Federal Deposit Insurance Corp. (FDIC), *Compliance and Consumer Affairs,* *550 17th St. N.W. 20429-9990; (202) 942-3100. Fax, (202) 942-3427. Donna J.*

Gambrell, Deputy Director. Information, (877) ASK-FDIC. TTY, (800) 925-4618.
General e-mail, consumer@fdic.gov
Web, www.fdic.gov

Coordinates and monitors complaints filed by consumers against federally insured state banks that are not members of the Federal Reserve System; handles complaints concerning truth-in-lending and other fair credit provisions, including charges of discrimination on the basis of sex or marital status; responds to general banking inquiries; answers questions on deposit insurance coverage.

Federal Deposit Insurance Corp. (FDIC), *Supervision and Consumer Protection,* *550 17th St. N.W. 20429; (202) 898-8946. Fax, (202) 898-3638. Michael J. Zamorski, Director.*

Examines and supervises federally insured state banks that are not members of the Federal Reserve System to ascertain their safety and soundness.

Federal Reserve System, *Consumer and Community Affairs,* *20th and C Sts. N.W., Stop 802 20551-0001; (202) 452-2631. Fax, (202) 872-4995. Dolores S. Smith, Director. Complaints, (202) 452-3693.*
Web, www.federalreserve.gov

Receives consumer complaints concerning truth-in-lending, fair credit billing, equal credit opportunity, electronic fund transfer, home mortgage disclosure, consumer leasing, and advertising; receives complaints about unregulated practices; refers complaints to district banks. The Federal Reserve monitors enforcement of fair lending laws with regard to state-chartered banks that are members of the Federal Reserve System.

Federal Trade Commission (FTC), *Financial Practices,* *601 New Jersey Ave. N.W., MS NJ 3158 20580; (202) 326-3224. Fax, (202) 326-3768. Joel Winston, Associate Director.*
Web, www.ftc.gov

Enforces truth-in-lending and fair credit billing provisions for creditors not handled by other agencies, such as retail stores and small loan companies; enforces the Fair Credit Reporting Act, which protects consumers from unfair credit ratings and practices; enforces the Fair Debt Collection Practices Act, Electronic Funds Transfer Act, Equal Credit Opportunity Act, Consumer Leasing Act, Holder in Due Course Rule, and Credit Practices Rule.

Justice Dept. (DOJ), *Civil Division: Consumer Litigation,* *1331 Pennsylvania Ave. N.W., #950N 20004; (202) 307-0066. Fax, (202) 514-8742. Eugene M. Thirolf, Director.*

Web, www.usdoj.gov

Files suits to enforce the Truth-in-Lending Act and other federal statutes protecting consumers, generally upon referral by client agencies.

National Credit Union Administration, *Examination and Insurance,* 1775 Duke St., Alexandria, VA 22314-3428; (703) 518-6360. Fax, (703) 518-6499. David M. Marquis, Director. Toll-free investment hotline, (800) 755-5999.

Web, www.ncua.gov

Oversees and enforces compliance by federally chartered credit unions with the Truth-in-Lending Act, the Equal Credit Opportunity Act, and other federal statutes protecting consumers.

Office of Thrift Supervision (OTS), *(Treasury Dept.),* *Compliance Policy,* 1700 G St. N.W. 20552; (202) 906-6134. Fax, (202) 906-6326. Richard Riese, Director. Consumer complaints, (800) 842-6929.

Web, www.ots.treas.gov

Prepares consumer protection regulations and compliance examination procedures. Sponsors a consumer complaint process that covers federal savings associations.

Small Business Administration (SBA), *Equal Employment Opportunity and Civil Rights Compliance,* 409 3rd St. S.W., #4600 20416; (202) 205-6751. Fax, (202) 205-7580. Carol L. Walker, Director. TTY, (202) 205-7150.

Web, www.sba.gov

Reviews complaints based on disability against the Small Business Administration by recipients of its assistance in cases of alleged discrimination in credit transactions; monitors recipients for civil rights compliance.

NONPROFIT

American Bankers Assn. (ABA), *Communications,* 1120 Connecticut Ave. N.W., 8th Floor 20036; (202) 663-7501. Fax, (202) 663-7578. Virginia Dean, Executive Director.

Web, www.aba.com

Provides information on a wide range of banking issues and financial management.

American Financial Services Assn. (AFSA), 919 18th St. N.W., #300 20006; (202) 296-5544. Fax, (202) 223-0321. H. Randy Lively, President.

General e-mail, afsa@afsamail.org

Web, www.afsaonline.org

Membership: consumer installment credit industry including consumer finance, sales finance, and industrial

banking companies. Conducts research; provides consumer finance education. Monitors legislation and regulations.

National Retail Federation, 325 7th St. N.W., #1100 20004-2802; (202) 783-7971. Fax, (202) 737-2849. Tracy Mullin, President.

Web, www.nrf.com

Membership: national and state associations of retailers and major retail corporations. Provides information on credit, truth-in-lending laws, and other fair credit practices.

Fire Prevention and Control

AGENCIES

Consumer Product Safety Commission (CPSC), *Hazard Identification and Reduction,* 4330 East-West Hwy., #702, Bethesda, MD 20814; (301) 504-7949. Fax, (301) 504-0407. Jacqueline Elder, Assistant Executive Director (Acting).

Web, www.cpsc.gov

Proposes, evaluates, and develops standards and test procedures for safety and fire resistance in accordance with the Flammable Fabrics Act and the Federal Hazardous Substances Act. Reports injuries resulting from use of products.

Federal Emergency Management Agency (FEMA), *National Fire Academy,* 16825 S. Seton Ave., Emmitsburg, MD 21727-8998; (301) 447-1117. Fax, (301) 447-1173. Denis Onieal, Superintendent.

Web, www.usfa.fema.gov/nfa

Trains fire officials and related professionals in fire prevention and management, current fire fighting technologies, and the administration of fire prevention organizations.

Forest Service *(Agriculture Dept.), Fire and Aviation Management,* 201 14th St. S.W. 20250 (mailing address: P.O. Box 96090 20090-6090); (202) 205-1483. Fax, (202) 205-1272. Jerry T. Williams, Director.

Web, www.fs.fed.us/fire

Responsible for aviation and fire management programs, including fire control planning and prevention, suppression of fires, and the use of prescribed fires. Provides state foresters with financial and technical assistance for fire protection in forests and on rural lands.

National Institute of Standards and Technology (NIST), *(Commerce Dept.), Building and Fire Research Laboratory,* 100 Bureau Dr., MS 8600, Gaithersburg, MD 20899-8600; (301) 975-6850. Fax, (301) 975-4032. Jack E. Snell, Director; James E. Hill, Deputy Director.

Web, www.bfrl.nist.gov

Conducts basic and applied research on fire and fire resistance of construction materials; develops testing methods, standards, design concepts, and technologies for fire protection and prevention.

National Institute of Standards and Technology (NIST), *(Commerce Dept.), Fire Research, 100 Bureau Dr., MS 8600, Gaithersburg, MD 20899-8600; (301) 975-6863. Fax, (301) 975-4052. William Grosshandler, Chief.*
Web, www.nist.gov

Conducts research on fire safety and metrology. Develops models to measure the behavior and mitigate the impact of large-scale fires. Operates the Fire Research Information Service, Fire Dynamics Group, and a large-scale fire test facility. Studies smoke components of flames, the burning of polymeric materials, and fire detection and suppression systems.

Occupational Safety and Health Administration (OSHA), *(Labor Dept.), Safety Standards, 200 Constitution Ave. N.W., #N3609 20210; (202) 693-2222. Fax, (202) 693-1663. Steven Witt, Director, (202) 693-1950.*

Administers regulations for fire safety standards; sponsors programs for maritime, fire protection, mechanical, and electrical industries.

U.S. Fire Administration *(Federal Emergency Management Agency), 16825 S. Seton Ave., Emmitsburg, MD 21727; (301) 447-1018. Fax, (301) 447-1270. R. David Paulison, Administrator.*
Web, www.usfa.fema.gov

Conducts research and collects, analyzes, and disseminates data on combustion, fire prevention, fire fighter safety, and the management of fire prevention organizations; studies and develops arson prevention programs and fire prevention codes; maintains the National Fire Data System.

NONPROFIT

International Assn. of Fire Chiefs, *4025 Fair Ridge Dr. #300, Fairfax, VA 22033-2868; (703) 273-0911. Fax, (703) 273-9363. Garry L. Briese, Executive Director.*
General e-mail, iafchq@iafc.org
Web, www.iafc.org

Membership: fire fighting chiefs and managers. Conducts research on fire control; testifies before congressional committees. Monitors legislation and regulations affecting fire safety codes.

International Assn. of Fire Fighters, *1750 New York Ave. N.W., 3rd Floor 20006; (202) 737-8484. Fax, (202) 737-8418. Harold A. Schaitberger, General President.*
Web, www.iaff.org

Membership: more than 225,000 professional fire fighters and emergency medical personnel. Assists members with contract negotiation and grievances; conducts training programs and workshops. Monitors legislation and regulations. (Affiliated with the AFL-CIO and the Canadian Labour Congress.)

National Fire Protection Assn., *Government Affairs, Washington Office, 1110 N. Glebe Rd., #210, Arlington, VA 22201; (703) 516-4346. Fax, (703) 516-4350. John C. Biechman, Vice President.*
General e-mail, wdc@nfpa.org
Web, www.nfpa.org

Membership: individuals and organizations interested in fire protection. Develops and updates fire protection codes and standards; sponsors technical assistance programs; collects fire data statistics. Monitors legislation and regulations. (Headquarters in Quincy, Mass.)

Labeling and Packaging

AGENCIES

Consumer Product Safety Commission (CPSC), *Hazard Identification and Reduction, 4330 East-West Hwy., #702, Bethesda, MD 20814; (301) 504-7949. Fax, (301) 504-0407. Jacqueline Elder, Assistant Executive Director (Acting).*
Web, www.cpsc.gov

Establishes labeling and packaging regulations. Develops standards in accordance with the Poison Prevention Packaging Act, the Federal Hazardous Substances Act, and the Consumer Products Safety Act.

Food and Drug Administration (FDA), *(Health and Human Services Dept.), Center for Food Safety and Applied Nutrition, 5100 Paint Branch Pkwy., College Park, MD 20740-3835; (301) 436-1600. Joseph A. Levitt, Director.*
Web, www.cfsan.fda.gov

Develops and enforces labeling regulations for foods (except meat and poultry but including fish) and cosmetics; develops and enforces standards on form and fill of packaging for foods and cosmetics; develops and enforces safety regulations for food and cosmetic packaging materials; recommends action to Justice Dept.

Food and Drug Administration (FDA), *(Health and Human Services Dept.), Drug Marketing, Advertising, and Communications, 5600 Fishers Lane, HFD-42, #17B-17, Rockville, MD 20857; (301) 827-2828. Fax, (301) 594-6771. Thomas Abrams, Director.*
Web, www.fda.gov/cder

Monitors prescription drug advertising and labeling; investigates complaints; conducts market research on health care communications and drug issues.

Food Safety and Inspection Service (*Agriculture Dept.*), *1400 Independence Ave. S.W., #331E 20250; (202) 720-7025. Fax, (202) 205-0158. Garry L. McKee, Administrator. Press, (202) 720-9113. Consumer inquiries, (800) 535-4555; in Washington, (202) 720-3333.*
Web, www.usda.gov/fsis

Inspects meat and poultry products and provides safe handling and labeling guidelines.

National Institute of Standards and Technology (NIST), (*Commerce Dept.*), *Weights and Measures, 100 Bureau Dr., MS 2600, Gaithersburg, MD 20899; (301) 975-4004. Fax, (301) 926-0647. Henry V. Opperman, Director.*
Web, www.nist.gov/owm

Promotes uniform standards among the states for packaging and labeling products and for measuring devices, including scales and commercial measurement instruments; advises manufacturers on labeling and packaging laws and on measuring device standards.

NONPROFIT

Flexible Packaging Assn., *971 Corporate Blvd., #403, Linthicum, MD 21090-2211; (410) 694-0800. Fax, (410) 694-0900. Marla Donahue, President.*
General e-mail, fpa@flexpack.org
Web, www.flexpack.org

Membership: companies that supply or manufacture flexible packaging. Collects and disseminates industry-related information. Monitors legislation and regulations.

Glass Packaging Institute, *515 King St., #420, Alexandria, VA 22314-3137; (703) 684-6359. Fax, (703) 684-6048. Joseph Cattaneo, President.*
Web, www.gpi.org

Membership: manufacturers of glass containers and their suppliers. Promotes industry policies to protect the environment, conserve natural resources, and reduce energy consumption; conducts research; monitors legislation affecting the industry. Interests include glass recycling.

Packaging Machinery Manufacturers Institute, *4350 N. Fairfax Dr., #600, Arlington, VA 22203; (703) 243-8555. Fax, (703) 243-8556. Chuck Yuska, President.*
General e-mail, pmmi@pmmi.org
Web, www.pmmi.org

Membership: manufacturers of packaging and packaging-related converting machinery. Provides industry information and statistics; offers educational programs to members.

Privacy

AGENCIES

Federal Communications Commission (FCC), *Wireline Competition Bureau, 445 12th St. S.W. 20554; (202) 418-1500. Fax, (202) 418-2825. William Maher, Chief.*
Web, www.fcc.gov/wcb

Creates rules and develops plans for numbering and network service issues, such as abbreviated dialing codes, local access and transport area boundary modifications, and toll-free numbers.

Federal Trade Commission (FTC), *Financial Practices, 601 New Jersey Ave. N.W., MS NJ 3158 20580; (202) 326-3224. Fax, (202) 326-3768. Joel Winston, Associate Director.*
Web, www.ftc.gov

Enforces the Fair Credit Reporting Act, which requires credit bureaus to furnish correct and complete information to businesses evaluating credit, insurance, or job applications.

Office of Management and Budget (OMB), (*Executive Office of the President*), *Information Policy and Technology, 725 17th St. N.W., #10236 20503; (202) 395-3785. Fax, (202) 395-5167. Dan Chenok, Chief.*
Web, www.whitehouse.gov/omb

Oversees implementation of the Privacy Act of 1974. Issues guidelines and regulations.

CONGRESS

House Judiciary Committee, *Subcommittee on the Constitution, 362 FHOB 20515; (202) 226-7680. Fax, (202) 225-3746. Rep. Steve Chabot, R-Ohio, Chair; Crystal Roberts, Chief Counsel.*
General e-mail, Judiciary@mail.house.gov
Web, www.house.gov/judiciary

Jurisdiction over legislation on the release of personal information by government agencies.

Senate Judiciary Committee, *Subcommittee on the Constitution, Civil Rights, and Property Rights, SD-524 20510; (202) 224-4135. Fax, (202) 228-0463. Sen. John Cornyn, R-Texas, Chair; James Ho, Chief Counsel.*
Web, Judiciary.senate.gov/subcommittees/constitution.cfm

Jurisdiction over legislation on the release of personal information by government agencies.

NONPROFIT

American Society for Industrial Security,
*1625 Prince St., Alexandria, VA 22314; (703) 519-6200.
Fax, (703) 519-6298. Michael Stack, Executive Director.
Web, www.asisonline.org*

Membership: security professionals worldwide. Interests include all aspects of security, with emphases on counterterrorism, computer security, privacy issues, government security, and the availability of job-related information for employers determining an employee's suitability for employment.

Assn. of Direct Response Fundraising Counsel,
*1612 K St. N.W., #510 20006-2802; (202) 293-9640. Fax,
(202) 887-9699. Robert S. Tigner, General Counsel.
General e-mail, adrfco@aol.com*

Membership: businesses in the direct response fundraising industry. Establishes standards of ethical practice in such areas as ownership of direct mail donor lists and mandatory disclosures by fundraising counsel. Educates nonprofit organizations and the public on direct mail fundraising.

Center for Democracy and Technology, *1634 Eye St.
N.W., #1100 20006; (202) 637-9800. Fax, (202) 637-0968.
James Dempsey, Executive Director.
General e-mail, info@cdt.org
Web, www.cdt.org*

Promotes civil liberties and democratic values in new computer and communications media, both in the United States and abroad. Interests include free speech, privacy, freedom of information, electronic commerce, and design of the information infrastructure. Monitors legislation and regulations.

Communications Workers of America, *501 3rd St.
N.W. 20001; (202) 434-1100. Fax, (202) 434-1279. Morton Bahr, President.
Web, www.cwa-union.org*

Membership: telecommunications, broadcast, and printing and publishing workers. Opposes electronic monitoring of productivity, eavesdropping by employers, and misuse of drug and polygraph tests.

Consumers Union of the United States, *Washington
Office, 1666 Connecticut Ave. N.W., #310 20009; (202)
462-6262. Fax, (202) 265-9548. Gene Kimmelman,
Director.
Web, www.consumersunion.org*

Consumer advocacy group active in protecting the privacy of consumers. Interests include credit report accuracy. (Headquarters in Yonkers, N.Y.)

Direct Marketing Assn., *Ethics and Consumer
Affairs: Government Affairs, Washington Office, 1111
19th St. N.W., #1100 20036; (202) 955-5030. Fax, (202)
955-0085. Jerry Cerasale, Senior Vice President.
Web, www.the-dma.org*

Membership: telemarketers; users, creators, and producers of direct mail; and suppliers to the industry. Evaluates direct marketing methods that make use of personal consumer information. Offers free service whereby consumers may remove their names from national mailing and telephone marketing lists. (Headquarters in New York.)

Electronic Privacy Information Center, *1718 Connecticut Ave. N.W., #200 20009; (202) 483-1140. Fax,
(202) 483-1248. Marc Rotenberg, Director.
General e-mail, info@epic.org
Web, www.epic.org*

Public interest research center. Conducts research and conferences on domestic and international civil liberties issues, including privacy, free speech, information access, computer security, and encryption; litigates cases. Monitors legislation and regulations.

National Assn. of State Utility Consumer Advocates, *8380 Colesville Rd., #101, Silver Spring, MD
20910; (301) 589-6313. Fax, (301) 589-6380. Charles
Acquard, Executive Director.
General e-mail, nasuca@nasuca.org
Web, www.nasuca.org*

Membership: public advocate offices authorized by states to represent ratepayer interests before state and federal utility regulatory commissions. Supports privacy protection for telephone customers.

National Consumers League, *1701 K St. N.W., #1200
20006; (202) 835-3323. Fax, (202) 835-0747. Linda F.
Golodner, President.
Web, www.nclnet.org*

Advocacy group concerned with privacy rights of consumers. Interests include credit and financial records, medical records, direct marketing, telecommunications, and workplace privacy.

U.S. Public Interest Research Group (USPIRG),
*218 D St. S.E. 20003; (202) 546-9707. Fax, (202) 546-
2461. Gene Karpinski, Executive Director.
General e-mail, uspirg@pirg.org
Web, www.uspirg.org*

Coordinates grassroots efforts to advance consumer protection laws. Works for the protection of privacy rights, particularly in the area of fair credit reporting.

Product Safety, Testing

AGENCIES

Consumer Product Safety Commission (CPSC),
4330 East-West Hwy., #519, Bethesda, MD 20814 (mailing address: Washington, DC 20207-0001); (301) 504-6816. Fax, (301) 504-0124. Hal Stratton, Chair; Thomas W. Murr, Executive Director. Information, (301) 504-7908. Library, (301) 504-0000. TTY, (800) 638-8270. Locator, (301) 504-6816. Product safety hotline, (800) 638-2772.
General e-mail, info@cpsc.gov
Web, www.cpsc.gov

Establishes and enforces product safety standards; collects data; studies the causes and prevention of product-related injuries; identifies hazardous products, including imports, and recalls them from the marketplace. Library open to the public.

Consumer Product Safety Commission (CPSC),
Compliance, *4330 East-West Hwy., #610, Bethesda, MD 20814; (301) 504-7912. Fax, (301) 504-0359. Alan H. Schoem, Director.*
Web, www.cpsc.gov

Identifies and acts on any defective consumer product already in distribution; conducts surveillance and enforcement programs to ensure industry compliance with existing safety standards; works to ensure that products imported to the United States comply with existing safety standards; conducts enforcement litigation. Participates in developing standards to ensure that the final result is enforceable; monitors recall of defective products and issues warnings to consumers when appropriate.

Consumer Product Safety Commission (CPSC),
Engineering Sciences, *4330 East-West Hwy., #611, Bethesda, MD 20814; (301) 504-7918. Fax, (301) 504-0533. Hugh M. McLaurin, Associate Executive Director.*
Web, www.cpsc.gov

Develops and evaluates consumer product safety standards, test methods, performance criteria, design specifications, and quality standards; conducts and evaluates engineering tests. Collects scientific and technical data to determine potential hazards of consumer products.

Consumer Product Safety Commission (CPSC),
Health Sciences, *4330 East-West Hwy., #600, Bethesda, MD 20814; (301) 504-7919. Fax, (301) 504-0079. Mary Ann Danello, Associate Executive Director.*
Web, www.cpsc.gov

Collects data on consumer product-related hazards and potential hazards; determines the frequency, severity, and distribution of various types of injuries and investigates their causes; assesses the effects of product safety standards and programs on consumer injuries; conducts epidemiological studies and research in the field of consumer product-related injuries.

National Injury Information Clearinghouse *(Consumer Product Safety Commission),* *4330 East-West Hwy., Bethesda, MD 20814; (301) 504-0424. Fax, (301) 504-0124. Ann DeTemple, Director. Fax-on-demand, (301) 504-0051. To report consumer product-related accidents or injuries, (800) 638-2772.*
General e-mail, clearinghouse@cpsc.gov
Web, www.cpsc.gov

Analyzes types and frequency of injuries resulting from consumer and recreational products. Collects injury information from consumer complaints, investigations, coroners' reports, death certificates, newspaper clippings, and statistically selected hospital emergency rooms nationwide.

NONPROFIT

American Academy of Pediatrics, *Washington Office, 601 13th St. N.W., #400N 20005; (202) 347-8600. Fax, (202) 393-6137. Jackie Noyes, Director. Information, (800) 336-5475.*
General e-mail, kids1st@aap.org
Web, www.aap.org

Promotes legislation and regulations concerning child health and safety. Committee on Injury and Poison Prevention drafts policy statements and publishes information on toy safety, poisons, and other issues that affect children and adolescents. (Headquarters in Elk Grove Village, Ill.)

Cosmetic Ingredient Review, *1101 17th St. N.W., #310 20036-4702; (202) 331-0651. Fax, (202) 331-0088. F. Alan Andersen, Director.*
General e-mail, cirinfo@cir-safety.org
Web, www.cir-safety.org

Voluntary self-regulatory program funded by the Cosmetic, Toiletry, and Fragrance Assn. Reviews and evaluates published and unpublished data to assess the safety of cosmetic ingredients.

Product Liability Alliance, *Government Relations, 1725 K St. N.W., #300 20006; (202) 872-0885. Fax, (202) 785-0586. James A. Anderson Jr., Vice President.*
Web, www.naw.org

Membership: manufacturers, product sellers and their insurers, and trade associations. Promotes enactment of federal product liability tort reform legislation.

Tobacco

AGENCIES

Alcohol and Tobacco Tax and Trade Bureau (TTB), *(Treasury Dept.),* *650 Massachusetts Ave. N.W. 20226; (202) 927-5000. Fax, (202) 927-5611. Arthur J. Libertucci, Administrator. Press, (202) 927-8262.*
Web, www.ttb.gov

Enforces and administers existing federal laws and tax code provisions relating to the production and taxation of tobacco.

Centers for Disease Control and Prevention *(Health and Human Services Dept.), Smoking and Health/Liaison,* *200 Independence Ave. S.W., #317B 20201; (202) 205-8500. Fax, (202) 205-8313. Alison Kelly, Director (Acting).*
Web, www.cdc.gov/tobacco

Produces and issues the surgeon general's annual report on smoking and health; conducts public information and education programs on smoking and health. Conducts epidemiological studies, surveys, and analyses on tobacco use. Serves as liaison between governmental and nongovernmental organizations that work on tobacco initiatives.

Federal Trade Commission (FTC), *Advertising Practices,* *601 Pennsylvania Ave. N.W., #S4002 20580; (202) 326-3090. Fax, (202) 326-3259. Mary Engle, Associate Director (Acting).*
Web, www.ftc.gov

Regulates advertising of tobacco products under the Federal Cigarette Labeling and Advertising Act and the Comprehensive Smokeless Tobacco Health Education Act. Regulates labeling and advertising of tobacco products; administers health warnings on packages; monitors and tests claims on tobacco products for validity. Works with the Justice Dept. in enforcing the ban on tobacco advertising in the broadcast media; investigates deceptive claims and violations of laws and may refer violations to the Justice Dept. for criminal prosecution.

NONPROFIT

Action on Smoking and Health (ASH), *2013 H St. N.W. 20006; (202) 659-4310. Fax, (202) 833-3921. John F. Banzhaf III, Executive Director.*
General e-mail, vd@ash.org
Web, www.ash.org

Educational and legal organization that works to protect nonsmokers from cigarette smoking; provides information about smoking hazards and nonsmokers' rights.

Bakery, Confectionery, Tobacco Workers, and Grain Millers International Union, *10401 Connecticut Ave., Kensington, MD 20895; (301) 933-8600. Fax, (301) 946-8452. Frank Hurt, President.*
Web, www.bctgm.org

Membership: approximately 120,000 workers from the bakery, grain miller, and tobacco industries. Helps members negotiate pay, benefits, and better working conditions; conducts training programs and workshops. Monitors legislation and regulations. (Affiliated with the AFL-CIO.)

National Center for Tobacco-Free Kids, *1400 Eye St. N.W., #1200 20005; (202) 296-5469. Fax, (202) 296-5427. Matthew Myers, President. Information, (800) 803-7178.*
Web, www.tobaccofreekids.org

Seeks to reduce tobacco use by children through public policy change and educational programs. Provides technical assistance to state and local programs.

PHILANTHROPY, PUBLIC SERVICE, AND VOLUNTARISM

AGENCIES

AmeriCorps *(Corporation for National and Community Service),* *1201 New York Ave. N.W. 20525; (202) 606-5000. Fax, (202) 565-2784. Rosie Mauk, Director. TTY, (800) 833-3722. Volunteer recruiting information, (800) 942-2677.*
General e-mail, questions@americorps.org
Web, www.americorps.org

Provides Americans age seventeen or older with opportunities to serve their communities on a full- or part-time basis. Participants work in the areas of education, public safety, human needs, and the environment and earn education awards for college or vocational training.

AmeriCorps *(Corporation for National and Community Service), National Civilian Community Corps,* *1201 New York Ave. N.W. 20525; (202) 606-5000. Fax, (202) 565-2792. Wendy Zenker, Director. TTY, (800) 833-3722. Volunteer recruiting information, (800) 942-2677.*
General e-mail, questions@americorps.org
Web, www.americorps.org/nccc

Provides a 10-month residential service and leadership program for men and women between the ages of eighteen and twenty-four of all social, economic, and educational backgrounds. Works to restore and preserve the environment. Members provide intensive disaster relief, fight forest fires, and restore homes and habitats after natural disasters.

AmeriCorps *(Corporation for National and Community Service), State and National Program, 1201 New York Ave. N.W. 20525; (202) 606-5000. John Foster-Bey, Director. Information, (800) 942-2677. TTY, (800) 833-3722.*
General e-mail, questions@americorps.org
Web, www.americorps.org

Administers and oversees Americorps funding that is distributed to governor-appointed state commissions, which distribute grants to local organizations and to national organizations such as Habitat for Humanity.

AmeriCorps *(Corporation for National and Community Service), Volunteers in Service to America (VISTA), 1201 New York Ave. N.W. 20525; (202) 606-5000. Fax, (202) 565-2789. David Caprara, Director. TTY, (800) 833-3722. Volunteer recruiting information, (800) 942-2677.*
General e-mail, questions@americorps.org
Web, www.americorps.org/vista

Assigns full-time volunteers to public and private nonprofit organizations for one year to alleviate poverty in local communities. Volunteers receive stipends.

Corporation for National and Community Service, *1201 New York Ave. N.W. 20525; (202) 606-5000. Fax, (202) 565-2799. Leslie Lenkowsky, Chief Executive Officer. TTY, (800) 833-3722. Volunteer recruiting information, (800) 942-2677.*
General e-mail, webmaster@cns.gov
Web, www.cns.gov

Independent corporation that administers federally sponsored domestic volunteer programs to provide disadvantaged citizens with services. Engages Americans of all ages and backgrounds in community-based service. Addresses U.S. education, human, public safety, and environmental needs. Works to foster civic responsibility and provide educational opportunity for those who make a substantial commitment to service. Programs include AmeriCorps, AmeriCorps-VISTA (Volunteers in Service to America), AmeriCorps-NCCC (National Civilian Community Corps), Learn and Serve America, and the National Senior Service Corps.

Learn and Serve America *(Corporation for National and Community Service), 1201 New York Ave. N.W. 20525; (202) 606-5000. Fax, (202) 565-2781. Amy Cohen, Director. TTY, (800) 833-3722. Volunteer recruiting information, (800) 942-2677.*

Coordinates school-based community service programs, including the K–12 Program, for school-age children; the Higher Education Program, for undergraduate and graduate students; and School and Community-based Programs, which support schools and nonprofit organizations that provide school-age children with community service opportunities.

National Senior Service Corps *(Corporation for National and Community Service), Retired and Senior Volunteer Program, Foster Grandparent Program, and Senior Companion Program, 1201 New York Ave. N.W. 20525; (202) 606-5000. Fax, (202) 565-2789. Tess Scannell, Director. TTY, (800) 833-3722. Volunteer recruiting information, (800) 424-8867.*
Web, www.seniorcorps.org

Network of programs that help older Americans find service opportunities in their communities, including the Retired and Senior Volunteer Program, which encourages older citizens to use their talents and experience in community service; the Foster Grandparent Program, which gives older citizens opportunities to work with exceptional children and children with special needs; and the Senior Companion Program, which recruits older citizens to help homebound adults, especially seniors, with special needs.

Peace Corps, *1111 20th St. N.W. 20526; (202) 692-2100. Fax, (202) 692-2101. Gaddi Vasquez, Director. Information, (800) 424-8580. Press, (202) 692-2234.*
Web, www.peacecorps.gov

Promotes world peace and mutual understanding between the United States and developing nations. Administers volunteer programs to assist developing countries in education, the environment, health, small business development, agriculture, and urban development.

USA Freedom Corps, *1600 Pennsylvania Ave. N.W. 20500; (877) USA-CORPS. John Bridgeland, Director.*
General e-mail, info@USAFreedomCorps.gov
Web, www.usafreedomcorps.gov

Works to engage Americans in meeting community needs. Provides prospective volunteers with information about opportunities to participate in a variety of service programs through the USA Freedom Corps Volunteer Network and Web site, a clearinghouse of volunteer opportunities. Supports nonprofit groups that are looking to recruit and use volunteers. Provides educators with a "Students in Service to America" guidebook. Tracks volunteerism levels among Americans.

CONGRESS

General Accounting Office (GAO), *Education, Work-force, and Income Security,* 441 G St. N.W., #5928 20548; (202) 512-7215. *Cynthia Fagnoni, Managing Director.*

Web, www.gao.gov

Independent, nonpartisan agency in the legislative branch. Audits, analyzes, and evaluates programs of the Corporation for National and Community Service; makes reports available to the public.

House Appropriations Committee, *Subcommittee on VA, HUD, and Independent Agencies,* H143 CAP 20515; (202) 225-3241. *Rep. James T. Walsh, R-N.Y., Chair; Tim Peterson, Staff Director.*

Web, www.house.gov/appropriations

Appropriates funds for programs of the Corporation for National and Community Service.

House Government Reform Committee, *Subcom-mittee on Criminal Justice, Drug Policy, and Human Resources,* B373 RHOB 20515; (202) 225-2577. *Fax, (202) 225-1154. Rep. Mark Souder, R-Ind., Chair; Christopher Donesa, Staff Director.*

Web, www.house.gov/reform

Oversight of the Corporation for National and Com-munity Service.

House Ways and Means Committee, *1102 LHOB 20515; (202) 225-3625. Fax, (202) 225-2610. Rep. Bill Thomas, R-Calif., Chair; Allison Giles, Chief of Staff.*

General e-mail, contactwaysandmeans@mail.house.gov

Web, waysandmeans.house.gov

Jurisdiction over legislation on tax-exempt founda-tions and charitable trusts.

Senate Appropriations Committee, *Subcommittee on Labor, Health and Human Services, Education, and Related Agencies,* SD-184 20510; (202) 224-3471. *Fax, (202) 224-8553. Sen. Arlen Specter, R-Pa., Chair; Bettilou Taylor, Clerk.*

Web, appropriations.senate.gov

Jurisdiction over legislation to appropriate funds for programs of the Corporation for National and Commu-nity Service.

Senate Finance Committee, *SD-219 20510; (202) 224-4515. Fax, (202) 228-0554. Sen. Charles E. Grassley, R-Iowa, Chair; Kolan L. Davis, Staff Director.*

Web, finance.senate.gov

Jurisdiction over legislation on tax-exempt founda-tions and charitable trusts.

Senate Health, Education, Labor, and Pensions Committee, *SD-428 20510; (202) 224-5375. Fax, (202) 228-5044. Sen. Judd Gregg, R-N.H., Chair; Sharon Soder-strom, Staff Director.*

Web, health.senate.gov

Oversight of the Corporation for National and Com-munity Service and domestic activities of the Red Cross.

NONPROFIT

Advocacy Institute, *1629 K St. N.W., #200 20006; (202) 777-7575. Fax, (202) 777-7577. Kathleen Sheekey, President.*

General e-mail, info@advocacy.org

Web, www.advocacy.org

Public interest organization that offers counseling and training in advocacy skills and strategies to non-profit groups interested in such issues as civil and human rights, public health, arms control, and environmental and consumer affairs. Aids groups in making better use of resources, such as access to the media and coalition building.

Arca Foundation, *1308 19th St. N.W. 20036; (202) 822-9193. Fax, (202) 785-1446. Donna Edwards, Executive Director.*

Web, www.arcafoundation.org

Seeks to inform and empower citizens to help shape public policy. Awards grants to nonprofit organizations in the areas of campaign finance reform, U.S. policy with Cuba and Central America, and international labor and education.

Assn. of Fund Raising Professionals (AFP), *1101 King St., #700, Alexandria, VA 22314; (703) 684-0410. Fax, (703) 684-0540. Paulette V. Maehara, Presi-dent. Information, (800) 666-3863.*

General e-mail, afp@afpnet.org

Web, afpnet.org

Membership: individuals who serve as fundraising executives for nonprofit institutions or as members of counseling firms engaged in fundraising management. Promotes ethical standards; offers workshops; certifies members; monitors legislation and regulations. AFP Foundation promotes philanthropy and voluntarism. Library open to the public by appointment.

Assn. of Junior Leagues International, *Washington Office,* 1319 F St. N.W., #604 20004; (202) 393-3364. *Fax, (202) 393-4519. Mary P. Douglass, Senior Associate.*

Web, www.ajli.org

Educational and charitable women's organization that promotes voluntarism and works for community improvement through leadership of trained volunteers;

includes leagues in Canada, Mexico, and Great Britain. Interests include children, women, domestic violence, aging, education, and child health issues. (Headquarters in New York.)

BoardSource, *1828 L St. N.W., #900 20036-5114; (202) 452-6262. Fax, (202) 452-6299. Judith O'Connor, President.*
Web, www.boardsource.org

Works to improve the effectiveness of nonprofit organizations by strengthening their boards of directors. Operates an information clearinghouse; publishes materials on governing nonprofit organizations; assists organizations in conducting training programs, workshops, and conferences for board members and chief executives.

Capital Research Center, *1513 16th St. N.W. 20036-1480; (202) 483-6900. Fax, (202) 483-6902. Terrence M. Scanlon, President.*
General e-mail, crc@capitalresearch.org
Web, www.capitalresearch.org

Researches funding sources of public interest and advocacy groups; analyzes the impact these groups have on public policy; publishes findings in newsletters and reports.

Caring Institute, *228 7th St. S.E. 20003; (202) 547-4273. Fax, (202) 547-3540. Val J. Halamandaris, Executive Director.*
General e-mail, inquiry@caring-institute.org
Web, www.caring-institute.org

Promotes selflessness and public service. Recognizes the achievements of individuals who have demonstrated a commitment to serving others. Operates the Frederick Douglass Museum and Hall of Fame for Caring Americans. Sponsors the National Caring Award and offers internships to high school and college students.

Center for a New American Dream, *6930 Carroll Ave., #900, Takoma Park, MD 20912; (301) 891-3683. Fax, (301) 891-3684. Diane Wood, Executive Director. Information, (877) 683-7326.*
General e-mail, newdream@newdream.org
Web, www.newdream.org

Promotes sustainable consumption; distributes educational materials.

The Congressional Award, *379 FHOB 20515 (mailing address: P.O. Box 77440 20013-8440); (202) 226-0130. Fax, (202) 226-0131. William E. Kelly, National Director.*
General e-mail, information@congressionalaward.org
Web, www.congressionalaward.org

Noncompetitive program established by Congress that recognizes the achievements of young people ages fourteen to twenty-three. Participants are awarded certificates or medals for setting and achieving goals in four areas: volunteer public service, personal development, physical fitness, and expeditions and exploration.

Council of Better Business Bureaus, *Wise Giving Alliance, 4200 Wilson Blvd., #800, Arlington, VA 22203-1838; (703) 276-0100. Fax, (703) 525-8277. Art Taylor, President.*
General e-mail, charities@cbbb.bbb.org
Web, www.give.org

Serves as a donor information service on national charities. Evaluates charities in relation to Better Business Bureau standards for charitable solicitation which address charity finances, solicitations, fundraising practices, and governance. Produces quarterly guide that summarizes these findings.

Council on Foundations, *1828 L St. N.W., #300 20036; (202) 466-6512. Fax, (202) 785-3926. Dorothy S. Ridings, President.*
Web, www.cof.org

Membership: independent community, family, and public and company-sponsored foundations; corporate giving programs; and foundations in other countries. Promotes responsible and effective philanthropy through educational programs, publications, government relations, and promulgation of a set of principles and practices for effective grant making.

Earth Share, *3400 International Dr. N.W., #2K 20008; (202) 537-7100. Fax, (202) 537-7101. Kalman Stein, President. Information, (800) 875-3863.*
General e-mail, info@earthshare.org
Web, www.earthshare.org

Federation of environmental and conservation organizations. Works with government and private payroll deduction programs to solicit contributions to member organizations for environmental research, education, and community programs. Provides information on establishing environmental giving options in the workplace.

Eugene and Agnes E. Meyer Foundation, *1400 16th St. N.W., #360 20036; (202) 483-8294. Fax, (202) 328-6850. Julie L. Rogers, President.*
General e-mail, meyer@meyerfdn.org
Web, www.meyerfoundation.org

Seeks to improve the quality of life in Washington, D.C. Awards grants to nonprofit organizations in seven program areas: arts and humanities, education, health, mental health, law and justice, neighborhood development and housing, and nonprofit-sector strengthening.

Eugene B. Casey Foundation, *800 S. Frederick Ave., #100, Gaithersburg, MD 20877-4150; (301) 948-4595. Betty Brown Casey, Chair.*

Philanthropic organization that supports the arts, education, and social services in the metropolitan Washington area.

Evangelical Council for Financial Accountability, *440 W. Jubal Early Dr., #130, Winchester, VA 22601-6319; (540) 535-0103. Fax, (540) 535-0533. Paul D. Nelson, President. Information, (800) 323-9473.*
Web, www.ecfa.org

Membership: charitable, religious, international relief, and educational nonprofit organizations committed to evangelical Christianity. Assists members in making appropriate public disclosure of their financial practices and accomplishments. Certifies organizations that conform to standards of financial integrity and Christian ethics.

Foundation Center, *Washington Office, 1627 K St. N.W., 3rd Floor 20006-1708; (202) 331-1400. Fax, (202) 331-1739. Anita H. Plotinsky, Director.*
General e-mail, feedback@fdncenter.org
Web, www.fdncenter.org

Publishes foundation guides. Serves as a clearinghouse on foundations and corporate giving, nonprofit management, fundraising, and grants for individuals. Provides training and seminars on fundraising and grant writing. Operates libraries in Atlanta, Cleveland, New York, San Francisco, and Washington, D.C.; libraries open to the public. (Headquarters in New York.)

General Federation of Women's Clubs, *1734 N St. N.W. 20036-2990; (202) 347-3168. Fax, (202) 835-0246. Gabrielle Smith, Executive Director.*
General e-mail, gfwc@gfwc.org
Web, www.gfwc.org

Nondenominational, nonpartisan international organization of women volunteers. Interests include conservation, education, international and public affairs, and the arts.

Gifts In Kind International, *333 N. Fairfax St., #100, Alexandria, VA 22314; (703) 836-2121. Fax, (703) 549-1481. Susan Corrigan, President.*
General e-mail, productdonations@giftsinkind.org
Web, www.giftsinkind.org

Encourages corporations to donate newly manufactured products to domestic and international charities. Works with companies to develop in-kind programs, coordinates the distribution of gifts to nonprofit agencies, collects tax documentation from recipients, and conducts communitywide public relations activities to encourage product giving. Serves schools and health, recreational, housing, arts, and environmental groups.

Grantmakers in Health, *1100 Connecticut Ave. N.W., 12th Floor 20036; (202) 452-8331. Fax, (202) 452-8340. Lauren LeRoy, President.*
Web, www.gih.org

Seeks to increase the capacity of private sector grantmakers to enhance public health. Fosters information exchange among grantmakers. Publications include a bulletin on current news in health and human services and the *Directory of Health Philanthropy.*

Habitat for Humanity International, *Washington Office, 1010 Vermont Ave. N.W., #900 20005; (202) 628-9171. Fax, (202) 628-9169. Thomas L. Jones, Managing Director.*
General e-mail, washingtonoffice@hfhi.org
Web, www.habitat.org

Ecumenical housing ministry that, with the help of volunteers, donors, and its own affiliate offices, builds affordable homes worldwide for low-income persons. (Headquarters in Americus, Ga.)

Independent Sector, *1200 18th St. N.W., #200 20036; (202) 467-6100. Fax, (202) 467-6101. Sara E. Melendez, President.*
Web, www.independentsector.org

Membership: corporations, foundations, and national voluntary, charitable, and philanthropic organizations. Encourages volunteering, giving, and not-for-profit initiatives by the private sector for public causes.

Institute for Justice, *1717 Pennsylvania Ave. N.W., #200 20006; (202) 955-1300. Fax, (202) 955-1329. Chip Mellor, President.*
General e-mail, general@ij.org
Web, www.ij.org

Sponsors seminars to train law students, grassroots activists, and practicing lawyers in applying advocacy strategies in public interest litigation. Seeks to protect individuals from arbitrary government interference in free speech, private property rights, parental school choice, and economic liberty. Litigates cases.

Lutheran Volunteer Corps, *1226 Vermont Ave. N.W., 2nd Floor 20005; (202) 387-3222. Fax, (202) 667-0037. Jennifer Maloney, Executive Director.*
General e-mail, staff@lvchome.org
Web, www.lvchome.org

Administers volunteer program in selected U.S. cities; coordinates activities with health and social service agencies, educational institutions, and environmental groups.

Mars Foundation, *6885 Elm St., McLean, VA 22101; (703) 821-4900. Fax, (703) 448-9678. O. O. Otih, Secretary-Treasurer.*

Awards grants to education, arts, and health care concerns.

Morris and Gwendolyn Cafritz Foundation, *1825 K St. N.W., #1400 20006; (202) 223-3100. Fax, (202) 296-7567. Calvin Cafritz, Chair.*
Web, www.cafritzfoundation.org

Awards grants to educational institutions, arts groups, and social services in the metropolitan Washington area.

National Assembly of Health and Human Service Organizations, *1319 F St. N.W., #601 20004; (202) 347-2080. Fax, (202) 393-4517. Irv Katz, President; Chuck Gould, Board Chair.*
General e-mail, nassembly@nassembly.org
Web, www.nassembly.org

Membership: national voluntary health and human service organizations. Provides collective leadership in the areas of health and human service. Provides members' professional staff and volunteers with a forum to share information. Supports public policies, programs, and resources that advance the effectiveness of health and human service organizations and their service delivery.

National Committee for Responsive Philanthropy, *2001 S St. N.W., #620 20009; (202) 387-9177. Fax, (202) 332-5084. Rick Cohen, Executive Director.*
General e-mail, info@ncrp.org
Web, www.ncrp.org

Directs philanthropic giving to benefit the socially, economically, and politically disenfranchised; advocates for groups that represent the poor, minorities, and women. Conducts research; organizes local coalitions; assists philanthropic groups in other countries. Monitors legislation and regulations.

Points of Light Foundation, *1400 Eye St. N.W., #800 20005; (202) 729-8000. Fax, (202) 729-8100. Robert Goodwin, President.*
Web, www.pointsoflight.org

Promotes mobilization of people for volunteer community service aimed at solving social problems. Offers technical assistance, training, and information services to nonprofit organizations, public agencies, corporations, and others interested in volunteering.

Progressive Policy Institute, *600 Pennsylvania Ave. S.E., #400 20003; (202) 547-0001. Fax, (202) 544-5014. Will Marshall, President.*
General e-mail, ppiinfo@dlcppi.org
Web, www.ppionline.org

Encourages civic participation in solving U.S. problems through voluntary national service, community-based institutions, and public-private partnerships.

Public Allies, *Washington Office, 1120 Connecticut Ave. N.W., #435 20036; (202) 293-3969. Fax, (202) 822-1199. Jay Kim, Executive Director.*
Web, www.publicallies.org

Works in partnership with nonprofit organizations, business, and government to place young adults aged eighteen to thirty in challenging paid positions, provide them with leadership training, and engage them in team projects that serve needs in local neighborhoods. (Headquarters in Milwaukee, Wis.)

United Way of America, *701 N. Fairfax St., Alexandria, VA 22314; (703) 836-7100. Fax, (703) 683-7840. Brian Gallagher, President.*
Web, national.unitedway.org

Service association for independent local United Way organizations in the United States. Services include staff training; fundraising, planning, and communications assistance; resource management; and national public service advertising.

W. O'Neil Foundation, *5454 Wisconsin Ave., #730, Chevy Chase, MD 20815; (301) 656-5848. Helene O'Neil Cobb, Vice Chair.*

Awards grants to Roman Catholic interests providing for basic needs of the poor both nationally and internationally.

Youth Service America, *1101 15th St. N.W., #200 20005; (202) 296-2992. Fax, (202) 296-4030. Steven A. Culbertson, President.*
General e-mail, info@ysa.org
Web, www.servenet.org

Advocates youth service at national, state, and local levels. Promotes opportunities for young people to be engaged in community service. Provides faith-based and community organizations with service and conservation corps and school- and university-based programs with technical assistance; acts as a clearinghouse on youth service.

⚖ PUBLIC INTEREST LAW

AGENCIES

Legal Services Corp., *750 1st St. N.E., 10th Floor 20002-4250; (202) 336-8800. Fax, (202) 336-8959. John Erlenborn, President. Information, (202) 336-8892. Library, (202) 336-8804.*
Web, www.lsc.gov

Independent federal corporation established by Congress. Awards grants to local agencies that provide the poor with legal services. Library open to the public.

CONGRESS

House Government Reform Committee, *Subcommittee on Criminal Justice, Drug Policy, and Human Resources, B373 RHOB 20515; (202) 225-2577. Fax, (202) 225-1154. Rep. Mark Souder, R-Ind., Chair; Christopher Donesa, Staff Director.*
Web, www.house.gov/reform

Oversees operations of the Legal Services Corp.

House Judiciary Committee, *Subcommittee on Commercial and Administrative Law, B353 RHOB 20515; (202) 225-2825. Rep. Christopher B. Cannon, R-Utah, Chair; Ray Smietanka, Chief Counsel.*
General e-mail, Judiciary@mail.house.gov
Web, www.house.gov/judiciary

Jurisdiction over legislation on legal services. Oversees the Legal Services Corp.

Senate Health, Education, Labor, and Pensions Committee, *SD-428 20510; (202) 224-5375. Fax, (202) 228-5044. Sen. Judd Gregg, R-N.H., Chair; Sharon Soderstrom, Staff Director.*
Web, health.senate.gov

Legislative and oversight jurisdiction over operations of the Legal Services Corp.

NONPROFIT

Alliance for Justice, *11 Dupont Circle N.W., 2nd Floor 20036-1213; (202) 822-6070. Fax, (202) 822-6068. Nan Aron, President.*
General e-mail, alliance@afj.org
Web, www.afj.org

Membership: public interest lawyers and advocacy, environmental, civil rights, and consumer organizations. Promotes reform of the legal system to ensure access to the courts; monitors selection of federal judges; works to preserve the rights of nonprofit organizations to advocate on behalf of their constituents.

American Bar Assn. (ABA), *Commission on Mental and Physical Disability Law, 740 15th St. N.W. 20005; (202) 662-1571. Fax, (202) 662-1032. John Parry, Director.*
Web, www.abanet.org/disability/home.html

Serves as a clearinghouse for information on mental and physical disability law and offers legal research services. Publishes law report on mental and physical disability law.

Bazelon Center for Mental Health Law, *1101 15th St. N.W., #1212 20005; (202) 467-5730. Fax, (202) 223-0409. Robert Bernstein, Executive Director.*
General e-mail, bazelon@webcom.com
Web, www.bazelon.org

Public interest law firm. Conducts test case litigation to defend rights of persons with mental disabilities. Monitors legislation and regulations.

Center for Law and Education, *Washington Office, 1875 Connecticut Ave. N.W., #510 20009-5728; (202) 986-3000. Fax, (202) 986-6648. Paul Weckstein, Co-Director. Publications, (202) 462-7688.*
General e-mail, cle@cleweb.org
Web, www.cleweb.org

Assists local legal services programs in matters concerning education, civil rights, and provision of legal services to low-income persons; litigates some cases for low-income individuals. (Headquarters in Boston, Mass.)

Center for Law and Social Policy, *1015 15th St. N.W., #400 20005; (202) 906-8000. Fax, (202) 842-2885. Alan W. Houseman, Director.*
Web, www.clasp.org

Public interest organization with expertise in law and policy affecting low-income Americans. Seeks to improve the economic conditions of low-income families with children and to secure access to the civil justice system for the poor.

Center for Study of Responsive Law, *1530 P St. N.W. 20005 (mailing address: P.O. Box 19367 20036); (202) 387-8030. Fax, (202) 234-5176. John Richard, Administrator.*
Web, www.csrl.org

Consumer interest clearinghouse that conducts research and holds conferences on public interest law. Interests include white-collar crime, the environment, occupational health and safety, the postal system, banking deregulation, insurance, freedom of information policy, and broadcasting.

Disability Rights Education and Defense Fund, *Governmental Affairs, Washington Office, 1629 K St. N.W., #802 20006; (202) 986-0375. Fax, (202) 775-7465. Pat Wright, Director.*

Law and policy center working to protect and advance the civil rights of people with disabilities through legislation, litigation, advocacy, and technical assistance. Educates and trains attorneys, advocates, persons with disabilities, and parents of children with disabilities. (Headquarters in Berkeley, Calif.)

Institute for Justice, *1717 Pennsylvania Ave. N.W., #200 20006; (202) 955-1300. Fax, (202) 955-1329. Chip Mellor, President.*
General e-mail, general@ij.org
Web, www.ij.org

Sponsors seminars to train law students, grassroots activists, and practicing lawyers in applying advocacy strategies in public interest litigation. Seeks to protect individuals from arbitrary government interference in free speech, private property rights, parental school choice, and economic liberty. Litigates cases.

Institute for Public Representation, *600 New Jersey Ave. N.W. 20001; (202) 662-9535. Fax, (202) 662-9634. Douglas L. Parker, Director. TTY, (202) 662-9538.*

Public interest law firm funded by Georgetown University Law Center that studies federal administrative law and federal court litigation. Interests include communications law, environmental protection, and disability rights.

Lawyers' Committee for Civil Rights Under Law, *1401 New York Ave. N.W., #400 20005; (202) 662-8600. Fax, (202) 783-0857. Barbara R. Arnwine, Executive Director.*
Web, www.lawyerscommittee.org

Provides minority groups and the poor with legal assistance in such areas as voting rights, employment discrimination, education, environment, and equal access to government services and benefits.

Migrant Legal Action Program, *1001 Connecticut Ave. N.W., #915 20036; (202) 775-7780. Fax, (202) 775-7784. Roger C. Rosenthal, Executive Director.*
General e-mail, mlap@mlap.org
Web, www.mlap.org

Provides both direct representation to farm workers and technical assistance and support to service providers, such as migrant legal services programs, education programs, and health programs. Monitors legislation and regulations.

National Consumer Law Center, *Washington Office, 1629 K St. N.W., #600 20006; (202) 986-6060. Fax, (202) 463-9462. Margot Saunders, Managing Attorney.*
General e-mail, consumerlaw@nclc.org
Web, www.consumerlaw.org

Provides lawyers funded by the Legal Services Corp. with research and assistance; researches problems of low-income consumers and develops alternative solutions. (Headquarters in Boston, Mass.)

National Health Law Program, *Washington Office, 1101 14th St. N.W., #405 20005; (202) 289-7661. Fax, (202) 289-7724. Lawrence M. Lavin, Director.*
General e-mail, nhelpdc@healthlaw.org
Web, www.healthlaw.org

Organization of lawyers representing the economically disadvantaged, minorities, and the elderly in issues concerning federal, state, and local health care programs. Offers technical assistance, workshops, seminars, and training for health law specialists. (Headquarters in Los Angeles, Calif.)

National Legal Aid and Defender Assn., *1625 K St. N.W., #800 20006; (202) 452-0620. Fax, (202) 872-1031. Clinton Lyons, President.*
General e-mail, info@nlada.org
Web, www.nlada.org

Membership: local organizations and individuals providing indigent clients, including prisoners, with legal aid and defender services. Serves as a clearinghouse for member organizations; publishes directory of legal aid and defender programs.

National Legal Center for the Public Interest, *1600 K St. N.W., #800 20006; (202) 466-9360. Fax, (202) 466-9366. Ernest B. Hueter, President.*
General e-mail, info@nlcpi.org
Web, www.nlcpi.org

Public interest law center and information clearinghouse. Studies judicial issues and the impact of the legal system on the private sector; sponsors seminars; does not litigate cases.

Public Citizen Litigation Group, *1600 20th St. N.W. 20009; (202) 588-1000. Fax, (202) 588-7795. Alan Morrison, Director of Litigation.*
Web, www.citizen.org

Conducts litigation for Public Citizen, a citizens' interest group, in the areas of consumer rights, employee rights, health and safety, government and corporate accountability, and separation of powers; represents other individuals and citizens' groups with similar interests.

Trial Lawyers for Public Justice, *1717 Massachusetts Ave. N.W., #800 20036; (202) 797-8600. Fax, (202) 232-7203. Arthur H. Bryant, Executive Director.*
General e-mail, tlpj@tlpj.org
Web, www.tlpj.org

Membership: consumer activists, trial lawyers, and public interest lawyers. Litigates to influence corporate and government decisions about products or activities adversely affecting health or safety. Interests include toxic torts, environmental protection, civil rights and civil liberties, workers' safety, consumer protection, and the preservation of the civil justice system.

 RELIGION AND ETHICS

NONPROFIT

Alban Institute, *7315 Wisconsin Ave., #1250 West, Bethesda, MD 20814-3211; (301) 718-4407. Fax, (301) 718-1958. Lee Nelson, Chief Financial Officer. Information, (800) 486-1318.*
Web, www.alban.org

Nondenominational research, consulting, and educational membership organization that provides church and synagogue congregations with support and services. Interests include planning and growth, conflict resolution, leadership and staff training, spiritual development, and mission and stewardship. Conducts continuing education programs.

American Assn. of Pastoral Counselors, *9504A Lee Hwy., Fairfax, VA 22031-2303; (703) 385-6967. Fax, (703) 352-7725. C. Roy Woodruff, Executive Director.*
General e-mail, info@aapc.org
Web, www.aapc.org

Membership: mental health professionals with training in both religion and the behavioral sciences. Nonsectarian organization that accredits pastoral counseling centers, certifies pastoral counselors, and approves training programs.

American Baptist Churches U.S.A., *Government Relations, Washington Office, 110 Maryland Ave. N.E., #505 20002-5694; (202) 544-3400. Fax, (202) 544-0277. Curtis Ramsey-Lucas, Director. Information, (800) 222-3872 (also rendered: 800-ABC-3USA).*
Web, www.nationalministries.org

Serves as liaison between American Baptist churches and government organizations. Interests include immigration, foreign and military policy, human services, employment, the environment, and civil rights. (Headquarters in Valley Forge, Pa.)

American Ethical Union (AEU), *Washington Ethical Action, Washington Office, 7750 16th St. N.W. 20012; (202) 882-6650. Fax, (202) 829-1354. Donald Montagna, Leader.*
General e-mail, aeucontact@aeu.org
Web, www.aeu.org

Federation of ethical culture societies in the United States. Interests include human rights, ethics, world peace, health, welfare, education, and civil and religious liberties. Monitors legislation and regulations. (Headquarters in New York.)

American Friends Service Committee (AFSC), *Washington Office, 1822 R St. N.W. 20009-1604; (202) 483-3341. Fax, (202) 232-3197. James H. Matlack, Director.*
Web, www.afsc.org

Education, outreach, and advocacy office for the AFSC, an independent organization affiliated with the Religious Society of Friends (Quakers) in America. Sponsors domestic and international service, development, justice, and peace programs. Interests include peace education; arms control and disarmament; social and economic justice; gay and lesbian rights, racism, sexism, and civil rights; refugees and immigration policy; crisis response and relief efforts; and international development efforts, especially in Central America, the Middle East, and southern Africa. (Headquarters in Philadelphia, Pa.)

American Jewish Committee, *Government and International Affairs, Washington Office, 1156 15th St. N.W., #1201 20005; (202) 785-4200. Fax, (202) 785-4115. Jason Isaacson, Director.*
Web, www.ajc.org

Human relations agency devoted to protecting civil and religious rights for all people. Interests include church-state issues, research on human behavior, Israel and the Middle East, Jews in the former Soviet Union, immigration, social discrimination, civil and women's rights, employment, education, housing, and international cooperation for peace and human rights. (Headquarters in New York.)

American Jewish Congress, *Washington Office, 1001 Connecticut Ave. N.W., #470 20036; (202) 466-9661. Fax, (202) 466-9665. Charles Brooks, Executive Director.*
General e-mail, washrep@ajcongress.org
Web, www.ajcongress.org

Jewish community relations and civil liberties organization. Seeks to combat anti-Semitism and other forms of bigotry in employment, education, housing, and voting. Areas of activity include church-state relations; government involvement in education; public school prayer; gun control policy; constitutional, minority, women's, and human rights; world Jewry; U.S. foreign policy in the Middle East; Arab investment in the United States; and the Arab boycott of Israel. Monitors legislation. (Headquarters in New York.)

American Muslim Council, *721-R 2nd St. N.E., #200 20002; (202) 543-0075. Fax, (202) 543-0095. Yahya Mossa Basha, Chair.*
General e-mail, amc@amconline.org
Web, www.amconline.org
Promotes equal rights and political empowerment for Muslims in the United States. Opposes discrimination against Muslims; fosters cultural understanding and cooperation among organizations. (Plans to merge with the American Muslim Alliance in summer 2003 to form the National American Muslim Federation.)

Americans United for Separation of Church and State, *518 C St. N.E. 20002; (202) 466-3234. Fax, (202) 466-2587. Barry W. Lynn, Executive Director.*
General e-mail, americansunited@au.org
Web, www.au.org
Citizens' interest group. Opposes federal and state aid to parochial schools; works to ensure religious neutrality in public schools; supports religious free exercise; initiates litigation; maintains speakers bureau. Monitors legislation and regulations.

Baptist Joint Committee on Public Affairs, *200 Maryland Ave. N.E., 3rd Floor 20002; (202) 544-4226. Fax, (202) 544-2094. J. Brent Walker, Executive Director.*
General e-mail, bjcpa@bjcpa.org
Web, www.bjcpa.org
Membership: Baptist conventions and conferences. Conducts research and operates an information service. Interests include religious liberty, separation of church and state, First Amendment religious issues, and government regulation of religious institutions.

Baptist World Alliance, *405 N. Washington St., Falls Church, VA 22046; (703) 790-8980. Fax, (703) 893-5160. Denton Lotz, General Secretary.*
General e-mail, bwa@bwanet.org
Web, www.bwanet.org
International Baptist organization. Conducts religious teaching and works to create a better understanding among nations. Organizes development efforts and disaster relief in less developed nations. Interests include human rights and religious liberty.

Becket Fund for Religious Liberty, *1350 Connecticut Ave. N.W., #605 20036; (202) 955-0095. Fax, (202) 955-0090. Kevin J. Hasson, President.*

Web, www.becketfund.org
Public interest law firm that promotes freedom of expression for religious Americans of all faiths. Works to ensure that religious people and institutions are entitled to a voice in public affairs.

B'nai B'rith International, *1640 Rhode Island Ave. N.W. 20036; (202) 857-6535. Fax, (202) 857-6609. Daniel S. Mariaschin, Executive Vice President.*
General e-mail, info@bnaibrith.org
Web, www.bbinet.org
Provides information and coordinates political action on public policy issues important to the international Jewish community. The B'nai B'rith Youth Organization offers educational and leadership training programs for teenagers and counseling and career guidance services. Other interests include community volunteer programs, senior citizen housing, and the security and development of Israel. Partially funds the Hillel: Foundation for Jewish Campus Life, which offers educational, religious, recreational, and social programs for Jewish college and university students. Operates the B'nai B'rith Klutznick National Jewish Museum.

Catholic Charities USA, *1731 King St., Alexandria, VA 22314; (703) 549-1390. Fax, (703) 549-1656. Rev. J. Bryan Hehir, President.*
Web, catholiccharitiesinfo.org
Member agencies and institutions provide persons of all backgrounds with social services, including adoption, education, counseling, food, and housing services. National office promotes public policies that address human needs and social injustice. Provides members with advocacy and professional support, including technical assistance, training, and resource development; disseminates publications.

Catholic Information Center, *1501 K St. N.W. 20005; (202) 783-2062. Fax, (202) 783-6667. C. John McCloskey III, Director.*
General e-mail, books@cic.org
Web, www.cicdc.org
Provides information on Roman Catholicism and the Catholic church. Offers free counseling services. Includes Catholic bookstore and chapel.

Christian Science Committee on Publication, *910 16th St. N.W., #700 20006; (202) 857-0427. Fax, (202) 331-0587. Robert D. Miller, Federal Representative.*
Public service organization that provides information on the religious convictions and practices of Christian Scientists; maintains a speakers bureau. Monitors legislation and regulations.

Church of the Brethren, *Washington Office,*
337 North Carolina Ave. S.E. 20003; (202) 546-3202. Fax,
(202) 544-5852. Greg Laszakovits, Coordinator.
General e-mail, washington_office_gb@brethren.org
Web, www.brethren.org/genbd/washofc

Organizes and coordinates political activities on
social policy issues of concern to the church. Interests
include military spending; civil rights and liberties;
health care; conditions for the poor; refugees and immigrants; world hunger; conditions in the Middle East,
Sudan, and Central America; and religious freedom.
Sponsors seminars. (Headquarters in Elgin, Ill.)

Churches' Center for Theology and Public Policy,
*4500 Massachusetts Ave. N.W. 20016-5690; (202) 885-
8648. Fax, (202) 885-8559. Barbara G. Green, Director.*
General e-mail, cctpp@wesleysem.edu

Studies the effect of Christian faith on political life
and public policy. Interests include arms control and disarmament, health care, minority rights, and world political economy. Sponsors the Nuclear Reduction/Disarma-
ment Initiative.

Episcopal Church, *Government Relations, 110 Maryland Ave. N.E., #309 20002; (202) 547-7300. Fax, (202)
547-4457. Thomas Hart, Director.*
Web, www.episcopalchurch.org/eppn

Informs Congress, the executive branch, and govern-
mental agencies about the actions and resolutions of the
Episcopal church. Monitors legislation and regulations.
(Headquarters in New York.)

Ethics and Public Policy Center, *Religion and Society
Program, 1015 15th St. N.W., #900 20005; (202) 682-1200.
Fax, (202) 408-0632. Hillel Fradkin, President (Acting).*
General e-mail, ethics@eppc.org
Web, www.eppc.org

Considers implications of Judeo-Christian moral tradition for domestic and foreign policy making.

Evangelical Lutheran Church in America, *Governmental Affairs, 122 C St. N.W., #125 20001; (202) 783-
7507. Fax, (202) 783-7502. Vacant, Director.*
General e-mail, loga@ecunet.org
Web, www.loga.org

Monitors and responds to legislation and regulations
on public policy issues of interest to the Lutheran
church, especially those of poor and oppressed people.
(Headquarters in Chicago, Ill.)

**Friends Committee on National Legislation
(FCNL),** *245 2nd St. N.E. 20002-5795; (202) 547-6000.
Fax, (202) 547-6019. Joe Volk, Executive Secretary.
Recorded information, (202) 547-4343.*

General e-mail, fcnl@fcnl.org
Web, www.fcnl.org

Advocates for economic justice, world disarmament,
international cooperation, and religious rights. Advocates on behalf of native Americans in such areas as
treaty rights, self-determination, and U.S. trust responsibilities. Conducts research and education activities
through the FCNL Education Fund. Opposes the death
penalty. Monitors national legislation and policy. Affiliated with the Religious Society of Friends (Quakers).

**General Board of Church and Society of the
United Methodist Church,** *100 Maryland Ave. N.E.
20002; (202) 488-5600. Fax, (202) 488-5619. James Win-
kler, General Secretary.*
General e-mail, gbcs@umc-gbcs.org
Web, www.umc-gbcs.org

Conducts research on social, political, and economic
issues. Interests include social welfare, the environment,
civil liberties, criminal justice, and foreign policy; assists
member churches.

General Conference of Seventh-day Adventists,
*12501 Old Columbia Pike, Silver Spring, MD 20904-6600;
(301) 680-6000. Fax, (301) 680-6090. Jan Paulsen, President.*
General e-mail, info@adventist.org
Web, www.adventist.org

World headquarters of the Seventh-day Adventist
church. Interests include education, health care, humanitarian relief, and development. Supplies educational
tools for the blind and the hearing-impaired. Operates
schools worldwide. Organizes community service-
oriented youth groups.

Institute on Religion and Democracy, *1110 Vermont
Ave. N.W., #1180 20005-3544; (202) 969-8430. Fax, (202)
969-8429. Diane L. Knippers, President.*
General e-mail, mail@ird-renew.org
Web, www.ird-renew.org

Interdenominational bipartisan organization that
supports democratic and constitutional forms of government consistent with the values of Christianity. Serves as
a resource center to promote Christian perspectives on
U.S. foreign policy questions. Interests include international conflicts, religious liberties, and the promotion of
democratic forms of government in the United States
and worldwide.

Interfaith Alliance, *1331 H St. N.W., 11th Floor 20005;
(202) 639-6370. Fax, (202) 639-6375. Rev. Dr. C. Welton
Gaddy, President.*
General e-mail, tia@interfaithalliance.org
Web, www.interfaithalliance.org

Membership: Protestant, Catholic, Jewish, and Muslim clergy, laity, and others who favor a positive, nonpartisan role for religious faith in public life. Advocates mainstream religious values; promotes tolerance and social opportunity; opposes the use of religion to promote political extremism at national, state, and local levels. Monitors legislation and regulations.

International Religious Liberty Assn., *12501 Old Columbia Pike, Silver Spring, MD 20904-6600; (301) 680-6680. Fax, (301) 680-6695. John Graz, Secretary General.*
General e-mail, 74532.240@compuserve.com
Web, www.irla.org

Seeks to preserve and expand religious liberty and freedom of conscience; advocates separation of church and state; sponsors international and domestic meetings and congresses.

Jesuit Conference, *Social and International Ministries, 1616 P St. N.W., #300 20036-1405; (202) 462-0400. Fax, (202) 328-9212. British Robinson, Director.*
General e-mail, mseneco@jesuit.org
Web, www.jesuit.org/JCOSIM

Information and advocacy organization of Jesuits and laypersons concerned with peace and social justice issues in the United States. Interests include peace and disarmament, economic justice, and issues affecting minorities, especially native Americans, Hispanics, and African Americans.

Leadership Conference of Women Religious,
8808 Cameron St., Silver Spring, MD 20910-4152; (301) 588-4955. Fax, (301) 587-4575. Carole Shinnick, Executive Director.

Membership: Roman Catholic women who are the principal administrators of their congregations in the United States and around the world. Offers programs and support to members; conducts research; serves as an information clearinghouse.

Loyola Foundation, *308 C St. N.E. 20002; (202) 546-9400. Albert G. McCarthy III, Executive Director.*

Assists overseas Catholic mission activities. Awards grants to international missionaries and Catholic dioceses for construction and capital projects.

Maryknoll Fathers and Brothers (Catholic Foreign Mission Society of America), *Washington Office, 4834 16th St. N.W. 20011; (202) 726-4252. Fax, (202) 726-0466. Richard Czajkowski, Regional Director.*
Web, www.maryknoll.org

Conducts religious teaching and other mission work for the poor in Africa, Asia, Latin America, China, Russia, and other countries. (Headquarters in Maryknoll, N.Y.)

Mennonite Central Committee, *Washington Office, 110 Maryland Ave. N.E., #502 20002-5626; (202) 544-6564. Fax, (202) 544-2820. J. Daryl Byler, Director.*
General e-mail, mccwash@mcc.org
Web, www.mcc.org

Christian organization engaged in service and development projects. Monitors legislation and regulations affecting issues of interest to Mennonite and Brethren in Christ churches. Interests include human rights in developing countries, military spending, the environment, world hunger, poverty, and civil and religious liberties. (Headquarters in Akron, Pa.)

National Assn. of Evangelicals, *718 Capitol Square Pl. S.W. 20024 (mailing address: P.O. Box 23269 20026); (202) 789-1011. Fax, (202) 842-0392. Leith Anderson, President (Interim).*
General e-mail, nae@nae.net
Web, www.nae.net

Represents fifty Christian evangelical denominations. Interests include religious liberty; economic policy; church-state relations; public health issues, including HIV and AIDS; and immigration and refugee policy. Monitors legislation and regulations.

National Council of Catholic Women, *1275 K St. N.W., #975 20005; (202) 682-0334. Fax, (202) 682-0338. Susan T. Muskett, Executive Director.*
General e-mail, nccw01@winstarmail.com
Web, www.nccw.org

Federation of Roman Catholic women's organizations. Provides a forum for Catholic women to research and discuss issues affecting the church and society; monitors legislation and regulations. Interests include employment, family life, abortion, care for the elderly, day care, world hunger, global water supplies, genetic engineering research, pornography legislation, and substance abuse. Special programs include volunteer respite care, leadership training for women, mentoring of mothers, and drug and alcohol abuse education.

National Council of Churches, *Washington Office, 110 Maryland Ave. N.E., #108 20002; (202) 544-2350. Fax, (202) 543-1297. Brenda Girton-Mitchell, Director.*
Web, www.ncccusa.org

Membership: Protestant, Anglican, and Eastern Orthodox churches. Interests include racial and social equality; social welfare, economic justice, and peace issues; church-state relations; prayer in public schools; and federal aid to private schools. (Headquarters in New York.)

National Council of Jewish Women, *Washington Office,* *1707 L St. N.W., #950 20036; (202) 296-2588. Fax, (202) 331-7792. Sammie Moshenberg, Director.*

General e-mail, action@ncjwdc.org

Web, www.ncjw.org

Jewish women's education, community service, and advocacy organization. Interests include economic equity for women; reproductive, civil, and constitutional rights; child care; education and welfare programs; Israel; aging issues; and work and family issues. (Headquarters in New York.)

NCSJ: Advocates on behalf of Jews in Russia, Ukraine, the Baltic States and Eurasia, *2020 K St. N.W., #7800 20006; (202) 898-2500. Fax, (202) 898-0822. Mark B. Levin, Executive Director.*

General e-mail, ncsj@ncsj.org

Web, www.ncsj.org

Advocacy group for the organized American Jewish community on issues concerning the former Soviet Union. Works with community and government leadership in the U.S. and in the former Soviet Union addressing issues of anti-Semitism, community relations, and promotion of democracy, tolerance, and U.S. engagement in the region.

NETWORK, *801 Pennsylvania Ave. S.E., #460 20003-2167; (202) 547-5556. Fax, (202) 547-5510. Kathy Thornton, National Coordinator.*

General e-mail, network@networklobby.org

Web, www.networklobby.org

Catholic social justice lobby that coordinates political activity and promotes economic and social justice. Monitors legislation and regulations.

Presbyterian Church (U.S.A.), *Washington Office, 110 Maryland Ave. N.E., #104 20002; (202) 543-1126. Fax, (202) 543-7755. Elenora Giddings Ivory, Director.*

General e-mail, ga_washington_office@pcusa.org

Web, www.pcusa.org/washington

Provides information on the views of the general assembly of the Presbyterian church on public policy issues; monitors legislation affecting issues of concern. Interests include arms control, budget priorities, foreign policy, civil rights, religious liberty, church-state relations, economic justice, and public policy issues affecting women. (Headquarters in Louisville, Ky.)

Progressive National Baptist Convention, *601 50th St. N.E. 20019; (202) 396-0558. Fax, (202) 398-4998. Tyrone S. Pitts, General Secretary.*

General e-mail, info@pnbc.org

Web, www.pnbc.org

Baptist denomination that supports missionaries, implements education programs, and advocates for civil and human rights.

Sojourners, *2401 15th St. N.W. 20009; (202) 328-8842. Fax, (202) 328-8757. James E. Wallis, Executive Director. Information, (800) 714-7474.*

General e-mail, sojourners@sojo.net

Web, www.sojo.net

Membership: Catholics, Protestants, Evangelicals, and other interested Christians. Grassroots network that focuses on the intersection of faith, politics, and culture.

Union of American Hebrew Congregations, *Religious Action Center of Reform Judaism, 2027 Massachusetts Ave. N.W. 20036; (202) 387-2800. Fax, (202) 667-9070. Rabbi David Saperstein, Director.*

General e-mail, rac@uahc.org

Web, www.rac.org

Religious and educational organization concerned with social justice and religious liberty. Mobilizes the American Jewish community and serves as its advocate on issues concerning Jews around the world, including economic justice, civil rights, and international peace.

Unitarian Universalist Assn. of Congregations in North America, *Washington Office, 1320 18th St. N.W., #300B 20036; (202) 296-4672. Fax, (202) 296-4673. Rev. Meg A. Riley, Director.*

General e-mail, uuawo@uua.org

Web, www.uua.org/uuawo

Monitors public policy and legislation. Interests include civil and religious liberties; the federal budget; international and interfaith affairs; human rights; and public policy affecting women, including reproductive rights policy. (Headquarters in Boston, Mass.)

United Church of Christ, *Washington Office, 110 Maryland Ave. N.E., #207 20002; (202) 543-1517. Fax, (202) 543-5994. Ron Stief, Director.*

General e-mail, jpmdc@ucc.org

Web, www.ucc.org

Studies public policy issues and promotes church policy on these issues; organizes political activity to implement church views. Interests include health care, international peace, economic justice, and civil rights. (Headquarters in Cleveland, Ohio.)

United Jewish Communities (UJC), *Washington Office, 1720 Eye St. N.W., #800 20006; (202) 785-5900. Fax, (202) 785-4937. Diana Aviv, Director.*

General e-mail, info@ujc.org

Web, www.ujc.org

Fundraising organization. Sustains and enhances the quality of Jewish life domestically and internationally. Advocates the needs of the Jewish community abroad. Offers marketing, communications, and public relations support; coordinates a speakers bureau and Israeli emissaries. (Headquarters in New York.)

U.S. Conference of Catholic Bishops (USCCB),
3211 4th St. N.E. 20017; (202) 541-3000. Fax, (202) 541-3322. Msgr. William P. Fay, General Secretary. Press, (202) 541-3200.
Web, www.usccb.org

Serves as a forum for bishops to exchange ideas, debate concerns of the church, and draft responses to religious and social issues. Provides information on doctrine and policies of the Roman Catholic church; develops religious education and training programs; formulates policy positions on social issues, including the economy, employment, federal budget priorities, voting rights, energy, health, housing, rural affairs, international military and political matters, human rights, the arms race, global economics, and immigration and refugee policy.

Women's Alliance for Theology, Ethics, and Ritual,
8035 13th St., Silver Spring, MD 20910-4803; (301) 589-2509. Fax, (301) 589-3150. Diann L. Neu, Co-Director; Mary E. Hunt, Co-Director.
General e-mail, water@hers.com
Web, www.hers.com/water

Feminist theological organization that focuses on issues concerning women and religion. Interests include social issues; work skills for women with disabilities; human rights in Latin America; and liturgies, rituals, counseling, and research.

2

Agriculture
and Nutrition

AGENCIES

Agricultural Marketing Service (AMS), *(Agriculture Dept.),* *1400 Independence Ave. S.W., #3071S 20250-0201; (202) 720-5115. Fax, (202) 720-8477. A. J. Yates, Administrator; Kenneth C. Clayton, Associate Administrator. Information, (202) 720-8998.*
Web, www.ams.usda.gov

Provides domestic and international marketing services to the agricultural industry. Administers marketing, standardization, grading, inspection, and regulatory programs; maintains a market news service to inform producers of price changes; conducts agricultural marketing research and development programs; studies agricultural transportation issues.

Agriculture Dept. (USDA), *1400 Independence Ave. S.W. 20250; (202) 720-3631. Fax, (202) 720-2166. Ann M. Veneman, Secretary; James R. Moseley, Deputy Secretary. Information, (202) 720-4623. Recorded news, (202) 488-8358. Locator, (202) 720-8732.*
Web, www.usda.gov

Serves as principal adviser to the president on agricultural policy; works to increase and maintain farm income and to develop markets abroad for U.S. agricultural products.

Agriculture Dept. (USDA), *Board of Contract Appeals, 1400 Independence Ave. S.W. #2916S 20250-0601; (202) 720-7023. Fax, (202) 720-3059. Howard A. Pollack, Chair.*
Web, www.usda.gov/bca

Considers appeals of decisions made by contracting officers involving agencies within the Agriculture Dept., including decisions on contracts for construction, property, and services.

Agriculture Dept. (USDA), *Chief Economist, 1400 Independence Ave. S.W., #112A, Whitten Building 20250-3810; (202) 720-5955. Fax, (202) 690-4915. Keith J. Collins, Chief Economist.*
Web, www.usda.gov/oce

Prepares economic and statistical analyses used to plan and evaluate short- and intermediate-range agricultural policy. Evaluates Agriculture Dept. policy, proposals, and legislation for their impact on the agricultural economy. Administers Agriculture Dept. economic agencies, including the Office of Risk Assessment and Cost-Benefit Analysis, the Office of Energy Policy and New Uses, the Global Change Program Office, and the World Agricultural Outlook Board.

Agriculture Dept. (USDA), *Food, Nutrition, and Consumer Services, 1400 Independence Ave. S.W., #240E 20250; (202) 720-7711. Fax, (202) 690-3100. Eric M. Bost, Under Secretary; Suzanne M. Biermann, Deputy Under Secretary.*
Web, www.fns.usda.gov/fncs

Oversees the Food and Nutrition Service, the Center for Nutrition Policy and Promotion, and the office of the consumer adviser for agricultural products.

Farm Service Agency (FSA), *(Agriculture Dept.), 1400 Independence Ave. S.W., #3086, MS 0501 20250-0501; (202) 720-3467. Fax, (202) 720-9105. James R. Little, Administrator. Information, (202) 720-5237.*
Web, www.fsa.usda.gov

Oversees farm commodity programs that provide crop loans and purchases. Administers price support programs that provide crop payments when market prices fall below specified levels; conducts programs to help obtain adequate farm and commercial storage and drying equipment for farm products; directs conservation and environmental cost sharing projects and programs to assist farmers during natural disasters and other emergencies.

CONGRESS

General Accounting Office (GAO), *Agriculture Issues, 441 G St. N.W., #2T23A 20548; (202) 512-9692. Lawrence J. Dyckman, Director.*
Web, www.gao.gov

Independent, nonpartisan agency in the legislative branch that audits the Agriculture Dept. and analyzes and reports on its handling of agriculture issues and food safety.

House Agriculture Committee, *1301 LHOB 20515; (202) 225-2171. Fax, (202) 225-0917. Rep. Robert W. Goodlatte, R-Va., Chair; Bill O'Conner, Staff Director.*
General e-mail, agriculture@mail.house.gov
Web, agriculture.house.gov

Jurisdiction over legislation on agriculture and forestry in general; agricultural trade matters and international commodity agreements; inspection and certification of livestock, poultry, meat products, and seafood; agricultural research; pests and pesticides; nutrition; and agricultural assistance programs. Oversees Agriculture Dept. operations.

House Agriculture Committee, *Subcommittee on Conservation, Credit, Rural Development, and Research, 1301 LHOB 20515; (202) 225-2171. Fax, (202) 225-0917. Rep. Frank Lucas, R-Okla., Chair; Ryan Weston, Staff Director.*

Web, agriculture.house.gov/cons.htm

Jurisdiction over legislation on rural development; oversight of Rural Utilities Service. Jurisdiction over legislation on soil conservation; small-scale stream channelization, watershed, and flood control programs; water and air quality; and agricultural credit programs.

House Appropriations Committee, *Subcommittee on Agriculture, Rural Development, FDA, and Related Agencies, 2362 RHOB 20515; (202) 225-2638. Rep. Henry Bonilla, R-Texas, Chair; Hank Moore, Staff Director.*

Web, www.house.gov/appropriations

Jurisdiction over legislation to appropriate funds for the Agriculture Dept. (except the Forest Service), the Commodity Futures Trading Commission, the Food and Drug Administration, and other agriculture-related services and programs.

House Government Reform Committee, *Subcommittee on Energy Policy, Natural Resources, and Regulatory Affairs, B377 RHOB 20515; (202) 225-4407. Fax, (202) 225-2441. Rep. Doug Ose, R-Calif., Chair; Dan Skopec, Staff Director.*

Web, www.house.gov/reform

Oversees operations of the Energy, Interior, and Transportation Depts. and the Environmental Protection Agency.

Senate Agriculture, Nutrition, and Forestry Committee, *SR-328A 20510; (202) 224-2035. Fax, (202) 224-1725. Sen. Thad Cochran, R-Miss., Chair; Hunt Shipman, Chief of Staff. TTY, (202) 224-2587.*

Web, agriculture.senate.gov

Jurisdiction over legislation on agriculture, agricultural economics and research, agricultural extension services and experiment stations, agricultural engineering, animal industry and diseases, forestry, pests and pesticides, rural issues, nutrition, and family farms; oversees Agriculture Dept. operations.

Senate Agriculture, Nutrition, and Forestry Committee, *Subcommittee on Forestry, Conservation, and Rural Revitalization, SR-328A 20510; (202) 224-2035. Sen. Michael D. Crapo, R-Idaho, Chair.*

Web, agriculture.senate.gov

Jurisdiction over legislation on family farming and rural development, including rural electrification and telephone development. Jurisdiction includes legislation on irrigation, soil conservation, stream channelization, watershed programs, and flood control programs involving structures of less than 4,000 acre-feet in storage capacity.

Senate Appropriations Committee, *Subcommittee on Agriculture, Rural Development, and Related Agencies, SD-136 20510; (202) 224-8090. Fax, (202) 228-2320. Sen. Robert F. Bennett, R-Utah, Chair; Pat Raymond, Clerk.*

Web, appropriations.senate.gov

Jurisdiction over legislation to appropriate funds for the Food and Drug Administration, Food Safety and Inspection Service, and Food and Consumer Service.

Senate Banking, Housing, and Urban Affairs Committee, *Subcommittee on Financial Institutions, SD-534 20510; (202) 224-7391. Fax, (202) 224-5137. Sen. Robert F. Bennett, R-Utah, Chair; Mike Nielson, Staff Contact.*

Web, banking.senate.gov

Jurisdiction over legislation on economic stabilization and growth, including regulatory relief issues, barriers to development in rural areas, price controls, and asset disposition policies.

NONPROFIT

American Farm Bureau Federation (AFBF), *Washington Office, 600 Maryland Ave. S.W., #800 20024-2520; (202) 484-3600. Fax, (202) 484-3604. Bob Stallman, President.*

Web, www.fb.org

Federation of state farm bureaus in fifty states and Puerto Rico. Promotes agricultural research. Interests include commodity programs, domestic production, marketing, education, research, financial assistance to the farmer, foreign assistance programs, rural development, the world food shortage, and inspection and certification of food. (Headquarters in Park Ridge, Ill., but relocating to Washington, D.C., by Sept. 2003.)

National Assn. of State Departments of Agriculture, *1156 15th St. N.W., #1020 20005-1711; (202) 296-9680. Fax, (202) 296-9686. Richard W. Kirchhoff, Executive Vice President.*

General e-mail, nasda@nasda.org

Web, www.nasda.org

Membership: agriculture commissioners from the fifty states, Puerto Rico, Guam, American Samoa, and the Virgin Islands. Serves as liaison between federal agencies and state governments to coordinate agricultural policies and laws. Seeks to protect consumers and the environment. Monitors legislation and regulations.

National Council of Agricultural Employers, *1112 16th St. N.W., #920 20036-4825; (202) 728-0300. Fax, (202) 728-0303. Sharon M. Hughes, Executive Vice President.*

General e-mail, info@ncaeonline.org

Web, www.ncaeonline.org

Membership: employers of agricultural labor. Encourages establishment and maintenance of conditions conducive to an adequate supply of domestic and foreign farm labor.

National Farmers Union (Farmers Educational and Cooperative Union of America), *Washington Office,* *400 N. Capitol St. N.W., #790 20001; (202) 554-1600. Fax, (202) 554-1654. Thomas P. Buis, Director.*

Web, www.nfu.org

Membership: family farmers belonging to state affiliates. Interests include commodity programs, domestic production, marketing, education, research, energy and natural resources, financial assistance to farmers, Social Security for farmers, foreign programs, rural development, the world food shortage, and inspection and certification of food. (Headquarters in Denver, Colo.)

National Grange, *1616 H St. N.W., 10th Floor 20006-4999; (202) 628-3507. Fax, (202) 347-1091. Kermit W. Richardson, President.*

Web, www.nationalgrange.org

Membership: farmers and others involved in agricultural production and rural community service activities. Coordinates community service programs with state grange organizations.

Rural Coalition, *1411 K St. N.W., #901 20005; (202) 628-7160. Fax, (202) 628-7165. Lorette Picciano, Executive Director.*

General e-mail, ruralco@ruralco.org

Web, www.ruralco.org

Alliance of organizations that develop public policies benefiting rural communities. Collaborates with community-based groups on agriculture and rural development issues, including health and the environment, minority farmers, farm workers, native Americans' rights, and rural community development. Provides rural groups with technical assistance.

Union of Concerned Scientists, *Government Relations, Washington Office, 1707 H St. N.W., #600 20006-3919; (202) 223-6133. Fax, (202) 223-6162. Alden Meyer, Director; Todd Perry, Washington Representative for Arms Control and International Security.*

General e-mail, ucs@ucsusa.org

Web, www.ucsusa.org

Advocates policies to encourage low-input sustainable agricultural practices and to reduce the environmental and health effects caused by conventional agri-

cultural practices and high-chemical inputs. Seeks to evaluate future role, risk, and benefits of biotechnology. Monitors legislation and regulations. (Headquarters in Cambridge, Mass.)

U.S. Chamber of Commerce, *Environment, Technology, and Regulatory Affairs, 1615 H St. N.W. 20062-2000; (202) 463-5533. Fax, (202) 887-3445. Bill Kovacs, Vice President.*

General e-mail, environment@uschamber.com

Web, www.uschamber.com

Develops policy on issues affecting food safety, pesticides, nutrition labeling, and the regulation of biotechnology.

Agricultural Research, Education

AGENCIES

Agricultural Research Service *(Agriculture Dept.), 1400 Independence Ave. S.W., #302A 20250-0300; (202) 720-3656. Fax, (202) 720-5427. Edward B. Knipling, Administrator (Acting).*

General e-mail, arsinfo@ars-grin.gov

Web, www.ars.usda.gov

Conducts research on crops, livestock, poultry, soil and water conservation, agricultural engineering, and control of insects and other pests; develops new uses for farm commodities.

Agriculture Dept. (USDA), *Employment Compliance and Technical Assistance, 1400 Independence Ave. S.W., #6420S, MS 440 20250-9400; (202) 720-7314. Fax, (202) 690-2345. Carol A. Fields, Chief.*

Web, www.usda.gov

Works with state governments to foster participation by minority and disabled individuals and institutions in food and agricultural research, teaching programs, and related areas. Assists the Agriculture Dept. in developing and improving opportunities in agricultural enterprises for minority individuals and institutions.

Agriculture Dept. (USDA), *National Agricultural Statistics Service Census and Survey, 1400 Independence Ave. S.W., #6306 20250-2000; (202) 720-4557. Marshall L. Dantzler, Director. Information, (800) 727-9540.*

General e-mail, nass@nass.usda.gov

Web, www.usda.gov/nass

Conducts a quinquennial agricultural census that provides data on crops, livestock, operator characteristics, land use, farm production expenditures, machinery and equipment, and irrigation for counties, states, regions, and the nation.

Agriculture Dept. (USDA), *Research, Education, and Economics, 1400 Independence Ave. S.W., #216W 20250-0110; (202) 720-5923. Fax, (202) 690-2842. Joseph J. Jen, Under Secretary; Dawn R. Riley, Director of Intergovernmental and Legislative Affairs.*

Web, www.usda.gov

Coordinates agricultural research, extension, and teaching programs in the food and agricultural sciences, including human nutrition, home economics, consumer services, agricultural economics, environmental quality, natural and renewable resources, forestry and range management, animal and plant production and protection, aquaculture, and the processing, distribution, marketing, and utilization of food and agricultural products. Oversees the Agricultural Research Service; the Cooperative State Research, Education, and Extension Service; the Economic Research Service; and the National Agricultural Statistics Service.

Cooperative State Research, Education, and Extension Service *(Agriculture Dept.), 1400 Independence Ave. S.W., #305A 20250-2201; (202) 720-4423. Fax, (202) 720-8987. Colien Hefferan, Administrator. Information, (202) 720-6133. TTY, (202) 690-1899.*

Web, www.reeusda.gov

Conducts educational programs to assist farmers, processors, and others in efficient production and marketing of agricultural products. Conducts educational programs on sustainable agriculture. Serves as national headquarters for the 4-H youth programs and coordinates activities with state and local clubs.

Cooperative State Research, Education, and Extension Service *(Agriculture Dept.), Competitive Research Grants and Awards Management, 800 9th St. S.W., #2256 20024-2240; (202) 401-1761. Fax, (202) 401-1782. Mark Poth, Deputy Administrator (Acting).*

Web, www.reeusda.gov/funding

Administers grants to colleges, universities, small businesses, and other organizations to promote research in food, agriculture, and related areas. Maintains administrative responsibility for programs in aquaculture, small-farm resource development, and higher education.

Cooperative State Research, Education, and Extension Service *(Agriculture Dept.), Science and Education Resources Development, 1400 Independence Ave. S.W., #3312 Waterfront Centre 20250-2250; (202) 401-2855. Fax, (202) 720-3945. K. Jane Coulter, Deputy Administrator.*

Web, www.reeusda.gov

Provides national leadership and coordination on issues relating to food and agricultural research, higher education, and extension; assists colleges and universities in developing and maintaining education programs in the food and agricultural sciences. Seeks to ensure that colleges and universities produce the requisite number of graduates to satisfy the nation's need for individuals trained in the field. Maintains research information system covering all publicly supported agriculture, food, human nutrition, and forestry research.

Economic Research Service *(Agriculture Dept.), 1800 M St. N.W., #5120N 20036; (202) 694-5200. Fax, (202) 694-5792. Susan E. Offutt, Administrator; Demcey Johnson, Chief, Field Crops, (202) 694-5300; Daniel L. Pick, Chief, Specialty Crops, (202) 694-5250.*

Web, www.ers.usda.gov

Conducts market research; studies and forecasts domestic supply-and-demand trends for fruits and vegetables.

National Agricultural Library *(Agriculture Dept.), 10301 Baltimore Ave., Beltsville, MD 20705; (301) 504-5248. Fax, (301) 504-7042. Peter R. Young, Director. TTY, (301) 504-6856. Reference desk, (301) 504-5755, 8:30 a.m.– 4:30 p.m.*

Web, www.nal.usda.gov

Makes agricultural information available to researchers, educators, policymakers, and the public; coordinates state land-grant and Agriculture Dept. field libraries; promotes international cooperation and exchange of information. Interests include food production, nutrition, animal and plant health, rural development, and agricultural trade.

National Agricultural Statistics Service *(Agriculture Dept.), 1400 Independence Ave. S.W., #4117S 20250-2001; (202) 720-2707. Fax, (202) 720-9013. R. Ronald Bosecker, Administrator. Information, (800) 727-9540. Publications, (202) 720-4021.*

General e-mail, nass@nass.usda.gov

Web, www.usda.gov/nass

Prepares estimates and reports on production, supply, prices, and other items relating to the U.S. agricultural economy. Reports include statistics on field crops, fruits and vegetables, cattle, hogs, poultry, and related products.

National Science and Technology Council *(Executive Office of the President), Dwight D. Eisenhower Executive Office Bldg., #430 20502-0001; (202) 456-6101. Fax, (202) 456-6026. Ann B. Carlson, Executive Secretary.*

General e-mail, information@ostp.eop.gov

Web, www.ostp.gov

AGRICULTURE DEPARTMENT

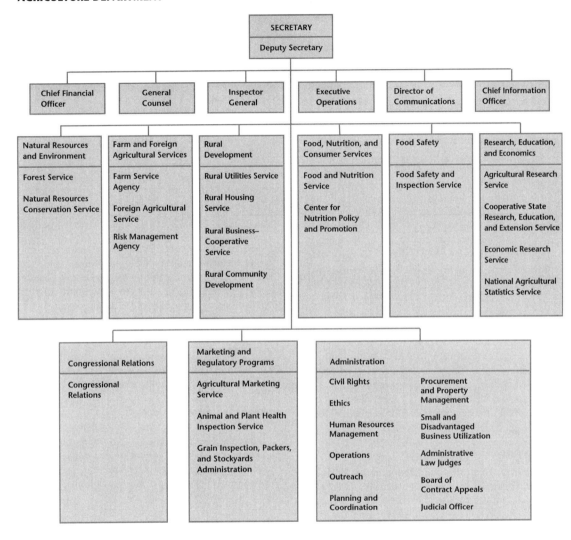

Coordinates research and development activities and programs that involve more than one federal agency. Concerns include food, agriculture, and forestry research.

Rural Business-Cooperative Service *(Agriculture Dept.), Cooperative Services,* 1400 Independence Ave. S.W., #4016S, STOP 3250 20250-3250; (202) 720-7558. Fax, (202) 720-4641. James E. Haskell, Deputy Administrator (Acting).

Conducts economic research and provides technical assistance to help farmers market their products and purchase supplies; helps people living in rural areas to obtain business services through cooperatives.

CONGRESS

House Agriculture Committee, *Subcommittee on Conservation, Credit, Rural Development, and Research,* 1301 LHOB 20515; (202) 225-2171. Fax, (202) 225-0917. Rep. Frank Lucas, R-Okla., Chair; Ryan Weston, Staff Director.
Web, agriculture.house.gov/cons.htm

Jurisdiction over legislation on agricultural research.

House Science Committee, *Subcommittee on Research,* *B374 RHOB 20515; (202) 225-7858. Fax, (202) 225-7815. Rep. Nick Smith, R-Mich., Chair; Peter Rooney, Staff Director.*
General e-mail, science@mail.house.gov
Web, www.house.gov/science/committeeinfo/members/research/index.htm

Jurisdiction over legislation concerning agricultural research and development.

Senate Agriculture, Nutrition, and Forestry Committee, *Subcommittee on Research, Nutrition, and General Legislation,* *SR-328A 20510; (202) 224-2035. Sen. Peter G. Fitzgerald, R-Ill., Chair; Vacant, Staff Director.*
Web, agriculture.senate.gov

Jurisdiction over legislation on agricultural education and research.

INTERNATIONAL ORGANIZATIONS

Consultative Group on International Agricultural Research (CGIAR), *1818 H St. N.W., #G6-601 20433; (202) 473-8951. Fax, (202) 473-8110. Francisco Jose Becker Reifschneider, Director.*
General e-mail, cgiar@cgiar.org
Web, www.cgiar.org

Promotes sustainable agriculture for food security in developing countries; supports a network of sixteen international agricultural research centers. Interests include agricultural productivity, environmental protection, and biodiversity; promotes effective public policy and strong national research programs.

NONPROFIT

Academy for Educational Development (AED), *Social Change,* *1825 Connecticut Ave. N.W., #800 20009-5721; (202) 884-8700. Fax, (202) 884-8701. William A. Smith, Executive Vice President. Information, (202) 884-8000.*
Web, www.aed.org

Conducts studies of international agricultural development on a contract basis; encourages exchange of agricultural information between researchers and farmers.

National Council of Farmer Cooperatives, *50 F St. N.W., #900 20001; (202) 626-8700. Fax, (202) 626-8722. David Graves, President.*
General e-mail, info@ncfc.org
Web, www.ncfc.org

Membership: cooperative businesses owned and operated by farmers. Conducts educational programs and encourages research on agricultural cooperatives;

provides statistics and analyzes trends; presents awards for research papers.

National FFA, *1410 King St., #400, Alexandria, VA 22314; (703) 838-5889. Fax, (703) 838-5888. Larry D. Case, Chief Executive Officer. Toll-free, (800) 772-0939.*
Web, www.ffa.org

Membership: local chapters of high school students enrolled in agricultural education and agribusiness programs. Coordinates leadership training and other activities with local chapters across the United States. Formerly known as the Future Farmers of America. (Headquarters in Indianapolis, Ind.)

National 4-H Council, *7100 Connecticut Ave., Chevy Chase, MD 20815-4999; (301) 961-2820. Fax, (301) 961-2894. Donald T. Floyd Jr., President. Press, (301) 961-2915.*
Web, www.fourhcouncil.edu

Educational organization incorporated to strengthen and complement the 4-H program (for young people ages seven to nineteen) of the Agriculture Dept.'s Cooperative Extension Service and state land-grant universities. Programs include citizenship and leadership training.

Fertilizer and Pesticides

AGENCIES

Agriculture Dept. (USDA), *Natural Resources Conservation Service: Pest Management,* *P.O. Box 2890 20013-2890; (202) 720-7838. Fax, (202) 720-2646. Benjamin F. Smallwood, Specialist.*
Web, www.nhq.nrcs.usda.gov/BCS/pest/pest.html

Formulates and recommends agency policy in coordination with the Environmental Protection Agency and other USDA agencies for the establishment of standards, procedures, and management of agronomic, forest, and horticultural use of pesticides.

Environmental Protection Agency (EPA), *Pesticide Programs,* *1921 Jefferson Davis Hwy., Arlington, VA 22202 (mailing address: 1200 Pennsylvania Ave. N.W. 20460-7101); (703) 305-7090. Fax, (703) 308-4776. Marcia Mulkey, Director. National Pesticide Information Center, (800) 858-7378.*
Web, www.epa.gov/pesticides

Evaluates data to determine the risks and benefits of pesticides; sets standards for safe use of pesticides, including those for use on foods. Develops rules that govern labeling and literature accompanying pesticide products.

Environmental Protection Agency (EPA), *Prevention, Pesticides, and Toxic Substances,* *1200 Pennsylva-*

nia Ave. N.W. 20460-7101; (202) 564-2902. Fax, (202) 564-0512. Stephen L. Johnson, Assistant Administrator. Pollution prevention and toxic substances control, (202) 564-3810.

Web, www.epa.gov

Studies and makes recommendations for regulating chemical substances under the Toxic Substances Control Act; compiles list of chemical substances subject to the act; registers, controls, and regulates use of pesticides and toxic substances.

CONGRESS

House Agriculture Committee, *Subcommittee on Department Operations, Oversight, Nutrition, and Forestry,* 1407 LHOB 20515; (202) 225-2171. Fax, (202) 225-4464. Rep. Gil Gutknecht, R-Minn., Chair; Samuel Diehl, Staff Director.

Web, agriculture.house.gov

Jurisdiction over legislation on environmental policy, including pesticides.

Senate Environment and Public Works Committee, *Subcommittee on Superfund and Waste Management,* SD-410 20510; (202) 224-6176. Fax, (202) 224-1273. Sen. Lincoln Chafee, R-R.I., Chair; Ted Michaels, Staff Contact.

Web, epw.senate.gov/super_108.htm

Jurisdiction over legislation on environmental policy, including pesticides.

NONPROFIT

Beyond Pesticides/National Coalition Against the Misuse of Pesticides, 701 E St. S.E., #200 20003; (202) 543-5450. Fax, (202) 543-4791. Jay Feldman, Executive Director.

General e-mail, info@beyondpesticides.org

Web, www.beyondpesticides.org

Coalition of family farmers, farm workers, consumers, home gardeners, physicians, lawyers, and others concerned about pesticide hazards and safety. Issues information to increase public awareness of environmental, public health, and economic problems caused by pesticide abuse; promotes alternatives to pesticide use, such as the integrated pest management program.

Croplife America, 1156 15th St. N.W., #400 20005; (202) 296-1585. Fax, (202) 463-0474. Jay J. Vroom, President.

General e-mail, webmaster@croplifeamerica.org

Web, www.croplifeamerica.org

Membership: pesticide manufacturers. Provides information on pesticide safety, development, and use.

Monitors legislation and regulations. (Formerly American Crop Protection Assn.)

Entomological Society of America, 9301 Annapolis Rd., #300, Lanham, MD 20706-3115; (301) 731-4535. Fax, (301) 731-4538. Paula Lettice, Executive Director.

General e-mail, esa@entsoc.org

Web, www.entsoc.org

Scientific association that promotes the science of entomology and the interests of professionals in the field. Advises on crop protection, food chain, and individual and urban health matters dealing with insect pests.

Fertilizer Institute, Union Center Plaza, 820 1st St. N.E., #430 20002; (202) 962-0490. Fax, (202) 962-0577. Kraig R. Naasz, President.

Web, www.tfi.org

Membership: manufacturers, dealers, and distributors of fertilizer. Provides statistical data and other information concerning the effects of fertilizer and its relationship to world food production, food supply, and the environment.

Migrant Legal Action Program, 1001 Connecticut Ave. N.W., #915 20036; (202) 775-7780. Fax, (202) 775-7784. Roger C. Rosenthal, Executive Director.

General e-mail, mlap@mlap.org

Web, www.mlap.org

Assists local legal services groups and private attorneys representing farm workers. Monitors legislation, regulations, and enforcement activities of the Environmental Protection Agency and the Occupational Safety and Health Administration in the area of pesticide use as it affects the health of migrant farm workers. Litigates cases concerning living and working conditions experienced by migrant farm workers. Works with local groups on implementation of Medicaid block grants.

National Agricultural Aviation Assn., 1005 E St. S.E. 20003; (202) 546-5722. Fax, (202) 546-5726. Andrew Moore, Executive Director.

General e-mail, information@agaviation.org

Web, www.agaviation.org

Membership: qualified agricultural pilots; operating companies that seed, fertilize, and spray land by air; and allied industries. Monitors legislation and regulations.

National Food Processors Assn., 1350 Eye St. N.W., #300 20005; (202) 639-5900. Fax, (202) 639-5932. John R. Cady, President. Press, (202) 639-5919.

General e-mail, nfpa@nfpa-food.org

Web, www.nfpa-food.org

Maintains an information clearinghouse on environmental and crop protection; analyzes products for pesticide residue. Monitors legislation and regulations.

National Pest Management Assn., *Government Affairs, 8100 Oak St., Dunn Loring, VA 22027-1026; (703) 573-8330. Fax, (703) 573-4116. Robert M. Rosenberg, Director.*
Web, www.pestworld.org

Membership: pest control operators. Monitors federal regulations that affect pesticide use; provides members with technical information.

Horticulture and Gardening

AGENCIES

National Arboretum *(Agriculture Dept.), 3501 New York Ave. N.E. 20002; (202) 245-2726. Fax, (202) 245-4575. Thomas S. Elias, Director. Library, (202) 245-4538.*
Web, www.usna.usda.gov

Maintains public display of plants on 446 acres; provides information and makes referrals concerning cultivated plants (exclusive of field crops and fruits); conducts plant breeding and research; maintains herbarium. Library open to the public by appointment.

Smithsonian Institution, *Botany and Horticulture Library, 10th St. and Constitution Ave. N.W., MRC 166 20560-0166; (202) 357-2715. Fax, (202) 357-1896. Ruth F. Schallert, Chief Librarian.*
General e-mail, libmail@si.edu
Web, www.si.edu

Collection includes books, periodicals, trade catalogs, and videotapes on horticulture, garden history, and landscape design. Specializes in American gardens and gardening of the late nineteenth and early twentieth centuries. Open to the public by appointment. (Housed at the National Museum of Natural History.)

CONGRESS

U.S. Botanic Garden, *245 1st St. S.W., (Conservatory address: 100 Maryland Ave. S.W.) 20024; (202) 225-8333. Fax, (202) 225-1561. Holly H. Shimizu, Executive Director.*
General e-mail, usbg@aoc.gov
Web, www.usbg.gov

Collects, cultivates, and grows various plants for public display and study; identifies botanic specimens and furnishes information on proper growing methods. Conducts horticultural classes and tours.

NONPROFIT

American Horticultural Society, *7931 E. Boulevard Dr., Alexandria, VA 22308-1300; (703) 768-5700. Fax,* *(703) 768-8700. Katy Moss Warner, President. Information, (800) 777-7931.*
Web, www.ahs.org

Promotes the expansion of horticulture in the United States through educational programs for amateur and professional horticulturists. Operates the Gardener's Information Service. Publishes gardening magazine. Oversees historic house and farm once owned by George Washington, with gardens maintained by plant societies; house and grounds are rented for special occasions.

American Nursery and Landscape Assn., *1000 Vermont Ave. N.W., 3rd Floor 20005-4914; (202) 789-2900. Fax, (202) 789-1893. Robert J. Dolibois, Executive Vice President.*
Web, www.anla.org

Membership: wholesale growers, garden center retailers, landscape firms, and suppliers to the horticultural community. Monitors legislation and regulations on agricultural, environmental, and small-business issues; conducts educational seminars on business management for members. (Affiliated with the National Assn. of Plant Patent Owners.)

American Society for Horticultural Science, *113 S. West St., #200, Alexandria, VA 22314; (703) 836-4606. Fax, (703) 836-2024. Michael W. Neff, Executive Director.*
General e-mail, ashs@ashs.org
Web, www.ashs.org

Membership: educators, government workers, firms, associations, and individuals interested in horticultural science. Promotes scientific research and education in horticulture, including international exchange of information.

National Assn. of Plant Patent Owners, *1000 Vermont Ave. N.W., 3rd Floor 20005-4914; (202) 789-2900. Fax, (202) 789-1893. Craig Regelbrugge, Administrator.*
Web, www.anla.org

Membership: owners of patents on newly propagated horticultural plants. Informs members of plant patents issued, provisions of patent laws, and changes in practice. Promotes the development, protection, production, and distribution of new varieties of horticultural plants. Works with international organizations of plant breeders on matters of common interest. (Affiliated with the American Nursery and Landscape Assn.)

Society of American Florists, *1601 Duke St., Alexandria, VA 22314; (703) 836-8700. Fax, (703) 836-8705. Drew Gruenburg, Senior Vice President.*
Web, www.safnow.org

Membership: growers, wholesalers, and retailers in the floriculture and ornamental horticulture industries. Interests include labor, pesticides, the environment, international trade, and toxicity of plants. Mediates industry problems.

Soil and Watershed Conservation

AGENCIES

Farm Service Agency (FSA), *(Agriculture Dept.), Conservation and Environmental Programs,* 1400 Independence Ave. S.W., MS-0513 20250-0513; (202) 720-6221. Fax, (202) 720-4619. Robert K. Stephenson, Director.
Web, www.fsa.usda.gov/pas

Directs conservation and environmental projects and programs to help farmers and ranchers prevent soil erosion and contamination of natural resources.

Interior Dept. (DOI), *Bird Habitat Conservation,* 4401 N. Fairfax Dr., MBSP 4075, Arlington, VA 22203; (703) 358-1784. Fax, (703) 358-2282. David A. Smith, Coordinator.
General e-mail, dbhc@fws.gov
Web, www.fws.gov

Membership: government and private-sector conservation experts. Works to protect, restore, and manage wetlands and other habitats for migratory birds and other animals and to maintain migratory bird and waterfowl populations.

Natural Resources Conservation Service *(Agriculture Dept.),* 1400 Independence Ave. S.W., #5105 20250 (mailing address: P.O. Box 2890 20013-2890); (202) 720-4525. Fax, (202) 720-7690. Bruce I. Knight, Chief. Information, (202) 720-7246.
Web, www.nrcs.usda.gov

Responsible for soil and water conservation programs, including watershed protection, flood prevention, river basin surveys, and resource conservation and development. Provides landowners, operators, state and local units of government, and community groups with technical assistance in carrying out local programs. Inventories and monitors soil, water, and related resource data and resource use trends. Provides information about soil surveys, farmlands, and other natural resources.

CONGRESS

House Agriculture Committee, *Subcommittee on Conservation, Credit, Rural Development, and Research,* 1301 LHOB 20515; (202) 225-2171. Fax, (202) 225-0917. Rep. Frank Lucas, R-Okla., Chair; Ryan Weston, Staff Director.
Web, agriculture.house.gov/cons.htm

Jurisdiction over legislation on soil conservation, watershed programs, and flood control programs.

Senate Agriculture, Nutrition, and Forestry Committee, *Subcommittee on Forestry, Conservation, and Rural Revitalization,* SR-328A 20510; (202) 224-2035. Sen. Michael D. Crapo, R-Idaho, Chair.
Web, agriculture.senate.gov

Jurisdiction over legislation on soil conservation, watershed programs, and flood control programs.

NONPROFIT

American Farmland Trust (AFT), 1200 18th St. N.W., #800 20036; (202) 331-7300. Fax, (202) 659-8339. Ralph Grossi, President.
General e-mail, info@farmland.org
Web, www.farmland.org

Works with farmers to promote farming practices that lead to a healthy environment. Interests include preservation of farmlands from urban development, establishment of safeguards against soil erosion, and agricultural resource conservation policy development at all government levels. Initiates local preservation efforts and assists individuals and organizations engaged in safeguarding agricultural properties.

Irrigation Assn., 6540 Arlington Blvd., Falls Church, VA 22042; (703) 536-7080. Fax, (703) 536-7019. Thomas H. Kimmell, Executive Director.
Web, www.irrigation.org

Membership: companies and individuals involved in irrigation, drainage, and erosion control worldwide. Seeks to improve the products and practices used to manage water resources; interests include economic development and environmental enhancement.

National Assn. of Conservation Districts, 509 Capitol Court N.E. 20002-4937; (202) 547-6223. Fax, (202) 547-6450. Ernest C. Shea, Chief Executive Officer.
General e-mail, washington@nacdnet.org
Web, www.nacdnet.org

Membership: conservation districts (local subdivisions of state government). Works to promote the conservation of land, forests, and other natural resources. Interests include erosion and sediment control; water quality; forestry, water, flood plain, and range management; rural development; and urban and community conservation.

Wallace Center for Agricultural and Environmental Policy at Winrock International, 1621 N. Kent St., #1200, Arlington, VA 22209; (703) 525-9430. Fax, (703) 525-1744. Kate Clancy, Executive Director.

General e-mail, wallacecenter@winrock.org

Web, www.wallacecenter.org

Supports the adoption of low-cost, resource-conserving, and environmentally sound farming methods. Provides scientific information and sponsors research and education programs on alternative agricultural methods. Monitors legislation and regulations.

COMMODITIES, FARM PRODUCE

AGENCIES

Agricultural Marketing Service (AMS), *(Agriculture Dept.), Seed Regulatory and Testing, Bldg. 306, BARC East, #209, Beltsville, MD 20705; (301) 504-9237. Fax, (301) 504-8098. Richard C. Payne, Chief.*

Web, www.ams.usda.gov/lsg/seed/ls-sd.htm

Administers interstate programs prohibiting false advertising and labeling of seeds. Regulates interstate shipment of seeds. Tests seeds for a fee under the Agricultural Marketing Act.

Agricultural Marketing Service (AMS), *(Agriculture Dept.), Transportation and Marketing, 1400 Independence Ave. S.W., #2510S, MS 0264 20250-0264; (202) 690-1300. Fax, (202) 690-0338. Barbara C. Robinson, Deputy Administrator; James A. Caron, Associate Deputy Administrator, Transportation Services, (202) 690-1304.*

Web, www.ams.usda.gov

Promotes efficient, cost-effective marketing and transportation for U.S. agricultural products; sets standards for domestic and international marketing of organic products. Provides exporters with market information, educational services, and regulatory representation.

Agricultural Research Service *(Agriculture Dept.), National Plant Germplasm and Genomes System, 5601 Sunnyside Ave., BLF-4-2200, Beltsville, MD 20705; (301) 504-6252. Fax, (301) 504-6191. Peter Bretting, National Program Leader.*

Web, www.ars-grin.gov

Network of organizations and individuals interested in preserving the genetic diversity of crop plants, including cotton, wheat and other grains, fruits and vegetables, rice, sugar, tobacco, and peanuts. Collects, preserves, evaluates, and catalogs germplasm and distributes it for specific purposes.

Agriculture Dept. (USDA), *Marketing and Regulatory Programs, 1400 Independence Ave. S.W., #228W, MS 0109 20250-0109; (202) 720-4256. Fax, (202) 720-5775.*

William T. Hawks, Under Secretary; Charles Lambert, Deputy Under Secretary.

Web, www.usda.gov

Administers inspection and grading services and regulatory programs for agricultural commodities through the Agricultural Marketing Service; Animal and Plant Health Inspection Service; and Grain Inspection, Packers, and Stockyards Administration.

Animal and Plant Health Inspection Service (APHIS), *(Agriculture Dept.), 1400 Independence Ave. S.W., #312E 20250 (mailing address: Ag. Box 3401 20250); (202) 720-3861. Fax, (202) 720-3054. Bobby R. Acord, Administrator.*

Web, www.aphis.usda.gov

Administers quarantine regulations governing imports of agricultural commodities into the United States; certifies that U.S. exports are free of pests and disease.

Commodity Credit Corp. *(Agriculture Dept.), 1400 Independence Ave. S.W., MS 0601 20250-0601; (202) 720-7711. Fax, (202) 690-3100. Eric M. Bost, Member, Board of Directors, and Under Secretary, Food, Nutrition and Consumer Services.*

Web, www.fsa.usda.gov/pas/about_us/mission.htm#ccc

Finances commodity stabilization programs, domestic and export surplus commodity disposal, foreign assistance, storage activities, and related programs.

Commodity Futures Trading Commission, *3 Lafayette Center, 1155 21st St. N.W. 20581; (202) 418-5050. Fax, (202) 418-5533. James E. Newsome, Chair; Madge A. Bolinger, Executive Director. Information, (202) 418-5080. Library, (202) 418-5255. Locator, (202) 418-5000.*

Web, www.cftc.gov

Oversees the Commodity Exchange Act, which regulates all commodity futures and options to prevent fraudulent trade practices.

Cooperative State Research, Education, and Extension Service *(Agriculture Dept.), 1400 Independence Ave. S.W., #305A 20250-2201; (202) 720-4423. Fax, (202) 720-8987. Colien Hefferan, Administrator. Information, (202) 720-6133. TTY, (202) 690-1899.*

Web, www.reeusda.gov

Conducts workshops on management of farmer cooperatives and educational programs on sustainable agriculture. Provides small farmers with management and marketing programs; offers training and assistance to rural communities and local officials.

Farm Service Agency (FSA), *(Agriculture Dept.),* *1400 Independence Ave. S.W., #3086, MS 0501 20250-0501; (202) 720-3467. Fax, (202) 720-9105. James R. Little, Administrator. Information, (202) 720-5237.*
Web, www.fsa.usda.gov

Administers farm commodity programs providing crop loans and purchases; provides crop payments when market prices fall below specified levels; sets acreage allotments and marketing quotas; assists farmers in areas affected by natural disasters.

Foreign Agricultural Service (FAS), *(Agriculture Dept.), 1400 Independence Ave. S.W., #5071S 20250-1001; (202) 720-3935. Fax, (202) 690-2159. A. Ellen Terpstra, Administrator; W. Kirk Miller, General Sales Manager. Information, (202) 720-3448. TTY, (202) 720-1786.*
Web, www.fas.usda.gov

Promotes exports of U.S. commodities and assists with trade negotiations; coordinates activities of U.S. representatives in foreign countries who report on crop and market conditions; sponsors trade fairs in foreign countries to promote export of U.S. agricultural products; analyzes world demand and production of various commodities; administers food aid programs; monitors sales by private exporters.

Foreign Agricultural Service (FAS), *(Agriculture Dept.), Commodity and Marketing Programs, 1400 Independence Ave. S.W., #5089 20250; (202) 720-4761. Fax, (202) 690-3606. Franklin D. Lee, Deputy Administrator.*
Web, www.fas.usda.gov/commodity.html

Works with nonprofit commodity and trade associations to increase and maintain exports of U.S. agricultural products. Studies and reports on markets for specific commodities and food products, both worldwide and in particular countries; assists with advertising and consumer promotions abroad.

Rural Business-Cooperative Service *(Agriculture Dept.), Cooperative Services, 1400 Independence Ave. S.W., #4016S, STOP 3250 20250-3250; (202) 720-7558. Fax, (202) 720-4641. James E. Haskell, Deputy Administrator (Acting).*

Provides cooperative enterprises that process and market farm products and other cooperatively owned, rural-based industries with technical and research assistance. Helps to develop new cooperatives.

State Dept., *Agricultural, Biotechnology, and Textile Trade Affairs, 2201 C St. N.W., #3526 20520; (202) 647-3090. Fax, (202) 647-2302. Hans G. Klemm, Chief.*
Web, www.state.gov

Negotiates bilateral textile trade agreements with foreign governments concerning cotton, wool, and synthetic textile and apparel products. Develops agricultural trade policy; handles questions pertaining to international negotiations on all agricultural products covered by the World Trade Organization (WTO).

CONGRESS

House Agriculture Committee, *1301 LHOB 20515; (202) 225-2171. Fax, (202) 225-0917. Rep. Robert W. Goodlatte, R-Va., Chair; Bill O'Conner, Staff Director.*
General e-mail, agriculture@mail.house.gov
Web, agriculture.house.gov

Jurisdiction over legislation on emergency commodity distribution. Jurisdiction over legislation on international commodity agreements, foreign agricultural trade of commodities, and foreign market development (jurisdiction shared with House International Relations Committee).

House Agriculture Committee, *Subcommittee on Conservation, Credit, Rural Development, and Research, 1301 LHOB 20515; (202) 225-2171. Fax, (202) 225-0917. Rep. Frank Lucas, R-Okla., Chair; Ryan Weston, Staff Director.*
Web, agriculture.house.gov/cons.htm

Jurisdiction over legislation on farm security and family farming matters.

House Agriculture Committee, *Subcommittee on Livestock and Horticulture, 1432P LHOB 20515; (202) 225-2171. Fax, (202) 225-0917. Rep. Robin Hayes, R-N.C., Chair; Pam Scott, Staff Director.*
Web, agriculture.house.gov/livestoc.htm

Jurisdiction over legislation on livestock, dairy, poultry, meat, seafood, and seafood products.

House Small Business Committee, *Subcommittee on Tax, Finance, and Exports, B363 RHOB 20515; (202) 226-2630. Fax, (202) 225-8950. Rep. Pat Toomey, R-Pa., Chair; Sean McGraw, Staff Director.*
General e-mail, smbiz@mail.house.gov
Web, www.house.gov/smbiz

Jurisdiction over legislation on export expansion and agricultural development as it relates to the small-business community.

Senate Agriculture, Nutrition, and Forestry Committee, *SR-328A 20510; (202) 224-2035. Fax, (202) 224-1725. Sen. Thad Cochran, R-Miss., Chair; Hunt Shipman, Chief of Staff. TTY, (202) 224-2587.*
Web, agriculture.senate.gov

Jurisdiction over legislation on food from fresh waters; inspection of livestock, meat, and agriculture products.

Senate Agriculture, Nutrition, and Forestry Committee, *Subcommittee on Marketing, Inspection, and Product Promotion, SR-328A 20510; (202) 224-2035. Sen. Jim Talent, R-Mo., Chair; Vacant, Staff Director.*
Web, agriculture.senate.gov

Jurisdiction over legislation on food production and distribution for foreign assistance programs under Public Law 480, including the Food for Peace program.

Senate Agriculture, Nutrition, and Forestry Committee, *Subcommittee on Production and Price Competitiveness, SR-328A 20510; (202) 224-2035. Fax, (202) 224-1725. Sen. Elizabeth Dole, R-N.C., Chair; Vacant, Staff Director.*
Web, agriculture.senate.gov

Jurisdiction over legislation on agricultural commodities, including cotton, dairy products, feed grains, wheat, tobacco, peanuts, sugar, wool, rice, oilseeds, and soybeans.

Senate Agriculture, Nutrition, and Forestry Committee, *Subcommittee on Research, Nutrition, and General Legislation, SR-328A 20510; (202) 224-2035. Sen. Peter G. Fitzgerald, R-Ill., Chair; Vacant, Staff Director.*
Web, agriculture.senate.gov

Jurisdiction over legislation relating to food, nutrition, and hunger.

Senate Finance Committee, *SD-219 20510; (202) 224-4515. Fax, (202) 228-0554. Sen. Charles E. Grassley, R-Iowa, Chair; Kolan L. Davis, Staff Director.*
Web, finance.senate.gov

Jurisdiction over some legislation on sugar, including sugar imports. (Jurisdiction shared with Senate Agriculture, Nutrition, and Forestry Committee.)

Senate Small Business and Entrepreneurship Committee, *SR-428A 20510; (202) 224-5175. Fax, (202) 228-1128. Sen. Olympia J. Snowe, R-Maine, Chair; Mark Warren, Staff Director.*
Web, sbc.senate.gov

Jurisdiction over legislation on export expansion and agricultural development as it relates to the small-business community.

NONPROFIT

Agribusiness Council, *1312 18th St. N.W., #300 20036; (202) 296-4563. Fax, (202) 887-9178. Nicholas E. Hollis, President.*

General e-mail, info@agribusinesscouncil.org
Web, www.agribusinesscouncil.org

Works to strengthen U.S. competitiveness in overseas agricultural markets. Promotes cooperation between private industry and government to improve international agricultural trade and development. Sponsors trade missions to developing countries. Helps to establish state and local agribusiness councils. (U.S. affiliate of Agri-Energy Roundtable.)

Agri-Energy Roundtable, *1312 18th St. N.W., #300 20036; (202) 887-0528. Fax, (202) 887-9178. Nicholas E. Hollis, Executive Director.*
Web, www.agribusinesscouncil.org

Membership: companies, international organizations, and affiliated agro-industry associations in emerging countries. International clearinghouse that encourages cooperation in energy and agricultural development between industrialized and developing nations.

American Seed Trade Assn., *225 Reinekers Lane, #650, Alexandria, VA 22314; (703) 837-8140. Fax, (703) 837-9365. Sonny Beck, Executive Vice President (Acting).*
Web, www.amseed.com

Membership: producers and merchandisers of seeds. Conducts seminars on research developments in corn, sorghum, soybean, garden seeds, and other farm seeds; promotes overseas seed market development.

International Assn. of Refrigerated Warehouses, *7315 Wisconsin Ave., #1200N, Bethesda, MD 20814; (301) 652-5674. Fax, (301) 652-7269. J. William Hudson, President.*
General e-mail, email@iarw.org
Web, www.iarw.org

Membership: owners and operators of public refrigerated warehouses. Interests include labor, transportation, taxes, environment, safety, regulatory compliance, and food distribution. Monitors legislation and regulations.

National Cooperative Business Assn., *1401 New York Ave. N.W., #1100 20005-2160; (202) 638-6222. Fax, (202) 638-1374. Paul Hazen, President.*
General e-mail, ncba@ncba.coop
Web, www.ncba.coop

Alliance of cooperatives, businesses, and state cooperative associations. Provides information about starting and managing agricultural cooperatives in the United States and in developing nations. Monitors legislation and regulations.

National Council of Farmer Cooperatives, *50 F St. N.W., #900 20001; (202) 626-8700. Fax, (202) 626-8722. David Graves, President.*

General e-mail, info@ncfc.org

Web, www.ncfc.org

Membership: cooperative businesses owned and operated by farmers. Encourages research on agricultural cooperatives; provides statistics and analyzes trends. Monitors legislation and regulations on agricultural trade, transportation, energy, and tax issues.

U.S. Agricultural Export Development Council, 6707 Old Dominion Dr., #315, McLean, VA 22101; (703) 556-9290. Fax, (703) 556-9301. Annie Durbin, Executive Director.

General e-mail, usaedc@msn.com

Web, www.usaedc.org

Membership: producer and agribusiness organizations. Works with the Foreign Agricultural Service on projects to create, expand, and maintain agricultural markets abroad. Sponsors seminars and workshops.

Cotton

AGENCIES

Agricultural Marketing Service (AMS), *(Agriculture Dept.)*, **Cotton**, *1400 Independence Ave. S.W., #2641, MS 0224 20250; (202) 720-3193. Fax, (202) 690-1718. Norma McDill, Administrator.*

Web, www.ams.usda.gov/cotton/index.htm

Administers cotton marketing programs; sets cotton grading standards and conducts quality inspections based on those standards. Maintains market news service to inform producers of daily price changes.

Farm Service Agency (FSA), *(Agriculture Dept.)*, **Fibers Analysis**, *1400 Independence Ave. S.W., MS 0515 20250-0515; (202) 720-3451. Fax, (202) 690-2186. Scott Sanford, Director.*

Web, www.fsa.usda.gov

Develops production adjustment and price support programs to balance supply and demand for cotton.

INTERNATIONAL ORGANIZATIONS

International Cotton Advisory Committee, *1629 K St. N.W., #702 20006; (202) 463-6660. Fax, (202) 463-6950. Terry P. Townsend, Executive Director.*

General e-mail, secretariat@icac.org

Web, www.icac.org

Membership: cotton producing and consuming countries. Provides information on cotton production, trade, consumption, stocks, and prices.

NONPROFIT

American Cotton Shippers Assn., *Washington Office*, *1725 K St. N.W., #1404 20006; (202) 296-7116.*

Fax, (202) 659-5322. Neal P. Gillen, Executive Vice President.

Web, www.acsa-cotton.org

Coalition of four regional cotton shippers' associations. Monitors legislation and regulations concerning international cotton trade. (Headquarters in Memphis, Tenn.)

Cotton Council International, *Washington Office*, *1521 New Hampshire Ave. N.W. 20036; (202) 745-7805. Fax, (202) 483-4040. Allen Terhaar, Executive Director.*

Web, www.cottonusa.org/index.htm

Division of National Cotton Council of America. Promotes U.S. raw cotton exports. (Headquarters in Memphis, Tenn.)

Cotton Warehouse Assn. of America, *499 S. Capitol St. S.W., #600 20003; (202) 554-1233. Fax, (202) 554-1230. Donald L. Wallace Jr., Executive Vice President.*

General e-mail, cwaa@cottonwarehouse.org

Web, www.cottonwarehouse.org

Membership: cotton compress and warehouse workers. Serves as a liaison between members and government agencies; monitors legislation and regulations.

National Cotton Council of America, *Washington Office*, *1521 New Hampshire Ave. N.W. 20036; (202) 745-7805. Fax, (202) 483-4040. John Maguire, Vice President.*

Web, www.cotton.org/ncc

Membership: all segments of the U.S. cotton industry. Provides statistics and information on such topics as cotton history and processing. (Headquarters in Memphis, Tenn.)

Dairy Products and Eggs

AGENCIES

Agricultural Marketing Service (AMS), *(Agriculture Dept.)*, **Dairy Programs**, *1400 Independence Ave. S.W., #2968 20250; (202) 720-4392. Fax, (202) 690-3410. Richard M. McKee, Deputy Administrator.*

Web, www.ams.usda.gov/dairy/index.htm

Administers dairy product marketing and promotion programs; grades dairy products; maintains market news service on daily price changes; sets minimum price that farmers receive for milk.

Farm Service Agency (FSA), *(Agriculture Dept.)*, **Dairy and Sweeteners Analysis**, *1400 Independence Ave. S.W., #3754S, MS-0516 20250-0516; (202) 720-6733. Fax, (202) 690-1346. Daniel Colacicco, Director.*

Web, www.fsa.usda.gov

Develops production adjustment and price support programs to balance supply and demand for certain commodities, including dairy products, sugar, and honey.

Farm Service Agency (FSA), *(Agriculture Dept.), Domestic Programs, 1400 Independence Ave. S.W., MS-0551 20250-0551; (202) 720-4037. Fax, (202) 690-0767. William March, Chief.*
Web, www.fsa.usda.gov

Administers processed commodities (cheese, feed grains and oils, cereals, and peanut butter) stabilization and price support programs, including purchases and dispositions of processed commodities acquired under price supports.

NONPROFIT

American Butter Institute, *2101 Wilson Blvd., #400, Arlington, VA 22201; (703) 243-5630. Fax, (703) 841-9328. Jerome J. Kozak, Executive Director.*
Web, www.nmpf.org

Membership: butter manufacturers, packagers, and distributors. Interests include dairy price supports and programs, packaging and labeling, and imports. Monitors legislation and regulations.

Egg Nutrition Center, *1050 17th St. N.W., #560 20036; (202) 833-8850. Fax, (202) 463-0102. Donald J. McNamara, Director.*
General e-mail, enc@enc-online.org
Web, www.enc-online.org

Provides information on egg nutrition and related health issues. Disseminates information on cholesterol and heart disease.

International Dairy Foods Assn., *1250 H St. N.W., #900 20005; (202) 737-4332. Fax, (202) 331-7820. E. Linwood Tipton, President.*
Web, www.idfa.org

Membership: processors, manufacturers, marketers, and distributors of dairy foods in the United States and abroad. Provides members with marketing, public relations, training, and management services. Monitors legislation and regulations. (Affiliated with the Milk Industry Foundation, the National Cheese Institute, and the International Ice Cream Assn.)

International Ice Cream Assn., *1250 H St. N.W., #900 20005; (202) 737-4332. Fax, (202) 331-7820. E. Linwood Tipton, President.*
Web, www.idfa.org

Membership: manufacturers and distributors of ice cream and other frozen desserts. Conducts market research. Monitors legislation and regulations.

Milk Industry Foundation, *1250 H St. N.W., #900 20005; (202) 737-4332. Fax, (202) 331-7820. E. Linwood Tipton, President.*
Web, www.idfa.org

Membership: processors of fluid milk and fluid-milk products. Conducts market research. Monitors legislation and regulations.

National Cheese Institute, *1250 H St. N.W., #900 20005; (202) 737-4332. Fax, (202) 331-7820. E. Linwood Tipton, President.*
Web, www.idfa.org

Membership: cheese manufacturers, packagers, processors, and distributors. Interests include dairy price supports and programs, packaging and labeling, and imports. Monitors legislation and regulations.

National Milk Producers Federation, *2101 Wilson Blvd., #400, Arlington, VA 22201; (703) 243-6111. Fax, (703) 841-9328. Jerome J. Kozak, Chief Executive Officer.*
General e-mail, nmpf@aol.com
Web, www.nmpf.org

Membership: dairy farmer cooperatives. Provides information on development and modification of sanitary regulations, product standards, and marketing procedures for dairy products.

United Egg Producers, *Government Relations, Washington Office, 1 Massachusetts Ave. N.W., #800 20001-1401; (202) 789-2499. Fax, (202) 682-0775. Ken Klippen, Vice President.*
Web, www.unitedegg.org

Membership: egg marketing cooperatives and egg producers. Monitors legislation and regulations. (Headquarters in Atlanta, Ga.)

Fruits and Vegetables

AGENCIES

Agricultural Marketing Service (AMS), *(Agriculture Dept.), Fruit and Vegetable Program, 1400 Independence Ave. S.W., #2077-S 20250; (202) 720-4722. Fax, (202) 720-0016. Robert C. Keeney, Deputy Administrator.*
Web, www.ams.usda.gov/fv/index.htm

Administers research, marketing, promotional, and regulatory programs for fruits, vegetables, nuts, ornamental plants, and other specialty crops; focus includes international markets. Sets grading standards for fresh and processed fruits and vegetables; conducts quality inspections; maintains market news service to inform producers of price changes.

Economic Research Service *(Agriculture Dept.),* *1800 M St. N.W., #5120N 20036; (202) 694-5200. Fax, (202) 694-5792. Susan E. Offutt, Administrator; Demcey Johnson, Chief, Field Crops, (202) 694-5300; Daniel L. Pick, Chief, Specialty Crops, (202) 694-5250.*
Web, www.ers.usda.gov

Conducts market research; studies and forecasts domestic supply-and-demand trends for fruits and vegetables.

NONPROFIT

International Banana Assn., *1901 Pennsylvania Ave. N.W., #1100 20006; (202) 303-3400. Fax, (202) 303-3433. Tim Debus, Vice President.*
Web, www.eatmorebananas.com

Works to improve global distribution and increased consumption of bananas; collects and disseminates information about the banana industry; serves as a liaison between the U.S. government and banana-producing countries on issues of concern to the industry.

United Fresh Fruit and Vegetable Assn., *1901 Pennsylvania Ave. N.W., #1100 20006; (202) 303-3400. Fax, (202) 303-3433. Tom Stenzel, President.*
Web, www.uffva.org

Membership: growers, shippers, wholesalers, retailers, food service operators, importers, and exporters involved in producing and marketing fresh fruits and vegetables. Represents the industry before the government and the public sector.

U.S. Apple Assn., *8233 Old Courthouse Rd., #200, Vienna, VA 22182; (703) 442-8850. Fax, (703) 790-0845. Nancy Foster, President.*
Web, www.usapple.org

Membership: U.S. commercial apple growers and processors, distributors, exporters, importers, and retailers of apples. Compiles statistics, including imports and exports; promotes research and marketing; provides information about apples and nutrition to educators. Monitors legislation and regulations.

Wine Institute, *Washington Office, 601 13th St. N.W., #580 South 20005; (202) 408-0870. Fax, (202) 371-0061. Robert P. Koch, Senior Vice President.*
Web, www.wineinstitute.org

Membership: California wineries and affiliated businesses. Seeks international recognition for California wines; conducts promotional campaigns in other countries. Monitors legislation and regulations. (Headquarters in San Francisco, Calif.)

Grains and Oilseeds

AGENCIES

Agricultural Marketing Service (AMS), *(Agriculture Dept.), Livestock and Seed, 1400 Independence Ave. S.W., #2092S, MS 0249 20250-0249; (202) 720-5705. Fax, (202) 720-3499. Barry L. Carpenter, Deputy Administrator.*
Web, www.ams.usda.gov/lsg/index.htm

Administers programs for marketing grain, including rice; maintains market news service to inform producers of grain market situation and daily price changes.

Farm Service Agency (FSA), *(Agriculture Dept.), Feed Grains and Oilseeds Analysis, 1400 Independence Ave. S.W., #3741S, MS-0532 20250-0532; (202) 720-3451. Fax, (202) 690-2186. Phil Scronce, Director.*
Web, www.fsa.usda.gov

Develops production adjustment and price support programs to balance supply and demand for certain commodities, including corn, soybeans, and other feed grains and oilseeds.

Farm Service Agency (FSA), *(Agriculture Dept.), Food Grains, 1400 Independence Ave. S.W., MS-0518 20250; (202) 720-2891. Fax, (202) 690-2186. Thomas F. Tice, Director.*
Web, www.fsa.usda.gov

Develops marketing loan and contract crop programs in support of food grain commodities, including wheat and rice.

Grain Inspection, Packers, and Stockyards Administration *(Agriculture Dept.), 1400 Independence Ave. S.W., MS 3601 20250-3601; (202) 720-0219. Fax, (202) 205-9237. Donna Reifschneider, Administrator. Information, (202) 720-5091.*
Web, www.usda.gov/gipsa

Administers inspection and weighing program for grain, soybeans, rice, sunflower seeds, and other processed commodities; conducts quality inspections based on established standards.

NONPROFIT

American Feed Industry Assn. (AFIA), *1501 Wilson Blvd., #1100, Arlington, VA 22209; (703) 524-0810. Fax, (703) 524-1921. David A. Bossman, President.*
General e-mail, afia@afia.org
Web, www.afia.org

Membership: feed manufacturers and ingredient suppliers. Conducts seminars on feed grain production, marketing, advertising, and quality control; interests include international trade.

American Soybean Assn., *Washington Office*, *600 Pennsylvania Ave. S.E., #320 20003; (202) 969-8900. Fax, (202) 969-7040. John Gordley, Washington Representative.*

Web, www.oilseeds.org/asa

Membership: soybean farmers. Promotes expanded world markets and research for the benefit of soybean growers; maintains a network of state and international offices. (Headquarters in St. Louis, Mo.)

Corn Refiners Assn., *1701 Pennsylvania Ave. N.W., #950 20006-5805; (202) 331-1634. Fax, (202) 331-2054. Audrae Erickson, President.*

General e-mail, details@corn.org

Web, www.corn.org

Promotes research on technical aspects of corn refining and product development; acts as a clearinghouse for members who award research grants to colleges and universities. Monitors legislation and regulations.

National Assn. of Wheat Growers, *415 2nd St. N.E., #300 20002; (202) 547-7800. Fax, (202) 546-2638. Daren Coppock, Chief Executive Officer.*

General e-mail, wheatworld@wheatworld.org

Web, www.wheatworld.org

Federation of state wheat grower associations. Sponsors annual wheat industry conference.

National Corn Growers Assn., *Public Policy, Washington Office,* *122 C St. N.W., #510 20001; (202) 628-7001. Fax, (202) 628-1933. John Doggett, Vice President.*

General e-mail, corninfo@ncga.com

Web, www.ncga.com

Represents the interests of U.S. corn farmers, including in international trade; promotes the use, marketing, and efficient production of corn; conducts research and educational activities; monitors legislation and regulations. (Headquarters in St. Louis, Mo.)

National Grain and Feed Assn., *1250 Eye St. N.W., #1003 20005; (202) 289-0873. Fax, (202) 289-5388. Kendell Keith, President.*

General e-mail, ngfa@ngfa.org

Web, www.ngfa.org

Membership: firms that process U.S. grains and oilseeds for domestic and export markets. Arbitration panel resolves disputes over trade and commercial regulations.

National Grain Trade Council, *1300 L St. N.W., #925 20005; (202) 842-0400. Fax, (202) 789-7223. Jula J. Kinnaird, President.*

Web, www.ngtc.org

Federation of grain exchanges and national associations of grain processors, handlers, merchandisers, distributors, exporters, and warehouse workers.

National Institute of Oilseed Products, *1156 15th St. N.W., #900 20005; (202) 785-8450. Fax, (202) 223-9741. Richard E. Cristol, Washington Representative.*

General e-mail, niop@assnhq.com

Web, www.oilseed.org

Membership: companies and individuals involved in manufacturing and trading oilseed products. Provides statistics on oilseed product imports and exports.

National Oilseed Processors Assn., *1255 23rd St. N.W., #200 20037-1174; (202) 452-8040. Fax, (202) 835-0400. Thomas A. Hammer, President.*

General e-mail, nopa@nopa.org

Web, www.nopa.org

Provides information on soybean crops, products, processing, and commodity programs; interests include international trade.

North American Export Grain Assn., *1250 Eye St. N.W., #1003 20005; (202) 682-4030. Fax, (202) 682-4033. Gary C. Martin, President.*

General e-mail, info@naega.org

Membership: grain exporting firms and others interested in the grain export industry. Provides information on grain export allowances, distribution, and current market trends; sponsors foreign seminars. Monitors legislation and regulations.

North American Millers Assn., *600 Maryland Ave. S.W., #305W 20024-2573; (202) 484-2200. Fax, (202) 488-7416. Betsy Faga, President.*

General e-mail, info@namamillers.org

Web, www.namamillers.org

Trade association representing the dry corn, wheat, oats, and rye milling industry. Seeks to inform the public, the industry, and government about issues affecting the domestic milling industry. Monitors legislation and regulations.

Soy Protein Council, *1255 23rd St. N.W., #200 20037-1174; (202) 467-6610. Fax, (202) 833-3636. David Saunders, Director.*

General e-mail, rpage@spcouncil.org

Web, www.spcouncil.org

Membership: firms that process and sell vegetable proteins or food products containing vegetable proteins. Provides information on the nutritional properties of vegetable proteins.

Transportation, Elevator, and Grain Merchants Assn., *1300 L St. N.W., #925 20005; (202) 842-0400. Fax, (202) 789-7223. Jula J. Kinnaird, Secretary.*
Web, www.ngtc.org

Membership: companies owning terminal elevators. Monitors legislation and regulations concerning grain inspection programs, transportation of grain, and general farm policy.

U.S. Grains Council, *1400 K St. N.W., #1200 20005; (202) 789-0789. Fax, (202) 898-0522. Kenneth Hobbie, President.*
General e-mail, grains@grains.org
Web, www.grains.org

Membership: feed grain producers and exporters; railroads; banks; and chemical, machinery, malting, and seed companies interested in feed grain exports. Promotes development of U.S. feed grain markets overseas.

U.S. Wheat Associates, *1620 Eye St. N.W., #801 20006; (202) 463-0999. Fax, (202) 785-1052. Alan Tracy, President.*
General e-mail, info@uswheat.org
Web, www.uswheat.org

Membership: wheat farmers. Develops export markets for the U.S. wheat industry; provides information on wheat production and marketing.

USA Rice Federation, *4301 N. Fairfax Dr., #425, Arlington, VA 22203-1616; (703) 236-2300. Fax, (703) 236-2301. Stuart Proctor Jr., President.*
Web, www.usarice.com

Membership: rice producers, millers, and related firms. Provides U.S. and foreign rice trade and industry information; assists in establishing quality standards for rice production and milling. Monitors legislation and regulations.

Sugar

Economic Research Service *(Agriculture Dept.), 1800 M St. N.W., #5120N 20036; (202) 694-5200. Fax, (202) 694-5792. Susan E. Offutt, Administrator; Demcey Johnson, Chief, Field Crops, (202) 694-5300; Daniel L. Pick, Chief, Specialty Crops, (202) 694-5250.*
Web, www.ers.usda.gov

Conducts market research; studies and forecasts domestic supply-and-demand trends for sugar and other sweeteners.

Farm Service Agency (FSA), *(Agriculture Dept.), Dairy and Sweeteners Analysis, 1400 Independence Ave.*
S.W., #3754S, MS 0516 20250-0516; (202) 720-6733. Fax, (202) 690-1346. Daniel Colacicco, Director.
Web, www.fsa.usda.gov

Develops production adjustment and price support programs to balance supply and demand for certain commodities, including dairy products, sugar, and honey.

House Agriculture Committee, *Subcommittee on Specialty Crops and Foreign Agriculture Programs, 1336 LHOB 20515; (202) 225-2171. Fax, (202) 225-0917. Rep. Bill Jenkins, R-Tenn., Chair; Pelham Straughn, Staff Director.*
Web, agriculture.house.gov/spec.htm

Jurisdiction over legislation on peanuts, sugar, tobacco, honey and bees, and marketing orders relating to such commodities. Jurisdiction over legislation on foreign agricultural assistance and trade promotion programs in general.

American Sugarbeet Growers Assn., *1156 15th St. N.W., #1101 20005; (202) 833-2398. Fax, (202) 833-2962. Luther Markwart, Executive Vice President.*
General e-mail, asga@aol.com
Web, members.aol.com/asga

Membership: sugarbeet growers associations. Serves as liaison to U.S. government agencies, including the Agriculture Dept. and the U.S. Trade Representative; interests include international trade. Monitors legislation and regulations.

Chocolate Manufacturers Assn./American Cocoa Research Institute, *8320 Old Courthouse Rd., #300, Vienna, VA 22182; (703) 790-5011. Fax, (703) 790-5752. Lawrence T. Graham, President.*
General e-mail, info@candyusa.org
Web, www.candyusa.org or www.eatcandy.com

Membership: U.S. chocolate manufacturers and distributors. Sponsors educational programs; offers grants for cocoa research.

National Confectioners Assn., *8320 Old Courthouse Rd., #300, Vienna, VA 22182; (703) 790-5750. Fax, (703) 790-5752. Lawrence T. Graham, President.*
General e-mail, info@candyusa.org
Web, www.candyusa.org or www.eatcandy.com

Membership: confectionery manufacturers and suppliers. Provides information on confectionery consumption and nutrition; sponsors educational programs and research on candy technology. Monitors legislation and regulations.

Sugar Assn., *1101 15th St. N.W., #600 20005; (202) 785-1122. Fax, (202) 785-5019. Richard Keelor, President.*

General e-mail, sugar@sugar.org

Web, www.sugar.org

Membership: sugar processors, growers, refiners, and planters. Provides nutritional information, public education, and research on sugar. Library open to the public by appointment.

U.S. Beet Sugar Assn., *1156 15th St. N.W., #1019 20005-1704; (202) 296-4820. Fax, (202) 331-2065. James W. Johnson, President.*

General e-mail, beetsugar@aol.com

Membership: beet sugar processors. Library open to the public by appointment.

U.S. Cane Sugar Refiners' Assn., *8215 Donset Dr., Springfield, VA 22152; (703) 451-2235. Fax, (703) 451-6444. Nicholas A. Kominus, President.*

General e-mail, sugarrefiner@aol.com

Membership: U.S. sugar cane refiners. Monitors legislation and regulations.

Tobacco and Peanuts

AGENCIES

Agricultural Marketing Service (AMS), *(Agriculture Dept.), Tobacco, 300 12th St. S.W., #502 Annex 20250; (202) 205-0567. Fax, (202) 205-0235. John P. Duncan III, Deputy Administrator.*

Web, www.ams.usda.gov/tob/index.htm

Administers tobacco marketing programs; sets standards for domestic and imported tobacco; tests imports for prohibited pesticides; conducts voluntary inspections of U.S. tobacco exports; maintains market news service to inform producers of price changes.

Economic Research Service *(Agriculture Dept.), 1800 M St. N.W., #5120N 20036; (202) 694-5200. Fax, (202) 694-5792. Susan E. Offutt, Administrator; Demcey Johnson, Chief, Field Crops, (202) 694-5300; Daniel L. Pick, Chief, Specialty Crops, (202) 694-5250.*

Web, www.ers.usda.gov

Conducts market research; studies and forecasts domestic supply-and-demand trends for tobacco.

Farm Service Agency (FSA), *(Agriculture Dept.), Tobacco, 1400 Independence Ave. S.W., MS 0514 20250; (202) 720-0156. Fax, (202) 690-2298. Thomas R. Burgess, Director (Acting).*

Web, www.fsa.usda.gov

Develops production adjustment and price support programs to balance supply and demand for tobacco.

CONGRESS

House Agriculture Committee, *Subcommittee on Specialty Crops and Foreign Agriculture Programs, 1336 LHOB 20515; (202) 225-2171. Fax, (202) 225-0917. Rep. Bill Jenkins, R-Tenn., Chair; Pelham Straughn, Staff Director.*

Web, agriculture.house.gov/spec.htm

Jurisdiction over legislation on peanuts, sugar, tobacco, honey and bees, and marketing orders relating to such commodities. Jurisdiction over legislation on foreign agricultural assistance and trade promotion programs in general.

NONPROFIT

American Peanut Council, *1500 King St., #301, Alexandria, VA 22314-2737; (703) 838-9500. Fax, (703) 838-9089. Jeannette H. Anderson, President.*

General e-mail, info@peanutsusa.com

Web, www.peanutsusa.com

Membership: peanut growers, shellers, brokers, and manufacturers, as well as allied companies. Provides information on economic and nutritional value of peanuts; coordinates research; promotes U.S. peanut exports, domestic production, and market development.

Cigar Assn. of America, *1707 H St. N.W., #800 20006-3919; (202) 223-8204. Fax, (202) 833-0379. Norman F. Sharp, President.*

Membership: growers and suppliers of cigar leaf tobacco and manufacturers, packagers, importers, and distributors of cigars. Monitors legislation and regulations.

Smokeless Tobacco Council, *1627 K St. N.W., #700 20006; (202) 452-1252. Fax, (202) 452-0118. Robert Y. Maples, President.*

Members: smokeless tobacco manufacturers. Monitors legislation and regulations.

Tobacco Associates, Inc., *1725 K St. N.W., #512 20006-1420; (202) 828-9144. Fax, (202) 828-9149. Kirk Wayne, President.*

General e-mail, taw@tobaccoassociatesinc.org

Web, www.tobaccoassociatesinc.org

Membership: producers of flue-cured tobacco. Promotes exports; provides information to encourage overseas market development.

FARM LOANS, INSURANCE, AND SUBSIDIES

AGENCIES

Commodity Credit Corp. *(Agriculture Dept.),* 1400 Independence Ave. S.W., MS 0601 20250-0601; (202) 720-7711. Fax, (202) 690-3100. Eric M. Bost, Member, Board of Directors, and Under Secretary, Food, Nutrition and Consumer Services.
Web, www.fsa.usda.gov/pas/about_us/mission.htm#ccc

Administers and finances the commodity stabilization program through loans, purchases, and supplemental payments; sells through domestic and export markets commodities acquired by the government under this program; administers some aspects of foreign food aid through the Food for Peace program; provides storage facilities.

Farm Credit Administration, 1501 Farm Credit Dr., McLean, VA 22102-5090; (703) 883-4000. Fax, (703) 734-5784. Michael M. Reyna, Chair. Information, (703) 883-4056. TTY, (703) 883-4444.
General e-mail, info-line@fca.gov
Web, www.fca.gov

Examines and regulates the cooperative Farm Credit System, which comprises federal land bank associations, production credit associations, federal land credit associations, agriculture credit associations, farm credit banks, and one agricultural credit bank. Oversees credit programs and related services for harvesters of aquatic products, farmers, ranchers, producers, and their associations.

Farm Credit Administration, *Examination,*
1501 Farm Credit Dr., McLean, VA 22102-5090; (703) 883-4160. Fax, (703) 893-2978. Roland E. Smith, Chief Examiner. Press, (703) 883-4056.
General e-mail, info-line@fca.gov
Web, www.fca.gov

Enforces and oversees compliance with the Farm Credit Act. Monitors cooperatively owned member banks' and associations' compliance with laws prohibiting discrimination in credit transactions.

Farm Service Agency (FSA), *(Agriculture Dept.),*
1400 Independence Ave. S.W., #3086, MS 0501 20250-0501; (202) 720-3467. Fax, (202) 720-9105. James R. Little, Administrator. Information, (202) 720-5237.
Web, www.fsa.usda.gov

Administers farm commodity programs providing crop loans and purchases; provides crop payments when market prices fall below specified levels; sets acreage allotments and marketing quotas; assists farmers in areas affected by natural disasters.

Farm Service Agency (FSA), *(Agriculture Dept.),* *Farm Loan Programs,* 1400 Independence Ave. S.W., MS 0520 20250-0520; (202) 720-4671. Fax, (202) 690-3573. Carolyn Cooksie, Deputy Administrator.
Web, www.fsa.usda.gov

Provides services and loans to beginning farmers and administers emergency farm loan programs.

Farm Service Agency (FSA), *(Agriculture Dept.),* *Minority and Socially Disadvantaged Farmers Assistance,* 1400 Independence Ave. S.W., MS 0501 20250-0501; (202) 720-1584. Fax, (202) 720-5398. Ronald Holling, Director. TTY, (202) 720-5132. Toll-free, 866-538-2610 (phone); 866-302-1760 (fax); 866-480-2824 (TTY).
General e-mail, msda@wdc.usda.gov
Web, www.fsa.usda.gov/pas/msda.htm

Works with minority and socially disadvantaged farmers who have concerns and questions about loan applications filed with local offices.

Farmer Mac, 1133 21st St. N.W., #600 20036; (202) 872-7700. Fax, (202) 872-7713. Nancy Corsiglia, Vice President.
Web, www.farmermac.com

Private corporation chartered by Congress to provide a secondary mortgage market for farm and rural housing loans. Guarantees principal and interest repayment on securities backed by farm and rural housing loans. (Farmer Mac stands for Federal Agricultural Mortgage Corp.)

Risk Management Agency *(Agriculture Dept.),* 1400 Independence Ave. S.W., #3053S 20250; (202) 690-2803. Fax, (202) 690-2818. Ross J. Davidson Jr., Administrator.
Web, www.rma.usda.gov

Provides farmers with insurance against crops lost because of bad weather, insects, disease, and other natural causes.

Rural Development *(Agriculture Dept.), Civil Rights,* 1400 Independence Ave. S.W. 20250-3220 (mailing address: Ag. Box 0703 20250-0703); (202) 692-0204. Fax, (202) 692-0276. Cheryl Prejean Greaux, Director.

Enforces compliance with the Equal Credit Opportunity Act, which prohibits discrimination on the basis of sex, marital status, race, color, religion, disability, or age, in public assistance for rural housing and utilities.

CONGRESS

House Agriculture Committee, 1301 LHOB 20515; (202) 225-2171. Fax, (202) 225-0917. Rep. Robert W. Goodlatte, R-Va., Chair; Bill O'Conner, Staff Director.

General e-mail, agriculture@mail.house.gov

Web, agriculture.house.gov

Jurisdiction over legislation on price supports, natural disaster assistance relating to the farm industry, and production adjustment programs.

House Agriculture Committee, *Subcommittee on General Farm Commodities and Risk Management,* 1301 LHOB 20515; (202) 225-2171. Fax, (202) 225-0917. Rep. Jerry Moran, R-Kan., Chair; Christy Seyfert, Staff Director.

Web, agriculture.house.gov/general.htm

Jurisdiction over legislation on commodity futures and crop insurance.

House Small Business Committee, 2361 RHOB 20515; (202) 225-5821. Fax, (202) 225-3587. Rep. Donald Manzullo, R-Ill., Chair; J. Matthew Szymanski, Chief of Staff.

General e-mail, smbiz@mail.house.gov

Web, www.house.gov/smbiz

Jurisdiction over rural economy and family farming legislation as it relates to the small-business community.

House Ways and Means Committee, *Subcommittee on Oversight,* 1136 LHOB 20515; (202) 225-7601. Fax, (202) 225-9680. Rep. Amo Houghton, R-N.Y., Chair; Kirk Walder, Staff Director.

Web, waysandmeans.house.gov

Oversees government-sponsored enterprises, including the Farm Credit Banks and the Federal Agricultural Mortgage Corp., with regard to the financial risk they pose to the federal government.

Senate Agriculture, Nutrition, and Forestry Committee, *Subcommittee on Forestry, Conservation, and Rural Revitalization,* SR-328A 20510; (202) 224-2035. Sen. Michael D. Crapo, R-Idaho, Chair.

Web, agriculture.senate.gov

Jurisdiction over legislation on agricultural credit, loans, natural disaster assistance, and insurance, including crop insurance.

Senate Agriculture, Nutrition, and Forestry Committee, *Subcommittee on Production and Price Competitiveness,* SR-328A 20510; (202) 224-2035. Fax, (202) 224-1725. Sen. Elizabeth Dole, R-N.C., Chair; Vacant, Staff Director.

Web, agriculture.senate.gov

Jurisdiction over legislation on price supports and production adjustment programs.

Senate Banking, Housing, and Urban Affairs Committee, SD-534 20510; (202) 224-7391. Fax, (202) 224-5137. Sen. Richard C. Shelby, R-Ala., Chair; Kathy Casey, Staff Director.

Web, banking.senate.gov

Oversees government-sponsored enterprises, including the Farm Credit Banks and the Federal Agricultural Mortgage Corp., with regard to the financial risk they pose to the federal government.

Senate Small Business and Entrepreneurship Committee, SR-428A 20510; (202) 224-5175. Fax, (202) 228-1128. Sen. Olympia J. Snowe, R-Maine, Chair; Mark Warren, Staff Director.

Web, sbc.senate.gov

Jurisdiction over rural economy and family farming legislation as it relates to the small-business community.

NONPROFIT

Environmental Working Group, 1436 U St. N.W., #100 20009; (202) 667-6982. Fax, (202) 232-2592. Kenneth A. Cook, President.

General e-mail, info@ewg.org

Web, www.ewg.org

Research and advocacy group that studies and publishes reports on a wide range of agricultural and environmental issues. Monitors legislation and regulations.

Farm Credit Council, 50 F St. N.W., #900 20001; (202) 626-8710. Fax, (202) 626-8718. Ken Auer, President.

Web, www.fccouncil.com

Represents the Farm Credit System, a national financial cooperative that makes loans to agricultural producers, rural homebuyers, farmer cooperatives, and rural utilities. Finances the export of U.S. agricultural commodities.

 FOOD AND NUTRITION

AGENCIES

Agricultural Marketing Service (AMS), *(Agriculture Dept.), Science and Technology,* 1400 Independence Ave. S.W., #5231 EPA West 20250; (202) 720-5231. Fax, (202) 720-6496. Robert L. Epstein, Deputy Administrator.

Web, www.ams.usda.gov/science/index.htm

Provides analytical testing to AMS divisions, federal and state agencies, and the private sector food industry; participates in international food safety organizations. Tests commodities traded with specific countries and regions, including butter, honey, eggs, nuts, poultry, and meat; analyzes nutritional value of U.S. military rations.

Agricultural Research Service *(Agriculture Dept.),* *1400 Independence Ave. S.W., #302A 20250-0300; (202) 720-3656. Fax, (202) 720-5427. Edward B. Knipling, Administrator (Acting).*
General e-mail, arsinfo@ars-grin.gov
Web, www.ars.usda.gov

Conducts studies on agricultural problems of domestic and international concern through nationwide network of research centers. Studies include research on human nutrition; livestock production and protection; crop production, protection, and processing; postharvest technology; and food distribution and market value.

Agriculture Dept. (USDA), *Food, Nutrition, and Consumer Services,* *1400 Independence Ave. S.W., #240E 20250; (202) 720-7711. Fax, (202) 690-3100. Eric M. Bost, Under Secretary; Suzanne M. Biermann, Deputy Under Secretary.*
Web, www.fns.usda.gov/fncs

Oversees the Food and Nutrition Service, the Center for Nutrition Policy and Promotion, and the office of the consumer adviser for agricultural products.

Animal and Plant Health Inspection Service (APHIS), *(Agriculture Dept.), 1400 Independence Ave. S.W., #312E 20250 (mailing address: Ag. Box 3401 20250); (202) 720-3861. Fax, (202) 720-3054. Bobby R. Acord, Administrator.*
Web, www.aphis.usda.gov

Administers animal disease control programs in cooperation with states; inspects imported animals, flowers, and plants; licenses the manufacture and marketing of veterinary biologics to ensure purity and effectiveness.

Cooperative State Research, Education, and Extension Service *(Agriculture Dept.), 1400 Independence Ave. S.W., #305A 20250-2201; (202) 720-4423. Fax, (202) 720-8987. Colien Hefferan, Administrator. Information, (202) 720-6133. TTY, (202) 690-1899.*
Web, www.reeusda.gov

Oversees county agents and operation of state offices that provide information on nutrition, diet, food purchase budgeting, food safety, home gardening, and other consumer concerns.

Food and Drug Administration (FDA), *(Health and Human Services Dept.), Center for Food Safety and Applied Nutrition,* *5100 Paint Branch Pkwy., College Park, MD 20740-3835; (301) 436-1600. Joseph A. Levitt, Director.*
Web, www.cfsan.fda.gov

Develops standards of composition and quality of foods (except meat and poultry but including fish);

develops safety regulations for food and color additives for foods, cosmetics, and drugs; monitors pesticide residues in foods; conducts food safety and nutrition research; develops analytical methods for measuring food additives, nutrients, pesticides, and chemical and microbiological contaminants; recommends action to Justice Dept.

Food and Drug Administration (FDA), *(Health and Human Services Dept.), Nutritional Products Labeling and Dietary Supplements,* *5100 Paint Branch Pkwy., College Park, MD 20740; (301) 436-2375. Fax, (301) 436-2639. Christine Taylor, Director.*
Web, www.cfsan.fda.gov

Scientific and technical component of the Center for Food Safety and Applied Nutrition. Conducts research on nutrients; develops regulations and labeling requirements on infant formulas, medical foods, and dietary supplements, including herbs.

Food and Nutrition Service *(Agriculture Dept.), 3101 Park Center Dr., #906, Alexandria, VA 22302; (703) 305-2062. Fax, (703) 305-2908. Roberto Salazar, Administrator. Information, (703) 305-2286.*
Web, www.fns.usda.gov/fns

Administers all Agriculture Dept. domestic food assistance, including the distribution of funds and food for school breakfast and lunch programs (preschool through secondary) to public and nonprofit private schools; the food stamp program; and a supplemental nutrition program for women, infants, and children (WIC).

Food and Nutrition Service *(Agriculture Dept.), Analysis, Nutrition, and Evaluation,* *3101 Park Center Dr., #1014, Alexandria, VA 22302; (703) 305-2585. Fax, (703) 305-2576. Alberta Frost, Director.*
Web, www.fns.usda.gov/oane

Administers the Nutrition Education and Training Program, which provides states with grants for disseminating nutrition information to children and for in-service training of food service and teaching personnel; administers the Child Nutrition Labeling Program, which certifies that foods served in school lunch and breakfast programs meet nutritional requirements; provides information and technical assistance in nutrition and food service management.

Food and Nutrition Service *(Agriculture Dept.), Child Nutrition,* *3101 Park Center Dr., #640, Alexandria, VA 22302; (703) 305-2590. Fax, (703) 305-2879. Stanley C. Garnett, Director. Press, (703) 305-2039.*
Web, www.fns.usda.gov

Administers the transfer of funds to state agencies for the National School Lunch Program; the School Breakfast Program; the Special Milk Program, which helps schools and institutions provide children who do not have access to full meals under other child nutrition programs with fluid milk; the Child and Adult Care Food Program, which provides children in nonresidential child-care centers and family day care homes with year-round meal service; and the Summer Food Service Program, which provides children from low-income families with meals during the summer months.

Food and Nutrition Service *(Agriculture Dept.), Food Distribution, 3101 Park Center Dr., #503, Alexandria, VA 22302; (703) 305-2680. Fax, (703) 305-1410. Rosalind S. Cleveland, Director (Acting).*
Web, www.fns.usda.gov

Administers the Emergency Food Assistance Program, under which butter, cheese, milk, rice, and other surplus commodities are distributed to the needy. Administers the National Commodity Processing Program, which facilitates distribution, at reduced prices, of processed foods to state agencies, including charitable institutions, child-care food programs, nutrition programs for the elderly, state correctional institutions, and summer food service programs.

Food and Nutrition Service *(Agriculture Dept.), Food Stamp Program, 3101 Park Center Dr., #808, Alexandria, VA 22302; (703) 305-2026. Fax, (703) 305-2454. Kate Coler, Deputy Administrator.*
Web, www.fns.usda.gov

Administers, through state welfare agencies, the Food Stamp Program, which provides needy persons with food coupons to increase food purchasing power. Provides matching funds to cover half the cost of coupon issuance.

Food and Nutrition Service *(Agriculture Dept.), Supplemental Food Programs, 3101 Park Center Dr., #520, Alexandria, VA 22302; (703) 305-2746. Fax, (703) 305-2196. Patricia N. Daniels, Director.*
Web, www.fns.usda.gov

Provides health departments and agencies with federal funding for food supplements and administrative expenses to make food, nutrition education, and health services available to infants, young children, and pregnant, nursing, and postpartum women.

Food Safety and Inspection Service *(Agriculture Dept.), 1400 Independence Ave. S.W., #331E 20250; (202) 720-7025. Fax, (202) 205-0158. Garry L. McKee, Administrator. Press, (202) 720-9113. Consumer inquiries, (800) 535-4555; in Washington, (202) 720-3333.*

Web, www.usda.gov/fsis

Inspects meat, poultry, and egg products moving in interstate commerce for use as human food to ensure that they are safe, wholesome, and accurately labeled. Provides safe handling and labeling guidelines.

National Agricultural Library *(Agriculture Dept.), Food and Nutrition Information Center, 10301 Baltimore Ave., #105, Beltsville, MD 20705-2351; (301) 504-5719. Fax, (301) 504-6409. Dennis Smith, Coordinator. TTY, (301) 504-6856.*
General e-mail, fnic@nal.usda.gov
Web, www.nal.usda.gov/fnic

Serves individuals and agencies seeking information or educational materials on food and human nutrition; lends books and audiovisual materials for educational purposes; maintains a database of food and nutrition software and multimedia programs; provides reference services; develops resource lists of health and nutrition publications. Center open to the public.

National Institute of Diabetes and Digestive and Kidney Diseases *(National Institutes of Health), Nutritional Sciences, 6707 Democracy Blvd., MSC 5450, Bethesda, MD 20892-5450; (301) 594-8883. Fax, (301) 480-8300. Dr. Van S. Hubbard, Chief.*
Web, www.nih.gov

Supports research on nutritional requirements, dietary fiber, obesity, eating disorders, energy regulation, clinical nutrition, trace minerals, and basic nutrient functions.

National Oceanic and Atmospheric Administration (NOAA), *(Commerce Dept.), Seafood Inspection Program, 1315 East-West Hwy. #10842, Silver Spring, MD 20910; (301) 713-2355. Fax, (301) 713-1081. Richard V. Cano, Director.*
Web, seafood.nmfs.noaa.gov

Administers voluntary inspection program for fish products and fish processing plants; certifies fish for wholesomeness, safety, and condition; grades for quality. Conducts training and workshops to help U.S. importers and foreign suppliers comply with food regulations.

CONGRESS

House Agriculture Committee, *Subcommittee on Department Operations, Oversight, Nutrition, and Forestry, 1407 LHOB 20515; (202) 225-2171. Fax, (202) 225-4464. Rep. Gil Gutknecht, R-Minn., Chair; Samuel Diehl, Staff Director.*
Web, agriculture.house.gov/departme.htm

Jurisdiction over legislation on nutrition and hunger issues, pesticides, food safety, food stamps, and consumer programs.

House Agriculture Committee, *Subcommittee on Livestock and Horticulture,* *1432P LHOB 20515; (202) 225-2171. Fax, (202) 225-0917. Rep. Robin Hayes, R-N.C., Chair; Pam Scott, Staff Director.*
Web, agriculture.house.gov/livestoc.htm
     Jurisdiction over legislation concerning inspection of aquacultural species (seafood), dairy products, meats, poultry, and livestock.

House Appropriations Committee, *Subcommittee on Agriculture, Rural Development, FDA, and Related Agencies,* *2362 RHOB 20515; (202) 225-2638. Rep. Henry Bonilla, R-Texas, Chair; Hank Moore, Staff Director.*
Web, www.house.gov/appropriations
     Jurisdiction over legislation to appropriate funds for the Food and Drug Administration, Food Safety and Inspection Service, and Food and Consumer Service.

House Education and the Workforce Committee, *Subcommittee on Education Reform,* *H2-230 FHOB 20515; (202) 225-6558. Fax, (202) 225-9571. Rep. Michael N. Castle, R-Del., Chair; Paula Nowakowski, Staff Director.*
Web, edworkforce.house.gov/members/108th/mem-edr.htm
     Jurisdiction over legislation on the National School Lunch Program; the School Breakfast Program; the Summer Food Program for Children; the Special Milk Program for Children; and the Special Supplemental Food Program for Women, Infants, and Children (WIC).

House Energy and Commerce Committee, *Subcommittee on Health,* *2125 RHOB 20515; (202) 225-2927. Fax, (202) 225-1919. Rep. Michael Bilirakis, R-Fla., Chair; David V. Marventano, Staff Director.*
General e-mail, commerce@mail.house.gov
Web, energycommerce.house.gov/108/subcommittees/ Health.htm
     Jurisdiction over legislation on vaccines; food and drugs; labeling and packaging, including tobacco products and alcohol beverages; and the use of vitamins. Oversight of the Food and Drug Administration.

House Government Reform Committee, *Subcommittee on Criminal Justice, Drug Policy, and Human Resources,* *B373 RHOB 20515; (202) 225-2577. Fax, (202) 225-1154. Rep. Mark Souder, R-Ind., Chair; Christopher Donesa, Staff Director.*
Web, www.house.gov/reform
     Oversees government food and consumer services, including the Food and Nutrition Service and the Food Safety and Inspection Service.

House Science Committee, *Subcommittee on Research,* *B374 RHOB 20515; (202) 225-7858. Fax, (202) 225-7815. Rep. Nick Smith, R-Mich., Chair; Peter Rooney, Staff Director.*
General e-mail, science@mail.house.gov
Web, www.house.gov/science/committeeinfo/members/ research/index.htm
     Jurisdiction over research and development involving government nutrition programs.

Senate Agriculture, Nutrition, and Forestry Committee, *Subcommittee on Research, Nutrition, and General Legislation,* *SR-328A 20510; (202) 224-2035. Sen. Peter G. Fitzgerald, R-Ill., Chair; Vacant, Staff Director.*
Web, agriculture.senate.gov
     Jurisdiction over legislation on food, nutrition, and hunger. Jurisdiction over commodity donations; food stamps; school lunch and breakfast programs; nutritional programs for the elderly; and the Special Supplemental Food Program for Women, Infants, and Children (WIC).

Senate Appropriations Committee, *Subcommittee on Agriculture, Rural Development, and Related Agencies,* *SD-188 20510; (202) 224-5270. Fax, (202) 228-2320. Sen. Robert F. Bennett, R-Utah, Chair; Pat Raymond, Clerk.*
Web, appropriations.senate.gov
     Jurisdiction over legislation to appropriate funds for the Food and Drug Administration, Food Safety and Inspection Service, and Food and Consumer Service.

Senate Commerce, Science, and Transportation Committee, *Subcommittee on Consumer Affairs and Product Safety,* *SH-428 20510; (202) 224-5183. Fax, (202) 228-0326. Sen. Peter G. Fitzgerald, R-Ill., Chair; Carlos Fierro, Senior Counsel.*
Web, commerce.senate.gov
     Jurisdiction over legislation on the Food and Drug Administration and over labeling and packaging legislation, including advertising and packaging of tobacco products and alcohol beverages.

Senate Health, Education, Labor, and Pensions Committee, *SD-428 20510; (202) 224-5375. Fax, (202) 228-5044. Sen. Judd Gregg, R-N.H., Chair; Sharon Soderstrom, Staff Director.*
Web, health.senate.gov
     Jurisdiction over legislation on vaccines, drug labeling and packaging, and the use of vitamins.

INTERNATIONAL ORGANIZATIONS

Codex Alimentarius Commission, *U.S. Codex Office,* *1400 Independence Ave. S.W., South Bldg., #4861 20250; (202) 205-7760. Fax, (202) 720-3157. F. Edward Scarbrough, U.S. Codex Manager.*
General e-mail, uscodex@fsis.usda.gov
Web, www.fsis.usda.gov/OA/codex

U.S. contact point for the principal U.N. agency concerned with food standards, food safety, and related regulation of international trade. Convenes committees in member countries to address specific commodities and issues including labeling, additives in food and veterinary drugs, pesticide residues and other contaminants, and systems for food inspection. (Located in the USDA Food Safety and Inspection Service; international headquarters in Rome.)

NONPROFIT

American Dietetic Assn. (ADA), *Washington Office,* *1120 Connecticut Ave. N.W., #480 20036-3989; (202) 775-8277. Fax, (202) 775-8284. Stephanie Patrick, Vice President.*
Web, www.eatright.org

Membership: dietitians and other nutrition professionals. Promotes public health and nutrition; accredits academic programs in clinical nutrition and food service management; sets standards of professional practice. Sponsors the National Center for Nutrition and Dietetics. (Headquarters in Chicago, Ill.)

American Herbal Products Assn., *8484 Georgia Ave., #370, Silver Spring, MD 20910; (301) 588-1171. Fax, (301) 588-1174. Michael McGuffin, President.*
General e-mail, ahpa@ahpa.org
Web, www.ahpa.org

Membership: U.S. companies and individuals that grow, manufacture, and distribute therapeutic herbs and herbal products; and associates in education, law, media, and medicine. Supports research; promotes standardization, consumer protection, competition, and self-regulation in the industry. Monitors legislation and regulations.

American Society for Clinical Nutrition, *9650 Rockville Pike, #L3300, Bethesda, MD 20814-3998; (301) 634-7110. Fax, (301) 571-1863. Sandra Schlicker, Executive Officer.*
General e-mail, secretar@ascn.faseb.org
Web, www.faseb.org/ascn

Membership: clinical nutritionists. Supports research on the role of human nutrition in health and disease; encourages undergraduate and graduate nutrition education. (Division of American Society for Nutritional Sciences.)

American Society for Nutritional Sciences, *9650 Rockville Pike, #L4500, Bethesda, MD 20814-3998; (301) 634-7050. Fax, (301) 571-1892. Richard G. Allison, Executive Officer.*
General e-mail, sec@asns.faseb.org
Web, www.faseb.org/asns

Membership: nutrition scientists. Conducts research in nutrition and related fields worldwide and promotes the exchange of information; promotes nutrition education; offers awards for research. Divisions include the Society for International Nutrition Research and the American Society for Clinical Nutrition.

American Society for Parenteral and Enteral Nutrition, *8630 Fenton St., #412, Silver Spring, MD 20910-3805; (301) 587-6315. Fax, (301) 587-2365. Robin V. Kriegel, Executive Director.*
General e-mail, aspen@nutr.org
Web, www.nutritioncare.org

Membership: health care professionals who provide patients with intravenous nutritional support during hospitalization and rehabilitation at home. Develops nutrition guidelines; provides educational materials; conducts annual meetings.

Center for Science in the Public Interest, *1875 Connecticut Ave. N.W., #300 20009-5728; (202) 332-9110. Fax, (202) 265-4954. Michael F. Jacobson, Executive Director.*
General e-mail, cspi@cspinet.org
Web, www.cspinet.org

Conducts research on food and nutrition. Interests include eating habits, food safety regulations, food additives, organically produced foods, alcohol beverages, and links between diet and disease. Monitors U.S. and international policy.

Child Nutrition Forum, *1875 Connecticut Ave. N.W., #540 20009-5728; (202) 986-2200. Fax, (202) 986-2525. Lynn Parker, Coordinator.*
General e-mail, comments@frac.org
Web, www.frac.org

Membership: agriculture, labor, education, and health and nutrition specialists; school food service officials; and consumer and religious groups. Supports federal nutrition programs for children; provides information on school nutrition programs. Monitors legislation and regulations concerning hunger issues.

Congressional Hunger Center, *229 1/2 Pennsylvania Ave. S.E. 20003; (202) 547-7022. Fax, (202) 547-7575. Edward Cooney, Executive Director.*
Web, www.hungercenter.org

Works to increase public awareness of hunger in the United States and abroad. Develops strategies and trains leaders to combat hunger and facilitates collaborative efforts between organizations.

Council for Responsible Nutrition, *1828 L St. N.W., #900 20036-5114; (202) 776-7929. Fax, (202) 204-7980. Annette Dickinson, President (Acting).*
Web, www.crnusa.org

Membership: manufacturers, distributors, and ingredient suppliers of dietary supplements. Provides information to members; monitors Food and Drug Administration, Federal Trade Commission, and Consumer Product Safety Commission regulations.

Food Research and Action Center (FRAC),
1875 Connecticut Ave. N.W., #540 20009-5728; (202) 986-2200. Fax, (202) 986-2525. James D. Weill, President.
General e-mail, comments@frac.org
Web, www.frac.org

Public interest advocacy, research, and legal center that works to end hunger and poverty in the United States; offers legal assistance, organizational aid, training, and information to groups seeking to improve or expand federal food programs, including food stamp, child nutrition, and WIC (women, infants, and children) programs; conducts studies relating to hunger and poverty; coordinates network of antihunger organizations. Monitors legislation and regulations.

International Food Information Council, *1100 Connecticut Ave. N.W., #430 20036; (202) 296-6540. Fax, (202) 296-6547. Sylvia Rowe, President.*
General e-mail, foodinfo@ific.health.org
Web, www.ific.org

Membership: food and beverage companies and manufacturers of food ingredients. Provides the media, health professionals, and consumers with scientific information about food safety, health, and nutrition. Interests include harmonization of international food safety standards.

International Life Sciences Institute, North America, *1 Thomas Circle N.W., 9th Floor 20005-5802; (202) 659-0074. Fax, (202) 659-3859. Lori Tiller, Vice President.*
General e-mail, ilsi@ilsi.org
Web, www.ilsi.org

Acts as liaison among scientists from international government agencies, concerned industries, research institutes, and universities regarding the safety of foods and chemical ingredients. Conducts research on caffeine, food coloring, oral health, human nutrition, and other food issues. Promotes international cooperation among scientists.

Physicians Committee for Responsible Medicine, *5100 Wisconsin Ave. N.W., #400 20016; (202) 686-2210. Fax, (202) 686-2216. Dr. Neal D. Barnard, President.*
General e-mail, pcrm@pcrm.org
Web, www.pcrm.org

Membership: health care professionals, medical students, and laypersons interested in preventive medicine, nutrition, and higher standards in research. Conducts clinical research, educational programs, and public information campaigns; advocates for more effective and compassionate health-related policies in government and in public and private institutions.

Public Citizen, *Health Research Group, 1600 20th St. N.W. 20009; (202) 588-1000. Fax, (202) 588-7796. Dr. Sidney M. Wolfe, Director.*
Web, www.citizen.org

Citizens' interest group that studies and reports on unsafe foods; monitors and petitions the Food and Drug Administration.

United Food and Commercial Workers International Union, *1775 K St. N.W. 20006; (202) 223-3111. Fax, (202) 466-1562. Douglas H. Dority, President.*
Web, www.ufcw.org

Membership: approximately 1.4 million workers in food-related industries, including supermarkets, department stores, insurance and finance, and packing houses and processing plants. Helps members negotiate pay, benefits, and better working conditions; conducts training programs and workshops. Monitors legislation and regulations. (Affiliated with the AFL-CIO and Canadian Labour Congress.)

Vegetarian Resource Group, *P.O. Box 1463, Baltimore, MD 21203; (410) 366-8343. Fax, (410) 366-8804. Charles Stahler, Co-Director; Debra Wasserman, Co-Director.*
General e-mail, vrg@vrg.org
Web, www.vrg.org

Works to educate the public on vegetarianism and issues of health, nutrition, ecology, ethics, and world hunger.

Vegetarian Union of North America, *P.O. Box 9710 20016; (202) 362-8349. Peter McQueen, President.*
General e-mail, vuna@ivu.org

Web, www.ivu.org/vuna/english.html

Promotes the vegetarian movement throughout North America. Part of a network of vegetarian groups throughout the U.S. and Canada that serve as a liaison with the worldwide vegetarian movement.

Beverages

AGENCIES

Alcohol and Tobacco Tax and Trade Bureau (TTB), *(Treasury Dept.),* *650 Massachusetts Ave. N.W. 20226; (202) 927-5000. Fax, (202) 927-5611. Arthur J. Libertucci, Administrator. Press, (202) 927-8262.*
Web, www.ttb.gov

Regulates the advertising and labeling of alcohol beverages, including the size of containers; enforces taxation of alcohol. Authorized to refer violations to Justice Dept. for criminal prosecution.

National Clearinghouse for Alcohol and Drug Information *(Health and Human Services Dept.), Center for Substance Abuse Prevention, 11426-28 Rockville Pike, #200, Rockville, MD 20852 (mailing address: P.O. Box 2345, Rockville, MD 20847-2345); (301) 468-2600. Fax, (301) 468-6433. John Noble, Director. Information, (800) 729-6686. TTY, (800) 487-4889.*
Web, www.health.org

Provides information, publications, and grant applications for programs to prevent alcohol and drug abuse.

NONPROFIT

American Beverage Licensees, *5101 River Rd., #108, Bethesda, MD 20816-1508; (301) 656-1494. Fax, (301) 656-7539. Harry G. Wiles, Executive Director.*
General e-mail, info@ablusa.org
Web, www.ablusa.org

Membership: state associations of on- and off-premise licensees. Sponsors program that trains bartenders and wait staff to serve alcohol in a responsible manner. Monitors legislation and regulations affecting the alcohol beverage industry. (Formerly National Assn. of Beverage Retailers and National Licensed Beverage Assn.)

Beer Institute, *122 C St. N.W., #750 20001; (202) 737-2337. Fax, (202) 737-7004. Jeffrey G. Becker, President.*
General e-mail, info@beerinstitute.org
Web, www.beerinstitute.org

Membership: domestic and international brewers and suppliers to the domestic brewing industry. Monitors legislation and regulations.

Center for Science in the Public Interest, *1875 Connecticut Ave. N.W., #300 20009-5728; (202) 332-9110. Fax, (202) 265-4954. Michael F. Jacobson, Executive Director.*
General e-mail, cspi@cspinet.org
Web, www.cspinet.org

Concerned with U.S. and international policy on food and alcohol, including marketing, labeling, and taxation. Opposes U.S. government promotion of alcohol products overseas.

Distilled Spirits Council of the United States, *1250 Eye St. N.W., #400 20005; (202) 628-3544. Fax, (202) 682-8888. Peter H. Cressy, President.*
Web, www.discus.org

Membership: manufacturers and marketers of distilled spirits sold in the United States. Provides consumer information on alcohol-related issues and topics. Monitors legislation and regulations.

International Bottled Water Assn., *1700 Diagonal Rd., #650, Alexandria, VA 22314; (703) 683-5213. Fax, (703) 683-4074. Joseph Doss, President.*
Web, www.bottledwater.org

Serves as a clearinghouse for industry-related consumer, regulatory, and technical information; interests include international trade. Monitors state and federal legislation and regulations.

Mothers Against Drunk Driving (MADD), *Washington Office, 1025 Connecticut Ave. N.W., #1200 20036; (202) 293-2270. Fax, (202) 293-0106. Karen Sprattler, Public Policy Director.*
Web, www.madd.org

Concerned with alcohol policy as it relates to motor vehicle safety. Supports implementation of a nationwide legal intoxication level of 0.08 blood alcohol content. (Headquarters in Irving, Texas.)

National Alcohol Beverage Control Assn., *4216 King St. West, Alexandria, VA 22302-1507; (703) 578-4200. Fax, (703) 820-3551. James M. Sgueo, Executive Director.*
General e-mail, nabca@nabca.org
Web, www.nabca.org

Membership: distilleries, trade associations, and state agencies that control the purchase, distribution, and sale of alcohol beverages. Serves as an information clearinghouse. Monitors legislation and regulations.

National Assn. of State Alcohol and Drug Abuse Directors, *808 17th St. N.W., #410 20006; (202) 293-0090. Fax, (202) 293-1250. Lewis E. Gallant, Executive Director.*

General e-mail, dcoffice@nasadad.org

Web, www.nasadad.org

Provides information on drug abuse treatment and prevention; contracts with federal and state agencies for design of programs to fight drug abuse.

National Beer Wholesalers Assn., *1101 King St., #600, Alexandria, VA 22314; (703) 683-4300. Fax, (703) 683-8965. David K. Rehr, President.*

General e-mail, info@nbwa.org

Web, www.nbwa.org

Works to enhance the independent beer wholesale industry. Advocates before government and the public; encourages responsible consumption of beer; sponsors programs and services to benefit members; monitors legislation and regulations.

National Soft Drink Assn., *1101 16th St. N.W. 20036-6396; (202) 463-6732. Fax, (202) 463-8172. William L. Ball III, President.*

Web, www.nsda.org

Membership: companies engaged in producing or distributing carbonated and non-carbonated soft drinks. Acts as industry liaison with government and the public.

Wine and Spirits Wholesalers of America, *805 15th St. N.W., #430 20005; (202) 371-9792. Fax, (202) 789-2405. Juanita D. Duggan, Executive Vice President.*

General e-mail, comments@wswa.org

Web, www.wswa.org

Membership: wholesale distributors of domestic and imported wine and distilled spirits. Provides information on drinking awareness.

Wine Institute, *Washington Office, 601 13th St. N.W., #580 South 20005; (202) 408-0870. Fax, (202) 371-0061. Robert P. Koch, Senior Vice President.*

Web, www.wineinstitute.org

Membership: California wineries and affiliated businesses. Seeks international recognition for California wines; conducts promotional campaigns in other countries. Monitors legislation and regulations. (Headquarters in San Francisco, Calif.)

Food Industries

NONPROFIT

American Bakers Assn. (ABA), *1350 Eye St. N.W., #1290 20005; (202) 789-0300. Fax, (202) 898-1164. Paul C. Abenante, President.*

General e-mail, info@americanbakers.org

Web, www.americanbakers.org

Membership: wholesale baking companies and their suppliers. Promotes increased consumption of baked goods; provides consumers with nutritional information; conducts conventions. Monitors legislation and regulations.

American Frozen Food Institute, *2000 Corporate Ridge, #1000, McLean, VA 22102; (703) 821-0770. Fax, (703) 821-1350. Leslie G. Sarasin, President.*

Web, www.affi.com

Membership: frozen food packers, distributors, and suppliers. Provides production statistics.

American Meat Institute, *1700 N. Moore St., #1600, Arlington, VA 22209; (703) 841-2400. Fax, (703) 527-0938. J. Patrick Boyle, President.*

Web, www.meatami.com

Membership: national and international meat and poultry packers, suppliers, and processors. Provides statistics on meat and poultry production and exports. Funds research projects and consumer education programs. Monitors legislation and regulations.

Bakery, Confectionery, Tobacco Workers, and Grain Millers International Union, *10401 Connecticut Ave., Kensington, MD 20895; (301) 933-8600. Fax, (301) 946-8452. Frank Hurt, President.*

Web, www.bctgm.org

Membership: approximately 120,000 workers from the bakery, grain miller, and tobacco industries. Helps members negotiate pay, benefits, and better working conditions; conducts training programs and workshops. Monitors legislation and regulations. (Affiliated with the AFL-CIO.)

Biscuit and Cracker Manufacturers' Assn., *8484 Georgia Ave., #700, Silver Spring, MD 20910; (301) 608-1552. Fax, (301) 608-1557. Frank P. Rooney, President.*

Web, www.thebcma.org

Membership: companies in the biscuit and cracker industry. Monitors legislation and regulations.

Food Marketing Institute, *655 15th St. N.W., #700 20005; (202) 452-8444. Fax, (202) 220-0877. Timothy Hammonds, President. Library, (202) 220-0687.*

Web, www.fmi.org

Trade association of food retailers and wholesalers. Conducts programs in research, education, industry relations, and public affairs; participates in international conferences. Library open to the public by appointment.

Food Processing Machinery and Supplies Assn., *200 Daingerfield Rd., Alexandria, VA 22314-2800; (703)*

684-1080. Fax, (703) 548-6563. George O. Melnykovich, President.

General e-mail, info@fpmsa.org

Web, www.processfood.com

Membership: manufacturers and suppliers of processing and packaging equipment to the food and beverage industries. Helps members market their products and services.

Grocery Manufacturers of America, 1010 Wisconsin Ave. N.W., #900 20007; (202) 337-9400. Fax, (202) 337-4508. C. Manly Molpus, President.

Web, www.gmabrands.com

Membership: manufacturers of products sold through the retail grocery trade. Monitors legislation and regulations.

Hotel Employees and Restaurant Employees International, 1219 28th St. N.W. 20007; (202) 393-4373. Fax, (202) 333-0468. John W. Wilhelm, President.

Web, www.hereunion.org

Membership: approximately 241,000 hotel and restaurant employees. Helps members negotiate pay, benefits, and better working conditions; conducts training programs and workshops. Monitors legislation and regulations. (Affiliated with the AFL-CIO.)

International Assn. of Food Industry Suppliers, 1451 Dolley Madison Blvd., #200, McLean, VA 22101-3850; (703) 761-2600. Fax, (703) 761-4334. Charles W. Bray, President.

Web, www.iafis.org

Membership: equipment manufacturers, suppliers, and servicers for the food and dairy processing industry. Co-sponsors food engineering scholarships and the biennial Worldwide Food Expo.

International Foodservice Distributors Assn., 201 Park Washington Court, Falls Church, VA 22046-4521; (703) 532-9400. Fax, (703) 538-4673. John Gray, President.

Web, www.ifdaonline.org

Trade association of grocery wholesale distribution companies that supply and service independent grocers throughout the United States and Canada. Provides members with research, technical, educational, and government service programs. (Formerly Food Distributors International.)

National Assn. of Convenience Stores, 1600 Duke St., #700, Alexandria, VA 22314; (703) 684-3600. Fax, (703) 836-4564. Kerley LeBoeuf, President.

General e-mail, nacs@nacsonline.com

Web, www.nacsonline.com

Membership: convenience store retailers and industry suppliers. Advocates industry position on labor, tax, environment, alcohol, and food-related issues; conducts research and training programs. Monitors legislation and regulations.

National Food Processors Assn., 1350 Eye St. N.W., #300 20005; (202) 639-5900. Fax, (202) 639-5932. John R. Cady, President. Press, (202) 639-5919.

General e-mail, nfpa@nfpa-food.org

Web, www.nfpa-food.org

Membership: manufacturers and suppliers of processed and packaged food, drinks, and juice. Promotes agricultural interests of food processors; provides research, technical services, education, communications, and crisis management for members. Monitors legislation and regulations.

National Pasta Assn., 1156 15th St. N.W., #900 20005; (202) 637-5888. Fax, (202) 637-5910. Robert Vermylen, Chair.

General e-mail, npa@ibm.net

Web, www.ilovepasta.org

Membership: U.S. pasta manufacturers, related suppliers, and allied industry representatives. Represents the industry on public policy issues; monitors and addresses technical issues; and organizes events and seminars for the industry.

National Restaurant Assn., 1200 17th St. N.W. 20036-3097; (202) 331-5900. Fax, (202) 331-2429. Steven C. Anderson, President.

General e-mail, info@dineout.org

Web, www.restaurant.org

Membership: restaurants, cafeterias, clubs, contract feeders, caterers, institutional food services, and other members of the food industry. Supports food service education and research. Monitors legislation and regulations.

Retailer's Bakery Assn., 14239 Park Center Dr., Laurel, MD 20707; (301) 725-2149. Fax, (301) 725-2187. Bernie Reynolds, Executive Vice President.

Web, www.rbanet.com

Membership: single- and multiunit retail bakeries and bakery-delis; donut and other specialty shops; supermarket in-store bakeries and bakery-delis; allied companies that offer equipment, ingredients, supplies, or services to these retailers; and students and teachers of secondary or postsecondary school baking programs. Provides business and training aids. Monitors legislation and regulations.

Snack Food Assn., *1711 King St., #1, Alexandria, VA 22314; (703) 836-4500. Fax, (703) 836-8262. James A. McCarthy, President.*

General e-mail, sfa@sfa.org

Web, www.sfa.org

Membership: snack food manufacturers and suppliers. Promotes industry sales; compiles statistics; conducts research and surveys; assists members with training and education; provides consumers with industry information. Monitors legislation and regulations.

Soyfoods Association of North America, *1723 U St. N.W. 20009; (202) 986-5600. Fax, (202) 387-5553. Tom Woodward, President.*

General e-mail, info@soyfoods.org

Web, www.soyfoods.org

Membership: large and small soyfood companies, growers and suppliers of soybeans, nutritionists, cookbook authors, equipment representatives, food scientists, and retailers. Promotes soybean consumption.

Women Grocers of America, *1005 N. Glebe Rd., #250, Arlington, VA 22201; (703) 516-0700. Fax, (703) 516-0115. Thomas K. Zaucha, President.*

General e-mail, info@nationalgrocers.org

Web, www.nationalgrocers.org

Supports the interests of women in the food distribution industry; sponsors seminars. (Affiliated with National Grocers Assn.)

Vegetarianism

NONPROFIT

FARM (Farm Animal Reform Movement), *P.O. Box 30654, Bethesda, MD 20824; (301) 530-1737. Fax, (301) 530-5747. Alex Hershaft, President.*

General e-mail, farm@farmusa.org

Web, www.farmusa.org

Works to end use of animals for food. Interests include animal protection, consumer health, agricultural resources, and environmental quality. Conducts national educational campaigns, including World Farm Animals Day and the Great American Meatout. Monitors legislation and regulations.

Great American Meatout, *P.O. Box 30654, Bethesda, MD 20824; (800) 632-8688. Laurelee Blanchard, Communications Director, (888) 348-6325.*

General e-mail, meatout@meatout.org

Web, www.meatout.org

Promotes the dietary elimination of meat. Facilitates information tables, exhibits, cooking demonstrations, and festivals nationwide. (Affiliated with Farm Animal Reform Movement.)

People for the Ethical Treatment of Animals (PETA), *501 Front St., Norfolk, VA 23510 (mailing address: P.O. Box 42516 20015); (757) 622-7382. Fax, (757) 622-0457. Ingrid Newkirk, President.*

General e-mail, info@peta.org

Web, www.peta.org

Educational and activist group supporting animal rights worldwide. Provides information on topics including laboratory research animals, factory farming, cosmetics, and vegetarianism. Monitors legislation; conducts workshops.

Vegetarian Resource Group, *P.O. Box 1463, Baltimore, MD 21203; (410) 366-8343. Fax, (410) 366-8804. Charles Stahler, Co-Director; Debra Wasserman, Co-Director.*

General e-mail, vrg@vrg.org

Web, www.vrg.org

Works to educate the public on vegetarianism and issues of health, nutrition, ecology, ethics, and world hunger.

Vegetarian Union of North America, *P.O. Box 9710 20016; (202) 362-8349. Peter McQueen, President.*

General e-mail, vuna@ivu.org

Web, www.ivu.org/vuna/english.html

Promotes the vegetarian movement throughout North America. Part of a network of vegetarian groups throughout the U.S. and Canada that serve as a liaison with the worldwide vegetarian movement.

World Food Assistance

AGENCIES

Foreign Agricultural Service (FAS), *(Agriculture Dept.), Export Credits, 1400 Independence Ave. S.W., #4083S 20250; (202) 720-6301. Fax, (202) 690-0727. Mary T. Chambliss, Deputy Administrator.*

Web, www.fas.usda.gov

Administers Commodity Credit Corporation commercial export programs, including export credit guarantee and export enhancement programs. Administers, with the Agency for International Development, U.S. foreign food aid programs.

Foreign Agricultural Service (FAS), *(Agriculture Dept.), International Cooperation and Development, 1400 Independence Ave. S.W., #3008S 20250-1081; (202) 690-0776. Fax, (202) 720-6103. Suzanne E. Heinen, Deputy Administrator (Acting).*

Web, www.fas.usda.gov

Coordinates and conducts the department's international cooperation and development programs in agriculture and related fields. Programs include technical assistance and training, scientific and technical cooperation, administration of collaborative research, representation of Agriculture Dept. and U.S. government interests in international organization affairs, and facilitation of private sector involvement in country and regional agricultural development. Programs are conducted cooperatively with other Agriculture Dept. and U.S. government agencies, universities, and the private sector.

State Dept., *Agricultural, Biotechnology, and Textile Trade Affairs: Agricultural Trade Policy and Programs,* *2201 C St. N.W., #3831A 20520; (202) 647-3090. Fax, (202) 647-1894. Hans Klemm, Director.*
Web, www.state.gov

Makes recommendations on international food policy issues such as the effects of U.S. food aid on foreign policy; studies and drafts proposals on the U.S. role in Food for Peace and World Food programs.

World Agricultural Outlook Board *(Agriculture Dept.), 1400 Independence Ave. S.W., #5143S 20250; (202) 720-6030. Fax, (202) 690-1805. Gerald A. Bange, Chair.*
Web, www.usda.gov/oce

Reports to the USDA chief economist. Coordinates the department's commodity forecasting program, which develops the official prognosis of supply, utilization, and prices for commodities worldwide. Works with the National Weather Service to monitor the impact of global weather on agriculture.

CONGRESS

House Agriculture Committee, *1301 LHOB 20515; (202) 225-2171. Fax, (202) 226-2831. Rep. Robert W. Goodlatte, R-Va., Chair; Bill O'Conner, Staff Director.*
General e-mail, agriculture@mail.house.gov
Web, agriculture.house.gov

Jurisdiction over international commodity donations and over legislation on U.S. domestic food production for foreign assistance programs under Public Law 480, including the Food for Peace program and the Foreign Agricultural Service. (House International Relations Committee has jurisdiction over legislation on overseas food distribution.)

House International Relations Committee,
2170 RHOB 20515; (202) 225-5021. Fax, (202) 226-2831. Rep. Henry J. Hyde, R-Ill., Chair; Thomas E. Mooney, Chief of Staff.
General e-mail, hirc@mail.house.gov
Web, www.house.gov/international_relations

Jurisdiction over legislation on overseas food distribution for foreign assistance programs under Public Law

480, including the Food for Peace program and the Foreign Agricultural Service. (House Agriculture Committee has jurisdiction over legislation on domestic food production for Public Law 480 programs.)

Senate Agriculture, Nutrition, and Forestry Committee, *Subcommittee on Marketing, Inspection, and Product Promotion, SR-328A 20510; (202) 224-2035. Sen. Jim Talent, R-Mo., Chair; Vacant, Staff Director.*
Web, agriculture.senate.gov

Jurisdiction over legislation on food production and distribution for foreign assistance programs under Public Law 480, including the Food for Peace program.

Senate Agriculture, Nutrition, and Forestry Committee, *Subcommittee on Research, Nutrition, and General Legislation, SR-328A 20510; (202) 224-2035. Sen. Peter G. Fitzgerald, R-Ill., Chair; Vacant, Staff Director.*
Web, agriculture.senate.gov

Jurisdiction over legislation on commodity donations, food, nutrition, and hunger in the United States and in foreign countries.

INTERNATIONAL ORGANIZATIONS

Food and Agriculture Organization of the United Nations (FAO), *Liaison Office for North America, 2175 K St. N.W., #300 20437-0001; (202) 653-2400. Fax, (202) 653-5760. Charles H. Riemenschneider, Director. Library, (202) 653-2402. Press, (202) 653-0011.*
Web, www.fao.org

Offers development assistance; collects, analyzes, and disseminates information; provides policy and planning advice to governments; acts as an international forum for debate on food and agricultural issues, including animal health and production, fisheries, and forestry; encourages sustainable agricultural development and a long-term strategy for the conservation and management of natural resources. (International headquarters in Rome.)

International Fund for Agricultural Development (IFAD), *North American Liaison Offices, 1775 K St. N.W., #410 20006; (202) 331-9099. Fax, (202) 331-9366. Vera P. Weill-Hallé, Director.*
Web, www.ifad.org

Specialized agency of the United Nations that provides the rural poor of developing nations with cost-effective ways of overcoming hunger, poverty, and malnutrition. Advocates a community-based approach to reducing rural poverty. (International headquarters in Rome.)

NONPROFIT

Agricultural Cooperative Development International (ACDI/VOCA), *50 F St. N.W., #1100 20001; (202) 638-4661. Fax, (202) 626-8726. Michael Deegan, President.*

Web, www.acdivoca.org

Membership: farm supply, processing, and marketing cooperatives; farm credit banks; national farmer organizations; and insurance cooperatives. Provides cooperatives with training and technical, management, and marketing assistance; supports farm credit systems, agribusiness, and government agencies in developing countries. Contracts with the Agency for International Development to start farm cooperatives in other countries. (Affiliated with the National Council of Farmer Cooperatives.)

American Red Cross, *National Headquarters, 430 17th St. N.W., 2nd Floor 20006-2401; (202) 737-8300. Fax, (202) 783-3432. Marsha Evans, Chief Executive Officer.*

Web, www.redcross.org

Humanitarian relief and health education organization chartered by Congress. Provides food and supplies to assist in major disaster and refugee situations worldwide.

Bread for the World/Bread for the World Institute, *50 F St. N.W., #500 20001; (202) 639-9400. Fax, (202) 639-9401. David Beckmann, President.*

General e-mail, bread@bread.org

Web, www.bread.org

Christian citizens' movement that works to eradicate world hunger. Organizes and coordinates political action on issues and public policy affecting the causes of hunger. Interests include domestic food assistance programs, international famine, and hunger relief.

CARE, *Washington Office, 1625 K St. N.W., #500 20006; (202) 595-2800. Fax, (202) 296-8695. Marianne M. Leach, Executive Director.*

General e-mail, info@care.org

Web, www.care.org

Assists the developing world's poor through emergency assistance and community self-help programs that focus on sustainable development, agriculture, agroforestry, water and sanitation, health, family planning, and income generation. (U.S. headquarters in Atlanta, Ga.; international headquarters in Brussels.)

International Food Policy Research Institute, *2033 K St. N.W., #400 20006; (202) 862-5600. Fax, (202)* *467-4439. Joachim Bon Braun, Director. Library, (202) 862-5615.*

General e-mail, ifpri@ifpri.org

Web, www.ifpri.org

Research organization that analyzes the world food situation and suggests ways of making food more available in developing countries. Provides various governments with information on national and international food policy. Sponsors conferences and seminars; publishes research reports. Library open to the public by appointment.

National Center for Food and Agricultural Policy, *1616 P St. N.W., #100 20036; (202) 328-5048. Fax, (202) 328-5133. Dale E. Hathaway, Director.*

General e-mail, ncfap@ncfap.org

Web, www.ncfap.org

Research and educational organization concerned with international food and agricultural issues. Examines public policy concerning agriculture, food safety and quality, natural resources, and the environment.

Oxfam America, *Policy, Washington Office, 1112 16th St., N.W., #600 20036; (202) 496-1180. Fax, (202) 496-1190. Jo Marie Griesgraber, Director; Bernice Romero, Humanitarian Affairs Advocate. Information, (800) 776-9326.*

Web, www.oxfamamerica.org

Funds disaster relief and self-help development projects, primarily at the international level, including food and agriculture programs; supports grassroots and community efforts to combat hunger; conducts an educational campaign and debt relief for foreign countries. (Headquarters in Boston, Mass.)

RESULTS, *440 1st St. N.W., #450 20001; (202) 783-7100. Fax, (202) 783-2818. Barbara Wallace, Executive Director.*

General e-mail, results@results.org

Web, www.results.org

Works to end world hunger; encourages grassroots and legislative support of programs and proposals dealing with hunger and hunger-related issues. Monitors legislation and regulations.

U.S. National Committee for World Food Day, *2175 K St. N.W. 20437-0001; (202) 653-2404. Fax, (202) 653-5760. Patricia Young, National Coordinator.*

Web, www.worldfooddayusa.org

Consortium of farm, religious, nutrition, education, consumer, relief, and development organizations. Coordinates widespread community participation in World Food Day. Distributes materials about food and hunger issues and encourages long-term action.

Winrock International, *Washington Office,*
1621 N. Kent St., #1200, Arlington, VA 22209; (703) 525-
9430. Fax, (703) 525-1744. Frank Tugwell, President.
Web, www.winrock.org

Works to increase economic opportunity; sustain natural resources; protect the environment; and increase long-term productivity, equity, and responsible resource management to benefit the world's poor and disadvantaged communities. Matches innovative approaches in agriculture, natural resources management, clean energy, and leadership development with the unique needs of its partners. Links local individuals and communities with new ideas and technology. (Headquarters in Morrilton, Ark.)

Worldwatch Institute, *1776 Massachusetts Ave. N.W., 8th Floor 20036; (202) 452-1999. Fax, (202) 296-7365. Christopher Flavin, President.*
General e-mail, worldwatch@worldwatch.org
Web, www.worldwatch.org

Research organization that studies the environmental origins of world population growth and health trends; interests include the food supply and malnutrition.

LIVESTOCK AND POULTRY

AGENCIES

Agricultural Marketing Service (AMS), *(Agriculture Dept.), Livestock and Seed, 1400 Independence Ave. S.W., #2092S, MS 0249 20250-0249; (202) 720-5705. Fax, (202) 720-3499. Barry L. Carpenter, Deputy Administrator.*
Web, www.ams.usda.gov/lsg/index.htm

Administers meat marketing program; maintains market news service to inform producers of meat market situation and daily price changes; develops, establishes, and revises U.S. standards for classes and grades of livestock and meat; grades, examines, and certifies meat and meat products.

Agricultural Marketing Service (AMS), *(Agriculture Dept.), Poultry Programs, 1400 Independence Ave. S.W., #3932S 20250; (202) 720-4476. Fax, (202) 720-5631. Howard M. Magwire, Deputy Administrator.*
Web, www.ams.usda.gov/poultry/index.htm

Sets poultry and egg grading standards. Provides promotion and market news services, including for international markets.

Food Safety and Inspection Service *(Agriculture Dept.), 1400 Independence Ave. S.W., #331E 20250; (202) 720-7025. Fax, (202) 205-0158. Garry L. McKee, Adminis-*
trator. Press, (202) 720-9113. Consumer inquiries, (800) 535-4555; in Washington, (202) 720-3333.
Web, www.usda.gov/fsis

Inspects meat and poultry products and provides safe handling and labeling guidelines.

Grain Inspection, Packers, and Stockyards Administration *(Agriculture Dept.), 1400 Independence Ave. S.W., MS 3601 20250-3601; (202) 720-0219. Fax, (202) 205-9237. Donna Reifschneider, Administrator. Information, (202) 720-5091.*
Web, www.usda.gov/gipsa

Maintains competition in the marketing of livestock, poultry, grain, and meat by prohibiting deceptive and monopolistic marketing practices; tests market scales and conducts check weighings for accuracy.

CONGRESS

House Agriculture Committee, *Subcommittee on Livestock and Horticulture, 1432P LHOB 20515; (202) 225-2171. Fax, (202) 225-0917. Rep. Robin Hayes, R-N.C., Chair; Pam Scott, Staff Director.*
Web, agriculture.house.gov/livestoc.htm

Jurisdiction over legislation on inspection and certification of meat, livestock, and poultry. Jurisdiction over animal welfare, including animals used for experimentation.

Senate Agriculture, Nutrition, and Forestry Committee, *Subcommittee on Marketing, Inspection, and Product Promotion, SR-328A 20510; (202) 224-2035. Sen. Jim Talent, R-Mo., Chair; Vacant, Staff Director.*
Web, agriculture.senate.gov

Jurisdiction over legislation on inspection and certification of meat, livestock, and poultry.

NONPROFIT

American Meat Institute, *1700 N. Moore St., #1600, Arlington, VA 22209; (703) 841-2400. Fax, (703) 527-0938. J. Patrick Boyle, President.*
Web, www.meatami.com

Membership: national and international meat and poultry packers and processors. Provides statistics on meat and poultry production and consumption, livestock, and feed grains. Funds meat research projects and consumer education programs; sponsors conferences and correspondence courses on meat production and processing. Monitors legislation and regulations.

American Sheep Industry Assn., *Washington Office, 412 1st St. S.E., #1 Lobby Level 20003; (202) 484-7134.*

Fax, (202) 484-0770. Fran Boyd, Washington Representative.

General e-mail, info@sheepusa.org

Web, www.sheepusa.org

Membership: sheep, wool, and mohair producers. Interests include sheep breeds, lamb and wool marketing, and wool research. Monitors legislation and regulations. (Headquarters in Denver, Colo.)

Animal Health Institute, *1325 G St. N.W., #700 20005-3104; (202) 637-2440. Fax, (202) 393-1667. Alexander S. Mathews, President.*

Web, www.ahi.org

Membership: manufacturers of drugs and other products (including vaccines, pesticides, and vitamins) for pets and food-producing animals. Monitors legislation and regulations.

FARM (Farm Animal Reform Movement), *P.O. Box 30654, Bethesda, MD 20824; (301) 530-1737. Fax, (301) 530-5747. Alex Hershaft, President.*

General e-mail, farm@farmusa.org

Web, www.farmusa.org

Works to end use of animals for food. Interests include animal protection, consumer health, agricultural resources, and environmental quality. Conducts national educational campaigns, including World Farm Animals Day and the Great American Meatout. Monitors legislation and regulations.

National Cattlemen's Beef Assn., *Government Affairs, Washington Office,* *1301 Pennsylvania Ave. N.W., #300 20004; (202) 347-0228. Fax, (202) 638-0607. Chandler Keys, Vice President.*

Web, www.beef.org

Membership: individual cattlemen, state cattlemen's groups, and breed associations. Provides information on beef research, agricultural labor, beef grading, foreign trade, taxes, marketing, cattle economics, branding, animal health, and environmental management. (Headquarters in Denver, Colo.)

National Chicken Council, *1015 15th St. N.W., #930 20005; (202) 296-2622. Fax, (202) 293-4005. George B. Watts, President.*

Web, www.eatchicken.com

Membership: producers and processors of chickens. Provides information on production, marketing, and consumption of chickens.

National Meat Canners Assn., *1700 N. Moore St., #1600, Arlington, VA 22209; (703) 841-3680. Fax, (703) 841-9656. James Hodges, Executive Secretary.*

Web, www.meatami.com

Membership: canners of prepared meats and meat food products. Provides information on the canned meat industry.

National Pork Producers Council, *Washington Office,* *122 C St. N.W., #875 20001; (202) 347-3600. Fax, (202) 347-5265. Kirk Ferrell, Vice President.*

General e-mail, pork@nppc.org

Web, www.nppc.org

Membership: pork producers and independent pork producer organizations. Interests include pork production, nutrition, the environment, trade, and federal regulations. Monitors legislation and regulations. (Headquarters in Des Moines, Iowa.)

National Renderers Assn., *801 N. Fairfax St., #207, Alexandria, VA 22314; (703) 683-0155. Fax, (703) 683-2626. Thomas M. Cook, President.*

General e-mail, renderers@nationalrenderers.com

Web, www.renderers.org

Membership: manufacturers of meat meal and tallow. Compiles industry statistics; sponsors research; conducts seminars and workshops. Monitors legislation and regulations.

National Turkey Federation, *1225 New York Ave. N.W., #400 20005; (202) 898-0100. Fax, (202) 898-0203. Alice L. Johnson, President.*

Web, www.eatturkey.com

Membership: turkey growers, hatcheries, breeders, and processors. Promotes turkey consumption. Monitors legislation and regulations.

North American Meat Processors Assn., *1910 Association Dr., Reston, VA 20191; (703) 758-1900. Fax, (703) 758-8001. Marty Holmes, Executive Vice President.*

Web, www.namp.com

Membership: meat, poultry, fish, and game companies specializing in the food service industry. Conducts seminars; interests include quality standards and procedures for handling meat, poultry, fish, and game.

U.S. Hide, Skin, and Leather Assn., *1700 N. Moore St., #1600, Arlington, VA 22209; (703) 841-5485. Fax, (703) 527-0938. John Reddington, President.*

Web, www.meatami.com

Membership: meatpackers, brokers, dealers, processors, and exporters of hides and skins. Maintains liaison with allied trade associations and participates in programs on export statistics, hide price reporting, and freight rates; conducts seminars and consumer information programs. (Division of American Meat Institute.)

3 Business and Economics

GENERAL POLICY

AGENCIES

Census Bureau *(Commerce Dept.), Economic Programs,* *Suitland and Silver Hill Rds., #2061-3, Suitland, MD 20746 (mailing address: MS 6000 #2061-3, Washington, DC 20233-6000); (301) 457-2112. Fax, (301) 457-8140. Frederick T. Knickerbocker, Associate Director.*
Web, www.census.gov

Compiles comprehensive statistics on the level and structure of U.S. economic activity and the characteristics of industrial and business establishments at the national, state, and local levels; collects and publishes foreign trade statistics.

Commerce Dept., *14th St. and Constitution Ave. N.W., #5854 20230; (202) 482-2112. Fax, (202) 482-2741. Donald L. Evans, Secretary; Samuel W. Bodman, Deputy Secretary. Information, (202) 482-3263. Library, (202) 482-5511. Press, (202) 482-4883.*
Web, www.doc.gov

Acts as principal adviser to the president on federal policy affecting industry and commerce; promotes national economic growth and development, competitiveness, international trade, and technological development; provides business and government with economic statistics, research, and analysis; encourages minority business; promotes tourism. Library reference service staff answers questions about commerce and business.

Commerce Dept., *Business Liaison, 14th St. and Constitution Ave. N.W., #5062 20230; (202) 482-1360. Fax, (202) 482-4054. Travis Thomas, Director.*
Web, www.doc.gov

Serves as the central office for business assistance. Handles requests for information and services as well as complaints and suggestions from businesses; provides a forum for businesses to comment on federal regulations; initiates meetings on policy issues with industry groups, business organizations, trade and small-business associations, and the corporate community.

Commerce Dept., *STAT-USA, 14th St. and Constitution Ave. N.W., #4886, MS 4885 20230; (202) 482-3429. Fax, (202) 482-3417. Forrest Williams, Director. Toll-free, (800) STAT-USA.*
General e-mail, stat-usa@doc.gov
Web, www.stat-usa.gov

Maintains and makes available for public use the National Trade Data Bank (NTDB) and Stat-USA-Internet.

Council of Economic Advisers *(Executive Office of the President), Dwight D. Eisenhower Executive Office Bldg., #94 20502; (202) 395-5042. Fax, (202) 395-6958. N. Gregory Mankiw, Chair (Designate); Phillip L. Swagel, Chief of Staff.*
Web, www.whitehouse.gov/cea

Advisory body consisting of three members and supporting staff of economists. Monitors and analyzes the economy and advises the president on economic developments, trends, and policies and on the economic implications of other policy initiatives. Prepares the annual *Economic Report of the President* for Congress. Assesses economic implications of international policy.

Economics and Statistics Administration *(Commerce Dept.), 14th St. and Constitution Ave. N.W., #4848 20230; (202) 482-3727. Fax, (202) 482-0432. Kathleen B. Cooper, Under Secretary. Information, (202) 482-2235.*
General e-mail, esa@doc.gov
Web, www.esa.doc.gov

Advises the secretary on economic policy matters, including consumer and capital spending, inventory status, and the short- and long-term outlook in output and unemployment. Seeks to improve economic productivity and growth. Serves as departmental liaison with the Council of Economic Advisers and other government agencies concerned with economic policy. Supervises and sets policy for the Census Bureau and the Bureau of Economic Analysis.

Federal Reserve System, *Board of Governors, 20th and C Sts. N.W., B2046 20551; (202) 452-3201. Fax, (202) 452-3819. Alan Greenspan, Chair; Roger W. Ferguson Jr., Vice Chair. Information, (202) 452-3215. Press, (202) 452-3204. Locator, (202) 452-3000; Publications, (202) 452-3245.*
Web, www.federalreserve.gov

Sets U.S. monetary policy. Supervises the Federal Reserve System and influences credit conditions through the buying and selling of treasury securities in the open market, by fixing the amount of reserves depository institutions must maintain, and by determining discount rates.

Federal Trade Commission (FTC), *6th St. and 600 Pennsylvania Ave. N.W., #440 20580; (202) 326-2100. Timothy J. Muris, Chair; Rosemarie Straight, Executive Director. Information, (202) 326-2222. Library, (202) 326-2395. Press, (202) 326-2180. Chair's fax, (202) 326-2396.*
Web, www.ftc.gov

Promotes policies designed to maintain strong competitive enterprise within the U.S. economic system. Monitors trade practices and investigates cases involving

COMMERCE DEPARTMENT

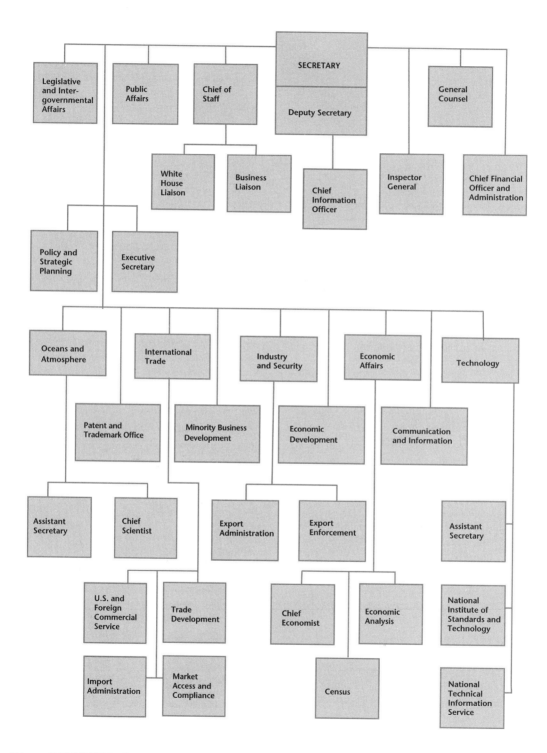

FEDERAL TRADE COMMISSION

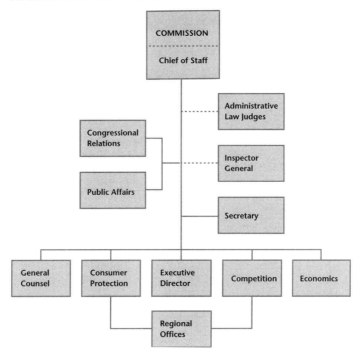

monopoly, unfair restraints, or deceptive practices. Enforces Truth in Lending and Fair Credit Reporting acts. Library open to the public.

Federal Trade Commission (FTC), *Economics, 6th St. and Pennsylvania Ave. N.W. 20580; (202) 326-3429. Fax, (202) 326-2380. David T. Scheffman, Director.*
Web, www.ftc.gov/ftc/economic.htm

Provides economic analyses for consumer protection and antitrust investigations, cases, and rulemakings; advises the commission on the effect of government regulations on competition and consumers in various industries; develops special reports on competition, consumer protection, and regulatory issues.

National Economic Council *(Executive Office of the President), The White House 20500; (202) 456-6630. Fax, (202) 456-2223. Stephen Friedman, National Economic Adviser.*
Web, www.whitehouse.gov/nec/

Comprised of cabinet members and other high-ranking executive branch officials. Coordinates domestic and international economic policy-making process to facili-

tate the implementation of the president's economic agenda.

National Institute of Standards and Technology (NIST), *(Commerce Dept.), Global Standards and Information, 100 Bureau Dr. MS-2160, Bldg. 820, #164, Gaithersburg, MD 20899; (301) 975-4040. Fax, (301) 926-1559. Carmina Londono, Group Leader. TTY, (301) 975-8295. Public Inquiries Unit, (301) 975-6478.*
General e-mail, gsig@nist.gov
Web, www.nist.gov

Serves as the national repository for information on voluntary industry standards and regulations for domestic and international products. Provides information on specifications, test methods, domestic and international technical regulations, codes, and recommended practices.

National Women's Business Council, *409 3rd St. S.W., #210 20024; (202) 205-3850. Fax, (202) 205-6825. Marilyn Carlson Nelson, Chair; Julie R. Weeks, Executive Director.*
Web, www.nwbc.gov

Membership: eight women business owners, six representatives of women business organizations, and one chair appointed by the president. Independent, congressionally mandated council established by the Women's Business Ownership Act of 1988. Reviews the status of women-owned businesses nationwide and makes policy recommendations to the president and Congress. Assesses the role of the federal government in aiding and promoting women-owned businesses.

Small Business Administration (SBA), *409 3rd St. S.W., #7000 20416; (202) 205-6605. Fax, (202) 205-6802. Hector Barreto, Administrator; Lisa Goeas, Chief of Staff. Library, (202) 205-7033. Press, (202) 205-6540. Toll-free information, (800) 827-5722. Locator, (202) 205-6600.* Web, www.sba.gov

Serves as the government's principal advocate of small-business interests through financial, investment, procurement, and management assistance and counseling; evaluates effect of federal programs on and recommends policies for small business.

Treasury Dept., *1500 Pennsylvania Ave. N.W., #3330 20220; (202) 622-1100. Fax, (202) 622-0073. John W. Snow, Secretary; Kenneth Dam, Deputy Secretary. Information, (202) 622-1260. Library, (202) 622-0990. Locator, (202) 622-2111.* Web, www.ustreas.gov

Serves as chief financial officer of the government and adviser to the president on economic policy. Formulates and recommends domestic and international financial, economic, tax, and broad fiscal policies; manages the public debt. Library open to the public by appointment.

Treasury Dept., *Economic Policy,* *1500 Pennsylvania Ave. N.W., #3454 20220; (202) 622-2200. Fax, (202) 622-2633. Richard H. Clarida, Assistant Secretary.* Web, www.ustreas.gov

Assists and advises the Treasury secretary in the formulation and execution of domestic and international economic policies and programs; helps prepare economic forecasts for the federal budget.

Treasury Dept., *Financial Management Service,* *401 14th St. S.W., #548 20227; (202) 874-7000. Fax, (202) 874-6743. Richard Gregg, Commissioner. Press, (202) 874-6604.* Web, www.ustreas.gov/fms

Serves as the government's central financial manager, responsible for cash management and investment of government trust funds, credit administration, and debt collection. Handles central accounting for government fiscal activities; promotes sound financial management prac-

tices and increased use of automated payments, collections, accounting, and reporting systems.

Treasury Dept., *Fiscal,* *1500 Pennsylvania Ave. N.W., #2112 20220; (202) 622-0560. Fax, (202) 622-0962. Donald V. Hammond, Fiscal Assistant Secretary.* Web, www.ustreas.gov

Administers Treasury Dept. financial operations. Supervises the Financial Management Service and the Bureau of the Public Debt.

CONGRESS

General Accounting Office (GAO), *441 G St. N.W. 20548; (202) 512-5500. Fax, (202) 512-5507. David M. Walker, Comptroller General. Information, (202) 512-4800. Library, (202) 512-5180. Documents, (202) 512-6000.* Web, www.gao.gov

Independent, nonpartisan agency in the legislative branch. Serves as the investigating agency for Congress; carries out legal, accounting, auditing, and claims settlement functions; makes recommendations for more effective government operations; publishes monthly lists of reports available to the public. Library open to the public by appointment.

House Appropriations Committee, *H218 CAP 20515; (202) 225-2771. Rep. C.W. Bill Young, R-Fla., Chair; James W. Dyer, Staff Director.* Web, www.house.gov/appropriations

Jurisdiction over legislation to appropriate funds for all government programs; responsible for rescissions of appropriated funds, transfers of surplus allocations, and new spending under the Congressional Budget Act. Maintains data on congressional appropriating process and government spending.

House Appropriations Committee, *Subcommittee on Commerce, Justice, State, and the Judiciary,* *H309 CAP 20515; (202) 225-3351. Rep. Frank R. Wolf, R-Va., Chair; Mike Ringler, Staff Director.* Web, www.house.gov/appropriations

Jurisdiction over legislation to appropriate funds for the Commerce Dept., the Securities and Exchange Commission, the Small Business Administration, the Competitiveness Policy Council, the Federal Trade Commission, the International Trade Commission, and the Office of the U.S. Trade Representative.

House Appropriations Committee, *Subcommittee on Transportation, Treasury, and Related Agencies,* *2358 RHOB 20515; (202) 225-2141. Fax, (202) 225-5895. Rep. Ernest Istook, R-Okla., Chair; Rich Efford, Clerk.* Web, www.house.gov/appropriations

Jurisdiction over legislation to appropriate funds for the Executive Office of the President, including the Council of Economic Advisers and the Office of Management and Budget; the Treasury Dept.; and the U.S. Tax Court.

House Energy and Commerce Committee, *2125 RHOB 20515; (202) 225-2927. Fax, (202) 225-1919. Rep. Billy Tauzin, R-La., Chair; David V. Marventano, Staff Director.*
General e-mail, commerce@mail.house.gov
Web, www.house.gov/commerce

Jurisdiction over measures relating to general management of the Energy Dept., the management and all functions of the Federal Energy Regulatory Commission, and national energy policy generally. Has a special oversight function with respect to all laws, programs, and government activities affecting nuclear and other energy, and nonmilitary nuclear energy and research and development, including the disposal of nuclear waste.

House Financial Services Committee, *2129 RHOB 20515; (202) 225-7502. Fax, (202) 226-6052. Rep. Michael G. Oxley, R-Ohio, Chair; Bob Foster, Staff Director.*
Web, financialservices.house.gov

Jurisdiction over legislation dealing with banks and banking, including deposit insurance and federal monetary policy; economic stabilization, defense production, renegotiation, and control of the price of commodities, rents, and services; financial aid to commerce and industry (other than transportation); insurance generally; international finance; money and credit, including currency and coinage; revaluation of the dollar; public and private housing; securities and exchanges; and urban development.

House Government Reform Committee, *2157 RHOB 20515; (202) 225-5074. Fax, (202) 225-3974. Rep. Thomas M. Davis III, R-Va., Chair; Peter Sirh, Staff Director.*
Web, www.house.gov/reform

Jurisdiction over legislation on government budget and accounting issues other than appropriations; oversight of General Accounting Office operations and of the Office of Management and Budget.

House Government Reform Committee, *Subcommittee on Energy Policy, Natural Resources, and Regulatory Affairs, B377 RHOB 20515; (202) 225-4407. Fax, (202) 225-2441. Rep. Doug Ose, R-Calif., Chair; Dan Skopec, Staff Director.*
Web, www.house.gov/reform

Oversees operations of the Commerce and Treasury departments, the Federal Reserve System, U.S. Tax Court,

and other federal agencies dealing with economic and monetary affairs (jurisdiction shared with House Banking and Financial Services Committee).

House Ways and Means Committee, *1102 LHOB 20515; (202) 225-3625. Fax, (202) 225-2610. Rep. Bill Thomas, R-Calif., Chair; Allison Giles, Chief of Staff.*
General e-mail, contactwaysandmeans@mail.house.gov
Web, waysandmeans.house.gov

Jurisdiction over legislation dealing with the debt ceiling; investment policy; and taxes, including taxation of savings, interest, and dividends. Oversees the Internal Revenue Service; sets excise tax rates for the Bureau of Alcohol, Tobacco, and Firearms.

Joint Economic Committee, *SD-G01 20510; (202) 224-5171. Sen. Robert F. Bennett, R-Utah, Chair; Donald Marron, Executive Director.*
General e-mail, jec@jec.house.gov
Web, jec.senate.gov

Studies and makes recommendations on economic policy. Maintains and analyzes data pertaining to aggregate economic activity; analyzes the president's annual economic report to Congress and communicates findings to the House and Senate.

Senate Appropriations Committee, *S128 CAP 20510; (202) 224-7363. Sen. Ted Stevens, R-Alaska, Chair; James Morhard, Staff Director.*
Web, appropriations.senate.gov

Jurisdiction over legislation to appropriate funds for all government programs; responsible for rescissions of appropriated funds, transfers of surplus allocations, and new spending under the Congressional Budget Act. Maintains data on congressional appropriating process and government spending.

Senate Appropriations Committee, *Subcommittee on Commerce, Justice, State, and the Judiciary, S-206 CAP 20510; (202) 224-7277. Fax, (202) 228-0587. Sen. Judd Gregg, R-N.H., Chair; James Morhard, Clerk.*
Web, appropriations.senate.gov/commerce

Jurisdiction over legislation to appropriate funds for the Commerce Dept., the Securities and Exchange Commission, the Small Business Administration, the Competitiveness Policy Council, the Federal Trade Commission, the International Trade Commission, and the Office of the U.S. Trade Representative.

Senate Appropriations Committee, *Subcommittee on Transportation, Treasury, and General Government, SD-196 20510; (202) 224-4869. Fax, (202) 228-1621. Sen. Richard C. Shelby, R-Ala., Chair; Paul Doerrer, Clerk.*

TREASURY DEPARTMENT

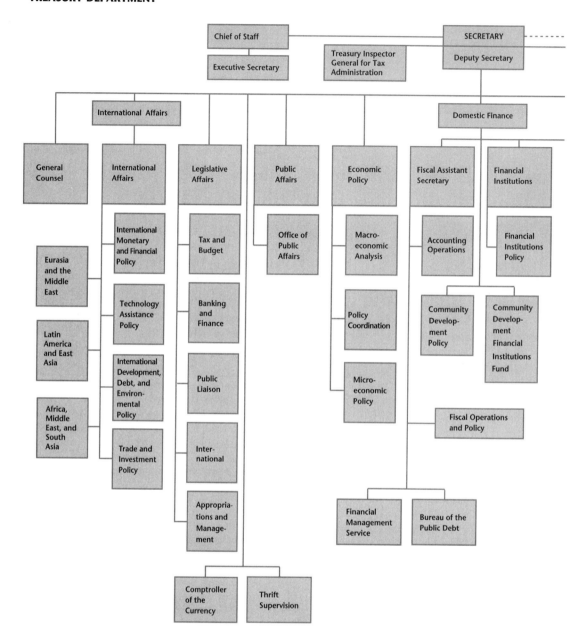

Web, appropriations.senate.gov

Jurisdiction over legislation to appropriate funds for the Executive Office of the President, including the Council of Economic Advisers and the Office of Management and Budget; the Treasury Dept.; and the U.S. Tax Court.

Senate Banking, Housing, and Urban Affairs Committee, *SD-534 20510; (202) 224-7391. Fax, (202) 224-5137. Sen. Richard C. Shelby, R-Ala., Chair; Kathy Casey, Staff Director.*

Web, banking.senate.gov

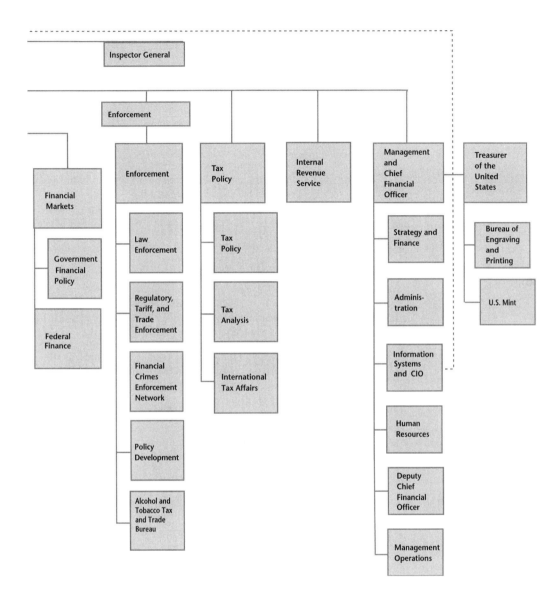

Inspector General

Enforcement

Financial Markets

Government Financial Policy

Federal Finance

Enforcement

Law Enforcement

Regulatory, Tariff, and Trade Enforcement

Financial Crimes Enforcement Network

Policy Development

Alcohol and Tobacco Tax and Trade Bureau

Tax Policy

Tax Policy

Tax Analysis

International Tax Affairs

Internal Revenue Service

Management and Chief Financial Officer

Strategy and Finance

Administration

Information Systems and CIO

Human Resources

Deputy Chief Financial Officer

Management Operations

Treasurer of the United States

Bureau of Engraving and Printing

U.S. Mint

Jurisdiction over legislation dealing with bank regulation, federal monetary policy, financial aid to commerce and industry, the measurement of economic activity, federal loan guarantees, economic development, and other economic stabilization measures (including wage and price controls); oversees the Treasury Dept.; oversees the Federal Reserve System.

Senate Commerce, Science, and Transportation Committee, *SD-508 20510; (202) 224-5115. Fax, (202) 228-0303. Sen. John McCain, R-Ariz., Chair; Jeanne Bumpus, Staff Director.*

Web, commerce.senate.gov

Jurisdiction over legislation on interstate and foreign commerce generally, including the Federal Trade Commission, and many operations of the Commerce Dept.

Senate Finance Committee, *SD-219 20510; (202) 224-4515. Fax, (202) 228-0554. Sen. Charles E. Grassley, R-Iowa, Chair; Kolan L. Davis, Staff Director.*

Web, finance.senate.gov

Jurisdiction over tax legislation; oversees the Internal Revenue Service and the U.S. Tax Court; sets excise tax rates for the Alcohol and Tobacco Tax and Trade Bureau.

Senate Finance Committee, *Subcommittee on Long-Term Growth and Debt Reduction,* SD-219 20510; (202) 224-4515. Fax, (202) 224-5920. Sen. Gordon H. Smith, R-Ore., Chair; Kolan L. Davis, Staff Director.*

Web, finance.senate.gov

Holds hearings on debt ceiling legislation.

Senate Finance Committee, *Subcommittee on Taxation and IRS Oversight,* SD-219 20510; (202) 224-4515. Sen. Don Nickles, R-Okla., Chair; Kolan L. Davis, Staff Director.*

Web, finance.senate.gov

Holds hearings on legislation relating to investment policy and taxation of savings, interest, and dividends.

Senate Governmental Affairs Committee, *SD-340 20510; (202) 224-4751. Fax, (202) 228-3792. Sen. Susan Collins, R-Maine, Chair; Michael Bopp, Staff Director.*

Web, www.senate.gov/~gov_affairs

Jurisdiction over legislation on government budget and accounting issues other than appropriations; oversight of General Accounting Office operations and of the Office of Management and Budget.

NONPROFIT

American Business Conference, *1828 L St. N.W., #908 20036; (202) 822-9300. Fax, (202) 467-4070. John Endean, President.*

General e-mail, abc@americanbusinessconference.org

Web, www.americanbusinessconference.org

Membership: chief executive officers of midsize, high-growth companies. Seeks a public policy role for growth companies. Studies capital formation, tax policy, regulatory reform, and international trade.

American Chamber of Commerce Executives, *4232 King St., Alexandria, VA 22302; (703) 998-0072. Fax, (703) 931-5624. Mick Fleming, President.*

General e-mail, adminacce@acce.org

Web, www.acce.org

Membership: executives of local, state, and international chambers of commerce. Conducts for members educational programs and conferences on topics of interest, including economic development, management symposiums, and membership drives. Sponsors special interest groups for members.

American Council for Capital Formation (ACCF), *1750 K St. N.W., #400 20006; (202) 293-5811. Fax, (202) 785-8165. Mark Bloomfield, President.*

General e-mail, info@accf.org

Web, www.accf.org

Advocates tax, trade, and environmental policies conducive to saving, investment, and economic growth. Affiliated with the ACCF Center for Policy Research, which conducts and funds research on capital formation topics.

American Enterprise Institute for Public Policy Research (AEI), *Economic Policy Studies,* 1150 17th St. N.W., #1100 20036; (202) 862-5800. Fax, (202) 862-7177. Christopher DeMuth, President.*

Web, www.aei.org

Research and educational organization. Interests include monetary, tax, trade, and regulatory policy and labor and social security issues.

American Management Assn. International, *Washington Office,* 440 1st St. N.W. 20001; (202) 347-3092. Fax, (202) 347-4549. Judy Doran, Executive Director.*

Web, www.amanet.org

Membership: managers and other corporate professionals. Offers training and education programs to members. (Headquarters in New York.)

American Society of Assn. Executives (ASAE), *1575 Eye St. N.W. 20005-1103; (202) 626-2723. Fax, (202) 371-8825. Michael S. Olson, President. Library, (202) 626-2742. Press, (202) 626-2733. TTY, (202) 626-2803.*

General e-mail, pr@asaenet.org

Web, www.asaenet.org

Conducts research and provides educational programs on association management, trends, and developments. Library open to the public.

The Brookings Institution, *Economic Studies Program,* 1775 Massachusetts Ave. N.W. 20036-2188; (202) 797-6111. Fax, (202) 797-6181. Robert E. Litan, Director. Information, (202) 797-6302.*

Web, www.brookings.edu

Sponsors economic research and publishes studies on domestic and international economics, worldwide economic growth and stability, public finance, urban economics, industrial organization and regulation, labor economics, social policy, and the economics of human resources.

The Business Council, *P.O. Box 20147 20041; (202) 298-7650. Fax, (202) 785-0296. Philip E. Cassidy, Executive Director.*
Web, www.businesscouncil.com
   Membership: current and former chief executive officers of major corporations. Serves as a forum for business and government to exchange views and explore public policy as it affects U.S. business interests.

Business–Higher Education Forum, *1 Dupont Circle N.W., #800 20036; (202) 939-9345. Fax, (202) 833-4723. Jeremiah L. Murphy, Director.*
General e-mail, bhef@ace.nche.edu
Web, www.bhef.com
   Membership: chief executive officers of major corporations, museums, colleges, and universities. Promotes cooperation between businesses and higher educational institutions. Interests include international economic competitiveness, education and training, research and development, science and technology, and global interdependence.

The Business Roundtable, *1615 L St. N.W., #1100 20036-5610; (202) 872-1260. Fax, (202) 466-3509. John J. Castellani, President.*
Web, www.brt.org
   Membership: chief executives of the nation's largest corporations. Examines issues of concern to business, including taxation, antitrust law, international trade, employment policy, and the federal budget.

Center for the Study of Public Choice *(George Mason University), Carrow Hall, #1D3, 4400 University Dr., Fairfax, VA 22030; (703) 993-2330. Fax, (703) 993-2323. W. Mark Crain, Director.*
Web, www.gmu.edu/departments/economics
   Promotes research in public choice, an interdisciplinary approach to the study of the relationship between economic and political institutions. Interests include constitutional economics, public finance, federalism and local government, econometrics, and trade protection and regulation. Sponsors conferences and seminars. Library open to the public.

Citizens for a Sound Economy, *1900 M St. N.W., #500 20036; (202) 783-3870. Fax, (202) 783-4687. Paul Beckner, President.*
Web, www.cse.org
   Citizens' advocacy group that promotes reduced taxes, free trade, and deregulation. Advocates deficit reduction through spending restraint, competitiveness in financial markets, and increased private involvement in providing public services. Encourages citizens to petition members of Congress.

Committee for Economic Development, *2000 L St. N.W., #700 20036; (202) 296-5860. Fax, (202) 223-0776. Everett M. Ehrlich, Senior Vice President.*
Web, www.ced.org
   Research organization that makes recommendations on domestic and international economic policy.

Competitive Enterprise Institute, *1001 Connecticut Ave. N.W., #1250 20036; (202) 331-1010. Fax, (202) 331-0640. Fred L. Smith, President.*
General e-mail, info@cei.org
Web, www.cei.org
   Advocates free enterprise and limited government. Produces policy analyses on tax, budget, financial services, antitrust, biotechnological, and environmental issues. Monitors legislation and litigates against restrictive regulations through its Free Market Legal Program.

The Conference Board, *Government Affairs, Washington Office, 1255 34th St. N.W. 20007; (202) 625-4733. Fax, (202) 462-4694. Meredith Whiting, Senior Research Fellow.*
Web, www.conference-board.org
   Membership: senior executives from various industries. Researches science and technology policy, environmental affairs, corporate governance and citizenship, management-related issues, the integrated market, and European business activities. Headquarters conducts research and provides economic data on business management, trends, and development. (Headquarters in New York.)

Council for Social and Economic Studies, *1133 13th St. N.W., #C2 20005-4297; (202) 371-2700. Fax, (202) 371-1523. Roger Pearson, Executive Director.*
Web, www.mankind.org
   Conducts research on domestic and international economic, social, and political issues. Publishes the *Journal of Social, Political, and Economic Studies.*

Council on Competitiveness, *1500 K St. N.W., #850 20005; (202) 682-4292. Fax, (202) 682-5150. Deborah Wince-Smith, President.*
General e-mail, council@compete.org
Web, www.compete.org
   Membership: executives from business, education, and labor. Seeks increased public awareness of economic competition. Works to set a national action agenda for U.S. competitiveness in global markets.

Economic Policy Institute, *1660 L St. N.W., #1200 20036; (202) 775-8810. Fax, (202) 775-0819. Lawrence Mishel, President.*
General e-mail, epi@epinet.org
Web, www.epinet.org

Research and educational organization that publishes analyses on economics, economic development, competitiveness, income distribution, industrial competitiveness, and investment. Conducts public conferences and seminars.

Ethics Resource Center, *1747 Pennsylvania Ave. N.W., #400 20006; (202) 737-2258. Fax, (202) 737-2227. Stuart C. Gilman, President. Information, (800) 777-1285. Press, (202) 872-4768.*
Web, www.ethics.org

Nonpartisan educational organization whose vision is an ethical world. Fosters ethical practices among individuals and institutions. Interests include research and knowledge building, education and advocacy, and consulting and technical assistance.

Financial Executives International, *Washington Office, 1629 K St. N.W., #1100 20006; (202) 785-6719. Fax, (202) 331-4212. Andrea Ball, Chapter Administrator.*
Web, www.fei.org/chapter/dc

Membership: senior financial executives of public and private companies worldwide. Provides conferences and professional development programs; publishes the *Financial Executive.* Monitors legislation and regulations affecting business. (Headquarters in Florham Park, N.J.)

Greater Washington Board of Trade, *1725 Eye St. N.W., #200 20006; (202) 857-5900. Fax, (202) 223-2648. Robert A. Peck, President.*
General e-mail, info@bot.org
Web, www.bot.org

Promotes and plans economic growth for the capital region. Supports business-government partnerships, technological training, and transportation planning; promotes international trade; works to increase economic viability of the city of Washington. Monitors legislation and regulations at local, state, and federal levels.

National Assn. of Corporate Directors, *1828 L St. N.W., #801 20036; (202) 775-0509. Fax, (202) 775-4857. Roger Raber, President.*
Web, www.nacdonline.org

Membership: executives of closely held and public companies, outside and inside directors, and stewards of corporate governance. Serves as a clearinghouse on corporate governance and current board practices. Conducts seminars; runs executive search service; sponsors insurance program for directors and officers.

National Assn. of Manufacturers (NAM), *1331 Pennsylvania Ave. N.W., #600 20004-1790; (202) 637-3000. Fax, (202) 637-3182. Jerry Jasinowski, President. Press, (202) 637-3094.*
General e-mail, manufacturing@nam.org
Web, www.nam.org

Represents industry views (mainly of manufacturers) to government on national and international issues. Reviews legislation, administrative rulings, and judicial decisions affecting industry. Sponsors the Human Resources Forum; operates a Web site for members and the public that provides information on legislative and other news; conducts programs on labor relations, occupational safety and health, regulatory and consumer affairs, environmental trade and technology, and other business issues.

National Assn. of State Budget Officers, *444 N. Capitol St. N.W., #642 20001-1501; (202) 624-5382. Fax, (202) 624-7745. Scott Pattison, Executive Director.*
Web, www.nasbo.org

Membership: state budget and financial officers. Publishes research reports on budget-related issues. (Affiliate of the National Governors' Assn.)

National Chamber Litigation Center, *1615 H St. N.W., #230 20062; (202) 463-5337. Fax, (202) 463-5346. Stephen A. Bokat, Executive Vice President.*
Web, www.uschamber.com/nclc

Public policy law firm of the U.S. Chamber of Commerce. Advocates business's positions in court on such issues as employment, environmental, and constitutional law. Provides businesses with legal assistance and representation in legal proceedings before federal courts and agencies.

National Cooperative Business Assn., *1401 New York Ave. N.W., #1100 20005-2160; (202) 638-6222. Fax, (202) 638-1374. Paul Hazen, President.*
General e-mail, ncba@ncba.coop
Web, www.ncba.coop

Alliance of cooperatives, businesses, and state cooperative associations. Supports development of cooperative businesses; promotes and develops trade among domestic and international cooperatives. Monitors legislation and regulations.

National Policy Assn., *1424 16th St. N.W., #700 20036; (202) 265-7685. Fax, (202) 797-5516. Anthony C. E. Quainton, President.*
General e-mail, npa@npa1.org
Web, www.npa1.org

Research organization that conducts studies on domestic and international economic policy issues.

Interests include agriculture, human resources, employment, international trade, investment and monetary policy, and U.S. economic competitiveness.

National Retail Federation, *325 7th St. N.W., #1100 20004-2802; (202) 783-7971. Fax, (202) 737-2849. Tracy Mullin, President.*
Web, www.nrf.com

Membership: international, national, and state associations of retailers and major retail corporations. Concerned with federal regulatory activities and legislation that affect retailers, including tax, employment, trade, and credit issues. Provides information on retailing through seminars, conferences, and publications.

National Venture Capital Assn., *1655 N. Fort Myer Dr., #850, Arlington, VA 22209; (703) 524-2549. Fax, (703) 524-3940. Mark Heesen, President.*
Web, www.nvca.org

Membership: venture capital organizations and individuals and corporate financiers. Promotes understanding of venture capital investment. Monitors legislation.

Private Sector Council, *1101 16th St. N.W., #300 20036-4813; (202) 822-3910. Fax, (202) 822-0638. A. W. Smith Jr., President.*
General e-mail, privsect@privsect.org
Web, www.privsect.org

Membership: large corporations and private businesses including financial and information technology organizations. Seeks to improve government efficiency, productivity, and management through a cooperative effort of the public and private sectors.

Society of Competitive Intelligence Professionals, *1700 Diagonal Rd., #600, Alexandria, VA 22314; (703) 739-0696. Fax, (703) 739-2524. William Weber, Executive Director.*
General e-mail, postmaster@scip.org
Web, www.scip.org

Promotes businesses' competitiveness through a greater understanding of competitive behaviors and future strategies as well as the market dynamics in which they conduct business. Conducts seminars and conferences. Publishes the *Competitive Intelligence Magazine.*

U.S. Business and Industry Council, *910 16th St. N.W., #300 20006; (202) 728-1980. Fax, (202) 728-1981. Kevin L. Kearns, President.*
General e-mail, council@usbusiness.org
Web, www.usbusiness.org

Advocates energy independence, reindustrialization, and effective use of natural resources and manufacturing

capacity. Current issues include business tax reduction, the liability crisis, defense and other federal spending, and the trade deficit. Media network distributes op-ed pieces to newspapers and radio stations.

U.S. Chamber of Commerce, *1615 H St. N.W. 20062-2000; (202) 659-6000. Fax, (202) 463-5328. Thomas J. Donohue, President. Press, (202) 463-5682. Publications, (800) 638-6582.*
Web, www.uschamber.com

Federation of businesses, trade, and professional associations; state and local chambers of commerce; and American chambers of commerce abroad. Develops policy on legislative issues important to American business; sponsors programs on management, business confidence, small business, consumer affairs, economic policy, minority business, and tax policy; maintains a business forecast and survey center and a trade negotiation information service. Monitors legislation and regulations.

U.S. Chamber of Commerce, *Congressional and Public Affairs, 1615 H St. N.W. 20062-2000; (202) 463-5600. Fax, (202) 887-3430. Rolf T. Lundberg, Senior Vice President.*
Web, www.uschamber.com

Advocates business's position on government and regulatory affairs. Monitors legislation and regulations on antitrust and corporate policy, product liability, and business-consumer relations.

U.S. Chamber of Commerce, *Economic Policy, 1615 H St. N.W. 20062-2000; (202) 463-5620. Fax, (202) 463-3174. Martin A. Regalia, Chief Economist. Press, (202) 463-5682.*
Web, www.uschamber.com

Represents business community's views on economic policy, including government spending, the federal budget, and tax issues. Forecasts the economy of the United States and other industrialized nations and projects the impact of major policy changes. Studies economic trends and analyzes their effect on the business community.

Coins and Currency

AGENCIES

Bureau of Engraving and Printing (BEP), *(Treasury Dept.), 14th and C Sts. S.W., #119M 20228; (202) 874-2002. Fax, (202) 874-3879. Thomas A. Ferguson, Director. Information, (202) 874-3019.*
Web, www.bep.treas.gov

Designs, engraves, and prints Federal Reserve notes, postage stamps, military certificates, White House invitations, presidential portraits, and special security documents for the federal government. Provides information on history, design, and engraving of currency; offers public tours; maintains reading room where materials are brought for special research (for appointment, write to the BEP's Historical Resource Center).

Bureau of Engraving and Printing (BEP), *(Treasury Dept.), Currency Standards, 14th and C Sts. S.W. 20228 (mailing address: P.O. Box 37048 20013); (202) 874-8897. Fax, (202) 874-5362. Carol L. Seegars, Chief. Information, (866) 575-2361. Mutilation redemption, (202) 874-2532. Unfit currency and destruction of currency, (202) 874-2176. Claims, (202) 874-2397.*

Redeems U.S. currency that has been mutilated; develops regulations and procedures for the destruction of unfit U.S. currency.

Federal Reserve System, *Board of Governors, 20th and C Sts. N.W., B2046 20551; (202) 452-3201. Fax, (202) 452-3819. Alan Greenspan, Chair; Roger W. Ferguson Jr., Vice Chair. Information, (202) 452-3215. Press, (202) 452-3204. Locator, (202) 452-3000; Publications, (202) 452-3245.*
Web, www.federalreserve.gov

Influences the availability of money as part of its responsibility for monetary policy; maintains reading room for inspection of records that are available to the public.

National Museum of American History *(Smithsonian Institution), National Numismatic Collection, 14th St. and Constitution Ave. N.W. 20013; (202) 357-1798. Fax, (202) 357-4840. Richard G. Doty, Curator.*
Web, www.si.edu

Develops and maintains collections of ancient, medieval, modern, U.S., and world coins; U.S. and world currencies; tokens; medals; orders and decorations; and primitive media of exchange. Conducts research and responds to public inquiries.

Treasury Dept., *1500 Pennsylvania Ave. N.W., #3330 20220; (202) 622-1100. Fax, (202) 622-0073. John W. Snow, Secretary; Kenneth Dam, Deputy Secretary. Information, (202) 622-1260. Library, (202) 622-0990. Locator, (202) 622-2111.*
Web, www.ustreas.gov

Oversees the manufacture of U.S. coins and currency; submits to Congress final reports on the minting of coins or any changes in currency. Library open to the public by appointment.

Treasury Dept., *Financial Management Service, 401 14th St. S.W., #548 20227; (202) 874-7000. Fax, (202) 874-6743. Richard Gregg, Commissioner. Press, (202) 874-6604.*

Web, www.ustreas.gov/fms

Prepares and publishes for the president, Congress, and the public monthly, quarterly, and annual statements of government financial transactions, including reports on U.S. currency and coins in circulation.

Treasury Dept., *Treasurer of the United States, 1500 Pennsylvania Ave. N.W., #2134 20220; (202) 622-0100. Fax, (202) 622-2258. Rosario Marin, Treasurer.*
Web, www.ustreas.gov

Spokesperson for the Treasury Dept. in matters dealing with currency, coinage, and savings bonds. Signs currency; promotes selling and holding of savings bonds; oversees operation of the U.S. Mint and the Bureau of Engraving and Printing.

U.S. Mint *(Treasury Dept.), 801 9th St. N.W. 20220; (202) 354-7200. Fax, (202) 756-6160. Henrietta Holsman Fore, Director. Information, (202) 354-7227.*
Web, www.usmint.gov

Manufactures and distributes all domestic coins; safeguards government's holdings of precious metals; manufactures and sells commemorative coins and medals of historic interest. Maintains a sales area at Union Station in Washington, D.C.

CONGRESS

House Financial Services Committee, *Subcommittee on Domestic and International Monetary Policy, Trade, and Technology, B304 RHOB 20515; (202) 225-7502. Rep. Peter T. King, R-N.Y., Chair; Bob Foster, Staff Director.*
Web, www.house.gov/financialservices

Jurisdiction over legislation on all matters relating to coins, currency, medals, proof and mint sets, and other special coins. Oversight of the U.S. Mint and the Bureau of Engraving and Printing.

Senate Banking, Housing, and Urban Affairs Committee, *SD-534 20510; (202) 224-7391. Fax, (202) 224-5137. Sen. Richard C. Shelby, R-Ala., Chair; Kathy Casey, Staff Director.*
Web, banking.senate.gov

Jurisdiction over legislation on coins and currency, medals, proof and mint sets, and other special coins.

Federal Budget

AGENCIES

Federal Financing Bank *(Treasury Dept.), 1500 Pennsylvania Ave. N.W. 20220; (202) 622-2470. Fax, (202) 622-0707. Gary H. Burner, Manager.*
Web, www.ustreas.gov/ffb

Coordinates federal agency borrowing by purchasing securities issued or guaranteed by federal agencies; funds its operations by borrowing from the Treasury.

Office of Management and Budget (OMB),
(Executive Office of the President), *Eisenhower Executive Office Bldg., #252 20503; (202) 395-4840. Fax, (202) 395-3888. Mitchell E. Daniels Jr., Director. Press, (202) 395-7254.*
Web, www.omb.gov

Prepares president's annual budget; works with the Council of Economic Advisers and the Treasury Dept. to develop the federal government's fiscal program; oversees administration of the budget; reviews government regulations; coordinates administration procurement and management policy.

Treasury Dept., *Bureau of the Public Debt,* *999 E St. N.W., #500 20239; (202) 691-3500. Fax, (202) 219-4163. Van Zeck, Commissioner. Press, (202) 691-3502. Savings bonds, (800) 487-2663.*
Web, www.publicdebt.treas.gov

Handles public debt securities, Treasury notes, and bonds; maintains all records on series EE and HH savings bonds.

Treasury Dept., *Federal Finance Policy Analysis,*
1500 Pennsylvania Ave. N.W., #5011 20220; (202) 622-2680. Fax, (202) 622-0974. Norman K. Carleton, Director.
Web, www.ustreas.gov

Analyzes and evaluates economic and financial development, problems and proposals in the areas of Treasury financing, public debt management, and related economic matters. Provides analysis and technical assistance on regulatory issues involving government securities and related markets. Monitors and analyzes foreign investment in Treasury securities.

Treasury Dept., *Government Financing,* *1500 Pennsylvania Ave. N.W., South Court #1 20220; (202) 622-2460. Fax, (202) 622-0427. Kerry Lanham, Director.*
Web, www.ustreas.gov

Analyzes federal credit program principles and standards, legislation, and proposals related to government borrowing, lending, and investment. Furnishes actuarial and mathematical analysis required for Treasury market financing, the Federal Financing Bank, and other government agencies. Manages the Federal Financing Bank.

Treasury Dept., *Market Finance,* *1500 Pennsylvania Ave. N.W., #5020 20220; (202) 622-2630. Fax, (202) 622-0244. Paul F. Malvey, Director.*
Web, www.ustreas.gov

Provides financial and economic analysis on government financing and Treasury debt management. Coordinates, analyzes, and reviews government borrowing, lending, and investment activities. Monitors the volume of funds raised and supplied in the credit market. Determines interest rates for government loan programs.

CONGRESS

Congressional Budget Office, *402 FHOB 20515; (202) 226-2700. Fax, (202) 225-7509. Douglas J. Holtz-Eakin, Director. Information, (202) 226-2600.*
Web, www.cbo.gov

Nonpartisan office that provides the House and Senate with budget-related information and analyses of alternative fiscal policies.

House Budget Committee, *309 CHOB 20515; (202) 226-7270. Fax, (202) 226-7174. Rep. Jim Nussle, R-Iowa, Chair; Rich Meade, Staff Director.*
General e-mail, budget@mail.house.gov
Web, budget.house.gov/budget

Jurisdiction over congressional budget resolutions, which set levels for federal spending, revenues, deficit, and debt. Jurisdiction over reconciliation bills, which alter existing programs to meet budget goals. Oversight of Congressional Budget Office. Studies budget matters; makes available statistics pertaining to budget proposals put forward by the president and Congress.

Senate Budget Committee, *SD-624 20510; (202) 224-0642. Fax, (202) 224-4835. Sen. Don Nickles, R-Okla., Chair; Hazen Marshall, Staff Director.*
Web, budget.senate.gov

Jurisdiction over congressional budget resolutions, which set levels for federal spending, revenues, deficit, and debt. Jurisdiction over reconciliation bills, which alter existing programs to meet budget goals. Oversight of the Congressional Budget Office. Studies budget matters; makes available statistics pertaining to budget proposals put forward by the president and Congress.

NONPROFIT

Committee for a Responsible Federal Budget,
220 1/2 E St. N.E. 20002; (202) 547-4484. Fax, (202) 547-4476. Carol Cox Wait, President.
General e-mail, crfb@aol.com
Web, www.crfb.org

Educational organization that works to support and improve the congressional budget process. Seeks to increase public awareness of the dangers of long-term financial imbalances. Offers seminars and symposia; commissions studies and policy analyses.

Concord Coalition, *1011 Arlington Blvd., #300, Arlington, VA 22209; (703) 894-6222. Fax, (703) 894-6231. Robert L. Bixby, Executive Director.*
General e-mail, concord@concordcoalition.org
Web, www.concordcoalition.org

Nonpartisan, grassroots organization advocating fiscal responsibility and ensuring Social Security, Medicare, and Medicaid are secure for all generations.

Institute for Policy Studies, *National Commission for Economic Conversion and Disarmament, 733 15th St. N.W., #1020 20005; (202) 234-9382. Fax, (202) 387-7915. Miriam Pemberton, Director.*
Web, www.webcom.com/ncecd

Supports cutbacks in the U.S. military budget and reallocation of funds for civilian economic development. Advocates investment in civilian research and development, transportation, housing, health, education, and the environment.

OMB Watch, *1742 Connecticut Ave. N.W. 20009; (202) 234-8494. Fax, (202) 234-8584. Gary D. Bass, Executive Director.*
General e-mail, ombwatch@ombwatch.org
Web, www.ombwatch.org

Research and advocacy organization that monitors and interprets the policies and activities of the Office of Management and Budget. Sponsors conferences and teaches the governmental decision-making process concerning accountability.

Statistics, Economic Projections

AGENCIES

Bureau of Economic Analysis *(Commerce Dept.), 1441 L St. N.W., #6006 20230; (202) 606-9600. Fax, (202) 606-5311. J. Steven Landefeld, Director. Information, (202) 606-9900.*
Web, www.bea.doc.gov

Compiles, analyzes, and publishes data on measures of aggregate U.S. economic activity, including gross national product; prices by type of expenditure; personal income and outlays; personal savings; corporate profits; capital stock; U.S. international transactions; and foreign investment. Provides estimates of personal income and employment by industry for regions, states, metropolitan areas, and counties. Refers specific inquiries to economic specialists in the field.

Bureau of Labor Statistics (BLS), *(Labor Dept.), 2 Massachusetts Ave. N.E. 20212; (202) 691-7800. Fax, (202) 691-7797. Kathleen P. Utgoff, Commissioner. Press, (202) 691-5902.*

General e-mail, blsdata_staff@bls.gov
Web, www.bls.gov

Provides statistical data on labor economics, including labor force, employment and unemployment, hours of work, wages, employee compensation, prices, living conditions, labor-management relations, productivity, technological developments, occupational safety and health, and structure and growth of the economy. Publishes reports on these statistical trends including the Consumer Price Index, Producer Price Index, and Employment and Earnings.

Census Bureau *(Commerce Dept.), Economic Programs, Suitland and Silver Hill Rds., #2061-3, Suitland, MD 20746 (mailing address: MS 6000 #2061-3, Washington, DC 20233-6000); (301) 457-2112. Fax, (301) 457-8140. Frederick T. Knickerbocker, Associate Director.*
Web, www.census.gov

Provides data and explains proper use of data on county business patterns, classification of industries and commodities, and business statistics. Compiles quarterly reports listing financial data for corporations in certain industrial sectors.

Census Bureau *(Commerce Dept.), Governments Division, 8905 Presidential Pkwy., Upper Marlboro, MD 20722 (mailing address: Washington Plaza II, #407, Washington, DC 20233-6800); (301) 763-1489. Fax, (301) 457-1423. Stephanie Brown, Chief (Acting).*
Web, www.census.gov

Provides data and explains proper use of data concerning state and local governments, employment, finance, governmental organization, and taxation.

Census Bureau *(Commerce Dept.), Manufacturing and Construction, 4401 Silver Hill Rd., Bldg FB4, #2102A, Suitland, MD 20746; (301) 763-4593. Fax, (301) 457-4583. William G. Bostic Jr., Chief.*
Web, www.census.gov

Collects and distributes manufacturing, construction, and mineral industry data. Reports are organized by commodity, industry, and geographic area.

Census Bureau *(Commerce Dept.), Service Sector Statistics Division, 4700 Silver Hill Rd., Bldg. 3, #2633, Suitland, MD 20746; (301) 763-2668. Fax, (301) 457-1343. Mark E. Wallace, Chief.*
Web, www.census.gov

Provides data of five-year census programs on retail, wholesale, and service industries. Conducts periodic monthly or annual surveys for specific items within these industries.

Council of Economic Advisers *(Executive Office of the President)*, **Statistical Office,** *Dwight D. Eisenhower Executive Office Bldg., #56 20502; (202) 395-5062. Fax, (202) 395-5630. Catherine H. Furlong, Senior Statistician.*
Web, www.whitehouse.gov/cea

Compiles and reports aggregate economic data, including national income and expenditures, employment, wages, productivity, production and business activity, prices, money stock, credit, finance, government finance, corporate profits and finance, agriculture, and international statistics, including balance of payments and import-export levels by commodity and area. Data published in the *Annual Economic Report* and the monthly *Economic Indicators,* published by the congressional Joint Economic Committee.

Economic Research Service *(Agriculture Dept.),* *1800 M St. N.W., #5120N 20036; (202) 694-5200. Fax, (202) 694-5792. Susan E. Offutt, Administrator; Demcey Johnson, Chief, Field Crops, (202) 694-5300; Daniel L. Pick, Chief, Specialty Crops, (202) 694-5250.*
Web, www.ers.usda.gov

Conducts market research; studies and forecasts domestic supply-and-demand trends for fruits and vegetables.

Federal Reserve System, *Monetary Affairs, 20th and C Sts. N.W., #B3022B 20551; (202) 452-3199. Fax, (202) 452-2301. Vincent R. Reinhart, Director.*
Web, www.federalreserve.gov

Analyzes monetary policy and issues related to open market operations, reserve requirements, and discount policy. Reports statistics associated with monetary aggregates; issues related to the government securities market; and economic aspects of other regulatory issues closely related to monetary policy, such as banking, loans, and securities.

Federal Reserve System, *Research and Statistics, 20th and C Sts. N.W., #B3048 20551; (202) 452-3301. Fax, (202) 452-5296. David J. Stockton, Director.*
Web, www.federalreserve.gov

Publishes statistical data on business finance, real estate credit, consumer credit, industrial production, construction, and flow of funds.

Internal Revenue Service (IRS), *(Treasury Dept.),* **Statistics of Income,** *500 N. Capitol St. N.W. 20001 (mailing address: P.O. Box 2608 20013-2608); (202) 874-0700. Fax, (202) 874-0983. Thomas B. Petska, Director. Publications, (202) 874-0410.*
Web, www.irs.ustreas.gov/prod/tax_stats

Provides the public and the Treasury Dept. with statistical information on tax laws. Prepares statistical information for the Commerce Dept. to use in formulating the gross national product (GNP). Publishes *Statistics of Income,* a series available at cost to the public.

International Trade Administration (ITA), *(Commerce Dept.),* **Trade and Economic Analysis,** *14th St. and Constitution Ave. N.W., #2815 20230; (202) 482-5145. Fax, (202) 482-4614. Jeffrey Lins, Director (Acting).*
Web, www.ita.doc.gov/tradestats

Monitors developments in major U.S. industrial sectors. Produces studies, including *U.S. Industrial Trade Outlook,* which reports business planning and marketing data on more than 350 industries and projects economic trends for selected industries.

National Agricultural Statistics Service *(Agriculture Dept.), 1400 Independence Ave. S.W., #4117S 20250-2001; (202) 720-2707. Fax, (202) 720-9013. R. Ronald Bosecker, Administrator. Information, (800) 727-9540. Publications, (202) 720-4021.*
General e-mail, nass@nass.usda.gov
Web, www.usda.gov/nass

Prepares estimates and reports on production, supply, prices, and other items relating to the U.S. agricultural economy. Reports include statistics on field crops, fruits and vegetables, cattle, hogs, poultry, and related products.

Office of Management and Budget (OMB), *(Executive Office of the President),* **Statistical Policy,** *New Executive Office Bldg., #10201 20503; (202) 395-3093. Fax, (202) 395-7245. Katherine K. Wallman, Chief.*
Web, www.whitehouse.gov/omb

Carries out the statistical policy and coordination functions under the Paperwork Reduction Act of 1995; develops long-range plans for improving federal statistical programs; develops policy standards and guidelines for statistical data collection, classification, and publication; evaluates statistical programs and agency performance.

Securities and Exchange Commission, *Economic Analysis, 450 5th St. N.W. 20549; (202) 942-8020. Fax, (202) 942-9657. Lawrence E. Harris, Chief Economist.*
Web, www.sec.gov

Publishes data on trading volume of the stock exchanges; compiles statistics on financial reports of brokerage firms.

U.S. International Trade Commission, *Industries, 500 E St. S.W., #504 20436; (202) 205-3296. Fax, (202) 205-3161. Vern Simpson, Director. Press, (202) 205-1819.*
Web, www.usitc.gov

Identifies, analyzes, and develops data on economic and technical matters related to the competitive position of the United States in domestic and world markets in agriculture and forest production, chemicals, textiles, energy, electronics, transportation, services and investments, minerals, metals, and machinery.

CONGRESS

Joint Economic Committee, SD-G01 20510; (202) 224-5171. Sen. Robert F. Bennett, R-Utah, Chair; Donald Marron, Executive Director.
General e-mail, jec@jec.house.gov
Web, jec.senate.gov

Maintains statistics on nearly all facets of economic activity; provides information to the public or refers individuals to office where information is available; provides statistics on economy pertaining to energy and environment; publishes monthly *Economic Indicators* from data supplied by the Council of Economic Advisers.

NONPROFIT

American Statistical Assn., 1429 Duke St., Alexandria, VA 22314; (703) 684-1221. Fax, (703) 684-2037. William B. Smith, Executive Director.
General e-mail, asainfo@amstat.org
Web, www.amstat.org

Membership: individuals interested in statistics and related quantitative fields. Advises government agencies on statistics and methodology in agency research; promotes development of statistical techniques for use in business, industry, finance, government, agriculture, and science.

Taxes and Tax Reform

AGENCIES

Alcohol and Tobacco Tax and Trade Bureau (TTB), *(Treasury Dept.), Field Operations,* 650 Massachusetts Ave. N.W., #8100 20226; (202) 927-7970. Fax, (202) 927-7756. Paul M. Sable, Assistant Director. Information, (202) 927-7777. Press, (202) 927-9510.
Web, www.atf.treas.gov

Enforces and administers revenue laws relating to firearms, explosives, alcohol, and tobacco.

Internal Revenue Service (IRS), *(Treasury Dept.),* 1111 Constitution Ave. N.W. 20224; (202) 622-4115. Fax, (202) 622-5756. Mark W. Everson, Commissioner. Information, (800) 829-1040. Press, (202) 622-4000. TTY, (800) 829-4059. National Taxpayer Advocates Helpline, (877) 777-4778.
Web, www.irs.gov

Administers and enforces internal revenue laws and related statutes (except those relating to firearms, explosives, alcohol, and tobacco).

Internal Revenue Service (IRS), *(Treasury Dept.), Taxpayer Advocate,* 1111 Constitution Ave. N.W. 20224; (202) 622-6100. Fax, (202) 622-7854. Nina E. Olson, National Taxpayer Advocate.
Web, www.irs.gov/advocate/index.html

Helps taxpayers resolve problems with the IRS and recommends changes to prevent the problems. Represents taxpayers' interests in the formulation of policies and procedures.

Justice Dept. (DOJ), *Tax Division,* 950 Pennsylvania Ave. N.W., #4141 20530; (202) 514-2901. Fax, (202) 514-5479. Eileen J. O'Connor, Assistant Attorney General.
Web, www.usdoj.gov/tax/tax.html

Acts as counsel for the Internal Revenue Service (IRS) in court litigation between the government and taxpayers (other than those handled by the IRS in the U.S. Tax Court).

Multistate Tax Commission, 444 N. Capitol St. N.W., #425 20001-1538; (202) 624-8699. Fax, (202) 624-8819. Dan R. Bucks, Executive Director.
General e-mail, mtc@mtc.gov
Web, www.mtc.gov

Membership: state governments that have enacted the Multistate Tax Compact. Promotes fair, effective, and efficient state tax systems for interstate and international commerce; works to preserve state tax sovereignty. Encourages uniform state tax laws and regulations for multistate and multinational enterprises. Maintains three regional audit offices that monitor compliance with state tax laws and encourage uniformity in taxpayer treatment. Administers program to identify businesses that do not file tax returns with states.

Treasury Dept., *Tax Policy,* 1500 Pennsylvania Ave. N.W., #3120 20220; (202) 622-0050. Fax, (202) 622-0605. Pamela F. Olson, Assistant Secretary.
Web, www.ustreas.gov/offices/tax-policy

Formulates and implements domestic and international tax policies and programs; conducts analyses of proposed tax legislation and programs; participates in international tax treaty negotiations; responsible for receipts estimates for the annual budget of the United States.

CONGRESS

Joint Committee on Taxation, 1015 LHOB 20515; (202) 225-3621. Fax, (202) 225-0832. Rep. Bill Thomas, R-Calif., Chair; George K. Yin, Chief of Staff.

Web, www.house.gov/jct

Performs staff work for House Ways and Means and Senate Finance committees on domestic and international tax matters in the Internal Revenue Code, the public debt limit, and savings bonds under the Second Liberty Bond Act. Provides those committees with general economic and budgetary analysis. Provides revenue estimates for all tax legislation.

JUDICIARY

U.S. Tax Court, *400 2nd St. N.W. 20217; (202) 606-8700. Fax, (202) 606-8958. Thomas B. Wells, Chief Judge; Charles S. Casazza, Clerk of the Court.*

Web, www.ustaxcourt.gov

Tries and adjudicates disputes involving income, estate, and gift taxes and personal holding company surtaxes in cases in which deficiencies have been determined by the Internal Revenue Service.

NONPROFIT

American Enterprise Institute for Public Policy Research (AEI), *Fiscal Policy Studies, 1150 17th St. N.W., #1100 20036; (202) 862-5800. Fax, (202) 862-7177. Marv Kosters, Director. Information, (202) 862-7158. Press, (202) 862-4871.*

Web, www.aei.org

Research and educational organization that conducts studies on fiscal policy, taxes, and budget issues.

Americans for Tax Reform, *1920 L St. N.W., #200 20036; (202) 785-0266. Fax, (202) 785-0261. Grover G. Norquist, President. Information, (888) 785-0266.*

General e-mail, info@atr.org

Web, www.atr.org

Advocates reduction of federal and state taxes; encourages candidates for public office to pledge their opposition to income tax increases through a national pledge campaign.

Citizens for a Sound Economy, *1900 M St. N.W., #500 20036; (202) 783-3870. Fax, (202) 783-4687. Paul Beckner, President.*

Web, www.cse.org

Citizens' advocacy group that promotes reduced taxes, free trade, and deregulation.

Citizens for Tax Justice, *1311 L St. N.W., #400 20005; (202) 626-3780. Fax, (202) 638-3486. Robert S. McIntyre, Director.*

Web, www.ctj.org

Coalition that works for progressive taxes at the federal, state, and local levels.

Federation of Tax Administrators, *444 N. Capitol St. N.W., #348 20001; (202) 624-5890. Fax, (202) 624-7888. Harley T. Duncan, Executive Director.*

Web, www.taxadmin.org

Membership: state tax agencies. Provides information upon written request on tax-related issues, including court decisions and legislation. Conducts research and sponsors workshops.

Institute for Research on the Economics of Taxation, *1710 Rhode Island Ave. N.W., 11th Floor 20036; (202) 463-1400. Fax, (202) 463-6199. Stephen Entin, Executive Director.*

General e-mail, iret@iret.org

Web, www.iret.org

Research organization that analyzes all aspects of taxation. Conducts research on the economic effects of federal tax policies; publishes studies on domestic and international economic policy issues.

National Assn. of Manufacturers (NAM), *Taxation, 1331 Pennsylvania Ave. N.W., #600 20004-1790; (202) 637-3073. Fax, (202) 637-3182. Monica McGuire, Senior Policy Director.*

Web, www.nam.org

Represents industry views (mainly of manufacturers) on federal tax and budget policies; conducts conferences. Monitors legislation and regulations.

National Taxpayers Union, *Communications, 108 N. Alfred St., 3rd Floor, Alexandria, VA 22314; (703) 683-5700. Fax, (703) 683-5722. Peter Sepp, Vice President.*

General e-mail, ntu@ntu.org

Web, www.ntu.org

Citizens' interest group that promotes tax and spending reduction at all levels of government. Supports constitutional amendments to balance the federal budget and limit taxes.

Tax Council, *1301 K St. N.W., #800W 20005; (202) 822-8062. Fax, (202) 414-1301. Roger J. LeMaster, Executive Director.*

General e-mail, thetaxcouncil@starpower.net

Web, www.thetaxcouncil.org

Organization of corporations concerned with tax policy and legislation. Interests include tax rate, capital formation, capital gains, foreign source income, and capital cost recovery.

Tax Executives Institute, *1200 G St. N.W., #300 20005-3814; (202) 638-5601. Fax, (202) 638-5607. Timothy J. McCormally, Executive Director.*

Web, www.tei.org

Membership: accountants, lawyers, and other corporate and business employees dealing with tax issues. Sponsors seminars and conferences on federal, state, local, and international tax issues. Develops and monitors tax legislation, regulations, and administrative procedures.

Tax Foundation, *1900 M St. N.W., #550 20036; (202) 464-6200. Fax, (202) 464-6201. Scott A. Hodge, Executive Director.*
General e-mail, tf@taxfoundation.org
Web, www.taxfoundation.org
Membership: individuals and businesses interested in federal, state, and local fiscal matters. Conducts research and prepares reports on taxes and government expenditures.

U.S. Conference of Mayors, *1620 Eye St. N.W., #400 20006; (202) 293-7330. Fax, (202) 293-2352. J. Thomas Cochran, Executive Director.*
General e-mail, uscm@cais.com
Web, www.usmayors.org/uscm
Membership: mayors of cities with populations of 30,000 or more. Monitors tax policy and legislation.

FINANCE AND INVESTMENTS

Banking

AGENCIES

Antitrust Division *(Justice Dept.), Networks and Technology Enforcement, 600 E St. N.W., #9500 20530; (202) 307-6122. Fax, (202) 616-8544. Renata B. Hesse, Chief.*
Web, www.usdoj.gov/atr
Investigates and litigates certain antitrust cases involving financial institutions, including securities, commodity futures, computer software, and insurance; participates in agency proceedings and rulemaking in these areas; monitors and analyzes legislation.

Comptroller of the Currency *(Treasury Dept.), 250 E St. S.W. 20219; (202) 874-4900. Fax, (202) 874-4950. John D. Hawke Jr., Comptroller. Information, (202) 874-5000. Library, (202) 874-4720. Press, (202) 874-5770.*
Web, www.occ.treas.gov
Regulates and examines operations of national banks; establishes guidelines for bank examinations; handles mergers of national banks with regard to antitrust law. Library open to the public.

Comptroller of the Currency *(Treasury Dept.), Washington Directed Licensing, 250 E St. S.W. 20219; (202) 874-5060. Fax, (202) 874-5293. Julie L. Williams, 1st Senior Deputy Comptroller and Chief Counsel. Library, (202) 874-4720.*
Web, www.occ.treas.gov
Advises the comptroller on policy matters and programs related to bank corporate activities and is the primary decision maker on national bank corporate applications, including charters, mergers, and acquisitions, conversions, and operating subsidiaries.

Federal Deposit Insurance Corp. (FDIC), *550 17th St. N.W. 20429; (202) 898-6974. Fax, (202) 898-3778. Donald E. Powell, Chair; John Reich, Vice Chair. Information, (800) 374-3405. Library, (202) 898-3631. Press, (202) 898-6993.*
Web, www.fdic.gov
Insures deposits in national banks, state banks, and savings and loans. Conducts examinations of insured state banks that are not members of the Federal Reserve System.

Federal Deposit Insurance Corp. (FDIC), *Resolutions and Receiverships, 1776 F St. N.W. 20429 (mailing address: 550 17th St. N.W. 20429); (202) 898-6779. Fax, (202) 898-7024. Gail Patelunas, Deputy Director.*
Web, www.fdic.gov
Plans, executes, and monitors the orderly and least cost resolution of failing FDIC insured institutions. Manages remaining liability of the federal savings and loan resolution fund.

Federal Deposit Insurance Corp. (FDIC), *Supervision and Consumer Protection, 550 17th St. N.W. 20429; (202) 898-8946. Fax, (202) 898-3638. Michael J. Zamorski, Director.*
Serves as the federal regulator and supervisor of insured state banks that are not members of the Federal Reserve System. Conducts regular examinations and investigations of banks under the jurisdiction of FDIC; advises bank managers on improving policies and practices. Administers the Bank Insurance Fund, which insures deposits in commercial and savings banks, and the Savings Assn. Insurance Fund, which insures deposits in savings and loan institutions.

Federal Reserve System, *Banking Supervision and Regulation, 20th and C Sts. N.W., #M3142 20551; (202) 452-2773. Fax, (202) 452-2770. Richard Spillenkothen, Director.*
Web, www.federalreserve.gov

FEDERAL DEPOSIT INSURANCE CORPORATION

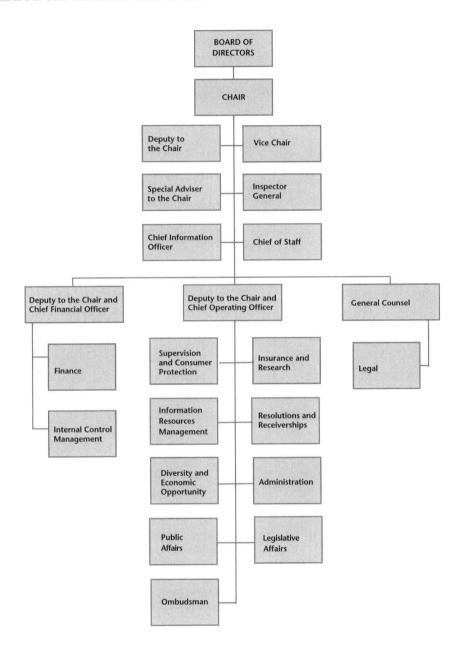

Supervises and regulates state banks that are members of the Federal Reserve System; supervises and inspects all bank holding companies; monitors banking practices; approves bank mergers, consolidations, and other changes in bank structure.

Federal Reserve System, *Board of Governors,*
20th and C Sts. N.W., B2046 20551; (202) 452-3201. Fax,
(202) 452-3819. Alan Greenspan, Chair; Roger W. Fergu-
son Jr., Vice Chair. Information, (202) 452-3215. Press,
(202) 452-3204. Locator, (202) 452-3000; Publications,
(202) 452-3245.

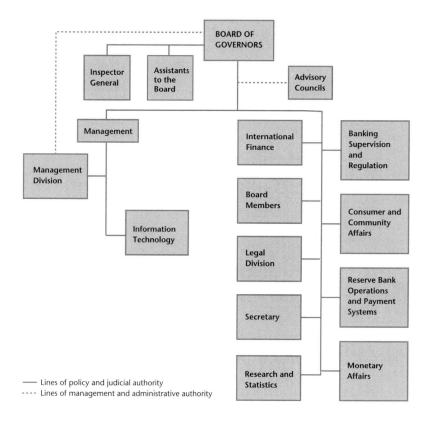

— Lines of policy and judicial authority
---- Lines of management and administrative authority

Web, www.federalreserve.gov

Serves as the central bank and fiscal agent for the government. Examines Federal Reserve banks and state member banks; supervises bank holding companies. Controls wire system transfer operations and supplies currency for depository institutions.

National Credit Union Administration, *1775 Duke St., Alexandria, VA 22314-3428; (703) 518-6300. Fax, (703) 518-6319. Dennis Dollar, Chair. Information, (703) 518-6330. Electronic bulletin board, (703) 518-6480.*
Web, www.ncua.gov

Regulates all federally chartered credit unions; charters new credit unions; supervises and examines federal credit unions and insures their member accounts up to $100,000. Insures state-chartered credit unions that apply and are eligible. Manages the Central Liquidity Facility, which supplies emergency short-term loans to members. Conducts research on economic trends and their effect on credit unions and advises the administration's board on economic and financial policy and regulations.

Office of Management and Budget (OMB), *(Executive Office of the President), Financial Institutions, New Executive Office Bldg., #9235 20503; (202) 395-7241. Fax, (202) 395-1292. James Boden, Chief.*
Web, www.whitehouse.gov/omb

Monitors the financial condition of deposit insurance funds including the Bank Insurance Fund, the Savings Assn. Insurance Fund, and the Federal Savings and Loan Insurance Corp. (FSLIC) Resolution Fund. Monitors the Securities and Exchange Commission. Has limited oversight over the Federal Housing Finance Board and the Federal Home Loan Bank System.

Office of Thrift Supervision (OTS), *(Treasury Dept.), 1700 G St. N.W. 20552; (202) 906-6590. Fax, (202) 898-0230. James E. Gilleran, Director. Information, (202) 906-6000. Library, (202) 906-6470. Press, (202) 906-6913. General e-mail, public.info@ots.treas.gov*
Web, www.ots.treas.gov

Charters, regulates, and examines the operations of savings and loan institutions. Library open to the public.

Securities and Exchange Commission, *Corporation Finance,* 450 5th St. N.W. 20549; (202) 942-2800. Fax, (202) 942-9525. Allen Beller, Director. Information, (202) 942-8088.
Web, www.sec.gov

Receives and examines disclosure statements and other information from publicly held companies, including bank holding companies.

Securities and Exchange Commission, *Economic Analysis,* 450 5th St. N.W. 20549; (202) 942-8020. Fax, (202) 942-9657. Lawrence E. Harris, Chief Economist.
Web, www.sec.gov

Provides the commission with economic analyses of proposed rule and policy changes and other information to guide the SEC in influencing capital markets. Evaluates the effect of policy and other factors on competition within the securities industry and among competing securities markets; compiles financial statistics on capital formation and the securities industry.

Treasury Dept., *Financial Institutions,* 1500 Pennsylvania Ave. N.W., #2326 20220; (202) 622-2610. Fax, (202) 622-2027. Wayne A. Abernathy, Assistant Secretary.
Web, www.ustreas.gov

Advises the under secretary for domestic finance and the Treasury secretary on financial institutions, banks, and thrifts.

CONGRESS

House Appropriations Committee, *Subcommittee on VA, HUD, and Independent Agencies,* H143 CAP 20515; (202) 225-3241. Rep. James T. Walsh, R-N.Y., Chair; Tim Peterson, Staff Director.
Web, www.house.gov/appropriations

Jurisdiction over legislation to appropriate funds for the National Credit Union Administration.

House Financial Services Committee, *Subcommittee on Financial Institutions and Consumer Credit,* 2129 RHOB 20515; (202) 225-7502. Rep. Spencer Bachus, R-Ala., Chair; Bob Foster, Staff Director.
Web, www.house.gov/financialservices/finin108.htm

Jurisdiction over legislation regulating banking and financial institutions.

House Government Reform Committee, *Subcommittee on Energy Policy, Natural Resources, and Regulatory Affairs,* B377 RHOB 20515; (202) 225-4407. Fax, (202) 225-2441. Rep. Doug Ose, R-Calif., Chair; Dan Skopec, Staff Director.

Web, www.house.gov/reform

Oversees federal bank regulatory agencies.

House Ways and Means Committee, *Subcommittee on Oversight,* 1136 LHOB 20515; (202) 225-7601. Fax, (202) 225-9680. Rep. Amo Houghton, R-N.Y., Chair; Kirk Walder, Staff Director.
Web, waysandmeans.house.gov

Oversees government-sponsored enterprises, including the Federal Home Loan Bank System, with regard to the financial risk posed to the federal government.

Senate Appropriations Committee, *Subcommittee on VA, HUD, and Independent Agencies,* SD-130 20510; (202) 224-8252. Fax, (202) 228-1624. Sen. Christopher S. Bond, R-Mo., Chair; Jon Kamarck, Clerk.
Web, appropriations.senate.gov

Jurisdiction over legislation to appropriate funds for the National Credit Union Administration.

Senate Banking, Housing, and Urban Affairs Committee, SD-534 20510; (202) 224-7391. Fax, (202) 224-5137. Sen. Richard C. Shelby, R-Ala., Chair; Kathy Casey, Staff Director.
Web, banking.senate.gov

Jurisdiction over legislation regulating banking and financial institutions. Oversees federal bank regulatory agencies, including the Federal Deposit Insurance Corp., National Credit Union Administration, and Office of Thrift Supervision; also oversees government-sponsored enterprises, including the Federal Home Loan Bank System, with regard to the financial risk posed to the federal government.

NONPROFIT

American Bankers Assn. (ABA), 1120 Connecticut Ave. N.W. 20036; (202) 663-5000. Fax, (202) 663-7533. Donald G. Ogilvie, Executive Vice President. Information, (800) BANKERS.
Web, www.aba.com

Membership: commercial banks. Operates schools to train banking personnel; conducts conferences; formulates government relations policies for the banking community.

American Council of State Savings Supervisors, P.O. Box 1904, Leesburg, VA 20177-1904; (703) 669-5440. Fax, (703) 669-5441. Andrea M. Falzarano, Executive Director.
Web, www.acsss.org

Membership: supervisors and regulators of state-chartered savings associations; associate members include state-chartered savings associations and state

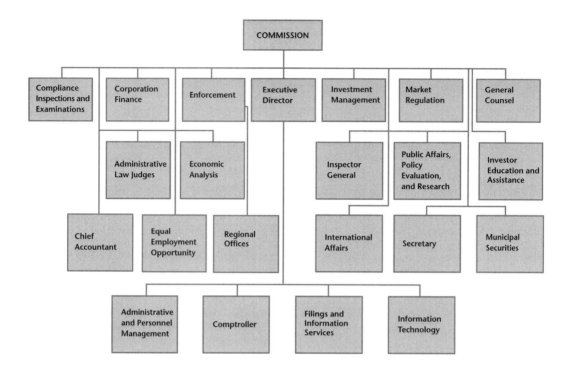

savings banks. Monitors legislation and regulations affecting the state-chartered thrift industry.

American Institute of Certified Public Accountants, *Washington Office,* 1455 Pennsylvania Ave. N.W., 4th Floor 20004-1081; (202) 737-6600. Fax, (202) 638-4512. James O'Malley, Senior Vice President. Press, (202) 434-9214.
Web, www.aicpa.org

Establishes voluntary professional and ethical regulations for the profession; sponsors conferences and training workshops. Answers technical auditing and accounting questions. (Headquarters in New York.)

American League of Financial Institutions, 900 19th St. N.W., #400 20006-2105; (202) 857-5094. Fax, (202) 296-8716. Dina Curtis, President.
Web, www.alfi.org

Membership: minority-controlled community savings banks and savings associations. Helps promote small business; offers on-site technical assistance. Monitors legislative and regulatory issues.

American Savings Education Council, 2121 K St. N.W., #600 20037; (202) 659-0670. Fax, (202) 775-6360. Don M. Blandin, President.
Web, www.asec.org

Seeks to raise public awareness about long-term personal financial independence and encourage retirement savings. Sponsors workshops.

America's Community Bankers, 900 19th St. N.W., #400 20006; (202) 857-3100. Fax, (202) 296-8716. Diane M. Casey, President. Press, (202) 857-3110.
General e-mail, info@acbankers.org
Web, www.acbankers.org

Membership: insured depository institutions involved in community finance. Provides information and statistics on issues that affect the industry; sponsors conferences with international banks and savings and loan institutions. Monitors economic issues affecting savings institutions. Monitors legislation and regulations.

Assn. for Financial Professionals, 7315 Wisconsin Ave., #600W, Bethesda, MD 20814; (301) 907-2862. Fax, (301) 907-2864. James A. Kaitz, President.

Web, www.afponline.org

Membership: more than 14,000 members from wide range of industries throughout all stages of their careers in various aspects of treasury and financial management. Acts as resource for continuing education, financial tools and publications, career development, certifications, research, representation to legislators and regulators, and the development of industry standards.

Bank Marketing Assn., *1120 Connecticut Ave. N.W., 3rd Floor 20036; (202) 663-5268. Fax, (202) 828-4540. Douglas Adamson, Managing Director. Information, (800) 433-9013.*
Web, www.bmanet.org

Membership: financial institutions and firms that provide products and services to the financial industry. (Affiliate of the American Bankers Assn.)

Bankers' Assn. for Finance and Trade, *1120 Connecticut Ave. N.W., 5th Floor 20036; (202) 663-5530. Fax, (202) 663-5538. Mary Condeelis, Executive Director.*
General e-mail, baft@baft.org
Web, www.baft.org

Membership: U.S. commercial banks with major international operations; foreign banks with U.S. operations are affiliated as nonvoting members. Monitors activities that affect the operation of U.S. commercial and international banks.

Conference of State Bank Supervisors, *1155 Connecticut Ave. N.W., #500 20036; (202) 296-2840. Fax, (202) 296-1928. Neil Milner, President.*
Web, www.csbs.org

Membership: state officials responsible for supervision of state-chartered banking institutions. Conducts educational programs. Monitors legislation.

Consumer Bankers Assn., *1000 Wilson Blvd., #2500, Arlington, VA 22209; (703) 276-1750. Fax, (703) 528-1290. Joe Belew, President. Press, (703) 276-3880.*
Web, www.cbanet.org

Membership: federally insured financial institutions. Provides information on retail banking, including industry trends. Operates the Graduate School of Retail Bank Management to train banking personnel; conducts research and analysis on retail banking trends; sponsors conferences.

Consumer Data Industry Assn., *1090 Vermont Ave. N.W., #200 20005-4905; (202) 371-0910. Fax, (202) 371-0134. Stuart Pratt, President. Press, (202) 408-7406.*
Web, www.cdiaonline.org

Membership: credit reporting, mortgage reporting, and collection service companies. Provides information

about credit rights to consumers. Monitors legislation and regulations. (Formerly Associated Credit Bureaus.)

Credit Union National Assn., *Washington Office, 601 Pennsylvania Ave. N.W., South Bldg., #600 20004; (202) 638-5777. Fax, (202) 638-7734. Daniel A. Mica, President.*
Web, www.cuna.org

Confederation of credit unions from every state, the District of Columbia, and Puerto Rico. Represents federal and state chartered credit unions. Monitors legislation and regulations. (Headquarters in Madison, Wis.)

Electronic Funds Transfer Assn., *950 Herndon Pkwy., #390, Herndon, VA 20170; (703) 435-9800. Fax, (703) 435-7157. H. Kurt Helwig, Executive Director.*
Web, www.efta.org

Membership: financial institutions, electronic funds transfer hardware and software providers, automatic teller machine networks, and others engaged in electronic commerce. Promotes electronic payments and commerce technologies; sponsors industry analysis. Monitors legislation and regulations.

Financial Services Roundtable, *805 15th St. N.W., #600 20005; (202) 289-4322. Fax, (202) 289-1903. Richard Whiting, Executive Director.*
Web, www.fsround.org

Membership: over one hundred integrated financial services companies. Provides banking, insurance, investment products, and services to American consumers.

Independent Community Bankers of America, *1 Thomas Circle N.W., #400 20005; (202) 659-8111. Fax, (202) 659-9216. Kenneth A. Guenther, President. Information, (800) 422-8439.*
General e-mail, info@icba.org
Web, www.icba.org

Membership: medium-sized and smaller community banks. Interests include farm credit, deregulation, interstate banking, deposit insurance, and financial industry standards.

Mortgage Bankers Assn. of America, *1919 Pennsylvania Ave. N.W., 8th Floor 20006; (202) 557-2700. Fax, (202) 721-0249. Jonathan Kempner, President.*
Web, www.mbaa.org

Membership: institutions involved in real estate finance. Maintains School of Mortgage Banking and sponsors educational seminars; collects statistics on the industry.

National Assn. of Federal Credit Unions (NAFCU), *3138 N. 10th St., Arlington, VA 22201; (703) 522-4770. Fax, (703) 524-1082. Fred Becker, President.*

Web, www.nafcu.org

Membership: federally chartered credit unions. Represents interests of federal credit unions before Congress and regulatory agencies and provides legislative alerts for its members. Sponsors educational meetings focusing on current financial trends, changes in legislation and regulations, and management techniques.

National Assn. of State Credit Union Supervisors, 1655 N. Fort Meyer Dr., #300, Arlington, VA 22209; (703) 528-8351. Fax, (703) 528-3248. Douglas Duerr, President.
General e-mail, offices@nascus.org
Web, www.nascus.org

Membership: state credit union supervisors, state-chartered credit unions, and credit union leagues. Interests include state regulatory systems; conducts educational programs for examiners.

National Automated Clearing House Assn., 13665 Dulles Technology Dr., #300, Herndon, VA 20171; (703) 561-1100. Fax, (703) 787-0996. Elliott C. McEntee, President.
Web, www.nacha.org

Membership: financial institutions involved in the ACH payment system. Establishes rules and standards for the ACH system; works for the development of technological and service innovation in electronic funds transfers; provides information for members. Sponsors workshops and seminars.

National Bankers Assn., 1513 P St. N.W. 20005; (202) 588-5432. Fax, (202) 588-5443. Norma Alexander Hart, President.
Web, www.nationalbankers.org

Membership: minority-owned banks and minority banking personnel. Monitors legislation and regulations affecting minority banking.

National Society of Accountants, 1010 N. Fairfax St., Alexandria, VA 22314-1574; (703) 549-6400. Fax, (703) 549-2984. John G. Ams, Executive Vice President.
Web, www.nsacct.org

Seeks to improve the accounting profession and to enhance the status of individual practitioners. Sponsors seminars and correspondence courses on accounting, auditing, business law, and estate planning; monitors legislation and regulations affecting accountants and their small-business clients.

Stocks, Bonds, and Securities

AGENCIES

Bureau of the Public Debt *(Treasury Dept.), Marketing,* 999 E St. N.W., #314 20226; (202) 691-3535. Fax,

(202) 208-1574. Paul Vogelzang, Executive Director. Information, (800) 4US-BOND.
Web, www.savingsbonds.gov

Promotes the sale and retention of U.S. savings bonds through educational and volunteer programs; administers the payroll savings plan for savings bonds.

Federal Reserve System, *Board of Governors,* 20th and C Sts. N.W., B2046 20551; (202) 452-3201. Fax, (202) 452-3819. Alan Greenspan, Chair; Roger W. Ferguson Jr., Vice Chair. Information, (202) 452-3215. Press, (202) 452-3204. Locator, (202) 452-3000; Publications, (202) 452-3245.
Web, www.federalreserve.gov

Regulates amount of credit that may be extended and maintained on certain securities in order to prevent excessive use of credit for purchase or carrying of securities.

Securities and Exchange Commission, 450 5th St. N.W. 20549; (202) 942-0100. Fax, (202) 942-9646. William H. Donaldson, Chair; James M. McConnell, Executive Director, (202) 942-4300. Press, (202) 942-0020. Investor Education and Assistance, (202) 942-7040. Locator, (202) 942-4150. Public Reference, (202) 942-8090.
Web, www.sec.gov

Requires public disclosure of financial and other information about companies whose securities are offered for public sale, traded on exchanges, or traded over the counter; issues and enforces regulations to prevent fraud in securities markets and investigates securities frauds and violations; supervises operations of stock exchanges and activities of securities dealers, investment advisers, and investment companies; regulates purchase and sale of securities, properties, and other assets of public utility holding companies and their subsidiaries; participates in bankruptcy proceedings involving publicly held companies; has some jurisdiction over municipal securities trading. Public Reference Section, (202) 942-8090, makes available corporation reports and statements filed with SEC. The information also is available via the Web (www.sec.gov/edgarhp.htm).

Securities and Exchange Commission, *Economic Analysis,* 450 5th St. N.W. 20549; (202) 942-8020. Fax, (202) 942-9657. Lawrence E. Harris, Chief Economist.
Web, www.sec.gov

Provides the commission with economic analyses of proposed rule and policy changes and other information to guide the SEC in influencing capital markets. Evaluates the effect of policy and other factors on competition within the securities industry and among competing securities markets; compiles financial statistics on capital formation and the securities industry.

Securities and Exchange Commission, *Market Regulation,* 450 5th St. N.W., MS 1001 20549; (202) 942-0090. Fax, (202) 942-9643. Annette L. Nazareth, Director. Library, (202) 942-7090.

Web, www.sec.gov

Oversees and regulates the operations of securities markets, brokers, dealers, and transfer agents. Promotes the establishment of a national system for clearing and settling securities transactions. Works for standards among and oversees self-regulatory organizations, such as national securities exchanges, registered clearing agencies, and the National Assn. of Securities Dealers. Facilitates the development of a national market system.

Treasury Dept., *Financial Institutions Policy,* 1500 Pennsylvania Ave. N.W., 3170 Annex Bldg. 20220; (202) 622-2740. Fax, (202) 622-0256. Edward DeMarco, Director.

Web, www.ustreas.gov

Coordinates department efforts on all legislation affecting financial institutions and the government agencies that regulate them. Develops department policy on all matters relating to agencies responsible for supervising financial institutions and financial markets.

CONGRESS

House Energy and Commerce Committee, *Subcommittee on Commerce, Trade, and Consumer Protection,* 2125 RHOB 20515; (202) 225-2927. Fax, (202) 225-1919. Rep. Cliff Stearns, R-Fla., Chair.

General e-mail, commerce@mail.house.gov

Web, energycommerce.house.gov/108/subcommittees/Commerce_Trade_and_Consumer_Protection.htm

Jurisdiction over interstate and foreign commerce, regulation of commercial practices, and the Federal Trade Commission.

House Government Reform Committee, *Subcommittee on Energy Policy, Natural Resources, and Regulatory Affairs,* B377 RHOB 20515; (202) 225-4407. Fax, (202) 225-2441. Rep. Doug Ose, R-Calif., Chair; Dan Skopec, Staff Director.

Web, www.house.gov/reform

Investigates investment fraud schemes and commodities and securities fraud. Jurisdiction over the Treasury Dept.

Senate Banking, Housing, and Urban Affairs Committee, *Subcommittee on Securities and Investment,* SD-534 20510; (202) 224-7391. Fax, (202) 224-2080. Sen. Michael B. Enzi, R-Wyo., Chair; Kathy Casey, Staff Director.

Web, banking.senate.gov/subcom.htm

Jurisdiction over stocks, bonds, stock exchanges, over-the-counter markets, mergers and acquisitions, and securities legislation; the Securities Investor Protection Corp.; and the Securities and Exchange Commission.

Senate Governmental Affairs Committee, *Permanent Subcommittee on Investigations,* SR-199 20510; (202) 224-3721. Sen. Norm Coleman, R-Minn., Chair; Mary Robertson, Chief Clerk.

General e-mail, PSI@govt-aff.senate.gov

Web, www.senate.gov/~gov_affairs/psi.htm

Investigates investment fraud schemes and commodities and securities fraud.

NONPROFIT

Bond Market Assn., Washington Office, 1399 New York Ave. N.W., 8th Floor 20005; (202) 434-8400. Fax, (202) 434-8456. John Vogt, Executive Vice President.

Web, www.bondmarkets.com

Membership: banks, dealers, and brokers who underwrite, trade, and sell municipal securities, mortgage-backed securities, and government and federal agency securities. Acts as an information and education center for the public securities industry. (Headquarters in New York.)

Council of Institutional Investors, 1730 Rhode Island Ave. N.W., #512 20036; (202) 822-0800. Fax, (202) 822-0801. Sarah Teslik, Executive Director.

Web, www.cii.org

Membership: public, union, and corporate pension funds. Studies investment issues that affect pension plan assets. Monitors legislation and regulations.

Futures Industry Assn., 2001 Pennsylvania Ave. N.W., #600 20006; (202) 466-5460. Fax, (202) 296-3184. John M. Damgard, President.

Web, www.futuresindustry.org

Membership: commodity futures brokerage firms and others interested in commodity futures. Serves as a forum for discussion of futures industry; provides market information and statistical data; offers educational programs; works to establish professional and ethical standards for members.

Investment Company Institute, 1401 H St. N.W., 12th Floor 20005-2148; (202) 326-5800. Fax, (202) 326-5806. Matthew P. Fink, President.

Web, www.ici.org

Membership: mutual funds and closed-end funds registered under the Investment Company Act of 1940 (including investment advisers to and underwriters of such companies) and the unit investment trust industry.

Conducts research and disseminates information on issues affecting mutual funds.

Investment Program Assn., *1101 17th St. N.W., #703 20036; (202) 775-9750. Fax, (202) 331-8446. Christopher L. Davis, President.*
Web, www.ipa-dc.org

Membership: broker/dealer organizations and sponsors, law and accounting firms, financial planners, and partnership consultants. Works to preserve limited partnerships and real estate investment trusts as a form of investment and a source of new capital for the economy. Conducts economic research. Monitors legislation and regulations, especially those concerning tax policy.

Investor Responsibility Research Center, *1350 Connecticut Ave. N.W., #700 20036-1702; (202) 833-0700. Fax, (202) 833-3555. Linda Crompton, President.*
Web, www.irrc.com

Research organization that reports on and analyzes business and public policy issues affecting corporations and investors.

Municipal Securities Rulemaking Board, *1900 Duke St., #600, Alexandria, VA 22314; (703) 797-6600. Fax, (703) 797-6700. Christopher A. Taylor, Executive Director.*
Web, www.msrb.org

Writes rules, subject to approval by the Securities and Exchange Commission, applicable to municipal securities brokers and dealers, in such areas as conduct, industry practices, and professional qualifications. Serves as a self-regulatory agency for the municipal securities industry.

National Assn. of Bond Lawyers, *Governmental Affairs, Washington Office, 601 13th St., #800-S 20005-3875; (202) 682-1498. Fax, (202) 637-0217. William L. Larsen, Director.*
Web, www.nabl.org

Membership: municipal finance lawyers. Provides members with information on laws relating to the borrowing of money by states and municipalities and to the issuance of state and local government bonds. Monitors legislation and regulations. (Headquarters in Chicago, Ill.)

National Assn. of Real Estate Investment Trusts, *1875 Eye St. N.W., #600 20006; (202) 739-9400. Fax, (202) 739-9401. Steven Wechsler, President.*
Web, www.nareit.com

Membership: real estate investment trusts and corporations, partnerships, and individuals interested in real estate securities and the industry. Monitors federal and state legislation, federal taxation, securities regulation,

standards and ethics, and housing and education; compiles industry statistics.

National Assn. of Securities Dealers (NASD), *1735 K St. N.W. 20006-1506; (202) 728-8000. Fax, (202) 728-8075. Robert Glauber, Chair. Member services, (301) 590-6500. Public disclosure, (800) 289-9999.*
Web, www.nasd.com

Membership: investment brokers and dealers authorized to conduct transactions of the investment banking and securities business under federal and state laws. Serves as the self-regulatory mechanism in the over-the-counter securities market. Operates speakers bureau. (Affiliated with NASD Regulation Inc.)

National Investor Relations Institute, *20 Towers Crescent Dr., #250, Vienna, VA 22182; (703) 506-3570. Fax, (703) 506-3571. Louis M. Thompson Jr., President.*
Web, www.niri.org

Membership: executives engaged in investor relations and financial communications. Provides publications, educational training sessions, and research on investor relations for members; offers conferences and workshops; maintains job placement and referral services for members.

New York Stock Exchange, *Washington Office, 801 Pennsylvania Ave. N.W., #630 20004; (202) 347-4300. Fax, (202) 347-4370. Richard Ribbentrop Sr., Vice President.*
Web, www.nyse.com

Provides limited information on operations of the New York Stock Exchange; Washington office monitors legislation and regulations. (Headquarters in New York.)

North American Securities Administrators Assn., *10 G St. N.E., #710 20002; (202) 737-0900. Fax, (202) 783-3571. Marc Beauchamp, Executive Director.*
Web, www.nasaa.org

Membership: state, provincial, and territorial securities administrators of the United States, Canada, and Mexico. Serves as the national representative of the state agencies responsible for investor protection. Works to prevent fraud in securities markets and provides a national forum to increase the efficiency and uniformity of state regulation of capital markets. Operates the Central Registration Depository, a nationwide computer link for agent registration and transfers, in conjunction with the National Assn. of Securities Dealers. Monitors legislation and regulations.

Securities Industry Assn., *Washington Office, 1401 Eye St. N.W., #1000 20005-2225; (202) 296-9410. Fax, (202) 296-9775. Marc E. Lackritz, President.*

General e-mail, info@sia.com

Web, www.sia.com

Membership: investment bankers, securities underwriters, and dealers in stocks and bonds. Represents all segments of the securities industry. Monitors legislation, regulations, and international agreements. (Headquarters in New York.)

Securities Investor Protection Corp., *805 15th St. N.W., #800 20005-2207; (202) 371-8300. Fax, (202) 371-6728. Debbie D. Branson, Chair.*

Web, www.sipc.org

Private corporation established by Congress to administer the Securities Investor Protection Act. Provides financial protection for customers of member broker-dealers that fail financially.

Tangible Assets

AGENCIES

Census Bureau *(Commerce Dept.),* **Manufacturing and Construction: Construction and Minerals,** *#2229, Bldg. 4 20233; (301) 763-4680. Fax, (301) 457-2059. Mary Susan Bucci, Chief.*

Web, www.census.gov/mcd

Collects, tabulates, and publishes statistics for the mining and construction sectors of the Economic Census; collects and tabulates data for Manufacturing Energy Consumption Survey for the Energy Dept. concerning combustible and non-combustible energy sources for the U.S. manufacturing sector.

Commodity Futures Trading Commission, *3 Lafayette Center, 1155 21st St. N.W. 20581; (202) 418-5050. Fax, (202) 418-5533. James E. Newsome, Chair; Madge A. Bolinger, Executive Director. Information, (202) 418-5080. Library, (202) 418-5255. Locator, (202) 418-5000.*

Web, www.cftc.gov

Enforces federal statutes relating to commodity futures and options, including gold and silver futures and options. Monitors and regulates gold and silver leverage contracts, which provide for deferred delivery of the commodity and the payment of an agreed portion of the purchase price on margin.

Defense Logistics Agency *(Defense Dept.),* **Defense National Stockpile Center,** *8725 John Jay Kingman Rd., #3229, Fort Belvoir, VA 22060-6223; (703) 767-5500. Fax, (703) 767-5538. Cornel A. Holder, Administrator.*

Web, www.dnsc.dla.mil

Manages the national defense stockpile of strategic and critical materials. Purchases strategic materials including beryllium and newly developed high-tech alloys. Disposes of excess materials including tin, silver, industrial diamond stones, tungsten, and vegetable tannin.

Federal Reserve System, *Planning and Control,* *20th and C Sts. N.W., MS-195 20551; (202) 452-3963. Fax, (202) 872-7574. Dorothy Lachapelle, Manager.*

Web, www.federalreserve.gov

Monitors gold certificate accounts and budgets of Federal Reserve Banks. (Gold certificate accounts are credits issued by the Treasury Dept. against gold held by the Treasury.)

U.S. Geological Survey (USGS), *(Interior Dept.),* **Metals,** *12201 Sunrise Valley Dr., MS 989, Reston, VA 20192; (703) 648-4967. Fax, (703) 648-7757. Michael J. McKinley, Chief; Earle B. Amey, Gold; Henry E. Hilliard, Silver and Platinum Group Metals; Daniel Edelstein, Copper.*

Web, minerals.usgs.gov/minerals

Collects, analyzes, and disseminates information on ferrous and non-ferrous metals, including gold, silver, platinum group metals, iron, iron ore, steel, chromium, and nickel. (CD-ROMs may be purchased from the Government Printing Office, [202] 512-1800.)

U.S. Mint *(Treasury Dept.),* *801 9th St. N.W. 20220; (202) 354-7200. Fax, (202) 756-6160. Henrietta Holsman Fore, Director. Information, (202) 354-7227.*

Web, www.usmint.gov

Produces gold, silver, and platinum coins for sale to investors.

CONGRESS

House Financial Services Committee, *Subcommittee on Domestic and International Monetary Policy, Trade, and Technology,* *B304 RHOB 20515; (202) 225-7502. Rep. Peter T. King, R-N.Y., Chair; Bob Foster, Staff Director.*

Web, www.house.gov/financialservices

Jurisdiction over legislation on all matters relating to coins, currency, medals, proof and mint sets, and other special coins. Oversight of the U.S. Mint and the Bureau of Engraving and Printing.

Senate Banking, Housing, and Urban Affairs Committee, *Subcommittee on International Trade and Finance,* *SD-534 20510; (202) 224-4224. Sen. Chuck Hagel, R-Neb., Chair; Dayna Cade, Staff Director.*

Web, banking.senate.gov

Jurisdiction over legislation to regulate international transactions in gold and precious metals.

Silver Institute, *1112 16th St. N.W., #240 20036; (202) 835-0185. Fax, (202) 835-0155. Paul Bateman, Executive Director.*

Web, www.silverinstitute.org

Membership: companies that mine, refine, fabricate, or manufacture silver or silver-containing products. Conducts research on new technological and industrial uses for silver. Compiles statistics by country on mine production of silver; coinage use; the production, distribution, and use of refined silver; and the conversion of refined silver into other forms, such as silverware and jewelry.

Silver Users Assn., *1730 M St. N.W., #911 20036-4505; (202) 785-3050. Fax, (202) 659-5760. Walter L. Frankland Jr., Executive Vice President.*

General e-mail, silverusers@aol.com

Web, www.silverusersassociation.org

Membership: users of silver, including the photographic industry, silversmiths, and other manufacturers. Conducts research on silver market; monitors government activities in silver; analyzes government statistics on silver consumption and production.

INDUSTRIAL PRODUCTION, MANUFACTURING

AGENCIES

Bureau of Export Administration *(Commerce Dept.), Strategic Industries and Economic Security, 14th St. and Constitution Ave. N.W., #3876 20230; (202) 482-4506. Fax, (202) 482-5650. Daniel O. Hill, Director.*

Web, www.bxa.doc.gov

Assists in providing for an adequate supply of strategic and critical materials for defense activities and civilian needs, including military requirements, and other domestic energy supplies; develops plans for industry to meet national emergencies. Studies the effect of imports on national security and recommends actions.

Census Bureau *(Commerce Dept.), Manufacturing and Construction, 4401 Silver Hill Rd., Bldg FB4, #2102A, Suitland, MD 20746; (301) 763-4593. Fax, (301) 457-4583. William G. Bostic Jr., Chief.*

Web, www.census.gov

Collects and distributes manufacturing, construction, and mineral industry data. Reports are organized by commodity, industry, and geographic area.

Economic Development Administration *(Commerce Dept.), Trade Adjustment and Technical Assistance, 14th St. and Constitution Ave. N.W., #7315 20230; (202) 482-2127. Fax, (202) 482-0466. Tony Meyer, Coordinator.*

Web, www.doc.gov/eda

Assists U.S. firms in increasing their competitiveness against foreign imports. Certifies eligibility and provides domestic firms and industries adversely affected by increased imports with technical assistance under provisions of the Trade Act of 1974. Administers ten regional Trade Adjustment Assistance Centers that offer services to eligible U.S. firms.

Economics and Statistics Administration *(Commerce Dept.), 14th St. and Constitution Ave. N.W., #4848 20230; (202) 482-3727. Fax, (202) 482-0432. Kathleen B. Cooper, Under Secretary. Information, (202) 482-2235.*

General e-mail, esa@doc.gov

Web, www.esa.doc.gov

Advises the secretary on economic policy matters, including consumer and capital spending, inventory status, and the short- and long-term outlook in output and unemployment. Seeks to improve economic productivity and growth. Serves as departmental liaison with the Council of Economic Advisers and other government agencies concerned with economic policy. Supervises and sets policy for the Census Bureau and the Bureau of Economic Analysis.

International Trade Administration (ITA), *(Commerce Dept.), Energy, Environment, and Materials, 14th St. and Constitution Ave. N.W., #4043 20230; (202) 482-0614. Fax, (202) 482-5666. Kevin W. Murphy, Deputy Assistant Secretary.*

Web, www.trade.gov

Analyzes and maintains data on domestic and international industries, including metals, materials, chemicals, construction, forest products, energy, automotives, and industrial machinery; responds to government and business inquiries about materials shortages in specific industries. Analyzes supply and demand, capacity and production capability, and capital formation requirements.

Technology Administration *(Commerce Dept.), Technology Competitiveness, 1401 Constitution Ave. N.W., #4418 20230; (202) 482-2100. Fax, (202) 219-8667. Karen Laney-Cummings, Director (Acting), (202) 482-6101. Library, (202) 482-1288. Press, (202) 482-8321. Publications request, (202) 482-1397.*

Web, www.ta.doc.gov/otpolicy

Encourages industrial research to promote U.S. competitiveness and economic security. Works with industry to promote domestic technological competitiveness.

Interests include technology development and transfer; business innovation; state and local efforts to promote technology-based economic growth; and workforce preparation for a technology-driven future.

NONPROFIT

American National Standards Institute, *Conformity Assessment, Washington Office, 1819 L St. N.W., #600 20036; (202) 293-8020. Fax, (202) 293-9287. Lane Hallenbeck, Vice President.*
Web, www.ansi.org

Administers and coordinates the voluntary standardization system for the U.S. private sector; maintains staff contacts for specific industries. Serves as U.S. member of the International Organization for Standardization (ISO) and hosts the U.S. National Committee of the International Electrotechnical Commission (IEC).

APICS, The Educational Society for Resource Management, *5301 Shawnee Rd., Alexandria, VA 22312; (703) 354-8851. Fax, (703) 354-8106. Jeffry Raynes, Executive Director.*
Web, www.apics.org

Membership: integrated resource management professionals in the manufacturing and service industries. Offers certification exams in production and inventory management and integrated resource management; provides job placement assistance; conducts workshops and symposia. Formerly the American Production and Inventory Control Society (APICS).

Assn. for Manufacturing Technology, *7901 Westpark Dr., McLean, VA 22102; (703) 893-2900. Fax, (703) 893-1151. Al Moore, President (Acting).*
Web, www.amtonline.org

Supports the U.S. manufacturing industry; sponsors workshops and seminars; fosters safety and technical standards. Monitors legislation and regulations.

Envelope Manufacturers Assn., *500 Montgomery St., #550, Alexandria, VA 22314-1565; (703) 739-2200. Fax, (703) 739-2209. Maynard H. Benjamin, President.*
Web, www.envelope.org

Membership: envelope manufacturers and suppliers. Monitors legislation and regulations.

Flexible Packaging Assn., *971 Corporate Blvd., #403, Linthicum, MD 21090-2211; (410) 694-0800. Fax, (410) 694-0900. Marla Donahue, President.*
General e-mail, fpa@flexpack.org
Web, www.flexpack.org

Researches packaging trends and technical developments; compiles industry statistics. Monitors legislation and regulations.

Independent Lubricant Manufacturers Assn., *651 S. Washington St., Alexandria, VA 22314; (703) 684-5574. Fax, (703) 836-8503. Celeste Powers, Executive Director.*
Web, www.ilma.org

Membership: U.S. and international companies that manufacture automotive, industrial, and metalworking lubricants; associates include suppliers and related businesses. Conducts workshops and conferences; compiles statistics. Monitors legislation and regulations.

Independent Office Products and Furniture Dealers Assn., *301 N. Fairfax St., #200, Alexandria, VA 22314; (703) 549-9040. Fax, (703) 683-7552. Jim McGarry, President. Information, (800) 542-6672.*
Web, www.iopfda.org

Membership: independent dealers of office products and office furniture. Serves independent dealers and works with their trading partners to develop programs and opportunities that help strengthen the dealer position in the marketplace.

Industrial Designers Society of America, *45195 Business Ct., #250, Dulles, VA 20166-6717; (703) 707-6000. Fax, (703) 787-8501. Kristina Goodrich, Executive Director.*
General e-mail, idsa@idsa.org
Web, www.idsa.org

Membership: designers of products, equipment, instruments, furniture, transportation, packages, exhibits, information services, and related services. Provides the Bureau of Labor Statistics with industry information. Monitors legislation and regulations.

Industrial Research Institute, *1550 M St. N.W., #1100 20005-1712; (202) 296-8811. Fax, (202) 776-0756. F. M. Ross Armbrecht, President.*
Web, www.iriinc.org

Membership: companies that maintain laboratories for industrial research. Seeks to improve the process of industrial research by promoting cooperative efforts among companies, between the academic and research communities, and between industry and the government. Monitors legislation and regulations concerning technology, industry, and national competitiveness.

International Sleep Products Assn., *501 Wythe St., Alexandria, VA 22314; (703) 683-8371. Fax, (703) 683-4503. Russell L. Abolt, President.*
General e-mail, info@sleepproducts.org
Web, www.sleepproducts.org

Membership: manufacturers of bedding and mattresses. Compiles statistics on the industry. (Affiliated with Sleep Products Safety Council and the Better Sleep Council.)

International Union of Electronic, Electrical, Salaried, Machine, and Furniture Workers, *1275 K St. N.W. 20005; (202) 513-6300. Fax, (202) 513-6357. Edward L. Fire, President.*
Web, www.iue-cwa.org

Membership: approximately 125,000 workers in the field of industrial electronics and furniture and general manufacturing. Helps members negotiate pay, benefits, and better working conditions; conducts training programs and workshops. (Affiliated with the AFL-CIO.)

Manufacturers' Alliance for Productivity and Innovation, *1525 Wilson Blvd., #900, Arlington, VA 22209; (703) 841-9000. Fax, (703) 841-9514. Thomas J. Duesterberg, President.*
Web, www.mapi.net

Membership: companies involved in high technology industries, including electronics, telecommunications, precision instruments, computers, and the automotive and aerospace industries. Seeks to increase industrial productivity. Conducts research; organizes discussion councils. Monitors legislation and regulations.

National Assn. of Manufacturers (NAM),
1331 Pennsylvania Ave. N.W., #600 20004-1790; (202) 637-3000. Fax, (202) 637-3182. Jerry Jasinowski, President. Press, (202) 637-3094.
General e-mail, manufacturing@nam.org
Web, www.nam.org

Represents industry views (mainly of manufacturers) to government on national and international issues. Reviews legislation, administrative rulings, and judicial decisions affecting industry. Sponsors the Human Resources Forum; operates a Web site for members and the public that provides information on legislative and other news; conducts programs on labor relations, occupational safety and health, regulatory and consumer affairs, environmental trade and technology, and other business issues.

National Coalition for Advanced Manufacturing,
2000 L St. N.W., #807 20036; (202) 429-2220. Fax, (202) 429-2422. Leo Reddy, President.
Web, www.nacfam.org

Seeks a public policy environment more supportive of advanced manufacturing and industrial modernization as keys to global economic competitiveness. Advocates greater national focus on industrial base modernization, increased investment in plants and equipment, accelerated development and deployment of advanced manufacturing technology, and reform of technical education and training.

National Industrial Council, *1331 Pennsylvania Ave. N.W., #600 20004-1790; (202) 637-3053. Fax, (202) 637-3182. Barry Buzby, Executive Director, State Associations, (202) 637-3054; Mark Stuart, Executive Director, Employer Associations, (202) 637-3052.*
Web, www.nam.org

Membership: employer associations at the regional, state, and local levels. Works to strengthen U.S. competitive enterprise system. Represents views of industry on business and economic issues; sponsors conferences and seminars. (Affiliated with the National Assn. of Manufacturers.)

Paper Allied-Industrial, Chemical, and Energy Workers International Union, *Government Relations, Washington Office, 727 15th St. N.W., #700 20005; (202) 293-7939. Fax, (202) 293-7888. Pete Strader, Legislative Director. Information, (800) 432-6229.*
Web, www.paceunion.org

Membership: approximately 310,000 workers in the energy, chemical, pharmaceutical, and allied industries. Assists members with contract negotiation and grievances; conducts training programs and workshops. Monitors legislation and regulations. (Headquarters in Nashville, Tenn.; affiliated with the AFL-CIO.)

Rubber Manufacturers Assn., *1400 K St. N.W., #900 20005; (202) 682-4800. Fax, (202) 682-4854. Donald Shea, President.*
Web, www.rma.org

Membership: manufacturers of tires, tubes, roofing, sporting goods, and mechanical and industrial products. Interests include recycling.

U.S. Business and Industry Council, *910 16th St. N.W., #300 20006; (202) 728-1980. Fax, (202) 728-1981. Kevin L. Kearns, President.*
General e-mail, council@usbusiness.org
Web, www.usbusiness.org

Advocates energy independence, reindustrialization, and effective use of natural resources and manufacturing capacity. Current issues include business tax reduction, the liability crisis, defense and other federal spending, and the trade deficit. Media network distributes op-ed pieces to newspapers and radio stations.

Clothing and Textiles

AGENCIES

Federal Trade Commission (FTC), *Consumer Protection, 600 Pennsylvania Ave. N.W., #466 20580; (202) 326-3665. Fax, (202) 326-3799. J. Howard Beales III, Director. Identity Fraud report line, (877) IDTHEFT.*

Web, www.ftc.gov

Enforces regulations dealing with unfair or deceptive business practices in advertising, credit, marketing, and service industries; educates consumers and business about these regulations; conducts investigations and litigation.

International Trade Administration (ITA), *(Commerce Dept.), Textiles, Apparel, and Consumer Goods Industries,* *14th St. and Constitution Ave. N.W., #3001A 20230; (202) 482-3737. Fax, (202) 482-2331. James C. Leonard III, Deputy Assistant Secretary.*

Web, otexa.ita.doc.gov

Participates in negotiating bilateral textile and apparel import restraint agreements; responsible for textile, apparel, and consumer goods export expansion programs and reduction of nontariff barriers; provides data on economic conditions in the domestic textile, apparel, and consumer goods markets, including impact of imports.

NONPROFIT

American Apparel and Footwear Assn. (AAFA), *1601 N. Kent St., Arlington, VA 22209; (703) 524-1864. Fax, (703) 522-6741. Kevin M. Burke, President.*

Web, www.apparelandfootwear.org

Membership: manufacturers of apparel, allied needle-trade products, footwear and their suppliers, importers, and distributors. Provides members with information on the industry, including import and export data. Interests include product flammability and trade promotion. Monitors legislation and regulations.

American Fiber Manufacturers Assn., *1530 Wilson Blvd., #690, Arlington, VA 22209; (703) 875-0432. Fax, (703) 875-0907. Paul T. O'Day, President.*

General e-mail, afma@afma.org

Web, www.fibersource.com

Membership: U.S. producers of manufactured (manmade) fibers, filaments, and yarns. Interests include international trade, education, and environmental and technical services. Monitors legislation and regulations.

American Textile Machinery Assn., *111 Park Pl., Falls Church, VA 22046; (703) 538-1789. Fax, (703) 241-5603. Harry W. Buzzerd Jr., President.*

General e-mail, atmahq@aol.com

Web, www.atmanet.org

Membership: U.S.-based manufacturers of textile machinery and related parts and accessories. Interests include competitiveness and expansion of foreign markets. Monitors legislation and regulations.

American Textile Manufacturers Institute, *1130 Connecticut Ave. N.W., #1200 20036-3954; (202) 862-0500. Fax, (202) 862-0570. Parks D. Shackelford, President.*

Web, www.atmi.org

Membership: U.S. companies that spin, weave, knit, or finish textiles from natural fibers, and associate members from affiliated industries. Interests include domestic and world markets. Monitors legislation and regulations.

Footwear Distributors and Retailers of America, *1319 F St. N.W., #700 20004; (202) 737-5660. Fax, (202) 638-2615. Peter T. Mangione, President.*

Web, www.fdra.org

Membership: companies that operate shoe retail outlets. Provides business support and government relations to members. Interests include intellectual property rights, ocean shipping rates, trade with China, and labeling regulations.

International Fabricare Institute, *12251 Tech Rd., Silver Spring, MD 20904; (301) 622-1900. Fax, (301) 236-9320. William E. Fisher, Executive Vice President.*

Web, www.ifi.org

Membership: dry cleaners and launderers. Conducts research and provides information on products and services. Monitors legislation and regulations.

National Cotton Council of America, *Washington Office,* *1521 New Hampshire Ave. N.W. 20036; (202) 745-7805. Fax, (202) 483-4040. John Maguire, Vice President.*

Web, www.cotton.org/ncc

Membership: all segments of the U.S. cotton industry. Formulates positions on trade policy and negotiations; seeks to improve competitiveness of U.S. exports; sponsors programs to educate the public about flammable fabrics. (Headquarters in Memphis, Tenn.)

Uniform and Textile Service Assn., *1300 N. 17th St., #750, Arlington, VA 22209; (703) 247-2600. Fax, (703) 841-4750. David F. Hobson, President.*

General e-mail, info@utsa.com

Web, www.utsa.com

Membership: companies that provide uniforms and textile products to commercial and government enterprises. Sponsors seminars and conferences; provides information on environmental policy and procedures to members. Monitors legislation and regulations.

Union of Needletrades Industrial and Textile Employees (UNITE), *Washington Office,* *888 16th St. N.W., #303 20006; (202) 347-7417. Fax, (202) 347-0708. Patricia Campos, Legislative Representative.*

General e-mail, stopsweatshops@uniteunion.org

Web, www.uniteunion.org

Membership: approximately 250,000 workers in basic apparel and textiles, millinery, shoe, laundry, retail, and related industries; and in auto parts and auto supply. Assists members with contract negotiation and grievances; conducts training programs and workshops. Monitors legislation and regulations. (Headquarters in New York; affiliated with the AFL-CIO.)

Electronics and Appliances

NONPROFIT

Consumer Electronics Assn., *2500 Wilson Blvd., Arlington, VA 22201-3834; (703) 907-7600. Fax, (703) 907-7601. Gary Shapiro, President.*
Web, www.ce.org
 Membership: U.S. consumer electronics manufacturers. Promotes the industry; sponsors seminars and conferences; conducts research; consults with member companies. Monitors legislation and regulations. (Affiliated with Electronic Industries Alliance.)

Electronic Industries Alliance, *2500 Wilson Blvd., #400, Arlington, VA 22201-3834; (703) 907-7500. Fax, (703) 907-7501. Dave McCurdy, President.*
Web, www.eia.org
 Membership: manufacturers, dealers, installers, and distributors of consumer electronics products. Provides consumer information and data on industry trends; advocates an open market. Monitors legislation and regulations.

Gas Appliance Manufacturers Assn., *2107 Wilson Blvd., #600, Arlington, VA 22201; (703) 525-7060. Fax, (703) 525-6790. Evan Gaddis, President.*
General e-mail, information@gamanet.org
Web, www.gamanet.org
 Membership: manufacturers of gas appliances and equipment for residential and commercial use and related industries. Advocates product improvement; provides market statistics. Monitors legislation and regulations.

National Electrical Contractors Assn., *3 Bethesda Metro Center, #1100, Bethesda, MD 20814; (301) 657-3110. Fax, (301) 215-4500. John Grau, Executive Vice President.*
Web, www.necanet.org
 Membership: electrical contractors who build and service electrical wiring, equipment, and appliances. Represents members in collective bargaining with union workers; sponsors research and educational programs.

Optoelectronics Industry Development Assn., *1133 Connecticut Ave., N.W., #600 20036; (202) 785-4426. Fax, (202) 785-4428. Fred Welsh, Executive Director.*

Web, www.oida.org
 Membership: users and suppliers of optoelectronics in North America. Promotes the global competitiveness of members; provides a forum for exchange of information; conducts workshops and conferences; sponsors research. Monitors legislation and regulations.

Steel, Metalworking, Machinery

NONPROFIT

American Boiler Manufacturers Assn., *4001 N. 9th St., #226, Arlington, VA 22203; (703) 522-7350. Fax, (703) 522-2665. Randall Rawson, President.*
Web, www.abma.com
 Membership: manufacturers of boiler systems and boiler-related products, including fuel-burning systems. Interests include energy and environmental issues.

American Gear Manufacturers Assn., *1500 King St., #201, Alexandria, VA 22314; (703) 684-0211. Fax, (703) 684-0242. Joe T. Franklin, President.*
Web, www.agma.org
 Membership: gear manufacturers, suppliers, and industry consultants. Conducts workshops, seminars, and conferences; develops industry standards; sponsors research. Monitors legislation and regulations.

American Institute for International Steel, *1325 G St. N.W., #980 20005; (202) 628-3878. Fax, (202) 737-3134. David Phelps, President.*
General e-mail, aiis@aiis.org
Web, www.aiis.org
 Membership: importers and exporters of steel. Conducts research on manufacturing processes. Holds annual conferences.

American Machine Tool Distributors Assn., *1445 Research Blvd., #450, Rockville, MD 20850; (301) 738-1200. Fax, (301) 738-9499. Ralph J. Nappi, President. Information, (800) 878-2683.*
Web, www.amtda.org
 Membership: distributors of machine tools. Supports advances in manufacturing and expansion of international trade. Monitors legislation and regulations.

American Wire Producers Assn., *801 N. Fairfax St., #211, Alexandria, VA 22314; (703) 299-4434. Fax, (703) 299-9233. Kimberly A. Korbel, Executive Director.*
General e-mail, info@awpa.org
Web, www.awpa.org
 Membership: companies that produce carbon, alloy, and stainless steel wire and wire products in the United States. Interests include imports of rod, wire, and wire products. Publishes survey of the domestic wire industry. Monitors legislation and regulations.

Cold Finished Steel Bar Institute, *111 Park Pl., Falls Church, VA 22046; (703) 538-3543. Fax, (703) 241-5603. Peter Murray, President.*

Web, www.cfsbi.com

Promotes the industry of cold finished steel bar production. Conducts research; sponsors annual award. Monitors legislation and regulations.

International Assn. of Bridge, Structural, Ornamental, and Reinforcing Iron Workers, *1750 New York Ave. N.W., #400 20006; (202) 383-4800. Fax, (202) 638-4856. Joseph J. Hunt, President.*

Web, www.ironworkers.org

Membership: approximately 82,000 iron workers. Helps members negotiate pay, benefits, and better working conditions; conducts training programs and workshops. Monitors legislation and regulations. (Affiliated with the AFL-CIO.)

International Assn. of Machinists and Aerospace Workers, *9000 Machinists Pl., Upper Marlboro, MD 20772-2687; (301) 967-4500. Fax, (301) 967-4588. Thomas Buffenbarger, President.*

Web, www.iamaw.org

Membership: machinists in more than 200 industries. Helps members negotiate pay, benefits, and better working conditions; conducts training programs and workshops. Monitors legislation and regulations. (Affiliated with the AFL-CIO, the Canadian Labour Congress, the Railway Labor Executives Assn., the International Metalworkers Federation, and the International Transport Workers' Federation.)

International Magnesium Assn., *900 17th St. N.W., #450 20006; (202) 466-6601. Fax, (202) 466-6678. Richard E. Opatick, Executive Director.*

General e-mail, info@intlmag.org

Web, www.intlmag.org

Membership: international magnesium producers, processors, recyclers, die casters, and suppliers. Promotes the magnesium industry. (Operates offices in Europe and China.)

Machinery Dealers National Assn., *315 S. Patrick St., Alexandria, VA 22314; (703) 836-9300. Fax, (703) 836-9303. Mark Robinson, Executive Vice President.*

General e-mail, office@mdna.org

Web, www.mdna.org

Membership: companies that buy and sell used capital equipment. Establishes a code of ethics for members; publishes a buyer's guide that lists members by types of machinery they sell.

National Tooling and Machining Assn., *9300 Livingston Rd., Ft. Washington, MD 20744-4998; (301) 248-6200. Fax, (301) 248-7104. Matthew B. Coffey, President.*

Web, www.ntma.org

Membership: members of the contract precision metalworking industry, including tool, die, mold, diecasting die, and special machining companies. Assists members in developing and expanding their domestic and foreign markets. Offers training program, insurance, and legal advice; compiles statistical information. Monitors legislation and regulations.

Outdoor Power Equipment Institute, *341 S. Patrick St., Alexandria, VA 22314; (703) 549-7600. Fax, (703) 549-7604. William G. Harley, President.*

Web, opei.mow.org

Membership: manufacturers of powered lawn and garden maintenance products, components and attachments, and their suppliers. Promotes safe use of outdoor power equipment; keeps statistics on the industry; fosters exchange of information. Monitors legislation and regulations.

Sheet Metal Workers' International Assn., *1750 New York Ave. N.W. 20006; (202) 783-5880. Fax, (202) 662-0880. Michael J. Sullivan, General President.*

Web, www.smwia.org

Membership: more than 150,000 U.S. and Canadian workers in the building and construction trades, manufacturing, and the railroad and shipyard industries. Assists members with contract negotiation and grievances; conducts training programs and workshops. Monitors legislation and regulations. (Affiliated with the Sheet Metal and Air Conditioning Contractors' Assn., the AFL-CIO, and the Canadian Labour Congress.)

Specialty Steel Industry of North America, *3050 K St. N.W., #400 20007; (202) 342-8630. Fax, (202) 342-8631. David Hartquist, Counsel.*

Web, www.ssina.com

Membership: manufacturers of products in stainless and other specialty steels. Establishes quality standards and manufacturing techniques; sponsors workshops; operates a hotline for technical questions.

Steel Manufacturers Assn., *1150 Connecticut Ave., N.W., #715 20036-3101; (202) 296-1515. Fax, (202) 296-2506. Thomas A. Danjczek, President.*

Web, www.steelnet.org

Membership: steel producers in North America and abroad. Helps members exchange information on technical matters; provides information on the steel industry to the public and government. Monitors legislation and regulations.

United Steelworkers of America, *Washington Office,* *1150 17th St. N.W., #300 20036; (202) 778-4384. Fax, (202) 293-5308. William J. Klinefelter, Legislative and Political Director.*

Web, www.uswa.org

Membership: more than 700,000 steelworkers in the United States and Canada. Helps members negotiate pay, benefits, and better working conditions; conducts training programs and workshops. Monitors legislation and regulations. (Headquarters in Pittsburgh, Pa.; affiliated with the AFL-CIO.)

 INSURANCE

AGENCIES

Federal Insurance and Mitigation Administration *(Federal Emergency Management Agency),* *500 C St. S.W., #430 20472; (202) 646-2781. Fax, (202) 646-7970. Anthony S. Lowe, Administrator.*

Web, www.fema.gov/nfip

Administers federal flood insurance programs, including the National Flood Insurance Program. Makes low-cost flood insurance available to eligible homeowners.

Small Business Administration (SBA), *Disaster Assistance,* *409 3rd St. S.W., #6050 20416; (202) 205-6734. Fax, (202) 205-7728. Herbert L. Mitchell, Associate Administrator.*

Web, www.sba.gov

Provides victims of physical disasters with disaster and economic injury loans for homes, businesses, and personal property. Lends funds to individual homeowners, business concerns of all sizes, and nonprofit institutions to repair or replace damaged structures and furnishings, business machinery, equipment, and inventory.

CONGRESS

House Financial Services Committee, *Subcommittee on Housing and Community Opportunity,* *B303 RHOB 20515; (202) 225-7502. Rep. Bob Ney, R-Ohio, Chair; Bob Foster, Staff Director.*

Web, www.house.gov/financialservices

Jurisdiction over federal flood, fire, and earthquake insurance programs; oversees activities of the insurance industry pertaining to these programs.

Senate Banking, Housing, and Urban Affairs Committee, *Subcommittee on Housing and Transporta-* *tion,* *SD-534 20510; (202) 224-7391. Fax, (202) 224-5137. Sen. Wayne Allard, R-Colo., Chair; Tewana Wilkerson, Staff Director.*

Web, banking.senate.gov/subcom.htm

Jurisdiction over federal flood, crime, fire, and earthquake insurance programs; oversees activities of the insurance industry pertaining to these programs.

NONPROFIT

Alliance of American Insurers, *Federal Affairs, Washington Office,* *1211 Connecticut Ave. N.W., #400 20036; (202) 822-8811. Fax, (202) 872-1885. David M. Farmer, Senior Vice President.*

Web, www.allianceai.org

Membership: property and casualty insurance companies. Provides educational and advisory services for members on insurance issues. (Headquarters in Downers Grove, Ill.)

American Academy of Actuaries, *1100 17th St. N.W., 7th Fl. 20036; (202) 223-8196. Fax, (202) 872-1948. Rick Lawson, Executive Director.*

Web, www.actuary.org

Membership: professional actuaries practicing in the areas of life, health, liability, property, and casualty insurance; pensions; government insurance plans; and general consulting. Provides information on actuarial matters, including insurance and pensions; develops professional standards; advises public policymakers.

American Council of Life Insurers, *101 Constitution Ave. N.W., #700 20001; (202) 624-2000. Fax, (202) 624-2319. Frank Keating, President. Press, (202) 624-2416. National Insurance Consumer Helpline, (800) 942-4242.*

Web, www.acli.com

Membership: life insurance companies authorized to do business in the United States. Conducts research and compiles statistics at state and federal levels. Monitors legislation and regulations.

American Insurance Assn., *1130 Connecticut Ave. N.W., #1000 20036; (202) 828-7100. Fax, (202) 293-1219. Robert E. Vagley, President. Library, (202) 828-7183. Press, (202) 828-7116.*

Web, www.aiadc.org

Membership: companies providing property and casualty insurance. Conducts public relations and educational activities; provides information on issues related to property and casualty insurance. Library open to the public by appointment.

American Society of Pension Actuaries, *4245 N. Fairfax Dr., #750, Arlington, VA 22203-1619; (703) 516-9300. Fax, (703) 516-9308. Brian Graff, Executive Director.*

Web, www.aspa.org

Membership: professional pension plan actuaries, administrators, consultants, and other benefits professionals. Sponsors educational programs to prepare actuaries and consultants for professional exams. Monitors legislation.

Assn. for Advanced Life Underwriting, *2901 Telstar Court, 4th Floor, Falls Church, VA 22042; (703) 641-9400. Fax, (703) 641-9885. David J. Stertzer, Executive Vice President.*

Web, www.aalu.org

Membership: specialized underwriters in the fields of estate analysis, charitable planning, business insurance, pension planning, and employee benefit plans. Monitors legislation and regulations on small-business taxes and capital formation.

Assn. of Trial Lawyers of America, *1050 31st St. N.W. 20007-4499; (202) 965-3500. Fax, (202) 342-5484. Thomas H. Henderson Jr., Executive Director.*

Web, www.atlanet.org

Membership: attorneys, judges, law professors, and students. Interests include aspects of legal and legislative activity relating to the adversary system and trial by jury, including property and casualty insurance.

Consumer Federation of America's Insurance Group, *1424 16th St. N.W., #604 20036; (202) 387-6121. Fax, (202) 265-7989. J. Robert Hunter, Director.*

Web, www.consumerfed.org

Public interest organization that conducts research and provides consumers with information on buying insurance. Interests include auto, homeowner, renter, and life insurance. Monitors legislation and regulations.

Council of Insurance Agents and Brokers, *701 Pennsylvania Ave. N.W., #750 20004; (202) 783-4400. Fax, (202) 783-4410. Ken A. Crerar, President.*

General e-mail, ciab@ciab.com

Web, www.ciab.com

Represents commercial property and casualty insurance agencies and brokerage firms. Members offer insurance products and risk management services to business, government, and the public.

ERISA Industry Committee, *1400 L St. N.W., #350 20005; (202) 789-1400. Fax, (202) 789-1120. Mark J. Ugoretz, President.*

General e-mail, eric@eric.org

Web, www.eric.org

Membership: major U.S. employers. Advocates members' positions on employee retirement, health care cov-

erage, and welfare benefit plans; promotes flexibility and cost-effectiveness in employee benefits. Monitors legislation and regulations.

GAMA International, *2901 Telstar Court, #140, Falls Church, VA 22042; (703) 770-8184. Fax, (703) 770-8182. MaryKay Myers, Director. Information, (800) 345-2687. Web, www.gamaweb.com*

Membership: general agents and managers who provide life insurance and related financial products and services. Provides information, education, and training for members.

Independent Insurance Agents of America, *Government Relations: Industry and State Relations, 127 S. Peyton St., Alexandria, VA 22314; (703) 683-4422. Fax, (703) 683-7556. Bob Rusbuldt, Executive Officer.*

Web, www.iiaa.org

Provides educational and advisory services; researches issues pertaining to auto, home, business, life, and health insurance; offers cooperative advertising program to members. Political action committee monitors legislation and regulations.

Insurance Information Institute, *Washington Office, 1730 Rhode Island Ave. N.W., #710 20036; (202) 833-1580. Fax, (202) 223-5779. Carolyn Gorman, Vice President.*

General e-mail, media@iii.org

Web, www.iii.org

Membership: property and casualty insurance companies. Monitors state and federal issues concerning insurance. Serves as a primary source for information, analysis, and referral concerning property and casualty insurance. (Headquarters in New York.)

Mortgage Insurance Companies of America, *727 15th St. N.W., 12th Floor 20005; (202) 393-5566. Fax, (202) 393-5557. Suzanne C. Hutchinson, Executive Vice President.*

Web, www.privatemi.com

Membership: companies that provide private mortgage guarantee insurance on residential mortgage loans.

National Assn. of Independent Insurers, *Government Relations, Washington Office, 444 N. Capitol St. N.W., #801 20001; (202) 639-0490. Fax, (202) 639-0494. Carl M. Parks, Senior Vice President.*

Web, www.naii.org

Membership: companies providing property and casualty insurance. Monitors legislation and compiles statistics; interests include auto and no-fault insurance and personal lines. (Headquarters in Des Plaines, Ill.)

National Assn. of Independent Life Brokerage Agencies, *12150 Monument Dr., #125, Fairfax, VA 22033; (703) 383-3081. Fax, (703) 383-6942. Joe Normandy, Executive Director.*
Web, www.nailba.org

Membership: owners of independent life insurance agencies. Fosters the responsible and effective distribution of life and health insurance and related financial services; provides a forum for exchange of information among members. Monitors legislation and regulations.

National Assn. of Insurance and Financial Advisors, *2901 Telstar Court, Falls Church, VA 22042; (703) 770-8100. Fax, (703) 770-8107. David F. Woods, Chief Executive Officer.*
General e-mail, membersupport@naifa.org
Web, www.naifa.org

Federation of affiliated state and local life underwriters. Provides information on life and health insurance and other financial services; sponsors education and training programs. Formerly the National Assn. of Life Underwriters.

National Assn. of Insurance Commissioners, *Washington Office, 444 N. Capitol St. N.W., #701 20001-1512; (202) 624-7790. Fax, (202) 624-8579. David Wetmore, Washington Director.*
Web, www.naic.org

Membership: state insurance commissioners, directors, and supervisors. Provides members with information on computer information services, legal and market conduct, and financial services; publishes research and statistics on the insurance industry. Monitors legislation and regulations. (Headquarters in Kansas City, Mo.)

National Assn. of Professional Insurance Agents, *400 N. Washington St., Alexandria, VA 22314-2353; (703) 836-9340. Fax, (703) 836-1279. Gary Eberhart, Executive Vice President; Peter J. Bizzozero, Assistant Vice President, Federal Affairs, (703) 518-1365. Information, (800) 742-6900. Press, (703) 518-1351.*
General e-mail, piaweb@pianet.org
Web, www.pianet.com

Membership: independent insurance agents and brokers. Operates schools to provide agents with basic training; offers seminars and provides educational materials. Monitors legislation and regulations.

Nonprofit Risk Management Center, *1001 Connecticut Ave. N.W., #410 20036; (202) 785-3891. Fax, (202) 296-0349. Melanie Herman, Executive Director.*
General e-mail, info@nonprofitrisk.org
Web, www.nonprofitrisk.org

Assists all groups engaged in charitable service, including nonprofit organizations, government entities, and corporate volunteer programs, to improve the quality of and reduce the cost of their insurance. Provides information on insurance and risk management issues through conferences and publications.

Product Liability Alliance, *Government Relations, 1725 K St. N.W., #300 20006; (202) 872-0885. Fax, (202) 785-0586. James A. Anderson Jr., Vice President.*
Web, www.naw.org

Membership: manufacturers, product sellers and their insurers, and trade associations. Promotes enactment of federal product liability tort reform legislation.

Reinsurance Assn. of America, *1301 Pennsylvania Ave. N.W., #900 20004; (202) 638-3690. Fax, (202) 638-0936. Franklin W. Nutter, President.*
Web, www.reinsurance.org

Membership: companies writing property and casualty reinsurance. Serves as an information clearinghouse.

PATENTS, COPYRIGHTS, AND TRADEMARKS

AGENCIES

Bureau of Customs and Border Protection *(Homeland Security Dept.), Intellectual Property Rights, 1300 Pennsylvania Ave. N.W., Mint Annex 20229; (202) 572-8710. Fax, (202) 572-8747. Joanne Roman Stump, Chief.*
Web, www.customs.gov

Responsible for Customs recordation of registered trademarks and copyrights. Enforces rules and regulations pertaining to intellectual property rights. Coordinates enforcement of International Trade Commission exclusion orders against unfairly competing goods. Determines admissibility of restricted merchandise and cultural properties. Provides support to and coordinates with international organizations and the Office of the U.S. Trade Representative.

Justice Dept. (DOJ), *Civil Division: Intellectual Property, 1100 L St. N.W., #11116 20005; (202) 514-7223. Fax, (202) 307-0345. Vito J. DiPietro, Director.*
Web, www.usdoj.gov

Represents the United States in patent, copyright, and trademark cases. Includes the defense of patent infringement suits; legal proceedings to establish government priority of invention; defense of administrative acts of the Register of Copyrights; and actions on behalf of the government involving the use of trademarks.

Patent and Trademark Office *(Commerce Dept.),* *2121 Crystal Dr., Crystal Park II, #906, Arlington, VA 22202; (703) 305-8600. Fax, (703) 305-8664. James E. Rogan, Under Secretary. Press, (703) 305-8341. TTY, (703) 305-7785. Toll-free, (800) 786-9199. Trademark search library, (703) 308-9800. Patent search library, (703) 305-4463. Copyright search library, (202) 707-3000.*
Web, www.uspto.gov

Grants patents, registers trademarks, and provides patent and trademark information. Scientific library and search file of U.S. and foreign patents available for public use.

State Dept., *Intellectual Property and Competition,* *2201 C St. N.W., #3638 20520-3638; (202) 647-3251. Fax, (202) 647-1537. Jack Felt, Division Chief.*
Web, www.state.gov

Handles multilateral and bilateral policy formulation involving patents, copyrights, and trademarks, and international industrial property of U.S. nationals.

CONGRESS

House Judiciary Committee, *Subcommittee on Courts, the Internet, and Intellectual Property,* *B351A RHOB 20515; (202) 225-5741. Fax, (202) 225-3673. Rep. Lamar Smith, R-Texas, Chair; Blaine Merritt, Chief Counsel.*
General e-mail, Judiciary@mail.house.gov
Web, www.house.gov/judiciary/submembers.htm

Jurisdiction over patent, trademark, and copyright legislation, including legislation on home audio and video taping, intellectual property rights, and financial syndication. Oversees the Patent and Trademark Office, Copyright Office, and Copyright Royalty Tribunal. (Some jurisdictions shared with House Science Committee.)

House Science Committee, *Subcommittee on Environment, Technology, and Standards,* *2319 RHOB 20515; (202) 225-8844. Fax, (202) 225-4438. Rep. Vernon J. Ehlers, R-Mich., Chair; Eric Webster, Staff Director.*
General e-mail, science@mail.house.gov
Web, www.house.gov/science

Jurisdiction over patent and intellectual property policies (shared with House Judiciary Committee).

Library of Congress, *Copyright Office,* *101 Independence Ave. S.E., #403 20540; (202) 707-8350. Fax, (202) 707-8366. Marybeth Peters, Register of Copyrights. Information, (202) 707-3000.*
Web, www.loc.gov/copyright

Provides information on copyright registration procedures and requirements, copyright law, and international copyrights; registers copyright claims and maintains public records of copyright registrations. Copyright record searches conducted on an hourly fee basis. Files open to public for research during weekday business hours. Does not give legal advice on copyright matters.

Senate Judiciary Committee, *SD-224 20510; (202) 224-5225. Fax, (202) 224-9102. Sen. Orrin G. Hatch, R-Utah, Chair; Makan Delrahim, Chief Counsel.*
Web, judiciary.senate.gov

Jurisdiction over patent, trademark, and copyright legislation, including legislation on home audio and video taping, intellectual property rights, and financial syndication.

JUDICIARY

U.S. Court of Appeals for the Federal Circuit, *717 Madison Pl. N.W. 20439; (202) 633-6556. Fax, (202) 633-6353. Haldane Robert Mayer, Chief Judge; Jan Horbaly, Clerk, (202) 633-9614. Electronic bulletin board, (202) 633-9608 or (202) 786-6584.*

Reviews decisions of U.S. Patent and Trademark Office on applications and interferences regarding patents and trademarks; hears appeals on patent infringement cases from district courts.

NONPROFIT

American Bar Assn. (ABA), *Intellectual Property Law,* *740 15th St. N.W., 9th Floor 20005; (202) 662-1772. Fax, (202) 662-1762. Hayden Gregory, Staff Legislative Consultant.*
Web, www.abanet.org

Membership: attorneys practicing intellectual property law, including patent, trademark, copyright, and related unfair competition law. Promotes development and improvement of intellectual property treaties, laws, and regulations, and monitors their enforcement; conducts continuing legal education programs.

American Intellectual Property Law Assn., *2001 Jefferson Davis Hwy., #203, Arlington, VA 22202; (703) 415-0780. Fax, (703) 415-0786. Michael K. Kirk, Executive Director.*
General e-mail, aipla@aipla.org
Web, www.aipla.org

Membership: lawyers practicing in the field of patents, trademarks, and copyrights (intellectual property law). Holds continuing legal education conferences.

Assn. of American Publishers, *Copyright and New Technology,* *50 F St. N.W., #400 20001; (202) 347-3375.*

Fax, (202) 347-3690. Allan Adler, Vice President, Legal and Government Affairs.

Web, www.publishers.org

Monitors copyright activity in government, Congress, and international forums and institutions; sponsors seminars open to the public for a fee.

Digital Futures Coalition, 105 Buxton Rd., Falls Church, VA 22046; (202) 628-9210. Fax, (703) 532-5669. Ruth Rodgers, Coordinator.

General e-mail, dfc@dfc.org

Web, www.dfc.org

Membership: educational, scholarly, library, and consumer groups as well as trade associations. Advocates a fair and balanced approach to implementing the World Intellectual Property Organization treaties. Monitors legislation and regulations.

Intellectual Property Owners, 1255 23rd St. N.W., #200 20037; (202) 466-2396. Fax, (202) 466-2893. Herbert C. Wamsley, Executive Director.

Web, www.ipo.org

Monitors legislation and conducts educational programs to protect intellectual property through patents, trademarks, copyrights, and trade secret laws.

National Assn. of Manufacturers (NAM), *Technology Policy,* 1331 Pennsylvania Ave. N.W., #600 20004-1790; (202) 637-3147. Fax, (202) 637-3182. David Peyton, Director.

Web, www.nam.org

Develops policy and legislation on patents, copyrights, trademarks, and trade secrets.

National School Boards Assn., 1680 Duke St., Alexandria, VA 22314; (703) 838-6722. Fax, (703) 683-7590. Anne Bryant, Executive Director; Julie Underwood, General Counsel.

Web, www.nsba.org

Promotes a broad interpretation of copyright law to permit legitimate scholarly use of published and musical works, videotaped programs, and materials for computer-assisted instruction.

Progress and Freedom Foundation, *Center for the Study of Digital Property,* 1401 H St. N.W., #1075 20005-2110; (202) 289-8928. Fax, (202) 289-6079. James V. DeLong, Director.

General e-mail, mail@pff.org

Web, www.pff.org

Conducts program of research and education on intellectual property issues related to the Internet and other digital technologies.

U.S. Chamber of Commerce, *Congressional and Public Affairs,* 1615 H St. N.W. 20062-2000; (202) 463-5600. Fax, (202) 887-3430. Rolf T. Lundberg, Senior Vice President.

Web, www.uschamber.com

Monitors legislation and regulations on patents, copyrights, and trademarks.

 # SALES AND SERVICES

AGENCIES

Bureau of Labor Statistics (BLS), *(Labor Dept.), Prices and Living Conditions,* 2 Massachusetts Ave. N.E., #3120 20212; (202) 691-6960. Fax, (202) 691-7080. Kenneth V. Dalton, Associate Commissioner.

Web, www.bls.gov

Collects, processes, analyzes, and disseminates data relating to prices and consumer expenditures; maintains the Consumer Price Index.

Census Bureau *(Commerce Dept.), Service Sector Statistics Division,* 4700 Silver Hill Rd., Bldg. 3, #2633, Suitland, MD 20746; (301) 763-2668. Fax, (301) 457-1343. Mark E. Wallace, Chief.

Web, www.census.gov

Provides data of five-year census programs on retail, wholesale, and service industries. Conducts periodic monthly or annual surveys for specific items within these industries.

NONPROFIT

American Wholesale Marketers Assn., 1128 16th St. N.W. 20036; (202) 463-2124. Fax, (202) 467-0559. Scott Raminger, President.

Web, www.awmanet.org

Membership: wholesalers, manufacturers, retailers, and brokers who sell or distribute convenience products. Conducts education programs. Monitors legislation and regulations.

Cosmetic, Toiletry, and Fragrance Assn., 1101 17th St. N.W., #300 20036; (202) 331-1770. Fax, (202) 331-1969. E. Edward Kavanaugh, President.

Web, www.ctfa.org

Membership: manufacturers and distributors of finished personal care products. Represents the industry at the local, state, and national levels. Interests include scientific research, legal issues, international trade, legislation, and regulatory policy.

Council of Better Business Bureaus, *4200 Wilson Blvd., #800, Arlington, VA 22203-1838; (703) 276-0100. Fax, (703) 525-8277. Kenneth Hunter, President. Web, www.bbb.org*

Membership: businesses and Better Business Bureaus in the United States and Canada. Promotes ethical business practices and truth in national advertising; mediates disputes between consumers and businesses.

Equipment Leasing Assn. of America, *4301 N. Fairfax Dr., #550, Arlington, VA 22203; (703) 527-8655. Fax, (703) 527-2649. Michael Fleming, Chief Executive Officer. Web, www.elaonline.com*

Promotes the interests of the equipment leasing and finance industry; assists in the resolution of industry problems; encourages standards. Monitors legislation and regulations.

Grocery Manufacturers of America, *1010 Wisconsin Ave. N.W., #900 20007; (202) 337-9400. Fax, (202) 337-4508. C. Manly Molpus, President. Web, www.gmabrands.com*

Membership: sales and marketing agents and retail merchandisers of food and consumer products worldwide. Sponsors research, training, and educational programs for members and their trading partners. Monitors legislation and regulations. (Merged with Assn. of Sales and Marketing Companies.)

International Cemetery and Funeral Assn., *1895 Preston White Dr., #220, Reston, VA 20191; (703) 391-8400. Fax, (703) 391-8416. Robert Fells, Chief Executive Officer. Information, (800) 645-7700. General e-mail, gen4@icfa.org Web, www.icfa.org*

Membership: owners and operators of cemeteries, funeral homes, mausoleums, and columbariums. Promotes the building and proper maintenance of modern interment places; promotes high ethical standards in the industry; encourages pre-arrangement of funerals.

International Council of Shopping Centers, Government Relations, Washington Office, *1033 N. Fairfax St., #404, Alexandria, VA 22314; (703) 549-7404. Fax, (703) 549-8712. Herb Tyson, Vice President. General e-mail, govrel@icsc.org Web, www.icsc.org*

Membership: shopping center owners, developers, managers, retailers, contractors, and others in the industry worldwide. Provides information, including research data. Monitors legislation and regulations. (Headquarters in New York.)

International Franchise Assn., *1350 New York Ave. N.W., #900 20005; (202) 628-8000. Fax, (202) 628-0812. Don J. DeBolt, President. General e-mail, ifa@franchise.org Web, www.franchise.org*

Membership: national and international franchisers. Sponsors seminars, workshops, trade shows, and conferences. Monitors legislation and regulations.

International Mass Retail Assn., *1700 N. Moore St., #2250, Arlington, VA 22209-1998; (703) 841-2300. Fax, (703) 841-1184. Sandy Kennedy, President. Web, www.imra.org*

Membership: discount, specialty, home center, wholesale club, and mass retailers in the United States and abroad. Interests include industry research, trade, and government relations. Monitors legislation and regulations.

National Assn. of Convenience Stores, *1600 Duke St., #700, Alexandria, VA 22314; (703) 684-3600. Fax, (703) 836-4564. Kerley LeBoeuf, President. General e-mail, nacs@nacsonline.com Web, www.nacsonline.com*

Membership: convenience store retailers and industry suppliers. Advocates industry position on labor, tax, environment, alcohol, and food-related issues; conducts research and training programs. Monitors legislation and regulations.

National Assn. of Wholesaler-Distributors, *1725 K St. N.W., #300 20006; (202) 872-0885. Fax, (202) 785-0586. Dirk Van Dongen, President. Web, www.naw.org*

Membership: wholesale distributors and trade associations. Provides members and government policymakers with research, education, and government relations information. Monitors legislation and regulations.

National Burglar and Fire Alarm Assn., *8300 Colesville Rd., #750, Silver Spring, MD 20910; (301) 585-1855. Fax, (301) 585-1866. Merlin J. Guilbeau, Executive Director. General e-mail, staff@alarm.org Web, www.alarm.org*

Promotes the electronic security industry. Conducts professional training and certification; compiles industry statistics; disseminates information to consumers regarding home security systems; sponsors seminars. Monitors legislation and regulations.

National Retail Federation, *325 7th St. N.W., #1100 20004-2802; (202) 783-7971. Fax, (202) 737-2849. Tracy Mullin, President.*

Web, www.nrf.com

Membership: international, national, and state associations of retailers and major retail corporations. Concerned with federal regulatory activities and legislation that affect retailers, including tax, employment, trade, and credit issues. Provides information on retailing through seminars, conferences, and publications.

Security Industry Assn., *635 Slaters Lane, #110, Alexandria, VA 22314; (703) 683-2075. Fax, (703) 683-2469. Richard Chace, Executive Director.*
Web, www.siaonline.org

Promotes expansion and professionalism in the security industry. Sponsors trade shows, develops industry standards, supports educational programs and job training, and publishes statistical research. Serves as an information source for the media and the industry.

Service Station Dealers of America and Allied Trades, *1532 Pointer Ridge Pl., Bowie, MD 20716; (301) 390-4405. Fax, (301) 390-3161. Robert Howard, President.*
Web, www.ssda-at.org

Membership: state associations of gasoline retailers. Interests include environmental issues, retail marketing, oil allocation, imports and exports, prices, and taxation.

Society of Consumer Affairs Professionals in Business, *675 N. Washington St., #200, Alexandria, VA 22314-1757; (703) 519-3700. Fax, (703) 549-4886. Louis Garcia, President.*
General e-mail, socap@socap.org
Web, www.socap.org

Membership: managers and supervisors who are responsible for consumer affairs, customer service, market research, and sales and marketing operations. Provides information on customer service techniques, market trends, and industry statistics; sponsors seminars and conferences. Monitors legislation and regulations.

Advertising

AGENCIES

Federal Highway Administration (FHWA), *(Transportation Dept.), Real Estate Services, 400 7th St. S.W., #3221 20590; (202) 366-0142. Fax, (202) 366-3713. Susan Lauffer, Director.*
Web, www.fhwa.dot.gov/realestate

Administers laws concerning outdoor advertising along interstate and federally aided primary highways.

Federal Trade Commission (FTC), *Advertising Practices, 601 Pennsylvania Ave. N.W., #S4002 20580; (202) 326-3090. Fax, (202) 326-3259. Mary Engle, Associate Director (Acting).*

Web, www.ftc.gov

Monitors advertising claims of products for validity; investigates allegations of deceptive advertising practices; handles complaints from consumers, public interest groups, businesses, and Congress regarding the truthfulness and fairness of advertising practices. Enforces statutes and rules preventing misrepresentations in print and broadcast advertising.

Food and Drug Administration (FDA), *(Health and Human Services Dept.), Drug Marketing, Advertising, and Communications, 5600 Fishers Lane, HFD-42, #17B-17, Rockville, MD 20857; (301) 827-2828. Fax, (301) 594-6771. Thomas Abrams, Director.*
Web, www.fda.gov/cder

Monitors prescription drug advertising and labeling; investigates complaints; conducts market research on health care communications and drug issues.

NONPROFIT

American Advertising Federation, *1101 Vermont Ave. N.W., #500 20005; (202) 898-0089. Fax, (202) 898-0159. Wallace Snyder, President.*
General e-mail, aaf@aaf.org
Web, www.aaf.org

Membership: advertising companies (ad agencies, advertisers, media, and services), clubs, associations, and college chapters. A founder of the National Advertising Review Board, a self-regulatory body. Sponsors annual awards for outstanding advertising.

American Assn. of Advertising Agencies, *Washington Office, 1203 19th St. N.W., 4th Floor 20036; (202) 331-7345. Fax, (202) 857-3675. Richard O'Brien, Executive Vice President.*
General e-mail, wash@aaaadc.org
Web, www.aaaa.org

Co-sponsors the National Advertising Review Board (a self-regulatory body), the Advertising Council, and the Media/Advertising Partnership for a Drug Free America. Monitors legislation and regulations. (Headquarters in New York.)

Color Marketing Group, *5904 Richmond Hwy., #408, Alexandria, VA 22303; (703) 329-8500. Fax, (703) 329-0155. Allen Ferrell, President.*
General e-mail, cmg@colormarketing.org
Web, www.colormarketing.org

Provides a forum for the exchange of noncompetitive information on color marketing. Holds meetings; sponsors special events in the United States as well as abroad.

Direct Marketing Assn., *Ethics and Consumer Affairs: Government Affairs, Washington Office,*

1111 19th St. N.W., #1100 20036; (202) 955-5030. Fax, (202) 955-0085. Jerry Cerasale, Senior Vice President.
Web, www.the-dma.org

Membership: telemarketers; users, creators, and producers of direct mail; and suppliers to the industry. Conducts research and promotes knowledge and use of direct response marketing; interests include international business. Handles consumer complaints about telephone and mail-order purchases. Operates a mail preference service, which removes consumer names from unwanted mailing lists, and a telephone preference service, which helps consumers handle unsolicited telephone sales calls. (Headquarters in Westchester, Ill.)

International Sign Assn., 707 N. Saint Asaph St., Alexandria, VA 22314; (703) 836-4012. Fax, (703) 836-8353. Dean Garritson, President.
Web, www.signs.org

Membership: manufacturers and distributors of signs. Promotes the sign industry; conducts workshops and seminars; sponsors annual competition.

Outdoor Advertising Assn. of America, 1850 M St. N.W., #1040 20036; (202) 833-5566. Fax, (202) 833-1522. Nancy Fletcher, President.
Web, www.oaaa.org

Membership: outdoor advertising companies, operators, suppliers, and affiliates. Serves as a clearinghouse for public service advertising campaigns. Monitors legislation and regulations.

SMALL AND DISADVANTAGED BUSINESS

AGENCIES

Agency for International Development (USAID), *Small and Disadvantaged Business Utilization/Minority Resource Center,* 1300 Pennsylvania Ave. N.W., #7.8-E 20523; (202) 712-1500. Fax, (202) 216-3056. Marilyn S. Marton, Director.
Web, www.usaid.gov/procurement_bus_opp/osdbu

Provides information and counseling to U.S. business firms seeking export sales and technical service contracts. Devotes special attention to assisting small businesses and minority-owned firms.

Commerce Dept., *Business Liaison,* 14th St. and Constitution Ave. N.W., #5062 20230; (202) 482-1360. Fax, (202) 482-4054. Travis Thomas, Director.
Web, www.doc.gov

Serves as the central office for business assistance. Handles requests for information and services as well as complaints and suggestions from businesses; provides a forum for businesses to comment on federal regulations; initiates meetings on policy issues with industry groups, business organizations, trade and small-business associations, and the corporate community.

Farm Service Agency (FSA), *(Agriculture Dept.), Minority and Socially Disadvantaged Farmers Assistance,* 1400 Independence Ave. S.W., MS 0501 20250-0501; (202) 720-1584. Fax, (202) 720-5398. Ronald Holling, Director. TTY, (202) 720-5132. Toll-free, 866-538-2610 (phone); 866-302-1760 (fax); 866-480-2824 (TTY).
General e-mail, msda@wdc.usda.gov
Web, www.fsa.usda.gov/pas/msda.htm

Works with minority and socially disadvantaged farmers who have concerns and questions about loan applications filed with local offices.

Federal Insurance and Mitigation Administration *(Federal Emergency Management Agency),* 500 C St. S.W., #430 20472; (202) 646-2781. Fax, (202) 646-7970. Anthony S. Lowe, Administrator.
Web, www.fema.gov/nfip

Administers federal crime and flood insurance programs. Makes available to eligible small businesses low-cost flood and crime insurance.

General Services Administration (GSA), *Enterprise Development,* 1800 F St. N.W., #6029 20405; (202) 501-1021. Fax, (202) 208-5938. Felipe Mendoza, Associate Administrator.
Web, www.gsa.gov/oed

Works to increase small-business procurement of government contracts. Provides policy guidance and direction for GSA Business Service Centers, which offer advice and assistance to businesses interested in government procurement.

Minority Business Development Agency *(Commerce Dept.),* 14th St. and Constitution Ave. N.W., #5055 20230; (202) 482-5061. Fax, (202) 482-2500. Ronald N. Langston, Director.
Web, www.mbda.gov

Assists minority business owners in obtaining federal loans and contract awards; produces an annual report on federal agencies' performance in procuring from minority-owned businesses.

National Science Foundation (NSF), *Small Business Innovation Research Program,* 4201 Wilson Blvd., #550, Arlington, VA 22230; (703) 292-8330. Fax, (703) 292-9056. Joseph Hennessy, Senior Adviser.
General e-mail, sbir@nsf.gov
Web, www.eng.nsf.gov/sbir

Serves as liaison between the small-business community and NSF offices awarding grants and contracts. Administers the Small Business Innovation Research Program, which funds research proposals from small science/high technology firms and offers incentives for commercial development of NSF-funded research.

National Women's Business Council, *409 3rd St. S.W., #210 20024; (202) 205-3850. Fax, (202) 205-6825. Marilyn Carlson Nelson, Chair; Julie R. Weeks, Executive Director.*
Web, www.nwbc.gov

Membership: eight women business owners, six representatives of women business organizations, and one chair appointed by the president. Independent, congressionally mandated council established by the Women's Business Ownership Act of 1988. Reviews the status of women-owned businesses nationwide and makes policy recommendations to the president and Congress. Assesses the role of the federal government in aiding and promoting women-owned businesses.

Securities and Exchange Commission, *Economic Analysis,* *450 5th St. N.W. 20549; (202) 942-8020. Fax, (202) 942-9657. Lawrence E. Harris, Chief Economist.*
Web, www.sec.gov

Provides the commission with economic analyses of proposed rule and policy changes and other information to guide the SEC in influencing capital markets. Evaluates the effect of policy and other factors on competition within the securities industry and among competing securities markets; compiles financial statistics on capital formation and the securities industry.

Small Business Administration (SBA), *409 3rd St. S.W., #7000 20416; (202) 205-6605. Fax, (202) 205-6802. Hector Barreto, Administrator; Lisa Goeas, Chief of Staff. Library, (202) 205-7033. Press, (202) 205-6540. Toll-free information (SBA Answer Desk), (800) 827-5722. Locator, (202) 205-6600.*
Web, www.sba.gov

Provides small businesses with financial and management assistance; offers loans to victims of floods, natural disasters, and other catastrophes; licenses, regulates, and guarantees some financing of small-business investment companies; conducts economic and statistical research on small businesses. SBA Answer Desk is an information and referral service. District or regional offices can be contacted for specific loan information.

Small Business Administration (SBA), *Advocacy,* *409 3rd St. S.W., #7800 20416; (202) 205-6533. Fax, (202) 205-6928. Thomas M. Sullivan, Chief Counsel.*

General e-mail, agh@adv.sba.gov
Web, www.sba.gov/ADVO

Acts as an advocate for small-business viewpoints in regulatory and legislative proceedings. Economic Research Office analyzes the effects of government policies on small business and documents the contributions of small business to the economy.

Small Business Administration (SBA), *Business and Community Initiatives,* *409 3rd St. S.W., #6100 20416; (202) 205-6665. Fax, (202) 205-7416. Ellen M. Thrasher, Associate Administrator.*
Web, www.sba.gov/BI

Provides small businesses with instruction and counseling in marketing, accounting, product analysis, production methods, research and development, and management problems.

Small Business Administration (SBA), *Capital Access,* *409 3rd St. S.W., #8200 20416; (202) 205-6657. Fax, (202) 205-7230. Ronald Bew, Associate Deputy Administrator.*
Web, www.sba.gov

Provides financial assistance to small business; focus includes surety guarantees, investment, and international trade. Makes microloans to start-up businesses and loans to established businesses for purchase of new equipment or facilities.

Small Business Administration (SBA), *Entrepreneurial Development,* *409 3rd St. S.W., #6200 20416; (202) 205-6706. Fax, (202) 205-6903. Kaaren Johnson Street, Associate Deputy Administrator.*
Web, www.sba.gov/ed

Responsible for business development programs of the Small Business Development Centers and the offices of Business Initiatives, native American Affairs, and Women's Business Ownership.

Small Business Administration (SBA), *Financial Assistance,* *409 3rd St. S.W., #8300 20416; (202) 205-6490. Fax, (202) 205-7722. James Rivera, Associate Administrator.*
Web, www.sba.gov/FA

Makes available guaranteed loans to aid in developing small businesses.

Small Business Administration (SBA), *Minority Enterprise Development,* *409 3rd St. S.W., #8000 20416; (202) 205-7340. Fax, (202) 205-7267. Delorice Ford, Associate Administrator.*
Web, www.sba.gov/MED

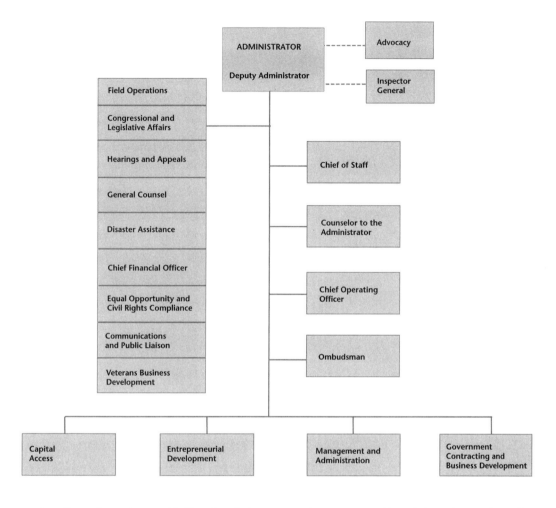

Coordinates the services provided by private industry, banks, the SBA, and other government agencies—such as business development and management and technical assistance—to increase the number of small businesses owned by socially and economically disadvantaged Americans.

Small Business Administration (SBA), *Women's Business Ownership,* 409 3rd St. S.W., 4th Floor 20416; (202) 205-6673. Fax, (202) 205-7287. Wilma Goldstein, Assistant Administrator.
Web, www.sba.gov/womeninbusiness

Advocates for current and potential women business owners throughout the federal government and in the private sector. Provides training and counseling; offers information on national and local resources.

CONGRESS

House Government Reform Committee, *Subcommittee on Energy Policy, Natural Resources, and Regulatory Affairs,* B377 RHOB 20515; (202) 225-4407. Fax, (202) 225-2441. Rep. Doug Ose, R-Calif., Chair; Dan Skopec, Staff Director.
Web, www.house.gov/reform

Reviews regulatory process and effect of specific regulations and paperwork on the small-business community. Oversees operations of the Small Business Administration. (Shared with House Small Business Committee.)

SMALL AND DISADVANTAGED BUSINESS CONTACTS AT FEDERAL AGENCIES

DEPARTMENTS

Agriculture, Jim House, (202) 720-7117

Commerce, T. J. Garcia, (202) 482-1472

Defense, Frank Ramos, (703) 588-8631

  Air Force, Joseph Diamond, (703) 696-1103

  Army, Tracey L. Pinson, (703) 695-9800

  Navy, Nancy Tarrant, (202) 685-6485

Education, Viola J. Jaramillo, (202) 708-9820

Energy, Theresa Speake, (202) 586-8383

Health and Human Services, Debbie Ridgely, (202) 690-7300

Housing and Urban Development, Jo Baylor, (202) 708-1428

Interior, Robert Faithful, (202) 208-2252

Justice, Ken Bryan, (202) 616-0521

State, Durie N. White, (703) 875-6824

Transportation, Sean M. Moss, (202) 366-1930

Treasury, Kevin Boshears, (202) 622-0376

  Office of Thrift Supervision, John Connors, (202) 906-6666

Veterans Affairs, Scott F. Denniston, (202) 565-8124

AGENCIES

Agency for International Development, Marilyn Marton, (202) 712-1500

Consumer Product Safety Commission, (301) 504-7904

Environmental Protection Agency, Jeanette L. Brown, (202) 564-4100

General Services Administration, Felipe Mendoza, (202) 501-1021

National Aeronautics and Space Administration, Ralph C. Thomas III, (202) 358-2088

Nuclear Regulatory Commission, Maurico Vera, (301) 415-7380

Social Security Administration, Tom Purdy, (410) 965-7467

House Small Business Committee, *2361 RHOB 20515; (202) 225-5821. Fax, (202) 225-3587. Rep. Donald Manzullo, R-Ill., Chair; J. Matthew Szymanski, Chief of Staff.*
General e-mail, smbiz@mail.house.gov
Web, www.house.gov/smbiz

Jurisdiction over legislation dealing with the Small Business Administration (shared with House Govern-

ment Reform Committee). Studies and makes recommendations on problems of American small business.

House Small Business Committee, *Subcommittee on Tax, Finance, and Exports, B363 RHOB 20515; (202) 226-2630. Fax, (202) 225-8950. Rep. Pat Toomey, R-Pa., Chair; Sean McGraw, Staff Director.*
General e-mail, smbiz@mail.house.gov
Web, www.house.gov/smbiz

Jurisdiction over legislation on programs affecting small business; studies impact of tax policy on small business.

House Small Business Committee, *Subcommittee on Workforce, Empowerment, and Government Programs, B363 RHOB 20515; (202) 226-2630. Fax, (202) 225-8950. Rep. Todd Akin, R-Mo., Chair; Nelson Crowther, Chief of Staff.*
General e-mail, smbiz@mail.house.gov
Web, www.house.gov/smbiz/subcommittees/index.html

Jurisdiction over development of economically depressed areas, including regulations and licensing policies that affect small businesses in high-risk communities.

Senate Small Business and Entrepreneurship Committee, *SR-428A 20510; (202) 224-5175. Fax, (202) 228-1128. Sen. Olympia J. Snowe, R-Maine, Chair; Mark Warren, Staff Director.*
Web, sbc.senate.gov

Jurisdiction over and oversight of the Small Business Administration. Studies and makes recommendations on problems of American small business and on programs involving minority enterprise. Reviews regulatory process and effect of specific regulations and paperwork on the small-business community.

NONPROFIT

Latin American Management Assn., *419 New Jersey Ave. S.E. 20003-4007; (202) 546-3803. Fax, (202) 546-3807. Stephen Denlinger, President.*
General e-mail, lamausa@bellatlantic.net

Membership: Hispanic manufacturing and technical firms. Promotes Hispanic enterprise, industry, and technology throughout the United States. Supports public policy beneficial to minority businesses. Monitors legislation and regulations.

Minority Business Enterprise Legal Defense and Education Fund, *419 New Jersey Ave. S.E. 20003; (202) 289-1700. Fax, (202) 289-1701. Anthony W. Robinson, President.*
Web, www.mbeldef.org

Acts as an advocate for the minority business community. Represents minority businesses in class action suits; conducts legal research; serves as an information clearinghouse on business and legal trends. Monitors legislation and regulations.

National Assn. of Investment Companies, *1300 Pennsylvania Ave. N.W., #700 20004; (202) 289-4336. Fax, (202) 289-4329. Angela L. West, Chief Administrator.*
General e-mail, NAICHQTRS@aol.com
Web, www.naichq.org

Membership: investment companies that provide minority-owned small businesses with venture capital and management guidance. Provides technical assistance; monitors legislation affecting small business.

National Assn. of Negro Business and Professional Women's Clubs, *1806 New Hampshire Ave. N.W. 20009; (202) 483-4206. Fax, (202) 462-7253. Cleopatra Vaughns, President.*
General e-mail, nanbpwc@aol.com
Web, www.nanbpwc.org

Promotes opportunities for African American women in business; sponsors workshops and scholarships; maintains a job bank. Monitors legislation and regulations.

National Assn. of Small Business Investment Companies, *666 11th St. N.W., #750 20001; (202) 628-5055. Fax, (202) 628-5080. Lee W. Mercer, President.*
General e-mail, nasbic@nasbic.org
Web, www.nasbic.org

Membership: companies licensed by the Small Business Administration to provide small businesses with advisory services, equity financing, and long-term loans.

National Federation of Independent Business (NFIB), *1201 F St. N.W., #200 20004-1221; (202) 554-9000. Fax, (202) 554-0496. Jackson Faris, President.*
Web, www.nfib.com

Membership: independent business and professional people. Monitors public policy issues and legislation affecting small and independent businesses, including taxation, government regulation, labor-management relations, and liability insurance.

National Small Business United, *1156 15th St. N.W., #1100 20005; (202) 293-8830. Fax, (202) 872-8543. Todd McCracken, President.*
General e-mail, nsbu@nsbu.org
Web, www.nsbu.org

Membership: manufacturing, wholesale, retail, service, and other small-business firms and regional small-business organizations. Represents the interests of small

business before Congress, the administration, and federal agencies. Services to members include a toll-free legislative hotline and group insurance.

Research Institute for Small and Emerging Business (RISE), *722 12th St. N.W. 20005; (202) 628-8382. Fax, (202) 628-8392. Mark Shultz, President.*
General e-mail, info@riseb.org
Web, www.riseb.org

Seeks to enhance the formation and growth of the small and emerging business sector by developing and sponsoring research on small and emerging businesses, and then ensuring its effective dissemination.

Service Corps of Retired Executives Assn., *409 3rd St. S.W., 6th Floor 20024; (202) 205-6762. Fax, (202) 205-7636. W. Kenneth Yancey Jr., Chief Executive Officer. Information, (800) 634-0245.*
General e-mail, contact.score@sba.gov
Web, www.score.org

Independent voluntary organization funded by the Small Business Administration through which retired, semiretired, and active business executives use their knowledge and experience to counsel small businesses.

Small Business Legislative Council, *1010 Massachusetts Ave. N.W., #400 20001; (202) 639-8500. Fax, (202) 296-5333. John S. Satagaj, President.*
General e-mail, email@sblc.org
Web, www.sblc.org

Membership: trade associations that represent small businesses in the manufacturing, wholesale, retail, service, and other sectors. Monitors and proposes legislation and regulations to benefit small businesses.

Small Business Survival Committee, *1920 L St. N.W., #200 20036; (202) 785-0238. Fax, (202) 822-8118. Darrell McKigney, President.*
Web, www.sbsc.org

Membership: small businesses throughout the United States. Promotes small business economic growth through limited government. Acts as an educational resource for members. Monitors legislation and regulations.

U.S. Chamber of Commerce, *Small Business Policy, 1615 H St. N.W. 20062-2000; (202) 463-5498. Fax, (202) 463-3174. Giovanni Coratolo, Director.*
Web, www.uschamber.com

Seeks to enhance visibility of small business within the national Chamber and the U.S. business community. Provides members with information on national small-business programs.

4 ⌨

Communications and the Media

⊞ GENERAL POLICY

AGENCIES

Federal Communications Commission (FCC), *445 12th St. S.W. 20554; (888) 225-5322. Fax, (202) 418-0232. Michael K. Powell, Chair. Press, (202) 418-0500. TTY, (888) 835-5322.*
General e-mail, fccinfo@fcc.gov
Web, www.fcc.gov

Regulates interstate and foreign communications by radio, television, wire, cable, microwave, and satellite; consults with other government agencies and departments on national and international matters involving wire and radio telecommunications and with state regulatory commissions on telegraph and telephone matters; reviews applications for construction permits and licenses for such services. Reference Information Center open to the public.

Federal Communications Commission (FCC), *Media Bureau: Policy Division, 445 12th St. S.W., 3rd Floor 20554; (202) 418-1440. Fax, (202) 418-2053. Robert Baker, Assistant Chief.*
Web, www.fcc.gov

Handles complaints and inquiries concerning the equal time rule, which requires equal broadcast opportunities for all legally qualified candidates for the same office, and other political broadcast, cable, and satellite rules. Interprets and enforces related Communications Act provisions, including the requirement for sponsorship identification of all paid political broadcast, cable, and satellite announcements.

National Telecommunications and Information Administration (NTIA), *(Commerce Dept.), 1401 Constitution Ave. N.W., #4898 20230; (202) 482-1840. Fax, (202) 482-1635. Nancy J. Victory, Administrator. Information, (202) 482-7002.*
Web, www.ntia.doc.gov

Develops domestic and international telecommunications policy for the executive branch; manages federal use of radio spectrum; conducts research on radiowave transmissions and other aspects of telecommunications; serves as information source for federal and state agencies on the efficient use of telecommunications resources; provides noncommercial telecommunications services with grants for construction of facilities.

CONGRESS

House Appropriations Committee, *Subcommittee on Commerce, Justice, State, and the Judiciary, H309 CAP*

20515; (202) 225-3351. Rep. Frank R. Wolf, R-Va., Chair; Mike Ringler, Staff Director.
Web, www.house.gov/appropriations

Jurisdiction over legislation to appropriate funds for the Federal Communications Commission and the Board for International Broadcasting.

House Appropriations Committee, *Subcommittee on Labor, Health and Human Services, Education, and Related Agencies, 2358 RHOB 20515; (202) 225-3508. Fax, (202) 225-3509. Rep. Ralph Regula, R-Ohio, Chair; Craig Higgins, Staff Director.*
Web, www.house.gov/appropriations

Jurisdiction over legislation to appropriate funds for the Corporation for Public Broadcasting.

House Energy and Commerce Committee, *Subcommittee on Telecommunications and the Internet, 2125 RHOB 20515; (202) 225-2927. Fax, (202) 225-1919. Rep. Fred Upton, R-Mich., Chair; David V. Marventano, Staff Director.*
General e-mail, commerce@mail.house.gov
Web, energycommerce.house.gov/108/subcommittees/ Telecommunications_and_the_Internet.htm

Jurisdiction over interstate and foreign telecommunications including, but not limited to, all telecommunication and information transmission by broadcast, radio, wire, microwave, satellite, or other mode.

House Government Reform Committee, *Subcommittee on Government Efficiency and Financial Management, 349C RHOB 20515; (202) 225-3741. Fax, (202) 225-2544. Rep. Todd R. Platts, R-Pa., Chair; Mike Hettinger, Staff Director.*
Web, www.house.gov/reform

Oversees operations of the National Telecommunications and Information Administration, the Federal Communications Commission, and the Board for International Broadcasting.

House Judiciary Committee, *2138 RHOB 20515; (202) 225-3951. Fax, (202) 225-7682. Rep. F. James Sensenbrenner Jr., R-Wis., Chair; Phil Kiko, Chief of Staff.*
General e-mail, Judiciary@mail.house.gov
Web, www.house.gov/judiciary

Jurisdiction over legislation related to anticompetitive practices and to monopolies in communications, including cable telecommunications and network practices.

Library of Congress, *Copyright Office: Licensing, 101 Independence Ave. S.E. 20557; (202) 707-8150. Fax, (202)*

707-0905. John E. Martin Jr., Chief, Licensing (Acting), (202) 707-8130. Information, (202) 707-3000.

Web, www.loc.gov/copyright/carp

Licenses cable television companies and satellite carriers; collects and distributes royalty payments under the copyright law. Distributes licenses for making and distributing phonorecords and for use of certain noncommercial broadcasting. Administers Section 115 licensing for making and distributing phonorecords.

Senate Appropriations Committee, *Subcommittee on Commerce, Justice, State, and the Judiciary,* S-206 CAP 20510; (202) 224-7277. Fax, (202) 228-0587. Sen. Judd Gregg, R-N.H., Chair; James Morhard, Clerk.

Web, appropriations.senate.gov

Jurisdiction over legislation to appropriate funds for the Commerce Dept., the Securities and Exchange Commission, the Small Business Administration, the Competitiveness Policy Council, the Federal Trade Commission, the International Trade Commission, and the Office of the U.S. Trade Representative.

Senate Appropriations Committee, *Subcommittee on Labor, Health and Human Services, Education, and Related Agencies,* SD-184 20510; (202) 224-3471. Fax, (202) 224-8553. Sen. Arlen Specter, R-Pa., Chair; Bettilou Taylor, Clerk.

Web, appropriations.senate.gov

Jurisdiction over legislation to appropriate funds for the Corporation for Public Broadcasting.

Senate Commerce, Science, and Transportation Committee, *Subcommittee on Communications,* SD-510 20510; (202) 224-5184. Fax, (202) 228-0326. Sen. Conrad Burns, R-Mont., Chair; Paul Martino, Counsel.

Web, commerce.senate.gov

Jurisdiction over legislation related to interstate and foreign communications, including television, cable television, local and long-distance telephone service, radio, wire, microwave, and satellite communications. Oversight of the Federal Communications Commission, the National Telecommunications and Information Administration, and the Corporation for Public Broadcasting.

Senate Foreign Relations Committee, *Subcommittee on International Operations and Terrorism,* SD-446 20510; (202) 224-4651. Sen. John E. Sununu, R-N.H., Chair; Vacant, Staff Director.

Web, foreign.senate.gov

Oversight of foreign broadcasting activities.

Senate Judiciary Committee, *Subcommittee on Antitrust, Competition Policy, and Consumer Rights,*

SD-161 20510; (202) 224-9494. Fax, (202) 228-0463. Sen. Mike DeWine, R-Ohio, Chair; Peter Levitas, Chief Counsel.

Web, judiciary.senate.gov

Jurisdiction over legislation related to anticompetitive practices and to monopolies in communications, including cable telecommunication and network practices.

INTERNATIONAL ORGANIZATIONS

Inter-American Telecommunications Commission (Organization of American States), 1889 F St. N.W., #552 20006; (202) 458-3004. Fax, (202) 458-6854. Clovis Baptista, Executive Secretary.

General e-mail, citel@oas.org

Web, www.oas.org

Works with the public and private sectors to facilitate the development of telecommunications in the Americas.

NONPROFIT

Accuracy in Media (AIM), 4455 Connecticut Ave. N.W., #330 20008; (202) 364-4401. Fax, (202) 364-4098. Reed J. Irvine, Board Chair.

General e-mail, ar@aim.org

Web, www.aim.org

Analyzes print and electronic news media for bias, omissions, and errors in news; approaches media with complaints. Maintains speakers bureau.

Alliance for Public Technology, 919 18th St. N.W., #900 20006; (202) 263-2970. Fax, (202) 263-2960. Sylvia Rosenthal, Executive Director. Main phone is voice and TTY accessible.

General e-mail, apt@apt.org

Web, www.apt.org

Membership: public groups and individuals concerned with developing affordable access to information services and telecommunications technology, particularly for the elderly, residential consumers, low-income groups, and people with disabilities.

Alliance for Telecommunications Industry Solutions, 1200 G St. N.W., #500 20005; (202) 628-6380. Fax, (202) 393-5453. Susan M. Miller, President.

General e-mail, atispr@atis.org

Web, www.atis.org

Promotes the timely resolution of national and international issues involving telecommunications standards and operational guidelines. Sponsors industry forums; serves as an information clearinghouse. Monitors legislation and regulations.

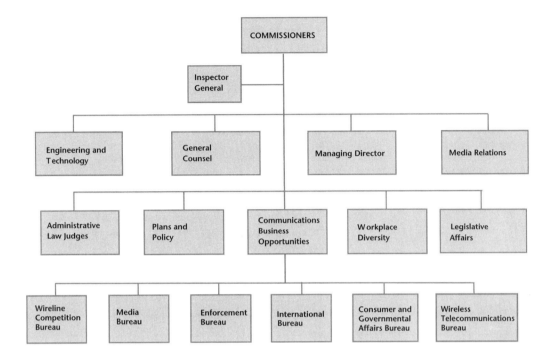

Center for Media and Public Affairs, *2100 L St. N.W., #300 20037-1525; (202) 223-2942. Fax, (202) 872-4014. Linda Ladas, Managing Director.*

Web, www.cmpa.com

Nonpartisan research and educational organization that studies media coverage of social and political issues and campaigns. Conducts surveys; publishes materials and reports.

Center for Media Education, *2120 L St. N.W., #200 20037; (202) 331-7833. Fax, (202) 331-7841. Kathryn C. Montgomery, President.*

Web, www.cme.org

Promotes public interest in media policies and access to new educational technologies for all children. Provides nonprofit groups with educational and informational services. Maintains a speakers bureau.

Computer and Communications Industry Assn., *666 11th St. N.W., #600 20001; (202) 783-0070. Fax, (202) 783-0534. Edward J. Black, President.*

General e-mail, ccia@ccianet.org

Web, www.ccianet.org

Membership: manufacturers and suppliers of computer data processing and communications-related products and services. Interests include telecommunications policy, capital formation and tax policy, federal procurement policy, communications and computer industry standards, intellectual property policies, encryption, international trade, and antitrust reform.

Institute for Public Representation, *600 New Jersey Ave. N.W. 20001; (202) 662-9535. Fax, (202) 662-9634. Douglas L. Parker, Director. TTY, (202) 662-9538.*

Public interest law firm funded by Georgetown University Law Center that specializes in communications regulatory policy. Assists citizens' groups that seek input into local and federal regulation of the electronic media; interests include freedom of information.

International Communications Industries Assn., *11242 Waples Mill Rd., #200, Fairfax, VA 22030; (703) 273-7200. Fax, (703) 278-8082. Randy Lemke, Executive Director. Information, (800) 659-7469.*

General e-mail, icia@infocomm.org

Web, www.infocomm.org

Membership: video and audiovisual dealers; manufacturers and producers; and individuals. Interests include international trade, small business issues, postal rates, copyright, education, and taxation. Monitors legislation and regulations.

Media Access Project, *1625 K St. N.W., #1118 20006; (202) 232-4300. Fax, (202) 466-7656. Andrew Jay Schwartzman, President.*
Web, www.mediaaccess.org

Public interest telecommunications law firm that represents the right of the public to speak and to receive information from the mass media. Interests include media ownership, access to new technologies, and the fairness doctrine.

Media Institute, *1000 Potomac St. N.W., #301 20007; (202) 298-7512. Fax, (202) 337-7092. Patrick D. Maines, President.*
General e-mail, info@mediainstitute.org
Web, www.mediainstitute.org

Conducts conferences, files court briefs and regulatory comments, and sponsors programs on communications topics. Advocates free-speech rights for individuals, media, and corporate speakers.

Media Research Center, *325 S. Patrick St., Alexandria, VA 22314; (703) 683-9733. Fax, (703) 683-9736. L. Brent Bozell III, President.*
General e-mail, mrc@mediaresearch.org
Web, www.mediaresearch.org

Media-watch organization working for balanced and responsible news coverage of political issues. Records and analyzes network news programs; analyzes print media; maintains profiles of media executives and library of recordings.

National Assn. of Broadcasters (NAB), *1771 N St. N.W. 20036-2891; (202) 429-5300. Fax, (202) 429-5343. Edward O. Fritts, President. Library, (202) 429-5490. Press, (202) 429-5350.*
Web, www.nab.org

Membership: radio and television broadcast stations and broadcast networks holding an FCC license or construction permit; associate members include producers of equipment and programs. Assists members in areas of management, engineering, and research. Interests include privatization abroad and related business opportunities. Monitors legislation and regulations.

National Assn. of Regulatory Utility Commissioners, *1101 Vermont Ave. N.W., #200 20005; (202) 898-*
2200. Fax, (202) 898-2213. Charles Gray, Executive Director. Press, (202) 898-2205.
Web, www.naruc.org

Membership: members of federal, state, municipal, and Canadian regulatory commissions that have jurisdiction over utilities and carriers. Interests include telecommunications regulation.

National Captioning Institute, *1900 Gallows Rd. #3000, Vienna, VA 22182; (703) 917-7600. Fax, (703) 917-9878. Jack Gates, President and Chief Operating Officer. Main phone is voice and TTY accessible.*
General e-mail, mail@ncicap.org
Web, www.ncicap.org

Captions television programs for the deaf and hard-of-hearing and produces audio description for the blind on behalf of public and commercial broadcast television networks, cable network companies, syndicators, program producers, advertisers, and home video distributors. Produces and disseminates information about the national closed-captioning service and audio description.

Telecommunications for the Deaf, *8630 Fenton St., #604, Silver Spring, MD 20910; (301) 589-3786. Fax, (301) 589-3797. Claude L. Stout, Executive Director. TTY, (301) 589-3006. Voice via relay, (800) 735-2258.*
General e-mail, adminasst@tdi-online.org
Web, www.tdi-online.org

Membership: individuals, organizations, and businesses using text telephone (TTY) equipment. Provides information on TTY equipment. Interests include closed captioning for television, emergency access (911), TTY relay services, visual alerting systems, and TTY/computer conversion. Publishes a national TTY telephone directory.

Telecommunications Industry Assn., *2500 Wilson Blvd., #300, Arlington, VA 22201-3834; (703) 907-7700. Fax, (703) 907-7727. Matthew J. Flanigan, President. Press, (703) 907-7723.*
General e-mail, tia@tia.eia.org
Web, www.tiaonline.org

Membership: telecommunications equipment manufacturers, suppliers, and distributors. Represents members in telecommunications manufacturing issues; helps to develop standards for products; sponsors a job-matching service; cohosts trade shows worldwide. (Affiliated with the communications sector of the Electronic Industries Assn.)

Cable Services

AGENCIES

Federal Communications Commission (FCC), *Media Bureau,* 445 12th St. S.W., 3rd Floor 20554; (202) 418-7200. Fax, (202) 418-2376. W. Kenneth Ferree, Chief, (202) 418-7200.
Web, www.fcc.gov/csb

Makes and enforces rules governing cable television and other video distribution services; promotes industry growth, competition, and availability to the public; ensures reasonable rates for consumers in areas that do not have competition in cable service.

Federal Communications Commission (FCC), *Media Bureau: Engineering,* 445 12th St. S.W., #4-C83 20554; (202) 418-7012. Fax, (202) 418-1189. John Wong, Chief.
Web, www.fcc.gov

Processes applications and notifications for licensing of cable television relay service stations (CARS); registers cable television systems; develops, administers, and enforces regulation of cable television and CARS.

NONPROFIT

Alliance for Community Media, 666 11th St. N.W., #740 20001; (202) 393-2650. Fax, (202) 393-2653. Bunnie Riedel, Executive Director.
General e-mail, acm@alliancecm.org
Web, www.alliancecm.org

Membership: cable television companies, programming managers and producers, independent producers, cable administrators and regulators, media access centers, and others involved in community communications. Promotes local programming and participation in cable television. Interests include freedom of expression, diversity of information, and developing technologies. Monitors legislation and regulations.

CTAM, 201 N. Union St., #440, Alexandria, VA 22314; (703) 549-4200. Fax, (703) 684-1167. Char Beales, President.
Web, www.ctam.com

Promotes innovation in the cable and related industries in areas of marketing, research, management, and new product development. Sponsors annual marketing conference; interests include international markets. CTAM stands for the Cable and Telecommunications Assn. for Marketing.

National Cable Television and Telecommunications Assn., 1724 Massachusetts Ave. N.W. 20036-1969; (202) 775-3550. Fax, (202) 775-3671. Robert Sachs, President.
Web, www.ncta.com

Membership: companies that operate cable television systems, cable television programmers, and manufacturers and suppliers of hardware and software for the industry. Represents the industry before federal regulatory agencies and Congress and in the courts; provides management and promotional aids and information on legal, legislative, and regulatory matters.

Enforcement, Judicial, and Legal Actions

AGENCIES

Antitrust Division *(Justice Dept.),* **Telecommunications,** 1401 H St. N.W., #8000 20530; (202) 514-5621. Fax, (202) 514-6381. Nancy Goodman, Chief. Information, (888) 736-5287.
Web, www.usdoj.gov/atr

Investigates and litigates antitrust cases dealing with communications and multimedia; participates in agency proceedings and rulemaking concerning communications and multimedia; monitors and analyzes legislation.

Federal Bureau of Investigation (FBI), *(Justice Dept.), CALEA Implementation Section,* 14800 Conference Center Dr., #300, Chantilly, VA 20151; (703) 814-4800. Fax, (703) 814-4750. Michael P. Clifford, Chief. Toll-free, (800) 551-0336.
Web, www.askcalea.net

Administers enforcement of the Communications Assistance for Law Enforcement Act (CALEA). Promotes cooperation between the telecommunications industry and law enforcement officials to develop intercept capabilities required by law enforcement.

Federal Communications Commission (FCC), *Administrative Law Judges,* 445 12th St. S.W. 20554; (202) 418-2280. Fax, (202) 418-0195. Richard L. Sippel, Chief Judge.
Web, www.fcc.gov/oalj

Presides over hearings and issues initial decisions in disputes over FCC regulations and applications for licensing.

Federal Communications Commission (FCC), *Enforcement Bureau,* 445 12th St. S.W. 20554-0001; (202) 418-7450. David H. Solomon, Chief. Information, (888) 225-5322. TTY, (888) 835-5322.
Web, www.fcc.gov/eb

Commission's primary enforcement organization responsible for compliance with the Communications Act of 1934, the FCC's rules, Commission orders, and the terms of licenses and other organizations. Promotes competition under the Telecommunications Act of 1996 and related regulations and ensures access to communications by the disabled.

NONPROFIT

Federal Communications Bar Assn., *1020 19th St. N.W., #325 20036; (202) 293-4000. Fax, (202) 293-4317. Stan Zenor, Executive Director.*
General e-mail, fcba@fcba.org
Web, www.fcba.org

Membership: attorneys, nonattorneys, and law students in communications law who practice before the Federal Communications Commission, the courts, and state and local regulatory agencies. Cooperates with the FCC and other members of the bar on legal aspects of communications issues.

International and Satellite Communications

AGENCIES

Federal Communications Commission (FCC), *International Bureau, 445 12th St. S.W., 6th Floor 20554; (202) 418-0437. Fax, (202) 418-2818. Donald Abelson, Chief.*
Web, www.fcc.gov/ib

Coordinates the FCC's collection and dissemination of information on communications and telecommunications policy, regulation, and market developments in other countries and the policies and regulations of international organizations. Coordinates the FCC's international policy activities; represents the FCC in international forums.

Federal Communications Commission (FCC), *Wireline Competition Bureau, 445 12th St. S.W. 20554; (202) 418-1500. Fax, (202) 418-2825. William Maher, Chief.*
Web, www.fcc.gov/wcb

Develops, recommends, and administers FCC policies involving common carriers (wireline facilities that furnish interstate communications services for hire). Interests include pricing policy, economic and technical aspects, numbering resources, and competition in telecommunications markets.

State Dept., *International Communications and Information Policy, 2201 C St. N.W., #4826, MC EB/CIP 20520-5818; (202) 647-5212. Fax, (202) 647-5957. David Gross, U.S. Coordinator.*
Web, www.state.gov/e/eb/cip

Develops and manages international communication and information policy for the State Dept. Acts as a liaison for other federal departments and agencies and the private sector in international communications issues.

Promotes advancement of information and communication technology; the creation of business opportunities at home and abroad in this sector; and the expansion of access to the technology by the world population. Trade-related telecommunications issues are handled by the Bureau of Economic and Business Affairs.

INTERNATIONAL ORGANIZATIONS

Intelsat, *3400 International Dr. N.W., VOC, Box 17 20008-3098; (202) 944-6800. Fax, (202) 944-8138. Conny Kullman, Chief Executive Officer.*
General e-mail, videosolutions@intelsat.com
Web, www.intelsat.com

Owns and operates a global satellite communications system. Serves customers in approximately 200 countries and territories.

NONPROFIT

Satellite Broadcasting and Communications Assn., *225 Reinekers Lane, #600, Alexandria, VA 22314; (703) 549-6990. Fax, (703) 549-7640. Andrew Wright, President. Fax-on-demand, (888) 629-7222.*
General e-mail, info@sbca.com
Web, www.sbca.com

Membership: owners, operators, manufacturers, dealers, and distributors of satellite receiving stations; software and program suppliers; and others in the home satellite industry. Promotes use of satellite earth stations for television programming and as part of the national and global information infrastructure. Monitors legislation and regulations.

Radio and Television

AGENCIES

Corporation for Public Broadcasting, *401 9th St. N.W. 20004-2129; (202) 879-9600. Fax, (202) 789-9700. Robert T. Coonrod, President. Comments, (800) 272-2190.*
General e-mail, comments@cpb.org
Web, www.cpb.org

Private corporation chartered by Congress under the Public Broadcasting Act of 1967 and funded by the federal government. Supports public broadcasting through grants for public radio and television stations; provides general support for national program production and operation; helps fund projects on U.S. and international news, culture, history, and natural history; studies emerging technologies, such as cable and satellite transmission, the Internet and broadband communication networks, for possible use by public telecommunications; supports training activities.

Federal Communications Commission (FCC),
Enforcement Bureau, 445 12th St. S.W. 20554-0001;
(202) 418-7450. David H. Solomon, Chief. Information,
(888) 225-5322. TTY, (888) 835-5322.
Web, www.fcc.gov/eb

Monitors the radio spectrum and inspects broadcast stations; ensures that U.S. radio laws and FCC rules are observed. Develops activities to inform, assist, and educate licensees; provides presentations and information. Manages the Emergency Alert System. Operates the National Call Center in Gettysburg, Pa.; toll-free (888) numbers handle inquiries and complaints.

Federal Communications Commission (FCC), *Engineering and Technology,* 445 12th St. S.W., 7th Floor 20554; (202) 418-2470. Fax, (202) 418-1944. Ed Thomas, Chief.
General e-mail, oetinfo@fcc.gov
Web, www.fcc.gov/oet

Advises the FCC on technical and spectrum matters and assists in developing U.S. telecommunications policy. Identifies and reviews developments in telecommunications and related technologies. Studies characteristics of radio frequency spectrum. Certifies radios and other electronic equipment to meet FCC standards.

Federal Communications Commission (FCC), *Media Bureau: Broadcast License Policy,* 455 12th St. S.W. 20554; (202) 418-2600. Fax, (202) 418-2828. Roy J. Stewart, Chief.
Web, www.fcc.gov/mb/broadcast_policy

Responsible for the regulation of analog and digital broadcast services. Licenses, regulates, and develops audio and video services in traditional broadcasting and emerging television delivery systems, including high-definition television; processes applications for licensing commercial and noncommercial radio and television broadcast equipment and facilities; handles renewals and changes of ownership; investigates public complaints.

National Endowment for the Arts (NEA), *(National Foundation on the Arts and the Humanities), Dance, Design, Media Arts, Museums, and Visual Arts,* 1100 Pennsylvania Ave. N.W., #726 20506-0001; (202) 682-5452. Fax, (202) 682-5721. Douglas Sonntag, Director, Dance; Robert Frankel, Director, Design (Acting); Ted Libbey, Director, Media Arts; Robert Frankel, Director, Museums and Visual Arts. TTY, (202) 682-5496.
Web, www.arts.gov

Awards grants to nonprofit organizations for film, video, and radio productions; supports arts programming broadcast nationally on public television and radio.

NONPROFIT

Assn. for Maximum Service Television, *1776 Massachusetts Ave. N.W., #310 20036; (202) 861-0344. Fax, (202) 861-0342. David Donovan, President.*
General e-mail, mstv@mstv.org
Web, www.mstv.org

Membership: commercial and educational television stations. Participates in FCC rulemaking proceedings; specializes in television engineering and other matters concerning the transmission structure of the nation's television system.

Electronic Industries Alliance, *2500 Wilson Blvd., #400, Arlington, VA 22201-3834; (703) 907-7500. Fax, (703) 907-7501. Dave McCurdy, President.*
Web, www.eia.org

Membership: U.S. electronics manufacturers. Interests include common distribution, government procurement, high-definition television, and home recording rights; promotes trade, competitiveness, and export expansion through the International Business Council. Monitors legislation and regulations.

National Assn. of Broadcasters (NAB), *1771 N St. N.W. 20036-2891; (202) 429-5300. Fax, (202) 429-5343. Edward O. Fritts, President. Library, (202) 429-5490. Press, (202) 429-5350.*
Web, www.nab.org

Membership: radio and television broadcast stations and broadcast networks holding an FCC license or construction permit; associate members include producers of equipment and programs. Assists members in areas of management, engineering, and research. Interests include privatization abroad and related business opportunities. Monitors legislation and regulations.

National Public Radio, *635 Massachusetts Ave. N.W. 20001-3753; (202) 513-2000. Fax, (202) 513-3329. Kevin Klose, President. Press, (202) 513-2300. Audience services (tapes, transcripts, and listener inquiries), (202) 414-3232.*
General e-mail, ombudsman@npr.org
Web, www.npr.org

Membership: public radio stations nationwide. Produces and distributes news and public affairs programming, congressional hearings, speeches, cultural and dramatic presentations, and programs for specialized audiences. Provides program distribution service via satellite. Represents member stations before Congress, the FCC, and other regulatory agencies.

Public Broadcasting Service, *1320 Braddock Pl., Alexandria, VA 22314; (703) 739-5000. Fax, (703) 739-0775. Pat Mitchell, President.*

General e-mail, pbs@pbs.org

Web, www.pbs.org

Membership: public television stations nationwide. Selects, schedules, promotes, and distributes national programs; provides public television stations with educational, instructional, and cultural programming; also provides news and public affairs, science and nature, fundraising, and children's programming. Assists members with technology development and fundraising.

TV-Turnoff Network, *1601 Connecticut Ave. N.W., #303 20009; (202) 518-5556. Fax, (202) 518-5560. Frank Vespe, Executive Director.*

General e-mail, email@tvturnoff.org

Web, www.tvturnoff.org

Promotes a voluntary and dramatic reduction in the amount of television watched by Americans. Sponsors National TV Turn-off Week.

Telephone and Telegraph

For cellular telephones, see Wireless Telecommunications

AGENCIES

Federal Communications Commission (FCC), *Wireline Competition Bureau, 445 12th St. S.W. 20554; (202) 418-1500. Fax, (202) 418-2825. William Maher, Chief.*

Web, www.fcc.gov/wcb

Develops, recommends, and administers FCC policies involving common carriers (wireline facilities that furnish interstate communications services for hire). Interests include pricing policy, economic and technical aspects, numbering resources, and competition in telecommunications markets.

General Services Administration (GSA), *Federal Technology Service, 10304 Eaton Pl., Fairfax, VA 22030; (703) 306-6000. Sandra N. Bates, Commissioner.*

Web, www.gsa.gov

Purchases and leases telecommunications equipment and services for the federal government. Monitors the transition from federal telecommunications direct service to private provider partnerships for government telephone service.

NONPROFIT

Assn. for Local Telecommunications Services, *888 17th St. N.W., #900 20006; (202) 969-2587. Fax, (202) 969-2581. John Windenhausen, President.*

General e-mail, info@alts.org

Web, www.alts.org

Members include telecommunication companies that build, own, and operate local competitive networks. Seeks to open local telecommunications market to full and fair facilities-based competition. Monitors legislation and regulations.

CompTel, *1900 M St. N.W., #800 20036; (202) 296-6650. Fax, (202) 296-7585. Russell Frisby, President.*

Web, www.comptel.org

Membership: providers of long-distance telecommunications services and suppliers to the industry. Analyzes domestic and international issues affecting competitive long-distance carriers, including mergers. Monitors legislation and regulations.

National Telephone Cooperative Assn., *4121 Wilson Blvd., 10th Floor, Arlington, VA 22203-1801; (703) 351-2000. Fax, (703) 351-2001. Michael E. Brunner, Executive Vice President.*

General e-mail, contact@ntca.org

Web, www.ntca.org

Membership: locally owned and controlled telecommunications cooperatives and companies serving rural and small-town areas. Offers educational seminars, workshops, technical assistance, and a benefits program to members. Monitors legislation and regulations.

Organization for the Promotion and Advancement of Small Telecommunication Companies, *21 Dupont Circle N.W., #700 20036; (202) 659-5990. Fax, (202) 659-4619. John N. Rose, President.*

General e-mail, opastco@opastco.org

Web, www.opastco.org

Membership: local exchange carriers with 100,000 or fewer access lines. Provides members with educational materials and information on regulatory, legislative, and judicial issues in the telecommunications industry. Operates Foundation for Rural Education and Development.

U.S. Telecom Assn. (USTA), *1401 H St. N.W., #600 20005; (202) 326-7300. Fax, (202) 326-7333. Walter B. McCormick Jr., President.*

Web, www.usta.org

Membership: telecommunication companies and manufacturers and suppliers for these companies. Provides members with information on the industry; conducts seminars; participates in FCC regulatory proceedings.

Wireless Telecommunications

AGENCIES

Federal Communications Commission (FCC), *Wireless Telecommunications Bureau, 445 12th St. S.W.*

20554; (202) 418-0600. Fax, (202) 418-0787. *Tom Sugrue, Chief.*

Web, www.fcc.gov/wtb

Regulates wireless communications, including cellular telephone, paging, personal communications services, public safety, air and maritime navigation, and other commercial and private radio services. Assesses new uses of wireless technologies, including electronic commerce. Gettysburg office handles all licensing applications and concerns: FCC Wireless Telecommunications Bureau, Licensing Division, 1270 Fairfield Rd., Gettysburg, PA 17325; (717) 338-2510.

U.S. Secret Service *(Homeland Security Dept.), Financial Crimes, 950 H St. N.W., #5300 20223; (202) 406-5850. Fax, (202) 406-5031. Timothy Caddigan, Special Agent in Charge.*

Web, www.secretservice.gov/financial_crimes.shtml

Investigates reports of cellular phone, computer, and credit fraud.

NONPROFIT

American Mobile Telecommunications Assn., *200 N. Glebe Rd., #1000, Arlington, VA 22203; (202) 331-7773. Fax, (202) 331-9062. Alan R. Shark, President.*

Web, www.amtausa.org

Membership: mobile telecommunications companies, including dispatch services. Serves as an information source on radio frequencies, licensing, new products and technology, and market conditions; offers research service of FCC records. Promotes the industry abroad through the International Mobile Telecommunications Assn. Monitors legislation and regulations.

Cellular Telecommunications and Internet Assn., *1250 Connecticut Ave. N.W., #800 20036; (202) 785-0081. Fax, (202) 776-0721. Thomas E. Wheeler, President.*

Web, www.wow-com.com

Membership: system operators, equipment manufacturers, engineering firms, and others engaged in the cellular telephone and mobile communications industry in domestic and world markets. Monitors legislation and regulations.

Council of Independent Communication Suppliers, *1110 N. Glebe Rd., #500, Arlington, VA 22201-5720; (703) 528-5115. Fax, (703) 524-1074. Laura Smith, President.*

General e-mail, customerservice@ita-relay.com

Web, www.ita-relay.com

Represents independent radio sales and service organizations, communications service providers, and telecommunications consultants and engineers serving the Private Land Mobile Radio Service industry. Informs members of FCC and industry activities; solicits members' views on FCC regulatory proceedings. (Affiliated with Industrial Telecommunications Assn.)

Industrial Telecommunications Assn., *1110 N. Glebe Rd., #500, Arlington, VA 22201-5720; (703) 528-5115. Fax, (703) 524-1074. Laura Smith, President.*

General e-mail, info@ita-relay.com

Web, www.ita-relay.com

Trade association whose objective is to preserve spectrum rights and access for private wireless licensees. FCC-certified frequency advisory committee. Coordinates process for applicants seeking FCC authority to operate business and industrial/land transportation radio stations on frequency assignments allocated between 30-900 MHz. Provides telecommunications services for members, including license preparation, engineering analysis, FCC research, radio protection and interference resolutions. Publishes monthly magazine.

Personal Communications Industry Assn., *500 Montgomery St., #700, Alexandria, VA 22314; (703) 739-0300. Fax, (703) 836-1608. E. B. "Jay" Kitchen Jr., President. Information, (800) 759-0300. Fax-on-demand, (800) 680-7242.*

Web, www.pcia.com

Membership: individuals; institutions; independent two-way radio dealers; FCC-licensed carriers who provide the public with personal communications services, including pagers, cellular telephones, and conventional radio telephones; and companies that own, develop, manage and operate facilities and infrastructure used to provide wireless, broadcasting, and telecommunications services, such as tower and antenna companies. Provides members with information, technical assistance, and educational programs. Serves as the FCC-recognized coordinator for frequencies in the Business Radio Service. Interests include technological standards and development of international markets. Library offers fee-based services by appointment. Monitors legislation and regulations.

United Telecom Council (UTC), *1901 Pennsylvania Ave., #500 20006; (202) 872-0030. Fax, (202) 872-1331. Bill Moroney, President.*

Web, www.utc.org

Membership: electric, gas, and water utility companies and natural gas pipelines. Participates in FCC rule-making proceedings. Interests include radio spectrum for fixed and mobile communication and technological, legislative, and regulatory developments affecting telecommunications operations of energy utilities.

Wireless Communications Assn. International,
1140 Connecticut Ave. N.W., #810 20036; (202) 452-7823.
Fax, (202) 452-0041. Andrew Kreig, President.
Web, www.wcai.com

Membership: system operators, program suppliers, equipment and service providers, engineers, and others involved in the wireless broadband industry (including stationary, nomadic, and portable access to broadband). Develops standards; promotes technological advancement and worldwide growth of the industry. Monitors legislation and regulations.

▣ GOVERNMENT INFORMATION

AGENCIES

General Services Administration (GSA), *Federal Relay Service, 10304 Eaton Pl., Fairfax, VA 22030; (703) 306-6308. Patricia Stevens, Program Manager. TTY, (800) 877-8845. Customer service, (800) 877-0996.*
Web, www.gsa.gov/frs

Assures that the federal telecommunications system is fully accessible to deaf, hearing-impaired, and speech-impaired individuals, including federal workers. Operates via relay, twenty-four hours a day, seven days a week. Produces a directory of TDD/TTY services within the federal government.

General Services Administration (GSA), *National Contact Center, P.O. Box 450, Camby, IN 46113-0450. Warren Snaider, Program Manager. Information, (800) 688-9889. TTY, (800) 326-2996.*
Web, fic.info.gov

Operates a toll-free hotline which provides information on all federal government agencies, programs, and services.

National Archives and Records Administration (NARA), *8601 Adelphi Rd., #4200, College Park, MD 20740-6001; (866) 272-6272. Fax, (301) 837-0483. John W. Carlin, Archivist of the United States; Lewis J. Bellardo, Deputy Archivist.*
Web, www.archives.gov

Identifies, preserves, and makes available federal government documents of historic value; administers a network of regional storage centers and archives and operates the presidential library system. Collections include photographs, graphic materials, and films; holdings include records generated by foreign governments (especially in wartime) and by international conferences, commissions, and exhibitions.

National Archives and Records Administration (NARA), *Center for Legislative Archives, 700 Pennsylvania Ave. N.W., #8E 20408; (202) 501-5350. Fax, (202) 219-2176. Michael L. Gillette, Director.*
Web,
http://www.archives.gov/records_of_congress/about_the_cla/about_the_cla.html

Collects and maintains records of congressional committees and legislative files from 1789 to the present. Publishes inventories and guides to these records.

National Archives and Records Administration (NARA), *Electronic and Special Media Records, 8601 Adelphi Rd., #5320, College Park, MD 20740-6001; (301) 837-3420. Fax, (301) 837-3861. Michael Carlson, Director.*
Web, www.archives.gov

Preserves, maintains, and makes available electronic records of the U.S. government in all subject areas. Provides researchers with magnetic tape copies of records on a cost-recovery basis. Distributes lists of holdings.

National Archives and Records Administration (NARA), *Federal Register, 800 N. Capitol St., #700 20001 (mailing address: 8601 Adelphi Rd., College Park, MD 20740-6001); (202) 741-6000. Fax, (202) 741-6012. Raymond Mosley, Director. TTY, (202) 741-6086. Public Laws Update Service (PLUS), (202) 523-6641.*
General e-mail, fedreg.info@nara.gov
Web, www.archives.gov/federal_register

Assigns public law numbers to enacted legislation, executive orders, and proclamations; responds to inquiries on public law numbers; assists inquirers in finding presidential signing or veto messages in the *Weekly Compilation of Presidential Documents* and the *Public Papers of the Presidents* series; compiles slip laws and annual *United States Statutes at Large;* compiles indexes for finding statutory provisions. Operates Public Laws Update Service (PLUS) and Public Law Electronic Notification System (PENS), which provides information by telephone or e-mail on new legislation. Publications available from the U.S. Government Printing Office.

National Archives and Records Administration (NARA), *Modern Records Program, 8601 Adelphi Rd., College Park, MD 20740; (301) 837-3570. Fax, (301) 837-3697. Howard Lowell, Director (Acting).*
General e-mail, Records.Management@arch2.nara.gov
Web, www.archives.gov

Administers programs that establish standards, guidelines, and procedures for agency records administration. Manages training programs; inspects records management practices; monitors certain records not contained in National Archives depositories.

CHIEF INFORMATION OFFICERS FOR FEDERAL AGENCIES

DEPARTMENTS

Agriculture, Scott Charbo, (202) 720-8833

Commerce, Thomas Pyke, (202) 482-4797

Defense, John Stenbit, (703) 695-0348

Air Force, John Gilligan, (703) 697-6361

Army, Lt. Gen. Peter Cuviello, (703) 697-7494

Navy, Daniel E. Porter, (703) 602-1800

Education, Craig Luygart, (202) 401-3200

Energy, Karen Evans, (202) 586-0166

Health and Human Services, Bill Clark, (202) 690-6162

Homeland Security, Steven I. Cooper (Designate), (202) 282-8000 (switchboard)

Housing and Urban Development, Gloria Parker, (202) 708-1008

Interior, Daryl W. White, (202) 208-6194

Justice, Vance Hitch, (202) 514-3101

Labor, Patrick Pizzella, (202) 693-4040

State, Fernando Burbano, (202) 647-2226

Transportation, Daniel P. Matthews, (202) 366-9201

Treasury, Jim Flyzik, (202) 622-1200

Veterans Affairs, John A. Gauss, (202) 273-8842

AGENCIES

Environmental Protection Agency, Alvin Pesachowitz, (202) 564-6665

Federal Emergency Management Agency, Ron Miller, (202) 646-3006

Federal Trade Commission, Stephen Warren, (202) 326-2898

General Accounting Office, Anthony Cicco, (202) 512-6623

General Services Administration, Mike Carlton, (202) 501-1000

Intelligence Community, John Young, (703) 482-1100

National Aeronautics and Space Administration, Lee Holcomb, (202) 358-1824

National Science Foundation, Linda Massaro, (703) 292-8100

Nuclear Regulatory Commission, Stuart Reiter, (301) 415-8700

Office of Personnel Management, Janet L. Barnes, (202) 606-2150

Securities and Exchange Commission, Ken Fogash (Acting), (202) 942-8800

Small Business Administration, Lawrence E. Barrett, (202) 205-6708

Social Security Administration, Dean Mesberharm (410) 965-9000

National Archives and Records Administration (NARA), *Presidential Libraries,* 8601 Adelphi Rd., #2200, College Park, MD 20740-6001; (301) 837-3250. Fax, (301) 837-3199. Richard L. Claypoole, Assistant Archivist.
Web, www.archives.gov/presidential_libraries

Directs all programs relating to acquisition, preservation, publication, and research use of materials in presidential libraries; conducts oral history projects; publishes finding aids for research sources; provides reference service, including information from and about documentary holdings.

National Archives and Records Administration (NARA), *Regional Records Services,* 8601 Adelphi Rd., #3600, College Park, MD 20740-6001; (301) 837-2950. Fax, (301) 837-1617. Thomas Mills, Assistant Archivist.
Web, www.archives.gov/records_center_program

Stores federal records and assists agencies in microfilming records, protecting vital operating records, improving filing and classification systems, and developing disposition schedules.

National Archives and Records Administration (NARA), *Textual Archives Services,* 8601 Adelphi Rd., #2600, College Park, MD 20740-6001; (301) 837-3480. Fax, (301) 837-1919. James J. Hastings, Director.
Web, www.archives.gov/research_room/obtain_copies/textual_archives_services

Provides reference service for unpublished civil and military federal government records. Maintains central catalog of all library materials. Compiles comprehensive bibliographies of materials related to archival administration and records management. Permits research in American history, archival science, and records management. Maintains collections of the papers of the Conti-

PUBLICATIONS OFFICES AT FEDERAL AGENCIES

DEPARTMENTS

Agriculture, Orders, (202) 720-2791

Commerce, Orders (via NTIS), (703) 605-6000

Defense, Orders, (703) 428-0711

   Army, Orders, (703) 325-6297

Energy, Orders, (202) 586-5575

Health and Human Services, Orders, (202) 619-0257

Housing and Urban Development, Orders, (800) 767-7468; Fax orders, (202) 708-2313

Justice, Orders, (202) 514-2007

Labor, Statistic orders, (202) 691-5200

State, Orders, (202) 647-6575; Fax-on-demand, (202) 736-7720

Transportation, Orders, (301) 322-4961; Fax orders, (301) 386-5394

Treasury, Orders, (202) 622-2970; Fax-on-demand, (202) 622-2040

Veterans Affairs, Orders, (202) 273-5700

AGENCIES

Census Bureau, Orders, (301) 457-4100

Commission on Civil Rights, Orders, (202) 376-8128

Consumer Product Safety Commission, Orders, (301) 504-7923

Corporation for National Service (AmeriCorps), Orders, (800) 942-2677

Energy Information Administration, Orders, (202) 586-8800

Environmental Protection Agency, Orders, (202) 260-5922

Equal Employment Opportunity Commission, Orders, (800) 669-3362

Federal Communications Commission, Fax-on-demand, (202) 418-2830

Federal Election Commission, Orders, (800) 424-9530

Federal Emergency Management Agency, Orders, (202) 646-3484

Federal Reserve System, Orders, (202) 452-3244

Federal Trade Commission, Orders, (202) 326-2222

General Accounting Office, Orders, (202) 512-6000

General Services Administration, Orders, (202) 501-1235

Government Printing Office, Orders, (202) 512-1800

International Bank for Reconstruction and Development (World Bank), Orders, (202) 473-1155

International Trade Administration
  Orders from NTIS and GPO, (202) 482-5487

National Aeronautics and Space Administration, Orders, (301) 621-0390

National Archives and Records Administration, Orders, (202) 501-5235; Toll-free, (800) 234-8861

National Endowment for the Humanities, Orders, (202) 606-8400

National Institute of Standards and Technology, Information (orders from NTIS and GPO), (301) 975-6478

National Labor Relations Board, Pamphlets, (202) 273-1991; Orders from GPO, (202) 512-1800

National Park Service, Information (orders by mail only), (202) 208-4747

National Science Foundation, Orders, (301) 947-2722

National Technical Information Service, Orders, (703) 605-6000

National Transportation Safety Board, Orders, (202) 314-6551

Nuclear Regulatory Commission, Orders from GPO, (202) 512-1800

Occupational Safety and Health Administration, Orders, (202) 693-1888

Office of Personnel Management, Information (orders from GPO), (202) 606-1822; Retirement and insurance information, (202) 606-0623

Peace Corps, Orders from NTIS, (703) 605-6000 or ERIC, (800) 538-3742

Securities and Exchange Commission, Information, (202) 942-4046; Orders, (202) 942-4040

Smithsonian Institution, Orders: Smithsonian books, recordings, videos, (800) 410-9815; Orders: Smithsonian Institution Press, (800) 782-4612

Social Security Administration, Orders, (410) 965-4155

U.S. Fish and Wildlife Service, Orders, (304) 876-7203

U.S. Geological Survey, Orders, (888) ASK-USGS

U.S. Institute of Peace, Book orders, (800) 868-8064; Other orders, (202) 457-1700

nental Congress (1774–1789), U.S. State Dept. diplomatic correspondence (1789–1963), and general records of the U.S. government.

National Technical Information Service (NTIS), (Commerce Dept.), 5285 Port Royal Rd., Springfield, VA 22161; (703) 605-6400. Fax, (703) 605-6715. Ronald E. Lawson, Director. TTY, (703) 605-6043. Sales center, (703) 605-6000; rush orders, (800) 553-6847.

Web, www.ntis.gov

Collects and organizes technical, scientific, engineering, and business-related information generated by U.S. and foreign governments and makes it available for commercial use in the private sector. Incorporates over 2 million works covering research and development, current events, business and management studies, translations of foreign reports, foreign and domestic trade, general statistics, environment and energy, health and social sciences, and hundreds of other areas. Provides computer software and computerized data files on tape, diskette, optical disk, and other multimedia materials.

Office of Global Communications (Executive Office of the President), Dwight D. Eisenhower Executive Office Bldg. 20501; (202) 456-4636. Fax, (202) 456-6180. Tucker Eskew, Director.

Web, www.whitehouse.gov/ogc

Advises U.S. government agencies on the direction and theme of the president's message. Assists in the development and coordination of communications programs that will disseminate consistent and accurate messages about U.S. government and policies to the global audience.

CONGRESS

General Accounting Office (GAO), Document Distribution Center, 441 G St. N.W., #1100 20548 (mailing address: P.O. Box 37050 20013); (202) 512-6000. Fax, (202) 512-6061. Gerry Mader, Manager. Press, (202) 512-4800. TTY, (202) 512-2537.

General e-mail, info@www.gao.gov

Web, www.gao.gov

Provides information to the public on many federal programs. GAO publications and information about GAO publications are available upon request.

Government Printing Office (GPO), 732 N. Capitol St. N.W. 20401; (202) 512-2034. Fax, (202) 512-1347. Bruce James, Public Printer. Press, (202) 512-1991. Congressional documents, (202) 512-1808. To order government publications, (202) 512-1800 or (866) 512-1800.

General e-mail, gpoinfo@gpo.gov

Web, www.gpo.gov

Prints, distributes, and sells selected publications of the U.S. Congress, government agencies, and executive departments. Makes available, for a fee, the Monthly Catalog of U.S. Government Publications, a comprehensive listing of all publications issued by the various departments and agencies each month. Publications are distributed to GPO Regional Depository Libraries; some titles also may be purchased at GPO bookstores in larger cities.

House Administration Committee, 1309 LHOB 20515; (202) 225-8281. Fax, (202) 225-9957. Rep. Bob W. Ney, R-Ohio, Chair; Paul Vinovich, Staff Director.

Web, www.house.gov/cha

Jurisdiction over the printing, cost of printing, binding, and distribution of congressional publications; jurisdiction (in conjunction with the Senate Rules and Administration Committee and the Joint Committee on Printing) over the Government Printing Office, executive papers, and depository libraries; jurisdiction over federal election law.

Joint Committee on Printing, SR-346 20515; (202) 224-3244. Fax, (202) 228-2186. Rep. Bob Ney, R-Ohio, Chair; Paul Vinovich, Staff Director.

Web, www.house.gov/jcp

Oversees public printing, binding, and distribution of government publications; executive papers and depository libraries; and activities of the Government Printing Office (in conjunction with the House Administration and Senate Rules and Administration committees).

Legislative Resource Center, B106 CHOB 20515-6612; (202) 226-5200. Fax, (202) 226-5204. Deborah Turner, Manager.

General e-mail, lrc@mail.house.gov

Web, clerk.house.gov/clerk/Offices_Services/lrc.php

Conducts historical research. Advises members on the disposition of their records and papers; maintains information on manuscript collections of former members; maintains biographical files on former members. Print publications include Biographical Directory of the United States Congress, 1774–1989; Guide to Research Collections of Former Members of the United States House of Representatives, 1789–1987; Black Americans in Congress, 1870–1989; and Women in Congress, 1917–1989.

Library of Congress, Federal Library and Information Center Committee, 101 Independence Ave. S.E., #LA217 20540-4935; (202) 707-4800. Fax, (202) 707-4818. Susan M. Tarr, Executive Director.

General e-mail, flicc@loc.gov

Web, lcweb.loc.gov/flicc

PUBLIC AFFAIRS CONTACTS FOR FEDERAL AGENCIES

DEPARTMENTS

Agriculture, Alisa Harrison, (202) 720-4623

Commerce, Emily Kertz, (202) 482-4883

Defense, Victoria Clarke, (703) 697-9312

Air Force, Brig. Gen. Ronald T. Rand, (703) 697-6061

Army, Maj. Gen. Larry D. Gottardi, (703) 695-5135

Marine Corps, Col. Marianne Crucidawson, (703) 614-2958

Navy, Adm. Stephen Pietropauli, (703) 697-7391

Education, Dan Langan, (202) 401-1576

Energy, Jeanne Lopatto, (202) 586-4940

Health and Human Services, Campbell Gardett, (202) 690-6343

Homeland Security, Susan K. Neely, (202) 282-8010

Housing and Urban Development, Nancy Segerdahl, (202) 708-0980

Interior, Eric Ruff, (202) 208-6416

Justice, Barbara Comstock, (202) 616-2777

Labor, Sue Hensley, (202) 693-4676

State, Phil Reeker, (202) 647-2492

Transportation, Bill Adams, (202) 366-4570

Treasury, Rob Nichols (Acting), (202) 622-2910

Veterans Affairs, Jeffrey E. Phillips, (202) 273-5750

AGENCIES

Agency for International Development, Joanne Giordano, (202) 712-4300

Commission on Civil Rights, Terri Dickerson (Acting), (202) 376-8312

Commodity Futures Trading Commission, Alan Sobba, (202) 418-5080

Consumer Product Safety Commission, Ken Giles, (301) 504-7052

Corporation for National Service, Sandy Scott, (202) 606-5000, ext. 255

Environmental Protection Agency, Thomas J. Basile, (202) 564-4455

Equal Employment Opportunity Commission, Vacant, (202) 663-4900

Export–Import Bank, Andrea Richardson, (202) 565-3237

Farm Credit Administration, Eileen M. McMahon, (202) 347-1184

Federal Communications Commission, David Fiske (Acting), (202) 418-0500

Federal Deposit Insurance Corporation, Philip Battey, (202) 898-7192

Federal Election Commission, Ronald M. Harris, (202) 694-1220

Federal Emergency Management Agency, Lara Shane, (202) 646-4600

Federal Labor Relations Authority, Vacant, (202) 482-6500

Federal Mediation and Conciliation Services, Cynthia Hedgepeth, (202) 606-8080

Federal Reserve System, Lynn Fox, (202) 452-3204

Membership: one representative from each major federal agency, one representative each from the Library of Congress and the national libraries of medicine and agriculture, and one representative from each of the major Federal Information Centers. Coordinates planning, development, operations, and activities among federal libraries.

Library of Congress, *Serial and Government Publications, 101 Independence Ave. S.E. 20540; (202) 707-5647. Fax, (202) 707-6128. Karen Renninger, Chief. Information, (202) 707-5690.*
Web, www.lcweb.loc.gov

Operates Newspaper and Periodical Reading Room; maintains library's collection of current domestic and foreign newspapers, current periodicals, and serially issued publications of federal, state, and foreign governments; has maintained full government publication depository since 1979. Responds to written or telephone requests for information on government publications.

Senate Historical Office, *SH-201 20510; (202) 224-6900. Fax, (202) 224-5329. Richard Baker, Historian. General e-mail, historian@sec.senate.gov*
Web, www.senate.gov

Serves as an information clearinghouse on Senate history, traditions, and members. Collects, organizes, and distributes to the public previously unpublished Senate documents; collects and preserves photographs

PUBLIC AFFAIRS CONTACTS FOR FEDERAL AGENCIES (continued)

Federal Trade Commission, Cathleen MacFarland, (202) 326-2180

General Accounting Office, Jeff Nelligan, (202) 512-4800

General Services Administration, Ed Larkin, (202) 501-0705

Government Printing Office, Andrew M. Sherman, (202) 512-1991

Institute of Museum and Library Services, Mary Ann Bittner, (202) 606-8536

National Aeronautics and Space Administration, Glen Mahone, (202) 358-1898

National Archives and Records Administration, Jeannetta Edwards-Ford, (301) 713-6000

National Capital Planning Commission, Denise H. Liebowitz, (202) 482-7200

National Credit Union Administration, Robert E. Loftus, (703) 518-6330

National Endowment for the Arts, Vacant, (202) 682-5570

National Endowment for the Humanities, Vacant, (202) 606-8446

National Labor Relations Board, David B. Parker, (202) 273-1991

National Science Foundation, Curtis Suplee, (703) 292-8070

National Transportation Safety Board, Ted Lopatkiewicz, (202) 314-6100

Nuclear Regulatory Commission, William M. Beecher, (301) 415-8200

Occupational Safety and Health Review Commission, Linda A. Whitsett, (202) 606-5398

Office of Personnel Management, Scott Hatch, (202) 606-1800

Office of Special Counsel, Jane McFarland, (202) 653-7984

Pension Benefit Guaranty Corporation, Bill Fitzgerald, (202) 326-4040

Securities and Exchange Commission, Christi Harlan, (202) 942-0020

Selective Service System, Richard S. Flahavan, (703) 605-4100

Small Business Administration, Patrick Rhode, (202) 205-6740, ext. 44

Social Security Administration, Annie White, (410) 965-2739

U.S. International Trade Commission, Margaret M. O'Laughlin, (202) 205-1819

U.S. Postal Service, Judy deTorok, (202) 268-3615

---

and pictures related to Senate history; conducts an oral history program; advises senators and Senate committees on the disposition of their noncurrent papers and records. Produces publications on the history of the Senate.

Senate Rules and Administration Committee, *SR-305 20510; (202) 224-6352. Fax, (202) 224-5400. Sen. Trent Lott, R-Miss., Chair; Susan Wells, Staff Director. Web, rules.senate.gov*

Jurisdiction over the printing, cost of printing, binding, and distribution of congressional publications; the Government Printing Office; executive papers; and depository libraries.

Freedom of Information

AGENCIES

Justice Dept. (DOJ), *Information and Privacy, 950 Pennsylvania Ave. N.W., #570 20530; (202) 514-3642. Fax, (202) 514-1009. Richard L. Huff, Co-Director; Daniel J. Metcalfe, Co-Director. Information, (202) 514-2000. TTY, (202) 514-1888.*
Web, www.usdoj.gov/oip/oip.html

Provides federal agencies with advice and policy guidance on matters related to implementing and interpreting the Freedom of Information Act (FOIA). Litigates selected FOIA and Privacy Act cases; adjudicates administrative appeals from Justice Dept. denials of

FREEDOM OF INFORMATION CONTACTS

DEPARTMENTS

Agriculture, Andrea Fowler, (202) 720-8164

Commerce, Brenda Dolan, (202) 482-4115

Defense, H. J. McIntyre, (703) 697-4026

  Air Force, Rhonda Jenkins, (703) 696-7263

  Army, Phyllis Walls, (703) 806-5698

  Navy, Doris M. Lama, (202) 685-6545

Education, Information, (202) 708-9263

Energy, Abel Lopez, (202) 586-6025

Health and Human Services, Rosario Cirrincione, (202) 690-7453

Housing and Urban Development, Marylee Byrd, (202) 708-3866

Interior, Alexandra Mallus, (202) 208-5342

Justice, Patricia D. Harris, (301) 436-1007

Labor, Miriam Miller, (202) 693-5500

State, Margaret Grafeld, (202) 261-8303

Transportation, Patricia Riep-Dice, (202) 366-4542

Treasury, Lana Johnson, (202) 622-0930

Veterans Affairs, Ernesto Castro, (202) 273-8135

AGENCIES

Agency for International Development, Information, (202) 712-0960

Central Intelligence Agency, Information, (703) 613-1287

Commission on Civil Rights, Emma Monroig, (202) 376-8351

Commodity Futures Trading Commission, Information, (202) 418-5105

Consumer Product Safety Commission, Todd A. Stevenson, (301) 504-7923

Environmental Protection Agency, Betty Lopez, (202) 566-1660

Equal Employment Opportunity Commission, Denise Austin, (202) 663-4669

Export-Import Bank, Howard Schweitzer, (202) 565-3229

Farm Credit Administration, Deborah Buccolo, (703) 883-4020

Federal Communications Commission, Patricia Quartey, (202) 418-0440

Federal Deposit Insurance Corp., Fred Fisch, (202) 736-0526

Federal Election Commission, Ron Harris, (202) 694-1220

Federal Emergency Management Agency, J. D. Schwartzkopf, (202) 646-3840

Federal Labor Relations Authority, David M. Smith, (202) 482-6620

Federal Maritime Commission, Bryant Van Brakle, (202) 523-5725

Federal Reserve, Jeanne McLaughlin, (202) 452-3684

Federal Trade Commission, William Golden, (202) 326-2494

General Services Administration, Yvonne Thompson, (202) 619-6200

Legal Services Corp., Patricia Batie, (202) 336-8922

Merit Systems Protection Board, Michael Hoxie, (202) 653-7200

National Aeronautics and Space Administration, Sharon Holgerson, (202) 358-0205

National Archives and Records Administration, Ramona Oliver, (301) 837-2024

National Credit Union Administration, Patricia Slye, (703) 518-6565

National Endowment for the Humanities, Laura Nelson, (202) 606-8322

National Labor Relations Board, John J. Toner, (202) 273-1944

National Mediation Board, Judy Femi, (202) 692-5040

National Science Foundation, Leslie Jensen, (703) 292-8060

National Transportation Safety Board, Joy White, (202) 314-6548

Nuclear Regulatory Commission, Carol Ann Reed, (301) 415-7169

Office of Personnel Management, Mary Beth Smith-Toomey, (202) 606-8358

Peace Corps, Mary Fausier, (202) 692-1125

Pension Benefit Guaranty Corp., Bill Fitzgerald, (202) 326-4040

Securities and Exchange Commission, Barry D. Walters, (202) 942-4320

Selective Service, Paula Sweeney, (703) 605-4046

Small Business Administration, Lisa J. Babcock, (202) 401-8203

Social Security Administration, Darrell Blevins, (410) 966-6645

U.S. International Trade Commission, Marilyn Abbott (Acting), (202) 205-2000

U.S. Postal Service, Robert Faruq, (202) 268-2608

public requests for access to documents; conducts FOIA training for government agencies.

National Archives and Records Administration (NARA), *Information Security Oversight,* 700 Pennsylvania Ave. N.W., #500 20408-0001; (202) 219-5250. Fax, (202) 219-5385. J. William Leonard, Director.
General e-mail, isoo@arch1.nara.gov
Web, www.archives.gov

Oversees government policy on security classification of documents for federal agencies and industry; reviews procedures; monitors declassification programs of federal agencies.

National Archives and Records Administration (NARA), *Initial Processing/Declassification,* 8601 Adelphi Rd., College Park, MD 20740; (301) 837-3440. Jeanne Schauble, Director.
Web, www.archives.gov

Directs the review and declassification of records and security-classified materials in the National Archives in accordance with Executive Order 12958 and the Freedom of Information Act; assists other federal archival agencies in declassifying security-classified documents in their holdings.

CONGRESS

House Government Reform Committee, *Subcommittee on Government Efficiency and Financial Management,* B349C RHOB 20515; (202) 225-3741. Fax, (202) 225-2544. Rep. Todd R. Platts, R-Pa., Chair; Mike Hettinger, Staff Director.
Web, www.house.gov/reform

Jurisdiction over Freedom of Information Act.

Senate Judiciary Committee, *Subcommittee on Terrorism, Technology, and Homeland Security,* SH-325 20510; (202) 224-6791. Fax, (202) 228-0542. Sen. Jon Kyl, R-Ariz., Chair; Stephen Higgins, Chief Counsel.
Web, judiciary.senate.gov

Jurisdiction over Freedom of Information Act.

NONPROFIT

American Civil Liberties Union (ACLU), *Washington Office,* 1333 H St. N.W., 10th Floor 20005; (202) 544-1681. Fax, (202) 546-0738. Laura Murphy, Legal Director.
Web, www.aclu.org

Initiates test court cases and advocates legislation to guarantee constitutional rights and civil liberties. Monitors agency compliance with the Privacy Act, and other access statutes. Produces publications. (Headquarters in New York maintains docket of cases.)

American Society of Access Professionals, 1444 Eye St. N.W., #700 20005; (202) 712-9054. Fax, (202) 216-9646. Claire Shanley, Executive Director.
General e-mail, asap@bostromdc.com
Web, www.accesspro.org

Membership: federal employees, attorneys, journalists, and others working with or interested in access-to-information laws. Seeks to improve the administration of the Freedom of Information Act, the Privacy Act, and other access statutes.

Center for National Security Studies, Gelman Library, 1120 19th St. N.W., #800 20036; (202) 721-5650. Fax, (202) 530-0128. Kate Martin, Director.
General e-mail, cnss@gwu.edu
Web, www.cnss.org

Specializes in the Freedom of Information Act as it relates to national security matters and access to government information issues in the United States and abroad.

Radio-Television News Directors Assn., 1600 K St. N.W. #700 20006-2838; (202) 659-6510. Fax, (202) 223-4007. Barbara Cochran, President.
General e-mail, rtnda@rtnda.org
Web, www.rtnda.org

Membership: local and network news executives in broadcasting, cable, and other electronic media. Operates the Freedom of Information Committee, which assists members with news access.

INTERNET AND RELATED TECHNOLOGIES

AGENCIES

Criminal Division *(Justice Dept.), Computer Crime and Intellectual Property,* 1301 New York Ave. N.W., #600 20530; (202) 514-1026. Fax, (202) 514-6113. Martha Stansell-Gamm, Chief.
Web, www.usdoj.gov/criminal/cybercrime

Investigates and litigates criminal and civil cases involving computers and the Internet; provides specialized technical and legal assistance to other Justice Dept. divisions; coordinates international efforts; formulates policies and proposes legislation on computer crime issues.

CyberSmuggling Center *(Treasury Dept.), U.S. Customs Service: Investigations,* 11320 Random Hills Rd., #400, Fairfax, VA 22030; (703) 293-8005. Fax, (703) 293-9127. Monty Price, Director (Acting).

WORLD WIDE WEB SITES OF FEDERAL AGENCIES

CONGRESS

General Accounting Office, www.gao.gov

House of Representatives, www.house.gov

Library of Congress, www.loc.gov

Senate, www.senate.gov

WHITE HOUSE

General Information, www.whitehouse.gov

DEPARTMENTS

Agriculture, www.usda.gov

Commerce, www.commerce.gov

Defense, www.defenselink.mil

  Air Force, www.af.mil

  Army, www.army.mil

  Marine Corps, www.usmc.mil

  Navy, www.navy.mil

Education, www.ed.gov

Energy, www.energy.gov

Health and Human Services, www.os.dhhs.gov

Homeland Security, www.dhs.gov

Housing and Urban Development, www.hud.gov

Interior, www.doi.gov

Justice, www.usdoj.gov

Labor, www.dol.gov

State, www.state.gov

Transportation, www.dot.gov

Treasury, www.ustreas.gov

Veterans Affairs, www.va.gov

AGENCIES

Consumer Product Safety Commission,
www.cpsc.gov

Corporation for Public Broadcasting, www.cpb.org

Drug Enforcement Administration,
www.usdoj.gov/dea

Environmental Protection Agency, www.epa.gov

Export-Import Bank, www.exim.gov

Federal Aviation Administration, www.faa.gov

Federal Bureau of Investigation, www.fbi.gov

Federal Communications Commission, www.fcc.gov

Federal Deposit Insurance Corporation,
www.fdic.gov

Federal Election Commission, www.fec.gov

Federal Emergency Management Agency,
www.fema.gov

Federal Energy Regulatory Commission,
www.ferc.fed.us

Federal Reserve System, www.federalreserve.gov

Federal Trade Commission, www.ftc.gov

Food and Drug Administration, www.fda.gov

General Services Administration, www.gsa.gov

Government Printing Office, www.gpo.gov

Internal Revenue Service, www.irs.ustreas.gov

National Aeronautics and Space Administration,
www.nasa.gov

National Archives and Records Administration,
www.nara.gov

National Institute of Standards and Technology,
www.nist.gov

National Institutes of Health, www.nih.gov

National Oceanic and Atmospheric Administration,
www.noaa.gov

National Park Service, www.nps.gov

National Railroad Passenger Corporation (Amtrak),
www.amtrak.com

National Science Foundation, www.nsf.gov

National Technical Information Service,
www.ntis.gov

National Transportation Safety Board, www.ntsb.gov

Nuclear Regulatory Commission, www.nrc.gov

Occupational Safety and Health Administration,
www.osha.gov

Patent and Trademark Office, www.uspto.gov

Peace Corps, www.peacecorps.gov

Pension Benefit Guaranty Corporation,
www.pbgc.gov

Securities and Exchange Commisssion, www.sec.gov

Small Business Administration, www.sba.gov

Smithsonian Institution, www.si.edu

Social Security Administration, www.ssa.gov

U.S. Fish and Wildlife Service, www.fws.gov

U.S. Geological Survey, www.usgs.gov

U.S. International Trade Commission, www.usitc.gov

U.S. Postal Service, www.usps.gov

General e-mail, c3@customs.treas.gov

Web, www.customs.ustreas.gov/enforcem/cyber.htm

Focuses U.S. Customs Service resources on the investigation of international Internet crimes such as money laundering, financing of terrorist activities, child exploitation, intellectual property rights violations, illegal arms trafficking, and stolen antiquities and art.

Defense Advanced Research Projects Agency (Defense Dept.), *3701 N. Fairfax Dr., Arlington, VA 22203-1714; (703) 696-2400. Fax, (703) 696-2209. Anthony J. Tether, Director. Press, (703) 696-2404.*

Web, www.darpa.mil

Helps maintain U.S. technological superiority in support of national security. Conducts ongoing research to develop the World Wide Web; funds Web-related research at other organizations.

Federal Bureau of Investigation (FBI), *(Justice Dept.), Financial Institution Fraud, 935 Pennsylvania Ave. N.W., #7373 20535; (202) 324-6336. Fax, (202) 324-6248. John V. Gillies, Chief. Press, (202) 324-3691.*

Web, www.fbi.gov

Investigates crimes of fraud, theft, or embezzlement within or against financial institutions. Priorities include mortgage and credit card fraud and identity theft.

Federal Communications Commission (FCC), *Plans and Policy: New Technology and Policy, 445 12th St. S.W., #7-C347 20554; (202) 418-2030. Fax, (202) 418-2807. Robert Pepper, Chief.*

Web, www.fcc.gov/opp

Monitors developments in expansion of the global Internet.

General Services Administration (GSA), *Electronic Government and Technology, 1800 F St. N.W. 20405; (202) 501-0202. Fax, (202) 219-1533. Mary Mitchell, Deputy Associate Administrator (Acting).*

General e-mail, estrategy.gov@gsa.gov

Web, www.gsa.gov

Reviews agencies' information resources management and procurement of information technology. Coordinates the development and use of technology to deliver government information and services.

National Science Foundation (NSF), *Computer and Information Sciences and Engineering, 4201 Wilson Blvd., Arlington, VA 22230; (703) 292-8900. Fax, (703) 292-9074. Peter Freeman, Assistant Director.*

Web, www.cise.nsf.gov

Directorate that promotes basic research and education in computer and information sciences and engi-

neering; helps maintain U.S. preeminence in these fields. Coordinates NSF involvement in the High-Performance Computing and Communications (HPCC) program; develops computer resources for scholarly communication, including links with foreign research and education networks; helps set Internet policy.

National Telecommunications and Information Administration (NTIA), *(Commerce Dept.), 1401 Constitution Ave. N.W., #4898 20230; (202) 482-1840. Fax, (202) 482-1635. Nancy J. Victory, Administrator. Information, (202) 482-7002.*

Web, www.ntia.doc.gov

Promotes private-sector development of the National Information Infrastructure (NII) and market access for U.S. firms in developing the Global Information Infrastructure (GII). Makes grants to public and nonprofit entities for innovative use of the Internet and related technologies.

Office of Management and Budget (OMB), *(Executive Office of the President), Information Policy and Technology, 725 17th St. N.W., #10236 20503; (202) 395-3785. Fax, (202) 395-5167. Dan Chenok, Chief.*

Web, www.whitehouse.gov/omb

Oversees implementation and policy development under the Information Technology Reform Act of 1996 and the Paperwork Reduction Act of 1995; focuses on information technology management and substantive information policy, including records management, privacy, and computer security.

CONGRESS

General Accounting Office (GAO), *Applied Research and Methods, 441 G St. N.W., #2037 20548; (202) 512-2700. Nancy Kingsbury, Managing Director.*

Web, www.gao.gov

Assesses the quality of the nation's major statistical databases and helps adapt the government's dissemination of information to a new technological environment. Conducts congressional studies that entail specialized analysis.

General Accounting Office (GAO), *Information Technology, 441 G St. N.W., #4T21 20548; (202) 512-6240. Fax, (202) 512-6450. Linda D. Koontz, Director.*

Web, www.gao.gov

Seeks to make the federal government more effective in its information management. Assesses practices in the public and private sectors; makes recommendations to government agencies. Interests include information security.

Senate Commerce, Science, and Transportation Committee, *Subcommittee on Communications, SD-510 20510; (202) 224-5184. Fax, (202) 228-0326. Sen. Conrad Burns, R-Mont., Chair; Paul Martino, Counsel. Web, commerce.senate.gov*

Jurisdiction over legislation on communications, including computer communications and the Internet.

NONPROFIT

AEA—Advancing the Business of Technology, Washington Office, *601 Pennsylvania Ave. N.W., North Bldg., #600 20004; (202) 682-9110. Fax, (202) 682-9111. William T. Archey, President. Web, www.aeanet.org*

Membership: companies in the software, electronics, telecommunications, and information technology industries. Interests include international trade and investment, export controls, and U.S. competitiveness internationally. Holds conferences. Monitors legislation and regulations. (Headquarters in Santa Clara, Calif.)

American Library Assn., *Information Technology Policy,* *1301 Pennsylvania Ave. N.W., #403 20004; (202) 628-8421. Fax, (202) 628-8424. Frederick Weingarten, Director. Information, (800) 941-8478. General e-mail, oitp@alawash.org Web, www.ala.org/oitp*

Provides policy analysis and development in technology and telecommunications; interests include free expression on the Internet, equitable access to new media, and treaty negotiations of the World Intellectual Property Organization.

American Society for Information Science and Technology, *1320 Fenwick Lane, #510, Silver Spring, MD 20910-3560; (301) 495-0900. Fax, (301) 495-0810. Richard Hill, Executive Director. General e-mail, asis@asis.org Web, www.asis.org*

Membership: librarians, computer scientists, management specialists, behavioral scientists, engineers, and individuals concerned with access to information. Conducts research and educational programs.

Assn. for Competitive Technology, *1413 K St. N.W., 12th Floor 20005; (202) 331-2130. Jonathan Zuck, President. General e-mail, info@ACTonline.org Web, www.actonline.org*

Membership: businesses that engage in or support the information technology industry; individuals who

are concerned about the future of the industry. Education and advocacy organization that engages in activities in support of information technology companies. Monitors legislation and regulations.

Assn. of Research Libraries, *21 Dupont Circle N.W., #800 20036; (202) 296-2296. Fax, (202) 872-0884. Duane Webster, Executive Director. Web, www.arl.org*

Membership: major research libraries, mainly at universities, in the United States and Canada. Interests include computer information systems and other bibliographic tools; publishing and scholarly communication; and worldwide policy on information, copyrights, and intellectual property.

Business Software Alliance, *1150 18th St. N.W., #700 20036; (202) 872-5500. Fax, (202) 872-5501. Robert Holleyman, President. Anti-piracy hotline, (800) 667-4722. General e-mail, software@bsa.org Web, www.bsa.org*

Membership: personal computer software publishing companies. Promotes growth of the software industry worldwide; helps develop electronic commerce. Operates a toll-free hotline to report software piracy; investigates claims of software theft within corporations, financial institutions, academia, state and local governments, and nonprofit organizations. Provides legal counsel and initiates litigation on behalf of members.

Capcon Library Network, *1990 M St. N.W., #200 20036; (202) 331-5771. Fax, (202) 331-5788. Robert Drescher, Executive Director. General e-mail, info@capcon.net Web, www.capcon.net*

Serves as a resource to libraries and other organizations on the information technology industry. Provides Internet access and training, education programs, and bibliographic services. Sponsors workshops and product demonstrations.

Center for Democracy and Technology, *1634 Eye St. N.W., #1100 20006; (202) 637-9800. Fax, (202) 637-0968. James Dempsey, Executive Director. General e-mail, info@cdt.org Web, www.cdt.org*

Promotes civil liberties and democratic values in new computer and communications media, both in the United States and abroad. Interests include free speech, privacy, freedom of information, electronic commerce, and design of the information infrastructure. Monitors legislation and regulations.

Center for Digital Democracy, *2120 L St. N.W., #200 20037; (202) 452-9898. Fax, (202) 331-7842. Jeffrey Chester, Executive Director.*
Web, www.democraticmedia.org

Promotes understanding of the changing U.S. digital media system by disseminating information about communications options and public-interest resources.

Computer and Communications Industry Assn., *666 11th St. N.W., #600 20001; (202) 783-0070. Fax, (202) 783-0534. Edward J. Black, President.*
General e-mail, ccia@ccianet.org
Web, www.ccianet.org

Membership: manufacturers and suppliers of computer data processing and communications-related products and services. Interests include telecommunications policy, capital formation and tax policy, federal procurement policy, communications and computer industry standards, intellectual property policies, encryption, international trade, and antitrust reform.

Computer Law Assn., *3028 Javier Rd., #402, Fairfax, VA 22031-4622; (703) 560-7747. Fax, (703) 207-7028. Barbara Fieser, Executive Director.*
General e-mail, clanet@aol.com
Web, www.cla.org

Membership: lawyers, law students, and nonattorneys concerned with the legal aspects of computers and computer communications. Sponsors programs and provides information on such issues as software protection, contracting, telecommunications, international distribution, financing, taxes, copyrights, patents, and electronic data interchange. Focus includes the Internet and e-commerce.

Cyber Security Policy and Research Institute, *George Washington University School of Engineering and Applied Science, 2033 K St. N.W. 20006; (202) 994-5513. Fax, (202) 994-5505. C. Dianne Martin, Director.*
General e-mail, cspri@gwu.edu
Web, www.cpi.seas.gwu.edu

Encourages and conducts interdisciplinary research on telecommunications delivery systems, management information systems, computer security and privacy, electronic commerce, tele-medicine, computer networks, compensation for electronic intellectual property, ethics and values among users of new media, and related cultural and geopolitical issues. Works with government and private organizations.

Data Interchange Standards Assn., *333 John Carlyle St., #600, Alexandria, VA 22314-5743; (703) 548-7005. Fax, (703) 548-5738. Jerry C. Connors, President.*

General e-mail, info@disa.org
Web, www.disa.org

Supports the development and the use of electronic data interchange standards in electronic commerce. Sponsors workshops, seminars, and conferences. Helps develop international standards.

Electronic Privacy Information Center, *1718 Connecticut Ave. N.W., #200 20009; (202) 483-1140. Fax, (202) 483-1248. Marc Rotenberg, Director.*
General e-mail, info@epic.org
Web, www.epic.org

Public interest research center. Conducts research and conferences on domestic and international civil liberties issues, including privacy, free speech, information access, computer security, and encryption; litigates cases. Monitors legislation and regulations.

Idea Alliance, *100 Daingerfield Rd., Alexandria, VA 22314-2888; (703) 837-1070. Fax, (703) 837-1072. David Steinhardt, President.*
Web, www.idealliance.org

Membership: firms and customers in printing, publishing, and related industries. Helps set industry standards for electronic commerce and conducts studies on new information technologies. (Affiliated with Printing Industries of America.)

Information Sciences Institute, *Washington Office, 3811 Fairfax Dr, #200, Arlington, VA 22203; (703) 243-9422. Fax, (703) 812-3712. Terri Shaulis, Senior Business Officer.*
Web, www.isi.edu or www.east.isi.edu

Conducts research in advanced computer, communications, and information processing technologies; serves as the Internet Assigned Numbers Authority (IANA). Specific projects support development of the Internet, related software, and electronic commerce. (Headquarters in Marina del Rey, Calif.; part of University of Southern California.)

Information Technology Assn. of America, *1401 Wilson Blvd., #1100, Arlington, VA 22209; (703) 284-5300. Fax, (703) 525-2279. Harris N. Miller, President.*
Web, www.itaa.org

Membership: organizations in the computer, communications, and data industries. Conducts research; holds seminars and workshops; interests include small business, government procurement, competitive practices, communications, software, trade, and international copyright issues. Monitors legislation and regulations.

Information Technology Industry Council, *1250 Eye St. N.W., #200 20005; (202) 737-8888. Fax, (202) 638-4922. Rhett Dawson, President. Press, (202) 626-5725.*
General e-mail, webmaster@itc.org
Web, www.itic.org

Membership: providers of information technology products and services. Promotes the global competitiveness of its members and advocates free trade. Seeks to protect intellectual property and encourages the use of voluntary standards.

Interactive Digital Software Assn., *1211 Connecticut Ave., #600 20036-2705; (202) 223-2400. Fax, (202) 223-2401. Douglas Lowenstein, President.*
General e-mail, idsa@idsa.com
Web, www.idsa.com

Membership: publishers of interactive entertainment software. Distributes marketing statistics and information. Administers an independent rating system for the industry and a worldwide anti-piracy program. Monitors legislation and regulations.

International Communications Industries Assn., *11242 Waples Mill Rd., #200, Fairfax, VA 22030; (703) 273-7200. Fax, (703) 278-8082. Randy Lemke, Executive Director. Information, (800) 659-7469.*
General e-mail, icia@infocomm.org
Web, www.infocomm.org

Membership: video and audiovisual dealers; manufacturers and producers; and individuals. Interests include international trade, small business issues, postal rates, copyright, education, and taxation. Monitors legislation and regulations.

International Telework Assn. and Council, *8403 Colesville Rd., #865, Silver Spring, MD 20901; (301) 650-2322. Fax, (301) 495-4959. Robert Smith, Executive Director.*
General e-mail, info@workingfromanywhere.org
Web, www.workingfromanywhere.org

Membership: individuals, corporations, government agencies, educators, consultants, and vendors involved in telecommuting. Promotes the economic, social, and environmental benefits of telecommuting. Seeks to facilitate the development of telecommuting programs internationally. (Headquarters in Wakefield, Mass.)

International Webcasting Assn., *2020 Pennsylvania Ave. N.W., #182 20006-1811. Roger Dean, Chair.*
General e-mail, info@webcasters.org
Web, www.webcasters.org

Promotes the art, technology, and commerce of Webcasting and streaming media; provides a forum to exchange ideas, and to promote and encourage the growth of Webcasting over the Internet and other networks; encourages common technical standards; develops educational programs and research for the community and works to identify issues that affect the Webcasting community and general public.

Internet Alliance, *1111 19th St. N.W., #1180 20036-3637; (202) 955-8091. Fax, (202) 955-8081. Emily Hackett, Executive Director.*
General e-mail, ia@internetalliance.org
Web, www.internetalliance.org

Membership: Internet and online companies, marketing agencies, consulting and research organizations, entrepreneurs, financial institutions, interactive service providers, software vendors, telecommunications companies, and service bureaus. Promotes consumer confidence and trust in the Internet and monitors the effect of public policy on the Internet and its users with a focus on privacy, taxation, children's online marketing, unsolicited e-mail, and content regulation.

Internet Content Rating Assn., *1130 Connecticut Ave. N.W., #1201 20036; (202) 331-8651. Fax, (202) 331-8652. Mary Lou Kenny, Director/North America.*
Web, www.rsac.org

Organization of Internet industry leaders that promotes safe and effective use of the Internet by children through education and information, while protecting the rights of content providers. Provides the public with information about the level of sex, nudity, and violence in software games and on the Internet. Assists parents through programs that label the content of software.

Internet Engineering Task Force, *Secretariat, 1895 Preston White Dr., #100, Reston, VA 20191-5434; (703) 620-8990. Fax, (703) 620-0913. Steve Coya, Executive Director.*
General e-mail, ietf-info@ietf.org
Web, www.ietf.org

Membership: network designers, operators, vendors, and researchers from around the world who are concerned with the evolution, smooth operation, and continuing development of the Internet. Establishes working groups to address technical concerns.

Internet Society, *1775 Wiehle Ave., #102, Reston, VA 20190-5108; (703) 326-9880. Fax, (703) 326-9881. Lynn St. Amour, President.*
General e-mail, isoc@isoc.org
Web, www.isoc.org

Membership: individuals, corporations, nonprofit organizations, and government agencies. Promotes development and availability of the Internet and its associated technologies and applications; promulgates international standards. Conducts research and educational programs; assists technologically developing countries in achieving Internet usage; provides information about the Internet.

Progress and Freedom Foundation, *1401 H St. N.W., #1075 20005-2110; (202) 289-8928. Fax, (202) 289-6079. Jeffrey A. Eisenach, President.*
General e-mail, mail@pff.org
Web, www.pff.org
Studies the impact of the digital revolution and its implications for public policy; sponsors seminars, conferences, and broadcasts.

Progress and Freedom Foundation, *Center for the Study of Digital Property, 1401 H St. N.W., #1075 20005-2110; (202) 289-8928. Fax, (202) 289-6079. James V. DeLong, Director.*
General e-mail, mail@pff.org
Web, www.pff.org
Conducts program of research and education on intellectual property issues related to the Internet and other digital technologies.

Public Service Telecommunications Corporation, *4900 Seminary Rd., #1120, Alexandria, VA 22311; (703) 998-1703. Fax, (703) 998-8480. Louis Bransford, President.*
General e-mail, info@pstc.net
Membership: educational and public service organizations. Represents the interests of members in the use of new and advanced technologies. Conducts telecommunications policy research.

Software and Information Industry Assn., *1090 Vermont Ave., 6th Floor 20005; (202) 289-7442. Fax, (202) 289-7097. Ken Wasch, President.*
Web, www.siia.net
Membership: software and digital information companies. Promotes the industry worldwide; conducts antipiracy program and other initiatives that protect members' intellectual property; collects market research data; sponsors conferences, seminars, and other events that focus on industry-wide and specific interests. Monitors legislation and regulations.

U.S. Internet Industry Assn., *815 Connecticut Ave. N.W., #620 20006 (mailing address: 5810 Kingstowne Center Blvd., Kingstowne, VA 22315); (703) 924-0006. Fax, (703) 924-4203. David P. McClure, President.*
General e-mail, info@usiia.org
Web, www.usiia.org

Membership: U.S. Internet access, business, and electronic commerce companies. Fosters the growth and development of online commerce and communications. Monitors legislation and regulations.

MEDIA PROFESSIONS AND RESOURCES

AGENCIES

Federal Communications Commission (FCC), *Communications Business Opportunity, 445 12th St. S.W., #7C207 20554; (202) 418-0990. Fax, (202) 418-0235. Carolyn Fleming Williams, Director.*
Web, www.fcc.gov/ocbo
Provides technical and legal guidance and assistance to the small, minority, and female business community in the telecommunications industry. Advises the FCC chair on small, minority, and female business issues. Serves as liaison between federal agencies, state and local governments, and trade associations representing small, minority, and female enterprises concerning FCC policies, procedures, and rulemaking activities.

Federal Communications Commission (FCC), *Equal Employment Opportunity, 445 12th St. S.W., #3A625 20554; (202) 418-1450. Fax, (202) 418-1797. Lewis Pulley, Director.*
Web, www.fcc.gov
Responsible for the annual certification of cable television equal employment opportunity compliance. Oversees broadcast employment practices. Publishes annual report on employment trends in cable television and broadcast industries.

NONPROFIT

American News Women's Club, *1607 22nd St. N.W. 20008; (202) 332-6770. Fax, (202) 265-6477. Karen James Cody, President.*
General e-mail, anwc@anwc.org
Web, www.anwc.org
Membership: writers, reporters, photographers, cartoonists, and professionals in print and broadcast media, government and private industry, publicity, and public relations. Promotes the advancement of women in all media. Sponsors professional receptions and seminars.

Communications Workers of America, *501 3rd St. N.W. 20001; (202) 434-1100. Fax, (202) 434-1279. Morton Bahr, President.*
Web, www.cwa-union.org

MEDIA CONTACTS IN WASHINGTON

MAGAZINES

CQ Weekly, 1255 22nd St. N.W. 20037; (202) 419-8500

National Journal, 1501 M St. N.W., #300 20005; (202) 739-8400

Newsweek, 1750 Pennsylvania Ave. N.W., #1220 20006; (202) 626-2000

Time, 555 12th St. N.W., #600 North 20004; (202) 861-4000

U.S. News & World Report, 1050 Thomas Jefferson St. N.W. 20007; (202) 955-2000

NEWSPAPERS

Baltimore Sun, 1627 K St. N.W., #1100 20006; (202) 452-8250

Christian Science Monitor, 910 16th St. N.W. 20006; (202) 785-4400

Los Angeles Times, 1875 Eye St. N.W., #1100 20006; (202) 293-4650

New York Times, 1627 Eye St. N.W. 20006; (202) 862-0300

USA Today, 7950 Jones Branch Dr., McLean, VA 22108; (703) 854-3400

Wall Street Journal, 1025 Connecticut Ave. N.W., #800 20036; (202) 862-9200

Washington Post, 1150 15th St. N.W. 20071; (202) 334-6000

Washington Times, 3600 New York Ave. N.E. 20002; (202) 636-3000

NEWS SERVICES

Agence France-Presse, 1015 15th St. N.W., #500 20005; (202) 289-0700

Associated Press, 2021 K St. N.W., 6th Floor 20006; (202) 776-9400

Gannett News Service, 7950 Jones Branch Dr., McLean, VA 22108; (703) 854-5800

Knight-Ridder Newspapers, 700 National Press Bldg., 529 14th St. N.W. 20045; (202) 383-6000

Newhouse News Service, 1101 Connecticut Ave. N.W., #300 20036; (202) 383-7800

Reuters, 1333 H St. N.W., #500 20005; (202) 898-8300

Scripps-Howard Newspapers, 1090 Vermont Ave. N.W., #1000 20005; (202) 408-1484

States News Service, 1331 Pennsylvania Ave. N.W., #232 20004; (202) 628-3100

United Press International, 1510 H St. N.W. 20005; (202) 898-8000

TELEVISION/RADIO NETWORKS

ABC News, 1717 DeSales St. N.W. 20036; (202) 222-7777

Cable News Network (CNN), 820 1st St. N.E. 20002; (202) 898-7900

CBS News, 2020 M St. N.W. 20036; (202) 457-4321

C-SPAN, 400 N. Capitol St. N.W., #650 20001; (202) 737-3220

Fox News, 400 N. Capitol St. N.W., #550 20001; (202) 824-6300

National Public Radio, 635 Massachusetts Ave. N.W. 20001; (202) 513-2000

NBC News, 4001 Nebraska Ave. N.W. 20016; (202) 885-4200

Public Broadcasting Service, 1320 Braddock Place, Alexandria, VA 22314; (703) 739-5000

Membership: approximately 600,000 workers in telecommunications, printing and news media, public service, cable television, electronics, and other fields. Assists members with contract negotiation and grievances; conducts training programs and workshops. Monitors legislation and regulations. (Affiliated with the AFL-CIO.)

Education and Research Institute, *800 Maryland Ave. N.E. 20002; (202) 546-1710. Fax, (202) 546-3489. M. Stanton Evans, Chair.*

Educational organization that conducts seminars to train interns in basic skills of media work.

Freedom Forum, *1101 Wilson Blvd., Arlington, VA 22209; (703) 528-0800. Fax, (703) 284-3770. Charles L. Overby, Chair. Toll-Free Inquiries, (888) 639-7386. General e-mail, newseum@freedomforum.org Web, www.freedomforum.org*

Sponsors conferences, educational activities, training, and research that promote free press, free speech, and freedom of information and that enhance the teaching and practice of journalism, both in the United States and abroad. Funds the Newseum, an interactive museum of news, scheduled to re-open in downtown Washington in 2006.

Fund for Investigative Journalism, *P.O. Box 60184 20039-0184; (202) 362-0260. Fax, (301) 422-7449. John Hyde, Executive Director.*
General e-mail, fundfij@aol.com
Web, www.fij.org

Provides investigative reporters with grants for articles, broadcasts, photojournalism, and books.

J-Lab, *7100 Baltimore Ave., #101, College Park, MD 20740-3637; (301) 985-4020. Fax, (301) 985-4021. Jan Schaffer, Executive Director.*
General e-mail, news@j-lab.org
Web, www.j-lab.org

Journalism center that facilitates innovative news experiments that use new technologies to help people engage in public policy issues. Affiliated with the University of Maryland Philip Merrill College of Journalism.

Matrix Foundation, *780 Richie Hwy., #28S, Severna Park, MD 21146; (410) 544-7558. Fax, (410) 544-4640. Pat Troy, Executive Director.*
Web, www.awcmatrix.com

Scholarship foundation that promotes the advancement of women in the communications profession by providing funds for education, research, and publications. Works in cooperation with the Assn. for Women in Communications to carry out its educational and charitable goals.

National Assn. of Black Journalists, *University of Maryland, 8701-A Adelphi Rd., Adelphi, MD 20783-1716; (301) 445-7100. Fax, (301) 445-7101. Tangie Newborn, Executive Director.*
General e-mail, nabj@nabj.org
Web, www.nabj.org

Membership: African American journalists working for radio and television stations, newspapers, and magazines, and others in the field of journalism. Works to increase recognition of the achievements of minority journalists, to expand opportunities for minority students entering the field, and to promote balanced coverage of the African American community by the media. Sponsors scholarships and internship program.

National Assn. of Government Communicators, *10366 Democracy Lane, #B, Fairfax, VA 22030; (703) 691-0377. Fax, (703) 691-0866. Gaye Farris, President.*
General e-mail, info@nagc.com
Web, www.nagc.com

National network of federal, state, and local government communications employees. Promotes high standards for the government communications profession and awards noteworthy service.

National Assn. of Hispanic Journalists, *1000 National Press Bldg., 529 14th St. N.W. 20045; (202) 662-7145. Fax, (202) 662-7144. Anna Lopez, Executive Director.*
Web, www.nahj.org

Membership: professional journalists, educators, students, and others interested in encouraging Hispanics to study and enter the field of journalism. Promotes fair representation of Hispanics by the news media. Provides professional development and computerized job referral service; compiles and updates national directory of Hispanics in the media; sponsors national high school essay contest, journalism awards, and scholarships.

National Lesbian and Gay Journalists Assn., *1420 K St. N.W., #910 20005; (202) 588-9888. Fax, (202) 588-1818. Steven Petrow, President.*
General e-mail, info@nlgja.org
Web, www.nlgja.org

Fosters fair and accurate coverage of lesbian and gay issues. Provides professional development support and networking services; sponsors conferences, seminars, and workshops.

National Press Foundation, *1211 Connecticut Ave. N.W., #310 20036; (202) 663-7280. Fax, (202) 530-2855. Bob Meyers, President.*
General e-mail, npf@nationalpress.org
Web, www.nationalpress.org

Works to enhance the professional competence of journalists through in-career education projects. Sponsors conferences, seminars, fellowships, and awards; conducts public forums and international exchanges. Supports the National Press Club library; includes the Washington Journalism Center.

Society for Technical Communication, *901 N. Stuart St., #904, Arlington, VA 22203-1822; (703) 522-4114. Fax, (703) 522-2075. William C. Stolgitis, Executive Director.*
General e-mail, stc@stc.org
Web, www.stc.org

Membership: writers, publishers, educators, editors, illustrators, and others involved in technical communication in the print and broadcast media. Encourages research and develops training programs for technical communicators; aids educational institutions in devising curricula; awards scholarships.

Statistical Assessment Service (STATS), *2100 L St. N.W., #300 20037; (202) 223-3193. Fax, (202) 872-4014. S. Robert Lichter, President.*
Web, www.stats.org

Promotes accurate use of statistical and quantitative data in public policy debate. Provides journalists with analysis of current statistical disputes.

Washington Press Club Foundation, *529 14th St. N.W., #1115 20045; (202) 393-0613. Fax, (202) 662-7040. Maryellen Holley, Executive Director.*

General e-mail, wpcf@erols.com

Web, www.wpcf.org

Seeks to advance professionalism in journalism. Awards minority grants and scholarships. Administers an oral history of women in journalism. Sponsors annual Salute to Congress Dinner in February to welcome Congress back into session. Maintains speakers bureau.

White House Correspondents Assn., *1067 National Press Bldg. 20045; (202) 737-2934. Fax, (202) 783-0841. Carl Cannon, President.*

General e-mail, whca@starpower.net

Web, www.whca.net

Membership: reporters who cover the White House. Acts as a link between reporters and White House staff.

Women's Institute for Freedom of the Press, *1940 Calvert St. N.W. 20009-1502; (202) 265-6707. Fax, (202) 986-6355. Martha Allen, Director.*

General e-mail, info@wifp.org

Web, www.wifp.org

Conducts research and publishes in areas of communications and the media that are of particular interest to women. Promotes freedom of the press. Publishes a free online directory of women in the media.

Accreditation in Washington

Most federal agencies and courts do not require special press credentials

AGENCIES

Defense Dept. (DoD), *Public Affairs, The Pentagon, #2E800 20301-1400; (703) 428-0711. Fax, (703) 697-3501. Victoria Clark, Assistant Secretary of Defense (Public Affairs). Press, (703) 697-5131.*

Web, www.defenselink.mil

Grants accreditation to Washington-based media organizations to form the National Media Pool. Selected staff of accredited groups are assigned to the media pool on a rotating basis and put on alert for short-notice deployment to the site of military operations.

Foreign Press Center *(State Dept.), 529 14th St. N.W., #800 20045; (202) 504-6300. Fax, (202) 504-6334. David Ballard, Director.*

Web, www.fpc.gov

Provides foreign journalists with access to news sources, including wire services and daily briefings from the White House, State Dept., and Pentagon. Holds live news conferences. Foreign journalists wishing to use the center must present a letter from their organization, a letter from the embassy of the country in which their paper is published, and two passport-size photographs.

Metropolitan Police Dept., *Police Public Information, 300 Indiana Ave. N.W., #4048 20001; (202) 727-4383. Fax, (202) 727-5306. Sgt. Joseph Gentile, Director.*

Web, www.mpdc.dc.gov

Serves as connection between the media and the police department. Handles Freedom of Information requests. Provides application forms and issues press passes required for crossing police lines within the city of Washington. Passes are issued on a yearly basis; applicants should allow four to six weeks for processing of passes.

National Park Service (NPS), *(Interior Dept.), National Capital Region, 1100 Ohio Dr. S.W., #336 20242; (202) 619-7000. Fax, (202) 619-7220. Terry Carlstrom, Regional Director. Recorded information, (202) 619-7275. Permits, (202) 619-7225.*

Web, www.nps.gov/ncro

Regional office that administers national parks, monuments, historic sites, and recreation areas in the Washington metropolitan area. Issues special permits required for commercial filming on public park lands. Media representatives covering public events that take place on park lands should notify the Office of Public Affairs and Tourism in advance. A White House or metropolitan police press pass is required in some circumstances.

State Dept., *Public Affairs Press Office, 2201 C St. N.W., #2109 20520; (202) 647-2492. Fax, (202) 647-0244. Charlotte Beers, Under Secretary for Public Diplomacy and Public Affairs. Fax-on-demand, (202) 736-7720.*

General e-mail, publicaffairs@panet.us-state.gov

Web, www.state.gov/press.cfm

U.S. journalists seeking building passes must apply in person with a letter from their editor or publisher and a passport-size photograph. In addition, foreign correspondents need a letter from the embassy of the country in which their organization is based. All journalists must reside in the Washington, D.C., area and must cover the State Dept.'s daily briefing on a regular basis. Applicants should allow three months for security clearance.

White House, *Press Office, 1600 Pennsylvania Ave. N.W. 20500; (202) 456-2580. Fax, (202) 456-6210. Ari Fleischer, Press Secretary. Comments and information, (202) 456-1111.*

Web, www.whitehouse.gov

Journalists seeking permanent accreditation must be accredited by the House or Senate press galleries, must be residents of the Washington, D.C., area, and must be full-time employees of a news-gathering organization, expecting to cover the White House on a nearly daily basis. A journalist's editor, publisher, or employer must write to the press office requesting accreditation. Journalists wishing temporary accreditation should have their assignment desk call a day ahead to be cleared for a one-day pass. Applicants must undergo a Secret Service investigation that takes approximately two months.

CONGRESS

House Periodical Press Gallery, *H304 CAP 20515; (202) 225-2941. Lorraine Woellert, Chair (Business Week). General e-mail, periodical.press@mail.house.gov*

Open by application to periodical correspondents whose chief occupation is gathering and reporting news for periodicals not affiliated with lobbying or membership organizations. Accreditation with the House Gallery covers accreditation with the Senate Gallery.

Press Photographers Gallery, *Standing Committee of Press Photographers, S317 CAP 20510; (202) 224-6548. Fax, (202) 224-0280. Tim Dillon, Chair (USA Today). Web, www.senate.gov/galleries/photo*

Open by application to bona fide news photographers and to heads of photographic bureaus. Accreditation by the standing committee covers both the House and Senate.

Senate Press Gallery, *Standing Committee of Correspondents, S316 CAP 20510; (202) 224-0241. Scott Shepard, Chair (Cox Newspapers). Web, www.senate.gov/galleries/daily/standing.htm*

Open by application to Washington-based reporters who earn more than half their income from news services or from newspapers published at least five times a week. Accreditation with the Senate Gallery covers accreditation with the House Gallery.

Senate Radio and Television Gallery, *Executive Committee of the Radio and Television Correspondents' Galleries, S325 CAP 20510; (202) 224-6421. Fax, (202) 224-4882. Annie Tin, Chair (C-SPAN). Web, www.senate.gov/galleries/radiotv/index.htm*

Open by application to Washington-based radio and television correspondents and technicians who earn more than half their income from or spend at least half their time in the news gathering profession. Accreditation with the Senate Gallery covers accreditation with the House Gallery.

CONGRESSIONAL NEWS MEDIA GALLERIES

The congressional news media galleries serve as liaisons between members of Congress and their staffs and accredited newspaper, magazine, and broadcasting correspondents. The galleries provide accredited correspondents with facilities to cover activities of Congress, and gallery staff members ensure that congressional press releases reach appropriate correspondents. Independent committees of correspondents working through the press galleries are responsible for accreditation of correspondents; see Accreditation in Washington, (pp. 144–145).

House Periodical Press Gallery, H304 CAP 20515; (202) 225-2941. Robert Zatkowski, Director.

House Press Gallery, H315 CAP 20515; (202) 225-3945. Jerry Gallegos, Superintendent.

House Radio and Television Gallery, H321 CAP 20515; (202) 225-5214. Tina Tate, Director.

Press Photographers Gallery, S317 CAP 20510; (202) 224-6548. Jeffrey Kent, Director.

Senate Periodical Press Gallery, S320 CAP 20510; (202) 224-0265. Edward Pesce, Superintendent.

Senate Press Gallery, S316 CAP 20510; (202) 224-0241. Joe Keenan, Superintendent.

Senate Radio and Television Gallery, S325 CAP 20510; (202) 224-6421. Larry Janezich, Director.

JUDICIARY

Supreme Court of the United States, *1 1st St. N.E. 20543; (202) 479-3000. William H. Rehnquist, Chief Justice; Kathleen Arberg, Public Information Officer, (202) 479-3050. Information, (202) 479-3211.*

Journalists seeking to cover the Court must be accredited by either the White House or the House or Senate press galleries. Contact the public information office to make arrangements.

Broadcasting

NONPROFIT

American Women in Radio and Television, *8405 Greenboro Dr., #800, McLean, VA 22102; (703) 506-3290. Fax, (703) 506-3266. Maria Brennan, Executive Director. General e-mail, info@awrt.org Web, www.awrt.org*

Membership: professionals in the electronic media and full-time students in accredited colleges and universities. Promotes industry cooperation and advancement of women. Maintains foundation for educational and charitable purposes.

Broadcast Education Assn., *1771 N St. N.W. 20036-2891; (202) 429-5354. Fax, (202) 775-2981. Louisa A. Nielsen, Executive Director. Information, (888) 380-7222.*
General e-mail, beainfo@beaweb.org
Web, www.beaweb.org

Membership: universities, colleges, and faculty members offering specialized training in radio and television broadcasting. Promotes improvement of curriculum and teaching methods. Fosters working relationships among academics, students, and professionals in the industry.

National Academy of Television Arts and Sciences, *Washington Office, 9405 Russell Rd., Silver Spring, MD 20910-1445; (301) 587-3993. Fax, (301) 587-3993. Dianne E. Bruno, Administrator.*
General e-mail, natasdc@aol.com
Web, www.natasdc.org

Membership: professionals in television and related fields and students in communications. Works to upgrade television programming; awards scholarship to a junior, senior, or graduate student in communications. Sponsors annual Emmy Awards. (Headquarters in New York.)

National Assn. of Black-Owned Broadcasters, *1155 Connecticut Ave. N.W., 6th Floor 20036; (202) 463-8970. Fax, (202) 429-0657. James L. Winston, Executive Director.*
General e-mail, info@nabob.org
Web, www.nabob.org

Membership: minority owners and employees of radio and television stations and telecommunications properties. Provides members and the public with information on the broadcast industry and the FCC. Provides members with legal and advertising research facilities. Monitors legislation and regulations.

National Assn. of Broadcast Employees and Technicians, *501 3rd St. N.W., 8th Floor 20001; (202) 434-1254. Fax, (202) 434-1426. John S. Clark, President.*
Web, www.nabetcwa.org

Membership: approximately 10,000 commercial broadcast and cable television and radio personnel. Helps members negotiate pay, benefits, and better working conditions; conducts training programs and workshops. Monitors legislation and regulations. (Broadcast and Cable Television Workers Sector of the Communications Workers of America.)

National Assn. of Broadcasters (NAB), *1771 N St. N.W. 20036-2891; (202) 429-5300. Fax, (202) 429-5343.*

Edward O. Fritts, President. Library, (202) 429-5490. Press, (202) 429-5350.
Web, www.nab.org

Membership: radio and television broadcast stations and broadcast networks holding an FCC license or construction permit; associate members include producers of equipment and programs. Assists members in areas of management, engineering, and research. Interests include privatization abroad and related business opportunities. Monitors legislation and regulations.

Radio and Television Correspondents Assn., *S-325 CAP 20510; (202) 224-6421. Fax, (202) 224-4882. Larry Janezich, Director.*
Web, www.senate.gov/galleries/radiotv

Membership: broadcast correspondents who cover the White House and Congress. Sponsors annual dinner.

Radio-Television News Directors Assn., *1600 K St. N.W. #700 20006-2838; (202) 659-6510. Fax, (202) 223-4007. Barbara Cochran, President.*
General e-mail, rtnda@rtnda.org
Web, www.rtnda.org

Membership: local and network news executives in broadcasting, cable, and other electronic media in more than thirty countries. Serves as information source for members; provides advice on legislative, political, and judicial problems of electronic journalism; conducts international exchanges.

Press Freedom

CONGRESS

House Judiciary Committee, *Subcommittee on the Constitution, 362 FHOB 20515; (202) 226-7680. Fax, (202) 225-3746. Rep. Steve Chabot, R-Ohio, Chair; Crystal Roberts, Chief Counsel.*
General e-mail, Judiciary@mail.house.gov
Web, www.house.gov/judiciary

Jurisdiction over press shield legislation.

Senate Judiciary Committee, *Subcommittee on the Constitution, Civil Rights, and Property Rights, SD-524 20510; (202) 224-4135. Fax, (202) 228-0463. Sen. John Cornyn, R-Texas, Chair; James Ho, Chief Counsel.*
Web, Judiciary.senate.gov

Jurisdiction over press shield legislation.

NONPROFIT

Reporters Committee for Freedom of the Press, *1815 N. Fort Myer Dr., #900, Arlington, VA 22209; (703) 807-2100. Fax, (703) 807-2109. Lucy A. Dalglish, Executive Director. Freedom of information hotline, (800) 336-4243.*

General e-mail, rcfp@rcfp.org

Web, www.rcfp.org

Membership: reporters, news editors, publishers, and lawyers from the print and broadcast media. Maintains a legal defense and research fund for members of the news media involved in freedom of the press court cases; interests include freedom of speech abroad, primarily as it affects U.S. citizens in the media industry.

Student Press Law Center, *1815 N. Fort Myer Dr., #900, Arlington, VA 22209; (703) 807-1904. Fax, (703) 807-2109. Mark Goodman, Executive Director.*

General e-mail, splc@splc.org

Web, www.splc.org

Collects, analyzes, and distributes information on free expression and freedom of information rights of student journalists (print and broadcast) and on violations of those rights in high schools and colleges. Provides free legal assistance to students and faculty advisers experiencing censorship.

World Press Freedom Committee, *11690-C Sunrise Valley Dr., Reston, VA 20191; (703) 715-9811. Fax, (703) 620-6790. Marilyn J. Greene, Executive Director.*

General e-mail, freepress@wpfc.org

Web, www.wpfc.org

Worldwide organization of print and broadcast groups. Promotes freedom of the press and opposes government censorship. Conducts training programs and assists journalists in central and eastern Europe and the developing world. Participates in international conferences.

Print Media

NONPROFIT

American Press Institute (API), *11690 Sunrise Valley Dr., Reston, VA 20191; (703) 620-3611. Fax, (703) 620-5814. William L. Winter, President.*

General e-mail, api@apireston.org

Web, www.americanpressinstitute.org

Promotes the continuing education and career development of newspaper men and women. Conducts seminars, workshops, and conferences. Programs include an intensive computerized newspaper management simulation.

American Society of Newspaper Editors, *11690-B Sunrise Valley Dr., Reston, VA 20191; (703) 453-1122. Fax, (703) 453-1133. Scott Bosley, Executive Director.*

General e-mail, asne@asne.org

Web, www.asne.org

Membership: directing editors of daily newspapers. Campaigns against government secrecy; works to improve the racial mix of newsroom staff; sponsors work/training program for journalists from developing countries; serves as information clearinghouse for newsrooms of daily newspapers; conducts initiative for high school students at www.highschooljournalism.org.

Assn. of American Publishers, *Copyright and New Technology, 50 F St. N.W., #400 20001; (202) 347-3375. Fax, (202) 347-3690. Allan Adler, Vice President, Legal and Government Affairs.*

Web, www.publishers.org

Membership: U.S. publishers of books, journals, tests, and software. Provides members with information on domestic and international trade and market conditions; interests include library and educational funding, educational reform, postal rates, new technology, taxes, copyright, censorship, and libel matters. Monitors legislation and regulations.

Document Management Industries Assn., *433 E. Monroe Ave., Alexandria, VA 22301-1693; (703) 836-6225. Fax, (703) 836-2241. Donald Calman, President.*

Web, www.dmia.org

Membership: manufacturers, suppliers, and distributors of business forms, labels, commercial printing, advertising specialties, electronic forms, or document products. Conducts workshops, seminars, and conferences; sponsors industry research. Monitors legislation and regulations.

Essential Information, *P.O. Box 19405 20036; (202) 387-8030. Fax, (202) 234-5176. John Richard, Director.*

General e-mail, info@essential.org

Web, www.essential.org

Provides writers and the public with information on public policy matters; awards grants to investigative reporters; sponsors conference on investigative journalism. Interests include activities of multinational corporations in developing countries.

Idea Alliance, *100 Daingerfield Rd., Alexandria, VA 22314-2888; (703) 837-1070. Fax, (703) 837-1072. David Steinhardt, President.*

Web, www.idealliance.org

Membership: firms and customers in printing, publishing, and related industries. Assists members in production of color graphics and conducts studies on print media management methods. (Affiliated with Printing Industries of America.)

Graphic Communications International Union,
1900 L St. N.W. 20036; (202) 462-1400. Fax, (202) 721-0600. George Tedeschi, President.
Web, www.gciu.org

Membership: approximately 150,000 members of the print industry, including lithographers, photoengravers, and bookbinders. Assists members with contract negotiation and grievances; conducts training programs and workshops. Monitors legislation and regulations. (Affiliated with the AFL-CIO.)

Greeting Card Assn., *1156 15th St. N.W. 20005; (202) 393-1778. Fax, (202) 331-2714. Richard Crystal, Director.*
Web, www.greetingcard.org

Membership: publishers, printers, and others interested in the greeting card industry. Monitors legislation and regulations.

International Newspaper Financial Executives,
21525 Ridgetop Circle, #200, Sterling, VA 20166; (703) 421-4060. Fax, (703) 421-4068. Robert J. Kasabian, Executive Vice President.
General e-mail, membership@infe.org
Web, www.infe.org

Membership: controllers and chief financial officers of newspapers. Disseminates information on financial aspects of publishing newspapers. Provides members with information on business office technology, including accounting software and spreadsheet applications. Produces publications, conducts seminars, and sponsors an annual convention.

Magazine Publishers of America, *Government Affairs, Washington Office, 1211 Connecticut Ave. N.W., #610 20036; (202) 296-7277. Fax, (202) 296-0343. Jim Cregan, Executive Vice President.*
Web, www.magazine.org

Washington office represents members in all aspects of government relations in Washington and state capitals. (Headquarters in New York.)

National Newspaper Assn., *Washington-Area Office, 510 N. Washington St., #400, Falls Church, VA 22046-3537 (mailing address: P.O. Box 5737, Arlington, VA 22205); (703) 534-1278. Fax, (703) 534-5751. Tonda Rush, Director, Public Policy.*
Web, www.nna.org

Membership: community, weekly, and daily newspapers. Provides members with advisory services; informs members of legislation and regulations that affect their business. Educational arm, the National Newspaper Foundation, conducts management seminars and conferences. (Headquarters in Columbia, Mo.)

National Newspaper Publishers Assn., *3200 13th St. N.W. 20010; (202) 588-8764. Fax, (202) 588-5029. George Curry, Executive Director (Interim); John T. Oliver Jr., President.*
General e-mail, nnpadc@nnpa.org
Web, www.nnpa.org

Membership: newspapers owned by African Americans serving an African American audience. Assists in improving management and quality of the African American press through workshops and merit awards.

Newsletter and Electronic Publishers Assn., *1501 Wilson Blvd., #509, Arlington, VA 22209; (703) 527-2333. Fax, (703) 841-0629. Patricia M. Wysocki, Executive Director.*
General e-mail, nepa@newsletters.org
Web, www.newsletters.org

Membership: newsletter publishers and specialized information services. Serves as information clearinghouse; interests include international marketing. Monitors legislation and regulations. Library open to the public.

Newspaper Assn. of America, *1921 Gallows Rd., #600, Vienna, VA 22182; (703) 902-1600. Fax, (703) 917-0636. John Sturm, President. Library, (703) 902-1692.*
Web, www.naa.org

Membership: daily and weekly newspapers and other papers published in the United States, Canada, other parts of the Western Hemisphere, and Europe. Conducts research and disseminates information on newspaper publishing, including labor relations, legal matters, government relations, technical problems and innovations, telecommunications, economic and statistical data, training programs, and public relations. Library open to the public.

NPES: Assn. for Suppliers of Printing, Publishing, and Converting Technologies, *Communications, 1899 Preston White Dr., Reston, VA 20191-4367; (703) 264-7200. Fax, (703) 620-0994. Carol J. Hurlburt, Marketing Director.*
General e-mail, npes@npes.org
Web, www.npes.org

Trade association representing companies that manufacture and distribute equipment, supplies, systems, software, and services for printing and publishing. (Founded as the National Printing Equipment Assn.)

Printing Industries of America, *100 Daingerfield Rd., Alexandria, VA 22314; (703) 519-8100. Fax, (703) 548-3227. Ray Roper, President.*
General e-mail, gain@printing.org
Web, www.gain.org/servlet/gateway/

Membership: printing firms and businesses that service printing industries. Represents members before Congress and regulatory agencies. Assists members with labor relations, human resources management, and other business management issues. Sponsors graphic arts competition. Monitors legislation and regulations. (Affiliated with Graphic Arts Technical Foundation.)

Screen Printing Technical Foundation, *10015 Main St., Fairfax, VA 22031-3489; (703) 385-1335. Fax, (703) 273-0456. John M. Crawford, Managing Director.*
General e-mail, sgia@sgia.org
Web, www.sgia.org

Provides screen printers, suppliers, manufacturers, and schools with technical support and training; conducts research on production practices and standards. Offers scholarships for college students, grants to schools and teachers, and workshops. (Affiliated with Screenprinting and Graphic Imaging Assn. International.)

Screenprinting and Graphic Imaging Assn. International, *10015 Main St., Fairfax, VA 22031-3489; (703) 385-1335. Fax, (703) 273-0456. Michael Robertson, President.*
General e-mail, sgia@sgia.org
Web, www.sgia.org

Provides screen printers, graphic imagers, digital imagers, suppliers, manufacturers, and educators with technical guidebooks, training videos, managerial support, and guidelines for safety programs. Monitors legislation and regulations.

Society for Service Professionals in Printing, *433 E. Monroe Ave., Alexandria, VA 22301-1693; (703) 684-0044. Fax, (703) 548-9137. Peter Colaianni, Executive Director. Toll-free, (877) 777-7398.*
General e-mail, ssppinfo@sspp.org
Web, www.sspp.org

Individual membership association that works to advance the education and recognition of customer service professionals in the printing industry.

Society of National Assn. Publications, *8405 Greensboro Dr., #800, McLean, VA 22102; (703) 506-3285. Fax, (703) 506-3266. Laura Skoff, Director.*
General e-mail, snapinfo@snaponline.org
Web, www.snaponline.org

Membership: publications owned or controlled by voluntary organizations. Works to develop high publishing standards, including high quality editorial and advertising content in members' publications. Compiles statistics; bestows editorial and graphics awards; monitors postal regulations.

Understanding Government, *School of Communication: American University,* *4400 Massachusetts Ave. N.W. 20016-8017; (202) 885-2665. Charles Peters, Director.*
Web, www.understandinggovt.org

Helps fund long-term journalistic projects on government. Seeks to stimulate more informed reporting and analyses of government agencies.

5 Culture and Recreation

☒ ARTS AND HUMANITIES

AGENCIES

Commission of Fine Arts, *National Building Museum, 401 F St. N.W., #312 20001; (202) 504-2200. Fax, (202) 504-2195. Harry G. Robinson III, Chair; Charles H. Atherton, Secretary.*

Advises the president, congressional committees, and government agencies on designs of public buildings, parks, and statuary.

General Services Administration (GSA), *Center for Design Excellence and the Arts: Office of the Chief Architect, 1800 F St. N.W. 20405; (202) 501-1888. Fax, (202) 501-3393. Marilyn Farley, Director.*

Administers the Art in Architecture Program, which commissions publicly scaled works of art for government buildings and landscapes, and the Fine Arts Program, which manages the GSA's collection of fine artwork that has been commissioned for use in government buildings.

General Services Administration (GSA), *Living Buildings Program, 18th and F Sts. 20405; (202) 501-0514. Fax, (202) 208-5912. Tim Turano, Building Management Specialist.*

Provides information on the opening of federal buildings for public use for cultural, educational, and recreational activities, including conferences, performing arts functions, and art exhibits.

John F. Kennedy Center for the Performing Arts, *2700 F St. N.W. 20566-0001; (202) 416-8000. Fax, (202) 416-8205. James A. Johnson, Chair; Michael Kaiser, President. Press, (202) 416-8841. TTY, (202) 416-8524. Performance and ticket information, (202) 467-4600; toll-free, (800) 444-1324.*
Web, www.kennedy-center.org

National cultural center created by Congress that operates independently; funded in part by federal dollars but primarily through private gifts and sales. Sponsors educational programs; presents American and international performances in theater, music, dance, and film; sponsors the John F. Kennedy Center Education Program, which produces the annual American College Theater Festival; presents and subsidizes events for young people.

National Endowment for the Arts (NEA), *(National Foundation on the Arts and the Humanities), 1100 Pennsylvania Ave. N.W. 20506-0001; (202) 682-5400. Fax, (202) 682-5611. Dana Gioia, Chair. Library, (202) 682-5485. Press, (202) 682-5570. TTY, (202) 682-5496.*
Web, www.arts.gov

Independent federal grant-making agency. Awards grants to nonprofit arts organizations for specified projects in five areas: creativity; arts learning access; heritage and preservation; challenge America; and organizational capacity. Organizations must choose one of the five theme areas for submission of project proposals. Library open to the public by appointment.

National Endowment for the Arts (NEA), *(National Foundation on the Arts and the Humanities), Arts Education, Music, Opera, Presenting, and Multidisciplinary, 1100 Pennsylvania Ave. N.W., #703 20506-0001; (202) 682-5438. Fax, (202) 682-5002. Jan Stunkard, Division Coordinator.*
Web, www.arts.gov

Awards grants to exceptional projects in the arts and arts education to arts organizations, art service organizations, federally recognized tribal communities, state or local government offices, and others.

National Endowment for the Arts (NEA), *(National Foundation on the Arts and the Humanities), Dance, Design, Media Arts, Museums, and Visual Arts, 1100 Pennsylvania Ave. N.W., #726 20506-0001; (202) 682-5452. Fax, (202) 682-5721. Douglas Sonntag, Director, Dance; Robert Frankel, Director, Design (Acting); Ted Libbey, Director, Media Arts; Robert Frankel, Director, Museums and Visual Arts. TTY, (202) 682-5496.*
Web, www.arts.gov

Grant-making theme program for the creation of new work and the presentation of new and existing works of any culture, period, or discipline.

National Endowment for the Arts (NEA), *(National Foundation on the Arts and the Humanities), Folk and Traditional Arts, Literature, Theater, Musical Theater, and Planning and Stabilization, 1100 Pennsylvania Ave. N.W. 20506-0001; (202) 682-5428. Fax, (202) 682-5669. Silvio Lim, Division Coordinator (Acting).*
Web, www.arts.gov

Awards grants to exceptional projects in the arts and arts education to arts organizations, art service organizations, federally recognized tribal communities, state or local government offices, and others.

National Endowment for the Arts (NEA), *(National Foundation on the Arts and the Humanities), Partnership, 1100 Pennsylvania Ave. N.W. 20506-0001; (202) 682-5429. Fax, (202) 682-5602. Jeff Watson, Division Coordinator.*
Web, www.arts.gov

Encourages and administers partnerships with other federal agencies, nonprofit organizations, and public and private funders that further the NEA's mission to increase access to the arts for all Americans and broaden the impact of the arts on American communities through support for artists and arts organizations.

National Endowment for the Humanities (NEH),
(National Foundation on the Arts and the Humanities), 1100 Pennsylvania Ave. N.W., #503 20506; (202) 606-8310. Fax, (202) 606-8588. Bruce Cole, Chair. Information, (202) 606-8400. Library, (202) 606-8244. Press, (202) 606-8446. TTY, (202) 606-8282.

General e-mail, info@neh.gov

Web, www.neh.gov

Independent federal grant-making agency. Awards grants to individuals and institutions for research, scholarship, educational programs, and public programs (including broadcasts, museum exhibitions, lectures, and symposia) in the humanities (defined as study of archeology; history; jurisprudence; language; linguistics; literature; philosophy; comparative religion; ethics; the history, criticism, and theory of the arts; and humanistic aspects of the social sciences). Funds preservation of books, newspapers, historical documents, and photographs.

President's Committee on the Arts and the Humanities, *1100 Pennsylvania Ave. N.W., #526 20506; (202) 682-5409. Fax, (202) 682-5668. Henry Moran, Executive Director.*

Recommends to the president, the National Endowment for the Arts, and the National Endowment for the Humanities ways to promote private sector support for the arts, humanities, and international cultural exchanges; analyzes the effectiveness of federal support.

CONGRESS

House Administration Committee, *1309 LHOB 20515; (202) 225-8281. Fax, (202) 225-9957. Rep. Bob W. Ney, R-Ohio, Chair; Paul Vinovich, Staff Director.*

Web, www.house.gov/cha

Jurisdiction over legislation related to and operations of the Smithsonian Institution.

House Appropriations Committee, *Subcommittee on Interior, B308 RHOB 20515; (202) 225-3081. Fax, (202) 225-9069. Rep. Charles H. Taylor, R-N.C., Chair; Deborah A. Weatherly, Staff Director.*

Web, www.house.gov/appropriations

Jurisdiction over legislation to appropriate funds for the Interior Dept. and government programs for the arts and the humanities, including the Smithsonian Institution, the National Foundation on the Arts and the Humanities, the Commission of Fine Arts, and the Advisory Council on Historic Preservation.

House Education and the Workforce Committee, *Subcommittee on Select Education, 2181 RHOB 20515; (202) 225-4527. Fax, (202) 225-9571. Rep. Peter Hoekstra, R-Mich., Chair; Paula Nowakowski, Staff Director.*

Web, edworkforce.house.gov/members/108th/mem-sed.htm

Jurisdiction over programs related to the arts and humanities, museum services, and arts and artifacts indemnity. Jurisdiction over the National Foundation on the Arts and Humanities Act.

House Government Reform Committee, *Subcommittee on Civil Service and Agency Organization, B373A RHOB 20515; (202) 225-5147. Fax, (202) 225-2373. Rep. Jo Ann Davis, R-Va., Chair; Garry Ewing, Staff Director.*

Web, www.house.gov/reform

Jurisdiction over legislation on holidays and celebrations.

Senate Appropriations Committee, *Subcommittee on Interior and Related Agencies, SD-131 20510; (202) 224-7233. Fax, (202) 228-4532. Sen. Conrad Burns, R-Mont., Chair; Bruce Evans, Clerk.*

Web, appropriations.senate.gov

Jurisdiction over legislation to appropriate funds for government programs for the arts and the humanities, including the Commission of Fine Arts; the National Foundation on the Arts and the Humanities; and the operations and programs of the Smithsonian Institution, the Institute of Museum and Library Services, and the Advisory Council on Historic Preservation.

Senate Health, Education, Labor, and Pensions Committee, *SD-428 20510; (202) 224-5375. Fax, (202) 228-5044. Sen. Judd Gregg, R-N.H., Chair; Sharon Soderstrom, Staff Director. TTY, (202) 224-1975.*

Web, health.senate.gov

Jurisdiction over legislation on government programs for the arts and the humanities, including the National Endowment for the Arts, the National Endowment for the Humanities, and the Institute of Museum and Library Services. Jurisdiction over the Library Services and Construction Act.

Senate Judiciary Committee, *SD-224 20510; (202) 224-5225. Fax, (202) 224-9102. Sen. Orrin G. Hatch, R-Utah, Chair; Makan Delrahim, Chief Counsel.*

Web, judiciary.senate.gov

Jurisdiction over legislation on holidays and celebrations.

Senate Rules and Administration Committee,
SR-305 20510; (202) 224-6352. Fax, (202) 224-5400. Sen. Trent Lott, R-Miss., Chair; Susan Wells, Staff Director.

Web, rules.senate.gov

Jurisdiction over legislation concerning the Smithsonian Institution and the U.S. Botanic Garden.

NONPROFIT

America the Beautiful Fund, *1730 K St. N.W., #1002 20006; (202) 638-1649. Fax, (202) 204-0028. Nanine Bilski, President.*
Web, www.america-the-beautiful.org

National service organization that promotes community self-help. Offers advisory services; grants; free seeds for civic and charitable volunteer programs; and national recognition awards to local community groups for activities that promote America's heritage, culture, environment, public parks, and human services.

American Arts Alliance, *1869 Park Rd. N.W. 20010; (202) 387-8300. Fax, (202) 797-9856. Rick Swartz, Executive Director.*
General e-mail, aaa@artswire.org
Web, www.artswire.org/~aaa

Membership: symphony orchestras; art museums; arts presenters; and theater, dance, and opera companies. Advocates national policies that recognize the important role played by the arts in American life.

Americans for the Arts, *1000 Vermont Ave. N.W., 6th Floor 20005; (202) 371-2830. Fax, (202) 371-0424. Robert L. Lynch, President.*
Web, www.AmericansForTheArts.org

Membership: groups and individuals dedicated to advancing the arts and culture in U.S. communities. Provides information on programs, activities, and administration of local arts agencies; on funding sources and guidelines; and on government policies and programs. Monitors legislation and regulations.

Aspen Institute, *Policy Programs, 1 Dupont Circle N.W., #700 20036; (202) 736-5800. Fax, (202) 467-0790. Charles M. Firestone, Director of Communications and Society Program.*
Web, www.aspeninst.org

Conducts seminars on Western civilization and other traditions and cultures; conducts studies and workshops on critical contemporary issues. Fields of interest include communications, energy, justice and the law, science and technology, education, international relations, social policies, rural economy, and the environment.

Assn. of Performing Arts Presenters, *1112 16th St. N.W., #400 20036; (202) 833-2787. Fax, (202) 833-1543. Sandra Gibson, President.*
General e-mail, artpres@artspresenters.org
Web, www.artspresenters.org

Connects performing artists to audiences and communities around the world. Facilitates the work of presenters, artist managers, and consultants through continuing education, regranting programs, and legislative advocacy.

Federation of State Humanities Councils, *1600 Wilson Blvd., #902, Arlington, VA 22209; (703) 908-9700. Fax, (703) 908-9706. Gail Leftwich, President.*
Web, www.acls.org/fshc.htm

Membership: humanities councils from U.S. states and territories. Provides members with information; forms partnerships with other organizations and with the private sector to promote the humanities. Monitors legislation and regulations.

International Network of Performing and Visual Arts Schools, *733 15th St. N.W., #330 20005; (202) 966-2216. Fax, (202) 638-7895. Catherine Thompson, President.*
Web, www.artsschoolsnetwork.org

Membership: schools of the arts, universities, and allied arts organizations from around the world. Supports and serves the leaders of specialized arts schools, fosters communication, and promotes development of new schools of the arts.

National Assembly of State Arts Agencies, *1029 Vermont Ave. N.W., 2nd Floor 20005; (202) 347-6352. Fax, (202) 737-0526. Jonathan Katz, Chief Executive Officer. TTY, (202) 347-5948.*
General e-mail, nasaa@nasaa-arts.org
Web, www.nasaa-arts.org

Membership: state and jurisdictional arts agencies. Provides members with information, resources, and representation. Interests include arts programs for rural and underserved populations, and the arts as a catalyst for economic development. Monitors legislation and regulations.

National Humanities Alliance, *21 Dupont Circle N.W., #604 20036; (202) 296-4994. Fax, (202) 872-0884. John H. Hammer, Director.*
Web, www.nhalliance.org

Represents scholarly and professional humanities associations; associations of museums, libraries, and historical societies; higher education institutions; state humanities councils; and independent and university-based research centers. Promotes the interests of individuals engaged in research, writing, and teaching.

National League of American Pen Women, *1300 17th St. N.W. 20036-1973; (202) 785-1997. Fax, (202) 452-6868. Bernice Reid, National President.*

Web, www.americanpenwomen.org

Promotes the development of the creative talents of professional women in the fields of art, letters, and music composition. Conducts and promotes literary, educational, and charitable activities. Offers scholarships, workshops, and discussion groups.

Wolf Trap Foundation for the Performing Arts,
1645 Trap Rd., Vienna, VA 22182; (703) 255-1900. Fax, (703) 255-1918. Terrence D. Jones, President.
Web, www.wolf-trap.org

Established by Congress to administer Wolf Trap Farm Park for the Performing Arts, today called Wolf Trap National Park for the Performing Arts. Sponsors performances in theater, music, and dance. Conducts educational programs for children, internships for college students, career-entry programs for young singers, and professional training for teachers and performers.

Education

AGENCIES

Education Dept., Arts in Education, *400 Maryland Ave. S.W. 20202-6341; (202) 260-2487. Fax, (202) 205-5630. Shelton Allen, Program Specialist.*
Web, www.ed.gov

Provides information on arts education programs. Awards grants to the Kennedy Center's arts and education program and to Very Special Arts, a program for the disabled.

John F. Kennedy Center for the Performing Arts,
Alliance for Arts Education Network, *2700 F St. N.W. 20566-0001; (202) 416-8845. Fax, (202) 416-8802. Kathi Levin, Director.*
General e-mail, kcaaen@kennedy-center.org
Web, www.kennedy-center.org/education/kcaaen

Supports state alliances with operating and program grants and information. Alliances are statewide arts education organizations that provide communities with services including teacher professional development, conferences, and arts education programming.

John F. Kennedy Center for the Performing Arts,
Education, *2700 F St. N.W. 20566-0004; (202) 416-8800. Fax, (202) 416-8802. Derek Gordon, Vice President.*
Web, www.kennedy-center.org/education

Establishes and supports state committees to encourage arts education in schools (Kennedy Center Alliance for Arts Education Network); promotes community partnerships between performing arts centers and school systems (Partners in Education); provides teachers with professional development opportunities; offers perfor-

mances for young people and families; arranges artist and company residencies in schools; sponsors the National Symphony Orchestra education program; presents lectures, demonstrations, and classes in the performing arts for the general public; offers internships in arts management and fellowships for visiting artists; and produces annually the Kennedy Center American College Theater Festival.

National Endowment for the Arts (NEA), *(National Foundation on the Arts and the Humanities), Arts Education, Music, Opera, Presenting, and Multidisciplinary,* *1100 Pennsylvania Ave. N.W., #703 20506-0001; (202) 682-5438. Fax, (202) 682-5002. Jan Stunkard, Division Coordinator.*
Web, www.arts.gov

Awards grants to state arts agencies and arts organizations to support arts education of students in grades pre-K through 12. Awards grants to nonprofit groups for development of community-based educational arts programs that reflect the culture of minority, inner city, rural, and tribal communities. Supports projects that create, present, or teach art. Awards grants to presenting organizations.

National Endowment for the Humanities (NEH), *(National Foundation on the Arts and the Humanities), Research and Education,* *1100 Pennsylvania Ave. N.W., #318 20506; (202) 606-8200. Fax, (202) 606-8394. James Herbert, Director.*
General e-mail, education@neh.gov
Web, www.neh.gov

Advocates the improvement of education in the humanities. Supports projects such as curricula and materials development and faculty training and development. Offers fellowships, stipends, seminars, and institutes for higher education faculty, school teachers, and independent scholars. Conducts research.

National Gallery of Art, *Education, 6th St. and Constitution Ave. N.W. 20565 (mailing address: 2000B S. Club Dr., Landover, MD 20785); (202) 842-6273. Fax, (202) 842-6935. Lynn Russell, Head. TTY, (202) 842-6176. Order desk, (202) 842-6263.*
General e-mail, EdResources@nga.gov
Web, www.nga.gov

Serves as an educational arm of the gallery; lends audiovisual educational materials free of charge to schools, colleges, community groups, libraries, and individuals on a free loan basis. Answers written and telephone inquiries about European and American art.

Smithsonian Center for Education and Museum Studies, *900 Jefferson Dr. S.W., #1163 20560 (mailing address: P.O. Box 37012, A&I 1163, MRC 402 20013-7012); (202) 357-2425. Fax, (202) 357-2116. Stephanie Norby, Executive Director. TTY, (202) 357-1696.*
General e-mail, educate@.si.edu
Web, educate.si.edu

Serves as the Smithsonian's central education office. Provides elementary and secondary teachers with programs, publications, audiovisual materials, regional workshops, and summer courses on using museums and primary source materials as teaching tools. Publishes books and other educational materials for teachers.

Smithsonian Institution, *Smithsonian Associates, 1100 Jefferson Dr. S.W., #3077 20560 (mailing address: P.O. Box 23293 20026-3293); (202) 357-3030. Fax, (202) 786-2034. Mara Mayor, Director. TTY, (202) 633-9467.*
General e-mail, www.smithsonianassociates.si.edu
Web, rap@tsa.si.edu

National cultural and educational membership organization that offers courses and lectures for adults and young people. Presents films and offers study tours on arts-, humanities-, and science-related subjects; sponsors performances, studio arts workshops, and research.

NONPROFIT

National Art Education Assn., *1916 Association Dr., Reston, VA 20191-1590; (703) 860-8000. Fax, (703) 860-2960. Thomas A. Hatfield, Executive Director.*
General e-mail, naea@dgs.dgsys.com
Web, www.naea-reston.org

Membership: art teachers (elementary through university), museum staff, and manufacturers and suppliers of art materials. Issues publications on art education theory and practice, research, and current trends; provides technical assistance to art educators. Sponsors awards.

National Assn. of Schools of Art and Design, *11250 Roger Bacon Dr., #21, Reston, VA 20190; (703) 437-0700. Fax, (703) 437-6312. Samuel Hope, Executive Director.*
General e-mail, info@arts-accredit.org
Web, www.arts-accredit.org

Accrediting agency for educational programs in art and design. Provides information on art and design programs at the postsecondary level; offers professional development for executives of art and design programs.

Young Audiences, *1330 New Hampshire Ave. N.W. 20036; (202) 887-0630. Fax, (202) 887-0633. Marie C. Barksdale, Executive Director.*

General e-mail, yadc4arted@aol.com
Web, www.youngaudiences.com

Sponsors professional musicians, actors, and dancers who present arts education programs in U.S. schools; promotes career opportunities in the performing arts. Seeks to enhance the education of students through exposure to the performing arts. Researches techniques and disseminates information on developing arts education programs.

Film, Photography, and Broadcasting

AGENCIES

American Film Institute (AFI), *Silver Theater and Cultural Center,* *8633 Colesville Rd., Silver Spring, MD 20910; (301) 495-6700. Fax, (301) 495-6777. Murray Horowitz, Director. Recorded information, (202) 833-2348.*
Web, www.afi.com

Preserves and catalogs films; supports research. Shows films of historical and artistic importance. AFI theater open to the public. Films also shown at the John F. Kennedy Center for the Performing Arts in Washington.

National Archives and Records Administration (NARA), *Motion Picture, Sound, and Video,* *8601 Adelphi Rd., #3340, College Park, MD 20740-6001; (301) 837-3520. Debra Lelansky, Manager.*
General e-mail, mopix@nara.gov
Web, www.archives.gov

Selects and preserves audiovisual records produced or acquired by federal agencies; maintains collections from private sector, including newsreels. Research room open to the public.

National Archives and Records Administration (NARA), *Still Pictures,* *8601 Adelphi Rd., #5360, College Park, MD 20740-6001; (301) 837-3530. Fax, (301) 837-3621. Robert E. Richardson, Director. Reference, (301) 837-0561.*
General e-mail, stillpix@nara.gov
Web, www.archives.gov/research_room/media_formats/photographs_in_college_park.html

Provides the public with copies of still pictures from around the world; supplies guides to these materials. Collection includes still pictures from more than 150 federal agencies.

National Endowment for the Arts (NEA), *(National Foundation on the Arts and the Humanities), Dance, Design, Media Arts, Museums, and Visual Arts,* *1100 Pennsylvania Ave. N.W., #726 20506-0001; (202)*

682-5452. Fax, (202) 682-5721. Douglas Sonntag, Director, Dance; Robert Frankel, Director, Design (Acting); Ted Libbey, Director, Media Arts; Robert Frankel, Director, Museums and Visual Arts. TTY, (202) 682-5496.
Web, www.arts.gov

Awards grants to nonprofit organizations for film, video, and radio productions; supports film and video exhibitions and workshops.

National Endowment for the Humanities (NEH), *(National Foundation on the Arts and the Humanities), Public Programs,* 1100 Pennsylvania Ave. N.W., #426 20506; (202) 606-8267. Fax, (202) 606-8557. Nancy Rodger, Director.
General e-mail, publicpgms@neh.gov
Web, www.neh.gov

Promotes public appreciation of the humanities through support of quality public programs of broad significance, reach, and impact. Awards grants for projects that meet NEH goals and standards, including excellence in content and format, broad public appeal, and wide access to diverse audiences.

CONGRESS

Library of Congress, *Motion Picture, Broadcasting, and Recorded Sound Division,* 101 Independence Ave. S.E. 20540-4690; (202) 707-5840. Fax, (202) 707-2371. Gregory Lukow, Chief (Acting). Recorded sound reference center, (202) 707-7833. Motion picture and television reading room, (202) 707-8572.
Web, www.loc.gov/rr/mopic

Collections include archives of representative motion pictures (1942–present); historic films (1894–1915); early American films (1898–1926); German, Italian, and Japanese features, newsreels, and documentary films (1930–1945); and a selected collection of stills, newspaper reviews, and U.S. government productions. Collection also includes television programs of all types (1948–present), radio broadcasts (1924–present), and sound recordings (1890–present). Tapes the library's concert series and other musical events for radio broadcast; produces recordings of music and poetry for sale to the public. American Film Institute film archives are interfiled with the division's collections. Use of collections restricted to scholars and researchers; reading room open to the public.

Library of Congress, *National Film Preservation Board,* 101 Independence Ave. S.E. 20540-4710; (202) 707-6240. Fax, (202) 707-2371. Gregory Lukow, Administrator. TTY, (202) 707-6362.

Web, www.loc.gov/film

Administers the National Film Preservation Plan. Establishes guidelines and receives nominations for the annual selection of twenty-five films of cultural, historical, or aesthetic significance; selections are entered in the National Film Registry to ensure archival preservation in their original form.

Library of Congress, *Prints and Photographs,* 101 Independence Ave. S.E. 20540-4730; (202) 707-5836. Fax, (202) 707-6647. Jeremy Adamson, Chief. TTY, (202) 707-9051. Reading room, (202) 707-6394.
Web, www.loc.gov/rr/print

Maintains Library of Congress's collection of pictorial material, not in book format, totaling more than 13.5 million items. U.S. and international collections include artists' prints; historical prints, posters, and drawings; photographs (chiefly documentary); political and social cartoons; and architectural plans, drawings, prints, and photographs. Reference service provided in the Prints and Photographs Reading Room. Reproductions of nonrestricted material available through the Library of Congress's Photoduplication Service; prints and photographs may be borrowed through the Exhibits Office for exhibits by qualified institutions. A portion of the collections and an overview of reference services are available on the World Wide Web.

NONPROFIT

Council on International Nontheatrical Events, 1112 16th St. N.W., #510 20036; (202) 785-1136. Fax, (202) 785-4114. David L. Weiss, Executive Director.
General e-mail, info@cine.org
Web, www.cine.org

Selects and enters nontheatrical films in international film festivals; holds semiannual screening competitions and annual showcase and awards ceremonies.

Library of American Broadcasting, *University of Maryland, Hornbake Library,* College Park, MD 20742; (301) 405-9160. Fax, (301) 314-2634. Chuck Howell, Curator.
General e-mail, bp50@umail.umd.edu
Web, www.lib.umd.edu/UMCP/LAB

Maintains library and archives on the history of radio and television. Open to the public.

Motion Picture Assn. of America, 1600 Eye St. N.W. 20006; (202) 293-1966. Fax, (202) 452-9823. Jack Valenti, President. Anti-piracy hotline, (800) 662-6797.
Web, www.mpaa.org

Membership: motion picture producers and distributors. Advises state and federal governments on copyrights, censorship, cable broadcasting, and other topics; administers volunteer rating system for motion pictures; works to prevent video piracy. (Headquarters in Encino, Calif.)

Language and Literature

AGENCIES

National Endowment for the Arts (NEA), *(National Foundation on the Arts and the Humanities), Folk and Traditional Arts, Literature, Theater, Musical Theater, and Planning and Stabilization,* 1100 Pennsylvania Ave. N.W. 20506-0001; (202) 682-5428. Fax, (202) 682-5669. Silvio Lim, Division Coordinator (Acting).
Web, www.arts.gov

Awards grants to published writers, poets, and translators of prose and poetry; awards grants to small presses and literary magazines that publish poetry and fiction.

CONGRESS

Library of Congress, *Center for the Book,* 101 Independence Ave. S.E., #650 20540-4920; (202) 707-5221. Fax, (202) 707-0269. John Y. Cole, Director.
General e-mail, cfbook@loc.gov
Web, www.loc.gov/loc/cfbook

Seeks to broaden public appreciation of books, reading, and libraries; sponsors lectures and conferences on the educational and cultural role of the book worldwide, including the history of books and printing, television and the printed word, and the publishing and production of books; cooperates with state centers and with other organizations. Projects and programs are privately funded except for basic administrative support from the Library of Congress.

Library of Congress, *Children's Literature Center,* 101 Independence Ave. S.E. 20540-4620; (202) 707-5535. Fax, (202) 707-4632. Sybille Jagusch, Chief.
Web, www.loc.gov

Provides reference and information services by telephone, by correspondence, and in person; maintains reference materials on all aspects of the study of children's literature. Sponsors lectures, symposia, and exhibits. Consultation by appointment only.

Library of Congress, *Poetry and Literature,* 101 Independence Ave. S.E. 20540-4861; (202) 707-5395. Fax, (202) 707-9946. Billy Collins, Poet Laureate. Recording, (202) 707-5394.
Web, www.loc.gov/poetry

Advises the library on public literary programs and on the acquisition of literary materials. Sponsors public poetry and fiction readings, lectures, symposia, occa-

sional dramatic performances, and other literary events. Arranges for poets to record readings of their work for the library's tape archive. The poet laureate is appointed by the Librarian of Congress on the basis of literary distinction.

NONPROFIT

Alliance Française de Washington DC, 2142 Wyoming Ave. N.W. 20008; (202) 234-7911. Fax, (202) 234-0125. Laurent Mellier, Executive Director.
General e-mail, alliance@francedc.org
Web, www.francedc.org

Offers courses in French language and literature; presents lectures and cultural events; maintains library of French-language publications for members; offers corporate language training programs.

American Councils for International Education, *American Council of Teachers of Russian,* 1776 Massachusetts Ave. N.W., #700 20036; (202) 833-7522. Fax, (202) 833-7523. Dan Davidson, President.
General e-mail, general@americancouncils.org
Web, www.actr.org

Conducts educational exchanges for high school, university, and graduate school students as well as scholars with the countries of the former Soviet Union and Eastern Europe. Assists the countries of the former Soviet Union in implementing education reforms, advises them on academic testing, and provides them with language instruction materials.

American Poetry and Literacy Project, P.O. Box 53445 20009; (202) 338-1109. Andrew Carroll, Executive Director.
Web, www.poets.org/aplp

Donates new books of poetry to schools, libraries, hospitals, homeless shelters, nursing homes, hotels, and other public places around the country to promote literacy.

Brazilian-American Cultural Institute, 4719 Wisconsin Ave. 20016-4609; (202) 362-8334. Fax, (202) 362-8337. José M. Neistein, Executive Director.
General e-mail, info@bacidc.org
Web, www.bacidc.org

Conducts courses in Portuguese language and Brazilian literature; sponsors art exhibitions, films, concerts, and other public presentations on Brazilian culture. Library open to the public.

Center for Applied Linguistics, 4646 40th St. N.W., #200 20016-1859; (202) 362-0700. Fax, (202) 362-3740. Donna Christian, President.

General e-mail, info@cal.org

Web, www.cal.org

Research and technical assistance organization that serves as clearinghouse on application of linguistics to practical language problems. Interests include English as a second language (ESL), teacher training and material development, language education, language proficiency test development, bilingual education, and sociolinguistics.

English First, 8001 Forbes Pl., #102, Springfield, VA 22151; (703) 321-8818. Fax, (703) 321-8408. Jim Boulet Jr., Executive Director.

Web, www.englishfirst.org

Seeks to make English the official language of the United States. Advocates policies which make English education available to all children. Monitors legislation and regulations. Opposes bilingual education and ballots and Clinton Executive Order 13166.

Folger Shakespeare Library, 201 E. Capitol St. S.E. 20003; (202) 544-4600. Fax, (202) 544-7520. Gail Kern Paster, Director.

Web, www.folger.edu

Administered by the trustees of Amherst College. Maintains major Shakespearean and Renaissance materials; awards fellowships for postdoctoral research; presents concerts, theater performances, poetry and fiction readings, exhibits, and other public events. Offers educational programs for elementary and secondary school students and teachers.

Hurston/Wright Foundation, 6525 Belcrest Rd., #531, Hyattsville, MD 20782; (301) 683-2134. Marita Golden, President.

General e-mail, info@hurston-wright.org

Web, www.hurston-wright.org

Supports the world community of writers of African descent. Presents monetary awards to writers and sponsors writers' workshops.

Japan-America Society of Washington, 1020 19th St. N.W., Lower Lobby #40 20036; (202) 833-2210. Fax, (202) 833-2456. JoAnna Phillips, Executive Director.

General e-mail, jaswdc@us-japan.org

Web, www.us-japan.org/dc

Assists Japanese performing artists; offers lectures and films on Japan; operates a Japanese-language school and an annual language competition for high school students; awards scholarships to college students studying in the Washington area. Maintains library for members.

Joint National Committee for Languages, 4646 40th St. N.W., #310 20016; (202) 966-8477. Fax, (202) 966-8310. J. David Edwards, Executive Director.

General e-mail, info@languagepolicy.org

Web, www.languagepolicy.org

Membership: translators, interpreters, and associations of language teachers (primary through postsecondary level). Supports a national policy on language study and international education. Provides forum and clearinghouse for professional language and international education associations. National Council for Languages and International Studies is the political arm.

Linguistic Society of America, 1325 18th St. N.W., #211 20036; (202) 835-1714. Fax, (202) 835-1717. Margaret W. Reynolds, Executive Director.

General e-mail, lsa@lsadc.org

Web, www.lsadc.org

Membership: individuals and institutions interested in the scientific analysis of language. Holds linguistic institutes every other year.

National Foreign Language Center (University of Maryland), 7100 Baltimore Ave., #300, College Park, MD 20740; (301) 403-1750. Fax, (301) 403-1754. Richard Brecht, Director.

General e-mail, info@nflc.org

Web, www.nflc.org

Research and policy organization that develops new strategies to strengthen foreign language competence in the United States. Conducts research on national language needs and assists policymakers in identifying priorities, allocating resources, and designing programs. Interests include the role of foreign language in higher education, national competence in critical languages, ethnic language maintenance, and K–12 and postsecondary language programs.

PEN/Faulkner Foundation, c/o Folger Shakespeare Library, 201 E. Capitol St. S.E. 20003-1094; (202) 675-0345. Fax, (202) 608-1719. Robert Stone, Chair; Janice Delaney, Executive Director.

Web, www.penfaulkner.org

Sponsors an annual juried award for American fiction. Brings authors to public schools to teach classes. Holds readings by authors of new American fiction.

U.S. English, 1747 Pennsylvania Ave. N.W., #1050 20006; (202) 833-0100. Fax, (202) 833-0108. Mauro E. Mujica, Chair.

General e-mail, info@us-english.org

Web, www.us-english.org

Advocates English as the official language of federal and state government. Affiliate U.S. English Foundation promotes English language education for immigrants.

The Writer's Center, *4508 Walsh St., Bethesda, MD 20815; (301) 654-8664. Fax, (301) 654-8667. Karen Goodwin, Executive Director.*
General e-mail, postmaster@writer.org
Web, www.writer.org

Membership: writers, editors, graphic artists, and interested individuals. Sponsors workshops in writing and graphic arts, and a reading series of poetry, fiction, and plays. Provides access to word processing, desktop publishing, and design equipment; maintains a book gallery.

Museums

AGENCIES

Anacostia Museum and Center for African American History and Culture *(Smithsonian Institution), 1901 Fort Place S.E. 20020 (mailing address: P.O. Box 37012, MRC 520 20013-7012); (202) 287-3306. Fax, (202) 287-3183. Steven Newsome, Director. TTY, (202) 357-1729.*
Web, anacostia.si.edu

Explores American history, society, and creative expression from an African American perspective and encourages the collection and preservation of materials that reflect that history and tradition.

Arthur M. Sackler Gallery *(Smithsonian Institution), 1050 Independence Ave. S.W. 20560-0707 (mailing address: P.O. Box 37012, MRC 707 20013-7012); (202) 357-4880. Fax, (202) 357-4911. Julian Raby, Director. Press, (202) 357-4880. TTY, (202) 357-1729. Public programs, (202) 357-2700 (recording).*
General e-mail, asiainfo@asia.si.edu
Web, www.asia.si.edu

Exhibits Asian and Near Eastern art drawn from collections in the United States and abroad; features international exhibitions and public programs. Presents films, lectures, and concerts. Library open to the public.

Federal Council on the Arts and the Humanities *(National Foundation on the Arts and the Humanities), 1100 Pennsylvania Ave. N.W. 20506; (202) 682-5574. Fax, (202) 682-5603. Alice M. Whelihan, Indemnity Administrator.*

Membership: leaders of federal agencies sponsoring arts-related activities. Administers the Arts and Artifacts Indemnity Act, which helps museums reduce the costs of commercial insurance for international exhibits.

Frederick Douglass National Historic Site, *1411 W St. S.E. 20020; (202) 426-5961. Fax, (202) 426-0880. Paul Gross, Site Manager (Acting).*
Web, www.nps.gov/frdo

Administered by the National Park Service. Museum of the life and work of abolitionist Frederick Douglass and his family. Offers tours of the home and special programs, such as documentary films, videos, and slide presentations; maintains visitors' center and bookstore. Reservations are required.

Freer Gallery of Art *(Smithsonian Institution), 1050 Independence Ave. S.W. 20560 (mailing address: P.O. Box 37012, MRC 707 20013-7012); (202) 357-4880. Fax, (202) 357-4911. Julian Raby, Director. TTY, (202) 357-1729. Public programs, (202) 357-2700 (recording).*
Web, www.asia.si.edu

Exhibits Asian art from the Mediterranean to Japan and late nineteenth and early twentieth century American art from its permanent collection, including works by James McNeill Whistler. Presents films, lectures, and concerts. Library open to the public.

Hirshhorn Museum and Sculpture Garden *(Smithsonian Institution), 7th St. and Independence Ave. S.W. 20560 (mailing address: P.O. Box 37012, HMSG, MRC 350 20013-7012); (202) 357-3091. Fax, (202) 786-2682. Ned Rifkin, Director. Information, (202) 357-2700. Press, (202) 357-1618. TTY, (202) 633-8043. Additional fax number, (202) 357-3151.*
General e-mail, inquiries@hmsg.si.edu
Web, www.hirshhorn.si.edu

Preserves and exhibits contemporary American and European paintings and sculpture. Offers films, lectures, concerts, and tours of the collection.

Institute of Museum and Library Services, *1100 Pennsylvania Ave. N.W. 20506; (202) 606-8536. Fax, (202) 606-8591. Robert S. Martin, Director. Information, (202) 606-8539. TTY, (202) 606-8636.*
General e-mail, info@imls.gov
Web, www.imls.gov

Independent agency established by Congress to assist museums and libraries in increasing and improving their services. Awards grants for general operating support, conservation projects, and museum assessment to museums of all disciplines and budget sizes; helps fund museum associations.

National Endowment for the Arts (NEA), *(National Foundation on the Arts and the Humanities), Dance, Design, Media Arts, Museums, and Visual Arts, 1100 Pennsylvania Ave. N.W., #726 20506-0001; (202)*

MUSEUM EDUCATION PROGRAMS

Alexandria Archaeology, (703) 838-4399

American Assn. of Museums, Museum Assessment Program, (202) 289-9118

Arlington Arts Center, (703) 797-4573

Assn. of Science-Technology Centers, (202) 783-7200

B'nai B'rith Klutznick Museum, (202) 857-6583

C & O Canal, (301) 739-4200

Capital Children's Museum, (202) 675-4120

Corcoran Gallery of Art, (202) 639-1700

Daughters of the American Revolution (DAR) Museum, (202) 879-3241

Decatur House, (202) 842-0915

Dumbarton Oaks, (202) 339-6409

Federal Reserve Board, (202) 452-3686

Folger Shakespeare Library, (202) 675-0306

Gadsby's Tavern Museum, (703) 838-4242

Historical Society of Washington, DC, (202) 785-2068

J.F.K. Center for the Performing Arts—Alliance for Arts Education, (202) 416-8800

Lyceum, (703) 838-4994

Mount Vernon, (703) 780-2000

National Arboretum, (202) 245-2726

National Archives, (202) 501-5210

National Building Museum, (202) 272-2448

National Gallery of Art, (202) 842-6246

National Museum of Women in the Arts, (202) 783-7370

Navy Museum, (202) 433-4882

Octagon Museum, (202) 638-3221

Phillips Collection, (202) 387-2151

Smithsonian Institution

  Central education office, (202) 357-2425

  Anacostia Museum, (202) 357-1300

  Arthur M. Sackler Gallery, (202) 357-4880

  Freer Gallery of Art, (202) 357-4880

  Friends of the National Zoo, (202) 673-4954

  Hirshhorn Museum and Sculpture Garden, (202) 357-3235

  National Air and Space Museum, (202) 786-2106

  National Museum of African Art, (202) 357-4600

  National Museum of American Art, (202) 357-1300

  National Museum of American History, (202) 357-3229

  National Museum of Natural History, (202) 357-2747

  National Portrait Gallery, (202) 357-2920

  Renwick Gallery, (202) 357-2531

Textile Museum, (202) 483-0981

Woodrow Wilson House, (202) 387-4062

682-5452. Fax, (202) 682-5721. *Douglas Sonntag, Director, Dance; Robert Frankel, Director, Design (Acting); Ted Libbey, Director, Media Arts; Robert Frankel, Director, Museums and Visual Arts.* TTY, (202) 682-5496.
Web, www.arts.gov

Awards grants to museums for installing and cataloging permanent and special collections; traveling exhibits; training museum professionals; conserving and preserving museum collections; and developing arts-related educational programs.

National Gallery of Art, *6th St. and Constitution Ave. N.W. 20565 (mailing address: 2000B S. Club Dr., Landover, MD 20785); (202) 737-4215. Fax, (202) 842-2356. Earl A. Powell III, Director. Press, (202) 842-6353. TTY, (202) 842-6176.*
Web, www.nga.gov

Created by a joint resolution of Congress, the museum is a public-private partnership that preserves and exhibits European and American paintings, sculpture, and decorative and graphic arts. Offers concerts,

demonstrations, lectures, symposia, films, tours, and teachers' workshops to enhance exhibitions, the permanent collection, and related topics. Lends art to museums in all fifty states and abroad through the National Lending Service. Publishes monthly calendar of events.

National Museum of African Art *(Smithsonian Institution), 950 Independence Ave. S.W. 20560-0708; (202) 357-4600. Fax, (202) 357-4879. Sharon Patton, Director. TTY, (202) 357-4814.*
Web, www.nmafa.si.edu/default.htm

Collects, studies, and exhibits traditional and contemporary arts of Africa. Exhibits feature objects from the permanent collection and from private and public collections worldwide. Library and photo archive open to the public by appointment.

National Museum of American History/Behring Center *(Smithsonian Institution), 14th St. and Constitution Ave. N.W. 20560-0622; (202) 357-2510. Fax, (202) 786-2624. Brent B. Glass, Director. Information, (202)*

357-3129. Library, (202) 357-2414. TTY, (202) 357-1563. General e-mail, viarcmx@sivm.si.edu

Web, www.americanhistory.si.edu

Collects and exhibits objects representative of American cultural history, applied arts, industry, national and military history, and science and technology. Library open to the public by appointment.

National Museum of Health and Medicine (*Defense Dept.*), *Walter Reed Medical Center, Bldg. 54 South 20307 (mailing address: 6825 16th St. N.W. 20036-6000); (202) 782-2200. Fax, (202) 782-3573. Dr. Adrianne Noe, Director.*

Web, www.natmedmuse.afip.org

Collects and exhibits medical models, tools, and teaching aids. Maintains permanent exhibits on the human body, AIDS, Civil War medicine, and military contributions to medicine; collects specimens illustrating a broad range of pathological conditions. Open to the public. Study collection available for scholars by appointment.

National Museum of the American Indian (*Smithsonian Institution*), *470 L'Enfant Plaza, #7102 20560; (202) 287-2523. Fax, (202) 287-2538. W. Richard West, Director.*

Web, www.americanindian.si.edu

Established by Congress in 1989 the museum, scheduled to open in 2004, will collect, preserve, study, and exhibit American Indian languages, literature, history, art, and culture.

National Portrait Gallery (*Smithsonian Institution*), *750 9th St. N.W., #8300 20560-0973 (mailing address: P.O. Box 37012, Victor Bldg., #8300, MRC 973 20013-7012); (202) 275-1738. Fax, (202) 275-1887. Marc Pachter, Director; Carolyn K. Carr, Deputy Director. Library, (202) 275-1913. TTY, (202) 357-1729.*

Web, www.npg.si.edu

Exhibits paintings, photographs, sculpture, drawings, and prints of individuals who have made significant contributions to the history, development, and culture of the United States. Library open to the public.

Renwick Gallery of the Smithsonian American Art Museum (*Smithsonian Institution*), *17th St. and Pennsylvania Ave. N.W. 20006 (mailing address: Washington, DC 20560-0510); (202) 357-2700. Kenneth Trapp, Curator-in-Charge. TTY, (202) 357-1729.*

Web, www.americanart.si.edu/collections/renwick/main.html

Curatorial department of the National Museum of American Art. Exhibits nineteenth to twenty-first-century American crafts.

Smithsonian American Art Museum (*Smithsonian Institution*), *8th and G Sts. N.W. 20560 (mailing address: Washington, DC 20560-0970); (202) 275-1500. Fax, (202) 357-2528. Elizabeth Broun, Director. Press, (202) 275-1594. TTY, (202) 357-1729.*

General e-mail, info@saam.si.edu

Web, www.americanart.si.edu

Exhibits and interprets American painting, sculpture, photographs, folk art, and graphic art from eighteenth century to present in permanent collection and temporary exhibition galleries.(Closed for renovation until fall 2004.)

Smithsonian Institution, *1000 Jefferson Dr. S.W., #205 20560 (mailing address: P.O. Box 37012, SI Bldg., #153, MRC 010 20013-7012); (202) 357-1846. Fax, (202) 786-2515. Lawrence M. Small, Secretary; David L. Evans, Under Secretary of Science; Sheila Burke, Under Secretary of National Museums and American Programs. Information, (202) 357-2700. Library, (202) 357-2240. Press, (202) 357-2627. TTY, (202) 357-1729. Recorded daily museum highlights, (202) 357-2020. Locator, (202) 357-1300.*

General e-mail, info@si.edu

Web, www.si.edu

Conducts research; publishes results of studies, explorations, and investigations; maintains study and reference collections on science, culture, and history; maintains exhibitions in the arts, American history, technology, aeronautics and space exploration, and natural history. Smithsonian Institution sites in Washington, D.C., include the Anacostia Museum, Archives of American Art, Arthur M. Sackler Gallery, Arts and Industries Building, Freer Gallery of Art, Hirshhorn Museum and Sculpture Garden, National Air and Space Museum, National Museum of African Art, National Museum of American Art, National Museum of American History, National Museum of Natural History, National Portrait Gallery, National Postal Museum, National Zoological Park, S. Dillon Ripley Center, Smithsonian Institution Building, and Renwick Gallery. Supports affiliates in New York, Arizona, Florida, Maryland, Massachusetts, and Panama. Autonomous bureaus affiliated with the Smithsonian Institution include John F. Kennedy Center for the Performing Arts, National Gallery of Art, and Woodrow Wilson International Center for Scholars. Libraries open to the public by appointment; library catalogs are available on the Web.

Smithsonian Institution, *Center for Education and Museum Studies, 900 Jefferson Dr. S.W. 20560-1163 (mailing address: P.O. Box 37012, A&I 1163, MRC 402 20013-7012); (202) 357-2425. Fax, (202) 357-2116. Stephanie Norby, Executive Director. Library, (202) 786-2271.*

General e-mail, educate@si.edu

Web, museumstudies.si.edu

Provides training, services, information, and assistance for the professional enhancement of museum personnel and institutions in the United States; sponsors museum training workshops; maintains museum reference center; offers career counseling.

Smithsonian Institution, *Fellowships,* *900 Jefferson Dr. S.W. 20560 (mailing address: P.O. Box 37012, Victor Bldg. 9300, MRC 902 20013-7012); (202) 275-0655. Fax, (202) 275-0489. Catherine F. Harris, Director.*

General e-mail, siofg@.si.edu

Web, www.si.edu/ofg

Provides internship placements to high school students over sixteen years of age, undergraduate and graduate students, and museum professionals. Emphasizes methods and current practices employed by museum professionals.

Smithsonian Institution, *International Relations,* *1100 Jefferson Dr. S.W., #3123 20560 (mailing address: P.O. Box 37012, Quad MRC 705 20013-7012); (202) 357-4282. Fax, (202) 786-2557. Francine C. Berkowitz, Director.*

Web, www.si.edu/intrel

Fosters the development and coordinates the international aspects of Smithsonian cultural activities; facilitates basic research in history and art and encourages international collaboration among individuals and institutions.

CONGRESS

Library of Congress, *Interpretive Programs,* *101 Independence Ave. S.E. 20540-4950; (202) 707-5223. Fax, (202) 707-9063. Irene Chambers, Interpretive Programs Officer.*

Web, www.loc.gov/exhibits

Handles exhibits within the Library of Congress; establishes and coordinates traveling exhibits; handles loans of library material.

NONPROFIT

American Assn. of Museums, *1575 Eye St. N.W., #400 20005-1105; (202) 289-1818. Fax, (202) 289-6578. Edward H. Able Jr., President. TTY, (202) 289-8439.*

General e-mail, aaminfo@aam-us.org

Web, www.aam-us.org

Membership: individuals, institutions, museums, and museum professionals. Accredits museums; conducts educational programs; promotes international professional exchanges.

Art Services International, *1319 Powhatan St., Alexandria, VA 22314; (703) 548-4554. Fax, (703) 548-3305. Lynn K. Rogerson, Director.*

Web, www.artservicesintl.org

Organizes and circulates fine arts exhibitions to museums worldwide.

Black Fashion Museum, *2007 Vermont Ave. N.W. 20001; (202) 667-0744. Fax, (202) 667-4379. Joyce Alexander Bailey, Executive Director.*

General e-mail, bfmdc@aol.com

Web, www.bfmdc.org

Researches, collects, and displays clothing by African Americans, from slave garments to contemporary fashions.

Capital Children's Museum, *800 3rd St. N.E. 20002; (202) 675-4120. Fax, (202) 675-4140. Kathy Dwyer Sutton, Executive Director. Press, (202) 675-4135.*

Web, www.ccm.org

Offers exhibits that involve participation by children. Integrates art, science, the humanities, and technology through "hands-on" learning experiences. (A program of the National Learning Center.)

Corcoran Gallery of Art, *500 17th St. N.W. 20006; (202) 639-1700. Fax, (202) 639-1768. David C. Levy, President.*

General e-mail, museum@corcoran.org

Web, www.corcoran.org

Exhibits paintings, sculpture, and drawings, primarily American. Collections include European art and works of local Washington artists. The affiliated Corcoran College of Art and Design offers a BFA degree and a continuing education program. Library open to the public by appointment.

Dumbarton Oaks, *1703 32nd St. N.W. 20007; (202) 339-6410. Edward L. Keenan, Director. Information, (202) 339-6400. Recorded information, (202) 339-6401.*

General e-mail, DumbartonOaks@doaks.org

Web, www.doaks.org

Administered by the trustees for Harvard University. Exhibits Byzantine and pre-Columbian art and artifacts; conducts advanced research and maintains publication programs and library in Byzantine and pre-Columbian studies and in landscape architecture. Gardens open to the public daily (except during inclement weather and on holidays; fee charged March 15 through October); library open to qualified scholars by advance application.

Freedom Forum Newseum, *1101 Wilson Blvd., 10th Floor, Arlington, VA 22209; (703) 284-3700. Fax, (703)*

284-3777. *Joe Urschel, Executive Director. Toll-free, (888) 639-7386.*

General e-mail, newseum@freedomforum.org

Web, www.newseum.org

World's only interactive museum of news. Collects items related to the history of news coverage; offers multimedia presentations and exhibits on the past, present, and future of news coverage; emphasizes the importance of the First Amendment to news coverage. (Museum is closed and will reopen in 2006 at 6th St. and Pennsylvania Ave. N.W. in Washington. Affiliated with Freedom Forum.)

Hillwood Museum and Gardens, *4155 Linnean Ave. N.W. 20008; (202) 686-8500. Fax, (202) 966-7846. Frederick Fisher, Director. TTY, (202) 363-3056.*

General e-mail, info@hillwoodmuseum.org

Web, www.hillwoodmuseum.org

Former residence of Marjorie Merriweather Post. Maintains and exhibits collection of French and Russian decorative arts, including portraits, liturgical objects, and furniture. Gardens and museum open to the public by reservation.

National Building Museum, *401 F St. N.W. 20001; (202) 272-2448. Fax, (202) 272-2564. Vacant, President. Press, (202) 272-3606.*

Web, www.nbm.org

Celebrates American achievements in building, architecture, urban planning, engineering, and historic preservation through educational programs, exhibitions, tours, lectures, workshops, and publications.

National Museum of Women in the Arts, *1250 New York Ave. N.W. 20005; (202) 783-5000. Fax, (202) 393-3235. Judy Larson, Director. Information, (800) 222-7270. Library, (202) 783-7365.*

Web, www.nmwa.org

Acquires, researches, and presents the works of women artists from the Renaissance to the present. Promotes greater representation and awareness of women in the arts. Library open for research to the public by appointment.

Octagon Museum, *1799 New York Ave. N.W. 20006-5291; (202) 638-3221. Fax, (202) 879-7764. Sherry Birk, Director.*

General e-mail, info@theoctagon.org

Web, www.theoctagon.org

Federal period house open for tours; served as the executive mansion following the War of 1812. Presents temporary exhibits on architecture, decorative arts, and Washington history. Sponsors lectures, scholarly research, publications, and educational programs. (Owned by the American Architectural Foundation.)

Phillips Collection, *1600 21st St. N.W. 20009; (202) 387-2151. Fax, (202) 387-2436. Jay Gates, Director. Membership, (202) 387-3036. Shop, (202) 387-2151, ext. 239.*

Web, www.phillipscollection.org

Maintains permanent collection of European and American paintings, primarily of the nineteenth and twentieth centuries, and holds special exhibits from the same period. Sponsors lectures, gallery talks, and special events, including Sunday concerts (September–May). Library open to researchers and members by appointment.

Textile Museum, *2320 S St. N.W. 20008; (202) 667-0441. Fax, (202) 483-0994. Ursula E. McCracken, Director.*

General e-mail, info@textilemuseum.org

Web, www.textilemuseum.org

Exhibits historic and handmade textiles and carpets. Sponsors symposia, conferences, workshops, lectures, and an annual rug convention. Library open to the public during restricted hours.

Trust for Museum Exhibitions, *1424 16th St. N.W., #600 20036; (202) 745-2566. Fax, (202) 745-0103. Ann Van Devanter Townsend, President.*

General e-mail, thetrust@tme.org

Web, www.tme.org

Provides lending and exhibiting institutions with traveling exhibition services, which include negotiating loans, engaging guest curators, scheduling tours, fundraising, and managing registrarial details and catalog production.

U.S. Holocaust Memorial Museum, *100 Raoul Wallenberg Pl. S.W. 20024-2126; (202) 488-0400. Fax, (202) 488-2690. Sara Bloomfield, Director. Library, (202) 488-9717. TTY, (202) 488-0406.*

General e-mail, visitorsmail@ushmm.org

Web, www.ushmm.org

Works to preserve documentation about the Holocaust; encourages research; provides educational resources, including conferences, publications, and public programming. Responsible for the annual Days of Remembrance of the Victims of the Holocaust. Library and archives are open to the public.

Woodrow Wilson House *(National Trust for Historic Preservation), 2340 S St. N.W. 20008; (202) 387-4062. Fax, (202) 483-1466. Frank Aucella, Director.*

General e-mail, sandrews@woodrowwilsonhouse.org

Web, www.woodrowwilsonhouse.org

Georgian Revival home that exhibits furnishings and memorabilia from President Woodrow Wilson's political and retirement years.

Music

AGENCIES

National Archives and Records Administration (NARA), *Museum Programs, 700 Pennsylvania Ave. N.W., #G13 20408; (202) 501-5210. Fax, (202) 501-5239. Marvin Pinkert, Director.*
Web, www.nara.gov

Plans and directs activities to acquaint the public with materials of the National Archives; conducts tours, workshops, and classes; stages exhibits; produces books and pamphlets; issues teaching packets using historic documents.

National Endowment for the Arts (NEA), *(National Foundation on the Arts and the Humanities), Arts Education, Music, Opera, Presenting, and Multidisciplinary, 1100 Pennsylvania Ave. N.W., #703 20506-0001; (202) 682-5438. Fax, (202) 682-5002. Jan Stunkard, Division Coordinator.*
Web, www.arts.gov

Awards grants to music professional training and career development institutions and to music performing, presenting, recording, and service organizations; awards fellowship grants to professional jazz musicians. Awards grants to professional opera and musical theater companies for regional touring and to organizations that provide services for opera and musical theater professionals.

National Museum of American History *(Smithsonian Institution), Cultural History, 12th St. and Constitution Ave. N.W. 20560-0616 (mailing address: P.O. Box 37012, NMAH 616 20013-7012); (202) 357-1707. Fax, (202) 786-2883. Rayna Green, Chair.*
General e-mail, info@info.si.edu
Web, www.americanhistory.si.edu

Handles exhibits, including construction, and audiovisual services. Presents concerts that feature jazz by regional artists and ensembles, American popular songs, and American theater music on topics related to the museum's collections and current exhibitions. The chamber music program uses a collection of historic European and American musical instruments in performances.

National Symphony Orchestra Education Program *(John F. Kennedy Center for the Performing Arts), 2700 F St. N.W. 20566-0004; (202) 416-8820. Fax, (202) 416-*

8802. *Carole J. Wysocki, Manager. TTY, (202) 416-8822.*
Web, www.kennedy-center.org/nso/nsoed

Presents concerts for students, grades K–12; sponsors fellowship program for talented high school musicians and a young associates program for high school students interested in arts management and professional music careers; holds an annual soloist competition open to college and high school pianists, orchestral instrumentalists, and college vocalists; sponsors Youth Orchestra Day for area youth orchestra members selected by their conductors.

CONGRESS

Library of Congress, *Motion Picture, Broadcasting, and Recorded Sound Division, 101 Independence Ave. S.E. 20540-4690; (202) 707-5840. Fax, (202) 707-2371. Gregory Lukow, Chief (Acting). Recorded sound reference center, (202) 707-7833. Motion picture and television reading room, (202) 707-8572.*
Web, www.loc.gov/rr/mopic

Maintains library's collection of musical and vocal recordings; tapes the library's concert series and other musical events for radio broadcast; produces recordings of music and poetry for sale to the public. Collection also includes sound recordings (1890–present). Reading room open to the public; listening and viewing by appointment.

Library of Congress, *Music Division, 101 Independence Ave. S.E., LM 113 20540-4710; (202) 707-5503. Fax, (202) 707-0621. Jon Newsom, Chief. Concert information, (202) 707-5502. Reading room, (202) 707-5507.*

Maintains and services, through the Performing Arts Reading Room, the library's collection of music manuscripts, sheet music, books, and instruments. Coordinates the library's chamber music concert series; produces radio broadcasts and, for sale to the public, recordings of concerts sponsored by the division; issues publications relating to the field of music and to division collections.

NONPROFIT

American Music Therapy Assn., *8455 Colesville Rd., #1000, Silver Spring, MD 20910; (301) 589-3300. Fax, (301) 589-5175. Andrea Farbman, Executive Director.*
General e-mail, info@musictherapy.org
Web, www.musictherapy.org

Promotes the therapeutic use of music by approving degree programs and clinical training sites for therapists, setting standards for certification of music therapists, and conducting research in the music therapy field.

American Symphony Orchestra League, Washington Office, 910 17th St. N.W. 20006; (202) 776-0215. Fax, (202) 776-0224. Heather Watts, Government Affairs Director.

Web, www.symphony.org

Service and educational organization dedicated to strengthening symphony and chamber orchestras. Monitors legislative activities affecting orchestras. Produces quarterly newsletter to keep league members informed of legislative developments. (Headquarters in New York.)

Music Educators National Conference, 1806 Robert Fulton Dr., Reston, VA 20191-4348; (703) 860-4000. Fax, (703) 860-1531. John J. Mahlmann, Executive Director. Information, (800) 336-3768.

Web, www.menc.org

Membership: music educators (preschool through university). Holds biennial conference. Publishes books and teaching aids for music educators.

National Assn. of Schools of Music, 11250 Roger Bacon Dr., #21, Reston, VA 20190; (703) 437-0700. Fax, (703) 437-6312. Samuel Hope, Executive Director.

General e-mail, info@arts-accredit.org

Web, www.arts-accredit.org/nasm/nasm.htm

Accrediting agency for educational programs in music. Provides information on music education programs; offers professional development for executives of music programs.

OPERA America, 1156 15th St. N.W., #810 20005-1704; (202) 293-4466. Fax, (202) 393-0735. Marc A. Scorca, President.

General e-mail, frontdesk@operaamerica.org

Web, www.operaamerica.org

Membership: professional opera companies in the United States and abroad, producing and presenting organizations, artists, and others affiliated with professional opera. Advises and assists opera companies in daily operations; encourages development of opera and musical theater; produces educational programs; implements programs to increase awareness and appreciation of opera and opera companies.

Recording Industry Assn. of America, 1330 Connecticut Ave. N.W., #300 20036; (202) 775-0101. Fax, (202) 775-7253. Hilary B. Rosen, President.

Web, www.riaa.com

Membership: creators, manufacturers, and marketers of sound recordings. Educates members about new technology in the music industry. Advocates copyright protection and opposes censorship. Works to prevent recording piracy, counterfeiting, bootlegging, and unau-

thorized record rental and imports. Certifies gold, platinum, and multiplatinum recordings. Publishes statistics on the recording industry.

Rhythm and Blues Foundation, 1555 Connecticut Ave. N.W., #401 20036-1111; (202) 588-5566. Fax, (202) 588-5549. Cecilia K. Carter, Executive Director.

General e-mail, randbfdn@aol.com

Web, www.rhythm-n-blues.org

Fosters wider recognition, financial support, and historic and cultural preservation of rhythm and blues music through various grants and programs in support of artists from the 1940s, '50s, and '60s.

Washington Area Music Assn., 1101 17th St. N.W., #1100 20036; (202) 338-1134. Fax, (703) 393-1028. Mike Schreibman, Executive Director. Information, (703) 368-3300.

General e-mail, dcmusic@wamadc.com

Web, www.wamadc.com

Membership: musicians, concert promoters, lawyers, recording engineers, managers, contractors, and other music industry professionals. Sponsors workshops on industry-related topics. Represents professionals from all musical genres. Serves as a liaison between the Washington-area music community and music communities nationwide.

Theater and Dance

AGENCIES

Ford's Theatre National Historic Site, 511 10th St. N.W. 20004; (202) 426-6924. Fax, (202) 426-1845. Claudia Anderson, Site Manager (Acting). TTY, (202) 426-1749. Recorded ticket information, (202) 347-4833.

General e-mail, NACC_FOTH_Interpretation@nps.gov

Web, www.nps.gov/foth

Administered by the National Park Service, which manages Ford's Theatre, Ford's Theatre Museum, and the Peterson House (house where Lincoln died; closed for renovation). Presents interpretive talks, exhibits, and tours; research library open by appointment. Functions as working stage for theatrical productions.

Fund for New American Plays (John F. Kennedy Center for the Performing Arts), 2700 F St. N.W. 20566; (202) 416-8024. Fax, (202) 416-8205. Rebecca Foster, Co-Manager; Max Woodward, Co-Manager.

Web, www.kennedy-center.org/fnap

Encourages playwrights to write and nonprofit professional theaters to produce new American plays; gives playwrights financial support and provides grants to cover some expenses that exceed standard production costs. Submissions must come from the producing theater.

National Endowment for the Arts (NEA), *(National Foundation on the Arts and the Humanities), Dance, Design, Media Arts, Museums, and Visual Arts,* 1100 Pennsylvania Ave. N.W., #726 20506-0001; (202) 682-5452. Fax, (202) 682-5721. Douglas Sonntag, Director, Dance; Robert Frankel, Director, Design (Acting); Ted Libbey, Director, Media Arts; Robert Frankel, Director, Museums and Visual Arts. TTY, (202) 682-5496.
Web, www.arts.gov

Awards grants to dance services organizations and companies.

National Endowment for the Arts (NEA), *(National Foundation on the Arts and the Humanities), Folk and Traditional Arts, Literature, Theater, Musical Theater, and Planning and Stabilization,* 1100 Pennsylvania Ave. N.W. 20506-0001; (202) 682-5428. Fax, (202) 682-5669. Silvio Lim, Division Coordinator (Acting).
Web, www.arts.gov

Awards grants to professional theater companies and theater service organizations.

Smithsonian Institution, *Discovery Theater,* 900 Jefferson Dr. S.W. 20560 (mailing address: Smithsonian Associates, P.O. Box 23293 20026-3293); (202) 357-1502. Fax, (202) 357-2588. Roberta Gasbarre, Director. Reservations, (202) 357-1500.
General e-mail, disc-th@tsa.si.edu
Web, www.discoverytheater.si.edu

Presents live theatrical performances, including storytelling, dance, music, puppetry, and plays, for young people and their families.

NONPROFIT

National Assn. of Schools of Dance, 11250 Roger Bacon Dr., #21, Reston, VA 20190; (703) 437-0700. Fax, (703) 437-6312. Samuel Hope, Executive Director.
General e-mail, info@arts-accredit.org
Web, www.arts-accredit.org/nasd/default.htm

Accrediting agency for educational programs in dance. Provides information on dance education programs; offers professional development for executives of dance programs.

National Assn. of Schools of Theatre, 11250 Roger Bacon Dr., #21, Reston, VA 20190; (703) 437-0700. Fax, (703) 437-6312. Samuel Hope, Executive Director.
General e-mail, info@arts-accredit.org
Web, www.arts-accredit.org/nast/default.htm

Accrediting agency for educational programs in the-

ater. Provides information on theater education programs; offers professional development for executives of theater programs.

National Conservatory of Dramatic Arts, 1556 Wisconsin Ave. N.W. 20007; (202) 333-2202. Fax, (202) 333-1753. Dennis A. Dulmage, President.
General e-mail, ncdadrama@aol.com
Web, www.theconservatory.org

Offers an accredited two-year program in postsecondary professional actor training and a one-year program in advanced professional training. Emphasizes both physical and mental preparedness for acting in the professional entertainment industry.

Shakespeare Theatre, 450 7th St. N.W. 20004 (mailing address: 516 8th St. S.E. 20003); (202) 547-3230. Fax, (202) 547-0226. Nicholas Goldsborough, Managing Director. TTY, (202) 638-3863. Box office, (202) 547-1122.
Web, www.shakespearetheatre.org

Professional resident theater that presents Shakespearean and other classical plays. Offers actor training program for youths, adults, and professional actors. Produces free outdoor summer Shakespeare plays and free Shakespeare plays for schools.

Visual Arts

AGENCIES

National Endowment for the Arts (NEA), *(National Foundation on the Arts and the Humanities), Dance, Design, Media Arts, Museums, and Visual Arts,* 1100 Pennsylvania Ave. N.W., #726 20506-0001; (202) 682-5452. Fax, (202) 682-5721. Douglas Sonntag, Director, Dance; Robert Frankel, Director, Design (Acting); Ted Libbey, Director, Media Arts; Robert Frankel, Director, Museums and Visual Arts. TTY, (202) 682-5496.
Web, www.arts.gov

Awards grants to nonprofit organizations for creative works and programs in the visual arts, including painting, sculpture, crafts, video, photography, printmaking, drawing, artists' books, and performance art.

National Endowment for the Arts (NEA), *(National Foundation on the Arts and the Humanities), Folk and Traditional Arts, Literature, Theater, Musical Theater, and Planning and Stabilization,* 1100 Pennsylvania Ave. N.W. 20506-0001; (202) 682-5428. Fax, (202) 682-5669. Silvio Lim, Division Coordinator (Acting).
Web, www.arts.gov

Awards grants for design arts projects in architecture; landscape architecture; urban design and planning; historic preservation; and interior, graphic, industrial, product, and costume and fashion design.

State Dept., *Art in Embassies,* M-OBO-OM-ART, Dept. of State 20052-0611; (703) 875-4202. Fax, (703) 875-4182. Anne Johnson, Director.
Web, aiep.state.gov

Exhibits American art in U.S. ambassadorial residences. Borrows art works from artists, collectors, galleries, and museums.

CONGRESS

Library of Congress, *Prints and Photographs,*
101 Independence Ave. S.E. 20540-4730; (202) 707-5836. Fax, (202) 707-6647. Jeremy Adamson, Chief. TTY, (202) 707-9051. Reading room, (202) 707-6394.
Web, www.loc.gov/rr/print

Maintains Library of Congress's collection of pictorial material, not in book format, totaling more than 13.5 million items. U.S. and international collections include artists' prints; historical prints, posters, and drawings; photographs (chiefly documentary); political and social cartoons; and architectural plans, drawings, prints, and photographs. Reference service provided in the Prints and Photographs Reading Room. Reproductions of nonrestricted material available through the Library of Congress's Photoduplication Service; prints and photographs may be borrowed through the Exhibits Office for exhibits by qualified institutions. A portion of the collections and an overview of reference services are available on the World Wide Web.

NONPROFIT

American Institute of Architects, 1735 New York Ave. N.W. 20006; (202) 626-7310. Fax, (202) 626-7426. Norman L. Koonce, Chief Executive Officer. Information, (202) 626-7300. Library, (202) 626-7492.
Web, www.aia.org

Membership: licensed American architects, interns, architecture faculty, engineers, planners, landscape architects, artists, and those in government, manufacturing, or other field in a capacity related to architecture. Works to advance the standards of architectural education, training, and practice. Promotes the aesthetic, scientific, and practical efficiency of architecture, urban design, and planning; monitors international developments. Offers continuing and professional education programs; sponsors scholarships, internships, and awards. Houses archival collection, including documents and drawings of American architects and architecture. Library open to the public. Monitors legislation and regulations.

Friends of Art and Preservation in Embassies,
1725 K St. N.W., #300 20006; (202) 349-3724. Fax, (202) 349-3727. Jennifer A. Duncan, Director.

General e-mail, fapeindc@aol.com
Web, www.fapeglobal.org

Foundation established to assist the State Dept.'s Office of Foreign Buildings and Art in Embassies programs. Acquires and exhibits American art and preserves high-value furnishings in U.S. embassies and other diplomatic facilities.

National Assn. of Schools of Art and Design,
11250 Roger Bacon Dr., #21, Reston, VA 20190; (703) 437-0700. Fax, (703) 437-6312. Samuel Hope, Executive Director.
General e-mail, info@arts-accredit.org
Web, www.arts-accredit.org

Accrediting agency for educational programs in art and design. Provides information on art and design programs at the postsecondary level; offers professional development for executives of art and design programs.

HISTORY AND PRESERVATION

AGENCIES

Most federal agencies have historic preservation officers who ensure that agencies protect historic buildings and other cultural resources that are on or eligible for nomination to the National Register of Historic Places, including nonfederal property that may be affected by agency activities.

Advisory Council on Historic Preservation,
1100 Pennsylvania Ave. N.W., #809 20004; (202) 606-8503. Fax, (202) 606-8672. John M. Fowler, Executive Director; John Nau, Chair.
General e-mail, achp@achp.gov
Web, www.achp.gov

Advises the president and Congress on historic preservation; reviews and comments on federal projects and programs affecting historic, architectural, archeological, and cultural resources.

Bureau of Land Management (BLM), *(Interior Dept.), Cultural Heritage, Wilderness, Special Areas, and Paleontology,* 1620 L St. N.W., #204 20036 (mailing address: 1849 C St. N.W., #204-LS 20240); (202) 452-0330. Fax, (202) 452-7701. Marilyn Nickels, Group Manager. TTY, (202) 452-0326.
Web, www.blm.gov

Develops bureau policy on historic preservation, archeological resource protection, consultation with native Americans, curation of artifacts and records, heritage education, and paleontological resource management.

National Archives and Records Administration (NARA), *Advisory Committee on Preservation,* 8601 Adelphi Rd., #2807, College Park, MD 20740-6001; (301) 837-1567. Fax, (301) 837-3701. Alan Calmes, Preservation Archivist.

Advises the archivist of the United States on preservation technology and research and on matters related to the continued preservation of records of the National Archives of the United States.

National Archives and Records Administration (NARA), *Cartographic and Architectural Branch,* 8601 Adelphi Rd., #3320, College Park, MD 20740-6001; (301) 837-3200. Robert E. Richardson, Director. General e-mail, carto@arch2.nara.gov Web, www.archives.gov

Preserves and makes available historical records of federal agencies, including maps, charts, aerial photographs, architectural drawings, patents, and ships' plans. Research room open to the public. Records may be reproduced for a fee.

National Archives and Records Administration (NARA), *Preservation Programs,* 8601 Adelphi Rd., #2800, College Park, MD 20740-6001; (301) 837-3435. Fax, (301) 837-3701. Doris A. Hamburg, Director. General e-mail, preserve@nara.gov Web, www.archives.gov/preservation

Responsible for conserving textual and nontextual records in the archives. Nontextual records include videotapes, sound recordings, motion pictures, still photos, and preservation microfilming. Conducts research and testing for materials purchased by and used in the archives.

National Capital Planning Commission, 401 9th St. N.W., #500N 20576; (202) 482-7200. Fax, (202) 482-7272. Patricia Gallagher, Executive Director. Web, www.ncpc.gov

Central planning agency for the federal government in the national capital region, which includes the District of Columbia and suburban Maryland and Virginia. Reviews and approves plans for the preservation of certain historic and environmental features in the national capital region, including the annual federal capital improvement plan.

National Endowment for the Arts (NEA), *(National Foundation on the Arts and the Humanities), Folk and Traditional Arts, Literature, Theater, Musical Theater, and Planning and Stabilization,* 1100 Pennsylvania Ave. N.W. 20506-0001; (202) 682-5428. Fax, (202) 682-5669. Silvio Lim, Division Coordinator (Acting). Web, www.arts.gov

Awards grants to exceptional projects in the arts and arts education to arts organizations, art service organizations, federally recognized tribal communities, state or local government offices, and others.

National Endowment for the Humanities (NEH), *(National Foundation on the Arts and the Humanities), Preservation and Access,* 1100 Pennsylvania Ave. N.W., #411 20506; (202) 606-8570. Fax, (202) 606-8639. George Farr, Director. General e-mail, preservation@neh.gov Web, www.neh.gov

Sponsors preservation and access projects, the stabilization and documentation of material culture collections, and the U.S. newspaper program.

National Museum of American History *(Smithsonian Institution), Cultural History,* 12th St. and Constitution Ave. N.W. 20560-0616 (mailing address: P.O. Box 37012, NMAH 616 20013-7012); (202) 357-1707. Fax, (202) 786-2883. Rayna Green, Chair. General e-mail, info@info.si.edu Web, www.americanhistory.si.edu

Collects and preserves artifacts related to U.S. cultural heritage; supports research, exhibits, performances, and educational programs. Areas of focus include ethnic and religious communities; sports, recreation, and leisure; popular entertainment and mass media; business and commercial culture; musical instruments; hand tools; and educational, civic, and voluntary organizations.

National Park Service (NPS), *(Interior Dept.), Cultural Resources,* 1849 C St. N.W., #3128 20240; (202) 208-7625. Fax, (202) 273-3237. Vacant, Associate Director. Web, www.cr.nps.gov

Oversees preservation of federal historic sites and administration of buildings programs. Programs include the National Register of Historic Places, National Historic and National Landmark Programs, Historic American Building Survey, Historic American Engineering Record, Archeology and Antiquities Act Program, and Technical Preservation Services. Gives grant and aid assistance and tax benefit information to properties listed in the National Register of Historic Places.

CONGRESS

House Resources Committee, *Subcommittee on National Parks, Recreation, and Public Lands,* 1333 LHOB 20515; (202) 226-7736. Fax, (202) 226-2301. Rep. George P. Radanovich, R-Calif., Chair; Casey Hammond, Clerk. General e-mail, parks.subcommittee@mail.house.gov Web, resourcescommittee.house.gov/108cong/assign08.htm

Jurisdiction over historic preservation legislation.

Senate Energy and Natural Resources Committee, Subcommittee on National Parks, SD-364 20510; (202) 224-4971. Fax, (202) 224-6163. Sen. Craig Thomas, R-Wyo., Chair; Tom Lillie, Professional Staff Member.
General e-mail, parks@energy.senate.gov
Web, energy.senate.gov

Jurisdiction over historic preservation legislation.

Senate Office of Conservation and Preservation, S410 CAP 20510; (202) 224-4550. Carl Fritter, Bookbinder.

Develops and coordinates programs related to the conservation and preservation of Senate records and materials for the Secretary of the Senate.

NONPROFIT

American Historical Assn., 400 A St. S.E. 20003; (202) 544-2422. Fax, (202) 544-8307. Arnita Jones, Executive Director.
General e-mail, aha@theaha.org
Web, www.theaha.org

Supports public access to government information; publishes original historical research, journal, bibliographies, historical directories, and job placement bulletin. Committee on Women Historians seeks to improve the status of women in the profession as well as promotes the teaching of women's history.

American Institute for Conservation of Historic and Artistic Works, 1717 K St. N.W., #200 20006; (202) 452-9545. Fax, (202) 452-9328. Elizabeth Jones, Executive Director.
General e-mail, info@aic-faic.org
Web, aic.stanford.edu

Membership: professional conservators, scientists, students, administrators, cultural institutions, and others. Promotes the knowledge and practice of the conservation of cultural property; supports research; and disseminates information on conservation.

American Studies Assn., 1120 19th St. N.W., #301 20036; (202) 467-4783. Fax, (202) 467-4786. John F. Stephens, Executive Director.
General e-mail, asastaff@theasa.net
Web, www.theasa.net

Fosters exchange of ideas about American life; supports and assists programs for teaching American studies abroad and encourages teacher and student exchanges; awards annual prizes for contributions to American studies; provides curriculum resources.

Civil War Preservation Trust, 1331 H St. N.W. 20005; (202) 367-1861. Fax, (202) 367-1865. O. James Lighthizer, President.

General e-mail, civilwartrust@civilwar.org
Web, www.civilwar.org

Promotes the appreciation and preservation of significant Civil War battlefields by protecting the land and educating the public about the role of the battlefields.

Council on America's Military Past—U.S.A., P.O. Box 1151, Fort Myer, VA 22211-1151; (703) 912-6124. Fax, (703) 912-5666. Herbert M. Hart, Executive Director. Information, (800) 398-4693.
Web, www.campjamp.org

Membership: historians, archeologists, curators, writers, and others interested in military history and preservation of historic military establishments and ships.

Heritage Preservation, 1625 K St. N.W., #700 20006; (202) 634-1422. Fax, (202) 634-1435. Larry Reger, President. Information, (888) 388-6789.
General e-mail, info@heritagepreservation.org
Web, www.heritagepreservation.org

Membership: museums, libraries, archives, historic preservation organizations, historical societies, and conservation groups. Advocates the conservation and preservation of works of art, anthropological artifacts, documents, historic objects, architecture, and natural science specimens. Programs include Save Outdoor Sculpture, which works to inventory all U.S. outdoor sculpture; the Conservation Assessment Program, which administers grants to museums for conservation surveys of their collections; the Heritage Health Index, which will document the condition of U.S. collections; and the Heritage Emergency Task Force, which helps institutions protect their collections from disasters and emergencies.

National Conference of State Historic Preservation Officers, 444 N. Capitol St. N.W., #342 20001-1512; (202) 624-5465. Fax, (202) 624-5419. Nancy Schamu, Executive Director.
Web, www.ncshpo.org

Membership: state and territorial historic preservation officers and deputy officers. Compiles statistics on programs; monitors legislation and regulations.

National Preservation Institute, P.O. Box 1702, Alexandria, VA 22313; (703) 765-0100. Fax, (703) 768-9350. Jere Gibber, Executive Director.
General e-mail, info@npi.org
Web, www.npi.org

Provides education and professional training for the management, development, and preservation of historic, cultural, and environmental resources.

National Society, Colonial Dames XVII Century,
1300 New Hampshire Ave. N.W. 20036; (202) 293-1700.
Fax, (202) 466-6099. Sandra Quimby, Office Manager.

Membership: American women who are lineal descendants of persons who rendered civil or military service and lived in America or one of the British colonies before 1701. Preserves records and shrines; encourages historical research; awards scholarships to undergraduate and graduate students and scholarships in medicine to persons of native American descent.

National Society, Daughters of the American Revolution, *1776 D St. N.W. 20006-5303; (202) 628-1776. Fax, (202) 879-3227. Linda Tinker Watkins, President.*
Web, www.dar.org

Membership: women descended from American Revolutionary War patriots. Conducts historical, educational, and patriotic activities; maintains a genealogical library, American museum, and documentary collection antedating 1830. Library open to the public (nonmembers charged fee for use).

National Society of the Children of the American Revolution, *1776 D St. N.W., #224 20006-5392; (202) 638-3153. Fax, (202) 737-3162. Julie Pearce, Office Manager.*
General e-mail, hq@nscar.org
Web, www.nscar.org

Membership: descendants, age twenty-two years and under, of American soldiers or patriots of the American Revolution. Conducts historical, educational, and patriotic activities; preserves places of historical interest.

National Society of the Colonial Dames of America, *2715 Que St. N.W. 20007; (202) 337-2288. Fax, (202) 337-0348. Bill Birdseye, Director.*
General e-mail, info@nscda.org
Web, www.nscda.org

Membership: descendants of colonists in America before 1750. Conducts historical and educational activities; maintains Dumbarton House, a museum open to the public.

National Trust for Historic Preservation, *1785 Massachusetts Ave. N.W. 20036-2117; (202) 588-6000. Fax, (202) 588-6038. Richard Moe, President. Information, (800) 944-6847.*
Web, www.nthp.org

Conducts seminars, workshops, and conferences on topics related to preservation, including neighborhood conservation, main street revitalization, rural conservation, and preservation law; offers financial assistance through loan and grant programs; provides advisory services; operates historic house museums, which are open to the public.

Preservation Action, *1054 31st St. N.W., #526 20007; (202) 298-6180. Fax, (202) 298-6182. Susan West Montgomery, President.*
General e-mail, mail@preservationaction.org
Web, www.preservationaction.org

Monitors legislation affecting historic preservation and neighborhood conservation; promotes effective management of historic preservation programs.

Society for American Archaeology, *900 2nd St. N.E., #12 20002; (202) 789-8200. Fax, (202) 789-0284. Tobi Brimsek, Executive Director.*
General e-mail, info@saa.org
Web, www.saa.org

Promotes greater awareness, understanding, and research of archaeology on the American continents; works to preserve and publish results of scientific data and research; serves as information clearinghouse for members.

Archives and Manuscripts

AGENCIES

National Archives and Records Administration (NARA), *8601 Adelphi Rd., #4200, College Park, MD 20740-6001; (866) 272-6272. Fax, (301) 837-0483. John W. Carlin, Archivist of the United States; Lewis J. Bellardo, Deputy Archivist.*
Web, www.archives.gov

Identifies, preserves, and makes available federal government documents of historic value; administers a network of regional storage centers and archives and operates the presidential library system. Collections include photographs, graphic materials, and films; holdings include records generated by foreign governments (especially in wartime) and by international conferences, commissions, and exhibitions.

National Archives and Records Administration (NARA), *Center for Legislative Archives, 700 Pennsylvania Ave. N.W., #8E 20408; (202) 501-5350. Fax, (202) 219-2176. Michael L. Gillette, Director.*
Web, http://www.archives.gov/records_of_congress/about_the_cla/about_the_cla.html

Collects and maintains records of congressional committees and legislative files from 1789 to the present. Publishes inventories and guides to these records.

National Archives and Records Administration (NARA), *Presidential Libraries, 8601 Adelphi Rd.,*

#2200, College Park, MD 20740-6001; (301) 837-3250. Fax, (301) 837-3199. Richard L. Claypoole, Assistant Archivist.
Web, www.archives.gov/presidential_libraries

Directs all programs relating to acquisition, preservation, publication, and research use of materials in presidential libraries; conducts oral history projects; publishes finding aids for research sources; provides reference service, including information from and about documentary holdings.

National Historical Publications and Records Commission (*National Archives and Records Administration*), *700 Pennsylvania Ave. N.W., #111 20408-0001; (202) 501-5610. Fax, (202) 501-5601. Max J. Evans, Executive Director.*
General e-mail, nhprc@nara.gov
Web, www.archives.gov/grants/index.html

Makes plans and recommendations and provides cost estimates for preserving and publishing documentation of U.S. history. Awards grants to government and private cultural institutions that preserve, arrange, edit, and publish documents of historical importance, including the papers of outstanding Americans.

National Museum of American History/Behring Center (*Smithsonian Institution*), *Archives Center, 12th St. and Constitution Ave. N.W., #C340 20560-0601 (mailing address: P.O. Box 37012, NMAH MRC 601 20013-7012); (202) 357-3270. Fax, (202) 786-2453. John A. Fleckner, Chief Archivist. TTY, (202) 357-1729.*
General e-mail, archivescenter@si.edu
Web, www.americanhistory.si.edu/archives/ac-i.htm

Acquires, organizes, preserves, and makes available for research the museum's archival and documentary materials relating to American history and culture. (Three-dimensional objects and closely related documents are in the care of curatorial divisions.)

Smithsonian Institution, *Archives of American Art, 750 9th St. N.W., #2200 20560 (mailing address: P.O. Box 37012, Victor Bldg. MRC 937 20013-7012); (202) 275-2156. Fax, (202) 275-1955. Richard J. Wattenmaker, Director. Reference desk, (202) 275-1961.*
Web, www.archivesofamericanart.si.edu

Collects and preserves manuscript items, such as notebooks, sketchbooks, letters, and journals; photos of artists and works of art; tape-recorded interviews with artists, dealers, and collectors; exhibition catalogs; directories; and biographies on the history of visual arts in the United States. Library open to scholars and researchers. Reference centers that maintain microfilm copies of a

selection of the Archives' collection include New York; Boston; San Francisco; and San Marino, Calif.

CONGRESS

Legislative Resource Center, *B106 CHOB 20515-6612; (202) 226-5200. Fax, (202) 226-5204. Deborah Turner, Manager.*
General e-mail, lrc@mail.house.gov
Web, clerk.house.gov/clerk/Offices_Services/lrc.php

Conducts historical research. Advises members on the disposition of their records and papers; maintains information on manuscript collections of former members; maintains biographical files on former members. Print publications include *Biographical Directory of the United States Congress, 1774–1989; Guide to Research Collections of Former Members of the United States House of Representatives, 1789–1987; Black Americans in Congress, 1870–1989;* and *Women in Congress, 1917–1989.*

Library of Congress, *Manuscript Division, 101 Independence Ave. S.E., #LM102 20540-4680; (202) 707-5383. Fax, (202) 707-6336. James H. Hutson, Chief. Reading room, (202) 707-5387.*
Web, www.loc.gov/rr/mss

Maintains, describes, and provides reference service on the library's manuscript collections, including the papers of U.S. presidents and other eminent Americans. Manuscript Reading Room primarily serves serious scholars and researchers; historians and reference librarians are available for consultation.

Library of Congress, *Rare Book and Special Collections Division, 101 Independence Ave. S.E., #239 20540-4740; (202) 707-5434. Fax, (202) 707-4142. Mark Dimunation, Chief. Reading room, (202) 707-3448.*
Web, lcweb.loc.gov/rr/rarebook

Maintains collections of incunabula (books printed before 1501) and other early printed books; early imprints of American history and literature; illustrated books; early Spanish American, Russian, and Bulgarian imprints; Confederate states imprints; libraries of famous personalities (including Thomas Jefferson, Woodrow Wilson, and Oliver Wendell Holmes); special format collections (miniature books, broadsides, almanacs, and pre-1870 copyright records); special interest collections; and special provenance collections. Reference assistance is provided in the Rare Book and Special Collections Reading Room.

Senate Historical Office, *SH-201 20510; (202) 224-6900. Fax, (202) 224-5329. Richard Baker, Historian.*
General e-mail, historian@sec.senate.gov
Web, www.senate.gov

Serves as an information clearinghouse on Senate history, traditions, and members. Collects, organizes, and distributes to the public previously unpublished Senate documents; collects and preserves photographs and pictures related to Senate history; conducts an oral history program; advises senators and Senate committees on the disposition of their noncurrent papers and records. Produces publications on the history of the Senate.

NONPROFIT

Assassination Archives and Research Center, *1003 K St. N.W., #640 20001; (202) 393-1921. Fax, (301) 657-3699. James Lesar, President.*
Web, www.aarclibrary.org

Acquires, preserves, and disseminates information on political assassinations. Available to the public by appointment only.

Council on Library and Information Resources, *1755 Massachusetts Ave. N.W., #500 20036-2124; (202) 939-4750. Fax, (202) 939-4765. Deanna B. Marcum, President.*
General e-mail, info@clir.org
Web, www.clir.org

Acts on behalf of the nation's libraries, archives, and universities to develop and encourage collaborative strategies for preserving the nation's intellectual heritage and strengthening its information system.

Moorland-Spingarn Research Center *(Howard University), 500 Howard Pl. N.W. 20059; (202) 806-7239. Fax, (202) 806-6405. Thomas C. Battle, Director.*
Web, www.howard.edu/library/moorland-spingarn

Collects, preserves, and makes available for study numerous artifacts, books, manuscripts, newspapers, photographs, prints, recordings, and other materials documenting black history and culture in the United States, Africa, Europe, Latin America, and the Caribbean. Maintains extensive collections of black newspapers and magazines; contains the works of African American and African scholars, poets, and novelists; maintains collections on the history of Howard University.

Genealogy

AGENCIES

National Archives and Records Administration (NARA), *Archives 1, Research Support Branch, 700 Pennsylvania Ave. N.W., #406 20408; (202) 501-5400. Fax, (202) 501-5005. Kenneth Hager, Branch Chief.*
Web, www.archives.gov

Assists individuals interested in researching record holdings of the National Archives, including genealogical records; issues research cards to prospective genealogical, biographical, and other researchers who present photo identification. Users must be fourteen. Still and motion picture research rooms located in College Park, Md.

National Archives and Records Administration (NARA), *Museum Programs, 700 Pennsylvania Ave. N.W., #G13 20408; (202) 501-5210. Fax, (202) 501-5239. Marvin Pinkert, Director.*
Web, www.nara.gov

Plans and directs activities to acquaint the public with materials of the National Archives; conducts tours, workshops, and classes; stages exhibits; produces books and pamphlets; issues teaching packets using historic documents.

CONGRESS

Library of Congress, *Local History and Genealogy Reading Room, 101 Independence Ave. S.E., #LJ-G42 20540-4660; (202) 707-5537. Fax, (202) 707-1957. Judith Roach, Head. TTY, (202) 707-9958.*
Web, www.loc.gov/rr/genealogy

Provides reference and referral service on topics related to local history, genealogy, and heraldry throughout the United States.

NONPROFIT

Family History Center, *Church of Jesus Christ of Latter-day Saints, 10000 Stoneybrook Dr., Kensington, MD 20895 (mailing address: P.O. Box 49, Kensington, MD 20895); (301) 587-0042. Susan Frazier, Director.*

Maintains genealogical library for research. Collection includes international genealogical index, family group record archives, microfiche registers, and the Family Search Computer Program (www.familysearch.org). Library open to the public.

National Genealogical Society, *4527 17th St. North, Arlington, VA 22207-2399; (703) 525-0050. Fax, (703) 525-0052. Wendy Herr, Executive Director. Information, (800) 473-0060.*
General e-mail, membership@ngsgenealogy.org
Web, www.ngsgenealogy.org

Encourages study of genealogy and publication of all records that are of genealogical interest. Maintains a genealogical library for research; provides an accredited home study online program; holds an annual conference. Member Resource Center open to the public by appointment.

National Society, Daughters of the American Colonists, *2205 Massachusetts Ave. N.W. 20008; (202) 667-3076. Jacquelyn Barnes, President.*

Web, www.nsdac.org

Membership: women descended from men and women who gave civil service to the colonies prior to the Revolutionary War. Maintains library of colonial and genealogical records.

National Society, Daughters of the American Revolution, *1776 D St. N.W. 20006-5303; (202) 628-1776. Fax, (202) 879-3227. Linda Tinker Watkins, President.*
Web, www.dar.org

Membership: women descended from American Revolutionary War patriots. Maintains a genealogical library, which is open to the public (nonmembers charged fee for use).

Specific Cultures

AGENCIES

Interior Dept. (DOI), *Indian Arts and Crafts Board,*
1849 C St. N.W. 20240-0001; (202) 208-3773. Fax, (202) 208-5196. Meredith Stanton, Director.
Web, www.doi.gov

Advises native American artisans and craft guilds; produces a source directory on arts and crafts of native Americans (including Alaskan natives); maintains museums of native crafts in Montana, South Dakota, and Oklahoma; provides information on native American crafts.

National Endowment for the Arts (NEA), *(National Foundation on the Arts and the Humanities), Folk and Traditional Arts, Literature, Theater, Musical Theater, and Planning and Stabilization, 1100 Pennsylvania Ave. N.W. 20506-0001; (202) 682-5428. Fax, (202) 682-5669. Silvio Lim, Division Coordinator (Acting).*
Web, www.arts.gov

Seeks to preserve and enhance multicultural artistic heritage through grants for folk arts projects.

National Museum of American History *(Smithsonian Institution), History Department, 12th St. and Constitution Ave. N.W., #4601 20560 (mailing address: P.O. Box 37012, NMAH 638 20013-7012); (202) 357-1963. Fax, (202) 633-8192. Jim Gardner, Assistant Director.*
Web, www.si.edu/nmah

Conducts research, develops collections, and creates exhibits on political, community, and domestic life, based on collections of folk and popular arts, ethnic and craft objects, textiles, coins, costumes and jewelry, ceramics and glass, graphic arts, musical instruments, photographs, appliances, and machines.

Smithsonian Institution, *Center for Folklife and Cultural Heritage, 750 9th St. N.W., #4100 20560-0953*
(mailing address: P.O. Box 37012, Victor Bldg. #4100, MRC 953 20013-7012); (202) 275-1150. Fax, (202) 275-1119. Richard Kurin, Director.
General e-mail, folklife-info@si.edu
Web, www.folklife.si.edu

Promotes and conducts research into traditional U.S. cultures and foreign folklife traditions; produces folkways recordings, films, monographs, and educational programs; presents annual Smithsonian Folklife Festival in Washington, D.C.

CONGRESS

Library of Congress, *American Folklife Center,*
101 Independence Ave. S.E. 20540-4610; (202) 707-5510. Fax, (202) 707-2076. Margaret Bulger, Director. Archive of Folk Culture, (202) 707-5510.
General e-mail, folklife@loc.gov
Web, www.loc.gov/folklife

Coordinates national, regional, state and local government, and private folklife activities; contracts with individuals and groups for research and field studies in American folklife and for exhibits and workshops; maintains the National Archive of Folk Culture (an ethnographic collection of American and international folklore, grassroots oral histories, and ethnomusicology) and the Veterans History Project (a collection of oral histories and documentary materials from veterans of World Wars I and II and the Korean, Vietnam, and Persian Gulf wars). Conducts internships at the archive; sponsors summer concerts of traditional and ethnic music.

NONPROFIT

American Indian Heritage Foundation, *6051 Arlington Blvd., Falls Church, VA 22044; (703) 237-7500. Fax, (703) 532-1921. Princess Pale Moon, President.*
Web, www.indians.org

Promotes national and international cultural programs for native Americans. Sponsors the National American Indian Heritage Month and the Miss Indian USA Scholarship Program; notes outstanding achievement among young native Americans; assists tribes in meeting emergency needs.

National Council for the Traditional Arts, *1320 Fenwick Lane, #200, Silver Spring, MD 20910; (301) 565-0654. Fax, (301) 565-0472. Joseph T. Wilson, Executive Director.*
General e-mail, info@ncta.net
Web, www.ncta.net

Presents and provides consultation for regional and national folk festivals; offers training programs for park officials on folk culture; conducts ethnocultural surveys;

NATIONAL PARK SERVICE SITES IN THE CAPITAL REGION

The National Park Service administers most parks, circles, and monuments in the District of Columbia, as well as sites in nearby Maryland, Virginia, and West Virginia. For information on facilities not listed here, call (202) 619-7000. Web, www.nps.gov/ncro/index.htm.

Antietam National Battlefield, (301) 432-5124

Arlington House, Robert E. Lee Memorial, (703) 235-1530

C & O Canal National Historic Park, (301) 739-4200

  Great Falls Area, Maryland, (301) 767-3714

Catoctin Mountain Park, (301) 663-9330

Clara Barton National Historic Site, (301) 492-6245

Ford's Theatre National Historic Site, (202) 426-6924

Fort Washington Park, (301) 763-4600 (includes Piscataway Park)

Frederick Douglass National Historic Site, (202) 426-5961

George Washington Parkway, (703) 289-2500 (includes memorials to Theodore Roosevelt, Lyndon Johnson, and U.S. Marine Corps)

Glen Echo Park, (301) 492-6229

Great Falls Park, Virginia, (703) 285-2966

Greenbelt Park, (301) 344-3948

Harpers Ferry National Historic Park, (304) 535-6298

Manassas National Battlefield Park, (703) 754-1861

Mary McLeod Bethune National Historic Site, (202) 673-2402

Monocacy National Battlefield, (301) 662-3515

National Mall, (202) 426-6841 (includes presidential and war memorials and Pennsylvania Avenue National Historic Site)

Prince William Forest Park, (703) 221-7181

Rock Creek Park, (202) 895-6070

Thomas Stone National Historic Site, (301) 392-1776

White House, (202) 456-7041

Wolf Trap Farm Park, (703) 255-1800

coordinates exhibitions and tours of traditional folk artists with the support of the National Endowment for the Arts. Produces films and videos on traditional arts; sponsors annual national folk festival.

National Italian American Foundation, *1860 19th St. N.W. 20009; (202) 387-0600. Fax, (202) 387-0800. John Salamone, Executive Director.*
Web, www.niaf.org

Membership: U.S. citizens of Italian ancestry. Promotes recognition of Italian American contributions to American society. Funds cultural events, educational symposia, antidefamation programs, and grants and scholarships. Represents the interests of Italian Americans before Congress. Serves as an umbrella organization for local Italian American clubs throughout the United States.

Washington Area

AGENCIES

National Park Service (NPS), *(Interior Dept.),* **National Capital Region,** *1100 Ohio Dr. S.W., #336 20242; (202) 619-7000. Fax, (202) 619-7220. Terry Carlstrom, Regional Director. Recorded information, (202) 619-7275. Permits, (202) 619-7225.*
Web, www.nps.gov/ncro

Provides visitors with information on Washington-area parks, monuments, and Civil War battlefields; offers press services for the media and processes special event applications and permits.

White House Visitors Center, *1450 Pennsylvania Ave. N.W., #1894 20230; (202) 208-1631. Fax, (202) 208-1643. Rachel Frantum, Manager. Information, (202) 456-7041. TTY, (202) 456-2121.*
General e-mail, WHHO_Presidents_Park@nps.gov
Web, www.nps.gov/whho

Administered by the National Park Service. Educates visitors about the White House through videos, exhibits, and historical artifacts. Tours are suspended indefinitely, except for youth groups, organized veteran groups, and school groups upon request through their member of Congress, on Tuesdays through Saturdays.

CONGRESS

Architect of the Capitol, *Office of the Curator,* **HT3 CAP 20515; (202) 228-1222. Fax, (202) 228-4602. Barbara A. Wolanin, Curator. Press, (202) 228-1205.**
Web, www.aoc.gov

Preserves artwork; maintains collection of drawings, photographs, and manuscripts on and about the Capitol and the House and Senate office buildings. Maintains records of the architect of the Capitol. Library open to the public.

Senate Commission on Art, *S411 CAP 20510-7102; (202) 224-2955. Fax, (202) 224-8799. Sen. Bill Frist, R-Tenn., Chair; Diane K. Skvarla, Curator of the Senate.*

General e-mail, curator@sec.senate.gov

Web, www.senate.gov/artandhistory/art/common/generic/senate_art.htm

Accepts artwork and historical objects for display in Senate office buildings and the Senate wing of the Capitol. Maintains and exhibits Senate collections (paintings, sculpture, furniture, and manuscripts); oversees and maintains old Senate and Supreme Court chambers.

NONPROFIT

Assn. for Preservation of Historic Congressional Cemetery, *1801 E St. S.E. 20003; (202) 543-0539. Fax, (202) 543-5966. Linda Harper, Chair.*

General e-mail, congressionalcemetery@att.net

Web, www.congressionalcemetery.org

Administers and maintains the Washington Parish Burial Ground (commonly known as the Congressional Cemetery).

D.C. Preservation League, *1815 Pennsylvania Ave. N.W., #200 20006; (202) 955-5616. Fax, (202) 955-5456. T. David Bell, President.*

General e-mail, info@dcpreservation.org

Web, www.dcpreservation.org

Participates in planning and preserving buildings and sites in Washington, D.C. Programs include protection and enhancement of the city's landmarks; educational lectures, tours, and seminars; and technical assistance to neighborhood groups. Monitors legislation and regulations.

Historical Society of Washington, D.C., *801 K St. N.W. 20001; (202) 785-2068. Fax, (202) 887-5785. Barbara Franco, President.*

General e-mail, info@hswdc.org

Web, www.hswdc.org

Maintains research collections on the District of Columbia, including photographs, manuscripts, archives, books, and prints and graphics of Washington (1790–present); publishes *Metro D.C. History News* and *Washington History* magazine; operates the newly opened City Museum in the Carnegie Library building in Mt. Vernon Square. Museum and library open to the public.

Martin Luther King Memorial Library, *Washingtoniana Division, 901 G St. N.W., #307 20001; (202) 727-1213. Fax, (202) 727-1129. Susan L. Malbin, Chief.*

Web, www.dclibrary.org/washingtoniana

Maintains reference collections of District of Columbia current laws and regulations, history, and culture. Collections include biographies; travel books; memoirs and diaries; family, church, government, and institu-

tional histories; maps (1612–present); plat books; city, telephone, and real estate directories (1822–present); census schedules; newspapers and periodicals (including the *Washington Star* collection of clippings and photographs, 1940–1981); photographs; and oral history materials on local neighborhoods, ethnic groups, and businesses.

National Assn. to Restore Pride in America's Capital, *4401 Boxwood Rd., Bethesda, MD 20816; (301) 229-6076. Fax, (301) 229-6077. Leonard Sullivan, President.*

General e-mail, lsnarpac@bellatlantic.net

Web, www.narpac.org

Operates as an information clearinghouse on the city's history and its major current issues.

Supreme Court Historical Society, *224 E. Capitol St. N.E., Opperman House 20003; (202) 543-0400. Fax, (202) 547-7730. David T. Pride, Executive Director.*

Web, www.supremecourthistory.org

Acquires, preserves, and displays historic items associated with the Court; conducts and publishes scholarly research. Conducts lecture programs; promotes and supports educational activities in the Court.

U.S. Capitol Historical Society, *200 Maryland Ave. N.E. 20002; (202) 543-8919. Fax, (202) 544-8244. Ron Sarasin, President. Information, (800) 887-9318. Library, (202) 543-8919, ext. 27.*

General e-mail, uschs@uschs.org

Web, www.uschs.org

Membership: members of Congress, individuals, and organizations interested in the preservation of the history and traditions of the U.S. Capitol. Conducts historical research; offers tours, lectures, and films; maintains information centers in the Capitol; publishes an annual historical calendar.

White House Historical Assn., *740 Jackson Pl. N.W. 20006; (202) 737-8292. Fax, (202) 789-0440. Neil W. Horstman, President.*

Web, www.whitehousehistory.org

Seeks to enhance the understanding and appreciation of the White House. Publishes books on the White House, including a historical guide, a description of ceremonial events, two volumes of biographical sketches and illustrations of the presidents and first ladies, a book on White House glassware, and a book on White House paintings and sculptures. Net proceeds from book sales go toward the purchase of historic items, such as paintings and furniture, for the White House permanent collection.

◧ RECREATION AND SPORTS

AGENCIES

Health and Human Services Dept. (HHS), *President's Council on Physical Fitness and Sports,* *Humphrey Bldg. #738H, 200 Independence Ave. S.W. 20201; (202) 690-9000. Fax, (202) 690-5211. Penny Royall, Executive Director (Acting).*
Web, www.fitness.gov

Provides schools, state and local governments, recreation agencies, and employers with information on designing and implementing physical fitness programs; conducts award programs for children and adults and for schools, clubs, and other institutions.

U.S. Armed Forces Sports Council, *4700 King St., 4th Floor, Alexandria, VA 22302-4418; (703) 681-7287. Fax, (703) 681-1616. Suba Saty, Secretariat.*
Web, www.armedforcessports.com

Membership: one representative from each of the four armed services. Administers and coordinates interservice, national, and international sports activities and competitions for military personnel from the intramural level to the world class-athlete program.

NONPROFIT

American Alliance for Health, Physical Education, Recreation, and Dance, *1900 Association Dr., Reston, VA 20191; (703) 476-3400. Fax, (703) 476-9527. Michael Davis, Chief Executive Officer.*
General e-mail, info@aahperd.org
Web, www.aahperd.org

Membership: teachers and others who work with school health, physical education, athletics, recreation, dance, and safety education programs (kindergarten through postsecondary levels). Member associations are American Assn. for Leisure and Recreation, National Assn. for Girls and Women in Sport, American Assn. for Health Education, National Dance Assn., National Assn. for Sport and Physical Education, and American Assn. for Active Lifestyles and Fitness.

American Canoe Assn., *7432 Alban Station Blvd., #B-232, Springfield, VA 22150; (703) 451-0141. Fax, (703) 451-2245. Pamela Dillon, Executive Director.*
General e-mail, aca@acanet.org
Web, www.acanet.org

Membership: individuals and organizations interested in the promotion of canoeing, kayaking, and other paddle sports. Works to preserve the nation's recreational waterways. Sponsors programs in safety education, competition, recreation, public awareness, conservation, and public policy. Monitors legislation and regulations.

American Gaming Assn., *555 13th St. N.W., #1010E 20004-1109; (202) 637-6500. Fax, (202) 637-6507. Frank J. Fahrenkopf Jr., President. Information, (202) 637-6500.*
Web, www.americangaming.org

Membership: casinos, casino and gaming equipment manufacturers, and financial services companies. Compiles statistics and serves as an information clearinghouse on the gaming industry. Administers a task force to study gambling addiction, raise public awareness, and develop assistance programs. Monitors legislation and regulations.

American Hiking Society, *1422 Fenwick Lane, Silver Spring, MD 20910; (301) 565-6704. Fax, (301) 565-6714. Mary Margaret Sloan, President.*
General e-mail, info@americanhiking.org
Web, www.americanhiking.org

Membership: individuals and clubs interested in preserving America's trail system and protecting the interests of hikers and other trail users. Sponsors research on trail construction and a trail maintenance summer program. Provides information on outdoor volunteer opportunities on public lands.

American Medical Athletic Assn., *4405 East-West Hwy., #405, Bethesda, MD 20814; (301) 913-9517. Fax, (301) 913-9520. David Watt, Executive Director. Information, (800) 776-2732.*
General e-mail, run@amaasportsmed.org
Web, www.amaasportsmed.org

Membership: sports medicine and allied health professionals. Assists members in promoting physical fitness to their patients and in developing their own physical fitness programs. Promotes and reports on sports medicine research and discussion. (Sister organization to American Running Assn.)

American Recreation Coalition, *1225 New York Ave. N.W., #450 20005; (202) 682-9530. Fax, (202) 682-9529. Derrick A. Crandall, President.*
General e-mail, arc@funoutdoors.com
Web, www.funoutdoors.com

Membership: organized recreationists, national and regional corporations offering recreational products and services, and recreation industry trade associations. Works to increase public and private sector activity in public recreation, land and water management, and energy policy. Provides information on innovative recreational planning.

American Resort Development Assn., *1201 15th St. N.W., #400 20005; (202) 371-6700. Fax, (202) 289-8544. Howard Nusbaum, President.*
Web, www.arda.org

Membership: U.S. and international developers, builders, financiers, marketing companies, and others involved in resort, recreational, and community development. Serves as an information clearinghouse; monitors federal and state legislation affecting land, time share, and community development industries.

American Running Assn., *4405 East-West Hwy., #405, Bethesda, MD 20814; (301) 913-9517. Fax, (301) 913-9520. David Watt, Executive Director. Information, (800) 776-2732.*
General e-mail, run@americanrunning.org
Web, www.americanrunning.org

Membership: athletes, health clubs, businesses, and individuals. Promotes proper nutrition and regular exercise. Provides members with medical advice and referrals, fitness information, and assistance in developing fitness programs. (Sister organization to American Medical Athletic Assn.)

American Sportfishing Assn., *225 Reinekers Lane, #420, Alexandria, VA 22314; (703) 519-9691. Fax, (703) 519-1872. Michael Nussman, President.*
General e-mail, info@asafishing.org
Web, www.asafishing.org

Works to ensure healthy and sustainable fish resources, to increase participation in sport fishing, and to make its members more profitable.

Bicycle Federation of America, *1506 21st St. N.W., #200 20036; (202) 463-6622. Fax, (202) 463-6625. William C. Wilkinson III, Executive Director.*
General e-mail, info@bikefed.org
Web, www.bikefed.org

Promotes bicycle use; conducts research, planning, and training projects; develops safety education and public information materials. Works to increase public awareness of the benefits and opportunities of bicycling and walking. Manages the Campaign to Make America Walkable.

Boat Owners Assn. of the United States, *Government and Public Affairs, 880 S. Pickett St., Alexandria, VA 22304; (703) 461-2864. Fax, (703) 461-2845. Michael Sciulla, Director.*
General e-mail, govtaffairs@boatus.com
Web, www.boatus.com

Membership: owners of recreational boats. Represents boat-owner interests before the federal govern-

ment; offers consumer protection and other services to members.

Disabled Sports USA, *451 Hungerford Dr., #100, Rockville, MD 20850; (301) 217-0960. Fax, (301) 217-0968. Kirk M. Bauer, Executive Director. TTY, (301) 217-0963.*
General e-mail, dsusa@dsusa.org
Web, www.disabledsportsusa.org

Conducts sports and recreation activities and physical fitness programs for people with disabilities and their families and friends; conducts workshops and competitions; participates in world championships.

Future Fisherman Foundation, *225 Reinekers Lane, #420, Alexandria, VA 22314; (703) 519-9691. Fax, (703) 519-1872. Anne Glick, Director.*
General e-mail, info@asafishing.org
Web, www.asafishing.org

Promotes sportfishing to youth through programs such as the Tackle Box Program, a resource for fishing equipment, and the Hooked on Fishing—Not on Drugs Campaign, a curriculum program. (Affiliated with the American Sportfishing Assn.)

National Aeronautic Assn., *1815 N. Fort Myer Dr., #500, Arlington, VA 22209; (703) 527-0226. Fax, (703) 527-0229. Donald J. Koranda, President.*
General e-mail, naa@naa-usa.org
Web, www.naa-usa.org

Membership: persons interested in development of general and sporting aviation. Supervises sporting aviation competitions; oversees and approves official U.S. aircraft, aeronautics, and astronautics records. Interests include aeromodeling, aerobatics, helicopters, ultralights, home-built aircraft, parachuting, soaring, hang gliding, and ballooning. Serves as U.S. representative to the International Aeronautical Federation in Lausanne, Switzerland.

National Assn. for Girls and Women in Sport, *1900 Association Dr., Reston, VA 20191-1599; (703) 476-3452. Fax, (703) 476-4566. Athena Yiamouyiannis, Director.*
General e-mail, nagws@aahperd.org
Web, www.nagws.org

Membership: students, coaches, physical education teachers, athletes, athletic directors, and trainers for girls' and women's sports programs. Seeks to increase sports opportunity for women and girls; provides information on laws relating to equality of sports funds and facilities for women; hosts training sites and rates officials; publishes sports guides; maintains speakers bureau.

National Collegiate Athletic Assn. (NCAA), *Government Relations, Washington Office,* 1 Dupont Circle N.W., #310 20036; (202) 293-3050. Fax, (202) 293-3075. *Abe L. Frank, Director.*
Web, www.ncaa.org

Membership: senior colleges and universities, conferences, and organizations interested in the administration of intercollegiate athletics. Certifies institutions' athletic programs; compiles records and statistics; produces publications and television programs; administers youth development programs; awards student athletes with postgraduate scholarships and degree-completion grants. (Headquarters in Indianapolis, Ind.)

National Football League Players Assn., 2021 L St. N.W., #600 20036; (202) 463-2200. Fax, (202) 857-0380. *Gene Upshaw, Executive Director.*
Web, www.nflplayers.com

Membership: professional football players. Represents members in matters concerning wages, hours, and working conditions. Provides assistance to charitable and community organizations. Sponsors programs and events to promote the image of professional football and its players.

National Recreation and Park Assn., 22377 Belmont Ridge Rd., Ashburn, VA 20148-4501; (703) 858-0784. Fax, (703) 858-0794. *John A. Thorner, Executive Director.*
General e-mail, info@nrpa.org
Web, www.nrpa.org

Membership: park and recreation professionals and interested citizens. Promotes support and awareness of park, recreation, and leisure services; facilitates development, expansion, and management of resources; provides technical assistance for park and recreational programs; and provides professional development to members.

National Spa and Pool Institute, 2111 Eisenhower Ave., Alexandria, VA 22314-4698; (703) 838-0083. Fax, (703) 549-0493. *Jack Cergol, Chief Staff Executive.*
Web, www.nspi.org

Membership: manufacturers, dealers, service companies, builders, and distributors of pools, spas, and hot tubs. Promotes the industry; compiles statistics; establishes construction standards for pools and spas. Monitors legislation and regulations.

Road Runners Club of America, 510 N. Washington St., Alexandria, VA 22314; (703) 836-0558. Fax, (703) 836-4430. *David Dobrzynski, Executive Director. Information,* (703) 683-7722.
General e-mail, office@rrca.org
Web, www.rrca.org

Develops and promotes road races and fitness programs, including the Children's Running Development Program. Issues guidelines on road races. Interests include safety, wheelchair participation, and baby joggers/strollers in races; facilitates communication between clubs. Supports running for people with disabilities.

Snowsports Industries America, 8377-B Greensboro Dr., McLean, VA 22102; (703) 556-9020. Fax, (703) 821-8276. *David Ingemie, President.*
General e-mail, siamail@snowsports.org
Web, www.snowlink.com

Membership: manufacturers and distributors of ski and other outdoor sports equipment, apparel, accessories, and footwear. Interests include international markets.

Society of State Directors of Health, Physical Education, and Recreation, 1900 Association Dr., #100, Reston, VA 20191; (703) 390-4599. Fax, (703) 476-0988. *Sharon Murray, Executive Director.*
General e-mail, info@thesociety.org
Web, www.thesociety.org

Membership: state directors, supervisors, and coordinators for physical and health education and recreation activities in state education departments, and other interested individuals. Seeks to improve school programs on comprehensive health, physical education, athletics, outdoor education, recreation, and safety.

Special Olympics International, 1325 G St. N.W., #500 20005; (202) 628-3630. Fax, (202) 824-0200. *Robert Sargent Shriver Jr., Chair.*
General e-mail, soimail@aol.com
Web, www.specialolympics.org

Offers individuals with mental retardation opportunities for year-round sports training; sponsors athletic competition worldwide in twenty-two individual and team sports.

U.S. Eventing Association (USEA), 525 Old Waterford Rd. N.W., Leesburg, VA 20176; (703) 779-0440. Fax, (703) 779-0550. *Jo Whitehouse, Executive Director.*
General e-mail, info@eventingusa.com
Web, www.eventingusa.com

Membership: individuals interested in eventing, an Olympic-recognized equestrian sport. Registers all national events to ensure that they meet the standards set by the USA Equestrian Assn. Sponsors three-day events for members from novice to Olympic levels. Provides educational materials on competition, riding, and care of horses.

U.S. Olympic Committee, *Washington Office,* 1150 18th St. N.W., #300 20036; (202) 466-3399. Fax, (202) 466-5068. *Stephen Bull, Director, Government Relations.*

Web, www.usolympicteam.com

Responsible for training, entering, and underwriting the full expenses for U.S. teams in the Olympic and Pan American Games. Supports the bid of U.S. cities to host the Olympic and Pan American Games; recognizes the national governing body of each sport in these games. Promotes international athletic competition. (Headquarters in Colorado Springs, Colo.)

U.S. Parachute Assn., *1440 Duke St., Alexandria, VA 22314; (703) 836-3495. Fax, (703) 836-2843. Christopher Needels, Executive Director. Information, (800) 371-8772. General e-mail, uspa@uspa.org*

Web, www.uspa.org

Membership: individuals and organizations interested in skydiving. Develops safety procedures; maintains training programs; issues skydiving licenses and ratings; certifies skydiving instructors; sanctions national competitions; and documents record attempts. Offers liability insurance to members. Monitors legislation and regulations.

 **TRAVEL AND TOURISM**

AGENCIES

Bureau of Citizenship and Immigration Services (BCIS), *(Homeland Security Dept.),* *Nebraska Ave. Complex, 3801 Nebraska Ave. N.W. 20395; (202) 282-8000 (switchboard). Eduardo Aguirre, Director (Acting). Automated information, (800) 375-5283 or TTY, (800) 767-1833.*

Web, www.bcis.gov

Clears aliens and U.S. citizens for entry into the United States. Compiles statistics on tourists.

International Trade Administration (ITA), *(Commerce Dept.), Tourism Industries, 14th St. and Constitution Ave. N.W., #7025 20230; (202) 482-0140. Fax, (202) 482-2887. Helen Marano, Director of Office, Travel and Tourism Industries.*

Web, tinet.ita.doc.gov

Fosters tourism trade development, including public-private partnerships; represents the United States in tourism-related meetings with foreign government officials. Assembles, analyzes, and disseminates data and statistics on travel and tourism.

State Dept., *Consular Affairs: Passport Services, 2201 C St. N.W., #6811 20520; (202) 955-0307. Fax, (202) 647-0341. Frank Moss, Deputy Assistant Secretary. Passport information, (900) 225-5674.*

Web, travel.state.gov/passport_services.html

Administers passport laws and issues passports. (Most branches of the U.S. Postal Service and most U.S. district and state courts are authorized to accept applications and payment for passports and to administer the required oath to U.S. citizens. Completed applications are sent from the post office or court to the nearest State Dept. regional passport office for processing.) Maintains a variety of records received from the Overseas Citizens Services, including consular certificates of witness to marriage and reports of birth and death. (Individuals wishing to apply for a U.S. passport may seek additional information via the phone number or Web address listed above.)

CONGRESS

House Energy and Commerce Committee, *Subcommittee on Commerce, Trade, and Consumer Protection, 2125 RHOB 20515; (202) 225-2927. Fax, (202) 225-1919. Rep. Cliff Stearns, R-Fla., Chair.*

General e-mail, commerce@mail.house.gov

Web, energycommerce.house.gov/108/subcommittees/ Commerce_Trade_and_Consumer_Protection.htm

Jurisdiction over legislation affecting tourism.

Senate Commerce, Science, and Transportation Committee, *Subcommittee on Competition, Foreign Commerce, and Infrastructure, SH-428 20510; (202) 224-5183. Fax, (202) 228-0326. Sen. Gordon H. Smith, R-Ore., Chair; Carlos Fierro, Senior Counsel.*

Web, commerce.senate.gov

Jurisdiction over legislation affecting tourism.

INTERNATIONAL ORGANIZATIONS

Organization of American States (OAS), *Inter-Sectoral Unit for Tourism, 1889 F St. N.W., #300A 20006; (202) 458-3196. Fax, (202) 458-3190. Cecil Miller, Director.*

General e-mail, tourism@oas.org

Web, www.oas.org/tourism

Responsible for matters related to tourism and its development in the hemisphere. Provides support to the Inter-American Travel Congress; works for sustainable tourism development; promotes cooperation among international, regional, and subregional tourism offices.

NONPROFIT

American Hotel and Lodging Assn., *1201 New York Ave. N.W., #600 20005-3931; (202) 289-3100. Fax, (202) 289-3199. Joseph McInerney, President.*

General e-mail, info@ahla.com

Web, www.ahla.com

Provides operations, technical, educational, marketing, and communications services to members; focus includes international travel. Monitors legislation and regulations.

American Society of Travel Agents, *1101 King St., #200, Alexandria, VA 22314; (703) 739-2782. Fax, (703) 684-8319. Richard M. Copland, President.*
General e-mail, askasta@astahq.com
Web, www.astanet.com
Membership: representatives of the travel industry. Works to safeguard the traveling public against fraud, misrepresentation, and other unethical practices. Offers training programs for travel agents. Consumer affairs department offers help for anyone with a travel complaint against a member of the association.

Hostelling International—American Youth Hostels, *8401 Colesville Rd., #600, Silver Spring, MD 20910; (301) 495-1240. Fax, (301) 495-6697. Russell Hedge, Executive Director.*
General e-mail, hiayhserv@hiayh.org
Web, www.hiayh.org
Provides opportunities for outdoor recreation and inexpensive educational travel through hostelling. Member of the International Youth Hostel Federation.

Hotel Employees and Restaurant Employees International, *1219 28th St. N.W. 20007; (202) 393-4373. Fax, (202) 333-0468. John W. Wilhelm, President.*
Web, www.hereunion.org
Membership: approximately 241,000 hotel and restaurant employees. Helps members negotiate pay, benefits, and better working conditions; conducts training programs and workshops. Monitors legislation and regulations. (Affiliated with the AFL-CIO.)

International Assn. of Amusement Parks and Attractions, *1448 Duke St., Alexandria, VA 22314; (703) 836-4800. Fax, (703) 836-4801. Clark Robinson, President. Fax-on-demand, (703) 836-9678.*
General e-mail, iaapa@iaapa.org
Web, www.iaapa.org
Membership: companies from around the world in the amusement parks and attractions industry. Conducts an international exchange program for members. Monitors legislation and regulations.

International Assn. of Convention and Visitor Bureaus, *2025 M St. N.W., #500 20036-3349; (202) 296-7888. Fax, (202) 296-7889. Michael Gehrisch, President.*
General e-mail, iacvb@iacvb.org
Web, www.iacvb.org

Membership: travel- and tourism-related businesses, convention and meeting professionals, and tour operators. Encourages business travelers and tourists to visit local historic, cultural, and recreational areas; assists in meeting preparations. Monitors legislation and regulations.

International Council of Cruise Lines, *2111 Wilson Blvd., 8th Floor, Arlington, VA 22201; (703) 522-8463. Fax, (703) 522-3811. Michael Crye, President.*
General e-mail, info@iccl.org
Web, www.iccl.org
Membership: Chief executives of sixteen cruise lines and other cruise industry professionals. Advises domestic and international regulatory organizations on shipping policy. Works with U.S. and international agencies to promote safety, public health, security, medical facilities, environmental awareness, and passenger protection. Monitors legislation and regulations about the cruise industry.

National Business Travel Assn., *110 N. Royal St., 4th Floor, Alexandria, VA 22314; (703) 684-0836. Fax, (703) 684-0263. Bill Connors, Executive Director.*
General e-mail, info@nbta.org
Web, www.nbta.org
Membership: corporate travel managers. Promotes educational advancement of members and provides a forum for exchange of information on U.S. and international travel. Monitors legislation and regulations.

Passenger Vessel Assn., *801 N. Quincy St., #200, Arlington, VA 22203; (703) 807-0100. Fax, (703) 807-0103. John R. Groundwater, Executive Director.*
Web, www.passengervessel.com
Membership: owners, operators, and suppliers for U.S. and Canadian passenger vessels; and international vessel companies. Interests include dinner and excursion boats, car and passenger ferries, overnight cruise ships, and riverboat casinos. Monitors legislation and regulations.

Travel Industry Assn. of America, *1100 New York Ave. N.W., #450W 20005; (202) 408-8422. Fax, (202) 408-1255. William S. Norman, President.*
Web, www.tia.org
Membership: business, professional, and trade associations of the travel industry and state and local associations (including official state government tourism offices) promoting tourism to a specific region or site. Encourages travel to and within the United States.

6 *ABC*

Education

AGENCIES

Education Dept., *400 Maryland Ave. S.W., #7W301 20202; (202) 401-3000. Fax, (202) 260-7867. Roderick R. Paige, Secretary; Philip Link, Director, Executive Secretariat; Brian Jones, General Counsel. Information, (202) 401-2000. TTY, (800) 437-0833. Toll-free, (800) 872-5327.*
Web, www.ed.gov

Establishes education policy and acts as principal adviser to the president on education matters; administers and coordinates most federal assistance programs on education.

Education Dept., *Intergovernmental and Interagency Affairs, 400 Maryland Ave. S.W., #5E317 20202-3500; (202) 401-0404. Fax, (202) 401-8607. Laurie M. Rich, Assistant Secretary. Press, (202) 401-1576. TTY, (800) 437-0833. Information, (800) USA-LEARN.*
Web, www.ed.gov/offices/OIIA

Disseminates information on government programs that encourage public understanding and support for improving American education. Engages government, business, religious, and community organizations, as well as families, students, and the general public. Oversees recognition programs (Presidential Scholars, President's Education Awards, No Child Left Behind Blue Ribbon Schools).

Education Dept., *National Center for Education Statistics: Assessment, 1990 K St. N.W., 8th Floor 20006-5574; (202) 502-7321. Fax, (202) 502-7440. Peggy G. Carr, Associate Commissioner.*
Web, www.nces.ed.gov/nationsreportcard/sitemap.asp

Assesses the abilities of U.S. students in various subject areas on national and state levels. Makes findings available to policymakers at the national, state, and local levels.

Education Dept., *School Support and Technology, 400 Maryland Ave. S.W., #3E115 20202-6400; (202) 401-0039. Fax, (202) 205-5870. Sylvia L. Wright, Director. Information, (800) 872-5327. Press, (202) 401-1576. TTY, (800) 437-0833.*
Web, www.ed.gov

Provides a coordinated strategy to focus federal resources on supporting improvements in schools; promotes development and implementation of comprehensive improvement plans that direct resources toward improved achievement for all students.

Educational Resources Information Center (ERIC), *(Education Dept.), 2277 Research Blvd., #4M, Rockville,*
MD 20850-3172; (301) 519-5157. Fax, (301) 519-6760. Lynn Smarte, Project Director. Information, (800) 538-3742.
General e-mail, accesseric@accesseric.org
Web, www.eric.ed.gov

Coordinates a national information system comprising sixteen clearinghouses on specific subjects. Documents available in microfiche form at most university libraries. Answers queries and offers referrals to individuals on all facets of education.

For a list of clearinghouses on the Web, see box (p. 185).

CONGRESS

General Accounting Office (GAO), *Education, Workforce, and Income Security, 441 G St. N.W., #5928 20548; (202) 512-7215. Cynthia Fagnoni, Managing Director.*
Web, www.gao.gov

Independent, nonpartisan agency in the legislative branch that audits, analyzes, and evaluates Health and Human Services Dept. programs, including Social Security; makes reports available to the public.

House Appropriations Committee, *Subcommittee on Labor, Health and Human Services, Education, and Related Agencies, 2358 RHOB 20515; (202) 225-3508. Fax, (202) 225-3509. Rep. Ralph Regula, R-Ohio, Chair; Craig Higgins, Staff Director.*
Web, www.house.gov/appropriations

Jurisdiction over legislation to appropriate funds for federal education programs (except native American education programs), including adult education, compensatory education, and education for the disadvantaged and disabled.

House Education and the Workforce Committee, *Subcommittee on Education Reform, 2181 RHOB 20515; (202) 225-4527. Fax, (202) 225-9571. Rep. Michael N. Castle, R-Del., Chair; Paula Nowakowski, Staff Director.*
Web, edworkforce.house.gov/members/108th/mem-edr.htm

Jurisdiction over legislation on preschool, elementary, and secondary education; vocational education; school lunch and child nutrition; special education programs including alcohol and drug abuse, education of the disabled, migrant and agricultural labor education, and education for the homeless; educational research and improvement; overseas dependent schools.

House Education and the Workforce Committee, *Subcommittee on Select Education, 2181 RHOB 20515; (202) 225-4527. Fax, (202) 225-9571. Rep. Peter Hoekstra, R-Mich., Chair; Paula Nowakowski, Staff Director.*

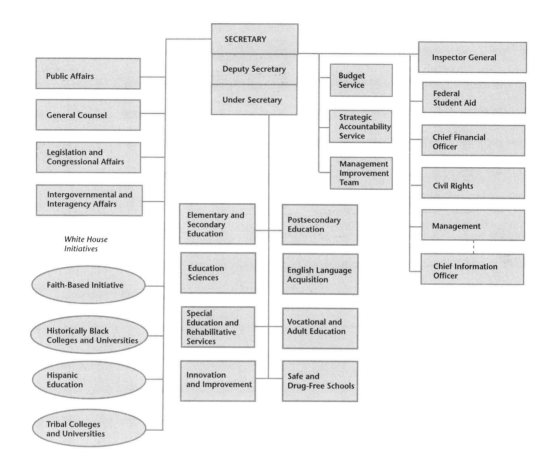

SECRETARY

Deputy Secretary

Under Secretary

Public Affairs

General Counsel

Legislation and Congressional Affairs

Intergovernmental and Interagency Affairs

White House Initiatives

Faith-Based Initiative

Historically Black Colleges and Universities

Hispanic Education

Tribal Colleges and Universities

Elementary and Secondary Education

Education Sciences

Special Education and Rehabilitative Services

Innovation and Improvement

Postsecondary Education

English Language Acquisition

Vocational and Adult Education

Safe and Drug-Free Schools

Budget Service

Strategic Accountability Service

Management Improvement Team

Inspector General

Federal Student Aid

Chief Financial Officer

Civil Rights

Management

Chief Information Officer

Web, edworkforce.house.gov/members/108th/mem-sed.htm

Jurisdiction over the School to Work Opportunities Act; library services and construction; environmental education; programs and services for at-risk youth; programs related to the arts and humanities.

House Education and the Workforce Committee, *Subcommittee on 21st Century Competitiveness,* *2181 RHOB 20515; (202) 225-4527. Fax, (202) 225-9571. Rep. Howard P. "Buck" McKeon, R-Calif., Chair; Paula Nowakowski, Staff Director.*
Web, edworkforce.house.gov/members/108th/mem-21st.htm

Jurisdiction over legislation on education beyond the high school level, including student assistance and employment services; training and apprenticeship; adult basic education (family literacy); rehabilitation; profes-

sional development; teacher training; and science and technology programs. Oversees the Robert A. Taft Institute and the Institute for Peace.

House Government Reform Committee, *Subcommittee on Criminal Justice, Drug Policy, and Human Resources, B373 RHOB 20515; (202) 225-2577. Fax, (202) 225-1154. Rep. Mark Souder, R-Ind., Chair; Christopher Donesa, Staff Director.*
Web, www.house.gov/reform

Oversees operations of the Education Dept.

Senate Appropriations Committee, *Subcommittee on Labor, Health and Human Services, Education, and Related Agencies, SD-184 20510; (202) 224-3471. Fax, (202) 224-8553. Sen. Arlen Specter, R-Pa., Chair; Bettilou Taylor, Clerk.*

Web, appropriations.senate.gov

Jurisdiction over legislation to appropriate funds for federal education programs, including adult education, compensatory education, and education for the disadvantaged and disabled.

Senate Health, Education, Labor, and Pensions Committee, SD-428 20510; (202) 224-5375. Fax, (202) 228-5044. Sen. Judd Gregg, R-N.H., Chair; Sharon Soderstrom, Staff Director. TTY, (202) 224-1975.
Web, health.senate.gov

Jurisdiction over legislation on preschool, elementary, secondary, and vocational education, including community schools, aid to private schools, the Office of Educational Research and Improvement, education technology, and drug and alcohol abuse education. Jurisdiction over legislation on postsecondary education, libraries, and education of people with disabilities; jurisdiction over legislation barring discrimination in education. Oversees operations of the Education Dept.

NONPROFIT

Annenberg Public Policy Center, 529 14th St. N.W., #320 20045; (202) 879-6700. Fax, (202) 879-6707. Lorie Slass, Director.
General e-mail, appcdc@appcpenn.org
Web, www.appcpenn.org

Supports research on public policy issues at the federal level. Sponsors lectures and conferences.

Capital Children's Museum, 800 3rd St. N.E. 20002; (202) 675-4120. Fax, (202) 675-4140. Kathy Dwyer Sutton, Executive Director. Press, (202) 675-4135.
Web, www.ccm.org

Designs, implements, and conducts studies in education. Interests include the creation and development of new educational methods, materials, and structures. Maintains the Options School.

Center for Education Reform, 1001 Connecticut Ave. N.W., #204 20036; (202) 822-9000. Fax, (202) 822-5077. Jeanne Allen, President.
General e-mail, cer@edreform.com
Web, www.edreform.com

Provides support and guidance to individuals, community and civic groups, policymakers, and others who are working to bring fundamental reforms to their schools.

Center for Law and Education, Washington Office, 1875 Connecticut Ave. N.W., #510 20009-5728; (202) 986-3000. Fax, (202) 986-6648. Paul Weckstein, Co-Director. Publications, (202) 462-7688.

General e-mail, cle@cleweb.org
Web, www.cleweb.org

Works to advance the right of all students, and low-income students in particular, to a high-quality education. Interests include testing and tracking; bilingual education; discriminatory discipline; special education; special needs for native Americans, migrants, and Hispanics; parent, community, and student participation in education; and vocational and compensatory education. (Headquarters in Boston, Mass.)

Charles F. Kettering Foundation, Washington Office, 444 N. Capitol St. N.W., #434 20001-1512; (202) 393-4478. Fax, (202) 393-7644. Phillip D. Lurie, Director (Acting).
Web, www.kettering.org

Works to improve the domestic policy-making process. Supports international program focusing on unofficial, citizen-to-citizen diplomacy. Encourages greater citizen involvement in formation of public policy. Interests include public education and at-risk youths. (Headquarters in Dayton, Ohio.)

Council for Advancement and Support of Education, 1307 New York Ave. N.W., #1000 20005; (202) 328-5900. Fax, (202) 387-4973. Vance Peterson, President.
General e-mail, info@case.org
Web, www.case.org

Membership: two- and four-year colleges, universities, and independent schools. Offers professional education and training programs to members; advises members on institutional advancement issues, including fundraising, alumni affairs, public relations programs, government relations, and management. Library open to the public by appointment.

Council for Advancement and Support of Education, Matching Gifts Clearinghouse, 1307 New York Ave. N.W., #1000 20005-4701; (202) 478-5634. Fax, (202) 387-4973. Matt Konetschni, Director.
General e-mail, matchinggifts@case.org
Web, www.case.org

Provides companies and educational institutions with information on matching gift programs, in which companies match employee contributions to educational and other nonprofit institutions.

Distributive Education Clubs of America, 1908 Association Dr., Reston, VA 20191-1594; (703) 860-5000. Fax, (703) 860-4013. Edward L. Davis, Executive Director.
General e-mail, decainc@aol.com
Web, www.deca.org

Educational organization that helps high school and college students develop skills in marketing, management, and entrepreneurship. Promotes business and education partnerships.

Education Policy Institute, *4401-A Connecticut Ave. N.W., PMB 294 20008-2322; (202) 244-7535. Fax, (202) 244-7584. Charlene K. Haar, President; Myron Lieberman, Chair.*
General e-mail, info@educationpolicy.org
Web, www.educationpolicy.org

Seeks to improve education through research, policy analysis, and the development of alternatives to current policies and practices. Promotes greater parental choice in education, a more competitive education industry, and an increase in the creative role of for-profit schools.

Ethics Resource Center, *1747 Pennsylvania Ave. N.W., #400 20006; (202) 737-2258. Fax, (202) 737-2227. Stuart C. Gilman, President. Information, (800) 777-1285. Press, (202) 872-4768.*
Web, www.ethics.org

Nonpartisan educational organization whose vision is an ethical world. Fosters ethical practices among individuals and institutions. Interests include research and knowledge building, education and advocacy, and consulting and technical assistance.

Institute for Educational Leadership, *1001 Connecticut Ave. N.W., #310 20036; (202) 822-8405. Fax, (202) 872-4050. Elizabeth Hale, President.*
General e-mail, iel@iel.org
Web, www.iel.org

Works with educators, human services personnel, government officials, and association executives to improve educational opportunities for youths; conducts research on education issues.

National Assn. of State Boards of Education,
277 S. Washington St., #100, Alexandria, VA 22314; (703) 684-4000. Fax, (703) 836-2313. Brenda L. Welburn, Executive Director.
General e-mail, boards@nasbe.org
Web, www.nasbe.org

Membership: members of state boards of education, state board attorneys, and executives to state boards. Interests include strengthening state leadership in educational policy making; promoting excellence in the education of all students; advocating equality of access to educational opportunity; and assuring continued citizen support for public education.

EDUCATIONAL RESOURCES INFORMATION CENTER (ERIC) CLEARINGHOUSES

ERIC, supported by the Education Dept.'s Office of Educational Research and Improvement and administered by the National Library of Education, provides users with access to a national information system of education-related literature. Its clearinghouses collect, abstract, index, and disseminate information in sixteen subject-specific categories.

Adult, Career, and Vocational Education
Web, ericacve.org

AskERIC
Web, ericir.syr.edu

Assessment and Evaluation
Web, ericae.net

Community College
Web, www.gseis.ucla.edu/ERIC/eric.html

Counseling and Student Services
Web, ericcass.uncg.edu

Disabilities and Gifted Education
Web, www.ericec.org

Educational Management
Web, eric.uoregon.edu

Elementary and Early Childhood Education
Web, ericeece.org

Higher Education
Web, www.eriche.org

Information and Technology
Web, ericir.syr.edu/ithome

Languages and Linguistics
Web, www.cal.org/ericcll

National Parent Information Network
Web, npin.org

Reading, English, and Communication
Web, www.indiana.edu/~eric_rec

Rural Education and Small Schools
Web, www.ael.org/eric

Science, Mathematics, and Environmental Education
Web, www.ericse.org

Social Studies/Social Science Education
Web, www.indiana.edu/~ssdc/eric_chess.htm

Teaching and Teacher Education
Web, www.ericsp.org

Urban Education
Web, eric-web.tc.columbia.edu

National Center for Education Information,
4401-A Connecticut Ave. N.W., PMB 212 20008; (202) 362-3444. Fax, (202) 362-3493. C. Emily Feistritzer, President.
General e-mail, cef@ncei.com
Web, www.ncei.com

Specializes in survey research and data analysis of alternative teacher preparation and certification. Conducts national and state surveys of teachers, school administrators, school board presidents, state departments of education, local school districts, and individuals interested in becoming teachers.

National Center on Education and the Economy,
America's Choice District and School Design, 1 Thomas Circle N.W., #700 20005; (202) 783-3668. Fax, (202) 783-3672. Larry Molinaro, Director.
General e-mail, info@ncee.org
Web, www.ncee.org

Partnership of states, school districts, corporations, foundations, and nonprofit organizations that provides tools and technical assistance to help school systems improve student performance. Areas of focus include standards, assessments, curriculum, and instruction.

National Community Education Assn., *3929 Old Lee Hwy., #91-A, Fairfax, VA 22030-2401; (703) 359-8973. Fax, (703) 359-0972. Starla Jewell-Kelly, Executive Director.*
General e-mail, ncea@ncea.com
Web, www.ncea.com

Works for greater recognition of community education programs, services, and personnel. Interests include business-education partnerships to improve schools; lifelong learning; school-site child care and latchkey programs; extended learning opportunities and after school programs; and parental involvement in public education.

National Humanities Institute (NHI), *P.O. Box 1387, Bowie, MD 20718-1387; (301) 464-4277. Fax, (301) 464-4277. Joseph F. Baldacchino, President. Phone and fax are the same number.*
General e-mail, mail@nhinet.org
Web, www.nhinet.org

Promotes research, publishing, and teaching in the humanities. Interests include the effect of the humanities on society.

National School Public Relations Assn., *15948 Derwood Rd., Rockville, MD 20855; (301) 519-0496. Fax, (301) 519-0494. Richard D. Bagin, Executive Director.*
General e-mail, nspra@nspra.org
Web, www.nspra.org

Membership: educators and individuals interested in improving communications in education. Works to improve communication between educators and the public on the needs of schools; provides educators with information on public relations and policy developments.

New American Schools, *675 N. Washington St., #220, Alexandria, VA 22314; (703) 647-1600. Fax, (703) 647-1700. Mary Anne Schmitt, President.*
General e-mail, info@nasdc.org
Web, www.newamericanschools.org

Promotes comprehensive school improvement strategies; provides services to education providers to strengthen their offerings to schools.

Internships, Fellowships, Grants

AGENCIES

Harry S. Truman Scholarship Foundation, *712 Jackson Pl. N.W., 3rd Floor 20006-4901; (202) 395-4831. Fax, (202) 395-6995. Louis H. Blair, Executive Secretary.*
General e-mail, office@truman.gov
Web, www.truman.gov

Memorial to Harry S. Truman established by Congress. Provides students preparing for careers in public service with scholarships. (Candidates are nominated by their respective colleges or universities while in their third year of undergraduate study.)

National Endowment for the Arts (NEA), *(National Foundation on the Arts and the Humanities), 1100 Pennsylvania Ave. N.W. 20506-0001; (202) 682-5400. Fax, (202) 682-5611. Dana Gioia, Chair. Library, (202) 682-5485. Press, (202) 682-5570. TTY, (202) 682-5496.*
Web, www.arts.gov

Independent federal grant-making agency. Awards grants to nonprofit arts organizations for specified projects in five areas: creativity; arts learning access; heritage and preservation; challenge America; and organizational capacity. Organizations must choose one of the five theme areas for submission of project proposals. Library open to the public by appointment.

National Endowment for the Humanities (NEH), *(National Foundation on the Arts and the Humanities), 1100 Pennsylvania Ave. N.W., #503 20506; (202) 606-8310. Fax, (202) 606-8588. Bruce Cole, Chair. Information, (202) 606-8400. Library, (202) 606-8244. Press, (202) 606-8446. TTY, (202) 606-8282.*
General e-mail, info@neh.gov
Web, www.neh.gov

Independent federal grant-making agency. Awards grants to individuals and institutions for research, scholarship, educational programs, and public programs (including broadcasts, museum exhibitions, lectures, and symposia) in the humanities (defined as study of archeology; history; jurisprudence; language; linguistics; literature; philosophy; comparative religion; ethics; the history, criticism, and theory of the arts; and humanistic aspects of the social sciences). Funds preservation of books, newspapers, historical documents, and photographs.

National Endowment for the Humanities (NEH), *(National Foundation on the Arts and the Humanities), Research and Education,* 1100 Pennsylvania Ave. N.W., #318 20506; (202) 606-8200. Fax, (202) 606-8394. *James Herbert, Director.*
General e-mail, education@neh.gov
Web, www.neh.gov

Offers fellowships, stipends, seminars, and institutes for higher education faculty, school teachers, and independent scholars. Conducts research.

National Science Foundation (NSF), *Graduate Education,* 4201 Wilson Blvd., #907, Arlington, VA 22230; (703) 292-8630. Fax, (703) 292-9048. *James Lightbourne, Director (Acting). TTY, (703) 306-0090.*
Web, www.nsf.gov/EHR/DGE/dge.htm

Supports activities to strengthen the education of research scientists and engineers; promotes career development; offers pre- and postdoctoral fellowships for study and research; manages the graduate fellowships and the travel awards for the NATO–Advanced Study Institute.

President's Commission on White House Fellowships, 712 Jackson Pl. N.W. 20503; (202) 395-4522. Fax, (202) 395-6179. *Jocelyn White, Director.*
General e-mail, info@whitehousefellows.gov
Web, www.whitehousefellows.gov

Nonpartisan commission that provides professionals from all sectors of national life with the opportunity to observe firsthand the processes of the federal government. Fellows work for one year as special assistants to cabinet members or to principal members of the White House staff. Qualified applicants have demonstrated superior accomplishments early in their careers and have a commitment to community service.

Smithsonian Institution, *Fellowships,* 900 Jefferson Dr. S.W. 20560 (mailing address: P.O. Box 37012, Victor Bldg. 9300, MRC 902 20013-7012); (202) 275-0655. Fax, (202) 275-0489. *Catherine F. Harris, Director.*

General e-mail, siofg@si.edu
Web, www.si.edu/ofg

Administers internships and fellowships in residence for study and research at the Smithsonian Institution in history of science and technology, American and cultural history, history of art, anthropology, evolutionary and systematic biology, environmental sciences, astrophysics and astronomy, earth sciences, and tropical biology.

Woodrow Wilson International Center for Scholars, *Fellowships,* 1300 Pennsylvania Ave. N.W. 20004-3027; (202) 691-4000. Fax, (202) 691-4001. *Rosemary Lyon, Director.*
General e-mail, fellowships@wwic.si.edu
Web, www.wilsoncenter.org

Awards fellowships to established scholars and professionals from the United States and abroad for humanities and social science research at the center. Publishes guides to scholarly research material in the Washington area.

NONPROFIT

American Assn. of University Women Educational Foundation, 1111 16th St. N.W. 20036; (202) 728-7602. Fax, (202) 463-7169. *Nancy Eynon Lark, Director.*
General e-mail, foundation@aauw.org
Web, www.aauw.org

Awards fellowships and grants to women for various areas of study and educational pursuit. Offers fellowships to foreign women coming to the United States for one year of graduate study. Awards grants to women returning to school for postbaccalaureate education or professional development. Administers the Eleanor Roosevelt Fund, which supports a teacher sabbatical program for women who teach girls math and science in grades K–12. (Affiliate of the American Assn. of University Women.)

American Institute of Architects, *American Architectural Foundation,* 1799 New York Ave. N.W. 20006; (202) 626-7500. Fax, (202) 626-7420. *Ronald E. Bogle, President (Acting). Library, (202) 626-7492.*
General e-mail, info@archfoundation.org
Web, www.archfoundation.org

Seeks to advance the quality of American architecture. Works to increase public awareness and understanding, and apply new technology to create more humane environments. Acts as liaison between the profession and the public; awards grants for architecture-oriented projects. Serves as the educational arm of the American Institute of Architects. Also operates the historic Octagon Museum.

INTERNSHIPS IN WASHINGTON

The following are some key organizations offering internships in the Washington area. For congressional internships, contact the individual member's office (see appendix).

Alexis de Tocqueville Institution, (202) 548-0006

American Civil Liberties Union, (202) 544-1681

American Enterprise Institute for Public Policy Research, (202) 862-5800

Amnesty International USA, (202) 544-0200

Brookings Institution, (202) 797-6096

C-SPAN, (202) 737-3220

Cato Institute, (202) 842-0200

Center for Defense Information, (202) 332-0600

Center for Policy Alternatives, (202) 387-6030

Center for Science in the Public Interest, (202) 332-9110

Center for Strategic and International Studies, (202) 887-0200

Center for Study of Responsive Law, (202) 387-8030

Central Intelligence Agency, (703) 482-1100

Children's Defense Fund, (202) 628-8787

Concord Coalition, (703) 894-6222

Conservative Caucus, (703) 938-9626

Democratic National Committee, (202) 863-8000

Empower America, (202) 452-8200

Environmental Protection Agency, (202) 564-1111

Fund for the Feminist Majority, (703) 522-2214

General Accounting Office, (202) 512-3429

The Heritage Foundation, (202) 546-4400

Institute for Policy Studies, (202) 234-9382

John F. Kennedy Center for the Performing Arts, (202) 416-8807

Joint Center for Political and Economic Studies, (202) 789-3500

Library of Congress, (202) 707-2087

National Audubon Society, (202) 861-2242

National Institutes of Health, (301) 402-2176

National Public Radio, (202) 513-2909

National Wildlife Federation, (202) 797-6800

Office of Personnel Management, (202) 606-2525

Progress and Freedom Foundation, (202) 289-8928

Public Defender Service, (800) 341-2582

Republican National Committee, (202) 863-8563

Smithsonian Institution, (202) 357-3102

State Dept., (703) 875-7490

Supreme Court of the United States, (202) 479-3412

The Urban Institute, (202) 833-7200

The White House, (202) 456-1414

American Political Science Assn. (APSA), *Congressional Fellowship Program, 1527 New Hampshire Ave. N.W. 20036-1206; (202) 483-2512. Fax, (202) 483-2657. Jeff Biggs, Program Director.*
General e-mail, cfp@apsanet.org
Web, www.apsanet.org/about/cfp

Places mid-career political scientists, journalists, faculty of medical schools (Robert Wood Johnson Fellowships), and federal executives in congressional offices and committees for nine-month fellowships. Individual government agencies nominate federal executive participants.

Business and Professional Women's Foundation,
1900 M St. N.W., #310 20036; (202) 293-1100. Fax, (202) 861-0298. Cindy Patterson, President.
General e-mail, ea@bpw.org
Web, www.bpwusa.org

Works to improve women's economic status by promoting their employment at all levels in all occupations. Provides mature women seeking training and education

with scholarships and loans to increase their job skills. Awards grants for doctoral research on women's economic issues. (Affiliate of Business and Professional Women U.S.A.)

Center for the Study of the Presidency, *1020 19th St. N.W., #250 20036; (202) 872-9800. Fax, (202) 872-9811. David M. Abshire, President.*
General e-mail, center@thepresidency.org
Web, www.thepresidency.org

Membership: college students, government officials, and business leaders interested in the presidency, government, and politics. Educational organization that conducts conferences, lectures, and symposiums on domestic, economic, and foreign policy issues. Publishes papers, essays, books, and reports on various aspects of a president or the presidency.

Congressional Black Caucus Foundation, *1004 Pennsylvania Ave. S.E. 20003; (202) 675-6730. Fax, (202) 547-3806. Weldon J. Rougeau, President.*

Web, www.cbcfinc.org

Conducts public policy research on issues of concern to African Americans. Sponsors fellowship programs in which professionals and academic candidates work on congressional committees and subcommittees. Sponsors internship and scholarship programs.

Council for International Exchange of Scholars, *3007 Tilden St. N.W., #5L 20008-3009; (202) 686-4000. Fax, (202) 362-3442. Patti McGill Peterson, Executive Director.*

General e-mail, apprequest@cies.iie.org

Web, www.cies.org

Cooperates with the U.S. government in administering Fulbright grants for university teaching and advanced research abroad. (Affiliated with the American Council of Learned Societies.)

Council on Foundations, *1828 L St. N.W., #300 20036; (202) 466-6512. Fax, (202) 785-3926. Dorothy S. Ridings, President.*

Web, www.cof.org

Membership: independent community, family, and public and company-sponsored foundations; corporate giving programs; and foundations in other countries. Acts as clearinghouse for information on private philanthropy; sponsors conferences and workshops on effective grant making.

Foundation Center, *Washington Office, 1627 K St. N.W., 3rd Floor 20006-1708; (202) 331-1400. Fax, (202) 331-1739. Anita H. Plotinsky, Director.*

General e-mail, feedback@fdncenter.org

Web, www.fdncenter.org

Publishes foundation guides. Serves as a clearinghouse on foundations and corporate giving, nonprofit management, fundraising, and grants for individuals. Provides training and seminars on fundraising and grant writing. Operates libraries in Atlanta, Cleveland, New York, San Francisco, and Washington, D.C.; libraries open to the public. (Headquarters in New York.)

Fund for American Studies, *1706 New Hampshire Ave. N.W. 20009; (202) 986-0384. Fax, (202) 986-0390. Roger R. Ream, President. Toll-free, (800) 741-6964 (outside D.C. area).*

General e-mail, feedback@tfas.org

Web, www.tfas.org

Educational foundation that sponsors summer and semester internships on comparative political and economic systems, business and government affairs, and political journalism; grants scholarships to qualified students for study-internship programs.

Institute of International Education, *National Security Education Program, 1400 K St. N.W., #650 20005-2403; (202) 326-7697. Fax, (202) 326-7698. Chris Powers, Deputy Director. Information, (800) 618-6737.*

General e-mail, nsep@iie.org

Web, www.iie.org/nsep

Provides scholarships, fellowships, and institutional grants to academics with an interest in foreign affairs and national security.

National Journalism Center, *800 Maryland Ave. N.E. 20002; (202) 546-1710. Fax, (202) 544-5368. Kenneth Grubbs, Director.*

Web, www.nationaljournalismcenter.org

Sponsors extensive internship program in journalism; provides a stipend for living expenses; offers job placement service.

The Washington Center, *2301 M St. N.W., 5th Floor 20037; (202) 336-7600. Fax, (202) 336-7609. William M. Burke, President. Information, (800) 486-8921.*

General e-mail, info@twc.edu

Web, www.twc.edu

Arranges congressional, agency, and public service internships for college students for credit. Fee for internship and housing assistance. Sponsors classes and lectures as part of the internship program. Scholarships and stipends available.

Washington Center for Politics and Journalism, *1901 L St. N.W., #300 20036 (mailing address: P.O. Box 15201 20003); (202) 296-8455. Fax, (800) 858-8365. Terry Michael, Executive Director.*

General e-mail, pol-jrn@wcpj.org

Web, www.wcpj.org

Offers internships in political journalism to undergraduate and graduate students; provides a stipend for living expenses. Sixteen-week fall and winter/spring sessions include full-time work in Washington news bureaus and seminars in campaign, governance, and interest group politics for future political reporters.

Women's Research and Education Institute, *1750 New York Ave. N.W., #350 20006; (202) 628-0444. Fax, (202) 628-0458. Susan Scanlan, President.*

General e-mail, wrei@wrei.org

Web, www.wrei.org

Analyzes policy-relevant information on issues that concern or affect women; serves as a resource for federal and state policymakers, the media, and the public. Sponsors Congressional Fellowships on Women and Public Policy for graduate students who are placed in congressional offices for one academic year to work on policy issues affecting women.

Youth Policy Institute, *1320 Fenwick Lane, #506, Silver Spring, MD 20910; (301) 585-0580. Fax, (301) 585-0584. David L. Hackett, Executive Director.*
General e-mail, corpsnet@mnsinc.com
Web, www.corpsnet.com

Seeks to involve everyone in public policy decision making.

Professional Interests and Benefits

NONPROFIT

AARP, *National Retired Teachers Assn.,* *601 E St. N.W. 20049; (202) 434-2380. Fax, (202) 434-6451. Annette S. Norsman, Director.*
General e-mail, aarpwrit@aol.com
Web, www.aarp.org/nrta

Membership: active and retired teachers and other school personnel (elementary through postsecondary) over age fifty. Provides members with information on relevant national issues. Provides state associations of retired school personnel with technical assistance.

American Assn. of Colleges for Teacher Education, *1307 New York Ave. N.W., #300 20005-4701; (202) 293-2450. Fax, (202) 457-8095. David G. Imig, President.*
Web, www.aacte.org

Membership: colleges and universities with teacher education programs. Informs members about state and federal policies affecting teacher education and about professional issues such as accreditation, certification, and assessment. Collects and analyzes information on education.

American Assn. of School Administrators, *1801 N. Moore St., Arlington, VA 22209-1813; (703) 528-0700. Fax, (703) 841-1543. Paul D. Houston, Executive Director.*
General e-mail, info@aasa.org
Web, www.aasa.org

Membership: chief school executives, administrators at district or higher level, and teachers of school administration. Promotes opportunities for minorities, women, and the disabled in educational administration and organization.

American Federation of School Administrators, *1729 21st St. N.W. 20009; (202) 986-4209. Fax, (202) 986-4211. Joe L. Greene, President.*
General e-mail, afsa@admin.org
Web, www.admin.org

Membership: approximately 12,000 school administrators, including principals, vice principals, directors, and superintendents. Helps members negotiate pay, benefits, and better working conditions; conducts training

programs and workshops. Monitors legislation and regulations. (Affiliated with the AFL-CIO.)

American Federation of Teachers (AFT), *555 New Jersey Ave. N.W., 10th Floor 20001; (202) 879-4400. Fax, (202) 879-4545. Sandra Feldman, President.*
General e-mail, online@aft.org
Web, www.aft.org

Membership: 1.2 million public and private school teachers, higher education faculty, school support staff, state and local government employees, and nurses and health care professionals. Assists members with contract negotiation and grievances; conducts training programs and workshops. Monitors legislation and regulations. (Affiliated with the AFL-CIO.)

American Political Science Assn. (APSA), *1527 New Hampshire Ave. N.W. 20036; (202) 483-2512. Fax, (202) 483-2657. Michael A. Brintrall, Executive Director.*
General e-mail, apsa@apsanet.org
Web, www.apsanet.org

Membership: political scientists, primarily college and university professors. Promotes scholarly inquiry into all aspects of political science, including international affairs and comparative government. Works to increase public understanding of politics; provides services to facilitate and enhance research, teaching, and professional development of its members. Acts as liaison with federal agencies, Congress, and the public. Seeks to improve the status of women and minorities in the profession. Offers congressional fellowships, workshops, and awards. Provides information on political science issues.

Assn. of School Business Officials International, *11401 N. Shore Dr., Reston, VA 20190-4232; (703) 478-0405. Fax, (703) 478-0205. Anne Miller, Executive Director.*
Web, www.asbointl.org

Membership: administrators, directors, and others involved in school business management. Works to educate members on tools, techniques, and procedures of school business management. Researches, analyzes, and disseminates information; conducts workshops.

Assn. of Teacher Educators, *1900 Association Dr., Reston, VA 20191-1502; (703) 620-3110. Fax, (703) 620-9530. Lynn Montgomery, Executive Director.*
General e-mail, ate1@aol.com
Web, www.ate1.org

Membership: individuals and public and private agencies involved with teacher education. Seeks to improve teacher education at all levels; conducts workshops and conferences; produces and disseminates publications.

Council of Chief State School Officers, *1 Massachusetts Ave. N.W., #700 20001-1431; (202) 408-5505. Fax, (202) 408-8072. G. Thomas Houlihan, Executive Director. Press, (202) 336-7005.*

General e-mail, info@ccsso.org

Web, www.ccsso.org

Membership: state superintendents and commissioners of education. Works to achieve equal education for all children and to improve ways to measure school performance; provides state education agency personnel and others with leadership, technical assistance, and training. Offers seminars, educational travel, and study programs for members.

Federal Education Assn., *1101 15th St. N.W., #1002 20005; (202) 822-7850. Fax, (202) 822-7816. Sheridan Pearce, President.*

General e-mail, fea@feaonline.org

Web, www.feaonline.org

Membership: teachers and personnel of Defense Dept. schools for military dependents in the United States and abroad. Helps members negotiate pay, benefits, and better working conditions. Monitors legislation and regulations.

International Test and Evaluation Assn., *4400 Fair Lakes Court, #104, Fairfax, VA 22033-3899; (703) 631-6220. Fax, (703) 631-6221. R. Alan Plishker, Executive Director.*

Web, www.itea.org

Membership: engineers, scientists, managers, and other industry, government, and academic professionals interested in testing and evaluating products and complex systems. Provides a forum for information exchange; monitors international research.

National Assn. of Biology Teachers, *12030 Sunrise Valley Dr., #110, Reston, VA 20191-3409; (703) 264-9696. Fax, (703) 264-7778. Wayne Carley, Executive Director. Information, (800) 406-0775.*

General e-mail, office@nabt.org

Web, www.nabt.org

Membership: biology teachers and others interested in biology and life sciences education at the elementary, secondary, and collegiate levels. Provides professional development opportunities through its publication program, summer workshops, conventions, and national award programs. Interests include teaching standards, science curriculum, and issues affecting biology and life sciences education.

National Assn. of School Psychologists, *4340 East-West Hwy., #402, Bethesda, MD 20814; (301) 657-0270.*

Fax, (301) 657-0275. Susan Gorin, Executive Director. TTY, (301) 657-4155.

Web, www.nasponline.org

Advocates for the mental health and educational needs of children; encourages professional growth of members. Monitors legislation and regulations.

National Business Education Assn., *1914 Association Dr., Reston, VA 20191-1596; (703) 860-8300. Fax, (703) 620-4483. Janet M. Treichel, Executive Director.*

General e-mail, nbea@nbea.org

Web, www.nbea.org

Membership: business education teachers and others interested in the field. Provides information on business education; offers teaching materials; sponsors conferences. Monitors legislation and regulations affecting business education.

National Certification Commission, *P.O. Box 15282, Chevy Chase, MD 20825; (301) 588-1212. Fax, (301) 588-1212. Richard C. Jaffeson, Executive Director.*

General e-mail, certification@usa.com

Web, pages.zdnet.com/washdc/certification

Provides information on the development and improvement of professional certification programs.

National Council for Accreditation of Teacher Education, *2010 Massachusetts Ave. N.W., #500 20036-1023; (202) 466-7496. Fax, (202) 296-6620. Arthur E. Wise, President.*

General e-mail, ncate@ncate.org

Web, www.ncate.org

Evaluates and accredits schools, colleges, and academic departments at higher education institutions; publishes list of accredited institutions and standards for accreditation.

National Council for the Social Studies, *8555 16th St., #500, Silver Spring, MD 20910; (301) 588-1800. Fax, (301) 588-2049. Susan Griffith, Executive Director. Publications, (800) 683-0812.*

General e-mail, information@ncss.org

Web, www.ncss.org

Membership: curriculum developers, educational administrators, state supervisors, and social studies educators, including teachers of history, political science, geography, economics, civics, psychology, sociology, and anthropology. Promotes the teaching of social studies; encourages research; sponsors publications; works with other organizations to advance social studies education.

National Council of Teachers of Mathematics, *1906 Association Dr., Reston, VA 20191-9988; (703) 620-*

9840. Fax, (703) 476-2970. James M. Rubillo, Executive Director.

General e-mail, infocentral@nctm.org

Web, www.nctm.org

Membership: teachers of mathematics in elementary and secondary schools and two-year colleges; university teacher education faculty; students; and other interested persons. Works for the improvement of classroom instruction at all levels. Serves as forum and information clearinghouse on issues related to mathematics education. Offers educational materials and conferences. Monitors legislation and regulations.

National Education Assn. (NEA), *1201 16th St. N.W., 8th Floor 20036; (202) 833-4000. Fax, (202) 822-7767. John Wilson, Executive Director.*

Web, www.nea.org

Membership: more than 2.5 million educators from preschool to university graduate programs. Promotes the interest of the profession of teaching and the cause of education in the United States. Monitors legislation and regulations at state and national levels.

National Science Resources Center, *Smithsonian Institution Arts and Industries Bldg., #1201 20560-0403; (202) 357-4892. Fax, (202) 633-9136. Sally Getz Schuler, Executive Director.*

General e-mail, outreach@nsrc.edu

Web, www.si.edu/nsrc

Sponsored by the Smithsonian Institution and the National Academy of Sciences. Works to establish effective science programs for all students. Disseminates research information; develops curriculum materials; seeks to increase public support for change of science education through the development of strategic partnerships.

National Science Teachers Assn., *1840 Wilson Blvd., Arlington, VA 22201-3000; (703) 243-7100. Fax, (703) 243-7177. Gerald Wheeler, Executive Director.*

General e-mail, publicinfo@nsta.org

Web, www.nsta.org

Membership: science teachers from elementary through college levels. Seeks to improve science education; provides forum for exchange of information. Monitors legislation and regulations.

NEA Foundation for the Improvement of Education, *1201 16th St. N.W., #416 20036-3207; (202) 822-7840. Fax, (202) 822-7779. Judith Rényi, President.*

General e-mail, info@nfie.org

Web, www.nfie.org

Educational and charitable organization created by the National Education Assn. Awards grants to teachers to improve teaching techniques and professional development; provides teachers with assistance to integrate computer and telecommunications technology into classroom instruction, curriculum management, and administration.

Teachers of English to Speakers of Other Languages (TESOL), *700 S. Washington St., #200, Alexandria, VA 22314-4287; (703) 836-0774. Fax, (703) 836-7864. Charles S. Amorosino, Executive Director. Publications, (888) 891-0041.*

General e-mail, tesol@tesol.org

Web, www.tesol.org

Promotes scholarship and provides information on instruction and research in the teaching of English to speakers of other languages. Offers placement service.

Research

AGENCIES

Education Dept., *Institute of Education Sciences, 555 New Jersey Ave. N.W., #600 20208; (202) 219-1385. Fax, (202) 219-1402. Russ Whitehurst, Director. Library, (202) 401-2199. Education statistics and trends, (202) 502-7300 or toll-free, (800) 424-1616.*

Web, www.ed.gov

Gathers, analyzes, and disseminates information, statistics, and research findings on the conditions and practices of American education. Supports nationally significant model projects, including the National Assessment of Educational Progress (the Nation's Report Card), a survey of the knowledge, skills, understanding, and attitudes of nine, thirteen, and seventeen year olds.

Education Dept., *National Center for Education Research, 555 New Jersey Ave. N.W., #510 20208; (202) 219-2079. Fax, (202) 219-2135. Vacant, Commissioner.*

Web, www.ed.gov/offices/IES/NCER

Supports fundamental research at every institutional level of education on topics such as the processes of teaching and learning; school organization and improvement; curriculum; and factors that contribute to excellence in education.

Education Dept., *National Center for Education Statistics, 1990 K St. N.W., #9000 20006; (202) 502-7300. Fax, (202) 502-7466. Val Plisko, Commissioner (Acting). Information, (800) 424-1616.*

Web, www.nces.ed.gov

Gathers, analyzes, synthesizes, and disseminates qualitative and quantitative data on the characteristics and effectiveness of American education. Helps state and local education agencies improve statistical gathering and processing methods.

Education Dept., *National Library of Education,* 400 Maryland Ave. S.W. 20202; (202) 205-5015. Fax, (202) 219-0955. Sheila McGarr, Director. Information, (800) 424-1616.
General e-mail, library@ed.gov
Web, www.ed.gov/NLE

Federal government's main resource center for education information. Dedicated to presenting information on education to the public. Houses publications produced or funded by the Education Dept., including Educational Resources Information Center (ERIC) materials. Provides information and answers questions on education statistics and research.

NONPROFIT

Academy for Educational Development (AED), 1825 Connecticut Ave. N.W., #800 20009; (202) 884-8000. Fax, (202) 884-8400. Stephen F. Moseley, President.
General e-mail, admin@aed.org
Web, www.aed.org

Conducts studies on domestic and international education, on a contract basis. Interests include finance; management of educational institutions; application of communications technology to health education, agricultural extension, and other development problems; exchange of information; and use of telecommunications for social services. Operates international exchange programs.

American Educational Research Assn., 1230 17th St. N.W. 20036; (202) 223-9485. Fax, (202) 775-1824. Felice Levine, Executive Officer.
Web, www.aera.net

Membership: educational researchers affiliated with universities and colleges, school systems, and federal and state agencies. Publishes original research in education; sponsors publication of reference works in educational research; conducts continuing education programs; studies status of women and minorities in the education field.

Council on Governmental Relations, 1200 New York Ave. N.W., #320 20005; (202) 289-6655. Fax, (202) 289-6698. Katharina Phillips, President.
Web, www.cogr.edu

Membership: research universities maintaining federally supported programs. Advises members and makes recommendations to government agencies regarding policies and regulations affecting university research.

Ethics and Public Policy Center, 1015 15th St. N.W., #900 20005; (202) 682-1200. Fax, (202) 408-0632. Hillel Fradkin, President.
General e-mail, ethics@eppc.org
Web, www.eppc.org

Conducts research and holds conferences on the role of formal education and morality in teaching facts, ideas, attitudes, and values.

National Assn. of Independent Colleges and Universities, *Research and Policy,* 1025 Connecticut Ave. N.W., #700 20036; (202) 785-8866. Fax, (202) 835-0003. Frank J. Balz, Vice President.
Web, www.naicu.edu

Conducts research on national attitudes and policies concerning independent higher education; surveys student aid programs and federal tax policies affecting institutional financing; acts as a clearinghouse for state associations.

National Education Knowledge Industry Assn., 1718 Connecticut Ave. N.W., #700 20009-1162; (202) 518-0847. Fax, (202) 785-3849. James Kohlmoos, President.
General e-mail, info@nekia.org
Web, www.nekia.org

Membership: regional educational laboratories and university-based educational research and development organizations. Serves as a clearinghouse for information on research conducted by members on various education issues. Formerly the Council for Educational Development and Research.

National Research Council (NRC), *Board on International Comparative Studies in Education,* 500 5th St. N.W., #1153 20001; (202) 334-3010. Fax, (202) 334-1294. Colette Chabbot, Director.
Web, www4.nationalacademies.org/dbasse/bicse.nsf

Helps plan and implement U.S. participation in comparative international research in education. Interests include the scope of specific projects, funding, and the supply and quality of U.S. statistics for use in research.

Rand Corporation, *Washington Office,* 1200 S. Hayes St., Arlington, VA 22202-5050; (703) 413-1100. Fax, (703) 413-8111. Bruce Hoffman, Director.
Web, www.rand.org

Research organization partially funded by federal agencies. Conducts research on education policy. (Headquarters in Santa Monica, Calif.)

LIBRARIES AND EDUCATIONAL MEDIA

AGENCIES

Institute of Museum and Library Services, *Library Services,* 1100 Pennsylvania Ave. N.W., #802 20506; (202) 606-8536. Fax, (202) 606-8591. Robert S. Martin, Director.
General e-mail, info@imls.gov
Web, www.imls.gov

Awards federal grants to support public, academic, research, school, and special libraries. Promotes access to information through electronic networks, links between libraries, and services to individuals having difficulty using a library. Provides funding for improved library services to native American tribal communities, Alaskan native villages, and native Hawaiian library users.

National Archives and Records Administration (NARA), *Presidential Libraries,* 8601 Adelphi Rd., #2200, College Park, MD 20740-6001; (301) 837-3250. Fax, (301) 837-3199. Richard L. Claypoole, Assistant Archivist.
Web, www.archives.gov/presidential_libraries

Directs all programs relating to acquisition, preservation, publication, and research use of materials in presidential libraries; conducts oral history projects; publishes finding aids for research sources; provides reference service, including information from and about documentary holdings.

National Commission on Libraries and Information Science, 1110 Vermont Ave. N.W., #820 20005-3552; (202) 606-9200. Fax, (202) 606-9203. Martha B. Gould, Chair; Joan B. Challinor, Vice Chair.
Web, www.nclis.gov

Advises Congress and the president on national and international information and library policy issues; works with other agencies, the private sector, libraries, and information networks to improve access to library and information resources for all Americans, including the elderly, disadvantaged, illiterate, and geographically isolated; promotes effective local use of information generated by the federal government.

National Endowment for the Humanities (NEH), *(National Foundation on the Arts and the Humanities), Division of Public Programs,* 1100 Pennsylvania Ave. N.W., #426 20506; (202) 606-8269. Fax, (202) 606-8557. Nancy Rogers, Program Officer.
General e-mail, info@neh.gov
Web, www.neh.gov

Awards grants to libraries, museums, special projects, and media for projects that enhance public appreciation and understanding of the humanities through books and other resources in American library collections. Projects include conferences, exhibitions, essays, documentaries, radio programs, and lecture series.

Smithsonian Institution, *Museum Studies and Reference Library,* 10th St. and Constitution Ave. N.W., MRC 154 20560; (202) 357-2139. Fax, (202) 786-2443. Amy E. Levin, Branch Librarian. TTY, (202) 357-2328.
Web, www.sil.si.edu

Maintains collection of general reference, biographical, and interdisciplinary materials; serves as an information resource on institution libraries and museum studies.

CONGRESS

House Administration Committee, 1309 LHOB 20515; (202) 225-8281. Fax, (202) 225-9957. Rep. Bob W. Ney, R-Ohio, Chair; Paul Vinovich, Staff Director.
Web, www.house.gov/cha

Oversight of and jurisdiction over legislation on the Library of Congress.

House Appropriations Committee, *Subcommittee on Legislative Branch,* H147 CAP 20515; (202) 226-7252. Rep. Jack Kingston, R-Ga., Chair; Elizabeth G. Dawson, Staff Director.
Web, www.house.gov/appropriations

Jurisdiction over legislation to appropriate funds for the Library of Congress, including the Congressional Research Service.

House Education and the Workforce Committee, *Subcommittee on Select Education,* 2181 RHOB 20515; (202) 225-4527. Fax, (202) 225-9571. Rep. Peter Hoekstra, R-Mich., Chair; Paula Nowakowski, Staff Director.
Web, edworkforce.house.gov/members/108th/mem-sed.htm

Jurisdiction over legislation on libraries, including the Library Services and Construction Act.

Joint Committee on the Library of Congress, S237 CAP 20515; (202) 224-1034. Fax, (202) 224-0075. Sen. Ted Stevens, R-Alaska, Chair; Jennifer Mies, Senate Staff Contact.

Studies and makes recommendations on legislation dealing with the Library of Congress.

Library of Congress, 101 Independence Ave. S.E. 20540-1000; (202) 707-5205. Fax, (202) 707-1714. James H. Billington, Librarian of Congress. Information, (202) 707-5000. Press, (202) 707-2905.

LIBRARY OF CONGRESS DIVISIONS AND PROGRAMS

African and Middle Eastern Division, (202) 707-7937

American Folklife Center, (202) 707-5510

Asian Division, (202) 707-5420

Cataloging Distribution Service, (202) 707-9797

The Center for the Book, (202) 707-5221

Children's Literature Center, (202) 707-5535

Computer Catalog Center, (202) 707-3370

Copyright Office, (202) 707-3000

European Division, (202) 707-5414

Federal Library and Information Center Committee, (202) 707-4800

Geography and Map Division, (202) 707-8530

Hispanic Division, (202) 707-5400

Humanities and Social Science Division, (202) 707-5530

Interlibrary Loans, (202) 707-5444

Interpretative Programs, (202) 707-5223

Law Library, (202) 707-5065

Law Library Reading Room, (202) 707-5079

Local History and Genealogy Reading Room, (202) 707-5537

Manuscript Division, (202) 707-5383

Mary Pickford Theater, (202) 707-5677

Microform Reading Room, (202) 707-5471

Motion Picture, Broadcasting, and Recorded Sound Division, (202) 707-5840

Music Division, (202) 707-5502

National Library Service for the Blind and Physically Handicapped, (202) 707-5104

Photoduplication Service, (202) 707-5640

Poetry and Literature Center, (202) 707-5394

Preservation Office, (202) 707-5213

Prints and Photographs Division, (202) 707-6394

Rare Book and Special Collections Division, (202) 707-5434

Science, Technology, and Business Division, (202) 707-5664

Serial and Government Publications Division, (202) 707-5647

Web, www.loc.gov

Main book repository of the United States.

Library of Congress, *Center for the Book,* 101 Independence Ave. S.E., #650 20540-4920; (202) 707-5221. Fax, (202) 707-0269. John Y. Cole, Director.

General e-mail, cfbook@loc.gov

Web, www.loc.gov/loc/cfbook

Seeks to broaden public appreciation of books, reading, and libraries; sponsors lectures and conferences on the educational and cultural role of the book worldwide, including the history of books and printing, television and the printed word, and the publishing and production of books; cooperates with state centers and with other organizations. Projects and programs are privately funded except for basic administrative support from the Library of Congress.

Library of Congress, *Federal Library and Information Center Committee,* 101 Independence Ave. S.E., #LA217 20540-4935; (202) 707-4800. Fax, (202) 707-4818. Susan M. Tarr, Executive Director.

General e-mail, flicc@loc.gov

Web, lcweb.loc.gov/flicc

Membership: one representative from each major federal agency, one representative each from the Library of Congress and the national libraries of medicine and agriculture, and one representative from each of the major Federal Information Centers. Coordinates planning, development, operations, and activities among federal libraries.

Library of Congress, *Preservation,* 101 Independence Ave. S.E., #G21 20540-4500; (202) 707-5213. Fax, (202) 707-3434. Mark Roosa, Director.

General e-mail, preserve@loc.gov

Web, www.loc.gov

Responsible for preserving book and paper materials in the library's collections.

Senate Appropriations Committee, *Subcommittee on Legislative Branch,* SD-115 20510; (202) 224-7328. Sen. Ben Nighthorse Campbell, R-Colo., Chair; Carolyn Apostolou, Clerk.

Web, appropriations.senate.gov

Jurisdiction over legislation to appropriate funds for the Library of Congress, including the Congressional Research Service.

Senate Health, Education, Labor, and Pensions Committee, SD-428 20510; (202) 224-5375. Fax, (202)

228-5044. *Sen. Judd Gregg, R-N.H., Chair; Sharon Soderstrom, Staff Director. TTY, (202) 224-1975. Web, health.senate.gov*

Jurisdiction over legislation on libraries, including the Library Services and Construction Act.

Senate Rules and Administration Committee,
SR-305 20510; (202) 224-6352. Fax, (202) 224-5400. Sen. Trent Lott, R-Miss., Chair; Susan Wells, Staff Director. Web, rules.senate.gov

Oversight of and jurisdiction over legislation on the Library of Congress.

NONPROFIT

American Chemical Society, *Project Bookshare,*
1155 16th St. N.W. 20036-4892; (202) 872-6285. Fax, (202) 872-6317. J. C. Torio, Coordinator. General e-mail, help@acs.org Web, www.acs.org/international

Collects used scientific books and journals; distributes the books to tribal libraries and other educational institutions in the United States and in other countries in need.

American Library Assn., *Washington Office,*
1301 Pennsylvania Ave. N.W., #403 20004; (202) 628-8410. Fax, (202) 628-8419. Emily Sheketoff, Executive Director. General e-mail, alawash@alawash.org Web, www.ala.org/washoff

Educational organization of librarians, trustees, and educators. Washington office monitors legislation and regulations on libraries and information science. (Headquarters in Chicago, Ill.)

American Society for Information Science and Technology, *1320 Fenwick Lane, #510, Silver Spring, MD 20910-3560; (301) 495-0900. Fax, (301) 495-0810. Richard Hill, Executive Director. General e-mail, asis@asis.org Web, www.asis.org*

Membership: librarians, computer scientists, management specialists, behavioral scientists, engineers, and individuals concerned with access to information. Conducts research and educational programs.

Assn. for Information and Image Management,
1100 Wayne Ave., #1100, Silver Spring, MD 20910; (301) 587-8202. Fax, (301) 587-2711. John F. Mancini, President. General e-mail, aiim@aiim.org Web, www.aiim.org

Membership: manufacturers and users of image-based information systems. Works to advance the profession of information management; develops standards on such technologies as microfilm and electronic imaging. Library open to the public.

Assn. of Research Libraries, *21 Dupont Circle N.W., #800 20036; (202) 296-2296. Fax, (202) 872-0884. Duane Webster, Executive Director. Web, www.arl.org*

Membership: major research libraries, mainly at universities, in the United States and Canada. Interests include development of library resources in all formats, subjects, and languages; computer information systems and other bibliographic tools; management of research libraries; preservation of library materials; worldwide information policy; and publishing and scholarly communication.

Council on Library and Information Resources,
1755 Massachusetts Ave. N.W., #500 20036-2124; (202) 939-4750. Fax, (202) 939-4765. Deanna B. Marcum, President. General e-mail, info@clir.org Web, www.clir.org

Acts on behalf of the nation's libraries, archives, and universities to develop and encourage collaborative strategies for preserving the nation's intellectual heritage and strengthening its information systems.

Gallaudet University, *Library, 800 Florida Ave. N.E. 20002; (202) 651-5217. Fax, (202) 651-5213. Vacant, University Librarian. Archives, (202) 651-5920 (TTY only). Some numbers require state relay service for voice transmission. General e-mail, library.reference@gallaudet.edu Web, library.gallaudet.edu*

Maintains extensive special collection on deafness, including archival materials relating to deaf cultural history and Gallaudet University.

International Communications Industries Assn.,
11242 Waples Mill Rd., #200, Fairfax, VA 22030; (703) 273-7200. Fax, (703) 278-8082. Randy Lemke, Executive Director. Information, (800) 659-7469. General e-mail, icia@infocomm.org Web, www.infocomm.org

Membership: manufacturers, dealers, and specialists in educational communications products. Provides educators with information on federal funding for audiovisual, video, and computer equipment and materials; monitors trends in educational technology; conducts educational software conference on microcomputers and miniaturization.

LIBRARIES AT FEDERAL AGENCIES

DEPARTMENTS

Agriculture, (301) 504-6778

Commerce, (202) 482-5511

Defense, (703) 697-4301

Education, (202) 205-5019

Energy, (202) 586-9534

Health and Human Services, (202) 619-0190

Housing and Urban Development, (202) 708-3728

Interior, (202) 208-5815

Justice, (202) 514-3775

Labor, (202) 693-6600

State, (202) 647-1099

Transportation, (202) 366-0746

Treasury, (202) 622-0990

Veterans Affairs, (202) 273-8523

  Law (202) 273-6558

AGENCIES

Agency for International Development, (202) 712-0579

Commission on Civil Rights, (202) 376-8110

Commodity Futures Trading Commission, (202) 418-5255

Consumer Product Safety Commission, (301) 504-6816

Drug Enforcement Administration, (202) 307-8932

Environmental Protection Agency, (202) 260-5922

Equal Employment Opportunity Commission, (202) 663-4630

Export-Import Bank, (202) 565-3980

Farm Credit Administration, (703) 883-4296

Federal Communications Commission, (202) 418-0450

Federal Deposit Insurance Corporation, (202) 898-3631

Federal Election Commission, (202) 694-1600

Federal Emergency Management Agency, (202) 646-3771

Federal Labor Relations Authority, (202) 482-6552

Federal Maritime Commission, (202) 523-5762

Federal Reserve System, (202) 452-3332

Federal Trade Commission, (202) 326-2395

General Accounting Office

  Law (202) 512-2585

  Technical (202) 512-5180

General Services Administration, (202) 501-0788

International Bank for Reconstruction and Development (World Bank) and International Monetary Fund, (202) 623-7054

Merit Systems Protection Board, (202) 653-7132

National Aeronautics and Space Administration, (202) 358-0168

National Credit Union Administration, (703) 518-6540

National Endowment for the Arts, (202) 682-5485

National Endowment for the Humanities, (202) 606-8244

National Labor Relations Board, (202) 273-3720

National Library of Medicine, (301) 496-5501

National Science Foundation, (703) 292-7830

Nuclear Regulatory Commission, (301) 415-5610

Occupational Safety and Health Review Commission, (202) 606-5100, ext. 261

Office of Personnel Management, (202) 606-1381

Office of Thrift Supervision (202) 906-6470

Overseas Private Investment Corporation, (202) 336-8565

Peace Corps, (202) 692-2635

Postal Rate Commission, (202) 789-6877

Public Health Library, (301) 443-2673

Securities and Exchange Commission, (202) 942-7090

Small Business Administration

  Main Library (202) 205-7033

  Law (202) 205-6849

Smithsonian Institution, (202) 357-2139

Social Security Administration

  Main Library (410) 965-6113

  Law (410) 965-6108

U.S. International Trade Commission

  Main Library (202) 205-2630

  Law (202) 205-3287

U.S. Postal Service, (202) 268-2904

Kidsnet, *6856 Eastern Ave. N.W., #208 20012-2165; (202) 291-1400. Fax, (202) 882-7315. Karen W. Jaffe, Executive Director.*
General e-mail, kidsnet@kidsnet.org
Web, www.kidsnet.org

Computerized clearinghouse for educational opportunities available from television, radio, and multimedia sources for preschool through high school. Publishes study and media guides for classroom use. Information available by subscription and electronically.

Society for Imaging Science and Technology,
7003 Kilworth Lane, Springfield, VA 22151; (703) 642-9090. Fax, (703) 642-9094. Calva A. Leonard, Executive Director.
General e-mail, info@imaging.org
Web, www.imaging.org

Membership: individuals and companies worldwide in fields of imaging science and technology, including photofinishing, nonimpact printing, electronic imaging, silver halide, image preservation, and hybrid imaging systems. Gathers and disseminates technical information; fosters professional development.

Special Libraries Assn., *1700 18th St. N.W. 20009-2514; (202) 234-4700. Fax, (202) 265-9317. Lynn Smith, Executive Director (Acting). Fax-on-demand, (888) 411-2856.*
General e-mail, sla@sla.org
Web, www.sla.org

Membership: librarians and information managers serving institutions that use or produce information in specialized areas, including business, engineering, law, the arts and sciences, government, museums, and universities. Conducts professional development programs, research projects, and annual conference; provides a consultation service; sponsors International Special Libraries Day. Monitors legislation and regulations.

 POSTSECONDARY EDUCATION

AGENCIES

Education Dept., *Fund for the Improvement of Postsecondary Education, 1990 K St. N.W., 8th Floor 20006-8544; (202) 502-7500. Fax, (202) 502-7877. Jeffrey R. Andrade, Director (Acting).*
Web, www.ed.gov/offices/OPE/FIPSE

Works to improve postsecondary education by administering grant competitions, including the Comprehensive Program for improvements in postsecondary

education; the European Community/United States (ECUS) Joint Consortia for Cooperation in Higher Education and Vocational Education; the Program for North American Mobility in Higher Education; and the U.S.-Brazil Higher Education Consortia Program.

Education Dept., *Postsecondary Education, 1990 K St. N.W., #7113 20006; (202) 502-7750. Fax, (202) 502-7677. Jeffrey R. Andrade, Deputy Assistant Secretary. TTY, (800) 848-0978.*
Web, www.ed.gov/offices/OPE

Administers federal assistance programs for public and private postsecondary institutions; provides financial support for faculty development, construction of facilities, and improvement of graduate, continuing, cooperative, and international education; awards grants and loans for financial assistance to eligible students.

CONGRESS

House Education and the Workforce Committee, *Subcommittee on 21st Century Competitiveness, 2181 RHOB 20515; (202) 225-4527. Fax, (202) 225-9571. Rep. Howard P. "Buck" McKeon, R-Calif., Chair; Paula Nowakowski, Staff Director.*
Web, edworkforce.house.gov/members/108th/mem-21st.htm

Jurisdiction over legislation on postsecondary education, including community and junior colleges, the Construction Loan Program, construction of school facilities, and financial aid, and over legislation barring discrimination in postsecondary education.

Senate Banking, Housing, and Urban Affairs Committee, *SD-534 20510; (202) 224-7391. Fax, (202) 224-5137. Sen. Richard C. Shelby, R-Ala., Chair; Kathy Casey, Staff Director.*
Web, banking.senate.gov

Oversees government-sponsored enterprises, including the Student Loan Marketing Assn. and the College Construction Loan Insurance Assn., with regard to the financial risk posed to the federal government.

Senate Health, Education, Labor, and Pensions Committee, *SD-428 20510; (202) 224-5375. Fax, (202) 228-5044. Sen. Judd Gregg, R-N.H., Chair; Sharon Soderstrom, Staff Director. TTY, (202) 224-1975.*
Web, health.senate.gov

Jurisdiction over legislation on postsecondary education, including community and junior colleges, the Construction Loan Program, construction of school facilities, and financial aid, and over legislation barring discrimination in postsecondary education, including the Women's Educational Equity Act of 1974 as it applies to postsecondary education.

NONPROFIT

ACT (American College Testing), *Washington Office,* *1 Dupont Circle N.W., #340 20036-1170; (202) 223-2318. Fax, (202) 293-2223. Anna Critz Rubin, Director.*
Web, www.act.org

Administers ACT Assessment entrance examination for colleges and universities. Provides colleges and universities with testing, counseling, research, student aid processing services, and a broad range of services for educational planning, career planning, and workforce development. (Headquarters in Iowa City, Iowa.)

American Assn. for Higher Education, *1 Dupont Circle N.W., #360 20036; (202) 293-6440. Fax, (202) 293-0073. Yolanda T. Moses, President.*
Web, www.aahe.org

Membership: college and university educators, students, public officials, and others interested in postsecondary education. Evaluates issues in higher education; interests include statewide and institutional assessment, school-college collaboration, improvement of teaching and learning, and student community service. Conducts studies, conferences, and an annual convention.

American Assn. of Colleges of Pharmacy, *1426 Prince St., Alexandria, VA 22314-2841; (703) 739-2330. Fax, (703) 836-8982. Lucinda L. Maine, Executive Vice President.*
Web, www.aacp.org

Represents and advocates for pharmacists in the academic community. Conducts programs and activities in cooperation with other national health and higher education associations.

American Assn. of Collegiate Registrars and Admissions Officers, *1 Dupont Circle N.W., #520 20036-1135; (202) 293-9161. Fax, (202) 872-8857. Jerry Sullivan, Executive Director.*
General e-mail, info@aacrao.org
Web, www.aacrao.org

Membership: degree-granting postsecondary institutions, government agencies, higher education coordinating boards, private education organizations, and education-oriented businesses. Promotes higher education and contributes to the professional development of members working in admissions, enrollment management, financial aid, institutional research, records, and registration.

American Assn. of Community Colleges, *1 Dupont Circle N.W., #410 20036-1176; (202) 728-0200. Fax, (202) 223-9390. George R. Boggs, President.*
Web, www.aacc.nche.edu

Membership: accredited, two-year community technical and junior colleges, corporate foundations, international associates, and institutional affiliates. Studies include policies for lifelong education, workforce training programs and partnerships, international curricula, enrollment trends, and cooperative programs with public schools and communities.

American Assn. of State Colleges and Universities, *1307 New York Ave. N.W., #500 20005; (202) 293-7070. Fax, (202) 296-5819. Constantine W. Curris, President.*
Web, www.aascu.org

Membership: presidents and chancellors of state colleges and universities. Promotes equity in education; fosters information exchange among members; interests include minority participation in higher education, student financial aid, international education programs, academic affairs, and teacher education. Monitors legislation and regulations.

American Assn. of University Professors (AAUP), *1012 14th St. N.W., #500 20005; (202) 737-5900. Fax, (202) 737-5526. Mary Burgan, General Secretary.*
General e-mail, aaup@aaup.org
Web, www.aaup.org

Membership: college and university faculty members. Defends faculties' academic freedom and tenure; advocates collegial governance; assists in the development of policies ensuring due process. Conducts workshops and education programs. Monitors legislation and regulations.

American Conference of Academic Deans, *1818 R St. N.W. 20009; (202) 387-3760. Fax, (202) 265-9532. Carol Geary Schneider, President.*
Web, www.acad-edu.org

Membership: academic deans of two- and four-year accredited colleges, universities, and community colleges (private and public). Fosters information exchange among members on college curricular and administrative issues.

American Council of Trustees and Alumni, *1726 M St. N.W., #800 20036-4525; (202) 467-6787. Fax, (202) 467-6784. Lynne V. Cheney, Chair Emeritus; Jerry L. Martin, President.*
General e-mail, info@goacta.org
Web, goacta.org

Membership: college and university alumni and trustees interested in promoting academic freedom and excellence. Seeks to help alumni and trustees direct their financial contributions to programs that will raise educational standards at their alma maters. Promotes the role

COLLEGES AND UNIVERSITIES IN WASHINGTON

Agriculture Dept. Graduate School, 1400 Independence Ave. S.W., #1031 20250

Switchboard: (202) 314-3686

Executive Director: Jerry Ice, (202) 720-2077

American University, 4400 Massachusetts Ave. N.W. 20016

Switchboard: (202) 885-1000

President: Benjamin Ladner, (202) 885-2121

Catholic University, 620 Michigan Ave. N.E. 20064

Switchboard: (202) 319-5000

President: Rev. David M. O'Connell C.M., (202) 319-5100

Columbia Union College, 7600 Flower Ave., Takoma Park, MD 20912

Switchboard: (800) 835-4212

President: Randal R. Whisbey, (301) 891-4128

Gallaudet University, 800 Florida Ave. N.E. 20002

Switchboard: (202) 651-5000 (voice and TTY)

President: I. King Jordan, (202) 651-5005 (voice and TTY)

George Mason University, 4400 University Dr., Fairfax, VA 22030

Switchboard: (703) 993-1000

President: Alan G. Merton, (703) 993-8700

George Washington University, 2121 Eye St. N.W. 20052

Switchboard: (202) 994-1000

President: Stephen Joel Trachtenberg, (202) 994-6500

George Washington University at Mount Vernon College, 2100 Foxhall Rd. N.W. 20007

Switchboard: (202) 242-6600

Executive Dean: Grae Baxter, (202) 242-6609

Georgetown University, 37th and O Sts. N.W. 20057

Switchboard: (202) 687-0100

President: John De Gioia, (202) 687-4134

Howard University, 2400 6th St. N.W. 20059

Switchboard: (202) 806-6100

President: H. Patrick Swygert, (202) 806-2500

Marymount University, 2807 N. Glebe Rd., Arlington, VA 22207

Switchboard: (703) 522-5600

President: James Bundschuh, (703) 284-1598

Paul H. Nitze School of Advanced International Studies (Johns Hopkins University), 1740 Massachusetts Ave. N.W. 20036

Switchboard: (202) 663-5600

Dean: Jessica P. Einhorn, (202) 663-5624

Southeastern University, 501 Eye St. S.W. 20024

Switchboard: (202) 488-8162

President: Charlene Drew Jarvis, (202) 488-8162

Trinity College, 125 Michigan Ave. N.E. 20017

Switchboard: (202) 884-9000

President: Patricia McGuire, (202) 884-9050

University of Maryland, Rt. 1, College Park Campus, College Park, MD 20742

Switchboard: (301) 405-1000

President: C.D. Mote Jr., (301) 405-5803

University of the District of Columbia, 4200 Connecticut Ave. N.W. 20008

Switchboard: (202) 274-5000

President: William L. Pollard, (202) 274-5100

University of Virginia/Virginia Tech Northern Virginia Center, 7054 Haycock Rd., Falls Church, VA 22043

UVA Switchboard: (703) 536-1100

UVA Director: Steve Gladis, (703) 536-1118

VT Switchboard: (703) 538-8324

VT Interim Administrator: Karen Akers, (703) 538-8310

Virginia Theological Seminary, 3737 Seminary Rd., Alexandria, VA 22304

Switchboard: (703) 370-6600

Dean: Martha J. Horne, (703) 461-1701

---

of alumni and trustees in shaping higher education policies.

American Council on Education (ACE), *1 Dupont Circle N.W., #800 20036-1193; (202) 939-9300. Fax, (202) 833-4760. David Ward, President. Library, (202) 939-9405. Press, (202) 939-9365.*

Web, *www.acenet.edu*

Membership: colleges, universities, education associations, students with disabilities, and businesses. Conducts and publishes research; maintains offices dealing with government relations, women and minorities in higher education, management of higher education institutions, adult learning and educational credentials (academic credit for nontraditional learning, especially in the armed forces), leadership development, and international education. Library open to the public by appointment.

Assn. for Supervision and Curriculum Development, *1703 N. Beauregard St., Alexandria, VA 22311-1714; (703) 578-9600. Fax, (703) 575-5400. Gene R. Carter, Executive Director. Information, (800) 933-2723.*
General e-mail, member@ascd.org
Web, www.ascd.org

Membership: teachers, supervisors, directors of instruction, school principals (kindergarten through secondary), university and college faculty, school board members, and individuals interested in curriculum development. Sponsors institutes and conferences. Monitors legislation and regulations.

Assn. of American Colleges and Universities (ACCU), *1818 R St. N.W. 20009; (202) 387-3760. Fax, (202) 265-9532. Carol Geary Schneider, President.*
Web, www.aacu-edu.org

Membership: public and private colleges, universities, and postsecondary consortia. Works to develop effective academic programs and improve undergraduate curricula and services. Seeks to encourage, enhance, and support the development of broadly based intellectual skills through the study of liberal arts and sciences.

Assn. of American Law Schools, *1201 Connecticut Ave. N.W., #800 20036; (202) 296-8851. Fax, (202) 296-8869. Carl C. Monk, Executive Director.*
General e-mail, aals@aals.org
Web, www.aals.org

Membership: schools of law, subject to approval by the association. Represents member organizations before federal government and private agencies; evaluates member institutions; conducts workshops on the teaching of law; assists law schools with faculty recruitment; publishes faculty placement bulletin and annual directory of law teachers.

Assn. of American Universities, *1200 New York Ave. N.W., #550 20005; (202) 408-7500. Fax, (202) 408-8184. Nils Hasselmo, President.*
Web, www.aau.edu

Membership: public and private universities with emphasis on graduate and professional education and research. Fosters information exchange among presidents of member institutions.

Assn. of Catholic Colleges and Universities, *1 Dupont Circle N.W., #650 20036; (202) 457-0650. Fax, (202) 728-0977. Monika K. Hellwig, Executive Director.*

General e-mail, accu@accunet.org
Web, www.accunet.org

Membership: regionally accredited Catholic colleges and universities and individuals interested in Catholic higher education. Acts as a clearinghouse for information on Catholic institutions of higher education. (Affiliated with the National Catholic Educational Assn.)

Assn. of Community College Trustees, *1233 20th St. N.W., #605 20036; (202) 775-4667. Fax, (202) 223-1297. Ray Taylor, President.*
Web, www.acct.org

Provides members of community college governing boards with training in educational programs. Monitors federal education programs.

Assn. of Governing Boards of Universities and Colleges, *1 Dupont Circle N.W., #400 20036-1190; (202) 296-8400. Fax, (202) 223-7053. Richard T. Ingram, President.*
Web, www.agb.org

Membership: presidents, boards of trustees, regents, commissions, and other groups governing colleges, universities, and institutionally related foundations. Interests include the relationship between the president and board of trustees and other subjects relating to governance. Zwingle Information Center open to the public.

Assn. of Higher Education Facilities Officers, *1643 Prince St., Alexandria, VA 22314-2818; (703) 684-1446. Fax, (703) 549-2772. E. Lander Medlin, Executive Vice President.*
General e-mail, info@appa.org
Web, www.appa.org

Membership: professionals involved in the administration, maintenance, planning, and development of buildings and facilities used by colleges and universities. Interests include maintenance and upkeep of housing facilities. Provides information on campus energy management programs and campus accessibility for people with disabilities.

Assn. of Jesuit Colleges and Universities, *1 Dupont Circle N.W., #405 20036-1140; (202) 862-9893. Fax, (202) 862-8523. Charles L. Currie (SJ), President.*
General e-mail, blkrobe@aol.com
Web, www.ajcunet.edu

Membership: American Jesuit colleges and universities. Monitors government regulatory and policy-making activities affecting higher education. Publishes directory of Jesuit colleges, universities, and high schools and monthly report on the state of higher education. Promotes international cooperation among Jesuit higher education institutions.

Business–Higher Education Forum, *1 Dupont Circle N.W., #800 20036; (202) 939-9345. Fax, (202) 833-4723. Jeremiah L. Murphy, Director.*

General e-mail, bhef@ace.nche.edu

Web, www.bhef.com

Membership: chief executive officers of major corporations, museums, colleges, and universities. Promotes cooperation between businesses and higher educational institutions. Interests include international economic competitiveness, education and training, research and development, science and technology, and global interdependence.

Career College Assn., *10 G St. N.E., #750 20002-4213; (202) 336-6700. Fax, (202) 336-6828. Nick Glakas, President.*

General e-mail, cca@career.org

Web, www.career.org

Membership: private postsecondary colleges and career schools in the United States. Works to expand the accessibility of postsecondary career education and to improve the quality of education offered by member schools.

College and University Professional Assn. for Human Resources, *1233 20th St. N.W., #301 20036-1250; (202) 429-0311. Fax, (202) 429-0149. Stephen J. Otzenberger, Executive Director.*

Web, www.cupahr.org

Membership: college and university human resource administrators. Conducts seminars and workshops; responds to inquiries on human resource administration. Monitors legislation and regulations.

College Board, *Communications and Government Relations, Washington Office, 1233 20th St. N.W., #600 20036-2304; (202) 822-5900. Fax, (202) 822-5920. Lezli Baskerville, Vice President.*

Web, www.collegeboard.com

Membership: colleges and universities, secondary schools, school systems, and education associations. Provides direct student support programs and professional development for educators; conducts policy analysis and research; and advocates public policy positions that support educational excellence and promote student access to higher education. Library open to the public. (Headquarters in New York.)

Council for Christian Colleges and Universities, *321 8th St. N.E. 20002; (202) 546-8713. Fax, (202) 546-8913. Robert C. Andringa, President.*

General e-mail, council@cccu.org

Web, www.cccu.org

Membership: accredited four-year Christian liberal arts colleges. Offers faculty development conferences on faith and the academic disciplines. Coordinates annual gathering of college administrators. Sponsors internship/seminar programs for students at member colleges. Interests include religious and educational freedom.

Council for Resource Development, *1 Dupont Circle N.W., #410 20036-1176; (202) 822-0750. Fax, (202) 822-5014. Joy Rafey, Executive Director; Perry Hammock, President.*

General e-mail, crd@aacc.nche.edu

Web, www.crdnet.org

Membership: college presidents, administrators, fundraisers, grant writers, and development officers at two-year colleges. Educates members on how to secure resources for their institution; conducts workshops and training programs. Monitors legislation and regulations. (Affiliated with the American Assn. of Community Colleges.)

Council of Graduate Schools, *1 Dupont Circle N.W., #430 20036-1173; (202) 223-3791. Fax, (202) 331-7157. Debra W. Stewart, President.*

Web, www.cgsnet.org

Membership: private and public colleges and universities with significant involvement in graduate education. Produces publications and information about graduate education; provides a forum for member schools to exchange information and ideas.

Council of Independent Colleges, *1 Dupont Circle N.W., #320 20036-1110; (202) 466-7230. Fax, (202) 466-7238. Richard Ekman, President.*

General e-mail, cic@cic.nche.edu

Web, www.cic.edu

Membership: private four-year liberal arts colleges. Sponsors management development institutes for college presidents and deans; conducts faculty development programs; sponsors national projects on leadership, curriculum development, and related topics. Holds workshops and produces publications.

Educational Testing Service (ETS), *Communications and Public Affairs, Washington Office, 1800 K St. N.W., #900 20006-2202; (202) 659-0616. Fax, (202) 659-8075. Les Francis, Vice President.*

Web, www.ets.org

Administers examinations for admission to educational programs and for graduate and licensing purposes; conducts instructional programs in testing, evaluation, and research in education fields. Washington office handles government and professional relations. Fee for services. (Headquarters in Princeton, N.J.)

National Assn. for College Admission Counseling, *1631 Prince St., Alexandria, VA 22314; (703) 836-2222. Fax, (703) 836-8015. Joyce Smith, Executive Director.*
Web, www.nacac.com

Membership: high school guidance counselors, independent counselors, college and university admissions officers, and financial aid officers. Assists counselors who serve students in the college admission process. Promotes and funds research on admission counseling and on the transition from high school to college. Advocates for the rights of students in the college admission process. Sponsors national college fairs and continuing education for members.

National Assn. of College and University Attorneys, *1 Dupont Circle N.W., #620 20036-1182; (202) 833-8390. Fax, (202) 296-8379. Kathleen Curray Santora, Chief Executive Officer.*
General e-mail, nacua@nacua.org
Web, www.nacua.org

Provides information on legal developments affecting postsecondary education. Operates a clearinghouse through which attorneys on campuses are able to network with their counterparts on current legal problems.

National Assn. of College and University Business Officers, *2501 M St. N.W., #400 20037-1308; (202) 861-2500. Fax, (202) 861-2583. James E. Morley Jr., President.*
General e-mail, webmaster@nacubo.org
Web, www.nacubo.org

Membership: chief business officers at higher education institutions. Provides members with information on financial management, federal regulations, and other subjects related to the business administration of universities and colleges; conducts workshops on issues such as student aid, institutional budgeting, and accounting.

National Assn. of Independent Colleges and Universities, *1025 Connecticut Ave. N.W., #700 20036-5405; (202) 785-8866. Fax, (202) 835-0003. David L. Warren, President.*
Web, www.naicu.edu

Membership: independent colleges and universities and related state associations. Counsels members on federal education programs and tax policy.

National Assn. of State Universities and Land Grant Colleges, *1307 New York Ave. N.W., #400 20005; (202) 478-6040. Fax, (202) 478-6046. C. Peter Magrath, President.*
Web, www.nasulgc.org

Membership: land grant colleges and state universities. Serves as clearinghouse on issues of public higher education.

National Assn. of Student Personnel Administrators, *1875 Connecticut Ave. N.W., #418 20009-5728; (202) 265-7500. Fax, (202) 797-1157. Gwen Dungy, Executive Director.*
General e-mail, office@naspa.org
Web, www.naspa.org

Membership: deans, student affairs administrators, faculty, and graduate students. Seeks to develop leadership and improve practices in student affairs administration. Initiates and supports programs and legislation to improve student affairs administration.

National Council of University Research Administrators, *1 Dupont Circle N.W., #220 20036; (202) 466-3894. Fax, (202) 223-5573. Kathleen Larmett, Executive Director.*
General e-mail, info@ncura.edu
Web, www.ncura.edu

Membership: individuals engaged in administering research, training, and educational programs, primarily at colleges and universities. Encourages development of effective policies and procedures in the administration of these programs.

U.S. Student Assn., *1413 K St. N.W., 9th Floor 20005; (202) 347-8772. Fax, (202) 393-5886. Jo'ie Taylor, President.*
General e-mail, comm@usstudents.org
Web, www.usstudents.org

Represents postsecondary students, student government associations, and state student lobby associations. Interests include civil rights on campus and the financing of higher education. Maintains student coalitions of women, racial, ethnic, and sexual minorities. Serves as clearinghouse for information on student problems, activities, and government; holds conferences emphasizing student lobbying techniques.

Washington Higher Education Secretariat, *1 Dupont Circle N.W., #800 20036; (202) 939-9336. Fax, (202) 833-4723. Ellen R. Babby, Executive Secretary.*
Web, www.whes.org

Membership: national higher education associations representing the different sectors and functions in postsecondary institutions. Provides forum for discussion on national and local education issues.

Women's College Coalition, *125 Michigan Ave. N.E. 20017-1094; (202) 234-0443. Fax, (202) 234-0445. Jadwiga S. Sebrechts, President.*

General e-mail, msm@trinitydc.edu

Web, www.womenscolleges.org

Membership: public and private, independent and church-related, two- and four-year women's colleges. Interests include the role of women's colleges as model institutions for educating women, gender equity issues, and retention of women in math, science, and engineering. Maintains an information clearinghouse on U.S. undergraduate women's colleges. Conducts research on gender equity issues in education and positive learning environments.

College Accreditation

Many college- or university-based and independent postsecondary education programs are accredited by member associations. See specific subject headings and associations within the chapter.

AGENCIES

Education Dept., *Accreditation State Liaison,* 1990 K St. N.W., #7105 20006-8509; (202) 219-7011. Fax, (202) 219-7005. John Barth, Director (Acting).

Web, www.ed.gov

Reviews accrediting agencies and state approval agencies that seek initial or renewed recognition by the secretary; provides the National Advisory Committee on Institutional Quality and Integrity with staff support.

NONPROFIT

American Academy for Liberal Education (AALE), 1710 Rhode Island Ave. N.W., 4th Floor 20036; (202) 452-8611. Fax, (202) 452-8620. Jeffrey D. Wallin, President.

General e-mail, info@aale.org

Web, www.aale.org

Accredits colleges and universities whose general education programs in the liberal arts meets the academy's accreditation requirements. Provides support for institutions that maintain substantial liberal arts programs and which desire to raise requirements to meet AALE standards.

Council for Higher Education Accreditation, 1 Dupont Circle N.W., #510 20036-1135; (202) 955-6126. Fax, (202) 955-6129. Judith S. Eaton, President.

General e-mail, chea@chea.org

Web, www.chea.org

Advocates voluntary self regulation of colleges and universities through accreditation; coordinates research, debate, and processes that improve accreditation; mediates disputes and fosters communications among accrediting bodies and the higher education community.

Financial Aid to Students

AGENCIES

Education Dept., *Federal Student Aid,* 830 1st St. N.E. 20202; (202) 377-3000. Fax, (202) 275-5000. Theresa Shaw, Chief Operating Officer. Student Aid Information Center, (800) 433-3243.

Web, www.ed.gov

Administers federal loan, grant, and work-study programs for postsecondary education to eligible individuals. Administers the Pell Grant Program, the Perkins Loan Program, the Stafford Student Loan Program (Guaranteed Student Loan)/PLUS Program, the College Work-Study Program, the Supplemental Loans for Students (SLS), and the Supplemental Educational Opportunity Grant Program.

NONPROFIT

Alliance to Save Student Aid, *Public Affairs,* c/o American Council on Education, 1 Dupont Circle N.W., #800 20036-1193; (202) 939-9365. Fax, (202) 833-4762. Vacant, Federal Relations Associate.

General e-mail, gpa@ace.nche.edu

Web, www.acenet.edu

Membership: more than sixty organizations representing students, administrators, and faculty members from all sectors of higher education. Seeks to ensure adequate funding of federal aid programs. Monitors legislation and regulations.

College Board, *Communications and Government Relations, Washington Office,* 1233 20th St. N.W., #600 20036-2304; (202) 822-5900. Fax, (202) 822-5920. Lezli Baskerville, Vice President.

Web, www.collegeboard.com

Membership: colleges and universities, secondary schools, school systems, and education associations. Provides direct student support programs and professional development for educators; conducts policy analysis and research; and advocates public policy positions that support educational excellence and promote student access to higher education. Library open to the public. (Headquarters in New York.)

College Parents of America, 8300 Boone Blvd., #500, Vienna, VA 22182; (703) 761-6702. Fax, (703) 761-6703. Richard M. Flaherty, President. Information, (888) 256-4627.

General e-mail, information@collegeparents.org

Web, www.collegeparents.org

Provides information on savings strategies and financial aid; offers advice on the evaluation, selection, and application process to families with children applying to college; provides information on meeting the opportunities and challenges of a child's college years. Monitors legislation and regulations on the national and state level.

Education Finance Council, *1155 15th St. N.W., #801 20005; (202) 466-8621. Fax, (202) 466-8643. Mark Powden, President.*
Web, www.efc.org

Membership: nonprofit educational loan secondary market organizations. Works to maintain and expand student access to higher education through tax-exempt funding for loans.

National Assn. of Student Financial Aid Administrators, *1129 20th St. N.W., #400 20036; (202) 785-0453. Fax, (202) 785-1487. Dallas A. Martin, President.*
General e-mail, ask@nasfaa.org
Web, www.nasfaa.org

Membership: more than 3,500 educational institutions, organizations, and individuals at postsecondary institutions who administer student financial aid. Works to ensure adequate funding for individuals seeking postsecondary education and to ensure proper management and administration of public and private financial aid funds.

National Council of Higher Education Loan Programs, *1100 Connecticut Ave. N.W., 12th Floor 20036; (202) 822-2106. Fax, (202) 822-2142. Brett E. Lief, President.*
Web, www.nchelp.org

Membership: agencies and organizations involved in making, servicing, and collecting Guaranteed Student Loans. Works with the Education Dept. to develop forms and procedures for administering the Federal Family Education Loan Program. Fosters information exchange among members.

Student Loan Marketing Assn. (Sallie Mae), *901 E St. N.W., #410 20004; (202) 969-8000. Fax, (202) 969-8030. Al L. Lord, Chief Executive Officer.*
Web, www.salliemae.com

Government-sponsored private corporation. Provides funds to financial and educational institutions (such as commercial banks, colleges, and universities) that make Stafford Student Loans and other educational loans administered by the Education Dept. available to students.

PRESCHOOL, ELEMENTARY, SECONDARY EDUCATION

AGENCIES

Education Dept., *Elementary and Secondary Education, 400 Maryland Ave. S.W., #3W300 20202-6100; (202) 401-0113. Fax, (202) 205-0303. Vacant, Assistant Secretary.*
Web, www.ed.gov

Administers federal assistance programs for elementary and secondary education (both public and private). Program divisions are Compensatory Education (including Chapter 1 aid for disadvantaged children); School Improvement; Migrant Education; Indian Education; Impact Aid; School Support and Technology Programs; and Safe, Drug-Free Schools.

Education Dept., *English Language Acquisition, 330 C St. S.W., #5086 20202-6510; (202) 205-5463. Fax, (202) 205-8737. Maria H. Ferrier, Director.*
Web, www.ed.gov/offices/OELA

Administers bilingual education programs in elementary and secondary schools to help students of limited English proficiency learn the English language. The program is designed to give students of limited English proficiency better opportunities to achieve academic success and meet grade promotion and graduation requirements. (Formerly the Office of Bilingual Education and Minority Languages Affairs.)

Education Dept., *Even Start, 400 Maryland Ave. S.W., #3W230 20202-6132; (202) 260-3718. Fax, (202) 260-7764. Patricia McKee, Coordinator, (202) 260-0991.*
Web, www.ed.gov/offices/OESE/CEP

Develops family-centered education projects to encourage parents of economic and educationally disadvantaged families to become involved in the education of their children; helps children reach their full potential as learners and offers literacy training to parents.

Education Dept., *Impact Aid, 400 Maryland Ave. S.W., #3E105 20202-6244; (202) 260-3858. Fax, (202) 205-0088. Catherine Schagh, Director.*
Web, www.ed.gov/offices/OESE/ImpactAid

Provides funds for elementary and secondary educational activities to school districts in federally impacted areas (where federal activities such as military bases enlarge staff and reduce taxable property).

Education Dept., *Safe and Drug-Free Schools, 400 Maryland Ave. S.W., #3E300 20202-6123; (202) 260-*

3954. Fax, (202) 260-7767. *William Modzeleski, Associate Deputy Under Secretary.*

Web, www.ed.gov/offices/OESE/SDFS

Develops policy for the department's drug and violence prevention initiatives for students in elementary and secondary schools and institutions of higher education. Coordinates education efforts in drug and violence prevention with those of other federal departments and agencies.

Environmental Protection Agency (EPA), *Pollution Prevention and Toxics, 1200 Pennsylvania Ave. N.W., #3166, EPA East Bldg. 20460; (202) 564-3810. Fax, (202) 564-0575. Charles M. Auer, Director. Information, (202) 554-1404.*

Web, www.epa.gov

Administers the Asbestos Loan and Grant Program by awarding loans and grants to needy public and private elementary and secondary schools to eliminate asbestos materials that pose a health threat to building occupants. Provides information on chemical risks.

Health and Human Services Dept. (HHS), *Head Start, 330 C St. S.W., 2nd Floor 20447; (202) 205-8572. Fax, (202) 260-9336. Windy Hill, Associate Commissioner.*

Web, www.headstartinfo.org

Awards grants to nonprofit organizations and local governments for operating community Head Start programs (comprehensive development programs for children, ages three to five, of low-income families); manages a limited number of parent and child centers for families with children up to age three. Conducts research and manages demonstration programs, including those under the Comprehensive Child Care Development Act of 1988; administers the Child Development Associate scholarship program, which trains individuals for careers in child development, often as Head Start teachers.

National Agricultural Library *(Agriculture Dept.), Food and Nutrition Information Center, 10301 Baltimore Ave., #105, Beltsville, MD 20705-2351; (301) 504-5719. Fax, (301) 504-6409. Dennis Smith, Coordinator. TTY, (301) 504-6856.*

General e-mail, fnic@nal.usda.gov

Web, www.nal.usda.gov/fnic

Serves as a resource center for school and child nutrition program personnel who need information on food service management and nutrition education. Center open to the public.

White House Commission on Presidential Scholars *(Education Dept.), 400 Maryland Ave. S.W., #5E225 20202-3500; (202) 401-0961. Fax, (202) 205-0676. Melissa Apostolides, Executive Director.*

Web, www.ed.gov/offices/OIIA/Recognition/PSP/index.html

Honorary recognition program that selects high school seniors of outstanding achievement in academics, community service, artistic ability, and leadership to receive the Presidential Scholars Award. Scholars travel to Washington during national recognition week to receive the award.

CONGRESS

House Education and the Workforce Committee, *Subcommittee on Education Reform, 2181 RHOB 20515; (202) 225-4527. Fax, (202) 225-9571. Rep. Michael N. Castle, R-Del., Chair; Paula Nowakowski, Staff Director.*

Web, edworkforce.house.gov/members/108th/mem-edr.htm

Jurisdiction over preschool, elementary, and secondary education legislation, including impact aid legislation and food programs for children in schools.

Senate Agriculture, Nutrition, and Forestry Committee, *Subcommittee on Research, Nutrition, and General Legislation, SR-328A 20510; (202) 224-2035. Sen. Peter G. Fitzgerald, R-Ill., Chair; Vacant, Staff Director.*

Web, agriculture.senate.gov

Jurisdiction over legislation on food programs for children in schools.

Senate Health, Education, Labor, and Pensions Committee, *SD-428 20510; (202) 224-5375. Fax, (202) 228-5044. Sen. Judd Gregg, R-N.H., Chair; Sharon Soderstrom, Staff Director. TTY, (202) 224-1975.*

Web, health.senate.gov

Jurisdiction over preschool, elementary, and secondary education legislation, including impact aid legislation; and legislation barring discrimination in schools. Oversight of the Follow Through Act, which aids children in making the transition from preschool to elementary grades.

NONPROFIT

American School Food Service Assn., *700 S. Washington St., #300, Alexandria, VA 22314-4287; (703) 739-3900. Fax, (703) 739-3915. Barbara Belmont, Executive Director. Information, (800) 877-8822.*

Web, www.asfsa.org

Membership: state and local food service workers and supervisors, school cafeteria managers, nutrition educators, industry members, and others interested in school food programs and child nutrition. Sponsors National School Lunch Week and National School Breakfast Week.

Assn. for Childhood Education International, *17904 Georgia Ave., #215, Olney, MD 20832; (301) 570-2111. Fax, (301) 570-2212. Gerald C. Odland, Executive Director. Information, (800) 423-3563.*
General e-mail, aceihq@aol.com
Web, www.acei.org

Membership: educators, parents, and professionals who work with children (infancy to adolescence). Works to promote the rights, education, and well-being of children worldwide. Holds annual conference.

Assn. for Supervision and Curriculum Development, *1703 N. Beauregard St., Alexandria, VA 22311-1714; (703) 578-9600. Fax, (703) 575-5400. Gene R. Carter, Executive Director. Information, (800) 933-2723.*
General e-mail, member@ascd.org
Web, www.ascd.org

Membership: teachers, supervisors, directors of instruction, school principals (kindergarten through secondary), university and college faculty, school board members, and individuals interested in curriculum development. Sponsors institutes and conferences. Monitors legislation and regulations.

Council for Basic Education, *1319 F St. N.W., #900 20004-1152; (202) 347-4171. Fax, (202) 347-5047. Raymond Bartlett, President.*
General e-mail, info@c-b-e.org
Web, www.c-b-e.org

Promotes liberal arts education in elementary and secondary schools; seeks to improve liberal arts instruction of teachers and administrators; conducts workshops, seminars, and independent summer study programs for elementary and secondary school teachers; works to establish and maintain high academic standards; serves as information clearinghouse on education issues.

Council of the Great City Schools, *1301 Pennsylvania Ave. N.W., #702 20004; (202) 393-2427. Fax, (202) 393-2400. Mike Casserly, Executive Director.*
Web, www.cgcs.org

Membership: superintendents and school board members of large urban school districts. Provides research, legislative, and support services for members; interests include elementary and secondary education and school finance.

Home and School Institute, *MegaSkills Education Center, 1500 Massachusetts Ave. N.W. 20005; (202) 466-3633. Fax, (202) 833-1400. Dorothy Rich, President.*
General e-mail, edstaff@megaskillshsi.org
Web, www.megaskillshsi.org

Works to improve the quality of education for children and parents by integrating the resources of the home, the school, and the community. Develops family training curricula and materials for home use, and training programs and conferences for professionals. Interests include special, bilingual, and career education; character development; and working, single, and teenage parents.

National Assessment Governing Board, *800 N. Capitol St. N.W., #825 20002-4233; (202) 357-6938. Fax, (202) 357-6945. Charles E. Smith, Executive Director.*
General e-mail, nagb@ed.gov
Web, www.nagb.org

Independent board of local, state, and federal officials, educators, and others appointed by the secretary of education and funded under the National Assessment of Educational Progress (NAEP) program. Sets policy for NAEP, a series of tests measuring achievements of U.S. students since 1969.

National Assn. for College Admission Counseling, *1631 Prince St., Alexandria, VA 22314; (703) 836-2222. Fax, (703) 836-8015. Joyce Smith, Executive Director.*
Web, www.nacac.com

Membership: high school guidance counselors, independent counselors, college and university admissions officers, and financial aid officers. Assists counselors who serve students in the college admission process. Promotes and funds research on admission counseling and on the transition from high school to college. Advocates for the rights of students in the college admission process. Sponsors national college fairs and continuing education for members.

National Assn. for the Education of Young Children, *1509 16th St. N.W. 20036-1426; (202) 232-8777. Fax, (202) 328-1846. Mark R. Ginsberg, Executive Director. Information, (800) 424-2460. Customer service, (866) 623-9248.*
Web, www.naeyc.org

Membership: teachers, parents, and directors of early childhood programs. Works to improve the education of and the quality of services to children from birth through age eight. Sponsors professional development opportunities for early childhood educators. Offers an accreditation program and conducts an annual conference; issues publications.

National Assn. of Elementary School Principals, *1615 Duke St., Alexandria, VA 22314-3483; (703) 684-3345. Fax, (703) 548-6021. Vincent Ferrandino, Executive Director.*
General e-mail, naesp@naesp.org
Web, www.naesp.org

Membership: elementary and middle school principals. Conducts workshops for members on federal and state policies and programs and on professional development. Offers assistance in contract negotiations.

National Assn. of Partners in Education, *901 N. Pitt St., #320, Alexandria, VA 22314; (703) 836-4880. Fax, (703) 836-6941. Daniel W. Merenda, President.*
General e-mail, napehq@napehq.org
Web, www.partnersineducation.org

Membership: teachers, administrators, volunteers, businesses, community groups, and others seeking to help students achieve academic excellence. Creates and strengthens volunteer and partnership programs. Advocates community involvement in schools.

National Assn. of Secondary School Principals, *1904 Association Dr., Reston, VA 20191-1537; (703) 860-0200. Fax, (703) 476-5432. Gerald Triozzi, Executive Director.*
Web, www.principals.org

Membership: principals and assistant principals of middle and senior high schools, both public and private, and college-level teachers of secondary education. Conducts training programs for members; serves as clearinghouse for information on secondary school administration. Student activities office provides student councils, student activity advisers, and national and junior honor societies with information on national associations.

National Congress of Parents and Teachers, *Legislation, Washington Office,* *1090 Vermont Ave. N.W., #1200 20005; (202) 289-6790. Fax, (202) 289-6791. Maribeth Oakes, Director.*
General e-mail, info@pta.org
Web, www.pta.org

Membership: parent-teacher associations at the preschool, elementary, and secondary levels. Washington office represents members' interests on education, funding for education, parent involvement, child protection and safety, comprehensive health care for children, AIDS, the environment, children's television and educational technology, child care, and nutrition. (Headquarters in Chicago, Ill.)

National Head Start Assn., *1651 Prince St., Alexandria, VA 22314; (703) 739-0875. Fax, (703) 739-0878. Sarah M. Greene, President.*
Web, www.nhsa.org

Membership: organizations that represents Head Start children, families, and staff. Recommends strategies on issues affecting Head Start programs; provides training and professional development opportunities. Monitors legislation and regulations.

National School Boards Assn., *1680 Duke St., Alexandria, VA 22314; (703) 838-6722. Fax, (703) 683-7590. Anne Bryant, Executive Director; Julie Underwood, General Counsel.*
Web, www.nsba.org

Federation of state school board associations. Interests include funding of public education, local governance, and quality of education programs. Sponsors seminars, an annual conference, and an information center. Monitors legislation and regulations. Library open to the public by appointment.

Reading Is Fundamental, *1825 Connecticut Ave. N.W., #400 20009-5726; (202) 673-1641. Fax, (202) 673-1649. Carol Rasco, President. Information, (877) RIF-READ.*
General e-mail, contactus@rif.org
Web, www.rif.org

Conducts programs and workshops to motivate young people to read. Provides young people with books and parents with services to encourage reading at home.

Teach for America, *Washington Office,* *1112 11th St. N.W., #B 20001; (202) 371-8111. Fax, (202) 371-9250. Miwa Powell, Executive Director. Information, (800) 832-1230.*
General e-mail, tfadcw@aol.com
Web, www.teachforamerica.org

A national teacher corps of recent college graduates from all academic majors and cultural backgrounds. Participants teach for a minimum of two years in underfunded urban and rural public schools. Promotes outstanding teaching and educational equity. Monitors legislation and regulations. (Headquarters in New York.)

Private, Parochial, and Home Schooling

AGENCIES

Education Dept., *Non-Public Education,* *400 Maryland Ave. S.W., #5E100 20202-3600; (202) 401-1365. Fax, (202) 401-1368. Jack Klenk, Director (Acting).*
Web, www.ed.gov

Acts as ombudsman for interests of teachers and students in non-public schools (elementary and secondary levels); reports to the secretary on matters relating to non-public education.

NONPROFIT

Americans United for Separation of Church and State, *518 C St. N.E. 20002; (202) 466-3234. Fax, (202) 466-2587. Barry W. Lynn, Executive Director.*
General e-mail, americansunited@au.org
Web, www.au.org

Citizens' interest group. Opposes federal and state aid to parochial schools; works to ensure religious neutrality in public schools; supports religious free exercise; initiates litigation; maintains speakers bureau. Monitors legislation and regulations.

Council for American Private Education, *13017 Wysteria Dr., #457, Germantown, MD 20874; (301) 916-8460. Fax, (301) 916-8485. Joe McTighe, Executive Director.*
General e-mail, cape@capenet.org
Web, www.capenet.org

Coalition of national private school associations serving private elementary and secondary schools. Acts as a liaison between private education and government, other educational organizations, the media, and the public. Seeks greater access to private schools for all families. Monitors legislation and regulations.

Home School Legal Defense Assn., *1 Patrick Henry Circle, Purcellville, VA 20132-3000 (mailing address: P.O. Box 3000, Purcellville, VA 20134); (540) 338-5600. Fax, (540) 338-2733. J. Michael Smith, President.*
General e-mail, info@hslda.org
Web, www.hslda.org

Membership: families who practice home schooling. Provides members with legal consultation and defense. Initiates civil rights litigation on behalf of members. Monitors legislation and regulations.

National Assn. of Independent Schools, *Government Relations, 1620 L St. N.W., #1100 20036-5605; (202) 973-9700. Fax, (202) 973-9790. Jefferson G. Burnett, Director. Press, (202) 973-9717.*
Web, www.nais.org

Membership: independent elementary and secondary schools in the United States and abroad. Provides statistical and educational information to members. Monitors legislation and regulations.

National Catholic Educational Assn., *1077 30th St. N.W., #100 20007-3852; (202) 337-6232. Fax, (202) 333-6706. Michael Guerra, President.*
General e-mail, admin@ncea.org
Web, www.ncea.org

Membership: Catholic schools (preschool through college and seminary) and school administrators. Provides consultation services to members for administration, curriculum, continuing education, religious education, campus ministry, boards of education, and union and personnel negotiations; conducts workshops and conferences; supports federal aid for private education. (Affiliated with the Assn. of Catholic Colleges and Universities.)

National Congress of Parents and Teachers, *Legislation, Washington Office, 1090 Vermont Ave. N.W., #1200 20005; (202) 289-6790. Fax, (202) 289-6791. Maribeth Oakes, Director.*
General e-mail, info@pta.org
Web, www.pta.org

Membership: parent-teacher associations at the preschool, elementary, and secondary levels. Coordinates the National Coalition for Public Education, which opposes tuition tax credits and vouchers for private education. (Headquarters in Chicago, Ill.)

National Council of Churches, *Washington Office, 110 Maryland Ave. N.E., #108 20002; (202) 544-2350. Fax, (202) 543-1297. Brenda Girton-Mitchell, Director.*
Web, www.ncccusa.org

Membership: Protestant, Anglican, and Eastern Orthodox churches. Opposes federal aid to private schools. (Headquarters in New York.)

National Home Education Research Institute, *Washington Office, 12221 Van Brady Rd., Upper Marlboro, MD 20772-7924; (301) 372-2889. William Lloyd, Manager.*
General e-mail, mail@nheri.org
Web, www.nheri.org

Serves as an information clearinghouse for researchers, home educators, attorneys, legislators, policymakers, and the public. Conducts research on home education. Monitors legislation and regulations. (Headquarters in Salem, Ore.)

U.S. Conference of Catholic Bishops (USCCB), *Education Dept., 3211 4th St. N.E. 20017; (202) 541-3130. Fax, (202) 541-3390. Glenn Anne McPhee, Education Secretary. Press, (202) 541-3200. TTY, (202) 740-0424.*
General e-mail, education@usccb.org
Web, www.usccb.org

Represents the Catholic church in the United States in educational matters; advises Catholic schools on federal programs; assists church organizations with religious education.

 ## SPECIAL GROUPS IN EDUCATION

Gifted and Talented

AGENCIES

Education Dept., *Gifted and Talented Education, 400 Maryland Ave. S.W. 20202; (202) 260-7813. Fax, (202) 219-2053. Patricia O'Connell Ross, Program Analyst.*
Web, www.ed.gov/offices/OESE/Javits

Awards grants for developing programs for gifted and talented students, including the limited-English-speaking, economically disadvantaged, and disabled. Oversees the National Research Center, which administers grants for research and analysis of gifted and talented programs. Conducts seminars and produces publications on issues related to gifted and talented programs.

NONPROFIT

Council for Exceptional Children, *1110 N. Glebe Rd., #300, Arlington, VA 22201; (703) 620-3660. Fax, (703) 620-4334. Nancy Safer, Executive Director. Information, (800) 224-6830. TTY, (866) 915-5000.*
Web, www.cec.sped.org

Provides information on gifted and talented education nationwide; maintains clearinghouse of information on the gifted; provides lawmakers with technical assistance. Monitors legislation and regulations affecting gifted and talented education. Library open to the public by appointment.

National Assn. for Gifted Children, *1707 L St. N.W., #550 20036; (202) 785-4268. Fax, (202) 785-4248. Peter D. Rosenstein, Executive Director.*
Web, www.nagc.org

Membership: teachers, administrators, state coordinators, and parents. Works for programs for intellectually and creatively gifted children in public and private schools.

Yes I Can! Foundation for Exceptional Children, *1110 N. Glebe Rd., #300, Arlington, VA 22201; (703) 264-9462. Fax, (703) 758-1896. Christine Mason, Executive Director (Acting).*
General e-mail, yesican@cec.sped.org
Web, yesican.sped.org

Provides information and assists educators and parents; works to protect the rights of gifted children and children with disabilities; develops education programs and faculty standards. Awards scholarships and grants. (Affiliated with Council for Exceptional Children.)

Learning and Physically Disabled

AGENCIES

Education Dept., *Special Education and Rehabilitative Services, 330 C St. S.W., #3006 20202-2500; (202) 205-5465. Fax, (202) 205-9252. Robert Pasternack, Assistant Secretary. TTY, (202) 205-0136. Main phone is voice and TTY accessible.*
Web, www.nochildleftbehind.gov

Administers federal assistance programs for the education and rehabilitation of people with disabilities, which are administered by the National Institute of Disability and Rehabilitation Research, the Office of Special Education Programs, and the Rehabilitation Services Administration; maintains a national information clearinghouse on people with disabilities.

Education Dept., *Special Education Programs, 330 C St. S.W., #3086 20202-2570; (202) 205-5507. Fax, (202) 260-0416. Stephanie Lee, Director.*
Web, www.ed.gov

Responsible for special education programs and services designed to meet the needs and develop the full potential of children with disabilities. Programs include support for training of teachers and other professional personnel; grants for research; financial aid to help states initiate and improve their resources; and media services and captioned films for hearing impaired persons.

Smithsonian Institution, *Accessibility Program, 900 Jefferson Dr. S.W., #1239 20560-0426; (202) 786-2942. Fax, (202) 786-2210. Elizabeth Ziebarth, Coordinator. Information, (888) 783-0001. TTY, (202) 786-2414.*
Web, www.si.edu

Coordinates Smithsonian efforts to improve accessibility of its programs and facilities to visitors and staff with disabilities. Serves as a resource for museums and individuals nationwide.

CONGRESS

House Education and the Workforce Committee, *Subcommittee on Education Reform, 2181 RHOB 20515; (202) 225-4527. Fax, (202) 225-9571. Rep. Michael N. Castle, R-Del., Chair; Paula Nowakowski, Staff Director.*
Web, edworkforce.house.gov/members/108th/mem-edr.htm

Jurisdiction over legislation on special education programs including, but not limited to, alcohol and drug abuse and education of the disabled.

Library of Congress, *National Library Service for the Blind and Physically Handicapped, 1291 Taylor St. N.W. 20542; (202) 707-5104. Fax, (202) 707-0712. Frank Kurt Cylke, Director. TTY, (202) 707-0744. Reference, (202) 707-5100; outside D.C. area, (800) 424-8567.*
General e-mail, nls@loc.gov
Web, www.loc.gov/nls

Administers a national program of free library services for persons with physical disabilities in cooperation with regional and subregional libraries. Produces and distributes full-length books and magazines in recorded form and in Braille. Reference section answers questions relating to blindness and physical disabilities and on library services available to persons with disabilities.

Senate Health, Education, Labor, and Pensions Committee, *SD-428 20510; (202) 224-5375. Fax, (202) 228-5044. Sen. Judd Gregg, R-N.H., Chair; Sharon Soderstrom, Staff Director. TTY, (202) 224-1975.*
Web, health.senate.gov

Jurisdiction over legislation on education of people with disabilities, including Gallaudet University and the National Technical Institute for the Deaf; jurisdiction over the Americans with Disabilities Act.

NONPROFIT

Assn. for Education and Rehabilitation of the Blind and Visually Impaired, *P.O. Box 22397, Alexandria, VA 22304; (703) 823-9690. Fax, (703) 823-9695. Mark Richard, Executive Director.*
General e-mail, aer@aerbvi.org
Web, www.aerbvi.org

Membership: professionals and paraprofessionals who work with the blind and visually impaired. Provides information on services for people who are blind and visually impaired and on employment opportunities for those who work with them. Works to improve quality of education and rehabilitation services. Monitors legislation and regulations.

Assn. of University Centers on Disabilities (AAUAP), *8630 Fenton St., #410, Silver Spring, MD 20910; (301) 588-8252. Fax, (301) 588-2842. George Jesien, Executive Director.*
Web, www.aucd.org

Network of facilities that diagnose and treat the developmentally disabled. Trains graduate students and professionals in the field; helps state and local agencies develop services. Interests include interdisciplinary training and services, early screening to prevent developmental disabilities, and development of equipment and programs to serve persons with disabilities.

Council for Exceptional Children, *1110 N. Glebe Rd., #300, Arlington, VA 22201; (703) 620-3660. Fax, (703) 620-4334. Nancy Safer, Executive Director. Information, (800) 224-6830. TTY, (866) 915-5000.*
Web, www.cec.sped.org

Provides information on the education of exceptional children; maintains clearinghouse of information on disabilities, learning disorders, and special education topics; provides lawmakers with technical assistance. Monitors legislation and regulations affecting special education. Library open to the public by appointment.

Gallaudet University, *800 Florida Ave. N.E. 20002-3695; (202) 651-5000. Fax, (202) 651-5508. I. King Jordan, President, (202) 651-5005. Phone numbers are voice and TTY accessible.*
Web, www.gallaudet.edu

Offers undergraduate, graduate, and doctoral degree programs for deaf, hard of hearing, and hearing students. Conducts research, maintains regional extension outreach centers, and demonstration secondary, elementary, and preschool programs (Laurent Clerc National Deaf Education Center). Sponsors the Center for Global Education, National Deaf Education Network and Clearinghouse, and the Cochlear Implant Education Center.

National Assn. of Private Special Education Centers, *1522 K St. N.W., #1032 20005-1202; (202) 408-3338. Fax, (202) 408-3340. Sherry L. Kolbe, Executive Director.*
General e-mail, napsec@aol.com
Web, www.napsec.com

Promotes greater education opportunities for children with disabilities; provides legislators and agencies with information and testimony; formulates and disseminates positions and statements on special education issues.

National Assn. of State Directors of Special Education, *1800 Diagonal Rd., #320, Alexandria, VA 22314; (703) 519-3800. Fax, (703) 519-3808. Bill East, Executive Director. TTY, (703) 519-7008.*
General e-mail, nasdse@nasdse.org
Web, www.nasdse.org

Membership: state education agency special education administrators, consultants, and supervisors. Monitors legislation and research developments in special education.

VSA Arts, *1300 Connecticut Ave. N.W., #700 20036; (202) 628-2800. Fax, (202) 737-0725. Soula Antoniou, Chief Executive Officer. Information, (800) 933-8721. TTY, (202) 737-0645.*
Web, www.vsarts.org

Initiates and supports research and program development providing arts training and demonstration for persons with disabilities. Provides technical assistance and training to VSA Arts state organizations; acts as an information clearinghouse for arts and persons with disabilities. Formerly known as Very Special Arts. (Affiliated with the Kennedy Center education office.)

Yes I Can! Foundation for Exceptional Children, *1110 N. Glebe Rd., #300, Arlington, VA 22201; (703) 264-9462. Fax, (703) 758-1896. Christine Mason, Executive Director (Acting).*

General e-mail, yesican@cec.sped.org

Web, yesican.sped.org

Provides information and assists educators and parents; works to protect the rights of gifted children and children with disabilities; develops education programs and faculty standards. Awards scholarships and grants. (Affiliated with Council for Exceptional Children.)

Minorities and Women

AGENCIES

Bureau of Indian Affairs (BIA), *(Interior Dept.),* **Indian Education Programs,** *1849 C St. N.W., #3512 20240; (202) 208-6123. Fax, (202) 208-3312. William M. Mehojah Jr., Director.*

Web, www.oiep.bia.edu

Operates schools for native Americans, including people with disabilities. Provides special assistance to native American pupils in public schools; aids native American college students; sponsors adult education programs.

Commission on Civil Rights, *Civil Rights Evaluation, 624 9th St. N.W., #740 20425; (202) 376-8582. Fax, (202) 376-7754. Terri A. Dickerson, Assistant Staff Director. Library, (202) 376-8110.*

Web, www.usccr.gov

Researches federal policy on education, including desegregation. Library open to the public.

Education Dept., *Civil Rights, 330 C St. S.W., #5000 20202-1100 (mailing address: 400 Maryland Ave. S.W. 20202-1100); (202) 205-5413. Fax, (202) 205-9862. Gerald Reynolds, Assistant Secretary.*

Web, www.ed.gov

Enforces laws prohibiting use of federal funds for education programs or activities that discriminate on the basis of race, color, sex, national origin, age, or disability; authorized to discontinue funding.

Education Dept., *Federal TRIO Programs, 1990 K St. N.W., #7000 20006-8510; (202) 502-7600. Fax, (202) 502-7857. Linda Byrd-Johnson, Team Leader. TTY, (202) 502-7600.*

Web, www.ed.gov

Administers programs for disadvantaged students, including Upward Bound, Talent Search, Student Support Services, the Ronald E. McNair Post-Baccalaureate Achievement Program, and educational opportunity centers; provides special programs personnel with training.

Education Dept., *Indian Education Programs, 400 Maryland Ave. S.W., #FB6 20202-6335; (202) 260-3774. Fax, (202) 260-7779. Victoria Vasques, Director.*

Web, www.ed.gov/offices/OESE/OIE

Aids local school districts with programs for native American students; funds schools operated by the Bureau of Indian Affairs and native American-controlled schools and programs.

Education Dept., *Migrant Education, 400 Maryland Ave. S.W., #3E317 20202-6135; (202) 260-1164. Fax, (202) 205-0089. Francisco Garcia, Director.*

Web, www.ed.gov/offices/OESE/MEP

Administers programs that fund education (preschool through postsecondary) for children of migrant workers.

Education Dept., *Student Achievement and Schools Accountability Program, 400 Maryland Ave. S.W., #3W230 20202-6132; (202) 260-0826. Fax, (202) 260-7764. Jacqueline Jackson, Director (Acting). Press, (202) 401-1008.*

Web, www.ed.gov

Administers the Chapter 1 federal assistance program for education of educationally deprived children (preschool through secondary), including native American children, homeless children, delinquents, and residents in state institutions. Administers the Even Start program.

Education Dept., *White House Initiative on Historically Black Colleges and Universities, 1990 K St. N.W., 8th Floor 20006; (202) 502-7900. Fax, (202) 502-7879. Leonard H. Spearman, Executive Director.*

Web, www.ed.gov/inits/commissionsboards/whhbcu/index.html

Supervises and seeks to increase involvement of the private sector in historically black colleges and universities. Works to eliminate barriers to the participation of these colleges and universities in federal and private programs.

Education Dept., *Women's Educational Equity Act Program, 400 Maryland Ave. S.W., #3E106 20202-6140; (202) 260-1393. Fax, (202) 205-5630. Edith Harvey, Program Specialist.*

Web, www.ed.gov

Administers the Women's Educational Equity Act; awards grants and contracts to higher education institutions, public and nonprofit private organizations, and individuals; promotes issues related to educational equity for women; maintains liaison with national women's organizations. (Program does not offer financial aid directly to students.)

Justice Dept. (DOJ), *Educational Opportunity,* 601 D St. N.W., #4300 20530; (202) 514-4092. Fax, (202) 514-8337. Ralph F. Boyd Jr., Assistant Attorney General.
Web, www.usdoj.gov/crt

Initiates litigation to ensure equal opportunities in public education; enforces laws dealing with civil rights in public education.

Office of Personnel Management (OPM), *Diversity,* 1900 E St. N.W., #2445 20415-0001; (202) 606-1059. Fax, (202) 606-0927. Maria Mercedes Olivieri, Director.
Web, www.opm.gov/disability

Develops and provides guidance to federal agencies on the employment of minorities and women. Administers the Federal Equal Opportunity Recruitment Program.

CONGRESS

House Appropriations Committee, *Subcommittee on Interior,* B308 RHOB 20515; (202) 225-3081. Fax, (202) 225-9069. Rep. Charles H. Taylor, R-N.C., Chair; Deborah A. Weatherly, Staff Director.
Web, www.house.gov/appropriations

Jurisdiction over legislation to appropriate funds for all native American education activities of the Education Dept. and for the Bureau of Indian Affairs.

House Education and the Workforce Committee, 2181 RHOB 20515; (202) 225-4527. Fax, (202) 225-9571. Rep. John A. Boehner, R-Ohio, Chair; Paula Nowakowski, Staff Director.
Web, edworkforce.house.gov

Jurisdiction over legislation pertaining to native American education; oversight of native American education programs (jurisdiction shared with the House Resources Committee).

House Education and the Workforce Committee, *Subcommittee on Select Education,* 2181 RHOB 20515; (202) 225-4527. Fax, (202) 225-9571. Rep. Peter Hoekstra, R-Mich., Chair; Paula Nowakowski, Staff Director.
Web, edworkforce.house.gov/members/108th/mem-sed.htm

Jurisdiction over legislation barring discrimination in education, including the Women's Educational Equity Act of 1974.

House Education and the Workforce Committee, *Subcommittee on 21st Century Competitiveness,* 2181 RHOB 20515; (202) 225-4527. Fax, (202) 225-9571. Rep. Howard P. "Buck" McKeon, R-Calif., Chair; Paula Nowakowski, Staff Director.
Web, edworkforce.house.gov/members/108th/mem-21st.htm

Jurisdiction over legislation barring discrimination in postsecondary education.

House Resources Committee, 1324 LHOB 20515; (202) 225-2761. Fax, (202) 225-5929. Rep. Richard W. Pombo, R-Calif., Chair; Steve Ding, Chief of Staff.
General e-mail, resources.committee@mail.house.gov
Web, resourcescommittee.house.gov

Jurisdiction over legislation pertaining to native American education; oversight of native American education programs (jurisdiction shared with House Education and the Workforce Committee).

Senate Appropriations Committee, *Subcommittee on Interior and Related Agencies,* SD-131 20510; (202) 224-7233. Fax, (202) 228-4532. Sen. Conrad Burns, R-Mont., Chair; Bruce Evans, Clerk.
Web, appropriations.senate.gov/interior

Jurisdiction over legislation to appropriate funds for all native American education activities and for the Bureau of Indian Affairs.

Senate Health, Education, Labor, and Pensions Committee, SD-428 20510; (202) 224-5375. Fax, (202) 228-5044. Sen. Judd Gregg, R-N.H., Chair; Sharon Soderstrom, Staff Director. TTY, (202) 224-1975.
Web, health.senate.gov

Jurisdiction over legislation barring discrimination in education, including the Women's Educational Equity Act of 1974.

Senate Indian Affairs Committee, SH-838 20510; (202) 224-2251. Fax, (202) 228-2589. Sen. Ben Nighthorse Campbell, R-Colo., Chair; Paul Moorehead, Staff Director.
Web, indian.senate.gov

Jurisdiction over legislation pertaining to native American education; oversight of native American education programs.

NONPROFIT

American Assn. of University Women (AAUW), 1111 16th St. N.W. 20036-4873; (202) 785-7700. Fax, (202) 872-1425. Jacqueline E. Woods, Executive Director. Library, (202) 785-7763. TTY, (202) 785-7777.
General e-mail, info@aauw.org
Web, www.aauw.org

Membership: graduates of accredited colleges, universities, and recognized foreign institutions. Interests include equity for women and girls in education, the workplace, health care, and the family. Library open to the public by appointment.

Aspira Assn., *1444 Eye St. N.W., #800 20005; (202) 835-3600. Fax, (202) 835-3613. Ronald Blackburn-Moreno, President.*
General e-mail, info@aspira.org
Web, www.aspira.org

Provides Latino youth with resources necessary for them to remain in school and contribute to their community. Interests include math, science, leadership development, parental involvement, and research. Monitors legislation and regulations.

Assn. of American Colleges and Universities (ACCU), *1818 R St. N.W. 20009; (202) 387-3760. Fax, (202) 265-9532. Carol Geary Schneider, President.*
Web, www.aacu-edu.org

Serves as clearinghouse for information on women professionals in higher education. Interests include women's studies, women's centers, and women's leadership and professional development.

Council for Opportunity in Education, *1025 Vermont Ave. N.W., #900 20005; (202) 347-7430. Fax, (202) 347-0786. Arnold L. Mitchem, President.*
General e-mail, trio@ed.gov
Web, www.trioprograms.org

Represents institutions of higher learning, administrators, counselors, teachers, and others committed to advancing equal educational opportunity in colleges and universities. Works to sustain and improve educational opportunity programs such as the federally funded TRIO program, designed to help low-income, first-generation immigrant, and physically disabled students enroll in and graduate from college.

East Coast Migrant Head Start Project, *4245 N. Fairfax Dr., #800, Arlington, VA 22203; (703) 243-7522. Fax, (703) 243-1259. Raphael Guerra, Executive Director.*
Web, www.ecmhsp.org

Establishes Head Start programs for migrant children and offers training and technical assistance to established centers that enroll migrant children.

League of United Latin American Citizens, *2000 L St. N.W., #610 20036; (202) 833-6130. Fax, (202) 833-6135. Brent Wilkes, Executive Director.*
Web, www.lulac.org

Seeks to increase the number of minorities, especially Hispanics, attending postsecondary schools; supports legislation to increase educational opportunities for Hispanics and other minorities; provides scholarship funds and educational and career counseling.

The Links Inc., *1200 Massachusetts Ave. N.W. 20005-4501; (202) 842-8686. Fax, (202) 842-4020. Mary Clark, Executive Director (Interim).*
Web, www.linksinc.org

Predominantly African American women's service organization that works with the educationally disadvantaged and culturally deprived; focuses on arts, services for youth, and national and international trends and services.

NAACP Legal Defense and Educational Fund, *Washington Office, 1444 Eye St. N.W., 10th Floor 20005; (202) 682-1300. Fax, (202) 682-1312. Leslie M. Proll, Senior Attorney.*

Civil rights litigation group that provides legal information about civil rights and advice on educational discrimination against women and minorities; monitors federal enforcement of civil rights laws. Not affiliated with the National Assn. for the Advancement of Colored People (NAACP). (Headquarters in New York.)

National Alliance of Black School Educators, *310 Pennsylvania Ave. S.E. 20003; (202) 608-6310. Fax, (202) 608-6319. Quentin R. Lawson, Executive Director.*
General e-mail, nabse@nabse.org
Web, www.nabse.org

Develops and recommends policy for and promotes the education of African American youth and adults; seeks to raise the academic achievement level of all African American students. Sponsors workshops and conferences on major issues in education affecting African American students and educators.

National Assn. for Equal Opportunity in Higher Education, *8701 Georgia Ave., #200, Silver Spring, MD 20910; (301) 650-2440. Fax, (301) 495-3306. Fredrick Humphries, President (Interim).*
Web, www.nafeo.org

Membership: historically and predominantly black colleges and universities. Works for increased federal and private support for member institutions and for increased minority representation in private and governmental education agencies; serves as a clearinghouse for information on federal contracts and grants for member institutions; collects, analyzes, and publishes data on member institutions; operates internship program.

National Assn. for the Advancement of Colored People (NAACP), *Washington Office, 1025 Vermont Ave. N.W., #1120 20005; (202) 638-2269. Fax, (202) 638-5936. Hilary O. Shelton, Director.*
Web, www.naacp.org

Membership: persons interested in civil rights for all minorities. Works for equal opportunity for minorities in all areas, including education; seeks to ensure a quality desegregated education for all through litigation and legislation. (Headquarters in Baltimore, Md.)

National Assn. of Colored Women's Clubs, *1601 R St. N.W. 20009; (202) 667-4080. Fax, (202) 667-4113. Margaret J. Cooper, President.*

Seeks to promote education; protect and enforce civil rights; raise the standard of family living; promote inter-racial understanding; and enhance leadership development. Awards scholarships; conducts programs in education, social service, and philanthropy.

National Assn. of State Universities and Land Grant Colleges, *Advancement of Public Black Colleges, 1307 New York Ave. N.W., #400 20005; (202) 478-6041. Fax, (202) 478-6046. Joyce Payne, Director.*
Web, www.nasulgc.org

Seeks to heighten awareness and visibility of public African American colleges; promotes institutional advancement. Conducts research and provides information on issues of concern; acts as a liaison with African American public colleges and universities, the federal government, and private associations. Monitors legislation and regulations.

National Clearinghouse for English Language Acquisition (NCELA), *Language Instruction Educational Programs, 2121 K St. N.W., #260 20037; (202) 467-0867. Fax, (202) 467-4283. Minerva Gorena, Director.*
General e-mail, askncela@ncela.gwu.edu
Web, www.ncela.gwu.edu

Collects, analyzes, and disseminates information relating to the effective education of linguistically and culturally diverse learners in the U.S. Interests include foreign language programs, ESL programs, Head Start, Title I, migrant education, and adult education programs.

National Council of La Raza, *1111 19th St. N.W., #1000 20036; (202) 785-1670. Fax, (202) 776-1792. Raul Yzaguirre, President.*
General e-mail, info@nclr.org
Web, www.nclr.org

Provides research, policy analysis, and advocacy on educational status and needs of Hispanics; promotes education reform benefiting Hispanics; develops and tests community-based models for helping Hispanic students succeed in school. Interests include counseling, testing, and bilingual, vocational, preschool through postsecondary, and migrant education.

National Women's Law Center, *11 Dupont Circle N.W., #800 20036; (202) 588-5180. Fax, (202) 588-5185. Marcia D. Greenberger, Co-President; Nancy Duff Campbell, Co-President.*
General e-mail, info@nwlc.org
Web, www.nwlc.org

Works to expand and protect women's legal rights in education through advocacy and public education.

United Negro College Fund, *8260 Willow Oaks Corporate Dr., Fairfax, VA 22031-4511 (mailing address: P.O. Box 10444, Fairfax, VA 22031-0444); (703) 205-3400. Fax, (703) 205-3575. William H. Gray III, President. Press, (703) 205-3553.*
Web, www.uncf.org

Membership: private colleges and universities with historically black enrollment. Raises money for member institutions; monitors legislation and regulations.

 SPECIAL TOPICS IN EDUCATION

Bilingual and Multicultural

AGENCIES

Education Dept., *English Language Acquisition, 330 C St. S.W., #5086 20202-6510; (202) 205-5463. Fax, (202) 205-8737. Maria H. Ferrier, Director.*
Web, www.ed.gov/offices/OELA

Provides school districts and state education agencies with grants to establish, operate, and improve programs for people with limited English proficiency; promotes development of resources for such programs, including training for parents and education personnel. Administers assistance programs for refugee and immigrant children. (Formerly the Office of Bilingual Education and Minority Languages Affairs.)

NONPROFIT

National Assn. for Bilingual Education, *1030 15th St. N.W., #470 20005-1503; (202) 898-1829. Fax, (202) 789-2866. Delia Pompa, Executive Director.*
General e-mail, NABE@nabe.org
Web, www.nabe.org

Membership: educators, policymakers, paraprofessionals, publications personnel, students, researchers, and interested individuals. Works to improve educational programs for non-English-speaking students and to promote bilingualism among American students. Conducts annual conference and workshops.

National MultiCultural Institute, *3000 Connecticut Ave. N.W., #438 20008-2556; (202) 483-0700. Fax, (202) 483-5233. Elizabeth P. Salett, President.*

General e-mail, nmci@nmci.org

Web, www.nmci.org

Encourages understanding and communication among people of various backgrounds; seeks to increase awareness of different perspectives and experiences; provides multicultural training, education, and counseling programs for organizations and institutions working with diverse cultural groups; conducts two conferences annually.

Teachers of English to Speakers of Other Languages (TESOL), *700 S. Washington St., #200, Alexandria, VA 22314-4287; (703) 836-0774. Fax, (703) 836-7864. Charles S. Amorosino, Executive Director. Publications, (888) 891-0041.*

General e-mail, tesol@tesol.org

Web, www.tesol.org

Promotes scholarship and provides information on instruction and research in the teaching of English to speakers of other languages. Offers placement service.

Citizenship Education

NONPROFIT

Close Up Foundation, *44 Canal Center Plaza, #500, Alexandria, VA 22314; (703) 706-3300. Fax, (703) 706-0000. Stephen A. Janger, President.*

Web, www.closeup.org

Sponsors week-long programs on American government for high school students, teachers, older Americans, new Americans, native Americans, Alaskan natives, and Pacific Islanders; offers fellowships for participation in the programs; produces television series for secondary schools; conducts First Vote, a voter registration program, and Active Citizenship Today, a program that promotes community service.

Horatio Alger Assn. of Distinguished Americans, *99 Canal Center Plaza, #320, Alexandria, VA 22314; (703) 684-9444. Fax, (703) 684-9445. Terrence J. Giroux, Executive Director.*

General e-mail, association@horatioalger.org

Web, www.horatioalger.org

Educates young people about the economic and personal opportunities available in the American free enterprise system. Conducts seminars on careers in public and community service; operates speakers bureau and internship program. Presents the Horatio Alger Youth Award to outstanding high school students and the Horatio Alger Award to professionals who have achieved suc-

cess in their respective fields. Awards college scholarships.

League of Women Voters Education Fund (LWV), *1730 M St. N.W., #1000 20036; (202) 429-1965. Fax, (202) 429-0854. Nancy Tate, Director.*

Web, www.lwv.org

Public foundation established by the League of Women Voters of the United States. Promotes citizen knowledge of and involvement in representative government; conducts citizen education on current public policy issues; seeks to increase voter registration and turnout; sponsors candidate forums and debates.

National 4-H Council, *7100 Connecticut Ave., Chevy Chase, MD 20815-4999; (301) 961-2820. Fax, (301) 961-2894. Donald T. Floyd Jr., President. Press, (301) 961-2915.*

Web, www.fourhcouncil.edu

Educational organization incorporated to expand and strengthen the 4-H program (for young people ages seven to nineteen) of the Cooperative Extension System and state land-grant universities. Programs include citizenship and leadership training.

Presidential Classroom for Young Americans, *119 Oronoco St., Alexandria, VA 22314-2015; (703) 683-5400. Fax, (703) 548-5728. Jack Buechner, President. Information, (800) 441-6533.*

General e-mail, info@presidentialclassroom.org

Web, www.presidentialclassroom.org

Offers civic education programs for high school students and volunteer opportunities for college students and adults. Provides week-long series of seminars featuring representatives of each branch of government, the diplomatic community, the military, the media, private interest groups, and both major political parties.

Washington Workshops Foundation, *3222 N St. N.W., #340 20007; (202) 965-3434. Fax, (202) 965-1018. Sharon E. Sievers, President. Information, (800) 368-5688.*

General e-mail, info@workshops.org

Web, www.workshops.org

Educational foundation that provides introductory seminars on American government and politics to junior and senior high school students; congressional seminars to secondary and postsecondary students; and seminars on diplomacy and global affairs to secondary students.

Consumer Education

AGENCIES

Agriculture Dept. (USDA), *Research, Education, and Economics, 1400 Independence Ave. S.W., #216W 20250-*

0110; (202) 720-5923. Fax, (202) 690-2842. Joseph J. Jen, Under Secretary; Dawn R. Riley, Director of Intergovernmental and Legislative Affairs.

Web, www.usda.gov

Coordinates agricultural research, extension, and teaching programs in the food and agricultural sciences, including human nutrition, home economics, consumer services, agricultural economics, environmental quality, natural and renewable resources, forestry and range management, animal and plant production and protection, aquaculture, and the production, distribution, and utilization of food and agricultural products. Oversees the Cooperative State Research, Education, and Extension Service.

Consumer Product Safety Commission (CPSC), Information and Public Affairs, 4330 East-West Hwy., #519, Bethesda, MD 20814 (mailing address: Washington, DC 20207-0001); (301) 504-7908. Fax, (301) 504-0862. Becky Bailey, Director. TTY, (800) 638-8270. Product safety hotline, (800) 638-2772.

General e-mail, info@cpsc.gov

Web, www.cpsc.gov

Provides information concerning consumer product safety; works with local and state governments, school systems, and private groups to develop product safety information and education programs. Toll-free hotline accepts consumer complaints on hazardous products and injuries associated with a product and offers recorded information on product recalls and CPSC safety recommendations.

Cooperative State Research, Education, and Extension Service (Agriculture Dept.), 1400 Independence Ave. S.W., #305A 20250-2201; (202) 720-4423. Fax, (202) 720-8987. Colien Hefferan, Administrator. Information, (202) 720-6133. TTY, (202) 690-1899.

Web, www.reeusda.gov

Oversees county agents and operation of state offices that provide information on home economics, including diet and nutrition, food budgeting, food safety, home gardening, clothing care, and other consumer concerns.

Federal Trade Commission (FTC), Consumer and Business Education, 601 New Jersey Ave. N.W., #2223 20001; (202) 326-3268. Fax, (202) 326-3574. Carolyn Shanoff, Director. TTY, (202) 326-2502. Consumer Response Center, (202) FTC-HELP or (877) FTC-HELP.

Web, www.ftc.gov

Develops educational material about FTC activities for consumers and businesses.

Food and Drug Administration (FDA), (Health and Human Services Dept.), Consumer Affairs, 5600 Fishers Lane, Rockville, MD 20857-0001; (301) 827-4422. Fax, (301) 443-9767. Patricia Kuntze, Associate Director (Acting). Consumer inquiries, (888) 463-6332.

Web, www.fda.gov/oca/oca.htm

Responds to inquiries on issues related to the FDA. Conducts consumer health education programs for specific groups, including women, the elderly, and the educationally and economically disadvantaged. Serves as liaison with national health and consumer organizations.

Food Safety and Inspection Service (Agriculture Dept.), 1400 Independence Ave. S.W., #331E 20250; (202) 720-7025. Fax, (202) 205-0158. Garry L. McKee, Administrator. Press, (202) 720-9113. Consumer inquiries, (800) 535-4555; in Washington, (202) 720-3333.

Web, www.usda.gov/fsis

Sponsors food safety educational programs to inform the public about measures to prevent foodborne illnesses; sponsors lectures, publications, public service advertising campaigns, exhibits, and audiovisual presentations. Toll-free hotline answers food safety questions.

NONPROFIT

American Assn. of Family and Consumer Sciences, 1555 King St., 4th Floor, Alexandria, VA 22314; (703) 706-4600. Fax, (703) 706-4663. Karen Tucker, Executive Director.

General e-mail, staff@aafcs.org

Web, www.aafcs.org

Membership: professional home economists. Supports family and consumer sciences education; develops accrediting standards for undergraduate family and consumer science programs; trains and certifies family and consumer science professionals. Monitors legislation and regulations concerning family and consumer issues.

Family, Career, and Community Leaders of America, 1910 Association Dr., Reston, VA 20191-1584; (703) 476-4900. Fax, (703) 860-2713. Alan T. Rains Jr., Executive Director.

General e-mail, nationalheadquarters@fcclainc.org

Web, www.fcclainc.org

National student organization that helps young men and women address personal, family, work, and social issues through family and consumer sciences education.

Literacy, Basic Skills

AGENCIES

AmeriCorps (Corporation for National and Community Service), Volunteers in Service to America (VISTA), 1201 New York Ave. N.W. 20525; (202) 606-5000. Fax, (202) 565-2789. David Caprara, Director. TTY,

(800) 833-3722. *Volunteer recruiting information,* (800) 942-2677.

General e-mail, questions@americorps.org

Web, www.americorps.org/vista

Assigns volunteers to local and state education departments, to public agencies, and to private, non-profit organizations that have literacy programs. Other activities include tutor recruitment and training and the organization and expansion of local literacy councils, workplace literacy programs, and intergenerational literacy programs.

Education Dept., *Adult Education and Literacy,* 330 C St. S.W., #4428 20202-7240 (mailing address: 400 Maryland Ave. S.W. 20202); (202) 205-8270. Fax, (202) 205-8973. *Cheryl L. Keenan, Director. Literacy clearinghouse,* (202) 205-9996.

Web, www.ed.gov/offices/OVAE

Provides state and local education agencies and the general public with information on establishing, expanding, improving, and operating adult education and literacy programs. Emphasizes basic and life skills attainment, English literacy, and high school completion. Awards grants to state education agencies for adult education and literacy programs, including workplace and family literacy.

Education Dept., *National Institute for Literacy,* 1775 Eye St. N.W., #730 20006; (202) 233-2025. Fax, (202) 233-2050. *Sandra Baxter, Director (Acting).*

Web, www.nifl.gov

Operates a literacy clearinghouse and an electronic national literacy and communications system; provides private literacy groups, educational institutions, and federal, state, and local agencies working on illiteracy with assistance; awards grants and fellowships to literacy programs and individuals pursuing careers in the literacy field.

CONGRESS

Library of Congress, *Center for the Book,* 101 Independence Ave. S.E., #650 20540-4920; (202) 707-5221. Fax, (202) 707-0269. *John Y. Cole, Director.*

General e-mail, cfbook@loc.gov

Web, www.loc.gov/loc/cfbook

Promotes family and adult literacy; encourages the study of books and stimulates public interest in books, reading, and libraries; sponsors publication of a directory describing national organizations that administer literacy programs. Affiliated state centers sponsor projects and hold events that call attention to the importance of literacy.

NONPROFIT

AFL-CIO Working for America Institute, 815 16th St. N.W. 20006; (202) 974-8128. Fax, (202) 974-8101. *Nancy Mills, Executive Director.*

General e-mail, info@workingforamerica.org

Web, www.workingforamerica.org

Provides labor unions, employers, education agencies, and community groups with technical assistance for workplace education programs focusing on adult literacy, basic skills, and job training. Interests include new technologies and workplace innovations.

American Poetry and Literacy Project, P.O. Box 53445 20009; (202) 338-1109. *Andrew Carroll, Executive Director.*

Web, www.poets.org/aplp

Donates new books of poetry to schools, libraries, hospitals, homeless shelters, nursing homes, hotels, and other public places around the country to promote literacy.

American Society for Training and Development (ASTD), 1640 King St., Box 1443, Alexandria, VA 22313-2043; (703) 683-8100. Fax, (703) 683-1523. *Tina Sung, President.*

Web, www.astd.org

Membership: trainers and human resource developers. Publishes information on workplace literacy.

Barbara Bush Foundation for Family Literacy, 1201 15th St. N.W., #420 20005; (202) 955-6183. Fax, (202) 955-8084. *Benita Somerfield, Executive Director.*

General e-mail, sooc@erols.com

Web, www.barbarabushfoundation.com

Seeks to establish literacy as a value in every family and to develop and expand family literacy programs nationwide. Encourages recognition of volunteers, educators, students, and effective programs. Awards grants and publishes materials that document effective literacy programs.

Center for Applied Linguistics, *National Clearinghouse for ESL Literacy Education,* 4646 40th St. N.W. 20016; (202) 362-0700. Fax, (202) 362-3740. *Donna Christian, President.*

General e-mail, ncle@cal.org

Web, www.cal.org

Provides information and referral service on literacy instruction for adults and out-of-school youth learning English as a second language. Operates English language training programs internationally.

First Book, *1319 F St. N.W., #1000 20004; (202) 393-1222. Fax, (202) 628-1258. Kyle Zimmer, President.*
General e-mail, staff@firstbook.org
Web, www.firstbook.org

Purchases and distributes new books to low-income families. Organizes fundraisers to support and promote local literacy programs.

General Federation of Women's Clubs, *1734 N St. N.W. 20036-2990; (202) 347-3168. Fax, (202) 835-0246. Gabrielle Smith, Executive Director.*
General e-mail, gfwc@gfwc.org
Web, www.gfwc.org

Nondenominational, nonpartisan international organization of women volunteers. Develops literacy projects in response to community needs; sponsors tutoring.

Newspaper Assn. of America Foundation, *Educational Programs, 1921 Gallows Rd., #600, Vienna, VA 22182; (703) 902-1600. Fax, (703) 917-0636. Jim Abbott, Manager.*
Web, www.naa.org

Publishes a handbook for starting newspaper literacy projects; promotes intergenerational literacy through its Family Focus program; acts as a clearinghouse for literacy information.

Reading Is Fundamental, *1825 Connecticut Ave. N.W., #400 20009-5726; (202) 673-1641. Fax, (202) 673-1649. Carol Rasco, President. Information, (877) RIF-READ.*
General e-mail, contactus@rif.org
Web, www.rif.org

Conducts programs and workshops to motivate young people to read. Provides young people with books and parents with services to encourage reading at home.

Science and Mathematics Education

AGENCIES

Education Dept., *Higher Education: Minority Science and Engineering Improvement, 1990 K St. N.W., 6th Floor 20006; (202) 502-7777. Fax, (202) 502-7861. Deborah Newkirk, Program Director.*
Web, www.ed.gov

Funds programs to improve science and engineering education in predominantly minority colleges and universities; promotes increased participation by minority students and faculty in science and engineering fields; encourages minority schools and universities to apply for grants that will generate precollege student interest in science.

National Museum of Natural History *(Smithsonian Institution), Naturalist Center, 741 Miller Dr. S.E., #G2,* *Leesburg, VA 20175; (703) 779-9712. Fax, (703) 779-9715. Richard H. Efthim, Manager. Information, (800) 729-7725.*
General e-mail, natcenter@aol.com
Web, www.mnh.si.edu/edu_resources.html#NC

Maintains natural history research and reference library with books and more than 36,000 objects, including minerals, rocks, plants, animals, shells and corals, insects, invertebrates, micro- and macrofossil materials, and microbiological and anthropological materials. Facilities include study equipment such as microscopes, dissecting instruments, and plant presses. Operates a teachers' reference center. Library open to the public. Reservations required for groups of six or more.

National Oceanic and Atmospheric Administration (NOAA), *(Commerce Dept.), National Sea Grant College Program, 1315 East-West Hwy., 11th Floor, Silver Spring, MD 20910; (301) 713-2448. Fax, (301) 713-0799. Ronald C. Baird, Director.*
Web, www.nsgo.seagrant.org

Provides grants, primarily to colleges and universities, for marine resource development; sponsors undergraduate and graduate education and the training of technicians at the college level.

National Science Foundation (NSF), *Education and Human Resources, 4201 Wilson Blvd., #805, Arlington, VA 22230; (703) 292-8600. Fax, (703) 292-9179. Judith A. Ramaley, Assistant Director.*
Web, www.ehr.nsf.gov

Directorate that develops and supports programs to strengthen science and mathematics education. Provides fellowships and grants for graduate research and teacher education, instructional materials, and studies on the quality of existing science and mathematics programs. Participates in international studies.

National Science Foundation (NSF), *Science Resources Statistics, 4201 Wilson Blvd., #965, Arlington, VA 22230; (703) 292-8780. Fax, (703) 292-9092. Lynda T. Carlson, Director.*
Web, www.nsf.gov/sbe/srs

Develops and analyzes U.S. and international statistics on training, use, and characteristics of scientists, engineers, and technicians.

Office of Science and Technology Policy (OSTP), *(Executive Office of the President), Science, Dwight D. Eisenhower Executive Office Bldg., #436 20502; (202) 456-6130. Fax, (202) 456-6027. Kathie Olsen, Associate Director.*
General e-mail, ostpinfo@ostp.eop.gov
Web, www.ostp.gov

Advises the president and others within the EOP on the impact of science and technology on domestic and international affairs; coordinates executive office and federal agency actions related to these issues. Evaluates the effectiveness of science education programs, which include environment, life sciences, physical sciences and engineering, and social, behavioral, and educational sciences. Provides technical support to Homeland Security Dept.

NONPROFIT

American Assn. for the Advancement of Science (AAAS), *Education and Human Resources Programs,* *1200 New York Ave. N.W., 6th Floor 20005; (202) 326-6670. Fax, (202) 371-9849. Shirley M. Malcom, Head. Main phone is voice and TTY accessible.*
Web, www.aaas.org

Membership: scientists, scientific organizations, and others interested in science and technology education. Works to increase and provide information on the status of women, minorities, and people with disabilities in the sciences and engineering; focuses on expanding science education opportunities for women, minorities, and people with disabilities.

American Assn. of Physics Teachers, *1 Physics Ellipse, College Park, MD 20740-3843; (301) 209-3300. Fax, (301) 209-0845. Bernard V. Khoury, Executive Officer.*
General e-mail, aapt@aapt.org
Web, www.aapt.org

Membership: physics teachers and others interested in physics education. Seeks to advance the institutional and cultural role of physics education. Sponsors seminars and conferences; provides educational information and materials. (Affiliated with the American Institute of Physics.)

American Society for Engineering Education, *1818 N St. N.W., #600 20036; (202) 331-3500. Fax, (202) 265-8504. Frank L. Huband, Executive Director. Press, (202) 331-3537.*
Web, www.asee.org

Membership: engineering faculty and administrators, professional engineers, government agencies, and engineering colleges, corporations, and professional societies. Conducts research, conferences, and workshops on engineering education. Monitors legislation and regulations.

Assn. of Science-Technology Centers, *Government and Public Relations, 1025 Vermont Ave. N.W., #500 20005-3516; (202) 783-7200. Fax, (202) 783-7207. Sean Smith, Director.*
General e-mail, info@astc.org
Web, www.astc.org

Membership: more than 500 science centers and science museums in forty-three countries. Strives to enhance the ability of its members to engage visitors in science activities and explorations of scientific phenomena. Sponsors conferences and informational exchanges on interactive exhibits, hands-on science experiences, and educational programs for children, families, and teachers; publishes journal; compiles statistics; provides technical assistance for museums; speaks for science centers before Congress and federal agencies.

Challenger Center for Space Science Education, *1250 N. Pitt St., Alexandria, VA 22314; (703) 683-9740. Fax, (703) 683-7546. Vance Ablott, President.*
Web, www.challenger.org

Educational organization designed to stimulate interest in science, math, and technology among middle school and elementary school students. Students participate in interactive mission simulations that require training and classroom preparation. Sponsors Challenger Learning Centers across the United States, Canada, and England.

Commission on Professionals in Science and Technology, *1200 New York Ave. N.W., #390 20005; (202) 326-7080. Fax, (202) 842-1603. Eleanor Babco, Executive Director.*
General e-mail, info@cpst.org
Web, www.cpst.org

Membership: scientific societies, corporations, academicians, and individuals. Analyzes and publishes data on scientific and engineering human resources in the United States. Interests include employment of minorities and women, salary ranges, and supply and demand of scientists and engineers.

Mathematical Assn. of America, *1529 18th St. N.W. 20036-1358; (202) 387-5200. Fax, (202) 265-2384. Tina H. Straley, Executive Director.*
General e-mail, maahq@maa.org
Web, www.maa.org

Membership: mathematics professors and individuals worldwide with a professional interest in mathematics. Seeks to improve the teaching of collegiate mathematics. Conducts professional development programs.

National Assn. of Biology Teachers, *12030 Sunrise Valley Dr., #110, Reston, VA 20191-3409; (703) 264-9696. Fax, (703) 264-7778. Wayne Carley, Executive Director. Information, (800) 406-0775.*
General e-mail, office@nabt.org
Web, www.nabt.org

Membership: biology teachers and others interested in biology and life sciences education at the elementary, secondary, and collegiate levels. Provides professional development opportunities through its publication program, summer workshops, conventions, and national award programs. Interests include teaching standards, science curriculum, and issues affecting biology and life sciences education.

National Council of Teachers of Mathematics, *1906 Association Dr., Reston, VA 20191-9988; (703) 620-9840. Fax, (703) 476-2970. James M. Rubillo, Executive Director.*

General e-mail, infocentral@nctm.org

Web, www.nctm.org

Membership: teachers of mathematics in elementary and secondary schools and two-year colleges; university teacher education faculty; students; and other interested persons. Works for the improvement of classroom instruction at all levels. Serves as forum and information clearinghouse on issues related to mathematics education. Offers educational materials and conferences. Monitors legislation and regulations.

National Geographic Society, *1145 17th St. N.W. 20036-4688; (202) 857-7000. Fax, (202) 775-6141. John M. Fahey, President. Information, (800) 647-5463. Library, (202) 857-7783. Press, (202) 857-7027. TTY, (202) 857-7198.*

Web, www.nationalgeographic.com

Educational and scientific organization. Publishes *National Geographic, Research and Exploration, National Geographic Traveler,* and *World* magazines; produces maps, books, and films; maintains an exhibit hall; offers film-lecture series; produces television specials. Library open to the public.

National Science Resources Center, *Smithsonian Institution Arts and Industries Bldg., #1201 20560-0403; (202) 357-4892. Fax, (202) 633-9136. Sally Getz Schuler, Executive Director.*

General e-mail, outreach@nsrc.edu

Web, www.si.edu/nsrc

Sponsored by the Smithsonian Institution and the National Academy of Sciences. Works to establish effective science programs for all students. Disseminates research information; develops curriculum materials; seeks to increase public support for change of science education through the development of strategic partnerships.

National Science Teachers Assn., *1840 Wilson Blvd., Arlington, VA 22201-3000; (703) 243-7100. Fax, (703) 243-7177. Gerald Wheeler, Executive Director.*

General e-mail, publicinfo@nsta.org

Web, www.nsta.org

Membership: science teachers from elementary through college levels. Seeks to improve science education; provides forum for exchange of information. Monitors legislation and regulations.

Science Service, *1719 N St. N.W. 20036; (202) 785-2255. Fax, (202) 331-1121. Donald R. Harless, President.*

Web, www.sciserv.org

Seeks to increase public understanding of science and to distribute scientific information. Publishes *Science News;* administers the Intel Science Talent Search and the Intel International Science and Engineering Fair.

World Future Society, *7910 Woodmont Ave., #450, Bethesda, MD 20814; (301) 656-8274. Fax, (301) 951-0394. Edward S. Cornish, President.*

General e-mail, info@wfs.org

Web, www.wfs.org

Scientific and educational organization interested in future social and technological developments on a global scale. Publishes magazines and journals.

Vocational and Adult

AGENCIES

Agriculture Dept. (USDA), *Graduate School, 1400 Independence Ave. S.W., #1031 20250; (202) 314-3686. Fax, (202) 690-3277. Jerry Ice, Executive Director; Deborah Smith, Communications Director. Information, (888) 744-GRAD.*

General e-mail, pubaffairs@grad.usda.gov

Web, www.grad.usda.gov

Self-supporting educational institution that is open to the public. Offers continuing education courses for career advancement and personal fulfillment; offers training at agency locations.

Education Dept., *High School, Postsecondary, and Career Education, 330 C St. S.W., #4317 20202-5175 (mailing address: 400 Maryland Ave. S.W. 20202-7241); (202) 205-9441. Fax, (202) 205-5522. Richard LaPointe, Director.*

Web, www.ed.gov/offices/OVAE

Provides state and local education agencies with information on establishment, expansion, improvement, and operation of vocational technical education programs. Awards grants to state education agencies for vocational technical education programs.

Education Dept., *Vocational and Adult Education, 330 C St. S.W., #4090 20202-5175 (mailing address: 400 Maryland Ave. S.W. 20202-7100); (202) 205-5451. Fax, (202) 205-8748. Carol D'Amico, Assistant Secretary.*

Web, www.ed.gov/offices/OVAE

Coordinates and recommends national policy for improving vocational and adult education. Administers grants, contracts, and technical assistance for programs in adult education, dropout prevention, literacy, and occupational training.

NONPROFIT

Accrediting Commission of Career Schools and Colleges of Technology, *2101 Wilson Blvd., #302, Arlington, VA 22201; (703) 247-4212. Fax, (703) 247-4533. Elise Scanlon, Executive Director.*
General e-mail, info@accsct.org
Web, www.accsct.org

Serves as the national accrediting agency for private, postsecondary institutions offering occupational and vocational programs. Sponsors workshops and meetings on academic excellence and ethical practices in career education.

American Assn. for Adult and Continuing Education, *4380 Forbes Blvd., Lanham, MD 20706; (301) 918-1913. Fax, (301) 918-1846. Fran Tracy-Mumford, President.*
General e-mail, aaace10@aol.com
Web, www.aaace.org

Membership: adult and continuing education professionals. Acts as an information clearinghouse; evaluates adult and continuing education programs; sponsors conferences, seminars, and workshops.

Assn. for Career and Technical Education, *1410 King St., Alexandria, VA 22314; (703) 683-3111. Fax, (703) 683-7424. Janet Bray, Executive Director. Information, (800) 826-9972.*
General e-mail, acte@acteonline.org
Web, www.acteonline.org

Membership: teachers, students, supervisors, administrators, and others working or interested in vocational education (middle school through postgraduate). Interests include the impact of high school graduation requirements on vocational education; private sector initiatives; and improving the quality and image of vocational education. Offers conferences, workshops, and an annual convention. Monitors legislation and regulations.

Career College Assn., *10 G St. N.E., #750 20002-4213; (202) 336-6700. Fax, (202) 336-6828. Nick Glakas, President.*
General e-mail, cca@career.org
Web, www.career.org

Acts as an information clearinghouse on trade and technical schools.

Distance Education and Training Council, *1601 18th St. N.W., #2 20009-2529; (202) 234-5100. Fax, (202) 332-1386. Michael P. Lambert, Executive Director.*
General e-mail, detc@detc.org
Web, www.detc.org

Membership: accredited correspondence schools. Accredits distance education institutions, many of which offer vocational training.

International Assn. for Continuing Education and Training, *1620 Eye St. N.W., #615 20006; (202) 463-2905. Fax, (202) 463-8498. James Clawson, Executive Director.*
General e-mail, iacet@moinc.com
Web, www.iacet.org

Membership: education and training organizations and individuals who use the Continuing Education Unit. (The C.E.U. is defined as ten contact hours of participation in an organized continuing education program that is noncredit.) Authorizes organizations that issue the C.E.U.; develops criteria and guidelines for use of the C.E.U.

International Technology Education Assn., *1914 Association Dr., #201, Reston, VA 20191-1539; (703) 860-2100. Fax, (703) 860-0353. Kendall N. Starkweather, Executive Director.*
General e-mail, itea@iris.org
Web, www.iteawww.org

Membership: technology education teachers, supervisors, teacher educators, and individuals studying to be technology education teachers. Technology education includes the curriculum areas of manufacturing, construction, communications, transportation, and energy.

National Assn. of State Directors of Career Technical Education Consortium, *444 N. Capitol St. N.W., #830 20001; (202) 737-0303. Fax, (202) 737-1106. Kimberly A. Green, Executive Director.*
General e-mail, nasdvtec@nasdvtec.org
Web, www.nasdvtec.org

Membership: state career education agency heads, senior staff, and business, labor, and other education officials. Advocates state and national policy to strengthen career technical education to create a foundation of skills for American workers and provide them with opportunities to acquire new and advanced skills.

National Institute for Work and Learning, *1825 Connecticut Ave. N.W., 7th Floor 20009-1202; (202) 884-8186. Fax, (202) 884-8422. Ivan Charner, Vice President.*
General e-mail, NIWL@aed.org
Web, www.niwl.org

Public policy research organization that seeks to improve collaboration between educational and business institutions. Conducts demonstration projects with communities throughout the country on employer-funded tuition aid, youth transition from school to work, and employee education and career development. Conducts research on education and work issues. Library open to the public. (Affiliated with the Academy for Educational Development.)

Skills USA-VICA, *14001 James Monroe Hwy., Leesburg, VA 20177 (mailing address: P.O. Box 3000, Leesburg, VA 20177-3000); (703) 777-8810. Fax, (703) 777-8999. Timothy W. Lawrence, Executive Director.*
Web, www.skillsusa.org

Membership: students, teachers, and administrators of trade, industrial, technical, and health occupations programs at public high schools, vocational schools, and two-year colleges. Promotes strong work skills, workplace ethics, understanding of free enterprise, and lifelong education. (Formerly Vocational Industrial Clubs of America.)

University Continuing Education Assn., *1 Dupont Circle N.W., #615 20036; (202) 659-3130. Fax, (202) 785-0374. Kay J. Kohl, Executive Director.*
Web, www.ucea.edu

Membership: higher education institutions and non-profit organizations involved in postsecondary continuing education. Prepares statistical analyses and produces data reports for members; recognizes accomplishments in the field. Monitors legislation and regulations.

7 ⏰

Employment and Labor

GENERAL POLICY

AGENCIES

Labor Dept. (DOL), *200 Constitution Ave. N.W., #S2018 20210; (202) 693-6000. Fax, (202) 693-6111. Elaine L. Chao, Secretary; D. Cameron Findlay, Deputy Secretary. Library, (202) 693-6600. Locator, (202) 693-5000. Toll-free, (866) 487-2365.*
Web, www.dol.gov

Promotes and develops the welfare of U.S. wage earners; administers federal labor laws; acts as principal adviser to the president on policies relating to wage earners, working conditions, and employment opportunities. Library open to the public.

Labor Dept. (DOL), *Administrative Law Judges, 800 K St. N.W., #400N 20001-8002; (202) 693-7300. Fax, (202) 693-7365. John Vittone, Chief Administrative Law Judge; Beverly Queen, Docket Clerk.*
Web, www.oalj.dol.gov

Presides over formal hearings to determine violations of minimum wage requirements, overtime payments, compensation benefits, employee discrimination, grant performance, alien certification, employee protection, and health and safety regulations set forth under numerous statutes, executive orders, and regulations. With few exceptions, hearings are required to be conducted in accordance with the Administrative Procedure Act.

Labor Dept. (DOL), *Administrative Review Board, 200 Constitution Ave. N.W., #S4309 20210; (202) 693-6200. Fax, (202) 693-6220. M. Cynthia Douglass, Chair.*
General e-mail, Contact-OAS@dol.gov
Web, www.dol.gov/arb/welcome.html

Issues final decisions on appeals under the Service Contract Act, the Comprehensive Employment and Training Act, the Job Training Partnership Act, the Davis-Bacon Act, the Trade Act, the Surface Transportation Assistance Act, the Energy Reorganization Act, and several environmental laws, unemployment insurance conformity proceedings, and cases brought by the Office of Federal Contract Compliance Programs.

CONGRESS

General Accounting Office (GAO), *Education, Workforce, and Income Security, 441 G St. N.W., #5928 20548; (202) 512-7215. Cynthia Fagnoni, Managing Director.*
Web, www.gao.gov

Independent, nonpartisan agency in the legislative branch. Audits, analyzes, and evaluates Labor Dept. programs; makes reports available to the public.

House Appropriations Committee, *Subcommittee on Labor, Health and Human Services, Education, and Related Agencies, 2358 RHOB 20515; (202) 225-3508. Fax, (202) 225-3509. Rep. Ralph Regula, R-Ohio, Chair; Craig Higgins, Staff Director.*
Web, www.house.gov/appropriations

Jurisdiction over legislation to appropriate funds for the Labor Dept., National Labor Relations Board, National Mediation Board, Federal Mediation and Conciliation Service, and other labor-related agencies.

House Education and the Workforce Committee, *2181 RHOB 20515; (202) 225-4527. Fax, (202) 225-9571. Rep. John A. Boehner, R-Ohio, Chair; Paula Nowakowski, Staff Director.*
Web, edworkforce.house.gov

Jurisdiction over labor and employment legislation.

Senate Appropriations Committee, *Subcommittee on Labor, Health and Human Services, Education, and Related Agencies, SD-184 20510; (202) 224-3471. Fax, (202) 224-8553. Sen. Arlen Specter, R-Pa., Chair; Bettilou Taylor, Clerk.*
Web, appropriations.senate.gov/labor

Jurisdiction over legislation to appropriate funds for the Labor Dept., National Labor Relations Board, National Mediation Board, Federal Mediation and Conciliation Service, and other labor-related agencies.

Senate Health, Education, Labor, and Pensions Committee, *Subcommittee on Employment, Safety, and Training, SH-607 20510; (202) 224-7229. Sen. Michael B. Enzi, R-Wyo., Chair; Raissa H. Geary, Staff Director.*
Web, health.senate.gov

Jurisdiction over labor and employment legislation, including public- and full-employment legislation.

NONPROFIT

AFL–CIO (American Federation of Labor–Congress of Industrial Organizations), *815 16th St. N.W. 20006; (202) 637-5000. Fax, (202) 637-5050. John J. Sweeney, President.*
Web, www.aflcio.org

Voluntary federation of national and international labor unions in the United States. Represents members before Congress and other branches of government. Each member union conducts its own contract negotiations. Library (located in Silver Spring, Md.) open to the public.

American Civil Liberties Union (ACLU), *National Capital Area, 1400 20th St. N.W., #119 20036; (202) 457-0800. Johnnie Barnes, Executive Director.*

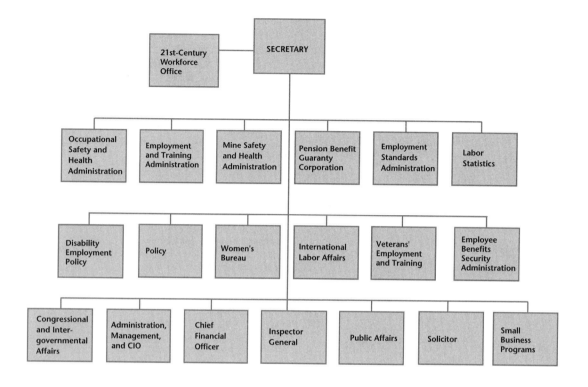

Protects the civil rights and liberties of the citizens, including federal employees, of the Washington metropolitan area. Interests include First Amendment rights, privacy, and due process.

American Enterprise Institute for Public Policy Research (AEI), *Economic Policy Studies, 1150 17th St. N.W., #1100 20036; (202) 862-5800. Fax, (202) 862-7177. Christopher DeMuth, President.*
Web, www.aei.org

Research and educational organization that studies trends in employment, earnings, the environment, health care, and income in the United States.

American Staffing Assn., *277 S. Washington St., #200, Alexandria, VA 22314; (703) 253-2020. Fax, (703) 253-2053. Richard Wahlquist, President.*
General e-mail, asa@staffingtoday.net
Web, www.natss.org

Membership: companies supplying other companies with workers on a temporary or permanent basis, with

outsourcing, with human resources, and with PEO arrangements. Monitors legislation and regulations. Encourages the maintenance of high ethical standards and provides public relations and educational support to members.

Campaign for America's Future, *1025 Connecticut Ave. N.W., #205 20036; (202) 955-5665. Fax, (202) 955-5606. Robert L. Borosage, Co-Director; Roger Hickey, Co-Director.*
General e-mail, info@ourfuture.org
Web, www.ourfuture.org

Operates the Campaign for America's Future and the Institute for America's Future. Advocates policies to help working people. Supports improved employee benefits, including health care, child care, and paid family leave; promotes life-long education and training of workers. Seeks full employment, higher wages, and increased productivity. Monitors legislation and regulations.

Employment Policy Foundation, *1015 15th St. N.W., #1200 20005; (202) 789-8685. Fax, (202) 789-8684. Edward E. Potter, President.*

General e-mail, info@epfnet.org

Web, www.epf.org

Research and education foundation. Seeks employment policy that facilitates U.S. economic growth; increases productivity, job creation, and job security; and raises the standard of living of the American workforce. Interests include global competitiveness.

International Telework Assn. and Council, 8403 Colesville Rd., #865, Silver Spring, MD 20901; (301) 650-2322. Fax, (301) 495-4959. Robert Smith, Executive Director.

General e-mail, info@workingfromanywhere.org

Web, www.workingfromanywhere.org

Membership: individuals, corporations, government agencies, educators, consultants, and vendors involved in telecommuting. Promotes the economic, social, and environmental benefits of telecommuting. Seeks to facilitate the development of telecommuting programs internationally. (Headquarters in Wakefield, Mass.)

Labor Policy Assn., 1015 15th St. N.W., #1200 20005; (202) 789-8670. Fax, (202) 789-0064. Jeffrey C. McGuiness, President.

General e-mail, info@lpa.org

Web, www.lpa.org

Membership: corporate vice presidents in charge of employee relations. Promotes research in employee relations, particularly in federal employment policy and implementation. Interests include international labor issues, including immigration and child labor.

National Assn. of Personnel Services (NAPS), 10905 Fort Washington Rd., #400, Fort Washington, MD 20744; (301) 203-6700. Fax, (301) 203-4346. Dianne Callis, President.

Web, www.napsweb.org

Membership: owners and managers of private personnel services companies, including permanent and temporary service firms. Monitors legislation and regulations concerning the personnel services industry.

National Assn. of Professional Employer Organizations, 901 N. Pitt St., #150, Alexandria, VA 22314; (703) 836-0466. Fax, (703) 836-0976. Milan P. Yager, Executive Vice President.

General e-mail, info@napeo.org

Web, www.napeo.org

Membership: professional employer organizations. Conducts research; sponsors seminars and conferences for members. Monitors legislation and regulations.

Society for Human Resource Management, 1800 Duke St., Alexandria, VA 22314; (703) 548-3440.

Fax, (703) 836-0367. Susan R. Meisinger, President. Information, (800) 283-7476. TTY, (703) 548-6999.

General e-mail, shrm@shrm.org

Web, www.shrm.org

Membership: human resource management professionals. Monitors legislation and regulations concerning recruitment, training, and employment practices; occupational safety and health; compensation and benefits; employee and labor relations; and equal employment opportunity. Sponsors seminars and conferences.

U.S. Chamber of Commerce, Economic Policy, 1615 H St. N.W. 20062-2000; (202) 463-5620. Fax, (202) 463-3174. Martin A. Regalia, Chief Economist. Press, (202) 463-5682.

Web, www.uschamber.com

Monitors legislation and regulations affecting the business community, including employee benefits, health care, legal and regulatory affairs, transportation and telecommunications infrastructure, defense conversion, and equal employment opportunity.

International Issues

AGENCIES

Bureau of Labor Statistics (BLS), (Labor Dept.), Foreign Labor Statistics, 2 Massachusetts Ave. N.E., #2150 20212; (202) 691-5654. Fax, (202) 691-5679. Wolodar Lysko, Division Chief (Acting).

Web, www.bls.gov/fls

Issues statistical reports on labor force, productivity, employment, prices, and labor costs in foreign countries adjusted to U.S. concepts.

Employment and Training Administration (Labor Dept.), Trade Adjustment Assistance, 200 Constitution Ave. N.W., #C5311 20210; (202) 693-3555. Edward A. Tomchick, Director.

Web, wdsc.doleta.gov/trade_act/taa_basic.asp

Assists American workers who are totally or partially unemployed because of increased imports; offers training, job search and relocation assistance, weekly benefits at state unemployment insurance levels, and other reemployment services.

Labor Dept. (DOL), Foreign Relations, 200 Constitution Ave. N.W., #S5303 20210; (202) 693-4785. Fax, (202) 693-4784. James Perlmutter, Director.

General e-mail, Contact-OFR@dol.gov

Web, www.dol.gov/ILAB/programs/ofr/main.htm

Provides foreign governments with technical assistance in labor-related activities on a reimbursable basis. (Funding is provided by the U.S. Agency for International Development, international organizations, and foreign governments.) Participates with the State Dept. in managing the U.S. labor attaché program; conducts the U.S. Foreign Visitors Program. Provides information on foreign labor developments, including foreign labor trends. Assists in developing and communicating U.S. foreign economic policy.

Labor Dept. (DOL), *International Labor Affairs,* 200 Constitution Ave. N.W., #C4325 20210; (202) 693-4770. Fax, (202) 693-4780. Thomas B. Moorhead, Deputy Under Secretary.

General e-mail, Contact-ILAB@dol.gov

Web, www.dol.gov/ilab

Assists in developing international economic policy relating to labor; helps represent the United States in multilateral and bilateral trade negotiations. Evaluates the effects of immigration policy on the wages and employment of U.S. workers.

Labor Dept. (DOL), *International Organizations,* 200 Constitution Ave. N.W., #S5317 20210; (202) 693-4855. Fax, (202) 693-4860. H. Charles Spring, Director, (202) 693-4852.

General e-mail, Contact-OIO@dol.gov

Web, www.dol.gov/ilab/programs/oio

Provides administrative support for U.S. participation in the International Labor Organization (ILO) and at the Paris-based Organization for Economic Cooperation and Development (OECD), which studies and reports on world economic issues.

Labor Dept. (DOL), *U.S. Foreign Visitors Program,* 200 Constitution Ave. N.W., #S5303 20210; (202) 693-4785. Fax, (202) 693-4784. James Perlmutter, Director.

Web, www.dol.gov

Works with the State Dept., the Agency for International Development, and other agencies in arranging visits and training programs for foreign officials interested in U.S. labor and trade unions.

President's Committee on the International Labor Organization *(Labor Dept.),* 200 Constitution Ave. N.W., #S5317 20210; (202) 693-4855. Fax, (202) 693-4860. Elaine L. Chao, Chair; Thomas B. Moorhead, Deputy Under Secretary for International Affairs.

Advisory committee of government, employer, and worker representatives, including secretaries of state, commerce, and labor, the president's national security adviser, the president of the U.S. Council for International Business, the president's national economic adviser, and the president of the AFL-CIO. Formulates and coordinates policy on the International Labor Organization (ILO); advises the president and the secretary of labor.

State Dept., *International Labor Affairs,* 2201 C St. N.W., #4829A 20520; (202) 647-3663. Fax, (202) 647-0431. George White, Director.

Web, www.state.gov

Uses bilateral and multilateral diplomacy and works with trade unions and the U.S. business community to promote worker rights around the world. Concerned with issues of core labor standards such as child labor, forced labor, and freedom of association.

State Dept., *International Organization Affairs,* 2201 C St. N.W., #6323 20520-6319; (202) 647-9600. Fax, (202) 736-4116. Kim R. Holmes, Assistant Secretary. Press, (202) 647-8490.

Web, www.state.gov/p/io

Responsible, with the Labor Dept. and the Commerce Dept., for U.S. policy in the United Nations, the UN's specialized agencies, and other international organizations, including government relations with the International Labor Organization (ILO).

CONGRESS

House Ways and Means Committee, *Subcommittee on Trade,* 1104 LHOB 20515; (202) 225-6649. Fax, (202) 226-0158. Rep. Philip M. Crane, R-Ill., Chair; Angela Ellard, Staff Director.

Web, waysandmeans.house.gov

Jurisdiction over legislation on foreign trade, including its impact on U.S. workers.

Senate Finance Committee, *Subcommittee on International Trade,* SD-219 20510; (202) 224-4515. Sen. Craig Thomas, R-Wyo., Chair; Everett Eissenstadt, Counsel.

Web, finance.senate.gov

Holds hearings on legislation concerning foreign trade, including its impact on U.S. workers.

INTERNATIONAL ORGANIZATIONS

International Labor Organization (ILO), *Washington Office,* 1828 L St. N.W., #600 20036; (202) 653-7652. Fax, (202) 653-7687. Anthony G. Freeman, Director.

Web, www.us.ilo.org

Specialized agency of the United Nations. Works to improve working conditions, create employment, and promote human rights worldwide. Establishes international labor standards; conducts training and technical assistance. Washington office serves as liaison between the ILO and U.S. government, employer, and worker groups. Library open to the public. (Headquarters in Geneva.)

American Center for International Labor Solidarity, *1925 K St. N.W., #300 20006; (202) 778-4500. Fax, (202) 778-4525. Harry Kamberis, Executive Director.*
General e-mail, info@solidaritycenter.org
Web, www.solidaritycenter.org

Provides assistance to free and democratic trade unions worldwide. Provides trade union leadership courses in collective bargaining, union organization, trade integration, labor-management cooperation, union administration, and political theories. Sponsors social and community development projects; focus includes child labor, human and worker rights, and the role of women in labor unions. (Affiliated with the AFL-CIO.)

International Labor Rights Fund, *733 15th St. N.W., #920 20005; (202) 347-4100. Fax, (202) 347-4885. Terry Collingsworth, Executive Director.*
General e-mail, laborrights@igc.org
Web, www.laborrights.org

Promotes the enforcement of international labor rights. Pursues legal and administrative actions on behalf of working people; advocates for better protection of workers. Concerns include child labor, sweatshops, and exploited workers. Monitors legislation and regulations on national and international levels.

Society for Human Resource Management, *Global Affairs, 1800 Duke St., Alexandria, VA 22314-3499; (703) 548-3440. Fax, (703) 836-0367. Brian Glade, Vice President.*
General e-mail, forum@shrm.org
Web, www.shrmglobal.org

Provides human resources professionals with specialized, timely information on the worldwide business environment and its implications on the human resources profession.

Labor Standards and Practices

AGENCIES

Bureau of Labor Statistics (BLS), *(Labor Dept.), Compensation and Working Conditions, 2 Massachusetts Ave. N.E., #4130 20212; (202) 691-6300. Fax, (202) 691-6310. Katrina Reut, Associate Commissioner.*
Web, www.bls.gov/bls/proghome.htm#ocwc

Conducts annual area wage surveys to determine occupational pay information in individual labor markets. Conducts industry wage surveys, which provide wage and employee benefit information; collects data on labor costs, job injuries and illnesses, and work stoppages.

Employment Standards Administration *(Labor Dept.), 200 Constitution Ave. N.W. 20210; (202) 693-0200. Fax, (202) 693-0218. Victoria Lipnic, Assistant Secretary.*
Web, www.dol.gov

Administers and enforces employment laws and regulations. Responsibilities include ensuring compliance among federal contractors, administering benefits claims for federal employees and other workers, and protecting workers' wages and working conditions.

Employment Standards Administration *(Labor Dept.), Child Labor and Special Employment, 200 Constitution Ave. N.W., #S3510 20210; (202) 693-0072. Fax, (202) 693-1432. Arthur M. Kerschner Jr., Team Leader.*
Web, www.dol.gov/esa/whd

Authorizes subminimum wages under the Fair Labor Standards Act for certain categories of workers, including full-time students, student learners, and workers with disabilities. Administers the Fair Labor Standards Act restrictions on working at home in certain industries. Administers special minimum wage provisions applicable in Puerto Rico and American Samoa.

Employment Standards Administration *(Labor Dept.), Fair Labor Standards Act Enforcement, 200 Constitution Ave. N.W., #S3516 20210; (202) 693-0067. Fax, (202) 693-1387. Barbara Relerford, Team Leader. Information, (866) 487-9243.*
Web, www.dol.gov/esa

Issues interpretations and rulings of the Fair Labor Standards Act of 1938, as amended (Federal Minimum Wage and Overtime Pay and Record Keeping Law).

Employment Standards Administration *(Labor Dept.), Federal Contract Compliance Programs, 200 Constitution Ave. N.W., #C3325 20210; (202) 693-0101. Fax, (202) 693-1304. Charles E. James Sr., Deputy Assistant Secretary.*
Web, www.dol.gov/esa/ofccp/index.htm

Monitors and enforces government contractors' compliance with federal laws and regulations on equal employment opportunities and affirmative action, including employment rights of minorities, women, persons with disabilities, and disabled and Vietnam-era veterans.

Employment Standards Administration *(Labor Dept.), Government Contracts Enforcement, 200 Constitution Ave. N.W., #S3018 20210; (202) 693-0064. Fax, (202) 693-1432. Timothy Helm, Team Leader.*
Web, www.dol.gov/esa/whd/contracts/index.htm

Enforces the Davis-Bacon Act, the Walsh-Healey Public Contracts Act, the Contract Work Hours and

Safety Standards Act, the Service Contract Act, and other related government contract labor standards statutes.

Employment Standards Administration *(Labor Dept.), Wage and Hour Division,* 200 Constitution Ave. N.W., #S3502 20210; (202) 693-0051. Fax, (202) 693-1406. Tammy D. McCutchen, Administrator.
Web, www.dol.gov/esa/whd

Enforces the minimum-wage, overtime, record keeping, and child labor provisions of the Fair Labor Standards Act. Also enforces certain labor standards of the Immigration and Nationality Act and other laws regarding employment standards with respect to polygraphs, leave from work, agricultural workers, and the construction industry.

Employment Standards Administration *(Labor Dept.), Wage Determinations,* 200 Constitution Ave. N.W. 20210; (202) 693-0062. Fax, (202) 693-1425. William Gross, Director.
Web, www.dol.gov/esa/whd

Issues prevailing wage determinations under the Service Contract Act of 1965, the Davis-Bacon Act, and other regulations pertaining to wage determination.

CONGRESS

House Education and the Workforce Committee, *Subcommittee on Workforce Protections,* 2181 RHOB 20515; (202) 225-4527. Fax, (202) 225-9571. Rep. Charlie Norwood, R-Ga., Chair; Paula Nowakowski, Staff Director.
Web, edworkforce.house.gov/members/108th/mem-wp.htm

Jurisdiction over legislation on minimum wage and wage and hour standards, including the Davis-Bacon Act, the Walsh-Healey Act, and the Fair Labor Standards Act; jurisdiction over mandated benefits, including those for government contractors. Jurisdiction over legislation on job discrimination by government contractors, electronic monitoring, and polygraph testing.

Senate Health, Education, Labor, and Pensions Committee, *Subcommittee on Employment, Safety, and Training,* SH-404A 20510; (202) 224-4925. Sen. Michael B. Enzi, R-Wyo., Chair; Raissa H. Geary, Staff Director.
Web, health.senate.gov

Jurisdiction over legislation on job discrimination by government contractors, minimum wage, wage and hour standards, and mandated benefits, including those for government contractors.

NONPROFIT

Fair Labor Assn. (FLA), 1505 22nd St. N.W. 20037; (202) 898-1000. Fax, (202) 898-9050. Auret Van Heerden, Executive Director.

Web, www.fairlabor.org

Membership: consumer, human, and labor rights groups; apparel and footwear manufacturers and retailers; and colleges and universities. Seeks to protect the rights of workers in the United States and worldwide. Concerns include sweatshop practices, forced labor, child labor, and worker health and benefits. Monitors workplace conditions and reports findings to the public.

Statistics and Information

AGENCIES

Bureau of Labor Statistics (BLS), *(Labor Dept.),* 2 Massachusetts Ave. N.E. 20212; (202) 691-7800. Fax, (202) 691-7797. Kathleen P. Utgoff, Commissioner. Press, (202) 691-5902.
General e-mail, blsdata_staff@bls.gov
Web, www.bls.gov

Collects, analyzes, and publishes data on labor economics, including employment, unemployment, hours of work, wages, employee compensation, prices, consumer expenditures, labor-management relations, productivity, technological developments, occupational safety and health, and structure and growth of the economy. Publishes reports on these statistical trends, including the Consumer Price Index, the Producer Price Index, and Employment and Earnings.

Bureau of Labor Statistics (BLS), *(Labor Dept.), Current Employment Statistics,* 2 Massachusetts Ave. N.E., #4860 20212; (202) 691-6555. Fax, (202) 691-6641. Patricia Getz, Chief, (202) 691-6521.
General e-mail, cesinfo@bls.gov
Web, stats.bls.gov/ces/home.htm

Analyzes and publishes national-level employment, hour, and earnings statistics based on data submitted by the states; develops statistical information on employment, hours, and earnings by industry for the nation, states, and metropolitan statistical areas.

Bureau of Labor Statistics (BLS), *(Labor Dept.), Employment and Unemployment Statistics,* 2 Massachusetts Ave. N.E., #4945 20212; (202) 691-6400. Fax, (202) 691-6425. John M. Galvin, Assistant Commissioner.
General e-mail, labstathelpdesk@bls.gov
Web, www.bls.gov

Monitors employment and unemployment trends on national and local levels; compiles data on worker and industry employment and earnings.

Bureau of Labor Statistics (BLS), *(Labor Dept.), Foreign Labor Statistics,* 2 Massachusetts Ave. N.E., #2150 20212; (202) 691-5654. Fax, (202) 691-5679. Wolodar Lysko, Division Chief (Acting).

Web, www.bls.gov/fls

Issues statistical reports on labor force, productivity, employment, prices, and labor costs in foreign countries adjusted to U.S. concepts.

Bureau of Labor Statistics (BLS), *(Labor Dept.),* *Local Area Unemployment Statistics, 2 Massachusetts Ave. N.E., #4675 20212; (202) 691-6392. Fax, (202) 691-6459. Sharon P. Brown, Chief.*
General e-mail, lausinfo@bls.gov
Web, www.bls.gov/lau

Issues labor force and unemployment statistics for states, metropolitan statistical areas, cities with populations of 25,000 or more, counties, and other areas covered under federal assistance programs.

Bureau of Labor Statistics (BLS), *(Labor Dept.),* *Occupational Statistics and Employment Projections, 2 Massachusetts Ave. N.E., #2135 20212; (202) 691-5700. Fax, (202) 691-5701. Michael Horrigan, Assistant Commissioner.*
Web, stats.bls.gov

Develops economic, industrial, and demographic employment projections according to industry and occupation. Provides career guidance material.

Bureau of Labor Statistics (BLS), *(Labor Dept.),* *Productivity and Technology, 2 Massachusetts Ave. N.E., #2150 20212; (202) 691-5600. Fax, (202) 691-5664. Marilyn E. Manser, Associate Commissioner. TTY, (202) 691-6034.*
Web, www.bls.gov

Develops and analyzes productivity measures for U.S. industries and total economy; adjusts productivity measures of foreign countries for comparison with U.S. standards; studies implications of technological changes on employment and occupational distribution.

Census Bureau *(Commerce Dept.), Demographic Surveys Division, 4700 Silver Hill Rd., Suitland, MD 20746; (301) 763-3773. Fax, (301) 763-2306. Chester E. Bowie, Chief.*

Conducts surveys and compiles official monthly employment and unemployment statistics for the Labor Dept.'s Bureau of Labor Statistics.

Employment and Training Administration *(Labor Dept.), Workforce Security, 200 Constitution Ave. N.W., #S4231 20210; (202) 693-3200. Cheryl Atkinson, Administrator.*
Web, workforcesecurity.doleta.gov

Provides information and advice on job searches and job training; provides guidance and oversight with respect to federal and state unemployment compensation. Compiles statistics on state unemployment insurance programs. Studies unemployment issues related to benefits.

Occupational Safety and Health Administration (OSHA), *(Labor Dept.), Statistical Analysis, 200 Constitution Ave. N.W., #N3507 20210; (202) 693-1702. Fax, (202) 693-1631. Joe DuBois, Director.*

Compiles and provides all statistical data for OSHA, such as occupational injury and illness records, which are used in setting standards and making policy.

CONGRESS

House Education and the Workforce Committee, *Subcommittee on Employer-Employee Relations, 2181 RHOB 20515; (202) 225-4527. Fax, (202) 225-9571. Rep. Sam Johnson, R-Texas, Chair; Paula Nowakowski, Staff Director.*
Web, edworkforce.house.gov/members/108th/mem-eer.htm

Jurisdiction over legislation on the Bureau of Labor Statistics.

Senate Health, Education, Labor, and Pensions Committee, *Subcommittee on Employment, Safety, and Training, SH-607 20510; (202) 224-7229. Sen. Michael B. Enzi, R-Wyo., Chair; Raissa H. Geary, Staff Director.*
Web, health.senate.gov

Jurisdiction over legislation on the Bureau of Labor Statistics.

Unemployment Benefits

AGENCIES

Employment and Training Administration *(Labor Dept.), Trade Adjustment Assistance, 200 Constitution Ave. N.W., #C5311 20210; (202) 693-3555. Edward A. Tomchick, Director.*
Web, wdsc.doleta.gov/trade_act/taa_basic.asp

Assists American workers who are totally or partially unemployed because of increased imports; offers training, job search and relocation assistance, weekly benefits at state unemployment insurance levels, and other reemployment services.

Employment and Training Administration *(Labor Dept.), Workforce Security, 200 Constitution Ave. N.W., #S4231 20210; (202) 693-3200. Cheryl Atkinson, Administrator.*
Web, workforcesecurity.doleta.gov

Directs and reviews the state-administered system that provides income support for unemployed workers nationwide; advises state and federal employment security agencies on wage-loss, worker dislocation, and adjustment assistance compensation programs.

CONGRESS

House Ways and Means Committee, *Subcommittee on Human Resources,* B317 RHOB 20515; (202) 225-1025. Fax, (202) 225-9480. Rep. Wally Herger, R-Calif., Chair; Matt Weidinger, Staff Director.
Web, waysandmeans.house.gov
Jurisdiction over unemployment benefits legislation.

Senate Finance Committee, *Subcommittee on Social Security and Family Policy,* SD-219 20510; (202) 224-4515. Sen. Rick Santorum, R-Pa., Chair; Kolan L. Davis, Staff Director.
Web, finance.senate.gov
Holds hearings on unemployment benefits legislation.

NONPROFIT

National Assn. of State Workforce Agencies, 444 N. Capitol St. N.W., #142 20001; (202) 434-8020. Fax, (202) 434-8033. Kathleen A. Cashen, Executive Director.
Web, www.naswa.org
Membership: state employment security administrators. Informs members of unemployment insurance programs and legislation. Provides unemployment insurance and reemployment professionals with opportunities for networking and information exchange.

▣ EMPLOYMENT AND TRAINING PROGRAMS

AGENCIES

Employment and Training Administration *(Labor Dept.),* 200 Constitution Ave. N.W., #S2307 20210; (202) 693-2700. Fax, (202) 693-2725. Emily Stover DeRocco, Assistant Secretary. Press, (202) 693-4650. TTY, (877) 889-5627. Toll-free, (877) 872-5627.
Web, www.doleta.gov
Responsible for employment, training, and trade adjustment programs for economically disadvantaged, unemployed, and dislocated workers. Administers and directs policy for the U.S. Employment Service, the Unemployment Insurance Service, and the Office of Work-Based Learning. Administers and directs programs for native Americans, migrants, youth, older workers, and workers with disabilities.

Employment and Training Administration *(Labor Dept.),* **Adults and Dislocated Workers,** 200 Constitution Ave. N.W., #N5325 20210; (202) 693-3502. John R. Beverly, Director.
Web, www.doleta.gov/layoff
Responsible for Worker Retraining and Adjustment programs (including the Trade Adjustment Assistance Program and the Economic Dislocation and Worker Adjustment Assistance Act); examines training initiatives and technology.

Employment and Training Administration *(Labor Dept.),* **U.S. Employment Service,** 200 Constitution Ave. N.W., #N4464 20210; (202) 693-3428. Gay Gilbert, Chief.
Web, www.doleta.gov/uses
Assists states in maintaining a nationwide system of one-stop centers for labor-employee exchange.

CONGRESS

House Education and the Workforce Committee, 2181 RHOB 20515; (202) 225-4527. Fax, (202) 225-9571. Rep. John A. Boehner, R-Ohio, Chair; Paula Nowakowski, Staff Director.
Web, edworkforce.house.gov
Jurisdiction over work incentive, education, and job training programs for youth and public assistance recipients, including the Job Opportunities and Basic Skills Training program and the Job Training Partnership Act.

House Education and the Workforce Committee, *Subcommittee on Select Education,* 2181 RHOB 20515; (202) 225-4527. Fax, (202) 225-9571. Rep. Peter Hoekstra, R-Mich., Chair; Paula Nowakowski, Staff Director.
Web, edworkforce.house.gov/members/108th/mem-sed.htm
Jurisdiction over legislation on employment training programs for elderly workers.

House Education and the Workforce Committee, *Subcommittee on 21st Century Competitiveness,* 2181 RHOB 20515; (202) 225-4527. Fax, (202) 225-9571. Rep. Howard P. "Buck" McKeon, R-Calif., Chair; Paula Nowakowski, Staff Director.
Web, edworkforce.house.gov/members/108th/mem-21st.htm
Jurisdiction over employment training legislation, including legislation on apprenticeship programs, on-the-job training, dislocated workers and plant shutdowns, displaced homemakers, rural workers, and vocational rehabilitation and education for workers with disabilities. Jurisdiction over youth and young adult conservation corps programs.

House Education and the Workforce Committee, *Subcommittee on Workforce Protections,* *2181 RHOB 20515; (202) 225-4527. Fax, (202) 225-9571. Rep. Charlie Norwood, R-Ga., Chair; Paula Nowakowski, Staff Director.*

Web, edworkforce.house.gov/members/108th/mem-wp.htm

Jurisdiction over legislation on minimum wage and wage and hour standards, including the Davis-Bacon Act, the Walsh-Healey Act, and the Fair Labor Standards Act; jurisdiction over mandated benefits, including those for government contractors.

House Judiciary Committee, *Subcommittee on Immigration, Border Security, and Claims,* *B370B RHOB 20515; (202) 225-5727. Fax, (202) 225-3672. Rep. John Hostettler, R-Ind., Chair; George Fishman, Chief Counsel.*

General e-mail, Judiciary@mail.house.gov

Web, www.house.gov/judiciary

Jurisdiction over legislation on foreign laborers once they are in the United States and on employer sanctions for not complying with the Immigration and Refugee Control Act of 1986.

Senate Finance Committee, *Subcommittee on Social Security and Family Policy,* *SD-219 20510; (202) 224-4515. Sen. Rick Santorum, R-Pa., Chair; Kolan L. Davis, Staff Director.*

Web, finance.senate.gov

Holds hearings on legislation affecting the Job Opportunities and Basic Skills Training Program.

Senate Health, Education, Labor, and Pensions Committee, *Subcommittee on Aging,* *SH-608 20510; (202) 224-2962. Sen. Christopher S. Bond, R-Mo., Chair; C. Kate Lambrew Hall, Staff Director.*

Web, health.senate.gov

Jurisdiction over legislation on employment training programs for elderly workers.

Senate Health, Education, Labor, and Pensions Committee, *Subcommittee on Employment, Safety, and Training,* *SH-607 20510; (202) 224-7229. Sen. Michael B. Enzi, R-Wyo., Chair; Raissa H. Geary, Staff Director.*

Web, health.senate.gov

Jurisdiction over education and job training programs for youth and public assistance recipients, including the Job Training Partnership Act and legislation on apprenticeship programs, on-the-job training, and displaced homemakers.

Senate Judiciary Committee, *Subcommittee on Immigration, Border Security, and Citizenship,* *SD-520 20510; (202) 224-7878. Fax, (202) 224-9516. Sen. Saxby Chambliss, R-Ga., Chair; David Neal, Chief Counsel.*

Web, judiciary.senate.gov

Jurisdiction over legislation on nonimmigrant foreign laborers once they are in the United States.

Senate Special Committee on Aging, *SD-G31 20510; (202) 224-5364. Fax, (202) 224-8660. Sen. Larry E. Craig, R-Idaho, Chair; Lupe Wissel, Staff Director.*

Web, aging.senate.gov

Studies and makes recommendations on legislation and federal programs affecting older Americans, including the areas of age discrimination, compensation, and unemployment; oversees Older Americans Act programs.

NONPROFIT

AFL-CIO Working for America Institute, *815 16th St. N.W. 20006; (202) 974-8128. Fax, (202) 974-8101. Nancy Mills, Executive Director.*

General e-mail, info@workingforamerica.org

Web, www.workingforamerica.org

Provides technical assistance to labor unions, employers, education agencies, and community groups for workplace programs focusing on dislocated workers, economically disadvantaged workers, and skill upgrading. Interests include new technologies and workplace innovations.

American Labor Education Center, *2000 P St. N.W., #300 20036; (202) 828-5170. Fax, (202) 785-3862. Karen Ohmans, Director.*

General e-mail, amlabor@mindspring.com

Produces materials for workers and unions. Interests include occupational health and safety, communication skills, and other labor issues.

American Society for Training and Development (ASTD), *1640 King St., Box 1443, Alexandria, VA 22313-2043; (703) 683-8100. Fax, (703) 683-1523. Tina Sung, President.*

Web, www.astd.org

Membership: trainers and human resource developers. Promotes workplace training programs and human resource development. Interests include productivity, job training and retraining, participative management, and unemployment. Holds conferences and provides information on technical and skills training.

Employee Relocation Council, *1717 Pennsylvania Ave. N.W., #800 20006; (202) 857-0857. Fax, (202) 659-8631. H. Cris Collie, Executive Vice President.*

Web, www.erc.org

Membership: corporations that relocate employees and moving, real estate, and relocation management companies. Researches and recommends policies that provide a smooth transition for relocated employees and their families. Holds conferences and issues publications on employee relocation issues.

National Assn. of Counties (NACo), *Employment and Training Program,* *440 1st St. N.W., 8th Floor 20001; (202) 393-6226. Fax, (202) 393-2630. Gary Gortenberg, Program Director.*
Web, www.naco.org

Oversees, directs, and offers technical assistance to members participating in federal job training programs; informs members of related legislation. Assists county officials, private industry councils, workforce development boards, and service delivery areas in implementing workforce development systems.

National Assn. of State Workforce Agencies, *444 N. Capitol St. N.W., #142 20001; (202) 434-8020. Fax, (202) 434-8033. Kathleen A. Cashen, Executive Director.*
Web, www.naswa.org

Membership: state employment security administrators. Informs members of federal legislation on job placement, veterans' affairs, and employment and training programs. Distributes labor market information; trains new state administrators and executive staff. Provides employment and training professionals with opportunities for networking and information exchange.

National Assn. of Workforce Boards, *1701 K St. N.W., #1000 20006; (202) 775-0960. Fax, (202) 775-0330. Robert F. Knight, President.*
General e-mail, nawb@nawb.org
Web, www.nawb.org

Membership: private industry councils and state job training coordinating councils established under the Job Training Partnership Act of 1982 (renamed Workforce Boards under the Workforce Investment Act). Interests include job training opportunities for youth and unemployed, economically disadvantaged, and dislocated workers; and private sector involvement in federal employment and training policy. Provides members with technical assistance; holds conferences and seminars.

National Assn. of Workforce Development Professionals, *810 1st St. N.W., #525 20002-4227; (202) 589-1790. Fax, (202) 589-1799. Paul Mendez, President.*
General e-mail, nawdp@aol.com
Web, www.nawdp.org

Membership: professionals and policymakers in the employment and training field. Promotes professionalism, information exchange, networking, and professional growth in the workforce development field.

National Center on Education and the Economy, *America's Choice District and School Design,* *1 Thomas Circle N.W., #700 20005; (202) 783-3668. Fax, (202) 783-3672. Larry Molinaro, Director.*
General e-mail, info@ncee.org
Web, www.ncee.org

Partnership of states, school districts, corporations, foundations, and nonprofit organizations that provides tools and technical assistance for school districts to improve education and training for the workplace.

National Governors Assn. (NGA), *Center for Best Practices: Employment and Vocational Training,* *444 N. Capitol St. N.W., #267 20001-1512; (202) 624-5345. Fax, (202) 624-5313. Martin Simon, Director. Press, (202) 624-5331.*
Web, www.nga.org

Provides information and technical assistance to members participating in federal job training programs, including programs authorized under the federal workforce development programs; informs members of related legislation. Provides technical assistance to members in areas of work and welfare programs, youth programs, employment services, dislocated workers, and dropout prevention.

National Institute for Work and Learning, *1825 Connecticut Ave. N.W., 7th Floor 20009-1202; (202) 884-8186. Fax, (202) 884-8422. Ivan Charner, Vice President.*
General e-mail, NIWL@aed.org
Web, www.niwl.org

Public policy research organization that seeks to improve collaboration between educational and business institutions. Conducts demonstration projects with communities throughout the country on employer-funded tuition aid, youth transition from school to work, and employee education and career development. Conducts research on education and work issues. Library open to the public. (Affiliated with the Academy for Educational Development.)

U.S. Chamber of Commerce, *Center for Workforce Preparation,* *1615 H St. N.W. 20062-2000; (202) 463-5525. Fax, (202) 463-5308. Beth B. Buehlman, Executive Director.*
Web, www.uschamber.com/cwp

Works with state and local chambers on workforce development issues, including educational reform, human resource, and job training.

U.S. Conference of Mayors, *Workforce Development,* *1620 Eye St. N.W., #400 20006; (202) 293-7330. Fax,*

(202) 293-2352. Joan Crigger, Assistant Executive Director.

Web, www.usmayors.org

Offers technical assistance to members participating in federal job training programs; monitors related legislation; acts as an information clearinghouse on employment and training programs.

Aliens

AGENCIES

Administration for Children and Families (ACF), *(Health and Human Services Dept.), Refugee Resettlement,* 901 D St. S.W., 6th Floor 20447; (202) 401-9246. Fax, (202) 401-0981. Nguyen Van Hanh, Director.

Web, www.acf.dhhs.gov

Directs a domestic resettlement program for refugees; reimburses states for costs incurred in giving refugees monetary and medical assistance; awards funds to private resettlement agencies for providing refugees with monetary assistance and case management; provides states and nonprofit agencies with grants for social services such as English and employment training.

Employment and Training Administration *(Labor Dept.), Foreign Labor Certification,* 200 Constitution Ave. N.W., #C4318 20210; (202) 693-3010. Dale M. Ziegler, Director.

Web, www.doleta.gov/employer/dflc.asp

Sets policies and guidelines for regional offices that certify applications for alien employment in the United States; determines whether U.S. citizens are available for those jobs and whether employment of aliens will adversely affect similarly employed U.S. citizens.

Apprenticeship Programs

AGENCIES

Employment and Training Administration *(Labor Dept.), Apprenticeship, Training, Employer and Labor Services,* 200 Constitution Ave. N.W., #N4649 20210; (202) 693-3812. Fax, (202) 693-3799. Anthony Swoope, Administrator, (202) 693-2796. Library, (202) 693-3812.

Web, www.doleta.gov/atels_bat

Promotes establishment of apprenticeship programs in private industry and the public sector.

Employment and Training Administration *(Labor Dept.), Federal Committee on Registered Apprenticeship,* 200 Constitution Ave. N.W., #N4649 20210; (202) 693-3812. Fax, (202) 693-3799. Anthony Swoope, Administrator, (202) 693-2796; Marion Winters, Program Analyst.

Web, www.doleta.gov/atels_bat

Advises the secretary of labor on the role of apprenticeship programs in employment training and on safety standards for those programs; encourages sponsors to include these standards in planning apprenticeship programs.

Dislocated Workers

AGENCIES

Employment and Training Administration *(Labor Dept.), Adults and Dislocated Workers,* 200 Constitution Ave. N.W., #N5325 20210; (202) 693-3502. John R. Beverly, Director.

Web, www.doleta.gov/layoff

Responsible for dislocated worker retraining programs.

NONPROFIT

National Assn. of Workforce Boards, 1701 K St. N.W., #1000 20006; (202) 775-0960. Fax, (202) 775-0330. Robert F. Knight, President.

General e-mail, nawb@nawb.org

Web, www.nawb.org

Membership: private industry councils and state job training coordinating councils established under the Job Training Partnership Act of 1982. Interests include job training opportunities for dislocated workers.

National Governors Assn. (NGA), *Center for Best Practices: Employment and Vocational Training,* 444 N. Capitol St. N.W., #267 20001-1512; (202) 624-5345. Fax, (202) 624-5313. Martin Simon, Director. Press, (202) 624-5331.

Web, www.nga.org

Provides technical assistance to members participating in employment and training activities for dislocated workers.

Migrant and Seasonal Farm Workers

AGENCIES

Employment and Training Administration *(Labor Dept.), Migrant and Seasonal Farm Worker Programs,* 200 Constitution Ave. N.W., #N4641 20210; (202) 693-3843. Fax, (202) 693-3818. Alicia Fernandez-Mott, Chief.

Web, wdsc.doleta.gov/msfw

Provides funds for programs that help seasonal farm workers and their families find better jobs in agriculture and other areas. Services include occupational training, education, and job development and placement.

Employment Standards Administration *(Labor Dept.), Farm Labor Programs,* 200 Constitution Ave.

N.W., #S3510 20210; (202) 693-0070. Fax, (202) 693-1432. Mary Ziegler, Chief.

Administers and enforces the Migrant and Seasonal Agricultural Worker Protection Act, which protects migrant and seasonal agricultural workers from substandard labor practices by farm labor contractors, agricultural employers, and agricultural associations.

NONPROFIT

Assn. of Farmworker Opportunity Programs, *4350 N. Fairfax Dr., #410, Arlington, VA 22203; (703) 528-4141. Fax, (703) 528-4145. David Strauss, Executive Director.*
General e-mail, afop@afop.org
Web, www.afop.org

Represents state-level organizations that provide services and support to migrant and guest workers. Monitors legislation and conducts research.

Migrant Legal Action Program, *1001 Connecticut Ave. N.W., #915 20036; (202) 775-7780. Fax, (202) 775-7784. Roger C. Rosenthal, Executive Director.*
General e-mail, mlap@mlap.org
Web, www.mlap.org

Supports and assists local legal services, migrant education, migrant health issues, and other organizations and private attorneys with respect to issues involving the living and working conditions of migrant farm workers. Monitors legislation and regulations.

Older Workers

AGENCIES

Employment and Training Administration *(Labor Dept.), Older Worker Programs, 200 Constitution Ave. N.W., #N4641 20210; (202) 693-3842. Fax, (202) 693-3817. Ria Moore Benedict, Chief (Acting).*
Web, wdsc.doleta.gov/seniors

Administers the Senior Community Service Employment Program, which provides funds for part-time, community service work-training programs; the programs pay minimum wage and are operated by national sponsoring organizations and state and territorial governments. The program is aimed at economically disadvantaged persons age fifty-five and over.

NONPROFIT

AARP, *Senior Community Service Employment Program, 601 E St. N.W. 20049; (202) 434-2020. Fax, (202) 434-6446. Jim Seits, Director. Information, (800) 424-3410.*
Web, www.aarp.org

Conducts a federally funded work-experience program for economically disadvantaged older persons; places trainees in community service jobs and helps them reenter the labor force.

National Council on the Aging, *Senior Community Service Employment Program, 300 D St. S.W., #801 20024; (202) 479-6631. Fax, (202) 479-0735. Donald Davis, Vice President. Information, (202) 479-1200. TTY, (202) 479-6674.*
General e-mail, info@ncoa.org
Web, www.ncoa.org

Works with the Labor Dept. under the authority of the Older Americans Act to provide workers age fifty-five and over with employment, community service, and training opportunities in their resident communities. Library open to the public.

Workers with Disabilities

AGENCIES

Committee for Purchase from People Who Are Blind or Severely Disabled, *1421 Jefferson Davis Hwy., #10800, Arlington, VA 22202-3259; (703) 603-7740. Fax, (703) 603-0655. Leon Wilson, Executive Director.*
Web, www.jwod.gov

Presidentially appointed committee. Determines which products and services are suitable for federal procurement from qualified nonprofit agencies that employ people who are blind or have other severe disabilities; seeks to increase employment opportunities for these individuals.

Employment Standards Administration *(Labor Dept.), Child Labor and Special Employment, 200 Constitution Ave. N.W., #S3510 20210; (202) 693-0072. Fax, (202) 693-1432. Arthur M. Kerschner Jr., Team Leader.*
Web, www.dol.gov/esa/whd

Administers certification of special lower minimum wage rates for workers with disabilities and impaired earning capacity; wage applies in industry, sheltered workshops, hospitals, institutions, and group homes.

Equal Employment Opportunity Commission (EEOC), *Interagency Committee on Employees with Disabilities, 1801 L St. N.W. 20507; (202) 663-4580. Fax, (202) 663-4388. Cari M. Dominguez, Co-Chair; Kay Coles James, Co-Chair; Ronald Ballard, Executive Secretary. TTY, (202) 663-4593.*

Established by the Rehabilitation Act of 1973, as amended, and co-chaired by the Office of Personnel Management and the EEOC. Works for increased employment of persons with disabilities, affirmative action by the federal government, and an equitable work environment for employees with mental and physical disabilities.

Office of Disability Employment Policy *(Labor Dept.),* 200 Constitution Ave., #S1303 20210; (202) 693-7880. Fax, (202) 693-7888. Roy Grizzard, Assistant Secretary; William Mea, Deputy Assistant Secretary. TTY, (202) 693-7881.

General e-mail, info@pcepd.gov

Web, www.dol.gov/odep

Promotes training, rehabilitation, and employment opportunities for people with disabilities.

Office of Personnel Management (OPM), *Diversity,* 1900 E St. N.W., #2445 20415-0001; (202) 606-1059. Fax, (202) 606-0927. Maria Mercedes Olivieri, Director.

Web, www.opm.gov/disability

Develops policies, programs, and procedures to promote opportunities for qualified workers with disabilities, including veterans, to obtain and advance in federal employment. Administers the Disabled Veterans Affirmative Action Program.

Rehabilitation Services Administration *(Education Dept.),* 330 C St. S.W. 20202-2531; (202) 205-5482. Fax, (202) 205-9874. Joanne Wilson, Commissioner. TTY, (202) 205-9295.

Web, www.ed.gov

Coordinates and directs federal services for eligible persons with physical or mental disabilities, with emphasis on programs that promote employment opportunities. Provides vocational training and job placement; supports projects with private industry; administers grants for the establishment of supported-employment programs.

NONPROFIT

Inter-National Assn. of Business, Industry, and Rehabilitation, P.O. Box 15242 20003; (202) 543-6353. Fax, (202) 546-2854. Charles Harles, Executive Director.

General e-mail, inabir@harles.com

Web, www.inabir.org

Membership: corporations, organized labor, state government agencies, rehabilitation service organizations, and other groups that work to provide competitive employment for persons with disabilities.

NISH, 2235 Cedar Lane, Vienna, VA 22182-5200; (703) 560-6800. Fax, (703) 849-8916. E. Robert Chamberlin, President. TTY, (703) 560-6512.

General e-mail, info@nish.org

Web, www.nish.org

Assists work centers that employ people with severe disabilities in obtaining federal contracts under the Javits-Wagner-O'Day Act; supports community rehabilitation programs employing persons with severe disabilities.

Youth

AGENCIES

Employment and Training Administration *(Labor Dept.), Job Corps,* 200 Constitution Ave. N.W., #N4463 20210; (202) 693-3000. Fax, (202) 693-2767. Richard Trigg, Director. Information, (800) 733-5627.

Web, jobcorps.doleta.gov

Administers with the Interior Dept. and Agriculture Dept. a national program of comprehensive job training for disadvantaged youth at residential centers. Most of the centers are managed and operated by corporations and nonprofit organizations.

Employment Standards Administration *(Labor Dept.), Child Labor and Special Employment,* 200 Constitution Ave. N.W., #S3510 20210; (202) 693-0072. Fax, (202) 693-1432. Arthur M. Kerschner Jr., Team Leader. Press, (202) 693-0023.

Web, www.dol.gov

Administers and enforces child labor, special minimum wage, and other provisions of Section 14 of the Fair Labor Standards Act. Administers the Work Experience and Career Exploration Program aimed at reducing the number of high school dropouts.

Forest Service *(Agriculture Dept.), Youth Conservation Corps,* 1621 N. Kent St., Arlington, VA 22209 (mailing address: P.O. Box 96090, Washington, DC 20090-6090); (703) 605-4854. Fax, (703) 605-5115. Ransom Hughes, Program Manager.

Administers with the National Park Service and the Fish and Wildlife Service the Youth Conservation Corps, a summer employment and training, public works program for youths ages fifteen to eighteen. The program is conducted in national parks, in national forests, and on national wildlife refuges.

NONPROFIT

Joint Action in Community Service, 5225 Wisconsin Ave. N.W., #404 20015-2021; (202) 537-0996. Fax, (202) 363-0239. Harvey Wise, Executive Director. Information, (800) 522-7773.

Web, www.jacsinc.org

Volunteer organization that works with the Labor Dept.'s Job Corps program for disadvantaged youths ages sixteen to twenty-four. Provides follow-up assistance to help these youths make the transition from training to jobs.

National Assn. of Service and Conservation Corps, *666 11th St. N.W., #1000 20001; (202) 737-6272. Fax, (202) 737-6277. Sally T. Prouty, President.*
General e-mail, nascc@nascc.org
Web, www.nascc.org

Membership: youth corps programs. Produces publications on starting and operating youth corps. Offers technical assistance to those interested in launching programs and sponsors professional development workshops. Holds annual conference. Monitors legislation and regulations.

Work, Achievement, Values, and Education (WAVE), *525 School St. S.W., #500 20024; (202) 484-0103. Fax, (202) 488-7595. Larry C. Brown, President.*
General e-mail, mail@waveinc.org
Web, www.waveinc.org

Public service corporation that provides high school dropouts and students at risk, ages twelve to twenty-one, with a program of education and employment services. Provides educational institutions with training and technical assistance.

▓ EQUAL EMPLOYMENT OPPORTUNITY

AGENCIES

Commission on Civil Rights, *Civil Rights Evaluation, 624 9th St. N.W., #740 20425; (202) 376-8582. Fax, (202) 376-7754. Terri A. Dickerson, Assistant Staff Director. Library, (202) 376-8110.*
Web, www.usccr.gov

Researches federal policy in areas of equal employment and job discrimination; monitors the economic status of minorities and women, including their employment and earnings. Library open to the public.

Employment Standards Administration *(Labor Dept.), Federal Contract Compliance Programs, 200 Constitution Ave. N.W., #C3325 20210; (202) 693-0101. Fax, (202) 693-1304. Charles E. James Sr., Deputy Assistant Secretary.*
Web, www.dol.gov/esa/ofccp/index.htm

Monitors and enforces government contractors' compliance with federal laws and regulations on equal employment opportunities and affirmative action, including employment rights of minorities, women, persons with disabilities, and disabled and Vietnam-era veterans.

Equal Employment Opportunity Commission (EEOC), *1801 L St. N.W., #10006 20507; (202) 663-4001. Fax, (202) 663-4110. Cari M. Dominguez, Chair. Information, (202) 663-4900. Library, (202) 663-4630. TTY, (202) 663-4494.*
Web, www.eeoc.gov

Works to end job discrimination by private and government employers based on race, color, religion, sex, national origin, disability, or age. Works to protect employees against reprisal for protest of employment practices alleged to be unlawful in hiring, promotion, firing, wages, and other terms and conditions of employment. Enforces Title VII of the Civil Rights Act of 1964, as amended, which includes the Pregnancy Discrimination Act; Americans with Disabilities Act; Age Discrimination in Employment Act; Equal Pay Act; and, in the federal sector, rehabilitation laws. Receives charges of discrimination; attempts conciliation or settlement; can bring court action to force compliance; has review and appeals responsibility in the federal sector.

Equal Employment Opportunity Commission (EEOC), *Field Programs, 1801 L St. N.W., #8002 20507; (202) 663-4801. Fax, (202) 663-7190. Reuben Daniels, Director (Acting).*

Provides guidance and technical assistance to employees who suspect discrimination and to employers who are working to comply with equal employment laws.

Justice Dept. (DOJ), *Civil Rights: Employment Litigation, 601 D St. N.W., #4040 20004 (mailing address: 950 Pennsylvania Ave. N.W., PHB 4040 20530); (202) 514-3831. Fax, (202) 514-1005. David Palmer, Chief. Library, (202) 616-5564.*
Web, www.usdoj.gov/crt

Investigates, negotiates, and litigates allegations of employment discrimination by public schools, universities, state and local governments, and federally funded employers; has enforcement power. Library open to the public on a limited basis by appointment.

Office of Personnel Management (OPM), *Diversity, 1900 E St. N.W., #2445 20415-0001; (202) 606-1059. Fax, (202) 606-0927. Maria Mercedes Olivieri, Director.*
Web, www.opm.gov/disability

Develops policies and guidelines for government recruiting programs, including diversity employment efforts related to women, minorities, persons with disabilities, and veterans. Collects and maintains statistics on the federal employment of these groups. Administers the Federal Equal Opportunity Recruitment Program.

CONGRESS

House Education and the Workforce Committee, *Subcommittee on Employer-Employee Relations,* 2181 RHOB 20515; (202) 225-4527. Fax, (202) 225-9571. Rep. Sam Johnson, R-Texas, Chair; Paula Nowakowski, Staff Director.

Web, edworkforce.house.gov/members/108th/mem-eer.htm

Jurisdiction over legislation on discrimination based on race, color, religion, sex, age, or national origin in employment where public funds are involved. Oversight of federal equal opportunity, age discrimination, and equal pay laws.

House Government Reform Committee, *Subcommittee on Criminal Justice, Drug Policy, and Human Resources,* B373 RHOB 20515; (202) 225-2577. Fax, (202) 225-1154. Rep. Mark Souder, R-Ind., Chair; Christopher Donesa, Staff Director.

Web, www.house.gov/reform

Oversees operations of the Equal Employment Opportunity Commission and the Commission on Civil Rights.

Office of Compliance, 110 2nd St. S.E., #LA-200 20540-1999; (202) 724-9250. Fax, (202) 426-1913. William W. Thompson II, Executive Director, (202) 724-9250. Information, (202) 724-9260. TTY, (202) 426-1912.

Web, www.compliance.gov

Provides general information to covered employees, applicants, and former employees of the legislative branch about their equal employment rights and protections under the Congressional Accountability Act of 1995.

Senate Governmental Affairs Committee, SD-340 20510; (202) 224-4751. Fax, (202) 228-3792. Sen. Susan Collins, R-Maine, Chair; Michael Bopp, Staff Director.

Web, govt-aff.senate.gov

Jurisdiction over legislation on discrimination based on race, color, religion, sex, age, or national origin in employment where federal employees are involved.

Senate Health, Education, Labor, and Pensions Committee, *Subcommittee on Employment, Safety, and Training,* SH-607 20510; (202) 224-7229. Sen. Michael B. Enzi, R-Wyo., Chair; Raissa H. Geary, Staff Director.

Web, health.senate.gov

Jurisdiction over legislation on discrimination based on race, color, religion, sex, age, or national origin in employment except where federal employees are involved. Oversight of federal equal pay laws and of fed-eral agencies concerned with racial and sexual discrimination in employment. Oversees operation of the Equal Employment Opportunity Commission.

NONPROFIT

Center for Equal Opportunity, 14 Pidgeon Hill Dr., #500, Sterling, VA 20165; (703) 421-5443. Fax, (703) 421-6401. Linda Chavez, President.

General e-mail, comment@ceousa.org

Web, www.ceousa.org

Research organization concerned with issues of race, ethnicity, and assimilation; opposes racial preferences in employment and education. Monitors legislation and regulations.

Equal Employment Advisory Council, 1015 15th St. N.W., #1200 20005; (202) 789-8650. Fax, (202) 789-2291. Jeffrey A. Norris, President. TTY, (202) 789-8645.

General e-mail, eeac@eeac.org

Web, www.eeac.org

Membership: principal equal employment officers and lawyers. Files amicus curiae (friend of the court) briefs; conducts research and provides information on equal employment law and policy. Monitors legislation and regulations.

NAACP Legal Defense and Educational Fund, *Washington Office,* 1444 Eye St. N.W., 10th Floor 20005; (202) 682-1300. Fax, (202) 682-1312. Leslie M. Proll, Senior Attorney.

Civil rights litigation group that provides legal information about civil rights legislation and advice on employment discrimination against women and minorities; monitors federal enforcement of equal opportunity rights laws. Not affiliated with the National Assn. for the Advancement of Colored People (NAACP). (Headquarters in New York.)

Minorities

AGENCIES

Bureau of Indian Affairs (BIA), *(Interior Dept.),* *Economic Development,* 1849 C St. N.W., #4642 20240; (202) 208-5324. Fax, (202) 208-7419. Ray Brown, Director (Acting).

Develops policies and programs to promote the achievement of economic goals for members of federally recognized tribes who live on or near reservations. Provides job training; assists those who have completed job training programs in finding employment; provides loan guarantees; enhances contracting opportunities for individuals and tribes.

Employment and Training Administration (*Labor Dept.*), *Indian and Native American Programs,* 200 Constitution Ave. N.W., #N4645 20210; (202) 693-3841. James DeLuca, Chief.

Web, www.wdsc.doleta/gov/dinap

Administers grants for training and employment-related programs to promote employment opportunity; provides unemployed, underemployed, and economically disadvantaged native Americans and Alaskan and Hawaiian natives with funds for training, job placement, and support services.

NONPROFIT

Coalition of Black Trade Unionists, *1625 L St. N.W. 20036 (mailing address: P.O. Box 66268 20035); (202) 429-1203. Fax, (202) 429-1102. Wil Duncan, Executive Director.*

Web, www.cbtu.org

Monitors legislation affecting African American and other minority trade unionists. Focuses on equal employment opportunity, unemployment, and voter education and registration.

Labor Council for Latin American Advancement, *888 16th St. N.W., #640 20006; (202) 347-4223. Fax, (202) 347-5095. Oscar Sanchez, Executive Director.*

General e-mail, headquarters@lclaa.org

Web, www.lclaa.org

Membership: Hispanic trade unionists. Encourages equal employment opportunity, voter registration and education, and participation in the political process. (Affiliated with the AFL-CIO.)

Mexican American Legal Defense and Educational Fund, *Washington Office,* 1717 K St. N.W., #311 20036; (202) 293-2828. Fax, (202) 293-2849. Marisa Demeo, Regional Counsel.

Web, www.maldef.org

Provides Mexican Americans and other Hispanics involved in class-action employment discrimination suits or complaints with legal assistance. Monitors legislation and regulations. (Headquarters in Los Angeles, Calif.)

National Assn. for the Advancement of Colored People (NAACP), *Washington Office,* 1025 Vermont Ave. N.W., #1120 20005; (202) 638-2269. Fax, (202) 638-5936. Hilary O. Shelton, Director.

Web, www.naacp.org

Membership: persons interested in civil rights for all minorities. Advises individuals with employment discrimination complaints. Seeks to eliminate job discrimination and to bring about full employment for all Amer-

icans through legislation and litigation. (Headquarters in Baltimore, Md.)

National Assn. of Negro Business and Professional Women's Clubs, *1806 New Hampshire Ave. N.W. 20009; (202) 483-4206. Fax, (202) 462-7253. Cleopatra Vaughns, President.*

General e-mail, nanbpwc@aol.com

Web, www.nanbpwc.org

Promotes opportunities for African American women in business; sponsors workshops and scholarships; maintains a job bank. Monitors legislation and regulations.

National Council of La Raza, *1111 19th St. N.W., #1000 20036; (202) 785-1670. Fax, (202) 776-1792. Raul Yzaguirre, President.*

General e-mail, info@nclr.org

Web, www.nclr.org

Provides research, policy analysis, and advocacy on Hispanic employment status and programs; provides Hispanic community-based groups with technical assistance to help develop effective employment programs with strong educational components. Works to promote understanding of Hispanic employment needs in the private sector. Interests include women in the workplace, affirmative action, equal opportunity employment, and youth employment. Monitors federal employment legislation and regulations.

National Urban League, *Washington Office,* 3501 14th Street N.W. 20010; (202) 265-8200. Fax, (202) 265-6122. Maudine R. Cooper, President.

Web, www.gwul.org

Social service organization concerned with the social welfare of African Americans and other minorities. Testifies before congressional committees and federal agencies on equal employment; studies and evaluates federal enforcement of equal employment laws and regulations. (Headquarters in New York.)

Women

AGENCIES

Agriculture Dept. (USDA), *Executive Leadership Program for Mid-Level Employers,* 600 Maryland Ave. S.W., #330 20024; (202) 314-3580. Fax, (202) 479-6813. Debra Eddington, Director.

Web, www.grad.usda.gov

Trains federally employed men and women with managerial potential for executive positions in the government. The program is geared toward GS-11 and GS-12 employees.

EQUAL EMPLOYMENT CONTACTS AT FEDERAL AGENCIES

DEPARTMENTS

Agriculture, David Winningham, (202) 720-5212

Commerce, Suzan Aramaki, (202) 482-0625

Defense, Clarence A. Johnson, (703) 695-0105

  Air Force, Shirley A. Martinez, (703) 697-6586

  Army, Luther L. Santiful, (703) 607-1976

  Marines, Deborah Summers, (703) 784-9379

  Navy, Betty Welch, (703) 695-2248

Education, James R. White, (202) 401-3560

Energy, Poli A. Marmolejos, (202) 586-2218

Health and Human Services, Robin Frohboese, (202) 619-0403

Homeland Security Dept., Daniel Sutherland (Designee), (202) 282-8000

Housing and Urban Development, Peggy J. Armstrong (Acting), (202) 708-5921

Interior, E. Melodee Stith, (202) 208-5693

Justice, Ted McBurrows, (202) 616-4800

Labor, Annabelle Lockhart, (202) 693-6503

State, Gail Neelon, (202) 647-9294

Transportation, Jeremy S. Wu, (202) 366-4648

Treasury, Mariam Harvey, (202) 622-1160

Veterans Affairs, Michael Dole, (202) 273-5888

AGENCIES

Commission on Civil Rights, Robert Anthony, (202) 376-8351

Commodity Futures Trading Commission, Vacant, (202) 418-5011

Consumer Product Safety Commission, Donna Marshall, (301) 504-7904

Corporation for National Service, Nancy Voss, (202) 606-5000, ext. 309

Environmental Protection Agency, Karen Higginbotham, (202) 564-7272

Equal Employment Opportunity Commission, Jean Watson, (202) 663-7081

Export-Import Bank, Kennie May, (202) 565-3590

Farm Credit Administration, Eric Howard, (703) 883-4481

Federal Communications Commission, Barbara Douglas, (202) 418-1799

Federal Deposit Insurance Corporation, D. Michael Collins, (202) 416-2172

Federal Election Commission, Patricia Brown, (202) 694-1228

Federal Emergency Management Agency, Pauline Campbell, (202) 646-4122

Federal Labor Relations Authority, Shelya White, (202) 482-6690

Federal Maritime Commission, Alice Blackman, (202) 523-5806

Federal Mediation and Conciliation Service, Information, (202) 606-5460

Federal Reserve Board, Sheila Clark, (202) 452-2883

Federal Trade Commission, Barbara B. Wiggs, (202) 326-2196

General Services Administration, Madeline Caliendo, (202) 501-0767

Merit Systems Protection Board, Janice E. Pirkle, (202) 653-6180

National Aeronautics and Space Administration, Dorothy Hayden-Watkins, (202) 358-2167

National Credit Union Administration, Robert French, (703) 518-6325

National Endowment for the Humanities, Willie McGhee, (202) 606-8233

National Labor Relations Board, Lori Suto-Goldsby, (202) 273-3891

National Science Foundation, Anna Ortiz, (703) 292-8020

National Transportation Safety Board, Fara Guest, (202) 314-6190

Nuclear Regulatory Commission, Corenthis Kelley, (301) 415-7380

Occupational Safety and Health Review Commission, Ledia E. Bernal, (202) 606-5390

Office of Personnel Management, Michelle Payton-Kenner, (202) 606-2460

Peace Corps, Shirley Everest, (202) 692-2159

Securities and Exchange Commission, Deborah Balducchi, (202) 942-0040

Small Business Administration, Loyola (Rose) Trujillo (Acting), (202) 205-6750

Smithsonian Institution, Era Marshall, (202) 275-0145

Social Security Administration, Miguel Torrado, (410) 965-8882

U.S. International Trade Commission, Jackie Waters, (202) 205-2240

U.S. Postal Service, Stephanie H. Webster, (202) 268-3658

Labor Dept. (DOL), *Women's Bureau, 200 Constitution Ave. N.W., #S3002 20210; (202) 693-6710. Fax, (202) 693-6725. Shinae Chun, Director. Information, (800) 827-5335.*
Web, www.dol.gov/wb

Monitors women's employment issues. Promotes employment opportunities for women; sponsors workshops, job fairs, symposia, demonstrations, and pilot projects. Offers technical assistance; conducts research and provides publications on issues that affect working women; represents working women in international forums.

Office of Personnel Management (OPM), *Diversity, 1900 E St. N.W., #2445 20415-0001; (202) 606-1059. Fax, (202) 606-0927. Maria Mercedes Olivieri, Director.*
Web, www.opm.gov/disability

Promotes opportunities for women to obtain and advance in federal employment; assists federal agencies in the recruitment and employment of women. Collects and maintains statistics on women's employment.

NONPROFIT

Business and Professional Women U.S.A., *1900 M St. N.W., #310 20036; (202) 293-1100. Fax, (202) 861-0298. Cindy Young, President.*
Web, www.bpwusa.org

Seeks to improve the status of working women through education, legislative action, and local projects. Sponsors Business and Professional Women's Foundation, which awards grants and loans, based on need, to mature women reentering the workforce or entering nontraditional fields.

Federally Employed Women, *1666 K St. N.W., #440 20006; (202) 898-0994. Fax, (202) 898-1535. Patricia M. Wolfe, President.*
Web, www.few.org

Membership: women and men who work for the federal government. Works to eliminate sex discrimination in government employment and to increase job opportunities for women; offers training program. Monitors legislation and regulations.

Institute for Women's Policy Research (IWPR), *1707 L St. N.W., #750 20036; (202) 785-5100. Fax, (202) 833-4362. Heidi I. Hartmann, President.*
General e-mail, iwpr@iwpr.org
Web, www.iwpr.org

Public policy research organization that focuses on women's issues, including welfare reform, family and work policies, employment and wages, and discrimination based on gender, race, or ethnicity.

National Women's Law Center, *11 Dupont Circle N.W., #800 20036; (202) 588-5180. Fax, (202) 588-5185. Nancy Duff Campbell, Co-President; Marcia D. Greenberger, Co-President.*
General e-mail, info@nwlc.org
Web, www.nwlc.org

Works to expand and protect women's legal rights in education through advocacy and public education.

Wider Opportunities for Women, *1000 Connecticut Ave. N.W., #930 20036; (202) 464-1596. Fax, (202) 464-1660. Joan Kuriansky, Executive Director.*
General e-mail, info@wowonline.org
Web, www.wowonline.org

Promotes equal employment opportunities for women through equal access to jobs and training, equal incomes, and an equitable workplace. Monitors public policy relating to jobs, affirmative action, vocational education, training opportunities, and welfare reform.

Women in Community Service, *1900 N. Beauregard St., #103, Alexandria, VA 22311; (703) 671-0500. Fax, (703) 671-4489. Jacquelyn L. Lendsey, President. Information, (800) 442-9427.*
General e-mail, wicsnatl@wics.org
Web, www.wics.org

Seeks to reduce the number of women living in poverty by promoting self-reliance and economic independence. Interests include job training and welfare reform. Holds contract with Labor Dept. for outreach, support service, and job placement for the Job Corps. Sponsors the Lifeskills Program to assist at-risk women in such areas as job training and money management.

Women Work!, *1625 K St. N.W., #300 20006; (202) 467-6346. Fax, (202) 467-5366. Jill Miller, Executive Director. Information, (800) 235-2732.*
General e-mail, womenwork@womenwork.org
Web, www.womenwork.org

Fosters the development of programs and services for former homemakers reentering the job market and provides information about public policy issues that affect displaced homemakers and single parents. Refers individuals to local services. Monitors legislation.

 LABOR-MANAGEMENT RELATIONS

AGENCIES

Bureau of Labor Statistics (BLS), *(Labor Dept.), Compensation and Working Conditions, 2 Massachu-*

setts Ave. N.E., #4130 20212; (202) 691-6300. Fax, (202) 691-6310. Katrina Reut, Associate Commissioner. Web, www.bls.gov/bls/proghome.htm#ocwc

Provides data on collective bargaining agreements, wage structures, industrial relations, and work stoppages. Compiles data for *Employment Cost Index,* published quarterly.

Criminal Division *(Justice Dept.), Organized Crime and Racketeering: Labor-Management Racketeering,* 1301 New York Ave., #510 20530; (202) 514-3666. Fax, (202) 514-9837. Gerald A. Toner, Assistant Chief.

Reviews and advises on prosecutions of criminal violations involving labor-management relations, the operation of employee pension and health care plans, and internal affairs of labor unions.

Employment Standards Administration *(Labor Dept.), Labor-Management Standards,* 200 Constitution Ave. N.W., #N5119 20210; (202) 693-0122. Fax, (202) 693-1340. Don Todd, Deputy Assistant Secretary. General e-mail, OLMS-Mail@dol-esa.gov Web, www.dol.gov/esa/olms_org.htm

Administers and enforces the Labor-Management Reporting and Disclosure Act of 1959 (Landrum-Griffin Act), which guarantees union members certain rights; sets rules for electing union officers, handling union funds, and using trusteeships; requires unions to file annual financial reports with the Labor Dept. Regulatory authority over relevant sections of the Civil Service Reform Act of 1980 and the Foreign Service Act of 1980.

Federal Mediation and Conciliation Service, 2100 K St. N.W. 20427; (202) 606-8100. Fax, (202) 606-4216. Peter J. Hurtgen, Director. Information, (202) 606-8080. Web, www.fmcs.gov

Assists labor and management representatives in resolving disputes in collective bargaining contract negotiation through voluntary mediation and arbitration services; awards competitive grants to joint labor-management initiatives; trains other federal agencies in mediating administrative disputes and formulating rules and regulations under the Administrative Dispute Resolution Act of 1996 and the Negotiated Rulemaking Act of 1996; provides training to unions and management in cooperative processes.

National Labor Relations Board (NLRB), 1099 14th St. N.W. 20570-0001; (202) 273-1000. Fax, (202) 273-4276. Robert J. Battista, Chair, (202) 273-1770; Lester Heltzer, Executive Secretary (Acting). Information, (202) 273-1991. Library, (202) 273-3720. Web, www.nlrb.gov

Administers the National Labor Relations Act. Works to prevent and remedy unfair labor practices by employers and labor unions; conducts elections among employees to determine whether they wish to be represented by a labor union for collective bargaining purposes. Library open to the public.

National Mediation Board, 1301 K St. N.W., #250E 20572; (202) 692-5000. Fax, (202) 692-5080. Francis J. Duggan, Chair; Benetta M. Mansfield, Chief of Staff, (202) 692-5030. Information, (202) 692-5000. Press, (202) 692-5050. TTY, (202) 692-5001. Web, www.nmb.gov

Mediates labor disputes in the railroad and airline industries; determines and certifies labor representatives for those industries.

CONGRESS

House Education and the Workforce Committee, *Subcommittee on Employer-Employee Relations,* 2181 RHOB 20515; (202) 225-4527. Fax, (202) 225-9571. Rep. Sam Johnson, R-Texas, Chair; Paula Nowakowski, Staff Director. Web, edworkforce.house.gov/members/108th/mem-eer.htm

Jurisdiction over legislation on labor-management issues and unfair labor practices and the National Labor Relations Act.

House Government Reform Committee, *Subcommittee on Civil Service and Agency Organization,* B373A RHOB 20515; (202) 225-5147. Fax, (202) 225-2373. Rep. Jo Ann Davis, R-Va., Chair; Garry Ewing, Staff Director. Web, www.house.gov/reform

Jurisdiction over legislation on federal civil service labor-management issues; oversees the Federal Labor Relations Authority.

House Government Reform Committee, *Subcommittee on Criminal Justice, Drug Policy, and Human Resources,* B373 RHOB 20515; (202) 225-2577. Fax, (202) 225-1154. Rep. Mark Souder, R-Ind., Chair; Christopher Donesa, Staff Director. Web, www.house.gov/reform

Oversight of the Federal Mediation and Conciliation Service, the Labor Dept., and the National Labor Relations Board.

House Government Reform Committee, *Subcommittee on Energy Policy, Natural Resources, and Regulatory Affairs,* B377 RHOB 20515; (202) 225-4407. Fax, (202) 225-2441. Rep. Doug Ose, R-Calif., Chair; Dan Skopec, Staff Director.

AFL-CIO

DEPARTMENTS

Civil, Human, and Women's Rights, Richard Womack, Director; (202) 637-5270

Field Mobilization, Marilyn Sneiderman, Director; (202) 637-5356

International Affairs, Barbara Shailor, Director; (202) 637-5050

Legal Dept., Jonathan Hiatt, General Counsel; (202) 637-5053

Legislation, Bill Samuel, Director; (202) 637-5320

Occupational Safety and Health, Peg Seminario, Director; (202) 637-5366

Organizing, Stewart Acuff, Director; (202) 639-6200

Political Dept., Karen Ackerman, Director; (202) 637-5102

Public Affairs, Denise Mitchell, Special Assistant to the President; (202) 637-5340

Public Policy, Christine Owens, Director; (202) 637-5178

Working Women, Karen Nussbaum, Director; (202) 637-5064

TRADE AND INDUSTRIAL DEPARTMENTS

Building and Construction Trades, Edward Sullivan, President; (202) 347-1461

Food and Allied Service Trades, Jeffrey Fiedler, President; (202) 737-7200

Maritime Trades, Michael Sacco, President; (202) 628-6300

Metal Trades, Ronald Ault, President; (202) 974-8030

Professional Employees, Paul E. Almeida, President; (202) 638-0320

Transportation Trades, Sonny Hall, President; (202) 628-9262

Union Label and Service Trades, Charles E. Mercer, President; (202) 628-2131

Web, www.house.gov/reform

Oversees operations of the National Mediation Board.

Senate Governmental Affairs Committee, *Subcommittee on Financial Management, the Budget, and International Security, SH-442 20510; (202) 224-2254. Sen. Peter G. Fitzgerald, R-Ill., Chair; Mitch Kugler, Staff Director.*

Web, govt-aff.senate.gov/subcom.htm

Jurisdiction over legislation on federal civil service labor-management issues, including classification, compensation, and benefits.

Senate Health, Education, Labor, and Pensions Committee, *Subcommittee on Employment, Safety, and Training, SH-607 20510; (202) 224-7229. Sen. Michael B. Enzi, R-Wyo., Chair; Raissa H. Geary, Staff Director.*

Web, health.senate.gov

Jurisdiction over the National Labor Relations Act and over legislation on labor-management issues and unfair labor practices. Oversight of the Labor Dept., the National Mediation Board, the Federal Mediation and Conciliation Service, and the National Labor Relations Board.

NONPROFIT

AFL–CIO (American Federation of Labor–Congress of Industrial Organizations), *815 16th St. N.W. 20006; (202) 637-5000. Fax, (202) 637-5050. John J. Sweeney, President.*

Web, www.aflcio.org

Voluntary federation of national and international labor unions in the United States. Represents members before Congress and other branches of government. Each member union conducts its own contract negotiations. Library (located in Silver Spring, Md.) open to the public.

American Arbitration Assn., *Federal Center for Dispute Resolution, 601 Pennsylvania Ave. N.W., #700 20004; (202) 737-1460. Fax, (202) 737-2418. S. Pierre Paret, Vice President, Government Relations.*

Web, www.adr.org

Provides dispute resolution services to the federal government. (American Arbitration Assn. headquarters in New York.)

American Federation of Musicians, *Washington Office, 1717 K St., #500 20036; (202) 463-0772. Fax, (202) 463-9009. Thomas Lee, President.*

Web, www.afm.org

Seeks to improve the working conditions and salary of musicians. Monitors legislation and regulations affecting musicians and the arts.

American Foreign Service Assn. (AFSA), *2101 E St. N.W. 20037; (202) 338-4045. Fax, (202) 338-6820. Susan Reardon, Executive Director.*

General e-mail, afsa@afsa.org

Web, www.afsa.org

Membership: active and retired foreign service employees of federal agencies. Represents active duty foreign service personnel in labor-management negotiations; seeks to ensure adequate resources for foreign service operations and personnel. Monitors legislation and regulations.

Coalition of Black Trade Unionists, *1625 L St. N.W. 20036 (mailing address: P.O. Box 66268 20035); (202) 429-1203. Fax, (202) 429-1102. Wil Duncan, Executive Director.*
Web, www.cbtu.org

Monitors legislation affecting African American and other minority trade unionists. Focuses on equal employment opportunity, unemployment, and voter education and registration.

Coalition of Labor Union Women, *1925 K St. N.W., #402 20006; (202) 223-8360. Fax, (202) 776-0537. Carol Rosenblatt, Executive Director.*
General e-mail, info@cluw.org
Web, www.cluw.org

Seeks to make unions more responsive to the needs of women in the workplace; advocates affirmative action and the active participation of women in unions. Monitors legislation and regulations.

George Meany Center for Labor Studies and the George Meany Memorial Archives, *10000 New Hampshire Ave., Silver Spring, MD 20903; (301) 431-6400. Fax, (301) 434-0371. Susan Sherman, Executive Director.*
Web, www.georgemeany.org

Educational institute that offers classes, workshops, graduate programs, and an undergraduate degree program to AFL-CIO–affiliated officers, representatives, and staff. Maintains the AFL-CIO archives and the Institute for the Study of Labor Organizations.

International Brotherhood of Teamsters, *25 Louisiana Ave. N.W. 20001; (202) 624-6800. Fax, (202) 624-6918. James P. Hoffa, President.*
Web, www.teamster.org

Membership: more than 1.4 million workers in the transportation and construction industries, factories, offices, hospitals, warehouses, and other workplaces. Helps members negotiate pay, benefits, and better working conditions; conducts training programs and workshops. Monitors legislation and regulations. (Affiliated with the AFL-CIO.)

Labor Council for Latin American Advancement, *888 16th St. N.W., #640 20006; (202) 347-4223. Fax, (202) 347-5095. Oscar Sanchez, Executive Director.*

General e-mail, headquarters@lclaa.org
Web, www.lclaa.org

Membership: Hispanic trade unionists. Encourages equal employment opportunity, voter registration and education, and participation in the political process. (Affiliated with the AFL-CIO.)

Laborers' International Union of North America, *905 16th St. N.W. 20006; (202) 737-8320. Fax, (202) 737-2754. Terence O'Sullivan, President.*
Web, www.liuna.org

Membership: over 800,000 construction workers; federal, state, and local government employees; health care professionals; mail handlers; custodial service personnel; shipbuilders; and hazardous waste handlers. Helps members negotiate pay, benefits, and better working conditions; conducts training programs and workshops. Monitors legislation and regulations. (Affiliated with the AFL-CIO.)

National Assn. of Manufacturers (NAM), *Human Resources Policy, 1331 Pennsylvania Ave. N.W., #600N 20004-1790; (202) 637-3134. Fax, (202) 637-3182. Pat Cleary, Senior Vice President.*
General e-mail, manufacturing@nam.org
Web, www.nam.org

Provides information on corporate industrial relations, including collective bargaining, labor standards, international labor relations, productivity, employee benefits, health care, and other current labor issues; monitors legislation and regulations.

National Public Employer Labor Relations Assn. (NPELRA), *1620 Eye St. N.W., 3rd Floor 20006; (800) 296-2230. Fax, (202) 293-2352. Roger E. Dahl, Executive Director.*
General e-mail, info@npelra.org
Web, www.npelra.org

Represents professional public employers in federal, state, and local governments and school and special districts in a wide range of areas including individual relationships with employees, state labor relations boards, and bargaining with employee unions and associations.

National Right to Work Committee, *8001 Braddock Rd., #500, Springfield, VA 22160; (703) 321-9820. Fax, (703) 321-7342. Mark Mix, Executive Vice President. Information, (800) 325-7892.*
General e-mail, info@nrtwc.org
Web, www.nrtwc.org

Citizens' organization opposed to compulsory union membership. Supports right-to-work legislation.

National Right to Work Legal Defense Foundation, *8001 Braddock Rd., #600, Springfield, VA 22160; (703) 321-8510. Fax, (703) 321-9613. Mark Mix, Executive Vice President. Toll-free, (800) 336-3600.*
General e-mail, info@nrtw.org
Web, www.nrtw.org

Provides free legal aid for employees in cases of compulsory union membership abuses.

Office and Professional Employees International Union, *Washington Office, 1660 L St. N.W., #801 20036; (202) 393-4464. Fax, (202) 347-0649. Michael Goodwin, President.*
Web, www.opeiu.org

Membership: 140,000 workers, including computer analysts, programmers, and data entry operators; copywriters; nurses and other health care personnel; attorneys; law enforcement officers and security guards; accountants; secretaries; bank employees; and insurance workers and agents. Helps members negotiate pay, benefits, and better working conditions; conducts training program and workshops. Monitors legislation and regulations. (Headquarters in New York; affiliated with the AFL-CIO and the Canadian Labour Congress.)

Public Service Research Foundation, *320D Maple Ave. East, Vienna, VA 22180; (703) 242-3575. Fax, (703) 242-3579. David Y. Denholm, President.*
General e-mail, info@psrf.org
Web, www.psrf.org

Independent, nonpartisan research and educational organization. Opposes collective bargaining, strikes, and binding arbitration in the public sector. Sponsors conferences and seminars. Library open to the public by appointment.

Service Employees International Union, *1313 L St. N.W. 20005; (202) 898-3200. Fax, (202) 898-3402. Andrew L. Stern, President.*
Web, www.seiu.org

Membership: more than one million service providers, including teachers; nurses, doctors, and other health care professionals; school bus drivers; janitors; and others. Helps members negotiate pay, benefits, and better working conditions; conducts training programs and workshops. Monitors legislation and regulations. (Affiliated with the AFL-CIO.)

United Auto Workers, *Washington Office, 1757 N St. N.W. 20036; (202) 828-8500. Fax, (202) 293-3457. Alan Reuther, Legislative Director.*
Web, www.uaw.org

Membership: approximately 750,000 active and 600,000 retired North American workers in aerospace, automotive, defense, manufacturing, steel, technical, and other industries. Assists members with contract negotiation and grievances; conducts training programs and workshops. Monitors legislation and regulations. (Headquarters in Detroit, Mich.; affiliated with the AFL-CIO.)

United Electrical, Radio and Machine Workers of America, *1800 Diagonal Rd., #600, Alexandria, VA 22314; (703) 684-3123. Fax, (703) 519-8982. Chris Townsend, Legislative Director.*
General e-mail, ue@ranknfile-ue.org
Web, www.ranknfile-ue.org/uewho.html

Represents over 35,000 workers in electrical, metal working, and plastic manufacturing public sector and private nonprofit sector jobs. Membership: manufacturing assembly workers, plastic injection molders, tool and die makers, sheet metal workers, truck drivers, warehouse workers, custodians, clerical workers, graduate instructors, graduate researchers, scientists, librarians, social workers, and day care workers.

United Steelworkers of America, *Washington Office, 1150 17th St. N.W., #300 20036; (202) 778-4384. Fax, (202) 293-5308. William J. Klinefelter, Legislative and Political Director.*
Web, www.uswa.org

Membership: more than 700,000 steelworkers in the United States and Canada. Helps members negotiate pay, benefits, and better working conditions; conducts training programs and workshops. Monitors legislation and regulations. (Headquarters in Pittsburgh, Pa.; affiliated with the AFL-CIO.)

U.S. Chamber of Commerce, *Labor, Immigration, and Employee Benefits, 1615 H St. N.W. 20062-2000; (202) 463-5522. Fax, (202) 463-5901. Randel K. Johnson, Vice President. Press, (202) 463-5682.*
Web, www.uschamber.org

Monitors legislation and regulations affecting labor-management relations, employee benefits, and immigration issues.

 PENSIONS AND BENEFITS

AGENCIES

Advisory Council on Employee Welfare and Pension Benefit Plans (ERISA Advisory Council) *(Labor Dept.), 200 Constitution Ave. N.W., #N5677 20210; (202) 693-8668. Fax, (202) 219-6531. Sharon Morrissey, Executive Secretary.*
Web, www.dol.gov/ebsa

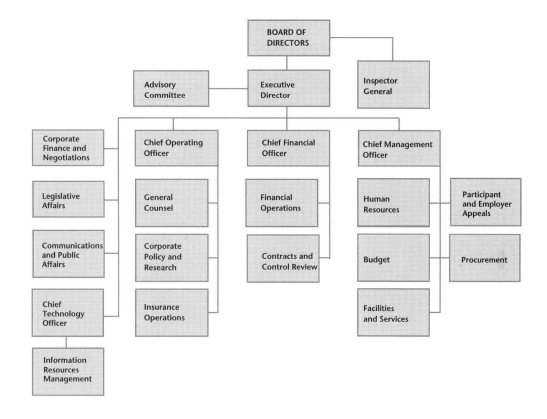

Advises and makes recommendations to the secretary of labor under the Employee Retirement Income Security Act of 1974 (ERISA).

Bureau of Labor Statistics (BLS), *(Labor Dept.), Compensation and Working Conditions,* 2 Massachusetts Ave. N.E., #4130 20212; (202) 691-6300. Fax, (202) 691-6310. Katrina Reut, Associate Commissioner.
Web, www.bls.gov/bls/proghome.htm#ocwc

Provides data on pensions and related work benefits.

Criminal Division *(Justice Dept.), Organized Crime and Racketeering: Labor-Management Racketeering,* 1301 New York Ave., #510 20530; (202) 514-3666. Fax, (202) 514-9837. Gerald A. Toner, Assistant Chief.

Reviews and advises on prosecutions of criminal violations concerning the operation of employee benefit plans in the private sector.

Employee Benefits Security Administration *(Labor Dept.),* 200 Constitution Ave. N.W., #S2524 20210; (202) 693-8300. Fax, (202) 219-5526. Ann L. Combs, Assistant Secretary, (202) 693-8300.
Web, www.dol.gov/ebsa

Administers, regulates, and enforces private employee benefit plan standards established by the Employee Retirement Income Security Act of 1974 (ERISA), with particular emphasis on fiduciary obligations; receives and maintains required reports from employee benefit plan administrators pursuant to ERISA.

Federal Retirement Thrift Investment Board, 1250 H St. N.W., #200 20005; (202) 942-1600. Fax, (202) 942-1674. James Petrick, Executive Director (Acting).
Web, www.frtib.gov

Administers the Thrift Savings Plan, a tax-deferred, defined contribution plan that permits federal employees to save for additional retirement security under a program similar to private 401(k) plans.

Joint Board for the Enrollment of Actuaries, 1111 Constitution Ave. N.W., N:C:SC:OPR, Internal Revenue Service 20224; (202) 694-1891. Fax, (202) 694-1876. Paulette Tino, Chair.

Web, www.irs.gov/taxpros/actuaries/index.html

Joint board, with members from the departments of Labor and Treasury and the Pension Benefit Guaranty Corp., established under the Employee Retirement Income Security Act of 1974 (ERISA). Promulgates regulations for the enrollment of pension actuaries; examines applicants and grants certificates of enrollment; disciplines enrolled actuaries who have engaged in misconduct in the discharge of duties under ERISA.

Office of Personnel Management (OPM), *Retirement Information,* 1900 E St. N.W. 20415-0001; (202) 606-0500. Fax, (202) 606-0145. Wellington Sadler, Chief. TTY, (800) 878-5707. Toll-free, (888) 767-6738.

General e-mail, retire@opm.gov

Web, www.opm.gov/retire/index.asp

Provides civil servants with information and assistance on federal retirement payments.

Pension Benefit Guaranty Corp., 1200 K St. N.W., #210 20005-4026; (202) 326-4010. Fax, (202) 326-4016. Steve Kandarian, Executive Director (Acting); Joseph Grant, Deputy Executive Director. Information, (202) 326-4000. Locator, (202) 326-4110.

Web, www.pbgc.gov

Self-financed U.S. government corporation. Insures private-sector, defined-benefit pension plans; guarantees payment of retirement benefits subject to certain limitations established in the Employee Retirement Income Security Act of 1974 (ERISA). Provides insolvent multiemployer pension plans with financial assistance to enable them to pay guaranteed retirement benefits.

CONGRESS

General Accounting Office (GAO), *Education, Workforce, and Income Security,* 441 G St. N.W., #5928 20548; (202) 512-7215. Cynthia Fagnoni, Managing Director.

Web, www.gao.gov

Independent, nonpartisan agency in the legislative branch. Audits, analyzes, and evaluates federal agency and private sector pension programs; makes reports available to the public.

House Education and the Workforce Committee, *Subcommittee on Employer-Employee Relations,* 2181 RHOB 20515; (202) 225-4527. Fax, (202) 225-9571. Rep. Sam Johnson, R-Texas, Chair; Paula Nowakowski, Staff Director.

Web, edworkforce.house.gov/members/108th/mem-eer.htm

Jurisdiction over pension plan, fringe benefit, and retirement income security legislation, including the

Employee Retirement Income Security Act of 1974 (ERISA) and the Labor-Management Reporting and Disclosure Act.

House Ways and Means Committee, 1102 LHOB 20515; (202) 225-3625. Fax, (202) 225-2610. Rep. Bill Thomas, R-Calif., Chair; Allison Giles, Chief of Staff.

General e-mail, contactwaysandmeans@mail.house.gov

Web, waysandmeans.house.gov

Jurisdiction over legislation concerning changes in enforcement of tax laws.

House Ways and Means Committee, *Subcommittee on Oversight,* 1136 LHOB 20515; (202) 225-7601. Fax, (202) 225-9680. Rep. Amo Houghton, R-N.Y., Chair; Kirk Walder, Staff Director.

Web, waysandmeans.house.gov

Oversees the Pension Benefit Guaranty Corp.

Senate Finance Committee, SD-219 20510; (202) 224-4515. Fax, (202) 228-0554. Sen. Charles E. Grassley, R-Iowa, Chair; Kolan L. Davis, Staff Director.

Web, finance.senate.gov

Jurisdiction over legislation related to taxation of pension contributions.

Senate Finance Committee, *Subcommittee on Taxation and IRS Oversight,* SD-219 20510; (202) 224-4515. Sen. Don Nickles, R-Okla., Chair; Kolan L. Davis, Staff Director.

Web, finance.senate.gov

Holds hearings on pension reform legislation; investigates private and self-employed pension plan problems. Oversees the Pension Benefit Guaranty Corp.

Senate Governmental Affairs Committee, *Permanent Subcommittee on Investigations,* SR-199 20510; (202) 224-3721. Sen. Norm Coleman, R-Minn., Chair; Mary Robertson, Chief Clerk.

General e-mail, PSI@govt-aff.senate.gov

Web, govt-aff.senate.gov/psi.htm

Investigates labor racketeering, including pension, health, and welfare fund frauds.

Senate Health, Education, Labor, and Pensions Committee, *Subcommittee on Employment, Safety, and Training,* SH-607 20510; (202) 224-7229. Sen. Michael B. Enzi, R-Wyo., Chair; Raissa H. Geary, Staff Director.

Web, health.senate.gov

Jurisdiction over pension plan and retirement income security legislation and over the Labor-Management Reporting and Disclosure Act.

Senate Special Committee on Aging, *SD-G31 20510; (202) 224-5364. Fax, (202) 224-9926. Sen. Larry E. Craig, R-Idaho, Chair; Lupe Wissel, Staff Director.*

Web, aging.senate.gov

Studies and makes recommendations on private and self-employed pension plan legislation and mandatory retirement.

NONPROFIT

AARP, *601 E St. N.W. 20049; (202) 434-2277. Fax, (202) 434-2320. William D. Novelli, Chief Executive Officer. Library, (202) 434-6240. Press, (202) 434-2560. TTY, (202) 434-6561.*

Web, www.aarp.org

Researches and testifies on private, federal, and other government employee pension legislation and regulations; conducts seminars; provides information on pre-retirement preparation. Library open to the public.

Alliance for Worker Retirement Security, *1331 Pennsylvania Ave. N.W., #600 20004-1290; (202) 637-3453. Fax, (202) 637-3182. Max Derrick, Executive Director.*

Coalition of forty organizations representing businesses of all sizes. Supports private retirement accounts.

American Academy of Actuaries, *1100 17th St. N.W., 7th Fl. 20036; (202) 223-8196. Fax, (202) 872-1948. Rick Lawson, Executive Director.*

Web, www.actuary.org

Membership: professional actuaries practicing in the areas of life, health, liability, property, and casualty insurance; pensions; government insurance plans; and general consulting. Provides information on actuarial matters, including insurance and pensions; develops professional standards; advises public policymakers.

American Benefits Council, *1212 New York Ave. N.W., #1250 20005; (202) 289-6700. Fax, (202) 289-4582. James A. Klein, President.*

General e-mail, info@abcstaff.org

Web, www.americanbenefitscouncil.org

Membership: employers, consultants, banks, and service organizations. Informs members of employee benefits, including private pension benefits and compensation.

American Society of Pension Actuaries, *4245 N. Fairfax Dr., #750, Arlington, VA 22203-1619; (703) 516-9300. Fax, (703) 516-9308. Brian Graff, Executive Director.*

Web, www.aspa.org

Membership: professional pension plan actuaries,

administrators, consultants, and other benefits professionals. Sponsors educational programs to prepare actuaries and consultants for professional exams. Monitors legislation.

Center for Economic Organizing, *1705 Desales St. N.W., #400 20036; (202) 775-9072. Fax, (202) 775-9074. Randy Barber, Director.*

Research, consulting, and training organization. Interests include the investment and control of pension funds and the role of unions and the private sector in administering these funds.

Employee Benefit Research Institute, *2121 K St. N.W., #600 20037; (202) 659-0670. Fax, (202) 775-6312. Dallas L. Salisbury, President.*

General e-mail, info@ebri.org

Web, www.ebri.org

Researches proposed policy changes on employee benefits. Sponsors studies on retirement income and on health, work, family, and other benefits.

Employers Council on Flexible Compensation, *927 15th St. N.W., #1000 20005; (202) 659-4300. Fax, (202) 371-1467. Kenneth E. Feltman, Executive Director.*

General e-mail, info@ecfc.org

Web, www.ecfc.org

Represents employers who have or are considering flexible compensation plans. Supports the preservation and expansion of employee choice in savings and pension plans. Monitors legislation and regulations. Interests include cafeteria plans and 401(k) plans.

ERISA Industry Committee, *1400 L St. N.W., #350 20005; (202) 789-1400. Fax, (202) 789-1120. Mark J. Ugoretz, President.*

General e-mail, eric@eric.org

Web, www.eric.org

Membership: major U.S. employers. Advocates members' positions on employee retirement, health care coverage, and welfare benefit plans; promotes flexibility and cost-effectiveness in employee benefits. Monitors legislation and regulations.

National Assn. of Manufacturers (NAM), *Human Resources Policy, 1331 Pennsylvania Ave. N.W., #600N 20004-1790; (202) 637-3134. Fax, (202) 637-3182. Pat Cleary, Senior Vice President.*

General e-mail, manufacturing@nam.org

Web, www.nam.org

Studies the Social Security system to ensure that its long-term status remains compatible with private sector retirement plans. Other interests include health care, pensions, cost containment, mandated benefits, and Medicare and other federal programs that affect employers. Opposed to government involvement in health care and proposed expansion of health care liability.

National Employee Benefits Institute, *1350 Connecticut Ave. N.W., #600 20036; (202) 822-6432. Fax, (202) 466-5109. Joseph Semo, Executive Director. Information, (888) 822-1344.*
Web, www.nebif.org
Membership: large self-insured companies interested in employee benefits. Provides a forum for members and serves as a clearinghouse for information on employee benefits. Monitors legislation and regulations.

Pension Rights Center, *1140 19th St. N.W., #602 20036-6608; (202) 296-3776. Fax, (202) 833-2472. Karen W. Ferguson, Director.*
General e-mail, PnsnRights@aol.com
Web, www.pensionrights.org
Works to preserve and expand pension rights; provides information and technical assistance on pensions.

Retirement Policy Institute, *2158 Florida Ave. N.W. 20008; (202) 483-3140. A. Haeworth Robertson, President.*
Researches and educates the public about retirement policy issues. Interests include trends, pension reform, Social Security, and policy alternatives.

Society of Professional Benefit Administrators, *2 Wisconsin Circle, #670, Chevy Chase, MD 20815-7003; (301) 718-7722. Fax, (301) 718-9440. Frederick D. Hunt Jr., President.*
Web, users.erols.com/spba
Membership: third-party administration firms that manage outside claims and benefit plans for client employers. Monitors government compliance requirements. Interests include pensions and retirement policy and funding, health funding, and the Employee Retirement Income Security Act of 1974 (ERISA).

United Mine Workers of America Health and Retirement Funds, *2121 K St. N.W. 20037; (202) 521-2200. Fax, (202) 521-2394. Vacant, Executive Director.*
Web, www.umwafunds.org
Labor/management trust fund that provides health and retirement benefits to coal miners. Health benefits are provided to pensioners, their dependents, and, in some cases, their survivors.

Women's Institute for a Secure Retirement (WISER), *1920 N St. N.W., #300 20036; (202) 393-5452. Fax, (202) 393-5890. Cindy Hounsell, Executive Director.*
General e-mail, wiserwomen@aol.org

Web, www.wiser.heinz.org
Provides information on women's retirement issues; conducts workshops and seminars. Monitors legislation and regulations.

WORKPLACE SAFETY AND HEALTH

AGENCIES

Bureau of Labor Statistics (BLS), *(Labor Dept.), Compensation and Working Conditions, 2 Massachusetts Ave. N.E., #4130 20212; (202) 691-6300. Fax, (202) 691-6310. Katrina Reut, Associate Commissioner.*
Web, www.bls.gov/bls/proghome.htm#ocwc
Compiles data on occupational safety and health.

Environment, Safety, and Health *(Energy Dept.), Safety and Health, 20300 Century Blvd., Germantown, MD 20874 (mailing address: 1000 Independence Ave. S.W., Washington, DC 20585-0270); (301) 903-5532. Fax, (301) 903-3189. Rick Jones, Deputy Assistant Secretary (Acting).*
Develops policy and establishes standards to ensure safety and health protection in all department activities.

Federal Mine Safety and Health Review Commission, *601 New Jersey Ave. N.W., #9500 20001; (202) 434-9900. Fax, (202) 434-9906. Vacant, Chair; Richard L. Baker, Executive Director, (202) 434-9905. Library, (202) 653-9935.*
Web, www.fmshrc.gov
Independent agency established by the Federal Mine Safety and Health Act of 1977. Holds fact-finding hearings and issues orders affirming, modifying, or vacating the labor secretary's enforcement actions regarding mine safety and health. Library open to the public.

Mine Safety and Health Administration *(Labor Dept.), 1000 Wilson Blvd., #2176, Arlington, VA 22209-3939; (202) 693-9899. Fax, (202) 693-9801. Dave D. Lauriske, Assistant Secretary.*
Web, www.msha.gov
Administers and enforces the health and safety provisions of the Federal Mine Safety and Health Act of 1977.

National Institute for Occupational Safety and Health (NIOSH), *(Centers for Disease Control and Prevention), 200 Independence Ave. S.W. 20201; (202) 401-6997. Fax, (202) 260-4464. Dr. John Howard, Director. Information, (800) 356-4674.*
Web, www.cdc.gov/niosh

Entity within the Centers for Disease Control and Prevention in Atlanta. Supports and conducts research on occupational safety and health issues; provides technical assistance and training; develops recommendations for the Labor Dept. Operates an occupational safety and health bibliographic database (mailing address: NIOSH Clearinghouse for Occupational Safety and Health Information, 4676 Columbia Pkwy., Cincinnati, OH 45226).

Occupational Safety and Health Administration (OSHA), *(Labor Dept.), 200 Constitution Ave. N.W., #S2315 20210; (202) 693-2000. Fax, (202) 693-2106. John L. Henshaw, Assistant Secretary.*
Web, www.osha.gov

Sets and enforces rules and regulations for workplace safety and health. Implements the Occupational Safety and Health Act of 1970. Provides federal agencies and private industries with compliance guidance and assistance.

Occupational Safety and Health Administration (OSHA), *(Labor Dept.), Construction, 200 Constitution Ave. N.W., #N3468 20210; (202) 693-2020. Fax, (202) 693-1689. Russell B. Swanson, Director.*
Web, www.osha.gov

Provides technical expertise to OSHA's enforcement personnel; initiates studies to determine causes of construction accidents; works with private sector to promote construction safety.

Occupational Safety and Health Administration (OSHA), *(Labor Dept.), Cooperative and State Programs, 200 Constitution Ave. N.W., #N3700 20210; (202) 693-2200. Fax, (202) 693-1671. Paula O. White, Director.*
Web, www.osha.gov/fso/DFSO.html

Makes grants to nonprofit organizations under the New Directions Grant Program to assist in providing education, training, and technical assistance to meet the workplace safety and health needs of employers and employees; administers state enforcement and consultation programs; trains federal and private employees, OSHA and state inspectors, and state consultants.

Occupational Safety and Health Administration (OSHA), *(Labor Dept.), Enforcements, 200 Constitution Ave. N.W., #N3119 20210; (202) 693-2100. Fax, (202) 693-1681. Richard Fairfax, Director.*
Web, www.osha.gov

Interprets compliance safety standards for agency field personnel and private employees and employers.

Occupational Safety and Health Administration (OSHA), *(Labor Dept.), Public Affairs, 200 Constitution Ave. N.W., #N3647 20210; (202) 693-1999. Fax, (202)*

693-1635. Bonnie Friedman, Director. Emergency hotline, (800) 321-OSHA.
Web, www.osha.gov

Conducts public hearings on proposed workplace safety and health standards; provides information, staff assistance, and support for the National Advisory Committee for Occupational Safety and Health and the Construction Advisory Committee. Advises the assistant secretary of labor for occupational safety and health on consumer affairs matters.

Occupational Safety and Health Administration (OSHA), *(Labor Dept.), Safety Standards, 200 Constitution Ave. N.W., #N3609 20210; (202) 693-2222. Fax, (202) 693-1663. Steven Witt, Director, (202) 693-1950.*

Develops new or revised occupational safety standards.

Occupational Safety and Health Administration (OSHA), *(Labor Dept.), Standards and Guidance, 200 Constitution Ave. N.W., #N3718 20210; (202) 693-1950. Fax, (202) 693-1678. Steven F. Witt, Director.*
Web, www.osha.gov

Develops new or revised occupational health standards for toxic, hazardous, and carcinogenic substances; biological hazards; or other harmful physical agents, such as vibration, noise, and radiation.

Occupational Safety and Health Review Commission, *1120 20th St. N.W., 9th Floor 20036-3419; (202) 606-5398. Fax, (202) 606-5050. W. Scott Railton, Chair; Patricia A. Randle, Executive Director. TTY, (202) 606-5386.*
Web, www.oshrc.gov

Independent executive branch agency that adjudicates disputes between private employers and the Occupational Safety and Health Administration arising under the Occupational Safety and Health Act of 1970.

Office of Personnel Management (OPM), *Work/Life Programs, 1900 E St. N.W., #7425 20415-2000; (202) 606-5520. Fax, (202) 606-2091. Bonnie Storm, Director. General e-mail, ehs@opm.gov*
Web, www.opm.gov/ehs/index.htm

Sets policy and guides federal agencies in establishing and maintaining programs on alcohol and drug abuse, drug-free workplaces, workplace violence, work and family issues, and fitness.

CONGRESS

House Appropriations Committee, *Subcommittee on Labor, Health and Human Services, Education, and Related Agencies, 2358 RHOB 20515; (202) 225-3508.*

OCCUPATIONAL SAFETY AND HEALTH ADMINISTRATION

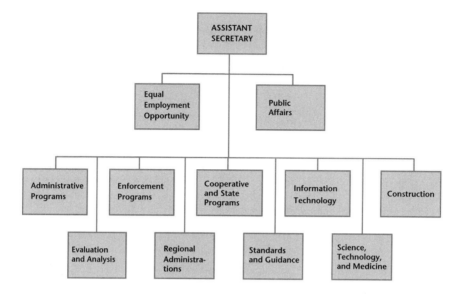

Fax, (202) 225-3509. Rep. Ralph Regula, R-Ohio, Chair; Craig Higgins, Staff Director.
Web, www.house.gov/appropriations

Jurisdiction over legislation to appropriate funds for the Federal Mine Safety and Health Review Commission and the Occupational Safety and Health Review Commission.

House Education and the Workforce Committee,
Subcommittee on Workforce Protections, 2181 RHOB 20515; (202) 225-4527. Fax, (202) 225-9571. Rep. Charlie Norwood, R-Ga., Chair; Paula Nowakowski, Staff Director.
Web, edworkforce.house.gov/members/108th/mem-wp.htm

Jurisdiction over legislation on workers' compensation and related wage loss; occupational safety and health; mine safety and health; youth camp safety; and migrant and agricultural labor health and safety.

House Small Business Committee, *Subcommittee on Regulatory Reform and Oversight, B363 RHOB 20515; (202) 226-2630. Fax, (202) 225-8950. Rep. Ed Schrock, R-Va., Chair; Rosario Palmieri, Staff Director.*
General e-mail, smbiz@mail.house.gov
Web, www.house.gov/smbiz/subcommittees

Jurisdiction over the Occupational Safety and Health Administration as it affects small business.

Senate Appropriations Committee, *Subcommittee on Labor, Health and Human Services, Education, and*

Related Agencies, SD-184 20510; (202) 224-3471. Fax, (202) 224-8553. Sen. Arlen Specter, R-Pa., Chair; Bettilou Taylor, Clerk.
Web, appropriations.senate.gov/labor

Jurisdiction over legislation to appropriate funds for the Federal Mine Safety and Health Review Commission and the Occupational Safety and Health Review Commission.

Senate Health, Education, Labor, and Pensions Committee, *SD-428 20510; (202) 224-5375. Fax, (202) 228-5044. Sen. Judd Gregg, R-N.H., Chair; Sharon Soderstrom, Staff Director. TTY, (202) 224-1975.*
Web, health.senate.gov

Jurisdiction over legislation on occupational safety and health.

Senate Small Business and Entrepreneurship Committee, *SR-428A 20510; (202) 224-5175. Fax, (202) 228-1128. Sen. Olympia J. Snowe, R-Maine, Chair; Mark Warren, Staff Director.*
Web, sbc.senate.gov

Jurisdiction over the Occupational Safety and Health Administration as it affects small business.

NONPROFIT

American Industrial Hygiene Assn., *2700 Prosperity Ave., #250, Fairfax, VA 22031; (703) 849-8888. Fax, (703) 207-3561. Steven Davis, Executive Director.*

Web, www.aiha.org

Membership: scientists and engineers who practice industrial hygiene in government, labor, academic institutions, and independent organizations. Promotes health and safety standards in the workplace and the community; conducts research to identify potential dangers; educates workers about job-related risks; monitors safety regulations. Interests include international standards and information exchange.

Fair Labor Assn. (FLA), *1505 22nd St. N.W. 20037; (202) 898-1000. Fax, (202) 898-9050. Auret Van Heerden, Executive Director.*
Web, www.fairlabor.org

Membership: consumer, human, and labor rights groups; apparel and footwear manufacturers and retailers; and colleges and universities. Seeks to protect the rights of workers in the United States and worldwide. Concerns include sweatshop practices, forced labor, child labor, and worker health and benefits. Monitors workplace conditions and reports findings to the public.

Institute for a Drug-Free Workplace, *1225 Eye St. N.W., #1000 20005; (202) 842-7400. Fax, (202) 842-0022. Mark A. de Bernardo, Executive Director.*
Web, www.drugfreeworkplace.org

Coalition of businesses, business organizations, and individuals. Seeks to increase productivity, improve safety, and control insurance costs through detection and treatment of drug and alcohol abuse. Promotes fair and consistent implementation of drug abuse prevention programs; supports the right of employers to test for drugs. Monitors legislation and regulations.

ISEA—The Safety Equipment Assn., *1901 N. Moore St., #808, Arlington, VA 22209; (703) 525-1695. Fax, (703) 528-2148. Daniel K. Shipp, President.*
General e-mail, isea@safetyequipment.org
Web, www.safetyequipment.org

Trade organization that drafts industry standards for employee personal safety and protective equipment; encourages development and use of proper equipment to deal with industrial hazards; works to influence international standards, especially in North America. Monitors legislation and regulations.

National Assn. of Manufacturers (NAM), *Human Resources Policy, 1331 Pennsylvania Ave. N.W., #600N 20004-1790; (202) 637-3134. Fax, (202) 637-3182. Pat Cleary, Senior Vice President.*
General e-mail, manufacturing@nam.org
Web, www.nam.org

Conducts research, develops policy, and informs members of toxic injury compensation systems, and occupational safety and health legislation, regulations, and standards internationally. Offers mediation service to business members.

National Safety Council, *Public Affairs, Washington Office, 1025 Connecticut Ave. N.W., #1200 20036; (202) 293-2270. Fax, (202) 293-0032. Charles A. Hurley, Vice President of Transportation Safety Group.*
Web, www.nsc.org

Chartered by Congress. Conducts research and provides educational and informational services on highway safety, child passenger safety, and occupational safety and health; promotes policies to reduce accidental deaths and injuries and preventable illnesses. Monitors legislation and regulations. (Headquarters in Itasca, Ill.)

Public Citizen, *Health Research Group, 1600 20th St. N.W. 20009; (202) 588-1000. Fax, (202) 588-7796. Dr. Sidney M. Wolfe, Director.*
Web, www.citizen.org

Citizens' interest group that studies and reports on occupational diseases; monitors the Occupational Safety and Health Administration and participates in OSHA enforcement proceedings.

Workers' Compensation

AGENCIES

Bureau of Labor Statistics (BLS), *(Labor Dept.), Compensation and Working Conditions: Occupational Safety and Health, 2 Massachusetts Ave. N.E., #4130 20212-0001; (202) 691-6162. Fax, (202) 691-6196. Kate Newman, Assistant Commissioner (Acting).*
Web, www.bls.gov/iif

Compiles and publishes statistics on occupational injuries, illnesses, and fatalities.

Employment Standards Administration *(Labor Dept.), Coal Mine Workers' Compensation, 200 Constitution Ave. N.W., #C3520 20210; (202) 693-0046. Fax, (202) 693-1395. James L. DeMarce, Director.*
Web, www.dol.gov/dol/esa

Provides direction for administration of the black lung benefits program. Adjudicates claims filed on or after July 1, 1973; certifies these benefit payments and maintains black lung beneficiary rolls.

(For claims filed before July 1, 1973, contact the Social Security Administration, Disability.)

Employment Standards Administration *(Labor Dept.), Workers' Compensation Programs, 200 Consti-*

tution Ave. N.W., #S3524 20210; (202) 693-0031. Fax, (202) 693-1378. Shelby Hallmark, Deputy Assistant Secretary.

Administers three federal workers' compensation laws: the Federal Employees' Compensation Act, the Longshore and Harbor Workers' Compensation Act and extensions, and Title IV (Black Lung Benefits Act) of the Federal Coal Mine Health and Safety Act; and the Division of Energy Employees Occupational Illness Compensation Program.

Labor Dept. (DOL), *Benefits Review Board,* 200 Constitution Ave. N.W., #N5101 20210 (mailing address: P.O. Box 37601 20013-7601); (202) 693-6300. Fax, (202) 693-6261. Nancy Dolder, Chief Administrative Appeals Judge.
Web, www.dol.gov/brb

Reviews appeals of workers seeking benefits under the Longshore and Harbor Workers' Compensation Act and its extensions, including the District of Columbia Workers' Compensation Act, and Title IV (Black Lung Benefits Act) of the Federal Coal Mine Health and Safety Act.

Labor Dept. (DOL), *Employees' Compensation Appeals Board,* 200 Constitution Ave. N.W., #N-2609 20210; (202) 693-6420. Fax, (202) 693-6367. Alec J. Koromilas, Chair.
Web, www.dol.gov/ecab

Reviews and determines appeals of final determinations of benefits claims made by the Office of Workers' Compensation Programs under the Federal Employees' Compensation Act.

NONPROFIT

American Insurance Assn., 1130 Connecticut Ave. N.W., #1000 20036; (202) 828-7100. Fax, (202) 293-1219. Robert E. Vagley, President. Library, (202) 828-7183. Press, (202) 828-7116.
Web, www.aiadc.org

Membership: companies providing property and casualty insurance. Offers information on workers' compensation legislation and regulations; conducts educational activities. Library open to the public by appointment.

National Assn. of Manufacturers (NAM), *Human Resources Policy,* 1331 Pennsylvania Ave. N.W., #600N 20004-1790; (202) 637-3134. Fax, (202) 637-3182. Pat Cleary, Senior Vice President.
General e-mail, manufacturing@nam.org
Web, www.nam.org

Conducts research, develops policy, and informs members of workers' compensation law; provides feedback to government agencies.

8 Energy

⬡ GENERAL POLICY

AGENCIES

Bureau of Land Management (BLM), *(Interior Dept.), Minerals, Realty, and Resource Protection,* 1849 C St. N.W., #3224 20240; (202) 208-4201. Fax, (202) 208-4800. Vacant, Assistant Director.
Web, www.blm.gov

Evaluates and classifies onshore oil, natural gas, geothermal resources, and all solid energy and mineral resources, including coal and uranium on federal lands. Develops and administers regulations for fluid and solid mineral leasing on national lands and on the subsurface of land where fluid and solid mineral rights have been reserved for the federal government.

Economic Research Service *(Agriculture Dept.),* 1800 M St. N.W., #5120N 20036; (202) 694-5200. Fax, (202) 694-5792. Susan E. Offutt, Administrator; Demcey Johnson, Chief, Field Crops, (202) 694-5300; Daniel L. Pick, Chief, Specialty Crops, (202) 694-5250.
Web, www.ers.usda.gov

Conducts market research; studies and forecasts domestic supply-and-demand trends for fruits and vegetables.

Energy Dept. (DOE), *1000 Independence Ave. S.W., #7A257 20585; (202) 586-6210. Fax, (202) 586-4403. Spencer Abraham, Secretary. Information, (202) 586-5575. Press, (202) 586-4940. Locator, (202) 586-5000.*
Web, www.energy.gov

Decides major energy policy issues and acts as principal adviser to the president on energy matters, including trade issues, strategic reserves, and nuclear power; acts as principal spokesperson for the department.

Energy Dept. (DOE), *1000 Independence Ave. S.W., #7B252 20585; (202) 586-5500. Fax, (202) 586-7644. Kyle E. McSlarrow, Deputy Secretary. Information, (202) 586-5575. Press, (202) 586-4940. Locator, (202) 586-5000.*
Web, www.energy.gov

Manages departmental programs in conservation and renewable energy, fossil energy, energy research, the Energy Information Administration, nuclear energy, civilian radioactive waste management, and the power marketing administrations.

Energy Dept. (DOE), *1000 Independence Ave. S.W. 20585; (202) 586-7700. Fax, (202) 586-0148. Robert G. Card, Under Secretary. Information, (202) 586-5575. Press, (202) 586-4940. Locator, (202) 586-5000.*
Web, www.energy.gov

Manages departmental programs in defense, environmental safety and health, and waste management (including radioactive and nuclear waste); responsible for all administration and management matters and for regulatory and information programs.

Energy Dept. (DOE), *Defense Nuclear Nonproliferation: National Nuclear Security Administration,* 1000 Independence Ave. S.W., #7A049 20585; (202) 586-0645. Fax, (202) 586-0862. Ambassador Linton F. Brooks, Administrator (Acting).
Web, www.nn.doe.gov

Provides intelligence community with technical and operational expertise on foreign nuclear and energy issues. Oversees programs to prevent the spread of nuclear, chemical, and biological weapons and missiles for their delivery. Partners with Russia and other former Soviet states to secure weapons of mass destruction materials and expertise; works to strengthen legal and institutional nonproliferation norms; builds technologies to detect proliferation activities; and promotes the safe use of nuclear power.

Energy Dept. (DOE), *Economic Impact and Diversity,* 1000 Independence Ave. S.W., #5B110 20585; (202) 586-8383. Fax, (202) 586-3075. Theresa Alvillar-Speake, Director.
Web, www.hr.doe.gov/ed/index.html

Researches the effects of government energy policies on minority businesses; offers technical and financial assistance to minority businesses, educational institutions, and developmental organizations to encourage their participation in energy research, development, and conservation; acts as an information clearinghouse.

Energy Dept. (DOE), *Emergency Operations,* 1000 Independence Ave. S.W., #GH060 20585; (202) 586-9892. Fax, (202) 586-3904. Richard Arkin, Director (Acting).
Web, www.energy.gov

Works to ensure coordinated Energy Dept. responses to energy-related emergencies. Recommends policies to mitigate the effects of energy supply crises on the United States; recommends government responses to energy emergencies.

Energy Dept. (DOE), *Inventions and Innovation,* 1000 Independence Ave. S.W., #6B056 20585; (202) 586-5772. Fax, (202) 586-3000. Lisa Barnet, Director.
Web, www.oit.doe.gov/inventions

Provides financial assistance for establishing technical performance and conducting early development of innovative ideas and inventions that have a significant energy

ENERGY DEPARTMENT

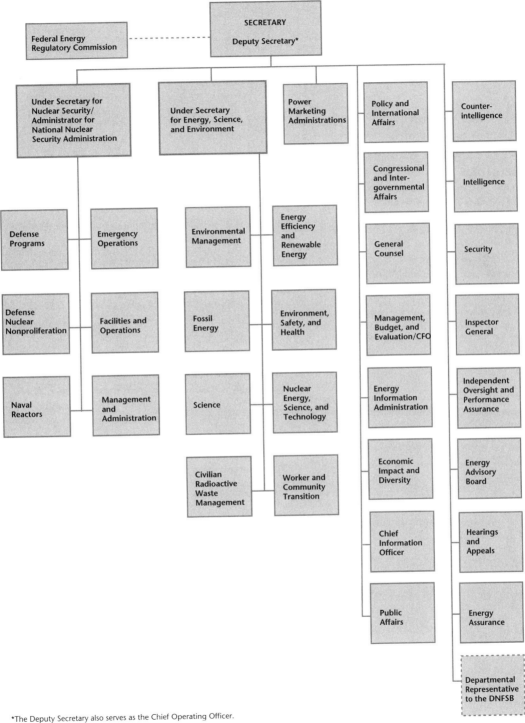

*The Deputy Secretary also serves as the Chief Operating Officer.

saving impact and future commercial market potential. Offers technical guidance and commercialization support to successful applicants.

Energy Dept. (DOE), *Policy, 1000 Independence Ave. S.W., #7C034 20585; (202) 586-5316. Fax, (202) 586-3047. Margot Anderson, Deputy Assistant Secretary.*
Web, www.osti.gov/policy

Serves as principal adviser to the secretary, deputy secretary, and undersecretary in formulating and evaluating departmental policy. Reviews programs, budgets, regulations, and legislative proposals to ensure consistency with departmental policy.

Energy Dept. (DOE), *Secretary of Energy Advisory Board, 1000 Independence Ave. S.W., #6F055 20585; (202) 586-7092. Fax, (202) 586-6279. Craig R. Reed, Executive Director.*
Web, www.hr.doe.gov/seab

Provides the secretary with advice and long-range guidance on the department's research and development, energy, environmental, and national defense-related activities.

Energy Information Administration (EIA), *(Energy Dept.), 1000 Independence Ave. S.W., #2H027 20585; (202) 586-4361. Fax, (202) 586-0329. Guy F. Caruso, Administrator (Acting).*
Web, www.eia.doe.gov

Collects and publishes data on national and international energy reserves, financial status of energy-producing companies, production, demand, consumption, and other areas; provides long- and short-term analyses of energy trends and data.

Energy Information Administration (EIA), *(Energy Dept.), Energy Markets and End Use, 1000 Independence Ave. S.W., #2G-090 20585; (202) 586-1617. Fax, (202) 586-9753. W. Calvin Kilgore, Director.*
General e-mail, infoctr@eia.doe.gov
Web, www.eia.doe.gov

Designs, develops, and maintains statistical and short-term forecasting information systems concerning consumption and other subjects that cut across energy sources. Formulates and administers financial data reporting requirements for major energy companies. Maintains survey on energy supply and use.

Energy Information Administration (EIA), *(Energy Dept.), Integrated Analysis and Forecasting, 1000 Independence Ave. S.W., EI-80, #2F081 20585; (202) 586-2222. Fax, (202) 586-3045. Mary J. Hutzler, Director. Library, (202) 586-9534.*
Web, www.eia.doe.gov

Analyzes and forecasts alternative energy futures. Develops, applies, and maintains modeling systems for analyzing the interactions of demand, conversion, and supply for all energy sources and their economic and environmental impacts. Concerned with emerging energy markets and U.S. dependence on petroleum imports.

Environment, Safety, and Health *(Energy Dept.), 1000 Independence Ave. S.W., #7A097 20585; (202) 586-6151. Fax, (202) 586-0956. Beverly Cook, Assistant Secretary.*
Web, www.eh.doe.gov

Ensures that Energy Dept. programs comply with federal policies and standards designed to protect the environment and government property. Approves all environmental impact statements prepared by the department. Oversees health and nonnuclear safety conditions at Energy Dept. facilities.

Federal Energy Regulatory Commission (FERC), *(Energy Dept.), 888 1st St. N.E., #11A 20426; (202) 502-8000. Fax, (202) 208-0064. Patrick Henry Wood III, Chair. Information, (202) 502-8200. Press, (202) 508-8680. Dockets, (202) 502-8714.*
Web, www.ferc.fed.us

Establishes and enforces interstate oil pipeline rates, charges, and valuations and rates and charges for wholesale electric power transmission, sale, and interconnection. Regulates the construction and operation of interstate natural gas facilities and the interstate rates for resale and transportation of natural gas. Issues licenses for nonfederal hydroelectric projects and establishes accounting rules and procedures for utilities.

Interior Dept. (DOI), *Land and Minerals Management, 1849 C St. N.W., #7328 20240; (202) 208-5676. Fax, (202) 208-3144. Rebecca Watson, Assistant Secretary.*
Web, www.doi.gov

Directs and supervises the Bureau of Land Management, the Minerals Management Service, and the Office of Surface Mining and Reclamation Enforcement. Supervises programs associated with land use planning, onshore and offshore minerals, surface mining reclamation and enforcement, and outer continental shelf minerals management.

Office of Management and Budget (OMB), *(Executive Office of the President), Energy and Science, New Executive Office Bldg., 725 17th St. N.W., #8002 20503; (202) 395-3404. Fax, (202) 395-3049. Mark Weatherly, Deputy Associate Director.*
Web, www.whitehouse.gov/omb

Advises and assists the president in preparing the budget for energy programs; coordinates OMB energy policy and programs.

Office of Science (*Energy Dept.*), *1000 Independence Ave. S.W., #7B058 20585; (202) 586-5430. Fax, (202) 586-4120. Raymond L. Orbach, Director.*
Web, www.science.doe.gov

Advises the secretary on the department's physical science research and energy research and development programs; the use of multipurpose laboratories (except weapons laboratories); and education and training for basic and applied research activities, including fellowships for university researchers. Manages the department's high energy and nuclear physics programs and the fusion energy program. Conducts environmental and health-related research and development programs, including studies of energy-related pollutants and hazardous materials.

Office of Science and Technology Policy (OSTP), (*Executive Office of the President*), *Dwight D. Eisenhower Executive Office Bldg. 20502; (202) 456-7116. Fax, (202) 456-6021. John H. Marburger III, Director.*
General e-mail, information@ostp.eop.gov
Web, www.ostp.gov

Provides the president with policy analysis on scientific and technological matters, including energy policy and technology issues; coordinates executive office and federal agency responses to these issues; evaluates the effectiveness of scientific and technological programs.

Treasury Dept., *Tax Analysis: Business Taxation, 1500 Pennsylvania Ave. N.W., #4025 20220; (202) 622-1782. Fax, (202) 622-2969. Geraldine Gerardi, Director.*
Web, www.ustreas.gov

Develops and provides economic analysis of business taxation policy relating to energy matters, including tax incentives for alternative energy usage and development, gasoline and automobile efficiency taxes, and tax incentives designed to encourage industrial conversion from oil to coal in industrial facilities.

CONGRESS

General Accounting Office (GAO), *Natural Resources and Environment, 441 G St. N.W., MS 2T23A 20548; (202) 512-9894. Fax, (202) 512-8774. Robert A. Robinson, Managing Director.*
Web, www.gao.gov

Independent, nonpartisan agency in the legislative branch. Audits, analyzes, and reports on efficiency and effectiveness of the Defense, Energy, and Interior Depts. Addresses governmentwide science issues and the pro-

duction, regulation, and consumption of all forms of energy.

House Appropriations Committee, *Subcommittee on Energy and Water Development, 2362 RHOB 20515; (202) 225-3421. Rep. David L. Hobson, R-Ohio, Chair; Robert Schmidt, Staff Director.*
Web, www.house.gov/appropriations

Jurisdiction over legislation to appropriate funds for the Energy Dept. (except for the Economic Regulatory Administration; Energy Information Administration; strategic petroleum reserve; naval petroleum and oil shale reserves; fossil energy research and development; energy conservation; alternative fuels production; and related matters), the Nuclear Regulatory Commission, the Tennessee Valley Authority, the Federal Energy Regulatory Commission, and the federal power marketing administrations.

House Appropriations Committee, *Subcommittee on Interior, B308 RHOB 20515; (202) 225-3081. Fax, (202) 225-9069. Rep. Charles H. Taylor, R-N.C., Chair; Deborah A. Weatherly, Staff Director.*
Web, www.house.gov/appropriations

Jurisdiction over legislation to appropriate funds for the Interior Dept.; strategic petroleum reserve and naval petroleum and oil shale reserves; clean coal technology; fossil energy research and development; energy conservation; alternate fuels production; and related matters.

House Energy and Commerce Committee, *2125 RHOB 20515; (202) 225-2927. Fax, (202) 225-1919. Rep. Billy Tauzin, R-La., Chair; David V. Marventano, Staff Director.*
General e-mail, commerce@mail.house.gov
Web, energycommerce.house.gov

Jurisdiction over measures relating to general management of the Energy Dept., the management and all functions of the Federal Energy Regulatory Commission, and national energy policy generally. Has a special oversight function with respect to all laws, programs, and government activities affecting nuclear and other energy, and nonmilitary nuclear energy and research and development, including the disposal of nuclear waste.

House Energy and Commerce Committee, *Subcommittee on Energy and Air Quality, 2125 RHOB 20515; (202) 225-2927. Fax, (202) 225-1919. Rep. Joe L. Barton, R-Texas, Chair; David V. Marventano, Staff Director.*
General e-mail, commerce@mail.house.gov
Web, energycommerce.house.gov

Jurisdiction over legislation on energy policy, regulation, conservation, exploration, production, distribution, storage, and pricing; commercialization and utilization of new technologies, including liquefied natural gas projects; and measures relating to the Energy Dept., and the Federal Energy Regulatory Commission.

House Government Reform Committee, *Subcommittee on Energy Policy, Natural Resources, and Regulatory Affairs,* B377 RHOB 20515; (202) 225-4407. Fax, (202) 225-2441. Rep. Doug Ose, R-Calif., Chair; Dan Skopec, Staff Director.

Web, www.house.gov/reform

Oversight of Energy Dept., Nuclear Regulatory Commission, and Tennessee Valley Authority.

House Resources Committee, *Subcommittee on Energy and Mineral Resources,* 1626 LHOB 20515; (202) 225-9297. Fax, (202) 225-5255. Rep. Barbara Cubin, R-Wyo., Chair; Jack Belcher, Staff Director.

General e-mail, energy.minerals@mail.house.gov

Web, resourcescommittee.house.gov

Jurisdiction over conservation of the U.S. uranium supply, the U.S. Geological Survey (except water-related programs), mineral land laws, mining, and mineral resources on public lands.

House Resources Committee, *Subcommittee on Water and Power,* 1522 LHOB 20515; (202) 225-8331. Fax, (202) 226-6953. Rep. Ken Calvert, R-Calif., Chair; Joshua Johnson, Staff Director.

General e-mail, water.power@mail.house.gov

Web, resourcescommittee.house.gov

Jurisdiction over water-related programs of the U.S. Geological Survey, saline water research and development, water resources research programs, and matters related to the Water Resources Planning Act.

House Science Committee, 2320 RHOB 20515; (202) 225-6371. Fax, (202) 226-0113. Rep. Sherwood Boehlert, R-N.Y., Chair; David Goldston, Staff Director.

General e-mail, science@mail.house.gov

Web, www.house.gov/science

Jurisdiction over legislation on all nonmilitary energy research and development.

House Small Business Committee, 2361 RHOB 20515; (202) 225-5821. Fax, (202) 225-3587. Rep. Donald Manzullo, R-Ill., Chair; J. Matthew Szymanski, Chief of Staff.

General e-mail, smbiz@mail.house.gov

Web, www.house.gov/smbiz

Studies and makes recommendations on energy allocation and marketing, and energy research and development contracts as they relate to small business.

House Ways and Means Committee, 1102 LHOB 20515; (202) 225-3625. Fax, (202) 225-2610. Rep. Bill Thomas, R-Calif., Chair; Allison Giles, Chief of Staff.

General e-mail, contactwaysandmeans@mail.house.gov

Web, waysandmeans.house.gov

Jurisdiction over legislation on taxes, tariffs, and trade measures relating to energy.

Joint Committee on Taxation, 1015 LHOB 20515; (202) 225-3621. Fax, (202) 225-0832. Rep. Bill Thomas, R-Calif., Chair; George Yin, Chief of Staff.

Web, www.house.gov/jct

Performs staff work for House Ways and Means and Senate Finance committees on legislation involving internal revenue, including taxation of energy producers, transporters, and consumers. Provides revenue estimates for all tax legislation.

Senate Appropriations Committee, *Subcommittee on Energy and Water Development,* SD-129 20510; (202) 224-7260. Fax, (202) 228-2322. Sen. Pete V. Domenici, R-N.M., Chair; Clay Sell, Clerk.

Web, appropriations.senate.gov

Jurisdiction over legislation to appropriate funds for the Energy Dept. (except for the Energy Regulatory Administration; Energy Information Administration; strategic petroleum reserve; fossil energy research, development, and construction; and energy conservation); the Federal Energy Regulatory Commission; the federal power marketing administrations; the Nuclear Regulatory Commission; and the Tennessee Valley Authority.

Senate Appropriations Committee, *Subcommittee on Interior and Related Agencies,* SD-131 20510; (202) 224-7233. Fax, (202) 228-4532. Sen. Conrad Burns, R-Mont., Chair; Bruce Evans, Clerk.

Web, appropriations.senate.gov

Jurisdiction over legislation to appropriate funds for the Energy Information Administration; economic regulation; strategic petroleum reserve; energy production, demonstration, and distribution; fossil energy research, development, and construction; energy conservation; civilian (nonnuclear) programs in the Energy Dept.; and related matters.

Senate Energy and Natural Resources Committee, SD-364 20510; (202) 224-4971. Fax, (202) 224-6163. Sen. Pete V. Domenici, R-N.M., Chair; Alex Flint, Staff Director.

General e-mail, committee@energy.senate.gov

Web, energy.senate.gov

Jurisdiction over legislation on energy policy, regulation, and conservation; research and development; nonmilitary development of nuclear energy; oil and gas production and distribution (including price); energy-related aspects of deepwater ports; hydroelectric power; coal production and distribution; mining, mineral land laws, and mineral conservation; leasing and the extraction of minerals from the ocean and outer continental shelf lands; and naval petroleum reserves in Alaska. Jurisdiction over legislation on the Federal Energy Regulatory Commission. Oversees the Energy Dept., Tennessee Valley Authority, and the U.S. Geological Survey.

Senate Energy and Natural Resources Committee, *Subcommittee on Energy, SD-364 20510; (202) 224-4971. Fax, (202) 224-6163. Sen. Lamar Alexander, R-Tenn., Chair; Scott O'Malia, Professional Staff Member.*
General e-mail, energy-sub@energy.senate.gov
Web, energy.senate.gov

Jurisdiction over legislation on regulatory functions of nuclear energy; nonmilitary energy research and development; commercialization and utilization of new technologies; global climate changes; energy conservation; and liquefied natural gas projects.

Senate Finance Committee, *SD-219 20510; (202) 224-4515. Fax, (202) 228-0554. Sen. Charles E. Grassley, R-Iowa, Chair; Kolan L. Davis, Staff Director.*
Web, finance.senate.gov

Holds hearings on legislation concerning taxes, tariffs, and trade measures relating to energy, such as oil import fees.

Senate Special Committee on Aging, *SD-G31 20510; (202) 224-5364. Fax, (202) 224-8660. Sen. Larry E. Craig, R-Idaho, Chair; Lupe Wissel, Staff Director.*
Web, aging.senate.gov

Studies and makes recommendations on the availability of energy to older people and on the adequacy of federal energy programs for the elderly.

NONPROFIT

American Assn. of Blacks in Energy, *927 15th St. N.W., #200 20005; (202) 371-9530. Fax, (202) 371-9218. Robert L. Hill, Executive Director.*
General e-mail, aabe@aabe.org
Web, www.aabe.org

Encourages participation of African Americans and other minorities in formulating energy policy.

American Boiler Manufacturers Assn., *4001 N. 9th St., #226, Arlington, VA 22203; (703) 522-7350. Fax, (703) 522-2665. Randall Rawson, President.*
Web, www.abma.com

Membership: manufacturers of boiler systems and boiler-related products, including fuel-burning systems. Interests include energy and environmental issues.

Consumer Energy Council of America, *2000 L St. N.W., #802 20036-4907; (202) 659-0404. Fax, (202) 659-0407. Ellen Berman, President.*
General e-mail, outreach@cecarf.org
Web, www.cecarf.org

Analyzes economic and social effects of energy policies; develops long-range conservation and load-management strategies for utilities; designs pilot programs for and conducts research on conservation initiatives. Builds consensus among public- and private-sector organizations, state and local groups, businesses, utilities, consumers, environmentalists, government agencies, and others on energy policy issues. Interests include transportation policies, transmission siting and certification, air pollution emissions trading, oil overcharge funds, and appliance rebate programs. Conducts consumer education campaigns.

Energy Bar Assn., *2175 K St. N.W., #600 20037-1828; (202) 223-5625. Fax, (202) 833-5596. Lorna Wilson, Administrator.*
General e-mail, admin@eba-net.org
Web, www.eba-net.org

Membership: lawyers interested in all areas of energy law. Interests include administration of laws covering production, development, conservation, transmission, and economic regulation of energy.

National Assn. of Energy Service Companies, *1615 M St. N.W., #800 20036; (202) 822-0950. Fax, (202) 822-0955. Terry E. Singer, Executive Director.*
Web, www.naesco.org

Membership: energy service companies, equipment manufacturers, affiliates of utilities, financial institutions, and governmental and other organizations involved in energy conservation and alternative energy projects. Acts as an energy information clearinghouse; sponsors conferences and seminars. Monitors legislation and regulations affecting the industry.

National Assn. of Regulatory Utility Commissioners, *1101 Vermont Ave. N.W., #200 20005; (202) 898-2200. Fax, (202) 898-2213. Charles Gray, Executive Director. Press, (202) 898-2205.*
Web, www.naruc.org

Membership: members of federal, state, municipal, and Canadian regulatory commissions that have jurisdiction over utilities and carriers. Interests include electricity, natural gas, and nuclear power.

National Governors Assn. (NGA), *Natural Resources,* 444 N. Capitol St. N.W., #267 20001-1512; (202) 624-5339. Fax, (202) 624-5313. Diane S. Shea, Staff Director.

General e-mail, webmaster@nga.org

Web, www.nga.org

Develops governors' recommendations on energy and environmental issues and presents these policies to Congress and federal agencies.

Paper Allied-Industrial, Chemical, and Energy Workers International Union, *Government Relations, Washington Office,* 727 15th St. N.W., #700 20005; (202) 293-7939. Fax, (202) 293-7888. Pete Strader, Legislative Director. Information, (800) 432-6229.

Web, www.paceunion.org

Membership: approximately 310,000 workers in the energy, chemical, pharmaceutical, and allied industries. Assists members with contract negotiation and grievances; conducts training programs and workshops. Monitors legislation and regulations. (Headquarters in Nashville, Tenn.; affiliated with the AFL-CIO.)

Southern States Energy Board, *Washington Office,* P.O. Box 34606 20043; (202) 667-7303. Fax, (202) 667-7313. Carolyn C. Drake, Director.

General e-mail, sseb@sseb.org

Web, www.sseb.org

Interstate compact organization that serves as regional representative of sixteen southern states, Puerto Rico, and the Virgin Islands for energy and environmental issues. (Headquarters in Norcross, Ga.)

SRI International, *Washington Office,* 1100 Wilson Blvd., #2800, Arlington, VA 22209; (703) 524-2053. Fax, (703) 247-8569. John Bramer, Director.

Web, www.sri.com

Research organization that conducts policy-related energy studies and scientific research. Projects include surveys of energy supply and demand; analyses of fossil fuel, solar, and nuclear energy; the environmental effects of advanced energy technology; and energy management. (Headquarters in Menlo Park, Calif.)

U.S. Chamber of Commerce, *Environment, Technology, and Regulatory Affairs,* 1615 H St. N.W. 20062-2000; (202) 463-5533. Fax, (202) 887-3445. Bill Kovacs, Vice President.

General e-mail, environment@uschamber.com

Web, www.uschamber.com

Develops policy on all issues affecting the production, use, and conservation of energy, including transportation, energy taxes, and on- and offshore mining of energy resources.

U.S. Conference of Mayors, *Municipal Waste Management Assn.,* 1620 Eye St. N.W., 6th Floor 20006; (202) 293-7330. Fax, (202) 429-0422. J. Thomas Cochran, Executive Director.

Web, www.usmayors.org/uscm/mwma

Membership: mayors of cities with populations of 30,000 or more. Brings together local government and other organizations with a common interest in the management of solid waste and broader environment issues related to environmental protection in the urban setting.

Utility Workers Union of America, 815 16th St. N.W. 20006; (202) 347-8105. Fax, (202) 974-8201. Donald E. Wightman, President.

Web, www.uwua.org

Membership: approximately 50,000 workers in utilities and related industries. Helps members negotiate pay, benefits, and better working conditions; conducts training programs and workshops. Monitors legislation and regulations. (Affiliated with the AFL-CIO.)

Energy Conservation

AGENCIES

Energy Efficiency and Renewable Energy *(Energy Dept.),* 1000 Independence Ave. S.W., #6C016 20585; (202) 586-9220. Fax, (202) 586-9260. David K. Garman, Assistant Secretary. Information, (800) 363-3732.

Web, www.eren.doe.gov

Develops and manages programs to improve foreign and domestic markets for renewable energy sources including solar, biomass, wind, geothermal, and hydropower and to increase efficiency of energy use among residential, commercial, transportation, utility, and industrial users. Administers financial and technical assistance for state energy programs, weatherization for low-income households, and implementation of energy conservation measures by schools, hospitals, local governments, and public care institutions.

Energy Efficiency and Renewable Energy *(Energy Dept.), Industrial Technologies,* 1000 Independence Ave. S.W., #5F065, EE2F 20585; (202) 586-9232. Fax, (202) 586-9234. Robert Garland, Program Manager.

Web, www.oit.doe.gov

Conducts research and disseminates information to increase energy end-use efficiency, promote renewable energy use and industrial applications, and reduce the volume of industrial and municipal waste.

Energy Efficiency and Renewable Energy *(Energy Dept.), Weatherization and Intergovernmental Programs,* 1000 Independence Ave. S.W., #EE2K, MS 5E-052

20585; (202) 586-1510. Fax, (202) 586-1233. John Millhone, Program Manager.
Web, www.eren.dot.gov

Supports private and government efforts to improve the energy efficiency of buildings and increase use of renewable energy sources. Conducts research to make information and energy technologies available. Administers weatherization assistance program that assists elderly and low-income persons to make their homes energy efficient.

Energy Information Administration (EIA), *(Energy Dept.), Energy Consumption,* 1000 Independence Ave. S.W., #2F065, MS 2G-090, EI-63 20585; (202) 586-1126. Fax, (202) 586-0018. Dwight K. French, Director.
Web, www.eia.doe.gov

Maintains data on energy consumption in the residential, commercial, industrial, and transportation sectors. Prepares analyses on energy consumption by sector and fuel type, including the impact of conservation measures.

Housing and Urban Development Dept. (HUD), *Community Viability,* 451 7th St. S.W., #7240 20410; (202) 708-2894. Fax, (202) 708-3363. Richard H. Broun, Director.
Web, www.hud.gov

Develops policies promoting energy efficiency, conservation, and renewable sources of supply in housing and community development programs, including district heating and cooling systems and waste-to-energy cogeneration projects.

National Institute of Standards and Technology (NIST), *(Commerce Dept.), Building and Fire Research Laboratory,* 100 Bureau Dr., MS 8600, Gaithersburg, MD 20899-8600; (301) 975-6850. Fax, (301) 975-4032. Jack E. Snell, Director; James E. Hill, Deputy Director.
Web, www.bfrl.nist.gov

Develops measurement techniques, test methods, and mathematical models to encourage energy conservation in large buildings. Interests include refrigeration, lighting, infiltration and ventilation, heating and air conditioning, indoor air quality, and heat transfer in the building envelope.

CONGRESS

House Energy and Commerce Committee, *Subcommittee on Energy and Air Quality,* 2125 RHOB 20515; (202) 225-2927. Fax, (202) 225-1919. Rep. Joe L. Barton, R-Texas, Chair; David V. Marventano, Staff Director.
General e-mail, commerce@mail.house.gov
Web, energycommerce.house.gov

Jurisdiction over legislation on proposals to label appliances to indicate energy consumption and on emergency fuel allocation. Jurisdiction over legislation on energy conservation measures in housing (jurisdiction shared with House Banking and Financial Service Committee).

House Science Committee, *Subcommittee on Energy,* 390 FHOB 20515; (202) 225-9662. Fax, (202) 226-6983. Rep. Judy Biggert, R-Ill., Chair; Gabor J. Rozsa, Staff Director.
General e-mail, science@mail.house.gov
Web, www.house.gov/science

Jurisdiction over legislation on research and development of energy sources and over Energy Dept. basic research programs, including those in energy conservation and utilization; jurisdiction over legislation related to the Energy Dept.'s transportation energy conservation programs.

Joint Economic Committee, *SD-G01 20510; (202) 224-5171. Sen. Robert F. Bennett, R-Utah, Chair; Donald Marron, Executive Director.*
General e-mail, jec@jec.house.gov
Web, jec.senate.gov

Studies and makes recommendations on the conservation and expansion of energy supplies.

Senate Energy and Natural Resources Committee, SD-364 20510; (202) 224-4971. Fax, (202) 224-6163. Sen. Pete V. Domenici, R-N.M., Chair; Alex Flint, Staff Director.
General e-mail, committee@energy.senate.gov
Web, energy.senate.gov

Jurisdiction over mineral conservation and over energy conservation measures, such as emergency fuel allocation, proposals to label appliances to indicate energy consumption, gasoline rationing, and coal conversion. Jurisdiction over legislation on energy research and development, including petroleum on public lands and the U.S. uranium supply.

NONPROFIT

Alliance to Save Energy, *1200 18th St. N.W., #900 20036; (202) 857-0666. Fax, (202) 331-9588. David Nemtzow, President.*
General e-mail, info@ase.org
Web, www.ase.org

Coalition of government, business, consumer, and labor leaders concerned with increasing the efficiency of energy use. Advocates efficient use of energy; conducts research, demonstration projects, and public education programs.

American Council for an Energy-Efficient Economy (ACEEE), *1001 Connecticut Ave. N.W., #801 20036-5525; (202) 429-8873. Fax, (202) 429-2248. Steve Nadel, Executive Director.*

General e-mail, info@aceee.org

Web, www.aceee.org

Independent research organization concerned with energy policy, technologies, and conservation. Interests include informing consumers, energy efficiency in buildings and appliances, improved transportation efficiency, industrial efficiency, utility issues, and conservation in developing countries.

Environmental Defense Fund, *Washington Office, 1875 Connecticut Ave. N.W., #600 20009-5728; (202) 387-3500. Fax, (202) 234-6049. Senta Boardley, Office Manager.*

Web, www.environmentaldefense.org

Citizens' interest group staffed by lawyers, economists, and scientists. Provides information on energy issues and advocates energy conservation measures. Interests include Antarctica and the Amazon rain forest. Provides utilities and environmental organizations with energy conservation computer models. (Headquarters in New York.)

Friends of the Earth (FOE), *1025 Vermont Ave. N.W., #300 20005-6303; (202) 783-7400. Fax, (202) 783-0444. Brent Blackwelder, President.*

General e-mail, foe@foe.org

Web, www.foe.org

Environmental advocacy group. Interests include conservation and renewable energy resources and air and water pollution, including international water projects. Specializes in federal budget and tax issues related to the environment; ozone layer and groundwater protection; and World Bank and International Monetary Fund reform. Library open to the public by appointment.

International Institute for Energy Conservation, *2131 K St. N.W., #700 20037-1810; (202) 785-6420. Fax, (202) 833-2604. Harvey M. Bernstein, President.*

Web, www.cerf.org/iiec

Works with developing nations to establish sustainable growth through efficient uses of energy. Seeks to counteract air and water pollution and the threat of global warming.

National Conference of States on Building Codes and Standards, *505 Huntmar Park Dr., #210, Herndon, VA 20170; (703) 437-0100. Fax, (703) 481-3596. Robert C. Wible, Executive Director.*

Web, www.ncsbcs.org

Membership: delegates appointed by the governors of the states and territories, and individuals and organizations concerned with building standards. Prepares code reports under contract. Works with national and state organizations and governmental agencies to promote the updating and adoption of model energy conservation codes for new and existing buildings. Serves as secretariat to National Alliance for Building Regulatory Reform in the Digital Age. Maintains library of national, state, and local government building codes including energy conservation codes. Library open to members.

National Insulation Assn., *99 Canal Center Plaza, #222, Alexandria, VA 22314; (703) 683-6422. Fax, (703) 549-4838. Michele M. Jones, Executive Vice President.*

General e-mail, niainfo@insulation.org

Web, www.insulation.org

Membership: companies in the commercial and industrial insulation and asbestos abatement industries. Monitors legislation and regulations.

North American Insulation Manufacturers Assn., *44 Canal Center Plaza, #310, Alexandria, VA 22314; (703) 684-0084. Fax, (703) 684-0427. Kenneth D. Mentzer, President.*

General e-mail, insulation@naima.org

Web, www.naima.org

Membership: manufacturers of insulation products for use in homes, commercial buildings, and industrial facilities. Provides information on the use of insulation for thermal efficiency, sound control, and fire safety; monitors research in the industry. Monitors legislation and regulations.

Resources for the Future, *1616 P St. N.W. 20036; (202) 328-5000. Fax, (202) 939-3460. Paul R. Portney, President. Library, (202) 328-5089.*

General e-mail, info@rff.org

Web, www.rff.org

Research organization that conducts studies on economic and policy aspects of energy, conservation, and development of natural resources, including effects on the environment. Interests include hazardous waste, the Superfund, and biodiversity.

Sierra Club, *Washington Office, 408 C St. N.E. 20002; (202) 547-1141. Fax, (202) 547-6009. Debbie Sease, Legislative Director. Legislative hotline, (202) 675-2394.*

General e-mail, information@sierraclub.org

Web, www.sierraclub.org

Citizens' interest group that promotes protection and responsible use of the Earth's ecosystems and its natural resources. Focuses on combating global warming/greenhouse effect through energy conservation, efficient use of renewable energy resources, auto efficiency, and constraints on deforestation. Monitors federal, state, and local legislation relating to the environment and natural resources. (Headquarters in San Francisco, Calif.)

Union of Concerned Scientists, *Government Relations, Washington Office,* 1707 H St. N.W., #600 20006-3919; (202) 223-6133. Fax, (202) 223-6162. Alden Meyer, Director; Todd Perry, Washington Representative for Arms Control and International Security.
General e-mail, ucs@ucsusa.org
Web, www.ucsusa.org

Independent group of scientists and others that advocates safe and sustainable international, national, and state energy policies. Conducts research, advocacy, and educational outreach focusing on market-based strategies for the development of renewable energy and alternative fuels, transportation policy, carbon reduction, global warming, and energy efficiency. (Headquarters in Cambridge, Mass.)

Worldwatch Institute, *1776 Massachusetts Ave. N.W., 8th Floor 20036; (202) 452-1999. Fax, (202) 296-7365. Christopher Flavin, President.*
General e-mail, worldwatch@worldwatch.org
Web, www.worldwatch.org

Research organization that focuses on interdisciplinary approach to solving global environmental problems. Interests include energy conservation, renewable resources, solar power, and energy use in developing countries.

International Trade and Cooperation

AGENCIES

Agency for International Development (USAID), *Center for Environment,* 1300 Pennsylvania Ave. N.W., #3.08-B, USAID/G/ENV 20523-3800; (202) 712-1750. Fax, (202) 216-3174. Jacqueline Schafer, Deputy Assistant Administrator.
Web, www.usaid.gov/environment

Assists with the economic growth of developing countries by providing policy, technical, and financial assistance for cost-effective, reliable, and environmentally sound energy programs. Focuses on the Global Warming Initiative, private initiatives, renewable energy, energy efficiency and conservation, technology innovation, and training officials in developing countries.

Census Bureau *(Commerce Dept.), Foreign Trade Statistics,* Suitland and Silver Hill Rds., Suitland, MD 20772; (301) 763-2255. Fax, (301) 457-2645. C. Harvey Monk Jr., Chief. Trade data inquiries, (301) 763-2227.
Web, www.census.gov/foreign-trade/www/index.html

Provides information on imports and exports of energy commodities, including coal, oil, and natural gas.

Commerce Dept., *Balance of Payments,* 1441 L St. N.W., #BE-58 20230; (202) 606-9545. Fax, (202) 606-5314. Christopher L. Bach, Chief.
Web, www.bea.gov

Provides statistics on U.S. balance of trade, including figures on energy commodities.

Energy Dept. (DOE), *Emergency Operations,* 1000 Independence Ave. S.W., #GH060 20585; (202) 586-9892. Fax, (202) 586-3904. Richard Arkin, Director (Acting).
Web, www.energy.gov

Monitors international energy situations as they affect domestic market conditions; recommends policies on and government responses to energy emergencies; represents the United States in the International Energy Agency's emergency programs and NATO civil emergency preparedness activities.

Energy Dept. (DOE), *Policy,* 1000 Independence Ave. S.W., #7C034 20585; (202) 586-5316. Fax, (202) 586-3047. Margot Anderson, Deputy Assistant Secretary.
Web, www.osti.gov/policy

Advises the secretary on developing and implementing international energy policies consistent with U.S. foreign policy. Evaluates Energy Dept. programs. Represents the department in international discussions on energy matters, including the Organization for Economic Cooperation and Development's International Energy Agency. Assesses world energy price and supply trends and technological developments; studies effects of international actions on U.S. energy supply.

Energy Dept. (DOE), *Policy and International Affairs,* 1000 Independence Ave. S.W., #7C016, PI-1 20585; (202) 586-5800. Fax, (202) 586-0861. Vicki A. Bailey, Assistant Secretary.
Web, www.international.energy.gov

Monitors and evaluates energy policies of foreign nations to determine the effect on international trade; works with industry associations and the Commerce Dept. on promoting U.S. energy exports.

Energy Information Administration (EIA), *(Energy Dept.), International Economic and Greenhouse Gases,* 1000 Independence Ave. S.W., #2F081, EI81 20585; (202) 586-1441. Fax, (202) 586-3045. John J. Conti, Director.
Web, www.eia.doe.gov

Compiles, interprets, and reports international energy statistics and U.S. energy data for international energy organizations. Analyzes international energy markets; makes projections concerning world prices and trade for energy sources, including oil, natural gas, coal, and electricity; monitors world petroleum market to determine U.S. vulnerability.

Fossil Energy *(Energy Dept.), Coal and Power Import and Export,* FE-27, 19901 Germantown Rd., Germantown, MD 20874-1290; (301) 903-3820. Fax, (301) 903-1591. Barbara N. McKee, Director.
Web, www.fe.doe.gov/international

Responsible for coal and technology import and export promotion activities for the Office of Fossil Energy; assesses fossil energy markets; evaluates international research development activities; regulates transporter electricity trade.

International Trade Administration (ITA), *(Commerce Dept.), Energy,* 14th St. and Constitution Ave. N.W., #4054 20230; (202) 482-0313. Fax, (202) 482-0170. Joseph Ayoub, Director.
Web, www.ita.doc.gov/td/energy

Conducts research on the effect of federal energy policy on the business community; monitors overseas trade and investment opportunities; promotes improved market competitiveness and participation in international trade by the basic energy fuels industries. Provides export counseling; develops strategies to remove foreign trade barriers; conducts conferences and workshops.

Nonproliferation *(Energy Dept.), International Nuclear Safety,* 1000 Independence Ave. S.W., #4F094 20585; (202) 586-6641. Fax, (202) 586-8272. James M. Turner, Assistant Deputy Administrator.

Seeks to improve the safety of nuclear activities internationally and coordinates other departmental offices and government agencies in the implementation of U.S. nonproliferation policy. Promotes nuclear safety in the former Soviet Union and Eastern Europe and assists in the shutdown of plutonium production reactors. Works with other agencies to open new markets for U.S. nuclear technology.

Nuclear Regulatory Commission, *International Programs,* MS 04E21 20555; (301) 415-2344. Fax, (301) 415-2395. Janice Dunn Lee, Director.
Web, www.nrc.gov

Coordinates application review process for exports and imports of nuclear materials, facilities, and components. Makes recommendations on licensing upon completion of review process. Conducts related policy reviews.

Office of Science *(Energy Dept.),* 1000 Independence Ave. S.W., #7B058 20585; (202) 586-5430. Fax, (202) 586-4120. Raymond L. Orbach, Director.
Web, www.science.doe.gov

Coordinates energy research, science, and technology programs among producing and consuming nations; analyzes existing international research and development activities; pursues international collaboration in research and in the design, development, construction, and operation of new facilities and major scientific experiments; participates in negotiations for international cooperation activities.

State Dept., *International Energy and Commodities Policy,* 2201 C St. N.W., #3529 20520; (202) 647-3036. Fax, (202) 647-4037. Stephen J. Gallogly, Director.
Web, www.state.gov

Coordinates U.S. international energy policy related to commodities, including energy supply, and U.S. participation in the International Energy Agency; monitors cooperative multilateral and bilateral agreements related to energy; coordinates energy-related aspects of U.S. relations with other countries.

State Dept., *Nuclear Energy Affairs,* 2201 C St. N.W., #3320 A 20520; (202) 647-3310. Fax, (202) 647-0775. Richard J. K. Stratford, Director.
Web, www.state.gov

Coordinates and supervises international nuclear energy policy for the State Dept. Advises the secretary on policy matters relating to nonproliferation and export controls, nuclear technology and safeguards, and nuclear safety. Promotes adherence to the Nuclear Nonproliferation Treaty and other international agreements. Chairs the Subgroup on Nuclear Export Coordination, the interagency group that reviews nuclear export license applications. Enforces the Atomic Energy Act.

Treasury Dept., *International Affairs: Middle East and South Asia,* 1500 Pennsylvania Ave. N.W., #5400 20220; (202) 622-5504. Fax, (202) 622-0037. Larry McDonald, Director.
Web, www.ustreas.gov

Represents the department in the World Bank, International Monetary Fund, and other international institutions that address energy matters. Analyzes oil market and provides economic analyses of Arabian peninsular and South Asian countries.

U.S. International Trade Commission, *Energy, Petroleum, Benzenoid, Chemicals, Rubber, and Plastics,* 500 E St. S.W., #513 20436; (202) 205-3368. Fax, (202) 205-2150. Edmund Cappuccilli, Chief.
Web, www.usitc.gov

Advisory fact-finding agency on tariffs, commercial policy, and foreign trade matters. Analyzes data on oil, petrochemical, coal, coke, and natural gas products traded internationally; investigates effects of tariffs on certain chemical and energy imports.

U.S. Trade Representative (*Executive Office of the President*), *600 17th St. N.W., #209 20508; (202) 395-6890. Fax, (202) 395-4549. Ambassador Robert B. Zoellick, U.S. Trade Representative. Information, (202) 395-8787. Press, (202) 395-3230.*

Web, www.ustr.gov

Serves as principal adviser to the president and primary trade negotiator on international trade policy. Develops and coordinates energy trade matters among government agencies.

CONGRESS

House International Relations Committee, *2170 RHOB 20515; (202) 225-5021. Fax, (202) 226-2831. Rep. Henry J. Hyde, R-Ill., Chair; Thomas E. Mooney, Chief of Staff.*

General e-mail, hirc@mail.house.gov

Web, www.house.gov/international_relations

Jurisdiction over most legislation on U.S. participation in international energy programs and legislation related to the economic aspects of trading nuclear technology and materials with foreign countries.

House Ways and Means Committee, *1102 LHOB 20515; (202) 225-3625. Fax, (202) 225-2610. Rep. Bill Thomas, R-Calif., Chair; Allison Giles, Chief of Staff.*

General e-mail, contactwaysandmeans@mail.house.gov

Web, waysandmeans.house.gov

Jurisdiction over legislation on taxes, tariffs, and trade measures relating to energy, such as oil import fees.

Senate Energy and Natural Resources Committee, *SD-364 20510; (202) 224-4971. Fax, (202) 224-6163. Sen. Pete V. Domenici, R-N.M., Chair; Alex Flint, Staff Director.*

General e-mail, committee@energy.senate.gov

Web, energy.senate.gov

Jurisdiction over legislation relating to U.S. participation in international energy programs. (Jurisdiction shared with Senate Foreign Relations Committee.)

Senate Finance Committee, *SD-219 20510; (202) 224-4515. Fax, (202) 228-0554. Sen. Charles E. Grassley, R-Iowa, Chair; Kolan L. Davis, Staff Director.*

Web, finance.senate.gov

Holds hearings on legislation concerning taxes, tariffs, and trade measures relating to energy, such as oil import fees.

Senate Foreign Relations Committee, *SD-450 20510; (202) 224-4651. Fax, (202) 228-1608. Sen. Richard G. Lugar, R-Ind., Chair; Kenneth A. Myers, Staff Director.*

Web, foreign.senate.gov

Jurisdiction over legislation related to the economic aspects of trading nuclear technology and materials. Jurisdiction over legislation relating to U.S. participation in international energy programs. (Jurisdiction shared with Senate Energy and Natural Resources Committee.)

INTERNATIONAL ORGANIZATIONS

European Commission, *Press and Public Affairs, Washington Office,* *2300 M St. N.W. 20037; (202) 862-9500. Fax, (202) 429-1766. Willy Helin, Director; Günter Burghardt, Ambassador.*

Web, www.eurunion.org

Provides information on European Union energy policy, initiatives, research activities, and selected statistics. Library open to the public by appointment. (Headquarters in Brussels.)

International Energy Agency (*Organization for Economic Cooperation and Development*), *Washington Office,* *2001 L St. N.W., #650 20036-4922; (202) 785-6323. Fax, (202) 785-0350. Matthew Brosius, Director.*

General e-mail, washington.contact@oecd.org

Web, www.oecdwash.org

Promotes cooperation in energy research among developed nations; assists developing countries in negotiations with energy-producing nations; prepares plans for international emergency energy allocation. Publishes statistics and analyses on most aspects of energy. Washington Center maintains reference library open to the public; offers for sale publications of the International Energy Agency. (Headquarters in Paris.)

United Nations Information Centre, *1775 K St. N.W., #400 20006; (202) 331-8670. Fax, (202) 331-9191. Catherine O'Neill, Director.*

Web, www.unicwash.org

Center for reference publications of the United Nations; publications include *World Energy Statistics, Energy Balances and Electricity Profiles,* and other statistical material on energy. Library open to the public.

NONPROFIT

Atlantic Council of the United States, *Energy and Environment Program,* *910 17th St. N.W., #1000 20006; (202) 778-4942. Fax, (202) 463-7241. Eliane Lomax, Associate Director. Information, (202) 463-7226.*

General e-mail, info@acus.org

Web, www.acus.org

Studies and makes policy recommendations on international energy relationships for all energy sources, including oil, natural gas, coal, synthetic and renewable fuels, and nuclear power.

U.S. Energy Assn., *1300 Pennsylvania Ave. N.W., #550, Mailbox 142 20004-3022; (202) 312-1230. Fax, (202) 682-1682. Barry K. Worthington, Executive Director.*
Web, www.usea.org

Membership: energy-related organizations, including professional, trade, and government groups. Participates in the World Energy Council (headquartered in London). Sponsors seminars and conferences on energy resources, policy management, technology, utilization, and conservation.

World Energy Efficiency Assn., *910 17th St. N.W., #1000 20006; (202) 778-4942. Fax, (202) 463-7241. Donald L. Guertin, Executive Director.*
General e-mail, info@weea.org
Web, www.weea.org

Assists developing countries in accessing information on energy efficiency programs, technologies, and measures; fosters international cooperation in energy efficiency efforts.

Statistics

AGENCIES

Bureau of Labor Statistics (BLS), *(Labor Dept.), Producer Price Index,* *2 Massachusetts Ave. N.E., #3840 20212-0001; (202) 691-7727. Fax, (202) 691-7754. Roger Hippen, Manager, Energy Programs. Information, (202) 691-7705.*
General e-mail, ppi-info@bls.gov
Web, www.bls.gov/ppi/home.htm

Compiles statistics on energy for the Producer Price Index; analyzes movement of prices for natural gas, petroleum, coal, and electric power in the primary commercial and industrial markets.

Energy Information Administration (EIA), *(Energy Dept.), National Energy Information Center,* *1000 Independence Ave. S.W., #1E238, EI-30 20585; (202) 586-8800. Fax, (202) 586-0727. Nancy Nicoletti, Chief.*
Web, www.eia.doe.gov

Catalogs and distributes energy data; acts as a clearinghouse for statistical information on energy; makes referrals for technical information. Reading room of EIA publications open to the public.

NONPROFIT

American Gas Assn., *Statistics,* *400 N. Capitol St. N.W., 4th Floor 20001; (202) 824-7000. Fax, (202) 824-7115. Paul Pierson, Manager.*
Web, www.aga.org

Issues statistics on the gas utility industry, including supply and reserves.

American Petroleum Institute, *Policy Analysis and Statistics,* *1220 L St. N.W. 20005; (202) 682-8532. Fax, (202) 682-8408. John Felmy, Chief Economist. Information, (202) 682-8520. Library, (202) 682-8042.*
General e-mail, statistics@api.org
Web, www.api.org

Provides basic statistical information on petroleum industry operations, market conditions, and environmental, health, and safety performance. Includes data on supply and demand of crude oil and petroleum products, exports and imports, refinery operations, drilling activities and costs, environmental expenditures, injuries, illnesses and fatalities, oil spills, and emissions.

Edison Electric Institute, *Statistics,* *701 Pennsylvania Ave. N.W. 20004; (202) 508-5574. Fax, (202) 508-5542. Steven Faruenheim, Manager.*
General e-mail, statistics@eei.org
Web, www.eei.org

Provides statistics on electric utility operations, including the *Statistical Yearbook of the Electric Utility Industry,* which contains data on the capacity, generation, sales, customers, revenue, and finances of the electric utility industry.

National Mining Assn., *Policy Analysis,* *101 Constitution Ave. N.W., #500E 20001; (202) 463-2600. Fax, (202) 463-2665. Constance D. Holmes, Senior Vice President.*
Web, www.nma.org

Collects, analyzes, and distributes statistics on the mining industry, including statistics on the production, transportation, and consumption of coal.

❄ ELECTRICITY

AGENCIES

Energy Dept. (DOE), *Bonneville Power Administration, Washington Office,* *1000 Independence Ave. S.W., #8G061 20585; (202) 586-5640. Fax, (202) 586-6762. Jeffrey K. Stier, Vice President.*
Web, www.bpa.gov

Coordinates marketing of electric power and energy for the Bonneville Power Administration; serves as liaison between the Bonneville Power Administration and Congress. (Headquarters in Portland, Ore.)

Energy Dept. (DOE), *Power Marketing Liaison Office,* 1000 Independence Ave. S.W., #8G027 20585; (202) 586-5581. Fax, (202) 586-6261. Robert M. Porter, Administrator.
Web, www.energy.gov

Serves as a liaison among the Southeastern, Southwestern, and Western area power administrations; other federal agencies; and Congress. Coordinates marketing of electric power from federally owned hydropower projects.

Energy Information Administration (EIA), *(Energy Dept.), Coal, Nuclear, Electric, and Alternate Fuels,* 950 L'Enfant Plaza S.W., #6070 20024 (mailing address: 1000 Independence Ave. S.W. 20585); (202) 287-1990. Fax, (202) 287-1933. Robert M. Schnaff, Director (Acting).
Web, www.eia.doe.gov

Prepares analyses and forecasts on electric power supplies, including the effects of government policies and regulatory actions on capacity, consumption, finances, and rates. Publishes statistics on electric power industry.

Tennessee Valley Authority, *Government Relations, Washington Office,* 1 Massachusetts Ave. N.W., #300 20001; (202) 898-2999. Fax, (202) 898-2998. Linda Whitestone, Vice President.
Web, www.tva.gov

Coordinates resource conservation, development, and land-use programs in the Tennessee River Valley. Produces and supplies wholesale power to municipal and cooperative electric systems, federal installations, and some industries. (Headquarters in Knoxville, Tenn.)

CONGRESS

House Energy and Commerce Committee, *Subcommittee on Energy and Air Quality,* 2125 RHOB 20515; (202) 225-2927. Fax, (202) 225-1919. Rep. Joe L. Barton, R-Texas, Chair; David V. Marventano, Staff Director.
General e-mail, commerce@mail.house.gov
Web, energycommerce.house.gov

Jurisdiction over legislation on electric utilities regulation, energy plant siting (including nuclear facilities), and proposals to label appliances to indicate energy consumption.

House Resources Committee, *Subcommittee on Water and Power,* 1522 LHOB 20515; (202) 225-8331. Fax, (202) 226-6953. Rep. Ken Calvert, R-Calif., Chair; Joshua Johnson, Staff Director.

General e-mail, water.power@mail.house.gov
Web, resourcescommittee.house.gov

Jurisdiction over legislation on the federal power administrations.

House Science Committee, *Subcommittee on Energy,* 390 FHOB 20515; (202) 225-9662. Fax, (202) 226-6983. Rep. Judy Biggert, R-Ill., Chair; Gabor J. Rozsa, Staff Director.
General e-mail, science@mail.house.gov
Web, www.house.gov/science

Jurisdiction over legislation on electric energy research and development.

House Transportation and Infrastructure Committee, *Subcommittee on Water Resources and Environment,* B376 RHOB 20515; (202) 225-4360. Fax, (202) 226-5435. Rep. John J. "Jimmy" Duncan Jr., R-Tenn., Chair; Susan Bodine, Staff Director.
General e-mail, transcomm@mail.house.gov
Web, www.house.gov/transportation

Jurisdiction over the Tennessee Valley Authority.

Senate Energy and Natural Resources Committee, *Subcommittee on Energy,* SD-364 20510; (202) 224-4971. Fax, (202) 224-6163. Sen. Lamar Alexander, R-Tenn., Chair; Scott O'Malia, Professional Staff Member.
General e-mail, energy-sub@energy.senate.gov
Web, energy.senate.gov

Jurisdiction over legislation on electric energy research and development.

Senate Energy and Natural Resources Committee, *Subcommittee on Water and Power,* SD-364 20510; (202) 224-4971. Fax, (202) 224-6163. Sen. Lisa Murkowski, R-Alaska, Chair; Colleen Deegan, Counsel.
General e-mail, water&power@energy.senate.gov
Web, energy.senate.gov

Jurisdiction over the federal power marketing administrations, hydroelectric power, and the impact of energy development on water resources.

Senate Environment and Public Works Committee, *Subcommittee on Clean Air, Climate Change, and Nuclear Safety,* SD-410 20510; (202) 224-6176. Fax, (202) 224-1273. Sen. George V. Voinovich, R-Ohio, Chair; Michael Whatley, Staff Director.
Web, epw.senate.gov

Jurisdiction over Tennessee Valley Authority legislation.

NONPROFIT

Center for Energy and Economic Development, *333 John Carlyle Dr., #530, Alexandria, VA 22314; (703) 684-6292. Fax, (703) 684-6297. Stephen L. Miller, President.*

Web, www.ceednet.org

Membership: coal, railroad, and electric utility companies and suppliers. Educates the public and policy-makers about economic, technological, and scientific research on energy resources employed in generating electricity.

Citizens for State Power, *122 S. Patrick St., Alexandria, VA 22314; (703) 739-5920. Fax, (703) 739-5924. Craig Shirley, Consulting Director.*

General e-mail, csp@sbpublicaffairs.com

Web, www.sbpublicaffairs.com

Coalition of conservative policy organizations that seeks to increase competition in the electric utility industry through federal and state deregulation.

Electric Power Supply Assn., *1401 New York Ave., 11th Floor 20005; (202) 628-8200. Fax, (202) 628-8260. Lynne H. Church, President.*

Web, www.epsa.org

Membership: power generators active in U.S. and global markets, power marketers, and suppliers of goods and services to the industry. Promotes competition in the delivery of electricity to consumers.

Electricity Consumers Resource Council, *1333 H St. N.W., West Tower, 8th Floor 20005; (202) 682-1390. Fax, (202) 289-6370. John A. Anderson, Executive Director.*

General e-mail, elcon@elcon.org

Web, www.elcon.org

Membership: large industrial users of electricity. Promotes development of coordinated federal, state, and local policies concerning electrical supply for industrial users; studies rate structures and their impact on consumers.

National Electrical Contractors Assn., *3 Bethesda Metro Center, #1100, Bethesda, MD 20814; (301) 657-3110. Fax, (301) 215-4500. John Grau, Executive Vice President.*

Web, www.necanet.org

Membership: electrical contractors who build and service electrical wiring, equipment, and appliances. Represents members in collective bargaining with union workers; sponsors research and educational programs.

National Electrical Manufacturers Assn., *1300 N. 17th St., #1847, Rosslyn, VA 22209; (703) 841-3200. Fax, (703) 841-3300. Malcolm O'Hagan, President.*

Web, www.nema.org

Membership: manufacturers of electrical products. Develops and promotes use of electrical standards; compiles and analyzes industry statistics. Interests include efficient energy management, product safety and liability, occupational safety, and the environment. Monitors international trade activities, legislation, and regulations.

National Hydropower Assn., *1 Massachusetts Ave. N.W., #850 20001; (202) 682-1700. Fax, (202) 682-9478. Linda Church Ciocci, Executive Director.*

General e-mail, help@hydro.org

Web, www.hydro.org

Membership: investor-owned utilities and municipal and independent companies that generate hydroelectric power; consulting, engineering, and law firms; and equipment suppliers and manufacturers. Focus includes regulatory relief, international marketing, and coalition building. Monitors legislation and regulations.

Public Utilities

AGENCIES

Federal Energy Regulatory Commission (FERC), *(Energy Dept.), Energy Project, 888 1st St. N.E., #6A01 20426; (202) 502-8700. Fax, (202) 219-0205. J. Mark Robinson, Director.*

Web, www.ferc.gov

Issues licenses, permits, and exemptions for hydroelectric power projects. Ensures safety of licensed dams and safeguards the environment.

Federal Energy Regulatory Commission (FERC), *(Energy Dept.), Markets, Tariffs, and Rates, 888 1st St. N.E., #8A-01 20426; (202) 502-6700. Fax, (202) 208-0193. Daniel L. Larcamp, Director.*

Web, www.ferc.gov

Establishes rates and power charges for electric energy transmission, sale, and interconnections. Regulates wholesale electric rates in interstate commerce.

Rural Utilities Service *(Agriculture Dept.), 1400 Independence Ave. S.W., #4055, MS-1510 20250-1500; (202) 720-9540. Fax, (202) 720-1725. Hilda Gay Legg, Administrator. Information, (202) 720-1255.*

Web, www.usda.gov/rus

Makes loans and loan guarantees to provide electricity, telecommunication systems, and water and waste disposal services to rural areas.

NONPROFIT

American Public Power Assn., *2301 M St. N.W. 20037; (202) 467-2900. Fax, (202) 467-2910. Alan H. Richardson, President. Library, (202) 467-2957.*

Membership: local, publicly owned electric utilities nationwide. Represents industry interests before Congress, federal agencies, and the courts; provides educational programs; collects and disseminates information; funds energy research and development projects. Library open to the public by appointment.

Edison Electric Institute, *701 Pennsylvania Ave. N.W. 20004; (202) 508-5000. Fax, (202) 508-5759. Thomas R. Kuhn, President.*
Web, www.eei.org

Membership: investor-owned electric power companies and electric utility holding companies. Interests include electric utility operation and concerns, including conservation and energy management, energy analysis, resources and environment, cogeneration and renewable energy resources, nuclear power, and research. Provides information and statistics relating to electric energy; aids member companies in generating and selling electric energy; and conducts information forums. Library open to the public by appointment.

National Assn. of Regulatory Utility Commissioners, *1101 Vermont Ave. N.W., #200 20005; (202) 898-2200. Fax, (202) 898-2213. Charles Gray, Executive Director. Press, (202) 898-2205.*
Web, www.naruc.org

Membership: members of federal, state, municipal, and Canadian regulatory commissions that have jurisdiction over utilities. Interests include electric utilities.

National Assn. of State Utility Consumer Advocates, *8380 Colesville Rd., #101, Silver Spring, MD 20910; (301) 589-6313. Fax, (301) 589-6380. Charles Acquard, Executive Director.*
General e-mail, nasuca@nasuca.org
Web, www.nasuca.org

Membership: public advocate offices authorized by states to represent ratepayer interests before state and federal utility regulatory commissions. Monitors legislation and regulatory agencies with jurisdiction over electric utilities, telecommunications, natural gas, and water; conducts conferences and workshops.

National Rural Electric Cooperative Assn., *4301 Wilson Blvd., Arlington, VA 22203-1860; (703) 907-5500. Fax, (703) 907-5516. Glenn English, Chief Executive Officer.*
Web, www.nreca.org

Membership: rural electric cooperative systems and public power and utility districts. Provides members with legislative, legal, and regulatory services. Supports

energy and environmental research and offers technical advice and assistance to developing countries.

Research and Development

AGENCIES

Energy Dept. (DOE), *Office of Science: Fusion Energy Sciences,* *19901 Germantown Rd., Germantown, MD 20874-1290; (301) 903-4941. Fax, (301) 903-8584. N. Anne Davies, Associate Director.*
Web, www.ofes.fusion.doe.gov

Conducts research and development on fusion energy for electric power generation.

National Institute of Standards and Technology (NIST), *(Commerce Dept.), Electricity Division,* *100 Bureau Dr., MS-8110, Gaithersburg, MD 20899-8110; (301) 975-2400. Fax, (301) 926-3972. Jim Olthoff, Chief.*
Web, www.eeel.nist.gov

Conducts research to characterize and define performance parameters of electrical/electronic systems, components, and materials; applies research to advance measurement instrumentation and the efficiency of electric power transmission and distribution; develops and maintains national electrical reference standards, primarily for power, energy, and related measurements, to assist in the development of new products and promote international competitiveness.

National Institute of Standards and Technology (NIST), *(Commerce Dept.), Electronics and Electrical Engineering Laboratory,* *100 Bureau Dr., Bldg. 220, #B358, MS 8100, Gaithersburg, MD 20899; (301) 975-2220. Fax, (301) 975-4091. William E. Anderson, Director.*
General e-mail, eeel@nist.gov
Web, www.eeel.nist.gov

Provides focus for research, development, and applications in the fields of electrical, electronic, quantum electric, and electromagnetic materials engineering. Interests include fundamental physical constants, practical data, measurement methods, theory, standards, technology, technical services, and international trade.

NONPROFIT

Electric Power Research Institute, *Washington Office,* *2000 L St. N.W., #805 20036; (202) 872-9222. Fax, (202) 293-2697. Barbara Bauman Tyran, Director, Government Relations.*
Web, www.epri.com

Membership: investor- and municipal-owned electric utilities and rural cooperatives. Conducts research and development in power generation and delivery technologies, including fossil fuel, nuclear, and renewable energy sources used by electric utilities. Studies energy management and utilization, including conservation and environmental issues. (Headquarters in Palo Alto, Calif.)

 **FOSSIL FUELS**

AGENCIES

Fossil Energy *(Energy Dept.), 1000 Independence Ave. S.W., #4G084 20585-1290; (202) 586-6660. Fax, (202) 586-7847. Carl Michael Smith, Assistant Secretary.*
Web, www.fe.doe.gov

Responsible for policy and management of high-risk, long-term research and development in recovering, converting, and using fossil energy, including coal, petroleum, oil shale, and unconventional sources of natural gas. Handles the petroleum reserve and the naval petroleum and oil shale reserve programs; oversees the Clean Coal Program to design and construct environmentally clean coal-burning facilities.

U.S. Geological Survey (USGS), *(Interior Dept.),* **Energy Resources Program,** *12201 Sunrise Valley Dr., Reston, VA 20192 (mailing address: 915A National Center, Reston, VA 20192); (703) 648-6641. Fax, (703) 648-5464. Vacant, Program Coordinator.*
Web, energy.usgs.gov

Conducts research on fossil energy resources of the United States and the world, including assessments of the quality, quantity, and geographic locations of natural gas, oil, and coal resources. Estimates energy resource availability and recoverability; anticipates and mitigates deleterious environmental impacts of energy resource extraction and use.

CONGRESS

House Energy and Commerce Committee, *Subcommittee on Energy and Air Quality, 2125 RHOB 20515; (202) 225-2927. Fax, (202) 225-1919. Rep. Joe L. Barton, R-Texas, Chair; David V. Marventano, Staff Director.*
General e-mail, commerce@mail.house.gov
Web, energycommerce.house.gov

Jurisdiction over legislation dealing with coal, oil, and natural gas, including proposed emergency presidential energy authority (such as rationing), proposals to create civilian petroleum reserves, petroleum and natural gas pricing and pipelines, natural gas imports, regulation of public utilities, energy plant siting, and low head hydro projects.

House Resources Committee, *Subcommittee on Energy and Mineral Resources, 1626 LHOB 20515; (202) 225-9297. Fax, (202) 225-5255. Rep. Barbara Cubin, R-Wyo., Chair; Jack Belcher, Staff Director.*
General e-mail, energy.minerals@mail.house.gov
Web, resourcescommittee.house.gov

Jurisdiction over legislation on mineral land laws; mining policy; coal, oil and gas, and mineral leasing on publicly owned land; and conservation and development of energy and natural resources in the ocean and outer continental shelf. Jurisdiction over oil and coal slurry pipelines (shared with House Transportation and Infrastructure Committee).

House Science Committee, *Subcommittee on Energy, 390 FHOB 20515; (202) 225-9662. Fax, (202) 226-6983. Rep. Judy Biggert, R-Ill., Chair; Gabor J. Rozsa, Staff Director.*
General e-mail, science@mail.house.gov
Web, www.house.gov/science

Jurisdiction over legislation on research and development of fossil fuel energy (including coal, petroleum, natural gas, oil shale, tar sand, and synthetic fuels such as liquefied and gasified coal) and over Energy Dept. basic research programs.

House Transportation and Infrastructure Committee, *Subcommittee on Economic Development, Public Buildings, and Emergency Management, 589 FHOB 20515; (202) 225-3014. Fax, (202) 226-1898. Rep. Steven C. LaTourette, R-Ohio, Chair; Matt Wallen, Staff Director.*
General e-mail, transcomm@mail.house.gov
Web, www.house.gov/transportation

Jurisdiction over legislation on oil and coal slurry pipelines. (Jurisdiction shared with House Resources Committee.)

Senate Commerce, Science, and Transportation Committee, *Subcommittee on Oceans, Fisheries, and Coast Guard, SH-227 20510; (202) 224-8172. Fax, (202) 224-9334. Sen. Olympia J. Snowe, R-Maine, Chair; Andrew Minkiewicz, Counsel Member.*
Web, commerce.senate.gov

Jurisdiction over legislation on production and development of deep seabed mining and deepwater ports. (Jurisdiction shared with Senate Energy and Natural Resources Committee.)

Senate Energy and Natural Resources Committee, *SD-364 20510; (202) 224-4971. Fax, (202) 224-6163. Sen. Pete V. Domenici, R-N.M., Chair; Alex Flint, Staff Director.*
General e-mail, committee@energy.senate.gov

Web, energy.senate.gov

Jurisdiction over legislation on fossil fuel research and development, including Energy Dept. programs; mining policy, including mineral leasing; and interstate aspects of production and distribution of coal, natural gas, and petroleum. Jurisdiction over deep seabed mining and deepwater ports. (Jurisdiction shared with Senate Commerce, Science, and Transportation Committee.)

Coal

AGENCIES

Bureau of Land Management (BLM), *(Interior Dept.), Solid Minerals Group, 1620 L St. N.W., #501 20036 (mailing address: 1849 C St. N.W., #LS501 20240); (202) 452-0350. Fax, (202) 653-7397. Brenda Aird, Group Manager.*
Web, www.blm.gov/nhp/300/wo320

Evaluates and classifies coal resources on federal lands; develops and administers leasing programs. Supervises coal mining operations on federal lands; oversees pre- and post-lease operations, including production phases of coal development. Oversees implementation of the Mining Law of 1872 and the Mineral Materials Act of 1955.

Energy Information Administration (EIA), *(Energy Dept.), Coal, Nuclear, Electric, and Alternate Fuels, 950 L'Enfant Plaza S.W., #6070 20024 (mailing address: 1000 Independence Ave. S.W. 20585); (202) 287-1990. Fax, (202) 287-1933. Robert M. Schnaff, Director (Acting).*
Web, www.eia.doe.gov

Collects data, compiles statistics, and prepares analyses and forecasts on domestic coal supply, including availability, production, costs, processing, transportation, and distribution. Publishes data on the export and import of coal; makes forecasts and provides analyses on coal imports and exports.

Federal Mine Safety and Health Review Commission, *601 New Jersey Ave. N.W., #9500 20001; (202) 434-9900. Fax, (202) 434-9906. Michael Duffy, Chair; Richard L. Baker, Executive Director, (202) 434-9905. Library, (202) 653-9935.*
Web, www.fmshrc.gov

Independent agency established by the Federal Mine Safety and Health Act of 1977. Holds fact-finding hearings and issues orders affirming, modifying, or vacating the labor secretary's enforcement actions regarding mine safety and health. Library open to the public.

Fossil Energy *(Energy Dept.), Coal Fuels and Industrial Systems, 19901 Germantown Rd., Germantown, MD 20874 (mailing address: 1000 Independence Ave. S.W., FE 24, GTN, Washington, DC 20585-1290); (301) 903-9451. Fax, (301) 903-2238. C. Lowell Miller, Director.*
Web, www.fe.doe.gov

Fosters the development and implementation of clean coal technologies in the private sector. Monitors economic and commercial efficiency program and disseminates results. Cofunded by private industry.

Interior Dept. (DOI), *Surface Mining Reclamation and Enforcement, 1951 Constitution Ave. N.W., #233 20240; (202) 208-4006. Fax, (202) 219-3106. Jeffrey D. Jarrett, Director.*
Web, www.osmre.gov/osm.htm

Administers the Surface Mining Control and Reclamation Act of 1977. Establishes and enforces national standards for the regulation and reclamation of surface coal mining and the surface effects of underground coal mining; oversees state implementation of these standards.

Mine Safety and Health Administration *(Labor Dept.), 1000 Wilson Blvd., #2176, Arlington, VA 22209-3939; (202) 693-9899. Fax, (202) 693-9801. Dave D. Lauriske, Assistant Secretary.*
Web, www.msha.gov

Administers and enforces the health and safety provisions of the Federal Mine Safety and Health Act of 1977. Monitors underground mining and processing operations of minerals, including minerals used in construction materials; produces educational materials in engineering; and assists with rescue operations following mining accidents.

CONGRESS

House Education and the Workforce Committee, *Subcommittee on Workforce Protections, 2181 RHOB 20515; (202) 225-4527. Fax, (202) 225-9571. Rep. Charlie Norwood, R-Ga., Chair; Paula Nowakowski, Staff Director.*
Web, edworkforce.house.gov

Jurisdiction over legislation on coal mining health and safety.

Senate Health, Education, Labor, and Pensions Committee, *SD-428 20510; (202) 224-5375. Fax, (202) 228-5044. Sen. Judd Gregg, R-N.H., Chair; Sharon Soderstrom, Staff Director. TTY, (202) 224-1975.*
Web, health.senate.gov

Jurisdiction over legislation on coal mining health and safety.

NONPROFIT

American Coke and Coal Chemicals Institute, *1255 23rd St. N.W., #200 20037; (202) 452-1140. Fax, (202) 833-3636. David A. Saunders, President.*

General e-mail, information@accci.org

Web, www.accci.org

Membership: producers of oven coke, metallurgical coal, and chemicals; coke sales agents; tar distillers; and builders of coke ovens and coke oven byproduct plants. Maintains committees on chemicals, coke, manufacturing and environment, safety and health, and traffic.

Assn. of Bituminous Contractors, *1815 Connecticut Ave. N.W., #620 20006; (202) 785-4440. Fax, (202) 331-8049. William H. Howe, General Counsel.*

Membership: independent and general contractors that build coal mines. Represents members before the Federal Mine Safety and Health Review Commission and in collective bargaining with the United Mine Workers of America.

Bituminous Coal Operators Assn., *1500 K St. N.W., #875 20005-1209; (202) 783-3195. Fax, (202) 783-4862. David M. Young, President.*

Membership: firms that mine bituminous coal. Represents members in collective bargaining with the United Mine Workers of America.

Coal Exporters Assn. of the United States, *101 Constitution Ave. N.W., #500E 20001; (202) 463-2654. Fax, (202) 463-2648. Constance D. Holmes, Executive Director.*

Web, www.nma.org

Membership: exporters of coal. Provides information on coal exports. Monitors legislation and regulations. (Affiliate of the National Mining Assn.)

National Coal Council, *1730 M St. N.W., #907 20036; (202) 223-1191. Fax, (202) 223-9031. Robert A. Beck, Executive Director.*

Web, www.nationalcoalcouncil.org

Membership: individuals appointed by the secretary of energy. Represents coal producers, transporters, women and minorities in mining, and manufacturers of coal-producing equipment. Makes recommendations to the secretary on issues involving coal. Monitors federal policies. Library open to the public.

National Mining Assn., *101 Constitution Ave. N.W., #500E 20001; (202) 463-2600. Fax, (202) 463-2665. Jack N. Gerard, President. Press, (202) 463-2651.*

General e-mail, nma@prime.planetcom.com

Web, www.nma.org

Membership: coal producers, coal sales and transportation companies, equipment manufacturers, consulting firms, coal resource developers and exporters, coal-burning electric utility companies, and other energy companies. Collects, analyzes, and distributes industry statistics; conducts special studies of competitive fuels, coal markets, production and consumption forecasts, and industry planning. Interests include exports, coal leasing programs, coal transportation, environmental issues, health and safety, national energy policy, slurry pipelines, and research and development, including synthetic fuels.

United Mine Workers of America, *8315 Lee Hwy., 5th Floor, Fairfax, VA 22031; (703) 208-7200. Fax, (703) 208-7132. Cecil E. Roberts, President.*

Web, www.umwa.org

Membership: coal miners and other mining workers. Represents members in collective bargaining with industry. Conducts educational, housing, and health and safety training programs; monitors federal coal mining safety programs.

Oil and Natural Gas

AGENCIES

Energy Information Administration (EIA), *(Energy Dept.), Collection and Dissemination, 1000 Independence Ave. S.W., #2E068, EI 30 20585; (202) 586-6134. Fax, (202) 586-4419. Kendrick E. Brown Jr., Director.*

General e-mail, infoctr@eia.doe.gov

Web, www.eia.doe.gov

Collects natural gas and petroleum publications; disseminates publications in print and via the Web; collects and disseminates EIA forms.

Energy Information Administration (EIA), *(Energy Dept.), Natural Gas, 1000 Independence Ave. S.W., #BE054 20585; (202) 586-5590. Fax, (202) 586-4420. Elizabeth E. Campbell, Director.*

General e-mail, infoctr@eia.doe.gov

Web, www.eia.doe.gov

Collects and publishes monthly and annual estimates of domestic crude oil, natural gas, and natural gas liquids. Performs analyses of the natural gas industry.

Energy Information Administration (EIA), *(Energy Dept.), Oil and Gas, 1000 Independence Ave. S.W., #2G024 20585; (202) 586-6401. Fax, (202) 586-9739. Kenneth A. Vagts, Director.*

General e-mail, infoctr@eia.doe.gov

Web, www.eia.doe.gov

Collects, interprets, and publishes data on domestic production, use, and distribution of oil and natural gas; analyzes and projects oil and gas reserves, resources, production, capacity, and supply; surveys and monitors alternative fuel needs during emergencies; publishes statistics.

Energy Information Administration (EIA), *(Energy Dept.), Petroleum Marketing,* 1000 Independence Ave. S.W., #2G051 20585; (202) 586-5986. Fax, (202) 586-3873. John S. Cook, Director.
General e-mail, infoctr@eia.doe.gov
Web, www.eia.doe.gov

Collects, compiles, interprets, and publishes data on domestic production, distribution, and prices of crude oil and refined petroleum products; analyzes and projects availability of petroleum supplies. Publishes statistics, including import and export data.

Fossil Energy *(Energy Dept.), Natural Gas and Petroleum Technology,* 1000 Independence Ave. S.W., #3E028 20585; (202) 586-5600. Fax, (202) 586-6221. James Slutz, Deputy Assistant Secretary.
Web, www.fe.doe.gov

Responsible for research and development programs in oil and gas exploration, production, processing, and storage; studies ways to improve efficiency of oil recovery in depleted reservoirs; coordinates and evaluates research and development among government, universities, and industrial research organizations.

Fossil Energy *(Energy Dept.), Naval Petroleum and Oil Shale Reserves,* 1000 Independence Ave. S.W., #3H076 20585; (202) 586-4685. Fax, (202) 586-4446. Anton R. Dammer, Director.
Web, www.fe.doe.gov

Develops, conserves, operates, and maintains oil fields for producing oil, natural gas, and other petroleum products. Operates Rocky Mountain Oil Field Testing Center.

Internal Revenue Service (IRS), *(Treasury Dept.), Passthrough and Special Industries, Branch 8,* 1111 Constitution Ave. N.W., #5314 20224; (202) 622-3130. Fax, (202) 622-4524. Frank Boland, Chief.
Web, www.irs.ustreas.gov

Administers excise tax programs, including taxes on diesel, gasoline, and special fuels. Advises district offices, internal IRS offices, and general inquirers on tax policy, rules, and regulations.

Minerals Management Service *(Interior Dept.), Engineering and Operations,* 381 Elden St., MS 4020, Herndon, VA 20170-4817; (703) 787-1598. Fax, (703) 787-1093. E. P. Danenberger, Chief.
Web, www.mms.gov

Administers the Outer Continental Shelf Land Act. Supervises oil and gas operations on outer continental shelf lands; oversees lease operations including exploration, drilling, and production phases of offshore oil

and gas development; administers lease provisions for offshore oil and gas.

National Oceanic and Atmospheric Administration (NOAA), *(Commerce Dept.), Policy and Strategic Planning,* 14th St. and Constitution Ave. N.W., #6121 20230; (202) 482-5181. Fax, (202) 501-3024. Jim Burgess, Director (Acting).
Web, www.noaa.gov

Makes recommendations to NOAA concerning environmental and ecological problems. Assesses the accuracy and coordinates the implementation of environmental impact statements for all federal projects, including offshore oil and natural gas facilities.

NONPROFIT

American Gas Assn., 400 N. Capitol St. N.W., 4th Floor 20001; (202) 824-7000. Fax, (202) 824-7115. David N. Parker, President.
Web, www.aga.org

Membership: natural gas utilities and pipeline companies. Interests include all technical and operational aspects of the gas industry. Publishes comprehensive statistical record of gas industry; conducts national standard testing for gas appliances. Monitors legislation and regulations.

American Petroleum Institute, 1220 L St. N.W., 9th Floor 20005; (202) 682-8100. Fax, (202) 682-8110. Red Cavaney, President. Library, (202) 682-8042. Press, (202) 682-8120.
Web, www.api.org

Membership: producers, refiners, marketers, and transporters of oil, natural gas, and related products such as gasoline. Provides information on the industry, including data on exports and imports, taxation, transportation, weekly refinery operations (stock levels, output, and input), and drilling activity and costs; conducts research on petroleum and publishes statistical and drilling reports.

American Petroleum Institute, *Taxation,* 1220 L St. N.W., 12th Floor 20005; (202) 682-8465. Fax, (202) 682-8049. Andy Yood, Director.
Web, www.api.org

Provides information on petroleum taxation.

American Public Gas Assn., 11094-D Lee Hwy., #102, Fairfax, VA 22030-5014; (703) 352-3890. Fax, (703) 352-1271. Robert S. Cave, President.
General e-mail, apga@apga.org
Web, www.apga.org

Membership: municipally owned gas distribution systems. Provides information on federal developments affecting natural gas. Promotes efficiency and works to protect the interests of public gas systems. Sponsors workshops and conferences.

Compressed Gas Assn., *4221 Walney Rd., 5th Floor, Chantilly, VA 20151-2923; (703) 788-2700. Fax, (703) 961-1831. Carl T. Johnson, President.*
General e-mail, cga@cganet.com
Web, www.cganet.com
Membership: all segments of the compressed gas industry, including producers and distributors of compressed and liquefied gases. Promotes and coordinates technical development and standardization of the industry. Monitors legislation and regulations.

Gas Appliance Manufacturers Assn., *2107 Wilson Blvd., #600, Arlington, VA 22201; (703) 525-7060. Fax, (703) 525-6790. Evan Gaddis, President.*
General e-mail, information@gamanet.org
Web, www.gamanet.org
Membership: manufacturers of gas appliances and equipment for residential and commercial use and related industries. Advocates product improvement; provides market statistics. Monitors legislation and regulations.

Gas Technology Institute, *Policy and Regulatory Affairs, Washington Office, 1225 Eye St. N.W., #350 20005; (202) 824-6640. Melanie Kenderdine, Vice President.*
Web, www.gastechnology.org
Membership: all segments of the natural gas industry, including producers, pipelines, and distributors. Conducts research and develops new technology for gas customers and the industry. (Headquarters in Des Plaines, Ill.)

Independent Liquid Terminals Assn., *1444 Eye St. N.W., #400 20005; (202) 842-9200. Fax, (202) 326-8660. David E. Doane, President.*
General e-mail, info@ilta.org
Web, www.ilta.org
Membership: commercial operators of for-hire bulk liquid terminals and tank storage facilities, including those for crude oil and petroleum. Promotes the safe and efficient handling of various types of bulk liquid commodities. Sponsors workshops and seminars; maintains speakers bureau; publishes directories. Monitors legislation and regulations.

Independent Petroleum Assn. of America, *1201 15th St. N.W., #300 20005; (202) 857-4722. Fax, (202) 857-4799. Barry Russell, President.*
Web, www.ipaa.org

Membership: independent oil and gas producers; land and royalty owners; and others with interests in domestic exploration, development, and production of oil and natural gas. Interests include leasing, prices and taxation, foreign trade, environmental restrictions, and improved recovery methods.

International Assn. of Drilling Contractors, *Government Affairs, Washington Office, 1901 L St. N.W., #702 20036-3506; (202) 293-0670. Fax, (202) 872-0047. Brian T. Petty, Senior Vice President.*
General e-mail, info@iadc.org
Web, www.iadc.org
Membership: drilling contractors, oil and gas producers, and others in the industry worldwide. Promotes safe exploration and production of hydrocarbons, advances in drilling technology, and preservation of the environment. Monitors legislation and regulations. (Headquarters in Houston, Texas.)

National Ocean Industries Assn., *1120 G St. N.W., #900 20005; (202) 347-6900. Fax, (202) 347-8650. Tom A. Fry, President.*
General e-mail, noia@noia.org
Web, www.noia.org
Membership: manufacturers, producers, suppliers, and support and service companies involved in marine, offshore, and ocean work. Interests include offshore oil and gas supply and production.

National Petrochemical and Refiners Assn., *1899 L St. N.W., #1000 20036-3896; (202) 457-0480. Fax, (202) 457-0486. Bob Slaughter, President.*
Web, www.npradc.org
Membership: petroleum, petrochemical, and refining companies. Interests include allocation, imports, refining technology, petrochemicals, and environmental regulations.

National Petroleum Council, *1625 K St. N.W., #600 20006; (202) 393-6100. Fax, (202) 331-8539. Marshall W. Nichols, Executive Director.*
General e-mail, info@npc.org
Web, www.npc.org
Advisory committee to the secretary of energy on matters relating to the petroleum industry, including oil and natural gas. Publishes reports concerning technical aspects of the oil and gas industries.

National Propane Gas Assn., *1150 17th St. N.W., #310 20036; (202) 466-7200. Fax, (202) 466-7205. Richard R. Roldan, President.*
General e-mail, info@npga.org
Web, www.npga.org

Membership: retail marketers, producers, wholesale distributors, appliance and equipment manufacturers, equipment fabricators, and distributors and transporters of liquefied petroleum gas. Conducts research, safety, and educational programs; provides statistics on the industry.

Natural Gas Supply Assn., *805 15th St. N.W., #510 20005; (202) 326-9300. Fax, (202) 326-9330. Ralph Horvath, President.*
Web, www.ngsa.org

Membership: major and independent producers of domestic natural gas. Interests include the production, consumption, marketing, and regulation of natural gas. Monitors legislation and regulations.

Natural Gas Vehicle Coalition, *400 N. Capitol St. N.W. 20001; (202) 824-7360. Fax, (202) 824-7367. Richard R. Kolodziej, President.*
Web, www.ngvc.org

Membership: natural gas distributors; pipeline, automobile, and engine manufacturers; environmental groups; research and development organizations; and state and local government agencies. Advocates installation of natural gas and hydrogen fuel stations and development of industry standards. Helps market new products and equipment related to natural gas and hydrogen-powered vehicles.

Petroleum Marketers Assn. of America, *1901 N. Fort Myer Dr., #1200, Arlington, VA 22209-1604; (703) 351-8000. Fax, (703) 351-9160. Dan Gilligan, President.*
General e-mail, info@pmaa.org
Web, www.pmaa.org

Membership: state and regional associations representing independent branded and nonbranded marketers of petroleum products. Provides information on all aspects of petroleum marketing. Monitors legislation and regulations.

Public Citizen, *Buyers Up, 1600 20th St. N.W. 20009; (202) 588-7780. Fax, (202) 588-7798. Bill Wilson, Program Manager.*
General e-mail, publiccitizen@citizen.org
Web, www.citizen.org/buyersup.htm

Administers cooperative purchasing program for consumers of heating oil and heating and cooling services. Promotes energy conservation; helps consumers save on energy bills.

Service Station Dealers of America and Allied Trades, *1532 Pointer Ridge Pl., Bowie, MD 20716; (301) 390-4405. Fax, (301) 390-3161. Robert Howard, President.*
Web, www.ssda-at.org

Membership: state associations of gasoline retailers. Interests include environmental issues, retail marketing, oil allocation, imports and exports, prices, and taxation.

Society of Independent Gasoline Marketers of America, *11911 Freedom Dr., #590, Reston, VA 20190; (703) 709-7000. Fax, (703) 709-7007. Kenneth A. Doyle, Executive Vice President.*
General e-mail, sigma@sigma.org
Web, www.sigma.org

Membership: marketers and wholesalers of brand and nonbrand gasoline. Seeks to ensure adequate supplies of gasoline at competitive prices. Monitors legislation and regulations affecting gasoline supply and price.

US Oil and Gas Assn., *901 F St. N.W., #601 20004; (202) 638-4400. Fax, (202) 638-5967. Wayne Gibbens, President.*

Membership: major and independent petroleum companies. Monitors legislation and regulations affecting the petroleum industry.

Pipelines

AGENCIES

Federal Energy Regulatory Commission (FERC), *(Energy Dept.), Markets, Tariffs, and Rates, 888 1st St. N.E., #8A-01 20426; (202) 502-6700. Fax, (202) 208-0193. Daniel L. Larcamp, Director.*
Web, www.ferc.gov

Establishes and enforces maximum rates and charges for oil and natural gas pipelines; establishes oil pipeline operating rules; issues certificates for and regulates construction, sale, and acquisition of natural gas pipeline facilities. Ensures compliance with the Natural Gas Policy Act, the Natural Gas Act, and other statutes.

National Transportation Safety Board, *Railroad, Pipeline, and Hazardous Material Investigations, 490 L'Enfant Plaza East S.W. 20594; (202) 314-6460. Fax, (202) 314-6482. Bob Chipkevich, Director.*
Web, www.ntsb.gov

Investigates railroad, natural gas, and petroleum pipeline accidents.

Research and Special Programs Administration *(Transportation Dept.), Hazardous Materials Safety, 400 7th St. S.W., #8321 20590; (202) 366-0656. Fax, (202) 366-5713. Robert McGuire, Associate Administrator.*
Web, hazmat.dot.gov

Designates fuels, chemicals, and other substances as hazardous materials and regulates their transportation in interstate commerce; coordinates international standards regulations.

Research and Special Programs Administration
*(Transportation Dept.), Pipeline Safety, 400 7th St.
S.W., #7128 20590; (202) 366-4595. Fax, (202) 366-4566.
Stacey Gerard, Associate Administrator.*
Web, www.ops.dot.gov

Issues and enforces federal regulations for oil, natural
gas, and petroleum products pipeline safety.

NONPROFIT

Assn. of Oil Pipe Lines, *1101 Vermont Ave. N.W., #604
20005; (202) 408-7970. Fax, (202) 408-7983. Ben Cooper,
Executive Director.*
General e-mail, aopl@aopl.org
Web, www.aopl.org

Membership: oil pipeline companies. Analyzes industry statistics. Monitors legislation and regulations.

Coal Technology Assn., *601 Suffield Dr., Gaithersburg,
MD 20878; (301) 294-6080. Fax, (301) 294-7480. Stuart
D. Serkin, Executive Director.*
Web, www.coaltechnologies.com

Membership: business professionals interested in
energy (coal technology), economic, and environmental
policies and regulations. Seeks to improve coal utilization technologies and to develop coal cleaning technologies. Facilitates the exchange of technical information on
coal technologies through annual international conference.

Interstate Natural Gas Assn. of America, *10 G St.
N.E., #700 20002; (202) 216-5900. Fax, (202) 216-0877.
Jerald V. Halvorsen, President.*
Web, www.ingaa.org

Membership: U.S. interstate and Canadian inter-
provincial natural gas pipeline companies. Commissions
studies and provides information on the natural gas
pipeline industry.

☢ NUCLEAR ENERGY

AGENCIES

Energy Information Administration (EIA), *(Energy
Dept.), Coal, Nuclear, Electric, and Alternate Fuels, 950
L'Enfant Plaza S.W., #6070 20024 (mailing address: 1000
Independence Ave. S.W. 20585); (202) 287-1990. Fax,
(202) 287-1933. Robert M. Schnapf, Director (Acting).*
Web, www.eia.doe.gov

Prepares analyses and forecasts on the availability,
production, prices, processing, transportation, and distribution of nuclear energy, both domestically and inter-

nationally. Collects and publishes data concerning the
uranium supply and market.

Nuclear Energy, Science, and Technology *(Energy
Dept.), 1000 Independence Ave. S.W., #5A-143 20585;
(202) 586-6450. Fax, (202) 586-8353. William D. Mag-
wood IV, Director.*
Web, www.nuclear.gov

Administers nuclear fission power generation and
fuel technology programs; develops and provides nuclear
power sources to meet national civilian requirements.
Develops, interprets, and coordinates nuclear safety policy for all Energy Dept. reactors and nuclear facilities.
Encourages public involvement in programs and provides information to increase public knowledge.

Nuclear Energy, Science, and Technology *(Energy
Dept.), Isotope Programs, 19901 Germantown Rd., #B-
432, NE-40, Germantown, MD 20874-1290; (301) 903-
5161. Fax, (301) 903-5434. Owen W. Lowe, Associate
Director.*
Web, www.nuclear.gov

Directs all isotope production and distribution activities within the Energy Dept.; ensures a reliable supply of
medical, research, and industrial isotopes consistent with
customer needs.

Nuclear Energy, Science, and Technology *(Energy
Dept.), Nuclear Facilities Management, 19901 German-
town Rd., #B-432, NE-40, Germantown, MD 20874-1290;
(301) 903-5161. Fax, (301) 903-5434. Owen W. Lowe,
Associate Director.*
Web, www.nuclear.gov

Manages the design, construction, and operation of
nuclear energy test facilities and Office of Energy
Research reactor and supporting facilities, assuring their
safe, reliable, and environmentally sound operation and
cost-effective use. Interests include international nuclear
safety.

Nuclear Regulatory Commission, *11555 Rockville
Pike, MS 016C1, Rockville, MD 20852; (301) 415-1759.
Fax, (301) 415-1757. Nils J. Diaz, Chair (Designate);
William D. Travers, Executive Director, (301) 415-1700.
Information, (301) 415-8200.*
General e-mail, opa@nrc.gov
Web, www.nrc.gov

Regulates commercial uses of nuclear energy; responsibilities include licensing, inspection, and enforcement;
monitors and regulates the imports and exports of
nuclear material and equipment.

Tennessee Valley Authority, *Government Relations,
Washington Office, 1 Massachusetts Ave. N.W., #300*

20001; (202) 898-2999. Fax, (202) 898-2998. Linda Whitestone, Vice President.

Web, www.tva.gov

Coordinates resource conservation, development, and land-use programs in the Tennessee River Valley. Produces and supplies wholesale power to municipal and cooperative electric systems, federal installations, and some industries; interests include nuclear power generation.

CONGRESS

House Energy and Commerce Committee, 2125 RHOB 20515; (202) 225-2927. Fax, (202) 225-1919. Rep. Billy Tauzin, R-La., Chair; David V. Marventano, Staff Director.

General e-mail, commerce@mail.house.gov

Web, energycommerce.house.gov

Jurisdiction over measures relating to general management of the Energy Dept., the management and all functions of the Federal Energy Regulatory Commission, and national energy policy generally. Has a special oversight function with respect to all laws, programs, and government activities affecting nuclear and other energy, and nonmilitary nuclear energy and research and development, including the disposal of nuclear waste.

House Energy and Commerce Committee, *Subcommittee on Energy and Air Quality,* 2125 RHOB 20515; (202) 225-2927. Fax, (202) 225-1919. Rep. Joe L. Barton, R-Texas, Chair; David V. Marventano, Staff Director.

General e-mail, commerce@mail.house.gov

Web, energycommerce.house.gov

Jurisdiction over regulation of commercial nuclear facilities and special oversight functions with respect to all laws, programs, and government activities affecting nonmilitary aspects of nuclear energy.

House Science Committee, *Subcommittee on Energy,* 390 FHOB 20515; (202) 225-9662. Fax, (202) 226-6983. Rep. Judy Biggert, R-Ill., Chair; Gabor J. Rozsa, Staff Director.

General e-mail, science@mail.house.gov

Web, www.house.gov/science

Jurisdiction over legislation and international cooperation on nuclear energy research and development. Oversight responsibilities over the uranium supply and the operation of nonmilitary Energy Dept. laboratories, including toxic waste cleanup.

Senate Energy and Natural Resources Committee, SD-364 20510; (202) 224-4971. Fax, (202) 224-6163. Sen. Pete V. Domenici, R-N.M., Chair; Alex Flint, Staff Director.

General e-mail, committee@energy.senate.gov

Web, energy.senate.gov

Jurisdiction over nonmilitary and nonregulatory aspects of nuclear energy.

Senate Energy and Natural Resources Committee, *Subcommittee on Energy,* SD-364 20510; (202) 224-4971. Fax, (202) 224-6163. Sen. Lamar Alexander, R-Tenn., Chair; Scott O'Malia, Professional Staff Member.

General e-mail, energy-sub@energy.senate.gov

Web, energy.senate.gov

Jurisdiction over nuclear energy research and development, including uranium enrichment and nuclear fuel cycle policy.

Senate Environment and Public Works Committee, *Subcommittee on Clean Air, Climate Change, and Nuclear Safety,* SD-410 20510; (202) 224-6176. Fax, (202) 224-1273. Sen. George V. Voinovich, R-Ohio, Chair; Michael Whatley, Staff Director.

Web, epw.senate.gov

Legislative jurisdiction over nonmilitary environmental regulation and control of nuclear energy, including plant licensing and siting, radiological health and safety, security and safeguards, nuclear waste disposal, and licensing of certain nuclear exports.

Senate Governmental Affairs Committee, SD-340 20510; (202) 224-4751. Fax, (202) 228-3792. Sen. Susan Collins, R-Maine, Chair; Michael Bopp, Staff Director.

Web, govt-aff.senate.gov

Jurisdiction over organization and management of nuclear export policy; jurisdiction over legislation on the reform of nuclear licensing procedures and nuclear waste and spent fuel policy, physical security at nuclear installations, and nuclear proliferation.

NONPROFIT

American Physical Society, *Public Information, Washington Office,* 529 14th St. N.W., #1050 20045; (202) 662-8700. Fax, (202) 662-8711. Robert L. Park, Director.

General e-mail, opa@aps.org

Web, www.aps.org

Scientific and educational society of educators, students, citizens, and scientists, including industrial scientists. Sponsors studies on issues of public concern related to physics, such as reactor safety and energy use. Informs members of national and international developments. (Headquarters in College Park, Md.)

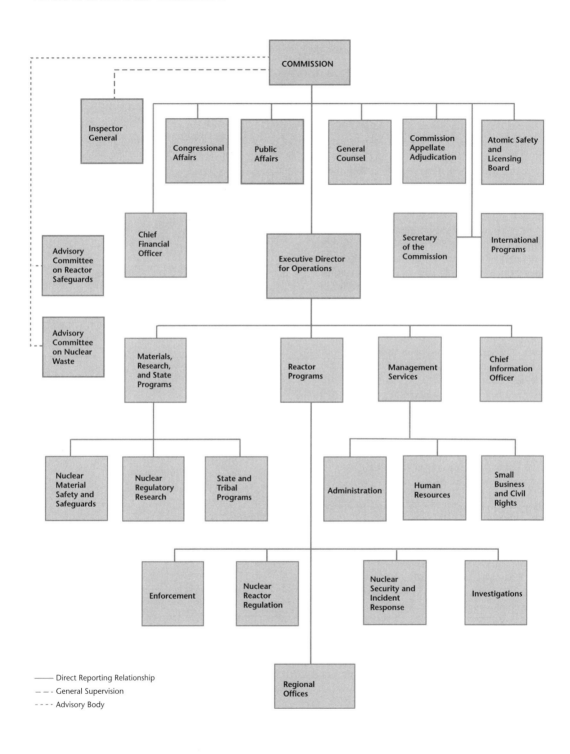

COMMISSION

Inspector General

Congressional Affairs

Public Affairs

General Counsel

Commission Appellate Adjudication

Atomic Safety and Licensing Board

Chief Financial Officer

Advisory Committee on Reactor Safeguards

Executive Director for Operations

Secretary of the Commission

International Programs

Advisory Committee on Nuclear Waste

Materials, Research, and State Programs

Reactor Programs

Management Services

Chief Information Officer

Nuclear Material Safety and Safeguards

Nuclear Regulatory Research

State and Tribal Programs

Administration

Human Resources

Small Business and Civil Rights

Enforcement

Nuclear Reactor Regulation

Nuclear Security and Incident Response

Investigations

Regional Offices

——— Direct Reporting Relationship

— — · General Supervision

- - - - Advisory Body

Nuclear Energy Institute, *1776 Eye St. N.W., #400 20006-3708; (202) 739-8000. Fax, (202) 785-4019. Joe Colvin, President.*

Web, www.nei.org

Membership: utilities; industries; labor, service, and research organizations; law firms; universities; and government agencies interested in peaceful uses of nuclear energy, including the generation of electricity. Acts as a spokesperson for the nuclear power industry; provides information on licensing and plant siting, research and development, safety and security, waste disposal, and legislative and policy issues.

Nuclear Information and Resource Service, *1424 16th St. N.W., #404 20036; (202) 328-0002. Fax, (202) 462-2183. Michael Mariotte, Executive Director.*

General e-mail, nirsnet@nirs.org

Web, www.nirs.org

Membership: organizations and individuals concerned about nuclear energy and nuclear waste. Information and networking clearinghouse on nuclear power plants, radioactive waste, and radiation and sustainable energy issues. Initiates large-scale organizing and public education campaigns and provides technical and strategic expertise to environmental groups. Library open to the public by appointment.

Public Citizen, *Critical Mass Energy Project,* *215 Pennsylvania Ave. S.E. 20003-1155; (202) 546-4996. Fax, (202) 547-7392. Wenonah Hauter, Director.*

General e-mail, pcmail@citizen.org

Web, www.citizen.org/cmep

Public interest group that promotes energy efficiency and renewable energy technologies; opposes nuclear energy. Interests include nuclear plant safety and energy policy issues.

Union of Concerned Scientists, *Government Relations, Washington Office,* *1707 H St. N.W., #600 20006-3919; (202) 223-6133. Fax, (202) 223-6162. Alden Meyer, Director; Todd Perry, Washington Representative for Arms Control and International Security.*

General e-mail, ucs@ucsusa.org

Web, www.ucsusa.org

Independent group of scientists and others concerned with U.S. energy policy, including nuclear policy and nuclear plant safety. (Headquarters in Cambridge, Mass.)

Licensing and Plant Siting

AGENCIES

Federal Emergency Management Agency (FEMA), *(Homeland Security Dept.), Preparedness,* *500 C St.* *S.W., #832 20472; (202) 646-4223. Fax, (202) 646-4557. R. David Paulison, Chief.*

Reviews off-site preparedness for commercial nuclear power facilities; evaluates emergency plans before plant licensing and submits findings to the Nuclear Regulatory Commission.

Nuclear Regulatory Commission, *Nuclear Material Safety and Safeguards,* *11555 Rockville Pike, MS-T8A28, Rockville, MD 20852; (301) 415-7800. Fax, (301) 415-5370. Martin J. Virgilio, Director.*

Web, www.nrc.gov

Licenses all nuclear facilities and materials except power reactors; directs principal licensing and regulation activities for the management of nuclear waste.

Nuclear Regulatory Commission, *Nuclear Reactor Regulation,* *11555 Rockville Pike, MS-O5E7, Rockville, MD 20852; (301) 415-1270. Fax, (301) 415-8333. Samuel J. Collins, Director.*

Web, www.nrc.gov

Licenses nuclear power plants and operators.

Research and Development

AGENCIES

Energy Dept. (DOE), *Office of Science: Fusion Energy Sciences,* *19901 Germantown Rd., Germantown, MD 20874-1290; (301) 903-4941. Fax, (301) 903-8584. N. Anne Davies, Associate Director.*

Web, www.ofes.fusion.doe.gov

Conducts research and development on fusion energy for electric power generation.

National Institute of Standards and Technology (NIST), *(Commerce Dept.), Physics Laboratory,* *100 Bureau Dr., Bldg. 221, #B160, Gaithersburg, MD 20899-8400; (301) 975-4200. Fax, (301) 975-3038. Katharine B. Gebbie, Director.*

Web, www.physics.nist.gov

Provides national standards for radiation measurement methods and technology. Conducts research in measurement science in the fields of electron physics; ionizing radiation dosimetry; neutron physics; and optical, ultraviolet, x-ray, gamma-ray, and infrared radiometry.

Nuclear Energy, Science, and Technology *(Energy Dept.), Management and Planning,* *1000 Independence Ave. S.W., NE-2.2 20585; (202) 586-6450. Fax, (202) 586-8353. Robert Knipp, Deputy Director.*

Web, www.nuclear.gov

Responsible for uranium activities and management of fuel cycle issues. Supplies reactor fuel to university reactors; manages conversion of university reactors from highly enriched uranium fuel to low enriched fuel; supports university reactor instrumentation and equipment upgrades; provides general support to nuclear engineering programs at U.S. universities.

Nuclear Energy, Science, and Technology *(Energy Dept.), Space and Defense Power Systems,* 19901 Germantown Rd., 2nd Floor, Germantown, MD 20874; (301) 903-3456. Fax, (301) 903-1510. Earl Wahlquist, Associate Director.

Web, www.nuclear.gov

Develops and produces radio isotopes power systems for space applications in support of NASA.

Nuclear Regulatory Commission, *Nuclear Regulatory Research,* 11545 Rockville Pike, Rockville, MD 20852-2738; (301) 415-6641. Fax, (301) 415-5153. Ashok C. Thadani, Director.

Web, www.nrc.gov

Plans, recommends, and implements nuclear regulatory research, standards development, and resolution of safety issues for nuclear power plants and other facilities regulated by the Nuclear Regulatory Commission; develops and promulgates all technical regulations.

Safety, Security, and Waste Disposal

AGENCIES

Defense Nuclear Facilities Safety Board, 625 Indiana Ave. N.W., #700 20004; (202) 694-7080. Fax, (202) 208-6518. John T. Conway, Chair. Information, (202) 694-7000.

Web, www.dnfsb.gov

Independent board created by Congress and appointed by the president to provide external oversight of Energy Dept. defense nuclear facilities and make recommendations to the secretary of energy regarding public health and safety.

Energy Dept. (DOE), *Civilian Radioactive Waste Management,* 1000 Independence Ave. S.W., #5A085 20585; (202) 586-6842. Fax, (202) 586-6638. Margaret F.Y. Chu, Director.

Web, www.ocrwm.doe.gov

Responsible for developing the waste disposal system for commercial spent nuclear fuels and some military high-level radioactive waste. Sites, licenses, constructs, and operates a permanent repository. Monitors and reports on the adequacy of congressional appropriations for the Nuclear Waste Fund to finance nuclear waste disposal through fees collected from private utility companies that generate electricity.

Energy Information Administration (EIA), *(Energy Dept.), Coal, Nuclear, Electric, and Alternate Fuels,* 950 L'Enfant Plaza S.W., #6070 20024 (mailing address: 1000 Independence Ave. S.W. 20585); (202) 287-1990. Fax, (202) 287-1933. Robert M. Schnaff, Director (Acting).

Web, www.eia.doe.gov

Directs collection of spent fuel data and validation of spent nuclear fuel discharge data for the Civilian Radioactive Waste Management Office.

Environment, Safety, and Health *(Energy Dept.), Environment,* 1000 Independence Ave. S.W., #7A075 20585; (202) 586-5680. Fax, (202) 586-2268. Raymond P. Berube, Deputy Assistant Secretary.

Web, www.eh.doe.gov

Establishes policies and guidance for environmental protection and compliance; provides technical assistance to departmental program and field offices in complying with environmental requirements.

Environment, Safety, and Health *(Energy Dept.), Health Studies,* 19901 Germantown Rd., EH-6/27OCC, Germantown, MD 20874-1290; (301) 903-5926. Fax, (301) 903-3445. Steven V. Carey, Deputy Assistant Secretary.

Evaluates and establishes standards related to radiation, industrial hygiene, and occupational medicine. Oversees epidemiologic studies.

Environment, Safety, and Health *(Energy Dept.), Safety and Health,* 20300 Century Blvd., Germantown, MD 20874 (mailing address: 1000 Independence Ave. S.W., Washington, DC 20585-0270); (301) 903-5532. Fax, (301) 903-3189. Rick Jones, Deputy Assistant Secretary (Acting).

Develops policy and establishes standards to ensure safety and health protection in all department activities.

Environmental Management *(Energy Dept.), Project Completion Environmental Management,* 1000 Independence Ave. S.W., #5B040 20585; (202) 586-0370. Fax, (202) 586-0449. Mark W. Frei, Deputy Assistant Secretary (Acting).

Web, www.em.doe.gov

Provides policy guidance for and oversees waste management operations.

Environmental Management *(Energy Dept.), Science and Technology,* 1000 Independence Ave. S.W., #5B014 20585; (202) 586-6382. Fax, (202) 586-6773. James Owendoff, Deputy Assistant Secretary.

Performs research, development, testing, demonstration, and evaluation for innovative, safe, and cost-effective solutions to the problems of hazardous waste and contamination of soils and groundwater.

Environmental Management *(Energy Dept.)*, *Site Closure,* 1000 Independence Ave. S.W., #5B050 20585; (202) 586-6331. Fax, (202) 586-6523. Mark W. Frei, Assistant Secretary.

Web, www.em.doe.gov

Manages Energy Dept. programs that treat and stabilize radioactive waste including the decontamination and decommissioning of nongovernment facilities and sites; works to develop a reliable national system for low-level waste management and techniques for treatment and immobilization of waste from former nuclear weapons complex sites.

Environmental Protection Agency (EPA), *Radiation and Indoor Air,* 1200 Pennsylvania Ave. N.W., MC 6601J 20460; (202) 564-9320. Fax, (202) 565-2043. Elizabeth Cotsworth, Director.

Web, www.epa.gov/oar/oria.html

Establishes standards to regulate the amount of radiation discharged into the environment from uranium mining and milling projects, and other activities that result in radioactive emissions; and to ensure the safe disposal of radioactive waste. Fields a Radiological Emergency Response Team to respond to radiological incidents.

Federal Emergency Management Agency (FEMA), *(Homeland Security Dept.),* 500 C St. S.W., #828 20472; (202) 646-3923. Fax, (202) 646-3930. Michael Brown, Director (Acting). Press, (202) 646-4600. Locator, (202) 646-2500. Disaster assistance, (800) 462-9029. Radio network, (800) 323-5248. Fax-on-demand, (202) 646-3362.

Web, www.fema.gov

Assists state and local governments in preparing for and responding to natural, technological, and attack-related emergencies, including accidents at nuclear power facilities and accidents involving transportation of radioactive materials; provides planning guidance in the event of such accidents; operates the National Emergency Training Center. Coordinates emergency preparedness, mitigation and response activities, and planning for all federal agencies and departments.

National Transportation Safety Board, *Railroad, Pipeline, and Hazardous Material Investigations,* 490 L'Enfant Plaza East S.W. 20594; (202) 314-6460. Fax, (202) 314-6482. Bob Chipkevich, Director.

Web, www.ntsb.gov

Investigates accidents involving the transportation of hazardous materials.

Nuclear Regulatory Commission, *Advisory Committee on Nuclear Waste,* 11545 Rockville Pike, Rockville, MD 20852 (mailing address: Nuclear Regulatory Commis-

sion, #T2E26, Washington, DC 20555-0001); (301) 415-7360. Fax, (301) 415-5589. John T. Larkins, Executive Director.

Web, www.nrc.gov/what-we-do/regulatory/advisory/acnw.html

Oversees handling and disposal of high- and low-level nuclear waste, especially the disposal of high-level waste in the Yucca Mountain Repository.

Nuclear Regulatory Commission, *Advisory Committee on Reactor Safeguards,* 11545 Rockville Pike, Rockville, MD 20852 (mailing address: Nuclear Regulatory Commission, #T2E26, Washington, DC 20555-0001); (301) 415-7360. Fax, (301) 415-5589. John T. Larkins, Executive Director.

Web, www.nrc.gov/what-we-do/regulatory/advisory/acrs.html

Established by Congress to review and report on safety aspects of proposed and existing nuclear reactor facilities and the adequacy of proposed reactor safety standards; directs the Safety Research Program.

Nuclear Regulatory Commission, *Nuclear Material Safety and Safeguards,* 11555 Rockville Pike, MS-T8A28, Rockville, MD 20852; (301) 415-7800. Fax, (301) 415-5370. Martin J. Virgilio, Director.

Web, www.nrc.gov

Develops and implements safeguards programs; directs licensing and regulation activities for the management and disposal of nuclear waste.

Nuclear Regulatory Commission, *Nuclear Reactor Regulation,* 11555 Rockville Pike, MS-O5E7, Rockville, MD 20852; (301) 415-1270. Fax, (301) 415-8333. Samuel J. Collins, Director.

Web, www.nrc.gov

Conducts safety inspections of nuclear reactors. Regulates nuclear materials used or produced at nuclear power plants.

Nuclear Regulatory Commission, *Nuclear Regulatory Research,* 11545 Rockville Pike, Rockville, MD 20852-2738; (301) 415-6641. Fax, (301) 415-5153. Ashok C. Thadani, Director.

Web, www.nrc.gov

Plans, recommends, and implements resolution of safety issues for nuclear power plants and other facilities regulated by the Nuclear Regulatory Commission.

Nuclear Waste Technical Review Board, 2300 Clarendon Blvd., #1300, Arlington, VA 22201-3367; (703) 235-4473. Fax, (703) 235-4495. William D. Barnard, Executive Director.

General e-mail, info@nwtrb.gov

Web, www.nwtrb.gov

Independent board of scientists and engineers appointed by the president to review, evaluate, and report on Energy Dept. development of waste disposal systems and repositories for spent fuel and high-level radioactive waste. Oversees siting, packaging, and transportation of waste, in accordance with the Nuclear Waste Policy Act of 1987.

Research and Special Programs Administration *(Transportation Dept.), Hazardous Materials Safety,* *400 7th St. S.W., #8321 20590; (202) 366-0656. Fax, (202) 366-5713. Robert McGuire, Associate Administrator.*

Web, hazmat.dot.gov

Issues safety regulations and exemptions for the transportation of hazardous materials; works with the International Atomic Energy Agency on standards for international shipments of radioactive materials.

⚡ RENEWABLE ENERGIES, ALTERNATIVE FUELS

AGENCIES

Energy Efficiency and Renewable Energy *(Energy Dept.), Clearinghouse,* *P.O. Box 3048, Merrifield, VA 22116-3048; (800) 363-3732. Fax, (703) 893-0400. Larry Goldberg, Project Manager. TTY, (800) 273-2957.*

General e-mail, doe.erec@nciinc.com

Web, www.eren.doe.gov/consumerinfo

Provides information on renewable energy and energy efficiency; makes referrals to other organizations for technical information on renewable energy resources. Serves as repository of information for the Federal Energy Management Program.

Energy Information Administration (EIA), *(Energy Dept.), Coal, Nuclear, Electric, and Alternate Fuels,* *950 L'Enfant Plaza S.W., #6070 20024 (mailing address: 1000 Independence Ave. S.W. 20585); (202) 287-1990. Fax, (202) 287-1933. Robert M. Schnaff, Director (Acting).*

Web, www.eia.doe.gov

Prepares analyses on the availability, production, costs, processing, transportation, and distribution of uranium and alternative energy supplies, including biomass, solar, wind, waste, wood, and alcohol.

Environmental Management *(Energy Dept.), Project Completion Environmental Management,* *1000 Independence Ave. S.W., #5B040 20585; (202) 586-0370. Fax,* *(202) 586-0449. Mark W. Frei, Deputy Assistant Secretary (Acting).*

Web, www.em.doe.gov

Conducts research on municipal waste conversion for use as an energy source.

CONGRESS

House Energy and Commerce Committee, *Subcommittee on Energy and Air Quality,* *2125 RHOB 20515; (202) 225-2927. Fax, (202) 225-1919. Rep. Joe L. Barton, R-Texas, Chair; David V. Marventano, Staff Director.*

General e-mail, commerce@mail.house.gov

Web, energycommerce.house.gov

Jurisdiction over legislation on regulation, commercialization, and utilization of hydroelectric power, synthetic and alcohol fuels, and renewable energy resources, including wind, solar, and ocean thermal energy.

House Resources Committee, *Subcommittee on Energy and Mineral Resources,* *1626 LHOB 20515; (202) 225-9297. Fax, (202) 225-5255. Rep. Barbara Cubin, R-Wyo., Chair; Jack Belcher, Staff Director.*

General e-mail, energy.minerals@mail.house.gov

Web, resourcescommittee.house.gov

Jurisdiction over legislation concerning the development and conservation of energy and natural resources found in the ocean and the outer continental shelf. Jurisdiction over legislation affecting the use of geothermal resources.

House Resources Committee, *Subcommittee on Water and Power,* *1522 LHOB 20515; (202) 225-8331. Fax, (202) 226-6953. Rep. Ken Calvert, R-Calif., Chair; Joshua Johnson, Staff Director.*

General e-mail, water.power@mail.house.gov

Web, resourcescommittee.house.gov

Jurisdiction over legislation on irrigation and reclamation projects and electrical power marketing administrations.

House Science Committee, *Subcommittee on Energy,* *390 FHOB 20515; (202) 225-9662. Fax, (202) 226-6983. Rep. Judy Biggert, R-Ill., Chair; Gabor J. Rozsa, Staff Director.*

General e-mail, science@mail.house.gov

Web, www.house.gov/science

Jurisdiction over Energy Dept. basic research programs, including legislation on research and development of solar, wind, geothermal, and fossil fuel energy (including synthetic fuels such as liquefied and gasified coal) and other nonfossil and nonnuclear energy sources.

Senate Commerce, Science, and Transportation Committee, *Subcommittee on Oceans, Fisheries, and Coast Guard,* SH-227 20510; (202) 224-8172. Fax, (202) 224-9334. Sen. Olympia J. Snowe, R-Maine, Chair; Andrew Minkiewicz, Counsel Member.

Web, commerce.senate.gov

Studies ocean resources development and conservation. (Subcommittee does not report legislation.)

Senate Energy and Natural Resources Committee, SD-364 20510; (202) 224-4971. Fax, (202) 224-6163. Sen. Pete V. Domenici, R-N.M., Chair; Alex Flint, Staff Director.

General e-mail, committee@energy.senate.gov

Web, energy.senate.gov

Jurisdiction over legislation on energy and nonfuel mineral resources, including hydroelectric power, irrigation and reclamation projects, power marketing administrations, and the impact of energy developments on water resources. Jurisdiction over legislation on synfuels research and development and over Energy Dept. basic research programs.

NONPROFIT

Electric Power Supply Assn., *1401 New York Ave., 11th Floor 20005; (202) 628-8200. Fax, (202) 628-8260. Lynne H. Church, President.*

Web, www.epsa.org

Membership: companies that generate electricity, steam, and other forms of energy using a broad spectrum of fossil fuel-fired and renewable technologies.

Energy Frontiers International, *1110 N. Glebe Rd., #610, Arlington, VA 22201; (703) 276-6655. Fax, (703) 276-7662. Michael S. Koleda, President.*

Web, www.energyfrontiers.org

Membership: companies interested in technologies for converting solid, liquid, and gaseous fossil fuels and biomass into other forms. Interests include coal gasification, combined cycle power generation, and liquid transportation fuels from coal, natural gas, and biomass.

Hearth, Patio, and Barbecue Assn., *1601 N. Kent St., #1001, Arlington, VA 22209; (703) 522-0086. Fax, (703) 522-0548. Carter E. Keithley, President.*

General e-mail, hpamail@hpba.org

Web, www.hpba.org

Membership: all sectors of the hearth products industry. Provides industry training programs to its members on the safe and efficient use of alternative fuels and appliances. Works with the Hearth Education Foundation, which certifies gas hearth, fireplace, pellet stove, and wood stove appliances and venting design specialists.

National Hydrogen Assn., *1800 M St. N.W., #300 20036; (202) 223-5547. Fax, (202) 223-5537. Karen Miller, Vice President.*

General e-mail, nha@ttcorp.com

Web, www.hydrogenus.com

Membership: industry, small businesses, universities, and research institutions. Promotes use of hydrogen as an energy carrier; fosters the development and application of hydrogen technologies.

Alcohol Fuels

AGENCIES

Alcohol and Tobacco Tax and Trade Bureau (TTB), *(Treasury Dept.), Regulations and Procedures,* 650 Massachusetts Ave. N.W., #5000 20226; (202) 927-8210. Fax, (202) 927-8602. William Foster, Chief.

Web, www.ttb.gov

Develops guidelines for regional offices responsible for issuing permits for producing gasohol and other ethyl alcohol fuels, whose uses include heating and operating machinery. Writes and interprets regulations for distilleries that produce ethyl alcohol fuels.

Rural Business-Cooperative Service *(Agriculture Dept.), Business Programs,* 1400 Independence Ave. S.W., #5050 20250-3220; (202) 720-7287. Fax, (202) 690-0097. John Rosso, Administrator, Business Programs.

Web, www.rurdev.usda.gov/rbs/busp/bpdir.htm

Makes loan guarantees to rural businesses, including those seeking to develop alcohol fuels production facilities.

NONPROFIT

Methanol Institute, *800 Connecticut Ave. N.W., #620 20006; (202) 467-5050. Fax, (202) 331-9055. John E. Lynn, President.*

General e-mail, mi@methanol.org

Web, www.methanol.org

Membership: methanol producers and related industries. Encourages use of methanol fuels and development of chemical-derivative markets. Monitors legislation and regulations.

Renewable Fuels Assn., *One Massachusetts Ave. N.W., #820 20001-1431; (202) 289-3835. Fax, (202) 289-7519. Bob Dinneen, President.*

General e-mail, info@ethanolrfa.org

Web, www.ethanolrfa.org

Membership: companies and state governments involved in developing the domestic ethanol industry. Distributes publications on ethanol performance.

Geothermal Energy

AGENCIES

Energy Efficiency and Renewable Energy *(Energy Dept.), Geothermal,* 1000 Independence Ave. S.W., #5H072, EE-12 20585-0121; (202) 586-5340. Fax, (202) 586-8185. Peter Goldman, Director (Acting).
Web, www.eere.energy.gov

Responsible for long-range research and technology development of geothermal energy resources.

U.S. Geological Survey (USGS), *(Interior Dept.), Volcano Hazards,* 12201 Sunrise Valley Dr., Reston, VA 20192 (mailing address: 904 National Center, Reston, VA 20192); (703) 648-6711. Fax, (703) 648-5483. John Pallister, Program Coordinator.
Web, volcanoes.usgs.gov

Provides staff support to the U.S. Geological Survey through programs in volcano hazards.

Solar, Ocean, and Wind Energy

AGENCIES

Energy Efficiency and Renewable Energy *(Energy Dept.), Solar Energy Technologies,* 1000 Independence Ave. S.W., #5H095 20585; (202) 586-1720. Fax, (202) 586-8148. Raymond A. Sutula, Program Director.
Web, www.eere.energy.gov

Supports research and development of solar technologies of all types through national laboratories and partnerships with industries and universities.

Energy Efficiency and Renewable Energy *(Energy Dept.), Wind and Hydropower Technologies,* 1000 Independence Ave. S.W., #5H072EE-12 20585; (202) 586-5348. Fax, (202) 586-8185. Peter Goldman, Director (Acting).
Web, www.eere.energy.gov

Conducts research on wind technologies. Works with U.S. industries to develop geothermal and wind technologies.

National Oceanic and Atmospheric Administration (NOAA), *(Commerce Dept.), Ocean and Coastal Resource Management,* 1305 East-West Hwy., SSMC4, Silver Spring, MD 20910; (301) 713-3155. Fax, (301) 713-4012. Douglas L. Brown, Director (Acting).
Web, www.nos.noaa.gov/programs/ocrm.html

Administers the Coastal Zone Management Act, the National Estuarine Research Reserve System, the National Marine Sanctuary Program, the Deep Seabed Hard Mineral Resources Act, and the Ocean Thermal Energy Conversion Act to carry out NOAA's goals for preservation, conservation, and restoration management of the ocean and coastal environment.

CONGRESS

House Science Committee, *Subcommittee on Environment, Technology, and Standards,* 2319 RHOB 20515; (202) 225-8844. Fax, (202) 225-4438. Rep. Vernon J. Ehlers, R-Mich., Chair; Eric Webster, Staff Director.
General e-mail, science@mail.house.gov
Web, www.house.gov/science

Jurisdiction over the National Oceanic and Atmospheric Administration, including all activities related to weather, weather services, climate, the atmosphere, marine fisheries, and oceanic research.

NONPROFIT

American Wind Energy Assn., 122 C St. N.W., #380 20001; (202) 383-2500. Fax, (202) 383-2505. Randall S. Swisher, Executive Director.
General e-mail, windmail@awea.org
Web, www.awea.org

Membership: manufacturers, developers, operators, and distributors of wind machines; utility companies; and others interested in wind energy. Advocates wind energy as an alternative energy source; makes industry data available to the public and to federal and state legislators. Promotes export of wind energy technology.

National Ocean Industries Assn., 1120 G St. N.W., #900 20005; (202) 347-6900. Fax, (202) 347-8650. Tom A. Fry, President.
General e-mail, noia@noia.org
Web, www.noia.org

Membership: manufacturers, producers, suppliers, and support and service companies involved in marine, offshore, and ocean work. Interests include ocean thermal energy and new energy sources.

Solar Electric Light Fund, 1775 K St. N.W., #595 20006; (202) 234-7265. Fax, (202) 328-9512. Robert A. Freling, Executive Director.
General e-mail, solarlight@self.org
Web, www.self.org

Promotes and develops solar rural electrification and energy self-sufficiency in developing countries. Assists developing world communities and governments in acquiring, financing, and installing decentralized household solar electric systems.

Solar Energy Industries Assn., 1616 H St. N.W., 8th Floor 20006; (202) 628-7745. Fax, (202) 628-7779. Glenn Hamer, Director.
General e-mail, info@seia.org
Web, www.seia.org

Membership: industries with interests in the production and use of solar energy. Promotes growth of U.S.

and international markets; interests include photovoltaic, solar thermal power, solar hot water, and solar space heating and cooling technologies. Monitors legislation and regulations. (Affiliated with National BioEnergy Industries Assn.)

Sustainable Buildings Industry Council, *1331 H St. N.W., #1000 20005; (202) 628-7400. Fax, (202) 393-5043. Helen English, Executive Director.*

General e-mail, sbic@sbicouncil.org
Web, www.sbicouncil.org

Membership: building industry associations, corporations, small businesses, and independent professionals. Provides information on sustainable design and construction. Interests include passive solar industry and related legislation, regulations, and programs.

9 ⬚

Environment and Natural Resources

GENERAL POLICY

AGENCIES

Agriculture Dept. (USDA), *Natural Resources and Environment,* 1400 Independence Ave. S.W., #217E 20250-0108; (202) 720-7173. Fax, (202) 720-0632. Mark Rey, Under Secretary.
Web, www.usda.gov

Formulates and promulgates policy relating to environmental activities and management of natural resources. Oversees the Forest Service and the Natural Resources Conservation Service.

Council on Environmental Quality *(Executive Office of the President),* 730 Jackson Pl. N.W. 20503; (202) 395-5750. Fax, (202) 456-6546. James Laurence Connaughton, Chair.
Web, www.whitehouse.gov/ceq

Advises the president on environmental issues and prepares annual report on environmental quality for Congress; develops regulations for implementation of environmental impact statement law; provides information on environmental affairs.

Environment, Safety, and Health *(Energy Dept.),* 1000 Independence Ave. S.W., #7A097 20585; (202) 586-6151. Fax, (202) 586-0956. Beverly Cook, Assistant Secretary.
Web, www.eh.doe.gov

Ensures that Energy Dept. programs comply with federal policies and standards designed to protect the environment and government property. Approves all environmental impact statements prepared by the department. Oversees health and nonnuclear safety conditions at Energy Dept. facilities.

Environmental Protection Agency (EPA), 1200 Pennsylvania Ave. N.W., #3000 20460; (202) 564-4700. Fax, (202) 501-1450. Christine Todd Whitman, Administrator; Linda Fisher, Deputy Administrator. Information, (202) 260-7751. Press, (202) 260-4355.
Web, www.epa.gov

Administers federal environmental policies, research, and regulations; provides information on environmental subjects, including water pollution, pollution prevention, hazardous and solid waste disposal, air and noise pollution, pesticides and toxic substances, and radiation.

Environmental Protection Agency (EPA), *Children's Health Protection,* 1200 Pennsylvania Ave. N.W., MS 1107A 20460; (202) 564-2188. Fax, (202) 564-2733. Joanne Rodman, Director (Acting).
Web, www.epa.gov

Supports and facilitates EPA's efforts to protect children's health from environmental threats.

Environmental Protection Agency (EPA), *National Center for Environmental Assessment,* 808 17th St. N.W., #400 20460; (202) 564-3322. Fax, (202) 565-0090. George W. Alapas, Director (Acting).
Web, www.epa.gov/ncea

Evaluates animal and human health data to define environmental health hazards and estimate risk to humans.

Environmental Protection Agency (EPA), *Policy,* 1200 Pennsylvania Ave. N.W., MS 1804 20460; (202) 564-4332. Fax, (202) 501-1688. Jessica L. Furey, Assistant Administrator.
Web, www.epa.gov

Coordinates agency policy development and standard-setting activities.

Environmental Protection Agency (EPA), *Research and Development,* 1200 Pennsylvania Ave. N.W., MS 8101R 20460; (202) 564-6620. Fax, (202) 565-2430. Paul Gilman, Assistant Administrator.
Web, www.epa.gov

Develops scientific data and methods to support EPA standards and regulations; conducts exposure and risk assessments; researches applied and long-term technologies to reduce risks from pollution.

Environmental Protection Agency (EPA), *Science Advisory Board,* 1200 Pennsylvania Ave. N.W., MC 1400A 20460; (202) 564-4533. Fax, (202) 501-0323. Vanessa Vu, Staff Director.
Web, www.epa.gov

Coordinates nongovernment scientists and engineers who advise the administrator on scientific and technical aspects of environmental problems and issues. Evaluates EPA research projects, the technical basis of regulations and standards, and policy statements.

Housing and Urban Development Dept. (HUD), *Community Viability,* 451 7th St. S.W., #7240 20410; (202) 708-2894. Fax, (202) 708-3363. Richard H. Broun, Director.
Web, www.hud.gov

Issues policies and sets standards for environmental and land-use planning and environmental management practices. Oversees HUD implementation of requirements on environment, historic preservation, archeology, flood plain management, coastal zone management, sole source aquifers, farmland protection, endangered species, airport clear zones, explosive hazards, radon, and noise.

Interior Dept. (DOI), *1849 C St. N.W., #6156 20240; (202) 208-7351. Fax, (202) 208-6956. Gale A. Norton, Secretary; Steven Griles, Deputy Secretary. Information, (202) 208-3100. Library, (202) 208-5815. Locator, (202) 208-3100.*
Web, www.doi.gov

Principal U.S. conservation agency. Manages most federal land; responsible for conservation and development of mineral and water resources; responsible for conservation, development, and use of fish and wildlife resources; operates recreation programs for federal parks, refuges, and public lands; preserves and administers the nation's scenic and historic areas; reclaims arid lands in the West through irrigation; administers native American lands and relationships with tribal governments.

Interior Dept. (DOI), *Policy Analysis, 1849 C St. N.W., #4411, MS 4426 20240; (202) 208-5978. Fax, (202) 208-4867. William D. Bettenberg, Director.*
Web, www.doi.gov

Analyzes how policies affect the department; makes recommendations and develops policy options for resolving natural resource problems.

Justice Dept. (DOJ), *Environment and Natural Resources, 950 Pennsylvania Ave. N.W., #2143 20530-0001; (202) 514-2701. Fax, (202) 514-0557. Thomas L. Sansonetti, Assistant Attorney General.*
Web, www.usdoj.gov/enrd

Handles civil suits involving the federal government in all areas of the environment and natural resources; handles some criminal suits involving pollution control.

National Institute of Environmental Health Sciences *(National Institutes of Health), Bldg. 31, #B1C02, 31 Center Dr., MSC 2256, Bethesda, MD 20892-2256; (301) 496-3511. Fax, (301) 496-0563. Kenneth Olden, Director; Chris Schonwalder, Director, International Programs.*
Web, www.niehs.nih.gov

Conducts and supports fundamental research on the effects of chemical, biological, and physical factors in the environment on human health. Participates in international research. (Most operations located in Research Triangle Park, N.C.)

National Oceanic and Atmospheric Administration (NOAA), *(Commerce Dept.), 14th St. and Constitution Ave. N.W., #5128 20230; (202) 482-3436. Fax, (202) 408-9674. Vice Admiral Conrad C. Lautenbacher Jr., Under Secretary. Information, (301) 713-4000. Press, (301) 482-6090.*

Web, www.noaa.gov

Conducts research in marine and atmospheric sciences; issues weather forecasts and warnings vital to public safety and the national economy; surveys resources of the sea; analyzes economic aspects of fisheries operations; develops and implements policies on international fisheries; provides states with grants to conserve coastal zone areas; protects marine mammals; maintains a national environmental center with data from satellite observations and other sources including meteorological, oceanic, geodetic, and seismological data centers; provides colleges and universities with grants for research, education, and marine advisory services; prepares and provides nautical and aeronautical charts and maps.

National Oceanic and Atmospheric Administration (NOAA), *(Commerce Dept.), National Environmental Satellite, Data, and Information Service, 1335 East-West Hwy., Silver Spring, MD 20910; (301) 713-3578. Fax, (301) 713-1249. Gregory W. Withee, Assistant Administrator.*
Web, www.nesdis.noaa.gov

Provides satellite observations of the environment by operating polar orbiting and geostationary satellites; develops satellite techniques; increases the utilization of satellite data in environmental services.

National Science and Technology Council *(Executive Office of the President), Dwight D. Eisenhower Executive Office Bldg., #430 20502-0001; (202) 456-6101. Fax, (202) 456-6026. Ann B. Carlson, Executive Secretary.*
General e-mail, information@ostp.eop.gov
Web, www.ostp.gov

Coordinates research and development activities and programs that involve more than one federal agency. Activities concern earth sciences, materials, forestry research, and radiation policy.

Office of Science and Technology Policy (OSTP), *(Executive Office of the President), Environment, Dwight D. Eisenhower Executive Office Bldg., #436 20502; (202) 456-6202. Fax, (202) 456-6027. Kathie L. Olsen, Assistant Director, Science.*
General e-mail, ostpinfo@ostp.eop.gov
Web, www.ostp.gov

Provides the president with policy analysis and assistance on issues related to the environment and natural resources.

Transportation Dept. (DOT), *Environmental Policies Team, 400 7th St. S.W., #10309 20590-0001; (202) 366-4861. Fax, (202) 366-7618. Camille H. Mittelholtz, Team Leader.*

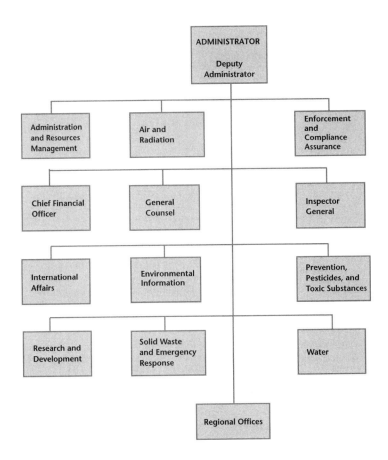

General e-mail, dot.comments@ost.dot.gov
Web, www.dot.gov

Develops environmental policy and makes recommendations to the secretary; monitors Transportation Dept. implementation of environmental legislation; serves as liaison with other federal agencies and state and local governments on environmental matters related to transportation.

U.S. Geological Survey (USGS), *(Interior Dept.),*
12201 Sunrise Valley Dr., MS 100, Reston, VA 20192;
(703) 648-7411. Fax, (703) 648-4454. Charles G. Groat,
Director. Library, (703) 648-4302. Press, (703) 648-4460.
Web, www.usgs.gov

Provides reports, maps, and databases that describe and analyze water, energy, biological, and mineral resources; the land surface; and the underlying geological structure and dynamic processes of the earth.

CONGRESS

General Accounting Office (GAO), *Natural Resources and Environment, 441 G St. N.W., MS 2T23A 20548; (202) 512-9894. Fax, (202) 512-8774. Robert A. Robinson, Managing Director.*
Web, www.gao.gov

Independent, nonpartisan agency in the legislative branch that audits, analyzes, and reports on efficiency and effectiveness of Interior Dept. programs concerned with managing natural resources.

House Appropriations Committee, *Subcommittee on Commerce, Justice, State, and the Judiciary*, H309 CAP 20515; (202) 225-3351. Rep. Frank R. Wolf, R-Va., Chair; Mike Ringler, Staff Director.

Web, www.house.gov/appropriations

Jurisdiction over legislation to appropriate funds for the Marine Mammal Commission and the Commerce Dept., including the National Oceanic and Atmospheric Administration.

House Appropriations Committee, *Subcommittee on Energy and Water Development*, 2362 RHOB 20515; (202) 225-3421. Rep. David L. Hobson, R-Ohio, Chair; Robert Schmidt, Staff Director.

Web, www.house.gov/appropriations

Jurisdiction over legislation to appropriate funds for the Bureau of Reclamation in the Interior Dept., the federal power marketing administrations in the Energy Dept., the civil programs of the Army Corps of Engineers, the Tennessee Valley Authority, and related agencies.

House Appropriations Committee, *Subcommittee on Interior*, B308 RHOB 20515; (202) 225-3081. Fax, (202) 225-9069. Rep. Charles H. Taylor, R-N.C., Chair; Deborah A. Weatherly, Staff Director.

Web, www.house.gov/appropriations

Jurisdiction over legislation to appropriate funds for the Interior Dept. (except the Bureau of Reclamation), the Forest Service in the Agriculture Dept., clean coal technology, fossil energy, naval petroleum and oil shale reserves, and other natural resources-related services and programs.

House Appropriations Committee, *Subcommittee on VA, HUD, and Independent Agencies*, H143 CAP 20515; (202) 225-3241. Rep. James T. Walsh, R-N.Y., Chair; Tim Peterson, Staff Director.

Web, www.house.gov/appropriations

Jurisdiction over legislation to appropriate funds for the Environmental Protection Agency, Office of Environmental Quality, Council on Environmental Quality, National Science Foundation, and other environment-related services and programs.

House Energy and Commerce Committee, *Subcommittee on Environment and Hazardous Materials*, 2125 RHOB 20515; (202) 225-2927. Fax, (202) 225-1919. Rep. Paul E. Gillmor, R-Ohio, Chair; David V. Marventano, Staff Director.

General e-mail, commerce@mail.house.gov

Web, energycommerce.house.gov

Jurisdiction over legislation on solid waste disposal, pollution, toxic substances, noise pollution control, and hazardous materials (except EPA research and development programs). Jurisdiction over the Comprehensive Environmental Response, Compensation, and Liability Act (Superfund); the Resource Conservation and Recovery Act; and the Toxic Substances Control Act (jurisdiction shared with House Science Committee).

House Government Reform Committee, *Subcommittee on Energy Policy, Natural Resources, and Regulatory Affairs*, B377 RHOB 20515; (202) 225-4407. Fax, (202) 225-2441. Rep. Doug Ose, R-Calif., Chair; Dan Skopec, Staff Director.

Web, www.house.gov/reform

Oversight of the Interior Dept., the Environmental Protection Agency, the Office of Environmental Policy, the Nuclear Regulatory Commission, the U.S. Fish and Wildlife Service, and the Council on Environmental Quality.

House Resources Committee, 1324 LHOB 20515; (202) 225-2761. Fax, (202) 225-5929. Rep. Richard W. Pombo, R-Calif., Chair; Steve Ding, Chief of Staff.

General e-mail, resources.committee@mail.house.gov

Web, resourcescommittee.house.gov

Jurisdiction over legislation on natural resource issues, including water control.

House Resources Committee, *Subcommittee on Fisheries, Conservation, Wildlife, and Oceans*, H2-188 FHOB 20515; (202) 226-0200. Fax, (202) 225-1542. Rep. Wayne T. Gilchrest, R-Md., Chair; Harry Burroughs, Staff Director.

General e-mail, fisheries.subcommittee@mail.house.gov

Web, resourcescommittee.house.gov

Jurisdiction over legislation on many natural resource issues, including conservation, marine sanctuaries, and wildlife resources.

House Science Committee, *Subcommittee on Environment, Technology, and Standards*, 2319 RHOB 20515; (202) 225-8844. Fax, (202) 225-4438. Rep. Vernon J. Ehlers, R-Mich., Chair; Eric Webster, Staff Director.

General e-mail, science@mail.house.gov

Web, www.house.gov/science

Jurisdiction over Environmental Protection Agency research and development programs.

House Small Business Committee, 2361 RHOB 20515; (202) 225-5821. Fax, (202) 225-3587. Rep. Donald Manzullo, R-Ill., Chair; J. Matthew Szymanski, Chief of Staff.

General e-mail, smbiz@mail.house.gov

Web, www.house.gov/smbiz

Studies and makes recommendations on environmental and pollution issues as they relate to small business.

Senate Agriculture, Nutrition, and Forestry Committee, *Subcommittee on Forestry, Conservation, and Rural Revitalization,* SR-328A 20510; (202) 224-2035. Sen. Michael D. Crapo, R-Idaho, Chair; Vacant, Staff Director.
Web, agriculture.senate.gov

Jurisdiction over legislation on many natural resource issues, including conservation, forestry, and water control; oversight of the Interior Dept. and the Agriculture Dept.'s Forest Service.

Senate Appropriations Committee, *Subcommittee on Commerce, Justice, State, and the Judiciary,* S-206 CAP 20510; (202) 224-7277. Fax, (202) 228-0587. Sen. Judd Gregg, R-N.H., Chair; James Morhard, Clerk.
Web, appropriations.senate.gov

Jurisdiction over legislation to appropriate funds for the Commerce Dept., including the National Oceanic and Atmospheric Administration, the National Institute of Standards and Technology, and the National Technical Information Service.

Senate Appropriations Committee, *Subcommittee on Energy and Water Development,* SD-129 20510; (202) 224-7260. Fax, (202) 228-2322. Sen. Pete V. Domenici, R-N.M., Chair; Clay Sell, Clerk.
Web, appropriations.senate.gov

Jurisdiction over legislation to appropriate funds for the Bureau of Reclamation in the Interior Dept., the federal power marketing administrations in the Energy Dept., the civil programs of the Army Corps of Engineers, the Tennessee Valley Authority, and related agencies.

Senate Appropriations Committee, *Subcommittee on Interior and Related Agencies,* SD-131 20510; (202) 224-7233. Fax, (202) 228-4532. Sen. Conrad Burns, R-Mont., Chair; Bruce Evans, Clerk.
Web, appropriations.senate.gov

Jurisdiction over legislation to appropriate funds for the Interior Dept., the Forest Service in the Agriculture Dept., the National Park Service, clean coal technology, fossil energy, naval petroleum and oil shale reserves, and other natural resources–related services and programs.

Senate Appropriations Committee, *Subcommittee on VA, HUD, and Independent Agencies,* SD-130 20510; (202) 224-8252. Fax, (202) 228-1624. Sen. Christopher S. Bond, R-Mo., Chair; Jon Kamarck, Clerk.
Web, appropriations.senate.gov

Jurisdiction over legislation to appropriate funds for the Environmental Protection Agency, Office of Environmental Quality, Council on Environmental Quality, National Science Foundation, and other environment-related services and programs.

Senate Energy and Natural Resources Committee, SD-364 20510; (202) 224-4971. Fax, (202) 224-6163. Sen. Pete V. Domenici, R-N.M., Chair; Alex Flint, Staff Director.
General e-mail, committee@energy.senate.gov
Web, energy.senate.gov

Jurisdiction over legislation on many aspects of natural resources, including research and development.

Senate Environment and Public Works Committee, SD-410 20510; (202) 224-6176. Fax, (202) 224-5167. Sen. James M. Inhofe, R-Okla., Chair; Andrew Wheeler, Staff Director.
General e-mail, guest1@epw.senate.gov
Web, epw.senate.gov

Jurisdiction over most legislation relating to environmental affairs, including global warming and Environmental Protection Agency research and development programs concerning air, water, noise, solid waste, hazardous materials, and toxic substances; jurisdiction over legislation relating to the National Environmental Policy Act, the Comprehensive Environmental Response, Compensation, and Liability Act (Superfund), the Resource Conservation and Recovery Act, and the Toxic Substances Control Act. Oversight of the Environmental Protection Agency, the Office of Environmental Policy, the Nuclear Regulatory Commission, the U.S. Fish and Wildlife Service, and the Council on Environmental Quality.

Senate Small Business and Entrepreneurship Committee, SR-428A 20510; (202) 224-5175. Fax, (202) 228-1128. Sen. Olympia J. Snowe, R-Maine, Chair; Mark Warren, Staff Director.
Web, sbc.senate.gov

Studies and makes recommendations on environmental and pollution issues as they relate to small businesses.

NONPROFIT

American Bar Assn. (ABA), *Standing Committee on Environmental Law,* 740 15th St. N.W. 20005; (202) 662-1694. Fax, (202) 638-3844. Elissa Lichtenstein, Director.
Web, www.abanet.org/publicserv/environmental.html

Conducts domestic and international projects in environmental law and policy; coordinates environmental law activities throughout the ABA.

Citizens for a Sound Economy, *1900 M St. N.W., #500 20036; (202) 783-3870. Fax, (202) 783-4687. Paul Beckner, President.*
Web, www.cse.org

Education and research organization that seeks market-oriented solutions to environmental problems. Develops initiatives to balance environmental and economic considerations; supports private efforts to manage wildlife habitats.

Concern, *1794 Columbia Rd. N.W., #6 20009; (202) 328-8160. Fax, (202) 387-3378. Susan F. Boyd, Executive Director.*
General e-mail, concern@igc.org
Web, www.sustainable.org

Environmental education organization interested in issues such as sustainable communities and smart growth issues.

The Conservation Fund, *1800 N. Kent St., #1120, Arlington, VA 22209-2156; (703) 525-6300. Fax, (703) 525-4610. Lawrence A. Selzer, President.*
General e-mail, postmaster@conservationfund.org
Web, www.conservationfund.org

Creates partnerships with the private sector, non-profit organizations, and public agencies to promote land and water conservation.

Co-op America, *1612 K St. N.W., #600 20006; (202) 872-5307. Fax, (202) 331-8166. Alisa Gravitz, Executive Director. Information, (800) 584-7336.*
General e-mail, info@coopamerica.org
Web, www.coopamerica.org

Educates consumers and businesses about social and environmental responsibility. Publishes a directory of environmentally and socially responsible businesses and a financial planning guide for investment.

Earth Share, *3400 International Dr. N.W., #2K 20008; (202) 537-7100. Fax, (202) 537-7101. Kalman Stein, President. Information, (800) 875-3863.*
General e-mail, info@earthshare.org
Web, www.earthshare.org

Federation of environmental and conservation organizations. Works with government and private payroll deduction programs to solicit contributions to member organizations for environmental research, education, and community programs. Provides information on establishing environmental giving options in the workplace.

Edison Electric Institute, *701 Pennsylvania Ave. N.W. 20004; (202) 508-5000. Fax, (202) 508-5759. Thomas R. Kuhn, President.*

Web, www.eei.org

Membership: investor-owned electric power companies and electric utility holding companies. Interests include electric utility operation and concerns, including conservation and energy management, energy analysis, resources and environment, cogeneration and renewable energy resources, nuclear power, and research. Library open to the public by appointment.

Environmental and Energy Study Institute, *122 C St. N.W., #630 20001-2109; (202) 628-1400. Fax, (202) 628-1825. Carol Werner, Director.*
General e-mail, eesi@eesi.org
Web, www.eesi.org

Nonpartisan policy education and analysis group established by members of Congress to foster informed debate on environmental and energy issues. Interests include policies for sustainable development, energy, climate change, transportation, and fiscal policy reform.

Environmental Council of the States, *444 N. Capitol St. N.W., #445 20001; (202) 624-3660. Fax, (202) 624-3666. R. Steven Brown, Executive Director.*
General e-mail, ecos@sso.org
Web, www.ecos.org

Works to improve the environment by providing for the exchange of ideas and experiences among states and territories; fosters cooperation and coordination among environmental management professionals.

Environmental Defense Fund, *Washington Office, 1875 Connecticut Ave. N.W., #600 20009-5728; (202) 387-3500. Fax, (202) 234-6049. Senta Boardley, Office Manager.*
Web, www.environmentaldefense.org

Citizens' interest group staffed by lawyers, economists, and scientists. Takes legal action on environmental issues; provides information on pollution prevention, environmental health, wetlands, toxic substances, acid rain, tropical rain forests, and litigation of water pollution standards. (Headquarters in New York.)

Environmental Law Institute, *1616 P St. N.W., #200 20036; (202) 939-3800. Fax, (202) 939-3868. J. William Futrell, President.*
General e-mail, law@eli.org
Web, www.eli.org

Research and education organization with an interdisciplinary staff of lawyers, economists, scientists, and journalists. Publishes materials on environmental issues, sponsors education and training courses, issues policy recommendations, and cosponsors conferences on environmental law.

Environmental Media Services, *1320 18th St., 5th Floor 20036; (202) 463-6670. Fax, (202) 463-6671. Arlie Schardt, President.*

Web, www.ems.org

Advocates expanded and improved coverage of environmental issues in the nation's media. Conducts educational workshops.

Environmental Working Group, *1436 U St. N.W., #100 20009; (202) 667-6982. Fax, (202) 232-2592. Kenneth A. Cook, President.*

General e-mail, info@ewg.org

Web, www.ewg.org

Research and advocacy organization that studies and reports on the presence of herbicides and pesticides in food and drinking water. Monitors legislation and regulations.

Friends of the Earth (FOE), *1025 Vermont Ave. N.W., #300 20005-6303; (202) 783-7400. Fax, (202) 783-0444. Brent Blackwelder, President.*

General e-mail, foe@foe.org

Web, www.foe.org

Environmental advocacy group concerned with environmental, public health, and energy-related issues, including clean air, water, and groundwater; energy conservation; international water projects; transportation of hazardous wastes; global warming; and toxic substances and pesticides. Specializes in federal budget and tax issues related to the environment; ozone layer and groundwater protection; and World Bank and International Monetary Fund reform. Library open to the public by appointment.

Izaak Walton League of America, *707 Conservation Lane, Gaithersburg, MD 20878-2983; (301) 548-0150. Fax, (301) 548-0146. Paul W. Hansen, Executive Director.*

General e-mail, general@iwla.org

Web, www.iwla.org

Grassroots organization that promotes conservation of natural resources and the environment. Interests include air and water pollution and wildlife habitat protection. Provides information on acid rain and stream cleanup efforts at the local level.

League of Conservation Voters (LCV), *1920 L St. N.W., #800 20036; (202) 785-8683. Fax, (202) 835-0491. Debra J. Callahan, President.*

General e-mail, lcv@lcv.org

Web, www.lcv.org

Works to support the environmental movement by helping elect environmentally concerned candidates to public office.

League of Women Voters Education Fund (LWV), *Natural Resources, 1730 M St. N.W., #1000 20036; (202) 429-1965. Fax, (202) 429-0854. Nancy Tate, Director.*

General e-mail, lwv@lwv.org

Web, www.lwv.org

Education foundation affiliated with the League of Women Voters. Promotes citizen understanding of nuclear and solid waste issues; holds regional workshops to educate community leaders on these issues.

National Assn. of Conservation Districts, *509 Capitol Court N.E. 20002-4937; (202) 547-6223. Fax, (202) 547-6450. Ernest C. Shea, Chief Executive Officer.*

General e-mail, washington@nacdnet.org

Web, www.nacdnet.org

Membership: conservation districts (local subdivisions of state government). Works to promote the conservation of land, forests, and other natural resources. Interests include erosion and sediment control; water quality; forestry, water, flood plain, and range management; rural development; and urban and community conservation.

National Audubon Society, *Public Policy, Washington Office, 1150 Connecticut Ave. N.W., #600 20036; (202) 861-2242. Fax, (202) 861-4290. Bob Perciasepe, Senior Vice President.*

Web, www.audubon.org

Citizens' interest group that promotes environmental preservation. Provides information on water resources, public lands, rangelands, forests, parks, wildlife and marine conservation, and the national wildlife refuge system. (Headquarters in New York.)

National Environmental Trust, *1200 18th St. N.W., #500 20036; (202) 887-8800. Fax, (202) 887-8877. Phil Clapp, President.*

General e-mail, netinfo@environet.org

Web, www.environet.org

Organization that identifies and publicizes environmental issues at the national and local levels. Interests include climate change, endangered species, hazardous chemicals, and campaign finance reform; opposes efforts to weaken environmental laws. Monitors legislation and regulations.

National Wilderness Institute, *805 King St., 4th Floor, Alexandria, VA 22314; (703) 836-7404. Fax, (703) 836-7405. Robert Gordon, Executive Director.*

General e-mail, nwi@nwi.org

Web, www.nwi.org

Works to inform the public, the media, educators, and public officials about environmental issues including endangered species, land use rights, and environmental regulations.

National Wildlife Federation, *11100 Wildlife Center Dr., Reston, VA 20190-5362; (703) 438-6000. Fax, (703) 438-3570. Mark Van Putten, President. Information, (800) 822-9919.*
General e-mail, info@nwf.org
Web, www.nwf.org

Promotes conservation of natural resources; provides information on the environment and resource management; takes legal action on environmental issues.

Natural Resources Defense Council, *Washington Office, 1200 New York Ave. N.W., #400 20005-4709; (202) 289-6868. Fax, (202) 289-1060. Rae Roach, Office Manager.*
General e-mail, nycnrdcinfo@nrdc.org
Web, www.nrdc.org

Environmental organization staffed by lawyers and scientists who undertake litigation and research. Interests include air, water, land use, forests, toxic materials, natural resources management and conservation, preservation of endangered plant species, and ozone pollution. (Headquarters in New York.)

Nature Conservancy, *4245 N. Fairfax Dr., #100, Arlington, VA 22203; (703) 841-5300. Fax, (703) 841-1283. Steven McCormick, President.*
Web, www.nature.org

Maintains an international system of natural sanctuaries; operates the Heritage Program, a cooperative effort with state governments to identify and inventory threatened and endangered plants and animals; acquires land to protect endangered species and habitats.

Population-Environment Balance, *2000 P St. N.W., #600 20036; (202) 955-5700. Fax, (202) 955-6161. Michelle Pheler, Coordinator.*
General e-mail, uspop@us.net
Web, www.balance.org

Grassroots organization that advocates U.S. population stabilization to safeguard the environment.

Resources for the Future, *1616 P St. N.W. 20036; (202) 328-5000. Fax, (202) 939-3460. Paul R. Portney, President. Library, (202) 328-5089.*
General e-mail, info@rff.org
Web, www.rff.org

Engages in research and education on environmental and natural resource issues, including forestry, multiple use of public lands, costs and benefits of pollution control, endangered species, environmental risk manage-

ment, energy and national security, and climate resources. Interests include hazardous waste, the Superfund, and biodiversity. Library open to the public.

Sierra Club, *Washington Office, 408 C St. N.E. 20002; (202) 547-1141. Fax, (202) 547-6009. Debbie Sease, Legislative Director. Legislative hotline, (202) 675-2394.*
General e-mail, information@sierraclub.org
Web, www.sierraclub.org

Citizens' interest group that promotes protection of natural resources. Interests include the Clean Air Act; the Arctic National Wildlife Refuge; protection of national forests, parks, and wilderness; toxins; global warming; promotion of responsible international trade; and international development lending reform. Monitors legislation and regulations. (Headquarters in San Francisco, Calif.)

Union of Concerned Scientists, *Government Relations, Washington Office, 1707 H St. N.W., #600 20006-3919; (202) 223-6133. Fax, (202) 223-6162. Alden Meyer, Director; Todd Perry, Washington Representative for Arms Control and International Security.*
General e-mail, ucs@ucsusa.org
Web, www.ucsusa.org

Membership: scientists and others who advocate a comprehensive approach to resolving global environmental and resource concerns. Educates and mobilizes citizens on the linkages between resource depletion, environmental degradation, climate changes, consumption patterns, and population growth. Fosters cooperative efforts between the scientific, environmental, and religious communities through the National Religious Partnership for the Environment. (Headquarters in Cambridge, Mass.)

U.S. Chamber of Commerce, *Environment, Technology, and Regulatory Affairs, 1615 H St. N.W. 20062-2000; (202) 463-5533. Fax, (202) 887-3445. Bill Kovacs, Vice President.*
General e-mail, environment@uschamber.com
Web, www.uschamber.com

Monitors operations of federal departments and agencies responsible for environmental programs, policies, regulatory issues, and food safety. Analyzes and evaluates legislation and regulations that affect the environment.

U.S. Public Interest Research Group (USPIRG), *218 D St. S.E. 20003; (202) 546-9707. Fax, (202) 546-2461. Gene Karpinski, Executive Director.*
General e-mail, uspirg@pirg.org
Web, www.uspirg.org

Coordinates grassroots efforts to advance environmental and consumer protection laws; conducts research on environmental issues, including toxic and solid waste, air and water pollution, pesticides, endangered species, forest and wildlife preservation, alternative energy sources, and energy conservation; compiles reports and disseminates information on such issues; drafts and monitors environmental laws; testifies on behalf of proposed environmental legislation.

The Wilderness Society, *1615 M St. N.W., 2nd Floor 20036; (202) 833-2300. Fax, (202) 429-3958. William H. Meadows III, President. Information, (202) 833-2300.*
General e-mail, tws@tws.org
Web, www.wilderness.org

Promotes preservation of wilderness and the responsible management of all federal lands, including national parks and forests, wilderness areas, wildlife refuges, and land administered by the Interior Dept.'s Bureau of Land Management.

International Issues

AGENCIES

Environmental Protection Agency (EPA), *International Affairs, 1200 Pennsylvania Ave. N.W., #31207 20460; (202) 564-6600. Fax, (202) 564-1450. Judith E. Ayres, Assistant Administrator.*
Web, www.epa.gov

Coordinates the agency's work on international environmental issues and programs, including management of bilateral agreements and participation in multilateral organizations and negotiations.

International Trade Administration (ITA), *(Commerce Dept.), Environmental Technologies Industries, 14th St. and Constitution Ave. N.W., #1003 20230; (202) 482-5225. Fax, (202) 482-5665. Carlos F. Montoulieu, Director.*
Web, www.environment.ita.doc.gov

Works to facilitate and increase exports of U.S. environmental technologies, including both goods and services. Conducts market analysis, business counseling, and trade promotion.

State Dept., *Ecology and Terrestrial Conservation, 2201 C St. N.W., #4333 20520; (202) 647-2418. Fax, (202) 736-7351. Doris K. Stephens, Director; Stephanie J. Caswell, Deputy Director.*
Web, www.state.gov

Represents the United States in international affairs relating to natural resources. Interests include wildlife, tropical forests, and biological diversity.

State Dept., *Environmental Policy, 2201 C St. N.W., #4325 20520; (202) 647-9266. Fax, (202) 647-5947. Jeff Lunstead, Director.*
Web, www.state.gov

Advances U.S. interests internationally regarding multilateral environmental organizations, chemical wastes and other pollutants, and bilateral and regional environmental policies.

State Dept., *Oceans and International Environmental and Scientific Affairs, 2201 C St. N.W., #7831 20520-7818; (202) 647-1554. Fax, (202) 647-0217. John F. Turner, Assistant Secretary. Press, (202) 647-3486.*
Web, www.state.gov

Concerned with foreign policy as it affects natural resources and the environment, human health, the global climate, energy production, and oceans and fisheries.

U.S.-Asia Environmental Partnership, *1819 H St. N.W., 7th Floor 20006; (202) 835-0333. Fax, (202) 835-0366. Julie Haines, Director.*
Web, www.usaep.org

Interagency program, led by the Agency for International Development (AID), that uses U.S. technology and services to help address environmental degradation and sustainable development issues in Asia and the Pacific. Focuses on pulp and paper, food processing, electroplating, petrochemical, and textile industries. (Secretariat located within the Asia and Near East Bureau at AID.)

CONGRESS

Senate Foreign Relations Committee, *Subcommittee on International Economic Policy, Export, and Trade Promotion, SD-446 20510; (202) 224-4651. Sen. Chuck Hagel, R-Neb., Chair; Mark Lagon, Professional Staff Member.*
Web, foreign.senate.gov

Jurisdiction over legislation on international environmental agreements and policy, including international marine affairs in the Antarctic and Arctic areas.

INTERNATIONAL ORGANIZATIONS

International Joint Commission, United States and Canada, *U.S. Section, 1250 23rd St. N.W., #100 20440; (202) 736-9000. Fax, (202) 736-9015. Dennis L. Schornack, Chair.*
Web, www.ijc.org/ijcweb-e.html

Deals with disputes between the United States and Canada on transboundary water and air resources. Investigates issues upon request of the governments of the United States and Canada. Reviews applications for water resource projects. (Canadian section in Ottawa.)

Organization of American States (OAS), *Sustainable Development and Environment, 1889 F St. N.W., #610 20006; (202) 458-6248. Fax, (202) 458-3560. Richard A. Meganck, Director.*
Web, www.oas.org

Provides support to OAS technical cooperation projects. Promotes integrated and sustainable development of natural resources; interests include international river basins, border areas, coastal zones, and emerging trade corridors.

World Conservation Union, *U.S. Office, Washington Office, 1630 Connecticut Ave. N.W., 3rd Floor 20009; (202) 387-4826. Fax, (202) 387-4823. Scott Hajost, Executive Director.*
General e-mail, postmaster@iucnus.org
Web, www.iucn.org

Membership: world governments, their environmental agencies, and nongovernmental organizations. Studies conservation issues from local to global levels; interests include protected areas, forests, oceans, polar regions, biodiversity, species survival, environmental law, sustainable use of resources, and the impact of trade on the environment. (Headquarters in Gland, Switzerland.)

NONPROFIT

Antarctica Project, *1630 Connecticut Ave. N.W., 3rd Floor 20009; (202) 234-2480. Fax, (202) 387-4823. Beth C. Clark, Director.*
General e-mail, antarctica@igc.org
Web, www.asoc.org

Promotes effective implementation of the Antarctic Treaty System; works to protect the environment of the Antarctic continent. Interests include depletion of ozone in polar regions.

Conservation International, *1919 M St. N.W., #600 20036; (202) 912-1000. Fax, (202) 912-1030. Russell Mittermeier, President. Information, (800) 429-5660.*
Web, www.conservation.org

Works to conserve tropical rain forests through economic development; promotes exchange of debt relief for conservation programs that involve local people and organizations. Provides private groups and governments with information and technical advice on conservation efforts; supports conservation data gathering in Latin America, Africa, Asia, and the Caribbean.

Greenpeace USA, *Washington Office, 702 H St. N.W., #300 20001; (202) 462-1177. Fax, (202) 462-4507. John Passacantando, Executive Director.*
General e-mail, greenpeace.usa@wdc.greenpeace.org
Web, www.greenpeaceusa.org

Seeks to expose global environmental problems and to promote solutions through non-violent direct action, lobbying, and creative communications. Interests include forests, oceans, toxics, global warming, nuclear energy, disarmament, and genetic engineering. (International office in Amsterdam, Netherlands.)

Pinchot Institute for Conservation, *1616 P St. N.W., #100 20036; (202) 797-6580. Fax, (202) 797-6583. V. Alaric Sample, President.*
General e-mail, pinchot@pinchot.org
Web, www.pinchot.org

Seeks to advance the conservation of natural resources nationally through policy research and analysis, convening and facilitation, and developing conservation leaders. Programs include Community-based Forest Stewardship, Conservation Policy and Organizational Change, Conservation Leadership and Executive Development, Conservation and the Arts, International Forest Policy and Planning, and the Milford Experimental Forest in Pennsylvania.

World Resources Institute, *10 G St. N.E., #800 20002; (202) 729-7600. Fax, (202) 729-7610. Jonathan Lash, President. Press, (202) 729-7736.*
General e-mail, front@wri.org
Web, www.wri.org

International organization that conducts research on environmental problems and studies the inter-relationships of natural resources, economic growth, and human needs. Interests include forestry and land use, renewable energy, fisheries, and sustainable agriculture. Assesses environmental policies of aid agencies.

World Wildlife Fund (WWF), *1250 24th St. N.W., #400 20037; (202) 293-4800. Fax, (202) 293-9211. Kathryn S. Fuller, President.*
Web, www.wwf.org

Conducts scientific research and analyzes policy on environmental and conservation issues, including pollution reduction, land use, forestry and wetlands management, parks, soil conservation, and sustainable development. Supports projects to promote biological diversity and to save endangered species and their habitats, including tropical forests in Latin America, Asia, and Africa. Awards grants and provides technical assistance to local conservation groups.

Worldwatch Institute, *1776 Massachusetts Ave. N.W., 8th Floor 20036; (202) 452-1999. Fax, (202) 296-7365. Christopher Flavin, President.*
General e-mail, worldwatch@worldwatch.org
Web, www.worldwatch.org

Research organization that focuses on interdisciplinary approach to solving global environmental problems. Interests include energy conservation, renewable resources, solar power, and energy use in developing countries.

ANIMALS AND PLANTS

AGENCIES

Animal and Plant Health Inspection Service (APHIS), *(Agriculture Dept.), Animal Care,* 4700 River Rd., Unit 84, Riverdale, MD 20737-1234; (301) 734-7833. Fax, (301) 734-4978. Dr. Chester Gipson, Deputy Administrator.
Web, www.aphis.usda.gov/ac

Administers laws that regulate the handling, breeding, and care of animals raised for sale, used in research, transported commercially, or exhibited to the public. Conducts inspections; works to prevent neglect and inhumane treatment.

Animal and Plant Health Inspection Service (APHIS), *(Agriculture Dept.), Investigative and Enforcement Services,* 4700 River Rd., Unit 85, Riverdale, MD 20737-1234; (301) 734-8684. Fax, (301) 734-4328. Alan Christian, Director.
Web, www.aphis.usda.gov/ies

Provides investigative and enforcement services and leadership, direction, and support for compliance activities within the service.

Food and Drug Administration (FDA), *(Health and Human Services Dept.), Center for Veterinary Medicine,* 7519 Standish Pl., Rockville, MD 20855-2764; (301) 827-2950. Fax, (301) 827-4401. Dr. Stephen F. Sundlof, Director.
Web, www.fda.gov/cvm

Regulates the manufacture and distribution of drugs, food additives, feed ingredients, and devices for animals, including both livestock and pets. Conducts research; works to ensure animal health and the safety of food derived from animals.

Health and Human Services Dept. (HHS), *(Health and Human Services Dept.), Human Research Protections,* 1101 Wootton Pkwy., #200, The Tower Building, Rockville, MD 20852; (301) 496-7005. Fax, (301) 402-2071. Bernard Schwetz, Director (Acting). Additional fax, (301) 402-0527.
General e-mail, ohrp@osophs.dhhs.gov
Web, ohrp.osophs.dhhs.gov

Monitors the use of human subjects in federally funded research to ensure that programs and procedures comply with Public Health Service and Health and Human Services Dept. regulations; conducts educational programs; evaluates the effectiveness of HHS policies and procedures concerning the protection of human subjects; helps domestic and international organizations address ethical issues involving human subjects' protection in medicine and research.

National Zoological Park *(Smithsonian Institution),* 3001 Connecticut Ave. N.W. 20008; (202) 673-4721. Fax, (202) 673-4607. Lucy H. Spelman, Director. Information, (202) 673-4821. Library, (202) 673-4771. TTY, (202) 673-4823. Recorded information, (202) 673-4800.
Web, www.nationalzoo.si.edu

Maintains a public zoo for exhibiting animals. Conducts research on animal behavior, ecology, nutrition, reproductive physiology, pathology, and veterinary medicine; operates an annex near Front Royal, Va., for the long-term propagation and study of endangered species. Houses a unit of the Smithsonian Institution library with volumes in zoology, biology, ecology, animal behavior, and veterinary medicine; makes interlibrary loans. Library open to qualified researchers by appointment.

CONGRESS

House Agriculture Committee, *Subcommittee on Livestock and Horticulture,* 1432P LHOB 20515; (202) 225-2171. Fax, (202) 225-0917. Rep. Robin Hayes, R-N.C., Chair; Pam Scott, Staff Director.
Web, agriculture.house.gov

Jurisdiction over legislation on inspection and certification of meat, livestock, and poultry. Jurisdiction over animal welfare, including animals used for experimentation.

Senate Agriculture, Nutrition, and Forestry Committee, *Subcommittee on Marketing, Inspection, and Product Promotion,* SR-328A 20510; (202) 224-2035. Sen. Jim Talent, R-Mo., Chair; Vacant, Staff Director.
Web, agriculture.senate.gov

Jurisdiction over legislation on inspection and certification of meat, livestock, and poultry.

NONPROFIT

American Herbal Products Assn., 8484 Georgia Ave., #370, Silver Spring, MD 20910; (301) 588-1171. Fax, (301) 588-1174. Michael McGuffin, President.
General e-mail, ahpa@ahpa.org
Web, www.ahpa.org

Membership: U.S. companies and individuals that grow, manufacture, and distribute therapeutic herbs and herbal products; and associates in education, law, media, and medicine. Supports research; promotes standardization, consumer protection, competition, and self-regulation in the industry. Monitors legislation and regulations.

American Horse Protection Assn., *1000 29th St. N.W., #T100 20007; (202) 965-0500. Fax, (202) 965-9621. Robin C. Lohnes, Executive Director.*
General e-mail, amhrseprot@aol.com
Membership: individuals, corporations, and foundations interested in protecting wild and domestic horses.

American Humane Assn., *Public Policy, Washington Office, 2007 N. 15th St., #201, Arlington, VA 22201; (703) 294-6690. Fax, (703) 294-4853. Suzanne Barnard, Director.*
Web, www.americanhumane.org
Membership: humane societies, government agencies, and individuals. Monitors legislation and regulations to ensure the proper treatment of all animals; assists local societies in establishing shelters and investigating cruelty cases; maintains training programs for humane society personnel; assists in public school education programs. (Headquarters in Denver, Colo.)

American Veterinary Medical Assn., *Governmental Relations, Washington Office, 1101 Vermont Ave. N.W., #710 20005-3521; (202) 789-0007. Fax, (202) 842-4360. Dr. Michael Chaddock, Director.*
General e-mail, avmagrg@avma.org
Web, www.avma.org
Monitors legislation and regulations affecting veterinary medicine. (Headquarters in Schaumburg, Ill.)

Americans for Medical Progress Educational Foundation, *908 King St., #301, Alexandria, VA 22314-3067; (703) 836-9595. Fax, (703) 836-9594. Jacqueline Calnan, President.*
General e-mail, amp@amprogress.org
Web, www.amprogress.org
Seeks to promote and protect animal-based medical research. Serves as a media resource by fact-checking claims of animal rights groups. Conducts public education campaign on the link between animal research and medical advances.

Animal Health Institute, *1325 G St. N.W., #700 20005-3104; (202) 637-2440. Fax, (202) 393-1667. Alexander S. Mathews, President.*
Web, www.ahi.org

Membership: manufacturers of drugs and other products (including vaccines, pesticides, and vitamins) for pets and food-producing animals. Monitors legislation and regulations.

Animal Welfare Institute, *P.O. Box 3650 20027; (202) 337-2332. Fax, (202) 338-9478. Cathy Liss, President.*
General e-mail, awi@awionline.org
Web, www.awionline.org
Educational group that opposes cruel treatment of animals used in research.

Assn. of American Veterinary Medical Colleges, *1101 Vermont Ave. N.W., #710 20005-3521; (202) 371-9195. Fax, (202) 842-0773. Dr. Lawrence E. Heider, Executive Director.*
Web, www.aavmc.org
Membership: U.S. and Canadian schools and colleges of veterinary medicine, departments of comparative medicine, and departments of veterinary science in agricultural colleges. Produces veterinary reports; sponsors continuing education programs and conferences on veterinary medical issues.

Compassion Over Killing, *P.O. Box 9773 20016; (301) 891-2458. Fax, (301) 891-6815. Paul Shapiro, Director.*
General e-mail, info@cok.net
Web, www.cok.net
Animal rights organization that primarily focuses on factory farming.

Fund for Animals, *Washington Office, 8121 Georgia Ave., #301, Silver Spring, MD 20910; (301) 585-2591. Fax, (301) 585-2595. Heidi Prescott, National Director.*
General e-mail, fundinfo@fund.org
Web, www.fund.org
Works for the humane treatment and protection of both domestic and wild animals. (Headquarters in New York.)

Humane Society of the United States, *2100 L St. N.W. 20037; (202) 452-1100. Fax, (202) 778-6132. Paul Irwin, Chief Executive.*
Web, www.hsus.org
Citizens' interest group that seeks to reduce suffering of animals used in medical research and testing. Promotes the use of nonanimal alternatives, elimination of unnecessary testing, and refinement of procedures to minimize pain. Interests include legislation regulating the use of live animals in research and testing.

National Assn. for Biomedical Research, *818 Connecticut Ave. N.W., #200 20006; (202) 857-0540. Fax, (202) 659-1902. Frankie L. Trull, President.*

General e-mail, info@nabr.org

Web, www.nabr.org

Membership: scientific and medical professional societies, academic institutions, and research-oriented corporations. Supports the humane use of animals in medical research, education, and product safety testing.

National Research Council (NRC), *Institute for Laboratory Animal Research,* 500 5th St. N.W., #NA687 20001; (202) 334-2590. Fax, (202) 334-1687. Joanne Zurlo, Director.

General e-mail, ILAR@nas.edu

Web, www.national-academies.org/ilar

Maintains an information center and answers inquiries concerning animal models for use in biomedical research, location of unique animal colonies, and availability of animals and genetic stocks from colonies and breeders. Develops guidelines on topics related to animal care and use in research, testing, and education; conducts conferences.

Physicians Committee for Responsible Medicine, 5100 Wisconsin Ave. N.W., #400 20016; (202) 686-2210. Fax, (202) 686-2216. Dr. Neal D. Barnard, President.

General e-mail, pcrm@pcrm.org

Web, www.pcrm.org

Membership: health care professionals, medical students, and laypersons interested in preventive medicine, nutrition, and higher standards in research. Investigates alternatives to animal use in medical research experimentation, product testing, and education.

Society for Animal Protective Legislation, P.O. Box 3719 20027; (703) 836-4300. Fax, (703) 836-0400. Cathy Liss, Legislative Director.

General e-mail, sapl@saplonline.org

Web, www.saplonline.org

Citizens' interest group that supports legislation to ensure the proper treatment of animals.

Fish

AGENCIES

Atlantic States Marine Fisheries Commission, 1444 Eye St. N.W., 6th Floor 20005; (202) 289-6400. Fax, (202) 289-6051. Vincent O'Shea, Executive Director.

Web, www.asmfc.org

Interstate compact commission of marine fisheries representatives from fifteen states along the Atlantic seaboard. Assists states in developing joint fisheries programs; works with other fisheries organizations and the federal government on environmental, natural resource, and conservation issues.

Interior Dept. (DOI), *Fish, Wildlife, and Parks,* 1849 C St. N.W., #3156 20240; (202) 208-4416. Fax, (202) 208-4684. Craig Manson, Assistant Secretary.

Web, www.doi.gov

Responsible for programs associated with the development, conservation, and use of fish, wildlife, recreational, historical, and national park system resources. Coordinates marine environmental quality and biological resources programs with other federal agencies.

Justice Dept. (DOJ), *Wildlife and Marine Resources,* 601 D St. N.W., 3rd Floor 20004 (mailing address: P.O. Box 7369, Ben Franklin Station 20044-7369); (202) 305-0210. Fax, (202) 305-0275. Jean E. Williams, Chief.

Web, www.usdoj.gov

Supervises both civil and criminal cases under federal maritime laws and other laws protecting marine fish and mammals. Focuses on smugglers and black market dealers of protected wildlife.

National Oceanic and Atmospheric Administration (NOAA), *(Commerce Dept.), National Marine Fisheries Service,* 1315 East-West Hwy., Silver Spring, MD 20910; (301) 713-2239. Fax, (301) 713-2258. William T. Hogarth, Assistant Administrator. Press, (301) 713-2370.

Web, www.nmfs.gov

Administers marine fishing regulations, including offshore fishing rights and international agreements; conducts marine resources research; studies use and management of these resources; administers the Magnuson Fishery Conservation and Management Act; manages and protects marine resources, especially endangered species and marine mammals, within the exclusive economic zone.

U.S. Fish and Wildlife Service *(Interior Dept.),* 1849 C St. N.W., #3256 20240; (202) 208-4717. Fax, (202) 208-6965. Stephen Williams, Director. Information, (202) 208-4131.

Web, www.fws.gov

Works with federal and state agencies and nonprofits to conserve, protect, and enhance fish and wildlife and their habitats for continuing benefit of the American people.

U.S. Fish and Wildlife Service *(Interior Dept.), Endangered Species Program,* 1849 C St. N.W., #3242 20240; (202) 208-4646. Fax, (202) 208-6916. Gary D. Frazer, Assistant Director.

Web, www.fws.gov

Monitors federal policy on fish and wildlife. Reviews all federal and federally licensed projects to determine environmental effect on fish and wildlife; responsible for maintaining the endangered species list and for protecting and restoring species to healthy numbers.

U.S. Fish and Wildlife Service *(Interior Dept.), Fisheries, 1849 C St. N.W., #3245 20240; (202) 208-6394. Fax, (202) 208-4674. Cathleen Short, Assistant Director.*
Web, www.fws.gov

Develops, manages, and protects interstate and international fisheries, including fisheries of the Great Lakes, fisheries on federal lands, aquatic ecosystems, endangered species of fish, and anadromous species. Administers the National Fish Hatchery System and the National Fish and Wildlife Resource Management Offices.

U.S. Geological Survey (USGS), *(Interior Dept.), Biological Resources, 12201 Sunrise Valley Dr., Reston, VA 20192; (703) 648-4050. Fax, (703) 648-4042. Vacant, Associate Director for Biology.*
Web, biology.usgs.gov

Performs research in support of biological resource management. Monitors and reports on the status of the nation's biotic resources, including fish resources. Conducts research on fish diseases, nutrition, and culture techniques; studies ecology of the Great Lakes and the effects of pesticides and herbicides on fish.

CONGRESS

House Resources Committee, *Subcommittee on Fisheries, Conservation, Wildlife, and Oceans, H2-188 FHOB 20515; (202) 226-0200. Fax, (202) 225-1542. Rep. Wayne T. Gilchrest, R-Md., Chair; Harry Burroughs, Staff Director.*
General e-mail, fisheries.subcommittee@mail.house.gov
Web, resourcescommittee.house.gov

Jurisdiction over legislation on fish and fish hatcheries, fisheries promotion, the Magnuson-Stevens Fishery Conservation and Management Act, fisheries research, aquaculture, and seafood safety.

Senate Commerce, Science, and Transportation Committee, *Subcommittee on Oceans, Fisheries, and Coast Guard, SH-227 20510; (202) 224-8172. Fax, (202) 224-9334. Sen. Olympia J. Snowe, R-Maine, Chair; Andrew Minkiewicz, Counsel Member.*
Web, commerce.senate.gov

Studies all aspects of fish and fish hatcheries, including the Magnuson-Stevens Fishery Conservation and Management Act, fisheries research, aquaculture, and seafood safety. (Subcommittee does not report legislation.)

NONPROFIT

American Fisheries Society (AFS), *5410 Grosvenor Lane, #110, Bethesda, MD 20814-2199; (301) 897-8616. Fax, (301) 897-8096. Gus Rassam, Executive Director.*

General e-mail, main@fisheries.org
Web, www.fisheries.org

Membership: biologists and other scientists interested in fisheries. Promotes the fisheries profession, the advancement of fisheries science, and conservation of renewable aquatic resources. Monitors legislation and regulations.

International Assn. of Fish and Wildlife Agencies, *444 N. Capitol St. N.W., #544 20001; (202) 624-7890. Fax, (202) 624-7891. John Baughman, Executive Vice President.*
General e-mail, iafwa@sso.org
Web, www.iafwa.org

Membership: federal, state, and provincial fish and wildlife management agencies in the United States, Canada, and Mexico. Encourages balanced fish and wildlife resource management.

National Fisheries Institute, *1901 N. Fort Myer Dr., #700, Arlington, VA 22209; (703) 524-8880. Fax, (703) 524-4619. John Connelly, President.*
General e-mail, office@nfi.org
Web, www.nfi.org

Membership: vessel owners and distributors, processors, wholesalers, importers, traders, and brokers of fish and shellfish. Monitors legislation and regulations on fisheries.

National Food Processors Assn., *1350 Eye St. N.W., #300 20005; (202) 639-5900. Fax, (202) 639-5932. John R. Cady, President. Press, (202) 639-5919.*
General e-mail, nfpa@nfpa-food.org
Web, www.nfpa-food.org

Membership: manufacturers and suppliers of processed and packaged food, drinks, and juice. Serves as industry liaison between seafood processors and the federal government.

Ocean Conservancy, *1725 DeSales St. N.W., #600 20036; (202) 429-5609. Fax, (202) 872-0619. Roger T. Rufe, President.*
General e-mail, ocean@oceanconservancy.org
Web, www.oceanconservancy.org

Works to prevent the overexploitation of living marine resources, including fisheries, and to restore depleted marine wildlife populations.

Trout Unlimited, *1500 Wilson Blvd., #310, Arlington, VA 22209-2404; (703) 522-0200. Fax, (703) 284-9400. Charles F. Gauvin, President.*
General e-mail, trout@tu.org
Web, www.tu.org

Membership: individuals interested in the protection and enhancement of cold-water fish and their habitat. Sponsors research projects with federal and state fisheries agencies; maintains programs for water quality surveillance and cleanup of streams and lakes.

U.S. Tuna Foundation, *1101 17th St. N.W., #609 20036; (202) 857-0610. Fax, (202) 331-9686. David G. Burney, Executive Director.*
Web, www.tunafacts.com

Membership: tuna processors, vessel owners, and fishermen's unions. Interests include fishing legislation and government relations.

Wildlife and Marine Mammals

AGENCIES

Animal and Plant Health Inspection Service (APHIS), *(Agriculture Dept.), Wildlife Services, 1400 Independence Ave. S.W., #1624S 20250-3402; (202) 720-2054. Fax, (202) 690-0053. William H. Clay, Deputy Administrator.*
Web, www.aphis.usda.gov/ws

Works to minimize damage caused by wildlife to crops and livestock, natural resources, and human health and safety. Removes or eliminates predators and nuisance birds; interests include aviation safety and coexistence of people and wildlife in suburban areas. Oversees the National Wildlife Research Center in Ft. Collins, Colo.

Forest Service *(Agriculture Dept.), Fish, Wildlife, Rare Plants, Air, and Watershed, 201 14th St. S.W. 20024 (mailing address: P.O. Box 96090 20090-6090); (202) 205-1205. Fax, (202) 205-1599. Jim Gladen, Director.*
Web, www.fs.fed.us

Provides national policy direction and management for watershed, fish, wildlife, air, and rare plants programs on lands managed by the Forest Service.

Interior Dept. (DOI), *Bird Habitat Conservation, 4401 N. Fairfax Dr., MBSP 4075, Arlington, VA 22203; (703) 358-1784. Fax, (703) 358-2282. David A. Smith, Coordinator.*
General e-mail, dbhc@fws.gov
Web, www.fws.gov

Membership: government and private-sector conservation experts. Works to protect, restore, and manage wetlands and other habitats for migratory birds and other animals and to maintain migratory bird and waterfowl populations.

Interior Dept. (DOI), *Fish, Wildlife, and Parks, 1849 C St. N.W., #3156 20240; (202) 208-4416. Fax, (202) 208-4684. Craig Manson, Assistant Secretary.*
Web, www.doi.gov

Responsible for programs associated with the development, conservation, and use of fish, wildlife, recreational, historical, and national park system resources. Coordinates marine environmental quality and biological resources programs with other federal agencies.

Justice Dept. (DOJ), *Wildlife and Marine Resources, 601 D St. N.W., 3rd Floor 20004 (mailing address: P.O. Box 7369, Ben Franklin Station 20044-7369); (202) 305-0210. Fax, (202) 305-0275. Jean E. Williams, Chief.*
Web, www.usdoj.gov

Responsible for criminal enforcement and civil litigation under federal fish and wildlife conservation statutes, including protection of wildlife, fish, and plant resources within U.S. jurisdiction; monitors interstate and foreign commerce of these resources.

Marine Mammal Commission, *4340 East-West Hwy., #905, Bethesda, MD 20814; (301) 504-0087. Fax, (301) 504-0099. David Cottingham, Executive Director; Timothy J. Ragen, Scientific Program Director.*

Established by Congress to ensure protection and conservation of marine mammals; conducts research and makes recommendations on federal programs that affect marine mammals.

Migratory Bird Conservation Commission, *4401 N. Fairfax Dr., #622, Arlington, VA 22203; (703) 358-1716. Fax, (703) 358-2223. Eric Alvarez, Secretary.*
Web, realty.fws.gov/mbcc.html

Established by the Migratory Bird Conservation Act of 1929. Decides which areas to purchase for use as migratory bird refuges and the price at which they are acquired.

National Oceanic and Atmospheric Administration (NOAA), *(Commerce Dept.), Protected Resources, 1315 East-West Hwy., #13701, Silver Spring, MD 20910; (301) 713-2332. Fax, (301) 713-0376. Laurie K. Allen, Director.*
Web, www.nmfs.gov/prot_res

Provides guidance on the conservation and protection of marine mammals and endangered species and on the conservation and restoration of their habitats. Develops national guidelines and policies for relevant research programs; prepares and reviews management and recovery plans and environmental impact analyses.

U.S. Fish and Wildlife Service *(Interior Dept.), 1849 C St. N.W., #3256 20240; (202) 208-4717. Fax, (202) 208-*

6965. Stephen Williams, Director. Information, (202) 208-4131.

Web, www.fws.gov

Works with federal and state agencies and nonprofits to conserve, protect, and enhance fish and wildlife and their habitats for continuing benefit of the American people.

U.S. Fish and Wildlife Service (*Interior Dept.*), *Bird Habitat Conservation,* 4401 N. Fairfax Dr., #110, Arlington, VA 22203; (703) 358-1784. Fax, (703) 358-2282. David A. Smith, Executive Director.

Web, www.fws.gov

Coordinates U.S. activities with Canada and Mexico to protect waterfowl habitats, restore waterfowl populations, and set research priorities under the North American Waterfowl Management Plan.

U.S. Fish and Wildlife Service (*Interior Dept.*), *Endangered Species Program,* 1849 C St. N.W., #3242 20240; (202) 208-4646. Fax, (202) 208-6916. Gary D. Frazer, Assistant Director.

Web, www.fws.gov

Monitors federal policy on fish and wildlife. Reviews all federal and federally licensed projects to determine environmental effect on fish and wildlife; responsible for maintaining the endangered species list and for protecting and restoring species to healthy numbers.

U.S. Fish and Wildlife Service (*Interior Dept.*), *National Wildlife Refuge System,* 1849 C St. N.W., #3251 20240; (202) 208-5333. Fax, (202) 208-3082. William F. Hartwig, Chief.

Web, www.fws.gov

Determines policy for the management of wildlife; manages the National Wildlife Refuge System; and manages land acquisition for wildlife refuges.

U.S. Geological Survey (USGS), (*Interior Dept.*), *Biological Resources,* 12201 Sunrise Valley Dr., Reston, VA 20192; (703) 648-4050. Fax, (703) 648-4042. Vacant, Associate Director for Biology.

Web, biology.usgs.gov

Performs research in support of biological resource management. Monitors and reports on the status of the nation's biotic resources. Conducts research on fish and wildlife, including the effects of disease and environmental contaminants on wildlife populations. Studies endangered and other species.

CONGRESS

House Government Reform Committee, *Subcommittee on Energy Policy, Natural Resources, and Regulatory Affairs,* B377 RHOB 20515; (202) 225-4407. Fax, (202) 225-2441. Rep. Doug Ose, R-Calif., Chair; Dan Skopec, Staff Director.

Web, www.house.gov/reform

Oversight of the U.S. Fish and Wildlife Service.

House Resources Committee, *Subcommittee on Fisheries, Conservation, Wildlife, and Oceans,* H2-188 FHOB 20515; (202) 226-0200. Fax, (202) 225-1542. Rep. Wayne T. Gilchrest, R-Md., Chair; Harry Burroughs, Staff Director.

General e-mail, fisheries.subcommittee@mail.house.gov

Web, resourcescommittee.house.gov

Jurisdiction over legislation on fisheries and wildlife, habitat preservation and research programs, endangered species and marine mammal protection, wildlife refuges, estuarine protection, wetlands conservation, and biological diversity. General oversight of the U.S. Fish and Wildlife Service, the National Marine Fisheries Service, the Office of Environmental Policy, the Marine Mammal Commission, and certain programs of the National Oceanic and Atmospheric Administration.

Senate Environment and Public Works Committee, *Subcommittee on Fisheries, Wildlife, and Water,* SH-407 20510; (202) 224-6176. Fax, (202) 224-1273. Sen. Michael D. Crapo, R-Idaho, Chair; Sharla Moffett-Beall, Staff Contact.

Web, epw.senate.gov

Jurisdiction over legislation on fisheries and wildlife, habitat preservation and research programs, endangered species and marine mammal protection, wildlife refuges, estuarine protection, wetlands conservation, and biological diversity; oversight of the U.S. Fish and Wildlife Service, the Office of Environmental Policy, and the Marine Mammal Commission.

NONPROFIT

Animal Welfare Institute, P.O. Box 3650 20027; (202) 337-2332. Fax, (202) 338-9478. Cathy Liss, President.

General e-mail, awi@awionline.org

Web, www.awionline.org

Educational group that opposes steel jaw leghold animal traps and supports the protection of marine mammals. Interests include preservation of endangered species, reform of cruel methods of raising food animals, and humane treatment of laboratory animals.

Defenders of Wildlife, 1101 14th St. N.W., #1400 20005; (202) 682-9400. Fax, (202) 682-1331. Rodger Schlickeisen, President.

General e-mail, info@defenders.org

Web, www.defenders.org

Advocacy group that works to protect wild animals and plants in their natural communities. Interests include endangered species and biodiversity. Monitors legislation and regulations.

Ducks Unlimited, *Governmental Affairs, Washington Office,* 1301 Pennsylvania Ave. N.W., #402 20004; (202) 347-1530. Fax, (202) 347-1533. Scott Sutherland, Director.
Web, www.ducks.org

Promotes waterfowl and other wildlife conservation through activities aimed at developing and restoring natural nesting and migration habitats. (Headquarters in Memphis, Tenn.)

Humane Society of the United States, *2100 L St. N.W. 20037; (202) 452-1100. Fax, (202) 778-6132. Paul Irwin, Chief Executive.*
Web, www.hsus.org

Works for the humane treatment and protection of animals. Interests include protecting endangered wildlife and marine mammals and their habitats and ending inhumane or cruel conditions in zoos.

International Assn. of Fish and Wildlife Agencies, *444 N. Capitol St. N.W., #544 20001; (202) 624-7890. Fax, (202) 624-7891. John Baughman, Executive Vice President.*
General e-mail, iafwa@sso.org
Web, www.iafwa.org

Membership: federal, state, and provincial fish and wildlife management agencies in the United States, Canada, and Mexico. Encourages balanced fish and wildlife resource management.

Jane Goodall Institute, *P.O. Box 14890, Silver Spring, MD 20911-4890; (301) 565-0086. Fax, (301) 565-3188. Fred Thompson, Executive Director.*
General e-mail, JGIinformation@janegoodall.org
Web, www.janegoodall.org

Seeks to increase primate habitat conservation, expand noninvasive primate research, and promote activities that ensure the well-being of primates. (Affiliated with Jane Goodall Institutes in Canada, Europe, Asia, and Africa.)

National Fish and Wildlife Foundation, *1120 Connecticut Ave. N.W., #900 20036; (202) 857-0166. Fax, (202) 857-0162. John Berry, Executive Director.*
General e-mail, nfwf@nfwf.org
Web, www.nfwf.org

Forges partnerships between the public and private sectors in support of national and international conservation activities that identify the root causes of environmental problems.

National Wildlife Federation, *11100 Wildlife Center Dr., Reston, VA 20190-5362; (703) 438-6000. Fax, (703) 438-3570. Mark Van Putten, President. Information, (800) 822-9919.*
General e-mail, info@nwf.org
Web, www.nwf.org

Educational organization that promotes preservation of natural resources; provides information on wildlife.

National Wildlife Refuge Assn., *1010 Wisconsin Ave. N.W., #200 20007; (202) 333-9075. Fax, (202) 333-9077. Evan Hirsche, President.*
General e-mail, nwra@refugenet.org
Web, www.refugenet.org

Works to improve management and protection of the Refuge System by providing information to administrators, Congress, and the public. Advocates adequate funding and improved policy guidance for the Refuge System; assists individual refuges with particular needs.

Nature Conservancy, *4245 N. Fairfax Dr., #100, Arlington, VA 22203; (703) 841-5300. Fax, (703) 841-1283. Steven McCormick, President.*
Web, www.nature.org

Maintains an international system of natural sanctuaries; operates the Heritage Program, a cooperative effort with state governments to identify and inventory threatened and endangered plants and animals; acquires land to protect endangered species and habitats.

Ocean Conservancy, *1725 DeSales St. N.W., #600 20036; (202) 429-5609. Fax, (202) 872-0619. Roger T. Rufe, President.*
General e-mail, ocean@oceanconservancy.org
Web, www.oceanconservancy.org

Works to conserve the diversity and abundance of life in the oceans and coastal areas, to prevent the overexploitation of living marine resources and the degradation of marine ecosystems, and to restore depleted marine wildlife populations and their ecosystems.

Wildlife Habitat Council, *8737 Colesville Rd., #800, Silver Spring, MD 20910; (301) 588-8994. Fax, (301) 588-4629. William W. Howard, President.*
General e-mail, whc@wildlifehc.org
Web, www.wildlifehc.org

Membership: corporations, conservation groups, and individuals. Supports use of underdeveloped private lands for the benefit of wildlife, fish, and plant life. Provides technical assistance and educational programs; fosters information sharing among members.

Wildlife Management Institute, *1101 14th St. N.W., #801 20005; (202) 371-1808. Fax, (202) 408-5059. Rollin D. Sparrowe, President.*
Web, www.wildlifemanagementinstitute.org

Research and consulting organization that provides technical services and information on natural resources, particularly on wildlife management. Interests include threatened and endangered species, nongame and hunted wildlife, waterfowl, large land mammals, and predators.

The Wildlife Society, *5410 Grosvenor Lane, #200, Bethesda, MD 20814-2144; (301) 897-9770. Fax, (301) 530-2471. Harry E. Hodgdon, Executive Director.*
General e-mail, tws@wildlife.org
Web, www.wildlife.org

Membership: wildlife biologists and resource management specialists. Provides information on management techniques; sponsors conferences; maintains list of job opportunities for members.

World Wildlife Fund (WWF), *1250 24th St. N.W., #400 20037; (202) 293-4800. Fax, (202) 293-9211. Kathryn S. Fuller, President.*
Web, www.wwf.org

International conservation organization that supports and conducts scientific research and conservation projects to promote biological diversity and to save endangered species and their habitats. Awards grants for habitat protection.

 POLLUTION AND TOXINS

AGENCIES

Environmental Protection Agency (EPA), *Enforcement and Compliance Assurance, 1200 Pennsylvania Ave. N.W., #3204 20460; (202) 564-2440. Fax, (202) 501-3842. John Peter Suarez, Assistant Administrator.*
Web, www.epa.gov

Principal adviser to the administrator on enforcement of standards for air, water, toxic substances and pesticides, hazardous and solid waste management, radiation, and emergency preparedness programs. Investigates criminal and civil violations of environmental standards; oversees federal facilities' environmental compliance and site cleanup; serves as EPA's liaison office for federal agency compliance with the National Environmental Policy Act; manages environmental review of other agencies' projects and activities; coordinates EPA native American environmental programs.

Justice Dept. (DOJ), *Environmental Crimes, 601 D St. N.W., #2102 20004 (mailing address: P.O. Box 23985 20026-3985); (202) 305-0321. Fax, (202) 305-0397. David M. Uhlmann, Chief.*
Web, www.usdoj.gov

Conducts criminal enforcement actions on behalf of the United States for all environmental protection statutes, including air, water, pesticides, hazardous wastes, wetland matters investigated by the Environmental Protection Agency, and other criminal environmental enforcement.

Justice Dept. (DOJ), *Environmental Defense, 601 D St. N.W., #8000 20004 (mailing address: P.O. Box 23986 20026-3986); (202) 514-2219. Fax, (202) 514-8865. Letitia J. Grishaw, Chief.*
Web, www.usdoj.gov

Conducts litigation on air, water, noise, pesticides, solid waste, toxic substances, Superfund, and wetlands in cooperation with the Environmental Protection Agency; represents the EPA in suits involving judicial review of EPA actions; represents the U.S. Army Corps of Engineers in cases involving dredge-and-fill activity in navigable waters and adjacent wetlands; represents the Coast Guard in oil and hazardous spill cases; defends all federal agencies in environmental litigation.

Justice Dept. (DOJ), *Environmental Enforcement, 1425 New York Ave. N.W., 13th Floor 20005 (mailing address: P.O. Box 7611, Ben Franklin Station 20044-7611); (202) 514-4624. Fax, (202) 514-0097. Bruce S. Gelber, Chief.*
Web, www.usdoj.gov

Conducts civil enforcement actions on behalf of the United States for all environmental protection statutes, including air, water, pesticides, hazardous waste, wetland matters investigated by the Environmental Protection Agency, and other civil environmental enforcement.

NONPROFIT

American Academy of Environmental Engineers, *130 Holiday Court, #100, Annapolis, MD 21401; (410) 266-3311. Fax, (410) 266-7653. William C. Anderson, Executive Director.*
General e-mail, academy@aaee.net
Web, www.aaee.net

Membership: state-licensed environmental engineers who have passed examinations in environmental engineering specialties, including general environment, air pollution control, solid waste management, hazardous waste management, industrial hygiene, radiation protection, water supply, and wastewater.

Environmental Industry Assns., *4301 Connecticut Ave. N.W., #300 20008; (202) 244-4700. Fax, (202) 966-4818. Bruce J. Parker, President.*

General e-mail, eia@envasns.org

Web, www.envasns.org

Membership: trade associations from the waste services and environmental technology industries. Represents the National Solid Waste Management Assn. and the Waste Equipment Technology Assn.

Air Pollution

AGENCIES

Environmental Protection Agency (EPA), *Air and Radiation,* *1200 Pennsylvania Ave. N.W., MC 6101A 20460; (202) 564-7400. Fax, (202) 501-0986. Jeffrey R. Holmstead, Assistant Administrator.*

Web, www.epa.gov

Administers air quality standards and planning programs of the Clean Air Act Amendment of 1990; operates the Air and Radiation Docket and Information Center. Supervises the Office of Air Quality Planning and Standards in Durham, N.C., which develops air quality standards and provides information on air pollution control issues, including industrial air pollution. Administers the Air Pollution Technical Information Center in Research Triangle Park, N.C., which collects and provides technical literature on air pollution.

Environmental Protection Agency (EPA), *Atmospheric Programs,* *1200 Pennsylvania Ave. N.W., #4410 20460; (202) 564-9140. Fax, (202) 565-2147. Brian McLean, Director.*

Web, www.epa.gov/airprogm/oar/oap.html

Responsible for acid rain and global protection programs; examines strategies for preventing atmospheric pollution and mitigating climate change.

Environmental Protection Agency (EPA), *Compliance Assessment and Media Programs,* *1200 Pennsylvania Ave. N.W., 7th Floor, MC 2223A 20460; (202) 564-2300. Fax, (202) 564-0050. Michael S. Alushin, Director.*

Web, www.epa.gov

Develops strategies and programs that help organize and explain, through inspection guidance and compliance monitoring techniques, environmental requirements that affect the regulated community. Provides program direction and support on compliance matters related to air, water, waste, oil pollution, and asbestos programs, and selected industrial sectors such as transportation, coal-fired utilities, and petroleum refining. Develops and recommends action on proposed programs, policies, and regulations.

Environmental Protection Agency (EPA), *Radiation and Indoor Air,* *1200 Pennsylvania Ave. N.W., MC 6601J 20460; (202) 564-9320. Fax, (202) 565-2043. Elizabeth Cotsworth, Director.*

Web, www.epa.gov/oar/oria.html

Administers indoor air quality control programs, including those regulating radon and environmental tobacco smoke; trains building managers in sound operation practices to promote indoor air quality.

Federal Aviation Administration (FAA), *(Transportation Dept.), Environment and Energy,* *800 Independence Ave. S.W., #900W 20591; (202) 267-3576. Fax, (202) 267-5594. Carl E. Burleson, Director.*

Web, www.faa.aee.gov

Develops government standards for aircraft noise and emissions.

U.S. Geological Survey (USGS), *(Interior Dept.), Energy Resources Program,* *12201 Sunrise Valley Dr., Reston, VA 20192 (mailing address: 915A National Center, Reston, VA 20192); (703) 648-6641. Fax, (703) 648-5464. Vacant, Program Coordinator.*

Web, energy.usgs.gov

Conducts research on fossil energy resources of the United States and the world; estimates energy resource availability and recoverability; anticipates and mitigates deleterious environmental impacts of energy resource extraction and use.

CONGRESS

Senate Environment and Public Works Committee, *Subcommittee on Clean Air, Climate Change, and Nuclear Safety,* *SD-410 20510; (202) 224-6176. Fax, (202) 224-1273. Sen. George V. Voinovich, R-Ohio, Chair; Michael Whatley, Staff Director.*

Web, epw.senate.gov

Jurisdiction over legislation on indoor and outdoor air pollution, including the Clean Air Act.

NONPROFIT

Alliance for Responsible Atmospheric Policy, *2111 Wilson Blvd., 8th Floor, Arlington, VA 22201; (703) 243-0344. Fax, (703) 243-2874. David Stirpe, Executive Director.*

General e-mail, alliance98@aol.com

Web, www.arap.org

Coalition of users and producers of chlorofluorocarbons (CFCs). Seeks further study of the ozone depletion theory.

Asbestos Information Assn./North America,
1235 Jefferson Davis Hwy., PMB-114, Arlington, VA 22202; (703) 560-2980. Fax, (703) 560-2981. B. J. Pigg, President.
General e-mail, aiabjpigg@aol.com

Membership: firms that manufacture, sell, and use products containing asbestos fiber and those that mine, mill, and sell asbestos. Provides information on asbestos and health and on industry efforts to eliminate problems associated with asbestos dust; serves as liaison between the industry and federal and state governments.

Assn. of Local Air Pollution Control Officials,
444 N. Capitol St. N.W., #307 20001; (202) 624-7864. Fax, (202) 624-7863. S. William Becker, Executive Director.
General e-mail, 4clnair@sso.org
Web, www.cleanairworld.org

Membership: local representatives of air pollution control programs nationwide that are responsible for implementing provisions of the Clean Air Act. Disseminates policy and technical information; analyzes air pollution issues; conducts seminars, workshops, and conferences. Monitors legislation and regulations.

Center for Auto Safety, *1825 Connecticut Ave. N.W., #330 20009; (202) 328-7700. Fax, (202) 387-0140. Clarence M. Ditlow III, Executive Director.*
Web, www.autosafety.org

Public interest organization that conducts research on air pollution caused by auto emissions; monitors fuel economy regulations.

Center for Clean Air Policy, *750 1st St. N.E., #940 20002; (202) 408-9260. Fax, (202) 408-8896. Edward Helme, Executive Director.*
General e-mail, general@ccap.org
Web, www.ccap.org

Membership: governors, corporations, environmentalists, and academicians. Analyzes economic and environmental effects of air pollution and related environmental problems. Serves as a liaison among government, corporate, community, and environmental groups.

Climate Institute, *333 1/2 Pennsylvania Ave. S.E., 3rd Floor 20003-1148; (202) 547-0104. Fax, (202) 547-0111. John C. Topping Jr., President.*
General e-mail, info@climate.org
Web, www.climate.org

Educates the public and policymakers on climate change (greenhouse effect, or global warming) and on the depletion of the ozone layer. Develops strategies on mitigating climate change in developing countries and in North America.

Environmental Defense Fund, *Washington Office, 1875 Connecticut Ave. N.W., #600 20009-5728; (202) 387-3500. Fax, (202) 234-6049. Senta Boardley, Office Manager.*
Web, www.environmentaldefense.org

Citizens' interest group staffed by lawyers, economists, and scientists. Conducts research and provides information on pollution prevention, environmental health, and protection of the Amazon rain forest and the ozone layer. (Headquarters in New York.)

Manufacturers of Emission Controls Assn., *1660 L St. N.W., #1100 20036; (202) 296-4797. Fax, (202) 331-1388. Dale L. McKinnon, Executive Director.*
General e-mail, info@meca.org
Web, www.meca.org

Membership: manufacturers of motor vehicle emission control equipment. Provides information on emission technology and industry capabilities.

State and Territorial Air Pollution Program Admin./Assn. of Local Air Pollution Control Officials, *444 N. Capitol St. N.W., #307 20001; (202) 624-7864. Fax, (202) 624-7863. S. William Becker, Executive Director.*
General e-mail, 4clnair@sso.org
Web, www.cleanairworld.org

Membership: state territorial and local officials responsible for implementing programs established under state and local legislation and the Clean Air Act. Disseminates policy and technical information and analyzes air quality issues; conducts seminars, workshops, and conferences. Monitors legislation and regulations.

Hazardous Materials

AGENCIES

Agency for Toxic Substances and Disease Registry (Health and Human Services Dept.), Washington Office, *200 Independence Ave. S.W., #719B 20201; (202) 690-7536. Fax, (202) 690-6985. Barbara A. Rogers, Associate Administrator.*
Web, www.atsdr.cdc.gov/legislation

Works with federal, state, and local agencies to minimize or eliminate adverse effects of exposure to toxic substances at spill and waste disposal sites; maintains a registry of persons exposed to hazardous substances and of diseases and illnesses resulting from exposure to hazardous or toxic substances; maintains inventory of hazardous substances; maintains registry of sites closed or restricted because of contamination by hazardous material. (Headquarters in Atlanta, Ga.)

Defense Dept. (DoD), *Installations and Environment,* 3400 Defense Pentagon, #3E792 20301-3400; (703) 697-8080. Fax, (703) 693-7011. Raymond F. DuBois, Deputy Under Secretary.
Web, www.acq.osd.mil/ie
Oversees and offers policy guidance for all Defense Dept. installations and environmental programs.

Environmental Protection Agency (EPA), *Chemical Control,* 1200 Pennsylvania Ave. N.W., MC 7405M 20460; (202) 564-4760. Fax, (202) 564-4745. Wardner Penberthy, Director (Acting).
Web, www.epa.gov
Selects and implements control measures for new and existing chemicals that present a risk to human health and the environment. Oversees and manages regulatory evaluation and decision-making processes. Evaluates alternative remedial control measures under the Toxic Substances Control Act and makes recommendations concerning the existence of unreasonable risk from exposure to chemicals. Develops generic and chemical-specific rules for new chemicals.

Environmental Protection Agency (EPA), *Chemical Emergency Preparedness and Prevention,* 1200 Pennsylvania Ave. N.W., #1448, MC 5104A 20460; (202) 564-8600. Fax, (202) 564-8222. Deborah Dietrich, Director. Toll-free hotline, (800) 535-0202.
Web, www.epa.gov
Develops and administers chemical emergency preparedness and prevention programs; reviews effectiveness of programs; prepares community right-to-know regulations. Provides guidance materials, technical assistance, and training. Implements the preparedness and community right-to-know provisions of the Superfund Amendments and Reauthorization Act of 1986.

Environmental Protection Agency (EPA), *Enforcement and Compliance Assurance,* 1200 Pennsylvania Ave. N.W., #3204 20460; (202) 564-2440. Fax, (202) 501-3842. John Peter Suarez, Assistant Administrator.
Web, www.epa.gov
Enforces laws that protect public health and the environment from hazardous materials, pesticides, and toxic substances.

Environmental Protection Agency (EPA), *Pollution Prevention and Toxics,* 1200 Pennsylvania Ave. N.W., #3166, EPA East Bldg. 20460; (202) 564-3810. Fax, (202) 564-0575. Charles M. Auer, Director. Information, (202) 554-1404.

Web, www.epa.gov
Assesses the health and environmental hazards of existing chemical substances and mixtures; collects information on chemical use, exposure, and effects; maintains inventory of existing chemical substances; reviews new chemicals and regulates the manufacture, distribution, use, and disposal of harmful chemicals.

Environmental Protection Agency (EPA), *Prevention, Pesticides, and Toxic Substances,* 1200 Pennsylvania Ave. N.W. 20460-7101; (202) 564-2902. Fax, (202) 564-0512. Stephen L. Johnson, Assistant Administrator. Pollution prevention and toxic substances control, (202) 564-3810.
Web, www.epa.gov
Studies and makes recommendations for regulating chemical substances under the Toxic Substances Control Act; compiles list of chemical substances subject to the act; registers, controls, and regulates use of pesticides and toxic substances.

Environmental Protection Agency (EPA), *Solid Waste and Emergency Response,* 1200 Pennsylvania Ave. N.W., MC 5101T 20460; (202) 566-0200. Fax, (202) 566-0207. Barry Breen, Principal Deputy Assistant Administrator. Superfund/Resource conservation and recovery hotline, (800) 424-9346; in Washington, (703) 412-9810. TTY, (800) 553-7672; in Washington, (703) 412-3323.
Web, www.epa.gov/swerrims
Administers and enforces the Superfund Act; manages the handling, cleanup, and disposal of hazardous wastes.

Housing and Urban Development Dept. (HUD), *Healthy Homes and Lead Hazard Control,* 451 7th St. S.W., #P3206 20410; (202) 755-1785. Fax, (202) 755-1000. David E. Jacobs, Director.
Web, www.hud.gov/lea
Advises HUD offices, other agencies, health authorities, and the housing industry on lead poisoning prevention. Develops regulations for lead-based paint; conducts research; makes grants to state and local governments for lead hazard reduction and inspection of housing.

Justice Dept. (DOJ), *Environmental Enforcement,* 1425 New York Ave. N.W., 13th Floor 20005 (mailing address: P.O. Box 7611, Ben Franklin Station 20044-7611); (202) 514-4624. Fax, (202) 514-0097. Bruce S. Gelber, Chief.
Web, www.usdoj.gov
Represents the United States in civil cases under environmental laws that involve the handling, storage, treatment, transportation, and disposal of hazardous waste. Recovers federal money spent to clean up hazardous

waste sites or sues defendants to clean up sites under Superfund.

National Response Center *(Homeland Security Dept.), 2100 2nd St. S.W., #2611 20593; (202) 267-2675. Fax, (202) 267-2165. Syed Qadir, Director, (202) 267-6352. Toll-free hotline, (800) 424-8802.*
Web, www.nrc.uscg.mil

Maintains twenty-four-hour hotline for reporting oil spills, hazardous materials accidents, chemical releases, or known or suspected terrorist threats. Notifies appropriate federal officials to reduce the effects of accidents.

National Transportation Safety Board, *Railroad, Pipeline, and Hazardous Material Investigations, 490 L'Enfant Plaza East S.W. 20594; (202) 314-6460. Fax, (202) 314-6482. Bob Chipkevich, Director.*
Web, www.ntsb.gov

Investigates railroad, natural gas, and liquid pipeline accidents and other accidents involving the transportation of hazardous materials.

Research and Special Programs Administration *(Transportation Dept.), 400 7th St. S.W., #8417 20590; (202) 366-4433. Fax, (202) 366-3666. Ellen G. Engleman, Administrator.*
Web, www.rspa.dot.gov

Coordinates research and development programs to improve safety of transportation systems; focus includes hazardous materials shipments, pipeline safety, and preparedness for transportation emergencies. Oversees Volpe National Transportation Systems Center in Cambridge, Mass., and the Transportation Safety Institute in Oklahoma City.

Research and Special Programs Administration *(Transportation Dept.), Hazardous Materials Safety, 400 7th St. S.W., #8321 20590; (202) 366-0656. Fax, (202) 366-5713. Robert McGuire, Associate Administrator.*
Web, hazmat.dot.gov

Designates substances as hazardous materials and regulates their transportation in interstate commerce; coordinates international standards regulations.

Research and Special Programs Administration *(Transportation Dept.), Pipeline Safety, 400 7th St. S.W., #7128 20590; (202) 366-4595. Fax, (202) 366-4566. Stacey Gerard, Associate Administrator.*
Web, ops.dot.gov

Issues and enforces federal regulations for hazardous liquids pipeline safety.

State Dept., *Environmental Policy, 2201 C St. N.W., #4325 20520; (202) 647-9266. Fax, (202) 647-5947. Jeff Lunstead, Director.*

Web, www.state.gov

Advances U.S. interests internationally regarding multilateral environmental organizations, chemical wastes and other pollutants, and bilateral and regional environmental policies.

CONGRESS

House Energy and Commerce Committee, *Subcommittee on Environment and Hazardous Materials, 2125 RHOB 20515; (202) 225-2927. Fax, (202) 225-1919. Rep. Paul E. Gillmor, R-Ohio, Chair; David V. Marventano, Staff Director.*
General e-mail, commerce@mail.house.gov
Web, energycommerce.house.gov

Jurisdiction over legislation on pollution; toxic substances, including the Toxic Substances Control Act; hazardous substances, including the Comprehensive Environmental Response, Compensation, and Liability Act (Superfund); and other hazardous materials programs. (Jurisdiction shared with House Science and House Transportation and Infrastructure committees.)

House Transportation and Infrastructure Committee, *Subcommittee on Water Resources and Environment, B376 RHOB 20515; (202) 225-4360. Fax, (202) 226-5435. Rep. John J. "Jimmy" Duncan Jr., R-Tenn., Chair; Susan Bodine, Staff Director.*
General e-mail, transcomm@mail.house.gov
Web, www.house.gov/transportation

Shares jurisdiction over the Comprehensive Environmental Response, Compensation, and Liability Act (Superfund) with the House Energy and Commerce and House Science committees.

Senate Environment and Public Works Committee, *Subcommittee on Superfund and Waste Management, SD-410 20510; (202) 224-6176. Fax, (202) 224-1273. Sen. Lincoln Chafee, R-R.I., Chair; Ted Michaels, Staff Contact.*
Web, epw.senate.gov

Jurisdiction over legislation on pollution, environmental research and development, pesticides, and toxic substances, including the Toxic Substances Control Act. Oversight of the Comprehensive Environmental Response, Compensation, and Liability Act (Superfund) and of hazardous materials programs.

NONPROFIT

Center for Health, Environment, and Justice, *150 S. Washington St., #300, Falls Church, VA 22046 (mailing address: P.O. Box 6806, Falls Church, VA 22040-6806); (703) 237-2249. Fax, (703) 237-8389. Lois Marie Gibbs, Executive Director.*

General e-mail, chej@chej.org

Web, www.chej.org

Provides citizens' groups, individuals, and municipalities with support and information on solid and hazardous waste. Sponsors workshops, speakers' bureau, leadership development conference, and convention. Operates a toxicity data bank on environmental and health effects of common chemical compounds; maintains a registry of technical experts to assist in solid and hazardous waste problems; gathers information on polluting corporations.

Chlorine Institute Inc., *1300 Wilson Blvd., Arlington, VA 22209; (703) 741-5760. Fax, (703) 741-6068. Robert G. Smerko, President.*

Web, www.cl2.com

Safety, health, and environmental protection center of the chlor-alkali (chlorine, caustic soda, caustic potash, and hydrogen chloride) industry. Interests include employee health and safety, resource conservation and pollution abatement, control of chlorine emergencies, product specifications, and public and community relations. Publishes technical pamphlets and drawings.

Consumer Specialty Products Assn., *900 17th St. N.W., #300 20006; (202) 872-8110. Fax, (202) 872-8114. Christopher Cathcart, President.*

General e-mail, info@cspa.org

Web, www.cspa.org

Membership: manufacturers, marketers, packagers, and suppliers in the chemical specialties industry. Specialties include cleaning compounds and detergents, insecticides, disinfectants, automotive and industrial products, polishes and floor finishes, antimicrobials, and aerosol products. Monitors scientific developments; conducts surveys and research; provides chemical safety information and consumer education programs; sponsors National Inhalants and Poisons Awareness and Aerosol Education Bureau. Monitors legislation and regulations.

Dangerous Goods Advisory Council, *1101 Vermont Ave. N.W., #301 20005; (202) 289-4550. Fax, (202) 289-4074. Alan Roberts, President.*

General e-mail, info@dgac.org

Web, dgac.org

Membership: shippers, carriers, container manufacturers, and emergency response and spill cleanup companies. Promotes safety in the domestic and international transportation of hazardous materials. Provides information and educational services; sponsors conferences, workshops, and seminars. Advocates uniform hazardous materials regulations. (Formerly Hazardous Materials Advisory Council.)

Environmental Technology Council, *734 15th St. N.W., #720 20005; (202) 783-0870. Fax, (202) 737-2038. David R. Case, Executive Director.*

General e-mail, mail@etc.org

Web, www.etc.org

Membership: environmental service firms. Interests include the recycling, detoxification, and disposal of hazardous and industrial waste and cleanup of contaminated industrial sites; works to encourage permanent and technology-based solutions to environmental problems. Provides the public with information.

International Assn. of Heat and Frost Insulators and Asbestos Workers, *9602 Martin Luther King Hwy., Lanham, MD 20706; (301) 731-9101. Fax, (301) 731-5058. James A. Grogan, President.*

Web, www.insulators.org

Membership: approximately 18,000 workers in insulation industries. Helps members negotiate pay, benefits, and better working conditions; conducts training programs and workshops. Monitors legislation and regulations. (Affiliated with the AFL-CIO.)

National Insulation Assn., *99 Canal Center Plaza, #222, Alexandria, VA 22314; (703) 683-6422. Fax, (703) 549-4838. Michele M. Jones, Executive Vice President.*

General e-mail, niainfo@insulation.org

Web, www.insulation.org

Membership: companies in the commercial and industrial insulation and asbestos abatement industries. Monitors legislation and regulations.

Rachel Carson Council, *P.O. Box 10779, Silver Spring, MD 20904; (301) 593-7507. Fax, (301) 593-6251. Diana Post, Executive Director.*

General e-mail, rccouncil@aol.com

Web, www.members.aol.com/rccouncil/ourpage

Acts as a clearinghouse for information on pesticides and alternatives to their use; maintains extensive data on toxicity and the effects of pesticides on humans, domestic animals, and wildlife. Library open to the public by appointment.

Radiation Protection

AGENCIES

Armed Forces Radiobiology Research Institute (Defense Dept.), *8901 Wisconsin Ave., Bethesda, MD 20889-5603; (301) 295-1210. Fax, (301) 295-4967. Col. Robert R. Eng (MS, USA), Director.*

Web, www.afrri.usuhs.mil

Serves as the principal ionizing radiation radiobiology research laboratory under the jurisdiction of the

Uniformed Services University of the Health Sciences. Participates in international conferences and projects. Library open to the public.

Environmental Protection Agency (EPA), *Radiation and Indoor Air,* 1200 Pennsylvania Ave. N.W., MC 6601J 20460; (202) 564-9320. Fax, (202) 565-2043. Elizabeth Cotsworth, Director.

Web, www.epa.gov/oar/oria.html

Establishes standards to regulate the amount of radiation discharged into the environment from uranium mining and milling projects and other activities that result in radioactive emissions; and to ensure safe disposal of radioactive waste. Fields a Radiological Emergency Response Team. Administers the nationwide Environmental Radiation Ambient Monitoring System (ERAMS), which analyzes environmental radioactive contamination.

Food and Drug Administration (FDA), *(Health and Human Services Dept.), Center for Devices and Radiological Health,* 9200 Corporate Blvd., #100E, Rockville, MD 20850; (301) 827-7975. Fax, (301) 594-1320. Dr. David W. Feigal Jr., Director. International Reference System, (301) 827-3993.

Web, www.fda.gov/cdrh

Administers national programs to control exposure to radiation; establishes standards for emissions from consumer and medical products; conducts factory inspections. Accredits and certifies mammography facilities and personnel; provides physicians and consumers with guidelines on radiation-emitting products. Conducts research, training, and educational programs. Library open to the public.

NONPROFIT

Institute for Science and International Security, 236 Massachusetts Ave. N.E., #500 20002; (202) 547-3633. Fax, (202) 547-3634. David Albright, Director.

General e-mail, isis@isis-online.org

Web, www.isis-online.org

Analyzes scientific and policy issues affecting national and international security, including the problems of war, regional and global arms races, the spread of nuclear weapons, and the environmental, health, and safety hazards of nuclear weapons production.

NAHB Research Center, *Radon Research and Indoor Air Quality: Laboratory Services,* 400 Prince George's Blvd., Upper Marlboro, MD 20774; (301) 249-4000. Fax, (301) 430-6180. Robert Hill, Director.

Web, www.nahbrc.org

Conducts building research to lower the cost and improve the quality of housing and other types of buildings; labels and certifies building products. (Affiliated with the National Assn. of Home Builders [NAHB].)

National Council on Radiation Protection and Measurements, 7910 Woodmont Ave., #400, Bethesda, MD 20814; (301) 657-2652. Fax, (301) 907-8768. William M. Beckner, Executive Director. Information, (800) 229-2652.

General e-mail, ncrp@ncrp.com

Web, www.ncrp.com

Nonprofit organization chartered by Congress that collects and analyzes information and provides recommendations on radiation protection and measurement. Studies radiation emissions from household items and from office and medical equipment. Holds annual conference; publishes reports on radiation protection and measurement.

Recycling and Solid Waste

AGENCIES

Environmental Protection Agency (EPA), *Solid Waste and Emergency Response,* 1200 Pennsylvania Ave. N.W., MC 5101T 20460; (202) 566-0200. Fax, (202) 566-0207. Barry Breen, Principal Deputy Assistant Administrator. Superfund/Resource conservation and recovery hotline, (800) 424-9346; in Washington, (703) 412-9810. TTY, (800) 553-7672; in Washington, (703) 412-3323.

Web, www.epa.gov/swerrims

Administers and enforces the Resource Conservation and Recovery Act.

CONGRESS

House Energy and Commerce Committee, *Subcommittee on Environment and Hazardous Materials,* 2125 RHOB 20515; (202) 225-2927. Fax, (202) 225-1919. Rep. Paul E. Gillmor, R-Ohio, Chair; David V. Marventano, Staff Director.

General e-mail, commerce@mail.house.gov

Web, energycommerce.house.gov

Jurisdiction over legislation on solid waste disposal, including the Resource Conservation and Recovery Act. (Jurisdiction shared with House Science and House Transportation and Infrastructure committees.)

House Transportation and Infrastructure Committee, *Subcommittee on Water Resources and Environment,* B376 RHOB 20515; (202) 225-4360. Fax, (202) 226-5435. Rep. John J. "Jimmy" Duncan Jr., R-Tenn., Chair; Susan Bodine, Staff Director.

General e-mail, transcomm@mail.house.gov

Web, www.house.gov/transportation

Shares jurisdiction over the Comprehensive Environmental Response, Compensation, and Liability Act (Superfund) with the House Energy and Commerce and House Science committees.

Senate Environment and Public Works Committee, *Subcommittee on Superfund and Waste Management,* SD-410 20510; (202) 224-6176. Fax, (202) 224-1273. Sen. Lincoln Chafee, R-R.I., Chair; Ted Michaels, Staff Contact.
Web, epw.senate.gov

Jurisdiction over research and development and legislation on solid waste disposal, including the Resource Conservation and Recovery Act.

NONPROFIT

Alliance of Foam Packaging Recyclers, 1298 Cronson St., #201, Crofton, MD 21114; (410) 451-8340. Fax, (410) 451-8343. Betsy Steiner, Executive Director. Information, (800) 944-8448.
Web, www.epspackaging.org

Membership: companies that recycle foam packaging material. Coordinates national network of collection centers for postconsumer foam packaging products; helps to establish new collection centers.

American Plastics Council, 1300 Wilson Blvd., Arlington, VA 22209; (703) 741-5000. Fax, (703) 741-6000. Greg Lebedev, President.
Web, www.plastics.org

Seeks to increase plastics recycling; conducts research on disposal of plastic products; sponsors research on waste-handling methods, incineration, and degradation; supports programs that test alternative waste management technologies. Monitors legislation and regulations. (Affiliated with the American Chemical Council.)

Assn. of State and Territorial Solid Waste Management Officials, 444 N. Capitol St. N.W., #315 20001; (202) 624-5828. Fax, (202) 624-7875. Thomas J. Kennedy, Executive Director.
General e-mail, swmtrina@sso.org
Web, www.astswmo.org

Membership: state and territorial solid waste management officials. Works with the Environmental Protection Agency to develop policy on solid and hazardous waste.

Container Recycling Institute, 1911 N. Fort Myer Dr., #702, Arlington, VA 22209-1603; (703) 276-9800. Fax, (703) 276-9587. Pat Franklin, Executive Director.
General e-mail, cri@container-recycling.org
Web, www.container-recycling.org

Studies alternatives for reducing container and packaging waste; researches container and packaging reuse and recycling options; serves as an information clearinghouse on container deposit legislation.

Environmental Industry Assns., 4301 Connecticut Ave. N.W., #300 20008; (202) 244-4700. Fax, (202) 966-4818. Bruce J. Parker, President.
General e-mail, eia@envasns.org
Web, www.envasns.org

Membership: organizations engaged in refuse collection, processing, and disposal. Provides information on solid and hazardous waste management and waste equipment; sponsors workshops.

Foodservice and Packaging Institute (FPI), 150 S. Washington St., #204, Falls Church, VA 22046; (703) 538-2800. Fax, (703) 538-2187. John Burke, President.
General e-mail, fpi@fpi.org
Web, www.fpi.org

Membership: manufacturers, suppliers, and distributors of disposable products used in food service, packaging, and consumer products. Promotes the use of disposables for commercial and home use.

Glass Packaging Institute, 515 King St., #420, Alexandria, VA 22314-3137; (703) 684-6359. Fax, (703) 684-6048. Joseph Cattaneo, President.
Web, www.gpi.org

Membership: manufacturers of glass containers and their suppliers. Promotes industry policies to protect the environment, conserve natural resources, and reduce energy consumption; conducts research; monitors legislation affecting the industry. Interests include glass recycling.

Institute for Local Self-Reliance, 2425 18th St. N.W. 20009-2096; (202) 232-4108. Fax, (202) 332-0463. Neil N. Seldman, President.
General e-mail, ilsr@igc.org
Web, www.ilsr.org

Conducts research and provides technical assistance on environmentally sound economic development for government, small businesses, and community organizations. Advocates the development of a materials policy at local, state, and regional levels to reduce per capita consumption of raw materials and to shift from dependence on fossil fuels to reliance on renewable resources.

Institute of Scrap Recycling Industries, Inc., 1325 G St. N.W., #1000 20005; (202) 737-1770. Fax, (202) 626-0900. Robin K. Wiener, President.
General e-mail, isri@isri.org
Web, www.isri.org

Represents processors, brokers, and consumers of scrap paper, glass, plastic, textiles, rubber, and ferrous and nonferrous metals.

Integrated Waste Services Assn., *1401 H St. N.W., #220 20005; (202) 467-6240. Fax, (202) 467-6225. Maria Zannes, President.*
General e-mail, iwsawte@aol.com
Web, www.wte.org

Membership: companies that design, build, and operate resource recovery facilities. Promotes integrated solutions to municipal solid waste management issues. Encourages the use of waste-to-energy technology.

National Recycling Coalition, *1325 G St. N.W., #1025 20005; (202) 347-0450. Fax, (202) 347-0449. Kate Krebs, Executive Director.*
General e-mail, info@nrc-recycle.org
Web, www.nrc-recycle.org

Membership: public officials; community recycling groups; local, state, and national agencies; environmentalists; waste haulers; solid waste disposal consultants; and private recycling companies. Encourages recycling to reduce waste, preserve resources, and promote economic development.

Polystyrene Packaging Council, *1300 Wilson Blvd., 13th Floor, Arlington, VA 22209-2321; (703) 741-5649. Fax, (703) 741-5651. Michael Levy, Executive Director.*
General e-mail, pspc@plastics.org
Web, www.polystyrene.org

Membership: manufacturers and suppliers of polystyrene foam products. Promotes effective use and recycling of polystyrene; studies and reports on solid waste disposal issues, including waste-to-energy incineration and use of landfills. Serves as an information clearinghouse. Monitors legislation and regulations.

Secondary Materials and Recycled Textiles Assn., *7910 Woodmont Ave., #1130, Bethesda, MD 20814; (301) 656-1077. Fax, (301) 656-1079. Bernard D. Brill, Executive Vice President.*
General e-mail, smartasn@erols.com
Web, www.smartasn.org

Membership: organizations and individuals involved in shipping and distributing recycled textiles and other textile products. Sponsors educational programs; publishes newsletters.

Solid Waste Assn. of North America, *1100 Wayne Ave., #700, Silver Spring, MD 20910 (mailing address: P.O. Box 7219, Silver Spring, MD 20907); (301) 585-2898. Fax, (301) 589-7068. John Skinner, Executive Director. Fax-on-demand, (877) 238-5555.*

Web, www.swana.org

Membership: government and private industry officials who manage municipal solid waste programs. Interests include waste reduction, collection, recycling, combustion, and disposal. Conducts training and certification programs. Operates solid waste information clearinghouse. Monitors legislation and regulations.

U.S. Conference of Mayors, *Municipal Waste Management Assn., 1620 Eye St. N.W., 6th Floor 20006; (202) 293-7330. Fax, (202) 429-0422. J. Thomas Cochran, Executive Director.*
Web, www.usmayors.org/uscm/mwma

Organization of local governments and private companies involved in planning and developing solid waste management programs, including pollution prevention, waste-to-energy, and recycling. Assists communities with financing, environmental assessments, and associated policy implementation.

Water Pollution

AGENCIES

Environmental Protection Agency (EPA), *Ground Water and Drinking Water, 1200 Pennsylvania Ave. N.W., #4601M, ICC Bldg. 20460; (202) 564-3750. Fax, (202) 564-3753. Cynthia Dougherty, Director. Toll-free hotline, (800) 426-4791.*
Web, www.epa.gov/ogwdw

Develops standards for the quality of drinking water supply systems; regulates underground injection of waste and protection of groundwater wellhead areas under the Safe Drinking Water Act; provides information on public water supply systems.

Environmental Protection Agency (EPA), *Municipal Support, 1200 Pennsylvania Ave. N.W., #7119A ICC Bldg., MC 4204 20460; (202) 564-0749. Fax, (202) 501-2346. Sheila E. Frace, Director.*
Web, www.epa.gov

Directs programs to assist in the design and construction of municipal sewage systems; develops programs to ensure efficient operation and maintenance of municipal wastewater treatment facilities; implements programs for prevention of water pollution.

Environmental Protection Agency (EPA), *Science and Technology, 1200 Pennsylvania Ave. N.W., #5231 ICC Bldg. 20460; (202) 566-0430. Fax, (202) 566-0441. Geoffrey H. Grubbs, Director.*
Web, www.epa.gov

Develops and coordinates water pollution control programs for the Environmental Protection Agency; monitors water quality nationwide and maintains a data collection system; assists state and regional agencies in establishing water quality standards and planning local water resources management; develops guidelines for industrial wastewater discharge.

Environmental Protection Agency (EPA), *Wastewater Management, 1200 Pennsylvania Ave. N.W., #7116A ICC Bldg., MC 4201M 20460; (202) 564-0748. Fax, (202) 501-2338. James Hanlon, Director.*
Web, www.epa.gov

Oversees the issuance of water permits. Responsible for the Pretreatment Program regulating industrial discharges to local sewage treatment. Oversees the State Revolving Funds Program, which provides assistance for the construction of wastewater treatment plants.

National Drinking Water Advisory Council, *1200 Pennsylvania Ave. N.W., #2140 20460; (202) 564-3791. Fax, (202) 564-3753. Brenda P. Johnson, Designated Federal Officer.*
Web, www.epa.gov/OGWDW

Advises the EPA administrator on activities, functions, and policies relating to implementation of the Safe Drinking Water Act.

National Oceanic and Atmospheric Administration (NOAA), *(Commerce Dept.), Office of Response and Restoration, 1305 East-West Hwy., 10th Floor, Bldg. 4, Silver Spring, MD 20910; (301) 713-2989. Fax, (301) 713-4389. David Kennedy, Director.*
Web, www.nos.noaa.gov/programs/orr.html

Provides information on damage to marine ecosystems caused by pollution. Offers information on spill trajectory projections and chemical hazard analyses. Researches trends of toxic contamination on U.S. coastal regions.

U.S. Coast Guard (USCG), *(Homeland Security Dept.), National Pollution Funds Center, 4200 Wilson Blvd., #1000, Arlington, VA 22203; (202) 493-6700. Fax, (202) 493-6900. Jan P. Lane, Director.*
Web, www.uscg.mil/hq/npfc/index.htm

Certifies the financial responsibility of vessels and companies involved in oil exploration and transportation in U.S. waters and on the outer continental shelf; manages the Oil Spill Liability Trust Fund under the Oil Pollution Act of 1990.

U.S. Coast Guard (USCG), *(Homeland Security Dept.), Response, 2100 2nd St. S.W., #2100 20593; (202) 267-0518. Fax, (202) 267-4085. Capt. David G. Westerholm, Chief.*
Web, www.uscg.mil/hq/g-m/mor/default.html

Oversees cleanup operations after spills of oil and other hazardous substances in U.S. waters, on the outer continental shelf, and in international waters. Reviews coastal zone management and enforces international standards for pollution prevention and response.

CONGRESS

House Resources Committee, *Subcommittee on Fisheries, Conservation, Wildlife, and Oceans, H2-188 FHOB 20515; (202) 226-0200. Fax, (202) 225-1542. Rep. Wayne T. Gilchrest, R-Md., Chair; Harry Burroughs, Staff Director.*
General e-mail, fisheries.subcommittee@mail.house.gov
Web, resourcescommittee.house.gov

Jurisdiction over legislation concerning coastal marine pollution, including the Magnuson-Stevens Fishery Conservation and Management Act, and elements of the Clean Water Act and the National Environmental Policy Act.

House Transportation and Infrastructure Committee, *Subcommittee on Coast Guard and Maritime Transportation, 507 FHOB 20515; (202) 226-3552. Fax, (202) 226-2524. Rep. Frank A. LoBiondo, R-N.J., Chair; Mark Zachares, Staff Director.*
General e-mail, transcomm@mail.house.gov
Web, www.house.gov/transportation

Jurisdiction over legislation on ocean dumping, oil spills and financial responsibility requirements, and marine pollution control and abatement. (Jurisdiction shared with the Subcommittee on Water Resources and Environment.)

House Transportation and Infrastructure Committee, *Subcommittee on Water Resources and Environment, B376 RHOB 20515; (202) 225-4360. Fax, (202) 226-5435. Rep. John J. "Jimmy" Duncan Jr., R-Tenn., Chair; Susan Bodine, Staff Director.*
General e-mail, transcomm@mail.house.gov
Web, www.house.gov/transportation

Jurisdiction over most legislation on water pollution, including the Clean Water Act. Shares jurisdiction on oil spills and financial responsibility requirements with the Subcommittee on Coast Guard and Maritime Transportation.

Senate Environment and Public Works Committee, *SD-410 20510; (202) 224-6176. Fax, (202) 224-5167. Sen. James M. Inhofe, R-Okla., Chair; Andrew Wheeler, Staff Director.*
General e-mail, guest1@epw.senate.gov
Web, epw.senate.gov

Jurisdiction over legislation on ocean dumping and ocean pollution research; drinking water purity; water pollution; oil spill laws and financial responsibility requirements; and marine pollution control and abatement. Jurisdiction over the Clean Water Act, National Environmental Policy Act, Safe Drinking Water Act, and Ocean Dumping Act.

NONPROFIT

Alliance for Environmental Technology, *1250 24th St. N.W., #300 20037; (202) 835-1688. Fax, (202) 835-1601. Douglas C. Pryke, Executive Director.*
General e-mail, info@aet.org
Web, www.aet.org

Membership: U.S. and Canadian chemical manufacturers and forest products companies. Seeks to improve environmental performance of the pulp and paper industry, particularly in waste water; supports use of chlorine dioxide to prevent pollution. Monitors legislation and regulations.

Assn. of State and Interstate Water Pollution Control Administrators, *750 1st St. N.E., #1010 20002; (202) 898-0905. Fax, (202) 898-0929. Roberta Haley Savage, Executive Director.*
General e-mail, admin1@asiwpca.org
Web, www.asiwpca.org

Membership: administrators of state water pollution agencies and related associations. Represents the states' concerns on implementation, funding, and reauthorization of the Clean Water Act. Monitors legislation and regulations.

Clean Water Action, *4455 Connecticut Ave. N.W., #A300 20008; (202) 895-0420. Fax, (202) 895-0438. David R. Zwick, President.*
General e-mail, cwa@essential.org
Web, www.cleanwateraction.org

Citizens' organization interested in clean, safe, and affordable water. Works to influence public policy through education, technical assistance, and grassroots organizing. Interests include toxins and pollution, drinking water, water conservation, sewage treatment, pesticides, mass burn incineration, bay and estuary protection, and consumer water issues. Monitors legislation and regulations.

League of Women Voters Education Fund (LWV), *Natural Resources, 1730 M St. N.W., #1000 20036; (202) 429-1965. Fax, (202) 429-0854. Nancy Tate, Director.*
General e-mail, lwv@lwv.org
Web, www.lwv.org

Education foundation affiliated with the League of Women Voters. Conducts a national project concerning community drinking water systems and groundwater. Sponsors research and develops educational materials on water issues; helps local leagues manage demonstration programs.

Ocean Conservancy, *1725 DeSales St. N.W., #600 20036; (202) 429-5609. Fax, (202) 872-0619. Roger T. Rufe, President.*
General e-mail, ocean@oceanconservancy.org
Web, www.oceanconservancy.org

Protects the health of oceans and seas. Advocates policies that restrict discharge of pollutants harmful to marine ecosystems.

Water Environment Federation, *601 Wythe St., Alexandria, VA 22314-1994; (703) 684-2400. Fax, (703) 684-2492. William Bertera, Executive Director. Fax-on-demand, (800) 444-2933.*
Web, www.wef.org

Membership: civil and environmental engineers, wastewater treatment plant operators, scientists, government officials, and others concerned with water quality. Works to preserve and improve water quality worldwide. Provides the public with technical information and educational materials. Monitors legislation and regulations.

 RESOURCES MANAGEMENT

AGENCIES

Bureau of Land Management (BLM), *(Interior Dept.), Renewable Resources and Planning, 1849 C St. N.W., #3326 20240; (202) 208-4896. Fax, (202) 208-5010. Ed Shephard, Assistant Director (Acting).*
Web, www.blm.gov

Develops and implements natural resource programs for renewable resources use and protection, including management of forested land, rangeland, wild horses and burros, wildlife habitats, endangered species, soil and water quality, rights of way, recreation, and cultural programs.

Interior Dept. (DOI), *1849 C St. N.W., #6156 20240; (202) 208-7351. Fax, (202) 208-6956. Gale A. Norton, Secretary; Steven Griles, Deputy Secretary. Information, (202) 208-3100. Library, (202) 208-5815. Locator, (202) 208-3100.*
Web, www.doi.gov

Manages most federal land through its component agencies; responsible for conservation and development of mineral, water, and fish and wildlife resources; operates recreation programs for federal parks, refuges, and public lands; preserves and administers scenic and historic areas; administers native American lands and relationships with tribal governments.

Tennessee Valley Authority, *Government Relations, Washington Office, 1 Massachusetts Ave. N.W., #300 20001; (202) 898-2999. Fax, (202) 898-2998. Linda Whitestone, Vice President.*
Web, www.tva.gov

Coordinates resource conservation, development, and land-use programs in the Tennessee River Valley. Activities include forestry and wildlife development.

NONPROFIT

National Assn. of Conservation Districts, *509 Capitol Court N.E. 20002-4937; (202) 547-6223. Fax, (202) 547-6450. Ernest C. Shea, Chief Executive Officer.*
General e-mail, washington@nacdnet.org
Web, www.nacdnet.org

Membership: conservation districts (local subdivisions of state government). Works to promote the conservation of land, forests, and other natural resources. Interests include erosion and sediment control; water quality; forestry, water, flood plain, and range management; rural development; and urban and community conservation.

Renewable Natural Resources Foundation,
5430 Grosvenor Lane, #220, Bethesda, MD 20814-2193; (301) 493-9101. Fax, (301) 493-6148. Robert D. Day, Executive Director.
General e-mail, info@rnrf.org
Web, www.rnrf.org

Consortium of professional, scientific, and education organizations working to advance scientific and public education in renewable natural resources. Encourages the application of sound scientific practices to resource management and conservation. Fosters interdisciplinary cooperation among its member organizations.

U.S. Chamber of Commerce, *Environment, Technology, and Regulatory Affairs, 1615 H St. N.W. 20062-2000; (202) 463-5533. Fax, (202) 887-3445. Bill Kovacs, Vice President.*
General e-mail, environment@uschamber.com
Web, www.uschamber.com

Develops policy on all issues affecting the production, use, and conservation of natural resources, including fuel and nonfuel minerals, timber, water, public lands, on- and offshore energy, wetlands, and endangered species.

Wildlife Management Institute, *1101 14th St. N.W., #801 20005; (202) 371-1808. Fax, (202) 408-5059. Rollin D. Sparrowe, President.*

Web, www.wildlifemanagementinstitute.org

Research and consulting organization that provides technical services and information about natural resources. Interests include forests, rangelands, and land, water, and wildlife resources.

Forests and Rangelands

AGENCIES

Forest Service *(Agriculture Dept.), 201 14th St. and Independence Ave. S.W., #4NW 20024 (mailing address: P.O. Box 96090 20090-6090); (202) 205-1661. Fax, (202) 205-1765. Dale Bosworth, Chief.*
Web, www.fs.fed.us

Manages national forests and grasslands for outdoor recreation and sustained yield of renewable natural resources, including timber, water, forage, fish, and wildlife. Cooperates with state and private foresters; conducts forestry research.

Forest Service *(Agriculture Dept.), International Programs, 201 14th St. S.W., #1NW 20024 (mailing address: P.O. Box 96090 20090-6090); (202) 205-1650. Fax, (202) 205-1603. Valdis Mezainis, Director.*
Web, www.fs.fed.us/global

Responsible for the Forest Service's involvement in international forest conservation efforts. Analyzes international resource issues; promotes information exchange; provides planning and technical assistance. Interests include tropical forests and sustainable forest management.

Forest Service *(Agriculture Dept.), National Forest System, 201 14th St. S.W., #3NW 20024 (mailing address: P.O. Box 96090 20090-6090); (202) 205-1523. Fax, (202) 205-1758. Tom L. Thompson, Deputy Chief.*
Web, www.fs.fed.us

Manages 191 million acres of forests and rangelands. Products and services from these lands include timber, water, forage, wildlife, minerals, and recreation.

Forest Service *(Agriculture Dept.), Research and Development, 201 14th St. S.W., #1NW 20024 (mailing address: P.O. Box 96090 20090-6090); (202) 205-1665. Fax, (202) 205-1530. Robert Lewis Jr., Deputy Chief.*
Web, www.fs.fed.us

Conducts biological, physical, and economic research related to forestry, including studies on harvesting methods, acid deposition, international forestry, the effects of global climate changes on forests, and forest products. Provides information on the establishment, improvement, and growth of trees, grasses, and other forest vegetation. Works to protect forest resources from fire, insects, diseases, and animal pests. Examines

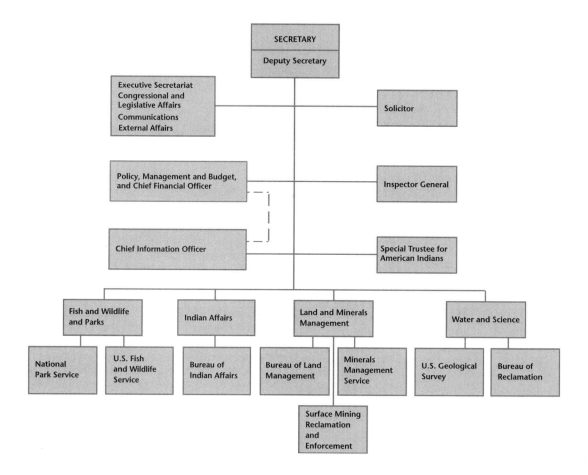

the effect of forest use activities on water quality, soil erosion, and sediment production. Conducts continuous forest survey and analyzes outlook for future supply and demand.

Forest Service *(Agriculture Dept.), State and Private Forestry, 201 14th St. S.W., # 2NW 20024 (mailing address: P.O. Box 96090 20090-6090); (202) 205-1657. Fax, (202) 205-1174. Joel D. Holtrop, Deputy Chief. Web, www.fs.fed.us*

Assists state and private forest owners with the protection and management of 574 million acres of forest and associated watershed lands. Assistance includes fire control, protecting forests from insects and diseases, land-use planning, developing multiple-use manage-

ment, and improving practices in harvesting, processing, and marketing of forest products.

Forest Service *(Agriculture Dept.), Youth Conservation Corps, 1621 N. Kent St., Arlington, VA 22209 (mailing address: P.O. Box 96090, Washington, DC 20090-6090); (703) 605-4854. Fax, (703) 605-5115. Ransom Hughes, Program Manager.*

Administers with the National Park Service and the Fish and Wildlife Service the Youth Conservation Corps, a summer employment and training, public works program for youths ages fifteen to eighteen. The program is conducted in national parks, in national forests, and on national wildlife refuges.

CONGRESS

House Agriculture Committee, *Subcommittee on Department Operations, Oversight, Nutrition, and Forestry,* 1407 LHOB 20515; (202) 225-2171. Fax, (202) 225-4464. Rep. Gil Gutknecht, R-Minn., Chair; Samuel Diehl, Staff Director.

Web, agriculture.house.gov

Jurisdiction over legislation on forestry in general and forest reserves acquired from state, local, or private sources. Oversight of Forest Service.

House Resources Committee, 1324 LHOB 20515; (202) 225-2761. Fax, (202) 225-5929. Rep. Richard W. Pombo, R-Calif., Chair; Steve Ding, Chief of Staff.

General e-mail, resources.committee@mail.house.gov

Web, resourcescommittee.house.gov

Jurisdiction over legislation on forest reserves and public lands in Alaska.

House Resources Committee, *Subcommittee on Forests and Forest Health,* 1337 LHOB 20515; (202) 225-0691. Fax, (202) 225-0521. Rep. Scott McInnis, R-Colo., Chair; Josh Penry, Staff Director.

General e-mail, forests.health@mail.house.gov

Web, resourcescommittee.house.gov

Jurisdiction over legislation on public forest lands (except in Alaska), including issues of forestry, wilderness preservation, forest reserve, water rights, national trails and rivers, and recreation.

House Resources Committee, *Subcommittee on National Parks, Recreation, and Public Lands,* 1333 LHOB 20515; (202) 226-7736. Fax, (202) 226-2301. Rep. George P. Radanovich, R-Calif., Chair; Casey Hammond, Clerk.

General e-mail, parks.subcommittee@mail.house.gov

Web, resourcescommittee.house.gov

Jurisdiction over legislation on public lands (except lands in Alaska and forests), the national park system, the establishment of wildlife refuges on public lands, and the Bureau of Land Management.

Senate Agriculture, Nutrition, and Forestry Committee, *Subcommittee on Forestry, Conservation, and Rural Revitalization,* SR-328A 20510; (202) 224-2035. Sen. Michael D. Crapo, R-Idaho, Chair; Vacant, Staff Director.

Web, agriculture.senate.gov

Jurisdiction over legislation on forestry in general and forest reserves acquired from state, local, or private sources.

Senate Energy and Natural Resources Committee, *Subcommittee on Public Lands and Forests,* SD-364

20510; (202) 224-4971. Fax, (202) 224-6163. Sen. Larry E. Craig, R-Idaho, Chair; Frank Gladics, Professional Staff Member.

Web, energy.senate.gov

Jurisdiction over legislation on forest reserves, public lands, the national forest system, the establishment of wildlife refuges on public lands, and the Bureau of Land Management.

NONPROFIT

American Forest and Paper Assn., *Regulatory Affairs,* 1111 19th St. N.W., #800 20036; (202) 463-2700. Fax, (202) 463-2423. Sharon Kneiss, Vice President.

Web, www.afandpa.org

Membership: manufacturers of wood and specialty products and related associations. Interests include tax, housing, environmental, international trade, natural resources, and land-use issues that affect the wood products industry.

American Forests, 910 17th St. N.W., #600 20006 (mailing address: P.O. Box 2000 20013-2000); (202) 955-4500. Fax, (202) 955-4588. Deborah Gangloff, Executive Vice President.

General e-mail, info@amfor.org

Web, www.amfor.org

Citizens' interest group that promotes protection and responsible management of forests and natural resources. Provides information on conservation, public land policy, urban forestry, and timber management. Runs an international tree planting campaign to help mitigate global warming.

American Hardwood Export Council, 1111 19th St. N.W., #800 20036; (202) 463-2720. Fax, (202) 463-2787. Michael S. Snow, Executive Director.

General e-mail, info@ahec.org

Web, www.ahec.org

Trade association of companies and associations that export hardwood products. Aids members in developing and expanding export capabilities in new and existing markets.

American Wood Preservers Institute, 12100 Sunset Hills Dr., #130, Reston, VA 20190; (703) 204-0500. Fax, (703) 204-4610. Bert Jones, Chair.

General e-mail, info@awpi.org

Web, www.preservedwood.com

Membership: wood preservers, including manufacturers, formulators of wood preservatives, wood treating companies, and environmental technology companies. Monitors legislation and regulations.

Forest Resources Assn., *600 Jefferson Plaza, #350, Rockville, MD 20852; (301) 838-9385. Fax, (301) 838-9481. Richard Lewis, President.*
General e-mail, fra@forestresources.org
Web, www.forestresources.org

Membership: logging contractors, pulpwood dealers, suppliers, and consumers. Administers programs to improve the productivity, safety, and efficiency of pulpwood harvesting and transport; provides information on new equipment, tools, and methods; works to ensure continued access to the timberland base. Monitors legislation and regulations.

International Wood Products Assn., *4214 King St., Alexandria, VA 22302; (703) 820-6696. Fax, (703) 820-8550. Wendy Baer, Executive Vice President.*
General e-mail, info@iwpawood.org
Web, www.iwpawood.org

Membership: companies that handle imported wood products. Encourages environmentally responsible forest management and international trade in wood products. Sponsors research and environmental education on tropical forestry. (Affiliated with the Tropical Forest Foundation.)

National Assn. of State Foresters, *444 N. Capitol St. N.W., #540 20001; (202) 624-5415. Fax, (202) 624-5407. Anne Heissenbuttel, Executive Director.*
General e-mail, nasf@sso.org
Web, www.stateforesters.org

Membership: directors of state forestry agencies from all states, the District of Columbia, and U.S. territories. Members manage and protect over two thirds of the nation's forests, as well as assist private landowners in managing their forests. Monitors legislation and regulations.

National Forest Foundation, *2715 M St. N.W., #100 20036; (202) 298-6740. Fax, (202) 298-6758. William Possiel, President.*
Web, www.natlforests.org

Established by Congress to support the U.S. Forest Service in its management of public lands. Promotes research and multiple-use, cooperative forestry. Interests include conservation, preservation, recreation, wildlife, and environmental education.

National Lumber and Building Material Dealers Assn., *40 Ivy St. S.E. 20003; (202) 547-2230. Fax, (202) 547-7640. Gary W. Donnelly, President.*
General e-mail, nlbmda@dealer.org
Web, www.dealer.org

Membership: federated associations of retailers in the lumber and building material industries. Monitors legislation and regulations.

Save America's Forests, *4 Library Court S.E. 20003; (202) 544-9219. Fax, (202) 544-7462. Carl Ross, Executive Director.*
General e-mail, forests@saveamericasforests.org
Web, www.saveamericasforests.org

Coalition of environmental and public interest groups, businesses, and individuals. Advocates comprehensive nationwide laws to prevent deforestation and to protect forest ecosystems.

Society of American Foresters, *5400 Grosvenor Lane, Bethesda, MD 20814-2198; (301) 897-8720. Fax, (301) 897-3690. Michael Goergen, Executive Vice President (Acting).*
General e-mail, safweb@safnet.org
Web, www.safnet.org

Association of forestry professionals. Provides technical information on forestry; accredits forestry programs in universities and colleges; and publishes scientific forestry journals.

Land Resources and Rights

AGENCIES

Bureau of Land Management (BLM), *(Interior Dept.), 1849 C St. N.W., MC 3314 20240; (202) 208-3801. Fax, (202) 208-5242. Kathleen Clarke, Director.*
Web, www.blm.gov

Manages public lands and federally owned mineral resources, including oil, gas, and coal. Resources managed and leased include wildlife habitats, timber, minerals, open space, wilderness areas, forage, and recreational resources. Surveys federal lands and maintains public land records.

Bureau of Land Management (BLM), *(Interior Dept.), Lands and Realty, 1620 L St. N.W. 20240 (mailing address: 1849 C St. N.W., MC 1000LS 20240); (202) 452-7773. Fax, (202) 452-7708. Donald A. Buhler, Manager (Acting).*
Web, www.blm.gov

Oversees use, acquisition, and disposal of public lands. Conducts the Public Lands Survey; authorizes rights-of-way on public lands, including roads and power lines.

Bureau of Reclamation *(Interior Dept.), 1849 C St. N.W., #7554 20240; (202) 513-0501. Fax, (202) 513-0312. John W. Keys III, Commissioner.*
Web, www.usbr.gov

Responsible for acquisition, administration, management, and disposal of lands in seventeen western states associated with bureau water resource development projects.

Interior Dept. (DOI), *Bird Habitat Conservation,* 4401 N. Fairfax Dr., MBSP 4075, Arlington, VA 22203; (703) 358-1784. Fax, (703) 358-2282. David A. Smith, Coordinator.
General e-mail, dbhc@fws.gov
Web, www.fws.gov

Membership: government and private-sector conservation experts. Works to protect, restore, and manage wetlands and other habitats for migratory birds and other animals and to maintain migratory bird and waterfowl populations.

Interior Dept. (DOI), *Board of Land Appeals,* 801 N. Quincy St., #300, Arlington, VA 22203; (703) 235-3750. Fax, (703) 235-8349. Bruce Harris, Chief Administrative Judge (Acting).
Web, www.doi.gov

Adjunct office of the interior secretary that decides appeals from decisions rendered by the Bureau of Land Management, the Minerals Management Service, the Office of Surface Mining, and the Bureau of Indian Affairs concerning the use and disposition of public lands and minerals; issues final decisions concerning the Surface Mining Control and Reclamation Act of 1977.

Interior Dept. (DOI), *Land and Minerals Management,* 1849 C St. N.W., #7328 20240; (202) 208-5676. Fax, (202) 208-3144. Rebecca Watson, Assistant Secretary.
Web, www.doi.gov

Directs and supervises the Bureau of Land Management, the Minerals Management Service, and the Office of Surface Mining and Reclamation Enforcement. Supervises programs associated with land use planning, onshore and offshore minerals, surface mining reclamation and enforcement, and outer continental shelf minerals management.

Interior Dept. (DOI), *Surface Mining Reclamation and Enforcement,* 1951 Constitution Ave. N.W., #233 20240; (202) 208-4006. Fax, (202) 219-3106. Jeffrey D. Jarrett, Director.
Web, www.osmre.gov/osm.htm

Regulates surface mining of coal and surface effects of underground coal mining. Responsible for reclamation of abandoned coal mine lands.

Natural Resources Conservation Service *(Agriculture Dept.),* 1400 Independence Ave. S.W., #5105 20250

(mailing address: P.O. Box 2890 20013-2890); (202) 720-4525. Fax, (202) 720-7690. Bruce I. Knight, Chief. Information, (202) 720-7246.
Web, www.nrcs.usda.gov

Responsible for soil and water conservation programs, including watershed protection, flood prevention, river basin surveys, and resource conservation and development. Provides landowners, operators, state and local units of government, and community groups with technical assistance in carrying out local programs.

Tennessee Valley Authority, *Government Relations, Washington Office,* 1 Massachusetts Ave. N.W., #300 20001; (202) 898-2999. Fax, (202) 898-2998. Linda Whitestone, Vice President.
Web, www.tva.gov

Coordinates resource conservation, development, and land-use programs in the Tennessee River Valley. Provides information on land usage in the region.

CONGRESS

House Resources Committee, *Subcommittee on Energy and Mineral Resources,* 1626 LHOB 20515; (202) 225-9297. Fax, (202) 225-5255. Rep. Barbara Cubin, R-Wyo., Chair; Jack Belcher, Staff Director.
General e-mail, energy.minerals@mail.house.gov
Web, resourcescommittee.house.gov

Jurisdiction over legislation on land use planning, including surface mining and development of public lands.

House Resources Committee, *Subcommittee on National Parks, Recreation, and Public Lands,* 1333 LHOB 20515; (202) 226-7736. Fax, (202) 226-2301. Rep. George P. Radanovich, R-Calif., Chair; Casey Hammond, Clerk.
General e-mail, parks.subcommittee@mail.house.gov
Web, resourcescommittee.house.gov

Jurisdiction over legislation on public lands (except in Alaska), the land and water conservation fund, and the Bureau of Land Management.

Senate Energy and Natural Resources Committee, SD-364 20510; (202) 224-4971. Fax, (202) 224-6163. Sen. Pete V. Domenici, R-N.M., Chair; Alex Flint, Staff Director.
General e-mail, committee@energy.senate.gov
Web, energy.senate.gov

Jurisdiction over legislation on public lands, the land and water conservation fund, the Bureau of Land Management, and the Alaska National Interest Lands Conservation Act.

Senate Energy and Natural Resources Committee, *Subcommittee on Energy, SD-364 20510; (202) 224-4971. Fax, (202) 224-6163. Sen. Lamar Alexander, R-Tenn., Chair; Scott O'Malia, Professional Staff Member.*
General e-mail, energy-sub@energy.senate.gov
Web, energy.senate.gov

Jurisdiction over legislation on land use planning, including surface mining; coal production, distribution, and utilization; and coal severance tax.

Senate Environment and Public Works Committee, *Subcommittee on Clean Air, Climate Change, and Nuclear Safety, SD-410 20510; (202) 224-6176. Fax, (202) 224-1273. Sen. George V. Voinovich, R-Ohio, Chair; Michael Whatley, Staff Director.*
Web, epw.senate.gov

Jurisdiction over legislation on wetlands.

NONPROFIT

American Geological Institute, *4220 King St., Alexandria, VA 22302; (703) 379-2480. Fax, (703) 379-7563. Marcus E. Milling, Executive Director.*
General e-mail, agi@agiweb.org
Web, www.agiweb.org

Membership: earth science societies and associations. Maintains computerized database of the world's geoscience literature (available to the public for a fee).

American Resort Development Assn., *1201 15th St. N.W., #400 20005; (202) 371-6700. Fax, (202) 289-8544. Howard Nusbaum, President.*
Web, www.arda.org

Membership: U.S. and international developers, builders, financiers, marketing companies, and others involved in resort, recreational, and community development. Serves as an information clearinghouse; monitors federal and state legislation affecting land, time share, and community development industries.

Defenders of Property Rights, *1350 Connecticut Ave. N.W., #410 20036; (202) 822-6770. Fax, (202) 822-6774. Nancie G. Marzulla, President; Roger Marzulla, Chair.*
General e-mail, mail@yourpropertyrights.org
Web, www.yourpropertyrights.org

Advocates private property rights. Works to ensure that federal and state governments compensate property owners for property seizures and for effects on property value due to government regulations. Conducts litigation on behalf of property owners.

Land Trust Alliance, *1331 H St. N.W., #400 20005-4734; (202) 638-4725. Fax, (202) 638-4730. Rand Wentworth, President.*
Web, www.lta.org

Membership: organizations and individuals who work to conserve land resources. Serves as a forum for the exchange of information; conducts research and public education programs. Monitors legislation and regulations.

National Assn. of Conservation Districts, *509 Capitol Court N.E. 20002-4937; (202) 547-6223. Fax, (202) 547-6450. Ernest C. Shea, Chief Executive Officer.*
General e-mail, washington@nacdnet.org
Web, www.nacdnet.org

Membership: conservation districts (local subdivisions of state government). Works to promote the conservation of land, forests, and other natural resources. Interests include erosion and sediment control; water quality; forestry, water, flood plain, and range management; rural development; and urban and community conservation.

Public Lands Council, *1301 Pennsylvania Ave. N.W., #300 20004-1701; (202) 347-5355. Fax, (202) 638-0607. Jeff Eisenberg, Executive Director, (202) 347-0228.*
Web, hill.beef.org

Membership: cattle and sheep ranchers who hold permits and leases to graze livestock on public lands.

Scenic America, *801 Pennsylvania Ave. S.E., #300 20003-2152; (202) 543-6200. Fax, (202) 543-9130. Meg Maguire, President.*
General e-mail, scenic@scenic.org
Web, www.scenic.org

Membership: national, state, and local groups concerned with land-use control, growth management, and landscape protection. Works to enhance the scenic quality of America's communities and countryside. Provides information and technical assistance on scenic byways, tree preservation, economics of aesthetic regulation, billboard and sign control, scenic areas preservation, and growth management.

Wallace Genetic Foundation, *4900 Massachusetts Ave. N.W., #220 20016; (202) 966-2932. Fax, (202) 966-3370. Patricia M. Lee, Co-Executive Director; Carolyn H. Sand, Co-Executive Director.*
General e-mail, wgfdn@aol.com
Web, www.wallacegenetic.org

Supports national and international nonprofits in the areas of agricultural research, land conservation and preservation, and environmental concerns.

Metals and Minerals

AGENCIES

Bureau of Land Management (BLM), *(Interior Dept.), Minerals, Realty, and Resource Protection,*

1849 C St. N.W., #3224 20240; (202) 208-4201. Fax, (202) 208-4800. Vacant, Assistant Director.
Web, www.blm.gov

Evaluates and classifies onshore oil, natural gas, geothermal resources, and all solid energy and mineral resources, including coal and uranium on federal lands. Develops and administers regulations for fluid and solid mineral leasing on national lands and on the subsurface of land where fluid and solid mineral rights have been reserved for the federal government.

Interior Dept. (DOI), *Board of Land Appeals,* 801 N. Quincy St., #300, Arlington, VA 22203; (703) 235-3750. Fax, (703) 235-8349. Bruce Harris, Chief Administrative Judge (Acting).
Web, www.doi.gov

Adjunct office of the interior secretary that decides appeals from decisions rendered by the Bureau of Land Management, the Minerals Management Service, the Office of Surface Mining, and the Bureau of Indian Affairs concerning the use and disposition of public lands and minerals; issues final decisions concerning the Surface Mining Control and Reclamation Act of 1977.

Interior Dept. (DOI), *Land and Minerals Management,* 1849 C St. N.W., #7328 20240; (202) 208-5676. Fax, (202) 208-3144. Rebecca Watson, Assistant Secretary.
Web, www.doi.gov

Directs and supervises the Bureau of Land Management, the Minerals Management Service, and the Office of Surface Mining and Reclamation Enforcement. Supervises programs associated with land use planning, onshore and offshore minerals, surface mining reclamation and enforcement, and outer continental shelf minerals management.

Interior Dept. (DOI), *Water and Science,* 1849 C St. N.W., #7412, MS 7428 20240; (202) 208-3186. Fax, (202) 208-3324. Bennett W. Raley, Assistant Secretary.
Web, www.doi.gov

Administers departmental water, scientific, and research activities. Directs and supervises the Bureau of Reclamation and the U.S. Geological Survey.

Minerals Management Service *(Interior Dept.),* 1849 C St. N.W., MS 4230 20240; (202) 208-3500. Fax, (202) 208-7242. Rejean Burton, Director.
Web, www.mms.gov

Collects and accounts for revenues from onshore and offshore minerals production; disburses royalties to the federal government and native American groups; oversees development of offshore resources, especially oil and natural gas.

Minerals Management Service *(Interior Dept.),* *Engineering and Operations,* 381 Elden St., MS 4020, Herndon, VA 20170-4817; (703) 787-1598. Fax, (703) 787-1093. E. P. Danenberger, Chief.
Web, www.mms.gov

Oversees postlease operations, including exploration, drilling, and production phases of oil and gas development. Ensures compliance with environmental statutes and regulations.

Minerals Management Service *(Interior Dept.),* *Minerals Revenue Management, Washington Office,* 1849 C St. N.W., #4226, MS 4230 20240; (202) 208-3512. Fax, (202) 501-0247. Cathy J. Hamilton, Chief of Staff.
Web, www.mms.gov

Collects and manages royalties on minerals produced on federal and native American lands. (Headquarters and accounting center in Denver, Colo.)

State Dept., *International Energy and Commodities Policy,* 2201 C St. N.W., #3529 20520; (202) 647-3036. Fax, (202) 647-4037. Stephen J. Gallogly, Director.
Web, www.state.gov

Coordinates U.S. international energy policy related to commodities, including energy supply, and U.S. participation in the International Energy Agency; monitors cooperative multilateral and bilateral agreements related to energy; coordinates energy-related aspects of U.S. relations with other countries.

U.S. Geological Survey (USGS), *(Interior Dept.),* *Mineral Resources Program,* 12201 Sunrise Valley Dr., #3A204, MS 913, Reston, VA 20192; (703) 648-6110. Fax, (703) 648-6057. Kathleen Johnson, Program Coordinator.
Web, www.usgs.gov

Coordinates mineral resource activities for the Geological Survey, including geochemical and geophysical instrumentation and application research.

CONGRESS

House Resources Committee, *Subcommittee on Energy and Mineral Resources,* 1626 LHOB 20515; (202) 225-9297. Fax, (202) 225-5255. Rep. Barbara Cubin, R-Wyo., Chair; Jack Belcher, Staff Director.
General e-mail, energy.minerals@mail.house.gov
Web, resourcescommittee.house.gov

Jurisdiction over legislation on metallic and nonmetallic minerals; oversight and legislative jurisdiction over the Minerals Management Service, mineral aspects of the Office of Surface Mining, mineral leasing of the Bureau of Land Management, and offshore hardrock mineral development programs.

Senate Energy and Natural Resources Committee, *Subcommittee on Public Lands and Forests, SD-364 20510; (202) 224-4971. Fax, (202) 224-6163. Sen. Larry E. Craig, R-Idaho, Chair; Frank Gladics, Professional Staff Member.*

Web, energy.senate.gov

Jurisdiction over legislation on metallic and non-metallic minerals, including mineral supply and leasing; oversight and legislative jurisdiction over the Minerals Management Service and offshore hardrock mineral development programs. Jurisdiction over the Bureau of Land Management.

NONPROFIT

Aluminum Assn., *900 19th St. N.W., #300 20006; (202) 862-5100. Fax, (202) 862-5164. J. Stephen Larkin, President.*

Web, www.aluminum.org

Represents the aluminum industry. Develops voluntary standards and technical data; compiles statistics concerning the industry.

American Iron and Steel Institute, *1140 Connecticut Ave. N.W., #705 20036; (202) 452-7100. Fax, (202) 463-6573. Andrew G. Sharkey III, President.*

Web, www.steel.org

Represents the iron and steel industry. Publishes statistics on iron and steel production; promotes the use of steel; conducts research. Monitors legislation and regulations.

American Zinc Assn., *2025 M St. N.W., #800 20036; (202) 367-1151. Fax, (202) 367-2100. George F. Vary, Executive Director.*

Web, www.zinc.org

Provides information on zinc. Monitors legislation and regulations.

Mineralogical Society of America, *1015 18th St. N.W., #601 20036; (202) 775-4344. Fax, (202) 775-0018. Doug Rumble, President.*

Web, www.minsocam.org

Membership: mineralogists, petrologists, crystallographers, geochemists, educators, students, and others interested in mineralogy. Conducts research; sponsors educational programs; promotes industrial application of mineral studies.

National Mining Assn., *101 Constitution Ave. N.W., #500E 20001; (202) 463-2600. Fax, (202) 463-2665. Jack N. Gerard, President. Press, (202) 463-2651.*

General e-mail, nma@prime.planetcom.com

Web, www.nma.org

Membership: domestic producers of coal and industrial-agricultural minerals and metals; manufacturers of mining equipment; engineering and consulting firms; and financial institutions. Interests include mine leasing programs, mine health and safety, research and development, public lands, and minerals availability. Monitors legislation and regulations.

Salt Institute, *700 N. Fairfax St., #600, Alexandria, VA 22314; (703) 549-4648. Fax, (703) 548-2194. Richard L. Hanneman, President.*

General e-mail, info@saltinstitute.org

Web, www.saltinstitute.org

Membership: North American salt companies and overseas companies that produce dry salt for use in food, animal feed, highway deicing, water softening, and chemicals. Sponsors education and training projects with the Bureau of Mines and the Food and Drug Administration. Monitors legislation and regulations.

Native American Trust Resources

AGENCIES

Bureau of Indian Affairs (BIA), *(Interior Dept.), Trust Responsibilities, 1849 C St. N.W., MS 4513 20240; (202) 208-5831. Fax, (202) 219-1255. Larry Scriver, Director (Acting).*

Web, www.doi.gov

Assists in developing and managing bureau programs involving native American trust resources (agriculture, minerals, forestry, wildlife, water, transportation, irrigation, energy, geographic data services, environmental services, and real property management).

Interior Dept. (DOI), *Office of the Solicitor: Indian Affairs, 1849 C St. N.W., MS 6456 20240; (202) 208-3401. Fax, (202) 219-1791. Edith Blackwell, Associate Solicitor (Acting).*

Web, www.doi.gov

Advises the Bureau of Indian Affairs and the secretary of interior on all legal matters, including its trust responsibilities toward native Americans and their natural resources.

Justice Dept. (DOJ), *Indian Resources, 601 D St. N.W., #3507 20530 (mailing address: P.O. Box 44378, L'Enfant Plaza 20026-4378); (202) 305-0269. Fax, (202) 305-0271. S. Craig Alexander, Chief.*

Web, www.usdoj.gov

Represents the United States in suits, including trust violations, brought on behalf of individual native Americans and native American tribes against the government. Also represents the United States as trustee for native

Americans in court actions involving protection of native American land and resources.

Minerals Management Service *(Interior Dept.), Minerals Revenue Management, Washington Office,* 1849 C St. N.W., #4226, MS 4230 20240; (202) 208-3512. Fax, (202) 501-0247. Cathy J. Hamilton, Chief of Staff.
Web, www.mms.gov

Collects and manages royalties on minerals produced on federal and native American lands. (Headquarters and accounting center in Denver, Colo.)

CONGRESS

House Resources Committee, 1324 LHOB 20515; (202) 225-2761. Fax, (202) 225-5929. Rep. Richard W. Pombo, R-Calif., Chair; Steve Ding, Chief of Staff.
General e-mail, resources.committee@mail.house.gov
Web, resourcescommittee.house.gov

Jurisdiction over native American legislation, including land management and trust responsibilities and claims against the United States.

Senate Indian Affairs Committee, SH-838 20510; (202) 224-2251. Fax, (202) 228-2589. Sen. Ben Nighthorse Campbell, R-Colo., Chair; Paul Moorehead, Staff Director.
Web, indian.senate.gov

Jurisdiction over native American legislation, including land management and trust responsibilities and claims against the United States.

NONPROFIT

Native American Rights Fund, *Washington Office,* 1712 N St. N.W. 20036; (202) 785-4166. Fax, (202) 822-0068. Tracy Lavin, Managing Attorney.
Web, www.narf.org

Provides native Americans and Alaskan natives with legal assistance in land claims, water rights, hunting, and other areas. (Headquarters in Boulder, Colo.)

Ocean Resources

AGENCIES

National Oceanic and Atmospheric Administration (NOAA), *(Commerce Dept.), Marine and Aviation Operations,* 1315 East-West Hwy., 12th Floor, Bldg. #3, Silver Spring, MD 20910-3282; (301) 713-1045. Fax, (301) 713-1541. Rear Adm. Evelyn J. Fields, Director.
Web, www.noaacorps.noaa.gov/index.html

Uniformed service of the Commerce Dept. that operates and manages NOAA's fleet of hydrographic, oceanographic, and fisheries research ships and aircraft. Supports NOAA's scientific programs.

National Oceanic and Atmospheric Administration (NOAA), *(Commerce Dept.), National Environmental Satellite, Data, and Information Service,* 1335 East-West Hwy., Silver Spring, MD 20910; (301) 713-3578. Fax, (301) 713-1249. Gregory W. Withee, Assistant Administrator.
Web, www.nesdis.noaa.gov

Disseminates worldwide environmental data through a system of meteorological, oceanographic, geophysical, and solar-terrestrial data centers.

National Oceanic and Atmospheric Administration (NOAA), *(Commerce Dept.), National Sea Grant College Program,* 1315 East-West Hwy., 11th Floor, Silver Spring, MD 20910; (301) 713-2448. Fax, (301) 713-0799. Ronald C. Baird, Director.
Web, www.nsgo.seagrant.org

Provides institutions with grants for marine research, education, and advisory services; provides marine environmental information.

National Oceanic and Atmospheric Administration (NOAA), *(Commerce Dept.), Ocean and Coastal Resource Management,* 1305 East-West Hwy., SSMC4, Silver Spring, MD 20910; (301) 713-3155. Fax, (301) 713-4012. Douglas L. Brown, Director (Acting).
Web, www.nos.noaa.gov/programs/ocrm.html

Administers the Coastal Zone Management Act, the National Estuarine Research Reserve System, the National Marine Sanctuary Program, the Deep Seabed Hard Mineral Resources Act, and the Ocean Thermal Energy Conversion Act to carry out NOAA's goals for preservation, conservation, and restoration management of the ocean and coastal environment.

National Oceanic and Atmospheric Administration (NOAA), *(Commerce Dept.), Sanctuaries,* 1305 East-West Hwy., 11th Floor, Silver Spring, MD 20910; (301) 713-3125. Fax, (301) 713-0404. Dan J. Basta, Director.
Web, www.noaa.gov

Administers the National Marine Sanctuary program, which seeks to protect the ecology and the recreational and cultural resources of marine and Great Lakes waters. Administers (in cooperation with state governments) the National Estuarine Research Reserve System, which helps to acquire, develop, and operate estuarine areas as natural field laboratories for research and education.

National Oceanic and Atmospheric Administration (NOAA), *(Commerce Dept.), Special Projects,* 1305 East-West Hwy., Silver Spring, MD 20910; (301) 713-3000. Fax, (301) 713-4384. Dan Farrow, Chief.
Web, www.nos.noaa.gov

Conducts national studies and develops policies on ocean management and use along the U.S. coastline and the exclusive economic zone.

CONGRESS

House Resources Committee, *Subcommittee on Fisheries, Conservation, Wildlife, and Oceans, H2-188 FHOB 20515; (202) 226-0200. Fax, (202) 225-1542. Rep. Wayne T. Gilchrest, R-Md., Chair; Harry Burroughs, Staff Director.*
General e-mail, fisheries.subcommittee@mail.house.gov
Web, resourcescommittee.house.gov

Jurisdiction over legislation concerning research on ocean life and the National Environmental Policy Act as it applies to ocean resources. Jurisdiction over ocean environment and charting, ocean engineering, coastal barriers, coastal zone management, Law of the Sea, Sea Grant programs and extension services, and all matters relating to the protection of coastal and marine environments.

Senate Commerce, Science, and Transportation Committee, *SD-508 20510; (202) 224-5115. Fax, (202) 228-0303. Sen. John McCain, R-Ariz., Chair; Jeanne Bumpus, Staff Director.*
Web, commerce.senate.gov

Jurisdiction over legislation concerning research on ocean life, the National Environmental Policy Act as it applies to ocean resources, deep seabed mining, ocean environment and charting, coastal zone management, Law of the Sea, Sea Grant programs and extension services, and commerce and transportation aspects of outer continental shelf lands.

Senate Commerce, Science, and Transportation Committee, *Subcommittee on Oceans, Fisheries, and Coast Guard, SH-227 20510; (202) 224-8172. Fax, (202) 224-9334. Sen. Olympia J. Snowe, R-Maine, Chair; Andrew Minkiewicz, Counsel Member.*
Web, commerce.senate.gov

Studies all aspects of ocean policy, including marine science funding and the outer continental shelf. Studies issues involving marine research, coastal zone management, ocean environment, and the Law of the Sea. Studies deep seabed mining, ocean charting, and the National Environmental Policy Act as it applies to ocean resources. (Subcommittee does not report legislation.)

NONPROFIT

Coastal States Organization, *444 N. Capitol St. N.W., #322 20001; (202) 508-3860. Fax, (202) 508-3843. Anthony B. MacDonald, Executive Director.*

General e-mail, cso@sso.org
Web, www.sso.org/cso

Nonpartisan organization that represents governors of U.S. coastal states, territories, and commonwealths on management of coastal, Great Lakes, and marine resources. Interests include ocean dumping, coastal pollution, wetlands preservation and restoration, national oceans policy, and the outer continental shelf. Gathers and analyzes data to assess state coastal needs; sponsors and participates in conferences and workshops.

Marine Technology Society, *5565 Sterrett Place, #108, Columbia, MD 21044; (410) 884-5330. Fax, (410) 884-9060. Judith Krauthamer, Executive Director.*
General e-mail, mtpubs@aol.com
Web, www.mtsociety.org

Membership: scientists, engineers, technologists, and others interested in marine science and technology. Provides information on marine science, technology, and education.

National Ocean Industries Assn., *1120 G St. N.W., #900 20005; (202) 347-6900. Fax, (202) 347-8650. Tom A. Fry, President.*
General e-mail, noia@noia.org
Web, www.noia.org

Membership: manufacturers, producers, suppliers, and support and service companies involved in marine, offshore, and ocean work. Interests include offshore oil and gas supply and production, deep-sea mining, ocean thermal energy, and new energy sources.

Outer Continental Shelf

AGENCIES

Minerals Management Service *(Interior Dept.), Offshore Minerals Management, 1849 C St. N.W., MS 4230 20240-0001; (202) 208-3530. Fax, (202) 208-6048. Thomas A. Readinger, Associate Director.*
Web, www.mms.gov

Administers the Outer Continental Shelf Lands Act. Evaluates, classifies, and supervises oil, gas, and other mineral reserves and operations on outer continental shelf lands; manages the submerged lands of the outer continental shelf.

Minerals Management Service *(Interior Dept.), Resources and Environmental Management, 381 Elden St., Herndon, VA 20170; (703) 787-1700. Fax, (703) 787-1209. Robert P. LaBelle, Deputy Associate Director.*
Web, www.mms.gov

Oversees prelease operations; administers offshore oil and gas leasing.

U.S. Geological Survey (USGS), *(Interior Dept.),* *Coastal and Marine Geology Program,* 12201 Sunrise Valley Dr., Reston, VA 20192 (mailing address: 915B National Center, Reston, VA 20192); (703) 648-6422. Fax, (703) 648-5464. John W. Haines, Program Coordinator.

Web, marine.usgs.gov

Handles resource assessment, exploration research, and marine geologic and environmental studies on U.S. coastal regions and the outer continental shelf.

CONGRESS

House Resources Committee, *Subcommittee on Energy and Mineral Resources,* 1626 LHOB 20515; (202) 225-9297. Fax, (202) 225-5255. Rep. Barbara Cubin, R-Wyo., Chair; Jack Belcher, Staff Director.

General e-mail, energy.minerals@mail.house.gov

Web, resourcescommittee.house.gov

Jurisdiction over legislation on leasing and development of the outer continental shelf under the Outer Continental Shelf Lands Act.

Senate Commerce, Science, and Transportation Committee, *Subcommittee on Oceans, Fisheries, and Coast Guard,* SH-227 20510; (202) 224-8172. Fax, (202) 224-9334. Sen. Olympia J. Snowe, R-Maine, Chair; Andrew Minkiewicz, Counsel Member.

Web, commerce.senate.gov

Studies outer continental shelf matters related to coastal zone management, marine research, and ocean environment. (Jurisdiction shared with the Senate Energy and Natural Resources and the Senate Environment and Public Works committees.)

Senate Energy and Natural Resources Committee, SD-364 20510; (202) 224-4971. Fax, (202) 224-6163. Sen. Pete V. Domenici, R-N.M., Chair; Alex Flint, Staff Director.

General e-mail, committee@energy.senate.gov

Web, energy.senate.gov

Jurisdiction over legislation on ocean environment and coastal zone matters, including leasing and development of the outer continental shelf under the Outer Continental Shelf Lands Act; and on the environmental impact of offshore drilling on the outer continental shelf (jurisdiction shared with Senate Commerce, Science, and Transportation and Senate Environment and Public Works committees).

Senate Environment and Public Works Committee, *Subcommittee on Clean Air, Climate Change, and Nuclear Safety,* SD-410 20510; (202) 224-6176. Fax, (202) 224-1273. Sen. George V. Voinovich, R-Ohio, Chair; Michael Whatley, Staff Director.

Web, epw.senate.gov

Jurisdiction over legislation on the environmental impact of offshore drilling on the outer continental shelf. (Jurisdiction shared with Senate Commerce, Science, and Transportation and Senate Energy and Natural Resources committees.)

Parks and Recreation Areas

AGENCIES

Bureau of Land Management (BLM), *(Interior Dept.), Cultural Heritage, Wilderness, Special Areas, and Paleontology,* 1620 L St. N.W., #204 20036 (mailing address: 1849 C St. N.W., #204-LS 20240); (202) 452-0330. Fax, (202) 452-7701. Marilyn Nickels, Group Manager. TTY, (202) 452-0326.

Web, www.blm.gov

Identifies and manages cultural heritage and recreation programs on public lands.

Bureau of Land Management (BLM), *(Interior Dept.), Recreation,* 1620 L St. N.W., #306 20036 (mailing address: 1849 C St. N.W., #306-LS 20240); (202) 452-5041. Fax, (202) 452-7709. Lee Larson, Manager.

Web, www.blm.gov

Develops recreation opportunities on public lands.

Bureau of Reclamation *(Interior Dept.),* 1849 C St. N.W., #7554 20240; (202) 513-0501. Fax, (202) 513-0312. John W. Keys III, Commissioner.

Web, www.usbr.gov

Responsible for acquisition, administration, management, and disposal of lands in seventeen western states associated with bureau water resource development projects. Provides overall policy guidance for land use, including agreements with public agencies for outdoor recreation, fish and wildlife enhancement, and land use authorizations such as leases, licenses, permits, and rights of way.

Forest Service *(Agriculture Dept.), Recreation Heritage and Wilderness Resources,* 201 14th St. S.W., 4th Floor Central 20250 (mailing address: P.O. Box 96090 20090-6090); (202) 205-1706. Fax, (202) 205-1145. David G. Holland, Director.

Web, www.fs.fed.us

Develops policy and sets guidelines on administering national forests and grasslands for recreational purposes. (The Forest Service administers some of the lands designated as national recreation areas.)

Interior Dept. (DOI), *Fish, Wildlife, and Parks,* 1849 C St. N.W., #3156 20240; (202) 208-4416. Fax, (202) 208-4684. Craig Manson, Assistant Secretary.

Web, www.doi.gov

Responsible for programs associated with the development, conservation, and use of fish, wildlife, recreational, historical, and national park system resources. Coordinates marine environmental quality and biological resources programs with other federal agencies.

National Park Service (NPS), *(Interior Dept.),* 1849 C St. N.W., #3112 20240; (202) 208-4621. Fax, (202) 208-7889. Fran P. Mainella, Director. Press, (202) 208-6843. Washington area activities, (202) 619-7275 (recording). Web, www.nps.gov

Administers national parks, monuments, historic sites, and recreation areas. Oversees coordination, planning, and financing of public outdoor recreation programs at all levels of government. Conducts recreation research surveys; administers financial assistance program to states for planning and development of outdoor recreation programs. (Some lands designated as national recreation areas are not under NPS jurisdiction.)

National Park Service (NPS), *(Interior Dept.), Policy,* 1849 C St. N.W., #7252 20240; (202) 208-7456. Fax, (202) 219-8835. Loran G. Fraser, Chief.
Web, www.nps.gov

Researches and develops management policy on matters relating to the National Park Service; makes recommendations on the historical significance of national trails and landmarks.

Tennessee Valley Authority, *Government Relations, Washington Office,* 1 Massachusetts Ave. N.W., #300 20001; (202) 898-2999. Fax, (202) 898-2998. Linda Whitestone, Vice President.
Web, www.tva.gov

Operates Land Between the Lakes, a national recreation and environmental education area located in western Kentucky and Tennessee.

U.S. Fish and Wildlife Service *(Interior Dept.), National Wildlife Refuge System,* 1849 C St. N.W., #3251 20240; (202) 208-5333. Fax, (202) 208-3082. William F. Hartwig, Chief.
Web, www.fws.gov

Manages the National Wildlife Refuge System. Most refuges are open to public use; activities include bird and wildlife watching, fishing, hunting, and environmental education.

CONGRESS

House Resources Committee, *Subcommittee on Forests and Forest Health,* 1337 LHOB 20515; (202) 225-0691. Fax, (202) 225-0521. Rep. Scott McInnis, R-Colo., Chair; Josh Penry, Staff Director.

General e-mail, forests.health@mail.house.gov
Web, resourcescommittee.house.gov

Jurisdiction over legislation on public forest lands (except in Alaska), including issues of forestry, wilderness preservation, forest reserve, water rights, national trails and rivers, and recreation.

House Resources Committee, *Subcommittee on National Parks, Recreation, and Public Lands,* 1333 LHOB 20515; (202) 226-7736. Fax, (202) 226-2301. Rep. George P. Radanovich, R-Calif., Chair; Casey Hammond, Clerk.
General e-mail, parks.subcommittee@mail.house.gov
Web, resourcescommittee.house.gov

Jurisdiction over legislation on the national park system, the Bureau of Land Management, and related parks and recreation.

Senate Energy and Natural Resources Committee, *Subcommittee on National Parks,* SD-364 20510; (202) 224-4971. Fax, (202) 224-6163. Sen. Craig Thomas, R-Wyo., Chair; Tom Lillie, Professional Staff Member.
General e-mail, parks@energy.senate.gov
Web, energy.senate.gov

Jurisdiction over legislation on national parks, recreation areas, wilderness areas, trails, wild and scenic rivers, historic sites, and military parks and battlefields.

NONPROFIT

American Hiking Society, 1422 Fenwick Lane, Silver Spring, MD 20910; (301) 565-6704. Fax, (301) 565-6714. Mary Margaret Sloan, President.
General e-mail, info@americanhiking.org
Web, www.americanhiking.org

Membership: individuals and clubs interested in preserving America's trail system and protecting the interests of trail users. Provides information on outdoor volunteer opportunities on public lands.

American Recreation Coalition, 1225 New York Ave. N.W., #450 20005; (202) 682-9530. Fax, (202) 682-9529. Derrick A. Crandall, President.
General e-mail, arc@funoutdoors.com
Web, www.funoutdoors.com

Membership: organized recreationists, national and regional corporations offering recreational products and services, and recreation industry trade associations. Works to increase public and private sector activity in public recreation, land and water management, and energy policy. Provides information on innovative recreational planning.

National Park Foundation, *11 Dupont Circle, 6th Floor 20036; (202) 238-4200. Fax, (202) 234-3103. James D. Maddy, President.*
Web, www.nationalparks.org

Chartered by Congress and chaired by the interior secretary. Encourages private-sector support of the national park system; provides grants and sponsors educational and cultural activities.

National Parks and Conservation Assn., *1300 19th St. N.W., #300 20036-6404; (202) 223-6722. Fax, (202) 659-0650. Tom Kiernan, President. Information, (800) 628-7275.*
General e-mail, npca@npca.org
Web, www.npca.org

Citizens' interest group that seeks to protect national parks and other park system areas.

National Recreation and Park Assn., *22377 Belmont Ridge Rd., Ashburn, VA 20148-4501; (703) 858-0784. Fax, (703) 858-0794. John A. Thorner, Executive Director.*
General e-mail, info@nrpa.org
Web, www.nrpa.org

Membership: park and recreation professionals and interested citizens. Promotes support and awareness of park, recreation, and leisure services; facilitates development, expansion, and management of resources; provides technical assistance for park and recreational programs; and provides professional development to members.

Rails-to-Trails Conservancy, *1100 17th St. N.W., 10th Floor 20036; (202) 331-9696. Fax, (202) 331-9680. Keith Laughlin, President.*
General e-mail, railtrails@transact.org
Web, www.railtrails.org

Promotes the conversion of abandoned railroad corridors into hiking and biking trails for public use. Provides public education programs and technical and legal assistance. Publishes trail guides. Monitors legislation and regulations.

Scenic America, *801 Pennsylvania Ave. S.E., #300 20003-2152; (202) 543-6200. Fax, (202) 543-9130. Meg Maguire, President.*
General e-mail, scenic@scenic.org
Web, www.scenic.org

Membership: national, state, and local groups concerned with land-use control, growth management, and landscape protection. Works to enhance the scenic quality of America's communities and countryside. Provides information and technical assistance on scenic byways, tree preservation, economics of aesthetic regulation, bill-board and sign control, scenic areas preservation, and growth management.

Student Conservation Assn., *Washington Office, 1800 N. Kent St., #102, Arlington, VA 22209; (703) 524-2441. Fax, (703) 524-2451. Gary King, Regional Vice President, Mid-Atlantic Southeast Region.*
Web, www.thesca.org

Educational organization that provides youth and adults with opportunities for training and work experience in natural resource management and conservation. Volunteers serve in national parks, forests, wildlife refuges, and other public lands. (Headquarters in Charlestown, N.H.)

World Wildlife Fund (WWF), *1250 24th St. N.W., #400 20037; (202) 293-4800. Fax, (202) 293-9211. Kathryn S. Fuller, President.*
Web, www.wwf.org

International conservation organization that provides funds and technical assistance for establishing and maintaining parks.

Water Resources

AGENCIES

Army Corps of Engineers *(Defense Dept.), 441 G St. N.W., #3K05 20314-1000; (202) 761-0001. Fax, (202) 761-4463. Lt. Gen. Robert B. Flowers (USACE), Chief of Engineers.*
Web, www.usace.army.mil

Provides local governments with disaster relief, flood control, navigation, and hydroelectric power services.

Bureau of Reclamation *(Interior Dept.), 1849 C St. N.W., #7554 20240; (202) 513-0501. Fax, (202) 513-0312. John W. Keys III, Commissioner.*
Web, www.usbr.gov

Administers federal programs for water and power resource development and management in seventeen western states; oversees municipal and industrial water supplies, hydroelectric power generation, irrigation, flood control, water quality improvement, river regulation, fish and wildlife enhancement, and outdoor recreation.

Environmental Protection Agency (EPA), *Wetlands Protection, 1200 Pennsylvania Ave. N.W., #6105C 20460; (202) 566-1348. Fax, (202) 566-1349. John W. Meagher, Director.*
General e-mail, wetlands.hotline@epamail.epa.gov
Web, www.epa.gov/owow/wetlands

Manages dredge-and-fill program under section 404 of the Clean Water Act. Coordinates federal policies affecting wetlands. Promotes public awareness of wetland preservation and management. Encourages the development of stronger wetland programs at the state level.

Interstate Commission on the Potomac River Basin, *6110 Executive Blvd., #300, Rockville, MD 20852; (301) 984-1908. Fax, (301) 984-5841. Joseph K. Hoffman, Executive Director.*
Web, www.potomacriver.org

Nonregulatory interstate compact commission established by Congress to control and reduce water pollution and to restore and protect living resources in the Potomac River and its tributaries. Monitors water quality; assists metropolitan water utilities; seeks innovative methods to solve water supply and land resource problems. Provides information and educational materials on the Potomac River basin.

Office of Management and Budget (OMB), *(Executive Office of the President), Water and Power,* New *Executive Office Bldg., #8002 20503; (202) 395-4590. Fax, (202) 395-4817. Gene Ebner, Chief.*
Web, www.whitehouse.gov/omb

Reviews all plans and budgets related to federal or federally assisted water power and related land resource projects.

Rural Utilities Service *(Agriculture Dept.), 1400 Independence Ave. S.W., #4055, MS-1510 20250-1500; (202) 720-9540. Fax, (202) 720-1725. Hilda Gay Legg, Administrator. Information, (202) 720-1255.*
Web, www.usda.gov/rus

Makes loans and provides technical assistance for development, repair, and replacement of water and waste disposal systems in rural areas.

Smithsonian Environmental Research Center *(Smithsonian Institution), 647 Contees Wharf Rd., Edgewater, MD 21037 (mailing address: P.O. Box 28, Edgewater, MD 21037); (443) 482-2200. Fax, (443) 482-2380. Ross B. Simons, Director.*
Web, www.serc.si.edu

Studies the interaction of the Rhode River with its watershed, the effect of humans on the system, and the long-term effects of water quality on the plant and animal population.

Tennessee Valley Authority, *Government Relations, Washington Office, 1 Massachusetts Ave. N.W., #300 20001; (202) 898-2999. Fax, (202) 898-2998. Linda Whitestone, Vice President.*
Web, www.tva.gov

Coordinates resource conservation, development, and land-use programs in the Tennessee River Valley. Operates the river control system; projects include flood control, navigation development, and multiple-use reservoirs.

U.S. Geological Survey (USGS), *(Interior Dept.), Water Resources, 12201 Sunrise Valley Dr., MS 409, Reston, VA 20192; (703) 648-5215. Fax, (703) 648-7031. Robert M. Hirsch, Associate Director for Water.*
Web, www.usgs.gov

Administers the Water Resources Research Act of 1990. Assesses the quantity and quality of surface and groundwater resources; collects, analyzes, and disseminates data on water use and the effect of human activity and natural phenomena on hydrologic systems. Provides federal agencies, state and local governments, international organizations, and foreign governments with scientific and technical assistance.

CONGRESS

House Agriculture Committee, *Subcommittee on Conservation, Credit, Rural Development, and Research, 1301 LHOB 20515; (202) 225-2171. Fax, (202) 225-0917. Rep. Frank Lucas, R-Okla., Chair; Ryan Weston, Staff Director.*
Web, agriculture.house.gov

Jurisdiction over legislation on small watershed programs, including stream channelization.

House Energy and Commerce Committee, *Subcommittee on Energy and Air Quality, 2125 RHOB 20515; (202) 225-2927. Fax, (202) 225-1919. Rep. Joe L. Barton, R-Texas, Chair; David V. Marventano, Staff Director.*
General e-mail, commerce@mail.house.gov
Web, energycommerce.house.gov

Jurisdiction over legislation on hydroelectric power and ocean thermal energy resource commercialization, utilization, and conversion.

House Resources Committee, *Subcommittee on Water and Power, 1522 LHOB 20515; (202) 225-8331. Fax, (202) 226-6953. Rep. Ken Calvert, R-Calif., Chair; Joshua Johnson, Staff Director.*
General e-mail, water.power@mail.house.gov
Web, resourcescommittee.house.gov

Jurisdiction over legislation on water rights, including federally reserved water rights on public lands; irrigation and reclamation projects; compacts relating to use and apportionment of interstate water resources; and power marketing administrations.

House Transportation and Infrastructure Committee, *Subcommittee on Water Resources and Environment,* *B376 RHOB 20515; (202) 225-4360. Fax, (202) 226-5435. Rep. John J. "Jimmy" Duncan Jr., R-Tenn., Chair; Susan Bodine, Staff Director.*
General e-mail, transcomm@mail.house.gov
Web, www.house.gov/transportation

Jurisdiction over legislation on water resources; watershed and flood control programs; U.S. Army Corps of Engineers water resources projects; wetlands protection; navigation and river basin programs; small watershed programs within the Agriculture Dept.; groundwater programs; construction, operation, and maintenance of harbors and inland waterways; and hydroelectric power.

Senate Agriculture, Nutrition, and Forestry Committee, *Subcommittee on Forestry, Conservation, and Rural Revitalization,* *SR-328A 20510; (202) 224-2035. Sen. Michael D. Crapo, R-Idaho, Chair; Vacant, Staff Director.*
Web, agriculture.senate.gov

Jurisdiction over legislation on family farming and rural development, including rural electrification and telephone development. Jurisdiction includes legislation on irrigation, soil conservation, stream channelization, watershed programs, and flood control programs involving structures of less than 4,000 acre-feet in storage capacity.

Senate Energy and Natural Resources Committee, *Subcommittee on Water and Power,* *SD-364 20510; (202) 224-4971. Fax, (202) 224-6163. Sen. Lisa Murkowski, R-Alaska, Chair; Colleen Deegan, Counsel.*
General e-mail, water&power@energy.senate.gov
Web, energy.senate.gov

Jurisdiction over legislation on hydroelectric power; irrigation and reclamation projects; water rights, including federally reserved water rights on public lands; compacts relating to use and apportionment of interstate water resources; and power marketing administrations.

Senate Environment and Public Works Committee, *SD-410 20510; (202) 224-6176. Fax, (202) 224-5167. Sen. James M. Inhofe, R-Okla., Chair; Andrew Wheeler, Staff Director.*
General e-mail, guest1@epw.senate.gov
Web, epw.senate.gov

Jurisdiction over water resources and water resources research legislation; watershed and flood control programs; U.S. Army Corps of Engineers water resources projects; navigation and river basin programs; small watershed programs of the Natural Resources Conserva-tion Service; wetlands protection and groundwater programs; and construction, operation, and maintenance of harbors.

NONPROFIT

American Rivers, *1025 Vermont Ave. N.W., #720 20005; (202) 347-7550. Fax, (202) 347-9240. Rebecca Wodder, President.*
General e-mail, amrivers@amrivers.org
Web, www.americanrivers.org

Works to preserve and protect the nation's river systems.

American Water Works Assn., *Washington Office,* *1401 New York Ave. N.W., #640 20005; (202) 628-8303. Fax, (202) 628-2846. Tom Curtis, Deputy Executive Director.*
Web, www.awwa.org

Membership: municipal water utilities, manufacturers of equipment for water industries, water treatment companies, and individuals. Provides information on drinking water treatment; publishes voluntary standards for the water industry. (Headquarters in Denver, Colo.)

Assn. of State Drinking Water Administrators, *1025 Connecticut Ave. N.W., #903 20036; (202) 293-7655. Fax, (202) 293-7656. James D. Taft, Executive Director.*
General e-mail, asdwa@erols.com
Web, www.asdwa.org

Membership: state officials responsible for the drinking water supply and enforcement of safety standards. Monitors legislation and regulations.

Environmental Defense Fund, *Washington Office,* *1875 Connecticut Ave. N.W., #600 20009-5728; (202) 387-3500. Fax, (202) 234-6049. Senta Boardley, Office Manager.*
Web, www.environmentaldefense.org

Citizens' interest group staffed by lawyers, economists, and scientists. Takes legal action on environmental issues; provides information on pollution prevention, environmental health, water resources, and water marketing. (Headquarters in New York.)

Irrigation Assn., *6540 Arlington Blvd., Falls Church, VA 22042; (703) 536-7080. Fax, (703) 536-7019. Thomas H. Kimmell, Executive Director.*
Web, www.irrigation.org

Membership: companies and individuals involved in irrigation, drainage, and erosion control worldwide. Seeks to improve the products and practices used to manage water resources; interests include economic development and environmental enhancement.

Izaak Walton League of America, *707 Conservation Lane, Gaithersburg, MD 20878-2983; (301) 548-0150. Fax, (301) 548-0146. Paul W. Hansen, Executive Director.*
General e-mail, general@iwla.org
Web, www.iwla.org

Grassroots organization that promotes conservation of natural resources and the environment. Coordinates a citizen action program to monitor and improve the condition of local streams.

National Assn. of Conservation Districts, *509 Capitol Court N.E. 20002-4937; (202) 547-6223. Fax, (202) 547-6450. Ernest C. Shea, Chief Executive Officer.*
General e-mail, washington@nacdnet.org
Web, www.nacdnet.org

Membership: conservation districts (local subdivisions of state government). Develops national policies and works to promote the conservation of water resources. Interests include erosion and sediment control and control of nonpoint source pollution.

National Assn. of Flood and Stormwater Management Agencies, *1299 Pennsylvania Ave. N.W., 8th Floor West 20004; (202) 218-4122. Fax, (202) 785-5277. Susan Gilson, Executive Director.*
Web, www.nafsma.org

Membership: state, county, and local governments concerned with management of water resources. Monitors legislation and regulations.

National Assn. of Regulatory Utility Commissioners, *1101 Vermont Ave. N.W., #200 20005; (202) 898-2200. Fax, (202) 898-2213. Charles Gray, Executive Director. Press, (202) 898-2205.*
Web, www.naruc.org

Membership: members of federal, state, municipal, and Canadian regulatory commissions that have jurisdiction over utilities. Interests include water.

National Assn. of Water Companies, *1725 K St. N.W., #1212 20006; (202) 833-8383. Fax, (202) 331-7442. Peter L. Cook, Executive Director.*
Web, www.nawc.org

Membership: privately owned, regulated water companies. Provides members with information on legislative and regulatory issues and other subjects.

National Rural Community Assistance Program, *1522 K St. N.W., #400 20005; (202) 408-1273. Fax, (202) 408-8165. Randolph A. Adams, Executive Director.*
General e-mail, rcap@rcap.org
Web, www.rcap.org

Federally funded organization that conducts programs to improve water delivery and disposal of waste water for rural residents, particularly low-income families.

National Utility Contractors Assn., *4301 N. Fairfax Dr., #360, Arlington, VA 22203-1627; (703) 358-9300. Fax, (703) 358-9307. Bill Hillman, Chief Executive Officer.*
Web, www.nuca.com

Membership: contractors who perform water, sewer, and other underground utility construction. Sponsors conferences; conducts surveys. Monitors public works legislation and regulations.

National Water Resources Assn., *3800 N. Fairfax Dr., #4, Arlington, VA 22203; (703) 524-1544. Fax, (703) 524-1548. Thomas F. Donnelly, Executive Vice President.*
General e-mail, nwra@nwra.org
Web, www.nwra.org

Membership: conservation and irrigation districts, municipalities, and others interested in water resources. Works for the development and maintenance of water resource projects in the western reclamation states. Represents interests of members before Congress and regulatory agencies.

River Network, *Washington Office, 4000 Albemarle St. N.W., #303 20016; (202) 364-2550. Fax, (202) 364-2520. Pat Munoz, Program Manager.*
General e-mail, dc@rivernetwork.org
Web, www.rivernetwork.org

Acquires and conserves watersheds of rivers used for drinking water supply, floodplain management, fish and wildlife habitats, and recreation. Works to build and support citizen watershed councils. (Headquarters in Portland, Ore.)

10 🏛

Government Operations

🏛 GENERAL POLICY

AGENCIES

Domestic Policy Council *(Executive Office of the President),* *The White House 20502; (202) 456-5594. Fax, (202) 456-5557. Margaret Spellings, Assistant to the President for Domestic Policy.*

Comprises cabinet officials and staff members. Coordinates the domestic policy-making process to facilitate the implementation of the president's domestic agenda in such areas as agriculture, education, energy, environment, health, housing, labor, and veterans affairs.

Federal Bureau of Investigation (FBI), *(Justice Dept.),* **Administrative Services,** *935 Pennsylvania Ave. N.W., #6012 20535; (202) 324-3514. Fax, (202) 324-1091. Sheri A. Farrar, Assistant Director.*

Performs background investigations of presidential appointees.

General Services Administration (GSA), *1800 F St. N.W., #6137 20405; (202) 501-0800. Stephen A. Perry, Administrator; Thurman M. Davis Sr., Deputy Administrator; Daniel R. Levinson, Inspector General. Library, (202) 501-0788. Press, (202) 501-1231.*
Web, www.gsa.gov

Establishes policies for managing federal government property, including construction and operation of buildings and procurement and distribution of supplies and equipment; manages transportation and telecommunications. Manages disposal of surplus federal property. Library open to the public.

General Services Administration (GSA), *Acquisition Policy,* *1800 F St. N.W., #4040 20405; (202) 501-1043. Fax, (202) 501-1986. David A. Drabkin, Deputy Associate Administrator.*
Web, www.gsa.gov

Develops and implements federal government acquisition policies and procedures; conducts preaward and postaward contract reviews; administers federal acquisition regulations for civilian agencies; suspends and debars contractors for unsatisfactory performance; coordinates and promotes governmentwide career management and training programs for contracting personnel.

General Services Administration (GSA), *Governmentwide Policy,* *1800 F St. N.W., #5240 20405; (202) 501-8880. Fax, (202) 501-8898. G. Martin Wagner, Associate Administrator.*
Web, www.policyworks.gov

Coordinates GSA policy-making activities; promotes collaboration between government and the private sector in developing policy and management techniques; works to integrate acquisition, management, and disposal of government property.

General Services Administration (GSA), *National Contact Center,* *P.O. Box 450, Camby, IN 46113-0450. Warren Snaider, Program Manager. Information, (800) 688-9889. TTY, (800) 326-2996.*
Web, fic.info.gov

Responds to inquiries about federal programs and services. Gives information or locates particular agencies or persons best suited to help with specific concerns.

National Archives and Records Administration (NARA), *Federal Register,* *800 N. Capitol St., #700 20001 (mailing address: 8601 Adelphi Rd., College Park, MD 20740-6001); (202) 741-6000. Fax, (202) 741-6012. Raymond Mosley, Director. TTY, (202) 741-6086. Public Laws Update Service (PLUS), (202) 523-6641.*
General e-mail, fedreg.info@nara.gov
Web, www.archives.gov/federal_register

Assigns public law numbers to enacted legislation, executive orders, and proclamations; responds to inquiries on public law numbers; assists inquirers in finding presidential signing or veto messages in the *Weekly Compilation of Presidential Documents* and the *Public Papers of the Presidents* series; compiles slip laws and annual *United States Statutes at Large;* compiles indexes for finding statutory provisions. Operates Public Laws Update Service (PLUS) and Public Law Electronic Notification System (PENS), which provides information by telephone or e-mail on new legislation. Publications available from the U.S. Government Printing Office.

Office of Administration *(Executive Office of the President),* *725 17th St. N.W., #147 20503; (202) 456-2861. Fax, (202) 456-6515. Tim Campen, Director.*
Web, www.whitehouse.gov/oa

Provides administrative support services to the Executive Office of the President, including personnel and financial management, data processing, library services, and general office operations.

Office of Management and Budget (OMB), *(Executive Office of the President), Federal Procurement Policy,* *Dwight D. Eisenhower Executive Office Bldg., #352 20503; (202) 395-5802. Fax, (202) 395-3242. Angela B. Styles, Administrator.*
Web, www.whitehouse.gov/omb

Coordinates government procurement policies, regulations, and procedures. Responsible for cost accounting rules governing federal contractors and subcontractors.

WHITE HOUSE OFFICES

OFFICE OF THE PRESIDENT

President, George W. Bush

  1600 Pennsylvania Ave. N.W. 20500;
    (202) 456-1414

  Web, www.whitehouse.gov

  E-mail, president@whitehouse.gov

Cabinet Affairs, Brian Montgomery, Cabinet
  Secretary, (202) 456-0165

Chief of Staff, Andrew H. Card Jr., Chief of Staff,
  (202) 456-6797

  Joshua Bolten (Policy), Joseph Hagin (Operations),
    Deputy Chiefs of Staff, (202) 456-6798

  Communications, Dan Bartlett, Director,
    (202) 456-7910

  Speechwriting, Michael Gerson, Director,
    (202) 456-2763

  General Counsel, Alberto Gonzales, Counsel,
    (202) 456-2632

Intergovernmental Affairs, Ruben Barrales, Director,
  (202) 456-2896

Legislative Affairs, David Hobbs, Director,
  (202) 456-2230

  House Liaison, Daniel Keniry, Director,
    (202) 456-6620

  Senate Liaison, Ziad Ojakli, Director,
    (202) 456-6493

Management and Administration, Hector Irastorza,
  Director, (202) 456-5400

  White House Intern Program, Michael Sanders,
    Coordinator, (202) 456-2500

  White House Military Office, Rear Adm. Michael
    H. Miller, Director, (202) 757-2151

Oval Office Operations, Linda Gambatesa, Director,
  (202) 456-1414

Political Affairs, Ken Mehlman, Director,
  (202) 456-6257

Presidential Personnel, Clay Johnson, Director,
  (202) 456-9713

Press Secretary, Ari Fleischer, Press Secretary,
  (202) 456-2673

  Media Affairs, Nicolle Devenish, Director,
    (202) 456-6238

Public Liaison, Lezlee Westine, Director,
  (202) 456-2930

Scheduling and Advance, Bradley A. Blakeman,
  Director, (202) 456-2514

Staff Secretary, Harriet Miers, Staff Secretary,
  (202) 456-2702

  Correspondence, Desiree Thompson Sayle, Director,
    (202) 456-5465

OFFICE OF THE FIRST LADY

First Lady, Laura Bush

  1600 Pennsylvania Ave. N.W. 20500;
    (202) 456-7064

  Web, www.whitehouse.gov/firstlady

  E-mail, first.lady@whitehouse.gov

Chief of Staff, Andrea Ball, Chief of Staff,
  (202) 456-7064

Communications, Noelia Rodriguez, Press Secretary,
  (202) 456-6313

OFFICE OF THE VICE PRESIDENT

Vice President, Richard B. Cheney

  Old Executive Office Bldg. 20501; (202) 456-7549

  Web, www.whitehouse.gov/vicepresident

  E-mail, vice-president@whitehouse.gov

Chief of Staff, I. Lewis Libby Jr., Chief of Staff,
  (202) 456-9000

Communications, Jennifer Millerwise, Press Secretary,
  (202) 456-0373

Mrs. Cheney, Lynne Cheney, Wife of the Vice President,
  (202) 456-7458

Office of Management and Budget (OMB), *(Executive Office of the President), Information and Regulatory Affairs,* *Dwight D. Eisenhower Executive Office Bldg., #262 20503; (202) 395-4852. Fax, (202) 395-3047. John D. Graham, Administrator.*
Web, www.whitehouse.gov/omb

  Oversees development of federal regulatory programs. Supervises agency information management activities in accordance with the Paperwork Reduction Act of 1995, as amended; reviews agency analyses of the effect of government regulatory activities on the U.S. economy.

Office of Management and Budget (OMB), *(Executive Office of the President), Personnel Policy, 725 17th St. N.W., #7236 20503; (202) 395-5017. Fax, (202) 395-5738. Lisa Fairhall, Chief.*
Web, www.whitehouse.gov/omb

Examines, evaluates, and suggests improvements for agencies and programs within the Office of Personnel Management, the U.S. Postal Service, and the Executive Office of the President.

Office of Management and Budget (OMB), *(Executive Office of the President), Treasury,* New Executive Office Bldg., #9236 20503; (202) 395-6156. Fax, (202) 395-6825. Mark Schwartz, Chief.
Web, www.whitehouse.gov/omb
Examines, evaluates, and suggests improvements for agencies and programs within the Treasury Dept. (including the Internal Revenue Service and the Customs Service), and the District of Columbia government.

Regulatory Information Service Center *(General Services Administration),* 1800 F St. N.W., #3039 20405; (202) 482-7349. Fax, (202) 482-7360. Ronald Kelly, Executive Director. Information, (202) 482-7340.
General e-mail, risc@gsa.gov
Web, www.gsa.gov
Provides the president, Congress, and the public with information on federal regulatory policies; recommends ways to make regulatory information more accessible to government officials and the public. Publishes the *Unified Agenda of Federal Regulatory and Deregulatory Action.*

CONGRESS

General Accounting Office (GAO), 441 G St. N.W. 20548; (202) 512-5500. Fax, (202) 512-5507. David M. Walker, Comptroller General. Information, (202) 512-4800. Library, (202) 512-5180. Documents, (202) 512-6000.
Web, www.gao.gov
Independent, nonpartisan agency in the legislative branch. Serves as the investigating agency for Congress; carries out legal, accounting, auditing, and claims settlement functions; makes recommendations for more effective government operations; publishes monthly lists of reports available to the public. Library open to the public by appointment.

House Appropriations Committee, *Subcommittee on Transportation, Treasury, and Related Agencies,* 2358 RHOB 20515; (202) 225-2141. Fax, (202) 225-5895. Rep. Ernest Istook, R-Okla., Chair; Richard Efford, Clerk.
Web, www.house.gov/appropriations
Jurisdiction over legislation to appropriate funds for the Office of Management and Budget, the General Services Administration (except the Consumer Information Center), the National Archives and Records Administration, and the Executive Office of the President.

House Government Reform Committee, 2157 RHOB 20515; (202) 225-5074. Fax, (202) 225-3974. Rep. Thomas M. Davis III, R-Va., Chair; Peter Sirh, Staff Director.
Web, www.house.gov/reform
Jurisdiction over legislation on all procurement practices. Also examines the efficiency of government operations, including federal regulations and program management.

House Government Reform Committee, *Subcommittee on Government Efficiency and Financial Management,* B349C RHOB 20515; (202) 225-3741. Fax, (202) 225-2544. Rep. Todd R. Platts, R-Pa., Chair; Mike Hettinger, Staff Director.
Web, www.house.gov/reform
Jurisdiction over legislation concerning the efficiency and management of government operations and activities; oversight responsibilities for operations of the White House, the Executive Office of the President, and the Office of Management and Budget. Jurisdiction over legislation for the General Services Administration and General Accounting Office.

Senate Appropriations Committee, *Subcommittee on Transportation, Treasury, and General Government,* SD-196 20510; (202) 224-4869. Fax, (202) 228-1621. Sen. Richard C. Shelby, R-Ala., Chair; Paul Doerrer, Clerk.
Web, appropriations.senate.gov
Jurisdiction over legislation to appropriate funds for the Office of Management and Budget, the General Services Administration (except the Consumer Information Center), the National Archives and Records Administration, and the Executive Office of the President.

Senate Environment and Public Works Committee, *Subcommittee on Transportation and Infrastructure,* SD-410 20510; (202) 224-6176. Fax, (202) 224-1273. Sen. Christopher S. Bond, R-Mo., Chair; Ellen Stein, Staff Director.
Web, epw.senate.gov
Oversight of the public buildings service of the General Services Administration.

Senate Governmental Affairs Committee, *Subcommittee on Oversight of Government Management, the Federal Workforce, and the District of Columbia,* SH-442 20510; (202) 224-3682. Sen. George V. Voinovich, R-Ohio, Chair; Andrew Richardson, Staff Director.
General e-mail, ogm@govt-aff.senate.gov
Web, govt-aff.senate.gov
Jurisdiction over legislation for the General Services Administration and the National Archives and Records

GENERAL ACCOUNTING OFFICE

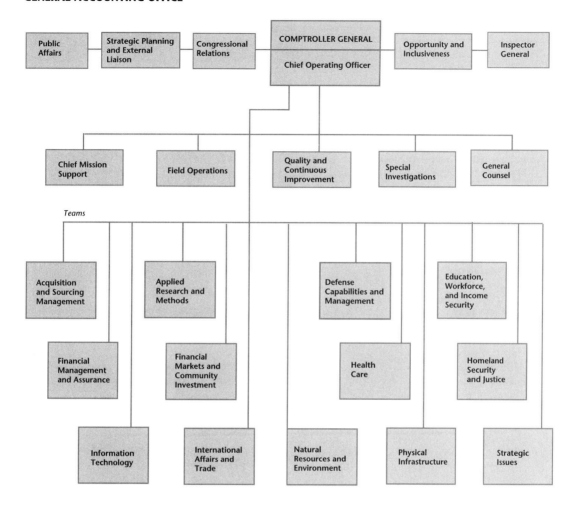

Administration; government procurement and legislation to reduce the volume of federal paperwork; and the improvement of federal information management. Oversight responsibilities for operations of the White House and the Office of Management and Budget. Jurisdiction over the Ethics and Government Act of 1978. Examines the efficiency of government operations, including federal regulations and program management.

NONPROFIT

The Brookings Institution, *Center for Public Service,* *1775 Massachusetts Ave. N.W. 20036; (202) 797-6090. Fax, (202) 797-6144. Paul Light, Director. Information, (202) 797-6000.*

General e-mail, gscomment@brook.edu
Web, www.brookings.edu/gs/cps/cps_hp.htm
   Conducts research on public service and critical problems of federal, state, and local governance; offers training programs in leadership and public service for government executives.

Center for the Study of the Presidency, *1020 19th St. N.W., #250 20036; (202) 872-9800. Fax, (202) 872-9811. David M. Abshire, President.*
General e-mail, center@thepresidency.org
Web, www.thepresidency.org
   Membership: college students, government officials, and business leaders interested in the presidency, government, and politics. Educational organization that con-

THE CABINET OF GEORGE W. BUSH

The president's cabinet includes the vice president and the heads of the fifteen executive departments. In addition, every president has discretion to elevate any number of other government officials to cabinet-rank status. The cabinet is primarily an advisory group. The members of George W. Bush's cabinet are listed below.

Richard B. Cheney, Vice President, (202) 456-7549
  Web, www.whitehouse.gov/vicepresident
  E-mail, vice-president@whitehouse.gov

**EXECUTIVE DEPT. CABINET MEMBERS
  (in alphabetical order by department)**

Agriculture Dept., Ann M. Veneman, Secretary,
  (202) 720-3631
  Web, www.usda.com
  E-mail, agsec@usda.gov

Commerce Dept., Donald L. Evans, Secretary,
  (202) 482-2112
  Web, www.doc.gov
  E-mail, devans@doc.gov

Defense Dept., Donald Rumsfeld, Secretary,
  (703) 692-7100
  Web, www.defenselink.mil

Education Dept., Roderick R. Paige, Secretary,
  (202) 401-3000
  Web, www.ed.gov
  E-mail, rod.paige@ed.gov

Energy Dept., Spencer Abraham, Secretary,
  (202) 586-6210
  Web, www.energy.gov
  E-mail, The.Secretary@hq.doe.gov

**Health and Human Services Dept., Tommy G.
  Thompson, Secretary,** (202) 690-7000
  Web, www.dhhs.gov

Homeland Security Dept., Tom Ridge, Secretary,
  (202) 282-8000
  Web, www.dhs.gov

**Housing and Urban Development Dept.,
  Mel Martinez, Secretary,** (202) 708-0417
  Web, www.hud.gov
  E-mail, Secretary_Mel_Martinez@hud.gov

Interior Dept., Gale A. Norton, Secretary,
  (202) 208-7351
  Web, www.doi.gov
  E-mail, gale_norton@ios.doi.gov

Justice Dept., John D. Ashcroft, Attorney General,
  (202) 514-2001
  Web, www.usdoj.gov
  E-mail, AskDOJ@usdoj.gov

Labor Dept., Elaine L. Chao, Secretary,
  (202) 693-6000
  Web, www.dol.gov

State Dept., Gen. Colin Powell, Secretary,
  (202) 647-5291
  Web, www.state.gov
  E-mail, secretary@state.gov

Transportation Dept., Norman Y. Mineta, Secretary,
  (202) 366-1111
  Web, www.dot.gov

Treasury Dept., John W. Snow, Secretary,
  (202) 622-1100
  Web, www.ustreas.gov

Veterans Affairs Dept., Anthony J. Principi, Secretary,
  (202) 273-4800
  Web, www.va.gov

**OTHER CABINET-RANK OFFICIALS
  (in alphabetical order by department)**

**Environmental Protection Agency, Christine Todd
  Whitman, Administrator,** (202) 564-4700
  Web, www.epa.gov

**Office of Management and Budget, Mitchell E.
  Daniels Jr., Director,** (202) 395-4840
  Web, www.omb.gov

**Office of National Drug Control Policy, John P.
  Walters, Director,** (202) 395-6700
  Web, www.whitehousedrugpolicy.gov

**Office of the U. S. Trade Representative, Robert B.
  Zoellick, U.S. Trade Representative,** (202) 395-6890
  Web, www.ustr.gov

**Office of the White House Chief of Staff, Andrew H.
  Card Jr., Chief of Staff,** (202) 456-6797
  Web, www.whitehouse.gov

---

ducts conferences, lectures, and symposiums on domestic, economic, and foreign policy issues. Publishes papers, essays, books, and reports on various aspects of a president or the presidency.

Council for Excellence in Government, *1301 K St. N.W., #450 West 20005; (202) 728-0418. Fax, (202) 728-0422. Patricia G. McGinnis, President.*
General e-mail, ceg@excelgov.org
Web, www.excelgov.org

Membership: business and professional leaders with previous executive-level government experience. Works to improve public-sector performance by strengthening federal leadership and management; seeks to build a public understanding of and confidence in government.

Federal Managers Assn., *1641 Prince St., Alexandria, VA 22314-2818; (703) 683-8700. Fax, (703) 683-8707. Didier Trinh, Government and Public Affairs Director.*
General e-mail, info@fedmanagers.org
Web, www.fedmanagers.org

Seeks to improve the effectiveness of federal supervisors and managers and the operations of the federal government.

Private Sector Council, *1101 16th St. N.W., #300 20036-4813; (202) 822-3910. Fax, (202) 822-0638. A. W. Smith Jr., President.*
General e-mail, privsect@privsect.org
Web, www.privsect.org

Membership: large corporations and private businesses including financial and information technology organizations. Seeks to improve government efficiency, productivity, and management through a cooperative effort of the public and private sectors.

Buildings and Services

AGENCIES

Federal Protective Service, *(Homeland Security Department), 1800 F St. N.W., #2341 20405; (202) 501-0907. Fax, (202) 208-5866. Wendell Schingler, Assistant Commissioner.*

Law enforcement agency. Oversees security and law enforcement for all buildings under charge and control of the General Services Administration.

General Services Administration (GSA), *Business Performance, 1800 F St. N.W., #4340 20405; (202) 501-0971. Fax, (202) 501-3296. Paul Lynch, Assistant Commissioner.*
Web, www.gsa.gov

Oversees safety programs for federal buildings, employees, and visitors to federal buildings.

General Services Administration (GSA), *Federal Acquisition Institute, 1800 F St. N.W. 20405. Gloria Sochon, Director, (202) 208-6726.*
General e-mail, Gloria.Sochon@gsa.gov
Web, www.gsa.gov/fai

Fosters development of a professional acquisition workforce governmentwide; collects and analyzes acquisition workforce data; helps agencies identify and recruit

candidates for the acquisitions field; develops instructional materials; evaluates training and career development programs.

General Services Administration (GSA), *Federal Supply Service, 1941 Jefferson Davis Hwy., Arlington, VA 22202; (703) 305-6667. Fax, (703) 305-5500. Donna D. Bennett, Commissioner.*
Web, www.fss.gsa.gov

Responsible for providing federal agencies with common-use goods and nonpersonal services and for procurement and supply, transportation and travel management, and disposal of surplus personal property.

General Services Administration (GSA), *National Capital Region, 7th and D Sts. S.W., #7022 20407; (202) 708-9100. Fax, (202) 708-9966. Donald C. Williams, Regional Administrator.*
Web, www.gsa.gov

Provides federal agencies with space, supplies, telecommunications, transportation, data processing, and construction services; has equal status with regional offices.

General Services Administration (GSA), *Public Buildings Service, 1800 F St. N.W., #6344 20405; (202) 501-1100. Fax, (202) 219-2310. Joseph Moravec, Commissioner.*
Web, www.gsa.gov

Administers the construction, maintenance, and operation of buildings owned or leased by the federal government. Manages and disposes of federal real estate.

General Services Administration (GSA), *Transportation and Property Management, 1941 Jefferson Davis Hwy., #815, Arlington, VA 22202; (703) 605-5600. Fax, (703) 305-6905. Joseph Jew, Assistant Commissioner.*
Web, www.gsa.gov

Manages governmentwide programs and activities relating to the use of excess personal property (except Automated Data Processing [ADP] equipment); provides transportation, travel, aircraft, mail, relocation, and vehicle fleet services. Produces *Federal Travel Regulations* and *Federal Travel Directory*.

Ethics in Government

AGENCIES

Office of Government Ethics, *1201 New York Ave. N.W., #500 20005-3917; (202) 208-8000. Fax, (202) 208-8037. Amy Comstock, Director; Jane Ley, Deputy Director.*
General e-mail, usoge@oge.gov
Web, www.usoge.gov

FINANCIAL OFFICERS FOR FEDERAL AGENCIES

DEPARTMENTS

Agriculture, Edward R. McPherson, (202) 720-5539

Commerce, Otto Wolff, (202) 482-4951

Defense, Dov Zakheim, (703) 695-3237

  Air Force, Michael Montelongo, (703) 693-6457

  Army, Erin Olmes, (703) 697-8121

  Navy, Dionel M. Aviles, (703) 697-2325

Education, Jack Martin, (202) 401-0085

Energy, Bruce M. Carnes, (202) 586-4171 (As of March 2003, Carnes was the designee to be the Homeland Security Dept.'s chief financial officer.)

Health and Human Services, Kerry N. Weems (Acting), (202) 690-6396

Homeland Security, Bruce M. Carnes (Designee), (202) 282-8000 (Switchboard)

Housing and Urban Development, Angela Antonelli, (202) 708-1946

Interior, Lynn Scarlett, (202) 208-4203

Justice, Paul R. Corts, (202) 514-3101

Labor, Samuel T. Mok, (202) 693-6800

State, Christopher B. Burnham, (202) 647-7490

Transportation, Donna McLean, (202) 366-9192

Treasury

  Chief Financial Officer, Teresa Ressel (Acting), (202) 622-0410

  Comptroller of the Currency, John D. Hawke Jr., (202) 874-4900

Veterans Affairs, William H. Campbell, (202) 273-5583

AGENCIES

Advisory Council on Historic Preservation, Carol McLain, (202) 606-8503

Agency for International Development, Susan J. Rabern, (202) 712-1980

Central Intelligence Agency, Mary Corrado, (703) 482-4456

Commission on Civil Rights, George Harbison, (202) 376-8356

Commodity Futures Trading Commission, Emory Bevill, (202) 418-5190

Consumer Product Safety Commission, Edward E. Quist, (301) 504-0029, ext. 2240

Corporation for National Service, Michelle Guillermin, (202) 606-5000, ext. 395

Corporation for Public Broadcasting, Elizabeth A. Griffith, (202) 879-9730

Environmental Protection Agency, Linda Combs, (202) 564-1151

Equal Employment Opportunity Commission, Jeffrey Smith, (202) 663-4200

Export-Import Bank, James K. Hess, (202) 565-3240

Farm Credit Administration, W. B. Erwin, (703) 883-4099

Federal Bureau of Investigation, Tina W. Jonas, (202) 324-1345

Federal Communications Commission, Mark Reger, (202) 418-1925

Federal Deposit Insurance Corporation, Steven O. App, (202) 898-8732

Federal Election Commission, Brian Duffy, (202) 694-1230

Federal Emergency Management Agency, Matt Jadacki (Acting), (202) 646-3545

Federal Energy Regulatory Commission, Thomas R. Herlihy, (202) 502-8300

Federal Home Loan Mortgage Corporation (Freddie Mac), Vaughn Clarke, (703) 903-2000

Federal Labor Relations Authority, Joan Hicks (Acting), (202) 482-6640

Federal Maritime Commission, Karon Douglass, (202) 523-5770

Federal Mediation and Conciliation Service, Fran Leonard, (202) 606-3661

Administers executive branch policies relating to financial disclosure, employee conduct, and conflict-of-interest laws.

Office of Special Counsel, *Congressional and Public Affairs, 1730 M St. N.W., #300 20036-4505; (202) 653-9001. Fax, (202) 653-5161. Elaine D. Kaplan, Special Counsel; Jane McFarland, Director. Information, (202)* 653-7188. TTY, (800) 877-8339. *Issues relating to the Hatch Act, (800) 854-2824.*

Web, www.osc.gov

Investigates allegations of prohibited personnel practices and prosecutes individuals who violate civil service regulations. Receives and refers federal employee disclosures of waste, fraud, inefficiency, mismanagement, and other violations in the federal government. Enforces the Hatch Act, which limits political activity by most federal and District of Columbia employees.

FINANCIAL OFFICERS FOR FEDERAL AGENCIES (continued)

Federal National Mortgage Association (Fannie Mae), Timothy Howard, (202) 752-7140

Federal Reserve System, Stephen J. Clark, (202) 452-2304

Federal Trade Commission, Henry Hoffman, (202) 326-2664

General Accounting Office, Sallyann Harper, (202) 512-5800

General Services Administration, Kathleen M. Turco, (202) 501-1721

International Bank for Reconstruction and Development (World Bank), Gary L. Perlin, (202) 458-9111

John F. Kennedy Center for the Performing Arts, Lynn Pratt, (202) 416-8603

Merit Systems Protection Board, Robert Lawshe, (202) 653-7263

National Academy of Sciences, Archie Turner, (202) 334-3110

National Aeronautics and Space Administration, Gwendolyn Brown (Acting), (202) 358-2262

National Archives and Records Administration, Valerie Spargo, (301) 837-3150

National Credit Union Administration, Dennis Winans, (703) 518-6571

National Endowment for the Arts, Sandra Stueckler, (202) 682-5407

National Endowment for the Humanities, Anthony A. Banko, (202) 606-8428

National Labor Relations Board, Karl Rohrbaugh, (202) 273-4230

National Mediation Board, June D. W. King, (202) 692-5010

National Railroad Passenger Corporation (Amtrak), Deno Bokas, (202) 906-3300

National Science Foundation, Thomas Coolay, (703) 292-8200

National Transportation Safety Board, Steven Goldberg, (202) 314-6210

Nuclear Regulatory Commission, Jesse L. Funches, (301) 415-7322

Occupational Safety and Health Review Commission, Ledia E. Bernal, (202) 606-5390

Office of Management and Budget, Robert O'Neill, (202) 395-6190

Office of Personnel Management, Clarence Crawford, (202) 606-1101

Overseas Private Investment Corporation, Gary A. Keel, (202) 336-8524

Peace Corps, Charles Caldwell, (202) 692-1600

Pension Benefit Guaranty Corporation, Hazel Broadnax, (202) 326-4170

Postal Rate Commission, Steven Williams, (202) 789-6850

Securities and Exchange Commission, Margaret Carpenter, (202) 942-0360

Small Business Administration, Thomas Dumaresq, (202) 205-6449

Smithsonian Institution, Alice C. Maroni, (202) 275-2020

Social Security Administration, Dale Sopper, (410) 965-2910

U.S. International Trade Commission, Patricia Katsourous, (202) 205-2678

U.S. Postal Service, Richard J. Strasser Jr., (202) 268-5272

CONGRESS

House Appropriations Committee, *Subcommittee on Transportation, Treasury, and Related Agencies, 2358 RHOB 20515; (202) 225-2141. Fax, (202) 225-5895. Rep. Ernest Istook, R-Okla., Chair; Richard Efford, Clerk. Web, www.house.gov/appropriations*

Jurisdiction over legislation to appropriate funds for the Office of Government Ethics.

House Government Reform Committee, *Subcommittee on Civil Service and Agency Organization, B373A RHOB 20515; (202) 225-5147. Fax, (202) 225-2373. Rep. Jo Ann Davis, R-Va., Chair; Garry Ewing, Staff Director. Web, www.house.gov/reform*

Jurisdiction over legislation on civil service issues, including code of ethics.

House Government Reform Committee, *Subcommittee on Government Efficiency and Financial Management,* B349C RHOB 20515; (202) 225-3741. Fax, (202) 225-2544. Rep. Todd R. Platts, R-Pa., Chair; Mike Hettinger, Staff Director.
Web, www.house.gov/reform

Oversight of the Office of Government Ethics.

Senate Appropriations Committee, *Subcommittee on Transportation, Treasury, and General Government,* SD-196 20510; (202) 224-4869. Fax, (202) 228-0249. Sen. Richard C. Shelby, R-Ala., Chair; Paul Doerrer, Clerk.
Web, appropriations.senate.gov

Jurisdiction over legislation to appropriate funds for the Office of Government Ethics.

Senate Governmental Affairs Committee, SD-340 20510; (202) 224-4751. Fax, (202) 228-3792. Sen. Susan Collins, R-Maine, Chair; Michael Bopp, Staff Director.
Web, govt-aff.senate.gov

Jurisdiction over legislation on civil service issues, including code of ethics and right to privacy. Oversight of the Office of Government Ethics.

NONPROFIT

Center for Public Integrity, 910 17th St. N.W., 7th Floor 20006; (202) 466-1300. Fax, (202) 466-1101. Charles Lewis, Executive Director.
General e-mail, contact@publicintegrity.org
Web, www.publicintegrity.org

Educational foundation supported by corporations, labor unions, foundations, and individuals. Publishes comprehensive reports concerning ethics-related issues.

Council for Citizens Against Government Waste, 1301 Connecticut Ave. N.W., #400 20036; (202) 467-5300. Fax, (202) 467-4253. Thomas A. Schatz, President. Information, (800) 232-6479.
Web, www.cagw.org

Nonpartisan organization that seeks to eliminate waste, mismanagement, and inefficiency in the federal government. Monitors legislation and regulations.

Fund for Constitutional Government (FCG), 122 Maryland Ave. N.E. 20002; (202) 546-3799. Fax, (202) 543-3156. Anne B. Zill, President.
General e-mail, FunForCon@aol.com
Web, www.fcgonline.org

Seeks to expose and correct corruption in the federal government and private sector through research and public education. Sponsors the Electronic Privacy Information Center, the Government Accountability Project, and the Project on Government Oversight.

Government Accountability Project, 1612 K St. N.W., #400 20006; (202) 408-0034. Fax, (202) 408-9855. Louis Clark, Executive Director.
Web, www.whistleblower.org

Membership: federal employees, union members, professionals, and interested citizens. Provides legal and strategic counsel to public and private employees who seek to expose corporate and government actions that are illegal, wasteful, or repressive; aids such employees in personnel action taken against them; assists grassroots organizations investigating corporate wrongdoing, government inaction, or corruption.

Project on Government Oversight, 666 11th St. N.W., #500 20001-4542; (202) 347-1122. Fax, (202) 347-1116. Danielle Brian, Executive Director.
General e-mail, pogo@pogo.org
Web, www.pogo.org

Public interest organization that works to expose waste, fraud, abuse, and conflicts of interest in all aspects of federal spending.

Executive Reorganization

AGENCIES

Office of Management and Budget (OMB), *(Executive Office of the President), President's Management Council,* Dwight D. Eisenhower Executive Office Bldg., #350 20503; (202) 395-5963. Fax, (202) 395-0331. Mark W. Everson, Chair.
Web, www.whitehouse.gov/omb

Membership: chief operating officers of federal government departments and agencies. Responsible for implementing the management improvement initiatives of the administration. Develops and oversees improved governmentwide management and administrative systems; formulates long-range plans to promote these systems; works to resolve interagency management problems and to implement reforms.

CONGRESS

General Accounting Office (GAO), *Information Technology,* 441 G St. N.W., #4T21 20548; (202) 512-6240. Fax, (202) 512-6450. Linda D. Koontz, Director.
Web, www.gao.gov

Seeks to make the federal government more effective in its information management. Assesses practices in the public and private sectors; makes recommendations to government agencies. Interests include information security.

INSPECTORS GENERAL FOR FEDERAL AGENCIES

Departmental and agency inspectors general are responsible for identifying and reporting program fraud and abuse, criminal activity, and unethical conduct in the federal government. In the legislative branch the General Accounting Office also has a fraud and abuse hotline: (202) 512-7470. Check www.ignet.gov for additional listings.

DEPARTMENTS

Agriculture, Phyllis K. Fong, (202) 720-8001

Hotline, (800) 424-9121; (202) 690-1622 in Washington

Commerce, Johnnie Frazier, (202) 482-4661

Hotline, (800) 424-5197; (202) 482-2495 in Washington

Defense, Joseph Schmitz, (703) 604-8300

Hotline, (800) 424-9098; (703) 604-8546 in Washington

Education, John P. Higgins Jr., (202) 205-5439

Hotline, (800) 647-8733

Energy, Gregory H. Friedman, (202) 586-4393

Hotline, (800) 541-1625; (202) 586-4073 in Washington

Health and Human Services, Vacant, (202) 619-3148

Hotline, (800) 447-8477

Homeland Security, Clark Kent Ervin (Nominee), (202) 282-8000 (switchboard)

Housing and Urban Development, Keith M. Donohue, (202) 708-0430

Hotline, (800) 347-3735; (202) 708-4200 in Washington

Interior, Earl D. Devaney, (202) 208-5745

Hotline, (800) 424-5081; (202) 208-5300 in Washington

Justice, Glenn A. Fine, (202) 514-3435

Hotline, (800) 869-4499

Labor, Gordon S. Heddell, (202) 693-5100

Hotline, (800) 347-3756; (202) 693-6999 in Washington

State, Anne Sigmund (Acting), (202) 647-9450

Hotline, (800) 409-9926; (202) 647-3320 in Washington

Transportation, Kenneth Mead, (202) 366-1959

Hotline, (800) 424-9071; (202) 366-1461 in Washington

Treasury, Jeffrey Rush, (202) 622-1090

Hotline, (800) 359-3898

Veterans Affairs, Richard Griffin, (202) 565-8620

Hotline, (800) 488-8244

AGENCIES

Agency for International Development, Everett L. Mosley, (202) 712-1150

Hotline, (800) 230-6539

Central Intelligence Agency, John Helgerson, (703) 874-2553

Hotline, (703) 874-2600

Environmental Protection Agency, Nikki Tinsley, (202) 566-0847

Hotline, (202) 566-2476

Federal Deposit Insurance Corporation, Gaston L. Gianni, (202) 416-2026

Hotline, (800) 964-3342

Federal Emergency Management Agency, Richard L. Skinner (Acting), (202) 646-3910

Hotline, (800) 323-8603

General Services Administration, Daniel Levinson, (202) 501-0450

Hotline, (800) 424-5210; (202) 501-1780 in Washington

National Aeronautics and Space Administration, Robert W. Cobb, (202) 358-1220

Hotline, (800) 424-9183

National Science Foundation, Christine Boesz, (703) 292-7100

Hotline, (800) 428-2189

Nuclear Regulatory Commission, Hubert Bell, (301) 415-5930

Hotline, (800) 233-3497

Office of Personnel Management, Patrick E. McFarland, (202) 606-1200

Hotline, (202) 606-2423

Small Business Administration, Peter McClintock (Acting), (202) 205-6580

Hotline, (800) 767-0385

Social Security Administration, James G. Huse Jr., (410) 966-8385

Hotline, (800) 269-0271

U.S. Postal Service, Karla Corcoran, (703) 248-2300

Hotline, (888) 877-7644; (202) 268-5746 in Washington

House Government Reform Committee, *Subcommittee on Civil Service and Agency Organization,* B373A RHOB 20515; (202) 225-5147. Fax, (202) 225-2373. Rep. Jo Ann Davis, R-Va., Chair; Garry Ewing, Staff Director.
Web, www.house.gov/reform

Studies the effect of reorganization of agencies on federal employees.

House Government Reform Committee, *Subcommittee on Government Efficiency and Financial Management,* B349C RHOB 20515; (202) 225-3741. Fax, (202) 225-2544. Rep. Todd R. Platts, R-Pa., Chair; Mike Hettinger, Staff Director.
Web, www.house.gov/reform

Jurisdiction over executive and legislative reorganization legislation.

Senate Governmental Affairs Committee, *SD-340 20510; (202) 224-4751. Fax, (202) 228-3792. Sen. Susan Collins, R-Maine, Chair; Michael Bopp, Staff Director.*
Web, govt-aff.senate.gov

Jurisdiction over executive and legislative reorganization legislation; studies the effect of reorganization of agencies on federal employees.

🏛 CENSUS, POPULATION DATA

The Census Bureau publishes a pamphlet, "Telephone Contacts for Data Users," that lists key Census Bureau personnel and their fields of specialty. Copies may be obtained from the Census Bureau, Customer Service, (301) 763-4100.

AGENCIES

Census Bureau *(Commerce Dept.), 4700 Silver Hill Rd., Suitland, MD 20746 (mailing address: Washington, DC 20233-0100); (301) 763-2135. Fax, (301) 457-3761. C. Louis Kincannon, Director. Information, (301) 763-4636. Library, (301) 763-2511. Press, (301) 763-3030.*
General e-mail, pio@census.gov
Web, www.census.gov

Conducts surveys and censuses (including the decennial census of population and housing; the economic census and census of governments every five years); collects and analyzes demographic, social, economic, housing, agricultural, and foreign trade data and data on governments; publishes statistics for use by Congress, business, state and local governments, planners, and the public. Library open to the public.

Census Bureau *(Commerce Dept.), Decennial Census,* 4700 Silver Hill Rd., Suitland, MD 20746 (mailing address: Washington, DC 20233-7000); (301) 763-3968. Fax, (301) 457-3024. Preston Jay Waite, Associate Director.
Web, www.census.gov

Provides data from the 2000 decennial census (including general plans and procedures) and conducts preparation for next census; economic, demographic, and population statistics; and information on trends.

Census Bureau *(Commerce Dept.), Demographic Surveys Division,* 4700 Silver Hill Rd., Suitland, MD 20746; (301) 763-3773. Fax, (301) 763-2306. Chester E. Bowie, Chief.

Provides and explains proper use of data on consumer spending, crime, employment and unemployment, income, and housing. Conducts surveys on various subjects, including population, prisoners, health, and travel.

Census Bureau *(Commerce Dept.), Housing and Household Economic Statistics,* 4700 Silver Hill Rd., Suitland, MD 20746 (mailing address: HHES, #10553, Washington, DC 20233-8500); (301) 763-3234. Fax, (301) 457-3248. Daniel H. Weinberg, Chief.
General e-mail, hhes-info@census.gov
Web, www.census.gov

Develops statistical programs for the decennial census and for other surveys on housing, income, poverty, and the labor force. Collects and explains the proper use of economic, social, and demographic data. Responsible for the technical planning, analysis, and publication of data from current surveys, including the decennial census, the American Housing Survey, Current Population Survey, and Survey of Income and Program Participation.

Census Bureau *(Commerce Dept.), Population,* 4700 Silver Hill Rd., Suitland, MD 20746 (mailing address: Bldg. 3, #2318, Washington, DC 20233); (301) 457-2071. Fax, (301) 457-2644. John F. Long, Chief.
General e-mail, pop@census.gov
Web, www.census.gov

Prepares population estimates and projections for national, state, and local areas and congressional districts. Provides data on demographic and social statistics in the following areas: families and households, marital status and living arrangements, farm population, migration and mobility, population distribution, ancestry, fertility, child care, race and ethnicity, language patterns, school enrollment, educational attainment, and voting.

CONGRESS

House Appropriations Committee, *Subcommittee on Commerce, Justice, State, and the Judiciary,* H309 CAP 20515; (202) 225-3351. Rep. Frank R. Wolf, R-Va., Chair; Mike Ringler, Staff Director.
Web, www.house.gov/appropriations

Jurisdiction over legislation to appropriate funds for the Commerce Dept., including the Census Bureau.

House Government Reform Committee, *Subcommittee on Technology, Information Policy, Intergovernmental Relations, and the Census,* B349A RHOB 20515; (202) 225-6751. Fax, (202) 225-4960. Rep. Adam H. Putnam, R-Fla., Chair; Robert Dix, Staff Director.
Web, www.house.gov/reform

Jurisdiction over census legislation and statistics collection, demography, and population issues; oversight of the Census Bureau.

Senate Appropriations Committee, *Subcommittee on Commerce, Justice, State, and the Judiciary,* S-206 CAP 20510; (202) 224-7277. Fax, (202) 228-0587. Sen. Judd Gregg, R-N.H., Chair; James Morhard, Clerk.
Web, appropriations.senate.gov

Jurisdiction over legislation to appropriate funds for the Commerce Dept., including the Census Bureau.

Senate Governmental Affairs Committee, SD-340 20510; (202) 224-4751. Fax, (202) 228-3792. Sen. Susan Collins, R-Maine, Chair; Michael Bopp, Staff Director.
Web, govt-aff.senate.gov

Jurisdiction over census legislation and statistics collection, demography, and population issues; oversight of the Census Bureau.

NONPROFIT

Population Assn. of America, 8630 Fenton St., #722, Silver Spring, MD 20910; (301) 565-6710. Fax, (301) 565-7850. Stephanie Dudley, Executive Director.
General e-mail, info@popassoc.org
Web, www.popassoc.org

Membership: university, government, and industry researchers in demography. Holds annual technical sessions to present papers on domestic and international population issues and statistics.

Population Reference Bureau, 1875 Connecticut Ave. N.W., #520 20009; (202) 483-1100. Fax, (202) 328-3937. Peter J. Donaldson, President.
General e-mail, popref@prb.org
Web, www.prb.org

Educational organization engaged in information dissemination, training, and policy analysis on domestic and international population trends and issues. Interests include international development and family planning programs, the environment, and U.S. social and economic policy. Library open to the public.

 CIVIL SERVICE

AGENCIES

National Archives and Records Administration (NARA), *Information Security Oversight,* 700 Pennsylvania Ave. N.W., #500 20408-0001; (202) 219-5250. Fax, (202) 219-5385. J. William Leonard, Director.
General e-mail, isoo@arch1.nara.gov
Web, www.archives.gov

Oversees the security classification system throughout the executive branch; reports to the president on implementation of the security classification system. Develops and disseminates security education materials. Oversees the Classified Information Nondisclosure Agreement, which bars federal employees from disclosing classified and sensitive government information.

Office of Personnel Management (OPM), 1900 E St. N.W., #5H09 20415-0001; (202) 606-1000. Fax, (202) 606-0082. Kay Coles James, Director. Press, (202) 606-2402. TTY, (202) 606-2532. Additional fax, (202) 606-2183.
Web, www.opm.gov

Administers civil service rules and regulations; sets policy for personnel management, labor-management relations, workforce effectiveness, and employment within the executive branch; manages federal personnel activities, including recruitment, pay comparability, and benefit programs. Library open to the public (10 a.m.–2 p.m., Monday–Friday).

Office of Personnel Management (OPM), *Human Capital, Leadership, and Merit Systems Accountability,* 1900 E St. N.W., #7470 20415-0001; (202) 606-1575. Fax, (202) 606-1798. Marta Brito Perez, Associate Director.
General e-mail, oversight@opm.gov
Web, www.opm.gov/ovrsight

Monitors federal agencies' personnel practices and ensures that they abide by the Merit Systems Principles. Develops policies and programs in human capital management.

Office of Personnel Management (OPM), *Pay and Performance Policy,* 1900 E St. N.W., #7H31 20415; (202) 606-2880. Fax, (202) 606-4264. Donald J. Winstead, Deputy Associate Director.

OFFICE OF PERSONNEL MANAGEMENT

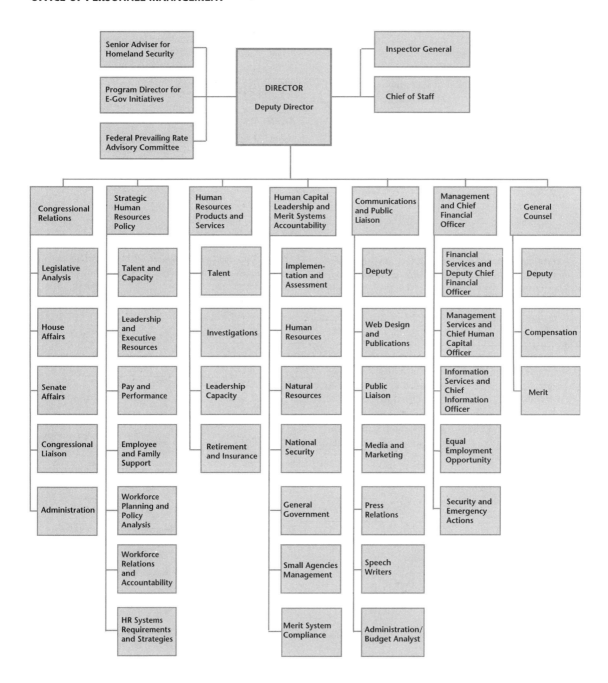

Web, www.opm.gov/oca

Responsible for policy development of compensation systems for about 1.8 million federal civilian white-collar and blue-collar employees.

Office of Personnel Management (OPM), *Workforce Information and Planning*, 1900 E St. N.W., #7439 20415-0001; (202) 606-1909. Fax, (202) 606-1719. Robert Heim, Chief (Acting).

Web, www.opm.gov

Produces information and analyses for the Office of Personnel Management, Congress, and the public on statistical aspects of the federal civilian workforce, including trends in composition, grade levels, minority employment, sizes of agencies, and salaries.

Office of Special Counsel, *Congressional and Public Affairs*, 1730 M St. N.W., #300 20036-4505; (202) 653-9001. Fax, (202) 653-5161. Elaine D. Kaplan, Special Counsel; Jane McFarland, Director. Information, (202) 653-7188. TTY, (800) 877-8339. Issues relating to the Hatch Act, (800) 854-2824.

Web, www.osc.gov

Interprets federal laws, including the Hatch Act, concerning political activities allowed by certain federal employees; investigates allegations of Hatch Act violations and conducts prosecutions. Investigates and prosecutes complaints under the Whistleblower Protection Act.

CONGRESS

House Appropriations Committee, *Subcommittee on Transportation, Treasury, and Related Agencies*, 2358 RHOB 20515; (202) 225-2141. Fax, (202) 225-5895. Rep. Ernest Istook, R-Okla., Chair; Richard Efford, Clerk.

Web, www.house.gov/appropriations

Jurisdiction over legislation to appropriate funds for the Office of Personnel Management and the Merit Systems Protection Board.

House Education and the Workforce Committee, *Subcommittee on Workforce Protections*, 2181 RHOB 20515; (202) 225-4527. Fax, (202) 225-9571. Rep. Charlie Norwood, R-Ga., Chair; Paula Nowakowski, Staff Director.

Web, edworkforce.house.gov

Jurisdiction over legislation on federal employees' compensation.

House Government Reform Committee, *Subcommittee on Civil Service and Agency Organization*, B373A RHOB 20515; (202) 225-5147. Fax, (202) 225-2373. Rep. Jo Ann Davis, R-Va., Chair; Garry Ewing, Staff Director.

Web, www.house.gov/reform

Jurisdiction over legislation on civil service labor-management issues, job classifications, hiring and recruiting, pay and compensation, benefits, retirement, rights of privacy, and code of ethics; and legislation related to the Hatch Act, which deals with the political activity of civil service employees. Oversight of the Senior Executive Service and intergovernmental personnel programs. Studies the effects of reorganization of agencies on federal employees.

House Government Reform Committee, *Subcommittee on Criminal Justice, Drug Policy, and Human Resources*, B373B RHOB 20515; (202) 225-2577. Fax, (202) 225-1154. Rep. Mark Souder, R-Ind., Chair; Christopher Donesa, Staff Director.

Web, www.house.gov/reform

Oversight of the Office of Personnel Management and the Merit Systems Protection Board.

Senate Appropriations Committee, *Subcommittee on Transportation, Treasury, and General Government*, SD-196 20510; (202) 224-4869. Fax, (202) 228-1621. Sen. Richard C. Shelby, R-Ala., Chair; Paul Doerrer, Clerk.

Web, appropriations.senate.gov

Jurisdiction over legislation to appropriate funds for the Office of Personnel Management and the Merit Systems Protection Board.

Senate Governmental Affairs Committee, SD-340 20510; (202) 224-4751. Fax, (202) 228-3792. Sen. Susan Collins, R-Maine, Chair; Michael Bopp, Staff Director.

Web, govt-aff.senate.gov

Jurisdiction over legislation on civil service labor-management issues; hiring, recruiting, and job classifications; compensation, including pay allowances and benefits; code of ethics; rights of privacy; intergovernmental personnel programs; effects of reorganization; leave and retirement; and legislation related to the Hatch Act, which deals with the political activity of civil service employees. Oversight of the Senior Executive Service, the Office of Personnel Management, and the Merit Systems Protection Board.

NONPROFIT

American Federation of Government Employees (AFGE), 80 F St. N.W. 20001; (202) 737-8700. Fax, (202) 639-6490. Bobby L. Harnage Sr., President. Membership, (202) 639-6411.

Web, www.afge.org

Membership: approximately 600,000 federal government employees. Provides legal services to members;

assists members with contract negotiations and grievances. Monitors legislation and regulations. (Affiliated with the AFL-CIO.)

Blacks in Government, *3005 Georgia Ave. N.W. 20001-5015; (202) 667-3280. Fax, (202) 667-3705. Greg Reeves, President.*
Web, www.bignet.org

Advocacy organization for public employees. Promotes equal opportunity and career advancement for African American government employees; provides career development information; seeks to eliminate racism in the federal workforce; sponsors programs, business meetings, and social gatherings; represents interests of African American government workers to Congress and the executive branch; promotes voter education and registration.

Council for Excellence in Government, *1301 K St. N.W., #450 West 20005; (202) 728-0418. Fax, (202) 728-0422. Patricia G. McGinnis, President.*
General e-mail, ceg@excelgov.org
Web, www.excelgov.org

Membership: business and professional leaders with previous executive-level government experience. Works to improve public-sector performance by strengthening federal leadership and management; seeks to build a public understanding of and confidence in government.

Federal Managers Assn., *1641 Prince St., Alexandria, VA 22314-2818; (703) 683-8700. Fax, (703) 683-8707. Didier Trinh, Government and Public Affairs Director.*
General e-mail, info@fedmanagers.org
Web, www.fedmanagers.org

Seeks to improve the effectiveness of federal supervisors and managers and the operations of the federal government.

Federally Employed Women, *1666 K St. N.W., #440 20006; (202) 898-0994. Fax, (202) 898-1535. Patricia M. Wolfe, President.*
Web, www.few.org

Membership: women and men who work for the federal government. Works to eliminate sex discrimination in government employment and to increase job opportunities for women; offers training program. Monitors legislation and regulations.

Public Employees Roundtable, *500 N. Capitol St., #1204 20001 (mailing address: P.O. Box 75248 20013-5248); (202) 927-4926. Fax, (202) 927-4920. Jeanne Van Vlandren, Executive Director.*
General e-mail, info@theroundtable.org
Web, www.theroundtable.org

Membership: professional and managerial associations and unions representing a wide range of public employees at all levels. Sponsors conferences, celebrations, and publicity events to educate the public about the contributions of public employees. Sponsors annual scholarship program for college students pursuing a public service career.

Senior Executives Assn., *P.O. Box 44808 20026-4808; (202) 927-7000. Fax, (202) 927-5192. Carol A. Bonosaro, President.*
Web, www.seniorexecs.com

Professional association representing Senior Executive Service members and other federal career executives. Sponsors professional education. Interests include management improvement. Monitors legislation and regulations.

Dismissals and Disputes

AGENCIES

Merit Systems Protection Board, *1615 M St. N.W., 5th Floor 20419; (202) 653-7200. Fax, (202) 653-7130. Suzanne Marshall, Chair, (202) 653-7105; Bentley M. Roberts, Clerk of the Board. TTY, (800) 877-8339. Toll-free, (800) 209-8960. MSPB hotline, (800) 424-9121.*
General e-mail, mspb@mspb.gov
Web, www.mspb.gov

Independent quasi-judicial agency that handles hearings and appeals involving federal employees; protects the integrity of federal merit systems and ensures adequate protection for employees against abuses by agency management. Library open to the public.

Merit Systems Protection Board, *Appeals Counsel, 1615 M St. N.W. 20419; (202) 653-8888. Fax, (202) 653-7130. John Murphy, Director (Acting).*
General e-mail, settlement@mspb.gov
Web, www.mspb.gov/offices/appeals.html

Analyzes and processes petitions for review of appeals decisions from the regional offices; prepares opinions and orders for board consideration; analyzes and processes cases that are reopened and prepares proposed dispositions.

Merit Systems Protection Board, *Policy and Evaluations, 1615 M St. N.W. 20419; (202) 653-8879. Fax, (202) 653-7211. Steve Nelson, Director. Information, (800) 209-8960. TTY, (800) 877-8339.*
General e-mail, studies@mspb.gov
Web, www.mspb.gov/studies/studies.html

Conducts studies on the civil service and other executive branch merit systems; reports to the president and Congress on whether federal employees are adequately protected against political abuses and prohibited personnel practices. Conducts annual oversight review of the Office of Personnel Management.

Merit Systems Protection Board, *Washington Regional Office, 1800 Diagonal Rd., #205, Alexandria, VA 22314-2840; (703) 756-6250. Fax, (703) 756-7112. P. J. Winzer, Director.*
General e-mail, washingtonregion@mspb.gov
Web, www.mspb.gov

Hears and decides appeals of adverse personnel actions (such as removals, suspensions for more than fourteen days, and reductions in grade or pay), retirement, and performance-related actions for federal civilian employees who work in the Washington area, Virginia, North Carolina, or in overseas areas not covered by other board regional offices. Federal civilian employees who work outside Washington should contact the Merit Systems Protection Board regional office in their area.

Office of Personnel Management (OPM), *Employee Accountability, 1900 E St. N.W. 20415-0001; (202) 606-1972. Fax, (202) 606-0967. Ken Bates, Chief.*
General e-mail, er@opm.gov
Web, www.opm.gov/er

Develops, implements, and interprets policy on governmentwide employee relations. Intervenes in or seeks reconsideration of erroneous third-party decisions. Provides technical advice and assistance on employee relations to agencies and the public.

Office of Personnel Management (OPM), *General Counsel, 1900 E St. N.W., #7353 20415-0001. Mark Robbins, General Counsel, (202) 606-1700.*
Web, www.opm.gov

Represents the federal government before the Merit Systems Protection Board, other administrative tribunals, and the courts.

Office of Special Counsel, *Congressional and Public Affairs, 1730 M St. N.W., #300 20036-4505; (202) 653-9001. Fax, (202) 653-5161. Elaine D. Kaplan, Special Counsel; Jane McFarland, Director. Information, (202) 653-7188. TTY, (800) 877-8339. Issues relating to the Hatch Act, (800) 854-2824.*
Web, www.osc.gov

Investigates allegations of prohibited personnel practices, including reprisals against whistleblowers (federal employees who disclose waste, fraud, inefficiency, and wrongdoing by supervisors of federal departments and agencies). Initiates necessary corrective or disciplinary action. Enforces the Hatch Act, which limits political activity by most federal and District of Columbia employees.

U.S. Court of Appeals for the Federal Circuit, *717 Madison Pl. N.W. 20439; (202) 633-6556. Fax, (202) 633-6353. Haldane Robert Mayer, Chief Judge; Jan Horbaly, Clerk, (202) 633-9614. Electronic bulletin board, (202) 633-9608 or (202) 786-6584.*

Reviews decisions of the Merit Systems Protection Board.

Hiring, Recruitment, and Training

AGENCIES

Office of Personnel Management (OPM), *Diversity, 1900 E St. N.W., #2445 20415-0001; (202) 606-1059. Fax, (202) 606-0927. Maria Mercedes Olivieri, Director.*
Web, www.opm.gov/disability

Develops policies and guidelines for government recruiting programs, including diversity employment efforts related to women, minorities, persons with disabilities, and veterans. Collects and maintains statistics on the federal employment of these groups. Administers the Federal Equal Opportunity Recruitment Program.

Office of Personnel Management (OPM), *Executive Resources Management, 1900 E St. N.W., #6484 20415-5100; (202) 606-1610. Fax, (202) 606-0557. William Collins, Director, (202) 606-2246.*
Web, www.opm.gov

Responsible for training and curriculum development programs for government executives and supervisors. Administers executive personnel systems, including those for the Senior Executive Service (SES) and personnel in executive positions not in SES.

Office of Personnel Management (OPM), *Intergovernmental Personnel Act Mobility Program, 1900 E St. N.W., #7463 20415-0001; (202) 606-1181. Fax, (202) 606-3577. Tony Ryan, Program Head.*
Web, www.opm.gov

Implements temporary personnel exchanges between federal agencies and nonfederal entities including state and local governments, institutions of higher education, and other organizations.

Office of Personnel Management (OPM), *Investigations Service, 1900 E St. N.W., #5416 20415-0001; (202) 606-1042. Fax, (202) 606-2390. Kathy Dillaman, Deputy Associate Director (Acting).*
Web, www.opm.gov/extra/investigate

Initiates and conducts investigations of new federal employees; determines whether applicants and appointees are suitable for positions other than those involving national security.

PERSONNEL OFFICES AT FEDERAL AGENCIES

Job seekers interested in additional information can explore federal government career opportunities through the government's official employment information system: (478) 757-3000; TTY, (478) 744-2299; Web, www.usajobs.opm.gov

DEPARTMENTS

Agriculture, (202) 720-3585

Commerce, (202) 482-4807; recording, (202) 482-5138

Defense (civilian), (703) 696-2720

  Air Force (civilian), (703) 697-3127

  Defense Logistics Agency, (703) 767-6445

  Navy (civilian), (703) 695-2633

Education, (202) 401-0553

Energy, (202) 586-5610

Health and Human Services, (301) 690-6191

  Food and Drug Administration, (301) 827-4120; recording, (301) 443-1969

  Health Resources and Services Administration, (301) 443-2747; recording, (301) 443-1230

  National Institutes of Health, (301) 496-3592

  Public Health and Science, (202) 619-0146

Homeland Security, (202) 282-8000 (switchboard)

  Federal Emergency Management Agency, (202) 646-4040; recording, (202) 646-3244

  Transportation Security Administration, (866) 274-6438

Housing and Urban Development, (202) 708-2000; recording, (202) 708-3203

Interior, (202) 208-4727; recording, (800) 336-4562

Justice, (202) 305-4976

Labor, (202) 693-7600

State, (202) 647-9898; civil service recording, (202) 647-7284; foreign service recording, (703) 875-7490

Transportation, (202) 366-4088; recording, (202) 366-9391; toll-free, (800) 525-2878

Treasury, (202) 622-3492

Veterans Affairs, (202) 273-4920

AGENCIES

Administrative Office of the U.S. Courts, (202) 502-3100; recording, (202) 502-1271

Commodity Futures Trading Commission, (202) 418-5003; recording (202) 418-5009

Consumer Product Safety Commission, (301) 504-7925

Corporation for National Service, (202) 606-5000, ext. 332

Environmental Protection Agency, (202) 564-4606

Equal Employment Opportunity Commission, (202) 663-4306

Export-Import Bank, (202) 565-3300; recording, (202) 565-3946

Farm Credit Administration, (703) 883-4135; recording, (703) 883-4139

Federal Communications Commission, (202) 418-0137; recording, (202) 418-0101

Federal Deposit Insurance Corporation, (202) 942-3311

Federal Election Commission, (202) 694-1080

Federal Labor Relations Authority, (202) 482-6660

Federal Mediation and Conciliation Service, (202) 606-5460

Federal Reserve Board, (202) 452-3880; recording, (202) 452-3038; toll-free, (800) 448-4894

Federal Trade Commission, (202) 326-2021; recording, (202) 326-2020

General Accounting Office, (202) 512-4500; recording, (202) 512-6092

General Services Administration, (202) 501-0398

Government Printing Office, (202) 512-1200

National Aeronautics and Space Administration, (202) 358-0520

National Archives and Records Administration, (301) 837-3710

National Credit Union Administration, (703) 518-6510

National Endowment for the Arts, (202) 682-5405

National Endowment for the Humanities, (202) 606-8415

National Labor Relations Board, (202) 273-3900

National Mediation Board, (202) 692-5008

National Science Foundation, (703) 292-8180

National Transportation Safety Board, (202) 314-6230; recording, (800) 573-0937

Nuclear Regulatory Commission, (301) 415-7516

Office of Personnel Management, recording, (202) 606-2440

Securities and Exchange Commission, (202) 942-4000; recording, (202) 942-4150

Small Business Administration, (202) 205-6780

Smithsonian Institution, (202) 275-1102; recording, (202) 287-3102

Social Security Administration, (410) 965-3324

U.S. International Trade Commission, (202) 205-2651

U.S. Postal Service, (202) 268-3646

Office of Personnel Management (OPM), *Standards, Competencies, and Assessments Development,* *1900 E St. N.W., #6H31 20415-0001; (202) 606-2950. Fax, (202) 606-4891. Leslie Pollack, Chief. Web, www.opm.gov/fedclass/index.htm*

Develops job classification standards for occupations in the general schedule and federal wage system.

Office of Personnel Management (OPM), *Strategic Human Resources Policy, 1900 E St. N.W., #6500 20415-0001; (202) 606-6500. Fax, (202) 606-1637. Ronald Sanders, Associate Director.*

Responsible for development of policy concerning human resources throughout the federal government covering the areas of pay and performance, employee and family support, workforce relations, and training and development. Also responsible for research and development of workforce information needed for policy making.

Labor-Management Relations

AGENCIES

Federal Labor Relations Authority, *607 14th St. N.W., #410 20424-0001; (202) 482-6500. Fax, (202) 482-6635. V. Dale Cabaniss, Chair; Kevin Copper, Executive Director. Web, www.flra.gov*

Oversees the federal labor-management relations program; administers the law that protects the right of federal employees to organize, bargain collectively, and participate through labor organizations of their own choosing.

Federal Service Impasses Panel *(Federal Labor Relations Authority), 607 14th St. N.W., #220 20424-0001; (202) 482-6670. Fax, (202) 482-6674. H. Joseph Schimansky, Executive Director; Becky P. Dunlop, Chair. Web, www.flra.gov*

Assists in resolving contract negotiation impasses between federal agencies and labor organizations representing federal employees.

Office of Personnel Management (OPM), *General Counsel, 1900 E St. N.W., #7353 20415-0001. Mark Robbins, General Counsel, (202) 606-1700. Web, www.opm.gov*

Advises the government on law and legal policy relating to federal labor-management relations; represents the government before the Merit Systems Protection Board.

Office of Personnel Management (OPM), *Workforce Relations and Accountability Policy, 1900 E St. N.W., #7H28 20415-0001; (202) 606-2639. Fax, (202) 606-2613. Jeffrey Sumberg, Deputy Associate Director.*

Web, www.opm.gov

Develops policy for government agencies and unions regarding employee- and labor-management relations.

NONPROFIT

National Alliance of Postal and Federal Employees, *1628 11th St. N.W. 20001; (202) 939-6325. Fax, (202) 939-6389. James M. McGee, President. General e-mail, napfe@patriot.net Web, www.napfe.com*

Membership: approximately 70,000 postal and federal employees. Helps members negotiate pay, benefits, and better working conditions; conducts training programs and workshops. Monitors legislation and regulations.

National Assn. of Government Employees, *Washington Office, 317 S. Patrick St., Alexandria, VA 22314; (703) 519-0300. Fax, (703) 519-0311. Vacant, Regional Director. General e-mail, nage@erols.com Web, www.nage.org*

Membership: approximately 200,000 federal government employees. Helps members negotiate pay, benefits, and better working conditions; conducts training programs and workshops. Monitors legislation and regulations. (Headquarters in Quincy, Mass.; affiliated with the AFL-CIO.)

National Federation of Federal Employees, *1016 16th St. N.W., #300 20036; (202) 862-4400. Fax, (202) 862-4432. Richard Brown, National President. Web, www.nffe.org*

Membership: federal government employees throughout various agencies within the federal government. Helps members negotiate pay, benefits, and better working conditions; conducts training programs and workshops. Monitors legislation and regulations.

National Treasury Employees Union, *901 E St. N.W., #600 20004; (202) 783-4444. Fax, (202) 783-4085. Colleen Kelly, President. General e-mail, nteuinfo@nteuhq1.nteu.org Web, www.nteu.org*

Membership: approximately 150,000 employees from the Treasury Dept. and eighteen other federal agencies. Helps members negotiate pay, benefits, and better working conditions; conducts training programs and workshops. Monitors legislation and regulations.

Public Service Research Foundation, *320D Maple Ave. East, Vienna, VA 22180; (703) 242-3575. Fax, (703) 242-3579. David Y. Denholm, President. General e-mail, info@psrf.org*

Web, www.psrf.org

Independent, nonpartisan research and educational organization. Opposes collective bargaining, strikes, and binding arbitration in the public sector. Sponsors conferences and seminars. Library open to the public by appointment.

Pay and Employee Benefits

AGENCIES

Bureau of Labor Statistics (BLS), *(Labor Dept.), Survey, Data Analysis, and Publications, 2 Massachusetts Ave. N.E., #4175 20212-0001; (202) 691-6199. Fax, (202) 691-6647. Wanda Davies, Project Manager.*
General e-mail, ocltinfo@bls.gov
Web, www.bls.gov

Develops occupational pay surveys on area and national industries; analyzes, distributes, and disseminates information.

Labor Dept. (DOL), *Federal Employees' Compensation, 200 Constitution Ave. N.W., #S3229 20210; (202) 693-0040. Fax, (202) 693-1497. Deborah Sanford, Director. General inquiries: toll-free, (866) 999-3322; TTY, (877) 889-5627. Specific claims: toll-free, (866) 692-7487 (customers should contact their district office first).*
Web, www.dol.gov/esa/owcp_org.htm

Administers the Federal Employees Compensation Act, which provides workers' compensation for federal employees.

Office of Personnel Management (OPM), *Federal Prevailing Rate Advisory Committee, 1900 E St. N.W., #5538 20415; (202) 606-1500. Fax, (202) 606-5104. Mary M. Rose, Chair.*

Advises OPM on pay systems for federal blue-collar workers.

Office of Personnel Management (OPM), *Insurance Services, 1900 E St. N.W., #3400 20415; (202) 606-0770. Fax, (202) 606-4640. Frank D. Titus, Assistant Director.*
Web, www.opm.gov/insure/index.html

Administers group life insurance for federal employees and retirees; negotiates rates and benefits with health insurance carriers; settles disputed claims. Administers the Federal Employees' Health Benefits (FEHB) and the Federal Employees' Group Life Insurance (FEGLI) programs.

Office of Personnel Management (OPM), *Pay and Performance Policy, 1900 E St. N.W., #7H31 20415; (202) 606-2880. Fax, (202) 606-4264. Donald J. Winstead, Deputy Associate Director.*
Web, www.opm.gov/oca

Administers governmentwide pay systems for federal civilian employees, family pay and leave policies, and assists federal agencies and employees in administering governmentwide compensation systems.

Office of Personnel Management (OPM), *Performance Management, 1900 E St. N.W., #7412 20415; (202) 606-2720. Fax, (202) 606-2395. Margaret M. Higgins, Manager, (202) 606-1758.*
Web, www.opm.gov/perform

Sets policy and implements the performance appraisal and pay-for-performance system for all federal employees. Consults with agencies to help them develop their own systems; reviews and approves agencies' plans before implementation. Sets policy for performance appraisal and awards for federal employees.

Office of Personnel Management (OPM), *Retirement and Insurance Services, 1900 E St. N.W., #4312 20415; (202) 606-0462. Fax, (202) 606-1163. Kathleen McGettigan, Deputy Associate Director.*
Web, www.opm.gov

Implements federal policy and regulations on retirement and insurance benefits.

Office of Personnel Management (OPM), *Retirement Information, 1900 E St. N.W. 20415-0001; (202) 606-0500. Fax, (202) 606-0145. Wellington Sadler, Chief. TTY, (800) 878-5707. Toll-free, (888) 767-6738.*
General e-mail, retire@opm.gov
Web, www.opm.gov/retire/index.asp

Responds to telephone inquiries on retirement law and health and life insurance; handles reports of annuitants' deaths; conducts interviews on individual cases; makes appropriate referrals.

Office of Personnel Management (OPM), *Retirement Services, 1900 E St. N.W., #3305 20415; (202) 606-0300. Fax, (202) 606-1998. Sidney M. Conley, Assistant Director.*
Web, www.opm.gov

Administers the civil service and federal employees' retirement systems; responsible for monthly annuity payments and other benefits; organizes and maintains retirement records; distributes information on retirement and on insurance programs for annuitants.

Office of Personnel Management (OPM), *Salary and Wage Systems, 1900 E St. N.W., #7H31 20415; (202) 606-2838. Fax, (202) 606-4264. Jerome D. Mikowicz, Manager.*
Web, www.opm.gov/oca/payrates/index.htm

Responsible for the annual pay adjustment review process and for local adjustment allowances (locality pay) for federal white-collar workers. Works jointly with the Office of Management and Budget and the Labor Dept. to aid the director of OPM in the role of "pay agent" for the president. Report available to the public after presidential consideration. Administers the federal wage system that establishes pay scales for federal blue-collar employees and the non-foreign area cost of living allowance program for federal employees in offshore areas. Responds to inquiries on federal blue-collar pay rates and pay administration matters.

NONPROFIT

National Assn. of Retired Federal Employees (NARFE), *606 N. Washington St., Alexandria, VA 22314; (703) 838-7760. Fax, (703) 838-7785. Charles L. Fallis, President. Member relations, (800) 456-8410.*
General e-mail, natlhq@narfe.org
Web, www.narfe.org

Works to preserve the integrity of the civil service retirement system. Provides members with information about benefits for retired federal employees and for survivors of deceased federal employees. Monitors legislation and regulations.

🏛 FEDERAL CONTRACTS AND PROCUREMENT

AGENCIES

Agencies and departments have their own procurement offices to deal with firms, organizations, and individuals seeking to sell goods and services to the government (see the list of procurement officers, this section). Federal business opportunities over $25,000 can be explored online through www.FedBizOpps.gov.

Committee for Purchase from People Who Are Blind or Severely Disabled, *1421 Jefferson Davis Hwy., #10800, Arlington, VA 22202-3259; (703) 603-7740. Fax, (703) 603-0655. Leon Wilson, Executive Director.*
Web, www.jwod.gov

Presidentially appointed committee. Determines which products and services are suitable for federal procurement from qualified nonprofit agencies that employ people who are blind or have other severe disabilities; seeks to increase employment opportunities for these individuals.

Comptroller of the Currency *(Treasury Dept.),* **Acquisition Management,** *250 E St. S.W. 20219; (202)*

874-5040. Fax, (202) 874-5625. Michael Stafford, Director.
Web, www.occ.treas.gov

Responsible for procuring all of the goods and services required by the Office of the Comptroller of the Currency through federal contracting, interagency agreements, and cooperative agreements. Ensures that small businesses owned and controlled by minorities, women, and individuals with disabilities are given the opportunity to participate in contracts with the Comptroller of the Currency.

General Services Administration (GSA), *Acquisition Policy, 1800 F St. N.W., #4040 20405; (202) 501-1043. Fax, (202) 501-1986. David A. Drabkin, Deputy Associate Administrator.*
Web, www.gsa.gov

Develops and implements federal government acquisition policies and procedures; conducts preaward and postaward contract reviews; administers federal acquisition regulations for civilian agencies; suspends and debars contractors for unsatisfactory performance; coordinates and promotes governmentwide career management and training programs for contracting personnel.

General Services Administration (GSA), *Board of Contract Appeals, 1800 F St. N.W., #7022 20405; (202) 501-0585. Fax, (202) 501-0664. Stephen M. Daniels, Chair. For filings, (202) 501-0116.*
Web, www.gsa.gov

Resolves disputes arising out of contracts with the General Services Administration, the Treasury Dept., the Education Dept., the Commerce Dept., and other independent agencies. Provides alternative dispute resolution services to other agencies.

General Services Administration (GSA), *Enterprise Development, 1800 F St. N.W., #6029 20405; (202) 501-1021. Fax, (202) 208-5938. Felipe Mendoza, Associate Administrator.*
Web, www.gsa.gov/oed

Works to increase small-business procurement of government contracts. Provides policy guidance and direction for GSA Business Service Centers, which offer advice and assistance to businesses interested in government procurement.

General Services Administration (GSA), *Federal Procurement Data Center, 7th and D Sts. S.W., #5652 20407; (202) 401-1529. Fax, (202) 401-1546. Jim Adams, Director.*
Web, www.fpdc.gov

PROCUREMENT OFFICERS FOR FEDERAL AGENCIES

DEPARTMENTS

Agriculture, W. R. Ashworth, (202) 720-9448

Commerce, Michael S. Sade, (202) 482-2773

Defense, Deidre A. Lee, (703) 695-7145

Education, Glenn Perry, (202) 708-8488

Energy, Richard H. Hopf, (202) 586-8613

Health and Human Services, Marc Weisman, (202) 401-6103

Homeland Security, Vacant, (202) 282-8000

Housing and Urban Development, Dexter J. Sidney, (202) 708-0600, ext. 5375

Interior, Debra Sonderman, (202) 208-6352

Justice, James W. Johnston, (202) 307-2000

Labor, Daniel P. Murphy, (202) 693-4570

State, Cathy Read, (703) 875-6639

Transportation, Mark Welch, (202) 366-4953

Treasury, Cory Rindner, (202) 622-0520

Veterans Affairs, Gary J. Krump, (202) 273-6029

AGENCIES

Consumer Product Safety Commission, Robert Frost, (301) 504-7928

Corporation for National Service, Simon Woodward, (202) 606-5000, ext. 114

Environmental Protection Agency, Judy Davis, (202) 564-4310

Export-Import Bank, Mark Pitra, (202) 565-3338

Farm Credit Administration, Peter McLean, (703) 883-4135

Federal Communications Commission, Sonna B. Stampone, (202) 418-0992

Federal Deposit Insurance Corporation, Rodney Cartwright, (202) 942-3680

Federal Emergency Management Agency, Patricia English, (202) 646-3757

Federal Maritime Commission, Michael Kilby, (202) 523-5900

Federal Mediation and Conciliation Service, Sam Baumgardner, (202) 606-8111

Federal Reserve System, Michael E. Kelly, (202) 452-3296

Federal Trade Commission, Jean Sefchick, (202) 326-2258

General Services Administration, David A. Drabkin, (202) 501-1043

National Aeronautics and Space Administration, Thomas Luedtke, (202) 358-2090

National Labor Relations Board, Angela Crawford, (202) 273-4040

National Mediation Board, Jan Smith, (202) 692-5010

National Science Foundation, Donna Fortunat, (703) 292-8240

Nuclear Regulatory Commission, Kathryn Greene, (301) 415-7305

Office of Personnel Management, Alfred Chatterton, (202) 606-2240

Securities and Exchange Commission, Kim Davis, (202) 942-4990

Small Business Administration, Sharon Gurley, (202) 205-6622

Social Security Administration, James Fornataro, (410) 965-9459

U.S. International Trade Commission, Michael Boling, (202) 205-2734

U.S. Postal Service, A. Keith Strange, (202) 268-4040

Makes available quarterly information about government procurement contracts over $25,000; collects and disseminates data on the amount of business that companies do with each federal department and agency.

General Services Administration (GSA), *Governmentwide Policy, 1800 F St. N.W., #5240 20405; (202) 501-8880. Fax, (202) 501-8898. G. Martin Wagner, Associate Administrator.*
Web, www.policyworks.gov

Coordinates GSA policy-making activities; promotes collaboration between government and the private sector in developing policy and management techniques; works to integrate acquisition, management, and disposal of government property.

Minority Business Development Agency *(Commerce Dept.), 14th St. and Constitution Ave. N.W., #5055 20230; (202) 482-5061. Fax, (202) 482-2500. Ronald N. Langston, Director.*

Web, www.mbda.gov

Assists minority business owners in obtaining federal loans and contract awards; produces an annual report on federal agencies' performance in procuring from minority-owned businesses.

Office of Management and Budget (OMB), *(Executive Office of the President), Federal Procurement Policy, Dwight D. Eisenhower Executive Office Bldg., #352 20503; (202) 395-5802. Fax, (202) 395-3242. Angela B. Styles, Administrator.*

Web, www.whitehouse.gov/omb

Coordinates government procurement policies, regulations, and procedures. Responsible for cost accounting rules governing federal contractors and subcontractors.

CONGRESS

General Accounting Office (GAO), *Procurement Law Division, 441 G St. N.W., #1139 20548; (202) 512-6071. Fax, (202) 512-9749. Daniel I. Gordon, Managing Associate General Counsel.*

Web, www.gao.gov

Considers and rules on the proposed or actual award of a government contract upon receipt of a written protest.

House Government Reform Committee, *Subcommittee on Government Efficiency and Financial Management, B349C RHOB 20515; (202) 225-3741. Fax, (202) 225-2544. Rep. Todd R. Platts, R-Pa., Chair; Mike Hettinger, Staff Director.*

Web, www.house.gov/reform

Jurisdiction over legislation on the federal procurement system; oversees rules and regulations concerning government procurement.

House Small Business Committee, *Subcommittee on Tax, Finance, and Exports, B363 RHOB 20515; (202) 226-2630. Fax, (202) 225-8950. Rep. Pat Toomey, R-Pa., Chair; Sean McGraw, Staff Director.*

General e-mail, smbiz@mail.house.gov

Web, www.house.gov/smbiz

Jurisdiction over legislation on programs affecting small business and the federal procurement system; oversees rules and regulations concerning government procurement.

Senate Governmental Affairs Committee, *Subcommittee on Oversight Government Management, the Federal Workforce, and the District of Columbia, SH-601 20510; (202) 224-3682. Sen. George V. Voinovich, R-Ohio, Chair; Andrew Richardson, Staff Director.*

General e-mail, ogm@govt-aff.senate.gov

Web, govt-aff.senate.gov

Jurisdiction over legislation on the federal procurement system; oversees rules and regulations concerning government procurement.

Senate Small Business and Entrepreneurship Committee, *SR-428A 20510; (202) 224-5175 Fax, (202) 228-1128. Sen. Olympia J. Snowe, R-Maine, Chair; Mark Warren, Staff Director.*

Web, sbc.senate.gov

Studies and makes recommendations on legislation concerning government procurement as it affects small business.

NONPROFIT

Some nongovernmental groups provide members with information about government contracts. Contact representative group for information.

Coalition for Government Procurement, *1990 M St. N.W., #400 20036; (202) 331-0975. Fax, (202) 822-9788. Bruce McLellan, Executive Director.*

General e-mail, info@coalgovpro.org

Web, www.coalgovpro.org

Alliance of business firms that sell to the federal government. Seeks equal opportunities for businesses to sell to the government; monitors practices of the General Services Administration and government procurement legislation and regulations.

Contract Services Assn. of America, *1000 Wilson Blvd., #1800, Arlington, VA 22209; (703) 243-2020. Fax, (703) 243-3601. Gary Engebretson, President.*

General e-mail, info@csa-dc.org

Web, www.csa-dc.org

Membership: companies that, under contract, provide federal, state, and local governments and other agencies with various technical and support services (particularly in defense, space, transportation, environment, energy, and health care). Analyzes the process by which the government awards contracts to private firms. Monitors legislation and regulations.

National Contract Management Assn., *8260 Greensboro Dr., #200, McLean, VA 22102; (703) 448-9231. Fax, (703) 448-0939. Neal J. Couture, Executive Director. Information, (800) 344-8096.*

Web, www.ncmahq.org

Membership: individuals concerned with administering, procuring, negotiating, and managing government and commercial contracts and subcontracts. Sponsors

Certified Professional Contracts Manager Program and various educational and professional programs.

National Institute of Governmental Purchasing,
151 Spring St., #300, Herndon, VA 20170-5223; (703) 736-8900. Fax, (703) 736-9644. Rick Grimm, Executive Vice President. Information, (800) 367-6447.
Web, www.nigp.org

Membership: governmental purchasing departments, agencies, and organizations at the federal, state, and local levels in the United States and Canada. Provides public procurement officers with technical assistance and information, training seminars, and professional certification.

Professional Services Council, *2101 Wilson Blvd., #750, Arlington, VA 22201; (703) 875-8059. Fax, (703) 875-8922. Stan Z. Soloway, President.*
Web, www.pscouncil.org

Membership: associations and firms that provide local, state, federal, and international governments with professional and technical services. Promotes reform of the procurement system; seeks to improve the compilation of data and statistics about the professional and technical services industry.

 **POSTAL SERVICE**

AGENCIES

U.S. Postal Service (USPS), *475 L'Enfant Plaza S.W. 20260-0001; (202) 268-2000. Fax, (202) 268-4860. John E. Potter, Postmaster General. Library, (202) 268-2904. Press, (202) 268-2155. Locator, (202) 268-2020.*
Web, www.usps.com

Offers postal service throughout the country as an independent establishment of the executive branch. Library open to the public.

U.S. Postal Service (USPS), *Inspection Service,*
475 L'Enfant Plaza S.W., #3100 20260-2100; (202) 268-4264. Fax, (202) 268-4563. Lee R. Heath, Chief Postal Inspector. Fraud and abuse hotline, (888) 877-7644.
Web, www.usps.com/postalinspectors

Investigates criminal violations of postal laws, such as theft of mail or posted valuables, assaults on postal employees, organized crime in postal-related matters, and prohibited mailings. Conducts internal audits; investigates postal activities to determine effectiveness of procedures; monitors compliance of individual post offices with postal regulations; functions as the inspector general for the U.S. Postal Service.

CONGRESS

House Appropriations Committee, *Subcommittee on Transportation, Treasury, and Related Agencies,*
2358 RHOB 20515; (202) 225-2141. Fax, (202) 225-5895. Rep. Ernest Istook, R-Okla., Chair; Richard Efford, Clerk.
Web, www.house.gov/appropriations

Jurisdiction over legislation to appropriate funds for the U.S. Postal Service and the Postal Rate Commission.

House Government Reform Committee,
2157 RHOB 20515; (202) 225-5074. Fax, (202) 225-3974. Rep. Thomas M. Davis III, R-Va., Chair; Peter Sirh, Staff Director.
Web, www.house.gov/reform

Jurisdiction over the U.S. Postal Service generally, including the transportation of mail.

Senate Appropriations Committee, *Subcommittee on Transportation, Treasury, and General Government,*
SD-196 20510; (202) 224-8244. Fax, (202) 228-1621. Sen. Richard C. Shelby, R-Ala., Chair; Paul Doerrer, Clerk.
Web, appropriations.senate.gov

Jurisdiction over legislation to appropriate funds for the U.S. Postal Service and the Postal Rate Commission.

Senate Governmental Affairs Committee, *Permanent Subcommittee on Investigations, SR-199 20510; (202) 224-3721. Sen. Norm Coleman, R-Minn., Chair; Mary Robertson, Chief Clerk.*
General e-mail, PSI@govt-aff.senate.gov
Web, govt-aff.senate.gov

Investigates postal fraud.

Senate Governmental Affairs Committee, *Subcommittee on Financial Management, the Budget, and International Security, SH-442 20510; (202) 224-2254. Sen. Peter G. Fitzgerald, R-Ill., Chair; Mitch Kugler, Staff Director.*
Web, govt-aff.senate.gov

Jurisdiction over postal service legislation, including legislation on postal service consumer protection, labor relations, automation of postal facilities, postal fraud, mail rates, and classifications for the postal service and philately; postal finances and expenditures; and mail transportation and military mail. Oversight of the U.S. Postal Service and the Postal Rate Commission. Analyzes the impact on federal jobs of the use of mail consultants and contractors by government agencies.

Consumer Services

AGENCIES

U.S. Postal Service (USPS), *Corporate Law*, 475 L'Enfant Plaza S.W. 20260-1135; (202) 268-4816. Fax, (202) 268-5418. George C. Davis, Chief Counsel.

Reviews and processes cases falling under the Program Fraud Civil Remedies Act of 1986.

U.S. Postal Service (USPS), *Customer Protection and Privacy*, 475 L'Enfant Plaza S.W., #6118 20260-1135; (202) 268-2965. Fax, (202) 268-5418. Elizabeth P. Martin, Chief Counsel.

Web, www.usps.gov

Initiates civil administrative proceedings to stop mail delivery that solicits money by lottery or misrepresentation; enforces statutes designed to prevent receipt of unwanted sexual material.

U.S. Postal Service (USPS), *Office of Consumer Advocate*, 475 L'Enfant Plaza S.W., #5821 20260-2200; (202) 268-2284. Fax, (202) 268-2304. Francia G. Smith, Vice President and Consumer Advocate. TTY, (877) 877-7833. Inquiries, (800) ASK-USPS or (800) 275-8777.

Web, www.usps.gov

Handles consumer complaints; oversees investigations into consumer problems; intercedes in local areas when problems are not adequately resolved; provides information on specific products and services; represents consumers' viewpoint before postal management bodies; initiates projects to improve the U.S. Postal Service.

U.S. Postal Service (USPS), *Service and Market Development*, 1735 N. Lynn St., Arlington, VA 22209-6004; (703) 292-3800. Fax, (703) 292-3737. John R. Wargo, Vice President of Service and Market Development.

Develops policies, plans, and programs for commercial mailers to improve customer satisfaction. Directs the Business Partners program. Activities include the local postal customer councils, the National Postal Forum, and the Mailers' Technical Advisory Committee.

U.S. Postal Service (USPS), *Stamp Acquisition and Distribution*, 475 L'Enfant Plaza S.W., #5826 20260-2436; (202) 268-2325. Fax, (202) 268-5978. Lawrence L. Lum, Acquisitions and Distribution Manager.

Web, www.usps.gov

Manufactures and distributes postage stamps and postal stationery; develops inventory controls.

Employee and Labor Relations

AGENCIES

U.S. Postal Service (USPS), *Diversity Development*, 475 L'Enfant Plaza S.W., #3901 20260-5600; (202) 268-6567. Fax, (202) 268-4263. Murry E. Weatherall, Vice President.

Responsible for policy and planning with regard to affirmative employment and supplier/vendor diversity.

U.S. Postal Service (USPS), *Employee Resource Management*, 475 L'Enfant Plaza S.W., #9840 20260-4200; (202) 268-3783. Fax, (202) 268-3803. DeWitt O. Harris, Vice President.

Drafts and implements employment policies and practices, safety and health guidelines, and training and development programs.

U.S. Postal Service (USPS), *Labor Relations*, 475 L'Enfant Plaza S.W., #9014 20260-4100; (202) 268-7853. Fax, (202) 268-3074. Anthony J. Vegliante, Vice President.

Handles collective bargaining and contract administration for the U.S. Postal Service and processes complaints regarding equal employment opportunity.

U.S. Postal Service (USPS), *Personnel Operations Support*, 475 L'Enfant Plaza S.W., #1831 20260-4261; (202) 268-4255. Fax, (202) 268-6195. Janet Qualters, Manager.

Web, www.usps.gov

Matches needs of U.S. Postal Service with career goals and job preferences of its executive employees.

NONPROFIT

American Postal Workers Union (APWU), 1300 L St. N.W. 20005; (202) 842-4200. Fax, (202) 842-4297. William Burrus, President.

Web, www.apwu.org

Membership: approximately 366,000 postal employees, including clerks, motor vehicle operators, special delivery messengers, and other employees. Assists members with contract negotiation and grievances; conducts training programs and workshops. Monitors legislation and regulations. (Affiliated with the Postal, Telegraph, and Telephone International and the AFL-CIO.)

National Alliance of Postal and Federal Employees, 1628 11th St. N.W. 20001; (202) 939-6325. Fax, (202) 939-6389. James M. McGee, President.

General e-mail, napfe@patriot.net

Web, www.napfe.com

Membership: approximately 70,000 postal and federal employees. Helps members negotiate pay, benefits, and better working conditions; conducts training programs and workshops. Monitors legislation and regulations.

National Assn. of Letter Carriers, 100 Indiana Ave. N.W. 20001-2144; (202) 393-4695. Fax, (202) 737-1540. William H. Yancy, President.

General e-mail, nalcinf@nalc.org

Web, www.nalc.org

Membership: approximately 307,000 city letter carriers working for, or retired from, the U.S. Postal Service. Assists members with contract negotiation and grievances; conducts training programs and workshops. Monitors legislation and regulations. (Affiliated with the AFL-CIO and the Union Network International.)

National Assn. of Postal Supervisors, *1727 King St., #400, Alexandria, VA 22314-2753; (703) 836-9660. Fax, (703) 836-9665. Vincent Palladino, President.*

General e-mail, napshq@naps.org

Web, www.naps.org

Membership: present and former postal supervisors. Cooperates with other postal management associations, unions, and the U.S. Postal Service to improve the efficiency of the postal service; promotes favorable working conditions and broader career opportunities for all postal employees; provides members with information on current functions and legislative issues of the postal service.

National Assn. of Postmasters of the United States, *8 Herbert St., Alexandria, VA 22305-2600; (703) 683-9027. Fax, (703) 683-6820. Charles Moser, Executive Director. Hotline, (703) 683-9038.*

General e-mail, napusinfo@napus.org

Web, www.napus.org

Membership: present and former postmasters of the United States. Promotes quality mail service and favorable relations between the postal service and the public; works with other postal groups and levels of management in the interest of postal matters and the welfare of its members.

National League of Postmasters, *1023 N. Royal St., Alexandria, VA 22314; (703) 548-5922. Fax, (703) 836-8937. Steve LeNoir, President. Hotline, (703) 683-0549.*

Web, www.postmasters.org

Membership: state and area postmaster associations. Promotes effective postal management; sponsors insurance plans for members; operates a 24-hour help line, which makes confidential referrals for those experiencing stress. Monitors legislation and regulations.

National Rural Letter Carriers' Assn., *1630 Duke St., 4th Floor, Alexandria, VA 22314-3465; (703) 684-5545. Fax, (703) 548-8735. Gus Baffa, President.*

Web, www.nrlca.org

Membership: approximately 100,000 rural letter carriers working for, or retired from, the U.S. Postal Service. Seeks to improve rural mail delivery. Helps members negotiate pay, benefits, and better working conditions;

conducts training programs and workshops. Monitors legislation and regulations.

National Star Route Mail Contractors Assn., *324 E. Capitol St. N.E. 20003-3897; (202) 543-1661. Fax, (202) 543-8863. John V. Maraney, Executive Director.*

General e-mail, info@starroutecontractors.org

Web, www.starroutecontractors.org

Membership: contractors for highway mail transport and selected rural route deliverers. Acts as liaison between contractors and the U.S. Postal Service, the Transportation Dept., and the Labor Dept. concerning contracts, wages, and other issues. Monitors legislation and regulations.

Mail Rates and Classification

AGENCIES

Postal Rate Commission, *1333 H St. N.W., #300 20268-0001; (202) 789-6800. Fax, (202) 789-6886. George Omas, Chair. TTY, (202) 789-6881.*

Web, www.prc.gov

Submits recommendations to the governors of the U.S. Postal Service concerning proposed changes in postage rates, fees, and mail classifications; issues advisory opinions on proposed changes in postal services; studies and submits recommendations on public complaints concerning postal rates and nationwide service. Reviews appeals of post office closings.

U.S. Postal Service (USPS), *Business Mail Acceptance, 1735 N. Lynn St., Arlington, VA 22209; (703) 292-3541. Fax, (703) 292-3738. John Sadler, Manager.*

Implements policies on and answers customer inquiries about domestic mail classification matters.

U.S. Postal Service (USPS), *Mailing Standards, 1735 N. Lynn St., #3025, Arlington, VA 22209-6038; (703) 292-3651. Fax, (703) 292-4058. Sherry Freda, Manager.*

Issues policy statements on domestic mail classification matters. Ensures the accuracy of policies developed by the Postal Rate Commission with respect to domestic mail classification schedules.

U.S. Postal Service (USPS), *Pricing and Classification, 1735 N. Lynn St., Arlington, VA 22209; (703) 292-3783. Fax, (703) 292-3794. Stephen Kearney, Vice President.*

Sets prices for U.S. Postal Service product lines using competitive pricing methods.

NONPROFIT

Alliance of Nonprofit Mailers, *1211 Connecticut Ave. N.W., #620 20036-2701; (202) 462-5132. Fax, (202) 462-0423. Neal Denton, Executive Director.*

General e-mail, alliance@nonprofitmailers.org

Web, www.nonprofitmailers.org

Works to maintain reasonable mail rates for non-profit organizations. Represents member organizations before Congress, the U.S. Postal Service, the Postal Rate Commission, and the courts on nonprofit postal rate and mail classification issues.

Assn. for Postal Commerce, *1901 N. Fort Myer Dr., #401, Arlington, VA 22209-1609; (703) 524-0096. Fax, (703) 524-1871. Gene A. Del Polito, President.*

Web, www.postcom.org

Membership: companies and organizations interested in advertising (Standard Mail A) mail. Provides members with information about postal policy, postal rates, and legislation regarding postal regulations.

Direct Marketing Assn., *Ethics and Consumer Affairs: Government Affairs, Washington Office,* 1111 19th St. N.W., #1100 20036; (202) 955-5030. Fax, (202) 955-0085. Jerry Cerasale, Senior Vice President.

Web, www.the-dma.org

Membership: telemarketers; users, creators, and producers of direct mail; and suppliers to the industry. Serves as liaison between members and the U.S. Postal Service. Monitors federal legislation and regulations concerning postal rates. (Headquarters in New York.)

DMA Nonprofit Federation, *1111 19th St. N.W., #1180 20036; (202) 628-4380. Fax, (202) 628-4383. Xenia Boone, Executive Director.*

General e-mail, nonprofitfederation@the-dma.org

Web, www.federationofnonprofits.org

Membership: educational, cultural, fraternal, religious, and scientific organizations that mail nonprofit second-, third-, or fourth-class mail. Serves as liaison between members and the U.S. Postal Service; represents nonprofit members' interests on the Mailers' Technical Advisory Committee. Monitors legislation and regulations. Sponsors education programs on direct-response fundraising. Formerly known as the National Federation of Nonprofits.

Mailing and Fulfillment Service Assn., *1421 Prince St., #410, Alexandria, VA 22314-2806; (703) 836-9200. Fax, (703) 548-8204. David A. Weaver, President.*

General e-mail, info@mfsanet.org

Web, www.mfsanet.org

Membership: U.S. and foreign letter and printing shops that engage in direct mail advertising. Serves as a clearinghouse for members on improving methods of using the mail for advertising.

Parcel Shippers Assn., *1211 Connecticut Ave. N.W., #610 20036; (202) 296-3690. Fax, (202) 296-0343. J. Pierce Myers, Executive Vice President.*

General e-mail, psa@parcelshippers.org

Web, www.parcelshippers.org

Voluntary organization of business firms concerned with the shipment of parcels. Works to improve parcel post rates and service; represents members before the Postal Rate Commission in matters regarding parcel post rates. Monitors legislation and regulations.

Stamps, Postal History

AGENCIES

Smithsonian Institute *(Smithsonian Institution),* **National Postal Museum,** *2 Massachusetts Ave. N.E., MRC 570 20002; (202) 357-2991. Fax, (202) 633-9393. Allen Kane, Director. TTY, (202) 633-9849.*

Web, www.si.edu/postal

Exhibits postal history and philatelic collections; provides information on world postal and philatelic history.

U.S. Postal Service (USPS), *Citizens' Stamp Advisory Committee,* 475 L'Enfant Plaza S.W., #5670 20260-2437; (202) 268-2313. Fax, (202) 268-2714. Virginia Noelke, Chair.

Web, www.usps.gov

Reviews stamp subject nominations. Develops the annual Stamp Program and makes subject and design recommendations to the Postmaster General.

U.S. Postal Service (USPS), *Stamp Acquisition and Distribution,* 475 L'Enfant Plaza S.W., #5826 20260-2436; (202) 268-2325. Fax, (202) 268-5978. Lawrence L. Lum, Acquisitions and Distribution Manager.

Web, www.usps.gov

Manufactures and distributes postage stamps and postal stationery.

U.S. Postal Service (USPS), *Stamp Development,* 475 L'Enfant Plaza S.W., #5670 20260-2437; (202) 268-2313. Fax, (202) 268-2714. Terry McCaffrey, Manager.

Manages the stamp selection function; develops the basic stamp pre-production design; manages relationship with philatelic community.

🏛 PUBLIC ADMINISTRATION

AGENCIES

Office of Management and Budget (OMB), *(Executive Office of the President), President's Management*

Council, *Dwight D. Eisenhower Executive Office Bldg., #350 20503; (202) 395-5963. Fax, (202) 395-0331. Mark W. Everson, Chair.*
Web, www.whitehouse.gov/omb

Membership: chief operating officers of federal government departments and agencies. Responsible for implementing the management improvement initiatives of the administration. Develops and oversees improved governmentwide management and administrative systems; formulates long-range plans to promote these systems; works to resolve interagency management problems and to implement reforms.

President's Commission on White House Fellowships, *712 Jackson Pl. N.W. 20503; (202) 395-4522. Fax, (202) 395-6179. Jocelyn White, Director.*
General e-mail, info@whitehousefellows.gov
Web, www.whitehousefellows.gov

Nonpartisan commission that provides professionals from all sectors of national life with the opportunity to observe firsthand the processes of the federal government. Fellows work for one year as special assistants to cabinet members or to principal members of the White House staff. Qualified applicants have demonstrated superior accomplishments early in their careers and have a commitment to community service.

CONGRESS

House Government Reform Committee, *Subcommittee on Energy Policy, Natural Resources, and Regulatory Affairs, B377 RHOB 20515; (202) 225-4407. Fax, (202) 225-2441. Rep. Doug Ose, R-Calif., Chair; Dan Skopec, Staff Director.*
Web, www.house.gov/reform

Jurisdiction over legislation involving the efficiency and management of government operations, including federal paperwork reduction.

House Government Reform Committee, *Subcommittee on Government Efficiency and Financial Management, B349C RHOB 20515; (202) 225-3741. Fax, (202) 225-2544. Rep. Todd R. Platts, R-Pa., Chair; Mike Hettinger, Staff Director.*
Web, www.house.gov/reform

Jurisdiction over legislation on all procurement practices. Also examines the efficiency of government operations, including federal regulations and program management.

House Standards of Official Conduct Committee, *HT-2 CAP 20515; (202) 225-7103. Fax, (202) 225-7392. Rep. Joel Hefley, R-Colo., Chair; John E. Vargo, Staff Director.*

Web, www.house.gov/ethics

Jurisdiction over the Ethics in Government Act of 1978.

Senate Governmental Affairs Committee, *Subcommittee on Oversight Government Management, the Federal Workforce, and the District of Columbia, SH-442 20510; (202) 224-3682. Sen. George V. Voinovich, R-Ohio, Chair; Andrew Richardson, Staff Director.*
General e-mail, ogm@govt-aff.senate.gov
Web, govt-aff.senate.gov

Jurisdiction over the Ethics in Government Act of 1978 and over legislation on all procurement practices. Examines the efficiency of government operations, including federal regulations and program management.

NONPROFIT

American Society for Public Administration, *1120 G St. N.W., #700 20005; (202) 393-7878. Fax, (202) 638-4952. Mary Hamilton, Executive Director.*
Web, www.aspanet.org

Membership: government administrators, public officials, educators, researchers, and others interested in public administration. Presents awards to distinguished professionals in the field; sponsors workshops and conferences; disseminates information about public administration. Promotes high ethical standards for public service.

Assn. of Government Accountants, *2208 Mount Vernon Ave., Alexandria, VA 22301; (703) 684-6931. Fax, (703) 548-9367. Charles W. Culkin Jr., Executive Director.*
Web, www.agacgfm.org

Membership: individuals engaged in government accounting, auditing, budgeting, and information systems.

Federally Employed Women, *1666 K St. N.W., #440 20006; (202) 898-0994. Fax, (202) 898-1535. Patricia M. Wolfe, President.*
Web, www.few.org

Membership: women and men who work for the federal government. Works to eliminate sex discrimination in government employment and to increase job opportunities for women; offers training program. Monitors legislation and regulations.

International City/County Management Assn., *777 N. Capitol St. N.E., #500 20002; (202) 289-4262. Fax, (202) 962-3500. Robert O'Neill, Executive Director.*
Web, www.icma.org

Membership: city and county managers, council of government directors, and municipal administrators.

Sponsors a professional development institute that offers courses and workshops in municipal administration; maintains an information service on local government management practices.

International Personnel Management Assn., *1617 Duke St., Alexandria, VA 22314; (703) 549-7100. Fax, (703) 684-0948. Neil Reichenberg, Executive Director. General e-mail, ipma@ipma-hr.org Web, www.ipma-hr.org*

Membership: personnel professionals from federal, state, and local governments. Provides information on training procedures, management techniques, and legislative developments on the federal, state, and local levels.

National Academy of Public Administration, *1100 New York Ave. N.W., #1090E 20005; (202) 347-3190. Fax, (202) 393-0993. Philip M. Burgess, President. General e-mail, academy@napawash.org Web, www.napawash.org*

Membership: scholars and administrators in public management. Offers assistance to federal, state, and local government agencies, public officials, foreign governments, foundations, and corporations on problems related to public administration.

National Assn. of Schools of Public Affairs and Administration, *1120 G St. N.W., #730 20005; (202) 628-8965. Fax, (202) 626-4978. Kenneth Tolo, Executive Director. General e-mail, office@naspaa.org Web, www.naspaa.org*

Membership: universities and government agencies interested in the advancement of education, research, and training in public management. Serves as a clearinghouse for information on public administration and public affairs programs in colleges and universities. Accredits master's degree programs.

National Women's Political Caucus, *1634 Eye St. N.W., #310 20006; (202) 785-1100. Fax, (202) 785-3605. Roselyn O'Connell, President. General e-mail, info@nwpc.org Web, www.nwpc.org*

Seeks to increase the number of women in policy-making positions in federal, state, and local government. Identifies, recruits, trains, and supports pro-choice women candidates for public office. Monitors agencies and provides names of qualified women for high- and mid-level appointments.

Women in Government Relations, *801 N. Fairfax St., #211, Alexandria, VA 22314-1757; (703) 299-8546. Fax, (703) 299-9233. Kimberly A. Korbel, Executive Director.*

General e-mail, info@wgr.org Web, www.wgr.org

Membership: professionals in business, trade associations, and government whose jobs involve governmental relations at the federal, state, or local level. Serves as a forum for exchange of information among its members.

🏛 STATE AND LOCAL GOVERNMENT

AGENCIES

Census Bureau *(Commerce Dept.),* **Governments Division,** *8905 Presidential Pkwy., Upper Marlboro, MD 20722 (mailing address: Washington Plaza II, #407, Washington, DC 20233-6800); (301) 763-1489. Fax, (301) 457-1423. Stephanie Brown, Chief (Acting). Web, www.census.gov*

Compiles annual *Federal Expenditures by State* (available to the public), which provides information on overall federal grants-in-aid expenditures to state and local governments; collects data on finances, employment, and structure of the public sector; and serves as national clearinghouse on state and local audit reports. Computer data obtainable from Data User Services, (301) 457-4100.

Executive Office of the President, *Intergovernmental Affairs, White House 20502; (202) 456-2896. Fax, (202) 456-7015. Ruben Barrales, Director.*

Serves as liaison with state, local, and tribal governments; provides information on administration programs and policies.

General Services Administration (GSA), *Federal Domestic Assistance Catalog Staff, 1800 F St. N.W., #4032 20405; (202) 208-1582. Fax, (202) 501-3341. Kathy Hospodar, Director, (202) 208-4052. Web, www.cfda.gov*

Prepares *Catalog of Federal Domestic Assistance* (published annually in June and updated in December), which lists all types of federal aid and explains types of assistance, eligibility requirements, application process, and suggestions for writing proposals. Copies may be ordered from the Superintendent of Documents, U.S. Government Printing Office 20402; (202) 512-1800 or toll-free, (866) 512-1800 or online at bookstore.gpo.gov. Also available on CD-ROM and floppy diskettes.

Housing and Urban Development Dept. (HUD), *Policy Development and Research, 451 7th St. S.W., #8100 20410-6000; (202) 708-1600. Fax, (202) 619-8000. Alberto Treviño, Assistant Secretary. Web, www.huduser.org*

Assesses urban economic development and the fiscal capacity of state and local governments.

Multistate Tax Commission, *444 N. Capitol St. N.W., #425 20001-1538; (202) 624-8699. Fax, (202) 624-8819. Dan R. Bucks, Executive Director.*
General e-mail, mtc@mtc.gov
Web, www.mtc.gov

Membership: state governments that have enacted the Multistate Tax Compact. Promotes fair, effective, and efficient state tax systems for interstate and international commerce; works to preserve state tax sovereignty. Encourages uniform state tax laws and regulations for multistate and multinational enterprises. Maintains three regional audit offices that monitor compliance with state tax laws and encourage uniformity in taxpayer treatment. Administers program to identify businesses that do not file tax returns with states.

Office of Management and Budget (OMB), *(Executive Office of the President), Federal Financial Management,* *New Executive Office Bldg., #6025 20503; (202) 395-3993. Fax, (202) 395-3952. Linda Springer, Controller.*
Web, www.whitehouse.gov/omb

Facilitates exchange of information on financial management standards, techniques, and processes among officers of state and local governments.

CONGRESS

General Accounting Office (GAO), *Education, Workforce, and Income Security,* *441 G St. N.W., #5928 20548; (202) 512-7215. Cynthia Fagnoni, Managing Director.*
Web, www.gao.gov

Independent, nonpartisan agency in the legislative branch. Responsible for intergovernmental relations activities. Reviews the effects of federal grants and regulations on state and local governments; works to reduce intergovernmental conflicts and costs; seeks to improve the allocation and targeting of federal funds to state and local governments through changes in federal funding formulas.

House Government Reform Committee, *Subcommittee on Criminal Justice, Drug Policy, and Human Resources,* *B373B RHOB 20515; (202) 225-2577. Fax, (202) 225-1154. Rep. Mark Souder, R-Ind., Chair; Christopher Donesa, Staff Director.*
Web, www.house.gov/reform

Jurisdiction over legislation dealing with the interrelationship among federal, state, and local governments.

Senate Finance Committee, *SD-219 20510; (202) 224-4515. Fax, (202) 228-0554. Sen. Charles E. Grassley, R-Iowa, Chair; Kolan L. Davis, Staff Director.*
Web, finance.senate.gov

Jurisdiction over legislation dealing with the interrelationship among federal, state, and local governments, including revenue sharing legislation. (Jurisdiction shared with Senate Governmental Affairs Committee.)

Senate Governmental Affairs Committee, *SD-340 20510; (202) 224-4751. Fax, (202) 228-3792. Sen. Susan Collins, R-Maine, Chair; Michael Bopp, Staff Director.*
Web, govt-aff.senate.gov

Jurisdiction over legislation dealing with the interrelationship among federal, state, and local governments, including revenue sharing legislation. (Jurisdiction shared with Senate Finance Committee.)

NONPROFIT

Academy for State and Local Government, *444 N. Capitol St. N.W., #345 20001; (202) 434-4850. Fax, (202) 434-4851. Vacant, Director.*

Offers technical assistance, training, and research to the Council of State Governments, International City/County Management Assn., National Assn. of Counties, National Conference of State Legislatures, National Governors' Assn., National League of Cities, and U.S. Conference of Mayors. Promotes cooperation among federal, state, and local governments; the private sector; and researchers. Interests include tax policy, finance, state and local relations, and homeland security. Works to improve state and local litigation in the Supreme Court. Promotes the exchange of information from overseas with state and local officials.

American Legislative Exchange Council, *1129 20th St. N.W., #500 20036; (202) 466-3800. Fax, (202) 466-3801. Duane Parde, Executive Director.*
General e-mail, info@alec.org
Web, www.alec.org

Bipartisan educational and research organization for state legislators. Conducts research and provides information and model state legislation on public policy issues. Supports the development of state policies to limit government, expand free markets, promote economic growth, and preserve individual liberty.

Assn. of Metropolitan Sewerage Agencies, *1816 Jefferson Pl. N.W. 20036; (202) 833-2672. Fax, (202) 833-4657. Ken Kirk, Executive Director.*
General e-mail, info@amsa-cleanwater.org
Web, www.amsa-cleanwater.org

Represents the interests of the country's publicly owned wastewater treatment works. Sponsors conferences. Monitors legislation and regulations.

Assn. of Public Treasurers of the United States and Canada, *1029 Vermont Ave. N.W., #710 20005; (202) 737-0660. Fax, (202) 737-0662. Stacey Crane, Executive Director.*
General e-mail, info@aptusc.org
Web, www.aptusc.org

Provides continuing education and certification programs. Monitors legislation and regulations.

Center for Policy Alternatives (CPA), *1875 Connecticut Ave. N.W., #710 20009-5728; (202) 387-6030. Fax, (202) 387-8529. Tim McFeeley, Executive Director.*
General e-mail, info@cfpa.org
Web, www.stateaction.org

Clearinghouse and research center that assists state legislators, state policy organizations, and state grassroots leaders in developing policy initiatives. Interests include state and local economic development and tax reform, governmental reform, health policy, leadership issues, voter registration, and women's rights issues. Provides technical assistance, leadership training, and network opportunities.

Coalition of Northeastern Governors (CONEG),
Policy Research Center, Inc., *400 N. Capitol St. N.W., #382 20001; (202) 624-8450. Fax, (202) 624-8463. Anne D. Stubbs, Executive Director.*
General e-mail, coneg@sso.org
Web, www.coneg.org

Membership: governors of eight northeastern states (Connecticut, Maine, Massachusetts, New Hampshire, New Jersey, New York, Rhode Island, and Vermont). Addresses common issues of concern such as energy, economic development, transportation, and the environment; serves as an information clearinghouse and liaison among member states and with the federal government.

Council of State Governments, *Washington Office, 444 N. Capitol St. N.W., #401 20001; (202) 624-5460. Fax, (202) 624-5452. James Brown, Director.*
General e-mail, csg-dc@csg.org
Web, www.csg.org

Membership: governing bodies of states, commonwealths, and territories. Promotes interstate, federal-state, and state-local cooperation; interests include education, transportation, human services, housing, natural resources, and economic development. Provides services to affiliates and associated organizations, including the National Assn. of State Treasurers, National Assn. of

Government Labor Officials, and other state administrative organizations in specific fields. Monitors legislation and executive policy. (Headquarters in Lexington, Ky.)

Government Finance Officers Assn., *Federal Liaison Center, Washington Office, 1750 K St. N.W., #350 20006; (202) 429-2750. Fax, (202) 429-2755. Susan Gaffney, Director.*
General e-mail, federalliaison@gfoa.org
Web, www.gfoa.org

Membership: state and local government finance managers. Offers training and publications in public financial management. Conducts research in public fiscal management, design and financing of government programs, and formulation and analysis of government fiscal policy. (Headquarters in Chicago, Ill.)

International Municipal Lawyers Assn., *1110 Vermont Ave. N.W., #200 20005; (202) 466-5424. Fax, (202) 785-0152. Henry W. Underhill Jr., General Counsel.*
General e-mail, info@imla.org
Web, www.imla.org

Membership: chief legal officers of cities and municipalities. Acts as a research service for members in all areas of municipal law; participates in litigation of municipal and constitutional law issues.

National Assn. of Bond Lawyers, *Governmental Affairs, Washington Office, 601 13th St., #800-S 20005-3875; (202) 682-1498. Fax, (202) 637-0217. William L. Larsen, Director.*
Web, www.nabl.org

Membership: municipal finance lawyers. Provides members with information on laws relating to the borrowing of money by states and municipalities and to the issuance of state and local government bonds. Monitors legislation and regulations. (Headquarters in Chicago, Ill.)

National Assn. of Counties (NACo), *440 1st St. N.W., 8th Floor 20001-2080; (202) 393-6226. Fax, (202) 942-4281. Larry Naake, Executive Director.*
Web, www.naco.org

Membership: county officials. Conducts research, provides information, and offers technical assistance on issues affecting counties. Monitors legislation and regulations.

National Assn. of Regional Councils, *1666 Connecticut Ave. N.W., #300 20009; (202) 986-1032. Fax, (202) 986-1038. Robert Sokolowski, Executive Director.*
Web, www.narc.org

Membership: regional councils of local governments and metropolitan planning councils. Works to improve local governments' ability to deal with common public needs, address regional issues, and reduce public expense. Interests include housing, urban and rural planning, transportation, the environment, workforce development, economic and community development, and aging.

National Assn. of State Budget Officers,
444 N. Capitol St. N.W., #642 20001-1501; (202) 624-5382. Fax, (202) 624-7745. Scott Pattison, Executive Director.
Web, www.nasbo.org
Membership: state budget and financial officers. Publishes research reports on budget-related issues. (Affiliate of the National Governors' Assn.)

National Assn. of Towns and Townships,
444 N. Capitol St. N.W., #397 20001-1202; (202) 624-3550. Fax, (202) 624-3554. Thomas Halicki, Executive Director.
General e-mail, natat@sso.org
Web, www.natat.org
Membership: towns, townships, small communities, and others interested in supporting small town government. Provides local government officials from small jurisdictions with technical assistance, educational services, and public policy support; conducts research and coordinates training for local government officials nationwide. Holds an annual conference. (Affiliated with National Center for Small Communities.)

National Black Caucus of State Legislators,
444 N. Capitol St. N.W., #622 20001; (202) 624-5457. Fax, (202) 508-3826. Khalil Abdulah, Executive Director.
General e-mail, staff@nbcsl.com
Web, www.nbcsl.com
Membership: African American state legislators. Promotes effective leadership among African American state legislators; serves as an information network and clearinghouse for members.

National Center for Small Communities,
444 N. Capitol St. N.W., #397 20001-1202; (202) 624-3550. Fax, (202) 624-3554. Thomas Halicki, Executive Director.
General e-mail, ncsc@sso.org
Web, www.natat.org/ncsc
Provides elected officials of small communities with technical assistance and information. Interests include job growth, leadership skills, financial resources, and natural resource preservation. (Affiliated with National Assn. of Towns and Townships.)

National Conference of State Legislatures, Washington Office,
444 N. Capitol St. N.W., #515 20001; (202) 624-5400. Fax, (202) 737-1069. Carl Tubbesing, Deputy Executive Director.
General e-mail, info@ncsl.org
Web, www.ncsl.org
Coordinates and represents state legislatures at the federal level; conducts research, produces videos, and publishes reports in areas of interest to state legislatures; conducts an information exchange program on intergovernmental relations; sponsors seminars for state legislators and their staffs. Monitors legislation and regulations. (Headquarters in Denver, Colo.)

National Governors Assn. (NGA),
444 N. Capitol St. N.W., #267 20001; (202) 624-5300. Fax, (202) 624-5313. Raymond C. Scheppach, Executive Director. Press, (202) 624-5364.
Web, www.nga.org
Membership: governors of states, commonwealths, and territories. Provides members with policy and technical assistance. Makes policy recommendations to Congress and the president in community and economic development; education; international trade and foreign relations; energy and the environment; health care and welfare reform; agriculture; transportation, commerce, and technology; communications; criminal justice; public safety; and workforce development.

National League of Cities,
1301 Pennsylvania Ave. N.W., #550 20004-1763; (202) 626-3000. Fax, (202) 626-3043. Donald J. Borut, Executive Director. Press, (202) 626-3158. Public Affairs, (202) 626-3120.
Web, www.nlc.org
Membership: cities and state municipal leagues. Provides city leaders with training, technical assistance, and publications; investigates needs of local governments in implementing federal programs that affect cities. Holds an annual conference; conducts research; sponsors awards. (Affiliates include National Black Caucus of Local Elected Officials.)

Public Risk Management Assn.,
1815 N. Fort Myer Dr., #1020, Arlington, VA 22209; (703) 528-7701. Fax, (703) 528-7966. Jim Hirt, Executive Director.
General e-mail, info@primacentral.org
Web, www.primacentral.org
Membership: state and local government risk management practitioners, including benefits and insurance managers. Develops and teaches cost-effective management techniques for handling public liability issues; promotes professional development of its members. Gathers and disseminates information about risk management to public and private sectors.

Public Technology, Inc., *1301 Pennsylvania Ave. N.W., #800 20004; (202) 626-2400. Fax, (202) 626-2498. Costis Toregas, President. Information, (800) 852-4934. Library, (202) 626-2456. Press, (202) 626-2412.*

General e-mail, press@pti.org

Web, www.pti.org

Cooperative research, development, and technology-transfer organization of cities and counties in North America. Assists local governments in increasing efficiency, reducing costs, improving services, and developing public enterprise programs to help local officials create revenues and serve citizens. Participates in international conferences.

Southern Governors' Assn., *444 N. Capitol St. N.W., #200 20001; (202) 624-5897. Fax, (202) 624-7797. Elizabeth G. Schneider, Executive Director.*

General e-mail, sga@sso.org

Web, www.southerngovernors.org

Membership: governors of sixteen southern states, plus the territories of Puerto Rico and the U.S. Virgin Islands. Provides a regional, bipartisan forum for governors to help formulate and implement national policy; works to enhance the region's competitiveness nationally and internationally.

U.S. Conference of Mayors, *1620 Eye St. N.W., #400 20006; (202) 293-7330. Fax, (202) 293-2352. J. Thomas Cochran, Executive Director.*

General e-mail, uscm@cais.com

Web, www.usmayors.org/uscm

Membership: mayors of cities with populations of 30,000 or more. Promotes city-federal cooperation; publishes reports and conducts meetings on federal programs, policies, and initiatives that affect urban and suburban interests. Serves as a clearinghouse for information on urban and suburban problems.

Western Governors' Assn., *Washington Office, 400 N. Capitol St. N.W., #388 20001; (202) 624-5402. Fax, (202) 624-7707. Kevin M. Moran, Director.*

Web, www.westgov.org

Independent, nonpartisan organization of governors from eighteen western states, two Pacific territories, and one commonwealth. Identifies and addresses key policy and governance issues in natural resources, the environment, human services, economic development, international relations, and public management. (Headquarters in Denver, Colo.)

Women In Government, *2600 Virginia Ave. N.W., #709 20037; (202) 333-0825. Fax, (202) 333-0875. Joy Newton, Executive Director.*

LOCAL GOVERNMENT IN THE WASHINGTON AREA

DISTRICT OF COLUMBIA

Executive Office of the Mayor
Anthony A. Williams, Mayor
John A. Wilson Building
1350 Pennsylvania Ave. N.W. 20004; (202) 727-2980; fax, (202) 727-9561
Web, www.dc.gov

MARYLAND

Montgomery County
Douglas M. Duncan, County Executive
101 Monroe St., 2nd Floor, Rockville, MD 20850; (240) 777-2500; fax, (240) 777-2517
Web, www.montgomerycountymd.gov

Prince George's County
Jack B. Johnson, County Executive
14741 Gov. Oden Bowie Dr., #5032, Upper Marlboro, MD 20772; (301) 952-4131; fax, (301) 952-3784
Web, www.co.pg.md.us

VIRGINIA

City of Alexandria
Kerry J. Donley, Mayor
301 King St., City Hall, Alexandria, VA 22314; (703) 838-4500; fax, (703) 838-6433
Web, www.ci.alexandria.va.us

Arlington County
Ron Carlee, County Manager
2100 Clarendon Blvd., #300, Arlington, VA 22201; (703) 228-3120; fax, (703) 228-7430
Web, www.co.arlington.va.us

Fairfax County
Anthony H. Griffin, County Executive
12000 Government Center Pkwy., #552, Fairfax, VA 22035; (703) 324-2531; fax, (703) 324-3956
Web, www.co.fairfax.va.us

City of Falls Church
Daniel E. McKeever, City Manager
300 Park Ave., Falls Church, VA 22046; (703) 248-5004; fax, (703) 248-5146
Web, www.ci.falls-church.va.us

General e-mail, wig@womeningovernment.org

Web, www.womeningovernment.org

Seeks to enhance the leadership role of women policymakers by providing issue education and leadership training. Sponsors seminars and conducts educational research.

Washington Area

CONGRESS

House Appropriations Committee, *Subcommittee on the District of Columbia,* H147 CAP 20515; (202) 226-7500. *Rep. Rodney Frelinghuysen, R-N.J., Chair; Carol Murphy, Staff Director.*
Web, www.house.gov/appropriations

Jurisdiction over legislation to appropriate funds for the District of Columbia.

House Government Reform Committee,
2157 RHOB 20515; (202) 225-5074. Fax, (202) 225-3974. Rep. Thomas M. Davis III, R-Va., Chair; Peter Sirh, Staff Director.
Web, www.house.gov/reform

Jurisdiction over all measures relating to the municipal affairs of the District of Columbia, other than appropriations.

Senate Appropriations Committee, *Subcommittee on the District of Columbia,* S128 CAP 20510; (202) 224-7643. *Sen. Mike DeWine, R-Ohio, Chair; Mary Dietrich, Clerk.*
Web, appropriations.senate.gov

Jurisdiction over legislation to appropriate funds for the District of Columbia and St. Elizabeth's Hospital.

Senate Governmental Affairs Committee, *Subcommittee on Oversight Government Management, the Federal Workforce, and the District of Columbia,* SH-601 20510; (202) 224-3682. *Sen. George V. Voinovich, R-Ohio, Chair; Andrew Richardson, Staff Director.*

General e-mail, ogm@govt-aff.senate.gov
Web, govt-aff.senate.gov

Jurisdiction over all measures relating to the municipal affairs of the District of Columbia, other than appropriations.

NONPROFIT

Metropolitan Washington Council of Governments, *777 N. Capitol St. N.E., #300 20002-4239; (202) 962-3200. Fax, (202) 962-3201. David Robertson, Executive Director (Interim). TTY, (202) 962-3213.*
General e-mail, infocntr@mwcog.org
Web, www.mwcog.org

Membership: local governments in the Washington area, plus members of the Maryland and Virginia legislatures and the U.S. Congress. Analyzes and develops regional responses to issues such as the environment, affordable housing, economic development, population growth, human and social services, public safety, and transportation.

Washington Convention Center Authority, *900 9th St. N.W. 20001; (202) 789-1600. Lewis H. Dawley III, Chief Executive Officer. Information, (800) 368-9000.*
Web, www.dcconvention.com

Promotes national and international conventions and trade shows; hosts local events; fosters redevelopment of downtown Washington.

11 Health

✚ GENERAL POLICY

AGENCIES

Agency for Health Care Research and Quality
(Health and Human Services Dept.), 2101 E. Jefferson St., #600, Rockville, MD 20852; (301) 594-6662. Fax, (301) 594-2168. Dr. Carolyn M. Clancy, Director. TTY, (888) 586-6340.
General e-mail, info@ahrq.gov
Web, www.ahrq.gov

Works to enhance the quality, appropriateness, and effectiveness of health care services and to improve access to services. Promotes improvements in clinical practices and in organizing, financing, and delivering health care services. Conducts and supports research, demonstration projects, evaluations, and training; disseminates information on a wide range of activities.

Centers for Disease Control and Prevention
(Health and Human Services Dept.), Washington Office, 200 Independence Ave. S.W., HHH Bldg., #746-G 20201-0004; (202) 690-8598. Fax, (202) 690-7519. Donald E. Shriber, Associate Director.
Web, www.cdc.gov/washington

Surveys national and international disease trends, epidemics, and environmental health problems; administers block grants to states for preventive health services; collects national health statistics; promotes national health education program; administers foreign quarantine program and occupational safety and health programs; assists state and local health departments and programs with control of sexually transmitted diseases, treatment of tuberculosis, childhood immunization, and health promotion regarding chronic diseases and injury. (Headquarters in Atlanta, Ga.: 1600 Clifton Rd. N.E. 30333. Public inquiries, [404] 639-3534.)

Food and Drug Administration (FDA), *(Health and Human Services Dept.),* 5600 Fishers Lane, #1471, Rockville, MD 20857; (301) 827-2410. Fax, (301) 443-3100. Dr. Mark B. McClellan, Commissioner. Information, (301) 827-6250. Press, (301) 827-6242.
Web, www.fda.gov

Conducts research and develops standards on the composition, quality, and safety of drugs, cosmetics, medical devices, radiation-emitting products, foods, food additives, and infant formulas, including imports. Develops labeling and packaging standards; conducts inspections of manufacturers; issues orders to companies to recall and/or cease selling or producing hazardous products; enforces rulings and recommends action to Justice Dept. when necessary. Library open to the public.

Food and Drug Administration (FDA), *(Health and Human Services Dept.), International Programs,* 5600 Fishers Lane, #15A55, Rockville, MD 20857; (301) 827-4553. Fax, (301) 827-1451. Melinda K. Plaisier, Assistant Commissioner.
Web, www.fda.gov/oia/homepage.htm

Serves as the principal FDA liaison with foreign counterpart agencies, international organizations, and U.S. government agencies on international issues. Coordinates agency involvement in international trade, harmonization, and technical assistance; administers programs for foreign scientists and other international visitors.

Food and Drug Administration (FDA), *(Health and Human Services Dept.), Regulatory Affairs,* 5600 Fishers Lane, #1490, #HFCO1, Rockville, MD 20857; (301) 827-3101. Fax, (301) 443-6591. John M. Taylor III, Associate Commissioner.
Web, www.fda.gov

Directs and coordinates the FDA's compliance activities; manages field offices; advises FDA commissioner on domestic and international regulatory policies.

Health and Human Services Dept. (HHS), *National Committee on Vital and Health Statistics,* 3311 Toledo Rd., #2402, Hyattsville, MD 20782; (301) 458-4200. Fax, (301) 458-4022. Marjorie S. Greenberg, Executive Secretary.
Web, www.ncvhs.hhs.gov

Advises the secretary on health problem statistics; works with agencies and committees of other nations on health problems of mutual concern.

Health and Human Services Dept. (HHS), *Planning and Evaluation,* 200 Independence Ave. S.W., #415F 20201; (202) 690-7858. Fax, (202) 690-7383. William Raub, Assistant Secretary (Acting).
Web, aspe.dhhs.gov

Provides policy advice and makes recommendations to the secretary on the full range of department planning, including Medicare, Medicaid, health care services, human resources, health care facilities development and financing, biomedical research, and health care planning.

Health and Human Services Dept. (HHS), *Public Health Emergency Preparedness,* 200 Independence Ave. S.W., #636-G 20201; (202) 401-4862. Fax, (202) 690-7412. Jerome M. Hauer, Assistant Secretary (Acting).
Web, www.hhs.gov/ophp

Directs activities of HHS relating to the protection of the civilian population from acts of bioterrorism and other public health emergencies. Serves as the secretary's

HEALTH AND HUMAN SERVICES DEPARTMENT

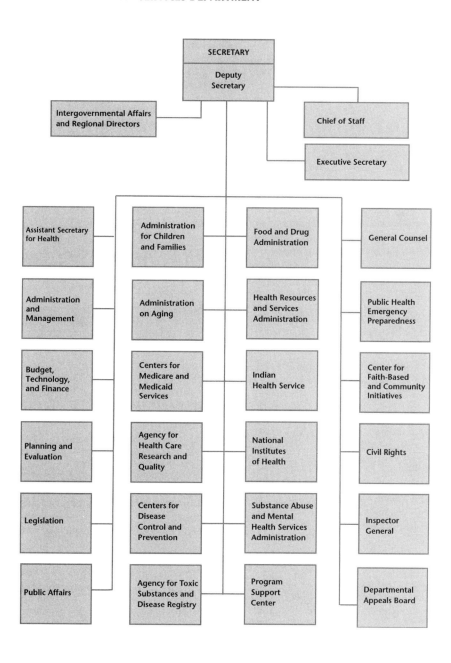

principal adviser on matters relating to bioterrorism and public health emergencies.

Health Resources and Services Administration *(Health and Human Services Dept.),* 5600 Fishers Lane, #1405, Rockville, MD 20857; (301) 443-2216. Fax, (301) 443-1246. Betty James Duke, Administrator. Information, (301) 443-3376. Press, (301) 443-3376.
Web, www.hrsa.gov

Administers federal health service programs related to access, quality, equity, and cost of health care. Supports state and community efforts to deliver care to underserved areas and groups with special health needs.

Health Resources and Services Administration *(Health and Human Services Dept.), Rural Health Policy,* 5600 Fishers Lane, #9A55, Rockville, MD 20857; (301) 443-0835. Fax, (301) 443-2803. Marsha K. Brand, Director.
Web, www.ruralhealth.hrsa.gov

Works with federal agencies, states, and the private sector to develop solutions to health care problems in rural communities. Administers grants to rural communities and supports rural health services research. Studies the effects of Medicare and Medicaid programs on rural access to health care. Provides the National Advisory Committee on Rural Health with staff support.

National Center for Health Statistics *(Centers for Disease Control and Prevention),* 3311 Toledo Rd., #7209, Hyattsville, MD 20782; (301) 458-4500. Fax, (301) 458-4020. Edward J. Sondik, Director. Information, (301) 458-4636.
Web, www.cdc.gov/nchs

Compiles, analyzes, and disseminates national statistics on population health characteristics, health facilities and human resources, health costs and expenditures, and health hazards. Interests include international health statistics.

National Clearinghouse for Primary Care Information *(Health and Human Services Dept.),* 2070 Chain Bridge Rd., #450, Vienna, VA 22182; (703) 821-8955. Fax, (703) 821-2098. Judy A. Cramer, Project Director. Information, (888) 275-4772.
Web, www.circlesolutions.com

Supports the planning, development, and delivery of ambulatory health care to urban and rural areas in need of medical personnel and services; gives information to health care providers, administrators, and other interested persons. (Clearinghouse managed by Circle Solutions, Inc.)

National Institute for Occupational Safety and Health (NIOSH), *(Centers for Disease Control and Prevention),* 200 Independence Ave. S.W. 20201; (202) 401-6997. Fax, (202) 260-4464. Dr. John Howard, Director. Information, (800) 356-4674.
Web, www.cdc.gov/niosh

Supports and conducts research on occupational safety and health issues; provides technical assistance and training; organizes international conferences and symposia; develops recommendations for the Labor Dept. Operates occupational safety and health bibliographic databases; publishes documents on occupational safety and health.

National Institutes of Health (NIH), *(Health and Human Services Dept.),* 1 Center Dr., Bldg. 1, #126, MSC-0148, Bethesda, MD 20892-0148; (301) 496-2433. Fax, (301) 402-2700. Elias A. Zerhouni, Director. Press, (301) 496-4461.
Web, www.nih.gov

Supports and conducts biomedical research into the causes and prevention of diseases and furnishes information to health professionals and the public. Comprises research institutes *(see Health Topics: Research and Advocacy, this chapter),* and other components (the National Library of Medicine, the Warren Grant Magnuson Clinical Center, the National Center for Research Resources, the John E. Fogarty International Center, the Division of Research Grants, and the Division of Computer Research and Technology). All institutes are located in Bethesda except the National Institute of Environmental Health Sciences, P.O. Box 12233, Research Triangle Park, NC 27709.

Public Health and Science *(Health and Human Services Dept.),* 5600 Fishers Lane, #18-66, Rockville, MD 20857; (301) 443-4000. Fax, (301) 443-3574. Richard H. Carmona, Surgeon General.
Web, www.surgeongeneral.gov

Directs activities of the Public Health Service. Serves as the secretary's principal adviser on health concerns; exercises specialized responsibilities in various health areas, including population affairs and international health.

Public Health and Science *(Health and Human Services Dept.), Disease Prevention and Health Promotion,* 200 Independence Ave. S.W., #738G 20201; (202) 401-6295. Fax, (202) 205-9478. Elizabeth Majestic, Director (Acting). Publications, (301) 468-5960.
Web, www.odphp.osophs.dhhs.gov

Develops national policies for disease prevention, clinical preventive services, and health promotion; assists the private sector and agencies with disease prevention, clinical preventive services, and health promotion activities.

Public Health and Science *(Health and Human Services Dept.), National Health Information Center,* *P.O. Box 1133 20013-1133; (301) 565-4167. Fax, (301) 984-4256. Sarah Baron, Project Director. Information, (800) 336-4797.*
General e-mail, info@nhic.org
Web, www.health.gov/nhic and www.healthfinder.gov

A project of the office of Disease Prevention and Health Promotion; provides referrals on health topics and resources.

Public Health and Science *(Health and Human Services Dept.), Surgeon General, 5600 Fishers Lane, #18-66, Rockville, MD 20857; (301) 443-4000. Fax, (301) 443-3574. Richard H. Carmona, Surgeon General.*
Web, www.surgeongeneral.gov

Advises the public on smoking, AIDS, immunization, diet, nutrition, disease prevention, and other general health issues, including responses to bioterrorism. Oversees activities of all members of the Public Health Service Commissioned Corps.

CONGRESS

General Accounting Office (GAO), *Education, Workforce, and Income Security, 441 G St. N.W., #5928 20548; (202) 512-7215. Cynthia Fagnoni, Managing Director.*
Web, www.gao.gov

Independent, nonpartisan agency in the legislative branch. Audits all federal government health programs, including those administered by the departments of Defense, Health and Human Services, and Veterans Affairs.

House Appropriations Committee, *Subcommittee on Agriculture, Rural Development, FDA, and Related Agencies, 2362 RHOB 20515; (202) 225-2638. Rep. Henry Bonilla, R-Texas, Chair; Hank Moore, Clerk.*
Web, www.house.gov/appropriations

Jurisdiction over legislation to appropriate funds for the Food and Drug Administration, Food Safety and Inspection Service, and Food and Consumer Service.

House Appropriations Committee, *Subcommittee on Labor, Health and Human Services, Education, and Related Agencies, 2358 RHOB 20515; (202) 225-3508. Fax, (202) 225-3509. Rep. Ralph Regula, R-Ohio, Chair; Craig Higgins, Staff Director.*
Web, www.house.gov/appropriations

Jurisdiction over legislation to appropriate funds for health agencies in the Health and Human Services Dept. (excluding the Food and Drug Administration and native American health and health facilities construction activities); the National Commission on Acquired Immune Deficiency Syndrome; and the National Council on Disability.

House Energy and Commerce Committee, *Subcommittee on Health, 2125 RHOB 20515; (202) 225-2927. Fax, (202) 225-1919. Rep. Michael Bilirakis, R-Fla., Chair; David V. Marventano, Staff Director.*
General e-mail, commerce@mail.house.gov
Web, energycommerce.house.gov

Jurisdiction over most health legislation, including Medicaid, national health insurance proposals (jurisdiction shared with the House Ways and Means Committee), public health and quarantine, alcohol abuse, drug abuse including medical and psychological rehabilitation programs for drug abusers, dental health, medical devices, long-term and nursing home care, orphan drugs, preventive health and emergency medical care, family planning, population research, mental health, and prenatal, maternal, and child health care.

House Government Reform Committee, *Subcommittee on Criminal Justice, Drug Policy, and Human Resources, B373B RHOB 20515; (202) 225-2577. Fax, (202) 225-1154. Rep. Mark Souder, R-Ind., Chair; Christopher Donesa, Staff Director.*
Web, www.house.gov/reform

Oversees operations of the Health and Human Services Dept.

House Ways and Means Committee, *Subcommittee on Health, 1136 LHOB 20515; (202) 225-3943. Fax, (202) 226-1765. Rep. Nancy L. Johnson, R-Conn., Chair; John E. McManus, Staff Director.*
Web, waysandmeans.house.gov

Jurisdiction over legislation dealing with health care research and delivery programs supported by tax revenues, including Medicare, and proposals to establish a national health insurance system (jurisdiction shared with the House Commerce Committee).

Senate Appropriations Committee, *Subcommittee on Agriculture, Rural Development, and Related Agencies, SD-188 20510; (202) 224-5270. Fax, (202) 228-2320. Sen. Robert F. Bennett, R-Utah, Chair; Pat Raymond, Clerk.*
Web, appropriations.senate.gov

Jurisdiction over legislation to appropriate funds for the Food and Drug Administration, Food Safety and Inspection Service, and Food and Consumer Service.

Senate Appropriations Committee, Subcommittee on Labor, Health and Human Services, Education, and Related Agencies, SD-184 20510; (202) 224-3471. Fax, (202) 224-8553. Sen. Arlen Specter, R-Pa., Chair; Bettilou Taylor, Clerk.

Web, appropriations.senate.gov

Jurisdiction over legislation to appropriate funds for health agencies in the Health and Human Services Dept. (excluding the Food and Drug Administration and native American health programs).

Senate Finance Committee, SD-219 20510; (202) 224-4515. Fax, (202) 228-0554. Sen. Charles E. Grassley, R-Iowa, Chair; Kolan L. Davis, Staff Director.

Web, finance.senate.gov

Jurisdiction over health programs supported by tax revenues, including Medicaid and Medicare.

Senate Health, Education, Labor, and Pensions Committee, SD-428 20510; (202) 224-5375. Fax, (202) 228-5044. Sen. Judd Gregg, R-N.H., Chair; Sharon Soderstrom, Staff Director. TTY, (202) 224-1975.

Web, health.senate.gov

Jurisdiction over most health legislation, including insurance, dental health, emergency medical care, mental health, medical devices, public health and quarantine, family planning, population research, prenatal, and some maternal and child health care legislation, including the dangers of lead-based paint and sudden infant death syndrome. Jurisdiction over legislation on radiation hazards of consumer products and machines used in industry. Jurisdiction over alcohol and drug abuse legislation. Oversees operations of the Health and Human Services Dept.

Senate Judiciary Committee, SD-224 20510; (202) 224-5225. Fax, (202) 224-9102. Sen. Orrin G. Hatch, R-Utah, Chair; Makan Delrahim, Chief Counsel.

Web, judiciary.senate.gov

Jurisdiction over legislation on drug abuse, which includes regulatory aspects of federal drug abuse programs and criminal justice system rehabilitation programs for juvenile drug abusers.

INTERNATIONAL ORGANIZATIONS

International Bank for Reconstruction and Development (World Bank), Human Development Network, 1818 H St. N.W., #G8 801 20433; (202) 473-3437. Fax, (202) 522-3235. Vacant, Vice President.

Web, www.worldbank.org

Provides member countries with support in education, health and nutrition, and population and social protection. (Works in conjunction with regional World Bank offices.)

Pan American Health Organization, 525 23rd St. N.W. 20037; (202) 974-3000. Fax, (202) 974-3608. Dr. Mirta Roses Periago, Director. Information, (202) 974-3458. Library, (202) 974-3305.

Web, www.paho.org

Regional office for the Americas of the World Health Organization, headquartered in Geneva, Switzerland. Works to extend health services to underserved populations of its member countries and to control or eradicate communicable diseases; promotes cooperation among governments to solve public health problems. Library open to the public by appointment.

World Federation of Public Health Assns., 800 Eye St. N.W. 20001-3710; (202) 777-2487. Fax, (202) 777-2534. Dr. Alan Jones, Executive Secretary.

General e-mail, comments@apha.org

Web, www.apha.org

International health organization composed of national public health associations whose membership includes health professionals and laypersons interested in improving community health. Sponsors triennial international congress.

NONPROFIT

American Clinical Laboratory Assn., 1250 H St. N.W., #880 20005; (202) 637-9466. Fax, (202) 637-2050. Dr. David N. Sundwall, President.

Web, www.clinical-labs.org

Membership: laboratories and laboratory service companies. Advocates laws and regulations that recognize the role of laboratory services in cost-effective health care. Works to ensure the confidentiality of patient test results. Provides education, information, and research materials to members.

American Public Health Assn., 800 Eye St. N.W. 20001; (202) 777-2742. Fax, (202) 777-2534. Dr. Georges Benjamin, Executive Director.

General e-mail, comments@apha.org

Web, www.apha.org

Membership: health care professionals, educators, environmentalists, social workers, industrial hygienists, and individuals. Interests include all aspects of health care and education. Establishes standards for scientific procedures in public health; conducts research on the causes and origin of communicable diseases. Produces data on the number of women and minority workers in public health and on their health status.

Assn. of State and Territorial Health Officials, 1275 K St. N.W., #800 20005-4006; (202) 371-9090. Fax, (202) 371-9797. George E. Hardy Jr., Executive Director.

Web, www.astho.org

Membership: executive officers of state and territorial health departments. Serves as legislative review agency and information source for members.

The Brookings Institution, *Economic Studies Program,* *1775 Massachusetts Ave. N.W. 20036-2188; (202) 797-6111. Fax, (202) 797-6181. Robert E. Litan, Director. Information, (202) 797-6302.*
Web, www.brookings.edu

Studies federal health care issues and health programs, including Medicare, Medicaid, and long-term care.

Center for Patient Advocacy, *1350 Beverly Rd., #108, McLean, VA 22101; (703) 748-0400. Fax, (703) 748-0402. Terre McFillen Hall, Executive Director. Information, (800) 846-7444.*
General e-mail, advocate@patientadvocacy.org
Web, www.patientadvocacy.org

Represents the interests of patients nationwide. Dedicated to ensuring that patients have timely access to state-of-the-art health care.

Forum for State Health Policy Leadership, *444 N. Capitol St. N.W., #515 20001; (202) 624-5400. Fax, (202) 737-1069. Richard E. Merritt, Director.*
Web, www.ncsl.org

Researches state health laws and programs. Provides health policymakers, administrators, and others with information on state health programs and policies. (Affiliated with the National Conference of State Legislatures.)

Global Health Council, *1701 K St. N.W., #600 20006; (202) 833-5900. Fax, (202) 833-0075. Dr. Nils Daulaire, President.*
General e-mail, ghc@globalhealth.org
Web, www.globalhealth.org

Membership: health care professionals, NGOs, foundations, corporations, government agencies, and academic institutions. Works to promote better health around the world by assisting those who work for improvement and equity in global health to secure the information and resources they need to work effectively.

Grantmakers in Health, *1100 Connecticut Ave. N.W., 12th Floor 20036; (202) 452-8331. Fax, (202) 452-8340. Lauren LeRoy, President.*
Web, www.gih.org

Seeks to increase the capacity of private sector grantmakers to enhance public health. Fosters information exchange among grantmakers. Publications include a bulletin on current news in health and human services and the *Directory of Health Philanthropy.*

Health Education Foundation, *2600 Virginia Ave. N.W., #502 20037; (202) 338-3501. Fax, (202) 965-6520. Dr. Morris E. Chafetz, President.*
General e-mail, hefmona@erols.com

Develops health information programs. Promotes responsible drinking behavior.

Healthcare Leadership Council, *900 17th St. N.W., #600 20006; (202) 452-8700. Fax, (202) 296-9561. Mary R. Grealy, President.*
Web, www.hlc.org

Membership: health care leaders who examine major health issues, including access and affordability. Works to implement new public policies.

Institute for Health Care Research and Policy, *2233 Wisconsin Ave. N.W., #525 20007; (202) 687-0880. Fax, (202) 687-3110. Harriet Komisar, Co-Director; Karen Pollitz, Co-Director.*
Web, www.georgetown.edu/research/ihcrp

Research branch of Georgetown University. Interests include quality of care, cost effectiveness, outcomes research, structure and impact of managed care, health privacy, and access to care.

National Assn. of Counties (NACo), *Health, 440 1st St. N.W., 8th Floor 20001-2028; (202) 393-6226. Fax, (202) 942-4281. Frank Kolb, Associate Legislative Director.*
Web, www.naco.org

Promotes federal understanding of county government's role in providing, funding, and overseeing health care services at the local level. Interests include indigent health care, Medicaid and Medicare, prevention of and services for HIV infection and AIDS, long-term care, mental health, maternal and child health, and traditional public health programs conducted by local health departments.

National Assn. of County and City Health Officials, *1100 17th St. N.W., 2nd Floor 20036; (202) 783-5550. Fax, (202) 783-1583. Patrick M. Libbey, Executive Director.*
General e-mail, info@naccho.org
Web, www.naccho.org

Represents local health departments. Promotes partnership among local, state, and federal health agencies. Works to improve the capacity of local health departments to assess health needs, develop public health policies, and ensure delivery of community services. Submits health policy proposals to the federal government.

National Governors Assn. (NGA), *Health Policy Studies,* 444 N. Capitol St. N.W., #267 20001; (202) 624-5343. Fax, (202) 624-5313. Joan Henneberry, Director. Information, (202) 624-5300.

Web, www.nga.org

Provides technical assistance regarding the Title 21 Program, state oversight of managed care, public/private efforts to improve health care quality, and long-term care services.

National Health Council, *1730 M St. N.W., #500 20036-4505; (202) 785-3910. Fax, (202) 785-5923. Myrl Weinberg, President.*

General e-mail, info@nhcouncil.org

Web, www.nhcouncil.org

Membership: voluntary health agencies, associations, and business, insurance, and government groups interested in health. Conducts research on health and health-related issues; serves as an information clearinghouse on health careers. Monitors legislation and regulations.

National Health Policy Forum, *2131 K St. N.W., #500 20037; (202) 872-1390. Fax, (202) 862-9837. Judith Miller Jones, Director.*

General e-mail, nhpf@gwu.edu

Web, www.nhpf.org

Nonpartisan policy analysis and research organization that provides executive branch and congressional staff with information on financing and delivery of health care services. Affiliated with George Washington University.

National Vaccine Information Center, *421-E Church St., Vienna, VA 22180; (703) 938-3783. Fax, (703) 938-5768. Barbara Loe Fisher, President. Information, (800) 909-SHOT.*

Web, www.909shot.com

Educates the public and provides research on vaccination safety procedures and effectiveness. Supports reform of the vaccination system; provides assistance to parents of children who have experienced vaccine reactions; and publishes information on diseases and vaccines. Monitors legislation and regulations.

Partnership for Prevention, *1015 18th St. N.W., #200 20036; (202) 833-0009. Fax, (202) 833-0113. John M. Clymer, President.*

Web, www.prevent.org

Seeks to make prevention a priority in national health policy and practice. Coordinates the prevention-oriented efforts of federal health agencies, corporations, states, and nonprofit organizations in order to achieve the Healthy People 2010 national prevention goals.

Public Citizen, *Health Research Group,* 1600 20th St. N.W. 20009; (202) 588-1000. Fax, (202) 588-7796. Dr. Sidney M. Wolfe, Director.

Web, www.citizen.org

Citizens' interest group that conducts policy-oriented research on health care issues. Interests include hospital quality and costs, doctors' fees, physician discipline and malpractice, state administration of Medicare programs, workplace safety and health, unnecessary surgery, comprehensive health planning, dangerous drugs, carcinogens, and medical devices. Favors a single-payer (Canadian-style), comprehensive health program.

Rand Corporation, *Health Program, Washington Office,* 1200 S. Hayes St., Arlington, VA 22202-5050; (703) 413-1100. Fax, (703) 413-8111. Bruce Hoffman, Director.

Web, www.rand.org

Research organization that assesses health issues, including alternative reimbursement schemes for health care. Monitors national and international trends. (Headquarters in Santa Monica, Calif.)

Regulatory Affairs Professionals Society, *11300 Rockville Pike, #1000, Rockville, MD 20852; (301) 770-2920. Fax, (301) 770-2924. Sherry Keramidas, Executive Director.*

General e-mail, raps@raps.org

Web, www.raps.org

Membership: regulatory professionals in the pharmaceutical, medical device, biologic, biotechnicology, and related industries. Fosters cooperation among health care regulatory professionals; sponsors seminars. Monitors legislation and regulations.

Robert Wood Johnson Foundation, *Center for Studying Health System Change,* 600 Maryland Ave. S.W., #550 20024-2512; (202) 484-5261. Fax, (202) 484-9258. Paul B. Ginsburg, President.

General e-mail, hscinfo@hschange.org

Web, www.hschange.org

Studies change in the health care system; conducts and monitors research; disseminates information to policymakers. Interests include access to health care, insurance coverage, and managed care. Sponsors workshops and conferences. (Foundation headquarters in Princeton, N.J.)

Health Insurance, Managed Care

AGENCIES

Centers for Medicare and Medicaid Services (CMS), *(Health and Human Services Dept.), Medicare*

Management, 7500 Security Blvd., C5-17-14, Baltimore, MD 21244; (410) 786-4164. Fax, (410) 786-0192. Thomas Grissom, Director.

Web, www.cms.hhs.gov

Sets national policies for federally qualified health maintenance organizations (HMOs) and competitive medical plans; monitors HMO compliance with federal regulations. Administers and promotes prepaid health plan participation in Medicare and Medicaid programs. (Formerly Health Care Financing Administration.)

CONGRESS

Congressional Budget Office, *Health and Human Resources,* 419 FHOB 20515; (202) 226-2668. Fax, (202) 225-3149. Steve Lieberman, Assistant Director.

Web, www.cbo.gov

Analyzes program and budget issues in the areas of health, education, employment and training, and social services. Examines the potential effects on the private sector of proposed federal mandates in those areas.

House Energy and Commerce Committee, *Subcommittee on Health,* 2125 RHOB 20515; (202) 225-2927. Fax, (202) 225-1919. Rep. Michael Bilirakis, R-Fla., Chair; David V. Marventano, Staff Director.

General e-mail, commerce@mail.house.gov

Web, energycommerce.house.gov

Jurisdiction over national health insurance proposals (jurisdiction shared with the House Ways and Means Committee) and legislation on malpractice insurance, Medicaid, and health maintenance organizations.

House Ways and Means Committee, *Subcommittee on Health,* 1136 LHOB 20515; (202) 225-3943. Fax, (202) 226-1765. Rep. Nancy L. Johnson, R-Conn., Chair; John E. McManus, Staff Director.

Web, waysandmeans.house.gov

Jurisdiction over national health insurance proposals (jurisdiction shared with the House Commerce Committee) and legislation on health insurance supported by tax revenues, including Medicare.

Senate Finance Committee, *Subcommittee on Health Care,* SD-219 20510; (202) 224-4515. Sen. Jon Kyl, R-Ariz., Chair; Linda Fishman, Counsel.

Web, finance.senate.gov

Holds hearings on national health insurance proposals (jurisdiction shared with the Senate Health, Education, Labor, and Pensions Committee) and on legislation on health insurance and Medicaid for low-income individuals.

Senate Health, Education, Labor, and Pensions Committee, SD-428 20510; (202) 224-5375. Fax, (202)

228-5044. Sen. Judd Gregg, R-N.H., Chair; Sharon Soderstrom, Staff Director. TTY, (202) 224-1975.

Web, health.senate.gov

Jurisdiction over national health insurance proposals (jurisdiction shared with the Senate Finance Committee) and legislation on malpractice insurance and health maintenance organizations.

NONPROFIT

Alliance for Health Reform, 1444 Eye St. N.W., #910 20005; (202) 789-2300. Fax, (202) 789-2233. Edward F. Howard, Executive Vice President.

General e-mail, frontdesk@allhealth.org

Web, www.allhealth.org

Nonpartisan organization that advocates health care reform, including cost containment and universal coverage. Sponsors conferences and seminars for journalists, business leaders, policymakers, and the public.

American Assn. of Health Plans, 1129 20th St. N.W., #600 20036-3421; (202) 778-3200. Fax, (202) 331-7487. Karen Ignagni, President. Press, (202) 778-8494.

General e-mail, aahp@aahp.org

Web, www.aahp.org

Membership: managed health care plans and organizations. Provides legal counsel and conducts educational programs. Conducts research and analysis of managed care issues; produces publications. Monitors legislation and regulations.

American Medical Assn. (AMA), *Public and Private Sector Advocacy, Washington Office,* 1101 Vermont Ave. N.W., 12th Floor 20005; (202) 789-7400. Fax, (202) 789-7485. Lee Stillwell, Senior Vice President.

Web, www.ama-assn.org

Membership: physicians, residents, and medical students. Provides information on health care. Monitors legislation and regulations. (Headquarters in Chicago, Ill.)

Blue Cross and Blue Shield Assn., *Washington Office,* 1310 G St. N.W. 20005; (202) 626-4780. Fax, (202) 626-4833. Scott Serota, President.

Web, www.bluecares.com

Membership: Blue Cross and Blue Shield insurance plans, which operate autonomously at the local level. Certifies member plans; acts as consultant to plans in evaluating new medical technologies and contracting with doctors and hospitals. Operates a national telecommunications network to collect, analyze, and disseminate data. (Headquarters in Chicago, Ill.)

Council for Affordable Health Insurance, 112 S. West St., #400, Alexandria, VA 22314; (703) 836-

6200. Fax, (703) 836-6550. Merrill Matthews Jr., Director.
General e-mail, mail@cahi.org
Web, www.cahi.org

Membership: insurance carriers in the small group, individual, and senior markets, business groups, doctors, actuaries, and insurance brokers. Research and advocacy organization devoted to free market solutions to America's health care problems. Promotes reform measures, including establishment of medical savings accounts, tax equity, universal access, medical price disclosure prior to treatment, and caps on malpractice awards. Serves as a liaison with businesses, provider organizations, and public interest groups. Monitors legislation and regulations at state and federal levels.

Employee Benefit Research Institute, 2121 K St. N.W., #600 20037; (202) 659-0670. Fax, (202) 775-6312. Dallas L. Salisbury, President.
General e-mail, info@ebri.org
Web, www.ebri.org

Conducts research on health insurance coverage, health care utilization, and health care cost containment; studies health care delivery and financing alternatives, including long-term care, flexible benefits, and retiree health financing options.

Employers Council on Flexible Compensation,
927 15th St. N.W., #1000 20005; (202) 659-4300. Fax, (202) 371-1467. Kenneth E. Feltman, Executive Director.
General e-mail, info@ecfc.org
Web, www.ecfc.org

Represents employers who have or are considering flexible compensation plans. Supports the preservation and expansion of employee choice in health insurance coverage. Monitors legislation and regulations.

Health Insurance Assn. of America, 1201 F St. N.W., #500 20004-1204; (202) 824-1600. Fax, (202) 824-1722. Donald A. Young, President.
General e-mail, info@hiaa.org
Web, www.hiaa.org

Membership: health insurance companies that write and sell health insurance policies. Promotes effective management of health care expenditures; provides statistical information on health insurance issues. Monitors legislation and regulations.

National Academy of Social Insurance, 1776 Massachusetts Ave. N.W., #615 20036-1904; (202) 452-8097. Fax, (202) 452-8111. Pamela J. Larson, Executive Vice President.
General e-mail, nasi@nasi.org
Web, www.nasi.org

Promotes research and education on Social Security, health care financing, and related public and private programs; assesses social insurance programs and their relationship to other programs; supports research and leadership development. Acts as a clearinghouse for social insurance information.

National Assn. of Health Underwriters,
2000 N. 14th St., #450, Arlington, VA 22201; (703) 276-0220. Fax, (703) 841-7797. Kevin Corcoran, Executive Vice President.
General e-mail, nahu@nahu.org
Web, www.nahu.org

Promotes the health insurance industry; certifies health underwriters; conducts advanced health insurance underwriting and research seminars at universities; maintains a speakers bureau.

National Assn. of Manufacturers (NAM), Human Resources Policy, 1331 Pennsylvania Ave. N.W., #600N 20004-1790; (202) 637-3134. Fax, (202) 637-3182. Pat Cleary, Senior Vice President.
General e-mail, manufacturing@nam.org
Web, www.nam.org

Interests include health care, Social Security, pensions, employee benefits, cost containment, mandated benefits, Medicare, and other federal programs that affect employers. Opposed to government involvement in health care.

National Health Care Anti-Fraud Assn., 1255 23rd St. N.W., #200 20037-1174; (202) 659-5955. Fax, (202) 785-6764. William J. Mahon, Executive Director.
General e-mail, fraud@nhcaa.org
Web, www.nhcaa.org

Membership: health insurance companies and regulatory and law enforcement agencies. Members work to identify, investigate, and prosecute individuals defrauding health care reimbursement systems.

Society of Professional Benefit Administrators,
2 Wisconsin Circle, #670, Chevy Chase, MD 20815-7003; (301) 718-7722. Fax, (301) 718-9440. Frederick D. Hunt Jr., President.
Web, users.erols.com/spba

Membership: third-party administration firms that manage employee benefit plans for client employers. Interests include health care and insurance legislation and regulations, revision of Medicare programs, and health care cost containment. Monitors industry trends, government compliance requirements, and developments in health care financing.

Washington Business Group on Health, *50 F St. N.W., #600 20001; (202) 628-9320. Fax, (202) 628-9244. Helen Darling, President.*

General e-mail, wbgh@wbgh.org

Web, www.wbgh.org

Membership: large corporations with an interest in health. Monitors health care legislation and regulations of interest to large corporations. Interests include reimbursement policies, Medicare, retiree medical cost, hospital cost containment, health planning, and corporate health education.

Hospitals

AGENCIES

Centers for Medicare and Medicaid Services (CMS), *(Health and Human Services Dept.), Survey and Certification, 7500 Security Blvd., S2-13-17, Baltimore, MD 21244; (410) 786-3160. Fax, (410) 786-0194. Steven Pelovitz, Director.*

Web, www.cms.hhs.gov

Enforces health care and safety standards for hospitals and other health care facilities. (Formerly Health Care Financing Administration.)

CONGRESS

House Energy and Commerce Committee, *Subcommittee on Health, 2125 RHOB 20515; (202) 225-2927. Fax, (202) 225-1919. Rep. Michael Bilirakis, R-Fla., Chair; David V. Marventano, Staff Director.*

General e-mail, commerce@mail.house.gov

Web, energycommerce.house.gov

Jurisdiction over legislation on health planning, health facilities construction, and government-run health care facilities, including Public Health Service hospitals.

Senate Banking, Housing, and Urban Affairs Committee, *SD-534 20510; (202) 224-7391. Fax, (202) 224-5137. Sen. Richard C. Shelby, R-Ala., Chair; Kathy Casey, Staff Director.*

Web, banking.senate.gov

Jurisdiction over secondary market organizations for home mortgages including the Federal National Mortgage Assn., Federal Home Loan Mortgage Corporation, and the Federal Agricultural Mortgage Corporation; the Office of Federal Housing Enterprise Oversight; the Federal Housing Finance Board; and the supervision and operation of the Federal Home Loan Banks.

Senate Health, Education, Labor, and Pensions Committee, *SD-428 20510; (202) 224-5375. Fax, (202)*

228-5044. Sen. Judd Gregg, R-N.H., Chair; Sharon Soderstrom, Staff Director. TTY, (202) 224-1975.

Web, health.senate.gov

Jurisdiction over legislation on health planning, health facilities construction, and government-run health care facilities, including Public Health Service hospitals.

NONPROFIT

American Hospital Assn., *325 7th St. N.W., #700 20004-2802; (202) 638-1100. Fax, (202) 626-2345. Richard J. Davidson, President.*

Web, www.aha.org

Membership: hospitals, other inpatient care facilities, outpatient centers, Blue Cross plans, areawide planning agencies, regional medical programs, hospital schools of nursing, and individuals. Conducts research and education projects in such areas as provision of comprehensive care, hospital economics, hospital facilities and design, and community relations; participates with other health care associations in establishing hospital care standards. Monitors legislation and regulations.

Assn. of Academic Health Centers, *1400 16th St. N.W., #720 20036; (202) 265-9600. Fax, (202) 265-7514. Dr. Roger J. Bulger, President.*

Web, www.ahcnet.org

Membership: academic health centers (composed of a medical school, a teaching hospital, and at least one other health professional school or program). Participates in studies and public debates on health professionals' training and education, patient care, and biomedical research.

Federation of American Hospitals, *801 Pennsylvania Ave. N.W., #245 20004-2604; (202) 624-1500. Fax, (202) 737-6462. Charles N. Kahn, President.*

Web, www.americashospitals.com

Membership: investor-owned, for-profit hospitals and health care systems. Interests include health care reform, cost containment, and Medicare and Medicaid reforms. Maintains speakers bureau; compiles statistics on investor-owned hospitals. Monitors legislation and regulations.

National Assn. of Children's Hospitals, *401 Wythe St., Alexandria, VA 22314; (703) 684-1355. Fax, (703) 684-1589. Lawrence A. McAndrews, President.*

Web, www.childrenshospitals.net

Membership: more than 100 children's hospitals nationwide. Assists member hospitals in addressing public policy issues that affect their ability to provide clinical care, education, research, and advocacy. (Affiliated with the National Assn. of Children's Hospitals and Related Institutions.)

National Assn. of Children's Hospitals and Related Institutions, *401 Wythe St., Alexandria, VA 22314; (703) 684-1355. Fax, (703) 684-1589. Lawrence A. McAndrews, President.*
Web, www.childrenshospitals.net

Advocates and promotes education and research on child health care related to children's hospitals; compiles statistics and provides information on pediatric hospitalizations. (Affiliated with the National Assn. of Children's Hospitals.)

National Assn. of Public Hospitals and Health Systems, *1301 Pennsylvania Ave. N.W., #950 20004; (202) 585-0100. Fax, (202) 585-0101. Larry S. Gage, President.*
General e-mail, naph@naph.org
Web, www.naph.org

Membership: city and county public hospitals, state universities, and hospital districts and authorities. Works to improve and expand health care in hospitals; interests include Medicaid patients and vulnerable populations, including AIDS patients, the homeless, the mentally ill, and non-English-speaking patients. Holds annual regional meetings. Monitors legislation and regulations.

Medicaid and Medicare

AGENCIES

Centers for Medicare and Medicaid Services (CMS), *(Health and Human Services Dept.),* *200 Independence Ave. S.W., #314G 20201; (202) 690-6726. Fax, (202) 690-6262. Thomas A. Scully, Administrator. Information, (202) 690-6105.*
Web, cms.hhs.gov

Administers Medicare (a health insurance program for persons with disabilities or age sixty-five or older, who are eligible to participate) and Medicaid (a health insurance program for persons judged unable to pay for health services). (Formerly Health Care Financing Administration.)

Centers for Medicare and Medicaid Services (CMS), *(Health and Human Services Dept.), Clinical Standards and Quality,* *7500 Security Blvd., S3-02-01, Baltimore, MD 21244; (410) 786-6842. Fax, (410) 786-6857. Robert Streimer, Director (Acting).*
Web, www.cms.hhs.gov

Develops, establishes, and enforces standards that regulate the quality of care of hospitals and other health care facilities under Medicare and Medicaid programs. Administers operations of survey and peer review organizations that enforce health care standards, primarily for institutional care. Oversees clinical laboratory improvement programs and end stage renal disease networks. Monitors providers' and suppliers' compliance with standards. (Formerly Health Care Financing Administration.)

Centers for Medicare and Medicaid Services (CMS), *(Health and Human Services Dept.), Disabled and Elderly Health Programs,* *7500 Security Blvd., S2-14-27, Baltimore, MD 21244; (410) 786-9493. Fax, (410) 786-9004. Thomas Hamilton, Director.*
Web, www.cms.hhs.gov

Approves state Medicaid plan amendments and waivers to serve disabled and elderly population. Organizes and administers grant programs that assist persons with disabilities to participate fully in communities. (Formerly Health Care Financing Administration.)

Centers for Medicare and Medicaid Services (CMS), *(Health and Human Services Dept.), Information Services,* *7500 Security Blvd., N3-15-25, Baltimore, MD 21244-1850; (410) 786-1800. Fax, (410) 786-1810. Timothy P. Love, Director.*
Web, www.cms.hhs.gov

Serves as primary federal statistical office for disseminating economic data on Medicare and Medicaid. (Formerly Health Care Financing Administration.)

Centers for Medicare and Medicaid Services (CMS), *(Health and Human Services Dept.), Medicaid,* *7500 Security Blvd., #C52223, Baltimore, MD 21244; (410) 786-3870. Fax, (410) 786-0025. Dennis Smith, Director. Alternate phone, (202) 205-3067.*
Web, www.cms.hhs.gov

Administers and monitors Medicaid programs to ensure program quality and financial integrity; promotes beneficiary awareness and access to services. (Formerly Health Care Financing Administration.)

Centers for Medicare and Medicaid Services (CMS), *(Health and Human Services Dept.), Medicare Contractor Management,* *7500 Security Blvd., C5014, Baltimore, MD 21244; (410) 786-0550. Fax, (410) 786-0192. Thomas Grissom, Director.*
Web, www.cms.hhs.gov

Manages the contractual framework for the Medicare program; establishes and enforces performance standards for contractors who process and pay Medicare claims. (Formerly Health Care Financing Administration.)

Centers for Medicare and Medicaid Services (CMS), *(Health and Human Services Dept.), Medicare*

Management, 7500 Security Blvd., C5-17-14, Baltimore, MD 21244; (410) 786-4164. Fax, (410) 786-0192. Thomas Grissom, Director.
Web, www.cms.hhs.gov

Issues regulations and guidelines for administration of the Medicare program. (Formerly Health Care Financing Administration.)

Health Resources and Services Administration (Health and Human Services Dept.), Rural Health Policy, 5600 Fishers Lane, #9A55, Rockville, MD 20857; (301) 443-0835. Fax, (301) 443-2803. Marsha K. Brand, Director.
Web, www.ruralhealth.hrsa.gov

Studies the effects of Medicare and Medicaid programs on rural access to health care.

NONPROFIT

Blue Cross and Blue Shield Assn., Washington Office, 1310 G St. N.W. 20005; (202) 626-4780. Fax, (202) 626-4833. Scott Serota, President.
Web, www.bluecares.com

Acts as the primary contractor for the federal government in administration of Medicare Part A, which covers hospitalization and institutional care for persons with disabilities and persons age sixty-five or older. (Headquarters in Chicago, Ill.)

Federation of American Hospitals, 801 Pennsylvania Ave. N.W., #245 20004-2604; (202) 624-1500. Fax, (202) 737-6462. Charles N. Kahn, President.
Web, www.americashospitals.com

Membership: investor-owned, for-profit hospitals and health care systems. Studies Medicaid and Medicare reforms. Maintains speakers bureau; compiles statistics on investor-owned hospitals. Monitors legislation and regulations.

National Committee to Preserve Social Security and Medicare, 10 G St. N.E., #600 20002; (202) 216-0420. Fax, (202) 216-0451. Barbara Kenelly, President.
Web, www.ncpssm.org

Educational and advocacy organization that focuses on Social Security and Medicare programs and on related income security and health issues. Interests include retirement income protection, health care reform, and the quality of life of seniors. Monitors legislation and regulations.

Medical Devices and Technology

AGENCIES

Food and Drug Administration (FDA), (Health and Human Services Dept.), Center for Devices and Radio-

logical Health, 9200 Corporate Blvd., #100E, Rockville, MD 20850; (301) 827-7975. Fax, (301) 594-1320. Dr. David W. Feigal Jr., Director. International Reference System, (301) 827-3993.
Web, www.fda.gov/cdrh

Evaluates safety, efficacy, and labeling of medical devices; classifies devices; establishes performance standards; assists in legal actions concerning medical devices; coordinates research and testing; conducts training and educational programs. Maintains an international reference system, to facilitate trade in devices. Library open to the public.

Food and Drug Administration (FDA), (Health and Human Services Dept.), Combination Products, 5600 Fishers Lane, #HF-7, Rockville, MD 20857; (301) 827-3390. Fax, (301) 480-8039. Mark D. Kramer, Director.
General e-mail, combination@fda.gov
Web, www.fda.gov/oc/combination

Created to streamline the processing of complex drug-device, drug-biologic, and device-biologic combination products. Responsibilities cover the entire regulatory life cycle of combination products, including jurisdiction decisions as well as the timeliness and effectiveness of pre-market review, and the consistency and appropriateness of post-market regulation.

Food and Drug Administration (FDA), (Health and Human Services Dept.), Small Manufacturers International and Consumer Assistance, 1350 Piccard Dr., HFZ-220, Rockville, MD 20850; (301) 443-6597. Fax, (301) 443-8818. John F. Stigi, Director. Information, (800) 638-2041. Fax-on-demand, (800) 899-0381.
General e-mail, dsma@cdrh.fda.gov
Web, www.fda.gov/cdrh

Serves as liaison between small-business manufacturers of medical devices and the FDA. Assists manufacturers in complying with FDA regulatory requirements; sponsors seminars.

NONPROFIT

Advanced Medical Technology Assn., 1200 G St. N.W., #400 20005-3814; (202) 783-8700. Fax, (202) 783-8750. Pamela G. Bailey, President.
General e-mail, info@advamed.org
Web, www.advamed.org

Membership: manufacturers of medical devices, diagnostic products, and health care information systems. Interests include safe and effective medical devices; conducts educational seminars. Monitors legislation, regulations, and international issues. (Formerly Health Industry Manufacturers Assn.)

American Assn. for Homecare, *625 Slaters Lane, #200, Alexandria, VA 22314-1171; (703) 836-6263. Fax, (703) 836-6730. Thomas A. Connaughton, President.*
General e-mail, info@aahomecare.org
Web, www.aahomecare.org
Membership: home medical equipment suppliers, manufacturers, and state associations. Promotes legislative and regulatory policy that improves access to quality home medical equipment.

American Institute of Ultrasound in Medicine, *14750 Sweitzer Lane, #100, Laurel, MD 20707-5906; (301) 498-4100. Fax, (301) 498-4450. Carmine Valente, Executive Director.*
General e-mail, admin@aium.org
Web, www.aium.org
Membership: medical professionals who use ultrasound technology in their practices. Promotes multidisciplinary research and education in the field of diagnostic ultrasound through conventions and educational programs. Monitors international research.

American Medical Informatics Assn., *4915 St. Elmo Ave., #401, Bethesda, MD 20814; (301) 657-1291. Fax, (301) 657-1296. Dennis Reynolds, Executive Director.*
General e-mail, mail@mail.amia.org
Web, www.amia.org
Membership: doctors and other medical professionals in the applied informatics field. Provides members information on medical systems and the use of computers in the health care field. Promotes use of computers and information systems in patient care; conducts and promotes research on medical technology; encourages development of universal standards, terminology, and coding systems.

American Orthotic and Prosthetic Assn., *330 John Carlyle St., #210, Alexandria, VA 22314; (571) 431-0876. Fax, (571) 431-0899. Tyler Wilson, Executive Director.*
Web, www.aopanet.org
Membership: companies that manufacture or supply artificial limbs and braces. Provides information on the profession.

American Roentgen Ray Society, *44211 Slatestone Court, Leesburg, VA 20176-5109; (703) 729-3353. Fax, (703) 729-4839. Susan B. Cappitelli, Executive Director. Toll-free, (800) 438-2777.*
General e-mail, staff@arrs.org
Web, www.arrs.org
Membership: physicians and researchers in radiology and allied sciences. Publishes research; conducts conferences; presents scholarships and awards; monitors international research.

Health Industry Distributors Assn., *310 Montgomery St., Alexandria, VA 22314-1516; (703) 549-4432. Matthew Rowan, President.*
General e-mail, mail@hida.org
Web, www.hidanetwork.com
Membership: medical products distributors and home health care providers. Administers educational programs and conducts training seminars. Monitors legislation and regulations.

Optical Society of America, *2010 Massachusetts Ave. N.W. 20036; (202) 223-8130. Fax, (202) 223-1096. Elizabeth Rogan, Executive Director.*
General e-mail, postmaster@osa.org
Web, www.osa.org
Membership: researchers, educators, manufacturers, students, and others interested in optics and photonics worldwide. Promotes research and information exchange; conducts conferences. Interests include use of optics in medical imaging and surgery.

Program for Appropriate Technology in Health, *Washington Office, 1800 K St. N.W., #800 20006; (202) 822-0033. Fax, (202) 457-1466. Anne Wilson, Director.*
General e-mail, info@path-dc.org
Web, www.path.org
Seeks to improve the safety and availability of health products and technologies worldwide, particularly in developing countries. Interests include reproductive health, immunization, maternal-child health, AIDS, and nutrition. (Headquarters in Seattle, Wash.)

Nursing Homes and Hospices

AGENCIES

Centers for Medicare and Medicaid Services (CMS), *(Health and Human Services Dept.), Nursing Homes and Continuing Care Services, 7500 Security Blvd., S2-12-25-07, Baltimore, MD 21244-1850; (410) 786-3870. Fax, (410) 786-6730. Steven Pelovitz, Director.*
Web, www.cms.hhs.gov
Monitors compliance of nursing homes, psychiatric hospitals, and long-term and intermediate care facilities with government standards. Focus includes quality of care, environmental conditions, and participation in Medicaid and Medicare programs. Coordinates health care programs for the mentally retarded. (Formerly Health Care Financing Administration.)

Centers for Medicare and Medicaid Services (CMS), *(Health and Human Services Dept.), Survey and Certification, 7500 Security Blvd., S2-13-17, Baltimore, MD 21244; (410) 786-3160. Fax, (410) 786-0194. Steven Pelovitz, Director.*

Web, www.cms.hhs.gov

Enforces health care and safety standards for nursing homes and other long-term care facilities. (Formerly Health Care Financing Administration.)

NONPROFIT

American College of Health Care Administrators,

300 N. Lee St., #301, Alexandria, VA 22314; (703) 739-7900. Fax, (703) 739-7901. Mary Tellis-Nayak, President.
General e-mail, info@achca.org
Web, www.achca.org

Membership: administrators of long-term health care organizations and facilities, including home health care programs, hospices, day care centers for the elderly, nursing and hospital facilities, retirement communities, and mental health care centers. Conducts research on statistical characteristics of nursing home and other medical administrators; conducts seminars and workshops; offers education courses; provides certification for administrators.

American Health Care Assn., *1201 L St. N.W. 20005; (202) 842-4444. Fax, (202) 842-3860. Charles H. Roadman II, President. Publication orders, (800) 321-0343.*
Web, www.ahca.org

Federation of associations representing assisted living nursing facilities and subacute care providers. Sponsors and provides educational programs and materials. Library open to the public by appointment.

Assisted Living Federation of America, *11200 Waples Mill Rd., #150, Fairfax, VA 22030; (703) 691-8100. Fax, (703) 691-8106. Dr. Paul R. Willging, President.*
General e-mail, info@alfa.org
Web, www.alfa.org

Represents over 7,000 providers of assisted living and continuing care facilities and others involved in the industry. Promotes the development of standards and increased awareness for the assisted living industry. Provides members with information on policy, funding access, and quality of care. Interests include funding alternatives to make assisted living available to all who need it and assuring a safe environment and caring and competent staff for residents. Monitors legislation and regulations.

Consumer Consortium on Assisted Living, *2342 Oak St., Falls Church, VA 22046; (703) 533-8121. Fax, (703) 533-8495. Karen Love, Executive Director.*
General e-mail, webmaster@ccal.org
Web, www.ccal.org

Educates consumers, advocates, and professionals on assisted living choices and needs.

Hospice Foundation of America, *Washington Office, 2001 S St. N.W., #300 20009; (202) 638-5419. Fax, (202) 638-5312. Judith Rensberger, Senior Program Officer. Toll-free, (800) 854-3402.*
General e-mail, questions@hospicefoundation.org
Web, www.hospicefoundation.org

Promotes hospice care for terminally ill people. Disseminates information; conducts education and training. (Headquarters in Miami Beach, Fla.)

National Assn. for Home Care and Hospice, *228 7th St. S.E. 20003; (202) 547-7424. Fax, (202) 547-3540. Val J. Halamandaris, President.*
General e-mail, webmaster@nahc.org
Web, www.nahc.org

Promotes high-quality hospice, home care, and other community services for those with chronic health problems or life-threatening illness. Conducts research and provides information on related issues. Works to educate the public concerning health and social policy matters. Monitors legislation and regulations.

National Citizens' Coalition for Nursing Home Reform, *1424 16th St. N.W., #202 20036-2211; (202) 332-2275. Fax, (202) 332-2949. Donna Lenhoff, Executive Director.*
Web, www.nursinghomeaction.org

Seeks to improve the long-term care system and quality of life for residents in nursing homes and other facilities for the elderly; coordinates the Campaign for Quality Care. Promotes citizen participation in all aspects of nursing homes; acts as clearinghouse for nursing home advocacy.

National Hospice and Palliative Care Organization, *1700 Diagonal Rd., #625, Alexandria, VA 22314; (703) 837-1500. Fax, (703) 837-1233. Don Schumacher, President. Toll-free information and referral helpline, (800) 646-6460.*
General e-mail, nhpco_info@nhpco.org
Web, www.nhpco.org

Membership: institutions and individuals providing hospice and palliative care and other interested organizations and individuals. Promotes supportive care for the terminally ill and their families; sets hospice program standards; provides information on hospices. Monitors legislation and regulations.

Pharmaceuticals

AGENCIES

Food and Drug Administration (FDA), *(Health and Human Services Dept.), Center for Drug Evaluation*

and Research, 1451 Rockville Pike, Rockville, MD 20852; (301) 594-5400. Fax, (301) 594-6197. Dr. Janet Woodcock, Director. Information, (301) 827-4573. Press, (301) 827-6242.

Web, www.fda.gov/cdr

Reviews and approves applications to investigate and market new drugs; monitors prescription drug advertising; works to harmonize drug approval internationally.

Food and Drug Administration (FDA), *(Health and Human Services Dept.), Generic Drugs, 7500 Standish Pl., Rockville, MD 20855; (301) 827-5845. Fax, (301) 594-0183. Gary Buehler, Director.*

Web, www.fda.gov/ogd

Oversees generic drug review process to ensure the safety and effectiveness of approved drugs.

National Institutes of Health (NIH), *(Health and Human Services Dept.), Dietary Supplements, 6100 Executive Blvd., #3B01, MSC-7517, Bethesda, MD 20892-7517; (301) 435-2920. Fax, (301) 480-1845. Paul M. Coates, Director.*

General e-mail, ods@nih.gov

Web, dietary-supplements.info.nih.gov

Provides accurate, up-to-date information on dietary supplements.

Public Health Service *(Health and Human Services Dept.), Orphan Products Development, 5600 Fishers Lane, #6A55, Rockville, MD 20857; (301) 827-3666. Fax, (301) 827-0017. Dr. Marlene E. Haffner, Director.*

Web, www.fda.gov/orphan

Promotes the development of drugs, devices, and alternative medical food therapies for rare diseases or conditions. Coordinates activities on the development of orphan drugs among federal agencies, manufacturers, and organizations representing patients.

NONPROFIT

American Assn. of Colleges of Pharmacy,
1426 Prince St., Alexandria, VA 22314-2841; (703) 739-2330. Fax, (703) 836-8982. Lucinda L. Maine, Executive Vice President.

Web, www.aacp.org

Represents and advocates for pharmacists in the academic community. Conducts programs and activities in cooperation with other national health and higher education associations.

American Assn. of Pharmaceutical Scientists, 2107 Wilson Blvd., #700, Arlington, VA 22201-3042; (703) 243-2800. Fax, (703) 243-9650. Maureen Downs, Executive Director (Interim).

General e-mail, aaps@aaps.org

Web, www.aaps.org

Membership: pharmaceutical scientists from biomedical, biotechnological, and health care fields. Promotes pharmaceutical sciences as an industry; represents scientific interests within academia and public and private institutions. Monitors legislation and regulations.

American Pharmaceutical Assn., 2215 Constitution Ave. N.W. 20037-2985; (202) 628-4410. Fax, (202) 783-2351. Dr. John A. Gans, Executive Vice President. Information, (800) 237-2742. Library, (202) 429-7524.

Web, www.aphanet.org

Membership: practicing pharmacists, pharmaceutical scientists, and pharmacy students. Promotes professional education and training; publishes scientific journals and handbook on nonprescription drugs; monitors international research. Library open to the public by appointment.

American Society for Pharmacology and Experimental Therapeutics, 9650 Rockville Pike, Bethesda, MD 20814-3995; (301) 634-7060. Fax, (301) 634-7061. Dr. Christine K. Carrico, Executive Officer.

General e-mail, info@aspet.org

Web, www.aspet.org

Membership: researchers and teachers involved in basic and clinical pharmacology primarily in the United States and Canada.

American Society of Health-System Pharmacists,
7272 Wisconsin Ave., Bethesda, MD 20814; (301) 657-3000. Fax, (301) 657-1251. Henri Manasse, Chief Executive Officer.

Web, www.ashp.org

Membership: pharmacists who practice in organized health care settings such as hospitals, health maintenance organizations, and long-term care facilities. Provides publishing and educational programs designed to help members improve pharmaceutical services; accredits pharmacy residency and pharmacy technician training programs. Monitors legislation and regulations.

Consumer Health Care Products Assn., 1150 Connecticut Ave. N.W., #1200 20036-4193; (202) 429-9260. Fax, (202) 223-6835. Linda Suydam, President.

Web, www.chpa-info.org

Membership: manufacturers and distributors of nonprescription medicines; associate members include suppliers, advertising agencies, and research and testing laboratories. Promotes the role of self-medication in health care. Monitors legislation and regulations.

FOOD AND DRUG ADMINISTRATION

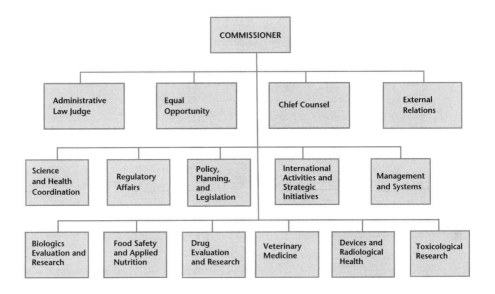

Drug Policy Alliance, *Washington Office, 925 15th St. N.W., 2nd Floor 20005; (202) 216-0035. Fax, (202) 216-0803. William D. McColl, Director.*
General e-mail, dc@drugpolicy.org
Web, www.drugpolicy.org

Seeks to broaden debate on drug policy to include consideration of alternatives to incarceration, expanding maintenance therapies, and restoring constitutional protections. Studies drug policy in other countries. Monitors legislation and regulations. (Headquarters in New York.)

Generic Pharmaceutical Assn., *1620 Eye St. N.W., #800 20006-4005; (202) 833-9070. Fax, (202) 833-9612. Kathleen D. Jaeger, Chief Executive Officer.*
General e-mail, info@gphaonline.org
Web, www.gphaonline.org

Represents the generic pharmaceutical industry in legislative, regulatory, scientific, and health care policy matters. Attempts to increase availability and public awareness of generic medicines.

Healthcare Distribution Management Assn.,
1821 Michael Faraday Dr., #400, Reston, VA 20190; (703) 787-0000. Fax, (703) 787-6930. Ronald J. Streck, President.
Web, www.healthcaredistribution.org

Membership: full-service drug wholesalers. Works to improve relations among supplier and customer industries; serves as a forum on major industry issues; researches and disseminates information on management practices for drug wholesalers. Monitors legislation and regulations. (Formerly the National Wholesale Druggists' Assn.)

National Assn. of Chain Drug Stores, *413 N. Lee St., Alexandria, VA 22314 (mailing address: P.O. Box 1417-D49, Alexandria, VA 22313); (703) 549-3001. Fax, (703) 836-4869. Craig L. Fuller, President.*
Web, www.nacds.org

Membership: chain drug retailers; associate members include manufacturers, suppliers, publishers, and advertising agencies. Provides information on the pharmacy profession, community pharmacy practice, and retail prescription drug economics.

National Community Pharmacists Assn.,
205 Daingerfield Rd., Alexandria, VA 22314; (703) 683-8200. Fax, (703) 683-3619. Bruce Roberts, Executive Vice President.
Web, www.ncpanet.org

Membership: independent drugstore owners and pharmacists working in retail drugstores. Interests include drug regulation and national health insurance.

Provides consumer information on such issues as prescription drugs, poison control, and mail order drug fraud.

National Council on Patient Information and Education, *4915 St. Elmo Ave., #505, Bethesda, MD 20814-6082; (301) 656-8565. Fax, (301) 656-4464. W. Ray Bullman, Executive Vice President.*
General e-mail, ncpie@erols.com
Web, www.talkaboutrx.org and www.bemedwise.org

Membership: organizations of health care professionals, pharmaceutical manufacturers, federal agencies, voluntary health organizations, and consumer groups. Works to improve communication between health care professionals and patients about the appropriate use of medicines; produces educational resources; conducts public affairs programs; sponsors awards program.

National Pharmaceutical Council, *1894 Preston White Dr., Reston, VA 20191-5433; (703) 620-6390. Fax, (703) 476-0904. Karen Williams, President.*
General e-mail, main@npcnow.org
Web, www.npcnow.org

Membership: pharmaceutical manufacturers that research and produce trade-name prescription medication and other pharmaceutical products. Provides information on the quality and cost-effectiveness of pharmaceutical products and the economics of drug programs.

Parenteral Drug Assn., *3 Bethesda Metro Center, #1500, Bethesda, MD 20814; (301) 986-0293. Fax, (301) 986-0296. Neal C. Koller, President.*
General e-mail, info@pda.org
Web, www.pda.org

Educates pharmaceutical professionals on parenteral and sterile-product technologies. Promotes pharmaceutical research. Serves as a liaison with pharmaceutical manufacturers, suppliers, users, academics, and government regulatory officials.

Pharmaceutical Care Management Assn., *2300 9th St. South, #210, Arlington, VA 22204-2320; (703) 920-8480. Fax, (703) 920-8491. LaVarne A. Burton, President.*
Web, www.pcmanet.org

Membership: companies providing managed care pharmacy and pharmacy benefits management. Promotes legislation, research, education, and practice standards that foster quality, affordable pharmaceutical care.

Pharmaceutical Research and Manufacturers of America, *1100 15th St. N.W., #900 20005; (202) 835-3400. Fax, (202) 835-3414. Alan F. Holmer, President.*
Web, www.phrma.org

Membership: companies that discover, develop, and manufacture prescription drugs. Provides consumer information on drug abuse, the safe and effective use of prescription medicines, and developments in important areas, including AIDS. Provides pharmaceutical industry statistics.

U.S. Pharmacopeial Convention, *12601 Twinbrook Pkwy., Rockville, MD 20852; (301) 881-0666. Fax, (301) 816-8299. Roger L. Williams, Executive Director.*
Web, www.usp.org

Establishes and revises standards for drug strength, quality, purity, packaging, labeling, and storage. Publishes drug use information, official drug quality standards, patient education materials, and consumer drug references. Interests include international standards.

 HEALTH PROFESSIONS

AGENCIES

Centers for Medicare and Medicaid Services (CMS), *(Health and Human Services Dept.), Clinical Standards and Quality, 7500 Security Blvd., S3-02-01, Baltimore, MD 21244; (410) 786-6842. Fax, (410) 786-6857. Robert Streimer, Director (Acting).*
Web, www.cms.hhs.gov

Oversees professional review and other medical review programs; establishes guidelines; prepares issue papers relating to legal aspects of professional review and quality assurance. (Formerly Health Care Financing Administration.)

Health Resources and Services Administration *(Health and Human Services Dept.), Health Education Assistance Loan Branch, 5600 Fishers Lane, #8-37, Parklawn Bldg., Rockville, MD 20857; (301) 443-1176. Fax, (301) 594-6911. Nancy Durham, Chief.*
Web, www.bhpr.hrsa.gov/dsa/healsite

Insures loans provided by private lenders to students attending eligible health professions schools under the Public Health Service Act.

Health Resources and Services Administration *(Health and Human Services Dept.), Health Professions, 5600 Fishers Lane, #805, Rockville, MD 20857; (301) 443-5794. Fax, (301) 443-2111. Kerry P. Nesseler, Associate Administrator.*
Web, www.hrsa.dhhs.gov/bhpr

Promotes primary care and public health education and practice. Advocates recruitment of health care professionals, including nursing and allied health professionals, for underserved populations. Administers categorical training programs, scholarship and loan programs, and minority and disadvantaged assistance programs. Oversees national practitioner data bank and vaccine injury compensation program.

Health Resources and Services Administration

(Health and Human Services Dept.), National Health Service Corps, 5600 Fishers lane, #8A55, Rockville, MD 20857; (301) 594-4130. Fax, (301) 594-4076. Dr. Donald L. Weaver, Director. Toll-free, (800) 221-9393.

Web, www.bphc.hrsa.gov/nhsc

Supplies communities experiencing a shortage of health care personnel with doctors and other medical professionals.

Health Resources and Services Administration

(Health and Human Services Dept.), National Practitioner Data Bank, 7519 Standish Pl., #300, Rockville, MD 20857; (301) 443-2300. Fax, (301) 443-6725. John Heyob, Director. Information, (800) 767-6732.

Web, www.npdb-hipdb.com

Provides information on reports of malpractice payments, adverse state licensure, clinical privileges, and society membership actions (only to eligible state licensing boards, hospitals, and other health care entities) about physicians, dentists, and other licensed health care practitioners.

National Institutes of Health (NIH), *(Health and Human Services Dept.), Minority Opportunities in Research,* 45 Center Dr., Bldg. 45, #2AS.37, Bethesda, MD 20892; (301) 594-3900. Fax, (301) 480-2753. Dr. Clifton A. Poodry, Director.

Web, www.nigms.nih.gov

Administers research and research training programs aimed at increasing the number of minority biomedical scientists. Funds grants, fellowships, faculty development awards, and development of research facilities.

Program Support Center, Human Resources Service *(Health and Human Services Dept.), Commissioned Personnel,* 5600 Fishers Lane, #4-04, Rockville, MD 20857; (301) 594-3000. Fax, (301) 443-8207. Rear Adm. R. Michael Davidson (CC), Director.

Web, dcp.psc.gov

Develops policies and procedures related to the personnel and payroll system of the Public Health Service Commissioned Corps.

CONGRESS

House Energy and Commerce Committee, *Subcommittee on Health,* 2125 RHOB 20515; (202) 225-2927.

Fax, (202) 225-1919. Rep. Michael Bilirakis, R-Fla., Chair; David V. Marventano, Staff Director.

General e-mail, commerce@mail.house.gov

Web, energycommerce.house.gov

Jurisdiction over legislation on the education, training, and distribution of health professionals.

House Ways and Means Committee, *Subcommittee on Health,* 1136 LHOB 20515; (202) 225-3943. Fax, (202) 226-1765. Rep. Nancy L. Johnson, R-Conn., Chair; John E. McManus, Staff Director.

Web, waysandmeans.house.gov

Jurisdiction over Professional Standards Review Organizations legislation.

Senate Health, Education, Labor, and Pensions Committee, SD-428 20510; (202) 224-5375. Fax, (202) 228-5044. Sen. Judd Gregg, R-N.H., Chair; Sharon Soderstrom, Staff Director. TTY, (202) 224-1975.

Web, health.senate.gov

Jurisdiction over legislation on the education, training, and distribution of health professionals.

NONPROFIT

AFT Healthcare, 555 New Jersey Ave. N.W. 20001; (202) 879-4491. Fax, (202) 879-4597. Sandra Feldman, President.

General e-mail, healthcare@aft.org

Web, www.aft.org/healthcare

Membership: nurses and other technical health care workers. Assists members with contract negotiation and grievances; conducts training programs and workshops. Monitors legislation and regulations. (Division of the American Federation of Teachers.)

American Assn. for Health Education, 1900 Association Dr., Reston, VA 20191-1599; (703) 476-3437. Fax, (703) 476-6638. Becky J. Smith, Executive Director.

General e-mail, aahe@aahperd.org

Web, www.aahperd.org/aahe

Membership: health educators and allied health professionals in community and volunteer health agencies, educational institutions, and businesses. Develops health education programs; monitors legislation.

American Assn. of Colleges of Pharmacy,
1426 Prince St., Alexandria, VA 22314-2841; (703) 739-2330. Fax, (703) 836-8982. Lucinda L. Maine, Executive Vice President.

Web, www.aacp.org

Membership: teachers and administrators representing colleges of pharmacy accredited by the American Council on Pharmaceutical Education. Sponsors educational programs; conducts research; provides career information; helps administer the Pharmacy College Admissions Test.

American College of Health Care Administrators, *300 N. Lee St., #301, Alexandria, VA 22314; (703) 739-7900. Fax, (703) 739-7901. Mary Tellis-Nayak, President.*
General e-mail, info@achca.org
Web, www.achca.org

Membership: administrators of long-term health care organizations and facilities, including home health care programs, hospices, day care centers for the elderly, nursing and hospital facilities, retirement communities, and mental health care centers. Conducts research on statistical characteristics of nursing home and other medical administrators; conducts seminars and workshops; offers education courses; provides certification for administrators.

American Health Lawyers Assn., *1025 Connecticut Ave. N.W., #600 20036; (202) 833-1100. Fax, (202) 833-1105. Doug Hastings, President.*
General e-mail, info@healthlawyers.org
Web, www.healthlawyers.org

Membership: corporate, institutional, and government lawyers interested in the health field; law students; and health professionals. Serves as an information clearinghouse on health law; sponsors health law educational programs and seminars.

American Medical Group Assn., *1422 Duke St., Alexandria, VA 22314-3430; (703) 838-0033. Fax, (703) 548-1890. Donald W. Fisher, Chief Executive Officer.*
Web, www.amga.org

Membership: medical and dental group practices. Compiles statistics on group practice; sponsors a foundation for research and education programs.

American Society of Consultant Pharmacists, *1321 Duke St., 4th Floor, Alexandria, VA 22314-3563; (703) 739-1300. Fax, (703) 739-1321. R. Tim Webster, Executive Director. Toll-free phone, (800) 355-ASCP. Toll-free fax, (800) 220-1321.*
General e-mail, info@ascp.com
Web, www.ascp.com

Membership: dispensing and clinical pharmacists who provide services to long-term care facilities. Makes grants and conducts research in the science and practice of consultant pharmacy. Monitors legislation and regulations.

American Speech-Language Hearing Assn. (ASHA), *10801 Rockville Pike, Rockville, MD 20852; (301) 897-5700. Fax, (301) 571-0457. Frederick T. Spahr, Executive*

Director. Press, (301) 897-0156. TTY, (301) 897-0157. Toll-free hotline (except Alaska, Hawaii, and Maryland), (800) 638-8255 (voice and TTY accessible).
General e-mail, actioncenter@asha.org
Web, www.asha.org

Membership: specialists in speech-language pathology and audiology. Sponsors professional education programs; acts as accrediting agent for graduate college programs and for public clinical education programs in speech-language pathology and audiology. Advocates the rights of the communicatively disabled; provides information on speech, hearing, and language problems. Provides referrals to speech-language pathologists and audiologists. Interests include national and international standards for bioacoustics and noise.

Assn. for Healthcare Philanthropy, *313 Park Ave., #400, Falls Church, VA 22046; (703) 532-6243. Fax, (703) 532-7170. William C. McGinly, President.*
General e-mail, ahp@ahp.org
Web, www.ahp.org

Membership: hospital and health care executives who manage fundraising activities.

Assn. of Reproductive Health Professionals, *2401 Pennsylvania Ave. N.W., #350 20037-1718; (202) 466-3825. Fax, (202) 466-3826. Wayne C. Shields, President.*
General e-mail, arhp@arhp.org
Web, www.arhp.org

Membership: obstetricians, gynecologists, other physicians, researchers, clinicians, educators, and others. Educates health professionals and the public on reproductive health issues, including family planning, contraception, HIV/AIDS, other sexually transmitted diseases, abortion, menopause, infertility, and cancer prevention and detection.

Assn. of Schools of Allied Health Professions, *1730 M St. N.W., #500 20036; (202) 293-4848. Fax, (202) 293-4852. Thomas W. Elwood, Executive Director.*
General e-mail, asahp1@asahp.org
Web, www.asahp.org

Membership: two- and four-year colleges and academic health science centers with allied health professional training programs; administrators, educators, and practitioners; and professional societies. Serves as information resource; works with the Health and Human Services Dept. to conduct surveys of allied health education programs. Interests include health promotion and disease prevention, ethics in health care, and the participation of women and persons with disabilities in allied health. Monitors legislation and regulations.

Assn. of Schools of Public Health, *1101 15th St. N.W., #910 20005; (202) 296-1099. Fax, (202) 296-1252. Harrison C. Spencer, President.*

General e-mail, info@asph.org

Web, www.asph.org

Membership: accredited graduate schools of public health. Promotes improved education and training of professional public health personnel; interests include international health.

Assn. of State and Territorial Health Officials, *1275 K St. N.W., #800 20005-4006; (202) 371-9090. Fax, (202) 371-9797. George E. Hardy Jr., Executive Director.*

Web, www.astho.org

Membership: executive officers of state and territorial health departments. Serves as legislative review agency and information source for members.

Assn. of Teachers of Preventive Medicine, *1660 L St. N.W., #208 20036; (202) 463-0550. Fax, (202) 463-0555. Barbara J. Calkins, Executive Director.*

General e-mail, info@atpm.org

Web, www.atpm.org

Membership: medical educators, practitioners, administrators, students, and health care agencies. Works to advance education in preventive medicine; interests include public health, international health, clinical prevention, and aerospace and occupational medicine. Promotes collaborative research and programs; fosters information exchange.

Assn. of University Programs in Health Administration, *730 11th St. N.W., 4th Floor 20001; (202) 638-1448. Fax, (202) 638-3429. Jeptha W. Dalston, President.*

General e-mail, aupha@aupha.org

Web, www.aupha.org

Membership: colleges and universities with programs in health administration, public health, and/or health care management. Offers consultation services to health administration programs; maintains task forces on undergraduate education, educational outcomes, ethics, epidemiology diversity, health law, health facilities, long-term care, international development, institutional research, information management, quality improvement, and technology assessment.

Council on Education for Public Health, *800 Eye St. N.W., #202 20001; (202) 789-1050. Fax, (202) 789-1895. Patricia P. Evans, Executive Director.*

Web, www.ceph.org

Accredits schools of public health and graduate programs in community health education and community health preventive medicine. Works to strengthen public health programs through consultation, research, and other services.

Healthcare Financial Management Assn., *Washington Office,* *1301 Connecticut Ave. N.W., #300 20036-5503; (202) 296-2920. Fax, (202) 223-9771. Richard Gundling, Vice President. Information, (800) 252-4362.*

Web, www.hfma.org

Membership: health care financial management specialists. Offers educational programs; provides information on financial management of health care. (Headquarters in Westchester, Ill.)

Hispanic Serving Health Professions Schools Inc., *1411 K St. N.W., #200 20005; (202) 783-5262. Fax, (202) 628-5898. Yanira Cruz, Executive Director.*

General e-mail, hshps@hshps.com

Web, www.hshps.com

Seeks to increase representation of Hispanics in all health care professions. Monitors legislation and regulations.

National Assn. of County and City Health Officials, *1100 17th St. N.W., 2nd Floor 20036; (202) 783-5550. Fax, (202) 783-1583. Patrick M. Libbey, Executive Director.*

General e-mail, info@naccho.org

Web, www.naccho.org

Membership: city, county, and district health officers. Provides members with information on national, state, and local health developments. Works to develop the technical competence, managerial capacity, and leadership potential of local public health officials.

National Assn. of Healthcare Access Management, *2025 M St. N.W., #800 20036-3309; (202) 367-1125. Fax, (202) 367-2125. Steven Kemp, Executive Director.*

General e-mail, info@naham.org

Web, www.naham.org

Promotes professional growth and recognition of health care patient access managers; provides instructional videotapes; sponsors educational programs.

National Center for Homeopathy, *801 N. Fairfax St., #306, Alexandria, VA 22314; (703) 548-7790. Fax, (703) 548-7792. Sharon Stevenson, Executive Director.*

General e-mail, info@homeopathic.org

Web, www.homeopathic.org

Educational organization for professionals, groups, associations, and individuals interested in homeopathy and homeotherapeutics. Promotes health through homeopathy; conducts education programs; holds annual conference.

National Organization for Competency Assurance, 2025 M St. N.W., #800 20036-3309; (202) 367-1165. Fax, (202) 367-2165. Wade Delk, Executive Director.
General e-mail, info@noca.org
Web, www.noca.org

Membership: certifying agencies and other groups that issue credentials to health professionals. Promotes public understanding of competency assurance certification programs for health professions and occupations. Oversees commission that establishes certification program standards. Monitors regulations.

Chiropractors

NONPROFIT

American Chiropractic Assn., 1701 Clarendon Blvd., 2nd Floor, Arlington, VA 22209; (703) 276-8800. Fax, (703) 243-2593. Gary F. Cuneo, Executive Vice President. Toll-free, (800) 986-4636.
General e-mail, memberinfo@amerchiro.org
Web, www.acatoday.org

Promotes professional growth and recognition for chiropractors. Interests include health care coverage, sports injuries, physical fitness, internal disorders, and orthopedics. Supports foundation for chiropractic education and research. Monitors legislation and regulations.

International Chiropractors Assn., 1110 N. Glebe Rd., #1000, Arlington, VA 22201; (703) 528-5000. Fax, (703) 528-5023. Ronald Hendrickson, Executive Director.
General e-mail, chiro@chiropractic.org
Web, www.chiropractic.org

Membership: chiropractors, students, educators, and laypersons. Seeks to increase public awareness of chiropractic care. Supports research on health issues; administers scholarship program; monitors legislation and regulations.

Dental Care

AGENCIES

National Institute of Dental and Craniofacial Research (*National Institutes of Health*), 31 Center Dr., Bldg. 31, #2C39, MSC-2290, Bethesda, MD 20892-2290; (301) 496-3571. Fax, (301) 402-2185. Lawrence A. Tabak, Director. Information, (301) 496-4261.
Web, www.nidcr.nih.gov

Conducts and funds research on the causes, prevention, and treatment of oral diseases and conditions. Monitors international research.

NONPROFIT

American College of Dentists, 839 Quince Orchard Blvd., Suite J, Gaithersburg, MD 20878; (301) 977-3223. Fax, (301) 977-3330. Stephen Ralls, Executive Director.
General e-mail, info@facd.org
Web, www.facd.org

Honorary society of dentists. Fellows are elected based on their contributions to education, research, dentistry, and community and civic organizations. Interests include ethics, professionalism, and dentistry in health care.

American Dental Assn. (ADA), *Government Relations, Washington Office,* 1111 14th St. N.W., #1100 20005; (202) 898-2400. Fax, (202) 898-2437. Dorothy Moss, Director.
Web, www.ada.org

Conducts research; provides dental education materials; compiles statistics on dentistry and dental care. Monitors legislation and regulations. (Headquarters in Chicago, Ill.)

American Dental Education Assn., 1625 Massachusetts Ave. N.W., #600 20036-2212; (202) 667-9433. Fax, (202) 667-0642. Dr. Richard W. Valachovic, Executive Director.
General e-mail, adea@adea.org
Web, www.adea.org

Membership: individuals interested in dental education; undergraduate and graduate schools of dentistry; hospital dental education programs; and allied dental education programs in the United States, Canada, and Puerto Rico. Provides information on dental teaching and research and on admission requirements of U.S. and Canadian dental schools; publishes a directory of dental educators.

American Dental Trade Assn., 4222 King St. West, Alexandria, VA 22302-1597; (703) 379-7755. Fax, (703) 931-9429. Gary W. Price, President.
Web, www.adta.com

Membership: dental laboratories and distributors and manufacturers of dental equipment and supplies. Collects and disseminates statistical and management information; conducts studies, programs, and projects of interest to the industry; acts as liaison with government agencies.

International Assn. for Dental Research, 1619 Duke St., Alexandria, VA 22314-3406; (703) 548-0066. Fax, (703) 548-1883. Dr. Christopher Fox, Executive Director. Toll-free, (800) 950-1150.
General e-mail, research@iadr.com
Web, www.iadr.com

Membership: professionals engaged in dental research worldwide. Conducts annual convention, conferences, and symposia.

National Dental Assn., *3517 16th St. N.W. 20010; (202) 588-1697. Fax, (202) 588-1244. Robert S. Johns, Executive Director.*
Web, www.ndaonline.org

Promotes the interests of African American and other minority dentists through educational services and federal legislation and programs.

Medical Researchers

NONPROFIT

American Assn. for Clinical Chemistry, *2101 L St. N.W., #202 20037-1526; (202) 857-0717. Fax, (202) 887-5093. Richard G. Flaherty, Executive Vice President.*
General e-mail, info@aacc.org
Web, www.aacc.org

International society of chemists, physicians, and other scientists specializing in clinical chemistry. Provides educational and professional development services; presents awards for outstanding achievement. Monitors legislation and regulations.

American Assn. of Immunologists, *9650 Rockville Pike, Bethesda, MD 20814-3994; (301) 530-7178. Fax, (301) 571-1816. M. M. Hogan, Executive Director.*
General e-mail, infoaai@aaifaseb.org
Web, www.aai.org

Membership: scientists working in virology, bacteriology, biochemistry, genetics, immunology, and related disciplines. Conducts training courses and workshops; compiles statistics; participates in international conferences.

American Society for Clinical Laboratory Science, *6701 Democracy Blvd., #300, Bethesda, MD 20817; (301) 657-2768. Fax, (301) 657-2909. Elissa Passiment, Executive Vice President.*
General e-mail, ascls@ascls.org
Web, www.ascls.org

Membership: laboratory technologists. Conducts continuing education programs for medical technologists and laboratory workers. Monitors legislation and regulations.

American Society for Clinical Pathology, Washington Office, *1225 New York Ave. N.W., #250 20005-6156; (202) 347-4450. Fax, (202) 347-4453. Robin E. Stombler, Vice President, Government Affairs. Information, (800) 621-4142.*

General e-mail, info@ascp.org
Web, www.ascp.org

Membership: pathologists, residents, and other physicians; clinical scientists; registered certified medical technologists; and technicians. Promotes continuing education, educational standards, and research in pathology. Monitors legislation, regulations, and international research. (Headquarters in Chicago, Ill.)

Assn. of Public Health Laboratories, *2025 M St. N.W., #550 20036; (202) 822-5227. Fax, (202) 887-5098. Dr. David Mills, President.*
Web, www.aphl.org

Membership: state and territorial public health laboratories. Administers the National Laboratory Training Network, which assesses, develops, and delivers continuing education for laboratory practitioners. Implements international training and assistance programs for developing nations. Acts as a liaison to the Centers for Disease Control.

Society of Toxicology, *1767 Business Center Dr., #302, Reston, VA 20190; (703) 438-3115. Fax, (703) 438-3113. Shawn Lamb, Executive Director.*
General e-mail, sothq@toxicology.org
Web, www.toxicology.org

Membership: scientists from academic institutions, government, and industry worldwide who work in toxicology. Promotes professional development, exchange of information, public health, and protection of the environment.

Nurses and Physician Assistants

AGENCIES

National Institute of Nursing Research *(National Institutes of Health), 31 Center Dr., Bldg. 31, #5B05, MSC-2178, Bethesda, MD 20892-2178; (301) 496-8230. Fax, (301) 594-3405. Dr. Patricia A. Grady, Director. Information, (301) 496-0207.*
Web, www.nih.gov/ninr

Provides grants and awards for nursing research and research training. Programs include research to prevent the onset of disease or disability and to find effective approaches to achieving and sustaining good health.

NONPROFIT

AFT Healthcare, *555 New Jersey Ave. N.W. 20001; (202) 879-4491. Fax, (202) 879-4597. Sandra Feldman, President.*
General e-mail, healthcare@aft.org
Web, www.aft.org/healthcare

Membership: nurses and other technical health care workers. Assists members with contract negotiation and grievances; conducts training programs and workshops. Monitors legislation and regulations. (Division of the American Federation of Teachers.)

American Academy of Physician Assistants (AAPA), *950 N. Washington St., Alexandria, VA 22314-1552; (703) 836-2272. Fax, (703) 684-1924. Stephen C. Crane, Executive Vice President.*
General e-mail, aapa@aapa.org
Web, www.aapa.org
Membership: physician assistants and people interested in physician assistant issues. Sponsors continuing medical education programs for recertification of physician assistants; offers malpractice insurance. Interests include federal support for physician assistants' education programs; health issues related to underserved populations, Medicare coverage of physician assistants' services, and state laws regulating practice. Maintains speakers bureau. Monitors legislation and regulations.

American Assn. of Colleges of Nursing, *1 Dupont Circle N.W., #530 20036-1120; (202) 463-6930. Fax, (202) 785-8320. Geraldine P. Bednash, Executive Director.*
Web, www.aacn.nche.edu
Promotes quality baccalaureate and graduate nursing education; works to secure federal support of nursing education, nursing research, and student financial assistance; operates databank providing information on enrollments, graduations, salaries, and other conditions in nursing higher education. Interests include international practices.

American College of Nurse-Midwives, *818 Connecticut Ave. N.W., #900 20006; (202) 728-9860. Fax, (202) 728-9897. Deanne Williams, Executive Director. Press, (202) 728-9875.*
General e-mail, info@acnm.org
Web, www.midwife.org
Membership: certified nurse-midwives who preside at deliveries. Interests include preventive health care for women.

American Nurses Assn., *600 Maryland Ave. S.W., #100W 20024-2571; (202) 651-7000. Fax, (202) 651-7001. Linda Stierle, Executive Director.*
General e-mail, info@ana.org
Web, www.nursingworld.org
Membership: registered nurses. Sponsors the American Nurses Foundation. Monitors legislation and regulations.

Physical and Occupational Therapy

NONPROFIT

American Occupational Therapy Assn., *4720 Montgomery Lane, Bethesda, MD 20814 (mailing address: P.O. Box 31220, Bethesda, MD 20824-1220); (301) 652-2682. Fax, (301) 652-7711. Joe Isaacs, Executive Director. TTY, (800) 377-8555.*
General e-mail, info@aota.org
Web, www.aota.org
Membership: registered occupational therapists, certified occupational therapy assistants, and students. Associate members include businesses and organizations supportive of occupational therapy. Accredits colleges and universities and certifies therapists.

American Physical Therapy Assn., *1111 N. Fairfax St., Alexandria, VA 22314-1488; (703) 684-2782. Fax, (703) 684-7343. Francis Mallon, Executive Vice President. Information, (800) 999-2782. Fax-on-demand, (800) 399-2782.*
General e-mail, svcctr@apta.org
Web, www.apta.org
Membership: physical therapists, assistants, and students. Establishes professional standards and accredits physical therapy programs; seeks to improve physical therapy education, practice, and research.

Physicians

NONPROFIT

American Academy of Family Physicians, Washington Office, *2021 Massachusetts Ave. N.W. 20036; (202) 232-9033. Fax, (202) 232-9044. Rosemarie Sweeney, Vice President.*
General e-mail, fp@aafp.org
Web, www.aafp.org
Membership: family physicians, family practice residents, and medical students. Sponsors continuing medical education programs; promotes family practice residency programs. Monitors legislation and regulations. (Headquarters in Leawood, Kan.)

American Academy of Otolaryngology–Head and Neck Surgery, *1 Prince St., Alexandria, VA 22314; (703) 836-4444. Fax, (703) 683-5100. Dr. G. Richard Holt, Executive Vice President. Press, (703) 519-1563. TTY, (703) 519-1585.*
Web, www.entnet.org
Coordinates research in ear, nose, and throat disorders and head and neck surgery; provides continuing education. Related interests include allergies, plastic and reconstructive surgery, and medical problems resulting

from the use of tobacco. Monitors legislation, regulations, and international research.

American Assn. of Colleges of Osteopathic Medicine, *5550 Friendship Blvd., #310, Chevy Chase, MD 20815-4101; (301) 968-4100. Fax, (301) 968-4101. Dr. Douglas L. Wood, President.*
General e-mail, mail@aacom.org
Web, www.aacom.org

Administers a centralized application service for osteopathic medical colleges; supports increase in the number of minority and economically disadvantaged students in osteopathic colleges; maintains an information database; sponsors recruitment and retention programs. Monitors legislation and regulations.

American College of Cardiology, *9111 Old Georgetown Rd., Bethesda, MD 20814-1699; (301) 897-5400. Fax, (301) 897-9745. Christine McEntee, Chief Executive Officer.*
General e-mail, resource@acc.org
Web, www.acc.org

Membership: physicians, surgeons, and scientists specializing in cardiovascular health care. Sponsors programs in continuing medical education; collaborates with national and international cardiovascular organizations. Library open to the public by appointment.

American College of Emergency Physicians, *Government Affairs, Washington Office, 2121 K St. N.W., #325 20037-1801; (202) 728-0610. Fax, (202) 728-0617. Gordon B. Wheeler, Director.*
General e-mail, pr@acep.org
Web, www.acep.org

Monitors legislation affecting emergency medicine and practitioners. Interests include Medicare and Medicaid legislation and regulations, graduate medical education, indigent care, prehospital care, drunk driving, public health, tax policy, domestic violence, and the ban on assault weapons. (Headquarters in Dallas, Texas.)

American College of Obstetricians and Gynecologists, *409 12th St. S.W. 20024 (mailing address: P.O. Box 96920 20090-6920); (202) 638-5577. Fax, (202) 484-5107. Dr. Ralph Hale, Executive Director. Press, (202) 863-2560.*
Web, www.acog.org

Membership: medical specialists in obstetrics and gynecology. Monitors legislation, regulations, and international research on maternal and child health care.

American College of Osteopathic Surgeons, *123 N. Henry St., Alexandria, VA 22314-2903; (703) 684-0416. Fax, (703) 684-3280. Guy D. Beaumont, Executive Director.*

General e-mail, info@theacos.org
Web, www.facos.org

Membership: osteopathic surgeons in disciplines of orthopedics, neurosurgery, thoracic surgery, cardiovascular surgery, urology, plastic surgery, and general surgery. Offers members continuing education programs.

American College of Preventive Medicine, *1307 New York Ave. N.W., #200 20005; (202) 466-2044. Fax, (202) 466-2662. Jordan Richland, Executive Director.*
General e-mail, info@acpm.org
Web, www.acpm.org

Membership: physicians in general preventive medicine, public health, international health, occupational medicine, and aerospace medicine. Provides educational opportunities; advocates public policies consistent with scientific principles of the discipline; supports the investigation and analysis of issues relevant to the field.

American College of Radiology, *1891 Preston White Dr., Reston, VA 20191; (703) 648-8900. Fax, (703) 295-6773. Harvey L. Neiman, Executive Director.*
General e-mail, info@acr.org
Web, www.acr.org

Membership: certified radiologists in the United States and Canada. Develops programs in radiation protection, technologist training, practice standards, and health care insurance; maintains a placement service for radiologists; participates in international conferences.

American College of Surgeons, *Washington Office, 1640 Wisconsin Ave. N.W. 20007; (202) 337-2701. Fax, (202) 337-4271. Cynthia A. Brown, Associate Director.*
General e-mail, ahp@facs.org
Web, www.facs.org

Monitors legislation and regulations concerning surgery; conducts continuing education programs and sponsors scholarships for graduate medical education. Interests include hospital cancer programs, trauma care, hospital accreditation, and international research. (Headquarters in Chicago, Ill.)

American Health Quality Assn., *1140 Connecticut Ave. N.W., #1050 20036; (202) 331-5790. Fax, (202) 331-9334. David G. Schulke, Director.*
General e-mail, ahqa@ahqa.org
Web, www.ahqa.org

Seeks to improve physicians' ability to assess the quality of medical care services through community-based, independent evaluation and improvement programs; assists in developing methods to monitor the appropriateness of medical care. Monitors legislation and regulations.

American Medical Assn. (AMA), *Public and Private Sector Advocacy, Washington Office, 1101 Vermont Ave. N.W., 12th Floor 20005; (202) 789-7400. Fax, (202) 789-7485. Lee Stillwell, Senior Vice President.*
Web, www.ama-assn.org

Membership: physicians, residents, and medical students. Provides information on the medical profession and health care; cooperates in setting standards for medical schools and hospital intern and residency training programs; offers physician placement service and counseling on management practices; provides continuing medical education. Interests include international research and peer review. Monitors legislation and regulations. (Headquarters in Chicago, Ill.)

American Medical Women's Assn., *801 N. Fairfax St., #400, Alexandria, VA 22314-1767; (703) 838-0500. Fax, (703) 549-3864. Linda Hallman, Executive Director.*
General e-mail, info@amwa-doc.org
Web, www.amwa-doc.org

Membership: female physicians, interns, residents, and medical students; interested members of the public can join as associate members. Promotes continuing education; evaluates manufacturers' research on products for women's health; provides student educational loans. Monitors legislation and regulations.

American Osteopathic Assn., *Washington Office, 1090 Vermont Ave. N.W., #510 20005; (202) 414-0140. Fax, (202) 544-3525. Sydney Olson, Director. Information, (800) 962-9008.*
Web, www.aoa-net.org

Membership: osteopathic physicians. Promotes general health and education; accredits osteopathic educational institutions. Monitors legislation and regulations. (Headquarters in Chicago, Ill.)

American Podiatric Medical Assn., *9312 Old Georgetown Rd., Bethesda, MD 20814-1698; (301) 581-9200. Fax, (301) 530-2752. Dr. Glenn Gastwirth, Executive Director.*
Web, www.apma.org

Membership: podiatrists. Interests include the status of podiatrists in the military, federally supported financial assistance for podiatric students, and national health care initiatives.

American Psychiatric Assn., *1000 Wilson Blvd., #1825, Arlington, VA 22209-3901; (703) 907-7300. Fax, (703) 907-1085. Dr. James Scully, Medical Director. Library, (703) 907-8648. Press, (703) 907-8540.*
General e-mail, apa@psych.org
Web, www.psych.org

Membership: psychiatrists. Promotes availability of high-quality psychiatric care; provides the public with information; assists state and local agencies; conducts educational programs for professionals and students in the field; participates in international meetings and research. Library open to members.

American Society of Addiction Medicine, *4601 N. Park Ave., Upper Arcade, #101, Chevy Chase, MD 20815-4520; (301) 656-3920. Fax, (301) 656-3815. Eileen McGrath, Executive Vice President.*
General e-mail, email@asam.org
Web, www.asam.org

Membership: physicians and medical students. Supports the study and provision of effective treatment and care for people with alcohol and drug dependencies; educates physicians; administers certification program in addiction medicine. Monitors legislation and regulations.

American Society of Nuclear Cardiology, *9111 Old Georgetown Rd., Bethesda, MD 20814-1699; (301) 493-2360. Fax, (301) 493-2376. Steve Carter, Executive Director.*
General e-mail, admin@asnc.org
Web, www.asnc.org

Membership: physicians, scientists, technologists, and other professionals engaged in nuclear cardiology practice or research. Provides professional education programs; establishes standards and guidelines for training and practice; promotes research worldwide. Works with agreement states to monitor user-licensing requirements of the Nuclear Regulatory Commission.

Assn. of American Medical Colleges, *2450 N St. N.W. 20037; (202) 828-0400. Fax, (202) 828-1125. Dr. Jordan J. Cohen, President.*
Web, www.aamc.org

Membership: U.S. schools of medicine, councils of deans, teaching hospitals, academic societies, medical students, and residents. Administers Medical College Admissions Test.

Assn. of Professors of Medicine, *2501 M St. N.W., #550 20037-1325; (202) 861-7700. Fax, (202) 861-9731. Tod Ibrahim, Executive Director.*
General e-mail, apm@im.org
Web, www.im.org/apm

Membership: chairs of internal medicine departments at all U.S. medical schools and several affiliated teaching hospitals.

Clerkship Directors in Internal Medicine, *2501 M St. N.W., #550 20037-1308; (202) 861-8600. Fax, (202) 861-9731. Tod Ibrahim, Executive Director.*
General e-mail, cdim@im.org
Web, www.im.org/cdim

Membership: directors of third- and fourth-year internal medicine clerkships at U.S. medical schools.

College of American Pathologists, *Washington Office, 1350 Eye St. N.W., #590 20005-3305; (202) 354-7100. Fax, (202) 354-7155. John Scott, Vice President. Information, (800) 392-9994.*
Web, www.cap.org

Membership: physicians who are board certified in clinical or anatomic pathology. Accredits laboratories and provides them with proficiency testing programs; promotes the practice of pathology and laboratory medicine worldwide. (Headquarters in Northfield, Ill.)

International Council of Societies of Pathology, *7001 Georgia Ave., Chevy Chase, MD 20815; (202) 782-2759. Fax, (202) 782-3056. Dr. F. K. Mostofi, Secretary-Treasurer.*

Seeks to develop and maintain international cooperative research and education programs in pathology. Assists the World Health Organization and other international organizations in the delivery of medical care.

National Medical Assn., *1012 10th St. N.W. 20001; (202) 347-1895. Fax, (202) 842-3293. Dr. James Barnes, Executive Director.*
Web, www.nmanet.org

Membership: minority physicians. Supports increased participation of minorities in the health professions, especially medicine.

Vision Care

AGENCIES

National Eye Institute *(National Institutes of Health), 31 Center Dr., Bldg. 31, #6A03, MSC-2510, Bethesda, MD 20892-2510; (301) 496-2234. Fax, (301) 496-9970. Dr. Paul A. Sieving, Director. Information, (301) 496-5248.*
Web, www.nei.nih.gov

Conducts and funds research on the eye and visual disorders. Participates in international research.

NONPROFIT

American Academy of Ophthalmology, *Governmental Affairs, Washington Office, 1101 Vermont Ave. N.W., #700 20005-3570; (202) 737-6662. Fax, (202) 737-7061. Cathy G. Cohen, Vice President.*
Web, www.aao.org

Membership: eye physicians and surgeons. Provides information on eye diseases. Monitors legislation, regulations, and international research. (Headquarters in San Francisco, Calif.)

American Academy of Optometry, *6110 Executive Blvd., #506, Rockville, MD 20852; (301) 984-1441. Fax, (301) 984-4737. Lois Schoenbrun, Executive Director.*
General e-mail, aaoptom@aol.com
Web, www.aaopt.org

Membership: optometrists and students of optometry. Conducts research and continuing education; participates in international meetings; interests include primary care optometry, contact lenses, low vision, and diseases of the eye.

American Board of Opticianry and National Contact Lens Examiners Board, *6506 Loisdale Rd., #209, Springfield, VA 22150; (703) 719-5800. Fax, (703) 719-9144. Michael Robey, Executive Manager.*
General e-mail, abo@abo-ncle.org
Web, www.abo-ncle.org

Establishes standards for opticians who dispense eyeglasses and contact lenses. Administers professional exams and awards certification; maintains registry of certified eyeglass and contact lens dispensers. Adopts and enforces continuing education requirements; assists state licensing boards; approves educational offerings for recertification requirements.

American Optometric Assn., *Washington Office, 1505 Prince St., #300, Alexandria, VA 22314; (703) 739-9200. Fax, (703) 739-9497. Jeffrey G. Mays, Director.*
Web, www.aoanet.org

Membership: optometrists, optometry students, and paraoptometric assistants and technicians. Monitors legislation and regulations and acts as liaison with international optometric groups and government optometrists; conducts continuing education programs for optometrists and provides information on eye care. (Headquarters in St. Louis, Mo.)

Assn. for Research in Vision and Ophthalmology, *12300 Twinbrook Pkwy., #250, Rockville, MD 20852; (240) 221-2900. Fax, (240) 221-0370. Joanne Angle, Executive Director.*
General e-mail, mem@arvo.org
Web, www.arvo.org

Promotes eye and vision research; issues awards for significant research and administers research grant program.

Assn. of Schools and Colleges of Optometry, 6110 Executive Blvd., #510, Rockville, MD 20852; (301) 231-5944. Fax, (301) 770-1828. Martin A. Wall, Executive Director.

General e-mail, admini@opted.org

Web, www.opted.org

Membership: U.S. and Puerto Rican optometry schools and colleges, and foreign affiliates. Provides information about the Optometry College Admissions Test to students. Monitors legislation and regulations.

Contact Lens Society of America, 441 Carlisle Dr., Herndon, VA 20170; (703) 437-5100. Fax, (703) 437-0727. Tina M. Schott, Executive Director.

General e-mail, clsa@patriot.net

Web, www.clsa.info

Membership: contact lens professionals. Conducts courses and continuing education seminars for contact lens fitters and technicians.

Eye Bank Assn. of America, 1015 18th St. N.W., #1010 20036-5504; (202) 775-4999. Fax, (202) 429-6036. Patricia Aiken-O'Neill, President.

General e-mail, info@restoresight.org

Web, www.restoresight.org

Membership: eye banks in Brazil, Canada, England, Italy, Japan, Saudi Arabia, Taiwan, and the United States. Sets and enforces medical standards for eye banking; seeks to increase donations to eye, tissue, and organ banks; conducts training and certification programs for eye bank technicians; compiles statistics; accredits eye banks.

International Eye Foundation, 10801 Connecticut Ave., Kensington, MD 20895; (240) 290-0263. Fax, (240) 290-0269. Victoria M. Sheffield, Executive Director.

General e-mail, ief@iefusa.org

Web, www.iefusa.org

Operates blindness prevention programs focusing on cataracts, trachoma, "river blindness," and childhood blindness, including vitamin A deficiency. Provides affordable ophthalmic medical and surgical equipment and supplies to ophthamologists and hospitals to help lower surgical costs. Works with the World Health Organization, the Ministries of Health, and indigenous nongovernmental organizations in Africa, Latin America, and Eastern Europe to promote eye care.

Optical Laboratories Assn., 11096B Lee Hwy., #102, Fairfax, VA 22030 (mailing address: P.O. Box 2000, Merrifield, VA 22116-2000); (703) 359-2830. Fax, (703) 359-2834. Robert L. Dziuban, Executive Director.

General e-mail, ola@ola-labs.org

Web, www.ola-labs.org

Membership: optical laboratories. Promotes the eyewear industry; sponsors conferences. Monitors legislation and regulations.

Opticians Assn. of America, 7023 Little River Turnpike, #207, Annandale, VA 22003; (703) 916-8856. Fax, (703) 916-7966. Mike Robey, Executive Director. Information, (800) 443-8997.

General e-mail, oaa@opticians.org

Web, www.oaa.org

Membership: independent retail optical firms, optical corporations, state societies of opticians, and individual optical dispensers. Conducts education programs for members. Monitors legislation and regulations.

Vision Council of America, 1700 Diagonal Rd., #500, Alexandria, VA 22314; (703) 548-4560. Fax, (703) 548-4580. Bill Thomas, Chief Executive Officer.

General e-mail, vca@visionsite.org

Web, www.visionsite.org

Sponsors trade shows and public relations programs for the ophthalmic industry. Educates the public on developments in the optical industry. Represents manufacturers and distributors of lenses and frames.

⊞✚ HEALTH SERVICES FOR SPECIAL GROUPS

AGENCIES

Administration for Children and Families (ACF), *(Health and Human Services Dept.),* 901 D St. S.W., #600 20447 (mailing address: 370 L'Enfant Promenade S.W. 20447); (202) 401-2337. Fax, (202) 401-4678. Wade F. Horn, Assistant Secretary. Information, (202) 401-9215.

Web, www.acf.dhhs.gov

Administers and funds programs for native Americans, children, youth, families, and those with developmental disabilities. Responsible for Social Services Block Grants to the states. Provides agencies with technical assistance; administers Head Start program; funds the National Runaway Switchboard, (800) 621-4000, the Domestic Violence Hotline, (800) 799-7233, and programs for abused children.

Centers for Medicare and Medicaid Services (CMS), *(Health and Human Services Dept.), Nursing Homes and Continuing Care Services,* 7500 Security Blvd., S2-12-25-07, Baltimore, MD 21244-1850; (410) 786-3870. Fax, (410) 786-6730. Steve Pelovitz, Director.

Web, www.cms.hhs.gov

Monitors compliance of nursing homes, psychiatric hospitals, and long-term and intermediate care facilities with government standards. Focus includes quality of care, environmental conditions, and participation in Medicaid and Medicare programs. Coordinates health care programs for the mentally retarded. (Formerly Health Care Financing Administration.)

Health Resources and Services Administration *(Health and Human Services Dept.), Community and Migrant Health,* 4350 East-West Hwy., 7th Floor, Bethesda, MD 20814; (301) 594-4300. Fax, (301) 594-4997. Richard C. Bohrer, Director.
Web, www.bphc.hrsa.gov

Awards grants to public and nonprofit migrant, community, and health care centers to provide direct health care services in areas that are medically underserved. Administers National Migrant Health Advisory Council.

Health Resources and Services Administration *(Health and Human Services Dept.), Immigration Health Services,* 1220 L St. N.W., #500 20005; (202) 514-3339. Fax, (202) 514-0095. Gene Migliaccio, Director.
Web, www.inshealth.org

Division of the Bureau of Primary Health Care. Works to improve the health of new immigrants and detained aliens in the United States; promotes increased access to comprehensive primary and preventive health care.

Health Resources and Services Administration *(Health and Human Services Dept.), Primary Health Care,* 4350 East-West Hwy., #11-10, Bethesda, MD 20814; (301) 594-4110. Fax, (301) 594-4072. Sam Shekar, Director.
Web, www.bphc.hrsa.gov

Advocates accessible primary health care for underserved communities and individuals. Promotes partnerships in public and private health care delivery communities. Researches and analyzes effectiveness of community-based systems of care.

Health Resources and Services Administration *(Health and Human Services Dept.), Primary Health Care: Special Populations,* 4350 East-West Hwy., West Towers Bldg., 9th Floor, Bethesda, MD 20814; (301) 594-4420. Fax, (301) 594-4989. Regan Crump, Director.
Web, www.bphc.hrsa.gov

Awards grants to community-based organizations to provide primary health care services to special populations, including HIV-infected persons, women considered to be at risk, homeless individuals, substance abusers, elderly people, and native Hawaiian and Pacific Basin residents. Focus includes Alzheimer's disease.

Indian Health Service *(Health and Human Services Dept.),* 801 Thompson Ave., #440, Rockville, MD 20852; (301) 443-1083. Fax, (301) 443-4794. Charles W. Grim, Director (Interim). Information, (301) 443-3593.
Web, www.ihs.gov

Operates hospitals and health centers that provide native Americans and Alaska natives with preventive and remedial health care. Provides or improves sanitation and water supply systems in native American communities.

National Institute of Child Health and Human Development *(National Institutes of Health), National Center for Medical Rehabilitation Research,* 6100 Executive Blvd., Bldg. 6100, #2A-03, Bethesda, MD 20892; (301) 402-2242. Fax, (301) 402-0832. Dr. Michael Weinrich, Director.
Web, www.nichd.nih.gov

Conducts and supports research to develop improved technologies, techniques, and prosthetic and orthotic devices for people with disabilities; promotes medical rehabilitation training.

National Institute on Deafness and Other Communication Disorders *(National Institutes of Health),* 31 Center Dr., #3C02, MSC-2320, Bethesda, MD 20892-2320; (301) 402-0900. Fax, (301) 402-1590. Dr. James F. Battey Jr., Director. Information, (301) 496-7243. TTY, (301) 496-6596.
Web, www.nidcd.nih.gov

Conducts and supports research and research training and disseminates information on hearing disorders and other communication processes, including diseases that affect hearing, balance, smell, taste, voice, speech, and language. Monitors international research.

Public Health and Science *(Health and Human Services Dept.), Minority Health,* 5515 Security Lane, #1000, Rockwall II Bldg., Rockville, MD 20852; (301) 443-5084. Fax, (301) 594-0767. Nathan Stinson, Deputy Assistant Secretary. Information, (800) 444-6472.
General e-mail, info@omhrc.gov
Web, www.omhrc.gov

Oversees the implementation of the secretary's Task Force on Black and Minority Health and legislative mandates; develops programs to meet the health care needs of minorities; awards grants to coalitions of minority community organizations and to minority AIDS education and prevention projects.

Rehabilitation Services Administration *(Education Dept.),* 330 C St. S.W. 20202-2531; (202) 205-5482. Fax, (202) 205-9874. Joanne Wilson, Commissioner. TTY, (202) 205-9295.

Web, www.ed.gov

Allocates funds to state agencies and nonprofit organizations for programs serving eligible physically and mentally disabled persons; services provided by these funds include medical and psychological treatment as well as establishment of supported-employment and independent-living programs.

CONGRESS

House Education and the Workforce Committee, *Subcommittee on Select Education, 2181 RHOB 20515; (202) 225-4527. Fax, (202) 225-9571. Rep. Peter Hoekstra, R-Mich., Chair; Paula Nowakowski, Staff Director.*
Web, edworkforce.house.gov

Jurisdiction over legislation on all matters dealing with programs and services for the elderly, including health and nutrition programs and the Older Americans Act.

House Education and the Workforce Committee, *Subcommittee on Workforce Protections, 2181 RHOB 20515; (202) 225-4527. Fax, (202) 225-9571. Rep. Charlie Norwood, R-Ga., Chair; Paula Nowakowski, Staff Director.*
Web, edworkforce.house.gov

Jurisdiction over workers' health and safety legislation, including migrant and agricultural labor matters.

House Energy and Commerce Committee, *Subcommittee on Health, 2125 RHOB 20515; (202) 225-2927. Fax, (202) 225-1919. Rep. Michael Bilirakis, R-Fla., Chair; David V. Marventano, Staff Director.*
General e-mail, commerce@mail.house.gov
Web, energycommerce.house.gov

Jurisdiction over legislation on the mentally retarded, migrant health care, the disabled, long-term and nursing home programs, health care for the poor (including Medicaid and national health insurance proposals), and medical research on aging. (Jurisdiction over native American health care shared with House Resources Committee.)

House Resources Committee, *1324 LHOB 20515; (202) 225-2761. Fax, (202) 225-5929. Rep. Richard W. Pombo, R-Calif., Chair; Steve Ding, Chief of Staff.*
General e-mail, resources.committee@mail.house.gov
Web, resourcescommittee.house.gov

Jurisdiction over legislation pertaining to native American health care and special services; oversight of native American health care programs. (Jurisdiction shared with House Commerce Committee.)

Senate Finance Committee, *Subcommittee on Health Care, SD-219 20510; (202) 224-4515. Sen. Jon Kyl, R-Ariz., Chair; Linda Fishman, Counsel.*
Web, finance.senate.gov

Holds hearings on health legislation for low-income individuals, including Medicaid and national health insurance proposals. (Jurisdiction shared with the Senate Health, Education, Labor, and Pensions Committee.)

Senate Health, Education, Labor, and Pensions Committee, *SD-428 20510; (202) 224-5375. Fax, (202) 228-5044. Sen. Judd Gregg, R-N.H., Chair; Sharon Soderstrom, Staff Director. TTY, (202) 224-1975.*
Web, health.senate.gov

Jurisdiction over legislation on migrant health care, health care for the poor and elderly (excluding Medicaid and Medicare), health care for individuals with physical and developmental disabilities, government-run health care facilities, and medical research on aging.

Senate Indian Affairs Committee, *SH-838 20510; (202) 224-2251. Fax, (202) 228-2589. Sen. Ben Nighthorse Campbell, R-Colo., Chair; Paul Moorehead, Staff Director.*
Web, indian.senate.gov

Jurisdiction over legislation pertaining to native American health care; oversight of native American health care programs.

Senate Special Committee on Aging, *SD-G31 20510; (202) 224-5364. Fax, (202) 224-8660. Sen. Larry E. Craig, R-Idaho, Chair; Lupe Wissel, Staff Director.*
Web, aging.senate.gov

Studies and makes recommendations on the overall health problems of the elderly, including quality and cost of long-term care, and on access to and quality of health care for minority elderly; oversight of federally funded programs for the elderly, including Medicare, Medicaid, and programs concerning day-to-day care.

NONPROFIT

Brain Injury Assn. of America, *105 N. Alfred St., Alexandria, VA 22314; (703) 236-6000. Fax, (703) 236-6001. Allan I. Bergman, President. Family helpline, (800) 444-6443.*
Web, www.biausa.org

Works to improve the quality of life for persons with traumatic brain injuries and for their families. Promotes the prevention of head injuries through public awareness and education programs. Offers state-level support services for individuals and their families. Monitors legislation and regulations.

Catholic Health Assn. of the United States, *1875 Eye St. N.W., #1000 20006; (202) 296-3993. Fax, (202) 296-3997. Michael D. Place, President.*
Web, www.chausa.org

Concerned with the health care needs of the poor and disadvantaged. Promotes health care reform, including universal insurance coverage, and more cost-effective, affordable health care.

Center on Disability and Health, *1522 K St. N.W., #800 20005; (202) 842-4408. Bob Griss, Director.*
General e-mail, bgrisscdh@aol.com

Promotes changes in the financing and delivery of health care to meet the needs of persons with disabilities and other chronic health conditions. Conducts research; provides technical assistance to disability groups and agencies. Monitors legislation and regulations.

Farm Worker Health Services, *1221 Massachusetts Ave. N.W., #5 20005-4526; (202) 347-7377. Fax, (202) 347-6385. Oscar C. Gomez, Executive Director.*
General e-mail, farmwlths@aol.com
Web, www.farmworkerhealth.org

Funded by the Health and Human Services Dept. Assigns health professionals and allied health care personnel to health facilities along the East Coast. Assists migrants in addressing health and social needs and familiarizes providers with migrants' special health care needs.

National Alliance for Hispanic Health, *1501 16th St. N.W. 20036; (202) 387-5000. Fax, (202) 265-8027. Dr. Jane L. Delgado, President.*
General e-mail, info@hispanichealth.org
Web, www.hispanichealth.org

Assists agencies and groups serving the Hispanic community in general health care and in targeting health and psychosocial problems; provides information, technical assistance, health care provider training, and policy analysis; coordinates and supports research. Interests include mental health, chronic diseases, substance abuse, maternal and child health, youth issues, juvenile delinquency, and access to care.

National Assn. of Community Health Centers, *7200 Wisconsin Ave., #210, Bethesda, MD 20814; (301) 347-0400. Fax, (301) 347-0459. Thomas Van Coverden, President.*
General e-mail, contact@nachc.com
Web, www.nachc.com

Membership: community health centers, migrant and homeless health programs, and other community health care programs. Provides the medically underserved with health services; seeks to ensure the continued development of community health care programs through policy analysis, research, technical assistance, publications, education, and training.

National Easter Seal Society, *Washington Office, 700 13th St. N.W., #200 20005; (202) 347-3066. Fax, (202) 737-7914. Joseph D. Romer, Executive Vice President. TTY, (202) 347-7385.*
Web, www.easter-seals.org

Federation of state and local groups with programs that help people with disabilities achieve independence. Washington office monitors legislation and regulations. Affiliates assist individuals with a broad range of disabilities, including muscular dystrophy, cerebral palsy, stroke, speech and hearing loss, blindness, amputation, and learning disabilities. Services include physical, occupational, vocational, and speech therapy; speech, hearing, physical, and vocational evaluation; psychological testing and counseling; personal and family counseling; and special education programs. (Headquarters in Chicago, Ill.)

National Health Law Program, *Washington Office, 1101 14th St. N.W., #405 20005; (202) 289-7661. Fax, (202) 289-7724. Lawrence M. Lavin, Director.*
General e-mail, nhelpdc@healthlaw.org
Web, www.healthlaw.org

Organization of lawyers representing the economically disadvantaged, minorities, and the elderly in issues concerning federal, state, and local health care programs. Offers technical assistance, workshops, seminars, and training for health law specialists. (Headquarters in Los Angeles, Calif.)

Spina Bifida Assn. of America, *4590 MacArthur Blvd. N.W., #250 20007-4226; (202) 944-3285. Fax, (202) 944-3295. Cindy Brownstein, Chief Executive Officer. Information, (800) 621-3141.*
General e-mail, sbaa@sbaa.org
Web, www.sbaa.org

Membership: individuals with spina bifida, their supporters, and concerned professionals. Offers educational programs, scholarships, and support services; acts as a clearinghouse; provides referrals. Serves as U.S. member of the International Federation for Hydrocephalus and Spina Bifida, which is headquartered in Geneva. Monitors legislation and regulations.

White House Initiative on Asian Americans and Pacific Islanders, *5600 Fishers Lane, #10-42, Rockville, MD 20857-0259; (301) 443-2492. Fax, (301) 443-0259. John Quoc Duong, Executive Director.*
General e-mail, aapi@hrsa.gov
Web, www.aapi.gov

Advises the HHS secretary on the implementation and coordination of federal programs and how they relate to Asian Americans and Pacific Islanders; oversees federal interagency working group and presidential advisory commission (advisory commission will serve until June 7, 2003). Interests include health, education, housing, and economic and community development.

Elderly

AGENCIES

National Institute on Aging *(National Institutes of Health),* *31 Center Dr., Bldg. 31, #5C35, MSC-2292, Bethesda, MD 20892-2292; (301) 496-9265. Fax, (301) 496-2525. Dr. Richard J. Hodes, Director. Information, (301) 496-1752.*
Web, www.nih.gov/nia

Conducts and funds research and disseminates information on the biological, medical, behavioral, and social aspects of aging and the common problems of the elderly. Participates in international research.

NONPROFIT

AARP, *Long-Term Care, Independent Living, and End of Life, 601 E St. N.W., #B4170 20049; (202) 434-2264. Fax, (202) 434-6466. Elinor Ginzler, Manager.*
Web, www.aarp.org

Assists older adults in making health care decisions and staying independent.

AARP Foundation, *601 E St. N.W. 20049; (202) 434-6200. Fax, (202) 434-6483. Kathleen Burch, Director.*
Web, www.aarp.org/foundation

Seeks to educate the public on aging issues; sponsors conferences and produces publications on age-related concerns. Interests include aging and living environments for older persons. Funds age-related research, educational grants, legal hotlines, senior employment programs, and reverse mortgage projects. (Affiliated with AARP.)

Alliance for Aging Research, *2021 K St. N.W., #305 20006; (202) 293-2856. Fax, (202) 785-8574. Daniel P. Perry, Executive Director.*
General e-mail, info@agingresearch.org
Web, www.agingresearch.org

Membership: senior corporate and foundation executives, science leaders, and congressional representatives. Citizen advocacy organization that seeks to improve the health and independence of older Americans through public and private research.

Alliance for Retired Americans, *888 16th St. N.W., #520 20006; (202) 974-8222. Fax, (202) 974-8256. George J. Kourpias, President. Information, (888) 373-6497.*

Web, www.retiredamericans.org

Supports expansion of Medicare, improved health programs, national health care, and reduced cost of drugs. Nursing Home Information Service provides information on nursing home standards and regulations. (Affiliate of the AFL-CIO.)

Alzheimer's Assn., *Public Policy, Washington Office, 1319 F St. N.W., #710 20004-1106; (202) 393-7737. Fax, (202) 393-2109. Stephen R. McConnell, Vice President. Information, (800) 272-3900.*
Web, www.alz.org

Offers family support services and educates the public about Alzheimer's disease, a neurological disorder mainly affecting the brain tissue in older adults. Promotes research and long-term care protection; maintains liaison with Alzheimer's associations abroad. Monitors legislation and regulations. (Headquarters in Chicago, Ill.)

American Assn. of Homes and Services for the Aging, *Policy and Governmental Affairs, 2519 Connecticut Ave. N.W. 20008-1520; (202) 783-2242. Fax, (202) 783-2255. Susan M. Weiss, Vice President.*
Web, www.aahsa.org

Membership: nonprofit homes, housing, and health-related facilities for the elderly sponsored by religious, fraternal, labor, private, and governmental organizations. Conducts research on long-term care for the elderly; sponsors institutes and workshops on accreditation, financing, and institutional life. Monitors legislation and regulations.

Gerontological Society of America, *1030 15th St. N.W., #250 20005-1503; (202) 842-1275. Fax, (202) 842-1150. Carol Schutz, Executive Director.*
General e-mail, geron@geron.org
Web, www.geron.org

Scientific organization of researchers, educators, and professionals in the field of aging. Promotes the study of aging and the application of research to public policy; interests include international aging and migration.

National Assn. for Home Care and Hospice, *228 7th St. S.E. 20003; (202) 547-7424. Fax, (202) 547-3540. Val J. Halamandaris, President.*
General e-mail, webmaster@nahc.org
Web, www.nahc.org

Membership: home care professionals and paraprofessionals. Advocates the rights of the elderly, infirm, and terminally ill to remain independent in their own homes as long as possible. Monitors legislation and regulations.

National Citizens' Coalition for Nursing Home Reform, *1424 16th St. N.W., #202 20036-2211; (202)*

332-2275. Fax, (202) 332-2949. *Donna Lenhoff, Executive Director.*

Web, www.nursinghomeaction.org

Seeks to improve the long-term care system and quality of life for residents in nursing homes and other facilities for the elderly; coordinates the Campaign for Quality Care. Promotes citizen participation in all aspects of nursing homes; acts as clearinghouse for nursing home advocacy.

National Council on the Aging, *300 D St. S.W., #801 20024; (202) 479-1200. Fax, (202) 479-0735. James P. Firman, President. Information, (202) 479-6653. Press, (202) 479-6975.*

General e-mail, info@ncoa.org

Web, www.ncoa.org

Promotes the physical, mental, and emotional health of older persons and studies adult day care and community-based long-term care. Monitors legislation and regulations.

National Hispanic Council on Aging, *2713 Ontario Rd. N.W. 20009; (202) 265-1288. Fax, (202) 745-2522. Marta Sotomayor, President.*

General e-mail, nhcoa@nhcoa.org

Web, www.nhcoa.org

Membership: senior citizens, health care workers, professionals in the field of aging, and others in the United States and Puerto Rico who are interested in topics related to Hispanics and aging.

National Long-Term Care Ombudsman Resource Center, *1424 16th St. N.W., #202 20036-2211; (202) 332-2275. Fax, (202) 332-2949. Alice Hedt, Director.*

General e-mail, ombudcenter@nccnhr.org

Web, www.ltcombudsman.org

Provides technical assistance, management guidance, policy analysis, and program development information on behalf of state and substate ombudsman programs. (Affiliate of the National Citizens' Coalition for Nursing Home Reform.)

National Osteoporosis Foundation, *1232 22nd St. N.W. 20037-1292; (202) 223-2226. Fax, (202) 223-2237. Judith Cranford, Executive Director.*

General e-mail, nofmail@nof.org

Web, www.nof.org

Seeks to reduce osteoporosis through educational programs, research, and patient advocacy. Monitors international research.

Prenatal, Maternal, and Child Health Care

AGENCIES

Centers for Disease Control and Prevention *(Health and Human Services Dept.), Washington Office, 200 Independence Ave. S.W., HHH Bldg., #746-G 20201-0004; (202) 690-8598. Fax, (202) 690-7519. Donald E. Shriber, Associate Director.*

Web, www.cdc.gov

Assists state and local health agencies that receive grants for the control of childhood diseases preventable by immunization. Studies childhood diseases worldwide. (Headquarters in Atlanta, Ga.: 1600 Clifton Rd. N.E. 30333. Public inquiries, [404] 639-3534.)

Centers for Medicare and Medicaid Services (CMS), *(Health and Human Services Dept.), Medicaid, 7500 Security Blvd., #C52223, Baltimore, MD 21244; (410) 786-3870. Fax, (410) 786-0025. Dennis Smith, Director. Alternate phone, (202) 205-3067.*

Web, www.cms.hhs.gov

Develops health care policies and programs for needy children under Medicaid; works with the Public Health Service and other related agencies to coordinate the department's child health resources. (Formerly Health Care Financing Administration.)

Environmental Protection Agency (EPA), *Children's Health Protection, 1200 Pennsylvania Ave. N.W., MS 1107A 20460; (202) 564-2188. Fax, (202) 564-2733. Joanne Rodman, Director (Acting).*

Web, www.epa.gov

Supports and facilitates EPA's efforts to protect children's health from environmental threats.

Health Resources and Services Administration *(Health and Human Services Dept.), Maternal and Child Health, 5600 Fishers Lane, #18-05, Rockville, MD 20857; (301) 443-2170. Fax, (301) 443-1797. Dr. Peter C. van Dyck, Associate Administrator.*

Web, www.hrsa.mchb.gov

Administers block grants to states for mothers and children and for children with special health needs; awards funding for research training, genetic disease testing, counseling and information dissemination, hemophilia diagnostic and treatment centers, and demonstration projects to improve the health of mothers and children. Interests also include pediatric AIDS health care and emergency medical services for children.

Health Resources and Services Administration *(Health and Human Services Dept.), National Mater-*

nal and Child Health Clearinghouse, *2070 Chain Bridge Rd., #450, Vienna, VA 22182; (703) 442-9051. Fax, (703) 821-2098. Jody Nurik, Project Director, (703) 902-1265.*
Web, www.nmchc.org

Disseminates information on various aspects of maternal and child health and genetics.

Health Resources and Services Administration *(Health and Human Services Dept.), National Sudden Infant Death Syndrome Resource Center, 2070 Chain Bridge Rd., #450, Vienna, VA 22182; (703) 821-8955. Fax, (703) 821-2098. Olivia Cowdrill, Director.*
General e-mail, sids@circlesolutions.com
Web, www.sidscenter.org

Provides information about sudden infant death syndrome (SIDS), apnea, and related issues; makes referrals to local SIDS programs and parent support groups; publishes educational information about SIDS; distributes literature for the National Institute of Child Health and Human Development's "Back to Sleep" campaign.

Health Resources and Services Administration *(Health and Human Services Dept.), National Vaccine Injury Compensation Program, 5600 Fishers Lane, Parklawn Bldg., #16C-17, Rockville, MD 20857; (301) 443-6593. Fax, (301) 443-8196. Thomas E. Balbier Jr., Director. Toll-free hotline, (800) 338-2382.*
Web, www.hrsa.gov/osp/vicp

Provides no-fault compensation to individuals injured by certain childhood vaccines (rotavirus vaccine; diphtheria and tetanus toxoids and pertussis vaccine; measles, mumps, and rubella vaccine; varicella, hepatitis B, HiB vaccine; and oral polio and inactivated polio vaccine).

National Institute of Child Health and Human Development *(National Institutes of Health), 31 Center Dr., Bldg. 31, #2A03, MSC-2425, Bethesda, MD 20892-2425; (301) 496-3454. Fax, (301) 402-1104. Dr. Duane F. Alexander, Director. Information, (301) 496-5133.*
Web, www.nichd.nih.gov

Conducts research and research training on biological and behavioral human development. Studies reproduction and population statistics, perinatal biology and infant mortality, congenital defects, nutrition, human learning and behavior, medical rehabilitation, and mental retardation. Interests include UNICEF and other international organizations.

National Institute of Child Health and Human Development *(National Institutes of Health), Center for Research for Mothers and Children, 6100 Executive*

Blvd., #4B05, Bethesda, MD 20892-7510; (301) 496-5097. Fax, (301) 480-7773. Anne Willoughby, Director.
Web, www.nichd.nih.gov

Supports biomedical and behavioral science research and training for maternal and child health care. Areas of study include fetal development, maternal-infant health problems, HIV-related diseases in childbearing women, roles of nutrients and hormones in child growth, developmental disabilities, and behavioral development.

Public Health and Science *(Health and Human Services Dept.), Adolescent Pregnancy Programs, 1101 Wootton Pkwy., 7th Floor, Rockville, MD 20852; (301) 594-4004. Fax, (301) 594-5981. Patrick J. Sheeran, Director.*
General e-mail, ops@opa.osophs.dhhs.gov
Web, opa.osophs.dhhs.gov

Awards, administers, and evaluates research and demonstration grants through the Adolescent Family Life Program, which funds community health care and pregnancy prevention programs. Administers a program that provides pregnant adolescents and children of teenage parents with comprehensive health education and social services, and a program that focuses on sexual abstinence. Interests include adolescent sexual behavior, adoption, and early childbearing.

NONPROFIT

Advocates for Youth, *1025 Vermont Ave. N.W., #200 20005; (202) 347-5700. Fax, (202) 347-2263. James Wagoner, Executive Director.*
General e-mail, info@advocatesforyouth.org
Web, www.advocatesforyouth.org

Seeks to reduce the incidence of unintended teenage pregnancy and AIDS through public education, training and technical assistance, research, and media programs.

Alan Guttmacher Institute, *Public Policy, Washington Office, 1120 Connecticut Ave. N.W., #460 20036-3902; (202) 296-4012. Fax, (202) 223-5756. Cory L. Richards, Senior Vice President.*
General e-mail, policyinfo@guttmacher.org
Web, www.guttmacher.org

Conducts research, policy analysis, and public education in reproductive health issues, including maternal and child health. (Headquarters in New York.)

Alliance to End Childhood Lead Poisoning, *227 Massachusetts Ave. N.E., #200 20002; (202) 543-1147. Fax, (202) 543-4466. Don Ryan, Executive Director.*
General e-mail, aeclp@aeclp.org
Web, www.aeclp.org

Works to increase awareness of childhood lead poisoning and to develop and implement prevention programs.

American Academy of Child and Adolescent Psychiatry, *3615 Wisconsin Ave. N.W., 2nd Floor 20016-3007; (202) 966-7300. Fax, (202) 966-2891. Virginia Q. Anthony, Executive Director.*

Web, www.aacap.org

Membership: psychiatrists working with children and adolescents. Sponsors annual meeting and review for medical board examinations; provides information on child abuse, youth suicide, and drug abuse; monitors international research and U.S. legislation concerning children with mental illness.

American Academy of Pediatrics, *Washington Office, 601 13th St. N.W., #400N 20005; (202) 347-8600. Fax, (202) 393-6137. Jackie Noyes, Director. Information, (800) 336-5475.*

General e-mail, kids1st@aap.org

Web, www.aap.org

Advocates for maternal and child health legislation and regulations. Interests include increased access and coverage for persons under age twenty-one, immunizations, injury prevention, environmental hazards, child abuse, emergency medical services, biomedical research, Medicaid, disabilities, pediatric AIDS, substance abuse, and nutrition. (Headquarters in Elk Grove Village, Ill.)

American Assn. of Children's Residential Centers, *51 Monroe Pl., #1603, Rockville, MD 20850; (301) 738-6460. Fax, (301) 738-6461. Tammy J. Eisenhart, Executive Director.*

General e-mail, info@aacrc-dc.net

Web, www.aacrc-dc.org

Membership: mental health out-of-home agencies and individuals interested in clinical practice in residential care for children with emotional disturbance. Represents interests of children with emotional disturbance and their families before the federal government; conducts educational conferences; provides information on residential treatment.

American College of Nurse-Midwives, *818 Connecticut Ave. N.W., #900 20006; (202) 728-9860. Fax, (202) 728-9897. Deanne Williams, Executive Director. Press, (202) 728-9875.*

General e-mail, info@acnm.org

Web, www.midwife.org

Membership: certified nurse-midwives who preside at deliveries. Interests include preventive health care for women.

American College of Obstetricians and Gynecologists, *409 12th St. S.W. 20024 (mailing address: P.O. Box 96920 20090-6920); (202) 638-5577. Fax, (202) 484-5107. Dr. Ralph Hale, Executive Director. Press, (202) 863-2560.*

Web, www.acog.org

Membership: medical specialists in obstetrics and gynecology. Monitors legislation, regulations, and international research on maternal and child health care.

Children's Defense Fund, *25 E St. N.W. 20001; (202) 628-8787. Fax, (202) 662-3510. Marian Wright Edelman, President.*

General e-mail, cdfinfo@childrensdefense.org

Web, www.childrensdefense.org

Advocacy group concerned with programs for children and youth. Assesses adequacy of the Early and Periodic Screening, Diagnosis, and Treatment Program for Medicaid-eligible children. Promotes adequate prenatal care for adolescent and lower-income women; works to prevent adolescent pregnancy.

Lamaze International, *2025 M St. N.W., #800 20036-3309; (202) 367-1128. Fax, (202) 367-2128. Linda Harmon, Executive Director. Information, (800) 368-4404.*

General e-mail, lamaze@dc.sba.com

Web, www.lamaze.org

Membership: supporters of the Lamaze method of childbirth, including parents, physicians, childbirth educators, and other health professionals. Trains and certifies Lamaze educators. Provides referral service for parents seeking Lamaze classes.

March of Dimes, *Government Affairs, Washington Office, 1146 19th St. N.W., #600 20036; (202) 659-1800. Fax, (202) 296-2964. Marina L. Weiss, Senior Vice President.*

Web, www.modimes.org

Works to prevent birth defects, low birth weight, and infant mortality. Awards grants for research and provides funds for treatment of birth defects. Medical services grantees provide prenatal counseling. Monitors legislation and regulations. (Headquarters in White Plains, N.Y.)

National Assn. of Children's Hospitals and Related Institutions, *401 Wythe St., Alexandria, VA 22314; (703) 684-1355. Fax, (703) 684-1589. Lawrence A. McAndrews, President.*

Web, www.childrenshospitals.net

Advocates and promotes education and research on child health care related to children's hospitals; compiles statistics and provides information on pediatric hospitalizations. (Affiliated with the National Assn. of Children's Hospitals.)

National Center for Education in Maternal and Child Health, 2115 Wisconsin Ave. N.W., #601 20007; (202) 784-9770. Fax, (202) 784-9777. Dr. Rochelle Mayer, Director.
General e-mail, info@ncemch.org
Web, www.ncemch.org

Collects and disseminates information about maternal and child health to health professionals and the general public. Carries out special projects for the U.S. Maternal and Child Health Bureau. Library open to the public by appointment. (Affiliated with Georgetown University.)

National Consortium for Child Mental Health Services, 3615 Wisconsin Ave. N.W., 2nd Floor 20016-2037; (202) 966-7300. Fax, (202) 966-2891. Virginia Q. Anthony, Executive Director.
Web, www.aacap.org

Membership: organizations interested in developing mental health services for children. Fosters information exchange; advises local, state, and federal agencies that develop children's mental health services. (Affiliated with American Academy of Child and Adolescent Psychiatry.)

National Organization on Adolescent Pregnancy, Parenting and Prevention, Inc., 2401 Pennsylvania Ave. N.W., #350 20037; (202) 293-8370. Fax, (202) 293-8805. Mary Martha Wilson, Co-Executive Director (Acting); Karen L. Canova, Co-Executive Director (Acting).
General e-mail, noappp@noappp.org
Web, www.noappp.org

Membership: health and social work professionals, community and state leaders, and individuals. Promotes services to prevent and resolve problems associated with adolescent sexuality, pregnancy, and parenting. Helps to develop stable and supportive family relationships through program support and evaluation. Monitors legislation and regulations.

National Organization on Fetal Alcohol Syndrome, 216 G St. N.E. 20002; (202) 785-4585. Fax, (202) 466-6456. Tom Donaldson, Executive Director. Information, (800) 666-6327.
General e-mail, information@nofas.org
Web, www.nofas.org

Works to eradicate fetal alcohol syndrome and alcohol-related birth defects through public education, conferences, medical school curricula, and partnerships with federal programs interested in fetal alcohol syndrome.

Zero to Three/National Center for Infants, Toddlers, and Families, 2000 M St. N.W., #200 20036; (202) 638-1144. Fax, (202) 638-0851. Matthew Melmed, Executive Director. Publications, (800) 899-4301.

General e-mail, 0to3@zerotothree.org
Web, www.zerotothree.org

Works to improve infant health, mental health, and development. Sponsors training programs for professionals; offers fellowships. Provides private and government organizations with information on infant development issues.

✚ HEALTH TOPICS: RESEARCH AND ADVOCACY

AGENCIES

Armed Forces Institute of Pathology (Defense Dept.), 6825 16th St. N.W., Bldg. 54 20306-6000; (202) 782-2100. Fax, (202) 782-9376. Capt. Glenn Wagner (USN), Director.
Web, www.afip.org

Maintains a central laboratory of pathology for consultation and diagnosis of pathologic tissue for the Defense Dept., other federal agencies, and civilian pathologists. Conducts research and provides instruction in advanced pathology and related subjects; monitors international research.

Armed Forces Radiobiology Research Institute (Defense Dept.), 8901 Wisconsin Ave., Bethesda, MD 20889-5603; (301) 295-1210. Fax, (301) 295-4967. Col. Robert R. Eng (MSUSA), Director.
Web, www.afrri.usuhs.mil

Serves as the principal ionizing radiation radiobiology research laboratory under the jurisdiction of the Uniformed Services of the Health Sciences. Participates in international conferences and projects.

Environment, Safety, and Health (Energy Dept.), **Health Studies,** 19901 Germantown Rd., Germantown, MD 20874-1290 (mailing address: 1000 Independence Ave. S.W, EH-6/270CC, Washington, DC 20585); (301) 903-5926. Fax, (301) 903-3445. Steven V. Carey, Deputy Assistant Secretary.
Web, www.tis.eh.doe.gov/health

Evaluates and establishes standards related to radiation, industrial hygiene, and occupational medicine. Oversees epidemiologic studies.

Fogarty International Center (National Institutes of Health), 9000 Rockville Pike, Bldg. 31, #B2C02, Bethesda, MD 20892-2220; (301) 496-1415. Fax, (301) 402-2173. Gerald T. Keusch, Director.
General e-mail, ficinfo@nih.gov
Web, www.fic.nih.gov

Promotes and supports international scientific research and training to reduce disparities in global health. Leads formulation and implementation of international biomedical research and policy. Supports the conduct of research in priority global health areas and helps build research capacity in the developing world.

Health and Human Services Dept. (HHS), *(Health and Human Services Dept.),* **Human Research Protections,** *1101 Wootton Pkwy., #200, The Tower Building, Rockville, MD 20852; (301) 496-7005. Fax, (301) 402-0527. Bernard Schwetz, Director (Acting).*
General e-mail, ohrp@osophs.dhhs.gov
Web, ohrp.osophs.dhhs.gov

Monitors the use of humans in research to ensure that programs and procedures comply with Public Health Service and Health and Human Services Dept. regulations; develops and conducts educational programs for the protection of human subjects; helps other organizations address ethical issues in medicine and research.

Health Resources and Services Administration *(Health and Human Services Dept.),* **Special Programs: Transplantation,** *5600 Fishers Lane, #16 C-17, Rockville, MD 20857; (301) 443-7577. Fax, (301) 443-1267. Joyce Somsak, Director (Acting).*
Web, www.organdonor.gov

Implements provisions of the National Organ Transplant Act. Provides information on federal, state, and private programs involved in transplantation; supports a national computerized network for organ procurement and matching; maintains information on transplant recipients; awards grants to organ procurement organizations. Administers the National Marrow Donor Program, which maintains a registry of potential unrelated bone marrow donors.

National Heart, Lung, and Blood Institute *(National Institutes of Health),* *31 Center Dr., Bldg. 31, #5A52, MSC-2486, Bethesda, MD 20892-2486; (301) 496-5166. Fax, (301) 402-0818. Dr. Claude Lenfant, Director. Press, (301) 496-4236.*
Web, www.nhlbi.nih.gov

Collects and disseminates information on diseases of the heart, lungs, and blood, on sleep disorders, and on transfusion medicine, with an emphasis on disease prevention. Conducts educational programs for scientists and clinicians; participates in international research.

National Institute of Diabetes and Digestive and Kidney Diseases *(National Institutes of Health),* *31 Center Dr., Bldg. 31, #9A52, MSC-2560, Bethesda, MD 20892-2560; (301) 496-5877. Fax, (301) 402-2125. Dr. Allen M. Spiegel, Director.*
Web, www.niddk.nih.gov

Conducts and supports research on kidney, urologic, hematologic, digestive, metabolic, and endocrine diseases, as well as on diabetes and nutrition. Provides health information to the public; participates in international research.

National Institute of General Medical Sciences *(National Institutes of Health),* *45 Center Dr., #2AN12B, MSC-6200, Bethesda, MD 20892-6200; (301) 594-2172. Fax, (301) 402-0156. Judith Greenberg, Director (Acting).*
Web, www.nigms.nih.gov

Supports basic biomedical research and training that are not targeted to specific diseases; focus includes cell biology, genetics, pharmacology, and systemic response to trauma and anesthesia.

National Institutes of Health (NIH), *(Health and Human Services Dept.),* *1 Center Dr., Bldg. 1, #126, MSC-0148, Bethesda, MD 20892-0148; (301) 496-2433. Fax, (301) 402-2700. Elias A. Zerhouni, Director. Press, (301) 496-4461.*
Web, www.nih.gov

Supports and conducts biomedical research on the causes and prevention of diseases; furnishes health professionals and the public with information.

National Institutes of Health (NIH), *(Health and Human Services Dept.),* **Center for Information Technology,** *12 South Dr., Bldg. 12A, #3033, MSC-5654, Bethesda, MD 20892-5654; (301) 496-6203. Fax, (301) 402-4437. Alan Graeff, Director.*
Web, www.cit.gov

Responsible for incorporating computers into biomedical research information, technology, security, and administrative procedures of NIH. Serves as the primary scientific and technological resource for NIH in the areas of high performance computing, database applications, mathematics, statistics, laboratory automation, engineering, computer science and technology, telecommunications, and information resources management.

National Institutes of Health (NIH), *(Health and Human Services Dept.),* **Center for Scientific Review,** *6701 Rockledge Dr., #3016, MSC-7776, Bethesda, MD 20892-7776; (301) 435-1114. Fax, (301) 480-3965. Dr. Ellie Ehrenfeld, Director.*
Web, www.csr.nih.gov

Conducts scientific merit review of research grant and fellowship applications submitted to NIH. Assists in formulating grant and award policies.

National Institutes of Health (NIH), *(Health and Human Services Dept.), Minority Opportunities in Research,* 45 Center Dr., Bldg. 45, #2AS.37, Bethesda, MD 20892; (301) 594-3900. Fax, (301) 480-2753. Dr. Clifton A. Poodry, Director.

Web, www.nigms.nih.gov

Administers research and research training programs aimed at increasing the number of minority biomedical scientists. Funds grants, fellowships, faculty development awards, and development of research facilities.

National Institutes of Health (NIH), *(Health and Human Services Dept.), National Center for Complementary and Alternative Medicine,* 31 Center Dr., Bldg. 31, #2B11, MSC-2182, Bethesda, MD 20892-2182; (301) 435-5042. Fax, (301) 435-6549. Dr. Stephen E. Straus, Director. Information, (888) 644-6226.

General e-mail, nccam-info@nccam.nih.gov

Web, www.nccam.nih.gov

Conducts and supports complementary and alternative medicine research and training; disseminates information to practitioners and the public; works with the Food and Drug Administration (FDA) to evaluate the current rules and regulations governing research on and the use of devices, acupuncture needles, herbs, and homeopathic remedies.

National Institutes of Health (NIH), *(Health and Human Services Dept.), National Center for Research Resources,* 9000 Rockville Pike, Bldg. 31, #3B11, MSC-2128, Bethesda, MD 20892-2128; (301) 496-5793. Fax, (301) 402-0006. Dr. Judith L. Vaitukaitis, Director.

Web, www.ncrr.nih.gov

Discovers, develops, and provides biomedical researchers with access to critical research technologies and resources, including sophisticated instrumentation, models of human disease, and clinical research environments.

National Institutes of Health (NIH), *(Health and Human Services Dept.), National Center on Minority Health and Health Disparities,* 2 Democracy Plaza, 6707 Democracy Blvd., #800, MSC-5465, Bethesda, MD 20892-5465; (301) 402-1366. Fax, (301) 480-4049. Dr. John Ruffin, Director.

Web, www.ncmhd.nih.gov

Coordinates the development of NIH policies and objectives related to minority health research and research training programs. Encourages minorities to work in the biomedical research field.

National Library of Medicine *(National Institutes of Health),* 8600 Rockville Pike, Bldg. 38, #2E17, MSC-0002, Bethesda, MD 20894-0002; (301) 496-6221. Fax, (301) 496-4450. Dr. Donald A. B. Lindberg, Director. Information, (800) 346-3656.

Web, www.nlm.nih.gov

Offers medical library services and computer-based reference service to the public, health professionals, libraries in medical schools and hospitals, and research institutions; operates a toxicology information service for the scientific community, industry, and federal agencies; assists medical libraries through the National Network of Libraries of Medicines with research in medical library science. Assists in the improvement of basic library resources.

National Library of Medicine *(National Institutes of Health), Health Information Programs Development,* 8600 Rockville Pike, Bldg. 38, #2S20, MSC-12, Bethesda, MD 20894; (301) 496-2311. Fax, (301) 496-4450. Elliot R. Siegel, Associate Director.

Web, www.nlm.nih.gov

Facilitates worldwide use of the library's medical databases, through agreements with individual nations, international organizations, and commercial vendors. Helps the library acquire and share international biomedical literature; promotes international collaboration in creating new databases. Conducts programs for international visitors.

Naval Medical Research Center *(Defense Dept.),* 503 Robert Grant Ave., #1W28, Silver Spring, MD 20910-7500; (301) 319-7400. Fax, (301) 319-7410. Capt. Richard B. Oberst, Commanding Officer.

Web, www.nmrc.navy.mil

Performs basic and applied biomedical research in areas of military importance, including infectious diseases, hyperbaric medicine, wound repair enhancement, environmental stress, and immunobiology. Provides support to field laboratories and naval hospitals; monitors research internationally.

Walter Reed Army Institute of Research *(Defense Dept.),* 503 Robert Grant Ave., Silver Spring, MD 20910-7500; (301) 319-9100. Fax, (301) 319-9227. Col. Charles E. McQueen, Director.

Web, www.wrair.army.mil

Provides research, education, and training in support of the Defense Dept.'s health care system. Develops vaccines and drugs to prevent and treat naturally occurring diseases. Interests include biochemistry, biometrics, pathology, veterinary medicine, naturally occurring infectious diseases of military importance, battle casualties, operational stress, sleep deprivation, and defense against biological and chemical agents.

NATIONAL INSTITUTES OF HEALTH

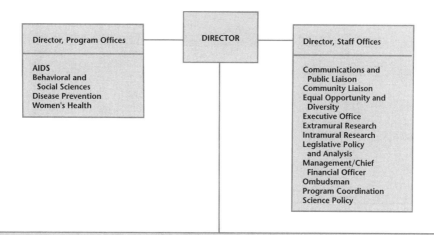

Warren Grant Magnuson Clinical Center *(National Institutes of Health)*, 10 Center Dr., Bldg. 10, #2C146, MSC-1504, Bethesda, MD 20892-1504; (301) 496-4114. Fax, (301) 402-0244. Dr. John I. Gallin, Director.
Web, www.cc.nih.gov

Serves as a clinical research center for the NIH; patients are referred by physicians and self-referred throughout the United States and overseas.

CONGRESS

House Energy and Commerce Committee, *Subcommittee on Health,* 2125 RHOB 20515; (202) 225-2927. Fax, (202) 225-1919. Rep. Michael Bilirakis, R-Fla., Chair; David V. Marventano, Staff Director.
General e-mail, commerce@mail.house.gov
Web, energycommerce.house.gov

Jurisdiction over legislation on health research, the treatment of cancer, AIDS, medical research on human

subjects, and developmental disabilities (including epilepsy, cerebral palsy, autism, and mental retardation).

House Science Committee, *Subcommittee on Research,* B374 RHOB 20515; (202) 225-7858. Fax, (202) 225-7815. Rep. Nick Smith, R-Mich., Chair; Peter Rooney, Staff Director.
General e-mail, science@mail.house.gov
Web, www.house.gov/science

Jurisdiction over legislation on research and development involving health, nutrition, and medical programs.

Senate Health, Education, Labor, and Pensions Committee, SD-428 20510; (202) 224-5375. Fax, (202) 228-5044. Sen. Judd Gregg, R-N.H., Chair; Sharon Soderstrom, Staff Director. TTY, (202) 224-1975.
Web, health.senate.gov

Jurisdiction over legislation on health research and health professions education. Oversight of public health programs, including the National Institutes of Health, Agency for Health Care Policy and Research, and Substance Abuse and Mental Health Services Administration.

NONPROFIT

AcademyHealth, *1801 K St. N.W., #701-L 20036; (202) 292-6700. Fax, (202) 292-6800. W. David Helms, Chief Executive Officer.*
Web, www.academyhealth.org

Membership: individuals and organizations with an interest in health services research, including universities, private research organizations, professional associations, consulting firms, advocacy organizations, insurers, managed care companies, health care systems, and pharmaceutical companies. Serves as an information clearinghouse on health services research; works to increase public and private funding for research. Monitors legislation and regulations. (Formerly Academy for Health Services Research and Health Policy.)

American Physiological Society, *9650 Rockville Pike, #4403, Bethesda, MD 20814-3991; (301) 634-7118. Fax, (301) 634-7242. Dr. Martin Frank, Executive Director.*
General e-mail, info@aps.faseb.org
Web, www.the-aps.org

Researches how the body and its organ systems function. Promotes scientific research, education, and dissemination of information through publication of peer-reviewed journals; monitors international research. Offers travel fellowships for scientific meetings; encourages minority participation in physiological research. Works to establish standards for the humane care and use of laboratory animals. Publishes fourteen scientific journals and a newsletter.

American Trauma Society, *8903 Presidential Pkwy., #512, Upper Marlboro, MD 20772-2656; (301) 420-4189. Fax, (301) 420-0617. Harry Teter, Executive Director.*
General e-mail, atstrauma@aol.com
Web, www.amtrauma.org

Seeks to prevent trauma and improve its treatment. Coordinates programs aimed at reducing the incidence and severity of trauma; sponsors research; provides training to nurses and others involved in the trauma field. Monitors legislation and regulations.

Center for Patient Advocacy, *1350 Beverly Rd., #108, McLean, VA 22101; (703) 748-0400. Fax, (703) 748-0402. Terre McFillen Hall, Executive Director. Information, (800) 846-7444.*
General e-mail, advocate@patientadvocacy.org
Web, www.patientadvocacy.org

Represents the interests of patients nationwide. Dedicated to ensuring that patients have timely access to state-of-the-art health care.

Foundation for the National Institutes of Health, *1 Cloister Court, #152, Bethesda, MD 20814-1460; (301) 402-5311. Amy McGuire, Executive Director.*
General e-mail, Foundation@FNIH.org
Web, www.fnih.org

Supports the NIH's mission of developing new knowledge through biomedical research. Works to foster collaborative relationships in education, research, and related activities between the NIH, industry, academia, and nonprofit organizations; supports basic and clinical research to advance medical knowledge; supports training and advanced education programs for future researchers; and invests in educational programs related to medical research.

Howard Hughes Medical Institute, *4000 Jones Bridge Rd., Chevy Chase, MD 20815-6789; (301) 215-8500. Fax, (301) 215-8663. Dr. Thomas R. Cech, President.*
Web, www.hhmi.org

Conducts biomedical research programs in major academic medical centers and universities. Areas of research include cell biology, genetics, immunology, neuroscience, and structural biology. Maintains a grants program in science education, including precollege, undergraduate, graduate, and postgraduate levels. Supports selected biomedical researchers in foreign countries.

Institute for Alternative Futures, *100 N. Pitt St., #235, Alexandria, VA 22314-3134; (703) 684-5880. Fax, (703) 684-0640. Dr. Clement Bezold, President.*
General e-mail, futurist@altfutures.com
Web, www.altfutures.com

Research and educational organization that explores the implications of scientific developments. Works with state and local governments, Congress, and associations; conducts seminars. Interests include pharmaceutical research, health care, telecommunications, artificial intelligence, energy, and the environment.

Institute of Medicine, *2101 Constitution Ave. N.W. 20418; (202) 334-3300. Fax, (202) 334-3851. Harvey V. Fineberg, President. Library, (202) 334-2125. Press, (202) 334-2138.*
General e-mail, iomwww@nas.edu
Web, www.iom.edu

Independent research organization chartered by the National Academy of Sciences. Studies policy issues related to health and medicine and issues position statements; interests include international health. National

Academy of Sciences library open to the public by appointment.

Johns Hopkins University Applied Physics Laboratory, *11100 Johns Hopkins Rd., Laurel, MD 20723-6099; (240) 228-5000. Fax, (240) 228-1093. Dr. Richard T. Roca, Director. Information, (240) 228-5021. Web, www.jhuapl.edu*

Organization that, with affiliated medical centers, conducts research and develops engineering-related biomedical programs and high technology systems to improve medical care.

National Sleep Foundation, *1522 K St. N.W., #500 20005-1253; (202) 347-3471. Fax, (202) 347-3472. Richard Gelula, Executive Director. General e-mail, nsf@sleepfoundation.org Web, www.sleepfoundation.org*

Promotes research to understand sleep disorders, including insomnia, sleep apnea, and narcolepsy. Works to prevent sleep-related accidents, especially those that involve driving.

Research!America, *1101 King St., #520, Alexandria, VA 22314-2944; (703) 739-2577. Fax, (703) 739-2372. Mary Woolley, President. Information, (800) 366-2873. General e-mail, info@researchamerica.org Web, www.researchamerica.org*

Membership: academic institutions, professional societies, voluntary health organizations, corporations, and individuals interested in promoting medical research. Provides information on the benefits of medical and health research and seeks to increase funding for research.

SRI International, *Washington Office, 1100 Wilson Blvd., #2800, Arlington, VA 22209; (703) 524-2053. Fax, (703) 247-8569. John Bramer, Director. Web, www.sri.com*

Research and consulting organization. Conducts studies on biotechnology, genetic engineering, drug metabolism, cancer, toxicology, disease control systems, and other areas of basic and applied research; monitors international research. (Headquarters in Menlo Park, Calif.)

Undersea and Hyperbaric Medical Society, *10531 Metropolitan Ave., Kensington, MD 20895-2627; (301) 942-2980. Fax, (301) 942-7804. Donald R. Chandler, Executive Director. General e-mail, uhms@uhms.org Web, www.uhms.org*

Membership: doctors and researchers in the diving and hyperbaric medical field. Works internationally to advance undersea and hyperbaric medicine and its supporting sciences. Interests include the effect of greater than normal atmospheric pressure on the human body. Serves as a forum for information exchange on scientific issues.

Whitaker Foundation, *1700 N. Moore St., #2200, Arlington, VA 22209; (703) 528-2430. Fax, (703) 528-2431. Dr. Peter G. Katona, President. General e-mail, info@whitaker.org Web, www.whitaker.org*

Dedicated to improving human health through the support of biomedical engineering. Awards grants and fellowships to universities in the fields of biomedical engineering research, development, and education.

AIDS and HIV

AGENCIES

Centers for Disease Control and Prevention *(Health and Human Services Dept.), Washington Office, 200 Independence Ave. S.W., HHH Bldg., #746-G 20201-0004; (202) 690-8598. Fax, (202) 690-7519. Donald E. Shriber, Associate Director. Web, www.cdc.gov*

Conducts research to prevent and control acquired immune deficiency syndrome (AIDS); promotes public awareness through guidelines for health care workers, educational packets for schools, and monthly reports on incidences of AIDS. (Headquarters in Atlanta, Ga.: 1600 Clifton Rd. N.E. 30333. Public inquiries, [404] 639-3534.)

Food and Drug Administration (FDA), *(Health and Human Services Dept.), Center for Biologics Evaluation and Research, 1401 Rockville Pike, #200 North, Rockville, MD 20852-1448; (301) 827-0372. Fax, (301) 827-0440. Dr. Jesse L. Goodman, Director. Press, (301) 827-2000. Web, www.fda.gov/cber*

Develops testing standards for vaccines, blood supply, and blood products and derivatives to prevent transmission of the human immunodeficiency virus (HIV); regulates biological therapeutics; helps formulate international standards. Serves as the focus for AIDS activities within the FDA.

Food and Drug Administration (FDA), *(Health and Human Services Dept.), Center for Drug Evaluation and Research, 1451 Rockville Pike, Rockville, MD 20852; (301) 594-5400. Fax, (301) 594-6197. Dr. Janet Woodcock, Director. Information, (301) 827-4573. Press, (301) 827-6242. Web, www.fda.gov/cdr*

Approves new drugs for AIDS and AIDS-related diseases. Reviews and approves applications to investigate and market new drugs; works to harmonize drug approval internationally.

Health Resources and Services Administration *(Health and Human Services Dept.), HIV/AIDS Bureau, 5600 Fishers Lane, #705, Rockville, MD 20857; (301) 443-1993. Fax, (301) 443-9645. Deborah L. Parham, Associate Administrator.*
Web, www.hab.hrsa.gov

Administers grants to support health care programs for AIDS patients, including those that reimburse low-income patients for drug expenses. Provides patients with AIDS and HIV-related disorders with ambulatory and community-based care. Conducts AIDS/HIV education and training activities for health professionals.

National Institute of Allergy and Infectious Diseases *(National Institutes of Health), AIDS, 6700-B Rockledge Dr., #4142, Bethesda, MD 20892-7620; (301) 496-0545. Fax, (301) 402-1505. Dr. Edmond C. Tramont, Director. Toll-free hotline, (800) 342-2437.*
Web, www.niaid.nih.gov/daids

Primary institute at NIH for AIDS research. Conducts a network of AIDS clinical trials and preclinical drug development research. Supports epidemiological studies and research into AIDS vaccines. Studies the pathogenesis of HIV infection.

National Institutes of Health (NIH), *(Health and Human Services Dept.), Office of AIDS Research, 2 Center Dr., Bldg. 2, Bethesda, MD 20892; (301) 496-0357. Fax, (301) 496-2119. Jack E. Whitescarver, Director.*
Web, www.nih.gov/od/oar/index.htm

Responsible for the scientific, budgetary, legislative, and policy elements of the NIH AIDS research program. Plans, coordinates, evaluates, and funds all NIH AIDS research.

Office of National AIDS Policy (ONAP), *(Executive Office of the President), 736 Jackson Pl. N.W. 20503; (202) 456-7320. Fax, (202) 456-7315. Dr. Joseph F. O'Neill, Director.*
Web, www.whitehouse.gov/onap/aids.html

Advises the president and formulates policy on matters related to AIDS and AIDS treatment.

Public Health and Science *(Health and Human Services Dept.), HIV/AIDS Policy, 200 Independence Ave. S.W., #736E 20201; (202) 690-5560. Fax, (202) 690-7560. Christopher H. Bates, Director (Acting).*
Web, www.dhhs.gov

Coordinates national AIDS policy, sets priorities, recommends funding, and helps implement all Public Health Service HIV programs. Monitors progress of prevention and control programs; serves as a liaison with governmental and private organizations.

Public Health and Science *(Health and Human Services Dept.), Minority Health, 5515 Security Lane, #1000, Rockwall II Bldg., Rockville, MD 20852; (301) 443-5084. Fax, (301) 594-0767. Nathan Stinson, Deputy Assistant Secretary. Information, (800) 444-6472.*
General e-mail, info@omhrc.gov
Web, www.omhrc.gov

Oversees the implementation of the secretary's Task Force on Black and Minority Health and legislative mandates; develops programs to meet the health care needs of minorities; awards grants to coalitions of minority community organizations and to minority AIDS education and prevention projects.

Walter Reed Army Institute of Research *(Defense Dept.), Combined Military Diagnostic Retrovirology Service, 13 Taft Court, Rockville, MD 20850-5318; (301) 251-5000. Fax, (301) 309-8346. Dr. Deborah Birx, Director.*
Web, www.hjf.org

Conducts and funds AIDS research for the military's retrovirus program; oversees AIDS testing for Defense Dept. personnel.

Warren Grant Magnuson Clinical Center *(National Institutes of Health), Transfusion Medicine, 10 Center Dr., Bldg. 10, #1C711, MSC-1184, Bethesda, MD 20892-1184; (301) 496-9702. Fax, (301) 594-1981. Dr. Harvey Klein, Chief. Information, (301) 496-4506.*
Web, www.cc.nih.gov/dtm/index.html

Supplies blood and blood components for patient care and research. Conducts research on diseases transmissible by blood, primarily AIDS and hepatitis.

NONPROFIT

AIDS Action, *1906 Sunderland Pl. N.W. 20036; (202) 530-8030. Fax, (202) 530-8031. Dr. Marsha A. Martin, Executive Director.*
General e-mail, aidsaction@aidsaction.org
Web, www.aidsaction.org

Promotes and monitors legislation on AIDS research and education and on related public policy issues.

AIDS Alliance for Children, Youth, and Families, *1600 K St. N.W., #200 20006; (202) 785-3564. Fax, (202) 785-3579. David C. Harvey, Executive Director.*
General e-mail, info@aids-alliance.org
Web, www.aids-alliance.org

Conducts research and disseminates information on health care and HIV issues. Develops and promotes policy aimed at improving the health and welfare of children, youth, and families affected by HIV. Provides training and technical assistance to health care providers and consumers.

American Foundation for AIDS Research (AmfAR), *Public Policy, Washington Office, 1828 L St. N.W., #802 20036; (202) 331-8600. Fax, (202) 331-8606. Leah Stevralia, Director (Acting). Information, (800) 392-6327.*
Web, www.amfar.org

Supports funding for basic biomedical and clinical AIDS research; promotes AIDS prevention education worldwide; advocates effective AIDS-related public policy. Monitors legislation, regulations, and international research. (Headquarters in New York.)

American Red Cross, *National Headquarters, 430 17th St. N.W., 2nd Floor 20006-2401; (202) 737-8300. Fax, (202) 783-3432. Marsha Evans, Chief Executive Officer.*
Web, www.redcross.org

Humanitarian relief and health education organization chartered by Congress. Conducts public education campaigns on AIDS.

Human Rights Campaign (HRC), *919 18th St. N.W., #800 20006; (202) 628-4160. Fax, (202) 347-5323. Elizabeth Birch, Executive Director.*
General e-mail, hrc@hrc.org
Web, www.hrc.org

Promotes legislation to fund AIDS research.

National AIDS Fund, *1030 15th St. N.W., #860 20005; (202) 408-4848. Fax, (202) 408-1818. Kandy Ferree, President. Toll-free, (888) 234-AIDS.*
General e-mail, info@aidsfund.org
Web, www.aidsfund.org

Channels resources to community-based organizations to fight HIV/AIDS at the local level. Provides grants and other support to nearly 500 organizations, principally for prevention efforts.

National Assn. of People with AIDS, *1413 K St. N.W., 7th Floor 20005; (202) 898-0414. Fax, (202) 898-0435. Terje Anderson, Executive Director.*
General e-mail, napwa@napwa.org
Web, www.napwa.org

Membership: people with AIDS or HIV disease. Provides persons infected by AIDS or HIV disease with information and social service referrals; contributes to educational campaigns about AIDS; maintains speakers bureau.

National Minority AIDS Council, *1931 13th St. N.W. 20009-4432; (202) 483-6622. Fax, (202) 483-1135. Paul A. Kawata, Executive Director.*
General e-mail, nmac@nmac.org
Web, www.nmac.org

Works to encourage leadership within minority communities responding to the HIV/AIDS epidemic; provides community-based AIDS programs with technical assistance. Disseminates information on AIDS, especially information on the impact of the disease on minority communities. Monitors legislation and regulations.

Arthritis

AGENCIES

National Institute of Arthritis and Musculoskeletal and Skin Diseases *(National Institutes of Health), 31 Center Dr., Bldg. 31, #4C32, MSC-2350, Bethesda, MD 20892-2350; (301) 496-4353. Fax, (301) 402-3607. Dr. Stephen I. Katz, Director. Information, (301) 496-8190.*
Web, www.niams.nih.gov

Conducts and funds research on arthritis, rheumatic, skin, muscle, and bone diseases and musculoskeletal disorders. Funds national arthritis centers.

National Institute of Arthritis and Musculoskeletal and Skin Diseases *(National Institutes of Health), Information Clearinghouse, 1 AMS Circle, Bethesda, MD 20892-3675; (301) 495-4484. Fax, (301) 718-6366. Sam Beatty, Project Manager. TTY, (301) 565-2966. Toll-free, (877) 226-4267.*
Web, www.niams.nih.gov

Provides physicians and the public with educational materials related to rheumatic, musculoskeletal, and skin diseases.

Blood and Bone Marrow

AGENCIES

Health Resources and Services Administration *(Health and Human Services Dept.), Special Programs: Transplantation, 5600 Fishers Lane, #16 C-17, Rockville, MD 20857; (301) 443-7577. Fax, (301) 443-1267. Joyce Somsak, Director (Acting).*
Web, www.organdonor.gov

Administers the National Marrow Donor Program, which maintains a registry of potential unrelated bone marrow donors.

National Heart, Lung, and Blood Institute *(National Institutes of Health), Blood Diseases and Resources, 6701 Rockledge Dr., #10160, MSC-7950, Bethesda, MD 20892-7950; (301) 435-0080. Fax, (301) 480-0867. Dr. Charles Peterson, Director.*

Web, www.nhlbi.nih.gov

Administers and conducts research and training programs to improve the diagnosis, prevention, and treatment of blood diseases and related disorders. Works to ensure the efficient and safe use and adequate supply of high-quality blood and blood products.

National Heart, Lung, and Blood Institute
(National Institutes of Health), Blood Resources Program, 6701 Rockledge Dr., #10162, MSC-7950, Bethesda, MD 20892-7950; (301) 435-0080. Fax, (301) 480-0867. *Dr. Jean Henslee-Downey, Director.*
Web, www.nhlbi.nih.gov

Promotes and supports research on bone marrow and stem cell transplantation technology and on transplantation procedure-related complications.

National Heart, Lung, and Blood Institute
(National Institutes of Health), Health Information Center, P.O. Box 30105, Bethesda, MD 20824-0105; (301) 592-8573. Fax, (301) 592-8563. *Larry Thomas, Operations Manager. Press, (301) 496-4236.*
General e-mail, nhlbiinfo@rover.nhlbi.nih.gov
Web, www.nhlbi.nih.gov

Acquires, maintains, and disseminates information on cholesterol and high blood pressure. Provides reference and referral services.

National Institute of Diabetes and Digestive and Kidney Diseases *(National Institutes of Health), Hematology,* 6707 Democracy Bldg., MSC-5458, Bethesda, MD 20892-5458; (301) 594-7717. Fax, (301) 480-3510. *David G. Badman, Director.*
Web, www.niddk.nih.gov

Supports basic research on and clinical studies of the states of blood cell formation, mobilization, and release. Interests include anemia associated with chronic diseases, iron and white blood cell metabolism, and genetic control of hemoglobin.

Warren Grant Magnuson Clinical Center *(National Institutes of Health), Transfusion Medicine,* 10 Center Dr., Bldg. 10, #1C711, MSC-1184, Bethesda, MD 20892-1184; (301) 496-9702. Fax, (301) 594-1981. *Dr. Harvey Klein, Chief. Information, (301) 496-4506.*
Web, www.cc.nih.gov/dtm/index.html

Supplies blood and blood components for research and patient care. Provides training programs and conducts research in the preparation and transfusion of blood and blood products. Research topics include hepatitis, automated cell separation, immunohematology, and AIDS transmittal through transfusions.

American Assn. of Blood Banks, *8101 Glenbrook Rd., Bethesda, MD 20814-2749; (301) 907-6977. Fax, (301) 907-6895. Karen Shoos Lipton, Executive Officer.*
General e-mail, aabb@aabb.org
Web, www.aabb.org

Membership: hospital and community blood centers, transfusion and transplantation services, and individuals involved in transfusion and transplantation medicine. Supports high medical standards, scientific investigation, clinical application, and education. Encourages the voluntary donation of blood and other tissues and organs through education and public information.

American Red Cross, *National Headquarters,*
430 17th St. N.W., 2nd Floor 20006-2401; (202) 737-8300. Fax, (202) 783-3432. Marsha Evans, Chief Executive Officer.
Web, www.redcross.org

Humanitarian relief and health education organization chartered by Congress; provides services in the United States and internationally. Collects blood and maintains blood centers; conducts research; operates the national bone marrow registry and a rare-donor registry; operates transfusion alternative program. Conducts training programs in nursing and first aid; trains volunteers. Serves as U.S. member of the International Federation of Red Cross and Red Crescent Societies.

Cancer

AGENCIES

National Cancer Institute *(National Institutes of Health), 31 Center Dr., Bldg. 31, #11A48, MSC-2590, Bethesda, MD 20892-2590; (301) 496-5615. Fax, (301) 402-0338. Dr. Andrew C. von Eschenbach, Director; Dr. Joe Harford, Associate Director, Special Projects, (301) 496-5534. Information, (301) 435-7782. Press, (301) 496-6641.*
Web, www.nci.nih.gov

Conducts and funds research on the causes, diagnosis, treatment, prevention, control, and biology of cancer and the rehabilitation of cancer patients; administers the National Cancer Program; coordinates international research activities. Sponsors regional and national cancer information services.

National Cancer Institute *(National Institutes of Health), Cancer Information Products and Systems,*
6116 Executive Blvd., #300A, Rockville, MD 20852; (301) 496-9096. Fax, (301) 480-8105. Dr. Gisele Sarosy, Associate Director (Acting).
Web, cancer.gov

Collects and disseminates scientific information on cancer biology, etiology, screening, prevention, treatment, and supportive care. Evaluates and develops new media formats for cancer information.

National Cancer Institute *(National Institutes of Health), Cancer Prevention, 6130 Executive Blvd., #2040, Bethesda, MD 20892; (301) 496-6616. Fax, (301) 496-9931. Dr. Peter Greenwald, Director.*
Web, www.nci.nih.gov

Funds projects for innovative and effective approaches to preventing and controlling cancer. Coordinates support for establishing multidisciplinary cancer care and clinical research activities in community hospitals. Supports cancer research training, clinical and continuing education, and career development.

National Cancer Institute *(National Institutes of Health), Organ Systems Branch, 6116 Executive Blvd., #7013, MSC-8347, Bethesda, MD 20892-8347; (301) 496-8528. Fax, (301) 402-5319. Dr. Jorge Gomez, Chief.*
Web, spores.nci.nih.gov

Encourages the study of organ-specific cancers and leukemia. Encourages multidisciplinary research linking laboratory and clinical medicine.

President's Cancer Panel, *c/o National Cancer Institute, 31 Center Dr., #3A-18, MSC-2440, Bethesda, MD 20892-2440; (301) 496-1148. Fax, (301) 402-1508. Dr. Maureen O. Wilson, Executive Secretary.*
General e-mail, prescan@nih.gov
Web, www.deainfo.nci.nih.gov/advisory/pop/pcp.htm

Presidentially appointed committee that monitors and evaluates the National Cancer Program; reports to the president and Congress.

NONPROFIT

American Cancer Society, *National Government Relations, Washington Office, 901 E St. N.W., #500 20004; (202) 661-5700. Fax, (202) 661-5750. Dan Smith, Director. Information, (800) 227-2345.*
Web, www.cancer.org

Nationwide community-based voluntary health organization dedicated to eliminating cancer as a major health problem by preventing cancer, saving lives, and diminishing suffering from cancer through research, education, advocacy, and service. Monitors legislation. (Headquarters in Atlanta, Ga.)

American Institute for Cancer Research, *1759 R St. N.W. 20009-2583; (202) 328-7744. Fax, (202) 328-7226. Marilyn Gentry, Executive Director. Information, (800) 843-8114.*

General e-mail, aicrweb@aicr.org
Web, www.aicr.org

Funds cancer research in areas of diet and nutrition; sponsors education programs. Library open to the public by appointment.

American Society for Therapeutic Radiology and Oncology, *12500 Fair Lakes Circle, #375, Fairfax, VA 22033-3882; (703) 502-1550. Fax, (703) 502-7852. Laura Thevenot, Executive Director. Toll-free, (800) 962-7876.*
General e-mail, info@astro.org
Web, www.astro.org

Seeks to advance the practice of radiation oncology; disseminates data on scientific research; sponsors workshops and conferences. Monitors legislation and regulations.

American Society of Clinical Oncology, *1900 Duke St., #200, Alexandria, VA 22314; (703) 299-0150. Fax, (703) 299-1044. Dr. Charles M. Balch, Executive Vice President.*
General e-mail, asco@asco.org
Web, www.asco.org

Membership: physicians and scientists specializing in cancer prevention, treatment, education, and research. Promotes exchange of information in clinical research and patient care relating to all stages of cancer; monitors international research.

Assn. of Community Cancer Centers, *11600 Nebel St., #201, Rockville, MD 20852-2538; (301) 984-9496. Fax, (301) 770-1949. Lee E. Mortenson, Executive Director.*
Web, www.accc-cancer.org

Membership: individuals from community hospitals involved in multidisciplinary cancer programs, including physicians, administrators, nurses, medical directors, pharmacists, and other members of the cancer care team.

Candlelighters Childhood Cancer Foundation, *3910 Warner St., Kensington, MD 20895; (301) 962-3520. Fax, (301) 962-3521. Ruth Hoffman, Executive Director. Information, (800) 366-2223.*
General e-mail, info@candlelighters.org
Web, www.candlelighters.org

Membership: families of children with cancer, survivors of childhood cancer, and health and education professionals. Serves as an information and educational network; sponsors self-help groups for parents of children and adolescents with cancer. Monitors legislation and regulations.

Leukemia and Lymphoma Society of America, *Washington Office, 5845 Richmond Hwy., #630, Alexan-*

dria, VA 22303; (703) 960-1100. Fax, (703) 960-0920. David M. Timko, Executive Director. Information, (800) 955-4572.

Web, www.leukemia-lymphoma.org

Seeks to fight and expand knowledge of blood-related cancers (leukemia, lymphoma, Hodgkins myeloma, and related diseases). Conducts research, provides research scholarships and fellowships, maintains speakers bureau. Local chapters provide leukemia and lymphoma patients with financial assistance, counseling, and referrals. (Headquarters in New York.)

National Breast Cancer Coalition, 1707 L St. N.W., #1060 20036; (202) 296-7477. Fax, (202) 265-6854. Frances M. Visco, President.

Web, www.stopbreastcancer.org

Membership: organizations, local coalitions, and individuals. Advocates increased funding for research to prevent and treat breast cancer; promotes better access to screening and care; conducts training for breast cancer activists.

National Coalition for Cancer Survivorship, 1010 Wayne Ave., #770, Silver Spring, MD 20910-5600; (301) 650-9127. Fax, (301) 565-9670. Ellen L. Stovall, President. Information, (888) 937-6227. Toll-free publications, (877) 622-7937.

General e-mail, info@canceradvocacy.org

Web, www.canceradvocacy.org

Membership: survivors of cancer (newly diagnosed to long-term), their families and friends, health care providers, and support organizations. Disseminates information about living with cancer; works to reduce cancer-based discrimination in employment and insurance; operates Cansearch, a guide to cancer resources on the Internet.

Diabetes, Digestive Diseases

AGENCIES

National Diabetes Information Clearinghouse *(National Institutes of Health),* 1 Information Way, Bethesda, MD 20892-3560; (301) 654-3327. Fax, (301) 907-8906. Vacant, Senior Information Specialist.

Web, www.niddk.nih.gov

Provides health professionals and the public with information on the symptoms, causes, treatments, and general nature of diabetes.

National Digestive Diseases Information Clearing-house *(National Institutes of Health),* 2 Information Way, Bethesda, MD 20892-3570; (301) 654-3810. Fax, (301) 907-8906. Vacant, Senior Information Specialist.

Web, www.niddk.nih.gov

Provides health professionals and the public with information on the symptoms, causes, treatments, and general nature of digestive ailments.

National Institute of Diabetes and Digestive and Kidney Diseases *(National Institutes of Health), Diabetes, Endocrinology, and Metabolic Diseases,* 31 Center Dr., #9A27, MSC-2560, Bethesda, MD 20892-2560; (301) 496-7348. Fax, (301) 480-6792. Judith E. Fradkin, Director.

Web, www.niddk.nih.gov

Awards grants and contracts to support basic and clinical research of diabetes mellitus and its complications.

National Institute of Diabetes and Digestive and Kidney Diseases *(National Institutes of Health), Digestive Diseases and Nutrition,* 31 Center Dr., #9A27, MSC-2560, Bethesda, MD 20892-2560; (301) 496-1333. Fax, (301) 480-7926. Dr. Jay H. Hoofnagle, Director.

Web, www.niddk.nih.gov

Awards grants and contracts to support basic and clinical research on digestive diseases.

NONPROFIT

American Diabetes Assn. (ADA), 1701 N. Beauregard St., Alexandria, VA 22311; (703) 549-1500. Fax, (703) 836-7439. John H. Graham IV, Chief Executive Officer. Information, (800) 232-3472.

Web, www.diabetes.org

Conducts and funds research on diabetes; monitors international research. Provides local affiliates with education, information, and referral services.

American Gastroenterological Assn., 4930 Del Ray Ave., Bethesda, MD 20814; (301) 654-2055. Fax, (301) 654-5920. Robert Greenberg, Executive Vice President.

General e-mail, members@gastro.org

Web, www.gastro.org

Membership: gastroenterology clinicians, scientists, health care professionals, and educators. Sponsors scientific research on digestive diseases; disseminates information on new methods of prevention and treatment. Monitors legislation and regulations. (Affiliated with the American Digestive Health Foundation.)

Endocrine Society, 4350 East-West Hwy., #500, Bethesda, MD 20814-4426; (301) 941-0200. Fax, (301) 941-0259. Scott Hunt, Executive Director.

Web, www.endo-society.org

Membership: scientists, doctors, health care educators, clinicians, nurses, and others interested in endocrine glands and their disorders. Promotes endocrinology research and clinical practice; sponsors seminars and conferences; gives awards and travel grants.

Juvenile Diabetes Research Foundation, *Governmental Relations, Washington Office, 1400 Eye St. N.W., #530 20005-2208; (202) 371-9746. Fax, (202) 371-2760. Lawrence Soler, Vice President. Information, (800) 533-1868.*
Web, www.jdrf.org

Conducts research, education, and public awareness programs aimed at improving the lives of people with diabetes and finding a cure for diabetes. Monitors legislation and regulations. (Headquarters in New York.)

Family Planning and Population

AGENCIES

Agency for International Development (USAID), *Population and Reproductive Health, 1300 Pennsylvania Ave. N.W., 3rd Floor 20523-3600; (202) 712-0540. Fax, (202) 216-3485. Margaret Neuse, Director.*
Web, www.info.usaid.gov/pop_health

Division of the AID Bureau for Global Health. Supports family planning and reproductive health programs; conducts research.

Census Bureau *(Commerce Dept.), Fertility and Family Statistics, 4700 Silver Hill Rd., Bldg. 3, #2351, Suitland, MD 20746-8800; (301) 763-2416. Fax, (301) 457-2396. Martin O'Connell, Chief.*
Web, www.census.gov

Provides data and statistics on fertility and family composition. Conducts census and survey research on the number of children, households and living arrangements, and current child spacing patterns of women in the United States, especially working mothers. Conducts studies on child care.

National Institute of Child Health and Human Development *(National Institutes of Health), Center for Population Research, 6100 Executive Blvd., #8B-07, Bethesda, MD 20892-7510; (301) 496-1101. Fax, (301) 496-0962. Dr. Florence P. Haseltine, Director.*
Web, www.nih.gov/nichd

Supports biomedical and behavioral research on reproductive processes influencing human fertility and infertility; develops methods for regulating fertility; evaluates the safety and effectiveness of contraceptive methods; conducts research on the reproductive motivation of individuals and the causes and consequences of population change.

Public Health and Science *(Health and Human Services Dept.), Population Affairs, 4350 East-West Hwy.,* *#200, Bethesda, MD 20814; (301) 594-4001. Fax, (301) 594-5980. Dr. Alma Golden, Deputy Assistant Secretary.*
Web, www.osophs.dhhs.gov

Responsible for planning, monitoring, and evaluating population research, voluntary family planning, and adolescent family life programs.

Public Health and Science *(Health and Human Services Dept.), Population Affairs: Clearinghouse, P.O. Box 30686, Bethesda, MD 20824-0686; (301) 654-6190. Fax, (301) 215-7731. Cathy J. House, Project Manager.*
General e-mail, clearinghouse@dhhsopa.net
Web, www.surgeongeneral.gov/ophs

Federally contracted program that collects and disseminates information on family planning, general reproductive health care and related topics, including adoption, adolescent pregnancy prevention, contraception, HIV/AIDS, sexually transmitted diseases, and abstinence. (Formerly Family Life Information Exchange.)

INTERNATIONAL ORGANIZATIONS

International Bank for Reconstruction and Development (World Bank), *Human Development Network, 1818 H St. N.W., #G8 801 20433; (202) 473-3437. Fax, (202) 522-3235. Vacant, Vice President.*
Web, www.worldbank.org

Provides member countries with support in education, health and nutrition, and population and social protection. (Works in conjunction with regional World Bank offices.)

NONPROFIT

Advocates for Youth, *1025 Vermont Ave. N.W., #200 20005; (202) 347-5700. Fax, (202) 347-2263. James Wagoner, Executive Director.*
General e-mail, info@advocatesforyouth.org
Web, www.advocatesforyouth.org

Seeks to reduce the incidence of unintended teenage pregnancy and AIDS through public education, training and technical assistance, research, and media programs.

Alan Guttmacher Institute, *Public Policy, Washington Office, 1120 Connecticut Ave. N.W., #460 20036-3902; (202) 296-4012. Fax, (202) 223-5756. Cory L. Richards, Senior Vice President.*
General e-mail, policyinfo@guttmacher.org
Web, www.guttmacher.org

Conducts research, policy analysis, and public education in reproductive health, fertility regulation, population, and related areas of U.S. and international health. (Headquarters in New York.)

National Abortion Federation (NAF), *1755 Massachusetts Ave. N.W., #600 20036; (202) 667-5881. Fax, (202) 667-5890. Vicki Saporta, Executive Director. Information, (800) 772-9100.*
General e-mail, naf@prochoice.org
Web, www.prochoice.org
     Federation of facilities providing abortion services. Offers information on medical, legal, and social aspects of abortion; sets quality standards for abortion care. Conducts training workshops and seminars. Monitors legislation and regulations.

National Family Planning and Reproductive Health Assn., *1627 K St. N.W., 12th Floor 20006-1702; (202) 293-3114. Fax, (202) 293-1990. Judith M. DeSarno, President.*
General e-mail, info@nfprha.org
Web, www.nfprha.org
     Membership: health professionals and others interested in family planning and reproductive health. Operates a network for information, referral, research, policy analysis, and training designed to improve and expand the delivery of family planning services and reproductive health care.

Planned Parenthood Federation of America, *Public Policy, Washington Office, 1780 Massachusetts Ave. N.W. 20036; (202) 973-4800. Fax, (202) 296-3762. Susanne Martinez, Vice President.*
Web, www.plannedparenthood.org
     Educational, research, and medical services organization. Washington office conducts research and monitors legislation on fertility-related health topics, including abortion, reproductive health, contraception, family planning, and international population control. (Headquarters in New York accredits affiliated local centers, which offer medical services, birth control, and family planning information.)

Population Action International, *1300 19th St. N.W., #200 20036; (202) 557-3400. Fax, (202) 728-4177. Amy Coen, President.*
General e-mail, pai@popact.org
Web, www.populationaction.org
     Promotes population stabilization through public education and universal access to voluntary family planning. Library open to the public by appointment.

Population Connection, *1400 16th St. N.W., #320 20036; (202) 332-2200. Fax, (202) 332-2302. Peter H. Kostmayer, President.*
General e-mail, info@populationconnection.org
Web, www.populationconnection.org

Membership: persons interested in sustainable world populations. Promotes the expansion of domestic and international family planning programs; supports a voluntary population stabilization policy and women's access to abortion and family planning services; works to protect the earth's resources and environment. (Formerly Zero Population Growth.)

Population-Environment Balance, *2000 P St. N.W., #600 20036; (202) 955-5700. Fax, (202) 955-6161. Michelle Pheler, Coordinator.*
General e-mail, uspop@us.net
Web, www.balance.org
     Grassroots organization that advocates U.S. population stabilization to safeguard the environment.

Population Institute, *107 2nd St. N.E. 20002; (202) 544-3300. Fax, (202) 544-0068. Werner Fornos, President.*
Web, www.populationinstitute.org
     Encourages leaders of developing nations to balance population growth through resource management; works with leaders of industrial nations to help achieve a balance between population and natural resources.

Population Reference Bureau, *1875 Connecticut Ave. N.W., #520 20009; (202) 483-1100. Fax, (202) 328-3937. Peter J. Donaldson, President.*
General e-mail, popref@prb.org
Web, www.prb.org
     Educational organization engaged in information dissemination, training, and policy analysis on domestic and international population trends and issues. Interests include international development and family planning programs, the environment, and U.S. social and economic policy. Library open to the public.

Genetic Disorders

AGENCIES

Health Resources and Services Administration *(Health and Human Services Dept.), Genetic Services, 5600 Fishers Lane, #18A19, Rockville, MD 20857; (301) 443-1080. Fax, (301) 443-8604. Dr. Michele A. Puryear, Chief.*
Web, www.mchb.hrsa.gov
     Awards funds, including demonstration grants, to develop or enhance regional, local, and state genetic screening, diagnostic, counseling, and follow-up programs; assists states in their newborn screening programs; provides funding for regional hemophilia treatment centers. Supports comprehensive care for individuals and families with Cooley's anemia, and those with sickle cell anemia identified through newborn screening. Supports educational programs.

National Heart, Lung, and Blood Institute
(National Institutes of Health), Blood Diseases Program, 6701 Rockledge Dr., 10th Floor, Bethesda, MD 20892-7950; (301) 435-0050. Fax, (301) 480-0868. Herman Branson, Director.

Web, www.nih.gov/nhlbi

Supports research into the diagnosis and treatment of genetic blood disorders and continuing education programs for professionals and the public.

National Human Genome Research Institute
(National Institutes of Health), 31 Center Dr., Bldg. 31, #4B09, MSC-2152, Bethesda, MD 20892-2152; (301) 496-0844. Fax, (301) 402-0837. Dr. Francis S. Collins, Director. Information, (301) 402-0911.

Web, www.genome.gov

Responsible, with the Energy Dept., for U.S. involvement in the international Human Genome Project, which seeks to map all genes in human DNA, as well as those of model organisms. Works to improve techniques for cloning, storing, and handling DNA and to enhance data processing and analysis; promotes exchange of information.

National Institute of Allergy and Infectious Diseases *(National Institutes of Health), Allergy, Immunology, and Transplantation,* 6700 B Rockledge Dr., #5142, Bethesda, MD 20892-7640; (301) 496-1886. Fax, (301) 402-0175. Dr. Daniel Rotrosen, Director. Information, (301) 496-5717.

Web, www.niaid.nih.gov/research/dait.htm

Focuses on the immune system as it functions to maintain health and as it malfunctions to produce disease; interests include allergies, asthma, immune deficiencies (other than AIDS), transplantation of organs and tissue, and genetics. Monitors international research.

National Institute of Diabetes and Digestive and Kidney Diseases *(National Institutes of Health), Hematology,* 6707 Democracy Bldg., MSC-5458, Bethesda, MD 20892-5458; (301) 594-7717. Fax, (301) 480-3510. David G. Badman, Director.

Web, www.niddk.nih.gov

Supports basic research on and clinical studies of the states of blood cell formation, mobilization, and release. Interests include anemia associated with chronic diseases, iron and white blood cell metabolism, and genetic control of hemoglobin.

National Institute of General Medical Sciences
(National Institutes of Health), Genetics and Developmental Biology, 45 Center Dr., #2AS25N, MSC-6200,

Bethesda, MD 20892-6200; (301) 594-0943. Fax, (301) 480-2228. Judith H. Greenberg, Director.

Web, www.nigms.nih.gov

Supports research and research training in genetics.

National Institutes of Health (NIH), *(Health and Human Services Dept.), Biotechnology Activities,* 6705 Rockledge Dr., #750, MSC-7985, Bethesda, MD 20892-7985; (301) 496-9838. Fax, (301) 496-9839. Amy P. Patterson, Director.

Web, www4.od.nih.gov/oba

Reviews requests submitted to NIH involving genetic testing, recombinant DNA technology, and xenotransplantation, and implements research guidelines.

NONPROFIT

Center for Sickle Cell Disease *(Howard University),* 2121 Georgia Ave. N.W. 20059; (202) 806-7930. Fax, (202) 806-4517. Dr. Oswaldo Castro, Director.

Web, www.huhosp.org

Screens and tests for sickle cell disease; conducts research; promotes public education and community involvement; provides counseling and patient care.

Cystic Fibrosis Foundation, 6931 Arlington Rd., #200, Bethesda, MD 20814; (301) 951-4422. Fax, (301) 951-6378. Robert J. Beall, President. Information, (800) 344-4823.

General e-mail, info@cff.org

Web, www.cff.org

Conducts research on cystic fibrosis, an inherited genetic disease affecting the respiratory and digestive systems. Provides funding for care centers; publishes and disseminates information on the disease.

Genetics Society of America, 9650 Rockville Pike, Bethesda, MD 20814; (301) 571-1825. Fax, (301) 530-7079. Elaine Strass, Executive Director.

General e-mail, society@genetics-gsa.org

Web, www.genetics-gsa.org

Encourages professional cooperation among persons working in genetics and related sciences; participates in international conferences.

Kennedy Institute of Ethics *(Georgetown University),* Healy Hall, 4th Floor, 37th and O Sts. N.W. 20057; (202) 687-8099. Fax, (202) 687-8089. G. Madison Powers, Director. Library, (800) 633-3849; in Washington, (202) 687-3885.

Web, www.georgetown.edu/research/kie

Sponsors research on medical ethics, including legal and ethical definitions of death, allocation of scarce health resources, and recombinant DNA and human gene therapy. Works with the National Library of Medicine to provide citations to bioethical issues; conducts international programs and free bibliographic searches. Library open to the public.

March of Dimes, Government Affairs, Washington Office, 1146 19th St. N.W., #600 20036; (202) 659-1800. Fax, (202) 296-2964. Marina L. Weiss, Senior Vice President.
Web, www.modimes.org
Works to prevent and treat birth defects. Awards grants for research and provides funds for treatment of birth defects. Monitors legislation and regulations. (Headquarters in White Plains, N.Y.)

Heart Disease, Strokes

AGENCIES

National Heart, Lung, and Blood Institute (National Institutes of Health), Health Information Center, P.O. Box 30105, Bethesda, MD 20824-0105; (301) 592-8573. Fax, (301) 592-8563. Larry Thomas, Operations Manager. Press, (301) 496-4236.
General e-mail, nhlbiinfo@rover.nhlbi.nih.gov
Web, www.nhlbi.nih.gov
Acquires, maintains, and disseminates information on cholesterol, high blood pressure, heart attack awareness, and asthma to the public and health professionals. Provides reference and referral services. Library open to the public.

National Heart, Lung, and Blood Institute (National Institutes of Health), Heart and Vascular Diseases, 6701 Rockledge Dr., #9160, Bethesda, MD 20892-7940; (301) 435-0466. Fax, (301) 480-7971. Dr. Stephen C. Mockrin, Director.
Web, www.nhlbi.nih.gov/index.hm
Conducts and funds research on the prevention, causes, and treatment of heart and vascular diseases.

National Institute of Neurological Disorders and Stroke (National Institutes of Health), 31 Center Dr., Bldg. 31, #8A52, MSC-2540, Bethesda, MD 20892-2540; (301) 496-9746. Fax, (301) 496-0296. Dr. Audrey S. Penn, Director (Acting). Information, (301) 496-5751.
Web, www.ninds.nih.gov
Conducts and funds stroke research. Monitors international research.

NONPROFIT

American Heart Assn., Washington Office, 1150 Connecticut Ave. N.W., #300 20036; (202) 785-7900. Fax, (202) 785-7950. Diane M. Canova, Vice President. Information, (800) 242-8721.

Web, www.americanheart.org
Membership: physicians, scientists, and other interested individuals. Supports cardiovascular research, treatment, and community service programs that provide information about heart disease and stroke; participates in international conferences and research. Monitors legislation and regulations. (Headquarters in Dallas, Texas.)

Infectious Diseases, Allergies

AGENCIES

National Institute of Allergy and Infectious Diseases (National Institutes of Health), 31 Center Dr., Bldg. 31, #7A03, MSC-2520, Bethesda, MD 20892-2520; (301) 496-2263. Fax, (301) 496-4409. Dr. Anthony S. Fauci, Director. Information, (301) 496-5717.
General e-mail, niaidoc@flash.niaid.nih.gov
Web, www.niaid.nih.gov
Conducts and funds research on infectious diseases, allergies, and other immunological disorders. Participates in international research, especially on AIDS and HIV.

NONPROFIT

Allergy and Asthma Network Mothers of Asthmatics, 2751 Prosperity Ave., #150, Fairfax, VA 22031-4397; (703) 641-9595. Fax, (703) 573-7794. Nancy Sander, President. Information, (800) 878-4403.
General e-mail, aanma@aol.com
Web, www.aanma.org
Membership: families dealing with asthma and allergies. Promotes research; provides information on treatments and therapies, new products, support groups, and coping techniques.

Asthma and Allergy Foundation of America, 1233 20th St. N.W., #402 20036; (202) 466-7643. Fax, (202) 466-8940. Bill McLin, Executive Director. Information, (800) 727-8462.
General e-mail, info@aafa.org
Web, www.aafa.org
Provides information on asthma and allergies; awards research grants to health care professionals; offers in-service training to allied health professionals, child care providers, and others.

National Foundation for Infectious Diseases, 4733 Bethesda Ave., #750, Bethesda, MD 20814-5228; (301) 656-0003. Fax, (301) 907-0878. William J. Martone, Senior Executive Director.
General e-mail, info@nfid.org
Web, www.nfid.org

Raises, receives, maintains, and disburses funds to support research on infectious diseases; educates the public and health professionals about infectious diseases; conducts prevention programs, including an annual adult immunization awareness campaign; coordinates activities for the National Coalition for Adult Immunization. Monitors international research.

Kidney Disease

AGENCIES

Centers for Medicare and Medicaid Services (CMS), *(Health and Human Services Dept.), Chronic Care Management, 7500 Security Blvd., C5-05-27, Baltimore, MD 21244-1850; (410) 786-4533. Fax, (410) 786-0765. Lana K. Price, Director.*
Web, www.cms.hhs.gov

Administers coverage policy for Medicare persons with renal disease, chronic kidney failure, and the program for all inclusive care for the elderly. Coordinates coverage under new treatment methods. (Formerly Health Care Financing Administration.)

National Institute of Allergy and Infectious Diseases *(National Institutes of Health), Allergy, Immunology, and Transplantation, 6700 B Rockledge Dr., #5142, Bethesda, MD 20892-7640; (301) 496-1886. Fax, (301) 402-0175. Dr. Daniel Rotrosen, Director. Information, (301) 496-5717.*
Web, www.niaid.nih.gov/research/dait.htm

Focuses on the immune system as it functions to maintain health and as it malfunctions to produce disease; interests include allergies, asthma, immune deficiencies (other than AIDS), transplantation of organs and tissue, and genetics. Monitors international research.

National Institute of Diabetes and Digestive and Kidney Diseases *(National Institutes of Health), Kidney, Urologic, and Hematologic Diseases, 31 Center Dr., Bldg. 31, #9A19, MSC-2560, Bethesda, MD 20892-2560; (301) 496-6325. Fax, (301) 402-4874. Dr. Josephine Briggs, Director. Information, (301) 496-3583.*
Web, www.niddk.nih.gov

Funds research on the prevention, diagnosis, and treatment of renal disorders. Conducts research and reviews grant proposals concerning maintenance therapy for persons with chronic renal disease.

National Institute of Diabetes and Digestive and Kidney Diseases *(National Institutes of Health), National Kidney and Urologic Diseases Information Clearinghouse, 3 Information Way, Bethesda, MD 20892-3580; (301) 654-4415. Fax, (301) 907-8906. Vacant, Senior Information Specialist.*

Web, www.niddk.nih.gov

Supplies health care providers and the public with information on the symptoms, causes, treatments, and general nature of kidney and urologic diseases.

NONPROFIT

American Kidney Fund, *6110 Executive Blvd., #1010, Rockville, MD 20852; (301) 881-3052. Fax, (301) 881-0898. Karen Sendelback, Executive Director. Information, (800) 638-8299.*
General e-mail, helpline@akfinc.org
Web, www.kidneyfund.org

Voluntary health organization that gives financial assistance to kidney disease victims. Disseminates public service announcements and public education materials; sponsors research grants and conferences for professionals; promotes organ donation for transplantation.

National Kidney Foundation, *Government Relations, Washington Office, 1522 K St. N.W., #825 20005; (202) 216-9257. Fax, (202) 216-9258. Troy Zimmerman, Director. Information, (800) 889-9559.*
General e-mail, info@kidney.org
Web, www.kidney.org

Supports funding for kidney dialysis and other forms of treatment for kidney disease; provides information on detection and screening of kidney diseases; supports organ transplantation programs. Monitors legislation, regulations, and international research. (Headquarters in New York.)

Lung Diseases

AGENCIES

National Heart, Lung, and Blood Institute *(National Institutes of Health), Health Information Center, P.O. Box 30105, Bethesda, MD 20824-0105; (301) 592-8573. Fax, (301) 592-8563. Larry Thomas, Operations Manager. Press, (301) 496-4236.*
General e-mail, nhlbiinfo@rover.nhlbi.nih.gov
Web, www.nhlbi.nih.gov

Acquires, maintains, and disseminates information on asthma and other lung ailments. Provides reference and referral services.

National Heart, Lung, and Blood Institute *(National Institutes of Health), Lung Diseases, 6701 Rockledge Dr., #10018, Bethesda, MD 20892; (301) 435-0233. Fax, (301) 480-3557. James P. Kiley, Director.*
Web, www.nhlbi.nih.gov

Plans and directs research and training programs in lung diseases including research on causes, treatments, prevention, and health education.

American Assn. for Respiratory Care (AARC), *Government Affairs, Washington Office,* 1100 Duke St., Alexandria, VA 22314; (703) 548-8538. Fax, (703) 548-8499. Jill Eicher, Director.

General e-mail, info@aarc.org

Web, www.aarc.org

   Membership: respiratory therapists, educators, and managers of respiratory and cardiopulmonary services. Monitors legislation and regulations. (Headquarters in Dallas, Texas.)

American Lung Assn., *Washington Office,* 1150 18th St. N.W., #900 20036-4502; (202) 785-3355. Fax, (202) 452-1805. Fran Du Melle, Director.

Web, www.lungusa.org

   Fights lung disease through research, educational programs, and public awareness campaigns. Interests include antismoking campaigns, lung-related biomedical research, air pollution, school health education, and all lung diseases, including tuberculosis and occupational lung diseases. Participates in international research. (Headquarters in New York.)

Cystic Fibrosis Foundation, 6931 Arlington Rd., #200, Bethesda, MD 20814; (301) 951-4422. Fax, (301) 951-6378. Robert J. Beall, President. Information, (800) 344-4823.

General e-mail, info@cff.org

Web, www.cff.org

   Conducts research on cystic fibrosis, an inherited genetic disease affecting the respiratory and digestive systems. Provides funding for care centers; publishes and disseminates information on the disease.

Minority Health

AGENCIES

Health and Human Services Dept. (HHS), *Civil Rights,* 200 Independence Ave. S.W., #522A 20201; (202) 619-0403. Fax, (202) 619-3437. Richard M. Campanelli, Director. TTY, (800) 537-7697. Toll-free hotline, (800) 368-1019.

Web, www.hhs.gov/ocr

   Administers and enforces laws prohibiting discrimination on the basis of race, color, sex, national origin, religion, age, or disability in programs receiving federal funds from the department; authorized to discontinue funding. Responsible for health information privacy under Health Insurance Portability and Accountability Act.

Health and Human Services Dept. (HHS), *Minority Health,* Rockwall II Bldg., #1000, 5515 Security Lane,

Rockville, MD 20852; (301) 443-5084. Fax, (301) 594-0767. Dr. Nathan Stinson Jr., Deputy Assistant Secretary. Information, (800) 444-6472.

General e-mail, info@omhrc.gov

Web, www.omhrc.gov

   Promotes improved health among racial and ethnic minority populations. Advises the secretary and the Office of Public Health and Science on public health program activities affecting American Indian and Alaska Native, African American, Asian American and Pacific Islander, and Hispanic populations.

Health and Human Services Dept. (HHS), *Minority Health Resource Center,* 1101 Wootton Pkwy., 6th Floor, Rockville, MD 20852 (mailing address: P.O. Box 37337, Washington, DC 20013-7337); (301) 230-7874. Fax, (301) 230-7198. Jose Tarcisio M. Carneiro, Director. Information, (800) 444-6472. TTY, (301) 230-7199.

General e-mail, info@omhrc.gov

Web, www.omhrc.gov

   Serves as a national resource and referral service on minority health issues. Distributes information on health topics such as substance abuse, cancer, heart disease, violence, diabetes, HIV/AIDS, and infant mortality. Provides free services, including customized database searches, publications, mailing lists, and referrals regarding American Indian and Alaska Native, African American, Asian American and Pacific Islander, and Hispanic populations.

Health Resources and Services Administration, *Minority Health,* 5600 Fishers Lane, #1049, Rockville, MD 20857; (301) 443-2964. Fax, (301) 443-7853. M. June Horner, Director.

General e-mail, comments@hrsa.gov

Web, www.hrsa.gov

   Sponsors programs and activities that address the special health needs of racial and ethnic minorities. Advises the administrator on minority health issues affecting the Health Resources and Services Administration (HRSA) and policy development; collects data on minority health activities within HRSA; represents HRSA programs affecting the health of racial and ethnic minorities to the health community, and organizations in the public, private, and international sectors.

Indian Health Service (*Health and Human Services Dept.*), 801 Thompson Ave., #440, Rockville, MD 20852; (301) 443-1083. Fax, (301) 443-4794. Charles W. Grim, Director (Interim). Information, (301) 443-3593.

Web, www.ihs.gov

   Operates hospitals and health centers that provide native Americans and Alaska natives with preventive and remedial health care. Provides or improves sanitation and water supply systems in native American communities.

National Institutes of Health (NIH), *(Health and Human Services Dept.), National Center on Minority Health and Health Disparities,* 2 Democracy Plaza, 6707 Democracy Blvd., #800, MSC-5465, Bethesda, MD 20892-5465; (301) 402-1366. Fax, (301) 480-4049. Dr. John Ruffin, Director.
Web, www.ncmhd.nih.gov

Coordinates the development of NIH policies and objectives related to minority health research and research training programs. Encourages minorities to work in the biomedical research field.

Public Health and Science *(Health and Human Services Dept.), Minority Health,* 5515 Security Lane, #1000, Rockwall II Bldg., Rockville, MD 20852; (301) 443-5084. Fax, (301) 594-0767. Nathan Stinson, Deputy Assistant Secretary. Information, (800) 444-6472.
General e-mail, info@omhrc.gov
Web, www.omhrc.gov

Oversees the implementation of the secretary's Task Force on Black and Minority Health and legislative mandates; develops programs to meet the health care needs of minorities; awards grants to coalitions of minority community organizations and to minority AIDS education and prevention projects.

NONPROFIT

National Alliance for Hispanic Health, 1501 16th St. N.W. 20036; (202) 387-5000. Fax, (202) 265-8027. Dr. Jane L. Delgado, President.
General e-mail, info@hispanichealth.org
Web, www.hispanichealth.org

Assists agencies and groups serving the Hispanic community in general health care and in targeting health and psychosocial problems; provides information, technical assistance, health care provider training, and policy analysis; coordinates and supports research. Interests include mental health, chronic diseases, substance abuse, maternal and child health, youth issues, juvenile delinquency, and access to care.

Neurological and Muscular Disorders

AGENCIES

National Institute of Neurological Disorders and Stroke *(National Institutes of Health),* 31 Center Dr., Bldg. 31, #8A52, MSC-2540, Bethesda, MD 20892-2540;

(301) 496-9746. Fax, (301) 496-0296. Dr. Audrey S. Penn, Director (Acting). Information, (301) 496-5751.
Web, www.ninds.nih.gov

Conducts and funds research on neurological diseases. Monitors international research.

NONPROFIT

Alzheimer's Assn., *Public Policy, Washington Office,* 1319 F St. N.W., #710 20004-1106; (202) 393-7737. Fax, (202) 393-2109. Stephen R. McConnell, Vice President. Information, (800) 272-3900.
Web, www.alz.org

Offers family support services and educates the public about Alzheimer's disease, a neurological disorder mainly affecting the brain tissue in older adults. Promotes research and long-term care protection; maintains liaison with Alzheimer's associations abroad. Monitors legislation and regulations. (Headquarters in Chicago, Ill.)

Epilepsy Foundation, 4351 Garden City Dr., #500, Landover, MD 20785; (301) 459-3700. Fax, (301) 577-2684. Eric Hargis, President. Information, (800) 332-1000. Library, (800) 332-4050.
General e-mail, postmaster@efa.org
Web, www.epilepsyfoundation.org

Promotes research and treatment of epilepsy; makes research grants; disseminates information and educational materials. Affiliates provide direct services for people with epilepsy and make referrals when necessary. Library open to the public by appointment.

Foundation for the Advancement of Chiropractic Tenets and Science, 1110 N. Glebe Rd., #1000, Arlington, VA 22201-5722; (703) 528-5000. Fax, (703) 528-5023. Ronald Hendrickson, Executive Director.
General e-mail, chiro@chiropractic.org
Web, www.chiropractic.org

Offers financial aid for education and research programs in colleges and independent institutions; studies chiropractic services in the United States; provides international relief and development programs. (Affiliate of the International Chiropractors Assn.)

International Rett Syndrome Assn., 9121 Piscataway Rd., #2B, Clinton, MD 20735; (301) 856-3334. Fax, (301) 856-3336. Kathy Hunter, President. Information, (800) 818-7388.
General e-mail, irsa@rettsyndrome.org
Web, www.rettsyndrome.org

Provides information and support to families of children with Rett syndrome, a severe neurological disorder causing mental and physical disabilities. Awards grants nationally and internationally. Promotes research on causes and treatment.

National Foundation for Brain Research, *6283 Dunaway Ct., McLean, VA 22101; (703) 821-1975. Fax, (703) 356-3631. Lawrence S. Hoffheimer, Executive Director. Web, www.brainnet.org/nfbr.htm*

Membership: professional societies, voluntary organizations, and businesses that support research into neurological and addictive brain disorders, including Alzheimer's disease, obsessive-compulsive behavior, dyslexia, drug addiction and alcoholism, stroke, Tay-Sachs disease, and depression. Sponsors programs that heighten public and professional awareness of brain disorders. Serves as a liaison with government agencies, medical and scientific societies, volunteer health organizations, and industry.

National Multiple Sclerosis Society, *Washington Office, 2021 K St. N.W., #715 20006-1003; (202) 296-9891. Fax, (202) 296-3425. Jeanne Oates Angulo, President.*

General e-mail, info@msandyou.org

Web, www.msandyou.org

Seeks to advance medical knowledge of multiple sclerosis, a disease of the central nervous system; disseminates information worldwide. Patient services include individual and family counseling, exercise programs, equipment loans, medical and social service referrals, transportation assistance, back-to-work training programs, and in-service training seminars for nurses, homemakers, and physical and occupational therapists. (Headquarters in New York.)

Neurofibromatosis Inc., *9320 Annapolis Rd., #300, Lanham, MD 20706-2924; (301) 918-4600. Fax, (301) 918-0009. Gwyneth A. Charest, Executive Director. Information, (800) 942-6825.*

General e-mail, nfinc1@aol.com

Web, www.nfinc.org

Provides information and assistance to health care professionals, individuals, and families affected by neurofibromatosis and related disorders. Promotes research; maintains a database of resources; makes referrals to physicians, service providers, and peer counselors.

Society for Neuroscience, *11 Dupont Circle N.W., #500 20036; (202) 462-6688. Fax, (202) 234-9770. Donald Price, President.*

General e-mail, info@sfn.org

Web, www.sfn.org

Membership: scientists and physicians worldwide who research the brain, spinal cord, and nervous system.

Interests include the molecular and cellular levels of the nervous system; systems within the brain, such as vision and hearing; and behavior produced by the brain. Promotes education in the neurosciences and the application of research to treat nervous system disorders.

United Cerebral Palsy Assns., *1660 L St. N.W., #700 20036-5602; (202) 776-0406. Fax, (202) 776-0414. Kirsten Nyrop, Executive Director. Information, (800) 872-5827. Main phone is voice and TTY accessible.*

General e-mail, ucpnatl@ucp.org

Web, www.ucpa.org

National network of state and local affiliates that assists individuals with cerebral palsy and other developmental disabilities and their families. Provides parent education, early intervention, employment services, family support and respite programs, therapy, assistive technology, and vocational training. Promotes research on cerebral palsy; supports the use of assistive technology and community-based living arrangements for persons with cerebral palsy and other developmental disabilities.

Skin Disorders

AGENCIES

National Institute of Arthritis and Musculoskeletal and Skin Diseases *(National Institutes of Health), 31 Center Dr., Bldg. 31, #4C32, MSC-2350, Bethesda, MD 20892-2350; (301) 496-4353. Fax, (301) 402-3607. Dr. Stephen I. Katz, Director. Information, (301) 496-8190. Web, www.niams.nih.gov*

Supports research on the causes and treatment of skin diseases, including psoriasis, eczema, and acne.

NONPROFIT

American Academy of Facial Plastic and Reconstructive Surgery, *310 S. Henry St., Alexandria, VA 22314; (703) 299-9291. Fax, (703) 299-8898. Stephen C. Duffy, Executive Vice President. Toll-free information and physician referral, (800) 332-3223.*

Web, www.aafprs.org

Promotes research and study in the field. Helps train residents in facial plastic and reconstructive surgery; offers continuing medical education. Sponsors scientific and medical meetings, international symposia, fellowship training program, seminars, and workshops. Provides videotapes on facial plastic and reconstructive surgery.

Substance Abuse

AGENCIES

Education Dept., *Safe and Drug-Free Schools, 400 Maryland Ave. S.W., #3E300 20202-6123; (202) 260-3954.*

Fax, (202) 260-7767. William Modzeleski, Associate Deputy Under Secretary.
Web, www.ed.gov/offices/OESE/SDFS

Develops policy for the department's drug and violence prevention initiatives for students in elementary and secondary schools and institutions of higher education. Coordinates education efforts in drug and violence prevention with those of other federal departments and agencies.

Health Resources and Services Administration
(Health and Human Services Dept.), Primary Health Care: Special Populations, 4350 East-West Hwy., West Towers Bldg., 9th Floor, Bethesda, MD 20814; (301) 594-4420. Fax, (301) 594-4989. Regan Crump, Director.
Web, www.bphc.hrsa.gov

Funds a program that links primary care and substance abuse treatment.

National Institute on Alcohol Abuse and Alcoholism *(National Institutes of Health), 6000 Executive Blvd., Willco Bldg., #400, MSC-7003, Bethesda, MD 20892-7003; (301) 443-3885. Fax, (301) 443-7043. Ting-Kai Li, Director. Information, (301) 443-3860.*
Web, www.niaaa.nih.gov

Supports basic and applied research on preventing and treating alcoholism and alcohol-related problems; conducts research and disseminates findings on alcohol abuse and alcoholism. Participates in international research.

National Institute on Drug Abuse *(National Institutes of Health), 6001 Executive Blvd., #5274, MSC-9581, Bethesda, MD 20892-9581; (301) 443-6480. Fax, (301) 443-9127. Dr. Nora Volkow, Director. Information, (301) 443-1124. Press, (301) 443-6245. TTY, (888) 889-6432. Toll-free fax-on-demand, (888) 644-6432.*
Web, www.nida.nih.gov

Conducts and sponsors research on the prevention, effects, and treatment of drug abuse. Monitors international policy and research.

Office of National Drug Control Policy (ONDCP), *(Executive Office of the President), 750 17th St. N.W. 20503; (202) 395-6700. Fax, (202) 395-6680. John P. Walters, Director.*
Web, www.whitehousedrugpolicy.gov

Establishes policies and oversees the implementation of a national drug control strategy; recommends changes to reduce demand for and supply of illegal drugs; advises the National Security Council on drug control policy.

Substance Abuse and Mental Health Services Administration *(Health and Human Services Dept.),*

5600 Fishers Lane, #12-105, Rockville, MD 20857; (301) 443-4795. Fax, (301) 443-0284. Charles G. Curie, Administrator. Information, (301) 443-8956.
Web, www.samhsa.gov

Coordinates activities of the Center for Substance Abuse Treatment, Center for Mental Health Services, and Center for Substance Abuse Prevention, which sponsors the National Clearinghouse for Alcohol and Drug Information.

Substance Abuse and Mental Health Services Administration *(Health and Human Services Dept.), Center for Substance Abuse Prevention, 5515 Security Lane, Rockwall 2, #900, Rockville, MD 20857 (mailing address: 5600 Fishers Lane, Rockwall II Bldg., Rockville, MD 20857); (301) 443-0365. Fax, (301) 443-5447. Elaine P. Parry, Director (Acting). TTY, (800) 487-4889. Clearinghouse, (800) 729-6686.*
Web, www.samhsa.gov

Promotes strategies to prevent alcohol and drug abuse. Operates the National Clearinghouse for Alcohol and Drug Information, which provides information, publications, and grant applications for programs to prevent substance abuse. (Clearinghouse address: P.O. Box 2345, Rockville, MD 29847.)

Substance Abuse and Mental Health Services Administration *(Health and Human Services Dept.), Center for Substance Abuse Treatment, 5515 Security Lane, Rockwall 2, #615, Rockville, MD 20852 (mailing address: 5600 Fishers Lane, Rockwall 2, Rockville, MD 20857); (301) 443-5700. Fax, (301) 443-8751. Dr. H. Westley Clark, Director. TTY, (800) 487-4889. Treatment referral, literature, and reports, (800) 662-4357.*
Web, www.samhsa.gov

Develops and supports policies and programs that improve and expand treatment services for alcoholism and substance abuse addiction. Administers grants that support private and public addiction prevention and treatment services. Conducts research on and evaluates alcohol treatment programs and other drug treatment programs and delivery systems.

INTERNATIONAL ORGANIZATIONS

International Commission for the Prevention of Alcoholism and Drug Dependency, *12501 Old Columbia Pike, Silver Spring, MD 20904; (301) 680-6719. Fax, (301) 680-6707. Dr. Peter N. Landless, Executive Director.*
General e-mail, the_icpa@hotmail.com
Web, www.adventist.org/ICPA

Membership: health officials, physicians, educators, clergy, and judges worldwide. Promotes scientific research on prevention of alcohol and drug dependencies; provides information about medical effects of alcohol and drugs; conducts world congresses.

NONPROFIT

American Society of Addiction Medicine, *4601 N. Park Ave., Upper Arcade, #101, Chevy Chase, MD 20815-4520; (301) 656-3920. Fax, (301) 656-3815. Eileen McGrath, Executive Vice President.*
General e-mail, email@asam.org
Web, www.asam.org
Membership: physicians and medical students. Supports the study and provision of effective treatment and care for people with alcohol and drug dependencies; educates physicians; administers certification program in addiction medicine. Monitors legislation and regulations.

Employee Assistance Professionals Assn., *2101 Wilson Blvd., #500, Arlington, VA 22201; (703) 387-1000. Fax, (703) 522-4585. Antoinette Samuel, Chief Executive Officer.*
General e-mail, info@eap-association.org
Web, www.eap-association.org
Represents professionals in the workplace who assist employees and their family members with personal and behavioral problems, including health, marital, family, financial, alcohol, drug, legal, emotional, stress, or other personal problems that adversely affect employee job performance and productivity.

National Assn. for Addiction Professionals, *901 N. Washington St., #600, Alexandria, VA 22314; (703) 741-7686. Fax, (703) 741-7698. Pat Ford-Roegner, Executive Director. Information, (800) 548-0497.*
General e-mail, naadac@naadac.org
Web, www.naadac.org
Provides information on drug dependency treatment, research, and resources. Works with private groups and federal agencies concerned with treating and preventing alcoholism and drug abuse; certifies addiction counselors; holds workshops and conferences for treatment professionals. (Formerly National Assn. of Alcoholism and Drug Abuse Counselors.)

National Assn. of State Alcohol and Drug Abuse Directors, *808 17th St. N.W., #410 20006; (202) 293-0090. Fax, (202) 293-1250. Lewis E. Gallant, Executive Director.*
General e-mail, dcoffice@nasadad.org
Web, www.nasadad.org

Provides information on drug abuse treatment and prevention; contracts with federal and state agencies for design of programs to fight drug abuse.

Therapeutic Communities of America, *1601 Connecticut Ave. N.W., #803 20009; (202) 296-3503. Fax, (202) 518-5475. Linda Hay Crawford, Executive Director.*
Web, www.tcanet.org
Membership: substance abuse treatment and rehabilitation agencies. Provides policy analysis and educates the public on substance abuse and treatment issues. Promotes the interests of therapeutic communities, their clients, and staffs. Monitors legislation and regulations.

Women's Health

AGENCIES

National Institutes of Health (NIH), *(Health and Human Services Dept.), Research on Women's Health, 9000 Rockville Pike, Bldg. 1, #200, MSC-0161, Bethesda, MD 20892-0161; (301) 402-1770. Fax, (301) 402-1798. Dr. Vivian W. Pinn, Director.*
Web, www4.od.nih.gov/orwh
Collaborates with NIH institutes and centers to establish NIH goals and policies for research related to women's health; supports expansion of research on diseases, conditions, and disorders that affect women; monitors inclusion of women and minorities in clinical research; develops opportunities and support for recruitment and advancement of women in biomedical careers.

Public Health and Science *(Health and Human Services Dept.), Women's Health, 200 Independence Ave. S.W., #730B 20201; (202) 690-7650. Fax, (202) 401-4005. Dr. Wanda K. Jones, Deputy Assistant Secretary.*
Web, www.4woman.gov
Coordinates HHS activities in women's health research and medical care, including professional education and advancement of women; works with other agencies and organizations; participates in international conferences. Oversees the National Women's Health Information Center; interests include breast cancer.

NONPROFIT

American Medical Women's Assn., *801 N. Fairfax St., #400, Alexandria, VA 22314-1767; (703) 838-0500. Fax, (703) 549-3864. Linda Hallman, Executive Director.*
General e-mail, info@amwa-doc.org
Web, www.amwa-doc.org
Membership: female physicians, interns, residents, and medical students; interested members of the public can join as associate members. Promotes continuing education; evaluates manufacturers' research on prod-

ucts for women's health; provides student educational loans. Monitors legislation and regulations.

Institute for Women's Policy Research (IWPR), *1707 L St. N.W., #750 20036; (202) 785-5100. Fax, (202) 833-4362. Heidi I. Hartmann, President.*
General e-mail, iwpr@iwpr.org
Web, www.iwpr.org

Public policy research organization that focuses on women's issues, including health care and comprehensive family and medical leave programs.

National Center for Policy Research for Women and Families, *1901 Pennsylvania Ave. N.W., #901 20006; (202) 223-4000. Fax, (202) 223-4242. Diana Zuckerman, Executive Director.*
General e-mail, info@center4policy.org
Web, www.center4policy.org

Utilizes scientific and medical research to improve the quality of women's lives and the lives of family members. Seeks to educate policymakers about medical and scientific research through hearings, meetings, and publications.

National Women's Health Network, *514 10th St. N.W., #400 20004-1410; (202) 347-1140. Fax, (202) 347-1168. Cynthia Pearson, Executive Director.*
Web, www.womenshealthnetwork.org

Acts as an information clearinghouse on women's health issues; monitors federal health policies and legislation. Interests include older women's health issues, contraception, breast cancer, abortion, unsafe drugs, and AIDS.

Society for Women's Health Research, *1828 L St. N.W., #625 20036; (202) 223-8224. Fax, (202) 833-3472. Phyllis Greenberger, President.*
General e-mail, info@womens-health.org
Web, www.womens-health.org

Promotes public and private funding for women's health research and changes in public policies affecting women's health. Seeks to advance women as leaders in the health professions and to inform policymakers, educators, and the public of research outcomes. Sponsors meetings; produces reports and educational videotapes.

 **MENTAL HEALTH**

AGENCIES
National Institute of Mental Health *(National Institutes of Health), 6001 Executive Blvd., #8235, Rockville,*
MD 20892; (301) 443-3673. Fax, (301) 443-2578. Dr. Thomas R. Insel, Director (Acting). Information, (301) 443-8410. Press, (301) 443-6330. TTY, (301) 443-8431.
Web, www.nimh.nih.gov

Conducts research on the cause, diagnosis, treatment, and prevention of mental disorders; provides information on mental health problems and programs. Participates in international research.

National Institute of Mental Health *(National Institutes of Health), Developmental Psychopathology and Prevention Research, 6001 Executive Blvd., #6200, Bethesda, MD 20892; (301) 443-5944. Fax, (301) 480-4415. Doreen Koretz, Chief.*
Web, www.nimh.nih.gov

Promotes research programs concerning the prevention of mental disorders and the promotion of mental health.

National Institute of Mental Health *(National Institutes of Health), Neuroscience and Basic Behavioral Science, 6001 Executive Blvd., #7204, Rockville, MD 20892; (301) 443-3563. Fax, (301) 443-1731. Steve L. Foote, Director.*
Web, www.nimh.nih.gov

Directs, plans, and supports programs of basic and clinical neuroscience research, genetics and therapeutics research, research training, resource development, and research dissemination to further understand the treatment and prevention of brain disorders. Interests include: behavioral and integrative neuroscience; molecular and cellular neuroscience; genetics; and preclinical and clinical therapeutics. Analyzes national needs and research opportunities.

National Institute of Mental Health *(National Institutes of Health), Special Populations, 6001 Executive Blvd., #8125, MSC-9659, Bethesda, MD 20892; (301) 443-2847. Fax, (301) 443-8022. Ernest Marquez, Director.*
Web, www.nimh.nih.gov

Sets research policy on women and under-represented racial and ethnic minorities. Administers the minority institutions programs, which support research on and research training for minorities in the mental health field.

Substance Abuse and Mental Health Services Administration *(Health and Human Services Dept.), 5600 Fishers Lane, #12-105, Rockville, MD 20857; (301) 443-4795. Fax, (301) 443-0284. Charles G. Curie, Administrator. Information, (301) 443-8956.*
Web, www.samhsa.gov

Coordinates activities of the Center for Substance Abuse Treatment, Center for Mental Health Services, and Center for Substance Abuse Prevention, which sponsors the National Clearinghouse for Alcohol and Drug Information.

Substance Abuse and Mental Health Services Administration *(Health and Human Services Dept.), Center for Mental Health Services, 5600 Fishers Lane, #17-99, Rockville, MD 20857; (301) 443-0001. Fax, (301) 443-1563. Gail P. Hutchings, Director. Information, (301) 443-2792. TTY, (301) 443-9006.*
Web, www.samhsa.gov

Works with federal agencies and state and local governments to demonstrate, evaluate, and disseminate service delivery models to treat mental illness, promote mental health, and prevent the developing or worsening of mental illness.

NONPROFIT

American Academy of Child and Adolescent Psychiatry, *3615 Wisconsin Ave. N.W., 2nd Floor 20016-3007; (202) 966-7300. Fax, (202) 966-2891. Virginia Q. Anthony, Executive Director.*
Web, www.aacap.org

Membership: psychiatrists working with children and adolescents. Sponsors annual meeting and review for medical board examinations; provides information on child abuse, youth suicide, and drug abuse; monitors international research and U.S. legislation concerning children with mental illness.

American Assn. of Pastoral Counselors, *9504A Lee Hwy., Fairfax, VA 22031-2303; (703) 385-6967. Fax, (703) 352-7725. C. Roy Woodruff, Executive Director.*
General e-mail, info@aapc.org
Web, www.aapc.org

Membership: mental health professionals with training in both religion and the behavioral sciences. Nonsectarian organization that accredits pastoral counseling centers, certifies pastoral counselors, and approves training programs.

American Assn. of Suicidology, *4201 Connecticut Ave. N.W., #408 20008; (202) 237-2280. Fax, (202) 237-2282. Dr. Alan L. Berman, Executive Director.*
General e-mail, info@suicidology.org
Web, www.suicidology.org

Membership: educators, researchers, suicide prevention centers, school districts, volunteers, and survivors affected by suicide. Works to understand and prevent suicide; serves as an information clearinghouse.

American Bar Assn. (ABA), *Commission on Mental and Physical Disability Law, 740 15th St. N.W. 20005; (202) 662-1571. Fax, (202) 662-1032. John Parry, Director.*
Web, www.abanet.org/disability/home.html

Serves as a clearinghouse for information on mental and physical disability law and offers legal research services. Publishes law report on mental and physical disability law.

American Mental Health Counselors Assn., *801 N. Fairfax St., #304, Alexandria, VA 22314; (703) 548-6002. Fax, (703) 548-4775. Dr. W. Mark Hamilton, Executive Director. Toll-free, (800) 326-2642.*
Web, www.amhca.org

Membership: professional counselors and graduate students in the mental health field. Sponsors leadership training and continuing education programs for members; holds annual conference. Monitors legislation and regulations. (Affiliated with the American Counseling Assn.)

American Psychiatric Assn., *1000 Wilson Blvd., #1825, Arlington, VA 22209-3901; (703) 907-7300. Fax, (703) 907-1085. Dr. James Scully, Medical Director. Library, (703) 907-8648. Press, (703) 907-8540.*
General e-mail, apa@psych.org
Web, www.psych.org

Membership: psychiatrists. Promotes availability of high-quality psychiatric care; provides the public with information; assists state and local agencies; conducts educational programs for professionals and students in the field; participates in international meetings and research. Library open to members.

American Psychological Assn., *750 1st St. N.E. 20002-4242; (202) 336-5500. Fax, (202) 336-6069. Raymond D. Fowler, Executive Vice President. Library, (202) 336-5640. TTY, (202) 336-6123.*
Web, www.apa.org

Membership: professional psychologists, educators, and behavioral research scientists. Supports research, training, and professional services; works toward improving the qualifications, competence, and training programs of psychologists. Monitors international research and U.S. legislation on mental health.

American Psychosomatic Society, *6728 Old McLean Village Dr., McLean, VA 22101; (703) 556-9222. Fax, (703) 556-8729. George K. Degnon, Executive Director.*
General e-mail, info@psychosomatic.org
Web, www.psychosomatic.org

Promotes and advances scientific understanding of relationships among biological, psychological, social, and behavioral factors in health and disease.

Anxiety Disorders Assn. of America, *8730 Georgia Ave., #600, Silver Spring, MD 20910; (240) 485-1001. Fax, (240) 485-1035. Alies Muskin, Chief Operating Officer. Web, www.adaa.org*

Membership: clinicians and researchers who treat and study anxiety disorders; individuals with anxiety disorders and their families; and other interested individuals. Promotes prevention, treatment, and cure of anxiety disorders by disseminating information, linking individuals with treatment facilities, and encouraging research and advancement of scientific knowledge.

Assn. of Black Psychologists, *P.O. Box 55999 20040-5999; (202) 722-0808. Fax, (202) 722-5941. Dr. Harvette Grey, President. General e-mail, abpsi@abpsi.org Web, www.abpsi.org*

Membership: psychologists, psychology students, and others in the mental health field. Develops policies to foster mental health in the African American community.

Bazelon Center for Mental Health Law, *1101 15th St. N.W., #1212 20005; (202) 467-5730. Fax, (202) 223-0409. Robert Bernstein, Executive Director. General e-mail, bazelon@webcom.com Web, www.bazelon.org*

Public interest law firm. Conducts test case litigation to defend rights of persons with mental disabilities. Monitors legislation and regulations.

International Assn. of Psychosocial Rehabilitation Services, *601 N. Hammonds Ferry Rd., #A, Linthicum, MD 21090; (410) 789-7054. Fax, (410) 789-7675. Ruth A. Hughes, Chief Executive Officer. TTY, (410) 730-1723. General e-mail, general@iapsrs.org Web, www.iapsrs.org*

Membership: agencies, mental health practitioners, policymakers, family groups, and consumer organizations. Supports the community adjustment of persons with psychiatric disabilities; promotes the role of rehabilitation in mental health systems; opposes discrimination based on mental disability.

National Alliance for the Mentally Ill, *2107 Wilson Blvd., Colonial Pl. III, #300, Arlington, VA 22201-3042; (703) 524-7600. Fax, (703) 524-9094. Dr. Rick Birkel, Executive Director. Helpline, (800) 950-6264. General e-mail, membership@nami.org Web, www.nami.org*

Membership: mentally ill individuals and their families and friends. Works to eradicate mental illness and improve the lives of those affected by brain disorders; sponsors public education and research. Monitors legislation and regulations.

National Assn. of Psychiatric Health Systems, *325 7th St. N.W., #625 20004-2802; (202) 393-6700. Fax, (202) 783-6041. Mark Covall, Executive Director. General e-mail, naphs@naphs.org Web, www.naphs.org*

Membership: behavioral health care systems that are committed to the delivery of responsive, accountable, and clinically effective treatment and prevention and care programs for children, adolescents, adults, and older adults with mental and substance use disorders.

National Assn. of School Psychologists, *4340 East-West Hwy., #402, Bethesda, MD 20814; (301) 657-0270. Fax, (301) 657-0275. TTY, (301) 657-4155. Susan Gorin, Executive Director. Web, www.nasponline.org*

Membership: persons currently working or credentialed as school psychologists; persons trained as school psychologists and working as consultants or supervisors of psychological services; persons engaged in the training of school psychologists at colleges or universities; and persons pursuing an advanced degree in school psychology. Works to promote educationally and psychologically healthy environments for children and youth by implementing research-based programs designed to prevent problems, enhance independence, and promote learning. Publications include *Communiqué* and *School Psychology Review*. Monitors legislation and regulations.

National Assn. of State Mental Health Program Directors, *66 Canal Center Plaza, #302, Alexandria, VA 22314-1591; (703) 739-9333. Fax, (703) 548-9517. Robert W. Glover, Executive Director. Web, www.nasmhpd.org*

Membership: officials in charge of state mental health agencies. Compiles data on state mental health programs. Fosters collaboration among members; provides technical assistance and consultation. Maintains research institute.

National Consortium for Child Mental Health Services, *3615 Wisconsin Ave. N.W., 2nd Floor 20016-2037; (202) 966-7300. Fax, (202) 966-2891. Virginia Q. Anthony, Executive Director. Web, www.aacap.org*

Membership: organizations interested in developing mental health services for children. Fosters information exchange; advises local, state, and federal agencies that develop children's mental health services. (Affiliated with American Academy of Child and Adolescent Psychiatry.)

National Council for Community Behavioral Healthcare, *12300 Twinbrook Pkwy., #320, Rockville, MD 20852; (301) 984-6200. Fax, (301) 881-7159. Charles G. Ray, Chief Executive Officer.*
Web, www.nccbh.org

Membership: community mental health agencies and state community mental health associations. Conducts research on community mental health activities; provides information, technical assistance, and referrals. Operates a job bank; publishes newsletters and a membership directory. Monitors legislation and regulations affecting community mental health facilities.

National Mental Health Assn., *2001 N. Beauregard St., 12th Floor, Alexandria, VA 22311; (703) 684-7722. Fax, (703) 684-5968. Michael Faenza, President. Information, (800) 969-6642.*
General e-mail, infoctr@nmha.org
Web, www.nmha.org

Works to increase accessible and appropriate care for adults and children with mental disorders. Informs and educates public about mental illnesses and available treatment. Supports research on illnesses and services.

12 Housing and Development

GENERAL POLICY

AGENCIES

Economic Development Administration *(Commerce Dept.), 14th St. and Constitution Ave. N.W., #7800 20230; (202) 482-5081. Fax, (202) 273-4781. David A. Sampson, Assistant Secretary. Information, (202) 482-2309.*
Web, www.doc.gov/eda

Advises the commerce secretary on domestic economic development. Administers development assistance programs that provide financial and technical aid to economically distressed areas to stimulate economic growth and create jobs. Awards public works and technical assistance grants to public institutions, nonprofit organizations, and native American tribes; assists state and local governments with economic adjustment problems caused by long-term or sudden economic dislocation.

General Services Administration (GSA), *Federal Domestic Assistance Catalog Staff, 1800 F St. N.W., #4032 20405; (202) 208-1582. Fax, (202) 501-3341. Kathy Hospodar, Director, (202) 208-4052.*
Web, www.cfda.gov

Prepares *Catalog of Federal Domestic Assistance* (published annually in June and updated in December), which lists all types of federal aid and explains types of assistance, eligibility requirements, application process, and suggestions for writing proposals. Copies may be ordered from the Superintendent of Documents, U.S. Government Printing Office 20402; (202) 512-1800 or toll-free, (866) 512-1800 or online at bookstore.gpo.gov. Also available on CD-ROM and floppy diskettes.

Housing and Urban Development Dept. (HUD), *451 7th St. S.W., #10000 20410; (202) 708-0417. Fax, (202) 619-8365. Mel Martinez, Secretary; Alfonso Jackson, Deputy Secretary. Information, (202) 708-0980. Library, (202) 708-1420. Press, (202) 708-0685. TTY, (202) 708-1455.*
Web, www.hud.gov

Responsible for federal programs concerned with housing needs, fair housing opportunity, and improving and developing the nation's urban and rural communities. Administers mortgage insurance, rent subsidy, preservation, rehabilitation, and antidiscrimination in housing programs. Advises the president on federal policy and makes legislative recommendations on housing and community development issues.

Housing and Urban Development Dept. (HUD), *HUD USER, P.O. Box 23268 20026-3268; (202) 708-3178. Fax, (202) 708-9981. Mel Adkins, Program Manager. Information, (800) 245-2691.*

General e-mail, helpdesk@huduser.org
Web, www.huduser.org

Research information service and clearinghouse for HUD research reports. Provides information on past and current HUD research; maintains HUD USER, an in-house database. Performs custom search requests for a nominal fee; blueprints available upon request. Some documents available online.

Housing and Urban Development Dept. (HUD), *Policy Development and Research, 451 7th St. S.W., #8100 20410-6000; (202) 708-1600. Fax, (202) 619-8000. Alberto Treviño, Assistant Secretary.*
Web, www.huduser.org

Studies ways to improve the effectiveness and equity of HUD programs; analyzes housing and urban issues, including national housing goals, the operation of housing financial markets, the management of housing assistance programs, and statistics on federal and housing insurance programs; conducts the American Housing Survey; develops policy recommendations to improve federal housing programs. Works to increase the affordability of rehabilitated and newly constructed housing through technological and regulatory improvements.

Housing and Urban Development Dept. (HUD), *Program Evaluation, 451 7th St. S.W., #8140 20410; (202) 708-0574. Fax, (202) 708-4250. Kevin J. Neary, Director.*
Web, www.hud.gov

Conducts research, program evaluations, and demonstrations for all HUD housing, community development, and fair housing and equal opportunity programs.

Office of Management and Budget (OMB), *(Executive Office of the President), Housing, New Executive Office Bldg., #9226 20503; (202) 395-4610. Fax, (202) 395-1307. F. Stevens Redburn, Chief.*
Web, www.whitehouse.gov/omb

Assists and advises the OMB director in budget preparation, reorganizations, and evaluations of Housing and Urban Development Dept. programs.

CONGRESS

House Appropriations Committee, *Subcommittee on VA, HUD, and Independent Agencies, H143 CAP 20515; (202) 225-3241. Rep. James T. Walsh, R-N.Y., Chair; Tim Peterson, Staff Director.*
Web, www.house.gov/appropriations

Jurisdiction over legislation to appropriate funds for all programs of the Housing and Urban Development Dept., the National Credit Union Administration, and the Neighborhood Reinvestment Corporation.

HOUSING AND URBAN DEVELOPMENT DEPARTMENT

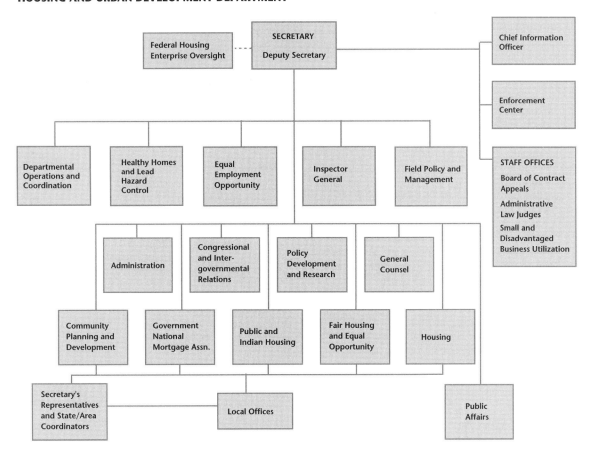

House Financial Services Committee, *Subcommittee on Housing and Community Opportunity,* B303 RHOB 20515; (202) 225-7502. Rep. Bob Ney, R-Ohio, Chair; Bob Foster, Staff Director.

Web, financialservices.house.gov

Jurisdiction over all housing legislation, including construction standards and materials, condominiums and cooperatives, home ownership aid, manufactured homes, single and multifamily housing, and rural housing; oversees the Rural Housing Service in the Agriculture Dept. and other housing-related services and programs.

House Government Reform Committee, *Subcommittee on Criminal Justice, Drug Policy, and Human Resources,* B373B RHOB 20515; (202) 225-2577. Fax, (202) 225-1154. Rep. Mark Souder, R-Ind., Chair; Christopher Donesa, Staff Director.

Web, www.house.gov/reform

Oversight of the Housing and Urban Development Dept.

House Small Business Committee, *Subcommittee on Workforce, Empowerment, and Government Programs,* B363 RHOB 20515; (202) 226-2630. Fax, (202) 225-8950. Rep. Todd Akin, R-Mo., Chair; Nelson Crowther, Chief of Staff.

General e-mail, smbiz@mail.house.gov

Web, www.house.gov/smbiz

Jurisdiction over development of economically depressed areas, including regulations and licensing policies that affect small businesses in high-risk communities.

Senate Appropriations Committee, *Subcommittee on VA, HUD, and Independent Agencies,* SD-130 20510;

(202) 224-8252. Fax, (202) 228-1624. Sen. Christopher S. Bond, R-Mo., Chair; Jon Kamarck, Clerk.

Web, appropriations.senate.gov

Jurisdiction over legislation to appropriate funds for all programs of the Housing and Urban Development Dept., the National Credit Union Administration, and the Neighborhood Reinvestment Corporation.

Senate Banking, Housing, and Urban Affairs Committee, *Subcommittee on Financial Institutions, SD-534 20510; (202) 224-7391. Fax, (202) 224-5137. Sen. Robert F. Bennett, R-Utah, Chair; Mike Nielson, Staff Contact.*

Web, banking.senate.gov

Jurisdiction over legislation on economic stabilization and growth, including regulatory relief issues and barriers to development in rural areas.

Senate Banking, Housing, and Urban Affairs Committee, *Subcommittee on Housing and Transportation, SD-534 20510; (202) 224-7391. Fax, (202) 224-5137. Sen. Wayne Allard, R-Colo., Chair; Tewana Wilkerson, Staff Director.*

Web, banking.senate.gov

Jurisdiction over legislation concerning housing issues, including rural housing, construction standards and materials, condominiums and cooperatives, home ownership aid, manufactured homes, and single and multifamily housing. Oversees the Housing and Urban Development Dept. and housing programs in the Agriculture Dept.

Senate Small Business and Entrepreneurship Committee, *SR-428A 20510; (202) 224-5175. Fax, (202) 228-1128. Sen. Olympia J. Snowe, R-Maine, Chair; Mark Warren, Staff Director.*

Web, sbc.senate.gov

Jurisdiction over small and disadvantaged business and related economic development.

NONPROFIT

Center for Housing Policy, *1801 K St. N.W., #M100 20006; (202) 466-2121. Fax, (202) 466-2122. Robert J. Reid, Executive Director.*

General e-mail, nhc@nhc.org

Web, www.nhc.org

Researches and develops fundamentals of housing policy. Seeks to create new policies that integrate housing into overall social and economic goals. Sponsors educational forums. (Affiliated with the National Housing Conference.)

Housing and Development Law Institute, *630 Eye St. N.W. 20001-3736; (202) 289-3400. Fax, (202) 289-3401. Tim Coyle, Director of Administration.*

General e-mail, hdli@hdli.org

Web, www.hdli.org

Assists public agencies that administer assisted housing and community development programs in addressing common legal concerns and problems; publishes legal periodicals concerning affordable housing issues; conducts seminars on legal issues and practices in the housing and community development field. (Affiliated with the National Assn. of Housing and Redevelopment Officials.)

Institute for Local Self-Reliance, *2425 18th St. N.W. 20009-2096; (202) 232-4108. Fax, (202) 332-0463. Neil N. Seldman, President.*

General e-mail, ilsr@igc.org

Web, www.ilsr.org

Conducts research and provides technical assistance on environmentally sound economic development for government, small businesses, and community organizations.

National Assn. of Housing and Redevelopment Officials, *630 Eye St. N.W. 20001; (202) 289-3500. Fax, (202) 289-8181. Saul Ramirez, Executive Director.*

Web, www.nahro.org

Membership: housing, community, and urban development practitioners and organizations, and state and local government agencies and personnel. Works with federal government agencies to improve community development and housing programs; conducts training programs.

Statistics

AGENCIES

Census Bureau *(Commerce Dept.), Governments Division, 8905 Presidential Pkwy., Upper Marlboro, MD 20722 (mailing address: Washington Plaza II, #407, Washington, DC 20233-6800); (301) 763-1489. Fax, (301) 457-1423. Stephanie Brown, Chief (Acting).*

Web, www.census.gov

Compiles the annual *Federal Expenditures by State,* which provides information on federal domestic spending, federal grants programs, and federal aid to states.

Census Bureau *(Commerce Dept.), Housing and Household Economic Statistics, 4700 Silver Hill Rd., Suitland, MD 20746 (mailing address: HHES, #10553, Washington, DC 20233-8500); (301) 763-3234. Fax, (301) 457-3248. Daniel H. Weinberg, Chief.*

General e-mail, hhes-info@census.gov

Web, www.census.gov

Publishes decennial census of housing and the American Housing Survey, which describe housing inventory characteristics. Also publishes a quarterly survey of market absorption. Survey on housing vacancy is available on the Internet.

Census Bureau *(Commerce Dept.), Manufacturing and Construction,* *4401 Silver Hill Rd., Bldg FB4, #2102A, Suitland, MD 20746; (301) 763-4593. Fax, (301) 457-4583. William G. Bostic Jr., Chief.*

Web, www.census.gov

Publishes statistics on the value of construction put in place; housing starts, sales, and completions; building permits; price index of single-family homes sold; characteristics of new housing; and expenditures for residential improvements. Conducts a census of construction industries every five years.

Housing and Urban Development Dept. (HUD), *Economic Affairs, 451 7th St. S.W., #8204 20410-6000; (202) 708-3080. Fax, (202) 708-1159. Harold Bunce, Deputy Assistant Secretary.*

Web, www.hud.gov

Directs research in public finance and urban economic development; assembles data on housing markets; conducts annual housing surveys; analyzes financial instruments used in housing.

International Trade Administration (ITA), *(Commerce Dept.), Energy, Environment, and Materials,* *14th St. and Constitution Ave. N.W., #4043 20230; (202) 482-0614. Fax, (202) 482-5666. Kevin W. Murphy, Deputy Assistant Secretary.*

Web, www.trade.gov

Analyzes and maintains data on international construction and engineering. Monitors production costs, prices, financial and labor conditions, technological changes, distribution, markets, trade patterns, and other aspects of these industries. Promotes international trade, develops competitive assessments, and assists engineering and construction companies in obtaining overseas construction projects.

Office of Thrift Supervision (OTS), *(Treasury Dept.), Financial Reporting, 1700 G St. N.W., 3rd Floor 20552-6720; (202) 906-6000. Fax, (202) 906-6527. Patrick G. Berbakos, Director.*

General e-mail, public.info@ots.treas.org

Web, www.ots.treas.gov

Provides housing and mortgage statistics, including terms and rates of conventional home mortgages, and asset and liability information for thrift institutions insured by the Savings Assn. Insurance Fund.

COMMUNITY AND REGIONAL DEVELOPMENT

AGENCIES

Administration for Children and Families (ACF), *(Health and Human Services Dept.), Office of Community Services, 901 D St. S.W., 5th Floor 20447 (mailing address: 370 L'Enfant Promenade S.W. 20447); (202) 401-9333. Fax, (202) 401-4694. Clarence H. Carter, Director.*

Web, www.acf.dhhs.gov

Administers the Community Services Block Grant and Discretionary Grant programs.

Administration for Native Americans *(Health and Human Services Dept.), 370 L'Enfant Promenade S.W., M.S. Aerospace Center, 8th Floor, West 20447-0002; (202) 690-7776. Fax, (202) 690-7441. Quanah Crossland Stamps, Commissioner.*

Web, www.acf.hhs.gov/programs/ana

Awards grants for locally determined social and economic development strategies; promotes native American economic and social self-sufficiency; funds tribes and native American and native Hawaiian organizations. Commissioner chairs the Intradepartmental Council on Indian Affairs, which coordinates native American-related programs.

Army Corps of Engineers *(Defense Dept.), 441 G St. N.W., #3K05 20314-1000; (202) 761-0001. Fax, (202) 761-4463. Lt. Gen. Robert B. Flowers (USACE), Chief of Engineers.*

Web, www.usace.army.mil

Provides local governments with disaster relief, flood control, navigation, and hydroelectric power services.

Defense Dept. (DoD), *Office of Economic Adjustment, 400 Army-Navy Dr., #200, Arlington, VA 22202-4704; (703) 604-6020. Fax, (703) 604-5843. Patrick J. O'Brien, Director.*

Web, www.acq.osd.mil/oea

Civilian office that helps community officials develop strategies and coordinate plans to alleviate the economic effect of major defense program changes, including base closings, reductions in forces, and contract cutbacks. Assists communities where defense activities are being expanded. Serves as the staff for the Economic Adjustment Committee, an interagency group that coordinates federal defense economic adjustment activities.

Empowerment Programs, *1400 Independence Ave. S.W., Stop 3203 20250; (202) 619-7980. Fax, (202) 401-7420. Rick Wetherill, Director. Information, (800) 645-4712. TTY, (202) 720-7807.*

Web, www.ezec.gov

Provides information about federal empowerment zones and enterprise communities in economically distressed urban and rural areas.

Housing and Urban Development Dept. (HUD), Block Grant Assistance, *451 7th St. S.W., #7286 20410; (202) 708-3587. Fax, (202) 401-2044. Richard Kennedy, Director. Press, (202) 708-0614.*

Web, www.hud.gov/cpd/cpdhome.html

Develops regulations and procedures for the Community Development Block Grant Program and the Section 108 Loan Guarantee Program.

Housing and Urban Development Dept. (HUD), Community Planning and Development, *451 7th St. S.W., #7100 20410; (202) 708-2690. Fax, (202) 708-3336. Roy A. Bernardi, Assistant Secretary.*

Web, www.hud.gov

Provides cities and states with community and economic development and housing assistance, including community development block grants. Encourages public-private partnerships in urban development and private sector initiatives. Oversees enterprise zone development program.

Housing and Urban Development Dept. (HUD), Community Viability, *451 7th St. S.W., #7240 20410; (202) 708-2894. Fax, (202) 708-3363. Richard H. Broun, Director.*

Web, www.hud.gov

Issues policies and sets standards for environmental and land-use planning and for environmental management practices. Develops policies promoting energy efficiency, conservation, and renewable sources of supply in housing and community development programs, including district heating and cooling systems and wastes-to-energy cogeneration projects.

Housing and Urban Development Dept. (HUD), Field Management, *451 7th St. S.W., #7150 20410; (202) 708-2565. Fax, (202) 401-9681. Nadab O. Bynum, Director.*

Web, www.hud.gov

Acts as liaison and coordinates all activities between the Office of Community Planning and Development and regional and field offices; evaluates the performance of regional and field offices. Conducts policy analyses and evaluations of community planning and development programs, including the Community Development

Block Grant Program, the Empowerment Zones/Enterprise Communities Program, and the McKinney Act programs.

Housing and Urban Development Dept. (HUD), State and Small Cities, *451 7th St. S.W., #7184 20410; (202) 708-1322. Fax, (202) 401-2044. Steve Johnson, Director.*

Web, www.hud.gov

Provides states with grants for distribution to small cities and counties with fewer than 50,000 persons that are not entitled to community development block grants; insular areas also are eligible. Funds community development programs in low- and moderate-income communities and communities with urgent needs.

Housing and Urban Development Dept. (HUD), Technical Assistance and Management, *451 7th St. S.W., #7216 20410; (202) 708-3176. Fax, (202) 619-5979. Jean Whaley, Director.*

Web, www.hud.gov

Develops program policies and designs and implements technical assistance plans for state and local governments for use in community planning and development programs.

CONGRESS

House Financial Services Committee, *Subcommittee on Housing and Community Opportunity, B303 RHOB 20515; (202) 225-7502. Rep. Bob Ney, R-Ohio, Chair; Bob Foster, Staff Director.*

Web, financialservices.house.gov

Jurisdiction over all community development legislation; urban planning, design, and research; urban redevelopment and relocation; and community development training and fellowships. Jurisdiction over Urban Development Action Grants and enterprise zones. Oversees the Housing and Urban Development Dept. and housing programs in the Agriculture Dept.

House Transportation and Infrastructure Committee, *Subcommittee on Economic Development, Public Buildings, and Emergency Management, 589 FHOB 20515; (202) 225-3014. Fax, (202) 226-1898. Rep. Steven C. LaTourette, R-Ohio, Chair; Matt Wallen, Staff Director.*

General e-mail, transcomm@mail.house.gov

Web, www.house.gov/transportation

Jurisdiction over legislation on development of economically depressed areas, including Appalachia, and legislation designed to create jobs, often with public works and water resource development projects; jurisdiction over the Economic Development Administration.

Senate Banking, Housing, and Urban Affairs Committee, *Subcommittee on Housing and Transportation,* SD-534 20510; (202) 224-7391. Fax, (202) 224-5137. Sen. Wayne Allard, R-Colo., Chair; Tewana Wilkerson, Staff Director.

Web, banking.senate.gov

Jurisdiction over community development legislation (including Urban Development Action Grants and enterprise zones); urban planning, design, and research; and urban redevelopment and relocation. Oversees the Housing and Urban Development Dept. and housing programs in the Agriculture Dept.

Senate Environment and Public Works Committee, SD-410 20510; (202) 224-6176. Fax, (202) 224-5167. Sen. James M. Inhofe, R-Okla., Chair; Andrew Wheeler, Staff Director.

General e-mail, guest1@epw.senate.gov

Web, epw.senate.gov

Jurisdiction over legislation on development of economically depressed areas, including Appalachia, and over legislation designed to create jobs, often with public works and water resource development projects; jurisdiction over the Economic Development Administration.

Senate Finance Committee, SD-219 20510; (202) 224-4515. Fax, (202) 228-0554. Sen. Charles E. Grassley, R-Iowa, Chair; Kolan L. Davis, Staff Director.

Web, finance.senate.gov

Jurisdiction over revenue-sharing legislation. (Jurisdiction shared with Senate Governmental Affairs Committee.)

Senate Governmental Affairs Committee, SD-340 20510; (202) 224-4751. Fax, (202) 228-3792. Sen. Susan Collins, R-Maine, Chair; Michael Bopp, Staff Director.

Web, govt-aff.senate.gov

Jurisdiction over revenue sharing legislation. (Jurisdiction shared with Senate Finance Committee.)

NONPROFIT

American Planning Assn., *1776 Massachusetts Ave. N.W., #400 20036-1904; (202) 872-0611. Fax, (202) 872-0643. Paul Farmer, Executive Director.*

Web, www.planning.org

Membership: professional planners and others interested in urban and rural planning. Serves as a clearinghouse for planners. Sponsors professional development workshops conducted by the American Institute of Certified Planners. Prepares studies and technical reports; conducts seminars and conferences.

American Resort Development Assn., *1201 15th St. N.W., #400 20005; (202) 371-6700. Fax, (202) 289-8544. Howard Nusbaum, President.*

Web, www.arda.org

Membership: U.S. and international developers, builders, financiers, marketing companies, and others involved in resort, recreational, and community development. Serves as an information clearinghouse; monitors federal and state legislation affecting land, time share, and community development industries.

Center for Community Change, *1000 Wisconsin Ave. N.W. 20007; (202) 342-0519. Fax, (202) 333-5462. Deepak Bhargava, Executive Director.*

General e-mail, info@communitychange.org

Web, www.communitychange.org

Provides community-based organizations serving minorities and the economically disadvantaged with technical assistance. Areas of assistance include housing, economic and resource development, rural development projects, and program planning.

Corporation for Enterprise Development, *777 N. Capitol St. N.E., #800 20002; (202) 408-9788. Fax, (202) 408-9793. Brian Dabson, President.*

General e-mail, cfed@cfed.org

Web, www.cfed.org

Research and consulting organization that promotes economic self-sufficiency among low-income people through enterprise development, including microbusinesses to generate self-employment for the unemployed. Provides technical assistance and policy analysis to state and local governments and community organizations.

Council of State Community Development Agencies, *1825 K St. N.W., #515 20006; (202) 293-5820. Fax, (202) 293-2820. Dianne E. Taylor, Executive Director.*

General e-mail, coscda@coscda.org

Web, www.coscda.org

Membership: directors and staff of state community development agencies. Promotes common interests among the states, including community and economic development, housing, homelessness, infrastructure, and state and local planning.

International Institute of Site Planning, *715 G St. S.E., Lower Level 20003; (202) 546-2322. Fax, (202) 546-2722. Beatriz de W. Coffin, Director.*

General e-mail, iisitep@aol.com

Web, www.iisitep.org

Directs research and provides information on site planning development and design of sites and buildings; conducts study/travel programs.

Land Trust Alliance, *1331 H St. N.W., #400 20005-4734; (202) 638-4725. Fax, (202) 638-4730. Rand Wentworth, President.*
Web, www.lta.org

Membership: organizations and individuals who work to conserve land resources. Serves as a forum for the exchange of information; conducts research and public education programs. Monitors legislation and regulations.

Local Initiatives Support Corp., *Washington Office, 1825 K St. N.W., #1100 20006; (202) 785-2908. Fax, (202) 835-8931. Michael Tierney, Executive Vice President.*
Web, www.liscnet.org

Provides community development corporations with financial and technical assistance to build affordable housing and revitalize distressed neighborhoods. (Headquarters in New York.)

National Assn. of Conservation Districts, *509 Capitol Court N.E. 20002-4937; (202) 547-6223. Fax, (202) 547-6450. Ernest C. Shea, Chief Executive Officer.*
General e-mail, washington@nacdnet.org
Web, www.nacdnet.org

Membership: conservation districts (local subdivisions of state government). Works to promote the conservation of land, forests, and other natural resources. Interests include erosion and sediment control; water quality; forestry, water, flood plain, and range management; rural development; and urban and community conservation.

National Assn. of Counties (NACo), *Community and Economic Development, 440 1st St. N.W., 8th Floor 20001-2028; (202) 393-6226. Fax, (202) 942-4281. Cassandra Matthews, Associate Legislative Director.*
Web, www.naco.org

Membership: county governments. Conducts research and provides information on community development block grants, assisted low-income housing, and other housing and economic development programs. Monitors legislation and regulations.

National Assn. of Development Organizations, *400 N. Capitol St. N.W., #390 20001; (202) 624-7806. Fax, (202) 624-8813. Aliceann Wohlbruck, Executive Director.*
General e-mail, info@nado.org
Web, www.nado.org

Membership: organizations interested in regional, local, and rural economic development. Provides information on federal, state, and local development programs and revolving loan funds; sponsors conferences and seminars.

National Assn. of Regional Councils, *1666 Connecticut Ave. N.W., #300 20009; (202) 986-1032. Fax, (202) 986-1038. Robert Sokolowski, Executive Director.*
Web, www.narc.org

Membership: regional councils of local governments and metropolitan planning councils. Works with member local governments to encourage areawide economic growth and cooperation between public and private sectors, with emphasis on community development.

National Community Development Assn., *522 21st St. N.W., #120 20006; (202) 293-7587. Fax, (202) 887-5546. Chandra Western, Executive Director.*
General e-mail, ncda@ncdaonline.org
Web, www.ncdaonline.org

Membership: local governments that administer federally supported community and economic development, housing, and human service programs.

National Congress for Community Economic Development, *1030 15th St. N.W., #325 20005; (202) 289-9020. Fax, (202) 289-7051. Roy Priest, President. Information, (877) 446-2233.*
General e-mail, mail@ncced.org
Web, www.ncced.org

Membership: organizations engaged in revitalizing economically distressed communities. Services include advocacy, fundraising and technical assistance, information and referrals, conferences, and training. Conducts research and compiles statistics on industry issues and trends. Library open to the public.

National Trust for Historic Preservation, *1785 Massachusetts Ave. N.W. 20036-2117; (202) 588-6000. Fax, (202) 588-6038. Richard Moe, President. Information, (800) 944-6847.*
Web, www.nthp.org

Conducts seminars, workshops, and conferences on topics related to preservation, including neighborhood conservation, main street revitalization, rural conservation, and preservation law; offers financial assistance through loan and grant programs; provides advisory services; operates historic house museums, which are open to the public.

Partners for Livable Communities, *1429 21st St. N.W., 2nd Floor 20036; (202) 887-5990. Fax, (202) 466-4845. Robert H. McNulty, President.*
Web, www.livable.com

Promotes working partnerships among public, private, and governmental sectors to improve the quality of life and economic development at local and regional levels. Conducts conferences and workshops; maintains referral clearinghouse.

Scenic America, *801 Pennsylvania Ave. S.E., #300 20003-2152; (202) 543-6200. Fax, (202) 543-9130. Meg Maguire, President.*

General e-mail, scenic@scenic.org

Web, www.scenic.org

Membership: national, state, and local groups concerned with land-use control, growth management, and landscape protection. Works to enhance the scenic quality of America's communities and countryside. Provides information and technical assistance on scenic byways, tree preservation, economics of aesthetic regulation, billboard and sign control, scenic areas preservation, and growth management.

Rural Areas

AGENCIES

Agriculture Dept. (USDA), *Rural Development, 1400 Independence Ave. S.W., #206W 20250; (202) 720-4581. Fax, (202) 720-2080. Thomas C. Dorr, Under Secretary. Information, (202) 720-4323.*

Web, www.rurdev.usda.gov

Acts as chief adviser to the secretary on agricultural credit and related matters; coordinates rural development policies and programs throughout the federal government; supervises the Rural Utilities Service, Rural Housing Service, and Rural Business-Cooperative Service.

Farm Service Agency (FSA), *(Agriculture Dept.),* **Farm Loan Programs,** *1400 Independence Ave. S.W., MS 0520 20250-0520; (202) 720-4671. Fax, (202) 690-3573. Carolyn Cooksie, Deputy Administrator.*

Web, www.fsa.usda.gov

Supports rural development through farm program loans, including real estate, farm production, and emergency loans.

Rural Business-Cooperative Service *(Agriculture Dept.), 1400 Independence Ave. S.W., #5045 20250-3201; (202) 690-4730. Fax, (202) 690-4737. John Rosso, Administrator.*

Web, www.rurdev.usda.gov/rbs

Promotes rural economic development by financing community facilities and assisting community businesses.

Rural Housing Service *(Agriculture Dept.), 1400 Independence Ave. S.W., #5014, STOP 0701 20250-0701; (202) 690-1533. Fax, (202) 690-0500. Arthur A. Garcia, Administrator.*

Web, www.rurdev.usda.gov/rhs

Offers financial assistance to apartment dwellers and homeowners in rural areas; provides funds to construct or improve community facilities.

Rural Utilities Service *(Agriculture Dept.), 1400 Independence Ave. S.W., #4055, MS-1510 20250-1500; (202) 720-9540. Fax, (202) 720-1725. Hilda Gay Legg, Administrator. Information, (202) 720-1255.*

Web, www.usda.gov/rus

Makes loans and loan guarantees to rural electric and telephone utilities providing service in rural areas. Administers the Rural Telephone Bank, which provides supplemental financing from federal sources. Makes loans for economic development and creation of jobs in rural areas, for water and waste disposal, and for distance learning and telemedicine.

CONGRESS

House Agriculture Committee, *Subcommittee on Conservation, Credit, Rural Development, and Research, 1301 LHOB 20515; (202) 225-2171. Fax, (202) 225-0917. Rep. Frank Lucas, R-Okla., Chair; Ryan Weston, Staff Director.*

Web, agriculture.house.gov

Jurisdiction over legislation on rural development; oversight of Rural Utilities Service. Jurisdiction over legislation on soil conservation; small-scale stream channelization, watershed, and flood control programs; water and air quality; and agricultural credit programs.

Senate Agriculture, Nutrition, and Forestry Committee, *Subcommittee on Forestry, Conservation, and Rural Revitalization, SR-328A 20510; (202) 224-2035. Sen. Michael D. Crapo, R-Idaho, Chair; Vacant, Staff Director.*

Web, agriculture.senate.gov

Jurisdiction over legislation on rural development; oversight of Rural Utilities Service. Jurisdiction over legislation on soil conservation; small-scale stream channelization, watershed, and flood control programs; water and air quality; and agricultural credit programs.

NONPROFIT

Farm Credit Council, *50 F St. N.W., #900 20001; (202) 626-8710. Fax, (202) 626-8718. Ken Auer, President.*

Web, www.fccouncil.com

Represents the Farm Credit System, a national financial cooperative that makes loans to agricultural producers, rural homebuyers, farmer cooperatives, and rural utilities. Finances the export of U.S. agricultural commodities.

Housing Assistance Council, *1025 Vermont Ave. N.W., #606 20005-3516; (202) 842-8600. Fax, (202) 347-3441. Moises Loza, Executive Director. Information, (800) 989-4422.*

General e-mail, hac@ruralhome.org

Web, www.ruralhome.org

Operates in rural areas and in cities of fewer than 25,000 citizens. Advises low-income and minority groups seeking federal assistance for improving rural housing and community facilities; studies and makes recommendations for state and local housing policies; makes low-interest loans for housing programs for low-income and minority groups living in rural areas, including native Americans and farm workers.

Irrigation Assn., *6540 Arlington Blvd., Falls Church, VA 22042; (703) 536-7080. Fax, (703) 536-7019. Thomas H. Kimmell, Executive Director.*

Web, www.irrigation.org

Membership: companies and individuals involved in irrigation, drainage, and erosion control worldwide. Seeks to improve the products and practices used to manage water resources; interests include economic development and environmental enhancement.

National Cooperative Business Assn., *1401 New York Ave. N.W., #1100 20005-2160; (202) 638-6222. Fax, (202) 638-1374. Paul Hazen, President.*

General e-mail, ncba@ncba.coop

Web, www.ncba.coop

Alliance of cooperatives, businesses, and state cooperative associations. Provides information about starting and managing agricultural cooperatives in the United States and in developing nations. Monitors legislation and regulations.

National Council of Farmer Cooperatives, *50 F St. N.W., #900 20001; (202) 626-8700. Fax, (202) 626-8722. David Graves, President.*

General e-mail, info@ncfc.org

Web, www.ncfc.org

Membership: cooperative businesses owned and operated by farmers. Encourages research on agricultural cooperatives; provides statistics and analyzes trends. Monitors legislation and regulations on agricultural trade, transportation, energy, and tax issues.

National Rural Community Assistance Program, *1522 K St. N.W., #400 20005; (202) 408-1273. Fax, (202) 408-8165. Randolph A. Adams, Executive Director.*

General e-mail, rcap@rcap.org

Web, www.rcap.org

Federally funded organization that conducts programs to improve water delivery and disposal of waste water for rural residents, particularly low-income families.

National Rural Electric Cooperative Assn., *4301 Wilson Blvd., Arlington, VA 22203-1860; (703) 907-5500. Fax, (703) 907-5516. Glenn English, Chief Executive Officer.*

Web, www.nreca.org

Membership: rural electric cooperative systems and public power and utility districts. Provides members with legislative, legal, and regulatory services.

National Telephone Cooperative Assn., *4121 Wilson Blvd., 10th Floor, Arlington, VA 22203-1801; (703) 351-2000. Fax, (703) 351-2001. Michael E. Brunner, Executive Vice President.*

General e-mail, contact@ntca.org

Web, www.ntca.org

Membership: locally owned and controlled telecommunications cooperatives and companies serving rural and small-town areas. Offers educational seminars, workshops, technical assistance, and a benefits program to members. Monitors legislation and regulations.

Rural Coalition, *1411 K St. N.W., #901 20005; (202) 628-7160. Fax, (202) 628-7165. Lorette Picciano, Executive Director.*

General e-mail, ruralco@ruralco.org

Web, www.ruralco.org

Alliance of organizations that develop public policies benefiting rural communities. Collaborates with community-based groups on agriculture and rural development issues, including health and the environment, minority farmers, farm workers, native Americans' rights, and rural community development. Provides rural groups with technical assistance.

Specific Regions

AGENCIES

Appalachian Regional Commission, *1666 Connecticut Ave. N.W., #600 20009; (202) 884-7660. Fax, (202) 884-7693. Thomas Hunter, Executive Director, (202) 884-7700; Anne B. Pope, Federal Co-Chair. Information, (202) 884-7773. Press, (202) 884-7770.*

Web, www.arc.gov

Federal-state-local partnership for economic development of the region including West Virginia and parts of Alabama, Georgia, Kentucky, Maryland, Mississippi, New York, North Carolina, Ohio, Pennsylvania, South Carolina, Tennessee, and Virginia. Plans and provides technical and financial assistance and coordinates federal and state efforts for economic development of Appalachia.

Bureau of Reclamation *(Interior Dept.)*, *1849 C St. N.W., #7554 20240; (202) 513-0501. Fax, (202) 513-0312. John W. Keys III, Commissioner.*
Web, www.usbr.gov

Administers federal programs for water and power resource development and management in seventeen western states; oversees municipal and industrial water supplies, hydroelectric power generation, irrigation, flood control, water quality improvement, river regulation, fish and wildlife enhancement, and outdoor recreation.

Interstate Commission on the Potomac River Basin, *6110 Executive Blvd., #300, Rockville, MD 20852; (301) 984-1908. Fax, (301) 984-5841. Joseph K. Hoffman, Executive Director.*
Web, www.potomacriver.org

Nonregulatory interstate compact commission established by Congress to control and reduce water pollution and to restore and protect living resources in the Potomac River and its tributaries. Monitors water quality; assists metropolitan water utilities; seeks innovative methods to solve water supply and land resource problems. Provides information and educational materials on the Potomac River basin.

National Capital Planning Commission, *401 9th St. N.W., #500N 20576; (202) 482-7200. Fax, (202) 482-7272. Patricia Gallagher, Executive Director.*
Web, www.ncpc.gov

Central planning agency for the federal government in the national capital region, which includes the District of Columbia and suburban Maryland and Virginia. Reviews and approves plans for the physical growth and development of the national capital area, using environmental, historic, and land-use criteria.

Tennessee Valley Authority, *Government Relations, Washington Office, 1 Massachusetts Ave. N.W., #300 20001; (202) 898-2999. Fax, (202) 898-2998. Linda Whitestone, Vice President.*
Web, www.tva.gov

Coordinates resource conservation, development, and land-use programs in the Tennessee River Valley. Produces and supplies wholesale power to municipal and cooperative electric systems, federal installations, and some industries. (Headquarters in Knoxville, Tenn.)

NONPROFIT

Greater Washington Board of Trade, *1725 Eye St. N.W., #200 20006; (202) 857-5900. Fax, (202) 223-2648. Robert A. Peck, President.*

General e-mail, info@bot.org
Web, www.bot.org

Promotes and plans economic growth for the capital region. Supports business-government partnerships, technological training, and transportation planning; promotes international trade; works to increase economic viability of the city of Washington. Monitors legislation and regulations at local, state, and federal levels.

New England Council, *Government Relations, Washington Office, 331 Constitution Ave. N.E. 20002; (202) 547-0048. Fax, (202) 547-9149. Deidre W. Savage, Vice President.*
General e-mail, newenglandcouncildc@msn.com
Web, www.newenglandcouncil.com

Provides information on business and economic issues concerning New England; serves as liaison between the New England congressional delegations and business community. (Headquarters in Boston, Mass.)

Northeast–Midwest Institute, *218 D St. S.E., 1st Floor 20003; (202) 544-5200. Fax, (202) 544-0043. Dick Munson, Executive Director.*
General e-mail, info@nemw.org
Web, www.nemw.org

Public policy research organization that promotes the economic vitality of the northeast and midwest regions. Interests include distribution of federal funding to regions, economic development, human resources, energy, and natural resources.

Urban Areas

AGENCIES

Housing and Urban Development Dept. (HUD), *Affordable Housing Programs, 451 7th St. S.W., #7164 20410; (202) 708-2685. Fax, (202) 708-1744. Mary Kolesar, Director.*
Web, www.hud.gov

Coordinates with cities to convey publicly owned, abandoned property to low-income families in exchange for their commitment to repair, occupy, and maintain property.

Housing and Urban Development Dept. (HUD), *Economic Development, 451 7th St. S.W., #7136 20410; (202) 708-2690. Fax, (202) 708-3336. Donald P. Mims, Deputy Assistant Secretary.*
Web, www.ezec.gov

Manages economic development programs, including Urban Development Action Grants, Empowerment Zones/Enterprise Communities, and YOUTHBUILD. Encourages private-public partnerships for development through neighborhood development corporations. Formulates policies and legislative proposals on economic development.

Neighborhood Reinvestment Corp., *1325 G St. N.W., #800 20005; (202) 220-2300. Fax, (202) 376-2600. Ellen Lazar, Executive Director.*

Web, www.nw.org

Chartered by Congress to assist localities in developing and operating local neighborhood-based programs designed to reverse decline in urban residential neighborhoods and rural communities. Oversees the National NeighborWorks Network, an association of local non-profit organizations concerned with urban and rural development.

NONPROFIT

International Downtown Assn., *1250 H St. N.W., 10th Floor 20006; (202) 393-6801. Fax, (202) 393-6869. David M. Feehan, President.*

General e-mail, question@ida-downtown.org

Web, www.ida-downtown.org

Membership: organizations, corporations, public agencies, and individuals interested in the development and management of city downtown areas. Supports cooperative efforts between the public and private sectors to revitalize downtowns and adjacent neighborhoods; provides members with information, technical assistance, and advice.

International Economic Development Council, *734 15th St. N.W., #900 20005; (202) 223-7800. Fax, (202) 223-4745. Jeffrey Finkle, President.*

General e-mail, mail@iedconline.org

Web, www.iedconline.org

Membership: public economic development directors, chamber of commerce staff, utility executives, academicians, and others who design and implement development programs. Provides information to members on job creation, attraction, and retention.

Milton S. Eisenhower Foundation, *1660 L St. N.W., #200 20036; (202) 429-0440. Fax, (202) 452-0169. Lynn A. Curtis, President.*

General e-mail, mseisenhower@msn.com

Web, www.eisenhowerfoundation.org

Strives to help inner city communities combat violence by supporting programs with proven records of success. Provides funding, technical assistance, evaluation, and supervision to communities wishing to replicate successful programs.

National Assn. for the Advancement of Colored People (NAACP), *Washington Office, 1025 Vermont Ave. N.W., #1120 20005; (202) 638-2269. Fax, (202) 638-5936. Hilary O. Shelton, Director.*

Web, www.naacp.org

Membership: persons interested in civil rights for all minorities. Works to eliminate discrimination in housing and urban affairs. Interests include programs for urban redevelopment, urban homesteading, and low-income housing. Supports programs that make affordable rental housing available to minorities and that maintain African American ownership of urban and rural land. (Headquarters in Baltimore, Md.)

National Assn. of Neighborhoods, *1300 Pennsylvania Ave. N.W., #700 20004; (202) 332-7766. Fax, (202) 332-2314. Ricardo C. Byrd, Executive Director.*

Web, www.nanworld.org

Federation of neighborhood groups that provides technical assistance to local governments, neighborhood groups, and businesses. Seeks to increase influence of grassroots groups on decisions affecting neighborhoods; sponsors training workshops promoting neighborhood awareness.

National Center for Neighborhood Enterprise, *1424 16th St. N.W., #300 20036; (202) 518-6500. Fax, (202) 588-0314. Robert L. Woodson Sr., President.*

General e-mail, info@ncne.com

Web, www.ncne.com

Provides community and faith-based organizations with training and technical assistance and links them to sources of support. Addresses issues such as homelessness and deteriorating neighborhoods.

National Center for Urban Ethnic Affairs, *P.O. Box 20, Cardinal Station 20064; (202) 319-6188. Fax, (202) 319-4463. John A. Kromkowski, President.*

Educational and research organization that preserves and revitalizes urban neighborhoods through community organization and development; provides technical support and encourages interethnic and interracial cooperation, particularly between recent and older immigrants, and fosters international cooperation. Publishes monographs.

National League of Cities, *1301 Pennsylvania Ave. N.W., #550 20004-1763; (202) 626-3000. Fax, (202) 626-3043. Donald J. Borut, Executive Director. Press, (202) 626-3158. Public Affairs, (202) 626-3120.*

Web, www.nlc.org

Membership: cities and state municipal leagues. Aids city leaders in developing programs; investigates needs of local governments in implementing federal community development programs.

National Neighborhood Coalition, *1030 15th St. N.W., #325 20005; (202) 408-8553. Fax, (202) 408-8551. Anne Pasmanick, Executive Director.*
General e-mail, nncnnc@erols.com
Web, www.neighborhoodcoalition.org

Membership: national and regional organizations that have neighborhood-based affiliates. Provides technical assistance to neighborhood groups, and conducts research on issues affecting neighborhoods. Monitors national programs and policies that affect inner-city neighborhoods; conducts monthly information forums.

National Urban League, *Washington Office, 3501 14th Street N.W. 20010; (202) 265-8200. Fax, (202) 265-6122. Maudine R. Cooper, President.*
Web, www.gwul.org

Social service organization concerned with the social welfare of African Americans and other minorities. Conducts legislative and policy analysis on housing and urban affairs. Operates a job bank. (Headquarters in New York.)

Urban Institute, *Metropolitan Housing and Communities Policy Center, 2100 M St. N.W., #500 20037; (202) 833-7200. Fax, (202) 872-9322. Margery Austin Turner, Director.*
Web, www.urban.org

Research organization that deals with urban problems. Researches federal, state, and local policies; focus includes community development block grants, neighborhood rehabilitation programs, and housing issues. Conducts economic research on the infrastructure of urban areas.

Urban Land Institute, *1025 Thomas Jefferson St. N.W., #500W 20007-5201; (202) 624-7000. Fax, (202) 624-7140. Richard Rosan, President. Information, (800) 321-5011. Library, (202) 624-7117.*
Web, www.uli.org

Membership: land developers, planners, state and federal agencies, financial institutions, home builders, consultants, and realtors. Provides responsible leadership in the use of land in order to enhance the total environment; monitors trends in new community development. Library open to the public by appointment for a fee.

U.S. Conference of Mayors, *1620 Eye St. N.W., #400 20006; (202) 293-7330. Fax, (202) 293-2352. J. Thomas Cochran, Executive Director.*
General e-mail, uscm@cais.com
Web, www.usmayors.org/uscm

Membership: mayors of cities with populations of 30,000 or more. Promotes city-federal cooperation; publishes reports and conducts meetings on federal programs, policies, and initiatives that affect urban and suburban interests. Serves as a clearinghouse for information on urban and suburban problems.

 # CONSTRUCTION

AGENCIES

Census Bureau *(Commerce Dept.), Manufacturing and Construction, 4401 Silver Hill Rd., Bldg FB4, #2102A, Suitland, MD 20746; (301) 763-4593. Fax, (301) 457-4583. William G. Bostic Jr., Chief.*
Web, www.census.gov

Publishes statistics on the value of construction put in place; housing starts, sales, and completions; building permits; price index of single-family homes sold; characteristics of new housing; and expenditures for residential improvements. Conducts a census of construction industries every five years.

General Services Administration (GSA), *Public Buildings Service, 1800 F St. N.W., #6344 20405; (202) 501-1100. Fax, (202) 219-2310. Joseph Moravec, Commissioner.*
Web, www.gsa.gov

Administers the construction, maintenance, and operation of buildings owned or leased by the federal government. Manages and disposes of federal real estate.

International Trade Administration (ITA), *(Commerce Dept.), Energy, Environment, and Materials, 14th St. and Constitution Ave. N.W., #4043 20230; (202) 482-0614. Fax, (202) 482-5666. Kevin W. Murphy, Deputy Assistant Secretary.*
Web, www.trade.gov

Analyzes and maintains data on international construction and engineering. Monitors production costs, prices, financial and labor conditions, technological changes, distribution, markets, trade patterns, and other aspects of these industries. Promotes international trade, develops competitive assessments, and assists engineering and construction companies in obtaining overseas construction projects.

NONPROFIT

American Public Works Assn., *Washington Office, 1401 K St. N.W., 11th Floor 20005; (202) 408-9541. Fax, (202) 408-9542. Peter B. King, Executive Director.*

General e-mail, apwa.dc@apwa.net

Web, www.apwa.net

Membership: engineers, architects, and others who maintain and manage public works facilities and services. Conducts research and promotes exchange of information on transportation and infrastructure-related issues. (Headquarters in Kansas City, Kan.)

American Subcontractors Assn., *1004 Duke St., Alexandria, VA 22314-3588; (703) 684-3450. Fax, (703) 836-3482. Colette Nelson, Executive Vice President.*

General e-mail, asaoffice@asa-hq.com

Web, www.asaonline.com

Membership: construction subcontractors, specialty contractors, and their suppliers. Addresses business, contract, and payment issues affecting all subcontractors. Interests include procurement laws, payment practices, and lien laws. Monitors legislation and regulations.

Associated Builders and Contractors, *1300 N. 17th St., 8th Floor, Arlington, VA 22209; (703) 812-2000. Fax, (703) 812-8202. M. Kirk Pickerel, Executive Vice President.*

General e-mail, info@abc.org

Web, www.abc.org

Membership: construction contractors engaged primarily in nonresidential construction, subcontractors, and suppliers. Sponsors apprenticeship, safety, and training programs. Provides labor relations information; compiles statistics. Monitors legislation and regulations.

Associated General Contractors of America, *333 John Carlyle St., #200, Alexandria, VA 22314; (703) 548-3118. Fax, (703) 548-3119. Steve E. Sandherr, Executive Vice President.*

Web, www.agc.org

Membership: general contractors engaged primarily in nonresidential construction; subcontractors; suppliers; accounting, insurance and bonding, and law firms. Conducts training programs, conferences, seminars, and market development activities for members. Produces position papers on construction issues. Monitors legislation and regulations.

Associated Landscape Contractors of America, *150 Elden St., #270, Herndon, VA 20170; (703) 736-9666. Fax, (703) 736-9668. Debra H. Holder, Executive Director.*

General e-mail, information@alca.org

Web, www.alca.org

Represents the interior and exterior landscape contracting industry. Monitors legislation and regulations.

Construction Management Assn. of America, *7918 Jones Branch Dr., #540, McLean, VA 22102; (703)*

356-2622. Fax, (703) 356-6388. Bruce D'Agostino, Executive Director.

General e-mail, info@cmaanet.org

Web, www.cmaanet.org

Promotes the development of construction management as a profession through publications, education, a certification program, and an information network. Serves as an advocate for construction management in the legislative, executive, and judicial branches of government.

Construction Specifications Institute, *99 Canal Center Plaza, #300, Alexandria, VA 22314-1588; (703) 684-0300. Fax, (703) 684-0465. Karl Borgstrom, Executive Director. Information, (800) 689-2900.*

General e-mail, membcustsrv@csinet.org

Web, www.csinet.org

Membership: architects, engineers, contractors, and others in the construction industry. Promotes construction technology; maintains speakers bureau; publishes reference materials to help individuals prepare construction documents; sponsors certification programs for construction specifiers and manufacturing representatives.

Mechanical Contractors Assn. of America, *1385 Piccard Dr., Rockville, MD 20850; (301) 869-5800. Fax, (301) 990-9690. John R. Gentille, Executive Vice President.*

Web, www.mcaa.org

Membership: mechanical contractors and members of related professions. Seeks to improve building standards and codes. Provides information, publications, and training programs; conducts seminars and annual convention. Monitors legislation and regulations.

National Assn. of Home Builders (NAHB), *1201 15th St. N.W. 20005-2800; (202) 266-8200. Fax, (202) 266-8374. Jerry Howard, Executive Vice President (Acting). Press, (202) 266-8254.*

General e-mail, info@nahb.org

Web, www.nahb.org

Membership: contractors, builders, architects, engineers, mortgage lenders, and others interested in home building and commercial real estate construction. Participates in updating and developing building codes and standards; offers technical information.

National Assn. of Minority Contractors, *666 11th St. N.W., #520 20001; (202) 347-8259. Fax, (202) 628-1876. Gerard Holder, Executive Director.*

Membership: minority businesses and related firms, associations, and individuals serving those businesses in the construction industry. Advises members on commercial and government business; develops resources for technical assistance and training; provides bid information on government contracts.

National Assn. of Plumbing-Heating-Cooling Contractors, *180 S. Washington St., Falls Church, VA 22046 (mailing address: P.O. Box 6808, Falls Church, VA 22040-6808); (703) 237-8100. Fax, (703) 237-7442. Information, (800) 533-7694.*

General e-mail, naphcc@naphcc.org

Web, www.phccweb.org

Provides education and training for plumbing, heating, and cooling contractors and their employees. Offers career information, internships, and scholarship programs for business and engineering students to encourage careers in the plumbing and mechanical contracting field.

National Electrical Contractors Assn., *3 Bethesda Metro Center, #1100, Bethesda, MD 20814; (301) 657-3110. Fax, (301) 215-4500. John Grau, Executive Vice President.*

Web, www.necanet.org

Membership: electrical contractors who build and service electrical wiring, equipment, and appliances. Represents members in collective bargaining with union workers; sponsors research and educational programs.

National Utility Contractors Assn., *4301 N. Fairfax Dr., #360, Arlington, VA 22203-1627; (703) 358-9300. Fax, (703) 358-9307. Bill Hillman, Chief Executive Officer.*

Web, www.nuca.com

Membership: contractors who perform water, sewer, and other underground utility construction. Sponsors conferences; conducts surveys. Monitors public works legislation and regulations.

Rebuild America Coalition, *c/o American Public Works Assn., 1401 K St. N.W., 11th Floor 20005; (202) 408-9541. Fax, (202) 408-9542. Jim Fahey, Coalition Manager.*

Web, www.rebuildamerica.org

Coalition of public and private organizations concerned with maintaining the infrastructure of the United States. Advocates government encouragement of innovative technology, financing, and public-private partnerships to build and rebuild public facilities.

Sheet Metal and Air Conditioning Contractors National Assn., *4201 Lafayette Center Dr., Chantilly, VA 20151-1209; (703) 803-2980. Fax, (703) 803-3732. John W. Sroka, Executive Vice President.*

General e-mail, info@smacna.org

Web, www.smacna.org

Membership: unionized sheet metal and air conditioning contractors. Provides information on standards and installation and fabrication methods.

Society for Marketing Professional Services, *99 Canal Center Plaza, #250, Alexandria, VA 22314-1588; (703) 549-6117. Fax, (703) 549-2498. Ronald Worth, Vice President. Information, (800) 292-7677.*

General e-mail, info@smps.org

Web, www.smps.org

Membership: individuals who provide professional services to the building industry. Assists individuals who market design services in the areas of architecture, engineering, planning, interior design, landscape architecture, and construction management. Provides seminars, workshops, and publications for members. Maintains job banks.

Architecture and Design

AGENCIES

General Services Administration (GSA), *Center for Design Excellence and the Arts: Office of the Chief Architect, 1800 F St. N.W. 20405; (202) 501-1888. Fax, (202) 501-3393. Marilyn Farley, Director.*

Administers the Art in Architecture Program, which commissions publicly scaled works of art for government buildings and landscapes, and the Fine Arts Program, which manages the GSA's collection of fine artwork that has been commissioned for use in government buildings.

National Endowment for the Arts (NEA), *(National Foundation on the Arts and the Humanities), Folk and Traditional Arts, Literature, Theater, Musical Theater, and Planning and Stabilization, 1100 Pennsylvania Ave. N.W. 20506-0001; (202) 682-5428. Fax, (202) 682-5669. Silvio Lim, Division Coordinator (Acting).*

Web, www.arts.gov

Awards grants for design arts projects in architecture; landscape architecture; urban design and planning; historic preservation; and interior, graphic, industrial, product, and costume and fashion design.

NONPROFIT

American Institute of Architects, *1735 New York Ave. N.W. 20006; (202) 626-7310. Fax, (202) 626-7426. Norman L. Koonce, Chief Executive Officer. Information, (202) 626-7300. Library, (202) 626-7492.*

Web, www.aia.org

Membership: licensed American architects, interns, architecture faculty, engineers, planners, landscape architects, artists, and those in government, manufacturing, or other field in a capacity related to architecture. Works to advance the standards of architectural education, training, and practice. Promotes the aesthetic, scientific, and practical efficiency of architecture, urban design, and planning; monitors international developments. Offers continuing and professional education programs; sponsors scholarships, internships, and awards. Houses archival collection, including documents and drawings of American architects and architecture. Library open to the public. Monitors legislation and regulations.

American Nursery and Landscape Assn., *1000 Vermont Ave. N.W., 3rd Floor 20005-4914; (202) 789-2900. Fax, (202) 789-1893. Robert J. Dolibois, Executive Vice President; Warren Quinn, Director.*
Web, www.anla.org

Serves as an information clearinghouse on the technical aspects of nursery and landscape business and design.

American Society of Interior Designers, *608 Massachusetts Ave. N.E. 20002-6006; (202) 546-3480. Fax, (202) 546-3240. Michael Alin, Executive Director.*
Web, www.asid.org

Offers certified professional development courses addressing the technical, professional, and business needs of designers; bestows annual scholarships, fellowships, and awards; supports licensing efforts at the state level.

American Society of Landscape Architects, *636 Eye St. N.W. 20001; (202) 898-2444. Fax, (202) 898-1185. Nancy Somerville, Executive Vice President.*
Web, www.asla.org

Membership: professional landscape architects. Advises government agencies on land-use policy and environmental matters. Accredits university-level programs in landscape architecture; conducts professional education seminars for members.

Assn. of Collegiate Schools of Architecture,
1735 New York Ave. N.W., #3 20006; (202) 785-2324. Fax, (202) 628-0448. Odile Henault, Executive Director.
General e-mail, info@acsa-arch.org
Web, www.acsa-arch.org

Conducts workshops and seminars for architecture school faculty; presents awards for student and faculty excellence in architecture; publishes directory of architecture professors and a guide to architecture schools in North America.

Industrial Designers Society of America,
45195 Business Ct., #250, Dulles, VA 20166-6717; (703) 707-6000. Fax, (703) 787-8501. Kristina Goodrich, Executive Director.

General e-mail, idsa@idsa.org
Web, www.idsa.org

Membership: designers of products, equipment, instruments, furniture, transportation, packages, exhibits, information services, and related services. Provides the Bureau of Labor Statistics with industry information. Monitors legislation and regulations.

Landscape Architecture Foundation, *818 18th St. N.W., #810 20006; (202) 331-7070. Fax, (202) 331-7079. Susan Everett, Executive Director.*
Web, www.lafoundation.org

Conducts research and provides educational and scientific information on landscape architecture and related fields. Awards scholarships and fellowships in landscape architecture.

National Architectural Accrediting Board,
1735 New York Ave. N.W. 20006; (202) 783-2007. Fax, (202) 783-2822. Sharon C. Matthews, Executive Director.
General e-mail, info@naab.org
Web, www.naab.org

Accredits Bachelor and Master of Architecture degree programs.

National Assn. of Schools of Art and Design,
11250 Roger Bacon Dr., #21, Reston, VA 20190; (703) 437-0700. Fax, (703) 437-6312. Samuel Hope, Executive Director.
General e-mail, info@arts-accredit.org
Web, www.arts-accredit.org

Accrediting agency for educational programs in art and design. Provides information on art and design programs at the postsecondary level; offers professional development for executives of art and design programs.

National Council of Architectural Registration Boards, *1801 K St. N.W., #1100-K 20006; (202) 783-6500. Fax, (202) 783-0290. Lenore M. Lucey, Executive Vice President.*
Web, www.ncarb.org

Membership: state architectural licensing boards. Develops examination used in U.S. states and territories for licensing architects; certifies architects.

Codes, Standards, and Research

AGENCIES

Architectural and Transportation Barriers Compliance Board (Access Board), *1331 F St. N.W., #1000 20004-1111; (202) 272-0080. Fax, (202) 272-0081. Lawrence W. Roffee, Executive Director. TTY, (202) 272-0082. Toll-free technical assistance, (800) 872-2253.*
General e-mail, info@access-board.gov

Enforces standards requiring that buildings and telecommunications and transportation systems be accessible to persons with disabilities; provides technical assistance and information on designing these facilities; sets accessibility guidelines for the Americans with Disabilities Act (ADA) and the Telecommunications Act of 1996.

Environmental Protection Agency (EPA), *Radiation and Indoor Air,* 1200 Pennsylvania Ave. N.W., MC 6601J 20460; (202) 564-9320. Fax, (202) 565-2043. Elizabeth Cotsworth, Director.
Web, www.epa.gov/oar/oria.html

Establishes standards for measuring radon; develops model building codes for state and local governments; provides states and building contractors with technical assistance and training on radon detection and mitigation.

Federal Housing Administration (FHA), *(Housing and Urban Development Dept.), Manufactured Housing Programs,* 451 7th St. S.W., #9152 20410; (202) 708-6423. Fax, (202) 708-4213. William W. Matchneer III, Administrator. Consumer complaints, (800) 927-2891.
Web, www.hud.gov/offices/hsg/sfh/mhs/mhshome.cfm

Establishes and maintains standards for selection of new materials and methods of construction; evaluates technical suitability of products and materials; develops uniform, preemptive, and mandatory national standards for manufactured housing; enforces standards through design review and quality control inspection of factories; administers a national consumer protection program.

Housing and Urban Development Dept. (HUD), *Affordable Housing Research and Technology,* 451 7th St. S.W., #8134 20410; (202) 708-4370. Fax, (202) 708-5873. David Engel, Director.
Web, www.hud.gov

Studies regulatory barriers to housing, such as land development and building codes and zoning. Conducts building technology research on housing affordability, environmental hazards, and energy efficiency. Reviews and assesses changes in building codes and standards. Conducts demonstrations on innovative building construction techniques.

Housing and Urban Development Dept. (HUD), *Healthy Homes and Lead Hazard Control,* 451 7th St. S.W., #P3206 20410; (202) 755-1785. Fax, (202) 755-1000. David E. Jacobs, Director.
Web, www.hud.gov/lea

Advises HUD offices, other agencies, health authorities, and the housing industry on lead poisoning prevention. Develops regulations for lead-based paint; conducts research; makes grants to state and local governments for lead hazard reduction and inspection of housing.

National Institute of Building Sciences, 1090 Vermont Ave. N.W., #700 20005-4905; (202) 289-7800. Fax, (202) 289-1092. David A. Harris, President.
General e-mail, nibs@nibs.org
Web, www.nibs.org

Public-private partnership authorized by Congress to improve the regulation of building construction, facilitate the safe introduction of innovative building technology, and disseminate performance criteria and other technical information.

National Institute of Standards and Technology (NIST), *(Commerce Dept.), Building and Fire Research Laboratory,* 100 Bureau Dr., MS 8600, Gaithersburg, MD 20899-8600; (301) 975-6850. Fax, (301) 975-4032. Jack E. Snell, Director; James E. Hill, Deputy Director.
Web, www.bfrl.nist.gov

Performs analytical, laboratory, and field research in the area of building technology and its applications for building usefulness, safety, and economy; produces performance criteria and evaluation, test, and measurement methods for building owners, occupants, designers, manufacturers, builders, and federal, state, and local regulatory authorities.

Occupational Safety and Health Administration (OSHA), *(Labor Dept.), Safety Standards,* 200 Constitution Ave. N.W., #N3609 20210; (202) 693-2222. Fax, (202) 693-1663. Steven Witt, Director, (202) 693-1950.

Administers regulations for fire safety standards; sponsors programs for maritime, fire protection, mechanical, and electrical industries.

U.S. Fire Administration *(Federal Emergency Management Agency),* 16825 S. Seton Ave., Emmitsburg, MD 21727; (301) 447-1018. Fax, (301) 447-1270. R. David Paulison, Administrator.
Web, www.usfa.fema.gov

Conducts research and collects, analyzes, and disseminates data on combustion, fire prevention, fire fighter safety, and the management of fire prevention organizations; studies and develops arson prevention programs and fire prevention codes; maintains the National Fire Data System.

NONPROFIT

Air Conditioning and Refrigeration Institute, *Legislative and Regulatory Affairs,* 4100 N. Fairfax Dr., #200, Arlington, VA 22203; (703) 524-8800. Fax, (703) 528-3816. Don Davis, Director.

General e-mail, ari@ari.org

Web, www.ari.org

Represents manufacturers of central air conditioning and commercial refrigeration equipment. Develops product performance rating standards and administers programs to verify manufacturers' certified ratings.

American Society of Civil Engineers, *1801 Alexander Bell Dr., Reston, VA 20191-4400; (703) 295-6300. Fax, (703) 295-6222. Patrick Natale, Executive Director. Information, (800) 548-2723.*

Web, www.asce.org

Membership: professionals and students in civil engineering. Develops and produces consensus standards for construction documents and building codes. Maintains the Civil Engineering Research Foundation, which focuses national attention and resources on the research needs of the civil engineering profession. Participates in international conferences.

American Society of Heating, Refrigerating, and Air Conditioning Engineers, *Government Affairs, 1828 L St. N.W., #906 20036-5104; (202) 833-1830. Fax, (202) 833-0118. Carlos R. (Chuck) Miro, Director.*

Web, www.ashrae.org

Membership: engineers for the heating and cooling industry in the United States and abroad, including students. Sponsors research, meetings, and educational activities. Develops industry standards; publishes technical data. Monitors legislation and regulations.

Center for Auto Safety, *1825 Connecticut Ave. N.W., #330 20009; (202) 328-7700. Fax, (202) 387-0140. Clarence M. Ditlow III, Executive Director.*

Web, www.autosafety.org

Monitors Federal Trade Commission warranty regulations and HUD implementation of federal safety and construction standards for manufactured mobile homes.

International Code Council, *5203 Leesburg Pike, #600, Falls Church, VA 22041; (703) 931-4533. Fax, (703) 379-1546. William Tangye, Chief Executive Officer.*

Web, www.iccsafe.org

Seeks to ensure consistency among model codes; encourages uniformity in administration of building regulations; maintains a one- and two-family dwelling code, a model energy code, and manufactured home construction and safety standards; provides review board for the American National Standards Institute disabled accessibility standards.

NAHB Research Center, *400 Prince George's Blvd., Upper Marlboro, MD 20774; (301) 249-4000. Fax, (301) 430-6180. Mike Luzier, President.*

Web, www.nahbrc.org

Conducts contract research and product labeling and certification for U.S. industry, government, and trade associations related to home building and light commercial industrial building. Interests include energy conservation, new technologies, international research, public health issues, affordable housing, special needs housing for the elderly and persons with disabilities, building codes and standards, land development, and environmental issues. (Affiliated with the National Assn. of Home Builders [NAHB].)

National Conference of States on Building Codes and Standards, *505 Huntmar Park Dr., #210, Herndon, VA 20170; (703) 437-0100. Fax, (703) 481-3596. Robert C. Wible, Executive Director.*

Web, www.ncsbcs.org

Membership: individuals and organizations concerned with building standards. Works with HUD to ensure that manufactured housing conforms to HUD standards and codes; assists states in improving their building codes, standards, and regulations; promotes local, state, and interstate cooperation.

National Fire Protection Assn., *Government Affairs, Washington Office, 1110 N. Glebe Rd., #210, Arlington, VA 22201; (703) 516-4346. Fax, (703) 516-4350. John C. Biechman, Vice President.*

General e-mail, wdc@nfpa.org

Web, www.nfpa.org

Membership: individuals and organizations interested in fire protection. Develops and updates fire protection codes and standards; sponsors technical assistance programs; collects fire data statistics. Monitors legislation and regulations. (Headquarters in Quincy, Mass.)

National Spa and Pool Institute, *2111 Eisenhower Ave., Alexandria, VA 22314-4698; (703) 838-0083. Fax, (703) 549-0493. Jack Cergol, Chief Staff Executive.*

Web, www.nspi.org

Membership: manufacturers, dealers, service companies, builders, and distributors of pools, spas, and hot tubs. Promotes the industry; compiles statistics; establishes construction standards for pools and spas. Monitors legislation and regulations.

Materials and Labor

NONPROFIT

American Forest and Paper Assn., *Regulatory Affairs, 1111 19th St. N.W., #800 20036; (202) 463-2700. Fax, (202) 463-2423. Sharon Kneiss, Vice President.*

Web, www.afandpa.org

Membership: manufacturers of wood and specialty products and related associations. Interests include tax, housing, environmental, international trade, natural resources, and land-use issues that affect the wood and paper products industry.

Architectural Woodwork Institute, *1952 Isaac Newton Square West, Reston, VA 20190; (703) 733-0600. Fax, (703) 733-0584. Judith B. Durham, Executive Vice President.*

Web, www.awinet.org

Promotes the use of architectural woodworking; establishes industry standards; conducts seminars and workshops; certifies professionals in the industry. Monitors legislation and regulations.

Asbestos Information Assn./North America, *1235 Jefferson Davis Hwy., PMB-114, Arlington, VA 22202; (703) 560-2980. Fax, (703) 560-2981. B. J. Pigg, President.*

General e-mail, aiabjpigg@aol.com

Membership: firms that manufacture, sell, and use products containing asbestos fiber and those that mine, mill, and sell asbestos. Provides information on asbestos and health and on industry efforts to eliminate problems associated with asbestos dust; serves as liaison between the industry and federal and state governments.

Asphalt Roofing Manufacturers Assn., *1156 15th St. N.W., #900 20005; (202) 207-0917. Fax, (202) 223-9741. Russell K. Snyder, Executive Vice President.*

Web, www.asphaltroofing.org

Membership: manufacturers of bitumen-based roofing products. Assists in developing local building codes and standards for asphalt roofing products. Provides technical information; supports research. Monitors legislation and regulations.

Assn. of the Wall and Ceiling Industries, *803 W. Broad St., #600, Falls Church, VA 22046-3108; (703) 534-8300. Fax, (703) 534-8307. Steven A. Etkin, Executive Vice President.*

Web, www.awci.org

Membership: contractors and suppliers working in the wall and ceiling industries. Sponsors conferences and seminars. Monitors legislation and regulations.

Brick Industry Assn., *11490 Commerce Park Dr., #300, Reston, VA 20191-1525; (703) 620-0010. Fax, (703) 620-3928. Greg Borchelt, President (Acting).*

Web, www.brickinfo.org

Membership: manufacturers of clay brick. Provides technical expertise and assistance; promotes bricklaying vocational education programs; maintains collection of technical publications on brick masonry construction. Monitors legislation and regulations.

Building Systems Councils of the National Assn. of Home Builders, *1201 15th St. N.W., 7th Floor 20005-2800; (202) 266-8576. Fax, (202) 266-8141. David Kaufman, Executive Director.*

Web, www.buildingsystems.org

Membership: manufacturers and suppliers of home building products and services. Represents all segments of the industry. Assists in developing National Assn. of Home Builders policies regarding building codes, legislation, and government regulations affecting manufacturers of model code complying, factory-built housing; sponsors educational programs; conducts plant tours of member operations.

Composite Panel Assn., *18922 Premiere Court, Gaithersburg, MD 20879; (301) 670-0604. Fax, (301) 840-1252. Thomas A. Julia, President.*

General e-mail, pbmdf@pbmdf.com

Web, www.pbmdf.com

Membership: manufacturers of particleboard and medium-density fiberboard. Promotes use of these materials; conducts industry education through the Composite Wood Council. Monitors legislation and regulations.

Door and Hardware Institute, *14150 Newbrook Dr., #200, Chantilly, VA 20151-1232; (703) 222-2010. Fax, (703) 222-2410. Jerry Heppes, Executive Director.*

Web, www.dhi.org

Membership: companies and individuals that manufacture or distribute doors and related fittings. Promotes the industry. Interests include building security, life safety and exit devices, and compliance with the Americans with Disabilities Act. Monitors legislation and regulations.

Gypsum Assn., *810 1st St. N.E., #510 20002; (202) 289-5440. Fax, (202) 289-3707. Jerry A. Walker, Executive Director.*

General e-mail, info@gypsum.org

Web, www.gypsum.org

Membership: manufacturers of gypsum wallboard and plaster. Assists members, code officials, builders, designers, and others with technical problems and building code questions; publishes *Fire Resistance Design Manual* referenced by major building codes; conducts safety programs for member companies. Monitors legislation and regulations.

Hardwood, Plywood, and Veneer Assn., *1825 Michael Faraday Dr., Reston, VA 20190-5350 (mail-*

ing address: P.O. Box 2789, Reston, VA 20195-0789); (703) 435-2900. Fax, (703) 435-2537. E. T. Altman, President.

General e-mail, hpva@hpva.org

Web, www.hpva.org

Membership: manufacturers, distributors, wholesalers, suppliers, and sales agents of plywood, veneer, and laminated wood floor. Disseminates business information; sponsors workshops and seminars; conducts research.

International Assn. of Bridge, Structural, Ornamental, and Reinforcing Iron Workers, 1750 New York Ave. N.W., #400 20006; (202) 383-4800. Fax, (202) 638-4856. Joseph J. Hunt, President.

Web, www.ironworkers.org

Membership: approximately 82,000 iron workers. Helps members negotiate pay, benefits, and better working conditions; conducts training programs and workshops. Monitors legislation and regulations. (Affiliated with the AFL-CIO.)

International Assn. of Heat and Frost Insulators and Asbestos Workers, 9602 Martin Luther King Hwy., Lanham, MD 20706; (301) 731-9101. Fax, (301) 731-5058. James A. Grogan, President.

Web, www.insulators.org

Membership: approximately 18,000 workers in insulation industries. Helps members negotiate pay, benefits, and better working conditions; conducts training programs and workshops. Monitors legislation and regulations. (Affiliated with the AFL-CIO.)

International Brotherhood of Boilermakers, Iron Ship Builders, Blacksmiths, Forgers, and Helpers, Legislative Affairs, Washington Office, 2722 Merrilee Dr., #360, Fairfax, VA 22031; (703) 560-1493. Fax, (703) 560-2584. Ande M. Abbott, Director.

Web, www.boilermakers.org

Membership: approximately 80,000 workers in construction, repair, maintenance, manufacturing, and related industries in the United States and Canada. Helps members negotiate pay, benefits, and better working conditions; conducts training programs and workshops. Monitors legislation and regulations. (Headquarters in Kansas City, Kan.; affiliated with the AFL-CIO.)

International Brotherhood of Electrical Workers (IBEW), 1125 15th St. N.W. 20005; (202) 833-7000. Fax, (202) 728-6099. Edwin D. Hill, President.

General e-mail, postmaster@ibew.org

Web, www.ibew.org

Helps members negotiate pay, benefits, and better working conditions; conducts training programs and

workshops. Monitors legislation and regulations. (Affiliated with the AFL-CIO.)

International Brotherhood of Teamsters, 25 Louisiana Ave. N.W. 20001; (202) 624-6800. Fax, (202) 624-6918. James P. Hoffa, President.

Web, www.teamster.org

Membership: more than 1.4 million workers in the transportation and construction industries, factories, offices, hospitals, warehouses, and other workplaces. Helps members negotiate pay, benefits, and better working conditions; conducts training programs and workshops. Monitors legislation and regulations. (Affiliated with the AFL-CIO.)

International Union of Bricklayers and Allied Craftworkers, 1776 Eye St. N.W., #600 20006; (202) 783-3788. Fax, (202) 393-0219. John J. Flynn, President.

Web, www.bacweb.org

Membership: bricklayers, stonemasons, and other skilled craftworkers in the building industry. Helps members negotiate pay, benefits, and better working conditions; conducts training programs and workshops. Monitors legislation and regulations. (Affiliated with the AFL-CIO and the International Masonry Institute.)

International Union of Operating Engineers, 1125 17th St. N.W. 20036; (202) 429-9100. Fax, (202) 778-2616. Frank Hanley, President.

Web, www.iuoe.org

Membership: approximately 400,000 operating engineers, including heavy equipment operators, mechanics, and surveyors in the construction industry, and stationary engineers, including operations and building maintenance staff. Helps members negotiate pay, benefits, and better working conditions; conducts training programs and workshops. Monitors legislation and regulations. (Affiliated with the AFL-CIO.)

International Union of Painters and Allied Trades, 1750 New York Ave. N.W., 8th Floor 20006; (202) 637-0700. Fax, (202) 637-0771. James A. Williams, President.

Web, www.ibpat.org

Membership: more than 130,000 painters, paint makers, drywall finishers, decorators, carpet and soft tile layers, scenic artists, and workers in allied trades. Helps members negotiate pay, benefits, and better working conditions; conducts training programs and workshops. Monitors legislation and regulations. (Affiliated with the AFL-CIO.)

Kitchen Cabinet Manufacturers Assn., 1899 Preston White Dr., Reston, VA 20191-5435; (703) 264-1690. Fax, (703) 620-6530. C. Richard Titus, Executive Vice President.

General e-mail, info@kcma.org

Web, www.kcma.org

Represents cabinet manufacturers and suppliers to the industry. Provides government relations, management statistics, marketing information, and plant tours. Administers cabinet testing and certification programs.

National Concrete Masonry Assn., *13750 Sunrise Valley Dr., Herndon, VA 20171-3499; (703) 713-1900. Fax, (703) 713-1910. Mark B. Hogan, President.*

General e-mail, receptionist@ncma.org

Web, www.ncma.org

Membership: producers of concrete masonry and suppliers of related goods and services. Conducts research; provides members with technical, marketing, government relations, and communications assistance.

National Glass Assn., *8200 Greensboro Dr., #302, McLean, VA 22102-3881; (703) 442-4890. Fax, (703) 442-0630. Phillip J. James, President.*

General e-mail, nga@glass.org

Web, www.glass.org

Membership: companies in flat (architectural and automotive) glass industry, including manufacturers, fabricators, distributors, retailers, and installers of glass used in a structure. Conducts conferences; provides information on industry codes. Monitors legislation and regulations.

National Insulation Assn., *99 Canal Center Plaza, #222, Alexandria, VA 22314; (703) 683-6422. Fax, (703) 549-4838. Michele M. Jones, Executive Vice President.*

General e-mail, niainfo@insulation.org

Web, www.insulation.org

Membership: companies in the commercial and industrial insulation and asbestos abatement industries. Monitors legislation and regulations.

National Lumber and Building Material Dealers Assn., *40 Ivy St. S.E. 20003; (202) 547-2230. Fax, (202) 547-7640. Gary W. Donnelly, President.*

General e-mail, nlbmda@dealer.org

Web, www.dealer.org

Membership: federated associations of retailers in the lumber and building material industries. Monitors legislation and regulations.

National Paint and Coatings Assn., *1500 Rhode Island Ave. N.W. 20005; (202) 462-6272. Fax, (202) 462-8549. J. Andrew Doyle, President.*

General e-mail, npca@paint.org

Web, www.paint.org

Membership: paint and coatings manufacturers, raw materials suppliers, and distributors. Provides educational and public outreach programs for the industry; interests include health, safety, and the environment. Monitor legislation and regulations.

North American Insulation Manufacturers Assn., *44 Canal Center Plaza, #310, Alexandria, VA 22314; (703) 684-0084. Fax, (703) 684-0427. Kenneth D. Mentzer, President.*

General e-mail, insulation@naima.org

Web, www.naima.org

Membership: manufacturers of insulation products for use in homes, commercial buildings, and industrial facilities. Provides information on the use of insulation for thermal efficiency, sound control, and fire safety; monitors research in the industry. Monitors legislation and regulations.

Operative Plasterers' and Cement Masons' International Assn. of the United States and Canada, *14405 Laurel Pl., #300, Laurel, MD 20707; (301) 470-4200. Fax, (301) 470-2502. John Dougherty, President.*

Web, www.opcmia.org

Membership: approximately 58,000 concrete masons and terrazzo workers. Helps members negotiate pay, benefits, and better working conditions; conducts training programs and workshops. Monitors legislation and regulations. (Affiliated with the AFL-CIO.)

Painting and Decorating Contractors of America, *3913 Old Lee Hwy., #33B, Fairfax, VA 22030; (703) 359-0826. Fax, (703) 359-2576. William Patrick Nichols, Executive Vice President (Interim).*

Web, www.pdca.org

Promotes the painting and decorating industry; sponsors workshops and seminars. Monitors legislation and regulations.

Portland Cement Assn., *1130 Connecticut Ave. N.W., #1250 20036; (202) 408-9494. Fax, (202) 408-0877. Richard C. Creighton, President.*

Web, www.cement.org

Membership: producers of portland cement. Monitors legislation and regulations.

Roof Coatings Manufacturers Assn., *1156 15th St. N.W. #900 20005; (202) 207-0919. Fax, (202) 331-8714. Russell K. Snyder, Executive Vice President.*

General e-mail, info@roofcoatings.org

Web, www.roofcoatings.org

Represents the manufacturers of cold-applied protective roof coatings, cements, and systems, and the suppliers of products, equipment, and services to and for the roof coating manufacturing industry.

Sheet Metal Workers' International Assn.,
1750 New York Ave. N.W. 20006; (202) 783-5880. Fax, (202) 662-0880. Michael J. Sullivan, General President. Web, www.smwia.org

Membership: more than 150,000 U.S. and Canadian workers in the building and construction trades, manufacturing, and the railroad and shipyard industries. Assists members with contract negotiation and grievances; conducts training programs and workshops. Monitors legislation and regulations. (Affiliated with the Sheet Metal and Air Conditioning Contractors' Assn., the AFL-CIO, and the Canadian Labour Congress.)

United Assn. of Journeymen and Apprentices of the Plumbing and Pipe Fitting Industry, *901 Massachusetts Ave. N.W. 20001-4397; (202) 628-5823. Fax, (202) 628-5024. Martin J. Maddaloni, General President. Web, www.ua.org*

Membership: approximately 300,000 workers who fabricate, install, and service piping systems. Assists members with contract negotiation and grievances; sponsors training programs, apprenticeships, and workshops. Monitors legislation and regulations. (Affiliated with the AFL-CIO and the Canadian Federation of Labour.)

United Brotherhood of Carpenters and Joiners of America, *101 Constitution Ave. N.W., 10th Floor 20001; (202) 546-6206. Fax, (202) 543-5724. Andris Silins, Secretary-Treasurer. Web, www.carpenters.org*

Membership: approximately 500,000 carpenters and joiners. Helps members negotiate pay, benefits, and better working conditions; conducts training programs and workshops. Monitors legislation and regulations. (Affiliated with the AFL-CIO.)

United Union of Roofers, Waterproofers, and Allied Workers, *1660 L St. N.W., #800 20036; (202) 463-7663. Fax, (202) 463-6906. Earl Kruse, International President. General e-mail, roofers@unionroofers.com Web, www.unionroofers.com*

Membership: approximately 25,000 roofers, waterproofers, and allied workers. Helps members negotiate pay, benefits, and better working conditions; conducts training programs and workshops. Monitor legislation and regulations. (Affiliated with the AFL-CIO.)

Utility Workers Union of America, *815 16th St. N.W. 20006; (202) 347-8105. Fax, (202) 974-8201. Donald E. Wightman, President. Web, www.uwua.org*

Membership: approximately 50,000 workers in utilities and related industries. Helps members negotiate pay, benefits, and better working conditions; conducts training programs and workshops. Monitors legislation and regulations. (Affiliated with the AFL-CIO.)

 HOUSING

AGENCIES

Federal Housing Administration (FHA), *(Housing and Urban Development Dept.), Multifamily Business Products,* *451 7th St. S.W., #6134 20410-8000; (202) 708-3000. Fax, (202) 708-3104. Willie Spearmon, Director. Web, www.hud.gov/fha/mfh/fhamfbus.html*

Establishes procedures for the development of housing under the multifamily mortgage insurance programs. Administers the mortgage insurance programs for rental, cooperative, and condominium housing.

Federal Housing Administration (FHA), *(Housing and Urban Development Dept.), Multifamily Housing Programs,* *451 7th St. S.W., #6106 20410; (202) 708-2495. Fax, (202) 708-2583. Federick Tombar III, Deputy Assistant Secretary (Acting). Web, www.hud.gov*

Determines risk and administers programs associated with government-insured mortgage programs, architectural procedures, and land development programs for multifamily housing. Administers the Rural Rental Housing Program and the development of congregate housing facilities that provide affordable housing, adequate space for meals, and supportive services.

Federal Housing Administration (FHA), *(Housing and Urban Development Dept.), Single Family Housing,* *451 7th St. S.W., #9282 20410; (202) 708-3175. Fax, (202) 708-2582. John Coonts, Deputy Assistant Secretary (Acting). Web, www.hud.gov*

Determines risk and administers programs associated with government-insured mortgage programs, architectural procedures, land development programs, and interstate land sales for single family housing. Administers requirements to obtain and maintain federal government approval of mortgages.

Housing and Urban Development Dept. (HUD), *Entitlement Communities,* *451 7th St. S.W., #7282 20410; (202) 708-1577. Fax, (202) 401-2044. Susan Miller, Director. Web, www.hud.gov*

Provides entitled cities and counties with block grants to provide housing and economic opportunity for low- and moderate-income people.

Housing and Urban Development Dept. (HUD), *Housing,* 451 7th St. S.W., #9100 20410; (202) 708-3600. Fax, (202) 708-2580. John C. Weicher, Assistant Secretary. Web, www.hud.gov/fha/fhahome.html

Administers housing programs including the production, financing, and management of housing; directs preservation and rehabilitation of the housing stock; manages regulatory programs.

Rural Housing Service *(Agriculture Dept.),* 1400 Independence Ave. S.W., #5014, STOP 0701 20250-0701; (202) 690-1533. Fax, (202) 690-0500. Arthur A. Garcia, Administrator. Web, www.rurdev.usda.gov/rhs

Offers financial assistance to apartment dwellers and homeowners in rural areas.

Rural Housing Service *(Agriculture Dept.),* **Housing Programs,** 1400 Independence Ave. S.W., #5013 20250-0780; (202) 720-5177. Fax, (202) 690-3025. David J. Villano, Deputy Administrator. Press, (202) 720-6903. Web, www.rurdev.usda.gov/rhs

Makes loans and grants in rural communities (population under 20,000) to low-income borrowers, including the elderly and persons with disabilities, for buying, building, or improving single-family houses. Makes grants to communities for rehabilitating single-family homes or rental units.

CONGRESS

House Financial Services Committee, *Subcommittee on Housing and Community Opportunity,* B303 RHOB 20515; (202) 225-7502. Rep. Bob Ney, R-Ohio, Chair; Bob Foster, Staff Director. Web, financialservices.house.gov

Jurisdiction over all housing legislation, including housing allowances, housing for the elderly and persons with disabilities, public housing, and subsidized housing.

House Judiciary Committee, *Subcommittee on the Constitution,* 362 FHOB 20515; (202) 226-7680. Fax, (202) 225-3746. Rep. Steve Chabot, R-Ohio, Chair; Crystal Roberts, Chief Counsel. General e-mail, Judiciary@mail.house.gov Web, www.house.gov/judiciary

Jurisdiction over fair housing legislation pertaining to discrimination against minorities.

Senate Banking, Housing, and Urban Affairs Committee, *Subcommittee on Housing and Transportation,* SD-534 20510; (202) 224-7391. Fax, (202) 224-5137. Sen. Wayne Allard, R-Colo., Chair; Tewana Wilkerson, Staff Director. Web, banking.senate.gov

Jurisdiction over all housing legislation, including housing allowances, housing for the elderly and persons with disabilities, public housing, and subsidized housing.

Senate Judiciary Committee, *Subcommittee on the Constitution, Civil Rights, and Property Rights,* SD-524 20510; (202) 224-4135. Fax, (202) 228-0463. Sen. John Cornyn, R-Texas, Chair; James Ho, Chief Counsel. Web, judiciary.senate.gov

Jurisdiction over fair housing legislation, including legislation pertaining to discrimination against minorities.

Senate Special Committee on Aging, SD-G31 20510; (202) 224-5364. Fax, (202) 224-8660. Sen. Larry E. Craig, R-Idaho, Chair; Lupe Wissel, Staff Director. Web, aging.senate.gov

Studies and makes recommendations on housing access for the elderly.

NONPROFIT

Center for Housing Policy, 1801 K St. N.W., #M100 20006; (202) 466-2121. Fax, (202) 466-2122. Robert J. Reid, Executive Director. General e-mail, nhc@nhc.org Web, www.nhc.org

Researches and develops fundamentals of housing policy. Seeks to create new policies that integrate housing into overall social and economic goals. Sponsors educational forums. (Affiliated with the National Housing Conference.)

Enterprise Foundation, 10227 Wincopin Circle, #500, Columbia, MD 21044; (410) 964-1230. Fax, (410) 964-1918. Tarri Montague, President. Web, www.enterprisefoundation.org

Works with local groups to help provide decent, affordable housing for low-income individuals and families.

Habitat for Humanity International, *Washington Office,* 1010 Vermont Ave. N.W., #900 20005; (202) 628-9171. Fax, (202) 628-9169. Thomas L. Jones, Managing Director. General e-mail, washingtonoffice@hfhi.org Web, www.habitat.org

Ecumenical housing ministry that, with the help of volunteers, donors, and its own affiliate offices, builds affordable homes worldwide for low-income persons. (Headquarters in Americus, Ga.)

Housing Assistance Council, *1025 Vermont Ave. N.W., #606 20005-3516; (202) 842-8600. Fax, (202) 347-3441. Moises Loza, Executive Director. Information, (800) 989-4422.*

General e-mail, hac@ruralhome.org

Web, www.ruralhome.org

Operates in rural areas and in cities of fewer than 25,000 citizens. Advises low-income and minority groups seeking federal assistance for improving rural housing and community facilities; studies and makes recommendations for state and local housing policies; makes low-interest loans for housing programs for low-income and minority groups living in rural areas, including native Americans and farm workers.

National Housing and Rehabilitation Assn., *1625 Massachusetts Ave. N.W., #601 20036-2244; (202) 939-1750. Fax, (202) 265-4435. Peter H. Bell, Executive Director.*

Web, www.housingonline.com

Membership: development firms and organizations and city, state, and local agencies concerned with affordable multifamily housing. Monitors government policies affecting multifamily development and rehabilitation.

National Housing Conference, *1801 K St. N.W., #M100 20006; (202) 466-2121. Fax, (202) 466-2122. Conrad Egan, Executive Director.*

General e-mail, nhc@nhc.org

Web, www.nhc.org

Membership: state and local housing officials, community development specialists, builders, bankers, lawyers, civic leaders, tenants, architects and planners, labor and religious groups, and national housing and housing-related organizations. Mobilizes public support for community development and affordable housing programs; conducts educational sessions.

National Leased Housing Assn., *1818 N St. N.W., #405 20036; (202) 785-8888. Fax, (202) 785-2008. Denise Muha, Executive Director.*

General e-mail, info@hudnlha.com

Web, www.hudnlha.com

Membership: public and private organizations and individuals concerned with multifamily, government-assisted housing programs. Conducts training seminars. Monitors legislation and regulations.

National Low Income Housing Coalition, *1012 14th St. N.W., #610 20005; (202) 662-1530. Fax, (202) 393-1973. Sheila Crowley, President.*

General e-mail, info@nlihc.org

Web, www.nlihc.org

Membership: individuals and organizations interested in low-income housing. Works for decent, affordable housing and freedom of housing choice for low-income citizens. Provides information and technical assistance through the Low Income Housing Information Service. Monitors legislation.

National Rural Housing Coalition, *1250 Eye St. N.W., #902 20005; (202) 393-5229. Fax, (202) 393-3034. Robert A. Rapoza, Legislative Director.*

Web, www.nrhcweb.org

Advocates improved housing for low-income rural families; works to increase public awareness of rural housing problems; monitors legislation.

Fair Housing, Special Groups

AGENCIES

Bureau of Indian Affairs (BIA), *(Interior Dept.), Housing Assistance, 1951 Constitution Ave. S.W., South Interior Bldg., #355E 20240; (202) 513-7260. Fax, (202) 208-2648. Vacant, Chief.*

Web, www.bia.gov

Provides assistance to native American families who have limited resources, live within designated service areas, and do not qualify or receive assistance from other housing programs.

Federal Housing Administration (FHA), *(Housing and Urban Development Dept.), Asset Management, 451 7th St. S.W., #6160 20410; (202) 708-3730. Fax, (202) 401-5978. Beverly J. Miller, Director.*

Web, www.hud.gov

Manages grants for housing for the elderly and the disabled under Sections 202 and 811 of the Housing Act of 1959.

Housing and Urban Development Dept. (HUD), *Fair Housing and Equal Opportunity, 451 7th St. S.W., #5100 20410; (202) 708-4252. Fax, (202) 708-4483. Carolyn Y. Peoples, Assistant Secretary. Housing discrimination hotline, (800) 669-9777.*

Web, www.hud.gov

Monitors compliance with legislation requiring equal opportunities in housing for minorities, persons with disabilities, and families with children. Monitors compliance with construction codes to accommodate people with disabilities in multifamily dwellings. Hotline answers inquiries about housing discrimination.

Housing and Urban Development Dept. (HUD), *FHIP/FHAP Support, 451 7th St. S.W., #5222 20410; (202) 708-2288. Fax, (202) 708-4445. Loretta A. Dixon, Director.*

Web, www.hud.gov

Awards grants to public and private organizations and to state and local agencies. Funds projects that educate the public about fair housing rights; programs are designed to prevent or eliminate discriminatory housing practices. Administers the Fair Housing Initiative and the Fair Housing Assistance Programs (FHIP/FHAP).

Housing and Urban Development Dept. (HUD), *Native American Programs, 451 7th St. S.W., #4126 20410; (202) 401-7914. Fax, (202) 401-7909. Rodger J. Boyd, Deputy Assistant Secretary.*
Web, www.hud.gov

Administers federal assistance for Native American tribes. Assistance programs focus on housing and community and economic development through competitive and formula grants. Funds for approved activities are provided directly to tribes or Alaska native villages or to a tribally designated housing authority.

Justice Dept. (DOJ), *Civil Rights, 950 Pennsylvania Ave. N.W., #3623 20530; (202) 514-2151. Fax, (202) 514-0293. Ralph F. Boyd Jr., Assistant Attorney General. Library, (202) 514-3010. Press, (202) 514-2007. TTY, (202) 514-0716.*
Web, www.usdoj.gov/crt

Enforces federal civil rights laws prohibiting discrimination on the basis of race, color, religion, sex, disability, age, or national origin in housing, public accommodations and facilities, and credit and federally assisted programs.

Office of Thrift Supervision (OTS), *(Treasury Dept.), Compliance Policy, 1700 G St. N.W. 20552; (202) 906-6134. Fax, (202) 906-6326. Richard Riese, Director. Consumer complaints, (800) 842-6929.*
Web, www.ots.treas.gov

Handles complaints of discrimination against minorities and women by savings and loan associations; assists minority-owned or minority-controlled savings and loan institutions.

Rural Development *(Agriculture Dept.), Civil Rights, 1400 Independence Ave. S.W. 20250-3220 (mailing address: Ag. Box 0703 20250-0703); (202) 692-0204. Fax, (202) 692-0276. Cheryl Prejean Greaux, Director.*

Enforces compliance with laws prohibiting discrimination in credit transactions on the basis of sex, marital status, race, color, religion, age, or disability. Ensures equal opportunity in granting Rural Economic and Community Development housing, farm ownership, and operating loans, and a variety of community and business program loans.

NONPROFIT

AARP, *Consumer Protection, 601 E St. N.W. 20049; (202) 434-6055. Fax, (202) 434-6470. Bridget Small, Director.*
Web, www.aarp.org

Supports affordable and appropriate housing for older Americans, including shared housing, continuing care, retirement and assisted living communities, and home equity conversion.

American Assn. of Homes and Services for the Aging, *Policy and Governmental Affairs, 2519 Connecticut Ave. N.W. 20008-1520; (202) 783-2242. Fax, (202) 783-2255. Susan M. Weiss, Vice President.*
Web, www.aahsa.org

Membership: nonprofit nursing homes, housing, and health-related facilities for the elderly. Provides research and technical assistance on housing and long-term care for the elderly; conducts certification program for retirement housing professionals. Operates a capital formation program to procure financing for new housing facilities for the elderly. Monitors legislation and regulations.

Assn. of Community Organizations for Reform Now (ACORN), *Washington Office, 739 8th St. S.E. 20003; (202) 547-2500. Fax, (202) 546-2483. Chris Saffert, Legislative Director.*
General e-mail, natacorndc@acorn.org
Web, www.acorn.org

Works to advance the interests of minority and low-income families through community organizing and action. Interests include jobs, living wages, housing, welfare reform, and community reinvestment. (Headquarters in New Orleans, La.)

B'nai B'rith International, *Senior Housing Committee, 2020 K St. N.W., 7th Floor 20006; (202) 857-2785. Fax, (202) 857-2782. Mark D. Olshan, Director.*
General e-mail, seniors@bnaibrith.org
Web, www.bbinet.org

Works with local groups to sponsor federally assisted housing for independent low-income senior citizens and persons with disabilities, regardless of race or religion.

Center for Community Change, *1000 Wisconsin Ave. N.W. 20007; (202) 342-0519. Fax, (202) 333-5462. Deepak Bhargava, Executive Director.*
General e-mail, info@communitychange.org
Web, www.communitychange.org

Provides community-based organizations serving minorities and the economically disadvantaged with technical assistance. Areas of assistance include housing, economic and resource development, rural development projects, and program planning.

National American Indian Housing Council, *900 2nd St. N.E., #305 20002; (202) 789-1754. Fax, (202) 789-1758. Gary Gordon, Executive Director.*
Web, www.naihc.net

Membership: native American housing authorities. Clearinghouse for information on native American housing issues; works for safe and sanitary dwellings for native American and Alaska native communities; monitors HUD policies and housing legislation; provides members with training and technical assistance in managing housing assistance programs.

National Assn. for the Advancement of Colored People (NAACP), *Washington Office, 1025 Vermont Ave. N.W., #1120 20005; (202) 638-2269. Fax, (202) 638-5936. Hilary O. Shelton, Director.*
Web, www.naacp.org

Membership: persons interested in civil rights for all minorities. Works to eliminate discrimination in housing and urban affairs. Supports programs that make affordable rental housing available to minorities and that maintain African American ownership of land. (Headquarters in Baltimore, Md.)

National Assn. of Real Estate Brokers, *9831 Greenbelt Rd., #309, Lanham, MD 20706; (301) 552-9340. Fax, (301) 552-9216. Edward London, President.*
General e-mail, nareb3@aol.com
Web, www.nareb.com

Membership: minority real estate brokers, appraisers, contractors, property managers, and salespersons. Works to prevent discrimination in housing policies and practices; conducts regional seminars on federal policy, legislation, and regulations; advises members on procedures for procuring federal contracts.

National Council of La Raza, *1111 19th St. N.W., #1000 20036; (202) 785-1670. Fax, (202) 776-1792. Raul Yzaguirre, President.*
General e-mail, info@nclr.org
Web, www.nclr.org

Helps Hispanic community-based groups obtain funds, develop and build low-income housing and community facilities, and develop and finance community economic development projects; conducts research and provides policy analysis on the housing status and needs of Hispanics; monitors legislation on fair housing and government funding for low-income housing.

National Council on the Aging, *300 D St. S.W., #801 20024; (202) 479-1200. Fax, (202) 479-0735. James P. Firman, President. Information, (202) 479-6653. Press, (202) 479-6975.*
General e-mail, info@ncoa.org
Web, www.ncoa.org

Serves as an information clearinghouse on aging. Works to ensure quality housing for older persons. Monitors legislation and regulations.

Public and Subsidized Housing

AGENCIES

Housing and Urban Development Dept. (HUD), *Public Housing and Voucher Program, 451 7th St. S.W., #4204 20410-5000; (202) 708-1380. Fax, (202) 708-0690. William O. Russell III, Deputy Assistant Secretary.*
Web, www.hud.gov

Establishes policies and procedures for low-income public housing and rental assistance programs, including special needs for the elderly and disabled, standards for rental and occupancy, utilities and maintenance engineering, and financial management.

Housing and Urban Development Dept. (HUD), *Public Housing Investments, 451 7th St. S.W., #4130 20410; (202) 401-8812. Fax, (202) 401-2370. Milan Ozdinec, Assistant Secretary.*
Web, www.hud.gov

Establishes development policies and procedures for low-income housing programs, including criteria for site approval and construction standards; oversees administration of the Comprehensive Improvement Assistance Program for modernizing existing public housing. Administers the HOPE 6 Program.

Public and Indian Housing *(Housing and Urban Development Dept.), Rental Assistance, 451 7th St. S.W., #4210 20410; (202) 708-0477. Fax, (202) 401-7974. Gerald Benoit, Director.*
Web, www.hudweb.hud.gov

Administers certificate, housing voucher programs, and moderate rehabilitation authorized by Section 8 of the Housing Act of 1937, as amended. Provides rental subsidies to lower income families.

NONPROFIT

Public Housing Authorities Directors Assn., *511 Capitol Court N.E., #200 20002-4937; (202) 546-5445. Fax, (202) 546-2280. Timothy G. Kaiser, Executive Director.*
Web, www.phada.org

Membership: executive directors of public housing authorities. Serves as liaison between members and the Housing and Urban Development Dept. and Congress;

conducts educational seminars and conferences. Monitors legislation and regulations.

Urban Institute, *Metropolitan Housing and Communities Policy Center,* 2100 M St. N.W., #500 20037; (202) 833-7200. Fax, (202) 872-9322. Margery Austin Turner, Director.

Web, www.urban.org

Research organization that deals with urban problems. Researches housing policy problems, including housing management, public housing programs, finance, and rent control.

 REAL ESTATE

AGENCIES

Federal Highway Administration (FHWA), *(Transportation Dept.), Real Estate Services,* 400 7th St. S.W., #3221 20590; (202) 366-0142. Fax, (202) 366-3713. Susan Lauffer, Director.

Web, www.fhwa.dot.gov/realestate

Funds and oversees acquisition of land by states for federally assisted highways; provides financial assistance to relocate people and businesses forced to move by highway construction; cooperates in administering program for the use of air rights in connection with federally aided highways; administers Highway Beautification Act to control billboards and junkyards along interstate and federally aided primary highways.

Federal Insurance and Mitigation Administration *(Federal Emergency Management Agency),* 500 C St. S.W., #430 20472; (202) 646-2781. Fax, (202) 646-7970. Anthony S. Lowe, Administrator.

Web, www.fema.gov/nfip

Administers federal flood insurance programs, including the National Flood Insurance Program. Makes low-cost flood insurance available to eligible homeowners.

General Services Administration (GSA), *Public Buildings Service,* 1800 F St. N.W., #6344 20405; (202) 501-1100. Fax, (202) 219-2310. Joseph Moravec, Commissioner.

Web, www.gsa.gov

Administers the construction, maintenance, and operation of buildings owned or leased by the federal government. Manages and disposes of federal real estate.

Housing and Urban Development Dept. (HUD), *Affordable Housing Programs,* 451 7th St. S.W., #7164 20410; (202) 708-2685. Fax, (202) 708-1744. Mary Kolesar, Director.

Web, www.hud.gov

Administers the Uniform Relocation Assistance and Real Property Acquisition Policies Act of 1970, as amended, and other laws requiring that relocation assistance be given to persons displaced by federally assisted housing and community development programs.

Housing and Urban Development Dept. (HUD), *Interstate Land Sales/RESPA (Real Estate Settlement Procedure Act),* 451 7th St. S.W., #9146 20410; (202) 708-0502. Fax, (202) 708-4559. Ivy Jackson, Director (Acting).

Web, www.hud.gov

Administers the Interstate Land Sales Full Disclosure Act, which requires land developers who sell undeveloped land through interstate commerce or the mail to disclose required information about the land to the purchaser prior to signing a sales contract and to file information with the federal government.

Small Business Administration (SBA), *Disaster Assistance,* 409 3rd St. S.W., #6050 20416; (202) 205-6734. Fax, (202) 205-7728. Herbert L. Mitchell, Associate Administrator.

Web, www.sba.gov

Provides victims of physical disasters with disaster and economic injury loans for homes, businesses, and personal property. Lends funds to individual homeowners, business concerns of all sizes, and nonprofit institutions to repair or replace damaged structures and furnishings, business machinery, equipment, and inventory.

CONGRESS

House Financial Services Committee, *Subcommittee on Financial Institutions and Consumer Credit,* 2129 RHOB 20515; (202) 225-7502. Rep. Spencer Bachus, R-Ala., Chair; Bob Foster, Staff Director.

Web, financialservices.house.gov

Jurisdiction over legislation on federal financial regulatory agencies and authorized activities of federally chartered and supervised financial institutions.

House Financial Services Committee, *Subcommittee on Housing and Community Opportunity,* B303 RHOB 20515; (202) 225-7502. Rep. Bob Ney, R-Ohio, Chair; Bob Foster, Staff Director.

Web, financialservices.house.gov

Jurisdiction over mortgage banking legislation, including mortgage insurance, secondary mortgage markets, and mortgage credit (except programs administered by the Veterans Affairs Dept.). Jurisdiction over federal insurance, including flood insurance.

House Ways and Means Committee, *Subcommittee on Oversight,* *1136 LHOB 20515; (202) 225-7601. Fax, (202) 225-9680. Rep. Amo Houghton, R-N.Y., Chair; Kirk Walder, Staff Director.*

Web, waysandmeans.house.gov

Oversees government-sponsored enterprises, including the Federal Home Loan Mortgage Corp. and the Federal National Mortgage Assn., with regard to the financial risk posed to the federal government.

Senate Banking, Housing, and Urban Affairs Committee, *SD-534 20510; (202) 224-7391. Fax, (202) 224-5137. Sen. Richard C. Shelby, R-Ala., Chair; Kathy Casey, Staff Director.*

Web, banking.senate.gov

Jurisdiction over legislation on federal financial regulatory agencies and authorized activities of federally chartered and supervised financial institutions. Oversees government-sponsored enterprises, including the Federal Home Loan Mortgage Corp. and the Federal National Mortgage Assn.

Senate Banking, Housing, and Urban Affairs Committee, *Subcommittee on Economic Policy,* *SD-534 20510; (202) 224-7391. Fax, (202) 224-5137. Sen. Jim Bunning, R-Ky., Chair; Steve Patterson, Staff Director.*

Web, banking.senate.gov

Jurisdiction over legislation on mortgage insurance and secondary mortgage markets.

NONPROFIT

American Homeowners Foundation, *6776 Little Falls Rd., Arlington, VA 22213-1213; (703) 536-7445. Fax, (703) 536-7079. Bruce Hahn, President. Information, (800) 489-7776.*

General e-mail, ahf@americanhomeowners.org

Web, www.americanhomeowners.org

Conducts research and compiles statistics on home ownership; sponsors seminars and workshops; publishes model contracts.

American Land Title Assn., *1828 L St. N.W., #705 20036; (202) 296-3671. Fax, (202) 223-5843. James R. Maher, Executive Vice President.*

General e-mail, service@alta.org

Web, www.alta.org

Membership: land title insurance underwriting companies, abstracters, and title insurance agents. Searches, reviews, and insures land titles to protect real estate investors, including home buyers and mortgage lenders;

provides industry information. Monitors legislation and regulations.

American Resort Development Assn., *1201 15th St. N.W., #400 20005; (202) 371-6700. Fax, (202) 289-8544. Howard Nusbaum, President.*

Web, www.arda.org

Membership: U.S. and international developers, builders, financiers, marketing companies, and others involved in resort, recreational, and community development. Serves as an information clearinghouse; monitors federal and state legislation.

American Society of Appraisers, *555 Herndon Pkwy., #125, Herndon, VA 20170 (mailing address: P.O. Box 17265, Washington, DC 20041); (703) 478-2228. Fax, (703) 742-8471. Edwin W. Baker, Executive Director. Information, (800) 272-8258.*

General e-mail, asainfo@appraisers.org

Web, www.appraisers.org

Membership: accredited appraisers of real property, including land, houses, and commercial buildings; businesses; machinery and equipment; yachts; aircraft; public utilities; personal property, including antiques, fine art, residential contents, gems, and jewelry. Affiliate members include students and professionals interested in appraising. Provides technical information; accredits appraisers; provides consumer information program.

Appraisal Foundation, *1029 Vermont Ave. N.W., #900 20005; (202) 347-7722. Fax, (202) 347-7727. David S. Bunton, Executive Vice President.*

General e-mail, info@appraisalfoundation.org

Web, www.appraisalfoundation.org

Seeks to ensure that appraisers are qualified to offer their services by promoting uniform appraisal standards and establishing education, experience, and examination requirements.

Appraisal Institute, *Public Affairs, Washington Office,* *2600 Virginia Ave. N.W., #123 20037; (202) 298-6449. Fax, (202) 298-5547. Donald E. Kelly, Vice President.*

Web, www.appraisalinstitute.org

Provides Congress, regulatory agencies, and the executive branch with information on appraisal matters. (Headquarters in Chicago, Ill.)

Assn. of Foreign Investors in Real Estate, *1300 Pennsylvania Ave. N.W., #880 20004-3020; (202) 312-1400. Fax, (202) 312-1401. James A. Fetgatter, Chief Executive.*

General e-mail, afireinfo@afire.org

Web, www.afire.org

Represents foreign institutions that are interested in the laws, regulations, and economic trends affecting the U.S. real estate market. Informs the public and the government of the contributions foreign investment makes to the U.S. economy. Examines current issues and organizes seminars for members.

International Real Estate Federation, *U.S. Chapter,* *2000 N. 15th St., #101, Arlington, VA 22201; (703) 524-4279. Fax, (703) 991-6256. Steven H. Podolsky, President.*
General e-mail, info@fiabci-usa.com
Web, www.fiabci-usa.com

Membership: real estate professionals in the fields of appraisal, brokerage, counseling, development, financing, and property management. Sponsors seminars, workshops, and conferences. (International headquarters in Paris.)

Investment Program Assn., *1101 17th St. N.W., #703 20036; (202) 775-9750. Fax, (202) 331-8446. Christopher L. Davis, President.*
Web, www.ipa-dc.org

Represents the partnership industry, public and private investments that employ partnerships, Real Estate Investment Trusts (REIT), limited liability companies, and other direct investment programs. Conducts conferences and seminars.

Manufactured Housing Institute, *2101 Wilson Blvd., #610, Arlington, VA 22201-3062; (703) 558-0400. Fax, (703) 558-0401. Christopher Stinebert, President.*
General e-mail, info@manufacturedhousing.org
Web, www.manufacturedhousing.org

Represents park owners, financial lenders, and builders, suppliers, and retailers of manufactured and modular homes. Provides information on manufactured and modular home construction standards, finance, site development, property management, and marketing.

National Assn. of Home Builders (NAHB), *1201 15th St. N.W. 20005-2800; (202) 266-8200. Fax, (202) 266-8374. Jerry Howard, Executive Vice President (Acting). Press, (202) 266-8254.*
General e-mail, info@nahb.org
Web, www.nahb.org

Membership: contractors, builders, architects, engineers, mortgage lenders, and others interested in home building and commercial real estate construction. Offers educational programs and information on housing policy and mortgage finance in the United States. Library open to the public by appointment.

National Assn. of Real Estate Brokers, *9831 Greenbelt Rd., #309, Lanham, MD 20706; (301) 552-9340. Fax, (301) 552-9216. Edward London, President.*
General e-mail, nareb3@aol.com
Web, www.nareb.com

Membership: minority real estate brokers, appraisers, contractors, property managers, and salespersons. Works to prevent discrimination in housing policies and practices; conducts regional seminars on federal policy, legislation, and regulations; advises members on procedures for procuring federal contracts.

National Assn. of Real Estate Investment Trusts, *1875 Eye St. N.W., #600 20006; (202) 739-9400. Fax, (202) 739-9401. Steven Wechsler, President.*
Web, www.nareit.com

Membership: real estate investment trusts and corporations, partnerships, and individuals interested in real estate securities and the industry. Monitors federal and state legislation, federal taxation, securities regulation, standards and ethics, and housing and education; compiles industry statistics.

National Assn. of Realtors, *Government Affairs, Washington Office, 700 11th St. N.W. 20001-4507; (202) 383-1238. Fax, (202) 383-7850. Jerry Giovaniello, Senior Vice President.*
Web, www.realtors.com

Sets standards of ethics for the real estate business; promotes education, research, and exchange of information. Monitors legislation and regulations. (Headquarters in Chicago, Ill.)

The Real Estate Roundtable, *1420 New York Ave. N.W., #1100 20005-2159; (202) 639-8400. Fax, (202) 639-8442. Jeffrey D. DeBoer, President.*
General e-mail, info@rer.org
Web, www.rer.org

Membership: real estate owners, advisers, builders, investors, lenders, and managers. Serves as forum for public policy issues including taxes, the environment, capital, credit, and investments.

Society of Industrial and Office Realtors, *700 11th St. N.W., #510 20001-4507; (202) 737-1150. Fax, (202) 737-8796. Pam Hinton, Executive Vice President.*
Web, www.sior.com

Membership: commercial and industrial real estate brokers worldwide. Certifies brokers; sponsors seminars and conferences; mediates and arbitrates business disputes for members; sponsors a speakers bureau. (Affiliated with the National Assn. of Realtors.)

Mortgages and Finance

AGENCIES

Fannie Mae, *3900 Wisconsin Ave. N.W. 20016; (202) 752-7000. Fax, (202) 752-3616. Franklin D. Raines, Chair; Daniel Mudd, Chief Operating Officer. Information, (800) 732-6643. Library, (202) 752-7750. Press, (202) 752-7111.*

Web, www.fanniemae.com

Congressionally chartered, shareholder-owned corporation. Makes mortgage funds available by buying conventional and government-insured mortgages in the secondary mortgage market; raises capital through sale of short- and long-term obligations, mortgages, and stock; issues and guarantees mortgage-backed securities. Library open to the public by appointment. (Fannie Mae stands for Federal National Mortgage Assn.)

Farmer Mac, *1133 21st St. N.W., #600 20036; (202) 872-7700. Fax, (202) 872-7713. Nancy Corsiglia, Vice President.*

Web, www.farmermac.com

Private corporation chartered by Congress to provide a secondary mortgage market for farm and rural housing loans. Guarantees principal and interest repayment on securities backed by farm and rural housing loans. (Farmer Mac stands for Federal Agricultural Mortgage Corp.)

Federal Housing Administration (FHA), *(Housing and Urban Development Dept.), Multifamily Business Products, 451 7th St. S.W., #6134 20410-8000; (202) 708-3000. Fax, (202) 708-3104. Willie Spearmon, Director.*

Web, www.hud.gov/fha/mfh/fhamfbus.html

Establishes procedures for the development of housing under the multifamily mortgage insurance programs. Administers the mortgage insurance programs for rental, cooperative, and condominium housing.

Federal Housing Administration *(Housing and Urban Development Dept.), Title I Insurance, 451 7th St. S.W., #9272 20410; (202) 708-6396. Fax, (202) 401-8951. Mary Worthy, Loan Specialist.*

Web, www.hud.gov

Sets policy for Title I loans on manufactured home and property improvement loans. Provides information to lenders on policy issues.

Federal Housing Enterprise Oversight *(Housing and Urban Development Dept.), 1700 G St. N.W., 4th Floor 20552-0100; (202) 414-3800. Fax, (202) 414-3823. Armando Falcon Jr., Director.*

Web, www.ofheo.gov

Works to ensure the financial soundness of Fannie Mae (Federal National Mortgage Assn.) and Freddie Mac (Federal Home Loan Mortgage Corp.).

Federal Housing Finance Board, *1777 F St. N.W. 20006; (202) 408-2587. Fax, (202) 408-2950. John T. Korsmo, Chair. Information, (202) 408-2500. Press, (202) 408-2817.*

General e-mail, fhfb@fhfb.org

Web, www.fhfb.gov

Regulates and supervises the credit and financing operations of the twelve Federal Home Loan Banks, which provide a flexible credit reserve for member institutions engaged in home mortgage lending. Member institutions of the Federal Home Loan Banks include savings and loans, savings banks, commercial banks, credit unions, insurance companies, and other financial intermediaries.

Freddie Mac, *8200 Jones Branch Dr., McLean, VA 22102-3107; (703) 903-3001. Fax, (703) 903-3495. Leland C. Brendsel, Chair; David W. Glenn, Vice Chair, (703) 903-2701. Information, (703) 903-2000. Press, (703) 903-2511.*

Web, www.fhlmc.com

Chartered by Congress to increase the flow of funds for residential mortgages by buying conforming mortgages and selling mortgage securities to major investors. (Freddie Mac stands for Federal Home Loan Mortgage Corp.)

Ginnie Mae *(Housing and Urban Development Dept.), 451 7th St. S.W., #6100 20410; (202) 708-0926. Fax, (202) 708-0490. Ronald Rosenfeld, President; George S. Anderson, Executive Vice President.*

Web, www.ginniemae.gov

Supports government housing objectives by establishing secondary markets for residential mortgages. Serves as a vehicle for channeling funds from the securities markets into the mortgage market through mortgage-backed securities programs and helps to increase the supply of credit available for housing. Guarantees privately issued securities backed by Federal Housing Administration, Veterans Affairs Dept., and Farmers Home Administration mortgages. (Ginnie Mae stands for Government National Mortgage Assn.)

Housing and Urban Development Dept. (HUD), *Housing, 451 7th St. S.W., #9100 20410; (202) 708-3600. Fax, (202) 708-2580. John C. Weicher, Assistant Secretary.*

Web, www.hud.gov/fha/fhahome.html

Administers all Federal Housing Administration (FHA) mortgage insurance programs; approves and monitors all lending institutions that conduct business with HUD.

Office of Thrift Supervision (OTS), *(Treasury Dept.),* *1700 G St. N.W. 20552; (202) 906-6590. Fax, (202) 898-0230. James E. Gilleran, Director. Information, (202) 906-6000. Library, (202) 906-6470. Press, (202) 906-6913.*
Web, www.ots.treas.gov

Charters, regulates, and examines the operations of savings and loan institutions; focus includes mortgage rates. Library open to the public.

CONGRESS

House Financial Services Committee, *Subcommittee on Capital Markets, Insurance, and Government-Sponsored Enterprises, 2129 RHOB 20515; (202) 225-7502. Rep. Richard H. Baker, R-La., Chair; Bob Foster, Staff Director.*
Web, financialservices.house.gov

Jurisdiction over secondary market organizations for home mortgages including Fannie Mae (Federal National Mortgage Assn.), Freddie Mac (Federal Home Loan Mortgage Corporation), and Farmer Mac (Federal Agricultural Mortgage Corporation); the Office of Federal Housing Enterprise Oversight; the Federal Housing Finance Board, and the supervision and operation of the Federal Home Loan Banks.

NONPROFIT

American League of Financial Institutions, *900 19th St. N.W., #400 20006-2105; (202) 857-5094. Fax, (202) 296-8716. Dina Curtis, President.*
Web, www.alfi.org

Membership: minority-controlled community savings associations and savings banks. Offers on-site technical assistance to resolve problems in operations. Encourages financing of low- and moderate-income housing and promotes community reinvestment activities. Monitors legislative and regulatory issues.

America's Community Bankers, *900 19th St. N.W., #400 20006; (202) 857-3100. Fax, (202) 296-8716. Diane M. Casey, President. Press, (202) 857-3110.*
General e-mail, info@acbankers.org
Web, www.acbankers.org

Membership: insured depository institutions involved in community finance. Provides information on issues that affect the industry. Monitors economic issues affecting savings institutions; publishes homebuyers survey. Monitors legislation and regulations.

Mortgage Bankers Assn. of America, *1919 Pennsylvania Ave. N.W., 8th Floor 20006; (202) 557-2700. Fax, (202) 721-0249. Jonathan Kempner, President.*

Web, www.mbaa.org

Membership: institutions involved in real estate finance. Maintains School of Mortgage Banking; collects statistics on the industry. Conducts seminars and workshops in specialized areas of mortgage finance. Monitors legislation and regulations.

Mortgage Insurance Companies of America, *727 15th St. N.W., 12th Floor 20005; (202) 393-5566. Fax, (202) 393-5557. Suzanne C. Hutchinson, Executive Vice President.*
Web, www.privatemi.com

Membership: companies that provide guarantee insurance on residential, high-ratio mortgage loans. Insures members against loss from default on low down payment home mortgages and provides coverage that acts as a credit enhancement on mortgage securities.

National Assn. of Affordable Housing Lenders, *1300 Connecticut Ave. N.W., #905 20036; (202) 293-9850. Fax, (202) 293-9852. Judith A. Kennedy, President.*
General e-mail, naahl@naahl.org
Web, www.naahl.org

Membership: lenders who specialize in providing financing for affordable housing and community development, including regulated financial institutions, insurance companies, mortgage banking companies, and loan funds. Serves as an information clearinghouse; provides education, training, and direct technical assistance. Monitors legislation and regulations.

National Assn. of Local Housing Finance Agencies, *2025 M St. N.W., #800 20036-3309; (202) 857-1197. Fax, (202) 367-2197. John C. Murphy, Executive Director.*
Web, www.nalhfa.org

Membership: professionals of city and county government that finance affordable housing. Provides professional development programs in new housing finance and other areas. Monitors legislation and regulations.

National Assn. of Mortgage Brokers, *8201 Greensboro Dr., #300, McLean, VA 22102; (703) 610-9009. Fax, (703) 610-9005. Mike Nizankiewicz, Executive Vice President.*
Web, www.namb.org

Membership: mortgage brokers. Seeks to improve the mortgage broker industry. Offers educational programs to members. Provides referrals. Monitors legislation and regulations.

National Council of State Housing Agencies, *444 N. Capitol St. N.W., #438 20001; (202) 624-7710. Fax, (202) 624-5899. Barbara J. Thompson, Executive Director.*
Web, www.ncsha.org

Membership: state housing finance agencies. Promotes greater opportunities for lower-income people to rent or buy affordable housing.

Property Management

AGENCIES

Bureau of Land Management (BLM), *(Interior Dept.), Lands and Realty, 1620 L St. N.W. 20240 (mailing address: 1849 C St. N.W., MC 1000LS 20240); (202) 452-7773. Fax, (202) 452-7708. Donald A. Buhler, Manager (Acting).*
Web, www.blm.gov

Oversees use, acquisition, and disposal of public lands. Conducts the Public Lands Survey; authorizes rights-of-way on public lands, including roads and power lines.

Federal Housing Administration (FHA), *(Housing and Urban Development Dept.), Asset Management, 451 7th St. S.W., #6160 20410; (202) 708-3730. Fax, (202) 401-5978. Beverly J. Miller, Director.*
Web, www.hud.gov

Services mortgages developed under HUD's multifamily mortgage insurance programs, including the Community Disposal Program; reviews management of multifamily housing projects and administers project-based subsidy programs; advises state housing agencies that administer multifamily projects.

Federal Housing Administration (FHA), *(Housing and Urban Development Dept.), Procurement Management, 451 7th St. S.W., #2220 20410; (202) 708-4466. Fax, (202) 708-3698. Don F. Schade, Director.*
Web, www.hud.gov

Develops and implements policies and procedures and conducts contract administration for the Office of Housing and the Federal Housing Administration headquarters' procurement actions.

NONPROFIT

Building Owners and Managers Assn. International, *1201 New York Ave. N.W., #300 20005; (202) 408-2662. Fax, (202) 371-0181. Henry Chamberlain, Executive Vice President.*
Web, www.boma.org

Membership: office building owners and managers. Reviews changes in model codes and building standards; conducts seminars and workshops on building operation and maintenance issues; sponsors educational and training programs. Monitors legislation and regulations.

Building Service Contractors Assn. International, *10201 Lee Hwy., #225, Fairfax, VA 22030; (703) 359-7090.*

Fax, (703) 352-0493. Carol A. Dean, Executive Vice President.
Web, www.bscai.org

Membership: building service contractors. Promotes industry practices that are professional and environmentally responsive.

CHF International, *8601 Georgia Ave., #800, Silver Spring, MD 20910; (301) 587-4700. Fax, (301) 587-7315. Michael E. Doyle, President.*
General e-mail, mailbox@chfhq.com
Web, www.chfhq.org

Works under contract with the Agency for International Development, United Nations, and World Bank to strengthen government housing departments abroad. Develops and strengthens nonprofit technical service organizations; conducts training workshops; assists tenant groups in converting units into cooperatives; conducts research. (CHF stands for Community Habitat and Finance.)

Community Associations Institute, *225 Reinekers Lane, #300, Alexandria, VA 22314; (703) 548-8600. Fax, (703) 684-1581. Tom Skiba, President. Fax-on-demand, (703) 836-6904.*
Web, www.caionline.org

Membership: homeowner associations, builders, lenders, owners, managers, realtors, insurance companies, and public officials. Provides members with information on creating, financing, and maintaining common facilities and services in condominiums and other planned developments.

NAIOP, National Assn. of Industrial and Office Properties (NAIOP), *2201 Cooperative Way, 3rd Floor, Herndon, VA 20171-3024; (703) 904-7100. Fax, (703) 904-7942. Thomas J. Bisacquino, President.*
Web, www.naiop.org

Membership: developers, planners, designers, builders, financiers, and managers of industrial and office properties. Provides research and continuing education programs. Monitors legislation and regulations on capital gains, real estate taxes, impact fees, growth management, environmental issues, and hazardous waste liability.

National Apartment Assn., *201 N. Union St., #200, Alexandria, VA 22314; (703) 518-6141. Fax, (703) 518-6191. Phil Carlock, President.*
Web, www.naahq.org

Membership: state and local associations of owners, managers, investors, developers, and builders of apartment houses or other rental properties; conducts educational and professional certification programs. Monitors legislation and regulations.

National Assn. of Home Builders (NAHB), *1201 15th St. N.W. 20005-2800; (202) 266-8200. Fax, (202) 266-8374. Jerry Howard, Executive Vice President (Acting). Press, (202) 266-8254.*
General e-mail, info@nahb.org
Web, www.nahb.org

Membership: contractors, builders, architects, engineers, mortgage lenders, and others interested in home building and commercial real estate construction. Offers a Registered Apartment Managers certification program; provides educational programs and information on apartment construction and management, condominiums and cooperatives, multifamily rehabilitation, and low-income and federally assisted housing. Library open to the public by appointment.

National Assn. of Housing and Redevelopment Officials, *630 Eye St. N.W. 20001; (202) 289-3500. Fax, (202) 289-8181. Saul Ramirez, Executive Director.*
Web, www.nahro.org

Membership: housing, community, and urban development practitioners and organizations, and state and local government agencies and personnel. Conducts studies and provides training and certification in the operation and management of rental housing; develops performance standards for low-income rental housing operations.

National Assn. of Housing Cooperatives, *1707 H St. N.W., #201 20006; (202) 737-0797. Fax, (202) 783-7869. Douglas M. Kleine, Executive Director.*
General e-mail, info@coophousing.org
Web, www.coophousing.org

Membership: housing cooperative professionals, developers, and individuals. Promotes housing cooperatives; sets standards; provides technical assistance in all phases of cooperative housing; sponsors educational programs and on-site training; monitors legislation; maintains an information clearinghouse on housing cooperatives.

National Center for Housing Management,
National Training Center, 1010 N. Glebe Rd., #160, Arlington, VA 22201; (703) 516-4070. Fax, (703) 516-4069. W. Glenn Stevens, President.

General e-mail, service@nchm.org
Web, www.nchm.org

Private corporation created by executive order to meet housing management and training needs. Conducts research, demonstrations, and educational and training programs in all types of multifamily housing management. Develops and implements certification systems for housing management programs.

National Cooperative Business Assn., *1401 New York Ave. N.W., #1100 20005-2160; (202) 638-6222. Fax, (202) 638-1374. Paul Hazen, President.*
General e-mail, ncba@ncba.coop
Web, www.ncba.coop

Alliance of cooperatives, businesses, and state cooperative associations. Provides information about starting and managing housing cooperatives. Monitors legislation and regulations.

National Multi Housing Council, *1850 M St. N.W., #540 20036; (202) 974-2300. Fax, (202) 775-0112. Douglas Bibby, President.*
General e-mail, info@nmhc.org
Web, www.nmhc.org

Membership: owners, financiers, managers, and developers of multifamily housing. Advocates policies and programs at the federal, state, and local levels to increase the supply and quality of multifamily units in the United States; serves as a clearinghouse on rent control, condominium conversion, taxes, fair housing, and environmental issues.

Property Management Assn., *7900 Wisconsin Ave., #305, Bethesda, MD 20814; (301) 657-9200. Fax, (301) 907-9326. Thomas B. Cohn, Executive Vice President.*
General e-mail, pma@erols.com
Web, www.pma-dc.org

Membership: property managers and firms that offer products and services needed in the property management field. Promotes information exchange on property management practices.

13 International Affairs

☀ GENERAL POLICY

AGENCIES

Defense Dept. (DoD), *International Security Affairs,* *The Pentagon, #4E838 20301-2400; (703) 695-4351. Fax, (703) 697-7230. Peter W. Rodman, Assistant Secretary. Web, www.defenselink.mil*

Advises the secretary of defense and recommends policies on regional security issues (except those involving countries of the former Soviet Union).

National Security Council (NSC), *(Executive Office of the President), International Economic Affairs,* *The White House 20504; (202) 456-9281. Fax, (202) 456-9280. John A. Cloud Jr., Special Assistant to the President. Web, www.whitehouse.gov/nsc*

Advises the president, the National Security Council, and the National Economic Council on all aspects of U.S. foreign policy dealing with U.S. international economic policies.

Office of Global Communications *(Executive Office of the President), Dwight D. Eisenhower Executive Office Bldg. 20502; (202) 456-4636. Fax, (202) 456-6180. Tucker Eskew, Director. Web, www.whitehouse.gov/ogc*

Advises U.S. government agencies on the direction and theme of the president's message. Assists in the development and coordination of communications programs that will disseminate consistent and accurate messages about U.S. government and policies to the global audience.

Office of Science and Technology Policy (OSTP), *(Executive Office of the President), Dwight D. Eisenhower Executive Office Bldg. 20502; (202) 456-7116. Fax, (202) 456-6021. Kathie L. Olsen, Associate Director, Science; Richard M. Russell, Associate Director, Technology. Web, www.ostp.gov*

Advises the president on international science and technology matters as they affect national security; coordinates international science and technology initiatives at the interagency level. Interests include nuclear materials, security, nuclear arms reduction, and counter terrorism.

President's Foreign Intelligence Advisory Board *(Executive Office of the President), Dwight D. Eisenhower Executive Office Bldg., #494 20502; (202) 456-2352. Fax, (202) 395-3403. Brent Scowcroft, Chair; Randy Deitering, Executive Director. Web, www.whitehouse.gov/pfiab*

Members appointed by the president. Assesses the quality, quantity, and adequacy of foreign intelligence collection and of counterintelligence activities by all government agencies; advises the president on matters concerning intelligence and national security.

State Dept., *2201 C St. N.W. 20520; (202) 647-5291. Fax, (202) 647-6434. Gen. Colin Powell, Secretary; Richard L. Armitage, Deputy Secretary. Information, (202) 647-4000. Press, (202) 647-2492. Web, www.state.gov*

Directs and coordinates U.S. foreign relations and interdepartmental activities of the U.S. government overseas.

State Dept., *Consular Affairs, 2201 C St. N.W., #6811 20520-4818; (202) 647-9576. Fax, (202) 647-0341. Maura Harty, Assistant Secretary. National Passport Information Center (fees are charged for calls to these numbers), (900) 225-5674 or (888) 362-8668 with credit card. Assistance to U.S. citizens overseas, (888) 407-4747 or (317) 472-2328 from overseas. Web, travel.state.gov*

Issues passports to U.S. citizens and visas to immigrants and nonimmigrants seeking to enter the United States. Provides protection, assistance, and documentation for American citizens abroad.

State Dept., *Global Affairs, 2201 C St. N.W., #7250 20520; (202) 647-6240. Fax, (202) 647-0753. Paula J. Dobriansky, Under Secretary. Web, www.state.gov*

Advises the secretary on international issues. Divisions include Democracy, Human Rights, and Labor; International Narcotics and Law Enforcement Affairs; Oceans and International Environmental and Scientific Affairs; and Population, Refugees, and Migration.

State Dept., *Intelligence and Research, 2201 C St. N.W., #6531 20520-6531; (202) 647-9177. Fax, (202) 736-4688. Carl W. Ford Jr., Assistant Secretary. Web, www.state.gov*

Coordinates foreign policy-related research, analysis, and intelligence programs for the State Dept. and other federal agencies.

State Dept., *International Conferences, 2201 C St. N.W., #1517 20520-6319; (202) 647-6875. Fax, (202) 647-5996. Frank R. Provyn, Managing Director. Web, www.state.gov*

Coordinates U.S. participation in international conferences.

State Dept., *International Organization Affairs,* *2201 C St. N.W., #6323 20520-6319; (202) 647-9600. Fax,*

(202) 736-4116. Kim R. Holmes, Assistant Secretary. Press, (202) 647-8490.

Web, www.state.gov/p/io

Coordinates and develops policy guidelines for U.S. participation in the United Nations and in other international organizations and conferences.

State Dept., *Management,* 2201 C St. N.W., #7207 20520; (202) 647-1500. Fax, (202) 647-0168. Grant S. Green Jr., Under Secretary.

Web, www.state.gov

Serves as principal adviser to the secretary on management matters, including budgetary, administrative, and personnel policies of the department and the Foreign Service.

State Dept., *Policy Planning Staff,* 2201 C St. N.W., #7311 20520; (202) 647-2372. Fax, (202) 647-4147. Richard N. Haass, Director.

Web, www.state.gov

Advises the secretary and other State Dept. officials on foreign policy matters.

State Dept., *Political Affairs,* 2201 C St. N.W., #7240 20520; (202) 647-2471. Fax, (202) 647-4780. Marc Grossman, Under Secretary.

Web, www.state.gov

Assists in the formulation and conduct of foreign policy and in the overall direction of the department; coordinates interdepartmental activities of the U.S. government abroad.

State Dept., *Public Diplomacy and Public Affairs,* 2201 C St. N.W., #7261 20520; (202) 647-9199. Fax, (202) 647-9140. Patricia S. Harrison, Under Secretary (Acting).

Web, www.press.state.gov

Seeks to broaden public affairs discussion on foreign policy with American citizens, media, and institutions. Provides cultural and educational exchange opportunities and international information programs to people in the United States and abroad.

State Dept., *Public Diplomacy and Public Affairs: Bureau of Educational and Cultural Affairs,* 301 4th St. S.W., #534 20547; (202) 619-4949. Fax, (202) 205-2457. Patricia S. Harrison, Assistant Secretary.

Web, exchanges.state.gov

Seeks to promote mutual understanding between the people of the United States and other countries through international educational and training programs. Promotes personal, professional, and institutional ties between private citizens and organizations in the U.S. and abroad; presents U.S. history, society, art, and culture to overseas audiences.

U.S. Institute of Peace, 1200 17th St. N.W., #200 20036-3011; (202) 457-1700. Fax, (202) 429-6063. Chester Crocker, Chair; Richard H. Solomon, President. TTY, (202) 457-1719.

General e-mail, usip_requests@usip.org

Web, www.usip.org

Independent organization created and funded by Congress to promote the peaceful resolution of international conflict through negotiation and mediation. Provides federal agencies and individuals with training, research programs, and information; awards grants to institutions and individuals; and provides fellowships to scholars from the United States and abroad. Library open to the public by appointment.

CONGRESS

General Accounting Office (GAO), *International Affairs and Trade,* 441 G St. N.W., #4T43 20548; (202) 512-3655. Fax, (202) 512-9088. Susan Westin, Managing Director.

Web, www.gao.gov

Independent, nonpartisan agency in the legislative branch. Audits, analyzes, and evaluates international programs; makes unclassified reports available to the public.

House Appropriations Committee, *Subcommittee on Commerce, Justice, State, and the Judiciary,* H309 CAP 20515; (202) 225-3351. Rep. Frank R. Wolf, R-Va., Chair; Mike Ringler, Staff Director.

Web, www.house.gov/appropriations

Jurisdiction over legislation to appropriate funds for the State Dept. (except antiterrorism, international narcotics control, international organizations and programs, nonproliferation, migration, and refugee assistance), the Commission on Security and Cooperation in Europe, and the Japan–United States Friendship Commission.

House Appropriations Committee, *Subcommittee on Foreign Operations, Export Financing, and Related Programs,* H150 CAP 20515; (202) 225-2041. Fax, (202) 226-7992. Rep. Jim Kolbe, R-Ariz., Chair; Charles O. Flickner, Staff Director.

Web, www.house.gov/appropriations

Jurisdiction over legislation to appropriate funds for foreign operations, including migration, refugee, economic, and military assistance programs of the State Dept.; the Export-Import Bank; the International Bank for Reconstruction and Development (World Bank); the Inter-American Development Bank; the International Monetary Fund; the Agency for International Development; the Peace Corps; and related international organizations.

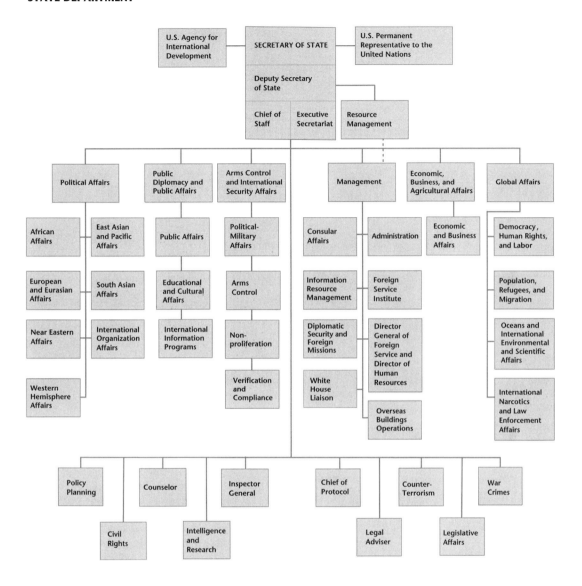

House Government Reform Committee, *Subcommittee on National Security, Emerging Threats, and International Relations, B372 RHOB 20515; (202) 225-2548. Fax, (202) 225-2382. Rep. Christopher Shays, R-Conn., Chair; Lawrence Halloran, Staff Director.*
Web, www.house.gov/reform

Oversees operations of the State Dept., the Peace Corps, the Agency for International Development, and other agencies concerned with foreign affairs.

House International Relations Committee,
2170 RHOB 20515; (202) 225-5021. Fax, (202) 226-2831. Rep. Henry J. Hyde, R-Ill., Chair; Thomas E. Mooney, Chief of Staff. Hearing notification line, (202) 225-3184.
General e-mail, hirc@mail.house.gov
Web, www.house.gov/international_relations

Jurisdiction over legislation on and operations of the State Dept. and U.S. foreign embassies. Jurisdiction over authorization of budget for the Agency for International Development and U.S. contributions to the United Nations and other international organizations. Oversight of State and Defense departments' operations regarding arms transfers, export licenses, sales, administration of security assistance, and foreign military training and advisory programs.

Library of Congress, *Serial and Government Publications,* *101 Independence Ave. S.E. 20540; (202) 707-5647. Fax, (202) 707-6128. Karen Renninger, Chief. Information, (202) 707-5690.*
Web, www.lcweb.loc.gov

Collects and maintains information on governmental and nongovernmental organizations that are internationally based, financed, and sponsored. Responds to written or telephone requests to provide information on the history, structure, operation, and activities of these organizations. Some book material available for interlibrary loan through the Library of Congress Loan Division.

Senate Appropriations Committee, *Subcommittee on Commerce, Justice, State, and the Judiciary,* *S-206 CAP 20510; (202) 224-7277. Fax, (202) 228-0587. Sen. Judd Gregg, R-N.H., Chair; James Morhard, Clerk.*
Web, appropriations.senate.gov

Jurisdiction over legislation to appropriate funds for the State Dept. (except counterterrorism, migration and refugee assistance, and international narcotics control), the Foreign Claims Settlement Commission, and other programs related to foreign policy and foreign aid.

Senate Appropriations Committee, *Subcommittee on Foreign Operations, SD-125 20510; (202) 224-2255. Fax, (202) 228-0280. Sen. Mitch McConnell, R-Ky., Chair; Paul Grove, Clerk.*
Web, appropriations.senate.gov

Jurisdiction over legislation to appropriate funds for foreign operations, including migration, refugee, development, economic, and military assistance programs of the State Dept.

Senate Foreign Relations Committee, *SD-450 20510; (202) 224-4651. Fax, (202) 228-1608. Sen. Richard G. Lugar, R-Ind., Chair; Kenneth A. Myers, Staff Director.*
Web, foreign.senate.gov

Jurisdiction over legislation on foreign affairs, including economic and military assistance programs. Oversight responsibilities for operations of the State Dept., the Foreign Service, U.S. participation in the United Nations, and other agencies concerned with foreign affairs.

Senate Foreign Relations Committee, *Subcommittee on Western Hemisphere, Peace Corps, and Narcotics Affairs, SD-446 20510; (202) 224-4651. Sen. Norm Coleman, R-Minn., Chair; Carl Meacham, Professional Staff Member.*
Web, foreign.senate.gov

Jurisdiction over foreign affairs legislation dealing with the Americas; oversight of all matters of the Peace Corps and the U.S. delegation to the Organization of American States.

INTERNATIONAL ORGANIZATIONS

European Commission, *Press and Public Affairs, Washington Office, 2300 M St. N.W. 20037; (202) 862-9500. Fax, (202) 429-1766. Willy Helin, Director; Günter Burghardt, Ambassador.*
Web, www.eurunion.org

Provides information on European Union energy policy, initiatives, research activities, and selected statistics. Library open to the public by appointment. (Headquarters in Brussels.)

International Bank for Reconstruction and Development (World Bank), *1818 H St. N.W., MC 12-750 20433; (202) 477-1234. Fax, (202) 522-3031. James D. Wolfensohn, President; Carole Brookins, U.S. Executive Director. Press, (202) 473-1800. Publications, (703) 661-1580.*
Web, www.worldbank.org

International development institution funded by membership subscriptions and borrowings on private capital markets. Encourages the flow of public and private foreign investment into developing countries through loans and technical assistance. Finances foreign economic development projects in agriculture, environmental protection, education, public utilities, telecommunications, water supply, sewerage, public health, and other areas.

International Crisis Group, *Washington Office, 1629 K St. N.W., #450 20006; (202) 785-1601. Fax, (202) 785-1630. Mark L. Schneider, Senior Vice President.*
General e-mail, icgwashington@crisisweb.org
Web, www.crisisweb.org

Private, multinational organization that seeks to prevent international conflict. Writes and distributes reports, and raises funds. (Headquarters in Brussels.)

International Monetary Fund (IMF), *700 19th St. N.W., #13-318 20431; (202) 623-7759. Fax, (202) 623-*

4940. Nancy P. Jacklin, U.S. Executive Director. Information, (202) 623-7300. Press, (202) 623-7100.
Web, www.imf.org

International organization that maintains funds, contributed and available for use by members, to promote world trade and aid members with temporary balance-of-payments problems.

Organization for Economic Cooperation and Development (OECD), *Washington Office*, 2001 L St. N.W., #650 20036-4922; (202) 785-6323. Fax, (202) 785-0350. Matthew Brosius, Co-Director; Sandra Wilson, Co-Director. Press, (202) 822-3866.
General e-mail, washington.contact@oecd.org
Web, www.oecdwash.org

Membership: thirty nations including Australia, Canada, Japan, Mexico, New Zealand, the United States, and western European nations. Serves as a forum for members to exchange information and attempt to coordinate their economic policies. Washington Center maintains reference library open to the public. (Headquarters in Paris.)

Organization of American States (OAS), *17th St. and Constitution Ave. N.W. 20006 (mailing address: 1889 F St. N.W. 20006); (202) 458-3000. Fax, (202) 458-3967. Cesar Gaviria, Secretary General. Library, (202) 458-6037.
Web, www.oas.org

Membership: the United States, Canada, and all independent Latin American and Caribbean countries. Funded by quotas paid by member states and by contributions to special multilateral funds. Works to promote democracy, eliminate poverty, and resolve disputes among member nations. Provides member states with technical and advisory services in cultural, educational, scientific, social, and economic areas. Library open to the public.

United Nations Information Centre, *1775 K St. N.W., #400 20006; (202) 331-8670. Fax, (202) 331-9191. Catherine O'Neill, Director.
Web, www.unicwash.org

Lead United Nations (U.N.) office in Washington. Center for reference publications of the U.N. Library, open to the public, includes all official U.N. records and publications.

NONPROFIT

American Enterprise Institute for Public Policy Research (AEI), *Foreign and Defense Policy Studies*, 1150 17th St. N.W., #1100 20036; (202) 862-5814. Fax, (202) 862-7177. Jeane Kirkpatrick, Director. Information, (202) 862-5800. Press, (202) 862-4871.
Web, www.aei.org

Research and educational organization that conducts conferences, seminars, and debates and sponsors research on international affairs.

Assn. on Third World Affairs, *1717 K St. N.W., #600 20036; (202) 973-0157. Fax, (202) 234-3201. Lorna Hahn, Executive Director.
General e-mail, info@atwa.org
Web, www.atwa.org

Membership: individuals and groups interested in developing nations and nations in transition. Promotes research projects; arranges lectures and conferences where members of Congress meet with ambassadors and other officials; sponsors student interns.

Assn. to Unite the Democracies, *P.O. Box 77164 20013-7164; (202) 347-9465. Fax, (202) 347-9464. Bob Frantz, President.
General e-mail, atunite@aol.com

Educational organization that promotes and conducts research on unity among the industrial democracies, including the United States, Japan, western European countries, and new and emerging democracies in the former Soviet bloc. Advocates a federation of these states.

Atlantic Council of the United States, *910 17th St. N.W., 10th Floor 20006; (202) 463-7226. Fax, (202) 463-7241. Christopher J. Makins, President.
General e-mail, info@acus.org
Web, www.acus.org

Conducts studies and makes policy recommendations on American foreign security and international economic policies in the Atlantic and Pacific communities; sponsors conferences and educational exchanges.

The Brookings Institution, *Foreign Policy Studies*, 1775 Massachusetts Ave. N.W. 20036; (202) 797-6400. Fax, (202) 797-6003. James B. Steinberg, Director. Information, (202) 797-6000. Press, (202) 797-6105. Publications, (202) 797-6258.
Web, www.brookings.edu

Conducts studies on foreign policy, national security, regional and global affairs, and economic policies. Includes three policy centers: Saban Center for Middle East Policy, the Center for Northeast Asian Policy Studies, and the Center on the United States and France.

Carnegie Endowment for International Peace, *1779 Massachusetts Ave. N.W. 20036; (202) 483-7600. Fax, (202) 483-1840. Jessica T. Mathews, President.
General e-mail, carnegie@ceip.org
Web, www.ceip.org

Conducts research on international affairs and American foreign policy. Program activities cover a broad range of military, political, and economic issues; sponsors panel discussions. (Affiliate office in Moscow.)

Center for Democracy, *1101 15th St. N.W., #505 20005-5002; (202) 429-9141. Fax, (202) 293-1768. Allen Weinstein, President.*
General e-mail, center@centerfordemocracy.org
Web, www.centerfordemocracy.org
Nonpartisan organization that works to promote the democratic process and strengthen democratic institutions in the United States and worldwide. Monitors elections and provides democratizing governments with technical and informational assistance.

Center for Strategic and International Studies, *1800 K St. N.W., #400 20006; (202) 887-0200. Fax, (202) 775-3199. John J. Hamre, President. Publications, (202) 775-3119.*
Web, www.csis.org
Independent nonpartisan research institute that studies international and domestic policy issues. Interests include science and technology, international business and economics, political-military affairs, arms control, international communications, and fiscal policy.

Center of Concern, *1225 Otis St. N.E. 20017; (202) 635-2757. Fax, (202) 832-9494. James Hug, President.*
General e-mail, coc@coc.org
Web, www.coc.org
Independent, interdisciplinary organization that conducts social analysis, theological reflection, policy advocacy, and public education on issues of international justice and peace.

Charles F. Kettering Foundation, *Washington Office, 444 N. Capitol St. N.W., #434 20001-1512; (202) 393-4478. Fax, (202) 393-7644. Phillip D. Lurie, Director (Acting).*
Web, www.kettering.org
Works to improve the domestic policy-making process. Supports international program focusing on unofficial, citizen-to-citizen diplomacy. Encourages greater citizen involvement in formation of public policy. Interests include public education and at-risk youths. (Headquarters in Dayton, Ohio.)

Citizens Network for Foreign Affairs, *1111 19th St. N.W., #900 20036; (202) 296-3920. Fax, (202) 296-3948. John H. Costello, President.*
General e-mail, info@cnfa.com
Web, www.cnfa.com

Public policy and education organization that works to involve Americans in the foreign policy process. Advocates a more collaborative partnership between the public and private sectors to promote global economic growth.

Council on Foreign Relations, *Washington Office, 1779 Massachusetts Ave. N.W. 20036; (202) 518-3400. Fax, (202) 986-2984. Robert Orr, Director.*
Web, www.cfr.org
Promotes understanding of U.S. foreign policy and international affairs. Awards research grants through its International Affairs Fellowship Program. (Headquarters in New York.)

Democracy International, *2803 Whirlaway Circle, Oak Hill, VA 20171; (703) 620-9258. Fax, (703) 620-0647. Ira Straus, Executive Director.*
Seeks to encourage democracy and protect human rights throughout the world.

Eisenhower Institute, *915 15th St. N.W., 8th Floor 20005; (202) 628-4444. Fax, (202) 628-4445. Susan Eisenhower, President.*
Web, www.eisenhowerinstitute.org
Sponsors public policy and educational programs for future leaders designed to improve understanding of the presidency and world affairs.

Friends Committee on National Legislation (FCNL), *245 2nd St. N.E. 20002-5795; (202) 547-6000. Fax, (202) 547-6019. Joe Volk, Executive Secretary. Recorded information, (202) 547-4343.*
General e-mail, fcnl@fcnl.org
Web, www.fcnl.org
Seeks to broaden public interest and affect legislation and policy concerning regional and global institutions, peace processes, international development, and the work of the United Nations. Affiliated with the Religious Society of Friends (Quakers).

Institute for Foreign Policy Analysis, *1725 DeSales St. N.W., #402 20036; (202) 463-7942. Fax, (202) 785-2785. Robert L. Pfaltzgraff Jr., President.*
Web, www.ifpa.org
Trains policy analysts in the fields of foreign policy and national security. Sponsors research and workshops.

Institute for Policy Studies, *733 15th St. N.W., #1020 20005; (202) 234-9382. Fax, (202) 387-7915. John Cavanagh, Director.*
Web, www.ips-dc.org
Research and educational organization. Interests include foreign policy, the U.S. military-industrial com-

plex, international development, human rights, and national security.

Institute of International Education, *National Security Education Program,* *1400 K St. N.W., #650 20005-2403; (202) 326-7697. Fax, (202) 326-7698. Chris Powers, Deputy Director. Information, (800) 618-6737.*
General e-mail, nsep@iie.org
Web, www.iie.org/nsep

Provides scholarships, fellowships, and institutional grants to academics with an interest in foreign affairs and national security.

Institute of World Politics, *1521 16th St. N.W. 20036; (202) 462-2101. Fax, (202) 462-7031. John Lenczowski, Director.*
General e-mail, info@iwp.edu
Web, www.iwp.edu

Offers master's degree in international affairs, foreign policy, methods of statecraft, and political philosophy.

International Center, *731 8th St. S.E. 20003; (202) 547-3800. Fax, (202) 546-4784. Lindsay Mattison, Executive Director.*
General e-mail, icnfp@erols.com
Web, www.internationalcenter.com

Research organization concerned with U.S. foreign policy. Sponsored U.S. delegation to more than twenty countries. Current projects include: Commission on U.S.-Russian Relations, New Forests Project, U.S.-Vietnam Trade Council, U.S.-Vietnam Forum, and the Korean Information Service on the Internet.

International Foundation for Election Systems, *1101 15th St. N.W., 3rd Floor 20005; (202) 828-8507. Fax, (202) 452-0804. Richard W. Soudriette, President.*
Web, www.ifes.org

Supports electoral and other democratic institutions in emerging democracies. Holds conferences; observes election activities in more than 120 countries. Provides technical assistance. Conducts education and training programs and conferences.

International Republican Institute, *1225 Eye St. N.W., #700 20005-3987; (202) 408-9450. Fax, (202) 408-9462. George Folsom, President.*
Web, www.iri.org

Created under the National Endowment for Democracy Act. Fosters democratic self-rule through closer ties and cooperative programs with political parties and other nongovernmental institutions overseas.

National Defense Council Foundation, *1220 King St., #230, Alexandria, VA 22314; (703) 836-3443. Fax, (703) 836-5402. Milton R. Copulos, President.*
General e-mail, ndcf@erols.com
Web, www.ndcf.org

Studies defense and foreign affairs issues that face the U.S. Informs Congress and the media on socioeconomic, political, and military issues that affect the U.S. Interests include low-intensity conflict, drug control, and energy concerns.

National Democratic Institute for International Affairs (NDI), *2030 M St. N.W., 5th Floor 20036; (202) 728-5500. Fax, (202) 728-5520. Kenneth Wollack, President.*
General e-mail, contactndi@ndi.org
Web, www.ndi.org

Conducts nonpartisan international programs to help maintain and strengthen democratic institutions worldwide. Focuses on party building, governance, and electoral systems.

National Endowment for Democracy, *1101 15th St. N.W., #700 20005-1650; (202) 293-9072. Fax, (202) 223-6042. Carl Gershman, President; Barbara Haig, Vice President for Program Planning and Evaluation.*
General e-mail, info@ned.org
Web, www.ned.org

Grant-making organization that receives funding from Congress. Awards grants to private organizations involved in democratic development abroad, including the areas of democratic political processes; pluralism; and education, culture, and communications.

National Peace Foundation, *666 11th St. N.W., #202 20001; (202) 783-7030. Fax, (202) 783-7040. Sarah Harder, President.*
General e-mail, npf@nationalpeace.org
Web, www.nationalpeace.org

Supports conflict resolution education and the U.S. Institute of Peace. Holds conferences and provides information on peace education and managing and resolving conflict.

National Security Archive, *Gelman Library, 2130 H St. N.W., #701 20037; (202) 994-7000. Fax, (202) 994-7005. Thomas Blanton, Executive Director.*
General e-mail, nsarchiv@gwu.edu
Web, www.nsarchive.org

Research institute and library that provides information on U.S. foreign and economic policy and national security affairs. Maintains collection of declassified and unclassified national security documents. Sponsors freedom of information legislation in Central Europe and elsewhere. Archive open to the public by appointment.

Paul H. Nitze School of Advanced International Studies, *1740 Massachusetts Ave. N.W. 20036; (202) 663-5624. Fax, (202) 663-5621. Jessica Einhorn, Dean. Information, (202) 663-5600. Press, (202) 663-5626.*
Web, www.sais-jhu.edu

Offers graduate programs in international relations and public policy. Sponsors the Johns Hopkins Foreign Policy Institute, the Center for Strategic Education, the International Energy and Environment Program, the Center for Transatlantic Relations, and centers for international business and public policy; central Asia and the Caucasus; and Canadian, Brazilian, East Asian, and Sino-American studies.

United Nations Assn. of the USA, *Washington Office, 1779 Massachusetts Ave. N.W., #610 20036; (202) 462-3446. Fax, (202) 462-3448. Steven A. Dimoff, Vice President.*
General e-mail, unadc@unausa.org
Web, www.unausa.org

Research and educational organization focusing on international institutions, multilateral diplomacy, U.S. foreign policy, and international economics. Coordinates Model United Nations program for high school and university students. Monitors legislation and regulations. (Headquarters in New York.)

U.S. Conference of Catholic Bishops (USCCB), *International Justice and Peace, 3211 4th St. N.E. 20017-1194; (202) 541-3199. Fax, (202) 541-3339. Gerard Powers, Director.*
Web, www.usccb.org

Works with the U.S. State Dept., foreign government offices, and international organizations on issues of peace, justice, and human rights.

Washington Institute of Foreign Affairs, *2121 Massachusetts Ave. N.W. 20008; (202) 966-1061. Fax, (202) 966-0945. Marina G. Fischer, Executive Secretary.*
General e-mail, wifa@erols.com
Web, wifadc.org

Membership: former government officials, retired military professionals, educators, and others concerned with foreign affairs. Seeks to promote greater understanding of foreign policy issues.

Women in International Security, *CPASS, School of Foreign Affairs, Georgetown University, Box 571145 20057; (202) 687-3366. Fax, (202) 687-3233. Sherry Gray, Executive Director.*

General e-mail, wiisinfo@georgetown.edu
Web, wiis.georgetown.edu

Seeks to advance women in the field of international relations. Maintains a database of women foreign and defense policy specialists worldwide; organizes conferences in Europe, the former Soviet Union, and Asia; disseminates information on jobs, internships, and fellowships for women in international affairs.

Women's Foreign Policy Group, *1875 Connecticut Ave. N.W., #720 20009-5728; (202) 884-8597. Fax, (202) 884-8487. Patricia Ellis, Executive Director.*
General e-mail, wfpg@wfpg.org
Web, www.wfpg.org

Promotes the leadership of women in international affairs professions. Conducts policy programs, mentoring, and research.

World Federalist Assn., *418-420 7th St. S.E. 20003-2796; (202) 546-3950. Fax, (202) 546-3749. John B. Anderson, President. Information, (800) 932-0123.*
General e-mail, information@wfa.org
Web, www.wfa.org

Sponsors projects and conducts research related to international affairs; seeks to broaden public support for world order organizations and a restructured United Nations.

Diplomats and Foreign Agents

AGENCIES

Foreign Service Institute *(State Dept.), School of Professional and Area Studies, 4000 Arlington Blvd., Arlington, VA 22204-1500; (703) 302-6940. Fax, (703) 302-6949. A. Ellen Shippy, Dean. Student messages and course information, (703) 302-7143.*

Provides training for U.S. government personnel involved in foreign affairs agencies, including employees of the State Dept., the Agency for International Development, the Defense Dept., and other agencies.

Justice Dept. (DOJ), *Foreign Agents Registration Unit, 1400 New York Ave. N.W., #100 20530; (202) 514-1216. Fax, (202) 514-2836. Heather H. Hunt, Chief (Acting).*
Web, www.usdoj.gov/criminal/fara

Receives and maintains the registration of agents representing foreign countries, companies, organizations, and individuals. Compiles semi-annual report on foreign agent registrations. Foreign agent registration files are open for public inspection.

State Dept., *Career Development and Assignments, 2201 C St. N.W., #2328 20520-6258 (mailing address:*

HR/CDA 20520-2810); (202) 647-1692. Fax, (202) 647-0277. Ralph Frank, Director.
Web, www.state.gov

Coordinates programs related to the professional development of American members of the Foreign Service, including career development and assignment counseling programs; training; and presidential appointments and resignations.

State Dept., *Diplomatic Security Bureau,* 2201 C St. N.W., #6316 20520; (202) 647-6290. Fax, (202) 647-0953. Francis X. Taylor, Assistant Secretary.
General e-mail, DSPublicAffairs@state.gov
Web, ds.state.gov

Provides a secure environment for conducting American diplomacy and promoting American interests abroad and in the United States.

State Dept., *Family Liaison,* 2201 C St. N.W., #1239 20520-0108; (202) 647-1076. Fax, (202) 647-1670. Faye G. Barnes, Director.
General e-mail, flo@state.gov
Web, www.state.gov/m/dghr/flo

Provides support for U.S. foreign affairs personnel and their families in Washington, D.C. and abroad. Maintains liaison offices that give support services to the U.S. foreign affairs community overseas. Services include dependent employment assistance and continuing education programs; educational assistance for families with children; and information on adoption and separation, regulations, allowance, and finances. Assists families in emergencies.

State Dept., *Foreign Missions,* 2201 C St. N.W., #2238 20520; (202) 647-4554. Fax, (202) 647-1919. Lynwood M. Dent Jr., Deputy Assistant Secretary.
Web, www.state.gov

Regulates the benefits, privileges, and immunities granted to foreign missions and their personnel in the United States on the basis of the treatment accorded U.S. missions abroad and considerations of national security and public safety.

State Dept., *Human Resources,* 2201 C St. N.W., #6218 20520; (202) 647-9898. Fax, (202) 647-5080. Ruth A. Davis, Director General of Foreign Service and Director of Human Resources.
Web, www.state.gov

Directs human resource policies of the State Dept. and Foreign Service.

State Dept., *Medical Services,* 2401 E St. N.W., #L209 20522-0102; (202) 663-1611. Fax, (202) 663-1613. Dr. Cedric E. Dumont, Medical Director.

Web, www.state.gov

Operates a worldwide primary health care system for American citizen employees, and eligible family members, of participating U.S. government agencies. Conducts physical examinations of Foreign Service officers and candidates; provides clinical services; assists with medical evacuation of patients overseas.

State Dept., *Protocol,* 2201 C St. N.W., #1238 20520; (202) 647-4543. Fax, (202) 647-3980. Donald B. Ensenat, Chief. Press, (202) 647-1685.
Web, www.state.gov

Serves as principal adviser to the president, vice president, the secretary, and other high-ranking government officials on matters of diplomatic procedure governed by law or international customs and practice.

CONGRESS

House International Relations Committee, *Subcommittee on International Terrorism, Nonproliferation, and Human Rights,* 2401A RHOB 20515; (202) 226-7820. Fax, (202) 225-7485. Rep. Elton Gallegly, R-Calif., Chair; Richard Mereu, Staff Director.
Web, www.house.gov/international_relations

Jurisdiction over legislation on the Foreign Service, the United Nations, other international organizations, and educational and cultural exchange programs.

Senate Foreign Relations Committee, *Subcommittee on International Operations and Terrorism,* SD-446 20510; (202) 224-4651. Sen. John E. Sununu, R-N.H., Chair; Vacant, Staff Director.
Web, foreign.senate.gov

Jurisdiction over legislation on the Foreign Service, the United Nations, other international organizations and conferences, and educational and cultural exchange programs.

NONPROFIT

American Foreign Service Assn. (AFSA), 2101 E St. N.W. 20037; (202) 338-4045. Fax, (202) 338-6820. Susan Reardon, Executive Director.
General e-mail, afsa@afsa.org
Web, www.afsa.org

Membership: active and retired foreign service employees of the State Dept., Agency for International Development, Foreign Commercial Service, and the Foreign Agricultural Service. Offers scholarship program; maintains club for members; represents active duty foreign service personnel in labor-management negotiations. Seeks to ensure adequate resources for foreign service operations and personnel. Interests include business-government collaboration and international trade. Monitors legislation and regulations.

Council of American Ambassadors, *888 17th St. N.W., #901 20006-3307; (202) 296-3757. Fax, (202) 296-0926. Keith L. Brown, President; Carolyn M. Gretzinger, Executive Director.*
General e-mail, council@his.com
Web,www.his.com/~council

Membership: U.S. ambassadors. Seeks to advance the understanding of the American ambassador's role in serving U.S. interests abroad.

Executive Council on Diplomacy, *818 Connecticut Ave. N.W., #1200 20006-2702; (202) 466-5199. Fax, (202) 872-8696. Kate Nelson, Deputy Director.*

Brings foreign diplomats from international organizations such as the United Nations and World Bank into contact with their American counterparts. Provides a forum for discussion on issues such as agriculture, international trade, education, and the arts.

Institute for the Study of Diplomacy *(Georgetown University),* *1316 36th St. N.W. 20007; (202) 965-5735. Fax, (202) 965-5811. Casimir A. Yost, Director.*
Web, cfdev.georgetown.edu/sfs/programs/isd

Part of the Edmund A. Walsh School of Foreign Service. Focuses on the practical implementation of foreign policy objectives; draws on academic research and the concrete experience of diplomats and other members of the policy community.

Humanitarian Aid

AGENCIES

Administration for Children and Families (ACF), *(Health and Human Services Dept.), Refugee Resettlement,* *901 D St. S.W., 6th Floor 20447; (202) 401-9246. Fax, (202) 401-0981. Nguyen Van Hanh, Director.*
Web, www.acf.dhhs.gov

Directs a domestic resettlement program for refugees; reimburses states for costs incurred in giving refugees monetary and medical assistance; awards funds to private resettlement agencies for providing refugees with monetary assistance and case management; provides states and nonprofit agencies with grants for social services such as English and employment training.

Agency for International Development (USAID), *Democracy, Conflict, and Humanitarian Assistance Bureau,* *1300 Pennsylvania Ave. N.W., #8.06C 20523-8601; (202) 712-0100. Fax, (202) 216-3397. Roger P. Winter, Assistant Administrator.*
Web, www.usaid.gov/pubs/cbj2003/cent_prog/dcha

Manages U.S. foreign disaster assistance, U.S. government food aid programs, grants to private voluntary and cooperative development organizations, and American sponsored schools and hospitals around the world.

Agency for International Development (USAID), *Global Health Bureau,* *1300 Pennsylvania Ave. N.W., GH 20523-3100; (202) 712-4120. Fax, (202) 216-3485. E. Anne Peterson, Assistant Administrator.*
General e-mail, globalhealth@phnip.com
Web, www.usaid.gov/pop_health

Participates in global efforts to stabilize world population growth and support women's reproductive rights. Focus includes family planning; reproductive health care; infant, child, and maternal health; and prevention of sexually transmitted diseases, especially AIDS. Conducts demographic and health surveys; educates girls and women.

Agency for International Development (USAID), *U.S. Foreign Disaster Assistance,* *1300 Pennsylvania Ave. N.W., #8.06A 20523-8600; (202) 712-0400. Fax, (202) 216-3707. Bernd McConnell, Director.*
Web, www.usaid.gov/hum_response/ofda

Office within the Democracy, Conflict, and Humanitarian Assistance Bureau. Administers disaster relief and preparedness assistance to foreign countries to save lives and alleviate human suffering. Aids displaced persons in disaster situations and helps other countries manage natural disasters and complex emergencies.

Defense Dept. (DoD), *Stability Operations,* *2500 Defense Pentagon, OASD 20301-2500; (703) 614-0446. Fax, (703) 697-4945. Joseph Collins, Deputy Assistant Secretary.*
Web, www.defenselink.mil

Develops policy and plans for department provision of humanitarian assistance, refugee affairs, U.S. international information programs, and international peacekeeping and peace enforcement activities. Develops policy related to creating, identifying, training, exercising, and committing military forces for peacekeeping and peace enforcement activities.

Public Health and Science *(Health and Human Services Dept.), Global Health Affairs,* *5600 Fishers Lane, #18105, Rockville, MD 20857-1750; (301) 443-1774. Fax, (301) 443-6288. Dr. William R. Steiger, Director.*
Web, www.globalhealth.gov

Represents the Health and Human Services Dept. before other governments, U.S. government agencies, international organizations, and the private sector on international and refugee health issues. Promotes international cooperation; provides health-related humanitarian and developmental assistance.

State Dept., *Population, Refugees, and Migration,*
2201 C St. N.W., #5824 20520-5824; (202) 647-7360. Fax,
(202) 647-8162. Arthur E. Dewey, Assistant Secretary.
Information, (202) 663-1071.
Web, www.state.gov/g/prm

Develops and implements policies and programs on
international refugee matters, including repatriation and
resettlement programs; funds and monitors overseas
relief, assistance, and repatriation programs; manages
refugee admission to the United States.

CONGRESS

House International Relations Committee,
2170 RHOB 20515; (202) 225-5021. Fax, (202) 226-2831.
Rep. Henry J. Hyde, R-Ill., Chair; Thomas E. Mooney,
Chief of Staff. Hearing notification line, (202) 225-3184.
General e-mail, hirc@mail.house.gov
Web, www.house.gov/international_relations

Jurisdiction over international disaster assistance legislation outside the Foreign Assistance Act.

House Judiciary Committee, *Subcommittee on Immi-*
gration, Border Security, and Claims, *B370B RHOB*
20515; (202) 225-5727. Fax, (202) 225-3672. Rep. John
Hostettler, R-Ind., Chair; George Fishman, Chief Counsel.
General e-mail, Judiciary@mail.house.gov
Web, www.house.gov/judiciary

Jurisdiction over legislation on immigration,
refugees, and repatriated Americans; oversight of private
immigration relief bills.

Senate Foreign Relations Committee, *SD-450 20510;*
(202) 224-4651. Fax, (202) 228-1608. Sen. Richard G.
Lugar, R-Ind., Chair; Kenneth A. Myers, Staff Director.
Web, foreign.senate.gov

Jurisdiction over international disaster assistance legislation, including the International Emergency Economic Powers Act.

Senate Judiciary Committee, *Subcommittee on*
Immigration, Border Security, and Citizenship, *SD-520*
20510; (202) 224-6098. Fax, (202) 228-0103. Sen. Saxby
Chambliss, R-Ga., Chair; David Neal, Chief Counsel.
Web, judiciary.senate.gov

Jurisdiction over legislation on refugees, repatriated
Americans, immigration, and naturalization. Oversight
of private immigration relief bills.

INTERNATIONAL ORGANIZATIONS

International Organization for Migration (IOM),
Washington Office, 1752 N St. N.W., #700 20036; (202)
862-1826. Fax, (202) 862-1879. Fran Sullivan, Regional
Representative.

General e-mail, mrfwashington@iom.int
Web, www.iom.int

Nonpartisan organization that plans and operates
refugee resettlement, national migration, and humanitarian assistance programs at the request of its member
governments. Recruits skilled professionals for developing countries. (Headquarters in Geneva.)

Pan American Health Organization, *525 23rd St.*
N.W. 20037; (202) 974-3000. Fax, (202) 974-3608. Dr.
Mirta Roses Periago, Director. Information, (202) 974-
3458. Library, (202) 974-3305.
Web, www.paho.org

Regional office for the Americas of the World Health
Organization, headquartered in Geneva, Switzerland.
Works to extend health services to underserved populations of its member countries and to control or eradicate
communicable diseases; promotes cooperation among
governments to solve public health problems. Library
open to the public by appointment.

United Nations High Commissioner for Refugees,
Washington Office, 1775 K St. N.W., #300 20006-1502;
(202) 296-5191. Fax, (202) 296-5660. Guenet Guebre-
Christos, Washington Representative.
General e-mail, usawa@unhcr.ch
Web, www.unhcr.ch

Works with governments and voluntary organizations to protect and assist refugees worldwide. Promotes
long-term alternatives to refugee camps, including voluntary repatriation, local integration, and resettlement
overseas. (Headquarters in Geneva.)

U.S. Fund for the United Nations Children's Fund,
Public Policy and Advocacy, Washington Office, 1775 K
St. N.W., #360 20006; (202) 296-4242. Fax, (202) 296-
4060. Martin S. Rendon, Vice President.
General e-mail, OPPA@unicefusa.org
Web, www.unicefusa.org

Serves as information reference service on UNICEF;
advocates policies to advance the well-being of the
world's children. Interests include international humanitarian assistance, U.S. voluntarism, child survival, and
international health. (Headquarters in New York.)

NONPROFIT

American Red Cross, *National Headquarters, 430 17th*
St. N.W., 2nd Floor 20006-2401; (202) 737-8300. Fax,
(202) 783-3432. Marsha Evans, Chief Executive Officer.
Web, www.redcross.org

Service organization chartered by Congress to provide domestic and international disaster relief and to act
as a medium of communication between the U.S. armed

forces and their families in time of war. Coordinates the distribution of supplies, funds, and technical assistance for relief in major foreign disasters through the International Federation of Red Cross and Red Crescent Societies and the International Committee of the Red Cross, both headquartered in Geneva.

Central American Resource Center, *1459 Columbia Rd. N.W. 20009; (202) 328-9799. Fax, (202) 328-0023. Saul Solorzano, Executive Director.*
General e-mail, info@carecendc.org
Web, dccarecen.org

Human rights organization that seeks recognition of Central American refugees' rights, including the right not to be deported. Provides legal representation for refugees seeking asylum; encourages church congregations to assist Central American refugees in applying for political asylum. Interests include civic participation, citizenship programs, community education, documentation of human rights abuses, and social services.

Christian Children's Fund, *Washington Office, 1717 N St. N.W. 20036; (202) 955-7951. Fax, (202) 955-6166. Ghassan Rubeiz, Director.*
Web, www.christianchildrensfund.org

Nonsectarian humanitarian organization that promotes improved child welfare standards and services worldwide by supporting long-term sustainable development. Provides children in emergency situations brought on by war, natural disaster, and other circumstances with education, medical care, food, clothing, and shelter. Provides aid and promotes the development potential of children of all backgrounds. (Headquarters in Richmond, Va.)

Health Volunteers Overseas, *1001 Connecticut Ave. N.W., #622 20036 (mailing address: Washington Station, P.O. Box 65157 20035-5157); (202) 296-0928. Fax, (202) 296-8018. Nancy Kelly, Executive Director.*
General e-mail, info@hvousa.org
Web, www.hvousa.org

Operates training programs in developing countries for health professionals who wish to teach low-cost health care delivery practices.

International Rescue Committee, *Government Relations, Washington Office, 1819 H St. N.W., #1200 20006; (202) 822-0166. Fax, (202) 822-0089. Sandra Mitchell, Vice President.*
Web, www.theirc.org/DC

Provides worldwide emergency aid, resettlement services, and educational support for refugees; recruits volunteers. (Headquarters in New York.)

Jesuit Refugee Service/USA, *1616 P St. N.W., #300 20036-1405; (202) 462-5200. Fax, (202) 328-9212. Armando Borja, Director of Programs and Management; Richard Ryscavage (SJ), National Coordinator, (202) 462-0400.*
General e-mail, aborja@jesuit.org
Web, www.jesref.org

U.S. Jesuit organization that aids refugees in Africa, Southeast Asia, Central America, and Mexico. Provides information on refugee problems; places individual Jesuits, and lay people in refugee work abroad. Monitors refugee- and immigration-related legislation. (International headquarters in Rome.)

Mental Disability Rights International, *1156 15th St. N.W., #1001 20005; (202) 296-0800. Fax, (202) 728-3053. Eric Rosenthal, Executive Director.*
General e-mail, mdri@mdri.org
Web, www.mdri.org

Challenges discrimination of and abuse faced by people with mental disabilities worldwide. Documents conditions, publishes reports.

National Council of Churches, *Washington Office, 110 Maryland Ave. N.E., #108 20002; (202) 544-2350. Fax, (202) 543-1297. Brenda Girton-Mitchell, Director.*
Web, www.ncccusa.org

Works to foster cooperation between Christian congregations across the nation in programs concerning poverty, racism, family, environment, and international humanitarian objectives. (Headquarters in New York.)

Program for Appropriate Technology in Health, *Washington Office, 1800 K St. N.W., #800 20006; (202) 822-0033. Fax, (202) 457-1466. Anne Wilson, Director.*
General e-mail, info@path-dc.org
Web, www.path.org

Seeks to improve the safety and availability of health products and technologies worldwide, particularly in developing countries. Interests include reproductive health, immunization, maternal-child health, AIDS, and nutrition. (Headquarters in Seattle, Wash.)

Refugee Women in Development, Inc., *5225 Wisconsin Ave. N.W., #502 20015; (703) 931-6442. Fax, (703) 931-5906. Sima Wali, President.*
General e-mail, refwid@erols.com
Web, www.refwid.org

Assists refugee, displaced, and returnee women from developing or war-torn countries, both in the United States and overseas. Heightens awareness of human rights abuses of refugee women around the world.

Southeast Asia Resource Action Center, *1628 16th St. N.W., 3rd Floor 20009; (202) 667-4690. Fax, (202) 667-6449. KaYing Yang, Executive Director.*
General e-mail, searac@searac.org
Web, www.searac.org

Assists Southeast Asians (from Cambodia, Laos, and Vietnam) in the United States with resettlement. Advocates for refugee rights. Interests include education, citizenship development, Indochinese self-help organizations, and economic development.

U.S. Committee for Refugees, *1717 Massachusetts Ave. N.W., #200 20036; (202) 347-3507. Fax, (202) 347-3418. Lavinia Limon, Executive Director.*
Web, www.refugees.org

Public information and educational organization that monitors the world refugee situation and informs the public about refugee issues. Interests include human rights abuses. Publishes position papers and an annual survey.

U.S. Conference of Catholic Bishops (USCCB), *Migration and Refugee Services, 3211 4th St. N.E. 20017; (202) 541-3352. Fax, (202) 722-8755. Mark Franken, Executive Director.*
General e-mail, mrs@usccb.org
Web, www.usccb.org/mrs

Advocate for immigrants, refugees, and migrants. Works with legislative and executive branches of U.S. government and with national and international organizations such as the U.N. High Commissioner for Refugees to promote fair and responsive immigration and refugee policy.

World Mercy Fund, *P.O. Box 227, Waterford, VA 22197-0227; (540) 882-4425. Fax, (540) 882-3226. Patrick Leonard, President.*

Provides the developing world with medical, educational, agricultural, and other forms of aid.

World Vision, *Washington Office, 220 Eye St. N.E., #270 20002; (202) 547-3743. Fax, (202) 547-4834. Bruce Wilkinson, Vice President.*
Web, www.worldvision.org

Provides children and families around the world with aid, including emergency disaster relief; helps impoverished communities become self-sustaining through agriculture, health care, community organization, food programming, nutritional training, income generation and credit, and other development projects. (Headquarters in Seattle, Wash.)

Information and Exchange Programs

AGENCIES

Broadcasting Board of Governors, *330 Independence Ave. S.W., #3360 20237; (202) 401-3736. Fax, (202) 401-6605. Kenneth Y. Tomlinson, Chair; Brian Conniff, Executive Director.*
Web, www.bbg.gov

Established by Congress to direct and supervise all U.S. government nonmilitary international broadcasting, including Voice of America, Radio and TV Marti, Worldnet Television, Radio Free Europe/Radio Liberty, and Radio Free Asia. Assesses the quality and effectiveness of broadcasts with regard to U.S. foreign policy objectives; reports annually to the president and to Congress.

USDA Graduate School *(Agriculture Dept.),* **International Institute,** *600 Maryland Ave. S.W., #320 20024-2520; (202) 314-3500. Fax, (202) 479-6803. John Maykoski, Director.*
General e-mail, intlinst@grad.usda.gov
Web, www.grad.usda.gov

Offers professional training and educational services to employees of foreign governments, international organizations, nongovernmental agencies, and employees of U.S. agencies engaged in international activities. Areas of concentration include governance and democratization, international conflict resolution, privatization, environmental management, and management skills and systems development. Conducts courses in Washington, D.C., San Francisco, and other locations worldwide.

Voice of America *(International Broadcasting Bureau),* *330 Independence Ave. S.W., #3300 20237; (202) 619-3375. Fax, (202) 260-2228. David S. Jackson, Director. Information, (202) 401-7000.*
Web, www.voa.gov

Official radio broadcast service of the International Broadcasting Bureau. Offers overseas broadcasts of news, editorials, and features dealing with developments in American foreign and domestic affairs. Operates African, East Asian and Pacific, European, Eurasian, Latin American, North African, and Near East and South Asian affairs offices, as well as the World English program.

NONPROFIT

Alliance for International Educational and Cultural Exchange, *1776 Massachusetts Ave. N.W., #620 20036; (202) 293-6141. Fax, (202) 293-6144. Michael McCarry, Executive Director.*
General e-mail, info@alliance-exchange.org
Web, www.alliance-exchange.org

Promotes public policies that support the growth of international exchange between the United States and other countries. Provides professional representation, resource materials, publications, and public policy research for those involved in international exchanges.

American Bar Assn. (ABA), *International Legal Exchange Program,* *740 15th St. N.W. 20005-1022; (202) 662-1660. Fax, (202) 662-1669. Leanne Pfautz, Director, International Law and Practice.*

Web, www.abanet.org/intlaw/ilex/home.html

Organizes the exchange of lawyers between the United States and other countries and arranges short-term placements for foreign lawyers with law firms nationwide. Serves as designated U.S. government sponsor for the J-1 visa and accepts applications from foreign lawyers.

American Council of Young Political Leaders, *1612 K St. N.W., #300 20006; (202) 857-0999. Fax, (202) 857-0027. Brad Minnick, Executive Director.*

General e-mail, info@acypl.org

Web, www.acypl.org

Bipartisan political education organization that promotes understanding of foreign policy between state and local leaders and their counterparts abroad. Sponsors conferences and political study tours for U.S. and foreign political leaders between the ages of twenty-five and forty.

Business–Higher Education Forum, *1 Dupont Circle N.W., #800 20036; (202) 939-9345. Fax, (202) 833-4723. Jeremiah L. Murphy, Director.*

General e-mail, bhef@ace.nche.edu

Web, www.bhef.com

Membership: chief executive officers of major corporations, museums, colleges, and universities. Promotes the development of industry-university alliances around the world. Provides countries in central and eastern Europe with technical assistance in enterprise development, management training, market economics, education, and infrastructure development.

Center for Intercultural Education and Development, *3307 M St. N.W., #202 20007 (mailing address: P.O. Box 579400, Georgetown University 20057-9400); (202) 687-1400. Fax, (202) 687-2555. Chantal Santelices, Director.*

Web, www.georgetown.edu/CIED

Designs and administers programs aimed at improving the quality of life of economically disadvantaged people; provides technical education, job training, leadership skill development, and business management

training; runs programs in Central America, the Caribbean, Central Europe, and Southeast Asia.

Council for International Exchange of Scholars, *3007 Tilden St. N.W., #5L 20008-3009; (202) 686-4000. Fax, (202) 362-3442. Patti McGill Peterson, Executive Director.*

General e-mail, apprequest@cies.iie.org

Web, www.cies.org

Cooperates with the U.S. government in administering Fulbright grants for university teaching and advanced research abroad. (Affiliated with the American Council of Learned Societies.)

Delphi International Program of World Learning, *1015 18th St. N.W., #1000 20036-5272; (202) 898-0950. Fax, (202) 842-0885. Peter Simpson, Director.*

General e-mail, pidt@worldlearning.org

Web, www.worldlearning.org/delphi

Assists public and private organizations engaged in international cooperation and business. Works with governments and private counterparts to support foreign professional exchanges. Develops technical training programs and educational curricula for foreign visitors. Provides technical expertise, management support, travel, and business development services. Administered by World Learning's Project in International Development division.

English-Speaking Union, *Washington Office,* *1785 Massachusetts Ave. N.W., #501 20036; (202) 234-4602. Fax, (202) 234-4639. John Andrews, Executive Director.*

General e-mail, esuwdc@msn.com

Web, www.esuwdc.org

International educational and cultural organization that promotes exchange programs with countries in which English is a major language; offers English conversational tutoring to persons for whom English is a second language; sponsors scholarships for studies in English-speaking countries; sponsors annual Shakespeare competition among Washington metropolitan area schools. (Headquarters in New York.)

Institute of International Education, *Washington Office,* *1400 K St. N.W., 6th Floor 20005-2403; (202) 898-0600. Fax, (202) 326-7835. Allan Goodman, President, (202) 326-7840.*

Web, www.iie.org/dc

Educational exchange, technical assistance, and training organization that arranges professional programs for international visitors; conducts training courses in energy, environment, journalism, human resource development, educational policy and administration, and business-related fields; provides developing countries with short- and long-term technical assistance in human resource development; arranges professional training and support for staff of human rights organizations; sponsors fellowships and applied internships for midcareer professionals from developing countries; manages programs sending U.S. teachers, undergraduate and graduate students, and professionals abroad; implements contracts and cooperative agreements for the State Dept., the U.S. Agency for International Development, foreign governments, philanthropic foundations, multilateral banks, and other organizations. (Headquarters in New York.)

International Research and Exchanges Board (IREX), *2121 K St. N.W., #700 20037; (202) 628-8188. Fax, (202) 628-8189. Mark G. Pomar, President.*
General e-mail, info@irex.org
Web, www.irex.org

Administers academic exchanges between the United States and Russia, the new independent states, central and eastern Europe, Mongolia, and China. Exchange efforts include professional training, institution building, technical assistance, media, and policy development.

Meridian International Center, *1630 Crescent Pl. N.W. 20009; (202) 667-6800. Fax, (202) 667-1475. Walter L. Cutler, President. Information, (202) 667-6670.*
General e-mail, info@meridian.org
Web, www.meridian.org

Conducts international educational and cultural programs; provides foreign visitors and diplomats in the United States with services, including cultural orientation, seminars, and language assistance. Offers world affairs programs and international exhibitions for Americans.

NAFSA: Assn. of International Educators, *1307 New York Ave. N.W., 8th Floor 20005-4701; (202) 737-3699. Fax, (202) 737-3657. Marlene Johnson, Executive Director. Publications, (800) 836-4994.*
General e-mail, inbox@nafsa.org
Web, www.nafsa.org

Membership: individuals, educational institutions, and others interested in international educational exchange. Seeks to increase awareness of and support for international education in colleges and universities, government, and the community. Provides information on evaluating exchange programs; assists members in complying with federal regulations affecting foreign students

and scholars; administers grant programs with an international education focus.

National Council for International Visitors, *1420 K St. N.W., #800 20005-2401; (202) 842-1414. Fax, (202) 289-4625. Sherry L. Mueller, Executive Director. Information, (800) 523-8101.*
Web, www.nciv.org

National network of nonprofit and community organizations that provides hospitality to international visitors. Seeks to improve international relations through professional and personal communications and exchanges. Provides training, networking, and information services.

Radio Free Europe/Radio Liberty, *Washington Office, 1201 Connecticut Ave. N.W., 4th Floor 20036; (202) 457-6900. Fax, (202) 457-6992. Jane Lester, Corporate Secretary, (202) 457-6914. Press, (202) 457-6947.*
Web, www.rferl.org

Independent radio broadcast service funded by federal grants to promote and support democracy. Radio Free Europe broadcasts programs to Afghanistan, Bulgaria, the Czech Republic, Estonia, Latvia, Lithuania, Poland, Romania, and Slovakia; programming includes entertainment, news, and specials on political developments in eastern Europe. Radio Liberty broadcasts similar programming to the former Soviet Union. Research materials available to the public by appointment. (Headquarters in Prague.)

Town Affiliation Assn. of the U.S., *Sister Cities International, 1301 Pennsylvania Ave. N.W., #850 20004; (202) 347-8630. Fax, (202) 393-6524. Tim Honey, Executive Director.*
General e-mail, info@sister-cities.org
Web, www.sister-cities.org

Assists U.S. and foreign cities in establishing formal city-to-city affiliations, including exchanges of people, ideas, and materials; serves as program coordinator and information clearinghouse; sponsors youth programs.

Youth for Understanding, *6400 Goldsboro Rd., #100, Bethesda, MD 20817; (240) 235-2100. Fax, (240) 895-2104. Michael Sinnell, President. TTY, (800) 787-8000. Teen Information, (800) TEENAGE.*
Web, www.youthforunderstanding.org

Educational organization that administers cross-cultural exchange programs for secondary school students. Administers scholarship programs that sponsor student exchanges, including the Congress-Bundestag Scholarship Program.

IMMIGRATION AND NATURALIZATION

AGENCIES

Administration for Children and Families (ACF), (Health and Human Services Dept.), Refugee Resettlement, 901 D St. S.W., 6th Floor 20447; (202) 401-9246. Fax, (202) 401-0981. Nguyen Van Hanh, Director. Web, www.acf.dhhs.gov

Directs a domestic resettlement program for refugees; reimburses states for costs incurred in giving refugees monetary and medical assistance; awards funds to private resettlement agencies for providing refugees with monetary assistance and case management; provides states and nonprofit agencies with grants for social services such as English and employment training.

Bureau of Citizenship and Immigration Services (BCIS), (Homeland Security Dept.), Nebraska Ave. Complex, 3801 Nebraska Ave. N.W. 20395; (202) 282-8000 (switchboard). Eduardo Aguirre, Director (Acting). Automated information, (800) 375-5283 or TTY, (800) 767-1833. Web, www.bcis.gov

Responsible for the administration of immigration and naturalization adjudication functions and establishing immigration services policies and priorities.

Justice Dept. (DOJ), Civil Division: Immigration Litigation, 1331 Pennsylvania Ave. N.W., #7025S 20530 (mailing address: P.O. Box 878, Ben Franklin Station 20044); (202) 616-4848. Fax, (202) 616-4948. Thomas W. Hussey, Director. Information, (202) 616-4900. Web, www.usdoj.gov/civil/oil

Handles most civil litigation arising under immigration and nationality laws.

Justice Dept. (DOJ), Executive Office for Immigration Review, 5107 Leesburg Pike, #2600, Falls Church, VA 22041; (703) 305-0169. Fax, (703) 305-0985. Kevin D. Rooney, Director. TTY, (800) 828-1120. Web, www.usdoj.gov/eoir

Quasi-judicial body that includes the Board of Immigration Appeals and offices of the chief immigration judge and the chief administration hearing officer. Interprets immigration laws; conducts hearings and hears appeals on immigration issues.

Justice Dept. (DOJ), Special Investigations, 10th St. and Constitution Ave. N.W., John C. Keeney Bldg, #200 20530; (202) 616-2492. Fax, (202) 616-2491. Eli M. Rosenbaum, Director.

Web, www.usdoj.gov

Identifies Nazi war criminals who illegally entered the United States after World War II. Handles legal action to ensure denaturalization and/or deportation.

State Dept., Visa Services, 2401 E St. N.W., SA-1 #L-703 20522-0106; (202) 663-1225. Fax, (202) 663-1247. Janice Jacobs, Deputy Assistant Secretary. Web, travel.state.gov/visa_services.html

Supervises visa issuance system, which is administered by U.S. consular offices abroad.

CONGRESS

House Judiciary Committee, Subcommittee on Immigration, Border Security, and Claims, B370B RHOB 20515; (202) 225-5727. Fax, (202) 225-3672. Rep. John Hostettler, R-Ind., Chair; George Fishman, Chief Counsel. General e-mail, Judiciary@mail.house.gov Web, www.house.gov/judiciary

Jurisdiction over immigration and naturalization legislation.

Senate Judiciary Committee, Subcommittee on Immigration, Border Security, and Citizenship, SD-520 20510; (202) 224-6098. Fax, (202) 228-0103. Sen. Saxby Chambliss, R-Ga., Chair; David Neal, Chief Counsel. Web, judiciary.senate.gov

Jurisdiction over legislation on refugees, immigration, and naturalization. Oversight of the immigration-related functions of the Homeland Security Dept., the Justice Dept., and the State Dept.; the U.S. Board of Immigration Appeals; international migration and refugee laws and policies; and private immigration relief bills.

INTERNATIONAL ORGANIZATIONS

International Organization for Migration (IOM), Washington Office, 1752 N St. N.W., #700 20036; (202) 862-1826. Fax, (202) 862-1879. Fran Sullivan, Regional Representative. General e-mail, mrfwashington@iom.int Web, www.iom.int

Nonpartisan organization that plans and operates refugee resettlement, national migration, and humanitarian assistance programs at the request of its member governments. Recruits skilled professionals for developing countries. (Headquarters in Geneva.)

NONPROFIT

Alexis de Tocqueville Institution, 1446 E St. S.E. 20003; (202) 548-0006. Kenneth N. Brown, President. General e-mail, kenbrown@adti.net

Web, www.adti.net

Works to increase public understanding of the cultural and economic benefits associated with legal immigration. Supports pro-immigration policy reform.

American Immigration Lawyers Assn., *918 F St. N.W. 20004; (202) 216-2400. Fax, (202) 783-7853. Jeanne Butterfield, Executive Director.*
Web, www.aila.org

Bar association for attorneys interested in immigration law. Provides information and continuing education programs on immigration law and policy; offers workshops and conferences. Monitors legislation and regulations.

Center for Immigration Studies, *1522 K St. N.W., #820 20005-1202; (202) 466-8185. Fax, (202) 466-8076. Mark Krikorian, Executive Director.*
General e-mail, center@cis.org
Web, www.cis.org

Nonpartisan organization that conducts research and policy analysis of the economic, social, demographic, and environmental impact of immigration on the United States. Sponsors symposiums.

Federation for American Immigration Reform,
1666 Connecticut Ave. N.W., #400 20009; (202) 328-7004. Fax, (202) 387-3447. Daniel A. Stein, Executive Director.
General e-mail, fair@fairus.org
Web, www.fairus.org

Organization of individuals interested in immigration reform. Monitors immigration laws and policies.

Immigration and Refugees Services of America,
1717 Massachusetts Ave. N.W., #200 20036; (202) 347-3507. Fax, (202) 347-3418. Lavinia Limon, Executive Director.
Web, www.refugees.org

Helps immigrants and refugees adjust to American society; assists in resettling recently arrived immigrants and refugees; offers information, counseling services, and temporary living accommodations through its member agencies nationwide; issues publications on immigration law, refugees, and refugee resettlement. Operates U.S. Committee for Refugees, which collects and disseminates information on refugee issues in the United States and abroad. Monitors legislation and regulations.

Lutheran Immigration and Refugee Service, *Washington Office, 122 C St. N.W., #125 20001-2172; (202) 783-7509. Fax, (202) 783-7502. Lynette Engelhardt Stott, Director, Government Relations.*
General e-mail, lstott@lirs.org
Web, www.lirs.org

Provides refugees in the United States with resettlement assistance, follow-up services, and immigration counseling. Funds local projects that provide social and legal services to all refugees, including undocumented persons. (Headquarters in Baltimore, Md.)

Migration Policy Institute, *1400 16th St. N.W., #300 20036; (202) 266-1940. Fax, (202) 266-1900. Kathleen Newland, Co-Director; Demetrios G. Papademetriou, Co-Director.*
General e-mail, info@migrationpolicy.org
Web, www.migrationpolicy.org

Studies the movement of people worldwide. Provides analysis, development, and evaluation of migration and refugee policies at local, national, and international levels.

National Council of La Raza, *1111 19th St. N.W., #1000 20036; (202) 785-1670. Fax, (202) 776-1792. Raul Yzaguirre, President.*
General e-mail, info@nclr.org
Web, www.nclr.org

Provides research, policy analysis, and advocacy relating to immigration policy and programs. Monitors federal legislation on immigration, legalization, employer sanctions, employment discrimination, and eligibility of immigrants for federal benefit programs. Assists community-based groups involved in immigration and education services and educates employers about immigration laws.

National Immigration Forum, *220 Eye St. N.E., #220 20002-4352; (202) 544-0004. Fax, (202) 544-1905. Frank Sharry, Executive Director.*
Web, www.immigrationforum.org

Pro-immigration organization that provides research, policy analysis, and updates on immigration policy developments to members. Conducts meetings and publishes newsletters on immigration issues. Assists in the rescue and resettlement of refugees fleeing persecution. Monitors legislation and regulations.

U.S. Conference of Catholic Bishops (USCCB), *Migration and Refugee Services, 3211 4th St. N.E. 20017; (202) 541-3352. Fax, (202) 722-8755. Mark Franken, Executive Director.*
General e-mail, mrs@usccb.org
Web, www.usccb.org/mrs

Advocate for immigrants, refugees, and migrants. Works with legislative and executive branches of U.S. government and with national and international organizations such as the U.N. High Commissioner for Refugees to promote fair and responsive immigration and refugee policy.

INTERNATIONAL LAW AND AGREEMENTS

AGENCIES

Commission on Security and Cooperation in Europe ***(Helsinki Commission),*** *234 FHOB, 3rd and D Sts. S.W. 20515; (202) 225-1901. Fax, (202) 226-4199. Sen. Ben Nighthorse Campbell, R-Colo., Chair; Rep. Christopher H. Smith, R-N.J., Co-Chair; Dorothy Douglas Taft, Chief of Staff.*
Web, www.csce.gov/helsinki.cfm

Independent agency created by Congress. Membership includes individuals from the executive and legislative branches. Monitors and encourages compliance with the Helsinki Accords, a series of agreements with provisions on security, economic, environmental, human rights, and humanitarian issues; conducts hearings; serves as an information clearinghouse for issues in eastern and western Europe, Canada, and the United States relating to the Helsinki Accords.

Federal Bureau of Investigation (FBI), ***(Justice Dept.), International Operations,*** *935 Pennsylvania Ave. N.W., #7443 20535; (202) 324-5904. Fax, (202) 324-5292. Roderick Beverly, Special Agent in Charge.*

Supports FBI involvement in international investigations; oversees liaison offices in U.S. embassies abroad. Maintains contacts with other federal agencies; Interpol; foreign police and security officers based in Washington, D.C.; and national law enforcement associations.

Securities and Exchange Commission, ***International Affairs,*** *450 5th St. N.W., #11-300 20549-1104; (202) 942-2770. Fax, (202) 942-9524. Ethiopis Tafara, Director (Acting).*
Web, www.sec.gov

Acts as liaison with enforcement and diplomatic officials abroad; coordinates international enforcement activities for the securities market; obtains evidence from abroad relating to investigations and litigation. Develops agreements with foreign countries to assist commission enforcement and regulatory efforts.

State Dept., ***International Claims and Investment Disputes,*** *2430 E St. N.W., #203 20037-2800; (202) 776-8360. Fax, (202) 776-8389. Mark A. Clodfelter, Assistant Legal Adviser.*
Web, www.state.gov

Handles claims by foreign governments and their nationals against the U.S. government, as well as claims against the State Dept. for negligence under the Federal Tort Claims Act. Administers the Iranian claims program and negotiates agreements with other foreign governments on claims settlements.

State Dept., ***Law Enforcement and Intelligence Affairs,*** *2201 C St. N.W., #5419 20520; (202) 647-7324. Fax, (202) 647-4802. Linda Jacobson, Assistant Legal Adviser.*
Web, www.state.gov

Negotiates extradition treaties, legal assistance treaties in criminal matters, and other agreements relating to international criminal matters.

State Dept., ***Legal Adviser,*** *2201 C St. N.W., #6423 20520-6310; (202) 647-9598. Fax, (202) 647-7096. William Howard Taft IV, Legal Adviser.*
Web, www.state.gov/s/l

Provides the department with legal advice on domestic and international problems; participates in international negotiations; represents the U.S. government in international litigation and in international conferences related to legal issues.

State Dept., ***Political-Military Affairs,*** *2201 C St. N.W., #6212 20520; (202) 647-9022. Fax, (202) 736-4779. Lincoln P. Bloomfield Jr., Assistant Secretary.*
Web, www.state.gov

Negotiates U.S. military base and operating rights overseas; acts as liaison between the Defense Dept. and State Dept.; controls military travel to sensitive or restricted areas abroad; arranges diplomatic clearance for overflights and ship visits.

State Dept., ***Treaty Affairs,*** *2201 C St. N.W., #5420 20520; (202) 647-1345. Fax, (202) 736-7541. Robert E. Dalton, Assistant Legal Adviser.*
Web, www.state.gov

Provides legal advice on treaties and other international agreements, including constitutional questions, drafting, negotiation, and interpretation of treaties; maintains records of treaties and executive agreements.

Technology Administration ***(Commerce Dept.), International Technology Policy,*** *14th St. and Constitution Ave. N.W., #4821 20230; (202) 482-6351. Fax, (202) 501-6849. Kathryn Sullivan, Director (Acting).*
Web, www.ta.doc.gov

Provides information on foreign research and development; coordinates, on behalf of the Commerce Dept., negotiation of international science and technology agreements.

Transportation Dept. (DOT), ***International Aviation,*** *400 7th St. S.W., #6402 20590; (202) 366-2423. Fax, (202) 366-3694. Paul L. Gretch, Director.*
Web, www.dot.gov

Responsible for international aviation regulation and negotiations, including fares, tariffs, and foreign licenses; represents the United States at international aviation meetings.

CONGRESS

House International Relations Committee, *2170 RHOB 20515; (202) 225-5021. Fax, (202) 226-2831. Rep. Henry J. Hyde, R-Ill., Chair; Thomas E. Mooney, Chief of Staff. Hearing notification line, (202) 225-3184.*
General e-mail, hirc@mail.house.gov
Web, www.house.gov/international_relations

Jurisdiction over legislation on international law enforcement, including narcotics control; boundaries; international terrorism (jurisdiction shared with House Judiciary Committee); international human rights, including implementation of the Universal Declaration of Human Rights; executive agreements; regional security agreements; protection of Americans abroad, including the Foreign Airports Security Act; embassy security; and United Nations organizations.

House Judiciary Committee, *Subcommittee on Immigration, Border Security, and Claims, B370B RHOB 20515; (202) 225-5727. Fax, (202) 225-3672. Rep. John Hostettler, R-Ind., Chair; George Fishman, Chief Counsel.*
General e-mail, Judiciary@mail.house.gov
Web, www.house.gov/judiciary

Jurisdiction over legislation on treaties, conventions, and international agreements; diplomatic immunity; foreign sovereign immunity; and admission and resettlement of refugees.

Senate Foreign Relations Committee, *SD-450 20510; (202) 224-4651. Fax, (202) 228-1608. Sen. Richard G. Lugar, R-Ind., Chair; Kenneth A. Myers, Staff Director.*
Web, foreign.senate.gov

Jurisdiction over legislation on human rights; international boundaries; regional security; executive agreements; international narcotics control; embassy security; international terrorism (jurisdiction shared with Senate Judiciary Committee); and exchange of prisoners with Canada and Mexico.

Senate Governmental Affairs Committee, *Permanent Subcommittee on Investigations, SR-199 20510; (202) 224-3721. Sen. Norm Coleman, R-Minn., Chair; Mary Robertson, Chief Clerk.*
General e-mail, PSI@govt-aff.senate.gov
Web, govt-aff.senate.gov

Investigates international narcotics trafficking.

INTERNATIONAL ORGANIZATIONS

INTERPOL, *Washington Office, INTERPOL-USNCB, U.S. Justice Dept. 20530; (202) 616-9000. Fax, (202) 616-8400. Edgar A. Adamson, Director.*
Web, www.usdoj.gov/usncb

U.S. national central bureau for INTERPOL; participates in international investigations on behalf of U.S. police; coordinates the exchange of investigative information on crimes, including drug trafficking, counterfeiting, missing persons, and terrorism. Coordinates law enforcement requests for investigative assistance in the United States and abroad. Assists with extradition processes. Serves as liaison between foreign and U.S. law enforcement agencies at federal, state, and local levels. (Headquarters in Lyons, France.)

NONPROFIT

American Arbitration Assn., *Federal Center for Dispute Resolution, 601 Pennsylvania Ave. N.W., #700 20004; (202) 737-1460. Fax, (202) 737-2418. S. Pierre Paret, Vice President, Government Relations.*
Web, www.adr.org

Provides dispute resolution services and information. Administers international arbitration and mediation systems. (Headquarters in New York.)

American Bar Assn. (ABA), *International Law and Practice, 740 15th St. N.W., 10th Floor 20005; (202) 662-1660. Fax, (202) 662-1669. Leanne Pfautz, Director.*
Web, www.abanet.org/intlaw

Monitors and makes recommendations concerning developments in the practice of international law that affect ABA members and the public. Conducts programs, including International Legal Exchange, and produces publications covering the practice of international law.

American Society of International Law, *2223 Massachusetts Ave. N.W. 20008-2864; (202) 939-6000. Fax, (202) 797-7133. Charlotte Ku, Executive Director.*
Web, www.asil.org

Membership: lawyers, political scientists, economists, government officials, and students. Conducts research and study programs on international law; sponsors the International Law Students Assn. Library open to the public.

Antarctica Project, *1630 Connecticut Ave. N.W., 3rd Floor 20009; (202) 234-2480. Fax, (202) 387-4823. Beth C. Clark, Director.*
General e-mail, antarctica@igc.org
Web, www.asoc.org

Promotes effective implementation of the Antarctic Treaty System; works to protect the environment of the Antarctic continent. Interests include depletion of ozone in polar regions.

Inter-American Bar Assn., *1211 Connecticut Ave. N.W., #202 20036; (202) 466-5944. Fax, (202) 466-5946. Louis Ferrand, Secretary General.*
General e-mail, iaba@iaba.org
Web, www.iaba.org

Membership: lawyers and bar associations in the Western Hemisphere with associate members in Europe and Asia. Works to promote uniformity of national and international laws; holds conferences; makes recommendations to national governments and organizations. Library open to the public.

World Jurist Assn., *1000 Connecticut Ave. N.W., #202 20036-5302; (202) 466-5428. Fax, (202) 452-8540. Margaret M. Henneberry, Executive Vice President.*
General e-mail, wja@worldjurist.org
Web, www.worldjurist.org

Membership: lawyers, law professors, judges, law students, and nonlegal professionals worldwide. Conducts research; promotes world peace through adherence to international law; holds biennial world conferences. (Affiliates, at same address, include World Assn. of Judges, World Assn. of Law Professors, World Assn. of Lawyers, and World Business Assn.)

Americans Abroad

AGENCIES

Administration for Children and Families (ACF), *(Health and Human Services Dept.), Repatriate Program,* *901 D St. S.W., 8th Floor 20447 (mailing address: 370 L'Enfant Promenade S.W. 20447); (202) 401-9246. Fax, (202) 401-5487. Nguyen Van Hanh, Director.*

Administers and operates a repatriation program available to State Dept.-certified U.S. citizens returning from foreign countries because of destitution, illness, or emergencies. Reimburses state and local governments and community-based organizations for transportation from port of entry and for the temporary costs of food, shelter, and clothing; and medical care, including hospitalization.

Foreign Claims Settlement Commission of the United States *(Justice Dept.), 600 E St. N.W., #6002 20579; (202) 616-6975. Fax, (202) 616-6993. Mauricio Tamargo, Chair; Judith H. Lock, Administrative Officer, (202) 616-6986.*
Web, www.usdoj.gov

Processes claims by U.S. nationals against foreign governments for property losses sustained.

State Dept., *American Citizens Services and Crisis Management, 2201 C St. N.W., #4811 20520-4818; (202) 647-5226. Fax, (202) 647-3732. Elizabeth Kirincich, Director (Acting). Recorded consular information, (202) 647-5225.*
Web, travel.state.gov

Handles matters involving protective services for Americans abroad, including arrests, assistance in death cases, loans, medical emergencies, welfare and whereabouts inquiries, travel warnings and consular information, nationality and citizenship determination, document issuance, judicial and notarial services, estates, property claims, third-country representation, and disaster assistance.

State Dept., *Children's Issues, 2201 C St. N.W., SA-22, #2100 20520-4818; (202) 312-9700. Fax, (202) 312-9743. Michele Bernier-Toth, Director. Recorded consular information, (202) 736-7000. Fax-on-demand, (202) 663-2674. Toll-free, (888) 407-4747.*
Web, travel.state.gov/children's_issues.html

Assists with consular aspects of children's services and fulfills U.S. treaty obligations relating to the abduction of children. Advises foreign service posts on international parental child abduction and transnational adoption.

State Dept., *Consular Affairs: Passport Services, 2201 C St. N.W., #6811 20520; (202) 955-0307. Fax, (202) 647-0341. Frank Moss, Deputy Assistant Secretary. Passport information, (900) 225-5674.*
Web, travel.state.gov/passport_services.html

Administers passport laws and issues passports. (Most branches of the U.S. Postal Service and most U.S. district and state courts are authorized to accept applications and payment for passports and to administer the required oath to U.S. citizens. Completed applications are sent from the post office or court to the nearest State Dept. regional passport office for processing.) Maintains a variety of records received from the Overseas Citizens Services, including consular certificates of witness to marriage and reports of birth and death. (Individuals wishing to apply for a U.S. passport may seek additional information via the phone number or Web address listed above.)

State Dept., *International Claims and Investment Disputes, 2430 E St. N.W., #203 20037-2800; (202) 776-8360. Fax, (202) 776-8389. Mark A. Clodfelter, Assistant Legal Adviser.*

Web, www.state.gov

Handles claims by U.S. government and citizens against foreign governments; handles claims by owners of U.S. flag vessels for reimbursements of fines, fees, licenses, and other direct payments for illegal seizures by foreign governments in international waters under the Fishermen's Protective Act.

State Dept., *Policy Review and Interagency Liaison,* 1800 G St. N.W., #2100 20006; (202) 312-9750. Fax, (202) 312-9744. Ed Betancourt, Director. Recorded consular information, (202) 647-5225. Toll-free, (888) 407-4747.

Web, www.state.gov

Offers guidance concerning the administration and enforcement of laws on citizenship and on the appropriate documentation of Americans traveling and residing abroad; gives advice on legislative matters, including implementation of new laws, and on treaties and agreements; reconsiders the acquisition and loss of U.S. citizenship in complex cases; and administers the overseas federal benefits program.

Boundaries

AGENCIES

Saint Lawrence Seaway Development Corp. *(Transportation Dept.),* 400 7th St. S.W., #5424 20590; (202) 366-0118. Fax, (202) 366-7147. Albert S. Jacquez, Administrator. Information, (202) 366-0091. Toll-free, (800) 785-2779.

Web, www.greatlakes-seaway.com

Operates and maintains the Saint Lawrence Seaway within U.S. territorial limits; conducts development programs and coordinates activities with its Canadian counterpart.

State Dept., *Mexican Affairs: U.S.-Mexico Border,* 2201 C St. N.W., #4258 20520-6258; (202) 647-8529. Fax, (202) 647-5752. Dennis M. Linskey, Border Coordinator.

Web, www.state.gov

Acts as liaison between the United States and Mexico in international boundary and water matters as defined by binational treaties and agreements.

INTERNATIONAL ORGANIZATIONS

International Boundary Commission, United States and Canada, *U.S. Section,* 1250 23rd St. N.W., #100 20037; (202) 736-9100. Fax, (202) 736-9015. Dennis L. Schornack, Commissioner.

Web, www.internationalboundarycommission.org

Defines and maintains the international boundary line between the United States and Canada. Rules on applications for approval of projects affecting boundary or transboundary waters. Assists the United States and Canada in protecting the transboundary environment. Alerts the governments to emerging issues that may give rise to bilateral disputes. Commissioners represent only the commission, not the government that appointed them. (Canadian section in Ottawa.)

International Joint Commission, United States and Canada, *U.S. Section,* 1250 23rd St. N.W., #100 20440; (202) 736-9000. Fax, (202) 736-9015. Dennis L. Schornack, Chair.

Web, www.ijc.org/ijcweb-e.html

Handles disputes concerning the use of boundary waters; negotiates questions dealing with the rights, obligations, and interests of the United States and Canada along the border; establishes procedures for the adjustment and settlement of questions. (Canadian section in Ottawa.)

Extradition

AGENCIES

Justice Dept. (DOJ), *International Affairs,* 1301 New York Ave. N.W., #800 20005 (mailing address: P.O. Box 27330 20038-7330); (202) 514-0000. Fax, (202) 514-0080. Mary Ellen Warlow, Director.

Web, www.usdoj.gov

Performs investigations necessary for extradition of fugitives from the United States and other nations. Handles U.S. and foreign government requests for legal assistance, including documentary evidence.

State Dept., *Law Enforcement and Intelligence Affairs,* 2201 C St. N.W., #5419 20520; (202) 647-7324. Fax, (202) 647-4802. Linda Jacobson, Assistant Legal Adviser.

Web, www.state.gov

Negotiates and approves extradition of fugitives between the United States and other nations.

NONPROFIT

Center for National Security Studies, *Gelman Library, 1120 19th St. N.W., #800 20036; (202) 721-5650. Fax, (202) 530-0128. Kate Martin, Director.*

General e-mail, cnss@gwu.edu

Web, www.cnss.org

Monitors and conducts research on extradition, intelligence, national security, and civil liberties.

Fishing, Law of the Sea

AGENCIES

National Oceanic and Atmospheric Administration (NOAA), *(Commerce Dept.), National Marine Fisheries Service, 1315 East-West Hwy., Silver Spring, MD 20910;*

(301) 713-2239. Fax, (301) 713-2258. William T. Hogarth, Assistant Administrator. Press, (301) 713-2370.
Web, www.nmfs.gov

Administers marine fishing regulations, including offshore fishing rights and international agreements.

State Dept., *Oceans and Fisheries,* 2201 C St. N.W., #7831 20520; (202) 647-2396. Fax, (202) 647-0217. Mary Beth West, Deputy Assistant Secretary.
Web, www.state.gov

Coordinates U.S. negotiations concerning international fishing and oceans issues. Handles both foreign fleets fishing in U.S. waters and U.S. fleets fishing in foreign waters or the open seas.

CONGRESS

House International Relations Committee,
2170 RHOB 20515; (202) 225-5021. Fax, (202) 226-2831. Rep. Henry J. Hyde, R-Ill., Chair; Thomas E. Mooney, Chief of Staff. Hearing notification line, (202) 225-3184.
General e-mail, hirc@mail.house.gov
Web, www.house.gov/international_relations

Jurisdiction over legislation concerning international fisheries agreements and Law of the Sea. (Jurisdiction shared with House Resources and House Transportation and Infrastructure committees.)

House Resources Committee, *Subcommittee on Fisheries, Conservation, Wildlife, and Oceans,*
H2-188 FHOB 20515; (202) 226-0200. Fax, (202) 225-1542. Rep. Wayne T. Gilchrest, R-Md., Chair; Harry Burroughs, Staff Director.
General e-mail, fisheries.subcommittee@mail.house.gov
Web, resourcescommittee.house.gov

Jurisdiction over legislation concerning international fisheries agreements and the U.N. Convention on the Law of the Sea. (Jurisdiction shared with House International Relations and House Transportation and Infrastructure committees.)

House Transportation and Infrastructure Committee, *Subcommittee on Coast Guard and Maritime Transportation,* 507 FHOB 20515; (202) 226-3552. Fax, (202) 226-2524. Rep. Frank A. LoBiondo, R-N.J., Chair; Mark Zachares, Staff Director.
General e-mail, transcomm@mail.house.gov
Web, www.house.gov/transportation

Jurisdiction over legislation concerning Law of the Sea, international arrangements to prevent collisions at sea, and enforcement of laws and treaties on marine pollution control and abatement. (Jurisdiction shared with House International Relations and House Resources committees.)

Senate Commerce, Science, and Transportation Committee, *Subcommittee on Oceans, Fisheries, and Coast Guard,* SH-227 20510; (202) 224-8172. Fax, (202) 224-9934. Sen. Olympia J. Snowe, R-Maine, Chair; Andrew Minkiewicz, Counsel Member.
Web, commerce.senate.gov

Studies issues concerning international fishing laws and Law of the Sea. (Jurisdiction shared with Senate Foreign Relations Committee. Subcommittee does not report legislation.)

Senate Foreign Relations Committee, SD-450 20510; (202) 224-4651. Fax, (202) 228-1608. Sen. Richard G. Lugar, R-Ind., Chair; Kenneth A. Myers, Staff Director.
Web, foreign.senate.gov

Oversight of Law of the Sea matters. (Jurisdiction shared with Senate Commerce, Science, and Transportation Committee.)

NONPROFIT

U.S. Tuna Foundation, 1101 17th St. N.W., #609 20036; (202) 857-0610. Fax, (202) 331-9686. David G. Burney, Executive Director.
Web, www.tunafacts.com

Membership: tuna processors, vessel owners, and fishermen's unions. Provides members with information and research on the tuna industry; offers advice on fisheries to the U.S. delegation to the United Nations Law of the Sea Conference and to other U.S. delegations.

Human Rights

AGENCIES

Commission on Security and Cooperation in Europe *(Helsinki Commission),* 234 FHOB, 3rd and D Sts. S.W. 20515; (202) 225-1901. Fax, (202) 226-4199. Sen. Ben Nighthorse Campbell, R-Colo., Chair; Rep. Christopher H. Smith, R-N.J., Co-Chair; Dorothy Douglas Taft, Chief of Staff.
Web, www.csce.gov/helsinki.cfm

Independent agency created by Congress. Membership includes individuals from the executive and legislative branches. Monitors and encourages compliance with the human rights provisions of the Helsinki Accords; conducts hearings; serves as an information clearinghouse for human rights issues in eastern and western Europe, Canada, and the United States relating to the Helsinki Accords.

Congressional–Executive Commission on China,
242 FHOB 20515; (202) 226-3766. Fax, (202) 226-3804. Rep. Jim Leach, R-Iowa, Chair; Sen. Chuck Hagel, R-Neb., Co-Chair; John Foarde, Staff Director.

General e-mail, infocecc@mail.house.gov

Web, www.cecc.gov

Independent agency created by Congress. Membership includes individuals from the executive and legislative branches. Monitors human rights and the development of the rule of law in the People's Republic of China. Submits an annual report to the president and Congress.

State Dept., *Democracy, Human Rights, and Labor,* 2201 C St. N.W., #7802 20520-7812; (202) 647-2126. Fax, (202) 647-5283. Lorne W. Craner, Assistant Secretary.

Web, www.state.gov/g/drl

Implements U.S. policies relating to human rights, labor, and religious freedom; prepares annual review of human rights worldwide; provides the Immigration and Naturalization Service with advisory opinions regarding asylum petitions.

State Dept., *Global Affairs: International Women's Issues,* 1800 G St. N.W., #2340 20520; (202) 312-9664. Fax, (202) 312-9663. April W. Parmelee, Senior Coordinator.

Web, www.state.gov/g/wi

Works to promote the human rights of women within U.S. foreign policy. Participates in international organizations and conferences; advises other U.S. agencies; disseminates information. Reports to under secretary for global affairs.

U.S. Commission on International Religious Freedom, 800 N. Capitol St. N.W., #790 20002; (202) 523-3240. Fax, (202) 523-5020. Joseph Crapa, Executive Director.

General e-mail, communications@uscirf.gov

Web, uscirf.gov

Agency created by the International Religious Freedom Act of 1998 to monitor religious freedom worldwide and to advise the president, the secretary of state, and Congress on how best to promote it.

CONGRESS

House International Relations Committee, *Subcommittee on International Terrorism, Nonproliferation, and Human Rights,* 2401A RHOB 20515; (202) 226-7820. Fax, (202) 225-7485. Rep. Elton Gallegly, R-Calif., Chair; Richard Mereu, Staff Director.

Web, www.house.gov/international_relations

Oversight of and legislation pertaining to implementation of the Universal Declaration of Human Rights and other matters relating to internationally-recognized human rights, including sanctions legislation aimed at the promotion of human rights and democracy generally.

NONPROFIT

Amnesty International USA, *Washington Office,* 600 Pennsylvania Ave. S.E., 5th Floor 20003; (202) 544-0200. Fax, (202) 546-7142. Maria Alexandra Arriaga, Director.

Web, www.amnestyusa.org

International organization that works for the release of men and women imprisoned anywhere in the world for their beliefs, political affiliation, color, ethnic origin, sex, language, or religion, provided they have neither used nor advocated violence. Opposes torture and the death penalty; urges fair and prompt trials for all political prisoners. (U.S. headquarters in New York.)

Center for Human Rights and Humanitarian Law, 4801 Massachusetts Ave. N.W. 20016-8084; (202) 274-4180. Fax, (202) 274-0783. Harder Harris, Executive Director.

Web, www.wcl.american.edu/pub/humright/info/info.html

Seeks to promote human rights and humanitarian law. Establishes training programs for judges, lawyers, and law schools; assists emerging democracies and other nations in developing laws and institutions that protect human rights; organizes conferences with public and private institutions; coordinates annual Inter-American moot court competition.

Human Rights Watch, *Washington Office,* 1630 Connecticut Ave. N.W., #500 20009; (202) 612-4321. Fax, (202) 612-4333. Anderson Allen, Office Manager.

General e-mail, hrwdc@hrw.org

Web, www.hrw.org

International, nonpartisan human rights organization that monitors human rights violations worldwide. Subdivided into five regional concentrations—Africa, Americas, Asia, Europe and Central Asia, and Middle East. Coordinates thematic projects on women's rights, arms sales, and prisons. Sponsors fact-finding missions to various countries; publicizes violations and encourages international protests; maintains file on human rights violations. (Headquarters in New York.)

International Assn. of Official Human Rights Agencies, 444 N. Capitol St. N.W., #536 20001; (202) 624-5410. Fax, (202) 624-8185. Shannon Bennett, Executive Director.

General e-mail, iaohra@sso.org

Web, www.sso.org/iaohra

Works with government and human rights agencies worldwide to identify needs common to civil rights enforcement. Offers management training for human rights executives and civil rights workshops for criminal justice agencies; develops training programs in investigative techniques, settlement and conciliation, and legal theory. Serves as an information clearinghouse on human rights laws and enforcement.

International Human Rights Law Group, *1200 18th St. N.W., #602 20036; (202) 822-4600. Fax, (202) 822-4606. Gay McDougall, Executive Director.*
General e-mail, humanrights@hrlawgroup.org
Web, www.hrlawgroup.org

Public interest law center concerned with promoting and protecting international human rights. Conducts educational programs and conferences; provides information and legal assistance regarding human rights violations; monitors the electoral and judicial process in several countries.

International Justice Mission, *P.O. Box 58147 20037-8147; (703) 465-5495. Fax, (703) 465-5499. Gary A. Haugen, President.*
General e-mail, contact@ijm.org
Web, www.ijm.org

Seeks to help people suffering injustice and oppression who cannot rely on local authorities for relief. Documents and monitors conditions of abuse and oppression, educates churches and the public about abuses, and mobilizes intervention on behalf of victims.

Lawyers Committee for Human Rights, *Washington Office, 100 Maryland Ave. N.E., #500 20002-5625; (202) 547-5692. Fax, (202) 543-5999. Elisa Massimino, Director.*
General e-mail, wdc@lchr.org
Web, www.lchr.org

Promotes human rights as guaranteed by the International Bill of Human Rights. Mobilizes the legal community to protect the rule of law. (Headquarters in New York.)

Robert F. Kennedy Memorial, *Center for Human Rights, 1367 Connecticut Ave. N.W., #200 20036-1859; (202) 463-7575. Fax, (202) 463-6606. Lynn Delaney, Executive Director; Todd Howland, Center Director.*
General e-mail, hrcenter@rfkmemorial.org
Web, www.rfkmemorial.org

Presents annual human rights award and carries out programs that support the work of the award laureates in their countries. Investigates and reports on human rights; campaigns to heighten awareness of these issues, stop abuses, and encourage governments, international organizations, and corporations to adopt policies that ensure respect for human rights.

Rugmark Foundation, *733 15th St. N.W., #912 20005; (202) 347-4205. Fax, (202) 347-4885. Nina Smith, Executive Director.*

General e-mail, info@rugmark.org
Web, www.rugmark.org

International human rights organization working to end child labor in Indian, Nepalese, and Pakistani carpet industries. Runs schools and rehabilitation centers for former child workers.

Narcotics Trafficking

AGENCIES

Defense Dept. (DoD), *Counternarcotics, 1510 Defense Pentagon 20301-1510; (703) 697-6000. Fax, (703) 697-3323. Andre Hollis, Deputy Assistant Secretary.*
Web, www.defenselink.mil/policy/solic/cn

Coordinates and monitors Defense Dept. support of civilian drug law enforcement agencies and interagency efforts to detect and monitor the maritime and aerial transit of illegal drugs into the United States. Represents the secretary on drug control matters outside the department.

Drug Enforcement Administration (DEA), *(Justice Dept.), 700 Army-Navy Dr., Arlington, VA 22202 (mailing address: Drug Enforcement Administration, 2401 Jefferson Davis Hwy., Alexandria, VA 22301); (202) 307-8000. Fax, (202) 307-7965. John J. Brown III, Administrator (Acting). Press, (202) 307-7977. Locator, (202) 307-4132.*
Web, www.dea.gov

Assists foreign narcotics agents; cooperates with the State Dept., embassies, the Agency for International Development, and international organizations to strengthen narcotics law enforcement and to reduce supply and demand in developing countries; trains and advises narcotics enforcement officers in developing nations.

State Dept., *International Narcotics and Law Enforcement Affairs, 2201 C St. N.W., #7333 20520-7512; (202) 647-8464. Fax, (202) 736-4885. Paul Simons, Assistant Secretary (Acting).*
Web, www.state.gov

Coordinates international drug control activities, including policy development, diplomatic initiatives, bilateral and multilateral assistance for crop control, interdiction and related enforcement activities in producer and transit nations, development assistance, technical assistance for demand reduction, and training for foreign personnel in narcotics enforcement and related procedures.

U.S. Coast Guard (USCG), *(Homeland Security Dept.), Law Enforcement, 2100 2nd St. S.W., #3110 20593-0001; (202) 267-1890. Fax, (202) 267-4082. Capt. Kenneth A. Ward, Chief.*

Web, www.uscg.mil/hq/g-o/g-opl/mle/welcome.htm

Enforces or assists in the enforcement of federal laws and treaties and other international agreements to which the United States is party, on, over, and under the high seas and waters subject to the jurisdiction of the United States; conducts investigations into suspected violations of laws and international agreements concerning narcotics and migration interdiction, and the enforcement of fisheries.

INTERNATIONAL TRADE AND DEVELOPMENT

AGENCIES

Advisory Committee for Trade Policy and Negotiations *(Executive Office of the President), 600 17th St. N.W., #100 20508; (202) 395-6120. Fax, (202) 395-3692. Christopher Padilla, Assistant U.S. Trade Representative for Intergovernmental Affairs, and Public Liaison.*

Serves as chief private sector advisory committee for the president, U.S. trade representative, and Congress on all matters concerning U.S. trade policy. Interests include the North American Free Trade Agreement (NAFTA) and the World Trade Organization (WTO).

Agency for International Development (USAID), *Global Trade and Technology Network, 1301 Pennsylvania Ave. N.W., #925 20004; (202) 628-9750. Fax, (202) 628-9740. Esen Senli, Program Director.*

Web, www.usgtn.net

Facilitates the transfer of U.S. technology and services to developing countries by matching a local company's needs with U.S. firms equipped to provide the appropriate technology and other solutions. Focuses primarily on agriculture, communications, information technology, environment and energy, and health technology industries. Implemented through cooperative agreement with International Executive Service Corp. business.

Antitrust Division *(Justice Dept.), Foreign Commerce, 601 D St. N.W., #10024 20530; (202) 514-2464. Fax, (202) 514-4508. Edward T. Hand, Chief.*

Web, www.usdoj.gov/atr

Acts as the division's liaison with foreign governments and international organizations including the European Union. Works with the State Dept. to exchange information with foreign governments concerning investigations involving foreign corporations and nationals.

Bureau of Customs and Border Protection *(Homeland Security Dept.), 1300 Pennsylvania Ave. N.W.,*

#4.4A 20229; (202) 927-2001. Fax, (202) 927-1380. Robert C. Bonner, Commissioner. Information, (202) 354-1000. Library, (202) 927-1350. Press, (202) 927-1790.

Web, www.customs.gov

Assesses and collects duties and taxes on imported merchandise; processes persons and baggage entering the United States; collects import and export data for international trade statistics; controls export carriers and goods to prevent fraud and smuggling. Library open to the public.

Bureau of Customs and Border Protection *(Homeland Security Dept.), Trade Compliance and Facilitation, 1300 Pennsylvania Ave. N.W., #5.2A 20229; (202) 927-0300. Fax, (202) 927-1096. Elizabeth Durant, Executive Director.*

Web, www.customs.gov

Enforces compliance with all commercial import requirements; collects import statistics; assesses and collects countervailing and antidumping duties after determinations have been made by the Commerce Dept. in conjunction with the U.S. International Trade Commission.

Bureau of Industry and Security *(Commerce Dept.), 14th St. and Constitution Ave. N.W., #3898 20230; (202) 482-1427. Fax, (202) 482-2387. Kenneth I. Juster, Under Secretary for Export Administration, (202) 482-1455. Press, (202) 482-2721. Export licensing information, (202) 482-4811.*

Web, www.bxa.doc.gov

Administers Export Administration Act; coordinates export administration programs of federal departments and agencies; maintains control lists and performs export licensing for the purposes of national security, foreign policy, and short supply. Monitors impact of foreign boycotts on the United States; ensures availability of goods and services essential to industrial performance on contracts for national defense. Assesses availability of foreign products and technology to maintain control lists and licensing.

Census Bureau *(Commerce Dept.), Foreign Trade Statistics, Suitland and Silver Hill Rds., Suitland, MD 20772; (301) 763-2255. Fax, (301) 457-2645. C. Harvey Monk Jr., Chief. Trade data inquiries, (301) 763-2227.*

Web, www.census.gov/foreign-trade/www/index.html

Provides data on all aspects of foreign trade in commodities.

Commerce Dept., *International Investment, 1441 L St. N.W., #7005 20230; (202) 606-9807. Fax, (202) 606-5318. Vacant, Chief. Information, (202) 606-9800.*

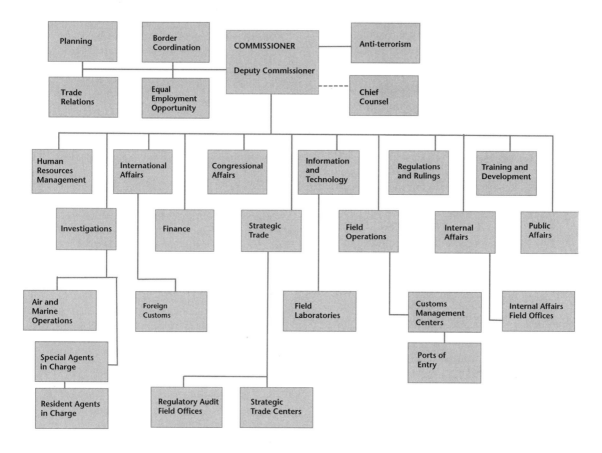

Web, www.bea.gov

Compiles statistics under the International Invest-ment and Trade in Services Survey Act for an ongoing study of foreign direct investment in the United States and direct investment abroad by the United States. (Visit www.bea.gov/bea/surveys/iussurv.htm for information on the surveys.)

Economic Development Administration *(Commerce Dept.), Trade Adjustment and Technical Assistance,* *14th St. and Constitution Ave. N.W., #7315 20230; (202) 482-2127. Fax, (202) 482-0466. Tony Meyer, Coordinator. Web, www.doc.gov/eda*

Assists U.S. firms in increasing their competitiveness against foreign imports. Certifies eligibility and provides domestic firms and industries adversely affected by increased imports with technical assistance under provi-sions of the Trade Act of 1974. Administers ten regional Trade Adjustment Assistance Centers that offer services to eligible U.S. firms.

Export-Import Bank of the United States, *811 Ver-mont Ave. N.W. 20571; (202) 565-3500. Fax, (202) 565-3513. Philip Merrill, Chair; Eduardo Aguirre, Vice Chair. Press, (202) 565-3200. TTY, (202) 565-3377. Toll-free hot-line, (800) 565-3946; in Washington, (202) 565-3946.* Web, www.exim.gov

Independent agency of the U.S. government. Aids in financing exports of U.S. goods and services; offers direct credit to borrowers outside the United States; guarantees export loans made by commercial lenders, working capi-tal guarantees, and export credit insurance; conducts an intermediary loan program. Hotline advises businesses in using U.S. government export programs.

Federal Trade Commission (FTC), *Competition: International Antitrust, 600 Pennsylvania Ave. N.W.,*

#H382 20580; (202) 326-3251. Fax, (202) 326-2884. Randolph W. Tritell, Assistant Director.
Web, www.ftc.gov

Assists in the enforcement of antitrust laws by arranging appropriate cooperation and coordination with foreign governments in international cases with the antitrust division of the Justice Dept.; negotiates bilateral and multilateral antitrust agreements and represents the U.S. in international antitrust policy forums.

Foreign Trade Zones Board *(Commerce Dept.),*
1401 Constitution Ave. N.W., FCB #4100W 20230; (202) 482-2862. Fax, (202) 482-0002. Dennis Puccinelli, Executive Secretary.
Web, www.ia.ita.doc.gov/ftzpage

Authorizes public and private corporations to establish foreign trade zones to which foreign and domestic goods can be brought without being subject to customs duties.

International Trade Administration (ITA), *(Commerce Dept.), 14th St. and Constitution Ave. N.W., #3850 20230; (202) 482-2867. Fax, (202) 482-4821. Grant D. Aldonas, Under Secretary. Information, (202) 482-3808. Press, (202) 482-3809. Publications, (202) 482-5487. Trade information, (800) 872-8723.*
Web, www.trade.gov

Serves as the focal point of operational responsibilities in nonagricultural world trade. Participates in formulating international trade policy and implements programs to promote world trade and strengthen the international trade and investment position of the United States. Library open to the public.

International Trade Administration (ITA), *(Commerce Dept.), Export Promotion Services, 14th St. and Constitution Ave. N.W., #2810 20230; (202) 482-6220. Fax, (202) 482-2526. Nealton J. Burnham, Deputy Assistant Secretary.*
Web, www.export.gov

Promotes and directs programs to expand exports abroad; manages overseas trade missions; conducts trade fair certification programs. Participates in trade fairs and technology seminars to introduce American products abroad. Provides the business community with sales and trade information through an automated system, which allows a direct connection between U.S. and overseas offices.

International Trade Administration (ITA), *(Commerce Dept.), Import Administration, 14th St. and Constitution Ave. N.W., #3099B 20230; (202) 482-1780. Fax, (202) 482-0947. Joe Spetrini, Assistant Secretary (Acting).*
Web, ia.ita.doc.gov

Enforces antidumping and countervailing duty statutes if foreign goods are subsidized or sold at less than fair market value. Evaluates and processes applications by U.S. international air- and seaport communities seeking to establish limited duty-free zones. Administers the Statutory Import Program, which governs specific tariff schedules and imports and determines whether property left abroad by U.S. agencies may be imported back into the United States.

International Trade Administration (ITA), *(Commerce Dept.), Market Access and Compliance, 14th St. and Constitution Ave. N.W., #3868A 20230; (202) 482-3022. Fax, (202) 482-5444. William H. Lash III, Assistant Secretary.*
Web, www.mac.doc.gov

Develops and implements trade and investment policies affecting countries, regions, or international organizations to improve U.S. market access abroad. Provides information and analyses of foreign business and economic conditions to the U.S. private sector; monitors consultation and renegotiation of the MTN (Multilateral Trade Negotiations) affecting specific areas; represents the United States in many other trade negotiations.

International Trade Administration (ITA), *(Commerce Dept.), NAFTA and Inter-American Affairs, 14th St. and Constitution Ave. N.W., #3024 20230; (202) 482-0393. Fax, (202) 482-5865. Juliet Bender, Director.*
Web, www.ita.doc.gov

Coordinates Commerce Dept. activities regarding NAFTA (North American Free Trade Agreement), FTAA (Free Trade Areas of the Americas), and U.S.–Chile Free Trade Agreement.

International Trade Administration (ITA), *(Commerce Dept.), Trade and Economic Analysis, 14th St. and Constitution Ave. N.W., #2815 20230; (202) 482-5145. Fax, (202) 482-4614. Jeffrey Lins, Director (Acting).*
Web, www.ita.doc.gov/tradestats

Monitors and analyzes U.S. international trade and competitive performance, foreign direct investment in the United States, and international economic factors affecting U.S. trade; identifies future trends and problems. Annual reports include *U.S. Industrial Trade Outlook* and *Foreign Direct Investment in the United States: Transactions.* Foreign Trade Reference Room open to the public.

International Trade Administration (ITA), *(Commerce Dept.), Trade Development, 14th St. and Constitution Ave. N.W., #3832 20230; (202) 482-1461. Fax, (202) 482-5697. Linda M. Conlin, Assistant Secretary.*
Web, www.ita.doc.gov/td/td_home/tdhome.html

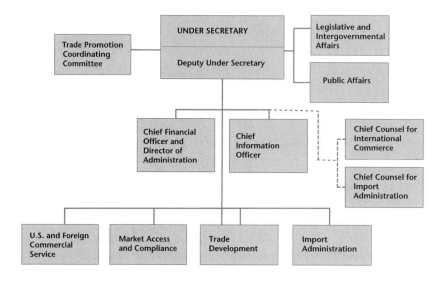

Seeks to strengthen the international competitiveness of U.S. businesses; coordinates export promotion programs and trade missions; compiles and analyzes trade data. Divisions focus on basic industries; service industries and finance; technology and aerospace; textiles, apparel, and consumer goods; tourism; and environmental technologies exports.

International Trade Administration (ITA), *(Commerce Dept.), Trade Information Center, 14th St. and Constitution Ave. N.W., #M800RRB 20230; (202) 482-0543. Fax, (202) 482-4473. Wendy Smith, Director. Information, (800) 872-8723.*
General e-mail, tic@ita.doc.gov
Web, www.trade.gov/td/tic

Counsels U.S. business firms on export matters and on programs and services provided by the agencies that are members of the Trade Promotion Coordinating Committee to facilitate exports. Agencies include the Agriculture and Commerce departments, Export-Import Bank, Overseas Private Investment Corp., Agency for International Development, and others.

International Trade Administration (ITA), *(Commerce Dept.), U.S. and Foreign Commercial Service, 14th St. and Constitution Ave. N.W., #3802 20230; (202) 482-5777. Fax, (202) 482-5013. Maria Cino, Assistant Secretary.*
Web, www.usatrade.gov

Promotes the export of U.S. goods and services; protects and advocates U.S. business interests abroad; provides counseling and information on overseas markets, international contacts, and trade promotion.

National Institute of Standards and Technology (NIST), *(Commerce Dept.), National Center for Standards and Certification Information, 100 Bureau Dr., MS 2150, Gaithersburg, MD 20899-2150; (301) 975-4040. Fax, (301) 926-1559. Carmina Londono, Chief.*
Web, ts.nist.gov/ts/htdocs/210/ncsci/ncsci.htm

Provides research services on standards, technical regulations, and conformity assessment procedures for nonagricultural products. Serves as central repository for standards-related information in the United States. Has access to U.S., foreign, and international documents and contact points through its role as the U.S. national inquiry point under the World Trade Organization Agreement on Technical Barriers to Trade. Standards Coordination and Conformity group receives submissions from selected countries of proposed standards for review by U.S. technical experts.

Overseas Private Investment Corp., *1100 New York Ave. N.W. 20527; (202) 336-8400. Fax, (202) 408-9859. Peter S. Watson, President; Ross J. Connelly, Executive Vice President. Press, (202) 336-8690.*
Web, www.opic.gov

Provides assistance through political risk insurance, direct loans, and loan guarantees to qualified U.S. private investors to support their investments in less developed countries. Offers preinvestment information and counseling. Provides insurance against the risks of inconvertibility of local currency; expropriation; and war, revolution, insurrection, or civil strife.

President's Export Council *(Commerce Dept.),* *14th St. and Constitution Ave. N.W., #2015B 20230; (202) 482-1124. Fax, (202) 482-4452. J. Marc Chittum, Director.*
Web, www.ita.doc.gov/pec

Advises the president on all aspects of export trade including export controls, promotion, and expansion.

Small Business Administration (SBA), *International Trade, 409 3rd St. S.W., 8th Floor 20416; (202) 205-6720. Fax, (202) 205-7272. Manuel A. Rosales, Assistant Administrator.*
Web, www.sba.gov/oit

Offers instruction, assistance, and information on exporting through counseling and conferences. Helps businesses gain access to export financing through loan guarantee programs.

State Dept., *Commercial and Business Affairs, 2201 C St. N.W., #2318 20520-5820; (202) 647-1625. Fax, (202) 647-3953. J. Frank Mermoud, Special Representative for Business Affairs.*
General e-mail, cbaweb@state.gov
Web, www.state.gov/e/eb/cba

Serves as primary contact in the State Dept. for U.S. businesses. Coordinates efforts to facilitate U.S. business interests abroad, ensures that U.S. business interests are given sufficient consideration in foreign policy, and provides assistance to firms with problems overseas (such as claims and trade complaints). Works with agencies in the Trade Promotion Coordinating Committee to support U.S. business interests overseas.

State Dept., *Economic and Business Affairs Bureau, 2201 C St. N.W., #6828 20520-5820; (202) 647-7971. Fax, (202) 647-5713. E. Anthony Wayne, Assistant Secretary.*
Web, www.state.gov/e/eb

Formulates and implements policies related to U.S. economic relations with foreign countries, including international business practices, communications and information, trade, finance, investment, development, natural resources, energy, and transportation.

State Dept., *Economic, Business, and Agricultural Affairs, 2201 C St. N.W., #7256 20520-5820; (202) 647-7575. Fax, (202) 647-9763. Alan Larson, Under Secretary.*
Web, www.state.gov/e

Advises the secretary on formulation and conduct of foreign economic policies and programs, including international monetary and financial affairs, trade, telecommunications, energy, agriculture, commodities, investments, and international transportation issues. Coordinates economic summit meetings.

State Dept., *Economic Sanctions Policy, 2201 C St. N.W., #4535 20520; (202) 647-7489. Fax, (202) 647-4064. George A. Glass, Director.*
Web, www.state.gov

Develops and implements U.S. foreign policy sanctions of embargo and terrorist listed countries. Coordinates U.S. participation in multilateral strategic trade control and revisions related to the export of strategically critical high-technology goods. Cooperates with the Commerce, Defense, and Treasury departments regarding export controls.

State Dept., *Investment Affairs, 2201 C St. N.W., #4820 20520-5820; (202) 736-4762. Fax, (202) 647-0320. Wesley S. Scholz, Director.*
Web, www.state.gov

Develops U.S. investment policy. Makes policy recommendations regarding multinational enterprises and the expropriation of and compensation for U.S. property overseas. Negotiates bilateral and multilateral investment agreements.

State Dept., *Trade Policy and Programs, 2201 C St. N.W., #6828, EB/TPP 20520-5820; (202) 647-5991. Fax, (202) 647-5713. Shaun Donnelly, Deputy Assistant Secretary.*
General e-mail, ebtpp@state.gov
Web, www.state.gov/e/eb/tpp

Develops and administers policies and programs on international trade, including trade negotiations and agreements, import relief, unfair trade practices, trade relations with developing countries, export development, and export controls (including controls imposed for national security or foreign policy purposes).

Trade Promotion Coordinating Committee, *14th St. and Constitution Ave. N.W., #3051 20230; (202) 482-5455. Fax, (202) 482-4139. Donald L. Evans, Chair; Jeri Jensen-Moran, Director.*

Coordinates all export promotion and export financing activities of the U.S. government. Composed of representatives from the departments of Commerce, State, Treasury, Defense, Interior, Agriculture, Labor, Transportation, and Energy, OMB, U.S. Trade Representative, U.S. Information Agency, Council of Economic Advisers, EPA, Small Business Administration, AID, Export-

Import Bank, Overseas Private Investment Corporation, and the U.S. Trade and Development Agency.

Treasury Dept., *Foreign Assets Control,* *1500 Pennsylvania Ave. N.W., Annex Bldg., #2233 20220; (202) 622-2500. Fax, (202) 622-1657. R. Richard Newcomb, Director. Fax-on-demand, (202) 622-0077.*
Web, www.ustreas.gov/ofac

Has authority under the revised Trading with the Enemy Act, the International Emergency Economic Powers Act, and the United Nations Participation Act to control financial and commercial dealings with certain countries and their foreign nationals in times of war or emergencies. Regulations involving foreign assets control, narcotics, nonproliferation, and commercial transactions currently apply in varying degrees to Angola, Cuba, Iran, Iraq, Libya, North Korea, Sierra Leone, Sudan, Taliban, and Yugoslavia.

Treasury Dept., *International Investment,* *1440 New York Ave. N.W., #4209 20220; (202) 622-1860. Fax, (202) 622-0391. Gay Hartwell Sills, Director.*
Web, www.ustreas.gov

Advises senior department officials on direct foreign investment.

Treasury Dept., *International Trade,* *1440 New York Ave. N.W., #4109 20005; (202) 622-0141. Fax, (202) 622-1731. Mary E. Chaves, Director.*
Web, www.ustreas.gov

Formulates Treasury Dept. foreign trade policies and coordinates them with other agencies through the U.S. Trade Representative.

U.S. International Trade Commission, *500 E St. S.W. 20436; (202) 205-2000. Fax, (202) 205-2698. Deanna Tanner Okun, Chair. Press, (202) 205-1819. Library Reference, (202) 205-2630.*
Web, www.usitc.gov

Provides Congress, the president, and government agencies with technical information and advice on trade and tariff matters. Determines the impact of imports on U.S. industries in antidumping and countervailing duty investigations. Directs actions against certain unfair trade practices, such as intellectual property infringement. Investigates and reports on U.S. industries and the global trends that affect them. Publishes the *Harmonized Tariff Schedule of the United States.* Library open to the public.

U.S. Trade and Development Agency, *1000 Wilson Blvd., #1660, Arlington, VA 22209-2131; (703) 875-4357. Fax, (703) 875-4009. Thelma J. Askey, Director.*

General e-mail, info@tda.gov
Web, www.tda.gov

Assists U.S. companies exporting to developing and middle-income countries. Provides grants for feasibility studies. Offers technical assistance and identifies commercial opportunities in these countries.

U.S. Trade Representative (*Executive Office of the President*), *600 17th St. N.W., #209 20508; (202) 395-6890. Fax, (202) 395-4549. Ambassador Robert B. Zoellick, U.S. Trade Representative. Information, (202) 395-8787. Press, (202) 395-3230.*
Web, www.ustr.gov

Serves as principal adviser to the president and primary trade negotiator on international trade policy. Develops and coordinates U.S. trade policy including commodity and direct investment matters; import remedies; East-West trade policy; U.S. export expansion policy; and the implementation of MTN (Multilateral Trade Negotiations) agreements. Conducts international trade negotiations and represents the United States in World Trade Organization (WTO) matters.

CONGRESS

House Appropriations Committee, *Subcommittee on Commerce, Justice, State, and the Judiciary,* H309 CAP 20515; (202) 225-3351. Rep. Frank R. Wolf, R-Va., Chair; Mike Ringler, Staff Director.*
Web, www.house.gov/appropriations

Jurisdiction over legislation to appropriate funds for the Commerce Dept., the Office of the U.S. Trade Representative, and the International Trade Commission.

House Energy and Commerce Committee, *Subcommittee on Commerce, Trade, and Consumer Protection,* 2125 RHOB 20515; (202) 225-2927. Fax, (202) 225-1919. Rep. Cliff Stearns, R-Fla., Chair.*
General e-mail, commerce@mail.house.gov
Web, energycommerce.house.gov

Jurisdiction over foreign commerce. Regulation of travel and tourism.

House Select Committee on Homeland Security, *2402 RHOB 20515; (202) 226-8417. Rep. Christopher Cox, R-Calif., Chair; John C. Gannon, Staff Director.*
Web, hsc.house.gov

Oversees the Bureau of Customs and Border Protection.

House Small Business Committee, *Subcommittee on Tax, Finance, and Exports,* B363 RHOB 20515; (202) 226-2630. Fax, (202) 225-8950. Rep. Pat Toomey, R-Pa., Chair; Sean McGraw, Staff Director.*

General e-mail, smbiz@mail.house.gov

Web, www.house.gov/smbiz

Jurisdiction over legislation on export expansion as it relates to small business.

House Ways and Means Committee, *Subcommittee on Trade,* 1104 LHOB 20515; (202) 225-6649. Fax, (202) 226-0158. Rep. Philip M. Crane, R-Ill., Chair; Angela Ellard, Staff Director.

Web, waysandmeans.house.gov

Jurisdiction over legislation on tariffs, trade, and customs. Authorizes budgets for the Bureau of Customs and Border Protection, U.S. International Trade Commission, and the Office of the U.S. Trade Representative.

Joint Economic Committee, SD-G01 20510; (202) 224-5171. Sen. Robert F. Bennett, R-Utah, Chair; Donald Marron, Executive Director.

General e-mail, jec@jec.house.gov

Web, jec.senate.gov

Studies and makes recommendations on international economic policy and programs, trade, and foreign investment policy; monitors economic policy in foreign countries.

Senate Appropriations Committee, *Subcommittee on Commerce, Justice, State, and the Judiciary,* S-206 CAP 20510; (202) 224-7277. Fax, (202) 228-0587. Sen. Judd Gregg, R-N.H., Chair; James Morhard, Clerk.

Web, appropriations.senate.gov

Jurisdiction over legislation to appropriate funds for the Commerce Dept., the Securities and Exchange Commission, the Small Business Administration, the Competitiveness Policy Council, the Federal Trade Commission, the International Trade Commission, and the Office of the U.S. Trade Representative.

Senate Banking, Housing, and Urban Affairs Committee, *Subcommittee on International Trade and Finance,* SD-534 20510; (202) 224-4224. Sen. Chuck Hagel, R-Neb., Chair; Dayna Cade, Staff Director.

Web, banking.senate.gov

Jurisdiction over legislation on international monetary and exchange rate policies, international capital flows, foreign investments in the United States, export control, foreign trade promotion, the Export-Import Bank, the Export Administration Act, and the revised Trading with the Enemy Act, which authorizes trade restrictions. (Some jurisdictions shared with Senate Finance and Foreign Relations committees.)

Senate Finance Committee, *Subcommittee on International Trade,* SD-219 20510; (202) 224-4515. Sen. Craig Thomas, R-Wyo., Chair; Everett Eissenstadt, Counsel.

Web, finance.senate.gov

Holds hearings on tariff and trade legislation; oversees the Bureau of Customs and Border Protection.

Senate Foreign Relations Committee, *Subcommittee on International Economic Policy, Export, and Trade Promotion,* SD-446 20510; (202) 224-4651. Sen. Chuck Hagel, R-Neb., Chair; Mark Lagon, Professional Staff Member.

Web, foreign.senate.gov

Jurisdiction over legislation to encourage foreign trade and to protect American business interests abroad. Jurisdiction over legislation affecting multinational corporations; balance of payments; the African Development Bank; the World Bank; the Asian Development Bank; the Inter-American Development Bank; the Overseas Private Investment Corp.; the Trade Development Agency; the International Monetary Fund, the Export-Import Bank, and other international monetary organizations; international economic and monetary policy as it relates to U.S. foreign policy. (Jurisdiction shared with the Senate Finance and Senate Banking, Housing, and Urban Affairs committees.)

Senate Small Business and Entrepreneurship Committee, SR-428A 20510; (202) 224-5175. Fax, (202) 228-1128. Sen. Olympia J. Snowe, R-Maine, Chair; Mark Warren, Staff Director.

Web, sbc.senate.gov

Jurisdiction over legislation on export expansion as it relates to small business.

INTERNATIONAL ORGANIZATIONS

European Commission, *Press and Public Affairs, Washington Office,* 2300 M St. N.W. 20037; (202) 862-9500. Fax, (202) 429-1766. Willy Helin, Director; Günter Burghardt, Ambassador.

Web, www.eurunion.org

Provides information on European Union energy policy, initiatives, research activities, and selected statistics. Library open to the public by appointment. (Headquarters in Brussels.)

Food and Agriculture Organization of the United Nations (FAO), *Liaison Office for North America,* 2175 K St. N.W., #300 20437-0001; (202) 653-2400. Fax, (202) 653-5760. Charles H. Riemenschneider, Director. Library, (202) 653-2402. Press, (202) 653-0011.

Web, www.fao.org

Offers development assistance; collects, analyzes, and disseminates information; provides policy and planning advice to governments; acts as an international forum for debate on food and agricultural issues, including animal health and production, fisheries, and forestry; encourages sustainable agricultural development and a long-term strategy for the conservation and management of natural resources. (International headquarters in Rome.)

Inter-American Development Bank, *1300 New York Ave. N.W. 20577; (202) 623-1100. Fax, (202) 623-3096. Enrique V. Iglesias, President; Jose Fourquet, U.S. Executive Director, (202) 623-1031. Information, (202) 623-1000. Library, (202) 623-3211. Press, (202) 623-1371. Web, www.iadb.org*

Promotes, through loans and technical assistance, the investment of public and private capital in member countries of Latin America and the Caribbean for social and economic development purposes. Facilitates economic integration of the Latin American region. Library open to the public by appointment.

International Bank for Reconstruction and Development (World Bank), *1818 H St. N.W., MC 12-750 20433; (202) 477-1234. Fax, (202) 522-3031. James D. Wolfensohn, President; Carole Brookins, U.S. Executive Director. Press, (202) 473-1800. Publications, (703) 661-1580. Web, www.worldbank.org*

International development institution funded by membership subscriptions and borrowings on private capital markets. Encourages the flow of public and private foreign investment into developing countries through loans and technical assistance; collects data on selected economic indicators, world trade, and external public debt. Finances economic development projects in agriculture, environmental protection, education, public utilities, telecommunications, water supply, sewerage, public health, and other areas.

International Centre for Settlement of Investment Disputes, *1818 H St. N.W., MSN MC6-611 20433; (202) 458-1534. Fax, (202) 522-2615. Ko-Yung Tung, Secretary General. Web, www.icsid.org*

World Bank affiliate that handles the conciliation and arbitration of investment disputes between contracting states and foreign investors.

International Development Assn., *1818 H St. N.W. 20433; (202) 458-5522. Fax, (202) 477-0861. Vacant, Director. Web, www.worldbank.org/ida*

Affiliate of the World Bank funded by membership contributions and transfers of funds from the World Bank. Provides long-term interest-free loans and grants to the poorest countries.

International Monetary Fund (IMF), *Statistics, 1825 Eye St. N.W. 20006 (mailing address: 700 19th St. N.W. 20431); (202) 623-7900. Fax, (202) 623-6460. Carol S. Carson, Director. Publications, (202) 623-7430. Web, www.imf.org*

Publishes monthly *International Financial Statistics (IFS)*, which includes comprehensive financial data for most countries, and *Direction of Trade Statistics*, a quarterly publication, which includes the distribution of exports and imports for 152 countries. Annual statistical publications include the *Balance of Payments Statistics Yearbook, Direction of Trade Statistics Yearbook, Government Finance Statistics Yearbook,* and *International Financial Statistics Yearbook*. Subscriptions available to the public. *IFS* also is available on CD-ROM and on the Internet at imf.largo.apdi.net.

Organization for Economic Cooperation and Development (OECD), *Washington Office, 2001 L St. N.W., #650 20036-4922; (202) 785-6323. Fax, (202) 785-0350. Matthew Brosius, Co-Director; Sandra Wilson, Co-Director. Press, (202) 822-3866. General e-mail, washington.contact@oecd.org Web, www.oecdwash.org*

Membership: thirty nations including Australia, Canada, Japan, Mexico, New Zealand, the United States, and western European nations. Funded by membership contributions. Serves as a forum for members to exchange information and coordinate their economic policies; compiles statistics. Washington Center sells OECD publications and software; maintains reference library that is open to the public. (Headquarters in Paris.)

United Nations Information Centre, *1775 K St. N.W., #400 20006; (202) 331-8670. Fax, (202) 331-9191. Catherine O'Neill, Director. Web, www.unicwash.org*

Lead United Nations (U.N.) office in Washington. Center for reference publications of the U.N.; publications include statistical compilations on international trade and development, national accounts, growth of world industry, and demographic statistics. Library open to the public.

JUDICIARY

U.S. Court of Appeals for the Federal Circuit, *717 Madison Pl. N.W. 20439; (202) 633-6556. Fax, (202) 633-6353. Haldane Robert Mayer, Chief Judge; Jan Horbaly, Clerk, (202) 633-9614. Electronic bulletin board, (202) 633-9608 or (202) 786-6584.*

Reviews decisions of U.S. Court of International Trade (located in New York) on classifications of and duties on imported merchandise; settles legal questions about unfair practices in import trade (such as antidumping cases) found by the U.S. International Trade Commission and on import duties found by the Commerce Dept.

NONPROFIT

Assn. of Foreign Investors in Real Estate, *1300 Pennsylvania Ave. N.W., #880 20004-3020; (202) 312-1400. Fax, (202) 312-1401. James A. Fetgatter, Chief Executive.*
General e-mail, afireinfo@afire.org
Web, www.afire.org

Represents foreign institutions that are interested in the laws, regulations, and economic trends affecting the U.S. real estate market. Informs the public and the government of the contributions foreign investment makes to the U.S. economy. Examines current issues and organizes seminars for members.

Assn. of Women in International Trade, *P.O. Box 65962 20035; (202) 785-9842. Barbara Tanner, President.*
Web, www.wiit.org

Membership: women and men from all sectors concerned with international trade, including import-export firms, government, corporations, and nonprofit organizations. Provides members with opportunities for professional development. Maintains job bank and sponsors mentoring program.

Business Alliance for International Economic Development, *1615 L St. N.W., #520 20036; (202) 429-8855. Fax, (202) 429-8857. Terrence L. Bracy, Executive Director.*
Web, www.fintrac.com/alliance

Studies the relation between foreign economic assistance and the expansion of U.S. exports and jobs. Supports proper implementation of foreign aid by the U.S. government and multilateral development banks.

Center for Global Development, *1776 Massachusetts Ave. N.W., #301 20036; (202) 416-0700. Fax, (202) 416-0750. Nancy Birdsall, President.*
General e-mail, info@cgdev.org
Web, www.cgdev.org

Works to reduce global poverty and inequality through policy-oriented research and active engagement on development issues with policymakers and the public.

Center for International Private Enterprise, *1155 15th St. N.W., #700 20005-2706; (202) 721-9200. Fax, (202) 721-9250. Thomas Donohue, President; John D. Sullivan, Executive Director.*

General e-mail, cipe@cipe.org
Web, www.cipe.org

Works to strengthen private voluntary business organizations worldwide and to promote participation in the formation of public policy. Cooperates with local, national, regional, and multilateral institutions promoting private enterprise. (Affiliate of the U.S. Chamber of Commerce.)

Coalition for Employment Through Exports, *1100 Connecticut Ave. N.W., #810 20036-4101; (202) 296-6107. Fax, (202) 296-9709. Edmund B. Rice, President.*
Web, www.usaexport.org

Membership: major U.S. exporters and banks. Works to ensure adequate lending authority for the Export-Import Bank and other trade finance facilities as well as aggressive export financing policies for the United States.

Consumers for World Trade, *1001 Connecticut Ave. N.W., #1110 20036; (202) 293-2944. Fax, (202) 293-0495. Robin W. Lanier, Executive Director.*
General e-mail, cwt@cwt.org
Web, www.cwt.org

Consumer organization that advocates open and competitive trade policies. Represents consumer views in the formulation of foreign trade policy.

Economic Strategy Institute, *1401 H St. N.W., #560 20005; (202) 289-1288. Fax, (202) 289-1319. Clyde V. Prestowitz Jr., President.*
Web, www.econstrat.org

Works to increase U.S. economic competitiveness through research on domestic and international economic policies, industrial and technological developments, and global security issues. Testifies before Congress and government agencies.

Emergency Committee for American Trade, *1211 Connecticut Ave. N.W., #801 20036-2703; (202) 659-5147. Fax, (202) 659-1347. Calman J. Cohen, President.*
Web, www.ecattrade.com

Membership: U.S. corporations and banks interested in international trade and investment. Supports liberalized trade and investment and opposes restrictions on U.S. exports and imports.

Federation of International Trade Assns., *11800 Sunrise Valley Dr., #210, Reston, VA 20191; (703) 620-1588. Fax, (703) 620-4922. Nelson T. Joyner, Chair. Toll-free, (800) 969-FITA.*
General e-mail, info@fita.org
Web, www.fita.org

Membership: local, regional, and national trade associations throughout North America that have an international mission. Works to increase North American exports.

G7 Council, *2099 Pennsylvania Ave. N.W., #950 20006; (202) 223-0774. Fax, (202) 861-0790. David Smick, Co-Chair; Manuel Johnson, Co-Chair.*

Membership: international economic policy experts and business leaders, including former G7 officials. Advocates promoting the international economy over national economies. Promotes cooperation and coordination among the G7 countries and other industrial nations.

Institute for International Economics (IIE), *1750 Massachusetts Ave. N.W. 20036; (202) 328-9000. Fax, (202) 328-5432. C. Fred Bergsten, Director.*
Web, www.iie.com

Conducts studies and makes policy recommendations on international monetary affairs, trade, investment, energy, exchange rates, commodities, and North-South and East-West economic relations.

International Management and Development Institute, *1615 L St. N.W., #900 20036; (202) 337-1022. Fax, (202) 337-6678. Don L. Bonker, President.*
General e-mail, imdimail@aol.com

Educational organization that works to improve government-business understanding and international economic and trade cooperation worldwide through policy seminars and research on international economic and trade issues.

National Assn. of Manufacturers (NAM), *International Economic Affairs, 1331 Pennsylvania Ave. N.W., #600 20004; (202) 637-3140. Fax, (202) 637-3182. Franklin J. Vargo, Vice President.*
Web, www.nam.org

Represents manufacturing business interests on international economic issues, including trade and technology, international investment and financial affairs, and multinational corporations.

National Customs Brokers and Forwarders Assn. of America, *1200 18th St. N.W., #901 20036; (202) 466-0222. Fax, (202) 466-0226. Barbara Reilly, Executive Vice President.*
General e-mail, staff@ncbfaa.org
Web, www.ncbfaa.org

Membership: customs brokers and freight forwarders in the United States. Fosters information exchange within the industry. Monitors legislation and regulations.

National Foreign Trade Council, *1625 K St. N.W., #200 20006-1604; (202) 887-0278. Fax, (202) 452-8160. William A. Reinsch, President.*
General e-mail, nftcinformation@nftc.org
Web, www.nftc.org

Membership: U.S. companies engaged in international trade and investment. Advocates open international trading, export expansion, and policies to assist U.S. companies competing in international markets. Provides members with information on international trade topics. Sponsors seminars and conferences.

National Policy Assn., *1424 16th St. N.W., #700 20036; (202) 265-7685. Fax, (202) 797-5516. Anthony C. E. Quainton, President.*
General e-mail, npa@npa1.org
Web, www.npa1.org

Research organization that conducts studies and makes policy recommendations on international economic issues, including international trade, investment, monetary policy, and U.S. economic competitiveness.

United States Council for International Business, *Washington Office, 1030 15th St. N.W., #800 20005; (202) 371-1316. Fax, (202) 371-8249. Timothy Deal, Senior Vice President.*
General e-mail, info@uscib.org
Web, www.uscib.org

Membership: multinational corporations, service companies, law firms, and business associations. Represents U.S. business positions before intergovernmental bodies, foreign governments, and business communities. Promotes an open system of world trade, finance, and investment. (Headquarters in New York.)

U.S. Chamber of Commerce, *International Division, 1615 H St. N.W. 20062-2000; (202) 463-5455. Fax, (202) 463-3114. Willard A. Workman, Senior Vice President. Information, (202) 463-5460.*
Web, www.uschamber.com

Provides liaison with network of American chambers of commerce abroad; administers bilateral business councils; responsible for international economic policy development; informs members of developments in international affairs, business economics, and trade; sponsors seminars and conferences.

Washington International Trade Assn., *1300 Pennsylvania Ave. N.W., #350 20004-3014; (202) 312-1600. Fax, (202) 312-1601. Libby Bingham, Executive Director.*
Web, www.wita.org

Membership: trade professionals. Conducts programs and provides neutral forums to discuss international trade issues. Monitors legislation and regulations.

Development Assistance

AGENCIES

Agency for International Development (USAID), *Economic Growth, Agriculture, and Trade,* 1300 Pennsylvania Ave. N.W., #3.09 20523-3900; (202) 712-0670. Emmy L. Simmons, Assistant Administrator.
Web, www.usaid.gov/pubs/cbj2003/cent_prog/egat

Works to foster increased capability of foreign missions to collaborate with governments, entrepreneurs, and other local institutions and individuals to encourage country-based assistance programs. Divisions focus on economic growth (including business, agriculture, microenterprise development, and institutional reform); the environment and energy use; human capacity development (including education and training); and women in development.

Agency for International Development (USAID), *Education,* 1300 Pennsylvania Ave. N.W., #3.09-036 20523-3901; (202) 712-4273. Fax, (202) 216-3229. Donald R. Mackenzie, Director.
Web, www.usaid.gov

Provides field support, technical leadership, and research to help foreign missions and countries manage and develop their human resources. Improves the means of basic and higher education as well as training. Administers the AID Participant Training Program, which provides students and midcareer professionals from developing countries with academic and technical training; the Entrepreneur International Initiative, a short-term training/trade program that matches developing country entrepreneurs with American counterparts to familiarize them with American goods, services, and technology.

Foreign Agricultural Service (FAS), *(Agriculture Dept.),* 1400 Independence Ave. S.W., #5071S 20250-1001; (202) 720-3935. Fax, (202) 690-2159. A. Ellen Terpstra, Administrator; W. Kirk Miller, General Sales Manager. Information, (202) 720-3448. TTY, (202) 720-1786.
Web, www.fas.usda.gov

Administers the U.S. foreign food aid program with the Agency for International Development. Responsible for Title I of the Food for Peace program, the Food for Progress program, and the Section 416(b) program, which provides developing countries with surplus commodities.

Peace Corps, 1111 20th St. N.W. 20526; (202) 692-2100. Fax, (202) 692-2101. Gaddi Vasquez, Director. Information, (800) 424-8580. Press, (202) 692-2234.
Web, www.peacecorps.gov

Promotes world peace and mutual understanding between the United States and developing nations.

Administers volunteer programs to assist developing countries in education, the environment, health, small business development, agriculture, and urban development.

State Dept., *Development Finance,* 2201 C St. N.W., #3425 20520-5820; (202) 647-9426. Fax, (202) 647-5585. Robert Reis Jr., Director.
Web, www.state.gov

Provides liaison between the International Bank for Reconstruction and Development (World Bank), regional development banks, and the U.S. Export-Import Bank to facilitate U.S. assistance to developing nations. Helps to formulate State Dept. and U.S. government positions on multilateral and bilateral lending.

Treasury Dept., *Multilateral Development Banks,* 1440 New York Ave. N.W., #3426 20220; (202) 622-1231. Fax, (202) 622-1228. Sara Paulson, Director. Information, (202) 622-1810.
Web, www.ustreas.gov

Provides support for U.S. participation in multilateral development banks: the World Bank Group, the Inter-American Development Bank, the African Development Bank/Fund, the Asian Development Bank, and the European Bank for Reconstruction and Development.

INTERNATIONAL ORGANIZATIONS

United Nations Development Programme (UNDP), *Washington Office,* 1775 K St. N.W., #420 20006; (202) 331-9130. Fax, (202) 331-9363. Michael Marek, Director.
Web, www.undp.org

Funded by voluntary contributions from member nations and by nonmember recipient nations. Administers and coordinates technical assistance programs provided through the United Nations system. Seeks to increase economic and social development in developing nations. (Headquarters in New York.)

NONPROFIT

Academy for Educational Development (AED), 1825 Connecticut Ave. N.W., #800 20009; (202) 884-8000. Fax, (202) 884-8400. Stephen F. Moseley, President.
General e-mail, admin@aed.org
Web, www.aed.org

Distributes information on basic education programs in developing countries and on education-related issues.

ACDI/VOCA, 50 F St. N.W., #1075 20001; (202) 383-4961. Fax, (202) 783-7204. Michael Deegan, President.
Web, www.acdivoca.org

Recruits professionals for voluntary, short-term technical assistance to cooperatives, environmental groups, and agricultural enterprises, upon request, in developing countries and emerging democracies. (ACDI/VOCA resulted from the 1997 merger of Agricultural Cooperative Development International and Volunteers in Overseas Cooperative Assistance.)

Adventist Development and Relief Agency International, *12501 Old Columbia Pike, Silver Spring, MD 20904; (301) 680-6380. Fax, (301) 680-6370. Charles Sandefur, President. Press, (800) 931-2372. Toll-free, (888) 237-2367.*
General e-mail, 104100.140@compuserve.com
Web, www.adra.org

Worldwide humanitarian agency of the Seventh-day Adventist church. Works to alleviate poverty in developing countries and responds to disasters. Sponsors activities that improve health, foster economic and social well-being, and build self-reliance.

Alliance for Communities in Action, *P.O. Box 30154, Bethesda, MD 20824-0154; (301) 229-7707. Fax, (301) 229-7707. Richard Schopfer, Executive Director.*

Collaborates with local and international development organizations to promote self-help projects for small Latin American communities and small-business projects for skilled workers. Arranges funding, technical assistance, and supplies for health, housing, food production, and water projects. Promotes microenterprise development projects.

Ashoka: Innovators for the Public, *1700 N. Moore St., #2000, Arlington, VA 22209; (703) 527-8300. Fax, (703) 527-8383. Sushmida Ghosh, President.*
General e-mail, USCanadaProgram@ashoka.org
Web, www.ashoka.org

Supports fellowships for individuals with ideas for social change in forty-three developing nations. Provides fellows with research support, organizational networking, legal counseling, economic support, and business consulting. Seeks to educate the public about the developing world and the work of its fellows.

CARE, *Washington Office, 1625 K St. N.W., #500 20006; (202) 595-2800. Fax, (202) 296-8695. Marianne M. Leach, Executive Director.*
General e-mail, info@care.org
Web, www.care.org

Assists the developing world's poor through emergency assistance and community self-help programs that focus on sustainable development, agriculture, agroforestry, water and sanitation, health, family planning,

and income generation. (U.S. headquarters in Atlanta, Ga.; international headquarters in Brussels.)

Center for Intercultural Education and Development, *3307 M St. N.W., #202 20007 (mailing address: P.O. Box 579400, Georgetown University 20057-9400); (202) 687-1400. Fax, (202) 687-2555. Chantal Santelices, Director.*
Web, www.georgetown.edu/CIED

Designs and administers programs aimed at improving the quality of life of economically disadvantaged people; provides technical education, job training, leadership skill development, and business management training; runs programs in Central America, the Caribbean, Central Europe, and Southeast Asia.

CHF International, *8601 Georgia Ave., #800, Silver Spring, MD 20910; (301) 587-4700. Fax, (301) 587-7315. Michael E. Doyle, President.*
General e-mail, mailbox@chfhq.com
Web, www.chfhq.org

Works under contract with the Agency for International Development, United Nations, and World Bank to strengthen local government housing departments abroad.

Citizens Development Corps, *1400 Eye St. N.W., #1125 20005; (202) 872-0933. Fax, (202) 872-0923. Michael Levett, President. Information, (800) 394-1945.*
General e-mail, info@cdc.org
Web, www.cdc.org

Mobilizes volunteers in the U.S. private sector to assist in the development of market economies and democratic societies worldwide. Through the Business Entrepreneur Program, American volunteers assist private and privatizing businesses and public and nonprofit institutions that support business development. (Formerly Citizens Democracy Corps.)

Development Group for Alternative Policies, *927 15th St. N.W., 4th Floor 20005; (202) 898-1566. Fax, (202) 898-1612. Douglas Hellinger, Executive Director.*
General e-mail, dgap@developmentgap.org
Web, www.developmentgap.org

Works with grassroots organizations in developing countries to promote changes in international economic policies to benefit the poor.

InterAction, *1717 Massachusetts Ave. N.W., #701 20036; (202) 667-8227. Fax, (202) 667-8236. Mary E. McClymont, President.*
General e-mail, ia@interaction.org
Web, www.interaction.org

Provides a forum for exchange of information among private U.S. voluntary agencies on development assistance issues, including food aid and other relief services, migration, and refugee affairs. Monitors legislation and regulations.

International Center for Research on Women, *1717 Massachusetts Ave. N.W., #302 20036; (202) 797-0007. Fax, (202) 797-0020. Geeta Rao Gupta, President. General e-mail, info@icrw.org*
Web, www.icrw.org

Seeks to advance women's rights and opportunities. Promotes social and economic development with participation of women; provides technical assistance on women's productive and reproductive roles; advocates with governments and agencies.

National Peace Corps Assn., *1900 L St. N.W., #205 20036-5002; (202) 293-7728. Fax, (202) 293-7554. Dane Smith, President.*
Web, www.rpcv.org

Membership: returned Peace Corps volunteers, staff, and interested individuals. Promotes a global perspective in the United States; seeks to educate the public about the developing world; supports Peace Corps programs; maintains network of returned volunteers.

Partners for Livable Communities, *1429 21st St. N.W., 2nd Floor 20036; (202) 887-5990. Fax, (202) 466-4845. Robert H. McNulty, President.*
Web, www.livable.com

Provides technical assistance, support services, and information to assist communities in creating better living environments. Works in the Caribbean, South America, and Europe on public/private partnerships and resource development to improve living environments. Conducts conferences and workshops; maintains referral clearinghouse.

Pax World Service, *1730 Rhode Island Ave. N.W., #707 20036; (202) 463-0486. Fax, (202) 463-7322. Landrum Bolling, President.*
General e-mail, info@paxworld.org
Web, www.paxworld.org

Initiates and supports community-based sustainable development projects. Supports educational activities and facilitates citizen diplomacy through people-to-people tours, a program that allows individuals to develop a better understanding of the culture and diverse viewpoints of people living in regions of conflict.

Planning Assistance, *50 F St. N.W., #1050 20001; (202) 879-0612. Fax, (202) 638-0026. Robert Learmonth, Executive Director.*

General e-mail, rlearmonth@planasst.org

Provides managerial assistance to governmental and nongovernmental organizations seeking to create, expand, or improve their social and economic development programs. Interests include health, family planning, environmental programming, and municipal development. Focuses on development in Africa, Asia, and Latin America.

Salvation Army World Service Office, *615 Slaters Lane, Alexandria, VA 22313 (mailing address: P.O. Box 269, Alexandria, VA 22313); (703) 684-5528. Fax, (703) 684-5536. Harden White, Executive Director.*
Web, www.salvationarmy.org

Works in Russia and the new independent states, Latin America, the Caribbean, Africa, Asia, and the South Pacific to provide technical assistance in support of local Salvation Army programs of health services (including HIV/AIDS), community development, education, institutional development, microenterprise, and relief and reconstruction assistance. (International headquarters in London.)

United Way International, *701 N. Fairfax St., Alexandria, VA 22314-2045; (703) 519-0092. Fax, (703) 519-0097. Robert Beggan, President.*
General e-mail, uwi@unitedway.org
Web, www.uwint.org

Membership: independent United Way organizations in other countries. Provides United Way fundraising campaigns with technical assistance; trains volunteers and professionals; operates an information exchange for affiliated organizations.

Vital Voices Global Partnership, *1050 Connecticut Ave. N.W., 10th Floor 20036; (202) 772-4162. Fax, (202) 772-2353. Theresa A. Loar, Director.*
Web, www.vitalvoices.org

Worldwide, nongovernmental organization of women leaders. Seeks to expand women's roles in politics and civil society, increase women's entrepreneurship, and fight human rights abuses.

Finance, Monetary Affairs

AGENCIES

Commerce Dept., *Balance of Payments,* *1441 L St. N.W., #BE-58 20230; (202) 606-9545. Fax, (202) 606-5314. Christopher L. Bach, Chief.*
Web, www.bea.gov

Compiles, analyzes, and publishes quarterly U.S. balance-of-payments figures.

Federal Reserve System, *International Finance, 20th and C Sts. N.W., #B1242C 20551-2345; (202) 452-2345. Fax, (202) 452-6424. Karen H. Johnson, Director.*
Web, www.federalreserve.gov

Provides the Federal Reserve's board of governors with economic analyses of international developments. Compiles data on exchange rates.

State Dept., *International Finance and Development, 2201 C St. N.W., #4820 20520; (202) 647-9496. Fax, (202) 647-0320. Janice Bay, Deputy Assistant Secretary.*
Web, www.state.gov

Formulates and implements policies related to multi-national investment and insurance; activities of the World Bank and regional banks in the financial development of various countries; bilateral aid; international monetary reform; international antitrust cases; and international debt, banking, and taxation.

State Dept., *Monetary Affairs, 2201 C St. N.W., #3425 20520; (202) 647-5935. Fax, (202) 647-7453. James Paul Reid, Director.*
Web, www.state.gov

Formulates balance-of-payments and debt reschedul-ing policies. Monitors balance-of-payments develop-ments in other countries.

Treasury Dept., *Foreign Exchange Operations, 1500 Pennsylvania Ave. N.W., #2409 20220; (202) 622-2650. Fax, (202) 622-2021. Timothy DuLaney, Director.*
Web, www.ustreas.gov

Monitors foreign exchange market developments; manages the Exchange Stabilization Fund to counter dis-ruptive market conditions and to provide developing countries with bridge loans.

Treasury Dept., *International Affairs, 1500 Pennsylva-nia Ave. N.W., #3430 20220; (202) 622-0656. Fax, (202) 622-0417. John B. Taylor, Under Secretary.*
Web, www.ustreas.gov

Coordinates and implements U.S. international eco-nomic and financial policy in cooperation with other government agencies. Works to improve the structure and stabilizing operations of the international monetary and investment system; monitors developments in inter-national gold and foreign exchange operations; coordi-nates policies and programs of development lending institutions; coordinates Treasury Dept. participation in direct and portfolio investment by foreigners in the United States; studies international monetary, economic, and financial issues; analyzes data on international trans-actions.

Treasury Dept., *Trade Finance, 1440 New York Ave., #4311 20220 (mailing address: 1500 Pennsylvania Ave. N.W. 20220); (202) 622-2120. Fax, (202) 622-0967. Steven F. Tvardek, Director, (202) 622-1749.*
Web, www.ustreas.gov

Reviews lending policies of the Export-Import Bank, the Commodity Credit Corp., and the Defense Dept.'s foreign military sales program. Serves as U.S. representa-tive to the Export Credits Group, a committee of the Organization for Economic Cooperation and Develop-ment, and negotiates international arrangements for export credits and participant groups.

CONGRESS

House Financial Services Committee, *Subcommittee on Domestic and International Monetary Policy, Trade, and Technology, B304 RHOB 20515; (202) 225-7502. Rep. Peter T. King, R-N.Y., Chair; Bob Foster, Staff Direc-tor.*
Web, financialservices.house.gov

Jurisdiction over legislation on international mone-tary policy, international capital flows, and foreign investment in the United States as they affect domestic monetary policy and the economy; exchange rates; the African, Asian, European, and Inter-American Develop-ment Banks; the World Bank; legislation on international trade, investment, and monetary policy and export expansion matters related to the International Monetary Fund and the Export-Import Bank.

Senate Banking, Housing, and Urban Affairs Com-mittee, *Subcommittee on International Trade and Finance, SD-534 20510; (202) 224-4224. Sen. Chuck Hagel, R-Neb., Chair; Dayna Cade, Staff Director.*
Web, banking.senate.gov

Jurisdiction over legislation on international mone-tary and exchange rate policies, international capital flows, foreign investments in the United States, export control, foreign trade promotion, the Export-Import Bank, the Export Administration Act, and the revised Trading with the Enemy Act, which authorizes trade restrictions. (Some jurisdictions shared with the Senate Finance and Foreign Relations committees.)

Senate Finance Committee, *SD-219 20510; (202) 224-4515. Fax, (202) 228-0554. Sen. Charles E. Grassley, R-Iowa, Chair; Kolan L. Davis, Staff Director.*
Web, finance.senate.gov

Jurisdiction over legislation on international mone-tary matters. (Shares jurisdiction with the Senate Foreign Relations and Banking, Housing, and Urban Affairs committees.)

Senate Foreign Relations Committee, *Subcommittee on International Economic Policy, Export, and Trade Promotion,* *SD-446 20510; (202) 224-4651. Sen. Chuck Hagel, R-Neb., Chair; Mark Lagon, Professional Staff Member.*

Web, foreign.senate.gov

Jurisdiction over legislation to encourage foreign trade and to protect American business interests abroad. Jurisdiction over legislation affecting multinational corporations; balance of payments; international monetary organizations; and international economic and monetary policy as it relates to U.S. foreign policy. (Jurisdiction shared with the Senate Finance and Senate Banking, Housing, and Urban Affairs committees.)

INTERNATIONAL ORGANIZATIONS

International Finance Corp., *2121 Pennsylvania Ave. N.W. 20433 (mailing address: 1818 H St. N.W., FIIK-1107 20433); (202) 477-1234. Fax, (202) 974-4359. Peter L. Woicke, Executive Vice President, (202) 473-0381; James D. Wolfensohn, President.*

Web, www.ifc.org

Promotes private enterprise in developing countries through direct investments in projects that establish new businesses or expand, modify, or diversify existing businesses; provides its own financing or recruits financing from other sources. Gives developing countries technical assistance in capital market development, privatization, corporate restructuring, and foreign investment. Affiliated with the World Bank.

International Monetary Fund (IMF), *700 19th St. N.W., #13-318 20431; (202) 623-7759. Fax, (202) 623-4940. Nancy P. Jacklin, U.S. Executive Director. Information, (202) 623-7300. Press, (202) 623-7100.*

Web, www.imf.org

International organization that maintains funds, contributed and available for use by members, to promote world trade and aid members with temporary balance-of-payments problems.

Multilateral Investment Guarantee Agency, *1800 G St. N.W., #1200 20433 (mailing address: 1818 H St. N.W. 20433); (202) 473-6138. Fax, (202) 522-2620. Motomichi Ikawa, Executive Vice President.*

Web, www.miga.org

World Bank affiliate that seeks to encourage foreign investment in developing countries. Provides guarantees against losses due to currency transfer, expropriation, war, civil disturbance, and breach of contract. Advises member developing countries on means of improving their attractiveness to foreign investors. Membership open to World Bank member countries and Switzerland.

NONPROFIT

Bankers' Assn. for Finance and Trade, *1120 Connecticut Ave. N.W., 5th Floor 20036; (202) 663-5530. Fax, (202) 663-5538. Mary Condeelis, Executive Director.*

General e-mail, baft@baft.org

Web, www.baft.org

Membership: U.S. commercial banks with major international operations; foreign banks with U.S. operations are affiliated as nonvoting members. Monitors activities that affect the operation of U.S. commercial and international banks.

Bretton Woods Committee, *1990 M St. N.W., #450 20036; (202) 331-1616. Fax, (202) 785-9423. James C. Orr, Executive Director.*

Web, www.brettonwoods.org

Works to increase public understanding of the World Bank, the regional development institutions, the International Monetary Fund, and the World Trade Organization.

Institute of International Finance, *2000 Pennsylvania Ave. N.W., #8500 20006-1812; (202) 857-3600. Fax, (202) 775-1430. Charles H. Dallara, Managing Director. Press, (202) 331-8183.*

General e-mail, info@iif.com

Web, www.iif.com

Membership: international commercial banks, multinational corporations, and official lending agencies. Promotes better understanding of international lending transactions by improving the availability and quality of financial information on major country borrowers. Collects and analyzes information to help members evaluate credit risks of public and private borrowers in developing and middle-income countries. Studies and develops alternative solutions to the developing-country debt problem. Examines factors affecting the future of international lending.

■ REGIONAL AFFAIRS

See also Foreign Embassies, U.S. Ambassadors, and Country Desk Offices (appendix).

Africa

For North Africa, see Near East and South Asia

AGENCIES

African Development Foundation (ADF), *1400 Eye St. N.W., 10th Floor 20005-2248; (202) 673-3916. Fax, (202) 673-3810. Nathaniel Fields, President.*

General e-mail, info@adf.gov

Web, www.adf.gov

Established by Congress to work with and fund organizations and individuals involved in development projects at the local level in Africa. Gives preference to projects involving extensive participation by local Africans.

Agency for International Development (USAID), *Africa Bureau,* 1300 Pennsylvania Ave. N.W., #4.08C 20523-4801; (202) 712-0500. Fax, (202) 216-3008. Constance Berry Newman, Assistant Administrator.

Web, www.usaid.gov/regions/afr

Advises AID administrator on U.S. policy toward developing countries in Africa.

State Dept., *Bureau of African Affairs,* 2201 C St. N.W., #6234A 20520; (202) 647-4440. Fax, (202) 647-6301. Walter H. Kansteiner III, Assistant Secretary. Press, (202) 647-7371.

Web, www.state.gov

Advises the secretary on U.S. policy toward sub-Saharan Africa. Directors, assigned to different regions in Africa, aid the assistant secretary.

State Dept., *Central African Affairs,* 2201 C St. N.W., #4246 20520-2902; (202) 647-2080. Fax, (202) 647-1726. Alan Eastham, Director.

Web, www.state.gov

Includes Burundi, Cameroon, Central African Republic, Chad, Congo, Democratic Republic of Congo, Equatorial Guinea, Gabon, Rwanda, and São Tomé and Principe.

State Dept., *East African Affairs,* 2201 C St. N.W., #5240 20520; (202) 647-9742. Fax, (202) 647-0810. Lauren Moriarty, Director.

Web, www.state.gov

Includes Comoros, Djibouti, Eritrea, Ethiopia, Kenya, Madagascar, Mauritius, Seychelles, Somalia, Sudan, Tanzania, Uganda, and Indian Ocean Territory.

State Dept., *Southern African Affairs,* 2201 C St. N.W., #4238 20520; (202) 647-9836. Fax, (202) 647-5007. Scott DeLisi, Director.

Web, www.state.gov

Includes Angola, Botswana, Lesotho, Malawi, Mozambique, Namibia, South Africa, Swaziland, Zambia, and Zimbabwe.

State Dept., *West African Affairs,* 2201 C St. N.W., #4250 20520-3430; (202) 647-3395. Fax, (202) 647-4855. Michael Arietti, Director.

Web, www.state.gov

Includes Benin, Burkina Faso, Cape Verde, Côte d'Ivoire, Gambia, Ghana, Guinea, Guinea-Bissau, Liberia, Mali, Mauritania, Niger, Nigeria, Senegal, Sierra Leone, and Togo.

CONGRESS

House International Relations Committee, *Subcommittee on Africa,* 255 FHOB 20515; (202) 226-7812. Fax, (202) 225-7491. Rep. Ed Royce, R-Calif., Chair; Thomas Sheehy, Staff Director.

Web, www.house.gov/international_relations

Jurisdiction over foreign affairs legislation dealing with Africa, with the exception of countries bordering on the Mediterranean Sea from Egypt to Morocco. Concurrent jurisdiction over matters assigned to the functional House International Relations subcommittees insofar as they affect the region.

Library of Congress, *African and Middle Eastern Division,* 110 2nd St. S.E., #220 20540; (202) 707-7937. Fax, (202) 252-3180. Beverly Gray, Chief.

Web, www.loc.gov

Maintains collections of African, Near Eastern, and Hebraic material. Prepares bibliographies and special studies relating to Africa and the Middle East. Reference service and reading rooms available to the public.

Senate Foreign Relations Committee, *Subcommittee on African Affairs,* SD-446 20510; (202) 224-4651. Sen. Lamar Alexander, R-Tenn., Chair; Michael Phelan, Professional Staff Member.

Web, foreign.senate.gov

Jurisdiction over foreign affairs legislation dealing with Africa, with the exception of countries bordering on the Mediterranean Sea from Egypt to Morocco.

INTERNATIONAL ORGANIZATIONS

International Bank for Reconstruction and Development (World Bank), *Africa,* 1818 H St. N.W., #J5093 20433; (202) 458-2858. Fax, (202) 477-0380. Callisto E. Madavo, Vice President, (202) 458-2856. Information, (202) 473-9156.

Web, www.worldbank.org

Encourages public and private foreign investment in the countries of sub-Saharan Africa through loans, loan guarantees, and technical assistance. Finances economic development projects in agriculture, environmental protection, education, public utilities, telecommunications, water supply, sewage treatment, public health, and other areas.

NONPROFIT

Africa-America Institute, *Washington Office,*
1625 Massachusetts Ave. N.W., #400 20036-2259; (202)
667-5636. Fax, (202) 265-6332. Paulette Nowden, Director, Education Outreach and Policy.
Web, www.aaionline.org

Designs exchange and visitor programs that bring
together African and American professionals and policy-makers to discuss areas of mutual concern. Sponsors policy studies program to educate Congress on African
issues. (Headquarters in New York.)

Africare, 440 R St. N.W. 20001; (202) 462-3614. Fax,
(202) 387-1034. Julius E. Coles, President.
General e-mail, africare@africare.org
Web, www.africare.org

Seeks to improve the quality of life in rural Africa
through development of water resources, increased food
production, and delivery of health services. Resource
center open to the public by appointment.

TransAfrica/TransAfrica Forum, *1426 21st St. N.W.*
20036; (202) 223-1960. Fax, (202) 223-1966. Bill Fletcher,
President.
General e-mail, info@transafricaforum.org
Web, www.transafricaforum.org

Focuses on U.S. foreign policy toward African
nations, the Caribbean, and peoples of African descent.
Provides members with information on foreign policy
issues. The Arthur R. Ashe Foreign Policy Library is open
to the public.

Washington Office on Africa, *212 E. Capitol St.*
20003; (202) 547-7503. Fax, (202) 547-7505. Leon P.
Spencer, Executive Director.
General e-mail, woa@igc.org
Web, www.woaafrica.org

Promotes a just American policy toward Africa. Monitors legislation and executive actions concerning Africa;
issues action alerts.

East Asia and the Pacific

AGENCIES

Agency for International Development (USAID),
Asia and Near East Bureau, 1300 Pennsylvania Ave.
N.W., #4.09-034 20523-4900; (202) 712-0200. Fax, (202)
216-3386. Wendy Chamberlin, Assistant Administrator.
Web, www.usaid.gov/regions/ane

Advises AID administrator on U.S. economic development policy in Asia and the Near East.

Defense Dept. (DoD), *Asian and Pacific Affairs,* The
Pentagon, #4C839 20301-2400; (703) 695-4175. Fax,

(703) 695-8222. Richard Lawless, Deputy Assistant Secretary.
Web, www.defenselink.mil

Advises the assistant secretary for international security affairs on matters dealing with Asia and the Pacific.

Japan-United States Friendship Commission,
110 Vermont Ave. N.W., #800 20005; (202) 418-9800. Fax,
(202) 418-9802. Eric J. Gangloff, Executive Director.
General e-mail, jusfc@jusfc.gov
Web, www.jusfc.gov

Independent agency established by Congress that
makes grants and administers funds and programs promoting educational and cultural exchanges between
Japan and the United States.

State Dept., *Bureau of East Asian and Pacific Affairs,*
2201 C St. N.W., #6205 20520-6205; (202) 647-9596. Fax,
(202) 647-7350. James Andrew Kelly, Assistant Secretary.
Press, (202) 647-2538.
Web, www.state.gov/p/eap

Advises the secretary on U.S. policy toward East
Asian and Pacific countries. Directors assigned to specific
countries within the bureau aid the assistant secretary.

State Dept., *Australia, New Zealand, and Pacific
Island Affairs,* 2201 C St. N.W., #4206 20520; (202) 736-
4741. Fax, (202) 647-0118. Terry Breese, Director.
Web, www.state.gov

State Dept., *Burma, Cambodia, Laos, Thailand, and
Vietnam Affairs,* 2201 C St. N.W., #5206 20520-6310;
(202) 647-4495. Fax, (202) 647-3069. Judith Strots, Director.
Web, www.state.gov

Handles issues related to Americans missing in action
in Indochina; serves as liaison with Congress, international organizations, and foreign governments on developments in these countries.

State Dept., *Chinese and Mongolian Affairs,* 2201 C
St. N.W., #4318 20520; (202) 647-6803. Fax, (202) 647-
6820. Stephen M. Young, Director.
Web, www.state.gov

State Dept., *Indonesia and East Timor Affairs,* 2201 C
St. N.W., #5210 20520; (202) 647-1221. Fax, (202) 736-
4559. Thomas Cynkin, Director.
Web, www.state.gov

State Dept., *Japanese Affairs,* 2201 C St. N.W., #4206
20520; (202) 647-2913. Fax, (202) 647-4402. Brian J.
Mohler, Director.
Web, www.state.gov

State Dept., *Korean Affairs,* 2201 C St. N.W., #5313 20520; (202) 647-7717. Fax, (202) 647-7388. W. David Straub, Director.
Web, www.state.gov

State Dept., *Philippines, Malaysia, Brunei, and Singapore Affairs,* 2201 C St. N.W., #5210 20520; (202) 647-3276. Fax, (202) 736-4559. Eunice Reddick, Director.
Web, www.state.gov

State Dept., *Taiwan Coordination Staff,* 2201 C St. N.W., #4312 20520; (202) 647-7712. Fax, (202) 647-0076. David Keegan, Director.
Web, www.state.gov

CONGRESS

House International Relations Committee, *Subcommittee on Asia and the Pacific,* B358 RHOB 20515; (202) 226-7825. Fax, (202) 226-7829. Rep. Jim Leach, R-Iowa, Chair; James W. McCormick, Staff Director.
Web, www.house.gov/international_relations

Jurisdiction over foreign affairs legislation dealing with Asia and the Pacific. Concurrent jurisdiction over matters assigned to the functional House International Relations subcommittees insofar as they affect the region.

Library of Congress, *Asian Division,* 101 Independence Ave. S.E., #LJ150 20540-4810; (202) 707-5420. Fax, (202) 707-1724. Hwa-wei Lee, Chief.
Web, www.lcweb.loc.gov/rr/asian

Maintains collections of Chinese, Korean, Japanese, Southeast Asian, and South Asian material. Reference service is provided in the Asian Reading Room.

Senate Foreign Relations Committee, *Subcommittee on East Asian and Pacific Affairs,* SD-446 20510; (202) 224-4651. Sen. Sam Brownback, R-Kan., Chair; Keith Luse, Professional Staff Member.
Web, foreign.senate.gov

Jurisdiction over foreign affairs legislation dealing with East Asia and the Pacific, including the mainland of Asia from China and Korea to Burma, Japan, the Philippines, Malaysia, Indonesia, Australia and New Zealand, Oceania, and the South Pacific islands.

INTERNATIONAL ORGANIZATIONS

International Bank for Reconstruction and Development (World Bank), *East Asia and Pacific,* 1818 H St. N.W., MC 9-910 20433; (202) 473-7723. Fax, (202) 477-0169. Jemal-ud-din Kassum, Vice President.
Web, www.worldbank.org

Encourages public and private investment in the countries of East Asia and the Pacific through loans, loan guarantees, and technical assistance. Finances economic development projects in agriculture, environmental protection, education, public utilities, telecommunications, water supply, sewerage, public health, and other areas.

NONPROFIT

American Institute in Taiwan, 1700 N. Moore St., #1700, Arlington, VA 22209; (703) 525-8474. Fax, (703) 841-1385. Barbara Schrage, Deputy Director.
Web, www.ait.org.tw

Chartered by Congress to coordinate commercial, cultural, and other activities between the people of the United States and Taiwan. Represents U.S. interests and maintains offices in Taiwan.

Asia Foundation, *Washington Office,* 1779 Massachusetts Ave. N.W., #815 20036; (202) 588-9420. Fax, (202) 588-9409. Nancy Yuan, Director.
Web, www.asiafoundation.org

Provides grants and technical assistance in Asia and the Pacific islands (excluding the Middle East). Seeks to strengthen legislatures, legal and judicial systems, market economies, the media, and nongovernmental organizations. (Headquarters in San Francisco, Calif.)

Asia Society, *Washington Office,* 1800 K St. N.W., #1102 20006; (202) 833-2742. Fax, (202) 833-0189. Joseph C. Snyder, Director.
General e-mail, dcinfo@asiasoc.org
Web, www.asiasociety.org

Membership: individuals interested in Asia and the Pacific (excluding the Middle East). Sponsors seminars and lectures on political, economic, and cultural issues. (Headquarters in New York.)

East-West Center, *Washington Office,* 1819 L St. N.W., #200 20036; (202) 293-3995. Fax, (202) 293-1402. Muthiah Alagappa, Director.
General e-mail, washington@eastwestcenter.org
Web, www.eastwestcenter.org

Promotes strengthening of relations and understanding among countries and peoples of Asia, the Pacific, and the United States. Plans to undertake substantive programming activities, including collaborative research, training, seminars, and outreach; publications; and congressional study groups. (Headquarters in Honolulu.)

Heritage Foundation, *Asian Studies Center,* 214 Massachusetts Ave. N.E. 20002; (202) 608-6081. Fax, (202) 675-1779. Peter Brookes, Director.
Web, www.asianstudies.org

Conducts research and provides information on U.S. policies in Asia and the Pacific. Interests include economic and security issues in the Asia Pacific region. Hosts speakers and visiting foreign policy delegations; sponsors conferences.

Japan-America Society of Washington, *1020 19th St. N.W., Lower Lobby #40 20036; (202) 833-2210. Fax, (202) 833-2456. JoAnna Phillips, Executive Director.*
General e-mail, jaswdc@us-japan.org
Web, www.us-japan.org/dc
Conducts programs on U.S.-Japan trade, politics, and economic issues. Cultural programs include lectures, films, a Japanese-language school, scholarships to college students studying in the Washington, D.C., area, and assistance to Japanese performing artists. Maintains library for members. Sponsors national Cherry Blossom Festival.

Japan Information Access Project, *2000 P St. N.W., #620 20036; (202) 822-6040. Fax, (202) 822-6044. Mindy Kotler, Director.*
General e-mail, access@jiaponline.org
Web, www.jiaponline.org
Studies Japanese and Northeast Asian security and public policy. Researches and analyzes issues affecting Japan's relationship with the West.

Japan Productivity Center for Socio-Economic Development, *Washington Office,* *1616 H St. N.W., #206 20006; (202) 737-2689. Fax, (202) 737-2753. Hiroshi Shinoda, Director.*
General e-mail, shinodah@email.msn.com
Promotes education and exchange of information between Japanese and American businesspeople by coordinating overseas meetings and visits for participating countries. (Headquarters in Tokyo.)

Pacific Economic Cooperation Council, *1819 L St. N.W., #200 20036; (202) 293-3995. Fax, (202) 293-1402. Mark Borthwick, Executive Director.*
General e-mail, uspecc@pecc.org
Web, www.pecc.org
Membership: business, government, and research representatives from twenty-two Asia-Pacific economies. Works on practical government and business policy issues to increase trade, investment, and economic development in the region. Serves as one of three observer organizations to the government forum on Asia Pacific Economic Cooperation (APEC). (Affiliated with East-West Center.)

Taipei Economic and Cultural Representative Office, *4201 Wisconsin Ave. N.W. 20016; (202) 895-1800.*

Fax, (202) 966-0825. C. J. Chen, Representative. Press, (202) 895-1850.
Represents political, economic, and cultural interests of the government of the Republic of China (Taiwan) in the United States; handles former embassy functions.

U.S.-Asia Institute, *232 E. Capitol St. N.E. 20003; (202) 544-3181. Fax, (202) 543-1748. Joji Konoshima, President.*
Organization of individuals interested in Asia. Encourages communication among political and business leaders in the United States and Asia. Interests include foreign policy, international trade, Asian and American cultures, education, and employment. Conducts research and sponsors conferences and workshops in cooperation with the State Dept. to promote greater understanding between the United States and Asian nations. Conducts programs that take congressional staff members to Japan and China.

U.S.-China Business Council, *1818 N St. N.W., #200 20036-2470; (202) 429-0340. Fax, (202) 775-2476. Robert A. Kapp, President.*
Web, www.uschina.org
Member-supported organization that represents U.S. companies engaged in business relations with the People's Republic of China. Participates in U.S. policy issues relating to China and other international trade. Publishes research reports. (Maintains offices in Beijing and Shanghai.)

Europe

(Includes the Baltic states)

AGENCIES

Agency for International Development (USAID), *Europe and Eurasia Bureau,* *1300 Pennsylvania Ave. N.W., #5.06 20523-5600; (202) 712-0290. Fax, (202) 216-3057. Kent R. Hill, Assistant Administrator.*
Web, www.usaid.gov/regions/europe_eurasia
Advises AID administrator on U.S. economic development policy in Europe and the new independent states.

Defense Dept. (DoD), *European and NATO Policy,* *The Pentagon, #4D800 20301-2900; (703) 697-7207. Fax, (703) 697-5992. Ian Brzezinski, Deputy Assistant Secretary.*
Web, www.defenselink.mil
Advises the assistant secretary for international security affairs on matters dealing with Europe and NATO.

International Trade Administration (ITA), *(Commerce Dept.), Central and Eastern Europe Business*

Information Center, 1300 Pennsylvania Ave. N.W. 20004 (mailing address: 1401 Constitution Ave. N.W., USA Trade Center Stop R-CEEBIC 20230); (202) 482-2645. Fax, (202) 482-3898. Jay Burgess, Director. Toll-free, (800) USATRADE.
General e-mail, ceebic@ita.doc.gov
Web, www.mac.doc.gov/ceebic

Provides information on trade and investment in central and eastern Europe, including the reconstruction of Kosovo and southeastern Europe. Disseminates information on potential trade partners, regulations and incentives, and trade promotion; encourages private enterprise in the region.

State Dept., *Bureau of European Affairs,* 2201 C St. N.W., #6226 20520; (202) 647-9626. Fax, (202) 647-5755. Amb. A. Elizabeth Jones, Assistant Secretary. Information, (202) 647-6925.
Web, www.state.gov

Advises the secretary on U.S. policy toward European and Eurasian countries. Directors assigned to specific countries within the bureau aid the assistant secretary.

State Dept., *European Security and Political Affairs,* 2201 C St. N.W., #6511 20520; (202) 647-1626. Fax, (202) 647-1369. John Schmidt, Director.
Web, www.state.gov

Coordinates and advises, with the Defense Dept. and other agencies, the U.S. mission to the North Atlantic Treaty Organization and the U.S. delegation to the Organization on Security and Cooperation in Europe regarding political, military, and arms control matters.

State Dept., *European Union and Regional Affairs,* 2201 C St. N.W., #5424 20520; (202) 647-3932. Fax, (202) 647-9959. Charles L. English, Director.
Web, www.state.gov

Handles all matters concerning the European Union, the Council of Europe, and the Organization for Economic Cooperation and Development, with emphasis on trade issues. Monitors export controls and economic activities for the North Atlantic Treaty Organization and the Conference on Security and Cooperation in Europe.

State Dept., *German, Austrian, and Swiss Affairs,* 2201 C St. N.W., #4228 20520; (202) 647-1484. Fax, (202) 647-5117. Carol Van Voorst, Director.
Web, www.state.gov

Includes Austria, Germany, Liechtenstein, and Switzerland.

State Dept., *Nordic and Baltic Affairs,* 2201 C St. N.W., #5218 20520; (202) 647-5669. Fax, (202) 736-4170. Judith B. Ceskin, Director.

Web, www.state.gov

Includes Denmark, Estonia, Finland, Iceland, Latvia, Lithuania, Norway, and Sweden.

State Dept., *North Central European Affairs,* 2201 C St. N.W., #5228 20520; (202) 647-4136. Fax, (202) 736-4853. Michael Mozur, Director.
Web, www.state.gov

Includes Czech Republic, Hungary, Poland, Romania, Slovakia, and Slovenia.

State Dept., *South Central European Affairs,* 2201 C St. N.W., #5221 20520; (202) 647-0608. Fax, (202) 647-0555. Paul A. Jones, Director.
Web, www.state.gov

Includes Albania, Bosnia-Herzegovina, Bulgaria, Croatia, Kosovo, Macedonia, Montenegro, and Serbia.

State Dept., *Southern European Affairs,* 2201 C St. N.W., #5511 20520; (202) 647-6112. Fax, (202) 647-5087. Douglas Hengel, Director.
Web, www.state.gov

Includes Cyprus, Greece, and Turkey.

State Dept., *United Kingdom, Benelux, and Ireland Affairs,* 2201 C St. N.W., #4513 20520; (202) 647-5687. Fax, (202) 647-3463. Alexander Karagiannis, Director.
Web, www.state.gov

Includes Belgium, Bermuda, Ireland, Luxembourg, the Netherlands, and the United Kingdom.

State Dept., *Western European Affairs,* 2201 C St. N.W., #5226 20520; (202) 647-3072. Fax, (202) 647-3459. Margaret Dean, Director.
Web, www.state.gov

Includes Andorra, France, Italy, Malta, Monaco, Portugal, Réunion, San Marino, Spain, and the Vatican.

CONGRESS

House International Relations Committee, *Subcommittee on Europe,* 2401A RHOB 20515; (202) 226-7820. Fax, (202) 226-2722. Rep. Doug Bereuter, R-Neb., Chair; Vince Morelli, Staff Director.
General e-mail, hirc@mail.house.gov
Web, www.house.gov/international_relations

Jurisdiction over foreign affairs legislation dealing with Europe. Concurrent jurisdiction over matters assigned to the functional House International Relations subcommittees insofar as they affect the region.

Library of Congress, *European Division,* 101 Independence Ave. S.E., Jefferson Bldg., #LJ-250 20540-4830; (202) 707-5414. Fax, (202) 707-8482. John Van Oudenaren, Chief. Reference desk, (202) 707-4515.

General e-mail, eurref@loc.gov

Web, www.lcweb.loc.gov/rr/european

Provides reference service on the library's European collections (except collections on Spain, Portugal, and the British Isles). Prepares bibliographies and special studies relating to European countries, including Russia and the new independent states. Maintains current unbound Slavic language periodicals and newspapers, which are available at the European Reference Desk.

Senate Foreign Relations Committee, *Subcommittee on European Affairs,* SD-446 20510; (202) 224-4651. *Sen. George Allen, R-Va., Chair; Jessica Fugate, Professional Staff Member.*

Web, foreign.senate.gov

Jurisdiction over foreign affairs legislation dealing with Europe (including Greece and Turkey), the United Kingdom, Greenland, Iceland, the former Soviet Union, and the North Polar region.

INTERNATIONAL ORGANIZATIONS

European Commission, *Press and Public Affairs, Washington Office,* 2300 M St. N.W. 20037; (202) 862-9500. Fax, (202) 429-1766. *Willy Helin, Director; Günter Burghardt, Ambassador.*

Web, www.eurunion.org

Information and public affairs office in the United States for the European Union, which includes the European Economic Community, the European Coal and Steel Community, and the European Atomic Energy Community. Provides social policy data on the European Union and provides statistics and documents on member countries, including those related to energy, economics, development and cooperation, commerce, agriculture, industry, and technology. Library open to the public by appointment. (Headquarters in Brussels.)

International Bank for Reconstruction and Development (World Bank), *Europe and Central Asia,* 600 19th St. N.W. 20431 (mailing address: 1818 H St. N.W., #H12211 20433); (202) 458-0602. Fax, (202) 522-2758. *Johannes F. Linn, Vice President.*

General e-mail, ecainformation@worldbank.org

Web, www.worldbank.org

Encourages public and private foreign investment in the countries of eastern Europe through loans, loan guarantees, and technical assistance. Finances economic development projects in agriculture, environmental protection, education, energy, public utilities, telecommunications, water supply, sewerage, public health, and other areas.

NONPROFIT

American Bar Assn. (ABA), *Central European and Eurasian Law Initiative,* 740 15th St. N.W., 8th Floor 20005-1022; (202) 662-1950. Fax, (202) 662-1597. *David Tolbert, Executive Director.*

General e-mail, ceeli@abanet.org

Web, www.abaceeli.org

Promotes the rule of law and specific legal reforms in the emerging democracies of central and eastern Europe, Russia, and the new independent states; recruits volunteer legal professionals from the United States and western Europe. Interests include civil, criminal, commercial, and environmental law; judicial restructuring; bar development; and legal education and research.

American Hellenic Institute, *1220 16th St. N.W. 20036; (202) 785-8430. Fax, (202) 785-5178. Eugene Rossides, General Counsel.*

General e-mail, info@ahiworld.org

Web, www.ahiworld.org

Works to strengthen trade and commerce between Greece and Cyprus and the United States and within the American Hellenic community.

British-American Business Assn., *P.O. Box 16482 20041; (202) 293-0010. Fax, (202) 296-3332. Don Neese, President.*

Web, www.babawashington.org

Membership: organizations dedicated to the development of business relations between the United Kingdom and the United States.

British American Security Information Council (BASIC), *1012 14th St. N.W., #900 20005; (202) 347-8340. Fax, (202) 347-4688. Ian Davis, Director.*

General e-mail, basicus@basicint.org

Web, www.basicint.org

Research organization that analyzes international security policy in Europe and North America. Promotes public awareness of defense and nonproliferation issues. Monitors and reports on the activities of Congress and the departments of State and Defense.

European-American Business Council, *1025 Connecticut Ave. N.W., #216 20036; (202) 728-0777. Fax, (202) 728-2937. Willard M. Berry, President.*

General e-mail, eabc@eabc.org

Web, www.eabc.org

Membership: American companies with operations in Europe and European companies with operations in the United States. Works for free and fair trade and investment between the United States and the European Union.

European Institute, *5225 Wisconsin Ave. N.W., #200 20015-2014; (202) 895-1670. Fax, (202) 362-1088. Jacqueline Grapin, President.*

Web, www.europeaninstitute.org

Membership: governments and multinational corporations. Provides an independent forum for business leaders, government officials, journalists, academics, and policy experts. Organizes seminars and conferences. Interests include international finance, economics, energy, telecommunications, defense and procurement policies, the integration of Central Europe into the European Union and NATO, and relations with Asia and Latin America.

French-American Chamber of Commerce,

3028 Javier Rd., Fairfax, VA 22031; (703) 560-6330. Fax, (703) 560-6310. Jeffrey Lenorovitz, President.

General e-mail, fachamber@aol.com

Web, www.faccwdc.org

Membership: small to large enterprises based in France and the United States. Promotes trade and investment between the United States and France. Provides seminars and various cultural events.

German American Business Council, *1524 18th St. N.W. 20036; (202) 332-7700. Fax, (202) 408-9369. Leo G. B. Welt, Executive Director.*

General e-mail, gabc.mail@worldnet.att.net

Web, www.washgabc.com

Promotes trade, investment, and business relationships between the United States and Germany. Provides seminars and opportunities for members to meet with industry leaders and government officials.

German Marshall Fund of the United States,

1744 R St. N.W. 20009; (202) 745-3950. Fax, (202) 265-1662. Craig Kennedy, President.

General e-mail, info@gmfus.org

Web, www.gmfus.org

American institution created by a gift from Germany as a permanent memorial to Marshall Plan aid. Seeks to stimulate exchange of ideas and promote cooperation between the United States and Europe. Awards grants to promote the study of international and domestic policies; supports comparative research and debate on key issues.

Irish American Unity Conference, *529 14th St. N.W., #837 20045; (800) 947-4282. Fax, (208) 441-1158. James J. Gallagher, President.*

General e-mail, iauc@iauc.org

Web, www.iauc.org

Nationwide organization that encourages nonviolent means of resolving conflict in Northern Ireland. Conducts symposia and provides information on Northern Ireland. Monitors legislation and regulations.

Irish National Caucus, *P.O. Box 15128 20003-0849; (202) 544-0568. Fax, (202) 488-7537. Sean McManus, President.*

General e-mail, info@irishnationalcaucus.org

Web, www.irishnationalcaucus.org

Educational organization concerned with protecting human rights in Northern Ireland. Seeks to end anti-Catholic discrimination in Northern Ireland through implementation of the McBride Principles, initiated in 1984. Advocates nonviolence. Monitors legislation and regulations.

Joint Baltic American National Committee,

400 Hurley Ave., Rockville, MD 20850; (301) 340-1954. Fax, (301) 309-1406. Vello Ederma, Chair; Karl Altau, Managing Director.

General e-mail, jbanc@jbanc.org

Web, www.jbanc.org

Washington representative of the Estonian, Latvian, and Lithuanian American communities in the United States; acts as a representative on issues affecting the Baltic states.

National Federation of Croatian Americans,

1329 Connecticut Ave. N.W. 20036; (202) 331-2830. Fax, (202) 331-0050. John Kraljic, President.

General e-mail, nfcahdq@aol.com

Membership: Croatian American organizations. Promotes independence, democracy, business and economic development, human rights, and a free-market economy in Croatia and Bosnia-Herzegovina. Supports equal rights in these countries regardless of ethnicity or religious beliefs.

Latin America, Canada, and the Caribbean

AGENCIES

Agency for International Development (USAID), *Latin America and the Caribbean Bureau, 1300 Pennsylvania Ave. N.W., #5.09 20523-5900; (202) 712-4800. Fax, (202) 216-3012. Adolfo Franco, Assistant Administrator.*

Web, www.usaid.gov/regions/lac

Advises AID administrator on U.S. policy toward developing Latin American and Caribbean countries. Designs and implements assistance programs for developing nations.

Defense Dept. (DoD), *Western Hemisphere Affairs,* *2400 Defense Pentagon 20301-2400; (703) 697-5884. Fax, (703) 695-8404. Rogello Pardo-Maurer, Deputy Assistant Secretary.*
Web, www.defenselink.mil

Advises the assistant secretary for international security affairs on inter-American matters; aids in the development of U.S. policy toward Latin America.

Inter-American Foundation, *901 N. Stuart St., 10th Floor, Arlington, VA 22203; (703) 306-4301. Fax, (703) 306-4365. David Valenzuela, President.*
Web, www.iaf.gov

Supports small-scale Latin American and Caribbean social and economic development efforts through grassroots development programs, grants, and fellowships.

International Trade Administration (ITA), *(Commerce Dept.), NAFTA and Inter-American Affairs,* *14th St. and Constitution Ave. N.W., #3024 20230; (202) 482-0393. Fax, (202) 482-5865. Juliet Bender, Director.*
Web, www.ita.doc.gov

Coordinates Commerce Dept. activities regarding NAFTA (North American Free Trade Agreement), FTAA (Free Trade Areas of the Americas), and U.S.-Chile Free Trade Agreement.

Panama Canal Commission, *Office of Transition Administration,* *1825 Eye St. N.W., #400 20006; (202) 775-4180. Fax, (202) 775-4184. William J. Connolly, Director.*

Established to close out the affairs of the Panama Canal Commission.

State Dept., *Bureau of Western Hemisphere Affairs,* *2201 C St. N.W., #6262 20520; (202) 647-5780. Fax, (202) 647-0791. J. Curtis Struble, Assistant Secretary (Acting).*
Web, www.state.gov

Advises the secretary on U.S. policy toward Canada, Latin America, and the Caribbean. Directors assigned to specific regions within the bureau aid the assistant secretary.

State Dept., *Andean Affairs,* *2201 C St. N.W., #4915 20520; (202) 647-1715. Fax, (202) 647-2628. Phillip Cicola, Director.*
Web, www.state.gov

Includes Bolivia, Colombia, Ecuador, Peru, and Venezuela.

State Dept., *Brazilian, Southern Cone Affairs,* *2201 C St. N.W., #5258 20520; (202) 647-2407. Fax, (202) 736-7481. James Carragher, Director.*
Web, www.state.gov

Includes Argentina, Brazil, Chile, Paraguay, and Uruguay.

State Dept., *Canadian Affairs,* *2201 C St. N.W., #3917 20520; (202) 647-3135. Fax, (202) 647-4088. Nancy M. Mason, Director.*
Web, www.state.gov

State Dept., *Caribbean Affairs,* *2201 C St. N.W., #4906 20520-6258; (202) 647-5088. Fax, (202) 647-4477. Mary Ellen Gilroy, Director.*
Web, www.state.gov

Includes Anguilla, Antigua and Barbuda, Aruba, Bahamas, Barbados, British Virgin Islands, Cayman Islands, Dominica, Dominican Republic, Grenada, Guyana, Haiti, Jamaica, Martinique, Montserrat, Netherlands Antilles, St. Kitts and Nevis, St. Lucia, St. Vincent and the Grenadines, Suriname, Trinidad and Tobago, and Turks and Caicos Islands.

State Dept., *Central American and Panamanian Affairs,* *2201 C St. N.W., #5908 20520-6258; (202) 647-4010. Fax, (202) 647-2597. Paul Trivelli, Director. Additional fax, (202) 647-0377.*
Web, www.state.gov

Includes Belize, Costa Rica, El Salvador, Guatemala, Honduras, Nicaragua, and Panama.

State Dept., *Cuban Affairs,* *2201 C St. N.W., #3234 20520; (202) 647-9272. Fax, (202) 736-4476. Kevin Whitaker, Director.*
Web, www.state.gov

State Dept., *Mexican Affairs: U.S.-Mexico Border,* *2201 C St. N.W., #4258 20520-6258; (202) 647-8529. Fax, (202) 647-5752. Dennis M. Linskey, Border Coordinator.*
Web, www.state.gov

Acts as liaison between the United States and Mexico in international boundary and water matters as defined by binational treaties and agreements.

State Dept., *U.S. Mission to the Organization of American States,* *2201 C St. N.W., #5914 20520-6258; (202) 647-9376. Fax, (202) 647-6973. Roger Noriega, U.S. Permanent Representative.*
Web, www.state.gov

Formulates U.S. policy and represents U.S. interests at the Organization of American States (OAS).

CONGRESS

House International Relations Committee, *Subcommittee on the Western Hemisphere,* *259A FHOB 20515; (202) 226-9980. Fax, (202) 225-7485. Rep. Cass Ballenger, R-N.C., Chair; Caleb McCarry, Staff Director.*

Web, www.house.gov/international_relations

Jurisdiction over foreign affairs legislation dealing with Latin America, the Caribbean, Mexico, and Canada. Concurrent jurisdiction over matters assigned to the functional House International Relations subcommittees insofar as they affect the region.

Library of Congress, *Hispanic Division, 101 Independence Ave. S.E., #LJ-240 20540-4850; (202) 707-5400. Fax, (202) 707-2005. Georgette M. Dorn, Chief. Reference staff and reading room, (202) 707-5397.*
Web, lcweb.loc.gov/rr/hispanic

Reading room staff (in the Hispanic Division Room) orients researchers and scholars in the area of Iberian, Latin American, Caribbean, and U.S. Latino studies. Primary and secondary source materials are available in the library's general collections for the study of all periods, from pre-Columbian to the present, including recordings of 640 authors reading their own material. All major subject areas are represented with emphasis on history, literature, and the social sciences; the "Archive of Hispanic Literature on Tape" is available in the reading room.

Senate Foreign Relations Committee, *Subcommittee on Western Hemisphere, Peace Corps, and Narcotics Affairs, SD-446 20510; (202) 224-4651. Sen. Norm Coleman, R-Minn., Chair; Carl Meacham, Professional Staff Member.*
Web, foreign.senate.gov

Jurisdiction over foreign affairs legislation dealing with Latin America, the Caribbean, Mexico, and Canada; oversight of all matters of the Peace Corps and the U.S. delegation to the Organization of American States.

INTERNATIONAL ORGANIZATIONS

Inter-American Development Bank, *1300 New York Ave. N.W. 20577; (202) 623-1100. Fax, (202) 623-3096. Enrique V. Iglesias, President; Jose Fourquet, U.S. Executive Director, (202) 623-1031. Information, (202) 623-1000. Library, (202) 623-3211. Press, (202) 623-1371.*
Web, www.iadb.org

Promotes, through loans and technical assistance, the investment of public and private capital in member countries of Latin America and the Caribbean for social and economic development purposes. Facilitates economic integration of the Latin American region. Library open to the public by appointment.

International Bank for Reconstruction and Development (World Bank), *Latin America and the Caribbean, 1850 Eye St. N.W. 20433 (mailing address: 1818 H St. N.W., MCI8-800 20433); (202) 473-8729. Fax, (202) 676-9271. David de Ferranti, Vice President.*

Web, www.worldbank.org

Encourages public and private foreign investment in the countries of Latin America and the Caribbean through loans, loan guarantees, and technical assistance. Finances economic development projects in agriculture, environmental protection, education, public utilities, telecommunications, water supply, sewerage, public health, and other areas.

Organization of American States (OAS), *17th St. and Constitution Ave. N.W. 20006 (mailing address: 1889 F St. N.W. 20006); (202) 458-3000. Fax, (202) 458-3967. Cesar Gaviria, Secretary General. Library, (202) 458-6037.*
Web, www.oas.org

Membership: the United States, Canada, and all independent Latin American and Caribbean countries. Funded by quotas paid by member states and by contributions to special multilateral funds. Works to promote democracy, eliminate poverty, and resolve disputes among member nations. Provides member states with technical and advisory services in cultural, educational, scientific, social, and economic areas. Library open to the public.

United Nations Economic Commission for Latin America and the Caribbean, *Washington Office, 1825 K St. N.W., #1120 20006; (202) 955-5613. Fax, (202) 296-0826. Inés Bustillo, Director.*
General e-mail, info@eclac.org
Web, www.eclac.org

Membership: Latin American and some industrially developed Western nations. Seeks to strengthen economic relations between countries both within and outside Latin America through research and analysis of socioeconomic problems, training programs, and advisory services to member governments. (Headquarters in Santiago, Chile.)

NONPROFIT

Caribbean/Latin American Action, *1818 N St. N.W., #310 20036; (202) 466-7464. Fax, (202) 822-0075. Frederico Sacasa, Executive Director.*
General e-mail, info@claa.org
Web, www.claa.org

Promotes trade and investment in Caribbean Basin countries; encourages democratic public policy in member countries and works to strengthen private initiatives.

Center for International Policy, *1717 Massachusetts Ave. N.W., #801 20036; (202) 232-3317. Fax, (202) 232-3440. William Goodfellow, Executive Director.*
General e-mail, cip@ciponline.org
Web, www.ciponline.org

Research and educational organization concerned with peace and security worldwide. Special interests include military spending, U.S. intelligence policy, and U.S. policy toward Columbia, Cuba, and Haiti. Publishes the *International Policy Report.*

Council of the Americas, Americas Society, *Washington Office,* *1310 G St. N.W., #690 20005; (202) 639-0724. Fax, (202) 639-0794. Eric Farnsworth, Vice President.*
Web, www.counciloftheamericas.org

Membership: businesses with interests and investments in Latin America. Seeks to expand the role of private enterprise in development of the region. (Headquarters in New York.)

Council on Hemispheric Affairs, *1730 M St. N.W., #1010 20036-4505; (202) 216-9261. Fax, (202) 223-6035. Larry R. Birns, Director.*
General e-mail, coha@coha.org
Web, www.coha.org

Seeks to expand interest in Inter-American relations and increase press coverage of Latin America and Canada. Monitors U.S., Latin American, and Canadian relations, with emphasis on human rights, trade, growth of democratic institutions, freedom of the press, and hemispheric economic and political developments; provides educational materials and analyzes issues. Issues annual survey on human rights and freedom of the press.

Cuban American National Foundation, *Washington Office,* *1822 Jefferson Place N.W. 20036; (202) 530-1894. Fax, (202) 530-2444. Dennis Hays, Director.*
General e-mail, canfhq@canf.org
Web, www.canf.org

Conducts research and provides information on Cuba; supports the establishment of a democratic government in Cuba. Library open to the public by appointment. (Headquarters in Miami, Fla.)

Guatemala Human Rights Commission/USA, *3321 12th St. N.E. 20017-4008; (202) 529-6599. Fax, (202) 526-4611. Phil Anderson, Coordinator.*
General e-mail, ghrc-usa@ghrc-usa.org
Web, www.ghrc-usa.org

Provides information and collects and makes available reports on human rights violations in Guatemala; publishes a bimonthly report of documented cases of specific abuses. Takes on special projects to further sensitize the public and the international community to human rights abuses in Guatemala.

Inter-American Dialogue, *1211 Connecticut Ave. N.W., #510 20036-2701; (202) 822-9002. Fax, (202) 822-9553. Peter Hakim, President.*
General e-mail, iad@thedialogue.org
Web, www.thedialogue.org

Serves as a forum for communication and exchange among leaders of the Americas. Provides analyses and policy recommendations on issues of hemispheric concern. Interests include economic integration, trade, and the strengthening of democracy in Latin America. Hosts private and public exchanges; sponsors conferences and seminars; publishes daily newsletter, *Latin America Advisor.*

Network in Solidarity with the People of Guatemala, *1830 Connecticut Ave. N.W. 20009; (202) 518-7638. Fax, (202) 223-8221. Sarah Aird, Executive Director.*
General e-mail, nisgua@igc.org
Web, www.nisgua.org

Membership: organizations interested in promoting social justice and human rights in Guatemala. Opposes U.S. intervention in Guatemala; seeks to inform the public about human rights and U.S. policy in Guatemala.

Pan American Development Foundation, *2600 16th St. N.W., 4th Floor 20009-4202; (202) 458-3969. Fax, (202) 458-6316. John Sanbrailo, Executive Director.*
Web, www.padf.org

Works with the public and private sectors to improve the quality of life throughout the Caribbean and Latin America. Associated with the Organization of American States (OAS).

Partners of the Americas, *1424 K St. N.W., #700 20005; (202) 628-3300. Fax, (202) 628-3306. Malcolm Butler, President, (202) 637-6203.*
Web, www.partners.net

Membership: individuals in the United States, Latin America, and the Caribbean. Sponsors technical assistance projects and exchanges between the United States, Latin America, and the Caribbean; supports self-help projects in agriculture, public health, education, and democratic participation.

Religious Task Force on Central America and Mexico, *3053 4th St. N.E. 20017; (202) 529-0441. Fax, (202) 529-0447. Margaret Swedish, Director.*
General e-mail, general@rtfcam.org
Web, www.rtfcam.org

Network of religious-based organizations and individuals concerned about Central America and Mexico. Provides information and promotes human rights and social justice in the region.

U.S.-Mexico Chamber of Commerce, *1300 Pennsylvania Ave. N.W., #270 20004-3021; (202) 371-8680. Fax, (202) 371-8686. Albert C. Zapanta, President.*
General e-mail, news-hq@usmcoc.org
Web, www.usmcoc.org

Promotes trade and investment between the United States and Mexico. Provides members with information and expertise on conducting business between the two countries. Serves as a clearinghouse for information.

Washington Office on Latin America, *1630 Connecticut Ave. N.W., #200 20009; (202) 797-2171. Fax, (202) 797-2172. Bill Spencer, Executive Director.*
General e-mail, wola@wola.org
Web, www.wola.org

Acts as a liaison between government policymakers and groups and individuals concerned with human rights and U.S. policy in Latin America and the Caribbean. Serves as an information resource center; monitors legislation.

Near East and South Asia

(Includes North Africa)

AGENCIES

Agency for International Development (USAID), *Asia and Near East Bureau, 1300 Pennsylvania Ave. N.W., #4.09-034 20523-4900; (202) 712-0200. Fax, (202) 216-3386. Wendy Chamberlin, Assistant Administrator.*
Web, www.usaid.gov/regions/ane

Advises AID administrator on U.S. economic development policy in Asia and the Near East.

Defense Dept. (DoD), *Near East and South Asia Affairs, The Pentagon, #4D765 20301; (703) 697-5146. Fax, (703) 693-6795. William J. Luti, Deputy Assistant Secretary.*
Web, www.defenselink.mil

Advises the assistant secretary for international security affairs on matters dealing with the Near East and South Asia.

State Dept., *Bureau of Near Eastern Affairs, 2201 C St. N.W., #6242 20520-6243; (202) 647-7209. Fax, (202) 736-4462. William J. Burns Jr., Assistant Secretary.*
Web, www.state.gov

Advises the secretary on U.S. policy toward countries of the Near East and North Africa. Directors, assigned to specific countries within the bureau, aid the assistant secretary.

State Dept., *Bureau of South Asian Affairs, 2201 C St. N.W., #6254 20520-6258; (202) 736-4325. Fax, (202) 736-4333. Christina B. Rocca, Assistant Secretary.*
Web, www.state.gov

Advises the secretary on U.S. policy toward South Asian countries. Directors, assigned to specific countries within the bureau, aid the assistant secretary.

State Dept., *Arabian Peninsula Affairs, 2201 C St. N.W., #4224 20520-6243; (202) 647-6184. Fax, (202) 736-4459. Deborah K. Jones, Director.*
Web, www.state.gov

Includes Bahrain, Kuwait, Oman, Qatar, Saudi Arabia, United Arab Emirates, and Yemen.

State Dept., *Egyptian and North African Affairs, 2201 C St. N.W., #5250 20520; (202) 647-2300. Fax, (202) 736-4458. William A. Stanton, Director.*
Web, www.state.gov

Includes Algeria, Egypt, Libya, Morocco, and Tunisia.

State Dept., *India, Nepal, Sri Lanka Affairs, 2201 C St. N.W., #5251 20520-6243; (202) 647-2141. Fax, (202) 736-4463. David Good, Director.*
Web, www.state.gov

Includes Bhutan, India, Maldives, Nepal, and Sri Lanka.

State Dept., *Israeli-Palestinian Affairs, 2201 C St. N.W., #6251 20520; (202) 647-3673. Fax, (202) 736-4461. David Hale, Director.*
Web, www.state.gov

State Dept., *Lebanon, Jordan, and Syria Affairs, 2201 C St. N.W., #6250 20520-6243; (202) 647-2670. Fax, (202) 647-0989. Stephen Seche, Director.*
Web, www.state.gov

State Dept., *Northern Gulf Affairs, 2201 C St. N.W., #4241 20520; (202) 647-5692. Fax, (202) 736-4464. Thomas Skrajeski, Director.*
Web, www.state.gov

Includes Iran and Iraq.

State Dept., *Pakistan, Afghanistan, and Bangladesh Affairs, 2201 C St. N.W., #5247 20520-6258; (202) 647-7593. Fax, (202) 647-3001. Gerry Fieriesine, Director.*
Web, www.state.gov

CONGRESS

House International Relations Committee, *Subcommittee on the Middle East and Central Asia, B359 RHOB 20515; (202) 226-9940. Fax, (202) 226-4684. Rep.*

Ileana Ros-Lehtinen, R-Fla., Chair; Yleem Poblete, Staff Director.

Web, www.house.gov/international_relations

Jurisdiction over foreign affairs legislation dealing with the Arab states, Israel, Bhutan, Bangladesh, India, Pakistan, Afghanistan, Nepal, Sri Lanka, and countries across North Africa from Egypt to Morocco. Concurrent jurisdiction over matters assigned to the functional House International Relations subcommittees insofar as they affect the region.

Library of Congress, *African and Middle Eastern Division,* 110 2nd St. S.E., #220 20540; (202) 707-7937. Fax, (202) 252-3180. Beverly Gray, Chief.

Web, www.loc.gov

Maintains collections of African, Near Eastern, and Hebraic material. Prepares bibliographies and special studies relating to Africa and the Middle East. Reference service and reading rooms available to the public.

Library of Congress, *Asian Division,* 101 Independence Ave. S.E., #LJ150 20540-4810; (202) 707-5420. Fax, (202) 707-1724. Hwa-wei Lee, Chief.

Web, www.lcweb.loc.gov/rr/asian

Maintains collections of Chinese, Korean, Japanese, Southeast Asian, and South Asian material. Reference service is provided in the Asian Reading Room.

Senate Foreign Relations Committee, *Subcommittee on Near Eastern and South Asian Affairs,* SD-446 20510; (202) 224-4651. Sen. Lincoln Chafee, R-R.I., Chair; Keith Luse, Professional Staff Member.

Web, foreign.senate.gov

Jurisdiction over foreign affairs legislation dealing with the Near East and South Asia, including the Arab states and Israel, Bhutan, Bangladesh, India, Pakistan, Afghanistan, Nepal, Sri Lanka, and across North Africa from Egypt to Morocco.

INTERNATIONAL ORGANIZATIONS

International Bank for Reconstruction and Development (World Bank), *Middle East and North Africa,* 600 19th St. N.W. 20433 (mailing address: 1818 H St. N.W., #H10-163 20433); (202) 473-4946. Fax, (202) 477-0810. Jean-Louis Sarbib, Vice President.

Web, www.worldbank.org

Encourages public and private foreign investment in the countries of the Middle East and North Africa through loans, loan guarantees, and technical assistance. Finances economic development projects in agriculture, education, public utilities, telecommunications, water supply, sewerage, and other areas.

International Bank for Reconstruction and Development (World Bank), *South Asia,* 1818 H St. N.W., MSN 10-1003 20433; (202) 458-0600. Fax, (202) 522-3707. Mieko Nishimizu, Vice President.

Web, www.worldbank.org

Encourages public and private foreign investment in the countries of South Asia through loans, loan guarantees, and technical assistance. Finances economic development projects in agriculture, environmental protection, education, public utilities, telecommunications, water supply, sewerage, public health, and other areas.

League of Arab States, *Washington Office,* 1100 17th St. N.W., #602 20036; (202) 265-3210. Fax, (202) 331-1525. Amb. Hussein Hassouna, Director.

General e-mail, arableague@aol.com

Membership: Arab countries in the Near East, North Africa, and the Indian Ocean. Coordinates members' policies in political, cultural, economic, and social affairs; mediates disputes among members and between members and third parties. Washington office maintains the Arab Information Center. (Headquarters in Cairo.)

NONPROFIT

American Israel Public Affairs Committee, 440 1st St. N.W., #600 20001; (202) 639-5200. Fax, (202) 347-4889. Howard Kohr, Executive Director.

General e-mail, help@aipac.org

Web, www.aipac.org

Works to maintain and improve relations between the United States and Israel.

American Jewish Congress, *Washington Office,* 1001 Connecticut Ave. N.W., #470 20036; (202) 466-9661. Fax, (202) 466-9665. Charles Brooks, Executive Director.

General e-mail, washrep@ajcongress.org

Web, www.ajcongress.org

National Jewish organization that advocates the maintenance and improvement of U.S.-Israeli relations through legislation, public education, and joint economic ventures. Interests include the Arab boycott of Israel and foreign investment in the United States. (Headquarters in New York.)

American Kurdish Information Network (AKIN), 2600 Connecticut Ave. N.W., #1 20008-1558; (202) 483-6444. Kani Xulam, Director.

General e-mail, akin@kurdistan.org

Web, www.kurdistan.org

Membership: Americans of Kurdish origin, recent Kurdish immigrants and refugees, and others. Collects and disseminates information about the Kurds, an ethnic group living in parts of Turkey, Iran, Iraq, and Syria. Monitors human rights abuses against Kurds; promotes self-determination in Kurdish homelands; fosters Kurdish American friendship and understanding.

American Near East Refugee Aid, *1522 K St. N.W., #202 20005-1270; (202) 347-2558. Fax, (202) 682-1637. Peter Gubser, President.*
General e-mail, anera@anera.org
Web, www.anera.org

Assists Palestinian, Jordanian, and Lebanese grassroots organizations in providing their communities with health and welfare services, employment, and educational opportunities. Provides relief in response to civilian emergencies. (Field offices in Jerusalem, Amman, and Gaza.)

AMIDEAST, *1730 M St. N.W., #1100 20036; (202) 776-9600. Fax, (202) 776-7000. William Rugh, President.*
Web, www.amideast.org

Promotes understanding and cooperation between Americans and the people of the Middle East and North Africa through education, information, and development programs. Produces educational material to help improve teaching about the Arab world in American schools and colleges.

Asia Foundation, *Washington Office, 1779 Massachusetts Ave. N.W., #815 20036; (202) 588-9420. Fax, (202) 588-9409. Nancy Yuan, Director.*
Web, www.asiafoundation.org

Provides grants and technical assistance in Asia and the Pacific islands (excluding the Middle East). Seeks to strengthen legislatures, legal and judicial systems, market economies, the media, and nongovernmental organizations. (Headquarters in San Francisco, Calif.)

Asia Society, *Washington Office, 1800 K St. N.W., #1102 20006; (202) 833-2742. Fax, (202) 833-0189. Joseph C. Snyder, Director.*
General e-mail, dcinfo@asiasoc.org
Web, www.asiasociety.org

Membership: individuals interested in Asia and the Pacific (excluding the Middle East). Sponsors seminars and lectures on political, economic, and cultural issues. (Headquarters in New York.)

Center for Contemporary Arab Studies *(Georgetown University), 241 Intercultural Center 20057-1020; (202) 687-5793. Fax, (202) 687-7001. Barbara Stowasser, Director.*
General e-mail, ccasinfo@georgetown.edu
Web, www.ccasonline.org

Sponsors lecture series, seminars, and conferences. Conducts a community outreach program that assists secondary school teachers in the development of instructional materials on the Middle East; promotes the study of the Arabic language in area schools.

Center for Middle East Peace and Economic Cooperation, *633 Pennsylvania Ave. N.W., 5th Floor 20004; (202) 624-0850. Fax, (202) 624-0855. S. Daniel Abraham, Chair.*
Web, www.centerpeace.org

Membership: Middle Eastern policymakers, American government officials, and international business leaders. Serves as a mediator to encourage a peaceful resolution to the Arab-Israeli conflict; sponsors travel to the region, diplomatic exchanges, and conferences for Middle Eastern and American leaders interested in the peace process.

Council on American-Islamic Relations, *453 New Jersey Ave. S.E. 20003; (202) 488-8787. Fax, (202) 488-0833. Nihad Awad, Executive Director.*
General e-mail, cair@cair-net.org
Web, www.cair-net.org

Promotes an Islamic perspective on issues of importance to the American public. Seeks to empower the Muslim community in America through political and social activism.

Foundation for Middle East Peace, *1761 N St. N.W. 20036; (202) 835-3650. Fax, (202) 835-3651. Amb. Philip C. Wilcox Jr., President.*
General e-mail, info@fmep.org
Web, www.fmep.org

Educational organization that seeks to promote understanding and resolution of the Israeli-Palestinian conflict. Publishes a bimonthly report, *Israeli Settlement in the Occupied Territories*; provides media with information; and awards grants to organizations and activities that contribute to the solution of the conflict.

Institute for Palestine Studies, *Washington Office, 3501 M St. N.W. 20007-2624; (202) 342-3990. Fax, (202) 342-3927. Linda Butler, Director (Acting).*
General e-mail, jps@palestine_studies.org
Web, www.ipsjps.org

Scholarly research institute that specializes in the history and development of the Palestine problem, the Arab-Israeli conflict, and their peaceful resolution. (Headquarters in Beirut, Lebanon.)

Institute of Turkish Studies *(Georgetown University), Georgetown University, Intercultural Center, Box*

571033 20057-1033; (202) 687-0295. Fax, (202) 687-3780. Sabri Sayari, Executive Director.

Web, www.turkishstudies.org

Supports and encourages the development of Turkish studies in American colleges and universities. Awards grants to individual scholars and educational institutions in the United States.

Kashmiri-American Council, 733 15th St. N.W., #1100 20005; (202) 628-6789. Fax, (202) 628-0062. Ghulam Nabi Fai, Executive Director.

Web, www.kashmiri.com

Promotes self-determination for Jammu and Kashmir, a region claimed by both India and Pakistan; monitors human rights violations in the region; fosters unity and social interaction among people of Kashmiri ancestry, regardless of religious or political affiliations.

Middle East Institute, 1761 N St. N.W. 20036-2882; (202) 785-1141. Fax, (202) 331-8861. Amb. Ned Walker Jr., President. Library, (202) 785-0183. Language Dept., (202) 785-2710.

General e-mail, mideasti@mideasti.org

Web, www.mideasti.org

Membership: individuals interested in the Middle East. Seeks to broaden knowledge of the Middle East through research, conferences and seminars, language classes, lectures, and exhibits. Library open to the public.

Middle East Policy Council, 1730 M St. N.W., #512 20036-4505; (202) 296-6767. Fax, (202) 296-5791. Charles W. Freeman Jr., President.

General e-mail, info@mepc.org

Web, www.mepc.org

Encourages public discussion and understanding of issues affecting U.S. policy in the Middle East. Sponsors conferences for the policy community; conducts workshops for high school teachers nationwide.

Middle East Research and Information Project, 1500 Massachusetts Ave. N.W., #119 20005; (202) 223-3677. Fax, (202) 223-3604. Christopher J. Toensing, Executive Director.

General e-mail, ctoensing@merip.org

Web, www.merip.org

Works to educate the public about the contemporary Middle East. Focuses on U.S. policy in the region and issues of human rights and social justice.

National Council on U.S.-Arab Relations, 1140 Connecticut Ave. N.W., #1210 20036; (202) 293-0801. Fax, (202) 293-0903. John Duke Anthony, President.

General e-mail, info@ncusar.org

Web, www.ncusar.org

Educational organization that works to improve mutual understanding between the United States and the Arab world. Serves as a clearinghouse on Arab issues and maintains speakers bureau. Coordinates trips for U.S. professionals and congressional delegations to the Arab world.

National U.S.-Arab Chamber of Commerce, 1023 15th St. N.W., 4th Floor 20005; (202) 289-5920. Fax, (202) 289-5938. Marjorie Adams, President.

Web, www.nusacc.org

Promotes trade between the United States and the Arab world. Offers members informational publications, research and certification services, and opportunities to meet with international delegations.

New Israel Fund, 1101 14th St. N.W., 6th Floor 20005-5639; (202) 842-0900. Fax, (202) 849-0991. Norman Rosenberg, Executive Director.

General e-mail, info@nif.org

Web, www.nif.org

International philanthropic partnership of North Americans, Israelis, and Europeans. Supports activities that defend civil and human rights, promote Jewish-Arab equality and coexistence, advance the status of women, nurture tolerance, bridge social and economic gaps, encourage government accountability, and assist citizen efforts to protect the environment. Makes grants and provides capacity-building assistance to Israeli public interest groups; trains civil rights and environmental lawyers.

United Palestinian Appeal, 1330 New Hampshire Ave. N.W., #104 20036; (202) 659-5007. Fax, (202) 296-0224. Makboula Yasin, Deputy Director.

General e-mail, contact@helpupa.com

Web, www.helpupa.com

Charitable organization dedicated to improving the quality of life for Palestinians in the Middle East, particularly those in the West Bank, the Gaza Strip, and refugee camps. Provides funding for community development projects, health care, education, children's services, and emergency relief. Funded by private donations from individuals and foundations in the United States and Arab world.

Washington Institute for Near East Policy, 1828 L St. N.W., #1050 20036; (202) 452-0650. Fax, (202) 223-5364. Robert Satloff, Executive Director.

General e-mail, info@washingtoninstitute.org

Web, www.washingtoninstitute.org

Research and educational organization that seeks to improve the effectiveness of American policy in the Near East by promoting debate among policymakers, journalists, and scholars.

Washington Kurdish Institute, *605 G St. S.W. 20024; (202) 484-0140. Fax, (202) 484-0142. Michael Amitay, Executive Director.*
General e-mail, wki@kurd.org
Web, www.kurd.org

Membership: scholars, human rights practitioners, Middle East and foreign policy experts, and Kurds from around the world.

Women's Alliance for Peace and Human Rights in Afghanistan, *P.O. Box 77057 20013-7057; (202) 882-1432. Fax, (202) 882-8125. Zieba Shorish-Shamley, Executive Director.*
General e-mail, zieba@aol.com
Web, www.wapha.org

United States–based organization that advocates for Afghan women's sociopolitical and economic rights. Seeks to achieve full restoration of Afghan women and girls' rights and Afghan women's full participation in the restoration of their country.

Russia and New Independent States

For the Baltic states, see Europe

AGENCIES

Agency for International Development (USAID), *Europe and Eurasia Bureau, 1300 Pennsylvania Ave. N.W., #5.06 20523-5600; (202) 712-0290. Fax, (202) 216-3057. Kent R. Hill, Assistant Administrator.*
Web, www.usaid.gov/regions/europe_eurasia

Advises AID administrator on U.S. economic development policy in Europe and the new independent states.

Kennan Institute for Advanced Russian Studies, *1300 Pennsylvania Ave. N.W. 20004-3027; (202) 691-4100. Fax, (202) 691-4247. Blair A. Ruble, Director.*
General e-mail, kiars@wwic.si.edu
Web, www.wilsoncenter.org

Offers residential research scholarships to academic scholars and to specialists from government, media, and the private sector for studies to improve American knowledge about Russia and the former Soviet Union. Sponsors lectures; publishes reports; promotes dialogue between academic specialists and policymakers. (Affiliated with the Woodrow Wilson International Center for Scholars.)

State Dept., *Ambassador-at-Large (NIS), 2201 C St. N.W., #4234 20520-7512; (202) 647-5067. Amb. Rudolf V. Perina, Special Negotiator.*
Web, www.state.gov

Handles regional conflicts among Nagorno-Karabakh and Russia's new independent states.

State Dept., *Caucasus and Central Asian Affairs, 2201 C St. N.W., #4217 20520-7512; (202) 647-9370. Fax, (202) 736-4710. Richard E. Hoagland, Director.*
Web, www.state.gov

Includes Armenia, Azerbaijan, Georgia, Kazakhstan, Kyrgyzstan, Tajikistan, Turkmenistan, and Uzbekistan.

State Dept., *Russian Affairs, 2201 C St. N.W., #4417 20520-7512; (202) 647-9806. Fax, (202) 647-8980. John Evans, Director.*
Web, www.state.gov

State Dept., *Ukraine, Moldova, and Belarus Affairs, 2201 C St. N.W., #4427 20520-7512; (202) 647-8671. Fax, (202) 647-3506. Mark Taplin, Director.*
Web, www.state.gov

CONGRESS

House International Relations Committee, *2170 RHOB 20515; (202) 225-5021. Fax, (202) 226-2831. Rep. Henry J. Hyde, R-Ill., Chair; Thomas E. Mooney, Chief of Staff. Hearing notification line, (202) 225-3184.*
General e-mail, hirc@mail.house.gov
Web, www.house.gov/international_relations

Jurisdiction over legislation dealing with Russia and the new independent states. Concurrent jurisdiction over matters assigned to the functional House International Relations subcommittees insofar as they affect the region.

Library of Congress, *European Division, 101 Independence Ave. S.E., Jefferson Bldg., #LJ-250 20540-4830; (202) 707-5414. Fax, (202) 707-8482. John Van Oudenaren, Chief. Reference desk, (202) 707-4515.*
General e-mail, eurref@loc.gov
Web, www.lcweb.loc.gov/rr/european

Provides reference service on the library's European collections (except collections on Spain, Portugal, and the British Isles). Prepares bibliographies and special studies relating to European countries, including Russia and the new independent states. Maintains current unbound Slavic language periodicals and newspapers, which are available at the European Reference Desk.

Senate Foreign Relations Committee, *SD-450 20510; (202) 224-4651. Fax, (202) 228-1608. Sen. Richard G. Lugar, R-Ind., Chair; Kenneth A. Myers, Staff Director. Web, foreign.senate.gov*

Jurisdiction over legislation dealing with Russia and the new independent states.

INTERNATIONAL ORGANIZATIONS

International Bank for Reconstruction and Development (World Bank), *Europe and Central Asia, 600 19th St. N.W. 20431 (mailing address: 1818 H St. N.W., #I12211 20433); (202) 458-0602. Fax, (202) 522-2758. Johannes F. Linn, Vice President. General e-mail, ecainformation@worldbank.org Web, www.worldbank.org*

Encourages public and private foreign investment in eastern Europe and central Asia, including the former Soviet Union, through loans, loan guarantees, and technical assistance. Finances economic development projects in agriculture, environmental protection, education, energy, public utilities, telecommunications, water supply, sewerage, public health, and other areas.

NONPROFIT

American Bar Assn. (ABA), *Central European and Eurasian Law Initiative, 740 15th St. N.W., 8th Floor 20005-1022; (202) 662-1950. Fax, (202) 662-1597. David Tolbert, Executive Director. General e-mail, ceeli@abanet.org Web, www.abaceeli.org*

Promotes the rule of law and specific legal reforms in the emerging democracies of central and eastern Europe, Russia, and the new independent states; recruits volunteer legal professionals from the United States and western Europe. Interests include civil, criminal, commercial, and environmental law; judicial restructuring; bar development; and legal education and research.

American Councils for International Education, *American Council of Teachers of Russian, 1776 Massachusetts Ave. N.W., #700 20036; (202) 833-7522. Fax, (202) 833-7523. Dan Davidson, President. General e-mail, general@americancouncils.org Web, www.actr.org*

Conducts educational exchanges for high school, university, and graduate school students as well as scholars with the countries of the former Soviet Union and Eastern Europe. Assists the countries of the former Soviet Union in implementing education reforms, advises them on academic testing, and provides them with language instruction materials.

Armenian Assembly of America, *122 C St. N.W., #350 20001; (202) 393-3434. Fax, (202) 638-4904. Ross Vartian, Executive Director. Web, www.armenianassembly.org*

Promotes public understanding and awareness of Armenian issues; advances research and data collection and disseminates information on the Armenian people; advocates greater Armenian American participation in the American democratic process; works to alleviate human suffering of Armenians.

Eurasia Foundation, *1350 Connecticut Ave. N.W., #1000 20036; (202) 234-7370. Fax, (202) 234-7377. Charles William Maynes, President. General e-mail, eurasia@eurasia.org Web, www.eurasia.org*

Grant-making organization that funds programs that build democratic and free market institutions in the new independent states. Interests include economic and governmental reform, development of the nonprofit sector, and projects in media and communications.

Free Congress Research and Education Foundation (FCF), *717 2nd St. N.E. 20002-4368; (202) 546-3000. Fax, (202) 543-5605. Marian E. Harrison, Chair. General e-mail, info@freecongress.org Web, www.freecongress.org*

Public policy research and education foundation. Through the Krieble Institute, provides citizens of the former Soviet bloc with training in democratic processes and free enterprise.

Institute for European, Russian, and Eurasian Studies *(George Washington University), 2013 G St. N.W., Stuart Hall #401 20052; (202) 994-6340. Fax, (202) 994-5436. James M. Goldgeier, Director. Web, www.ieres.org*

Studies and researches European, Russian, and Eurasian affairs.

ISAR: Initiative for Social Action and Renewal in Eurasia, *1601 Connecticut Ave. N.W., #301 20009; (202) 387-3034. Fax, (202) 667-3291. Eliza K. Klose, Executive Director. Web, www.isar.org*

Encourages cooperation between America and the former Soviet Union. Operates an information clearinghouse on issues such as agriculture and the environment. Library open to the public.

Jamestown Foundation, *4516 43rd St. N.W. 20016; (202) 483-8888. Fax, (202) 483-8337. Barbara Abbott, President.*

Web, www.jamestown.org

Promotes development of democracy, civil liberty, and free enterprise. Publishes news and analysis of events in the Russian Federation, the Baltic states, Ukraine, Belarus, Moldova, Central Asia, and the Caucasus, as well as on Chechnya and China.

NCSJ: Advocates on behalf of Jews in Russia, Ukraine, the Baltic States and Eurasia, *2020 K St. N.W., #7800 20006; (202) 898-2500. Fax, (202) 898-0822. Mark B. Levin, Executive Director.*
General e-mail, ncsj@ncsj.org
Web, www.ncsj.org

Membership: national Jewish organizations and local federations. Coordinates efforts by members to aid Jews in the former Soviet Union, including Jewish families attempting to emigrate.

Ukrainian National Information Service, *Washington Office, 311 Massachusetts Ave. N.E., Lower Level 20002; (202) 547-0018. Fax, (202) 543-5502. Michael Sawkiw Jr., Director and President.*
General e-mail, unis@ucca.org
Web, www.ucca.org

Information bureau of the Ukrainian Congress Committee of America in New York. Provides information and monitors U.S. policy on Ukraine and the Ukrainian community in the United States and abroad. (Headquarters in New York.)

U.S.-Russia Business Council, *1701 Pennsylvania Ave. N.W., #520 20006; (202) 739-9180. Fax, (202) 659-5920. Eugene K. Lawson, President. Press, (202) 739-9184.*
Web, www.usrbc.org

Membership: U.S. companies involved in trade and investment in Russia. Promotes commercial ties between the United States and Russia.

U.S. Territories and Associated States

AGENCIES

Interior Dept. (DOI), *Insular Affairs, 1849 C St. N.W., #4311, Mail Drop 4311A 20240; (202) 208-4736. Fax, (202) 219-1989. Nik Pula, Director.*
Web, www.doi.gov

Promotes economic, social, and political development of U.S. territories (Guam, American Samoa, the Virgin Islands, and the Commonwealth of the Northern Mariana Islands). Supervises federal programs for the freely associated states (Federated States of Micronesia, Republic of the Marshall Islands, and Republic of Palau).

CONGRESS

American Samoa's Delegate to Congress, *2422 RHOB 20515; (202) 225-8577. Fax, (202) 225-8757. Del. Eni F. H. Faleomavaega, D-Am. Samoa, Delegate.*
General e-mail, Faleomavaega@mail.house.gov
Web, www.house.gov/faleomavaega

Represents American Samoa in Congress.

Guam's Delegate to Congress, *427 CHOB 20515; (202) 225-1188. Fax, (202) 226-0341. Del. Madeleine Z. Bordallo, D-Guam, Delegate.*
General e-mail, madeleine.bordallo@mail.house.gov
Web, www.house.gov/bordallo

Represents Guam in Congress.

House Appropriations Committee, *Subcommittee on Interior, B308 RHOB 20515; (202) 225-3081. Fax, (202) 225-9069. Rep. Charles H. Taylor, R-N.C., Chair; Deborah A. Weatherly, Staff Director.*
Web, www.house.gov/appropriations

Jurisdiction over legislation to appropriate funds for territorial affairs.

House Resources Committee, *1324 LHOB 20515; (202) 225-2761. Fax, (202) 225-5929. Rep. Richard W. Pombo, R-Calif., Chair; Steve Ding, Chief of Staff.*
General e-mail, resources.committee@mail.house.gov
Web, resourcescommittee.house.gov

Jurisdiction, oversight, and investigative authority over activities, policies, and programs for U.S. territories (Guam, American Samoa, Puerto Rico, the Northern Mariana Islands, and the Virgin Islands) and for the freely associated states (Federated States of Micronesia, Republic of the Marshall Islands, Republic of Palau).

Puerto Rican Resident Commissioner, *2443 RHOB 20515; (202) 225-2615. Fax, (202) 225-2154. Del. Aníbal Acevedo-Vilá, D-P.R., Resident Commissioner.*
General e-mail, Anibal@mail.house.gov
Web, www.house.gov/acevedo-vila

Represents the Commonwealth of Puerto Rico in Congress.

Senate Appropriations Committee, *Subcommittee on Interior and Related Agencies, SD-131 20510; (202) 224-7233. Fax, (202) 228-4532. Sen. Conrad Burns, R-Mont., Chair; Bruce Evans, Clerk.*
Web, appropriations.senate.gov

Jurisdiction over legislation to appropriate funds for territorial and Pacific island affairs.

Senate Energy and Natural Resources Committee,
SD-364 20510; (202) 224-4971. Fax, (202) 224-6163. Sen.
Pete V. Domenici, R-N.M., Chair; Alex Flint, Staff Director.
General e-mail, committee@energy.senate.gov
Web, energy.senate.gov

Jurisdiction, oversight, and investigative authority over activities, policies, and programs for U.S. territories (Guam, American Samoa, Puerto Rico, the Northern Mariana Islands, and the Virgin Islands) and for the freely associated states (Federated States of Micronesia, Republic of the Marshall Islands, and Republic of Palau).

Virgin Islands Delegate to Congress, 1510 LHOB 20515; (202) 225-1790. Fax, (202) 225-5517. Del. Donna M. C. Christensen, D-Virgin Is., Delegate.
Web, www.house.gov/christian-christensen

Represents the Virgin Islands in Congress.

NONPROFIT

Puerto Rico Federal Affairs Administration,
1100 17th St. N.W., #800 20036; (202) 778-0710. Fax, (202) 632-1288. Mari Carmen Aponte, Executive Director.
Web, www.prfaa.com

Represents the governor and the government of the Commonwealth of Puerto Rico before Congress and the executive branch; conducts research; serves as official press information center for the Commonwealth of Puerto Rico. Monitors legislation and regulations.

U.S. Virgin Islands Department of Tourism, Washington Office, 444 N. Capitol St. N.W., #305 20001; (202) 624-3590. Fax, (202) 624-3594. Claude Richards, Manager.
Web, www.usvi.org/tourism

Provides information about the U.S. Virgin Islands; promotes tourism. (Headquarters in St. Thomas.)

14 ⚖

Law and Justice

⚖ GENERAL POLICY

AGENCIES

Executive Office for U.S. Attorneys *(Justice Dept.)*, *950 Pennsylvania Ave. N.W., #2621 20530; (202) 514-2121. Fax, (202) 616-2278. Guy A. Lewis, Director. Information, (202) 514-1020.*
Web, www.usdoj.gov/usao/eousa

Provides the offices of U.S. attorneys with technical assistance and supervision in areas of legal counsel, personnel, and training. Publishes the *U.S. Attorneys' Manual.* Administers the Attorney General's Advocacy Institute, which conducts workshops and seminars to develop the litigation skills of the department's attorneys in criminal and civil trials. Develops and implements Justice Dept. procedures and policy for collecting criminal fines.

Justice Dept. (DOJ), *950 Pennsylvania Ave. N.W., #5137 20530-0001; (202) 514-2001. Fax, (202) 307-6777. John D. Ashcroft, Attorney General; Larry D. Thompson, Deputy Attorney General; Jay B. Stephens, Associate Attorney General. Information, (202) 514-2000.*
Web, www.usdoj.gov

Investigates and prosecutes violations of federal laws; represents the government in federal cases and interprets laws under which other departments act. Supervises federal corrections system; administers immigration and naturalization laws. Justice Dept. organization includes divisions on antitrust, civil law, civil rights, criminal law, environment and natural resources, and tax, as well as the Federal Bureau of Investigation, Federal Bureau of Prisons, Office of Legal Counsel, Office of Policy Development, Office of Professional Responsibility, U.S. Parole Commission, Immigration and Naturalization Service, Board of Immigration Appeals, Executive Office for Immigration Review, Drug Enforcement Administration, Foreign Claims Settlement Commission of the United States, Office of Justice Programs, U.S. Marshals Service, and U.S. Trustees.

Justice Dept. (DOJ), *Legal Policy, 950 Pennsylvania Ave. N.W., #4234 20530; (202) 514-4601. Fax, (202) 514-2424. Viet D. Dinh, Assistant Attorney General.*
Web, www.usdoj.gov/olp

Studies, develops, and coordinates Justice Dept. policy. Drafts and reviews legislative proposals. Oversees implementation of the Freedom of Information and Privacy acts.

Justice Dept. (DOJ), *Professional Responsibility, 20 Massachusetts Ave. N.W., #5100 20530; (202) 514-3365. Fax, (202) 514-5050. H. Marshall Jarrett, Counsel.*
Web, www.usdoj.gov/opr

Receives and reviews allegations of misconduct by Justice Dept. attorneys; refers cases that warrant further review to appropriate investigative agency or unit; makes recommendations to the attorney general for action on certain misconduct cases.

Justice Dept. (DOJ), *Solicitor General, 950 Pennsylvania Ave. N.W., #5143 20530; (202) 514-2201. Fax, (202) 514-9769. Theodore B. Olson, Solicitor General. Information on pending cases, (202) 514-2218.*
Web, www.usdoj.gov/osg

Represents the federal government before the Supreme Court of the United States.

Office of Justice Programs (OJP), *(Justice Dept.), 810 7th St. N.W., #6100 20531; (202) 307-5933. Fax, (202) 514-7805. Deborah J. Daniels, Assistant Attorney General.*
Web, www.ojp.usdoj.gov

Sets program policy, provides staff support, and coordinates administration for the National Institute of Justice, which conducts research on criminal justice; the Bureau of Justice Statistics, which gathers and evaluates national crime data; the Office for Victims of Crime, which funds state victim compensation and assistance programs; the Office of Juvenile Justice and Delinquency Prevention, which administers federal juvenile delinquency programs; and the Bureau of Justice Assistance, which provides funds for anticrime programs.

CONGRESS

General Accounting Office (GAO), *Homeland Security and Justice, 441 G St. N.W., #2A38 20548; (202) 512-8777. Fax, (202) 512-8692. Norm Rabkin and Randall Yim, Managing Directors. Documents, (202) 512-6000.*
Web, www.gao.gov

Independent, nonpartisan agency in the legislative branch. Audits, analyzes, and evaluates federal administration of justice programs and activities; makes some reports available to the public.

House Appropriations Committee, *Subcommittee on Commerce, Justice, State, and the Judiciary, H309 CAP 20515; (202) 225-3351. Rep. Frank R. Wolf, R-Va., Chair; Mike Ringler, Staff Director.*
Web, www.house.gov/appropriations

Jurisdiction over legislation to appropriate funds for the Justice Dept., the federal judiciary, the Legal Services Corp., the State Justice Institute, juvenile justice and delinquency prevention, district courts, and other judicial-related services and programs.

House Government Reform Committee, *Subcommittee on Criminal Justice, Drug Policy, and Human*

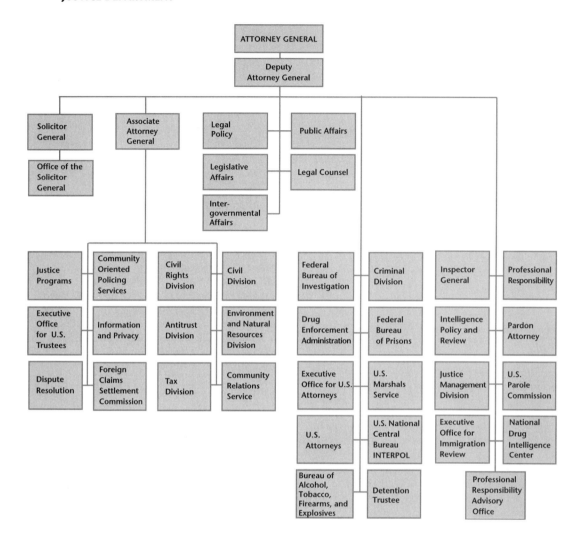

Resources, *B373B RHOB 20515; (202) 225-2577. Fax, (202) 225-1154. Rep. Mark Souder, R-Ind., Chair; Christopher Donesa, Staff Director.*
Web, www.house.gov/reform

Oversees operations of the Justice Dept., the federal judiciary (except the U.S. Tax Court), the Legal Services Corp., and the State Justice Institute.

House Judiciary Committee, *2138 RHOB 20515; (202) 225-3951. Fax, (202) 225-7682. Rep. F. James Sensenbrenner Jr., R-Wis., Chair; Phil Kiko, Chief of Staff.*
General e-mail, Judiciary@mail.house.gov
Web, www.house.gov/judiciary

Jurisdiction over legislation on judicial proceedings; constitutional amendments; civil liberties; ethics in government; federal judiciary; federal corrections system; interstate compacts; patents; copyrights and trademarks; bankruptcy; mutiny; espionage and counterfeiting; immigration and naturalization; revision and codification of the statutes of the United States; internal security; local courts in the territories and possessions; protection of trade and commerce against unlawful restraints and monopolies; legislation relating to claims against the United States; and state and territorial boundary lines.

House Judiciary Committee, *Subcommittee on Courts, the Internet, and Intellectual Property,* B351A RHOB 20515; (202) 225-5741. Fax, (202) 225-3673. Rep. Lamar Smith, R-Texas, Chair; Blaine Merritt, Chief Counsel.

General e-mail, Judiciary@mail.house.gov

Web, www.house.gov/judiciary

Jurisdiction over legislation on court administration and management and over rules of civil judicial procedure. Oversees the Administrative Office of the U.S. Courts.

Senate Appropriations Committee, *Subcommittee on Commerce, Justice, State, and the Judiciary,* S-206 CAP 20510; (202) 224-7277. Fax, (202) 228-0587. Sen. Judd Gregg, R-N.H., Chair; James Morhard, Clerk.

Web, appropriations.senate.gov

Jurisdiction over legislation to appropriate funds for the Commerce Dept., the Securities and Exchange Commission, the Small Business Administration, the Competitiveness Policy Council, the Federal Trade Commission, the International Trade Commission, and the Office of the U.S. Trade Representative.

Senate Judiciary Committee, SD-224 20510; (202) 224-5225. Fax, (202) 224-9102. Sen. Orrin G. Hatch, R-Utah, Chair; Makan Delrahim, Chief Counsel.

Web, judiciary.senate.gov

Jurisdiction over legislation on judicial proceedings, constitutional amendments, civil liberties, ethics in government, federal judiciary, federal corrections system, interstate compacts, government information, patents, copyrights and trademarks, bankruptcy, mutiny, espionage and counterfeiting, immigration and naturalization, revision and codification of the statutes of the United States, internal security, local courts in the territories and possessions, protection of trade and commerce against unlawful restraints and monopolies, legislation relating to claims against the United States, and state and territorial boundary lines. Oversees operations of the Justice Dept., the federal judiciary (except the U.S. Tax Court), the Legal Services Corp., and the State Justice Institute.

Senate Judiciary Committee, *Subcommittee on Administrative Oversight and the Courts,* SD-323 20510; (202) 224-7572. Fax, (202) 228-0545. Sen. Jeff Sessions, R-Ala., Chair; William Smith, Chief Counsel.

Web, judiciary.senate.gov

Jurisdiction over legislation on court administration and management and over rules of civil judicial procedure.

JUDICIARY

Administrative Office of the U.S. Courts, 1 Columbus Circle N.E., #7-400 20544; (202) 273-3000. Leonidas Ralph Mecham, Director. Information, (202) 502-2600.

Web, www.uscourts.gov

Provides administrative support to the federal courts including the procurement of supplies and equipment; the administration of personnel, budget, and financial control services; and the compilation and publication of statistical data and reports on court business. Implements the policies of the Judicial Conference of the United States and supports its committees. Recommends plans and strategies to manage court business. Supports judicial officers, including active and senior appellate and district court judges, bankruptcy judges, and magistrate judges.

Federal Judicial Center, 1 Columbus Circle N.E. 20002-8003; (202) 502-4160. Fax, (202) 502-4099. Fern M. Smith, Director. Library, (202) 502-4153.

Web, www.fjc.gov

Conducts research on the operations of the federal court system; develops and conducts continuing education and training programs for judges and judicial personnel; and makes recommendations to improve the administration of the courts.

Judicial Conference of the United States, 1 Columbus Circle N.E., #7-425 20544; (202) 502-2400. Fax, (202) 502-1144. William H. Rehnquist, Chief Justice of the United States, Chair; Leonidas Ralph Mecham, Secretary.

Web, www.uscourts.gov

Serves as the policy-making and governing body for the administration of the federal judicial system; advises Congress on the creation of new federal judgeships. Interests include international judicial relations.

Supreme Court of the United States, 1 1st St. N.E. 20543; (202) 479-3000. William H. Rehnquist, Chief Justice. Information, (202) 479-3211.

Web, www.supremecourtus.gov

Highest appellate court in the federal judicial system. Interprets the U.S. Constitution, federal legislation, and treaties. Provides information on new cases filed, the status of pending cases, and admissions to the Supreme Court Bar. Library open to Supreme Court bar members only.

NONPROFIT

Alliance for Justice, 11 Dupont Circle N.W., 2nd Floor 20036-1213; (202) 822-6070. Fax, (202) 822-6068. Nan Aron, President.

General e-mail, alliance@afj.org

Web, www.afj.org

Membership: public interest lawyers and advocacy, environmental, civil rights, and consumer organizations. Promotes reform of the legal system to ensure access to the courts; monitors selection of federal judges; works to preserve the rights of nonprofit organizations to advocate on behalf of their constituents.

American Bar Assn. (ABA), *Washington Office,* *740 15th St. N.W. 20005-1019; (202) 662-1000. Fax, (202) 662-1032. Robert D. Evans, Director. Information, (202) 662-1010. Library, (202) 662-1011.*

Web, www.abanet.org

Comprised of the Public Service Division, the Government and Public Sector Division, International Law and Practice Section, Criminal Justice Section, Taxation Section, Individual Rights and Responsibilities Section, Dispute Resolution Section, Administrative Law and Regulatory Practice Section, and others. Acts as a clearinghouse for the association's legislative activities and communicates the status of important bills and regulations to state and local bar associations and to all sections concerned with major governmental activities that affect the legal profession. (Headquarters in Chicago, Ill.)

American Tort Reform Assn., *1101 Connecticut Ave. N.W., #400 20036-5803; (202) 682-1163. Fax, (202) 682-1022. Sherman Joyce, President.*

General e-mail, atra@atra.org

Web, www.atra.org

Membership: businesses, associations, trade groups, professional societies, and individuals interested in reforming the civil justice system in the United States. Develops model state legislation and position papers on tort reform. Works with state coalitions in support of tort reform legislation.

Assn. of Trial Lawyers of America, *1050 31st St. N.W. 20007-4499; (202) 965-3500. Fax, (202) 342-5484. Thomas H. Henderson Jr., Executive Director.*

Web, www.atlanet.org

Membership: attorneys, judges, law professors, and students. Works to strengthen the civil justice system and the right to trial by jury. Interests include victims' rights, property and casualty insurance, revisions of federal rules of evidence, criminal code, jurisdictions of courts, juries, and consumer law.

Center for Study of Responsive Law, *1530 P St. N.W. 20005 (mailing address: P.O. Box 19367 20036); (202) 387-8030. Fax, (202) 234-5176. John Richard, Administrator.*

Web, www.csrl.org

Consumer interest clearinghouse that conducts research and holds conferences on public interest law. Interests include white-collar crime, the environment, occupational health and safety, the postal system, banking deregulation, insurance, freedom of information policy, and broadcasting.

Death Penalty Information Center, *1320 18th St. N.W., 2nd Floor 20036; (202) 293-6970. Fax, (202) 822-4787. Richard Dieter, Executive Director.*

General e-mail, dpic@deathpenaltyinfo.org

Web, www.deathpenaltyinfo.org

Provides the media and public with analysis and information on issues concerning capital punishment. Conducts briefings for journalists; prepares reports; issues press releases.

Federal Bar Assn., *2215 M St. N.W. 20037; (202) 785-1614. Fax, (202) 785-1568. Jack D. Lockridge, Executive Director.*

General e-mail, fba@fedbar.org

Web, www.fedbar.org

Membership: attorneys employed by the federal government or practicing before federal courts or agencies. Conducts research and programs in fields including tax, native American, antitrust, immigration, and international law; concerns include professional ethics, legal education (primarily continuing education), and legal services.

The Federalist Society, *1015 18th St. N.W., #425 20036; (202) 822-8138. Fax, (202) 296-8061. Eugene B. Meyer, Director.*

General e-mail, fedsoc@radix.net

Web, www.fed-soc.org

Promotes awareness of federalist principles among lawyers, judges, law professors, law students, and the general public. Sponsors lectures and seminars.

HALT—An Organization of Americans for Legal Reform, *1612 K St. N.W., #510 20006; (202) 887-8255. Fax, (202) 887-9699. James C. Turner, Executive Director.*

Web, www.halt.org

Public interest organization concerned with legal reform. Conducts research on alternative dispute resolution programs for delivery of legal services, including arbitration, legal clinics, and mediation services; provides educational and self-help manuals on the use of the legal system.

Lawyers for Civil Justice, *1140 Connecticut Ave. N.W., #503 20036; (202) 429-0045. Fax, (202) 429-6982. Barry Bauman, Executive Director.*

Web, www.lfcj.com

Membership: defense trial lawyers and corporate and insurance attorneys. Interests include tort reform, litigation cost containment, and tort and product liability. Monitors legislation and regulations affecting the civil justice system.

National Assn. for the Advancement of Colored People (NAACP), *Washington Office,* 1025 Vermont Ave. N.W., #1120 20005; (202) 638-2269. Fax, (202) 638-5936. Hilary O. Shelton, Director.
Web, www.naacp.org

Membership: persons interested in civil rights for all minorities. Seeks, through litigation, to end discrimination in all areas, including discriminatory practices in the administration of justice. Studies and recommends policy on court administration and jury selection. Maintains branch offices in many state and federal prisons. (Headquarters in Baltimore, Md.)

National Bar Assn., 1225 11th St. N.W. 20001-4217; (202) 842-3900. Fax, (202) 289-6170. John Crump, Executive Director.
Web, www.nationalbar.org

Membership: primarily minority attorneys, legal professionals, judges, and law students. Interests include legal education and improvement of the judicial process. Sponsors legal education seminars in all states that require continuing legal education for lawyers.

National Center for State Courts, *Government Relations,* 2425 Wilson Blvd., #350, Arlington, VA 22201; (703) 841-0200. Fax, (703) 841-0206. Thomas A. Henderson, Executive Director.
Web, www.ncsconline.org

Works to improve state court systems through research, technical assistance, and training programs. Monitors legislation affecting court systems; interests include state-federal jurisdiction and automated information systems. Serves as secretariat for several state court organizations, including the Conference of Chief Justices, Conference of State Court Administrators, American Judges Assn., and National Assn. for Court Management.

National Legal Center for the Public Interest, 1600 K St. N.W., #800 20006; (202) 466-9360. Fax, (202) 466-9366. Ernest B. Hueter, President.
General e-mail, info@nlcpi.org
Web, www.nlcpi.org

Public interest law center and information clearinghouse. Studies judicial issues and the impact of the legal system on the private sector; sponsors seminars; does not litigate cases.

National Whistleblower Center, *P.O. Box 3768 20007; (202) 342-1902. Fax, (202) 342-1904. Kris Kolesnik, Executive Director.*
Web, www.whistleblowers.org

Supports and represents employee whistleblowers. Works to ensure that whistleblower disclosures about improper government and industry actions that are harmful to the environment and the public health are defended and heard. Operates attorney referral service through National Whistleblower Legal Defense and Education Fund.

Rand Corporation, *Washington Office,* 1200 S. Hayes St., Arlington, VA 22202-5050; (703) 413-1100. Fax, (703) 413-8111. Bruce Hoffman, Director.
Web, www.rand.org

Analyzes current problems of the American civil and criminal justice systems and evaluates recent and pending changes and reforms. (Headquarters in Santa Monica, Calif.)

State Justice Institute, 1650 King St., #600, Alexandria, VA 22314; (703) 684-6100. Fax, (703) 684-7618. David I. Tevelin, Executive Director.
Web, www.statejustice.org

Nonprofit organization that awards grants to state courts and to state agencies working to improve judicial administration in the state courts. Interests include judicial education, court technology, victim assistance, prevention of violence against women, and federal-state relations.

U.S. Chamber of Commerce, *Congressional and Public Affairs,* 1615 H St. N.W. 20062-2000; (202) 463-5600. Fax, (202) 887-3430. Rolf T. Lundberg, Senior Vice President.
Web, www.uschamber.com

Federation of individuals; firms; corporations; trade and professional associations; and local, state, and regional chambers of commerce. Monitors legislation and regulations in administrative law, antitrust policy, civil justice reform, and product liability reform.

Washington Legal Foundation, 2009 Massachusetts Ave. N.W. 20036; (202) 588-0302. Fax, (202) 588-0386. Daniel J. Popeo, General Counsel.
General e-mail, administration@wlf.org
Web, www.wlf.org

Public interest law and policy center. Interests include constitutional law, government regulation, media law, and criminal justice; litigates on behalf of small businesses, members of Congress, and victims of violent crimes who bring civil suits against their attackers.

GENERAL COUNSELS FOR FEDERAL AGENCIES

DEPARTMENTS

Agriculture, Nancy S. Bryson, (202) 720-3351

Commerce, Theodore W. Kassinger, (202) 482-4772

Defense, William J. Hayes II, (703) 695-3341

  Air Force, Mary L. Walker, (703) 697-0941

  Army, Steven J. Morello, (703) 697-9235

  Navy, Alberto J. Mora, (703) 614-1994

Education, Brian W. Jones, (202) 401-6000

Energy, Lee Liberman Otis, (202) 586-6732

Health and Human Services, Alex M. Azar II, (202) 690-7741

Homeland Security, Joe D. Whitley (Designee), (202) 282-8000 (switchboard)

Housing and Urban Development, Richard A. Hauser, (202) 708-2244

Interior, William G. Myers, (202) 208-4423

Justice, Vacant, (202) 514-2051

Labor, Howard M. Radzely (Acting), (202) 693-5260

State, William H. Taft IV, (202) 647-9598

Transportation, Kirk K. Van Tine, (202) 366-4702

Treasury, David D. Aufhauser, (202) 622-0283

Veterans Affairs, Tim McClain, (202) 273-6660

AGENCIES

Advisory Council on Historic Preservation, Javier Marques, (202) 606-8503

Agency for International Development, John Gardner, (202) 712-0900

Central Intelligence Agency, John Rizzo, (703) 482-1951

Commission on Civil Rights, Debra Carr, (202) 376-8351

Commodity Futures Trading Commission, Patrick McCarty, (202) 418-5120

Consumer Product Safety Commission, William H. DuRoss, (301) 504-7922

Corporation for National Service, Frank Trinity, (202) 606-5000, ext. 290

Environmental Protection Agency, Robert Fabricant, (202) 564-8040

Equal Employment Opportunity Commission, Nicholas Inzeo (Acting), (202) 663-4702

Export-Import Bank, Peter Saba, (202) 565-3430

Farm Credit Administration, Philip Shebest (Acting), (703) 883-4020

Federal Communications Commission, Jane Mago, (202) 418-1700

Federal Deposit Insurance Corporation, William F. Kroener III, (202) 898-3680

Federal Election Commission, Lawrence Norton, (202) 694-1650

Federal Emergency Management Agency, Mark Wallace, (202) 646-4105

Federal Energy Regulatory Commission, Cynthia Marlette, (202) 502-6000

Federal Labor Relations Authority, David Feter (Acting), (202) 482-6680

Federal Maritime Commission, David Miles (Acting), (202) 523-5740

Women's Bar Assn., *1717 K St. N.W., #503 20036; (202) 639-8880. Fax, (202) 639-8889. Kimberly Knight, Executive Director.*
Web, www.wbadc.org

Membership: women and men who are judges, attorneys in the public and private sectors, law students, and lawyers at home who remain professionally active. Promotes appointment of members to positions in government and legislative policies that assist women in the workplace.

World Jurist Assn., *1000 Connecticut Ave. N.W., #202 20036-5302; (202) 466-5428. Fax, (202) 452-8540. Margaret M. Henneberry, Executive Vice President.*

General e-mail, wja@worldjurist.org
Web, www.worldjurist.org

Membership: lawyers, law professors, judges, law students, and nonlegal professionals worldwide. Conducts research; promotes world peace through adherence to international law; holds biennial world conferences. (Affiliates, at same address, include World Assn. of Judges, World Assn. of Law Professors, World Assn. of Lawyers, and World Business Assn.)

Dispute Resolution

AGENCIES

Justice Dept. (DOJ), *Dispute Resolution, 950 Pennsylvania Ave. N.W., #4617 20530; (202) 616-9471. Fax, (202) 616-9570. Linda A. Cinciotta, Senior Counsel.*

GENERAL COUNSELS FOR FEDERAL AGENCIES (continued)

Federal Mediation and Conciliation Service, Arthur Pearlstein, (202) 606-5444

Federal Reserve System, J. Virgil Mattingly Jr., (202) 452-3430

Federal Trade Commission, William E. Kovacic, (202) 326-2424

General Services Administration, Raymond J. McKenna, (202) 501-2200

International Bank for Reconstruction and Development (World Bank), Kuyung Tung, (202) 473-3701

Merit Systems Protection Board, Martha Schneider, (202) 653-7171

National Aeronautics and Space Administration, Paul G. Pastorek, (202) 358-2450

National Credit Union Administration, Robert M. Fenner, (703) 518-6540

National Endowment for Humanities, Daniel C. Schneider, (202) 606-8322

National Endowment for the Arts, Hope O'Keeffe, (202) 682-5418

National Labor Relations Board, Arthur F. Rosenfeld (Acting), (202) 273-3700

National Mediation Board, Mary Johnson, (202) 692-5040

National Railroad Passenger Corporation (Amtrak), Alicia Serfaty (Acting), (202) 906-2198

National Science Foundation, Lawrence Rudolph, (703) 292-8060

National Transportation Safety Board, Ronald S. Battocchi, (202) 314-6080

Nuclear Regulatory Commission, Karen D. Cyr, (301) 415-1743

Occupational Safety and Health Review Commission, Earl R. Ohman Jr., (202) 606-5410

Office of Personnel Management, Mark A. Robbins, (202) 606-1700

Overseas Private Investment Corporation, Mark Garfinkel, (202) 336-8410

Peace Corps, Tyler L. Posey, (202) 692-2150

Pension Benefit Guaranty Corporation, James Keightley, (202) 326-4020

Postal Rate Commission, Stephen Sharfman, (202) 789-6820

Securities and Exchange Commission, Giovanni P. Prezioso, (202) 942-0900

Small Business Administration, David Javdan, (202) 205-6642

Smithsonian Institution, John E. Huerta, (202) 357-1997

Social Security Administration, Lisa de Soto, (410) 965-0600

U.S. International Trade Commission, Lyn M. Schlitt, (202) 205-3061

U.S. Postal Service, Maryanne Gibbons, (202) 268-2950

Web, www.usdoj.gov/odr

Division of the office of the associate attorney general. Coordinates Justice Dept. activities related to dispute resolution.

NONPROFIT

American Arbitration Assn., *Federal Center for Dispute Resolution,* 601 Pennsylvania Ave. N.W., #700 20004; (202) 737-1460. Fax, (202) 737-2418. S. Pierre Paret, Vice President, Government Relations.
Web, www.adr.org

Provides dispute resolution services to the federal government. (American Arbitration Assn. headquarters in New York.)

American Bar Assn. (ABA), *Dispute Resolution,* 740 15th St. N.W., 9th Floor 20005; (202) 662-1680. Fax, (202) 662-1683. Jack Hanna, Director.
Web, www.abanet.org/dispute

Acts as a clearinghouse on dispute resolution; supports methods for resolving disputes other than litigation; provides technical assistance.

Assn. for Conflict Resolution, 1527 New Hampshire Ave. N.W., 3rd Floor 20036; (202) 667-9700. Fax, (202) 265-1968. David Hart, Director.
General e-mail, acr@acresolution.org
Web, www.acresolution.org

Promotes knowledge and public awareness of the value of alternative dispute resolution methods including mediation, negotiation, and arbitration. Fosters the use of such processes and programs in new arenas locally, nationally, and internationally; stimulates innovative approaches to the resolution of future conflict. Provides educators and conflict resolution professionals with information and technical assistance regarding the use of dispute resolution processes. Develops approaches to youth conflict and alternatives to violence. Offers referrals for mediation. (The Assn. for Conflict Resolution is a merged organization comprised of the Academy of Family Mediators, the Conflict Resolution Education Network, and the Society of Professional and Dispute Resolution.)

Center for Dispute Settlement, *1666 Connecticut Ave. N.W., #500 20009; (202) 265-9572. Fax, (202) 332-3951. Linda R. Singer, Executive Director.*
General e-mail, cds@cdsusa.org
Web, www.cdsusa.org

Designs, implements, and evaluates alternative and nonjudicial methods of dispute resolution; mediates disputes; provides training in dispute resolution.

Council of Better Business Bureaus, *Alternative Dispute Resolution, 4200 Wilson Blvd., #800, Arlington, VA 22203; (703) 276-0100. Fax, (703) 276-0634. Charles I. Underhill, Senior Vice President.*
General e-mail, bbb@bbb.org
Web, www.bbb.org/complaints

Administers mediation and arbitration programs through Better Business Bureaus nationwide to assist in resolving disputes between businesses and consumers. Assists with unresolved disputes between car owners and automobile manufacturers. Maintains pools of certified arbitrators nationwide. Provides mediation training.

HALT—An Organization of Americans for Legal Reform, *1612 K St. N.W., #510 20006; (202) 887-8255. Fax, (202) 887-9699. James C. Turner, Executive Director.*
Web, www.halt.org

Public interest organization concerned with legal reform. Conducts research on alternative dispute resolution programs for delivery of legal services, including arbitration, legal clinics, and mediation services; provides educational and self-help manuals on the use of the legal system.

National Assn. for Community Mediation, *1527 New Hampshire Ave. N.W., 4th Floor 20036-1206; (202) 667-9700. Fax, (202) 667-8629. Linda Baron, Executive Director.*

General e-mail, nafcm@nafcm.org
Web, www.nafcm.org

Supports the maintenance and growth of community-based mediation programs and processes. Provides information on the development and practice of community mediation; encourages regional and national collaborative projects among community mediation programs.

Judicial Appointments

AGENCIES

Justice Dept. (DOJ), *Legal Policy, 950 Pennsylvania Ave. N.W., #4234 20530; (202) 514-4601. Fax, (202) 514-2424. Viet D. Dinh, Assistant Attorney General.*
Web, www.usdoj.gov/olp

Investigates and processes prospective candidates for presidential appointment (subject to Senate confirmation) to the federal judiciary.

CONGRESS

House Judiciary Committee, *Subcommittee on Courts, the Internet, and Intellectual Property, B351A RHOB 20515; (202) 225-5741. Fax, (202) 225-3673. Rep. Lamar Smith, R-Texas, Chair; Blaine Merritt, Chief Counsel.*
General e-mail, Judiciary@mail.house.gov
Web, www.house.gov/judiciary

Jurisdiction over legislation on federal judicial appointments, which includes legislation to create new federal judgeships.

Senate Judiciary Committee, *SD-224 20510; (202) 224-5225. Fax, (202) 224-9102. Sen. Orrin G. Hatch, R-Utah, Chair; Makan Delrahim, Chief Counsel.*
Web, judiciary.senate.gov

Jurisdiction over legislation on federal judicial appointments, which includes legislation to create new federal judgeships; conducts hearings on presidential appointees to federal judgeships, including Supreme Court nominees.

JUDICIARY

Administrative Office of the U.S. Courts, *1 Columbus Circle N.E., #7-400 20544; (202) 273-3000. Leonidas Ralph Mecham, Director. Information, (202) 502-2600.*
Web, www.uscourts.gov

Supervises all administrative matters of the federal court system, except the Supreme Court. Transmits to Congress the recommendations of the Judicial Conference of the United States concerning creation of federal judgeships and other legislative proposals.

Judicial Conference of the United States, *1 Columbus Circle N.E., #7-425 20544; (202) 502-2400. Fax, (202) 502-1144. William H. Rehnquist, Chief Justice of the United States, Chair; Leonidas Ralph Mecham, Secretary. Web, www.uscourts.gov*

Serves as the policy-making and governing body for the administration of the federal judicial system; advises Congress on the creation of new federal judgeships. Interests include international judicial relations.

NONPROFIT

Alliance for Justice, *Judicial Selection Project, 11 Dupont Circle N.W., #200 20036-6919; (202) 822-6070. Fax, (202) 822-6068. Elaine Weiss, Director. General e-mail, alliance@afj.org Web, www.afj.org*

Monitors candidates for vacancies in the federal judiciary; independently reviews nominees' records; maintains statistics on the judiciary.

⚖ BUSINESS AND TAX LAW

Antitrust

AGENCIES

Antitrust Division *(Justice Dept.), 950 Pennsylvania Ave. N.W., #3109 20530; (202) 514-2401. Fax, (202) 616-2645. R. Hewitt Pate, Assistant Attorney General. Web, www.usdoj.gov/atr*

Enforces antitrust laws to prevent monopolies and unlawful restraint of trade; has civil and criminal jurisdiction; coordinates activities with Bureau of Competition of the Federal Trade Commission.

Antitrust Division *(Justice Dept.), Civil Task Force, 325 7th St. N.W., #300 20530; (202) 616-5935. Fax, (202) 514-7308. James R. Wade, Chief. Web, www.usdoj.gov/atr*

Investigates and litigates certain antitrust cases involving movies, radio, TV, newspapers, performing arts, sports, toys, and credit and debit cards. Handles certain violations of antitrust laws that involve patents, copyrights, and trademarks.

Antitrust Division *(Justice Dept.), Documents, 325 7th St. N.W., #215 20530; (202) 514-2481. Fax, (202) 514-3763. Janie Ingalls, Chief. Web, www.usdoj.gov/atr*

Maintains files and handles requests for information on federal civil and criminal antitrust cases; provides the president and Congress with copies of statutory reports prepared by the division on a variety of competition-related issues; issues opinion letters on whether certain business activity violates antitrust laws.

Antitrust Division *(Justice Dept.), Networks and Technology Enforcement, 600 E St. N.W., #9500 20530; (202) 307-6122. Fax, (202) 616-8544. Renata B. Hesse, Chief. Web, www.usdoj.gov/atr*

Investigates and litigates certain antitrust cases involving either communications industries or financial institutions, including securities, commodity futures, and insurance firms; participates in agency proceedings and rulemaking in these areas.

Antitrust Division *(Justice Dept.), Transportation, Energy, and Agriculture, 325 7th St. N.W., #500 20530; (202) 307-6351. Fax, (202) 307-2784. Roger W. Fones, Chief. Web, www.usdoj.gov/atr*

Enforces antitrust laws in the airline, railroad, motor carrier, barge line, ocean carrier, and energy industries; litigates antitrust cases pertaining to agriculture and related commodities.

Comptroller of the Currency *(Treasury Dept.), 250 E St. S.W. 20219; (202) 874-4900. Fax, (202) 874-4950. John D. Hawke Jr., Comptroller. Information, (202) 874-5000. Library, (202) 874-4720. Press, (202) 874-5770. Web, www.occ.treas.gov*

Regulates and examines operations of national banks; establishes guidelines for bank examinations; handles mergers of national banks with regard to antitrust law. Library open to the public.

Federal Communications Commission (FCC), *Wireline Competition Bureau, 445 12th St. S.W. 20554; (202) 418-1500. Fax, (202) 418-2825. William Maher, Chief. Web, www.fcc.gov/wcb*

Regulates mergers involving common carriers (wireline facilities that furnish interstate communications services).

Federal Deposit Insurance Corp. (FDIC), *Supervision and Consumer Protection, 550 17th St. N.W. 20429; (202) 898-8946. Fax, (202) 898-3638. Michael J. Zamorski, Director.*

Studies and analyzes applications for mergers, consolidations, acquisitions, and assumption transactions between insured banks.

Federal Energy Regulatory Commission (FERC), *(Energy Dept.), 888 1st St. N.E., #11A 20426; (202) 502-8000. Fax, (202) 208-0064. Patrick Henry Wood III, Chair. Information, (202) 502-8200. Press, (202) 508-8680. Dockets, (202) 502-8714.*

Web, www.ferc.fed.us

Regulates mergers, consolidations, and acquisitions of electric utilities; regulates the acquisition of interstate natural gas pipeline facilities.

Federal Maritime Commission, *800 N. Capitol St. N.W., #1046 20573-0001; (202) 523-5725. Fax, (202) 523-0014. Steven R. Blust, Chair; Bruce A. Dombrowski, Executive Director. Library, (202) 523-5762. TTY, (800) 877-8339. Locator, (202) 523-5773.*
Web, www.fmc.gov

Regulates foreign ocean shipping of the United States; reviews agreements (on rates, schedules, and other matters) filed by common carriers for compliance with shipping statutes and grants limited antitrust immunity. Library open to the public.

Federal Reserve System, *Banking Supervision and Regulation, 20th and C Sts. N.W., #M3142 20551; (202) 452-2773. Fax, (202) 452-2770. Richard Spillenkothen, Director.*
Web, www.federalreserve.gov

Approves bank mergers, consolidations, and other alterations in bank structure.

Federal Trade Commission (FTC), *Competition, 600 Pennsylvania Ave. N.W., #H374 20580; (202) 326-2555. Fax, (202) 326-2884. Joseph J. Simons, Director (Acting). Information, (202) 326-2180.*
Web, www.ftc.gov

Enforces antitrust laws and investigates possible violations, including international cases; seeks voluntary compliance and pursues civil judicial remedies; reviews premerger filings; coordinates activities with Antitrust Division of the Justice Dept.

Surface Transportation Board *(Transportation Dept.), 1925 K St. N.W., #810 20423-0001; (202) 565-1510. Fax, (202) 565-9004. Roger Nober, Chair; Wayne O. Burkes, Vice Chair. Information, (202) 565-1674.*
Web, www.stb.dot.gov

Regulates rail rate disputes, railroad consolidations, rail line construction proposals, line abandonments, and rail car service.

CONGRESS

House Financial Services Committee, *Subcommittee on Financial Institutions and Consumer Credit, 2129 RHOB 20515; (202) 225-7502. Rep. Spencer Bachus, R-Ala., Chair; Bob Foster, Staff Director.*
Web, financialservices.house.gov

Jurisdiction over legislation on mergers, acquisitions, consolidations, and conversions of financial institutions.

House Judiciary Committee, *2138 RHOB 20515; (202) 225-3951. Fax, (202) 225-7682. Rep. F. James Sensenbrenner Jr., R-Wis., Chair; Phil Kiko, Chief of Staff.*
General e-mail, Judiciary@mail.house.gov
Web, www.house.gov/judiciary

Jurisdiction over legislation affecting anticompetitive and monopolistic practices and over Justice Dept. antitrust enforcement policies. Oversight of the Sherman Act and the Clayton Act.

House Small Business Committee, *Subcommittee on Regulatory Reform and Oversight, B363 RHOB 20515; (202) 226-2630. Fax, (202) 225-8950. Rep. Ed Schrock, R-Va., Chair; Rosario Palmieri, Staff Director.*
General e-mail, smbiz@mail.house.gov
Web, www.house.gov/smbiz

Investigates anticompetitive and monopolistic practices.

Senate Judiciary Committee, *Subcommittee on Antitrust, Competition Policy, and Consumer Rights, SD-161 20510; (202) 224-9494. Fax, (202) 228-0463. Sen. Mike DeWine, R-Ohio, Chair; Peter Levitas, Chief Counsel.*
Web, judiciary.senate.gov

Jurisdiction over legislation affecting anticompetitive and monopolistic practices and over Justice Dept. antitrust enforcement polices. Oversight of the Sherman Act and the Clayton Act.

Senate Small Business and Entrepreneurship Committee, *SR-428A 20510; (202) 224-5175. Fax, (202) 228-1128. Sen. Olympia J. Snowe, R-Maine, Chair; Mark Warren, Staff Director.*
Web, sbc.senate.gov

Investigates antitrust matters relating to small business; investigates anticompetitive and monopolistic practices.

NONPROFIT

American Antitrust Institute (AAI), *2919 Ellicott St. N.W., #1000 20008-1022; (202) 276-6002. Fax, (202) 966-8711. Albert A. Foer, President.*
General e-mail, antitrustinstitute@antitrustinstitute.org
Web, www.antitrustinstitute.org

Pro-antitrust organization that provides research and policy analysis to journalists, academic researchers, lawyers, economists, businesspeople, government officials, and the general public. Seeks to educate the public on fair competition. Monitors legislation and regulations on competition-oriented policies.

American Corporate Counsel Assn., *1025 Connecticut Ave. N.W., #200 20036-5425; (202) 293-4103. Fax, (202) 293-4701. Frederick J. Krebs, President.*

Web, www.acca.com

Membership: practicing attorneys in corporate law departments. Provides information on corporate law issues, including securities, health and safety, the environment, intellectual property, litigation, international legal affairs, pro bono work, and labor benefits. Monitors legislation and regulations, with primary focus on issues affecting in-house attorneys' ability to practice law.

The Business Roundtable, *1615 L St. N.W., #1100 20036-5610; (202) 872-1260. Fax, (202) 466-3509. John J. Castellani, President.*

Web, www.brt.org

Membership: chief executives of the nation's largest corporations. Examines issues of concern to business, including antitrust law.

Bankruptcy

AGENCIES

Executive Office for U.S. Trustees *(Justice Dept.), 20 Massachusettes Ave. N.W., #8000 20530; (202) 307-1391. Fax, (202) 307-0672. Lawrence A. Friedman, Director.*

Web, www.usdoj.gov/ust

Handles the administration and oversight of bankruptcy and liquidation cases filed under the Bankruptcy Reform Act. Provides individual U.S. trustee offices with administrative and management support.

Justice Dept. (DOJ), *Legal Policy, 950 Pennsylvania Ave. N.W., #4234 20530; (202) 514-4601. Fax, (202) 514-2424. Viet D. Dinh, Assistant Attorney General.*

Web, www.usdoj.gov/olp

Studies and develops policy for improvement of the criminal and civil justice systems, including bankruptcy reform policy.

CONGRESS

House Judiciary Committee, *Subcommittee on Commercial and Administrative Law, B353 RHOB 20515; (202) 225-2825. Rep. Christopher B. Cannon, R-Utah, Chair; Ray Smietanka, Chief Counsel.*

General e-mail, Judiciary@mail.house.gov

Web, www.house.gov/judiciary

Jurisdiction over bankruptcy legislation. Oversees the bankruptcy court.

Senate Judiciary Committee, *Subcommittee on Administrative Oversight and the Courts, SD-323 20510; (202) 224-7572. Fax, (202) 228-0545. Sen. Jeff Sessions, R-Ala., Chair; William Smith, Chief Counsel.*

Web, judiciary.senate.gov

Jurisdiction over bankruptcy legislation.

JUDICIARY

Administrative Office of the U.S. Courts, *Bankruptcy Judges Division, 1 Columbus Circle N.E., #4-250 20544; (202) 502-1900. Fax, (202) 502-1988. Francis F. Szczebak, Chief.*

Web, www.uscourts.gov

Provides administrative assistance and support in the operation of the U.S. Bankruptcy Courts.

NONPROFIT

American Bankruptcy Institute, *44 Canal Center Plaza, #404, Alexandria, VA 22314-1592; (703) 739-0800. Fax, (703) 739-1060. Samuel Gerdano, Executive Director.*

General e-mail, info@abiworld.org

Web, www.abiworld.org

Membership: lawyers; federal and state legislators; and representatives of accounting and financial services firms, lending institutions, credit organizations, and consumer groups. Provides information and educational services on insolvency, reorganization, and bankruptcy issues; sponsors conferences, seminars, and workshops.

Tax Violations

AGENCIES

Internal Revenue Service (IRS), *(Treasury Dept.), Procedures and Administration, 1111 Constitution Ave. N.W., #4050 20224; (202) 622-7800. Fax, (202) 622-7722. Curtis G. Wilson, Assistant Chief Counsel.*

Web, www.irs.ustreas.gov

Oversees field office litigation of civil cases that involve underpayment of taxes when the taxpayer chooses to challenge the determinations of the Internal Revenue Service (IRS) in the U.S. Tax Court, or when the taxpayer chooses to pay the amount in question and sue the IRS for a refund. Reviews briefs and defense letters prepared by field offices for tax cases; prepares tax litigation advice memoranda; formulates litigation strategy. Makes recommendations concerning appeal and certiorari. Litigates insurance and declaratory judgment cases in the U.S. Tax Court.

Justice Dept. (DOJ), *Tax Division, 950 Pennsylvania Ave. N.W., #4141 20530; (202) 514-2901. Fax, (202) 514-5479. Eileen J. O'Connor, Assistant Attorney General.*

Web, www.usdoj.gov/tax/tax.html

Authorizes prosecution of all criminal cases involving tax violations investigated and developed by the Internal Revenue Service (IRS); represents IRS in civil litigation except in U.S. Tax Court proceedings; represents other agencies, including the departments of Defense and Interior, in cases with state or local tax authorities.

CONGRESS

House Ways and Means Committee, *1102 LHOB 20515; (202) 225-3625. Fax, (202) 225-2610. Rep. Bill Thomas, R-Calif., Chair; Allison Giles, Chief of Staff.*
General e-mail, contactwaysandmeans@mail.house.gov
Web, waysandmeans.house.gov

Jurisdiction over legislation concerning changes in enforcement of tax laws.

Senate Finance Committee, *Subcommittee on Taxation and IRS Oversight, SD-219 20510; (202) 224-4515. Sen. Don Nickles, R-Okla., Chair; Kolan L. Davis, Staff Director.*
Web, finance.senate.gov

Holds hearings on legislation concerning changes in enforcement of tax laws.

JUDICIARY

U.S. Tax Court, *400 2nd St. N.W. 20217; (202) 606-8700. Fax, (202) 606-8958. Thomas B. Wells, Chief Judge; Charles S. Casazza, Clerk of the Court.*
Web, www.ustaxcourt.gov

Tries and adjudicates disputes involving income, estate, and gift taxes and personal holding company surtaxes in cases in which deficiencies have been determined by the Internal Revenue Service.

NONPROFIT

American Bar Assn. (ABA), *Taxation Section, 740 15th St. N.W., 10th Floor 20005-1022; (202) 662-8675. Fax, (202) 662-8682. Christine A. Brunswick, Director.*
Web, www.abanet.org

Studies and recommends policies on taxation; provides information on tax issues; sponsors continuing legal education programs; monitors tax laws and legislation.

⚖ CONSTITUTIONAL LAW AND CIVIL LIBERTIES

AGENCIES

Commission on Civil Rights, *624 9th St. N.W., #700 20425; (202) 376-7700. Fax, (202) 376-7672. Mary*

Frances Berry, Chair; Cruz Reynoso, Vice Chair. Library, (202) 376-8110. Press, (202) 376-8312. TTY, (202) 376-8116. Locator, (202) 376-8177. Complaints, (800) 552-6843; in Washington, (202) 376-8582.
Web, www.usccr.gov

Assesses federal laws and policies of government agencies and reviews legal developments to determine the nature and extent of denial of equal protection on the basis of race, color, religion, sex, national origin, age, or disability; investigates complaints of denials of voting rights. Library open to the public.

Education Dept., *Civil Rights, 330 C St. S.W., #5000 20202-1100 (mailing address: 400 Maryland Ave. S.W. 20202-1100); (202) 205-5413. Fax, (202) 205-9862. Gerald Reynolds, Assistant Secretary.*
Web, www.ed.gov

Enforces laws prohibiting use of federal funds for education programs or activities that discriminate on the basis of race, color, sex, national origin, age, or disability; authorized to discontinue funding.

Health and Human Services Dept. (HHS), *Civil Rights, 200 Independence Ave. S.W., #522A 20201; (202) 619-0403. Fax, (202) 619-3437. Richard M. Campanelli, Director. TTY, (800) 537-7697. Toll-free hotline, (800) 368-1019.*
Web, www.hhs.gov/ocr

Administers and enforces laws prohibiting discrimination on the basis of race, color, sex, national origin, religion, age, or disability in programs receiving federal funds from the department; authorized to discontinue funding. Responsible for health information privacy under Health Insurance Portability and Accountability Act.

Justice Dept. (DOJ), *Civil Rights, 950 Pennsylvania Ave. N.W., #3623 20530; (202) 514-2151. Fax, (202) 514-0293. Ralph F. Boyd Jr., Assistant Attorney General. Library, (202) 514-3010. Press, (202) 514-2007. TTY, (202) 514-0716.*
Web, www.usdoj.gov/crt

Enforces federal civil rights laws prohibiting discrimination on the basis of race, color, religion, sex, disability, age, or national origin in voting, education, employment, credit, housing, public accommodations and facilities, and federally assisted programs.

Justice Dept. (DOJ), *Legal Counsel, 950 Pennsylvania Ave. N.W., #5229 20530; (202) 514-2041. Fax, (202) 514-0539. Jay S. Bybee, Assistant Attorney General.*
Web, www.usdoj.gov

Advises the attorney general, the president, and executive agencies on questions regarding constitutional law.

Labor Dept. (DOL), *Civil Rights Center,* *200 Constitution Ave. N.W., #N4123 20210; (202) 693-6500. Fax, (202) 693-6505. Annabelle T. Lockhart, Director. TTY, (202) 693-6515.*
Web, www.dol.gov/oasam/programs/crc/crcwelcome.htm

Resolves complaints of discrimination on the basis of race, color, religion, sex, national origin, age, or disability in programs funded by the department.

CONGRESS

House Government Reform Committee, *Subcommittee on Human Rights and Wellness, B371C RHOB 20515; (202) 225-6427. Fax, (202) 225-2392. Rep. Dan Burton, R-Ind., Chair; Mark Walker, Staff Director.*
Web, www.house.gov/reform

Oversees operations of the Commission on Civil Rights.

House Judiciary Committee, *2138 RHOB 20515; (202) 225-3951. Fax, (202) 225-7682. Rep. F. James Sensenbrenner Jr., R-Wis., Chair; Phil Kiko, Chief of Staff.*
General e-mail, Judiciary@mail.house.gov
Web, www.house.gov/judiciary

Jurisdiction over legislation on proposed amendments to the Constitution; subcommittee jurisdiction determined by subject of proposed amendment.

House Judiciary Committee, *Subcommittee on the Constitution, 362 FHOB 20515; (202) 226-7680. Fax, (202) 225-3746. Rep. Steve Chabot, R-Ohio, Chair; Crystal Roberts, Chief Counsel.*
General e-mail, Judiciary@mail.house.gov
Web, www.house.gov/judiciary

Jurisdiction over legislation dealing with civil rights enforcement, civil liberties, and constitutional issues. Oversees the Justice Dept.'s Civil Rights Division and the Commission on Civil Rights.

Senate Judiciary Committee, *Subcommittee on the Constitution, Civil Rights, and Property Rights, SD-524 20510; (202) 224-4135. Fax, (202) 228-0463. Sen. John Cornyn, R-Texas, Chair; James Ho, Chief Counsel.*
Web, judiciary.senate.gov

Jurisdiction over legislation on proposed amendments to the Constitution, civil rights enforcement, the Voting Rights Act and affirmative action, civil liberties (including the First Amendment, excluding computers), constitutional issues involving criminal law, habeas corpus, the death penalty, and the exclusionary rule; oversees operations of the Commission on Civil Rights.

SUPREME COURT JUSTICES

CHIEF JUSTICE
William H. Rehnquist

Appointed Associate Justice by President Nixon, sworn in Jan. 7, 1972; appointed Chief Justice by President Reagan, sworn in Sept. 26, 1986.

ASSOCIATE JUSTICES
in order of appointment

John Paul Stevens

Appointed by President Ford, sworn in Dec. 17, 1975.

Sandra Day O'Connor

Appointed by President Reagan, sworn in Sept. 25, 1981.

Antonin Scalia

Appointed by President Reagan, sworn in Aug. 17, 1986.

Anthony M. Kennedy

Appointed by President Reagan, sworn in Feb. 18, 1988.

David H. Souter

Appointed by President Bush, sworn in Oct. 9, 1990.

Clarence Thomas

Appointed by President Bush, sworn in Oct. 23, 1991.

Ruth Bader Ginsburg

Appointed by President Clinton, sworn in Aug. 19, 1993.

Stephen G. Breyer

Appointed by President Clinton, sworn in Aug. 3, 1994.

JUDICIARY

Supreme Court of the United States, *1 1st St. N.E. 20543; (202) 479-3000. William H. Rehnquist, Chief Justice. Information, (202) 479-3211.*
Web, www.supremecourtus.gov

Highest appellate court in the federal judicial system. Interprets the U.S. Constitution, federal legislation, and treaties. Provides information on new cases filed, the status of pending cases, and admissions to the Supreme Court Bar. Library open to Supreme Court bar members only.

NONPROFIT

American Civil Liberties Union (ACLU), *Washington Office,* 1333 H St. N.W., 10th Floor 20005; (202) 544-1681. Fax, (202) 546-0738. Laura Murphy, Legal Director.
Web, www.aclu.org

Initiates test court cases and advocates legislation to guarantee constitutional rights and civil liberties. Focuses on First Amendment rights, minority and women's rights, gay and lesbian rights, and privacy; supports legalized abortion, opposes government-sponsored school prayer and legislative restrictions on television content. Washington office monitors legislative and regulatory activities and public policy. Library open to the public by appointment. (Headquarters in New York maintains docket of cases.)

Center for Individual Rights, 1233 20th St. N.W., #300 20036; (202) 833-8400. Fax, (202) 833-8410. Terry Pell, President.
General e-mail, cir@mail.wdn.com
Web, www.cir-usa.org

Public interest law firm that supports reform of the civil justice system on the basis of private rights and individual responsibility. Interests include economic regulation, freedom of speech, and libel law.

Ethics and Public Policy Center, 1015 15th St. N.W., #900 20005; (202) 682-1200. Fax, (202) 408-0632. Hillel Fradkin, President.
General e-mail, ethics@eppc.org
Web, www.eppc.org

Examines current issues of jurisprudence, especially those relating to constitutional interpretation.

Institute for Justice, 1717 Pennsylvania Ave. N.W., #200 20006; (202) 955-1300. Fax, (202) 955-1329. Chip Mellor, President.
General e-mail, general@ij.org
Web, www.ij.org

Sponsors seminars to train law students, grassroots activists, and practicing lawyers in applying advocacy strategies in public interest litigation. Seeks to protect individuals from arbitrary government interference in free speech, private property rights, parental school choice, and economic liberty. Litigates cases.

Legal Affairs Council Freedom Center, 10560 Main St., #217, Fairfax, VA 22030; (703) 591-7767. Fax, (703) 273-4514. Richard A. Delgaudio, President.
Web, www.stardot.com/lac/lac.html

Reports on and provides limited financial assistance to defendants in high profile courtroom battles concerning constitutional and judicial system issues.

NAACP Legal Defense and Educational Fund, *Washington Office,* 1444 Eye St. N.W., 10th Floor 20005; (202) 682-1300. Fax, (202) 682-1312. Leslie M. Proll, Senior Attorney.

Civil rights litigation group that provides legal information on civil rights issues, including employment, housing, and educational discrimination; monitors federal enforcement of civil rights laws. Not affiliated with the National Assn. for the Advancement of Colored People (NAACP). (Headquarters in New York.)

National Assn. for the Advancement of Colored People (NAACP), *Washington Office,* 1025 Vermont Ave. N.W., #1120 20005; (202) 638-2269. Fax, (202) 638-5936. Hilary O. Shelton, Director.
Web, www.naacp.org

Membership: persons interested in civil rights for all minorities. Works for the political, educational, social, and economic equality and empowerment of minorities through legal, legislative, and direct action. (Headquarters in Baltimore, Md.)

National Organization for Women (NOW), 733 15th St. N.W., 2nd Floor 20005; (202) 628-8669. Fax, (202) 785-8576. Kim Gandy, President. TTY, (202) 331-9002.
General e-mail, now@now.org
Web, www.now.org

Membership: women and men interested in civil rights for women. Works to end discrimination based on gender, to preserve abortion rights, and to pass an equal rights amendment to the Constitution.

Abortion and Reproductive Issues

CONGRESS

House Judiciary Committee, *Subcommittee on the Constitution,* 362 FHOB 20515; (202) 226-7680. Fax, (202) 225-3746. Rep. Steve Chabot, R-Ohio, Chair; Crystal Roberts, Chief Counsel.
General e-mail, Judiciary@mail.house.gov
Web, www.house.gov/judiciary

Jurisdiction over proposed abortion amendments to the Constitution.

Senate Judiciary Committee, *Subcommittee on the Constitution, Civil Rights, and Property Rights,* SD-524 20510; (202) 224-4135. Fax, (202) 228-0463. Sen. John Cornyn, R-Texas, Chair; James Ho, Chief Counsel.
Web, judiciary.senate.gov

Jurisdiction over proposed abortion amendments to the Constitution.

NONPROFIT

Assn. of Reproductive Health Professionals,
2401 Pennsylvania Ave. N.W., #350 20037-1718; (202) 466-3825. Fax, (202) 466-3826. Wayne C. Shields, President.

General e-mail, arhp@arhp.org

Web, www.arhp.org

Membership: obstetricians, gynecologists, other physicians, researchers, clinicians, educators, and others. Educates health professionals and the public on reproductive health issues, including family planning, contraception, HIV/AIDS, other sexually transmitted diseases, abortion, menopause, infertility, and cancer prevention and detection.

Catholics for a Free Choice,
1436 U St. N.W., #301 20009-3997; (202) 986-6093. Fax, (202) 332-7995. Frances Kissling, President.

General e-mail, cffc@catholicsforchoice.org

Web, www.catholicsforchoice.org

Works to change church positions and public policies that limit individual freedom, particularly those related to sexuality and reproduction. Provides the public, policymakers, and groups working for change with information and analysis.

Feminists for Life of America,
733 15th St. N.W., #1100 20005; (202) 737-3352. Fax, (202) 737-0414. Serrin M. Foster, President.

General e-mail, info@feministsforlife.org

Web, www.feministsforlife.org

Membership: women and men who advocate classical feminism, including its pro-life position. Opposes abortion, euthanasia, and capital punishment; seeks to redress economic and social conditions that cause women to choose abortion.

March for Life Fund,
P.O. Box 90300 20090; (202) 543-3377. Fax, (202) 543-8202. Nellie J. Gray, President.

Web, www.marchforlife.org

Membership: individuals and organizations that support government action prohibiting abortion. Sponsors annual march in Washington each January 22. Monitors legislation and regulations.

NARAL Pro-Choice America,
1156 15th St. N.W., 7th Floor 20005; (202) 973-3000. Fax, (202) 973-3096. Kate Michelman, President. Press, (202) 973-3032.

Web, www.naral.org

Membership: persons favoring legalized abortion. Promotes grassroots support of political candidates in favor of legalized abortion. (Formerly National Abortion and Reproductive Rights Action League.)

National Abortion Federation (NAF),
1755 Massachusetts Ave. N.W., #600 20036; (202) 667-5881. Fax, (202) 667-5890. Vicki Saporta, Executive Director. Information, (800) 772-9100.

General e-mail, naf@prochoice.org

Web, www.prochoice.org

Membership: abortion providers. Seeks to preserve and enhance the quality and accessibility of abortion care.

National Committee for a Human Life Amendment,
733 15th St. N.W., #926 20005; (202) 393-0703. Fax, (202) 347-1383. Michael A. Taylor, Executive Director.

General e-mail, info@nchla.org

Web, www.nchla.org

Supports legislation and a constitutional amendment prohibiting abortion.

National Right to Life Committee,
512 10th St. N.W. 20004; (202) 626-8800. Fax, (202) 347-6121. David N. O'Steen, Executive Director.

General e-mail, nrlc@nrlc.org

Web, www.nrlc.org

Association of fifty state right-to-life organizations. Opposes abortion, infanticide, and euthanasia; supports legislation prohibiting abortion except when the life of the mother is endangered. Operates an information clearinghouse and speakers bureau. Monitors legislation and regulations.

National Women's Health Network,
514 10th St. N.W., #400 20004-1410; (202) 347-1140. Fax, (202) 347-1168. Cynthia Pearson, Executive Director.

Web, www.womenshealthnetwork.org

Advocacy organization interested in women's health. Seeks to preserve legalized abortion; monitors legislation and regulations; testifies before Congress.

National Women's Political Caucus,
1630 Connecticut Ave. N.W., #201 20009; (202) 785-1100. Fax, (202) 785-3605. Roselyn O'Connell, President.

General e-mail, info@nwpc.org

Web, www.nwpc.org

Advocacy group that seeks greater involvement of women in politics. Supports legalized abortion.

Operation Rescue, Press Relations, Washington Office,
2020 Pennsylvania Ave. N.W., #CCN 20006; (202) 546-0054. Gary L. McCullough, Director, Press Relations.

General e-mail, info@maranatha.tv

Web, www.maranatha.tv

Advocates active stand against abortion. Seeks repeal of the Freedom of Access to Clinic Entrances law. Monitors legislation and regulations. (Headquarters in Concord, N.C.)

Religious Coalition for Reproductive Choice, 1025 Vermont Ave. N.W., #1130 20005; (202) 628-7700. Fax, (202) 628-7716. Carlton Wadsworth Veazey, President.
General e-mail, info@rcrc.org
Web, www.rcrc.org

Coalition of religious groups favoring legalized abortion. Opposes constitutional amendments and federal and state legislation restricting access to abortion services.

U.S. Conference of Catholic Bishops (USCCB), *Secretariat for Pro-Life Activities,* 3211 4th St. N.E. 20017-1194; (202) 541-3070. Fax, (202) 541-3054. Gail Quinn, Executive Director.
General e-mail, plreceptionist@usccb.org
Web, www.usccb.org/prolife

Provides information on the position of the Roman Catholic Church on abortion; monitors legislation on abortion and related issues; provides alternatives to abortion through Catholic charities.

Voters for Choice, 1115 Massachusetts Ave. N.W. 20005; (202) 944-5080. Fax, (202) 944-5081. Maureen Britell, Executive Director.
General e-mail, info@voters4choice.org
Web, www.voters4choice.org

Independent, nonpartisan political action committee that supports candidates favoring legalized abortion. Provides candidates at all levels of government with campaign strategy information; opposes constitutional amendments and legislation restricting abortion.

Claims Against the Government

AGENCIES

Justice Dept. (DOJ), *Civil Division: National Courts,* 1100 L St. N.W., #12124 20530; (202) 514-7300. Fax, (202) 307-0972. David M. Cohen, Director.
Web, www.usdoj.gov

Represents the United States in the U.S. Court of Federal Claims, except in cases involving taxes, lands, or native American claims.

Justice Dept. (DOJ), *Environment and Natural Resources,* 950 Pennsylvania Ave. N.W., #2143 20530-0001; (202) 514-2701. Fax, (202) 514-0557. Thomas L. Sansonetti, Assistant Attorney General.

Web, www.usdoj.gov/enrd

Represents the United States in the U.S. Court of Federal Claims in cases arising from acquisition of property or related matters.

Justice Dept. (DOJ), *Tax Division,* 950 Pennsylvania Ave. N.W., #4141 20530; (202) 514-2901. Fax, (202) 514-5479. Eileen J. O'Connor, Assistant Attorney General.
Web, www.usdoj.gov/tax/tax.html

Represents the United States and its officers in all civil and criminal litigation arising under the internal revenue laws, other than proceedings in the United States Tax Court.

State Dept., *International Claims and Investment Disputes,* 2430 E St. N.W., #203 20037-2800; (202) 776-8360. Fax, (202) 776-8389. Mark A. Clodfelter, Assistant Legal Adviser.
Web, www.state.gov

Handles claims by U.S. government and citizens against foreign governments, as well as claims by foreign governments and their nationals against the U.S. government; negotiates international claims agreements. Handles claims against the State Dept. for negligence (under the Federal Tort Claims Act) and claims by owners of U.S. flag vessels due to illegal seizures by foreign governments in international waters (under the Fishermen's Protective Act).

CONGRESS

House Judiciary Committee, *Subcommittee on Immigration, Border Security, and Claims,* B370B RHOB 20515; (202) 225-5727. Fax, (202) 225-3672. Rep. John Hostettler, R-Ind., Chair; George Fishman, Chief Counsel.
General e-mail, Judiciary@mail.house.gov
Web, www.house.gov/judiciary

Jurisdiction over legislation related to claims against the United States.

Senate Judiciary Committee, SD-224 20510; (202) 224-5225. Fax, (202) 224-9102. Sen. Orrin G. Hatch, R-Utah, Chair; Makan Delrahim, Chief Counsel.
Web, judiciary.senate.gov

Jurisdiction over legislation related to claims against the United States.

JUDICIARY

U.S. Court of Federal Claims, 717 Madison Pl. N.W. 20005; (202) 219-9657. Fax, (202) 219-9593. Edward J. Damich, Chief Judge; Margaret Ernest, Clerk.

Renders judgment on any nontort claims for monetary damages against the United States founded upon the

Constitution, statutes, government regulations, and government contracts. Examples include compensation for taking of property, claims arising under construction and supply contracts, certain patent cases, and cases involving the refund of federal taxes. Hears cases involving native American claims.

Interstate Compacts

CONGRESS

House Judiciary Committee, *Subcommittee on Commercial and Administrative Law,* B353 RHOB 20515; (202) 225-2825. Rep. Christopher B. Cannon, R-Utah, Chair; Ray Smietanka, Chief Counsel.
General e-mail, Judiciary@mail.house.gov
Web, www.house.gov/judiciary

Jurisdiction over all interstate compacts, including hazardous waste transportation, water rights, and boundaries. (Congressional approval of interstate compacts is required by the Constitution.)

Senate Judiciary Committee, *Subcommittee on the Constitution, Civil Rights, and Property Rights,* SD-524 20510; (202) 224-4135. Fax, (202) 228-0463. Sen. John Cornyn, R-Texas, Chair; James Ho, Chief Counsel.
Web, judiciary.senate.gov

Jurisdiction over interstate compacts dealing with such matters as hazardous waste transportation, water rights, and boundaries. (Congressional approval of interstate compacts is required by the Constitution.)

Religious Freedom

CONGRESS

House Judiciary Committee, *Subcommittee on the Constitution,* 362 FHOB 20515; (202) 226-7680. Fax, (202) 225-3746. Rep. Steve Chabot, R-Ohio, Chair; Crystal Roberts, Chief Counsel.
General e-mail, Judiciary@mail.house.gov
Web, www.house.gov/judiciary

Jurisdiction over proposed constitutional amendments; oversight of the First Amendment right to religious freedom.

Senate Judiciary Committee, *Subcommittee on the Constitution, Civil Rights, and Property Rights,* SD-524 20510; (202) 224-4135. Fax, (202) 228-0463. Sen. John Cornyn, R-Texas, Chair; James Ho, Chief Counsel.
Web, judiciary.senate.gov

Jurisdiction over proposed constitutional amendments; oversight of the First Amendment right to religious freedom.

NONPROFIT

American Jewish Congress, *Washington Office,* 1001 Connecticut Ave. N.W., #470 20036; (202) 466-9661. Fax, (202) 466-9665. Charles Brooks, Executive Director.
General e-mail, washrep@ajcongress.org
Web, www.ajcongress.org

Advocacy organization that seeks to uphold civil and constitutional rights. Litigates cases involving prayer in public schools, tuition tax credits, equal access, and religious symbols on public property. (Headquarters in New York.)

Americans for Religious Liberty, *P.O. Box 6656, Silver Spring, MD 20916; (301) 260-2988. Fax, (301) 260-2989. Edd Doerr, President.*
General e-mail, arlinc@erols.com
Web, www.arlinc.org

Educational organization concerned with issues involving the separation of church and state. Opposes government-sponsored school prayer and tax support for religious institutions; supports religious neutrality in public education; defends abortion rights. Provides legal services in litigation cases. Maintains speakers bureau.

Americans United for Separation of Church and State, *518 C St. N.E. 20002; (202) 466-3234. Fax, (202) 466-2587. Barry W. Lynn, Executive Director.*
General e-mail, americansunited@au.org
Web, www.au.org

Citizens' interest group that opposes government-sponsored prayer in public schools and tax aid for parochial schools.

Christian Legal Society, *4208 Evergreen Lane, #222, Annandale, VA 22003; (703) 642-1070. Fax, (703) 642-1075. Samuel B. Casey, Chief Executive Director.*
General e-mail, clshq@clsnet.org
Web, www.clsnet.org

Membership: attorneys, judges, law professors, law students, and others. Seeks to create and mobilize a national grassroots network of Christians to advocate equal access to justice for the poor, religious freedom, the sanctity of human life, and biblical conflict reconciliation.

International Religious Liberty Assn., *12501 Old Columbia Pike, Silver Spring, MD 20904-6600; (301) 680-6680. Fax, (301) 680-6695. John Graz, Secretary General.*
General e-mail, 74532.240@compuserve.com
Web, www.irla.org

Seeks to preserve and expand religious liberty and freedom of conscience; advocates separation of church and state; sponsors international and domestic meetings and congresses.

National Assn. of Evangelicals, *718 Capitol Square Pl. S.W. 20024 (mailing address: P.O. Box 23269 20026); (202) 789-1011. Fax, (202) 842-0392. Leith Anderson, President (Interim).*
General e-mail, nae@nae.net
Web, www.nae.net

Membership: evangelical churches, organizations (including schools), and individuals. Supports religious freedom. Monitors legislation and regulations.

National Council of Churches, *Washington Office, 110 Maryland Ave. N.E., #108 20002; (202) 544-2350. Fax, (202) 543-1297. Brenda Girton-Mitchell, Director.*
Web, www.ncccusa.org

Membership: Protestant, Anglican, and Orthodox churches. Opposes government-sponsored prayer in public schools. Provides information on the school prayer issue. (Headquarters in New York.)

Separation of Powers

CONGRESS

House Government Reform Committee, *Subcommittee on Criminal Justice, Drug Policy, and Human Resources, B373B RHOB 20515; (202) 225-2577. Fax, (202) 225-1154. Rep. Mark Souder, R-Ind., Chair; Christopher Donesa, Staff Director.*
Web, www.house.gov/reform

Jurisdiction over legislation on some aspects of executive privilege and separation of powers. (Jurisdiction over separation of powers shared with House Judiciary Committee.)

House Judiciary Committee, *2138 RHOB 20515; (202) 225-3951. Fax, (202) 225-7682. Rep. F. James Sensenbrenner Jr., R-Wis., Chair; Phil Kiko, Chief of Staff.*
General e-mail, Judiciary@mail.house.gov
Web, www.house.gov/judiciary

Jurisdiction over legislation dealing with separation of powers and presidential succession. (Jurisdiction over separation of powers shared with House Government Reform Committee.)

Senate Judiciary Committee, *Subcommittee on the Constitution, Civil Rights, and Property Rights, SD-524 20510; (202) 224-4135. Fax, (202) 228-0463. Sen. John Cornyn, R-Texas, Chair; James Ho, Chief Counsel.*
Web, judiciary.senate.gov

Jurisdiction over legislation on separation of powers, presidential succession, and some aspects of executive privilege.

Public Citizen Litigation Group, *1600 20th St. N.W. 20009; (202) 588-1000. Fax, (202) 588-7795. Alan Morrison, Director of Litigation.*
Web, www.citizen.org

Conducts litigation for Public Citizen, a citizens' interest group, in cases involving separation of powers; represents individuals and groups with similar interests.

⚖ CRIMINAL LAW

AGENCIES

Criminal Division *(Justice Dept.), 950 Pennsylvania Ave. N.W., #2107 20530; (202) 514-2601. Fax, (202) 514-9412. Michael Chertoff, Assistant Attorney General.*
Web, www.usdoj.gov/criminal

Enforces all federal criminal laws except those specifically assigned to the antitrust, civil rights, environment and natural resources, and tax divisions of the Justice Dept. Supervises and directs U.S. attorneys in the field on criminal matters and litigation; supervises international extradition proceedings. Coordinates federal enforcement efforts against white-collar crime, fraud, and child pornography; handles civil actions under customs, liquor, narcotics, gambling, and firearms laws; coordinates enforcement activities against organized crime. Directs the National Asset Forfeiture Program for seizing the proceeds of criminal activity. Investigates and prosecutes criminal offenses involving public integrity and subversive activities, including treason, espionage, and sedition; Nazi war crimes; and related criminal offenses. Handles all civil cases relating to internal security and counsels federal departments and agencies regarding internal security matters. Drafts responses on proposed and pending criminal law legislation.

Criminal Division *(Justice Dept.), Enforcement Operations: International Prisoner Transfers, P.O. Box 7600, Ben Franklin Station 20044-7600; (202) 514-3173. Fax, (202) 514-9003. Paula A. Wolf, Chief.*
Web, www.usdoj.gov/criminal/oeo/index.htm

Implements prisoner transfer treaties with foreign countries.

Federal Bureau of Investigation (FBI), *(Justice Dept.), 935 Pennsylvania Ave. N.W., #7176 20535; (202) 324-3444. Fax, (202) 323-2079. Robert S. Mueller III, Director. Information, (202) 324-3000.*
Web, www.fbi.gov

Investigates all violations of federal criminal laws except those assigned specifically to other federal agencies. Exceptions include alcohol, counterfeiting, tobacco, and customs violations (Judiciary and Commerce Depts,); postal violations (U.S. Postal Service); and illegal entry of aliens (Homeland Security Dept.). Priorities include organized crime, drugs, counterterrorism, white-collar crime, foreign counterintelligence, and violent crime. Services provided to other law enforcement agencies include fingerprint identification, laboratory services, police training, and the National Crime Information Center (communications network among FBI, state, and local police agencies).

Office of Justice Programs (OJP), *(Justice Dept.),* ***National Institute of Justice,*** *810 7th St. N.W., 7th Floor 20531; (202) 307-2942. Fax, (202) 307-6394. Sarah V. Hart, Director.*
Web, www.ojp.usdoj.gov/nij

Conducts research on all aspects of criminal justice, including crime prevention, enforcement, adjudication, and corrections; evaluates programs; develops model programs using new techniques. Serves as an affiliated institute of the United Nations Crime Prevention and Criminal Justice Programme (UNCPCJ); studies transnational issues, especially within the Western Hemisphere. Maintains the National Criminal Justice Reference Service, which provides information on criminal justice research: (800) 851-3420; in Maryland, (301) 251-5500; Web, www.ncjrs.org.

Office of Justice Programs (OJP), *(Justice Dept.),* ***Victims of Crime,*** *810 7th St. N.W., 8th Floor 20531; (202) 307-5983. Fax, (202) 514-6383. John W. Gillis, Director. TTY, (202) 514-7908. Resource Center, (800) 627-6872. Alternate Fax: (202) 305-2440.*
Web, www.ojp.usdoj.gov/ovc

Provides funds to state victim compensation and assistance programs, including counseling for victims of rape, child abuse, and spouse abuse; supports victim assistance programs for native Americans. Operations are financed by the crime victims fund, which is financed by federal criminal fines, penalties, and bond forfeitures. Provides information on victim and witness services.

CONGRESS

House Education and the Workforce Committee, *Subcommittee on Select Education, 2181 RHOB 20515; (202) 225-6558. Fax, (202) 225-9571. Rep. Peter Hoekstra, R-Mich., Chair; Paula Nowakowski, Staff Director.*
Web, edworkforce.house.gov

Jurisdiction over legislation on juvenile justice and related issues, including the role of children in the courts (jurisdiction shared with House Judiciary Committee). Oversight of the Juvenile Justice and Delinquency Prevention Act, the Runaway Youth Act, and juvenile justice programs administered by the Office of Justice Programs.

House Energy and Commerce Committee, *Subcommittee on Health, 2125 RHOB 20515; (202) 225-2927. Fax, (202) 225-1919. Rep. Michael Bilirakis, R-Fla., Chair; David V. Marventano, Staff Director.*
General e-mail, commerce@mail.house.gov
Web, energycommerce.house.gov

Jurisdiction over legislation on drug abuse and rehabilitation of drug abusers, including narcotics addicts who have had contact (arrest or conviction) with the federal criminal justice system.

House Judiciary Committee, *2138 RHOB 20515; (202) 225-3951. Fax, (202) 225-7682. Rep. F. James Sensenbrenner Jr., R-Wis., Chair; Phil Kiko, Chief of Staff.*
General e-mail, Judiciary@mail.house.gov
Web, www.house.gov/judiciary

Jurisdiction over internal security legislation.

House Judiciary Committee, *Subcommittee on Crime, Terrorism, and Homeland Security, 207 CHOB 20515; (202) 225-3926. Fax, (202) 225-3737. Rep. Howard Coble, R-N.C., Chair; Jay Apperson, Chief Counsel.*
General e-mail, Judiciary@mail.house.gov
Web, www.house.gov/judiciary

Responsible for all aspects of criminal law and procedure, and revision of the U.S. criminal code (jurisdiction over juvenile justice and the role of children in the courts shared with House Education and the Workforce Committee). Oversees federal law enforcement agencies, including the Federal Bureau of Investigation; the Drug Enforcement Administration; the Bureau of Alcohol, Tobacco, Firearms, and Explosives; the Federal Bureau of Prisons; the U.S. Parole Commission; the U.S. Marshals Service; and the Secret Service. Jurisdiction over legislation concerning the Criminal Division of the Justice Dept.

House Permanent Select Committee on Intelligence, *H405 CAP 20515; (202) 225-4121. Fax, (202) 225-1991. Rep. Porter J. Goss, R-Fla., Chair; Tim Sample, Staff Director.*

Jurisdiction over the Central Intelligence Agency and intelligence and intelligence-related activities of other departments and agencies.

Senate Foreign Relations Committee, *Subcommittee on Western Hemisphere, Peace Corps, and Narcotics Affairs,* *SD-446 20510; (202) 224-4651. Sen. Norm Coleman, R-Minn., Chair; Carl Meacham, Professional Staff Member.*

Web, foreign.senate.gov

Jurisdiction over legislation dealing with the international flow of illegal drugs.

Senate Governmental Affairs Committee, *Permanent Subcommittee on Investigations,* *SR-199 20510; (202) 224-3721. Sen. Norm Coleman, R-Minn., Chair; Mary Robertson, Chief Clerk.*

General e-mail, PSI@govt-aff.senate.gov

Web, govt-aff.senate.gov

Investigates organized criminal activity, national and international narcotics trafficking, postal fraud, prison crime, child pornography, government contracts fraud, insurance fraud, entitlement fraud, fraud involving the use of computers, and securities theft and fraud. Investigates federal arson prevention and control activities.

Senate Health, Education, Labor, and Pensions Committee, *SD-428 20510; (202) 224-5375. Fax, (202) 228-5044. Sen. Judd Gregg, R-N.H., Chair; Sharon Soderstrom, Staff Director. TTY, (202) 224-1975.*

Web, health.senate.gov

Jurisdiction over legislation on drug abuse and rehabilitation of drug abusers, including narcotics addicts who have had contact (arrest or conviction) with the federal criminal justice system.

Senate Judiciary Committee, *SD-224 20510; (202) 224-5225. Fax, (202) 224-9102. Sen. Orrin G. Hatch, R-Utah, Chair; Makan Delrahim, Chief Counsel.*

Web, judiciary.senate.gov

Responsible for all aspects of criminal law and procedure and revision of the U.S. criminal code. Jurisdiction over legislation on internal security, speedy trials and pretrial procedures, grand juries, federal trial juries, federal corrections institutions (including prisoner health care), sentences, parole, pardons, the U.S. Parole Commission, and capital punishment. Jurisdiction over legislation dealing with organized crime, including the Racketeer Influenced and Corrupt Organizations Act (RICO); judicial ethics; gun control; control of domestic terrorism; some aspects of narcotics abuse, including control, enforcement, and criminal penalties; and regulation of trade.

Senate Select Committee on Intelligence, *SH-211 20510; (202) 224-1700. Sen. Pat Roberts, R-Kans., Chair; Bill Duhnke, Staff Contact.*

Web, intelligence.senate.gov

Studies, makes recommendations, and proposes legislation on intelligence agencies' activities, policies, and funds; oversees the Central Intelligence Agency, National Security Agency, Defense Intelligence Agency, the intelligence activities of the Federal Bureau of Investigation, and other intelligence operations of the U.S. government to ensure conformity with the U.S. Constitution and laws; authorizes appropriations for the intelligence community. Oversight of directives and procedures governing intelligence activities affecting the rights of Americans abroad.

INTERNATIONAL ORGANIZATIONS

INTERPOL, *Washington Office,* *INTERPOL-USNCB, U.S. Justice Dept. 20530; (202) 616-9000. Fax, (202) 616-8400. Edgar A. Adamson, Director.*

Web, www.usdoj.gov/usncb

U.S. national central bureau for INTERPOL; participates in international investigations on behalf of U.S. police; coordinates the exchange of investigative information on crimes, including drug trafficking, counterfeiting, missing persons, and terrorism. Coordinates law enforcement requests for investigative assistance in the United States and abroad. Assists with extradition processes. Serves as liaison between foreign and U.S. law enforcement agencies at federal, state, and local levels. (Headquarters in Lyons, France.)

NONPROFIT

American Bar Assn. (ABA), *Criminal Justice, Washington Office,* 740 15th St. N.W. 20005-1019; (202) 662-1500. Fax, (202) 662-1501. Thomas C. Smith, Director.

Web, www.abanet.org/crimjust

Responsible for all matters pertaining to criminal law and procedure for the association. Studies and makes recommendations on all facets of the criminal and juvenile justice system, including sentencing, juries, pretrial procedures, grand juries, white-collar crime, and the Racketeer Influenced and Corrupt Organizations Act (RICO). (Headquarters in Chicago, Ill.)

American Prosecutors Research Institute, *99 Canal Center Plaza, #510, Alexandria, VA 22314; (703) 549-4253. Fax, (703) 836-3195. Steven D. Dillingham, Chief Administrator.*

Web, www.ndaa-apri.org

Conducts research, provides information, and analyzes policies related to improvements in criminal prosecution. (Affiliated with the National District Attorneys' Assn.)

Justice Policy Institute, *4455 Connecticut Ave. N.W., #B500 20008; (202) 363-7847. Fax, (202) 363-8677. Vincent Schiraldi, President.*

General e-mail, info@justicepolicy.org

Web, www.justicepolicy.org

Research, advocacy, and policy development organization. Analyzes current and emerging criminal justice problems; works to develop new initiatives; educates the public about criminal justice issues. Interests include new prison construction, alternatives to incarceration, and curfew laws.

National Assn. of Attorneys General, *750 1st St. N.E., #1100 20002; (202) 326-6053. Fax, (202) 408-7014. Lynne M. Ross, Executive Director. Press, (202) 326-6047.*

General e-mail, feedback@naag.org

Web, www.naag.org

Membership: attorneys general of the states, territories, and commonwealths. Fosters interstate cooperation on legal and law enforcement issues, conducts policy research and analysis, and facilitates communication between members and all levels of government.

(For a list of state attorneys general, see Governors and Other State Officials in the appendix.)

National Assn. of Crime Victim Compensation Boards, *P.O. Box 16003, Alexandria, VA 22302-8003; (703) 313-9500. Fax, (703) 313-0546. Dan Eddy, Executive Director.*

Web, www.nacvcb.org

Provides state compensation agencies with training and technical assistance. Provides public information on victim compensation.

National Assn. of Criminal Defense Lawyers, *1025 Connecticut Ave. N.W., #901 20036; (202) 872-8600. Fax, (202) 872-8690. Ralph Grunewald, Executive Director.*

General e-mail, assist@nacdl.org

Web, www.nacdl.org

Membership: criminal defense attorneys. Provides members with continuing legal education programs, a brief bank, an ethics hotline, and specialized assistance in areas such as DNA and Section 8300 cash reporting requirements. Offers free legal assistance to members who are harassed, charged with contempt, or receive a bar grievance for providing ethical but aggressive representation. Interests include eliminating mandatory minimum sentencing, reforming the FBI laboratories, opposing the death penalty, and minimizing the effect on civil liberties of the war on drugs. Monitors legislation and regulations.

National Center For Victims of Crime, *2000 M St. N.W., #480 22036; (202) 467-8700. Fax, (202) 467-8701. Susan Herman, Executive Director.*

General e-mail, mail@ncvc.org

Web, www.ncvc.org

Works with victims' groups and criminal justice agencies to protect the rights of crime victims through state and federal statutes and policies. Promotes greater responsiveness to crime victims through training and education; provides research and technical assistance in the development of victim-related legislation.

National Crime Prevention Council, *1000 Connecticut Ave. N.W., 13th Floor 20036; (202) 466-6272. Fax, (202) 296-1356. John A. Calhoun, President. Fulfillment office, (800) 627-2911.*

Web, www.weprevent.org

Educates public on crime prevention through media campaigns, supporting materials, and training workshops; sponsors McGruff public service campaign; runs demonstration programs in schools.

National District Attorneys' Assn., *99 Canal Center Plaza, #510, Alexandria, VA 22314; (703) 549-9222. Fax, (703) 836-3195. Newman Flanagan, Executive Director.*

Web, www.ndaa-apri.org

Sponsors conferences and workshops on criminal justice; provides information on district attorneys, criminal justice, the courts, child abuse, environmental crime, and national traffic laws.

National Organization for Victim Assistance, *1730 Park Rd. N.W. 20010; (202) 232-6682. Fax, (202) 462-2255. Marlene A. Young, Executive Director. Toll-free information hotline, (800) 879-6682; (202) 232-6682 in the Washington area.*

General e-mail, nova@try-nova.org

Web, www.try-nova.org

Membership: persons involved with victim and witness assistance programs, criminal justice professionals, researchers, crime victims, and others interested in victims' rights. Monitors legislation; provides victims and victim support programs with technical assistance, referrals, and program support; provides information on victims' rights.

Child Abuse, Domestic Violence, and Sexual Assault

AGENCIES

Administration on Children, Youth, and Families *(Health and Human Services Dept.), Family and Youth Services, 330 C St. S.W., #2040 20447 (mailing address: P.O. Box 1182 20013-1182); (202) 205-8102. Fax, (202) 260-9330. Harry Wilson, Associate Commissioner.*

Web, www.acf.dhhs.gov/programs/fysb

Administers federal discretionary grant programs for projects serving runaway and homeless youth and for projects that deter youth involvement in gangs. Provides youth service agencies with training and technical assistance. Monitors federal policies, programs, and legislation. Supports research on youth development issues, including gangs, runaways, and homeless youth. Operates national clearinghouse on families and youth.

Criminal Division *(Justice Dept.), Child Exploitation and Obscenity Section,* 1400 New York Ave. N.W., #6400 20530; (202) 514-5780. Fax, (202) 514-1793. Andrew Oosterbaan, Chief.
Web, www.usdoj.gov/criminal/CEOS

Enforces federal obscenity and child pornography laws; prosecutes cases involving violations of these laws. Maintains collection of briefs, pleadings, and other material for use by federal, state, and local prosecutors.

Office of Justice Programs (OJP), *(Justice Dept.), National Institute of Justice,* 810 7th St. N.W., 7th Floor 20531; (202) 307-2942. Fax, (202) 307-6394. Sarah V. Hart, Director.
Web, www.ojp.usdoj.gov/nij

Conducts research on all aspects of criminal justice, including AIDS issues for law enforcement officials. Studies on rape and domestic violence available from the National Criminal Justice Reference Service: (800) 851-3420; in Maryland, (301) 251-5500; Web, www.ncjrs.org.

Office of Justice Programs (OJP), *(Justice Dept.), Violence Against Women,* 810 7th St. N.W., #920 20531; (202) 307-6026. Fax, (202) 307-3911. Diane Stuart, Director. National Domestic Violence Hotline, (800) 799-SAFE.
Web, www.usdoj.gov/vawo

Seeks more effective policies and services to combat domestic violence, sexual assault, stalking, and other crimes against women. Helps administer grants to states to fund shelters, crisis centers, and hotlines, and to hire law enforcement officers, prosecutors, and counselors specializing in cases of sexual violence and other violent crimes against women.

NONPROFIT

American Bar Assn. (ABA), *Center on Children and the Law,* 740 15th St. N.W., 9th Floor 20005-1022; (202) 662-1720. Fax, (202) 662-1755. Howard Davidson, Director.
General e-mail, ctrchildlaw@abanet.org
Web, www.abanet.org/child

Provides state and private child welfare organizations with training and technical assistance. Interests include child abuse and neglect, adoption, foster care, and medical neglect.

National Center for Prosecution of Child Abuse, 99 Canal Center Plaza, #510, Alexandria, VA 22314; (703) 549-4253. Fax, (703) 836-3195. Victor Vieth, Director.
General e-mail, ncpca@ndaa-apri.org
Web, www.ndaa-apri.org

Provides prosecutors involved in child abuse cases with training, technical assistance, and information. Monitors legislation concerning child abuse. (Affiliated with the National District Attorneys' Assn.)

Rape, Abuse, and Incest National Network (RAINN), 635-B Pennsylvania Ave. S.E. 20003-4303; (202) 544-1034. Fax, (202) 544-3556. Scott Berkowitz, President. National Sexual Assault Hotline, (800) 656-HOPE.
General e-mail, info@rainn.org
Web, www.rainn.org

Links sexual assault victims to confidential local services through national sexual assault hotline. Provides extensive public outreach and education programs nationwide.

Drug Control

AGENCIES

Bureau of Customs and Border Protection *(Homeland Security Dept.), Investigations,* 1300 Pennsylvania Ave. N.W., #6.5EA 20229; (202) 927-1600. Fax, (202) 927-1948. Richard Hoglund, Assistant Commissioner (Acting).
Web, www.customs.gov

Interdicts and seizes contraband, including narcotics and other dangerous drugs smuggled into the United States.

Criminal Division *(Justice Dept.), Narcotic and Dangerous Drugs,* 1400 New York Ave. N.W., #1100 20530; (202) 514-0917. Fax, (202) 514-6112. Jodi L. Avergun, Chief.
Web, www.usdoj.gov/criminal

Investigates and prosecutes participants in criminal syndicates involved in the large-scale importation, manufacture, shipment, or distribution of illegal narcotics and other dangerous drugs. Trains agents and prosecutors in the techniques of major drug litigation.

Defense Dept. (DoD), *Counternarcotics,* 1510 Defense Pentagon 20301-1510; (703) 697-6000. Fax, (703) 697-3323. Andre Hollis, Deputy Assistant Secretary.
Web, www.defenselink.mil/policy/solic/cn

Advises the secretary on Defense Dept. policies and programs in support of federal counternarcotics operations and the implementation of the president's National Drug Control Policy.

Drug Enforcement Administration (DEA), *(Justice Dept.), 700 Army-Navy Dr., Arlington, VA 22202 (mailing address: Drug Enforcement Administration, 2401 Jefferson Davis Hwy., Alexandria, VA 22301); (202) 307-8000. Fax, (202) 307-7965. John J. Brown III, Administrator (Acting). Press, (202) 307-7977. Locator, (202) 307-4132.*
Web, www.dea.gov

Enforces federal laws and statutes relating to narcotics and other dangerous drugs, including addictive drugs, depressants, stimulants, and hallucinogens; manages the National Narcotics Intelligence System in cooperation with federal, state, and local officials; investigates violations and regulates legal trade in narcotics and dangerous drugs. Provides school and community officials with drug abuse policy guidelines. Provides information on drugs and drug abuse.

Federal Bureau of Investigation (FBI), *(Justice Dept.), 935 Pennsylvania Ave. N.W., #7176 20535; (202) 324-3444. Fax, (202) 323-2079. Robert S. Mueller III, Director. Information, (202) 324-3000.*
Web, www.fbi.gov

Shares responsibility with the Drug Enforcement Administration for investigating violations of federal criminal drug laws; investigates organized crime involvement with illegal narcotics trafficking.

Food and Drug Administration (FDA), *(Health and Human Services Dept.), Center for Drug Evaluation and Research, 1451 Rockville Pike, Rockville, MD 20852; (301) 594-5400. Fax, (301) 594-6197. Dr. Janet Woodcock, Director. Information, (301) 827-4573. Press, (301) 827-6242.*
Web, www.fda.gov/cdr

Makes recommendations to the Justice Dept.'s Drug Enforcement Administration on narcotics and dangerous drugs to be controlled.

Interior Dept. (DOI), *Managing Risk and Public Safety, 1849 C St. N.W., #3458 20240-4108; (202) 208-7702. Fax, (202) 208-5078. L. Michael Kaas, Director.*
Web, www.doi.gov/mrps

Administers drug and law enforcement programs for the Interior Dept., including programs in national parks, ranges, and fish and wildlife refuges. Cooperates with local law enforcement agencies, state park rangers, and other drug enforcement agencies.

Office of Justice Programs (OJP), *(Justice Dept.), Justice Assistance, 810 7th St. N.W., #4427 20531; (202) 616-6500. Fax, (202) 305-1367. Richard R. Nedelkoff, Director.*
Web, www.ojp.usdoj.gov/bja

Awards grants and provides eligible state and local governments with training and technical assistance to enforce laws relating to narcotics and other dangerous drugs.

Office of National Drug Control Policy (ONDCP), *(Executive Office of the President), 750 17th St. N.W. 20503; (202) 395-6700. Fax, (202) 395-6680. John P. Walters, Director.*
Web, www.whitehousedrugpolicy.gov

Establishes policies and oversees the implementation of a national drug control strategy; recommends changes to reduce demand for and supply of illegal drugs; advises the National Security Council on drug control policy.

U.S. Coast Guard (USCG), *(Homeland Security Dept.), Law Enforcement, 2100 2nd St. S.W., #3110 20593-0001; (202) 267-1890. Fax, (202) 267-4082. Capt. Kenneth A. Ward, Chief.*
Web, www.uscg.mil/hq/g-o/g-opl/mle/welcome.htm

Combats smuggling of narcotics and other dangerous drugs into the United States via the Atlantic and Pacific oceans and the Gulf of Mexico; works with the Bureau of Customs and Border Protection on drug law enforcement; interdicts illegal migrants; enforces fisheries.

NONPROFIT

Common Sense for Drug Policy, *3220 N St. N.W., #141 20007; (202) 299-9780. Fax, (202) 518-4028. Kevin B. Zeese, President.*
General e-mail, info@csdp.org
Web, www.csdp.org

Provides comprehensive information on drug policy related questions to media and other interested parties. Offers technical assistance, fundraising, and public relations advice to groups that promote health-based strategies of drug control. Seeks to encourage development of an effective drug policy and to reduce drug-related harms, including spread of AIDS and other diseases, crime and violence, and social dysfunction; focus includes international drug policy.

Drug Policy Alliance, *Washington Office, 925 15th St. N.W., 2nd Floor 20005; (202) 216-0035. Fax, (202) 216-0803. William D. McColl, Director.*
General e-mail, dc@drugpolicy.org
Web, www.drugpolicy.org

Supports reform of current drug control policy. Advocates medical treatment to control drug abuse; opposes random drug testing. Sponsors the International Conference on Drug Policy Reform annually. (Headquarters in New York.)

Marijuana Policy Project, *P.O. Box 77492 20013; (202) 462-5747. Fax, (202) 232-0442. Robert D. Kampia, Executive Director.*
General e-mail, mpp@mpp.org
Web, www.mpp.org

Promotes reform of marijuana policies and regulations. Opposes the prohibition of responsible growing and use of marijuana by adults. Interests include allowing doctors to prescribe marijuana to seriously ill patients and removing criminal penalties for marijuana use.

National Assn. of State Alcohol and Drug Abuse Directors, *808 17th St. N.W., #410 20006; (202) 293-0090. Fax, (202) 293-1250. Lewis E. Gallant, Executive Director.*
General e-mail, dcoffice@nasadad.org
Web, www.nasadad.org

Provides information on drug abuse treatment and prevention; contracts with federal and state agencies for design of programs to fight drug abuse.

National Organization for the Reform of Marijuana Laws (NORML), *1600 K St. N.W., #501 20006; (202) 483-5500. Fax, (202) 483-0057. R. Keith Stroup, Executive Director.*
General e-mail, norml@norml.org
Web, www.norml.org

Works to reform federal, state, and local marijuana laws and policies. Educates the public and conducts litigation on behalf of marijuana consumers. Monitors legislation and regulations.

Rand Corporation, *Drug Policy Research Center, Washington Office, 1200 S. Hayes St., Arlington, VA 22202-5050; (703) 413-1100. Fax, (703) 413-8111. Barbara Williams, Senior Adviser.*
Web, www.rand.org/centers/dprc

Studies and analyzes the nation's drug problems and policies; interests include international policy, trafficking, and interdiction. Provides policymakers with information. (Headquarters in Santa Monica, Calif.)

Gun Control

AGENCIES

Bureau of Alcohol, Tobacco, Firearms, and Explosives (ATF), *(Justice Dept.), 650 Massachusetts Ave.*

N.W., #8000 20226; (202) 927-8700. Bradley A. Buckles, Director. Information, (202) 927-7777.
Web, www.atf.gov

Enforces and administers laws to eliminate illegal possession and use of firearms. Investigates criminal violations and regulates legal trade, including imports and exports. (To report illegal firearms activity, (800) ATF-GUNS; firearms theft hotline, (800) 800-3855; firearms tracing center, (800) 788-7133.)

NONPROFIT

Brady Campaign United with the Million Mom March, *1225 Eye St. N.W., #1100 20005; (202) 898-0792. Fax, (202) 371-9615. Sarah Brady, Chair.*
Web, www.bradycampaign.org

Public interest organization that works for handgun control legislation and serves as an information clearinghouse.

Brady Center to Prevent Gun Violence, *1225 Eye St. N.W., #1100 20005; (202) 289-7319. Fax, (202) 408-1851. Michael Barnes, President.*
Web, www.bradycenter.org

Educational, research, and legal action organization that seeks to allay gun violence, especially among children, through gun control legislation. (Affiliated with Brady Campaign United with the Million Mom March.)

Citizens Committee for the Right to Keep and Bear Arms, *Publications and Public Affairs, Washington Office, 1090 Vermont Ave. N.W., #800 20005; (202) 326-5259. Fax, (202) 898-1939. John M. Snyder, Director.*
General e-mail, gundean@aol.com
Web, www.ccrkba.org

Concerned with rights of gun owners. Maintains National Advisory Council, comprising members of Congress and other distinguished Americans, which provides advice on issues concerning the right to keep and bear arms. (Headquarters in Bellevue, Wash.)

Coalition to Stop Gun Violence, *1023 15th St. N.W., #600 20005; (202) 408-0061. Fax, (202) 408-0062. Michael K. Beard, President.*
General e-mail, webmaster@csgv.org
Web, www.csgv.org

Membership: 44 national organizations and 100,000 individuals. Works to reduce gun violence by fostering effective community and national action.

Educational Fund to Stop Gun Violence, *1023 15th St. N.W., #600 20005; (202) 408-7560. Fax, (202) 406-0062. Joshua Horwitz, Executive Director.*
General e-mail, webmaster@efsgv.org

Web, www.efsgv.org

Works to reduce handgun violence through education; assists schools and organizations in establishing antiviolence programs; maintains a firearms litigation clearinghouse.

Gun Owners of America, *8001 Forbes Pl., #102, Springfield, VA 22151; (703) 321-8585. Fax, (703) 321-8408. Lawrence D. Pratt, Executive Director.*
General e-mail, goamail@gunowners.org
Web, www.gunowners.org

Seeks to preserve the right to bear arms and to protect the rights of law-abiding gun owners. Administers foundation that provides gun owners with legal assistance in suits against the federal government. Monitors legislation, regulations, and international agreements.

National Rifle Assn. of America (NRA),
11250 Waples Mill Rd., Fairfax, VA 22030; (703) 267-1000. Fax, (703) 267-3976. Wayne LaPierre Jr., Executive Vice President. Press, (703) 267-3820.
Web, www.nra.org

Membership: target shooters, hunters, gun collectors, gunsmiths, police officers, and others interested in firearms. Promotes shooting sports and recreational shooting and safety; studies and makes recommendations on firearms laws. Opposes gun control legislation.

Juvenile Justice

AGENCIES

Education Dept., *Student Achievement and Schools Accountability Program, 400 Maryland Ave. S.W., #3W230 20202-6132; (202) 260-0826. Fax, (202) 260-7764. Jacqueline Jackson, Director (Acting). Press, (202) 401-1008.*
Web, www.ed.gov

Funds state and local institutions responsible for providing neglected or delinquent children with free public education.

Office of Justice Programs (OJP), *(Justice Dept.), Juvenile Justice and Delinquency Prevention, 810 7th St. N.W. 20531; (202) 307-5911. Fax, (202) 307-2093. John Robert Flores, Administrator. Technical information, (202) 307-0751. Clearinghouse, (800) 638-8736.*
Web, www.ncjrs.org/ojjhome.htm

Administers federal programs related to prevention and treatment of juvenile delinquency, missing and exploited children, child victimization, and research and evaluation of juvenile justice system; coordinates with youth programs of the departments of Agriculture, Education, Housing and Urban Development, Interior, and Labor, and of the Substance Abuse and Mental Health Services Administration, including the Center for Studies of Crime and Delinquency. Operates the Juvenile Justice Clearinghouse.

NONPROFIT

Coalition for Juvenile Justice, *1211 Connecticut Ave. N.W., #414 20036; (202) 467-0864. Fax, (202) 887-0738. David Doi, Executive Director.*
General e-mail, info@juvjustice.org
Web, www.juvjustice.org

Represents state juvenile justice advisory groups. Promotes the improvement of the juvenile justice system and the prevention of juvenile delinquency.

Robert F. Kennedy Memorial, *National Youth Project, 1367 Connecticut Ave. N.W., #200 20036-1819; (202) 463-7575. Fax, (202) 463-6606. Lynn Delaney, Director.*
General e-mail, info@rfkmemorial.org
Web, www.rfkmemorial.org

Develops new approaches to the problems of drug and alcohol addiction, crime and violence, school failures, and family disorder. Develops youth leadership skills through service and training programs, including the RFK Fellowship Program.

Organized Crime

AGENCIES

Criminal Division *(Justice Dept.), Narcotic and Dangerous Drugs, 1400 New York Ave. N.W., #1100 20530; (202) 514-0917. Fax, (202) 514-6112. Jodi L. Avergun, Chief.*
Web, www.usdoj.gov/criminal

Investigates and prosecutes participants in criminal syndicates involved in the large-scale importation, manufacture, shipment, or distribution of illegal narcotics and other dangerous drugs. Trains agents and prosecutors in the techniques of major drug litigation.

Criminal Division *(Justice Dept.), Organized Crime and Racketeering, 1301 New York Ave. N.W., #700 20005; (202) 514-3594. Fax, (202) 514-3601. Bruce G. Ohr, Chief.*
Web, www.usdoj.gov/criminal

Enforces federal criminal laws when subjects under investigation are alleged racketeers or part of syndicated criminal operations; coordinates efforts of federal, state, and local law enforcement agencies against organized crime, including emerging international groups. Cases include infiltration of legitimate businesses and labor unions, public corruption, labor-management racketeering, and violence that disrupts the criminal justice process.

Other Violations

AGENCIES

Bureau of Alcohol, Tobacco, Firearms, and Explosives (ATF), *(Justice Dept.),* *650 Massachusetts Ave. N.W., #8000 20226; (202) 927-8700. Bradley A. Buckles, Director. Information, (202) 927-7777.*
Web, www.atf.gov

Performs law enforcement functions relating to alcohol (beer, wine, distilled spirits), tobacco, arson, explosives, and destructive devices; investigates criminal violations and regulates legal trade.

Bureau of Customs and Border Protection *(Homeland Security Dept.),* **Investigations,** *1300 Pennsylvania Ave. N.W., #6.5EA 20229; (202) 927-1600. Fax, (202) 927-1948. Richard Hoglund, Assistant Commissioner (Acting).*
Web, www.customs.gov

Combats smuggling and the unreported transportation of funds in excess of $10,000; enforces statutes relating to the processing and regulation of people, carriers, cargo, and mail into and out of the United States. Investigates counterfeiting, child pornography, commercial fraud, and Internet crimes.

Criminal Division *(Justice Dept.),* **Asset Forfeiture and Money Laundering,** *1400 New York Ave. N.W., #10100 20530; (202) 514-1263. Fax, (202) 514-5522. John Roth, Chief.*
Web, www.usdoj.gov/criminal

Investigates and prosecutes money laundering and criminal and civil forfeiture offenses involving illegal transfer of funds within the United States and from the United States to other countries. Oversees and coordinates legislative policy proposals. Advises U.S. attorney's offices in multidistrict money laundering and criminal and civil forfeiture prosecutions. Represents Justice Dept. in international anti–money laundering and criminal and civil forfeiture initiatives.

Criminal Division *(Justice Dept.),* **Counterterrorism,** *601 D St. N.W., #6500 20530; (202) 514-0849. Fax, (202) 514-8714. Barry Sabin, Chief.*
Web, www.usdoj.gov/criminal/tvcs.html

Investigates and prosecutes incidents of international and domestic terrorism involving U.S. interests, domestic violent crime, firearms, and explosives violations. Provides legal advice on federal statutes relating to murder, assault, kidnapping, threats, robbery, weapons and explosives control, malicious destruction of property, and aircraft and sea piracy.

Criminal Division *(Justice Dept.),* **Fraud,** *1400 New York Ave. N.W., #4100 20005; (202) 514-0640. Fax, (202) 514-7021. Joshua R. Hochberg, Chief.*
Web, www.usdoj.gov/criminal/fraud

Administers federal enforcement activities related to fraud and white-collar crime. Focuses on frauds against government programs, transnational and multidistrict fraud, and cases involving the security and commodity exchanges, banking practices, and consumer victimization.

Federal Bureau of Investigation (FBI), *(Justice Dept.),* **Economic Crimes,** *935 Pennsylvania Ave. N.W., #7373 20535; (202) 324-6352. Fax, (202) 324-8072. Gary L. Dagan, Chief. Press, (202) 324-3691.*
Web, www.fbi.gov

Investigates crimes of fraud, theft, or embezzlement within or against the national or international financial community, excluding frauds against financial institutions. Priorities include insurance, securities and commodities, bankruptcy, and Internet and telemarketing fraud.

U.S. Postal Service (USPS), *Inspection Service, 475 L'Enfant Plaza S.W., #3100 20260-2100; (202) 268-4264. Fax, (202) 268-4563. Lee R. Heath, Chief Postal Inspector. Fraud and abuse hotline, (888) 877-7644.*
Web, www.usps.com/postalinspectors

Protects mail, postal funds, and property from violations of postal laws, such as mail fraud or distribution of obscene materials.

U.S. Secret Service *(Homeland Security Dept.),* *950 H St. N.W., #8000 20223; (202) 406-5700. Fax, (202) 406-5246. W. Ralph Basham, Director. Information, (202) 406-5708.*
Web, www.secretservice.gov

Enforces and administers counterfeiting and forgery laws. Investigates electronic fund transfer, credit card, and other types of access fraud, and threats against the president, vice president, and foreign heads of state visiting the United States.

Sentencing and Corrections

AGENCIES

Federal Bureau of Prisons *(Justice Dept.),* *320 1st St. N.W., #654 20534; (202) 307-3250. Fax, (202) 514-6878. Harley G. Lappin, Director. Press, (202) 307-3198. Inmate locator service, (202) 307-3126.*
Web, www.bop.gov

Supervises operations of federal correctional institutions and community treatment facilities, and commitment and management of federal inmates; oversees contracts with local institutions for confinement and support of federal prisoners. Regional offices are responsible for administration; central office in Washington coordinates operations and issues standards and policy guidelines. Central office includes Federal Prison Industries, a government corporation providing prison-manufactured goods and services for sale to federal agencies, and the National Institute of Corrections, an information and technical assistance center on state and local corrections programs.

Federal Bureau of Prisons *(Justice Dept.), Health Services,* *320 1st St. N.W., #1054 20534; (202) 307-3055. Fax, (202) 307-0826. Mary Ellen Thoms, Assistant Director; Dr. Newton E. Kendig, Medical Director.*
Web, www.bop.gov
Administers health care and treatment programs for prisoners in federal institutions.

Federal Bureau of Prisons *(Justice Dept.), Industries, Education, and Vocational Training—UNICOR,* *400 1st St. N.W. 20534 (mailing address: 320 1st St. N.W. 20534); (202) 305-3500. Fax, (202) 305-7340. Steve Schwalb, Chief Operating Officer.*
Web, www.unicor.gov
Administers program whereby inmates in federal prisons produce goods and services that are sold to the federal government.

Federal Bureau of Prisons *(Justice Dept.), National Institute of Corrections,* *320 1st St. N.W., #5007 20534; (202) 307-3106. Fax, (202) 307-3361. Morris L. Thigpen, Director. Inmate locator service (202) 307-3126.*
Web, www.nicic.org
Offers technical assistance and training for upgrading state and local corrections systems through staff development, research, and evaluation of correctional operations and programs. Acts as a clearinghouse on correctional information.

Justice Dept. (DOJ), *Pardon Attorney, 500 1st St. N.W., #400 20530; (202) 616-6070. Fax, (202) 616-6069. Roger C. Adams, Pardon Attorney.*
Web, www.usdoj.gov/pardon
Receives and reviews petitions to the president for all forms of executive clemency, including pardons and sentence reductions; initiates investigations and prepares the deputy attorney general's recommendations to the president on petitions.

Office of Justice Programs (OJP), *(Justice Dept.), Justice Assistance, 810 7th St. N.W., #4427 20531; (202)* 616-6500. Fax, (202) 305-1367. Richard R. Nedelkoff, Director.
Web, www.ojp.usdoj.gov/bja
Provides states and communities with funds and technical assistance for corrections demonstration projects.

Office of Justice Programs (OJP), *(Justice Dept.), National Institute of Justice, 810 7th St. N.W., 7th Floor 20531; (202) 307-2942. Fax, (202) 307-6394. Sarah V. Hart, Director.*
Web, www.ojp.usdoj.gov/nij
Conducts research on all aspects of criminal justice, including crime prevention, enforcement, adjudication, and corrections. Maintains the National Criminal Justice Reference Service, which provides information on corrections research: (800) 851-3420; in Maryland, (301) 251-5500; Web, www.ncjrs.org.

U.S. Parole Commission *(Justice Dept.), 5550 Friendship Blvd., #420, Chevy Chase, MD 20815-7286; (301) 492-5990. Fax, (301) 492-5307. Edward F. Reilly Jr., Chair.*
Web, www.usdoj.gov/uspc
Makes release decisions for all federal prisoners serving sentences of more than one year; jurisdiction over paroled federal prisoners and over other prisoners on mandatory release under the "good time" statutes. U.S. probation officers supervise parolees and mandatory releases.

U.S. Sentencing Commission, *1 Columbus Circle N.E., #2-500 South Lobby 20002-8002; (202) 502-4500. Fax, (202) 502-4699. Diana E. Murphy, Chair.*
Web, www.ussc.gov
Establishes sentencing guidelines and policy for all federal courts, including guidelines prescribing the appropriate form and severity of punishment for those convicted of federal crimes. Provides training and research on sentencing-related issues. Serves as an information resource.

JUDICIARY

Administrative Office of the U.S. Courts, *1 Columbus Circle N.E., #7-400 20544; (202) 273-3000. Leonidas Ralph Mecham, Director. Information, (202) 502-2600.*
Web, www.uscourts.gov
Supervises all administrative matters of the federal court system, except the Supreme Court; collects statistical data on business of the courts.

Administrative Office of the U.S. Courts, *Probation and Pretrial Services, 1 Columbus Circle N.E., #4-300*

20544; (202) 502-1600. Fax, (202) 502-1677. John M. Hughes, Assistant Director.

Supervises federal probation and pretrial services officers, subject to primary control by the respective district courts in which they serve. Responsible for general oversight of field offices; tests new probation programs such as probation teams and deferred prosecution.

NONPROFIT

American Bar Assn. (ABA), *Criminal Justice, Washington Office,* 740 15th St. N.W. 20005-1019; (202) 662-1500. Fax, (202) 662-1501. Thomas C. Smith, Director.
Web, www.abanet.org/crimjust
Studies and makes recommendations on all aspects of the correctional system, including overcrowding in prisons and the privatization of prisons and correctional institutions. (Headquarters in Chicago, Ill.)

American Civil Liberties Union Foundation, *National Prison Project,* 733 15th St. N.W., #620 20005-6016; (202) 393-4930. Fax, (202) 393-4931. Elizabeth Alexander, Executive Director.
Litigates on behalf of prisoners through class action suits. Seeks to improve prison conditions and the penal system; serves as resource center for prisoners' rights; operates an AIDS education project.

American Correctional Assn. (ACA), 4380 Forbes Blvd., Lanham, MD 20706-4322; (301) 918-1800. Fax, (301) 918-1900. James A. Gondles Jr., Executive Director. Information, (800) 222-5646.
Web, www.aca.org
Membership: corrections administrators and staff in juvenile and adult institutions, community corrections facilities, and jails; affiliates include state and regional corrections associations in the United States and Canada. Conducts and publishes research; provides state and local governments with technical assistance; certifies corrections professionals. Interests include criminal justice issues, correctional standards, and accreditation programs. Library open to the public.

Amnesty International USA, *Washington Office,* 600 Pennsylvania Ave. S.E., 5th Floor 20003; (202) 544-0200. Fax, (202) 546-7142. Maria Alexandra Arriaga, Director.
Web, www.amnestyusa.org
International organization that opposes retention or reinstitution of the death penalty; advocates humane treatment of all prisoners. (U.S. headquarters in New York.)

Correctional Education Assn., 4380 Forbes Blvd., Lanham, MD 20706-4322; (301) 918-1915. Fax, (301) 918-1846. Stephen J. Steurer, Executive Director.
General e-mail, ceaoffice@aol.com
Web, www.ceanational.org
Membership: educators and administrators who work with students in correctional settings. Provides members with information and technical assistance to improve quality of educational programs and services offered in correctional settings. Interests include postsecondary and vocational education, special education, jail education, and libraries and literacy.

Families Against Mandatory Minimums, 1612 K St. N.W., #700 20006; (202) 822-6700. Fax, (202) 822-6704. Julie Stewart, President.
General e-mail, famm@famm.org
Web, www.famm.org
Seeks to repeal statutory mandatory minimum prison sentences. Works to increase public awareness of inequity of mandatory minimum sentences through grassroots efforts and media outreach programs.

NAACP Legal Defense and Educational Fund, *Washington Office,* 1444 Eye St. N.W., 10th Floor 20005; (202) 682-1300. Fax, (202) 682-1312. Leslie M. Proll, Senior Attorney.
Civil rights litigation group that supports abolition of capital punishment; assists attorneys representing prisoners on death row; focuses public attention on race discrimination in the application of the death penalty. Not affiliated with the National Assn. for the Advancement of Colored People (NAACP). (Headquarters in New York.)

National Center on Institutions and Alternatives, 3125 Mt. Vernon Ave., Alexandria, VA 22305; (703) 684-0373. Fax, (703) 684-6037. Jerome G. Miller, President.
General e-mail, info@ncianet.org
Web, www.sentencing.org
Seeks to reduce incarceration as primary form of punishment imposed by criminal justice system; advocates use of extended community service, work-release, and halfway house programs; operates residential programs; provides defense attorneys and courts with specific recommendations for sentencing and parole.

National Coalition to Abolish the Death Penalty, 920 Pennsylvania Ave. S.E. 20003; (202) 543-9577. Fax, (202) 543-7798. Steven Hawkins, Executive Director.
General e-mail, info@ncadp.org
Web, www.ncadp.org
Membership: organizations and individuals opposed to the death penalty. Maintains collection of death

penalty research. Provides training, resources, and conferences. Works with families of murder victims; tracks execution dates. Monitors legislation and regulations.

Prison Fellowship Ministries, *1856 Old Reston Ave., Reston, VA 20190-3321 (mailing address: P.O. Box 17500, Washington, DC 20041-0500); (703) 478-0100. Fax, (703) 478-0452. Mark Early, President.*
Web, www.prisonfellowship.org

Religious organization that ministers to prisoners and ex-prisoners, victims, and the families involved. Offers counseling, seminars, and postrelease support for readjustment; works to increase the fairness and effectiveness of the criminal justice system.

The Sentencing Project, *514 10th St. N.W., #1000 20004; (202) 628-0871. Fax, (202) 628-1091. Malcolm C. Young, Executive Director.*
General e-mail, staff@sentencingproject.org
Web, www.sentencingproject.org

Develops and promotes sentencing programs that reduce reliance on incarceration; provides technical assistance to sentencing programs; compares domestic and international rates of incarceration; publishes research and information on criminal justice policy.

⚖ LAW ENFORCEMENT

AGENCIES

Criminal Division *(Justice Dept.), Computer Crime and Intellectual Property, 1301 New York Ave. N.W., #600 20530; (202) 514-1026. Fax, (202) 514-6113. Martha Stansell-Gamm, Chief.*
Web, www.usdoj.gov/criminal/cybercrime

Investigates and litigates criminal and civil cases involving computers and the Internet; provides specialized technical and legal assistance to other Justice Dept. divisions; coordinates international efforts; formulates policies and proposes legislation on computer crime issues.

Federal Law Enforcement Training Center *(Homeland Security Dept.), Washington Office, 555 11th St. N.W., #400 20004; (202) 927-8940. Fax, (202) 927-8782. John C. Dooher, Senior Associate Director.*
Web, www.fletc.gov

Trains federal law enforcement personnel from seventy-four agencies, excluding the Federal Bureau of Investigation and the Drug Enforcement Administration. (Headquarters in Glynco, Ga.)

National Institute of Standards and Technology (NIST), *(Commerce Dept.), Law Enforcement Standards, 100 Bureau Dr., Bldg. 225, #A323, MS-8102, Gaithersburg, MD 20899-8102; (301) 975-2757. Fax, (301) 948-0978. Kathleen M. Higgins, Director.*
General e-mail, oles@nist.gov
Web, www.nist.gov

Answers inquiries and makes referrals concerning the application of science and technology to the criminal justice community; maintains information on standards and current research; prepares reports and formulates standards for the National Institute of Justice, the Federal Bureau of Investigation, and the National Highway Traffic Safety Administration.

Office of Justice Programs (OJP), *(Justice Dept.), Justice Assistance, 810 7th St. N.W., #4427 20531; (202) 616-6500. Fax, (202) 305-1367. Richard R. Nedelkoff, Director.*
Web, www.ojp.usdoj.gov/bja

Provides funds to eligible state and local governments and to nonprofit organizations for criminal justice programs, primarily those that combat drug trafficking and other drug-related crime.

Treasury Dept., *Financial Crimes Enforcement Network, 2070 Chain Bridge Rd., #200, Vienna, VA 22183 (mailing address: P.O. Box 39, Vienna, VA 22183-0039); (703) 905-3591. Fax, (703) 905-3690. James F. Sloan, Director.*
Web, www.fincen.gov

Administers an information network in support of federal, state, and local law enforcement agencies in the prevention and detection of money-laundering operations and other financial crimes.

U.S. Marshals Service *(Justice Dept.), 600 Army-Navy Dr., #1200, Arlington, VA 22202; (202) 307-9001. Fax, (202) 307-5040. Benigno G. Reyna, Director. TTY, (800) 423-0719. Public Affairs, (202) 307-9065.*
Web, www.usdoj.gov/marshals

Provides the federal judiciary system and the attorney general with support services, including court and witness security, prisoner custody and transportation, prisoner support, maintenance and disposal of seized and forfeited property, and special operations. Administers the Federal Witness Protection program. Apprehends fugitives, including those wanted by foreign nations and believed to be in the United States; oversees the return of fugitives apprehended abroad and wanted by U.S. law enforcement.

CONGRESS

House Judiciary Committee, *Subcommittee on Crime, Terrorism, and Homeland Security,* 207 CHOB 20515; (202) 225-3926. Fax, (202) 225-3737. Rep. Howard Coble, R-N.C., Chair; Jay Apperson, Chief Counsel.

General e-mail, Judiciary@mail.house.gov
Web, www.house.gov/judiciary

Jurisdiction over legislation on federal criminal laws including terrorism, prisons, corrections, death penalty procedures, and the Federal Bureau of Investigation.

House Judiciary Committee, *Subcommittee on the Constitution,* 362 FHOB 20515; (202) 226-7680. Fax, (202) 225-3746. Rep. Steve Chabot, R-Ohio, Chair; Crystal Roberts, Chief Counsel.

General e-mail, Judiciary@mail.house.gov
Web, www.house.gov/judiciary

Jurisdiction over legislation dealing with the use, collection, evaluation, and release of U.S. and international criminal justice data. Oversight of legislation on information policy, electronic privacy, computer security, and trade and licensing.

Senate Judiciary Committee, SD-224 20510; (202) 224-5225. Fax, (202) 224-9102. Sen. Orrin G. Hatch, R-Utah, Chair; Makan Delrahim, Chief Counsel.

Web, judiciary.senate.gov

Jurisdiction over legislation related to Office of Justice Programs, which includes the Bureau of Justice Assistance, Bureau of Justice Statistics, National Institute of Justice, Office of Juvenile Justice and Delinquency Prevention, and the Office for Victims of Crime.

Senate Judiciary Committee, *Subcommittee on Terrorism, Technology, and Homeland Security,* SH-325 20510; (202) 224-6791. Fax, (202) 228-0542. Sen. Jon Kyl, R-Ariz., Chair; Stephen Higgins, Chief Counsel.

Web, judiciary.senate.gov

Jurisdiction over legislation dealing with the use, collection, evaluation, and release of U.S. and international criminal justice data. Oversight of legislation on information policy, electronic privacy, computer security, and trade and licensing.

NONPROFIT

American Federation of Police, *Washington Office,* 1090 Vermont Ave. N.W., #800 20005; (202) 293-9088. Fax, (305) 573-9819. Donna Shepherd, Director.
Web, www.aphf.org/nacop.html

Membership: governmental and private law enforcement officers. Provides members with insurance benefits

and training programs. (Affiliated with the National Police Hall of Fame in Titusville, Fla.)

International Assn. of Chiefs of Police, 515 N. Washington St., Alexandria, VA 22314-2357; (703) 836-6767. Fax, (703) 836-4543. Daniel N. Rosenblatt, Executive Director.
Web, www.theiacp.org

Membership: foreign and U.S. police executives and administrators. Consults and conducts research on all aspects of police activity; conducts training programs and develops educational aids; conducts public education programs.

International Union of Police, 1421 Prince St., #400, Alexandria, VA 22314; (703) 549-7473. Fax, (703) 683-9048. Sam Cabral, President.

General e-mail, iupa@iupa.org
Web, www.iupa.org

Membership: about 80,000 law enforcement officers and personnel. Helps members negotiate pay, benefits, and better working conditions; conducts training programs and workshops; offers legal services to members. Monitors legislation and regulations. (Affiliated with the AFL-CIO.)

Law Enforcement Alliance of America, 7700 Leesburg Pike, #421, Falls Church, VA 22043; (703) 847-2677. Fax, (703) 556-6485. James J. Fotis, Executive Director.

General e-mail, info@leaa.org
Web, www.leaa.org

Membership: law enforcement professionals, citizens, and victims of crime. Advocacy group on law and order issues.

National Black Police Assn., 3251 Mt. Pleasant St. N.W., 2nd Floor 20010-2103; (202) 986-2070. Fax, (202) 986-0410. Ronald Hampton, Executive Director.

General e-mail, nbpanatofc@worldnet.att.net
Web, www.blackpolice.org

Membership: local, state, and regional African American police associations. Works to improve the relationship between police departments and minorities; to evaluate the effect of criminal justice policies and programs on the minority community; to recruit minority police officers; to eliminate police corruption, brutality, and racial discrimination; and to educate and train police officers.

National Criminal Justice Assn., 720 7th St. N.W., 3rd Floor 20001-3716; (202) 628-8550. Fax, (202) 628-0080. Cabell C. Cropper, Executive Director.

General e-mail, info@ncja.org
Web, www.ncja.org

Membership: criminal justice organizations and professionals. Provides members and interested individuals with technical assistance and information.

National Law Enforcement Council, *888 16th St. N.W., #700 20006; (202) 835-8020. Fax, (202) 331-4291. Donald Baldwin, Executive Director.*

Membership: national law enforcement organizations. Fosters information exchange and explores the effects of public policy on law enforcement. Monitors legislation and regulations.

National Organization of Black Law Enforcement Executives, *4609 Pine Crest Office Park Dr., Suite F, Alexandria, VA 22312-1442; (703) 658-1529. Fax, (703) 658-9479. Jessie Lee, Executive Director (Interim).*
Web, www.noblenational.org

Membership: minority police chiefs and senior law enforcement executives. Works to increase community involvement in the criminal justice system and to enhance the role of minorities in law enforcement. Provides urban police departments with assistance in police operations, community relations, and devising strategies to combat urban and hate crimes.

National Sheriffs' Assn., *1450 Duke St., Alexandria, VA 22314; (703) 836-7827. Fax, (703) 683-6541. Thomas N. Faust, Executive Director. Information, (800) 424-7827. Web, www.sheriffs.org*

Membership: sheriffs and other municipal, state, and federal law enforcement officers. Conducts research and training programs for members in law enforcement, court procedures, and corrections. Publishes \ magazine.

Police Executive Research Forum, *1120 Connecticut Ave. N.W., #930 20036; (202) 466-7820. Fax, (202) 466-7826. Chuck Wexler, Executive Director.*
General e-mail, perf@policeforum.org
Web, www.policeforum.org

Membership: law enforcement executives from moderate to large police departments. Conducts research on law enforcement issues and methods of disseminating criminal justice and law enforcement information.

Police Foundation, *1201 Connecticut Ave. N.W., #200 20036; (202) 833-1460. Fax, (202) 659-9149. Hubert Williams, President.*
General e-mail, pfinfo@policefoundation.org
Web, www.policefoundation.org

Research and education foundation that conducts studies to improve police procedures; provides technical assistance for innovative law enforcement strategies, including community-oriented policing. Houses the National Center for the Study of Police and Civil Disorder.

⚖ LEGAL PROFESSIONS AND RESOURCES

NONPROFIT

American Bar Assn. (ABA), *International Law and Practice, 740 15th St. N.W., 10th Floor 20005; (202) 662-1660. Fax, (202) 662-1669. Leanne Pfautz, Director.*
Web, www.abanet.org/intlaw

Monitors and makes recommendations concerning developments in the practice of international law that affect ABA members and the public. Conducts programs, including International Legal Exchange, and produces publications covering the practice of international law.

American Blind Lawyers Assn., *1155 15th St. N.W., #1004 20005; (202) 467-5081. Fax, (202) 467-5085. Christopher Gray, President.*
General e-mail, info@acb.org
Web, www.acb.org

Membership: blind lawyers and law students. Provides members with legal information; acts as an information clearinghouse on legal materials available in Braille, in large print, on computer disc, and on tape. (Affiliated with American Council of the Blind.)

American Health Lawyers Assn., *1025 Connecticut Ave. N.W., #600 20036; (202) 833-1100. Fax, (202) 833-1105. Doug Hastings, President.*
General e-mail, info@healthlawyers.org
Web, www.healthlawyers.org

Membership: corporate, institutional, and government lawyers interested in the health field; law students; and health professionals. Serves as an information clearinghouse on health law; sponsors health law educational programs and seminars.

American Inns of Court Foundation, *127 S. Peyton St., #201, Alexandria, VA 22314; (703) 684-3590. Fax, (703) 684-3607. Don Stumbaugh, Executive Director.*
General e-mail, info@innsofcourt.org
Web, www.innsofcourt.org

Promotes professionalism, ethics, civility, and legal skills of judges, lawyers, academicians, and law students in order to improve the quality and efficiency of the justice system.

Assn. of American Law Schools, *1201 Connecticut Ave. N.W., #800 20036; (202) 296-8851. Fax, (202) 296-8869. Carl C. Monk, Executive Director.*

General e-mail, aals@aals.org

Web, www.aals.org

Membership: schools of law, subject to approval by the association. Represents member organizations before federal government and private agencies; evaluates member institutions; conducts workshops on the teaching of law; assists law schools with faculty recruitment; publishes faculty placement bulletin and annual directory of law teachers.

Friends of the Jessup, *1615 New Hampshire Ave. N.W. 20009; (202) 299-9101. Fax, (202) 299-9102. Michael Peil, Executive Director.*

General e-mail, ilsa@iamdigex.net

Web, www.foj.org

Membership: supporters and former participants of the Philip C. Jessup International Law Moot Court Competition. Raises funds for the competition, helps to organize and support teams from disadvantaged countries, and conducts educational programs for competition participants. (Affiliated with the International Law Students Assn.)

Hispanic National Bar Fund, *815 Connecticut Ave. N.W., #500 20006; (202) 223-4777. Carmen M. Feliciano, Executive Director.*

General e-mail, info@hnba.com

Web, www.hnba.com

Membership: Hispanic American attorneys, judges, professors, and law students. Seeks to increase professional opportunities in law for Hispanic Americans and to increase Hispanic American representation in law school. (Affiliated with National Hispanic Leadership Agenda and the American Bar Assn.)

International Law Institute, *1615 New Hampshire Ave. N.W., #100 20009-2520; (202) 483-3036. Fax, (202) 483-3029. Stuart Kerr, Executive Director.*

General e-mail, administrator@ili.org

Web, www.ili.org

Performs scholarly research, offers training programs, and provides technical assistance in the area of international law. Sponsors international conferences.

International Law Students Assn., *1615 New Hampshire Ave. N.W. 20009; (202) 299-9101. Fax, (202) 299-9102. Michael Peil, Executive Director.*

General e-mail, ilsa@ilsa.org

Web, www.ilsa.org

Promotes the study and understanding of international law and related issues. Encourages communication and cooperation among law students and lawyers internationally; works to expand opportunities for learning about legal systems worldwide.

National Consumer Law Center, *Washington Office, 1629 K St. N.W., #600 20006; (202) 986-6060. Fax, (202) 463-9462. Margot Saunders, Managing Attorney.*

General e-mail, consumerlaw@nclc.org

Web, www.consumerlaw.org

Provides lawyers funded by the Legal Services Corp. with research and assistance; provides lawyers with training in consumer and energy law. (Headquarters in Boston, Mass.)

National Court Reporters Assn., *8224 Old Courthouse Rd., Vienna, VA 22182-3808; (703) 556-6272. Fax, (703) 556-6291. Mark J. Golden, Executive Director. TTY, (703) 556-6289. Membership Service and Information, (800) 272-6272.*

Web, www.ncraonline.org

Membership organization that certifies and offers continuing education for court reporters. Acts as a clearinghouse on technology and information for and about court reporters; certifies legal video specialists.

Street Law, Inc., *1600 K St. N.W., #602 20006-2801; (202) 293-0088. Fax, (202) 293-0089. Edward L. O'Brien, Executive Director.*

General e-mail, clearinghouse@streetlaw.org

Web, www.streetlaw.org

Educational organization that promotes public understanding of the law and the legal system, particularly through citizen participation. Provides information, curriculum materials, training, and technical assistance to public and private school systems at elementary and secondary levels, law schools, departments of corrections, local juvenile justice systems, bar associations, community groups, and state and local governments interested in establishing law-related education programs, including mediation.

Data and Research

AGENCIES

Office of Justice Programs (OJP), *(Justice Dept.), Bureau of Justice Statistics, 810 7th St. N.W., #2400 20531; (202) 307-0765. Fax, (202) 307-5846. Lawrence A. Greenfeld, Director.*

Web, www.ojp.usdoj.gov/bjs

Collects, evaluates, publishes, and provides statistics on criminal justice. Data available from the National Criminal Justice Reference Service, P.O. Box 6000, Rockville, MD 20857; toll-free, (800) 732-3277; in Maryland, (301) 519-5500.

Office of Justice Programs (OJP), *(Justice Dept.),* *National Institute of Justice,* 810 7th St. N.W., 7th Floor 20531; (202) 307-2942. Fax, (202) 307-6394. Sarah V. Hart, Director.

Web, www.ojp.usdoj.gov/nij

Conducts research on all aspects of criminal justice, including crime prevention, enforcement, adjudication, and corrections; evaluates programs; develops model programs using new techniques. Serves as an affiliated institute of the United Nations Crime Prevention and Criminal Justice Programme (UNCPCJ); studies transnational issues. Maintains the National Criminal Justice Reference Service, which provides information on criminal justice, including activities of the Office of National Drug Control Policy and law enforcement in Latin America: (800) 851-3420 or (301) 251-5500; Web, www.ncjrs.org.

CONGRESS

Library of Congress, *Law Library,* 101 Independence Ave. S.E., #LM240 20540; (202) 707-5065. Fax, (202) 707-1820. Rubens Medina, Law Librarian. Reading room, (202) 707-5080.

Web, www.loc.gov

Maintains collections of foreign, international, and comparative law organized jurisdictionally by country; covers all legal systems—common, civil, Roman, canon, religious, and ancient and medieval law. Services include a public reading room; a microtext facility, with readers and printers for microfilm and microfiche; and foreign law/rare book reading areas. Staff of legal specialists is competent in approximately forty languages; does not provide advice on legal matters.

JUDICIARY

Administrative Office of the U.S. Courts, 1 Columbus Circle N.E., #7-400 20544; (202) 273-3000. Leonidas Ralph Mecham, Director. Information, (202) 502-2600.

Web, www.uscourts.gov

Supervises all administrative matters of the federal court system, except the Supreme Court; prepares statis-tical data and reports on the business of the courts, including reports on juror utilization, caseloads of federal, public, and community defenders, and types of cases adjudicated.

Administrative Office of the U.S. Courts, *Statistics,* 1 Columbus Circle N.E., #2-250 20544; (202) 502-1440. Fax, (202) 502-1411. Steven R. Schlesinger, Chief. Press, (202) 502-2600.

Web, www.uscourts.gov

Compiles information and statistics from civil, criminal, appeals, and bankruptcy cases. Publishes statistical reports on court management; juror utilization; federal offenders; equal access to justice; the Financial Privacy Act; caseloads of federal, public, and community defenders; and types of cases adjudicated.

Supreme Court of the United States, *Library,* 1 1st St. N.E. 20543; (202) 479-3037. Fax, (202) 479-3477. Shelley L. Dowling, Librarian.

Web, www.supremecourtus.gov

Maintains collection of Supreme Court documents dating from the mid-1800s. Records, briefs, and depository documents available for public use.

NONPROFIT

Justice Research and Statistics Assn., 777 N. Capitol St. N.E., #801 20002; (202) 842-9330. Fax, (202) 842-9329. Joan C. Weiss, Executive Director.

General e-mail, cjinfo@jrsa.org

Web, www.jrsa.org

Provides information on the collection, analysis, dissemination, and use of data concerning crime and criminal justice at the state level; serves as liaison between the Justice Dept. Bureau of Justice Statistics and the states; develops standards for states on the collection, analysis, and use of statistics. Offers courses in criminal justice software and in research and evaluation methodologies in conjunction with its annual conference.

15

Military Personnel and Veterans

GENERAL POLICY

AGENCIES

Air Force Dept. *(Defense Dept.), Force Management and Personnel,* 1660 Air Force Pentagon, #5E977 20330-1660; (703) 614-4751. Fax, (703) 693-4244. Kelly Craven, Deputy Assistant Secretary.
Web, www.af.mil

Civilian office that coordinates military and civilian personnel policies of the Air Force Dept. Focus includes pay; health care; education and training; commissaries, PXs, and service clubs; recruitment; retirement; and veterans affairs.

Air Force Dept. *(Defense Dept.), Personnel,* 1040 Air Force Pentagon, #4E194 20330-1040; (703) 697-6088. Fax, (703) 697-6091. Lt. Gen. Richard E. Brown III, Deputy Chief of Staff. Toll-free casualty assistance, (800) 433-0048.
Web, www.af.mil

Military office that coordinates military and civilian personnel policies of the Air Force Dept.

Army Dept. *(Defense Dept.), G-1,* 300 Army Pentagon, #2E460 20310-0300; (703) 697-8060. Fax, (703) 692-9000. Lt. Gen. John La Moyne, Deputy Chief of Staff, G-1.
Web, www.army.mil

Military office that coordinates military and civilian personnel policies of the Army Dept.

Army Dept. *(Defense Dept.), Human Resources Directorate,* 300 Army Pentagon 20310-0300; (703) 693-1850. Fax, (703) 695-6964. Brig. Gen. Steven Schook, Director.
Web, www.army.mil

Military office that coordinates military personnel policies of the Army. Focus includes pay; health care; equal opportunity; drug and alcohol abuse; recruitment; retirement; and commissaries, PXs, and service clubs.

Army Dept. *(Defense Dept.), Manpower and Reserve Affairs,* 111 Army Pentagon, #2E468 20310-0111; (703) 697-9253. Fax, (703) 692-9000. Reginald J. Brown, Assistant Secretary.
Web, www.asamra.army.pentagon.mil

Civilian office that reviews policies and programs for Army personnel and reserves; makes recommendations to the secretary of the Army.

Defense Dept. (DoD), *Military Personnel Policy,* 4000 Defense Pentagon, #3E767 20301-4000; (703) 697-4166. Fax, (703) 614-7046. Bill Carr, Deputy Assistant Secretary (Acting).

Web, www.defenselink.mil

Military office that coordinates military personnel policies of the Defense Dept. and reviews military personnel policies of the individual services.

Defense Dept. (DoD), *Personnel and Readiness,* 4000 Defense Pentagon, #3E764 20301-4000; (703) 695-5254. Fax, (703) 693-0171. David S. C. Chu, Under Secretary (Acting).
Web, www.defenselink.mil

Coordinates civilian and military personnel policies of the Defense Dept. and reviews personnel policies of the individual services. Handles equal opportunity policies; serves as focal point for all readiness issues.

Defense Dept. (DoD), *Public Inquiry and Analysis,* 1400 Defense Pentagon, #3A750 20301-1400; (703) 428-0711. Fax, (703) 428-1982. Harold Heilsnis, Director.
Web, www.defenselink.mil

Responds to public inquiries on Defense Dept. personnel.

Navy Dept. *(Defense Dept.), Manpower and Reserve Affairs,* 1000 Navy Pentagon, #4E789 20350-1000; (703) 697-2180. Fax, (703) 614-4103. William A. Navas Jr., Assistant Secretary.
Web, www.navy.mil

Civilian office that coordinates military personnel policies of the Navy and the Marine Corps. Focus includes pay, health care, education and training, family services, recruitment, retirement, and veterans affairs.

Navy Dept. *(Defense Dept.), Military Personnel Plans and Policy Division N13,* 2 Navy Annex, #3070 20370; (703) 614-5571. Fax, (703) 614-5595. Rear Adm. Joseph G. Henry, Director.
Web, www.navy.mil

Military office that coordinates naval personnel policies, including promotions, professional development, and compensation, for officers and enlisted personnel.

Navy Dept. *(Defense Dept.), Naval Personnel,* 2 Navy Annex 20370; (703) 614-1101. Fax, (703) 693-1746. Vice Adm. Norbert R. Ryan Jr., Chief.
Web, www.navy.mil

Military office that coordinates Navy Dept.'s military personnel policies of the Navy Dept.

Selective Service System, 1515 Wilson Blvd., Arlington, VA 22209-2425; (703) 605-4010. Fax, (703) 605-4006. Lewis Brodsky, Deputy Director. Locator, (703) 605-4000.
Web, www.sss.gov

Supplies the armed forces with manpower when authorized; registers male citizens of the United States ages eighteen to twenty-five. In an emergency, would institute a draft and would provide alternative service assignments to men classified as conscientious objectors.

U.S. Coast Guard (USCG), *(Homeland Security Dept.), Human Resources, 2100 2nd St. S.W., #5410 20593-0001; (202) 267-0905. Fax, (202) 267-4205. Rear Adm. Kenneth T. Venuto, Assistant Commissioner.*
Web, www.uscg.mil/hq/g-w/hrhome.htm

Responsible for hiring, recruiting, and training all military and nonmilitary Coast Guard personnel.

CONGRESS

House Armed Services Committee, *Subcommittee on Total Force, 2340 RHOB 20515; (202) 225-7560. Fax, (202) 226-0789. Rep. John M. McHugh, R-N.Y., Chair; John Chapla, Staff Director.*
Web, www.house.gov/hasc

Responsible for military personnel policy, reserve component integration, employment issues, military health care, military education, and POW/MIA matters. Responsible for morale, welfare, and recreation issues and programs.

Senate Armed Services Committee, *Subcommittee on Personnel, SR-228 20510; (202) 224-3871. Fax, (202) 228-0036. Sen. Saxby Chambliss, R-Ga., Chair; Dick Walsh, Staff Director.*
Web, www.senate.gov/~armed_services

Jurisdiction over legislation on military personnel, including drug and alcohol abuse, equal opportunity, banking and insurance, family services, medical care and benefits, Americans missing in action (MIAs), education of overseas dependents, pay and compensation, recruitment, military reserve strength, and retirement benefits. Jurisdiction over legislation on civilian personnel of the armed forces.

NONPROFIT

Air Force Assn., *1501 Lee Hwy., Arlington, VA 22209-1198; (703) 247-5800. Fax, (703) 247-5853. Donald L. Peterson, Executive Director. Information, (800) 727-3337. Library, (703) 247-5829. Press, (703) 247-5850.*
General e-mail, custserv@afa.org
Web, www.afa.org

Membership: civilians and active, reserve, retired, and cadet personnel of the Air Force. Informs members and the public of developments in the aerospace field. Monitors legislation and Defense Dept. policies. Library on aviation history open to the public by appointment.

Air Force Sergeants Assn., *5211 Auth Rd., Suitland, MD 20746; (301) 899-3500. Fax, (301) 899-8136. James D. Staton, Executive Director.*
Web, www.afsahq.org

Membership: active duty, reserve, National Guard, and retired enlisted Air Force personnel. Monitors defense policies and legislation on issues such as the proposed phasing out of federal subsidies for medical and retirement benefits and commissaries.

Assn. of the United States Army, *2425 Wilson Blvd., Arlington, VA 22201; (703) 841-4300. Fax, (703) 525-9039. Gordon R. Sullivan, President. Information, (800) 336-4570.*
Web, www.ausa.org

Membership: civilians and active and retired members of the armed forces. Conducts symposia on defense issues and researches topics that affect the military.

Center on Conscience & War, *1830 Connecticut Ave. N.W. 20009; (202) 483-2220. Fax, (202) 483-1246. J. E. McNeil, Executive Director.*
General e-mail, nisbco@nisbco.org
Web, www.nisbco.org

Seeks to defend and extend the rights of conscientious objectors. Provides information and advocacy about the military draft and national selective service. Offers counseling and information to military personnel seeking discharge or transfer to noncombatant positions within the military.

Fleet Reserve Assn., *125 N. West St., Alexandria, VA 22314-2754; (703) 683-1400. Fax, (703) 549-6610. Joseph L. Barnes, National Executive Secretary. Information, (800) 372-1924.*
General e-mail, news-fra@fra.org
Web, www.fra.org

Membership: active duty, reserve, and retired Navy, Marine Corps, and Coast Guard personnel. Works to safeguard the compensation, benefits, and entitlements of Sea Services personnel. Recognized by the Veterans Affairs Dept. to assist veterans and widows of veterans with benefit claims.

Marine Corps League, *8626 Lee Hwy., #201, Fairfax, VA 22031 (mailing address: P.O. Box 3070, Merrifield, VA 22116); (703) 207-9588. Fax, (703) 207-0047. William "Brooks" Corley Jr., Executive Director. Information, (800) 625-1775.*
General e-mail, mcl@mcleague.org
Web, www.mcleague.org

Membership: active duty, retired, and reserve Marine Corps groups. Promotes the interests of the Marine

Corps and works to preserve its traditions; assists veterans and their survivors. Monitors legislation and regulations.

Military Order of the World Wars, *435 N. Lee St., Alexandria, VA 22314; (703) 683-4911. Fax, (703) 683-4501. Roger C. Bultman, Chief of Staff.*
General e-mail, mowwhq@aol.com
Web, www.militaryorder.org

Membership: retired and active duty commissioned officers, warrant officers, and flight officers. Supports a strong national defense; supports patriotic education in schools; presents awards to outstanding Reserve Officers Training Corps (ROTC) cadets.

National Assn. for Uniformed Services, *5535 Hempstead Way, Springfield, VA 22151-4094; (703) 750-1342. Fax, (703) 354-4380. Richard D. Murray, President. Information, (800) 842-3451.*
Web, www.naus.org

Membership: active, reserve, and retired officers and enlisted personnel of all uniformed services and their families and survivors. Supports legislation that benefits military personnel and veterans. (Affiliated with the Society of Military Widows.)

Navy League of the United States, *2300 Clarendon Blvd., #705, Arlington, VA 22201 (mailing address: 2300 Wilson Blvd., Arlington, VA 22201); (703) 528-1775. Fax, (703) 528-2333. Charles L. Robinson, National Executive Director.*
General e-mail, mail@navyleague.org
Web, www.navyleague.org

Membership: retired and reserve military personnel and civilians interested in the U.S. Navy, Marine Corps, Coast Guard, and Merchant Marine. Distributes literature, provides speakers, and conducts seminars to promote interests of the sea services. Monitors legislation.

Noncommissioned Officers Assn., *Washington Office, 610 Madison St., Alexandria, VA 22314; (703) 549-0311. Fax, (703) 549-0245. David W. Sommers, President.*
Web, www.ncoausa.org

Congressionally chartered fraternal organization of active and retired enlisted military personnel. Sponsors job fairs to assist members in finding employment. (Headquarters in San Antonio, Texas.)

United Service Organizations (USO), *1008 Eberle Pl. S.E., #301, Washington Navy Yard, DC 20374-5096; (202) 610-5700. Fax, (202) 610-5701. Edward A. Powell, President.*
Web, www.uso.org

Voluntary civilian organization chartered by Congress. Provides military personnel and their families in the United States and overseas with social, educational, and recreational programs.

U.S. Army Warrant Officers Assn., *462 Herndon Pkwy., #207, Herndon, VA 20170-5235; (703) 742-7727. Fax, (703) 742-7728. Raymond A. Bell, Executive Director.*
General e-mail, usawoa@erols.com
Web, www.penfed.org/usawoa

Membership: active duty, guard, reserve, and retired and former warrant officers. Monitors and makes recommendations to Defense Dept., Army Dept., and Congress on policies and programs affecting Army warrant officers and their families.

DEFENSE PERSONNEL

Chaplains

AGENCIES

Air Force Dept. *(Defense Dept.), Chief of the Chaplain Service, Bolling Air Force Base, 112 Luke Ave. 20332-9050; (202) 767-4577. Fax, (202) 404-7841. Maj. Gen. Lorraine Potter, Chief.*
Web, www.usafhc.af.mil

Oversees chaplains and religious services with the Air Force; maintains liaison with religious denominations.

Armed Forces Chaplain Board *(Defense Dept.), 4000 Defense Pentagon, #2E341 20301-4000; (703) 697-9015. Fax, (703) 663-2280. Maj. Gen. Lorraine Potter (USAF), Executive Director; Maj. Gen. Gaylord T. Gunhus, Chair.*

Membership: chiefs and deputy chiefs of chaplains of the armed services; works to coordinate religious policies and services among the military branches.

Army Dept. *(Defense Dept.), Chief of Chaplains, 2700 Army Pentagon, #1E721 20310-2700; (703) 695-1133. Fax, (703) 695-9834. Maj. Gen. Gaylord T. Gunhus, Chief.*
Web, www.chapnet.army.mil

Oversees chaplains and religious services within the Army; maintains liaison with religious denominations.

Marine Corps *(Defense Dept.), Chaplain, 2 Navy Annex, #3024 20380-1775; (703) 614-5630. Fax, (703) 614-4491. Rear Adm. Louis V. Iasiello, Chaplain.*
Web, www2.hqmc.usmc.mil/chaplain/chaplain.nsf/chaplainmain

Oversees chaplains and religious services within the Marine Corps; maintains liaison with religious denominations.

National Guard Bureau *(Defense Dept.), Air National Guard: Chaplain Service,* 1411 Jefferson Davis Hwy., Arlington, VA 22202-3231; (703) 607-5278. Fax, (703) 607-5295. Col. John B. Ellington Jr., Chief.
Web, www.ang.af.mil

Oversees chaplains and religious services within the Air National Guard; maintains liaison with religious denominations.

National Guard Bureau *(Defense Dept.), Army National Guard: Chaplain Service,* 1411 Jefferson Davis Hwy., #9500, Arlington, VA 22202-3231; (703) 607-7072. Fax, (703) 607-5295. Col. Donald W. Hill, Chief.

Oversees chaplains and religious services with the Army National Guard; maintains liaison with religious denominations; serves as policy leader for chaplains.

Navy Dept. *(Defense Dept.), Chief of Chaplains,* N097, 2 Navy Annex, #1056 20370-0400; (703) 614-4043. Fax, (703) 693-2907. Rear Adm. Barry C. Black, Chief.
Web, www.chaplain.navy.mil

Oversees chaplains and religious services within the Navy; maintains liaison with religious denominations.

NONPROFIT

Military Chaplains Assn. of the United States of America, P.O. Box 7056, Arlington, VA 22207; (703) 276-2189. David E. White, Executive Director.
General e-mail, chaplains@mca-usa.org
Web, www.mca-usa.org

Membership: chaplains of all faiths in all branches of the armed services and chaplains of veterans affairs and civil air patrol. Sponsors workshops and conventions; coordinates a speakers' bureau.

National Conference on Ministry to the Armed Forces, 4141 N. Henderson Rd., Arlington, VA 22203; (703) 276-7905. Fax, (703) 276-7906. Jack Williamson, Executive Director.
Web, www.ncmaf.org

Offers support to the Armed Forces Chaplains Board and the chief of chaplains of each service; disseminates information on matters affecting service personnel welfare.

Civilian Employees

AGENCIES

Air Force Dept. *(Defense Dept.), Civilian Policy,* 1040 Air Force Pentagon 20330-1040; (703) 695-7381. Fax, (703) 692-9939. Sarah Bonilla, Chief.
Web, www.af.mil

Civilian office that monitors and reviews Air Force equal employment opportunity programs and policies, benefits and entitlements, civilian pay, career programs, and external and internal placement of staff.

Air Force Dept. *(Defense Dept.), Personnel Policy,* 1040 Air Force Pentagon, #4E228 20330-1040; (703) 695-6770. Fax, (703) 614-8523. Maj. Gen. John M. Speigel, Director.
Web, www.af.mil

Implements and evaluates Air Force civilian personnel policies; serves as the principal adviser to the Air Force personnel director on civilian personnel matters and programs.

Army Dept. *(Defense Dept.), Civilian Personnel Policy,* 300 Army Pentagon, #2C453 20310-0300; (703) 695-5701. Fax, (703) 695-6997. David L. Snyder, Assistant G-1.
Web, www.army.mil

Develops and reviews Army civilian personnel policies and advises the Army leadership on civilian personnel matters.

Army Dept. *(Defense Dept.), Equal Employment Opportunity Agency,* Crystal Mall 4, #207, 1941 Jefferson Davis Hwy., Arlington, VA 22202-4508; (703) 607-1976. Fax, (703) 607-2042. Luther L. Santiful, Director. Main phone is voice and TTY accessible.
General e-mail, luther.santiful@hqda.army.mil
Web, eeoa.army.pentagon.mil

Civilian office that administers equal employment opportunity programs and policies for civilian employees of the Army.

Defense Dept. (DoD), *Civilian Assistance and Re-Employment (CARE),* 1400 Key Blvd., #B-200, Arlington, VA 22209-5144; (703) 696-1799. Fax, (703) 696-5416. G. Jorge Araiza, Chief.
Web, www.cpms.osd.mil/care/index.html

Manages transition programs for Defense Dept. civilians, including placement, early retirement, and transition assistance programs.

Marine Corps *(Defense Dept.), Human Resources and Organizational Management,* 1213, Code ARH, Arlington, VA 20380; (703) 614-1300. Fax, (703) 697-7682. William T. Catsonis, Personnel Officer; Vacant, Deputy Equal Employment Opportunities Officer.
Web, www.chro.usmc.mil

Develops and implements personnel and equal employment opportunity programs for civilian employees of the Marine Corps.

Navy Dept. *(Defense Dept.), Civilian Human Resources,* 1000 Navy Pentagon, #4E789 20350-1000;

(703) 695-2633. Fax, (703) 614-4103. Vacant, Deputy Assistant Secretary.

Web, www.donhr.navy.mil

Civilian office that develops and reviews Navy and Marine Corps civilian personnel and equal opportunity programs and policies.

U.S. Coast Guard (USCG), *(Homeland Security Dept.), Civil Rights: Military Equal Opportunity,* 2100 2nd St. S.W., #2400 20593-0001; (202) 267-0042. Fax, (202) 267-4282. Cruz Sedillo, Director.

Administers the Affirmative Employment Program relating to civilian Coast Guard positions; processes complaints.

Equal Opportunity

AGENCIES

Air Force Dept. *(Defense Dept.), Military Equal Opportunity,* 1040 Air Force Pentagon, #5C238 20330-1040; (703) 614-8488. Fax, (703) 695-4083. Maj. Jay Doherty, Chief.

Web, www.af.mil

Military office that develops and administers Air Force equal opportunity programs and policies.

Army Dept. *(Defense Dept.), Equal Employment Opportunity Agency,* Crystal Mall 4, #207, 1941 Jefferson Davis Hwy., Arlington, VA 22202-4508; (703) 607-1976. Fax, (703) 607-2042. Luther L. Santiful, Director. Main phone is voice and TTY accessible.

General e-mail, luther.santiful@hqda.army.mil

Web, eeoa.army.pentagon.mil

Develops policy and conducts program review for the Dept. of Army Civilian Equal Employment Opportunity and Affirmative Employment Programs.

Defense Dept. (DoD), *Defense Advisory Committee on Women in the Services,* 4000 Defense Pentagon, #3D769 20301-4000; (703) 697-2122. Fax, (703) 614-6233. Col. Denise Dailey (U.S. Army), Military Director.

General e-mail, dacowits@osd.mil

Web, www.dtic.mil/dacowits

Advises the secretary of defense on matters relating to women in the military, including recruitment, retention, treatment, employment, and integration.

Defense Dept. (DoD), *Equal Opportunity,* 4000 Defense Pentagon, #3A272 20301-4000; (703) 697-6381. Fax, (703) 697-7534. Vacant, Director.

Web, www.dod.gov

Formulates equal employment opportunity policy for the Defense Dept. Evaluates civil rights complaints from

military personnel including issues of sexual harassment and recruitment.

Marine Corps *(Defense Dept.), Manpower Equal Opportunity,* HQMC, MNRA (MPE), 3280 Russell Rd., Quantico, VA 22134-5103; (703) 784-9371. Fax, (703) 784-9814. Col. L. D. Gonzales, Head.

Web, www.usmc.mil

Military office that develops, monitors, and administers Marine Corps equal opportunity programs.

Navy Dept. *(Defense Dept.), Minority Affairs,* Navy Annex 20370; (703) 695-2897. Fax, (703) 695-9922. Cmdr. Sid Abernethy, Special Assistant.

Web, www.navy.mil

Military office that develops and administers Navy minority programs and policies.

U.S. Coast Guard (USCG), *(Homeland Security Dept.), Civil Rights: Military Equal Opportunity,* 2100 2nd St. S.W., #2400 20593-0001; (202) 267-0042. Fax, (202) 267-4282. Cruz Sedillo, Director.

Administers equal opportunity regulations for Coast Guard military personnel.

NONPROFIT

Human Rights Campaign (HRC), 919 18th St. N.W., #800 20006; (202) 628-4160. Fax, (202) 347-5323. Elizabeth Birch, Executive Director.

General e-mail, hrc@hrc.org

Web, www.hrc.org

Promotes legislation affirming the rights of lesbians and gays. Focus includes discrimination in the military.

Minerva Center, 20 Granada Rd., Pasadena, MD 21122-2708; (410) 437-5379. Linda Grant De Pauw, Director.

Web, www.minervacenter.com

Encourages the study of women in the military. Focus includes current U.S. servicewomen; women veterans; women, war, and military abroad; and the preservation of artifacts, oral history, and first-hand accounts of women's experience in military service.

Servicemembers Legal Defense Network (SLDN), P.O. Box 65301 20035-5301; (202) 328-3244. Fax, (202) 797-1635. C. Dixon Osburn, Executive Director.

General e-mail, sldn@sldn.org

Web, www.sldn.org

Provides legal assistance to individuals affected by the military's policy on gays and lesbians. Monitors legislation and regulations.

Family Services

AGENCIES

Air Force Dept. *(Defense Dept.), Family Matters,* 1040 Air Force Pentagon, #5C238, Headquarters AF/DPPFF 20330-1040; (703) 697-4720. Fax, (703) 695-4083. Linda Smith, Chief.
Web, www.af.mil

Military policy office that monitors and reviews services provided to Air Force families and civilian employees with family concerns; oversees family support centers.

Air Force Dept. *(Defense Dept.), Personnel,* 1040 Air Force Pentagon, #4E194 20330-1040; (703) 697-6088. Fax, (703) 697-6091. Lt. Gen. Richard E. Brown III, Deputy Chief of Staff. Toll-free casualty assistance, (800) 433-0048.
Web, www.af.mil

Military office that responds to inquiries concerning deceased Air Force personnel and their beneficiaries; refers inquiries to the Military Personnel Center at Randolph Air Force Base in San Antonio, Texas.

Army Dept. *(Defense Dept.), Casualty Operations,* 2461 Eisenhower Ave., #920, Alexandria, VA 22332-0481; (703) 325-7990. Fax, (703) 325-0134. Lt. Col. Tracy Nicholson, Chief.
Web, www.army.mil

Verifies beneficiaries of deceased Army personnel for benefits distribution.

Army Dept. *(Defense Dept.), Community and Family Support Center,* 4700 King St., Alexandria, VA 22302-4401; (703) 681-7469. Fax, (703) 681-7446. Brig. Gen. Robert L. Decker, Commanding General.
Web, www.armymwr.com

Military office that directs operations of Army recreation, community service, child development, and youth activity centers. Handles dependent education in conjunction with the Defense Dept.

Defense Dept. (DoD), *Education Activity,* 4040 N. Fairfax Dr., Arlington, VA 22203-1635; (703) 696-4247. Fax, (703) 696-8918. Joseph Tafoya, Director.
Web, www.odedodea.edu

Civilian office that maintains school system for dependents of all military personnel and eligible civilians in the U.S. and abroad; advises the secretary of defense on overseas education matters; supervises selection of teachers in schools for military dependents.

Defense Dept. (DoD), *Quality of Life,* 4000 Defense Pentagon, #3B916 20301-4000; (703) 697-7191. Fax, (703) 695-1977. Jane C. Burke, Director.

Web, www.defenselink.mil

Coordinates policies of the individual services relating to the families of military personnel.

Marine Corps *(Defense Dept.), Casualty Section,* HQUSMC, 3280 Russell Rd., Quantico, VA 22134-5103; (703) 784-9580. Fax, (703) 784-9823. Ann Hammers, Head.
Web, www.usmc.mil

Confirms beneficiaries of deceased Marine Corps personnel for benefits distribution.

Marine Corps *(Defense Dept.), Personnel and Family Readiness Division,* HQUSMC, M and RA, 3280 Russell Rd., Quantico, VA 22134-5103; (703) 784-9501. Fax, (703) 784-9816. Michael Downs, Director.
Web, www.usmc-mccs.org

Sponsors family service centers located on major Marine Corps installations. Oversees the administration of policies affecting the quality of life of Marine Corps military families. Administers relocation assistance programs.

Navy Dept. *(Defense Dept.), Personal Readiness and Community Support: Personnel 6/N15 Washington Liaison,* Navy Annex, #1612 20370-5000; (703) 614-4259. Fax, (703) 614-4199. Bruce Sherman, Liaison.
Web, www.persnet.navy.mil/pers6det

Oversees Navy family service centers; provides naval personnel and families being sent overseas with information and support; addresses problems of abuse and sexual assault within families; helps Navy spouses find employment; facilitates communication between Navy families and Navy officials. Assists in relocating Navy families during transition from military to civilian life.

Navy Dept. *(Defense Dept.), Personnel Readiness and Community Support,* 1000 Navy Pentagon, #5D800 20350-1000; (703) 693-0484. Fax, (703) 693-4957. Buster Tate, Director.
Web, www.navy.mil

Civilian office that oversees the administration of all policies affecting the quality of life of families of Navy military personnel.

U.S. Coast Guard (USCG), *(Homeland Security Dept.), Individual and Family Support,* 2100 2nd St. S.W., #6320 20593-0001; (202) 267-6263. Fax, (202) 267-4798. Capt. Ruth I. Torres, Chief.

Offers broad array of human services to individuals in the Coast Guard and their families, including child care, elderly care, educational services, domestic violence counseling, health care, and special needs.

CONGRESS

House Armed Services Committee, *Subcommittee on Total Force,* 2340 RHOB 20515; (202) 225-7560. Fax, (202) 226-0789. Rep. John M. McHugh, R-N.Y., Chair; John Chapla, Staff Director.
Web, www.house.gov/hasc

Jurisdiction over legislation on education of overseas military dependents. (Jurisdiction shared with House Education and the Workforce Committee.)

House Education and the Workforce Committee, *Subcommittee on Select Education,* H2-230 FHOB 20515; (202) 225-6558. Fax, (202) 225-9571. Rep. Peter Hoekstra, R-Mich., Chair; Paula Nowakowski, Staff Director.
Web, edworkforce.house.gov

Jurisdiction over legislation concerning overseas and domestic military dependents' education programs. (Jurisdiction shared with House Armed Services Committee.)

Senate Armed Services Committee, *Subcommittee on Personnel,* SR-228 20510; (202) 224-3871. Fax, (202) 228-0036. Sen. Saxby Chambliss, R-Ga., Chair; Dick Walsh, Staff Director.
Web, www.senate.gov/~armed_services

Jurisdiction over legislation concerning military dependents' education programs.

NONPROFIT

Air Force Aid Society Inc., *1745 Jefferson Davis Hwy., #202, Arlington, VA 22202-3410; (703) 607-3072. Fax, (703) 607-3022. Gen. Michael D. McGinty, Director.*
Web, www.afas.org

Membership: Air Force active duty, reserve, and retired military personnel and their dependents. Provides active duty and retired Air Force military personnel with personal emergency loans for basic needs, travel, or dependents' health expenses; assists families of active, deceased, or retired Air Force personnel with postsecondary education loans and grants.

American Red Cross, *Armed Forces Emergency Services,* 2025 E St. N.W. 20006; (703) 206-7481. Sue A. Richter, Vice President.
Web, www.redcross.org/services/afes

Provides emergency services for active duty armed forces personnel and their families, including reporting and communications, financial assistance, information and referral, and counseling. (Moving from Virginia to the Washington address above in summer 2003.)

American Red Cross, *Emergency Communications,* 2025 E St. N.W. 20006; (703) 206-7430. Rick Davis, Director.
Web, www.redcross.org/services/afes/comm.html

Mandated by Congress. Contacts military personnel in family emergencies; provides military personnel with verification of family situations for emergency leave applications. (Moving from Virginia to the Washington address above in summer 2003.)

Armed Forces Hostess Assn., *The Pentagon, #1D110, #3A145 20310-6604; (703) 697-3180. Fax, (703) 693-9510. Gayl Taylor, President.*

Volunteer office staffed by wives of military personnel of all services. Serves as an information clearinghouse for military and civilian Defense Dept. families; maintains information on military bases in the United States and abroad; issues information handbook for families in the Washington area.

Army Distaff Foundation, *6200 Oregon Ave. N.W. 20015-1543; (202) 541-0105. Fax, (202) 364-2856. Maj. Gen. Donald C. Hilbert, Executive Director. Information, (800) 541-4255.*
Web, www.armydistaff.org

Nonprofit continuing care retirement community for career military officers and their families. Provides retirement housing and health care services.

EX-POSE, Ex-partners of Servicemembers for Equality, *P.O. Box 11191, Alexandria, VA 22312; (703) 941-5844. Fax, (703) 212-6951. Vacant, Director.*
General e-mail, ex-pose@juno.com

Membership: former partners of military members, both officers and enlisted, and other interested parties. Seeks federal laws to restore to ex-spouses benefits lost through divorce, including retirement pay; survivors' benefits; and medical, commissary, and exchange benefits. Provides information concerning legal resources and related federal laws and regulations. Serves as an information clearinghouse.

Federal Education Assn., *1101 15th St. N.W., #1002 20005; (202) 822-7850. Fax, (202) 822-7816. Sheridan Pearce, President.*
General e-mail, fea@feaonline.org
Web, www.feaonline.org

Membership: teachers and personnel of Defense Dept. schools for military dependents in the United States and abroad. Helps members negotiate pay, benefits, and better working conditions. Monitors legislation and regulations.

National Military Family Assn., *2500 N. Van Dorn St., #102, Alexandria, VA 22302-1601; (703) 931-6632. Fax, (703) 931-4600. Barbara Lee Williams, President.*
General e-mail, families@nmfa.org
Web, www.nmfa.org

Membership: active duty and retired military, National Guard, and reserve personnel of all U.S. uniformed services, civilian personnel, families, and other interested individuals. Works to improve the quality of life for military families.

Naval Services FamilyLine, *1254 9th St. S.E., #104, Washington Navy Yard, DC 20374-5067; (202) 433-2333. Fax, (202) 433-4622. David F. Tuma, Chair.*
General e-mail, nsfamline@aol.com
Web, www.lifelines2000.org

Offers support services to spouses of Navy, Marine Corps, and Coast Guard personnel; disseminates information on all aspects of military life; fosters sense of community among naval personnel and their families.

Navy–Marine Corps Relief Society, *801 N. Randolph St., #1228, Arlington, VA 22203-1978; (703) 696-4904. Fax, (703) 696-0144. Jerome L. Johnson, President.*
Web, www.nmcrs.org

Assists active and retired Navy and Marine Corps personnel and their families in times of need. Disburses interest-free loans and grants. Provides educational scholarships and loans, visiting nurse services, thrift shops, food lockers, budget counseling, and volunteer training.

Financial Services

AGENCIES

Air Force Dept. *(Defense Dept.),* **Financial Management and Comptroller,** *1130 Air Force Pentagon, #4E984 20330-1130; (703) 697-1974. Fax, (703) 693-1996. Michael Montelongo, Assistant Secretary.*
Web, www.saffm.hq.af.mil

Advises the secretary of the Air Force on policies relating to financial services for military and civilian personnel.

Defense Dept. (DoD), *Accounting and Finance Policy Analysis, 1100 Defense Pentagon, #3A882 20301-1100; (703) 697-3200. Fax, (703) 697-4608. Terri McKay, Director.*
Web, www.defenselink.mil

Develops accounting policy for the Defense Dept. federal management regulation.

CONGRESS

House Financial Services Committee, *Subcommittee on Financial Institutions and Consumer Credit, 2129 RHOB 20515; (202) 225-7502. Rep. Spencer Bachus, R-Ala., Chair; Bob Foster, Staff Director.*
Web, financialservices.house.gov

Jurisdiction over legislation regulating banking and credit unions on military bases. (Jurisdiction shared with Subcommittee on Oversight and Investigations.)

House Financial Services Committee, *Subcommittee on Oversight and Investigations, H2-137 FHOB 20515; (202) 225-7502. Rep. Sue W. Kelly, R-N.Y., Chair; Bob Foster, Staff Director.*
Web, financialservices.house.gov

Oversight of banking and credit unions on military bases. (Jurisdiction shared with Subcommittee on Financial Institutions and Consumer Credit.)

Senate Banking, Housing, and Urban Affairs Committee, *SD-534 20510; (202) 224-7391. Fax, (202) 224-5137. Sen. Richard C. Shelby, R-Ala., Chair; Kathy Casey, Staff Director.*
Web, banking.senate.gov

Oversees and has jurisdiction over legislation regulating banking and credit unions on military bases.

NONPROFIT

Armed Forces Benefit Assn., *909 N. Washington St., Alexandria, VA 22314; (703) 549-4455. Fax, (703) 548-6497. C. C. Blanton, President.*
General e-mail, info@afba.com
Web, www.afba.com

Membership: active and retired personnel of the uniformed services, federal civilian employees, government contractors, first responders, and dependents. Offers low-cost health and life insurance and financial, banking, and investment services worldwide.

Army and Air Force Mutual Aid Assn., *102 Sheridan Ave., Fort Myer, VA 22211-1110; (703) 522-3060. Fax, (703) 522-1336. Maj. Walt Lincoln, President. Information, (800) 336-4538.*
General e-mail, info@aafmaa.com
Web, www.aafmaa.com

Private service organization that offers member and family insurance services to active duty and reserve Army and Air Force officers, warrant officers, noncommissioned officers, and retired officers under age sixty-six.

Defense Credit Union Council, *601 Pennsylvania Ave. N.W., South Bldg., #600 20004-2601; (202) 638-3950. Fax, (202) 638-3410. Roland Arteaga, President.*
General e-mail, dcuc1@cuna.com
Web, www.dcuc.org

Trade association of credit unions serving the Defense Dept.'s military and civilian personnel. Works with the National Credit Union Administration to solve problems concerning the operation of credit unions for the military community; maintains liaison with the Defense Dept.

Health Care

AGENCIES

Air Force Dept. *(Defense Dept.), Health Benefits Policy,* 110 Luke Ave., Bldg. 5681, #400, Bolling Air Force Base 20332-7050; (202) 767-4699. Fax, (202) 767-1455. Charles Wolak, Chief.
Web, www.af.mil

Military office that develops and administers health benefits and policies for Air Force military personnel. Oversees modernization of Air Force medical facilities.

Air Force Dept. *(Defense Dept.), Surgeon General,* 110 Luke Ave., Bldg. 5681, #400, Bolling Air Force Base 20332-7050; (202) 767-4444. Fax, (202) 767-1456. Lt. Gen. (Dr.) George Peach Taylor, Surgeon General.
Web, www.airforcemedicine.afms.mil

Directs the provision of medical and dental services for Air Force personnel and their dependents.

Army Dept. *(Defense Dept.), Individual Readiness Policy,* The Pentagon, #2B659 20310-0300; (703) 614-7959. Lt. Col. Margaret Flott, Chief.
Web, www.army.mil

Military office that develops Army policies on HIV-positive Army personnel, suicide prevention, and general health promotion. Develops policies for combating alcohol and drug abuse; monitors and evaluates programs of the major Army commands.

Army Dept. *(Defense Dept.), Surgeon General,* 5109 Leesburg Pike, #672, Falls Church, VA 22041-3258; (703) 681-3000. Fax, (703) 681-3167. Lt. Gen. James B. Peake, Surgeon General.
Web, www.armymedicine.army.mil

Directs the provision of medical and dental services for Army personnel and their dependents.

Defense Dept. (DoD), *Health Affairs: Clinical Program Policy,* 1200 Defense Pentagon, #3E1082 20301-1200; (703) 697-2111. Fax, (703) 697-4197. Dr. William Winkenwerder Jr., Assistant Secretary.
Web, www.defenselink.mil

Administers the medical benefits programs for active duty and retired military personnel and dependents in the Defense Dept.; develops policies relating to medical programs.

Marine Corps *(Defense Dept.), Personnel and Family Readiness Division,* HQUSMC, M and RA, 3280 Russell Rd., Quantico, VA 22134-5103; (703) 784-9501. Fax, (703) 784-9816. Michael Downs, Director.
Web, www.usmc-mccs.org

Military office that directs Marine Corps health care, family violence, and drug and alcohol abuse policies and programs.

Naval Medical Research Center *(Defense Dept.),* 503 Robert Grant Ave., #1W28, Silver Spring, MD 20910-7500; (301) 319-7400. Fax, (301) 319-7410. Capt. Richard B. Oberst, Commanding Officer.
Web, www.nmrc.navy.mil

Performs basic and applied biomedical research in areas of military importance, including infectious diseases, hyperbaric medicine, wound repair enhancement, environmental stress, and immunobiology. Provides support to field laboratories and naval hospitals; monitors research internationally.

Navy Dept. *(Defense Dept.), Health Affairs,* 1000 Navy Pentagon, #5D825 20350-1000; (703) 693-0238. Fax, (703) 693-4959. Cmdr. Catherine Simpson, Director.
Web, www.navy.mil

Reviews medical programs for Navy and Marine Corps military personnel and develops and reviews policies relating to these programs.

Navy Dept. *(Defense Dept.), Patient Administration,* 23rd and E Sts. N.W. 20372-5300; (202) 762-3152. Fax, (202) 762-3743. Cmdr. Edward Piskura, Head.
Web, www.navy.mil

Military office that interprets and oversees the implementation of Navy health care policy. Assists in the development of eligibility policy for medical benefits programs for Navy and Marine Corps military personnel.

Navy Dept. *(Defense Dept.), Surgeon General,* 23rd and E Sts. N.W., #1215 20372-5120; (202) 762-3701. Fax, (202) 762-3750. Vice Adm. Michael L. Cowan, Surgeon General.
Web, www.navy.mil

Directs the provision of medical and dental services for Navy and Marine Corps personnel and their dependents; oversees the Navy's Bureau of Medicine and Surgery.

U.S. Coast Guard (USCG), *(Homeland Security Dept.), Health and Safety,* 2100 2nd St. S.W., G-WK 20593-0001; (202) 267-1098. Fax, (202) 267-4512. Rear Adm. Joyce M. Johnson, Director.

Oversees all health and safety aspects of the Coast Guard, including the operation of medical and dental clinics, sick bays on ships, and mess halls and galleys.

Investigates Coast Guard accidents, such as the grounding of ships and downing of aircraft.

Walter Reed Army Institute of Research *(Defense Dept.),* 503 Robert Grant Ave., Silver Spring, MD 20910-7500; (301) 319-9100. Fax, (301) 319-9227. Col. Charles E. McQueen, Director.
Web, www.wrair.army.mil

Provides research, education, and training in support of the Defense Dept.'s health care system. Develops vaccines and drugs to prevent and treat naturally occurring diseases. Interests include biochemistry, biometrics, pathology, veterinary medicine, naturally occurring infectious diseases of military importance, battle casualties, operational stress, sleep deprivation, and defense against biological and chemical agents.

NONPROFIT

Assn. of Military Surgeons of the United States, 9320 Old Georgetown Rd., Bethesda, MD 20814-1653; (301) 897-8800. Fax, (301) 530-5446. Frederic G. Sanford, Executive Director.
General e-mail, amsus@amsus.org
Web, www.amsus.org

Membership: health professionals, including nurses, dentists, pharmacists, and physicians, who work or have worked for the U.S. Public Health Service, the VA, or the Army, Navy, or Air Force, and students. Works to improve all phases of federal health services.

Commissioned Officers Assn. of the U.S. Public Health Service, 8201 Corporate Dr., #560, Landover, MD 20785; (301) 731-9080. Fax, (301) 731-9084. Gerard M. Farrell, Executive Director.
Web, www.coausphs.org

Membership: commissioned officers of the U.S. Public Health Service. Supports expansion of federal health care facilities, including military facilities.

Missing in Action, Prisoners of War

AGENCIES

Air Force Dept. *(Defense Dept.), Personnel,* 1040 Air Force Pentagon, #4E194 20330-1040; (703) 697-6088. Fax, (703) 697-6091. Lt. Gen. Richard E. Brown III, Deputy Chief of Staff. Toll-free casualty assistance, (800) 433-0048.
Web, www.af.mil

Military office that responds to inquiries about missing in action (MIA) personnel for the Air Force; refers inquiries to the Military Personnel Center at Randolph Air Force Base in San Antonio, Texas.

Army Dept. *(Defense Dept.), Repatriation and Family Affairs: POWs and MIAs,* 2461 Eisenhower Ave., Alexandria, VA 22331-0482; (703) 325-5305. Fax, (703) 325-1808. Lt. Col. Suzanne Walker, Chief.
Web, www.army.mil

Military office responsible for policy regarding prisoner of war (POW) and missing in action (MIA) personnel for the Army. Responds to inquiries and distributes information about Army POWs and MIAs to the next of kin.

Defense Dept. (DoD), *Prisoners of War and Missing Personnel,* 1745 Jefferson Davis Hwy., Crystal Square, #800, Arlington, VA 22202; (703) 602-2102. Fax, (703) 602-4375. Jerry Jennings, Deputy Assistant Secretary.
Web, www.dtic.mil/dpmo

Civilian office responsible for policy matters relating to prisoners of war and missing personnel issues. Represents the Defense Dept. before Congress, the media, veterans organizations, and prisoner of war and missing personnel families.

Defense Dept. (DoD), *Public Inquiry and Analysis,* 1400 Defense Pentagon, #3A750 20301-1400; (703) 428-0711. Fax, (703) 428-1982. Harold Heilsnis, Director.
Web, www.defenselink.mil

Responds to public inquiries on Defense Dept. personnel.

Marine Corps *(Defense Dept.), Casualty Section,* HQUSMC, 3280 Russell Rd., Quantico, VA 22134-5103; (703) 784-9580. Fax, (703) 784-9823. Ann Hammers, Head.
Web, www.usmc.mil

Military office that responds to inquiries about missing in action (MIA) personnel for the Marine Corps and distributes information about Marine Corps MIAs to the next of kin.

Navy Dept. *(Defense Dept.), Naval Personnel,* 2 Navy Annex 20370; (703) 614-1101. Fax, (703) 693-1746. Vice Adm. Norbert R. Ryan Jr., Chief.
Web, www.navy.mil

Military office that responds to inquiries about missing in action (MIA) personnel for the Navy and distributes information about Navy MIAs.

State Dept., *Burma, Cambodia, Laos, Thailand, and Vietnam Affairs,* 2201 C St. N.W., #5206 20520-6310; (202) 647-4495. Fax, (202) 647-3069. Judith Strots, Director.
Web, www.state.gov

Handles issues related to Americans missing in action in Indochina; serves as liaison with Congress, international organizations, and foreign governments on developments in these countries.

CONGRESS

House Armed Services Committee, *Subcommittee on Total Force,* 2340 RHOB 20515; (202) 225-7560. Fax, (202) 226-0789. Rep. John M. McHugh, R-N.Y., Chair; John Chapla, Staff Director.
Web, www.house.gov/hasc

Jurisdiction over legislation on Americans missing in action (MIAs).

Senate Armed Services Committee, *Subcommittee on Personnel,* SR-228 20510; (202) 224-3871. Fax, (202) 228-0036. Sen. Saxby Chambliss, R-Ga., Chair; Dick Walsh, Staff Director.
Web, www.senate.gov/~armed_services

Jurisdiction over legislation on Americans missing in action (MIAs).

NONPROFIT

American Defense Institute (ADI), *Pride in America,* 1055 N. Fairfax St., #200, Alexandria, VA 22314; (703) 519-7000. Fax, (703) 519-8627. Eugene B. McDaniel, President.
General e-mail, rdt2@americandefinst.org

Nonpartisan organization that seeks to educate young Americans on matters of national security and foreign policy, including POW/MIA issues.

National League of Families of American Prisoners and Missing in Southeast Asia, 1005 N. Glebe Rd., #170, Arlington, VA 22201; (703) 465-7432. Fax, (703) 465-7433. Ann Mills Griffiths, Executive Director.
General e-mail, info@pow.miafamilies.org
Web, www.pow-miafamilies.org

Membership: family members of MIAs and POWs and returned POWs of the Vietnam War. Works for the release of all prisoners of war, an accounting of the missing, and repatriation of the remains of those who have died serving their country in Southeast Asia. Works to raise public awareness of these issues; maintains regional and state coordinators; sponsors an annual recognition day.

Pay and Compensation

AGENCIES

Air Force Dept. *(Defense Dept.),* **Legislation and Benefits Policy,** 1040 Air Force Pentagon, #4E188 20330-1040; (703) 695-0060. Fax, (703) 614-0099. Lt. Col. William Cain, Chief.

Web, www.af.mil

Military office that develops and administers Air Force military and civilian personnel pay and compensation policies and legislation.

Army Dept. *(Defense Dept.),* **Military Compensation and Entitlements,** 111 Army Pentagon, #2B683 20310-0111; (703) 693-7617. Lt. Victor Burdette, Assistant Deputy.
Web, www.army.mil

Military office that provides oversight of the development and administration of Army military personnel pay and compensation policies.

Defense Dept. (DoD), *Compensation,* 4000 Defense Pentagon, #2B279 20301-4000; (703) 695-3176. Fax, (703) 697-8725. Capt. Chris Kopang (USN), Director.
Web, www.defenselink.mil

Coordinates military pay and compensation policies with the individual service branches and advises the secretary of defense on compensation policy.

Marine Corps *(Defense Dept.),* **Manpower Policy,** 3280 Russell Rd., Quantico, VA 22134-5103; (703) 784-9386. Fax, (703) 784-9815. Lt. Col. Jeff Sharrock, Director; Maj. Christina McCloskey, Compensation/Incentive Officer.

Military office that develops and administers Marine Corps personnel pay and compensation policies.

Navy Dept. *(Defense Dept.),* **Military Compensation and Policy Coordination,** 2 Navy Annex, #3608 20370-5000; (703) 614-7797. Fax, (703) 695-3311. Cmdr. Jeri B. Busch, Director (Acting).
Web, www.navy.mil

Military office that develops and administers Navy military pay, compensation, and personnel policies.

Recruitment

AGENCIES

Air Force Dept. *(Defense Dept.),* **Accession Retention Policy,** 1040 Air Force Pentagon, #4E161 20330-1040; (703) 697-2388. Fax, (703) 614-1436. Lt. Col. Mary Purdue, Chief.
Web, www.af.mil

Military office that establishes Air Force recruitment and retention policies.

Army Dept. *(Defense Dept.),* **Army Career and Alumni Program,** 200 Stovall St., #7S07, Alexandria, VA 22332-0476; (703) 325-3591. Fax, (703) 325-8092. James T. Hoffman, Chief.
Web, www.acap.army.mil

Military office that provides Army military personnel and Defense Dept. civilian personnel with information concerning transition benefits and job assistance for those separating service members, civilian personnel, and their families.

Army Dept. *(Defense Dept.), Enlisted Accessions,* 300 Army Pentagon, #2C632 20310-0300; (703) 614-7675. Col. Anthony Parker, Chief.
Web, www.army.mil

Military office that develops policies and administers Army recruitment programs.

Defense Dept. (DoD), *Accession Policy,* 4000 Defense Pentagon, #2B271 20301-4000; (703) 695-5525. Fax, (703) 614-9272. Curtis Gilroy, Director.
Web, www.defenselink.mil

Military office that develops Defense Dept. recruiting programs and policies, including advertising, market research, and enlistment standards. Coordinates with the individual services on recruitment of military personnel.

Marine Corps *(Defense Dept.), Recruiting Command,* 3280 Russell Rd., Quantico, VA 22134-5103; (703) 784-9400. Fax, (703) 784-9863. Maj. Gen. Christopher Carter, Commanding General.
Web, www.mcrc.usmc.mil

Military office that administers and develops policies for Marine Corps officer and enlisted recruitment programs.

Retirement

AGENCIES

Armed Forces Retirement Home—Washington, 3700 N. Capitol St. N.W. 20317; (202) 730-3229. Fax, (202) 730-3127. Col. Arnold Smith, Director. Information, (202) 730-3556.
Web, www.afrh.gov

Gives domiciliary and medical care to retired members of the armed services or career service personnel unable to earn a livelihood. Formerly known as U.S. Soldiers' and Airmen's Home. (Armed Forces Retirement—Gulfport, Miss., also serves all branches of the armed services.)

Army Dept. *(Defense Dept.), Retirement Services,* DAPE-RS0, 200 Stovall St., #3N33, Alexandria, VA 22332-0470; (703) 325-9158. Fax, (703) 325-8947. John W. Radke, Chief Army Retirement Services.
Web, www.odcsper.army.mil/retire

Military office that administers retirement programs for Army military personnel.

Defense Dept. (DoD), *Compensation,* 4000 Defense Pentagon, #2B279 20301-4000; (703) 695-3176. Fax, (703) 697-8725. Capt. Chris Kopang (USN), Director.

Web, www.defenselink.mil

Develops retirement policies and reviews administration of retirement programs for all Defense Dept. military personnel.

Marine Corps *(Defense Dept.), Retired Activities,* 3280 Russell Rd., Quantico, VA 22134-5103; (703) 784-9310. Fax, (703) 784-9834. Dennis Dahnert, Head.

Military office that administers retirement programs and benefits for Marine Corps retirees and the Marine Corps retirement community survivor benefit plan.

Marine Corps *(Defense Dept.), Separation and Retirement,* 3280 Russell Rd., Quantico, VA 22134-5103; (703) 784-9304. Fax, (703) 784-9834. James P. Rathbun Jr., Head.

Military office that processes Marine Corps military personnel retirements but does not administer benefits.

NONPROFIT

Army Distaff Foundation, 6200 Oregon Ave. N.W. 20015-1543; (202) 541-0105. Fax, (202) 364-2856. Maj. Gen. Donald C. Hilbert, Executive Director. Information, (800) 541-4255.
Web, www.armydistaff.org

Nonprofit continuing care retirement community for career military officers and their families. Provides retirement housing and health care services.

MILITARY EDUCATION AND TRAINING

AGENCIES

Air Force Dept. *(Defense Dept.), Air Force Academy Admissions Liaison,* HQ USAFA/OL-C, The Pentagon, #4C174 20330-1040; (703) 697-6505. Fax, (703) 695-7999. Karen E. Parker, Director.
Web, www.af.mil

Military office that receives congressional nominations for the Air Force Academy; counsels congressional offices on candidate selection.

Air Force Dept. *(Defense Dept.), Force Management and Personnel,* 1660 Air Force Pentagon, #5E977 20330-1660; (703) 614-4751. Fax, (703) 693-4244. Kelly Craven, Deputy Assistant Secretary.
Web, www.af.mil

Civilian office that monitors and reviews education policies of the U.S. Air Force Academy at Colorado Springs and officer candidates' training and Reserve Officers Training Corps (ROTC) programs for the Air Force.

Advises the secretary of the Air Force on education matters, including graduate education, voluntary education programs, and flight, specialized, and recruit training.

Air Force Dept. *(Defense Dept.), Personnel Policy,* 1040 Air Force Pentagon, #4E228 20330-1040; (703) 695-6770. Fax, (703) 614-8523. Maj. Gen. John M. Speigel, Director.
Web, www.af.mil

Supervises operations and policies of all professional military education, including continuing education programs. Oversees operations and policies of Air Force service schools, including technical training for newly enlisted Air Force personnel.

Army Dept. *(Defense Dept.), Collective Training Division,* 400 Army Pentagon, #1E533 20310-0400; (703) 697-4107. Col. Arthur Finehout, Chief.
Web, www.army.mil

Military office that plans and monitors program resources for civilian and military training readiness programs.

Army Dept. *(Defense Dept.), Education,* 200 Stovall St., Attn.: TAPC-PDE #3N07, Alexandria, VA 22332; (703) 325-9800. Fax, (703) 325-7476. Dian L. Stoskopf, Chief.
Web, www.army.mil

Military office that manages the operations and policies of voluntary education programs for active Army personnel. Administers the tuition assistance program and basic army special skills program.

Army Dept. *(Defense Dept.), Military Personnel Management,* 300 Army Pentagon, #2C640 20310-0300; (703) 614-7055. Brig. Gen. Henry B. Axon, Director.
Web, www.army.mil

Military office that supervises operations and policies of the U.S. Military Academy and officer candidates' training and Reserve Officers Training Corps (ROTC) programs. Advises the chief of staff of the Army on academy and education matters.

Civil Air Patrol, *National Capital Wing, Washington Office,* Bolling Air Force Base, 200 McChord St., #122 20032-0000; (202) 767-4405. Fax, (202) 767-5695. Col. Franklin F. McConnell Jr., Wing Commander.

Official auxiliary of the U.S. Air Force. Sponsors a cadet training and education program for junior and senior high school age students. Cadets who have earned the Civil Air Patrol's Mitchell Award are eligible to enter the Air Force at an advanced pay grade. Conducts an aerospace education program for adults. (Headquarters at Maxwell Air Force Base, Ala.)

Defense Acquisition University *(Defense Dept.),* 9820 Belvoir Rd., Fort Belvoir, VA 22060-5565. Fax, (703) 805-2639. Frank J. Anderson Jr., President, (703) 805-5051. Toll-free, (800) 845-7606; Registrar, (703) 805-3003. Web, www.dau.mil

Academic institution that offers courses to military and civilian personnel who specialize in acquisition and procurement. Conducts research to support and improve management of defense systems acquisition programs.

Defense Dept. (DoD), *Accession Policy,* 4000 Defense Pentagon, #2B271 20301-4000; (703) 695-5525. Fax, (703) 614-9272. Curtis Gilroy, Director.
Web, www.defenselink.mil

Reviews and develops education policies of the service academies, service schools, graduate and voluntary education programs, education programs for active duty personnel, tuition assistance programs, and officer candidates' training and Reserve Officers Training Corps (ROTC) programs for the Defense Dept. Advises the secretary of defense on education matters.

Defense Dept. (DoD), *Readiness and Training,* 4000 Defense Pentagon, #1C757 20301-4000; (703) 695-2618. Fax, (703) 693-7382. Daniel E. Gardner, Director.
Web, www.defenselink.mil

Develops, reviews, and analyzes legislation, policies, plans, programs, resource levels, and budgets for the training of military personnel and military units. Develops the substantive-based framework, working collaboratively across the defense, federal, academic, and private sectors for the global digital knowledge environment. Manages with other government agencies the sustainability and modernization of DOD ranges.

Industrial College of the Armed Forces *(Defense Dept.),* Fort Lesley J. McNair, 408 4th Ave., Bldg. #59 20319-5062; (202) 685-4333. Fax, (202) 685-4175. Maj. Gen. Harold Mashburn, Commandant.
Web, www.ndu.edu

Division of National Defense University. Offers professional level courses for senior military officers and senior civilian government officials. Academic program focuses on management of national resources, mobilization, and industrial preparedness.

Marine Corps *(Defense Dept.), Training and Education,* 3300 Russell Rd., Command MCCDC (C46), Quantico, VA 22134-5001; (703) 784-3730. Fax, (703) 784-3724. Maj. Gen. T. S. Jones, Commanding General.

Military office that develops and implements training and education programs for regular and reserve personnel and units.

National Defense University *(Defense Dept.), Fort Lesley J. McNair, 300 5th Ave. 20319-5066; (202) 685-3922. Fax, (202) 685-3931. Vice Adm. Paul G. Gaffney, President. Help Desk, (202) 685-3824.*

Web, www.ndu.edu

Specialized university sponsored by the Joint Chiefs of Staff to prepare individuals for senior executive duties in the national security establishment. Offers master of science degrees in national resource strategy and national security strategy, as well as nondegree programs and courses.

National War College *(Defense Dept.), Fort Lesley J. McNair, 300 5th Ave., Bldg. #61 20319-5078; (202) 685-4341. Fax, (202) 685-3993. Maj. Gen. Reginal Clemmons, Commandant. Information, (202) 685-3713.*

Web, www.ndu.edu/ndu/nducat22.html

Division of National Defense University. Offers professional level courses for senior military officers, senior civilian government officials, and foreign officers. Academic program focuses on the formulation and implementation of national security policy and military strategy.

Navy Dept. *(Defense Dept.), Manpower and Reserve Affairs, 1000 Navy Pentagon, #4E789 20350-1000; (703) 697-2180. Fax, (703) 614-4103. William A. Navas Jr., Assistant Secretary.*

Web, www.navy.mil

Civilian office that reviews policies of the U.S. Naval Academy, Navy and Marine Corps service schools, and officer candidates' training and Reserve Officer Training Corps (ROTC) programs. Advises the secretary of the Navy on education matters, including voluntary education programs.

Navy Dept. *(Defense Dept.), Naval Education and Training, 2000 Navy Pentagon 20350-2000; (703) 692-9823. Fax, (703) 692-9830. Vice Adm. Alfred G. Harms Jr., Chief.*

Web, www.navy.mil

Develops and implements naval training policies. Oversees Navy service college and graduate school programs. Administers training programs for Naval Reserve Officer Training Corps, Naval Junior ROTC, and officer and enlisted personnel.

Uniformed Services University of the Health Sciences *(Defense Dept.), 4301 Jones Bridge Rd., Bethesda, MD 20814-4799; (301) 295-3013. Fax, (301) 295-1960. Dr. James A. Zimble, President. Information, (301) 295-3166. Registrar, (301) 295-3101.*

Web, www.usuhs.mil

Fully accredited four-year medical school under the auspices of the Defense Dept. Awards doctorates and master's degrees in health- and science-related fields. The Graduate School of Nursing awards a masters of science (nursing).

U.S. Coast Guard (USCG), *(Homeland Security Dept.), Human Resources, 2100 2nd St. S.W., #5410 20593-0001; (202) 267-0905. Fax, (202) 267-4205. Rear Adm. Kenneth T. Venuto, Assistant Commissioner.*

Web, www.uscg.mil/hq/g-w/hrhome.htm

Responsible for hiring, recruiting, and training all military and nonmilitary Coast Guard personnel.

U.S. Naval Academy *(Defense Dept.), 121 Blake Rd., Annapolis, MD 21402-5000; (410) 293-1500. Fax, (410) 293-2303. Vice Adm. Richard Naughton, Superintendent, (410) 293-1500; David A. Vetter, Dean of Admissions, (410) 293-1801. Visitor information, (410) 263-6933; candidate guidance, (410) 293-4361; Public Affairs, (410) 293-2291.*

General e-mail, navy@nadn.navy.mil

Web, www.usna.navy.mil

Provides undergraduate education for young men and women who have been nominated by members of their state's congressional delegation, or, in some cases, the president or vice president of the United States. Graduates receive bachelor of science degrees and are commissioned as either an ensign in the U.S. Navy or a second lieutenant in the U.S. Marine Corps.

CONGRESS

House Armed Services Committee, *Subcommittee on Total Force, 2340 RHOB 20515; (202) 225-7560. Fax, (202) 226-0789. Rep. John M. McHugh, R-N.Y., Chair; John Chapla, Staff Director.*

Web, www.house.gov/hasc

Jurisdiction over legislation on precommissioning programs and on military service academies and schools.

Senate Armed Services Committee, *Subcommittee on Personnel, SR-228 20510; (202) 224-3871. Fax, (202) 228-0036. Sen. Saxby Chambliss, R-Ga., Chair; Dick Walsh, Staff Director.*

Web, www.senate.gov/~armed_services

Jurisdiction over legislation on precommissioning programs and on military service academies and schools.

NONPROFIT

Assn. of Military Colleges and Schools of the U.S., *9429 Garden Court, Potomac, MD 20854-3964; (301) 765-0695. Fax, (301) 983-0583. Lewis Sorley (USA, ret.), Executive Director.*

Web, www.amcsus.org

Membership: nonfederal military colleges, junior colleges, and secondary schools that emphasize character development, leadership, and knowledge. Interests include Reserve Officers Training Corps (ROTC); publishes a newsletter; sponsors an annual meeting and outreach activities.

George and Carol Olmsted Foundation, *103 W. Broad St., #330, Falls Church, VA 22046; (703) 536-3500. Fax, (703) 536-5020. Larry R. Marsh, President. Web, www.olmstedfoundation.org*

Administers grants for two years of graduate study overseas for selected officers of the armed forces.

Military Order of the World Wars, *435 N. Lee St., Alexandria, VA 22314; (703) 683-4911. Fax, (703) 683-4501. Roger C. Bultman, Chief of Staff. General e-mail, mowwhq@aol.com Web, www.militaryorder.org*

Membership: retired and active duty commissioned officers, warrant officers, and flight officers. Presents awards to outstanding Reserve Officers Training Corps (ROTC) cadets; gives awards to Boy Scouts and Girl Scouts; conducts youth leadership conferences.

Navy League of the United States, *2300 Clarendon Blvd., #705, Arlington, VA 22201 (mailing address: 2300 Wilson Blvd., Arlington, VA 22201); (703) 528-1775. Fax, (703) 528-2333. Charles L. Robinson, National Executive Director. General e-mail, mail@navyleague.org Web, www.navyleague.org*

Sponsors Naval Sea Cadet Corps and Navy League Sea Cadet Corps for young people ages eleven through eighteen years. Graduates are eligible to enter the Navy at advanced pay grades.

Servicemembers Opportunity Colleges, *1307 New York Ave. N.W., 5th Floor 20005-4701; (202) 667-0079. Fax, (202) 667-0622. Steve F. Kime, Director. Information, (800) 368-5622. General e-mail, socmail@aascu.org Web, www.soc.aascu.org*

Partnership of higher education associations, educational institutions, the Defense Dept., and the military services. Offers credit courses and degree programs to military personnel and their families stationed in the United States and around the world.

MILITARY GRIEVANCES AND DISCIPLINE

AGENCIES

Air Force Dept. *(Defense Dept.), Air Force Personnel Council, 1535 Command Dr., EE Wing, 3rd Floor, Andrews AFB, MD 20762-7002; (240) 857-5739. Fax, (240) 857-1814. Wayne Newman, Director. Web, www.af.mil*

Military office that administers boards that review appeal cases. Administers the Air Force Board of Review, Disability Review Board, Clemency and Parole Board, Discharge Review Board, Decorations Board, Personnel Board, and the Physical Disability Appeal Board.

Air Force Dept. *(Defense Dept.), Air Force Review Boards Agency, 1535 Command Dr., #E302, Andrews AFB, MD 20762-7002; (240) 857-3137. Fax, (240) 857-3136. Joe G. Lineberger, Director. Web, www.af.mil*

Civilian office that responds to complaints from Air Force military and civilian personnel and assists in seeking corrective action.

Air Force Dept. *(Defense Dept.), Inquiries Directorate, 1140 Air Force Pentagon, #4E1084 20330-1140; (703) 588-1531. Fax, (703) 696-2555. James N. Worth, Chief. Web, www.af.mil*

Military office that handles complaints and requests for assistance from civilians and Air Force and other military personnel.

Army Dept. *(Defense Dept.), Army Review Boards Agency, 1941 Jefferson Davis Hwy., 2nd Floor, Arlington, VA 22202-4508; (703) 607-1607. Fax, (703) 602-2420. Karl F. Schneider, Deputy Assistant Secretary. Information, (703) 607-1600. Web, arba.army.pentagon.mil*

Civilian office that administers boards that review appeal cases. Administers the Ad Hoc Board, Army Grade Determination Board, Army Board for Correction of Military Records, Army Active Duty Board, Disability Rating Review Board, Discharge Review Board, Elimination Review Board, Security Review Board, Physical Disability Review Board, and Physical Disability Appeal Board.

Army Dept. *(Defense Dept.), Human Resources Directorate, 300 Army Pentagon 20310-0300; (703) 693-1850. Fax, (703) 695-6964. Brig. Gen. Steven Schook, Director. Web, www.army.mil*

Military office that receives complaints from Army military personnel and assists in seeking corrective action.

Defense Dept. (DoD), *Equal Opportunity,* *4000 Defense Pentagon, #3A272 20301-4000; (703) 697-6381. Fax, (703) 697-7534. Vacant, Director.*
Web, www.dod.gov

Formulates equal employment opportunity policy for the Defense Dept. Evaluates civil rights complaints from military personnel including issues of sexual harassment and recruitment.

Defense Dept. (DoD), *Legal Policy, 4000 Defense Pentagon, #4C759 20301-4000; (703) 697-3387. Fax, (703) 693-6708. Col. Steve Strong, Director.*
Web, www.defenselink.mil

Coordinates policy for the Board for the Correction of Military Records and the discharge review boards of the armed services.

Marine Corps *(Defense Dept.), Inspector General of the Marine Corps, 2 Navy Annex 20380-1775 (mailing address: Headquarters, U.S. Marine Corps, Code IG 20380-1775); (703) 614-1533. Fax, (703) 697-6690. Brig. Gen. Duane D. Thiessen, Inspector General.*
Web, www.hqmc.usmc.mil/ig/ig.nsf

Military office that investigates complaints from Marine Corps personnel and assists in seeking corrective action.

Navy Dept. *(Defense Dept.), Manpower and Reserve Affairs, 1000 Navy Pentagon 20350-1000; (703) 697-2180. Fax, (703) 614-4103. William A. Navas Jr., Assistant Secretary.*
Web, www.navy.mil

Civilian office that receives complaints from Navy and Marine Corps military personnel and assists in seeking corrective action.

Navy Dept. *(Defense Dept.), Naval Council of Personnel Boards, 720 Kennon St. S.E., #309, Washington Navy Yard, DC 20374-5023; (202) 685-6408. Fax, (202) 685-6610. Capt. William F. Eckert, Director.*
Web, www.navy.mil

Military office that administers boards that review appeal cases for the Navy and the Marine Corps. Composed of the Physical Evaluation Boards, the Naval Discharge Review Board, and the Naval Clemency and Parole Board.

CONGRESS

House Armed Services Committee, *Subcommittee on Total Force, 2340 RHOB 20515; (202) 225-7560. Fax,* *(202) 226-0789. Rep. John M. McHugh, R-N.Y., Chair; John Chapla, Staff Director.*
Web, www.house.gov/hasc

Jurisdiction over legislation on military personnel matters, including courts martial and appeals and military grievance procedures.

Senate Armed Services Committee, *Subcommittee on Personnel, SR-228 20510; (202) 224-3871. Fax, (202) 228-0036. Sen. Saxby Chambliss, R-Ga., Chair; Dick Walsh, Staff Director.*
Web, www.senate.gov/~armed_services

Jurisdiction over legislation on military personnel matters, including courts martial and appeals and military grievance procedures.

NONPROFIT

Center on Conscience & War, *1830 Connecticut Ave. N.W. 20009; (202) 483-2220. Fax, (202) 483-1246. J. E. McNeil, Executive Director.*
General e-mail, nisbco@nisbco.org
Web, www.nisbco.org

Seeks to defend and extend the rights of conscientious objectors. Provides information and advocacy about the military draft and national selective service. Offers counseling and information to military personnel seeking discharge or transfer to noncombatant positions within the military.

National Institute of Military Justice, *c/o Feldesman, Tucker, 2001 L St. N.W., #200 20036; (202) 466-8960. Fax, (202) 293-8103. Eugene R. Fidell, President.*
General e-mail, efidell@feldesmantucker.com

Advances the administration of military justice within the U.S. armed services; fosters improved public understanding of the military justice system.

Servicemembers Legal Defense Network (SLDN), *P.O. Box 65301 20035-5301; (202) 328-3244. Fax, (202) 797-1635. C. Dixon Osburn, Executive Director.*
General e-mail, sldn@sldn.org
Web, www.sldn.org

Provides legal assistance to individuals affected by the military's policy on gays and lesbians. Monitors legislation and regulations.

Correction of Military Records

AGENCIES

Air Force Dept. *(Defense Dept.), Board for the Correction of Military Records, 1535 Command Dr., EE Wing, 3rd Floor, Andrews AFB, MD 20762-7002; (240) 857-3502. Fax, (240) 857-9207. Mack Burton, Executive Director.*

Web, www.af.mil

Civilian board that reviews appeals for corrections to Air Force personnel records and makes recommendations to the secretary of the Air Force.

Army Dept. *(Defense Dept.), Board for the Correction of Military Records,* 1941 Jefferson Davis Hwy., 2nd Floor, Arlington, VA 22202-4508; (703) 607-1621. Fax, (703) 607-2036. Carl W. S. Chun, Director.

Web, arba.army.pentagon.mil

Civilian board that reviews appeals for corrections to Army personnel records and makes recommendations to the secretary of the Army.

Defense Dept. (DoD), *Legal Policy,* 4000 Defense Pentagon, #4C759 20301-4000; (703) 697-3387. Fax, (703) 693-6708. Col. Steve Strong, Director.

Web, www.defenselink.mil

Coordinates policy for armed services boards charged with correcting military records.

Navy Dept. *(Defense Dept.), Board for Correction of Naval Records,* 2 Navy Annex, #2432 20370-5100; (703) 614-1402. Fax, (703) 614-9857. W. Dean Pfeiffer, Executive Director.

Web, www.navy.mil

Civilian board that reviews appeals for corrections to Navy and Marine Corps personnel records and makes recommendations to the secretary of the Navy.

U.S. Coast Guard (USCG), *(Homeland Security Dept.), Board for Correction of Military Records,* 400 7th St. S.W., #4100 20590-0001; (202) 366-9335. Fax, (202) 366-7152. Dorothy J. Ulmer, Chair.

General e-mail, bcmrcg@ost.dot.gov

Web, www.dot.gov/ost/ogc/org/bcmr/index.html

Civilian board (an adjunct to the U.S. Coast Guard) that reviews appeals for corrections to Coast Guard personnel records and makes recommendations to the general counsel of the Homeland Security Dept.

Legal Proceedings

AGENCIES

Air Force Dept. *(Defense Dept.), Air Force Personnel Council,* 1535 Command Dr., EE Wing, 3rd Floor, Andrews AFB, MD 20762-7002; (240) 857-5739. Fax, (240) 857-1814. Wayne Newman, Director.

Web, www.af.mil

Military office that administers review boards, including the Clemency and Parole Board, which in turn reviews cases of military prisoners and makes recommendations to the secretary of the Air Force.

Air Force Dept. *(Defense Dept.), Judge Advocate General,* 1420 Air Force Pentagon 20330-1420; (703) 614-5732. Fax, (703) 614-8894. Maj. Gen. Thomas J. Fiscus, Judge Advocate General.

Web, www.af.mil

Military office that prosecutes and defends Air Force personnel during military legal proceedings. Gives legal advice and assistance to Air Force staff.

Army Dept. *(Defense Dept.), Army Clemency and Parole Board,* Crystal Mall 4, 1941 Jefferson Davis Hwy., #109A, Arlington, VA 22202-4508; (703) 607-1504. Fax, (703) 607-2047. James E. Vick, Chair.

Web, www.army.mil

Civilian and military board that reviews cases of military prisoners and makes recommendations to the secretary of the Army; reviews suspension of less-than-honorable discharges and restoration of prisoners to active duty or parole.

Army Dept. *(Defense Dept.), Judge Advocate General,* 2200 Army Pentagon 20310-2200; (703) 697-5151. Fax, (703) 693-0600. Maj. Gen. Thomas J. Romig, Judge Advocate General.

Web, www.army.mil

Military policy office for the field offices that prosecute and defend Army personnel during military legal proceedings. Serves as an administrative office for military appeals court, which hears legal proceedings involving Army personnel.

Defense Dept. (DoD), *U.S. Court of Appeals for the Armed Forces,* 450 E St. N.W. 20442-0001; (202) 761-1448. Fax, (202) 761-4672. William DeCicco, Clerk of the Court. Library, (202) 761-1466.

Web, www.defenselink.mil

Serves as the appellate court for cases involving dishonorable or bad conduct discharges, confinement of a year or more, and the death penalty, and for cases certified to the court by the judge advocate general of an armed service. Less serious cases are reviewed by the individual armed services. Library open to the public.

Marine Corps *(Defense Dept.), Judge Advocate,* 1775 Marine Corps Pentagon, #5E611 20380-1775; (703) 614-2737. Fax, (703) 614-5775. Brig. Gen. Kevin M. Sandkuhler, Staff Judge Advocate.

Web, www.hqmc.usmc.mil

Military office that administers legal proceedings involving Marine personnel.

Navy Dept. *(Defense Dept.), Judge Advocate General,* 1322 Patterson Ave. S.E., #3000, Washington Navy Yard,

DC 20374-5066; (703) 614-7420. Fax, (703) 697-4610. Rear Adm. Michael F. Lohr, Judge Advocate General.
Web, www.jag.navy.mil

Military office that administers the Judge Advocate Generals' Corps, which conducts legal proceedings involving Navy and Marine personnel.

Navy Dept. *(Defense Dept.), Naval Clemency and Parole Board,* 720 Kennon St. S.E., Bldg. 36, #322 20374-5023; (202) 685-6455. Fax, (202) 685-6629. Lt. Col. David Francis, President.
Web, www.navy.mil

Military board that reviews cases of Navy and Marine Corps prisoners and makes recommendations to the secretary of the Navy.

Military Police and Corrections

AGENCIES

Army Dept. *(Defense Dept.), Security Force Protection and Law Enforcement,* 400 Army Pentagon, DAMO-ODL, #BF758 20310-0400; (703) 614-1061. Fax, (703) 693-6580. Col. Douglas Watson, Chief.
Web, www.army.mil

Develops policies and supports military police and corrections programs in all branches of the U.S. military. Operates the Military Police Management Information System (MPMIS), which automates incident reporting and tracks information on facilities, staff, and inmates, including enemy prisoners of war.

Defense Dept. (DoD), *Legal Policy,* 4000 Defense Pentagon, #4C759 20301-4000; (703) 697-3387. Fax, (703) 693-6708. Col. Steve Strong, Director.
Web, www.defenselink.mil

Coordinates and reviews Defense Dept. policies and programs relating to deserters.

Marine Corps *(Defense Dept.), Corrections,* CMC HQMC POS-40, 2 Navy Annex 20380-1775; (703) 614-1375. Fax, (703) 614-3499. Gregory Stroebel, Head.

Military office that develops Marine Corps policies and responds to inquiries relating to deserters. Oversees Marine Corps brigs (correctional facilities).

⬛ MILITARY HISTORY AND HONORS

AGENCIES

Air Force Dept. *(Defense Dept.), Air Force History,* Bolling Air Force Base, B-3 Brookley Ave. 20032-5000; (202) 404-2167. Fax, (202) 404-2270. William Heimdahl,

Historian (Acting). Library, (202) 404-2264.
Web, www.af.mil

Publishes histories, studies, monographs, and reference works; directs worldwide Air Force History Program and provides guidance to the Air Force Historical Research Agency at Maxwell Air Force Base in Alabama; supports Air Force Air Staff agencies and responds to inquiries from the public and the U.S. government. Library open to the public.

Army Dept. *(Defense Dept.), Institute of Heraldry,* 9325 Gunston Rd., Bldg. 1466, #S-112, Fort Belvoir, VA 22060-5579; (703) 806-4969. Fax, (703) 806-4964. Fred N. Eichorn, Director. Information, (703) 806-4972.

Furnishes heraldic services to the Armed Forces and other U.S. government agencies, including the Executive Office of the President. Responsible for research, design, development, and standardization of official symbolic items, including seals, decorations, medals, insignias, badges, flags, and other items awarded to or authorized for official wear or display by government personnel and agencies. Limited research and information services on these items are provided to the general public.

Army Dept. *(Defense Dept.), U.S. Center of Military History,* 103 3rd Ave., Bldg. 35, Fort Lesley J. McNair 20319-5058; (202) 685-2706. Fax, (202) 685-4570. Brig. Gen. John S. Brown, Chief. Information, (202) 685-2194. Library, (202) 685-4042.
Web, www.army.mil/cmh-pg

Publishes the official history of the Army. Provides information on Army history; coordinates Army museum system and art program. Works with Army school system to ensure that history is included in curriculum. Sponsors professional appointments, fellowships, and awards. Collections and library facilities open to the public by appointment.

Defense Dept. (DoD), *Historical Office,* 1777 N. Kent St., #5000, Arlington, VA 22209; (703) 588-7890. Fax, (703) 588-7572. Alfred Goldberg, Historian.
Web, www.odam.osd.mil/hist/index.htm

Collects, compiles, and publishes documents and data on the history of Defense Dept. and the office of the secretary; coordinates historical activities of the Defense Dept. and prepares special studies at the request of the secretary.

Defense Dept. (DoD), *Joint History Office,* 9999 Defense Pentagon, #1A466 20318-9999; (703) 695-2114. Fax, (703) 614-6243. Brig. Gen. David A. Armstrong (USA, ret.), Director.
Web, www.defenselink.mil

Provides historical support services to the chair of the Joint Chiefs of Staff and the Joint Staff, including research; writes the official history of the Joint Chiefs.

Marine Corps *(Defense Dept.), Historical Center,* *1254 Charles Morris St. S.E., Washington Navy Yard, DC 20374-5040; (202) 433-0731. Fax, (202) 433-7265. Col. John W. Ripley, Director. Information, (202) 433-3840. Library, (202) 433-3447. Reference, (202) 433-3483. Web, www.usmc.mil*

Maintains official Marine Corps archives; writes official histories of the corps for government agencies and the public; answers inquiries about Marine Corps history; maintains museum; conducts prearranged tours of the historical center and museum. Library open to the public.

National Archives and Records Administration (NARA), *Textual Archives Services, 8601 Adelphi Rd., #2600, College Park, MD 20740-6001; (301) 837-3480. Fax, (301) 837-1919. James J. Hastings, Director. Web, www.archives.gov/research_room/obtain_copies/textual_archives_services*

Contains Army records from the Revolutionary War to the Vietnam War, Navy records from the Revolutionary War to the Korean War, and Air Force records from 1947–1954. Handles records captured from enemy powers at the end of World War II and a small collection of records captured from the Vietnamese. Conducts research in response to specific inquiries; makes records available for reproduction or examination in research room.

National Museum of American History *(Smithsonian Institution), Armed Forces History Collections, 14th St. and Constitution Ave. N.W., NMAH-4012, MRC 620 20560-0620; (202) 357-1883. Fax, (202) 357-1853. Jennifer Locke Jones, Assistant Chair. Web, www.si.edu/organiza/museums/nmah/csr/cadht.htm*

Maintains collections relating to the history of the U.S. armed forces and the American flag; includes manuscripts, documents, correspondence, uniforms, ordnance material of European and American origin, and other personal memorabilia of armed forces personnel of all ranks.

National Museum of Health and Medicine *(Defense Dept.), Walter Reed Medical Center, Bldg. 54 South 20307 (mailing address: 6825 16th St. N.W. 20036-6000); (202) 782-2200. Fax, (202) 782-3573. Dr. Adrianne Noe, Director. Web, www.natmedmuse.afip.org*

Maintains exhibits related to pathology and the history of medicine, particularly military medicine during the Civil War. Open to the public. Study collection available for scholars by appointment.

National Park Service (NPS), *(Interior Dept.), 1849 C St. N.W., #3112 20240; (202) 208-4621. Fax, (202) 208-7889. Fran P. Mainella, Director. Press, (202) 208-6843. Washington area activities, (202) 619-7275 (recording). Web, www.nps.gov*

Administers national parks, monuments, historic sites, and recreation areas. Responsible for national battlefields, selected historic forts, and other sites associated with U.S. military history.

Navy Dept. *(Defense Dept.), Naval Historical Center, 805 Kidder Breese St. S.E. 20374-5060; (202) 433-2210. Fax, (202) 433-3593. William S. Dudley, Director. Library, (202) 433-4132. Museum, (202) 433-6897. Art Gallery, (202) 433-3815. Archives, (202) 433-3224. Web, www.history.navy.mil*

Produces publications on naval history. Maintains historical files on Navy ships, operations, shore installations, and aviation. Collects Navy art, artifacts, and photographs. Library and archives open to the public.

U.S. Coast Guard (USCG), *(Homeland Security Dept.), Historian, 2100 2nd St. S.W., #B-717 20593-0001; (202) 267-2596. Fax, (202) 267-4309. Robert M. Browning, Chief Historian. Web, www.uscg.mil/hq/g-cp/history/collect.html*

Collects and maintains Coast Guard historical materials, including service artifacts, documents, photographs, and books. Archives are available to the public by appointment only.

NONPROFIT

Aerospace Education Foundation, *1501 Lee Hwy., Arlington, VA 22209; (703) 247-5839. Fax, (703) 247-5853. Donald L. Peterson, Executive Director. Information, (800) 727-3337. General e-mail, aefstaff@aef.org Web, www.aef.org*

Promotes knowledge and appreciation of U.S. civilian and military aerospace development and history. (Affiliated with the Air Force Assn.)

Air Force Historical Foundation, *1535 Command Dr., #A-122, Andrews AFB, MD 20762; (301) 736-1959. Fax, (301) 981-3574. Col. Joseph A. Marston, Executive Director. Web, www.afhistoricalfoundation.com*

Membership: individuals interested in the history of the U.S. Air Force and U.S. air power. Bestows awards on Air Force Academy and Air War College students and to other active duty personnel. Funds research and publishes books on aviation and Air Force history.

Council on America's Military Past—U.S.A.,
P.O. Box 1151, Fort Myer, VA 22211-1151; (703) 912-6124. Fax, (703) 912-5666. Herbert M. Hart, Executive Director. Information, (800) 398-4693.
Web, www.campjamp.org

Membership: historians, archeologists, curators, writers, and others interested in military history and preservation of historic military establishments and ships.

National Museum of American Jewish History, *1811 R St. N.W. 20009; (202) 265-6280. Fax, (202) 234-5662. Herb Rosenbleeth, Executive Director.*
Web, www.jwv.org

Collects, preserves, and displays memorabilia of Jewish men and women in the military; conducts research; sponsors seminars; provides information on the history of Jewish participation in the U.S. armed forces.

Naval Historical Foundation, *1306 Dahlgren Ave. S.E., Washington Navy Yard, DC 20374-5055; (202) 678-4333. Fax, (202) 889-3565. Vice Adm. Robert F. Dunn (Ret.), President.*
General e-mail, nhfwny@navyhistory.org
Web, www.navyhistory.org

Collects private documents and artifacts relating to naval history; maintains collection on deposit with the Library of Congress for public reference; conducts oral history and heritage speakers programs; raises funds to support the Navy Museum and historical programs.

Cemeteries and Memorials

AGENCIES

American Battle Monuments Commission,
2300 Clarendon Blvd., #500, Arlington, VA 22201-3367; (703) 696-6900. Fax, (703) 696-6666. John P. Herrling, Secretary.
Web, www.abmc.gov

Maintains military cemeteries and memorials on foreign soil and certain memorials in the United States; provides next of kin with grave site and related information.

Army Dept. *(Defense Dept.), Arlington National Cemetery: Interment Services, Arlington, VA 22211; (703) 695-3250. Fax, (703) 614-6339. Vicki Tanner, Chief.*
Web, www.arlingtoncemetery.org

Arranges interment services and provides eligibility information for burials at Arlington National Cemetery.

Veterans Affairs Dept. (VA), *National Cemetery Administration, 810 Vermont Ave. N.W., #400 20420;*
(202) 273-5146. Fax, (202) 273-6709. Eric Benson, Under Secretary for Memorial Affairs (Acting). Information on burial eligibility, (800) 827-1000.
Web, www.cem.va.gov

Administers VA national cemeteries; furnishes markers and headstones for deceased veterans; administers state grants to establish, expand, and improve veterans' cemeteries. Provides presidential memorial certificates to next of kin.

CONGRESS

House Appropriations Committee, *Subcommittee on VA, HUD, and Independent Agencies, H143 CAP 20515; (202) 225-3241. Rep. James T. Walsh, R-N.Y., Chair; Tim Peterson, Staff Director.*
Web, www.house.gov/appropriations

Jurisdiction over legislation to appropriate funds for the American Battle Monuments Commission and for cemeterial expenses for the Army Dept., including Arlington National Cemetery.

House Veterans' Affairs Committee, *Subcommittee on Benefits, 337 CHOB 20515; (202) 225-9164. Fax, (202) 225-5486. Rep. Henry E. Brown Jr., R-S.C., Chair; Darryl Kehrer, Staff Director.*
Web, veterans.house.gov

Jurisdiction over legislation on national cemeteries, including Arlington National Cemetery.

Senate Appropriations Committee, *Subcommittee on VA, HUD, and Independent Agencies, SD-130 20510; (202) 224-8252. Fax, (202) 228-1624. Sen. Christopher S. Bond, R-Mo., Chair; Jon Kamarck, Clerk.*
Web, appropriations.senate.gov

Jurisdiction over legislation to appropriate funds for the American Battle Monuments Commission and for cemeterial expenses for the Army Dept., including Arlington National Cemetery.

Senate Veterans' Affairs Committee, *SR-412 20510; (202) 224-9126. Fax, (202) 224-9575. Sen. Arlen Specter, R-Pa., Chair; William Tuerk, Chief Counsel.*
Web, veterans.senate.gov

Jurisdiction over legislation on national cemeteries, including Arlington National Cemetery.

NONPROFIT

Air Force Memorial Foundation, *1501 Lee Hwy., #120, Arlington, VA 22209-1109; (703) 247-5808. Fax, (703) 247-5819. Maj. Gen. Edward F. Grillo Jr., President.*
Web, www.airforcememorial.org

Plans to design and construct an Air Force Memorial to honor the achievements of men and women who have served in the U.S. Air Force, or its predecessors, such as the Army Air Forces.

The Black Revolutionary War Patriots Foundation, *1612 K St. N.W., #1104 20006-2802; (202) 452-1776. Fax, (202) 728-0770. Mark A. Gresham, President. Toll-free, (800) 888-9811.*
General e-mail, blackpatriots@blackpatriots.org
Web, www.blackpatriots.org

Private corporation authorized by Congress to fund and build a national memorial to honor black patriots who served in the militia or provided civilian assistance during the American Revolution.

No Greater Love, *1750 New York Ave. N.W. 20006; (202) 783-4665. Fax, (202) 783-1168. Benjamin Barbin, Executive Director.*
General e-mail, remembrance@ngl.org
Web, www.ngl.org

Provides programs of remembrance, friendship, and care for families of Americans killed in war or by acts of terrorism.

U.S. Navy Memorial Foundation, *701 Pennsylvania Ave. N.W., #123 20004-2608; (202) 737-2300. Fax, (202) 737-2308. Henry C. McKinney, President.*
General e-mail, ahoy@lonesailor.org
Web, www.lonesailor.org

Educational foundation authorized by Congress. Focuses on American naval history; built and supports the national Navy memorial to honor those who serve or have served in the naval services.

Women in Military Service for America Memorial Foundation, *5510 Columbia Pike, #302, Arlington, VA 22204-3123 (mailing address: Dept. 560, Washington, DC 20042-0560); (703) 533-1155. Fax, (703) 931-4208. Wilma L. Vaught, President. Information, (800) 222-2294.*
General e-mail, wimsa@aol.com
Web, www.womensmemorial.org

Authorized by Congress to create, support, and build the national memorial to honor women who serve or have served in the U.S. armed forces from the revolutionary war to the present.

Ceremonies, Military Bands

AGENCIES

Air Force Dept. *(Defense Dept.), Air Force Band: Bolling Air Force Base, 201 McChord St. 20332-0202; (202) 767-9253 (Band Scheduler). Fax, (202) 767-0686. Col. Dennis Layendecker, Commander. Concerts, (202) 767-5658; Public Affairs, (202) 767-4310.*
General e-mail, bandpublicaffairs@bolling.af.mil

Web, www.bolling.af.mil/band

Supports the Air Force by providing musical services for official military ceremonies and community events.

Air Force Dept. *(Defense Dept.), Air Force Bands, 901 N. Stuart St., #803, Arlington, VA 22203; (703) 696-9161. Lt. Col. Mark R. Peterson, Chief.*
Web, www.af.mil/band/home.shtml

Disseminates information to the public regarding various Air Force bands; coordinates their schedules and performances.

Army Dept. *(Defense Dept.), Army Field Band, 4214 Field Band Dr., Fort Meade, MD 20755-5330; (301) 677-6231. Fax, (301) 677-7980. Col. Finley R. Hamilton, Commander.*
Web, www.mdw.army.mil/fband/usafb.htm

Supports the Army by providing musical services for official military ceremonies and community events. Sponsors vocal and instrumental clinics for high school and college students.

Army Dept. *(Defense Dept.), Ceremonies and Special Events, Fort Lesley J. McNair, 4th and P Sts. S.W. 20319-5050; (202) 685-2983. Fax, (202) 685-3379. Boyd Sarratt, Special Events Coordinator.*
Web, www.army.mil

Coordinates and schedules public ceremonies and special events, including appearances of all armed forces bands and honor guards.

Army Dept. *(Defense Dept.), The U.S. Army Band, Attn: ANAB, Bldg. 400, 204 Lee Ave., Fort Myer, VA 22211-1199; (703) 696-3647. Fax, (703) 696-3904. Col. Gary F. Lamb, Commander.*
Web, www.army.mil/armyband

Supports the Army by providing musical services for official military ceremonies and community events.

Defense Dept. (DoD), *Community Relations and Public Liaison, 1400 Defense Pentagon, 1E776 20301-1400; (703) 695-2733. Fax, (703) 697-2577. Brent Krueger, Director; Lt. Col. Archie Davis, Military Public Affairs Officer, (703) 695-3381; Michael W. Byers, Civilian Public Affairs Officer, (703) 695-6108.*
Web, www.defenselink.mil

Provides armed forces bands with policy guidance for related public events.

Marine Corps *(Defense Dept.), Marine Band, 8th and Eye Sts. S.E. 20390; (202) 433-4045. Fax, (202) 433-4752. Col. T. W. Foley, Director.*
Web, www.marineband.usmc.mil

Supports the Marines by providing musical services for official military ceremonies and community events.

Navy Dept. *(Defense Dept.)*, *Navy Band,* 617 Warrington Ave. S.E., Washington Navy Yard, DC 20374-5054; (202) 433-3366. Fax, (202) 433-4108. Capt. Ralph M. Gambone, Officer in Charge.
Web, www.navyband.navy.mil

Supports the Navy by providing musical services for official military ceremonies and community events.

U.S. Naval Academy *(Defense Dept.)*, *Band,* 121 Blake Rd., Annapolis, MD 21402-5080; (410) 293-1258. Fax, (410) 293-2116. Lt. Cmdr. Donald H. Keller, Director. Concert information, (410) 293-0263.
Web, www.nadn.navy.mil/USNABand

The Navy's oldest continuing musical organization. Supports the Navy by providing musical services for official military ceremonies and community events.

U.S. Naval Academy *(Defense Dept.)*, *Drum and Bugle Corps,* c/o U.S. Naval Academy, Stop 3A, Annapolis, MD 21402; (410) 293-4508. Jeff Weir, Civilian Director.
General e-mail, drumbug@nadn.navy.mil
Web, www.usna.edu/USNADB

The oldest drum and bugle corps in existence in the United States. Plays for Brigade of Midshipmen at sporting events, pep rallies, parades, and daily formations. Supports the Navy by providing musical services for official military ceremonies and community events.

🔲 RESERVES AND NATIONAL GUARD

AGENCIES

Air Force Dept. *(Defense Dept.)*, *Air Force Reserve,* 1150 Air Force Pentagon, #5C916 20330-1150; (703) 695-9225. Fax, (703) 695-8959. Lt. Gen. James E. Sherrard III, Chief.
Web, www.afreserve.com

Military office that coordinates and directs Air Force Reserve matters (excluding the Air National Guard).

Air Force Dept. *(Defense Dept.)*, *Reserve Affairs,* 1660 Air Force Pentagon, #5C938 20330-1660; (703) 697-6375. Fax, (703) 695-2701. John C. Truesdell, Deputy Assistant Secretary.
Web, www.af.mil

Civilian office that reviews and monitors Air Force Reserve, Air National Guard, and Civil Air Patrol policies.

Army Dept. *(Defense Dept.)*, *Army Reserve,* 2400 Army Pentagon, #1E729 20310-2400; (703) 697-1784. Fax, (703) 697-1891. Lt. Gen. James R. Helmly, Chief.

Web, www.army.mil

Military office that coordinates and directs Army Reserve matters (excluding the Army National Guard).

Army Dept. *(Defense Dept.)*, *Reserve Affairs, Mobilization, Readiness, and Training,* 111 Army Pentagon, #2C635 20310-0111; (703) 692-1294. Vacant, Assistant Deputy.
Web, www.army.mil

Oversees training, military preparedness, and mobilization for all active and reserve members of the Army.

Defense Dept. (DoD), *Reserve Affairs,* 1500 Defense Pentagon, #2D201 20301-1500; (703) 697-6631. Fax, (703) 697-1682. Thomas F. Hall, Assistant Secretary.
Web, www.defenselink.mil

Civilian office that addresses national guard and reserve component issues.

Marine Corps *(Defense Dept.)*, *Manpower and Reserve Affairs,* 3280 Russell Rd., Quantico, VA 22134-5103; (703) 784-9102. Fax, (703) 784-9805. Maj. Gen. Arnold L. Punaro, Assistant Deputy Commandant.
Web, www.usmc.mil

Military office that coordinates and directs Marine Corps Reserve matters.

National Guard Bureau *(Defense Dept.)*, 1411 Jefferson Davis Hwy., Arlington, VA 22202-3231; (703) 607-2200. Fax, (703) 607-3671. Vacant, Chief.
Web, www.ngb.dtic.mil

Military office that oversees and coordinates activities of the Air National Guard and Army National Guard.

National Guard Bureau *(Defense Dept.)*, *Air National Guard,* NGB/CF 1411 Jefferson Davis Hwy., Arlington, VA 22202-3231; (703) 607-2370. Fax, (703) 607-3678. Lt. Gen. Daniel James, Director.
Web, www.ang.af.mil

Military office that coordinates and directs Air National Guard matters.

National Guard Bureau *(Defense Dept.)*, *Air National Guard: Chaplain Service,* 1411 Jefferson Davis Hwy., Arlington, VA 22202-3231; (703) 607-5278. Fax, (703) 607-5295. Col. John B. Ellington Jr., Chief.
Web, www.ang.af.mil

Oversees chaplains and religious services within the Air National Guard; maintains liaison with religious denominations.

National Guard Bureau *(Defense Dept.)*, *Army National Guard,* 1411 Jefferson Davis Hwy., Arlington, VA 22202-3231; (703) 607-2365. Fax, (703) 607-7088. Lt. Gen. Roger C. Schultz, Director.

Web, www.ngb.army.mil

Military office that coordinates and directs Army National Guard matters.

National Guard Bureau *(Defense Dept.), Army National Guard: Chaplain Service,* 1411 Jefferson Davis Hwy., #9500, Arlington, VA 22202-3231; (703) 607-7072. Fax, (703) 607-5295. Col. Donald W. Hill, Chief.

Oversees chaplains and religious services with the Army National Guard; maintains liaison with religious denominations; serves as policy leader for chaplains.

Navy Dept. *(Defense Dept.), Naval Reserve,* 2000 Navy Pentagon, CNO-N095, #4E446 20350-2000; (703) 693-5758. Fax, (703) 693-5760. Vice Adm. John B. Totushek, Director.

Web, www.navy.mil

Military office that coordinates and directs Naval Reserve matters.

Navy Dept. *(Defense Dept.), Reserve Affairs,* 1000 Navy Pentagon, #5D833 20350-1000; (703) 614-1327. Fax, (703) 693-4959. Harvey C. Barnum Jr., Deputy Assistant Secretary.

Web, www.navy.mil

Civilian office that reviews Navy and Marine Corps Reserve policies.

U.S. Coast Guard (USCG), *(Homeland Security Dept.), Reserve and Training,* 2100 2nd St. S.W., #5100 20593-0001; (202) 267-2350. Fax, (202) 267-4243. Rear Adm. Robert Papp Jr., Director.

Web, www.uscg.mil/reserve

Oversees and ensures Coast Guard readiness to perform its peacetime mission and its wartime role. Responsible for training all reserve and active duty forces.

NONPROFIT

Adjutants General Assn. of the United States, 1 Massachusetts Ave. N.W. 20001-1431; (202) 789-0031. Fax, (202) 682-9358. Maj. Gen. John F. Kane, President.

Web, www.agaus.org

Organization of the adjutants general of the National Guard. Works to promote a strong national defense and National Guard with the Congress, governors, and Defense Dept.

Assn. of Civilian Technicians, 12620 Lake Ridge Dr., Lake Ridge, VA 22192-2354; (703) 690-1330. Fax, (703) 494-0961. Thomas G. Bastas, President.

Web, www.actnat.com

Membership: federal civil service employees of the National Guard. Represents members before federal agencies and Congress.

Enlisted Assn. of the National Guard of the United States, 3133 Mt. Vernon Ave., Alexandria, VA 22305; (703) 519-3846. Fax, (703) 519-3849. Michael P. Cline, Executive Director. Information, (800) 234-3264.

General e-mail, eangus@eangus.org

Web, www.eangus.org

Membership: active and retired enlisted members and veterans of the National Guard. Promotes a strong national defense and National Guard. Sponsors scholarships, conducts seminars, and provides information concerning members and their families.

Marine Corps Reserve Officers Assn., 337 Potomac Ave., Quantico, VA 22314; (703) 630-3772. Fax, (703) 630-1904. Vernon J. Leubecker, Executive Director (Acting). Information, (800) 927-6270.

Web, www.mcroa.com

Membership: active and retired Marine Corps Reserve officers. Promotes the interests of the Marine Corps and the Marine Corps Reserve.

National Guard Assn. of the United States, 1 Massachusetts Ave. N.W. 20001-1431; (202) 789-0031. Fax, (202) 682-9358. Maj. Gen. Richard C. Alexander, Executive Director.

General e-mail, ngaus@ngaus.org

Web, www.ngaus.org

Membership: active duty and retired officers of the National Guard. Works to promote a strong national defense and to maintain a strong, ready National Guard.

Naval Reserve Assn., 1619 King St., Alexandria, VA 22314-2793; (703) 548-5800. Fax, (703) 683-3647. Stephen T. Keith, Executive Director.

Web, www.navy-reserve.org

Membership: active duty, inactive, and retired Navy and Naval Reserve officers. Supports and promotes U.S. military and naval policies, particularly the interests of the Navy and Naval Reserve. Offers education programs for naval reservists and potential naval commissioned officers. Provides the public with information on national security issues. Assists members with Naval Reserve careers, military retirement, and veterans' benefits.

Reserve Officers Assn. of the United States, 1 Constitution Ave. N.E. 20002-5655; (202) 479-2200. Fax, (202) 479-0416. Robert A. McIntosh, Executive Director. Information, (800) 809-9448.

Web, www.roa.org

Membership: active and inactive commissioned officers of all uniformed services. Supports continuation of a reserve force to enhance national security.

⚔ VETERANS

AGENCIES

Armed Forces Retirement Home—Washington, *3700 N. Capitol St. N.W. 20317; (202) 730-3229. Fax, (202) 730-3127. Col. Arnold Smith, Director. Information, (202) 730-3556.*
Web, www.afrh.gov

Gives domiciliary and medical care to retired members of the armed services or career service personnel unable to earn a livelihood. Formerly known as U.S. Soldiers' and Airmen's Home. (Armed Forces Retirement—Gulfport, Miss., also serves all branches of the armed services.)

Center for Women Veterans *(Veterans Affairs Dept.), 810 Vermont Ave. N.W., #435 20420; (202) 273-6193. Fax, (202) 273-7092. Irene Trowell-Harris, Director.*
Web, www.va.gov/womenvet

Advises the secretary and promotes research on matters related to women veterans; seeks to ensure that women veterans receive benefits and services on par with men.

Veterans Affairs Dept. (VA), *810 Vermont Ave. N.W. 20420; (202) 273-4800. Fax, (202) 273-4877. Anthony J. Principi, Secretary; Leo S. Mackay, Deputy Secretary. Locator, (202) 273-5400.*
Web, www.va.gov

Administers programs benefiting veterans, including disability compensation, pensions, education, home loans, insurance, vocational rehabilitation, medical care at veterans' hospitals and outpatient facilities, and burial benefits.

Veterans Affairs Dept. (VA), *Compensation and Pension Service, 810 Vermont Ave. N.W., MC 21 20420; (202) 273-7203. Fax, (202) 275-5661. Ronald J. Henke, Director.*
Web, www.vabenefits.vba.va.gov

Administers disability payments; handles claims for burial and plot allowances by veterans' survivors. Provides information on and assistance with benefits legislated by Congress for veterans of active military, naval, or air service.

Veterans Affairs Dept. (VA), *National Cemetery Administration, 810 Vermont Ave. N.W., #400 20420; (202) 273-5146. Fax, (202) 273-6709. Eric Benson, Under Secretary for Memorial Affairs (Acting). Information on burial eligibility, (800) 827-1000.*
Web, www.cem.va.gov

Administers VA national cemeteries; furnishes markers and headstones for deceased veterans; administers state grants to establish, expand, and improve veterans' cemeteries. Provides presidential memorial certificates to next of kin.

Veterans Affairs Dept. (VA), *Policy, 810 Vermont Ave. N.W., #300 20420; (202) 273-5182. Fax, (202) 273-5993. David J. Balland, Deputy Assistant Secretary.*
Web, www.va.gov

Serves as the single, departmentwide repository, clearinghouse, and publication source for veterans' demographic and statistical information.

Veterans Affairs Dept. (VA), *Policy and Planning, 810 Vermont Ave. N.W., #300 MC 008 20420; (202) 273-5033. Fax, (202) 273-5993. Claude M. Kicklighter, Assistant Secretary.*
Web, www.va.gov

Manages policy and planning processes; supplies policymakers with analytical reports on improving services for veterans and their families.

Veterans Benefits Administration (VBA), *(Veterans Affairs Dept.), 810 Vermont Ave. N.W., #520, MC 20 20420; (202) 273-6761. Fax, (202) 275-3591. Daniel L. Cooper, Under Secretary. Information, (202) 418-4343. Toll-free insurance hotline, (800) 669-8477.*
Web, www.vba.va.gov

Administers nonmedical benefits programs for veterans and their dependents and survivors. Benefits include veterans' compensation and pensions, survivors' benefits, education and rehabilitation assistance, home loan benefits, insurance coverage, and burials. (Directs benefits delivery nationwide through regional offices and veterans' insurance offices in Philadelphia and St. Paul.)

CONGRESS

General Accounting Office (GAO), *Education, Workforce, and Income Security, 441 G St. N.W., #5928 20548; (202) 512-7215. Cynthia Fagnoni, Managing Director.*
Web, www.gao.gov

Independent, nonpartisan agency in the legislative branch that audits, analyzes, and evaluates Veterans Affairs Dept. programs; makes reports available to the public.

House Appropriations Committee, *Subcommittee on VA, HUD, and Independent Agencies, H143 CAP 20515; (202) 225-3241. Rep. James T. Walsh, R-N.Y., Chair; Tim Peterson, Staff Director.*
Web, www.house.gov/appropriations

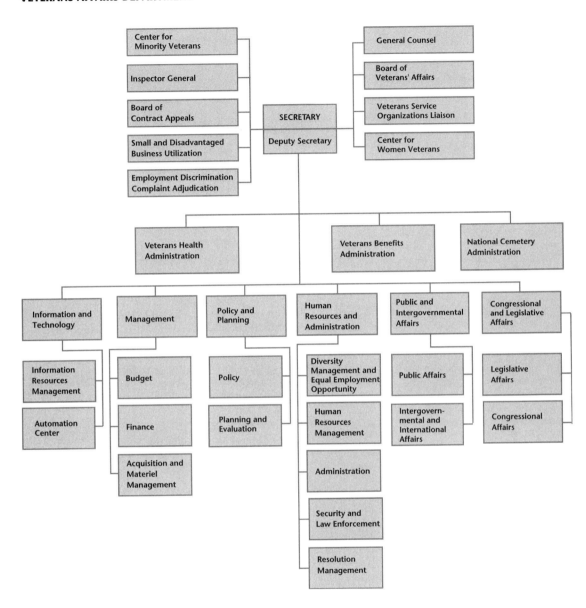

Jurisdiction over legislation to appropriate funds for the Veterans Affairs Dept., the Board of Veterans Appeals, the U.S. Court of Veterans Appeals, and other veterans' programs.

House Government Reform Committee, *Subcommittee on Criminal Justice, Drug Policy, and Human*

Resources, B373B RHOB 20515; (202) 225-2577. *Fax, (202) 225-1154. Rep. Mark Souder, R-Ind., Chair; Christopher Donesa, Staff Director.*
Web, www.house.gov/reform

Oversight jurisdiction of the Veterans Affairs Dept. (Shares oversight jurisdiction with the House Veterans' Affairs Committee.)

House Veterans' Affairs Committee, *335 CHOB 20515; (202) 225-3527. Fax, (202) 225-5486. Rep. Christopher H. Smith, R-N.J., Chair; Patrick Ryan, Staff Director.*
Web, veterans.house.gov

Jurisdiction over the Veterans Affairs Dept. (Jurisdiction shared with House Government Reform Committee.)

House Veterans' Affairs Committee, *Subcommittee on Benefits, 337 CHOB 20515; (202) 225-9164. Fax, (202) 225-5486. Rep. Henry E. Brown Jr., R-S.C., Chair; Darryl Kehrer, Staff Director.*
Web, veterans.house.gov

Jurisdiction over legislation on veterans' pensions and life insurance; service-connected disability payments to veterans, survivors, and dependents; and burial benefits for veterans. Jurisdiction over legislation on education, training, vocational rehabilitation, employment, housing loans, special housing for paraplegics, readjustment to civilian life for veterans and disabled veterans and educational assistance for survivors of deceased veterans.

Senate Appropriations Committee, *Subcommittee on VA, HUD, and Independent Agencies, SD-130 20510; (202) 224-8252. Fax, (202) 228-1624. Sen. Christopher S. Bond, R-Mo., Chair; Jon Kamarck, Clerk.*
Web, appropriations.senate.gov

Jurisdiction over legislation to appropriate funds for the Veterans Affairs Dept., the Board of Veterans Appeals, the U.S. Court of Veterans Appeals, and other veterans' programs.

Senate Veterans' Affairs Committee, *SR-412 20510; (202) 224-9126. Fax, (202) 224-9575. Sen. Arlen Specter, R-Pa., Chair; William Tuerk, Chief Counsel.*
Web, veterans.senate.gov

Jurisdiction over veterans' legislation, including pensions; service-connected disability payments to veterans, survivors, and dependents; education and training; vocational rehabilitation for disabled veterans; veterans' life insurance, hospitals, medical programs, and outpatient programs; construction of medical facilities; readjustment to civilian life; housing loans and special housing loans for paraplegics; employment; cemetery and burial benefits; state veterans' homes; and educational assistance for survivors of deceased veterans. Oversight of and legislative jurisdiction over the Veterans Affairs Dept.

NONPROFIT

American Legion National Headquarters, *1608 K St. N.W. 20006; (202) 861-2700. Fax, (202) 861-2728. John F. Sommer Jr., Executive Director.*

Web, www.legion.org

Membership: honorably discharged wartime veterans of World War I, World War II, the Korean War, the Vietnam War, or conflicts in Lebanon, Grenada, Panama, and the Persian Gulf. Chartered by Congress to assist veterans with claims for benefits.

American Red Cross, *Armed Forces Emergency Services, 2025 E St. N.W. 20006; (703) 206-7481. Sue A. Richter, Vice President.*
Web, www.redcross.org/services/afes

Assists veterans and their dependents with claims for benefits on a limited basis; provides emergency services for active duty armed forces personnel and their families. (Moving from Virginia to the Washington address above in summer 2003.)

American Veterans of World War II, Korea, and Vietnam (Amvets), *4647 Forbes Blvd., Lanham, MD 20706-4380; (301) 459-9600. Fax, (301) 459-7924. Jim King, Executive Director.*
Web, www.amvets.org

Membership: those who served honorably in the military after September 15, 1940. Helps members obtain benefits; participates in community programs; operates a volunteer service that donates time to hospitalized veterans. Monitors legislation and regulations.

Blinded Veterans Assn., *477 H St. N.W. 20001-2699; (202) 371-8880. Fax, (202) 371-8258. Thomas H. Miller, Director. Information, (800) 669-7079.*
General e-mail, bva@bva.org
Web, www.bva.org

Chartered by Congress to assist veterans with claims for benefits. Seeks out blinded veterans to make them aware of benefits and services available to them.

Catholic War Veterans U.S.A., *441 N. Lee St., Alexandria, VA 22314-2301; (703) 549-3622. Fax, (703) 684-5196. Leo J. Krichten, Executive Director.*
Web, www.cwv.org

Recognized by the Veterans Affairs Dept. to assist veterans with claims for benefits. Conducts community service programs; offers scholarships for children; supports benefits for Vietnam veterans commensurate with those received by World War II veterans.

Disabled American Veterans, *807 Maine Ave. S.W. 20024-2410; (202) 554-3501. Fax, (202) 554-3581. Arthur H. Wilson, National Adjutant.*
Web, www.dav.org

Chartered by Congress to assist veterans with claims for benefits; represents veterans seeking to correct alleged errors in military records. Assists families of veterans with disabilities.

Jewish War Veterans of U.S.A., *1811 R St. N.W. 20009; (202) 265-6280. Fax, (202) 234-5662. Herb Rosenbleeth, National Executive Director.*
Web, www.jwv.org

Recognized by the Veterans Affairs Dept. to assist veterans with claims for benefits. Offers programs in community relations and services, foreign affairs, national defense, and veterans' affairs. Monitors legislation and regulations that affect veterans.

Marine Corps League, *8626 Lee Hwy., #201, Fairfax, VA 22031 (mailing address: P.O. Box 3070, Merrifield, VA 22116); (703) 207-9588. Fax, (703) 207-0047. William "Brooks" Corley Jr., Executive Director. Information, (800) 625-1775.*
General e-mail, mcl@mcleague.org
Web, www.mcleague.org

Membership: active duty, retired, and reserve Marine Corps groups. Chartered by Congress to assist veterans with claims for benefits. Operates a volunteer service program in VA hospitals.

Military Officers Assn. of America, *201 N. Washington St., Alexandria, VA 22314-2539; (703) 549-2311. Fax, (703) 838-8173. Norbert R. Ryan Jr., President. Information, (800) 234-6622.*
General e-mail, msc@moaa.org
Web, www.moaa.org

Membership: officers, former officers, and surviving spouses of officers of the uniformed services. Assists members, their dependents, and survivors with military personnel matters, including service status and retirement problems; provides employment assistance. Monitors legislation affecting active duty officers, retirees, and veterans affairs, health, and military compensation issues.

Military Order of the Purple Heart of the U.S.A., *5413-B Backlick Rd., Springfield, VA 22151-3960; (703) 642-5360. Fax, (703) 642-2054. Jay H. Phillips, Adjutant General.*
General e-mail, info@purpleheart.org
Web, www.purpleheart.org

Membership: veterans awarded the Purple Heart for combat wounds. Chartered by Congress to assist veterans with claims for benefits. Conducts service and welfare work on behalf of disabled and needy veterans and their families.

National Coalition for Homeless Veterans, *333 1/2 Pennsylvania Ave. S.E. 20003-1148; (202) 546-1969. Fax, (202) 546-2063. Linda J. Boone, Executive Director.*

General e-mail, nchv@nchv.org
Web, www.nchv.org

Provides technical assistance to service providers; advocates on behalf of homeless veterans.

National Veterans Legal Services Program, *2001 S St. N.W., #610 20009; (202) 265-8305. Fax, (202) 328-0063. David F. Addlestone, Joint Executive Director; Barton F. Stichman, Joint Executive Director.*
General e-mail, nvlsp@nvlsp.org
Web, www.nvlsp.org

Represents the interests of veterans through educational programs, advocacy, public policy programming, and litigation.

Noncommissioned Officers Assn., *Washington Office,* *610 Madison St., Alexandria, VA 22314; (703) 549-0311. Fax, (703) 549-0245. David W. Sommers, President.*
Web, www.ncoausa.org

Congressionally chartered and accredited by the Veterans Affairs Dept. to assist veterans and widows of veterans with claims for benefits. (Headquarters in San Antonio, Texas.)

Paralyzed Veterans of America, *801 18th St. N.W. 20006-3517; (202) 872-1300. Fax, (202) 785-4452. Delatorro (Del) McNeal, Executive Director. Information, (800) 424-8200. TTY, (202) 416-7622.*
General e-mail, info@pva.org
Web, www.pva.org

Congressionally chartered organization that assists veterans with claims for benefits. Distributes information on special education for paralyzed veterans; advocates for quality care and supports and raises funds for medical research.

Retired Enlisted Assn., *Washington Office,* *909 N. Washington St., #301, Alexandria, VA 22314-1555; (703) 684-1981. Fax, (703) 548-4876. Deidre Park Holleman, National Legislative Director. Toll-free, (800) 554-8732.*
General e-mail, treadmin@treadc.org
Web, www.trea.org

Membership: enlisted personnel who have retired for length of service or medical reasons from the active, reserve, or guard components of the armed forces. Runs scholarship, legislative, and veterans service programs. (Headquarters in Aurora, Colo.)

Veterans of Foreign Wars of the United States, *National Veterans Service, 200 Maryland Ave. N.E. 20002; (202) 543-2239. Fax, (202) 547-3196. Bill Bradshaw Jr., Director.*

General e-mail, vfw@vfwdc.org
Web, www.vfw.org

Chartered by Congress to assist veterans with claims for benefits, including disability compensation, education, and pensions. Inspects VA health care facilities and cemeteries. Monitors medical updates and employment practices regarding veterans.

Veterans of the Battle of the Bulge, *P.O. Box 11129, Arlington, VA 22210-2129; (703) 528-4058. Nancy Monson, Administrative Director.*

Membership: veterans who were awarded the Ardennes Campaign battle star and their families; historians; and other interested individuals. Maintains historical data on the Battle of the Bulge; sponsors reunions, memorial services, and educational programs; fosters international peace.

Veterans of World War I of the U.S.A., *P.O. Box 8027, Alexandria, VA 22306; (703) 780-5660. Fax, (703) 780-8465. Muriel Sue Parkhurst, Executive Director.*

Fraternal organization of veterans of wartime service in World War I. Chartered by Congress to assist veterans with claims for benefits. Maintains representatives in VA hospitals.

Vietnam Veterans of America, *8605 Cameron St., #400, Silver Spring, MD 20910-3710; (301) 585-4000. Fax, (301) 585-0519. Thomas Corey, President. Information, (800) VVA-1316.*
General e-mail, vva@vva.org
Web, www.vva.org

Congressionally chartered membership organization that provides information on legislation that affects Vietnam era veterans and their families. Engages in legislative and judicial advocacy in areas relevant to Vietnam era veterans. Provides information concerning benefits and initiates programs that ensure access to education and employment opportunities. Promotes full accounting of POWs and MIAs.

Appeals of VA Decisions

AGENCIES

Defense Dept. (DoD), *Legal Policy, 4000 Defense Pentagon, #4C759 20301-4000; (703) 697-3387. Fax, (703) 693-6708. Col. Steve Strong, Director.*
Web, www.defenselink.mil

Coordinates policy for armed services boards charged with correcting military records and reviewing discharges.

Veterans Affairs Dept. (VA), *Board of Veterans Appeals, 810 Vermont Ave. N.W., #845 20420; (202) 565-5001. Fax, (202) 565-5587. Eligah Dane Clark, Chair.*

Web, www.va.gov

Final appellate body within the department; reviews claims for veterans' benefits on appeal from agencies of original jurisdiction. Decisions of the board are subject to review by the U.S. Court of Veterans Appeals.

JUDICIARY

U.S. Court of Appeals for the Federal Circuit, *717 Madison Pl. N.W. 20439; (202) 633-6556. Fax, (202) 633-6353. Haldane Robert Mayer, Chief Judge; Jan Horbaly, Clerk, (202) 633-9614. Electronic bulletin board, (202) 633-9608 or (202) 786-6584.*

Reviews decisions concerning the Veteran's Judicial Review Provisions.

U.S. Court of Appeals for Veterans Claims, *625 Indiana Ave. N.W., #900 20004-2950; (202) 501-5970. Fax, (202) 501-5849. Kenneth B. Kramer, Chief Judge.*
Web, www.vetapp.uscourts.gov

Independent court that reviews decisions of the VA's Board of Veterans Appeals concerning benefits. Focuses primarily on disability benefits claims.

NONPROFIT

American Legion National Organization, *Operations and Training, 1608 K St. N.W. 20006; (202) 861-2700. Fax, (202) 861-2728. Philip R. Wilkerson, Deputy Manager.*
Web, www.legion.org

Membership: honorably discharged wartime veterans of World War I, World War II, the Korean War, the Vietnam War, or conflicts in Lebanon, Grenada, Panama, and the Persian Gulf. Assists veterans with appeals before the Veterans Affairs Dept. for benefits claims.

American Legion National Organization, *Review and Correction Boards Unit, 1608 K St. N.W. 20006-2847; (202) 861-2700. Fax, (202) 861-2728. John Zangas and Ray Spencer, Supervisors.*
Web, www.legion.org

Membership: honorably discharged wartime veterans of World War I, World War II, the Korean War, the Vietnam War, or conflicts in Lebanon, Grenada, Panama, and the Persian Gulf. Represents before the Defense Dept. former military personnel seeking to upgrade less-than-honorable discharges and to correct alleged errors in military records.

National Veterans Legal Services Program, *2001 S St. N.W., #610 20009; (202) 265-8305. Fax, (202) 328-0063. David F. Addlestone and Barton F. Stichman, Joint Executive Directors.*

General e-mail, nvlsp@nvlsp.org

Web, www.nvlsp.org

Represents the interests of veterans through educational programs, advocacy, public policy programming, and litigation.

Veterans of Foreign Wars of the United States, Appeals, 200 Maryland Ave. N.E. 20002; (202) 543-2239. Fax, (202) 547-3196. George Estry, Representative to U.S. Court of Veterans Appeals for Veterans Claims, (202) 608-8366.

Web, www.vfwdc.org

Assists veterans and their dependents and survivors with appeals before the Veterans Affairs Dept. for benefits claims. Assists with cases in the U.S. Court of Veterans Appeals.

Veterans of Foreign Wars of the United States, Washington Regional Office, 1722 Eye St. N.W., #235 20421; (202) 530-9385. Fax, (202) 775-9475. William G. Crawford, Supervisor.

Web, www.vfwdc.org

Represents before the Military Service Review Board and Correction Board veterans seeking to upgrade less-than-honorable discharges.

Education, Economic Opportunity

AGENCIES

Office of Personnel Management (OPM), Diversity, 1900 E St. N.W., #2445 20415-0001; (202) 606-1059. Fax, (202) 606-0927. Maria Mercedes Olivieri, Director.

Web, www.opm.gov/disability

Responsible for government recruiting policies and guidelines. Advises and assists federal agency offices in the recruitment and employment of minorities, women, veterans, and people with disabilities. Collects and maintains statistics on the federal employment of these groups. Administers the Disabled Veterans Affirmative Action Program.

Small Business Administration (SBA), Veterans Business Development Affairs, 409 3rd St. S.W., 5th Floor 20416; (202) 205-6773. Fax, (202) 205-7292. William D. Elmore, Associate Administrator. TTY, (202) 205-6189.

Web, www.sba.gov

Coordinates programs to give special consideration to veterans in loan, counseling, procurement, and training programs and in transition training sessions.

Veterans Affairs Dept. (VA), Education Service, 1800 G St. N.W., #601B 20006 (mailing address: 810 Vermont Ave. N.W. 20420); (202) 273-7132. Fax, (202) 275-1653.

Judith A. Caden, Director. GI Bill information, (888) 442-4551.

General e-mail, wasco22@vba.va.gov

Web, www.va.gov/education

Administers VA's education program, including financial support for veterans' education and for spouses and dependent children of disabled and deceased disabled veterans; provides eligible veterans and dependents with educational assistance under the G.I. Bill and Veterans Educational Assistance Program. Provides postsecondary institutions with funds, based on their eligible veterans' enrollment.

Veterans Affairs Dept. (VA), Loan Guaranty Service, 810 Vermont Ave. N.W., #525 20420; (202) 273-7332. Fax, (202) 275-3523. R. Keith Pedigo, Director.

Web, www.va.gov

Guarantees private institutional financing of home loans (including manufactured home loans) for veterans; provides disabled veterans with direct loans and grants for specially adapted housing; administers a direct loan program for native American veterans living on trust land.

Veterans Affairs Dept. (VA), Vocational Rehabilitation and Employment Service, 1800 G St. N.W., #501 20006 (mailing address: 810 Vermont Ave. N.W. 20420); (202) 273-7419. Fax, (202) 275-5122. Julius M. Williams Jr., Director.

Web, www.va.gov

Administers VA's vocational rehabilitation and employment program, which provides service-disabled veterans with services and assistance; helps veterans to become employable and to obtain and maintain suitable employment.

Veterans' Employment and Training Service (Labor Dept.), 200 Constitution Ave. N.W., #S1325 20210; (202) 693-4700. Fax, (202) 693-4754. Frederico Juarbe Jr., Assistant Secretary, (202) 693-4700.

Web, www.dol.gov/vets

Works with and monitors state employment offices to see that preference is given to veterans seeking jobs; advises the secretary on veterans' issues.

Veterans' Employment and Training Service (Labor Dept.), Operations and Programs, 200 Constitution Ave. N.W., #S1316 20210; (202) 693-4707. Fax, (202) 693-4755. Gordon Burke, Chief Operating Officer.

Web, www.dol.gov/vets

Investigates veterans' complaints of job or benefits loss because of active or reserve duty military service. Operates in conjunction with state offices to create employment opportunities for veterans.

NONPROFIT

Blinded Veterans Assn., *477 H St. N.W. 20001-2699; (202) 371-8880. Fax, (202) 371-8258. Thomas H. Miller, Director. Information, (800) 669-7079.*
General e-mail, bva@bva.org
Web, www.bva.org

Provides blind and disabled veterans with vocational rehabilitation and employment services.

National Assn. of State Workforce Agencies, *444 N. Capitol St. N.W., #142 20001; (202) 434-8020. Fax, (202) 434-8033. Kathleen A. Cashen, Executive Director.*
Web, www.naswa.org

Membership: state employment security administrators. Provides veterans' employment and training professionals with opportunities for networking and information exchange. Monitors legislation and regulations that affect veterans' employment and training programs involving state employment security agencies.

Paralyzed Veterans of America, *801 18th St. N.W. 20006-3517; (202) 872-1300. Fax, (202) 785-4452. Delatorro (Del) McNeal, Executive Director. Information, (800) 424-8200. TTY, (202) 416-7622.*
General e-mail, info@pva.org
Web, www.pva.org

Congressionally chartered organization that assists veterans with claims for benefits. Promotes access to educational and public facilities and to public transportation for people with disabilities; seeks modification of workplaces.

Health Care, VA Hospitals

AGENCIES

Defense Dept. (DoD), *Deployment Health Support, 5113 Leesburg Pike, #901, Falls Church, VA 22041-3226; (703) 578-8500. Fax, (703) 578-8501. Dr. Michael E. Kilpatrick, Special Assistant. Incident reporting line, (800) 497-6261.*
Web, www.gulflink.osd.mil

Coordinates Defense Dept. investigation of illnesses suffered by Gulf War veterans. Researches links between these illnesses and possible exposure to Iraqi nerve agents. Responds to inquiries from veterans and their families.

Public Health and Science *(Health and Human Services Dept.), Military Liaison and Veterans Affairs, 200 Independence Ave. S.W., #730E 20201; (202) 205-1840. Fax, (202) 205-2107. Capt. Mary Lambert, Director.*
Web, www.osophs.dhhs.gov/ophs/ovaml.htm

Advises the assistant secretary on health issues that affect veterans and military personnel. Works to identify the health-related needs of veterans and their families and to facilitate the delivery of services.

Veterans Health Administration (VHA), *(Veterans Affairs Dept.), 810 Vermont Ave. N.W., #800 20420; (202) 273-5781. Fax, (202) 273-5787. Dr. Robert H. Roswell, Under Secretary for Health.*
Web, www.va.gov/health_benefits

Recommends policy and administers medical and hospital services for eligible veterans. Publishes guidelines on treatment of veterans exposed to Agent Orange.

Veterans Health Administration (VHA), *(Veterans Affairs Dept.), Academic Affiliations, 810 Vermont Ave. N.W., #475 20420; (202) 273-8946. Fax, (202) 273-9031. Stephanie Pincus, Chief Academic Affiliations Officer.*

Administers education and training programs for health professionals, students, and residents through partnerships with affiliated academic institutions.

Veterans Health Administration (VHA), *(Veterans Affairs Dept.), Dentistry, 810 Vermont Ave. N.W., MC 112-D 20420; (202) 273-8503. Fax, (202) 273-9105. Dr. Robert T. Frame, Assistant Under Secretary.*

Administers VA oral health care programs; coordinates oral research, education, and training of VA oral health personnel and outpatient dental care in private practice.

Veterans Health Administration (VHA), *(Veterans Affairs Dept.), Facilities Management, 810 Vermont Ave. N.W., MC 18 20420; (202) 565-5009. Fax, (202) 565-4155. C. V. Yarbrough, Chief Facilities Management Officer.*

Reviews construction policies for VA hospitals.

Veterans Health Administration (VHA), *(Veterans Affairs Dept.), Geriatrics and Extended Care, 810 Vermont Ave. N.W., MC 114 20420; (202) 273-8540. Fax, (202) 273-9131. Dr. James F. Burris, Chief Consultant.*
Web, www.va.gov

Administers research, educational, and clinical health care programs in geriatrics, including VA and community nursing homes, personal care homes, VA domiciliaries, state veterans' homes, and hospital-based home care.

Veterans Health Administration (VHA), *(Veterans Affairs Dept.), Mental Health Strategic Health Care Group, 810 Vermont Ave. N.W., MC 116 20420; (202) 273-8440. Fax, (202) 273-9069. Dr. Laurent S. Lehmann, Chief Consultant.*

Develops ambulatory and inpatient psychiatry and psychology programs for the mentally ill and for drug and alcohol abusers; programs are offered in VA facilities and twenty-two Veterans Integrated Service Networks. Incorporates special programs for veterans suffering from post-traumatic stress disorders, serious mental illness, addictive disorders, and homelessness.

Veterans Health Administration (VHA), *(Veterans Affairs Dept.), Patient Care Services,* 810 Vermont Ave. N.W., MC 11 20420; (202) 273-8474. Fax, (202) 273-9274. Dr. Thomas Holohan, Chief Officer.
Web, www.va.gov

Manages clinical programs of the VA medical care system.

Veterans Health Administration (VHA), *(Veterans Affairs Dept.), Policy and Planning,* 810 Vermont Ave. N.W., MC 105 20420; (202) 273-8932. Fax, (202) 273-9030. Greg A. Pane, Chief Policy and Planning Officer.
Web, www.va.gov

Coordinates and develops departmental planning to distribute funds to VA field facilities.

Veterans Health Administration (VHA), *(Veterans Affairs Dept.), Readjustment Counseling,* 810 Vermont Ave. N.W., MC 15 20420; (202) 273-8967. Fax, (202) 273-9071. Alfonso R. Batres, Chief.
Web, www.va.gov/rcs

Responsible for community-based centers for veterans nationwide. Provides outreach and counseling services for war-related psychological problems and transition to civilian life.

Veterans Health Administration (VHA), *(Veterans Affairs Dept.), Research and Development,* 810 Vermont Ave. N.W., MC 12 20420; (202) 254-0183. Fax, (202) 254-0460. Dr. Nelda Wray, Chief Medical Director.
Web, www.va.gov

Formulates and implements policy for the research and development program of the Veterans Health Administration; advises the undersecretary for health on research-related matters and on management of the VA's health care system; represents the VA in interactions with external organizations in matters related to biomedical and health services research.

Veterans Health Administration (VHA), *(Veterans Affairs Dept.), Voluntary Service,* 810 Vermont Ave. N.W., MC 10C2 20420; (202) 273-8952. Fax, (202) 273-9040. Jim W. Delgado, Director.
Web, www.va.gov/volunteer

Supervises volunteer programs in VA medical centers.

CONGRESS

House Veterans' Affairs Committee, *Subcommittee on Health,* 338 CHOB 20515; (202) 225-9154. Fax, (202) 226-4536. Rep. Rob Simmons, R-Conn., Chair; John Bradley, Staff Director.
Web, veterans.house.gov

Jurisdiction over legislation on veterans' hospitals, medical programs, outpatient programs, state veterans' homes, and construction of medical facilities.

Senate Veterans' Affairs Committee, SR-412 20510; (202) 224-9126. Fax, (202) 224-9575. Sen. Arlen Specter, R-Pa., Chair; William Tuerk, Chief Counsel.
Web, veterans.senate.gov

Jurisdiction over legislation on veterans' hospitals, medical programs, outpatient programs, state veterans' homes, and construction of medical facilities.

NONPROFIT

National Assn. of VA Physicians and Dentists, 11 Canal Center Plaza, #110, Alexandria, VA 22314; (703) 548-0280. Fax, (703) 683-7939. C. William Booher, Executive Director.
General e-mail, navapd@dgsys.com
Web, www.navapd.org

Seeks to improve the quality of care and conditions at VA hospitals. Monitors legislation and regulations on veterans' health care.

National Conference on Ministry in the Armed Forces, *Endorsers Conference for Veterans Affairs Chaplaincy,* 4141 N. Henderson Rd., #13, Arlington, VA 22203; (703) 276-7905. Fax, (703) 276-7906. Jack Williamson, Executive Director.

Encourages religious ministry to veterans in VA hospitals, centers, and the department of defense.

National Gulf War Resource Center, 8605 Cameron St., #400, Silver Spring, MD 20910; (301) 585-4000. Fax, (301) 515-4963. Steve Robinson, Executive Director; Michael Woods, President. Information, (800) 882-1316, ext. 162.
General e-mail, hq@ngwrc.org
Web, www.ngwrc.org

Supports grassroots efforts of national and international Gulf War veterans associations. Provides information and referrals on health and benefits. Monitors legislation and regulations.

Paralyzed Veterans of America, 801 18th St. N.W. 20006-3517; (202) 872-1300. Fax, (202) 785-4452. Delatorro (Del) McNeal, Executive Director. Information, (800) 424-8200. TTY, (202) 416-7622.

General e-mail, info@pva.org

Web, www.pva.org

Congressionally chartered veterans' service organization. Consults with the Veterans Affairs Dept. on the establishment and operation of spinal cord injury treatment centers.

Spouses, Dependents, and Survivors

AGENCIES

Air Force Dept. *(Defense Dept.), Personnel,* 1040 Air Force Pentagon, #4E194 20330-1040; (703) 697-6088. Fax, (703) 697-6091. Lt. Gen. Richard E. Brown III, Deputy Chief of Staff. Toll-free casualty assistance, (800) 433-0048.

Web, www.af.mil

Military office that responds to inquiries concerning deceased Air Force personnel and their beneficiaries; refers inquiries to the Military Personnel Center at Randolph Air Force Base in San Antonio, Texas.

Army Dept. *(Defense Dept.), Casualty Operations,* 2461 Eisenhower Ave., #920, Alexandria, VA 22332-0481; (703) 325-7990. Fax, (703) 325-0134. Lt. Col. Tracy Nicholson, Chief.

Web, www.army.mil

Verifies beneficiaries of deceased Army personnel for benefits distribution.

Marine Corps *(Defense Dept.), Casualty Section,* HQUSMC, 3280 Russell Rd., Quantico, VA 22134-5103; (703) 784-9580. Fax, (703) 784-9823. Ann Hammers, Head.

Web, www.usmc.mil

Confirms beneficiaries of deceased Marine Corps personnel for benefits distribution.

NONPROFIT

American Gold Star Mothers Inc., 2128 LeRoy Pl. N.W. 20008-1893; (202) 265-0991. Fax, (202) 265-6963. Dorothy Ovendine, National President; Ann Wolcott, Washington Representative.

General e-mail, agsmoms@aol.com

Web, www.goldstarmoms.com

Membership: mothers who have lost sons or daughters in military service. (World War I to the present). Members serve as volunteers in VA hospitals.

Army and Air Force Mutual Aid Assn., 102 Sheridan Ave., Fort Myer, VA 22211-1110; (703) 522-3060. Fax, (703) 522-1336. Maj. Walt Lincoln, President. Information, (800) 336-4538.

General e-mail, info@aafmaa.com

Web, www.aafmaa.com

Private service organization that offers member and family insurance services to Army and Air Force officers. Recognized by the Veterans Affairs Dept. to assist veterans and their survivors with claims for benefits.

Army Distaff Foundation, 6200 Oregon Ave. N.W. 20015-1543; (202) 541-0105. Fax, (202) 364-2856. Maj. Gen. Donald C. Hilbert, Executive Director. Information, (800) 541-4255.

Web, www.armydistaff.org

Nonprofit continuing care retirement community for career military officers and their families. Provides retirement housing and health care services.

EX-POSE, Ex-partners of Servicemembers for Equality, P.O. Box 11191, Alexandria, VA 22312; (703) 941-5844. Fax, (703) 212-6951. Vacant, Director.

General e-mail, ex-pose@juno.com

Membership: former partners of military members, both officers and enlisted, and other interested parties. Seeks federal laws to restore to ex-spouses benefits lost through divorce, including retirement pay; survivors' benefits; and medical, commissary, and exchange benefits. Provides information concerning legal resources and related federal laws and regulations. Serves as an information clearinghouse.

National Assn. of Military Widows, 4023 N. 25th Rd., Arlington, VA 22207; (703) 527-4565. Fax, (703) 527-2881. Jean Arthurs, President.

Provides military widows with referral information on survivor benefit programs; helps locate widows eligible for benefits. Interests include health and education. Monitors legislation.

No Greater Love, 1750 New York Ave. N.W. 20006; (202) 783-4665. Fax, (202) 783-1168. Benjamin Barbin, Executive Director.

General e-mail, remembrance@ngl.org

Web, www.ngl.org

Provides programs of remembrance, friendship, and care for families of Americans killed in war or by acts of terrorism.

Society of Military Widows, 5535 Hempstead Way, Springfield, VA 22151; (703) 750-1342. Fax, (703) 354-4380. Clara Sasser, President.

Web, www.militarywidows.org

Serves the interests of widows of servicemen who died while in active military service; provides support programs and information. Monitors legislation concerning military widows' benefits. (Affiliated with the National Assn. for Uniformed Services.)

16

National and Homeland Security

🖾 GENERAL POLICY

AGENCIES

Air Force Dept. *(Defense Dept.),* *1670 Air Force Pentagon, #4E874 20330-1670; (703) 697-7376. Fax, (703) 695-8809. Peter B. Teets, Under Secretary. Information, (703) 695-0640.*

Web, www.af.mil

Civilian office that develops and reviews Air Force national security policies in conjunction with the chief of staff of the Air Force and the secretary of defense.

Air Force Dept. *(Defense Dept.), **Chief of Staff,** 1670 Air Force Pentagon, #4E924 20330-1670; (703) 697-9225. Fax, (703) 693-9297. Gen. John P. Jumper, Chief of Staff.*

Web, www.hq.af.mil

Military office that develops and directs Air Force national security policies in conjunction with the secretary of the Air Force and the secretary of defense.

Army Dept. *(Defense Dept.), 101 Army Pentagon, #3E700 20310-0101; (703) 697-3211. Fax, (703) 697-8036. James G. Roche, Secretary (Designate). Press, (703) 697-4200.*

Web, www.army.mil

Civilian office that develops and reviews Army national security policies in conjunction with the chief of staff of the Army and the secretary of defense.

Army Dept. *(Defense Dept.), **Chief of Staff,** 200 Army Pentagon, #3E668 20310-0200; (703) 695-2077. Fax, (703) 614-5268. Eric K. Shinseki, Chief of Staff. Press, (703) 697-8719.*

Web, www.army.mil

Military office that develops and administers Army national security policies in conjunction with the secretary of the Army and the secretary of defense.

Defense Dept. (DoD), *1000 Defense Pentagon, #3E880 20301-1000; (703) 692-7100. Fax, (703) 697-9080. Donald Rumsfeld, Secretary; Paul D. Wolfowitz, Deputy Secretary. Information, (703) 428-0711. Press, (703) 697-5131. Tours, (703) 697-1776.*

Web, www.defenselink.mil

Civilian office that develops national security policies and has overall responsibility for administering national defense; responds to public and congressional inquiries about national defense matters.

Defense Dept. (DoD), *Homeland Defense, 2000 Defense Pentagon 20301-1000; (703) 697-7200. Paul McHale, Assistant Secretary.*

Web, www.defenselink.mil

Serves as primary liaison between the Defense Dept. and the Homeland Security Dept. Supervises all Defense Dept. homeland defense activities.

Defense Dept. (DoD), *Installations and Environment, 3400 Defense Pentagon, #3E792 20301-3400; (703) 697-8080. Fax, (703) 693-7011. Raymond F. DuBois, Deputy Under Secretary.*

Web, www.acq.osd.mil/ie

Oversees and offers policy guidance for all Defense Dept. installations and environmental programs.

Defense Dept. (DoD), *International Security Policy, 2900 Defense Pentagon, #4E817 20301-2900; (703) 697-7728. Fax, (703) 693-9146. J. D. Crouch II, Assistant Secretary.*

Web, www.defenselink.mil

Develops and coordinates national security and defense strategies and advises on the resources, forces, and contingency plans necessary to implement those strategies. Ensures the integration of defense strategy into the department's resource allocation, force structure development, weapons system acquisition, and budgetary processes. Evaluates the capability of forces to accomplish defense strategy.

Defense Dept. (DoD), *Joint Chiefs of Staff, 9999 Defense Pentagon, #2E872 20318-9999; (703) 697-9121. Gen. Richard B. Myers, Chair.*

Web, www.dtic.mil/jcs

Joint military staff office that assists the president, the National Security Council, and the secretary of defense in developing national security policy and in coordinating operations of the individual armed services.

Defense Dept. (DoD), *Policy, 2000 Defense Pentagon, #4E830 20301-2000; (703) 697-7200. Fax, (703) 697-6602. Douglas J. Feith, Under Secretary.*

Web, www.defenselink.mil/policy/index.html

Civilian office responsible for policy matters relating to international security issues and political-military affairs. Oversees such areas as arms control, foreign military sales, intelligence collection and analysis, and NATO and regional security affairs.

Defense Dept. (DoD), *Special Operations and Low-Intensity Conflict, 2500 Defense Pentagon, #2E258 20301-2500; (703) 693-2895. Fax, (703) 693-6335. Vacant, Assistant Secretary; Marshall S. Billingslea, Principal Deputy Assistant Secretary.*

Web, www.defenselink.mil

Serves as special staff assistant and civilian adviser to the secretary of defense on matters related to special

DEFENSE DEPARTMENT

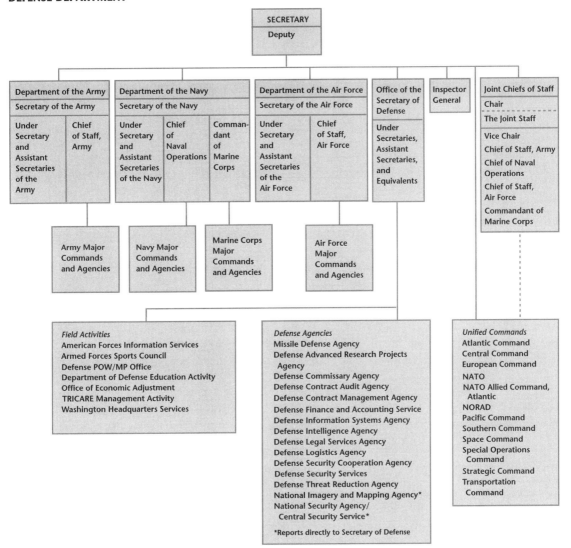

operations and low-intensity conflict. Responsible for the Army's Green Berets, the Navy Seals, and other special operations forces. Oversees counterdrug efforts and humanitarian and refugee affairs for the Defense Dept.

Homeland Security Dept. (DHS), *Nebraska Ave. Complex, 3801 Nebraska Ave. N.W. 20395; (202) 282-8000. Thomas J. Ridge, Secretary; Gordon R. England, Deputy Secretary.*
Web, www.dhs.gov

Responsible for the development and coordination of a comprehensive national strategy to protect the United States against terrorist attacks. Coordinates the strategy of the executive branch together with state and local governments and private entities to detect, prepare for, protect against, respond to, and recover from terrorist attacks in the United States.

Homeland Security Dept. (DHS), *Science and Technology Directorate, Nebraska Ave. Complex, 3801 Nebraska Ave. N.W. 20395; (202) 282-8000. Charles E. McQueary, Under Secretary.*

HOMELAND SECURITY DEPARTMENT

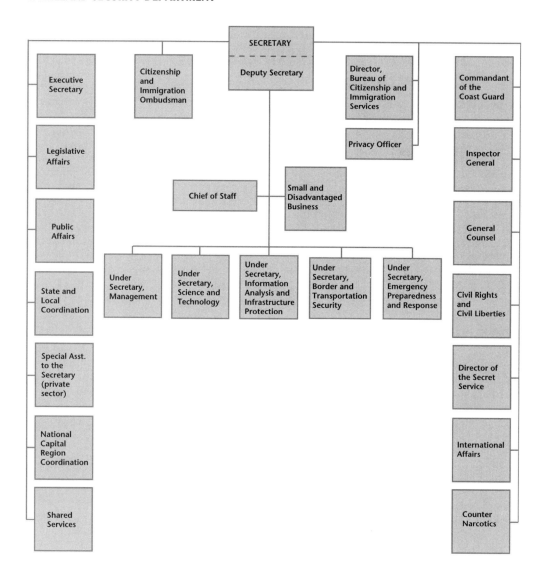

Web, www.dhs.gov

Responsible for oversight and coordination of the development and augmentation of homeland security technology.

Marine Corps *(Defense Dept.), **Commandant,** Navy Annex 20370 (mailing address: Marine Corps Headquarters 20380-1775); (703) 614-2500. Fax, (703) 697-7246. Michael W. Hagee, Commandant. Information, (703) 614-8010. Press, (703) 614-1492.*
Web, www.hqmc.usmc.mil

Military office that develops and directs Marine Corps national security policies in conjunction with the secretary of defense and the secretary of the Navy.

National Security Council (NSC), *(Executive Office of the President), **Combating Terrorism,** Dwight D. Eisenhower Executive Office Bldg., #303 20504; (202) 456-9361. Gen. John A. Gordon, National Director and Deputy National Security Adviser.*
Web, www.whitehouse.gov/nsc

Advises the president on combating global terrorism.

Navy Dept. *(Defense Dept.),* 1000 Navy Pentagon, #4E686 20350-1000; (703) 695-3131. Fax, (703) 697-3991. Vacant, Under Secretary; H. T. Johnson, Secretary *(Acting). Information, (703) 697-7491. Press, (703) 695-0911.*

Web, www.navy.mil

Civilian office that develops and reviews Navy and Marine Corps national security policies in conjunction with the chief of naval operations, the commandant of the Marine Corps, and the secretary of defense.

Navy Dept. *(Defense Dept.), Naval Operations,* 2000 Navy Pentagon, #4E660 20350-2000; (703) 695-6007. Fax, (703) 693-9408. Adm. Vern Clark, Chief. Information, (703) 692-5306.

Web, www.navy.mil

Military office that develops Navy national security policies in conjunction with the secretary of defense and the secretary of the Navy and in cooperation with the commandant of the Marine Corps.

State Dept., *Foreign Missions,* 2201 C St. N.W., #2238 20520; (202) 647-4554. Fax, (202) 647-1919. Lynwood M. Dent Jr., Deputy Assistant Secretary.

Web, www.state.gov

Authorized to control the numbers, locations, and travel privileges of foreign diplomats and diplomatic staff in the United States.

State Dept., *Political-Military Affairs,* 2201 C St. N.W., #6212 20520; (202) 647-9022. Fax, (202) 736-4779. Lincoln P. Bloomfield Jr., Assistant Secretary.

Web, www.state.gov

Responsible for security affairs policy; acts as a liaison between the Defense Dept. and the State Dept.

U.S. Coast Guard (USCG), *(Homeland Security Dept.),* 2100 2nd St. S.W. 20593-0001; (202) 267-2390. Fax, (202) 267-4158. Adm. Thomas H. Collins, Commandant. Information, (202) 267-1587.

Web, www.uscg.mil

Provides homeland security for U.S. harbors, ports, and coastlines. Implements heightened security measures for commercial, tanker, passenger, and merchant vessels. Enforces federal laws on the high seas and navigable waters of the United States and its possessions; maintains a state of military readiness to assist the Navy in time of war or when directed by the president.

CONGRESS

House Appropriations Committee, *Subcommittee on Defense,* H149 CAP 20515; (202) 225-2847. Fax, (202) 225-2822. Rep. Jerry Lewis, R-Calif., Chair; Kevin M. Roper, Staff Director.

Web, www.house.gov/appropriations

Jurisdiction over legislation to appropriate funds for the Defense Dept., excluding Army Corps of Engineers; defense agencies, excluding military construction, civil defense, and Military to Military Program; the Central Intelligence Agency; and the intelligence community.

House Appropriations Committee, *Subcommittee on Homeland Security,* B307 RHOB 20515; (202) 225-5834. Rep. Harold Rogers, R-Ky., Chair; Michelle Mrdeza, Staff Director.

Web, www.house.gov/appropriations

Jurisdiction over legislation to appropriate funds for the Homeland Security Dept.; Animal and Plant Health Inspection Service; Bureau of Citizenship and Immigration Services; Bureau of Customs and Border Protection; Defense National Stockpile Center; Federal Emergency Management Agency; Federal Flight Deck Officer Program; Federal Law Enforcement Training Center; Federal Protective Service; first responder programs (police officers, firefighters, emergency medical teams); Homeland Security Advisory System; metropolitan medical response systems; National Communications Systems and Bio-Weapons Defense Center; National Disaster Medical System; National Homeland Security Council; National Infrastructure Protection Center; Office of Emergency Preparedness; Transportation Security Administration; U.S. Coast Guard; U.S. Secret Service.

House Appropriations Committee, *Subcommittee on Transportation, Treasury, and Related Agencies,* 2358 RHOB 20515; (202) 225-2141. Fax, (202) 225-5895. Rep. Ernest Istook, R-Okla., Chair; Richard Efford, Clerk.

Web, www.house.gov/appropriations

Jurisdiction over legislation to appropriate funds for the Executive Office of the President, including the National Security Council.

House Armed Services Committee, 2120 RHOB 20515; (202) 225-4151. Fax, (202) 225-9077. Rep. Duncan Hunter, R-Calif., Chair; Robert S. Rangel, Staff Director.

Web, www.house.gov/hasc

Jurisdiction over defense legislation. Oversight of the Defense Dept., including the Army, Navy, and Air Force Depts.

House Government Reform Committee, *Subcommittee on National Security, Emerging Threats, and International Relations,* B372 RHOB 20515; (202) 225-2548. Fax, (202) 225-2382. Rep. Christopher Shays, R-Conn., Chair; Lawrence Halloran, Staff Director.

Web, www.house.gov/reform

Jurisdiction includes the efficiency and management of government operations and activities, specifically within agencies responsible for the nation's defense.

House Select Committee on Homeland Security, *2402 RHOB 20515; (202) 226-8417. Rep. Christopher Cox, R-Calif., Chair; John C. Gannon, Staff Director. Web, hsc.house.gov*

Reviews and studies on a continuing basis laws, programs, and government activities relating to homeland security.

Senate Appropriations Committee, *Subcommittee on Defense, SD-119 20510; (202) 224-7255. Sen. Ted Stevens, R-Alaska, Chair; Sid Ashworth, Clerk. Web, appropriations.senate.gov*

Jurisdiction over legislation to appropriate funds for the Defense Dept., the Central Intelligence Agency, and the intelligence community.

Senate Appropriations Committee, *Subcommittee on Homeland Security, SD-136 20510; (202) 224-4319. Fax, (202) 224-8553. Sen. Thad Cochran, R-Miss., Chair; Rebecca Davies, Clerk. Web, appropriations.senate.gov*

Jurisdiction over legislation to appropriate funds for the Homeland Security Dept.; Animal and Plant Health Inspection Service; Bio-Weapons Defense Center; Bureau of Citizenship and Immigration Services; Bureau of Customs and Border Protection; Federal Emergency Management Agency; Federal Flight Deck Officer Program; Federal Law Enforcement Training Center; Federal Protective Service; first responder programs (police officers, firefighters, emergency medical teams); Homeland Security Advisory System; Metropolitan Medical Response Systems; National Communications Systems; National Disaster Medical System; National Homeland Security Council; Office of Emergency Preparedness; Transportation Security Administration; U.S. Coast Guard; and U.S. Secret Service.

Senate Appropriations Committee, *Subcommittee on Transportation, Treasury, and General Government, SD-196 20510; (202) 224-4869. Fax, (202) 228-1621. Sen. Richard C. Shelby, R-Ala., Chair; Paul Doerrer, Clerk. Web, appropriations.senate.gov*

Jurisdiction over legislation to appropriate funds for the Executive Office of the President, including the National Security Council.

Senate Armed Services Committee, *SR-228 20510; (202) 224-3871. Fax, (202) 228-0036. Sen. John W. Warner, R-Va., Chair; Judy Ansley, Staff Director. Web, armed-services.senate.gov*

Jurisdiction over defense legislation. Oversight of the Defense Dept., including the Army, Navy, and Air Force Depts.

Senate Governmental Affairs Committee, *SD-340 20510; (202) 224-4751. Fax, (202) 224-9682. Sen. Susan Collins, R-Maine, Chair; Michael Bopp, Staff Director. Web, govt-aff.senate.gov*

Jurisdiction includes the efficiency and economy of all branches of government and the effectiveness of present national security methods.

NONPROFIT

Air Force Assn., *1501 Lee Hwy., Arlington, VA 22209-1198; (703) 247-5800. Fax, (703) 247-5853. Donald L. Peterson, Executive Director. Information, (800) 727-3337. Library, (703) 247-5829. Press, (703) 247-5850. General e-mail, custserv@afa.org Web, www.afa.org*

Membership: civilians and active, reserve, retired, and cadet personnel of the Air Force. Informs members and the public of developments in the aerospace field. Monitors legislation and Defense Dept. policies. Library on aviation history open to the public by appointment.

American Conservative Union (ACU), *1007 Cameron St., Alexandria, VA 22314; (703) 836-8602. Fax, (703) 836-8606. Stephen Thayer, Executive Director. Information, (800) 228-7345. General e-mail, acu@conservative.org Web, www.conservative.org*

Legislative interest organization concerned with national defense policy, legislation related to nuclear weapons, U.S. strategic position vis-à-vis the former Soviet Union, missile defense programs, U.S. troops under U.N. command, and U.S. strategic alliance commitments.

American Defense Institute (ADI), *Pride in America, 1055 N. Fairfax St., #200, Alexandria, VA 22314; (703) 519-7000. Fax, (703) 519-8627. Eugene B. McDaniel, President. General e-mail, rdt2@americandefinst.org*

Nonpartisan organization that advocates a strong national defense. Acts as an information clearinghouse on issues related to national security. Seeks to educate young Americans on matters of defense and foreign policy.

American Enterprise Institute for Public Policy Research (AEI), *Foreign and Defense Policy Studies, 1150 17th St. N.W., #1100 20036; (202) 862-5814. Fax, (202) 862-7177. Jeane Kirkpatrick, Director. Information, (202) 862-5800. Press, (202) 862-4871.*

Web, www.aei.org

Research and educational organization that conducts conferences, seminars, and debates and sponsors research on national security, defense policy, and arms control.

American Security Council, *201A N. Main St., Culpepper, VA 22713; (540) 829-8005. Fax, (540) 829-8333. Dr. Henry A. Fischer, Chair.*

Bipartisan organization that advocates continuation of the strategic modernization program and stable funding for the space program, new technologies, and conventional forces. Monitors legislation and conducts educational activities.

ANSER Institute for Homeland Security, *2900 S. Quincy St., #800, Arlington, VA 22206-2233; (703) 416-3597. Fax, (703) 416-4451. Randy Larsen, Director. General e-mail, homelandsecurity@anser.org*
Web, www.homelandsecurity.org

Public-service research organization that examines the homeland security challenges faced by the United States in the twenty-first century. Explores issues, conducts research, works to promote dialogue, and provides executive education through workshops, conferences, publications, and outreach programs.

Assn. of the United States Army, *2425 Wilson Blvd., Arlington, VA 22201; (703) 841-4300. Fax, (703) 525-9039. Gordon R. Sullivan, President. Information, (800) 336-4570.*
Web, www.ausa.org

Membership: civilians and active and retired members of the armed forces. Conducts symposia on defense issues and researches topics that affect the military.

Atlantic Council of the United States, *910 17th St. N.W., 10th Floor 20006; (202) 463-7226. Fax, (202) 463-7241. Christopher J. Makins, President.*
General e-mail, info@acus.org
Web, www.acus.org

Conducts studies and makes policy recommendations on American foreign security and international economic policies in the Atlantic and Pacific communities; sponsors conferences and educational exchanges.

The Brookings Institution, *Foreign Policy Studies, 1775 Massachusetts Ave. N.W. 20036; (202) 797-6400. Fax, (202) 797-6003. James B. Steinberg, Director. Information, (202) 797-6000. Press, (202) 797-6105. Publications, (202) 797-6258.*
Web, www.brookings.edu

Research and educational organization that focuses on major national security topics, including U.S. armed forces, weapons decisions, terrorism threats, employment policies, and the security aspects of U.S. foreign relations.

Business Executives for National Security, *1717 Pennsylvania Ave. N.W., #350 20006; (202) 296-2125. Fax, (202) 296-2490. Charles G. Boyd, Chief Executive Officer.*
Web, www.bens.org

Monitors legislation on national security issues from a business perspective; holds conferences, congressional forums, and other meetings on national security issues; works with other organizations on defense policy issues.

Center for Defense Information, *1779 Massachusetts Ave. N.W., #615 20036; (202) 332-0600. Fax, (202) 462-4559. Bruce Blair, President. Information, (800) 234-3334.*
General e-mail, info@cdi.org
Web, www.cdi.org

Educational organization that advocates a strong defense while opposing excessive expenditures for weapons and policies that increase the risk of war. Interests include the defense budget, weapons systems, and troop levels. Provides Congress, the Pentagon, State Dept., media, and public with appraisals of military matters.

Center for Naval Analyses, *4825 Mark Center Dr., Alexandria, VA 22311; (703) 824-2000. Fax, (703) 824-2942. Robert J. Murray, President.*
Web, www.cna.org

Conducts research on weapons acquisitions, tactical problems, and naval operations.

Center for Security Policy, *1920 L St. N.W., #210 20036; (202) 835-9077. Fax, (202) 835-9066. Frank J. Gaffney Jr., Director.*
General e-mail, info@centerforsecuritypolicy.org
Web, www.centerforsecuritypolicy.org

Educational institution concerned with U.S. defense and foreign policy. Interests include relations between the United States and the former Soviet Union, arms control compliance and verification policy, and technology transfer policy.

Conservative Caucus, *450 Maple Ave. East, #309, Vienna, VA 22180; (703) 938-9626. Fax, (703) 281-4108. Howard Phillips, Chair.*
Web, www.conservativeusa.org

Legislative interest organization that promotes grassroots activity on national defense and foreign policy.

Defense Orientation Conference Assn., *9271 Old Keene Mill Rd., #200, Burke, VA 22015-4202; (703) 451-1200. Fax, (703) 451-1201. John W. Ohlsen, Executive Vice President.*

General e-mail, info@doca.org

Web, www.doca.org

Membership: citizens interested in national defense. Under the auspices of the Defense Dept., promotes continuing education of members on national security issues through visits to embassies and tours of defense installations in the United States and abroad.

Ethics and Public Policy Center, *Foreign Policy Program, 1015 15th St. N.W., #900 20005; (202) 682-1200. Fax, (202) 408-0632. Hillel Fradkin, President.*

General e-mail, ethics@eppc.org

Web, www.eppc.org

Considers implications of Judeo-Christian moral tradition for domestic and foreign policy making. Conducts research and holds conferences on foreign policy, including the role of the U.S. military abroad.

Henry L. Stimson Center, *11 Dupont Circle N.W., 9th Floor 20036; (202) 223-5956. Fax, (202) 238-9604. Ellen Laipson, President.*

General e-mail, info@stimson.org

Web, www.stimson.org

Research and educational organization that studies arms control and international security, focusing on policy, technology, and politics.

Hudson Institute, *National Security Studies, Washington Office, 1015 18th St. N.W., #300 20036; (202) 223-7770. Fax, (202) 223-8537. William E. Odom, Director.*

Web, www.hudson.org

Public policy research organization that conducts studies on U.S. overseas bases, U.S.-NATO relations, and missile defense programs. Focuses on long-range implications for U.S. national security. (Headquarters in Indianapolis, Ind.)

Institute for Foreign Policy Analysis, *1725 DeSales St. N.W., #402 20036; (202) 463-7942. Fax, (202) 785-2785. Robert L. Pfaltzgraff Jr., President.*

Web, www.ifpa.org

Trains policy analysts in the fields of foreign policy and national security. Sponsors research and workshops.

Institute of International Education, *National Security Education Program, 1400 K St. N.W., #650 20005-2403; (202) 326-7697. Fax, (202) 326-7698. Chris Powers, Deputy Director. Information, (800) 618-6737.*

General e-mail, nsep@iie.org

Web, www.iie.org/nsep

Provides scholarships, fellowships, and institutional grants to academics with an interest in foreign affairs and national security.

Jewish Institute for National Security Affairs (JINSA), *1779 Massachusetts Ave. N.W., #515 20036; (202) 667-3900. Fax, (202) 669-0601. Tom Neumann, Executive Director.*

General e-mail, info@jinsa.org

Web, www.jinsa.org

Seeks to educate the public about the importance of effective U.S. defense capability and inform the U.S. defense and foreign affairs community about Israel's role in Mediterranean and Middle Eastern affairs. Sponsors lectures and conferences; facilitates dialogue between security policymakers, military officials, diplomats, and the general public.

Marine Corps League, *8626 Lee Hwy., #201, Fairfax, VA 22031 (mailing address: P.O. Box 3070, Merrifield, VA 22116); (703) 207-9588. Fax, (703) 207-0047. William "Brooks" Corley Jr., Executive Director. Information, (800) 625-1775.*

General e-mail, mcl@mcleague.org

Web, www.mcleague.org

Membership: active duty, retired, and reserve Marine Corps groups. Promotes the interests of the Marine Corps and works to preserve its traditions; assists veterans and their survivors. Monitors legislation and regulations.

National Institute for Public Policy, *3031 Javier Rd., #300, Fairfax, VA 22031; (703) 698-0563. Fax, (703) 698-0566. Keith B. Payne, President.*

Web, www.nipp.org

Studies public policy and its relation to national security. Interests include arms control, strategic weapons systems and planning, and foreign policy.

Navy League of the United States, *2300 Clarendon Blvd., #705, Arlington, VA 22201 (mailing address: 2300 Wilson Blvd., Arlington, VA 22201); (703) 528-1775. Fax, (703) 528-2333. Charles L. Robinson, National Executive Director.*

General e-mail, mail@navyleague.org

Web, www.navyleague.org

Membership: retired and reserve military personnel and civilians interested in the U.S. Navy, Marine Corps, Coast Guard, and Merchant Marine. Distributes literature, provides speakers, and conducts seminars to promote interests of the sea services. Monitors legislation.

Rand Corporation, *Washington Office,* 1200 S. Hayes St., Arlington, VA 22202-5050; (703) 413-1100. Fax, (703) 413-8111. Bruce Hoffman, Director.

Web, www.rand.org

Conducts research on national security issues, including political/military affairs of the former Soviet Union and U.S. strategic policy. (Headquarters in Santa Monica, Calif.)

Civil Rights and Liberties

AGENCIES

Homeland Security Dept. (DHS), *Chief Privacy Officer,* Nebraska Ave. Complex, 3801 Nebraska Ave. N.W. 20395; (202) 282-8000. Nuala O'Connor Kelly, Director.

Web, www.dhs.gov

Responsible for ensuring that department policies and use of technology do not erode individual privacy. Required to make annual report to Congress and to enforce the provisions of the 1974 Privacy Act, which bars the government from using personal, private information collected for one purpose for a different purpose.

Justice Dept. (DOJ), *Information and Privacy,* 950 Pennsylvania Ave. N.W., #570 20530; (202) 514-3642. Fax, (202) 514-1009. Richard L. Huff, Co-Director; Daniel J. Metcalfe, Co-Director. Information, (202) 514-2000. TTY, (202) 514-1888.

Web, www.usdoj.gov/oip/oip.html

Provides federal agencies with advice and policy guidance on matters related to implementing and interpreting the Freedom of Information Act (FOIA). Litigates selected FOIA and Privacy Act cases; adjudicates administrative appeals from Justice Dept. denials of public requests for access to documents; conducts FOIA training for government agencies.

Office of Management and Budget (OMB), *(Executive Office of the President), Information Policy and Technology,* New Executive Office Bldg., #10236 20503; (202) 395-3785. Fax, (202) 395-5167. Dan Chenok, Chief.

Web, www.whitehouse.gov/omb

Oversees implementation of the Privacy Act of 1974. Issues guidelines and regulations.

CONGRESS

House Government Reform Committee, *Subcommittee on Criminal Justice, Drug Policy, and Human Resources,* B373B RHOB 20515; (202) 225-2577. Fax, (202) 225-1154. Rep. Mark Souder, R-Ind., Chair; Christopher Donesa, Staff Director.

Web, www.house.gov/reform

Reviews policies related to border agencies and immigration, including the accessibility of the U.S.

immigration system and the effects of security measures on civil and individual rights.

House Government Reform Committee, *Subcommittee on Government Efficiency and Financial Management,* B349C RHOB 20515; (202) 225-3741. Fax, (202) 225-2544. Rep. Todd R. Platts, R-Pa., Chair; Mike Hettinger, Staff Director.

Web, www.house.gov/reform

Jurisdiction over the Freedom of Information Act.

House Judiciary Committee, *Subcommittee on the Constitution,* 362 FHOB 20515; (202) 226-7680. Fax, (202) 225-3746. Rep. Steve Chabot, R-Ohio, Chair; Crystal Roberts, Chief Counsel.

General e-mail, Judiciary@mail.house.gov

Web, www.house.gov/judiciary

Jurisdiction over constitutional issues associated with the war on terrorism and homeland security measures.

House Select Committee on Homeland Security, *Subcommittee on Intelligence and Counterterrorism,* 2402 RHOB 20515; (202) 226-8417. Rep. Jim Gibbons, R-Nev., Chair.

Web, hsc.house.gov

Jurisdiction includes the preservation of civil liberties, individual rights, and privacy as it relates to the activities of the Homeland Security Dept.

Senate Judiciary Committee, *Subcommittee on Terrorism, Technology, and Homeland Security,* SH-325 20510; (202) 224-6791. Fax, (202) 228-0542. Sen. Jon Kyl, R-Ariz., Chair; Stephen Higgins, Chief Counsel.

Web, judiciary.senate.gov

Jurisdiction includes laws related to government information policy, electronic privacy and security of computer information, and the Freedom of Information Act; espionage laws and their enforcement.

Senate Judiciary Committee, *Subcommittee on the Constitution, Civil Rights, and Property Rights,* SH-327 20510; (202) 224-2934. Fax, (202) 228-2856. Sen. John Cornyn, R-Texas, Chair; James Ho, Chief Counsel.

Web, judiciary.senate.gov

Jurisdiction includes civil rights, property rights, and individual rights.

NONPROFIT

American Civil Liberties Union (ACLU), *Washington Office,* 1333 H St. N.W., 10th Floor 20005; (202) 544-1681. Fax, (202) 546-0738. Laura Murphy, Legal Director.

Web, www.aclu.org

Initiates test court cases and advocates legislation to guarantee constitutional rights and civil liberties. Monitors agency compliance with the Privacy Act and other access statutes. Produces publications. (Headquarters in New York maintains docket of cases.)

American Society of Access Professionals, *1444 Eye St. N.W., #700 20005; (202) 712-9054. Fax, (202) 216-9646. Claire Shanley, Executive Director.*
General e-mail, asap@bostromdc.com
Web, www.accesspro.org
    Membership: federal employees, attorneys, journalists, and others working with or interested in access-to-information laws. Seeks to improve the administration of the Freedom of Information Act, the Privacy Act, and other access statutes.

Center for Democracy and Technology, *1634 Eye St. N.W., #1100 20006; (202) 637-9800. Fax, (202) 637-0968. James Dempsey, Executive Director.*
General e-mail, info@cdt.org
Web, www.cdt.org
    Promotes civil liberties and democratic values in computer and communications media, both in the United States and abroad. Interests include free speech, privacy, and freedom of information. Monitors legislation and regulations.

Center for National Security Studies, *Gelman Library, 1120 19th St. N.W., #800 20036; (202) 721-5650. Fax, (202) 530-0128. Kate Martin, Director.*
General e-mail, cnss@gwu.edu
Web, www.cnss.org
    Specializes in the Freedom of Information Act as it relates to national security matters and access to government information issues in the United States and abroad.

Electronic Privacy Information Center, *1718 Connecticut Ave. N.W., #200 20009; (202) 483-1140. Fax, (202) 483-1248. Marc Rotenberg, Director.*
General e-mail, info@epic.org
Web, www.epic.org
    Public interest research center. Conducts research and conferences on domestic and international civil liberties issues, including privacy, free speech, information access, computer security, and encryption; litigates cases. Monitors legislation and regulations.

Radio-Television News Directors Assn., *1600 K St. N.W., #700 20006-2838; (202) 659-6510. Fax, (202) 223-4007. Barbara Cochran, President.*
General e-mail, rtnda@rtnda.org
Web, www.rtnda.org
    Membership: local and network news executives in broadcasting, cable, and other electronic media. Oper-

ates the Freedom of Information Committee, which assists members with news access.

Reporters Committee for Freedom of the Press, *1815 N. Fort Myer Dr., #900, Arlington, VA 22209; (703) 807-2100. Fax, (703) 807-2109. Lucy A. Dalglish, Executive Director. Legal defense hotline, (800) 336-4243.*
General e-mail, rcfp@rcfp.org
Web, www.rcfp.org
    Membership: reporters, news editors, publishers, and lawyers from the print and broadcast media. Maintains a legal defense and research fund for members of the news media involved in freedom of the press court cases; interests include access to information and privacy issues faced by journalists covering antiterrorism initiatives and military actions abroad.

Defense and Homeland Security Budgets

AGENCIES

Defense Contract Audit Agency *(Defense Dept.),* *8725 John Jay Kingman Rd., #2135, Fort Belvoir, VA 22060-6219; (703) 767-3200. Fax, (703) 767-3267. William H. Reed, Director; Michael J. Thibault, Deputy Director, (703) 767-3272.*
Web, www.dcaa.mil
    Performs all contract audits for the Defense Dept. Provides Defense Dept. personnel responsible for procurement and contract administration with accounting and financial advisory services regarding the negotiation, administration, and settlement of contracts and subcontracts.

Defense Dept. (DoD), *Comptroller, 1100 Defense Pentagon, #3E822 20301-1100; (703) 695-3237. Fax, (703) 693-0582. Dov S. Zakheim, Comptroller.*
Web, www.defenselink.mil
    Supervises and reviews the preparation and implementation of the defense budget. Advises the secretary of defense on fiscal matters. Collects and distributes information on the department's management of resources.

Homeland Security Dept. (DHS), *Chief Financial Officer, Nebraska Ave. Complex, 3801 Nebraska Ave. N.W. 20395; (202) 282-8000. Bruce M. Carnes, Chief Financial Officer.*
Web, www.dhs.gov
    Responsible for the Homeland Security Dept.'s budget, budget justifications, supplemental spending bill figures, and five-year financial blueprint.

Homeland Security Dept. (DHS), *Management Directorate,* *Nebraska Ave. Complex, 3801 Nebraska Ave. N.W. 20395; (202) 282-8000. Janet Hale, Under Secretary.*
Web, www.dhs.gov

Responsible for Homeland Security Dept. budget, appropriations, expenditure of funds, accounting and finance, procurement, human resources and personnel, information technology systems, facilities, property, equipment and all material resources, and performance measurement.

Office of Management and Budget (OMB), *(Executive Office of the President), Homeland Security,* *New Executive Office Bldg., #9028 20503; (202) 395-5090. David Haun, Chief.*
Web, www.whitehouse.gov/omb

Assists and advises the OMB director on budget preparation, proposed legislation, and evaluations of Homeland Security Dept. programs, policies, and activities.

Office of Management and Budget (OMB), *(Executive Office of the President), National Security,* *New Executive Office Bldg., #10001 20503; (202) 395-3884. Fax, (202) 395-3307. Kathleen Peroff, Deputy Associate Director.*
Web, www.whitehouse.gov/omb

Supervises preparation of the Defense Dept.'s portion of the federal budget.

CONGRESS

General Accounting Office (GAO), *Defense Capabilities and Management,* *441 G St. N.W., #4035 20548; (202) 512-4300. Fax, (202) 512-7686. Henry L. Hinton Jr., Managing Director.*
Web, www.gao.gov

Independent, nonpartisan agency in the legislative branch. Audits, analyzes, and evaluates defense spending programs; makes unclassified reports available to the public.

General Accounting Office (GAO), *Homeland Security and Justice,* *441 G St. N.W., #2A38 20548; (202) 512-8777. Fax, (202) 512-8692. Norm Rabkin, Managing Director; Randall Yim, Managing Director, National Preparedness. Documents, (202) 512-6000.*
Web, www.gao.gov

Independent, nonpartisan agency in the legislative branch. Audits, analyzes, and evaluates federal administration of justice programs and initiatives related to national preparedness. Makes some reports available to the public.

NONPROFIT

Center for Strategic and Budgetary Assessments, *1730 Rhode Island Ave., #912 20036; (202) 331-7990. Fax, (202) 331-8019. Andrew F. Krepinevich, Executive Director.*
Web, www.csbaonline.org

Conducts detailed analyses of defense spending; makes results available to members of Congress, the executive branch, the media, academics, other organizations, and the general public.

Institute for Policy Studies, *National Commission for Economic Conversion and Disarmament,* *733 15th St. N.W., #1020 20005; (202) 234-9382. Fax, (202) 387-7915. Miriam Pemberton, Director.*
Web, www.webcom.com/ncecd

Supports cutbacks in the U.S. military budget and reallocation of funds for civilian economic development. Advocates investment in civilian research and development, transportation, housing, health, education, and the environment.

National Campaign for a Peace Tax Fund, *2121 Decatur Pl. N.W. 20008; (202) 483-3751. Fax, (202) 986-0667. Marian Franz, Executive Director. Toll-free, (888) 732-2382.*
General e-mail, info@peacetaxfund.org
Web, www.peacetaxfund.org

Supports legislation permitting taxpayers who are conscientiously opposed to military expenditures to have the military portion of their income tax money placed in a separate, nonmilitary fund.

Women's Action for New Directions, *Washington Office,* *322 4th St. N.E. 20002; (202) 543-8505. Fax, (202) 675-6469. Darcy Scott Martin, Director.*
General e-mail, wand@wand.org
Web, www.wand.org

Seeks to redirect federal spending priorities from military spending toward domestic needs; works to develop citizen expertise through education and political involvement; provides educational programs and material about nuclear and conventional weapons; monitors defense legislation, budget policy legislation, and legislation affecting women. (Headquarters in Arlington, Mass.)

Military Aid and Peacekeeping

AGENCIES

Commission on Security and Cooperation in Europe *(Helsinki Commission),* *234 FHOB, 3rd and D Sts. S.W. 20515; (202) 225-1901. Fax, (202) 226-4199. Sen. Ben Nighthorse Campbell, R-Colo., Chair; Rep.*

Christopher H. Smith, R-N.J., Co-Chair; Dorothy Douglas Taft, Chief of Staff.

Web, www.csce.gov/helsinki.cfm

Independent agency created by Congress. Membership includes individuals from the executive and legislative branches. Studies and evaluates international peacekeeping and peace enforcement operations, particularly as they relate to the Helsinki Accords.

Defense Dept. (DoD), *Defense Security Cooperation Agency,* Crystal Gateway North, #303, 1111 Jefferson Davis Hwy., Arlington, VA 22202-4306; (703) 604-6604. Fax, (703) 602-5403. Lt. Gen. Tome H. Walters Jr., Director. Information, (703) 604-6633.

Web, www.dsca.mil

Develops budgetary proposals and Defense Dept. policies on arms transfers. Selects and manages U.S. personnel in security assistance assignments overseas; manages weapons systems sales; maintains special defense acquisition funds and priority defense items information systems. Administers foreign military sales programs.

Defense Dept. (DoD), *European and NATO Policy,* The Pentagon, #4D800 20301-2900; (703) 697-7207. Fax, (703) 697-5992. Ian Brzezinski, Deputy Assistant Secretary.

Web, www.defenselink.mil

Advises the assistant secretary for international security affairs on matters dealing with Europe and NATO.

Defense Dept. (DoD), *International Security Affairs,* The Pentagon, #4E838 20301-2400; (703) 695-4351. Fax, (703) 697-7230. Peter W. Rodman, Assistant Secretary.

Web, www.defenselink.mil

Advises the secretary of defense and recommends policies on regional security issues (except those involving countries of the former Soviet Union).

State Dept., *Arms Control and International Security,* 2201 C St. N.W., #7208 20520-7512; (202) 647-1049. Fax, (202) 736-4397. John Robert Bolton, Under Secretary.

Web, www.state.gov

Works with the secretary of state to develop policy on foreign security assistance programs and technology transfer.

State Dept., *European Security and Political Affairs,* 2201 C St. N.W., #6511 20520; (202) 647-1626. Fax, (202) 647-1369. John Schmidt, Director.

Web, www.state.gov

Coordinates and advises, with the Defense Dept. and other agencies, the U.S. mission to NATO and the U.S. delegation to the Organization on Security and Cooperation in Europe regarding political, military, and arms control matters.

State Dept., *International Organization Affairs,* 2201 C St. N.W., #6323 20520-6319; (202) 647-9600. Fax, (202) 736-4116. Kim R. Holmes, Assistant Secretary. Press, (202) 647-8490.

Web, www.state.gov/p/io

Coordinates and develops policy guidelines for U.S. participation in the United Nations and in other international organizations and conferences.

State Dept., *Policy Planning Staff,* 2201 C St. N.W., #7311 20520; (202) 647-2372. Fax, (202) 647-4147. Richard N. Haass, Director.

Web, www.state.gov

Advises the secretary and other State Dept. officials on foreign policy matters, including international peacekeeping and peace enforcement operations.

State Dept., *Political-Military Affairs,* 2201 C St. N.W., #6212 20520; (202) 647-9022. Fax, (202) 736-4779. Lincoln P. Bloomfield Jr., Assistant Secretary.

Web, www.state.gov

Responsible for security affairs policy and operations for the non-European area.

State Dept., *United Nations Political Affairs,* 2201 C St. N.W., #6334 20520-6319; (202) 647-2392. Fax, (202) 647-0039. Marcie B. Ries, Director.

Web, www.state.gov

Deals with United Nations political and institutional matters and international security affairs.

U.S. Institute of Peace, 1200 17th St. N.W., #200 20036-3011; (202) 457-1700. Fax, (202) 429-6063. Chester Crocker, Chair; Richard H. Solomon, President. TTY, (202) 457-1719.

General e-mail, usip_requests@usip.org

Web, www.usip.org

Independent organization created and funded by Congress to promote the peaceful resolution of international conflict through negotiation and mediation. Provides federal agencies and individuals with training, research programs, and information. Awards grants to institutions and individuals and provides fellowships to scholars from the United States and abroad. Library open to the public by appointment.

CONGRESS

General Accounting Office (GAO), *Defense Capabilities and Management,* 441 G St. N.W., #4035 20548; (202) 512-4300. Fax, (202) 512-7686. Henry L. Hinton Jr., Managing Director.

Web, www.gao.gov

Independent, nonpartisan agency in the legislative branch. Audits, analyzes, and evaluates international programs, including U.S. participation in international peacekeeping and peace enforcement operations; makes unclassified reports available to the public.

House Appropriations Committee, *Subcommittee on Foreign Operations, Export Financing, and Related Programs,* *H150 CAP 20515; (202) 225-2041. Fax, (202) 226-7992. Rep. Jim Kolbe, R-Ariz., Chair; Charles O. Flickner, Staff Director.*
Web, www.house.gov/appropriations

Jurisdiction over legislation to appropriate funds for foreign operations, including military assistance programs of the State Dept.; the Export-Import Bank; the International Bank for Reconstruction and Development (World Bank); the Inter-American Development Bank; the International Monetary Fund; the Agency for International Development; the Peace Corps; and related international organizations.

House Appropriations Committee, *Subcommittee on Labor, Health and Human Services, Education, and Related Agencies,* *2358 RHOB 20515; (202) 225-3508. Fax, (202) 225-3509. Rep. Ralph Regula, R-Ohio, Chair; Craig Higgins, Staff Director.*
Web, www.house.gov/appropriations

Jurisdiction over legislation to appropriate funds for the U.S. Institute of Peace.

Senate Appropriations Committee, *Subcommittee on Foreign Operations,* *SD-142 20510; (202) 224-2255. Fax, (202) 224-8553. Sen. Mitch McConnell, R-Ky., Chair; Paul Grove, Clerk.*
Web, appropriations.senate.gov

Jurisdiction over legislation to appropriate funds for foreign operations, including economic and military assistance programs of the State Dept.

Senate Appropriations Committee, *Subcommittee on Labor, Health and Human Services, Education, and Related Agencies,* *SD-184 20510; (202) 224-3471. Fax, (202) 224-8553. Sen. Arlen Specter, R-Pa., Chair; Bettilou Taylor, Clerk.*
Web, appropriations.senate.gov

Jurisdiction over legislation to appropriate funds for the U.S. Institute of Peace.

Senate Armed Services Committee, *Subcommittee on Airland,* *SR-228 20510; (202) 224-3871. Fax, (202) 228-0036. Sen. Jeff Sessions, R-Ala., Chair; Tom MacKenzie, Staff Director.*
Web, armed-services.senate.gov

Jurisdiction over issues of peacekeeping and peace enforcement.

INTERNATIONAL ORGANIZATIONS

Inter-American Defense Board, *2600 16th St. N.W. 20441; (202) 939-6600. Fax, (202) 387-2880. Maj. Gen. Carl H. Freeman, Chair.*
Web, www.jid.org

Membership: military officers from twenty-six countries of the Western Hemisphere. Plans for the collective self-defense of the American continents. Develops procedures for standardizing military organization and operations; operates the Inter-American Defense Board and Inter-American Defense College.

Joint Mexican–United States Defense Commission, U.S. Section, *The Pentagon, #2D967, 5134 Joint Staff 20318-5134; (703) 695-8162. Fax, (703) 614-8945. Maj Gen. Michael M. Dunn, Chair.*

Composed of military delegates of the two countries. Studies problems concerning the common defense of the United States and Mexico.

NONPROFIT

National Peace Foundation, *666 11th St. N.W., #202 20001; (202) 783-7030. Fax, (202) 783-7040. Sarah Harder, President.*
General e-mail, npf@nationalpeace.org
Web, www.nationalpeace.org

Supports conflict resolution education and the U.S. Institute of Peace. Holds conferences and provides information on peace education and managing and resolving conflict.

ARMS CONTROL, DISARMAMENT, AND THREAT REDUCTION

AGENCIES

Defense Dept. (DoD), *Chemical and Biological Defense Programs,* *3050 Defense Pentagon, #3C257 20301-3050; (703) 693-9410. Fax, (703) 695-0476. Anna Johnson-Winegar, Director.*
Web, www.acq.osd.mil/cp/index.html

Coordinates, integrates, and provides oversight for the Joint Services Chemical and Biological Defense Program. Provides oversight for the Chemical Weapons Demilitarization Program.

Defense Dept. (DoD), *International Security Policy,* *2900 Defense Pentagon, #4E817 20301-2900; (703) 697-*

7728. Fax, (703) 693-9146. J. D. Crouch II, Assistant Secretary.

Web, www.defenselink.mil

Advises the secretary on reducing and countering nuclear, biological, chemical, and missile threats to the United States and its forces and allies; arms control negotiations, implementation, and verification policy; nuclear weapons policy, denuclearization, threat reduction, and nuclear safety and security; and technology transfer.

Defense Dept. (DoD), *Resources and Plans,*
2900 Defense Pentagon, #4B940 20301-2900; (703) 697-6963. Fax, (703) 693-5193. Christopher J. Lamb, Deputy Assistant Secretary.

Web, www.defenselink.mil

Formulates national policies to prevent and counter the proliferation of nuclear, chemical, and biological weapons; missiles; and conventional technologies. Devises arms control agreements, export controls, technology transfer policies, and military planning policies.

Defense Threat Reduction Agency *(Defense Dept.),*
8725 John Jay Kingman Rd., MS 6201, Fort Belvoir, VA 22060; (703) 767-4883. Fax, (703) 767-5830. Stephen M. Younger, Director; Vacant, Deputy Director.
General e-mail, (Chem-Bio): cb@dtra.mil; (Cooperative Threat Reduction): ct@dtra.mil

Web, www.dtra.mil

Seeks to reduce the threat to the United States and its allies from nuclear, biological, chemical, conventional, and special weapons; conducts technology security activities, cooperative threat reduction programs, arms control treaty monitoring, and on-site inspection; provides technical support on weapons of mass destruction matters to the Defense Dept. components.

Energy Dept. (DOE), *Defense Nuclear Nonproliferation: National Nuclear Security Administration,*
1000 Independence Ave. S.W., #7A049 20585; (202) 586-0645. Fax, (202) 586-0862. Amb. Linton F. Brooks, Administrator (Acting).

Web, www.nn.doe.gov

Provides intelligence community with technical and operational expertise on foreign nuclear and energy issues. Oversees programs to prevent the spread of nuclear, chemical, and biological weapons and missiles for their delivery. Partners with Russia and other former Soviet states to secure weapons of mass destruction materials and expertise; works to strengthen legal and institutional nonproliferation norms; builds technologies to detect proliferation activities; and promotes the safe use of nuclear power.

Proliferation Strategy, Counterproliferation, and Homeland Defense *(Executive Office of the President),*
Dwight D. Eisenhower Executive Office Bldg., #302 20506; (202) 456-9181. Fax, (202) 456-9180. Robert G. Joseph, Special Assistant to the President and Senior Director.

Responsible for policies concerning arms proliferation and control in the context of homeland security.

State Dept., *Bureau of Nonproliferation,* 2201 C St. N.W., #7531 20520; (202) 647-8699. Fax, (202) 736-4863. John S. Wolf, Assistant Secretary.

Web, www.state.gov/t/np

Leads the U.S. effort to curb the spread of weapons of mass destruction and their missile delivery systems; to secure the nuclear materials in the former Soviet Union; and to promote nuclear safety and the responsible transfer of conventional arms and technology. Interests include nuclear weapon–free zones.

State Dept., *Policy, Plans, and Analysis,* 2201 C St. N.W., #5827 20520; (202) 647-7775. Fax, (202) 647-8998. Elena Kim-Mitchell, Director (Acting); Michele Markoff, Deputy Director (Acting).

Web, www.state.gov

Develops policies related to nuclear and conventional arms control, strategic defenses, nuclear testing, and assistance to the former Soviet Union aimed toward eliminating weapons of mass destruction.

CONGRESS

House Armed Services Committee, 2120 RHOB 20515; (202) 225-4151. Fax, (202) 225-9077. Rep. Duncan Hunter, R-Calif., Chair; Robert S. Rangel, Staff Director.

Web, www.house.gov/hasc

Oversight of international arms control and disarmament matters. (Jurisdiction shared with House International Relations Committee.)

House International Relations Committee, *Subcommittee on International Terrorism, Nonproliferation, and Human Rights,* 2401A RHOB 20515; (202) 226-7820. Fax, (202) 226-2831. Rep. Elton Gallegly, R-Calif., Chair; Richard Mereu, Staff Director.

Web, www.house.gov/international_relations

Jurisdiction over arms control, disarmament, and nuclear nonproliferation legislation. Oversight of State Dept. and Defense Dept. activities involving arms transfers and arms sales.

Senate Armed Services Committee, SR-228 20510; (202) 224-3871. Fax, (202) 228-0036. Sen. John W. Warner, R-Va., Chair; Judy Ansley, Staff Director.

Oversight of arms control and disarmament matters. (Jurisdiction shared with Senate Foreign Relations Committee.)

Senate Foreign Relations Committee, *SD-450 20510; (202) 224-4651. Fax, (202) 224-0836. Sen. Richard G. Lugar, R-Ind., Chair; Kenneth A. Myers, Staff Director.* Web, foreign.senate.gov

Jurisdiction over arms control, disarmament, and nuclear nonproliferation legislation. (Jurisdiction shared with Senate Armed Services Committee.)

NONPROFIT

Arms Control Assn., *1726 M St. N.W., #201 20036; (202) 463-8270. Fax, (202) 463-8273. Daryl Kimball, Executive Director.*
General e-mail, aca@armscontrol.org
Web, www.armscontrol.org

Nonpartisan organization interested in arms control. Seeks to broaden public interest in arms control, disarmament, and national security policy.

Center for Defense Information, *1779 Massachusetts Ave. N.W., #615 20036; (202) 332-0600. Fax, (202) 462-4559. Bruce Blair, President. Information, (800) 234-3334.*
General e-mail, info@cdi.org
Web, www.cdi.org

Educational organization that advocates a strong defense while opposing excessive expenditures for weapons and policies that increase the risk of war. Interests include the defense budget, weapons systems, and troop levels. Provides Congress, the Pentagon, State Dept., media, and public with appraisals of military matters.

Chemical and Biological Arms Control Institute, *1747 Pennsylvania Ave. N.W., 7th Floor 20006; (202) 296-3550. Fax, (202) 296-3574. Michael L. Moodie, President.*
General e-mail, cbaci@cbaci.org
Web, www.cbaci.org

Promotes arms control, nonproliferation, and the elimination of chemical, biological, and other weapons of mass destruction through research, analysis, technical support, and education.

Council for a Livable World, *322 4th St. N.E. 20002; (202) 543-4100. Fax, (202) 543-6297. John D. Isaacs, President.*
General e-mail, clw@clw.org
Web, www.clw.org

Citizens' interest group that supports arms control treaties, reduced military spending, peacekeeping, and tight restrictions on international arms sales.

Federation of American Scientists, *1717 K St. N.W., #209 20036; (202) 546-3300. Fax, (202) 675-1010. Henry Kelly, President.*
General e-mail, fas@fas.org
Web, www.fas.org

Opposes the global arms race and supports nuclear disarmament and limits on government secrecy. Conducts studies and monitors legislation on U.S. weapons policy; provides the public with information on arms control and related issues; promotes learning technologies.

Friends Committee on National Legislation (FCNL), *245 2nd St. N.E. 20002-5795; (202) 547-6000. Fax, (202) 547-6019. Joe Volk, Executive Secretary. Recorded information, (202) 547-4343.*
General e-mail, fcnl@fcnl.org
Web, www.fcnl.org

Supports world disarmament; international cooperation; domestic, economic, peace, and social justice issues; and improvement in relations between the United States and the former Soviet Union. Opposes conscription. Affiliated with the Religious Society of Friends (Quakers).

High Frontier, *2800 Shirlington Rd., #405, Arlington, VA 22206-3601; (703) 671-4111. Fax, (703) 931-6432. Henry Cooper, Chair.*
General e-mail, high.frontier@verizon.net
Web, www.highfrontier.org

Educational organization that provides information on missile defense programs and proliferation. Advocates development of a single-stage-to-orbit space vehicle and development of a layered missile defense system. Operates speakers bureau, monitors defense legislation.

Lawyers Alliance for World Security, *1901 Pennsylvania Ave. N.W., #201 20006; (202) 745-2450. Fax, (202) 667-0444. Thomas Graham Jr., President.*
General e-mail, info@lawscns.org
Web, www.lawscns.org

Public education organization that seeks to broaden interest in and understanding of arms control and disarmament with regard to nuclear, conventional, chemical, and biological weapons. Sponsors educational programs for government officials, including legislators from the Commonwealth of Independent States.

Nuclear Threat Initiative (NTI), *1747 Pennsylvania Ave. N.W., 7th Floor 20006; (202) 296-4810. Fax, (202) 296-4811. Charles B. Curtis, President.*
General e-mail, contact@nti.org
Web, www.nti.org

Works to reduce threats from nuclear, biological, and chemical weapons.

Peace Action, *1819 H St. N.W., #420 20006-3603; (202) 862-9740. Fax, (202) 862-9762. Kevin Martin, Executive Director.*

Web, www.peace-action.org

Grassroots organization that supports a negotiated comprehensive test ban treaty. Seeks a reduction in the military budget and a transfer of those funds to nonmilitary programs. Works for an end to international arms trade. (Formerly Sane/Freeze.)

Physicians for Social Responsibility, *1875 Connecticut Ave., #1012 20009; (202) 667-4260. Fax, (202) 898-4201. Robert K. Musil, Executive Director.*

General e-mail, psrnatl@psr.org

Web, www.psr.org

Membership: doctors, dentists, and other individuals. Works toward the elimination of nuclear and other weapons of mass destruction, the achievement of a sustainable environment, and the reduction of violence and its causes. Conducts public education programs, monitors policy decisions on arms control, and serves as a liaison with other concerned groups.

Union of Concerned Scientists, *Government Relations, Washington Office, 1707 H St. N.W., #600 20006-3919; (202) 223-6133. Fax, (202) 223-6162. Alden Meyer, Director; Todd Perry, Washington Representative for Arms Control and International Security.*

General e-mail, ucs@ucsusa.org

Web, www.ucsusa.org

Works to advance the international security policies and agreements that restrict the spread of weapons of mass destruction and reduce the risk of war. Promotes international nonproliferation through reductions in fissile materials and through arms control measures including a comprehensive nuclear testing ban, restrictions on ballistic missile defenses, and dismantlement of nuclear warheads. Encourages the use of collective security forces such as the United Nations to alleviate conflicts. (Headquarters in Cambridge, Mass.)

Nuclear Weapons and Power

AGENCIES

Energy Dept. (DOE), *Defense Programs, 1000 Independence Ave. S.W., #4A019 20585; (202) 586-2179. Fax, (202) 586-1567. Everet H. Beckner, Deputy Administrator.*

Web, www.dp.doe.gov/dp_web

Responsible for nuclear weapons research, development, and engineering; performs laser fusion research and development.

Energy Dept. (DOE), *Naval Reactors, 1240 Isaac Hull Ave. S.E., Washington Navy Yard, DC 20376-8010; (202) 781-6174. Fax, (202) 781-6405. Adm. Frank L. Bowman, Director.*

Web, www.energy.gov

Designs, develops, and maintains naval nuclear propulsion plants.

Energy Dept. (DOE), *Nonproliferation and International Security: Export Control Policy and Cooperation, 1000 Independence Ave. S.W. 20585-0001; (202) 586-2331. Fax, (202) 586-1348. Adam M. Scheinman, Director.*

Web, www.energy.gov

Develops and implements policies concerning nuclear materials and equipment; participates in international negotiations involving nuclear policy; supports activities of the International Atomic Energy Agency; develops policies concerning nuclear reprocessing requests.

National Security Council (NSC), *(Executive Office of the President), Defense Policy and Arms Control, The White House 20504; (202) 456-9191. Fax, (202) 456-9190. Frank Miller, Senior Director.*

Web, www.whitehouse.gov/nsc

Advises the assistant to the president for national security affairs on matters concerning nuclear weapons policy.

Navy Dept. *(Defense Dept.), Naval Nuclear Propulsion, 1240 Isaac Hull Ave. S.E., Washington Navy Yard, DC 20376-8010; (202) 781-6174. Adm. Frank L. Bowman, Director.*

Web, www.navy.mil

Responsible for naval nuclear propulsion.

State Dept., *Nuclear Energy Affairs, 2201 C St. N.W., #3320 A 20520; (202) 647-3310. Fax, (202) 647-0775. Richard J. K. Stratford, Director.*

Web, www.state.gov

Coordinates U.S. government activities that support safeguards against proliferation of nuclear weapons.

CONGRESS

House Appropriations Committee, *Subcommittee on Energy and Water Development, 2362 RHOB 20515; (202) 225-3421. Rep. David L. Hobson, R-Ohio, Chair; Robert Schmidt, Staff Director.*

Web, www.house.gov/appropriations

Jurisdiction over legislation to appropriate funds for atomic energy defense activities within the Energy Dept.,

Defense Nuclear Facilities Safety Board, Nuclear Regulatory Commission, Nuclear Waste Technical Review Board, and Nuclear Safety Oversight Commission.

House Armed Services Committee, *Subcommittee on Strategic Forces,* 2340 RHOB 20515; (202) 226-7173. Fax, (202) 225-9077. Rep. Terry Everett, R-Ala., Chair. Web, www.house.gov/hasc

Jurisdiction over military applications of nuclear energy.

Senate Appropriations Committee, *Subcommittee on Energy and Water Development,* SD-129 20510; (202) 224-7260. Fax, (202) 228-2322. Sen. Pete V. Domenici, R-N.M., Chair; Clay Sell, Clerk. Web, appropriations.senate.gov

Jurisdiction over legislation to appropriate funds for the Nuclear Regulatory Commission, Nuclear Waste Technical Review Board, Defense Nuclear Facilities Safety Board, and atomic energy defense activities within the Energy Dept.

Senate Armed Services Committee, SR-228 20510; (202) 224-3871. Fax, (202) 228-0036. Sen. John W. Warner, R-Va., Chair; Judy Ansley, Staff Director. Web, armed-services.senate.gov

Jurisdiction over national security aspects of nuclear energy.

NONPROFIT

Institute for Science and International Security, 236 Massachusetts Ave. N.E., #500 20002; (202) 547-3633. Fax, (202) 547-3634. David Albright, Director. General e-mail, isis@isis-online.org Web, www.isis-online.org

Conducts research and analysis on nuclear weapons production and nonproliferation issues.

Nuclear Control Institute, 1000 Connecticut Ave. N.W., #410 20036; (202) 822-8444. Fax, (202) 452-0892. Edwin Lyman, President. General e-mail, nci@nci.org Web, www.nci.org

Promotes nuclear nonproliferation; works to prevent the use of nuclear explosive materials (plutonium and highly enriched uranium) as reactor fuels; advocates terminating the export of nuclear technologies and facilities that could be used in the manufacture of nuclear weaponry; works to reduce the nuclear arsenals of nuclear weapons states; studies and recommends measures to prevent nuclear terrorism.

BORDERS, CUSTOMS, AND IMMIGRATION

AGENCIES

Bureau of Citizenship and Immigration Services (BCIS), *(Homeland Security Dept.),* Nebraska Ave. Complex, 3801 Nebraska Ave. N.W. 20395; (202) 282-8000 (switchboard). Eduardo Aguirre, Director (Acting). Automated information, (800) 375-5283 or TTY, (800) 767-1833. Web, www.bcis.gov

Responsible for the delivery of immigration and citizenship services. Priorities include the promotion of national security, the elimination of immigration adjudications backlog, and the implementation of measures to improve service delivery.

Bureau of Customs and Border Protection *(Homeland Security Dept.),* 1300 Pennsylvania Ave. N.W., #4.4A 20229; (202) 927-2001. Fax, (202) 927-1380. Robert C. Bonner, Commissioner. Information, (202) 354-1000. Library, (202) 927-1350. Press, (202) 927-1790. Web, www.customs.gov

Responsible for enforcing all laws at U.S. borders and for protecting the perimeter of the United States (the border ports of entry and the areas between the ports of entry). Possesses an extensive air, land, and marine interdiction force and its own intelligence branch.

Bureau of Customs and Border Protection *(Homeland Security Dept.), Agricultural Inspection Policy and Programs,* 1300 Pennsylvania Ave. N.W., #5.4C 20229; (202) 927-3298. Mary Neal, Associate Commissioner. Web, www.dhs.gov

Responsible for safeguarding the nation's animal and natural resources from pests and disease through inspections at ports of entry and beyond.

Bureau of Customs and Border Protection *(Homeland Security Dept.), Border Patrol,* 1300 Pennsylvania Ave. N.W., #6.3D 20229; (202) 927-2050. Gustavo De LaVina, Chief. Web, www.customs.gov

Mobile uniformed law enforcement arm of the Homeland Security Dept. Primary mission is to detect and prevent the illegal trafficking of people and contraband across U.S. borders.

Bureau of Immigration and Customs Enforcement *(Homeland Security Dept.),* 425 Eye St. N.W., #7100 20772; (202) 514-1900. Fax, (202) 307-9911. Michael Garcia, Assistant Secretary.

Web, www.bice.immigration.gov

Assembles the resources of several former security and border agencies (from such former agencies as the Immigration and Naturalization Service and the U.S. Customs Service) to focus on the enforcement of immigration and customs laws within the United States; on the protection of specified federal buildings; and on air and marine enforcement. Focus areas include immigration investigations, customs investigations, customs air and marine interdiction, and the federal protective service.

Federal Law Enforcement Training Center *(Homeland Security Dept.), Washington Office,* 555 11th St. N.W., #400 20004; (202) 927-8940. Fax, (202) 927-8782. *John C. Dooher, Senior Associate Director.*
Web, www.fletc.gov

Trains law enforcement personnel from seventy-four federal agencies. Areas of enforcement include customs, other import and export restrictions, drug control, immigration, financial crimes, transportation, and extradition. (Headquarters in Glynco, Ga.)

Homeland Security Dept. (DHS), *Border and Transportation Security Directorate,* Nebraska Ave. Complex, 3801 Nebraska Ave. N.W. 20395; (202) 282-8000. *Asa Hutchinson, Under Secretary.*
Web, www.dhs.gov

Responsible for border security and the enforcement of immigration laws. Coordinated endeavor of former INS Border Patrol agents and investigators, U.S. Customs Service agents, and enforcement personnel from the Transportation Security Administration and other agencies to protect U.S. borders. Mission includes the securing of borders against illicit drugs, unlawful commerce, and the entry of terrorists and the instruments of terrorism.

CONGRESS

House Appropriations Committee, *Subcommittee on Homeland Security,* B307 RHOB 20515; (202) 225-5834. *Rep. Harold Rogers, R-Ky., Chair; Michelle Mrdeza, Staff Director.*
Web, www.house.gov/appropriations

Jurisdiction over legislation to appropriate funds for the Bureau of Citizenship and Immigration Services; the Bureau of Customs and Border Protection; the Bureau of Immigration and Customs Enforcement; the Transportation Security Administration; and the U.S. Coast Guard.

House Government Reform Committee, *Subcommittee on Criminal Justice, Drug Policy, and Human Resources,* B373B RHOB 20515; (202) 225-2577. *Fax, (202) 225-1154. Rep. Mark Souder, R-Ind., Chair; Christopher Donesa, Staff Director.*

Web, www.house.gov/reform

Reviews policies related to border agencies and immigration.

House Judiciary Committee, *Subcommittee on Crime, Terrorism, and Homeland Security,* 207 CHOB 20515; (202) 225-3926. Fax, (202) 225-3737. *Rep. Howard Coble, R-N.C., Chair; Jay Apperson, Chief Counsel.*
General e-mail, Judiciary@mail.house.gov
Web, www.house.gov/judiciary

Conducts oversight of the law enforcement components of the Homeland Security Dept., including the U.S. Coast Guard and the Bureau of Customs and Border Protection.

House Judiciary Committee, *Subcommittee on Immigration, Border Security, and Claims,* B370B RHOB 20515; (202) 225-5727. Fax, (202) 225-3672. *Rep. John Hostettler, R-Ind., Chair; George Fishman, Chief Counsel.*
General e-mail, Judiciary@mail.house.gov
Web, www.house.gov/judiciary

Jurisdiction over immigration and naturalization legislation and border security issues. Conducts oversight on implementation of the immigration-related provisions of the USA PATRIOT Act and the Enhanced Border Security and Visa Entry Reform Act.

House Select Committee on Homeland Security, 2402 RHOB 20515; (202) 226-8417. *Rep. Christopher Cox, R-Calif., Chair; John C. Gannon, Staff Director.*
Web, hsc.house.gov

Oversees the Bureau of Customs and Border Protection.

House Select Committee on Homeland Security, *Subcommittee on Infrastructure and Border Security,* 2402 RHOB 20515; (202) 226-8417. *Rep. Dave Camp, R-Mich., Chair.*
Web, hsc.house.gov

Jurisdiction includes border security, including prevention of importation of illicit weapons, pathogens, narcotics, and other contraband; illegal entry by foreign nationals; land borders, ports, and airspace; and integration of federal, state, and local immigration law enforcement.

Senate Appropriations Committee, *Subcommittee on Homeland Security,* SD-136 20510; (202) 224-4319. *Fax, (202) 224-8553. Sen. Thad Cochran, R-Miss., Chair; Rebecca Davies, Clerk.*
Web, appropriations.senate.gov

Jurisdiction over legislation to appropriate funds for the Bureau of Citizenship and Immigration Services; the

Bureau of Customs and Border Protection; the Bureau of Immigration and Customs Enforcement; the Transportation Security Administration; and the U.S. Coast Guard.

Senate Governmental Affairs Committee, *SD-340 20510; (202) 224-4751. Fax, (202) 224-9682. Sen. Susan Collins, R-Maine, Chair; Michael Bopp, Staff Director.*
Web, govt-aff.senate.gov

Reviews policies related to border agencies and immigration.

Senate Judiciary Committee, *Subcommittee on Immigration, Border Security, and Citizenship, SD-520 20510; (202) 224-6098. Fax, (202) 228-0103. Sen. Saxby Chambliss, R-Ga., Chair; David Neal, Chief Counsel.*
Web, judiciary.senate.gov

Oversight responsibility for the immigration-related functions of the Homeland Security Dept., the Justice Dept., and the State Dept.

Senate Judiciary Committee, *Subcommittee on Terrorism, Technology, and Homeland Security, SH-325 20510; (202) 224-6791. Fax, (202) 228-0542. Sen. Jon Kyl, R-Ariz., Chair; Stephen Higgins, Chief Counsel.*
Web, judiciary.senate.gov

Oversight responsibility for State Dept. consular operations as they relate to antiterrorism enforcement and policy.

🗂 DEFENSE TRADE AND TECHNOLOGY

AGENCIES

Bureau of Industry and Security *(Commerce Dept.), 14th St. and Constitution Ave. N.W., #3898 20230; (202) 482-1427. Fax, (202) 482-2387. Kenneth I. Juster, Under Secretary for Export Administration, (202) 482-1455. Press, (202) 482-2721. Export licensing information, (202) 482-4811.*
Web, www.bxa.doc.gov

Administers Export Administration Act; maintains control lists and performs export licensing for the purposes of national security, foreign policy, and prevention of short supply.

Bureau of Industry and Security *(Commerce Dept.), Export Enforcement, 14th St. and Constitution Ave. N.W., #3721 20230; (202) 482-3618. Fax, (202) 482-4173. Lisa A. Prager, Assistant Secretary (Acting).*
Web, www.bxa.doc.gov

Enforces dual-use export controls on exports of U.S. goods and technology for purposes of national security, nonproliferation, counterterrorism, foreign policy, and short supply. Enforces the antiboycott provisions of the Export Administration Regulations.

Defense Dept. (DoD), *Chemical and Biological Defense Information Analysis Center, Aberdeen Proving Ground–Edgewood Area, P.O. Box 196, Aberdeen, MD 21010-0196; (410) 676-9030. Fax, (410) 676-9703. Ronald L. Evans, Director.*
General e-mail, evansrl@battelle.org
Web, www.cbiac.apgea.army.mil

Defense Dept. information analysis center operated by Battelle Memorial Institute. Serves as Defense Dept.'s focal point for chemical and biological defense technology. Collects and analyzes information pertaining to chemical and biological warfare and defense. Identifies and implements high-priority research and development projects. Disseminates technical information to planners, scientists, and military field personnel.

Defense Dept. (DoD), *International Cooperation, 3070 Defense Pentagon, #3A280 20301-3070; (703) 697-4172. Fax, (703) 693-2026. Alfred G. Volkman, Director.*
Web, www.acq.osd.mil/ic

Advises the under secretary of defense on cooperative research and development, production, procurement, and follow-on support programs with foreign nations; monitors the transfer of secure technologies to foreign nations.

Energy Dept. (DOE), *Nonproliferation and International Security: Export Control Policy and Cooperation, 1000 Independence Ave. S.W. 20585-0001; (202) 586-2331. Fax, (202) 586-1348. Adam M. Scheinman, Director.*
Web, www.energy.gov

Develops policies concerning nuclear material and equipment exports, nuclear material transfers and retransfers, and regional nonproliferation.

Export Administration Review Board *(Commerce Dept.), 14th St. and Constitution Ave. N.W., #2639 20230; (202) 482-5863. Fax, (202) 501-2815. Carol A. Kalinoski, Executive Secretary.*
Web, www.bxa.doc.gov

Committee of cabinet-level secretaries and heads of other government offices. Considers export licensing policies and actions, especially those concerning national security and other major policy matters; advises the secretary of commerce on export licensing; reviews export licensing applications.

National Security Council (NSC), *(Executive Office of the President), International Economic Affairs, The White House 20504; (202) 456-9281. Fax, (202) 456-9280. John A. Cloud Jr., Special Assistant to the President.*

Web, www.whitehouse.gov/nsc

Advises the president, the National Security Council, and the National Economic Council on all aspects of U.S. foreign policy dealing with U.S. international economic policies.

Nuclear Regulatory Commission, *International Programs, MS 04E21 20555; (301) 415-2344. Fax, (301) 415-2395. Janice Dunn Lee, Director.*

Web, www.nrc.gov

Coordinates application review process for exports and imports of nuclear materials, facilities, and components. Makes recommendations on licensing upon completion of review process. Conducts related policy reviews.

President's Export Council *(Commerce Dept.), Subcommittee on Export Administration, 14th St. and Constitution Ave. N.W., #3876 20230; (202) 482-2583. Fax, (202) 482-3195. Lee Ann Carpenter, Committee Control Officer.*

Advises the president and secretary of commerce on matters related to the Export Administration Act of 1979, which deals with controlling trade for reasons of national security, foreign policy, and short supply. Seeks ways to minimize the negative effect of export controls while protecting U.S. national security and foreign policy interests.

State Dept., *Bureau of Nonproliferation, 2201 C St. N.W., #7531 20520; (202) 647-8699. Fax, (202) 736-4863. John S. Wolf, Assistant Secretary.*

Web, www.state.gov/t/np

Leads the U.S. effort to curb the spread of weapons of mass destruction and their missile delivery systems; to secure the nuclear materials in the former Soviet Union; and to promote nuclear safety and the responsible transfer of conventional arms and technology. Interests include nuclear weapon–free zones.

State Dept., *Defense Trade Controls, 2401 E St. N.W., SA-1, #H1200 20037 (mailing address: PM/DDTC, SA-1, 12th Floor, Bureau of Political Military Affairs 20522-0112); (202) 663-2700. Fax, (202) 261-8199. Robert Maggi, Managing Director.*

Web, www.pmdtc.org

Controls the commercial export of defense articles, services, and related technical data; authorizes the permanent export and temporary import of such items.

State Dept., *Economic Sanctions Policy, 2201 C St. N.W., #4535 20520; (202) 647-7489. Fax, (202) 647-4064. George A. Glass, Director.*

Web, www.state.gov

Develops and implements U.S. foreign policy sanctions of embargo and terrorist listed countries. Coordinates U.S. participation in multilateral strategic trade control and revisions related to the export of strategically critical high-technology goods. Cooperates with the Commerce, Defense, and Treasury departments regarding export controls.

Treasury Dept., *Foreign Assets Control, 1500 Pennsylvania Ave. N.W., Annex Bldg., #2233 20220; (202) 622-2500. Fax, (202) 622-1657. R. Richard Newcomb, Director. Fax-on-demand, (202) 622-0077.*

Web, www.ustreas.gov/ofac

Authorized under the revised Trading with the Enemy Act, the International Emergency Economic Powers Act, and the United Nations Participation Act to control financial and commercial dealings with certain countries and their foreign nationals in times of war or emergencies. Regulations involving foreign assets control, narcotics, nonproliferation, and commercial transactions currently apply in varying degrees to Angola, Cuba, Iran, Iraq, Libya, North Korea, Sierra Leone, Sudan, the Taliban, and Yugoslavia.

CONGRESS

House Armed Services Committee, *Subcommittee on Terrorism, Unconventional Threats and Capabilities, 2120 RHOB 20515; (202) 225-4151. Fax, (202) 225-9077. Rep. H. James Saxton, R-N.J., Chair.*

Web, www.house.gov/hasc

Jurisdiction over legislation on antiproliferation and antiterrorism programs; the Defense Advanced Research Projects Agency; and information technology policy and programs.

House International Relations Committee, *Subcommittee on International Terrorism, Nonproliferation, and Human Rights, 2401A RHOB 20515; (202) 226-7820. Fax, (202) 226-2831. Rep. Elton Gallegly, R-Calif., Chair; Richard Mereu, Staff Director.*

Web, www.house.gov/international_relations

Jurisdiction over legislation on transfers of arms and technology between the United States and foreign countries. (Jurisdiction shared with House Science Committee.)

House Science Committee, *Subcommittee on Environment, Technology, and Standards, 2319 RHOB 20515; (202) 225-8844. Fax, (202) 225-4438. Rep. Vernon J. Ehlers, R-Mich., Chair; Eric Webster, Staff Director.*

General e-mail, science@mail.house.gov

Web, www.house.gov/science

Jurisdiction over legislation on transfers of arms and technology between the United States and foreign countries. (Jurisdiction shared with House International Relations Committee.)

Senate Armed Services Committee, *Subcommittee on Emerging Threats and Capabilities,* SR-228 20510; (202) 224-3871. Fax, (202) 228-0036. Sen. Pat Roberts, R-Kan., Chair; Lynn Rusten, Staff Director.

Web, armed-services.senate.gov

Jurisdiction over legislation on antiproliferation and antiterrorism programs; information warfare and technology-based issues; foreign military sales and technology; and weapons export policies.

Senate Banking, Housing, and Urban Affairs Committee, *Subcommittee on International Trade and Finance,* SD-534 20510; (202) 224-4224. Sen. Chuck Hagel, R-Neb., Chair; Dayna Cade, Staff Director.

Web, banking.senate.gov

Jurisdiction over foreign trade legislation and legislation related to export control, including the Export Administration Act and the revised Trading with the Enemy Act, which authorize trade restrictions.

Senate Foreign Relations Committee, SD-450 20510; (202) 224-4651. Fax, (202) 224-0836. Sen. Richard G. Lugar, R-Ind., Chair; Kenneth A. Myers, Staff Director.

Web, foreign.senate.gov

Oversight of State and Defense Dept. operations regarding arms transfers, export licenses, and sales.

Senate Governmental Affairs Committee, *Permanent Subcommittee on Investigations,* SR-199 20510; (202) 224-3721. Sen. Norm Coleman, R-Minn., Chair; Mary Robertson, Chief Clerk.

General e-mail, PSI@govt-aff.senate.gov

Web, govt-aff.senate.gov

Investigates transfers of technology between the United States and foreign countries.

Research and Development

AGENCIES

Air Force Dept. *(Defense Dept.), Acquisition,* 1060 Air Force Pentagon, #4E964 20330-1060; (703) 697-6361. Fax, (703) 693-6400. Marvin R. Sambur, Assistant Secretary.

Web, www.af.mil

Civilian office that directs and reviews Air Force research, development, and acquisition of weapons systems.

Air Force Dept. *(Defense Dept.), Scientific Research,* 4015 Wilson Blvd., #713, Arlington, VA 22203-1954; (703) 696-7554. Fax, (703) 696-9556. Lyle H. Schwartz, Director.

Web, www.afosr.af.mil

Sponsors and sustains basic research; assists in the transfer of research results to the fleet; supports Air Force goals of control and maximum utilization of air and space.

Army Corps of Engineers *(Defense Dept.), Research and Development,* 441 G St. N.W., #3210 20314-1000; (202) 761-1839. Fax, (202) 761-0907. Michael J. O'Connor, Director.

Web, www.usace.army.mil

Coordinates the Corps of Engineers' research efforts; acts as advocate for its research laboratories in the Pentagon and with Congress; develops management procedures for laboratories.

Army Dept. *(Defense Dept.), Acquisition, Logistics, and Technology,* 103 Army Pentagon, #2E672 20310-0103; (703) 695-6153. Fax, (703) 697-4003. Claude M. Bolton Jr., Assistant Secretary.

Web, www.saalt.army.mil

Civilian office that directs and reviews Army acquisition research and development of weapons systems and missiles.

Army Dept. *(Defense Dept.), Research and Technology,* 103 Army Pentagon, #3E620 20310-0103; (703) 692-1830. Fax, (703) 692-1836. A. Michael Andrews II, Deputy Assistant Secretary.

Web, www.army.mil

Sponsors and supports basic research at Army laboratories, universities, and other public and private organizations; assists in the transfer of research and technology to the field.

Defense Advanced Research Projects Agency *(Defense Dept.),* 3701 N. Fairfax Dr., Arlington, VA 22203-1714; (703) 696-2400. Fax, (703) 696-2209. Anthony J. Tether, Director. Press, (703) 696-2404.

Web, www.darpa.mil

Helps maintain U.S. technological superiority and guard against unforeseen technological advances by potential adversaries; determines which proposals for future projects related to national security deserve further research.

Defense Dept. (DoD), *Defense Research and Engineering,* 3030 Defense Pentagon, #3E1014 20301-3030; (703) 697-5776. Fax, (703) 693-7167. Dr. Ronald M. Sega, Director.

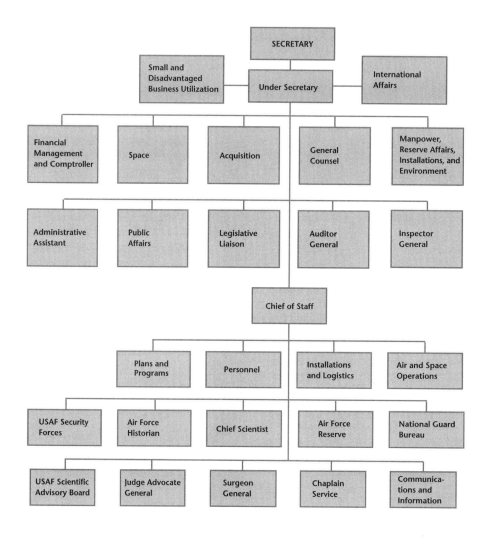

Web, www.dod.mil/ddre

Civilian office responsible for policy, guidance, and oversight of the Defense Dept.'s Science and Technology Program. Serves as focal point for in-house laboratories, university research, and other science and technology matters.

Defense Dept. (DoD), *Missile Defense Agency,*
7100 Defense Pentagon 20301-7100; (703) 695-8743. Fax, (703) 614-7059. Lt. Gen. Ronald T. Kadish (USAF), Director; Maj. Gen. Peter C. Franklin (USA), Deputy Director.

Web, www.acq.osd.mil/bmdo

Manages and directs the ballistic missile defense acquisition and research and development programs. Seeks to deploy improved theater missile defense systems and to develop options for effective national missile defenses while increasing the contribution of defensive systems to U.S. and allied security. (Formerly Ballistic Missile Defense Organization.)

Defense Technical Information Center *(Defense Dept.), 8725 John Jay Kingman Rd., #0944, Fort Belvoir, VA 22060-6218; (703) 767-9100. Fax, (703) 767-9183.*

ARMY DEPARTMENT

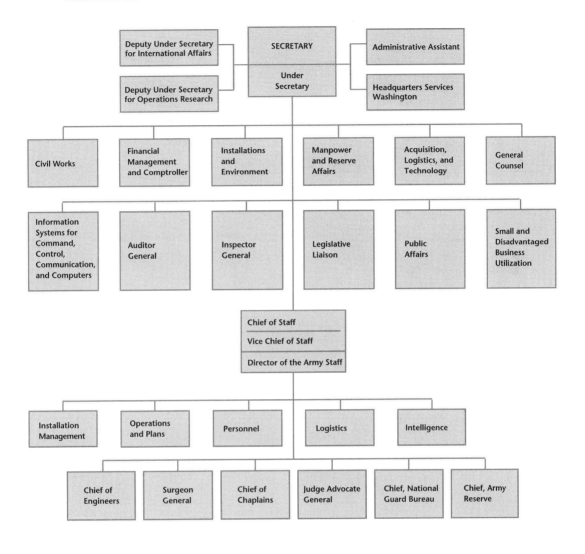

Kurt N. Molholm, Administrator. Registration, (703) 767-8200.
Web, www.dtic.mil

Acts as a central repository for the Defense Dept.'s collection of current and completed research and development efforts in all fields of science and technology. Disseminates research and development information to contractors, grantees, and registered organizations working on government research and development projects, particularly for the Defense Dept. Users must register with the center.

Marine Corps *(Defense Dept.), Systems Command,*
2033 Barnett Ave., #315, Quantico, VA 22134-5010; (703) 784-2411. Fax, (703) 784-3792. Brig. Gen. James M. Feigley, Commander.

Military office that directs Marine Corps research, development, and acquisition.

Naval Research Laboratory *(Defense Dept.), Research,*
4555 Overlook Ave. S.W. 20375-5320; (202) 767-3301. Fax, (202) 404-2676. John Montgomery, Director.
Web, www.nrl.navy.mil

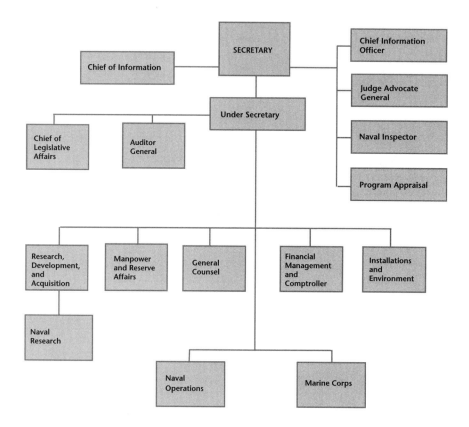

Conducts scientific research and develops advanced technology for the Navy. Areas of research include radar systems, radiation technology, tactical electronic warfare, and weapons guidance systems.

Navy Dept. *(Defense Dept.), Naval Research,*
800 N. Quincy St., #907, Arlington, VA 22217-5660; (703)
696-4767. Fax, (703) 696-4065. Rear Adm. Jay M. Cohen,
Chief.
Web, www.onr.navy.mil

Oversees the offices of Naval Research, Naval Technology, and Advanced Technology; works to ensure transition of research and technology to the fleet; sponsors and supports basic research at Navy laboratories, universities, and other public and private organizations.

Navy Dept. *(Defense Dept.), Research, Development,*
and Acquisition, 1000 Navy Pentagon, #4E741 20350-
1000; (703) 695-6315. Fax, (703) 697-0172. John J. Young,
Assistant Secretary.
Web, www.navy.mil

Civilian office that directs and reviews Navy and Marine Corps research and development of weapons systems.

Navy Dept. *(Defense Dept.), Test and Evaluation and*
Technology Requirements, 2000 Navy Pentagon 20350-
2000; (703) 601-1870. Fax, (703) 601-2011. Rear Adm.
Jay M. Cohen, Director.
Web, www.onr.navy.mil

Military office that directs Navy testing, evaluation, and science and technology.

Office of Science and Technology Policy (OSTP),
(Executive Office of the President), Dwight D. Eisenhower Executive Office Bldg. 20502; (202) 456-7116. Fax,
(202) 456-6027. Kathie L. Olsen, Associate Director, Science; Richard M. Russell, Associate Director, Technology.
Web, www.ostp.gov

Advises the president on international science and technology matters as they affect national security; coordinates international science and technology initiatives at the interagency level. Interests include nuclear materials, security, nuclear arms reduction, and counter terrorism.

President's National Security Telecommunications Advisory Committee, *c/o National Communications System, 701 S. Courthouse Rd., Arlington, VA 22204-2198; (703) 607-6221. Fax, (703) 607-4826. Janet S. Jefferson, Program Manager.*
Web, www.ncs.gov

Advises the president on specific measures to improve national security telecommunications.

State Dept., *Intelligence and Research, 2201 C St. N.W., #6531 20520-6531; (202) 647-9177. Fax, (202) 736-4688. Carl W. Ford Jr., Assistant Secretary.*
Web, www.state.gov

Coordinates foreign policy–related research, analysis, and intelligence programs for the State Dept. and other federal agencies.

U.S. Coast Guard (USCG), *(Homeland Security Dept.), Systems, 2100 2nd St. S.W., #6120 20593-0001; (202) 267-1844. Fax, (202) 267-4245. Rear Adm. J. A. Kinghorn, Assistant Commandant.*

Develops and maintains engineering standards for the building of ships and other Coast Guard craft.

CONGRESS

House Appropriations Committee, *Subcommittee on Defense, H149 CAP 20515; (202) 225-2847. Fax, (202) 225-2822. Rep. Jerry Lewis, R-Calif., Chair; Kevin M. Roper, Staff Director.*
Web, www.house.gov/appropriations

Jurisdiction over legislation to appropriate funds for the Defense Advanced Research Projects Agency.

House Armed Services Committee, *Subcommittee on Terrorism, Unconventional Threats and Capabilities, 2120 RHOB 20515; (202) 225-4151. Fax, (202) 225-9077. Rep. H. James Saxton, R-N.J., Chair.*
Web, www.house.gov/hasc

Responsible for the Defense Advanced Research Projects Agency.

Senate Appropriations Committee, *Subcommittee on Defense, SD-119 20510; (202) 224-7255. Sen. Ted Stevens, R-Alaska, Chair; Sid Ashworth, Clerk.*
Web, appropriations.senate.gov

Jurisdiction over legislation to appropriate funds for the Defense Advanced Research Projects Agency.

Senate Armed Services Committee, *SR-228 20510; (202) 224-3871. Fax, (202) 228-0036. Sen. John W. Warner, R-Va., Chair; Judy Ansley, Staff Director.*

Web, armed-services.senate.gov

Jurisdiction over military research and development legislation.

NONPROFIT

American Society of Naval Engineers, *1452 Duke St., Alexandria, VA 22314-3458; (703) 836-6727. Fax, (703) 836-7491. Dennis K. Kruse, Executive Director.*
General e-mail, asnehq@navalengineers.org
Web, www.navalengineers.org

Membership: civilian, active duty, and retired naval engineers. Provides forum for an exchange of information between industry and government involving all phases of naval engineering.

ANSER (Analytic Services), *2900 S. Quincy St., Arlington, VA 22206; (703) 416-2000. Fax, (703) 416-3050. Ruth David, President. Information, (800) 368-4173.*
Web, www.anser.org

Systems analysis organization funded by government contracts. Conducts weapons systems analysis.

Armed Forces Communications and Electronics Assn., *4400 Fair Lakes Court, Fairfax, VA 22033-3899; (703) 631-6100. Fax, (703) 631-4693. Adm. Herbert Browne, President. Information, (800) 336-4583.*
Web, www.afcea.com

Membership: industrial organizations, scientists, and military and government personnel in the fields of communications, electronics, computers, and electrical engineering. Consults with the Defense Dept. and other federal agencies on design and maintenance of command, control, communications, computer, and intelligence systems; holds shows displaying latest communications products.

Institute for Defense Analyses, *4850 Mark Center Dr., Alexandria, VA 22311-1882; (703) 845-2000. Fax, (703) 845-2569. Larry D. Welch, President.*
Web, www.ida.org

Federally funded research and development center that focuses on national security and defense. Conducts research, systems evaluation, and policy analysis for Defense Dept. and other agencies.

Johns Hopkins University Applied Physics Laboratory, *11100 Johns Hopkins Rd., Laurel, MD 20723-6099; (240) 228-5000. Fax, (240) 228-1093. Dr. Richard T. Roca, Director. Information, (240) 228-5021.*
Web, www.jhuapl.edu

Research and development organization that conducts research for the Defense Dept. (primarily the Navy) and other state and federal agencies. Interests include weapons systems and satellites.

Logistics Management Institute, *2000 Corporate Ridge, McLean, VA 22102-7805; (703) 917-9800. Fax, (703) 917-7597. Adm. Donald Pilling, President. Library, (703) 917-7249.*

Web, www.lmi.org

Conducts research on military and nonmilitary logistics, including transportation, supply and maintenance, force management, weapons support, acquisition, health systems, international programs, energy and environment, mathematical modeling, installations, operations, and information systems.

Military Operations Research Society, *1703 N. Beauregard St., #450, Alexandria, VA 22311; (703) 933-9070. Fax, (703) 933-9066. Brian Engler, Executive Vice President.*

Web, www.mors.org

Membership: professional analysts of military operations. Fosters information exchange; promotes professional development and high ethical standards; educates members on emerging issues, analytical techniques, and applications of research.

The Society of American Military Engineers, *607 Prince St., Alexandria, VA 22314-3117; (703) 549-3800. Fax, (703) 684-0231. Robert D. Wolff, Executive Director. Information, (800) 336-3097.*

Web, www.same.org

Membership: military and civilian engineers and architects. Conducts research, workshops, and conferences on subjects related to military engineering.

SRI International, *Washington Office, 1100 Wilson Blvd., #2800, Arlington, VA 22209; (703) 524-2053. Fax, (703) 247-8569. John Bramer, Director.*

Web, www.sri.com

Research organization supported by government and private contracts. Conducts research on military technology, including lasers and computers. Other interests include strategic planning and armed forces interdisciplinary research. (Headquarters in Menlo Park, Calif.)

🔲 EMERGENCY PREPAREDNESS AND RESPONSE

AGENCIES

Army Corps of Engineers *(Defense Dept.), Civil Emergency Management, 441 G St. N.W. 20314-1000; (202) 761-4603. Fax, (202) 761-1618. Bill Irwin, Chief (Acting).*

Web, www.usace.army.mil

Assists in repairing and restoring damaged flood control structures and federally authorized hurricane and shore protection projects damaged by wind or water; provides emergency assistance during floods or coastal storms. Supplies emergency power, removes debris, provides temporary housing, rebuilds public infrastructure, and performs other services at request of the Federal Emergency Management Agency.

Civil Air Patrol, *National Capital Wing, Washington Office, Bolling Air Force Base, 200 McChord St., #122 20032-0000; (202) 767-4405. Fax, (202) 767-5695. Col. Franklin F. McConnell Jr., Wing Commander.*

Official auxiliary of the U.S. Air Force. Conducts search-and-rescue missions for the Air Force; participates in emergency airlift and disaster relief missions. (Headquarters at Maxwell Air Force Base, Ala.)

Energy Dept. (DOE), *Emergency Operations, 1000 Independence Ave. S.W., #GH060 20585; (202) 586-9892. Fax, (202) 586-3904. Richard Arkin, Director (Acting).*

Web, www.energy.gov

Works to ensure coordinated Energy Dept. responses to energy-related emergencies. Recommends policies to mitigate the effects of energy supply crises on the United States; recommends government responses to energy emergencies.

Federal Emergency Management Agency (FEMA), *(Homeland Security Dept.), 500 C St. S.W., #828 20472; (202) 646-3923. Fax, (202) 646-3930. Michael Brown, Director (Acting). Press, (202) 646-4600. Locator, (202) 646-2500. Disaster assistance, (800) 462-9029. Radio network, (800) 323-5248. Fax-on-demand, (202) 646-3362.*

Web, www.fema.gov

Assists state and local governments in preparing for and responding to natural, man-made, and national security–related emergencies. Develops plans and policies for hazard mitigation, preparedness planning, emergency response, and recovery. Coordinates emergency preparedness, mitigation and response activities, and planning for all federal agencies and departments.

Federal Emergency Management Agency (FEMA), *(Homeland Security Dept.), National Preparedness, 500 C St. S.W. 20472; (202) 646-3700. Fax, (202) 646-4053. Charles E. Biggs, Director (Acting).*

Web, www.fema.gov

Dispenses money and provides training to police, firefighters, emergency workers, and citizen groups in preparation for and the event of terrorist attack.

FEDERAL EMERGENCY MANAGEMENT AGENCY

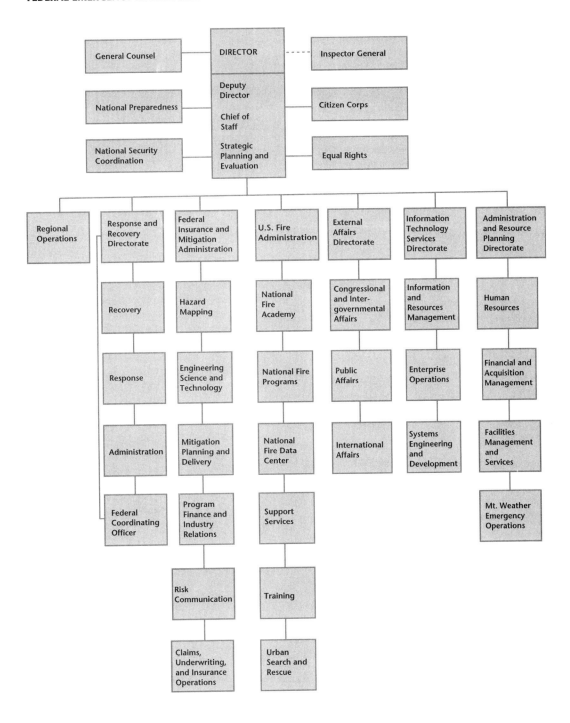

Federal Emergency Management Agency (FEMA), *(Homeland Security Dept.), National Security Division,* 500 C St. S.W. 20472; (202) 646-3700. Fax, (202) 646-4691. Reynold Hoover, Director.
Web, www.fema.gov

Responsible for the coordination of all Federal Emergency Management Agency national security programs.

Federal Emergency Management Agency (FEMA), *(Homeland Security Dept.), Preparedness,* 500 C St. S.W. 20472; (202) 646-4223. R. David Paulison, Chief.
Web, www.fema.gov

Responsible for coordination of the national emergency preparedness program.

Federal Emergency Management Agency (FEMA), *(Homeland Security Dept.), Recovery,* 500 C St. S.W. 20472; (202) 646-3642. Larry Zensinger, Director.
Web, www.fema.gov

Responsible for coordination of the president's disaster relief program.

Federal Emergency Management Agency (FEMA), *(Homeland Security Dept.), Response,* 500 C St. S.W. 20472; (202) 646-3692. Fax, (202) 646-4060. Eric Tolbert, Director. Press, (202) 646-4600.
Web, www.fema.gov

Responsible for coordination of federal response assets in the event of emergency.

Federal Insurance and Mitigation Administration *(Federal Emergency Management Agency),* 500 C St. S.W., #430 20472; (202) 646-2781. Fax, (202) 646-7970. Anthony S. Lowe, Administrator.
Web, www.fema.gov/nfip

Administers federal flood insurance programs, including the National Flood Insurance Program. Makes low-cost flood insurance available to eligible homeowners.

Homeland Security Dept. (DHS), *Emergency Preparedness and Response Directorate,* Nebraska Ave. Complex, 3801 Nebraska Ave. N.W. 20395; (202) 282-8000. Michael D. Brown, Under Secretary.
Web, www.dhs.gov

Responsible for implementing a comprehensive, risk-based emergency management program of preparedness, prevention, response, and recovery from catastrophe, whether natural disaster or terrorist attack. Handles development and management of a national training and evaluation system to design curriculums and to set standards and evaluate and reward performance in local, state, and federal training efforts.

National Response Center *(Homeland Security Dept.),* 2100 2nd St. S.W., #2611 20593; (202) 267-2675. Fax, (202) 267-2165. Syed Qadir, Director, (202) 267-6352. Toll-free hotline, (800) 424-8802.
Web, www.nrc.uscg.mil

Maintains twenty-four-hour hotline for reporting oil spills, hazardous materials accidents, chemical releases, or known or suspected terrorist threats. Notifies appropriate federal officials to reduce the effects of accidents.

Public Health and Science *(Health and Human Services Dept.), Emergency Response,* 12300 Twinbrook Pkwy., #360, Rockville, MD 20852; (301) 443-1167. Fax, (301) 443-5146. Dr. Kevin S. Yeskey, Director.
Web, www.oep-ndms.dhhs.gov

Works with the Federal Emergency Management Agency and other federal agencies and departments to develop plans and maintain operational readiness for responding to requests for assistance during presidentially declared disasters such as terrorist attack; develops and coordinates medical equipment and training plans for catastrophic disasters; maintains logistical plans and communications networks with federal, state, and local emergency preparedness organizations.

Research and Special Programs Administration *(Transportation Dept.), Emergency Transportation,* 400 7th St. S.W., #8417 20590-0001; (202) 366-5270. Fax, (202) 366-3769. Janet Benini, Director (Acting).
Web, www.rspa.dot.gov/oet

Develops, coordinates, and reviews transportation emergency preparedness programs for use in emergencies affecting national defense and in emergencies caused by natural disasters and crisis situations.

Small Business Administration (SBA), *Disaster Assistance,* 409 3rd St. S.W., #6050 20416; (202) 205-6734. Fax, (202) 205-7728. Herbert L. Mitchell, Associate Administrator.
Web, www.sba.gov

Provides victims of physical disasters with disaster and economic injury loans for homes, businesses, and personal property. Lends funds to individual homeowners, business concerns of all sizes, and nonprofit institutions to repair or replace damaged structures and furnishings, business machinery, equipment, and inventory.

U.S. Coast Guard (USCG), *(Homeland Security Dept.), Defense Operations,* 2100 2nd St. S.W., #3121 20593-0001; (202) 267-1502. Capt. Wayne Buchanan, Chief.

Ensures that the Coast Guard can mobilize effectively during national emergencies, including those resulting from enemy military attack.

CONGRESS

House Appropriations Committee, *Subcommittee on Homeland Security,* B307 RHOB 20515; (202) 225-5834. Rep. Harold Rogers, R-Ky., Chair; Michelle Mrdeza, Staff Director.

Web, www.house.gov/appropriations

Jurisdiction over legislation to appropriate funds for the Homeland Security Dept., including the Federal Emergency Management Agency, the Office of Emergency Preparedness, the National Disaster Medical System, and first responder programs.

House Armed Services Committee, *Subcommittee on Readiness,* 2120 RHOB 20515; (202) 225-6288. Fax, (202) 225-9077. Rep. Joel Hefley, R-Colo., Chair.

Web, www.house.gov/hasc

Jurisdiction over legislation concerning civil defense, emergency mobilization of merchant fleets, and national defense stockpiles, including military, civilian, and industrial requirements.

House Financial Services Committee, *Subcommittee on Housing and Community Opportunity,* B303 RHOB 20515; (202) 225-7502. Rep. Bob Ney, R-Ohio, Chair; Bob Foster, Staff Director.

Web, financialservices.house.gov

Jurisdiction over federal flood, fire, and earthquake insurance programs; oversees activities of the insurance industry pertaining to these programs.

House Select Committee on Homeland Security, *Subcommittee on Emergency Preparedness and Response,* 2402 RHOB 20515; (202) 226-8417. Rep. John Shadegg, R-Ariz., Chair.

Web, hsc.house.gov

Jurisdiction over preparation for and response to chemical, biological, radiological, and other attacks on civilian populations; protection of physical infrastructure and industrial assets against terrorist attack; public health issues related to such attacks; disaster preparedness; and coordination of emergency response with and among state and local governments and the private sector.

House Transportation and Infrastructure Committee, *Subcommittee on Economic Development, Public Buildings, and Emergency Management,* 589 FHOB 20515; (202) 225-3014. Fax, (202) 226-1898. Rep. Steven C. LaTourette, R-Ohio, Chair; Matt Wallen, Staff Director. General e-mail, transcomm@mail.house.gov

Web, www.house.gov/transportation

Responsible for the authorization and oversight of programs relating to the federal management of emergencies and disasters.

Senate Appropriations Committee, *Subcommittee on Homeland Security,* SD-136 20510; (202) 224-4319. Fax, (202) 224-8553. Sen. Thad Cochran, R-Miss., Chair; Rebecca Davies, Clerk.

Web, appropriations.senate.gov

Jurisdiction over legislation to appropriate funds for the Homeland Security Dept., the Federal Emergency Management Agency, the Office of Emergency Preparedness, the National Disaster Medical System, first responder programs, the Transportation Security Administration, the U.S. Coast Guard, the Bureau of Customs and Border Protection, and the U.S. Secret Service.

Senate Armed Services Committee, *Subcommittee on Readiness and Management Support,* SR-228 20510; (202) 224-3871. Fax, (202) 228-0036. Sen. John Ensign, R-Nev., Chair; Lucian Niemeyer, Professional Staff Member.

Web, armed-services.senate.gov

Jurisdiction over legislation concerning national defense stockpiles, including military, civilian, and industrial requirements. Jurisdiction over emergency preparedness legislation, including civil defense, emergency mobilization of merchant fleets, emergency communications, and industrial planning and mobilization.

Senate Banking, Housing, and Urban Affairs Committee, *Subcommittee on Housing and Transportation,* SD-534 20510; (202) 224-7391. Fax, (202) 224-5137. Sen. Wayne Allard, R-Colo., Chair; Tewana Wilkerson, Staff Director.

Web, banking.senate.gov

Jurisdiction over federal flood, crime, fire, and earthquake insurance programs; oversees activities of the insurance industry pertaining to these programs.

Senate Environment and Public Works Committee, *Subcommittee on Clean Air, Climate Change, and Nuclear Safety,* SD-410 20510; (202) 224-6176. Fax, (202) 224-1273. Sen. George V. Voinovich, R-Ohio, Chair; Michael Whatley, Staff Director.

Web, epw.senate.gov

Jurisdiction over the Federal Emergency Management Agency.

NONPROFIT

American Red Cross, *Disaster Services,* 2025 E St. N.W. 20006. Terry Sicilia, Executive Vice President.

Web, www.redcross.org/disaster

Chartered by Congress to administer disaster relief. Provides disaster victims with food, clothing, shelter, first aid, and medical care; promotes disaster preparedness and prevention.

International Assn. of Chiefs of Police, *Advisory Committee for Patrol and Tactical Operations,* 515 N. Washington St., Alexandria, VA 22314-2357; (703) 836-6767. Fax, (703) 836-4543. Matt Snyder, Staff Liaison.
Web, www.theiacp.org

Membership: foreign and U.S. police executives and administrators. Maintains liaison with civil defense and emergency service agencies; prepares guidelines for police cooperation with emergency and disaster relief agencies during emergencies.

National Assn. of State EMS Directors (NASEMSD), *111 Park Place, Falls Church, VA 22046-4513; (703) 538-1799. Fax, (703) 241-5603. Elizabeth B. Armstrong, Executive Director.*
General e-mail, info@nasemsd.org
Web, www.nasemsd.org

Works to provide leadership and support for the development of effective emergency medical services (EMS) systems throughout the United States; to formulate national EMS policy; and to foster communication and sharing among state EMS directors.

National Voluntary Organizations Active in Disaster (NVOAD), *14253 Ballinger Terrace, Burtonsville, MD 20866; (301) 890-2119. Fax, (253) 541-4915. John Gavin, Executive Secretary.*
Web, www.nvoad.org

Seeks to promote communication, cooperation, coordination, and collaboration among voluntary agencies that participate in disaster response nationally.

The Salvation Army Disaster Service, *2626 Pennsylvania Ave. N.W. 20037; (202) 756-2600. Fax, (202) 756-2663. Otis Childs, Divisional Secretary.*
Web, www.salvationarmyusa.org

Provides disaster victims and rescuers with emergency support, including food, clothing, and counseling services.

Coordination and Partnerships

AGENCIES

Federal Emergency Management Agency (FEMA), *(Homeland Security Dept.), Emergency Management Institute,* 16825 S. Seton Ave., Emmitsburg, MD 21727; (301) 447-1286. Fax, (301) 447-1497. Stephen Sharrow, Superintendent.
Web, www.fema.gov

Provides federal, state, and local government personnel and some private organizations engaged in emergency management with technical, professional, and vocational training. Educational programs include haz-

ard mitigation, emergency preparedness, and disaster response.

Homeland Security Dept. (DHS), *Information Analysis and Infrastructure Protection Directorate,* Nebraska Ave. Complex, 3801 Nebraska Ave. N.W. 20395; (202) 282-8000. Frank Libutti, Under Secretary (Designate).
Web, www.dhs.gov

Assigned the lead responsibility for coordinating the collection and analysis of intelligence and information pertaining to threats against U.S. infrastructure. Handles the merging of capabilities to identify and assess current and future threats to homeland infrastructure; identifies and assesses vulnerabilities, takes preventive action, and issues timely warnings. Develops partnerships and communication lines with state and local governments and the private sector.

Homeland Security Dept. (DHS), *Office for Domestic Preparedness,* Nebraska Ave. Complex, 3801 Nebraska Ave. N.W. 20395; (202) 282-8000. Andy Mitchell, Director (Acting).
Web, www.ojp.usdoj.gov/odp/welcome.html

Responsible for enhancing the capacity of state and local jurisdictions to respond to and mitigate the consequences of incidents of domestic terrorism. Facilitates the acquisition by state and local public safety personnel of specialized training and equipment necessary for management of terrorist incidents involving weapons of mass destruction. (Formerly Office for State and Local Domestic Preparedness Support within the Justice Dept.)

Homeland Security Dept. (DHS), *Office of the Secretary,* Nebraska Ave. Complex, 3801 Nebraska Ave. N.W. 20395; (202) 282-8000. Michael F. Byrne, National Capital Region Coordinator for Emergency Response.
Web, www.dhs.gov

Oversees and coordinates federal programs for emergency preparedness and response and relationships with state, local, and regional authorities in the national capital region.

Homeland Security Dept. (DHS), *Office of the Secretary,* Nebraska Ave. Complex, 3801 Nebraska Ave. N.W. 20395; (202) 282-8000. Alfonso Martinez-Fonts, Special Assistant to the Secretary for the Private Sector.
Web, www.dhs.gov

Works to facilitate outreach to industry and flow of information between industry and the department on security topics ranging from protecting critical infrastructure from sabotage to securing computer networks from hackers.

Homeland Security Dept. (DHS), *State and Local Coordination,* Nebraska Ave. Complex, 3801 Nebraska Ave. N.W. 20395; (202) 282-8000. Josh Filler, Director.
Web, www.dhs.gov

Responsible for outreach to state and local government officials and associations. Coordinates activities of the Homeland Security Dept. that relate to state and local governments.

CONGRESS

House Government Reform Committee, *Subcommittee on Technology, Information Policy, Intergovernmental Relations, and the Census,* B349A RHOB 20515; (202) 225-6751. Fax, (202) 225-4960. Rep. Adam H. Putnam, R-Fla., Chair; Robert Dix, Staff Director.
Web, www.house.gov/reform

Reviews coordinative efforts between state and federal governments in the area of homeland security.

House Judiciary Committee, *Subcommittee on Crime, Terrorism, and Homeland Security,* 207 CHOB 20515; (202) 225-3926. Fax, (202) 225-3737. Rep. Howard Coble, R-N.C., Chair; Jay Apperson, Chief Counsel.
General e-mail, Judiciary@mail.house.gov
Web, www.house.gov/judiciary

Oversees information sharing between federal, state, and local authorities, including implementation of USA PATRIOT Act and Homeland Security Act powers.

Senate Governmental Affairs Committee, SD-340 20510; (202) 224-4751. Fax, (202) 224-9682. Sen. Susan Collins, R-Maine, Chair; Michael Bopp, Staff Director.
Web, govt-aff.senate.gov

Jurisdiction includes intergovernmental relations and the efficiency and economy of all branches of government.

INFORMATION SHARING AND ANALYSIS CENTERS

A 1998 decision directive issued by President Bill Clinton defined various infrastructure industries critical to the national economy and public well-being. The directive proposed the creation of Information Sharing and Analysis Centers (ISACs), which would be established by each critical infrastructure industry to communicate with its members, its government partners, and other ISACs about threat indications, vulnerabilities, and protection strategies. Several such ISACs have taken shape, each led by a government agency or private entity. ISACs led by Washington-based agencies or companies are listed below.

Chemical Sector ISAC, *c/o American Chemistry Council,* 1300 Wilson Blvd., Arlington, VA 22209; (703) 741-5503. Timothy Butters, Director.
Web, chemicalisac.chemtrec.com

Cooperative arrangement between Chemtrec (the chemical industry's twenty-four-hour emergency communications center), the American Chemistry Council, and the Information Analysis and Information Protection Directorate at the Homeland Security Dept. that works to provide the chemistry industry with timely and critical information concerning potential or actual threats against it. Serves as a key centralized resource that gathers, analyzes, and disseminates threat information about cyber, physical, and contamination issues relevant to the chemical sector community.

Emergency Fire Services ISAC, *Critical Infrastructure Protection Information Center,* 16825 S. Seton Ave., Emmitsburg, MD 21727; (301) 447-1325. Hugh Wood, Response Branch Chief, USFA, (301) 447-1087.
General e-mail, usfacipc@fema.gov
Web, www.usfa.fema.gov/fire-service/cipc.cfm

Disseminates information to support the infrastructure protection efforts of emergency first responders throughout the U.S. Researches current physical and cyber protection issues, operates an information center, issues alerts and messages, and prepares instructional materials relevant to the emergency services community.

Emergency Law Enforcement ISAC, *935 Pennsylvania Ave. N.W. 20535-0001; (202) 323-3205. Fax, (202) 323-2079.*

A partnership of the Information Analysis and Infrastructure Protection Directorate at the Homeland Security Dept., the designated lead entity for the Emergency Law Enforcement Sector (ELES), and the ELES Forum, a group of senior law enforcement executives from state, local, and non-Federal Bureau of Investigation federal agencies. Serves as national advocate for emergency law enforcement issues and conducts liaison activities with the ELES community. Identifies the sector's most critical assets, assesses their vulnerability to attack, and develops remediation and mitigation plans. Operates a threat alert and notification system and security-related training programs.

Energy Sector ISAC, *c/o American Petroleum Institute,* 1220 L St., #900 20005; (202) 682-8286. Bobby Gillham (ConocoPhilips), ISAC Chair; Lisa Soda (American Petroleum Institute), ISAC Coordinator. International, 010 (1) (703) 480-3554.
Web, www.energyisac.com

Clearinghouse for the energy sector administered by the American Petroleum Institute. Provides information on threats, vulnerabilities, solutions, and best practices to members. Provides increased understanding of the threats and vulnerabilities to energy businesses so they can take appropriate action.

Financial Services ISAC, *c/o Global Integrity,* *220 Spring St., #400, Herndon, VA 20170; (888) 660-0134. Suzanne Gorman, Chair; Byron Yancey, Program Manager.*
Web, www.fsisac.com

Provides a confidential venue for sharing security vulnerabilities and solutions, including data obtained from sources such as other ISACs, law enforcement agencies, technology providers, and security associations. Works to facilitate trust, cooperation, and information sharing among its participants and assesses proactive means of mitigating cybersecurity risks.

Food Industry ISAC, *c/o Food Marketing Institute,* *655 15th St. N.W. 20005; (202) 220-0604. Fax, (202) 220-0870. Tim Hammonds, President, Food Marketing Institute.*
General e-mail, foodisac@fmi.org
Web, www.fmi.org/isac

Assembles information and analysis that enables the food industry to report, identify, and reduce its vulnerabilities to malicious attack and to recover from attack; helps the information analysis and infrastructure protection directorate at the Homeland Security Dept. and the Federal Bureau of Investigation's weapons of mass destruction operations unit identify credible threats and craft alerts to the industry; provides experts in threat assessment to the FBI.

Surface Transportation ISAC, *c/o EWA Information and Infrastructure Technologies, Inc.,* *13873 Park Center Rd., #200, Herndon, VA 20171; (866) 784-7221. Fax, (703) 478-7654. Paul G. Wolfe, Director.*
Web, www.surfacetransportationisac.org

Collects, analyzes, and distributes critical security and threat information from worldwide resources; shares best security practices and provides 24/7 immediate physical and cyberthreat warnings.

Telecommunications ISAC, *c/o National Coordinating Center for Communications (NCS),* *701 S. Courthouse Rd., Arlington, VA 22204; (703) 607-4900. Fred Herr, Chief, Critical Infrastructure Protection Division, NCC.*
General e-mail, ncs@ncs.gov
Web, www.ncs.gov/ncc

Supports the national critical infrastructure protection goals of government and industry. Facilitates voluntary collaboration and information sharing among its participants; gathers information on vulnerabilities, threats, intrusions, and anomalies from telecommunications industry, government, and other sources; develops baseline statistics and analyzes the data to avert or mitigate impact upon the telecommunications infrastructure.

Water ISAC, *1620 Eye St. N.W., #500 20006; (202) 331-0479. Susan Tramposch, Manager.*
Web, www.waterisac.org

Gathers, analyzes, and disseminates threat information concerning the water community from utilities' security incident reports and agencies of the federal government. Provides the water community with access to sensitive information and resources about cyber, physical, and contamination threats.

NONPROFIT

International Assn. of Chiefs of Police, *Advisory Committee for Patrol and Tactical Operations,* *515 N. Washington St., Alexandria, VA 22314-2357; (703) 836-6767. Fax, (703) 836-4543. Matt Snyder, Staff Liaison.*
Web, www.theiacp.org

Membership: foreign and U.S. police executives and administrators. Maintains liaison with civil defense and emergency service agencies; prepares guidelines for police cooperation with emergency and disaster relief agencies during emergencies.

National Governors Assn., *Center for Best Practices: Homeland Security and Emergency Management,* *444 N. Capitol St. N.W. 20001-1512; (202) 624-5300. Ann Beauchesne, Director.*
Web, www.nga.org/center

Provides support to governors in responding to the challenges of homeland security through technical assistance, policy research, and by facilitating their participation in national discussion and initiatives.

National Voluntary Organizations Active in Disaster (NVOAD), *14253 Ballinger Terrace, Burtonsville, MD 20866; (301) 890-2119. Fax, (253) 541-4915. John Gavin, Executive Secretary.*
Web, www.nvoad.org

Seeks to promote communication, cooperation, coordination, and collaboration among voluntary agencies that participate in disaster response nationally.

Emergency Communications

AGENCIES

Air Force Dept. *(Defense Dept.), Warfighting Integration,* *1800 Air Force Pentagon, #4E212 20330-1800; (703)*

695-6324. Fax, (703) 614-0156. Lt. Gen. Leslie Kenne, Deputy Chief.

Web, www.af.mil

Responsible for policy making, planning, programming, and evaluating performance of the Air Force's command, control, communications, and computers (C-4) system.

Army Dept. *(Defense Dept.), Chief Information Officer,* 107 Army Pentagon, #1A271 20310-0107; (703) 695-4366. Fax, (703) 695-3091. Lt. Gen. Peter M. Cuviello, Chief Information Officer.

Web, www.army.mil

Oversees policy and budget for the Army's information systems and programs.

Defense Dept. (DoD), *Command, Control, Communications, and Computer Systems,* 6000 Joint Staff Pentagon 20318-6000; (703) 695-6478. Fax, (703) 614-2945. Lt. Gen. Joseph K. Kellogg Jr., Director; Rear Adm. Nancy Brown, Vice Director.

Web, www.defenselink.mil

Military office that sets policy throughout the Defense Dept. for command, control, communications, and computers (C-4) matters.

Defense Dept. (DoD), *Command, Control, Communications, and Intelligence,* 6000 Defense Pentagon, #3E172 20301-6000; (703) 695-0348. Fax, (703) 614-8060. John P. Stenbit, Assistant Secretary.

Web, www.c3i.osd.mil

Civilian office with policy oversight for all command, control, communications, and intelligence matters.

Defense Dept. (DoD), *White House Communications Agency,* U.S. Naval Station—Anacostia Annex, 2743 Defense Blvd. S.W., #220 20373-5815; (202) 757-5530. Fax, (202) 757-5529. Col. Michael D. McDonald, Commander.

Web, www.defenselink.mil

Responsible for presidential communications.

Federal Communications Commission (FCC), *Emergency Alert System,* 445 12th St. S.W. 20554; (202) 418-1160. Fax, (202) 418-2790. Bonnie Gay, EAS Coordinator.

Web, www.fcc.gov/eb/eas

Develops rules and regulations for the Emergency Alert System, which is the national warning system the president would use to communicate with the public during a national emergency in the event that access to normal media outlets becomes unavailable. It is also used by state and local officials for weather-related and man-made emergencies.

National Communications System *(Homeland Security Dept.),* 701 S. Courthouse Rd., Arlington, VA 22204-2199; (703) 607-6001. Fax, (703) 607-4802. Vacant, Manager. Information, (703) 607-6900.

Web, www.ncs.gov

Ensures that the federal government has the necessary communications capabilities to permit its continued operation during a national emergency, including war; provides the Federal Emergency Management Agency with communications support as it directs the nation's recovery from a major disaster.

National Response Center *(Homeland Security Dept.),* 2100 2nd St. S.W., #2611 20593; (202) 267-2675. Fax, (202) 267-2165. Syed Qadir, Director, (202) 267-6352. Toll-free hotline, (800) 424-8802.

Web, www.nrc.uscg.mil

Maintains twenty-four-hour hotline for reporting oil spills, hazardous materials accidents, chemical releases, or known or suspected terrorist threats. Notifies appropriate federal officials to reduce the effects of accidents.

National Security Council (NSC), *(Executive Office of the President), Critical Infrastructure Protection,* Dwight D. Eisenhower Executive Office Bldg., #302 20506; (202) 456-9351. Paul Kurtz, Special Assistant to the President and Senior Director.

Web, www.whitehouse.gov/nsc

Coordinates the protection of critical national infrastructure systems in the event of terrorist attack; advises the president on all matters relating to cybersecurity.

Navy Dept. *(Defense Dept.), Naval Network Operations and Space Detachment Command,* 4234 Seminary Dr. N.W., #19122 20394-5460; (202) 764-0550. Fax, (202) 764-0357. Gerda Edwards, Officer in Charge.

Web, www.navy.mil

Provides, operates, and maintains all Navy global telecommunications, information, and space systems and services in support of operations, training, and education.

President's National Security Telecommunications Advisory Committee, *c/o National Communications System, 701 S. Courthouse Rd., Arlington, VA 22204-2198; (703) 607-6221. Fax, (703) 607-4826. Janet S. Jefferson, Program Manager.*

Web, www.ncs.gov

Advises the president on specific measures to improve national security telecommunications.

Industrial and Military Planning and Mobilization

AGENCIES

Bureau of Export Administration (*Commerce Dept.*), *Strategic Industries and Economic Security,* 14th St. and Constitution Ave. N.W., #3876 20230; (202) 482-4506. Fax, (202) 482-5650. Daniel O. Hill, Director.
Web, www.bxa.doc.gov

Administers the Defense Production Act and provides industry with information on the allocation of resources falling under the jurisdiction of the act; conducts studies on industrial mobilization for the federal government.

Defense Logistics Agency (*Defense Dept.*), *Logistics Operations,* 8725 John Jay Kingman Rd., Fort Belvoir, VA 22060-6221; (703) 767-1600. Fax, (703) 767-1588. Maj. Gen. Hawthorne L. Proctor, Director. Information, (703) 767-6200.
Web, www.supply.dla.mil

Oversees procurement, management, storage, and distribution of items used to support Defense Dept. logistics.

Maritime Administration (*Transportation Dept.*), *National Security Plans,* 400 7th St. S.W., #7130 20590; (202) 366-5900. Fax, (202) 366-5904. Thomas M. P. Christensen, Director.
Web, marad.dot.gov

Plans for the transition of merchant shipping from peacetime to wartime operations under the direction of the National Shipping Authority. (The National Shipping Authority is a stand-by organization that is activated upon the declaration of a war or other national emergency.)

Maritime Administration (*Transportation Dept.*), *Ship Operations,* 400 7th St. S.W., #2122 20590; (202) 366-1875. Fax, (202) 366-3954. William F. Trost, Director.
Web, marad.dot.gov

Maintains the National Defense Reserve Fleet, a fleet of older vessels traded in by U.S. flag operators that are called into operation during emergencies; manages and administers the Ready Reserve Force, a fleet of ships available for operation within four to twenty days, to meet the nation's sealift readiness requirements.

CONGRESS

House Armed Services Committee, *Subcommittee on Readiness,* 2120 RHOB 20515; (202) 225-6288. Fax, (202) 225-9077. Rep. Joel Hefley, R-Colo., Chair.
Web, www.house.gov/hasc

Jurisdiction over legislation concerning civil defense, emergency mobilization of merchant fleets, and national defense stockpiles, including military, civilian, and industrial requirements.

Senate Armed Services Committee, *Subcommittee on Readiness and Management Support,* SR-228 20510; (202) 224-3871. Fax, (202) 228-0036. Sen. John Ensign, R-Nev., Chair; Lucian Niemeyer, Professional Staff Member.
Web, armed-services.senate.gov

Jurisdiction over legislation concerning national defense stockpiles, including military, civilian, and industrial requirements. Jurisdiction over emergency preparedness legislation, including civil defense, emergency mobilization of merchant fleets, emergency communications, and industrial planning and mobilization.

NONPROFIT

National Defense Industrial Assn., 2111 Wilson Blvd., #400, Arlington, VA 22201-3061; (703) 522-1820. Fax, (703) 522-1885. Gen. Lawrence Farrell, President.
Web, www.ndia.org

Membership: U.S. citizens and businesses interested in national security. Also open to individuals and businesses in nations that have defense agreements with the United States. Provides information and expertise on defense preparedness issues; works to increase public awareness of national defense preparedness through education programs; serves as a forum for dialogue between the defense industry and the government.

National Defense Transportation Assn., 50 S. Pickett St., #222, Alexandria, VA 22304-7296; (703) 751-5011. Fax, (703) 823-8761. Kenneth Wykle, President.
Web, www.ndtahq.com

Membership: transportation service companies. Maintains liaison with the Defense Dept., Transportation Dept., and Federal Emergency Management Agency to prepare emergency transportation plans.

Shipbuilders Council of America, 1455 F St. N.W., #225 20005; (202) 347-5462. Fax, (202) 347-5464. Allen Walker, President.
Web, www.shipbuilders.org

Membership: commercially focused shipyards that repair and build ships, and allied industries and associations. National trade association representing the competitive shipyard industry that makes up the core shipyard industrial base in the United States. Monitors legislation and regulations.

Infrastructure Protection

See also Information Sharing and Analysis Centers on pp. 615–616.

AGENCIES

Energy Dept. (DOE), *Energy Assurance, 1000 Independence Ave. S.W. 20585; (202) 287-1808. Fax, (202) 287-1804. James F. McDonnell, Director.*
General e-mail, oea@hq.doe.gov
Web, www.oea.dis.anl.gov

Applies science and technology to improve security of critical energy infrastructure and protect against the use of this infrastructure as a means of terrorism. Works with states and industry to ensure a reliable flow of energy to homes, industry, public services, and transportation. Takes measures to minimize vulnerabilities and risks to the economy and public health safety including the testing of nuclear plants and major electric providers. Conducts Federal Liaison Officer Program to assist other agencies with critical energy infrastructure protection.

Federal Protective Service (FPS), *(Homeland Security Dept.), 1800 F St. N.W., #2341 20405; (202) 501-0907. Fax, (202) 208-5866. Wendell Shingler, Assistant Commissioner.*
Web, www.bice.immigration.gov

Works to ensure that appropriate levels of security are in place in General Services Administration–managed facilities throughout the United States. Conducts assessments on all GSA-controlled facilities to evaluate threats and tailor appropriate security countermeasures. Has enforcement capability to detain and arrest people, seize goods or conveyances, obtain arrest and search warrants, respond to incidents and emergency situations, provide protection during demonstrations or civil unrest, and to be deputized for law enforcement response in special situations.

Homeland Security Dept. (DHS), *Critical Infrastructure Assurance Office, 1401 Constitution Ave. N.W., #6095 20230; (202) 482-7473. Fax, (202) 482-7498. Nancy Wong, Director (Acting).*
General e-mail, Public.Affairs@ciao.gov
Web, www.ciao.gov and www.dhs.gov

Coordinates and implements the national strategy (which encompasses both public and private sectors) to protect critical infrastructure, including agriculture, food, water, public health, emergency services, government, the defense industrial base, information and telecommunications, energy, transportation, banking and finance, the chemical industry and hazardous materials, and the postal and shipping sectors.

Homeland Security Dept. (DHS), *Federal Computer Incident Response Center, 7th and D Sts. S.W. 20407. Lawrence C. Hale, Director. Nontechnical inquiries: (202)*
708-5060; fax, (202) 708-5869; secure fax, (202) 205-0799. Incident reports and technical inquiries: (888) 282-0870; fax, (703) 326-9461; secure fax, (703) 326-9413.
General e-mail, info@fedcirc.gov
Web, www.fedcirc.gov

Partnership of computer-incident response teams, security and law enforcement professionals, and academic and private-sector specialists who provide services in computer security incident prevention, reporting, analysis, and recovery.

Homeland Security Dept. (DHS), *Information Analysis and Infrastructure Protection Directorate, Nebraska Ave. Complex, 3801 Nebraska Ave. N.W. 20395; (202) 282-8000. Frank Libutti, Under Secretary (Designate).*
Web, www.dhs.gov

Assigned the lead responsibility for coordinating the collection and analysis of intelligence and information pertaining to threats against U.S. infrastructure. Handles the merging of capabilities to identify and assess current and future threats to homeland infrastructure; identifies and assesses vulnerabilities, takes preventive action, and issues timely warnings. Develops partnerships and communication lines with state and local governments and the private sector. Administers the Homeland Security Advisory System, which conveys threat information.

National Institute of Standards and Technology (NIST), *Computer Security, 100 Bureau Dr., MS 8930, Gaithersburg, MD 20899-8930; (301) 975-2934. Fax, (301) 926-2733. Edward Roback, Chief.*
Web, www.csrc.nist.gov

Works to improve information systems security by raising awareness of information technology risks, vulnerabilities, and protection requirements; researches and advises government agencies of risks; devises measures for cost-effective security and privacy of sensitive federal systems.

National Security Council (NSC), *(Executive Office of the President), Critical Infrastructure Protection, Dwight D. Eisenhower Executive Office Bldg., #302 20506; (202) 456-9351. Paul Kurtz, Special Assistant to the President and Senior Director.*
Web, www.whitehouse.gov/nsc

Coordinates the protection of critical national infrastructure systems in the event of terrorist attack; advises the president on all matters relating to cybersecurity.

Transportation Security Administration (TSA), *(Homeland Security Dept.), 701 S. 12th St., #1203 North, Arlington, VA 22202 (mailing address: 400 7th St. S.W., Washington, DC 20590); (571) 227-2800. Fax, (571) 227-2555. James M. Loy, Under Secretary.*

General e-mail, tsawebmaster@ost.dot.gov

Web, www.tsa.gov

Responsible for aviation, rail, land, and maritime transportation security. Programs and interests include the stationing of federal security directors and federal passenger screeners at airports, the Federal Air Marshal Program, improved detection of explosives, and enhanced port security.

Treasury Dept., *Critical Infrastructure Protection and Compliance Policy,* *1500 Pennsylvania Ave. N.W. 20220; (202) 622-0101. Michael A. Dawson, Deputy Assistant Secretary.*

General e-mail, OCIP@do.treas.gov

Web, www.treas.gov

Responsible for strengthening safeguards against terrorist activities and financial crimes.

U.S. Coast Guard (USCG), *(Homeland Security Dept.), Marine Safety, Security, and Environmental Protection,* *2100 2nd St. S.W., #2408 20593; (202) 267-2200. Fax, (202) 267-4839. Rear Adm. Paul J. Pluta, Assistant Commandant.*

Web, www.uscg.mil/hq/g-m/gmhome.htm

Establishes and enforces regulations for port safety; environmental protection; vessel safety, inspection, design, documentation, and investigation; licensing of merchant vessel personnel; and shipment of hazardous materials.

U.S. Secret Service *(Homeland Security Dept.), Financial Crimes,* *950 H St. N.W., #5300 20223; (202) 406-5850. Fax, (202) 406-5031. Timothy Caddigan, Special Agent in Charge.*

Web, www.secretservice.gov/financial_crimes.shtml

Investigates crimes associated with financial institutions. Jurisdiction includes bank fraud, access device fraud involving credit and debit cards, telecommunications and computer crimes, fraudulent identification, fraudulent government and commercial securities, and electronic funds transfer fraud.

CONGRESS

House Government Reform Committee, *Subcommittee on Technology, Information Policy, Intergovernmental Relations, and the Census,* *B349A RHOB 20515; (202) 225-6751. Fax, (202) 225-4960. Rep. Adam H. Putnam, R-Fla., Chair; Robert Dix, Staff Director.*

Web, www.house.gov/reform

Reviews technology security issues, including the safety of federal employees and their workplaces. Reviews security threats to telecommunications networks.

House Select Committee on Homeland Security, *Subcommittee on Cybersecurity, Science, and Research and Development,* *2402 RHOB 20515; (202) 226-8417. Rep. William M. "Mac" Thornberry, R-Texas, Chair.*

Web, hsc.house.gov

Jurisdiction over legislation related to the security of computer, telecommunications, information technology, electronic infrastructure and data systems, including science, research, and development related thereto; protection of government and private networks and computer systems from domestic and foreign attack; prevention of injury to civilian populations and physical infrastructure caused by cyberattack.

House Select Committee on Homeland Security, *Subcommittee on Infrastructure and Border Security,* *2402 RHOB 20515; (202) 226-8417. Rep. Dave Camp, R-Mich., Chair.*

Web, hsc.house.gov

Jurisdiction includes the protection of highways, bridges, waterways, airports and air transportation, energy supplies, and other critical infrastructure from attack; preservation of critical government, business, and financial institutions.

House Transportation and Infrastructure Committee, *2165 RHOB 20515; (202) 225-9446. Fax, (202) 225-6782. Rep. Don Young, R-Alaska, Chair; Lloyd Jones, Chief of Staff.*

General e-mail, transcomm@mail.house.gov

Web, www.house.gov/transportation

Jurisdiction over legislation on transportation and transportation infrastructure, including civil aviation, railroads, water transportation; transportation safety (except automobile safety); water power; the U.S. Coast Guard; federal management of emergencies and natural disasters; inspection of merchant marine vessels; measures, other than appropriations, that relate to construction, maintenance, and safety of roads, bridges, and dams.

Senate Commerce, Science, and Transportation Committee, *SD-508 20510; (202) 224-1251. Fax, (202) 224-1259. Sen. John McCain, R-Ariz., Chair; Jeanne Bumpus, Staff Director.*

Web, commerce.senate.gov

Jurisdiction over legislation on interstate commerce and transportation generally; communications systems; transportation safety, including aviation, rail, motor carrier industries; hazardous materials transportation.

Senate Governmental Affairs Committee, *SD-340 20510; (202) 224-4751. Fax, (202) 224-9682. Sen. Susan Collins, R-Maine, Chair; Michael Bopp, Staff Director.*

Jurisdiction includes the efficiency and economy of all branches of government and the effectiveness of present national security methods.

Public Health and Environment

AGENCIES

Centers for Disease Control and Prevention (CDC), *(Health and Human Services Dept.), Washington Office,* 200 Independence Ave. S.W., HHH Bldg., #746-G 20201-0004; (202) 690-8598. Fax, (202) 690-7519. Donald E. Shriber, Associate Director.

Web, www.cdc.gov/washington

Supports the CDC's Bioterrorism and Preparedness and Response Program, which ensures the rapid development of federal, state, and local capacity to respond to bioterrorism. (Headquarters in Atlanta, Ga.: 1600 Clifton Rd. N.E. 30333. Public inquiries, [404] 639-3534.)

Environmental Protection Agency (EPA), *Chemical Emergency Preparedness and Prevention,* 1200 Pennsylvania Ave. N.W., #1448, MC 5104A 20460; (202) 564-8600. Fax, (202) 564-8222. Deborah Dietrich, Director. Toll-free hotline, (800) 535-0202.

Web, www.epa.gov/ceppo

Responsible for planning for and responding to the harmful effects of the release or dissemination of toxic poisonous chemicals. Areas of responsibility include helping state and local responders plan for emergencies; coordinating with key federal partners; training first responders; and providing resources in the event of a terrorist incident.

Health and Human Services Dept. (HHS), *Public Health Emergency Preparedness,* 200 Independence Ave. S.W., #636-G 20201; (202) 401-4862. Fax, (202) 690-7412. Jerome M. Hauer, Assistant Secretary (Acting).

General e-mail, Jerome.Hauer@hhs.gov

Web, www.hhs.gov/ophp

Responsible for coordinating U.S. medical and public health preparedness and response to emergencies, including acts of biological, chemical, and nuclear terrorism. Oversees bioterrorism preparedness grant funding for state and local governments.

National Disaster Medical System, *12300 Twinbrook Pkwy., #360, Rockville, MD 20852; (301) 443-1167. Fax, (301) 443-5146. Tracy Williams, Director, (301) 443-9456. Toll-free, (800) USA-NDMS.*

Web, ndms.dhhs.gov/NDMS/ndms.html

Cooperative, federally coordinated program for federal, state, and local governments, private businesses, and civilian volunteers that works to ensure the availability of medical resources following a disaster.

National Institute of Allergy and Infectious Diseases *(National Institutes of Health), 31 Center Dr., Bldg. 31, #7A03, MSC-2520, Bethesda, MD 20892-2520; (301) 496-2263. Fax, (301) 496-4409. Dr. Anthony S. Fauci, Director. Information, (301) 496-5717.*

General e-mail, niaidoc@flash.niaid.nih.gov

Web, www.niaid.nih.gov

Responsible for basic research and development of new medical tools to detect and counter a bioterrorist attack. Conducts research aimed at understanding the organisms that might be used as agents of bioterrorism and the human immune system's response to them. Initiatives include the development of safer, next-generation smallpox vaccines. Shares capabilities and resources with the U.S. Army Medical Research Institute of Infectious Diseases at Fort Detrick, Md.

Public Health and Science *(Health and Human Services Dept.), Emergency Response, 12300 Twinbrook Pkwy., #360, Rockville, MD 20852; (301) 443-1167. Fax, (301) 443-5146. Dr. Kevin S. Yeskey, Director.*

Web, www.oep-ndms.dhhs.gov

Works with the Federal Emergency Management Agency and other federal agencies and departments to develop plans and maintain operational readiness for responding to requests for assistance during presidentially declared disasters such as terrorist attack; develops and coordinates medical equipment and training plans for catastrophic disasters; maintains logistical plans and communications networks with federal, state, and local emergency preparedness organizations.

CONGRESS

House Appropriations Committee, *Subcommittee on VA, HUD, and Independent Agencies, H143 CAP 20515; (202) 225-3241. Rep. James T. Walsh, R-N.Y., Chair; Tim Peterson, Staff Director.*

Web, www.house.gov/appropriations

Jurisdiction over legislation to appropriate funds for the Environmental Protection Agency, Office of Environmental Quality, Council on Environmental Quality, National Science Foundation, and other environment-related services and programs.

House Energy and Commerce Committee, *Subcommittee on Health, 2125 RHOB 20515; (202) 225-2927. Fax, (202) 225-1919. Rep. Michael Bilirakis, R-Fla., Chair; David V. Marventano, Staff Director.*

General e-mail, commerce@mail.house.gov

Web, energycommerce.house.gov

Jurisdiction over legislation regarding public health and health protection in general; quarantine; and vaccines.

Senate Appropriations Committee, *Subcommittee on VA, HUD, and Independent Agencies, SD-130 20510; (202) 224-8252. Fax, (202) 228-1624. Sen. Christopher S. Bond, R-Mo., Chair; Jon Kamarck, Clerk.*
Web, appropriations.senate.gov

Jurisdiction over legislation to appropriate funds for the Environmental Protection Agency, Office of Environmental Quality, Council on Environmental Quality, National Science Foundation, and other environment-related services and programs.

Senate Health, Education, Labor, and Pensions Committee, *SD-428 20510; (202) 224-5375. Fax, (202) 228-5044. Sen. Judd Gregg, R-N.H., Chair; Sharon Soderstrom, Staff Director. TTY, (202) 224-1975.*
Web, health.senate.gov

Jurisdiction over legislation regarding public health and health protection in general; quarantine; and vaccines.

NONPROFIT

American Red Cross, *Disaster Services, 2025 E St. N.W. 20006. Terry Sicilia, Executive Vice President.*
Web, www.redcross.org/disaster

Chartered by Congress to administer disaster relief. Provides disaster victims with food, clothing, shelter, first aid, and medical care; promotes disaster preparedness and prevention.

National Assn. of State EMS Directors (NASEMSD), *111 Park Place, Falls Church, VA 22046-4513; (703) 538-1799. Fax, (703) 241-5603. Elizabeth B. Armstrong, Executive Director.*
General e-mail, info@nasemsd.org
Web, www.nasemsd.org

Works to provide leadership and support for the development of effective emergency medical services (EMS) systems throughout the United States; to formulate national EMS policy; and to foster communication and sharing among state EMS directors.

National Vaccine Information Center, *421-E Church St., Vienna, VA 22180; (703) 938-3783. Fax, (703) 938-5768. Barbara Loe Fisher, President. Information, (800) 909-SHOT.*
Web, www.909shot.com

Educates the public and provides research on vaccination safety procedures and effectiveness; supports reform of the vaccination system; publishes information

on diseases and vaccines; and monitors legislation and regulations. Areas of recent interest include provisions of the Homeland Security Act relating to vaccination laws, and vaccination campaigns for anthrax and smallpox.

Selective Service

AGENCIES

Selective Service System, *1515 Wilson Blvd., Arlington, VA 22209-2425; (703) 605-4010. Fax, (703) 605-4006. Lewis Brodsky, Deputy Director. Locator, (703) 605-4000.*
Web, www.sss.gov

Supplies the armed forces with manpower when authorized; registers male citizens of the United States ages eighteen to twenty-five. In an emergency, would institute a draft and would provide alternative service assignments to men classified as conscientious objectors.

CONGRESS

House Appropriations Committee, *Subcommittee on VA, HUD, and Independent Agencies, H143 CAP 20515; (202) 225-3241. Rep. James T. Walsh, R-N.Y., Chair; Tim Peterson, Staff Director.*
Web, www.house.gov/appropriations

Jurisdiction over legislation to appropriate funds for the Selective Service System.

House Armed Services Committee, *Subcommittee on Total Force, 2340 RHOB 20515; (202) 225-7560. Fax, (202) 226-0789. Rep. John M. McHugh, R-N.Y., Chair; John Chapla, Staff Director.*
Web, www.house.gov/hasc

Jurisdiction over Selective Service legislation.

House Government Reform Committee, *Subcommittee on National Security, Emerging Threats, and International Relations, B372 RHOB 20515; (202) 225-2548. Fax, (202) 225-2382. Rep. Christopher Shays, R-Conn., Chair; Lawrence Halloran, Staff Director.*
Web, www.house.gov/reform

Oversees operations of the Selective Service System.

Senate Appropriations Committee, *Subcommittee on VA, HUD, and Independent Agencies, SD-130 20510; (202) 224-8252. Fax, (202) 228-1624. Sen. Christopher S. Bond, R-Mo., Chair; Jon Kamarck, Clerk.*
Web, appropriations.senate.gov

Jurisdiction over legislation to appropriate funds for the Selective Service System.

Senate Armed Services Committee, *Subcommittee on Personnel, SR-228 20510; (202) 224-3871. Fax, (202) 228-0036. Sen. Saxby Chambliss, R-Ga., Chair; Dick Walsh, Staff Director.*

Oversees operations of the Selective Service System.

NONPROFIT

Center on Conscience & War, *1830 Connecticut Ave. N.W. 20009; (202) 483-2220. Fax, (202) 483-1246. J. E. McNeil, Executive Director.*
General e-mail, nisbco@nisbco.org
Web, www.nisbco.org

Seeks to defend and extend the rights of conscientious objectors. Provides information and advocacy about the military draft and national selective service. Offers counseling and information to military personnel seeking discharge or transfer to noncombatant positions within the military.

Strategic Stockpiles

AGENCIES

Defense Dept. (DoD), *Industrial Policy, 3300 Defense Pentagon, #3E1060 20301-3300; (703) 695-7178. Fax, (703) 695-4277. Suzanne D. Patrick, Under Secretary.*
Web, www.acq.osd.mil/ip

Develops and oversees strategic, industrial, and critical materials policies including oversight of the National Defense Stockpile.

Defense Logistics Agency *(Defense Dept.), Defense National Stockpile Center, 8725 John Jay Kingman Rd., #3229, Fort Belvoir, VA 22060-6223; (703) 767-5500. Fax, (703) 767-5538. Cornel A. Holder, Administrator.*
Web, www.dnsc.dla.mil

Manages the national defense stockpile of strategic and critical materials. Purchases strategic materials including beryllium and newly developed high-tech alloys. Disposes of excess materials including tin, silver, industrial diamond stones, tungsten, and vegetable tannin.

Fossil Energy *(Energy Dept.), Naval Petroleum and Oil Shale Reserves, 1000 Independence Ave. S.W., #3H076 20585; (202) 586-4685. Fax, (202) 586-4446. Anton R. Dammer, Director.*
Web, www.fe.doe.gov

Develops, conserves, operates, and maintains oil fields for producing oil, natural gas, and other petroleum products. Operates Rocky Mountain Oil Field Testing Center.

National Institute of Standards and Technology (NIST), *(Commerce Dept.), Materials Science and Engineering Laboratory, 100 Bureau Dr., MS 8500, Gaithersburg, MD 20899-8500; (301) 975-5658. Fax, (301) 975-5012. Leslie E. Smith, Director.*
Web, www.nist.gov

Advises the secretary and Congress on strategic resources issues. Conducts studies; coordinates development of departmental positions on federal policies and programs; and develops and maintains consultation program with business interests.

CONGRESS

House Armed Services Committee, *Subcommittee on Readiness, 2120 RHOB 20515; (202) 225-6288. Fax, (202) 225-9077. Rep. Joel Hefley, R-Colo., Chair.*
Web, www.house.gov/hasc

Jurisdiction over legislation concerning civil defense, emergency mobilization of merchant fleets, and national defense stockpiles, including military, civilian, and industrial requirements.

Senate Armed Services Committee, *Subcommittee on Readiness and Management Support, SR-228 20510; (202) 224-3871. Fax, (202) 228-0036. Sen. John Ensign, R-Nev., Chair; Lucian Niemeyer, Professional Staff Member.*
Web, armed-services.senate.gov

Jurisdiction over legislation concerning national defense stockpiles, including military, civilian, and industrial requirements. Jurisdiction over emergency preparedness legislation, including civil defense, emergency mobilization of merchant fleets, emergency communications, and industrial planning and mobilization.

INTELLIGENCE AND COUNTERTERRORISM

AGENCIES

Air Force Dept. (ISR), *(Defense Dept.), Intelligence, Surveillance, and Reconnaissance, 1480 Air Force Pentagon, #4A932 20330-1480; (703) 695-5613. Fax, (703) 697-4903. Ronald Sams, Director.*
Web, www.af.mil

Military office that directs Air Force intelligence activities and coordinates activities with other intelligence agencies.

Army Dept. *(Defense Dept.), Intelligence, 1000 Army Pentagon, #2E408 20310-1000; (703) 695-3033. Fax, (703) 697-7605. Lt. Gen. Robert W. Noonan Jr., Deputy Chief of Staff.*
Web, www.army.mil

Military office that directs Army intelligence activities and coordinates activities with other intelligence agencies.

Bureau of Customs and Border Protection *(Homeland Security Dept.), Anti-terrorism,* 1300 Pennsylvania Ave. N.W., #4.2D 20229; (202) 927-2230. Fax, (202) 927-5506. William Parrish, Director.
General e-mail, anti-terrorism@customs.treas.gov
Web, www.customs.gov

Coordinates the effort to prevent the introduction of weapons of mass destruction into the United States and to prevent international terrorists from obtaining weapons of mass destruction materials, technologies, arms, funds, and other support.

Central Intelligence Agency (CIA), *CIA Headquarters, Langley, VA 20505; (703) 482-1100. Fax, (703) 482-1739. George J. Tenet, Director. Information, (703) 482-0623.*
Web, www.cia.gov

Coordinates the intelligence functions of government agencies as they relate to national security and advises the National Security Council on those functions; gathers and evaluates intelligence relating to national security and distributes the information to government agencies in the national security field.

Central Intelligence Agency (CIA), *National Intelligence Council, CIA Headquarters, Langley, VA 20505; (703) 482-6724. Fax, (703) 482-8632. Robert L. Hutchings, Chair.*
Web, www.cia.gov/nic

Supports the director of central intelligence and serves as the intelligence community's center for midterm and long-term strategic thinking. Provides a focal point for policymakers' inquiries and needs. Establishes contacts with private sector and academic experts in the intelligence field.

Criminal Division *(Justice Dept.), Counterterrorism,* 601 D St. N.W., #6500 20530; (202) 514-0849. Fax, (202) 514-8714. Barry Sabin, Chief.
Web, www.usdoj.gov/criminal/tvcs.html

Investigates and prosecutes incidents of international and domestic terrorism involving U.S. interests, domestic violent crime, firearms, and explosives violations. Provides legal advice on federal statutes relating to murder, assault, kidnapping, threats, robbery, weapons and explosives control, malicious destruction of property, and aircraft and sea piracy.

Defense Dept. (DoD), *Command, Control, Communications, and Intelligence,* 6000 Defense Pentagon, #3E172 20301-6000; (703) 695-0348. Fax, (703) 614-8060. John P. Stenbit, Assistant Secretary.
Web, www.c3i.osd.mil

Civilian office that advises and makes recommendations to the secretary of defense on the management of all Defense Dept. intelligence and communications programs, resources, and activities.

Defense Dept. (DoD), *Intelligence,* 5000 Defense Pentagon 20301-5000; (703) 695-0971. Fax, (703) 693-5706. Stephen A. Cambone, Under Secretary.
Web, www.defenselink.mil

Responsible for ensuring the secretary of defense access to intelligence information.

Defense Dept. (DoD), *Intelligence Oversight,* 4035 Ridgetop Rd., #210, Fairfax, VA 22030; (703) 275-6552. Fax, (703) 275-6590. George B. Lotz II, Assistant to the Secretary.
Web, www.dtic.mil/atsdio

Responsible for the independent oversight of all Defense Dept. intelligence, counterintelligence, and related activities, and for the formulation of intelligence oversight policy; reviews intelligence operations and investigates and reports on possible violations of federal law or regulations.

Defense Dept. (DoD), *Special Operations and Low-Intensity Conflict,* 2500 Defense Pentagon, #2E258 20301-2500; (703) 693-2895. Fax, (703) 693-6335. Vacant, Assistant Secretary; Marshall S. Billingslea, Principal Deputy Assistant Secretary.
Web, www.defenselink.mil

Serves as special staff assistant and civilian adviser to the secretary of defense on matters related to special operations and international terrorism.

Defense Information Systems Agency (DISA), *(Defense Dept.),* 701 S. Courthouse Rd., Arlington, VA 22204-2199; (703) 607-6001. Fax, (703) 607-4802. Lt. Gen. Harry D. Raduege Jr., Director. Information, (703) 607-6900.
Web, www.disa.mil

The Defense Dept. agency responsible for information technology and the central manager for major portions of the defense information infrastructure. Units include the White House Communications Agency; the DISA director is also manager of the National Communications System.

Defense Intelligence Agency *(Defense Dept.),* 7400 Defense Pentagon, #3E258 20301-7400; (703) 695-7353. Fax, (703) 614-8115. Lowell Jacoby, Director.
Web, www.dia.mil

Collects and evaluates foreign military-related intelligence information to satisfy the requirements of the secretary of defense, Joint Chiefs of Staff, selected components of the Defense Dept., and other authorized agencies.

Energy Dept. (DOE), *Office of Intelligence: Intelligence Support Division,* 1000 Independence Ave. S.W., #GA-301 20585; (202) 586-2610. Fax, (202) 586-0751. John A. Russack, Director.
Web, www.energy.gov

Gathers and maintains information as it relates to national security, including military applications of nuclear energy.

Federal Bureau of Investigation (FBI), *(Justice Dept.), Awareness of National Security Issues and Response,* 935 Pennsylvania Ave. N.W. 20535-0001; (202) 324-3000. To report suspected intelligence information or terrorism activity to ANSIR coordinator at local Washington field office of FBI, (202) 278-2000.
General e-mail, ansir@leo.gov
Web, www.fbi.gov/hq/ci/ansir/ansirhome.htm

Disseminates unclassified national security threat and warning information to U.S. corporations, law enforcement, and other government agencies to make potential targets of intelligence and terrorist activities less vulnerable through awareness; responds to activity when identified.

Federal Bureau of Investigation (FBI), *(Justice Dept.), Command Center,* 935 Pennsylvania Ave. N.W., #7110 20535; (202) 323-3300. David Szady, Assistant Director. Information, (202) 324-3000. Press, (202) 324-3691.

Investigates violations of federal law relating to sabotage, espionage, treason, sedition, and other matters affecting national security. Conducts counterespionage activities against hostile intelligence services and their agents in the United States.

Federal Bureau of Investigation (FBI), *(Justice Dept.), International Terrorism Operations,* 935 Pennsylvania Ave. N.W., #5222 20535; (202) 324-4664. Fax, (202) 324-4624. Arthur Cummings, Chief. Press, (202) 324-3691.

Federal law enforcement agency with primary jurisdiction over the U.S. government's counterterrorism activities. Responsible for preventing, interdicting, and investigating the criminal activities of international terrorist groups and individuals.

Homeland Security Dept. (DHS), *Nebraska Ave. Complex,* 3801 Nebraska Ave. N.W. 20395; (202) 282-8000. Thomas J. Ridge, Secretary; Gordon R. England, Deputy Secretary.

Web, www.dhs.gov

Responsible for the development and coordination of a comprehensive national strategy to protect the United States against terrorist attacks. Coordinates the strategy of the executive branch together with state and local governments and private entities to detect, prepare for, protect against, respond to, and recover from terrorist attacks in the United States.

Homeland Security Dept. (DHS), *Terrorist Threat Integration Center,* CIA Headquarters, Langley, VA 20505; (703) 482-1100. John O. Brennan, Director. Public Affairs, (703) 482-0623.
Web, www.dhs.gov

A joint Federal Bureau of Investigation-Central Intelligence Agency-Homeland Security Dept. intelligence analysis unit. Designed to enable full integration of information and analysis related to terrorist threats against the U.S. government and to promote unfettered sharing of relevant information across department lines.

Justice Dept. (DOJ), *Counterespionage Section,* 1400 New York Ave. N.W., 9th Floor 20530; (202) 514-1187. Fax, (202) 514-2836. John J. Dion, Chief.
Web, www.usdoj.gov

Enforces criminal statutes relating to national security, including treason, espionage, sedition, sabotage, and the export of military and strategic commodities and technology; supervises registration requirements of the Foreign Agents Registration Act.

Justice Dept. (DOJ), *Intelligence Policy and Review,* 950 Pennsylvania Ave. N.W., #6150 20530; (202) 514-5600. Fax, (202) 514-7858. James A. Baker, Counsel.
Web, www.usdoj.gov

Provides the attorney general with legal advice and recommendations on national security matters. Reviews executive orders, directives, and procedures relating to the intelligence community; approves certain intelligence-gathering activities. Provides interpretations and applications of the Constitution, statutes, regulations, and directives relating to U.S. national security activities. Represents the United States before the Foreign Intelligence Surveillance Court.

Marine Corps *(Defense Dept.), Intelligence,* 2 Navy Annex 20380-1775; (703) 614-2522. Fax, (703) 614-5888. Brig. Gen. Michael E. Ennis, Director.

Military office that directs Marine Corps intelligence activities and coordinates activities with other intelligence agencies.

National Commission on Terrorist Attacks Upon the United States (9-11 Commission), *(202) 331-*

4060. Fax, (202) 296-5545. Thomas Kean, Chair; Philip D. Zelikow, Executive Director.

General e-mail, info@9-11Commission.gov

Web, www.9-11commission.gov

Independent ten-person commission chartered by Congress and the president to prepare a full account of the circumstances surrounding the September 11, 2001, terrorist attacks on the United States. Mandated also to provide recommendations designed to guard against future attacks.

National Imagery and Mapping Agency *(Defense Dept.),* *4600 Sangamore Rd., #378, Bethesda, MD 20816; (301) 227-7300. Fax, (301) 227-3696. Lt. Gen. James R. Clapper Jr., Director.*

Web, www.nima.mil

Combat support agency that provides imagery and geospatial information to national policymakers and military forces in support of national defense objectives; incorporates the missions and functions of the former Defense Mapping Agency, Central Imaging Office, and Defense Dissemination Program Office.

National Reconnaissance Office *(Defense Dept.),* *14675 Lee Rd., Chantilly, VA 20151-1715; (703) 808-1198. Fax, (703) 808-1171. Peter B. Teets, Director. Public Affairs, (703) 808-1015.*

Web, www.nro.gov

Researches, develops, and operates intelligence satellites. Gathers intelligence for various purposes, including indications and warning, monitoring of arms control agreements, military operations and exercises, and monitoring of natural disasters and other environmental issues.

National Security Agency (NSA), *(Defense Dept.),* *9800 Savage Rd., Fort Meade, MD 20755-6000; (301) 688-6524. Fax, (301) 688-6198. Lt. Gen. Michael V. Hayden Jr., (USAF) Director; William B. Black, Deputy Director. Information, (301) 688-6524.*

Web, www.nsa.gov

Intercepts and analyzes foreign communication signals and protects U.S. national security–related information systems from exploitation through interception, unauthorized access, or related technical intelligence threats.

National Security Council (NSC), *(Executive Office of the President),* **International Economic Affairs,** *The White House 20504; (202) 456-9281. Fax, (202) 456-9280. John A. Cloud Jr., Special Assistant to the President.*

Web, www.whitehouse.gov/nsc

Advises the president, the National Security Council, and the National Economic Council on all aspects of U.S. foreign policy dealing with U.S. international economic policies.

Navy Dept. *(Defense Dept.),* **Naval Intelligence,** *2000 Navy Pentagon, #4E362 20350-2000; (703) 614-0281. Fax, (703) 697-6800. Rear Adm. Richard Porterfield, Director.*

Web, www.navy.mil

Military office that directs Navy intelligence activities and coordinates activities with other intelligence agencies.

President's Foreign Intelligence Advisory Board *(Executive Office of the President),* *Dwight D. Eisenhower Executive Office Bldg., #494 20502; (202) 456-2352. Fax, (202) 395-3403. Brent Scowcroft, Chair; Randy Deitering, Executive Director.*

Web, www.whitehouse.gov/pfiab

Members appointed by the president. Assesses the quality, quantity, and adequacy of foreign intelligence collection and of counterintelligence activities by all government agencies; advises the president on matters concerning intelligence and national security.

State Dept., *Counterterrorism,* *2201 C St. N.W., #2507 20520; (202) 647-9892. Fax, (202) 647-0221. Cofer Black, Coordinator. Press, (202) 647-8682.*

Web, www.state.gov

Implements U.S. counterterrorism policy and coordinates activities with foreign governments; responds to terrorist acts; works to promote a stronger counterterrorism stance worldwide.

State Dept., *Diplomatic Security Bureau,* *2201 C St. N.W., #6316 20520; (202) 647-6290. Fax, (202) 647-0953. Francis X. Taylor, Assistant Secretary.*

General e-mail, DSPublicAffairs@state.gov

Web, ds.state.gov

Conducts the Anti-Terrorism Assistance Program, which provides training to foreign governments fighting terrorism.

State Dept., *Intelligence and Research,* *2201 C St. N.W., #6531 20520-6531; (202) 647-9177. Fax, (202) 736-4688. Carl W. Ford Jr., Assistant Secretary.*

Web, www.state.gov

Coordinates foreign policy–related research, analysis, and intelligence programs for the State Dept. and other federal agencies.

Transportation Dept. (DOT), *Intelligence and Security,* *400 7th St. S.W., #10401 20590; (202) 366-6535. Fax, (202) 366-7261. Rear Adm. Stephen W. Rochon, Director.*

Web, www.dot.gov

Advises the secretary on transportation intelligence and security policy. Acts as liaison with the intelligence community, federal agencies, corporations, and interest groups; administers counterterrorism strategic planning processes.

Treasury Dept., *Executive Office for Terrorist Financing and Financial Crimes, 1500 Pennsylvania Ave. N.W. 20220; (202) 622-1466. Juan Zarate, Deputy Assistant Secretary.*
Web, www.treas.gov
Sets strategy and policy for combating the financing of terrorism both domestically and internationally.

U.S. Coast Guard (USCG), *(Homeland Security Dept.), Intelligence, 2100 2nd St. S.W., #3300 20593-0001; (202) 267-2126. Fax, (202) 267-6954. Frances Fragos-Townsend, Chief.*
Web, www.uscg.mil
Manages all Coast Guard intelligence activities and programs.

CONGRESS

House Appropriations Committee, *Subcommittee on Defense, H149 CAP 20515; (202) 225-2847. Fax, (202) 225-2822. Rep. Jerry Lewis, R-Calif., Chair; Kevin M. Roper, Staff Director.*
Web, www.house.gov/appropriations
Jurisdiction over legislation to appropriate funds for the Central Intelligence Agency and the intelligence community.

House Armed Services Committee, *Subcommittee on Terrorism, Unconventional Threats and Capabilities, 2120 RHOB 20515; (202) 225-4151. Fax, (202) 225-9077. Rep. H. James Saxton, R-N.J., Chair.*
Web, www.house.gov/hasc
Responsible for Defense Dept. counterterrorism programs and initiatives. Also responsible for Special Operations Forces, information technology policy and programs, force protection policy and oversight, and related intelligence support.

House Government Reform Committee, *Subcommittee on National Security, Emerging Threats, and International Relations, B372 RHOB 20515; (202) 225-2548. Fax, (202) 225-2382. Rep. Christopher Shays, R-Conn., Chair; Lawrence Halloran, Staff Director.*
Web, www.house.gov/reform
Oversight responsibilities for the operations of agencies related to intelligence and security, including the Defense Dept., Central Intelligence Agency, National Security Agency, and Defense Intelligence Agency.

House International Relations Committee, *2170 RHOB 20515; (202) 225-5021. Fax, (202) 226-2831. Rep. Henry J. Hyde, R-Ill., Chair; Thomas E. Mooney, Chief of Staff. Hearing notification line, (202) 225-3184.*
General e-mail, hirc@mail.house.gov
Web, www.house.gov/international_relations
Jurisdiction over legislation on international terrorism, including counterterrorism policy, embassy security, and the Anti-Terrorism Assistance Program. (Jurisdiction shared with House Judiciary Committee and House Select Committee on Homeland Security.)

House International Relations Committee, *Subcommittee on International Terrorism, Nonproliferation, and Human Rights, 2401A RHOB 20515; (202) 226-7820. Fax, (202) 226-2831. Rep. Elton Gallegly, R-Calif., Chair; Richard Mereu, Staff Director.*
Web, www.house.gov/international_relations
Oversight over and legislative responsibilities for U.S. efforts to manage and coordinate international programs to combat terrorism, as coordinated by the State Dept. and other agencies.

House Judiciary Committee, *2138 RHOB 20515; (202) 225-3951. Fax, (202) 225-7682. Rep. F. James Sensenbrenner Jr., R-Wis., Chair; Phil Kiko, Chief of Staff.*
General e-mail, Judiciary@mail.house.gov
Web, www.house.gov/judiciary
Jurisdiction over legislation on control of international terrorism (shared with House International Relations Committee and House Select Committee on Homeland Security).

House Judiciary Committee, *Subcommittee on Crime, Terrorism, and Homeland Security, 207 CHOB 20515; (202) 225-3926. Fax, (202) 225-3737. Rep. Howard Coble, R-N.C., Chair; Jay Apperson, Chief Counsel.*
General e-mail, Judiciary@mail.house.gov
Web, www.house.gov/judiciary
Jurisdiction over legislation on federal criminal laws including terrorism, prisons, corrections, death penalty procedures, and the Federal Bureau of Investigation. Oversight responsibility for the law enforcement components of the Homeland Security Dept., including the U.S. Secret Service, the U.S. Coast Guard, and the Bureau of Customs and Border Protection.

House Permanent Select Committee on Intelligence, *H405 CAP 20515; (202) 225-4121. Fax, (202) 225-1991. Rep. Porter J. Goss, R-Fla., Chair; Tim Sample, Staff Director.*
Web, intelligence.house.gov

Studies, makes recommendations, and proposes legislation on intelligence agencies' activities and policies, including the attorney general's implementation of guidelines for Federal Bureau of Investigation intelligence activities and the conduct of electronic surveillance for foreign intelligence purposes; oversees the Central Intelligence Agency, National Security Agency, Defense Intelligence Agency, and other intelligence activities of the U.S. government to ensure conformity with the U.S. Constitution and laws; authorizes budgets for the intelligence community.

House Permanent Select Committee on Intelligence, *Subcommittee on Terrorism and Homeland Security,* H-405 CAP 20510; (202) 225-4121. Fax, (202) 225-1991. Rep. Ray LaHood, R-Ill., Chair; Jay Jakub, Staff Director.
Web, intelligence.house.gov

Investigates the problem and threat of terrorism within the United States and evaluates terrorist threats, U.S. vulnerability, counterterrorism resources and capabilities, and all manner of domestic preparedness.

House Select Committee on Homeland Security, *Subcommittee on Intelligence and Counterterrorism,* 2402 RHOB 20515; (202) 226-8417. Rep. Jim Gibbons, R-Nev., Chair.
Web, hsc.house.gov

Jurisdiction includes the prevention and interdiction of terrorist attacks on U.S. territory; liaison and integration of the Homeland Security Dept. with the intelligence community and with law enforcement; collection, analysis, and sharing of intelligence among agencies and levels of government as it relates to homeland security; threat identification, assessment, and prioritization; and integration of intelligence analysis.

Senate Appropriations Committee, *Subcommittee on Defense,* SD-119 20510; (202) 224-7255. Sen. Ted Stevens, R-Alaska, Chair; Sid Ashworth, Clerk.
Web, appropriations.senate.gov

Jurisdiction over legislation to appropriate funds for the Central Intelligence Agency, the Defense Intelligence Agency, and the National Security Agency.

Senate Armed Services Committee, *Subcommittee on Strategic Forces,* SR-228 20510; (202) 224-3871. Fax, (202) 228-0036. Sen. Wayne Allard, R-Colo., Chair; Brian Green, Professional Staff Member.
Web, armed-services.senate.gov

Jurisdiction over military intelligence activities affecting national security.

Senate Foreign Relations Committee, SD-450 20510; (202) 224-4651. Fax, (202) 224-0836. Sen. Richard G. Lugar, R-Ind., Chair; Kenneth A. Myers, Staff Director.
Web, foreign.senate.gov

Oversight of foreign intelligence activities. Jurisdiction over international counterterrorism policy, including the Anti-Terrorism Assistance Program. (Jurisdiction shared with the Senate Judiciary Committee.)

Senate Foreign Relations Committee, *Subcommittee on International Operations and Terrorism,* SD-446 20510; (202) 224-4651. Sen. John E. Sununu, R-N.H., Chair; Vacant, Staff Director.
Web, foreign.senate.gov

Oversees all U.S. foreign policy, programs, and cooperative efforts to combat international terrorism.

Senate Judiciary Committee, SD-224 20510; (202) 224-5225. Fax, (202) 224-9102. Sen. Orrin G. Hatch, R-Utah, Chair; Makan Delrahim, Chief Counsel.
Web, judiciary.senate.gov

Jurisdiction over legislation relating to the control of international terrorism. (Jurisdiction shared with the Senate Foreign Relations Committee.)

Senate Judiciary Committee, *Subcommittee on Terrorism, Technology, and Homeland Security,* SH-325 20510; (202) 224-6791. Fax, (202) 228-0542. Sen. Jon Kyl, R-Ariz., Chair; Stephen Higgins, Chief Counsel.
Web, judiciary.senate.gov

Jurisdiction includes antiterrorism enforcement and policy; Homeland Security Dept. functions and State Dept. consular operations as they relate to antiterrorism enforcement and policy; laws related to government information policy, electronic privacy and security of computer information, and Freedom of Information Act; espionage laws and their enforcement.

Senate Select Committee on Intelligence, SH-211 20510; (202) 224-1700. Sen. Pat Roberts, R-Kan., Chair; Bill Duhnke, Staff Contact.
Web, intelligence.senate.gov

Studies, makes recommendations, and proposes legislation on intelligence agencies' activities, policies, and funds; oversees the Central Intelligence Agency, National Security Agency, Defense Intelligence Agency, the intelligence activities of the Federal Bureau of Investigation, and other intelligence operations of the U.S. government to ensure conformity with the U.S. Constitution and laws; authorizes appropriations for the intelligence community. Oversight of directives and procedures governing intelligence activities affecting the rights of Americans abroad.

INTERNATIONAL ORGANIZATIONS

INTERPOL, *Washington Office,* *INTERPOL-USNCB, U.S. Justice Dept. 20530; (202) 616-9000. Fax, (202) 616-8400. Edgar A. Adamson, Director.*
Web, www.usdoj.gov/usncb

U.S. national central bureau for INTERPOL; interacts in international investigations of terrorism on behalf of U.S. police. Serves as liaison between foreign and U.S. law enforcement agencies. Headquarters office sponsors forums enabling foreign governments to discuss counterterrorism policy. (Headquarters in Lyons, France.)

NONPROFIT

American Society for Industrial Security,
1625 Prince St., Alexandria, VA 22314; (703) 519-6200. Fax, (703) 519-6298. Michael Stack, Executive Director.
Web, www.asisonline.org

Membership: security administrators from around the world who protect the assets and personnel of private and public organizations. Sponsors seminars and workshops on counterterrorism.

Assn. of Former Intelligence Officers, *6723 Whittier Ave., #303A, McLean, VA 22101; (703) 790-0320. Fax, (703) 790-0264. Roy K. Jonkers, Executive Director.*
General e-mail, afio@afio.com
Web, www.afio.com

Membership: former military and civilian intelligence officers. Encourages public support for intelligence agencies; supports increased intelligence education in colleges and universities.

Center for National Security Studies, *Gelman Library, 1120 19th St. N.W., #800 20036; (202) 721-5650. Fax, (202) 530-0128. Kate Martin, Director.*
General e-mail, cnss@gwu.edu
Web, www.cnss.org

Monitors and conducts research on civil liberties and intelligence and national security, including activities of the Central Intelligence Agency and the Federal Bureau of Investigation.

Foundation for the Defense of Democracies, *1020 19th St. N.W., #340 20036; (202) 207-0190. Fax, (202) 207-0191. Clifford D. May, President; Eleana Gordon, Policy Director.*
General e-mail, info@defenddemocracy.org
Web, www.defenddemocracy.org

Conducts research and education related to the war on terrorism.

National Security Archive, *Gelman Library, 2130 H St. N.W., #701 20037; (202) 994-7000. Fax, (202) 994-7005. Thomas Blanton, Executive Director.*
General e-mail, nsarchiv@gwu.edu
Web, www.nsarchive.org

Research institute and library that provides information on U.S. foreign and economic policy and national security affairs. Maintains collection of declassified and unclassified national security documents. Sponsors freedom of information legislation in Central Europe and elsewhere. Archive open to the public by appointment.

Potomac Institute for Policy Studies, *International Center for Terrorism Studies (ICTS),* *901 N. Stuart St., #200, Arlington, VA 22203; (703) 525-0770. Fax, (703) 525-0299. Yonah Alexander, Director.*
Web, www.potomacinstitute.org

Public policy research institute that conducts studies on key science and technology issues. Areas of focus for the ICTS include the potential for terrorism in the form of biological, chemical, or nuclear violence, as well as information warfare and cyberterrorism.

Terrorism Research Center, *5765 F-Burke Center Pkwy., PBM 331, Burke, VA 22015; (877) 635-0816. Matthew G. Devost, President.*
General e-mail, TRC@terrorism.com
Web, www.terrorism.com

Independent institute dedicated to research in the areas of terrorism and homeland security.

Internal (Agency) Security

AGENCIES

Air Force Dept. *(Defense Dept.), Special Investigations,* *1140 Air Force Pentagon, #4E1081 20330-1140; (703) 697-1955. Fax, (703) 695-4346. Col. Michael P. McConnell, Director.*
Web, www.af.mil

Develops and implements policy on investigations of foreign intelligence, terrorism, and other crimes as they relate to Air Force security.

Army Dept. *(Defense Dept.), Counterintelligence, Foreign Disclosure, and Security,* *1000 Army Pentagon 20301-1000; (703) 695-1007. Fax, (703) 695-3149. Tom Dillon, Director.*

Responsible for policy formation, planning, programming, oversight, and representation for counterintelligence, human intelligence, and security countermeasures of the Army.

Defense Dept. (DoD), *Counterintelligence,*
6000 Defense Pentagon, #3C260 20301-6000; (703) 697-
9639. Col. Steve Coppinger, Director.
Web, www.defenselink.mil

Develops policy regarding counterintelligence as a means to protect against espionage and other foreign intelligence activities, sabotage, international terrorist activities, and assassination efforts of foreign powers, organizations, or persons directed against the Defense Dept.

Defense Security Service *(Defense Dept.), 1340 Brad-*
dock Pl., Alexandria, VA 22314-1651; (703) 325-5308.
Fax, (703) 325-7426. William A. Curtis, Director (Acting).
Web, www.dss.mil

Administers programs to protect classified government information and resources, including the Personnel Security Investigations and Defense Industrial Security programs. Serves the Defense Dept. and other executive departments and agencies. Operates DSS Academy to educate, train, and enhance awareness of security matters.

Energy Dept. (DOE), *Counterintelligence, 1000 Inde-*
pendence Ave. S.W. 20585; (202) 586-5901. Fax, (202)
586-5295. Stephen W. Dillard, Director.
Web, www.energy.gov

Identifies, neutralizes, and deters intelligence threats directed at Energy Dept. facilities, personnel, information, and technology.

National Archives and Records Administration (NARA), *Information Security Oversight, 700 Pennsyl-*
vania Ave. N.W., #500 20408-0001; (202) 219-5250. Fax,
(202) 219-5385. J. William Leonard, Director.
General e-mail, isoo@arch1.nara.gov
Web, www.archives.gov

Administers governmentwide national security classification program under which information is classified, declassified, and safeguarded for national security purposes.

National Security Agency (NSA), *(Defense Dept.),*
9800 Savage Rd., Fort Meade, MD 20755-6000; (301)
688-6524. Fax, (301) 688-6198. Lt. Gen. Michael V. Hay-
den Jr., (USAF) Director; William B. Black, Deputy Direc-
tor. Information, (301) 688-6524.
Web, www.nsa.gov

Maintains and operates the Defense Dept.'s Computer Security Center; ensures communications and computer security within the government.

Navy Dept. *(Defense Dept.), Naval Criminal Investiga-*
tive Service, Bldg. 111, 716 Sicard St. S.E., Washington

Navy Yard, DC 20388-5380; (202) 433-8800. Fax, (202)
433-9619. David L. Brant, Director. Information, (202)
433-9624.
Web, www.ncis.navy.mil

Handles investigative responsibilities for naval counterintelligence and security; processes security clearances for the Navy.

State Dept., *Countermeasures and Information Secu-*
rity, 2121 Virginia Ave. N.W. 20037; (202) 663-0538. Fax,
(202) 663-0653. W. Ray Williams, Deputy Assistant Secre-
tary.
Web, www.state.gov

Safeguards all electronic information and systems in the State Dept., both domestically and abroad. Also responsible for Physical Security Program for State Dept. officials and for the Diplomatic Courier Service.

State Dept., *Diplomatic Security Service: Intelligence*
and Threat Analysis, 2121 Virginia Ave. N.W. 20520;
(202) 663-0787. Fax, (202) 663-0852. John Rendeiro,
Director.
Web, www.state.gov

Oversees the safety and security of all U.S. government employees at U.S. embassies and consulates abroad. Responsible for the safety of the secretary of state and all foreign dignitaries. Conducts background investigations of potential government employees, investigates passport and visa fraud, and warns government employees of any counterintelligence dangers they might encounter.

 MILITARY INSTALLATIONS

AGENCIES

Air Force Dept. *(Defense Dept.), Bases and Units,*
1260 Air Force Pentagon, #4B267 20330-1260; (703) 697-
7356. Fax, (703) 697-5143. Lt. Col. Susan Mitchell, Chief.
Web, www.af.mil

Manages Air Force bases and units worldwide.

Army Dept. *(Defense Dept.), Installations and Hous-*
ing, 110 Army Pentagon, #3E475 20310-0110; (703) 697-
8161. Fax, (703) 614-7394. Joseph W. Whitaker, Deputy
Assistant Secretary.
Web, www.army.mil

Civilian office that manages all Army installations.

Defense Dept. (DoD), *Installations and Environment,*
3400 Defense Pentagon, #3E792 20301-3400; (703) 697-
8080. Fax, (703) 693-7011. Raymond F. DuBois, Deputy
Under Secretary.
Web, www.acq.osd.mil/ie

Oversees and offers policy guidance for all Defense Dept. installations and environmental programs.

Defense Dept. (DoD), *International Security Affairs,* *The Pentagon, #4E838 20301-2400; (703) 695-4351. Fax, (703) 697-7230. Peter W. Rodman, Assistant Secretary.* *Web, www.defenselink.mil*

Negotiates and monitors defense cooperation agreements, including base rights, access and prepositioning, exchange programs, and status of forces agreements with foreign governments in assigned geographic areas of responsibility.

CONGRESS

House Armed Services Committee, *Subcommittee on Readiness, 2120 RHOB 20515; (202) 225-6288. Fax, (202) 225-9077. Rep. Joel Hefley, R Colo., Chair.* *Web, www.house.gov/hasc*

Jurisdiction over legislation on military base operations and closings, military construction, military housing, and military real estate leasing and buying.

Senate Armed Services Committee, *Subcommittee on Readiness and Management Support, SR-228 20510; (202) 224-3871. Fax, (202) 228-0036. Sen. John Ensign, R-Nev., Chair; Lucian Niemeyer, Professional Staff Member.* *Web, armed-services.senate.gov*

Jurisdiction over legislation on military base operations and closings, military construction, military housing, and military real estate leasing and buying.

Base Closings, Economic Impact

AGENCIES

Air Force Dept. *(Defense Dept.), Base Transition, 1665 Air Force Pentagon 20330-1665; (703) 697-2995. Fax, (703) 695-2815. Wellington Selden, Chief.* *Web, www.af.mil*

Military office that plans for the transition of Air Force bases from functioning to no longer open.

Air Force Dept. *(Defense Dept.), Installations, 1665 Air Force Pentagon, #4C940, SAF/IEI 20330-1665; (703) 695-3592. Fax, (703) 693-7568. Fred W. Kuhn, Deputy Assistant Secretary.* *Web, www.af.mil*

Civilian office that plans and reviews the closing of Air Force bases.

Army Dept. *(Defense Dept.), Policy and Program Development, 200 Stovall St., #148, Alexandria, VA 22322; (703) 325-9989. Ann McFadden, Chief.* *Web, www.army.mil*

Military office responsible for employment policies to assist civilian personnel in cases of Defense Dept. program changes, including base closings.

Defense Dept. (DoD), *Civilian Assistance and Re-Employment (CARE), 1400 Key Blvd., #B-200, Arlington, VA 22209-5144; (703) 696-1799. Fax, (703) 696-5416. G. Jorge Araiza, Chief.* *Web, www.cpms.osd.mil/care/index.html*

Manages transition programs for Defense Dept. civilians, including placement, early retirement, and transition assistance programs.

Defense Dept. (DoD), *Office of Economic Adjustment, 400 Army-Navy Dr., #200, Arlington, VA 22202-4704; (703) 604-6020. Fax, (703) 604-5843. Patrick J. O'Brien, Director.* *Web, www.acq.osd.mil/oea*

Civilian office that helps community officials develop strategies and coordinate plans to alleviate the economic effect of major defense program changes, including base closings, reductions in forces, and contract cutbacks. Assists communities where defense activities are being expanded. Serves as the staff for the Economic Adjustment Committee, an interagency group that coordinates federal defense economic adjustment activities.

Marine Corps *(Defense Dept.), Land Use and Military Construction, 2 Navy Annex 20380-1775; (703) 695-8202. Fax, (703) 614-4773. Col. William J. Anderson, Head.*

Military office that reviews studies on base closings.

Commissaries, PXs, and Service Clubs

AGENCIES

Air Force Dept. *(Defense Dept.), Defense Commissary Agency, Washington Office, 4100 Defense Pentagon 20301-4100; (703) 695-3265. Fax, (703) 695-3650. Dan W. Sclater, Chief.* *Web, www.af.mil*

Serves as a liaison for defense commissary services. Monitors legislation and regulations.

Defense Dept. (DoD), *Army and Air Force Exchange, Washington Office, 2511 Jefferson Davis Hwy., #11600, Arlington, VA 22202-3922; (703) 604-7523. Fax, (703) 604-7510. Robert Ellis, Director.* *Web, www.aafes.com*

Coordinates Army and Air Force PX matters with other Defense Dept. offices. (Headquarters in Dallas, Texas.)

Navy Dept. *(Defense Dept.), Manpower and Reserve Affairs, 1000 Navy Pentagon 20350-1000; (703) 697-*

2180. Fax, (703) 614-4103. William A. Navas Jr., Assistant Secretary.

Web, www.navy.mil

Civilian office that develops policies for Navy and Marine Corps commissaries, exchanges, and service clubs and reviews their operations.

Navy Dept. *(Defense Dept.), Navy Exchange Service Command, Washington Office,* 1213 Jefferson Davis Hwy., #1400, Arlington, VA 22202; (703) 607-0072. Fax, (703) 607-1167. Alexander Douvres, Director.

Web, www.navy-nex.com

Civilian office that serves as a liaison among the Navy Exchange Service Command, the Navy Supply Systems Command, Congress, and the Defense Dept. (Headquarters in Virginia Beach, Va.)

CONGRESS

House Armed Services Committee, *Subcommittee on Total Force,* 2340 RHOB 20515; (202) 225-7560. Fax, (202) 226-0789. Rep. John M. McHugh, R-N.Y., Chair; John Chapla, Staff Director.

Web, www.house.gov/hasc

Oversight responsibility for military commissaries, PXs, and service clubs.

Senate Armed Services Committee, *Subcommittee on Personnel,* SR-228 20510; (202) 224-3871. Fax, (202) 228-0036. Sen. Saxby Chambliss, R-Ga., Chair; Dick Walsh, Staff Director.

Web, armed-services.senate.gov

Jurisdiction over legislation on military commissaries, PXs, and service clubs.

NONPROFIT

American Logistics Assn., 1133 15th St. N.W., #640 20005; (202) 466-2520. Fax, (202) 785-3826. Alan Burton, President.

Web, www.ala-national.org

Membership: suppliers of military commissaries, PXs, and service clubs. Acts as liaison between the Defense Dept. and service contractors; monitors legislation and testifies on issues of interest to members.

United Service Organizations (USO), 1008 Eberle Pl. S.E., #301, Washington Navy Yard, DC 20374-5096; (202) 610-5700. Fax, (202) 610-5701. Edward A. Powell, President.

Web, www.uso.org

Voluntary civilian organization chartered by Congress. Provides military personnel and their families in the United States and overseas with social, educational, and recreational programs.

Construction, Housing, and Real Estate

AGENCIES

Air Force Dept. *(Defense Dept.), Civil Engineering,* Headquarters USAF/ILE, 1260 Air Force Pentagon 20330-1260; (703) 607-0200. Fax, (703) 604-0610. Maj. Gen. Ernest O. Robbins II, Director.

Web, www.af.mil

Military office that plans and directs construction of Air Force facilities (except housing) in the United States and overseas.

Air Force Dept. *(Defense Dept.), Housing,* Crystal Gateway 1, 1235 Jefferson Davis Hwy., Arlington, VA 22202; (703) 601-0478. Fax, (703) 604-2484. Col James P. Holland, Director.

Web, www.af.mil

Military office that plans and manages construction of Air Force housing on military installations in the United States and overseas.

Air Force Dept. *(Defense Dept.), Installations,* 1665 Air Force Pentagon, #4C940, SAF/IEI 20330-1665; (703) 695-3592. Fax, (703) 693-7568. Fred W. Kuhn, Deputy Assistant Secretary.

Web, www.af.mil

Civilian office that plans and reviews construction policies and programs of Air Force military facilities (including the Military Construction Program), housing programs, and real estate buying, selling, and leasing in the United States.

Air Force Dept. *(Defense Dept.), Real Property,* 1700 N. Moore St., #2300, Arlington, VA 22209-2802; (703) 696-5552. Fax, (202) 696-8828. Richard D. Jenkins, Director.

Web, www.af.mil

Acquires, manages, and disposes of land for the Air Force worldwide. Maintains a complete land and facilities inventory; establishes instructions and operating procedures.

Army Corps of Engineers *(Defense Dept.),* 441 G St. N.W., #3K05 20314-1000; (202) 761-0001. Fax, (202) 761-4463. Lt. Gen. Robert B. Flowers (USACE), Chief of Engineers.

Web, www.usace.army.mil

Military office that establishes policy and designs, directs, and manages civil works and military construction projects of the Army Corps of Engineers; directs the Army's real estate leasing and buying for military installations and civil works projects.

Army Dept. *(Defense Dept.), Army Housing,* DAIM-FDH, 7701 Telegraph Rd., Alexandria, VA 22315-3802; (703) 428-6401. Fax, (703) 428-8359. George F. McKimmie, Chief.

Web, www.hqda.army.mil

Military office that plans, directs, and administers the construction and maintenance of Army family housing. Also responsible for unaccompanied personnel.

Army Dept. *(Defense Dept.), Installations and Housing,* 110 Army Pentagon, #3E475 20310-0110; (703) 697-8161. Fax, (703) 614-7394. Joseph W. Whitaker, Deputy Assistant Secretary.

Web, www.army.mil

Civilian office that reviews housing programs, the construction of Army military facilities, and the buying and leasing of real estate in the United States and overseas.

Defense Dept. (DoD), *Installations Requirements and Management,* 400 Army-Navy Dr., #206, Arlington, VA 22202-2884; (703) 604-5774. Fax, (703) 604-5934. Douglas Hansen, Director.

Web, www.defenselink.mil

Determines requirements and policies for military construction; facility sustainment, restoration, and modernization; and base operations except for housing. Prepares and defends the annual military construction bill before Congress; manages real property; and reports on base structure.

Marine Corps *(Defense Dept.), Facilities,* 3250 Catlin Ave., #235, Quantico, VA 22134-5001; (703) 784-2331. Fax, (703) 784-2332. E. C. Rushing Jr., Director.

Web, www.usmc.mil

Control point for the Marine Corps divisions of public works, family housing, and natural resources and environmental affairs.

Marine Corps *(Defense Dept.), Land Use and Military Construction,* 2 Navy Annex 20380-1775; (703) 695-8202. Fax, (703) 614-4773. Col. William J. Anderson, Head.

Military office responsible for military construction and the acquisition, management, and disposal of Marine Corps real property.

Navy Dept. *(Defense Dept.), Installations and Facilities,* 1000 Navy Pentagon, #4E765 20350-1000; (703) 693-4527. Fax, (703) 693-2734. Wayne Arny, Deputy Assistant Secretary.

Web, www.navy.mil

Civilian office that monitors and reviews construction of Navy military facilities and housing and the buying and leasing of real estate in the United States and overseas.

Navy Dept. *(Defense Dept.), Naval Facilities Engineering Command,* 1322 Patterson Ave. S.E., #1000, Washington Navy Yard, DC 20374-5065; (202) 685-9499. Fax, (202) 685-1463. Rear Adm. Michael Johnson (USN), Commander.

Web, www.navy.mil

Military command that plans, designs, and constructs facilities for Navy and other Defense Dept. activities around the world and manages Navy public works, utilities, environmental, real estate, and housing programs.

Navy Dept. *(Defense Dept.), Real Estate,* 1322 Patterson Ave. S.E., #1000, Washington Navy Yard, DC 20374-5065; (202) 685-9198. Howard D. Kelsey, Director.

Web, www.navy.mil

Military office that directs the Navy's real estate leasing, buying, and disposition for military installations.

U.S. Coast Guard (USCG), *(Homeland Security Dept.), Housing Programs,* G-WPM-4, 2100 2nd St. S.W. 20593-0001; (202) 267-2223. Fax, (202) 267-4862. David R. Pomeroy, Chief; Carol McFadden, Chief Warrant Officer, (202) 267-2228.

Provides temporary housing for active personnel and their families.

CONGRESS

House Appropriations Committee, *Subcommittee on Military Construction,* B300 RHOB 20515; (202) 225-3047. Rep. Joe Knollenberg, R-Mich., Chair; Valerie Baldwin, Staff Director.

Web, www.house.gov/appropriations

Jurisdiction over legislation to appropriate funds for military construction, including family housing and NATO infrastructure.

House Armed Services Committee, *Subcommittee on Readiness,* 2120 RHOB 20515; (202) 225-6288. Fax, (202) 225-9077. Rep. Joel Hefley, R-Colo., Chair.

Web, www.house.gov/hasc

Jurisdication over military construction, including NATO infrastructure and military family housing budget accounts.

Senate Appropriations Committee, *Subcommittee on Military Construction,* SD-140 20510; (202) 224-5245. Sen. Kay Bailey Hutchison, R-Texas, Chair; Dennis Ward, Clerk.

Web, appropriations.senate.gov

Jurisdiction over legislation to appropriate funds for military construction, including family housing and NATO infrastructure.

Web, armed-services.senate.gov

Jurisdiction over military construction, including NATO infrastructure and military family housing budget accounts.

🔲 PROCUREMENT, ACQUISITION, AND LOGISTICS

AGENCIES

Air Force Dept. *(Defense Dept.), Acquisition,* 1060 Air Force Pentagon, #4E964 20330-1060; (703) 697-6361. Fax, (703) 693-6400. Marvin R. Sambur, Assistant Secretary.
Web, www.af.mil

Civilian office that directs and reviews Air Force procurement policies and programs.

Air Force Dept. *(Defense Dept.), Contracting,* 1060 Air Force Pentagon, #700 20330-1060; (703) 588-7004. Fax, (703) 588-1067. Charlie Williams, Deputy Assistant Secretary.
Web, www.af.mil

Develops, implements, and enforces contracting policies on Air Force acquisitions worldwide, including research and development services, weapons systems, logistics services, and operational contracts.

Air Force Dept. *(Defense Dept.), Global Power Programs,* 1060 Air Force Pentagon 20330-1060; (703) 588-7170. Fax, (703) 588-6196. Vacant, Director.
Web, www.af.mil

Military office that directs Air Force acquisition and development programs within the tactical arena.

Army Dept. *(Defense Dept.), Operations Research,* 102 Army Pentagon, #2E660 20310-0102; (703) 695-0083. Fax, (703) 693-3897. Walter W. Hollis, Deputy Under Secretary.
Web, www.odusa-or.army.mil

Establishes policy for operations research and systems analysis activities for the Army. Supports acquisition review committees within the Army and the Defense Dept.

Army Dept. *(Defense Dept.), Procurement,* The Pentagon 20310-0103; (703) 695-4101. Fax, (703) 695-9386. Tina Ballard, Deputy Assistant Secretary (Acting), (703) 695-2488.

Web, www.army.mil

Directs and reviews Army procurement policies and programs.

Criminal Division *(Justice Dept.), Federal Procurement Fraud,* 10th and Constitution Ave. N.W., #3100 20530; (202) 616-0440. Fax, (202) 514-0152. Barbara Corprew, Deputy Chief.

Interdepartmental unit that investigates fraud in federal procurement contracting.

Defense Acquisition University *(Defense Dept.),* 9820 Belvoir Rd., Fort Belvoir, VA 22060-5565. Fax, (703) 805-2639. Frank J. Anderson Jr., President, (703) 805-5051. Toll-free, (800) 845-7606; Registrar, (703) 805-3003.
Web, www.dau.mil

Academic institution that offers courses to military and civilian personnel who specialize in acquisition and procurement. Conducts research to support and improve management of defense systems acquisition programs.

Defense Contract Audit Agency *(Defense Dept.),* 8725 John Jay Kingman Rd., #2135, Fort Belvoir, VA 22060-6219; (703) 767-3200. Fax, (703) 767-3267. William H. Reed, Director; Michael J. Thibault, Deputy Director, (703) 767-3272.
Web, www.dcaa.mil

Performs all contract audits for the Defense Dept. Provides Defense Dept. personnel responsible for procurement and contract administration with accounting and financial advisory services regarding the negotiation, administration, and settlement of contracts and subcontracts.

Defense Dept. (DoD), *Acquisition, Technology, and Logistics,* 3010 Defense Pentagon, #3E933 20301-3010; (703) 695-2381. Fax, (703) 693-2576. E. C. "Pete" Aldridge Jr., Under Secretary.
Web, www.acq.osd.mil

Formulates and directs policy relating to the department's purchasing system, research and development, logistics, advanced technology, international programs, environmental security, industrial base, and nuclear, biological, and chemical programs. Oversees all defense procurement and acquisition programs.

Defense Dept. (DoD), *Armed Services Board of Contract Appeals,* Skyline 6, 7th Floor, 5109 Leesburg Pike, Falls Church, VA 22041-3208; (703) 681-8500. Fax, (703) 681-8535. Paul Williams, Chair.
Web, www.law.gwu.edu/asbca

Adjudicates disputes arising under Defense Dept. contracts.

Defense Dept. (DoD), *Defense Acquisition Regulations Council,* 3062 Defense Pentagon 20301-3062; (703) 602-0302. Fax, (703) 602-0350. Ronald Poussard, Director.

Web, www.defenselink.mil

Develops procurement regulations for the Defense Dept.

Defense Dept. (DoD), *Defense Procurement and Acquisition Policy,* 3060 Defense Pentagon, #3E1044 20301-3060; (703) 695-7145. Fax, (703) 693-1142. Deidre A. Lee, Director.

Web, www.acq.osd.mil/dpap

Responsible for all acquisition and procurement policy matters for the Defense Dept. Serves as principal adviser to the under secretary of defense for acquisition, technology, and logistics on strategies relating to all major weapon systems programs, major automated information systems programs, and services acquisitions.

Defense Dept. (DoD), *Logistics and Material Readiness,* 3500 Defense Pentagon, #3E808 20301-3500; (703) 697-5530. Fax, (703) 693-0555. Diane K. Morales, Deputy Under Secretary.

Web, www.defenselink.mil

Formulates and implements department policies and programs regarding spare parts management. Helps determine Defense Dept. spare parts requirements and oversees acquisition of spare parts.

Defense Dept. (DoD), *Operational Test and Evaluation,* 1700 Defense Pentagon, #3A1073 20301-1700; (703) 697-3654. Fax, (703) 693-5248. Thomas P. Christie, Director.

Web, www.dote.osd.mil

Ensures that major acquisitions, including weapons systems, are operationally effective and suitable prior to full-scale investment. Provides the secretary of defense and Congress with independent assessment of these programs.

Defense Logistics Agency *(Defense Dept.),* 8725 John Jay Kingman Rd., #2533, Fort Belvoir, VA 22060-6221; (703) 767-5200. Fax, (703) 767-5207. Vice Adm. Keith W. Lippert, Director. Information, (703) 767-6200.

Web, www.dla.mil

Administers defense contracts; acquires, stores, and distributes food, clothing, medical, and other supplies used by the military services and other federal agencies; administers programs related to logistical support for the military services; and assists military services with developing, acquiring, and using technical information and defense materiel and disposing of materiel no longer needed.

Marine Corps *(Defense Dept.),* **Installations and Logistics, Contracts Division,** 2 Navy Annex 20380-1775; (703) 695-6326. Fax, (703) 695-6382. Shari Durand, Assistant Deputy Commandant.

Military office that directs Marine Corps procurement programs.

Navy Dept. *(Defense Dept.),* **Acquisition Management,** 2211 S. Clark Pl., #578, Arlington, VA 22202-3738; (703) 602-2338. Fax, (703) 602-4643. Rear Adm. Robert E. Cowley II, Deputy.

Web, www.navy.mil

Directs and reviews Navy acquisition and procurement policy.

Navy Dept. *(Defense Dept.),* **Military Sealift Command,** Bldg. 210, Washington Navy Yard, DC 20398-5540; (202) 685-5001. Fax, (202) 685-5020. Vice Adm. David L. Brewer, Commander.

Web, www.msc.navy.mil

Transports Defense Dept. and other U.S. government cargo by sea; operates ships that maintain supplies for the armed forces and scientific agencies; transports fuels for the Energy Dept.

U.S. Coast Guard (USCG), *(Homeland Security Dept.),* **Acquisition,** 2100 2nd St. S.W., #5120 20593-0001; (202) 267-2007. Fax, (202) 267-4279. Adm. Charles Wurster, Chief.

Web, www.uscg.mil

Administers all procurement made through the Acquisition Contract Support division.

U.S. Coast Guard (USCG), *(Homeland Security Dept.),* **Logistics Management,** 2100 2nd St. S.W. 20593-0001; (202) 267-1407. Fax, (202) 267-4516. Vacant, Chief.

Web, www.uscg.mil

Sets policy and procedures for the procurement, distribution, maintenance, and replacement of materiel and personnel.

CONGRESS

General Accounting Office (GAO), *Defense Capabilities and Management,* 441 G St. N.W., #4035 20548; (202) 512-4300. Fax, (202) 512-7686. Henry L. Hinton Jr., Managing Director.

Web, www.gao.gov

Independent, nonpartisan agency in the legislative branch. Audits, analyzes, and evaluates Defense Dept. acquisition programs; makes unclassified reports available to the public.

House Armed Services Committee, *Subcommittee on Readiness,* *2120 RHOB 20515; (202) 225-6288. Fax, (202) 225-9077. Rep. Joel Hefley, R-Colo., Chair.*
Web, www.house.gov/hasc

Jurisdiction over military logistics and maintenance issues and programs.

House Armed Services Committee, *Subcommittee on Tactical Air and Land Forces,* *2120 RHOB 20515; (202) 225-4151. Fax, (202) 226-0105. Rep. Curt Weldon, R-Pa., Chair; Doug Roach, Professional Staff Member.*
Web, www.house.gov/hasc

Responsible for all Army and Air Force acquisition programs (except strategic weapons and lift programs, special operations, and information technology accounts).

House Government Reform Committee, *Subcommittee on National Security, Emerging Threats, and International Relations,* *B372 RHOB 20515; (202) 225-2548. Fax, (202) 225-2382. Rep. Christopher Shays, R-Conn., Chair; Lawrence Halloran, Staff Director.*
Web, www.house.gov/reform

Oversight of defense procurement.

Senate Armed Services Committee, *SR-228 20510; (202) 224-3871. Fax, (202) 228-0036. Sen. John W. Warner, R-Va., Chair; Judy Ansley, Staff Director.*
Web, armed-services.senate.gov

Jurisdiction over legislation on military procurement (excluding construction), naval petroleum reserves, and military contract services.

NONPROFIT

Contract Services Assn. of America, *1000 Wilson Blvd., #1800, Arlington, VA 22209; (703) 243-2020. Fax, (703) 243-3601. Gary Engebretson, President.*
General e-mail, info@csa-dc.org
Web, www.csa-dc.org

Membership: companies that, under contract, provide federal, state, and local governments and other agencies with various technical and support services (particularly in defense, space, transportation, environment, energy, and health care). Analyzes the process by which the government awards contracts to private firms. Monitors legislation and regulations.

Council of Defense and Space Industry Assns., *2111 Wilson Blvd., #400, Arlington, VA 22201; (703) 247-9490. Fax, (703) 243-8539. Timothy Olsen, Administrative Officer.*
General e-mail, codsia@ndia.org
Web, www.codsia.org

Makes recommendations on federal procurement policies. Interests include estimating and accounting systems, contract clauses, defective pricing data, industrial security, management systems control, patents and technical data, property acquisition and control, and contract cost principles.

Government Electronic Industries Alliance, *2500 Wilson Blvd., #400, Arlington, VA 22201-3834; (703) 907-7566. Fax, (703) 907-7968. Dan C. Heinemeier, President; Jim Serafin, Vice President, Marketing and Government Relations.*
Web, www.geia.org

Membership: companies engaged in the research, development, integration, or manufacture of electronic equipment or services for government applications. Provides industry trends, forecasts, and information on standards. Monitors federal policy and practices in acquiring electronic products and services; represents the industry's views on acquisition regulations in federal agencies; serves as the focal point through which the government communicates with the electronics industry on procurement policy and other matters affecting the business-government relationship.

National Defense Transportation Assn., *50 S. Pickett St., #222, Alexandria, VA 22304-7296; (703) 751-5011. Fax, (703) 823-8761. Kenneth Wykle, President.*
Web, www.ndtahq.com

Membership: transportation users, manufacturers, and mode carriers; information technology firms; and related military, government, and civil interests worldwide. Promotes a strong U.S. transportation capability through coordination of private industry, government, and the military.

17

Science and Technology

GENERAL POLICY

AGENCIES

National Museum of Natural History *(Smithsonian Institution)*, *10th St. and Constitution Ave. N.W. 20560-0106 (mailing address: P.O. Box 37012 20013-7012); (202) 357-2664. Fax, (202) 357-4779. Cristian Samper, Director.*
Web, www.nmnh.si.edu

Conducts research and maintains exhibitions and collections relating to the natural sciences. Collections are organized into seven research and curatorial departments: anthropology, botany, entomology, invertebrate zoology, mineral sciences, paleobiology, and vertebrate zoology.

National Science and Technology Council *(Executive Office of the President)*, *Dwight D. Eisenhower Executive Office Bldg., #430 20502-0001; (202) 456-6101. Fax, (202) 456-6026. Ann B. Carlson, Executive Secretary.*
General e-mail, information@ostp.eop.gov
Web, www.ostp.gov

Coordinates research and development activities and programs that involve more than one federal agency. Activities concern biotechnology; earth sciences; human subjects; international science; engineering and technology; life sciences; food, agriculture, and forestry; and research, computing, materials, and radiation policy coordination.

National Science Board *(National Science Foundation)*, *4201 Wilson Blvd., #1220, Arlington, VA 22230; (703) 292-7000. Fax, (703) 292-9008. Warren M. Washington, Chair; Gerard R. Glaser, Executive Officer.*
Web, www.nsf.gov

Formulates policy for the National Science Foundation; advises the president on national science policy.

National Science Foundation (NSF), *4201 Wilson Blvd., #1205, Arlington, VA 22230; (703) 292-5111. Fax, (703) 292-9232. Rita R. Colwell, Director, (703) 292-8000. Library, (703) 292-7830. Publications, (301) 947-2722. Government Affairs, (703) 292-8070.*
General e-mail, info@nsf.gov
Web, www.nsf.gov

Sponsors scientific and engineering research; develops and helps implement science and engineering education programs; fosters dissemination of scientific information; promotes international cooperation within the scientific community; and assists with national science policy planning.

National Science Foundation (NSF), *Science Resources Statistics, 4201 Wilson Blvd., #965, Arlington, VA 22230; (703) 292-8780. Fax, (703) 292-9092. Lynda T. Carlson, Director.*
Web, www.nsf.gov/sbe/srs

Projects national scientific and technical resources and requirements.

Office of Management and Budget (OMB), *(Executive Office of the President)*, *Energy and Science, New Executive Office Bldg., #8002 20503; (202) 395-3404. Fax, (202) 395-3049. Mark Weatherly, Deputy Associate Director.*
Web, www.whitehouse.gov/omb

Assists and advises the OMB director in budget preparation; analyzes and evaluates programs in space and science, including the activities of the National Science Foundation and the National Aeronautics and Space Administration; coordinates OMB science, energy, and space policies and programs.

Office of Science *(Energy Dept.)*, *1000 Independence Ave. S.W., #7B058 20585; (202) 586-5430. Fax, (202) 586-4120. Raymond L. Orbach, Director.*
Web, www.science.doe.gov

Advises the secretary on the department's physical science and energy research and development programs; the management of the nonweapons multipurpose laboratories; and education and training activities required for basic and applied research activities. Manages the department's high energy physics, nuclear physics, fusion energy sciences, basic energy sciences, health and environmental research, and computational and technology research. Provides and operates the large-scale facilities required for research in the physical and life sciences.

Office of Science and Technology Policy (OSTP), *(Executive Office of the President)*, *Dwight D. Eisenhower Executive Office Bldg. 20502; (202) 456-7116. Fax, (202) 456-6021. John H. Marburger III, Director.*
General e-mail, information@ostp.eop.gov
Web, www.ostp.gov

Serves as the president's principal adviser on science and technology policy. Assists with review of research and development budgets of federal agencies, including the departments of Energy, Commerce, and Health and Human Services; the National Science Foundation; and the National Aeronautics and Space Administration. Works with the Office of Management and Budget, other executive offices, Congress, and federal agencies to develop research programs consistent with the president's science and technology goals. Administers the Federal Coordinating Council for Science, Engineering, and Technology.

Office of Science and Technology Policy (OSTP), *(Executive Office of the President), Science,* Dwight D. Eisenhower Executive Office Bldg., #436 20502; (202) 456-6130. Fax, (202) 456-6027. Kathie Olsen, Associate Director.

General e-mail, ostpinfo@ostp.eop.gov

Web, www.ostp.gov

Analyzes policies and advises the president and others within the Executive Office of the President on biological, physical, social, and behavioral sciences and on engineering; coordinates executive office and federal agency actions related to these issues. Evaluates the effectiveness of government science programs.

Office of Science and Technology Policy (OSTP), *(Executive Office of the President), Technology,* Dwight D. Eisenhower Executive Office Bldg., #431 20502; (202) 456-6046. Fax, (202) 456-6021. Richard M. Russell, Associate Director.

Web, www.ostp.gov/Technology/html/Technology.html

Analyzes policies and advises the president on technology and related issues of physical, computational, and space sciences; coordinates executive office and federal agency actions related to these issues.

Technology Administration *(Commerce Dept.),* 14th St. and Constitution Ave. N.W., #4824 20230; (202) 482-1575. Fax, (202) 501-2492. Phillip J. Bond, Under Secretary.

Web, www.ta.doc.gov

Seeks to enhance U.S. competitiveness by encouraging the development of new technologies and the conversion of technological knowledge into products and services. Oversees the National Institute of Standards and Technology and the National Technical Information Service.

CONGRESS

House Administration Committee, *1309 LHOB 20515; (202) 225-8281. Fax, (202) 225-9957. Rep. Bob W. Ney, R-Ohio, Chair; Paul Vinovich, Staff Director.*

Web, www.house.gov/cha

Jurisdiction over legislation related to and operations of the Smithsonian Institution.

House Appropriations Committee, *Subcommittee on Commerce, Justice, State, and the Judiciary,* H309 CAP 20515; (202) 225-3351. Rep. Frank R. Wolf, R-Va., Chair; Mike Ringler, Staff Director.

Web, www.house.gov/appropriations

Jurisdiction over legislation to appropriate funds for the Commerce Dept., including the National Oceanic and Atmospheric Administration, the National Institute of Standards and Technology, and the National Technical Infomation Service.

House Appropriations Committee, *Subcommittee on Interior,* B308 RHOB 20515; (202) 225-3081. Fax, (202) 225-9069. Rep. Charles H. Taylor, R-N.C., Chair; Deborah A. Weatherly, Staff Director.

Web, www.house.gov/appropriations

Jurisdiction over legislation to appropriate funds for the Smithsonian Institution and the U.S. Geological Survey.

House Appropriations Committee, *Subcommittee on VA, HUD, and Independent Agencies,* H143 CAP 20515; (202) 225-3241. Rep. James T. Walsh, R-N.Y., Chair; Tim Peterson, Staff Director.

Web, www.house.gov/appropriations

Jurisdiction over legislation to appropriate funds for the National Science Foundation and the Office of Science and Technology Policy.

House Science Committee, *2320 RHOB 20515; (202) 225-6371. Fax, (202) 226-0113. Rep. Sherwood Boehlert, R-N.Y., Chair; David Goldston, Staff Director.*

General e-mail, science@mail.house.gov

Web, www.house.gov/science

Jurisdiction over legislation on scientific research and development; science scholarships, programs, policy, resources, employment, and exploration; and technology.

House Science Committee, *Subcommittee on Environment, Technology, and Standards,* 2319 RHOB 20515; (202) 225-8844. Fax, (202) 225-4438. Rep. Vernon J. Ehlers, R-Mich., Chair; Eric Webster, Staff Director.

General e-mail, science@mail.house.gov

Web, www.house.gov/science

Jurisdiction over technology policy (including technology transfer), cooperative research and development, patent and intellectual property policy, biotechnology, and recombinant DNA research. Legislative jurisdiction over the National Institute of Standards and Technology and the National Technical Information Service.

House Science Committee, *Subcommittee on Research,* B374 RHOB 20515; (202) 225-7858. Fax, (202) 225-7815. Rep. Nick Smith, R-Mich., Chair; Peter Rooney, Staff Director.

General e-mail, science@mail.house.gov

Web, www.house.gov/science

Jurisdiction over legislation on the National Science Foundation and the Office of Science and Technology Policy; science research and development programs; math, science, and engineering education; international scientific cooperation; and nuclear research and development projects.

Senate Appropriations Committee, *Subcommittee on Commerce, Justice, State, and the Judiciary, S-206 CAP 20510; (202) 224-7277. Fax, (202) 228-0587. Sen. Judd Gregg, R-N.H., Chair; James Morhard, Clerk. Web, appropriations.senate.gov*

Jurisdiction over legislation to appropriate funds for the Commerce Dept., including the National Oceanic and Atmospheric Administration, the National Institute of Standards and Technology, and the National Technical Information Service.

Senate Appropriations Committee, *Subcommittee on Interior and Related Agencies, SD-132 20510; (202) 224-7233. Fax, (202) 228-4532. Sen. Conrad Burns, R-Mont., Chair; Bruce Evans, Clerk. Web, appropriations.senate.gov*

Jurisdiction over legislation to appropriate funds for the Smithsonian Institution and the U.S. Geological Survey.

Senate Appropriations Committee, *Subcommittee on VA, HUD, and Independent Agencies, SD-130 20510; (202) 224-8252. Fax, (202) 228-1624. Sen. Christopher S. Bond, R-Mo., Chair; Jon Kamarck, Clerk. Web, appropriations.senate.gov*

Jurisdiction over legislation to appropriate funds for the National Science Foundation and the Office of Science and Technology Policy.

Senate Commerce, Science, and Transportation Committee, *SD-508 20510; (202) 224-1251. Fax, (202) 224-1259. Sen. John McCain, R-Ariz., Chair; Jeanne Bumpus, Staff Director. Web, commerce.senate.gov*

Jurisdiction over legislation on the Commerce Dept. and its scientific activities and science aspects of the Office of Science and Technology Policy.

Senate Commerce, Science, and Transportation Committee, *Subcommittee on Science, Technology, and Space, SH-227 20510; (202) 224-8172. Fax, (202) 224-9934. Sen. Sam Brownback, R-Kan., Chair; Floyd Deschamps, Counsel. Web, commerce.senate.gov*

Oversight of the National Institute of Standards and Technology and other departments and agencies with an emphasis on science. Jurisdiction over scientific research

and development; science fellowships, scholarships, grants, programs, policy, resources, employment, and exploration; and technology. Jurisdiction over international scientific cooperation, technology transfer, and cooperative research and development (including global change and the space station); resolutions of joint cooperation with foreign governments on science and technology.

Senate Health, Education, Labor, and Pensions Committee, *SD-428 20510; (202) 224-5375. Fax, (202) 224-5128. Sen. Judd Gregg, R-N.H., Chair; Sharon Soderstrom, Staff Director. TTY, (202) 224-1975. Web, health.senate.gov*

Oversees and has jurisdiction over legislation on the National Science Foundation.

Senate Rules and Administration Committee, *SR-305 20510; (202) 224-6352. Fax, (202) 224-5400. Sen. Trent Lott, R-Miss., Chair; Susan Wells, Staff Director. Web, rules.senate.gov*

Jurisdiction over legislation concerning the Smithsonian Institution and the U.S. Botanic Garden.

NONPROFIT

American Assn. for Laboratory Accreditation, *5301 Buckeystown Pike, #350, Frederick, MD 21704; (301) 644-3248. Fax, (301) 662-2974. Peter Unger, President. Web, www.a2la.org*

Accredits and monitors laboratories that test construction materials and perform acoustics and vibration, biological, chemical, electrical, geotechnical, nondestructive, environmental, mechanical, metals and metal fasteners, calibration, asbestos, radon, and thermal testing. Registers laboratory quality systems.

American Assn. for the Advancement of Science (AAAS), *1200 New York Ave. N.W., 12th Floor 20005; (202) 326-6640. Fax, (202) 371-9526. Alan I. Leshner, Executive Officer. Information, (202) 326-6400. Web, www.aaas.org*

Membership: scientists, affiliated scientific organizations, and individuals interested in science. Fosters scientific education; monitors and seeks to influence public policy and public understanding of science and technology; encourages scientific literacy among minorities and women. Sponsors national and international symposia, workshops, and meetings; publishes *Science* magazine.

American Assn. for the Advancement of Science (AAAS), *Scientific Freedom, Responsibility, and Law Program, 1200 New York Ave. N.W. 20005; (202) 326-6600. Fax, (202) 289-4950. Mark S. Frankel, Director. Web, www.aaas.org/spp/dspp/SFRL/SFRL.htm*

Focuses on professional ethics and law in science and engineering and on the social implications of science and technology. Collaborates with other professional groups on these activities; provides technical assistance to organizations developing codes of ethics or educational programs on research integrity.

American Council of Independent Laboratories (ACIL), *1629 K St. N.W., #400 20006; (202) 887-5872. Fax, (202) 887-0021. Joan Walsh Cassedy, Executive Director. Laboratory Referral Service, (202) 887-5872.*
General e-mail, info@acil.org
Web, www.acil.org

Membership: independent commercial laboratories. Promotes professional and ethical business practices in providing analysis, testing, and research in engineering, microbiology, analytical chemistry, life sciences, and environmental geosciences.

Assn. for Women in Science, *1200 New York Ave. N.W., #650 20005; (202) 326-8940. Fax, (202) 326-8960. Catherine J. Didion, Executive Director.*
General e-mail, awis@awis.org
Web, www.awis.org

Promotes equal opportunity for women in scientific professions; provides career and funding information. Interests include international development.

Council of Scientific Society Presidents, *1550 M St. N.W. 20005 (mailing address: 1155 16th St. N.W., #0-1015 20036); (202) 872-6230. Fax, (202) 872-4079. Martin Apple, President.*
General e-mail, cssp@acs.org
Web, www.science-presidents.org

Membership: presidents, presidents-elect, and immediate past presidents of professional scientific societies and federations. Supports professional science education. Serves as a forum for discussion of emerging scientific issues, formulates national science policy, and develops the nation's scientific leadership.

Federation of American Scientists, *1717 K St. N.W., #209 20036; (202) 546-3300. Fax, (202) 675-1010. Henry Kelly, President.*
General e-mail, fas@fas.org
Web, www.fas.org

Conducts studies and monitors legislation on issues and problems related to science and technology, especially U.S. nuclear arms policy, energy, arms transfer, and civil aerospace issues.

George C. Marshall Institute, *1625 K St. N.W., #1050 20006; (202) 296-9655. Fax, (202) 296-9714. William O'Keefe, President.*

General e-mail, info@marshall.org
Web, www.marshall.org

Analyzes the technical and scientific aspects of public policy issues; produces publications on environmental science, space, national security, bioterrorism, and technology policy.

Government-University-Industry Research Roundtable, *500 5th St. N.W. #W525 20001; (202) 334-3486. Fax, (202) 334-1369. Merrilea Mayo, Executive Director.*
General e-mail, guirr@nas.edu
Web, www.national-academies.org

Forum sponsored by the National Academy of Sciences, National Academy of Engineering, and Institute of Medicine. Provides scientists, engineers, and members of government, academia, and industry with an opportunity to discuss ways of improving the infrastructure for science and technology research.

National Academy of Sciences (NAS), *2101 Constitution Ave. N.W. 20418; (202) 334-2000. Fax, (202) 334-2419. Bruce M. Alberts, President; James S. Langer, Vice President. Library, (202) 334-2125. Press, (202) 334-2138. Publications, (888) 624-8373; in Washington, (202) 334-3313.*
General e-mail, news@nas.edu
Web, www.nationalacademies.org

Congressionally chartered independent organization that advises the federal government on questions of science, technology, and health. Library open to the public by appointment. (Affiliated with the National Academy of Engineering, the Institute of Medicine, and the National Research Council.)

National Geographic Society, *Committee for Research and Exploration, 1145 17th St. N.W. 20036-4688; (202) 857-7161. Fax, (202) 429-5729. Peter H. Raven, Chair. TTY, (800) 548-9797.*
Web, www.nationalgeographic.com/research

Sponsors basic research grants in the sciences, including anthropology, archeology, astronomy, biology, botany, ecology, physical and human geography, geology, oceanography, paleontology, and zoology. To apply for grants, see Web site.

National Research Council (NRC), *500 5th St. N.W., #1153 20001; (202) 334-2000. Fax, (202) 334-2419. Bruce M. Alberts, President. Library, (202) 334-2125. Press, (202) 334-2138. Publications, (888) 624-8373; in Washington, (202) 334-3313.*
General e-mail, news@nas.edu
Web, www.nationalacademies.org/nrc

Serves as the principal operating agency of the National Academy of Sciences, National Academy of

Engineering, and Institute of Medicine. Program units focus on physical, social, and life sciences; applications of science including medicine, transportation, and education; international affairs; and U.S. government policy. Library open to the public by appointment.

SAMA Group of Assns., *225 Reinekers Lane, #625, Alexandria, VA 22314-2875; (703) 836-1360. Fax, (703) 836-6644. Mike Duff, Executive Director.*

Membership: manufacturers and distributors of high-technology scientific and industrial instruments and laboratory apparatus. Works to increase worldwide demand for products. (Affiliated with the Analytical and Life Science Systems Assn., the Opto-Precision Instrument Assn., and the Laboratory Products Assn.)

Society of Research Administrators, *1901 N. Moore St., #1004, Arlington, VA 22209; (703) 741-0140. Fax, (703) 741-0142. John Feather, Executive Director.*
General e-mail, info@srainternational.org
Web, www.srainternational.org

Membership: scientific and medical research administrators in the United States and other countries. Educates the public about the profession; offers professional development services; sponsors mentoring and awards programs. Monitors legislation and regulations.

Data, Statistics, and Reference

AGENCIES

National Aeronautics and Space Administration (NASA), *National Space Science Data Center, Goddard Space Flight Center, Code 633, Greenbelt, MD 20771; (301) 286-7355. Fax, (301) 286-1771. Donald Sawyer, Head (Acting).*
Web, nssdc.gsfc.nasa.gov

Acquires, catalogs, and distributes NASA mission data to the international space science community, including research organizations, universities, and other interested organizations worldwide. Provides software tools and network access to promote collaborative data analysis. (Mail data requests to above address, attention: Code 633.4/Request Coordination Office, or phone [301] 286-6695.)

National Aeronautics and Space Administration (NASA), *Space Science Data Operations, Goddard Space Flight Center, Code 630, Greenbelt, MD 20771; (301) 286-7354. Fax, (301) 286-1771. James L. Green, Chief. Information, (301) 286-6695.*
Web, ssdoo.gsfc.nasa.gov

Develops and operates systems for processing, archiving, and disseminating space physics and astrophysics data.

National Institute of Standards and Technology (NIST), *(Commerce Dept.), Information Services, 100 Bureau Dr., Stop 2500, Gaithersburg, MD 20899-2500; (301) 975-3052. Fax, (301) 869-8071. Mary-Diedre Coraggio, Director.*
Web, www.nvl.nist.gov

Conducts publications program for the institute and maintains a research information center, which includes material on engineering, chemistry, physics, mathematics, and the materials and computer sciences.

National Institute of Standards and Technology (NIST), *(Commerce Dept.), Measurement Services, 820 W. Diamond Ave., Bldg. 820, #306, MS 2000, Gaithersburg, MD 20899; (301) 975-8424. Fax, (301) 971-2183. Richard F. Kayser, Director.*
Web, www.nist.gov

Disseminates physical, chemical, and engineering measurement standards and provides services to ensure accurate and compatible measurements, specifications, and codes on a national and international scale.

National Institute of Standards and Technology (NIST), *(Commerce Dept.), Standard Reference Data, 820 W. Diamond Ave., Bldg. 820, #113, MS 2310, Gaithersburg, MD 20899-2310; (301) 975-2200. Fax, (301) 926-0416. John R. Rumble Jr., Chief. Information and publications, (301) 975-2208.*
General e-mail, srdata@nist.gov
Web, www.nist.gov/srd

Collects and disseminates critically evaluated physical, chemical, and materials properties data in the physical sciences and engineering for use by industry, government, and academic laboratories. Develops databases in a variety of formats, including disk, CD-ROM, online, and magnetic tape.

National Institute of Standards and Technology (NIST), *(Commerce Dept.), Statistical Engineering, 820 W. Diamond Ave., Bldg. 820, #353, MS 8980, Gaithersburg, MD 20899-8980; (301) 975-2839. Fax, (301) 990-4127. Nell Sedransk, Chief.*
Web, www.nist.gov/itl/div898

Promotes within industry and government the use of effective statistical techniques for planning analysis of experiments in the physical sciences; interprets experiments and data collection programs.

National Museum of American History *(Smithsonian Institution), Library, 14th St. and Constitution Ave. N.W., MRC 630 20560-0630; (202) 357-2414. Fax, (202) 357-4256. Jane Sanchez, Chief Librarian.*
Web, www.sil.si.edu

Collection includes materials on the history of science and technology, with concentrations in engineering, transportation, and applied science. Maintains collection of trade catalogs and materials about expositions and world fairs. Open to the public by appointment.

National Oceanic and Atmospheric Administration (NOAA), *(Commerce Dept.), Library and Information Services,* 1315 East-West Hwy., 2nd Floor, SSMC3, Silver Spring, MD 20910; (301) 713-2607. Fax, (301) 713-4598. Janice A. Beattie, Director. Reference service, (301) 713-2600.
General e-mail, library.reference@noaa.gov
Web, www.lib.noaa.gov

Collection includes reports, journals, monographs, photographs, and microforms on atmospheric and oceanic science. Maintains bibliographic database of other NOAA libraries, an online service, and reference materials on CD-ROM. Makes interlibrary loans; open to the public.

National Oceanic and Atmospheric Administration (NOAA), *(Commerce Dept.), National Environmental Satellite, Data, and Information Service,* 1335 East-West Hwy., Silver Spring, MD 20910; (301) 713-3578. Fax, (301) 713-1249. Gregory W. Withee, Assistant Administrator.
Web, www.nesdis.noaa.gov

Acquires and disseminates global environmental (marine, atmospheric, solid earth, and solar-terrestrial) data. Operates the following data facilities: National Climatic Data Center, Asheville, N.C.; National Geophysical Data Center, Boulder, Colo.; and National Oceanographic Data Center, Washington, D.C. Maintains comprehensive data and information referral service.

National Oceanic and Atmospheric Administration (NOAA), *(Commerce Dept.), National Oceanographic Data Center,* 1315 East-West Hwy., 4th Floor, SSMC3, Silver Spring, MD 20910-3282; (301) 713-3270. Fax, (301) 713-3300. H. Lee Dantzler, Director; Kurt Schnebele, Deputy Director. Information and requests, (301) 606-4549.
General e-mail, services@nodc.noaa.gov
Web, www.noaa.gov

Offers a wide range of oceanographic data on the Web, disk, CD-ROM, and hard copy; provides research scientists with data processing services; prepares statistical summaries and graphical data products. (Fee charged for some services.)

National Technical Information Service (NTIS), *(Commerce Dept.),* 5285 Port Royal Rd., Springfield, VA 22161; (703) 605-6400. Fax, (703) 605-6715. Ronald E.

Lawson, Director. TTY, (703) 605-6043. Sales center, (703) 605-6000; rush orders, (800) 553-6847.
Web, www.ntis.gov

Collects and organizes technical, scientific, engineering, and business-related information generated by U.S. and foreign governments and makes it available for commercial use in the private sector. Incorporates over 2 million works covering research and development, current events, business and management studies, translations of foreign reports, foreign and domestic trade, general statistics, environment and energy, health and social sciences, and hundreds of other areas. Provides computer software and computerized data files on tape, diskette, optical disk, and other multimedia materials.

Smithsonian Institution, *Dibner Library of the History of Science and Technology,* 14th St. and Constitution Ave. N.W., NMAH 1041/MRC 672 20560; (202) 357-1577. Fax, (202) 633-9102. Ronald Brashear, Curator.
General e-mail, libmail@si.edu
Web, www.sil.si.edu

Collection includes major holdings in the history of science and technology dating from the fifteenth to the twentieth centuries. Extensive collections in natural history, archeology, almanacs, physical and mathematical sciences, and scientific instrumentation. Open to the public by appointment.

Smithsonian Institution, *Museum Studies and Reference Library,* 10th St. and Constitution Ave. N.W., MRC 154 20560; (202) 357-2139. Fax, (202) 786-2443. Amy E. Levin, Branch Librarian. TTY, (202) 357-2328.
Web, www.sil.si.edu

Maintains collection of general reference, biographical, and interdisciplinary materials; serves as an information resource on institution libraries, a number of which have collections in scientific subjects, including horticulture, botany, science and technology, and anthropology.

U.S. Geological Survey (USGS), *(Interior Dept.), Earth Science Information Center,* 507 National Center, Reston, VA 20192-1507; (703) 648-5920. Fax, (703) 648-5548. Sherry Gwynn, Chief (Acting). U.S. maps, (888) 275-8747.
Web, www.usgs.gov

Collects, organizes, and distributes cartographic, geographic, hydrologic, and other earth science information; offers maps, reports, and other publications, digital cartographic data, aerial photographs, and space imagery and manned spacecraft photographs for sale. Acts as clearinghouse on cartographic and geographic data.

U.S. Geological Survey (USGS), *(Interior Dept.), Library Services,* 12201 Sunrise Valley Dr., MS 950,

Reston, VA 20192; (703) 648-4305. Fax, (703) 648-6373. Nancy Blair, Chief Librarian.

Web, library.usgs.gov

Maintains collection of books, periodicals, serials, maps, and technical reports on geology, mineral and water resources, mineralogy, paleontology, petrology, soil and environmental sciences, and physics and chemistry as they relate to earth sciences. Open to the public; makes interlibrary loans.

CONGRESS

General Accounting Office (GAO), *Document Distribution Center,* 441 G St. N.W., #1100 20548 (mailing address: P.O. Box 37050 20013); (202) 512-6000. Fax, (202) 512-6061. Gerry Mader, Manager. Press, (202) 512-4800. TTY, (202) 512-2537.

General e-mail, info@www.gao.gov

Web, www.gao.gov

Provides information to the public on many federal programs. GAO publications and information about GAO publications are available upon request.

Library of Congress, *Science, Technology, and Business,* 10 1st St. S.E. 20540-4750; (202) 707-5664. Fax, (202) 707-1925. William J. Sittig, Chief. Science reading room, (202) 707-6401. Technical reports, (202) 707-5655.

Web, lcweb.loc.gov/rr/scitech

Offers reference service by telephone, by correspondence, and in person. Maintains a collection of more than 3 million technical reports.

NONPROFIT

American Statistical Assn., 1429 Duke St., Alexandria, VA 22314; (703) 684-1221. Fax, (703) 684-2037. William B. Smith, Executive Director.

General e-mail, asainfo@amstat.org

Web, www.amstat.org

Membership: individuals interested in statistics and related quantitative fields. Advises government agencies on statistics and methodology in agency research; promotes development of statistical techniques for use in business, industry, finance, government, agriculture, and science.

Commission on Professionals in Science and Technology, 1200 New York Ave. N.W., #390 20005; (202) 326-7080. Fax, (202) 842-1603. Eleanor Babco, Executive Director.

General e-mail, info@cpst.org

Web, www.cpst.org

Membership: scientific societies, corporations, academicians, and individuals. Analyzes and publishes data on scientific and engineering human resources in the United States. Interests include employment of minorities and women, salary ranges, and supply and demand of scientists and engineers.

International Programs

AGENCIES

International Trade Administration (ITA), *(Commerce Dept.), Transportation and Machinery,* 14th St. and Constitution Ave. N.W., #2800A 20230; (202) 482-1872. Fax, (202) 482-0856. Joseph H. Bogosian, Deputy Assistant Secretary.

Web, www.ita.doc.gov

Conducts analyses and competitive assessments of high-tech industries, including aerospace, automotive, and industrial machinery. Develops trade policies for these industries, negotiates market access for U.S. companies, assists in promoting exports through trade missions, shows, and fairs in major overseas markets.

National Institute of Standards and Technology (NIST), *(Commerce Dept.), International and Academic Affairs,* Route I-270 and Quince Orchard Rd., Bldg. 222, #B224, Gaithersburg, MD 20899-1090; (301) 975-4119. Fax, (301) 975-3530. B. Stephen Carpenter, Director.

Web, www.nist.gov/oiaa/oiaa1.htm

Represents the institute in international functions; coordinates programs with foreign institutions; assists scientists from foreign countries who visit the institute for consultation. Administers a postdoctoral research associates program.

National Oceanic and Atmospheric Administration (NOAA), *(Commerce Dept.), National Environmental Satellite, Data, and Information Service,* 1335 East-West Hwy., Silver Spring, MD 20910; (301) 713-3578. Fax, (301) 713-1249. Gregory W. Withee, Assistant Administrator.

Web, www.nesdis.noaa.gov

Acquires and disseminates global environmental data: marine, atmospheric, solid earth, and solar-terrestrial. Participates, with National Meteorological Center, in the World Weather Watch Programme developed by the World Meteorological Organization. Manages U.S. civil earth-observing satellite systems and atmospheric, oceanographic, geophysical, and solar data centers. Provides the public, businesses, and government agencies with environmental data and information products and services.

National Science Foundation (NSF), *International Science and Engineering,* 4201 Wilson Blvd., #935,

Arlington, VA 22230; (703) 292-8710. Fax, (703) 292-9067. Kerri-Ann Jones, Director.
Web, www.nsf.gov/sbe/int

Coordinates and manages the foundation's international scientific activities and cooperative research and exchange programs; promotes new partnerships between U.S. scientists and engineers and their foreign colleagues; provides support for U.S. participation in international scientific organizations.

National Weather Service *(National Oceanic and Atmospheric Administration), National Center for Environmental Prediction,* 5200 Auth Rd., #101, Camp Springs, MD 20746; (301) 763-8016. Fax, (301) 763-8434. Louis W. Uccellini, Director.
Web, www.ncep.noaa.gov

The National Center for Environmental Prediction and the National Environmental Satellite, Data, and Information Service are part of the World Weather Watch Programme developed by the United Nations' World Meteorological Organization. Collects data and exchanges it with other nations; provides other national weather service offices, private meteorologists, and government agencies with products, including forecast guidance products.

Office of Science and Technology Policy (OSTP), *(Executive Office of the President),* Dwight D. Eisenhower Executive Office Bldg. 20502. Fax, (202) 456-6027. Kathie L. Olsen, Associate Director, Science; Richard M. Russell, Associate Director, Technology.
Web, www.ostp.gov

Advises the president on international science and technology matters as they affect national security; coordinates international science and technology initiatives at the interagency level. Interests include nuclear materials, security, nuclear arms reduction, and counterterrorism.

Smithsonian Institution, *International Relations,* 1100 Jefferson Dr. S.W., #3123 20560 (mailing address: P.O. Box 37012, Quad MRC 705 20013-7012); (202) 357-4282. Fax, (202) 786-2557. Francine C. Berkowitz, Director.
Web, www.si.edu/intrel

Fosters the development and coordinates the international aspects of Smithsonian scientific activities; facilitates basic research in the natural sciences and encourages international collaboration among individuals and institutions.

State Dept., *Oceans and International Environmental and Scientific Affairs,* 2201 C St. N.W., #7831 20520-7818; (202) 647-1554. Fax, (202) 647-0217. John F. Turner, Assistant Secretary. Press, (202) 647-3486.

Web, www.state.gov

Formulates and implements policies and proposals for U.S. international scientific, technological, environmental, oceanic and marine, arctic and Antarctic, and space programs; coordinates international science and technology policy with other federal agencies.

State Dept., *Technological and Specialized Agencies Programs,* 2201 C St. N.W., #5332 20520; (202) 647-1044. Fax, (202) 647-8902. Donald E. Booth, Director.
Web, www.state.gov

Oversees U.S. participation in international scientific and technical organizations, including the International Atomic Energy Agency; the United Nations Environment Programme; the Commission on Sustainable Development; and the United Nations Educational, Scientific, and Cultural Organization. Works to ensure that United Nations agencies follow United Nations Conference on Environment and Development recommendations on sustainable growth.

Technology Administration *(Commerce Dept.), International Technology Policy,* 14th St. and Constitution Ave. N.W., #4821 20230; (202) 482-6351. Fax, (202) 501-6849. Kathryn Sullivan, Director (Acting).
Web, www.ta.doc.gov

Develops and implements policies to enhance the competitiveness of U.S. technology-based industry. Provides information on foreign research and development; coordinates, on behalf of the Commerce Dept., negotiation of international science and technology agreements. Manages the Japan Technology program, which seeks to ensure access for U.S. researchers and industry to Japanese science and technology.

INTERNATIONAL ORGANIZATIONS

InterAcademy Panel on International Issues, 2101 Constitution Ave. N.W., NAS 243 20418 (mailing address: 500 5th St. N.W. 20001); (202) 334-2800. Fax, (202) 334-2139. John Boright, Executive Director.
Web, www.national-academies.org

Membership: academies of science in countries worldwide. Promotes communication among leading authorities in the natural and social sciences; advises governments and international organizations; interests include scientific aspects of population, sustainable development, energy and other resources, and environmental protection. (National Academy of Sciences is U.S. member.)

NONPROFIT

American Assn. for the Advancement of Science (AAAS), *International Programs,* 1200 New York Ave.

N.W., 7th Floor 20005; (202) 326-6650. Fax, (202) 289-4958. Shere Abbott, Director.

General e-mail, int@aaas.org

Web, www.aaas.org/international

Administers programs concerned with international science and engineering; works to further understanding of global problems with scientific and technological components; provides policymakers at national and international levels with information from the scientific community.

Japan Information Access Project, *2000 P St. N.W., #620 20036; (202) 822-6040. Fax, (202) 822-6044. Mindy Kotler, Director.*

General e-mail, access@jiaponline.org

Web, www.jiaponline.org

Studies Japanese and Northeast Asian security and public policy. Researches and analyzes issues affecting Japan's relationship with the West.

National Research Council (NRC), *International Affairs, 2101 Constitution Ave. N.W., FO 2045 20418; (202) 334-2800. Fax, (202) 334-3094. John Boright, Executive Director.*

Web, www4.nationalacademies.org/oia/oiahome.nsf

Serves the international interests of the National Research Council, National Academy of Sciences, National Academy of Engineering, and Institute of Medicine. Promotes effective application of science and technology to the economic and social problems of industrialized and developing countries; advises U.S. government agencies; participates in international organizations, conferences, and cooperative activities.

Research Applications

AGENCIES

Defense Technical Information Center *(Defense Dept.), 8725 John Jay Kingman Rd., #0944, Fort Belvoir, VA 22060-6218; (703) 767-9100. Fax, (703) 767-9183. Kurt N. Molholm, Administrator. Registration, (703) 767-8200.*

Web, www.dtic.mil

Acts as a central repository for the Defense Dept.'s collection of current and completed research and development efforts in all fields of science and technology. Disseminates research and development information to contractors, grantees, and registered organizations working on government research and development projects, particularly for the Defense Dept. Users must register with the center.

National Aeronautics and Space Administration (NASA), *Space Science, 300 E St. S.W. 20546 (mailing address: NASA Headquarters, Mail Code S 20546); (202) 358-1409. Fax, (202) 358-3092. Edward J. Weiler, Associate Administrator.*

Web, spacescience.nasa.gov

Provides information on technology developed during NASA's activities that have practical applications in other fields; maintains a data bank. (Accepts written requests for specific technical information.)

National Institute of Standards and Technology (NIST), *(Commerce Dept.), 100 Bureau Dr., Bldg. 101, #A1134, Gaithersburg, MD 20899-1000 (mailing address: 100 Bureau Dr., MS 1000, Gaithersburg, MD 20899); (301) 975-2300. Fax, (301) 869-8972. Arden L. Bement Jr., Director.*

Web, www.nist.gov

Nonregulatory agency that serves as national reference and measurement laboratory for the physical and engineering sciences. Works with industry, government agencies, and academia; conducts research in electronics, manufacturing, physics, chemistry, radiation, materials science, applied mathematics, computer science and technology, and engineering sciences.

National Institute of Standards and Technology (NIST), *Advanced Technology Program, 100 Bureau Dr., Bldg. 101, #A333, Gaithersburg, MD 20899-4700; (301) 975-3104. Fax, (301) 869-1150. Marc Stanley, Director (Acting).*

General e-mail, atp@nist.gov

Web, www.atp.nist.gov

Fosters partnerships among government, industry, and academia to support technological research. Projects focus on the technological needs of U.S. industry, not those of government.

National Science Foundation (NSF), *Human Resource Development, 4201 Wilson Blvd., #815, Arlington, VA 22230; (703) 292-4666. Fax, (703) 292-9018. Dr. Donald Thompson, Director.*

Web, www.ehr.nsf.gov/EHR/HRD

Supports and encourages participation in scientific and engineering research by women, minorities, and people with disabilities. Awards grants and scholarships.

Technology Administration *(Commerce Dept.), Technology Policy, 14th St. and Constitution Ave. N.W., #4814C 20230; (202) 482-5687. Fax, (202) 482-4817. Bruce P. Mehlman, Assistant Secretary.*

Web, www.ta.doc.gov

Promotes the removal of barriers to the commercialization of technology; analyzes federal research and development funding; acts as an information clearinghouse.

American National Standards Institute, *Conformity Assessment, Washington Office,* *1819 L St. N.W., #600 20036; (202) 293-8020. Fax, (202) 293-9287. Lane Hallenbeck, Vice President.*

Web, www.ansi.org

Administers and coordinates the voluntary standardization system for the U.S. private sector; maintains staff contacts for specific industries. Serves as U.S. member of the International Organization for Standardization (ISO) and hosts the U.S. National Committee of the International Electrotechnical Commission (IEC).

National Center for Advanced Technologies,

1000 Wilson Blvd., #1700, Arlington, VA 22209; (703) 358-1006. Fax, (703) 358-1012. Stan Siegel, President.

General e-mail, ncat@ncat.com

Web, www.ncat.com

Encourages U.S. competition in the world market by uniting government, industry, and university efforts to develop advanced technologies. (Affiliated with the Aerospace Industries Assn. of America.)

Public Technology, Inc., *1301 Pennsylvania Ave. N.W., #800 20004; (202) 626-2400. Fax, (202) 626-2498. Costis Toregas, President. Information, (800) 852-4934. Library, (202) 626-2456. Press, (202) 626-2412.*

General e-mail, press@pti.org

Web, www.pti.org

Cooperative research, development, and technology-transfer organization of cities and counties in North America. Applies available technological innovations and develops other methods to improve public services. Participates in international conferences.

Rand Corporation, *Washington Office,* *1200 S. Hayes St., Arlington, VA 22202-5050; (703) 413-1100. Fax, (703) 413-8111. Bruce Hoffman, Director.*

Web, www.rand.org

Research organization. Interests include energy, emerging technologies and critical systems, space and transportation, technology policies, international cooperative research, water resources, ocean and atmospheric sciences, and other technologies in defense and nondefense areas. (Headquarters in Santa Monica, Calif.)

SRI International, *Washington Office,* *1100 Wilson Blvd., #2800, Arlington, VA 22209; (703) 524-2053. Fax, (703) 247-8569. John Bramer, Director.*

Web, www.sri.com

Research and consulting organization that conducts basic and applied research for government, industry, and business. Interests include engineering, physical and life

sciences, and international research. (Headquarters in Menlo Park, Calif.)

Scientific Research Practices

AGENCIES

Education Dept., *Grants Policy and Oversight Staff: Protection of Human Subjects in Research,* *7th and D Sts. S.W., #3652 20202-4248; (202) 260-5353. Fax, (202) 205-0667. Helene Deramond, Coordinator.*

General e-mail, ocfoweb@ed.gov

Web, www.ed.gov/offices/OCFO/humansub.html

Advises the grantees and applicants on the regulations for the protection of human subjects and provides guidance to the Education Dept. on the requirements for complying with the regulations. Serves as the primary Education Dept. contact for matters concerning the protection of human subjects in research.

Energy Dept. (DOE), *Human Subjects Research Program,* *19901 Germantown Rd., #SC-72, Germantown, MD 20874-1290; (301) 903-4731. Fax, (301) 903-8521. Susan L. Rose, Program Manager.*

Web,

www.sc.doe.gov/production/ober/humsubj/index.html

Works to protect the rights and welfare of human research subjects by establishing guidelines and regulations on scientific research that uses human subjects; acts as an educational and technical resource to investigators, administrators, and institutional research boards. Interests include Energy Dept. health-related studies that use workers as subjects.

Health and Human Services Dept. (HHS), *(Health and Human Services Dept.), Human Research Protections,* *1101 Wootton Pkwy., #200, The Tower Building, Rockville, MD 20852; (301) 496-7005. Fax, (301) 402-0527. Bernard Schwetz, Director (Acting).*

General e-mail, ohrp@osophs.dhhs.gov

Web, ohrp.osophs.dhhs.gov

Monitors the use of humans in research to ensure that programs and procedures comply with Public Health Service and Health and Human Services Dept. regulations; develops and conducts educational programs for the protection of human subjects; helps other organizations address ethical issues in medicine and research.

Health and Human Services Dept. (HHS), *Research Integrity,* *5515 Security Lane, #700, Rockville, MD 20852; (301) 443-3400. Fax, (301) 443-5351. Chris B. Pascal, Director.*

Web, ori.hhs.gov

Seeks to promote the quality of Public Health Service extramural and intramural research programs. (Extramural programs provide funding to research institutions that are not part of the federal government. Intramural programs provide funding for research conducted within federal government facilities.) Develops policies and regulations that protect from retaliation individuals who disclose information about scientific misconduct; administers assurance program; provides technical assistance to institutions during inquiries and investigations of scientific misconduct; reviews institutional findings and recommends administrative actions to the assistant secretary of Health and Human Services; sponsors educational programs and activities for professionals interested in research integrity.

NONPROFIT

Do No Harm: The Coalition of Americans for Research Ethics, *200 Daingerfield Rd., #100, Alexandria, VA 22314; (703) 684-8352. Fax, (703) 684-5813. Gene Tarne, Communications Director.*
Web, www.stemcellresearch.org

Membership: researchers and health care, bioethic, and legal professionals opposed to scientific research conducted on human embryos. Seeks to educate policymakers and the public about the development of medical treatments and therapies that do not utilize human embryos.

Humane Society of the United States, *Animal Research Issues, 2100 L St. N.W. 20037; (301) 258-3043. Fax, (301) 258-7760. Martin Stephens, Vice President.*
Web, www.hsus.org/ace/11348

Seeks to end the suffering of animals in harmful research. Promotes the use of alternatives that replace, refine; or reduce the use of animals in scientific research, education, and consumer product testing. Conducts outreach programs aimed toward the public and the scientific community.

🔬 BIOLOGY AND LIFE SCIENCES

AGENCIES

Armed Forces Radiobiology Research Institute *(Defense Dept.), 8901 Wisconsin Ave., Bethesda, MD 20889-5603; (301) 295-1210. Fax, (301) 295-4967. Col. Robert R. Eng (MS, USA), Director.*
Web, www.afrri.usuhs.mil

Serves as the principal ionizing radiation radiobiology research laboratory under the jurisdiction of the Uniformed Services of the Health Sciences. Participates in international conferences and projects.

National Aeronautics and Space Administration **(NASA),** *Bioastronautics Research, 300 E St. S.W., #AP15 20546; (202) 358-2530. Fax, (202) 358-4168. Guy Fogleman, Director (Acting).*
Web, www.hq.nasa.gov

Conducts NASA's life sciences research.

National Institute of General Medical Sciences *(National Institutes of Health), 45 Center Dr., #2AN12B, MSC-6200, Bethesda, MD 20892-6200; (301) 594-2172. Fax, (301) 402-0156. Judith Greenberg, Director (Acting).*
Web, www.nigms.nih.gov

Supports basic biomedical research and training that are not targeted to specific diseases; focus includes cell biology, genetics, pharmacology, and systemic response to trauma and anesthesia.

National Museum of Natural History *(Smithsonian Institution), Library, 10th St. and Constitution Ave. N.W., #51 20560-0154 (mailing address: P.O. Box 37012 20013-7012); (202) 357-1496. Fax, (202) 357-1896. Ann Juneau, Chief Librarian.*
Web, www.sil.si.edu

Maintains reference collections covering anthropology, ethnology, botany, biology, ecology, biodiversity, and zoology; permits on-site use of the collections. Open to the public by appointment; makes interlibrary loans.

National Museum of Natural History *(Smithsonian Institution), Naturalist Center, 741 Miller Dr. S.E., #G2, Leesburg, VA 20175; (703) 779-9712. Fax, (703) 779-9715. Richard H. Efthim, Manager. Information, (800) 729-7725.*
General e-mail, natcenter@aol.com
Web, www.mnh.si.edu/edu_resources.html#NC

Maintains natural history research and reference library with books and more than 36,000 objects, including minerals, rocks, plants, animals, shells and corals, insects, invertebrates, micro- and macrofossil materials, and microbiological and anthropological materials. Facilities include study equipment such as microscopes, dissecting instruments, and plant presses. Operates a teachers' reference center. Library open to the public. Reservations required for groups of six or more.

National Oceanic and Atmospheric Administration **(NOAA),** *(Commerce Dept.), National Marine Fisheries Service, 1315 East-West Hwy., Silver Spring, MD 20910; (301) 713-2239. Fax, (301) 713-2258. William T. Hogarth, Assistant Administrator. Press, (301) 713-2370.*
Web, www.nmfs.gov

Conducts research and collects data on marine ecology and biology; collects, analyzes, and provides information through the Marine Resources Monitoring, Assessment, and Prediction Program. Administers the Magnuson Fishery Conservation and Management Act and marine mammals and endangered species protection programs. Works with the Army Corps of Engineers on research into habitat restoration and conservation.

National Science Foundation (NSF), *Biological Sciences,* 4201 Wilson Blvd., #605, Arlington, VA 22230; (703) 292-8400. Fax, (703) 292-9154. Mary E. Clutter, Assistant Director. Information, (703) 292-5111.
Web, www.nsf.gov/bio

Directorate that provides grants for research in the cellular and molecular biosciences, environmental biology, integrative biology and neuroscience, and biological infrastructure. Monitors international research.

Naval Medical Research Center *(Defense Dept.),* 503 Robert Grant Ave., #1W28, Silver Spring, MD 20910-7500; (301) 319-7400. Fax, (301) 319-7410. Capt. Richard B. Oberst, Commanding Officer.
Web, www.nmrc.navy.mil

Performs basic and applied biomedical research in areas of military importance, including infectious diseases, hyperbaric medicine, wound repair enhancement, environmental stress, and immunobiology. Provides support to field laboratories and naval hospitals; monitors research internationally.

U.S. Geological Survey (USGS), *(Interior Dept.),* Biological Resources, 12201 Sunrise Valley Dr., Reston, VA 20192; (703) 648-4050. Fax, (703) 648-4042. Vacant, Associate Director for Biology.
Web, biology.usgs.gov

Performs research in support of biological resource management. Monitors and reports on the status of the nation's biotic resources. Conducts research on wildlife, fish, insects, and plants, including the effects of disease and environmental contaminants on endangered and other species.

NONPROFIT

American Institute of Biological Sciences, 1444 Eye St. N.W., #200 20005; (202) 628-1500. Fax, (202) 628-1509. Richard O'Grady, Executive Director. Information, (800) 992-2427.
General e-mail, admin@aibs.org
Web, www.aibs.org

Membership: biologists, biological associations, industrial research laboratories, and others interested in biology. Promotes interdisciplinary cooperation among members engaged in biological research and education; conducts educational programs for members; sponsors Congressional Science Fellowship; administers projects supported by government grants. Monitors legislation and regulations.

American Society for Biochemistry and Molecular Biology, 9650 Rockville Pike, Bethesda, MD 20814; (301) 634-7145. Fax, (301) 634-7126. Charles C. Hancock, Executive Officer.
General e-mail, asbmb@asbmb.faseb.org
Web, www.asbmb.org

Professional society of biological chemists; membership by election. Participates in International Union of Biochemistry and Molecular Biology (headquartered in Berlin). Monitors legislation and regulations.

American Society for Cell Biology, 8120 Woodmont Ave., #750, Bethesda, MD 20814-2762; (301) 347-9300. Fax, (301) 347-9310. Elizabeth Marincola, Executive Director.
General e-mail, ascbinfo@ascb.org
Web, www.ascb.org

Membership: scientists who have education or research experience in cell biology or an allied field. Promotes scientific exchange worldwide; organizes courses, workshops, and symposia. Monitors legislation and regulations.

American Society for Microbiology, 1752 N St. N.W. 20036; (202) 737-3600. Fax, (202) 942-9333. Michael I. Goldberg, Executive Director. Press, (202) 942-9297.
General e-mail, oed@asmusa.org
Web, www.asmusa.org

Membership: microbiologists. Encourages education, training, scientific investigation, and application of research results in microbiology and related subjects; participates in international research.

American Type Culture Collection, 10801 University Blvd., Manassas, VA 20110-2209; (703) 365-2700. Fax, (703) 365-2750. Raymond H. Cypress, President. Toll-free, (800) 638-6597.
General e-mail, help@atcc.org
Web, www.atcc.org

Provides biological products, technical services, and educational programs to government agencies, academic institutions, and private industry worldwide. Serves as a repository of living cultures and genetic material.

AOAC International, 481 N. Frederick Ave., #500, Gaithersburg, MD 20877; (301) 924-7077. Fax, (301) 924-7089. E. James Bradford, Executive Director. Information, (800) 379-2622.

General e-mail, aoac@aoac.org

Web, www.aoac.org

International association of analytical science professionals, companies, government agencies, nongovernmental organizations, and institutions. Promotes methods validation and quality measurements in the analytical sciences. Supports the development, testing, validation, and publication of reliable chemical and biological methods of analyzing foods, drugs, feed, fertilizers, pesticides, water, forensic materials, and other substances.

Biophysical Society, *9650 Rockville Pike, #L0512, Bethesda, MD 20814-3998; (301) 530-7114. Fax, (301) 530-7133. Rosalba Kampman, Executive Director.*

Web, www.biophysics.org

Membership: scientists, professors, and researchers engaged in biophysics or related fields. Encourages development and dissemination of knowledge in biophysics.

Carnegie Institution of Washington, *1530 P St. N.W. 20005-1910; (202) 387-6400. Fax, (202) 387-8092. Dr. Richard Meserve, President.*

Web, www.carnegieinstitution.org

Conducts research in the physical and biological sciences at the following centers: the observatories of the Carnegie Institution with headquarters in Pasadena, Calif.; Geophysical Laboratory and Dept. of Terrestrial Magnetism in Washington, D.C.; Dept. of Plant Biology in Stanford, Calif.; Dept. of Embryology in Baltimore, Md; and Dept. of Global Ecology in Pasadena, Calif. Refers specific inquiries to appropriate department. Library open to the public by appointment.

Ecological Society of America, *1707 H St. N.W., 4th Floor 20006-3916; (202) 833-8773. Fax, (202) 833-8775. Katherine S. McCarter, Executive Director.*

General e-mail, esahq@esa.org

Web, www.esa.org

Promotes research in ecology, the scientific study of the relationship between organisms and their past, present, and future environments. Interests include biotechnology; management of natural resources, habitats, and ecosystems to protect biological diversity; and ecologically sound public policies.

Federation of American Societies for Experimental Biology, *9650 Rockville Pike, Bethesda, MD 20814-3998; (301) 530-7090. Fax, (301) 571-0686. Sidney H. Golub, Executive Director. Information, (301) 571-0657.*

Web, www.faseb.org

Federation of twenty-one scientific and educational groups: American Physiological Society, American Society for Biochemistry and Molecular Biology, American Society for Pharmacology and Experimental Therapeutics, American Society for Investigative Pathology, American Society for Nutritional Sciences, American Assn. of Immunologists, Biophysical Society, The Protein Society, American Assn. of Anatomists, American Society for Bone and Mineral Research, Society for Developmental Biology, American Peptide Society, Assn. of Biomolecular Resource Facilities, American Society for Clinical Investigation, Endocrine Society, American Society of Human Genetics, Radiation Research Society, Society for Gynecologic Investigation, Environmental Mutagen Society, Society for the Study of Reproduction, and Teratology Society. Serves as support group for member societies; participates in international conferences.

Biotechnology

AGENCIES

Cooperative State Research, Education, and Extension Service *(Agriculture Dept.), Competitive Research Grants and Awards Management, 800 9th St. S.W., #2256 20024-2240; (202) 401-1761. Fax, (202) 401-1782. Mark Poth, Deputy Administrator (Acting).*

Web, www.reeusda.gov/funding

Administers competitive research grants for biotechnology in the agricultural field. Oversees research in biotechnology.

Environmental Protection Agency (EPA), *Prevention, Pesticides, and Toxic Substances, 1200 Pennsylvania Ave. N.W. 20460-7101; (202) 564-2902. Fax, (202) 564-0512. Stephen L. Johnson, Assistant Administrator. Pollution prevention and toxic substances control, (202) 564-3810.*

Web, www.epa.gov

Studies and makes recommendations for regulating chemical substances under the Toxic Substances Control Act; compiles list of chemical substances subject to the act; registers, controls, and regulates use of pesticides and toxic substances.

National Institutes of Health (NIH), *(Health and Human Services Dept.), Biotechnology Activities, 6705 Rockledge Dr., #750, MSC-7985, Bethesda, MD 20892-7985; (301) 496-9838. Fax, (301) 496-9839. Amy P. Patterson, Director.*

Web, www4.od.nih.gov/oba

Reviews requests submitted to NIH involving genetic testing, recombinant DNA technology, and xenotransplantation, and implements research guidelines.

National Library of Medicine *(National Institutes of Health), National Center for Biotechnology Informa-*

tion, 8600 Rockville Pike, Bldg. 38A, 8th Floor, Bethesda, MD 20894; (301) 496-2475. Fax, (301) 480-9241. Dr. David J. Lipman, Director.

General e-mail, info@ncbi.nlm.nih.gov

Web, www.ncbi.nlm.nih.gov

Creates automated systems for storing and analyzing knowledge of molecular biology and genetics. Develops new information technologies to aid in understanding the molecular processes that control human health and disease. Conducts basic research in computational molecular biology.

Office of Science and Technology Policy (OSTP), *(Executive Office of the President), Biotechnology Subcommittee of the Committee on Science,* 4201 Wilson Blvd., #605, Arlington, VA 22230; (703) 292-8400. Fax, (703) 292-9154. Mary E. Clutter, Chair.

Web, www.nsf.gov

Serves as a forum for addressing biotechnology research issues, sharing information, identifying gaps in scientific knowledge, and developing consensus among concerned federal agencies. Facilitates continuing cooperation among federal agencies on topical issues.

NONPROFIT

Biotechnology Industry Organization, 1225 Eye St. N.W., #400 20005; (202) 962-9200. Fax, (202) 962-9201. Carl B. Feldbaum, President.

General e-mail, bio@bio.org

Web, www.bio.org

Membership: U.S. and international companies engaged in biotechnology. Monitors government activities at all levels; promotes educational activities; conducts workshops.

Friends of the Earth (FOE), 1025 Vermont Ave. N.W., #300 20005-6303; (202) 783-7400. Fax, (202) 783-0444. Brent Blackwelder, President.

General e-mail, foe@foe.org

Web, www.foe.org

Monitors legislation and regulations on issues related to seed industry consolidation and patenting laws and on business developments in agricultural biotechnology and their effect on farming, food production, genetic resources, and the environment.

Kennedy Institute of Ethics *(Georgetown University),* Healy Hall, 4th Floor, 37th and O Sts. N.W. 20057; (202) 687-8099. Fax, (202) 687-8089. G. Madison Powers, Director. Library, (800) 633-3849; in Washington, (202) 687-3885.

Web, www.georgetown.edu/research/kie

Sponsors research on medical ethics, including legal and ethical definitions of death, allocation of scarce health resources, and recombinant DNA and human gene therapy. Works with the National Library of Medicine to provide citations to bioethical issues; conducts international programs and free bibliographic searches. Library open to the public.

Botany

AGENCIES

National Arboretum *(Agriculture Dept.),* 3501 New York Ave. N.E. 20002; (202) 245-2726. Fax, (202) 245-4575. Thomas S. Elias, Director. Library, (202) 245-4538.

Web, www.usna.usda.gov

Maintains public display of plants on 446 acres; provides information and makes referrals concerning cultivated plants (exclusive of field crops and fruits); conducts plant breeding and research; maintains herbarium. Library open to the public by appointment.

National Museum of Natural History *(Smithsonian Institution), Botany,* 10th St. and Constitution Ave. N.W., MRC 166 20560-0166 (mailing address: P.O. Box 37012 20013-7012); (202) 357-2534. Fax, (202) 786-2563. W. John Kress, Chair.

Web, www.nmnh.si.edu/departments/botany.html

Conducts botanical research worldwide; furnishes information on the identification, distribution, and local names of flowering plants; studies threatened and endangered plant species.

Smithsonian Institution, *Botany and Horticulture Library,* 10th St. and Constitution Ave. N.W., MRC 166 20560-0166; (202) 357-2715. Fax, (202) 357-1896. Ruth F. Schallert, Chief Librarian.

General e-mail, libmail@si.edu

Web, www.si.edu

Collections include taxonomic botany, plant morphology, general botany, history of botany, grasses, and algae. Permits on-site use of collections (appointment preferred); makes interlibrary loans. (Housed at the National Museum of Natural History.)

CONGRESS

U.S. Botanic Garden, 245 1st St. S.W., (Conservatory address: 100 Maryland Ave. S.W.) 20024; (202) 225-8333. Fax, (202) 225-1561. Holly H. Shimizu, Executive Director.

General e-mail, usbg@aoc.gov

Web, www.usbg.gov

Collects, cultivates, and grows various plants for public display and study; identifies botanic specimens and furnishes information on proper growing methods. Conducts horticultural classes and tours.

NONPROFIT

American Society for Horticultural Science,
113 S. West St., #200, Alexandria, VA 22314; (703) 836-4606. Fax, (703) 836-2024. Michael W. Neff, Executive Director.
General e-mail, ashs@ashs.org
Web, www.ashs.org
Membership: educators, government workers, firms, associations, and individuals interested in horticultural science. Promotes scientific research and education in horticulture, including international exchange of information.

American Society of Plant Biologists, *15501 Monona Dr., Rockville, MD 20855-2768; (301) 251-0560. Fax, (301) 279-2996. John Lisack, Executive Director.*
Web, www.aspb.org
Membership: plant physiologists, plant biochemists, and molecular biologists. Seeks to educate and promote public interest in plant physiology. Publishes journals; provides placement service for members; sponsors annual meeting of plant scientists.

National Assn. of Plant Patent Owners, *1000 Vermont Ave. N.W., 3rd Floor 20005-4914; (202) 789-2900. Fax, (202) 789-1893. Craig Regelbrugge, Administrator.*
Web, www.anla.org
Membership: owners of patents on newly propagated horticultural plants. Informs members of plant patents issued, provisions of patent laws, and changes in practice. Promotes the development, protection, production, and distribution of new varieties of horticultural plants. Works with international organizations of plant breeders on matters of common interest. (Affiliated with the American Nursery and Landscape Assn.)

Zoology

AGENCIES

National Museum of Natural History *(Smithsonian Institution), Entomology, 10th St. and Constitution Ave. N.W., MRC 105 20560-0105 (mailing address: P.O. Box 37012 20013-7012); (202) 357-2078. Fax, (202) 786-3141. Wayne Mathis, Section Head. Library, (202) 357-2354.*
Web, www.nmnh.si.edu
Conducts worldwide research in entomology. Maintains the national collection of insects; lends insect specimens to specialists for research and classification. Library open to the public by appointment.

National Museum of Natural History *(Smithsonian Institution), Invertebrate Zoology, 10th St. and Constitution Ave. N.W., MRC 163 20560-0163 (mailing address: P.O. Box 37012 20013-7012); (202) 357-3027. Fax, (202) 357-3043. David Pawson, Section Head.*
Web, www.nmnh.si.edu
Conducts research on the identity, morphology, histology, life history, distribution, classification, and ecology of marine, terrestrial, and fresh water invertebrate animals (except insects); maintains the national collection of invertebrate animals; aids exhibit and educational programs; conducts pre- and postdoctoral fellowship programs; provides facilities for visiting scientists in the profession.

National Museum of Natural History *(Smithsonian Institution), Vertebrate Zoology, 10th St. and Constitution Ave. N.W., MRC 109 20560-0109 (mailing address: P.O. Box 37012 20013-7012); (202) 357-2740. Fax, (202) 786-2979. Lynne R. Parenti, Section Head.*
Web, www.nmnh.si.edu
Conducts research worldwide on the systematics, ecology, and behavior of mammals, birds, reptiles, amphibians, and fish; maintains the national collection of specimens.

NONPROFIT

American Zoo and Aquarium Assn., *8403 Colesville Rd., #710, Silver Spring, MD 20910; (301) 562-0777. Fax, (301) 562-0888. Sydney J. Butler, Executive Director.*
Web, www.aza.org
Membership: interested individuals and professionally run zoos and aquariums in North America. Administers professional accreditation program; participates in worldwide conservation, education, and research activities.

Entomological Society of America, *9301 Annapolis Rd., #300, Lanham, MD 20706-3115; (301) 731-4535. Fax, (301) 731-4538. Paula Lettice, Executive Director.*
General e-mail, esa@entsoc.org
Web, www.entsoc.org
Scientific association that promotes the science of entomology and the interests of professionals in the field. Advises on crop protection, food chain, and individual and urban health matters dealing with insect pests.

Jane Goodall Institute, *P.O. Box 14890, Silver Spring, MD 20911-4890; (301) 565-0086. Fax, (301) 565-3188. Fred Thompson, Executive Director.*
General e-mail, JGIinformation@janegoodall.org
Web, www.janegoodall.org

Seeks to increase primate habitat conservation, expand noninvasive primate research, and promote activities that ensure the well-being of primates. (Affiliated with Jane Goodall Institutes in Canada, Europe, Asia, and Africa.)

 ## ENGINEERING

AGENCIES

National Institute of Standards and Technology (NIST), *(Commerce Dept.), Electronics and Electrical Engineering Laboratory,* *100 Bureau Dr., Bldg. 220, #B358, MS 8100, Gaithersburg, MD 20899; (301) 975-2220. Fax, (301) 975-4091. William E. Anderson, Director.*

General e-mail, eeel@nist.gov

Web, www.eeel.nist.gov

Provides focus for research, development, and applications in the fields of electrical, electronic, quantum electric, and electromagnetic materials engineering. Interests include fundamental physical constants, practical data, measurement methods, theory, standards, technology, technical services, and international trade.

National Institute of Standards and Technology (NIST), *(Commerce Dept.), Manufacturing Engineering Laboratory,* *100 Bureau Dr., Bldg. 220, #B322, Gaithersburg, MD 20899; (301) 975-3400. Fax, (301) 948-5668. Dale Hall, Director.*

Web, www.mel.nist.gov

Collects technical data, develops standards in production engineering, and publishes findings; produces the technical base for proposed standards and technology for industrial and mechanical engineering; provides instrument design, fabrication, and repair. Helps establish international standards.

National Science Foundation (NSF), *Engineering,* *4201 Wilson Blvd., #505N, Arlington, VA 22230; (703) 292-8300. Fax, (703) 292-9013. Esin Gulari, Assistant Director (Acting).*

Web, www.eng.nsf.gov

Directorate that supports fundamental research and education in engineering through grants and special equipment awards. Programs are designed to enhance international competitiveness and to improve the quality of engineering in the United States. Oversees the following divisions: Electrical and Communications Systems; Chemical and Transport Systems; Engineering Education and Centers; Civil and Mechanical Systems; Design, Manufacture, and Industrial Innovation; and Bioengineering and Environmental Systems.

NONPROFIT

American Assn. of Engineering Societies, *1828 L St. N.W., #906 20036-5110; (202) 296-2237. Fax, (202) 296-1151. Tom Price, Executive Director.*

General e-mail, aaes@aaes.org

Web, www.aaes.org

Federation of engineering societies; members work in industry, construction, government, academia, and private practice. Advances the knowledge, understanding, and practice of engineering. Serves as delegate to the World Federation of Engineering Organizations.

American Council of Engineering Consultants, *1015 15th St. N.W., #802 20005; (202) 347-7474. Fax, (202) 898-0068. David Raymond, Executive Vice President.*

General e-mail, acec@acec.org

Web, www.acec.org

Membership: practicing consulting engineering firms and state, local, and regional consulting engineers councils. Serves as an information clearinghouse for member companies in such areas as legislation, legal cases, marketing, management, professional liability, business practices, and insurance. Monitors legislation and regulations.

American Council of Engineering Consultants, *Research and Management Foundation,* *1015 15th St. N.W., #802 20005; (202) 347-7474. Fax, (202) 898-0068. Florian Kogelnik, Director.*

General e-mail, acec@acec.org

Web, www.acec.org

Conducts research and educational activities to improve engineering practices, professional cooperation, and ties to government. Provides information and training to member organizations on research and analysis, management training, access to international markets, and community involvement.

American Society for Engineering Education, *1818 N St. N.W., #600 20036; (202) 331-3500. Fax, (202) 265-8504. Frank L. Huband, Executive Director. Press, (202) 331-3537.*

Web, www.asee.org

Membership: engineering faculty and administrators, professional engineers, government agencies, and engineering colleges, corporations, and professional societies. Conducts research, conferences, and workshops on engineering education. Monitors legislation and regulations.

American Society of Civil Engineers, *1801 Alexander Bell Dr., Reston, VA 20191-4400; (703) 295-6300. Fax, (703) 295-6222. Patrick Natale, Executive Director. Information, (800) 548-2723.*

Web, www.asce.org

Membership: professionals and students in civil engineering. Develops and produces consensus standards for construction documents and building codes. Maintains the Civil Engineering Research Foundation, which focuses national attention and resources on the research needs of the civil engineering profession. Participates in international conferences.

American Society of Mechanical Engineers, *Public Affairs, Washington Office, 1828 L St. N.W., #906 20036; (202) 785-3756. Fax, (202) 429-9417. Philip W. Hamilton, Managing Director.*

General e-mail, grdept@asme.org

Web, www.asme.org

Serves as a clearinghouse for sharing of information among federal, state, and local governments and the engineering profession. Monitors legislation and regulations. (Headquarters in New York.)

ASFE, *8811 Colesville Rd., #G106, Silver Spring, MD 20910; (301) 565-2733. Fax, (301) 589-2017. John P. Bachner, Executive Vice President.*

General e-mail, info@asfe.org

Web, www.asfe.org

Membership: consulting geotechnical and geoenvironmental engineering firms. Conducts seminars and a peer review program on quality control policies and procedures in geotechnical engineering. (Formerly the Assn. of Soil and Foundation Engineers).

Institute of Electrical and Electronics Engineers—United States Activities, *Professional Activities, Washington Office, 1828 L St. N.W., #1202 20036-5104; (202) 785-0017. Fax, (202) 785-0835. W. Thomas Suttle, Managing Director.*

General e-mail, ieeeusa@ieee.org

Web, www.ieee.org

U.S. arm of an international technological and professional organization concerned with all areas of electrotechnology policy, including aerospace, computers, communications, biomedicine, electric power, and consumer electronics. (Headquarters in New York.)

International Federation of Professional and Technical Engineers, *8630 Fenton St., #400, Silver Spring, MD 20910; (301) 565-9016. Fax, (301) 565-0018. Gregory J. Junemann, President.*

Web, www.ifpte.org

Membership: approximately 75,000 technicians, engineers, scientists, professionals, and other workers, including government employees. Helps members negotiate pay, benefits, and better working conditions; conducts

training programs and workshops. Monitors legislation and regulations. (Affiliated with the AFL-CIO and the Canadian Labour Congress.)

International Microelectronics and Packaging Society, *611 2nd St. N.E. 20002; (202) 548-4001. Fax, (202) 548-6115. Richard Breck, Executive Director. Information, (888) 464-6277.*

General e-mail, imaps@imaps.org

Web, www.imaps.org

Membership: persons involved in the microelectronics industry worldwide. Integrates disciplines of science and engineering; fosters exchange of information among complementary technologies, including ceramics, thin and thick films, surface mounts, semiconductor packaging, discrete semiconductor devices, monolithic circuits, and multichip modules; disseminates technical knowledge.

International Test and Evaluation Assn., *4400 Fair Lakes Court, #104, Fairfax, VA 22033-3899; (703) 631-6220. Fax, (703) 631-6221. R. Alan Plishker, Executive Director.*

Web, www.itea.org

Membership: engineers, scientists, managers, and other industry, government, and academic professionals interested in testing and evaluating products and complex systems. Provides a forum for information exchange; monitors international research.

National Academy of Engineering, *2101 Constitution Ave. N.W., #218 20418; (202) 334-3201. Fax, (202) 334-1680. William A. Wulf, President. Library, (202) 334-2125. Publications, (800) 624-6242; in Washington, (202) 334-3313.*

Web, www.nae.edu

Independent society whose members are elected in recognition of important contributions to the field of engineering and technology. Shares responsibility with the National Academy of Sciences for examining questions of science and technology at the request of the federal government; promotes international cooperation. Library open to the public by appointment. (Affiliated with the National Academy of Sciences.)

National Society of Professional Engineers (NSPE), *1420 King St., Alexandria, VA 22314-2794; (703) 684-2800. Fax, (703) 836-4875. Albert C. Gray, Executive Director.*

Web, www.nspe.org

Membership: U.S. licensed professional engineers from all disciplines. Holds engineering seminars; operates an information center; interests include international practice of engineering.

ENVIRONMENTAL AND EARTH SCIENCES

AGENCIES

National Aeronautics and Space Administration
(NASA), *Earth Science, 300 E St. S.W. 20546 (mailing address: NASA Headquarters, Mail Code Y 20546); (202) 358-2165. Fax, (202) 358-2921. Ghassem R. Asrar, Associate Administrator.*

Web, www.earth.nasa.gov

Conducts programs dealing with the earth as observed from space; conducts upper atmospheric and terrestrial studies and meteorological and ocean research.

National Oceanic and Atmospheric Administration
(NOAA), *(Commerce Dept.), 14th St. and Constitution Ave. N.W., #5128 20230; (202) 482-3436. Fax, (202) 408-9674. Vice Admiral Conrad C. Lautenbacher Jr., Under Secretary. Information, (301) 713-4000. Press, (301) 482-6090.*

Web, www.noaa.gov

Conducts research in marine and atmospheric sciences; issues weather forecasts and warnings vital to public safety and the national economy; surveys resources of the sea; analyzes economic aspects of fisheries operations; develops and implements policies on international fisheries; provides states with grants to conserve coastal zone areas; protects marine mammals; maintains a national environmental center with data from satellite observations and other sources including meteorological, oceanic, geodetic, and seismological data centers; provides colleges and universities with grants for research, education, and marine advisory services; prepares and provides nautical and aeronautical charts and maps.

National Oceanic and Atmospheric Administration
(NOAA), *(Commerce Dept.), Library and Information Services, 1315 East-West Hwy., 2nd Floor, SSMC3, Silver Spring, MD 20910; (301) 713-2607. Fax, (301) 713-4598. Janice A. Beattie, Director. Reference service, (301) 713-2600.*

General e-mail, library.reference@noaa.gov
Web, www.lib.noaa.gov

Collection includes reports, journals, monographs, photographs, and microforms on atmospheric and oceanic science. Maintains bibliographic database of other NOAA libraries, an online service, and reference materials on CD-ROM. Makes interlibrary loans; open to the public.

National Science Foundation (NSF),
Geosciences, 4201 Wilson Blvd., #705N, Arlington, VA 22230; (703)

292-8500. Fax, (703) 292-9042. Margaret S. Leinen, Assistant Director.

Web, www.geo.nsf.gov

Directorate that supports research about the earth, including its atmosphere, continents, oceans, and interior. Works to improve the education and human resource base for the geosciences; participates in international and multidisciplinary activities, especially to study changes in the global climate.

National Science Foundation (NSF),
Polar Programs, 4201 Wilson Blvd., #755S, Arlington, VA 22230; (703) 292-8032. Fax, (703) 292-9081. Karl A. Erb, Director; Dennis Peacock, Science Head, Antarctica Science, (703) 292-8033.

Web, www.nsf.gov/od/opp

Funds and manages U.S. activity in Antarctica; provides grants for arctic programs in polar biology and medicine, earth sciences, atmospheric sciences, meteorology, ocean sciences, and glaciology. The Polar Information Program serves as a clearinghouse for polar data and makes referrals on specific questions.

Smithsonian Environmental Research Center
(Smithsonian Institution), *647 Contees Wharf Rd., Edgewater, MD 21037 (mailing address: P.O. Box 28, Edgewater, MD 21037); (443) 482-2200. Fax, (443) 482-2380. Ross B. Simons, Director.*

Web, www.serc.si.edu

Performs laboratory and field research that measures physical, chemical, and biological interactions to determine the mechanisms of environmental responses to humans' use of air, land, and water. Evaluates properties of the environment that affect the functions of living organisms. Maintains research laboratories, public education program, facilities for controlled environments, and estuarine and terrestrial lands.

United States Arctic Research Commission,
4350 N. Fairfax Dr., #630, Arlington, VA 22203; (703) 525-0111. Fax, (703) 525-0114. Garrett W. Brass, Executive Director.

Web, www.arctic.gov

Presidential advisory commission that develops policy for arctic research; assists the interagency Arctic Research Policy Committee in implementing a national plan of arctic research; recommends improvements in logistics, data management, and dissemination of arctic information.

U.S. Geological Survey (USGS),
(Interior Dept.), 12201 Sunrise Valley Dr., MS 100, Reston, VA 20192; (703) 648-7411. Fax, (703) 648-4454. Charles G. Groat, Director. Library, (703) 648-4302. Press, (703) 648-4460.

Web, www.usgs.gov

Provides reports, maps, and databases that describe and analyze water, energy, biological, and mineral resources; the land surface; and the underlying geological structure and dynamic processes of the earth.

U.S. Geological Survey (USGS), *(Interior Dept.),* **Library Services,** *12201 Sunrise Valley Dr., MS 950, Reston, VA 20192; (703) 648-4305. Fax, (703) 648-6373. Nancy Blair, Chief Librarian.*

Web, library.usgs.gov

Maintains collection of books, periodicals, serials, maps, and technical reports on geology, mineral and water resources, mineralogy, paleontology, petrology, soil and environmental sciences, and physics and chemistry as they relate to earth sciences. Open to the public; makes interlibrary loans.

CONGRESS

House Government Reform Committee, *Subcommittee on Energy Policy, Natural Resources, and Regulatory Affairs, B377 RHOB 20515; (202) 225-4407. Fax, (202) 225-2441. Rep. Doug Ose, R-Calif., Chair; Dan Skopec, Staff Director.*

Web, www.house.gov/reform

Oversees operations of the National Oceanic and Atmospheric Administration.

House Resources Committee, *Subcommittee on Energy and Mineral Resources, 1626 LHOB 20515; (202) 225-9297. Fax, (202) 225-5255. Rep. Barbara Cubin, R-Wyo., Chair; Jack Belcher, Staff Director.*

General e-mail, energy.minerals@mail.house.gov

Web, resourcescommittee.house.gov

Jurisdiction over U.S. Geological Survey legislation, except water-related programs.

House Resources Committee, *Subcommittee on Fisheries, Conservation, Wildlife, and Oceans, H2-188 FHOB 20515; (202) 226-0200. Fax, (202) 225-1542. Rep. Wayne T. Gilchrest, R-Md., Chair; Harry Burroughs, Staff Director.*

General e-mail, fisheries.subcommittee@mail.house.gov

Web, resourcescommittee.house.gov

Jurisdiction over legislation on most oceanographic matters, including ocean engineering, ocean charting, and certain programs of the National Oceanic and Atmospheric Administration.

House Resources Committee, *Subcommittee on Water and Power, 1522 LHOB 20515; (202) 225-8331. Fax, (202) 226-6953. Rep. Ken Calvert, R-Calif., Chair; Joshua Johnson, Staff Director.*

General e-mail, water.power@mail.house.gov

Web, resourcescommittee.house.gov

Jurisdiction over water-related programs of the U.S. Geological Survey, saline water research and development, water resources research programs, and matters related to the Water Resources Planning Act.

Senate Commerce, Science, and Transportation Committee, *SD-508 20510; (202) 224-1251. Fax, (202) 224-1259. Sen. John McCain, R-Ariz., Chair; Jeanne Bumpus, Staff Director.*

Web, commerce.senate.gov

Jurisdiction over legislation on most oceanographic matters, including ocean charting and the National Oceanic and Atmospheric Administration.

Senate Commerce, Science, and Transportation Committee, *Subcommittee on Oceans, Fisheries, and Coast Guard, SH-227 20510; (202) 224-8172. Fax, (202) 224-9334. Sen. Olympia J. Snowe, R-Maine, Chair; Andrew Minkiewicz, Counsel Member.*

Web, commerce.senate.gov

Studies national ocean policy and programs, including ocean-specific satellite and atmospheric systems of the National Oceanic and Atmospheric Administration. (Subcommittee does not report legislation.)

Senate Energy and Natural Resources Committee, *Subcommittee on Public Lands and Forests, SD-364 20510; (202) 224-7556. Fax, (202) 224-7970. Sen. Larry E. Craig, R-Idaho, Chair; Frank Gladics, Professional Staff Member.*

General e-mail, plf@energy.senate.gov

Web, energy.senate.gov

Jurisdiction over legislation on the U.S. Geological Survey.

NONPROFIT

American Geophysical Union, *2000 Florida Ave. N.W. 20009-1277; (202) 462-6900. Fax, (202) 328-0566. A. F. Spilhaus Jr., Executive Director.*

General e-mail, service@agu.org

Web, www.agu.org

Membership: scientists and technologists who study the environments and components of the earth, sun, and solar system. Promotes international cooperation; disseminates information.

Atmospheric Sciences

AGENCIES

National Science Foundation (NSF), *Atmospheric Sciences, 4201 Wilson Blvd., #775, Arlington, VA 22230;*

(703) 292-8520. Fax, (703) 292-9022. Jarvis Moyers, Director.

Web, www.geo.nsf.gov/atm

Supports research on the earth's atmosphere and the sun's effect on it, including studies of the physics, chemistry, and dynamics of the earth's upper and lower atmospheres and its space environment; climate processes and variations; and the natural global cycles of gases and particles in the earth's atmosphere.

National Weather Service *(National Oceanic and Atmospheric Administration), 1325 East-West Hwy., #18150, Silver Spring, MD 20910; (301) 713-0689. Fax, (301) 713-0662. Jack Kelly, Administrator.*

Web, www.nws.noaa.gov

Issues warnings of hurricanes, severe storms, and floods; provides weather forecasts and services for the general public and for aviation and marine interests. National Weather Service forecast office, (703) 260-0107; weather forecast for Washington, D.C., and vicinity, (703) 260-0307; marine forecast, (703) 260-0505; recreational forecast, (703) 260-0705; climate data, (703) 271-4800; river stages, (703) 260-0305; pilot weather, (800) 992-7433.

National Weather Service *(National Oceanic and Atmospheric Administration), National Center for Environmental Prediction, 5200 Auth Rd., #101, Camp Springs, MD 20746; (301) 763-8016. Fax, (301) 763-8434. Louis W. Uccellini, Director.*

Web, www.ncep.noaa.gov

The National Center for Environmental Prediction and the National Environmental Satellite, Data, and Information Service are part of the World Weather Watch Programme developed by the United Nations' World Meteorological Organization. Collects data and exchanges data with other nations; provides other national weather service offices, private meteorologists, and government agencies with products, including forecast guidance products.

U.S. Geological Survey (USGS), *(Interior Dept.), Earth Surface Dynamics Program, 12201 Sunrise Valley Dr., MS 906, Reston, VA 20192; (703) 648-5330. Fax, (703) 648-6647. Martha Garcia, Program Coordinator.*

Web, geochange.er.usgs.gov

Conducts research on climate fluctuations and documents the variability of the climate system in the past and future; provides information on global change and its effects on society; examines terrestrial and marine processes and the natural history of global change.

Alliance for Responsible Atmospheric Policy, *2111 Wilson Blvd., 8th Floor, Arlington, VA 22201; (703) 243-0344. Fax, (703) 243-2874. David Stirpe, Executive Director.*

General e-mail, alliance98@aol.com

Web, www.arap.org

Coalition of users and producers of chlorofluorocarbons (CFCs). Seeks further study of the ozone depletion theory.

Climate Institute, *333 1/2 Pennsylvania Ave. S.E., 3rd Floor 20003-1148; (202) 547-0104. Fax, (202) 547-0111. John C. Topping Jr., President.*

General e-mail, info@climate.org

Web, www.climate.org

Educates the public and policymakers on climate change (greenhouse effect, or global warming) and on the depletion of the ozone layer. Develops strategies on mitigating climate change in developing countries and in North America.

Geology and Earth Sciences

AGENCIES

National Museum of Natural History *(Smithsonian Institution), Mineral Sciences, 10th St. and Constitution Ave. N.W., MRC 119 20560; (202) 357-2060. Fax, (202) 357-2476. James F. Luhr, Chair.*

Web, www.volcano.si.edu

Conducts research on meteorites. Interests include mineralogy, petrology, volcanology, and geochemistry. Maintains the Global Volcanism Network, which reports worldwide volcanic and seismic activity.

National Museum of Natural History *(Smithsonian Institution), Naturalist Center, 741 Miller Dr. S.E., #G2, Leesburg, VA 20175; (703) 779-9712. Fax, (703) 779-9715. Richard H. Efthim, Manager. Information, (800) 729-7725.*

General e-mail, natcenter@aol.com

Web, www.mnh.si.edu/edu_resources.html#NC

Maintains natural history research and reference library with books and more than 36,000 objects, including minerals, rocks, plants, animals, shells and corals, insects, invertebrates, micro- and macrofossil materials, and microbiological and anthropological materials. Facilities include study equipment such as microscopes, dissecting instruments, and plant presses. Operates a teachers' reference center. Library open to the public. Reservations required for groups of six or more.

National Museum of Natural History, *Paleobiology,*
10th St. and Constitution Ave. N.W., MRC 121 20560
(mailing address: P.O. Box 37012, NHB MRC 121 20013-
7012); (202) 357-2162. Fax, (202) 786-2832. Douglas
Erwin, Chair, (202) 357-2053.
General e-mail, paleo_dept@nmnh.si.edu
Web, www.nmnh.si.edu/paleo

Conducts research worldwide on invertebrate paleontology, paleobotany, sedimentology, and vertebrate
paleontology; provides information on paleontology.
Maintains national collection of fossil organisms and
sediment samples.

National Science Foundation (NSF), *Earth Sciences,*
4201 Wilson Blvd., #785, Arlington, VA 22230; (703) 292-
8550. Fax, (703) 292-9025. Herman B. Zimmerman,
Director.
Web, www.geo.nsf.gov/ear

Provides grants for research in geology, geophysics,
geochemistry, and related fields, including tectonics,
hydrologic sciences, and continental dynamics.

U.S. Geological Survey (USGS), *(Interior Dept.),*
Earthquake Hazards, 12201 Sunrise Valley Dr., Reston,
VA 20192 (mailing address: 905 National Center, Reston,
VA 20192); (703) 648-6714. Fax, (703) 648-6717. John
Filson, Program Coordinator.
Web, www.usgs.gov

Manages geologic, geophysical, and engineering
investigations, including assessments of hazards from
earthquakes and landslides; conducts research on the
mechanisms and occurrences of earthquakes worldwide
and their relationship to the behavior of the crust and
upper mantle; develops methods for predicting the time,
place, and magnitude of earthquakes; conducts engineering and geologic studies on landslides and ground failures.

U.S. Geological Survey (USGS), *(Interior Dept.),*
Geology, 12201 Sunrise Valley Dr., MS 911, Reston, VA
20192; (703) 648-6600. Fax, (703) 648-7031. P. Patrick
Leahy, Associate Director.
Web, geology.usgs.gov

Conducts onshore and offshore geologic research and
investigation. Produces information on geologic hazards,
such as earthquakes and volcanoes; geologic information
for use in the management of public lands and national
policy determinations; information on the chemistry and
physics of the earth; and geologic, geophysical, and geochemical maps and analyses to address environmental,
resource, and geologic hazards concerns. Participates in
international research.

U.S. Geological Survey (USGS), *(Interior Dept.),*
National Cooperative Geologic Mapping Program,
12201 Sunrise Valley Dr., MS 908, Reston, VA 20192;
(703) 648-6943. Fax, (703) 648-6937. Peter Little, Pro-
gram Coordinator.
Web, www.usgs.gov

Produces geologic maps; makes maps available to
public and private organizations.

U.S. Geological Survey (USGS), *(Interior Dept.), Vol-*
cano Hazards, 12201 Sunrise Valley Dr., Reston, VA
20192 (mailing address: 904 National Center, Reston, VA
20192); (703) 648-6711. Fax, (703) 648-5483. John Pallis-
ter, Program Coordinator.
Web, volcanoes.usgs.gov

Manages geologic, geophysical, and engineering
investigations, including assessments of hazards from
volcanoes; conducts research worldwide on the mechanisms of volcanoes and on igneous and geothermal systems. Issues warnings of potential volcanic hazards.

NONPROFIT

American Geological Institute, *4220 King St., Alexan-*
dria, VA 22302; (703) 379-2480. Fax, (703) 379-7563.
Marcus E. Milling, Executive Director.
General e-mail, agi@agiweb.org
Web, www.agiweb.org

Membership: earth science societies and associations.
Maintains a computerized database with worldwide
information on geology, engineering and environmental
geology, oceanography, and other geological fields (available to the public for a fee).

Oceanography

AGENCIES

National Museum of Natural History *(Smithsonian*
Institution), Botany, 10th St. and Constitution Ave.
N.W., MRC 166 20560-0166 (mailing address: P.O. Box
37012 20013-7012); (202) 357-2534. Fax, (202) 786-2563.
Ernani Menez, Marine Biologist.
Web, www.nmnh.si.edu/departments/botany.html

Investigates the biology, evolution, and classification
of tropical and subtropical marine algae and seagrasses.
Acts as curator of the national collection in this field.
Develops and participates in scholarly programs.

National Museum of Natural History *(Smithsonian*
Institution), Crustaceans, 10th St. and Constitution Ave.
N.W., #W115 20560 (mailing address: P.O. Box 37012
20013-7012); (202) 357-4673. Fax, (202) 357-3043.
Rafael Lemaitre, Curator.

Conducts worldwide research and answers scientific inquiries on the Smithsonian's marine invertebrate collections; engages in taxonomic identification, community analysis, and specimen and sample data management.

National Museum of Natural History *(Smithsonian Institution), Library, 10th St. and Constitution Ave. N.W., #51 20560-0154 (mailing address: P.O Box 37012 20013-7012); (202) 357-1496. Fax, (202) 357-1896. Ann Juneau, Chief Librarian.*
Web, www.sil.si.edu

Maintains reference collections covering anthropology, ethnology, botany, biology, ecology, biodiversity, and zoology; permits on-site use of the collections. Open to the public by appointment; makes interlibrary loans.

National Museum of Natural History *(Smithsonian Institution), Vertebrate Zoology, 10th St. and Constitution Ave. N.W., MRC 109 20560-0109 (mailing address: P.O. Box 37012 20013-7012); (202) 357-2740. Fax, (202) 786-2979. Lynne R. Parenti, Section Head.*
Web, www.nmnh.si.edu

Processes, sorts, and distributes to scientists specimens of marine vertebrates; engages in taxonomic sorting, community analysis, and specimen and sample data management.

National Oceanic and Atmospheric Administration (NOAA), *(Commerce Dept.), Marine and Aviation Operations, 1315 East-West Hwy., 12th Floor, Bldg. #3, Silver Spring, MD 20910-3282; (301) 713-1045. Fax, (301) 713-1541. Rear Adm. Evelyn J. Fields, Director.*
Web, www.noaacorps.noaa.gov/index.html

Uniformed service of the Commerce Dept. that operates and manages NOAA's fleet of hydrographic, oceanographic, and fisheries research ships and aircraft. Supports NOAA's scientific programs.

National Oceanic and Atmospheric Administration (NOAA), *(Commerce Dept.), National Ocean Service, 1305 East-West Hwy., SSMC4, Silver Spring, MD 20910; (301) 713-3074. Fax, (301) 713-4269. Jamison Hawkins, Assistant Administrator (Acting).*
Web, www.nos.noaa.gov

Manages charting and geodetic services, oceanography and marine services, coastal resource coordination, and marine survey operations.

National Oceanic and Atmospheric Administration (NOAA), *(Commerce Dept.), National Oceanographic Data Center, 1315 East-West Hwy., 4th Floor, SSMC3, Silver Spring, MD 20910-3282; (301) 713-3270. Fax,* *(301) 713-3300. H. Lee Dantzler, Director; Kurt Schnebele, Deputy Director. Information and requests, (301) 606-4549.*
General e-mail, services@nodc.noaa.gov
Web, www.noaa.gov

Offers a wide range of oceanographic data on the Web, disk, CD-ROM, and hard copy; provides research scientists with data processing services; prepares statistical summaries and graphical data products. (Fee charged for some services.)

National Science Foundation (NSF), *Ocean Sciences Research, 4201 Wilson Blvd., #725, Arlington, VA 22230; (703) 292-8582. Fax, (703) 292-9085. James A. Yoder, Director.*
Web, www.geo.nsf.gov/oce

Awards grants to academic institutions and private corporations for research in all areas of the marine sciences, including biological, chemical, and physical oceanography, marine geology, and marine geophysics.

National Science Foundation (NSF), *Oceanographic Centers and Facilities, 4201 Wilson Blvd., #725, Arlington, VA 22230; (703) 292-8583. Fax, (703) 292-9085. Lawrence H. Clark, Head.*
Web, www.geo.nsf.gov/oce/

Awards grants and contracts for acquiring, upgrading, and operating oceanographic research facilities that lend themselves to shared usage. Facilities supported include ships, submersibles, and shipboard and shore-based data logging and processing equipment. Supports development of new drilling techniques and systems.

U.S. Geological Survey (USGS), *(Interior Dept.), Coastal and Marine Geology Program, 12201 Sunrise Valley Dr., Reston, VA 20192 (mailing address: 915B National Center, Reston, VA 20192); (703) 648-6422. Fax, (703) 648-5464. John W. Haines, Program Coordinator.*
Web, marine.usgs.gov

Surveys the continental margins and the ocean floor to provide information on the mineral resources potential of submerged lands.

NONPROFIT

Marine Technology Society, *5565 Sterrett Place, #108, Columbia, MD 21044; (410) 884-5330. Fax, (410) 884-9060. Judith Krauthamer, Executive Director.*
General e-mail, mtpubs@aol.com
Web, www.mtsociety.org

Membership: scientists, engineers, technologists, and others interested in marine science and technology. Provides information on marine science, technology, and education.

National Ocean Industries Assn., *1120 G St. N.W., #900 20005; (202) 347-6900. Fax, (202) 347-8650. Tom A. Fry, President.*

General e-mail, noia@noia.org

Web, www.noia.org

Membership: manufacturers, producers, suppliers, and support and service companies involved in marine, offshore, and ocean work. Interests include offshore oil and gas supply and production, deep-sea mining, ocean thermal energy, and new energy sources.

MATHEMATICAL, COMPUTER, AND PHYSICAL SCIENCES

AGENCIES

National Institute of Standards and Technology (NIST), *(Commerce Dept.), 100 Bureau Dr., Bldg. 101, #A1134, Gaithersburg, MD 20899-1000 (mailing address: 100 Bureau Dr., MS 1000, Gaithersburg, MD 20899); (301) 975-2300. Fax, (301) 869-8972. Arden L. Bement Jr., Director.*

Web, www.nist.gov

Nonregulatory agency that serves as national reference and measurement laboratory for the physical and engineering sciences. Works with industry, government agencies, and academia; conducts research in electronics, manufacturing, physics, chemistry, radiation, materials science, applied mathematics, computer science and technology, and engineering sciences.

National Institute of Standards and Technology (NIST), *(Commerce Dept.), Information Technology Laboratory, 100 Bureau Dr., Bldg. 225, #B264, Gaithersburg, MD 20899-8900; (301) 975-2900. Fax, (301) 840-1357. Susan F. Zevin, Director (Acting).*

Web, www.itl.nist.gov

Offers support in mathematical and computer sciences to all institute programs and federal agencies; provides consultations, methods, and research supporting the institute's scientific and engineering projects. Manages and operates NIST central computing facilities.

National Science Foundation (NSF), *Mathematical and Physical Sciences, 4201 Wilson Blvd., #1025, Arlington, VA 22230; (703) 292-5324. Fax, (703) 292-9032. John B. Hunt, Assistant Director. Information, (703) 292-5111.*

Web, www.nsf.gov/mps

Directorate that supports research in the mathematical and physical sciences; divisions focus on physics, chemistry, materials research, mathematical sciences, and astronomical sciences. Works to improve the education and human resource base for these fields; participates in international and multidisciplinary activities.

NONPROFIT

Carnegie Institution of Washington, *1530 P St. N.W. 20005-1910; (202) 387-6400. Fax, (202) 387-8092. Dr. Richard Meserve, President.*

Web, www.carnegieinstitution.org

Conducts research in the physical and biological sciences at the following centers: the observatories of the Carnegie Institution with headquarters in Pasadena, Calif.; Geophysical Laboratory and Dept. of Terrestrial Magnetism in Washington, D.C.; Dept. of Plant Biology in Stanford, Calif.; Dept. of Embryology in Baltimore, Md; and Dept. of Global Ecology in Pasadena, Calif. Refers specific inquiries to appropriate department. Library open to the public by appointment.

Chemistry

AGENCIES

National Institute of Standards and Technology (NIST), *(Commerce Dept.), Chemical Science and Technology Laboratory, 100 Bureau Dr., Bldg. 227, #A311, Gaithersburg, MD 20899; (301) 975-3145. Fax, (301) 975-3845. Hratch G. Semerjian, Director.*

Web, www.nist.gov

Develops uniform chemical measurement methods; provides federal agencies and industry with advisory and research services in the areas of analytical chemistry, biotechnology, chemical engineering, and physical chemistry; conducts interdisciplinary research efforts with other NIST laboratories.

National Institute of Standards and Technology (NIST), *(Commerce Dept.), Materials Science and Engineering Laboratory, 100 Bureau Dr., MS 8500, Gaithersburg, MD 20899-8500; (301) 975-5658. Fax, (301) 975-5012. Leslie E. Smith, Director.*

Web, www.nist.gov

Provides measurements, data, standards, reference materials, concepts, and technical information fundamental to the processing, microstructure, properties, and performance of materials; addresses the scientific basis for new advanced materials; operates a research nuclear reactor for advanced materials characterization measurements; operates four materials data centers.

National Science Foundation (NSF), *Chemistry, 4201 Wilson Blvd., #1055, Arlington, VA 22230; (703) 292-8840. Fax, (703) 292-9037. Art Ellis, Director. Toll-free fax, (800) 338-3128.*

Web, www.nsf.gov/chem

Awards grants to research programs in organic and macromolecular chemistry, materials chemistry, physical chemistry, analytical and surface chemistry, and inorganic, bioinorganic, and organometallic chemistry; provides funds for instruments needed in chemistry research; coordinates interdisciplinary programs. Monitors international research.

National Science Foundation (NSF), *Materials Research,* 4201 Wilson Blvd., #1065, Arlington, VA 22230; (703) 292-8810. Fax, (703) 292-9035. Thomas A. Weber, Director.

Web, www.nsf.gov

Provides grants for research in condensed matter physics; solid state chemistry and polymers; metals, ceramics, and electronic materials; and materials theory. Provides major instrumentation for these activities. Supports multidisciplinary research in these areas through materials research science and engineering centers. Supports national facilities and instrumentation in the areas of synchrotron radiation and high magnetic fields. Monitors international research.

NONPROFIT

American Assn. for Clinical Chemistry, 2101 L St. N.W., #202 20037-1526; (202) 857-0717. Fax, (202) 887-5093. Richard G. Flaherty, Executive Vice President.

General e-mail, info@aacc.org

Web, www.aacc.org

International society of chemists, physicians, and other scientists specializing in clinical chemistry. Provides educational and professional development services; presents awards for outstanding achievement. Monitors legislation and regulations.

American Chemical Society, 1155 16th St. N.W. 20036; (202) 872-4600. Fax, (202) 872-4615. John K. Crum, Executive Director. Information, (800) 227-5558. Library, (202) 872-6000.

General e-mail, help@acs.org

Web, www.chemistry.org

Membership: professional chemists and chemical engineers. Maintains educational programs, including those that evaluate college chemistry departments and high school chemistry curricula. Administers grants and fellowships for basic research; sponsors international exchanges; presents achievement awards. Library open to the public by appointment.

American Chemical Society, *Petroleum Research Fund,* 1155 16th St. N.W. 20036; (202) 872-4481. Fax, (202) 872-6319. Lawrence A. Funke, Administrator.

Web, www.chemistry.org/prf

Makes grants to nonprofit institutions for advanced scientific education and fundamental research related to the petroleum industry (chemistry, geology, engineering).

American Chemistry Council, 1300 Wilson Blvd., Arlington, VA 22209; (703) 741-5000. Fax, (703) 741-6000. Greg Lebedev, President.

Web, www.americanchemistry.com

Membership: manufacturers of basic industrial chemicals. Provides members with technical research, communications services, and legal affairs counseling. Interests include environmental safety and health, transportation, energy, and international trade. Monitors legislation and regulations.

American Institute of Chemical Engineers, 1300 Eye St. N.W., #1090 East 20005-3314; (202) 962-8690. Fax, (202) 962-8699. Vacant, Director.

General e-mail, dc@aiche.org

Web, www.aiche.org

Membership: professionals from industry, government, academia, and consulting, including students and retirees. Sponsors research in chemical engineering and promotes public understanding of the profession.

AOAC International, 481 N. Frederick Ave., #500, Gaithersburg, MD 20877; (301) 924-7077. Fax, (301) 924-7089. E. James Bradford, Executive Director. Information, (800) 379-2622.

General e-mail, aoac@aoac.org

Web, www.aoac.org

International association of analytical science professionals, companies, government agencies, nongovernmental organizations, and institutions. Promotes methods validation and quality measurements in the analytical sciences. Supports the development, testing, validation, and publication of reliable chemical and biological methods of analyzing foods, drugs, feed, fertilizers, pesticides, water, forensic materials, and other substances.

Society of the Plastics Industry, 1801 K St. N.W., #600K 20006; (202) 974-5200. Fax, (202) 296-7005. Donald K. Duncan, President.

Web, www.plasticsindustry.org

Promotes the plastics industry. Monitors legislation and regulations.

Synthetic Organic Chemical Manufacturers Assn., 1850 M St. N.W., #700 20036; (202) 721-4100. Fax, (202) 296-8120. Edmund Fording, President.

Web, www.socma.com

Membership: companies that manufacture, distribute, and market organic chemicals, and providers of custom chemical services. Interests include international trade, environmental and occupational safety, and health issues; conducts workshops and seminars. Promotes commercial opportunities for members. Monitors legislation and regulations.

Computer Sciences

AGENCIES

National Coordination Office for Information, Technology Research, and Development, *4201 Wilson Blvd., #II-405, Arlington, VA 22230; (703) 292-4873. Fax, (703) 292-9097. David Nelson, Director.*
Web, www.itrd.gov

Coordinates multi-agency research and development projects that involve computing, communications, and technology research and development. Reports to the National Science and Technology Council; provides information to Congress, U.S. and foreign organizations, and the public. (Successor to the High Performance Computing and Communications [HPCC] Program.)

National Institute of Standards and Technology (NIST), *(Commerce Dept.), Information Technology Laboratory, 100 Bureau Dr., Bldg. 225, #B264, Gaithersburg, MD 20899-8900; (301) 975-2900. Fax, (301) 840-1357. Susan F. Zevin, Director (Acting).*
Web, www.itl.nist.gov

Advises federal agencies on automatic data processing management and use of information technology; helps federal agencies maintain up-to-date computer technology support systems, emphasizing computer security techniques; recommends federal information processing standards; conducts research in computer science and technology.

National Science Foundation (NSF), *Computer and Information Sciences and Engineering, 4201 Wilson Blvd., Arlington, VA 22230; (703) 292-8900. Fax, (703) 292-9074. Peter Freeman, Assistant Director.*
Web, www.cise.nsf.gov

Directorate that promotes basic research and education in computer and information sciences and engineering; helps maintain U.S. preeminence in these fields. Coordinates NSF involvement in the High-Performance Computing and Communications (HPCC) program; develops computer resources for scholarly communication, including links with foreign research and education networks; helps set Internet policy.

National Science Foundation (NSF), *Computer Communications Research, 4201 Wilson Blvd., #1145, Arlington, VA 22230; (703) 292-8918. Fax, (703) 292-9059. Julia Abrahams, Director.*
Web, www.cise.nsf.gov/ccr

Awards grants for research in computer science and engineering, including programs in computer and computation theory; numeric, symbolic, and geometric computation; computer systems; and software engineering.

National Science Foundation (NSF), *Information and Intelligence Systems, 4201 Wilson Blvd., #1115, Arlington, VA 22230; (703) 292-8930. Fax, (703) 292-9073. Michael Pazzini, Director.*
Web, www.cise.nsf.gov/iis

Supports research on designing, developing, managing, and using information systems, including database and expert systems, knowledge models and cognitive systems, machine intelligence and robotics, information technology and organizations, and interactive systems.

NONPROFIT

American Electronics Association, *601 Pennsylvania Ave. N.W., North Bldg., #600 20004; (202) 682-9110. Fax, (202) 682-9111. William Archey, Chief Executive Officer.*
Web, aeanet.org

High-tech nonprofit organization with an emphasis on software, Internet technology, advanced electronics, and telecommunications. Monitors and influences legislation, trade activities, and regulations.

Computer and Communications Industry Assn., *666 11th St. N.W., #600 20001; (202) 783-0070. Fax, (202) 783-0534. Edward J. Black, President.*
General e-mail, ccia@ccianet.org
Web, www.ccianet.org

Membership: manufacturers and suppliers of computer data processing and communications-related products and services. Interests include telecommunications policy, capital formation and tax policy, federal procurement policy, communications and computer industry standards, intellectual property policies, encryption, international trade, and antitrust reform.

Computer Law Assn., *3028 Javier Rd., #402, Fairfax, VA 22031-4622; (703) 560-7747. Fax, (703) 207-7028. Barbara Fieser, Executive Director.*
General e-mail, clanet@aol.com
Web, www.cla.org

Membership: lawyers, law students, and nonattorneys concerned with the legal aspects of computers and computer communications. Sponsors programs and provides information on such issues as software protection, contracting, telecommunications, international distribution, financing, taxes, copyrights, patents, and electronic data interchange. Focus includes the Internet and e-commerce.

Council on the Future of Technology and Public Policy, *1800 K St. N.W., #400 20006; (202) 887-0200. Fax, (202) 775-3199. John J. Hamre, Chief Executive Officer.*

Web, www.csis.org

Membership: chief executives of high-tech businesses and government. Sponsored by the Center for Strategic and International Studies. Conducts and publishes research on technology-related systems including authenticity, privacy issues, and Internet public policy.

Industry Advisory Council, *11350 Random Hills Rd., #120, Fairfax, VA 22030; (703) 218-1965. Fax, (703) 218-1960. Vivian Ronen, Executive Director (Acting).*

Web, www.iaconline.org

Membership: producers of computer hardware and software and systems integrators. Serves as liaison between government and industry; offers programs on development and acquisition of information technology. Monitors legislation and regulations. (Affiliated with the Federation of Government Information Processing Councils.)

Information Technology Assn. of America, *1401 Wilson Blvd., #1100, Arlington, VA 22209; (703) 284-5300. Fax, (703) 525-2279. Harris N. Miller, President.*

Web, www.itaa.org

Membership: personal computer software publishing companies. Promotes growth of the software industry worldwide; helps develop electronic commerce. Operates a toll-free hotline to report software piracy; investigates claims of software theft within corporations, financial institutions, academia, state and local governments, and nonprofit organizations. Provides legal counsel and initiates litigation on behalf of members.

Information Technology Industry Council, *1250 Eye St. N.W., #200 20005; (202) 737-8888. Fax, (202) 638-4922. Rhett Dawson, President. Press, (202) 626-5725.*

General e-mail, webmaster@itc.org

Web, www.itic.org

Membership: providers of information technology products and services. Promotes the global competitiveness of its members and advocates free trade. Seeks to protect intellectual property and encourages the use of voluntary standards.

Institute of Electrical and Electronics Engineers— United States Activities, *Professional Activities, Washington Office, 1828 L St. N.W., #1202 20036-5104; (202) 785-0017. Fax, (202) 785-0835. W. Thomas Suttle, Managing Director.*

General e-mail, ieeeusa@ieee.org

Web, www.ieee.org

U.S. arm of an international technological and professional organization. Interests include promoting career and technology policy interests of members. (Headquarters in New York.)

Software and Information Industry Assn., *1090 Vermont Ave., 6th Floor 20005; (202) 289-7442. Fax, (202) 289-7097. Ken Wasch, President.*

Web, www.siia.net

Membership: software and digital information companies. Promotes the industry worldwide; conducts anti-piracy program and other initiatives that protect members' intellectual property; collects market research data; sponsors conferences, seminars, and other events that focus on industry-wide and specific interests. Monitors legislation and regulations.

Mathematics

AGENCIES

National Institute of Standards and Technology (NIST), *(Commerce Dept.), Information Technology Laboratory, 100 Bureau Dr., Bldg. 225, #B264, Gaithersburg, MD 20899-8900; (301) 975-2900. Fax, (301) 840-1357. Susan F. Zevin, Director (Acting).*

Web, www.itl.nist.gov

Develops improved mathematical and statistical models and computational methods; consults on their use. Manages and operates NIST central computing facilities.

National Science Foundation (NSF), *Mathematical and Physical Sciences, 4201 Wilson Blvd., #1025, Arlington, VA 22230; (703) 292-5324. Fax, (703) 292-9032. John B. Hunt, Assistant Director. Information, (703) 292-5111.*

Web, www.nsf.gov/mps

Provides grants for research in the mathematical sciences in the following areas: classical and modern analysis, geometric analysis, topology and foundations, algebra and number theory, applied and computational mathematics, and statistics and probability. Maintains special projects program, which supports scientific computing equipment for mathematics research and several research institutes. Sponsors conferences, workshops, and postdoctoral research fellowships. Monitors international research.

NONPROFIT

American Statistical Assn., *1429 Duke St., Alexandria, VA 22314; (703) 684-1221. Fax, (703) 684-2037. William B. Smith, Executive Director.*
General e-mail, asainfo@amstat.org
Web, www.amstat.org

Membership: individuals interested in statistics and related quantitative fields. Advises government agencies on statistics and methodology in agency research; promotes development of statistical techniques for use in business, industry, finance, government, agriculture, and science.

Conference Board of the Mathematical Sciences, *1529 18th St. N.W. 20036; (202) 293-1170. Fax, (202) 293-3412. Ronald C. Rosier, Administrative Officer.*
Web, www.cbmsweb.org

Membership: presidents of fifteen mathematical sciences professional societies. Serves as a forum for discussion of issues of concern to the mathematical sciences community.

Mathematical Assn. of America, *1529 18th St. N.W. 20036-1358; (202) 387-5200. Fax, (202) 265-2384. Tina H. Straley, Executive Director.*
General e-mail, maahq@maa.org
Web, www.maa.org

Membership: mathematics professors and individuals worldwide with a professional interest in mathematics. Seeks to improve the teaching of collegiate mathematics. Conducts professional development programs.

Physics

AGENCIES

National Institute of Standards and Technology (NIST), *(Commerce Dept.), Materials Science and Engineering Laboratory, 100 Bureau Dr., MS 8500, Gaithersburg, MD 20899-8500; (301) 975-5658. Fax, (301) 975-5012. Leslie E. Smith, Director.*
Web, www.nist.gov

Provides measurements, data, standards, reference materials, concepts, and technical information fundamental to the processing, microstructure, properties, and performance of materials; addresses the scientific basis for new advanced materials; operates a research nuclear reactor for advanced materials characterization measurements; operates four materials data centers.

National Institute of Standards and Technology (NIST), *(Commerce Dept.), Physics Laboratory, 100 Bureau Dr., Bldg. 221, #B160, Gaithersburg, MD 20899-8400; (301) 975-4200. Fax, (301) 975-3038. Katharine B. Gebbie, Director.*

Web, www.physics.nist.gov

Conducts research to improve measurement capability and quantitative understanding of basic physical processes that underlie measurement science; investigates structure and dynamics of atoms and molecules; provides national standards for time and frequency and for measurement of radiation; develops radiometric and wavelength standards; analyzes national measurement needs.

National Science Foundation (NSF), *Materials Research, 4201 Wilson Blvd., #1065, Arlington, VA 22230; (703) 292-8810. Fax, (703) 292-9035. Thomas A. Weber, Director.*
Web, www.nsf.gov

Provides grants for research in condensed matter physics; solid state chemistry and polymers; metals, ceramics, and electronic materials; and materials theory. Provides major instrumentation for these activities. Supports multidisciplinary research in these areas through materials research science and engineering centers. Supports national facilities and instrumentation in the areas of synchrotron radiation and high magnetic fields. Monitors international research.

National Science Foundation (NSF), *Physics, 4201 Wilson Blvd., #1015, Arlington, VA 22230; (703) 292-8890. Fax, (703) 292-9078. Joseph L. Dehmer, Director.*
Web, www.nsf.gov/mps/phy

Awards grants for research and special programs in atomic, molecular, and optical physics; elementary particle physics; and nuclear, theoretical, and gravitational physics. Monitors international research.

Science *(Energy Dept.), High Energy and Nuclear Physics, 19901 Germantown Rd., Germantown, MD 20874-1290 (mailing address: 1000 Independence Ave. S.W., Washington, DC 20585-1290); (301) 903-3713. Fax, (301) 903-5079. S. Peter Rosen, Associate Director.*
Web, www.science.doe.gov

Provides grants and facilities for research in high energy and nuclear physics. Constructs, operates, and maintains particle accelerators used in high energy and nuclear physics research.

NONPROFIT

American Institute of Physics, *1 Physics Ellipse, College Park, MD 20740-3843; (301) 209-3000. Fax, (301) 209-0843. Marc H. Brodsky, Executive Director.*
Web, www.aip.org

Fosters cooperation within the physics community; improves public understanding of science; disseminates information on scientific research.

American Physical Society, *Public Information, Washington Office,* 529 14th St. N.W., #1050 20045; (202) 662-8700. Fax, (202) 662-8711. Robert L. Park, Director.

General e-mail, opa@aps.org

Web, www.aps.org

Scientific and educational society of educators, students, citizens, and scientists, including industrial scientists. Sponsors studies on issues of public concern related to physics, such as reactor safety and energy use. Informs members of national and international developments. (Headquarters in College Park, Md.)

Optical Society of America, 2010 Massachusetts Ave. N.W. 20036; (202) 223-8130. Fax, (202) 223-1096. Elizabeth Rogan, Executive Director.

General e-mail, postmaster@osa.org

Web, www.osa.org

Membership: researchers, educators, manufacturers, students, and others interested in optics and photonics worldwide. Promotes research and information exchange; conducts conferences. Interests include use of optics in medical imaging and surgery.

Weights and Measures, Metric System

AGENCIES

National Conference on Weights and Measures, 15245 Shady Grove Rd., #130, Rockville, MD 20850; (240) 632-9454. Fax, (301) 990-9771. Beth W. Palys, Executive Director.

General e-mail, ncwm@mgmtsol.com

Web, www.ncwm.net

Membership: state and local officials who deal with weights and measures, industry and business representatives, individuals, and associations. Serves as a national forum on issues related to weights and measures administration; develops consensus on uniform laws and regulations, specifications, and tolerances for weighing and measuring devices.

National Institute of Standards and Technology (NIST), *(Commerce Dept.), Laws and Metric Group,* 100 Bureau Dr., MS 2000, Gaithersburg, MD 20899; (301) 975-3690. Fax, (301) 948-1416. Henry Hoppermann, Director.

General e-mail, metric_prg@nist.gov

Web, www.nist.gov/metric

Coordinates federal metric conversion transition to ensure consistency; provides the public with technical and general information about the metric system; assists state and local governments, businesses, and educators with metric conversion activities.

National Institute of Standards and Technology (NIST), *(Commerce Dept.), Measurement Services,* 820 W. Diamond Ave., Bldg. 820, #306, MS 2000, Gaithersburg, MD 20899; (301) 975-8424. Fax, (301) 971-2183. Richard F. Kayser, Director.

Web, www.nist.gov

Disseminates physical, chemical, and engineering measurement standards and provides services to ensure accurate and compatible measurements, specifications, and codes on a national and international scale.

National Institute of Standards and Technology (NIST), *(Commerce Dept.), Weights and Measures,* 100 Bureau Dr., MS 2600, Gaithersburg, MD 20899; (301) 975-4004. Fax, (301) 926-0647. Henry V. Opperman, Director.

Web, www.nist.gov/owm

Promotes uniformity in weights and measures law and enforcement. Provides weights and measures agencies with training and technical assistance; assists state and local agencies in adapting their weights and measures to meet national standards; conducts research; sets uniform standards and regulations.

CONGRESS

House Science Committee, *Subcommittee on Environment, Technology, and Standards,* 2319 RHOB 20515; (202) 225-8844. Fax, (202) 225-4438. Rep. Vernon J. Ehlers, R-Mich., Chair; Eric Webster, Staff Director.

General e-mail, science@mail.house.gov

Web, www.house.gov/science

Jurisdiction over legislation on weights and measurement systems; monitors the National Institute of Standards and Technology.

Senate Commerce, Science, and Transportation Committee, *Subcommittee on Science, Technology, and Space,* SH-227 20510; (202) 224-8172. Fax, (202) 224-9934. Sen. Sam Brownback, R-Kan., Chair; Floyd Deschamps, Counsel.

Web, commerce.senate.gov

Jurisdiction over legislation on weights and measurement systems; monitors the National Institute of Standards and Technology.

 ## SOCIAL SCIENCES

AGENCIES

National Museum of Natural History *(Smithsonian Institution), Anthropology,* 10th St. and Constitution Ave. N.W., MRC 112 20560-0012 (mailing address: P.O.

Box 37012 20013-7012); (202) 357-2363. Fax, (202) 357-2208. William Fitzhugh, Chair. Information, (202) 357-1592.

Web, www.nmnh.si.edu/departments/anthro.html

Conducts research on paleo-Indian archeology and prehistory, New World origins, and paleoecology. Maintains anthropological and human studies film archives. Museum maintains public exhibitions of human cultures.

National Museum of Natural History (*Smithsonian Institution*), **Library,** *10th St. and Constitution Ave. N.W., #51 20560-0154 (mailing address: P.O Box 37012 20013-7012); (202) 357-1496. Fax, (202) 357-1896. Ann Juneau, Chief Librarian.*

Web, www.sil.si.edu

Maintains reference collections covering anthropology, ethnology, botany, biology, ecology, biodiversity, and zoology; permits on-site use of the collections. Open to the public by appointment; makes interlibrary loans.

National Science Foundation (NSF), *Social, Behavioral, and Economic Sciences, 4201 Wilson Blvd., #905, Arlington, VA 22230; (703) 292-8700. Fax, (703) 292-9083. Norman M. Bradburn, Assistant Director.*

Web, www.nsf.gov/sbe

Directorate that awards grants for research in behavioral and cognitive sciences, social and economic sciences, science resources studies, and international programs. Provides support for workshops, symposia, and conferences.

NONPROFIT

American Anthropological Assn., *2200 Wilson Blvd., #600, Arlington, VA 22201; (703) 528-1902. Fax, (703) 528-3546. William E. Davis III, Executive Director.*

Web, www.aaanet.org

Membership: anthropologists, educators, students, and others interested in anthropological studies. Publishes research studies of member organizations, sponsors workshops, and disseminates to members information concerning developments in anthropology worldwide.

American Institutes for Research, *1000 Thomas Jefferson St. N.W., #400 20007; (202) 944-5300. Fax, (202) 944-5454. Sol Pelavin, President.*

General e-mail, info-cbo@air.org

Web, www.air.org

Conducts research and analysis in the behavioral and social sciences, including education and health research and data analysis to assess fairness and equity in the workplace; assists in designing and writing documents;

assesses usability of software, systems, and other products; studies human-machine interface.

American Psychological Assn., *750 1st St. N.E. 20002-4242; (202) 336-5500. Fax, (202) 336-6069. Raymond D. Fowler, Executive Vice President. Library, (202) 336-5640. TTY, (202) 336-6123.*

Web, www.apa.org

Membership: professional psychologists, educators, and behavioral research scientists. Supports research, training, and professional services; works toward improving the qualifications, competence, and training programs of psychologists. Monitors international research and U.S. legislation on mental health.

American Sociological Assn., *1307 New York Ave. N.W., #700 20005; (202) 383-9005. Fax, (202) 638-0882. Sally Hillsman, Executive Officer. TTY, (202) 872-0486.*

General e-mail, executive.office@asanet.org

Web, www.asanet.org

Membership: sociologists, social scientists, and others interested in research, teaching, and application of sociology in the United States and internationally. Sponsors professional development program, teaching resources center, and education programs; offers fellowships for minorities.

Consortium of Social Science Assns., *1522 K St. N.W., #836 20005; (202) 842-3525. Fax, (202) 842-2788. Howard J. Silver, Executive Director.*

General e-mail, cossa@cossa.org

Web, www.cossa.org

Consortium of associations in the fields of anthropology, criminology, economics, history, political science, psychology, sociology, statistics, geography, linguistics, law, and social science. Advocates support for research and monitors federal funding in the social and behavioral sciences; conducts seminars.

Human Resources Research Organization, *66 Canal Center Plaza, #400, Alexandria, VA 22314; (703) 549-3611. Fax, (703) 549-9025. Lauress L. Wise II, President.*

Web, www.humrro.org

Research and development organization in the fields of industrial and behavioral psychology. Studies, designs, develops, surveys, and evaluates personnel systems, chiefly in the workplace. Interests include personnel selection and promotion, career progression, performance appraisal, training, and program evaluation.

Institute for the Study of Man, *1133 13th St. N.W., #C2 20005-4297; (202) 371-2700. Fax, (202) 371-1523. Roger Pearson, Executive Director.*

General e-mail, iejournal@aol.com

Web, www.jies.org

Publishes academic journals, books, and monographs in areas related to anthropology, archeology, linguistics, cultural history, and mythology.

Geography and Mapping

AGENCIES

Census Bureau *(Commerce Dept.), Geography,* 8903 Presidential Pkwy., #651, Upper Marlboro, MD 20772 (mailing address: 4700 Silver Hill Rd., Stop 7400, Washington, DC 20233-7400); (301) 763-2131. Fax, (301) 457-4710. Carol Van Horn, Chief (Acting).

Web, www.census.geo.gov

Manages the TIGER system, a nationwide geographic database; prepares maps for use in conducting censuses and surveys and for showing their results geographically; determines names and current boundaries of legal geographic units; defines names and boundaries of selected statistical areas; develops geographic code schemes; maintains computer files of area measurements, geographic boundaries, and map features with address ranges.

National Archives and Records Administration (NARA), *Cartographic and Architectural Branch,* 8601 Adelphi Rd., #3320, College Park, MD 20740-6001; (301) 837-3200. Robert E. Richardson, Director.

General e-mail, carto@arch2.nara.gov

Web, www.archives.gov

Makes information available on federal government cartographic records, architectural drawings, and aerial mapping films; prepares descriptive guides and inventories of records. Library open to the public. Records may be reproduced for a fee.

National Imagery and Mapping Agency *(Defense Dept.),* 4600 Sangamore Rd., #378, Bethesda, MD 20816; (301) 227-7300. Fax, (301) 227-3696. Lt. Gen. James R. Clapper Jr., Director.

Web, www.nima.mil

Combat support agency that provides imagery and geospatial information to national policymakers and military forces in support of national defense objectives; incorporates the missions and functions of the former Defense Mapping Agency, Central Imaging Office, and Defense Dissemination Program Office.

National Oceanic and Atmospheric Administration (NOAA), *(Commerce Dept.), National Geodetic Survey,* 1315 East-West Hwy., N-NGS, SSMC3, #8657, Silver Spring, MD 20910-3282; (301) 713-3222. Fax, (301) 713-4175. Charles W. Challstrom, Director.

Web, www.ngs.noaa.gov

Develops and maintains the National Spatial Reference System, a national geodetic reference system which serves as a common reference for latitude, longitude, height, scale, orientation, and gravity measurements. Maps the nation's coastal zone and waterways; conducts research and development programs to improve the collection, distribution, and use of spatial data; coordinates the development and application of new surveying instrumentation and procedures; and assists state, county, and municipal agencies through a variety of cooperative programs.

State Dept., *Office of the Geographer and Global Issues,* 2201 C St. N.W., #2911 20520; (202) 647-2021. Fax, (202) 647-0504. Lee R. Schwartz, Director (Acting).

Web, www.state.gov

Advises the State Dept. and other federal agencies on geographic and cartographic matters. Furnishes technical and analytical research and advice in the field of geography.

U.S. Board on Geographic Names, *12201 Sunrise Valley Dr., Reston, VA 20192-0523 (mailing address: 523 National Center, Reston, VA 20192); (703) 648-4544. Fax, (703) 648-4549. Roger L. Payne, Executive Secretary, Board and Domestic Names Committee; Randall Flynn, Executive Secretary, Foreign Names Committee, (301) 227-3055.*

Web, geonames.usgs.gov

Interagency organization established by Congress to standardize geographic names. Board members are representatives from the departments of Agriculture, Commerce, Defense, Interior, and State; the Central Intelligence Agency; the Government Printing Office; the Library of Congress; and the U.S. Postal Service. Sets policy governing the use of both domestic and foreign geographic names as well as undersea and Antarctic feature names.

U.S. Geological Survey (USGS), *(Interior Dept.), Earth Science Information Center,* 507 National Center, Reston, VA 20192-1507; (703) 648-5920. Fax, (703) 648-5548. Sherry Gwynn, Chief (Acting). U.S. maps, (888) 275-8747.

Web, www.usgs.gov

Collects, organizes, and distributes cartographic, geographic, hydrologic, and other earth science information; offers maps, reports, and other publications, digital cartographic data, aerial photographs, and space imagery and manned spacecraft photographs for sale. Acts as clearinghouse on cartographic and geographic data.

U.S. Geological Survey (USGS), *(Interior Dept.),* *Geography Information,* 12201 Sunrise Valley Dr., Reston, VA 20192 (mailing address: 159 National Center, Reston, VA 20192); (703) 648-5780. Fax, (703) 648-6821. Hedy J. Rossmeissl, Senior Adviser.

Web, www.usgs.gov

Plans and coordinates information dissemination activities.

U.S. Geological Survey (USGS), *(Interior Dept.),* *National Mapping Program,* 12201 Sunrise Valley Dr., MS 516, Reston, VA 20192; (703) 648-7413. Fax, (703) 648-5792. Barbara J. Ryan, Associate Director for Geography.

Web, www.usgs.gov

Provides government agencies and the public with geographic and cartographic information, maps, and technical assistance; conducts research; collects, compiles, and analyzes information about features of the earth's surface; develops and maintains a digital geographic/cartographic database and assists users in applying spatial data; coordinates federal mapping activities; encourages the development of surveying and mapping techniques.

CONGRESS

Library of Congress, *Geography and Map Division,* 101 Independence Ave. S.E., #B02 20540-4650; (202) 707-8530. Fax, (202) 707-8531. John R. Hébert, Chief. Reference, (202) 707-6277.

Web, www.loc.gov

Maintains cartographic collection of maps, atlases, globes, and reference books. Reference service provided; reading room open to the public. Interlibrary loans available through the library's loan division; photocopies, when not limited by copyright or other restriction, available through the library's photoduplication service.

NONPROFIT

American Congress on Surveying and Mapping, 6 Montgomery Village Ave., #403, Gaithersburg, MD 20879; (240) 632-9716. Fax, (240) 632-1321. Curtis W. Sumner, Executive Director.

General e-mail, info@acsm.net

Web, www.acsm.net

Membership: professionals working worldwide in surveying, cartography, geodesy, and geographic/land information systems (computerized mapping systems used in urban, regional, and environmental planning). Sponsors workshops and seminars for surveyors and mapping scientists; participates in accreditation of college and university surveying and related degree pro-

grams; grants fellowships; develops and administers certification programs for hydrographers and technician surveyors. Monitors legislation and regulations.

Assn. of American Geographers, 1710 16th St. N.W. 20009-3198; (202) 234-1450. Fax, (202) 234-2744. Douglas Richardson, Executive Director.

General e-mail, gaia@aag.org

Web, www.aag.org

Membership: educators, students, business executives, government employees, and scientists in the field of geography. Seeks to advance professional studies in geography and encourages the application of geographic research in education, government, and business.

National Geographic Maps, 1145 17th St. N.W. 20036-4688; (202) 857-7799. Fax, (202) 429-5704. Allen Carroll, Chief Cartographer. Library, (202) 857-7083. Map orders, (800) 962-1643.

Web, www.nationalgeographic.com

Educational and scientific organization. Supports and conducts research on cartography, mapping, and geography. Produces and sells to the public political, physical, and thematic maps, atlases, and globes. (Affiliated with National Geographic Society.)

SPACE SCIENCES

AGENCIES

Air Force Dept. *(Defense Dept.), Military Space,* 1670 Air Force Pentagon, #4C1000 20330-1640; (703) 693-5799. Fax, (703) 614-0403. Robert S. Dickman, Deputy for Space.

Web, www.af.mil

Manages the planning, programming, and acquisition of space systems for the Air Force and other military services.

Commerce Dept., *Space Commercialization,* 14th St. and Constitution Ave. N.W., #4800-B 20230; (202) 482-6125. Fax, (202) 501-4178. Benjamin H. Wu, Director (Acting).

General e-mail, spaceinfo@ta.doc.gov

Web, www.ta.doc.gov/space

Promotes private investment in space activities; seeks to remove legal, policy, and institutional impediments to space commerce; represents private sector interests at the federal level; coordinates commercial space policy for the Commerce Dept. Monitors international developments.

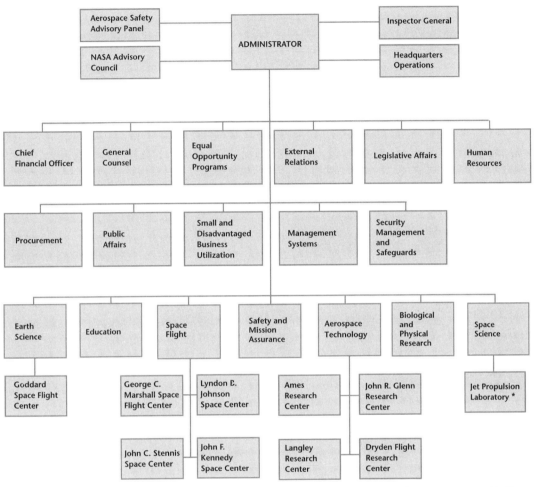

* JPL is a contractor-operated facility.

Federal Aviation Administration (FAA), *(Transportation Dept.), Commercial Space Transportation,* 800 Independence Ave. S.W., #331, AST-1 20591; (202) 267-7793. Fax, (202) 267-5450. Patricia Grace Smith, Associate Administrator.

Web, ast.faa.gov

Promotes and facilitates the operation of commercial expendable space launch vehicles by the private sector; licenses and regulates these activities.

National Aeronautics and Space Administration (NASA), 300 E St. S.W. 20546 (mailing address: NASA Headquarters, Mail Code A 20546); (202) 358-1010. Fax, (202) 358-2811. Sean O'Keefe, Administrator. Information, (202) 358-0000. TTY, (800) 877-8339. Locator, (202) 358-0000.

Web, www.hq.nasa.gov

Conducts research on problems of flight within and outside the earth's atmosphere; develops, constructs, tests, and operates experimental aeronautical and space vehicles; conducts activities for manned and unmanned exploration of space; maintains information center.

National Aeronautics and Space Administration (NASA), *Aerospace Technology,* 300 E St. S.W., #6A70 20546 (mailing address: NASA Headquarters, Mail Code R 20546); (202) 358-4600. Fax, (202) 358-2920. Murray S. Hirschbein, Associate Administrator.

Web, www.aero-space.nasa.gov

Conducts research in aerodynamics, materials, structures, avionics, propulsion, high-performance computing, human factors, aviation safety, and space transportation in support of national space and aeronautical research and technology goals. Manages the following NASA research centers: Ames (Moffett, Calif.); Dryden (Edwards, Calif.); Langley (Hampton, Va.); and Glenn (Cleveland, Ohio).

National Aeronautics and Space Administration (NASA), *Goddard Space Flight Center,* Code 100, Greenbelt, MD 20771; (301) 286-5121. Fax, (301) 286-1714. Al Diaz, Director. Information, (301) 286-8955.

Web, pao.gsfc.nasa.gov

Conducts space and earth science research; performs advanced planning for space missions; develops and manages spacecraft and scientific instrumentation; functions as the control center for earth orbital satellites; operates the NASA tracking and data relay satellite system.

National Aeronautics and Space Administration (NASA), *International Space Station and Space Shuttle,* 300 E St. S.W., #7A70 20546 (mailing address: NASA Headquarters, Mail Code M-1 20546); (202) 358-4424. Fax, (202) 358-2848. Michael Kostelnik, Deputy Associate Administrator.

Web, spaceflight.nasa.gov

Responsible for developing a permanently manned orbiting space station to serve as a research facility for scientific, technological, and commercial activities. Directs policy related to operation of the space shuttle program, including U.S.-Russia cooperative programs and commercial uses of the shuttle.

National Aeronautics and Space Administration (NASA), *NASA Advisory Council,* 300 E St. S.W. 20546 (mailing address: NASA Headquarters, Mail Code Z 20546); (202) 358-0732. Fax, (202) 358-4329. Charles F. Kennel, Chair.

Web, www.policy.nasa.gov/poladvisor.html

Advises the administrator on NASA's aeronautics and space plans and programs. The council comprises the following advisory committees: Aeronautics, Technology and Commercialization, Biological and Physical Research, Space Science, International Space Station, Minority Business Resource, and Earth Systems Science and Applications.

National Aeronautics and Space Administration (NASA), *National Space Science Data Center,* Goddard Space Flight Center, Code 633, Greenbelt, MD 20771; (301) 286-7355. Fax, (301) 286-1771. Donald Sawyer, Head (Acting).

Web, nssdc.gsfc.nasa.gov

Acquires, catalogs, and distributes NASA mission data to the international space science community, including research organizations, universities, and other interested organizations worldwide. Provides software tools and network access to promote collaborative data analysis. (Mail data requests to above address, attention: Code 633.4/Request Coordination Office, or phone [301] 286-6695.)

National Aeronautics and Space Administration (NASA), *Office of Biological and Physical Research,* 300 E St. S.W., #8F39 20546 (mailing address: NASA Headquarters, Mail Code U 20546); (202) 358-0122. Fax, (202) 358-4174. Mary E. Kicza, Associate Administrator.

Web, www.hq.nasa.gov/office/olmsa

Conducts all in-orbit exploration of space. Areas of research include life sciences (people, animals, and plants), materials (crystals and minerals), and microgravity effects observed in space. Participates in international projects and conferences.

National Aeronautics and Space Administration (NASA), *Safety and Mission Assurance,* 300 E St. S.W., #5W21 20546 (mailing address: NASA Headquarters, Mail Code Q 20546); (202) 358-2406. Fax, (202) 358-2699. Brian D. O'Connor, Associate Administrator (Acting).

Web, www.hq.nasa.gov/office/codeq

Evaluates the safety and reliability of NASA systems and programs. Alerts officials to technical execution and physical readiness of NASA projects.

National Aeronautics and Space Administration (NASA), *Space Communications,* 300 E St. S.W. 20546 (mailing address: NASA Headquarters, Mail Code M-3 20546); (202) 358-2020. Fax, (202) 358-2865. Robert Spearing, Director.

Web, www.hq.nasa.gov

Plans, develops, and operates worldwide tracking, data acquisition, data processing, and communications systems, facilities, and services essential to the agency's space flight missions, including the Space Tracking Data Network at Goddard Space Flight Center in Greenbelt, Md., and the Deep Space Network operated by the Jet Propulsion Laboratory in Pasadena, Calif. Gives support to planetary spacecraft, earth-orbiting satellites, shuttle missions, sounding rockets, balloons, and aeronautical test vehicles.

National Aeronautics and Space Administration (NASA), *Space Flight,* 300 E St. S.W. 20546 (mailing address: NASA Headquarters, Mail Code M 20546); (202) 358-2015. Fax, (202) 358-2848. William Readdy, Associate Administrator.

Web, www.hq.nasa.gov/osf

Responsible for space transportation systems operations, including U.S. participation in international missions. Manages the Johnson Space Center, Kennedy Space Center, Marshall Space Flight Center, and Stennis Space Center. Administers the development, testing, and production phases of the space shuttle. Manages the shuttle space lab program and the space station.

National Aeronautics and Space Administration (NASA), *Space Science,* 300 E St. S.W. 20546 (mailing address: NASA Headquarters, Mail Code S 20546); (202) 358-1409. Fax, (202) 358-3092. Edward J. Weiler, Associate Administrator.

Web, spacescience.nasa.gov

Makes information available on technological developments that have resulted from NASA programs. (Accepts written requests for specific technical information.)

National Aeronautics and Space Administration (NASA), *Space Science and Aeronautics,* 300 E St. S.W. 20546 (mailing address: NASA Headquarters, Mail Code IS 20546); (202) 358-0900. Fax, (202) 358-3030. P. Diane Rausch, Director.

Web, www.hq.nasa.gov

Acts as liaison with space agencies of foreign countries; negotiates and implements international agreements for cooperation in space; works with other U.S. government agencies on international issues regarding space and aeronautics.

National Air and Space Museum *(Smithsonian Institution),* 6th St. and Independence Ave. S.W. 20560-0310; (202) 633-2350. Fax, (202) 357-2426. Gen. John R. Dailey, Director. Library, (202) 633-2316. TTY, (202) 357-1505. Education office, (202) 633-2540. Tours, (202) 357-1400.

Web, www.nasm.si.edu

Collects, preserves, and exhibits astronautical objects and equipment of historical interest, including manned spacecraft and communications and weather satellites. Library open to the public by appointment.

CONGRESS

House Appropriations Committee, *Subcommittee on VA, HUD, and Independent Agencies,* H143 CAP 20515; (202) 225-3241. Rep. James T. Walsh, R-N.Y., Chair; Tim Peterson, Staff Director.

Web, www.house.gov/appropriations

Jurisdiction over legislation to appropriate funds for the National Aeronautics and Space Administration.

House Government Reform Committee, *Subcommittee on Technology, Information Policy, Intergovernmental Relations, and the Census,* B349A RHOB 20515; (202) 225-6751. Fax, (202) 225-4960. Rep. Adam H. Putnam, R-Fla., Chair; Robert Dix, Staff Director.

Web, www.house.gov/reform

Oversees operations of the National Aeronautics and Space Administration. (Jurisdiction shared with the House Science Committee.)

House Science Committee, *Subcommittee on Space and Aeronautics,* B374 RHOB 20515; (202) 225-7858. Fax, (202) 225-6415. Rep. Dana Rohrabacher, R-Calif., Chair; Bill Adkins, Staff Director.

General e-mail, science@mail.house.gov

Web, www.house.gov/science

Jurisdiction over legislation on space programs, national research and development in space exploration, space commercialization, earth-observing systems, the National Aeronautics and Space Administration (jurisdiction shared with House Government Reform Committee), and space-related activities of the Transportation and Commerce departments.

Senate Appropriations Committee, *Subcommittee on VA, HUD, and Independent Agencies,* SD-130 20510; (202) 224-8252. Fax, (202) 228-1624. Sen. Christopher S. Bond, R-Mo., Chair; Jon Kamarck, Clerk.

Web, appropriations.senate.gov

Jurisdiction over legislation to appropriate funds for the National Aeronautics and Space Administration.

Senate Commerce, Science, and Transportation Committee, *Subcommittee on Science, Technology, and Space,* SH-227 20510; (202) 224-8172. Fax, (202) 224-9934. Sen. Sam Brownback, R-Kan., Chair; Floyd Deschamps, Counsel.

Web, commerce.senate.gov

Jurisdiction over legislation on nonmilitary space programs, national research and development in space exploration, space commercialization, and earth-observing systems. Oversight and legislative jurisdiction over the National Aeronautics and Space Administration.

INTERNATIONAL ORGANIZATIONS

European Space Agency (ESA), *Washington Office,* 955 L'Enfant Plaza S.W., #7800 20024; (202) 488-4158. Fax, (202) 488-4930. Frederick Nordlund, Head.

Web, www.esa.int

Intergovernmental agency that promotes international collaboration in space research and development and the use of space technology for peaceful purposes. Members include Austria, Belgium, Denmark, Finland, France, Germany, Ireland, Italy, the Netherlands, Norway, Portugal, Spain, Sweden, Switzerland, and the United Kingdom; Canada participates in some programs. (Headquarters in Paris.)

NONPROFIT

Aerospace Education Foundation, *1501 Lee Hwy., Arlington, VA 22209; (703) 247-5839. Fax, (703) 247-5853. Donald L. Peterson, Executive Director. Information, (800) 727-3337.*
General e-mail, aefstaff@aef.org
Web, www.aef.org
Promotes knowledge and appreciation of U.S. civilian and military aerospace development and history. (Affiliated with the Air Force Assn.)

Aerospace Industries Assn. (AIA), *1000 Wilson Blvd., #1700, Arlington, VA 22209; (703) 358-1000. Fax, (703) 358-1012. John W. Douglass, President. Press, (703) 358-1076.*
General e-mail, aia@aia-aerospace.org
Web, www.aia-aerospace.org
Represents U.S. manufacturers of commercial, military, and business aircraft; helicopters; aircraft engines; missiles; spacecraft; and related components and equipment. Interests include international standards and trade.

American Astronautical Society, *6352 Rolling Mill Pl., #102, Springfield, VA 22152; (703) 866-0020. Fax, (703) 866-3526. James R. Kirkpatrick, Executive Director.*
General e-mail, info@astronautical.org
Web, www.astronautical.org
Scientific and technological society of researchers, scientists, astronauts, and other professionals in the field of astronautics and spaceflight engineering. Organizes national and local meetings and symposia; promotes international cooperation.

American Institute of Aeronautics and Astronautics (AIAA), *1801 Alexander Bell Dr., #500, Reston, VA 20191; (703) 264-7500. Fax, (703) 264-7551. Cort Durocher, Executive Director. Information, (800) 639-2422.*
General e-mail, custserv@aiaa.org
Web, www.aiaa.org
Membership: engineers, scientists, and students in the fields of aeronautics and astronautics. Holds work-

shops on aerospace technical issues for congressional subcommittees; sponsors international conferences. Offers computerized database through its Technical Information Service.

National Research Council (NRC), *Aeronautics and Space Engineering Board, 5000 5th St. N.W., 10th Floor 20001; (202) 334-2855. Fax, (202) 334-2482. George M. Levin, Director. Library, (202) 334-2125. Press, (202) 334-2138. Publications, (202) 334-2855.*
Web, www7.nationalacademies.org/aseb
Membership: aeronautics and space experts. Advises government agencies on aeronautics and space engineering research, technology, experiments, international programs, and policy. Library open to the public by appointment.

National Research Council (NRC), *Space Studies Board, 2001 Wisconsin Ave. N.W. 20007 (mailing address: 2101 Constitution Ave. N.W., #HA584 20418); (202) 334-3477. Fax, (202) 334-3701. Joseph K. Alexander, Director. Library, (202) 334-2125. Press, (202) 334-2138.*
General e-mail, ssb@nas.edu
Web, www.nas.edu/ssb
Provides assessments for NASA and other federal agencies on space science and applications, including international programs; provides research assessments and long-term research strategies. Interests include astronomy, lunar and planetary exploration, solar and space physics, earth science, space biology and medicine, and microgravity materials research. Library open to the public by appointment.

National Space Society, *600 Pennsylvania Ave. S.E., #201 20003-4316; (202) 543-1900. Fax, (202) 546-4189. Brian Chase, Executive Director.*
General e-mail, nsshq@nss.org
Web, www.nss.org
Membership: individuals interested in space programs and applications of space technology. Provides information on NASA, commercial space activities, and international cooperation; promotes public education on space exploration and development; conducts conferences and workshops. Monitors legislation and regulations.

Resources for the Future, *1616 P St. N.W. 20036; (202) 328-5000. Fax, (202) 939-3460. Paul R. Portney, President. Library, (202) 328-5089.*
General e-mail, info@rff.org
Web, www.rff.org
Examines the economic aspects of U.S. space policy, including policy on the space shuttle, unmanned rockets,

communications satellites, and the space station. Focuses on the role of private business versus that of government.

Space Policy Institute *(George Washington University)*, *1957 Eye St. N.W., #403 20052; (202) 994-7292. Fax, (202) 994-1639. John M. Logsdon, Director.*
General e-mail, spi@gwu.edu
Web, www.gwu.edu/~spi

Conducts research on space policy issues; organizes seminars, symposia, and conferences. Focuses on civilian space activities, including competitive and cooperative interactions on space between the United States and other countries.

Young Astronaut Council, *5200 27th St. N.W. 20015; (301) 617-0923. Fax, (301) 776-0858. T. Wendell Butler, President.*
General e-mail, YoungAstronauts@aol.com
Web, www.youngastronauts.com

Promotes improved math and science skills through aerospace activities for children ages three to sixteen. Encourages children to pursue careers in aerospace fields.

Astronomy

AGENCIES

National Aeronautics and Space Administration (NASA), *Space Science, 300 E St. S.W. 20546 (mailing address: NASA Headquarters, Mail Code S 20546); (202) 358-1409. Fax, (202) 358-3092. Edward J. Weiler, Associate Administrator.*
Web, spacescience.nasa.gov

Administers programs that study the composition, energy, mass, position, size, and properties of celestial bodies within the universe, as observed from Earth; participates in international research efforts. Administers NASA's rocket programs.

National Science Foundation (NSF), *Astronomical Sciences, 4201 Wilson Blvd., #1045, Arlington, VA 22230; (703) 292-8820. Fax, (703) 292-9034. G. Wayne Van Citters, Director.*
Web, www.nsf.gov/MPS/ast

Provides grants for ground-based astronomy and astronomical research on planetary astronomy, stellar astronomy and astrophysics, galactic astronomy, extra-

galactic astronomy and cosmology, and advanced technologies and instrumentation. Maintains astronomical facilities; participates in international projects.

U.S. Naval Observatory *(Defense Dept.), 3450 Massachusetts Ave. N.W. 20392-5420; (202) 762-1467. Fax, (202) 762-1489. David W. Gillard, Superintendent, (202) 762-1538. Information, (202) 762-1438.*
Web, www.usno.navy.mil

Determines the precise positions and motions of celestial bodies. Operates the U.S. master clock. Provides the U.S. Navy and Defense Dept. with astronomical and timing data for navigation, precise positioning, and command, control, and communications.

NONPROFIT

American Astronomical Society, *2000 Florida Ave. N.W., #400 20009-1231; (202) 328-2010. Fax, (202) 234-2560. Robert W. Milkey, Executive Officer. Press, (301) 286-5154.*
General e-mail, aas@aas.org
Web, www.aas.org

Membership: astronomers and other professionals interested in the advancement of astronomy in the United States, Canada, and Mexico. Holds scientific meetings; participates in international organizations; awards research grants.

American Geophysical Union, *2000 Florida Ave. N.W. 20009-1277; (202) 462-6900. Fax, (202) 328-0566. A. F. Spilhaus Jr., Executive Director.*
General e-mail, service@agu.org
Web, www.agu.org

Membership: scientists and technologists who study the environments and components of the earth, sun, and solar system. Promotes international cooperation; disseminates information.

Assn. of Universities for Research in Astronomy, *1200 New York Ave. N.W., #350 20005; (202) 483-2101. Fax, (202) 483-2106. William S. Smith, President.*
Web, www.aura-astronomy.org

Consortium of universities. Manages three ground-based observatories and the international Gemini Project for the National Science Foundation and manages the Space Telescope Science Institute for the National Aeronautics and Space Administration.

 **GENERAL POLICY**

AGENCIES

Administration for Children and Families (ACF), *(Health and Human Services Dept.), 901 D St. S.W., #600 20447 (mailing address: 370 L'Enfant Promenade S.W. 20447); (202) 401-2337. Fax, (202) 401-4678. Wade F. Horn, Assistant Secretary. Information, (202) 401-9215.*
Web, www.acf.hhs.gov

Administers and funds programs for native Americans, low-income families and individuals, and persons with disabilities. Responsible for Social Services Block Grants to the states; coordinates Health and Human Services Dept. policy and regulations on child protection, day care, foster care, adoption services, child abuse and neglect, and special services for those with disabilities. Administers Head Start program and funds the National Runaway Switchboard, (800) 621-4000, and the Domestic Violence Hotline, (800) 799-7233; TTY, (800) 787-3224.

Administration for Children and Families (ACF), *(Health and Human Services Dept.), Office of Community Services, 901 D St. S.W., 5th Floor 20447 (mailing address: 370 L'Enfant Promenade S.W. 20447); (202) 401-9333. Fax, (202) 401-4694. Clarence H. Carter, Director.*
Web, www.acf.dhhs.gov

Administers the Community Services Block Grant and Discretionary Grant programs and the Low Income Home Energy Assistance Block Grant Program for heating, cooling, and weatherizing low-income households.

Administration for Native Americans *(Health and Human Services Dept.), 370 L'Enfant Promenade S.W., M.S. Aerospace Center, 8th Floor, West 20447-0002; (202) 690-7776. Fax, (202) 690-7441. Quanah Crossland Stamps, Commissioner.*
Web, www.acf.hhs.gov/programs/ana

Awards grants for locally determined social and economic development strategies; promotes native American economic and social self-sufficiency; funds tribes and native American and native Hawaiian organizations. Commissioner chairs the Intradepartmental Council on Indian Affairs, which coordinates native American-related programs.

AmeriCorps *(Corporation for National and Community Service), Volunteers in Service to America (VISTA), 1201 New York Ave. N.W. 20525; (202) 606-5000. Fax, (202) 565-2789. David Caprara, Director. TTY, (800) 833-3722. Volunteer recruiting information, (800) 942-2677.*

General e-mail, questions@americorps.org
Web, www.americorps.org/vista

Assigns full-time volunteers to public and private nonprofit organizations for one year to alleviate poverty in local communities. Volunteers receive stipends.

Bureau of Indian Affairs (BIA), *(Interior Dept.), Social Services, 1849 C St. N.W., MS 320-SIB 20240-4001; (202) 208-2479. Fax, (202) 208-5113. Larry R. Blair, Chief. Information, (202) 208-3710.*
Web, www.doi.gov/bureau-indian-affairs.html

Gives assistance, in accordance with state payment standards, to American Indians and Alaska natives of federally recognized tribes. Provides family and individual counseling and child welfare services. Administers the Indian Child Welfare Act grants to native American tribes and organizations to establish and operate native American child protection services.

Corporation for National and Community Service, *1201 New York Ave. N.W. 20525; (202) 606-5000. Fax, (202) 565-2799. Leslie Lenkowsky, Chief Executive Officer. TTY, (800) 833-3722. Volunteer recruiting information, (800) 942-2677.*
General e-mail, webmaster@cns.gov
Web, www.cns.gov

Independent corporation that administers federally sponsored domestic volunteer programs that provide disadvantaged citizens with services, including AmeriCorps, AmeriCorps-VISTA (Volunteers in Service to America), AmeriCorps-NCCC (National Civilian Community Corps), Learn and Serve America, and the National Senior Service Corps.

Food and Nutrition Service *(Agriculture Dept.), 3101 Park Center Dr., #906, Alexandria, VA 22302; (703) 305-2062. Fax, (703) 305-2908. Roberto Salazar, Administrator. Information, (703) 305-2286.*
Web, www.fns.usda.gov/fns

Administers all Agriculture Dept. domestic food assistance, including the distribution of funds and food for school breakfast and lunch programs (preschool through secondary) to public and nonprofit private schools; the food stamp program; and a supplemental nutrition program for women, infants, and children (WIC).

Food and Nutrition Service *(Agriculture Dept.), Food Distribution, 3101 Park Center Dr., #503, Alexandria, VA 22302; (703) 305-2680. Fax, (703) 305-1410. Rosalind S. Cleveland, Director (Acting).*
Web, www.fns.usda.gov

Administers the purchasing and distribution of food to state agencies for child care centers, public and private schools, public and nonprofit charitable institutions, and summer camps. Coordinates the distribution of special commodities, including surplus cheese and butter. Administers the National Commodity Processing Program, which facilitates distribution, at reduced prices, of processed foods to state agencies.

Food and Nutrition Service *(Agriculture Dept.), Food Stamp Program,* *3101 Park Center Dr., #808, Alexandria, VA 22302; (703) 305-2026. Fax, (703) 305-2454. Kate Coler, Deputy Administrator.*
Web, www.fns.usda.gov

Administers, through state welfare agencies, the Food Stamp Program, which provides needy persons with food coupons to increase food purchasing power. Provides matching funds to cover half the cost of coupon issuance.

Health and Human Services Dept. (HHS), *200 Independence Ave. S.W., #615F 20201; (202) 690-7000. Fax, (202) 690-7203. Tommy G. Thompson, Secretary; Claude A. Allen, Deputy Secretary. Press, (202) 690-6343. TTY, (800) 877-8339. Locator, (202) 619-0257.*
Web, www.hhs.gov

Acts as principal adviser to the president on health and welfare plans, policies, and programs of the federal government. Encompasses the Health Care Financing Administration, the Administration for Children and Families, the Public Health Service, and the Centers for Disease Control and Prevention.

Health and Human Services Dept. (HHS), *Disability, Aging, and Long-Term Care Policy,* *200 Independence Ave. S.W., #424E 20201; (202) 690-6443. Fax, (202) 401-7733. John S. Hoff, Deputy Assistant Secretary.*
Web, aspe.hhs.gov/daltcp/home.shtml

Responsible for the development of financing and service organization/delivery policy—including planning, policy and budget analysis, review of regulations and formulation of legislation—and for the development and coordination of research and evaluation on issues related to disability, aging, and long-term care policy.

Health and Human Services Dept. (HHS), *Human Services Policy: Economic Support for Families,* *200 Independence Ave. S.W., #404E 20201; (202) 690-7148. Fax, (202) 690-6562. Canta Pian, Director.*
Web, www.hhs.gov

Collects and disseminates information on human services programs that provide nonelderly populations, including families and their children, with cash, employment, training, and related assistance.

Office of Faith-Based and Community Initiatives *(Executive Office of the President),* *708 Jackson Pl. 20502; (202) 456-6708. Jim Towey, Director.*
General e-mail, info@faithbasedcommunityinitiatives.org
Web, www.whitehouse.gov/infocus/faith-based

Educates and assists new and existing faith-based and community initiatives to apply and qualify for competitive federal funding. Works in conjunction with the Agriculture Dept., Education Dept., Health and Human Services Dept., Housing and Urban Development Dept., Justice Dept., Labor Dept., and U.S. Agency for International Development to make federal programs more friendly to faith-based and community solutions and to make federal funding more accessible nationwide.

CONGRESS

General Accounting Office (GAO), *Education, Workforce, and Income Security,* *441 G St. N.W., #5928 20548; (202) 512-7215. Cynthia Fagnoni, Managing Director.*
Web, www.gao.gov

Independent, nonpartisan agency in the legislative branch. Audits, analyzes, and evaluates Health and Human Services Dept. and Corporation for National and Community Service programs; makes reports available to the public.

House Agriculture Committee, *Subcommittee on Department Operations, Oversight, Nutrition, and Forestry,* *1407 LHOB 20515; (202) 225-2171. Fax, (202) 225-4464. Rep. Gil Gutknecht, R-Minn., Chair; Samuel Diehl, Staff Director.*
Web, agriculture.house.gov

Jurisdiction over food stamp legislation.

House Appropriations Committee, *Subcommittee on Labor, Health and Human Services, Education, and Related Agencies,* *2358 RHOB 20515; (202) 225-3508. Fax, (202) 225-3509. Rep. Ralph Regula, R-Ohio, Chair; Craig Higgins, Staff Director.*
Web, www.house.gov/appropriations

Jurisdiction over legislation to appropriate funds for the Health and Human Services Dept. (except the Food and Drug Administration and native American health programs), Corporation for National Service programs, and the National Council on Disability.

House Education and the Workforce Committee, *2181 RHOB 20515; (202) 225-4527. Fax, (202) 225-9571. Rep. John A. Boehner, R-Ohio, Chair; Paula Nowakowski, Staff Director. TTY, (202) 226-3372.*
Web, edworkforce.house.gov

Jurisdiction over legislation on Community Services Block Grant Program, Head Start, native Americans programs, antipoverty programs, applications of the Older Americans Act (including volunteer older Americans programs under the Corporation for National and Community Service) and related legislation, runaway youth, child and youth development, Child Care Development Block Grant, and child-family services.

House Ways and Means Committee, *Subcommittee on Human Resources,* B317 RHOB 20515; (202) 225-1025. Fax, (202) 225-9480. Rep. Wally Herger, R-Calif., Chair; Matt Weidinger, Staff Director.
Web, waysandmeans.house.gov

Jurisdiction over legislation on welfare programs, child support enforcement, child welfare, child care, foster care, adoption assistance, supplemental security income, unemployment compensation and insurance, low-income energy assistance, eligibility of welfare recipients for food stamps, and social services for the elderly and persons with disabilities.

Senate Agriculture, Nutrition, and Forestry Committee, SR-328A 20510; (202) 224-2035. Fax, (202) 224-1725. Sen. Thad Cochran, R-Miss., Chair; Hunt Shipman, Chief of Staff. TTY, (202) 224-2587.
Web, agriculture.senate.gov

Jurisdiction over legislation on low-income energy assistance programs.

Senate Appropriations Committee, *Subcommittee on Labor, Health and Human Services, Education, and Related Agencies,* SD-184 20510; (202) 224-3471. Fax, (202) 224-8553. Sen. Arlen Specter, R-Pa., Chair; Bettilou Taylor, Clerk.
Web, appropriations.senate.gov

Jurisdiction over legislation to appropriate funds for the Health and Human Services Dept. (except the Food and Drug Administration and native American health programs), Corporation for National and Community Service, and the National Council on Disability.

Senate Finance Committee, *Subcommittee on Social Security and Family Policy,* SD-219 20510; (202) 224-4515. Sen. Rick Santorum, R-Pa., Chair; Kolan L. Davis, Staff Director.
Web, finance.senate.gov

Holds hearings on legislation concerning welfare programs, child support enforcement, child welfare, child care, foster care, adoption assistance, supplemental security income, unemployment compensation and insurance, and social services for the elderly and persons with disabilities.

NONPROFIT

American Enterprise Institute for Public Policy Research (AEI), *Social and Individual Responsibility Project,* 1150 17th St. N.W. 20036; (202) 862-5904. Fax, (202) 862-5802. Douglas J. Besharov, Director.
Web, www.aei.org

Research and education organization that conducts studies on social welfare policies, including family and welfare policies. Interests include children, child abuse and neglect, divorce, drug abuse, family breakdown, poverty, out-of-wedlock births, and welfare programs.

American Public Human Services Assn., 810 1st St. N.E., #500 20002-4267; (202) 682-0100. Fax, (202) 289-6555. Jerry Friedman, Executive Director.
Web, www.aphsa.org

Membership: state and local human services administrators. Dedicated to developing, promoting, and implementing public human services policies that improve the health and well-being of families, children, and adults. Provides training and technical assistance; operates a job bank.

Assn. of Community Organizations for Reform Now (ACORN), *Washington Office,* 739 8th St. S.E. 20003; (202) 547-2500. Fax, (202) 546-2483. Chris Saffert, Legislative Director.
General e-mail, natacorndc@acorn.org
Web, www.acorn.org

Works to advance the interests of minority and low-income families through community organizing and action. Interests include jobs, living wages, housing, welfare reform, and community reinvestment. (Headquarters in New Orleans, La.)

Catholic Charities USA, 1731 King St., Alexandria, VA 22314; (703) 549-1390. Fax, (703) 549-1656. Rev. J. Bryan Hehir, President.
Web, catholiccharitiesinfo.org

Member agencies and institutions provide persons of all backgrounds with social services, including adoption, education, counseling, food, and housing services. National office promotes public policies that address human needs and social injustice. Provides members with advocacy and professional support, including technical assistance, training, and resource development; disseminates publications.

Center for Community Change, 1000 Wisconsin Ave. N.W. 20007; (202) 342-0519. Fax, (202) 333-5462. Deepak Bhargava, Executive Director.
General e-mail, info@communitychange.org
Web, www.communitychange.org

Provides community-based organizations serving minorities and the economically disadvantaged with technical assistance. Areas of assistance include housing, economic and resource development, rural development projects, and program planning.

Center for Law and Social Policy, *1015 15th St. N.W., #400 20005; (202) 906-8000. Fax, (202) 842-2885. Alan W. Houseman, Director.*
Web, www.clasp.org

Public interest organization with expertise in law and policy affecting low-income Americans. Seeks to improve the economic conditions of low-income families with children and to secure access to the civil justice system for the poor.

Center for the Study of Social Policy, *1575 Eye St. N.W., #500 20005-3922; (202) 371-1565. Fax, (202) 371-1472. Frank Farrow, Director.*
Web, www.cssp.org

Assists states and communities in organizing, financing, and delivering human services, with a focus on children and families. Helps build capacity for local decision making; helps communities use informal supports in the protection of children; promotes nonadversarial approach to class action litigation on behalf of dependent children.

Center on Budget and Policy Priorities, *820 1st St. N.E., #510 20002; (202) 408-1080. Fax, (202) 408-1056. Robert Greenstein, Executive Director.*
Web, www.cbpp.org

Research group that analyzes federal, state, and local government policies affecting low- and moderate-income Americans.

Christian Relief Services, *8815 Telegraph Rd., Lorton, VA 22079; (703) 550-2472. Fax, (703) 550-2473. Eugene L. Krizek, President. Information, (800) 33-RELIEF.*
General e-mail, info@christianrelief.org
Web, www.christianrelief.org

Promotes economic development and the alleviation of poverty in urban areas of the United States, native American reservations, and Africa. Donates medical supplies and food; administers housing, hospital, and school construction programs; provides affordable housing for low-income individuals and families.

Coalition on Human Needs, *1120 Connecticut Ave. N.W., #910 20036; (202) 223-2532. Fax, (202) 223-2538. Stuart P. Campbell, Executive Director.*
General e-mail, chn@chn.org
Web, www.chn.org

Promotes public policies that address the needs of low-income Americans. Members include civil rights, religious, labor, and professional organizations and individuals concerned with the well-being of children, women, the elderly, and people with disabilities.

Community Action Partnership, *1100 17th St. N.W., #500 20036; (202) 265-7546. Fax, (202) 265-8850. Derrick Span, National President.*
General e-mail, info@communityactionpartnership.com
Web, www.communityactionpartnership.com

Provides community action agencies with information, training, and technical assistance; advocates, at all levels of government, for low-income people.

Council on Social Work Education, *1725 Duke St., #500, Alexandria, VA 22314-3457; (703) 683-8080. Fax, (703) 683-8099. Julia Watkins, Executive Director.*
General e-mail, info@cswe.org
Web, www.cswe.org

Promotes quality education in social work. Accredits social work programs.

Food Research and Action Center (FRAC), *1875 Connecticut Ave. N.W., #540 20009-5728; (202) 986-2200. Fax, (202) 986-2525. James D. Weill, President.*
General e-mail, comments@frac.org
Web, www.frac.org

Public interest advocacy, research, and legal center that works to end hunger and poverty in the United States; offers legal assistance, organizational aid, training, and information to groups seeking to improve or expand federal food programs, including food stamp, child nutrition, and WIC (women, infants, and children) programs; conducts studies relating to hunger and poverty; coordinates network of antihunger organizations. Monitors legislation and regulations.

Goodwill Industries International, *9200 Rockville Pike, Bethesda, MD 20814-3896; (301) 530-6500. Fax, (301) 530-1516. George Kessinger, President.*
Web, www.goodwill.org

Membership: 182 autonomous organizations that provide disabled and disadvantaged individuals with Goodwill Industries services, which include vocational rehabilitation evaluation, job training, employment, and placement services.

Grameen Foundation USA, *1029 Vermont Ave. N.W., #400 20005; (202) 628-3560. Fax, (202) 628-3880. Alex Counts, President.*
General e-mail, info@gfusa.org
Web, www.gfusa.org

Seeks to eliminate poverty through collaboration with public and private institutions; supports and promotes antipoverty programs of the Grameen Bank; educates policymakers about microcredit programs for the poor; offers support services to agencies starting or expanding microcredit programs. Microcredit loans are small amounts of credit given to poor people for self-employment projects.

Hudson Institute, *National Security Studies, Washington Office, 1015 18th St. N.W., #300 20036; (202) 223-7770. Fax, (202) 223-8537. William E. Odom, Director.*
Web, www.hudson.org

Studies welfare policy; helps states create welfare reform programs. (Headquarters in Indianapolis, Ind.)

Institute for Women's Policy Research (IWPR), *1707 L St. N.W., #750 20036; (202) 785-5100. Fax, (202) 833-4362. Heidi I. Hartmann, President.*
General e-mail, iwpr@iwpr.org
Web, www.iwpr.org

Public policy research organization that focuses on women's issues, including welfare reform, family and work policies, employment and wages, and discrimination based on gender, race, or ethnicity.

National Assn. for the Advancement of Colored People (NAACP), *Washington Office, 1025 Vermont Ave. N.W., #1120 20005; (202) 638-2269. Fax, (202) 638-5936. Hilary O. Shelton, Director.*
Web, www.naacp.org

Membership: persons interested in civil rights for all minorities. Interests include welfare reform and related social welfare matters. Administers programs that create employment and affordable housing opportunities, and that improve health care. Monitors legislation and regulations. (Headquarters in Baltimore, Md.)

National Assn. of Social Workers, *750 1st St. N.E., #700 20002-4241; (202) 408-8600. Fax, (202) 336-8310. Elizabeth Clark, Executive Director.*
General e-mail, nasw@capcon.net
Web, www.socialworkers.org

Membership: graduates of accredited social work education programs and students in accredited programs. Promotes the interests of social workers and their clients; promotes professional standards; certifies members of the Academy of Certified Social Workers; conducts research.

National Community Action Foundation, *810 1st St. N.E., #530 20002; (202) 842-2092. Fax, (202) 842-2095. David A. Bradley, Executive Director.*

General e-mail, info@ncaf.org
Web, www.ncaf.org

Organization for community action agencies concerned with issues that affect the poor. Provides information on Community Services Block Grant, low-income energy assistance, employment and training, weatherization for low-income housing, nutrition, and the Head Start program.

National Urban League, *Washington Office, 3501 14th Street N.W. 20010; (202) 265-8200. Fax, (202) 265-6122. Maudine R. Cooper, President.*
Web, www.gwul.org

Social service organization concerned with the social welfare of African Americans and other minorities. (Headquarters in New York.)

Poverty and Race Research Action Council, *3000 Connecticut Ave. N.W., #200 20008; (202) 387-9887. Fax, (202) 387-0764. Chester W. Hartman, Executive Director.*
General e-mail, info@prrac.org
Web, www.prrac.org

Facilitates cooperative links between researchers and activists who work on race and poverty issues. Provides nonprofit organizations with funding for research on race and poverty.

Public Welfare Foundation, *1200 U St. N.W. 20009; (202) 965-1800. Fax, (202) 265-8851. Larry Kressley, Executive Director.*
Web, www.publicwelfare.org

Seeks to assist disadvantaged populations overcome barriers to full participation in society. Awards grants to nonprofits in the following areas: criminal justice, disadvantaged elderly and youths, the environment, health care, population and reproductive health, human rights and global security, technology, and community and economic development.

Salvation Army, *615 Slaters Lane, Alexandria, VA 22314-0269 (mailing address: P.O. Box 269, Alexandria, VA 22313-0269); (703) 684-5500. Fax, (703) 684-3478. W. Todd Bassett, National Commander.*
Web, www.salvationarmyusa.org

International religious social welfare organization that provides social services, including counseling, youth and senior citizens' services, emergency help, foster care, settlement and day care, tutoring for the retarded, programs for people with disabilities, prison work, summer camps, community centers, employment services, rehabilitation programs for alcoholics, missing persons bureaus, and residences for the homeless. (International headquarters in London.)

United Jewish Communities (UJC), *Washington Office,* *1720 Eye St. N.W., #800 20006; (202) 785-5900. Fax, (202) 785-4937. Diana Aviv, Director.*
General e-mail, info@ujc.org
Web, www.ujc.org
  Fundraising organization. Sustains and enhances the quality of Jewish life domestically and internationally. Advocates the needs of the Jewish community abroad. Offers marketing, communications, and public relations support; coordinates a speakers bureau and Israeli emissaries. (Headquarters in New York.)

Urban Institute, *2100 M St. N.W. 20037; (202) 833-7200. Fax, (202) 728-0232. Robert D. Reischauer, President. Information, (202) 261-5702. Library, (202) 261-5534.*
General e-mail, paffairs@ui.urban.org
Web, www.urban.org
  Nonpartisan, public policy research and education organization. Interests include states' use of federal funds; delivery of social services to specific groups, including children of mothers in welfare reform programs; retirement policy, income, and community-based services for the elderly; job placement and training programs for welfare recipients; health care cost containment and access; food stamps; child nutrition; the homeless; housing; immigration; and tax policy. Library open to the public by appointment.

U.S. Conference of City Human Services Officials, *1620 Eye St. N.W., #400 20006; (202) 861-6707. Fax, (202) 293-2352. Crystal Swann, Assistant Executive Director.*
Web, www.usmayors.org
  Promotes improved social services for specific urban populations through meetings, technical assistance, and training programs for members; fosters information exchange among federal, state, and local governments, human services experts, and other groups concerned with human services issues. (Affiliate of the U.S. Conference of Mayors.)

 CHILDREN AND FAMILIES

AGENCIES

Administration for Children and Families (ACF), *(Health and Human Services Dept.), 901 D St. S.W., #600 20447 (mailing address: 370 L'Enfant Promenade S.W. 20447); (202) 401-2337. Fax, (202) 401-4678. Wade F. Horn, Assistant Secretary. Information, (202) 401-9215.*
Web, www.acf.hhs.gov

  Plans, manages, and coordinates national assistance programs that promote stability, economic security, responsibility, and self-support for families; supervises programs and use of funds to provide the most needy with aid and to increase alternatives to public assistance. Programs include Temporary Assistance to Needy Families, Child Welfare, Head Start, Child Support Enforcement, Low-Income Home Energy Assistance, Community Services Block Grant, and Refugee Resettlement Assistance.

Administration for Children and Families (ACF), *(Health and Human Services Dept.), Child Support Enforcement, 901 D St. S.W. 20447 (mailing address: 370 L'Enfant Promenade S.W. 20447); (202) 401-9370. Fax, (202) 401-3450. Sherrie Heller, Commissioner. Information, (202) 401-9373.*
Web, www.acf.hhs.gov/programs/cse
  Helps states develop, manage, and operate child support programs. Maintains the Federal Parent Locator Service, which provides state and local child support agencies with information for locating absent parents. State enforcement agencies locate absent parents, establish paternity, establish and enforce support orders, and collect child support payments.

Administration for Children and Families (ACF), *(Health and Human Services Dept.), Family Assistance, 901 D St. S.W. 20447 (mailing address: 370 L'Enfant Promenade S.W. 20447); (202) 401-9275. Fax, (202) 205-5887. Andrew Bush, Director.*
Web, www.acf.hhs.gov/programs/ofa
  Provides leadership, direction, and technical guidance to the states and territories on administration of the TANF (Temporary Assistance to Needy Families) Block Grant. Focuses efforts to increase economic independence and productivity for families. Provides direction and guidance in collection and dissemination of performance and other data for these programs.

Administration on Children, Youth, and Families *(Health and Human Services Dept.), Children's Bureau, 330 C St. S.W., #2068 20447; (202) 205-8618. Fax, (202) 260-9345. Susan Orr, Associate Commissioner.*
Web, www.acf.hhs.gov/programs/cb
  Administers grants to agencies and institutes of higher learning for research projects and for training personnel in the child welfare field. Administers formula grants to strengthen child welfare services provided by state and local public welfare agencies. Provides states with technical assistance in group and foster care, adoption, and family services. Maintains clearinghouse of programs for preventing and treating child abuse.

Administration on Children, Youth, and Families *(Health and Human Services Dept.), Family and Youth Services,* 330 C St. S.W., #2040 20447 (mailing address: P.O. Box 1182 20013-1182); (202) 205-8102. Fax, (202) 260-9330. Harry Wilson, Associate Commissioner. Web, www.acf.dhhs.gov/programs/fysb

Administers federal discretionary grant programs for projects serving runaway and homeless youth and for projects that deter youth involvement in gangs. Provides youth service agencies with training and technical assistance. Monitors federal policies, programs, and legislation. Supports research on youth development issues, including gangs, runaways, and homeless youth. Operates national clearinghouse on families and youth.

Cooperative State Research, Education, and Extension Service *(Agriculture Dept.), Families, 4-H, and Nutrition,* 800 9th St. S.W. 20250 (mailing address: P.O. Box 2225 20250-2225); (202) 720-2908. Fax, (202) 690-2469. K. Jane Coulter, Deputy Administrator. Web, www.reeusda.gov/f4hn/pro4h.htm

Administers education programs with state land-grant universities and county governments for rural and urban youth ages five to nineteen. Projects provide youth with development skills and experience in the fields of science and technological literacy, nutrition, environment, natural resources, health, leadership, citizenship, service, and personal growth and responsibility.

Food and Nutrition Service *(Agriculture Dept.), Analysis, Nutrition, and Evaluation,* 3101 Park Center Dr., #1014, Alexandria, VA 22302; (703) 305-2585. Fax, (703) 305-2576. Alberta Frost, Director. Web, www.fns.usda.gov/oane

Administers the Nutrition Education and Training Program, which provides states with grants for disseminating nutrition information to children and for in-service training of food service and teaching personnel; administers the Child Nutrition Labeling Program, which certifies that foods served in school lunch and breakfast programs meet nutritional requirements; provides information and technical assistance in nutrition and food service management.

Food and Nutrition Service *(Agriculture Dept.), Child Nutrition,* 3101 Park Center Dr., #640, Alexandria, VA 22302; (703) 305-2590. Fax, (703) 305-2879. Stanley C. Garnett, Director. Press, (703) 305-2039. Web, www.fns.usda.gov

Administers the transfer of funds to state agencies for the National School Lunch Program; the School Breakfast Program; the Special Milk Program, which helps schools and institutions provide children who do not have access to full meals under other child nutrition programs with fluid milk; the Child and Adult Care Food Program, which provides children in nonresidential child-care centers and family day care homes with year-round meal service; and the Summer Food Service Program, which provides children from low-income families with meals during the summer months.

Food and Nutrition Service *(Agriculture Dept.), Supplemental Food Programs,* 3101 Park Center Dr., #520, Alexandria, VA 22302; (703) 305-2746. Fax, (703) 305-2196. Patricia N. Daniels, Director. Web, www.fns.usda.gov

Provides health departments and agencies with federal funding for food supplements and administrative expenses to make food, nutrition education, and health services available to infants, young children, and pregnant, nursing, and postpartum women.

Health and Human Services Dept. (HHS), *Head Start,* 330 C St. S.W., 2nd Floor 20447; (202) 205-8572. Fax, (202) 260-9336. Windy Hill, Associate Commissioner. Web, www.headstartinfo.org

Awards grants to nonprofit organizations and local governments for operating community Head Start programs (comprehensive development programs for children, ages three to five, of low-income families); manages a limited number of parent and child centers for families with children up to age three. Conducts research and manages demonstration programs, including those under the Comprehensive Child Care Development Act of 1988; administers the Child Development Associate scholarship program, which trains individuals for careers in child development, often as Head Start teachers.

Health and Human Services Dept. (HHS), *Human Services Policy: Children and Youth Policy,* 200 Independence Ave. S.W., #450G 20201; (202) 690-6461. Fax, (202) 690-5514. Martha Morehouse, Director. Web, www.hhs.gov

Develops policies and procedures for programs that benefit children, youth, and families. Interests include child protection, domestic violence, family support, gang violence, child care and development, and care for drug-exposed, runaway, and homeless children and their families.

National Institute of Child Health and Human Development *(National Institutes of Health), Center for Research for Mothers and Children,* 6100 Executive Blvd., #4B05, Bethesda, MD 20892-7510; (301) 496-5097. Fax, (301) 480-7773. Anne Willoughby, Director. Web, www.nichd.nih.gov

Supports biomedical and behavioral science research and training for maternal and child health care. Areas of study include fetal development, maternal-infant health problems, HIV-related diseases in childbearing women, roles of nutrients and hormones in child growth, developmental disabilities, and behavioral development.

Office of Justice Programs (OJP), *(Justice Dept.),* *Juvenile Justice and Delinquency Prevention,* *810 7th St. N.W. 20531; (202) 307-5911. Fax, (202) 307-2093. John Robert Flores, Administrator. Technical information, (202) 307-0751. Clearinghouse, (800) 638-8736.*
Web, www.ncjrs.org/ojjhome.htm

Administers federal programs related to prevention and treatment of juvenile delinquency, missing and exploited children, child victimization, and research and evaluation of juvenile justice system; coordinates with youth programs of the departments of Agriculture, Education, Housing and Urban Development, Interior, and Labor, and of the Substance Abuse and Mental Health Services Administration, including the Center for Studies of Crime and Delinquency. Operates the Juvenile Justice Clearinghouse.

Office of Justice Programs (OJP), *(Justice Dept.),* *Violence Against Women,* *810 7th St. N.W., #920 20531; (202) 307-6026. Fax, (202) 307-3911. Diane Stuart, Director. National Domestic Violence Hotline, (800) 799-SAFE.*
Web, www.usdoj.gov/vawo

Seeks more effective policies and services to combat domestic violence, sexual assault, stalking, and other crimes against women. Helps administer grants to states to fund shelters, crisis centers, and hotlines, and to hire law enforcement officers, prosecutors, and counselors specializing in cases of sexual violence and other violent crimes against women.

CONGRESS

House Education and the Workforce Committee, *Subcommittee on Education Reform,* *H2-230 FHOB 20515; (202) 225-6558. Fax, (202) 225-9571. Rep. Michael N. Castle, R-Del., Chair; Paula Nowakowski, Staff Director.*
Web, edworkforce.house.gov

Jurisdiction over legislation on the National School Lunch Program; the School Breakfast Program; the Summer Food Program for Children; the Special Milk Program for Children; and the Special Supplemental Food Program for Women, Infants, and Children (WIC).

Senate Agriculture, Nutrition, and Forestry Committee, *Subcommittee on Research, Nutrition, and*

General Legislation, *SR-328A 20510; (202) 224-2035. Sen. Peter G. Fitzgerald, R-Ill., Chair; Vacant, Staff Director.*
Web, agriculture.senate.gov

Jurisdiction over legislation on commodity donations; the Food Stamp Program; the National School Lunch Program; the School Breakfast Program; the Summer Food Program for Children; the Special Milk Program for Children; the Special Supplemental Food Program for Women, Infants, and Children (WIC); and nutritional programs for the elderly.

Senate Health, Education, Labor, and Pensions Committee, *Subcommittee on Children and Families,* *SH-632 20510; (202) 224-5800. Sen. Lamar Alexander, R-Tenn., Chair; Marguerite Sallee, Staff Director.*
Web, health.senate.gov

Jurisdiction over legislation on day care, child abuse and domestic violence, family and medical leave, low-income energy assistance, adoption reform, Community Services Block Grant Program, Head Start, youth, child and youth development, Child Care Development Block Grant, and child-family services.

NONPROFIT

Adoption Service Information Agency, *8555 16th St., #600, Silver Spring, MD 20910; (301) 587-7068. Fax, (301) 587-3869. Theodore Kim, President.*
General e-mail, info@asia-adopt.org
Web, www.asia-adopt.org

Provides information on international and domestic adoption; sponsors seminars and workshops for adoptive and prospective adoptive parents.

Alliance for Children and Families, *Washington Office,* *1319 F St. N.W., #400 20004; (202) 393-3570. Fax, (202) 393-3571. Carmen Delgado Votaw, Senior Vice President, Public Policy.*
General e-mail, policy@alliance1.org
Web, www.alliance1.org

Membership: 350 children and family service agencies in the United States and Canada. Provides families with support services and counseling. Promotes affordable and accessible family-centered health and mental health care, education and job training, family and child welfare, and fiscal and workplace policies that strengthen family viability. Monitors legislation. (Headquarters in Milwaukee, Wis.)

American Assn. for Marriage and Family Therapy, *112 S. Alfred St., Alexandria, VA 22314; (703) 838-9808. Fax, (703) 838-9805. Michael Bowers, Executive Director.*
Web, www.aamft.org

Membership: professional marriage and family therapists. Promotes professional standards in marriage and family therapy through training programs; provides the public with educational material and referral service for marriage and family therapy.

American Bar Assn. (ABA), *Center on Children and the Law,* 740 15th St. N.W., 9th Floor 20005-1022; (202) 662-1720. Fax, (202) 662-1755. Howard Davidson, Director.
General e-mail, ctrchildlaw@abanet.org
Web, www.abanet.org/child

Works to increase lawyer representation of children; sponsors speakers and conferences; monitors legislation. Interests include child sexual abuse and exploitation, missing and runaway children, parental kidnapping, child support, foster care, and adoption of children with special needs.

American Humane Assn., *Public Policy, Washington Office,* 2007 N. 15th St., #201, Arlington, VA 22201; (703) 294-6690. Fax, (703) 294-4853. Suzanne Barnard, Director.
Web, www.americanhumane.org

Membership: humane societies, individuals, and government agencies concerned with child and animal protection laws. Prepares model state legislation on child abuse and its prevention; publishes surveys on child and animal abuse and state abuse laws. (Headquarters in Denver, Colo.)

American Youth Work Center, 1200 17th St. N.W., 4th Floor 20036; (202) 785-0764. Fax, (202) 728-0657. William Treanor, Executive Director.
Web, www.youthtoday.org

Publishes *Youth Today: The Newspaper on Youth Work.* Coverage includes juvenile justice and community-based youth services, including runaway shelters, hotlines, crisis intervention centers, drug programs, alternative education, and job training and placement. Provides youth programs with information on dealing effectively with young people.

America's Promise–The Alliance for Youth, 909 N. Washington St., #400, Alexandria, VA 22314-1556; (703) 684-4500. Fax, (703) 535-3900. Harris Wofford, Chair; Peter A. Gallagher, President.
General e-mail, commit@americaspromise.org
Web, www.americaspromise.org

Works with national and local organizations to mobilize individuals, groups, and organizations to build and strengthen the character and competence of America's youth; encourages volunteerism and community service among young people; provides information to individuals about state and local mentorship opportunities.

Boy Scouts of America, *Washington Office,* 9190 Rockville Pike, Bethesda, MD 20814; (301) 530-9360. Fax, (301) 564-3648. Ron L. Carroll, Scout Executive.
Web, www.bsa.scouting.org

Educational services organization for boys ages seven to seventeen. Promotes citizen participation and physical fitness. The Explorers Program, which includes young men and women ages fourteen to twenty, provides vocational opportunities. (Headquarters in Irving, Texas.)

Boys and Girls Clubs of America, *Washington Office,* 600 Jefferson Plaza, #401, Rockville, MD 20852-1150; (301) 251-6676. Fax, (301) 294-3052. Robbie Callaway, Senior Vice President.
Web, www.bgca.org

Educational service organization for boys and girls, most from disadvantaged circumstances. Works to prevent juvenile delinquency; promotes youth employment, health and fitness, leadership, and citizenship. Interests include child care, child safety and protection, drug and alcohol abuse prevention, runaway and homeless youth, youth employment, child nutrition, tax reform and charitable contributions, and other issues that affect disadvantaged youth. (Headquarters in Atlanta, Ga.)

Child Nutrition Forum, 1875 Connecticut Ave. N.W., #540 20009-5728; (202) 986-2200. Fax, (202) 986-2525. Lynn Parker, Coordinator.
General e-mail, comments@frac.org
Web, www.frac.org

Membership: agriculture, labor, education, and health and nutrition specialists; school food service officials; and consumer and religious groups. Supports federal nutrition programs for children; provides information on school nutrition programs. Monitors legislation and regulations concerning hunger issues.

Child Welfare League of America, 440 1st St. N.W., 3rd Floor 20001-2085; (202) 638-2952. Fax, (202) 638-4004. Shay Bilchik, Chief Executive Officer.
Web, www.cwla.org

Membership: public and private child welfare agencies. Develops standards for the field; provides information on adoption, day care, foster care, group home services, child protection, residential care for children and youth, services to pregnant adolescents and young parents, and other child welfare issues.

Children's Defense Fund, 25 E St. N.W. 20001; (202) 628-8787. Fax, (202) 662-3510. Marian Wright Edelman, President.

General e-mail, cdfinfo@childrensdefense.org
Web, www.childrensdefense.org

Advocacy group concerned with programs and policies for children and youth, particularly poor and minority children. Interests include health care, education, child care, job training and employment, and family support; works to ensure educational and job opportunities for youth.

Children's Defense Fund, *Child Care Division,* 25 E St. N.W. 20001; (202) 628-8787. Fax, (202) 662-3560. Helen Blank, Director.
Web, www.childrensdefense.org

Advocacy group concerned with federal and state programs for children and youth; provides parents and child-care advocates with information on child-care policy.

Children's Foundation, *725 15th St. N.W., #505 20005-2109; (202) 347-3300. Fax, (202) 347-3382. Kay Hollestelle, Executive Director.*
General e-mail, info@childrensfoundation.net
Web, www.childrensfoundation.net

Advocacy group for children and those who care for them. Works to improve available child care; promotes enforcement of child support; offers information, technical assistance, and professional training to child-care providers and parents.

Children's Rights Council, *6200 Editors Park Dr., #103, Hyattsville, MD 20782; (301) 559-3120. Fax, (301) 559-3124. David L. Levy, President.*
Web, www.gocrc.com

Membership: parents and professionals. Works to strengthen families through education and advocacy. Supports family formation and preservation. Conducts conferences and serves as an information clearinghouse. Interests include children whose parents are separated, unwed, or divorced.

Christian Children's Fund, *Washington Office,* 1717 N St. N.W. 20036; (202) 955-7951. Fax, (202) 955-6166. Ghassan Rubeiz, Director.
Web, www.christianchildrensfund.org

Works internationally to ensure the survival, protection, and development of children. Promotes the improvement in quality of life of children within the context of family, community, and culture. Helps children in unstable situations brought on by war, natural disasters, and other high-risk circumstances. (Headquarters in Richmond, Va.)

Council for Professional Recognition, *Child Development Associate National Credentialing Program,*

2460 16th St. N.W. 20009-3575; (202) 265-9090. Fax, (202) 265-9161. Carol Brunson Day, President. Information, (800) 424-4310.
Web, www.cdacouncil.org

Promotes and establishes standards for quality child care through an accrediting program. Awards credentials to family day care, preschool, home visitor, and infant-toddler caregivers.

Every Child Matters, *440 1st St. N.W., Fifth Floor 20001-2080. Fax, (202) 661-8871. Michael Petit, President, (202) 393-4053.*
General e-mail, info@everychildmatters.org
Web, www.everychildmatters.org

Works to make children's needs a national priority through public education activities.

Family and Home Network, *9493-C Silver King Court, Fairfax, VA 22031-4713; (703) 352-1072. Fax, (703) 352-1076. Cathy Meyers, Executive Director. Information, (866) 352-1075. Press, (703) 866-4164.*
General e-mail, fahn@familyandhome.org
Web, www.familyandhome.org

Provides information and support for parents who stay home, or who would like to stay home, to raise their children, in the United States and abroad. Monitors legislation and regulations relating to family issues. (Formerly Mothers at Home.)

Girl Scouts of the U.S.A., *Government Relations, Washington Office,* 1025 Connecticut Ave. N.W., #309 20036; (202) 659-3780. Fax, (202) 331-8065. Laurie Westley, Vice President.
Web, www.girlscouts.org

Educational service organization for girls ages five to seventeen. Promotes personal development through social action, leadership, and other projects. Interests include career education, youth camp safety, prevention of child sexual exploitation, child health care, runaways, and juvenile justice. (Headquarters in New York.)

National Assn. for the Education of Young Children, *1509 16th St. N.W. 20036-1426; (202) 232-8777. Fax, (202) 328-1846. Mark R. Ginsberg, Executive Director. Information, (800) 424-2460. Customer service, (866) 623-9248.*
Web, www.naeyc.org

Membership: early childhood professionals and parents. Works to improve the quality of early childhood care and education. Administers national accreditation system for early childhood programs. Maintains information service.

National Assn. of Child Advocates, *1522 K St. N.W., #600 20005; (202) 289-0777. Fax, (202) 289-0776. Tamara Lucas Copeland, President.*

General e-mail, naca@childadvocacy.org

Web, www.childadvocacy.org

Membership: private, nonprofit, state- and community-based child advocacy organizations. Works for safety, security, health, and education for all children by strengthening and building child advocacy organizations.

National Black Child Development Institute, *1101 15th St. N.W., #900 20005; (202) 833-2220. Fax, (202) 833-8222. Evelyn K. Moore, President.*

General e-mail, moreinfo@nbcdi.org

Web, www.nbcdi.org

Advocacy group for African American children, youth, and families. Interests include child care, foster care, adoption, health, and education. Provides information on government policies that affect African American children, youth, and families.

National Campaign to Prevent Teen Pregnancy, *1776 Massachusetts Ave. N.W., #200 20036; (202) 478-8500. Fax, (202) 478-8588. Sarah S. Brown, Director.*

General e-mail, campaign@teenpregnancy.org

Web, www.teenpregnancy.org

Nonpartisan initiative that seeks to reduce the U.S. teen pregnancy rate by one-third by the year 2005.

National Center for Missing and Exploited Children, *699 Prince St., Alexandria, VA 22314; (703) 274-3900. Fax, (703) 274-2200. Ernest Allen, President. TTY, (800) 826-7653. Toll-free hotline, (800) 843-5678.*

Web, www.missingkids.org

Private organization funded primarily by the Justice Dept. Assists parents and citizens' groups in locating and safely returning missing children; offers technical assistance to law enforcement agencies; coordinates public and private missing children programs; maintains database that coordinates information on missing children.

National Child Support Enforcement Assn., *444 N. Capitol St. N.W., #414 20001-1512; (202) 624-8180. Fax, (202) 624-8828. James Hollan, Executive Director.*

General e-mail, ncsea@sso.org

Web, www.ncsea.org

Promotes enforcement of child support obligations and educates professionals on child support issues; fosters exchange of ideas among child support professionals. Monitors legislation and regulations.

National Collaboration for Youth, *1319 F St. N.W. 20004; (202) 347-2080. Fax, (202) 393-4517. Irv Katz, Executive Director.*

Web, www.nassembly.org

Membership: national youth-serving organizations. Works to improve members' youth development programs through information exchange and other support. Raises public awareness of youth issues. Monitors legislation and regulations. (Affiliate of the National Assembly of Health and Human Service Organizations.)

National Congress of Parents and Teachers, Legislation, Washington Office, *1090 Vermont Ave. N.W., #1200 20005; (202) 289-6790. Fax, (202) 289-6791. Maribeth Oakes, Director.*

General e-mail, info@pta.org

Web, www.pta.org

Membership: parent-teacher associations at the preschool, elementary, and secondary levels. Supports school lunch and breakfast programs; works as an active member of the Child Nutrition Forum, which supports federally funded nutrition programs for children. (Headquarters in Chicago, Ill.)

National Council for Adoption, *225 N. Washington St., Alexandria, VA 22314; (703) 299-6633. Fax, (703) 299-6004. Patrick D. Purtill, President.*

Web, www.adoptioncouncil.org

Organization of individuals, national and international agencies, and corporations interested in adoption. Supports adoption through legal, ethical agencies; advocates the right to confidentiality in adoption. Conducts research and holds conferences; provides information; supports pregnancy counseling, maternity services, and counseling for infertile couples.

National Family Caregivers Assn., *10400 Connecticut Ave., #500, Kensington, MD 20895-3944; (301) 942-6430. Fax, (301) 942-2302. Suzanne Mintz, President. Information, (800) 896-3650.*

General e-mail, info@nfcacares.org

Web, www.nfcacares.org

Seeks to increase the quality of life of family caregivers by providing support and information; works to raise public awareness of caregiving through educational activities.

National 4-H Council, *7100 Connecticut Ave., Chevy Chase, MD 20815-4999; (301) 961-2820. Fax, (301) 961-2894. Donald T. Floyd Jr., President. Press, (301) 961-2915.*

Web, www.fourhcouncil.edu

Educational organization incorporated to expand and strengthen the 4-H program (for young people ages seven to nineteen) of the Cooperative Extension System and state land-grant universities. Programs include citizenship and leadership training.

National Head Start Assn., *1651 Prince St., Alexandria, VA 22314; (703) 739-0875. Fax, (703) 739-0878. Sarah M. Greene, President.*
Web, www.nhsa.org

Membership: organizations that represents Head Start children, families, and staff. Recommends strategies on issues affecting Head Start programs; provides training and professional development opportunities. Monitors legislation and regulations.

National Network for Youth, *1319 F St. N.W., #401 20004; (202) 783-7949. Fax, (202) 783-7955. Gretchen Noll, Executive Director (Acting).*
General e-mail, nn4youth@nn4youth.org
Web, www.nn4youth.org

Membership: providers of services related to runaway and homeless youth. Offers technical assistance to new and existing youth projects. Monitors legislation and regulations.

National Urban League, *Washington Office, 3501 14th Street N.W. 20010; (202) 265-8200. Fax, (202) 265-6122. Maudine R. Cooper, President.*
Web, www.gwul.org

Social service organization concerned with the social welfare of African Americans and other minorities. Youth Development division provides local leagues with technical assistance for youth programs and seeks training opportunities for youth within Urban League programs. (Headquarters in New York.)

National Youth Advocate Program, *P.O. Box 39127 20016 (mailing address: 4545 42nd St. N.W., #209 20016); (202) 244-6410. Fax, (202) 244-6396. Mubarak E. Awad, Director.*
General e-mail, nyap@nyap.org
Web, www.nyap.org

Supports the development and operation of community-based services for at-risk youth and their families. (Affiliated with Youth Advocate Program International.)

Orphan Foundation of America, *Tall Oak Village Center, 12020-D N. Shore Dr., Reston, VA 20190-4977; (571) 203-0270. Fax, (571) 203-0273. Eileen McCaffrey, Executive Director. Information, (800) 950-4673.*
General e-mail, help@orphan.org
Web, www.orphan.org

Advocates for orphaned, abandoned, and homeless teenage youths. Provides scholarships, research, information, emergency cash grants, volunteer programs, guidance, and support. Interests include the rights of orphaned children, transition from youth foster care to young adult independence, and breaking the welfare cycle. Learning center provides training and educational materials.

Rape, Abuse, and Incest National Network (RAINN), *635-B Pennsylvania Ave. S.E. 20003-4303; (202) 544-1034. Fax, (202) 544-3556. Scott Berkowitz, President. National Sexual Assault Hotline, (800) 656-HOPE.*
General e-mail, info@rainn.org
Web, www.rainn.org

Links sexual assault victims to confidential local services through national sexual assault hotline. Provides extensive public outreach and education programs nationwide.

Stand for Children, *1420 Columbia Rd. N.W., 3rd Floor 20009; (202) 234-0095. Fax, (202) 234-0217. Jonah Martin Edelman, Executive Director. Toll-free, (800) 663-4032.*
General e-mail, tellstand@stand.org
Web, www.stand.org

Works with chapters nationwide to promote the growth, health, education, and safety of children. Provides information to the public about policies that affect children and families. Organizes meetings between parents and community leaders. (Affiliated with the Children's Defense Fund.)

Elderly

AGENCIES

Administration on Aging (AoA), *(Health and Human Services Dept.), 330 Independence Ave. S.W., #4716 20201; (202) 619-0724. Fax, (202) 357-3555. Josefina Carbonell, Assistant Secretary. Press, (202) 401-4541.*
General e-mail, AoAInfo@aoa.gov
Web, www.aoa.gov

Advocacy agency for older Americans and their concerns. Collaborates with state and area agencies on aging, tribal organizations, and local community and national organizations to implement grant programs and services designed to improve the quality of life for older Americans, such as information and referral, adult day care, elder abuse prevention, home-delivered meals, in-home care, transportation, and services for caregivers.

National Senior Service Corps *(Corporation for National and Community Service), Retired and Senior Volunteer Program, Foster Grandparent Program, and Senior Companion Program, 1201 New York Ave. N.W.*

20525; (202) 606-5000. Fax, (202) 565-2789. Tess Scannell, Director. TTY, (800) 833-3722. Volunteer recruiting information, (800) 424-8867.

Web, www.seniorcorps.org

Network of programs that help older Americans find service opportunities in their communities, including the Retired and Senior Volunteer Program, which encourages older citizens to use their talents and experience in community service; the Foster Grandparent Program, which gives older citizens opportunities to work with exceptional children and children with special needs; and the Senior Companion Program, which recruits older citizens to help homebound adults, especially seniors, with special needs.

CONGRESS

House Education and the Workforce Committee, *Subcommittee on Select Education,* H2-230 FHOB 20515; (202) 225-6558. Fax, (202) 225-9571. Rep. Peter Hoekstra, R-Mich., Chair; Paula Nowakowski, Staff Director.

Web, edworkforce.house.gov

Jurisdiction over legislation on all matters dealing with programs and services for the elderly, including health and nutrition programs and the Older Americans Act.

Senate Health, Education, Labor, and Pensions Committee, *Subcommittee on Aging,* SH-608 20510; (202) 224-2962. Sen. Christopher S. Bond, R-Mo., Chair; C. Kate Lambrew Hall, Staff Director.

Web, health.senate.gov

Jurisdiction over applications of the Older Americans Act and related legislation.

Senate Special Committee on Aging, SD-G31 20510; (202) 224-5364. Fax, (202) 224-8660. Sen. Larry E. Craig, R-Idaho, Chair; Lupe Wissel, Staff Director.

Web, aging.senate.gov

Oversight of all matters affecting older Americans. Studies and reviews public and private policies and programs that affect the elderly, including retirement income and maintenance, housing, health, welfare, employment, education, recreation, and participation in family and community life; provides other Senate committees with information. Cannot report legislation.

NONPROFIT

AARP, 601 E St. N.W. 20049; (202) 434-2277. Fax, (202) 434-2320. William D. Novelli, Chief Executive Officer. Library, (202) 434-6240. Press, (202) 434-2560. TTY, (202) 434-6561.

Web, www.aarp.org

Conducts educational and counseling programs in areas concerning the elderly such as widowed persons services, health promotion, housing, and consumer protection. Library open to the public.

Alliance for Retired Americans, 888 16th St. N.W., #520 20006; (202) 974-8222. Fax, (202) 974-8256. George J. Kourpias, President. Information, (888) 373-6497.

Web, www.retiredamericans.org

Seeks to strengthen benefits to the elderly, including improved Social Security payments, increased employment, and education and health programs. (Affiliate of the AFL-CIO.)

Families USA, 1334 G St. N.W., #300 20005; (202) 737-6340. Fax, (202) 347-2417. Ron Pollack, Executive Director.

General e-mail, info@familiesusa.org

Web, www.familiesusa.org

Organization of American families whose interests include health care and long-term care, Social Security, Medicare, and Medicaid. Monitors legislation and regulations affecting the elderly.

Jewish Council for the Aging of Greater Washington, 11820 Parklawn Dr., #200, Rockville, MD 20852; (301) 881-8782. Fax, (301) 231-9360. David N. Gamse, Executive Director. TTY, (301) 881-5263.

General e-mail, jcagw@jcagw.org

Web, www.jcagw.org

Nonsectarian organization that provides programs and services to help older people continue living independent lives. Offers employment-related services, computer training, adult day care, in-home care, transportation, information and referrals, physical fitness, volunteer opportunities, and consultation.

National Assn. of Area Agencies on Aging, 927 15th St. N.W., 6th Floor 20005; (202) 296-8130. Fax, (202) 296-8134. Sandy Markwood, Chief Executive Officer.

Web, www.n4a.org

Works to establish an effective national policy on aging; provides local agencies with training and technical assistance; disseminates information to these agencies and the public. Monitors legislation and regulations.

National Assn. of Area Agencies on Aging, *Eldercare Locator,* 927 15th St. N.W., 6th Floor 20005; (800) 677-1116. Fax, (202) 296-8134. Angela Heath, Project Officer. TTY, (202) 855-1234 or with operator, (202) 855-1000. TTY is not toll free.

Web, www.eldercare.gov

National toll-free directory assistance service that helps older people and caregivers locate local support resources for aging Americans. Refers people to agencies or organizations that deal with meal services, home care transportation, housing alternatives, home repair, recreation, social activities, and legal services. (Provided by the National Administration on Aging and administered by the National Assn. of Area Agencies on Aging and the National Assn. of State Units on Aging.)

National Assn. of State Units on Aging, *1201 15th St. N.W., #350 20005-2800; (202) 898-2578. Fax, (202) 898-2583. Daniel A. Quirk, Executive Director.*
General e-mail, staff@nasua.org
Web, www.nasua.org
Membership: state and territorial governmental units that deal with the elderly. Provides members with information, technical assistance, and professional training. Monitors legislation and regulations.

National Caucus and Center on Black Aged, *1220 L St. N.W., #800 20005-2407; (202) 637-8400. Fax, (202) 347-0895. Samuel J. Simmons, President.*
General e-mail, info@ncba-aged.org
Web, www.ncba-blackaged.org
Concerned with issues that affect elderly African Americans. Sponsors employment and housing programs for the elderly and education and training for professionals in gerontology. Monitors legislation and regulations.

National Council on the Aging, *300 D St. S.W., #801 20024; (202) 479-1200. Fax, (202) 479-0735. James P. Firman, President. Information, (202) 479-6653. Press, (202) 479-6975.*
General e-mail, info@ncoa.org
Web, www.ncoa.org
Serves as an information clearinghouse on training, technical assistance, advocacy, and research on every aspect of aging. Provides information on social services for older persons. Monitors legislation and regulations.

National Hispanic Council on Aging, *2713 Ontario Rd. N.W. 20009; (202) 265-1288. Fax, (202) 745-2522. Marta Sotomayor, President.*
General e-mail, nhcoa@nhcoa.org
Web, www.nhcoa.org
Membership: senior citizens, health care workers, professionals in the field of aging, and others in the United States and Puerto Rico who are interested in topics related to Hispanics and aging. Provides research training, policy analysis, consulting, and technical assistance; sponsors seminars, workshops, and management internships.

 **DISABILITIES**

AGENCIES

Administration for Children and Families (ACF), *(Health and Human Services Dept.), Administration on Developmental Disabilities, 200 Independence Ave. S.W., #300F 20201; (202) 690-6590. Fax, (202) 690-6904. Patricia A. Morrissey, Commissioner. TTY, (202) 690-6415.*
Web, www.acf.hhs.gov/programs/add
Establishes state protection and advocacy systems for people with developmental disabilities, including persons with mental retardation, cerebral palsy, epilepsy, and autism; awards discretionary grants to university-affiliated programs and to programs of national significance. Administers formula grants to states for persons who incurred developmental disabilities before the age of twenty-two.

Architectural and Transportation Barriers Compliance Board (Access Board), *1331 F St. N.W., #1000 20004-1111; (202) 272-0080. Fax, (202) 272-0081. Lawrence W. Roffee, Executive Director. TTY, (202) 272-0082. Toll-free technical assistance, (800) 872-2253.*
General e-mail, info@access-board.gov
Web, www.access-board.gov
Enforces standards requiring that buildings and telecommunications and transportation systems be accessible to persons with disabilities; provides technical assistance and information on designing these facilities; sets accessibility guidelines for the Americans with Disabilities Act (ADA) and the Telecommunications Act of 1996.

Committee for Purchase from People Who Are Blind or Severely Disabled, *1421 Jefferson Davis Hwy., #10800, Arlington, VA 22202-3259; (703) 603-7740. Fax, (703) 603-0655. Leon Wilson, Executive Director.*
Web, www.jwod.gov
Presidentially appointed committee. Determines which products and services are suitable for federal procurement from qualified nonprofit agencies that employ people who are blind or have other severe disabilities; seeks to increase employment opportunities for these individuals.

Education Dept., *Special Education and Rehabilitative Services, 330 C St. S.W., #3006 20202-2500; (202) 205-5465. Fax, (202) 205-9252. Robert Pasternack, Assistant Secretary. TTY, (202) 205-0136. Main phone is voice and TTY accessible.*
Web, www.nochildleftbehind.gov

Provides information on federal legislation and programs and national organizations concerning individuals with disabilities.

Employment Standards Administration *(Labor Dept.), Coal Mine Workers' Compensation, 200 Constitution Ave. N.W., #C3520 20210; (202) 693-0046. Fax, (202) 693-1395. James L. DeMarce, Director.*
Web, www.dol.gov/dol/esa

Provides direction for administration of the black lung benefits program. Adjudicates claims filed on or after July 1, 1973; certifies these benefit payments and maintains black lung beneficiary rolls.

(For claims filed before July 1, 1973, contact Social Security Administration, Disability.)

Equal Employment Opportunity Commission (EEOC), *Americans with Disabilities Act Policy Division, 1801 L St. N.W., #6027 20507; (202) 663-4665. Fax, (202) 663-7176. Christopher J. Kuczynski, Director. TTY, (202) 663-7026.*

Division of the Office of Legal Counsel. Provides interpretations, opinions, and technical assistance on the ADA provisions relating to employment.

Justice Dept. (DOJ), *Disability Rights, 1425 New York Ave. N.W., #4039 20005; (202) 307-0663. Fax, (202) 307-1198. John L. Wodatch, Chief. Information, (800) 514-0301. TTY, (800) 514-0383.*
Web, www.usdoj.gov/disabilities.htm

Litigates cases under Title II and III of the Americans with Disabilities Act, which prohibits discrimination on the basis of disability in places of public accommodation and in all activities of state and local government. Provides technical assistance to business and individuals affected by the law.

National Council on Disability, *1331 F St. N.W., #850 20004-1107; (202) 272-2004. Fax, (202) 272-2022. Lex Frieden, Chair.*
Web, www.ncd.gov

Reviews and reports to the president on all laws, programs, and policies of the federal government affecting individuals with disabilities.

National Institute of Child Health and Human Development *(National Institutes of Health), National Center for Medical Rehabilitation Research, 6100 Executive Blvd., Bldg. 6100, #2A-03, Bethesda, MD 20892; (301) 402-2242. Fax, (301) 402-0832. Dr. Michael Weinrich, Director.*
Web, www.nichd.nih.gov

Conducts and supports research to develop improved technologies, techniques, and prosthetic and orthotic devices for people with disabilities; promotes medical rehabilitation training.

National Institute on Disability and Rehabilitation Research *(Education Dept.), 330 C St. S.W., #3060 20202-2572 (mailing address: 400 Maryland Ave. S.W., #3060 20202); (202) 205-8134. Fax, (202) 205-8997. Steven J. Tingus, Director.*
Web, www.ed.gov/offices/OSERS/NIDRR/index.html

Assists research programs in rehabilitating people with disabilities; provides information on developments in the field; awards grants and contracts for scientific, technical, and methodological research; coordinates federal research programs on rehabilitation; offers fellowships to individuals conducting research in the field.

Office of Disability Employment Policy *(Labor Dept.), 200 Constitution Ave., #S1303 20210; (202) 693-7880. Fax, (202) 693-7888. Roy Grizzard, Assistant Secretary; William Mea, Deputy Assistant Secretary. TTY, (202) 693-7881.*
General e-mail, info@pcepd.gov
Web, www.dol.gov/odep

Seeks to eliminate physical and psychological barriers to the disabled through education and information programs; promotes education, training, rehabilitation, and employment opportunities for people with disabilities.

Rehabilitation Services Administration *(Education Dept.), 330 C St. S.W. 20202-2531; (202) 205-5482. Fax, (202) 205-9874. Joanne Wilson, Commissioner. TTY, (202) 205-9295.*
Web, www.ed.gov

Coordinates and directs major federal programs for eligible physically and mentally disabled persons. Administers distribution of grants for training and employment programs and for establishing supported-employment and independent-living programs. Provides vocational training and job placement.

Smithsonian Institution, *Accessibility Program, 900 Jefferson Dr. S.W., #1239 20560-0426; (202) 786-2942. Fax, (202) 786-2210. Elizabeth Ziebarth, Coordinator. Information, (888) 783-0001. TTY, (202) 786-2414.*
Web, www.si.edu

Coordinates Smithsonian efforts to improve accessibility of its programs and facilities to visitors and staff with disabilities. Serves as a resource for museums and individuals nationwide.

Social Security Administration (SSA), *Disability, 3570 Annex Bldg., 6501 Security Blvd., Baltimore, MD*

21235; (410) 965-3424. Fax, (410) 965-6503. Lenore Carlson, Associate Commissioner. Information, (410) 965-7700.

Web, www.ssa.gov/disability

Administers and regulates the disability insurance program and disability provisions of the Supplemental Security Income (SSI) program.

CONGRESS

House Appropriations Committee, *Subcommittee on Transportation, Treasury, and Related Agencies,* 2358 RHOB 20515; (202) 225-2141. Fax, (202) 225-5895. Rep. Ernest Istook, R-Okla., Chair; Richard Efford, Clerk.

Web, www.house.gov/appropriations

Jurisdiction over legislation to appropriate funds for the Architectural and Transportation Barriers Compliance Board.

House Education and the Workforce Committee, *Subcommittee on Education Reform,* H2-230 FHOB 20515; (202) 225-6558. Fax, (202) 225-9571. Rep. Michael N. Castle, R-Del., Chair; Paula Nowakowski, Staff Director.

Web, edworkforce.house.gov

Jurisdiction over legislation on special education programs including, but not limited to, alcohol and drug abuse and education of the disabled.

House Energy and Commerce Committee, *Subcommittee on Health,* 2125 RHOB 20515; (202) 225-2927. Fax, (202) 225-1919. Rep. Michael Bilirakis, R-Fla., Chair; David V. Marventano, Staff Director.

General e-mail, commerce@mail.house.gov

Web, energycommerce.house.gov

Jurisdiction over developmental disability legislation.

Library of Congress, *National Library Service for the Blind and Physically Handicapped,* 1291 Taylor St. N.W. 20542; (202) 707-5104. Fax, (202) 707-0712. Frank Kurt Cylke, Director. TTY, (202) 707-0744. Reference, (202) 707-5100; outside D.C. area, (800) 424-8567.

General e-mail, nls@loc.gov

Web, www.loc.gov/nls

Administers a national program of free library services for persons with physical disabilities in cooperation with regional and subregional libraries. Produces and distributes full-length books and magazines in recorded form and in Braille. Reference section answers questions relating to blindness and physical disabilities and on library services available to persons with disabilities.

Senate Appropriations Committee, *Subcommittee on Transportation, Treasury, and General Government,*

SD-196 20510; (202) 224-4869. Fax, (202) 228-0249. Sen. Richard C. Shelby, R-Ala., Chair; Paul Doerrer, Clerk.

Web, appropriations.senate.gov

Jurisdiction over legislation to appropriate funds for the Architectural and Transportation Barriers Compliance Board.

Senate Health, Education, Labor, and Pensions Committee, SD-428 20510; (202) 224-5375. Fax, (202) 224-5128. Sen. Judd Gregg, R-N.H., Chair; Sharon Soderstrom, Staff Director. TTY, (202) 224-1975.

Web, health.senate.gov

Jurisdiction over legislation on people with disabilities, including vocational rehabilitation for people with physical and developmental disabilities. Jurisdiction over the Americans with Disabilities Act.

NONPROFIT

American Assn. of People with Disabilities, 1629 K St. N.W., #503 20006; (202) 457-0046. Fax, (202) 457-0473. Andrew Imparato, President. TTY, (202) 457-0046.

General e-mail, aapd@aol.com

Web, www.aapd-dc.org/docs/info.html

Works to further the productivity and independence of persons with disabilities through programs on employment, independent living, and assistive technology. Seeks to educate the public and policymakers on issues affecting persons with disabilities. Works in coalition with other organizations toward full enforcement of disability and antidiscrimination laws.

American Bar Assn. (ABA), *Commission on Mental and Physical Disability Law,* 740 15th St. N.W. 20005; (202) 662-1571. Fax, (202) 662-1032. John Parry, Director.

Web, www.abanet.org/disability/home.html

Serves as a clearinghouse for information on mental and physical disability law and offers legal research services. Publishes law report on mental and physical disability law.

American Counseling Assn., *Rehabilitation,* 5999 Stevenson Ave., Alexandria, VA 22304-3300; (703) 823-9800. Fax, (703) 823-0252. Richard Yep, Executive Director. Information, (800) 347-6647. TTY, (703) 823-6862.

Web, www.counseling.org

Membership: counselors, counselor educators and graduate students in the rehabilitation field, and other interested persons. Establishes counseling and research standards; encourages establishment of rehabilitation facilities; conducts leadership training and continuing education programs; serves as a liaison between counselors and clients. Monitors legislation and regulations. Library open to the public.

American Medical Rehabilitation Providers Assn., *1710 N St. N.W. 20006; (202) 223-1920. Fax, (202) 223-1925. Carolyn Zollar, Vice President, Government Relations. Information, (888) 346-4624.*
Web, www.amrpa.org

Membership: freestanding rehabilitation hospitals and rehabilitation units of general hospitals, outpatient rehabilitation facilities, skilled nursing facilities, and others. Provides leadership, advocacy, and resources to develop medical rehabilitation services and supports for persons with disabilities and others in need of services. Acts as a clearinghouse for information to members on the nature, kind, and availability of services.

American Network of Community Options and Resources, *1101 King St., #380, Alexandria, VA 22314; (703) 535-7850. Fax, (703) 535-7860. Renee Pietrangelo, Managing Director.*
General e-mail, ancor@ancor.org
Web, www.ancor.org

Membership: privately operated agencies and corporations that provide support and services to people with disabilities. Advises and works with regulatory and consumer agencies that serve people with disabilities; provides information and sponsors seminars and workshops; publishes directory that lists services offered by member agencies. Monitors legislation and regulations.

American Occupational Therapy Assn., *4720 Montgomery Lane, Bethesda, MD 20814 (mailing address: P.O. Box 31220, Bethesda, MD 20824-1220); (301) 652-2682. Fax, (301) 652-7711. Joe Isaacs, Executive Director. TTY, (800) 377-8555.*
General e-mail, info@aota.org
Web, www.aota.org

Membership: registered occupational therapists, certified occupational therapy assistants, and students. Associate members include businesses and organizations supportive of occupational therapy. Accredits colleges and universities and certifies therapists.

American Orthotic and Prosthetic Assn., *330 John Carlyle St., #210, Alexandria, VA 22314; (571) 431-0876. Fax, (571) 431-0899. Tyler Wilson, Executive Director.*
Web, www.aopanet.org

Membership: companies that manufacture or supply artificial limbs and braces. Provides information on the profession.

American Physical Therapy Assn., *1111 N. Fairfax St., Alexandria, VA 22314-1488; (703) 684-2782. Fax,*
(703) 684-7343. Francis Mallon, Executive Vice President. Information, (800) 999-2782. Fax-on-demand, (800) 399-2782.
General e-mail, svcctr@apta.org
Web, www.apta.org

Membership: physical therapists, assistants, and students. Establishes professional standards and accredits physical therapy programs; seeks to improve physical therapy education, practice, and research.

American Speech-Language Hearing Assn. (ASHA), *10801 Rockville Pike, Rockville, MD 20852; (301) 897-5700. Fax, (301) 571-0457. Frederick T. Spahr, Executive Director. Press, (301) 897-0156. TTY, (301) 897-0157. Toll-free hotline (except Alaska, Hawaii, and Maryland), (800) 638-8255 (voice and TTY accessible).*
General e-mail, actioncenter@asha.org
Web, www.asha.org

Membership: specialists in speech-language pathology and audiology. Sponsors professional education programs; acts as accrediting agent for graduate college programs and for public clinical education programs in speech-language pathology and audiology. Advocates the rights of the communicatively disabled; provides information on speech, hearing, and language problems. Provides referrals to speech-language pathologists and audiologists. Interests include national and international standards for bioacoustics and noise.

Assn. of University Centers on Disabilities (AAUAP), *8630 Fenton St., #410, Silver Spring, MD 20910; (301) 588-8252. Fax, (301) 588-2842. George Jesien, Executive Director.*
Web, www.aucd.org

Network of facilities that diagnose and treat the developmentally disabled. Trains graduate students and professionals in the field; helps state and local agencies develop services. Interests include interdisciplinary training and services, early screening to prevent developmental disabilities, and development of equipment and programs to serve persons with disabilities.

Brain Injury Assn. of America, *105 N. Alfred St., Alexandria, VA 22314; (703) 236-6000. Fax, (703) 236-6001. Allan I. Bergman, President. Family helpline, (800) 444-6443.*
Web, www.biausa.org

Works to improve the quality of life for persons with traumatic brain injuries and for their families. Promotes the prevention of head injuries through public awareness and education programs. Offers state-level support services for individuals and their families. Monitors legislation and regulations.

Center on Disability and Health, *1522 K St. N.W., #800 20005; (202) 842-4408. Bob Griss, Director.*
General e-mail, bgrisscdh@aol.com

Promotes changes in the financing and delivery of health care to meet the needs of persons with disabilities and other chronic health conditions. Conducts research; provides technical assistance to disability groups and agencies. Monitors legislation and regulations.

Consortium for Citizens with Disabilities, *1331 H St. N.W., #301 20005; (202) 783-2229. Fax, (202) 783-8250. Tony Young, Chair.*
General e-mail, info@c-c-d.org
Web, www.c-c-d.org

Coalition of national disability organizations. Advocates national public policy that ensures the self-determination, independence, empowerment, and integration in all aspects of society for children and adults with disabilities.

Disability Resource Center, *4400 University Dr., MS 5C9, Fairfax, VA 22030; (703) 993-2474. Fax, (703) 993-4306. Deborah Wyne, Director. TTY, (703) 993-2476.*

Advocates for the rights of people with physical and mental disabilities; seeks to educate the public about these rights; conducts research. Monitors legislation and regulations.

Disability Rights Education and Defense Fund, *Governmental Affairs, Washington Office, 1629 K St. N.W., #802 20006; (202) 986-0375. Fax, (202) 775-7465. Pat Wright, Director.*

Law and policy center working to protect and advance the civil rights of people with disabilities through legislation, litigation, advocacy, and technical assistance. Educates and trains attorneys, advocates, persons with disabilities, and parents of children with disabilities. (Headquarters in Berkeley, Calif.)

Disabled American Veterans, *807 Maine Ave. S.W. 20024-2410; (202) 554-3501. Fax, (202) 554-3581. Arthur H. Wilson, National Adjutant.*
Web, www.dav.org

Chartered by Congress to assist veterans with claims for benefits; represents veterans seeking to correct alleged errors in military records. Assists families of veterans with disabilities.

Disabled Sports USA, *451 Hungerford Dr., #100, Rockville, MD 20850; (301) 217-0960. Fax, (301) 217-0968. Kirk M. Bauer, Executive Director. TTY, (301) 217-0963.*
General e-mail, dsusa@dsusa.org
Web, www.disabledsportsusa.org

Conducts sports and recreation activities and physical fitness programs for people with disabilities and their families and friends; conducts workshops and competitions; participates in world championships.

Epilepsy Foundation, *4351 Garden City Dr., #500, Landover, MD 20785; (301) 459-3700. Fax, (301) 577-2684. Eric Hargis, President. Information, (800) 332-1000. Library, (800) 332-4050.*
General e-mail, postmaster@efa.org
Web, www.epilepsyfoundation.org

Promotes research and treatment of epilepsy; makes research grants; disseminates information and educational materials. Affiliates provide direct services for people with epilepsy and make referrals when necessary. Library open to the public by appointment.

Girl Scouts of the U.S.A., *Government Relations, Washington Office, 1025 Connecticut Ave. N.W., #309 20036; (202) 659-3780. Fax, (202) 331-8065. Laurie Westley, Vice President.*
Web, www.girlscouts.org

Educational service organization for girls ages five to seventeen. Promotes personal development through social action, leadership, and programs such as Girl Scouting for Handicapped Girls. (Headquarters in New York.)

Goodwill Industries International, *9200 Rockville Pike, Bethesda, MD 20814-3896; (301) 530-6500. Fax, (301) 530-1516. George Kessinger, President.*
Web, www.goodwill.org

Membership: 182 autonomous organizations that provide disabled and disadvantaged individuals with Goodwill Industries services, which include vocational rehabilitation evaluation, job training, employment, and placement services.

Helen A. Kellar Institute for Human Disabilities, *George Mason University, 4400 University Dr., MS 1F2, Fairfax, VA 22030; (703) 993-3670. Fax, (703) 993-3681. Michael M. Behrmann, Director.*
Web, kihd.gmu.edu

Combines resources from local, state, national, public, and private affiliations to develop products, services, and programs for persons with disabilities.

International Code Council, *5203 Leesburg Pike, #600, Falls Church, VA 22041; (703) 931-4533. Fax, (703) 379-1546. William Tangye, Chief Executive Officer.*
Web, www.iccsafe.org

Provides review board for the American National Standards Institute accessibility standards, which ensure that buildings are accessible to persons with physical disabilities.

National Assn. of Developmental Disabilities Councils, *1234 Massachusetts Ave. N.W., #103 20005; (202) 347-1234. Fax, (202) 347-4023. Mary M. Kelley, Executive Director (Acting).*
General e-mail, naddc@naddc.org
Web, www.naddc.org

Membership: state and territorial councils authorized by the Development Disabilities Act, which promotes the interests of people with developmental disabilities and their families. Monitors legislation and regulations.

National Council on Independent Living, *1916 Wilson Blvd., #209, Arlington, VA 22201; (703) 525-3406. Fax, (703) 525-3409. Anne-Marie Hughey, Executive Director. TTY, (703) 525-4153.*
General e-mail, ncil@ncil.org
Web, www.ncil.org

Membership: independent living centers, their staff and volunteers, and individuals with disabilities. Seeks to strengthen independent living centers; facilitates the integration of people with disabilities into society; provides training and technical assistance; sponsors referral service and speakers' bureau.

National Easter Seal Society, *Washington Office, 700 13th St. N.W., #200 20005; (202) 347-3066. Fax, (202) 737-7914. Joseph D. Romer, Executive Vice President. TTY, (202) 347-7385.*
Web, www.easter-seals.org

Federation of state and local groups with programs that help people with disabilities achieve independence. Washington office monitors legislation and regulations. Affiliates assist individuals with a broad range of disabilities, including muscular dystrophy, cerebral palsy, stroke, speech and hearing loss, blindness, amputation, and learning disabilities. Services include physical, occupational, vocational, and speech therapy; speech, hearing, physical, and vocational evaluation; psychological testing and counseling; personal and family counseling; supported employment; special education programs; social clubs and day and residential camps; and transportation, referral, and follow-up programs. (Headquarters in Chicago, Ill.)

National Information Center for Children and Youth with Disabilities, *1825 Connecticut Ave. N.W., 7th Floor 20009 (mailing address: P.O. Box 1492 20013-1492); (202) 884-8200. Fax, (202) 884-8441. Suzanne Ripley, Director. Information, (800) 695-0285.*
Web, www.nichcy.org

Federally funded clearinghouse that provides information in Spanish and English to parents, educators, caregivers, advocates, and others who help children and youth with disabilities become active participants in school, work, and the community. Offers personal responses to specific questions, referrals to other organizations, prepared information packets, and technical assistance to families and professional groups.

National Multiple Sclerosis Society, *Washington Office, 2021 K St. N.W., #715 20006-1003; (202) 296-9891. Fax, (202) 296-3425. Jeanne Oates Angulo, President.*
General e-mail, info@msandyou.org
Web, www.msandyou.org

Seeks to advance medical knowledge of multiple sclerosis, a disease of the central nervous system; disseminates information worldwide. Patient services include individual and family counseling, exercise programs, equipment loans, medical and social service referrals, transportation assistance, back-to-work training programs, and in-service training seminars for nurses, homemakers, and physical and occupational therapists. (Headquarters in New York.)

National Organization on Disability, *910 16th St. N.W., #600 20006-2988; (202) 293-5960. Fax, (202) 293-7999. Allen A. Reich, President. TTY, (202) 293-5968.*
Web, www.nod.org

Administers the Community Partnership Program, a network of communities that works to remove barriers and address educational, employment, social, and transportation needs of people with disabilities. Provides members with information and technical assistance; sponsors annual community awards competition; makes referrals. Monitors legislation and regulations.

National Rehabilitation Assn., *633 S. Washington St., Alexandria, VA 22314; (703) 836-0850. Fax, (703) 836-0848. Michelle Vaughan, Executive Director. TTY, (703) 836-0849.*
Web, www.nationalrehab.org

Membership: administrators, counselors, therapists, disability examiners, vocational evaluators, instructors, job placement specialists, disability managers in the corporate sector, and others interested in rehabilitation of the physically and mentally disabled. Sponsors conferences and workshops. Monitors legislation and regulations.

National Rehabilitation Information Center, *4200 Forbes Blvd., #202, Lanham, MD 20706; (301) 459-5900. Fax, (301) 459-4263. Mark Odum, Director. Information, (800) 346-2742. TTY, (301) 459-5984.*

General e-mail, naricinfo@heitechservices.com

Web, www.naric.com

Provides information on disability and rehabilitation research. Acts as referral agency for disability and rehabilitation facilities and programs.

Paralyzed Veterans of America, *801 18th St. N.W. 20006-3517; (202) 872-1300. Fax, (202) 785-4452. Delatorro (Del) McNeal, Executive Director. Information, (800) 424-8200. TTY, (202) 416-7622.*

General e-mail, info@pva.org

Web, www.pva.org

Congressionally chartered organization that assists veterans with claims for benefits. Distributes information on special education for paralyzed veterans; advocates for quality care and supports and raises funds for medical research.

RESNA, *1700 N. Moore St., #1540, Arlington, VA 22209-1903; (703) 524-6686. Fax, (703) 524-6630. Larry Pencak, Executive Director. TTY, (703) 524-6639.*

General e-mail, membership@resna.org

Web, www.resna.org

Membership: engineers, health professionals, persons with disabilities, and others concerned with rehabilitation engineering and assistive technology. Promotes and supports developments in rehabilitation engineering; acts as an information clearinghouse.

Special Olympics International, *1325 G St. N.W., #500 20005; (202) 628-3630. Fax, (202) 824-0200. Robert Sargent Shriver Jr., Chair.*

General e-mail, soimail@aol.com

Web, www.specialolympics.org

Offers individuals with mental retardation opportunities for year-round sports training; sponsors athletic competition worldwide in twenty-two individual and team sports.

Spina Bifida Assn. of America, *4590 MacArthur Blvd. N.W., #250 20007-4226; (202) 944-3285. Fax, (202) 944-3295. Cindy Brownstein, Chief Executive Officer. Information, (800) 621-3141.*

General e-mail, sbaa@sbaa.org

Web, www.sbaa.org

Membership: individuals with spina bifida, their supporters, and concerned professionals. Offers educational programs, scholarships, and support services; acts as a clearinghouse; provides referrals. Serves as U.S. member of the International Federation for Hydrocephalus and Spina Bifida, which is headquartered in Geneva. Monitors legislation and regulations.

United Cerebral Palsy Assns., *1660 L St. N.W., #700 20036-5602; (202) 776-0406. Fax, (202) 776-0414. Kirsten Nyrop, Executive Director. Information, (800) 872-5827. Main phone is voice and TTY accessible.*

General e-mail, ucpnatl@ucp.org

Web, www.ucpa.org

National network of state and local affiliates that assists individuals with cerebral palsy and other developmental disabilities and their families. Provides parent education, early intervention, employment services, family support and respite programs, therapy, assistive technology, and vocational training. Promotes research on cerebral palsy; supports the use of assistive technology and community-based living arrangements for persons with cerebral palsy and other developmental disabilities.

VSA Arts, *1300 Connecticut Ave. N.W., #700 20036; (202) 628-2800. Fax, (202) 737-0725. Soula Antoniou, Chief Executive Officer. Information, (800) 933-8721. TTY, (202) 737-0645.*

Web, www.vsarts.org

Initiates and supports research and program development providing arts training and demonstration for persons with disabilities. Provides technical assistance and training to VSA Arts state organizations; acts as an information clearinghouse for arts and persons with disabilities. Formerly known as Very Special Arts. (Affiliated with the Kennedy Center education office.)

Blind and Visually Impaired

AGENCIES

Committee for Purchase from People Who Are Blind or Severely Disabled, *1421 Jefferson Davis Hwy., #10800, Arlington, VA 22202-3259; (703) 603-7740. Fax, (703) 603-0655. Leon Wilson, Executive Director.*

Web, www.jwod.gov

Presidentially appointed committee. Determines which products and services are suitable for federal procurement from qualified nonprofit agencies that employ people who are blind or have other severe disabilities; seeks to increase employment opportunities for these individuals.

CONGRESS

Library of Congress, *National Library Service for the Blind and Physically Handicapped, 1291 Taylor St. N.W. 20542; (202) 707-5104. Fax, (202) 707-0712. Frank Kurt Cylke, Director. TTY, (202) 707-0744. Reference, (202) 707-5100; outside D.C. area, (800) 424-8567.*

General e-mail, nls@loc.gov

Web, www.loc.gov/nls

Administers a national program of free library services for persons with physical disabilities in cooperation with regional and subregional libraries. Produces and distributes full-length books and magazines in recorded form and in Braille. Reference section answers questions relating to blindness and physical disabilities and on library services available to persons with disabilities.

NONPROFIT

American Blind Lawyers Assn., *1155 15th St. N.W., #1004 20005; (202) 467-5081. Fax, (202) 467-5085. Christopher Gray, President.*
General e-mail, info@acb.org
Web, www.acb.org

Membership: blind lawyers and law students. Provides members with legal information; acts as an information clearinghouse on legal materials available in Braille, in large print, on computer disc, and on tape. (Affiliated with American Council of the Blind.)

American Council of the Blind (ACB), *1155 15th St. N.W., #1004 20005-2706; (202) 467-5081. Fax, (202) 467-5085. Charles Crawford, Executive Director. Toll-free, 2:00–5:00 p.m. EST, (800) 424-8666.*
Web, www.acb.org

Membership organization serving blind and visually impaired individuals. Interests include Social Security, telecommunications, rehabilitation services, transportation, education, and architectural access. Provides blind individuals with information and referral services, including legal referrals; advises state organizations and agencies serving the blind; sponsors scholarships for the blind and visually impaired.

American Foundation for the Blind, *Governmental Relations, Washington Office, 820 1st St. N.E., #400 20002; (202) 408-0200. Fax, (202) 289-7880. Paul W. Schroeder, Vice President, Government Relations.*
General e-mail, afbgov@afb.net
Web, www.afb.org/gov.asp

Advocates equality of access and opportunity for the blind and visually impaired. Conducts research and provides consulting; develops and implements public policy and legislation. Maintains the Helen Keller Archives and M. C. Migel Memorial Library at its headquarters in New York.

Assn. for Education and Rehabilitation of the Blind and Visually Impaired, *P.O. Box 22397, Alexandria, VA 22304; (703) 823-9690. Fax, (703) 823-9695. Mark Richard, Executive Director.*
General e-mail, aer@aerbvi.org
Web, www.aerbvi.org

Membership: professionals and paraprofessionals who work with the blind and visually impaired. Provides information on services for people who are blind and visually impaired and on employment opportunities for those who work with them. Works to improve quality of education and rehabilitation services. Monitors legislation and regulations.

Blinded Veterans Assn., *477 H St. N.W. 20001-2699; (202) 371-8880. Fax, (202) 371-8258. Thomas H. Miller, Director. Information, (800) 669-7079.*
General e-mail, bva@bva.org
Web, www.bva.org

Chartered by Congress to assist veterans with claims for benefits. Seeks out blinded veterans to make them aware of benefits and services available to them.

National Industries for the Blind, *1901 N. Beauregard St., #200, Alexandria, VA 22311-1727; (703) 998-0770. Fax, (703) 671-9053. Pat Beattie, Director, Public Policy.*
Web, www.nib.org

Works to develop and improve opportunities for evaluating, training, employing, and advancing people who are blind and multidisabled blind. Develops business opportunities in the federal, state, and commercial marketplaces for organizations employing people with severe vision disabilities.

Prevention of Blindness Society, *1775 Church St. N.W. 20036; (202) 234-1010. Fax, (202) 234-1020. Michele Hartlove, Executive Director.*
General e-mail, mail@youreyes.org
Web, www.youreyes.org

Conducts preschool and elementary school screening program and glaucoma testing; provides information and referral service on eye health care; assists low-income persons in obtaining eye care and provides eyeglasses for a nominal fee to persons experiencing financial stress; conducts macular degeneration support group.

Deaf and Hearing Impaired

AGENCIES

General Services Administration (GSA), *Federal Relay Service, 10304 Eaton Pl., Fairfax, VA 22030; (703) 306-6308. Patricia Stevens, Program Manager. TTY, (800) 877-8845. Customer service, (800) 877-0996.*
Web, www.gsa.gov/frs

Assures that the federal telecommunications system is fully accessible to deaf, hearing-impaired, and speech-impaired individuals, including federal workers. Operates via relay, twenty-four hours a day, seven days a week. Produces a directory of TDD/TTY services within the federal government.

National Institute on Deafness and Other Communication Disorders *(National Institutes of Health),* *31 Center Dr., #3C02, MSC-2320, Bethesda, MD 20892-2320; (301) 402-0900. Fax, (301) 402-1590. Dr. James F. Battey Jr., Director. Information, (301) 496-7243. TTY, (301) 496-6596.*

Web, www.nidcd.nih.gov

Conducts and supports research and research training and disseminates information on hearing disorders and other communication processes, including diseases that affect hearing, balance, smell, taste, voice, speech, and language. Monitors international research.

NONPROFIT

Alexander Graham Bell Assn. for the Deaf and Hard of Hearing, *3417 Volta Pl. N.W. 20007-2778; (202) 337-5220. Fax, (202) 337-8314. Todd Houston, Executive Director. Main phone is voice and TTY accessible.*

General e-mail, info@agbell.org

Web, www.agbell.org

Provides hearing-impaired children in the United States and abroad with information and special education programs; works to improve employment opportunities for deaf persons; acts as a support group for parents of deaf persons.

American Academy of Audiology, *11730 Plaza America Dr., #300, Reston, VA 20190; (703) 790-8466. Fax, (703) 790-8631. Laura F. Doyle, Executive Director. Toll-free, (800) 222-2236.*

Web, www.audiology.org

Membership: audiologists. Provides consumer information on testing and treatment for hearing loss; sponsors research, awards, and continuing education for audiologists.

American Speech-Language Hearing Assn. (ASHA), *10801 Rockville Pike, Rockville, MD 20852; (301) 897-5700. Fax, (301) 571-0457. Frederick T. Spahr, Executive Director. Press, (301) 897-0156. TTY, (301) 897-0157. Toll-free hotline (except Alaska, Hawaii, and Maryland), (800) 638-8255 (voice and TTY accessible).*

General e-mail, actioncenter@asha.org

Web, www.asha.org

Membership: specialists in speech-language pathology and audiology. Sponsors professional education programs; acts as accrediting agent for graduate college programs and for public clinical education programs in speech-language pathology and audiology. Advocates the rights of the communicatively disabled; provides information on speech, hearing, and language problems. Provides referrals to speech-language pathologists and audiologists. Interests include national and international standards for bioacoustics and noise.

Better Hearing Institute, *515 King St., #420, Alexandria, VA 22314-3137; (703) 684-3391. Fax, (703) 684-6048. John Olive, Executive Director. Hearing helpline, (800) 327-9355. Main phone is voice and TTY accessible.*

Web, www.betterhearing.org

Educational organization that conducts national public information programs on hearing loss, hearing aids, and other treatments.

Gallaudet University, *800 Florida Ave. N.E. 20002-3695; (202) 651-5000. Fax, (202) 651-5508. I. King Jordan, President, (202) 651-5005. Phone numbers are voice and TTY accessible.*

Web, www.gallaudet.edu

Offers undergraduate, graduate, and doctoral degree programs for deaf, hard of hearing, and hearing students. Conducts research; maintains regional extension outreach centers and demonstration secondary, elementary, and preschool programs (Laurent Clerc National Deaf Education Center). Sponsors the Center for Global Education, National Deaf Education Network and Clearinghouse, and the Cochlear Implant Education Center.

Hearing Industries Assn., *515 King St., #420, Alexandria, VA 22314; (703) 684-5744. Fax, (703) 684-6048. Carole M. Rogin, President.*

Web, www.hearing.org

Membership: hearing aid manufacturers and companies that supply hearing aid components. Provides information on hearing loss and hearing aids.

Laurent Clerc National Deaf Education Center, *Publications and Information, 800 Florida Ave. N.E., #3400 20002-3695; (202) 651-5340 (Voice and TTY). Fax, (202) 651-5708. Margaret Hallau, Director. TTY, (800) 526-9105.*

General e-mail, Clearinghouse.Infotogo@gallaudet.edu

Web, clerccenter.gallaudet.edu/clearinghouse/index.html

Provides information on topics dealing with hearing loss and deafness for children and young adults up to age twenty-one. (Affiliated with Gallaudet University.)

National Assn. of the Deaf, *814 Thayer Ave., #250, Silver Spring, MD 20910-4500; (301) 587-1788. Fax, (301) 587-1791. Nancy J. Bloch, Executive Director. TTY, (301) 587-1789.*

General e-mail, nadinfo@nad.org

Web, www.nad.org

Safeguards the accessibility and civil rights of deaf and hard-of-hearing citizens in education, employment, health care, and telecommunications. Focuses on grassroots advocacy and empowerment, captioned media, deafness-related information and publications, legal assistance, policy development and research, public awareness, and youth leadership development.

Registry of Interpreters for the Deaf, *333 Commerce St., Alexandria, VA 22314; (703) 838-0030. Fax, (703) 838-0454. Ben Hall, President. TTY, (703) 838-0459.*
General e-mail, info@rid.org
Web, www.rid.org

Trains and certifies interpreters; maintains registry of certified interpreters; establishes certification standards. Sponsors training workshops and conferences.

Self Help for Hard of Hearing People, *7910 Woodmont Ave., #1200, Bethesda, MD 20814; (301) 657-2248. Fax, (301) 913-9413. Terry Portis, Executive Director. TTY, (301) 657-2249.*
General e-mail, national@shhh.org
Web, www.shhh.org

Promotes understanding of the nature, causes, and remedies of hearing loss. Provides hearing-impaired people with support and information. Seeks to educate the public about hearing loss and the problems of the hard of hearing. Provides travelers with information on assistive listening devices in museums, theaters, and places of worship.

Telecommunications for the Deaf, *8630 Fenton St., #604, Silver Spring, MD 20910; (301) 589-3786. Fax, (301) 589-3797. Claude L. Stout, Executive Director. TTY, (301) 589-3006. Voice via relay, (800) 735-2258.*
General e-mail, adminasst@tdi-online.org
Web, www.tdi-online.org

Membership: individuals, organizations, and businesses using text telephone (TTY) equipment. Provides information on TTY equipment. Interests include closed captioning for television, emergency access (911), TTY relay services, visual alerting systems, and TTY/computer conversion. Publishes a national TTY telephone directory.

Mental Disabilities

AGENCIES

Administration for Children and Families (ACF), *(Health and Human Services Dept.), Administration on Developmental Disabilities, 200 Independence Ave. S.W., #300F 20201; (202) 690-6590. Fax, (202) 690-6904. Patricia A. Morrissey, Commissioner. TTY, (202) 690-6415.*
Web, www.acf.hhs.gov/programs/add

Establishes state protection and advocacy systems for people with developmental disabilities, including persons with mental retardation, cerebral palsy, epilepsy, and autism; awards discretionary grants to university-affiliated programs and to programs of national significance. Administers formula grants to states for persons who incurred developmental disabilities before the age of twenty-two.

NONPROFIT

AAMR (American Assn. on Mental Retardation), *444 N. Capitol St. N.W., #846 20001-1512; (202) 387-1968. Fax, (202) 387-2193. Doreen Croser, Executive Director. Information, (800) 424-3688.*
Web, www.aamr.org

Membership: physicians, educators, administrators, social workers, psychologists, psychiatrists, lawyers, students, and others interested in mental retardation and related developmental disabilities. Provides information on legal rights, services, and facilities for people (including children) with mental retardation. Monitors international research.

The Arc, *Governmental Affairs, Washington Office, 1331 H St., #301 20005; (202) 783-2229. Fax, (202) 783-8250. Paul Marchand, Director.*
General e-mail, GAOinfo@thearc.org
Web, www.thearc.org

Membership: individuals interested in assisting people with mental retardation. Provides information on government programs and legislation concerning mental retardation; oversees and encourages support for local groups that provide direct services for people with mental retardation. (Headquarters in Silver Spring, Md.)

Autism Society of America, *7910 Woodmont Ave., #300, Bethesda, MD 20814-3067; (301) 657-0881. Fax, (301) 657-0869. Robert L. Beck, President. Information, (800) 328-8476.*
General e-mail, info@autism-society.org
Web, www.autism-society.org

Monitors legislation and regulations affecting support, education, training, research, and other services for individuals with autism. Offers referral service and information to the public.

Best Buddies International, *Washington Office, 401 9th St. N.W., #750 20004; (202) 266-2295. Fax, (202) 266-2260. Lisa Derx, Director. Information, (800) 892-8339.*
Web, www.bestbuddies.org

Volunteer organization that provides friends and jobs to people with intellectual disabilities worldwide. (Headquarters in Miami, Fla.)

International Assn. of Psychosocial Rehabilitation Services, *601 N. Hammonds Ferry Rd., #A, Linthicum, MD 21090; (410) 789-7054. Fax, (410) 789-7675. Ruth A. Hughes, Chief Executive Officer. TTY, (410) 730-1723.*
General e-mail, general@iapsrs.org
Web, www.iapsrs.org

Membership: agencies, mental health practitioners, policymakers, family groups, and consumer organizations. Supports the community adjustment of persons with psychiatric disabilities; promotes the role of rehabilitation in mental health systems; opposes discrimination based on mental disability.

Joseph P. Kennedy Jr. Foundation, *1325 G St. N.W., #500 20005-4709; (202) 393-1250. Fax, (202) 824-0351. Sue Swenson, Executive Director.*
Web, www.jpkf.org

Seeks to enhance the quality of life of persons with mental retardation and to prevent retardation by identifying and eliminating its causes. Awards grants for social services and medical research.

National Assn. of Protection and Advocacy Systems, *900 2nd St. N.E., #211 20002; (202) 408-9514. Fax, (202) 408-9520. Curtis Decker, Executive Director. TTY, (202) 408-9521.*
General e-mail, info@napas.org
Web, www.napas.org

Membership: agencies working for the rights of the mentally ill or developmentally disabled and clients of the vocational rehabilitation system. Provides state agencies with training and technical assistance; maintains an electronic mail network. Monitors legislation and regulations.

National Assn. of State Directors of Developmental Disability Services, *113 Oronoco St., Alexandria, VA 22314; (703) 683-4202. Fax, (703) 684-1395. Robert M. Gettings, Executive Director.*
Web, www.nasddds.org

Membership: chief administrators of state mental retardation programs. Coordinates exchange of information on mental retardation programs among the states; provides information on state programs.

National Children's Center, *6200 2nd St. N.W. 20011; (202) 722-2300. Fax, (202) 722-2383. Arthur Ginsberg, Executive Director.*
Web, www.washingtonpost.com/yp/ncc

Provides educational, social, and clinical services to infants, children, and adults with mental retardation and other developmental disabilities. Services provided through a 24-hour intensive treatment program, group

homes and independent living programs, educational services, adult treatment programs, and early intervention programs for infants with disabilities or infants at high risk. Operates a child development center for children with and without disabilities.

 HOMELESSNESS

AGENCIES

Education Dept., *Adult Education and Literacy, 330 C St. S.W., #4428 20202-7240 (mailing address: 400 Maryland Ave. S.W. 20202); (202) 205-8270. Fax, (202) 205-8973. Cheryl L. Keenan, Director. Literacy clearinghouse, (202) 205-9996.*
Web, www.ed.gov/offices/OVAE

Provides state and local agencies and community-based organizations with assistance in establishing education programs for homeless adults.

Education Dept., *Education for Homeless Children and Youth, 400 Maryland Ave. S.W., #3W214 20202; (202) 260-0994. Fax, (202) 260-7764. Gary Rutkin, Program Specialist, (202) 260-4412.*
Web, www.ed.gov

Provides formula grants to education agencies in the states and Puerto Rico to educate homeless children and youth and to establish an office of coordinator of education for homeless children and youth in each jurisdiction.

Emergency Food and Shelter National Board Program, *701 N. Fairfax St., #310, Alexandria, VA 22314-2064; (703) 706-9660. Fax, (703) 706-9677. Sharon Bailey, Director; Berl Jones, Program Chief, (202) 646-2778.*
Web, www.efsp.unitedway.org

Public/private partnership that administers the Emergency Food and Shelter Program under the McKinney Act. Gives supplemental assistance to programs that provide the homeless and persons in need with shelter, food, and support services.

Housing and Urban Development Dept. (HUD), *Community Planning and Development, 451 7th St. S.W., #7100 20410; (202) 708-2690. Fax, (202) 708-3336. Roy A. Bernardi, Assistant Secretary.*
Web, www.hud.gov

Gives supplemental assistance to facilities that aid the homeless; awards grants for innovative programs that address the needs of homeless families with children.

Housing and Urban Development Dept. (HUD), *Special Needs Assistance Programs, 451 7th St. S.W.,*

#7262 20410; (202) 708-4300. Fax, (202) 708-3617. *John D. Garrity, Director.*

Web, www.hud.gov

Advises and represents the secretary on homelessness matters; promotes cooperation among federal agencies on homelessness issues; coordinates assistance programs for the homeless under the McKinney Act. Trains HUD field staff in administering homelessness programs. Distributes funds to eligible nonprofit organizations, cities, counties, tribes, and territories for shelter, care, transitional housing, and permanent housing for the disabled homeless. Programs provide for acquisition and rehabilitation of buildings, prevention of homelessness, counseling, and medical care. Administers the Federal Surplus Property Program and spearheads the initiative to lease HUD-held homes to the homeless.

NONPROFIT

Housing Assistance Council, *1025 Vermont Ave. N.W., #606 20005-3516; (202) 842-8600. Fax, (202) 347-3441. Moises Loza, Executive Director. Information, (800) 989-4422.*

General e-mail, hac@ruralhome.org

Web, www.ruralhome.org

Provides low-income housing development groups in rural areas with seed money loans and technical assistance; assesses programs designed to respond to rural housing needs; makes recommendations for federal and state involvement; publishes technical guides and reports on rural housing issues.

National Alliance to End Homelessness, *1518 K St. N.W., #206 20005; (202) 638-1526. Fax, (202) 638-4664. Nan Roman, President.*

General e-mail, naeh@naeh.org

Web, www.endhomelessness.org

Seeks to form a corporate public-private partnership to alleviate problems of the homeless; promotes policies and programs that reduce the homeless population.

National Coalition for Homeless Veterans,
333½ Pennsylvania Ave. S.E. 20003-1148; (202) 546-1969. Fax, (202) 546-2063. Linda J. Boone, Executive Director.

General e-mail, nchv@nchv.org

Web, www.nchv.org

Provides technical assistance to service providers; advocates on behalf of homeless veterans.

National Coalition for the Homeless, *1012 14th St. N.W., #600 20005-3471; (202) 737-6444. Fax, (202) 737-6445. Donald Whitehead, Executive Director.*

General e-mail, info@nationalhomeless.org

Web, www.nationalhomeless.org

Advocacy network of persons who are or have been homeless, state and local coalitions, other activists, service providers, housing developers, and others. Seeks to create the systemic and attitudinal changes necessary to end homelessness. Works to meet the needs of persons who are homeless or at risk of becoming homeless.

National Law Center on Homelessness and Poverty, *1411 K St. N.W., #1400 20005; (202) 638-2535. Fax, (202) 628-2737. Maria Foscarinis, Executive Director.*

General e-mail, nlchp@nlchp.org

Web, www.nlchp.org

Legal advocacy group that works to protect and expand the rights of the homeless through impact litigation, and conducts research on homelessness issues. Acts as a clearinghouse for legal information and technical assistance. Monitors legislation and regulations.

Salvation Army, *615 Slaters Lane, Alexandria, VA 22314-0269 (mailing address: P.O. Box 269, Alexandria, VA 22313-0269); (703) 684-5500. Fax, (703) 684-3478. W. Todd Bassett, National Commander.*

Web, www.salvationarmyusa.org

International religious social welfare organization that provides the homeless with residences and social services, including counseling, emergency help, and employment services. (International headquarters in London.)

Share Our Strength, *733 15th St. N.W., #640 20005; (202) 393-2925. Fax, (202) 347-5868. Bill Shore, Executive Director. Information, (800) 969-4767.*

General e-mail, info@strength.org

Web, www.strength.org

Works to alleviate and prevent hunger and poverty in the United States and around the world. Meets immediate demands for food by providing food assistance; treats malnutrition and other consequences of hunger; promotes economic independence among people in need, while seeking long-term solutions to hunger and poverty. Helps mobilize industries, organizations, and individuals to contribute their talents to antihunger efforts.

U.S. Conference of Mayors, *Task Force on Hunger and Homelessness,* *1620 Eye St. N.W. 20006; (202) 861-6713. Fax, (202) 293-2352. Eugene T. Lowe, Assistant Executive Director.*

Web, www.usmayors.org/uscm

Tracks trends in hunger, homelessness, and community programs that address homelessness and hunger in U.S. cities; issues reports. Monitors legislation and regulations.

▦ SOCIAL SECURITY

AGENCIES

Employment Standards Administration *(Labor Dept.), Coal Mine Workers' Compensation, 200 Constitution Ave. N.W., #C3520 20210; (202) 693-0046. Fax, (202) 693-1395. James L. DeMarce, Director. Web, www.dol.gov/dol/esa*

Provides direction for administration of the black lung benefits program. Adjudicates claims filed on or after July 1, 1973; certifies these benefit payments and maintains black lung beneficiary rolls.

(For claims filed before July 1, 1973, contact Social Security Administration, Disability.)

Social Security Administration (SSA), *6401 Security Blvd., Baltimore, MD 21235; (410) 965-3120. Fax, (410) 966-1463. Jo Anne B. Barnhart, Commissioner; James B. Lockhart, Deputy Commissioner. Information, (800) 772-1213. Press, (410) 965-8904. TTY, (800) 325-0778. Web, www.ssa.gov*

Administers national Social Security programs and the Supplemental Security Income program.

Social Security Administration (SSA), *Central Operations, 1500 Woodlawn Dr., Baltimore, MD 21241; (410) 966-7000. Fax, (410) 966-6005. W. Burnell Hurt, Associate Commissioner. Information, (800) 772-1213.*

Reviews and authorizes claims for benefits under the disability insurance program and all claims for beneficiaries living abroad; certifies benefits payments; maintains beneficiary rolls.

Social Security Administration (SSA), *Disability, 3570 Annex Bldg., 6501 Security Blvd., Baltimore, MD 21235; (410) 965-3424. Fax, (410) 965-6503. Lenore Carlson, Associate Commissioner. Information, (410) 965-7700. Web, www.ssa.gov/disability*

Provides direction for administration of the disability insurance program, which is paid out of the Social Security Trust Fund. Administers disability and blindness provisions of the Supplemental Security Income (SSI) program. Responsible for claims filed under black lung benefits program before July 1, 1973.

Social Security Administration (SSA), *Hearings and Appeals, 5107 Leesburg Pike, #1600, Falls Church, VA 22041-3255; (703) 605-8200. Fax, (703) 605-8201. A. Jacy Thurmond Jr., Associate Commissioner. Web, www.ssa.gov*

Administers a nationwide system of administrative law judges who conduct hearings and decide appealed cases concerning benefits provisions. Reviews decisions for appeals council action, if necessary, and renders the secretary's final decision. Reviews benefits cases on health insurance, disability, retirement and survivors' benefits, and supplemental security income.

Social Security Administration (SSA), *Income Security Program, 6401 Security Blvd., #760, Baltimore, MD 21235; (410) 965-5961. Fax, (410) 965-8582. Nancy Veillon, Associate Commissioner.*

Develops policies and procedures for administering the retirement and survivors' insurance programs. Provides direction and technical guidance for administration of the Supplemental Security Income (SSI) program for the elderly, blind, and disabled. Provides guidance on administration of state supplementary benefits programs; monitors state compliance with mandatory minimum federal supplements.

Social Security Administration (SSA), *Operations, 6401 Security Blvd., West High Rise, #1204, Baltimore, MD 21235; (410) 965-3143. Fax, (410) 966-7941. Linda S. McMahon, Deputy Commissioner. Information, (800) 772-1213. TTY, (410) 965-4404.*

Issues Social Security numbers, maintains earnings and beneficiary records, authorizes claims, certifies benefits, and makes postadjudicative changes in beneficiary records for retirement, survivors', and disability insurance and black lung claims. Maintains toll-free number for workers who want information on future Social Security benefits.

Social Security Administration (SSA), *Research, Evaluation, and Statistics, 6401 Security Blvd., Operations Building, #4C-15, Baltimore, MD 21235; (410) 965-2841. Fax, (410) 965-3308. Susan Grad, Associate Commissioner (Acting). Publications, (202) 358-6263.*

Compiles statistics on beneficiaries; conducts research on the economic status of beneficiaries and the relationship between Social Security, the American people, and the economy; analyzes the effects of proposed Social Security legislation, especially on lower- and middle-income individuals and families; disseminates results of research and statistical programs through publications.

CONGRESS

General Accounting Office (GAO), *Education, Workforce, and Income Security, 441 G St. N.W., #5928 20548; (202) 512-7215. Cynthia Fagnoni, Managing Director.*

SOCIAL SECURITY ADMINISTRATION

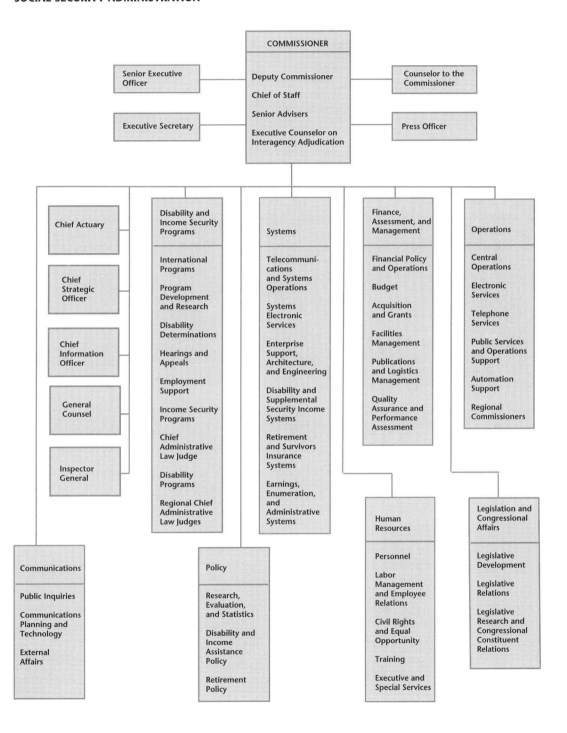

Web, www.gao.gov

Independent, nonpartisan agency in the legislative branch that audits, analyzes, and evaluates Health and Human Services Dept. programs, including Social Security; makes reports available to the public.

House Appropriations Committee, *Subcommittee on Labor, Health and Human Services, Education, and Related Agencies, 2358 RHOB 20515; (202) 225-3508. Fax, (202) 225-3509. Rep. Ralph Regula, R-Ohio, Chair; Craig Higgins, Staff Director.*
Web, www.house.gov/appropriations

Jurisdiction over legislation to appropriate funds for the Social Security Administration.

House Ways and Means Committee, *Subcommittee on Human Resources, B317 RHOB 20515; (202) 225-1025. Fax, (202) 225-9480. Rep. Wally Herger, R-Calif., Chair; Matt Weidinger, Staff Director.*
Web, waysandmeans.house.gov

Jurisdiction over legislation on supplemental security income for the elderly, blind, and disabled.

House Ways and Means Committee, *Subcommittee on Social Security, B316 RHOB 20515; (202) 225-9263. Fax, (202) 225-9480. Rep. E. Clay Shaw Jr., R-Fla., Chair; Kim Hildred, Staff Director.*
Web, waysandmeans.house.gov

Jurisdiction over Social Security disability and retirement and survivors' legislation.

Senate Appropriations Committee, *Subcommittee on Labor, Health and Human Services, Education, and Related Agencies, SD-184 20510; (202) 224-3471. Fax, (202) 224-8553. Sen. Arlen Specter, R-Pa., Chair; Bettilou Taylor, Clerk.*
Web, appropriations.senate.gov

Jurisdiction over legislation to appropriate funds for the Social Security Administration.

Senate Finance Committee, *Subcommittee on Social Security and Family Policy, SD-219 20510; (202) 224-4515. Sen. Rick Santorum, R-Pa., Chair; Kolan L. Davis, Staff Director.*
Web, finance.senate.gov

Holds hearings on supplemental security income for the elderly, blind, and disabled; Social Security disability; and retirement and survivors' legislation.

Senate Special Committee on Aging, *SD-G31 20510; (202) 224-5364. Fax, (202) 224-8660. Sen. Larry E. Craig, R-Idaho, Chair; Lupe Wissel, Staff Director.*
Web, aging.senate.gov

Studies and makes recommendations on Social Security and other retirement benefits for the elderly.

NONPROFIT

AARP, *601 E St. N.W. 20049; (202) 434-2277. Fax, (202) 434-2320. William D. Novelli, Chief Executive Officer. Library, (202) 434-6240. Press, (202) 434-2560. TTY, (202) 434-6561.*
Web, www.aarp.org

Membership organization that works to address the needs and interests of persons ages fifty and older through education, advocacy, and service. Monitors legislation and regulations and disseminates information on issues affecting older Americans, including issues related to Social Security. (Formerly the American Assn. of Retired Persons.)

National Academy of Social Insurance, *1776 Massachusetts Ave. N.W., #615 20036-1904; (202) 452-8097. Fax, (202) 452-8111. Pamela J. Larson, Executive Vice President.*
General e-mail, nasi@nasi.org
Web, www.nasi.org

Promotes research and education on Social Security, health care financing, and related public and private programs; assesses social insurance programs and their relationship to other programs; supports research and leadership development. Acts as a clearinghouse for social insurance information.

National Committee to Preserve Social Security and Medicare, *10 G St. N.E., #600 20002; (202) 216-0420. Fax, (202) 216-0451. Barbara Kenelly, President.*
Web, www.ncpssm.org

Educational and advocacy organization that focuses on Social Security and Medicare programs and on related income security and health issues. Interests include retirement income protection, health care reform, and the quality of life of seniors. Monitors legislation and regulations.

2030 Center, *1025 Connecticut Ave. N.W., #205 20036; (202) 822-6526. Fax, (202) 955-5606. Hans Riemer, Chair.*
General e-mail, 2030@2030.org
Web, www.2030.org

Public policy research and advocacy organization. Promotes policies that ensure the long-term viability of the Social Security system and expanded economic opportunities for younger Americans.

19 Transportation

AGENCIES

Architectural and Transportation Barriers Compliance Board (Access Board), *1331 F St. N.W., #1000 20004-1111; (202) 272-0080. Fax, (202) 272-0081. Lawrence W. Roffee, Executive Director. TTY, (202) 272-0082. Toll-free technical assistance, (800) 872-2253.*
General e-mail, info@access-board.gov
Web, www.access-board.gov

Enforces standards requiring that buildings and telecommunications and transportation systems be accessible to persons with disabilities; provides technical assistance and information on designing these facilities; sets accessibility guidelines for the Americans with Disabilities Act (ADA) and the Telecommunications Act of 1996.

Bureau of Customs and Border Protection *(Homeland Security Dept.), Field Operations, 1300 Pennsylvania Ave. N.W., #5.5C 20229; (202) 927-0774. Fax, (202) 927-0837. Jayson Ahern, Assistant Commissioner, (202)927-0100.*
Web, www.customs.gov

Enforces statutes relating to the processing and regulation of people, baggage, cargo, and mail in and out of the United States; assesses and collects customs duties, excise taxes, fees, and penalties due on imported merchandise; administers certain navigation laws.

Bureau of Transportation Statistics *(Transportation Dept.), 400 7th St. S.W., #3103 20590; (202) 366-1270. Fax, (202) 366-3640. Rick Kowaleski, Director (Acting). Information, (202) 366-3282.*
Web, www.bts.gov

Works to improve public awareness of the nation's transportation systems. Compiles, analyzes, and makes accessible information on transportation.

Census Bureau *(Commerce Dept.), Service Sector Statistics Division: Vehicle Inventory and Use Survey, Suitland and Silver Hill Rds., Suitland, MD 20746 (mailing address: MS 6500, Washington, DC 20233); (301) 457-2797. Fax, (301) 457-8345. David Lassman, Survey Statistician.*
Web, www.census.gov/econ/www/viusmain.html

Provides data and explains proper use of data for the bureau's Truck Inventory and Use Survey.

National Transportation Safety Board, *490 L'Enfant Plaza East S.W. 20594; (202) 314-6010. Fax, (202) 314-6018. Ellen G. Engelman, Chair.*
Web, www.ntsb.gov

Promotes transportation safety through independent investigations of accidents and other safety problems. Makes recommendations for safety improvement.

National Transportation Safety Board, *Research and Engineering, 490 L'Enfant Plaza East S.W. 20594; (202) 314-6500. Fax, (202) 314-6599. Vernon S. Ellingstad, Director.*
Web, www.ntsb.gov

Evaluates effectiveness of federal, state, and local safety programs. Identifies transportation safety issues not addressed by government or industry. Conducts studies on specific safety problems.

Office of Management and Budget (OMB), *(Executive Office of the President), Transportation, New Executive Office Bldg., #9002 20503; (202) 395-5704. Fax, (202) 395-4797. Steven Mertens, Chief.*
Web, www.whitehouse.gov/omb

Assists and advises the OMB director on budget preparation, proposed legislation, and evaluations of Transportation Dept. programs, policies, and activities.

Research and Special Programs Administration *(Transportation Dept.), 400 7th St. S.W., #8417 20590; (202) 366-4433. Fax, (202) 366-3666. Ellen G. Engleman, Administrator.*
Web, www.rspa.dot.gov

Coordinates research and development programs to improve safety of transportation systems; focus includes hazardous materials shipments, pipeline safety, and preparedness for transportation emergencies. Oversees Volpe National Transportation Systems Center in Cambridge, Mass., and the Transportation Safety Institute in Oklahoma City.

Research and Special Programs Administration *(Transportation Dept.), Emergency Transportation, 400 7th St. S.W., #8417 20590-0001; (202) 366-5270. Fax, (202) 366-3769. Janet Benini, Director (Acting).*
Web, www.rspa.dot.gov/oet

Develops, coordinates, and reviews transportation emergency preparedness programs for use in emergencies affecting national defense and in emergencies caused by natural disasters and crisis situations.

Research and Special Programs Administration *(Transportation Dept.), Innovation, Research, and Education, 400 7th St. S.W., #7108 20590; (202) 366-4434. Fax, (202) 366-3671. Timothy A. Klein, Associate Administrator.*
Web, www.rspa.dot.gov/dra

Supports transportation innovation research, engineering, education, and safety training. Focus includes

TRANSPORTATION DEPARTMENT

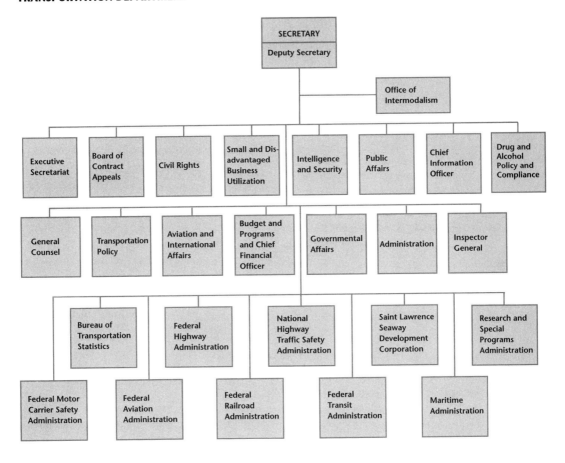

intermodal transportation; partnerships among government, universities, and industry; and economic growth and competitiveness through use of new technologies. Monitors international research.

Transportation Dept. (DOT), *400 7th St. S.W., #10200 20590; (202) 366-2222. Fax, (202) 366-7202. Norman Y. Mineta, Secretary; Michael P. Jackson, Deputy Secretary. Press, (202) 366-4570. Locator, (202) 366-4000.*
Web, www.dot.gov

Deals with most areas of transportation. Comprises the Bureau of Transportation Statistics, Federal Aviation Administration, Federal Highway Administration, Federal Motor Carrier Safety Administration, Federal Railroad Administration, Maritime Administration, National Highway Traffic Safety Administration, Research and Special Programs Administration, Federal Transit Administration, and Saint Lawrence Seaway Development Corp.

Transportation Dept. (DOT), *Aviation and International Affairs, 400 7th St. S.W., #10232 20590; (202) 366-4551. Fax, (202) 493-2005. Read C. Van de Water, Assistant Secretary.*
Web, www.dot.gov/ost/aviation

Formulates domestic aviation policy. Formulates international aviation, maritime, and across-the-border railroad and trucking policy.

Transportation Dept. (DOT), *Aviation Consumer Protection, 400 7th St. S.W., #4107 20590 (mailing address: Transportation Dept., C75, #4107 20590); (202) 366-2220. Fax, (202) 366-5944. Norman Strickman, Assistant Director.*
General e-mail, airconsumer@ost.dot.gov
Web, www.dot.gov/airconsumer

Refers consumer complaints to appropriate departmental offices; advises the secretary on consumer issues; coordinates citizen participation activities and promotes joint projects with consumer interest groups; serves as ombudsman for consumer protection affairs; publishes educational materials.

Transportation Dept. (DOT), *Environmental Policies Team,* 400 7th St. S.W., #10309 20590-0001; (202) 366-4861. Fax, (202) 366-7618. Camille H. Mittelholtz, Team Leader.
General e-mail, dot.comments@ost.dot.gov
Web, www.dot.gov

Develops environmental policy and makes recommendations to the secretary; monitors Transportation Dept. implementation of environmental legislation; serves as liaison with other federal agencies and state and local governments on environmental matters related to transportation.

Transportation Dept. (DOT), *Intelligence and Security,* 400 7th St. S.W., #10401 20590; (202) 366-6535. Fax, (202) 366-7261. Rear Adm. Stephen W. Rochon, Director.
Web, www.dot.gov

Advises the secretary on transportation intelligence and security policy. Acts as liaison with the intelligence community, federal agencies, corporations, and interest groups; administers counterterrorism strategic planning processes.

Transportation Dept. (DOT), *Transportation Policy Development,* 400 7th St. S.W., #10317 20590; (202) 366-4416. Fax, (202) 366-3393. Linda L. Lawson, Director.
Web, www.dot.gov

Develops, coordinates, and evaluates public policy with respect to safety, environmental, energy, and accessibility issues affecting all aspects of transportation. Assesses the economic and institutional implications of domestic transportation matters. Oversees legislative and regulatory proposals affecting transportation. Provides advice on research and development requirements. Develops policy proposals to improve the performance, safety, and efficiency of the transportation system.

CONGRESS

General Accounting Office (GAO), *Physical Infrastructure Team,* 441 G St. N.W., #2T23 20548; (202) 512-2834. Fax, (202) 512-3766. Michael Gryszkowiecz, Managing Director.
Web, www.gao.gov

Independent, nonpartisan agency in the legislative branch. Audits, analyzes, and evaluates performance of the Transportation Dept. and its component agencies; makes reports available to the public.

House Appropriations Committee, *Subcommittee on Transportation, Treasury, and Related Agencies,*
2358 RHOB 20515; (202) 225-2141. Fax, (202) 225-5895. Rep. Ernest Istook, R-Okla., Chair; Richard Efford, Clerk.
Web, www.house.gov/appropriations

Jurisdiction over legislation to appropriate funds for the Transportation Dept. and related agencies.

House Select Committee on Homeland Security, *Subcommittee on Infrastructure and Border Security,* 2402 RHOB 20515; (202) 226-8417. Rep. Dave Camp, R-Mich., Chair.
Web, hsc.house.gov

Jurisdiction includes border security, land borders, ports, and airspace; protection of highways, bridges, waterways, airports, and air transportation.

House Transportation and Infrastructure Committee, 2165 RHOB 20515; (202) 225-9446. Fax, (202) 225-6782. Rep. Don Young, R-Alaska, Chair; Lloyd Jones, Chief of Staff.
General e-mail, transcomm@mail.house.gov
Web, www.house.gov/transportation

Jurisdiction over legislation on transportation.

Senate Appropriations Committee, *Subcommittee on Transportation, Treasury, and General Government,* SD-196 20510; (202) 224-4869. Fax, (202) 228-0249. Sen. Richard C. Shelby, R-Ala., Chair; Paul Doerrer, Clerk.
Web, appropriations.senate.gov

Jurisdiction over legislation to appropriate funds for the Transportation Dept. and related agencies.

Senate Commerce, Science, and Transportation Committee, SD-508 20510; (202) 224-5115. Fax, (202) 224-1259. Sen. John McCain, R-Ariz., Chair; Jeanne Bumpus, Staff Director.
Web, commerce.senate.gov

Jurisdiction over legislation on transportation; oversight of the Transportation Dept. and the National Transportation Safety Board.

Senate Special Committee on Aging, SD-G31 20510; (202) 224-5364. Fax, (202) 224-8660. Sen. Larry E. Craig, R-Idaho, Chair; Lupe Wissel, Staff Director.
Web, aging.senate.gov

Studies and makes recommendations on the availability of transportation for the elderly.

NONPROFIT

American Public Works Assn., *Washington Office,* 1401 K St. N.W., 11th Floor 20005; (202) 408-9541. Fax, (202) 408-9542. Peter B. King, Executive Director.
General e-mail, apwa.dc@apwa.net
Web, www.apwa.net

Membership: engineers, architects, and others who maintain and manage public works facilities and services. Conducts research and promotes exchange of information on transportation and infrastructure-related issues. (Headquarters in Kansas City, Kan.)

Assn. for Transportation Law, Logistics, and Policy, *3 Church Circle, PMB 250, Annapolis, MD 21401; (410) 267-0023. Fax, (410) 267-7546. Michael Krissoff, Executive Director.*

Provides members with continuing educational development in transportation law and practice. Interests include railroad, motor, energy, pipeline, antitrust, labor, logistics, safety, environmental, air, and maritime matters.

Assn. of Metropolitan Planning Organizations, *Transportation, 1730 Rhode Island Ave. N.W., #608 20036; (202) 296-7051. Fax, (202) 296-7054. G. Alexander Taft, Director.*
General e-mail, staff@ampo.org
Web, www.ampo.org

Membership: more than 340 metropolitan planning organizations, which are councils of elected officials and transportation professionals that are responsible for planning local transportation systems. Provides a forum for professional and organizational development; sponsors conferences and training programs.

Institute of Navigation, *3975 University Dr., #390, Fairfax, VA 22030; (703) 383-9688. Fax, (703) 383-9689. Lisa Beaty, Director of Operations.*
General e-mail, membership@ion.org
Web, www.ion.org

Membership: individuals and organizations interested in navigation. Encourages research in navigation and establishment of uniform practices in navigation operations and education; conducts symposia on air, space, marine, and land navigation.

Institute of Transportation Engineers, *1099 14th St. N.W., #300 20005; (202) 289-0222. Fax, (202) 289-7722. Philip J. Caruso, Deputy Executive Director.*
General e-mail, ite_staff@ite.org
Web, www.ite.org

Membership: international professional transportation engineers. Conducts research, seminars, and training sessions; provides professional and scientific information on transportation standards and recommended practices.

International Brotherhood of Teamsters, *25 Louisiana Ave. N.W. 20001; (202) 624-6800. Fax, (202) 624-6918. James P. Hoffa, President.*

Web, www.teamster.org

Membership: more than 1.4 million workers in the transportation and construction industries, factories, offices, hospitals, warehouses, and other workplaces. Helps members negotiate pay, benefits, and better working conditions; conducts training programs and workshops. Monitors legislation and regulations. (Affiliated with the AFL-CIO.)

National Defense Transportation Assn., *50 S. Pickett St., #222, Alexandria, VA 22304-7296; (703) 751-5011. Fax, (703) 823-8761. Kenneth Wykle, President.*
Web, www.ndtahq.com

Membership: transportation users, manufacturers, and mode carriers; information technology firms; and related military, government, and civil interests worldwide. Promotes a strong U.S. transportation capability through coordination of private industry, government, and the military.

National Research Council (NRC), *Transportation Research Board, 500 5th St. N.W. 20001; (202) 334-2933. Fax, (202) 334-2003. Robert E. Skinner Jr., Executive Director. Information, (202) 334-2933. Library, (202) 334-2989. Publications, (202) 334-3213. Toll-free, (800) 424-9818.*
Web, www.nationalacademies.org/trb

Promotes research in transportation systems planning and administration and in the design, construction, maintenance, and operation of transportation facilities. Provides information to state and national highway and transportation departments; operates research information services; conducts special studies, conferences, and workshops; publishes technical reports. Library open to the public by appointment.

Rebuild America Coalition, *c/o American Public Works Assn., 1401 K St. N.W., 11th Floor 20005; (202) 408-9541. Fax, (202) 408-9542. Jim Fahey, Coalition Manager.*
Web, www.rebuildamerica.org

Coalition of public and private organizations concerned with maintaining the infrastructure of the United States. Advocates government encouragement of innovative technology, financing, and public-private partnerships to build and rebuild public facilities, including highways, ports, airports, and transit systems.

Sheet Metal Workers' International Assn., *1750 New York Ave. N.W. 20006; (202) 783-5880. Fax, (202) 662-0880. Michael J. Sullivan, General President.*
Web, www.smwia.org

Membership: more than 150,000 U.S. and Canadian workers in the building and construction trades, manufacturing, and the railroad and shipyard industries. Assists members with contract negotiation and grievances; conducts training programs and workshops. Monitors legislation and regulations. (Affiliated with the Sheet Metal and Air Conditioning Contractors' Assn., the AFL-CIO, and the Canadian Labour Congress.)

Surface Transportation Policy Project, *1100 17th St. N.W., 10th Floor 20036; (202) 466-2636. Fax, (202) 466-2247. Anne P. Canby, President.*
General e-mail, stpp@transact.org
Web, www.transact.org

Advocates transportation policy and investments that conserve energy, protect environmental and aesthetic quality, strengthen the economy, promote social equity, and make communities more livable.

Union of Concerned Scientists, *Government Relations, Washington Office, 1707 H St. N.W., #600 20006-3919; (202) 223-6133. Fax, (202) 223-6162. Alden Meyer, Director; Todd Perry, Washington Representative for Arms Control and International Security.*
General e-mail, ucs@ucsusa.org
Web, www.ucsusa.org

Develops and promotes market-based strategies to reduce the adverse environmental, economic, and public health effects of the U.S. transportation system. Advocates price incentives to promote transportation reform; development of cleaner, more fuel-efficient vehicles; and advancement of transportation technology and alternative fuels. (Headquarters in Cambridge, Mass.)

United Transportation Union, *Washington Office, 304 Pennsylvania Ave. S.E. 20003; (202) 543-7714. Fax, (202) 543-0015. James M. Brunkenhoefer, Legislative Director.*
General e-mail, utunld@aol.com
Web, www.utu.org

Membership: approximately 150,000 workers in the transportation industry. Helps members negotiate pay, benefits, and better working conditions; conducts training programs and workshops. Monitors legislation and regulations. (Headquarters in Cleveland, Ohio.)

Freight and Intermodalism

AGENCIES

Federal Railroad Administration *(Transportation Dept.), Policy and Program Development, 1120 Vermont Ave. N.W., #7075 20590 (mailing address: 400 7th St. S.W., Stop 15 20590); (202) 493-6400. Fax, (202) 493-6401. Vacant, Associate Administrator.*
Web, www.fra.dot.gov

Promotes intermodal movement of freight involving rail transportation; studies economics and industry practices.

Maritime Administration *(Transportation Dept.), Intermodal Development, 400 7th St. S.W., #7209 20590; (202) 366-8888. Fax, (202) 366-6988. Richard L. Walker, Director.*
Web, marad.dot.gov

Promotes development and improved use of marine-related intermodal transportation systems; provides technical information and advice to other agencies and organizations concerned with intermodal development.

Surface Transportation Board *(Transportation Dept.), 1925 K St. N.W., #810 20423-0001; (202) 565-1510. Fax, (202) 565-9004. Roger Nober, Chair; Wayne O. Burkes, Vice Chair. Information, (202) 565-1674.*
Web, www.stb.dot.gov

Regulates rates for water transportation and intermodal connections in noncontiguous domestic trade (between the mainland and Alaska, Hawaii, or U.S. territories).

Transportation Dept. (DOT), *Intermodalism, 400 7th St. S.W., #6316 20590; (202) 366-5781. Fax, (202) 366-0263. Richard Biter, Deputy Director.*
Web, www.dot.gov

Coordinates departmental efforts to develop an intermodal transportation system to move people and goods; promotes energy efficiency and optimal use of national transportation resources.

NONPROFIT

American Moving and Storage Assn., *1611 Duke St., Alexandria, VA 22314; (703) 683-7410. Fax, (703) 683-7527. Joseph Harrison, President.*
Web, www.moving.org

Represents members' views before the Transportation Dept. and other government agencies. Conducts certification and training programs. Provides financial support for research on the moving and storage industry.

Distribution and LTL Carriers Assn., *2200 Mill Rd., #600, Alexandria, VA 22314; (703) 838-1806. Fax, (703) 684-8143. Kevin M. Williams, President.*
General e-mail, dltlca@aol.com
Web, www.dltlca.org

Membership: movers of general freight. Provides networking opportunities; conducts workshops and seminars. Monitors legislation and regulations.

Intermodal Assn. of North America, *7501 Greenway Center Dr., #720, Greenbelt, MD 20770; (301) 982-3400. Fax, (301) 982-4815. Joni Casey, President.*

General e-mail, IANA@intermodal.org

Web, www.intermodal.org

Membership: railroads, stacktrain operators, water carriers, motor carriers, marketing companies, and suppliers to the intermodal industry. Promotes intermodal transportation of freight. Monitors legislation and regulations.

National Assn. of Chemical Distributors (NACD), *1560 Wilson Blvd., #1250, Arlington, VA 22209; (703) 527-6223. Fax, (703) 527-7747. James L. Kolstad, President.*

General e-mail, publicaffairs@nacd.com

Web, www.nacd.com

Membership: firms involved in purchasing, processing, blending, storing, transporting, and marketing of chemical products. Provides members with information on such topics as training, safe handling and transport of chemicals, liability insurance, and environmental issues. Manages the NACD Educational Foundation. Monitors legislation and regulations.

National Customs Brokers and Forwarders Assn. of America, *1200 18th St. N.W., #901 20036; (202) 466-0222. Fax, (202) 466-0226. Barbara Reilly, Executive Vice President.*

General e-mail, staff@ncbfaa.org

Web, www.ncbfaa.org

Membership: customs brokers and freight forwarders in the United States. Fosters information exchange within the industry. Monitors legislation and regulations.

National Industrial Transportation League, *1700 N. Moore St., #1900, Arlington, VA 22209-1904; (703) 524-5011. Fax, (703) 524-5017. Peter Gattie, President (Acting).*

General e-mail, info@nitl.org

Web, www.nitl.org

Membership: air, water, and surface shippers and receivers, including industries, corporations, chambers of commerce, and trade associations. Monitors legislation and regulations.

AIR TRANSPORTATION

AGENCIES

Civil Air Patrol, *National Capital Wing, Washington Office,* Bolling Air Force Base, 200 McChord St., #122

20032-0000; (202) 767-4405. Fax, (202) 767-5695. Col. Franklin F. McConnell Jr., Wing Commander.

Official civilian auxiliary of the U.S. Air Force. Primary function is to conduct search-and-rescue missions for the Air Force. Maintains an aerospace education program for adults and a cadet program for junior and senior high school students. (Headquarters at Maxwell Air Force Base, Ala.)

Federal Aviation Administration (FAA), *(Transportation Dept.), 800 Independence Ave. S.W., #1010A 20591; (202) 267-3111. Fax, (202) 267-5047. Marion C. Blakey, Administrator. Press, (202) 267-3883.*

Web, www.faa.gov

Regulates air commerce to improve aviation safety; promotes development of a national system of airports; develops and operates a common system of air traffic control and air navigation for both civilian and military aircraft; prepares the annual National Aviation System Plan.

Federal Aviation Administration (FAA), *(Transportation Dept.), Aviation Policy and Plans, 800 Independence Ave. S.W., #939, APO-1 20591; (202) 267-3274. Fax, (202) 267-3278. John M. Rodgers, Director.*

Web, www.api.hq.faa.gov

Responsible for economic and regulatory policy and analysis, aviation activity forecasts, and strategic planning within the FAA.

Federal Aviation Administration (FAA), *(Transportation Dept.), Environment and Energy, 800 Independence Ave. S.W., #900W 20591; (202) 267-3576. Fax, (202) 267-5594. Carl E. Burleson, Director.*

Web, www.faa.aee.gov

Responsible for environmental affairs and energy conservation for aviation, including implementation and administration of various aviation-related environmental acts.

Federal Aviation Administration (FAA), *(Transportation Dept.), International Aviation, 800 Independence Ave. S.W., #1028, AIA-1 20591; (202) 267-3213. Fax, (202) 267-5032. Ava L. Wilkerson, Director.*

Web, www.faa.gov

Coordinates all activities of the FAA that involve foreign relations; acts as liaison with the State Dept. and other agencies concerning international aviation; provides other countries with technical assistance on civil aviation problems; formulates international civil aviation policy for the United States.

Federal Aviation Administration (FAA), *(Transportation Dept.), Research and Acquisitions, 800 Inde-*

pende Ave. S.W., #1019, ARA-1 20591; (202) 267-7222. Fax, (202) 267-5085. Charles E. Keegan, Associate Administrator.

Web, www.faa.gov/ara/arahome.htm

Advises and assists in developing concepts for applying new technologies to meet long-range national airspace system requirements and for system acquisition, engineering, and management activities.

Federal Aviation Administration (FAA), *(Transportation Dept.), Statistics and Forecast,* 800 Independence Ave. S.W., #935, APO-110 20591; (202) 267-3355. Fax, (202) 267-5370. Robert L. Bowles, Manager.

Web, www.faa.gov

Maintains statistics relating to civil aircraft, airports, and air personnel, including age and type of pilots, passenger data, activity counts at FAA air traffic control facilities, and related information. Forecasts demand at FAA facilities and demand for commercial and general aviation sectors; holds annual forecast conference.

Federal Aviation Administration (FAA), *(Transportation Dept.), System Architecture and Investment Analysis,* 1250 Maryland Ave. S.W. 20202-5175 (mailing address: 800 Independence Ave. S.W., ASD-1 20591); (202) 385-7100. Fax, (202) 385-7105. John Scardina, Director.

Web, www.faa.gov

Advises and assists in developing advanced technologies to meet National Airspace System Development requirements. Works with internal FAA customers, other government agencies, and the aviation industry to understand and respond to user requirements.

Justice Dept. (DOJ), *Civil Division: Torts Branch, Aviation/Admiralty Litigation,* 1425 New York Ave. N.W., #10100 20530 (mailing address: P.O. Box 14271 20044-4271); (202) 616-4000. Fax, (202) 616-4002. Gary W. Allen, Director.

Web, www.usdoj.gov

Represents the federal government in civil suits arising from aviation incidents and accidents. Handles tort litigation for the government's varied activities in the operation of the air traffic control system, the regulation of air commerce, weather services, aeronautical charting, and the government's operation of its own civil and military aircraft.

National Aeronautics and Space Administration (NASA), *Aerospace Technology,* 300 E St. S.W., #6A70 20546 (mailing address: NASA Headquarters, Mail Code R 20546); (202) 358-4600. Fax, (202) 358-2920. Murray S. Hirschbein, Associate Administrator.

Web, www.aero-space.nasa.gov

Conducts research in aerodynamics, materials, structures, avionics, propulsion, high performance computing, human factors, aviation safety, and space transportation in support of national space and aeronautical research and technology goals. Manages the following NASA research centers: Ames (Moffett, Calif.); Dryden (Edwards, Calif.); Langley (Hampton, Va.); and Glenn (Cleveland, Ohio).

National Air and Space Museum *(Smithsonian Institution),* 6th St. and Independence Ave. S.W. 20560-0310; (202) 633-2350. Fax, (202) 357-2426. Gen. John R. Dailey, Director. Library, (202) 633-2316. TTY, (202) 357-1505. Education office, (202) 633-2540. Tours, (202) 357-1400.

Web, www.nasm.si.edu

Maintains exhibits and collections on aeronautics, pioneers of flight, and early aircraft through modern air technology. Library open to the public by appointment.

National Mediation Board, 1301 K St. N.W., #250E 20572; (202) 692-5000. Fax, (202) 692-5080. Francis J. Duggan, Chair; Stephen E. Crable, Chief of Staff, (202) 692-5030. Information, (202) 692-5000. Press, (202) 692-5050. TTY, (202) 692-5001.

Web, www.nmb.gov

Mediates labor disputes in the airline industry; determines and certifies labor representatives for the industry.

Transportation Dept. (DOT), *Airline Information,* 400 7th St. S.W., #4125, MC K-14 20590; (202) 366-9059. Fax, (202) 366-3383. Donald W. Bright, Assistant Director of Airline Information.

Web, www.bts.gov/oai

Develops, interprets, and enforces accounting and reporting regulations for the aviation industry; issues air carrier reporting instructions, waivers, and due-date extensions.

Transportation Dept. (DOT), *Aviation Analysis,* 400 7th St. S.W., #6401, X-50 20590; (202) 366-5903. Fax, (202) 366-7638. Randall D. Bennett, Director.

Web, www.dot.gov

Analyzes essential air service needs of communities; directs subsidy policy and programs; guarantees air service to small communities; conducts research for the department on airline mergers, international route awards, and employee protection programs; administers the air carrier fitness provisions of the Federal Aviation Act; registers domestic and foreign air carriers; enforces charter regulations for tour operators.

Transportation Dept. (DOT), *Aviation and International Affairs,* 400 7th St. S.W., #10232 20590; (202) 366-

4551. Fax, (202) 493-2005. Read C. Van de Water, Assistant Secretary.

Web, www.dot.gov/ost/aviation

Formulates domestic and international aviation policy. Assesses the performance of the U.S. aviation network in meeting public needs. Studies the social and economic conditions of the aviation industry, including airline licensing, antitrust concerns, and the effect of government policies.

Transportation Dept. (DOT), *Aviation Consumer Protection,* 400 7th St. S.W., #4107 20590 (mailing address: Transportation Dept., C75, #4107 20590); (202) 366-2220. Fax, (202) 366-5944. Norman Strickman, Assistant Director.

General e-mail, airconsumer@ost.dot.gov

Web, www.dot.gov/airconsumer

Addresses complaints about airline service and consumer-protection matters. Conducts investigations, provides assistance, and reviews regulations affecting air carriers.

Transportation Dept. (DOT), *Financial Information Technology,* 400 7th St. S.W., #9228, JA-20 20590; (202) 366-1496. Fax, (202) 366-3530. Vacant, Director.

Web, www.dot.gov

Provides auditing services for airline economic programs.

CONGRESS

House Appropriations Committee, *Subcommittee on Transportation, Treasury, and Related Agencies,* 2358 RHOB 20515; (202) 225-2141. Fax, (202) 225-5895. Rep. Ernest Istook, R-Okla., Chair; Richard Efford, Clerk.

Web, www.house.gov/appropriations

Jurisdiction over legislation to appropriate funds for the Federal Aviation Administration.

House Science Committee, *Subcommittee on Environment, Technology, and Standards,* 2319 RHOB 20515; (202) 225-8844. Fax, (202) 225-4438. Rep. Vernon J. Ehlers, R-Mich., Chair; Eric Webster, Staff Director.

General e-mail, science@mail.house.gov

Web, www.house.gov/science

Jurisdiction over legislation on civil aviation research and development, including research programs of the Federal Aviation Administration.

House Science Committee, *Subcommittee on Space and Aeronautics,* B374 RHOB 20515; (202) 225-7858. Fax, (202) 225-6415. Rep. Dana Rohrabacher, R-Calif., Chair; Bill Adkins, Staff Director.

General e-mail, science@mail.house.gov

Web, www.house.gov/science

Legislative jurisdiction over the Transportation Dept. (relating to space activities and aeronautics) and the National Aeronautics and Space Administration.

House Select Committee on Homeland Security, *Subcommittee on Infrastructure and Border Security,* 2402 RHOB 20515; (202) 226-8417. Rep. Dave Camp, R-Mich., Chair.

Web, hsc.house.gov

Jurisdiction includes the safety and security of air space, airports, and air transportation.

House Transportation and Infrastructure Committee, *Subcommittee on Aviation,* 2251 RHOB 20515; (202) 226-3220. Fax, (202) 225-4629. Rep. John L. Mica, R-Fla., Chair; David Schaffer, Counsel.

General e-mail, transcomm@mail.house.gov

Web, www.house.gov/transportation

Jurisdiction over legislation on civil aviation, including airport-improvement funding, airline deregulation, safety issues, the National Transportation Safety Board, and the Federal Aviation Administration (except research and development). Jurisdiction over aviation noise pollution legislation.

Senate Appropriations Committee, *Subcommittee on Transportation, Treasury, and General Government,* SD-196 20510; (202) 224-4869. Fax, (202) 228-0249. Sen. Richard C. Shelby, R-Ala., Chair; Paul Doerrer, Clerk.

Web, appropriations.senate.gov

Jurisdiction over legislation to appropriate funds for the Federal Aviation Administration.

Senate Commerce, Science, and Transportation Committee, SD-508 20510; (202) 224-5115. Fax, (202) 224-1259. Sen. John McCain, R-Ariz., Chair; Jeanne Bumpus, Staff Director.

Web, commerce.senate.gov

Jurisdiction over legislation on the National Aeronautics and Space Administration, including nonmilitary aeronautical research and development.

Senate Commerce, Science, and Transportation Committee, *Subcommittee on Aviation,* SH-427 20510; (202) 224-4852. Fax, (202) 228-0326. Sen. Trent Lott, R-Miss., Chair; Rob Chamberlin, Senior Counsel.

Web, commerce.senate.gov

Jurisdiction over legislation on civil aviation, including airport-improvement funding, airline deregulation, safety issues, research and development, the National Transportation Safety Board, and the Federal Aviation Administration. Jurisdiction over aviation noise pollution legislation.

NONPROFIT

Aeronautical Repair Station Assn., *121 N. Henry St., Alexandria, VA 22314-2903; (703) 739-9543. Fax, (703) 739-9488. Sarah MacLeod, Executive Director.*
General e-mail, arsa@arsa.org
Web, www.arsa.org

Membership: Federal Aviation Administration–certificated repair stations; associate members are suppliers and distributors of components and parts. Works to improve relations between repair stations and manufacturers. Interests include establishing uniformity in the application, interpretation, and enforcement of FAA regulations. Monitors legislation and regulations.

Aerospace Education Foundation, *1501 Lee Hwy., Arlington, VA 22209; (703) 247-5839. Fax, (703) 247-5853. Donald L. Peterson, Executive Director. Information, (800) 727-3337.*
General e-mail, aefstaff@aef.org
Web, www.aef.org

Promotes knowledge and appreciation of U.S. civilian and military aerospace development and history. (Affiliated with the Air Force Assn.)

Aerospace Industries Assn. (AIA), *1000 Wilson Blvd., #1700, Arlington, VA 22209; (703) 358-1000. Fax, (703) 358-1012. John W. Douglass, President. Press, (703) 358-1076.*
General e-mail, aia@aia-aerospace.org
Web, www.aia-aerospace.org

Represents U.S. manufacturers of commercial, military, and business aircraft; helicopters; aircraft engines; missiles; spacecraft; and related components and equipment. Interests include international standards and trade.

AIR Conference (Airline Industrial Relations Conference), *1300 19th St. N.W., #750 20036-1651; (202) 861-7550. Fax, (202) 861-7557. Robert J. DeLucia, Vice President.*
General e-mail, office@aircon.org
Web, www.aircon.org

Membership: domestic and international scheduled air carriers. Monitors developments and collects data on trends in airline labor relations.

Air Line Pilots Assn. International, *535 Herndon Parkway, Herndon, VA 20170; (703) 689-2270. Fax, (703) 689-4370. Duane E. Woerth, President. Press, (703) 481-4440.*
Web, www.alpa.org

Membership: airline pilots in the United States and Canada. Promotes air travel safety; assists investigations of aviation accidents. Monitors legislation and regulations. (Affiliated with the AFL-CIO.)

Air Transport Assn. of America, *1301 Pennsylvania Ave. N.W., #1100 20004; (202) 626-4000. Fax, (202) 626-4166. Carol B. Hallett, President.*
General e-mail, ata@airlines.org
Web, www.airlines.org

Membership: U.S. scheduled air carriers. Promotes aviation safety and the facilitation of air transportation for passengers and cargo. Monitors legislation and regulations.

American Helicopter Society, *217 N. Washington St., Alexandria, VA 22314; (703) 684-6777. Fax, (703) 739-9279. Morris E. Rhett Flater, Executive Director.*
General e-mail, staff@vtol.org
Web, www.vtol.org

Membership: individuals and organizations interested in vertical flight. Acts as an information clearinghouse for technical data on helicopter design improvement, aerodynamics, and safety. Awards the Vertical Flight Foundation Scholarship to students interested in helicopter technology.

American Institute of Aeronautics and Astronautics (AIAA), *1801 Alexander Bell Dr., #500, Reston, VA 20191; (703) 264-7500. Fax, (703) 264-7551. Cort Durocher, Executive Director. Information, (800) 639-2422.*
General e-mail, custserv@aiaa.org
Web, www.aiaa.org

Membership: engineers, scientists, and students in the fields of aeronautics and astronautics. Holds workshops on aerospace technical issues for congressional subcommittees; sponsors international conferences. Offers computerized database through its Technical Information Service.

AOPA Legislative Affairs, *Washington Office, 601 Pennsylvania Ave. N.W., #875 South Bldg. 20004; (202) 737-7950. Fax, (202) 737-7951. Julia Krauss, Vice President.*
Web, www.aopa.org

Membership: owners and pilots of general aviation aircraft. Washington office monitors legislation and regulations. Headquarters office provides members with maps, trip planning, speakers bureau, and other services; issues airport directory and handbook for pilots; sponsors the Air Safety Foundation. (Headquarters in Frederick, Md.)

Assn. of Flight Attendants, *1275 K St. N.W., #500 20005-4006; (202) 712-9799. Fax, (202) 712-9798. Patricia A. Friend, President.*

General e-mail, afatalk@afanet.org

Web, www.afanet.org

Membership: approximately 47,000 flight attendants. Helps members negotiate pay, benefits, and better working conditions; conducts training programs and workshops. Monitors legislation and regulations. (Affiliated with the AFL-CIO.)

Aviation Consumer Action Project, *529 14th St. N.W., #923 20045 (mailing address: P.O. Box 19029 20036); (202) 638-4000. Fax, (202) 638-0746. Paul S. Hudson, Executive Director.*

General e-mail, acap1971@aol.com

Web, www.acap1971.org

Consumer advocacy organization that represents interests of airline passengers before the Federal Aviation Administration on safety issues and before the Transportation Dept. on economic and regulatory issues; testifies before Congress.

Cargo Airline Assn., *1220 19th St. N.W., #400 20036; (202) 293-1030. Fax, (202) 293-4377. Stephen A. Alterman, President.*

Membership: cargo airlines and other firms interested in the development and promotion of air freight.

General Aviation Manufacturers Assn., *1400 K St. N.W., #801 20005; (202) 393-1500. Fax, (202) 842-4063. Edward M. Bolen, President.*

General e-mail, info@generalaviation.org

Web, www.generalaviation.org

Membership: manufacturers of business, commuter, and personal aircraft and manufacturers of engines, avionics, and equipment. Monitors legislation and regulations; sponsors safety and public information programs. Interests include international affairs.

Helicopter Assn. International, *1635 Prince St., Alexandria, VA 22314; (703) 683-4646. Fax, (703) 683-4745. Roy Resavage, President.*

General e-mail, rotor@rotor.com

Web, www.rotor.com

Membership: owners, manufacturers, and operators of helicopters, and affiliated companies in the civil helicopter industry. Provides information on use and operation of helicopters; offers business management and aviation safety courses; sponsors annual industry exposition. Monitors legislation and regulations.

International Assn. of Machinists and Aerospace Workers, *9000 Machinists Pl., Upper Marlboro, MD*

20772-2687; (301) 967-4500. Fax, (301) 967-4588. Thomas Buffenbarger, President.

Web, www.iamaw.org

Membership: machinists in more than 200 industries. Helps members negotiate pay, benefits, and better working conditions; conducts training programs and workshops. Monitors legislation and regulations. (Affiliated with the AFL-CIO, the Canadian Labour Congress, the Railway Labor Executives Assn., the International Metalworkers Federation, and the International Transport Workers' Federation.)

National Aeronautic Assn., *1815 N. Fort Myer Dr., #500, Arlington, VA 22209; (703) 527-0226. Fax, (703) 527-0229. Donald J. Koranda, President.*

General e-mail, naa@naa-usa.org

Web, www.naa-usa.org

Membership: persons interested in development of general and sporting aviation. Supervises sporting aviation competitions; oversees and approves official U.S. aircraft, aeronautics, and astronautics records. Interests include aeromodeling, aerobatics, helicopters, ultralights, home-built aircraft, parachuting, soaring, hang gliding, and ballooning. Serves as U.S. representative to the International Aeronautical Federation in Lausanne, Switzerland.

National Agricultural Aviation Assn., *1005 E St. S.E. 20003; (202) 546-5722. Fax, (202) 546-5726. Andrew Moore, Executive Director.*

General e-mail, information@agaviation.org

Web, www.agaviation.org

Membership: qualified agricultural pilots; operating companies that seed, fertilize, and spray land by air; and allied industries. Monitors legislation and regulations.

National Air Carrier Assn., *910 17th St. N.W., #800 20006; (202) 833-8200. Fax, (202) 659-9479. Juan Priddy, President.*

Web, www.naca.cc

Membership: air carriers certified for charter and scheduled operations. Monitors legislation and regulations.

National Air Transportation Assn., *4226 King St., Alexandria, VA 22302-1507; (703) 845-9000. Fax, (703) 845-8176. James K. Coyne, President. Information, (800) 808-6282.*

General e-mail, info@nata-online.org

Web, www.nata-online.org

Membership: companies that provide on-demand air charter, aircraft sales, flight training, maintenance and repair, avionics, and other services. Manages education foundation; compiles statistics; provides business assistance programs. Monitors legislation and regulations.

National Assn. of State Aviation Officials,
8401 Colesville Rd., #505, Silver Spring, MD 20910; (301) 588-0587. Fax, (301) 585-1803. Henry M. Ogrodzinski, President.
Web, www.nasao.org

Membership: state aeronautics agencies that deal with aviation issues, including regulation. Seeks uniform aviation laws; manages an aviation research and education foundation.

National Business Aviation Assn., *1200 18th St. N.W., #400 20036; (202) 783-9000. Fax, (202) 331-8364. John W. Olcott, President.*
General e-mail, info@nbaa.org
Web, www.nbaa.org

Membership: companies owning and operating aircraft for business use, suppliers, and maintenance and air fleet service companies. Conducts seminars and workshops in business aviation management. Sponsors annual civilian aviation exposition. Monitors legislation and regulations.

Regional Airline Assn., *2025 M St. N.W., #800 20036; (202) 367-1170. Fax, (202) 367-2170. Deborah McElroy, President.*
General e-mail, raa@dc.sba.com
Web, www.raa.org

Membership: regional airlines that provide passenger, scheduled cargo, and mail service. Issues annual report on the industry.

RTCA, *1828 L St. N.W., #805 20036; (202) 833-9339. Fax, (202) 833-9434. David S. Watrous, President.*
General e-mail, info@rtca.org
Web, www.rtca.org

Membership: federal agencies, aviation organizations, and commercial firms interested in aeronautical systems. Develops and publishes standards for aviation, including minimum operational performance standards for specific equipment; conducts research, makes recommendations, and issues reports on the field of aviation electronics and telecommunications. (Formerly the Radio Technical Commission for Aeronautics.)

Airports

AGENCIES

Animal and Plant Health Inspection Service (APHIS), *(Agriculture Dept.), Wildlife Services, 1400 Independence Ave. S.W., #1624S 20250-3402; (202) 720-*
2054. Fax, (202) 690-0053. William H. Clay, Deputy Administrator.
Web, www.aphis.usda.gov/ws

Works to minimize damage caused by wildlife to human health and safety. Interests include aviation safety; works with airport managers to reduce the risk of bird strikes. Oversees the National Wildlife Research Center in Ft. Collins, Colo.

Bureau of Land Management (BLM), *(Interior Dept.), Lands and Realty, 1620 L St. N.W. 20240 (mailing address: 1849 C St. N.W., MC 1000LS 20240); (202) 452-7773. Fax, (202) 452-7708. Donald A. Buhler, Manager (Acting).*
Web, www.blm.gov

Operates the Airport Lease Program, which leases public lands for use as public airports.

Federal Aviation Administration (FAA), *(Transportation Dept.), Airports, 800 Independence Ave. S.W., #600E, ARP-1 20591; (202) 267-9471. Fax, (202) 267-5301. Woodie Woodward, Associate Administrator.*
Web, www.faa.gov/arp/arphome.htm

Makes grants for development and improvement of publicly operated and owned airports and some privately owned airports; certifies safety design standards for airports; administers the congressional Airport Improvement Program; oversees construction and accessibility standards for people with disabilities. Questions about local airports are usually referred to a local FAA field office.

Maryland Aviation Administration, *P.O. Box 8766, Baltimore, MD 21240; (410) 859-7060. Fax, (410) 850-4729. Paul J. Wiedefeld, Executive Director.*
Web, www.bwiairport.com

Responsible for aviation operations, planning, instruction, and safety in Maryland; operates Baltimore/Washington International Airport (BWI).

Metropolitan Washington Airports Authority,
1 Aviation Circle 20001-6000; (703) 417-8610. Fax, (703) 417-8949. James E. Bennett, President (Acting). Press, (703) 417-8745.
Web, www.mwaa.com

Independent interstate agency created by Virginia and the District of Columbia with the consent of Congress; operates Washington Dulles International Airport and Ronald Reagan Washington National Airport.

NONPROFIT

Airports Council International (ACI), *1775 K St. N.W., #500 20006; (202) 293-8500. Fax, (202) 331-1362. David Z. Plavin, President.*

General e-mail, postmaster@aci-na.org

Web, www.aci-na.org

Membership: authorities, boards, commissions, and municipal departments operating public airports. Serves as liaison with government agencies and other aviation organizations; works to improve passenger and freight facilitation; acts as clearinghouse on engineering and operational aspects of airport development. Monitors legislation and regulations.

American Assn. of Airport Executives, *601 Madison St., #400, Alexandria, VA 22314; (703) 824-0500. Fax, (703) 820-1395. Charles M. Barclay, President.*

Web, www.airportnet.org

Membership: airport managers, superintendents, consultants, authorities and commissions, government officials, and others interested in the construction, management, and operation of airports. Conducts examination for and awards the professional designation of Accredited Airport Executive.

Aviation Safety and Security

AGENCIES

Federal Aviation Administration (FAA), *(Transportation Dept.), Accident Investigation, 800 Independence Ave. S.W., AAI-1 20591; (202) 267-9612. Fax, (202) 267-5043. Steven Wallace, Director.*

Web, www.faa.gov/avr/aai/aii/home.htm

Investigates aviation accidents and incidents to detect unsafe conditions and trends in the national airspace system and to coordinate corrective action.

Federal Aviation Administration (FAA), *(Transportation Dept.), Aerospace Medicine, 800 Independence Ave. S.W., #800W, AAM-1 20591; (202) 267-3535. Fax, (202) 267-5399. Dr. Jon L. Jordan, Federal Air Surgeon.*

Web, www.faa.gov

Responsible for the medical activities and policies of the FAA; designates, through regional offices, aviation medical examiners who conduct periodic medical examinations of all air personnel; regulates and oversees drug and alcohol testing programs for pilots, air traffic controllers, and others who hold safety-sensitive positions; maintains a Civil Aerospace Medical Institute in Oklahoma City.

Federal Aviation Administration (FAA), *(Transportation Dept.), Air Traffic Services, 800 Independence Ave. S.W., ATS-1 20591; (202) 267-7111. Fax, (202) 267-5621. Steven J. Brown, Associate Administrator.*

Web, www.faa.gov/ats/atshome.htm

Operates the national air traffic control system; employs air traffic controllers at airport towers, en route air traffic control centers, and flight service stations; maintains the National Flight Data Center.

Federal Aviation Administration (FAA), *(Transportation Dept.), Aircraft Certification Service, 800 Independence Ave. S.W., #800E, AIR-1 20591; (202) 267-8235. Fax, (202) 267-5364. John Hickey, Director.*

Web, www.faa.gov

Certifies all aircraft for airworthiness; approves designs and specifications for new aircraft, aircraft engines, propellers, and appliances; supervises aircraft manufacturing and testing.

Federal Aviation Administration (FAA), *(Transportation Dept.), Airway Facilities, 800 Independence Ave. S.W., #700E, AAF-1 20591; (202) 267-8181. Fax, (202) 267-5015. Steven B. Zaidman, Director.*

Web, www.faa.gov/ats/aaf

Conducts research and development programs aimed at providing procedures, facilities, and devices needed for a safe and efficient system of air navigation and air traffic control.

Federal Aviation Administration (FAA), *(Transportation Dept.), Flight Standards Service, 800 Independence Ave. S.W., #821, AFS-1 20591; (202) 267-8237. Fax, (202) 267-5230. James J. Ballough, Director.*

Web, www.faa.gov/avr/afshome.htm

Sets certification standards for air carriers, commercial operators, air agencies, and air personnel (except air traffic control tower operators); directs and executes certification and inspection of flight procedures, operating methods, air personnel qualification and proficiency, and maintenance aspects of airworthiness programs; manages the registry of civil aircraft and all official air personnel records; supports law enforcement agencies responsible for drug interdiction.

Federal Aviation Administration (FAA), *(Transportation Dept.), System Safety, 800 Independence Ave. S.W., #1040A, ASY-1 20591; (202) 267-3611. Fax, (202) 267-5496. Christopher A. Hart, Assistant Administrator.*

Web, www.nasdac.faa.gov

Responsible for safety promotion and for the quality and integrity of safety-data studies and analyses.

Federal Bureau of Investigation (FBI), *(Justice Dept.), Criminal Investigative Division, 935 Pennsylvania Ave. N.W., #5012 20535; (202) 324-4260. Fax, (202) 324-0027. Grant D. Ashley, Assistant Director.*

Web, www.fbi.gov

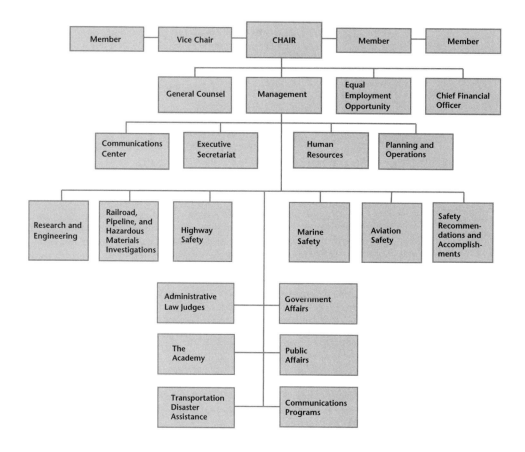

Investigates cases of aircraft hijacking, destruction of aircraft, and air piracy. Works with FAA to ensure security of national air carrier systems in areas of violent crime, organized crime, civil rights, corruption, and financial crimes.

Federal Communications Commission (FCC), *Enforcement Bureau, 445 12th St. S.W. 20554-0001; (202) 418-7450. David H. Solomon, Chief. Information, (888) 225-5322. TTY, (888) 835-5322.*
Web, www.fcc.gov/eb

Provides technical services to aid the Federal Aviation Administration in locating aircraft in distress; provides interference resolution for air traffic control radio frequencies.

National Oceanic and Atmospheric Administration (NOAA), *(Commerce Dept.), National Ocean Service,*

1305 East-West Hwy., SSMC4, Silver Spring, MD 20910; (301) 713-3074. Fax, (301) 713-4269. Jamison Hawkins, Assistant Administrator (Acting).
Web, www.nos.noaa.gov

Manages charting and geodetic services, oceanography and marine services, coastal resource coordination, and marine survey operations.

National Transportation Safety Board, *Aviation Safety, 490 L'Enfant Plaza East S.W., #5400 20594; (202) 314-6300. Fax, (202) 314-6309. John Clark, Director.*
Web, www.ntsb.gov

Responsible for management, policies, and programs in aviation safety and for aviation accident investigations. Manages programs on special investigations, safety issues, and safety objectives. Acts as U.S. representative in international investigations.

Transportation Security Administration (TSA), *(Homeland Security Dept.), 701 S. 12th St., #1203 North, Arlington, VA 22202 (mailing address: TSA Headquarters, 400 7th St. S.W., Washington, DC 20590); (571) 227-2800. Fax, (571) 227-2555. James M. Loy, Under Secretary. Feedback/complaints regarding travel experiences can be submitted to the TSA Consumer Response Center, toll-free, (866) 289-9673.*

General e-mail, tellTSA@tsa.gov

Web, www.tsa.gov

Protects the nation's transportation system. Performs and oversees airport security, including passenger and baggage screeners, airport federal security directors, and air marshals.

NONPROFIT

Aerospace Medical Assn., *320 S. Henry St., Alexandria, VA 22314-3579; (703) 739-2240. Fax, (703) 739-9652. Dr. Russell B. Rayman, Executive Director.*

Web, www.asma.org

Membership: physicians, flight surgeons, aviation medical examiners, flight nurses, scientists, technicians, and specialists in clinical, operational, and research fields of aerospace medicine. Promotes programs to improve aerospace medicine and maintain safety in aviation by examining and monitoring the health of aviation personnel; participates in aircraft investigation and cockpit design.

Air Traffic Control Assn., *2300 Clarendon Blvd., #711, Arlington, VA 22201; (703) 522-5717. Fax, (703) 527-7251. Gabriel A. Hartl, President.*

General e-mail, info@atca.org

Web, www.atca.org

Membership: air traffic controllers, flight service station specialists, pilots, aviation engineers and manufacturers, and others interested in air traffic control systems. Compiles and publishes information and data concerning air traffic control; provides information to members, Congress, and federal agencies; acts as liaison between members and Congress.

Flight Safety Foundation, *601 Madison St., #300, Alexandria, VA 22314; (703) 739-6700. Fax, (703) 739-6708. Stuart Matthews, President.*

Web, www.flightsafety.org

Membership: aerospace manufacturers, domestic and foreign airlines, energy and insurance companies, educational institutions, and organizations and corporations interested in flight safety. Sponsors seminars and conducts studies and safety audits on air safety for governments and industries. Administers award programs that

recognize achievements in air safety. Operates the Q-STAR program, which is a charter-provider verification service.

International Society of Air Safety Investigators, *Park Center, 107 E. Holly Ave., #11, Sterling, VA 20164; (703) 430-9668. Fax, (703) 430-4970. Ann Schull, Office Manager.*

General e-mail, isasi@erols.com

Web, www.isasi.org

Membership: specialists who investigate and seek to define the causes of aircraft accidents. Encourages improvement of air safety and investigative procedures.

National Air Traffic Controllers Assn., *1325 Massachusetts Ave. N.W. 20005; (202) 628-5451. Fax, (202) 628-5767. John Carr, President.*

Web, www.natca.org

Seeks to increase air traffic controller staffing levels, improve working conditions, and encourage procurement of more modern, reliable equipment. Concerned with airport safety worldwide.

National Assn. of Air Traffic Specialists, *11303 Amherst Ave., #4, Wheaton, MD 20902; (301) 933-6228. Fax, (301) 933-3902. Walter W. Pike, President.*

General e-mail, naatshq@aol.com

Web, www.naats.org

Membership: flight service station controllers from the FAA. Assists members with contract negotiations and grievances; conducts training programs and workshops. Monitors legislation and regulations.

 # MARITIME TRANSPORTATION

AGENCIES

Army Corps of Engineers *(Defense Dept.), 441 G St. N.W., #3K05 20314-1000; (202) 761-0001. Fax, (202) 761-4463. Lt. Gen. Robert B. Flowers (USACE), Chief of Engineers.*

Web, www.usace.army.mil

Provides local governments with navigation, flood control, disaster relief, and hydroelectric power services.

Federal Maritime Commission, *800 N. Capitol St. N.W., #1046 20573-0001; (202) 523-5725. Fax, (202) 523-0014. Steven R. Blust, Chair; Bruce A. Dombrowski, Executive Director. Library, (202) 523-5762. TTY, (800) 877-8339. Locator, (202) 523-5773.*

Web, www.fmc.gov

Regulates foreign ocean shipping of the United States; enforces maritime shipping laws and regulations regarding rates and charges, freight forwarding, passengers, and port authorities. Library open to the public.

Federal Maritime Commission, *Trade Analysis,* *800 N. Capitol St. N.W., 9th Floor 20573; (202) 523-5796. Fax, (202) 523-4372. Florence A. Carr, Director.*
Web, www.fmc.gov

Regulates the rates charged for shipping in foreign commerce; licenses and enforces regulations concerning ocean freight forwarders; issues certificates of financial responsibility to ensure that carriers refund fares and meet their liability in case of death, injury, or nonperformance.

Justice Dept. (DOJ), *Civil Division: Torts Branch, Aviation/Admiralty Litigation,* *1425 New York Ave. N.W., #10100 20530 (mailing address: P.O. Box 14271 20044-4271); (202) 616-4000. Fax, (202) 616-4002. Gary W. Allen, Director.*
Web, www.usdoj.gov

Represents the federal government in civil suits concerning the maritime industry, including ships, shipping, and merchant marine personnel. Handles civil cases arising from admiralty incidents and accidents, including oil spills.

Maritime Administration *(Transportation Dept.),* *400 7th St. S.W., #7206, MAR-100 20590; (202) 366-5823. Fax, (202) 366-3890. Capt. William G. Schubert, Maritime Administrator. Information, (202) 366-5807.*
Web, marad.dot.gov

Conducts research on shipbuilding and operations; administers subsidy programs; provides financing guarantees and a tax-deferred fund for shipbuilding; promotes the maritime industry; operates the U.S. Merchant Marine Academy in Kings Point, N.Y.

Maritime Administration *(Transportation Dept.),* *Financial and Rate Approvals,* *400 7th St. S.W., #8117, MAR-560 20590; (202) 366-2324. Fax, (202) 366-9580. Michael P. Ferris, Director.*
Web, marad.dot.gov

Conducts financial analysis of commercial shipping and calculates guideline rates for carriage of preference cargoes.

Maritime Administration *(Transportation Dept.),* *Financial Approvals and Cargo Preference,* *400 7th St. S.W., #8114, MAR-500 20590; (202) 366-0364. Fax, (202) 366-9580. James J. Zok, Associate Administrator.*
Web, marad.dot.gov

Administers financial approval and cargo preference programs.

Maritime Administration *(Transportation Dept.),* *Insurance and Shipping Analysis,* *400 7th St. S.W., #8117, MAR-780 20590; (202) 366-2400. Fax, (202) 366-7901. Edmond J. Fitzgerald, Director.*
Web, marad.dot.gov

Administers war risk insurance. Performs economic soundness analysis for Title XI Program.

Maritime Administration *(Transportation Dept.),* *Maritime Education,* *400 7th St. S.W., #7302, MAR-400 20590; (202) 366-5755. Fax, (202) 493-2288. Bruce J. Carlton, Director.*
Web, marad.dot.gov

Supports the training of merchant marine officers at the U.S. Merchant Marine Academy in Kings Point, N.Y., and at maritime academies in California, Maine, Massachusetts, Michigan, New York, and Texas.

Maritime Administration *(Transportation Dept.),* *Maritime Subsidy Board,* *400 7th St. S.W., #7210, MAR-120 20590; (202) 366-5746. Fax, (202) 366-9206. Joel C. Richard, Secretary.*
Web, marad.dot.gov

Administers subsidy contracts for the construction and operation of U.S.-flag ships engaged in foreign trade.

Maritime Administration *(Transportation Dept.),* *Policy and International Trade,* *400 7th St. S.W., #7123, MAR-400 20590; (202) 366-5772. Fax, (202) 366-7403. Bruce J. Carlton, Associate Administrator.*
Web, marad.dot.gov

Conducts economic analyses and makes policy recommendations to the administrator. Negotiates multilateral and bilateral maritime agreements; directs the agency's strategic planning; manages collection and dissemination of official government statistics on oceanborne foreign commerce; formulates government positions in international maritime policy matters.

Maritime Administration *(Transportation Dept.),* *Research and Development,* *400 7th St. S.W., #7307, MAR-500.5 20590; (202) 366-1923. Fax, (202) 493-2288. Alexander C. Landsburg, Coordinator.*
Web, marad.dot.gov

Conducts technology assessment activities related to the development and use of water transportation systems for commercial and national security purposes. Makes recommendations concerning future trends in such areas as trade, technologies, fuels, and materials.

Maritime Administration *(Transportation Dept.),* *Ship Financing,* 400 7th St. S.W., #8122, MAR-770 20590; (202) 366-5744. Fax, (202) 366-7901. Mitchell D. Lax, Director.
Web, marad.dot.gov

Provides ship financing guarantees and administers the Capital Construction Fund Program.

Maritime Administration *(Transportation Dept.),* *Shipbuilding,* 400 7th St. S.W., #8126, MAR-700 20590; (202) 366-5737. Fax, (202) 366-7901. Jean E. McKeever, Associate Administrator.
Web, marad.dot.gov

Works with private industry to develop standardized ship designs and improved shipbuilding techniques and materials.

Navy Dept. *(Defense Dept.), Military Sealift Command,* Bldg. 210, Washington Navy Yard, DC 20398-5540; (202) 685-5001. Fax, (202) 685-5020. Vice Adm. David L. Brewer, Commander.
Web, www.msc.navy.mil

Transports Defense Dept. and other U.S. government cargo by sea; operates ships that maintain supplies for the armed forces and scientific agencies; transports fuels for the Energy Dept.

Surface Transportation Board *(Transportation Dept.),* 1925 K St. N.W., #810 20423-0001; (202) 565-1510. Fax, (202) 565-9004. Roger Nober, Chair; Wayne O. Burkes, Vice Chair. Information, (202) 565-1674.
Web, www.stb.dot.gov

Regulates rates for water transportation and intermodal connections in noncontiguous domestic trade (between the mainland and Alaska, Hawaii, or U.S. territories).

U.S. Coast Guard (USCG), *(Homeland Security Dept.),* 2100 2nd St. S.W. 20593-0001; (202) 267-2390. Fax, (202) 267-4158. Adm. Thomas H. Collins, Commandant. Information, (202) 267-1587.
Web, www.uscg.mil

Carries out search-and-rescue missions in and around navigable waters and on the high seas; enforces federal laws on the high seas and navigable waters of the United States and its possessions; conducts marine environmental protection programs; administers boating safety programs; inspects and regulates construction, safety, and equipment of merchant marine vessels; establishes and maintains a system of navigation aids; carries out domestic icebreaking activities; maintains a state of military readiness to assist the Navy in time of war or when directed by the president.

U.S. Coast Guard (USCG), *(Homeland Security Dept.), Investigations and Analysis,* 2100 2nd St. S.W., #2404, G-MOA 20593; (202) 267-1430. Fax, (202) 267-1416. Capt. Michael Karr, Chief.
Web, www.uscg.mil/hq/g-m/moa/isn.htm

Handles disciplinary proceedings for merchant marine personnel. Compiles and analyzes records of marine casualties.

U.S. Coast Guard (USCG), *(Homeland Security Dept.), National Maritime Center, Licensing and Evaluation,* 4200 Wilson Blvd., #630, NMC-4C, Arlington, VA 22203-1804; (202) 493-1048. Fax, (202) 493-1062. Stewart A. Walker, Chief.
Web, www.uscg.mil/nmc

Provides guidance to marine licensing and documentation efforts and regional examination centers regarding evaluation of personnel qualifications, licensing, certification, shipment, and discharge of merchant mariners. Monitors operation of the Regional Examination Center; evaluates requests for medical waivers, vessel manning scales, and exemptions from citizenship requirements; advises the State Dept. concerning merchant marine personnel procedures abroad.

U.S. Coast Guard (USCG), *(Homeland Security Dept.), Strategic Analysis,* 2100 2nd St. S.W., #2316B 20593-0001; (202) 267-1265. Fax, (202) 267-4234. Capt. Robert Ross, Chief.
Web, www.uscg.mil

Makes five-to-fifteen-year projections on trends in politics, economics, sociology, technology, and society and how those trends will affect the Coast Guard.

CONGRESS

House Appropriations Committee, *Subcommittee on Energy and Water Development,* 2362 RHOB 20515; (202) 225-3421. Rep. David L. Hobson, R-Ohio, Chair; Robert Schmidt, Staff Director.
Web, www.house.gov/appropriations

Jurisdiction over legislation to appropriate funds for the civil programs of the Army Corps of Engineers.

House Appropriations Committee, *Subcommittee on Homeland Security,* B307 RHOB 20515; (202) 225-5834. Rep. Harold Rogers, R-Ky., Chair; Michelle Mrdeza, Staff Director.
Web, www.house.gov/appropriations

Jurisdiction over legislation to appropriate funds for the Panama Canal Commission, the Saint Lawrence Seaway Development Corp., and the U.S. Coast Guard.

House Government Reform Committee, *Subcommittee on Energy Policy, Natural Resources, and Regulatory Affairs,* B377 RHOB 20515; (202) 225-4407. Fax, (202) 225-2441. Rep. Doug Ose, R-Calif., Chair; Dan Skopec, Staff Director.
Web, www.house.gov/reform

Oversees operations of the Federal Maritime Commission.

House Science Committee, *Subcommittee on Environment, Technology, and Standards,* 2319 RHOB 20515; (202) 225-8844. Fax, (202) 225-4438. Rep. Vernon J. Ehlers, R-Mich., Chair; Eric Webster, Staff Director.
General e-mail, science@mail.house.gov
Web, www.house.gov/science

Oversight of research and development activities of the U.S. Coast Guard and the Maritime Administration.

House Transportation and Infrastructure Committee, *Subcommittee on Coast Guard and Maritime Transportation,* 507 FHOB 20515; (202) 226-3552. Fax, (202) 226-2524. Rep. Frank A. LoBiondo, R-N.J., Chair; Mark Zachares, Staff Director.
General e-mail, transcomm@mail.house.gov
Web, www.house.gov/transportation

Jurisdiction over legislation on most merchant marine matters, including government subsidies and assistance; merchant marine personnel programs; port regulation, safety, and security; and ship and freight regulation and rates. Jurisdiction over legislation on maritime safety, marine pollution control and abatement, U.S. Coast Guard, and the Saint Lawrence Seaway. (Jurisdiction shared with the Subcommittee on Water Resources and Environment.)

House Transportation and Infrastructure Committee, *Subcommittee on Water Resources and Environment,* B376 RHOB 20515; (202) 225-4360. Fax, (202) 226-5435. Rep. John J. "Jimmy" Duncan Jr., R-Tenn., Chair; Susan Bodine, Staff Director.
General e-mail, transcomm@mail.house.gov
Web, www.house.gov/transportation

Jurisdiction over legislation on deepwater ports and the Saint Lawrence Seaway, including the Saint Lawrence Seaway Development Corp. (Jurisdiction shared with the Subcommittee on Coast Guard and Maritime Transportation.)

Senate Appropriations Committee, *Subcommittee on Energy and Water Development,* SD-129 20510, (202) 224-7260. Fax, (202) 228-2322. Sen. Pete V. Domenici, R-N.M., Chair; Clay Sell, Clerk.
Web, appropriations.senate.gov

Jurisdiction over legislation to appropriate funds for the Civil Corps of Engineers.

Senate Appropriations Committee, *Subcommittee on Homeland Security,* S128 CAP 20510; (202) 224-3471. Fax, (202) 224-8553. Sen. Thad Cochran, R-Miss., Chair; Rebecca Davies, Clerk.
Web, appropriations.senate.gov

Jurisdiction over legislation to appropriate funds for the Panama Canal Commission, the Saint Lawrence Seaway Development Corp., and the U.S. Coast Guard.

Senate Commerce, Science, and Transportation Committee, SD-508 20510; (202) 224-5115. Fax, (202) 224-1259. Sen. John McCain, R-Ariz., Chair; Jeanne Bumpus, Staff Director.
Web, commerce.senate.gov

Oversight of and legislative jurisdiction over the U.S. Coast Guard, the Maritime Administration, maritime safety, and ports, including security and regulation; oversight of the Federal Maritime Commission.

Senate Commerce, Science, and Transportation Committee, *Subcommittee on Oceans, Fisheries, and Coast Guard,* SH-227 20510; (202) 224-8172. Fax, (202) 224-9334. Sen. Olympia J. Snowe, R-Maine, Chair; Andrew Minkiewicz, Counsel Member.
Web, commerce.senate.gov

Studies issues involving deepwater ports. (Jurisdiction shared with Senate Energy and Natural Resources and Senate Environment and Public Works committees.) Studies legislation on the U.S. Coast Guard. (Subcommittee does not report legislation.)

Senate Commerce, Science, and Transportation Committee, *Subcommittee on Surface Transportation and Merchant Marine,* SH-427 20510; (202) 224-4852. Fax, (202) 228-0326. Sen. Kay Bailey Hutchison, R-Texas, Chair; Robert Freeman, Senior Professional Staff.
Web, commerce.senate.gov

Jurisdiction over legislation on Saint Lawrence Seaway and merchant marine matters, including ship and freight regulation and rates, merchant marine personnel programs, and government subsidies and assistance to foreign and U.S. vessels; jurisdiction over the Federal Maritime Commission and the Maritime Administration.

Senate Energy and Natural Resources Committee, *Subcommittee on Water and Power,* SD-364 20510; (202) 224-7556. Fax, (202) 224-7970. Sen. Lisa Murkowski, R-Alaska, Chair; Colleen Deegan, Counsel.
General e-mail, water&power@energy.senate.gov
Web, energy.senate.gov

Jurisdiction over legislation on deepwater ports (jurisdiction shared with Senate Commerce, Science, and Transportation and Senate Environment and Public Works committees).

Senate Environment and Public Works Committee, *Subcommittee on Transportation and Infrastructure,* SD-410 20510; (202) 224-6176. Fax, (202) 224-1273. Sen. Christopher S. Bond, R-Mo., Chair; Ellen Stein, Staff Director.
Web, epw.senate.gov

Jurisdiction over legislation authorizing construction, operation, and maintenance of inland waterways and harbors.

NONPROFIT

AFL-CIO Maritime Committee, *1150 17th St. N.W., #700 20036; (202) 835-0404. Fax, (202) 872-0912. Talmage E. Simpkins, Executive Director.*

Membership: AFL-CIO maritime unions. Provides information on the maritime industry and unions. Interests include seamen's service contracts and pension plans, maritime safety, U.S. merchant marine, and the rights of Panama Canal residents. Monitors legislation and regulations.

American Maritime Congress, *1300 Eye St. N.W., #250W 20005-3314; (202) 842-4900. Fax, (202) 842-3492. Gloria Cataneo Tosi, President.*
Web, www.americanmaritime.org

Organization of U.S.-flag carriers engaged in oceanborne transportation. Conducts research and provides information on the U.S.-flag merchant marine.

Boat Owners Assn. of the United States, *Government and Public Affairs, 880 S. Pickett St., Alexandria, VA 22304; (703) 461-2864. Fax, (703) 461-2845. Michael Sciulla, Director.*
General e-mail, govtaffairs@boatus.com
Web, www.boatus.com

Membership: owners of recreational boats. Represents boat-owner interests before the federal government; offers consumer protection and other services to members.

Chamber of Shipping of America, *1730 M St. N.W., #407 20036; (202) 775-4399. Fax, (202) 659-3795. Joseph J. Cox, President.*

Represents U.S.-based companies that own, operate, or charter oceangoing tankers, container ships, and other merchant vessels engaged in domestic and international trade.

Maritime Institute for Research and Industrial Development, *1775 K St. N.W., #200 20006; (202) 463-6505. Fax, (202) 223-9093. C. James Patti, President.*
General e-mail, cpatti@miraid.org

Membership: U.S.-flag ship operators. Promotes the development of the U.S. Merchant Marine. Interests include bilateral shipping agreements, the use of private commercial merchant vessels by the Defense Dept., and enforcement of cargo preference laws for U.S.-flag ships.

National Marine Manufacturers Assn., *Government Relations, Washington Office, 1819 L St. N.W., #700 20036; (202) 721-1600. Fax, (202) 861-1181. Monita Fontaine, Vice President.*
Web, www.nmma.org

Membership: recreational marine equipment manufacturers. Promotes boating safety and the development of boating facilities. Serves as liaison with Congress and regulatory agencies. Monitors legislation and regulations. (Headquarters in Chicago, Ill.)

Shipbuilders Council of America, *1455 F St. N.W., #225 20005; (202) 347-5462. Fax, (202) 347-5464. Allen Walker, President.*
Web, www.shipbuilders.org

Membership: commercially focused shipyards that repair and build ships, and allied industries and associations. National trade association representing the competitive shipyard industry that makes up the core shipyard industrial base in the United States. Monitors legislation and regulations.

Transportation Institute, *5201 Auth Way, Camp Springs, MD 20746; (301) 423-3335. Fax, (301) 423-0634. James L. Henry, Chair and President.*
Web, www.trans-inst.org

Membership: U.S.-flag maritime shipping companies. Conducts research on freight regulation and rates, government subsidies and assistance, domestic and international maritime matters, maritime safety, ports, Saint Lawrence Seaway, shipbuilding, and regulation of shipping.

Maritime Safety

AGENCIES

Federal Communications Commission (FCC), *Enforcement Bureau, 445 12th St. S.W. 20554-0001; (202) 418-7450. David H. Solomon, Chief. Information, (888) 225-5322. TTY, (888) 835-5322.*
Web, www.fcc.gov/eb

Provides technical services to the U.S. Coast Guard for locating ships in distress. Provides policy and program support for maritime radiotelegraph inspection.

National Oceanic and Atmospheric Administration (NOAA), *(Commerce Dept.), National Ocean Service: Coast Survey,* 1315 East-West Hwy., #6147, SSMC3, Silver Spring, MD 20910-3282; (301) 713-2770. Fax, (301) 713-4019. Capt. David B. MacFarland, Director.
Web, www.chartmaker.ncd.noaa.gov

Directs programs and conducts research to support fundamental scientific and engineering activities and resource development for safe navigation of the nation's waterways and territorial seas. Constructs, prints, and distributes nautical charts.

National Response Center *(Homeland Security Dept.),* 2100 2nd St. S.W., #2611 20593; (202) 267-2675. Fax, (202) 267-2165. Syed Qadir, Director, (202) 267-6352. Toll-free hotline, (800) 424-8802.
Web, www.nrc.uscg.mil

Maintains twenty-four-hour hotline for reporting oil spills, hazardous materials accidents, chemical releases, or known or suspected terrorist threats. Notifies appropriate federal officials to reduce the effects of accidents.

National Transportation Safety Board, *Marine Safety,* 490 L'Enfant Plaza East S.W., #6313 20594; (202) 314-6450. Fax, (202) 314-6454. Marjorie Murtagh, Director.
Web, www.ntsb.gov

Investigates selected marine transportation accidents, including major marine accidents that involve U.S. Coast Guard operations or functions. Determines the facts upon which the board establishes probable cause; makes recommendations on matters pertaining to marine transportation safety and accident prevention.

Occupational Safety and Health Administration (OSHA), *(Labor Dept.), General Industry Enforcement,* 200 Constitution Ave. N.W., #N3107, MS-N3603 20210; (202) 693-1850. Fax, (202) 693-1628. Arthur T. Buchanan, Director.
Web, www.osha.gov

Interprets maritime compliance safety and health standards.

U.S. Coast Guard (USCG), *(Homeland Security Dept.), Boating Safety,* 2100 2nd St. S.W., G-OPB 20593-0001; (202) 267-1077. Fax, (202) 267-4285. Capt. Scott H. Evans, Chief.
Web, www.uscgboating.org

Establishes and enforces safety standards for recreational boats and associated equipment; sets boater education standards; coordinates nationwide public awareness and information programs.

U.S. Coast Guard (USCG), *(Homeland Security Dept.), Design and Engineering Standards,* 2100 2nd St. S.W., #1218, G-MSE 20593; (202) 267-2967. Fax, (202) 267-4816. Capt. Jeffrey G. Lantz, Chief.
Web, www.uscg.mil

Develops standards; responsible for general vessel arrangements, naval architecture, vessel design and construction, and transport of bulk dangerous cargoes. Supports national advisory committees and national professional organizations to achieve industry standards.

U.S. Coast Guard (USCG), *(Homeland Security Dept.), Investigations and Analysis,* 2100 2nd St. S.W., #2404, G-MOA 20593; (202) 267-1430. Fax, (202) 267-1416. Capt. Michael Karr, Chief.
Web, www.uscg.mil/hq/g-m/moa/isn.htm

Compiles and analyzes records of accidents involving commercial vessels that result in loss of life, serious injury, or substantial damage.

U.S. Coast Guard (USCG), *(Homeland Security Dept.), Marine Safety Center,* 400 7th St. S.W., #6302 20590; (202) 366-6480. Fax, (202) 366-3877. Alan Peek, Commanding Officer.
Web, www.uscg.mil

Reviews and approves commercial vessel plans and specifications to ensure technical compliance with federal safety and pollution abatement standards.

U.S. Coast Guard (USCG), *(Homeland Security Dept.), Marine Safety, Security, and Environmental Protection,* 2100 2nd St. S.W., #2408 20593; (202) 267-2200. Fax, (202) 267-4839. Rear Adm. Paul J. Pluta, Assistant Commandant.
Web, www.uscg.mil/hq/g-m/gmhome.htm

Establishes and enforces regulations for port safety; environmental protection; vessel safety, inspection, design, documentation, and investigation; licensing of merchant vessel personnel; and shipment of hazardous materials.

U.S. Coast Guard (USCG), *(Homeland Security Dept.), Operations Policy Directorate,* 2100 2nd St. S.W., 3100-D 20593-0001 (mailing address: Commandant G-OP 20593); (202) 267-2267. Fax, (202) 267-4674. Rear Adm. Jeffrey J. Hathaway, Director.
Web, www.uscg.mil

Administers Long Range and Short Range Aids to Navigation programs; regulates the construction, maintenance, and operation of bridges across U.S. navigable waters. Conducts search-and-rescue and polar and domestic ice-breaking operations. Regulates waterways under U.S. jurisdiction. Operates the Coast Guard Command Center; participates in defense operations and homeland security; enforces boating safety; assists with law enforcement/drug interdictions.

NONPROFIT

International Council of Cruise Lines, *2111 Wilson Blvd., 8th Floor, Arlington, VA 22201; (703) 522-8463. Fax, (703) 522-3811. Michael Crye, President.*
General e-mail, info@iccl.org
Web, www.iccl.org

Membership: Chief executives of sixteen cruise lines and other cruise industry professionals. Advises domestic and international regulatory organizations on shipping policy. Works with U.S. and international agencies to promote safety, public health, security, medical facilities, environmental awareness, and passenger protection. Monitors legislation and regulations about the cruise industry.

U.S. Coast Guard Auxiliary, *2100 2nd St. S.W. 20593-0001; (202) 267-1001. Fax, (202) 267-4460. Capt. David B. Hill, Chief Director.*
Web, www.cgaux.org

Volunteer, nonmilitary organization created by Congress to assist the Coast Guard in promoting water safety. Offers public education programs; administers the Courtesy Marine Examination Program, a safety equipment check free to the public; works with the Coast Guard and state boating officials to maintain marine safety.

Ports and Waterways

AGENCIES

Army Corps of Engineers *(Defense Dept.), Civil Works, 441 G St. N.W. 20314; (202) 761-0099. Fax, (202) 761-8992. Maj. Gen. Robert H. Griffin, Director.*
Web, www.usace.army.mil

Coordinates field offices that oversee harbors, dams, levees, waterways, locks, reservoirs, and other construction projects designed to facilitate transportation and flood control. Major projects include the Mississippi, Missouri, and Ohio Rivers.

Federal Maritime Commission, *Agreements, 800 N. Capitol St. N.W., #940 20573; (202) 523-5793. Fax, (202) 523-4372. Jeremiah D. Hospital, Chief.*
Web, www.fmc.gov

Analyzes agreements between terminal operators and shipping companies for docking facilities and agreements between ocean common carriers.

Maritime Administration *(Transportation Dept.), Port, Intermodal, and Environmental Activities, 400 7th St. S.W., #7214, MAR-800 20590; (202) 366-4721.*

Fax, (202) 366-6988. Margaret Blum, Associate Administrator.
Web, marad.dot.gov

Responsible for direction and administration of port and intermodal transportation development and port readiness for national defense.

Panama Canal Commission, *Office of Transition Administration, 1825 Eye St. N.W., #400 20006; (202) 775-4180. Fax, (202) 775-4184. William J. Connolly, Director.*

Established to close out the affairs of the Panama Canal Commission.

Saint Lawrence Seaway Development Corp. *(Transportation Dept.), 400 7th St. S.W., #5424 20590; (202) 366-0118. Fax, (202) 366-7147. Albert S. Jacquez, Administrator. Information, (202) 366-0091. Toll-free, (800) 785-2779.*
Web, www.greatlakes-seaway.com

Operates and maintains the Saint Lawrence Seaway within U.S. territorial limits; conducts development programs and coordinates activities with its Canadian counterpart.

Tennessee Valley Authority, *Government Relations, Washington Office, 1 Massachusetts Ave. N.W., #300 20001; (202) 898-2999. Fax, (202) 898-2998. Linda Whitestone, Vice President.*
Web, www.tva.gov

Coordinates resource conservation, development, and land-use programs in the Tennessee River Valley. Operates the river control system; projects include flood control, navigation development, and multiple-use reservoirs.

U.S. Coast Guard (USCG), *(Homeland Security Dept.), 2100 2nd St. S.W. 20593-0001; (202) 267-2390. Fax, (202) 267-4158. Adm. Thomas H. Collins, Commandant. Information, (202) 267-1587.*
Web, www.uscg.mil

Enforces rules and regulations governing the safety and security of ports and anchorages and the movement of vessels in U.S. waters. Supervises cargo transfer operations, storage, and stowage; conducts harbor patrols and waterfront facility inspections; establishes security zones and monitors vessel movement.

NONPROFIT

American Assn. of Port Authorities, *1010 Duke St., Alexandria, VA 22314; (703) 684-5700. Fax, (703) 684-6321. Kurt J. Nagle, President.*
General e-mail, info@aapa-ports.org
Web, www.aapa-ports.org

Membership: port authorities in the Western Hemisphere. Provides technical and economic information on port finance, construction, operation, and security.

American Waterways Operators, *801 N. Quincy St., #200, Arlington, VA 22203; (703) 841-9300. Fax, (703) 841-0389. Thomas A. Allegretti, President.*
Web, www.americanwaterways.com

Membership: commercial shipyard owners and operators of barges, tugboats, and towboats on navigable coastal and inland waterways. Monitors legislation and regulations; acts as liaison with Congress, the U.S. Coast Guard, the Army Corps of Engineers, and the Maritime Administration. Monitors legislation and regulations.

International Longshore and Warehouse Union, *Washington Office, 1775 K St. N.W., #200 20006; (202) 463-6265. Fax, (202) 467-4875. Lindsay McLaughlin, Legislative Director.*
General e-mail, ilwu@patriot.net
Web, www.ilwu.org

Membership: approximately 45,000 longshore and warehouse personnel. Helps members negotiate pay, benefits, and better working conditions; conducts training programs and workshops. Monitors legislation and regulations. (Headquarters in San Francisco, Calif.; affiliated with the AFL-CIO.)

International Longshoremen's Assn., *Washington Office, 1101 17th St. N.W., #400 20036; (202) 955-6304. Fax, (202) 955-6048. John Bowers Jr., Legislative Director.*
General e-mail, iladc@aol.com

Membership: approximately 61,000 longshore personnel. Helps members negotiate pay, benefits, and better working conditions; conducts training programs and workshops. Monitors legislation and regulations. (Headquarters in New York; affiliated with the AFL-CIO.)

National Assn. of Waterfront Employers, *2011 Pennsylvania Ave. N.W., #301 20006; (202) 296-2810. Fax, (202) 331-7479. Charles T. Carroll Jr., Executive Director.*

Membership: private stevedore companies and marine terminal operators, their subsidiaries, and other waterfront-related employers. Legislative interests include trade, antitrust, insurance, port security, and user-fee issues. Monitors legislation and regulations.

National Waterways Conference, *1130 17th St. N.W., #200 20036-4676; (202) 296-4415. Fax, (202) 835-3861. Worth Hager, Executive Director.*
General e-mail, info@waterways.org
Web, www.waterways.org

Membership: petroleum, coal, chemical, electric power, building materials, iron and steel, and grain companies; port authorities; water carriers; and others interested or involved in waterways. Conducts research on the economics of water transportation; sponsors educational programs on waterways. Monitors legislation and regulations.

Passenger Vessel Assn., *801 N. Quincy St., #200, Arlington, VA 22203; (703) 807-0100. Fax, (703) 807-0103. John R. Groundwater, Executive Director.*
Web, www.passengervessel.com

Membership: owners, operators, and suppliers for U.S. and Canadian passenger vessels; and international vessel companies. Interests include dinner and excursion boats, car and passenger ferries, overnight cruise ships, and riverboat casinos. Monitors legislation and regulations.

 MOTOR VEHICLES

AGENCIES

Federal Highway Administration (FHWA), *(Transportation Dept.), 400 7th St. S.W., #4218 20590; (202) 366-0650. Fax, (202) 366-3244. Mary E. Peters, Administrator. Information, (202) 366-0660.*
Web, www.fhwa.dot.gov

Administers federal-aid highway programs with money from the Highway Trust Fund; works to improve highway and motor vehicle safety; coordinates research and development programs on highway and traffic safety, construction costs, and the environmental impact of highway transportation; administers regional and territorial highway building programs and the highway beautification program.

Federal Motor Carrier Safety Administration *(Transportation Dept.), Bus and Truck Standards and Operations, 400 7th St. S.W., #8300 20590; (202) 366-5370. Fax, (202) 366-8842. Robert Proferes, Director.*
Web, www.fmcsa.dot.gov

Regulates motor vehicle size and weight on federally aided highways; conducts studies on issues relating to motor carrier transportation; promotes uniformity in state and federal motor carrier laws and regulations.

CONGRESS

House Appropriations Committee, *Subcommittee on Transportation, Treasury, and Related Agencies, 2358*

RHOB 20515; (202) 225-2141. Fax, (202) 225-5895. Rep. Ernest Istook, R-Okla., Chair; Richard Efford, Clerk.
Web, www.house.gov/appropriations

Jurisdiction over legislation to appropriate funds for the Transportation Dept., including the Federal Highway Administration and the National Highway Traffic Safety Administration.

House Energy and Commerce Committee, *Subcommittee on Commerce, Trade, and Consumer Protection,* 2125 RHOB 20515; (202) 225-2927. Fax, (202) 225-1919. Rep. Cliff Stearns, R-Fla., Chair.
General e-mail, commerce@mail.house.gov
Web, energycommerce.house.gov

Jurisdiction over motor vehicle safety legislation and the National Highway Traffic Safety Administration. (Jurisdiction shared with House Transportation and Infrastructure Committee.)

House Science Committee, *Subcommittee on Environment, Technology, and Standards,* 2319 RHOB 20515; (202) 225-8844. Fax, (202) 225-4438. Rep. Vernon J. Ehlers, R-Mich., Chair; Eric Webster, Staff Director.
General e-mail, science@mail.house.gov
Web, www.house.gov/science

Special oversight of surface transportation research and development programs of executive branch departments and agencies.

House Transportation and Infrastructure Committee, *Subcommittee on Highways, Transit, and Pipelines,* B370A RHOB 20515; (202) 225-6715. Fax, (202) 225-4623. Rep. Tom Petri, R-Wis., Chair; Levon Boyagian, Staff Director.
General e-mail, transcomm@mail.house.gov
Web, www.house.gov/transportation

Jurisdiction over legislation on regulation of commercial vehicles and interstate surface transportation, including the Federal Highway Administration, National Highway Traffic Safety Administration (jurisdiction shared with House Energy and Commerce Committee), federal aid to highways, and highway trust fund programs and activities.

Senate Appropriations Committee, *Subcommittee on Transportation, Treasury, and General Government,* SD-196 20510; (202) 224-4869. Fax, (202) 228-0249. Sen. Richard C. Shelby, R-Ala., Chair; Paul Doerrer, Clerk.
Web, appropriations.senate.gov

Jurisdiction over legislation to appropriate funds for the Transportation Dept., including the Federal Highway Administration and National Highway Traffic Safety Administration.

Senate Commerce, Science, and Transportation Committee, SD-508 20510; (202) 224-5115. Fax, (202) 224-1259. Sen. John McCain, R-Ariz., Chair; Jeanne Bumpus, Staff Director.
Web, commerce.senate.gov

Jurisdiction over motor vehicle safety legislation; oversight of the Surface Transportation Board.

Senate Commerce, Science, and Transportation Committee, *Subcommittee on Surface Transportation and Merchant Marine,* SH-427 20510; (202) 224-4852. Fax, (202) 228-0326. Sen. Kay Bailey Hutchison, R-Texas, Chair; Robert Freeman, Senior Professional Staff.
Web, commerce.senate.gov

Jurisdiction over legislation on regulation of commercial motor carriers and interstate buses. Oversight of surface transportation research and development, including Federal Highway Administration activities (but excluding federal highway construction).

Senate Environment and Public Works Committee, *Subcommittee on Transportation and Infrastructure,* SD-410 20510; (202) 224-6176. Fax, (202) 224-1273. Sen. Christopher S. Bond, R-Mo., Chair; Ellen Stein, Staff Director.
Web, epw.senate.gov

Jurisdiction over legislation on the Federal Highway Administration, the National Highway Traffic Safety Administration, highway trust fund programs, and federal aid to highways.

NONPROFIT

American Assn. of Motor Vehicle Administrators (AAMVA), 4301 Wilson Blvd., #400, Arlington, VA 22203; (703) 522-4200. Fax, (703) 522-1553. Linda Lewis, President.
Web, www.aamva.org

Membership: officials responsible for administering and enforcing motor vehicle and traffic laws in the United States and Canada. Promotes uniform laws and regulations for vehicle registration, drivers' licenses, and motor carrier services; provides administrative evaluation services for safety equipment.

American Automobile Assn. (AAA), *Washington Office,* 1440 New York Ave. N.W., #200 20005-2111; (202) 942-2050. Fax, (202) 783-4798. Mantill Williams, Director, Public Affairs.
Web, www.aaa.com

Membership: state and local automobile associations. Provides members with travel services. Interests include all aspects of highway transportation, travel and tourism, safety, drunk driving, economics, federal aid, and legislation that affects motorists. (Headquarters in Heathrow, Fla.)

American Bus Assn., *1100 New York Ave. N.W., #1050 20005-3934; (202) 842-1645. Fax, (202) 842-0850. Peter J. Pantuso, President.*
General e-mail, abainfo@buses.org
Web, www.buses.org

Membership: intercity privately owned bus companies, state associations, travel/tourism businesses, bus manufacturers, and those interested in the bus industry. Monitors legislation and regulations.

American Trucking Assns., *2200 Mill Rd., Alexandria, VA 22314-4677; (703) 838-1700. Fax, (703) 684-4326. Bill Graves, President. Press, (703) 838-7935.*
General e-mail, membership@trucking.org
Web, www.truckline.com

Membership: state trucking associations, individual trucking and motor carrier organizations, and related supply companies. Maintains departments on industrial relations, law, management systems, research, safety, traffic, state laws, taxation, communications, legislation, economics, and engineering.

Electric Drive Transportation Assn., *701 Pennsylvania Ave., 3rd Floor, East Bldg. 20004; (202) 508-5995. Fax, (202) 508-5924. Kateri Callahan, Executive Director.*
General e-mail, info@electricdrive.org
Web, www.electricdrive.org

Membership: auto and vehicle companies and manufacturers, electric utilities, electrical vehicle (EV) component suppliers, research institutions, and government agencies. Works to advance electric vehicles and supporting infrastructure through policy, information, and market development initiatives in the United States.

Highway Loss Data Institute, *1005 N. Glebe Rd., #800, Arlington, VA 22201; (703) 247-1600. Fax, (703) 247-1595. Brian O'Neill, President.*
Web, www.highwaysafety.org

Research organization that gathers, processes, and publishes data on the ways in which insurance losses vary among different kinds of vehicles. (Affiliated with Insurance Institute for Highway Safety.)

International Parking Institute, *701 Kenmore Ave., #200, Fredericksburg, VA 22401 (mailing address: P.O. Box 7167, Fredericksburg, VA 22404-7167); (540) 371-7535. Fax, (540) 371-8022. David Ivey, President.*
General e-mail, ipi@parking.org
Web, www.parking.org

Membership: operators, designers, and builders of parking lots and structures. Provides leadership to the parking industry; supports professional development; works with transportation and related fields.

Motor Freight Carriers Assn., *499 S. Capitol St. S.W., #502A 20003; (202) 554-3060. Fax, (202) 554-3160. Timothy P. Lynch, President.*
General e-mail, mfca@mfca.org
Web, www.mfca.org

Represents trucking employers. Negotiates and administers labor contracts with the Teamsters Union.

Motorcycle Industry Council, *Government Relations, Washington Office, 1235 Jefferson Davis Hwy., #600, Arlington, VA 22202; (703) 416-0444. Fax, (703) 416-2269. Kathy Van Kleeck, Vice President.*
Web, www.mic.org

Membership: manufacturers and distributors of motorcycles, mopeds and related parts, accessories, and equipment. Monitors legislation and regulations. (Headquarters in Irvine, Calif.)

National Assn. of Regulatory Utility Commissioners, *1101 Vermont Ave. N.W., #200 20005; (202) 898-2200. Fax, (202) 898-2213. Charles Gray, Executive Director. Press, (202) 898-2205.*
Web, www.naruc.org

Membership: members of federal, state, municipal, and Canadian regulatory commissions that have jurisdiction over motor and common carriers. Interests include motor carriers.

National Institute for Automotive Service Excellence, *101 Blue Seal Dr. S.E., #101, Leesburg, VA 20175; (703) 669-6600. Fax, (703) 669-6122. Ronald H. Weiner, President.*
Web, www.asecert.org

Administers program for testing and certifying automotive technicians; researches methods to improve technician training.

National Motor Freight Traffic Assn., *2200 Mill Rd., 4th Floor, Alexandria, VA 22314; (703) 838-1810. Fax, (703) 683-1094. William W. Pugh, Executive Director.*
General e-mail, nmfta@nmfta.org
Web, www.nmfta.org

Membership: motor carriers of general goods in interstate and intrastate commerce. Publishes *National Motor Freight Classification.*

National Parking Assn., *1112 16th St. N.W., #300 20036; (202) 296-4336. Fax, (202) 331-8523. Martin L. Stein, Executive Director.*
General e-mail, info@npapark.org
Web, www.npapark.org

Membership: parking garage owners, operators, and consultants and university municipalities. Offers information and research services; sponsors seminars and educational programs on garage design and equipment. Monitors legislation and regulations.

National Private Truck Council, *2200 Mill Rd., #350, Alexandria, VA 22314; (703) 683-1300. Fax, (703) 683-1217. Gary F. Petty, President.*
Web, www.nptc.org
Membership: manufacturers, producers, distributors, and retail establishments that operate fleets of vehicles incidental to their nontransportation businesses. Interests include truck safety, maintenance, and economics. Supports economic deregulation of the trucking industry and uniformity in state taxation of the industry. NPTC Institute conducts continuing education, truck research, and certification programs.

National Tank Truck Carriers (NTTC), *2200 Mill Rd., Alexandria, VA 22314; (703) 838-1960. Fax, (703) 684-5753. Cliff Harvison, President.*
General e-mail, inquiries@tanktruck.org
Web, www.tanktruck.net
Focuses on issues of the tank truck industry and represents the industry before Congress and federal agencies.

NATSO, Inc., *1199 N. Fairfax St., #801, Alexandria, VA 22314; (703) 549-2100. Fax, (703) 684-4525. William Fay, President.*
General e-mail, headquarters@natso.com
Web, www.natso.com
Membership: travel plaza and truck stop operators and suppliers to the truck stop industry. Provides credit information and educational training programs. Monitors legislation and regulations. Operates the NATSO Foundation, which promotes highway safety.

Natural Gas Vehicle Coalition, *400 N. Capitol St. N.W. 20001; (202) 824-7360. Fax, (202) 824-7367. Richard R. Kolodziej, President.*
Web, www.ngvc.org
Membership: natural gas distributors; pipeline, automobile, and engine manufacturers; environmental groups; research and development organizations; and state and local government agencies. Advocates installation of natural gas and hydrogen fuel stations and development of industry standards. Helps market new products and equipment related to natural gas and hydrogen-powered vehicles.

Truckload Carriers Assn., *2200 Mill Rd., Alexandria, VA 22314; (703) 838-1950. Fax, (703) 836-6610. Robert Hirsch, President.*
General e-mail, tca@truckload.org
Web, www.truckload.org
Represents intercity common and contract trucking companies before Congress, federal agencies, courts, and the media.

Highways

AGENCIES

Federal Highway Administration (FHWA), *(Transportation Dept.), Infrastructure,* 400 7th St. S.W., #3212 20590; (202) 366-0371. Fax, (202) 366-3043. King W. Gee, Associate Administrator.*
Web, www.fhwa.dot.gov
Provides guidance and oversight for planning, design, construction, and maintenance operations relating to federal aid, direct federal construction, and other highway programs; establishes design guidelines and specifications for highways built with federal funds.

Federal Highway Administration (FHWA), *(Transportation Dept.), National Highway Institute,* 4600 N. Fairfax Dr., #800, Arlington, VA 22203; (703) 235-0500. Fax, (703) 235-0593. Moges Ayele, Director.*
Web, www.nhi.fhwa.dot.gov
Develops and administers, in cooperation with state highway departments, training programs for agency, state, and local highway department employees.

Federal Highway Administration (FHWA), *(Transportation Dept.), Policy,* 400 7th St. S.W., #3317 20590; (202) 366-0585. Fax, (202) 366-3590. Charles D. Nottingham, Associate Administrator.*
Web, www.fhwa.dot.gov
Develops policy and administers the Federal Highway Administration's international programs. Conducts policy studies and analyzes legislation; makes recommendations; compiles and reviews highway-related data. Represents the administration at international conferences; administers foreign assistance programs.

Federal Highway Administration (FHWA), *(Transportation Dept.), Real Estate Services,* 400 7th St. S.W., #3221 20590; (202) 366-0142. Fax, (202) 366-3713. Susan Lauffer, Director.*
Web, www.fhwa.dot.gov/realestate
Funds and oversees acquisition of land by states for federally assisted highways; provides financial assistance to relocate people and businesses forced to move by highway construction; cooperates in administering pro-

gram for the use of air rights in connection with federally aided highways; administers Highway Beautification Act to control billboards and junkyards along interstate and federally aided primary highways.

Federal Highway Administration (FHWA), *(Transportation Dept.), Research, Development and Technology, 6300 Georgetown Pike, #T306, McLean, VA 22101; (202) 493-3999. Fax, (202) 493-3170. Dennis C. Judycki, Director.*
Web, www.fhwa.dot.gov

Conducts highway research and development programs; studies safety, location, design, construction, operation, and maintenance of highways; cooperates with state and local highway departments in utilizing results of research.

U.S. Coast Guard (USCG), *(Homeland Security Dept.), 2100 2nd St. S.W. 20593-0001; (202) 267-2390. Fax, (202) 267-4158. Adm. Thomas H. Collins, Commandant. Information, (202) 267-1587.*
Web, www.uscg.mil

Regulates the construction, maintenance, and operation of bridges across U.S. navigable waters.

NONPROFIT

American Assn. of State Highway and Transportation Officials, *444 N. Capitol St. N.W., #249 20001; (202) 624-5800. Fax, (202) 624-5806. John Horsley, Executive Director.*
Web, www.aashto.org

Membership: the Federal Highway Administration and transportation departments of the states, District of Columbia, Guam, and Puerto Rico. Maintains committees on transportation planning, finance, maintenance, safety, and construction.

American Road and Transportation Builders Assn., *1010 Massachusetts Ave. N.W., 6th Floor 20001; (202) 289-4434. Fax, (202) 289-4435. T. Peter Ruane, President.*
General e-mail, artbadc@aol.com
Web, www.artba-hq.org

Membership: highway and transportation contractors; federal, state, and local engineers and officials; construction equipment manufacturers and distributors; and others interested in the transportation construction industry. Serves as liaison with government; provides information on highway engineering and construction developments.

Intelligent Transportation Society of America, *400 Virginia Ave. S.W., #800 20024-2730; (202) 484-4847. Fax, (202) 484-3483. Neil Schuster, President. Publications, (202) 484-4548.*

Web, www.itsa.org

Advocates application of electronic, computer, and communications technology to make surface transportation more efficient and to save lives, time, and money. Coordinates research, development, and implementation of intelligent transportation systems by government, academia, and industry.

International Bridge, Tunnel, and Turnpike Assn., *1146 19th St. N.W., #800 20036-3703; (202) 659-4620. Fax, (202) 659-0500. Patrick D. Jones, Executive Director.*
General e-mail, ibtta@ibtta.org
Web, www.ibtta.org

Membership: public and private operators of toll facilities and associated industries. Conducts research; compiles statistics.

International Road Federation, *1010 Massachusetts Ave. N.W., #410 20001; (202) 371-5544. Fax, (202) 371-5565. C. Patrick Sankey, Director General.*
General e-mail, info@irfnet.org
Web, www.irfnet.org

Membership: road associations and automobile construction and related industries. Administers fellowship program that allows foreign engineering students to study at U.S. graduate schools. Maintains interest in roads and highways worldwide.

Road Information Program, *1726 M St. N.W., #401 20036; (202) 466-6706. Fax, (202) 785-4722. William M. Wilkins, Executive Director.*
General e-mail, trip@tripnet.org
Web, www.tripnet.org

Organization of transportation specialists; conducts research on economic and technical transportation issues; promotes consumer awareness of the condition of the national road and bridge system.

Manufacturing and Sales

AGENCIES

International Trade Administration (ITA), *(Commerce Dept.), Automotive Affairs, 14th St. and Constitution Ave. N.W., #4036 20230; (202) 482-0554. Fax, (202) 482-0674. Henry P. Misisco, Director.*
Web, www.trade.gov/td/auto

Promotes the export of U.S. automotive products; compiles and analyzes auto industry data; seeks to secure a favorable position for the U.S. auto industry in global markets through policy and trade agreements.

NONPROFIT

American Automotive Leasing Assn., *675 N. Washington St., #410, Alexandria, VA 22314; (703) 548-0777.*

Fax, (703) 548-1925. Pamela Sederholm, Executive Director.

Web, www.aalafleet.com

Membership: automotive commercial fleet leasing and management companies. Monitors legislation and regulations.

American International Automobile Dealers Assn., 211 N. Union St., #300, Alexandria, VA 22314; (703) 519-7800. Fax, (703) 519-7810. Marianne McInerney, President.

General e-mail, goaiada@aiada.org

Web, www.aiada.org

Promotes a free market for international nameplate automobiles in the United States. Monitors legislation and regulations.

Assn. of International Automobile Manufacturers, 1001 N. 19th St., #1200, Arlington, VA 22209; (703) 525-7788. Fax, (703) 525-8817/8938. Timothy C. MacCarthy, President.

Web, www.aiam.org

Membership: importers of cars and automotive equipment. Serves as an information clearinghouse on import regulations at the state and federal levels.

Automotive Aftermarket Industry Assn., 4600 East-West Hwy., #300, Bethesda, MD 20814; (301) 654-6664. Fax, (301) 654-3299. Alfred L. Gaspar, President.

General e-mail, aaia@aftermarket.org

Web, www.aftermarket.org

Membership: domestic and international manufacturers, manufacturers' representatives, retailers, and distributors in the automotive aftermarket industry, which involves service of a vehicle after it leaves the dealership. Offers educational programs, conducts research, and provides members with technical and international trade services; acts as liaison with government; sponsors annual marketing conference and trade shows.

Automotive Parts Rebuilders Assn., 14160 Newbrook Dr., #210, Chantilly, VA 20151; (703) 968-2772. Fax, (703) 968-2878. William C. Gager, President.

General e-mail, mail@apra.org

Web, www.apra.org

Membership: rebuilders of automotive parts. Conducts educational programs on transmission, brake, clutch, water pump, air conditioning, electrical parts, heavy-duty brake, and carburetor rebuilding.

Automotive Recyclers Assn., 3975 Fair Ridge Dr., #20 Terrace Level North, Fairfax, VA 22033-2924; (703) 385-1001. Fax, (703) 385-1494. William P. Steinkuller, Executive Vice President.

Web, www.autorecyc.org

Membership: retail and wholesale firms selling recycled auto and truck parts. Works to increase the efficiency of businesses in the automotive recycling industry. Cooperates with public and private agencies to encourage further automotive recycling efforts.

Electronic Industries Alliance, 2500 Wilson Blvd., #400, Arlington, VA 22201-3834; (703) 907-7500. Fax, (703) 907-7501. Dave McCurdy, President.

Web, www.eia.org

Membership: manufacturers, dealers, installers, and distributors of consumer electronics products. Provides consumer information and data on industry trends; advocates an open market. Monitors legislation and regulations.

Japan Automobile Manufacturers Assn., *Washington Office,* 1050 17th St. N.W., #410 20036; (202) 296-8537. Fax, (202) 872-1212. William C. Duncan, General Director.

General e-mail, jama@jama.org

Web, www.jama.org

Membership: Japanese motor vehicle manufacturers. Interests include energy, market, trade, and environmental issues. (Headquarters in Tokyo.)

National Automobile Dealers Assn., 8400 Westpark Dr., McLean, VA 22102-3591; (703) 821-7000. Fax, (703) 821-7075. Phillip Brady, President.

General e-mail, nada@nada.org

Web, www.nada.org

Membership: domestic and imported franchised new car and truck dealers. Publishes the *National Automobile Dealers Used Car Guide* (Blue Book).

Recreation Vehicle Dealers Assn. of North America, 3930 University Dr., Fairfax, VA 22030-2515; (703) 591-7130. Fax, (703) 591-0734. Michael A. Molino, President. Information, (800) 336-0355.

General e-mail, info@rvda.org

Web, www.rvda.org

Serves as liaison between the recreation vehicle industry and government; interests include government regulation of safety, trade, warranty, and franchising; provides members with educational services; works to improve service standards for consumers.

Recreation Vehicle Industry Assn., 1896 Preston White Dr., Reston, VA 20191 (mailing address: P.O. Box 2999, Reston, VA 20195-0999); (703) 620-6003. Fax, (703) 620-5071. David J. Humphreys, President.

General e-mail, rvia@rvia.org

Web, www.rvia.org

Membership: manufacturers of recreation vehicles and their suppliers. Compiles shipment statistics and other technical data; provides consumers and the media with information on the industry. Assists members' compliance with American National Standards Institute requirements for recreation vehicles. Monitors legislation and regulations.

Tire Assn. of North America, *11921 Freedom Dr., #550, Reston, VA 20190; (703) 736-8082. Fax, (703) 904-4339. Roy Littlefield, Executive Vice President. Information, (800) 876-8372.*

Web, www.tana.net

Membership: independent tire dealers and retreaders. Conducts seminars and market research. Monitors federal and state legislation and regulations.

Tire Industry Assn., *1532 Pointer Ridge Pl., Suite E, Bowie, MD 20716; (301) 430-7280. Fax, (301) 430-7283. Roy Littlefield, Executive Vice President.*

Web, www.tireindustry.org

Membership: all segments of the tire industry, including those that manufacture, repair, recycle, sell, service, or use new or retreaded tires and also suppliers that furnish equipment or services to the industry. Interests include environmental and small-business issues and quality control in the industry. Promotes government procurement of retreaded tires. Monitors legislation and regulations. (Created July 2002 by the merger of the International Tire and Rubber Assn. and the Tire Assn. of North America.)

Truck Renting and Leasing Assn., *675 N. Washington St., #410, Alexandria, VA 22314; (703) 299-9120. Fax, (703) 299-9115. Peter J. Vroom, President.*

Web, www.trala.org

Membership: truck renting and leasing companies and system suppliers to the industry. Acts as liaison with legislative bodies and regulatory agencies. Interests include federal motor carrier safety issues, highway funding, operating taxes and registration fees at the state level, and uniformity of state taxes.

Truck Trailer Manufacturers Assn., *1020 Princess St., Alexandria, VA 22314; (703) 549-3010. Fax, (703) 549-3014. Richard P. Bowling, President.*

Web, www.ttmanet.org

Membership: truck trailer manufacturing and supply companies. Serves as liaison between its members and government agencies; works to improve safety standards and industry efficiency.

Union of Needletrades Industrial and Textile Employees (UNITE), *Washington Office, 888 16th St.*

N.W., #303 20006; (202) 347-7417. Fax, (202) 347-0708. Patricia Campos, Legislative Representative.

General e-mail, stopsweatshops@uniteunion.org

Web, www.uniteunion.org

Membership: approximately 250,000 workers in basic apparel and textiles, millinery, shoe, laundry, retail, and related industries; and in auto parts and auto supply. Assists members with contract negotiation and grievances; conducts training programs and workshops. Monitors legislation and regulations. (Headquarters in New York; affiliated with the AFL-CIO.)

United Auto Workers, *Washington Office, 1757 N St. N.W. 20036; (202) 828-8500. Fax, (202) 293-3457. Alan Reuther, Legislative Director.*

Web, www.uaw.org

Membership: approximately 750,000 active and 600,000 retired North American workers in aerospace, automotive, defense, manufacturing, steel, technical, and other industries. Assists members with contract negotiation and grievances; conducts training programs and workshops. Monitors legislation and regulations. (Headquarters in Detroit, Mich.; affiliated with the AFL-CIO.)

Traffic Safety

AGENCIES

Federal Highway Administration (FHWA), *(Transportation Dept.), Operations, 400 7th St. S.W., #3401, HOP-1 20590; (202) 366-0408. Fax, (202) 366-3302. Jeffrey F. Paniati, Associate Administrator.*

Web, www.its.dot.gov

Fosters the efficient operation of streets and highways. Facilitates the deployment of transportation management and traveler information ITS technologies. Includes offices of Travel Management, Operations Technology Services, Freight Management and Operations, and Intelligent Transportation Systems ITS.

Federal Motor Carrier Safety Administration *(Transportation Dept.), 400 7th St. S.W., #8202 20590; (202) 366-2519. Fax, (202) 366-3224. Annette M. Sandberg, Administrator (Acting).*

Web, www.fmcsa.dot.gov

Develops roadway safety standards, including standards for traffic control systems and devices. Administers program to make safety improvements to highways. Monitors the federal and state Motor Carrier Safety Assistance programs to improve commercial vehicle safety on U.S. highways.

Federal Motor Carrier Safety Administration *(Transportation Dept.), Bus and Truck Standards and*

Operations, 400 7th St. S.W., #8300 20590; (202) 366-5370. Fax, (202) 366-8842. Robert Proferes, Director. Web, www.fmcsa.dot.gov

Interprets and disseminates national safety regulations regarding commercial drivers' qualifications, maximum hours of service, accident reporting, and transportation of hazardous materials. Sets minimum levels of financial liability for trucks and buses. Responsible for Commercial Driver's License Information Program.

National Highway Traffic Safety Administration *(Transportation Dept.),* 400 7th St. S.W., #5220 20590; (202) 366-1836. Fax, (202) 366-2106. Dr. Jeffrey William Runge, Administrator, (202) 366-2105. Information, (202) 366-9550. Toll-free 24-hour hotline, (800) 424-9393; in Washington, (202) 366-0123. Web, www.nhtsa.dot.gov

Implements motor vehicle safety programs; issues federal motor vehicle safety standards; conducts testing programs to determine compliance with these standards; funds local and state motor vehicle and driver safety programs; conducts research on motor vehicle development, equipment, and auto and traffic safety. The Auto Safety Hotline provides safety information and handles consumer problems and complaints involving safety-related defects.

National Highway Traffic Safety Administration *(Transportation Dept.),* **National Driver Register,** 400 7th St. S.W., #6124 20590; (202) 366-4800. Fax, (202) 366-2746. Glenn Karr, Chief. Web, www.nhtsa.dot.gov/people/perform/driver

Maintains and operates the National Driver Register, a program in which states exchange information on motor vehicle driving records to ensure that drivers with suspended licenses in one state cannot obtain licenses in any other state.

National Transportation Safety Board, *Highway Safety,* 490 L'Enfant Plaza East S.W., HS-1 20594; (202) 314-6440. Fax, (202) 314-6406. Joseph G. Osterman, Director. Web, www.ntsb.gov

In cooperation with states, investigates selected highway transportation accidents to compile the facts upon which the board determines probable cause; works to prevent similar recurrences; makes recommendations on matters pertaining to highway safety and accident prevention.

NONPROFIT

AAA Foundation for Traffic Safety, *1440 New York Ave. N.W., #201 20005; (202) 638-5944. Fax, (202) 638-*

5943. J. Peter Kissinger, President. Fulfillment, (800) 305-7233. Web, www.aaafoundation.org

Sponsors "human factor" research on traffic safety issues, including bicycle and pedestrian safety; supplies traffic safety educational materials to elementary and secondary schools, commercial driving schools, law enforcement agencies, motor vehicle administrations, and programs for older drivers.

Advocates for Highway and Auto Safety, *750 1st St. N.E., #901 20002; (202) 408-1711. Fax, (202) 408-1699.* Judith Lee Stone, President. General e-mail, advocates@saferoads.org Web, www.saferoads.org

Coalition of insurers, citizens' groups, and public health and safety organizations. Advocates public policy designed to reduce deaths, injuries, and economic costs associated with motor vehicle crashes and fraud and theft involving motor vehicles. Interests include safety belts and child safety seats, air bags, drunk driving abuse, motorcycle helmets, vehicle crashworthiness, and speed limits. Monitors legislation and regulations.

American Highway Users Alliance, *1 Thomas Circle N.W., 10th Floor 20005; (202) 857-1200. Fax, (202) 857-1220.* Diane Steed, President. Web, www.highways.org

Membership: companies and associations representing major industry and highway user groups. Develops information, analyzes public policy, and advocates legislation to improve roadway safety and efficiency and to increase the mobility of the American public. (Affiliated with the Roadway Safety Foundation.)

American Trucking Assns., *Safety and Operations Policy,* 2200 Mill Rd., Alexandria, VA 22314; (703) 838-1847. Fax, (703) 683-1398. David J. Osiecki, Vice President. Web, www.trucking.org

Membership: state trucking associations, individual trucking and motor carrier organizations, and related supply companies. Provides information on safety for the trucking industry. Develops safety training programs for motor carriers and drivers.

Center for Auto Safety, *1825 Connecticut Ave. N.W., #330 20009; (202) 328-7700. Fax, (202) 387-0140.* Clarence M. Ditlow III, Executive Director. Web, www.autosafety.org

Public interest organization that receives written consumer complaints against auto manufacturers; monitors federal agencies responsible for regulating and enforcing auto and highway safety rules.

Commercial Vehicle Safety Alliance, *1101 17th St. N.W., #803 20036; (202) 775-1623. Fax, (202) 775-1624. Stephen C. Campbell, Executive Director.*
General e-mail, cvsahq@cvsa.org
Web, www.cvsa.org

Membership: U.S., Canadian, and Mexican officials responsible for administering and enforcing commercial motor carrier safety laws. Works to increase on-highway inspections, prevent duplication of inspections, improve the safety of equipment operated on highways, and improve compliance with hazardous materials transportation regulations.

Governors Highway Safety Assn., *750 1st St. N.E., #720 20002-4241; (202) 789-0942. Fax, (202) 789-0946. Barbara L. Harsha, Executive Director.*
General e-mail, headquarters@statehighwaysafety.org
Web, www.statehighwaysafety.org

Membership: state officials who manage highway safety programs. Maintains information clearinghouse on state highway safety programs; interprets technical data concerning highway safety. Represents the states in policy debates on national highway safety issues.

Institute of Transportation Engineers, *1099 14th St. N.W., #300 20005; (202) 289-0222. Fax, (202) 289-7722. Philip J. Caruso, Deputy Executive Director.*
General e-mail, ite_staff@ite.org
Web, www.ite.org

Membership: international professional transportation engineers. Interests include safe and efficient surface transportation; provides professional and scientific information on transportation standards and recommended practices.

Insurance Institute for Highway Safety,
1005 N. Glebe Rd., #800, Arlington, VA 22201; (703) 247-1600. Fax, (703) 247-1678. Brian O'Neill, President.
Web, www.highwaysafety.org

Membership: property and casualty insurance associations and individual insurance companies. Conducts research and provides data on highway safety; seeks ways to reduce losses from vehicle crashes. (Affiliated with Highway Loss Data Institute.)

Mothers Against Drunk Driving (MADD), *Washington Office, 1025 Connecticut Ave. N.W., #1200 20036; (202) 293-2270. Fax, (202) 293-0106. Karen Sprattler, Public Policy Director.*
Web, www.madd.org

Concerned with alcohol policy as it relates to motor vehicle safety. Supports implementation of a nationwide legal intoxication level of 0.08 blood alcohol content. (Headquarters in Irving, Texas.)

National Commission Against Drunk Driving (NCADD), *8403 Colesville Rd., #370, Silver Spring, MD 20910; (240) 247-6004. Fax, (240) 247-7012. John V. Moulden, President.*
General e-mail, ncadd@ncadd.com
Web, www.ncadd.com

Works to increase public awareness of the problem of drunk and impaired drivers. Sponsors the Commission Communities Project, which targets male drivers between the ages of twenty-one and thirty-four. Administers work-site traffic safety programs for corporate managers. Monitors the implementation of recommendations made by the Presidential Commission Against Drunk Driving.

National Crash Analysis Center *(George Washington University), 20101 Academic Way, Ashburn, VA 20147; (703) 726-8362. Fax, (703) 726-8359. Azim Eskandarian, Director.*
Web, www.ncac.gwu.edu

Conducts advanced research on transportation safety. Serves as a resource for the transportation research community on all Federal Highway Administration and National Highway Traffic Safety Administration crash test films and documentation. Research interests include biomechanics, crash-related injury, vehicle dynamics, and vehicle-to-object analysis.

National Safety Council, *Public Affairs, Washington Office, 1025 Connecticut Ave. N.W., #1200 20036; (202) 293-2270. Fax, (202) 293-0032. Charles A. Hurley, Vice President of Transportation Safety Group.*
Web, www.nsc.org

Chartered by Congress. Conducts research and provides educational and informational services on highway safety, child passenger safety, and motor vehicle crash prevention; promotes policies to reduce accidental deaths and injuries. Monitors legislation and regulations. (Headquarters in Itasca, Ill.)

National School Transportation Assn., *625 Slaters Lane, #205, Alexandria, VA 22314; (703) 684-3200. Fax, (703) 684-3212. Jeffrey Kulick, Executive Director.*
General e-mail, info@schooltrans.com
Web, www.yellowbuses.org

Membership: private owners who operate school buses on contract, bus manufacturers, and allied companies. Primary area of interest and research is school bus safety.

Network of Employers for Traffic Safety, *8150 Leesburg Pike, #410, Vienna, VA 22182; (703) 891-6005. Fax, (703) 891-6010. Kathryn A. Lusby-Treber, Executive Director.*

General e-mail, nets@trafficsafety.org

Web, www.trafficsafety.org

Dedicated to reducing the human and economic cost associated with highway crashes. Helps employers develop and implement workplace highway safety programs. Provides technical assistance.

Roadway Safety Foundation, *1 Thomas Circle, 10th Floor 20005; (202) 857-1200. Fax, (202) 857-1220. Diane Steed, Executive Director (Acting).*

Web, www.roadwaysafety.org

Conducts highway safety programs to reduce automobile-related accidents and deaths. (Affiliated with American Highway Users Alliance.)

Rubber Manufacturers Assn., *1400 K St. N.W., #900 20005; (202) 682-4800. Fax, (202) 682-4854. Donald Shea, President.*

General e-mail, info@rma.org

Web, www.rma.org

Membership: American tire manufacturers. Provides consumers with information on tire care and safety.

United Motorcoach Assn., *113 S. West St., 4th Floor, Alexandria, VA 22314-2824; (703) 838-2929. Fax, (703) 838-2950. Victor S. Parra, Chief Executive Officer.*

General e-mail, webmaster@uma.org

Web, www.uma.org

Provides information, offers technical assistance, conducts research, and monitors legislation. Interests include insurance, safety programs, and credit.

 **RAIL TRANSPORTATION**

AGENCIES

Federal Railroad Administration *(Transportation Dept.), 1120 Vermont Ave., 7th Floor 20590; (202) 493-6014. Fax, (202) 493-6009. Allan Rutter, Administrator.*

Web, www.fra.dot.gov

Develops national rail policies; enforces rail safety laws; administers financial assistance programs available to states and the rail industry; conducts research and development on improved rail safety.

Federal Railroad Administration *(Transportation Dept.), Policy and Program Development, 1120 Vermont Ave. N.W., #7075 20590 (mailing address: 400 7th St. S.W., Stop 15 20590); (202) 493-6400. Fax, (202) 493-6401. Vacant, Associate Administrator.*

Web, www.fra.dot.gov

Plans, coordinates, and administers activities related to railroad economics, finance, traffic and network

analysis, labor management, and transportation planning, as well as intermodal, environmental, emergency response, and international programs.

Federal Railroad Administration *(Transportation Dept.), Railroad Development, 1120 Vermont Ave. N.W., 7th Floor 20590; (202) 493-6381. Fax, (202) 493-6330. Mark E. Yachmetz, Associate Administrator.*

Web, www.fra.dot.gov

Administers federal assistance programs for national, regional, and local rail services, including freight service assistance, service continuation, and passenger service. Conducts research and development on new rail technologies.

Federal Railroad Administration *(Transportation Dept.), Safety, 1120 Vermont Ave. N.W., 6th Floor 20590; (202) 493-6300. Fax, (202) 493-6309. George A. Gavalla, Associate Administrator.*

Web, www.fra.dot.gov

Administers and enforces federal laws and regulations that promote railroad safety, including track maintenance, inspection and equipment standards, operating practices, and transportation of explosives and other hazardous materials. Conducts inspections and reports on railroad equipment facilities and accidents.

National Mediation Board, *1301 K St. N.W., #250E 20572; (202) 692-5000. Fax, (202) 692-5080. Francis J. Duggan, Chair; Benetta M. Mansfield, Chief of Staff, (202) 692-5030. Information, (202) 692-5000. Press, (202) 692-5050. TTY, (202) 692-5001.*

Web, www.nmb.gov

Mediates labor disputes in the railroad industry; determines and certifies labor representatives in the industry.

National Railroad Passenger Corp. (Amtrak), *60 Massachusetts Ave. N.E. 20002; (202) 906-3000. Fax, (202) 906-3865. David Gunn, President. Press, (202) 906-3860. Consumer relations/complaints, (202) 906-2121; Travel and ticket information, (800) 872-7245.*

Web, www.amtrak.com

Quasi-public corporation created by the Rail Passenger Service Act of 1970 to improve and develop intercity passenger rail service.

National Transportation Safety Board, *Railroad Safety, 490 L'Enfant Plaza East S.W. 20594; (202) 314-6460. Fax, (202) 314-6497. Bob Chipkevich, Director.*

Web, www.ntsb.gov

Investigates passenger train accidents, including rapid rail transit and rail commuter systems, and freight rail accidents with substantial damage to determine probable cause; investigates all employee and passenger fatalities; makes recommendations on rail transportation safety and accident prevention.

Railroad Retirement Board, *Legislative Affairs, Washington Office,* 1310 G St. N.W., #500 20005-3004; (202) 272-7742. Fax, (202) 272-7728. Margaret Lindsley, Director.
Web, www.rrb.gov

Assists congressional offices with inquiries on retirement, spouse, survivor, and unemployment benefits for railroad employees and retirees. Assists with legislation. (Headquarters in Chicago, Ill.)

Surface Transportation Board *(Transportation Dept.),* 1925 K St. N.W., #810 20423-0001; (202) 565-1510. Fax, (202) 565-9004. Roger Nober, Chair; Wayne O. Burkes, Vice Chair. Information, (202) 565-1674.
Web, www.stb.dot.gov

Regulates rail rate disputes, railroad consolidations, rail line construction proposals, line abandonments, and rail car service.

Surface Transportation Board *(Transportation Dept.), Congressional and Public Services,* 1925 K St. N.W., #840 20423-0001; (202) 565-1592. Fax, (202) 565-9016. Dan G. King, Director.
Web, www.stb.dot.gov

Informs members of Congress, the public, and the media of board actions. Prepares testimony for hearings; comments on proposed legislation; assists the public in matters involving transportation regulations.

U.S. Coast Guard (USCG), *(Homeland Security Dept.),* 2100 2nd St. S.W. 20593-0001; (202) 267-2390. Fax, (202) 267-4158. Adm. Thomas H. Collins, Commandant. Information, (202) 267-1587.
Web, www.uscg.mil

Regulates the construction, maintenance, and operation of bridges across U.S. navigable waters, including railway bridges.

CONGRESS

House Appropriations Committee, *Subcommittee on Transportation, Treasury, and Related Agencies,* 2358 RHOB 20515; (202) 225-2141. Fax, (202) 225-5895. Rep. Ernest Istook, R-Okla., Chair; Richard Efford, Clerk.
Web, www.house.gov/appropriations

Jurisdiction over legislation to appropriate funds for the Federal Railroad Administration, the National Railroad Passenger Corp. (Amtrak), and the Surface Transportation Board.

House Transportation and Infrastructure Committee, *Subcommittee on Railroads,* 589 FHOB 20515; (202) 226-0727. Fax, (202) 226-3475. Rep. Jack Quinn, R-N.Y., Chair; Glenn Scammel, Staff Director.
General e-mail, transcomm@mail.house.gov
Web, www.house.gov/transportation

Jurisdiction over freight railroads; passenger rail service, including Amtrak; high-speed rail systems; railroad labor; railroad safety; railroad retirement; railroad workers' compensation; and railroad unemployment insurance.

Senate Appropriations Committee, *Subcommittee on Transportation, Treasury, and General Government,* SD-196 20510; (202) 224-4869. Fax, (202) 228-0249. Sen. Richard C. Shelby, R-Ala., Chair; Paul Doerrer, Clerk.
Web, appropriations.senate.gov

Jurisdiction over legislation to appropriate funds for the Federal Railroad Administration, the National Railroad Passenger Corp. (Amtrak), and the Surface Transportation Board.

Senate Commerce, Science, and Transportation Committee, *Subcommittee on Surface Transportation and Merchant Marine,* SH-427 20510; (202) 224-4852. Fax, (202) 228-0326. Sen. Kay Bailey Hutchison, R-Texas, Chair; Robert Freeman, Senior Professional Staff.
Web, commerce.senate.gov

Jurisdiction over railroad legislation (except railroad labor and retirement); oversees the Federal Railroad Administration, Surface Transportation Board, and National Railroad Passenger Corp. (Amtrak).

Senate Health, Education, Labor, and Pensions Committee, SD-428 20510; (202) 224-5375. Fax, (202) 224-5128. Sen. Judd Gregg, R-N.H., Chair; Sharon Soderstrom, Staff Director. TTY, (202) 224-1975.
Web, health.senate.gov

Jurisdiction over legislation on railroad labor and retirement.

NONPROFIT

American Short Line and Regional Railroad Assn., 50 F St. N.W., #7020 20001; (202) 628-4500. Fax, (202) 628-6430. Richard F. Timmons, President.
General e-mail, aslrra@aslrra.org
Web, www.aslrra.org

Membership: independently owned short line and regional railroad systems. Assists members with technical and legal questions; compiles information on laws, regulations, and other matters affecting the industry.

Assn. of American Railroads, *50 F St. N.W., 4th Floor 20001; (202) 639-2100. Fax, (202) 639-2558. Edward R. Hamberger, President. Library, (202) 639-2333. Press, (202) 639-2555.*

General e-mail, info@aar.org

Web, www.aar.org

Provides information on freight railroad operations, safety and maintenance, economics and finance, management, and law and legislation; conducts research; issues statistical reports. Library open to the public by appointment.

Brotherhood of Maintenance of Way Employees, Washington Office, *10 G St. N.E., #460 20002; (202) 638-2135. Fax, (202) 737-3085. Mac A. Fleming, President.*

Web, www.bmwe.org

Membership: rail industry workers and others. Assists members with contract negotiation and grievances; conducts training programs and workshops. Monitors legislation and regulations. (Headquarters in Southfield, Mich.; affiliated with the AFL-CIO.)

National Assn. of Railroad Passengers, *900 2nd St. N.E., #308 20002-3557; (202) 408-8362. Fax, (202) 408-8287. Ross B. Capon, Executive Director.*

General e-mail, narp@narprail.org

Web, www.narprail.org

Consumer organization. Works to expand and improve U.S. intercity and commuter rail passenger service, increase federal funds for mass transit, ensure fair treatment for rail freight transportation, and address environmental concerns pertaining to mass transit. Opposes subsidies for intercity trucking; works with Amtrak on scheduling, new services, fares, and advertising.

National Assn. of Regulatory Utility Commissioners, *1101 Vermont Ave. N.W., #200 20005; (202) 898-2200. Fax, (202) 898-2213. Charles Gray, Executive Director. Press, (202) 898-2205.*

Web, www.naruc.org

Membership: members of federal, state, municipal, and Canadian regulatory commissions that have jurisdiction over motor and common carriers. Interests include railroads.

National Railway Labor Conference, *1901 L St. N.W., #500 20036; (202) 862-7200. Fax, (202) 862-7230. Robert F. Allen, Chair.*

Assists member railroad lines with labor matters; negotiates with railroad labor representatives.

Railway Supply Institute, *700 N. Fairfax St., #601, Alexandria, VA 22314; (703) 836-2332. Fax, (703) 548-0058. Thomas D. Simpson, Executive Director.*

General e-mail, rpi@rpi.org

Web, www.rpi.org

Membership: railroad and rail rapid transit suppliers. Conducts research on safety and new technology; monitors legislation.

Transportation Communications International Union, *3 Research Pl., Rockville, MD 20850; (301) 948-4910. Fax, (301) 948-1872. Robert A. Scardelletti, President.*

Web, www.tcunion.org

Membership: approximately 120,000 railway workers. Assists members with contract negotiation and grievances; conducts training programs and workshops. Monitors legislation and regulations. (Affiliated with the AFL-CIO and Canadian Labour Congress.)

 TRANSIT SYSTEMS

AGENCIES

Federal Transit Administration *(Transportation Dept.), 400 7th St. S.W., #9328 20590; (202) 366-4040. Fax, (202) 366-9854. Jennifer L. Dorn, Administrator. Information, (202) 366-4319.*

Web, www.fta.dot.gov

Responsible for developing improved mass transportation facilities, equipment, techniques, and methods; assists state and local governments in financing mass transportation systems.

Federal Transit Administration *(Transportation Dept.), Budget and Policy, 400 7th St. S.W., #9310 20590; (202) 366-4050. Fax, (202) 366-7116. Robert Tuccillo, Associate Administrator (Acting).*

Web, www.fta.dot.gov/office/budget

Develops budgets, programs, legislative proposals, and policies for the federal transit program; evaluates program proposals and their potential impact on local communities; coordinates private sector initiatives of the agency.

Federal Transit Administration *(Transportation Dept.), Program Management, 400 7th St. S.W., #9315 20590; (202) 366-4020. Fax, (202) 366-7951. Hiram J. Walker, Associate Administrator.*

Web, www.fta.dot.gov/office/program

Administers capital planning and operating assistance grants and loan activities; monitors transit projects in such areas as environmental impact, special provisions for the elderly and people with disabilities, efficiency, and investment.

Federal Transit Administration *(Transportation Dept.), Research, Demonstration, and Innovation, 400 7th St. S.W., #9401 20590; (202) 366-4052. Fax, (202) 366-3765. Barbara A. Sisson, Associate Administrator.*
Web, www.fta.dot.gov/office/research

Provides industry and state and local governments with contracts, cooperative agreements, and grants for testing, developing, and demonstrating methods of improved mass transportation service and technology. Supports security, safety, and drug control efforts in transit systems.

Maryland Transit Administration, *6 St. Paul St., Baltimore, MD 21202; (410) 767-3943. Fax, (410) 333-3279. Robert L. Smith, Administrator (Acting). Information, (888) 218-2267. TTY, (410) 539-3497. Wheelchair accessibility, (410) MTA-LIFT.*
Web, www.mtamaryland.com

Responsible for mass transit programs in Maryland; provides MARC commuter rail service between Baltimore, Washington, and suburbs in Maryland and West Virginia. (Mailing address for MARC: 5 Amtrak Way, P.O. Box 8718, Baltimore, MD 21240-8718.)

National Transportation Safety Board, *Railroad Safety, 490 L'Enfant Plaza East S.W. 20594; (202) 314-6460. Fax, (202) 314-6497. Bob Chipkevich, Director.*
Web, www.ntsb.gov

Investigates passenger train accidents, including rapid rail transit and rail commuter systems, and freight rail accidents with substantial damage to determine probable cause; investigates all employee and passenger fatalities; makes recommendations on rail transportation safety and accident prevention.

Surface Transportation Board *(Transportation Dept.), 1925 K St. N.W., #810 20423-0001; (202) 565-1510. Fax, (202) 565-9004. Roger Nober, Chair; Wayne O. Burkes, Vice Chair. Information, (202) 565-1674.*
Web, www.stb.dot.gov

Regulates mergers and through-route requirements for the intercity bus industry.

Virginia Railway Express, *1500 King St., #202, Alexandria, VA 22314; (703) 684-1001. Fax, (703) 684-1313. Peter Sklannik Jr., Chief Operating Officer. Information, (703) 684-0400. TTY, (703) 684-0551. Toll-free, (800) 743-3873.*
General e-mail, gotrains@vre.org
Web, www.vre.org

Regional transportation partnership that provides commuter rail service from Fredericksburg and Manassas, Va., to Washington, D.C.

Washington Metropolitan Area Transit Authority (Metro), *600 5th St. N.W. 20001; (202) 962-1234. Fax, (202) 962-1133. Richard A. White, General Manager. Information, (202) 637-7000.*
Web, www.metroopensdoors.com

Provides bus and rail transit service to Washington, D.C., and the neighboring Maryland and Virginia communities; assesses and plans for transportation needs. Provides fare, schedule, and route information; promotes accessibility for persons with disabilities and the elderly.

CONGRESS

House Appropriations Committee, *Subcommittee on Transportation, Treasury, and Related Agencies, 2358 RHOB 20515; (202) 225-2141. Fax, (202) 225-5895. Rep. Ernest Istook, R-Okla., Chair; Richard Efford, Clerk.*
Web, www.house.gov/appropriations

Jurisdiction over legislation to appropriate funds for the Federal Transit Administration and intercity mass transit systems, including the Washington Metropolitan Area Transit Authority.

House Transportation and Infrastructure Committee, *Subcommittee on Highways, Transit, and Pipelines, B370A RHOB 20515; (202) 225-6715. Fax, (202) 225-4623. Rep. Tom Petri, R-Wis., Chair; Levon Boyagian, Staff Director.*
General e-mail, transcomm@mail.house.gov
Web, www.house.gov/transportation

Jurisdiction over legislation on urban mass transportation and intercity mass transit systems.

Senate Appropriations Committee, *Subcommittee on Transportation, Treasury, and General Government, SD-196 20510; (202) 224-4869. Fax, (202) 228-0249. Sen. Richard C. Shelby, R-Ala., Chair; Paul Doerrer, Clerk.*
Web, appropriations.senate.gov

Jurisdiction over legislation to appropriate funds for the Federal Transit Administration, urban mass transportation, and intercity mass transit systems, including the Washington Metropolitan Area Transit Authority.

Senate Banking, Housing, and Urban Affairs Committee, *SD-534 20510; (202) 224-7391. Fax, (202) 224-5137. Sen. Richard C. Shelby, R-Ala., Chair; Kathy Casey, Staff Director.*
Web, banking.senate.gov

Jurisdiction over legislation on urban mass transportation and intercity mass transit systems.

NONPROFIT

Amalgamated Transit Union (ATU), *5025 Wisconsin Ave. N.W., 3rd Floor 20016-4139; (202) 537-1645. Fax, (202) 244-7824. Jim La Sala, President.*
Web, www.atu.org

Membership: transit workers in the United States and Canada, including bus, van, subway, and light rail operators; clerks, baggage handlers, and maintenance employees in urban transit, over-the-road, and school bus industries; and municipal workers. Assists members with contract negotiations and grievances; conducts training programs and seminars. Monitors legislation and regulations. (Affiliated with the AFL-CIO.)

American Bus Assn., *1100 New York Ave. N.W., #1050 20005-3934; (202) 842-1645. Fax, (202) 842-0850. Peter J. Pantuso, President.*
General e-mail, abainfo@buses.org
Web, www.buses.org

Membership: intercity privately owned bus companies, state associations, travel/tourism businesses, bus manufacturers, and those interested in the bus industry. Monitors legislation and regulations.

American Public Transportation Assn. (APTA),
1666 K St. N.W., #1100 20006; (202) 496-4800. Fax, (202) 496-4324. William W. Millar, President. Information, (202) 496-4889.
General e-mail, apta@apta.com
Web, www.apta.com

Membership: rapid rail and motor bus systems and manufacturers, suppliers, and consulting firms. Compiles data on the industry; promotes research. Monitors legislation and regulations.

Assn. for Commuter Transportation, *P.O. Box 15542 20003-0542; (202) 393-3497. Fax, (202) 546-2196. Stuart Anderson, Executive Director.*
General e-mail, act@act-hq.com
Web, www.actweb.org

Membership: corporations, public agencies, transit authorities, transport management associations, vanpool management companies, and individuals. Serves as a clearinghouse for ride-sharing information and materials. Monitors legislation and regulations.

Community Transportation Assn. of America,
1341 G St. N.W., 10th Floor 20005; (202) 628-1480. Fax, (202) 737-9197. Dale J. Marsico, Executive Director. Information, (800) 527-8279.
Web, www.ctaa.org

Works to improve mobility for the elderly, the poor, and persons with disabilities; concerns include rural, small-city, and specialized transportation.

National Assn. of Railroad Passengers, *900 2nd St. N.E., #308 20002-3557; (202) 408-8362. Fax, (202) 408-8287. Ross B. Capon, Executive Director.*
General e-mail, narp@narprail.org
Web, www.narprail.org

Consumer organization. Works to expand and improve U.S. intercity and commuter rail passenger service, increase federal funds for mass transit, ensure fair treatment for rail freight transportation, and address environmental concerns pertaining to mass transit. Opposes subsidies for intercity trucking; works with Amtrak on scheduling, new services, fares, and advertising.

National Research Council (NRC), *Transportation Research Board Library, 500 5th St. N.W. 20001; (202) 334-2989. Fax, (202) 334-2527. Barbara Post, Librarian.*
Web, www.trb.org

Provides access to the National Research Council's research projects and publications covering such topics as public transportation technology and management, elderly and disabled passenger needs, and rural transport systems. Fee for services.

United Motorcoach Assn., *113 S. West St., 4th Floor, Alexandria, VA 22314-2824; (703) 838-2929. Fax, (703) 838-2950. Victor S. Parra, Chief Executive Officer.*
General e-mail, webmaster@uma.org
Web, www.uma.org

Provides information, offers technical assistance, conducts research, and monitors legislation. Interests include insurance, safety programs, and credit.

20

U.S. Congress and Politics

ACCESS TO CONGRESSIONAL INFORMATION

AGENCIES

National Archives and Records Administration (NARA), *Federal Register, 800 N. Capitol St., #700 20001 (mailing address: 8601 Adelphi Rd., College Park, MD 20740-6001); (202) 741-6000. Fax, (202) 741-6012. Raymond Mosley, Director. TTY, (202) 741-6086. Public Laws Update Service (PLUS), (202) 523-6641.*
General e-mail, fedreg.info@nara.gov
Web, www.archives.gov/federal_register

Assigns public law numbers to enacted legislation, executive orders, and proclamations; responds to inquiries on public law numbers; assists inquirers in finding presidential signing or veto messages in the *Weekly Compilation of Presidential Documents* and the *Public Papers of the Presidents* series; compiles slip laws and annual *United States Statutes at Large;* compiles indexes for finding statutory provisions. Operates Public Laws Update Service (PLUS) and Public Law Electronic Notification System (PENS), which provides information by telephone or e-mail on new legislation. Publications available from the U.S. Government Printing Office.

CONGRESS

Government Printing Office (GPO), *Documents, 732 N. Capitol St. N.W. 20401 (mailing address: Superintendent of Documents, Government Printing Office, MS-SD 20401); (202) 512-0571. Fax, (202) 512-1434. Judith C. Russell, Superintendent. Congressional order desk and publications, (202) 512-1808; fax for orders, (202) 512-2250. Toll-free, (866) 512-1800.*
General e-mail, orders@gpo.gov
Web, www.gpo.gov/su_docs

Prints, distributes, and sells congressional documents, prints, public laws, reports, and House calendars. Orders, P.O. Box 371954, Pittsburgh, PA 15250-7954.

House Administration Committee, *1309 LHOB 20515; (202) 225-8281. Fax, (202) 225-9957. Rep. Bob W. Ney, R-Ohio, Chair; Paul Vinovich, Staff Director.*
Web, www.house.gov/cha

Jurisdiction over the printing, cost of printing, binding, and distribution of congressional publications; jurisdiction (in conjunction with the Senate Rules and Administration Committee and the Joint Committee on Printing) over the Government Printing Office, executive papers, and depository libraries; jurisdiction over federal election law.

Joint Committee on Printing, *SR-346 20515; (202) 224-3244. Fax, (202) 228-2186. Rep. Bob Ney, R-Ohio, Chair; Paul Vinovich, Staff Director.*
Web, www.house.gov/jcp

Controls arrangement and style of the *Congressional Record;* determines which congressional prints, documents, and reports are inserted; oversees public printing, binding, and distribution of government publications; oversees activities of the Government Printing Office (in conjunction with the House Administration and Senate Rules and Administration committees).

Legislative Resource Center, *B106 CHOB 20515-6612; (202) 226-5200. Fax, (202) 226-5204. Deborah Turner, Manager.*
General e-mail, lrc@mail.house.gov
Web, clerk.house.gov/clerk/Offices_Services/lrc.php

Conducts historical research. Advises members on the disposition of their records and papers; maintains information on manuscript collections of former members; maintains biographical files on former members. Print publications include *Biographical Directory of the United States Congress, 1774–1989; Guide to Research Collections of Former Members of the United States House of Representatives, 1789–1987; Black Americans in Congress, 1870–1989;* and *Women in Congress, 1917–1989.*

Legislative Resource Center, *Records and Registration, B106 CHOB 20515-6612; (202) 226-5200. Fax, (202) 226-5208. Deborah Turner, Director.*
Web, clerkweb.house.gov/clerk/office_services/lrc.php

Maintains and distributes House bills, reports, public laws, and documents to members' offices, committee staffs, and the general public. (Telephone requests are accepted.)

Senate Document Room, *SH-B04 20510-7106; (202) 224-7860. Fax, (202) 228-2815. Karen Moore, Director.*

Maintains and distributes Senate bills, reports, public laws, and documents. (To obtain material send a self-addressed mailing label or fax with request. Telephone orders are not accepted, but telephone inquiries concerning availability will be answered.)

Senate Executive Clerk, *S138 CAP 20510; (202) 224-4341. Michelle Haynes, Executive Clerk.*

Maintains and distributes copies of treaties submitted to the Senate for ratification; provides information on submitted treaties and nominations. (Shares distribution responsibility with Senate Document Room, [202] 224-7860.)

Senate Historical Office, *SH-201 20510; (202) 224-6900. Fax, (202) 224-5329. Richard Baker, Historian.*

General e-mail, historian@sec.senate.gov

Web, www.senate.gov

Serves as an information clearinghouse on Senate history, traditions, and members. Collects, organizes, and distributes to the public previously unpublished Senate documents; collects and preserves photographs and pictures related to Senate history; conducts an oral history program; advises senators and Senate committees on the disposition of their noncurrent papers and records. Produces publications on the history of the Senate.

Senate Office of Conservation and Preservation, *S410 CAP 20510; (202) 224-4550. Carl Fritter, Bookbinder.*

Develops and coordinates programs related to the conservation and preservation of Senate records and materials for the Secretary of the Senate.

Senate Rules and Administration Committee, *SR-305 20510; (202) 224-6352. Fax, (202) 224-5400. Sen. Trent Lott, R-Miss., Chair; Susan Wells, Staff Director.*

Web, rules.senate.gov

Jurisdiction (in conjunction with the Joint Committee on Printing) over the Government Printing Office and legislation on printing of and corrections to the *Congressional Record.*

NONPROFIT

White House Correspondents Assn., *1067 National Press Bldg. 20045; (202) 737-2934. Fax, (202) 783-0841. Carl Cannon, President.*

General e-mail, whca@starpower.net

Web, www.whca.net

Membership: reporters who cover the White House. Acts as a link between reporters and White House staff.

NEWS SERVICES

Congressional Quarterly Inc., *1255 22nd St. N.W. 20037; (202) 419-8500. Robert W. Merry, President.*

Web, www.cq.com

Provides news, analysis, and information on government. Products include the *CQ Weekly,* online legislative tracking services, print and electronic news updates, and abstracts and full text of the *Congressional Record.* CQ Press publishes the Congressional Staff Directory, the *CQ Researcher,* and books on government. (Affiliated with the *St. Petersburg Times.*)

Congressional Record

The Congressional Record, *published daily when Congress is in session, is a printed account of proceedings on the floor of the House and Senate. A Daily*

Digest section summarizes the day's action on the floor and in committees, and lists committee meetings scheduled for the following day. An index is published monthly and at the close of sessions of Congress. Since January 1995, House members have not been allowed to edit their remarks before they appear in the Record, *but senators retain this privilege. Material not spoken on the floor may be inserted through unanimous consent to revise or extend a speech, and is published in a distinctive typeface. Grammatical, typographical, and technical corrections are also permitted.*

CONGRESS

Government Printing Office Main Bookstore (GPO), *Congressional Order Desk, 710 N. Capitol St. N.W. 20401 (mailing address: Superintendent of Documents, GPO, P.O. Box 371954, Pittsburgh, PA 15250-7954); (202) 512-1808. Fax, (202) 512-2250. Bookstore, (202) 512-1800.*

Web, www.access.gpo.gov/su_docs or bookstore.gpo.gov

Sells copies of and subscriptions to the *Congressional Record.* Orders, P.O. Box 371954, Pittsburgh, PA 15250-7954. The *Congressional Record* from 1995 to the present is available online at access.gpo.gov/su_docs .

Library of Congress, *Law Library, 101 Independence Ave. S.E., #LM240 20540; (202) 707-5065. Fax, (202) 707-1820. Rubens Medina, Law Librarian. Reading room, (202) 707-5080.*

Web, www.loc.gov

Copies of the *Congressional Record* are available for reading. Terminals in the reading room provide access to a computer system containing bill digests from the 93rd Congress to date.

NONPROFIT

Martin Luther King Jr. Memorial Library, *901 G St. N.W. 20001; (202) 727-1101. Fax, (202) 727-1129. Molly Raphael, Director. Information, (202) 727-0321. Hours of operation, (202) 727-1111 (recording).*

Web, www.dclibrary.org/mlk

Maintains collection of *Congressional Record* paperback volumes (1980 to date), bound volumes (1939–1976), microfilm (1827–1964), and microfiche (1977–1985).

Schedules, Status of Legislation

Information can also be obtained from the Congressional Record *(Daily Digest) and from individual congressional committees (see 108th Congress, p. 777)*

CONGRESS

Calendars of the U.S. House of Representatives and History of Legislation, *Clerk of the House of Representatives: Office of Legislative Operations,* mailing address: H154 CAP 20515-6601; (202) 225-7000. Fax, (202) 225-1776. Jeff Trandahl, Clerk.
Web, clerk.house.gov

Issued daily when the House is in session. Provides capsule legislative history of all measures reported by House and Senate committees; provides additional reference material in the *Congressional Record.* Subject index included in each Monday edition or in the edition published on the first day the House is in session. (Also available from the Superintendent of Documents, Government Printing Office 20402; [202] 512-1808.)

House Democratic Cloakroom, *H222 CAP 20515;* (202) 225-7330. Barry K. Sullivan, Manager. House floor action, (202) 225-7400. Legislative program, (202) 225-1600.

Provides information about House floor proceedings.

House Republican Cloakroom, *H223 CAP 20515;* (202) 225-7350. Timothy J. Harroun, Manager. House floor action, (202) 225-7430. Legislative program, (202) 225-2020.

Provides information about House floor proceedings.

Legislative Resource Center, *Legislative Information Service,* B106 CHOB 20515; (202) 225-1772. Fax, (202) 226-5208. Deborah Turner, Chief.

Records, stores, and provides legislative status information on all bills and resolutions pending in Congress. Provides information through LEGIS, a computer-based service, on all legislation introduced since the 96th Congress. Measures that became law (public or private) between the 93rd and 96th Congress are also available.

Legislative Resource Center, *Records and Registration,* B106 CHOB 20515-6612; (202) 226-5200. Fax, (202) 226-5208. Deborah Turner, Director.
Web, clerkweb.house.gov/clerk/office_services/lrc.php

Provides videotapes of House floor proceedings.

Library of Congress, *Main Reading Room,* 101 Independence Ave. 20540; (202) 707-5534. Fax, (202) 707-1957. Barbara Moreland, Head.
Web, www.loc.gov

Makes available a computer system containing information on all legislation introduced since the 93rd Congress (1973), arranged by member's name, subject, committee, and bill or resolution number.

Senate Democratic Cloakroom, *S225 CAP 20510;* (202) 224-4691. Joe Lapia, Manager. Senate floor action, (202) 224-8541.

Provides information about Senate floor proceedings.

Senate Republican Cloakroom, *S226 CAP 20510;* (202) 224-6191. Noel Ringel, Manager. Senate floor action, (202) 224-8601.

Provides information about Senate floor proceedings.

NEWS SERVICES

Associated Press, *Washington Office,* 2021 K St. N.W., #600 20006-1082; (202) 776-9400. Fax, (202) 776-9570. Sandy Johnson, Bureau Chief.
Web, www.wire.ap.org

Publishes daybook that lists congressional committee meetings and hearings and their location and subject matter. No fee for listing events in daybook. (Headquarters in New York.)

CQ Today, *1255 22nd St. N.W. 20037; (202) 419-8621. Fax, (202) 835-1635. Subscriptions, (202) 419-8515.*
Web, www.cq.com

Provides daily news and analysis about Congress; lists daily committee meetings and hearings, complete witness list, floor proceedings, and future scheduled committee meetings and hearings. Fee for services. (A publication of Congressional Quarterly Inc.)

CQ.com, *1255 22nd St. N.W. 20037; (202) 419-8511. Subscriptions and demonstrations, (202) 419-8279.*
Web, www.cq.com

Provides online congressional news and analysis, including legislative summaries, votes, testimony, and archival and reference materials. Provides hearing and markup schedules, including time and location, meeting agendas, and full witness listings. Fee for services. (Affiliated with Congressional Quarterly Inc.)

United Press International (UPI), *1510 H St. N.W., #700 20005; (202) 898-8000. Fax, (202) 898-8057.*
Web, www.upi.com

Wire service that lists congressional committee meetings and hearings, location, and subject matter. Fee for services.

Washington Post, *1150 15th St. N.W. 20071; (202) 334-7410. Information, (202) 334-6000.*
Web, www.washingtonpost.com

Lists congressional committee meetings and hearings, locations, and subject matter.

CAMPAIGNS AND ELECTIONS

AGENCIES

Federal Communications Commission (FCC), *Media Bureau: Policy Division, 445 12th St. S.W., 3rd Floor 20554; (202) 418-1440. Fax, (202) 418-2053. Robert Baker, Assistant Chief.*
Web, www.fcc.gov

Handles complaints and inquiries concerning the equal time rule, which requires equal broadcast opportunities for all legally qualified candidates for the same office, and other political broadcast, cable, and satellite rules. Interprets and enforces related Communications Act provisions, including the requirement for sponsorship identification of all paid political broadcast, cable, and satellite announcements.

Federal Election Commission (FEC), *999 E St. N.W. 20463; (202) 694-1000. Fax, (202) 219-3880. Ellen Weintraub, Chair. Information, (202) 694-1100. Library, (202) 694-1600. Press, (202) 694-1220. Toll-free information, (800) 424-9530.*
Web, www.fec.gov

Formulates, administers, and enforces policy with respect to the Federal Election Campaign Act of 1971 as amended, including campaign disclosure requirements, contribution and expenditure limitations, and public financing of presidential nominating conventions and campaigns. Receives campaign finance reports; makes rules and regulations; conducts audits and investigations. Serves as an election information clearinghouse. Copies of campaign finance reports available for inspection. Library open to the public.

Federal Election Commission (FEC), *Election Administration, 999 E St. N.W. 20463; (202) 694-1095. Fax, (202) 219-8500. Penelope Bonsall, Director. Information, (800) 424-9530.*
Web, www.fec.gov

Conducts studies on voter registration, voting procedures, and election administration; serves as an information clearinghouse on election administration; provides information on National Voter Registration Act of 1993; provides updates on performance standards for electronic voting systems; produces research publications, which are available through the Government Printing Office.

Federal Election Commission (FEC), *Public Records, 999 E St. N.W. 20463; (202) 694-1120. Fax, (202) 501-0693. Patricia Young, Assistant Staff Director. Information, (800) 424-9530.*

General e-mail, pubrec@fec.gov
Web, www.fec.gov

Makes available for public inspection and copying the detailed campaign finance reports on contributions and expenditures filed by candidates for federal office, their supporting political committees, and individuals and committees making expenditures on behalf of a candidate. Maintains copies of all reports and statements filed since 1972.

Justice Dept. (DOJ), *Election Crimes, 1400 New York Ave. N.W. 20005; (202) 514-1421. Fax, (202) 514-3003. Craig C. Donsanto, Director.*
Web, www.usdoj.gov

Supervises enforcement of federal criminal laws related to campaigns and elections. Oversees investigation of deprivation of voting rights; intimidation and coercion of voters; denial or promise of federal employment or other benefits; illegal political contributions, expenditures, and solicitations; and all other election violations referred to the division.

CONGRESS

House Administration Committee, *1309 LHOB 20515; (202) 225-8281. Fax, (202) 225-9957. Rep. Bob W. Ney, R-Ohio, Chair; Paul Vinovich, Staff Director.*
Web, www.house.gov/cha

Jurisdiction over legislation and other matters related to all federal elections, including campaign finance; corrupt practices; contested House elections; voter registration; overseas voters; and broadcast of early election projections. Oversees operations of the Federal Election Commission.

House Appropriations Committee, *Subcommittee on Transportation, Treasury, and Related Agencies, 2358 RHOB 20515; (202) 225-2141. Fax, (202) 225-5895. Rep. Ernest Istook, R-Okla., Chair; Richard Efford, Clerk.*
Web, www.house.gov/appropriations

Jurisdiction over legislation to appropriate funds for the Federal Election Commission.

House Commission on Congressional Mailing Standards (Franking Commission), *1338 LHOB 20515; (202) 225-9337. Fax, (202) 226-0047. Rep. Bob W. Ney, R-Ohio, Chair; Jack Dail, Staff Director.*
Web, www.house.gov/cha/nfrankingcommission1.htm

Receives complaints, conducts investigations, and issues decisions on disputes arising from the alleged abuse of franked mail by House members.

House Government Reform Committee, *2157 RHOB 20515; (202) 225-5074. Fax, (202) 225-3974.*

FEDERAL ELECTION COMMISSION

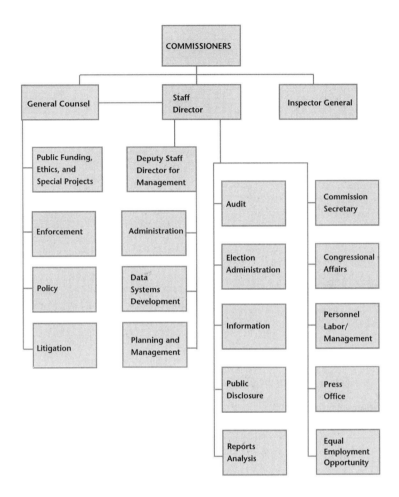

Rep. Thomas M. Davis III, R-Va., Chair; Peter Sirh, Staff Director.

Web, www.house.gov/reform

Oversight of election laws in the District of Columbia.

House Judiciary Committee, *Subcommittee on the Constitution,* 362 FHOB 20515; (202) 226-7680. Fax, (202) 225-3746. Rep. Steve Chabot, R-Ohio, Chair; Crystal Roberts, Chief Counsel.

General e-mail, Judiciary@mail.house.gov

Web, www.house.gov/judiciary

Jurisdiction over proposed constitutional amendments related to the electoral college, campaign reform, and presidential succession.

House Ways and Means Committee, 1102 LHOB 20515; (202) 225-3625. Fax, (202) 225-2610. Rep. Bill Thomas, R-Calif., Chair; Allison Giles, Chief of Staff.

General e-mail, contactwaysandmeans@mail.house.gov

Web, waysandmeans.house.gov

Jurisdiction over legislation on taxes and credits for public financing of federal elections.

Legislative Resource Center, *Records and Registration,* B106 CHOB 20515-6612; (202) 226-5200. Fax, (202) 226-5208. Deborah Turner, Director.

Web, clerkweb.house.gov/clerk/office_services/lrc.php

Receives reports of campaign receipts and expenditures of House candidates and committees. Open for public inspection.

Secretary of the Senate, *Public Records: Campaign Financing,* SH-232 20510; (202) 224-0761. Fax, (202) 224-1851. Raymond Davis, Chief.

Receives reports of campaign receipts and expenditures of Senate candidates and committees. Open for public inspection.

Senate Appropriations Committee, *Subcommittee on Transportation, Treasury, and General Government,* SD-196 20510; (202) 224-4869. Fax, (202) 228-0249. Sen. Richard C. Shelby, R-Ala., Chair; Paul Doerrer, Clerk.
Web, appropriations.senate.gov

Jurisdiction over legislation to appropriate funds for the Federal Election Commission.

Senate Finance Committee, SD-219 20510; (202) 224-4515. Fax, (202) 228-0554. Sen. Charles E. Grassley, R-Iowa, Chair; Kolan L. Davis, Staff Director.
Web, finance.senate.gov

Jurisdiction over legislation on taxes and credits for public financing of federal elections.

Senate Governmental Affairs Committee, *Subcommittee on Oversight of Government Management, the Federal Workforce, and the District of Columbia,* SH-442 20510; (202) 224-3682. Sen. George V. Voinovich, R-Ohio, Chair; Andrew Richardson, Staff Director.
General e-mail, ogm@govt-aff.senate.gov
Web, govt-aff.senate.gov

Oversight of election laws in the District of Columbia.

Senate Judiciary Committee, *Subcommittee on the Constitution, Civil Rights, and Property Rights,* SH-327 20510; (202) 224-2934. Fax, (202) 228-2856. Sen. John Cornyn, R-Texas, Chair; James Ho, Chief Counsel.
Web, judiciary.senate.gov

Jurisdiction over proposed constitutional amendments related to the electoral college, campaign reform, and presidential succession.

Senate Rules and Administration Committee, SR-305 20510; (202) 224-6352. Fax, (202) 224-5400. Sen. Trent Lott, R-Miss., Chair; Susan Wells, Staff Director.
Web, rules.senate.gov

Jurisdiction over legislation and other matters related to all federal elections, including presidential succession; campaign finance; corrupt practices; political action committees; election law changes; and broadcast of early election projections. Oversees voter registration by mail and operations of the Federal Election Commission.

NONPROFIT

Alliance for Better Campaigns, 1150 17th St. N.W., #600 20036; (202) 659-1300. Fax, (202) 659-1743. Meredith McGehee, Executive Director (Interim).
General e-mail, alliance@bettercampaigns.org
Web, www.bettercampaigns.org

Dedicated to improving the elections process by promoting voluntary, realistic standards of campaign conduct.

American Assn. of Political Consultants, 600 Pennsylvania Ave. S.E., #330 20003; (202) 544-9815. Fax, (202) 544-9816. Nancy Todd Tyner, President.
General e-mail, info@theaapc.org
Web, www.theaapc.org

Membership: political consultants, media specialists, campaign managers, corporate public affairs officers, pollsters, public officials, academicians, fundraisers, lobbyists, college students, and congressional staffers. Focuses on ethics of the profession; provides members with opportunities to meet industry leaders and learn new techniques and emerging technologies.

American Bar Assn. (ABA), *Standing Committee on Election Law,* 740 15th St. N.W. 20005; (202) 662-1692. Fax, (202) 638-3844. Elizabeth M. Yang, Director.
Web, www.abanet.org

Studies ways to improve the U.S. election and campaign process.

Center for Responsive Politics, 1101 14th St. N.W., #1030 20005; (202) 857-0044. Fax, (202) 857-7809. Larry Noble, Executive Director.
Web, www.opensecrets.org

Conducts research on Congress and related issues, with particular interest in campaign finance and congressional operations.

Commission on Presidential Debates, 1200 New Hampshire Ave. N.W., #445 20036; (202) 872-1020. Fax, (202) 783-5923. Frank J. Fahrenkopf Jr., Co-Chair; Paul G. Kirk, Co-Chair.
Web, www.debates.org

Independent, nonpartisan organization established to sponsor general election presidential and vice presidential debates, and to undertake educational and research activities related to the debates.

Common Cause, 1250 Connecticut Ave. N.W., #600 20036; (202) 833-1200. Fax, (202) 659-3716. Chellie Pingree, Director. Press, (202) 736-5770.
Web, www.commoncause.org

Citizens' legislative interest group. Records and analyzes campaign contributions to congressional candidates and campaign committees, particularly those from political action committees, and soft money contributions to national political parties.

Public Campaign, *1320 19th St. N.W., #M1 20036; (202) 293-0222. Fax, (202) 293-0202. Nick Nyhart, Executive Director.*
General e-mail, info@publicampaign.org
Web, www.publicampaign.org

National grassroots organization interested in campaign finance reform. Supports the Clean Money Campaign, a voluntary program in which candidates receive a set amount of public financing for elections if they reject private money and limit spending.

Election Statistics and Apportionment

AGENCIES

Census Bureau *(Commerce Dept.),* **Customer Services Center,** *4700 Silver Hill Rd., FB3, #1587, Suitland, MD 20746-8500 (mailing address: Customer Service, Bureau of the Census, MS-0801, Washington, DC 20233); (301) 763-4636. Fax, (301) 457-3842. Les Solomon, Chief. Fax after hours (orders only), (301) 457-3842.*
Web, www.census.gov

Provides for sale census data on counties, municipalities, and other small areas to state legislatures for use in redrawing congressional district boundaries.

Census Bureau *(Commerce Dept.),* **Population,**
4700 Silver Hill Rd., Suitland, MD 20746 (mailing address: Bldg. 3, #2318, Washington, DC 20233); (301) 457-2071. Fax, (301) 457-2644. John F. Long, Chief.
General e-mail, pop@census.gov
Web, www.census.gov

Computes every ten years the population figures that determine the number of representatives each state may have in the House of Representatives.

Census Bureau *(Commerce Dept.),* **Redistricting Data Center,** *4700 Silver Hill Rd., Suitland, MD 20746 (mailing address: Redistricting Data Center, Bureau of the Census, Washington, DC 20233); (301) 763-4039. Fax, (301) 457-4348. Catherine C. McCully, Chief.*
Web, www.census.gov/clo/www/redistricting.html

Provides state legislatures with population figures for use in legislative redistricting.

CONGRESS

Clerk of the House of Representatives, *H154 CAP 20515; (202) 225-7000. Fax, (202) 225-1776. Jeff Trandahl, Clerk.*

Web, clerkweb.house.gov

Publishes biennial compilation of statistics on congressional and presidential elections. Receives population figures compiled by the Census Bureau that form the basis for reapportionment of the House; informs state governors of new apportionment figures.

House Judiciary Committee, *2138 RHOB 20515; (202) 225-3951. Fax, (202) 225-7682. Rep. F. James Sensenbrenner Jr., R-Wis., Chair; Phil Kiko, Chief of Staff.*
General e-mail, Judiciary@mail.house.gov
Web, www.house.gov/judiciary

Jurisdiction over reapportionment legislation.

Senate Judiciary Committee, *SD-224 20510; (202) 224-5225. Fax, (202) 224-9102. Sen. Orrin G. Hatch, R-Utah, Chair; Makan Delrahim, Chief Counsel.*
Web, judiciary.senate.gov

Jurisdiction over reapportionment legislation.

Senate Rules and Administration Committee,
SR-305 20510; (202) 224-6352. Fax, (202) 224-5400. Sen. Trent Lott, R-Miss., Chair; Susan Wells, Staff Director.
Web, rules.senate.gov

Distributes *Senate Election Law Guidebook,* a compilation of Senate campaign information, including federal and state laws governing election to the U.S. Senate. Available from the Senate Document Room.

NONPROFIT

Common Cause, *State Organization,* *1250 Connecticut Ave. N.W., #600 20036; (202) 833-1200. Fax, (202) 659-3716. Ed Davis, Director.*
Web, www.commoncause.org

Citizens' interest group. Seeks to alter procedures governing redistricting by the establishment of independent redistricting commissions. Serves as an information clearinghouse; provides research and support for regional field offices.

Voting, Political Participation

NONPROFIT

AARP Grassroots and Elections, *601 E St. N.W. 20049; (202) 434-3730. Fax, (202) 434-3745. Kevin Donnellan, Director.*
Web, www.aarp.org

Nonpartisan voter education program of the AARP. Maintains nationwide volunteer network that raises issues of concern to older persons in political campaigns.

Arab American Institute, *1600 K St. N.W., #601 20006; (202) 429-9210. Fax, (202) 429-9214. James J. Zogby, President.*

General e-mail, aai@aaiusa.org

Web, www.aaiusa.org

Advocacy group concerned with political issues affecting Arab Americans. Seeks to involve the Arab American community in party politics and the electoral process.

Center for Civic Education, *Government Relations, Washington Office,* *1743 Connecticut Ave. N.W. 20009; (202) 861-8800. Fax, (202) 861-8811. Mark J. Molli, Director.*

General e-mail, centereast@civiced.org

Web, www.civiced.org

Fosters participation in civic life by citizens. Interests include the U.S. Constitution, American political traditions, and the rights and responsibilities of citizens. Develops curriculum and national standards for elementary and secondary school students; administers international civic education programs. (Headquarters in Calabasas, Calif.)

Center for Voting and Democracy, *6930 Carroll Ave., #610, Tacoma Park, MD 20912 (mailing address: P.O. Box 60037, Washington, DC 20039); (301) 270-4616. Fax, (301) 270-4133. Robert Richie, Executive Director.*

General e-mail, cvd@fairvote.org

Web, www.fairvote.org

Studies how voting systems affect participation, representation, and governance. Advocates proportional representation for legislative elections and instant runoff voting for executive elections.

Coalition of Black Trade Unionists, *1625 L St. N.W. 20036 (mailing address: P.O. Box 66268 20035); (202) 429-1203. Fax, (202) 429-1102. Wil Duncan, Executive Director.*

Web, www.cbtu.org

Monitors legislation affecting African American and other minority trade unionists. Focuses on equal employment opportunity, unemployment, and voter education and registration.

Committee for the Study of the American Electorate, *601 Pennsylvania Ave. N.W., #900, PMB #294 20004; (202) 546-3221. Fax, (202) 546-3571. Curtis Gans, Director.*

Web, www.gspm.org/csae

Nonpartisan research group that studies issues involving low and declining American voter participation.

Democracy 21, *1825 Eye St. N.W., #400 20006; (202) 429-2008. Fax, (202) 293-2660. Fred Wertheimer, President.*

General e-mail, info@Democracy21.org

Web, www.democracy21.org

Focuses on using the communications revolution to strengthen democracy and on eliminating the influence of big money in American politics.

Democratic National Committee (DNC), *Campaign Division,* *430 S. Capitol St. S.E. 20003; (202) 863-8000. Fax, (202) 863-8063. Terry McAuliffe, National Chair.*

Web, www.democrats.org

Responsible for electoral activities at the federal, state, and local levels; sponsors workshops to recruit Democratic candidates and to provide instruction in campaign techniques; conducts party constituency outreach programs; coordinates voter registration.

Joint Center for Political and Economic Studies, *1090 Vermont Ave. N.W., #1100 20005-4928; (202) 789-3500. Fax, (202) 789-6390. Eddie N. Williams, President.*

Web, www.jointcenter.org

Documents and analyzes the political and economic status of African Americans and other minority populations, focusing on economic advancement, social policy, political participation, and international affairs. Publishes an annual profile of African American elected officials in federal, state, and local government; disseminates information through forums, conferences, publications, and the Internet.

Labor Council for Latin American Advancement, *888 16th St. N.W., #640 20006; (202) 347-4223. Fax, (202) 347-5095. Oscar Sanchez, Executive Director.*

General e-mail, headquarters@lclaa.org

Web, www.lclaa.org

Membership: Hispanic trade unionists. Conducts nonpartisan voter registration and education programs; encourages increased participation by Hispanic workers in the political process. (Affiliated with the AFL-CIO.)

League of Women Voters of the United States (LWV), *1730 M St. N.W., #1000 20036; (202) 429-1965. Fax, (202) 429-0854. Nancy Tate, Executive Director.*

Web, www.lwv.org

Membership: women and men interested in nonpartisan political action and study. Works to increase participation in government; provides information on voter registration and balloting. Interests include social policy, natural resources, international relations, and representative government.

National Assn. of Latino Elected and Appointed Officials Educational Fund, *Washington Office,* *311 Massachusetts Ave. N.E. 20002; (202) 546-2536. Fax, (202) 546-4121. Larry Gonzalez, Director.*

Web, www.naleo.org

Research and advocacy group that provides civic affairs information and assistance on legislation affecting Hispanics. Encourages Hispanic participation in local, state, and national politics. Interests include the health and social, economic, and educational welfare of Hispanics. (Headquarters in Los Angeles, Calif.)

National Black Caucus of Local Elected Officials,
c/o National League of Cities, 1301 Pennsylvania Ave. N.W., #550 20004; (202) 626-3191. Fax, (202) 626-3043. E. W. Cromartie II. Press, (202) 626-3000.
Web, www.nbc-leo.org

Membership: elected officials at the local level and other interested individuals. Concerned with issues affecting African Americans, including housing, economics, the family, and human rights.

National Black Caucus of State Legislators,
444 N. Capitol St. N.W., #622 20001; (202) 624-5457. Fax, (202) 508-3826. Khalil Abdulah, Executive Director.
General e-mail, staff@nbcsl.com
Web, www.nbcsl.com

Membership: African American state legislators. Promotes effective leadership among African American state legislators; serves as an information network and clearinghouse for members.

National Coalition on Black Civic Participation,
1025 Vermont Ave. N.W., #1010 20005; (202) 659-4929. Fax, (202) 659-5025. Melanie L. Campbell, Executive Director.
General e-mail, ncbcp@ncbcp.org
Web, www.bigvote.org

Seeks to increase black voter civic participation to eliminate barriers to political participation for African Americans. Sponsors Operation Big Vote, Black Youth Vote, and Black Women's Roundtable that conducts voter education, registration, and get-out-the-vote activities in African American communities. Operates an information resource center. Monitors legislation and regulations.

National Political Congress of Black Women,
8484 Georgia Ave., #420, Silver Spring, MD 20910; (301) 562-8000. Fax, (301) 562-8303. C. DeLores Tucker, Chair.
General e-mail, info@npcbw.org
Web, www.npcbw.org

Nonpartisan political organization that encourages African American women to participate in the political process. Advocates nonpartisan voter registration and encourages African American women to engage in other political activities. Develops positions and participates in platform development and strategies that address the needs of communities at every level of government.

National Women's Political Caucus, *1634 Eye St. N.W., #310 20006; (202) 785-1100. Fax, (202) 785-3605. Roselyn O'Connell, President.*
General e-mail, info@nwpc.org
Web, www.nwpc.org

Advocacy group that seeks greater involvement of women in politics. Seeks to identify, recruit, and train women for elective and appointive political office, regardless of party affiliation; serves as an information clearinghouse on women in politics, particularly during election campaigns; publishes directory of women holding federal and state offices.

Republican National Committee (RNC), *Political Operations, 310 1st St. S.E. 20003; (202) 863-8600. Fax, (202) 863-8657. Blaise Hazelwood, Director.*
General e-mail, info@rnchq.org
Web, www.rnc.org

Responsible for electoral activities at the federal, state, and local levels; operates party constituency outreach programs; coordinates voter registration.

 CAPITOL

Capitol switchboard, (202) 224-3121. See also 108th Congress (p. 777) for each member's office.

CONGRESS

Architect of the Capitol, *SB15 CAP 20515; (202) 228-1793. Fax, (202) 228-1893. Alan M. Hantman, Architect.*
Web, www.aoc.gov

Maintains the Capitol and its grounds, the House and Senate office buildings, Capitol power plant, Robert A. Taft Memorial, and buildings and grounds of the Supreme Court and the Library of Congress; operates the Botanic Garden and Senate restaurants. Acquires property and plans and constructs buildings for Congress, the Supreme Court, and the Library of Congress. Assists in deciding which artwork, historical objects, and exhibits are to be accepted for display in the Capitol. Flag office flies American flags over the Capitol at legislators' request.

Architect of the Capitol, *Office of the Curator, HT3 CAP 20515; (202) 228-1222. Fax, (202) 228-4602. Barbara A. Wolanin, Curator. Press, (202) 228-1205.*
Web, www.aoc.gov

Preserves artwork; maintains collection of drawings, photographs, and manuscripts on and about the Capitol and the House and Senate office buildings. Maintains records of the architect of the Capitol. Library open to the public.

Capitol Police, *119 D St. N.E. 20510; (202) 224-9806. Fax, (202) 228-2592. Terrance W. Gainer, Chief. Web, www.uscapitolpolice.gov*

Responsible for security for the Capitol, House and Senate office buildings, and Botanic Garden; approves demonstration permits.

House Administration Committee, *1309 LHOB 20515; (202) 225-8281. Fax, (202) 225-9957. Rep. Bob W. Ney, R-Ohio, Chair; Paul Vinovich, Staff Director. Web, www.house.gov/cha*

Responsible for all matters related to security of the House office buildings and the House wing of the Capitol; jurisdiction over operations of the Botanic Garden, Library of Congress, Smithsonian Institution, and Capitol art collection (in conjunction with the Joint Committee on the Library of Congress).

House Appropriations Committee, *Subcommittee on Legislative Branch, H147 CAP 20515; (202) 226-7252. Rep. Jack Kingston, R-Ga., Chair; Elizabeth G. Dawson, Staff Director. Web, www.house.gov/appropriations*

Jurisdiction over legislation to appropriate funds for the House of Representatives, the Architect of the Capitol (except Senate items), the Botanic Garden, the Library of Congress, and House offices.

House Office Building Commission, *H232 CAP 20515; (202) 225-0600. Fax, (202) 226-0337. Rep. J. Dennis Hastert, R-Ill., Chair; Ted Van Der Meid, Staff Contact.*

Studies and approves all matters related to construction and alterations of House office buildings. Assigns office space to House committees.

House Transportation and Infrastructure Committee, *Subcommittee on Economic Development, Public Buildings, and Emergency Management, 589 FHOB 20515; (202) 225-3014. Fax, (202) 226-1898. Rep. Steven C. LaTourette, R-Ohio, Chair; Matt Wallen, Staff Director. General e-mail, transcomm@mail.house.gov Web, www.house.gov/transportation*

Jurisdiction over legislation relating to the Capitol and House office buildings, including naming of buildings and facilities. Oversees planning, construction, renovation, maintenance, and care of the grounds and buildings of the Capitol, House, Library of Congress, and Botanic Garden (in conjunction with the Joint Committee on the Library of Congress). Participates with other House committees in the oversight of security.

Joint Committee on the Library of Congress, *S237 CAP 20515; (202) 224-1034. Fax, (202) 224-0075. Sen. Ted Stevens, R-Alaska, Chair; Jennifer Mies, Senate Staff Contact.*

Oversees the placing of all works of art in the Capitol (in conjunction with the House Administration and Senate Rules and Administration committees); oversees development and maintenance of the Botanic Garden and the Library of Congress (in conjunction with the House Transportation and Infrastructure and Senate Rules and Administration committees).

Senate Appropriations Committee, *Subcommittee on Legislative Branch, SD-115 20510; (202) 224-7238. Sen. Ben Nighthorse Campbell, R-Colo., Chair; Carolyn Apostolou, Clerk. Web, appropriations.senate.gov*

Jurisdiction over legislation to appropriate funds for the Senate, the Architect of the Capitol (except House items), the Botanic Garden, the Library of Congress, and Senate offices.

Senate Commission on Art, *S411 CAP 20510-7102; (202) 224-2955. Fax, (202) 224-8799. Sen. Bill Frist, R-Tenn., Chair; Diane K. Skvarla, Curator of the Senate. General e-mail, curator@sec.senate.gov Web, www.senate.gov/artandhistory/art/common/generic/senate_art.htm*

Accepts artwork and historical objects for display in Senate office buildings and the Senate wing of the Capitol. Maintains and exhibits Senate collections (paintings, sculpture, furniture, and manuscripts); oversees and maintains old Senate and Supreme Court chambers.

Senate Rules and Administration Committee, *SR-305 20510; (202) 224-6352. Fax, (202) 224-5400. Sen. Trent Lott, R-Miss., Chair; Susan Wells, Staff Director. Web, rules.senate.gov*

Responsible for all matters related to the Senate office buildings, including oversight of alterations, and the Senate wing of the Capitol; jurisdiction over authorization of funds for constructing and acquiring additional office space; oversees the maintenance and care of the grounds and buildings of the Botanic Garden and the Library of Congress and the placement of all works of art in the Capitol (in conjunction with the Joint Committee on the Library of Congress). Assigns office space to Senate members and committees.

Superintendent of the House Office Buildings,
B341 RHOB 20515; (202) 225-4141. Fax, (202) 225-3003. Frank Tiscione, Superintendent.

Oversees construction, maintenance, and operation of House office buildings; assigns office space to House members under rules of procedure established by the Speaker's office and the House Office Building Commission.

Superintendent of the Senate Office Buildings,
SD-G45 20510; (202) 224-3141. Fax, (202) 224-0652. Larry R. Stoffel, Superintendent.

Oversees construction, maintenance, and operation of Senate office buildings.

U.S. Botanic Garden, *245 1st St. S.W., (Conservatory address: 100 Maryland Ave. S.W.) 20024; (202) 225-8333. Fax, (202) 225-1561. Holly H. Shimizu, Executive Director.*
General e-mail, usbg@aoc.gov
Web, www.usbg.gov

Collects, cultivates, and grows various plants for public display and study.

NONPROFIT

U.S. Capitol Historical Society, *200 Maryland Ave. N.E. 20002; (202) 543-8919. Fax, (202) 544-8244. Ron Sarasin, President. Information, (800) 887-9318. Library, (202) 543-8919, ext. 27.*
General e-mail, uschs@uschs.org
Web, www.uschs.org

Membership: members of Congress, individuals, and organizations interested in the preservation of the history and traditions of the U.S. Capitol. Conducts historical research; offers tours, lectures, and films; maintains information centers in the Capitol; publishes an annual historical calendar.

Tours and Events

CONGRESS

The House and Senate public galleries are open when Congress is in session. Free gallery passes are available from any congressional office.

Capitol Guide Service, *ST13 CAP 20510; (202) 224-3235. Sharon Nevitt, Director (Acting); David Hauck, Assistant Director, Special Services, (202) 224-4048. TTY, (202) 224-4049. Visitor information, (202) 225-6827.*

Offers the general public free guided tours of the interior of the U.S. Capitol. Provides accommodations for visitors with special needs. (As of April 2003 tours have been suspended indefinitely; visitors should call the information line.)

Capitol Police, *Protective Services, 119 D St. N.E., #605 20510; (202) 224-9596. Fax, (202) 224-0919. Steven D. Bahrns, Deputy Chief.*

Handles administrative and protective aspects of all special events held on the Capitol grounds. Accepts applications for demonstration permits and for visiting musical performances and submits them to the police board for approval. Coordinates all VIP arrivals.

Sergeant at Arms of the Senate, *S151 CAP 20510-7200; (202) 224-2341. Fax, (202) 224-7690. Bill Pickle, Sergeant at Arms.*

Enforces rules and regulations of the Senate public gallery. Responsible for security of the Capitol and Senate buildings. Approves visiting band performances on the Senate steps. (To arrange for performances, contact your senator.)

NONPROFIT

U.S. Capitol Historical Society, *200 Maryland Ave. N.E. 20002; (202) 543-8919. Fax, (202) 544-8244. Ron Sarasin, President. Information, (800) 887-9318. Library, (202) 543-8919, ext. 27.*
General e-mail, uschs@uschs.org
Web, www.uschs.org

Offers tours, lectures, and films; maintains information centers in the Capitol.

CAUCUSES: ORGANIZATIONS OF MEMBERS

HOUSE AND SENATE

Ad Hoc Congressional Committee for Irish Affairs,
436 CHOB 20515; (202) 225-7896. Fax, (202) 226-2279. Rep. Peter T. King, R-N.Y., Co-Chair; Rep. Joseph Crowley, D-N.Y., Co-Chair; Rep. Richard E. Neal, D-Mass., Co-Chair; Adam Paulson, Staff Contact.

California Democratic Congressional Delegation,
1221 LHOB 20515; (202) 225-2861. Fax, (202) 225-6791. Rep. Sam Farr, D-Calif., Chair; Rochelle Dornatt, Staff Contact.

Commission on Security and Cooperation in Europe *(Helsinki Commission), 234 FHOB, 3rd and D Sts. S.W. 20515; (202) 225-1901. Fax, (202) 226-4199. Sen. Ben Nighthorse Campbell, R-Colo., Chair; Rep. Christopher H. Smith, R-N.J., Co-Chair; Dorothy Douglas Taft, Chief of Staff.*
Web, www.csce.gov/helsinki.cfm

Independent agency created by Congress. Membership includes individuals from the executive and legislative branches. Monitors and encourages compliance with the Helsinki Accords, a series of agreements with provisions on security, economic, environmental, human rights, and humanitarian issues; conducts hearings; serves as an information clearinghouse for issues in eastern and western Europe, Canada, and the United States relating to the Helsinki Accords.

Congressional Arts Caucus, *2469 RHOB 20515; (202) 225-3615. Fax, (202) 225-7822. Rep. Louise M. Slaughter, D-N.Y., Chair; Sherrye Henry, Staff Contact.*

Congressional Asian Pacific American Caucus, *1023 LHOB 20515; (202) 225-0855. Fax, (202) 225-9497. Rep. David Wu, D-Ore., Chair; Ted Liu, Legislative Assistant.*

Congressional Black Caucus, *1632 LHOB 20515; (202) 226-9776. Fax, (202) 226-1477. Rep. Elijah E. Cummings, D-Md., Chair; Paul Brathwaite, Policy Director.*
Web, www.house.gov/cummings/cbc/cbchome.htm

Congressional Competitiveness Caucus, *c/o CELI, 201 Massachusetts Ave. N.E., #C-6 20002; (202) 546-5007. Fax, (202) 546-7037. Sen. Max Baucus, D-Mont., Co-Chair; Sen. Jeff Bingaman, D-N.M., Co-Chair; Sen. Charles E. Grassley, R-Iowa, Co-Chair; Rep. Marcy Kaptur, D-Ohio, Co-Chair; Rep. Jim Kolbe, R-Ariz., Co-Chair; Sen. Gordon H. Smith, R-Ore., Co-Chair; Joleen L. Worsley, Staff Contact.*
Web, www.celi.org/caucus.htm

Congressional Fire Services Caucus, *SH-309 20510; (202) 224-4524. Fax, (202) 224-1651. Sen. Paul S. Sarbanes, D-Md., Chair; Jim Woods, Staff Contact.*

Congressional Fire Services Institute, *900 2nd St. N.E., #303 20002; (202) 371-1277. Fax, (202) 682-3473. Sen. Paul S. Sarbanes, D-Md., Chair; William Webb, Executive Director.*
General e-mail, info@cfsi.org
Web, www.cfsi.org

Congressional Hispanic Caucus, *1507 LHOB 20515; (202) 225-1640. Fax, (202) 225-1641. Rep. Ciro D. Rodriguez, D-Texas, Chair; Alejandro Perez, Executive Director.*
Web, rodriguez.house.gov/chc/index.asp

Congressional Silk Road Caucus, *204 CHOB 20515; (202) 225-2411. Rep. Joe Pitts, R-Pa., Co-Chair; Rep. Gary L. Ackerman, D-N.Y., Co-Chair; Sen. Sam Brownback,*

R-Kan., Co-Chair; Sen. Mary L. Landrieu, D-La., Co-Chair; Ken Miller, Staff Contact.
Web, www.house.gov/pitts/silkroad.htm

Works to encourage economic, cultural, and political exchange and improved relations between the United States and the countries of central and south Asia and the Caucasus.

Congressional Task Force on International HIV/AIDS, *1035 LHOB 20515; (202) 225-3106. Fax, (202) 225-6197. Rep. Jim McDermott, D-Wash., Chair; Susanne Leach, Staff Contact.*

Studies the spread of HIV/AIDS in the developing world; helps plan the U.S. government response.

Fine Arts Board, *SH-522 20510; (202) 224-3004. Fax, (202) 224-2354. Sen. Ted Stevens, R-Alaska, Vice Chair; Jennifer Mies, Staff Contact.*

Global Legislators Organization for a Balanced Environment U.S.A., *1636 R St. N.W., 3rd Floor 20009; (202) 265-8283. Fax, (202) 265-8291. Rep. Christopher Shays, R-Conn., Chair; William R. Singleton, Executive Director.*
General e-mail, info@globeusa.org
Web, www.globeusa.org

Educates and encourages cooperation among environmentally concerned legislators around the world. Promotes the development of informed, balanced approaches to emerging environmental challenges.

Internet Caucus, *2240 RHOB 20515; (202) 225-5431. Rep. Rick Boucher, D-Va., Co-Chair; Sen. Conrad Burns, R-Mont., Co-Chair; Rep. Robert W. Goodlatte, R-Va., Co-Chair; Sen. Patrick J. Leahy, D-Vt., Co-Chair; Shelley Husband, Staff Contact.*
Web, www.netcaucus.org

Promotes growth of the Internet, including government participation; educates members and congressional staff about the Internet.

Long Island Congressional Delegation, *2243 RHOB 20515; (202) 225-2601. Fax, (202) 225-1589. Rep. Gary L. Ackerman, D-N.Y., Chair; Jedd Moskowitz, Chief of Staff.*

New York Bipartisan Congressional Delegation, *2354 RHOB 20515; (202) 225-4365. Fax, (202) 225-0816. Rep. Charles B. Rangel, D-N.Y., Chair; George Dalley, Staff Contact.*

Pennsylvania Congressional Delegation, *2123 RHOB 20515; (202) 225-2065. Fax, (202) 225-5709. Rep. John P. Murtha, D-Pa., Chair; Debra Tekavec, Staff Contact.*

Porkbusters Coalition, *2202 RHOB 20515; (202) 225-4111. Fax, (202) 226-0325. Rep. Ed Royce, R-Calif., Co-Chair; Sen. John McCain, R-Ariz., Co-Chair; Rep. Peter A. DeFazio, D-Ore., Co-Chair; Darrin Schrader, Staff Contact.*

U.S. Assn. of Former Members of Congress,
233 Pennsylvania Ave. S.E., #200 20003-1107; (202) 543-8676. Fax, (202) 543-7145. Larry LaRocco, President.

Nonpartisan organization of former members of Congress. Acts as a congressional alumni association; sponsors educational projects, including the Congress to Campus program, which provides support for colleges and universities to host visits of former representatives and senators.

U.S. Holocaust Memorial Council, *Council Relations, 100 Raoul Wallenberg Pl. S.W. 20024; (202) 488-0490. Fax, (202) 314-7881. Jane Rizer, Director.*

U.S. Interparliamentary Group—Canada, *SH-808 20510; (202) 224-3047. Fax, (202) 224-2373. Rep. Amo Houghton, R-N.Y., Chair; Sally Walsh, Director.*

Vietnam Veterans in Congress, *2211 RHOB 20515; (202) 225-5905. Fax, (202) 225-5396. Rep. David E. Bonior, D-Mich., Co-Chair; Sen. Tom Daschle, D-S.D., Co-Chair; Rep. Lane Evans, D-Ill., Co-Chair; Sen. John Kerry, D-Mass., Co-Chair; Tom O'Donnell, Staff Contact.*

Women's Policy Inc., *409 12th St. S.W., #310 20024; (202) 554-2323. Fax, (202) 554-2346. Cindy Hall, Executive Director.*
Web, www.womenspolicy.org

Nonpartisan organization that provides legislative analysis and information services on congressional actions affecting women and their families.

HOUSE

Albanian Issues Caucus, *2264 RHOB 20515; (202) 225-2464. Fax, (202) 225-5513. Rep. Eliot L. Engel, D-N.Y., Co-Chair; Rep. Sue W. Kelly, R-N.Y., Co-Chair; Jason Steinbaum, Staff Contact.*

Army Caucus, *2333 RHOB 20515; (202) 225-4611. Fax, (202) 226-0621. Rep. Chet Edwards, D-Texas, Co-Chair; Rep. John M. McHugh, R-N.Y., Co-Chair; Anne Lemay, Staff Contact.*

Biofuels Caucus, *507 CHOB 20515; (202) 225-6435. Fax, (202) 226-1385. Rep. Lane Evans, D-Ill., Co-Chair; Rep. Dennis Moore, D-Kan., Co-Chair; Rep. Tom Osborne, R-Neb., Co-Chair; Christina Muedeking, Staff Contact.*

Congressional Aerospace Caucus, *2347 RHOB 20515; (202) 225-3671. Fax, (202) 225-3516. Rep. Dave Weldon, R-Fla., Co-Chair; Brendan Curry, Staff Contact.*

Congressional Automotive Caucus, *2332 RHOB 20515; (202) 225-3401. Rep. Sherrod Brown, D-Ohio, Co-Chair; Rep. Marcy Kaptur, D-Ohio, Co-Chair; Rep. Dan Burton, R-Ind., Co-Chair; Rep. Fred Upton, R-Mich., Co-Chair; Rep. Dale E. Kildee, D-Mich., Co-Chair; Diana Brown, Staff Contact.*

Congressional Bearing Caucus, *2113 RHOB 20515; (202) 225-4476. Fax, (202) 225-4488. Rep. Nancy L. Johnson, R-Conn., Co-Chair; Rep. John M. Spratt Jr., D-S.C., Co-Chair; Douglas Lathrop, Staff Contact.*

Congressional Blue Dog Coalition, *1024 LHOB 20515; (202) 225-5315. Rep. Baron P. Hill, D-Ind., Co-Chair; Rep. Charles W. Stenholm, D-Texas, Co-Chair; Rep. Dennis Moore, D-Kan., Co-Chair; Rep. Jim Turner, D-Texas, Co-Chair; Scott Downes, Staff Contact.*

Congressional Caucus for Women's Issues,
1213 LHOB 20515; (202) 225-3515. Fax, (202) 225-9420. Rep. Judy Biggert, R-Ill., Co-Chair; Rep. Juanita Millender-McDonald, D-Calif., Co-Chair; Rep. Shelley Moore Capito, R-W.Va., Co-Chair; Rep. Louise M. Slaughter, D-N.Y., Co-Chair; Jaimie Vickery, Staff Contact.

Congressional Caucus on Korea, *1232 LHOB 20515; (202) 225-5111. Rep. Michael E. Capuano, D-Mass., Co-Chair; Rep. Vito J. Fossella, R-N.Y., Co-Chair; Robert E. Primus, Staff Contact.*

Congressional Children's Working Group, *2352 RHOB 20515; (202) 225-3915. Fax, (202) 225-6798. Rep. Tim Roemer, D-Ind., Chair; Sarah Schultz, Staff Contact.*

Congressional Friends of Animals, *2413 RHOB 20515; (202) 225-3531. Fax, (202) 226-9789. Rep. Tom Lantos, D-Calif., Co-Chair; Rep. Christopher Shays, R-Conn., Co-Chair; Guido Zucconi, Director.*

Congressional Hispanic Caucus Institute, *504 C St. N.E. 20002; (202) 543-1771. Fax, (202) 546-2143. Rep. Ciro D. Rodriguez, D-Texas, Chair; Ingrid Duran, President. Toll-free college scholarship information, (800) 392-3532.*

Develops educational and leadership programs to familiarize Hispanic students with policy-related careers and to encourage their professional development. Aids in the developing of future Latino leaders. Provides scholarship, internship, and fellowship opportunities.

Congressional Human Rights Caucus, *2413 RHOB 20515; (202) 225-3531. Rep. Tom Lantos, D-Calif., Co-Chair; Rep. Frank R. Wolf, R-Va., Co-Chair; Hans Hogrefe, Staff Contact.*

Congressional Older Americans Caucus, *2306 RHOB 20515; (202) 225-3876. Fax, (202) 225-3059. Rep. Ralph Regula, R-Ohio, Co-Chair; Rep. Bill Delahunt, D-Mass., Co-Chair; Rep. Shelley Berkley, D-Nev., Co-Chair; Jason Grove, Staff Contact.*

Congressional Social Security Caucus, *2408 RHOB 20515; (202) 225-3026. Fax, (202) 225-9764. Rep. E. Clay Shaw Jr., R-Fla., Chair; Christine Pollack, Staff Contact.*

Congressional Steel Caucus, *1410 LHOB 20515; (202) 225-5406. Fax, (202) 225-3103. Rep. Phil English, R-Pa., Co-Chair; Rep. Peter J. Visclosky, D-Ind., Co-Chair; David Stewart, Staff Contact.*

Congressional Task Force on Haiti, *2309 RHOB 20515; (202) 225-6231. Fax, (202) 226-0112. Rep. Major R. Owens, D-N.Y., Chair; Jacqueline Ellis, Staff Contact.*

Congressional Task Force on International HIV/AIDS, *1035 LHOB 20515; (202) 225-3106. Fax, (202) 225-6197. Rep. Jim McDermott, D-Wash., Chair; Susanne Leach, Staff Contact.*

Congressional Task Force on Tobacco and Health, *2229 RHOB 20515; (202) 225-3411. Fax, (202) 226-0771. Rep. Todd R. Platts, R-Pa., Co-Chair; Rep. Martin T. Meehan, D-Mass., Co-Chair; Suzy duMont, Staff Contact.*

Congressional Task Force to End the Arab Boycott, *2160 RHOB 20515; (202) 225-3931. Fax, (202) 225-5620. Rep. Ileana Ros-Lehtinen, R-Fla., Chair; Frederick Ratliff, Staff Contact.*

Congressional Urban Caucus, *1610 LHOB 20515; (202) 225-2261. Rep. Carolyn Cheeks Kilpatrick, D-Mich., Co-Chair; Rep. Deborah Pryce, D-Ohio, Co-Chair; Erica Woods-Warrior, Staff Contact.*

Congressional Working Group on China, *241 CHOB 20515; (202) 225-5136. Fax, (202) 225-0437. Rep. Frank R. Wolf, R-Va., Co-Chair; Daniel Scandling, Staff Contact.*

House Pro-Life Caucus, *2373 RHOB 20515; (202) 225-7669. Fax, (202) 225-7768. Rep. Christopher H. Smith, R-N.J., Co-Chair; John Cusey, Director.*

Medical Technology Caucus, *103 CHOB 20515; (202) 225-2871. Fax, (202) 225-6351. Rep. Anna G. Eshoo, D-Calif., Co-Chair; Rep. Jim Ramstad, R-Minn., Co-Chair; Karin Hope, Staff Contact.*

Northeast Agricultural Caucus, *2246 RHOB 20515; (202) 225-3665. Fax, (202) 225-1891. Rep. Sherwood Boehlert, R-N.Y., Co-Chair; Rep. Tim Holden, D-Pa., Co-Chair; Amy Chiang, Staff Contact.*

Permanent U.S. Congressional Delegation to the European Parliament, *2413 RHOB 20515; (202) 225-3531. Rep. Tom Lantos, D-Calif., Co-Chair; Kay Atkinson King, Staff Contact.*

Republican Study Committee, *306 CHOB 20515; (202) 225-3361. Fax, (202) 225-3462. Rep. John Shadegg, R-Ariz., Chair; Neil Bradley, Executive Director, (202) 226-9717.*

Rural Health Care Coalition, *1519 LHOB 20515; (202) 225-2715. Fax, (202) 225-5124. Rep. Mike McIntyre, D-N.C., Co-Chair; Rep. Jerry Moran, R-Kan., Co-Chair; Kim Rullman, Staff Contact.*

SENATE

Democratic Technology and Communications Committee, *SH-619 20510; (202) 224-1430. Fax, (202) 224-1431. Sen. John D. Rockefeller IV, D-W.Va., Chair; Sean R. Richardson, Staff Contact.*

Northeast–Midwest Senate Coalition, *SH-320 20510; (202) 224-0606. Fax, (202) 224-4680. Sen. Susan Collins, R-Maine, Co-Chair; Sen. Jack Reed, D-R.I., Co-Chair; Kris Sarri, Legislative Director.*

Senate Auto Caucus, *SR-269 20510; (202) 224-6221. Fax, (202) 224-1388. Sen. Carl Levin, D-Mich., Co-Chair; Sen. Mike DeWine, R-Ohio, Co-Chair; Sen. Debbie Stabenow, D-Mich., Co-Chair; Sen. George V. Voinovich, R-Ohio, Co-Chair; Alison Pascale, Staff Contact.*

Senate Cancer Coalition, *SH-303 20510; (202) 224-6521. Fax, (202) 228-1265. Sen. Sam Brownback, R-Kan., Co-Chair; Sen. Dianne Feinstein, D-Calif., Co-Chair; Glen Chambers, Staff Contact.*

Senate Democratic Task Force on Hispanic Issues, *SH-703 20510; (202) 224-5521. Fax, (202) 224-2852. Sen. Jeff Bingaman, D-N.M., Chair; Bernie Toon, Chief of Staff.*

Senate Rural Health Caucus, *SH-731 20510; (202) 224-3254. Fax, (202) 224-9369. Sen. Tom Harkin, D-Iowa, Co-Chair; Sen. Craig Thomas, R-Wyo., Co-Chair; Adam Gluck, Staff Contact.*

Senate Steel Caucus, *SH-711 20510; (202) 224-4254. Fax, (202) 228-1229. Sen. John D. Rockefeller IV, D-W.Va., Co-Chair; Sen. Arlen Specter, R-Pa., Co-Chair; Patrick Robertson, Staff Contact, (202) 224-6472.*

Senate Textile Caucus, *SR-125 20510; (202) 224-6121. Fax, (202) 228-0303. Sen. Ernest F. Hollings, D-S.C., Chair; Greg Elias, Staff Contact.*

U.S. Interparliamentary Group—British/American, *SH-808 20510; (202) 224-3047. Fax, (202) 224-2373. Vacant, Chair; Sally Walsh, Director.*

U.S. Interparliamentary Group—Mexico, *SH-808 20510; (202) 224-3047. Fax, (202) 224-2373. Sen. Christopher J. Dodd, D-Conn., Chair; Sally Walsh, Director.*

U.S. Interparliamentary Group—NATO/ U.S. Parliamentary Assembly, *SH-808 20510; (202) 224-3047. Fax, (202) 224-2373. Sen. Joseph R. Biden, D-Del., Chair; Sally Walsh, Director.*

U.S. Senate—Interparliamentary Services, *SH-808 20510; (202) 224-3047. Fax, (202) 224-2373. Sally Walsh, Director.*

Western States Senate Coalition, *SH-511 20510; (202) 224-2651. Fax, (202) 228-3687. Sen. Max Baucus, D-Mont., Co-Chair; Sen. Dianne Feinstein, D-Calif., Co-Chair; Sen. Ted Stevens, R-Alaska, Co-Chair; Sen. Orrin G. Hatch, R-Utah, Co-Chair; Sen. Byron L. Dorgan, D-N.D., Co-Chair; Sen. Ben Nighthorse Campbell, R-Colo., Co-Chair; Zak Anderson, Staff Contact.*

 CONGRESS AT WORK

See 108th Congress (p. 777) for individual members' offices and committee assignments and for rosters of congressional committees and subcommittees.

CONGRESS

House Recording Studio, *Communications Media, B310 RHOB 20515; (202) 225-3941. Fax, (202) 225-0707. Gary Denick, Director.*
Web, www.onlinecao.house.gov

Assists House members in making tape recordings. Provides daily gavel-to-gavel television coverage of House floor proceedings.

House Rules Committee, *H312 CAP 20515; (202) 225-9191. Fax, (202) 225-6763. Rep. David Dreier, R-Calif., Chair; Billy Pitts, Staff Director.*
Web, www.house.gov/rules

Sets rules for floor debate on legislation reported by regular standing committees; grants emergency waivers, under the House rules and the Congressional Budget Act of 1974, of required reporting dates for bills and resolutions authorizing new budget authority; has jurisdiction

over resolutions creating committees; has legislative authority to recommend changes in the rules of the House; has jurisdiction over recesses and final adjournments of Congress.

Office of Photography, *B302 RHOB 20515; (202) 225-2840. Dwight Comedy, Director.*

Provides House members with photographic assistance.

Parliamentarian of the House of Representatives, *H209 CAP 20515; (202) 225-7373. Charles W. Johnson III, Parliamentarian.*

Advises presiding officers on parliamentary procedures and committee jurisdiction over legislation; prepares and maintains a compilation of the precedents of the House.

Parliamentarian of the Senate, *S133 CAP 20510; (202) 224-6128. Alan S. Frumin, Parliamentarian.*

Advises presiding officers on parliamentary procedures and committee jurisdiction over legislation; prepares and maintains a compilation of the precedents of the Senate.

Senate Rules and Administration Committee, *SR-305 20510; (202) 224-6352. Fax, (202) 224-5400. Sen. Trent Lott, R-Miss., Chair; Susan Wells, Staff Director. Web, rules.senate.gov*

Jurisdiction over all matters related to the rules governing the conduct of business in the Senate, including floor, committee, and gallery procedures. Also studies and makes recommendations on computer and other technical services in the Senate; oversees operation of the computer information system for the Senate.

Sergeant at Arms of the Senate, *Senate Photographic Studio, SDG85 CAP 20510; (202) 224-6000. Fax, (202) 228-3584. Bill Allen, Supervisor.*

Provides Senate members with photographic assistance.

Sergeant at Arms of the Senate, *Senate Recording Studio, SC5 CAP 20510; (202) 224-4977. Fax, (202) 224-8701. David Bass, Manager.*

Assists Senate members in making radio and video tape recordings and live satellite broadcasts; televises Senate floor proceedings for broadcast by C-SPAN (Cable-Satellite Public Affairs Network).

Leadership

HOUSE

House Democratic Caucus, *1420 LHOB 20515; (202) 226-3210. Fax, (202) 225-9253. Rep. Robert Menendez, D-N.J., Chair; James Datri, Executive Director.*

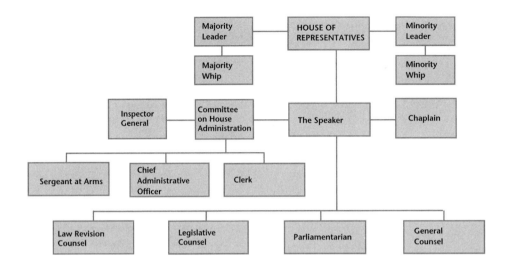

Web, dcaucusweb.house.gov

Membership: House Democrats. Selects Democratic leadership; formulates party rules and floor strategy; considers caucus members' recommendations on major issues; votes on the Democratic Steering and Policy Committee's recommendations for Democratic committee assignments.

House Democratic Policy Committee, *H301 CAP 20515; (202) 225-6760. Fax, (202) 226-0938. Rep. Nancy Pelosi, D-Calif., Chair; Craig Hanna, Executive Director.*
Web, democraticleader.house.gov

Makes recommendations to the Democratic leadership on party policy and priorities with assistance in decision making by the House Democratic leadership.

House Democratic Steering Committee, *H204 CAP 20515; (202) 225-0100. Fax, (202) 225-7414. Rep. Nancy Pelosi, D-Calif., Chair; Rep. Rosa DeLauro, D-Conn., Co-Chair; George Crawford, Sr. Adviser.*
Web, democraticleader.house.gov

Makes Democratic committee assignments, subject to approval by the House Democratic Caucus.

House Republican Conference, *1010 LHOB 20515; (202) 225-5107. Fax, (202) 225-0809. Rep. Deborah Pryce, R-Ohio, Chair; Kathryn Lehman, Chief of Staff.*
Web, www.gop.gov

Membership: House Republicans. Selects Republican leadership; formulates party rules and floor strategy, and

considers party positions on major legislation; votes on Republican Committee on Committees' recommendations for House committee chairs and Republican committee assignments; publishes *Weekly Floor Briefing* and *Daily Floor Briefing,* which analyzes pending legislation.

House Republican Policy Committee, *2471 RHOB 20515; (202) 225-6168. Fax, (202) 225-0931. Rep. Christopher Cox, R-Calif., Chair; Paul Wilkinson, Executive Director.*
Web, policy.house.gov

Studies legislation and makes recommendations on House Republican policies and positions on proposed legislation.

House Republican Steering Committee, *H209 CAP 20515; (202) 225-2204. Rep. J. Dennis Hastert, R-Ill., Chair; Karen Haas, Staff Contact.*

Makes Republican committee assignments and nominates committee chairmen subject to approval by the House Republican Conference and entire House of Representatives.

Majority Leader of the House of Representatives, *H107 CAP 20515; (202) 225-4000. Fax, (202) 225-5117. Rep. Tom DeLay, R-Tex., Majority Leader; Danielle Simonetta, Senior Floor Assistant.*
Web, majorityleader.gov

Serves as chief strategist and floor spokesperson for the majority party in the House.

Majority Whip of the House of Representatives, H329 CAP 20515; (202) 225-0197. Fax, (202) 225-5117. Rep. Roy Blunt, R-Mo., Majority Whip; Gregg L. Hartley, Chief of Staff.

General e-mail, majoritywhip.house.gov/contact.asp

Web, majoritywhip.house.gov

Serves as assistant majority leader in the House; helps marshal majority forces in support of party strategy.

Minority Leader of the House of Representatives, H204 CAP 20515-6502; (202) 225-0100. Fax, (202) 225-4188. Rep. Nancy Pelosi, D-Calif., Minority Leader; Jerry Hartz, Executive Floor Assistant.

Web, democraticleader.house.gov

Serves as chief strategist and floor spokesperson for the minority party in the House.

Minority Whip of the House of Representatives, H307 CAP 20515; (202) 225-3130. Fax, (202) 225-4188. Rep. Steny H. Hoyer, D-Md., Minority Whip; Cory Alexander, Chief of Staff.

Web, democraticwhip.house.gov

Serves as assistant minority leader in the House; helps marshal minority forces in support of party strategy.

Speaker of the House of Representatives, *Speaker's Office,* H232 CAP 20515; (202) 225-0600. Fax, (202) 226-1996. Rep. J. Dennis Hastert, R-Ill., Speaker; Scott B. Palmer, Chief of Staff.

General e-mail, speaker@mail.house.gov

Web, speaker.house.gov

Presides over the House while in session; preserves decorum and order; announces vote results; recognizes members for debate and introduction of bills, amendments, and motions; refers bills and resolutions to committees; decides points of order; appoints House members to conference committees; votes at own discretion.

See House Leadership and Partisan Committees (p. 801)

SENATE

Majority Leader of the Senate, SH-230 20510-4205; (202) 224-3135. Fax, (202) 224-4639. Sen. Bill Frist, R-Tenn., Majority Leader; Mitch Bainwol, Chief of Staff.

Web, frist.senate.gov

Serves as chief strategist and floor spokesperson for the majority party in the Senate.

Majority Whip of the Senate, S321 CAP 20510-1702; (202) 224-2708. Fax, (202) 224-3913. Sen. Mitch McConnell, R-Ky., Majority Whip; Vacant, Chief of Staff.

Web, mcconnell.senate.gov

Serves as assistant majority leader in the Senate; helps marshal majority forces in support of party strategy.

Minority Leader of the Senate, SH-221 20510-4103; (202) 224-5556. Fax, (202) 224-6603. Sen. Tom Daschle, D-S.D., Minority Leader; Peter Rouse, Chief of Staff.

General e-mail, daschle.senate.gov/webform.html

Web, daschle.senate.gov

Serves as chief strategist and floor spokesperson for the Republican party in the Senate.

Minority Whip of the Senate, S528 CAP 20510-2803; (202) 224-2158. Fax, (202) 224-7362. Sen. Harry Reid, D-Nev., Minority Whip; Susan McCue, Chief of Staff.

General e-mail, reid.senate.gov/email_form.cfm

Web, reid.senate.gov

Serves as assistant minority leader in the Senate; helps marshal minority forces in support of party strategy.

President Pro Tempore of the Senate, SH-522 20510; (202) 224-3004. Fax, (202) 224-0002. Sen. Ted Stevens, R-Alaska, President Pro Tempore.

Web, stevens.senate.gov

Presides over the Senate in the absence of the vice president.

Senate Democratic Conference, S309 CAP 20510; (202) 224-3735. Sen. Tom Daschle, D-S.D., Chair; Sen. Barbara A. Mikulski, D-Md., Secretary; Martin P. Paone, Secretary for the Majority.

Membership: Democratic senators. Selects Democratic leadership; formulates party rules and floor strategy and considers party positions on major legislation; votes on Democratic Steering Committee's recommendations for Democratic committee assignments.

Senate Democratic Policy Committee, SH-419 20510; (202) 224-3232. Sen. Byron L. Dorgan, D-N.D., Chair; Chuck Cooper, Staff Director.

General e-mail, postmaster@dpc.senate.gov

Web, www.senate.gov/~dpc

Studies and makes recommendations to the Democratic leadership on legislation for consideration by the Senate.

Senate Democratic Steering and Coordination Committee, SH-712 20510; (202) 224-9048. Sen. Hillary Rodham Clinton, R-N.Y., Chair; Jodi Sakol, Staff Director.

Makes Democratic committee assignments subject to approval by the Senate Democratic Conference.

Senate Republican Committee on Committees, SH-520 20510; (202) 224-2752. Fax, (202) 228-1067. Sen.

Larry E. Craig, R-Idaho, Chair; Michael Ware, Staff Contact.

Makes Republican committee assignments and selects committee chairs, subject to approval by the Senate Republican Conference. (The committee convenes once every two years at the beginning of each new Congress.)

Senate Republican Conference, *SH-405 20510; (202) 224-2764. Sen. Rick Santorum, R-Pa., Chair; Mark D. Rodgers, Staff Director.*
Web, www.senate.gov/~src/home/index.cfm

Membership: Republican senators. Serves as caucus and central coordinating body of the party. Organizes and elects Senate Republican leadership; votes on Republican Committee on Committees' recommendations for Senate committee chairs and Republican committee assignments. Staff provides various support and media services for Republican members.

Senate Republican Policy Committee, *SR-347 20510; (202) 224-2946. Fax, (202) 224-1235. Sen. Jon Kyl, R-Ariz., Chair; Lawrence Wilcox, Staff Director.*
Web, www.senate.gov/~rpc

Studies and makes recommendations to the majority leader on the priorities and scheduling of legislation on the Senate floor; prepares policy papers and develops Republican policy initiatives.

Vice President of the United States, *President of the Senate, S212 CAP 20510; (202) 224-2424. Richard B. Cheney, President of the Senate; Candida Wolff, Assistant to the Vice President. White House Office, (202) 456-6774.*
General e-mail, vice.president@whitehouse.gov
Web, www.whitehouse.gov/vicepresident

Presides over the Senate while in session; preserves decorum and order; announces vote results; recognizes members for debate and introduction of bills, amendments, and motions; decides points of order; votes only in the case of a tie. (President pro tempore of the Senate presides in the absence of the vice president.)

See Senate Leadership and Partisan Committees (p. 867)

Officers

HOUSE

Chaplain of the House of Representatives,
HB25 CAP 20515; (202) 225-2509. Fax, (202) 225-1776. Rev. Daniel Coughlin, Chaplain.
Web, chaplain.house.gov

Opens each day's House session with a prayer and offers other religious services to House members, their families, and staffs. (Prayer sometimes offered by visiting chaplain.)

Chief Administrative Officer of the House of Representatives,
HB30 CAP 20515; (202) 225-6900. Fax, (202) 226-6300. James M. "Jay" Eagen III, Human Resources Chief Administrative Officer.

Responsible for all administrative functions of the House, including services related to employee assistance, placement, finance, payroll, benefits, food service, information resources, telecommunications, furniture, procurement, photography, postal operations, office supplies and equipment, child care center, barber and beauty shop, and press galleries.

Clerk of the House of Representatives,
H154 CAP 20515; (202) 225-7000. Fax, (202) 225-1776. Jeff Trandahl, Clerk.
Web, clerkweb.house.gov

Responsible for direction of duties of House employees; receives lobby registrations and reports of campaign expenditures and receipts of House candidates; disburses funds appropriated for House expenditures; responsible for other activities necessary for the continuing operation of the House.

Floor Assistant to the Speaker of the House of Representatives,
HB13 CAP 20515; (202) 225-4768. Fax, (202) 225-1488. Jay Pierson and John Russell, Floor Assistants to the Speaker.

Assists the majority leadership and members on legislative matters.

General Counsel of the House of Representatives,
219 CHOB 20515; (202) 225-9700. Fax, (202) 226-1360. Geraldine R. Gennet, General Counsel.

Advises House members and committees on legal matters.

Inspector General of the House of Representatives,
385 FHOB 20515-9990; (202) 226-1250. Fax, (202) 225-4240. Steven A. McNamara, Inspector General; Chris Hendricks, Deputy Inspector General.
Web, www.house.gov/IG

Conducts periodic audits of the financial and administrative functions of the House and joint entities.

Legislative Counsel of the House of Representatives,
136 CHOB 20515; (202) 225-6060. Fax, (202) 225-3437. Pope Barrow, Legislative Counsel.
General e-mail, legcoun@mail.house.gov

Assists House members and committees in drafting legislation.

U.S. SENATE

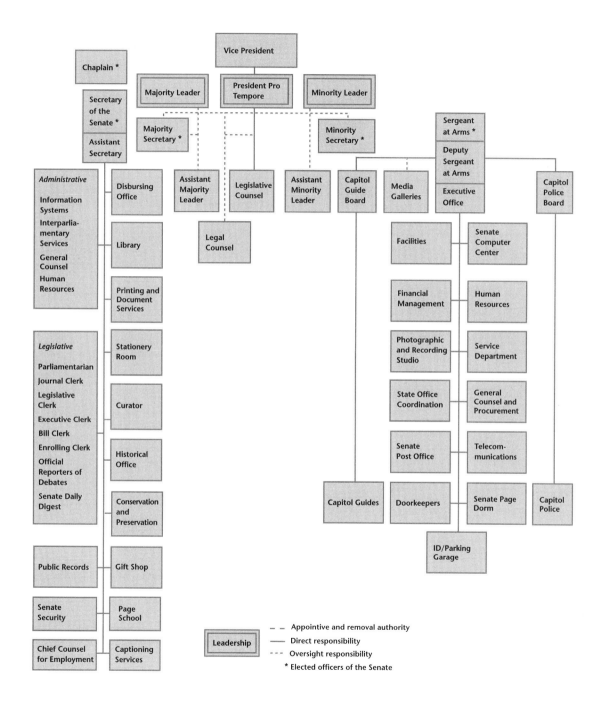

Vice President

Chaplain *

Majority Leader — President Pro Tempore — Minority Leader

Secretary of the Senate *

Assistant Secretary

Majority Secretary *

Minority Secretary *

Sergeant at Arms *

Deputy Sergeant at Arms

Administrative

Information Systems

Interparlia-mentary Services

General Counsel

Human Resources

Disbursing Office

Library

Printing and Document Services

Assistant Majority Leader

Legislative Counsel

Legal Counsel

Assistant Minority Leader

Capitol Guide Board

Media Galleries

Executive Office

Capitol Police Board

Legislative

Parliamentarian

Journal Clerk

Legislative Clerk

Executive Clerk

Bill Clerk

Enrolling Clerk

Official Reporters of Debates

Senate Daily Digest

Stationery Room

Curator

Historical Office

Conservation and Preservation

Facilities

Senate Computer Center

Financial Management

Human Resources

Photographic and Recording Studio

Service Department

State Office Coordination

General Counsel and Procurement

Senate Post Office

Telecom-munications

Public Records

Gift Shop

Senate Security

Page School

Chief Counsel for Employment

Captioning Services

Capitol Guides

Doorkeepers

Senate Page Dorm

Capitol Police

ID/Parking Garage

Leadership

- - Appointive and removal authority
— Direct responsibility
- - - Oversight responsibility
* Elected officers of the Senate

CONGRESSIONAL LIAISONS AT FEDERAL AGENCIES

DEPARTMENTS

Agriculture, Mary Kirtley Waters, (202) 720-7095

Commerce, Brenda Becker, (202) 482-3663

Defense, Powell Moore, (703) 697-6210

  Air Force, Maj. Gen. Leroy Barnidge Jr., (703) 697-8153

  Army, Brig. Gen. Guy Swan, (703) 697-6767

  Navy, Rear Adm. Gary Roughead, (703) 697-7146

Education, Karen Johnson (Nominee), (202) 401-0020

Energy, Shannon Henderson (Acting), (202) 586-5450

Health and Human Services, Paul L. Powell, (202) 690-6786

Homeland Security Dept., Wendy Grubbs (Senate) and Julie Nichols (House), (202) 282-8000

Housing and Urban Development, William Himpler, (202) 708-0380

Interior, David Bernhardt, (202) 208-7693

Justice, William Moschella (Nominee), (202) 514-2141

Labor, Kristina A. Iverson, (202) 693-4600

State, Michael Polt, (202) 647-4204

Transportation, Sean O'Hollaren, (202) 366-9714

Treasury, John Duncan, (202) 622-1900

Veterans Affairs, Vacant, (202) 273-5615

AGENCIES

Agency for International Development, Dorothy Rayburn, (202) 712-4340

Commission on Civil Rights, Less Jin, (202) 376-8317

Commodity Futures Trading Commission, Vacant, (202) 418-5075

Consumer Product Safety Commission, John Horner, (301) 504-0515

Corporation for National Service, Katherine Hoehn, (202) 606-5000, ext. 421

Environmental Protection Agency, John McKinnon, (202) 564-5200

Equal Employment Opportunity Commission, Sylvia Anderson, (202) 663-4900

Export-Import Bank, Anthony Welcher, (202) 565-3925

Farm Credit Administration, Hal DeCell III, (703) 883-4235

Federal Communications Commission, Martha Johnston, (202) 418-1900

Federal Deposit Insurance Corporation, Alice C. Goodman, (202) 898-8730

Federal Election Commission, Christina VanBrakle, (202) 694-1006

Federal Emergency Management Agency, Michele White, (202) 646-4500

Federal Labor Relations Authority, Jill Crumpacker, (202) 482-6500

Federal Maritime Commission, Amy Larson, (202) 523-5740

Federal Mediation and Conciliation Service, Kim Beg, (202) 606-8150

Federal Reserve System, Donald J. Winn, (202) 452-3456

Sergeant at Arms of the House of Representatives, H124 CAP 20515; (202) 225-2456. Fax, (202) 225-3233. Wilson L. "Bill" Livingood, Sergeant at Arms. Web, www.house.gov

Maintains order on the House floor; executes orders from the Speaker of the House. Serves on the Capitol Police Board and Capitol Guide Board; oversees Capitol security (with Senate Sergeant at Arms) and protocol.

SENATE

Chaplain of the Senate, S332 CAP 20510; (202) 224-2510. Fax, (202) 224-9686. Vacant, Chaplain.

Opens each day's Senate session with a prayer and offers other religious services to Senate members, their families, and staffs. (Prayer sometimes offered by visiting chaplain.)

Legal Counsel of the Senate, SH-642 20510; (202) 224-4435. Fax, (202) 224-3391. Patricia Mack Bryan, Legal Counsel.

Advises Senate members and committees on legal matters.

Legislative Counsel of the Senate, SD-668 20510; (202) 224-6461. Fax, (202) 224-0567. James W. Fransen, Legislative Counsel.

Assists Senate members and committees in drafting legislation.

Legislative Resource Center, *Legislative Counsel of the Senate,* SD-668 20510; (202) 224-6461. Fax, (202) 224-0567. James W. Fransen, Legislative Counsel.

Assists Senate members and committees in drafting legislation.

CONGRESSIONAL LIAISONS AT FEDERAL AGENCIES (continued)

Federal Trade Commission, Anna Davis, (202) 326-2195

General Services Administration, Shawn McBurney, (202) 501-0563

Legal Services Corporation, Mauricio Vivero, (202) 336-8862

Merit Systems Protection Board, Rosalyn Wilcots, (202) 653-7171

National Aeronautics and Space Administration, Mary D. Kerwin, (202) 358-1948

National Credit Union Administration, Clifford Northrup, (703) 518-6330

National Endowment for the Arts, Ann Guthrie Hingston, (202) 682-5434

National Endowment for the Humanities, Cherie Harder, (202) 606-8328

National Labor Relations Board, John Toner, (202) 273-1944

National Mediation Board, Benetta M. Mansfield, (202) 692-5040

National Science Foundation, David Stonner, (703) 292-8070

National Transportation Safety Board, Brenda Yager, (202) 314-6120

Nuclear Regulatory Commission, Dennis K. Rathbun, (301) 415-1776

Occupational Safety and Health Review Commission, Patricia A. Randle, (202) 606-5380

Office of Personnel Management, John C. Gartland, (202) 606-1300

Office of Special Counsel, Jane McFarland, (202) 653-5163

Pension Benefit Guaranty Corporation, Vince Snowbarger, (202) 326-4010

Postal Rate Commission, Vacant, (202) 789-6840

Securities and Exchange Commission, Jane Cobb, (202) 942-0010

Selective Service System, Richard S. Flahavan, (703) 605-4100

Small Business Administration, Richard Spence, (202) 205-6700

Smithsonian Institution, Nell Payne, (202) 357-2962

Social Security Administration, Diane Garro, (410) 965-3737

Surface Transportation Board, Dan King, (202) 565-1594

Tennessee Valley Authority, Jimmy Johnston, (202) 898-2999

U.S. International Trade Commission, Nancy Carman, (202) 205-3151

U.S. Postal Service, Ralph J. Moden, (202) 268-2506

Majority Secretary of the Senate, *S337 CAP 20510; (202) 224-3835. David Schiappa, Secretary; Denise Greenlaw Ramonas, Assistant Secretary.*

Assists the majority leader and majority party in the Senate.

Minority Secretary of the Senate, *S309 CAP 20510; (202) 224-3735. Martin P. Paone, Secretary; Lula J. Davis, Assistant Secretary.*

Assists the minority leader and the minority party in the Senate.

Secretary of the Senate, *S312 CAP 20510; (202) 224-3622. Emily Reynolds, Secretary of the Senate; Grant Kevin Lane, Administrative Assistant. Information, (202) 224-2115.*

Web, www.senate.gov/reference/office/secretary_of_senate.htm

Chief administrative officer of the Senate. Responsible for direction of duties of Senate employees and administration of oaths; receives lobby registrations and reports of campaign expenditures and receipts of Senate candidates; responsible for other day-to-day Senate activities.

Sergeant at Arms of the Senate, *S151 CAP 20510-7200; (202) 224-2341. Fax, (202) 224-7690. Bill Pickle, Sergeant at Arms.*

Oversees the Senate wing of the Capitol; doormen; Senate pages; and telecommunication, photographic, supply, and janitorial services. Maintains order on the Senate floor and galleries; oversees Capitol security (with House Sergeant at Arms); sits on the Capitol Police Board and Capitol Guide Board.

Pay and Perquisites

CONGRESS

Attending Physician, *H166 CAP 20515; (202) 225-5421. Christopher R. Picaut, Chief of Staff; Dr. John F. Eisold, Attending Physician.*

Provides members with primary care, first-aid, emergency care, and environmental/occupational health services; provides House and Senate employees, visiting dignitaries, and tourists with first-aid and emergency care.

Clerk of the House of Representatives, *H154 CAP 20515; (202) 225-7000. Fax, (202) 225-1776. Jeff Trandahl, Clerk.*
Web, clerkweb.house.gov

Prepares and submits quarterly reports covering the receipts and expenditures of the House for three months, including disbursements by each committee and each member's office and staff. Reports available from the House Document Room, (202) 225-3456.

House Administration Committee, *1309 LHOB 20515; (202) 225-8281. Fax, (202) 225-9957. Rep. Bob W. Ney, R-Ohio, Chair; Paul Vinovich, Staff Director.*
Web, www.house.gov/cha

Responsible for all matters related to the House's internal operational budget, including members' allowances and expenses, remuneration of House employees, and such unforeseen expenditures as special investigations. Oversight of the Franking Commission.

House Commission on Congressional Mailing Standards (Franking Commission), *1338 LHOB 20515; (202) 225-9337. Fax, (202) 226-0047. Rep. Bob W. Ney, R-Ohio, Chair; Jack Dail, Staff Director.*
Web, www.house.gov/cha/nfrankingcommission1.htm

Oversight of the use of franked mail by House members.

House Government Reform Committee, *Subcommittee on Government Efficiency and Financial Management, B349C RHOB 20515; (202) 225-3741. Fax, (202) 225-2373. Rep. Todd R. Platts, R-Pa., Chair; Mike Hettinger, Staff Director.*
Web, www.house.gov/reform

Jurisdiction over proposed changes in the salary of members of Congress.

Secretary of the Senate, *S312 CAP 20510; (202) 224-3622. Emily Reynolds, Secretary of the Senate; Grant Kevin Lane, Administrative Assistant. Information, (202) 224-2115.*
Web, www.senate.gov/reference/office/secretary_of_senate.htm

Prepares and submits semiannual reports covering the receipts and expenditures of the Senate for six months, including data on each committee and each member's office and staff. Reports available from the Government Printing Office, (202) 275-3030.

Senate Governmental Affairs Committee, *SD-340 20510; (202) 224-4751. Fax, (202) 224-9682. Sen. Susan Collins, R-Maine, Chair; Michael Bopp, Staff Director.*
Web, govt-aff.senate.gov

Jurisdiction over proposed changes in the salary of members of Congress.

Senate Rules and Administration Committee, *SR-305 20510; (202) 224-6352. Fax, (202) 224-5400. Sen. Trent Lott, R-Miss., Chair; Susan Wells, Staff Director.*
Web, rules.senate.gov

Responsible for all matters related to the Senate's internal operational budget, including members' allowances and expenses, remuneration of Senate employees, and such unforeseen expenditures as special investigations. Oversees budgets of the Secretary of the Senate, the Sergeant at Arms, and the Architect of the Capitol. Jurisdiction over Senate use of the franking privilege.

Senate Select Committee on Ethics, *SH-220 20510; (202) 224-2981. Fax, (202) 224-7416. Sen. George V. Voinovich, R-Ohio, Chair; Robert Walker, Staff Director.*
Web, ethics.senate.gov

Oversight of the use of franked mail by Senate members; takes action on misuse of the frank.

NONPROFIT

National Taxpayers Union, *Communications, 108 N. Alfred St., 3rd Floor, Alexandria, VA 22314; (703) 683-5700. Fax, (703) 683-5722. Peter Sepp, Vice President. General e-mail, ntu@ntu.org*
Web, www.ntu.org

Citizens' interest group that publishes reports on congressional pay and perquisites, including pensions and the franking privilege.

Standards of Conduct

AGENCIES

Justice Dept. (DOJ), *Public Integrity, 10th St. and Constitution Ave. N.W. 20530; (202) 514-1412. Fax, (202) 514-3003. Noel L. Hillman, Chief.*
Web, www.usdoj.gov

Conducts investigations of wrongdoing in selected cases that involve alleged corruption of public office or violations of election law by public officials, including members of Congress.

House Standards of Official Conduct Committee, *HT-2 CAP 20515; (202) 225-7103. Fax, (202) 225-7392. Rep. Joel Hefley, R-Colo., Chair; John E. Vargo, Staff Director (Acting).*
Web, www.house.gov/ethics

Enforces the House Code of Official Conduct (rules governing the behavior of House members and employees); has full legislative jurisdiction over all matters under that code; reviews members' financial disclosures.

Legislative Resource Center, *Records and Registration,* *B106 CHOB 20515-6612; (202) 226-5200. Fax, (202) 226-5208. Deborah Turner, Director.*
Web, clerkweb.house.gov/clerk/office_services/lrc.php

Receives and maintains the financial disclosure records of House members, officers, employees, candidates, and certain legislative organizations. Receives reports from committee chairs on foreign travel by members and staff. Records open for public inspection.

Secretary of the Senate, *Public Records: Ethics,* *SH-232 20510; (202) 224-0322. Pamela Gavin, Superintendent of Records.*

Receives and maintains the financial disclosure records of Senate members, officers, employees, candidates, and legislative organizations. Receives reports from committee chairs on foreign travel by senators and staff. Records open for public inspection.

Senate Select Committee on Ethics, *SH-220 20510; (202) 224-2981. Fax, (202) 224-7416. Sen. George V. Voinovich, R-Ohio, Chair; Robert Walker, Staff Director.*
Web, ethics.senate.gov

Receives complaints and investigates allegations of improper conduct; administers the code of official conduct; recommends disciplinary action; makes recommendations to the Senate on additional laws, rules, and regulations that may be necessary; investigates allegations of unauthorized disclosure of classified information and documents by members, officers, and employees of the Senate.

🏛 CONGRESSIONAL SUPPORT GROUPS

CONGRESS

Congressional Budget Office, *402 FHOB 20515; (202) 226-2700. Fax, (202) 225-7509. Douglas J. Holtz-Eakin, Director. Information, (202) 226-2600.*
Web, www.cbo.gov

Nonpartisan office that provides the House and Senate with budget-related information and analyses of alternative fiscal policies.

General Accounting Office (GAO), *441 G St. N.W. 20548; (202) 512-5500. Fax, (202) 512-5507. David M. Walker, Comptroller General. Information, (202) 512-4800. Library, (202) 512-5180. Documents, (202) 512-6000.*
Web, www.gao.gov

Independent, nonpartisan agency in the legislative branch. Serves as the investigating agency for Congress; carries out legal, accounting, auditing, and claims settlement functions; makes recommendations for more effective government operations; publishes monthly lists of reports available to the public. Library open to the public by appointment.

Law Revision Counsel, *H2-304 FHOB 20515; (202) 226-2411. Fax, (202) 225-0010. John R. Miller, Law Revision Counsel.*
Web, uscode.house.gov

Develops and updates an official classification of U.S. laws. Codifies, cites, and publishes the U.S. Code.

Legislative Counsel of the House of Representatives, *136 CHOB 20515; (202) 225-6060. Fax, (202) 225-3437. Pope Barrow, Legislative Counsel.*
General e-mail, legcoun@mail.house.gov

Assists House members and committees in drafting legislation.

Legislative Resource Center, *Legislative Counsel of the Senate,* *SD-668 20510; (202) 224-6461. Fax, (202) 224-0567. James W. Fransen, Legislative Counsel.*

Assists Senate members and committees in drafting legislation.

Library of Congress, *Congressional Research Service,* *101 Independence Ave. S.E. 20540; (202) 707-5775. Fax, (202) 707-2615. Daniel P. Mulhollan, Director. Information, (202) 707-5700. Services not available to public.*

Provides members of Congress and committees with general reference assistance; prepares upon request background reports, analytical studies, reading lists, bibliographies, and pros and cons of policy issues; conducts public issue seminars and workshops for committees, members, and staffs; makes available the services of subject specialists.

Liaison Offices

CONGRESS

Office of Personnel Management (OPM), *Congressional Liaison,* *B332 RHOB 20515; (202) 225-4955. Fax, (202) 632-0832. Charlene E. Luskey, Chief.*

Provides House and Senate members with information on federal civil service matters, especially those pertaining to federal employment, retirement, and health benefits programs.

HOUSE

Air Force Liaison, *B322 RHOB 20515; (202) 225-6656. Fax, (202) 685-2592. Col. Laura Shoaf, Chief (Acting).*

Provides House members with services and information on all matters related to the U.S. Air Force.

Army Liaison, *B325 RHOB 20515; (202) 225-3853. Fax, (202) 685-2674. Michael D. Young, Chief.*

Provides House members with services and information on all matters related to the U.S. Army.

Navy–Marine Corps Liaison, *B324 RHOB 20515; (202) 225-7124. Fax, (202) 685-6077. Capt. Dale Lumme, Navy Director; Col. Mike Shupp, Marine Corps Director.*

Provides House members with services and information on all matters related to the U.S. Navy and the U.S. Marine Corps.

U.S. Coast Guard Liaison, *B320 RHOB 20515; (202) 225-4775. Fax, (202) 426-6081. Cmdr. Karl Schultz, Chief.*

Provides House members with services and information on all matters related to the U.S. Coast Guard.

Veterans Affairs Dept., *Congressional Liaison Service,* *B328 RHOB 20515; (202) 225-2280. Fax, (202) 453-5225. Patricia Covington, Director.*
Web, www.va.gov

Provides House members with services and information on all matters related to veterans' benefits and services.

White House Legislative Affairs, *White House 20502; (202) 456-1414. Fax, (202) 456-1806. Dan Keniry, Deputy Assistant (House); David Hobbs, Assistant to the President for Legislative Affairs; Eric Pelletier, Deputy Assistant to the President for Legislative Affairs.*

Serves as a liaison between the president and the House of Representatives.

SENATE

Air Force Liaison, *SR-182 20510; (202) 224-2481. Fax, (202) 685-2575. Col. Bob Edmonds, Chief.*

Provides senators with services and information on all matters related to the U.S. Air Force.

Army Liaison, *SR-183 20510; (202) 224-2881. Fax, (202) 685-2570. Col. John Schorsch, Chief.*

Provides senators with services and information on all matters related to the U.S. Army.

Navy–Marine Corps Liaison, *SR-182 20510; (202) 224-4681. Fax, (202) 685-6005. Capt. Mark Ferguson, Navy Director; Col. Art White, Marine Corps Director.*

Provides senators with services and information on all matters related to the U.S. Navy and the U.S. Marine Corps.

U.S. Coast Guard Liaison, *SR-183 20510; (202) 224-2913. Fax, (202) 755-1695. Cmd. Tim Cook, Chief.*

Provides senators with services and information on all matters related to the U.S. Coast Guard.

Veterans Affairs Dept., *Congressional Liaison Service,* *SH-321 20510; (202) 224-5351. Fax, (202) 453-5218. Patricia Covington, Director; Paul L. Downs, Assistant Director.*

Provides senators with services and information on all matters related to veterans' benefits and services.

White House Legislative Affairs, *White House 20502; (202) 456-1414. Fax, (202) 456-1806. David Hobbs, Assistant to the President for Legislative Affairs; Eric Pelletier, Deputy Assistant to the President for Legislative Affairs; Ziad Ojakli, Deputy Assistant (Senate).*

Serves as a liaison between the president and the Senate.

Libraries

CONGRESS

House Administration Committee, *1309 LHOB 20515; (202) 225-8281. Fax, (202) 225-9957. Rep. Bob W. Ney, R-Ohio, Chair; Paul Vinovich, Staff Director.*
Web, www.house.gov/cha

Jurisdiction over legislation on the House library; manages, in conjunction with the Joint Library and the Senate Rules and Administration committees, policies and programs of the Library of Congress.

Joint Committee on the Library of Congress, *S237 CAP 20515; (202) 224-1034. Fax, (202) 224-0075. Sen. Ted Stevens, R-Alaska, Chair; Jennifer Mies, Senate Staff Contact.*

Studies and makes recommendations on legislation dealing with the Library of Congress.

Legislative Resource Center, *Library of the House,* *B106 CHOB 20515; (202) 226-5200. Fax, (202) 226-5207. Stephen R. Mayer, Senior Library Assistant.*

Serves as the statutory and official depository of House reports, hearings, prints, and documents for the Clerk of the House.

Library of Congress, *Congressional Research Service,* *101 Independence Ave. S.E. 20540; (202) 707-5775. Fax,*

(202) 707-2615. Daniel P. Mulhollan, Director. Information, (202) 707-5700. Services not available to public.

Provides members of Congress and committees with general reference assistance.

Library of Congress, *Law Library,* *101 Independence Ave. S.E., #LM240 20540; (202) 707-5065. Fax, (202) 707-1820. Rubens Medina, Law Librarian. Reading room, (202) 707-5080.*
Web, www.loc.gov

Maintains collections of foreign, international, and comparative law organized jurisdictionally by country; covers all legal systems—common, civil, Roman, canon, religious, and ancient and medieval law. Services include a public reading room; a microtext facility, with readers and printers for microfilm and microfiche; and foreign law/rare book reading areas. Staff of legal specialists is competent in approximately forty languages; does not provide advice on legal matters.

Library of the Senate, *SR-B15 20510; (202) 224-7106. Gregory Harness, Librarian.*

Maintains special collection for Senate private use of primary source legislative materials, including reports, hearings, prints, documents, and debate proceedings. (Not open to the public.)

Senate Rules and Administration Committee, *SR-305 20510; (202) 224-6352. Fax, (202) 224-5400. Sen. Trent Lott, R-Miss., Chair; Susan Wells, Staff Director.*
Web, rules.senate.gov

Manages, in conjunction with the House Administration and the Joint Library committees, policies and programs of the Library of Congress.

Pages

CONGRESS

House of Representatives Page Board, *H154 CAP 20515; (202) 225-7000. Fax, (202) 225-1776. Rep. John Shimkus, R-Ill., Chair; Grace Crews, Coordinator.*

Oversees and enforces rules and regulations concerning the House page program.

House of Representatives Page School, *LJ-A11, Library of Congress 20540-9996; (202) 225-9000. Fax, (202) 225-9001. Linda Miranda, Principal.*

Provides pages of the House with junior year high school education.

Senate Page School, *U.S. Senate 20510-7248; (202) 224-3926. Fax, (202) 224-1838. Kathryn S. Weeden, Principal.*

Provides education for pages of the Senate.

Sergeant at Arms of the Senate, *S151 CAP 20510-7200; (202) 224-2341. Fax, (202) 224-7690. Bill Pickle, Sergeant at Arms.*

Oversees and enforces rules and regulations concerning Senate pages after they have been appointed.

Staff

CONGRESS

House Administration Committee, *1309 LHOB 20515; (202) 225-8281. Fax, (202) 225-9957. Rep. Bob W. Ney, R-Ohio, Chair; Paul Vinovich, Staff Director.*
Web, www.house.gov/cha

Jurisdiction over employment of persons by the House. Handles issues of compensation, retirement, and other benefits for members, officers, and employees. Oversight of the House contingent fund, office equipment, and police, parking, restaurant, and other related services.

Human Resources, *House Resume Referral Service, 263 CHOB 20515-6610; (202) 225-2450. Fax, (202) 225-5969. James M. "Jay" Eagen III, Chief Administrative Officer; Susan Marone, Coordinator.*

Provides members, committees, and administrative offices of the House of Representatives, as well as job applicants, with placement and referral services. Produces weekly employment bulletin.

Office of Compliance, *110 2nd St. S.E., #LA-200 20540-1999; (202) 724-9250. Fax, (202) 426-1913. William W. Thompson II, Executive Director, (202) 724-9250. Information, (202) 724-9260. TTY, (202) 426-1912.*
Web, www.compliance.gov

Provides general information to covered employees, applicants, and former employees of the legislative branch about their equal employment rights and protections under the Congressional Accountability Act of 1995.

Senate Placement Office, *SH-142 20510; (202) 224-9167. Brian Bean, Manager. TTY, (202) 224-4215.*

Provides members, committees, and administrative offices of the Senate with placement and referral services. Compiles *Senate Employment Bulletin,* a weekly listing of available jobs. (Printed version available on Tuesdays.)

Senate Rules and Administration Committee, *SR-305 20510; (202) 224-6352. Fax, (202) 224-5400. Sen. Trent Lott, R-Miss., Chair; Susan Wells, Staff Director.*
Web, rules.senate.gov

Jurisdiction over Senate contingent fund, which provides salaries for professional committee staff members and general funds for personal Senate staffs.

NONPROFIT

Administrative Assistants Assn. of the U.S. House of Representatives, *2263 CHOB 20515; (202) 225-5161. Fax, (202) 225-3402. Nora Baumeister Matus, President.*

Professional and social organization of House administrative assistants and chiefs of staff. Meets to discuss mutual concerns and exchange information. Sponsors orientation program for new chiefs of staff. Meets with administrative, congressional, and international personnel for off-the-record briefings.

Congressional Legislative Staff Assn., *2230 RHOB 20515; (202) 225-4422. Fax, (202) 225-5615. Marcus Dunn, President.*

Nonpartisan professional organization of legislative assistants, legislative directors, legal counsels, and committee staff. Meets to discuss mutual concerns, exchange information, and hear guest speakers; holds seminars on issues pending on the House floor.

Congressional Management Foundation, *513 Capitol Court N.E., #300 20002; (202) 546-0100. Fax, (202) 547-0936. Richard Shapiro, Executive Director.*
General e-mail, cmf@cmfweb.org
Web, www.cmfweb.org

Nonpartisan organization that provides members of Congress and their staffs with management information and services through seminars, consultation, research, and publications.

Federal Bar Assn., *2215 M St. N.W. 20037; (202) 785-1614. Fax, (202) 785-1568. Jack D. Lockridge, Executive Director.*
General e-mail, fba@fedbar.org
Web, www.fedbar.org

Organization of bar members who are present or former staff members of the House, Senate, Library of Congress, Supreme Court, General Accounting Office, or Government Printing Office, or attorneys in legislative practice before federal courts or agencies.

Senate Press Secretaries Assn., *SH-405 20510; (202) 224-2764. Fax, (202) 224-6984. Robert Traynham, President.*
General e-mail, contact@usspsa.org
Web, www.usspsa.org

Bipartisan organization of present and former senatorial press secretaries and assistant press secretaries. Meets to discuss mutual concerns and to hear guest speakers.

 POLITICAL ADVOCACY

AGENCIES

Justice Dept. (DOJ), *Foreign Agents Registration Unit, 1400 New York Ave. N.W., #100 20530; (202) 514-1216. Fax, (202) 514-2836. Heather H. Hunt, Chief (Acting).*
Web, www.usdoj.gov/criminal/fara

Receives and maintains the registration of agents representing foreign countries, companies, organizations, and individuals. Compiles semi-annual report on foreign agent registrations. Foreign agent registration files are open for public inspection.

CONGRESS

House Judiciary Committee, *Subcommittee on the Constitution, 362 FHOB 20515; (202) 226-7680. Fax, (202) 225-3746. Rep. Steve Chabot, R-Ohio, Chair; Crystal Roberts, Chief Counsel.*
General e-mail, Judiciary@mail.house.gov
Web, www.house.gov/judiciary

Jurisdiction over legislation on regulation of lobbying and disclosure requirements for registered lobbyists.

Legislative Resource Center, *Records and Registration, B106 CHOB 20515-6612; (202) 226-5200. Fax, (202) 226-5208. Deborah Turner, Director.*
Web, clerkweb.house.gov/clerk/office_services/lrc.php

Receives and maintains lobby registrations and quarterly financial reports of lobbyists. Administers the statutes of the Federal Regulation of Lobbying Act of 1995 and counsels lobbyists. Receives and maintains agency filings made under the requirements of Section 319 of the Interior Dept. and Related Agencies Appropriations Act for fiscal 1990 (known as the Byrd amendment). Open for public inspection.

Secretary of the Senate, *Public Records: Campaign Financing, SH-232 20510; (202) 224-0761. Fax, (202) 224-1851. Raymond Davis, Information Specialist.*

Receives and maintains campaign expenditures of Senate members. Open for public inspection.

Senate Governmental Affairs Committee, *SD-340 20510; (202) 224-4751. Fax, (202) 224-9682. Sen. Susan Collins, R-Maine, Chair; Michael Bopp, Staff Director.*
Web, govt-aff.senate.gov

Jurisdiction over legislation on regulation of lobbying and disclosure requirements for registered lobbyists.

NONPROFIT

American League of Lobbyists, *P.O. Box 30005, Alexandria, VA 22310; (703) 960-3011. Patti Jo Baber, Executive Director.*
General e-mail, info@alldc.org
Web, www.alldc.org

Membership: lobbyists and government relations and public affairs professionals. Works to improve the skills, ethics, and public image of lobbyists. Monitors lobby legislation; conducts educational programs on public issues, lobbying techniques, and other topics of interest to membership.

Political Action Committees

The following are some key political action committees (PACs) based in Washington. Note that many other organizations listed in this book operate their own PACs.

LABOR

Active Ballot Club *(United Food and Commercial Workers International Union, AFL-CIO), 1775 K St. N.W. 20006; (202) 223-3111. Fax, (202) 728-1802. Joseph T. Hansen, Treasurer.*

Air Line Pilots Assn. PAC, *1625 Massachusetts Ave. N.W., 8th Floor 20036; (202) 797-4033. Fax, (202) 797-4030. Dennis Dolan, Treasurer.*
Web, www.alpa.org

Amalgamated Transit Union—Cope, *5025 Wisconsin Ave. N.W., 3rd Floor 20016; (202) 537-1645. Fax, (202) 244-7824. Oscar Owens, Treasurer.*
Web, www.atu.org

American Federation of State, County, and Municipal Employees—PEOPLE, Qualified (AFSCME), *1625 L St. N.W. 20036; (202) 429-1000. Fax, (202) 429-1102. William Lucy, Treasurer.*
Web, www.afscme.org

American Federation of Teachers Committee on Political Education, *555 New Jersey Ave. N.W. 20001; (202) 879-4436. Fax, (202) 393-6375. Edward J. McElroy, Treasurer.*
Web, www.aft.org

Carpenters' Legislative Improvement Committee *(United Brotherhood of Carpenters and Joiners of America, AFL-CIO), 101 Constitution Ave. N.W. 20001; (202) 546-6206. Fax, (202) 546-3873. Monte L. Byers, Treasurer.*
Web, www.carpenters.org

Committee on Letter Carriers Political Education *(National Assn. of Letter Carriers), 100 Indiana Ave. N.W. 20001; (202) 393-4695. Fax, (202) 756-7400. Florence Johnson, Treasurer.*

Committee on Political Action of the American Postal Workers Union, AFL-CIO, *1300 L St. N.W. 20005; (202) 842-4210. Fax, (202) 682-2528. Robert Tunstall, Treasurer.*
Web, www.apw.org

CWA-COPE Political Contributions Committee *(Communications Workers of America, AFL-CIO), 501 3rd St. N.W., #1070 20001; (202) 434-1410. Fax, (202) 434-1318. Barbara J. Easterling, Treasurer.*

Democratic Republican Independent Voter Education Committee (DRIVE), *(International Brotherhood of Teamsters, Chauffeurs, Warehousemen, and Helpers of America), 25 Louisiana Ave. N.W. 20001; (202) 624-8741. Fax, (202) 624-8973. Mike Mathis, Director.*

Engineers Political Education Committee/International Union of Operating Engineers, *1125 17th St. N.W. 20036; (202) 429-9100. Fax, (202) 778-2688. Vincent Giblin, Treasurer.*

International Brotherhood of Electrical Workers Committee on Political Education, *1125 15th St. N.W., #120 20005; (202) 728-6046. Fax, (202) 728-6144. Rick Diegel, Director, Political and Legislative Affairs; Jerry J. O'Connor, Secretary-Treasurer.*

Ironworkers Political Action League, *1750 New York Ave. N.W., #400 20006; (202) 383-4800. Fax, (202) 347-3569. Frank Voyack, Treasurer.*

Laborers' Political League of Laborers' International Union of North America, *905 16th St. N.W. 20006; (202) 737-8320. Fax, (202) 737-2754. Donald Kaniewski, Legislative and Political Director; Armand E. Sabitoni, Secretary and Treasurer.*

Machinists Non-Partisan Political League *(International Assn. of Machinists and Aerospace Workers, AFL-CIO), 9000 Machinists Pl., Upper Marlboro, MD 20772; (301) 967-4500. Fax, (301) 967-4595. Richard Michalski, Legislative and Political Director; Donald E. Wharton, Treasurer.*
Web, www.iamaw.org

National Education Assn., *Government Relations, 1201 16th St. N.W. 20036; (202) 822-7300. Fax, (202) 822-7741. Diane Shust, Director.*
Web, www.nea.org

RATINGS OF MEMBERS

The following organizations either publish voting records on selected issues or annually rate members of Congress; organizations marked with an asterisk (*) rate members biennially.

AFL–CIO, 815 16th St. N.W. 20006; (202) 637-5000.
Web, www.aflcio.org

American Conservative Union, 1007 Cameron St., Alexandria, VA 22314; (703) 836-8602.
Web, www.conservative.org

***American Farm Bureau Federation,** 600 Maryland Ave. S.W., #800 20024; (202) 484-3600.
Web, www.fb.com

Americans for Democratic Action, 1625 K St. N.W., #210 20006; (202) 785-5980.
Web, www.adaaction.org

***Common Cause,** 1250 Connecticut Ave. N.W., #600 20036; (202) 833-1200.
Web, www.commoncause.org

Competitive Enterprise Institute, 1001 Connecticut Ave. N.W., #1250 20036; (202) 331-1010.
Web, www.cei.org

Consumer Federation of America, 1424 16th St. N.W., #604 20036; (202) 387-6121.
Web, www.consumerfed.org

Human Rights Campaign, 919 18th St. N.W., #800 20006; (202) 628-4160.
Web, www.hrc.org

Leadership Conference on Civil Rights, 1629 K St. N.W., #1010 20006; (202) 466-3311.
Web, www.lccr.org

League of Conservation Voters, 1920 L St. N.W., #800 20036; (202) 785-8683.
Web, www.lcv.org

National Abortion and Reproductive Rights Action League-Political Action Committee (NARAL-PAC), 1156 15th St. N.W., 7th Floor 20005; (202) 973-3000.
Web, www.naral.org

***National Assn. for the Advancement of Colored People (NAACP),** 1025 Vermont Ave. N.W., #1120 20005; (202) 638-2269.
Web, www.naacp.org

National Assn. of Social Workers-PACE (Political Action for Candidate Election), 750 1st St. N.E., #700 20002; (202) 408-8600.
Web, www.socialworkers.org/pace

National Federation of Independent Business, 1201 F St. N.W., #200 20004-1221; (202) 554-9000.
Web, www.nfib.com

National Gay and Lesbian Task Force Policy Institute, 1325 Massachusetts Ave. N.W., #600 20005; (202) 393-5177.
Web, www.ngltf.org

National Taxpayers Union, 108 N. Alfred St., Alexandria, VA 22314; (703) 683-5700.
Web, www.ntu.org

National Women's Political Caucus, 1634 Eye St. N.W., #310 20006; (202) 785-1100.
Web, www.nwpc.org

Public Citizen, Congress Watch, 215 Pennsylvania Ave. S.E., 3rd Floor 20003; (202) 546-4996.
Web, www.citizen.org

U.S. Chamber of Commerce Legislative and Public Affairs, 1615 H St. N.W. 20062; (202) 463-5604.
Web, www.uschamber.com

U.S. Student Assn., 1413 K St. N.W., 9th Floor 20005; (202) 347-8772.
Web, www.usstudents.org

***Zero Population Growth,** 1400 16th St. N.W., #320 20036; (202) 332-2200
Web, www.zpg.org

Seafarers Political Activity Donation *(Seafarers International Union of North America), 5201 Auth Way, Camp Springs, MD 20746; (301) 899-0675. Fax, (301) 899-7355. David Heindel, Chair; Terry Turner, National Director, Political Action and Governmental Relations.*
Web, www.seafarers.org

Sheet Metal Workers International Assn. Political Action League, *1750 New York Ave. N.W., 6th Floor 20006; (202) 662-0887. Fax, (202) 662-0880. Vince Panvini, Political Director; Tom Kelly, Treasurer.*

United Mine Workers of America, *Coal Miners Political Action Committee, 8315 Lee Hwy., Fairfax, VA 22031; (703) 208-7200. Fax, (703) 208-7264. Carlo Tarley, Secretary-Treasurer.*

NONCONNECTED

American AIDS PAC, *1224 M St. N.W., #300 20005; (202) 628-7770. Fax, (202) 628-7773. Thomas F. Sheridan, Treasurer.*
Web, www.aidspac.org

American Sugarbeet Growers Assn. Political Action Committee, 1156 15th St. N.W., #1101 20005; (202) 833-2398. Fax, (202) 833-2962. Luther Markwart, Treasurer.

Automotive Free International Trade PAC, 1625 Prince St., #225, Alexandria, VA 22314; (703) 684-8880. Fax, (703) 684-8920. Mary Drape Hanagan, Executive Director.

Black America's PAC, 2029 P St. N.W., #202 20036; (202) 785-9619. Fax, (202) 785-9621. Alvin Williams, President.
General e-mail, bampac@bampac.org
Web, www.bampac.org

Council for a Livable World, 322 4th St. N.E. 20002; (202) 543-4100. Fax, (202) 543-6297. John D. Isaacs, President.
General e-mail, clw@clw.org
Web, www.clw.org
Supports congressional candidates who advocate arms control and cutting the military budget.

Deloitte and Touche LLP Federal Political Action Committee, 555 12th St. N.W., #500 20004; (202) 879-5600. Fax, (202) 879-5309. Cindy Stevens, Director.

EMILY's List, 1120 Connecticut Ave. N.W., 11th Floor, 20036; (202) 326-1400. Fax, (202) 326-1415. Ellen Malcolm, Treasurer.
Web, www.emilyslist.org
Raises money to support pro-choice Democratic women candidates for political office.

Ernst and Young PAC, 8484 Westpark Dr., McLean, VA 22102; (703) 747-1918. Fax, (703) 747-0132. Allen W. Urban, Treasurer.

GOPAC, 122 C St. N.W., #505 20001; (202) 464-5170. Fax, (202) 464-5177. J. C. Watts, National Chairman; Michele Miller, Executive Director; Tony Moonis, Treasurer.
Web, www.gopac.com
Promotes conservative Republican candidates for local and state office.

KPMG PAC, P.O. Box 18254 20036; (202) 533-5816. Fax, (202) 533-8516. Stephen E. Allis, Treasurer.

National Committee for an Effective Congress, 122 C St. N.W., #650 20001; (202) 639-8300. Fax, (202) 639-5038. James E. Byron, Treasurer.
Web, www.ncec.org
Supports liberal or progressive candidates in marginal races.

National PAC, 600 Pennsylvania Ave. S.E., #207 20003; (202) 879-7710. Fax, (202) 879-7728. Marvin Josephson, Treasurer.
Supports candidates who advocate close U.S.-Israeli relations.

New Republican Majority Fund, 201 N. Union St., #530, Alexandria, VA 22314; (703) 299-6600. Fax, (703) 548-5954. Tom H. Anderson, Treasurer; Bret Boyles, Executive Director.
General e-mail, nrmf2001@aol.com

PricewaterhouseCoopers PAC, 1900 K St. N.W., #900 20006; (202) 822-4222. Fax, (202) 822-5640. Allen J. Weltmann, Treasurer.

Voters for Choice, 1115 Massachusetts Ave. N.W. 20005; (202) 944-5080. Fax, (202) 944-5081. Mary Jean Collins, Treasurer.
General e-mail, info@voters4choice.org
Web, www.voters4choice.org
Independent, nonpartisan political action committee that supports candidates favoring legalized abortion. Provides candidates at all levels of government with campaign strategy information; opposes constitutional amendments and legislation restricting abortion.

WISH List, 499 S. Capitol St. S.W., #408 20003; (202) 479-1230. Fax, (202) 479-1231. Pat Carpenter, Executive Director.
General e-mail, WISH@thewishlist.org
Web, www.thewishlist.org
Raises money for pro-choice Republican women candidates.

TRADE, MEMBERSHIP, AND HEALTH

Action Committee for Rural Electrification, 4301 Wilson Blvd., Arlington, VA 22203; (703) 907-5500. Fax, (703) 907-6826. Michael Whalen, Manager.
Web, www.nreca.org

American Bankers Assn. BankPAC, 1120 Connecticut Ave. N.W., 8th Floor 20036; (202) 663-5113. Fax, (202) 663-7544. Gary W. Fields, Treasurer.
Web, www.aba.com

American Dental PAC, 1111 14th St. N.W., 11th Floor 20005; (202) 898-2424. Fax, (202) 898-2437. Ed Vigna, Treasurer.
Web, www.ada.org

American Health Care Assn. Political Action Committee (AHC-PAC), 1201 L St. N.W. 20005; (202) 842-

4444. Fax, (202) 842-3860. Ana Lee, Political Action Director.

Web, www.ahca.org

American Medical Assn. PAC, 1101 Vermont Ave. N.W., #1200 20005; (202) 789-7400. Fax, (202) 789-7469. Kevin Walker, Treasurer.

Web, www.ama-assn.org

Assn. of Trial Lawyers of America PAC, 1050 31st St. N.W. 20007; (202) 965-3500. Fax, (202) 338-8709. Heather Tureen, Director.

Build PAC of the National Assn. of Home Builders, 1201 15th St. N.W. 20005; (202) 266-8470. Fax, (202) 266-8572. Peter Rintye, Vice President, Political Affairs.

Web, www.nahb.com

Credit Union Legislative Action Council, 601 Pennsylvania Ave. N.W., #600, South Bldg. 20004; (202) 638-5777. Fax, (202) 638-7734. Karen Kincer, Political Affairs Director.

Web, www.cuna.org

Dealers Election Action Committee of the National Automobile Dealers Assn., 8400 Westpark Dr., McLean, VA 22102; (703) 821-7110. Fax, (703) 442-3168. Scott Spurgeon, Director.

Web, www.nada.org

Human Rights Campaign PAC (HRC), 919 18th St. N.W., #800 20006; (202) 628-4160. Fax, (202) 347-5323. Elizabeth Birch, Executive Director.

General e-mail, hrc@hrc.org

Web, www.hrc.org

Supports candidates for state and federal office who favor gay and lesbian rights.

Independent Insurance Agents of America Political Action Committee (INSURPAC), 412 1st St. S.E., #300 20003; (202) 863-7000. Fax, (202) 863-7015. Maria Bertoud, Vice President; Nathan Riedel, Political Director.

Web, www.independentagent.com

National Assn. of Broadcasters Television and Radio Political Action Committee, 1771 N St. N.W. 20036; (202) 429-5301. Fax, (202) 775-2157. John Orlando, Senior Vice President.

Web, www.nab.org

National Assn. of Insurance and Financial Advisors PAC, 2901 Telestar Ct., Falls Church, VA 22042-1205; (703) 770-8100. Fax, (703) 770-8151. Magenta Ishak, Director.

Web, www.naifa.org

National Assn. of Retired Federal Employees PAC (NARFE), 606 N. Washington St., Alexandria, VA 22314; (703) 838-7760. Fax, (703) 838-7782. Charles Fallis, President. Member relations, (800) 456-8410.

General e-mail, hq@narfe.org

Web, www.narfe.org

National Assn. of Social Workers Political Action for Candidate Election, 750 1st St. N.E., #700 20002; (202) 408-8600. Fax, (202) 336-8311. David Dempsey, Manager, Government Relations and Political Action, (202) 336-8278.

General e-mail, info@naswdc.org

Web, www.socialworkers.org

National Beer Wholesalers' Assn. PAC, 1101 King St., #600, Alexandria, VA 22314-2944; (703) 683-4300. Fax, (703) 683-8965. Linda Auglis, Director.

Web, www.nbwa.org

National Committee to Preserve Social Security and Medicare PAC, 10 G St. N.E., #600 20002; (202) 216-0420. Fax, (202) 216-0446. Shelly C. Shapiro, Treasurer.

Web, www.ncpssm.org

NRA Political Victory Fund, 11250 Waples Mill Rd., Fairfax, VA 22030; (703) 267-1000. Fax, (703) 267-3918. Wilson Phillips, Treasurer.

Web, www.nra.org

Physical Therapy Political Action Committee (PT-PAC), 1111 N. Fairfax St., Alexandria, VA 22314; (703) 684-2782. Fax, (703) 684-7343. Michael Matlack, Director. Fax-on-demand, (800) 399-2782.

Web, www.apta.org

Women's Campaign Fund, 734 15th St. N.W., #500 20005; (202) 393-8164. Fax, (202) 393-0649. Lynn Martin, Treasurer.

Web, www.wcfonline.org

Political Interest Groups

NONPROFIT

Alexis de Tocqueville Institution, 1446 E St. S.E. 20003; (202) 548-0006. Kenneth N. Brown, President.

General e-mail, kenbrown@adti.net

Web, www.adti.net

Public policy research organization that conducts, sponsors, and publishes research and analysis. Advocates individual political and economic freedom, limited government, and free markets.

American Conservative Union (ACU), *1007 Cameron St., Alexandria, VA 22314; (703) 836-8602. Fax, (703) 836-8606. Stephen Thayer, Executive Director. Information, (800) 228-7345.*

General e-mail, acu@conservative.org

Web, www.conservative.org

Legislative interest organization that focuses on defense, foreign policy, economics, the national budget, taxes, and legal and social issues. Monitors legislation and regulations.

Americans for Democratic Action, *1625 K St. N.W., #210 20006; (202) 785-5980. Fax, (202) 785-5969. Amy F. Isaacs, National Director; Jim McDermott, President.*

General e-mail, adaction@ix.netcom.com

Web, www.adaction.org

Legislative interest organization that seeks to strengthen civil, constitutional, women's, family, workers', and human rights.

The Brookings Institution, *1775 Massachusetts Ave. N.W. 20036; (202) 797-6000. Fax, (202) 797-6004. Strobe Talbott, President.*

General e-mail, brookinfo@brookings.edu

Web, www.brookings.edu

Public policy research organization that seeks to improve the performance of American institutions, the effectiveness of government programs, and the quality of public policy through research and analysis. Sponsors lectures, debates, and policy forums.

Campaign for America's Future, *1025 Connecticut Ave. N.W., #205 20036; (202) 955-5665. Fax, (202) 955-5606. Robert L. Borosage, Co-Director; Roger Hickey, Co-Director.*

General e-mail, info@ourfuture.org

Web, www.ourfuture.org

Operates the Campaign for America's Future and the Institute for America's Future. Advocates policies to help working people. Supports improved employee benefits, including health care, child care, and paid family leave; promotes life-long education and training of workers. Seeks full employment, higher wages, and increased productivity. Monitors legislation and regulations.

Cato Institute, *1000 Massachusetts Ave. N.W. 20001-5403; (202) 842-0200. Fax, (202) 842-3490. Edward H. Crane III, President.*

General e-mail, cato@cato.org

Web, www.cato.org

Public policy research organization that advocates limited government and individual liberty. Interests include privatization and deregulation, low and simple taxes, and reduced government spending. Encourages voluntary solutions to social and economic problems.

Center for National Policy, *1 Massachusetts Ave. N.W., #333 20001; (202) 682-1800. Fax, (202) 682-1818. Maureen Steinbruner, President.*

General e-mail, thecenter@cnponline.org

Web, www.cnponline.org

Public policy research and educational organization that serves as a forum for development of national policy alternatives. Studies issues of national and international concern including problems of governance; sponsors conferences and symposia.

Christian Coalition, *P.O. Box 37030 20013; (202) 479-6900. Fax, (202) 479-4260. Roberta Combs, President.*

Web, www.cc.org

Membership: individuals who support traditional, conservative Christian values. Represents members' views to all levels of government and to the media.

Common Cause, *1250 Connecticut Ave. N.W., #600 20036; (202) 833-1200. Fax, (202) 659-3716. Chellie Pingree, Director. Press, (202) 736-5770.*

Web, www.commoncause.org

Citizens' legislative interest group that works for institutional reform in federal and state government. Advocates partial public financing of congressional election campaigns, ethics in government, nuclear arms control, oversight of defense spending, tax reform, and a reduction of political action committee influence in Congress.

Concerned Women for America, *1015 15th St. N.W., #1100 20005; (202) 488-7000. Fax, (202) 488-0806. George Tryfiates, Executive Director.*

Web, www.cwfa.org

Educational organization that seeks to protect the rights of the family and preserve Judeo-Christian values. Monitors legislation affecting family and religious issues.

Concord Coalition, *1011 Arlington Blvd., #300, Arlington, VA 22209; (703) 894-6222. Fax, (703) 894-6231. Robert L. Bixby, Executive Director.*

General e-mail, concord@concordcoalition.org

Web, www.concordcoalition.org

Nonpartisan, grassroots organization advocating fiscal responsibility and ensuring Social Security, Medicare, and Medicaid are secure for all generations.

Congressional Economic Leadership Institute, *201 Massachusetts Ave. N.E., #C6 20002; (202) 546-5007. Fax, (202) 546-7037. Jolene L. Worsley, President.*

Web, www.celi.org

Nonpartisan educational group that serves as a forum for the discussion of economic issues between Congress and the private sector.

Congressional Institute for the Future, *444 N. Capitol St. N.W., #601D, Hall of the States 20001; (202) 393-0016. Fax, (202) 393-8889. Elaine Wicker, Executive Director.*
General e-mail, info@futuretrends.org
Web, www.futuretrends.org
Nonpartisan educational organization that offers information about emerging issues and trends to leaders in business and government. Conducts research; sponsors seminars and conferences; compiles and analyzes public opinion data.

Conservative Caucus, *450 Maple Ave. East, #309, Vienna, VA 22180; (703) 938-9626. Fax, (703) 281-4108. Howard Phillips, Chair.*
Web, www.conservativeusa.org
Legislative interest organization that promotes grassroots activity on issues such as national defense and economic and tax policy. The Conservative Caucus Research, Analysis, and Education Foundation studies public issues including Central American affairs, defense policy, and federal funding of political advocacy groups.

Council for Citizens Against Government Waste, *1301 Connecticut Ave. N.W., #400 20036; (202) 467-5300. Fax, (202) 467-4253. Thomas A. Schatz, President. Information, (800) 232-6479.*
Web, www.cagw.org
Nonpartisan organization that seeks to eliminate waste, mismanagement, and inefficiency in the federal government. Monitors legislation and regulations.

Eagle Forum, *Washington Office, 316 Pennsylvania Ave. S.E., #203 20003; (202) 544-0353. Fax, (202) 547-6996. Lori Waters, Executive Director.*
General e-mail, eagle@eagleforum.org
Web, www.eagleforum.org
Legislative interest group that supports conservative, pro-family policies at all levels of government. Concerns include abortion, affirmative action, education, national defense, and taxes. (Headquarters in St. Louis, Mo.)

Empower America, *1801 K St. N.W., #410 20006; (202) 452-8200. Fax, (202) 833-0388. James R. Taylor, President.*
General e-mail, empower1@empower.org
Web, www.empower.org
Public policy research organization that seeks to encourage economic growth through lower taxes, less government spending, and regulatory reform. Interests

include social policy and the moral impact of popular culture.

Family Research Council, *801 G St. N.W. 20001; (202) 393-2100. Fax, (202) 393-2134. Kenneth L. Connor, President.*
Web, www.frc.org
Legislative interest organization that analyzes issues affecting the family and seeks to ensure that the interests of the family are considered in the formulation of public policy.

Feminist Majority Foundation, *1600 Wilson Blvd., #801, Arlington, VA 22209; (703) 522-2214. Fax, (703) 522-2219. Eleanor Smeal, President.*
General e-mail, femmaj@feminist.org
Web, www.feminist.org
Legislative interest group that seeks to increase the number of feminists running for public office; promotes a national feminist agenda.

Foundation for Public Affairs, *2033 K St. N.W., #700 20006; (202) 872-1790. Fax, (202) 835-8343. Leslie Swift-Rosenzweig, Executive Director.*
Web, www.pac.org
Public policy research and educational foundation that serves as an information clearinghouse on interest groups and corporate public affairs programs. Monitors the activities of public policy groups and advises on methods of operation, staff, budget size, and other administrative topics. Provides third-party commentary on groups' effectiveness and political orientation. Library open to the public by appointment. (Affiliated with the Public Affairs Council.)

Free Congress Research and Education Foundation (FCF), *717 2nd St. N.E. 20002-4368; (202) 546-3000. Fax, (202) 543-5605. Marian E. Harrison, Chair.*
General e-mail, info@freecongress.org
Web, www.freecongress.org
Research and education foundation that promotes traditional values, conservative governance, and institutional reform. Studies judicial/political issues, electoral process, and public policy. Trains citizens to participate in a democracy.

Frontiers of Freedom, *12011 Lee Jackson Memorial Hwy., #310, Fairfax, VA 22033; (703) 246-0110. Fax, (703) 246-0129. George Landrith, President.*
General e-mail, info@ff.org
Web, www.ff.org
Seeks to increase personal freedom through a reduction in the size of government. Interests include property

rights, regulatory and tax reform, global warming, national missile defense, Internet regulation, school vouchers, and second amendment rights. Monitors legislation and regulations.

The Heritage Foundation, *214 Massachusetts Ave. N.E. 20002-4999; (202) 546-4400. Fax, (202) 546-8328. Edwin J. Feulner Jr., President.*
General e-mail, info@heritage.org
Web, www.heritage.org
Public policy research organization that conducts research and analysis and sponsors lectures, debates, and policy forums advocating individual freedom, limited government, the free market system, and a strong national defense.

Interfaith Alliance, *1331 H St. N.W., 11th Floor 20005; (202) 639-6370. Fax, (202) 639-6375. Rev. Dr. C. Welton Gaddy, President.*
General e-mail, tia@interfaithalliance.org
Web, www.interfaithalliance.org
Membership: Protestant, Catholic, Jewish, and Muslim clergy, laity, and others who favor a positive, nonpartisan role for religious faith in public life. Advocates mainstream religious values; promotes tolerance and social opportunity; opposes the use of religion to promote political extremism at national, state, and local levels. Monitors legislation and regulations.

Log Cabin Republicans, *1607 17th St. N.W. 20009; (202) 347-5306. Fax, (202) 347-5224. Patrick Guerriero, Executive Director.*
General e-mail, info@lcr.org
Web, www.lcr.org
Membership: lesbian and gay Republicans. Educates conservative politicians and voters on gay and lesbian issues; disseminates information; conducts seminars for members. Raises campaign funds. Monitors legislation and regulations.

Millennium Institute, *2200 Wilson Blvd., #650, Arlington, VA 22201; (703) 841-0048. Fax, (703) 841-0050. Gerald O. Barney, President.*
General e-mail, info@millenniuminstitute.net
Web, www.millenniuminstitute.net
Research and development firm that provides computer modeling services for planning and building a sustainable economic and ecological future.

National Center for Policy Analysis, *Washington Office, 601 Pennsylvania Ave. N.W., 900 South 20004; (202) 628-6671. Fax, (202) 628-6474. Michael Cannon, Government Affairs Director.*
General e-mail, ncpa@ncpa.org
Web, www.ncpa.org

Conducts research and policy analysis; disseminates others' outside research in the areas of tax reform, health care, the environment, criminal justice, education, social security, and welfare reform. (Headquarters in Dallas, Texas.)

National Jewish Democratic Council, *P.O. Box 75308 20013-5308; (202) 216-9060. Fax, (202) 216-9061. Ira Forman, Executive Director.*
General e-mail, njdc@njdc.org
Web, www.njdc.org
Encourages Jewish involvement in the Democratic party and its political campaigns. Monitors and analyzes domestic and foreign policy issues that concern the American Jewish community.

National Organization for Women (NOW), *733 15th St. N.W., 2nd Floor 20005; (202) 628-8669. Fax, (202) 785-8576. Kim Gandy, President. TTY, (202) 331-9002.*
General e-mail, now@now.org
Web, www.now.org
Advocacy organization that works for women's civil rights. Acts through demonstrations, court cases, and legislative efforts to improve the status of all women. Interests include increasing the number of women in elected and appointed office, improving women's economic status and health coverage, ending violence against women, preserving abortion rights, and abolishing discrimination based on gender, race, age, and sexual orientation.

National Taxpayers Union, *Communications, 108 N. Alfred St., 3rd Floor, Alexandria, VA 22314; (703) 683-5700. Fax, (703) 683-5722. Peter Sepp, Vice President.*
General e-mail, ntu@ntu.org
Web, www.ntu.org
Citizens' interest group that promotes tax and spending reduction at all levels of government. Supports constitutional amendments to balance the federal budget and limit taxes.

National Woman's Party, *144 Constitution Ave. N.E. 20002; (202) 546-1210. Fax, (202) 546-3997. Marty Langelan, President; Angela Gilchrist, Executive Director.*
Web, www.sewallbelmont.org
Membership: women seeking equality under the law. Supports the Equal Rights Amendment and other legislation to eliminate discrimination against women.

New America Foundation, *1630 Connecticut Ave. N.W., 7th Floor 20009; (202) 986-2700. Fax, (202) 986-3696. Ted Halstead, President.*
General e-mail, info@newamerica.net
Web, www.newamerica.net

Ideologically diverse public policy institute that seeks to nurture the next generation of public intellectuals. Sponsors research, writing, conferences, and events.

People for the American Way (PFAW), *2000 M St. N.W., #400 20036; (202) 467-4999. Fax, (202) 293-2672. Ralph G. Neas, President.*
General e-mail, pfaw@pfaw.org
Web, www.pfaw.org
Nonpartisan organization that promotes protection of First Amendment rights through a national grassroots network of members and volunteers. Conducts public education programs on constitutional issues. Provides radio, television, and newspaper advertisements; maintains speakers bureau. Library open to the public by appointment.

Progress and Freedom Foundation, *1401 H St. N.W., #1075 20005-2110; (202) 289-8928. Fax, (202) 289-6079. Jeffrey A. Eisenach, President.*
General e-mail, mail@pff.org
Web, www.pff.org
Studies the impact of the digital revolution and its implications for public policy; sponsors seminars, conferences, and broadcasts.

Progressive Policy Institute, *600 Pennsylvania Ave. S.E., #400 20003; (202) 547-0001. Fax, (202) 544-5014. Will Marshall, President.*
General e-mail, ppiinfo@dlcppi.org
Web, www.ppionline.org
Public policy research and educational organization that supports individual opportunity, equal justice under the law, and popular government.

Public Advocate of the U.S., *5613 Leesburg Pike, #17, Falls Church, VA 22041; (703) 845-1808. Eugene Delgaudio, Executive Director.*
Web, www.publicadvocateusa.org
Educational grassroots organization that promotes a limited role for the federal government and conservative life choices. Opposes federal gay rights laws.

Public Affairs Council, *2033 K St. N.W., #700 20006; (202) 872-1790. Fax, (202) 835-8343. Douglas G. Pinkham, President.*
General e-mail, pac@pac.org
Web, www.pac.org
Membership: public affairs executives. Informs and counsels members on public affairs programs. Sponsors conferences on election issues, government relations, and political trends. Sponsors the Foundation for Public Affairs.

Public Citizen, *Congress Watch, 215 Pennsylvania Ave. S.E., 3rd Floor 20003; (202) 546-4996. Fax, (202) 547-7392. Frank Clemente, Director.*
Web, www.citizen.org
Citizens' interest group. Interests include consumer protection, financial services, public health and safety, government reform, trade, and the environment.

Rainbow PUSH Coalition, *1131 8th St. N.E. 20007-3601; (202) 547-3235. Fax, (202) 547-7397. Jesse L. Jackson Sr., President.*
General e-mail, info@rainbowpush.org
Web, www.rainbowpush.org
Independent political organization concerned with U.S. domestic and foreign policy. Interests include D.C. statehood, civil rights, defense policy, agriculture, AIDS/HIV, poverty, the economy, energy, the environment, hate crimes, and social justice.

Republican Jewish Coalition, *50 F St. N.W. 20001; (202) 638-6688. Fax, (202) 638-6694. Matthew Brooks, Executive Director.*
General e-mail, rjc@rjchq.org
Web, www.rjchq.org
Legislative interest group that works to build support among Republican party decision makers on issues of concern to the Jewish community; studies domestic and foreign policy issues affecting the Jewish community; supports a strong relationship between the United States and Israel.

Traditional Values Coalition, *Washington Office, 139 C St. S.E. 20003; (202) 547-8570. Fax, (202) 546-6403. Andrea Sheldon Lafferty, Executive Director.*
General e-mail, tvcwashdc@traditionalvalues.org
Web, www.traditionalvalues.org
Legislative interest group that supports religious liberties and traditional, conservative Judeo-Christian values. Interests include pro-life issues, pornography, decreased federal funding for the arts, parental rights, and the promotion of school prayer. Opposes gay rights legislation. (Headquarters in Anaheim, Calif.)

20/20 Vision, *1828 Jefferson Pl. N.W. 20036; (202) 833-2020. Fax, (202) 833-5307. James K. Wyerman, Executive Director.*
General e-mail, vision@2020vision.org
Web, www.2020vision.org
Prodemocracy advocacy group that encourages members to spend twenty minutes each month in communicating their opinions to policymakers. Targets legislative issues in particular districts and provides infor-

mation on current issues. Interests include ending the production of weapons of mass destruction and protecting the environment.

Urban Institute, *2100 M St. N.W. 20037; (202) 833-7200. Fax, (202) 728-0232. Robert D. Reischauer, President. Information, (202) 261-5702. Library, (202) 261-5534.*

General e-mail, paffairs@ui.urban.org

Web, www.urban.org

Public policy research and education organization. Investigates U.S. social and economic problems; encourages discussion on solving society's problems, improving and implementing government decisions, and increasing citizens' awareness of public choices. Library open to the public by appointment.

U.S. Chamber of Commerce, *Grassroots and Advocacy Program, 1615 H St. N.W. 20062-2000; (202) 463-5604. Fax, (202) 463-3190. R. Bruce Josten, Senior Vice President. Press, (202) 463-5682.*

Web, www.uschamber.com

Federation that works to enact probusiness legislation; tracks election law legislation; coordinates the chamber's candidate endorsement program and its grassroots lobbying activities.

U.S. Term Limits, *10 G St. N.E., #410 20002; (202) 379-3000. Fax, (202) 379-3010. Stacie Rumenap, Executive Director.*

Web, www.termlimits.org

Works with state and local activists to place initiatives before voters; supports term limits at all levels of government; seeks limits of three terms in the House and two in the Senate. Monitors legislation and regulations.

The Woman Activist, *2310 Barbour Rd., Falls Church, VA 22043; (703) 573-8716. Flora Crater, President.*

Advocacy group that conducts research on individuals and groups in elective and appointive office, especially those who make decisions affecting women and minorities. Publishes the *Almanac of Virginia Politics.*

Women Legislators' Lobby (WiLL), *Policy and Programs, 322 4th St. N.E. 20002; (202) 544-5055. Fax, (202) 544-7612. Darcy Scott Martin, Washington Director.*

General e-mail, info@wand.org

Web, www.wand.org

Bipartisan group of women state legislators. Sponsors conferences, training workshops, issue briefings, and seminars; provides information and action alerts on ways federal policies affect states. Interests include violence against women and children, federal budget priori-

ties, national security, and arms control. Monitors related legislation and regulations. (Affiliated with Women's Action for New Directions.)

POLITICAL PARTY ORGANIZATIONS

Democratic

Democratic Congressional Campaign Committee, *430 S. Capitol St. S.E. 20003; (202) 863-1500. Fax, (202) 485-3512. Rep. Robert T. Matsui, D-Calif., Chair; Jim Bonham, Executive Director.*

Web, www.dccc.org

Provides Democratic House candidates with financial and other campaign services.

Democratic Governors' Assn., *499 S. Capitol St. S.W., #422 20003; (202) 772-5600. Fax, (202) 772-5602. Gov. Gary Locke, D-Wash., Chair; B. J. Thornberry, Executive Director.*

Web, www.democraticgovernors.org

Serves as a liaison between governors' offices and Democratic party organizations; assists Democratic gubernatorial candidates.

Democratic Leadership Council, *600 Pennsylvania Ave. S.E., #400 20003; (202) 546-0007. Fax, (202) 544-5002. Sen. Evan Bayh, D-Ind., Chair; Bruce Reed, President; Alvin From, Chief Executive Officer.*

Web, www.ndol.org

Organization of Democratic members of Congress, governors, state and local officials, and concerned citizens. Builds consensus within the Democratic party on public policy issues, including economic growth, national security, national service, and expansion of opportunity for all Americans.

Democratic National Committee (DNC), *430 S. Capitol St. S.E. 20003; (202) 863-8000. Fax, (202) 863-8063. Terry McAuliffe, National Chair. Press, (202) 863-8148.*

Web, www.democrats.org

Formulates and promotes Democratic party policies and positions; assists Democratic candidates for state and national office; organizes national political activities; works with state and local officials and organizations.

Democratic National Committee (DNC), *Assn. of State Democratic Chairs, 430 S. Capitol St. S.E. 20003; (202) 488-5015. Fax, (202) 479-5123. Ann Fishman, Executive Director.*

Web, www.democrats.org

Acts as a liaison between state parties and the DNC; works to strengthen state parties for national, state, and local elections; conducts fundraising activities for state parties.

Democratic National Committee (DNC), *Communications,* 430 S. Capitol St. S.E. 20003; (202) 863-8148. Fax, (202) 863-7194. Jim Mulhall, Director.
Web, www.democrats.org

Assists federal, state, and local Democratic candidates and officials in delivering a coordinated message on current issues; works to improve and expand relations with the press and to increase the visibility of Democratic officials and the Democratic party.

Democratic National Committee (DNC), *Finance,* 430 S. Capitol St. S.E. 20003; (202) 863-8000. Fax, (202) 863-8082. Jay Dunn, Director.
Web, www.democrats.org

Responsible for developing the Democratic party's financial base. Coordinates fundraising efforts for and gives financial support to Democratic candidates in national, state, and local campaigns.

Democratic National Committee (DNC), *Research,* 430 S. Capitol St. S.E. 20003; (202) 479-5130. Fax, (202) 488-5056. Jason Miner, Director.
Web, www.democrats.org

Provides Democratic elected officials, candidates, state party organizations, and the general public with information on Democratic party policy and programs.

Democratic Senatorial Campaign Committee, 120 Maryland Ave. N.E. 20002; (202) 224-2447. Fax, (202) 485-3120. Sen. Jon Corzine, D-N.J., Chair; Andy Grossman, Executive Director.
Web, www.dscc.org

Provides Democratic senatorial candidates with financial, research, and consulting services.

Women's National Democratic Club, *Committee on Public Policy,* 1526 New Hampshire Ave. N.W. 20036; (202) 232-7363. Fax, (202) 986-2791. Sandra Bieri, President.
General e-mail, womansndc@aol.com
Web, www.democraticwoman.org

Studies issues and presents views to congressional committees, the Democratic Party Platform Committee, Democratic leadership groups, elected officials, and other interested groups.

Republican

College Republican National Committee, 600 Pennsylvania Ave. S.E., #215 20003; (202) 608-1411. Fax, (202) 608-1429. Eric D. Hoplin, Executive Director.
General e-mail, info@crnc.org
Web, www.crnc.org

Membership: Republican college students. Promotes grassroots support for the Republican party and provides campaign assistance.

National Federation of Republican Women, 124 N. Alfred St., Alexandria, VA 22314; (703) 548-9688. Fax, (703) 548-9836. Heidi Smith, President.
General e-mail, mail@nfrw.org
Web, www.nfrw.org

Political education and volunteer arm of the Republican party. Organizes volunteers for support of Republican candidates for national, state, and local offices; encourages candidacy of Republican women; sponsors campaign management schools. Recruits Republican women candidates for office.

National Republican Congressional Committee, 320 1st St. S.E. 20003; (202) 479-7000. Fax, (202) 863-0693. Rep. Thomas M. Reynolds, R-N.Y., Chair; Sally Vastola, Executive Director.
Web, www.nrcc.org

Provides Republican House candidates with campaign assistance, including financial, public relations, media, and direct mail services.

National Republican Senatorial Committee (NRSC), 425 2nd St. N.E. 20002; (202) 675-6000. Fax, (202) 675-6058. Sen. George Allen, R-Va., Chair; Jay Timmons, Executive Director.
General e-mail, nrsc@nrsc.org
Web, www.nrsc.org

Provides Republican senatorial candidates with financial and public relations services.

Republican Governors Assn., 555 11th St. N.W., #700 20004; (202) 662-4140. Fax, (202) 662-4923. Gov. Bill Owens, R-Colo., Chair; Ed Tobin, Executive Director.
Web, www.rga.org

Serves as a liaison between governors' offices and Republican party organizations; assists Republican candidates for governor.

Republican Main Street Partnership, 1350 I St. N.W., #560 20005; (202) 682-3143. Fax, (202) 682-3943. Sarah Chamberlain-Resnick, Executive Director.

General e-mail, republicanmainst@mindspring.com

Web, www.republicanmainstreet.org

Membership: centrist Republican Party members and public officials. Develops and promotes moderate Republican policies.

Republican National Committee (RNC), *310 1st St. S.E. 20003; (202) 863-8500. Fax, (202) 863-8820. Marc Racicot, Chair. Press, (202) 863-8550.*

General e-mail, info@rnc.org

Web, www.rnc.org

Develops and promotes Republican party policies and positions; assists Republican candidates for state and national office; sponsors workshops to recruit Republican candidates and provide instruction in campaign techniques; organizes national political activities; works with state and local officials and organizations.

Republican National Committee (RNC), *Communications, 310 1st St. S.E. 20003; (202) 863-8614. Fax, (202) 863-8773. Jim Dyke, Director.*

General e-mail, info@rnc.org

Web, www.rnc.org

Assists federal, state, and local Republican candidates and officials in delivering a coordinated message on current issues; works to improve and expand relations with the press and to increase the visibility of Republican officials and the Republican message.

Republican National Committee (RNC), *Counsel, 310 1st St. S.E. 20003; (202) 863-8500. Fax, (202) 863-8820. Tom Josefiak, Chief Counsel. Press, (202) 863-8550.*

General e-mail, info@rnc.org

Web, www.rnc.org

Responsible for legal affairs of the RNC, including equal time and fairness cases before the Federal Communications Commission. Advises the RNC and state parties on redistricting and campaign finance law compliance.

Republican National Committee (RNC), *Finance, 310 1st St. S.E. 20003; (202) 863-8720. Fax, (202) 863-8690. Beverly Shea, Director.*

General e-mail, info@rnc.org

Web, www.rnc.org

Responsible for developing the Republican party's financial base. Coordinates fundraising efforts for and gives financial support to Republican candidates in national, state, and local campaigns.

Republican National Committee (RNC), *Republican National Hispanic Assembly, P.O. Box 1882 20013-1882; (202) 544-6700. Fax, (202) 544-6869. Massey Villarreal, Chair.*

General e-mail, info@rnha.org

Web, www.rnha.org

Seeks to develop a strong, effective, and informed Hispanic Republican constituency. Encourages Hispanic Americans to seek office at all levels of government; provides information and offers advisory services to Republican candidates, officeholders, and party organizations.

Ripon Society, *501 Capitol Court N.E., #300 20002; (202) 546-1292. Fax, (202) 547-6560. Lori Harju, Executive Director.*

Web, www.riponsociety.org

Membership: moderate Republicans. Works for the adoption of moderate policies within the Republican party.

Other Political Parties

Libertarian Party, *2600 Virginia Ave. N.W., #100 20037; (202) 333-0008. Fax, (202) 333-0072. Steve Dasbach, National Director; Geoff Neale, National Chair.*

Web, www.lp.org

Nationally organized political party. Seeks to bring libertarian ideas into the national political debate. Believes in the primacy of the individual over government; supports property rights, free trade, and eventual elimination of taxes.

Natural Law Party, *Washington Office, 347 Clouds Mill Dr., Alexandria, VA 22304; (703) 823-6933. Fax, (703) 823-6934. Sarina Grosswald, Government Liaison.*

General e-mail, info@natural-law.org

Web, www.natural-law.org

Nationally organized political party that seeks to infuse natural law philosophies with emphasis on prevention and proven solutions into the U.S. political debate. Supports preventive medicine programs, use and development of renewable energy resources, sustainable agricultural practices, and alternative approaches to criminal justice. (Headquarters in Fairfield, Iowa.)

108th Congress

PRONUNCIATION GUIDE TO MEMBERS' NAMES

The following is an informal guide for some of the most-often mispronounced names of members of Congress.

SENATE

Evan Bayh, D-Ind. – BY
John B. Breaux, D-La. – BRO
Lincoln Chafee, R-R.I. – CHAY-fee
Saxby Chambliss, R-Ga. – SAX-bee CHAM-bliss
John Cornyn, R-Texas – CORE-nin
Jon Corzine, D-N.J. – COR-zyne
Michael D. Crapo, R-Idaho – CRAY-poe
Tom Daschle, D-S.D. – DASH-el
Pete V. Domenici, R-N.M. – doe-MEN-ih-chee
Michael B. Enzi, R-Wyo. – EN-zee
Russell D. Feingold, D-Wis. – FINE-gold
Dianne Feinstein, D-Calif. – FINE-stine
James M. Inhofe, R-Okla. – IN-hoff
Daniel K. Inouye, D-Hawaii – in-NO-ay
Mary L. Landrieu, D-La. – LAN-drew
Rick Santorum, R-Pa. – san-TORE-um
Debbie Stabenow, D-Mich. – STAB-uh-now

HOUSE

Anibal Acevedo-Vilá, D-P.R. – AH-nee-baahl
  Ah-sah-VAY-dough VEE-la
Robert B. Aderholt, R-Ala. – ADD-er-holt
Spencer Bachus, R-Ala. – BACK-us
Bob Beauprez, R-Colo. – bo-PRAY
Xavier Becerra, D-Calif. – HAH-vee-air beh-SEH-ra
Doug Bereuter, R-Neb. – BEE-right-er
Michael Bilirakis, R-Fla. – bil-la-RACK-us
Earl Blumenauer, D-Ore. – BLUE-men-hour
Sherwood Boehlert, R-N.Y. – BO-lert
John A. Boehner, R-Ohio – BAY-ner
Henry Bonilla, R-Texas – bo-NEE-uh
John Boozman, R-Ark. – BOZE-man
Madeleine Z. Bordallo, D-Guam – bore-DAHL-ee-oh
Rick Boucher, D-Va. – BOUGH-cher
Steve Buyer, R-Ind. – BOO-yer
Michael E. Capuano, D-Mass. – KAP-you-AH-no
Steve Chabot, R-Ohio – SHAB-butt
Chris Chocola, R-Ind. – cha-KO-luh
Joseph Crowley, D-N.Y. – KRAU-lee
Barbara Cubin, R-Wyo. – CUE-bin
Peter A. DeFazio, D-Ore. – da-FAH-zee-o
Diana DeGette, D-Colo. – de-GET
Bill Delahunt, D-Mass. – DELL-a-hunt
Rosa DeLauro, D-Conn. – da-LAUR-o
Jim DeMint, R-S.C. – da-MENT
Peter Deutsch, D-Fla. – DOYCH
Lincoln Diaz-Balart, R-Fla. – DEE-az ba-LART
Mario Diaz-Balart, R-Fla. – DEE-az ba-LART
Lincoln Diaz-Balart, R-Fla. – DEE-az ba-LART
Vernon J. Ehlers, R-Mich. – AY-lurz
Anna G. Eshoo, D-Calif. – EH-shoo
Eni F.H. Faleomavaega, D-Am. Samoa – EN-ee
  FOL-ee-oh-mav-ah-ENG-uh
Chaka Fattah, D-Pa. – SHOCK-ah fa-TAH
Vito J. Fossella, R-N.Y. – VEE-toe Fuh-SELL-ah
Rodney Frelinghuysen, R-N.J. – FREE-ling-high-zen
Elton Gallegly, R-Calif. – GAL-uh-glee
Jim Gerlach, R-Pa. – GUR-lock

Virgil H. Goode Jr., R-Va. – GOOD (rhymes with "food")
Robert W. Goodlatte, R-Va. – GOOD-lat
Raúl M. Grijalva, D-Ariz. – gree-HAHL-va
Luis V. Gutierrez, D-Ill. – loo-EES goo-tee-AIR-ez
Gil Gutknecht, R-Minn. – GOOT-neck
Jeb Hensarling, R-Texas – HENN-sur-ling
Ruben Hinojosa, D-Texas – ru-BEN ee-na-HO-suh
Joseph M. Hoeffel, D-Pa. – HUFF-ull
Peter Hoekstra, R-Mich. – HOOK-struh
John Hostettler, R-Ind. – HO-stet-lur
Amo Houghton, R-N.Y. – HO-tun
Kenny Hulshof, R-Mo. – HULLZ-hoff
Darrell Issa, R-Calif. – EYE-sah
Ernest Istook, R-Okla. – IZ-took
Gerald D. Kleczka, D-Wis. – KLETCH-kuh
Jim Kolbe, R-Ariz. – COLE-bee
Dennis J. Kucinich, D-Ohio – ku-SIN-itch
Jim Langevin, D-R.I. – LAN-juh-vin
Steven C. LaTourette, R-Ohio – la-tuh-RETT
Frank A. LoBiondo, R-N.J. – lo-bee-ON-dough
Zoe Lofgren, D-Calif. – ZO
Nita M. Lowey, D-N.Y. – LOW-ee
Denise L. Majette, D-Ga. – muh-JET
Donald Manzullo, R-Ill. – man-ZOO-low
Michael H. Michaud, D-Maine – ME-shoo
Jerrold Nadler, D-N.Y. – NAD-ler
Bob Ney, R-Ohio – NAY
David R. Obey, D-Wis. – OH-bee
Doug Ose, R-Calif. – OH-see
Frank Pallone Jr., D-N.J. – puh-LOAN
Bill Pascrell Jr., D-N.J. – pas-KRELL
Ed Pastor, D-Ariz. – pas-TORE
Nancy Pelosi, D-Calif. – pa-LOH-see
Tom Petri, R-Wis. – PEA-try
Richard W. Pombo, R-Calif. – POM-bo
George P. Radanovich, R-Calif. – ruh-DON-o-vitch
Ralph Regula, R-Ohio – REG-you-luh
Denny Rehberg, R-Mont. – REE-berg
Silvestre Reyes, D-Texas – sil-VES-treh RAY-ess (rolled 'R')
Dana Rohrabacher, R-Calif. – ROAR-ah-BAH-ker
Ileana Ros-Lehtinen, R-Fla. – il-ee-AH-na ross-LAY-tin-nen
Jan Schakowsky, D-Ill. – shuh-KOW-ski
José E. Serrano, D-N.Y. – ho-ZAY sa-RAH-no (rolled 'R')
John Shadegg, R-Ariz. – SHAD-egg
John Shimkus, R-Ill. – SHIM-kus
Hilda L. Solis, D-Calif. – soh-LEEZ
Mark Souder, R-Ind. – SOW (rhymes with "now")-dur
Bart Stupak, D-Mich. – STU-pack
Tom Tancredo, R-Colo. – tan-CRAY-doe
Ellen O. Tauscher, D-Calif. – TAU (rhymes with "how")-sher
Billy Tauzin, R-La. – TOE-zan
Todd Tiahrt, R-Kan. – TEE-hart
Pat Tiberi, R-Ohio – TEA-berry
Nydia M. Velázquez, D-N.Y. – NID-ee-uh veh-LASS-kez
Peter J. Visclosky, D-Ind. – vis-KLOSS-key
Anthony Weiner, D-N.Y. – WEE-ner
Lynn Woolsey, D-Calif. – WOOL-zee

Delegations to the 108th Congress

Listed below are the names of senators and representatives of each state delegation for the 108th Congress, as of April 23, 2003. The senators are listed by seniority and the representatives by district. Italicized names indicate members serving in their freshman term. "AL" indicates an at-large member.

Alabama

Richard C. Shelby (R)
Jeff Sessions (R)
   1. *Jo Bonner (R)*
   2. Terry Everett (R)
   3. *Mike D. Rogers (R)*
   4. Robert B. Aderholt (R)
   5. Robert E. "Bud" Cramer (D)
   6. Spencer Bachus (R)
   7. *Artur Davis (D)*

Alaska

Ted Stevens (R)
Lisa Murkowski (R)
   AL Don Young (R)

American Samoa

   AL Eni F. H. Faleomavaega (D)

Arizona

John McCain (R)
Jon Kyl (R)
   1. *Rick Renzi (R)*
   2. *Trent Franks (R)*
   3. John Shadegg (R)
   4. Ed Pastor (D)
   5. J. D. Hayworth (R)
   6. Jeff Flake (R)
   7. *Raul M. Grijalva (D)*
   8. Jim Kolbe (R)

Arkansas

Blanche Lincoln (D)
Mark Pryor (D)

   1. Marion Berry (D)
   2. Vic Snyder (D)
   3. John Boozman (R)
   4. Mike Ross (D)

California

Dianne Feinstein (D)
Barbara Boxer (D)
   1. Mike Thompson (D)
   2. Wally Herger (R)
   3. Doug Ose (R)
   4. John T. Doolittle (R)
   5. Robert T. Matsui (D)
   6. Lynn Woolsey (D)
   7. George Miller (D)
   8. Nancy Pelosi (D)
   9. Barbara Lee (D)
   10. Ellen O. Tauscher (D)
   11. Richard W. Pombo (R)
   12. Tom Lantos (D)
   13. Pete Stark (D)
   14. Anna G. Eshoo (D)
   15. Michael M. Honda (D)
   16. Zoe Lofgren (D)
   17. Sam Farr (D)
   18. *Dennis Cardoza (D)*
   19. George P. Radanovich (R)
   20. Cal Dooley (D)
   21. *Devin Nunes (R)*
   22. Bill Thomas (R)
   23. Lois Capps (D)
   24. Elton Gallegly (R)
   25. Howard P. "Buck" McKeon (R)
   26. David Dreier (R)
   27. Brad Sherman (D)

   28. Howard L. Berman (D)
   29. Adam B. Schiff (D)
   30. Henry A. Waxman (D)
   31. Xavier Becerra (D)
   32. Hilda L. Solis (D)
   33. Diane Watson (D)
   34. Lucille Roybal-Allard (D)
   35. Maxine Waters (D)
   36. Jane Harman (D)
   37. Juanita Millender-McDonald (D)
   38. Grace F. Napolitano (D)
   39. *Linda T. Sanchez (D)*
   40. Ed Royce (R)
   41. Jerry Lewis (R)
   42. Gary G. Miller (R)
   43. Joe Baca (D)
   44. Ken Calvert (R)
   45. Mary Bono (R)
   46. Dana Rohrabacher (R)
   47. Loretta Sanchez (D)
   48. Christopher Cox (R)
   49. Darrell Issa (R)
   50. Randy "Duke" Cunningham (R)
   51. Bob Filner (D)
   52. Duncan Hunter (R)
   53. Susan A. Davis (D)

Colorado

Ben Nighthorse Campbell (R)
Wayne Allard (R)
   1. Diana DeGette (D)
   2. Mark Udall (D)
   3. Scott McInnis (R)
   4. *Marilyn Musgrave (R)*
   5. Joel Hefley (R)

6. Tom Tancredo (R)
7. *Bob Beauprez (R)*

Connecticut

Christopher J. Dodd (D)
Joseph I. Lieberman (D)
  1. John B. Larson (D)
  2. Rob Simmons (R)
  3. Rosa DeLauro (D)
  4. Christopher Shays (R)
  5. Nancy L. Johnson (R)

Delaware

Joseph R. Biden Jr. (D)
Thomas R. Carper (D)
  AL Michael N. Castle (R)

District of Columbia

  AL Eleanor Holmes Norton (D)

Florida

Bob Graham (D)
Bill Nelson (D)
  1. Jeff Miller (R)
  2. Allen Boyd (D)
  3. Corrine Brown (D)
  4. Ander Crenshaw (R)
  5. *Ginny Brown-Waite (R)*
  6. Cliff Stearns (R)
  7. John L. Mica (R)
  8. Ric Keller (R)
  9. Michael Bilirakis (R)
  10. C. W. Bill Young (R)
  11. Jim Davis (D)
  12. Adam H. Putnam (R)
  13. *Katherine Harris (R)*
  14. Porter J. Goss (R)
  15. Dave Weldon (R)
  16. Mark Foley (R)
  17. *Kendrick B. Meek (D)*
  18. Ileana Ros-Lehtinen (R)
  19. Robert Wexler (D)
  20. Peter Deutsch (D)
  21. Lincoln Diaz-Balart (R)
  22. E. Clay Shaw Jr. (R)
  23. Alcee L. Hastings (D)
  24. *Tom Feeney (R)*
  25. *Mario Diaz-Balart (R)*

Georgia

Zell Miller (D)
Saxby Chambliss (R)

1. Jack Kingston (R)
2. Sanford D. Bishop Jr. (D)
3. *Jim Marshall (D)*
4. *Denise L. Majette (D)*
5. John Lewis (D)
6. Johnny Isakson (R)
7. John Linder (R)
8. Mac Collins (R)
9. Charlie Norwood (R)
10. Nathan Deal (R)
11. *Phil Gingrey (R)*
12. *Max Burns (R)*
13. *David Scott (D)*

Guam

  AL *Madeleine Z. Bordallo (D)*

Hawaii

Daniel K. Inouye (D)
Daniel K. Akaka (D)
  1. Neil Abercrombie (D)
  2. *Ed Case (D)*

Idaho

Larry E. Craig (R)
Michael D. Crapo (R)
  1. C. L. "Butch" Otter (R)
  2. Mike Simpson (R)

Illinois

Richard J. Durbin (D)
Peter G. Fitzgerald (R)
  1. Bobby L. Rush (D)
  2. Jesse L. Jackson Jr. (D)
  3. William O. Lipinski (D)
  4. Luis V. Gutierrez (D)
  5. *Rahm Emanuel (D)*
  6. Henry J. Hyde (R)
  7. Danny K. Davis (D)
  8. Philip M. Crane (R)
  9. Jan Schakowsky (D)
  10. Mark Steven Kirk (R)
  11. Jerry Weller (R)
  12. Jerry F. Costello (D)
  13. Judy Biggert (R)
  14. J. Dennis Hastert (R)
  15. Timothy V. Johnson (R)
  16. Donald Manzullo (R)
  17. Lane Evans (D)
  18. Ray LaHood (R)
  19. John Shimkus (R)

Indiana

Richard G. Lugar (R)
Evan Bayh (D)
  1. Peter J. Visclosky (D)
  2. *Chris Chocola (R)*
  3. Mark Souder (R)
  4. Steve Buyer (R)
  5. Dan Burton (R)
  6. Mike Pence (R)
  7. Julia Carson (D)
  8. John Hostettler (R)
  9. Baron P. Hill (D)

Iowa

Charles E. Grassley (R)
Tom Harkin (D)
  1. Jim Nussle (R)
  2. Jim Leach (R)
  3. Leonard L. Boswell (D)
  4. Tom Latham (R)
  5. *Steve King (R)*

Kansas

Sam Brownback (R)
Pat Roberts (R)
  1. Jerry Moran (R)
  2. Jim Ryun (R)
  3. Dennis Moore (D)
  4. Todd Tiahrt (R)

Kentucky

Mitch McConnell (R)
Jim Bunning (R)
  1. Edward Whitfield (R)
  2. Ron Lewis (R)
  3. Anne M. Northup (R)
  4. Ken Lucas (D)
  5. Harold Rogers (R)
  6. Ernie Fletcher (R)

Louisiana

John B. Breaux (D)
Mary L. Landrieu (D)
  1. David Vitter (R)
  2. William J. Jefferson (D)
  3. Billy Tauzin (R)
  4. Jim McCrery (R)
  5. *Rodney Alexander (D)*
  6. Richard H. Baker (R)
  7. Chris John (D)

Maine

Olympia J. Snowe (R)
Susan Collins (R)
1. Tom Allen (D)
2. *Michael H. Michaud (D)*

Maryland

Paul S. Sarbanes (D)
Barbara A. Mikulski (D)
1. Wayne T. Gilchrest (R)
2. *C. A. Dutch Ruppersberger (D)*
3. Benjamin L. Cardin (D)
4. Albert R. Wynn (D)
5. Steny H. Hoyer (D)
6. Roscoe G. Bartlett (R)
7. Elijah E. Cummings (D)
8. *Chris Van Hollen (D)*

Massachusetts

Edward M. Kennedy (D)
John Kerry (D)
1. John W. Olver (D)
2. Richard E. Neal (D)
3. Jim McGovern (D)
4. Barney Frank (D)
5. Martin T. Meehan (D)
6. John F. Tierney (D)
7. Edward J. Markey (D)
8. Michael E. Capuano (D)
9. Stephen F. Lynch (D)
10. Bill Delahunt (D)

Michigan

Carl Levin (D)
Debbie Stabenow (D)
1. Bart Stupak (D)
2. Peter Hoekstra (R)
3. Vernon J. Ehlers (R)
4. Dave Camp (R)
5. Dale E. Kildee (D)
6. Fred Upton (R)
7. Nick Smith (R)
8. Mike Rogers (R)
9. Joe Knollenberg (R)
10. *Candice S. Miller (R)*
11. *Thaddeus McCotter (R)*
12. Sander M. Levin (D)
13. Carolyn Cheeks Kilpatrick (D)
14. John Conyers Jr. (D)
15. John D. Dingell (D)

Minnesota

Mark Dayton (D)
Norm Coleman (R)
1. Gil Gutknecht (R)
2. *John Kline (R)*
3. Jim Ramstad (R)
4. Betty McCollum (D)
5. Martin Olav Sabo (D)
6. Mark Kennedy (R)
7. Collin C. Peterson (D)
8. James L. Oberstar (D)

Mississippi

Thad Cochran (R)
Trent Lott (R)
1. Roger Wicker (R)
2. Bennie Thompson (D)
3. Charles W. "Chip" Pickering Jr. (R)
4. Gene Taylor (D)

Missouri

Christopher S. Bond (R)
Jim Talent (R)
1. William Lacy Clay (D)
2. Todd Akin (R)
3. Richard A. Gephardt (D)
4. Ike Skelton (D)
5. Karen McCarthy (D)
6. Sam Graves (R)
7. Roy Blunt (R)
8. Jo Ann Emerson (R)
9. Kenny Hulshof (R)

Montana

Max Baucus (D)
Conrad Burns (R)
AL Denny Rehberg (R)

Nebraska

Chuck Hagel (R)
Ben Nelson (D)
1. Doug Bereuter (R)
2. Lee Terry (R)
3. Tom Osborne (R)

Nevada

Harry Reid (D)
John Ensign (R)
1. Shelley Berkley (D)
2. Jim Gibbons (R)
3. *Jon Porter (R)*

New Hampshire

Judd Gregg (R)
John E. Sununu (R)
1. *Jeb Bradley (R)*
2. Charles Bass (R)

New Jersey

Jon Corzine (D)
Frank R. Lautenberg (D)
1. Robert E. Andrews (D)
2. Frank A. LoBiondo (R)
3. H. James Saxton (R)
4. Christopher H. Smith (R)
5. *Scott Garrett (R)*
6. Frank Pallone Jr. (D)
7. Mike Ferguson (R)
8. Bill Pascrell Jr. (D)
9. Steven R. Rothman (D)
10. Donald M. Payne (D)
11. Rodney Frelinghuysen (R)
12. Rush D. Holt (D)
13. Robert Menendez (D)

New Mexico

Pete V. Domenici (R)
Jeff Bingaman (D)
1. Heather A. Wilson (R)
2. *Steve Pearce (R)*
3. Tom Udall (D)

New York

Charles E. Schumer (D)
Hillary Rodham Clinton (D)
1. *Timothy H. Bishop (D)*
2. Steve Israel (D)
3. Peter T. King (R)
4. Carolyn McCarthy (D)
5. Gary L. Ackerman (D)
6. Gregory W. Meeks (D)
7. Joseph Crowley (D)
8. Jerrold Nadler (D)
9. Anthony Weiner (D)
10. Edolphus Towns (D)
11. Major R. Owens (D)
12. Nydia M. Velazquez (D)
13. Vito J. Fossella (R)
14. Carolyn B. Maloney (D)
15. Charles B. Rangel (D)
16. Jose E. Serrano (D)
17. Eliot L. Engel (D)
18. Nita M. Lowey (D)
19. Sue W. Kelly (R)

20. John E. Sweeney (R)
21. Michael R. McNulty (D)
22. Maurice D. Hinchey (D)
23. John M. McHugh (R)
24. Sherwood Boehlert (R)
25. James T. Walsh (R)
26. Thomas M. Reynolds (R)
27. Jack Quinn (R)
28. Louise M. Slaughter (D)
29. Amo Houghton (R)

North Carolina
John Edwards (D)
Elizabeth Dole (R)
  1. *Frank W. Ballance Jr. (D)*
  2. Bob Etheridge (D)
  3. Walter B. Jones (R)
  4. David E. Price (D)
  5. Richard M. Burr (R)
  6. Howard Coble (R)
  7. Mike McIntyre (D)
  8. Robin Hayes (R)
  9. Sue Myrick (R)
10. Cass Ballenger (R)
11. Charles H. Taylor (R)
12. Melvin Watt (D)
13. *Brad Miller (D)*

North Dakota
Kent Conrad (D)
Byron L. Dorgan (D)
  AL Earl Pomeroy (D)

Ohio
Mike DeWine (R)
George V. Voinovich (R)
  1. Steve Chabot (R)
  2. Rob Portman (R)
  3. *Michael R. Turner (R)*
  4. Michael G. Oxley (R)
  5. Paul E. Gillmor (R)
  6. Ted Strickland (D)
  7. David L. Hobson (R)
  8. John A. Boehner (R)
  9. Marcy Kaptur (D)
10. Dennis J. Kucinich (D)
11. Stephanie Tubbs Jones (D)
12. Pat Tiberi (R)
13. Sherrod Brown (D)
14. Steven C. LaTourette (R)
15. Deborah Pryce (R)
16. Ralph Regula (R)

17. *Tim Ryan (D)*
18. Bob Ney (R)

Oklahoma
Don Nickles (R)
James M. Inhofe (R)
  1. John Sullivan (R)
  2. Brad Carson (D)
  3. Frank D. Lucas (R)
  4. *Tom Cole (R)*
  5. Ernest Istook (R)

Oregon
Ron Wyden (D)
Gordon H. Smith (R)
  1. David Wu (D)
  2. Greg Walden (R)
  3. Earl Blumenauer (D)
  4. Peter A. DeFazio (D)
  5. Darlene Hooley (D)

Pennsylvania
Arlen Specter (R)
Rick Santorum (R)
  1. Robert A. Brady (D)
  2. Chaka Fattah (D)
  3. Phil English (R)
  4. Melissa A. Hart (R)
  5. John E. Peterson (R)
  6. *Jim Gerlach (R)*
  7. Curt Weldon (R)
  8. James C. Greenwood (R)
  9. Bill Shuster (R)
10. Don Sherwood (R)
11. Paul E. Kanjorski (D)
12. John P. Murtha (D)
13. Joseph M. Hoeffel (D)
14. Mike Doyle (D)
15. Patrick J. Toomey (R)
16. Joe Pitts (R)
17. Tim Holden (D)
18. *Tim Murphy (R)*
19. Todd R. Platts (R)

Puerto Rico
  AL Anibal Acevedo-Vila (D)

Rhode Island
Jack Reed (D)
Lincoln Chafee (R)
  1. Patrick J. Kennedy (D)
  2. Jim Langevin (D)

South Carolina
Ernest F. Hollings (D)
Lindsey Graham (R)
  1. Henry E. Brown Jr. (R)
  2. Joe Wilson (R)
  3. *J. Gresham Barrett (R)*
  4. Jim DeMint (R)
  5. John M. Spratt Jr. (D)
  6. James E. Clyburn (D)

South Dakota
Tom Daschle (D)
Tim Johnson (D)
  AL *Bill Janklow (R)*

Tennessee
Bill Frist (R)
Lamar Alexander (R)
  1. Bill Jenkins (R)
  2. John J. "Jimmy" Duncan Jr. (R)
  3. Zach Wamp (R)
  4. *Lincoln Davis (D)*
  5. *Jim Cooper (D)*
  6. Bart Gordon (D)
  7. *Marsha Blackburn (R)*
  8. John Tanner (D)
  9. Harold E. Ford Jr. (D)

Texas
Kay Bailey Hutchison (R)
John Cornyn (R)
  1. Max Sandlin (D)
  2. Jim Turner (D)
  3. Sam Johnson (R)
  4. Ralph M. Hall (D)
  5. *Jeb Hensarling (R)*
  6. Joe L. Barton (R)
  7. John Culberson (R)
  8. Kevin Brady (R)
  9. Nick Lampson (D)
10. Lloyd Doggett (D)
11. Chet Edwards (D)
12. Kay Granger (R)
13. William M. "Mac"
    Thornberry (R)
14. Ron Paul (R)
15. Ruben Hinojosa (D)
16. Silvestre Reyes (D)
17. Charles W. Stenholm (D)
18. Sheila Jackson-Lee (D)
19. Vacant

20. Charlie Gonzalez (D)
21. Lamar Smith (R)
22. Tom DeLay (R)
23. Henry Bonilla (R)
24. Martin Frost (D)
25. *Chris Bell (D)*
26. *Michael C. Burgess (R)*
27. Solomon P. Ortiz (D)
28. Ciro D. Rodriguez (D)
29. Gene Green (D)
30. Eddie Bernice Johnson (D)
31. *John Carter (R)*
32. Pete Sessions (R)

Utah

Orrin G. Hatch (R)
Robert F. Bennett (R)
1. *Rob Bishop (R)*
2. Jim Matheson (D)
3. Chris Cannon (R)

Vermont

Patrick J. Leahy (D)
James M. Jeffords (I)
AL Bernard Sanders (I)

Virgin Islands

AL Donna M. C. Christensen (D)

Virginia

John W. Warner (R)
George Allen (R)
1. Jo Ann Davis (R)
2. Ed Schrock (R)
3. Robert C. Scott (D)
4. J. Randy Forbes (R)
5. Virgil H. Goode Jr. (R)
6. Robert W. Goodlatte (R)
7. Eric Cantor (R)
8. James P. Moran (D)
9. Rick Boucher (D)
10. Frank R. Wolf (R)
11. Thomas M. Davis III (R)

Washington

Patty Murray (D)
Maria Cantwell (D)
1. Jay Inslee (D)
2. Rick Larsen (D)
3. Brian Baird (D)
4. Doc Hastings (R)
5. George Nethercutt (R)
6. Norm Dicks (D)
7. Jim McDermott (D)
8. Jennifer Dunn (R)
9. Adam Smith (D)

West Virginia

Robert C. Byrd (D)
John D. Rockefeller IV (D)
1. Alan B. Mollohan (D)
2. Shelley Moore Capito (R)
3. Nick J. Rahall II (D)

Wisconsin

Herb Kohl (D)
Russell D. Feingold (D)
1. Paul D. Ryan (R)
2. Tammy Baldwin (D)
3. Ron Kind (D)
4. Gerald D. Kleczka (D)
5. F. James Sensenbrenner Jr. (R)
6. Tom Petri (R)
7. David R. Obey (D)
8. Mark Green (R)

Wyoming

Craig Thomas (R)
Michael B. Enzi (R)
AL Barbara Cubin (R)

House Committees

The standing and select committees of the U.S. House of Representatives are listed below. The listing includes the room number, telephone and fax numbers, Web address, e-mail address if available, key majority and minority staff members, jurisdiction for each full committee, and party ratio. Subcommittees are listed alphabetically under each committee. Membership is listed in order of seniority on the committee or subcommittee.

Members of the majority party, Republicans, are shown in roman type; members of the minority party, Democrats, are shown in italic type. Bernard Sanders, I-Vt., caucuses with Democrats and accrues committee seniority with Democrats. The word vacancy indicates that a committee or subcommittee seat had not been filled as of April 23, 2003. Subcommittee vacancies do not necessarily indicate vacancies on full committees, or vice versa. The partisan committees of the House are listed on pp. 801–802. All area codes are (202). Larry Combest is resigning effective May 31, 2003.

AGRICULTURE

Office: 1301 LHOB
Phone: 225-2171 **Fax:** 225-0917
Web: agriculture.house.gov
E-mail: agriculture@mail.house.gov
Majority Staff Director: Bill O'Conner
Minority Staff Director: Stephen Haterius 225-0317 1305 LHOB

Agriculture generally; forestry in general, and forest reserves other than those created from the public domain; adulteration of seeds, insect pests, and protection of birds and animals in forest reserves; agricultural and industrial chemistry; agricultural colleges and experiment stations; agricultural economics and research; agricultural education extension services; agricultural production and marketing and stabilization of prices of agricultural products, and commodities (not including distribution outside of the United States); animal industry and diseases of animals; commodities exchanges; crop insurance and soil conservation; dairy industry; entomology and plant quarantine; extension of farm credit and farm security; inspection of livestock, poultry, meat products, seafood and seafood products; human nutrition and home economics; plant industry, soils, and agricultural engineering; rural electrification; rural development; water conservation related to activities of the Agriculture Dept. The Chair and ranking minority member are voting members ex officio of all subcommittees of which they are not regular members.
Party Ratio: R 27–D 24

Robert W. Goodlatte, Va., Chair
Larry Combest, Texas
John A. Boehner, Ohio, Vice Chair
Richard W. Pombo, Calif.
Nick Smith, Mich.
Terry Everett, Ala.
Frank D. Lucas, Okla.
Jerry Moran, Kan.
Bill Jenkins, Tenn.
Gil Gutknecht, Minn.
Doug Ose, Calif.
Robin Hayes, N.C.
Charles W. "Chip" Pickering Jr., Miss.
Timothy V. Johnson, Ill.
Tom Osborne, Neb.
Mike Pence, Ind.
Denny Rehberg, Mont.
Sam Graves, Mo.
Adam H. Putnam, Fla.
Bill Janklow, S.D.
Max Burns, Ga.
Jo Bonner, Ala.
Mike D. Rogers, Ala.
Steve King, Iowa
Chris Chocola, Ind.
Marilyn Musgrave, Colo.
Devin Nunes, Calif.

Charles W. Stenholm, Texas, Ranking Minority Member
Collin C. Peterson, Minn.
Cal Dooley, Calif.
Tim Holden, Pa.
Bennie Thompson, Miss.
Mike McIntyre, N.C.
Bob Etheridge, N.C.
Baron P. Hill, Ind.
Joe Baca, Calif.
Mike Ross, Ark.
Anibal Acevedo-Vila, P.R.
Ed Case, Hawaii
Rodney Alexander, La.
Frank W. Ballance Jr., N.C.
Dennis Cardoza, Calif.
David Scott, Ga.
Jim Marshall, Ga.
Earl Pomeroy, N.D.
Leonard L. Boswell, Iowa
Ken Lucas, Ky.
Mike Thompson, Calif.
Mark Udall, Colo.
Rick Larsen, Wash.
Lincoln Davis, Tenn.

Subcommittees

Conservation, Credit, Rural Development, and Research
Office: 1301 LHOB **Phone:** 225-2171

AGRICULTURE (continued)

Lucas (Okla.; Chair), Combest, Moran (Kan.), Osborne (Vice Chair), Graves, Putnam, Burns, Bonner, Rogers (Ala.), King (Iowa)

Holden (Ranking Minority Member), Case, Ballance, Peterson (Minn.), Dooley, Etheridge, Acevedo-Vila, Marshall, McIntyre

Department Operations, Oversight, Nutrition, and Forestry

Office: 1407 LHOB   **Phone:** 225-2171

Gutknecht (Chair), Pombo, Smith (Mich.), Ose, Rehberg (Vice Chair), Putnam, Janklow, Bonner, King (Iowa), Nunes

Dooley (Ranking Minority Member), Baca, Acevedo-Vila, Cardoza, Holden, Hill, Ballance, Thompson (Calif.), Davis (Tenn.)

General Farm Commodities and Risk Management

Office: 1336 LHOB   **Phone:** 225-2171

Moran (Kan.; Chair), Combest, Boehner, Smith (Mich.; Vice Chair), Everett, Lucas (Okla.), Jenkins, Pickering, Johnson (Ill.), Pence, Rehberg, Graves, Burns, Chocola, Musgrave

Peterson (Minn.; Ranking Minority Member), Thompson (Miss.), Alexander, Ross, Dooley, Pomeroy, Boswell, Etheridge, Hill, Case, Cardoza, Marshall, Larsen, Davis (Tenn.)

Livestock and Horticulture

Office: 1741P LHOB   **Phone:** 225-2171

Hayes (Chair), Pombo, Ose (Vice Chair), Pickering, Osborne, Pence, Putnam, Janklow, Rogers (Ala.), Chocola, Musgrave

Ross (Ranking Minority Member), Cardoza, Scott (Ga.), Peterson (Minn.), Alexander, Lucas (Ky.), Boswell, Udall (N.M.), Larsen, Baca

Specialty Crops and Foreign Agriculture

Office: 1336 LHOB   **Phone:** 225-2171

Jenkins (Chair), Combest, Everett (Vice Chair), Gutknecht, Hayes, Rehberg, Rogers (Ala.), Nunes

McIntyre (Ranking Minority Member), Etheridge, Hill, Scott (Ga.), Marshall, Thompson (Miss.), Alexander

APPROPRIATIONS

Office: H-218 CAP   **Phone:** 225-2771
Web: www.house.gov/appropriations
Majority Staff Director: James W. Dyer
Minority Staff Director: R. Scott Lilly 225-3481 1016 LHOB

Appropriation of the revenue for the support of the government; rescissions of appropriations contained in appropriation acts; transfers of unexpended balances; new spending authority under the Congressional Budget Act. The Chair and ranking minority member are voting members ex officio of all subcommittees of which they are not regular members.
Party Ratio: R 36–D 29

C. W. Bill Young, Fla., Chair
Ralph Regula, Ohio
Jerry Lewis, Calif.
Harold Rogers, Ky.
Frank R. Wolf, Va.
Jim Kolbe, Ariz.
James T. Walsh, N.Y.
Charles H. Taylor, N.C.
David L. Hobson, Ohio
Ernest Istook, Okla.
Henry Bonilla, Texas
Joe Knollenberg, Mich.
Jack Kingston, Ga.
Rodney Frelinghuysen, N.J.
Roger Wicker, Miss.
George Nethercutt, Wash.
Randy "Duke"
   Cunningham, Calif.
Todd Tiahrt, Kan.
Zach Wamp, Tenn.
Tom Latham, Iowa
Anne M. Northup, Ky.
Robert B. Aderholt, Ala.
Jo Ann Emerson, Mo.
Kay Granger, Texas
John E. Peterson, Pa.
Virgil H. Goode Jr., Va.
John T. Doolittle, Calif.
Ray LaHood, Ill.
John E. Sweeney, N.Y.
David Vitter, La.
Don Sherwood, Pa.
Dave Weldon, Fla.
Mike Simpson, Idaho
John Culberson, Texas
Mark Steven Kirk, Ill.
Ander Crenshaw, Fla.

David R. Obey, Wis.,
   Ranking Minority
   Member
John P. Murtha, Pa.
Norm Dicks, Wash.
Martin Olav Sabo, Minn.
Steny H. Hoyer, Md.
Alan B. Mollohan, W.Va.
Marcy Kaptur, Ohio
Peter J. Visclosky, Ind.
Nita M. Lowey, N.Y.
Jose E. Serrano, N.Y.
Rosa DeLauro, Conn.
James P. Moran, Va.
John W. Olver, Mass.
Ed Pastor, Ariz.
David E. Price, N.C.
Chet Edwards, Texas
Robert E. "Bud" Cramer,
   Ala.
Patrick J. Kennedy, R.I.
James E. Clyburn, S.C.
Maurice D. Hinchey, N.Y.
Lucille Roybal-Allard, Calif.
Sam Farr, Calif.
Jesse L. Jackson Jr., Ill.
Carolyn Cheeks, Kilpatrick,
   Mich.
Allen Boyd, Fla.
Chaka Fattah, Pa.
Steven R. Rothman, N.J.
Sanford D. Bishop Jr., Ga.
Marion Berry, Ark.

Subcommittees

Agriculture, Rural Development, FDA, and Related Agencies

Office: 2362A RHOB   **Phone:** 225-2638

Bonilla (Chair), Walsh, Kingston, Nethercutt, Latham (Vice Chair), Emerson, Goode, LaHood

Kaptur (Ranking Minority Member), DeLauro, Hinchey, Farr, Boyd

Commerce, Justice, State, and Judiciary

Office: H-309 CAP   **Phone:** 225-3351

Wolf (Chair), Rogers (Ky.), Kolbe, Taylor (N.C.), Regula, Vitter (Vice Chair), Sweeney, Kirk

Serrano (Ranking Minority Member), Mollohan, Cramer, Kennedy (R.I.), Sabo

Defense

Office: H-149 CAP   **Phone:** 225-2847

APPROPRIATIONS (continued)

Lewis (Calif.; Chair), Young (Fla.), Hobson, Bonilla, Nethercutt (Vice Chair), Cunningham, Frelinghuysen, Tiahrt, Wicker

Murtha (Ranking Minority Member), Dicks, Sabo, Visclosky, Moran (Va.)

District of Columbia
Office: H-147 CAP **Phone:** 225-5338

Frelinghuysen (Chair), Istook, Cunningham (Vice Chair), Doolittle, Weldon (Fla.), Culberson

Fattah (Ranking Minority Member), Pastor, Cramer

Energy and Water Development
Office: 2362 RHOB **Phone:** 225-3421

Hobson (Chair), Frelinghuysen, Latham, Wamp (Vice Chair), Emerson, Doolittle, Peterson (Pa.), Simpson

Visclosky (Ranking Minority Member), Edwards, Pastor, Clyburn, Berry

Foreign Operations, Export Financing, and Related Programs
Office: H-B28 CAP **Phone:** 225-2041

Kolbe (Chair), Knollenberg, Lewis (Calif.), Wicker (Vice Chair), Bonilla, Vitter, Crenshaw, Kirk

Lowey (Ranking Minority Member), Jackson, Kilpatrick, Rothman, Kaptur

Homeland Security
Office: B307 RHOB **Phone:** 225-5834

Rogers (Ky.; Chair), Young (Fla.; Vice Chair), Wolf, Wamp, Latham, Emerson, Granger, Sweeney, Sherwood

Sabo (Ranking Minority Member), Price, Serrano, Roybal-Allard, Berry, Mollohan

Interior
Office: B-308 RHOB **Phone:** 225-3081

Taylor (N.C.; Chair), Regula, Kolbe, Nethercutt, Wamp, Peterson (Pa.; Vice Chair), Sherwood, Crenshaw

Dicks (Ranking Minority Member), Murtha, Moran (Va.), Hinchey, Olver

Labor, Health and Human Services, and Education
Office: 2358 RHOB **Phone:** 225-3508

Regula (Chair), Istook, Wicker, Northup (Vice Chair), Cunningham, Granger, Peterson (Pa.), Sherwood, Weldon (Fla.), Simpson

Obey (Ranking Minority Member), Hoyer, Lowey, DeLauro, Jackson, Kennedy (R.I.), Roybal-Allard

Legislative Branch
Office: H-147 CAP **Phone:** 225-5338

Kingston (Chair), LaHood (Vice Chair), Tiahrt, Culberson, Kirk

Moran (Va., Ranking Minority Member), Price, Clyburn

Military Construction
Office: B-300 RHOB **Phone:** 225-3047

Knollenberg (Chair), Walsh, Aderholt (Vice Chair), Granger, Goode, Vitter, Kingston, Crenshaw

Edwards (Ranking Minority Member), Farr, Boyd, Bishop (Ga.), Dicks

Transportation, Treasury, and Related Agencies
Office: 2358 RHOB **Phone:** 225-2141

Istook (Chair), Wolf, Lewis (Calif.), Rogers (Ky.), Tiahrt (Vice Chair), Northup, Aderholt, Sweeney, Culberson

Hoyer (Ranking Minority Member), Olver, Pastor, Kilpatrick, Clyburn, Rothman

Veterans Affairs, Housing and Urban Development, and Independent Agencies
Office: H-143 CAP **Phone:** 225-3241

Walsh (Chair), Hobson, Knollenberg, Northup, Goode (Vice Chair), Aderholt LaHood, Weldon (Fla.), Simpson

Mollohan (Ranking Minority Member), Kaptur, Price, Cramer, Fattah, Bishop (Ga.)

ARMED SERVICES

Office: 2120 RHOB **Phone:** 225-4151
Fax: 225-9077
Web: www.house.gov/hasc
Majority Staff Director: Robert S. Rangel
Minority Staff Director: Jim Schweiter 225-4158 2340 RHOB

Ammunition depots; forts; arsenals; Army, Navy, and Air Force reservations and establishments; common defense generally; conservation, development, and use of naval petroleum and oil shale reserves; Defense Dept. generally, including the Army, Navy, and Air Force Depts. generally; interoceanic canals generally, including measures relating to the maintenance, operation, and administration of interoceanic canals; Merchant Marine Academy, and State Maritime Academies; military applications of nuclear energy; tactical intelligence and intelligence related activities of the Defense Dept.; national security aspects of merchant marine, including financial assistance for the construction and operation of vessels, the maintenance of the U.S. shipbuilding and ship repair industrial base, cabotage, cargo preference, and merchant marine officers and seamen as these matters relate to the national security; pay, promotion, retirement, and other benefits and privileges of members of the armed forces; scientific research and development in support of the armed services; selective service; size and composition of the Army, Navy, Marine Corps, and Air Force; soldiers' and sailors' homes; strategic and critical materials necessary for the common defense.
Party Ratio: R 33–D 28

Duncan Hunter, Calif., Chair	*Ike Skelton, Mo., Ranking Minority Member*
Curt Weldon, Pa.	*John M. Spratt Jr., S.C.*
Joel Hefley, Colo.	*Solomon P. Ortiz, Texas*
H. James Saxton, N.J.	*Lane Evans, Ill.*
John M. McHugh, N.Y.	*Gene Taylor, Miss.*
Terry Everett, Ala.	*Neil Abercrombie, Hawaii*
Roscoe G. Bartlett, Md.	*Martin T. Meehan, Mass.*

Howard P. "Buck" McKeon, Calif.
William M. "Mac" Thornberry, Texas
John Hostettler, Ind.
Walter B. Jones, N.C.
Jim Ryun, Kan.
Jim Gibbons, Nev.
Robin Hayes, N.C.
Heather A. Wilson, N.M.
Ken Calvert, Calif.
Rob Simmons, Conn.
Jo Ann Davis, Va.
Ed Schrock, Va.
Todd Akin, Mo.
J. Randy Forbes, Va.
Jeff Miller, Fla.
Joe Wilson, S.C.
Frank A. LoBiondo, N.J.
Tom Cole, Okla.
Jeb Bradley, N.H.
Rob Bishop, Utah
Michael R. Turner, Ohio
John Kline, Minn.
Candice S. Miller, Mich.
Phil Gingrey, Ga.
Mike D. Rogers, Ala.
Trent Franks, Ariz.

Silvestre Reyes, Texas
Vic Snyder, Ark.
Jim Turner, Texas
Adam Smith, Wash.
Loretta Sanchez, Calif.
Mike McIntyre, N.C.
Ciro D. Rodriguez, Texas
Ellen O. Tauscher, Calif.
Robert A. Brady, Pa.
Baron P. Hill, Ind.
John B. Larson, Conn.
Susan A. Davis, Calif.
Jim Langevin, R.I.
Steve Israel, N.Y.
Rick Larsen, Wash.
Jim Cooper, Tenn.
Jim Marshall, Ga.
Kendrick B. Meek, Fla.
Madeleine Z. Bordallo, Guam
Rodney Alexander, La.
Tim Ryan, Ohio

Subcommittees

Projection Forces
Office: 2340 RHOB   **Phone:** 225-1967

Bartlett (Chair), Simmons, Davis (Va.), Schrock, Saxton, Hostettler, Calvert, Bradley, Kline

Taylor (Miss.; Ranking Minority Member), Abercrombie, Tauscher, Langevin, Israel, Marshall, Alexander

Readiness
Office: 2120 RHOB   **Phone:** 225-6288

Hefley (Chair), McKeon, Hostettler, Jones (N.C.), Ryun, Hayes, Wilson (N.M.), Calvert, Forbes, Miller (Fla.), Cole, Bishop (Utah), Miller (Mich.), Rogers (Ala.), Franks, McHugh

Ortiz (Ranking Minority Member), Evans, Taylor (Miss.), Abercrombie, Reyes, Snyder, Rodriguez, Brady (Pa.), Hill, Larson, Davis (Calif.), Larsen, Marshall, Bordallo

Strategic Forces
Office: 2340 RHOB   **Phone:** 226-7173

Everett (Chair), Thornberry, Weldon (Pa.), Wilson (N.M.), Bishop (Utah), Turner (Ohio), Rogers (Ala.), Franks

Reyes (Ranking Minority Member), Spratt, Sanchez (Calif.), Tauscher, Meek, Ryan (Ohio)

Tactical Air and Land Forces
Office: 2120 RHOB   **Phone:** 225-4151

Weldon (Pa.; Chair), Gibbons, Akin, Bradley, Turner (Ohio,) Gingrey, Everett, McKeon, Jones (N.C.), Ryun, Simmons, Schrock, Forbes, Hefley, Wilson (S.C.), LoBiondo

Abercrombie (Ranking Minority Member), Skelton, Spratt, Ortiz, Evans, Turner (Texas), Smith (Wash.), McIntyre, Brady (Pa.), Larson, Israel, Cooper, Meek, Alexander

Terrorism, Unconventional Threats, and Capabilities
Office: 2120 RHOB   **Phone:** 225-4151

Saxton (Chair), Wilson (S.C.), LoBiondo, Kline, Miller (Fla.), Bartlett, Thornberry, Gibbons, Hayes, Davis (Va.), Akin, Hefley

Meehan (Ranking Minority Member), Turner (Texas), Smith (Wash.), McIntyre, Rodriguez, Hill, Davis (Calif.), Langevin, Larsen, Cooper

Total Force
Office: 2340 RHOB   **Phone:** 225-7560

McHugh (Chair), Cole, Miller (Mich.), Gingrey, Saxton, Ryun, Schrock, Hayes

Snyder (Ranking Minority Member), Meehan, Sanchez (Calif.), Tauscher, Cooper, Bordallo

BUDGET

Office: 309 CHOB   **Phone:** 226-7270
Fax: 226-7174
Web: budget.house.gov
E-mail: budget@mail.house.gov
Majority Chief of Staff: Rich Meade
Minority Staff Director: Thomas S. Kahn 226-7200 B-71 CHOB

Congressional budget process generally; concurrent budget resolutions; measures relating to special controls over the federal budget; Congressional Budget Office.

Party Ratio: R 24–D 19

Jim Nussle, Iowa, Chair
Christopher Shays, Conn., Vice Chair
Gil Gutknecht, Minn.
William M. "Mac" Thornberry, Texas
Jim Ryun, Kan.
Patrick J. Toomey, Pa.
Doc Hastings, Wash.
Rob Portman, Ohio
Ed Schrock, Va.
Henry E. Brown Jr., S.C.
Ander Crenshaw, Fla.
Adam H. Putnam, Fla.
Roger Wicker, Miss.
Kenny Hulshof, Mo.
Tom Tancredo, Colo.
David Vitter, La.
Jo Bonner, Ala.
Trent Franks, Ariz.
Scott Garrett, N.J.

John M. Spratt Jr., S.C., Ranking Minority Member
James P. Moran, Va.
Darlene Hooley, Ore.
Tammy Baldwin, Wis.
Dennis Moore, Kan.
John Lewis, Ga.
Richard E. Neal, Mass.
Rosa DeLauro, Conn.
Chet Edwards, Texas
Robert C. Scott, Va.
Harold E. Ford Jr., Tenn.
Lois Capps, Calif.
Mike Thompson, Calif.
Brian Baird, Wash.
Jim Cooper, Tenn.
Rahm Emanuel, Ill.
Artur Davis, Ala.
Denise L. Majette, Ga.
Ron Kind, Wis.

BUDGET (continued)

J. Gresham Barrett, S.C.
Thaddeus McCotter, Mich.
Mario Diaz-Balart, Fla.
Jeb Hensarling, Texas
Ginny Brown-Waite, Fla.

EDUCATION AND THE WORKFORCE

Office: 2181 RHOB   **Phone:** 225-4527
Fax: 225-9571
Web: edworkforce.house.gov
Majority Staff Director: Paula Nowakowski
Minority Staff Director: John Lawrence 225-3725 2101
   RHOB

Measures relating to education or labor generally; child labor; Columbia Institution for the Deaf, Dumb, and Blind; Howard University; Freedmen's Hospital; convict labor and the entry of goods made by convicts into interstate commerce; food programs for children in schools; labor standards and statistics; mediation and arbitration of labor disputes; regulation or prevention of importation of foreign laborers under contract; U.S. Employees' Compensation Commission; vocational rehabilitation; wages and hours of labor; welfare of miners; work incentive programs. The Chair and ranking minority member are non-voting members ex officio of all subcommittees of which they are not regular members.

Party Ratio: R 27–D 22

John A. Boehner, Ohio, Chair	*George Miller, Calif., Ranking Minority Member*
Tom Petri, Wis., Vice Chair	*Dale E. Kildee, Mich.*
Cass Ballenger, N.C.	*Major R. Owens, N.Y.*
Peter Hoekstra, Mich.	*Donald M. Payne, N.J.*
Howard P. "Buck" McKeon, Calif.	*Robert E. Andrews, N.J.*
Michael N. Castle, Del.	*Lynn Woolsey, Calif.*
Sam Johnson, Texas	*Ruben Hinojosa, Texas*
James C. Greenwood, Pa.	*Carolyn McCarthy, N.Y.*
Charlie Norwood, Ga.	*John F. Tierney, Mass.*
Fred Upton, Mich.	*Ron Kind, Wis.*
Vernon J. Ehlers, Mich.	*Dennis J. Kucinich, Ohio*
Jim DeMint, S.C.	*David Wu, Ore.*
Johnny Isakson, Ga.	*Rush D. Holt, N.J.*
Judy Biggert, Ill.	*Susan A. Davis, Calif.*
Todd R. Platts, Pa.	*Betty McCollum, Minn.*
Pat Tiberi, Ohio	*Danny K. Davis, Ill.*
Ric Keller, Fla.	*Ed Case, Hawaii*
Tom Osborne, Neb.	*Raul M. Grijalva, Ariz.*
Joe Wilson, S.C.	*Denise L. Majette, Ga.*
Tom Cole, Okla.	*Chris Van Hollen, Md.*
Jon Porter, Nev.	*Tim Ryan, Ohio*
John Kline, Minn.	*Timothy H. Bishop, N.Y*
John Carter, Texas	
Marilyn Musgrave, Colo.	

Marsha Blackburn, Tenn.
Phil Gingrey, Ga.
Max Burns, Ga.

Subcommittees

Education Reform
Office: H2-230 FHOB   **Phone:** 225-6558

Castle (Chair), Osborne (Vice Chair), Greenwood, Upton, Ehlers, DeMint, Biggert, Platts, Keller, Wilson (S.C.), Musgrave
   Woolsey (Ranking Minority Member), Davis (Calif.), Davis (Ill.), Case, Grijalva, Kind, Kucinich, Van Hollen, Majette

Employer-Employee Relations
Office: 2181 RHOB   **Phone:** 225-7101

Johnson (Texas; Chair), DeMint (Vice Chair), Boehner, Ballenger, McKeon, Platts, Tiberi, Wilson (S.C.), Cole, Kline, Carter, Musgrave, Blackburn
   Andrews (Ranking Minority Member), Payne, McCarthy (N.Y.), Kildee, Tierney, Wu, Holt, McCollum, Case, Grijalva

Select Education
Office: H2-230 FHOB   **Phone:** 225-6558

Hoekstra (Chair), Porter (Vice Chair), Greenwood, Norwood, Gingrey, Burns
   Hinojosa (Ranking Minority Member), Davis (Calif.), Davis (Ill.), Ryan (Ohio)

21st Century Competitiveness
Office: H2-230 FHOB   **Phone:** 225-6558

McKeon (Chair), Isakson (Vice Chair), Boehner, Petri, Castle, Johnson (Texas), Upton, Ehlers, Tiberi, Keller, Osborne, Cole, Porter, Carter, Gingrey, Burns
   Kildee (Ranking Minority Member), Tierney, Kind, Wu, Holt, McCollum, McCarthy (N.Y.), Van Hollen, Ryan (Ohio), Owens, Payne, Andrews, Hinojosa

Workforce Protections
Office: 2181 RHOB   **Phone:** 225-7101

Norwood (Chair), Biggert (Vice Chair), Ballenger, Hoekstra, Isakson, Keller, Kline, Blackburn
   Owens (Ranking Minority Member), Kucinich, Woolsey, Majette, Payne, Bishop (N.Y.)

ENERGY AND COMMERCE

Office: 2125 RHOB   **Phone:** 225-2927
Fax: 225-1919
Web: energycommerce.house.gov
E-mail: energycommerce@mail.house.gov
Majority Staff Director: David V. Marventano
Minority Staff Director: Reid Stuntz 225-3641
   2322 RHOB

Interstate and foreign commerce generally; biomedical research and development; consumer affairs and consumer protection; health and health facilities, except health care supported by payroll deductions; interstate energy compacts; measures relating to the exploration, production, storage, supply, marketing, pricing, and regulation of energy resources, including all fossil fuels, solar energy, and other unconventional or renewable energy resources; measures relating to the conservation of energy resources; measures relating to energy information generally; measures relating to (A) the generation and marketing of power (except by federally chartered or federal regional power marketing authorities), (B) the reliability and interstate transmission of, and ratemaking for, all power, and (C) the siting of generation facilities, except the installation of interconnections between government water power projects; measures relating to general management of the Energy Dept., and the management and all functions of the Federal Energy Regulatory Commission; national energy policy generally; public health and quarantine; regulation of the domestic nuclear energy industry, including regulation of research and development reactors and nuclear regulatory research; regulation of interstate and foreign communications; travel and tourism; nuclear and other energy. The Chair and ranking minority member are voting members ex officio of all subcommittees of which they are not regular members.

Party Ratio: R 31–D 26

Billy Tauzin, La., Chair	*John D. Dingell, Mich.,*
Michael Bilirakis, Fla.	*Ranking Minority*
Joe L. Barton, Texas	*Member*
Fred Upton, Mich.	
Cliff Stearns, Fla.	*Henry A. Waxman, Calif.*
Paul E. Gillmor, Ohio	*Edward J. Markey, Mass.*
James C. Greenwood, Pa.	*Ralph M. Hall, Texas*
Christopher Cox, Calif.	*Rick Boucher, Va.*
Nathan Deal, Ga.	*Edolphus Towns, N.Y.*
Richard M. Burr, N.C., Vice	*Frank Pallone Jr., N.J.*
Chair	*Sherrod Brown, Ohio*
Edward Whitfield, Ky.	*Bart Gordon, Tenn.*
Charlie Norwood, Ga.	*Peter Deutsch, Fla.*
Barbara Cubin, Wyo.	*Bobby L. Rush, Ill.*
John Shimkus, Ill.	*Anna G. Eshoo, Calif.*
Heather A. Wilson, N.M.	*Bart Stupak, Mich.*
John Shadegg, Ariz.	*Eliot L. Engel, N.Y.*
Charles W. "Chip" Pickering	*Albert R. Wynn, Md.*
Jr., Miss.	*Gene Green, Texas*
Vito J. Fossella, N.Y.	*Karen McCarthy, Mo.*
Roy Blunt, Mo.	*Ted Strickland, Ohio*
Steve Buyer, Ind.	*Diana DeGette, Colo.*
George P. Radanovich,	*Lois Capps, Calif.*
Calif.	*Mike Doyle, Pa.*
Charles Bass, N.H.	*Chris John, La.*
Joe Pitts, Pa.	*Tom Allen, Maine*
Mary Bono, Calif.	*Jim Davis, Fla.*
Greg Walden, Ore.	*Jan Schakowsky, Ill.*
Lee Terry, Neb.	*Hilda L. Solis, Calif.*
Ernie Fletcher, Ky.	
Mike Ferguson, N.J.	

Mike Rogers, Mich.
Darrell Issa, Calif.
C. L. "Butch" Otter, Idaho

Subcommittees

Commerce, Trade, and Consumer Protection
Office: 2125 RHOB   **Phone:** 225-2927

Stearns (Chair), Upton, Whitfield, Cubin, Shimkus, Shadegg (Vice Chair), Radanovich, Bass, Pitts, Bono, Terry, Fletcher, Ferguson, Issa, Otter
Schakowsky (Ranking Minority Member), Solis, Markey, Towns, Brown (Ohio), Davis (Fla.), Deutsch, Stupak, Green (Texas), McCarthy (Mo.), Strickland, DeGette

Energy and Air Quality
Office: 2125 RHOB   **Phone:** 225-2927

Barton (Chair), Cox, Burr, Whitfield, Norwood, Shimkus (Vice Chair), Wilson (N.M.), Shadegg, Pickering, Fossella, Buyer, Radanovich, Bono, Walden, Rogers, (Mich.), Issa, Otter
Boucher (Ranking Minority Member), Wynn, Allen, Waxman, Markey, Hall (Texas), Pallone, Brown (Ohio), Rush, McCarthy (Mo.), Strickland, Capps, Doyle, John

Environment and Hazardous Materials
Office: 2125 RHOB   **Phone:** 225-2927

Gillmor (Chair), Greenwood, Shimkus, Wilson (N.M.), Fossella (Vice Chair), Buyer, Radanovich, Bass, Pitts, Bono, Terry, Fletcher, Issa, Rogers (Mich.), Otter
Solis (Ranking Minority Member), Allen, Pallone, Doyle, Davis (Fla.), Schakowsky, Deutsch, Rush, Stupak, Wynn, Green (Texas), DeGette

Health
Office: 2125 RHOB   **Phone:** 225-2927

Bilirakis (Chair), Barton, Upton, Greenwood, Deal, Burr, Whitfield, Norwood (Vice Chair), Cubin, Wilson (N.M.), Shadegg, Pickering, Buyer, Pitts, Fletcher, Ferguson, Rogers (Mich.)
Brown (Ohio; Ranking Minority Member), Waxman, Hall (Texas), Towns, Pallone, Eshoo, Stupak, Engel, Green (Texas), Strickland, Capps, Gordon, DeGette, John

Oversight and Investigations
Office: 2125 RHOB   **Phone:** 225-2927

Greenwood (Chair), Bilirakis, Stearns, Burr, Bass, Walden (Vice Chair), Ferguson, Rogers (Mich.)
Deutsch (Ranking Minority Member), DeGette, Davis (Fla.), Schakowsky, Waxman, Rush

Telecommunications and the Internet
Office: 2125 RHOB   **Phone:** 225-2927

Upton (Chair), Bilirakis, Barton, Stearns (Vice Chair), Gillmor, Cox, Deal, Whitfield, Cubin, Shimkus, Wilson (N.M.), Pickering, Fossella, Bass, Bono, Walden, Terry
Markey (Ranking Minority Member), Rush, McCarthy (Mo.), Doyle, Davis (Fla.), Boucher, Towns, Gordon, Deutsch, Eshoo, Stupak, Engel, Wynn, Green (Texas)

FINANCIAL SERVICES

Office: 2129 RHOB **Phone:** 225-7502
Fax: 226-6052
Web: financialservices.house.gov
Majority Staff Director: Bob Foster
Minority Staff Director: Jeanne Roslanowick 225-4247
B-371A RHOB

Banks and banking, including deposit insurance and federal monetary policy; economic stabilization, defense production, renegotiation, and control of the price of commodities, rents, and services; financial aid to commerce and industry (other than transportation); insurance generally; international finance; international financial and monetary organizations; money and credit, including currency and the issuance of notes and redemption thereof; gold and silver, including the coinage thereof; valuation and revaluation of the dollar; public and private housing; securities and exchanges; and urban development. Chair and ranking minority member are non-voting members ex officio of all subcommittees of which they are not regular members.
Party Ratio: R 37–D 32–I 1

Michael G. Oxley, Ohio, Chair	*Barney Frank, Mass., Ranking Minority Member*
Jim Leach, Iowa	
Doug Bereuter, Neb.	*Paul E. Kanjorski, Pa.*
Richard H. Baker, La.	*Maxine Waters, Calif.*
Spencer Bachus, Ala.	**Bernard Sanders, I-Vt.**
Michael N. Castle, Del.	*Carolyn B. Maloney, N.Y.*
Peter T. King, N.Y.	*Luis V. Gutierrez, Ill.*
Ed Royce, Calif.	*Nydia M. Velazquez, N.Y.*
Frank D. Lucas, Okla.	*Melvin Watt, N.C.*
Bob Ney, Ohio	*Gary L. Ackerman, N.Y.*
Sue W. Kelly, N.Y., Vice Chair	*Darlene Hooley, Ore.*
	Julia Carson, Ind.
Ron Paul, Texas	*Brad Sherman, Calif.*
Paul E. Gillmor, Ohio	*Gregory W. Meeks, N.Y.*
Jim Ryun, Kan.	*Barbara Lee, Calif.*
Steven C. LaTourette, Ohio	*Jay Inslee, Wash.*
Donald Manzullo, Ill.	*Dennis Moore, Kan.*
Walter B. Jones, N.C.	*Charlie Gonzalez, Texas*
Doug Ose, Calif.	*Michael E. Capuano, Mass.*
Judy Biggert, Ill.	*Harold E. Ford Jr., Tenn.*
Mark Green, Wis.	*Ruben Hinojosa, Texas*
Patrick J. Toomey, Pa.	*Ken Lucas, Ky.*
Christopher Shays, Conn.	*Joseph Crowley, N.Y.*
John Shadegg, Ariz.	*William Lacy Clay, Mo.*
Vito J. Fossella, N.Y.	*Steve Israel, N.Y.*
Gary G. Miller, Calif.	*Mike Ross, Ark.*
Melissa A. Hart, Pa.	*Carolyn McCarthy, N.Y.*
Shelley Moore Capito, W.Va.	*Joe Baca, Calif.*
	Jim Matheson, Utah
Pat Tiberi, Ohio	*Stephen F. Lynch, Mass.*
Mark Kennedy, Minn.	*Brad Miller, N.C.*
Tom Feeney, Fla.	*Rahm Emanuel, Ill.*

Jeb Hensarling, Texas	*David Scott, Ga.*
Scott Garrett, N.J.	*Artur Davis, Ala.*
Tim Murphy, Pa.	
Ginny Brown-Waite, Fla.	
J. Gresham Barrett, S.C.	
Katherine Harris, Fla.	
Rick Renzi, Ariz.	

Subcommittees

Capital Markets, Insurance, and Government-Sponsored Enterprises
Office: 2129 RHOB **Phone:** 225-7502

Baker (Chair), Ose (Vice Chair), Shays, Gillmor, Bachus, Castle, King (N.Y.), Lucas (Okla.), Royce, Manzullo, Kelly, Ney, Shadegg, Ryun, Fossella, Biggert, Green (Wis.), Miller (Calif.), Toomey, Capito, Hart, Kennedy (Minn.), Tiberi, Brown-Waite, Harris, Renzi

Kanjorski (Ranking Minority Member), Ackerman, Hooley, Sherman, Meeks, Inslee, Moore, Gonzalez, Capuano, Ford, Hinojosa, Lucas (Ky.), Crowley, Israel, Ross, Clay, McCarthy (N.Y.), Baca, Matheson, Lynch, Miller (N.C.), Emanuel, Scott (Ga.)

Domestic and International Monetary Policy, Trade, and Technology
Office: 2129 RHOB **Phone:** 225-7502

King (N.Y.; Chair), Biggert (Vice Chair), Leach, Castle, Paul, Manzullo, Ose, Shadegg, Kennedy (Minn.), Feeney, Hensarling, Murphy, Barrett, Harris

Maloney (N.Y.; Ranking Minority Member), **Sanders (I),** *Watt, Waters, Lee, Kanjorski, Sherman, Hooley, Gutierrez, Velazquez, Baca, Emanuel*

Financial Institutions and Consumer Credit
Office: 2129 RHOB **Phone:** 225-7502

Bachus (Chair), LaTourette (Vice Chair), Bereuter, Baker, Castle, Royce, Lucas (Okla.), Kelly, Gillmor, Ryun, Jones (N.C.), Biggert, Toomey, Fossell, Hart, Capito, Tiberi, Kennedy (Minn.), Feeney, Hensarling, Garrett, Murphy, Brown-Waite, Barrett, Renzi

Sanders (I; Ranking Minority Member), *Maloney (N.Y.), Watt, Ackerman, Sherman, Meeks, Gutierrez, Moore, Gonzalez, Kanjorski, Waters, Velazquez, Hooley, Carson (Ind.), Ford, Hinojosa, Lucas (Ky.), Crowley, Israel, Ross, McCarthy (N.Y.), Davis (Ala.)*

Housing and Community Opportunity
Office: B-303 RHOB **Phone:** 225-7502

Ney (Chair), Green (Wis.; Vice Chair), Bereuter, Baker, King, (N.Y.), Jones (N.C.), Ose, Toomey, Shays, Miller (Calif.), Hart, Tiberi, Harris, Renzi

Waters (Ranking Minority Member), Velazquez, Carson (Ind.), Lee, Capuano, **Sanders (I),** *Watt, Clay, Lynch, Miller (N.C.), Scott (Ga.), Davis (Ala.)*

Oversight and Investigations
Office: H2-137-9 FHOB   **Phone:** 225-7502

Kelly (Chair), Paul (Vice Chair), LaTourette, Green (Wis.), Shadegg, Fossella, Hensarling, Garrett, Murphy, Brown-Waite, Barrett

Gutierrez (Ranking Minority Member), Inslee, Moore, Crowley, Maloney (N.Y.), Gonzalez, Hinojosa, Matheson, Lynch

GOVERNMENT REFORM

Office: 2157 RHOB   **Phone:** 225-5074
Fax: 225-3974
Web: www.house.gov/reform
Majority Staff Director: Peter Sirh
Minority Staff Director: Phil Schiliro 225-5051
B-350-A RHOB

Civil service, including intergovernmental personnel; the status of officers and employees of the United States, including their compensation, classification, and retirement; measures relating to the municipal affairs of the District of Columbia in general, other than appropriations; federal paperwork reduction; budget and accounting measures, generally; holidays and celebrations; overall economy, efficiency, and management of government operations and activities, including federal procurement; National Archives; population and demography generally, including the census; Postal Service generally, including the transportation of mail; public information and records; relationship of the federal government to the states and municipalities generally; reorganizations in the executive branch of the government. The Chair and ranking minority member are voting members ex officio of all subcommittees of which they are not regular members.

Party Ratio: R 24–D 19–I 1

Thomas M. Davis III, Va., Chair	*Henry A. Waxman, Calif., Ranking Minority Member*
Dan Burton, Ind.	
Christopher Shays, Conn., Vice Chair	*Tom Lantos, Calif.*
Ileana Ros-Lehtinen, Fla.	*Major R. Owens, N.Y.*
John M. McHugh, N.Y.	*Edolphus Towns, N.Y.*
John L. Mica, Fla.	*Paul E. Kanjorski, Pa.*
Mark Souder, Ind.	**Bernard Sanders, I-Vt.**
Steven C. LaTourette, Ohio	*Carolyn B. Maloney, N.Y.*
Doug Ose, Calif.	*Elijah E. Cummings, Md.*
Ron Lewis, Ky.	*Dennis J. Kucinich, Ohio*
Jo Ann Davis, Va.	*Danny K. Davis, Ill.*
Todd R. Platts, Pa.	*John F. Tierney, Mass.*
Chris Cannon, Utah	*William Lacy Clay, Mo.*
Adam H. Putnam, Fla.	*Diane Watson, Calif.*
Ed Schrock, Va.	*Stephen F. Lynch, Mass.*
John J. "Jimmy" Duncan Jr., Tenn.	*Chris Van Hollen, Md.*
John Sullivan, Okla.	*Linda T. Sanchez, Calif.*
Nathan Deal, Ga.	*C. A. Dutch Ruppersberger, Md.*
	Eleanor Holmes Norton, D.C.

Candice S. Miller, Mich.	*Jim Cooper, Tenn.*
Tim Murphy, Pa.	*Chris Bell, Texas*
Michael R. Turner, Ohio	
John Carter, Texas	
Bill Janklow, S.D.	
Marsha Blackburn, Tenn.	

Subcommittees

Civil Service and Agency Organization
Office: B373A RHOB   **Phone:** 225-5147

Davis (Va.; Chair), Murphy (Vice Chair), Mica, Souder, Putnam, Deal, Blackburn
Davis (Ill.; Ranking Minority Member), Owens, Van Hollen, Norton, Cooper

Criminal Justice, Drug Policy, and Human Resources
Office: B-373 RHOB   **Phone:** 225-2577

Souder (Chair), Deal (Vice Chair), McHugh, Mica, Ose, Davis (Va.), Schrock, Carter, Blackburn
Cummings (Ranking Minority Member), Davis (Ill.), Clay, Sanchez (Calif.), Ruppersberger, Norton, Bell

Energy Policy, Natural Resources, and Regulatory Affairs
Office: B-377 RHOB   **Phone:** 225-4407

Ose (Chair), Janklow (Vice Chair), Shays, McHugh, Cannon, Sullivan, Deal, Miller (Mich.)
Tierney (Ranking Minority Member), Lantos, Kanjorski, Kucinich, Van Hollen, Cooper

Government Efficiency and Financial Management
Office: B-349C RHOB   **Phone:** 225-3741

Platts (Chair), Blackburn (Vice Chair), LaTourette, Sullivan, Miller (Mich.), Turner (Ohio)
Towns (Ranking Minority Member), Kanjorski, Owens, Maloney (N.Y.)

Human Rights and Wellness
Office: B371C RHOB   **Phone:** 225-6427

Burton (Chair), Cannon (Vice Chair), Shays, Ros-Lehtinen
Watson (Ranking Minority Member), **Sanders (I),** *Cummings*

National Security, Emerging Threats, and International Relations
Office: B-372 RHOB   **Phone:** 225-2548

Shays (Chair), Turner (Ohio; Vice Chair), Burton, LaTourette, Lewis (Ky.), Platts, Putnam, Schrock, Duncan, Murphy, Janklow
Kucinich (Ranking Minority Member), Lantos, **Sanders (I),** *Lynch, Maloney (N.Y.), Sanchez (Calif.), Ruppersberger, Bell, Tierney*

Technology, Information Policy, Intergovernmental Relations, and the Census
Office: B-349A RHOB   **Phone:** 225-6751

GOVERNMENT REFORM (continued)

Putnam (Chair), Miller (Mich.; Vice Chair), Ose, Murphy, Turner (Ohio)

Clay (Ranking Minority Member), Watson, Lynch

HOUSE ADMINISTRATION

Office: 1309 LHOB   **Phone:** 225-8281
Fax: 225-9957
Web: www.house.gov/cha
Majority Staff Director: Paul Vinovich
Minority Staff Director: George Shevlin 225-2061
   1216 LHOB

Accounts of the House generally; assignment of office space for members and committees; disposition of useless executive papers; matters relating to the election of the president, vice president, or members of Congress; corrupt practices; contested elections; credentials and qualifications; federal elections generally; appropriations from accounts for committee salaries and expenses (except for the Appropriations Committee), House Information Systems, and allowances and expenses of members, House officers, and administrative offices of the House; auditing and settling of all such accounts; expenditure of such accounts; employment of persons by the House, including clerks for members and committees, and reporters of debates; Library of Congress and the House Library; statuary and pictures; acceptance or purchase of works of art for the Capitol; the Botanic Garden; management of the Library of Congress; purchase of books and manuscripts; Smithsonian Institution and the incorporation of similar institutions; Franking Commission; printing and correction of the Congressional Record; services to the House, including the House restaurant, parking facilities, and administration of the House office buildings and of the House wing of the Capitol; travel of members of the House; raising, reporting, and use of campaign contributions for candidates for office of representative in the House of Representatives, of delegate, and of resident commissioner to the United States from Puerto Rico; compensation, retirement, and other benefits of the members, officers, and employees of the Congress.

Party Ratio: R 6–D 3

Bob Ney, Ohio, Chair	*John B. Larson, Conn.,*
Vernon J. Ehlers, Mich.	*Ranking Minority*
John L. Mica, Fla.	*Member*
John Linder, Ga.	*Juanita Millender-*
John T. Doolittle, Calif.	*McDonald, Calif.*
Thomas M. Reynolds, N.Y.	*Robert A. Brady, Pa.*

INTERNATIONAL RELATIONS

Office: 2170 RHOB   **Phone:** 225-5021
Fax: 226-2831
Web: www.house.gov/international_relations
E-mail: HIRC@mail.house.gov
Majority Staff Director: Thomas E. Mooney
Minority Staff Director: Bob King 225-6735 B-360 RHOB

Relations of the United States with foreign nations generally; acquisition of land and buildings for embassies and legations in foreign countries; establishment of boundary lines between the United States and foreign nations; export controls, including nonproliferation of nuclear technology and nuclear hardware; foreign loans; international commodity agreements (other than those involving sugar) including all agreements for cooperation in the export of nuclear technology and nuclear hardware; international conferences and congresses; international education; intervention abroad and declarations of war; measures relating to the diplomatic service; measures to foster commercial intercourse with foreign nations and to safeguard American business interests abroad; measures relating to international economic policy; neutrality; protection of American citizens abroad and expatriation; American National Red Cross; trading with the enemy; U.N. organizations. The Chair and ranking minority member are non-voting members ex officio of all subcommittees of which they are not regular members.

Party Ratio: R 26–D 23

Henry J. Hyde, Ill., Chair	*Tom Lantos, Calif., Ranking*
Jim Leach, Iowa	*Minority Member*
Doug Bereuter, Neb.	*Howard L. Berman, Calif.*
Christopher H. Smith, N.J., Vice Chair	*Gary L. Ackerman, N.Y.*
	Eni F. H. Faleomavaega,
Dan Burton, Ind.	*Am. Samoa*
Elton Gallegly, Calif.	*Donald M. Payne, N.J.*
Ileana Ros-Lehtinen, Fla.	*Robert Menendez, N.J.*
Cass Ballenger, N.C.	*Sherrod Brown, Ohio*
Dana Rohrabacher, Calif.	*Brad Sherman, Calif.*
Ed Royce, Calif.	*Robert Wexler, Fla.*
Peter T. King, N.Y.	*Eliot L. Engel, N.Y.*
Steve Chabot, Ohio	*Bill Delahunt, Mass.*
Amo Houghton, N.Y.	*Gregory W. Meeks, N.Y.*
John M. McHugh, N.Y.	*Barbara Lee, Calif.*
Tom Tancredo, Colo.	*Joseph Crowley, N.Y.*
Ron Paul, Texas	*Joseph M. Hoeffel, Pa.*
Nick Smith, Mich.	*Earl Blumenauer, Ore.*
Joe Pitts, Pa.	*Shelley Berkley, Nev.*
Jeff Flake, Ariz.	*Grace F. Napolitano, Calif.*
Jo Ann Davis, Va.	*Adam B. Schiff, Calif.*
Mark Green, Wis.	*Diane Watson, Calif.*
Jerry Weller, Ill.	*Adam Smith, Wash.*
Mike Pence, Ind.	*Betty McCollum, Minn.*
Thaddeus McCotter, Mich.	*Chris Bell, Texas*
Bill Janklow, S.D.	
Katherine Harris, Fla.	

Subcommittees

Africa
Office: 255 FHOB   **Phone:** 226-7812

Royce (Chair), Houghton, Tancredo, Flake, Green (Wis.)
Payne (Ranking Minority Member), Meeks, Lee, McCollum

Asia and the Pacific
Office: B-358 RHOB   **Phone:** 226-7825

Leach (Chair), Burton, Bereuter, Smith (N.J.), Rohrabacher, Royce, Chabot, Paul, Flake, Weller, Tancredo

Faleomavaega (Ranking Minority Member), Brown (Ohio), Blumenauer, Watson, Smith (Wash.), Ackerman, Sherman, Wexler, Meeks

Europe
Office: 2401-A RHOB   **Phone:** 226-7820

Bereuter (Chair), Burton, Gallegly, King (N.Y.), Davis (Va.), McCotter, Janklow

Wexler (Ranking Minority Member), Engel, Delahunt, Lee, Hoeffel, Blumenauer

International Terrorism, Nonproliferation, and Human Rights
Office: 2401-A RHOB   **Phone:** 226-7820

Gallegly (Chair), Smith (N.J.), Rohrabacher, King (N.Y.), Pitts, Green (Wis.), Ballenger, Tancredo, Smith (Mich.), Pence

Sherman (Ranking Minority Member), Menendez, Crowley, Berkley, Napolitano, Schiff, Watson, Bell

Middle East and Central Asia
Office: B-359 RHOB   **Phone:** 226-9940

Ros-Lehtinen (Chair), Chabot, McHugh, Smith (Mich.), Davis (Va.), Pence, McCotter, Janklow, Pitts, Harris

Ackerman (Ranking Minority Member), Berman, Engel, Crowley, Hoeffel, Berkley, Schiff, Bell

Western Hemisphere
Office: 259A FHOB   **Phone:** 226-9980

Ballenger (Chair), Paul, Weller, Harris, Leach, Ros-Lehtinen

Menendez (Ranking Minority Member), Delahunt, Napolitano, Faleomavaega, Payne

JUDICIARY

Office: 2138 RHOB   **Phone:** 225-3951
Fax: 225-7682
Web: www.house.gov/judiciary
E-mail: Judiciary@mail.house.gov
Majority Chief of Staff: Phil Kiko
Minority Chief Counsel: Perry Apelbaum 225-6504
  2142 RHOB

The judiciary and judicial proceedings, civil and criminal; administrative practice and procedure; apportionment of representatives; bankruptcy, mutiny, espionage, and counterfeiting; civil liberties; constitutional amendments; federal courts and judges, and local courts in the territories and possessions; immigration and naturalization; interstate compacts, generally; measures relating to claims against the United States; meetings of Congress, attendance of members, and their acceptance of incompatible offices; national penitentiaries; patents, the Patent Office, copyrights, and trademarks; presidential succession; protection of trade and commerce against unlawful restraints and monopolies; revision and codification of the Statutes of the United States; state and territorial boundaries; subversive activities affecting the internal security of the United States. Chair and ranking minority member are non-voting members ex officio of all subcommittees of which they are not regular members.

Party Ratio: R 21–D 16

F. James Sensenbrenner Jr., Wis., Chair	John Conyers Jr., Mich., *Ranking Minority Member*
Henry J. Hyde, Ill.	
Howard Coble, N.C.	*Howard L. Berman, Calif.*
Lamar Smith, Texas	*Rick Boucher, Va.*
Elton Gallegly, Calif.	*Jerrold Nadler, N.Y.*
Robert W. Goodlatte, Va.	*Robert C. Scott, Va.*
Steve Chabot, Ohio	*Melvin Watt, N.C.*
Bill Jenkins, Tenn.	*Zoe Lofgren, Calif.*
Chris Cannon, Utah	*Sheila Jackson-Lee, Texas*
Spencer Bachus, Ala.	*Maxine Waters, Calif.*
John Hostettler, Ind.	*Martin T. Meehan, Mass.*
Mark Green, Wis.	*Bill Delahunt, Mass.*
Ric Keller, Fla.	*Robert Wexler, Fla.*
Melissa A. Hart, Pa.	*Tammy Baldwin, Wis.*
Jeff Flake, Ariz.	*Anthony Weiner, N.Y.*
Mike Pence, Ind.	*Adam B. Schiff, Calif.*
J. Randy Forbes, Va.	*Linda T. Sanchez, Calif.*
Steve King, Iowa	
John Carter, Texas	
Tom Feeney, Fla.	
Marsha Blackburn, Tenn.	

Subcommittees

Commercial and Administrative Law
Office: B-353 RHOB   **Phone:** 225-2825

Cannon (Chair), Coble, Flake, Carter, Blackburn, Chabot, Feeney

Watt (Ranking Minority Member), Nadler, Baldwin, Delahunt, Weiner

Constitution
Office: 362 FHOB   **Phone:** 226-7680

Chabot (Chair), King (Iowa), Jenkins, Bachus, Hostettler, Hart, Feeney, Forbes

Nadler (Ranking Minority Member), Conyers, Scott (Va.), Watt, Schiff

Courts, the Internet, and Intellectual Property
Office: B-351A RHOB   **Phone:** 225-5741

Smith (Texas; Chair), Hyde, Gallegly, Goodlatte, Jenkins, Bachus, Green (Wis.), Keller, Hart, Pence, Forbes, Carter

Berman (Ranking Minority Member), Conyers, Boucher, Lofgren, Waters, Meehan, Delahunt, Wexler, Baldwin, Weiner

Crime, Terrorism, and Homeland Security
Office: 207 CHOB   **Phone:** 225-3926

Coble (Chair), Feeney, Goodlatte, Chabot, Green (Wis.), Keller, Pence, Forbes

JUDICIARY (continued)

Scott (Va.; Ranking Minority Member), Schiff, Jackson-Lee, Waters, Meehan

Immigration, Border Security, and Claims
Office: B-370B RHOB   **Phone:** 225-5727

Hostettler (Chair), Flake, Blackburn, Smith (Texas), Gallegly, Cannon, King (Iowa), Hart

Jackson-Lee (Ranking Minority Member), Sanchez (Calif.), Lofgren, Berman, Conyers

RESOURCES

Office: 1324 LHOB   **Phone:** 225-2761
Fax: 225-5929
Web: resourcescommittee.house.gov
E-mail: resources.committee@mail.house.gov
Majority Chief of Staff: Steve Ding
Minority Staff Director: James "Jim" Zoia 225-6065
   1329 LHOB

Public lands generally, including entry, easements, and grazing; mining interests generally; fisheries and wildlife, including research, restoration, refuges, and conservation; forest reserves and national parks created from the public domain; forfeiture of land grants and alien ownership, including alien ownership of mineral lands; Geological Survey; international fishing agreements; interstate compacts relating to apportionment of waters for irrigation purposes; irrigation and reclamation, including water supply for reclamation projects, easements of public lands for irrigation projects, and acquisition of private lands when necessary to complete irrigation projects; measures relating to the care and management of Native Americans, including the care and allotment of Native American lands and general and special measures relating to claims which are paid out of Native American funds; measures relating generally to the insular possessions of the United States, except those affecting revenue and appropriations; military parks and battlefields, national cemeteries administered by the secretary of the Interior, parks within the District of Columbia, and the erection of monuments to the memory of individuals; mineral land laws and claims and entries thereunder; mineral resources of the public lands; mining schools and experimental stations; marine affairs (including coastal zone management), except for measures relating to oil and other pollution of navigable waters; oceanography; petroleum conservation on the public lands and conservation of the radium supply in the United States; preservation of prehistoric ruins and objects of interest on the public domain; relations of the United States with Native Americans and Native American tribes; disposition of oil transported by the Trans-Alaska Oil Pipeline, except rate-making. The Chair and ranking minority member are non-voting members ex officio of all subcommittees of which they are not regular members.

Party Ratio: R 28–D 24

Richard W. Pombo, Calif., Chair
Don Young, Alaska
Billy Tauzin, La.
H. James Saxton, N.J.
Elton Gallegly, Calif.
John J. "Jimmy" Duncan Jr., Tenn.
Wayne T. Gilchrest, Md.
Ken Calvert, Calif.
Scott McInnis, Colo.
Barbara Cubin, Wyo.
George P. Radanovich, Calif.
Walter B. Jones, N.C.
Chris Cannon, Utah
John E. Peterson, Pa.
Jim Gibbons, Nev., Vice Chair
Mark Souder, Ind.
Greg Walden, Ore.
Tom Tancredo, Colo.
J. D. Hayworth, Ariz.
Tom Osborne, Neb.
Jeff Flake, Ariz.
Denny Rehberg, Mont.
Rick Renzi, Ariz.
Tom Cole, Okla.
Steve Pearce, N.M.
Rob Bishop, Utah
Devin Nunes, Calif.
Vacancy

Nick J. Rahall II, W.Va., Ranking Minority Member
Dale E. Kildee, Mich.
Eni F. H. Faleomavaega, Am. Samoa
Neil Abercrombie, Hawaii
Solomon P. Ortiz, Texas
Frank Pallone Jr., N.J.
Cal Dooley, Calif.
Donna M. C. Christensen, Virgin Is.
Ron Kind, Wis.
Jay Inslee, Wash.
Grace F. Napolitano, Calif.
Tom Udall, N.M.
Mark Udall, Colo.
Anibal Acevedo-Vila, P.R.
Brad Carson, Okla.
Raul M. Grijalva, Ariz.
Dennis Cardoza, Calif.
Madeleine Z. Bordallo, Guam
George Miller, Calif.
Edward J. Markey, Mass.
Ruben Hinojosa, Texas
Ciro D. Rodriguez, Texas
Joe Baca, Calif.
Betty McCollum, Minn.

Subcommittees

Energy and Mineral Resources
Office: 1626 LHOB   **Phone:** 225-9297

Cubin (Chair), Tauzin, Cannon, Gibbons, Souder, Rehberg, Cole, Pearce, Bishop (Utah), Nunes

Kind (Ranking Minority Member), Faleomavaega, Ortiz, Napolitano, Udall (N.M.), Carson (Okla.), Markey, Vacancy

Fisheries Conservation, Wildlife, and Oceans
Office: H2-188 FHOB   **Phone:** 226-0200

Gilchrest (Chair), Young (Alaska), Tauzin, Saxton, Souder, Jones (N.C.)

Pallone (Ranking Minority Member), Faleomavaega, Abercrombie, Ortiz, Bordallo

Forests and Forest Health
Office: 1337 LHOB   **Phone:** 225-0691

McInnis (Chair), Duncan, Jones (N.C.), Peterson (Pa.), Tancredo, Hayworth, Flake, Rehberg, Renzi, Pearce

Inslee (Ranking Minority Member), Kildee, Udall (N.M.), Udall (Colo.), Acevedo-Vila, Carson (Okla.), McCollum, Vacancy, Vacancy

National Parks, Recreation, and Public Lands
Office: 1333 LHOB   **Phone:** 226-7736

Radanovich (Chair), Gallegly, Duncan, Gilchrest, Cubin, Jones (N.C.), Cannon, Peterson (Pa.), Gibbons, Souder, Bishop, (Utah)

Christensen (Ranking Minority Member), Kildee, Kind, Udall (N.M.), Udall (Colo.), Acevedo-Vila, Grijalva, Cardoza, Bordallo

Water and Power
Office: 1522 LHOB   **Phone:** 225-8331

Calvert (Chair), Radanovich, Walden, Tancredo, Hayworth, Osborne, Renzi, Pearce, Nunes

Napolitano (Ranking Minority Member), Dooley, Inslee, Grijalva, Cardoza, Miller, Rodriguez, Baca

RULES

Office: H-312 CAP   **Phone:** 225-9191
Fax: 225-6763
Web: www.house.gov/rules
Majority Staff Director: Billy Pitts
Minority Staff Director: Kristi Walseth 225-9091
   H-152 CAP

Rules and joint rules (other than rules or joint rules relating to the Code of Official Conduct) and order of business of the House; recesses and final adjournments of Congress.
Party Ratio: R 9–D 4

David Dreier, Calif., Chair
Porter J. Goss, Fla.
John Linder, Ga.
Deborah Pryce, Ohio
Lincoln Diaz-Balart, Fla.
Doc Hastings, Wash.
Sue Myrick, N.C.
Pete Sessions, Texas
Thomas M. Reynolds, N.Y.

Martin Frost, Texas, Ranking Minority Member
Louise M. Slaughter, N.Y.
Jim McGovern, Mass.
Alcee L. Hastings, Fla.

Subcommittees

Legislative and Budget Process
Office: 421 CHOB   **Phone:** 225-2015

Pryce (Chair), Diaz-Balart (Fla.; Vice Chair), Goss, Hastings (Wash.), Dreier
Slaughter (Ranking Minority Member), Frost

Technology and the House
Office: 421 CHOB   **Phone:** 225-4272

Linder (Chair), Myrick (Vice Chair), Sessions, Reynolds, Dreier
McGovern (Ranking Minority Member), Hastings (Fla.)

SCIENCE

Office: 2320 RHOB   **Phone:** 225-6371
Fax: 226-0113
Web: www.house.gov/science
E-mail: science@mail.house.gov

Majority Chief of Staff: David Goldston
Minority Staff Director: Robert Palmer 225-6375
   394 FHOB

All energy research, development, demonstration, and projects therefor, and all federally owned or operated non-military energy laboratories; astronautical research and development, including resources, personnel, equipment, and facilities; civil aviation research and development; environmental research and development; marine research; measures relating to the commercial application of energy technology; National Institute of Standards and Technology, standardization of weights and measures and the metric system; National Aeronautics and Space Administration (NASA); National Space Council; National Science Foundation; National Weather Service; outer space, including exploration and control thereof; science scholarships; scientific research, development, demonstration, and projects therefor. The Chair and ranking minority member are members ex officio of all subcommittees of which they are not regular members.
Party Ratio: R 25–D 22

Sherwood Boehlert, N.Y., Chair
Lamar Smith, Texas
Curt Weldon, Pa.
Dana Rohrabacher, Calif.
Joe L. Barton, Texas
Ken Calvert, Calif.
Nick Smith, Mich.
Roscoe G. Bartlett, Md.
Vernon J. Ehlers, Mich.
Gil Gutknecht, Minn.
George Nethercutt, Wash.
Frank D. Lucas, Okla.
Judy Biggert, Ill.
Wayne T. Gilchrest, Md.
Todd Akin, Mo.
Timothy V. Johnson, Ill.
Melissa A. Hart, Pa.
John Sullivan, Okla.
J. Randy Forbes, Va.
Phil Gingrey, Ga.
Rob Bishop, Utah
Michael C. Burgess, Texas
Jo Bonner, Ala.
Tom Feeney, Fla.
Vacancy

Ralph M. Hall, Texas, Ranking Minority Member
Bart Gordon, Tenn.
Jerry F. Costello, Ill.
Eddie Bernice Johnson, Texas
Lynn Woolsey, Calif.
Nick Lampson, Texas
John B. Larson, Conn.
Mark Udall, Colo.
David Wu, Ore.
Michael M. Honda, Calif.
Chris Bell, Texas
Brad Miller, N.C.
Lincoln Davis, Tenn.
Sheila Jackson-Lee, Texas
Zoe Lofgren, Calif.
Brad Sherman, Calif.
Brian Baird, Wash.
Dennis Moore, Kan.
Anthony Weiner, N.Y.
Jim Matheson, Utah
Dennis Cardoza, Calif.
Vacancy

Subcommittees

Energy
Office: 390 FHOB   **Phone:** 225-9662

Biggert (Chair), Weldon (Pa.), Bartlett, Ehlers, Nethercutt, Akin, Hart, Gingrey, Bonner
Lampson (Ranking Minority Member), Costello, Woolsey, Wu, Honda, Miller (N.C.), Davis (Tenn.)

SCIENCE (continued)
Environment, Technology, and Standards
Office: 2319 RHOB   **Phone:** 225-8844

Ehlers (Chair), Smith (Mich.), Gutknecht, Biggert, Gilchrest, Johnson (Ill.), Burgess, Vacancy

Udall (Colo.; Ranking Minority Member), Miller (N.C.), Davis (Tenn.), Baird, Matheson, Lofgren

Research
Office: B-374 RHOB   **Phone:** 225-7858

Smith (Mich.; Chair), Smith (Texas), Rohrabacher, Gutknecht, Lucas (Okla.), Akin, Johnson (Ill.), Hart, Sullivan, Gingrey

Johnson (Texas; Ranking Minority Member), Honda, Lofgren, Cardoza, Sherman, Moore, Matheson, Jackson-Lee

Space and Aeronautics
Office: B-374 RHOB   **Phone:** 225-7858

Rohrabacher (Chair), Smith (Texas), Weldon (Pa.), Barton, Calvert, Bartlett, Nethercutt, Lucas (Okla.), Sullivan, Forbes, Bishop (Utah), Burgess, Bonner, Feeney

Gordon (Ranking Minority Member), Larson, Bell, Lampson, Udall (Colo.), Wu, Johnson (Texas), Jackson-Lee, Sherman, Moore, Weiner, Vacancy

SELECT HOMELAND SECURITY

Office: 2402 RHOB   **Phone:** 226-8417
Web: hsc.house.gov
Majority Staff Director: John Gannon
Minority Staff Director: Steve Cash 225-2401 330 CHOB

Develops recommendations and reports to the House by bill or otherwise on such matters that relate to the Homeland Security Act of 2002 as may be referred to it by the Speaker; reviews and studies on a continuing basis laws, programs, and activities relating to homeland security; conducts a thorough and complete study of the operation and implementation of the rules of the House, including Rule X, with respect to issues of homeland security.
Party Ratio: R 27–D 23

Christopher Cox, Calif., Chair	*Jim Turner, Texas, Ranking Minority Member*
Jennifer Dunn, Wash.	*Bennie Thompson, Miss.*
C. W. Bill Young, Fla.	*Loretta Sanchez, Calif.*
Don Young, Alaska	*Edward J. Markey, Mass.*
F. James Sensenbrenner Jr., Wis.	*Norm Dicks, Wash.*
	Barney Frank, Mass.
Billy Tauzin, La.	*Jane Harman, Calif.*
David Dreier, Calif.	*Benjamin L. Cardin, Md.*
Duncan Hunter, Calif.	*Louise M. Slaughter, N.Y.*
Harold Rogers, Ky.	*Peter A. DeFazio, Ore.*
Sherwood Boehlert, N.Y.	*Nita M. Lowey, N.Y.*
Christopher Shays, Conn.	*Robert E. Andrews, N.J.*
Lamar Smith, Texas	*Eleanor Holmes Norton, D.C.*
Curt Weldon, Pa.	
Porter J. Goss, Fla.	*Zoe Lofgren, Calif.*
Dave Camp, Mich.	*Karen McCarthy, Mo.*

Lincoln Diaz-Balart, Fla.	*Sheila Jackson-Lee, Texas*
Robert W. Goodlatte, Va.	*Bill Pascrell Jr., N.J.*
Ernest Istook, Okla.	*Donna M. C. Christensen, Virgin Is.*
Peter T. King, N.Y.	
John Linder, Ga.	*Bob Etheridge, N.C.*
John Shadegg, Ariz.	*Charlie Gonzalez, Texas*
Mark Souder, Ind.	*Ken Lucas, Ky.*
William M. "Mac" Thornberry, Texas	*Jim Langevin, R.I.*
	Kendrick B. Meek, Fla.
Jim Gibbons, Nev.	
Kay Granger, Texas	
Pete Sessions, Texas	
John E. Sweeney, N.Y.	

Subcommittees

Cybersecurity, Science, and Research and Development
Office: 2402 RHOB   **Phone:** 226-8417

Thornberry (Chair), Sessions (Vice Chair), Boehlert, Smith (Texas), Weldon (Pa.), Camp, Goodlatte, King (N.Y.), Linder, Souder, Gibbons, Granger

Lofgren (Ranking Minority Member), Sanchez (Calif.), Andrews, Jackson-Lee, Christensen, Etheridge, Gonzalez, Lucas (Ky.), Langevin, Meek

Emergency Preparedness and Response
Office: 2402 RHOB   **Phone:** 226-8417

Shadegg (Chair), Weldon (Pa.; Vice Chair), Tauzin, Shays, Camp, Diaz-Balart (Fla.), King (N.Y.), Souder, Thornberry, Gibbons, Granger, Sessions

Thompson (Miss.; Ranking Minority Member), Harman, Cardin, DeFazio, Lowey, Norton, Pascrell, Christensen, Etheridge, Lucas (Ky.)

Infrastructure and Border Security
Office: 2402 RHOB   **Phone:** 226-8417

Camp (Chair), Granger (Vice Chair), Dunn, Young (Alaska), Hunter, Smith (Texas), Diaz-Balart (Fla.), Goodlatte, Istook, Shadegg, Souder, Sweeney

Sanchez (Calif.; Ranking Minority Member), Markey, Dicks, Frank, Cardin, Slaughter, DeFazio, Jackson-Lee, Pascrell, Gonzalez

Intelligence and Counterterrorism
Office: 2402 RHOB   **Phone:** 226-8417

Gibbons (Chair), Sweeney (Vice Chair), Dunn, Young (Fla.), Rogers (Ky.), Shays, Smith (Texas), Goss, King (N.Y.), Linder, Shadegg, Thornberry

Langevin (Ranking Minority Member), Markey, Dicks, Frank, Harman, Lowey, Andrews, Norton, McCarthy (Mo.), Meek

Rules
Office: 2402 RHOB   **Phone:** 226-8417

Diaz-Balart (Fla.; Chair), Dunn, Sensenbrenner, Dreier, Weldon (Pa.), Goss, Linder, Sessions

Slaughter (Ranking Minority Member), Thompson (Miss.), Sanchez (Calif.), Lofgren, McCarthy (Mo.), Meek

SELECT INTELLIGENCE

Office: H-405 CAP   **Phone:** 225-4121
Fax: 225-1991
Web: intelligence.house.gov
Majority Staff Director: Tim Sample
Minority Chief Counsel: Christine Healey H-405 CAP

Legislative and budget authority over the National Security Agency and the director of central intelligence, the Defense Intelligence Agency, the National Security Agency, intelligence activities of the Federal Bureau of Investigation and other components of the federal intelligence community. The Speaker of the House and minority leader are non-voting members ex officio of the full committee, as are the committee chair and ranking minority member.

Party Ratio: R 11–D 9

Porter J. Goss, Fla., Chair	*Jane Harman, Calif.,*
Doug Bereuter, Neb., Vice Chair	*Ranking Minority Member*
Sherwood Boehlert, N.Y.	*Alcee L. Hastings, Fla.*
Jim Gibbons, Nev.	*Silvestre Reyes, Texas*
Ray LaHood, Ill.	*Leonard L. Boswell, Iowa*
Randy "Duke" Cunningham, Calif.	*Collin C. Peterson, Minn.*
Peter Hoekstra, Mich.	*Robert E. "Bud" Cramer, Ala.*
Richard M. Burr, N.C.	*Anna G. Eshoo, Calif.*
Terry Everett, Ala.	*Rush D. Holt, N.J.*
Elton Gallegly, Calif.	*C. A. Dutch Ruppersberger, Md.*
Mac Collins, Ga.	

Subcommittees

Human Intelligence, Analysis, and Counterintelligence
Office: H-405 CAP   **Phone:** 225-4121

Gibbons (Chair), Boehlert (Vice Chair), Cunningham, Hoekstra, Burr, Everett, Collins
Boswell (Ranking Minority Member), Ruppersberger, Reyes, Peterson (Minn.), Cramer

Intelligence Policy and National Security
Office: H-405 CAP   **Phone:** 225-4121

Bereuter (Chair), LaHood (Vice Chair), Cunningham, Hoekstra, Burr, Gallegly
Eshoo (Ranking Minority Member), Hastings (Fla.), Holt, Ruppersberger

Technical and Tactical Intelligence
Office: H-405 CAP   **Phone:** 225-4121

Hoekstra (Chair), Boehlert (Vice Chair), Gibbons, Cunningham, Everett, Gallegly, Collins
Cramer (Ranking Minority Member), Holt, Eshoo, Peterson (Minn.), Ruppersberger

Terrorism and Homeland Security
Office: H-405 CAP   **Phone:** 225-4121

LaHood (Chair), Bereuter (Vice Chair), Gibbons, Burr, Everett, Gallegly, Collins

Hastings (Fla.; Ranking Minority Member), Reyes, Peterson (Minn.), Boswell, Cramer

SMALL BUSINESS

Office: 2361 RHOB   **Phone:** 225-5821
Fax: 225-3587
Web: www.house.gov/smbiz
E-mail: smbiz@mail.house.gov
Majority Chief of Staff: J. Matthew Szymanski
Minority Staff Director: Michael Day 225-4038
B-343C RHOB

Assistance to and protection of small business, including financial aid, regulatory flexibility, and paperwork reduction; participation of small business enterprises in federal procurement and government contracts.

Party Ratio: R 19–D 17

Donald Manzullo, Ill., Chair	*Nydia M. Velazquez, N.Y., Ranking Minority Member*
Larry Combest, Texas	*Juanita Millender-McDonald, Calif.*
Roscoe G. Bartlett, Md.	
Sue W. Kelly, N.Y.	*Tom Udall, N.M.*
Steve Chabot, Ohio	*Frank W. Ballance Jr., N.C.*
Patrick J. Toomey, Pa.	*Donna M. C. Christensen, Virgin Is.*
Jim DeMint, S.C.	
Sam Graves, Mo.	*Danny K. Davis, Ill.*
Ed Schrock, Va.	*Charlie Gonzalez, Texas*
Todd Akin, Mo.	*Grace F. Napolitano, Calif.*
Shelley Moore Capito, W.Va.	*Anibal Acevedo-Vila, P.R.*
Bill Shuster, Pa.	*Ed Case, Hawaii*
Marilyn Musgrave, Colo.	*Madeleine Z. Bordallo, Guam*
Trent Franks, Ariz.	
Jim Gerlach, Pa.	*Denise L. Majette, Ga.*
Jeb Bradley, N.H.	*Jim Marshall, Ga.*
Bob Beauprez, Colo.	*Michael H. Michaud, Maine*
Chris Chocola, Ind.	*Linda T. Sanchez, Calif.*
Steve King, Iowa	*Eni F. H. Faleomavaega, Am. Samoa*
	Vacancy

Subcommittees

Regulatory Reform and Oversight
Office: B-363 RHOB   **Phone:** 226-2630

Schrock (Chair), Bartlett, Kelly, Franks, Bradley, King (Iowa), Vacancy
Brady (Ranking Minority Member), Pascrell, Gonzalez, Langevin, Acevedo-Vila, Vacancy

Rural Enterprises, Agriculture, and Technology
Office: 2361 RHOB   **Phone:** 225-5821

Graves (Chair), Shuster, Kelly, Capito, Musgrave, Toomey
Ballance (Ranking Minority Member), Michaud, Christensen, Case, Bordallo

SMALL BUSINESS (continued)

Tax, Finance, and Exports
Office: B-363 RHOB   **Phone:** 226-2630

Toomey (Chair), Chabot, Musgrave, Gerlach, Beauprez, Franks, DeMint, Chocola

Millender-McDonald (Ranking Minority Member), Marshall, Ballance, Davis (Ill.), Acevedo-Vila, Majette, Michaud

Workforce, Empowerment, and Government Programs
Office: 2361 RHOB   **Phone:** 225-5821

Akin (Chair), Combest, DeMint, Capito, Bradley, Chocola, King

Udall (N.M.; Ranking Minority Member), Davis (Ill.), Gonzalez, Napolitano, Case, Bordallo

STANDARDS OF OFFICIAL CONDUCT

Office: HT-2 CAP   **Phone:** 225-7103
Fax: 225-7392
Web: www.house.gov/ethics
Majority Staff Director: John Vargo

All bills, resolutions, and other matters relating to the Code of Official Conduct adopted under House Rule XXIV. With respect to Members, officers, and employees of the U.S. House of Representatives, the committee is the supervising ethics office for the U.S. House of Representatives and is authorized to: (1) recommend administrative actions to establish or enforce standards of official conduct; (2) investigate violations of the Code of Official Conduct or of any applicable rules, laws, or regulations governing the performance of official duties or the discharge of official responsibilities (such reports must be approved by the House or by an affirmative vote of two-thirds of the committee); (3) report to appropriate federal or state authorities substantial evidence of a violation of any law applicable to the performance of official duties that may have been disclosed in a committee investigation; (4) render advisory opinions regarding the propriety of any current or proposed conduct of a Member, officer, or employee, and issue general guidance on such matters as necessary; and (5) consider requests for written waivers of the gift rule (clause 5 of House Rule XXVI).

Party Ratio: R 5–D 5

Joel Hefley, Colo., Chair	*Alan B. Mollohan, W.Va.,*
Doc Hastings, Wash.	*Ranking Minority*
Judy Biggert, Ill.	*Member*
Kenny Hulshof, Mo.	*Stephanie Tubbs Jones, Ohio*
Steven C. LaTourette, Ohio	*Gene Green, Texas*
	Lucille Roybal-Allard, Calif.
	Mike Doyle, Pa.

TRANSPORTATION AND INFRASTRUCTURE

Office: 2165 RHOB   **Phone:** 225-9446
Fax: 225-6782
Web: www.house.gov/transportation
E-mail: transcomm@mail.house.gov
Majority Chief of Staff: Lloyd Jones
Minority Staff Director: David Heymsfeld 225-4472
2163 RHOB

Transportation, including civil aviation, railroads, water transportation, transportation safety (except automobile safety), transportation infrastructure, transportation labor, and railroad retirement and unemployment (except revenue measures); water power; the Coast Guard; federal management of emergencies and natural disasters; flood control and improvement of waterways; inspection of merchant marine vessels; navigation and related laws; rules and international arrangements to prevent collisions at sea; measures, other than appropriations, that relate to construction, maintenance, and safety of roads; buildings and grounds of the Botanic Gardens, the Library of Congress, and the Smithsonian Institution and other governmental buildings within the District of Columbia; post offices, customhouses, federal courthouses, and the merchant marine, except for national security aspects; pollution of navigable waters; and bridges and dams and related transportation regulatory agencies. The Chair and ranking minority member are voting members ex officio of all subcommittees of which they are not regular members.

Party Ratio: R 41–D 34

Don Young, Alaska, Chair	*James L. Oberstar, Minn.,*
Tom Petri, Wis., Vice Chair	*Ranking Minority*
Sherwood Boehlert, N.Y.	*Member*
Howard Coble, N.C.	*Nick J. Rahall II, W.Va.*
John J. "Jimmy" Duncan Jr.,	*William O. Lipinski, Ill.*
Tenn.	*Peter A. DeFazio, Ore.*
Wayne T. Gilchrest, Md.	*Jerry F. Costello, Ill.*
John L. Mica, Fla.	*Eleanor Holmes Norton,*
Peter Hoekstra, Mich.	*D.C.*
Jack Quinn, N.Y.	*Jerrold Nadler, N.Y.*
Vernon J. Ehlers, Mich.	*Robert Menendez, N.J.*
Spencer Bachus, Ala.	*Corrine Brown, Fla.*
Steven C. LaTourette, Ohio	*Bob Filner, Calif.*
Sue W. Kelly, N.Y.	*Eddie Bernice Johnson, Texas*
Richard H. Baker, La.	*Gene Taylor, Miss.*
Bob Ney, Ohio	*Juanita Millender-*
Frank A. LoBiondo, N.J.	*McDonald, Calif.*
Jerry Moran, Kan.	*Elijah E. Cummings, Md.*
Gary G. Miller, Calif.	*Earl Blumenauer, Ore.*
Jim DeMint, S.C.	*Ellen O. Tauscher, Calif.*
Doug Bereuter, Neb.	*Bill Pascrell Jr., N.J.*
Johnny Isakson, Ga.	*Leonard L. Boswell, Iowa*
Robin Hayes, N.C.	*Nick Lampson, Texas*
Rob Simmons, Conn.	*Brian Baird, Wash.*
Shelley Moore Capito,	*Shelley Berkley, Nev.*
W.Va.	*Brad Carson, Okla.*

Henry E. Brown Jr., S.C.
Timothy V. Johnson, Ill.
Denny Rehberg, Mont.
Todd R. Platts, Pa.
Sam Graves, Mo.
Mark Kennedy, Minn.
Bill Shuster, Pa.
John Boozman, Ark.
John Sullivan, Okla.
Chris Chocola, Ind.
Bob Beauprez, Colo.
Michael C. Burgess, Texas
Max Burns, Ga.
Steve Pearce, N.M.
Jim Gerlach, Pa.
Mario Diaz-Balart, Fla.
Jon Porter, Nev.

Jim Matheson, Utah
Michael M. Honda, Calif.
Rick Larsen, Wash.
Michael E. Capuano, Mass.
Anthony Weiner, N.Y.
Julia Carson, Ind.
Joseph M. Hoeffel, Pa.
Mike Thompson, Calif.
Timothy H. Bishop, N.Y.
Michael H. Michaud, Maine
Lincoln Davis, Tenn.

Subcommittees

Aviation
Office: 2251 RHOB   **Phone:** 226-3220

Mica (Chair), Petri, Duncan, Quinn, Ehlers, Bachus, Kelly, Baker, LoBiondo, Moran (Kan.), Isakson, Hayes, Johnson (Ill.), Rehberg, Graves, Kennedy (Minn.), Shuster, Boozman, Sullivan, Chocola (Vice Chair), Beauprez, Pearce, Gerlach, Diaz-Balart (Fla.), Porter

DeFazio (Ranking Minority Member), Boswell, Lipinski, Costello, Norton, Menendez, Brown (Fla.), Johnson (Texas), Millender-McDonald, Tauscher, Pascrell, Holden, Berkley, Carson (Okla.), Matheson, Honda, Larsen, Capuano, Weiner, Rahall, Filner

Coast Guard and Maritime Transportation
Office: 507 FHOB   **Phone:** 226-3552

LoBiondo (Chair), Coble, Gilchrest, Hoekstra, DeMint, Simmons, Diaz-Balart (Fla.; Vice Chair)

Filner (Ranking Minority Member), DeFazio, Brown (Fla.), Millender-McDonald, Lampson, Thompson (Calif.)

Economic Development, Public Buildings, and Emergency Management
Office: 589 FHOB   **Phone:** 225-3014

LaTourette (Chair), Capito, Burgess, Burns (Vice Chair), Gerlach

Norton (Ranking Minority Member), Davis (Tenn.), Carson (Okla.), Michaud

Highways, Transit, and Pipelines
Office: B-370A RHOB   **Phone:** 225-6715

Petri (Chair), Boehlert, Coble, Duncan, Mica, Hoekstra, Quinn, LaTourette, Kelly, Baker, Ney, LoBiondo, Moran (Kan.), DeMint, Bereuter, Isakson, Hayes, Simmons, Capito, Brown (S.C.), Johnson (Ill.), Rehberg, Platts, Graves, Kennedy (Minn.), Shuster, Boozman, Beauprez (Vice Chair), Burgess, Burns

Lipinski (Ranking Minority Member), Rahall, Nadler, Johnson (Texas), Taylor (Miss.), Millender-McDonald, Cum-

mings, Tauscher, Pascrell, Holden, Baird, Berkley, Carson (Okla.), Matheson, Honda, Larsen, Capuano, Blumenauer, Lampson, Weiner, Carson (Ind.), Hoeffel, Thompson (Calif.), Bishop (N.Y.), Michaud

Railroads
Office: 589 FHOB   **Phone:** 226-0727

Quinn (Chair), Petri, Boehlert, Coble, Mica, Bachus, Moran (Kan.), Miller (Calif.), DeMint, Simmons, Capito, Platts, Graves, Porter (Vice Chair)

Brown (Fla.; Ranking Minority Member), Rahall, DeFazio, Nadler, Filner, Cummings, Blumenauer, Boswell, Carson (Ind.), Michaud, Lipinski, Costello

Water Resources and Environment
Office: B-376 RHOB   **Phone:** 225-4360

Duncan (Chair), Boehlert, Gilchrest, Ehlers, LaTourette, Kelly, Baker, Ney, Miller (Calif.), Isakson, Hayes, Brown (S.C.), Shuster, Boozman, Sullivan, Chocola, Pearce (Vice Chair), Gerlach, Diaz-Balart (Fla.)

Costello (Ranking Minority Member), Menendez, Taylor (Miss.), Lampson, Baird, Hoeffel, Thompson (Calif.), Bishop (N.Y.), Davis (Tenn.), Norton, Nadler, Johnson (Texas), Blumenauer, Tauscher, Pascrell

VETERANS' AFFAIRS

Office: 335 CHOB   **Phone:** 225-3527
Fax: 225-5486
Web: veterans.house.gov
Majority Staff Director: Patrick Ryan
Minority Staff Director: Michael Durishin 225-9756
    333 CHOB

Veterans' measures generally; cemeteries of the United States in which veterans of any war or conflict are or may be buried, whether in the United States or abroad, except cemeteries administered by the secretary of the Interior; compensation, vocational rehabilitation, and education of veterans; life insurance issued by the government on account of service in the armed forces; pensions of all the wars of the United States; readjustment of armed service members to civil life; soldiers' and sailors' civil relief; veterans' hospitals; medical care and treatment of veterans.

Party Ratio: R 17–D 14

Christopher H. Smith, N.J., Chair
Michael Bilirakis, Fla., Vice Chair
Terry Everett, Ala.
Steve Buyer, Ind.
Jack Quinn, N.Y.
Cliff Stearns, Fla.
Jerry Moran, Kan.
Richard H. Baker, La.
Rob Simmons, Conn.
Henry E. Brown Jr., S.C.
Jeff Miller, Fla.

Lane Evans, Ill., Ranking Minority Member
Bob Filner, Calif.
Luis V. Gutierrez, Ill.
Corrine Brown, Fla.
Vic Snyder, Ark.
Ciro D. Rodriguez, Texas
Michael H. Michaud, Maine
Darlene Hooley, Ore.
Silvestre Reyes, Texas
Ted Strickland, Ohio
Shelley Berkley, Nev.

VETERANS' AFFAIRS (continued)

Bob Beauprez, Colo.
Ginny Brown-Waite, Fla.
Rick Renzi, Ariz.
Tim Murphy, Pa.

Tom Udall, N.M.
Susan A. Davis, Calif.
Tim Ryan, Ohio

Subcommittees

Benefits
Office: 337 CHOB   **Phone:** 225-9164

Brown (S.C.; Chair), Quinn, Miller (Fla.), Bradley, Brown-Waite
Michaud (Ranking Minority Member), Davis (Calif.), Reyes, Brown (Fla.)

Health
Office: 338 CHOB   **Phone:** 225-9154

Simmons (Chair), Moran (Kan.), Baker, Miller (Fla.), Boozman, Bradley, Beauprez, Brown-Waite, Renzi, Stearns, Murphy
Rodriguez (Ranking Minority Member), Filner, Snyder, Strickland, Berkley, Ryan (Ohio), Gutierrez, Brown (Fla.), Hooley

Oversight and Investigations
Office: 337A CHOB   **Phone:** 225-3569

Buyer (Chair), Bilirakis, Everett, Boozman, Vacancy
Hooley (Ranking Minority Member), Evans, Filner, Rodriguez

WAYS AND MEANS

Office: 1102 LHOB   **Phone:** 225-3625
Fax: 225-2610
Web: waysandmeans.house.gov
E-mail: contactwaysandmeans@mail.house.gov
Majority Chief of Staff: Allison Giles
Minority Chief Counsel: Janice Mays 225-4021
    1106 LHOB

Revenue measures generally; reciprocal trade agreements; customs, collection districts, and ports of entry and delivery; revenue measures relating to the insular possessions; bonded debt of the United States; deposit of public moneys; transportation of dutiable goods; tax-exempt foundations and charitable trusts; national Social Security, except (A) health care and facilities programs that are supported from general revenues as opposed to payroll deductions and (B) work incentive programs. The Chair and ranking minority member are non-voting members ex officio of all subcommittees of which they are not regular members.

Party Ratio: R 24–D 17

Bill Thomas, Calif., Chair
Philip M. Crane, Ill.
E. Clay Shaw Jr., Fla.
Nancy L. Johnson, Conn.
Amo Houghton, N.Y.
Wally Herger, Calif.

Charles B. Rangel, N.Y., Ranking Minority Member
Pete Stark, Calif.
Robert T. Matsui, Calif.
Sander M. Levin, Mich.

John Boozman, Ark.
Jeb Bradley, N.H.
Jim McCrery, La.
Dave Camp, Mich.
Jim Ramstad, Minn.
Jim Nussle, Iowa
Sam Johnson, Texas
Jennifer Dunn, Wash.
Mac Collins, Ga.
Rob Portman, Ohio
Phil English, Pa.
J. D. Hayworth, Ariz.
Jerry Weller, Ill.
Kenny Hulshof, Mo.
Scott McInnis, Colo.
Ron Lewis, Ky.
Mark Foley, Fla.
Kevin Brady, Texas
Paul D. Ryan, Wis.
Eric Cantor, Va.

Benjamin L. Cardin, Md.
Jim McDermott, Wash.
Gerald D. Kleczka, Wis.
John Lewis, Ga.
Richard E. Neal, Mass.
Michael R. McNulty, N.Y.
William J. Jefferson, La.
John Tanner, Tenn.
Xavier Becerra, Calif.
Lloyd Doggett, Texas
Earl Pomeroy, N.D.
Max Sandlin, Texas
Stephanie Tubbs Jones, Ohio

Subcommittees

Health
Office: 1136 LHOB   **Phone:** 225-3943

Johnson (Conn.; Chair), McCrery, Crane, Johnson (Texas), Camp, Ramstad, English, Dunn
Stark (Ranking Minority Member), Kleczka, Lewis (Ga.), McDermott, Doggett

Human Resources
Office: B-317 RHOB   **Phone:** 225-1025

Herger (Chair), Johnson (Conn.), McInnis, McCrery, Camp, English, Lewis (Ky.), Cantor
Cardin (Ranking Minority Member), Stark, Levin, McDermott, Rangel

Oversight
Office: 1136 LHOB   **Phone:** 225-7601

Houghton (Chair), Portman, Weller, McInnis, Foley, Johnson (Texas), Ryan (Wis.), Cantor
Pomeroy (Ranking Minority Member), Kleczka, McNulty, Tanner, Sandlin

Select Revenue Measures
Office: 1135 LHOB   **Phone:** 226-5911

McCrery (Chair), Hayworth, Weller, Lewis (Ky.), Foley, Brady (Texas), Ryan (Wis.), Collins
McNulty (Ranking Minority Member), Jefferson, Sandlin, Doggett, Jones (Ohio)

Social Security
Office: B-316 RHOB   **Phone:** 225-9263

Shaw (Chair), Johnson (Texas), Collins, Hayworth, Hulshof, Lewis (Ky.), Brady (Texas), Ryan (Wis.)
Matsui (Ranking Minority Member), Cardin, Pomeroy, Becerra, Jones (Ohio)

Trade
Office: 1104 LHOB   **Phone:** 225-6649

Crane (Chair), Shaw, Houghton, Camp, Ramstad, Dunn, Herger, English, Nussle

Levin (Ranking Minority Member), Rangel, Neal, Jefferson, Becerra, Tanner

HOUSE LEADERSHIP AND PARTISAN COMMITTEES

REPUBLICAN LEADERS
Speaker of the House: J. Dennis Hastert, Ill.
Majority Leader: Tom DeLay, Texas
Majority Whip: Roy Blunt, Mo.
Conference Chair: Deborah Pryce, Ohio
Conference Vice Chair: Jack Kingston, Ga.
Conference Secretary: John T. Doolittle, Calif.
Chief Deputy Whip: Eric Cantor, Va.

REPUBLICAN PARTISAN COMMITTEES

National Republican Congressional Committee
Office: 320 1st St. S.E. 20003   **Phone:** 479-7000
Web: www.nrcc.org
Thomas M. Reynolds, N.Y., Chair
Other Leadership (in alphabetical order)
Phil English, Pa., Incumbent Development Chair
Howard P. "Buck" McKeon, Calif., Grassroots Mobilization Chair
Sue Myrick, N.C., Executive Committee Chair
Bob Ney, Ohio, Incumbent Review Chair
Mike Pence, Ind., Communications Chair
Mike Rogers, Mich., Finance Chair
Pete Sessions, Texas, Coalitions Chair
John Shadegg, Ariz., Education and Training Chair
John E. Sweeney, N.Y., Candidate Recruitment Chair
Jerry Weller, Ill., Community Partnerships Chair

Republican Policy Committee
Office: 2471 RHOB   **Phone:** 225-6168
Web: policy.house.gov
Christopher Cox, Calif., Chair
Members (in alphabetical order)

Bob Beauprez, Colo.	Lincoln Diaz-Balart, Fla.
Roy Blunt, Mo.	John T. Doolittle, Calif.
Kevin Brady, Texas	David Dreier, Calif.
Michael C. Burgess, Texas	Ernie Fletcher, Ky.
Eric Cantor, Va.	Wayne T. Gilchrest, Md.
Shelley Moore Capito, W.Va.	Phil Gingrey, Ga.
John Carter, Texas	Robert W. Goodlatte, Va.
Ander Crenshaw, Fla.	Katherine Harris, Fla.
John Culberson, Texas	Melissa A. Hart, Pa.
Tom DeLay, Texas	J. Dennis Hastert, Ill.
Jim DeMint, S.C.	Kenny Hulshof, Mo.
	Darrell Issa, Calif.

Jack Kingston, Ga.	Thomas M. Reynolds, N.Y.
Joe Knollenberg, Mich.	John Shadegg, Ariz.
Tom Latham, Iowa	Nick Smith, Mich.
Ron Lewis, Ky.	Billy Tauzin, La.
Bob Ney, Ohio	Bill Thomas, Calif.
Jim Nussle, Iowa	Patrick J. Toomey, Pa.
Mike Pence, Ind.	David Vitter, La.
Todd R. Platts, Pa.	Jerry Weller, Ill.
Jon Porter, Nev.	Roger Wicker, Miss.
Rob Portman, Ohio	Heather A. Wilson, N.M.
Deborah Pryce, Ohio	Joe Wilson, S.C.
Adam H. Putnam, Fla.	C. W. Bill Young, Fla.

Republican Steering Committee
Office: H-209 CAP   **Phone:** 225-2204
J. Dennis Hastert, Ill., Chair
Members (in alphabetical order)

Joe L. Barton, Texas	Jack Kingston, Ga.
Roy Blunt, Mo.	Tom Latham, Iowa
Ken Calvert, Calif.	John M. McHugh, N.Y.
Dave Camp, Mich.	Deborah Pryce, Ohio
Eric Cantor, Va.	Adam H. Putnam, Fla.
John Carter, Texas	Ralph Regula, Ohio
Mac Collins, Ga.	Thomas M. Reynolds, N.Y.
Christopher Cox, Calif.	Harold Rogers, Ky.
John Culberson, Texas	John Shadegg, Ariz.
Thomas M. Davis III, Va.	Billy Tauzin, La.
Tom DeLay, Texas	Bill Thomas, Calif.
John T. Doolittle, Calif.	Curt Weldon, Pa.
David Dreier, Calif.	C. W. Bill Young, Fla.
Doc Hastings, Wash.	Don Young, Alaska

DEMOCRATIC LEADERS

Minority Leader: *Nancy Pelosi, Calif.*
Minority Whip: *Steny H. Hoyer, Md.*
Caucus Chair: *Robert Menendez, N.J.*
Caucus Vice Chair: *James E. Clyburn, S.C.*
Assistant to the Leader: *John M. Spratt Jr., S.C.*
Senior Chief Deputy Whip: *John Lewis, Ga.*

DEMOCRATIC PARTISAN COMMITTEES

Democratic Congressional Campaign Committee
Office: 499 S. Capitol St. S.W. 20003 (temporary address during renovations to permanent offices at 430 S. Capitol St. S.E. 20003)   **Phone:** 863-1500
Web: www.dccc.org
Robert T. Matsui, Calif., Chair
Other Leadership (in alphabetical order)
John D. Dingell, Mich., Chair's Council
Rahm Emanuel, Ill., Vice Chair
Charlie Gonzalez, Texas, Vice Chair
Bart Gordon, Tenn., Recruitment Chair

Edward J. Markey, Mass., Vice Chair
Kendrick B. Meek, Fla., Vice Chair
Charles B. Rangel, N.Y., Executive Board Chair
Lucille Roybal-Allard, Calif., Vice Chair
Jan Schakowsky, Ill., Women Lead Project Chair
Mike Thompson, Calif., Business Council Chair

Democratic Steering Committee
Office: H-204 CAP   **Phone:** 225-0100
Nancy Pelosi, Calif., Chair
Other Leadership (in alphabetical order)
Rosa DeLauro, Conn., Co-Chair
George Miller, Calif., Co-Chair
Jose E. Serrano, N.Y., Vice Chair
John Tanner, Tenn., Vice Chair
Maxine Waters, Calif., Vice Chair
Members (in alphabetical order)
Earl Blumenauer, Ore.
Sherrod Brown, Ohio
Michael E. Capuano, Mass.
Benjamin L. Cardin, Md.
James E. Clyburn, S.C.
Jerry F. Costello, Ill.

Joseph Crowley, N.Y.
Jim Davis, Fla.
John D. Dingell, Mich.
Martin Frost, Texas
Baron P. Hill, Ind.
Steny H. Hoyer, Md.
Sheila Jackson-Lee, Texas
Chris John, La.
Carolyn Cheeks Kilpatrick, Mich.
John B. Larson, Conn.
John Lewis, Ga.
Zoe Lofgren, Calif.
Nita M. Lowey, N.Y.
Robert T. Matsui, Calif.
Carolyn McCarthy, N.Y.
Betty McCollum, Minn.
Robert Menendez, N.J.
Alan B. Mollohan, W.VA.
John P. Murtha, Pa.

David R. Obey, Wis.
Ed Pastor, Ariz.
Donald M. Payne, N.J.
Collin C. Peterson, Minn.
Earl Pomeroy, N.D.
Nick J. Rahall II, W.Va.
Charles B. Rangel, N.Y.
Ciro D. Rodriguez, Texas
Mike Ross, Ark.
C. A. Dutch Ruppersberger, Md.
Max Sandlin, Texas
Jan Schakowsky, Ill.
Hilda L. Solis, Calif.
John M. Spratt Jr., S.C.
Mike Thompson, Calif.
John F. Tierney, Mass.
Jim Turner, Texas
Tom Udall, N.M.

House Members' Offices

Listed below are the names of House members and their party, state, and district affiliation, followed by the address and telephone number for their Washington office. (The area code for all telephone numbers in Washington, D.C., is [202]). Also listed are the name of a top administrative aide for each member, and Web and e-mail addresses for each member.

The address, telephone and fax numbers, and name of a key aide for the members' district office(s) are also listed. And finally, each representative's committee assignments are given. (For partisan committee assignments, see page 801.)

As of April 23, 2003, there were 229 Republicans, 205 Democrats, and 1 Independent in the House of Representatives.

ABERCROMBIE, NEIL, D-HAWAII (1)

Capitol Hill Office: 1502 LHOB 20515; 225-2726; Fax: 225-4580; *Chief of Staff:* Cathy Mangino
Web: www.house.gov/abercrombie
E-mail: neil.abercrombie@mail.house.gov
District Office(s): 300 Ala Moana Blvd., #4104, Honolulu 96850; (808) 541-2570; Fax: (808) 533-0133; *District Director:* Alan Furuno
Committee Assignment(s): Armed Services; Resources

ACEVEDO-VILA, ANIBAL, D-P.R. (AT LARGE)

Capitol Hill Office: 126 CHOB 20515; 225-2615; Fax: 225-2154; *Administrative Assistant:* Carlos Dalmau
Web: www.house.gov/acevedo-vila
E-mail: anibal@mail.house.gov
District Office(s): Casa Alcaldia, Box 447, Mayaguez 00681; (787) 831-3400; *Office Director:* Ladislao Olmeda
La Rambla Plaza, #203, Ponce 00731; (787) 841-3209; Fax: (787) 841-3229; *Office Director:* Omar Santiago
Tercer Piso, Departamento de Estado, P.O. Box 9023958, San Juan 00902; (787) 723-6333; Fax: (787) 729-7738; *Chief of Staff:* Carlos Ruiz
Committee Assignment(s): Agriculture; Resources; Small Business

ACKERMAN, GARY L., D-N.Y. (5)

Capitol Hill Office: 2243 RHOB 20515; 225-2601; Fax: 225-1589; *Chief of Staff:* Jedd Moskowitz
Web: www.house.gov/ackerman
E-mail: gary_ackerman@mail.house.gov
District Office(s): 218-14 Northern Blvd., Bayside 11361; (718) 423-2154; Fax: (718) 423-5053; *District Administrator:* Moya Berry
Committee Assignment(s): Financial Services; International Relations

ADERHOLT, ROBERT B., R-ALA. (4)

Capitol Hill Office: 1433 LHOB 20515; 225-4876; Fax: 225-5587; *Chief of Staff:* Mark Busching
Web: www.house.gov/aderholt
E-mail: robert@mail.house.gov
District Office(s): 1710 Alabama Ave., #247, Jasper 35501; (205) 221-2310; Fax: (205) 221-9035; *Deputy Chief of Staff:* Bill Harris
205 4th Ave. N.E., #104, Cullman 35055; (256) 734-6043; Fax: (256) 737-0885; *Constituent Services Representative:* Evelyn Stevens
600 Broad St., #107, Gadsden 35901; (256) 546-0201; Fax: (256) 546-8778; *Field Representative:* Kevin Rosamond
Committee Assignment(s): Appropriations

AKIN, TODD, R-MO. (2)

Capitol Hill Office: 117 CHOB 20515; 225-2561; Fax: 225-2563; *Chief of Staff:* Robert Schwarzwalder
Web: www.house.gov/akin
E-mail: rep.akin@mail.house.gov
District Office(s): 301 Sovereign Court, #201, St. Louis 63141; (314) 590-0029; Fax: (314) 590-0037; *District Director:* Patrick Werner
820 S. Main St., #206, St. Charles 63301; (636) 949-6826; Fax: (636) 949-3832; *District Representative:* Debbie Cochran
Committee Assignment(s): Armed Services; Science; Small Business

ALEXANDER, RODNEY, D-LA. (5)

Capitol Hill Office: 316 CHOB 20515; 225-8490; Fax: 225-5639; *Chief of Staff:* Wooten Johnson
Web: www.house.gov/alexander
E-mail: rodney.alexander@mail.house.gov
District Office(s): 1900 Stubbs Ave., Suite B, Monroe 71201; (318) 322-3500; Fax: (318) 245-8218; *District Director:* Linda Blount

1412 Center Court, #402, Alexandria 71308; (318) 445-0818; Fax: (318) 445-3776; *District Representative:* Tommie Seaton

Committee Assignment(s): Agriculture; Armed Services

ALLEN, TOM, D-MAINE (1)

Capitol Hill Office: 1717 LHOB 20515; 225-6116; Fax: 225-5590; *Chief of Staff:* Jackie Potter

Web: www.house.gov/allen

E-mail: rep.tomallen@mail.house.gov

District Office(s): 234 Oxford St., Portland 04101; (207) 774-5019; Fax: (207) 871-0720; *Communications Director:* Mark Sullivan

Committee Assignment(s): Energy and Commerce

ANDREWS, ROBERT E., D-N.J. (1)

Capitol Hill Office: 2439 RHOB 20515; 225-6501; Fax: 225-6583; *Chief of Staff:* Matt Walker

Web: www.house.gov/andrews

E-mail: rob.andrews@mail.house.gov

District Office(s): 506 A White Horse Pike, Haddon Heights 08035; (856) 546-5100; Fax: (856) 546-9529; *Office Manager:* Christina Morales

63 N. Broad St., Woodbury 08096; (856) 848-3900; Fax: (856) 848-8341; *District Representative:* Leanne Hasbrouck

Committee Assignment(s): Education and Workforce; Select Homeland Security

BACA, JOE, D-CALIF. (43)

Capitol Hill Office: 328 CHOB 20515; 225-6161; Fax: 225-8671; *Chief of Staff:* Linda Macias

Web: www.house.gov/baca

E-mail: www.house.gov/writerep

District Office(s): 201 N. E St., #102, San Bernardino 92401; (909) 885-2222; Fax: (909) 888-5959; *District Director:* Mike Trujillo

Committee Assignment(s): Agriculture; Financial Services; Resources

BACHUS, SPENCER, R-ALA. (6)

Capitol Hill Office: 442 CHOB 20515; 225-4921; Fax: 225-2082; *Chief of Staff:* Larry Lavender

Web: www.house.gov/bachus

E-mail: www.house.gov/bachus/citizendirect.htm

District Office(s): 3500 McFarland Blvd., P.O. Box 569, Northport 35476; (205) 333-9894; Fax: (205) 333-9812; *District Office Manager:* Margaret Pyle

703 2nd Ave. North, Clanton 35045; (205) 755-1522; Fax: (205) 755-1161; *Field Representative:* Betty Bennett

1900 International Park Dr., #107, Birmingham 35243; (205) 969-2296; Fax: (205) 969-3958; *District Director:* Jeff Emerson

Committee Assignment(s): Financial Services; Judiciary; Transportation and Infrastructure

BAIRD, BRIAN, D-WASH. (3)

Capitol Hill Office: 1421 LHOB 20515; 225-3536; Fax: 225-3478; *Chief of Staff:* Ryan Hedgepeth

Web: www.house.gov/baird

E-mail: www.house.gov/baird/contact.htm

District Office(s): 120 Union Ave., #105, Olympia 98501; (360) 352-9768; Fax: (360) 352-9241; *District Representative:* Kasey Schiewe

1220 Main St., #360, Vancouver 98660; (360) 695-6292; Fax: (360) 695-6197; *District Director:* Thesesa Weil

Committee Assignment(s): Budget; Science; Transportation and Infrastructure

BAKER, RICHARD H., R-LA. (6)

Capitol Hill Office: 341 CHOB 20515; 225-3901; Fax: 225-7313; *Administrative Assistant:* Paul Sawyer

Web: www.house.gov/baker

E-mail: www.house.gov/writerep

District Office(s): 5555 Hilton Ave., #100, Baton Rouge 70808; (225) 929-7711; Fax: (225) 929-7688; *Chief of Staff:* Christy Casteel

Committee Assignment(s): Financial Services; Transportation and Infrastructure; Veterans' Affairs

BALDWIN, TAMMY, D-WIS. (2)

Capitol Hill Office: 1022 LHOB 20515; 225-2906; Fax: 225-6942; *Chief of Staff:* Bill Murat

Web: tammybaldwin.house.gov

E-mail: tammy.baldwin@mail.house.gov

District Office(s): 400 E. Grand Ave., #402, Beloit 53511; (608) 362-2800; Fax: (608) 362-2838; *Office Manager:* Helen Forbeck

10 E. Doty St., #405, Madison 53703; (608) 258-9800; Fax: (608) 258-9808; *District Director:* Mark Webster

Committee Assignment(s): Budget; Judiciary

BALLANCE, FRANK W. JR., D-N.C. (1)

Capitol Hill Office: 413 CHOB 20515; 225-3101; Fax: 225-3354; *Chief of Staff:* Corlis James

Web: www.house.gov/ballance

E-mail: frank.ballance@mail.house.gov

District Office(s): Warren Corners Shopping Center, #7, Route One, Norlina 27563; (252) 456-3091; Fax: (252) 456-3052; *District Director:* Dollie Burwell

415 E. Blvd., #100, Williamston 27892; (252) 789-4939; Fax: (252) 792-8113; *District Representative:* Ann Huggins

Committee Assignment(s): Agriculture; Small Business

BALLENGER, CASS, R-N.C. (10)

Capitol Hill Office: 2182 RHOB 20515; 225-2576; Fax: 225-0316; *Chief of Staff:* Dan Gurley

Web: www.house.gov/ballenger

E-mail: cass.ballenger@mail.house.gov

District Office(s): 361 10th Ave. Dr. N.E., #102, P.O. Box 1830, Hickory 28603; (828) 327-6100; Fax: (828) 327-8311; *District Director:* Thomas D. Luckadoo

Committee Assignment(s): Education and Workforce; International Relations

BARRETT, J. GRESHAM, R-S.C. (3)

Capitol Hill Office: 1523 LHOB 20515; 225-5301; Fax: 225-3216; *Chief of Staff:* Lance Williams

Web: www.house.gov/barrett

District Office(s): 315 S. McDuffie St., Anderson 29622; (864) 224-7401; Fax: (864) 225-7049; *District Director:* Darryl Broome

115 Enterprise Court, Suite B, Greenwood 29649; (864) 223-8251; Fax: (864) 223-1679; *District Representative:* Janice McCord

233 Pendleton St. N.W., Aiken 29801; (803) 649-5571; Fax: (803) 648-9038; *District Representative:* Ginny Allen

Committee Assignment(s): Budget; Financial Services

BARTLETT, ROSCOE G., R-MD. (6)

Capitol Hill Office: 2412 RHOB 20515; 225-2721; Fax: 225-2193; *Chief of Staff:* Gregg Cox

Web: bartlett.house.gov

E-mail: www.house.gov/writerep

District Office(s): 15 E. Main St., #110, Westminster 21157; (410) 857-1115; Fax: (410) 857-1329; *Projects Administrator:* Phil Straw

7360 Guilford Dr., #101, Frederick 21704; (301) 694-3030; Fax: (301) 694-6674; *District Director:* Sallie Taylor

1 Frederick St., Cumberland 21502; (301) 724-3105; Fax: (301) 724-3538; *Caseworker:* Brenda Frantz

11377 Robinwood Dr., Hagerstown 21742; (301) 797-6043; Fax: (301) 797-2385; *Caseworker:* Marci Cosens

Committee Assignment(s): Armed Services; Science; Small Business

BARTON, JOE L., R-TEXAS (6)

Capitol Hill Office: 2109 RHOB 20515; 225-2002; Fax: 225-3052; *Chief of Staff:* Heather Couri

Web: www.house.gov/barton

E-mail: www.house.gov/barton/IMA/get_address.htm

District Office(s): 303 W. Knox St., #201, Ennis 75119; (817) 543-1000; Fax: (972) 875-1907; *District Manager:* Linda Gillespie

805 Washington Dr., Suite F, Arlington 76011; (817) 543-1000; Fax: (817) 548-7029; *District Director:* Ron Wright

Committee Assignment(s): Energy and Commerce; Science

BASS, CHARLES, R-N.H. (2)

Capitol Hill Office: 2421 RHOB 20515; 225-5206; Fax: 225-2946; *Legislative Director:* Tad Furtado.

Web: www.house.gov/bass

E-mail: cbass@mail.house.gov

District Office(s): 170 Main St., Nashua 03060; (603) 889-8772; Fax: (603) 889-6890; *Constituent Services Representative:* Madeline Saulnier

142 N. Main St., Concord 03301; (603) 226-0249; Fax: (603) 226-0476; *Chief of Staff:* Darwin Cusack

76 Main St., #2C, Littleton 03561; (603) 444-1271; Fax: (603) 444-5343; *Constituent Services Representative:* Bill Williams

1 West St., #208, Keene 03431; (603) 358-4094; Fax: (603) 358-5092; *Constituent Services Representative:* Jane Lane

Committee Assignment(s): Energy and Commerce

BEAUPREZ, BOB, R-COLO. (7)

Capitol Hill Office: 511 CHOB 20515; 225-2645; Fax: 225-5278; *Chief of Staff:* Sean Murphy

Web: www.house.gov/beauprez

District Office(s): 4251 Kipling St., #370, Wheat Ridge 80033; (303) 940-5821; Fax: (303) 940-5831; *District Director:* Colin Campbell

Committee Assignment(s): Small Business; Transportation and Infrastructure; Veterans' Affairs

BECERRA, XAVIER, D-CALIF. (31)

Capitol Hill Office: 1119 LHOB 20515; 225-6235; Fax: 225-2202; *Chief of Staff:* Krista Atteberry

Web: www.house.gov/becerra

E-mail: www.house.gov/writerep

District Office(s): 1910 Sunset Blvd., #560, Los Angeles 90026; (213) 483-1425; Fax: (213) 483-1429; *District Director:* Laura Arciniega

Committee Assignment(s): Ways and Means

BELL, CHRIS, D-TEXAS (25)

Capitol Hill Office: 216 CHOB 20515; 225-7508; Fax: 225-2947; *Chief of Staff:* John Gonzalez

Web: www.house.gov/bell

District Office(s): 7707 Fannin St., #203, Houston 77054; *District Director:* Laurence Payne

1001 E. Southmore Ave., #810, Pasadena 77502; (713) 473-4334; Fax: (713) 475-8887; *Office Manager:* Lisa Hallford

Committee Assignment(s): Government Reform; International Relations; Science

BEREUTER, DOUG, R-NEB. (1)

Capitol Hill Office: 2184 RHOB 20515; 225-4806; Fax: 225-5686; *Chief of Staff:* Susan Olson

Web: www.house.gov/bereuter

District Office(s): P.O. Box 377, 629 N. Broad St., Fremont 68025; (402) 727-0888; Fax: (402) 727-9130; *Caseworker:* Jon Peterson

301 S. 13th St., #100, Lincoln 68508; (402) 438-1598; Fax: (402) 438-1604; *District Director:* Roger Massey

Committee Assignment(s): Financial Services; International Relations; Select Intelligence; Transportation and Infrastructure

BERKLEY, SHELLEY, D-NEV. (1)

Capitol Hill Office: 439 CHOB 20515; 225-5965; Fax: 225-3119; *Chief of Staff:* Richard Urey
Web: www.house.gov/berkley
E-mail: shelley.berkley@mail.house.gov
District Office(s): 2340 Paseo Del Prado, #D-106, Las Vegas 89102; (702) 220-9823; Fax: (702) 220-9841; *District Director:* Tod J. Story
Committee Assignment(s): International Relations; Transportation and Infrastructure; Veterans' Affairs

BERMAN, HOWARD L., D-CALIF. (28)

Capitol Hill Office: 2221 RHOB 20515; 225-4695; Fax: 225-3196; *Chief of Staff:* Gene Smith
Web: www.house.gov/berman
E-mail: howard.berman@mail.house.gov
District Office(s): 14546 Hamlin St., #202, Van Nuys 91411; (818) 994-7200; *District Director:* Bob Blumenfield
Committee Assignment(s): International Relations; Judiciary

BERRY, MARION, D-ARK. (1)

Capitol Hill Office: 1113 LHOB 20515; 225-4076; Fax: 225-5602; *Chief of Staff:* H. Thad Huguley
Web: www.house.gov/berry
E-mail: www.house.gov/writerep
District Office(s): 108 E. Huntington Ave., Jonesboro 72401; (870) 972-4600; Fax: (870) 972-4605; *District Director:* Jason R. Willette
116 N. 1st St., #C-1, Cabot 72023; (501) 843-3043; Fax: (501) 843-4955; *District Representative:* Jeffery Weaver
Committee Assignment(s): Appropriations

BIGGERT, JUDY, R-ILL. (13)

Capitol Hill Office: 1213 LHOB 20515; 225-3515; Fax: 225-9420; *Chief of Staff:* Kathy Lydon
Web: www.house.gov/biggert
E-mail: www.house.gov/writerep
District Office(s): 115 W. 55th St., #100, Clarendon Hills 60514; (630) 655-2052; Fax: (630) 655-1061; *District Office Manager:* Sandra Henrichs
Committee Assignment(s): Education and Workforce; Financial Services; Science; Standards of Official Conduct

BILIRAKIS, MICHAEL, R-FLA. (9)

Capitol Hill Office: 2269 RHOB 20515; 225-5755; Fax: 225-4085; *Chief of Staff:* Rebecca Hyder
Web: www.house.gov/bilirakis
E-mail: www.house.gov/writerep
District Office(s): 10330 N. Dale Mabry, #205, Tampa 33608; (813) 960-8173; *District Director:* Sonja B. Stefanadis
Committee Assignment(s): Energy and Commerce; Veterans' Affairs

BISHOP, ROB, R-UTAH (1)

Capitol Hill Office: 124 CHOB 20515; 225-0453; Fax: 225-5857; *Chief of Staff:* Scott Parker
Web: www.house.gov/robbishop
District Office(s): 1017 Federal Bldg., 324 25th St., Ogden 84401; (801) 625-5677; *District Director:* Peter Jenks
Committee Assignment(s): Armed Services; Resources; Science

BISHOP, SANFORD D. JR., D-GA. (2)

Capitol Hill Office: 2429 RHOB 20515; 225-3631; Fax: 225-2203; *Chief of Staff:* Nadine Chapman
Web: www.house.gov/bishop
E-mail: bishop.email@mail.house.gov
District Office(s): 401 N. Patterson St., #255, Valdosta 31601; (229) 247-9705; Fax: (229) 241-1035; *Field Representative:* Michael Bryant
Albany Towers, 235 Roosevelt Ave., #114, Albany 31701; (229) 439-8067; Fax: (229) 436-2099; *District Director:* Kenneth Cutts
City Hall, 101 S. Main St., Dawson 31701; (229) 995-3991; Fax: (229) 995-4894; *Field Representative:* Elaine Gillispie
Committee Assignment(s): Appropriations

BISHOP, TIMOTHY H., D-N.Y. (1)

Capitol Hill Office: 1133 LHOB 20515; 225-3826; Fax: 225-3143; *Chief of Staff:* Doug Dodson
Web: www.house.gov/timbishop
E-mail: tim.bishop@mail.house.gov
District Office(s): 3680 Route 112, Suite C, Coram 11727; (631) 696-6500; Fax: (631) 696-4520; *District Director:* Luis Rosero
Committee Assignment(s): Education and Workforce; Transportation and Infrastructure

BLACKBURN, MARSHA, R-TENN. (7)

Capitol Hill Office: 509 CHOB 20515; 225-2811; Fax: 225-2989; *Chief of Staff:* Steve Brophy
Web: www.house.gov/blackburn
E-mail: www.house.gov/writerep
District Office(s): 109 3rd Ave. South, #117, Franklin 37064; (615) 591-5161; Fax: (615) 599-2916; *District Director:* H. Steven Allbrooks
1850 Memorial Dr., Clarksville 37043; (931) 503-0391; Fax: (931) 503-0393; *Caseworker:* Woody Parker
7975 Stage Hills Blvd., #1, Memphis 38133; (901) 382-5811; Fax: (901) 373-8215; *Field Representative:* Susan McCord
Committee Assignment(s): Education and Workforce; Government Reform; Judiciary

BLUMENAUER, EARL, D-ORE. (3)

Capitol Hill Office: 2446 RHOB 20515; 225-4811; Fax: 225-8941; *Chief of Staff:* Maria Zimmerman
Web: www.house.gov/blumenauer
E-mail: write.earl@mail.house.gov

District Office(s): 729 N.E. Oregon St., #115, Portland 97232; (503) 231-2300; Fax: (503) 230-5413; *District Director:* Julia Pomeroy

Committee Assignment(s): International Relations; Transportation and Infrastructure

BLUNT, ROY, R-MO. (7)

Capitol Hill Office: 217 CHOB 20515; 225-6536; Fax: 225-5604; *Chief of Staff (leadership):* Gregg Hartley *Chief of Staff (personal):* Amy Field

Web: www.house.gov/blunt

E-mail: www.house.gov/blunt/guest.htm

District Office(s): 2740-B E. Sunshine St., Springfield 65804; (417) 889-1800; Fax: (417) 889-4915; *District Director:* Sharon Nahon

Northpark Mall, 101 Rangeline Rd., Joplin 64801; (417) 781-1041; *Field Representative:* Steve McIntosh

Committee Assignment(s): Energy and Commerce

BOEHLERT, SHERWOOD, R-N.Y. (24)

Capitol Hill Office: 2246 RHOB 20515; 225-3665; Fax: 225-1891; *Chief of Staff:* Dean Patrick D'Amore

Web: www.house.gov/boehlert

E-mail: rep.boehlert@mail.house.gov

District Office(s): 21 Lincoln St., Auburn 13021; (315) 225-0649; *District Representative:* Sue Dwyer

10 Broad St., #200, Utica 13501; (315) 793-8146; Fax: (315) 798-4099; *District Director:* Jeanne Donalty

Committee Assignment(s): Science; Select Homeland Security; Select Intelligence; Transportation and Infrastructure

BOEHNER, JOHN A., R-OHIO (8)

Capitol Hill Office: 1011 LHOB 20515; 225-6205; Fax: 225-0704; *Chief of Staff:* Michael Sommers

Web: johnboehner.house.gov

E-mail: john.boehner@mail.house.gov

District Office(s): 8200 Beckett Park Dr., Rd. 202, Hamilton 45011; (513) 870-0300; Fax: (513) 870-0151; *District Chief of Staff:* William C. Krieger II

12 S. Plum St., Troy 45373; (937) 339-1524; Fax: (937) 339-1878; *Field Representative:* Kelly Smith

Committee Assignment(s): Agriculture; Education and Workforce

BONILLA, HENRY, R-TEXAS (23)

Capitol Hill Office: 2458 RHOB 20515; 225-4511; Fax: 225-2237; *Chief of Staff:* Marcus Lubin

Web: www.house.gov/bonilla

E-mail: www.house.gov/writerep

District Office(s): 107 W. Ave. E, Rd. 14, Alpine 79830; (915) 837-1313; *District Representative:* Vacant

1300 Matamoros St., Rd. 113B, Laredo 78040; (956) 726-4682; Fax: (956) 726-4684; *Constituent Liaison:* Viola Martinez

11120 Wurzbach Rd., Rd. 300, San Antonio 78230; (210) 697-9055; Fax: (210) 697-9185; *District Director:* Phil Ricks

111 E. Broadway, #101, Del Rio 78840; (830) 774-6547; Fax: (830) 774-5693; *Constituent Liaison:* Ida Gutierrez

Committee Assignment(s): Appropriations

BONNER, JO, R-ALA. (1)

Capitol Hill Office: 315 CHOB 20515; 225-4931; Fax: 225-0562; *Chief of Staff:* Al Spencer

Web: www.house.gov/bonner

E-mail: www.house.gov/bonner/ima/get_address.htm

District Office(s): 1141 Montlimar Dr., Rd. 3010, Mobile 36609; (251) 690-2811; Fax: (251) 342-0404; *District Director:* Eliska Morgan

Committee Assignment(s): Agriculture; Budget; Science

BONO, MARY, R-CALIF. (45)

Capitol Hill Office: 404 CHOB 20515; 225-5330; Fax: 225-2961; *Chief of Staff:* Frank W. Cullen

Web: www.house.gov/bono

E-mail: www.house.gov/writerep

District Office(s): 707 E. Tahquitz Canyon Way, #9, Palm Springs 92264; (760) 320-1076; Fax: (760) 320-0596; *District Director:* Lou Penrose

1600 E. Florida Ave., #301, Hemet 92544; (909) 658-2312; Fax: (909) 652-2562; *Field Representative:* Alta Armstrong

Committee Assignment(s): Energy and Commerce

BOOZMAN, JOHN, R-ARK. (3)

Capitol Hill Office: 1708 LHOB 20515; 225-4301; Fax: 225-5713; *Chief of Staff:* Matt Sagely

Web: www.house.gov/boozman

E-mail: www.house.gov/writerep

District Office(s): 402 N. Walnut St., #210, Harrison 72601; (870) 741-6900; Fax: (870) 741-7741; *District Representative:* Sarah Hartley

30 S. 6th St., #240, Fort Smith 72901; (501) 782-7787; Fax: (501) 783-7662; *District Representative:* Kathy J. Watson

207 W. Center St., Fayetteville 72701; (501) 442-5258; Fax: (501) 442-0937; *Chief of Staff:* Steve Gray

Committee Assignment(s): Transportation and Infrastructure; Veterans' Affairs

BORDALLO, MADELEINE Z., D-GUAM (AT LARGE)

Capitol Hill Office: 427 CHOB 20515; 225-1188; Fax: 226-0341; *Chief of Staff:* John Whitt

Web: www.house.gov/bordallo

E-mail: madeleine.bordallo@mail.house.gov

District Office(s): 120 Father Duenas Ave., #107, Hagatna 96910; (671) 477-4272; Fax: (671) 477-2587; *District Director:* Joaquin Perez

Committee Assignment(s): Armed Services; Resources; Small Business

BOSWELL, LEONARD L., D-IOWA (3)

Capitol Hill Office: 1427 LHOB 20515; 225-3806; Fax: 225-5608; *Administrative Assistant:* E. H. "Ned" Michalek
Web: www.house.gov/boswell
E-mail: rep.boswell.ia03@mail.house.gov
District Office(s): 709 Furnas Dr., #1, Osceola 50213; (641) 342-4801; Fax: (641) 342-4354; *District Director:* Jay Byers
Committee Assignment(s): Agriculture; Select Intelligence; Transportation and Infrastructure

BOUCHER, RICK, D-VA. (9)

Capitol Hill Office: 2187 RHOB 20515; 225-3861; Fax: 225-0442; *Deputy Chief of Staff:* Laura Vaught
Web: www.house.gov/boucher
E-mail: ninthnet@mail.house.gov
District Office(s): 188 E. Main St., Abingdon 24210; (276) 628-1145; Fax: (276) 628-2203; *District Director:* Linda DiYorio
1 Cloverleaf Square, #C-1, Big Stone Gap 24219; (276) 523-5450; Fax: (276) 523-1412; *Casework Specialist:* Eloise Lawson
106 N. Washington Ave., Pulaski 24301; (540) 980-4310; Fax: (540) 980-0529; *Casework Supervisor:* Becki Gunn
Committee Assignment(s): Energy and Commerce; Judiciary

BOYD, ALLEN, D-FLA. (2)

Capitol Hill Office: 107 CHOB 20515; 225-5235; Fax: 225-5615; *Administrative Assistant:* Libby Greer
Web: www.house.gov/boyd
E-mail: www.house.gov/writerep
District Office(s): 301 S. Monroe St., #108, Tallahassee 32301; (850) 561-3979; Fax: (850) 681-2902; *District Director:* Jerry Smithwick
30 W. Government St., #203, Panama City 32401; (850) 785-0812; Fax: (850) 763-3764; *District Representative:* Bobby Pickles
Committee Assignment(s): Appropriations

BRADLEY, JEB, R-N.H. (1)

Capitol Hill Office: 1218 LHOB 20515; 225-5456; Fax: 225-5822; *Chief of Staff:* Debra Vanderbeek
Web: www.house.gov/bradley
E-mail: www.house.gov/bradley/contact.html
District Office(s): 1095 Elm St., Manchester 03101; (603) 641-3895; Fax: (603) 641-9561; *District Director:* Jeff Rose
104 Washington St., Dover 03820; (603) 743-4813; Fax: (603) 743-5956; *District Representative:* Olga Clough
Committee Assignment(s): Armed Services; Small Business; Veterans' Affairs

BRADY, KEVIN, R-TEXAS (8)

Capitol Hill Office: 428 CHOB 20515; 225-4901; Fax: 225-5524; *Chief of Staff:* Doug Centilli
Web: www.house.gov/brady
E-mail: rep.brady@mail.house.gov
District Office(s): 200 River Pointe Dr., #304, Conroe 77304; (936) 441-5700; Fax: (936) 441-5757; *District Director:* Heather Montgomery
616 FM 1960 West, #220, Houston 77090; (281) 895-8892; Fax: (281) 895-8912; *Casework Director:* June Kenyon
Committee Assignment(s): Ways and Means

BRADY, ROBERT A., D-PA. (1)

Capitol Hill Office: 206 CHOB 20515; 225-4731; Fax: 225-0088; *Chief of Staff:* Stan White
Web: www.house.gov/robertbrady
E-mail: www.house.gov/writerep
District Office(s): 500 Ritner St., 1st Floor, Philadelphia 19148; (215) 551-5357; Fax: (215) 551-5483; *Office Manager:* Jim Summers
1907 S. Broad St., Philadelphia 19148; (215) 389-4627; Fax: (215) 389-4636; *District Director:* Shirley Gregory
1510 W. Cecil B. Moore Ave., #304, Philadelphia 19121; (215) 236-5430; Fax: (215) 236-5472; *Office Manager:* Isabella Fitzgerald
511-13 Welsh St., 1st Floor, Chester 19013; (610) 874-7094; Fax: (610) 874-7193; *Office Manager:* Carl Fitzgerald
Committee Assignment(s): Armed Services; House Administration; Joint Printing

BROWN, CORRINE, D-FLA. (3)

Capitol Hill Office: 2444 RHOB 20515; 225-0123; Fax: 225-2256; *Chief of Staff:* Elias Ronnie Simmons
Web: www.house.gov/corrinebrown
E-mail: www.house.gov/writerep
District Office(s): 101 E. Union St., #202, Jacksonville 32202; (904) 354-1652; Fax: (904) 354-2721; *District Director:* Glenel Bowden
219 Lime Ave., Orlando 32805; (407) 872-0656; Fax: (407) 872-5763; *Area Director:* Ronita Sanders
Committee Assignment(s): Transportation and Infrastructure; Veterans' Affairs

BROWN, HENRY E. JR., R-S.C. (1)

Capitol Hill Office: 1124 LHOB 20515; 225-3176; Fax: 225-3407; *Chief of Staff:* W. Stovall Witte Jr.
Web: www.house.gov/henrybrown
E-mail: www.house.gov/writerep
District Office(s): 1800 N. Oak St., Suite C, Myrtle Beach 29577; (843) 445-6459; Fax: (843) 445-6418; *Field Representative:* Katherin Jenrette
5900 Core Ave., #401, N. Charleston 29406; (843) 747-4175; Fax: (843) 747-4711; *District Director:* Kathy Crawford
Committee Assignment(s): Budget; Transportation and Infrastructure; Veterans' Affairs

BROWN, SHERROD, D-OHIO (13)

Capitol Hill Office: 2332 RHOB 20515; 225-3401; Fax: 225-2266; *Chief of Staff:* Donna Pignatelli
Web: www.house.gov/sherrodbrown
E-mail: sherrod@mail.house.gov
District Office(s): 1655 W. Market St., Suite E, Akron 44313; (330) 865-8450; Fax: (330) 865-8470; *Community Liaison:* Pam Walker
5201 Abbe Rd., Elyria 44035; (440) 934-5100; Fax: (440) 934-5145; *District Director:* Elizabeth Thames
Committee Assignment(s): Energy and Commerce; International Relations

BROWN-WAITE, GINNY, R-FLA. (5)

Capitol Hill Office: 1516 LHOB 20515; 225-1002; Fax: 226-6559; *Chief of Staff:* Brian Walsh
Web: www.house.gov/brown-waite
E-mail: www.house.gov/writerep
District Office(s): 20 N. Main St., #200, Brooksville 34601; (352) 799-8354; Fax: (352) 799-8776; *District Director:* Shirley Anderson
38008 Meridian Ave., Suite A, Dade City 33525; (352) 567-6707; Fax: (352) 567-6259; *District Representative:* Joy Hampton
Committee Assignment(s): Budget; Financial Services; Veterans' Affairs

BURGESS, MICHAEL C., R-TEXAS (26)

Capitol Hill Office: 1721 LHOB 20515; 225-7772; Fax: 225-2919; *Chief of Staff:* Barry Brown
Web: www.house.gov/burgess
E-mail: www.house.gov/writerep
District Office(s): 1660 S. Stemmons Freeway, #230, Lewisville 75067; (972) 434-9700; Fax: (972) 434-9705; *District Director:* John Gonzales
Committee Assignment(s): Science; Transportation and Infrastructure

BURNS, MAX, R-GA. (12)

Capitol Hill Office: 512 CHOB 20515; 225-2823; Fax: 225-3377; *Chief of Staff:* Chris Ingram
Web: www.house.gov/burns
E-mail: www.house.gov/burns/html/contact_email.html
District Office(s): 2743 Perimeter Pkwy., Bldg. 200, #130, Augusta 30909; (706) 854-4595; Fax: (706) 854-7876; *District Director:* Nancy Bobbitt
6605 Abercorn St., #102, Savannah 31405; (912) 352-1736; Fax: (912) 352-4896; *District Representative:* Roland Stubbs
Committee Assignment(s): Agriculture; Education and Workforce; Transportation and Infrastructure

BURR, RICHARD M., R-N.C. (5)

Capitol Hill Office: 1526 LHOB 20515; 225-2071; Fax: 225-2995; *Chief of Staff:* Vacant

Web: www.house.gov/burr
E-mail: richard.burrnc05@mail.house.gov
District Office(s): Piedmont Plaza Two, 2000 W. 1st St., #508, Winston Salem 27104; (336) 631-5125; Fax: (336) 725-4493; *District Director:* L. Dean Myers
Committee Assignment(s): Energy and Commerce; Select Intelligence

BURTON, DAN, R-IND. (5)

Capitol Hill Office: 2185 RHOB 20515; 225-2276; Fax: 225-0016; *Chief of Staff:* Mark Walker
Web: www.house.gov/burton
E-mail: www.house.gov/writerep
District Office(s): 209 S. Washington St., Marion 46952; (765) 662-6770; Fax: (765) 662-6775; *Special Assistant:* Tresa Baker
8900 Keystone at the Crossing, #1050, Indianapolis 46240; (317) 848-0201; Fax: (317) 846-7306; *District Director:* Michael A. Delph
Committee Assignment(s): Government Reform; International Relations

BUYER, STEVE, R-IND. (4)

Capitol Hill Office: 2230 RHOB 20515; 225-5037; Fax: 225-2267; *Chief of Staff:* Mike Copher
Web: www.house.gov/buyer
E-mail: www.house.gov/writerep
District Office(s): 148 N. Perry Rd., Plainfield 46168; (317) 838-0404; *District Director:* Jim Huston
100 S. Main St., Monticello 47960; (219) 583-9819; Fax: (219) 583-9867; *District Operations Director:* Brandt Hershman
Committee Assignment(s): Energy and Commerce; Veterans' Affairs

CALVERT, KEN, R-CALIF. (44)

Capitol Hill Office: 2201 RHOB 20515; 225-1986; Fax: 225-2004; *Chief of Staff:* Dave Ramey
Web: www.house.gov/calvert
E-mail: www.house.gov/writerep
District Office(s): 3400 Central Ave., #200, Riverside 92506; (909) 784-4300; Fax: (909) 784-5255; *District Director:* Linda Fisher
Committee Assignment(s): Armed Services; Resources; Science

CAMP, DAVE, R-MICH. (4)

Capitol Hill Office: 137 CHOB 20515; 225-3561; Fax: 225-9679; *Chief of Staff:* Jim Brandell
Web: www.house.gov/camp
E-mail: www.house.gov/writerep
District Office(s): 121 E. Front St, #202, Traverse City 49684; (231) 929-4711; Fax: (231) 929-4776
135 Ashman Dr., Midland 48640; (989) 631-2552; Fax: (989) 631-6271; *District Director:* Eric Friedman

Committee Assignment(s): Select Homeland Security; Ways and Means

CANNON, CHRIS, R-UTAH (3)

Capitol Hill Office: 118 CHOB 20515; 225-7751; Fax: 225-5629; *Chief of Staff:* Chris MacKay
Web: www.house.gov/cannon
E-mail: cannon.ut03@mail.house.gov
District Office(s): 51 S. University Ave., #317, Provo 84606; (801) 379-2500; Fax: (801) 379-2509; *District Director:* Dee Dee Rose
Committee Assignment(s): Government Reform; Judiciary; Resources

CANTOR, ERIC, R-VA. (7)

Capitol Hill Office: 329 CHOB 20515; 225-2815; Fax: 225-0011; *Chief of Staff:* Boyd Marcus
Web: cantor.house.gov
E-mail: cantor.house.gov/email
District Office(s): 763 Madison Rd., #207, Culpeper 22701; (540) 825-8960; Fax: (540) 825-8964; *District Representative:* Barbara Taylor
5040 Sadler Place, #110, Glen Allen 23060; (804) 747-4073; Fax: (804) 747-5308; *District Director:* Kristi Way
Committee Assignment(s): Ways and Means

CAPITO, SHELLEY MOORE, R-W.VA. (2)

Capitol Hill Office: 1431 LHOB 20515; 225-2711; Fax: 225-7856; *Chief of Staff:* Mark G. Johnson
Web: www.house.gov/capito
E-mail: www.house.gov/writerep
District Office(s): 4815 MacCorkle Ave. S.E., Charleston 25304; (304) 925-5964; Fax: (304) 926-8912; *District Director:* Anne McCuskey
222 W. John St., Martinsburg 25401; (304) 264-8810; Fax: (304) 264-8815; *District Representative:* John Reisenweber
Committee Assignment(s): Financial Services; Small Business; Transportation and Infrastructure

CAPPS, LOIS, D-CALIF. (23)

Capitol Hill Office: 1707 LHOB 20515; 225-3601; Fax: 225-5632; *Chief of Staff:* Jeremy Rabinovitz
Web: www.house.gov/capps
E-mail: www.house.gov/writerep
District Office(s): 1216 State St., #405, Santa Barbara 93101; (805) 730-1710; Fax: (805) 730-9153; *District Director:* Sharon Siegel
1411 Marsh St., #205, San Luis Obispo 93401; (805) 546-8348; Fax: (805) 546-8368; *District Representative:* Betsey Umhofer
141 S. A St., #204, Oxnard 93030; (805) 385-3440; Fax: (805) 385-3399; *District Representative:* Chris Henson
Committee Assignment(s): Budget; Energy and Commerce

CAPUANO, MICHAEL E., D-MASS. (8)

Capitol Hill Office: 1232 LHOB 20515; 225-5111; Fax: 225-9322; *Chief of Staff:* Robert Primus
Web: www.house.gov/capuano
E-mail: www.house.gov/writerep
District Office(s): 110 1st St., Cambridge 02141; (617) 621-6208; Fax: (617) 621-8628; *District Director:* Mike Gorman
Roxbury Community College, Administration Bldg., #110, Roxbury 02120; (617) 621-6208; Fax: (617) 541-6909; *District Representative:* Ego Ezedi
Committee Assignment(s): Financial Services; Transportation and Infrastructure

CARDIN, BENJAMIN L., D-MD. (3)

Capitol Hill Office: 2207 RHOB 20515; 225-4016; Fax: 225-9219; *Chief of Staff:* Christopher Lynch
Web: www.house.gov/cardin
E-mail: rep.cardin@mail.house.gov
District Office(s): 600 Wyndhurst Ave., #230, Baltimore 21210; (410) 433-8886; Fax: (410) 433-2110; *District Office Director:* Bailey E. Fine
Committee Assignment(s): Select Homeland Security; Ways and Means

CARDOZA, DENNIS, D-CALIF. (18)

Capitol Hill Office: 503 CHOB 20515; 225-6131; Fax: 225-0819; *Administrative Assistant:* Jennifer Walsh
Web: www.house.gov/cardoza
E-mail: www.house.gov/writerep
District Office(s): 415 W. 18th St., Merced 95340; (209) 383-4455; Fax: (209) 726-1065; *Chief of Staff:* Mark Garrett
1321 I St., #1, Modesto 95354; (209) 527-1914; Fax: (209) 527-5748; *Field Representative:* Lisa Mantarro Moore
445 W. Weber Ave., #240, Stockton 95203; (209) 946-0361; Fax: (209) 946-0347; *Field Representative:* Angela Brady
Committee Assignment(s): Agriculture; Resources; Science

CARSON, BRAD, D-OKLA. (2)

Capitol Hill Office: 317 CHOB 20515; 225-2701; Fax: 225-3038; *Chief of Staff:* Chebon Marshall
Web: carson.house.gov
E-mail: brad.carson@mail.house.gov
District Office(s): 403 W. 1st St., #100, Claremore 74017; (918) 341-9336; Fax: (918) 341-9437; *District Director:* Marguerite McKinney
215 State St., #815, Muskogee 74401; (918) 687-2533; Fax: (918) 682-8503; *District Director:* Sue Bollinger
Committee Assignment(s): Resources; Transportation and Infrastructure

CARSON, JULIA, D-IND. (7)

Capitol Hill Office: 1535 LHOB 20515; 225-4011; Fax: 225-5633; *Deputy Chief of Staff:* Daren Roberson
Web: www.house.gov/carson
E-mail: rep.carson@mail.house.gov
District Office(s): 300 E. Fall Creek Pkwy., #201, Indianapolis 46205; (317) 283-6516; Fax: (317) 283-6567; *District Director:* Melody Barber
Committee Assignment(s): Financial Services; Transportation and Infrastructure

CARTER, JOHN, R-TEXAS (31)

Capitol Hill Office: 408 CHOB 20515; 225-3864; Fax: 225-5886; *Chief of Staff:* Chris Giblin
Web: www.house.gov/carter
E-mail: www.house.gov/writerep
District Office(s): 1111 University Dr. East, #216, College Station 77840; (979) 846-6068; Fax: (979) 260-2916; *Regional Director:* Jason Schneider
1 Financial Center, Hwy. 35, #303, Round Rock 78664; (512) 246-1600; Fax: (512) 246-1620; *District Director:* Travis Lucas
Committee Assignment(s): Education and Workforce; Government Reform; Judiciary

CASE, ED, D-HAWAII (2)

Capitol Hill Office: 128 CHOB 20515; 225-4906; Fax: 225-4987; *Chief of Staff:* Esther Kiaaina
Web: www.house.gov/case
E-mail: ed.case@mail.house.gov
District Office(s): 5104 Prince Kuhio Federal Bldg., 300 Ala Moana Blvd., Honolulu 96580; (808) 541-1986; Fax: (808) 538-0233; *District Director:* Jimmy Nakatani
Committee Assignment(s): Agriculture; Education and Workforce; Small Business

CASTLE, MICHAEL N., R-DEL. (AT LARGE)

Capitol Hill Office: 1233 LHOB 20515; 225-4165; Fax: 225-2291; *Chief of Staff:* Paul Leonard
Web: www.house.gov/castle
E-mail: delaware@mail.house.gov
District Office(s): 201 N. Walnut St., #107, Wilmington 19801; (302) 428-1902; Fax: (302) 428-1950; *District Director:* Jeffrey A. Dayton
300 S. New St., #2005, Dover 19904; (302) 736-1666; Fax: (302) 736-6580; *Field Representative:* Kate Rohrer
Committee Assignment(s): Education and Workforce; Financial Services

CHABOT, STEVE, R-OHIO (1)

Capitol Hill Office: 129 CHOB 20515; 225-2216; Fax: 225-3012; *Legislative Director:* Kevin Fitzpatrick
Web: www.house.gov/chabot
E-mail: www.house.gov/writerep

District Office(s): 441 Vine St., #3003, Cincinnati 45202; (513) 684-2723; Fax: (513) 421-8722; *District Director:* Mike Cantwell
Committee Assignment(s): International Relations; Judiciary; Small Business

CHOCOLA, CHRIS, R-IND. (2)

Capitol Hill Office: 510 CHOB 20515; 225-3915; Fax: 225-6798; *Chief of Staff:* Brooks Kochvar
Web: www.house.gov/chocola
E-mail: www.house.gov/chocola/webmail.html
District Office(s): 100 E. Wayne St., #330, South Bend 46601; (574) 251-0896; Fax: (574) 251-1066; *District Director:* Christopher Faulkner
444 Mall Rd., Logansport 46947; (574) 753-4700; Fax: (574) 753-4730; *District Representative:* Penny Titus
Committee Assignment(s): Agriculture; Small Business; Transportation and Infrastructure

CHRISTENSEN, DONNA M. C., D-VIRGIN IS. (AT LARGE)

Capitol Hill Office: 1510 LHOB 20515; 225-1790; Fax: 225-5517; *Chief of Staff:* Monique Clendinen
Web: www.house.gov/christian-christensen
E-mail: donna.christensen@mail.house.gov
District Office(s): Nisky Business Center, #207, 2nd Floor, St. Thomas 00801; (340) 774-4408; Fax: (340) 774-8033; *Office Manager:* Shawn Malone
P.O. Box 5980, Space #3 Mini Mall, Sunny Isle Shopping Center, St. Croix 00823; (340) 778-5900; Fax: (340) 778-5111; *District Director:* Claire Roker
Committee Assignment(s): Resources; Select Homeland Security; Small Business

CLAY, WILLIAM LACY, D-MO. (1)

Capitol Hill Office: 131 CHOB 20515; 225-2406; Fax: 225-1725; *Chief of Staff:* Harriet Grigsby
Web: www.house.gov/clay
E-mail: www.house.gov/writerep
District Office(s): 625 N. Euclid St., #200, St. Louis 63108; (314) 367-1970; *District Director:* Darryl Piggee
8525 Page Blvd., St. Louis 63114; (314) 890-0349; *District Manager:* Edwilla Massey
Committee Assignment(s): Financial Services; Government Reform

CLYBURN, JAMES E., D-S.C. (6)

Capitol Hill Office: 2135 RHOB 20515; 225-3315; Fax: 225-2313; *Chief of Staff:* Yelberton Watkins
Web: www.house.gov/clyburn
E-mail: jclyburn@mail.house.gov
District Office(s): 1703 Gervais St., Columbia 29201; (803) 799-1100; Fax: (803) 799-9060; *District Director:* Robert M. Nance

2106 Mount Pleasant St., #7, Charleston 29405; (843) 965-5578; Fax: (843) 965-5581; *Area Director:* Davis Marshall Business and Technology Center, 181 E. Evans St., #314, Florence 29506; (843) 662-1212; Fax: (843) 662-8474; *Area Director:* Charlene Lowery

Committee Assignment(s): Appropriations

COBLE, HOWARD, R-N.C. (6)

Capitol Hill Office: 2468 RHOB 20515; 225-3065; Fax: 225-8611; *Chief of Staff:* Missy Branson
Web: www.house.gov/coble
E-mail: howard.coble@mail.house.gov
District Office(s): 124 Elm St., P.O. Box 812, Graham 27253; (336) 229-0159; Fax: (336) 228-7974; *District Representative:* Janine Osborne
2727D Old Concord Rd., Salisbury 28144; (704) 645-8082; Fax: (704) 645-0896; *District Representative:* Terri Welch
241 Sunset Ave., #101, Asheboro 27203; (336) 626-3060; Fax: (336) 629-7819; *District Representative:* Rebecca Redding
2102 N. Elm St., Suite B, Greensboro 27408; (336) 333-5005; Fax: (336) 333-5048; *Office Manager:* Chris Beaman
155 Northpoint Ave., #200-B, High Point 27262; (336) 886-5106; Fax: (336) 886-8740; *District Representative:* Nancy Mazza

Committee Assignment(s): Judiciary; Transportation and Infrastructure

COLE, TOM, R-OKLA. (4)

Capitol Hill Office: 501 CHOB 20515; 225-6165; Fax: 225-3512; *Chief of Staff:* Leslie Sowell
Web: www.house.gov/cole
E-mail: tom.cole@mail.house.gov
District Office(s): 2420 Springer Dr., #120, Norman 73069; (405) 329-6500; Fax: (405) 321-7369; *District Director:* John Woods

Committee Assignment(s): Armed Services; Education and Workforce; Resources

COLLINS, MAC, R-GA. (8)

Capitol Hill Office: 1131 LHOB 20515; 225-5901; Fax: 225-2515; *Administrative Assistant:* Bo Bryant
Web: www.house.gov/maccollins
E-mail: www.house.gov/maccollins/authen.html
District Office(s): 1125 Meredith Park Dr., McDonough 30252; (678) 583-6500; Fax: (678) 583-6535; *Regional District Director:* Fred Chitwood
5820 Veterans Pkwy., #305, Columbus 31904; (706) 327-7228; Fax: (706) 324-7969; *Constituent Representative:* Ted Jones
20 Baker Rd., #9, Newnan 30265; (770) 683-4622; Fax: (770) 683-4630; *Constituent Representative:* Martin Smith

Committee Assignment(s): Select Intelligence; Ways and Means

COMBEST, LARRY, R-TEXAS (19)

Capitol Hill Office: 1026 LHOB 20515; 225-4005; Fax: 225-9615; *Chief of Staff:* Rob Lehman
Web: www.house.gov/combest
E-mail: www.house.gov/writerep
District Office(s): 5809 S. Western Ave., #205, Amarillo 79110; (806) 353-3945; Fax: (806) 353-6107; *Staff Assistant:* Jessica Detten
1205 Texas Ave., #810, Lubbock 79401; (806) 763-1611; Fax: (806) 767-9168; *District Representative:* Jimmy Clark
3800 E. 42nd St., #205, Odessa 79762; (915) 550-0743; Fax: (915) 550-0852; *Office Manager:* Jenny Welch

Committee Assignment(s): Agriculture; Small Business

CONYERS, JOHN JR., D-MICH. (14)

Capitol Hill Office: 2426 RHOB 20515; 225-5126; Fax: 225-0072; *Legislative Director:* Cynthia Martin
Web: www.house.gov/conyers
E-mail: john.conyers@mail.house.gov
District Office(s): 231 W. Lafayette Blvd., #669, Detroit 48226; (313) 961-5670; Fax: (313) 226-2085; *Chief of Staff:* Ray Plowden

Committee Assignment(s): Judiciary

COOPER, JIM, D-TENN. (5)

Capitol Hill Office: 1536 LHOB 20515; 225-4311; Fax: 226-1035; *Chief of Staff:* Greg Hinote
Web: www.house.gov/cooper
E-mail: jim.cooper@mail.house.gov
District Office(s): 706 Church St., #101, Nashville 37203; (615) 736-5295; Fax: (615) 736-7479; *Office Manager:* Kathy Floyd-Buggs

Committee Assignment(s): Armed Services; Budget; Government Reform

COSTELLO, JERRY F., D-ILL. (12)

Capitol Hill Office: 2454 RHOB 20515; 225-5661; Fax: 225-0285; *Chief of Staff:* David C. Gillies
Web: www.house.gov/costello
E-mail: www.house.gov/writerep
District Office(s): 1363 Neidringhaus Ave., Granite City 62040; (618) 451-7065; Fax: (618) 451-2126; *Staff Assistant:* David Cueto
8787 State St., East St. Louis 62203; (618) 397-8833; Fax: (618) 233-8765; *Staff Assistant:* Mel Frierson
155 Lincoln Place Court, Belleville 62221; (618) 233-8026; Fax: (618) 233-8765; *District Manager:* Frank Miles
250 W. Cherry St., Carbondale 62901; (618) 529-3791; Fax: (618) 233-8765; *Staff Assistant:* Alice Tucker
1330 Swanwick St., Chester 62233; (618) 826-3043; Fax: (618) 233-8765; *Staff Assistant:* Patsie Travelstead
201 W. Nolen St., West Frankfort 62896; (618) 937-6402; Fax: (618) 937-3307; *Staff Assistant:* Vacant

Committee Assignment(s): Science; Transportation and Infrastructure

COX, CHRISTOPHER, R-CALIF. (48)

Capitol Hill Office: 2402 RHOB 20515; 225-5611; Fax: 225-9177; *Chief of Staff:* Peter Uhlmann
Web: cox.house.gov
E-mail: christopher.cox@mail.house.gov
District Office(s): 1 Newport Place, #1010, Newport Beach 92660; (949) 756-2244; Fax: (949) 251-9309; *District Director:* Jim Fournier
Committee Assignment(s): Energy and Commerce; Select Homeland Security

CRAMER, ROBERT E. "BUD," D-ALA. (5)

Capitol Hill Office: 2368 RHOB 20515; 225-4801; Fax: 225-4392; *Chief of Staff:* Carter Wells
Web: www.house.gov/cramer
E-mail: budmail@mail.house.gov
District Office(s): Morgan County Courthouse, 302 Lee St., 5th Floor, #86, Decatur 35601; (256) 355-9400; Fax: (256) 355-9406; *Caseworker:* Peggy Allen
The Bevill Center for Advanced Technology, 1011 George Wallace Blvd., Tuscumbia 35674; (256) 381-3450; Fax: (256) 381-7659; *Caseworker:* Gary Chandler
626 Clinton Ave. West, Huntsville 35801; (256) 551-0190; Fax: (256) 551-0194; *District Director:* Howell Lee
Committee Assignment(s): Appropriations; Select Intelligence

CRANE, PHILIP M., R-ILL. (8)

Capitol Hill Office: 233 CHOB 20515; 225-3711; Fax: 225-7830; *Chief of Staff:* Jim Hayes
Web: www.house.gov/crane
District Office(s): 300 N. Milwaukee Ave., Suite C, Lake Villa 60046; (847) 265-9000; Fax: (847) 265-9028; *Caseworker:* Carol Toft
1100 W. Northwest Hwy., Palatine 60067; (847) 358-9160; Fax: (847) 358-9185; *Caseworker:* Linda Reed
Committee Assignment(s): Joint Taxation; Ways and Means

CRENSHAW, ANDER, R-FLA. (4)

Capitol Hill Office: 127 CHOB 20515; 225-2501; Fax: 225-2504; *Chief of Staff:* John Ariale
Web: www.house.gov/crenshaw
E-mail: www.house.gov/writerep
District Office(s): 1061 Riverside Ave., #100, Jacksonville 32204; (904) 598-0481; Fax: (904) 598-0486; *District Director:* Jackie Smith
Committee Assignment(s): Appropriations; Budget

CROWLEY, JOSEPH, D-N.Y. (7)

Capitol Hill Office: 312 CHOB 20515; 225-3965; Fax: 225-1909; *Chief of Staff:* Christopher McCannell
Web: www.house.gov/crowley
E-mail: write2joecrowley@mail.house.gov

District Office(s): 3425 E. Tremont Ave., #1-3, Bronx 10465; (718) 931-1400; Fax: (718) 931-1340; *Office Manager:* Fran Mahoney
177 Dreiser Loop, #3, Bronx 10475; (718) 320-2390
82-11 37th Ave., #607, Jackson Heights 11372; (718) 779-1400; Fax: (718) 505-0156; *District Director:* Annemarie Anzalone
Committee Assignment(s): Financial Services; International Relations

CUBIN, BARBARA, R-WYO. (AT LARGE)

Capitol Hill Office: 1114 LHOB 20515; 225-2311; Fax: 225-3057; *Chief of Staff:* Tom Wiblemo
Web: www.house.gov/cubin
E-mail: barbara.cubin@mail.house.gov
District Office(s): 2120 Capital Ave., #2015, Cheyenne 82001; (307) 772-2595; Fax: (307) 772-2597; *Field Representative:* Katie Legerski
100 E. B St., #4003, Casper 82601; (307) 261-6595; Fax: (307) 261-6597; *State Director:* Kyra Hageman
2515 Foothills Blvd., #204, Rock Springs 82901; (307) 362-4095; Fax: (307) 362-4097; *Field Representative:* Bonnie Cannon
Committee Assignment(s): Energy and Commerce; Resources

CULBERSON, JOHN, R-TEXAS (7)

Capitol Hill Office: 1728 LHOB 20515; 225-2571; Fax: 225-4381; *Administrative Assistant:* Tony Essalih
Web: www.culberson.house.gov
E-mail: www.house.gov/writerep
District Office(s): 10000 Memorial Dr., #620, Houston 77024; (713) 682-8828; Fax: (713) 680-8070; *District Director:* Jan Crow
Committee Assignment(s): Appropriations

CUMMINGS, ELIJAH E., D-MD. (7)

Capitol Hill Office: 1632 LHOB 20515; 225-4741; Fax: 225-3178; *Chief of Staff:* Vernon Simms
Web: www.house.gov/cummings
E-mail: www.house.gov/writerep
District Office(s): 1010 Park Ave., #105, Baltimore 21201; (410) 685-9199; Fax: (410) 685-9399; *Chief of Staff:* Vernon Simms
754 Frederick Rd., Catonsville 21228; (410) 719-8777; Fax: (410) 455-0110; *Special Assistant:* Frank Amtmann
Committee Assignment(s): Government Reform; Transportation and Infrastructure

CUNNINGHAM, RANDY "DUKE," R-CALIF. (50)

Capitol Hill Office: 2350 RHOB 20515; 225-5452; Fax: 225-2558; *Chief of Staff:* David Heil
Web: www.house.gov/cunningham
E-mail: www.house.gov/cunningham/IMA/get_address3.htm

District Office(s): 613 W. Valley Pkwy., #320, Escondido 92025; (760) 737-8438; Fax: (760) 737-9132; *District Director:* Nathan Fletcher

Committee Assignment(s): Appropriations; Select Intelligence

DAVIS, ARTUR, D-ALA. (7)

Capitol Hill Office: 208 CHOB 20515; 225-2665; Fax: 226-9567; *Chief of Staff:* Dana Gresham

Web: www.house.gov/arturdavis

District Office(s): 1728 N. 3rd Ave., #400B-2, Birmingham 35203; (205) 254-1960; Fax: (205) 254-1974; *District Director:* Sharon Rose

102 E. Washington St., Suite F, Demopolis 36732; (334) 287-8060; Fax: (334) 287-0870; *Field Representative:* Audrey Haskin

205 N. Washington St., #236-237, Livingston 35470; (205) 652-5834; Fax: (205) 625-5935; *Field Representative:* Kay Presley

908 Alabama Ave., #109, Selma 36701; (334) 877-4414; Fax: (334) 877-4489; *Field Representative:* Kobi Little

1118 Greensboro Ave., #336, Tuscaloosa 35401; (205) 752-5380; Fax: (205) 752-5899; *Field Representative:* Cynthia Burton

Committee Assignment(s): Budget; Financial Services

DAVIS, DANNY K., D-ILL. (7)

Capitol Hill Office: 1222 LHOB 20515; 225-5006; Fax: 225-5641; *Chief of Staff:* Richard Boykin

Web: www.house.gov/davis

E-mail: www.house.gov/writerep

District Office(s): 3333 W. Arthington St., #130, Chicago 60624; (773) 533-7520; Fax: (773) 533-7530; *District Director:* F. Daniel Cantrell

Committee Assignment(s): Education and Workforce; Government Reform; Small Business

DAVIS, JIM, D-FLA. (11)

Capitol Hill Office: 409 CHOB 20515; 225-3376; Fax: 225-5652; *Chief of Staff:* Karl Koch

Web: www.house.gov/jimdavis

E-mail: www.house.gov/writerep

District Office(s): 3315 Henderson Blvd., #100, Tampa 33609; (813) 354-9217; Fax: (813) 354-9514; *District Director:* John Keynes

Committee Assignment(s): Energy and Commerce

DAVIS, JO ANN, R-VA. (1)

Capitol Hill Office: 1123 LHOB 20515; 225-4261; Fax: 225-4382; *Chief of Staff:* Chris Connelly

Web: www.house.gov/joanndavis

E-mail: www.house.gov/writerep

District Office(s): 1623 Tappahannock Blvd., Tappahannock 22560; (804) 443-0668; Fax: (804) 443-0671; *District Representative:* Ruth Jessie

450 Plank Rd., #105A, Fredericksburg 22401; (540) 548-1086; Fax: (540) 548-1658; *District Representative:* John Goolrick

4904-B George Washington Memorial Hwy., Yorktown 23692; (757) 874-6687; Fax: (757) 874-7164; *District Director:* Joe Schumacher

Committee Assignment(s): Armed Services; Government Reform; International Relations

DAVIS, LINCOLN, D-TENN. (4)

Capitol Hill Office: 504 CHOB 20515; 225-6831; Fax: 226-5172; *Chief of Staff:* Beecher Frasier

Web: www.house.gov/lincolndavis

E-mail: www.house.gov/writerep

District Office(s): 1804 Carmack Blvd., Suite A, Columbia 38401; (931) 490-8699; Fax: (931) 490-8675; *Constituent Services Coordinator:* Bill Mason

629 N. Main St., Jamestown 38556; (931) 879-2361; Fax: (931) 879-2389; *Field Representative:* John Robbins

1064 N. Gateway Ave., Rockwood 37854; (865) 354-3323; Fax: (865) 354-3316; *Constituent Services Representative:* Sammy Lowdermilk

Committee Assignment(s): Agriculture; Science; Transportation and Infrastructure

DAVIS, SUSAN A., D-CALIF. (53)

Capitol Hill Office: 1224 LHOB 20515; 225-2040; Fax: 225-2948; *Chief of Staff:* Lisa Sherman

Web: www.house.gov/susandavis

E-mail: susan.davis@mail.house.gov

District Office(s): 4305 University Ave., #515, San Diego 92110; (619) 280-5353; Fax: (619) 280-5311; *District Director:* Todd Alona

Committee Assignment(s): Armed Services; Education and Workforce; Veterans' Affairs

DAVIS, THOMAS M. III, R-VA. (11)

Capitol Hill Office: 2348 RHOB 20515; 225-1492; Fax: 225-3071; *Chief of Staff:* Peter Sirh

Web: www.house.gov/tomdavis

E-mail: tom.davis@mail.house.gov

District Office(s): 4115 Annandale Rd., #103, Annandale 22003; (703) 916-9610; Fax: (703) 916-9617; *District Director:* Dave Foreman

13546 Minnieville Rd., Woodbridge 22192; (703) 590-4599; Fax: (703) 590-4740; *Constituent Services Representative:* Brian Gordon

Committee Assignment(s): Government Reform

DEAL, NATHAN, R-GA. (10)

Capitol Hill Office: 2437 RHOB 20515; 225-5211; Fax: 225-8272; *Chief of Staff:* Chris Riley

Web: www.house.gov/deal

E-mail: www.house.gov/writerep

District Office(s): 340 Jesse Jewell Pkwy., #520, Gainesville 30503; (770) 535-2592; Fax: (770) 535-2765; *District Director:* Jim Adams

415 E. Walnut Ave., #108, Dalton 30721; (706) 226-5320; Fax: (706) 278-0840; *Staff Assistant:* Vivian Campbell

108 W. Lafayette Square, #102, Lafayette 30728; (706) 638-7042; Fax: (706) 638-7049; *Staff Assistant:* Lonna Hightower

Committee Assignment(s): Energy and Commerce; Government Reform

DEFAZIO, PETER A., D-ORE. (4)

Capitol Hill Office: 2134 RHOB 20515; 225-6416; Fax: 225-0032; *Administrative Assistant:* Penny Dodge

Web: www.house.gov/defazio

E-mail: www.house.gov/writerep

District Office(s): 151 W. 7th Ave., #400, Eugene 97401; (541) 465-6732; Fax: (541) 465-6458; *District Director:* Karmen Fore

P.O. Box 1557, 125 Central, #250, Coos Bay 97420; (541) 269-2609; Fax: (541) 269-5760; *Field Representative:* Ron Kresky

P.O. Box 2460, 612 S.E. Jackson St. #9, Roseburg 97470; (541) 440-3523; Fax: (541) 440-3525; *Field Representative:* Chris Conroy

Committee Assignment(s): Select Homeland Security; Transportation and Infrastructure

DEGETTE, DIANA, D-COLO. (1)

Capitol Hill Office: 1530 LHOB 20515; 225-4431; Fax: 225-5657; *Chief of Staff:* Lisa Cohen

Web: www.house.gov/degette

E-mail: degette@mail.house.gov

District Office(s): 1600 Downing St., #550, Denver 80218; (303) 844-4988; Fax: (303) 844-4996; *District Director:* Greg Diamond

Committee Assignment(s): Energy and Commerce

DELAHUNT, BILL, D-MASS. (10)

Capitol Hill Office: 1317 LHOB 20515; 225-3111; Fax: 225-5658; *Chief of Staff:* Steve Schwadron

Web: www.house.gov/delahunt

E-mail: william.delahunt@mail.house.gov

District Office(s): 1250 Hancock St., #802-N, Quincy 02169; (617) 770-3700; Fax: (617) 770-2984; *District Director:* Corinne Young

146 Main St., Hyannis 02601; (508) 771-0666; Fax: (508) 790-1959; *Regional Representative:* Mark Forest

Committee Assignment(s): International Relations; Judiciary

DELAURO, ROSA, D-CONN. (3)

Capitol Hill Office: 2262 RHOB 20515; 225-3661; Fax: 225-4890; *Chief of Staff:* Richard Woodruff

Web: www.house.gov/delauro

E-mail: www.house.gov/delauro/message.html

District Office(s): 59 Elm St., 2nd Floor, New Haven 06510; (203) 562-3718; Fax: (203) 772-2260; *District Director:* Jennifer Emra

Committee Assignment(s): Appropriations; Budget

DELAY, TOM, R-TEXAS (22)

Capitol Hill Office: 242 CHOB 20515; 225-5951; Fax: 225-5241; *Chief of Staff:* Timothy Berry

Web: majorityleader.gov

E-mail: www.house.gov/writerep

District Office(s): 10701 Corporate Dr., #118, Stafford 77477; (281) 240-3700; Fax: (281) 240-2959; *District Director:* Ann Travis

Committee Assignment(s): No committee assignments

DEMINT, JIM, R-S.C. (4)

Capitol Hill Office: 432 CHOB 20515; 225-6030; Fax: 226-1177; *Chief of Staff:* Matt Hoskins

Web: www.demint.house.gov

E-mail: www.house.gov/writerep

District Office(s): P.O. Box 1169, Union 29379; (864) 427-2205; *Field Representative:* Kelly Long

300 E. Washington St., #101, Greenville 29601; (864) 232-1141; Fax: (864) 233-2160; *District Director:* Jason Elliott

Business Technology Center, 145 N. Church St., #302, Spartanburg 29301; (864) 582-6722; Fax: (864) 233-2160; *Field Representative:* Kelly Long

Committee Assignment(s): Education and Workforce; Small Business; Transportation and Infrastructure

DEUTSCH, PETER, D-FLA. (20)

Capitol Hill Office: 2303 RHOB 20515; 225-7931; Fax: 225-8456; *Chief of Staff:* Marcus Jadotte

Web: www.house.gov/deutsch

E-mail: www.house.gov/writerep

District Office(s): 10100 Pines Blvd., Pembroke Pines 33026; (954) 437-3936; Fax: (954) 437-4776; *District Director:* Jennifer Irving

1010 Kennedy Dr., #310, Key West 33040; (305) 294-5815; Fax: (305) 294-4193; *Monroe County Representative:* Becky Iannotta

Committee Assignment(s): Energy and Commerce

DIAZ-BALART, LINCOLN, R-FLA. (21)

Capitol Hill Office: 2244 RHOB 20515; 225-4211; Fax: 225-8576; *Chief of Staff:* Stephen Vermillion

Web: www.house.gov/diaz-balart

E-mail: www.house.gov/writerep

District Office(s): 8525 N.W. 53rd Terrace, #102, Miami 33166; (305) 470-8555; Fax: (305) 470-8575; *District Director:* Ana M. Carbonell

Committee Assignment(s): Rules; Select Homeland Security

DIAZ-BALART, MARIO, R-FLA. (25)

Capitol Hill Office: 313 CHOB 20515; 225-2778; Fax: 226-0346; *Chief of Staff:* Omar Franco
Web: www.house.gov/mariodiaz-balart
E-mail: www.house.gov/writerep
District Office(s): 12851 S.W. 42nd St., #131, Miami 33175; (305) 225-6866; Fax: (305) 225-7432; *District Director:* Miguel Otero
4715 Golden Gate Pkwy., #1, Naples 34116; (239) 348-1620; Fax: (239) 348-3569; *District Representative:* Stephen Hart
Committee Assignment(s): Budget; Transportation and Infrastructure

DICKS, NORM, D-WASH. (6)

Capitol Hill Office: 2467 RHOB 20515; 225-5916; Fax: 226-1176; *Office Manager:* Donna Taylor
Web: www.house.gov/dicks
E-mail: www.house.gov/writerep
District Office(s): 332 E. 5th St., Port Angeles 98362; (360) 452-3370; *District Representative:* Mary Schuneman
500 Pacific Ave., #301, Bremerton 98310; (360) 479-4011; Fax: (360) 553-7445; *County Director:* Cheri Williams
1717 Pacific Ave., #2244, Tacoma 98402; (253) 593-6536; Fax: (253) 593-6551; *District Director:* Bryan McConaughy
Committee Assignment(s): Appropriations; Select Homeland Security

DINGELL, JOHN D., D-MICH. (15)

Capitol Hill Office: 2328 RHOB 20515; 225-4071; Fax: 226-0371; *Chief of Staff:* Vacant
Web: www.house.gov/dingell
E-mail: www.house.gov/writerep
District Office(s): 19855 W. Outer Dr., #103E, Dearborn 48124; (313) 278-2936; Fax: (313) 278-3914; *District Administrator:* Terrance Spryzsak
23 E. Front St., #103, Monroe 48161; (734) 243-1849; Fax: (734) 243-5559; *Office Manager:* Donna Hoffer
Committee Assignment(s): Energy and Commerce

DOGGETT, LLOYD, D-TEXAS (10)

Capitol Hill Office: 201 CHOB 20515; 225-4865; Fax: 225-3073; *Chief of Staff:* Michael Mucchetti
Web: www.house.gov/doggett
E-mail: lloyd.doggett@mail.house.gov
District Office(s): 300 E. 8th St., #763, Austin 78701; (512) 916-5921; Fax: (512) 916-5108; *District Director:* Kristi A. Willis
Committee Assignment(s): Ways and Means

DOOLEY, CAL, D-CALIF. (20)

Capitol Hill Office: 1201 LHOB 20515; 225-3341; Fax: 225-9308; *Chief of Staff:* Lisa Quigley
Web: dooley.house.gov

E-mail: www.house.gov/writerep
District Office(s): 1060 Fulton Mall, #1015, Fresno 93721; (559) 441-7496; Fax: (559) 441-0587; *District Director:* Sarah Woolf
Committee Assignment(s): Agriculture; Resources

DOOLITTLE, JOHN T., R-CALIF. (4)

Capitol Hill Office: 2410 RHOB 20515; 225-2511; Fax: 225-5444; *Chief of Staff:* David Lopez
Web: www.house.gov/doolittle
E-mail: www.house.gov/doolittle/email_doolittle1.html
District Office(s): 4230 Douglas Blvd., #200, Granite Bay 95746; (916) 786-5560; Fax: (916) 786-6364; *Chief of Staff:* David Lopez
Committee Assignment(s): Appropriations; House Administration; Joint Printing

DOYLE, MIKE, D-PA. (14)

Capitol Hill Office: 401 CHOB 20515; 225-2135; Fax: 225-3084; *Chief of Staff:* David G. Lucas
Web: www.house.gov/doyle
E-mail: rep.doyle@mail.house.gov
District Office(s): 225 Ross St., #5, Pittsburgh 15219; (412) 261-5091; *District Director:* Paul D'Alesandro
627 Lysle Blvd., McKeesport 15132; (412) 664-4049; Fax: (412) 664-4053; *Office Liaison:* Alan Smith
11 Duff Rd., Penn Hills 15235; (412) 241-6055; Fax: (412) 241-6820; *Caseworker:* Jamel Iddriss
Committee Assignment(s): Energy and Commerce; Standards of Official Conduct

DREIER, DAVID, R-CALIF. (26)

Capitol Hill Office: 237 CHOB 20515; 225-2305; Fax: 225-7018; *Chief of Staff:* Brad Smith
Web: www.house.gov/dreier
E-mail: www.house.gov/writerep
District Office(s): 2220 E. Route 66, #225, Glendora 91740; (626) 852-2626; Fax: (626) 963-9842; *District Director:* Mark S. Harmsen
Committee Assignment(s): Rules; Select Homeland Security

DUNCAN, JOHN J. "JIMMY" JR., R-TENN. (2)

Capitol Hill Office: 2267 RHOB 20515; 225-5435; Fax: 225-6440; *Legislative Director:* Bert Robinson
Web: www.house.gov/duncan
E-mail: www.house.gov/writerep
District Office(s): 6 E. Madison Ave., Athens 37303; (423) 745-4671; Fax: (423) 745-6025; *Office Manager:* Linda Higdon
800 Market St., #110, Knoxville 37902; (865) 523-3772; Fax: (865) 544-0728; *Chief of Staff:* Bob Griffitts
262 E. Broadway, Maryville 37804; (423) 984-5464; Fax: (423) 984-0521; *Office Manager:* Vickie Flynn
Committee Assignment(s): Government Reform; Resources; Transportation and Infrastructure

DUNN, JENNIFER, R-WASH. (8)

Capitol Hill Office: 1501 LHOB 20515; 225-7761; Fax: 225-8673; *Chief of Staff:* Sarah Hildebrand
Web: www.house.gov/dunn
E-mail: dunnwa08@mail.house.gov
District Office(s): 2737 78th Ave. S.E., #202, Mercer Island 98040; (206) 275-3438; Fax: (206) 275-3437; *District Director:* Travis Sines
Committee Assignment(s): Joint Economic; Select Homeland Security; Ways and Means

EDWARDS, CHET, D-TEXAS (11)

Capitol Hill Office: 2459 RHOB 20515; 225-6105; Fax: 225-0350; *Administrative Assistant:* Chris Chwastyk
Web: www.house.gov/edwards
E-mail: www.house.gov/writerep
District Office(s): 625 S. Austin Ave., #220, Georgetown 78626; (512) 864-3186; Fax: (512) 864-3192
St. Charles Place, 600 Austin Ave., #29, Waco 76706; (254) 752-9600; Fax: (254) 752-7769; *Deputy District Director:* Myrtle Thompson
116 S. East St., Belton 76513; (254) 933-2904; Fax: (254) 933-2913; *District Director:* Sam Murphey
Committee Assignment(s): Appropriations; Budget

EHLERS, VERNON J., R-MICH. (3)

Capitol Hill Office: 1714 LHOB 20515; 225-3831; Fax: 225-5144; *Chief of Staff:* Bill McBride
Web: www.house.gov/ehlers
E-mail: www.house.gov/writerep
District Office(s): 110 Michigan St., #166, Grand Rapids 49503; (616) 451-8383; Fax: (616) 454-5630; *Constituent Services Director:* Nancy Ostapowicz
Committee Assignment(s): Education and Workforce; House Administration; Joint Library; Science; Transportation and Infrastructure

EMANUEL, RAHM, D-ILL. (5)

Capitol Hill Office: 1319 LHOB 20515; 225-4061; Fax: 225-5603; *Chief of Staff:* Elizabeth Sears Smith
Web: www.house.gov/emanuel
E-mail: rahm.emanuel@mail.house.gov
District Office(s): 3742 W. Irving Park Rd., Chicago 60618; (773) 267-5962; Fax: (773) 267-6583; *District Director:* John L. Borovicka IV
Committee Assignment(s): Budget; Financial Services

EMERSON, JO ANN, R-MO. (8)

Capitol Hill Office: 2440 RHOB 20515; 225-4404; Fax: 226-0326; *Administrative Assistant:* Jordan Bernstein
Web: www.house.gov/emerson
E-mail: www.house.gov/writerep
District Office(s): 339 Broadway, #246, Cape Girardeau 63701; (573) 335-0101; Fax: (573) 335-1931; *Chief of Staff:* Lloyd Smith

612 Pine St., Rolla 65401; (573) 364-2455; Fax: (573) 364-1053; *District Office Director:* Iris Bernhardt
22 E. Columbia St., Farmington 63640; (573) 756-9755; Fax: (573) 756-9762; *District Office Director:* Heather Garner
Committee Assignment(s): Appropriations

ENGEL, ELIOT L., D-N.Y. (17)

Capitol Hill Office: 2264 RHOB 20515; 225-2464; Fax: 225-5513; *Chief of Staff:* Jason Steinbaum
Web: www.house.gov/engel
E-mail: www.house.gov/writerep
District Office(s): 3655 Johnson Ave., Bronx 10463; (718) 796-9700; Fax: (718) 796-5134; *Chief of Staff:* Bill Weitz
Committee Assignment(s): Energy and Commerce; International Relations

ENGLISH, PHIL, R-PA. (3)

Capitol Hill Office: 1410 LHOB 20515; 225-5406; Fax: 225-3103; *Chief of Staff:* Robert Holste
Web: www.house.gov/english
E-mail: phil.english@mail.house.gov
District Office(s): Modern Tool Square, 310 French St., #107, Erie 16507; (814) 456-2038; Fax: (814) 454-0163; *District Director:* Regina Smith
900 N. Hermitage Rd., #6, Hermitage 16148; (724) 342-6132; Fax: (724) 342-6219; *Office Manager:* Marilyn Magnato
101 E. Diamond St., #213, Butler 16001; (724) 285-7005; Fax: (724) 285-5616; *Office Manager:* Marci Mustello
312 Chestnut St., #114, Meadville 16335; (814) 724-8414; Fax: (814) 333-8829; *District Representative:* Dianne Merchbaker
Committee Assignment(s): Joint Economic; Ways and Means

ESHOO, ANNA G., D-CALIF. (14)

Capitol Hill Office: 205 CHOB 20515; 225-8104; Fax: 225-8890; *Chief of Staff:* Eric Olson
Web: www.house.gov/eshoo
E-mail: annagram@mail.house.gov
District Office(s): 698 Emerson St., Palo Alto 94301; (650) 323-2984; Fax: (650) 323-3498; *District Director:* Karen Chapman
Committee Assignment(s): Energy and Commerce; Select Intelligence

ETHERIDGE, BOB, D-N.C. (2)

Capitol Hill Office: 1533 LHOB 20515; 225-4531; Fax: 225-5662; *Chief of Staff:* Julie Dwyer
Web: www.house.gov/etheridge
E-mail: www.house.gov/etheridge/contactbob.htm
District Office(s): 225 Hillsborough St., #490, Raleigh 27603; (919) 829-9122; Fax: (919) 829-9883; *District Director:* Russ Swindell

609 N. 1st St., P.O. Box 1059, Lillington 27546; (910) 814-0335; Fax: (910) 814-2264; *Senior Caseworker:* Amy Hornbuckle

Committee Assignment(s): Agriculture; Select Homeland Security

EVANS, LANE, D-ILL. (17)

Capitol Hill Office: 2211 RHOB 20515; 225-5905; Fax: 225-5396; *Administrative Assistant:* Dennis J. King

Web: www.house.gov/evans

E-mail: lane.evans@mail.house.gov

District Office(s): 1535 47th Ave., #5, Moline 61265; (309) 793-5760; Fax: (309) 762-9193; *District Representative:* Philip G. Hare

261 N. Broad St., #5, Galesburg 61401; (309) 342-4411; Fax: (309) 342-9749; *Office Manager:* Joyce Bean

236 N. Water St., #765, Decatur 62523; (217) 795-2003; Fax: (217) 795-4894; *Staff Assistant:* Patricia Dawson

Committee Assignment(s): Armed Services; Veterans' Affairs

EVERETT, TERRY, R-ALA. (2)

Capitol Hill Office: 2312 RHOB 20515; 225-2901; Fax: 225-8913; *Chief of Staff:* Wade Heck

Web: www.house.gov/everett

E-mail: terry.everett@mail.house.gov

District Office(s): 3500 Eastern Blvd., #250, Montgomery 36116; (334) 277-9113; Fax: (334) 277-8534; *District Director:* Thomas Paramore

256 Honeysuckle Rd., #15, Dothan 36305; (334) 794-9680; Fax: (334) 671-1480; *District Aide:* Joe Williams

108 N. Main St., Opp 36467; (334) 493-9253; Fax: (334) 493-6666; *Staff Assistant:* Frances Spurlin

Committee Assignment(s): Agriculture; Armed Services; Select Intelligence; Veterans' Affairs

FALEOMAVAEGA, ENI F. H., D-AM. SAMOA (AT LARGE)

Capitol Hill Office: 2422 RHOB 20515; 225-8577; Fax: 225-8757; *Legislative Director:* Leilani Judy

Web: www.house.gov/faleomavaega

E-mail: faleomavaega@mail.house.gov

District Office(s): P.O. Drawer X, Pago Pago 96799; (684) 633-1372; Fax: (684) 633-2680; *Legislative Assistant:* Oreta M. Togafau *Chief of Staff:* Alexander Godinet

Committee Assignment(s): International Relations; Resources; Small Business

FARR, SAM, D-CALIF. (17)

Capitol Hill Office: 1221 LHOB 20515; 225-2861; Fax: 225-6791; *Chief of Staff:* Rochelle Dornatt

Web: www.house.gov/farr

E-mail: samfarr@mail.house.gov

District Office(s): 100 W. Alisal St., Salinas 93901; (831) 424-2229; Fax: (831) 424-7099; *District Director:* Alec Arago

701 Ocean St., #318, Santa Cruz 95060; (831) 429-1976; Fax: (831) 424-7099; *Congressional Aide:* Rachel Dann

Committee Assignment(s): Appropriations

FATTAH, CHAKA, D-PA. (2)

Capitol Hill Office: 2301 RHOB 20515; 225-4001; Fax: 225-5392; *Chief of Staff:* Michelle Anderson Lee

Web: www.house.gov/fattah

E-mail: www.house.gov/writerep

District Office(s): 4104 Walnut St., Philadelphia 19104; (215) 387-6404; Fax: (215) 387-6407; *District Director:* Bonnie Bowser

6632 Germantown Ave., Philadelphia 19119; (215) 848-9386; Fax: (215) 848-3884; *Caseworker:* Phyllis Goode

Committee Assignment(s): Appropriations

FEENEY, TOM, R-FLA. (24)

Capitol Hill Office: 323 CHOB 20515; 225-2706; Fax: 226-6299; *Chief of Staff:* Jason C. Roe

Web: www.house.gov/feeney

E-mail: tomfeeney@mail.house.gov

District Office(s): 12424 Research Pkwy., #135, Orlando 32826; (407) 208-1106; Fax: (407) 208-1108; *District Director:* Cheryl Moore

1000 City Center Circle, 2nd Floor, Port Orange 32129; (386) 756-9798; Fax: (386) 756-9903; *District Representative:* Barbara Kotch

400 South St., #413, Titusville 32780; (321) 264-6113; Fax: (321) 264-6227; *District Representative:* Todd Sykes

Committee Assignment(s): Financial Services; Judiciary; Science

FERGUSON, MIKE, R-N.J. (7)

Capitol Hill Office: 214 CHOB 20515; 225-5361; Fax: 225-9460; *Chief of Staff:* Chris Jones

Web: www.house.gov/ferguson

E-mail: www.house.gov/writerep

District Office(s): 792 Chimney Rock Rd., Suite E, Martinsville 08836; (908) 757-7835; Fax: (908) 757-7841; *District Director:* Marcus Rayner

Committee Assignment(s): Energy and Commerce

FILNER, BOB, D-CALIF. (51)

Capitol Hill Office: 2428 RHOB 20515; 225-8045; Fax: 225-9073; *Chief of Staff:* Tony Buckles

Web: www.house.gov/filner

E-mail: www.house.gov/writerep

District Office(s): 333 F St., Suite A, Chula Vista 91910; (619) 422-5963; Fax: (619) 422-7290; *District Director:* Inez Gonzalez

Committee Assignment(s): Transportation and Infrastructure; Veterans' Affairs

FLAKE, JEFF, R-ARIZ. (6)

Capitol Hill Office: 424 CHOB 20515; 225-2635; Fax: 226-4386; *Chief of Staff:* Steven Voeller

Web: www.house.gov/flake
E-mail: jeff.flake@mail.house.gov
District Office(s): 1640 S. Stapley Dr., #215, Mesa 85204; (480) 833-0092; Fax: (480) 833-6314; *Chief of Staff:* Steve Voeller
Committee Assignment(s): International Relations; Judiciary; Resources

FLETCHER, ERNIE, R-KY. (6)

Capitol Hill Office: 1117 LHOB 20515; 225-4706; Fax: 225-2122; *Chief of Staff:* Pamela Mattox
Web: www.house.gov/fletcher
E-mail: www.house.gov/writerep
District Office(s): 860 Corporate Dr., #105, Lexington 40503; (859) 219-1366; Fax: (859) 219-3437; *District Director:* John Roach
Committee Assignment(s): Energy and Commerce

FOLEY, MARK, R-FLA. (16)

Capitol Hill Office: 104 CHOB 20515; 225-5792; Fax: 225-3132; *Administrative Assistant:* Kirk Fordham
Web: www.house.gov/foley
E-mail: www.house.gov/foley/mail.htm
District Office(s): 4440 PGA Blvd., #406, Palm Beach Gardens 33410; (561) 627-6192; Fax: (561) 626-4749; *District Director:* Don Kiselewski
250 N.W. Country Club Dr., Port St. Lucie 34986; (772) 878-3181; Fax: (772) 871-0651; *District Manager:* Ann Decker
Committee Assignment(s): Ways and Means

FORBES, J. RANDY, R-VA. (4)

Capitol Hill Office: 307 CHOB 20515; 225-6365; Fax: 226-1170; *Chief of Staff:* Dee Gilmore
Web: www.house.gov/forbes
E-mail: www.house.gov/writerep
District Office(s): 636 Cedar Rd., #200, Chesapeake 23322; (757) 382-0080; Fax: (757) 382-0780; *District Representative:* Ryan Mottley
2903 Boulevard, Suite B, Colonial Heights 23834; (804) 526-4969; Fax: (804) 520-7486; *District Representative:* Jason Gray
425H S. Main St., Emporia 23847; (434) 634-5575; Fax: (434) 634-0511; *District Representative:* Rick Franklin
Committee Assignment(s): Armed Services; Judiciary; Science

FORD, HAROLD E. JR., D-TENN. (9)

Capitol Hill Office: 325 CHOB 20515; 225-3265; Fax: 225-5663; *Chief of Staff:* Mark Schuermann
Web: www.house.gov/ford
E-mail: rep.harold.ford.jr@mail.house.gov
District Office(s): 167 N. Main St., #369, Memphis 38103; (901) 544-4131; Fax: (901) 544-4329; *District Director:* Nichole A. Francis
Committee Assignment(s): Budget; Financial Services

FOSSELLA, VITO J., R-N.Y. (13)

Capitol Hill Office: 1239 LHOB 20515; 225-3371; Fax: 226-1272; *Chief of Staff:* Tom Quaadman
Web: www.house.gov/fossella
E-mail: vito.fossella@mail.house.gov
District Office(s): 4434 Amboy Rd., 2nd Floor, Staten Island 10312; (718) 356-8400; Fax: (718) 356-1928; *District Director:* Sherry Diamond
9818 4th Ave., Brooklyn 11209; (718) 630-5277; Fax: (718) 630-5388; *Office Manager:* Eileen Long
Committee Assignment(s): Energy and Commerce; Financial Services

FRANK, BARNEY, D-MASS. (4)

Capitol Hill Office: 2252 RHOB 20515; 225-5931; Fax: 225-0182; *Chief of Staff:* Peter Kovar
Web: www.house.gov/frank
E-mail: www.house.gov/writerep
District Office(s): 29 Crafts St., Newton 02458; (617) 332-3920; Fax: (617) 332-2822; *District Director:* Dorothy M. Reichard
558 Pleasant St., #309, New Bedford 02740; (508) 999-6462; Fax: (508) 674-3030; *Office Manager:* Elsie Souza
29 Broadway St., Taunton 02780; *Office Manager:* Garth Patterson
Committee Assignment(s): Financial Services; Select Homeland Security

FRANKS, TRENT, R-ARIZ. (2)

Capitol Hill Office: 1237 LHOB 20515; 225-4576; Fax: 225-6328; *Chief of Staff:* John Graves
Web: www.house.gov/franks
E-mail: www.house.gov/writerep
District Office(s): 7121 W. Bell Rd., #200, Glendale 85308; (623) 776-7911; Fax: (623) 776-7832; *District Director:* Daniel Hay
Committee Assignment(s): Armed Services; Budget; Small Business

FRELINGHUYSEN, RODNEY, R-N.J. (11)

Capitol Hill Office: 2442 RHOB 20515; 225-5034; Fax: 225-3186; *Chief of Staff:* Nancy Fox
Web: www.house.gov/frelinghuysen
E-mail: rodney.frelinghuysen@mail.house.gov
District Office(s): 30 Schuyler Place, 2nd Floor, Morristown 07960; (973) 984-0711; Fax: (973) 292-1569; *District Director:* Mark Broadhurst
Committee Assignment(s): Appropriations

FROST, MARTIN, D-TEXAS (24)

Capitol Hill Office: 2256 RHOB 20515; 225-3605; Fax: 225-4951; *Chief of Staff:* Matt Angle
Web: www.house.gov/frost
E-mail: martin.frost@mail.house.gov

District Office(s): 101 E. Randol Mill Rd., #108, Arlington 76011; (817) 303-1530; Fax: (817) 303-9084; *Office Manager:* Lisa Hunsaker Turner

400 S. Zang Blvd., #506, Dallas 75208; (214) 948-3401; Fax: (214) 948-3468; *Office Manager:* Marsha Steever-Patykiewicz

3020 S.E. Loop 820, Fort Worth 76140; (817) 293-9231; Fax: (817) 293-0526; *District Director:* Cinda M. Crawford

Committee Assignment(s): Rules

GALLEGLY, ELTON, R-CALIF. (24)

Capitol Hill Office: 2427 RHOB 20515; 225-5811; Fax: 225-1100; *Chief of Staff:* Patrick Murphy

Web: www.house.gov/gallegly

E-mail: www.house.gov/writerep

District Office(s): 2829 Townsgate Rd., #315, Thousand Oaks 91361; (805) 497-2224; Fax: (805) 497-0039; *District Director:* Paula Sheil

485 Alisal Rd., #G-1A, Solvang 93463; (805) 686-2525; Fax: (805) 686-2566; *District Representative:* Tina Cobb

Committee Assignment(s): International Relations; Judiciary; Resources; Select Intelligence

GARRETT, SCOTT, R-N.J. (5)

Capitol Hill Office: 1641 LHOB 20515; 225-4465; Fax: 225-9048; *Chief of Staff:* Evan Kozlow

Web: www.house.gov/garrett

E-mail: www.house.gov/garrett/contact.html

District Office(s): 210 Route 4 East, #206, Paramus 07652; (201) 712-0330; Fax: (201) 712-0930; *District Representative:* Ellen Leahey

93 Main St., Newton 07860; (973) 300-2000; Fax: (973) 300-1051; *District Representative:* Rudy Solar

Committee Assignment(s): Budget; Financial Services

GEPHARDT, RICHARD A., D-MO. (3)

Capitol Hill Office: 1236 LHOB 20515; 225-2671; Fax: 225-7452; *Legislative Director:* Sean Kennedy

Web: dickgephardt.house.gov

E-mail: www.house.gov/writerep

District Office(s): 11140 S. Towne Square, #201, St. Louis 63123; (314) 894-3400; Fax: (314) 845-8675; *Administrative Assistant:* Mary Renick

998 E. Gannon Dr., P.O. Box 392, Festus 63208; (636) 937-6399; Fax: (636) 937-8098; *County Coordinator:* Chuck Banks

Committee Assignment(s): No committee assignments

GERLACH, JIM, R-PA. (6)

Capitol Hill Office: 1541 LHOB 20515; 225-4315; Fax: 225-8440; *Chief of Staff:* Linda Pedigo

Web: www.house.gov/gerlach

E-mail: www.house.gov/gerlach/zipauth.htm

District Office(s): 1230 Pottstown Pike, Glenmoore 19343; (310) 458-8010; Fax: (310) 458-8393; *District Director:* Edward Schmid

580 Main St., #4, Trappe 19426; (610) 409-2780; Fax: (610) 409-7988; *District Representative:* Jason Carver

501 N. Park Rd., Wyomissing 19160; (610) 376-7630; Fax: (670) 376-7633; *District Representative:* Patrick Beck

Committee Assignment(s): Small Business; Transportation and Infrastructure

GIBBONS, JIM, R-NEV. (2)

Capitol Hill Office: 100 CHOB 20515; 225-6155; Fax: 225-5679; *Chief of Staff:* Robert Uithoven

Web: www.house.gov/gibbons

E-mail: mail.gibbons@mail.house.gov

District Office(s): 400 S. Virginia St., #502, Reno 89501; (775) 686-5760; Fax: (775) 686-5711; *District Scheduler:* Deanna Lazovich

600 Las Vegas Blvd., #680, Las Vegas 89101; (702) 255-1651; Fax: (702) 255-1927; *Regional Field Representative:* Judy Ray

491 4th St., Elko 89801; (775) 777-7920; Fax: (775) 777-7922; *District Director:* Betty Jo Gerber

Committee Assignment(s): Armed Services; Resources; Select Homeland Security; Select Intelligence

GILCHREST, WAYNE T., R-MD. (1)

Capitol Hill Office: 2245 RHOB 20515; 225-5311; Fax: 225-0254; *Chief of Staff:* Tony Caligiuri

Web: www.house.gov/gilchrest

E-mail: www.house.gov/writerep

District Office(s): 1 Plaza East, Salisbury 21801; (410) 749-3184; Fax: (410) 749-8458; *District Director:* Cathy Bassett

315 High St., #105, Chestertown 21620; (410) 778-9407; Fax: (410) 778-9560; *District Office Manager:* Karen Willis

45 N. Main St., #3, Bel Air 21014; (410) 838-2517; Fax: (410) 838-7823; *Office Manager:* Shirley Stoyer

Committee Assignment(s): Resources; Science; Transportation and Infrastructure

GILLMOR, PAUL E., R-OHIO (5)

Capitol Hill Office: 1203 LHOB 20515; 225-6405; Fax: 225-1985; *Administrative Assistant:* Mark S. Wellman

Web: www.house.gov/gillmor

E-mail: www.house.gov/writerep

District Office(s): 96 S. Washington St., #400, Tiffin 44883; (419) 448-9016; *Office Manager:* Christina Strumsky

613 W. 3rd St., Defiance 43512; (419) 782-1996; Fax: (419) 784-9808; *Office Manager:* Kathy Shaver

Committee Assignment(s): Energy and Commerce; Financial Services

GINGREY, PHIL, R-GA. (11)

Capitol Hill Office: 1118 LHOB 20515; 225-2931; Fax: 225-2944; *Chief of Staff:* Mitch Hunter

Web: www.house.gov/gingrey

E-mail: gingrey.ga@mail.house.gov

District Office(s): 219 Roswell St. N.E., Marietta 30060; (770) 429-1776; Fax: (770) 795-9551; *District Representative:* Terri Wylie

600 E. 1st St., Rome 30161; (706) 290-1776; Fax: (706) 232-7864; *District Representative:* Janet Byington

207 Newnan St., Suite A, Carrollton 30117; (770) 836-8130; Fax: (770) 214-3655; *District Representative:* Jan Wylie

Committee Assignment(s): Armed Services; Education and Workforce; Science

GONZALEZ, CHARLIE, D-TEXAS (20)

Capitol Hill Office: 327 CHOB 20515; 225-3236; Fax: 225-1915; *Chief of Staff:* Kevin Kimble

Web: www.house.gov/gonzalez

E-mail: www.house.gov/writerep

District Office(s): 727 E. Durango Blvd., #B-124, San Antonio 78206; (210) 472-6195; Fax: (210) 472-4009; *District Director:* Mary Jessie Rogue

Committee Assignment(s): Financial Services; Select Homeland Security; Small Business

GOODE, VIRGIL H. JR., R-VA. (5)

Capitol Hill Office: 1520 LHOB 20515; 225-4711; Fax: 225-5681; *Chief of Staff:* Candace Friel

Web: www.house.gov/goode

E-mail: www.house.gov/writerep

District Office(s): 437 Main St., Danville 24541; (434) 792-1280; Fax: (434) 797-5942; *Press Secretary:* Linwood Duncan

104 S. 1st St., Charlottesville 22902; (434) 295-6372; Fax: (434) 295-6059; *District Office Manager:* Esther Page

70 E. Court St., #215, Rocky Mount 24151; (540) 484-1254; Fax: (540) 484-1459; *Staff Assistant:* Marilyn Mattox

103 S. Main St., Farmville 23901; (434) 392-8331; Fax: (434) 392-6448; *Caseworker:* Sarah Terry

Committee Assignment(s): Appropriations

GOODLATTE, ROBERT W., R-VA. (6)

Capitol Hill Office: 2240 RHOB 20515; 225-5431; Fax: 225-9681; *Chief of Staff:* Shelley Hanger

Web: www.house.gov/goodlatte

E-mail: talk2bob@mail.house.gov

District Office(s): 2 S. Main St., 1st Floor, Suite A, Harrisonburg 22801; (540) 432-2391; Fax: (540) 432-6593; *District Representative:* Ande Banks

10 Franklin Rd. S.E., #540, Roanoke 24011; (540) 857-2672; Fax: (540) 857-2675; *District Director:* Pete S. Larkin

916 Main St., #300, Lynchburg 24504; (434) 845-8306; Fax: (434) 845-8245; *District Representative:* Clarkie Featherstone

114 N. Central Ave., Staunton 24401; (540) 885-3861; Fax: (540) 885-3930; *District Representative:* Pat Haley

Committee Assignment(s): Agriculture; Judiciary; Select Homeland Security

GORDON, BART, D-TENN. (6)

Capitol Hill Office: 2304 RHOB 20515; 225-4231; Fax: 225-6887; *Chief of Staff:* Chuck Atkins

Web: www.house.gov/gordon

E-mail: www.house.gov/writerep

District Office(s): 101 5th Ave. West, Suite D, Springfield 37172; (615) 382-9712

106 S. Maple St., Murfreesboro 37130; (615) 896-1986; Fax: (615) 896-8218; *Chief of Staff:* Kent Syler

15 S. Jefferson Ave., Cookeville 38501; (931) 528-5907; Fax: (931) 528-1165; *Field Representative:* Billy Smith

Committee Assignment(s): Energy and Commerce; Science

GOSS, PORTER J., R-FLA. (14)

Capitol Hill Office: 108 CHOB 20515; 225-2536; Fax: 225-6820; *Chief of Staff:* Sheryl V. Wooley

Web: www.house.gov/goss

E-mail: porter.goss@mail.house.gov

District Office(s): 2000 Main St., #303, Fort Myers 33901; (941) 332-4677; Fax: (941) 332-1743; *Chief of Staff:* Sheryl V. Wooley

3301 Tamiami Trail East, Bldg. F, #212, Naples 34112; (941) 774-8060; Fax: (941) 774-7262; *County Liaison:* John Barretto

75 Taylor St., Punta Gorda 33950; (941) 639-0051; Fax: (941) 639-0714; *District Director:* Linda Uhler

Committee Assignment(s): Rules; Select Homeland Security; Select Intelligence

GRANGER, KAY, R-TEXAS (12)

Capitol Hill Office: 435 CHOB 20515; 225-5071; Fax: 225-5683; *Chief of Staff:* Barrett Karr

Web: www.house.gov/granger

E-mail: texas.granger@mail.house.gov

District Office(s): 1701 River Run Rd., #407, Ft. Worth 76107; (817) 338-0909; Fax: (817) 335-5852; *District Director:* Barbara Ragland

Committee Assignment(s): Appropriations; Select Homeland Security

GRAVES, SAM, R-MO. (6)

Capitol Hill Office: 1513 LHOB 20515; 225-7041; Fax: 225-8221; *Chief of Staff:* Jeff Roe

Web: www.house.gov/graves

E-mail: sam.graves@mail.house.gov

District Office(s): 113 Blue Jay Dr., #200, Liberty 64068; (816) 792-3976; Fax: (816) 792-0694; *District Press Secretary:* Jacob DiPietre

U.S. Post Office, 201 S. 8th St., #330, St. Joseph 64501; (816) 233-9818; Fax: (816) 233-9848; *District Director:* Dean Brookshier

Committee Assignment(s): Agriculture; Small Business; Transportation and Infrastructure

GREEN, GENE, D-TEXAS (29)

Capitol Hill Office: 2335 RHOB 20515; 225-1688; Fax: 225-9903; *Chief of Staff:* Marc Gonzales
Web: www.house.gov/green
E-mail: www.house.gov/writerep
District Office(s): 256 N. Sam Houston Pkwy. East, #29, Houston 77060; (281) 999-5879; Fax: (281) 999-5716; *District Director:* Rhonda Jackson
11811 I-10 East, #430, Houston 77029; (713) 330-0761; Fax: (713) 330-0807; *Caseworker:* Marlene Clowers
Committee Assignment(s): Energy and Commerce; Standards of Official Conduct

GREEN, MARK, R-WIS. (8)

Capitol Hill Office: 1314 LHOB 20515; 225-5665; Fax: 225-5729; *Chief of Staff:* Mark Graul
Web: www.house.gov/markgreen
E-mail: mark.green@mail.house.gov
District Office(s): 609A W. College Ave., Appleton 54911; (920) 380-0061; Fax: (920) 380-0051; *Caseworker:* Kathy McCarthy
700 E. Walnut St., Green Bay 54301; (920) 437-1954; Fax: (920) 437-1978; *District Director:* Chad Weininger
Committee Assignment(s): Financial Services; International Relations; Judiciary

GREENWOOD, JAMES C., R-PA. (8)

Capitol Hill Office: 2436 RHOB 20515; 225-4276; Fax: 225-9511; *Chief of Staff:* Jordan "Pete" Krauss
Web: www.house.gov/greenwood
E-mail: www.house.gov/writerep
District Office(s): 69 E. Oakland Ave., Doylestown 18901; (215) 348-7511; Fax: (215) 348-7658; *District Representative:* Linda Prosek
1 Oxford Valley, #800, Langhorne 19047; (215) 752-7711; Fax: (215) 750-8014; *District Director:* Vacant
Committee Assignment(s): Education and Workforce; Energy and Commerce

GRIJALVA, RAUL M., D-ARIZ. (7)

Capitol Hill Office: 1440 LHOB 20515; 225-2435; Fax: 226-6846; *Chief of Staff:* Anna Ma
Web: www.house.gov/grijalva
E-mail: raul.grijalva@mail.house.gov
District Office(s): 810 E. 22nd St., #122, Tucson 85713; (520) 622-6788; Fax: (520) 622-0198; *District Director:* Richard M. Martinez
Committee Assignment(s): Education and Workforce; Resources

GUTIERREZ, LUIS V., D-ILL. (4)

Capitol Hill Office: 2367 RHOB 20515; 225-8203; Fax: 225-7810; *Chief of Staff:* Jennice Fuentes
Web: luisgutierrez.house.gov
E-mail: www.house.gov/gutierrez/contact.html

District Office(s): 3455 W. North Ave., Chicago 60647; (773) 384-1655; Fax: (773) 384-1685; *District Director:* Mireya Hurtado
1310 W. 18th St., Chicago 60608; (312) 666-3882; Fax: (312) 666-3894; *Community Outreach Director:* Salvador Cerna
Committee Assignment(s): Financial Services; Veterans' Affairs

GUTKNECHT, GIL, R-MINN. (1)

Capitol Hill Office: 425 CHOB 20515; 225-2472; Fax: 225-3246; *Chief of Staff:* Stephanie Brand
Web: www.gil.house.gov
E-mail: gil@mail.house.gov
District Office(s): 109 E. 2nd St., Fairmont 56031; (507) 238-2835; *Field Representative:* Cally Eckles
1530 Greenview Dr. S.W., #108, Rochester 55902; (507) 252-9841; Fax: (507) 252-9915; *District Director:* Doug Altrichter
Committee Assignment(s): Agriculture; Budget; Science

HALL, RALPH M., D-TEXAS (4)

Capitol Hill Office: 2405 RHOB 20515; 225-6673; Fax: 225-3332; *Chief of Staff:* Janet Poppleton
Web: www.house.gov/ralphhall
E-mail: rmhall@mail.house.gov
District Office(s): 104 N. San Jacinto St., Rockwall 75087; (972) 771-9118; Fax: (972) 722-0907; *District Assistant:* Christy Holcomb
101 E. Pecan St., #119, Sherman 75090; (903) 892-1112; Fax: (903) 868-0264; *District Assistant:* Judy Rowton
211 W. Ferguson St., #211, Tyler 75702; (903) 597-3729; Fax: (903) 597-0726; *District Assistant:* Martha Glover
Committee Assignment(s): Energy and Commerce; Science

HARMAN, JANE, D-CALIF. (36)

Capitol Hill Office: 2400 RHOB 20515; 225-8220; Fax: 226-7290; *Chief of Staff:* John Hess
Web: www.house.gov/harman
E-mail: jane.harman@mail.house.gov
District Office(s): 2321 E. Rosecrans Ave., #3270, El Segundo 90245; (310) 643-3636; Fax: (310) 643-6445; *District Director:* Linda Rottblat-Wolin
544 N. Avalon Blvd., #307, Wilmington 90744; (310) 549-8282; Fax: (310) 549-8250; *Field Representative:* Kelly Calkin
Committee Assignment(s): Select Homeland Security; Select Intelligence

HARRIS, KATHERINE, R-FLA. (13)

Capitol Hill Office: 116 CHOB 20515; 225-5015; Fax: 226-0828; *Chief of Staff:* Dan Berger
Web: www.house.gov/harris
E-mail: katherine.harris@mail.house.gov

District Office(s): 1991 Main St., #181, Sarasota 34236; (941) 951-6643; Fax: (941) 951-2972; *District Director:* Nancie Kalin

1112 W. Manatee Ave., #902, Bradenton 34205; (941) 747-9081; Fax: (941) 749-5310; *District Representative:* Laura Griffin

Committee Assignment(s): Financial Services; International Relations

HART, MELISSA A., R-PA. (4)

Capitol Hill Office: 1508 LHOB 20515; 225-2565; Fax: 226-2274; *Chief of Staff:* Bill Ries

Web: hart.house.gov

E-mail: rep.hart@mail.house.gov

District Office(s): 4655 Route 8, #124G, Allison Park 15101; (412) 492-0161; Fax: (414) 492-0178; *District Director:* Patrick Geho

501 Lawrence Ave., Ellwood City 16117; (724) 752-0490; Fax: (724) 752-0494; *District Representative:* Cherith Brewer

Committee Assignment(s): Financial Services; Judiciary; Science

HASTERT, J. DENNIS, R-ILL. (14)

Capitol Hill Office: 235 CHOB 20515; 225-2976; Fax: 225-0697; *Chief of Staff:* Scott B. Palmer

Web: www.house.gov/hastert

E-mail: dhastert@mail.house.gov

District Office(s): 27 N. River St., Batavia 60510; (630) 406-1114; Fax: (630) 406-1808; *District Director:* Bryan Hardin

Committee Assignment(s): No committee assignments

HASTINGS, ALCEE L., D-FLA. (23)

Capitol Hill Office: 2235 RHOB 20515; 225-1313; Fax: 225-1171; *Chief of Staff:* Fred Turner

Web: www.house.gov/alceehastings

E-mail: alcee.pubhastings@mail.house.gov

District Office(s): 2701 W. Oakland Park Blvd., #200, Ft. Lauderdale 33311; (954) 733-2800; Fax: (954) 735-9444; *Chief of Staff:* Art W. Kennedy

5725 Corporate Way, #208, West Palm Beach 33407; (561) 684-0565; Fax: (561) 684-3613; *Congressional Aide:* Mikel Jones

Committee Assignment(s): Rules; Select Intelligence

HASTINGS, DOC, R-WASH. (4)

Capitol Hill Office: 1323 LHOB 20515; 225-5816; Fax: 225-3251; *Chief of Staff:* Ed Cassidy

Web: www.house.gov/hastings

E-mail: www.house.gov/hastings/get_address.htm

District Office(s): 2715 St. Andrews Loop, Suite D, Pasco 99302; (509) 543-9396; Fax: (509) 545-1972; *District Director:* Joyce Olson

302 E. Chestnut St., Yakima 98901; (509) 452-3243; Fax: (509) 452-3438; *Staff Assistant:* Ranie Haas

Committee Assignment(s): Budget; Rules; Standards of Official Conduct

HAYES, ROBIN, R-N.C. (8)

Capitol Hill Office: 130 CHOB 20515; 225-3715; Fax: 225-4036; *Chief of Staff:* Andrew Duke

Web: www.house.gov/hayes

E-mail: www.house.gov/writerep

District Office(s): 230 E. Franklin St., Rockingham 28379; (910) 997-2070; Fax: (910) 997-7987; *Constituent Liaison:* Paulette Burgess

137 Union St. South, Concord 28025; (704) 786-1612; Fax: (704) 782-1004; *District Director:* Richard Hudson

Committee Assignment(s): Agriculture; Armed Services; Transportation and Infrastructure

HAYWORTH, J. D., R-ARIZ. (5)

Capitol Hill Office: 2434 RHOB 20515; 225-2190; Fax: 225-3263; *Chief of Staff:* Joseph Eule

Web: www.house.gov/hayworth

E-mail: jdhayworth@mail.house.gov

District Office(s): 14300 N. Northsight Blvd., #101, Scottsdale 85260; (480) 926-4151; Fax: (480) 926-3998; *District Director:* Brian Murray

Committee Assignment(s): Resources; Ways and Means

HEFLEY, JOEL, R-COLO. (5)

Capitol Hill Office: 2372 RHOB 20515; 225-4422; Fax: 225-1942; *Legislative Director:* Lawrence Hojo

Web: www.house.gov/hefley

E-mail: www.house.gov/writerep

District Office(s): 104 S. Cascade Ave., #105, Colorado Springs 80903; (719) 520-0055; Fax: (719) 520-0840; *Chief of Staff:* Connie Solomon

Committee Assignment(s): Armed Services; Standards of Official Conduct

HENSARLING, JEB, R-TEXAS (5)

Capitol Hill Office: 423 CHOB 20515; 225-3484; Fax: 226-4888; *Chief of Staff:* Brian C. Thomas

Web: www.house.gov/hensarling

District Office(s): 10675 E. Northwest Hwy., #1685, Dallas 75238; (214) 349-9996; Fax: (214) 349-0738; *District Director:* Clifton Wiegand

100 E. Corsicana St., #208, Athens 75751; (903) 675-8288; Fax: (903) 675-8357; *Regional Director:* Richard Sanders

Committee Assignment(s): Budget; Financial Services

HERGER, WALLY, R-CALIF. (2)

Capitol Hill Office: 2268 RHOB 20515; 225-3076; Fax: 225-1740; *Administrative Assistant:* John P. Magill

Web: www.house.gov/herger

E-mail: www.house.gov/writerep

District Office(s): 55 Independence Circle, #104, Chico 95926; (530) 893-8363; *District Office Manager:* Fran Peace

410 Hemsted Dr., #115, Redding 96002; (530) 223-5898; *Field Representative:* David Meurer

Committee Assignment(s): Ways and Means

HILL, BARON P., D-IND. (9)

Capitol Hill Office: 1024 LHOB 20515; 225-5315; Fax: 226-6866; *Administrative Assistant:* Ryan Guthrie

Web: www.house.gov/baronhill

E-mail: www.house.gov/writerep

District Office(s): 590 Missouri Ave., #203, Jeffersonville 47130; (812) 288-3999; Fax: (812) 288-3877; *District Director:* Luke H. Clippinger

501 N. Morton St., #205, Bloomington 47404; (812) 334-7893; Fax: (812) 334-8272; *Deputy District Director:* Todd Lane

Committee Assignment(s): Agriculture; Armed Services; Joint Economic

HINCHEY, MAURICE D., D-N.Y. (22)

Capitol Hill Office: 2431 RHOB 20515; 225-6335; Fax: 226-0774; *Chief of Staff:* Wendy Darwell

Web: www.house.gov/hinchey

E-mail: mhinchey@mail.house.gov

District Office(s): 291 Wall St., Kingston 12401; (845) 331-4466; Fax: (845) 331-7456; *District Representative:* Dan Ahouse

123 S. Cayuga St., #201, Ithaca 14850; (607) 273-1388; Fax: (607) 273-8847; *District Representative:* Dan Lamb

18 Anawana Lake Rd., Monticello 12701; (845) 791-7116; Fax: (607) 498-5379; *Community Liaison:* Julie Allen

15 Henry St., #100A, Binghamton 13901; (607) 773-2768; Fax: (607) 773-3176; *Federal Liaison:* Robin Malloy

Committee Assignment(s): Appropriations

HINOJOSA, RUBEN, D-TEXAS (15)

Capitol Hill Office: 2463 RHOB 20515; 225-2531; Fax: 225-5688; *Chief of Staff:* Roy A. Dye

Web: www.house.gov/hinojosa

E-mail: rep.hinojosa@mail.house.gov

District Office(s): 311 N. 15th St., McAllen 78501; (956) 682-5545; Fax: (956) 682-0141; *District Director:* Salomon Torres

107 S. Saint Mary's St., Beeville 78102; (361) 358-8400; Fax: (361) 358-8407; *District Director:* Judy McAda

Committee Assignment(s): Education and Workforce; Financial Services; Resources

HOBSON, DAVID L., R-OHIO (7)

Capitol Hill Office: 2346 RHOB 20515; 225-4324; *Chief of Staff:* Wayne Struble

Web: www.house.gov/hobson

E-mail: www.house.gov/hobson/formmail.htm

District Office(s): 212 S. Broad St., #55, Lancaster 43130; (740) 654-5149; Fax: (740) 654-7825; *District Representative:* Talitha Elsea

5 W. North St., #200, P.O. Box 269, Springfield 45501; (937) 325-0474; Fax: (937) 325-9188; *District Director:* Eileen Austria

Committee Assignment(s): Appropriations

HOEFFEL, JOSEPH M., D-PA. (13)

Capitol Hill Office: 426 CHOB 20515; 225-6111; Fax: 226-0611; *Chief of Staff:* Jack Dempsey

Web: www.house.gov/hoeffel

E-mail: www.house.gov/writerep

District Office(s): 1768 Markley St., Norristown 19401; (610) 272-8400; Fax: (610) 272-8532; *District Director:* Joan Nagel

Committee Assignment(s): International Relations; Transportation and Infrastructure

HOEKSTRA, PETER, R-MICH. (2)

Capitol Hill Office: 2234 RHOB 20515; 225-4401; Fax: 226-0779; *Chief of Staff:* John Van Fossen

Web: www.house.gov/hoekstra

E-mail: tellhoek@mail.house.gov

District Office(s): 184 S. River Ave., Holland 49423; (616) 395-0030; Fax: (616) 395-0271; *District Representative:* Beatriz Mancilla

900 3rd St., #203, Muskegon 49440; (231) 722-8386; Fax: (231) 722-0176; *District Representative:* Holly Nolan

210 1/2 N. Mitchell St., Cadillac 49601; (231) 775-0050; Fax: (231) 775-0298; *Area Representative:* Jill Brown

Committee Assignment(s): Education and Workforce; Select Intelligence; Transportation and Infrastructure

HOLDEN, TIM, D-PA. (17)

Capitol Hill Office: 2417 RHOB 20515; 225-5546; Fax: 226-0996; *Chief of Staff:* Trish Reilly-Hudock

Web: www.house.gov/holden

E-mail: www.house.gov/writerep

District Office(s): 47 S. 8th St., Lebanon 17042; (717) 270-1395; Fax: (717) 270-1095; *Constituent Services Representative:* Sara Lopez

1721 N. Front St., Harrisburg 17102; (717) 234-5904; Fax: (717) 234-5918; *District Director:* Tim Smith

101 N. Centre St., #303, Pottsville 17901; (570) 622-4212; Fax: (570) 628-2561; *Field Representative:* Frank Ratkiewicz

Berks Corporate Center, 280 Corporate Dr., Reading 19605; (610) 916-6363; Fax: (610) 916-6337; *Executive Assistant:* Marge Lawler

Committee Assignment(s): Agriculture; Transportation and Infrastructure

HOLT, RUSH D., D-N.J. (12)

Capitol Hill Office: 1019 LHOB 20515; 225-5801; Fax: 225-6025; *Chief of Staff:* Jim Papa

Web: holt.house.gov

E-mail: holt.house.gov/feedback.cfm?campaign=holt

District Office(s): 50 Washington Rd., West Windsor 08550; (609) 750-9365; Fax: (609) 750-0618; *District Director:* Leslie Potter

Committee Assignment(s): Education and Workforce; Select Intelligence

HONDA, MICHAEL M., D-CALIF. (15)

Capitol Hill Office: 1713 LHOB 20515; 225-2631; Fax: 225-2699; *Chief of Staff:* Jennifer Vanderheide

Web: www.house.gov/honda

E-mail: mike.honda@mail.house.gov

District Office(s): 1999 S. Bascom Ave., #815, Campbell 95008; (408) 558-8085; Fax: (408) 558-8086; *District Director:* Meri Maben

Committee Assignment(s): Science; Transportation and Infrastructure

HOOLEY, DARLENE, D-ORE. (5)

Capitol Hill Office: 2430 RHOB 20515; 225-5711; Fax: 225-5699; *Chief of Staff:* Joan Mooney

Web: www.house.gov/hooley

E-mail: darlene@mail.house.gov

District Office(s): 315 Mission St., #101, Salem 97302; (503) 588-9100; Fax: (503) 588-5517; *District Director:* Willie Smith

21570 Willamette Dr., West Linn 97068; (503) 557-1324; Fax: (503) 557-1981; *District Aide:* Jean Eggers

Committee Assignment(s): Budget; Financial Services; Veterans' Affairs

HOSTETTLER, JOHN, R-IND. (8)

Capitol Hill Office: 1214 LHOB 20515; 225-4636; Fax: 225-3284; *Chief of Staff:* Carl Little

Web: www.house.gov/hostettler

E-mail: john.hostettler@mail.house.gov

District Office(s): 101 N.W. Martin Luther King Jr. Blvd., #124, Evansville 47708; (812) 465-6484; Fax: (812) 422-4761; *District Representative:* Nancy Wilder

328 N. 2nd St., #304, Vincennes 47591; (812) 882-0632; Fax: (812) 882-4298; *District Director:* Eric Holcomb

Committee Assignment(s): Armed Services; Judiciary

HOUGHTON, AMO, R-N.Y. (29)

Capitol Hill Office: 1111 LHOB 20515; 225-3161; Fax: 225-5574; *Chief of Staff:* William R. McKenney

Web: www.house.gov/houghton

E-mail: www.house.gov/writerep

District Office(s): 20 Pleasant St., #100, Canandaigua 14424; (585) 394-0220; Fax: (585) 394-7185; *Office Manager:* Sarah Blumer

32 Denison Pkwy. West, Corning 14830; (607) 937-3333; Fax: (607) 937-6047; *District Director:* Brandon Gardner

Committee Assignment(s): International Relations; Ways and Means

HOYER, STENY H., D-MD. (5)

Capitol Hill Office: 1705 LHOB 20515; 225-4131; Fax: 225-4300; *Chief of Staff:* Cory Alexander

Web: www.house.gov/hoyer

E-mail: www.house.gov/hoyer/letstalk.htm

District Office(s): 401 Post Office Rd., #202, Waldorf 20602; (301) 843-1577; Fax: (301) 843-1331; *Senior Adviser:* John Bohanan

6500 Cherrywood Lane, #310, Greenbelt 20770; (301) 474-0119; Fax: (301) 474-4697; *District Director:* Betsy Bossart

Committee Assignment(s): Appropriations

HULSHOF, KENNY, R-MO. (9)

Capitol Hill Office: 412 CHOB 20515; 225-2956; Fax: 225-5712; *Administrative Assistant:* Matt Miller

Web: www.house.gov/hulshof

E-mail: www.house.gov/writerep

District Office(s): 33 E. Broadway St., #280, Columbia 65203; (573) 449-5111; Fax: (573) 449-5312; *District Director:* Eric W. Feltner

201 N. 3rd St., #240, Hannibal 63401; (573) 221-1200; Fax: (573) 221-5349; *District Representative:* Scott Callicott

516 Jefferson St., Washington 63090; (636) 239-4001; Fax: (636) 239-1987; *District Representative:* Chris Haddox

Committee Assignment(s): Budget; Standards of Official Conduct; Ways and Means

HUNTER, DUNCAN, R-CALIF. (52)

Capitol Hill Office: 2265 RHOB 20515; 225-5672; Fax: 225-0235; *Chief of Staff:* Victoria J. Middleton

Web: www.house.gov/hunter

E-mail: www.house.gov/writerep

District Office(s): 366 S. Pierce St., El Cajon 92020; (619) 579-3001; Fax: (619) 579-2251; *District Chief of Staff:* Wendell Cutting

Committee Assignment(s): Armed Services; Select Homeland Security

HYDE, HENRY J., R-ILL. (6)

Capitol Hill Office: 2110 RHOB 20515; 225-4561; Fax: 225-1166; *Chief of Staff:* Judy Wolverton

Web: www.house.gov/hyde

E-mail: www.house.gov/writerep

District Office(s): 50 E. Oak St., #200, Addison 60101; (630) 832-5950; Fax: (630) 832-5969; *Executive Assistant:* Alice Horstman

Committee Assignment(s): International Relations; Judiciary

INSLEE, JAY, D-WASH. (1)

Capitol Hill Office: 308 CHOB 20515; 225-6311; Fax: 226-1606; *Chief of Staff:* Joby Shimomura

Web: www.house.gov/inslee

E-mail: jay.inslee@mail.house.gov

District Office(s): 17791 Fjord Dr. N.E., Door 112, Poulsbo 98370; (360) 598-2342; Fax: (360) 598-3650; *District Representative:* Clarence Moriwaki

21905 64th Ave. West, #101, Mountlake Terrace 98043; (425) 640-0233; Fax: (425) 776-7168; *District Director:* Kennie Endelman

Committee Assignment(s): Financial Services; Resources

ISAKSON, JOHNNY, R-GA. (6)

Capitol Hill Office: 132 CHOB 20515; 225-4501; Fax: 225-4656; *Legislative Director:* Glee Smith

Web: www.house.gov/isakson

E-mail: ga06@mail.house.gov

District Office(s): 6000 Lake Forest Dr., #110, Atlanta 30328; (404) 252-5239; Fax: (404) 303-1260; *Chief of Staff:* Heath Garrett

Committee Assignment(s): Education and Workforce; Transportation and Infrastructure

ISRAEL, STEVE, D-N.Y. (2)

Capitol Hill Office: 429 CHOB 20515; 225-3335; Fax: 225-4669; *Chief of Staff:* Mark Siegel

Web: www.house.gov/israel

E-mail: www.house.gov/writerep

District Office(s): 150 Motor Pkwy., #108, Hauppauge 11788; (631) 951-2210; Fax: (631) 951-3308; *District Director:* Holly Dunayer

Committee Assignment(s): Armed Services; Financial Services

ISSA, DARRELL, R-CALIF. (49)

Capitol Hill Office: 211 CHOB 20515; 225-3906; Fax: 225-3303; *Chief of Staff:* Dale Neugebauer

Web: www.house.gov/issa

E-mail: www.house.gov/writerep

District Office(s): 1800 Thibodo Rd., #310, Vista 92083; (760) 599-5000; Fax: (760) 599-1178; *District Director:* Andy Gharakhani

Committee Assignment(s): Energy and Commerce

ISTOOK, ERNEST, R-OKLA. (5)

Capitol Hill Office: 2404 RHOB 20515; 225-2132; Fax: 226-1463; *Administrative Assistant:* John C. Albaugh

Web: www.house.gov/istook

E-mail: istook@mail.house.gov

District Office(s): 29 E. 9th St., #301, Shawnee 74801; (405) 273-6202; Fax: (405) 273-2574

211 E. Broadway, Seminole 74868; (405) 303-2868; Fax: (405) 303-2847

5400 N. Grand Blvd., #505, Oklahoma City 73112; (405) 942-3636; Fax: (405) 942-3792; *District Director:* Steven Jones

Committee Assignment(s): Appropriations; Select Homeland Security

JACKSON, JESSE L. JR., D-ILL. (2)

Capitol Hill Office: 2419 RHOB 20515; 225-0773; Fax: 225-0899; *Chief of Staff:* Kenneth A. Edmonds

Web: www.jessejacksonjr.org

E-mail: webmaster@jessejacksonjr.org

District Office(s): 17926 S. Halsted St., Homewood 60430; (708) 798-6000; Fax: (708) 798-6160; *District Administrator:* Richard J. Bryant

Committee Assignment(s): Appropriations

JACKSON-LEE, SHEILA, D-TEXAS (18)

Capitol Hill Office: 2435 RHOB 20515; 225-3816; Fax: 225-3317; *Chief of Staff:* Leon Buck

Web: www.house.gov/jacksonlee

E-mail: tx18@mail.house.gov

District Office(s): 1919 Smith St., #1180, Houston 77002; (713) 655-0050; Fax: (713) 655-1612; *District Director:* Cynthia Buggage

420 W. 19th St., Houston 77008; (713) 861-4070; Fax: (713) 861-4323; *District Representative:* Betsy Love

6719 W. Montgomery Rd., #204, Houston 77091; (713) 691-4882; Fax: (713) 699-8292; *District Representative:* Dorothy Hubbard

Committee Assignment(s): Judiciary; Science; Select Homeland Security

JANKLOW, BILL, R-S.D. (AT LARGE)

Capitol Hill Office: 1504 LHOB 20515; 225-2801; Fax: 225-5823; *Chief of Staff:* Chris Braendlin

Web: www.house.gov/janklow

E-mail: billjanklow@mail.house.gov

District Office(s): 2600 S. Minnesota Ave., #100, Sioux Falls 57105; (605) 367-8371; Fax: (605) 367-8373; *District Director:* Dave Volk

2525 W. Main St., #210, Rapid City 57702; (605) 394-5280; Fax: (605) 394-5282; *Field Representative:* Jill Westbrook

10 6th Ave. S.W., Aberdeen 57401; (605) 626-3440; Fax: (605) 626-3441; *Field Representative:* Judy Vrchota

Committee Assignment(s): Agriculture; Government Reform; International Relations

JEFFERSON, WILLIAM J., D-LA. (2)

Capitol Hill Office: 240 CHOB 20515; 225-6636; Fax: 225-1988; *Chief of Staff:* Lionel R. Collins Jr.

Web: www.house.gov/jefferson

E-mail: jeffersonmc@mail.house.gov

District Office(s): 501 Magazine St., #1012, New Orleans 70130; (504) 589-2274; Fax: (504) 589-4513; *Executive Assistant:* Stephanie Butler

Committee Assignment(s): Ways and Means

JENKINS, BILL, R-TENN. (1)

Capitol Hill Office: 1207 LHOB 20515; 225-6356; Fax: 225-5714; *Chief of Staff:* Brenda Otterson

Web: www.house.gov/jenkins
E-mail: www.house.gov/writerep
District Office(s): 320 W. Center St., #157, Kingsport 37662; (423) 247-8161; Fax: (423) 247-1834; *Field Director:* Bill Snodgrass
Committee Assignment(s): Agriculture; Judiciary

JOHN, CHRIS, D-LA. (7)

Capitol Hill Office: 403 CHOB 20515; 225-2031; Fax: 225-5724; *Chief of Staff:* Lynn Hershey
Web: www.house.gov/john
E-mail: christopher.john@mail.house.gov
District Office(s): 800 Lafayette St., #1400, Lafayette 70501; (337) 235-6322; Fax: (337) 235-6072; *District Director:* Stephen Stefanski
1011 Lakeshore Dr., #306, Lake Charles 70601; (337) 433-1747; Fax: (337) 433-0974; *Executive Assistant:* Lynn Jones
Committee Assignment(s): Energy and Commerce

JOHNSON, EDDIE BERNICE, D-TEXAS (30)

Capitol Hill Office: 1511 LHOB 20515; 225-8885; Fax: 226-1477; *Chief of Staff:* Beverly Fields
Web: www.house.gov/ebjohnson
E-mail: rep.e.b.johnson@mail.house.gov
District Office(s): 2501 Cedar Springs Rd., #550, Dallas 75201; (214) 922-8885; Fax: (214) 922-7028; *District Director:* Roscoe Smith
1634-B W. Irving Blvd., Irving 75061; (972) 253-8885; Fax: (972) 253-3034; *Special Assistant:* Mardi Chev
Committee Assignment(s): Science; Transportation and Infrastructure

JOHNSON, NANCY L., R-CONN. (5)

Capitol Hill Office: 2113 RHOB 20515; 225-4476; Fax: 225-4488; *Chief of Staff:* Dave Karvelas
Web: www.house.gov/nancyjohnson
E-mail: www.house.gov/writerep
District Office(s): 480 Myrtle St., #200, New Britain 06053; (860) 223-8412; Fax: (860) 827-9009; *District Director:* Ken Hiscoe
20 E. Main St., #222, Waterbury 06702; (203) 573-1418; Fax: (203) 573-9329 *Constituent Services Director:* Terri Wilson;
Committee Assignment(s): Ways and Means

JOHNSON, SAM, R-TEXAS (3)

Capitol Hill Office: 1211 LHOB 20515; 225-4201; Fax: 225-1485; *Chief of Staff:* Cody Lusk
Web: www.house.gov/samjohnson
E-mail: www.house.gov/writerep
District Office(s): 801 E. Campbell Rd., #425, Richardson 75081; (972) 470-0892; Fax: (972) 470-9937; *District Director:* Mary Lynn Murrell
Committee Assignment(s): Education and Workforce; Ways and Means

JOHNSON, TIMOTHY V., R-ILL. (15)

Capitol Hill Office: 1229 LHOB 20515; 225-2371; Fax: 226-0791; *Chief of Staff:* Jerome Clarke
Web: www.house.gov/timjohnson
E-mail: www.house.gov/writerep
District Office(s): 1 Brickyard Dr., #201, Bloomington 61701; (309) 663-7049; Fax: (309) 663-9880; *District Aide:* Beth Harding
120 N. Vermilion St., Suite A, Danville 61832; (217) 431-8230; Fax: (217) 431-5338; *District Aide:* John Morris
2004 Fox Dr., Champaign 61820; (217) 403-4690; Fax: (217) 403-4691; *District Director:* Jeremy Cirks
1001 Market St., #102, Mt. Carmel 62863; (618) 262-8719; Fax: (618) 262-8859; *District Aide:* Craig Snow
655 W. Lincoln Ave., Unit B, Charleston 61920; (217) 348-6759; Fax: (217) 348-3761; *District Aide:* John Morris
Committee Assignment(s): Agriculture; Science; Transportation and Infrastructure

JONES, STEPHANIE TUBBS, D-OHIO (11)

Capitol Hill Office: 1009 LHOB 20515; 225-7032; Fax: 225-1339; *Chief of Staff:* Patrice Willoughby
Web: www.house.gov/tubbsjones
E-mail: stephanie.tubbs.jones@mail.house.gov
District Office(s): 3645 Warrensville Center Rd., #204, Shaker Heights 44122; (216) 522-4900; Fax: (216) 522-4908; *District Director:* Betty K. Pinkney
Committee Assignment(s): Standards of Official Conduct; Ways and Means

JONES, WALTER B., R-N.C. (3)

Capitol Hill Office: 422 CHOB 20515; 225-3415; Fax: 225-3286; *Administrative Assistant:* Glen Downs
Web: www.house.gov/jones
E-mail: congjones@mail.house.gov
District Office(s): 1105-C Corporate Dr., Greenville 27858; (252) 931-1003; Fax: (252) 931-1002; *District Director:* Millie Lilley
Committee Assignment(s): Armed Services; Financial Services; Resources

KANJORSKI, PAUL E., D-PA. (11)

Capitol Hill Office: 2353 RHOB 20515; 225-6511; Fax: 225-0764; *Chief of Staff:* Karen M. Feather
Web: www.house.gov/kanjorski
E-mail: paul.kanjorski@mail.house.gov
District Office(s): 7 N. Wilkes-Barre Blvd., #400 M, Wilkes-Barre 18702; (570) 825-2200; Fax: (570) 825-8685; *District Director:* Thomas P. Williams
Committee Assignment(s): Financial Services; Government Reform

KAPTUR, MARCY, D-OHIO (9)

Capitol Hill Office: 2366 RHOB 20515; 225-4146; Fax: 225-7711; *Chief of Staff:* Roger Szemraj

Web: www.house.gov/kaptur
E-mail: rep.kaptur@mail.house.gov
District Office(s): RHOB 43604; 259-7500; Fax: 255-9623
Committee Assignment(s): Appropriations

KELLER, RIC, R-FLA. (8)

Capitol Hill Office: 419 CHOB 20515; 225-2176; Fax: 225-0999; *Chief of Staff:* Jason Miller
Web: www.house.gov/keller
E-mail: www.house.gov/writerep
District Office(s): 605 E. Robinson St., #650, Orlando 32801; (407) 872-1962; Fax: (407) 872-1944; *District Director:* Mike Miller
Committee Assignment(s): Education and Workforce; Judiciary

KELLY, SUE W., R-N.Y. (19)

Capitol Hill Office: 1127 LHOB 20515; 225-5441; Fax: 225-3289; *Chief of Staff:* Michael Giuliani
Web: www.house.gov/suekelly
E-mail: dearsue@mail.house.gov
District Office(s): 21 Old Main St., #107, Fishkill 12524; (845) 897-5200; Fax: (845) 897-5800; *District Director:* Jerry Nappi
116 Radio Circle Dr., #301, Mount Kisco 10549; (914) 241-6340; Fax: (914) 241-3502; *District Representative:* Nicole Scova
Committee Assignment(s): Financial Services; Small Business; Transportation and Infrastructure

KENNEDY, MARK, R-MINN. (6)

Capitol Hill Office: 1415 LHOB 20515; 225-2331; Fax: 225-6475; *Chief of Staff:* Pat Shortridge
Web: markkennedy.house.gov
E-mail: mark.kennedy@mail.house.gov
District Office(s): 14669 Fitzgerald Ave. North, #100, Hugo 55038; (651) 653-5933; *Field Representative:* Kristin Flom
1111 Hwy. 25 North, #204, Buffalo 55313; (763) 684-1600; Fax: (763) 684-1730; *District Director:* Mark Matuska
22 Wilson Ave. N.E., #104, St. Cloud 56304; (320) 259-0099; Fax: (320) 259-0786; *Field Representative:* Chris Swedzinski
Committee Assignment(s): Financial Services; Transportation and Infrastructure

KENNEDY, PATRICK J., D-R.I. (1)

Capitol Hill Office: 407 CHOB 20515; 225-4911; Fax: 225-3290; *Chief of Staff:* Sean Richardson
Web: www.house.gov/patrickkennedy
E-mail: patrick.kennedy@mail.house.gov
District Office(s): 249 Roosevelt Ave., #200, Pawtuckct 02860; (401) 729-5600; Fax: (401) 729-5608; *District Director:* George Zainyeh
Committee Assignment(s): Appropriations

KILDEE, DALE E., D-MICH. (5)

Capitol Hill Office: 2107 RHOB 20515; 225-3611; Fax: 225-6393; *Chief of Staff:* Christopher Mansour
Web: www.house.gov/kildee
E-mail: www.house.gov/writerep
District Office(s): 432 N. Saginaw St., #410, Flint 48502; (810) 239-1437; Fax: (810) 239-1439; *District Director:* Tiffany Anderson-Flynn
Committee Assignment(s): Education and Workforce; Resources

KILPATRICK, CAROLYN CHEEKS, D-MICH. (13)

Capitol Hill Office: 1610 LHOB 20515; 225-2261; Fax: 225-5730; *Chief of Staff:* Kimberly Rudolph
Web: www.house.gov/kilpatrick
E-mail: www.house.gov/writerep
District Office(s): 1274 Library St., #1B, Detroit 48226; (313) 965-9004; Fax: (313) 965-9006; *District Director:* Wayne Powell
Committee Assignment(s): Appropriations

KIND, RON, D-WIS. (3)

Capitol Hill Office: 1406 LHOB 20515; 225-5506; Fax: 225-5739; *Chief of Staff:* Cindy Brown
Web: www.house.gov/kind
E-mail: ron.kind@mail.house.gov
District Office(s): 205 5th Ave. South, #227, La Crosse 54601; (608) 782-2558; Fax: (608) 782-4588; *District Director:* Loren J. Kannenberg
131 S. Barstow St., #301, Eau Claire 54701; (715) 831-9214; Fax: (715) 831-9272; *Caseworker:* Mark Aumann
Committee Assignment(s): Budget; Education and Workforce; Resources

KING, PETER T., R-N.Y. (3)

Capitol Hill Office: 436 CHOB 20515; 225-7896; Fax: 226-2279; *Chief of Staff:* Robert F. O'Connor
Web: www.house.gov/king
E-mail: pete.king@mail.house.gov
District Office(s): 1003 Park Blvd., Massapequa Park 11762; (516) 541-4225; Fax: (516) 541-6602; *District Director:* Anne Rosenfeld
Committee Assignment(s): Financial Services; International Relations; Select Homeland Security

KING, STEVE, R-IOWA (5)

Capitol Hill Office: 1432 LHOB 20515; 225-4426; Fax: 225-3193; *Chief of Staff:* Chuck Launder
Web: www.house.gov/steveking
E-mail: steve.king@mail.house.gov
District Office(s): 526 Nebraska St., Sioux City 51101; (712) 224-4692; Fax: (712) 224-4653; *District Representative:* Sandy Larvick
607 Lake Ave., Storm Lake 50588; (712) 732-4197; Fax: (712) 732-4217; *District Representative:* Dave Ehler

Committee Assignment(s): Agriculture; Judiciary; Small Business

KINGSTON, JACK, R-GA. (1)

Capitol Hill Office: 2242 RHOB 20515; 225-5831; Fax: 226-2269; *Chief of Staff:* Adam J. Sullivan
Web: www.house.gov/kingston
E-mail: jack.kingston@mail.house.gov
District Office(s): 805 Gloucester St., #304, Brunswick 31520; (912) 265-9010; Fax: (912) 265-9013; *District Representative:* Rob Asbell
P.O. Box 40, Baxley 31515; (912) 367-7403; Fax: (912) 367-7404; *District Manager:* Shiela Elliott
1 Diamond Causeway, #7, Savannah 31406; (912) 352-0101; Fax: (912) 352-0105; *District Representative:* Peggy Lee Mowers
Committee Assignment(s): Appropriations; Joint Library

KIRK, MARK STEVEN, R-ILL. (10)

Capitol Hill Office: 1531 LHOB 20515; 225-4835; Fax: 225-0837; *Chief of Staff:* Douglas S. O'Brien
Web: www.house.gov/kirk
E-mail: rep.kirk@mail.house.gov
District Office(s): 102 Wilmot Rd., #200, Deerfield 60015; (847) 940-0202; Fax: (847) 940-7143; *District Director:* Lenore MacDonald
20 S. Martin Luther King Jr. Dr., Waukegan 60085; (847) 662-0101; Fax: (847) 662-7519; *District Representative:* Roy Czajkowski
Committee Assignment(s): Appropriations

KLECZKA, GERALD D., D-WIS. (4)

Capitol Hill Office: 2217 RHOB 20515; 225-4572; Fax: 225-8135; *Administrative Assistant:* Winfield Boerckel
Web: www.house.gov/kleczka
E-mail: www.house.gov/writerep
District Office(s): 5032 W. Forest Home Ave., Milwaukee 53219; (414) 297-1140; Fax: (414) 327-6151; *Chief of Staff:* Kathryn A. Hein
Committee Assignment(s): Ways and Means

KLINE, JOHN, R-MINN. (2)

Capitol Hill Office: 1429 LHOB 20515; 225-2271; Fax: 225-2595; *Chief of Staff:* Steven Sutton
Web: www.house.gov/kline
E-mail: john.kline@mail.house.gov
District Office(s): 101 W. Burnsville Pkwy., #201, Burnsville 55337; (952) 808-1213; Fax: (952) 808-1261; *District Director:* Mike Osskopp
Committee Assignment(s): Armed Services; Education and Workforce

KNOLLENBERG, JOE, R-MICH. (9)

Capitol Hill Office: 2349 RHOB 20515; 225-5802; Fax: 226-2356; *Chief of Staff:* Jeff Onizuk

Web: www.house.gov/knollenberg
E-mail: rep.knollenberg@mail.house.gov
District Office(s): 312 Town Center Dr., Troy 48084; (248) 619-0531; *Staff Assistant:* Jessica Hallmark
30833 N. Western Hwy., #100, Farmington Hills 48334; (248) 851-1366; Fax: (248) 851-0418; *District Field Director:* Shawn Ciavattone
Committee Assignment(s): Appropriations

KOLBE, JIM, R-ARIZ. (8)

Capitol Hill Office: 2266 RHOB 20515; 225-2542; Fax: 225-0378; *Chief of Staff:* Frances C. McNaught
Web: www.house.gov/kolbe
E-mail: www.house.gov/writerep
District Office(s): 77 Calle Portal, #B-160, Sierra Vista 85635; (520) 459-3115; Fax: (520) 459-5419; *District Aide:* Bernadette Polley
1661 N. Swan Rd., #112, Tucson 85712; (520) 881-3588; Fax: (520) 322-9490; *District Director:* Patricia Klein
Committee Assignment(s): Appropriations

KUCINICH, DENNIS J., D-OHIO (10)

Capitol Hill Office: 1730 LHOB 20515; 225-5871; Fax: 225-5745; *Administrative Director:* Doug Gordon
Web: www.house.gov/kucinich
E-mail: www.house.gov/writerep
District Office(s): 5983 W. 54th St., Parma 44129; (440) 845-2707; Fax: (440) 845-2743; *District Representative:* Lynn Vittardi
14400 Detroit Ave., Lakewood 44107; (216) 228-8850; Fax: (216) 228-6465; *District Director:* Patricia Vecchio
Committee Assignment(s): Education and Workforce; Government Reform

LAHOOD, RAY, R-ILL. (18)

Capitol Hill Office: 1424 LHOB 20515; 225-6201; Fax: 225-9249; *Chief of Staff:* Diane R. Liesman
Web: www.house.gov/lahood
E-mail: www.house.gov/writerep
District Office(s): 100 N.E. Monroe St., Peoria 61602; (309) 671-7027; Fax: (309) 671-7309; *District Chief of Staff:* Brad McMillan
209 W. State St., Jacksonville 62650; (217) 245-1431; Fax: (217) 243-6852; *Office Manager:* Barb Baker
3050 Montvale Dr., Suite D, Springfield 62704; (217) 793-0808; Fax: (217) 793-9724; *Press Secretary:* Tim Butler
Committee Assignment(s): Appropriations; Select Intelligence

LAMPSON, NICK, D-TEXAS (9)

Capitol Hill Office: 405 CHOB 20515; 225-6565; Fax: 225-5547; *Chief of Staff:* Tom Combs
Web: www.house.gov/lampson
E-mail: www.house.gov/lampson/zipauth.htm

District Office(s): 1350 NASA Rd. One, #224, Houston 77058; (281) 333-4884; Fax: (281) 333-4355; *Special Projects:* Peter Tyler

300 Willow St., #322, Beaumont 77701; (409) 838-0061; Fax: (409) 832-0738; *District Director:* Jackie Savoy

601 Rosenberg St., #216, Galveston 77550; (409) 762-5877; Fax: (409) 763-4133; *Galveston Director:* Dorethea Lewis

Committee Assignment(s): Science; Transportation and Infrastructure

LANGEVIN, JIM, D-R.I. (2)

Capitol Hill Office: 109 CHOB 20515; 225-2735; Fax: 225-5976; *Chief of Staff:* Kristin E. Nicholson

Web: www.house.gov/langevin

E-mail: james.langevin@mail.house.gov

District Office(s): 300 Centreville Rd., #200, Warwick 02886; (401) 732-9400; Fax: (401) 737-2982; *District Director:* C. Kenneth Wild Jr.

Committee Assignment(s): Armed Services; Select Homeland Security

LANTOS, TOM, D-CALIF. (12)

Capitol Hill Office: 2413 RHOB 20515; 225-3531; Fax: 226-9789; *Chief of Staff:* Robert R. King

Web: www.house.gov/lantos

E-mail: www.house.gov/writerep

District Office(s): 400 El Camino Real, #410, San Mateo 94402; (650) 342-0300; Fax: (650) 375-8270; *District Representative:* Evelyn Szelenyi

Committee Assignment(s): Government Reform; International Relations

LARSEN, RICK, D-WASH. (2)

Capitol Hill Office: 1529 LHOB 20515; 225-2605; Fax: 225-4420; *Chief of Staff:* Jeff Bjornstad

Web: www.house.gov/larsen

E-mail: rick.larsen@mail.house.gov

District Office(s): 2930 Wetmore Ave., #9-E, Everett 98201; (425) 252-3188; Fax: (425) 252-6606; *District Director:* Jill McKinnie

104 W. Magnolia, #303, Bellingham 98201; (360) 733-4500; Fax: (360) 733-5144; *District Representative:* Andy Anderson

Committee Assignment(s): Agriculture; Armed Services; Transportation and Infrastructure

LARSON, JOHN B., D-CONN. (1)

Capitol Hill Office: 1005 LHOB 20515; 225-2265; Fax: 225-1031; *Legislative Director:* Jonathan Renfrew

Web: www.house.gov/larson

E-mail: www.house.gov/writerep

District Office(s): 221 Main St., 4th Floor, Hartford 06106; (860) 278-8888; Fax: (860) 278-2111; *District Director:* Maureen Moriarty

Committee Assignment(s): Armed Services; House Administration; Joint Library; Joint Printing; Science

LATHAM, TOM, R-IOWA (4)

Capitol Hill Office: 440 CHOB 20515; 225-5476; Fax: 225-3301; *Chief of Staff:* Michael Gruber

Web: www.house.gov/latham

E-mail: tom.latham@mail.house.gov

District Office(s): #238, 205 S. East St., Fort Dodge 50501; (515) 573-2738; Fax: (515) 576-7141; *Regional Representative:* Jim Oberhelman

213 N. Duff Ave., #1, Ames 50010; (515) 232-2885; Fax: (515) 232-2844; *District Director:* Clark Scanlon

812 Hwy. 18 East, Clear Lake 50428; (641) 357-5225; Fax: (641) 357-5226; *Regional Representative:* Louis Clark

Committee Assignment(s): Appropriations

LATOURETTE, STEVEN C., R-OHIO (14)

Capitol Hill Office: 2453 RHOB 20515; 225-5731; Fax: 225-3307; *Chief of Staff:* Jennifer Laptook

Web: www.house.gov/latourette

E-mail: www.house.gov/writerep

District Office(s): 1 Victoria Place, #320, Painesville 44077; (440) 352-3939; Fax: (440) 352-3622; *District Director:* Tom Intorcio

Committee Assignment(s): Financial Services; Government Reform; Standards of Official Conduct; Transportation and Infrastructure

LEACH, JIM, R-IOWA (2)

Capitol Hill Office: 2186 RHOB 20515; 225-6576; Fax: 226-1278; *Administrative Assistant:* Bill Tate

Web: www.house.gov/leach

E-mail: talk2jim@mail.house.gov

District Office(s): 129 12th St. S.E., Cedar Rapids 52403; (319) 363-4773; Fax: (319) 363-5008; *Staff Assistant:* Gary Grant

214 Jefferson St., Burlington 52601; (319) 754-1106; Fax: (319) 754-1107; *Staff Assistant:* Sue Zimmerman

125 S. Dubuque St., Iowa City 52240; (319) 351-0789; Fax: (319) 351-5789; *Staff Assistant:* Jenny Mitchell

105 E. 3rd St., #201, Ottumwa 52501; (641) 684-4024; Fax: (641) 684-1843; *Staff Assistant:* Deb McCurren

Committee Assignment(s): Financial Services; International Relations

LEE, BARBARA, D-CALIF. (9)

Capitol Hill Office: 1724 LHOB 20515; 225-2661; Fax: 225-9817; *Legislative Director:* Julie Little

Web: www.house.gov/lee

E-mail: barbara.lee@mail.house.gov

District Office(s): 1301 Clay St., #1000N, Oakland 94612; (510) 763-0370; Fax: (510) 763-6538; *Chief of Staff:* Sandre Swanson

Committee Assignment(s): Financial Services; International Relations

LEVIN, SANDER M., D-MICH. (12)

Capitol Hill Office: 2300 RHOB 20515; 225-4961; Fax: 226-1033; *Chief of Staff:* Hilarie Chambers
Web: www.house.gov/levin
E-mail: www.house.gov/levin/zipauth.htm
District Office(s): 25900 Greenfield Rd., #212, Oak Park 48237; (248) 968-2025; Fax: (248) 968-1405
27085 Gratiot Ave., Roseville 48066; (586) 498-7122; Fax: (586) 498-7123; *District Representative:* Diana McBroom
Committee Assignment(s): Ways and Means

LEWIS, JERRY, R-CALIF. (41)

Capitol Hill Office: 2112 RHOB 20515; 225-5861; Fax: 225-6498; *Administrative Assistant:* Arlene Willis
Web: www.house.gov/jerrylewis
E-mail: www.house.gov/writerep
District Office(s): 1150 Brookside Ave., #J5, Redlands 92373; (909) 862-6030; Fax: (909) 335-9155; *District Representative:* Janet Scott
Committee Assignment(s): Appropriations

LEWIS, JOHN, D-GA. (5)

Capitol Hill Office: 343 CHOB 20515; 225-3801; Fax: 225-0351; *Chief of Staff:* Michael Collins
Web: www.house.gov/johnlewis
E-mail: www.house.gov/writerep
District Office(s): 100 Peachtree St. N.W., #1920, Atlanta 30303; (404) 659-0116; Fax: (404) 331-0947; *Constituent Services Director:* Love Williams
Committee Assignment(s): Budget; Ways and Means

LEWIS, RON, R-KY. (2)

Capitol Hill Office: 2418 RHOB 20515; 225-3501; Fax: 226-2019; *Chief of Staff:* Helen Devlin
Web: www.house.gov/ronlewis
E-mail: www.house.gov/writerep
District Office(s): Warren County Justice Center, 1001 Center St., #300, Bowling Green 42101; (270) 842-9896; Fax: (270) 842-9081; *District Representative:* Phyllis Causey
1690 Ring Rd., #260, Elizabethtown 42701; (270) 765-4360; Fax: (270) 766-1580; *District Director:* Keith Rogers
1100 Walnut St., #P15B, Owensboro 42301; (270) 688-8858; Fax: (270) 688-8372; *District Representative:* Reagan Barnum
Committee Assignment(s): Government Reform; Ways and Means

LINDER, JOHN, R-GA. (7)

Capitol Hill Office: 1727 LHOB 20515; 225-4272; Fax: 225-4696; *Chief of Staff:* Rob Woodall
Web: linder.house.gov
E-mail: john.linder@mail.house.gov
District Office(s): 90 North St., #360, Canton 30114; (770) 479-1888; Fax: (770) 479-2999; *District Representative:* Victoria Benefield
2805 Peachtree Industrial Blvd., #213, Duluth 30097; (770) 232-3005; Fax: (770) 232-2909; *District Director:* Deborah Kearns
Committee Assignment(s): House Administration; Joint Printing; Rules; Select Homeland Security

LIPINSKI, WILLIAM O., D-ILL. (3)

Capitol Hill Office: 2188 RHOB 20515; 225-5701; Fax: 225-1012; *Administrative Assistant:* Michael McLaughlin
Web: www.house.gov/lipinski
E-mail: www.house.gov/writerep
District Office(s): 5239 W. 95th St., Oak Lawn 60453; (708) 952-0860; Fax: (708) 952-0862; *Caseworker:* Lenore Goodfriend
5832 S. Archer Ave., Chicago 60638; (312) 886-0481; Fax: (773) 767-9395; *District Director:* Jerry Hurkes
19 W. Hillgrove Ave., LaGrange 60525; (708) 352-0524; Fax: (708) 352-0927; *Staff Assistant:* Vacant
Committee Assignment(s): Transportation and Infrastructure

LOBIONDO, FRANK A., R-N.J. (2)

Capitol Hill Office: 225 CHOB 20515; 225-6572; Fax: 225-3318; *Chief of Staff:* Mary Annie Harper
Web: www.house.gov/lobiondo
E-mail: lobiondo@mail.house.gov
District Office(s): 5914 Main St., Mays Landing 08330; (609) 625-5008; Fax: (609) 625-5071; *District Director:* Joan Dermanoski
Committee Assignment(s): Armed Services; Transportation and Infrastructure

LOFGREN, ZOE, D-CALIF. (16)

Capitol Hill Office: 102 CHOB 20515; 225-3072; Fax: 225-3336; *Chief of Staff:* David Thomas
Web: www.house.gov/lofgren
E-mail: zoe.lofgren@mail.house.gov
District Office(s): 635 N. 1st St., Suite B, San Jose 95112; (408) 271-8700; Fax: (408) 271-8713; *District Director:* Sandra Soto
Committee Assignment(s): Judiciary; Science; Select Homeland Security

LOWEY, NITA M., D-N.Y. (18)

Capitol Hill Office: 2329 RHOB 20515; 225-6506; Fax: 225-0546; *Chief of Staff:* Clare Coleman
Web: www.house.gov/lowey
E-mail: nita.lowey@mail.house.gov
District Office(s): 222 Mamaroneck Ave., #310, White Plains 10605; (914) 428-1707; Fax: (914) 328-1505; *District Director:* Patricia Keegan

15 3rd St., #2, New City 10956; (845) 639-3485; Fax: (845) 639-3487; *District Representative:* David Fried

Committee Assignment(s): Appropriations; Select Homeland Security

LUCAS, FRANK D., R-OKLA. (3)

Capitol Hill Office: 2342 RHOB 20515; 225-5565; Fax: 225-8698; *Administrative Assistant:* Nicole Scott

Web: www.house.gov/lucas

E-mail: www.house.gov/writerep

District Office(s): 10952 N.W. Expressway, Suite B, Yukon 73099; (405) 373-1958; Fax: (405) 373-2046; *Chief of Staff:* Stacey Glasscock

720 S. Husband St., #7, Stillwater 74075; (405) 624-6407; Fax: (405) 624-6467; *Field Representative:* Julie Arntz

2728 Williams Ave., Suite F, Woodward 73801; (580) 256-5752; Fax: (580) 254-3047

Committee Assignment(s): Agriculture; Financial Services; Science

LUCAS, KEN, D-KY. (4)

Capitol Hill Office: 1205 LHOB 20515; 225-3465; Fax: 225-0003; *Chief of Staff:* Cheryl Brownell

Web: www.house.gov/kenlucas

E-mail: www.house.gov/writerep

District Office(s): 277 Buttermilk Pike, Ft. Mitchell 41017; (859) 426-0080; Fax: (859) 426-0061; *District Director:* Angie Cain

1405 Greenup Ave., #236, Ashland 41101; (606) 324-9898; Fax: (606) 325-9866; *District Representative:* Marilyn Mason

Committee Assignment(s): Agriculture; Financial Services; Select Homeland Security

LYNCH, STEPHEN F., D-MASS. (9)

Capitol Hill Office: 319 CHOB 20515; 225-8273; Fax: 225-3984; *Chief of Staff:* Kevin Ryan

Web: www.house.gov/lynch

E-mail: stephen.lynch@mail.house.gov

District Office(s): 1 Courthouse Way, #3110, Boston 02210; (617) 428-2000; Fax: (617) 428-2011; *District Director:* Stacey Walker

166 Main St., Brockton 02301; (508) 586-5555; Fax: (508) 580-4692; *District Representative:* Jim Gordon

Committee Assignment(s): Financial Services; Government Reform

MAJETTE, DENISE L., D-GA. (4)

Capitol Hill Office: 1517 LHOB 20515; 225-1605; Fax: 226-0691; *Chief of Staff:* Mike Williams

Web: www.house.gov/majette

E-mail: www.house.gov/majette/contact.shtml

District Office(s): 2050 Lawrenceville Hwy., #D-46, Decatur 30033; (404) 633-0927; *District Director:* Jeff Schoenberg

Committee Assignment(s): Budget; Education and Workforce; Small Business

MALONEY, CAROLYN B., D-N.Y. (14)

Capitol Hill Office: 2331 RHOB 20515; 225-7944; Fax: 225-4709; *Chief of Staff:* Ben Chevat

Web: www.house.gov/maloney

E-mail: rep.carolyn.maloney@mail.house.gov

District Office(s): 1651 3rd Ave., #311, New York 10128; (212) 860-0606; Fax: (212) 860-0704; *Chief of Staff:* Minna Elias

28-11 Astoria Blvd., Astoria 11102; (718) 932-1804; Fax: (718) 932-1805; *District Representative:* Mary Marangos

Committee Assignment(s): Financial Services; Government Reform; Joint Economic

MANZULLO, DONALD, R-ILL. (16)

Capitol Hill Office: 2228 RHOB 20515; 225-5676; Fax: 225-5284; *Chief of Staff:* Adam Magary

Web: www.house.gov/manzullo

E-mail: www.house.gov/writerep

District Office(s): 181 Virginia Ave., Crystal Lake 60014; (815) 356-9800; Fax: (815) 356-9803; *District Representative:* Nada Gebbes

415 S. Mulford Rd., Rockford 61108; (815) 394-1231; Fax: (815) 394-3930; *District Director:* Pamela Sexton

Committee Assignment(s): Financial Services; Small Business

MARKEY, EDWARD J., D-MASS. (7)

Capitol Hill Office: 2108 RHOB 20515; 225-2836; Fax: 226-0092; *Chief of Staff:* David Moulton

Web: www.house.gov/markey

E-mail: www.house.gov/writerep

District Office(s): 5 High St., #101, Medford 02155; (781) 396-2900; Fax: (781) 396-3220; *District Administrative Assistant:* Carol Lederman

188 Concord St., #102, Framingham 01702; (508) 875-2900; *Congressional Aide:* Roberto Pena

Committee Assignment(s): Energy and Commerce; Resources; Select Homeland Security

MARSHALL, JIM, D-GA. (3)

Capitol Hill Office: 502 CHOB 20515; 225-6531; Fax: 225-3013; *Chief of Staff:* John Kirincich

Web: www.house.gov/marshall

E-mail: jim.marshall@mail.house.gov

District Office(s): 682 Cherry St., #300, Macon 31201; (478) 464-0255; Fax: (478) 464-0277; *District Director:* Hobby Stripling

Committee Assignment(s): Agriculture; Armed Services; Small Business

MATHESON, JIM, D-UTAH (2)

Capitol Hill Office: 410 CHOB 20515; 225-3011; Fax: 225-5638; *Chief of Staff:* Stacey Alexander
Web: www.house.gov/matheson
E-mail: www.house.gov/writerep
District Office(s): 125 S. State St., #2311, Salt Lake City 84138; (801) 524-4394; Fax: (801) 524-5994; *District Director:* Alene Bentley
Committee Assignment(s): Financial Services; Science; Transportation and Infrastructure

MATSUI, ROBERT T., D-CALIF. (5)

Capitol Hill Office: 2310 RHOB 20515; 225-7163; Fax: 225-0566; *Chief of Staff:* Charles Brimmer
Web: www.house.gov/matsui
E-mail: www.house.gov/writerep
District Office(s): 12-600 Federal Courthouse, 501 I St., Sacramento 95814; (916) 498-5600; Fax: (916) 444-6117; *District Director:* Anne Sanger
Committee Assignment(s): Ways and Means

MCCARTHY, CAROLYN, D-N.Y. (4)

Capitol Hill Office: 106 CHOB 20515; 225-5516; Fax: 225-5758; *Chief of Staff:* Jim Hart
Web: www.house.gov/carolynmccarthy
E-mail: www.house.gov/writerep
District Office(s): 200 Garden City Plaza, #320, Garden City 11530; (516) 739-3008; Fax: (516) 739-2973; *District Director:* Mary Ellen Mendelsohn
Committee Assignment(s): Education and Workforce; Financial Services

MCCARTHY, KAREN, D-MO. (5)

Capitol Hill Office: 1436 LHOB 20515; 225-4535; Fax: 225-4403; *Chief of Staff:* Phil Scaglia
Web: www.house.gov/karenmccarthy
E-mail: www.house.gov/writerep
District Office(s): 400 E. 9th St., #9350, Kansas City 64106; (816) 842-4545; Fax: (816) 471-5215; *Chief of Staff:* Phil Scaglia
301 W. Lexington Ave., #217, Independence 64050; (816) 833-4545; Fax: (816) 833-2991; *District Aide:* Nicki Caldwell
Committee Assignment(s): Energy and Commerce; Select Homeland Security

MCCOLLUM, BETTY, D-MINN. (4)

Capitol Hill Office: 1029 LHOB 20515; 225-6631; Fax: 225-1968; *Chief of Staff:* Bill Harper
Web: www.house.gov/mccollum
E-mail: www.house.gov/writerep
District Office(s): 165 Western Ave. North, #17, St. Paul 55102; (651) 224-9191; Fax: (651) 224-3056; *District Director:* Joshua Stratka
Committee Assignment(s): Education and Workforce; International Relations; Resources

MCCOTTER, THADDEUS, R-MICH. (11)

Capitol Hill Office: 415 CHOB 20515; 225-8171; Fax: 225-2667; *Chief of Staff:* Kara Moore
Web: www.house.gov/mccotter
E-mail: thaddeus.mccotter@mail.house.gov
District Office(s): 17197 N. Laurel Park Dr., #161, Livonia 48152; (734) 632-0314; Fax: (734) 632-0373; *District Representative:* Paul Seewald
Committee Assignment(s): Budget; International Relations

MCCRERY, JIM, R-LA. (4)

Capitol Hill Office: 2104 RHOB 20515; 225-2777; Fax: 225-8039; *Chief of Staff:* Bob Brooks
Web: www.house.gov/mccrery
E-mail: jim.mccrery@mail.house.gov
District Office(s): 6425 Youree Dr., #350, Shreveport 71105; (318) 798-2254; Fax: (318) 798-2063; *District Manager:* Linda Sentell Wright
1606 S. 5th St., Leesville 71446; (337) 238-0778; Fax: (337) 238-0566; *Caseworker:* Lee Turner
Committee Assignment(s): Ways and Means

MCDERMOTT, JIM, D-WASH. (7)

Capitol Hill Office: 1035 LHOB 20515; 225-3106; Fax: 225-6197; *Chief of Staff:* Jan Shinpoch
Web: www.house.gov/mcdermott
E-mail: www.house.gov/writerep
District Office(s): 1809 7th Ave., #1212, Seattle 98101; (206) 553-7170; Fax: (206) 553-7175; *District Director:* Jane Sanders
Committee Assignment(s): Ways and Means

MCGOVERN, JIM, D-MASS. (3)

Capitol Hill Office: 430 CHOB 20515; 225-6101; Fax: 225-5759; *Chief of Staff:* Ed Augustus
Web: www.house.gov/mcgovern
E-mail: www.house.gov/mcgovern/send.htm
District Office(s): 34 Mechanic St., 1st Floor, Worcester 01608; (508) 831-7356; Fax: (508) 754-0982; *District Director:* Gladys Rodriguez-Parker
218 S. Main St., #204, Fall River 02721; (508) 677-0140; Fax: (508) 677-0992; *District Representative:* Patrick Norton
1 Park St., Attleboro 02703; (508) 431-8025; Fax: (508) 431-8017; *District Representative:* Shirley Coelho
255 Main St., #104, Marlborough 01752; (508) 460-9292; Fax: (508) 460-6869; *District Representative:* Matthew Pacheco
Committee Assignment(s): Rules

MCHUGH, JOHN M., R-N.Y. (23)

Capitol Hill Office: 2333 RHOB 20515; 225-4611; Fax: 226-0621; *Chief of Staff:* Robert G. Taub
Web: www.house.gov/mchugh
E-mail: www.house.gov/writerep

District Office(s): 205 S. Peterboro St, Canastota 13032; (315) 697-2063; Fax: (315) 697-2064

28 N. School St., P.O. Box 800, Mayfield 12117; (518) 661-6486; Fax: (518) 661-5704; *District Representative:* Diane Henderson

Federal Bldg., #104, Plattsburgh 12901; (518) 563-1406; Fax: (518) 561-9723; *District Representative:* Ruth Mary Ortloff

120 Washington St., #200, Watertown 13601; (315) 782-3150; Fax: (315) 782-1291; *District Representative:* Elaine Grabiec

Committee Assignment(s): Armed Services; Government Reform; International Relations

MCINNIS, SCOTT, R-COLO. (3)

Capitol Hill Office: 320 CHOB 20515; 225-4761; Fax: 226-0622; *Chief of Staff:* Mike Hesse
Web: www.house.gov/mcinnis
E-mail: www.house.gov/writerep
District Office(s): 134 W. B St., Pueblo 81003; (719) 543-8200; Fax: (719) 543-8204; *District Representative:* Susan Smith

1060 Main Ave., #102, Durango 81301; (970) 259-2754; Fax: (970) 259-2762; *District Representative:* Bob Moomaw

Hotel Colorado, 526 Pine St., #111, Glenwood Springs 81601; (970) 928-0637; Fax: (970) 928-0630; *Staff Assistant:* Lynne Kerst

225 N. 5th St., #702, Grand Junction 81501; (970) 245-7107; Fax: (970) 245-2194; *Office Manager:* Bill Endriss

Committee Assignment(s): Resources; Ways and Means

MCINTYRE, MIKE, D-N.C. (7)

Capitol Hill Office: 228 CHOB 20515; 225-2731; Fax: 225-5773; *Chief of Staff:* Dean Mitchell
Web: www.house.gov/mcintyre
E-mail: congmcintyre@mail.house.gov
District Office(s): 301 Green St., #218, Fayetteville 28301; (910) 323-0260; Fax: (910) 323-0069; *District Director:* Martha Ann McLean

201 N. Front St., #410, Wilmington 28401; (910) 815-4959; Fax: (910) 815-4543; *Constituent Services Assistant:* Pam Campbell-Dereef

701 N. Elm St., Lumberton 28358; (910) 671-6223; Fax: (910) 739-5085; *District Constituent Services Director:* Marie Thompson

Committee Assignment(s): Agriculture; Armed Services

MCKEON, HOWARD P. "BUCK," R-CALIF. (25)

Capitol Hill Office: 2351 RHOB 20515; 225-1956; Fax: 226-0683; *Chief of Staff:* Bob Cochran
Web: www.house.gov/mckeon
E-mail: tellbuck@mail.house.gov
District Office(s): 23929 W. Valencia Blvd., #410, Santa Clarita 91355; (661) 254-2111; Fax: (661) 254-2380; *District Director:* Scott Wilk

1008 W. Ave. M-14, #E-1, Palmdale 93551; (661) 274-9688; Fax: (661) 274-8744; *Field Representative:* Lew Stults
Committee Assignment(s): Armed Services; Education and Workforce

MCNULTY, MICHAEL R., D-N.Y. (21)

Capitol Hill Office: 2210 RHOB 20515; 225-5076; Fax: 225-5077; *Chief of Staff:* David Torian
Web: www.house.gov/mcnulty
E-mail: mike.mcnulty@mail.house.gov
District Office(s): 223 W. Main St., #10, Johnstown 12095
2490 Riverfront Center, Amsterdam 12010; (518) 843-3400; Fax: (518) 843-8874; *Staff Assistant:* Kathleen Joyce
U.S. Post Office, 29 Jay St., Schenectady 12305; (518) 374-4547; Fax: (518) 374-7908; *District Representative:* Bob Carr
1 Clinton Ave., #827, Albany 12207; (518) 465-0700; Fax: (518) 427-5107; *District Chief of Staff:* Charles Diamond
33 2nd St., Troy 12180; (518) 271-0822; Fax: (518) 273-6150; *District Representative:* Tom Matthews
Committee Assignment(s): Ways and Means

MEEHAN, MARTIN T., D-MASS. (5)

Capitol Hill Office: 2229 RHOB 20515; 225-3411; Fax: 226-0771; *Chief of Staff:* Bill McCann
Web: www.house.gov/meehan
E-mail: martin.meehan@mail.house.gov
District Office(s): Haverhill City Hall, 4 Summer St., #201 A, Haverhill 01830; (978) 521-1845; Fax: (978) 521-1843; *Congressional Aide:* Chris Doherty
11 Kearney Square, Lowell 01852; (978) 459-0101; Fax: (978) 459-1907; *District Director:* Pat Cook
305 Essex St., 4th Floor, Lawrence 01840; (978) 681-6200; Fax: (978) 682-6070; *Area Coordinator:* June Black
Committee Assignment(s): Armed Services; Judiciary

MEEK, KENDRICK B., D-FLA. (17)

Capitol Hill Office: 1039 LHOB 20515; 225-4506; Fax: 226-0777; *Chief of Staff:* John Shelby
Web: www.house.gov/kenmeek
District Office(s): 111 N.W. 183rd St., #315, Miami 33169; (305) 690-5905; Fax: (305) 690-5951; *District Director:* Anthony Williams
Committee Assignment(s): Armed Services; Select Homeland Security

MEEKS, GREGORY W., D-N.Y. (6)

Capitol Hill Office: 1710 LHOB 20515; 225-3461; Fax: 226-4169; *Chief of Staff:* Jameel W. Aalim-Johnson
Web: www.house.gov/meeks
E-mail: congmeeks@mail.house.gov
District Office(s): 106-11 Liberty Ave., Richmond Hill 11417; (718) 738-4200; Fax: (718) 738-5588; *Community Liaison:* Erline Nelson
196-06 Linden Blvd., St. Albans 11412; (718) 949-5600; Fax: (718) 949-5972; *District Director:* Patrick Jenkins

1931 Mott Ave., #305, Far Rockaway 11691; (718) 327-9791; Fax: (718) 327-4722; *Community Liaison:* Ed Williams

Committee Assignment(s): Financial Services; International Relations

MENENDEZ, ROBERT, D-N.J. (13)

Capitol Hill Office: 2238 RHOB 20515; 225-7919; Fax: 226-0792; *Chief of Staff:* Vacant

Web: menendez.house.gov

E-mail: menendez@mail.house.gov

District Office(s): 3109 Bergenline Ave., 2nd Floor, Union City 07087; (201) 558-0800; Fax: (201) 617-1612; *Congressional Aide:* Maritza Argudo

654 Ave. C, Bayonne 07002; (201) 823-2900; Fax: (201) 858-7139; *Congressional Aide:* Bob Burrows

911 Bergen Ave., Jersey City 07306; (201) 222-2828; Fax: (201) 222-0188; *District Director:* Nicholas Chiaravalloti

263 Hobart St., Perth Amboy 08861; (732) 324-6212; Fax: (732) 324-7470; *Congressional Aide:* Annette Polidura

Committee Assignment(s): International Relations; Transportation and Infrastructure

MICA, JOHN L., R-FLA. (7)

Capitol Hill Office: 2445 RHOB 20515; 225-4035; Fax: 226-0821; *Chief of Staff:* Russell Roberts

Web: www.house.gov/mica

E-mail: john.mica@mail.house.gov

District Office(s): 1000 City Center Circle, 2nd Floor, Port Orange 32129; (386) 756-9798; Fax: (386) 756-9903; *District Aide:* Barbara Koch

1211 Semoran Blvd., #117, Casselberry 32707; (407) 657-8080; Fax: (407) 657-5353; *District Representative:* Dick Harkey

840 Deltona Blvd., Suite G, Deltona 32725; (386) 860-1499; Fax: (386) 860-5730; *District Aide:* Janet Mines

Committee Assignment(s): Government Reform; House Administration; Transportation and Infrastructure

MICHAUD, MICHAEL H., D-MAINE (2)

Capitol Hill Office: 437 CHOB 20515; 225-6306; Fax: 225-2943; *Chief of Staff:* Peter Chandler

Web: www.house.gov/michaud

E-mail: www.housc.gov/writcrcp

District Office(s): 202 Harlow St., #235, Bangor 04401; (207) 942-6935; Fax: (207) 942-5907; *District Director:* Rosemary Winslow

179 Lisbon St., Lewiston 04240; (207) 782-3704; Fax: (207) 782-5330; *District Representative:* Andrea Quaid

445 Main St., Presque Isle 04769; (207) 764-1036; Fax: (207) 764-1060; *District Representative:* Marcia Gartley

Committee Assignment(s): Small Business; Transportation and Infrastructure; Veterans' Affairs

MILLENDER-MCDONALD, JUANITA, D-CALIF. (37)

Capitol Hill Office: 1514 LHOB 20515; 225-7924; Fax: 225-7926; *Chief of Staff:* Shirley Cooks

Web: www.house.gov/millender-mcdonald

E-mail: millender.mcdonald@mail.house.gov

District Office(s): 970 W. 190th St., E. Tower, #900, Torrance 90502; (310) 538-1190; Fax: (310) 538-9672; *District Director:* Carmen Taylor

Committee Assignment(s): House Administration; Joint Library; Small Business; Transportation and Infrastructure

MILLER, BRAD, D-N.C. (13)

Capitol Hill Office: 1505 LHOB 20515; 225-3032; Fax: 225-0181; *Chief of Staff:* Mark Harkins

Web: www.house.gov/bradmiller

E-mail: www.house.gov/writerep

District Office(s): 100 E. Forks Rd., #309, Raleigh 27609; (919) 781-9101; Fax: (919) 781-0649; *District Director:* Stephanie Bass

Committee Assignment(s): Financial Services; Science

MILLER, CANDICE S., R-MICH. (10)

Capitol Hill Office: 508 CHOB 20515; 225-2106; Fax: 226-1169; *Chief of Staff:* Jamie Roe

Web: www.house.gov/candicemiller

E-mail: candice.miller@mail.house.gov

District Office(s): 48653 Van Dyke Ave., Shelby Township 48317; (586) 997-5010; Fax: (586) 997-5013; *District Director:* Karen Czernel

Committee Assignment(s): Armed Services; Government Reform

MILLER, GARY G., R-CALIF. (42)

Capitol Hill Office: 1037 LHOB 20515; 225-3201; Fax: 226-6962; *Chief of Staff:* John Rothrock

Web: www.house.gov/garymiller

E-mail: publicCA41@mail.house.gov

District Office(s): 1800 E. Lambert Rd., #150, Brea 92821; (714) 257-1142; Fax: (714) 257-9242; *District Director:* Steve Thornton

Committee Assignment(s): Financial Services; Transportation and Infrastructure

MILLER, GEORGE, D-CALIF. (7)

Capitol Hill Office: 2205 RHOB 20515; 225-2095; Fax: 225-5609; *Administrative Assistant:* Daniel Weiss

Web: www.house.gov/georgemiller

E-mail: george.miller@mail.house.gov

District Office(s): 1333 Willow Pass Rd., #203, Concord 94520; (925) 602-1880; Fax: (925) 674-0983; *Deputy District Director:* Carol Hatch

3220 Blume Dr., #281, Richmond 94806; (510) 262-6500; Fax: (510) 222-1306; *Staff Assistant:* Hank Royal

375 G St., #1, Vallejo 94592; (707) 645-1888; Fax: (707) 645-1870; *Staff Assistant:* Katherine Hoffman

Committee Assignment(s): Education and Workforce; Resources

MILLER, JEFF, R-FLA. (1)

Capitol Hill Office: 331 CHOB 20515; 225-4136; Fax: 225-3414; *Chief of Staff:* Daniel McFaul
Web: www.house.gov/jeffmiller
E-mail: jeff.miller@mail.house.gov
District Office(s): 4300 Bayou Blvd., #17C, Pensacola 32503; (850) 479-1183; Fax: (850) 479-9394; *District Representative:* Kris Tande
348 S.W. Miracle Strip Pkwy., Unit 21, Fort Walton Beach 32548; (850) 664-1266; Fax: (850) 664-0851; *District Representative:* Lois Hoyt
Committee Assignment(s): Armed Services; Veterans' Affairs

MOLLOHAN, ALAN B., D-W.VA. (1)

Capitol Hill Office: 2302 RHOB 20515; 225-4172; Fax: 225-7564; *Chief of Staff:* Colleen McCarthy
Web: www.house.gov/mollohan
District Office(s): #316, 1125 Chapline St., Wheeling 26003; (304) 232-5390; Fax: (304) 232-5722; *Area Representative:* Cathy Abraham
Post Office Bldg., #209, Clarksburg 26302; (304) 623-4422; Fax: (304) 623-0571; *Area Representative:* Jane Merandi
Federal Bldg., #232, Morgantown 26507; (304) 292-3019; Fax: (304) 292-3027; *Area Representative:* Lotta Neer
425 Juliana St., #2040, Parkersburg 26101; (304) 428-0493; Fax: (304) 428-5980; *Caseworker:* Betsy Moore
Committee Assignment(s): Appropriations; Standards of Official Conduct

MOORE, DENNIS, D-KAN. (3)

Capitol Hill Office: 431 CHOB 20515; 225-2865; Fax: 225-2807; *Chief of Staff:* Howard Bauleke
Web: www.house.gov/moore
E-mail: dennis.moore@mail.house.gov
District Office(s): 8417 Santa Fe Dr., #101, Overland Park 66212; (913) 383-2013; Fax: (913) 383-2088; *District Director:* Kaye Cleaver
647 Massachusetts St., #212, Lawrence 66044; (785) 842-9313; Fax: (785) 843-3289; *Constituent Services Coordinator:* Becky Fast
500 State Ave., #176, Kansas City 66101; (913) 621-0832; Fax: (913) 621-1533; *Constituent Services Aide:* Paul Davidson
Committee Assignment(s): Budget; Financial Services; Science

MORAN, JAMES P., D-VA. (8)

Capitol Hill Office: 2239 RHOB 20515; 225-4376; Fax: 225-0017; *Chief of Staff:* Melissa Koloszar
Web: www.house.gov/moran
E-mail: www.house.gov/moran/letstalk.htm
District Office(s): 5115 Franconia Rd., Suite B, Alexandria 22310; (703) 971-4700; Fax: (703) 922-9436; *District Director:* Susie Warner
Committee Assignment(s): Appropriations; Budget

MORAN, JERRY, R-KAN. (1)

Capitol Hill Office: 1519 LHOB 20515; 225-2715; Fax: 225-5124; *Chief of Staff:* Jon Hixson
Web: www.house.gov/moranks01
E-mail: jerry.moran@mail.house.gov
District Office(s): 1200 Main St., #402, Hays 67601; (785) 628-6401; Fax: (785) 628-3791; *Constituent Services Representative:* Lisa Dethloff
1 N. Main St., #525, Hutchinson 67501; (620) 665-6138; Fax: (620) 665-6360; *District Director:* Kirk Johnson
Committee Assignment(s): Agriculture; Transportation and Infrastructure; Veterans' Affairs

MURPHY, TIM, R-PA. (18)

Capitol Hill Office: 226 CHOB 20515; 225-2301; Fax: 225-1844; *Chief of Staff:* Patrick Sheehan
Web: www.house.gov/murphy
E-mail: murphy@mail.house.gov
District Office(s): 504 Washington Rd., Mt. Lebanon 15228; (412) 344-5583; Fax: (412) 429-5092; *District Director:* David Uzelac
Committee Assignment(s): Financial Services; Government Reform; Veterans' Affairs

MURTHA, JOHN P., D-PA. (12)

Capitol Hill Office: 2423 RHOB 20515; 225-2065; Fax: 225-5709; *Administrative Assistant:* William Allen
Web: www.house.gov/murtha
E-mail: murtha@mail.house.gov
District Office(s): 647 Main St., #400, Johnstown 15907; (814) 535-2642; Fax: (814) 539-6229; *District Administrative Assistant:* John A. Hugya
Committee Assignment(s): Appropriations

MUSGRAVE, MARILYN, R-COLO. (4)

Capitol Hill Office: 1208 LHOB 20515; 225-4676; Fax: 225-5870; *Chief of Staff:* Guy Short
Web: www.house.gov/musgrave
E-mail: rep.musgrave@mail.house.gov
District Office(s): 5401 Stone Creek Circle, #240, Loveland 80538; (970) 663-3536; Fax: (970) 663-5270; *District Director:* B. J. Nikkel
5400 11th St., Greeley 80634; (970) 352-4037; Fax: (970) 521-9684; *District Representative:* Mark Fauth
332 Ambassador Thompson Blvd., Las Animas 81054; (719) 456-0925; Fax: (719) 456-0911; *District Representative:* Jace Ratzlaff
705 S. Division Ave., Sterling 80751; (970) 522-7188; Fax: (970) 521-9685; *District Representative:* Deb Carlstrom
Committee Assignment(s): Agriculture; Education and Workforce; Small Business

MYRICK, SUE, R-N.C. (9)

Capitol Hill Office: 230 CHOB 20515; 225-1976; Fax: 225-3389; *Administrative Assistant:* Ashley Hoy
Web: myrick.house.gov
E-mail: myrick@mail.house.gov
District Office(s): 318 South St., Suite B, Gastonia 28052; (704) 861-1976; Fax: (704) 864-2445; *District Representative:* Sandy Sigurdson
6525 Morrison Blvd., #402, Charlotte 28211; (704) 362-1060; Fax: (704) 367-0852; *Chief of Staff:* Hal Weatherman
Committee Assignment(s): Rules

NADLER, JERROLD, D-N.Y. (8)

Capitol Hill Office: 2334 RHOB 20515; 225-5635; Fax: 225-6923; *Legislative Director:* John Doty
Web: www.house.gov/nadler
E-mail: jerrold.nadler@mail.house.gov
District Office(s): 201 Varick St., #669, New York 10014; (212) 367-7350; Fax: (212) 367-7356; *Chief of Staff:* Amy Rutkin
445 Neptune Ave., Brooklyn 11224; (718) 373-3198; Fax: (718) 996-0039; *Regional Director:* Robert M. Gottheim
Committee Assignment(s): Judiciary; Transportation and Infrastructure

NAPOLITANO, GRACE F., D-CALIF. (38)

Capitol Hill Office: 1609 LHOB 20515; 225-5256; Fax: 225-0027; *Chief of Staff:* Kate Krause
Web: www.house.gov/napolitano
E-mail: grace@mail.house.gov
District Office(s): 11627 E. Telegraph Rd., #100, Santa Fe Springs 90670; (562) 801-2134; Fax: (562) 949-9144; *Office Manager:* Rose Stevens
Committee Assignment(s): International Relations; Resources; Small Business

NEAL, RICHARD E., D-MASS. (2)

Capitol Hill Office: 2133 RHOB 20515; 225-5601; Fax: 225-8112; *Chief of Staff:* Ann Jablon
Web: www.house.gov/neal
E-mail: www.house.gov/writerep
District Office(s): 1550 Main St., Springfield 01103; (413) 785-0325; Fax: (413) 747-0604; *District Director:* James Leydon
4 Congress St., Milford 01757; (508) 634-8198; Fax: (508) 634-8398; *Office Manager:* Virginia Purcell
Committee Assignment(s): Budget; Ways and Means

NETHERCUTT, GEORGE, R-WASH. (5)

Capitol Hill Office: 2443 RHOB 20515; 225-2006; Fax: 225-3392; *Chief of Staff:* Amy Flachbart
Web: www.house.gov/nethercutt
E-mail: www.house.gov/nethercutt/get_address.htm

District Office(s): W. 920 Riverside, #594, Spokane 99201; (509) 353-2374; Fax: (509) 353-2412; *Caseworker:* Don Gillespie
555 S. Main St., Colville 99114; (509) 684-3481; Fax: (509) 684-3482; *Legislative Representative:* Shelly Short
29 S. Palouse St., Walla Walla 99362; (509) 529-9358; Fax: (509) 529-9379; *Legislative Representative:* Scott Gruber
Committee Assignment(s): Appropriations; Science

NEY, BOB, R-OHIO (18)

Capitol Hill Office: 2438 RHOB 20515; 225-6265; Fax: 225-3394; *Chief of Staff:* Will Heaton
Web: www.house.gov/ney
E-mail: bobney@mail.house.gov
District Office(s): 126 E. 2nd St., Suite D, Chillicothe 45601; (740) 779-1634; Fax: (740) 779-1641; *Field Representative:* Carrie Mytinger
200 Broadway, Jackson 45640; (740) 288-1430; Fax: (740) 286-7630
146A W. Main St., St. Clairsville 43950; (740) 699-2704; Fax: (740) 699-2769; *District Director:* John Poe
152 2nd St. N.E., #200, New Philadelphia 44663; (330) 364-6380; Fax: (330) 364-7675; *Field Representative:* Lesley Applegarth
38 N. 4th St., #502, Zanesville 43701; (740) 452-7023; Fax: (740) 452-7191; *Office Director:* Joseph Rose
Committee Assignment(s): Financial Services; House Administration; Joint Library; Joint Printing; Transportation and Infrastructure

NORTHUP, ANNE M., R-KY. (3)

Capitol Hill Office: 1004 LHOB 20515; 225-5401; Fax: 225-5776; *Chief of Staff:* Terry Carmack
Web: northup.house.gov
E-mail: northup.house.gov/Contact.asp
District Office(s): 600 Martin Luther King Place, #216, Louisville 40202; (502) 582-5129; Fax: (502) 582-5897; *District Director:* Sherri Craig
Committee Assignment(s): Appropriations

NORTON, ELEANOR HOLMES, D-D.C. (AT LARGE)

Capitol Hill Office: 2136 RHOB 20515; 225-8050; Fax: 225-3002; *Chief of Staff:* Julia Hudson
Web: www.norton.house.gov
E-mail: www.norton.house.gov/feedback.cfm?campaign=norton&type=Contact%20Me
District Office(s): 529 14th St. N.W., #900, 20045; 783-5065; Fax: 783-5211; *District Office Director:* Sheila Bunn
2041 Martin Luther King Jr. Ave. S.E., #300, 20020; 678-8900; Fax: 678-8844; *District Liaison:* Aaron Ward
Committee Assignment(s): Government Reform; Select Homeland Security; Transportation and Infrastructure

NORWOOD, CHARLIE, R-GA. (9)

Capitol Hill Office: 2452 RHOB 20515; 225-4101; Fax: 226-5995; *Chief of Staff:* John S. Walker
Web: www.house.gov/norwood
E-mail: www.house.gov/writerep
District Office(s): 1056 Claussen Rd., #226, Augusta 30907; (706) 733-7066; Fax: (706) 733-7725; *District Director:* Michael Shaffer
Committee Assignment(s): Education and Workforce; Energy and Commerce

NUNES, DEVIN, R-CALIF. (21)

Capitol Hill Office: 1017 LHOB 20515; 225-2523; Fax: 225-3404; *Chief of Staff:* Johnny Amaral
Web: nunes.house.gov
E-mail: www.house.gov/writerep
District Office(s): 113 N. Church St., #208, Visalia 93291; (559) 733-3861; Fax: (559) 733-3865; *District Director:* Robert Jennings
264 Clovis Ave., #206, Clovis 93612; (559) 323-5235; Fax: (559) 323-5528; *District Representative:* Kevin Shakespeare
Committee Assignment(s): Agriculture; Resources

NUSSLE, JIM, R-IOWA (1)

Capitol Hill Office: 303 CHOB 20515; 225-2911; Fax: 225-9129; *Chief of Staff:* Rich Meade
Web: www.house.gov/nussle
E-mail: nussleia@mail.house.gov
District Office(s): 209 W. 4th St., Davenport 52801; (563) 326-1841; Fax: (563) 326-5464; *District Representative:* Jason Gordon
712 W. Main St., Manchester 52057; (563) 927-5141; Fax: (563) 927-5087; *District Administrator:* Cheryl Madlom
2255 John F. Kennedy Rd., Dubuque 52002; (563) 557-7740; Fax: (563) 557-1097; *District Representative:* Cindy Kholmann
3641 Kimball Ave., Waterloo 50702; (319) 235-1109; Fax: (319) 235-1260; *District Representative:* Matt Carrothers
Committee Assignment(s): Budget; Ways and Means

OBERSTAR, JAMES L., D-MINN. (8)

Capitol Hill Office: 2365 RHOB 20515; 225-6211; Fax: 225-0699; *Administrative Assistant:* William G. Richard
Web: www.house.gov/oberstar
E-mail: www.house.gov/writerep
District Office(s): 38625 14th Ave., #300B, N. Branch 55056; (651) 277-1234; Fax: (651) 277-1235; *Staff Assistant:* Deven Nelson
Duluth Federal Bldg., #231, Duluth 55802; (218) 727-7474; Fax: (218) 727-8270; *District Office Director:* Jackie Morris
501 Laurel St., Brainerd 56401; (218) 828-4400; Fax: (218) 828-1412; *Staff Assistant:* Ken Hasskamp
316 Lake St., Chisholm 55719; (218) 254-5761; Fax: (218) 254-5132; *Staff Assistant:* Peter Makowski

Committee Assignment(s): Transportation and Infrastructure

OBEY, DAVID R., D-WIS. (7)

Capitol Hill Office: 2314 RHOB 20515; 225-3365; Fax: 225-3240; *Staff Director:* William Stone
Web: www.house.gov/obey
E-mail: www.house.gov/writerep
District Office(s): 1401 Tower Ave., #307, Superior 54880; (715) 398-4426; Fax: (715) 398-4428; *District Representative:* Don Garner-Gerhardt
401 5th St., #406A, Wausau 54403; (715) 842-5606; Fax: (715) 842-4488; *District Director:* Doug Hill
Committee Assignment(s): Appropriations

OLVER, JOHN W., D-MASS. (1)

Capitol Hill Office: 1027 LHOB 20515; 225-5335; Fax: 226-1224; *Chief of Staff:* Hunter Ridgway
Web: www.house.gov/olver
E-mail: www.house.gov/olver/emailme.html
District Office(s): 47 Suffolk St., #310, Holyoke 01040; (413) 532-7010; Fax: (413) 532-6543; *District Director:* John Niedzielski
78 Center St., Pittsfield 01201; (413) 442-0946; Fax: (413) 443-2792; *District Aide:* Rhonda Serre
463 Main St., Fitchburg 01420; (978) 342-8722; Fax: (978) 343-8156; *District Aide:* Patricia Paulsen
Committee Assignment(s): Appropriations

ORTIZ, SOLOMON P., D-TEXAS (27)

Capitol Hill Office: 2470 RHOB 20515; 225-7742; Fax: 226-1134; *Chief of Staff:* Florencio Rendon
Web: www.house.gov/ortiz
E-mail: www.house.gov/writerep
District Office(s): 3649 Leopard St., #510, Corpus Christi 78408; (361) 883-5868; Fax: (361) 884-9201; *Office Manager:* Gerald Sawyer
3505 Boca Chica Blvd., #200, Brownsville 78521; (956) 541-1242; Fax: (956) 544-6915; *District Director:* Denise Blanchard
Committee Assignment(s): Armed Services; Resources

OSBORNE, TOM, R-NEB. (3)

Capitol Hill Office: 507 CHOB 20515; 225-6435; Fax: 226-1385; *Deputy Chief of Staff:* Christina Muedeking
Web: www.house.gov/osborne
E-mail: www.house.gov/writerep
District Office(s): 819 Diers Ave., #3, Grand Island 68803; (308) 381-5555; Fax: (308) 381-5557; *Chief of Staff:* Bruce Rieker
21 E. 20th St., Scottsbluff 69361; (308) 632-3333; Fax: (308) 635-3049; *Office Manager:* Scot Blehm
Committee Assignment(s): Agriculture; Education and Workforce; Resources

OSE, DOUG, R-CALIF. (3)

Capitol Hill Office: 236 CHOB 20515; 225-5716; Fax: 226-1298; *Chief of Staff:* Marko Mlikotin
Web: www.house.gov/ose
E-mail: www.house.gov/ose/Forms/messageform.htm
District Office(s): 4400 Auburn Blvd., #110, Sacramento 95841; (916) 489-3684; Fax: (916) 489-4911; *District Director:* Dan Sharp
Committee Assignment(s): Agriculture; Financial Services; Government Reform

OTTER, C. L. "BUTCH," R-IDAHO (1)

Capitol Hill Office: 1711 LHOB 20515; 225-6611; Fax: 225-3029; *Chief of Staff:* Jeff Malmen
Web: www.house.gov/otter
E-mail: www.house.gov/otter/email.htm
District Office(s): 802 W. Bannock St., #101, Boise 83702; (208) 336-9831; Fax: (208) 336-9891; *District Director:* Tana Cory
111 Main St., #170, Lewiston 83501; (208) 298-0030; Fax: (208) 298-0032; *District Representative:* Sherri Rothfusz
610 W. Hubbard, #206, Coeur D'Alene 83814; (208) 667-0127; Fax: (208) 667-0310; *District Representative:* Mark Compton
Committee Assignment(s): Energy and Commerce

OWENS, MAJOR R., D-N.Y. (11)

Capitol Hill Office: 2309 RHOB 20515; 225-6231; Fax: 226-0112; *Administrative Assistant:* Jacqueline Ellis
Web: www.house.gov/owens
E-mail: major.owens@mail.house.gov
District Office(s): 289 Utica Ave., Brooklyn 11213; (718) 773-3100; Fax: (718) 735-7143; *District Director:* Vacant
1414 Cortelyou Rd., Brooklyn 11226; (718) 940-3213; Fax: (718) 940-3217; *Office Director:* Nathan Spzilzinger
Committee Assignment(s): Education and Workforce; Government Reform

OXLEY, MICHAEL G., R-OHIO (4)

Capitol Hill Office: 2308 RHOB 20515; 225-2676; *Chief of Staff:* Jim Conzelman
Web: www.house.gov/oxley
E-mail: mike.oxley@mail.house.gov
District Office(s): 24 W. 3rd St., #314, Mansfield 44902; (419) 522-5757; Fax: (419) 525-2805; *District Representative:* R. Philip Holloway
100 E. Main Cross St., Findlay 45840; (419) 423-3210; Fax: (419) 422-2838; *District Representative:* Bonnie Dunbar
3121 W. Elm Plaza, Lima 45805; (419) 999-6455; Fax: (419) 999-4238; *District Representative:* Kelly Kirk
Committee Assignment(s): Financial Services

PALLONE, FRANK JR., D-N.J. (6)

Capitol Hill Office: 420 CHOB 20515; 225-4671; Fax: 225-9665; *Chief of Staff:* Jeffrey Carroll
Web: www.house.gov/pallone
E-mail: frank.pallone@mail.house.gov
District Office(s): 1390 Hwy. 36, #104, Hazlet 07730; (732) 264-9104; Fax: (732) 739-4668; *Staff Assistant:* Wanda Pettiford
504 Broadway, Long Branch 07740; (732) 571-1140; Fax: (732) 870-3890; *District Director:* Paul Dement
Kilmer Square, 67-69 Church St., New Brunswick 08901; (732) 249-8892; Fax: (732) 249-1335; *District Representative:* Gira Desai
Committee Assignment(s): Energy and Commerce; Resources

PASCRELL, BILL JR., D-N.J. (8)

Capitol Hill Office: 1722 LHOB 20515; 225-5751; Fax: 225-5782; *Chief of Staff:* Edward Farmer
Web: www.house.gov/pascrell
E-mail: bill.pascrell@mail.house.gov
District Office(s): 200 Federal Plaza, #500, Paterson 07505; (973) 523-5152; Fax: (973) 523-0637; *Chief of Staff:* Ed Farmer
Committee Assignment(s): Select Homeland Security; Transportation and Infrastructure

PASTOR, ED, D-ARIZ. (4)

Capitol Hill Office: 2465 RHOB 20515; 225-4065; Fax: 225-1655; *Legislative Director:* Eve Young
Web: www.house.gov/pastor
E-mail: www.house.gov/writerep
District Office(s): 411 N. Central Ave., #150, Phoenix 85004; (602) 256-0551; Fax: (602) 257-9103; *District Director:* Ron Piceno
Committee Assignment(s): Appropriations

PAUL, RON, R-TEXAS (14)

Capitol Hill Office: 203 CHOB 20515; 225-2831; Fax: 226-4871; *Chief of Staff:* Tom Lizardo
Web: www.house.gov/paul
E-mail: rep.paul@mail.house.gov
District Office(s): 200 W. 2nd St., #210, Freeport 77541; (979) 230-0000; Fax: (979) 230-0030; *Office Manager:* Dianna Kile
312 S. Main St., #228, Victoria 77901; (361) 576-1231; Fax: (361) 576-0381; *Casework Director:* Jackie Gloor
Committee Assignment(s): Financial Services; International Relations; Joint Economic

PAYNE, DONALD M., D-N.J. (10)

Capitol Hill Office: 2209 RHOB 20515; 225-3436; Fax: 225-4160; *Chief of Staff:* Kerry McKenney
Web: www.house.gov/payne
E-mail: donald.payne@mail.house.gov
District Office(s): 50 Walnut St., #1016, Newark 07102; (973) 645-3213; Fax: (973) 645-5902; *Chief of Staff:* Maxine James

333 N. Broad St., Elizabeth 07208; (908) 629-0222; Fax: (908) 629-0221; *Special Assistant:* Andrew Crawford

Committee Assignment(s): Education and Workforce; International Relations

PEARCE, STEVE, R-N.M. (2)

Capitol Hill Office: 1408 LHOB 20515; 225-2365; Fax: 225-9559; *Chief of Staff:* Jim Richards

Web: www.house.gov/pearce

E-mail: www.house.gov/pearce/contact.shtml

District Office(s): 1923 N. Dal Paso St., Hobbs 88240; (505) 392-8352; Fax: (505) 433-8325; *District Representative:* Glenda Carter

400 N. Telshor Blvd., Suite E, Las Cruces 88011; (505) 522-2219; Fax: (505) 522-3099; *District Representative:* Patty Dominguez

1717 W. 2nd St., Roswell 88201; (505) 622-0055; Fax: (505) 622-9608; *District Representative:* Cindy Willard

111 School of Mines Rd., Socorro 87801; (505) 838-7516; Fax: (505) 838-4027; *District Representative:* Barbara Romero

Committee Assignment(s): Resources; Transportation and Infrastructure

PELOSI, NANCY, D-CALIF. (8)

Capitol Hill Office: 2371 RHOB 20515; 225-4965; Fax: 225-8259; *Chief of Staff:* Judith Lemons

Web: www.house.gov/pelosi

E-mail: sf.nancy@mail.house.gov

District Office(s): 450 Golden Gate Ave., 14th Floor, San Francisco 94102; (415) 556-4862; Fax: (415) 861-1670; *District Director:* Catherine Dodd

Committee Assignment(s): No committee assignments

PENCE, MIKE, R-IND. (6)

Capitol Hill Office: 1605 LHOB 20515; 225-3021; Fax: 225-3382; *Chief of Staff:* Bill Smith

Web: mikepence.house.gov

E-mail: mike.pence@mail.house.gov

District Office(s): 1134 Meridian St., Anderson 46016; (765) 640-2919; Fax: (765) 640-2922; *District Director:* Lani Czarniecki

220 E. Main St., Muncie 47305; (765) 747-5566; Fax: (765) 747-5586; *Office Director:* Kim Orlosky

Committee Assignment(s): Agriculture; International Relations; Judiciary

PETERSON, COLLIN C., D-MINN. (7)

Capitol Hill Office: 2159 RHOB 20515; 225-2165; Fax: 225-1593; *Chief of Staff:* Mark Brownell

Web: www.house.gov/collinpeterson

E-mail: www.house.gov/writerep

District Office(s): 320 4th St. S.W., Willmar 56201; (320) 235-1061; Fax: (320) 235-2651; *Staff Assistant:* Mary Bertram

2603 Wheat Dr., Red Lake Falls 56750; (218) 253-4356; Fax: (218) 253-4373; *Staff Assistant:* Deb Hams

714 Lake Ave., #107, Detroit Lakes 56501; (218) 847-5056; Fax: (218) 847-5109; *Staff Assistant:* Sharon Josephson

Committee Assignment(s): Agriculture; Select Intelligence

PETERSON, JOHN E., R-PA. (5)

Capitol Hill Office: 123 CHOB 20515; 225-5121; Fax: 225-5796; *Chief of Staff:* Jordan Clark

Web: www.house.gov/johnpeterson

E-mail: john.peterson@mail.house.gov

District Office(s): 127 W. Spring St., Suite C, Titusville 16354; (814) 827-3985; Fax: (814) 827-7307; *District Director:* Peter Winkler

1524 W. College Ave., #208, State College 16801; (814) 238-1776; Fax: (814) 238-1918; *District Representative:* Mike Glazer

Committee Assignment(s): Appropriations; Resources

PETRI, TOM, R-WIS. (6)

Capitol Hill Office: 2462 RHOB 20515; 225-2476; Fax: 225-2356; *Chief of Staff:* Debbie Gephardt

Web: www.house.gov/petri

E-mail: www.house.gov/writerep

District Office(s): 115 Washington Ave., Oshkosh 54901; (920) 231-6333; Fax: (920) 231-0464; *Field Representative:* Melissa Kok

490 W. Rolling Meadows Dr., Suite B, Fond du Lac 54937; (920) 922-1180; Fax: (920) 922-4498; *District Director:* Sue Kerkman-Jung

Committee Assignment(s): Education and Workforce; Transportation and Infrastructure

PICKERING, CHARLES W. "CHIP" JR., R-MISS. (3)

Capitol Hill Office: 229 CHOB 20515; 225-5031; Fax: 225-5797; *Chief of Staff:* Susan Butler

Web: www.house.gov/pickering

E-mail: www.house.gov/writerep

District Office(s): 823 22nd Ave., Meridian 39301; (601) 693-6681; Fax: (601) 693-1801; *Special Assistant:* Lynne Compton

2080 Airport Rd., Suite D, Columbus 39702; (662) 327-2766; Fax: (662) 328-4570; *District Representative:* Hank Moseley

110-D Airport Rd., Pearl 39208; (601) 932-2410; Fax: (601) 965-4598; *District Director:* Stanley Shows

Committee Assignment(s): Agriculture; Energy and Commerce

PITTS, JOE, R-PA. (16)

Capitol Hill Office: 204 CHOB 20515; 225-2411; Fax: 225-2013; *Chief of Staff:* Gabe Neville

Web: www.house.gov/pitts

E-mail: www.house.gov/pitts/service/correspond.htm

District Office(s): 50 N. Duke St., Lancaster 17602; (717) 393-0667; Fax: (717) 393-0924; *District Director:* Tom P. Tillett

P.O. Box 837, Unionville 19375; (610) 444-4581; Fax: (610) 444-5750; *Executive Assistant:* Elizabeth Leaman

Committee Assignment(s): Energy and Commerce; International Relations

PLATTS, TODD R., R-PA. (19)

Capitol Hill Office: 1032 LHOB 20515; 225-5836; Fax: 226-1000; *Chief of Staff:* Bryan Tate

Web: www.house.gov/platts

E-mail: www.house.gov/writerep

District Office(s): 59 W. Louther St., Carlisle 17013; (717) 249-0190; Fax: (717) 218-0190; *Legislative Assistant:* Jay "Buck" Swisher

22 Chambersburg St., Gettysburg 17325; (717) 338-1919; Fax: (717) 334-6314; *Legislative Assistant:* Robert Reilly

2209 E. Market St., York 17402; (717) 600-1919; Fax: (717) 757-5001; *District Director:* Todd Abrisch

Committee Assignment(s): Education and Workforce; Government Reform; Transportation and Infrastructure

POMBO, RICHARD W., R-CALIF. (11)

Capitol Hill Office: 2411 RHOB 20515; 225-1947; Fax: 226-0861; *Chief of Staff:* Jessica Carter

Web: www.house.gov/pombo

E-mail: rpombo@mail.house.gov

District Office(s): 2495 W. March Lane, #104, Stockton 95207; (209) 951-3091; Fax: (209) 951-1910; *District Director:* Nicole Goehring

3000 Executive Pkwy., #216, San Ramon 94583; (925) 866-7040; Fax: (925) 866-7064; *District Representative:* Mike Pucci

315 W. Pine St., #11, Lodi 95240; (209) 482-1697; Fax: (916) 361-1683; *District Representative:* Nicole Goehring

Committee Assignment(s): Agriculture; Resources

POMEROY, EARL, D-N.D. (AT LARGE)

Capitol Hill Office: 1110 LHOB 20515; 225-2611; Fax: 226-0893; *Chief of Staff:* Bob Siggins

Web: www.house.gov/pomeroy

E-mail: rep.earl.pomeroy@mail.house.gov

District Office(s): 657 2nd Ave. North, #266, Fargo 58102; (701) 235-9760; Fax: (701) 235-9767; *Eastern Field Director:* Joan Carlson

220 E. Rosser Ave., #328, Bismarck 58501; (701) 224-0355; Fax: (701) 224-0431; *State Director:* Gail Skaley

Committee Assignment(s): Agriculture; Ways and Means

PORTER, JON, R-NEV. (3)

Capitol Hill Office: 218 CHOB 20515; 225-3252; Fax: 225-2185; *Chief of Staff:* Winsor Freemyer

Web: www.house.gov/porter

E-mail: www.house.gov/writerep

District Office(s): 2501 N. Green Valley Pkwy., #112 D, Henderson 89014; (702) 387-4941; Fax: (702) 434-1378; *District Director:* Kay Finfrock

Committee Assignment(s): Education and Workforce; Transportation and Infrastructure

PORTMAN, ROB, R-OHIO (2)

Capitol Hill Office: 238 CHOB 20515; 225-3164; Fax: 225-1992; *Chief of Staff:* Rob Lehman

Web: www.house.gov/portman

E-mail: portmail@mail.house.gov

District Office(s): 175 E. Main St., Batavia 45103; (513) 732-2948; Fax: (513) 732-3196; *District Representative:* Helen Heistand

8044 Montgomery Rd., #540, Cincinnati 45236; (513) 791-0381; Fax: (513) 791-1696; *District Representative:* Nan Cahall

Committee Assignment(s): Budget; Ways and Means

PRICE, DAVID E., D-N.C. (4)

Capitol Hill Office: 2162 RHOB 20515; 225-1784; Fax: 225-2014; *Chief of Staff:* Jean-Louise Beard

Web: www.house.gov/price

E-mail: www.house.gov/price/Email_David.htm

District Office(s): 5400 Trinity Rd., #205, Raleigh 27607; (919) 859-5999; Fax: (919) 859-5998; *District Director:* Rose Auman

411 W. Chapel Hill St., 6th Floor, Durham 27701; (919) 688-3004; Fax: (919) 688-0940; *District Liaison:* Tracy Lovett

88 Vilcom Center, #140, Chapel Hill 27514; (919) 967-7924; Fax: (919) 967-8324; *District Representative:* Gay Eddy

Committee Assignment(s): Appropriations

PRYCE, DEBORAH, R-OHIO (15)

Capitol Hill Office: 221 CHOB 20515; 225-2015; Fax: 225-3529; *Chief of Staff (personal):* Lori Salley; *Chief of Staff (leadership):* Kathryn Lehman

Web: www.house.gov/pryce

E-mail: pryce.oh15@mail.house.gov

District Office(s): 500 S. Front St., #1130, Columbus 43215; (614) 469-5614; Fax: (614) 469-7469; *District Director:* Marcee C. McCreary

Committee Assignment(s): Rules

PUTNAM, ADAM H., R-FLA. (12)

Capitol Hill Office: 506 CHOB 20515; 225-1252; Fax: 226-0585; *Chief of Staff:* John Hambel

Web: www.house.gov/putnam

E-mail: www.house.gov/putnam/pages/contact.html

District Office(s): 650 E. Davidson St., Bartow 33830; (863) 534-3530; Fax: (863) 534-3559; *District Director:* Mathew Joyner

Committee Assignment(s): Agriculture; Budget; Government Reform; Joint Economic

QUINN, JACK, R-N.Y. (27)

Capitol Hill Office: 2448 RHOB 20515; 225-3306; Fax: 226-0347; *Legislative Director:* Beth Thompson
Web: www.house.gov/quinn
E-mail: www.house.gov/writerep
District Office(s): 403 Main St., #240, Buffalo 14203; (716) 845-5257; Fax: (716) 847-0323; *Administrative Assistant:* Mary Lou Palmer
Committee Assignment(s): Transportation and Infrastructure; Veterans' Affairs

RADANOVICH, GEORGE P., R-CALIF. (19)

Capitol Hill Office: 438 CHOB 20515; 225-4540; Fax: 225-3402; *Chief of Staff:* John McCamman
Web: www.house.gov/radanovich
E-mail: www.house.gov/writerep
District Office(s): 2350 W. Shaw Ave., #137, Fresno 93711; (559) 449-2490; Fax: (559) 449-2499; *District Director:* Debbie Hurley
121 Main St., Suite D, Turlock 95380; (209) 656-8660; Fax: (209) 656-8649; *Field Representative:* Lacey Kiriakou
Committee Assignment(s): Energy and Commerce; Resources

RAHALL, NICK J. II, D-W.VA. (3)

Capitol Hill Office: 2307 RHOB 20515; 225-3452; Fax: 225-9061; *Administrative Assistant:* Kent Keyser
Web: www.house.gov/rahall
E-mail: nrahall@mail.house.gov
District Office(s): 601 Federal St., #1005, Bluefield 24701; (304) 325-6222; Fax: (304) 325-0552; *Community Relations:* Deborah Stevens
R. K. Bldg., Logan 25601; (304) 752-4934; Fax: (304) 752-8797; *Community Relations:* Debrina Workman
106 Main St., Beckley 25801; (304) 252-5000; Fax: (304) 252-9803; *Community Relations:* Kim McMillion
845 5th Ave., P.O. Box S, Huntington 25701; (304) 522-6425; Fax: (304) 529-5716; *Development Director:* Kelly Dyke
Committee Assignment(s): Resources; Transportation and Infrastructure

RAMSTAD, JIM, R-MINN. (3)

Capitol Hill Office: 103 CHOB 20515; 225-2871; Fax: 225-6351; *Chief of Staff:* Dean P. Peterson
Web: www.house.gov/ramstad
E-mail: mn03@mail.house.gov
District Office(s): 1809 Plymouth Rd. South, #300, Minnetonka 55305; (952) 738-8200; Fax: (952) 738-9362; *District Director:* Lance Olson
Committee Assignment(s): Ways and Means

RANGEL, CHARLES B., D-N.Y. (15)

Capitol Hill Office: 2354 RHOB 20515; 225-4365; Fax: 225-0816; *Administrative Assistant:* George Dalley
Web: www.house.gov/rangel
E-mail: www.house.gov/writerep
District Office(s): 163 W. 125th St., #737, New York 10027; (212) 663-3900; Fax: (212) 663-4277; *District Director:* James Capel
Committee Assignment(s): Joint Taxation; Ways and Means

REGULA, RALPH, R-OHIO (16)

Capitol Hill Office: 2306 RHOB 20515; 225-3876; Fax: 225-3059; *Chief of Staff:* Connie Ann Veillette
Web: www.house.gov/regula
E-mail: www.house.gov/writerep
District Office(s): 124 W. Washington St., #1A, Medina 44256; (330) 722-3793; Fax: (330) 723-1319; *Staff Assistant:* Michelle Connors
4150 Belden Village St. N.W., #408, Canton 44718; (330) 489-4414; Fax: (330) 489-4448; *District Director:* Rob Mullen
Committee Assignment(s): Appropriations

REHBERG, DENNY, R-MONT. (AT LARGE)

Capitol Hill Office: 516 CHOB 20515; 225-3211; Fax: 225-5687; *Chief of Staff:* Erik Iverson
Web: www.house.gov/rehberg
E-mail: denny.rehberg@mail.house.gov
District Office(s): 950 N. Montana Ave., Helena 59601; (406) 443-7878; Fax: (406) 443-8890; *Field Director:* Jeff Gerrard
105 Smelter Ave. N.E., #116, Great Falls 59404; (406) 454-1066; Fax: (406) 454-1130; *Constituent Services Director:* Sharon Westlake
218 E. Main St., Suite B, Missoula 59802; (406) 543-9550; Fax: (406) 543-0663; *Field Representative:* Teri Dinnell
1201 Grand Ave., #1, Billings 59102; (406) 256-1019; Fax: (406) 256-4934; *District Director:* Randy Vogel
Committee Assignment(s): Agriculture; Resources; Transportation and Infrastructure

RENZI, RICK, R-ARIZ. (1)

Capitol Hill Office: 418 CHOB 20515; 225-2315; Fax: 226-9739; *Chief of Staff:* Jimmy Jayne
Web: www.house.gov/renzi
E-mail: rick.renzi@mail.house.gov
District Office(s): 2707 S. White Mountain Rd., Suite E, Show Low 85901; (928) 537-2800; Fax: (928) 532-5088; *District Director:* Teri Grier
Committee Assignment(s): Financial Services; Resources; Veterans' Affairs

REYES, SILVESTRE, D-TEXAS (16)

Capitol Hill Office: 1527 LHOB 20515; 225-4831; Fax: 225-2016; *Chief of Staff:* Perry Finney Brody
Web: www.house.gov/reyes
E-mail: talk2silver@mail.house.gov

District Office(s): 310 N. Mesa St., #400, El Paso 79901; (915) 534-4400; Fax: (915) 534-7426; *Deputy Chief of Staff:* Salvador Payan

Committee Assignment(s): Armed Services; Select Intelligence; Veterans' Affairs

REYNOLDS, THOMAS M., R-N.Y. (26)

Capitol Hill Office: 332 CHOB 20515; 225-5265; Fax: 225-5910; *Chief of Staff:* Michael Brady

Web: www.house.gov/reynolds

E-mail: www.house.gov/writerep

District Office(s): 500 Essjay Rd., #260, Williamsville 14221; (716) 634-2324; Fax: (716) 631-7610; *District Director:* Chris Knospe

1577 W. Ridge Rd., Rochester 14615; (585) 663-5570

Committee Assignment(s): House Administration; Rules

RODRIGUEZ, CIRO D., D-TEXAS (28)

Capitol Hill Office: 1507 LHOB 20515; 225-1640; Fax: 225-1641; *Chief of Staff:* Jeff Mendelsohn

Web: www.house.gov/rodriguez

E-mail: www.house.gov/writerep

District Office(s): 1313 S.E. Military Dr., #115, San Antonio 78214; (210) 924-7383; Fax: (210) 927-6222; *District Director:* Norma Reyes

400 E. Gravis St., 2nd Floor, San Diego 78384; (361) 279-3907; Fax: (361) 279-8117; *S. Texas Liaison:* J. M. Rodriguez

301 Lincoln St., Roma 78584; (956) 847-1111; Fax: (956) 849-3871; *Constituent Services Liaison:* Norma Pena

Committee Assignment(s): Armed Services; Resources; Veterans' Affairs

ROGERS, HAROLD, R-KY. (5)

Capitol Hill Office: 2406 RHOB 20515; 225-4601; Fax: 225-0940; *Chief of Staff:* William Smith

Web: www.house.gov/rogers

E-mail: talk2hal@mail.house.gov

District Office(s): 119 College St., Suite 2, #212, Pikeville 41501; (606) 432-4388; Fax: (606) 432-4262; *Caseworker:* Deborah Dodge

601 Main St., Hazard 41701; (606) 439-0794; Fax: (606) 439-4647; *Field Representative:* Heath Preston

551 Clifty St., Somerset 42501; (606) 679-8346; Fax: (606) 678-4856; *District Administrator:* Robert L. Mitchell

Committee Assignment(s): Appropriations; Select Homeland Security

ROGERS, MIKE, R-MICH. (8)

Capitol Hill Office: 133 CHOB 20515; 225-4872; Fax: 225-5820; *Chief of Staff:* Matt Strawn

Web: www.house.gov/mikerogers

E-mail: www.house.gov/mikerogers/zipauth.htm

District Office(s): 1327 E. Michigan Ave., Lansing 48912; (517) 702-8000; Fax: (517) 702-8642; *District Director:* Anne Belser

Committee Assignment(s): Energy and Commerce

ROGERS, MIKE D., R-ALA. (3)

Capitol Hill Office: 514 CHOB 20515; 225-3261; Fax: 226-8485; *Chief of Staff:* Rob Jesmer

Web: www.house.gov/mike-rogers

District Office(s): 1129 Noble St., #104, Anniston 36201; (256) 236-5655; Fax: (256) 237-9203; *District Director:* Tripp Skipper

2216 Executive Park Dr., Opelika 36801; (334) 745-6221; Fax: (334) 742-0109; *Field Representative:* Cheryl Cunningham

7550 Halcyon Summit Dr., Montgomery 36117; (334) 277-4210; Fax: (334) 277-4257; *Field Representative:* Dan Webster

Committee Assignment(s): Agriculture; Armed Services

ROHRABACHER, DANA, R-CALIF. (46)

Capitol Hill Office: 2338 RHOB 20515; 225-2415; Fax: 225-0145; *Chief of Staff:* Rick Dykema

Web: www.house.gov/rohrabacher

E-mail: dana@mail.house.gov

District Office(s): 101 Main St., #380, Huntington Beach 92648; (714) 960-6483; Fax: (714) 960-7806; *District Director:* Kathleen Hollingsworth

Committee Assignment(s): International Relations; Science

ROS-LEHTINEN, ILEANA, R-FLA. (18)

Capitol Hill Office: 2160 RHOB 20515; 225-3931; Fax: 225-5620; *Chief of Staff:* Arthur Estopinan

Web: www.house.gov/ros-lehtinen

E-mail: www.house.gov/writerep

District Office(s): 9210 Sunset Dr., #100, Miami 33173; (305) 275-1800; Fax: (305) 275-1801; *District Director:* Debra Zimmerman

Committee Assignment(s): Government Reform; International Relations

ROSS, MIKE, D-ARK. (4)

Capitol Hill Office: 314 CHOB 20515; 225-3772; Fax: 225-1314; *Chief of Staff:* Cori Smith

Web: www.house.gov/ross

E-mail: www.house.gov/writerep

District Office(s): 112 Buena Vista, Hot Springs 71913; (501) 520-5892; Fax: (501) 520-5873; *Staff Member:* Donna Blackwood

1617 Olive St., Pine Bluff 71601; (870) 536-3376; Fax: (870) 536-4058; *District Director:* Chris Massingill

204 Northwest St., #202, El Dorado 71730; (870) 881-0681; Fax: (870) 881-0683; *Staff Member:* Patricia Herring

221 W. Main St., Prescott 71857; (870) 887-6787; Fax: (870) 887-6799; *Staff Member:* Aaron Stewart

Committee Assignment(s): Agriculture; Financial Services

ROTHMAN, STEVEN R., D-N.J. (9)

Capitol Hill Office: 1607 LHOB 20515; 225-5061; Fax: 225-5851; *Chief of Staff:* Charles L. Young

Web: www.house.gov/rothman

E-mail: www.house.gov/rothman/contact_steve.htm

District Office(s): 25 Main St., Court Plaza North, Hackensack 07601; (201) 646-0808; Fax: (201) 646-1944; *District Director:* Brendan Gill

130 Central Ave., Jersey City 07306; (201) 798-1366; Fax: (201) 798-1725; *Staff Assistant:* Al Zampella

Committee Assignment(s): Appropriations

ROYBAL-ALLARD, LUCILLE, D-CALIF. (34)

Capitol Hill Office: 2330 RHOB 20515; 225-1766; Fax: 226-0350; *Chief of Staff:* Ellen E. Riddleberger

Web: www.house.gov/roybal-allard

E-mail: www.house.gov/writerep

District Office(s): 255 E. Temple, #1860, Los Angeles 90012; (213) 628-9230; Fax: (213) 628-8578; *District Director:* Ana Figueroa-Davis

Committee Assignment(s): Appropriations; Standards of Official Conduct

ROYCE, ED, R-CALIF. (40)

Capitol Hill Office: 2202 RHOB 20515; 225-4111; Fax: 226-0335; *Chief of Staff:* Amy Porter

Web: www.house.gov/royce

E-mail: www.house.gov/writerep

District Office(s): 305 N. Harbor Blvd., #300, Fullerton 92832; (714) 992-8081; Fax: (714) 992-1668; *District Director:* Jennifer Cowen

Committee Assignment(s): Financial Services; International Relations

RUPPERSBERGER, C. A. DUTCH, D-MD. (2)

Capitol Hill Office: 1630 LHOB 20515; 225-3061; Fax: 225-3094; *Chief of Staff:* Jim Cavley

Web: www.house.gov/ruppersberger

E-mail: www.house.gov/writerep

District Office(s): 375 W. Padonia Rd., #200, Timonium 21093; (410) 628-2701; Fax: (410) 628-2708; *District Director:* Tara Linnehan Ousler

Committee Assignment(s): Government Reform; Select Intelligence

RUSH, BOBBY L., D-ILL. (1)

Capitol Hill Office: 2416 RHOB 20515; 225-4372; Fax: 226-0333; *Chief of Staff:* Kimberly C. Parker

Web: www.house.gov/rush

E-mail: www.house.gov/writerep

District Office(s): 700 E. 79th St., Chicago 60619; (773) 224-6500; Fax: (773) 224-9624; *District Director:* Sheila Jackson

Committee Assignment(s): Energy and Commerce

RYAN, PAUL D., R-WIS. (1)

Capitol Hill Office: 1217 LHOB 20515; 225-3031; Fax: 225-3393; *Administrative Assistant:* Joyce Yamat Meyer

Web: www.house.gov/ryan

E-mail: www.house.gov/ryan/email.html

District Office(s): 20 S. Main St., #10, Janesville 53545; (608) 752-4050; Fax: (608) 752-4711; *Chief of Staff:* Andy Speth

5712 7th Ave., Kenosha 53140; (262) 654-1901; Fax: (262) 654-2156; *Office Administrator:* Judi Pannozo

304 6th St., Racine 53403; (262) 637-0510; Fax: (262) 637-5689; *Field Representative:* Teresa Mora

Committee Assignment(s): Joint Economic; Ways and Means

RYAN, TIM, D-OHIO (17)

Capitol Hill Office: 222 CHOB 20515; 225-5261; Fax: 225-3719; *Chief of Staff:* Mary Ann Walsh

Web: www.house.gov/timryan

E-mail: tim.ryan@mail.house.gov

District Office(s): 241 Federal Plaza West, Youngstown 44503; (330) 740-0193; Fax: (330) 740-0182; *District Director:* Rick Leonard

Committee Assignment(s): Armed Services; Education and Workforce; Veterans' Affairs

RYUN, JIM, R-KAN. (2)

Capitol Hill Office: 2433 RHOB 20515; 225-6601; Fax: 225-7986; *Chief of Staff:* Mark Kelly

Web: ryun.house.gov

E-mail: jim.ryun@mail.house.gov

District Office(s): 800 S.W. Jackson, #100, Topeka 66612; (785) 232-4500; Fax: (785) 232-4512; *District Director:* Michelle Butler

701 N. Broadway, Pittsburg 66762; (316) 232-6100; Fax: (316) 232-6105; *Regional Representative:* Jim Allen

Committee Assignment(s): Armed Services; Budget; Financial Services

SABO, MARTIN OLAV, D-MINN. (5)

Capitol Hill Office: 2336 RHOB 20515; 225-4755; Fax: 225-4886; *Chief of Staff:* Michael S. Erlandson

Web: www.house.gov/sabo

E-mail: martin.sabo@mail.house.gov

District Office(s): 250 2nd Ave. South, #286, Minneapolis 55401; (612) 664-8000; Fax: (612) 664-8004; *Office Director:* Kathleen C. Anderson

Committee Assignment(s): Appropriations

SANCHEZ, LINDA T., D-CALIF. (39)

Capitol Hill Office: 1007 LHOB 20515; 225-6676; Fax: 226-1012; *Chief of Staff:* Janice Morris
Web: www.house.gov/lindasanchez
E-mail: www.house.gov/lindasanchez/contact.shtml
District Office(s): 4007 Paramount Blvd., Lakewood 90712; (562) 429-8499; Fax: (562) 938-1948; *District Director:* Bill Grady
Committee Assignment(s): Government Reform; Judiciary; Small Business

SANCHEZ, LORETTA, D-CALIF. (47)

Capitol Hill Office: 1230 LHOB 20515; 225-2965; Fax: 225-5859; *Chief of Staff:* Lee Godown
Web: www.house.gov/sanchez
E-mail: loretta@mail.house.gov
District Office(s): 12397 Lewis St., #101, Garden Grove 92840; (714) 621-0102; Fax: (714) 621-0401; *District Director:* Raul Luna
Committee Assignment(s): Armed Services; Select Homeland Security

SANDERS, BERNARD, I-VT. (AT LARGE)

Capitol Hill Office: 2233 RHOB 20515; 225-4115; Fax: 225-6790; *Chief of Staff:* Jeff Weaver
Web: bernie.house.gov
E-mail: bernie@mail.house.gov
District Office(s): 167 Main St., #410, Brattleboro 05301; (802) 254-8732; Fax: (802) 254-9207; *District Representative:* Sam Haskins
1 Church St., 2nd Floor, Burlington 05401; (802) 862-0697; Fax: (802) 860-6370; *District Representative:* Gretchen Bailey
Committee Assignment(s): Financial Services; Government Reform

SANDLIN, MAX, D-TEXAS (1)

Capitol Hill Office: 324 CHOB 20515; 225-3035; Fax: 225-5866; *Chief of Staff:* Paul F. Rogers
Web: www.house.gov/sandlin
E-mail: www.house.gov/writerep
District Office(s): 1300 E. Pinecrest Dr., #30, Marshall 75670; (903) 938-8386; Fax: (903) 935-5772; *District Director:* Bill Brannon
320 Church St., #132, Sulphur Springs 75482; (903) 885-8682; Fax: (903) 885-2976; *District Assistant:* Debbie Aikin
700 James Bowie Dr., New Boston 75570; (903) 628-5594; Fax: (903) 628-3155; *District Assistant:* Marie Martin
Committee Assignment(s): Ways and Means

SAXTON, H. JAMES, R-N.J. (3)

Capitol Hill Office: 339 CHOB 20515; 225-4765; Fax: 225-0778; *Chief of Staff:* Mark O'Connell
Web: www.house.gov/saxton
E-mail: www.house.gov/writerep
District Office(s): 1 Maine Ave., Cherry Hill 08002; (856) 428-0520; Fax: (856) 428-2384; *Staff Assistant:* Dee Denton
100 High St., #301, Mt. Holly 08060; (609) 261-5800; Fax: (609) 261-1275; *District Director:* Sandra R. Condit
247 Main St., Toms River 08753; (732) 914-2020; Fax: (732) 914-8351; *Staff Assistant:* Patricia Brogan
Committee Assignment(s): Armed Services; Joint Economic; Resources

SCHAKOWSKY, JAN, D-ILL. (9)

Capitol Hill Office: 515 CHOB 20515; 225-2111; Fax: 226-6890; *Chief of Staff:* Cathy Hurwit
Web: www.house.gov/schakowsky
E-mail: jan.schakowsky@mail.house.gov
District Office(s): 820 Davis St., #105, Evanston 60201; (847) 328-3399; Fax: (847) 328-3425; *Suburban Director:* Ra Joy
5533 Broadway St., Chicago 60640; (773) 506-7100; Fax: (773) 506-9202; *District Director:* Leslie Combs
6767 N. Milwaukee Ave., #101, Niles 60714; (847) 647-6955; Fax: (847) 647-6954; *District Representative:* Marie Anne Limjoco
Committee Assignment(s): Energy and Commerce

SCHIFF, ADAM B., D-CALIF. (29)

Capitol Hill Office: 326 CHOB 20515; 225-4176; Fax: 225-5828; *Chief of Staff:* Gail Ravnitzky
Web: www.house.gov/schiff
E-mail: www.house.gov/writerep
District Office(s): 35 S. Raymond Ave., #205, Pasadena 91105; (626) 304-2727; Fax: (626) 304-0572; *District Director:* Ann Peifer
Committee Assignment(s): International Relations; Judiciary

SCHROCK, ED, R-VA. (2)

Capitol Hill Office: 322 CHOB 20515; 225-4215; Fax: 225-4218; *Chief of Staff:* Rob Catron
Web: schrock.house.gov
E-mail: schrock.house.gov/contact.asp
District Office(s): 23386 Front St., Accomac 23301; (757) 787-7836; Fax: (757) 787-9540; *District Representative:* Sylvia Milliner
4966 Euclid Rd., #109, Virginia Beach 23462; (757) 497-6859; Fax: (757) 497-5474; *District Director:* Jim DeAngio
Committee Assignment(s): Armed Services; Budget; Government Reform; Small Business

SCOTT, DAVID, D-GA. (13)

Capitol Hill Office: 417 CHOB 20515; 225-2939; Fax: 225-4628; *Chief of Staff:* Rob Griner

Web: www.house.gov/davidscott

E-mail: david.scott@mail.house.gov

District Office(s): 173 N. Main St., Jonesboro 30236; (770) 210-5073; Fax: (770) 210-5673; *District Director:* Sheila Edwards

Committee Assignment(s): Agriculture; Financial Services

SCOTT, ROBERT C., D-VA. (3)

Capitol Hill Office: 2464 RHOB 20515; 225-8351; Fax: 225-8354; *Chief of Staff:* Joni L. Ivey

Web: www.house.gov/scott

E-mail: www.house.gov/writerep

District Office(s): 501 N. 2nd St., #401, Richmond 23219; (804) 644-4845; Fax: (804) 648-6026; *Legislative Assistant:* Nkechi George

2600 Washington Ave., #1010, Newport News 23607; (757) 380-1000; Fax: (757) 928-6694; *District Manager:* Gisele P. Russell

Committee Assignment(s): Budget; Judiciary

SENSENBRENNER, F. JAMES JR., R-WIS. (5)

Capitol Hill Office: 2449 RHOB 20515; 225-5101; Fax: 225-3190; *Deputy Chief of Staff:* Rich Zipperer

Web: www.house.gov/sensenbrenner

E-mail: sensenbrenner@mail.house.gov

District Office(s): 120 Bishops Way, #154, Brookfield 53005; (262) 784-1111; Fax: (262) 784-9437; *Chief of Staff:* Thomas Schreibel

Committee Assignment(s): Judiciary; Select Homeland Security

SERRANO, JOSE E., D-N.Y. (16)

Capitol Hill Office: 2227 RHOB 20515; 225-4361; Fax: 225-6001; *Chief of Staff:* Ellyn M. Toscano

Web: www.house.gov/serrano

E-mail: jserrano@mail.house.gov

District Office(s): 890 Grand Concourse, Bronx 10451; (718) 538-5400; Fax: (718) 588-3652; *District Director:* Cheryl Simmons-Oliver

Committee Assignment(s): Appropriations

SESSIONS, PETE, R-TEXAS (32)

Capitol Hill Office: 1318 LHOB 20515; 225-2231; Fax: 225-5878; *Chief of Staff:* Guy Harrison

Web: www.house.gov/sessions

E-mail: petes@mail.house.gov

District Office(s): 10675 E. Northwest Hwy., #1685, Dallas 75238; (214) 349-9996; Fax: (214) 349-0738; *District Director:* Charles Bauer

Committee Assignment(s): Rules; Select Homeland Security

SHADEGG, JOHN, R-ARIZ. (3)

Capitol Hill Office: 306 CHOB 20515; 225-3361; Fax: 225-3462; *Chief of Staff:* Elise Finley

Web: www.house.gov/shadegg

E-mail: j.shadegg@mail.house.gov

District Office(s): 301 E. Bethany Home Rd., #C178, Phoenix 85012; (602) 263-5300; Fax: (602) 248-7733; *District Chief of Staff:* Sean D. Noble

Committee Assignment(s): Energy and Commerce; Financial Services; Select Homeland Security

SHAW, E. CLAY JR., R-FLA. (22)

Capitol Hill Office: 2408 RHOB 20515; 225-3026; Fax: 225-8398; *Chief of Staff:* Eric Eikenberg

Web: www.house.gov/shaw

E-mail: www.house.gov/writerep

District Office(s): 222 Lakeview Ave., #162, West Palm Beach 33401; (561) 832-3007; Fax: (561) 832-0227; *District Representative:* Kathy Newell

1512 E. Broward Blvd., #101, Ft. Lauderdale 33301; (954) 522-1800; Fax: (954) 768-0511; *District Director:* George L. Caldwell

Committee Assignment(s): Joint Taxation; Ways and Means

SHAYS, CHRISTOPHER, R-CONN. (4)

Capitol Hill Office: 1126 LHOB 20515; 225-5541; Fax: 225-9629; *Chief of Staff:* Betsy Wright Hawkings

Web: www.house.gov/shays

E-mail: rep.shays@mail.house.gov

District Office(s): 10 Middle St., 11th Floor, Bridgeport 06604; (203) 579-5870; Fax: (203) 579-0771; *District Director:* Paul Pimentel

888 Washington Blvd., Stamford 06901; (203) 357-8277; Fax: (203) 357-1050; *District Representative:* Chris Albert

Committee Assignment(s): Budget; Financial Services; Government Reform; Select Homeland Security

SHERMAN, BRAD, D-CALIF. (27)

Capitol Hill Office: 1030 LHOB 20515; 225-5911; Fax: 225-5879; *Chief of Staff:* Ronnie P. Carleton

Web: www.house.gov/sherman

E-mail: brad.sherman@mail.house.gov

District Office(s): 5000 Van Nuys Blvd., #420, Sherman Oaks 91403; (818) 501-9200; Fax: (818) 501-1554; *District Director:* Mike Gatto

Committee Assignment(s): Financial Services; International Relations; Science

SHERWOOD, DON, R-PA. (10)

Capitol Hill Office: 1223 LHOB 20515; 225-3731; Fax: 225-9594; *Chief of Staff:* John S. Enright

Web: www.house.gov/sherwood

E-mail: www.house.gov/writerep

District Office(s): 330 Pine St., #202, Williamsport 17701; (570) 327-8161; Fax: (570) 327-9359; *District Representative:* Ruth Grieco

1146 Northern Blvd., Clarks Summit 18411; (570) 585-8190; Fax: (570) 586-8538; *District Director:* Jerry Morgan

Committee Assignment(s): Appropriations

SHIMKUS, JOHN, R-ILL. (19)

Capitol Hill Office: 513 CHOB 20515; 225-5271; Fax: 225-5880; *Chief of Staff:* Craig A. Roberts

Web: www.house.gov/shimkus

E-mail: www.house.gov/writerep

District Office(s): 3130 Chatham Rd., Suite C, Springfield 62704; (217) 492-5090; Fax: (217) 492-5096; *Office Manager:* Rodney Davis

221 E. Broadway, #102, Centralia 62801; (618) 532-9676; Fax: (618) 344-4215; *District Aide:* Matt Flanigan

508 W. Main St., Collinsville 62234; (618) 344-3065; Fax: (618) 344-4215; *Executive Assistant:* Dora Rohan

110 E. Locust St., #12, Harrisburg 62946; (618) 252-8271; Fax: (618) 252-8317; *District Aide:* Holly Linder

Committee Assignment(s): Energy and Commerce

SHUSTER, BILL, R-PA. (9)

Capitol Hill Office: 1108 LHOB 20515; 225-2431; Fax: 225-2486; *Chief of Staff:* Alex Mistri

Web: www.house.gov/shuster

E-mail: www.house.gov/writerep

District Office(s): 310 Penn St., Hollidaysburg 16648; (814) 696-6318; Fax: (814) 696-6726; *District Director:* Rob Young

179 E. Queen St., Chambersburg 17201; (717) 264-8308; Fax: (717) 264-0269; *District Aide:* Peggy Shank

Committee Assignment(s): Small Business; Transportation and Infrastructure

SIMMONS, ROB, R-CONN. (2)

Capitol Hill Office: 215 CHOB 20515; 225-2076; Fax: 225-4977; *Chief of Staff:* Todd Mitchell

Web: www.house.gov/simmons

E-mail: www.house.gov/writerep

District Office(s): 2 Courthouse Square, 5th Floor, Norwich 06360; (860) 886-0139; Fax: (860) 886-2974; *District Director:* Jane Dauphinais

Committee Assignment(s): Armed Services; Transportation and Infrastructure; Veterans' Affairs

SIMPSON, MIKE, R-IDAHO (2)

Capitol Hill Office: 1339 LHOB 20515; 225-5531; Fax: 225-8216; *Chief of Staff:* Lindsay Slater

Web: www.house.gov/simpson

E-mail: www.house.gov/writerep

District Office(s): 802 W. Bannock, #600, Boise 83702; (208) 334-1953; Fax: (208) 334-9533; *Casework Director:* Marcia Bain

1201 Falls Ave. East, #25, Twin Falls 83301; (208) 734-7219; Fax: (208) 734-7244; *Field Director:* Charles Barnes

490 Memorial Dr., #103, Idaho Falls 83402; (208) 523-6701; Fax: (208) 523-2384; *Field Director:* Laurel Hall

801 E. Sherman St., #194, Pocatello 83201; (208) 478-4160; Fax: (208) 478-4162; *Staff Assistant:* Kitty Kunz

Committee Assignment(s): Appropriations

SKELTON, IKE, D-MO. (4)

Capitol Hill Office: 2206 RHOB 20515; 225-2876; Fax: 225-2695; *Administrative Assistant:* Whitney D. Frost

Web: www.house.gov/skelton

E-mail: ike.skelton@mail.house.gov

District Office(s): 514-B N.W. Seven Hwy., Blue Springs 64014; (816) 228-4242; Fax: (816) 228-4814; *Chief of Staff:* Robert D. Hagedorn

1401 Southwest Blvd., #101, Jefferson City 65109; (573) 635-3499; Fax: (573) 635-8545; *Staff Assistant:* Carol Scott

219 N. Adams St., Lebanon 65536; (417) 532-7964; Fax: (417) 532-7975; *Staff Assistant:* Melissa Richardson

908 Thompson Blvd., Sedalia 65301; (660) 826-2675; Fax: (660) 827-5192; *Staff Assistant:* Arletta Garrett

Committee Assignment(s): Armed Services

SLAUGHTER, LOUISE M., D-N.Y. (28)

Capitol Hill Office: 2469 RHOB 20515; 225-3615; Fax: 225-7822; *Chief of Staff:* Cynthia M. Pellegrini

Web: www.house.gov/slaughter

E-mail: louiseny@mail.house.gov

District Office(s): 465 Main St., #105, Buffalo 14203; (716) 853-5813; Fax: (716) 853-6347; *District Aide:* Patricia Larke

1910 Pine Ave., Niagara Falls 14301; (716) 282-1274; Fax: (716) 282-2479; *District Aide:* Jane Schroeder

100 State St., #3120, Rochester 14614; (585) 232-4850; Fax: (585) 232-1954; *District Aide:* Chris Rumfola

Committee Assignment(s): Rules; Select Homeland Security

SMITH, ADAM, D-WASH. (9)

Capitol Hill Office: 227 CHOB 20515; 225-8901; Fax: 225-5893; *Chief of Staff:* Alixandria L. Wade

Web: www.house.gov/adamsmith

E-mail: adam.smith@mail.house.gov

District Office(s): 1717 Pacific Ave., #2135, Tacoma 98402; (253) 593-6600; Fax: (253) 593-6776; *District Director:* Linda Danforth

Committee Assignment(s): Armed Services; International Relations

SMITH, CHRISTOPHER H., R-N.J. (4)

Capitol Hill Office: 2373 RHOB 20515; 225-3765; Fax: 225-7768; *Chief of Staff:* Mary McDermott Noonan

Web: www.house.gov/chrissmith

E-mail: www.house.gov/writerep

District Office(s): 108 Lacey Rd., #38 A, Whiting 08759; (732) 350-2300; Fax: (732) 350-6260; *Regional Director:* Lorretta Charbonneau

1540 Kuser Rd., #A-9, Hamilton 08619; (609) 585-7878; Fax: (609) 585-9155; *Regional Director:* Joyce Golden

Committee Assignment(s): International Relations; Veterans' Affairs

SMITH, LAMAR, R-TEXAS (21)

Capitol Hill Office: 2231 RHOB 20515; 225-4236; Fax: 225-8628; *Chief of Staff:* John Lampmann

Web: www.house.gov/lamarsmith

E-mail: www.house.gov/writerep

District Office(s): 1006 Junction Hwy., Kerrville 78028; (830) 895-1414; Fax: (830) 895-2091; *District Representative:* Anne Overby

1100 N.E. Loop 410, #640, San Antonio 78209; (210) 821-5024; Fax: (210) 821-5947; *District Director:* O'Lene Stone

Committee Assignment(s): Judiciary; Science; Select Homeland Security

SMITH, NICK, R-MICH. (7)

Capitol Hill Office: 2305 RHOB 20515; 225-6276; Fax: 225-6281; *Chief of Staff:* Kurt Schmautz

Web: www.house.gov/nicksmith

E-mail: www.house.gov/nicksmith/email.htm

District Office(s): 110 1st St., Suite A, Jackson 49201; (517) 783-4486; Fax: (517) 783-3012; *District Director:* Keith Brown

249 W. Michigan Ave., Battle Creek 49017; (616) 965-9066; Fax: (616) 965-9036; *Field Representative:* Greg Moore

Committee Assignment(s): Agriculture; International Relations; Science

SNYDER, VIC, D-ARK. (2)

Capitol Hill Office: 1330 LHOB 20515; 225-2506; Fax: 225-5903; *Chief of Staff:* Edward D. Fry II

Web: www.house.gov/snyder

E-mail: snyder.congress@mail.house.gov

District Office(s): 700 W. Capitol Ave., #3118, Little Rock 72201; (501) 324-5941; Fax: (501) 324-6029; *District Director:* Amanda Nixon White

Committee Assignment(s): Armed Services; Veterans' Affairs

SOLIS, HILDA L., D-CALIF. (32)

Capitol Hill Office: 1725 LHOB 20515; 225-5464; Fax: 225-5467; *Chief of Staff:* Laura Rodriguez

Web: solis.house.gov

E-mail: www.house.gov/writerep

District Office(s): 4716 Cesar Chavez Ave., Bldg. A, East Los Angeles 90022; (323) 307-9904; Fax: (303) 307-9906; *District Representative:* Adele Andrade-Stadler

4401 Santa Anita Ave., #211, El Monte 91731; (626) 448-1271; Fax: (626) 448-8062; *District Chief of Staff:* Yvette Martinez

Committee Assignment(s): Energy and Commerce

SOUDER, MARK, R-IND. (3)

Capitol Hill Office: 1227 LHOB 20515; 225-4436; Fax: 225-3479; *Chief of Staff:* Angela Flood

Web: www.house.gov/souder

E-mail: souder@mail.house.gov

District Office(s): 1300 S. Harrison St., #3105, Fort Wayne 46802; (260) 424-3041; Fax: (260) 424-4042; *District Director:* Mark A. Wickersham

Committee Assignment(s): Government Reform; Resources; Select Homeland Security

SPRATT, JOHN M. JR., D-S.C. (5)

Capitol Hill Office: 1401 LHOB 20515; 225-5501; Fax: 225-0464; *Chief of Staff:* Ellen Wallace Buchanan

Web: www.house.gov/spratt

E-mail: www.house.gov/spratt/contact/email_john.htm

District Office(s): 39 E. Calhoun St., Sumter 29150; (803) 773-3362; Fax: (803) 773-7662; *District Aide:* Carolyn McCoy

88 Public Square, Darlington 29532; (843) 393-3998; Fax: (843) 393-8060; *District Aide:* Joanne Langley

Thomas S. Gettys Bldg., P.O. Box 350, Rock Hill 29731; (803) 327-1114; Fax: (803) 327-4330; *District Administrator:* Robert H. Hopkins

Committee Assignment(s): Armed Services; Budget

STARK, PETE, D-CALIF. (13)

Capitol Hill Office: 239 CHOB 20515; 225-5065; Fax: 226-3805; *Chief of Staff:* Debbie Curtis

Web: www.house.gov/stark

E-mail: www.house.gov/writerep

District Office(s): 39300 Civic Center Dr., #220, Fremont 94538; (510) 494-1388; Fax: (510) 494-5852; *District Director:* Jo Cazenave

Committee Assignment(s): Joint Economic; Joint Taxation; Ways and Means

STEARNS, CLIFF, R-FLA. (6)

Capitol Hill Office: 2370 RHOB 20515; 225-5744; Fax: 225-3973; *Chief of Staff:* Jack Seum

Web: www.house.gov/stearns

E-mail: www.house.gov/writerep

District Office(s): 115 S.E. 25th Ave., Ocala 34471; (352) 351-8777; Fax: (352) 351-8011; *District Director:* Judy Moore

1726 Kingsley Ave., #8, Orange Park 32073; (904) 269-3203; Fax: (904) 269-3343; *Staff Assistant:* Mary Johnson

100 S. 11th St., #102, Leesburg 34748; (352) 326-8285; Fax: (352) 326-9430; *Staff Assistant:* Vacant

Committee Assignment(s): Energy and Commerce; Veterans' Affairs

STENHOLM, CHARLES W., D-TEXAS (17)

Capitol Hill Office: 2409 RHOB 20515; 225-6605; Fax: 225-2234; *Chief of Staff:* Stephen Haterius
Web: www.house.gov/stenholm
E-mail: www.house.gov/writerep
District Office(s): 2121 Knickerbocker Rd., #318, San Angelo 76904; (915) 942-8881; Fax: (915) 942-8808; *District Representative:* Chandra Ford
1501-A Columbia, P.O. Box 1237, Stamford 79553; (915) 773-3623; Fax: (915) 773-2833; *District Manager:* Mark Lundgren
1500 Industrial Blvd., #101, Abilene 79602; (915) 673-7221; Fax: (915) 676-9547; *Office Manager:* Shandl Newman
Committee Assignment(s): Agriculture

STRICKLAND, TED, D-OHIO (6)

Capitol Hill Office: 336 CHOB 20515; 225-5705; Fax: 225-5907; *Chief of Staff:* John Haseley
Web: www.house.gov/strickland
E-mail: www.house.gov/writerep
District Office(s): 11692 Gallia Pike, Suite A, Wheelersburg 45694; (740) 574-2676; Fax: (740) 574-5337; *Field Representative:* Judy Newman
254 Front St., Marietta 45750; (740) 376-0868; Fax: (740) 376-0886; *District Director:* Jess Goode
374 Boardman-Poland Rd., Boardman 44512; (330) 965-4220; Fax: (330) 965-4224; *Field Representative:* Louis Gentile
35 S. 5th St., Martins Ferry 43935; (740) 633-2275; Fax: (740) 633-2280
Committee Assignment(s): Energy and Commerce; Veterans' Affairs

STUPAK, BART, D-MICH. (1)

Capitol Hill Office: 2352 RHOB 20515; 225-4735; Fax: 225-4744; *Chief of Staff:* Scott Schloegel
Web: www.house.gov/stupak
E-mail: stupak@mail.house.gov
District Office(s): 512 E. Houghton Ave., West Branch 48661; (989) 345-2258; Fax: (989) 345-2285; *Congressional Aide:* Lori Shelltron
200 Division St., Petoskey 49770; (231) 348-0657; Fax: (231) 348-0653; *Congressional Aide:* Heather Grobaski
111 E. Chisholm St., Alpena 49707; (989) 356-0690; Fax: (989) 356-0923; *Congressional Aide:* Sue Norkowski
1229 W. Washington St., Marquette 49855; (906) 228-3700; Fax: (906) 228-2305; *District Administrator:* Tom Baldini
902 Ludington St., Escanaba 49829; (906) 786-4504; Fax: (906) 786-4534; *Congressional Aide:* Sue McCarthy
2 S. 6th St., #3, Crystal Falls 49920; (906) 875-3751; Fax: (906) 875-3889; *Congressional Aide:* Jim Dellies
Committee Assignment(s): Energy and Commerce

SULLIVAN, JOHN, R-OKLA. (1)

Capitol Hill Office: 114 CHOB 20515; 225-2211; Fax: 225-9187; *Chief of Staff:* Elizabeth Bartheld
Web: sullivan.house.gov
E-mail: ok01.sullivan@mail.house.gov
District Office(s): 2424 E. 21st St., #510, Tulsa 74114; (918) 749-0014; Fax: (918) 749-0781; *District Director:* Richard Hedgecock
Committee Assignment(s): Government Reform; Science; Transportation and Infrastructure

SWEENEY, JOHN E., R-N.Y. (20)

Capitol Hill Office: 416 CHOB 20515; 225-5614; Fax: 225-6234; *Chief of Staff:* Martin Torrey
Web: www.house.gov/sweeney
E-mail: john.sweeney@mail.house.gov
District Office(s): 939 Route 146, #430, Clifton Park 12065; (518) 371-8839; Fax: (518) 371-9509; *Caseworker:* Barbara Palmer *Chief of Staff:* Marty Torrey
21 Bay St., Glens Falls 12801; (518) 792-3031; Fax: (518) 792-3181; *Caseworker:* Charlene Aspland
560 Warren St., Hudson 12534; (518) 828-0181; Fax: (518) 828-1657; *Caseworker:* Patricia Hart
Committee Assignment(s): Appropriations; Select Homeland Security

TANCREDO, TOM, R-COLO. (6)

Capitol Hill Office: 1130 LHOB 20515; 225-7882; Fax: 226-4623; *Chief of Staff:* Jacque Ponder
Web: www.house.gov/tancredo
E-mail: tom.tancredo@mail.house.gov
District Office(s): 5901 S. Middlefield Rd., #100, Littleton 80123; (720) 283-9772; Fax: (720) 283-9776; *Staff Assistant:* Carol Koppen
Committee Assignment(s): Budget; International Relations; Resources

TANNER, JOHN, D-TENN. (8)

Capitol Hill Office: 1226 LHOB 20515; 225-4714; Fax: 225-1765; *Chief of Staff:* Vickie Walling
Web: www.house.gov/tanner
E-mail: www.house.gov/tanner/letstalk.htm
District Office(s): 8120 Hwy. 51 North, #3, Millington 38053; (901) 873-5690; Fax: (901) 873-5692; *Caseworker:* Margaret Black
Federal Bldg., #B-7, Jackson 38301; (731) 423-4848; Fax: (731) 427-1537; *Constituent Services Director:* Shirlene Mercer
203 W. Church St., Union City 38261; (731) 885-7070; Fax: (731) 885-7094; *District Director:* Joe H. Hill
Committee Assignment(s): Ways and Means

TAUSCHER, ELLEN O., D-CALIF. (10)

Capitol Hill Office: 1034 LHOB 20515; 225-1880; Fax: 225-5914; *Chief of Staff:* Peter Muller
Web: www.house.gov/tauscher
E-mail: www.house.gov/writerep

District Office(s): 1801 N. California Blvd., #103, Walnut Creek 94596; (925) 932-8899; Fax: (925) 932-8159; *District Director:* Julie Hoffman

Committee Assignment(s): Armed Services; Transportation and Infrastructure

TAUZIN, BILLY, R-LA. (3)

Capitol Hill Office: 2183 RHOB 20515; 225-4031; Fax: 225-0563; *Chief of Staff:* Mimi Simoneaux

Web: www.house.gov/tauzin

E-mail: www.house.gov/writerep

District Office(s): 423 Lafayette St., #107, Houma 70360; (985) 876-3033; Fax: (985) 872-4449; *District Representative:* Jeri Theriot

828 S. Irma Blvd., #212A, Gonzales 70737; (225) 621-8490; Fax: (225) 621-8493; *Chief of Operations:* Martin Cancienne

8201 W. Judge Perez Dr., Chalmette 70043; (504) 271-1707; Fax: (504) 271-1756; *District Representative:* Justin Stevens

210 E. Main St., New Iberia 70560; (337) 367-8231; Fax: (337) 369-7084; *District Representative:* Vacant

Committee Assignment(s): Energy and Commerce; Resources; Select Homeland Security

TAYLOR, CHARLES H., R-N.C. (11)

Capitol Hill Office: 231 CHOB 20515; 225-6401; Fax: 226-6422; *Chief of Staff:* Roger France

Web: www.house.gov/charlestaylor

E-mail: www.house.gov/charlestaylor/email.htm

District Office(s): 515 S. Haywood St., #118, Waynesville 28786; (828) 456-7559; *District Representative:* Beverly Edwards

111 W. 2nd St., #100, Rutherfordton 28139; (828) 286-8750; *District Representative:* Larry Ford

22 S. Pack Square, #330, Asheville 28801; (828) 251-1988; *Office Manager:* Nancy Day

75 Peachtree St., P.O. Box 1271, Murphy 28906; (828) 837-3249; *District Representative:* Judy Edwards

Committee Assignment(s): Appropriations

TAYLOR, GENE, D-MISS. (4)

Capitol Hill Office: 2311 RHOB 20515; 225-5772; Fax: 225-7074; *Chief of Staff:* Wayne Weidie

Web: www.house.gov/genetaylor

E-mail: www.house.gov/writerep

District Office(s): 527 Central Ave., Laurel 39440; (601) 425-3905; *Caseworker:* Faye Heathcock

701 Main St., #215, Hattiesburg 39401; (601) 582-3246; Fax: (601) 582-3247; *District Representative:* Jerry Martin

2424 14th St., Gulfport 39501; (228) 864-7670; Fax: (228) 864-3099; *District Manager:* Beau Gex

1314 Government St., Ocean Springs 39564; (228) 872-7950; Fax: (228) 872-7949; *Caseworker:* Nancy Mathieu

Committee Assignment(s): Armed Services; Transportation and Infrastructure

TERRY, LEE, R-NEB. (2)

Capitol Hill Office: 1524 LHOB 20515; 225-4155; Fax: 226-5452; *Chief of Staff:* Eric Hultman

Web: leeterry.house.gov

E-mail: talk2lee@mail.house.gov

District Office(s): 11640 Arbor St., #100, Omaha 68114; (402) 397-9944; Fax: (402) 397-8787; *District Director:* Molly Lloyd

Committee Assignment(s): Energy and Commerce

THOMAS, BILL, R-CALIF. (22)

Capitol Hill Office: 2208 RHOB 20515; 225-2915; Fax: 225-8798; *Chief of Staff:* Mary Sue Englund

Web: www.house.gov/billthomas

E-mail: bill.thomas@mail.house.gov

District Office(s): 4100 Truxtun Ave., #220, Bakersfield 93309; (661) 327-3611; Fax: (661) 631-9535; *District Representative:* Billie Jo Medders

Committee Assignment(s): Joint Taxation; Ways and Means

THOMPSON, BENNIE, D-MISS. (2)

Capitol Hill Office: 2432 RHOB 20515; 225-5876; Fax: 225-5898; *Administrative Assistant:* Marsha G. McCraven

Web: www.house.gov/thompson

E-mail: thompsonms2nd@mail.house.gov

District Office(s): 335 Peach St., Marks 38646; (662) 326-9003; *Field Representative:* Samuel McCray

107 W. Madison St., Bolton 39041; (601) 866-9003; Fax: (601) 866-9036; *District Director:* Charlie Horhn

910 Courthouse Lane, Greenville 38701; (662) 335-9003; Fax: (662) 334-1304; *Office Manager:* Juliet Thomas

106 W. Green St., #134, Mound Bayou 38762; (662) 741-9003; Fax: (662) 741-9002; *Field Representative:* Geri Adams

509 Hwy. 82 West, Greenwood 38930; (662) 455-9003; Fax: (662) 453-0118; *Office Manager:* Trina George

Committee Assignment(s): Agriculture; Select Homeland Security

THOMPSON, MIKE, D-CALIF. (1)

Capitol Hill Office: 119 CHOB 20515; 225-3311; Fax: 225-4335; *Chief of Staff:* Ed Matovcik

Web: www.house.gov/mthompson

E-mail: www.house.gov/writerep

District Office(s): 317 3rd St., #1, Eureka 95501; (707) 269-9595; Fax: (707) 269-9598; *District Representative:* Liz Murguia

430 N. Franklin St., P.O. Box 2208, Ft. Bragg 95437; (707) 962-0933; Fax: (707) 962-0934; *Field Representative:* Kendall Smith

1040 Main St., #101, Napa 94559; (707) 226-9898; Fax: (707) 251-9800; *District Representative:* Cheryl Diehm

712 Main St., #1, Woodland 95695; (530) 662-5272; Fax: (530) 662-5163; *District Representative:* Elly Fairclough

Committee Assignment(s): Agriculture; Budget; Transportation and Infrastructure

THORNBERRY, WILLIAM M. "MAC," R-TEXAS (13)

Capitol Hill Office: 2457 RHOB 20515; 225-3706; Fax: 225-3486; *Administrative Assistant:* Lou Zickar

Web: www.house.gov/thornberry

E-mail: www.house.gov/writerep

District Office(s): 905 S. Fillmore St., #905, Amarillo 79101; (806) 371-8844; Fax: (806) 371-7044; *Chief of Staff:* Sylvia Nugent

4245 Kemp Blvd., #315, Wichita Falls 76308; (940) 692-1700; Fax: (940) 692-0593; *Office Manager:* Brent Oden

Committee Assignment(s): Armed Services; Budget; Select Homeland Security

TIAHRT, TODD, R-KAN. (4)

Capitol Hill Office: 2441 RHOB 20515; 225-6216; Fax: 225-3489; *Chief of Staff:* Jeff Kahrs

Web: www.house.gov/tiahrt

E-mail: www.house.gov/tiahrt/email.htm

District Office(s): 155 N. Market St., #400, Wichita 67202; (316) 262-8992; Fax: (316) 262-5309; *District Director:* Robert Noland

Committee Assignment(s): Appropriations

TIBERI, PAT, R-OHIO (12)

Capitol Hill Office: 113 CHOB 20515; 225-5355; Fax: 226-4523; *Chief of Staff:* Chris Zeigler

Web: www.house.gov/tiberi

E-mail: www.house.gov/writerep

District Office(s): 2700 E. Dublin-Granville Rd., #525, Columbus 43231; (614) 523-2555; Fax: (614) 818-0887; *District Director:* Sally Testa

Committee Assignment(s): Education and Workforce; Financial Services

TIERNEY, JOHN F., D-MASS. (6)

Capitol Hill Office: 120 CHOB 20515; 225-8020; Fax: 225-5915; *Chief of Staff:* Christine Pelosi

Web: www.house.gov/tierney

E-mail: www.house.gov/writerep

District Office(s): 17 Peabody Square, Peabody 01960; (978) 531-1669; Fax: (978) 531-1996; *District Director:* Gary Barrett

Lynn City Hall, #514, Lynn 01902; (781) 595-7375; Fax: (781) 595-7492; *Constituent Representative:* Rose Mary Sargent

Committee Assignment(s): Education and Workforce; Government Reform

TOOMEY, PATRICK J., R-PA. (15)

Capitol Hill Office: 224 CHOB 20515; 225-6411; Fax: 226-0778; *Chief of Staff:* Mark Dion

Web: www.house.gov/toomey

E-mail: rep.toomey.pa15@mail.house.gov

District Office(s): 553 Main St., Pennsburg 18073; (215) 541-1423; Fax: (215) 541-1424; *Constituent Services Representative:* Ethel Ritchie

2040 Hay Terrace, Wilson Borough 18042; (610) 515-1906; Fax: (610) 515-1907

2020 Hamilton St., Allentown 18104; (610) 439-8861; Fax: (610) 439-1918; *District Director:* Morrie Pulley

Committee Assignment(s): Budget; Financial Services; Small Business

TOWNS, EDOLPHUS, D-N.Y. (10)

Capitol Hill Office: 2232 RHOB 20515; 225-5936; Fax: 225-1018; *Chief of Staff:* Brenda Pillors

Web: www.house.gov/towns

E-mail: congressmantowns@mail.house.gov

District Office(s): 1110 Pennsylvania Ave., Store Five, Brooklyn 11207; (718) 272-1175; Fax: (718) 272-1203; *Special Assistant:* Anthony Foreman

26 Court St., #1510, Brooklyn 11241; (718) 855-8018; Fax: (718) 858-4542; *Chief of Staff:* Karen Johnson

1670 Fulton St., Brooklyn 11213; (718) 774-5682; Fax: (718) 774-5730; *District Scheduler:* Sabrina Evans

Committee Assignment(s): Energy and Commerce; Government Reform

TURNER, JIM, D-TEXAS (2)

Capitol Hill Office: 330 CHOB 20515; 225-2401; Fax: 225-5955; *Chief of Staff:* Elizabeth Hurley Burks

Web: www.house.gov/turner

E-mail: www.house.gov/writerep

District Office(s): 1202 Sam Houston Ave., #5, Huntsville 77340; (936) 291-3097; Fax: (936) 291-3086

701 N. 1st St., #201, Lufkin 75901; (936) 637-1770; Fax: (936) 632-8588; *District Director:* Jerry Huffman

420 W. Green Ave., Orange 77630; (409) 883-4990; Fax: (409) 883-5149; *Field Representative:* Ann Gray

Committee Assignment(s): Armed Services; Select Homeland Security

TURNER, MICHAEL R., R-OHIO (3)

Capitol Hill Office: 1740 LHOB 20515; 225-6465; Fax: 225-6754; *Chief of Staff:* Stacey Barton

Web: www.house.gov/miketurner

E-mail: oh03.wyr@mail.house.gov

District Office(s): 120 W. 3rd St., #305, Dayton 45402; (937) 225-2843; Fax: (937) 225-2752; *District Director:* John Shaw

15 E. Main St., Wilmington 45177; (937) 383-8931; Fax: (937) 383-8910; *District Representative:* Jennifer Taylor

Committee Assignment(s): Armed Services; Government Reform

UDALL, MARK, D-COLO. (2)

Capitol Hill Office: 115 CHOB 20515; 225-2161; Fax: 226-7840; *Chief of Staff:* Alan Salazar
Web: www.house.gov/markudall
E-mail: www.house.gov/writerep
District Office(s): 1333 W. 120th Ave., #210, Westminster 80234; (303) 457-4500; Fax: (303) 457-4504; *Chief of Staff:* Alan Salazar *Scheduler:* Lisa Carpenter
Committee Assignment(s): Agriculture; Resources; Science

UDALL, TOM, D-N.M. (3)

Capitol Hill Office: 1414 LHOB 20515; 225-6190; Fax: 226-1331; *Chief of Staff:* Tom Nagle
Web: www.house.gov/tomudall
E-mail: tom.udall@mail.house.gov
District Office(s): 321 N. Connelly St., Clovis 88101; (505) 763-7616; Fax: (505) 763-7642; *District Representative:* Vacant
800 Municipal Dr., Farmington 87401; (505) 324-1005; Fax: (505) 324-1026; *District Representative:* Pete Valencia
3900 Southern Blvd. S.E., #105-A, Rio Rancho 87124; (505) 994-0499; Fax: (505) 994-0550; *District Representative:* Sarah Cobb
110 W. Aztec Ave., Gallup 87301; (505) 863-0582; Fax: (505) 863-0678; *District Representative:* Rose Custer
1700 N. Grand Ave., Las Vegas 87701; (505) 454-4080; Fax: (505) 454-4078; *District Representative:* Thomas Garcia
811 St. Michael's Dr., #104, Santa Fe 87505; (505) 984-8950; Fax: (505) 986-5047; *District Director:* Michele Jacquez-Ortiz
Committee Assignment(s): Resources; Small Business; Veterans' Affairs

UPTON, FRED, R-MICH. (6)

Capitol Hill Office: 2161 RHOB 20515; 225-3761; Fax: 225-4986; *Chief of Staff:* Joan Hillebrands
Web: www.house.gov/upton
E-mail: talk2.fsu@mail.house.gov
District Office(s): 157 S. Kalamazoo Mall, #180, Kalamazoo 49007; (616) 385-0039; Fax: (616) 385-2888; *District Manager:* Ed Sackley
800 Ship St., #106, St. Joseph 49085; (616) 982-1986; Fax: (616) 982-0237; *District Director:* John Proos
Committee Assignment(s): Education and Workforce; Energy and Commerce

VAN HOLLEN, CHRIS, D-MD. (8)

Capitol Hill Office: 1419 LHOB 20515; 225-5341; Fax: 225-0375; *Chief of Staff:* Kay Casstevens
Web: www.house.gov/vanhollen
E-mail: chris.vanhollen@mail.house.gov
District Office(s): 51 Monroe St., #507, Rockville 20850; (301) 424-3501; Fax: (301) 424-5992; *District Director:* Joan Kleinman

Committee Assignment(s): Education and Workforce; Government Reform

VELAZQUEZ, NYDIA M., D-N.Y. (12)

Capitol Hill Office: 2241 RHOB 20515; 225-2361; Fax: 226-0327; *Chief of Staff:* Michael Day
Web: www.house.gov/velazquez
E-mail: www.house.gov/writerep
District Office(s): 268 Broadway, 2nd Floor, Brooklyn 11211; (718) 599-3658; Fax: (718) 599-4537; *District Director:* Vacant
16 Court St., #1006, Brooklyn 11201; (718) 222-5819; Fax: (718) 222-5830; *Community Coordinator:* Daniel Wiley
173 Ave. B, New York 10009; (212) 673-3997; Fax: (212) 473-5242; *Community Coordinator:* Michael Santos
Committee Assignment(s): Financial Services; Small Business

VISCLOSKY, PETER J., D-IND. (1)

Capitol Hill Office: 2313 RHOB 20515; 225-2461; Fax: 225-2493; *Chief of Staff:* Richard Kaelin
Web: www.house.gov/visclosky
E-mail: www.house.gov/writerep
District Office(s): 701 E. 83rd Ave., #9, Merrillville 46410; (219) 795-1844; Fax: (219) 795-1850; *District Director:* Mark Savinski
Committee Assignment(s): Appropriations

VITTER, DAVID, R-LA. (1)

Capitol Hill Office: 414 CHOB 20515; 225-3015; Fax: 225-0739; *Chief of Staff:* Kyle Ruckert
Web: vitter.house.gov
E-mail: david.vitter@mail.house.gov
District Office(s): 2800 Veterans Blvd., #201, Metairie 70002; (504) 589-2753; Fax: (504) 589-2607; *District Director:* David Doss
300 E. Thomas St., Hammond 70401; (985) 542-9616; Fax: (985) 542-9577; *Staff Assistant:* Peggy Breland
Committee Assignment(s): Appropriations; Budget

WALDEN, GREG, R-ORE. (2)

Capitol Hill Office: 1404 LHOB 20515; 225-6730; Fax: 225-5774; *Chief of Staff:* Brian MacDonald
Web: www.walden.house.gov
E-mail: greg.walden@mail.house.gov
District Office(s): 131 N.W. Hawthorne St., #211, Bend 97701; (541) 389-4408; Fax: (541) 389-4452; *District Representative:* Justen Rainey
843 E. Main St., #400, Medford 97504; (541) 776-4646; Fax: (541) 779-0204; *District Director:* John Snider
Committee Assignment(s): Energy and Commerce; Resources

WALSH, JAMES T., R-N.Y. (25)

Capitol Hill Office: 2369 RHOB 20515; 225-3701; Fax: 225-4042; *Administrative Assistant:* Arthur Jutton
Web: www.house.gov/walsh
E-mail: rep.james.walsh@mail.house.gov
District Office(s): 1180 Canandaigua Rd., Palmyra 14522; (315) 597-6138; Fax: (315) 597-6631; *Staff Assistant:* Nora Yancey
100 S. Clinton St., #1340, Syracuse 13261; (315) 423-5657; Fax: (315) 423-5669; *District Manager:* Ginny Carmody
Committee Assignment(s): Appropriations

WAMP, ZACH, R-TENN. (3)

Capitol Hill Office: 2447 RHOB 20515; 225-3271; Fax: 225-3494; *Chief of Staff:* Helen Hardin
Web: www.house.gov/wamp
E-mail: www.house.gov/wamp/IMA/get_address4.htm
District Office(s): 200 Administration Rd., #100, Oak Ridge 37830; (865) 576-1976; Fax: (865) 576-3221; *District Director:* Linda Ponce
900 Georgia Ave., #126, Chattanooga 37402; (423) 756-2342; Fax: (423) 756-6613; *District Director:* Sarah Bryan
Committee Assignment(s): Appropriations

WATERS, MAXINE, D-CALIF. (35)

Capitol Hill Office: 2344 RHOB 20515; 225-2201; Fax: 225-7854; *Chief of Staff:* Vacant
Web: www.house.gov/waters
District Office(s): 10124 S. Broadway, #1, Los Angeles 90003; (323) 757-8900; Fax: (323) 757-9506; *District Director:* Mike Murase
Committee Assignment(s): Financial Services; Judiciary

WATSON, DIANE, D-CALIF. (33)

Capitol Hill Office: 125 CHOB 20515; 225-7084; Fax: 225-2422; *Chief of Staff:* Rodney Emery
Web: www.house.gov/watson
E-mail: www.house.gov/writerep
District Office(s): 4322 Wilshire Blvd., #302, Los Angeles 90010; (323) 965-1422; Fax: (323) 965-1113; *District Director:* Paullette Starks
Committee Assignment(s): Government Reform; International Relations

WATT, MELVIN, D-N.C. (12)

Capitol Hill Office: 2236 RHOB 20515; 225-1510; Fax: 225-1512; *Chief of Staff:* Joyce Brayboy
Web: www.house.gov/watt
E-mail: nc12.public@mail.house.gov
District Office(s): 301 S. Greene St., #210, Greensboro 27401; (336) 275-9950; Fax: (336) 379-9951; *District Director:* Pamlyn C. Stubbs
1230 W. Morehead St., #306, Charlotte 28208; (704) 344-9950; Fax: (704) 344-9971; *District Liaison:* Teresa Gore

Committee Assignment(s): Financial Services; Joint Economic; Judiciary

WAXMAN, HENRY A., D-CALIF. (30)

Capitol Hill Office: 2204 RHOB 20515; 225-3976; Fax: 225-4099; *Chief of Staff:* Philip Schiliro
Web: www.house.gov/waxman
E-mail: www.house.gov/writerep
District Office(s): 8436 W. 3rd St., #600, Los Angeles 90048; (323) 651-1040; Fax: (323) 655-0502; *District Office Director:* Lisa Pinto
Committee Assignment(s): Energy and Commerce; Government Reform

WEINER, ANTHONY, D-N.Y. (9)

Capitol Hill Office: 1122 LHOB 20515; 225-6616; Fax: 226-7253; *Chief of Staff:* Veronica Sullivan
Web: www.house.gov/weiner
E-mail: weiner@mail.house.gov
District Office(s): 80-02 Kew Gardens Rd., #5000, Kew Gardens 11415; (718) 520-9001; *District Director:* Veronica Sullivan
90-16 Rockaway Beach Blvd., Rockaway 11693; (718) 318-9255; *District Director:* Veronica Sullivan
1800 Sheepshead Bay Rd., Brooklyn 11235; (718) 520-9001; Fax: (718) 332-9010; *District Director:* Veronica Sullivan
Committee Assignment(s): Judiciary; Science; Transportation and Infrastructure

WELDON, CURT, R-PA. (7)

Capitol Hill Office: 2466 RHOB 20515; 225-2011; Fax: 225-8137; *Chief of Staff:* Michael Conallen
Web: www.house.gov/curtweldon
E-mail: curtpa07@mail.house.gov
District Office(s): 1554 Garrett Rd., Upper Darby 19082; (610) 259-0700; Fax: (215) 596-4665; *District Director:* Kelly Daniel
Committee Assignment(s): Armed Services; Science; Select Homeland Security

WELDON, DAVE, R-FLA. (15)

Capitol Hill Office: 2347 RHOB 20515; 225-3671; Fax: 225-3516; *Chief of Staff:* Dana G. Gartzke
Web: www.house.gov/weldon
E-mail: www.house.gov/writerep
District Office(s): Bldg. C, 2725 Judge Fran Jamison Way, Melbourne 32940; (321) 632-1776; Fax: (321) 639-8595; *District Director:* Brian Chase
2000 16th Ave., #157, Vero Beach 32960; (561) 778-3534; Fax: (561) 562-5543; *Caseworker:* Janel Young
Committee Assignment(s): Appropriations

WELLER, JERRY, R-ILL. (11)

Capitol Hill Office: 1210 LHOB 20515; 225-3635; Fax: 225-3521; *Administrative Assistant:* Jeanette Forcash

Web: www.house.gov/weller
E-mail: www.house.gov/writerep
District Office(s): 2701 Black Rd., #201, Joliet 60435; (815) 740-2028; Fax: (815) 740-2037; *District Director:* Reed Wilson
Committee Assignment(s): International Relations; Ways and Means

WEXLER, ROBERT, D-FLA. (19)

Capitol Hill Office: 213 CHOB 20515; 225-3001; Fax: 225-5974; *Chief of Staff:* Eric Johnson
Web: www.house.gov/wexler
E-mail: www.house.gov/writerep
District Office(s): 2500 N. Military Trail, #100, Boca Raton 33431; (561) 988-6302; Fax: (561) 988-6423; *District Director:* Wendi Lipsich
5790 Margate Blvd., Margate 33063; (954) 972-6454; Fax: (954) 974-3191; *Area Coordinator:* Lynne Brenes
Committee Assignment(s): International Relations; Judiciary

WHITFIELD, EDWARD, R-KY. (1)

Capitol Hill Office: 301 CHOB 20515; 225-3115; Fax: 225-3547; *Chief of Staff:* Karen Long
Web: www.house.gov/whitfield
E-mail: www.house.gov/writerep
District Office(s): Monroe County Courthouse, P.O. Box 717, Tompkinsville 42167; (270) 487-9509; Fax: (270) 487-0019; *Field Representative:* Sandy Simpson
1403 S. Main St., Hopkinsville 42240; (270) 885-8079; Fax: (270) 885-8598; *District Director:* Michael Pape
222 1st St., #307, Henderson 42420; (270) 826-4180; Fax: (270) 826-6783; *Field Representative:* Ed West
100 Fountain Ave., #104, Paducah 42001; (270) 442-6901; Fax: (270) 442-6805; *Field Representative:* David Mast
Committee Assignment(s): Energy and Commerce

WICKER, ROGER, R-MISS. (1)

Capitol Hill Office: 2455 RHOB 20515; 225-4306; Fax: 225-3549; *Chief of Staff:* John Keast
Web: www.house.gov/wicker
E-mail: roger.wicker@mail.house.gov
District Office(s): P.O. Box 1482, 500 W. Main St., #210, Tupelo 38802; (662) 844-5437; Fax: (662) 844-9096; *District Director:* Bubba Lollar
P.O. Box 70, 8700 Northwest Dr., #102, Southaven 38671; (662) 342-3942; Fax: (662) 342-3883; *District Director:* Kim Chamberlin
Committee Assignment(s): Appropriations; Budget

WILSON, HEATHER A., R-N.M. (1)

Capitol Hill Office: 318 CHOB 20515; 225-6316; Fax: 225-4975; *Chief of Staff:* Bryce Dustman
Web: wilson.house.gov
E-mail: ask.heather@mail.house.gov

District Office(s): 625 Silver Ave. S.W., #340, Albuquerque 87102; (505) 346-6781; Fax: (505) 346-6723; *District Director:* Julie Dreike
Committee Assignment(s): Armed Services; Energy and Commerce

WILSON, JOE, R-S.C. (2)

Capitol Hill Office: 212 CHOB 20515; 225-2452; Fax: 225-2455; *Chief of Staff:* Eric Dell
Web: www.house.gov/joewilson
E-mail: joe.wilson@mail.house.gov
District Office(s): 1700 Sunset Blvd., #1, West Columbia 29169; (803) 939-0041; Fax: (803) 939-0078; *District Director:* Mary T. Howard
903 Port Republic St., P.O. Box 1538, Beaufort 29901; (843) 521-2530; Fax: (843) 521-2535; *Field Representative:* Ted Felder
Committee Assignment(s): Armed Services; Education and Workforce

WOLF, FRANK R., R-VA. (10)

Capitol Hill Office: 241 CHOB 20515; 225-5136; Fax: 225-0437; *Chief of Staff:* Daniel Scandling
Web: www.house.gov/wolf
E-mail: www.house.gov/writerep
District Office(s): 13873 Park Center Rd., #130, Herndon 20171; (703) 709-5800; Fax: (703) 709-5802; *Constituent Services Director:* Judy McCary
110 N. Cameron St., Winchester 22601; (540) 667-0990; Fax: (540) 678-0402; *Constituent Services Assistant:* Donna Crowley
Committee Assignment(s): Appropriations

WOOLSEY, LYNN, D-CALIF. (6)

Capitol Hill Office: 2263 RHOB 20515; 225-5161; Fax: 225-5163; *Chief of Staff:* Nora Matus
Web: www.house.gov/woolsey
E-mail: woolsey.house.gov/emailform.asp
District Office(s): 1050 Northgate Dr., #140, San Rafael 94903; (415) 507-9554; Fax: (415) 507-9601; *Field Representative:* Anita Fronzi
1101 College Ave., #200, Santa Rosa 95404; (707) 542-7182; Fax: (707) 542-2745; *District Director:* Wendy Friefeld
Committee Assignment(s): Education and Workforce; Science

WU, DAVID, D-ORE. (1)

Capitol Hill Office: 1023 LHOB 20515; 225-0855; Fax: 225-9497; *Chief of Staff:* Julie Tippens
Web: www.house.gov/wu
E-mail: www.house.gov/wu/generalform.htm
District Office(s): 620 S.W. Main St., #606, Portland 97205; (503) 326-2901; Fax: (503) 326-5066; *District Director:* Mary K. Elliott
Committee Assignment(s): Education and Workforce; Science

WYNN, ALBERT R., D-MD. (4)

Capitol Hill Office: 434 CHOB 20515; 225-8699; Fax: 225-8714; *Chief of Staff:* Curt S. Clifton
Web: www.house.gov/wynn
E-mail: www.house.gov/writerep
District Office(s): 9200 Basil Court, #221, Largo 20774; (301) 773-4094; Fax: (301) 925-9694; *District Director:* Adrian Jones
18200 Georgia Ave., Suite E, Olney 20832; (301) 929-3462; Fax: (301) 929-3466; *Community Liaison:* Craig Zucker
Committee Assignment(s): Energy and Commerce

YOUNG, C. W. BILL, R-FLA. (10)

Capitol Hill Office: 2407 RHOB 20515; 225-5961; Fax: 225-9764; *Administrative Assistant:* Harry J. Glenn
Web: www.house.gov/young
E-mail: bill.young@mail.house.gov
District Office(s): 801 W. Bay Dr., #606, Largo 33770; (727) 581-0980; Fax: (727) 893-3126; *District Assistant:* George N. Cretekos
360 Central Ave., #1480, St. Petersburg 33701; (727) 893-3191; *District Assistant:* Sharon Ghezzi
Committee Assignment(s): Appropriations; Select Homeland Security

YOUNG, DON, R-ALASKA (AT LARGE)

Capitol Hill Office: 2111 RHOB 20515; 225-5765; Fax: 225-0425; *Administrative Assistant:* Michael Anderson
Web: www.house.gov/donyoung
E-mail: www.house.gov/writerep
District Office(s): 130 Trading Bay Rd., #350, Kenai 99611; (907) 283-5808; Fax: (907) 283-4363; *Staff Assistant:* Becky Hultberg
Box 10, 101 12th Ave., Fairbanks 99701; (907) 456-0210; Fax: (907) 456-0279; *Special Assistant:* Royce Chapman
Federal Bldg., #401, P.O. Box 21247, Juneau 99802; (907) 586-7400; Fax: (907) 586-8922; *Staff Assistant:* Connie McKenzie
540 Water St., #101, Ketchikan 99901; (907) 225-6880; Fax: (907) 225-0390; *Staff Assistant:* Sherrie Slick
222 W. 7th Ave., #3, Anchorage 99513; (907) 271-5978; Fax: (907) 271-5950; *District Director:* Bill Sharrow
851 E. Westpoint Dr., #307, Wasilla 99654; (907) 376-7665; Fax: (907) 376-8526; *Staff Assistant:* Carol Gustafson
Committee Assignment(s): Resources; Select Homeland Security; Transportation and Infrastructure

Joint Committees of Congress

The joint committees of Congress are listed below. The listing includes room number, telephone and fax numbers, Web address(es), key staff names, committee jurisdiction, and membership (in seniority order) for each committee. Members are drawn from both the Senate and House and from both parties. Members of the majority party, Republicans, are shown in roman type; members of the minority party, Democrats, are shown in italic type. When a senator serves as chair, the vice chair usually is a representative, and vice versa. The location of chair usually rotates from one chamber to the other at the beginning of each Congress. The area code for all telephone numbers listed below is (202).

JOINT ECONOMIC

Office: SD-G01   **Phone:** 224-5171
Fax: 224-0240
Web: jec.senate.gov and www.house.gov/jec
Senate Staff Director: Donald Marron 224-5171 SH-805
House Staff Director: Chris Frenze 225-3923 1538 LHOB

Study and investigation of all recommendations in the president's annual Economic Report to Congress. Reporting of findings and recommendations to the House and Senate.

Senate Members

Republicans	Democrats
Robert F. Bennett, Utah, Chair	*Jack Reed, R.I.*
Sam Brownback, Kan.	*Edward M. Kennedy, Mass.*
Jeff Sessions, Ala.	*Paul S. Sarbanes, Md.*
John E. Sununu, N.H.	*Jeff Bingaman, N.M.*
Lamar Alexander, Tenn.	
Susan Collins, Maine	

House Members

Republicans	Democrats
H. James Saxton, N.J., Vice Chair	*Pete Stark, Calif., Ranking Minority Member*
Paul D. Ryan, Wis.	*Carolyn B. Maloney, N.Y.*
Jennifer Dunn, Wash.	*Melvin Watt, N.C.*
Phil English, Pa.	*Baron P. Hill, Ind.*
Adam H. Putnam, Fla.	
Ron Paul, Texas	

JOINT LIBRARY OF CONGRESS

Office: S240 CAP   **Phone:** 224-1034
Fax: 224-0075
Senate Staff Contact: Jennifer Mies 224-1034 S237 CAP
House Staff Contact: Bill McBride 225-3831 1714 LHOB

Management and expansion of the Library of Congress; receipt of gifts for the benefit of the library; development and maintenance of the Botanic Garden; placement of statues and other works of art in the Capitol.

Senate Members

Republicans	Democrats
Ted Stevens, Alaska, Chair	*Christopher J. Dodd, Conn.*
Trent Lott, Miss.	*Charles E. Schumer, N.Y.*
Thad Cochran, Miss.	

House Members

Republicans	Democrats
Vernon J. Ehlers, Mich., Vice Chair	*John B. Larson, Conn.*
Bob Ney, Ohio	*Juanita Millender-McDonald, Calif.*
Jack Kingston, Ga.	

JOINT PRINTING

Office: 1309 LHOB   **Phone:** 225-8281

Fax: 225-9957

Web: www.house.gov/jcp

Majority Staff Director: Maria Robinson 225-8281 1309 LHOB

Minority Staff Director: Matthew McGowan 224-3244 SR-346

Government Printing Office; inefficiency and waste in the printing, binding, and distribution of federal government publications; arrangement and style of the Congressional Record.

Senate Members

Republicans	Democrats
Saxby Chambliss, Ga., Vice Chair	*Mark Dayton, Minn., Ranking Minority Member*
Thad Cochran, Miss	
Gordon H. Smith, Ore.	*Daniel K. Inouye, Hawaii*

House Members

Republicans	Democrats
Bob Ney, Ohio, Chair	*John B. Larson, Conn.*
John T. Doolittle, Calif.	*Robert A. Brady, Pa.*
John Linder, Ga.	

JOINT TAXATION

Office: 1015 LHOB   **Phone:** 225-3621

Fax: 225-0832

Web: www.house.gov/jct

Chief of Staff: George Yin 225-3621 LHOB 1015

Operation, effects, and administration of the federal system of taxation; measures and methods for simplification of taxes.

Senate Members

Republicans	Democrats
Charles E. Grassley, Iowa, Vice Chair	*Max Baucus, Mont., Ranking Minority Member*
Orrin G. Hatch, Utah	*John D. Rockefeller IV, W.Va.*
Don Nickles, Okla.	

House Members

Republicans	Democrats
Bill Thomas, Calif., Chair	*Charles B. Rangel, N.Y.*
Philip M. Crane, Ill.	*Pete Stark, Calif.*
E. Clay Shaw Jr., Fla.	

Senate Committees

The standing and select committees of the U.S. Senate are listed below. The listing includes the room number, telephone and fax numbers, Web address, e-mail address if available, key majority and minority staff members, jurisdiction for each full committee, and party ratio. Subcommittees are listed alphabetically under each committee. Membership is listed in order of seniority on the committee or subcommittee.

Members of the majority party, Republicans, are shown in roman type; members of the minority party, Democrats, are shown in italic type. James M. Jeffords, I-Vt., caucuses with Democrats and accrues committee seniority with Democrats. The partisan committees of the Senate are listed on pp. 867–868. The area code for all phone and fax numbers listed below is (202).

AGRICULTURE, NUTRITION, AND FORESTRY

Office: SR-328A **Phone:** 224-2035
Fax: 224-9278
Web: agriculture.senate.gov
Majority Staff Director: Hunt Shipman
Minority Staff Director: Mark Halverson 224-2035
SR-328A

Agriculture in general; animal industry and diseases; crop insurance and soil conservation; farm credit and farm security; food from fresh waters; food stamp programs; forestry in general; home economics; human nutrition; inspection of livestock, meat, and agricultural products; pests and pesticides; plant industry, soils, and agriculture engineering; rural development, rural electrification, and watersheds; school nutrition programs. The Chair and ranking minority member are members ex officio of all subcommittees of which they are not regular members.

Party Ratio: R 11–D 10

Thad Cochran, Miss., Chair	*Tom Harkin, Iowa, Ranking*
Richard G. Lugar, Ind.	*Minority Member*
Mitch McConnell, Ky.	*Patrick J. Leahy, Vt.*
Pat Roberts, Kan.	*Kent Conrad, N.D.*
Peter G. Fitzgerald, Ill.	*Tom Daschle, S.D.*
Saxby Chambliss, Ga.	*Max Baucus, Mont.*
Norm Coleman, Minn.	*Blanche Lincoln, Ark.*
Michael D. Crapo, Idaho	*Zell Miller, Ga.*
Jim Talent, Mo.	*Debbie Stabenow, Mich.*
Elizabeth Dole, N.C.	*Ben Nelson, Neb.*
Charles E. Grassley, Iowa	*Mark Dayton, Minn.*

Subcommittees

Forestry, Conservation, and Rural Revitalization
Office: SR-328A **Phone:** 224-2035

Crapo (Chair), Lugar, Coleman, Talent, McConnell, Roberts
Lincoln (Ranking Minority Member), Dayton, Leahy, Daschle, Nelson (Neb.)

Marketing, Inspection, and Product Promotion
Office: SR-328A **Phone:** 224-2035

Talent (Chair), Roberts, Fitzgerald, Chambliss, Grassley
Baucus (Ranking Minority Member), Nelson (Neb.), Conrad, Stabenow

Production and Price Competitiveness
Office: SR-328A **Phone:** 224-2035

Dole (Chair), McConnell, Roberts, Chambliss, Coleman, Grassley
Conrad (Ranking Minority Member), Daschle, Miller, Baucus, Lincoln

Research, Nutrition, and General Legislation
Office: SR-328A **Phone:** 224-2035

Fitzgerald (Chair), Lugar, McConnell, Crapo, Dole
Leahy (Ranking Minority Member), Miller, Stabenow, Dayton

APPROPRIATIONS

Office: S-128 CAP **Phone:** 224-7363
Fax: 224-8553
Web: appropriations.senate.gov
Majority Staff Director: James Morhard
Minority Staff Director: Terrence E. Sauvain 224-7292
S-125 CAP

Appropriation of revenue; rescission of appropriations; new spending authority under the Congressional Budget Act. The Chair and ranking minority member are nonvoting members ex officio of all subcommittees of which they are not regular members.

Party Ratio: R 15–D 14

Ted Stevens, Alaska, Chair	*Robert C. Byrd, W.Va.,*
Thad Cochran, Miss.	*Ranking Minority Member*
Arlen Specter, Pa.	*ber*
Pete V. Domenici, N.M.	*Daniel K. Inouye, Hawaii*
Christopher S. Bond, Mo.	*Ernest F. Hollings, S.C.*
Mitch McConnell, Ky.	*Patrick J. Leahy, Vt.*
Conrad Burns, Mont.	*Tom Harkin, Iowa*
Richard C. Shelby, Ala.	*Barbara A. Mikulski, Md.*

Judd Gregg, N.H.
Robert F. Bennett, Utah
Ben Nighthorse Campbell, Colo.
Larry E. Craig, Idaho
Kay Bailey Hutchison, Texas
Mike DeWine, Ohio
Sam Brownback, Kan.

Harry Reid, Nev.
Herb Kohl, Wis.
Patty Murray, Wash.
Byron L. Dorgan, N.D.
Dianne Feinstein, Calif.
Richard J. Durbin, Ill.
Tim Johnson, S.D.
Mary L. Landrieu, La.

Subcommittees

Agriculture, Rural Development, and Related Agencies
Office: SD-188   **Phone:** 224-5270

Bennett (Chair), Cochran, Specter, Bond, McConnell, Burns, Craig, Brownback
Kohl (Ranking Minority Member), Harkin, Dorgan, Feinstein, Durbin, Johnson, Landrieu

Commerce, Justice, State, and Judiciary
Office: S-206 CAP   **Phone:** 224-7277

Gregg (Chair), Stevens, Domenici, McConnell, Hutchison, Campbell, Brownback
Hollings (Ranking Minority Member), Inouye, Mikulski, Leahy, Kohl, Murray

Defense
Office: SD-119   **Phone:** 224-7255

Stevens (Chair), Cochran, Specter, Domenici, Bond, McConnell, Shelby, Gregg, Hutchison, Burns
Inouye (Ranking Minority Member), Hollings, Byrd, Leahy, Harkin, Dorgan, Durbin, Reid, Feinstein

District of Columbia   **Office:** S-128 CAP
Phone: 224-6933

DeWine (Chair), Hutchison, Brownback
Landrieu (Ranking Minority Member), Durbin

Energy and Water Development
Office: SD-127   **Phone:** 224-7260

Domenici (Chair), Cochran, McConnell, Bennett, Burns, Craig, Bond
Reid (Ranking Minority Member), Byrd, Hollings, Murray, Dorgan, Feinstein

Foreign Operations
Office: SD-142   **Phone:** 224-2255

McConnell (Chair), Specter, Gregg, Shelby, Bennett, Campbell, Bond, DeWine
Leahy (Ranking Minority Member), Inouye, Harkin, Mikulski, Durbin, Johnson, Landrieu

Homeland Security
Office: SD-135   **Phone:** 224-4319

Cochran (Chair), Stevens, Specter, Domenici, McConnell, Shelby, Gregg, Campbell, Craig
Byrd (Ranking Minority Member), Inouye, Hollings, Leahy, Harkin, Mikulski, Kohl, Murray

Interior
Office: SD-132   **Phone:** 224-7233

Burns (Chair), Stevens, Cochran, Domenici, Bennett, Gregg, Campbell, Brownback
Dorgan (Ranking Minority Member), Byrd, Leahy, Hollings, Reid, Feinstein, Mikulski

Labor, Health and Human Services, and Education
Office: SD-184   **Phone:** 224-3471

Specter (Chair), Cochran, Gregg, Hutchison, Craig, Stevens, DeWine, Shelby
Harkin (Ranking Minority Member), Hollings, Inouye, Reid, Kohl, Murray, Landrieu

Legislative Branch
Office: SD-127   **Phone:** 224-7238

Campbell (Chair), Bennett, Stevens
Durbin (Ranking Minority Member), Johnson

Military Construction
Office: SD-140   **Phone:** 224-5245

Hutchison (Chair), Burns, Craig, DeWine, Brownback
Feinstein (Ranking Minority Member), Inouye, Johnson, Landrieu

Transportation, Treasury, and General Government
Office: SD-133   **Phone:** 224-4869

Shelby (Chair), Specter, Bond, Bennett, Campbell, Hutchison, DeWine, Brownback
Murray (Ranking Minority Member), Byrd, Mikulski, Reid, Kohl, Durbin, Dorgan

VA, HUD, and Independent Agencies
Office: SD-130   **Phone:** 224-8252

Bond (Chair), Burns, Shelby, Craig, Domenici, DeWine, Hutchison
Mikulski (Ranking Minority Member), Leahy, Harkin, Byrd, Johnson, Reid

ARMED SERVICES

Office: SR-228   **Phone:** 224-3871
Fax: 228-0036
Web: armed-services.senate.gov
Majority Staff Director: Judy Ansley
Minority Staff Director: Rick DeBobes 224-7530 SR-228

Defense and defense policy generally; aeronautical and space activities peculiar to or primarily associated with the development of weapons systems or military operations; the common defense; the Defense Dept., the Army Dept., the Navy Dept., and the Air Force Dept., generally; maintenance and operation of the Panama Canal including administration, sanitation, and government of the Canal Zone; military research and development; national security aspects of nuclear energy; naval petroleum reserves, except those in Alaska; pay, promotion, retirement, and other benefits and privileges of members of the Armed Forces, including overseas education of civilian and military depen-

ARMED SERVICES (continued)

dents; selective service system; strategic and critical materials necessary for the common defense; comprehensive study and review of matters relating to the common defense policy of the United States. The Chair and ranking minority member are nonvoting members ex officio of all subcommittees of which they are not regular members.

Party Ratio: R 13–D 12

John W. Warner, Va. (Chair)	*Carl Levin, Mich. (Ranking Minority Member)*
John McCain, Ariz.	
James M. Inhofe, Okla.	*Edward M. Kennedy, Mass.*
Pat Roberts, Kan.	*Robert C. Byrd, W.Va.*
Wayne Allard, Colo.	*Joseph I. Lieberman, Conn.*
Jeff Sessions, Ala.	*Jack Reed, R.I.*
Susan Collins, Maine	*Daniel K. Akaka, Hawaii*
John Ensign, Nev.	*Bill Nelson, Fla.*
Jim Talent, Mo.	*Ben Nelson, Neb.*
Saxby Chambliss, Ga.	*Mark Dayton, Minn.*
Lindsey Graham, S.C.	*Evan Bayh, Ind.*
Elizabeth Dole, N.C.	*Hillary Rodham Clinton, N.Y.*
John Cornyn, Texas	*Mark Pryor, Ark.*

Subcommittees

Airland
Office: S-228   **Phone:** 224-3871

Sessions (Chair), McCain, Inhofe, Roberts, Talent, Chambliss, Dole
Lieberman (Ranking Minority Member), Akaka, Dayton, Bayh, Clinton, Pryor

Emerging Threats and Capabilities
Office: SR-228   **Phone:** 224-3871

Roberts (Chair), Allard, Collins, Ensign, Talent, Chambliss, Graham (S.C.), Dole, Cornyn
Reed (Ranking Minority Member), Kennedy, Byrd, Lieberman, Akaka, Nelson (Fla.), Bayh, Clinton

Personnel
Office: SR-228   **Phone:** 224-3871

Chambliss (Chair), Collins, Dole, Cornyn
Nelson (Neb.; Ranking Minority Member), Kennedy, Pryor

Readiness and Management Support
Office: SR-228   **Phone:** 224-3871

Ensign (Chair), McCain, Inhofe, Roberts, Allard, Sessions, Talent, Chambliss, Cornyn
Akaka (Ranking Minority Member), Byrd, Nelson (Fla.), Nelson (Neb.), Dayton, Bayh, Clinton, Pryor

Seapower
Office: SR-228   **Phone:** 224-3871

Talent (Chair), McCain, Collins, Graham (S.C.)
Kennedy (Ranking Minority Member), Lieberman, Reed

Strategic Forces
Office: SR-228   **Phone:** 224-3871

Allard (Chair), Inhofe, Sessions, Ensign, Graham (S.C.), Cornyn
Nelson (Fla.; Ranking Minority Member), Byrd, Reed, Nelson (Neb.), Dayton

BANKING, HOUSING, AND URBAN AFFAIRS

Office: SD-534   **Phone:** 224-7391
Fax: 224-5137
Web: banking.senate.gov
Majority Staff Director: Kathy Casey
Minority Staff Director: Steven Harris 224-7391 SD-542

Banks, banking, and financial institutions; price controls; deposit insurance; economic stabilization and growth; defense production; export and foreign trade promotion; export controls; federal monetary policy, including Federal Reserve System; financial aid to commerce and industry; issuance and redemption of notes; money and credit, including currency and coinage; nursing home construction; public and private housing, including veterans' housing; renegotiation of government contracts; urban development and mass transit; international economic policy.

Party Ratio: R 11–D 10

Richard C. Shelby, Ala., Chair	*Paul S. Sarbanes, Md., Ranking Minority Member*
Robert F. Bennett, Utah	
Wayne Allard, Colo.	*Christopher J. Dodd, Conn.*
Michael B. Enzi, Wyo.	*Tim Johnson, S.D.*
Chuck Hagel, Neb.	*Jack Reed, R.I.*
Rick Santorum, Pa.	*Charles E. Schumer, N.Y.*
Jim Bunning, Ky.	*Evan Bayh, Ind.*
Michael D. Crapo, Idaho	*Zell Miller, Ga.*
John E. Sununu, N.H.	*Thomas R. Carper, Del.*
Elizabeth Dole, N.C.	*Debbie Stabenow, Mich.*
Lincoln Chafee, R.I.	*Jon Corzine, N.J.*

Subcommittees

Economic Policy
Office: SD-534   **Phone:** 224-7391

Bunning (Chair), Dole, Shelby
Schumer (Ranking Minority Member), Miller

Financial Institutions
Office: SD-534   **Phone:** 224-7391

Bennett (Chair), Dole, Chafee, Allard, Santorum, Hagel, Bunning, Crapo
Johnson (Ranking Minority Member), Miller, Carper, Dodd, Reed, Bayh, Stabenow

Housing and Transportation
Office: SD-534   **Phone:** 224-7391

Allard (Chair), Santorum, Bennett, Chafee, Enzi, Sununu, Shelby

Reed (Ranking Minority Member), Stabenow, Corzine, Dodd, Carper, Schumer

International Trade and Finance
Office: SD-534　**Phone:** 224-7391

Hagel (Chair), Enzi, Crapo, Sununu, Dole, Chafee,
Bayh (Ranking Minority Member), Miller, Johnson, Carper, Corzine

Securities and Investment
Office: SD-534　**Phone:** 224-7391

Enzi (Chair), Crapo, Sununu, Hagel, Bunning, Bennett, Allard, Santorum
Dodd (Ranking Minority Member), Johnson, Reed, Schumer, Bayh, Stabenow, Corzine

BUDGET

Office: SD-624　**Phone:** 224-0642
Fax: 224-4835
Web: budget.senate.gov
Majority Staff Director: Hazen Marshall
Minority Staff Director: Mary Naylor 224-0862 SD-624
Federal budget generally; concurrent budget resolutions; Congressional Budget Office.
Party Ratio: R 12–D 11

Don Nickles, Okla., Chair	*Kent Conrad, N.D., Ranking*
Pete V. Domenici, N.M.	*Minority Member*
Charles E. Grassley, Iowa	*Ernest F. Hollings, S.C.*
Judd Gregg, N.H.	*Paul S. Sarbanes, Md.*
Wayne Allard, Colo.	*Patty Murray, Wash.*
Conrad Burns, Mont.	*Ron Wyden, Ore.*
Michael B. Enzi, Wyo.	*Russell D. Feingold, Wis.*
Jeff Sessions, Ala.	*Tim Johnson, S.D.*
Jim Bunning, Ky.	*Robert C. Byrd, W.Va.*
Michael D. Crapo, Idaho	*Bill Nelson, Fla.*
John Ensign, Nev.	*Debbie Stabenow, Mich.*
John Cornyn, Texas	*Jon Corzine, N.J.*

COMMERCE, SCIENCE, AND TRANSPORTATION

Office: SD-508　**Phone:** 224-5115
Fax: 224-1259
Web: commerce.senate.gov
Majority Staff Director: Jeanne Bumpus
Minority Staff Director: Kevin Kayes 224-0411 SD-560
Interstate commerce and transportation generally; Coast Guard; coastal zone management; communications; highway safety; inland waterways, except construction; marine fisheries; Merchant Marine and navigation; nonmilitary aeronautical and space sciences; oceans, weather, and atmospheric activities; interoceanic canals generally; regulation of consumer products and services; science, engineering, and technology research, development, and policy; sports; standards and measurement; transportation and commerce aspects of outer continental shelf lands. The Chair and ranking minority member are nonvoting members ex officio of all subcommittees of which they are not regular members.
Party Ratio: R 12–D 11

John McCain, Ariz., Chair	*Ernest F. Hollings, S.C.,*
Ted Stevens, Alaska	*Ranking Minority*
Conrad Burns, Mont.	*Member*
Trent Lott, Miss.	*Daniel K. Inouye, Hawaii*
Kay Bailey Hutchison, Texas	*John D. Rockefeller IV, W.Va.*
Olympia J. Snowe, Maine	*John Kerry, Mass.*
Sam Brownback, Kan.	*John B. Breaux, La.*
Gordon H. Smith, Ore.	*Byron L. Dorgan, N.D.*
Peter G. Fitzgerald, Ill.	*Ron Wyden, Ore.*
John Ensign, Nev.	*Barbara Boxer, Calif.*
George Allen, Va.	*Bill Nelson, Fla.*
John E. Sununu, N.H.	*Maria Cantwell, Wash.*
	Frank R. Lautenberg, N.J.

Subcommittees

Aviation
Office: SH-427　**Phone:** 224-4852

Lott (Chair), Stevens, Burns, Hutchison, Snowe, Brownback, Smith, Fitzgerald, Ensign, Allen, Sununu
Rockefeller (Ranking Minority Member), Hollings, Inouye, Breaux, Dorgan, Wyden, Nelson (Fla.), Boxer, Cantwell, Lautenberg

Communications
Office: SH-428　**Phone:** 224-5184

Burns (Chair), Stevens, Lott, Hutchison, Snowe, Brownback, Smith, Fitzgerald, Ensign, Allen, Sununu
Hollings (Ranking Minority Member), Inouye, Rockefeller, Kerry, Breaux, Dorgan, Wyden, Boxer, Nelson (Fla.), Cantwell

Competition, Foreign Commerce, and Infrastructure
Office: SH-428　**Phone:** 224-5183

Smith (Chair), Burns, Brownback, Fitzgerald, Ensign, Sununu
Dorgan (Ranking Minority Member), Boxer, Nelson (Fla.), Cantwell, Lautenberg

Consumer Affairs and Product Safety
Office: SH-428　**Phone:** 224-5183

Fitzgerald (Chair), Burns, Smith
Wyden (Ranking Minority Member), Dorgan

Oceans, Fisheries, and Coast Guard
Office: SH-227　**Phone:** 224-8172

Snowe (Chair), Stevens, Lott, Hutchison, Smith, Sununu
Kerry (Ranking Minority Member), Hollings, Inouye, Breaux, Cantwell

Science, Technology, and Space
Office: SH-227　**Phone:** 224-8172

Brownback (Chair), Stevens, Burns, Lott, Hutchison, Ensign, Allen, Sununu
Breaux (Ranking Minority Member), Rockefeller, Kerry, Dorgan, Wyden, Nelson (Fla.), Lautenberg

Surface Transportation and Merchant Marine
Office: SH-427　**Phone:** 224-4852

Hutchison (Chair), Stevens, Burns, Lott, Snowe, Brownback, Smith, Allen

COMMERCE, SCIENCE, AND TRANSPORTATION (continued)

Inouye (Ranking Minority Member), Rockefeller, Kerry, Breaux, Wyden, Boxer, Lautenberg (N.J.)

ENERGY AND NATURAL RESOURCES

Office: SD-364   **Phone:** 224-4971
Fax: 224-6163
Web: energy.senate.gov
E-mail: committee@energy.senate.gov
Majority Staff Director: Alex Flint
Minority Staff Director: Robert "Bob" Simon 224-9201 SD-312

Energy policy, regulation, conservation, research, and development; coal; energy-related aspects of deep-water ports; hydroelectric power, irrigation, and reclamation; mines, mining, and minerals generally; national parks, recreation areas, wilderness areas, wild and scenic rivers, historic sites, military parks and battlefields; naval petroleum reserves in Alaska; nonmilitary development of nuclear energy; oil and gas production and distribution; public lands and forests; solar energy systems; territorial possessions of the United States.

Party Ratio: R 12–D 11

Pete V. Domenici, N.M., Chair	*Jeff Bingaman, N.M., Ranking Minority Member*
Don Nickles, Okla.	*Daniel K. Akaka, Hawaii*
Larry E. Craig, Idaho	*Byron L. Dorgan, N.D.*
Ben Nighthorse Campbell, Colo.	*Bob Graham, Fla.*
	Ron Wyden, Ore.
Craig Thomas, Wyo.	*Tim Johnson, S.D.*
Lamar Alexander, Tenn.	*Mary L. Landrieu, La.*
Lisa Murkowski, Alaska	*Evan Bayh, Ind.*
Jim Talent, Mo.	*Dianne Feinstein, Calif.*
Conrad Burns, Mont.	*Charles E. Schumer, N.Y.*
Gordon H. Smith, Ore.	*Maria Cantwell, Wash.*
Jim Bunning, Ky.	
Jon Kyl, Ariz.	

Subcommittees

Energy
Office: SD-364   **Phone:** 224-4971

Alexander (Chair), Nickles (Vice Chair), Talent, Bunning, Thomas, Murkowski, Craig, Burns
Graham (Fla.; Ranking Minority Member), Akaka, Johnson, Landrieu, Bayh, Schumer, Cantwell

National Parks
Office: SD-364   **Phone:** 224-4971

Thomas (Chair), Nickles (Vice Chair), Campbell, Alexander, Burns, Smith, Kyl
Akaka (Ranking Minority Member), Dorgan, Graham (Fla.), Landrieu, Bayh, Schumer

Public Lands and Forests
Office: SD-364   **Phone:** 224-4971

Craig (Chair), Burns (Vice Chair), Smith, Kyl, Campbell, Alexander, Murkowski, Talent
Wyden (Ranking Minority Member), Akaka, Dorgan, Johnson, Landrieu, Bayh, Feinstein

Water and Power
Office: SD-364   **Phone:** 224-4971

Murkowski (Chair), Campbell (Vice Chair), Smith, Kyl, Craig, Talent, Bunning, Thomas
Dorgan (Ranking Minority Member), Graham (Fla.), Wyden, Johnson, Feinstein, Schumer

ENVIRONMENT AND PUBLIC WORKS

Office: SD-410   **Phone:** 224-6176
Fax: 224-1273
Web: epw.senate.gov
E-mail: guest1@epw.senate.gov
Majority Staff Director: Andrew Wheeler
Minority Staff Director: Ken Connolly 224-8832 SD-456

Environmental policy, research, and development; air, water, and noise pollution; construction and maintenance of highways; environmental aspects of outer continental shelf lands; environmental effects of toxic substances other than pesticides; fisheries and wildlife; flood control and improvements of rivers and harbors; nonmilitary environmental regulation and control of nuclear energy; ocean dumping; public buildings and grounds; public works, bridges, and dams; regional economic development; solid waste disposal and recycling; water resources.

Party Ratio: R 10–D 8–I 1

James M. Inhofe, Okla., Chair	**James M. Jeffords, I-Vt., Ranking Minority Member**
John W. Warner, Va.	*Max Baucus, Mont.*
Christopher S. Bond, Mo.	*Harry Reid, Nev.*
George V. Voinovich, Ohio	*Bob Graham, Fla.*
Michael D. Crapo, Idaho	*Joseph I. Lieberman, Conn.*
Lincoln Chafee, R.I.	*Barbara Boxer, Calif.*
John Cornyn, Texas	*Ron Wyden, Ore.*
Lisa Murkowski, Alaska	*Thomas R. Carper, Del.*
Craig Thomas, Wyo.	*Hillary Rodham Clinton, N.Y.*
Wayne Allard, Colo.	

Subcommittees

Clean Air, Climate Change, and Nuclear Safety
Office: SD-410   **Phone:** 224-6176

Voinovich (Chair), Crapo, Bond, Cornyn, Thomas
Carper (Ranking Minority Member), Lieberman, Reid, Clinton

Fisheries, Wildlife, and Water
Office: SD-410   **Phone:** 224-6176

Crapo (Chair), Warner, Murkowski, Thomas, Allard

Graham (Fla.; Ranking Minority Member), Baucus, Wyden, Clinton

Superfund and Waste Management
Office: SD-410   **Phone:** 224-6176

Chafee (Chair), Warner, Allard, Bond
Boxer (Ranking Minority Member), Wyden, Carper

Transportation and Infrastructure
Office: SD-410   **Phone:** 224-6176

Bond (Chair), Warner, Voinovich, Chafee, Cornyn, Murkowski
Reid (Ranking Minority Member), Baucus, Graham (Fla.), Lieberman, Boxer

FINANCE

Office: SD-219   **Phone:** 224-4515
Fax: 228-0554
Web: finance.senate.gov
Majority Staff Director: Kolan L. Davis
Minority Staff Director: Jeff Forbes 224-4515 SD-219

Revenue measures generally; taxes; tariffs and import quotas; reciprocal trade agreements; customs; revenue sharing; federal debt limit; Social Security; health programs financed by taxes or trust funds. The Chair and ranking minority member are nonvoting members ex officio of all subcommittees of which they are not regular members.
Party Ratio: R 11–D 9–I 1

Charles E. Grassley, Iowa, Chair	*Max Baucus, Mont., Ranking Minority Member*
Orrin G. Hatch, Utah	
Don Nickles, Okla.	*John D. Rockefeller IV, W.Va.*
Trent Lott, Miss.	*Tom Daschle, S.D.*
Olympia J. Snowe, Maine	*John B. Breaux, La.*
Jon Kyl, Ariz.	*Kent Conrad, N.D.*
Craig Thomas, Wyo.	*Bob Graham, Fla.*
Rick Santorum, Pa.	**James M. Jeffords, I-Vt.**
Bill Frist, Tenn.	*Jeff Bingaman, N.M.*
Gordon H. Smith, Ore.	*John Kerry, Mass.*
Jim Bunning, Ky.	*Blanche Lincoln, Ark.*

Subcommittees

Health Care
Office: SD-219   **Phone:** 224-4515

Kyl (Chair), Snowe, Frist, Bunning, Nickles, Thomas, Santorum, Smith, Hatch, Lott
Rockefeller (Ranking Minority Member), Daschle, Graham (Fla.), **Jeffords (I-Vt.),** *Bingaman, Kerry, Lincoln, Breaux, Baucus*

International Trade
Office: SD-219   **Phone:** 224-4515

Thomas (Chair), Hatch, Grassley, Smith, Snowe, Frist, Lott, Bunning

Baucus (Ranking Minority Member), Rockefeller, Conrad, Graham (Fla.), **Jeffords (I-Vt.),** Daschle, Kerry

Long-Term Growth and Debt Reduction
Office: SD-219   **Phone:** 224-4515

Smith (Chair), Lott, Kyl
Graham (Fla.; Ranking Minority Member), Conrad

Social Security and Family Policy
Office: SD-219   **Phone:** 224-4515

Santorum (Chair), Grassley, Kyl, Bunning, Nickles, Snowe, Frist
Breaux (Ranking Minority Member), Daschle, Kerry, Rockefeller, Bingaman, Lincoln

Taxation and IRS Oversight
Office: SD-219   **Phone:** 224-4515

Nickles (Chair), Hatch, Lott, Snowe, Thomas, Santorum, Smith
Conrad (Ranking Minority Member), Bingaman, Lincoln, Breaux, Baucus, **Jeffords (I-Vt.)**

FOREIGN RELATIONS

Office: SD-450   **Phone:** 224-4651
Fax: 224-0836
Web: foreign.senate.gov
Majority Staff Director: Kenneth A. Myers
Minority Staff Director: Antony J. Blinken 224-3953 SD-439

Relations of the United States with foreign nations generally; treaties; foreign economic, military, technical, and humanitarian assistance; foreign loans; diplomatic service; International Red Cross; international aspects of nuclear energy; International Monetary Fund; intervention abroad and declarations of war; foreign trade; national security; oceans and international environmental and scientific affairs; protection of U.S. citizens abroad; United Nations; World Bank and other development assistance organizations. The Chair and ranking minority member are nonvoting members ex officio of all subcommittees of which they are not regular members.
Party Ratio: R 10–D 9

Richard G. Lugar, Ind., Chair	*Joseph R. Biden Jr., Del., Ranking Minority Member*
Chuck Hagel, Neb.	*Paul S. Sarbanes, Md.*
Lincoln Chafee, R.I.	*Christopher J. Dodd, Conn.*
George Allen, Va.	*John Kerry, Mass.*
Sam Brownback, Kan.	*Russell D. Feingold, Wis.*
Michael B. Enzi, Wyo.	*Barbara Boxer, Calif.*
George V. Voinovich, Ohio	*Bill Nelson, Fla.*
Lamar Alexander, Tenn.	*John D. Rockefeller IV, W.Va.*
Norm Coleman, Minn.	*Jon Corzine, N.J.*
John E. Sununu, N.H.	

FOREIGN RELATIONS (continued)
Subcommittees

African Affairs
Office: SD-446 **Phone:** 224-4651

Alexander (Chair), Brownback, Coleman, Sununu
Feingold (Ranking Minority Member), Dodd, Nelson (Fla.)

East Asian and Pacific Affairs
Office: SD-446 **Phone:** 224-4651

Brownback (Chair), Alexander, Hagel, Allen, Voinovich
Kerry (Ranking Minority Member), Rockefeller, Feingold, Corzine

European Affairs
Office: SD-446 **Phone:** 224-4651

Allen (Chair), Voinovich, Hagel, Sununu, Chafee
Biden (Ranking Minority Member), Sarbanes, Dodd, Kerry

International Economic Policy, Export, and Trade Promotion
Office: SD-446 **Phone:** 224-4651

Hagel (Chair), Chafee, Enzi, Alexander, Coleman
Sarbanes (Ranking Minority Member), Rockefeller, Corzine, Dodd

International Operations and Terrorism
Office: SD-446 **Phone:** 224-4651

Sununu (Chair), Enzi, Allen, Voinovich, Brownback
Nelson (Fla.; Ranking Minority Member), Biden, Feingold, Boxer

Near Eastern and South Asian Affairs
Office: SD-446 **Phone:** 224-4651

Chafee (Chair), Hagel, Brownback, Voinovich, Coleman
Boxer (Ranking Minority Member), Corzine, Rockefeller, Sarbanes

Western Hemisphere, Peace Corps, and Narcotics Affairs
Office: SD-446 **Phone:** 224-4651

Coleman (Chair), Chafee, Allen, Enzi, Sununu
Dodd (Ranking Minority Member), Boxer, Nelson (Fla.), Biden, Kerry

GOVERNMENTAL AFFAIRS

Office: SD-340 **Phone:** 224-4751
Fax: 224-9682
Web: govt-aff.senate.gov
Majority Staff Director: Michael Bopp
Minority Staff Director: Joyce Rechtschaffen 224-2627
SD-604

Archives of the United States; budget and accounting measures; census and statistics; federal civil service; congressional organization; intergovernmental relations; government information; District of Columbia; organization and management of nuclear export policy; executive branch organization and reorganization; Postal Service; efficiency,

economy, and effectiveness of government. The Chair and ranking minority member are nonvoting members ex officio of all subcommittees of which they are not regular members.
Party Ratio: R 9–D 8

Susan Collins, Maine, Chair	*Joseph I. Lieberman, Conn.,*
Ted Stevens, Alaska	*Ranking Minority*
George V. Voinovich, Ohio	*Member*
Norm Coleman, Minn.	*Carl Levin, Mich.*
Arlen Specter, Pa.	*Daniel K. Akaka, Hawaii*
Robert F. Bennett, Utah	*Richard J. Durbin, Ill.*
Peter G. Fitzgerald, Ill.	*Thomas R. Carper, Del.*
John E. Sununu, N.H.	*Mark Dayton, Minn.*
Richard C. Shelby, Ala.	*Frank R. Lautenberg, N.J.*
	Mark Pryor, Ark.

Subcommittees

Financial Management, the Budget, and International Security
Office: SH-442 **Phone:** 224-2254

Fitzgerald (Chair), Stevens, Voinovich, Specter, Bennett, Shelby, Sununu
Akaka (Ranking Minority Member), Levin, Dayton, Lautenberg, Pryor, Carper

Government Management, the Federal Workforce, and the District of Columbia
Office: SH-442 **Phone:** 224-3682

Voinovich (Chair), Stevens, Coleman, Bennett, Fitzgerald, Sununu
Durbin (Ranking Minority Member), Akaka, Carper, Lautenberg, Pryor

Permanent Investigations
Office: SR-199 **Phone:** 224-3721

Coleman (Chair), Stevens, Voinovich, Specter, Bennett, Fitzgerald, Sununu, Shelby
Levin (Ranking Minority Member), Akaka, Durbin, Carper, Dayton, Lautenberg, Pryor

HEALTH, EDUCATION, LABOR, AND PENSIONS

Office: SD-428 **Phone:** 224-5375
Fax: 224-5128
Web: health.senate.gov
Majority Staff Director: Sharon Soderstrom
Minority Staff Director: J. Michael Myers 224-0767
SD-644

Education, labor, health, and public welfare in general; aging; arts and humanities; biomedical research and development; child labor; convict labor; domestic activities of the Red Cross; equal employment opportunity; handicapped people; labor standards and statistics; mediation and arbitration of labor disputes; occupational safety and health; private pensions; public health; railway labor and retirement; regulation of foreign laborers; student loans;

wages and hours; agricultural colleges; Gallaudet University; Howard University; St. Elizabeth's Hospital in Washington, D.C. The Chair and ranking minority member are nonvoting members ex officio of all subcommittees of which they are not regular members.

Party Ratio: R 11–D 9–I 1

Judd Gregg, N.H., Chair
Bill Frist, Tenn.
Michael B. Enzi, Wyo.
Lamar Alexander, Tenn.
Christopher S. Bond, Mo.
Mike DeWine, Ohio
Pat Roberts, Kan.
Jeff Sessions, Ala.
John Ensign, Nev.
Lindsey Graham, S.C.
John W. Warner, Va.

*Edward M. Kennedy, Mass.,
    Ranking Minority
    Member*
Christopher J. Dodd, Conn.
Tom Harkin, Iowa
Barbara A. Mikulski, Md.
James M. Jeffords, I-Vt.
Jeff Bingaman, N.M.
Patty Murray, Wash.
Jack Reed, R.I.
John Edwards, N.C.
*Hillary Rodham Clinton,
    N.Y.*

Subcommittees

Aging
Office: SH-615   **Phone:** 224-2962

Bond (Chair), Alexander, DeWine, Roberts, Ensign, Warner
Mikulski (Ranking Minority Member), Kennedy, Murray, Edwards, Clinton

Children and Families
Office: SH-632   **Phone:** 224-5800

Alexander (Chair), Enzi, Bond, DeWine, Roberts, Sessions, Ensign, Graham (S.C.), Warner
Dodd (Ranking Minority Member), Harkin, **Jefford**s **(I-Vt.),** *Bingaman, Murray, Reed, Edwards, Clinton*

Employment, Safety, and Training
Office: SH-615   **Phone:** 224-7229

Enzi (Chair), Alexander, Bond, Roberts, Sessions
Murray (Ranking Minority Member), Dodd, Harkin, **Jefford**s **(I-Vt.)**

Substance Abuse and Mental Health Services
Office: SH-607   **Phone:** 224-2315

DeWine (Chair), Enzi, Sessions, Ensign
Kennedy (Ranking Minority Member), Bingaman, Reed

INDIAN AFFAIRS

Office: SH-838
Phone: 224-2251   **Fax:** 228-2589
Web: indian.senate.gov
Majority Staff Director: Paul Moorehead
Minority Staff Director: Patricia Zell 224-2251 SH-838

Problems and opportunities of Indians, including Indian land management and trust responsibilities, education, health, special services, loan programs, and claims

against the United States. Reports findings and makes recommendations to the Senate but cannot report legislation.

Party Ratio: R 8–D 7

Ben Nighthorse Campbell,
    Colo., Chair
John McCain, Ariz.
Pete V. Domenici, N.M.
Craig Thomas, Wyo.
Orrin G. Hatch, Utah
James M. Inhofe, Okla.
Gordon H. Smith, Ore.
Lisa Murkowski, Alaska

*Daniel K. Inouye, Hawaii,
    Ranking Minority
    Member*
Kent Conrad, N.D.
Harry Reid, Nev.
Daniel K. Akaka, Hawaii
Byron L. Dorgan, N.D.
Tim Johnson, S.D.
Maria Cantwell, Wash.

JUDICIARY

Office: SD-224   **Phone:** 224-5225
Fax: 224-9102
Web: judiciary.senate.gov
Majority Staff Director: Makan Delrahim
Minority Staff Director: Bruce Cohen 224-7703 SD-152

Civil and criminal judicial proceedings in general; national penitentiaries; bankruptcy, mutiny, espionage, and counterfeiting; civil liberties; constitutional amendments; apportionment of representatives; government information; immigration and naturalization; interstate compacts in general; claims against the United States; patents, copyrights, and trademarks; monopolies and unlawful restraints of trade; holidays and celebrations; revision and codification of the statutes of the United States; state and territorial boundary lines. The Chair and ranking minority member are nonvoting members ex officio of all subcommittees of which they are not regular members.

Party Ratio: R 10–D 9

Orrin G. Hatch, Utah,
    Chair
Charles E. Grassley, Iowa
Arlen Specter, Pa.
Jon Kyl, Ariz.
Mike DeWine, Ohio
Jeff Sessions, Ala.
Lindsey Graham, S.C.
Larry E. Craig, Idaho
Saxby Chambliss, Ga.
John Cornyn, Texas

*Patrick J. Leahy, Vt.,
    Ranking Minority
    Member*
Edward M. Kennedy, Mass.
Joseph R. Biden Jr., Del.
Herb Kohl, Wis.
Dianne Feinstein, Calif.
Russell D. Feingold, Wis.
Charles E. Schumer, N.Y.
Richard J. Durbin, Ill.
John Edwards, N.C.

Subcommittees

Administrative Oversight and the Courts
Office: SD-323   **Phone:** 224-7572

Sessions (Chair), Grassley, Specter, Craig, Cornyn
Schumer (Ranking Minority Member), Leahy, Feingold, Durbin

Antitrust, Competition Policy, and Consumer Rights
Office: SD-161   **Phone:** 224-9494

JUDICARY (continued)

DeWine (Chair), Hatch, Specter, Graham (S.C.), Chambliss

Kohl (Ranking Minority Member), Leahy, Feingold, Edwards

Constitution, Civil Rights, and Property Rights
Office: SH-327   **Phone:** 224-2934

Cornyn (Chair), Kyl, Graham (S.C.), Craig, Chambliss

Feingold (Ranking Minority Member), Kennedy, Schumer, Durbin

Crime, Corrections, and Victims' Rights
Office: SD-224   **Phone:** 224-5564

Graham (S.C.; Chair), Hatch, Grassley, Sessions, Craig, Cornyn

Biden (Ranking Minority Member), Kohl, Feinstein, Durbin, Edwards

Immigration, Border Security, and Citizenship
Office: SD-524   **Phone:** 224-6098

Chambliss (Chair), Grassley, Kyl, DeWine, Sessions, Craig, Cornyn

Kennedy (Ranking Minority Member), Leahy, Feinstein, Schumer, Durbin, Edwards

Terrorism, Technology, and Homeland Security
Office: SH-325   **Phone:** 224-6791

Kyl (Chair), Hatch, Specter, DeWine, Sessions, Chambliss

Feinstein (Ranking Minority Member), Kennedy, Biden, Kohl, Edwards

RULES AND ADMINISTRATION

Office: SR-305   **Phone:** 224-6352
Fax: 224-5400
Web: rules.senate.gov
Majority Staff Director: Susan Wells
Minority Staff Director: Kennie L. Gill 224-6351 SR-479

Senate rules and regulations; Senate administration in general; corrupt practices; qualifications of senators; contested elections; federal elections in general; Government Printing Office; Congressional Record; meetings of Congress and attendance of members; presidential succession; the Capitol, congressional office buildings, the Library of Congress, the Smithsonian Institution, and the Botanic Garden; purchases of books and manuscripts; and erection of monuments to the memory of individuals.

Party Ratio: R 10–D 9

Trent Lott, Miss., Chair	*Christopher J. Dodd, Conn.,*
Ted Stevens, Alaska	*Ranking Minority*
Mitch McConnell, Ky.	*Member*
Thad Cochran, Miss.	*Robert C. Byrd, W.Va.*
Rick Santorum, Pa.	*Daniel K. Inouye, Hawaii*
Don Nickles, Okla.	*Dianne Feinstein, Calif.*
Kay Bailey Hutchison, Texas	*Charles E. Schumer, N.Y.*
Bill Frist, Tenn.	*John B. Breaux, La.*

Gordon H. Smith, Ore.	*Tom Daschle, S.D.*
Saxby Chambliss, Ga.	*Mark Dayton, Minn.*
	Richard J. Durbin, Ill.

SELECT ETHICS

Office: SH-220   **Phone:** 224-2981
Fax: 224-7416
Web: ethics.senate.gov
Staff Director: Robert Walker 224-2981 SH-220

Studies and investigates standards and conduct of Senate members and employees and may recommend remedial action.

Party Ratio: R 3–D 3

George V. Voinovich, Ohio, Chair	*Harry Reid, Nev., Vice Chair*
Pat Roberts, Kan.	*Daniel K. Akaka, Hawaii*
Craig Thomas, Wyo.	*Blanche Lincoln, Ark.*

SELECT INTELLIGENCE

Office: SH-211   **Phone:** 224-1700
Fax: 224-1772
Web: intelligence.senate.gov
Majority Staff Director: Bill Duhnke
Minority Staff Director: Christopher Mellon 224-1700 SH-211

Legislative and budgetary authority over the Central Intelligence Agency, the Defense Intelligence Agency, the National Security Agency, and intelligence activities of the Federal Bureau of Investigation and other components of the federal intelligence community. The majority leader and minority leader are members ex officio of the committee.

Party Ratio: R 9–D 8

Pat Roberts, Kan., Chair	*John D. Rockefeller IV,*
Orrin G. Hatch, Utah	*W.Va., Vice Chair*
Mike DeWine, Ohio	*Carl Levin, Mich.*
Christopher S. Bond, Mo.	*Dianne Feinstein, Calif.*
Trent Lott, Miss.	*Ron Wyden, Ore.*
Olympia J. Snowe, Maine	*Richard J. Durbin, Ill.*
Chuck Hagel, Neb.	*Evan Bayh, Ind.*
Saxby Chambliss, Ga.	*John Edwards, N.C.*
John W. Warner, Va.	*Barbara A. Mikulski, Md.*

SMALL BUSINESS AND ENTREPRENEURSHIP

Office: SR-428A   **Phone:** 224-5175
Fax: 228-1128
Web: sbc.senate.gov
Majority Staff Director: Mark Warren
Minority Staff Director: Patricia R. Forbes 224-8496 SR-428A

Problems of small business; Small Business Administration.

Party Ratio: R 10–D 9

Olympia J. Snowe, Maine,
Chair
Christopher S. Bond, Mo.
Conrad Burns, Mont.
Robert F. Bennett, Utah
Michael B. Enzi, Wyo.
Peter G. Fitzgerald, Ill.
Michael D. Crapo, Idaho
George Allen, Va.
John Ensign, Nev.
Norm Coleman, Minn.

John Kerry, Mass., Ranking
Minority Member
Carl Levin, Mich.
Tom Harkin, Iowa
Joseph I. Lieberman, Conn.
Mary L. Landrieu, La.
John Edwards, N.C.
Maria Cantwell, Wash.
Evan Bayh, Ind.
Mark Pryor, Ark.

Jim Bunning, Ky.
John Ensign, Nev.
Lindsey Graham, S.C.
Lisa Murkowski, Alaska

Patty Murray, Wash.
Zell Miller, Ga.
Ben Nelson, Neb.

SPECIAL AGING

Office: SD-G31   **Phone:** 224-5364
Fax: 224-8660
Web: aging.senate.gov
Majority Staff Director: Lupe Wissel
Minority Staff Director: Michelle Easton 224-1467
SH-628

Problems and opportunities of older people including health, income, employment, housing, and care and assistance. Reports findings and makes recommendations to the Senate but cannot report legislation.
Party Ratio: R 11–D 9–I 1

Larry E. Craig, Idaho, Chair
Richard C. Shelby, Ala.
Michael B. Enzi, Wyo.
Susan Collins, Maine
Gordon H. Smith, Ore.
Jim Talent, Mo.
Peter G. Fitzgerald, Ill.
Orrin G. Hatch, Utah
Elizabeth Dole, N.C.
Ted Stevens, Alaska
Rick Santorum, Pa.

John B. Breaux, La., Ranking
Minority Member
Harry Reid, Nev.
Herb Kohl, Wis.
James M. Jeffords, I-Vt.
Russell D. Feingold, Wis.
Ron Wyden, Ore.
Evan Bayh, Ind.
Blanche Lincoln, Ark.
Thomas R. Carper, Del.
Debbie Stabenow, Mich.

VETERANS' AFFAIRS

Office: SR-412   **Phone:** 224-9126
Fax: 224-9575
Web: veterans.senate.gov
Majority Chief Counsel: William Tuerk
Minority Staff Director: Bryant Hall 224-2074 SH-202

Veterans' measures in general; compensation; life insurance issued by the government on account of service in the armed forces; national cemeteries; pensions; readjustment benefits; veterans' hospitals, medical care and treatment; vocational rehabilitation and education; soldiers' and sailors' civil relief.
Party Ratio: R 8–D 6–I 1

Arlen Specter, Pa., Chair
Ben Nighthorse Campbell,
Colo.
Larry E. Craig, Idaho
Kay Bailey Hutchison, Texas

Bob Graham, Fla., Ranking
Minority Member
John D. Rockefeller IV, W.Va.
James M. Jeffords, I-Vt.
Daniel K. Akaka, Hawaii

SENATE LEADERSHIP AND PARTISAN COMMITTEES

REPUBLICAN LEADERS

President of the Senate: Vice President Dick Cheney
President Pro Tempore: Ted Stevens, Alaska
Majority Floor Leader: Bill Frist, Tenn.
Assistant Majority Leader: Mitch McConnell, Ky.
Conference Chair: Rick Santorum, Pa.
Conference Vice Chair: Kay Bailey Hutchison, Texas
Chief Deputy Whip: Robert F. Bennett, Utah
Policy Committee Chair: Jon Kyl, Ariz.
Committee on Committees Chair: Larry E. Craig, Idaho
National Republican Senatorial Committee Chair:
George Allen, Va.
Counsel to the Majority Leader: Olympia J. Snowe,
Maine

REPUBLICAN PARTISAN COMMITTEES

National Republican Senatorial Committee
Office: 425 2nd St. N.E. 20002   **Phone:** 675-6000
Web: www.nrsc.org
George Allen, Va., Chair
Executive Committee
Elizabeth Dole, N.C., Chair, Inner Circle
Christopher S. Bond, Mo., Chair,
Republican Senate Council
Lindsey Graham, S.C., Chair, Presidential Roundtable

Republican Policy Committee
Office: SR-347   **Phone:** 224-2946
Web: www.senate.gov/~rpc
Jon Kyl, Ariz., Chair

Republican Steering Committee
Office: SR-493   **Phone:** 224-4124
Jeff Sessions, Ala., Chair

DEMOCRATIC LEADERS

Minority Floor Leader: *Tom Daschle, S.D.*
Assistant Minority Leader: *Harry Reid, Nev.*
Conference Chair: *Tom Daschle, S.D.*
Conference Secretary: *Barbara A. Mikulski, Md.*
Chief Deputy Whip: *John B. Breaux, La.*
Assistant Floor Leader: *Richard J. Durbin, Ill.*
Policy Committee Chair: *Byron L. Dorgan, N.D.*
Steering and Coordination Committee Chair: *Hillary*
Rodham Clinton, N.Y.

DEMOCRATIC LEADERS (continued)

Technology and Communications Committee Chair:
Tom Daschle, S.D.

Chief Deputy for Strategic Outreach: Barbara Boxer, Calif.

Democratic Senatorial Campaign Committee Chair:
Jon Corzine, N.J.

DEMOCRATIC PARTISAN COMMITTEES

Democratic Policy Committee

Office: SH-419   **Phone:** 224-3232
Byron L. Dorgan, N.D., Chair
Mary L. Landrieu, La., Regional Chair
Patty Murray, Wash., Regional Chair
Jack Reed, R.I., Regional Chair
Members (in alphabetical order)

Daniel K. Akaka, Hawaii	Joseph I. Lieberman, Conn.
Evan Bayh, Ind.	Blanche Lincoln, Ark.
Tom Daschle, S.D.	John D. Rockefeller IV, W.Va.
Russell D. Feingold, Wis.	Paul S. Sarbanes, Md.
Dianne Feinstein, Calif.	Charles E. Schumer, N.Y.
Ernest F. Hollings, S.C.	Ron Wyden, Ore.
Tim Johnson, S.D.	

Democratic Senatorial Campaign Committee

Office: 120 Maryland Ave. N.E. 20002   **Phone:** 224-2447
Web: www.dscc.org
Jon Corzine, N.J., Chair
Debbie Stabenow, Mich., Vice Chair
Program Chairs (in alphabetical order)

Jeff Bingaman, N.M.	Patrick J. Leahy, Vt.
John B. Breaux, La.	Blanche Lincoln, Ark.
Thomas R. Carper, Del.	Barbara A. Mikulski, Md.
Mark Dayton, Minn.	Ben Nelson, Neb.
John Edwards, N.C.	Jack Reed, R.I.
Dianne Feinstein, Ca.	Harry Reid, Nev.
Daniel K. Inouye, Hawaii	John D. Rockefeller IV, W.Va.
Tim Johnson, S.D.	Charles E. Schumer, N.Y.
Edward M. Kennedy, Mass.	Ron Wyden, Ore.

Democratic Steering and Coordination Committee

Office: SH-712   **Phone:** 224-9048
Hillary Rodham Clinton, N.Y., Chair
Members (in alphabetical order)

Max Baucus, Mont.	John Edwards, N.C.
Joseph R. Biden Jr., Del.	Bob Graham, Fla.
Jeff Bingaman, N.M.	Tom Harkin, Iowa
Barbara Boxer, Calif.	Daniel K. Inouye, Hawaii
John B. Breaux, La.	Edward M. Kennedy, Mass.
Robert C. Byrd, W.Va.	Herb Kohl, Wis.
Kent Conrad, N.D.	Patrick J. Leahy, Vt.
Tom Daschle, S.D.	Carl Levin, Mich.
Christopher J. Dodd, Conn.	Harry Reid, Nev.
Richard J. Durbin, Ill.	Paul S. Sarbanes, Md.

Democratic Technology and Communications Committee

Office: SH-619   **Phone:** 224-1430
Web: democrats.senate.gov/dtcc.html
Tom Daschle, S.D., Chair
John D. Rockefeller IV, W.Va., Co-Chair
Members (in alphabetical order)

Jeff Bingaman, N.M.	John Edwards, N.C.
Hillary Rodham Clinton, N.Y.	Ernest F. Hollings, S.C.
	Tim Johnson, S.D.
Kent Conrad, N.D.	Patty Murray, Wash.
Christopher J. Dodd, Conn.	

Senate Members' Offices

Listed below are the names of Senate members and their party and state, followed by the address and telephone and fax numbers for their Washington office (the area code for all telephone numbers in Washington, D.C., is [202]). Also listed for each senator are the name of a top administrative aide and Web and e-mail addresses.

The address, telephone and fax numbers, and name of a key aide for the senators' district office(s) are also listed. And finally, each senator's committee assignments are given. (For partisan committee assignments, see page 867.)

As of April 23, 2003, there were 51 Republicans, 48 Democrats, and 1 Independent in the Senate.

AKAKA, DANIEL K., D-HAWAII

Capitol Hill Office: SH-141 20510; 224-6361; Fax: 224-2126; *Administrative Assistant:* James K. Sakai
Web: akaka.senate.gov
E-mail: senator@akaka.senate.gov
District Office(s): 300 Ala Moana Blvd., #3-106, Honolulu 96850; (808) 522-8970; Fax: (808) 545-4683; *State Director:* Mike Kitamura
101 Aupuni St., Hilo 96720; (808) 935-1114; Fax: (808) 935-9064; *Staff Assistant:* Kim Sasaki
Committee Assignment(s): Armed Services; Energy and Natural Resources; Governmental Affairs; Indian Affairs; Select Ethics; Veterans' Affairs

ALEXANDER, LAMAR, R-TENN.

Capitol Hill Office: SH-302 20510; 224-4944; Fax: 228-3398; *Chief of Staff:* Tom Ingram
Web: alexander.senate.gov
E-mail: alexander.senate.gov/contact.cfm
District Office(s): 800 Market St., #112, Knoxville 37902; (865) 545-4253; Fax: (865) 545-4252; *State Director:* Patrick Jaynes
167 N. Main St., #1068, Memphis 38103; (901) 544-4224; Fax: (901) 544-4227; *Field Representative:* Lora Jobe
3322 W. End Ave., #120, Nashville 37203; (615) 736-5129; Fax: (615) 269-4803; *State Director:* Anne Locke
900 Georgia Ave., #260, Chattanooga 37402; (423) 752-5337; Fax: (423) 752-5342; *Field Representative:* Lyndsay Botts
109 S. Highland St., #B-9, Jackson 38301; (731) 423-9344; Fax: (731) 423-8918; *Field Representative:* Matt Varino
Tri-Cities Regional Airport, Terminal Bldg., #101, 2525 Highway 75, Blountville 37663; (423) 325-6240; Fax: (423) 325-6236; *Field Representative:* Jon Grayson
Committee Assignment(s): Energy and Natural Resources; Foreign Relations; Health, Education, Labor, and Pensions; Joint Economic

ALLARD, WAYNE, R-COLO.

Capitol Hill Office: SD-525 20510; 224-5941; Fax: 224-6471; *Chief of Staff:* Sean Conway
Web: allard.senate.gov
E-mail: allard.senate.gov/contactme/index.cfm
District Office(s): 7340 E. Caley, #215, Englewood 80111; (303) 220-7414; Fax: (303) 220-8126; *State Director:* Andy Merritt
3400 W. 16th St., #3Q, Greeley 80634; (970) 351-7582; Fax: (970) 351-7585; *Area Director:* Carol Salisbury
228 N. Cascade Ave., #106, Colorado Springs 80903; (719) 634-6071; Fax: (719) 636-2590; *Area Director:* Vicki Broerman
411 Thatcher Bldg., 511 N. Main St., Pueblo 81003; (719) 545-9751; Fax: (719) 545-3832; *Area Director:* Doris Morgan
400 Rood Ave., #215, Grand Junction 81501; (970) 245-9553; Fax: (970) 245-9523; *Area Director:* Derek Wagner
Committee Assignment(s): Armed Services; Banking, Housing, and Urban Affairs; Budget; Environment and Public Works

ALLEN, GEORGE, R-VA.

Capitol Hill Office: SR-204 20510; 224-4024; Fax: 224-5432; *Chief of Staff:* Michael Thomas
Web: allen.senate.gov
E-mail: allen.senate.gov/email.html
District Office(s): 507 E. Franklin St., Richmond 23219; (804) 771-2221; Fax: (804) 771-8313; *State Director:* Mike Thomas
3140 Chaparral Dr., Bldg. C, #101, Roanoke 24018; (540) 772-4236; Fax: (540) 772-6870; *Regional Representative:* Charles "Chaz" Evans-Haywood
222 Central Park Ave., #120, Virginia Beach 23462; (757) 518-1674; Fax: (757) 518-1679; *Regional Representative:* Elizabeth "Bizzie" Level
332 Cummings St., Suite C, Abingdon 24210; (276) 676-2646; Fax: (276) 676-2588; *Regional Representative:* Marty Hall
2214 Rock Hill Rd., #100, Herndon 20170; (703) 435-0039; (703) 435-3446; *Regional Representative:* John Putney
Committee Assignment(s): Commerce, Science, and Transportation; Foreign Relations; Small Business and Entrepreneurship

BAUCUS, MAX, D-MONT.

Capitol Hill Office: SH-511 20510; 224-2651; Fax: 228-3687; *Chief of Staff:* Zak Anderson

Web: baucus.senate.gov

E-mail: max@baucus.senate.gov

District Office(s): 222 N. 32nd St., #100, Billings 59101; (406) 657-6790; Fax: (406) 657-6793; *State Director:* Sharon Peterson

32 E. Babcock St., #114, Bozeman 59715; (406) 586-6104; Fax: (406) 586-9177; *Field Director:* Patty Bean

19 2nd St. East, Kalispell 59901; (406) 756-1150; Fax: (406) 756-1152; *Field Director:* Rebecca Manna

211 N. Higgins Ave., #102, Missoula 59802; (406) 329-3123; *State Chief of Staff:* Jim Foley

125 W. Granite St., Butte 59701; (406) 782-8700; Fax: (406) 782-6553; *Field Director:* Kim Krueger

113 3rd St. North, Great Falls 59401; (406) 761-1574; *Field Director:* Kim Falcon

225 Cruse Ave., Suite D, Helena 59601; (406) 449-5480; Fax: (406) 449-5484; *Communications Director:* Bill Lombardi

Committee Assignment(s): Agriculture, Nutrition, and Forestry; Environment and Public Works; Finance; Joint Taxation

BAYH, EVAN, D-IND.

Capitol Hill Office: SR-463 20510; 224-5623; Fax: 228-1377; *Chief of Staff:* Tom Sugar

Web: bayh.senate.gov

E-mail: senator@bayh.senate.gov

District Office(s): 10 W. Market St., #1650, Indianapolis 46204; (317) 554-0750; Fax: (317) 554-0760; *State Director:* Dan Parker

101 Martin Luther King Blvd., #110, Evansville 47708; (812) 465-6501; Fax: (812) 465-6503; *Regional Director:* Andrew Cullen

1300 S. Harrison St., #3161, Fort Wayne 46802; (260) 426-3151; Fax: (260) 420-0060; *Regional Director:* Amy Whitehouse

5400 Federal Plaza, #3200, Hammond 46320; (219) 852-2763; Fax: (219) 852-2787; *Regional Director:* David Rozmanich

1201 E. 10th St., #106, Jeffersonville 47130; (812) 218-2317; Fax: (812) 218-2370; *Regional Director:* Heidi Inman

130 S. Main St., #101, South Bend 46601; (574) 236-8302; Fax: (574) 236-8319; *Regional Director:* Hodge Patel

Committee Assignment(s): Armed Services; Banking, Housing, and Urban Affairs; Energy and Natural Resources; Select Intelligence; Small Business and Entrepreneurship; Special Aging

BENNETT, ROBERT F., R-UTAH

Capitol Hill Office: SD-431 20510; 224-5444; Fax: 228-1168; *Chief of Staff:* Paul Yost

Web: bennett.senate.gov

E-mail: bennett.senate.gov/e-mail_form.html

District Office(s): 125 S. State St., #4225, Salt Lake City 84138; (801) 524-5933; Fax: (801) 524-5730; *State Director:* Tim Sheehan

324 25th St., #1410, Ogden 84401; (801) 625-5676; Fax: (801) 394-0137; *Area Liaison:* Glenn Mecham

196 E. Tabernacle St., #42, St. George 84770; (435) 628-5514; Fax: (435) 624-4160; *Area Director:* Quinn Warnick

2390 W. Highway 56, #4B, Cedar City 84720; (435) 865-1335; Fax: (435) 865-1481; *Area Director:* Quinn Warnick

51 S. University Ave., #310, Provo 84601; (801) 379-2525; Fax: (801) 375-3432; *Central Utah Area Director:* Donna Sackett

Committee Assignment(s): Appropriations; Banking, Housing, and Urban Affairs; Governmental Affairs; Joint Economic; Small Business and Entrepreneurship

BIDEN, JOSEPH R. JR., D-DEL.

Capitol Hill Office: SR-221 20510; 224-5042; Fax: 224-0139; *Chief of Staff:* Danny O'Brien

Web: biden.senate.gov

E-mail: senator@biden.senate.gov

District Office(s): 1105 N. Market St., #2000, Wilmington 19801; (302) 573-6345; Fax: (302) 573-6351; *State Director:* John Dorsey

24 N.W. Front St., #101, Milford 19963; (302) 424-8090; Fax: (302) 494-8098; *Kent-Sussex County Coordinator:* Kevin Smith

Committee Assignment(s): Foreign Relations; Judiciary

BINGAMAN, JEFF, D-N.M.

Capitol Hill Office: SH-703 20510; 224-5521; Fax: 224-2852; *Chief of Staff:* Bernard R. Toon

Web: bingaman.senate.gov

E-mail: senator_bingaman@bingaman.senate.gov

District Office(s): 625 Silver Ave. S.W., #130, Albuquerque 87102; (505) 346-6601; Fax: (505) 346-6780; *State Director:* Terry Brunner

105 W. 3rd, #409, Roswell 88201; (505) 622-7113; Fax: (505) 622-3538; *Field Representative:* Lynn Ditto

118 Bridge St., #3, Las Vegas 87701; (505) 454-8824; Fax: (505) 454-8959; *Constituent Services Representative:* Laura Montoya

148 Loretto Towne Center, 505 S. Main, Las Cruces 88001; (505) 523-6561; Fax: (505) 523-6584; *Office Manager:* Rosalie Moralez

119 E. Marcy St., #101, Santa Fe 87501; (505) 988-6647; Fax: (505) 992-8435; *State Scheduler:* Helen Dorado-Gray

Committee Assignment(s): Energy and Natural Resources; Finance; Health, Education, Labor, and Pensions; Joint Economic

BOND, CHRISTOPHER S., R-MO.

Capitol Hill Office: SR-274 20510; 224-5721; Fax: 224-8149; *Chief of Staff:* Julie Dammann

Web: bond.senate.gov

E-mail: kit_bond@bond.senate.gov

District Office(s): 339 Broadway, #140, Cape Girardeau 63701; (573) 334-7044; Fax: (573) 334-7352; *District Office Director:* Tom Schulte

1700 S. Campbell, Suite E, Springfield 65807; (417) 864-8258; Fax: (417) 864-7519; *District Office Director:* Stacy Burks

911 Main St., #2224, Kansas City 64105; (816) 471-7141; Fax: (816) 471-7338; *District Office Director:* Matt Roney

308 E. High St., #202, Jefferson City 65101; (573) 634-2488; Fax: (573) 634-6005; *Deputy Chief of Staff:* Jason Van Eaton

7700 Bonhomme Ave., #615, St. Louis 63105; (314) 725-4484; Fax: (314) 727-3548; *District Office Director:* Charles Barnes

Committee Assignment(s): Appropriations; Environment and Public Works; Health, Education, Labor, and Pensions; Select Intelligence; Small Business and Entrepreneurship

BOXER, BARBARA, D-CALIF.

Capitol Hill Office: SH-112 20510; 224-3553; Fax: 228-1338; *Administrative Assistant:* Karen Olick

Web: boxer.senate.gov

E-mail: boxer.senate.gov/contact/webform.html

District Office(s): 312 N. Spring St., #1748, Los Angeles 90012; (213) 894-5000; Fax: (213) 894-5012; *State Director:* Rose Kapolczynski

1700 Montgomery St., #240, San Francisco 94111; (415) 403-0100; Fax: (415) 956-6701; *Chief of Staff:* Sam Chapman

501 I St., #7600, Sacramento 95814; (916) 448-2787; Fax: (916) 448-2563; *Field Representative:* Stacey Lybeck

1130 O St., #2450, Fresno 93721; (559) 497-5109; Fax: (559) 497-5111; *Deputy State Director:* Tom Bohigian

600 B St., #2240, San Diego 92101; (619) 239-3884; Fax: (619) 239-5719; *Field Representative:* Humberto Peraza

201 N. E St., #210, San Bernardino 92401; (909) 888-8525; Fax: (909) 888-8613; *Field Representative:* Alton Garrett

Committee Assignment(s): Commerce, Science, and Transportation; Environment and Public Works; Foreign Relations

BREAUX, JOHN B., D-LA.

Capitol Hill Office: SH-503 20510; 224-4623; Fax: 228-2577; *Chief of Staff:* Fred Hatfield

Web: breaux.senate.gov

E-mail: senator@breaux.senate.gov

District Office(s): 501 Magazine St., #1005, New Orleans 70130; (504) 589-2531; Fax: (504) 589-2533; *Constituent Services Representative:* Shantrice Norman-Dial

1900 N. 18th St., #805, Monroe 71201; (318) 325-3320; Fax: (318) 325-8740; *Executive Assistant:* Jean Bates

800 Lafayatte St., #1300, Lafayette 70501; (337) 262-6871; Fax: (337) 262-6874; *Executive Assistant:* Raymond Cordova

2237 S. Acadian Thruway, #802, Baton Rouge 70808; (225) 248-0104; Fax: (225) 248-8227; *State Director:* Robert Mann

Committee Assignment(s): Commerce, Science, and Transportation; Finance; Rules and Administration; Special Aging

BROWNBACK, SAM, R-KAN.

Capitol Hill Office: SH-303 20510; 224-6521; Fax: 228-1265; *Chief of Staff:* David Kensinger

Web: brownback.senate.gov

E-mail: sam_brownback@brownback.senate.gov

District Office(s): 612 S. Kansas Ave., Topeka 66603; (785) 233-2503; Fax: (785) 233-2616; *Executive Assistant:* Denise Coatney

11111 W. 95th St., #245, Overland Park 66214; (913) 492-6378; Fax: (913) 492-7253; *Deputy State Director:* George Stafford

225 N. Market St., #120, Wichita 67202; (316) 264-8066; Fax: (316) 264-9078; *Regional Director:* Chuck Alderson

1001-C N. Broadway, Pittsburg 66762; (620) 231-6040; Fax: (620) 231-6347; *Projects Director:* Anne Emerson

811 N. Main St., Suite A, Garden City 67846; (620) 275-1124; Fax: (620) 275-1837; *Regional Director:* Dennis Mesa

Committee Assignment(s): Appropriations; Commerce, Science, and Transportation; Foreign Relations; Joint Economic

BUNNING, JIM, R-KY.

Capitol Hill Office: SH-316 20510; 224-4343; Fax: 228-1373; *Chief of Staff:* Jon Deuser

Web: bunning.senate.gov

E-mail: bunning.senate.gov/guestbook.htm

District Office(s): 601 Main St., #2, Hazard 41701; (606) 435-2390; Fax: (606) 435-1761; *Field Representative:* Darlynn Barber

1100 S. Main St., #12, Hopkinsville 42240; (270) 885-1212; Fax: (270) 881-3975; *Field Representative:* T. C. Freeman

600 Dr. Martin Luther King Jr. Place, #1072 B, Louisville 40202; (502) 582-5341; Fax: (502) 582-5344; *Field Representative:* Colley W. Bell III

423 Frederica St., #305, Owensboro 42301; (270) 689-9085; Fax: (270) 689-9158; *Field Representative:* Jim Askins

771 Corporate Dr., #105, Lexington 40503; (859) 219-2239; Fax: (859) 219-3269; *Field Representative:* Bill Lambdin

1717 Dixie Highway, #220, Fort Wright 41011; (859) 341-2602; Fax: (859) 331-7445; *State Director:* Debbie McKinney

Committee Assignment(s): Banking, Housing, and Urban Affairs; Budget; Energy and Natural Resources; Finance; Veterans' Affairs

BURNS, CONRAD, R-MONT.

Capitol Hill Office: SD-187 20510; 224-2644; Fax: 224-8594; *Chief of Staff:* Will Brook

Web: burns.senate.gov

E-mail: www.senate.gov/~burns/mailform.htm

District Office(s): 222 N. 32nd St., #400, Billings 59101; (406) 252-0550; Fax: (406) 252-7768; *State Director:* Todd Casper

208 N. Montana Ave., #202A, Helena 59601; (406) 449-5401; Fax: (406) 449-5462; *Field Representative:* Betsy Allen

211 Haggerty Lane, Suite A and B, Bozeman 59715; (406) 586-4450; Fax: (406) 586-7647; *Field Representative:* Laura Brasen

1845 U.S. Highway 93 South, #210, Kalispell 59901; (406) 257-3360; Fax: (406) 257-3974; *Field Representative:* Megan Morris

200 E. Broadway, P.O. Box 7729, Missoula 59807; (406) 329-3528; Fax: (406) 728-2193; *Field Representative:* Erin Ballas

125 W. Granite St., #211, Butte 59701; (406) 723-3277; Fax: (406) 782-4717; *Field Representative:* Cindy Perdue Dolan

321 1st Ave. North, Great Falls 59401; (406) 452-9585; Fax: (406) 452-9586; *Deputy State Director:* Mike Brown

324 W. Towne St., Glendive 59330; (406) 365-2391; Fax: (406) 365-8836; *Field Representative:* Pamela Tierney Crisafulli

Committee Assignment(s): Appropriations; Budget; Commerce, Science, and Transportation; Energy and Natural Resources; Small Business and Entrepreneurship

BYRD, ROBERT C., D-W.VA.

Capitol Hill Office: SH-311 20510; 224-3954; Fax: 228-0002; *Chief of Staff:* Barbara Videnieks

Web: byrd.senate.gov

E-mail: byrd.senate.gov/byrd_email.html

District Office(s): 300 Virginia St. East, #2630, Charleston 25301; (304) 342-5855; Fax: (304) 343-7144; *State Director:* Anne S. Barth

Committee Assignment(s): Appropriations; Armed Services; Budget; Rules and Administration

CAMPBELL, BEN NIGHTHORSE, R-COLO.

Capitol Hill Office: SR-380 20510; 224-5852; Fax: 224-1933; *Chief of Staff:* Ginnie Kontnik

Web: campbell.senate.gov

E-mail: campbell.senate.gov/email.htm

District Office(s): 6950 E. Belleview Ave., #200, Greenwood Village 80111; (303) 843-4100; Fax: (303) 843-4116; *Senate Aide:* Amy Agler

3500 John F. Kennedy Parkway, #209, Ft. Collins 80525; (970) 206-1788; Fax: (970) 206-1082; *District Director:* Keith Johnson

212 N. Wahsatch Ave., #203, Colorado Springs 80903; (719) 636-9092; Fax: (719) 636-9165; *District Director:* Catherine Lawton

400 Rood Ave., #213, Grand Junction 81501; (970) 241-6631; Fax: (970) 241-8313; *District Director:* Georgean Rossman

503 N. Main St., #648, Pueblo 81003; (719) 542-6987; Fax: (719) 542-2515; *State Director:* Dave Devendorf

679 E. 2nd Ave., Suite B, Durango 81301; (970) 385-9877; Fax: (970) 385-9882; *District Director:* Katie Aggeler

Committee Assignment(s): Appropriations; Energy and Natural Resources; Indian Affairs; Veterans' Affairs

CANTWELL, MARIA, D-WASH.

Capitol Hill Office: SH-717 20510; 224-3441; Fax: 228-0514; *Chief of Staff:* Caroline Fredrickson

Web: cantwell.senate.gov

E-mail: maria@cantwell.senate.gov

District Office(s): 1313 Officers Row, Vancouver 98661; (360) 696-7838; Fax: (360) 696-7844; *Area Director:* Liz Luce

W. 920 Riverside Ave., #697, Spokane 99201; (509) 353-2507; Fax: (509) 353-2547; *Area Director:* Robert Thoms

915 2nd Ave., #3206, Seattle 98174; (206) 220-6400; Fax: (206) 220-6404; *State Director:* Kurt Beckett

825 Jadwin Ave., G-58-A, Richland 99352; (509) 946-8106; Fax: (509) 946-6937; *Area Director:* Clark Mather

Committee Assignment(s): Commerce, Science, and Transportation; Energy and Natural Resources; Indian Affairs; Small Business and Entrepreneurship

CARPER, THOMAS R., D-DEL.

Capitol Hill Office: SH-513 20510; 224-2441; Fax: 228-2190; *Chief of Staff:* Jonathon Jones

Web: carper.senate.gov

E-mail: carper.senate.gov/email-form.html

District Office(s): 844 King St., #3021, Wilmington 19801; (302) 573-6291; Fax: (302) 573-6434; *Regional Director:* Tyrone Jones

12 The Circle, Georgetown 19947; (302) 856-7690; Fax: (302) 856-3001; *Regional Director:* Mark Lally

300 S. New St., #2215, Dover 19904; (302) 674-3308; Fax: (302) 674-5464; *State Director:* Brian Bushweller

Committee Assignment(s): Banking, Housing, and Urban Affairs; Environment and Public Works; Governmental Affairs; Special Aging

CHAFEE, LINCOLN, R-R.I.

Capitol Hill Office: SR-141-A 20510; 224-2921; Fax: 228-2853; *Chief of Staff:* David Griswold

Web: chafee.senate.gov

E-mail: chafee.senate.gov/webform.htm

District Office(s): 170 Westminster St., #1100, Providence 02903; (401) 453-5294; Fax: (401) 453-5085; *State Director:* Peder Schaefer

Committee Assignment(s): Banking, Housing, and Urban Affairs; Environment and Public Works; Foreign Relations

CHAMBLISS, SAXBY, R-GA.

Capitol Hill Office: SR-416 20510; 224-3521; Fax: 224-0072; *Chief of Staff:* Krister Holladay

E-mail: saxby_chambliss@chambliss.senate.gov

District Office(s): 100 Galleria Parkway S.E., #1340, Atlanta 30339; (770) 763-9090; Fax: (770) 226-8633; *State Director:* Greg Wright

6501 Peake Rd., Bldg. 950, Macon 31210; (478) 476-0788; Fax: (478) 476-0735; *Regional Representative:* Bill Stembridge

419-A S. Main St., Moultrie 31776; (229) 985-2112; Fax: (229) 985-2123; *Regional Representative:* Eric Betts

Committee Assignment(s): Agriculture, Nutrition, and Forestry; Armed Services; Joint Printing; Judiciary; Rules and Administration; Select Intelligence

CLINTON, HILLARY RODHAM, D-N.Y.

Capitol Hill Office: SR-476 20510; 224-4451; Fax: 228-0282; *Chief of Staff:* Tamera S. Luzzatto

Web: clinton.senate.gov

E-mail: senator@clinton.senate.gov

District Office(s): 780 3rd Ave., #2601, New York 10017; (212) 688-6262; Fax: (212) 688-7444; *State Director:* Karen Persichilli Keogh

100 S. Clinton St., Syracuse 13261; (315) 448-0470; Fax: (315) 448-0476; *Regional Director:* Cathy Calhoun

28 Church St., #208, Buffalo 14202; (716) 854-9725; Fax: (716) 854-9731; *Regional Director:* Jim Keane

1 Clinton Square, #821, Albany 12207; (518) 431-0120; Fax: (518) 431-0128; *Scheduler:* Ken Mackintosh

155 Pinelawn Rd., #250 North, Melville 11747; (631) 249-2825; Fax: (631) 249-2847; *Regional Director:* Resi Cooper

P.O. Box 617, Hartsdale 10530; (914) 725-9294; Fax: (914) 472-5073; *Regional Director:* Jeri Shapiro

100 State St., #3280, Rochester 14614; (716) 263-6250; Fax: (716) 263-6247; *Regional Director:* Sarah Anderson

P.O. Box 273, Lowville 13367; (315) 376-6118; Fax: (315) 376-6221; *Regional Director:* Sue Merrell

Committee Assignment(s): Armed Services; Environment and Public Works; Health, Education, Labor, and Pensions

COCHRAN, THAD, R-MISS.

Capitol Hill Office: SD-113 20510; 224-5054; Fax: 224-9450; *Chief of Staff:* Mark Keenum

Web: cochran.senate.gov

E-mail: senator@cochran.senate.gov

District Office(s): 911 E. Jackson Ave., #249, Oxford 38655; (662) 236-1018; Fax: (662) 236-7618; *Office Manager:* Mindy Buchanan

188 E. Capitol St., #614, Jackson 39201; (601) 965-4459; Fax: (601) 965-4919; *State Field Representative:* Christopher Richardson

14094 Customs Blvd., #201, Gulfport 39503; (228) 867-9710; Fax: (228) 867-9798; *Office Manager:* Susan Case

Committee Assignment(s): Agriculture, Nutrition, and Forestry; Appropriations; Joint Library; Joint Printing; Rules and Administration

COLEMAN, NORM, R-MINN.

Capitol Hill Office: SH-320 20510; 224-5641; Fax: 224-8438; *Chief of Staff:* Tom Mason

Web: coleman.senate.gov

E-mail: www.senate.gov/~coleman/contact/index.cfm

District Office(s): 2550 University Ave. West, #100N, St. Paul 55114; (651) 645-0323; Fax: (651) 645-3110; *State Director:* Erich Mische

Committee Assignment(s): Agriculture, Nutrition, and Forestry; Foreign Relations; Governmental Affairs; Small Business and Entrepreneurship

COLLINS, SUSAN, R-MAINE

Capitol Hill Office: SR-172 20510; 224-2523; Fax: 224-2693; *Chief of Staff:* Steve Abbott

Web: collins.senate.gov

E-mail: senator@collins.senate.gov

District Office(s): 202 Harlow St., #204, P.O. Box 655, Bangor 04402; (207) 945-0417; Fax: (207) 990-4604; *State Office Representative:* Judy Cuddy

168 Capitol St., Augusta 04330; (207) 622-8414; Fax: (207) 622-5884; *State Office Representative:* Randy Bumps

160 Main St., Biddeford 04005; (207) 283-1101; Fax: (207) 283-4054; *State Office Representative:* William Vail

11 Lisbon St., Lewiston 04240; (207) 784-6969; Fax: (207) 782-6475; *State Director:* Randy Bumps

1 City Center, #100, Portland 04101; (207) 780-3575; Fax: (207) 828-0380; *Office Representative:* William Vail

25 Sweden St., Suite A, Caribou 04736; (207) 493-7873; Fax: (207) 493-7810; *State Office Representative:* Phil Bosse

Committee Assignment(s): Armed Services; Governmental Affairs; Joint Economic; Special Aging

CONRAD, KENT, D-N.D.

Capitol Hill Office: SH-530 20510; 224-2043; Fax: 224-7776; *Chief of Staff:* Robert "Bob" Van Heuvelen

Web: conrad.senate.gov

E-mail: senator@conrad.senate.gov

District Office(s): 657 2nd Ave. North, #306, Fargo 58102; (701) 232-8030; Fax: (701) 232-6449; *State Representative:* Lois E. Schneider

100 1st St. S.W., #105, Minot 58701; (701) 852-0703; Fax: (701) 838-8196; *State Representative:* Gail Bergstad

220 E. Rosser Ave., #228, Bismarck 58501; (701) 258-4648; Fax: (701) 258-1254; *State Director:* Lynn J. Clancy

102 N. 4th St., #104, Grand Forks 58201; (701) 775-9601; Fax: (701) 746-1990; *State Representative:* James S. Hand

Committee Assignment(s): Agriculture, Nutrition, and Forestry; Budget; Finance; Indian Affairs

CORNYN, JOHN, R-TEXAS

Capitol Hill Office: SH-517 20510; 224-2934; Fax: 228-2856; *Chief of Staff:* Pete Olson

Web: cornyn.senate.gov

E-mail: cornyn.senate.gov/contact/contact.cfm

District Office(s): 2323 Bryan St., #2150, Dallas 75201; (214) 767-3000; Fax: (214) 767-8754; *Constituent Services Director:* Linda Bazaco

P.O. Box 684827, Austin 78768; *State Director:* Jennifer Lustina

Committee Assignment(s): Armed Services; Budget; Environment and Public Works; Judiciary

CORZINE, JON, D-N.J.

Capitol Hill Office: SH-502 20510; 224-4744; Fax: 228-2197; *Chief of Staff:* Tom Shea

Web: corzine.senate.gov

E-mail: corzine.senate.gov/comment.html

District Office(s): 1 Gateway Center, 11th Floor, Newark 07102; (973) 645-3030; Fax: (973) 645-0502; *State Director:* Maggie Moran

208 White Horse Pike, #18, Barrington 08007; (856) 757-5353; Fax: (856) 546-1526; Deputy *State Director:* Karin Elkis

Committee Assignment(s): Banking, Housing, and Urban Affairs; Budget; Foreign Relations

CRAIG, LARRY E., R-IDAHO

Capitol Hill Office: SH-520 20510; 224-2752; Fax: 228-1067; *Chief of Staff:* Michael O. Ware

Web: craig.senate.gov

E-mail: craig.senate.gov/webform.html

District Office(s): 801 E. Sherman St., #193, Pocatello 83201; (208) 236-6817; Fax: (208) 236-6820; Regional Assistant: Francoise Cleveland

846 Main St., Lewiston 83501; (208) 743-0792; Fax: (208) 746-7275; *Regional Director:* Leann Bifford

304 N. 8th St., #149, Boise 83702; (208) 342-7985; Fax: (208) 343-2458; *Regional Director:* Ken Burgess

610 Hubbard St., #121, Coeur D'Alene 83814; (208) 667-6130; Fax: (208) 765-1743; *State Director:* Sandra Patano

490 Memorial Dr., #101, Idaho Falls 83402; (208) 523-5541; Fax: (208) 522-0135; *Regional Director:* Knut Meyerin

1292 Addison Ave. East, Twin Falls 83301; (208) 734-6780; Fax: (208) 734-3905; *Regional Director:* Michael Mathews

Committee Assignment(s): Appropriations; Energy and Natural Resources; Judiciary; Special Aging; Veterans' Affairs

CRAPO, MICHAEL D., R-IDAHO

Capitol Hill Office: SR-111 20510; 224-6142; Fax: 228-1375; *Administrative Assistant:* Peter Fischer

Web: crapo.senate.gov

E-mail: crapo.senate.gov/email.htm

District Office(s): 202 Falls Ave., #2, Twin Falls 83301; (208) 734-2515; Fax: (208) 733-0414; *Senior Regional Director:* Linda Norris

490 Memorial Dr., #102, Idaho Falls 83404; (208) 522-9779; Fax: (208) 529-8367; *District Representative:* Leslie Huddleston

304 N. 8th St., #338, Boise 83702; (208) 334-1776; Fax: (208) 334-9044; *Chief of Staff:* John Hoehne

801 E. Sherman St., Pocatello 83201; (208) 236-6775; Fax: (208) 236-6935; *Regional Director:* John Atkins

524 E. Cleveland Blvd., #220, Caldwell 83605; (208) 455-0360; Fax: (208) 455-0358; *Regional Director:* Jake Ball

1000 Northwest Blvd., #100, Coeur D'Alene 83814; (208) 664-5490; Fax: (208) 664-0889; *Regional Director:* Matt Elsworth

111 Main St., #140, Lewiston 83501; (208) 743-1492; Fax: (208) 743-6484; *Regional Director:* Mary Hasenoehrl

Committee Assignment(s): Agriculture, Nutrition, and Forestry; Banking, Housing, and Urban Affairs; Budget; Environment and Public Works; Small Business and Entrepreneurship

DASCHLE, TOM, D-S.D.

Capitol Hill Office: SH-509 20510; 224-2321; Fax: 224-2047; *Chief of Staff:* Peter Rouse

Web: daschle.senate.gov

E-mail: tom_daschle@daschle.senate.gov

District Office(s): 320 N. Main Ave., Suite B, Sioux Falls 57101; (605) 334-9596; Fax: (605) 334-2591; *State Director:* Steve Erpenbach

320 S. 1st St., #101, Aberdeen 57402; (605) 225-8823; Fax: (605) 225-8468; *Area Director:* Beth Smith

1313 W. Main St., Rapid City 57709; (605) 348-7551; Fax: (605) 348-7208; *Area Director:* Ace Gallagher

Committee Assignment(s): Agriculture, Nutrition, and Forestry; Finance; Rules and Administration

DAYTON, MARK, D-MINN.

Capitol Hill Office: SR-346 20510; 224-3244; Fax: 228-2186; *Chief of Staff:* Sarah Dahlin

Web: dayton.senate.gov

E-mail: dayton.senate.gov/webform.html

District Office(s): Federal Bldg., #298, Fort Snelling 55111; (612) 727-5220; Fax: (612) 727-5223; *State Director:* Jim Gelbmann

401 DeMers Ave., East Grand Forks 56721; (218) 773-1110; Fax: (218) 773-1993; *District Representative:* Valerie Gravesetti

222 Main St., #200, P.O. Box 937, Biwabik 55708; (218) 865-4480; Fax: (218) 865-4667; *District Representative:* Steve Bradach

Committee Assignment(s): Agriculture, Nutrition, and Forestry; Armed Services; Governmental Affairs; Joint Printing; Rules and Administration

DEWINE, MIKE, R-OHIO

Capitol Hill Office: SR-140 20510; 224-2315; Fax: 224-6519; *Legislative Director:* Paul Palagyi

Web: dewine.senate.gov

E-mail: senator_dewine@dewine.senate.gov

District Office(s): 37 W. Broad St., #300, Columbus 43215; (614) 469-6774; Fax: (614) 469-7419; *Chief of Staff:* Laurel Dawson

600 E. Superior Ave., #2450, Cleveland 44114; (216) 522-7272; Fax: (216) 522-2239; *Regional Director:* Michelle Gillcrist

121 Putnam St., #102, Marietta 45750; (740) 373-2317; Fax: (740) 373-8689; *District Representative:* Karen Sloan

100 W. Main St., 2nd Floor, Suite C, Xenia 45385; (937) 376-3080; Fax: (937) 376-3387; *State Director:* Barbara Briggs Schenck

420 Madison Ave., #1225, Toledo 43604; (419) 259-7535; Fax: (419) 259-7575; *District Representative:* Scott Noyes

312 Walnut St., #2030, Cincinnati 45202; (513) 763-8260; Fax: (513) 763-8268; *Regional Director:* Shannon Jones

Committee Assignment(s): Appropriations; Health, Education, Labor, and Pensions; Judiciary; Select Intelligence

DODD, CHRISTOPHER J., D-CONN.

Capitol Hill Office: SR-448 20510; 224-2823; Fax: 224-1683; *Chief of Staff:* Sheryl Cohen

Web: dodd.senate.gov

E-mail: senator@dodd.senate.gov

District Office(s): 100 Great Meadow Rd., Wethersfield 06109; (860) 258-6940; Fax: (860) 258-6958; *State Director:* Ed Mann

Committee Assignment(s): Banking, Housing, and Urban Affairs; Foreign Relations; Health, Education, Labor, and Pensions; Joint Library; Rules and Administration

DOLE, ELIZABETH, R-N.C.

Capitol Hill Office: SR-120 20510; 224-6342; Fax: 228-1339; *Chief of Staff:* Frank Hill

Web: dole.senate.gov

E-mail: dole.senate.gov/index.cfm?FuseAction=ContactMe.Home

District Office(s): 310 New Bern Ave., #122, Raleigh 27601; (919) 856-4630; Fax: (919) 856-4053; *Deputy State Director:* Reginald Ronald Holley

Federal Bldg., #210, Hickory 28603; (828) 322-5170; Fax: (828) 322-1255; *Staff Director:* Jo Murrat

225 N. Main St., #404, Salisbury 28144; (704) 633-5011; Fax: (704) 633-2937; *State Director:* Margaret Kluttz

Committee Assignment(s): Agriculture, Nutrition, and Forestry; Armed Services; Banking, Housing, and Urban Affairs; Special Aging

DOMENICI, PETE V., R-N.M.

Capitol Hill Office: SH-328 20510; 224-6621; Fax: 228-0900; *Chief of Staff:* Steve Bell

Web: domenici.senate.gov

E-mail: senator_domenici@domenici.senate.gov

District Office(s): 625 Silver Ave. S.W., #330, Albuquerque 87102; (505) 346-6791; *Communications Director:* Lisa Breeden

505 S. Main, #118, Las Cruces 88001; (505) 526-5475; Fax: (505) 523-6589; *Office Manager:* Susie Cordero

120 S. Federal Place, #302, Santa Fe 87501; (505) 988-6511; *Office Manager:* Maggie Murray

500 N. Richardson Ave., #140, Roswell 88201; (505) 623-6170; Fax: (505) 625-2547; *Regional Director:* Poe R. Corn

Committee Assignment(s): Appropriations; Budget; Energy and Natural Resources; Indian Affairs

DORGAN, BYRON L., D-N.D.

Capitol Hill Office: SH-713 20510; 224-2551; Fax: 224-1193; *Chief of Staff:* James A. Messina

Web: dorgan.senate.gov

E-mail: senator@dorgan.senate.gov

District Office(s): 112 Roberts St., #110, P.O. Box 2250, Fargo 58107; (701) 239-5389; Fax: (701) 239-5512; *Area Coordinator:* Kevin Carvell

220 E. Rosser Ave., #312, Bismarck 58501; (701) 250-4618; Fax: (701) 250-4484; *State Coordinator:* Bob Valeu

100 1st St. S.W., #105, Minot 58701; (701) 852-0703; Fax: (701) 838-8196; *State Representative:* Gail Bergstad

102 N. 4th St., Grand Forks 58201; (701) 746-8972; Fax: (701) 746-9122

Committee Assignment(s): Appropriations; Commerce, Science, and Transportation; Energy and Natural Resources; Indian Affairs

DURBIN, RICHARD J., D-ILL.

Capitol Hill Office: SD-332 20510; 224-2152; Fax: 228-0400; *Chief of Staff:* Ed Greelegs

Web: durbin.senate.gov

E-mail: dick@durbin.senate.gov

District Office(s): 525 S. 8th St., Springfield 62703; (217) 492-4062; Fax: (217) 492-4382; *Area Director:* Bill Houlihan

230 S. Dearborn St., 38th Floor, Chicago 60604; (312) 353-4952; Fax: (312) 353-0150; *State Director:* Michael Daly

701 N. Court St., Marion 62959; (618) 998-8812; Fax: (618) 997-0176; *Staff Assistant:* Donna Eastman

Committee Assignment(s): Appropriations; Governmental Affairs; Judiciary; Rules and Administration; Select Intelligence

EDWARDS, JOHN, D-N.C.

Capitol Hill Office: SD-225 20510; 224-3154; Fax: 228-1374; *Chief of Staff:* Miles Lackey

Web: edwards.senate.gov

E-mail: edwards.senate.gov/mailform.html

District Office(s): 301 Century Post Office Bldg., 300 Fayetteville St. Mall, Raleigh 27601; (919) 856-4245; Fax: (919) 856-4408; *State Director:* Alice Garland

151 Patton Ave., #200, Asheville 28801; (828) 285-0760; *Area Representative:* Jewell Wilson

401 W. Trade St., #219, Charlotte 28202; (704) 344-6154; Fax: (704) 344-6161; *Area Director:* Kevin Monroe

125 S. Elm St., #401, Greensboro 27409; (336) 333-5311; *Area Representative:* Judith Rossabi

401 W. 1st St., #1-C, Greenville 27401; (252) 931-1111; *Area Representative:* Joyce Mitchell

Committee Assignment(s): Health, Education, Labor, and Pensions; Judiciary; Select Intelligence; Small Business and Entrepreneurship

ENSIGN, JOHN, R-NEV.

Capitol Hill Office: SR-379A 20510; 224-6244; Fax: 228-2193; *Chief of Staff:* Scott Bensing

Web: ensign.senate.gov

E-mail: ensign.senate.gov/contact_john/contactjohn_email.html

District Office(s): 333 S. Las Vegas Blvd., #8203, Las Vegas 89101; (702) 388-6605; Fax: (702) 388-6501; *State Director:* Sonia Joya

400 S. Virginia St., #738, Reno 89501; (775) 686-5770; Fax: (775) 686-5729; *Area Director:* Verita Black Prothro

600 E. William St., #304, Carson City 89701; (775) 885-9111; Fax: (775) 883-5590; *Area Coordinator:* Kevin Kirkeby

Committee Assignment(s): Armed Services; Budget; Commerce, Science, and Transportation; Health, Education, Labor, and Pensions; Small Business and Entrepreneurship; Veterans' Affairs

ENZI, MICHAEL B., R-WYO.

Capitol Hill Office: SR-379A 20510; 224-3424; Fax: 228-0359; *Chief of Staff:* Flip McConnaughey

Web: enzi.senate.gov

E-mail: senator@enzi.senate.gov

District Office(s): 2120 Capitol Ave., #2007, Cheyenne 82001; (307) 772-2477; Fax: (307) 772-2480; *Field Representative:* Debbie McCann

400 S. Kendrick Ave., #303, Gillette 82716; (307) 682-6268; Fax: (307) 682-6501; *State Director:* Robin Bailey

100 E. B St., #3201, Casper 82601; (307) 261-6572; Fax: (307) 261-6574; *Field Representative:* Cherie Hilderbrand

1285 Sheridan Ave., #210, Cody 82414; (307) 527-9444; Fax: (307) 527-9476; *Field Representative:* Karen McCreery

545 W. Broadway, Jackson 83002; (307) 739-9507; Fax: (307) 739-9520; *Field Representative:* Lyn Shanaghy

Committee Assignment(s): Banking, Housing, and Urban Affairs; Budget; Foreign Relations; Health, Education, Labor, and Pensions; Small Business and Entrepreneurship; Special Aging

FEINGOLD, RUSSELL D., D-WIS.

Capitol Hill Office: SH-506 20510; 224-5323; Fax: 224-2725; *Chief of Staff:* Mary Irvine

Web: feingold.senate.gov

E-mail: feingold.senate.gov/contact.html

District Office(s): 517 E. Wisconsin Ave., #408, Milwaukee 53202; (414) 276-7282; *Regional Coordinator:* Cecilia B. Smith-Robertson

401 5th St., #410, Wausau 54403; (715) 848-5660; *Regional Coordinator:* Karen Graff

1600 Aspen Commons, #100, Middleton 53562; (608) 828-1200; Fax: (608) 828-1203; *State Director:* Janet Piraino

425 State St., #225, La Crosse 54601; (608) 782-5585; *Regional Coordinator:* Matt Nikolay

1640 Main St., Green Bay 54302; (920) 465-7508; *Regional Coordinator:* Bob Schweder

Committee Assignment(s): Budget; Foreign Relations; Judiciary; Special Aging

FEINSTEIN, DIANNE, D-CALIF.

Capitol Hill Office: SH-331 20510; 224-3841; Fax: 228-3954; *Chief of Staff:* Mark Kadesh

Web: feinstein.senate.gov

E-mail: feinstein.senate.gov/email.html

District Office(s): 11111 Santa Monica Blvd., #915, Los Angeles 90025; (310) 914-7300; Fax: (310) 914-7318; *Deputy State Director:* Guillermo Gonzalez

750 B St., #1030, San Diego 92101; (619) 231-9712; Fax: (619) 231-1108; *District Director:* James Peterson

1130 O St., #2446, Fresno 93721; (559) 485-7430; Fax: (559) 485-9689; *District Director:* Shelly Abajian

1 Post St., #2450, San Francisco 94104; (415) 393-0707; Fax: (415) 393-0710; *State Director:* Jim Molinari

Committee Assignment(s): Appropriations; Energy and Natural Resources; Judiciary; Rules and Administration; Select Intelligence

FITZGERALD, PETER G., R-ILL.

Capitol Hill Office: SD-555 20510; 224-2854; Fax: 228-1372; *Chief of Staff:* Gregory J. Gross

Web: fitzgerald.senate.gov

E-mail: senator_fitzgerald@fitzgerald.senate.gov

District Office(s): 230 S. Dearborn St., #3900, Chicago 60604; (312) 886-3506; Fax: (312) 886-3514; *State Director:* Maggie Hickey

520 S. 8th St., Springfield 62703; (217) 492-5089; Fax: (217) 492-5099; *Central Illinois Director:* David Curtin

Ginger Creek Village #7B, Glen Carbon 62034; (618) 692-0364; Fax: (618) 692-1499; *Southern Illinois Director:* Christine Sullivan

115 W. 1st St. #100, Dixon 61021; (815) 288-3140; Fax: (815) 288-3147; *Northern Illinois Director:* Jason Anderson

Committee Assignment(s): Agriculture, Nutrition, and Forestry; Commerce, Science, and Transportation; Governmental Affairs; Small Business and Entrepreneurship; Special Aging

FRIST, BILL, R-TENN.

Capitol Hill Office: SR-416 20510; 224-3344; Fax: 228-1264; *Chief of Staff:* Howard Liebengood; *Chief of Staff* (leadership): Mitch Bainwol

Web: frist.senate.gov

E-mail: frist.senate.gov/Contact/contact.html

District Office(s): 28 White Bridge Rd., #211, Nashville 37205; (615) 352-9411; Fax: (615) 352-9985; *State Director:* Bart Verhulst

735 Broad St., #701, Chattanooga 37402; (423) 756-2757; Fax: (423) 756-5313; *Field Representative:* Tyler Owens

200 E. Main St., #111, Jackson 38301; (731) 424-9655; Fax: (731) 424-8322; *Field Representative:* Jim Humphreys

10368 Wallace Alley St., #7, Kingsport 37663; (423) 323-1252; Fax: (423) 323-0358; *Field Representative:* Tim Whaley

Twelve Oaks Executive Park, Bldg. 1, #170, 5401 Kingston Pike, Knoxville 37919; (865) 602-7977; Fax: (865) 602-7979; *Senior Field Representative:* Carolyn Jensen

5100 Poplar Ave., #514, Memphis 38137; (901) 683-1910; Fax: (901) 683-3610; *Field Representative:* Ken Scroggs

Committee Assignment(s): Finance; Health, Education, Labor, and Pensions; Rules and Administration

GRAHAM, BOB, D-FLA.

Capitol Hill Office: SH-524 20510; 224-3041; Fax: 224-2237; *Chief of Staff:* Buddy Menn

Web: graham.senate.gov

E-mail: bob_graham@graham.senate.gov

District Office(s): 2252 Killearn Center Blvd., 3rd Floor, Tallahassee 32309; (850) 907-1100; Fax: (850) 894-3222; *State Director:* Mary Chiles

150 S.E. 2nd Ave., #1025, Miami 33131; (305) 536-7293; Fax: (305) 536-6949; *Regional Director:* Ellen Roth

625 E. Twiggs St., #500, Tampa 33930; (813) 228-2476; Fax: (813) 228-2479; *Regional Director:* Susan McGinn

Committee Assignment(s): Energy and Natural Resources; Environment and Public Works; Finance; Veterans' Affairs

GRAHAM, LINDSEY, R-S.C.

Capitol Hill Office: SR-290 20510; 224-5972; Fax: 224-1300; *Chief of Staff:* Richard Perry

Web: lgraham.senate.gov

E-mail: lgraham.senate.gov/email/email.htm

District Office(s): 508 Hampton St., #202, Columbia 29201; (803) 933-0112; Fax: (803) 933-0957; *Area Director:* Sara Snell

401 W. Evans St., #226B, Florence 29501; (843) 669-1505; Fax: (843) 669-9015; *Area Director:* Celia McLaughlin

101 E. Washington St., #220, Greenville 29601; (864) 250-1417; Fax: (864) 250-4322; *State Director:* Jane Goolsby

530 Johnnie Dodds Blvd., #203, Mt. Pleasant 29464; (843) 849-3887; Fax: (843) 971-3669; *Area Director:* Patricia Sykes

Committee Assignment(s): Armed Services; Health, Education, Labor, and Pensions; Judiciary; Veterans' Affairs

GRASSLEY, CHARLES E., R-IOWA

Capitol Hill Office: SH-135 20510; 224-3744; Fax: 224-6020; *Chief of Staff:* Kenneth C. Cunningham

Web: grassley.senate.gov

E-mail: chuck_grassley@grassley.senate.gov

District Office(s): 210 Walnut St., #721, Des Moines 50309; (515) 284-4890; Fax: (515) 284-4069; *State Director:* Henry Wulff

8 S. 6th St., #307, Council Bluffs 51501; (712) 322-7103; Fax: (712) 322-7196; *Regional Director:* Donna Barry

101 1st St. S.E., #206, Cedar Rapids 52401; (319) 363-6832; Fax: (319) 363-7179; *Regional Director:* Mary Day

131 W. 3rd St., #180, Davenport 52801; (563) 322-4331; Fax: (563) 322-8552; *Regional Director:* Penny Vacek

531 Commercial St., #210, Waterloo 50701; (319) 232-6657; Fax: (319) 232-9965; *Regional Director:* Valerie Nehl

320 6th St., #103, Sioux City 51101; (712) 233-1860; Fax: (712) 233-1634; *Regional Director:* Marliss De Jong

Committee Assignment(s): Agriculture, Nutrition, and Forestry; Budget; Finance; Joint Taxation; Judiciary

GREGG, JUDD, R-N.H.

Capitol Hill Office: SR-393 20510; 224-3324; Fax: 224-4952; *Administrative Assistant:* Vasiliki Christopoulos

Web: gregg.senate.gov

E-mail: mailbox@gregg.senate.gov

District Office(s): 41 Hooksett Rd., Manchester 03104; (603) 622-7979; Fax: (603) 622-0422; *Caseworker:* Peg Ouellette

60 Pleasant St., Berlin 03570; (603) 752-2604; Fax: (603) 752-7351; *Caseworker:* Janet Woodward

16 Pease Blvd., Portsmouth 03801; (603) 431-2171; Fax: (603) 431-1916; *Projects Assistant:* John Cavanaugh

125 N. Main St., Concord 03301; (603) 225-7115; Fax: (603) 224-0198; *Chief of Staff:* Joel Maiola

Committee Assignment(s): Appropriations; Budget; Health, Education, Labor, and Pensions

HAGEL, CHUCK, R-NEB.

Capitol Hill Office: SR-248 20510; 224-4224; Fax: 224-5213; *Chief of Staff:* Lou Ann Linehan

Web: hagel.senate.gov

E-mail: chuck_hagel@hagel.senate.gov

District Office(s): 11301 Davenport St., #2, Omaha 68154; (402) 758-8981; Fax: (402) 758-9165; *State Director:* Thomas Janssen

100 Centennial Mall North, #294, Lincoln 68508; (402) 476-1400; Fax: (402) 476-0605; *Constituent Services Director:* Dorothy Anderson

4009 6th Ave., #9, Kearney 68847; (308) 236-7602; Fax: (308) 236-7473; *Constituent Services Representative:* Julie Brooker

115 Railway St., #C102, Scottsbluff 69361; (308) 632-6032; Fax: (308) 632-6295; *Constituent Services Representative:* Krisa Hall

Committee Assignment(s): Banking, Housing, and Urban Affairs; Foreign Relations; Select Intelligence

HARKIN, TOM, D-IOWA

Capitol Hill Office: SH-731 20510; 224-3254; Fax: 224-9369; *Chief of Staff:* Peter Reinecke

Web: harkin.senate.gov

E-mail: tom_harkin@harkin.senate.gov

District Office(s): 210 Walnut St., #733, Des Moines 50309; (515) 284-4574; Fax: (515) 284-4937; *State Administrator:* Dianne Liepa

1606 Brady St., #323, Davenport 52803; (563) 322-1338; Fax: (563) 322-0417; *Regional Representative:* Rita Vargas

150 1st Ave. N.E., #370, Cedar Rapids 52401; (319) 365-4504; Fax: (319) 393-4683; *Regional Administrator:* Beth Freeman

350 W. 6th St., #315, Dubuque 52001; (563) 582-2130; Fax: (563) 582-2342; *Regional Representative:* Linda Lucy

320 6th St., #110, Sioux City 51101; (712) 252-1550; Fax: (712) 252-1638; *Regional Administrator:* Maureen Wilson

Committee Assignment(s): Agriculture, Nutrition, and Forestry; Appropriations; Health, Education, Labor, and Pensions; Small Business and Entrepreneurship

HATCH, ORRIN G., R-UTAH

Capitol Hill Office: SH-104 20510; 224-5251; Fax: 224-6331; *Chief of Staff:* Patricia Knight

Web: hatch.senate.gov

E-mail: senator_hatch@hatch.senate.gov

District Office(s): 125 S. State St., #8402, Salt Lake City 84138; (801) 524-4380; Fax: (801) 524-4379; *State Director:* Melanie Bowen

324 25th St., #1006, Ogden 84401; (801) 625-5672; Fax: (801) 625-5590; *Area Director:* Sandra Kester

51 S. University Ave., #320, Provo 84606; (801) 375-7881; Fax: (801) 374-5005; *Area Director:* Ronald Dean

2390 W. Highway 56, P.O. Box 99, Cedar City 84720; (435) 586-8435; Fax: (435) 586-2147; *Area Director:* Jeannine Holt

197 E. Tabernacle, #2, St. George 84770; (435) 634-1795; Fax: (435) 634-1796; *Area Director:* Jeannine Holt

Committee Assignment(s): Finance; Indian Affairs; Joint Taxation; Judiciary; Select Intelligence; Special Aging

HOLLINGS, ERNEST F., D-S.C.

Capitol Hill Office: SR-125 20510; 224-6121; Fax: 224-4293; *Chief of Staff:* Joey Lesesne

Web: hollings.senate.gov

E-mail: hollings.senate.gov/webform.html

District Office(s): 1835 Assembly St., #1551, Columbia 29201; (803) 765-5731; Fax: (803) 765-5742; *State Director:* Sam B. "Trip" King

300 E. Washington St., #126, Greenville 29603; (864) 233-5366; Fax: (864) 233-2923; *Area Representative:* John Funderburk

200 E. Bay St., #112, Charleston 29401; (843) 727-4525; Fax: (843) 722-4923; *Area Representative:* Joe S. Maupin

Committee Assignment(s): Appropriations; Budget; Commerce, Science, and Transportation

HUTCHISON, KAY BAILEY, R-TEXAS

Capitol Hill Office: SR-284 20510; 224-5922; Fax: 224-0776; *Chief of Staff:* Ruth Cymber

Web: hutchison.senate.gov

E-mail: senator@hutchison.senate.gov

District Office(s): 10440 N. Central Expressway, Lock Box 606, #1160, Dallas 75231; (214) 361-3500; Fax: (214) 361-3502; *Regional Director:* Cynthia Hall

1919 Smith St., #800, Houston 77002; (713) 653-3456; Fax: (713) 209-3459; *Community Affairs Director:* Mary Schneider

8023 Vantage Dr., #460, San Antonio 78230; (210) 340-2885; Fax: (210) 349-6753; *Regional Director:* George Antuna

300 E. 8th St., #961, Austin 78701; (512) 916-5834; Fax: (512) 916-5839; *State Director:* Lindsey Howe Parham

500 Chestnut St., #1570, Abilene 79602; (915) 676-2839; Fax: (915) 676-2937; *Regional Director:* Shea Woodard

Committee Assignment(s): Appropriations; Commerce, Science, and Transportation; Rules and Administration; Veterans' Affairs

INHOFE, JAMES M., R-OKLA.

Capitol Hill Office: SR-453 20510; 224-4721; Fax: 228-0380; *Chief of Staff:* Glenn Powell

Web: inhofe.senate.gov

E-mail: inhofe.senate.gov/contactus.htm

District Office(s): 1924 S. Utica St., #530, Tulsa 74104; (918) 748-5111; Fax: (918) 748-5119; *Field Representative:* Curt Price

1900 N.W. Expressway, #1210, Oklahoma City 73118; (405) 608-4381; Fax: (405) 608-4120; *State Director:* Ragon Gentry

100 S. Main St., McAlester 74502; (918) 426-0933; Fax: (918) 426-0935; *Field Representative:* Tim Gaines

302 N. Independence, #104, Enid 73701; (580) 234-5105; Fax: (580) 234-0929; *Field Representative:* Michael Jackson

Committee Assignment(s): Armed Services; Environment and Public Works; Indian Affairs

INOUYE, DANIEL K., D-HAWAII

Capitol Hill Office: SH-722 20510; 224-3934; Fax: 224-6747; *Administrative Assistant:* Patrick DeLeon

Web: inouye.senate.gov

E-mail: inouye.senate.gov/abtform.html

District Office(s): 300 Ala Moana Blvd., #7-212, Honolulu 96850; (808) 541-2542; Fax: (808) 541-2549; *Chief of Staff:* Jennifer Goto Sabas

24 N. Church St., #407, Wailuku 96793; (808) 242-9702; Fax: (808) 242-7233; *Field Representative:* Ryther Barbin

101 Aupuni St., #205, Hilo 96720; (808) 935-0844; Fax: (808) 961-5163; *Field Representative:* William Kikuchi

P.O. Box 573, Kaunakakai 96748; (808) 642-0203; Fax: (808) 560-3385; *Field Representative:* William Akutagawa

P.O. Box 41, Kealakekua 96750; (808) 935-0844; Fax: (808) 961-5163; *Field Representative:* Wayne Tanaka

1840A Leleiona St., P.O. Box 311, Kauai 96766; (808) 245-4611; Fax: (808) 246-9515; *Field Representative:* Ron Sakoda

Committee Assignment(s): Appropriations; Commerce, Science, and Transportation; Indian Affairs; Joint Printing; Rules and Administration

JEFFORDS, JAMES M., I-VT.

Capitol Hill Office: SH-728 20510; 224-5141; Fax: 228-0776; *Chief of Staff:* Susan Boardman Russ

Web: jeffords.senate.gov

E-mail: vermont@jeffords.senate.gov

District Office(s): 30 Main St., #350, Burlington 05401; (802) 658-6001; Fax: (802) 860-7624; *Office Coordinator:* Cathy Zaccone

453 Stone Cutters Way, #1, Montpelier 05602; (802) 223-5273; Fax: (802) 223-0416; *State Director:* Bill Kurtz

2 S. Main St., 2nd Floor, Rutland 05701; (802) 773-3875; *Office Coordinator:* Marie Pomainville

Committee Assignment(s): Environment and Public Works; Finance; Health, Education, Labor, and Pensions; Special Aging; Veterans' Affairs

JOHNSON, TIM, D-S.D.

Capitol Hill Office: SH-324 20510; 224-5842; Fax: 228-5765; *Chief of Staff:* Drey Samuelson

Web: johnson.senate.gov

E-mail: tim@johnson.senate.gov

District Office(s): 715 S. Minnesota Ave., Sioux Falls 57104; (605) 332-8896; Fax: (605) 332-2824; *State Director:* Sharon Boysen

320 S. 1st St., #103, Aberdeen 57401; (605) 226-3440; Fax: (605) 226-2439; *Area Director:* Sharon Stroschein

405 E. Omaha St., Suite B, Rapid City 57701; (605) 341-3990; Fax: (605) 341-2207; *Area Service Representative:* Darrell Shoemaker

Committee Assignment(s): Appropriations; Banking, Housing, and Urban Affairs; Budget; Energy and Natural Resources; Indian Affairs

KENNEDY, EDWARD M., D-MASS.

Capitol Hill Office: SR-317 20510; 224-4543; Fax: 224-2417; *Chief of Staff:* Mary Beth Cahill

Web: kennedy.senate.gov

E-mail: senator@kennedy.senate.gov

District Office(s): John F. Kennedy Federal Bldg., #2400, Boston 02203; (617) 565-3170; Fax: (617) 565-3183; *Staff Director:* Barbara Souliotis

Committee Assignment(s): Armed Services; Health, Education, Labor, and Pensions; Joint Economic; Judiciary

KERRY, JOHN, D-MASS.

Capitol Hill Office: SR-304 20510; 224-2742; Fax: 224-8525; *Chief of Staff:* David McKean

Web: kerry.senate.gov

E-mail: john_kerry@kerry.senate.gov

District Office(s): 1350 Main St., 12th Floor, Springfield 01103; (413) 785-4610; Fax: (413) 736-1049; *Regional Director:* Michael Vito

1 Bowdoin Square, 10th Floor, Boston 02114; (617) 565-8519; Fax: (617) 248-3870; *State Director:* Drew O'Brien

90 Madison Place, #205, Worcester 01608; (508) 831-7380; Fax: (508) 831-7381; *Regional Director:* Michael Vito

222 Milliken Place, #311, Fall River 02722; (508) 677-0522; Fax: (508) 677-0275; *Regional Director:* Janet Label

Committee Assignment(s): Commerce, Science, and Transportation; Finance; Foreign Relations; Small Business and Entrepreneurship

KOHL, HERB, D-WIS.

Capitol Hill Office: SH-330 20510; 224-5653; Fax: 224-9787; *Chief of Staff:* Paul Bock

Web: kohl.senate.gov

E-mail: senator_kohl@kohl.senate.gov

District Office(s): 310 W. Wisconsin Ave., #950, Milwaukee 53203; (414) 297-4451; Fax: (414) 297-4455; *State Director:* JoAnne Anton

14 W. Mifflin St., #207, Madison 53703; (608) 264-5338; Fax: (608) 264-5473; *Area Director:* Darcy Luoma

402 Graham Ave., #206, Eau Claire 54701; (715) 832-8424; Fax: (715) 832-8492; *Regional Representative:* Marjorie Bunce

4321 W. College Ave., #235, Appleton 54914; (920) 738-1640; Fax: (920) 738-1643; *Regional Representative:* Marlene Mielke

425 State St., #202, La Crosse 54601; (608) 796-0045; Fax: (608) 796-0089; *Regional Representative:* Kim Cates

Committee Assignment(s): Appropriations; Judiciary; Special Aging

KYL, JON, R-ARIZ.

Capitol Hill Office: SH-730 20510; 224-4521; Fax: 224-2207; *Chief of Staff:* Tim Glazewski

Web: kyl.senate.gov

E-mail: info@kyl.senate.gov

District Office(s): 2200 E. Camelback Rd., #120, Phoenix 85016; (602) 840-1891; Fax: (602) 957-6838; *State Director:* Kimberly Wold

7315 N. Oracle Rd., #220, Tucson 85704; (520) 575-8633; Fax: (520) 797-3232; *Regional Director:* Hank Kenski

Committee Assignment(s): Energy and Natural Resources; Finance; Judiciary

LANDRIEU, MARY L., D-LA.

Capitol Hill Office: SH-724 20510; 224-5824; Fax: 224-9735; *Chief of Staff:* Norma Jane Sabiston

Web: landrieu.senate.gov

E-mail: landrieu.senate.gov/newsite/webform.html

District Office(s): 501 Magazine St., #1010, New Orleans 70130; (504) 589-2427; Fax: (504) 589-4023; *Office Manager:* Richard Cortizas

707 Florida St., #326, Baton Rouge 70801; (225) 389-0395; Fax: (225) 389-0660; *State Director:* T. Bradley Keith

300 Fannin St., #2240, Shreveport 71101; (318) 676-3085; Fax: (318) 676-3100; *Office Manager:* Tari Bradford

1 Lakeshore Dr., #1260, Lake Charles 70629; (337) 436-6650; Fax: (337) 439-3762; *Regional Manager:* Rowdy Gaudet

Committee Assignment(s): Appropriations; Energy and Natural Resources; Small Business and Entrepreneurship

LAUTENBERG, FRANK R., D-N.J.

Capitol Hill Office: SH-324 20510; 224-3224; Fax: 224-8567; *Chief of Staff:* Tim Yehl

Web: lautenberg.senate.gov

E-mail: frank_lautenberg@lautenberg.senate.gov

District Office(s): 1 Gateway Center, 1st Floor, Newark 07102; (973) 639-8700; *State Director:* Sharon Harrington

Committee Assignment(s): Commerce, Science, and Transportation; Governmental Affairs

LEAHY, PATRICK J., D-VT.

Capitol Hill Office: SR-433 20510; 224-4242; Fax: 224-3479; *Chief of Staff:* Luke Albee

Web: leahy.senate.gov

E-mail: senator_leahy@leahy.senate.gov

District Office(s): 199 Main St., Burlington 05401; (802) 863-2525; Fax: (802) 658-1009; *Office Director:* Charles Ross

87 State St., #338, P.O. Box 933, Montpelier 05602; (802) 229-0569; Fax: (802) 229-1915; *Office Director:* Robert Paquin

Committee Assignment(s): Agriculture, Nutrition, and Forestry; Appropriations; Judiciary

LEVIN, CARL, D-MICH.

Capitol Hill Office: SR-269 20510; 224-6221; Fax: 224-1388; *Chief of Staff:* David Lyles

Web: levin.senate.gov

E-mail: senator2@levin.senate.gov

District Office(s): 30500 VanDyke Ave., #206, Warren 48093; (586) 573-9145; Fax: (586) 573-8260; *Regional Representative:* Eunice Confer

145 Water St., #102, Alpena 49707; (989) 354-5520; Fax: (989) 356-3216; *Community Affairs Specialist:* T. J. Thusat

623 Ludington St., #200B, Escanaba 49829; (906) 789-0052; Fax: (906) 789-0015; *Regional Representative:* Diana Charles

207 Grandview Parkway, #104, Traverse City 49684; (231) 947-9569; Fax: (231) 947-9518; *Regional Representative:* Harold Chase

110 Michigan Ave. N.W., #720, Grand Rapids 49503; (616) 456-2531; Fax: (616) 456-5147; *Regional Representative:* Paul Troost

477 Michigan Ave., #1860, Detroit 48226; (313) 226-6020; Fax: (313) 226-6948; *State Director:* Cassandra Woods

301 E. Genesee St., #101, Saginaw 48607; (989) 754-2494; Fax: (989) 754-2920; *Community Affairs Specialist:* Mary Washington

1810 Michigan National Tower, 124 W. Allegan St., Lansing 48933; (517) 377-1508; Fax: (517) 377-1506; *Regional Representative:* James J. Turner

Committee Assignment(s): Armed Services; Governmental Affairs; Select Intelligence; Small Business and Entrepreneurship

LIEBERMAN, JOSEPH I., D-CONN.

Capitol Hill Office: SH-706 20510; 224-4041; Fax: 224-9750; *Chief of Staff:* Clarine Nardi Riddle

Web: lieberman.senate.gov

E-mail: lieberman.senate.gov/newsite/contact.cfm

District Office(s): 1 Constitution Plaza, 7th Floor, Hartford 06103; (860) 549-8463; Fax: (860) 549-8478; *State Director:* Laura Cahill

Committee Assignment(s): Armed Services; Environment and Public Works; Governmental Affairs; Small Business and Entrepreneurship

LINCOLN, BLANCHE, D-ARK.

Capitol Hill Office: SD-355 20510; 224-4843; Fax: 228-1371; *Chief of Staff:* Steve Patterson

Web: lincoln.senate.gov

E-mail: blanche_lincoln@lincoln.senate.gov

District Office(s): 912 W. 4th St., Little Rock 72201; (501) 375-2993; Fax: (501) 375-7064; *Office Manager:* Cydney Pearce

615 S. Main St., #315, Jonesboro 72401; (870) 910-6896; Fax: (870) 910-6898; *Field Representative:* Roger Fisher

210 S. Main St., Monticello 71655; (870) 367-6925; Fax: (870) 367-7093; *Field Representative:* Raymond Frazier

6700 McKennon Blvd., #103-A, Fort Smith 72903; (479) 782-9215; Fax: (479) 782-9310; *Field Representative:* John Hicks

400 Laurel St., #101, Texarkana 71854; (870) 774-3106; Fax: (870) 774-7627; *Field Representative:* Ed French

Committee Assignment(s): Agriculture, Nutrition, and Forestry; Finance; Select Ethics; Special Aging

LOTT, TRENT, R-MISS.

Capitol Hill Office: SR-487 20510; 224-6253; Fax: 224-2262; *Chief of Staff:* William Gottshall

Web: lott.senate.gov

E-mail: senatorlott@lott.senate.gov

District Office(s): 911 Jackson Ave., #127, Oxford 38655; (662) 234-3774; Fax: (662) 234-1744; *Staff Assistant:* Geneise Hitt

200 E. Washington St., #145, Greenwood 38930; (662) 453-5681; Fax: (662) 453-8974; *Staff Assistant:* Carolyn Overstreet

245 E. Capitol St., #226, Jackson 39201; (601) 965-4644; Fax: (601) 965-4007; *State Director:* Guy Hovis

3100 Pascagoula St., Pascagoula 39567; (228) 762-5400; Fax: (228) 762-0137; *Field Representative:* Bill Pope

1 Government Plaza, #428, Gulfport 39501; (228) 863-1988; Fax: (228) 863-9960; *Staff Assistant:* Myrtis Franks

Committee Assignment(s): Commerce, Science, and Transportation; Finance; Joint Library; Rules and Administration; Select Intelligence

LUGAR, RICHARD G., R-IND.

Capitol Hill Office: SH-306 20510; 224-4814; Fax: 228-0360; *Chief of Staff:* Marty Morris

Web: lugar.senate.gov

E-mail: senator_lugar@lugar.senate.gov

District Office(s): 1180 Market Tower, 10 W. Market St., Indianapolis 46204; (317) 226-5555; *State Director:* Lesley Reser

1300 S. Harrison St., #3158, Fort Wayne 46802; (219) 422-1505; *Office Director:* Philip Shaull

1201 E. 10th St., #103, Jeffersonville 47130; (812) 288-3377; *Regional Director:* Pat McClain

101 N.W. Martin Luther King Jr. Blvd., #122, Evansville 47708; (812) 465-6313; *Office Director:* Larry Ordner

175 W. Lincolnway, #G-1, Valparaiso 46383; (219) 548-8035; *Office Director:* Tim Sanders

Committee Assignment(s): Agriculture, Nutrition, and Forestry; Foreign Relations

MCCAIN, JOHN, R-ARIZ.

Capitol Hill Office: SR-241 20510; 224-2235; Fax: 228-2862; *Administrative Assistant:* Mark Salter

Web: mccain.senate.gov

E-mail: john_mccain@mccain.senate.gov

District Office(s): 2400 E. Arizona Biltmore Circle, #1150, Bldg. 1, Phoenix 85016; (602) 952-2410; Fax: (602) 952-8702; *State Director:* Bettina Nova

4450 S. Rural Rd., #B-130, Tempe 85282; (480) 897-6289; Fax: (480) 897-8389; *Office Manager:* Deborah Jacobus

450 W. Paseo Redondo, #200, Tucson 85701; (520) 670-6334; Fax: (520) 670-6637; *Office Manager:* Rosemary Alexander

Committee Assignment(s): Armed Services; Commerce, Science, and Transportation; Indian Affairs

MCCONNELL, MITCH, R-KY.

Capitol Hill Office: SR-361A 20510; 224-2541; Fax: 224-2499; *Chief of Staff:* Billy Pipper; *Chief of Staff* (leadership): Kyle Simmons

Web: mcconnell.senate.gov

E-mail: senator@mcconnell.senate.gov

District Office(s): 601 W. Broadway, #630, Louisville 40202; (502) 582-6304; Fax: (502) 582-5326; *State Director:* Larry E. Cox

301 S. Main St., Suite N, London 40741; (606) 864-2026; Fax: (606) 864-2035; *Field Representative:* Rebecca Webster

1885 Dixie Highway, #345, Fort Wright 41011; (859) 578-0188; Fax: (859) 578-0488; *Field Representative:* Kelly White

241 E. Main St., #102, Bowling Green 42101; (270) 781-1673; Fax: (270) 782-1884; *Field Representative:* Leanne Boling

2320 Broadway, #100, Paducah 42001; (270) 442-4554; Fax: (270) 443-3102; *Field Representative:* Tim Thomas

771 Corporate Dr., #530, Lexington 40503; (859) 224-8286; Fax: (859) 224-9673; *Field Representative:* Kevin Atkins

Committee Assignment(s): Agriculture, Nutrition, and Forestry; Appropriations; Rules and Administration

MIKULSKI, BARBARA A., D-MD.

Capitol Hill Office: SH-709 20510; 224-4654; Fax: 224-8858; *Chief of Staff:* Jenny Luray

Web: mikulski.senate.gov

E-mail: mikulski.senate.gov/mailform.htm

District Office(s): 6404 Ivy Lane, #406, Greenbelt 20770; (301) 345-5517; Fax: (301) 345-7573; *Assistant to the Senator:* Pam College

1629 Thames St., #400, Baltimore 21231; (410) 962-4510; Fax: (410) 962-4760; *State Director:* Mike Morrill

60 West St., #202, Annapolis 21401; (410) 263-1805; Fax: (410) 263-5949; *Office Director:* Denise Nooe

1201 Pemberton Dr., #1E, Bldg. B, Salisbury 21801; (410) 546-7711; Fax: (410) 546-9324; *Outreach Representative:* Cindy Betts

94 W. Washington St., #301, Hagerstown 21740; (301) 797-2826; Fax: (301) 797-2241; *Outreach Representative:* Amy Short

Committee Assignment(s): Appropriations; Health, Education, Labor, and Pensions; Select Intelligence

MILLER, ZELL, D-GA.

Capitol Hill Office: SD-257 20510; 224-3643; Fax: 228-2090; *Chief of Staff:* Alex Albert

Web: miller.senate.gov

E-mail: miller.senate.gov/email.htm

District Office(s): 1175 Peachtree St. N.E., #300, Atlanta 30361; (404) 347-2202; Fax: (404) 347-2243; *State Director:* Toni Brown

2 E. Bryan St., Savannah 31401; (912) 238-3244; Fax: (912) 238-1240; *Field Representative:* Jared Downs

22 N. Main St., P.O. Box 1330, Moultrie 31768; (229) 985-8113; Fax: (229) 985-8018; *Field Representative:* Jody Redding

687 Main St., #2, Young Harris 30582; (706) 379-9950; Fax: (706) 379-4053; *Field Representative:* John Stacy

1090 Washington Ave., #110, Macon 31204; (478) 745-6025; Fax: (478) 747-0762; *Field Representative:* Bob Ensley

Committee Assignment(s): Agriculture, Nutrition, and Forestry; Banking, Housing, and Urban Affairs; Veterans' Affairs

MURKOWSKI, LISA, R-ALASKA

Capitol Hill Office: SH-322 20510; 224-6665; Fax: 224-5301; *Chief of Staff:* Justin Stiefel

Web: murkowski.senate.gov

E-mail: murkowski.senate.gov/index.htm

District Office(s): 510 L. St., #550, Anchorage 99501; (907) 271-3735; Fax: (907) 276-4081; *State Director:* Patricia B. Heller

130 Trading Bay Rd., #350, Kenai 99611; (907) 283-5808; Fax: (907) 283-4363; *Special Assistant:* Margaret Gilman

709 W. 9th St., #971, Juneau 99802; (907) 586-7400; Fax: (907) 586-8922; *Special Assistant:* Connie McKenzie

851 E. Westpoint Dr., #307, Wasilla 99654; (907) 376-7665; Fax: (907) 376-8526; *Special Assistant:* Carol Gustafson

540 Water St., #101, Ketchikan 99901; (907) 283-5808; Fax: (907) 225-0390; *Special Assistant:* Sherrie Slick

101 12th Ave., #216, Fairbanks 99701; (907) 456-0233; Fax: (907) 451-7146; *Special Assistant:* Althea St. Martin

Committee Assignment(s): Energy and Natural Resources; Environment and Public Works; Indian Affairs; Veterans' Affairs

MURRAY, PATTY, D-WASH.

Capitol Hill Office: SR-173 20510; 224-2621; Fax: 224-0238; *Chief of Staff:* Rick Desimone

Web: murray.senate.gov

E-mail: senator_murray@murray.senate.gov

District Office(s): 915 2nd Ave., #2988, Seattle 98174; (206) 553-5545; Fax: (206) 553-0891; *State Director:* John Engber

402 E. Yakima Ave., #390, Yakima 98901; (509) 453-7462; Fax: (509) 453-7731; *Regional Director:* Mary McBride

1323 Officer's Row, Vancouver 98661; (360) 696-7797; Fax: (360) 696-7798; *Regional Representative:* Mindi Lindquist

601 W. Main Ave., #1213, Spokane 99204; (509) 624-9515; Fax: (509) 624-9561; *Regional Coordinator:* Judy Olson

2930 Wetmore Ave., #903, Everett 98201; (425) 259-6515; Fax: (425) 259-7152; *Regional Coordinator:* Rachelle Hein

Committee Assignment(s): Appropriations; Budget; Health, Education, Labor, and Pensions; Veterans' Affairs

NELSON, BEN, D-NEB.

Capitol Hill Office: SH-720 20510; 224-6551; Fax: 228-0012; *Chief of Staff:* Tim Becker

Web: bennelson.senate.gov

E-mail: bennelson.senate.gov/email.html

District Office(s): 7602 Pacific St., #205, Omaha 68114; (402) 391-3411; Fax: (402) 391-4725; *Field Representative:* Sonny Foster

100 Centennial Mall North, #287, Lincoln 68508; (402) 441-4600; Fax: (402) 476-8753; *State Director:* Don Nelson

Committee Assignment(s): Agriculture, Nutrition, and Forestry; Armed Services; Veterans' Affairs

NELSON, BILL, D-FLA.

Capitol Hill Office: SH-716 20510; 224-5274; Fax: 228-2183; *Chief of Staff:* Peter J. Mitchell

Web: billnelson.senate.gov

E-mail: billnelson.senate.gov/contact/index.cfm

District Office(s): 2925 Salzedo St., Miami 33134; (305) 536-5999; Fax: (305) 536-5991; *Regional Director:* Emelio Vazquez

801 N. Florida Ave., 4th Floor, Tampa 33602; (813) 225-7040; Fax: (813) 225-7050; *Regional Director:* Sue Loftin

111 N. Adams St., Tallahassee 32301; (850) 942-8415; Fax: (850) 942-8450; *Regional Director:* Lynn Bannister

225 E. Robinson St., #410, Orlando 32801; (407) 872-7161; Fax: (407) 872-7165; *Regional Director:* Sherry Davich

500 Australian Ave., #125, West Palm Beach 33401; (561) 514-0189; Fax: (561) 514-4078; *Regional Director:* Michelle Oyola

1301 Riverplace Blvd., #2218, Jacksonville 32207; (904) 346-4500; Fax: (904) 346-4506; *Regional Director:* Joanelle Mulrain

3416 S. University Dr., Ft. Lauderdale 33328; (954) 693-4851; Fax: (954) 693-4862; *Regional Director:* Willowstine Lawson

Committee Assignment(s): Armed Services; Budget; Commerce, Science, and Transportation; Foreign Relations

NICKLES, DON, R-OKLA.

Capitol Hill Office: SH-133 20510; 224-5754; Fax: 224-6008; *Administrative Assistant:* Bret Bernhardt

Web: nickles.senate.gov

E-mail: senator@nickles.senate.gov

District Office(s): 100 N. Broadway, #1820, Oklahoma City 73102; (405) 231-4941; *Field Representative:* Mike Osburn

711 S.W. D Ave., #202, Lawton 73501; (580) 357-9878; *Field Representative:* Mary Eichinger

3310 Mid-Continent Tower, 409 S. Boston Ave., Tulsa 74103; (918) 581-7651; *Manager:* Sharon K. Keasler

1914 Lake Rd., Ponca City 74601; (580) 767-1270; *State Director:* Joey Bradford

Committee Assignment(s): Budget; Energy and Natural Resources; Finance; Joint Taxation; Rules and Administration

PRYOR, MARK, D-ARK.

Capitol Hill Office: SR-217 20510; 224-2353; Fax: 228-3973; *Chief of Staff:* Bob Russell

Web: pryor.senate.gov

E-mail: mark_pryor@pryor.senate.gov

District Office(s): 700 W. Capitol, #2527, Little Rock 72201; (501) 324-6336; Fax: (501) 324-5320; *State Director:* Randy Massanelli

Committee Assignment(s): Armed Services; Governmental Affairs; Small Business and Entrepreneurship

REED, JACK, D-R.I.

Capitol Hill Office: SH-320 20510; 224-4642; Fax: 224-4680; *Administrative Assistant:* J. B. Poersch

Web: reed.senate.gov

E-mail: jack@reed.senate.gov

District Office(s): 201 Hillside Rd., #200, Cranston 02920; (401) 943-3100; Fax: (401) 464-6837; *Chief of Staff:* Raymond Simone

1 Exchange Terrace, #408, Providence 02903; (401) 528-5200; Fax: (401) 528-5242; *Policy Director:* Nancy Langrall

Committee Assignment(s): Armed Services; Banking, Housing, and Urban Affairs; Health, Education, Labor, and Pensions; Joint Economic

REID, HARRY, D-NEV.

Capitol Hill Office: SH-528 20510; 224-3542; Fax: 224-7327; *Chief of Staff:* Susan McCue

Web: reid.senate.gov

E-mail: reid.senate.gov/email_form.cfm

District Office(s): 333 Las Vegas Blvd. South, #8016, Las Vegas 89101; (702) 388-5020; Fax: (702) 388-5030; *Regional Manager:* Jerry Reynoldson

600 E. William St., #302, Carson City 89701; (775) 882-7343; Fax: (775) 883-1980; *Regional Representative:* Yolanda Garcia

400 S. Virginia St., #902, Reno 89501; (775) 686-5750; Fax: (775) 686-5757; *State Director:* Mary Conelly

Committee Assignment(s): Appropriations; Environment and Public Works; Indian Affairs; Select Ethics; Special Aging

ROBERTS, PAT, R-KAN.

Capitol Hill Office: SH-302 20510; 224-4774; Fax: 224-3514; *Chief of Staff:* Leroy Towns

Web: roberts.senate.gov

E-mail: pat_roberts@roberts.senate.gov

District Office(s): 155 N. Market St., #120, Wichita 67202; (316) 263-0416; Fax: (316) 263-0273; *District Director:* Karin Wisdom

100 Military Plaza, #203, P.O. Box 550, Dodge City 67801; (620) 227-2244; Fax: (620) 227-2264; *District Director:* Debbie Pugh

4200 Somerset Dr., #152, Prairie Village 66208; (913) 648-3103; Fax: (913) 648-3106; *State Director:* Chad Tenenny

444 S.E. Quincy St., #392, Topeka 66683; (785) 295-2745; Fax: (785) 235-3665; *District Director:* Gilda Lintz

Committee Assignment(s): Agriculture, Nutrition, and Forestry; Armed Services; Health, Education, Labor, and Pensions; Select Ethics; Select Intelligence

ROCKEFELLER, JOHN D. IV, D-W.VA.

Capitol Hill Office: SH-531 20510; 224-6472; Fax: 224-7665; *Chief of Staff:* Katherine "Kerry" Ates

Web: rockefeller.senate.gov

E-mail: senator@rockefeller.senate.gov

District Office(s): 207 W. Prince St., Beckley 25801; (304) 253-9704; Fax: (304) 253-2578; *Caseworker:* Jenny Pennington

118 Adams St., #301, Fairmont 26554; (304) 367-0122; Fax: (304) 367-0822; *Area Coordinator:* Larry Lemon

405 Capitol St., #308, Charleston 25301; (304) 347-5372; Fax: (304) 347-5371; *State Director:* Lou Ann Johnson

225 W. King St., #307, Martinsburg 25401; (304) 262-9285; Fax: (304) 262-9288; *Area Coordinator:* Penny Porter

Committee Assignment(s): Commerce, Science, and Transportation; Finance; Foreign Relations; Joint Taxation; Select Intelligence; Veterans' Affairs

SANTORUM, RICK, R-PA.

Capitol Hill Office: SR-120 20510; 224-6324; Fax: 228-0604; *Chief of Staff:* Mike Hershey

Web: santorum.senate.gov

E-mail: santorum.senate.gov/emailrjs.html

District Office(s): Regency Square, #202, Altoona 16601; (814) 946-7023; Fax: (814) 946-7025; *Field Representative:* Julia Bowser

1705 W. 26th St., Erie 16508; (814) 454-7114; Fax: (814) 459-2096; *Field Representative:* Stephanie Lindenberger

333 Market St., Harrisburg 17101; (717) 231-7540; Fax: (717) 231-7542; *Economic Development Director:* Emmet Mahon

504 W. Hamilton St., #3804, Allentown 18101; (610) 770-0142; Fax: (610) 770-0911; *Community Affairs Director:* Vince Galko

1 Station Square, #250, Pittsburgh 15219; (412) 562-0533; Fax: (412) 562-4313; *Regional Director:* Keith Schmidt

527 Linden St., Scranton 18503; (570) 344-8799; Fax: (570) 344-8906; *Regional Director:* Mike Narcavage

1 S. Penn Square, #960, Philadelphia 19107; (215) 864-6900; Fax: (215) 864-6910; *Regional Director:* Jeff Haberkern

81 Marvin Hill Rd., Coudersport 16915; (814) 274-9773; Fax: (814) 274-2253; *Field Representative:* Patti Bowman

Committee Assignment(s): Banking, Housing, and Urban Affairs; Finance; Rules and Administration; Special Aging

SARBANES, PAUL S., D-MD.

Capitol Hill Office: SH-309 20510; 224-4524; Fax: 224-1651; *Chief of Staff:* Julie Kehrli

Web: sarbanes.senate.gov

E-mail: senator@sarbanes.senate.gov

District Office(s): 141 Baltimore St., #206, Cumberland 21502; (301) 724-0695; Fax: (301) 724-4660; *Western Maryland Representative:* Tim Magrath

110 W. Church St., Suite D, Salisbury 21801; (410) 860-2131; Fax: (410) 860-2134; *Eastern Shore Representative:* Lee Whaley

113 Baltimore St., #201, Baltimore 21201; (410) 962-4436; Fax: (410) 962-4156; *State Office Manager:* Sharon Faraone

1110 Bonifant St., #450, Silver Spring 20910; (301) 589-0797; Fax: (301) 589-0598; *Field Representative:* Jeanie Lazerov

Committee Assignment(s): Banking, Housing, and Urban Affairs; Budget; Foreign Relations; Joint Economic

SCHUMER, CHARLES E., D-N.Y.

Capitol Hill Office: SH-313 20510; 224-6542; Fax: 228-3027; *Chief of Staff:* Michael Lynch

Web: schumer.senate.gov

E-mail: schumer.senate.gov/webform.html

District Office(s): 757 3rd Ave., #17-02, New York 10017; (212) 486-4430; Fax: (212) 486-7693; *State Director:* Martin Brennan

Leo O'Brien Bldg., #420, Albany 12207; (518) 431-4070; Fax: (518) 431-4076; *Regional Representative:* Stephen Mann

100 S. Clinton St., #841, Syracuse 13261; (315) 423-5471; Fax: (315) 423-5185; *Regional Representative:* Jill Harvey

100 State St., #3040, Rochester 14614; (585) 263-5866; Fax: (585) 263-3173; *Regional Representative:* Joe Hamm

111 W. Huron St., #620, Buffalo 14202; (716) 846-4111; Fax: (716) 846-4113; *Regional Representative:* Scott Sroka

15 Henry St., #B-6, Binghamton 13901; (607) 772-6792; Fax: (607) 772-8124; *Regional Representative:* Amanda Pasquale

145 Pine Lawn Rd., #300N, Melville 11747; (631) 753-0978; Fax: (631) 753-0997; *Regional Representative:* Chris Hahn

Committee Assignment(s): Banking, Housing, and Urban Affairs; Energy and Natural Resources; Joint Library; Judiciary; Rules and Administration

SESSIONS, JEFF, R-ALA.

Capitol Hill Office: SR-493 20510; 224-4124; Fax: 224-3149; *Chief of Staff:* David Armand DeKeyser

Web: sessions.senate.gov

E-mail: senator@sessions.senate.gov

District Office(s): 1 Court Square, #248, Montgomery 36104; (334) 265-9507; Fax: (334) 834-2823; *State Director:* John Kennedy

1800 5th Ave. North, #341, Birmingham 35203; (205) 731-1500; Fax: (205) 731-0221; *Field Representative:* Shannon McClure

200 Clinton Ave. N.W., #802, Huntsville 35801; (256) 533-0979; Fax: (256) 533-0745; *Field Representative:* Lisa Ramsey

41 N. Beltline Highway, #187, Mobile 36608; (251) 414-3083; Fax: (251) 414-5845; *Field Representative:* Phillip May

Committee Assignment(s): Armed Services; Budget; Health, Education, Labor, and Pensions; Joint Economic; Judiciary

SHELBY, RICHARD C., R-ALA.

Capitol Hill Office: SH-110 20510; 224-5744; Fax: 224-3416; *Chief of Staff:* Phil Rivers

Web: shelby.senate.gov

E-mail: senator@shelby.senate.gov

District Office(s): 1800 5th Ave. North, #321, Birmingham 35203; (205) 731-1384; Fax: (205) 731-1386; *District Representative:* Blair Agricola

113 St. Joseph St., #308, Mobile 36602; (251) 694-4164; Fax: (251) 694-4166; *District Representative:* Laura Breland

1118 Greensboro Ave., Tuscaloosa 35401; (205) 759-5047; Fax: (205) 759-5067; *District Representative:* Melissa Davis

15 Lee St., #B-28, Montgomery 36104; (334) 223-7303; Fax: (334) 223-7317; *State Director:* Goodloe Sutton

Huntsville International Airport, 1000 Glenn Hearn Blvd., P.O. Box 20127, Huntsville 35824; (256) 772-0460; Fax: (256) 772-8387; *District Representative:* LeFreeda Jordan

Committee Assignment(s): Appropriations; Banking, Housing, and Urban Affairs; Governmental Affairs; Special Aging

SMITH, GORDON H., R-ORE.

Capitol Hill Office: SR-404 20510; 224-3753; Fax: 228-3997; *Chief of Staff:* John Easton

Web: gsmith.senate.gov

E-mail: gsmith.senate.gov/webform.htm

District Office(s): 121 S.W. Salmon St., #1250, Portland 97204; (503) 326-3386; Fax: (503) 326-2900; *State Director:* Kerry Tymchuk

211 E. 7th Ave., #202, Eugene 97401; (541) 465-6750; Fax: (541) 465-6808; *Regional Representative:* Terri Moffett

131 N.W. Hawthorne Ave., #208, Bend 97701; (541) 318-1298; Fax: (541) 318-1396; *Regional Representative:* Susan Fitch

1175 E. Main St., #2D, Medford 97504; (541) 608-9102; Fax: (541) 608-9104; *Regional Representative:* Esther Kennedy

116 S. Main St., #3, Pendleton 97801; (541) 278-1129; Fax: (541) 278-4109; *Regional Representative:* Linda Hamilton

Committee Assignment(s): Commerce, Science, and Transportation; Energy and Natural Resources; Finance; Indian Affairs; Joint Printing; Rules and Administration; Special Aging

SNOWE, OLYMPIA J., R-MAINE

Capitol Hill Office: SR-154 20510; 224-5344; Fax: 224-1946; *Chief of Staff:* Jane Calderwood

Web: snowe.senate.gov

E-mail: olympia@snowe.senate.gov

District Office(s): 231 Main St., #2, Biddeford 04005; (207) 282-4144; Fax: (207) 284-2358; *Regional Representative:* Peter Morin

3 Canal Plaza, #601, Portland 04112; (207) 874-0883; Fax: (207) 874-7631; *State Director:* Charles Summers

40 Western Ave., #408C, Augusta 04330; (207) 622-8292; Fax: (207) 622-7295; *Regional Representative:* John Cummings

169 Academy St., #3, Presque Isle 04769; (207) 764-5124; Fax: (207) 764-6420; *Regional Representative:* Ken White

1 Cumberland Place, #306, Bangor 04401; (207) 945-0432; Fax: (207) 941-9525; *Regional Representative:* Gail Kelly

2 Great Falls Plaza, #7B, Auburn 04210; (207) 786-2451; Fax: (207) 782-1438; *Regional Representative:* Diane Jackson

Committee Assignment(s): Commerce, Science, and Transportation; Finance; Select Intelligence; Small Business and Entrepreneurship

SPECTER, ARLEN, R-PA.

Capitol Hill Office: SH-711 20510; 224-4254; Fax: 228-1229; *Chief of Staff:* Carey Lackman

Web: specter.senate.gov

E-mail: specter.senate.gov/webform.htm

District Office(s): 1000 Liberty Ave., #2031, Pittsburgh 15222; (412) 644-3400; Fax: (412) 644-4871; *Executive Director:* Doug Saltzman

617 State St., #107, Erie 16501; (814) 453-3010; Fax: (814) 455-9925; *Executive Director:* Kim Green

504 W. Hamilton St., #3814, Allentown 18101; (610) 434-1444; Fax: (610) 434-1844; *Executive Director:* Mary Jo Bierman

228 Walnut St., #1159, Harrisburg 17101; (717) 782-3951; Fax: (717) 782-4920; *Executive Director:* Gayle Mills

600 Arch St., #9400, Philadelphia 19106; (215) 597-7200; Fax: (215) 597-0406; *State Director:* Anthony Cunningham

116 S. Main St., #306, Wilkes-Barre 18701; (570) 826-6265; Fax: (570) 826-6266; *Executive Director:* Andrew Wallace

310 Spruce St., #201, Scranton 18503; (570) 346-2006; Fax: (570) 346-8499; *Executive Director:* Andrew Wallace

Committee Assignment(s): Appropriations; Governmental Affairs; Judiciary; Veterans' Affairs

STABENOW, DEBBIE, D-MICH.

Capitol Hill Office: SH-702 20510; 224-4822; Fax: 228-0325; *Chief of Staff:* Sander Lurie

Web: stabenow.senate.gov

E-mail: senator@stabenow.senate.gov

District Office(s): 243 W. Congress, #550, Detroit 48226; (313) 961-4330; Fax: (313) 961-7566; *Regional Director:* Barbara McCallahan

109 S. Union, #305, Traverse City 49684; (231) 929-1031; Fax: (231) 929-1250; *Regional Director:* Brandon Fewins

3230 Broadmoor St., Suite B, Grand Rapids 49512; (616) 975-0052; Fax: (616) 975-5764; *Regional Director:* Mary Judnich

280 E. Saginaw St., East Lansing 48823; (517) 203-1760; Fax: (517) 203-1778; *State Director:* Teresa Plachetka

1901 W. Ridge, Marquette 49855; (906) 228-8756; Fax: (906) 228-9162; *Regional Director:* Sheri Davie

2503 S. Linden Rd., Flint 48532; (810) 720-4172; Fax: (810) 720-4178; *Regional Director:* Connie Feuerstein

Committee Assignment(s): Agriculture, Nutrition, and Forestry; Banking, Housing, and Urban Affairs; Budget; Special Aging

STEVENS, TED, R-ALASKA

Capitol Hill Office: SH-522 20510; 224-3004; Fax: 224-2354; *Chief of Staff:* David Russell

Web: stevens.senate.gov

E-mail: stevens.senate.gov/webform.htm

District Office(s): 222 W. 7th Ave., #2, Anchorage 99513; (907) 271-5915; Fax: (907) 258-9305; *State Director:* Marie Nash

130 Trading Bay Rd., #350, Kenai 99611; (907) 283-5808; Fax: (907) 283-4363; *Staff Assistant:* Margaret Gilman

Federal Bldg., #971, P.O. Box 020149, Juneau 99802; (907) 586-7400; Fax: (907) 586-8922; *Staff Assistant:* Connie McKenzie

540 Water St., #101, Ketchikan 99901; (907) 225-6880; Fax: (907) 225-0390; *Staff Assistant:* Sherrie Slick

101 12th Ave., #206, P.O. Box 4, Fairbanks 99701; (907) 456-0261; Fax: (907) 451-7290; *Staff Assistant:* Ruth Burnett

851 E. Westpoint Dr., #307, Wasilla 99654; (907) 376-7665; Fax: (907) 376-8526; *Staff Assistant:* Carol Gustafson

Committee Assignment(s): Appropriations; Commerce, Science, and Transportation; Governmental Affairs; Joint Library; Rules and Administration; Special Aging

SUNUNU, JOHN E., R-N.H.

Capitol Hill Office: SR-111 20510; 224-2841; Fax: 224-1353; *Chief of Staff:* Paul Collins

E-mail: mailbox@sununu.senate.gov

District Office(s): 1015 Elm St., #201, Manchester 03101; (603) 625-5585; Fax: (603) 625-6670; *Area Director:* Kathy Schneiderot

1 New Hampshire Ave., #120, Portsmouth 03801; (603) 430-9560; Fax: (603) 430-0058; *State Director:* Pam Kocher

Committee Assignment(s): Banking, Housing, and Urban Affairs; Commerce, Science, and Transportation; Foreign Relations; Governmental Affairs; Joint Economic

TALENT, JIM, R-MO.

Capitol Hill Office: SR-493 20510; 224-6154; Fax: 228-1518; *Chief of Staff:* Mark Strand

Web: talent.senate.gov

E-mail: senator_talent@talent.senate.gov

District Office(s): 122 E. High St., 2nd Floor, Jefferson City 65101; (573) 636-1070; Fax: (573) 638-3891; *State Director:* Donna Sprickert

400 E. 9th St., #40, Kansas City 64106; (816) 421-1639; Fax: (816) 421-2562; *District Representative:* Jo Keatley

339 Broadway, #520, Cape Girardeau 63701; (573) 651-0964; Fax: (573) 334-4278; *District Representative:* Jeff Glenn

300 John Q. Hammons Parkway, #111, Springfield 65806; (417) 831-2735; Fax: (417) 831-2407; *District Representative:* Terry Campbell

111 S. 10th St., #23.360, St. Louis 63102; (314) 436-3416; Fax: (314) 436-9640; *District Representative:* Kacky Garner

Committee Assignment(s): Agriculture, Nutrition, and Forestry; Armed Services; Energy and Natural Resources; Special Aging

THOMAS, CRAIG, R-WYO.

Capitol Hill Office: SH-109 20510; 224-6441; Fax: 224-1724; *Chief of Staff:* Chris Jahn

Web: thomas.senate.gov

E-mail: craig@thomas.senate.gov

District Office(s): 2120 Capitol Ave., #2013, Cheyenne 82001; (307) 772-2451; Fax: (307) 638-3512; *State Scheduler:* Mary Paxson

325 W. Main St., Suite F, Riverton 82501; (307) 856-6642; Fax: (307) 856-5901; *Field Representative:* Pam Buline

100 E. B St., #2201, Casper 82601; (307) 261-6413; Fax: (307) 265-6706; *State Director:* Bobbi Brown

2632 Foothill Blvd., #101, Rock Springs 82901; (307) 362-5012; Fax: (307) 362-5129; *Field Representative:* Pati Smith

2 N. Main St., #206, Sheridan 82801; (307) 672-6456; Fax: (307) 672-8227; *Field Representative:* Matt Jones

Committee Assignment(s): Energy and Natural Resources; Environment and Public Works; Finance; Indian Affairs; Select Ethics

VOINOVICH, GEORGE V., R-OHIO

Capitol Hill Office: SH-317 20510; 224-3353; Fax: 228-1382; *Chief of Staff:* Ted Hollingsworth

Web: voinovich.senate.gov

E-mail: senator_voinovich@voinovich.senate.gov

District Office(s): 420 Madison Ave., #1210, Toledo 43604; (419) 259-3895; Fax: (419) 259-3899; *District Representative:* Dennis Filgor

36 E. 7th St., #2615, Cincinnati 45202; (513) 684-3265; Fax: (513) 684-3269; *District Representative:* Tony Condia

1240 E. 9th St., #2955, Cleveland 44199; (216) 522-7095; Fax: (216) 522-7097; *District Director:* Nicholas Gattozzi

37 W. Broad St., #310, Columbus 43215; (614) 469-6697; Fax: (614) 469-7733; *State Director:* Beth Hansen

Committee Assignment(s): Environment and Public Works; Foreign Relations; Governmental Affairs; Select Ethics

WARNER, JOHN W., R-VA.

Capitol Hill Office: SR-225 20510; 224-2023; Fax: 224-6295; *Chief of Staff:* Susan Magill

Web: warner.senate.gov

E-mail: senator@warner.senate.gov

District Office(s): 600 E. Main St., 18th Floor, Richmond 23219; (804) 771-2579; Fax: (804) 782-2131; *Office Manager:* Aljean Peterson

World Trade Center, #4900, Norfolk 23510; (757) 441-3079; Fax: (757) 441-6250; *Office Manager:* Loretta Tate

180 W. Main St., #235, P.O. Box 887, Abingdon 24210; (276) 628-8158; Fax: (276) 628-1036; *Office Manager:* Cathie Gollehon

213 S. Jefferson St., #1003, Roanoke 24011; (540) 857-2676; Fax: (540) 857-2800; *Caseworker:* Camellia Crowder

Committee Assignment(s): Armed Services; Environment and Public Works; Health, Education, Labor, and Pensions; Select Intelligence

WYDEN, RON, D-ORE.

Capitol Hill Office: SH-516 20510; 224-5244; Fax: 228-2717; *Deputy Chief of Staff:* Jeff Michels

Web: wyden.senate.gov

E-mail: wyden.senate.gov/mail.htm

District Office(s): 151 W. 7th Ave., #435, Eugene 97401; (541) 431-0229; *Field Representative:* Emily Williams

310 W. 6th St., #118, Medford 97501; (541) 858-5122; *Field Representative:* Traci Dow

131 N.W. Hawthorne Ave., #107, Bend 97701; (541) 330-9142; *Field Representative:* David Blair

700 N.E. Multnomah St., #405, Portland 97232; (503) 326-7525; Fax: (503) 326-7528; *Chief of Staff:* Josh Kardon

105 Fir St., #210, La Grande 97850; (541) 962-7691; *Field Representative:* Wayne Kinney

707 13th St. S.E., #110, Salem 97301; (503) 589-4555; *Field Representative:* Scott Winkels

Committee Assignment(s): Budget; Commerce, Science, and Transportation; Energy and Natural Resources; Environment and Public Works; Select Intelligence; Special Aging

Ready Reference

Directory of Government Information on the Internet

Listed below are Web addresses that lead to executive, legislative, and judicial information on the Internet. These addresses were active as of April 2003. Government information can also be explored online through the **FirstGov.gov** Web site, which is the U.S. government's official Internet portal to Web pages for federal and state governments, the District of Columbia, and U.S. territories.

EXECUTIVE BRANCH

The White House

Main: www.whitehouse.gov
News: www.whitehouse.gov/news
President's Bio:
www.whitehouse.gov/president/gwbbio.html
Vice President's Bio:
www.whitehouse.gov/vicepresident/vpbio.html
First Lady's Bio:
www.whitehouse.gov/firstlady/flbio.html
Contacting the White House:
www.whitehouse.gov/contact

Agriculture Dept.

Main: www.usda.gov
About the Agriculture Dept.: www.usda.gov/welcome
News: www.usda.gov/newsroom.html
Secretary's Bio:
www.usda.gov/agencies/gallery/veneman.htm
Employee Directory:
dc-directory.hqnet.usda.gov/phone.php
List of Regional Offices: offices.usda.gov
Department Budget: www.usda.gov/agency/obpa/
Budget-Summary/2003/2003budsum.htm

Commerce Dept.

Main: www.commerce.gov
About the Commerce Dept.:
www.commerce.gov/history.html
News: www.commerce.gov/opa/index.html
Secretary's Bio:
www.commerce.gov/bios/evans_bio.html
Employee Directory: dir.commerce.gov
List of Regional Offices:
　Census Bureau:
www.census.gov/contacts/www/c-regoff.html

Economic Development Administration:
www.osec.doc.gov/eda/HTML/1c_regloffices.htm
Department Budget: www.osec.doc.gov/bmi/budget

Defense Dept.

Main: www.defenselink.mil
About the Defense Dept.:
www.defenselink.mil/pubs/dod101
News: www.defenselink.mil/news
Secretary's Bio:
www.defenselink.mil/bios/secdef_bio.html
Directory of Senior Defense Officials:
www.defenselink.mil/faq/pis/dod_addresses.html
Department Budget:
www.dtic.mil/comptroller/budgetindex.html

Education Dept.

Main: www.ed.gov/index.jsp
About the Education Dept.:
www.ed.gov/about/welcome.jsp
News: www.ed.gov/moreNews.jsp
Secretary's Bio: www.ed.gov/offices/OPA/paigebio.html
Employee Directory: web99.ed.gov/EDLocator
List of Regional Offices:
www.ed.gov/Programs/bastmp/SRR.htm
Department Budget:
www.ed.gov/offices/OUS/budget.html

Energy Dept.

Main: www.energy.gov
About the Energy Dept.:
www.energy.gov/aboutus/index.html
News: www.energy.gov/press/index.html
Secretary's Bio:
www.energy.gov/aboutus/history/abraham.html
Employee Directory: phonebook.doe.gov/callup.html
List of Regional Offices:
www.energy.gov/aboutus/org/regional_offices.html

Department Budget: www.cfo.doe.gov/budget/
index.htm

Health and Human Services Dept.

Main: www.dhhs.gov
About the Health and Human Services Dept.:
www.hhs.gov/about
News: www.hhs.gov/news
Secretary's Bio: www.hhs.gov/about/bios/dhhssec.html
Employee Directory: directory.psc.gov/employee.htm
List of Regional Offices:
www.hhs.gov/about/regionmap.html
Department Budget:
www.hhs.gov/budget/docbudget.htm

Homeland Security Dept.

Main: www.dhs.gov
About the Homeland Security Dept.:
www.dhs.gov/dhspublic/theme_home1.jsp
News: www.dhs.gov/dhspublic/theme_home8.jsp
Secretary's Bio: www.dhs.gov/dhspublic/
display?theme=11&content=13
Leadership Directory: www.dhs.gov/dhspublic/
display?theme=11&page=2
List of Regional Offices:
Bureau of Citizenship and Immigration Services:
http://www.immigration.gov/graphics/
fieldoffices/index.htm
Federal Emergency Management Agency:
www.fema.gov/regions
U.S. Secret Service:
www.secretservice.gov/field_offices.shtml
Department Budget:
www.dhs.gov/dhspublic/display?theme=12

Housing and Urban Development Dept.

Main: www.hud.gov
About the Housing and Urban Development Dept.:
www.hud.gov/about/index.cfm
News: www.hud.gov/news/index.cfm
Secretary's Bio:
www.hud.gov/about/secretary/martinezbio.cfm
Employee Directory:
http://www5.hud.gov:19542/netlocator
List of Regional Offices: www.hud.gov/local
Department Budget:
www.hud.gov/offices/cfo/reports/cforept.cfm

Interior Dept.

Main: www.doi.gov
About the Interior Dept.: www.doi.gov/about.html
News: www.doi.gov/doipress

Secretary's Bio: www.doi.gov/secretary/biography.html
Employee Directory:
momentum.doi.gov/email/doi.cfm
List of Regional Offices:
Bureau of Indian Affairs: Temporarily unavailable
due to litigation. For general information, (202)
208-3710.
Bureau of Land Management:
www.blm.gov/nhp/directory/index.htm
National Park Service:
www.nps.gov/legacy/regions.html
Office of Surface Mining:
www.osmre.gov/field.htm
U.S. Fish and Wildlife Service: www.fws.gov/where
U.S. Geological Survey:
interactive2.usgs.gov/contact_us/index.asp
Department Budget: www.doi.gov/budget

Justice Dept.

Main: www.usdoj.gov
About the Justice Dept.:
www.usdoj.gov/02organizations/index.html
News: www.usdoj.gov/03press/index.html
Attorney General's Bio:
www.usdoj.gov/ag/ashcroftbio.html
List of Regional Offices:
Drug Enforcement Administration:
www.usdoj.gov/dea/agency/domestic.htm
Federal Bureau of Investigation:
www.fbi.gov/contact/fo/fo.htm
Federal Bureau of Prisons:
www.bop.gov/facilnot.html
Department Budget:
www.usdoj.gov/02organizations/02_3.html

Labor Dept.

Main: www.dol.gov
About the Labor Dept.:
www.dol.gov/dol/aboutdol/main.htm
News: www.dol.gov/dol/media/main.htm
Secretary's Bio: www.dol.gov/_sec/aboutosec/chao.htm
Employee Directory: www.dol.gov/dol/contact/
contact-phonekeypersonnel.htm
List of Regional Offices:
Bureau of Labor Statistics:
www.bls.gov/bls/regnhome.htm
Employment and Training Administration:
wdr.doleta.gov/contacts
Occupational Safety and Health Administration:
www.osha-slc.gov/html/RAmap.html
Department Budget:
www.dol.gov/_sec/budget2004/overview-toc.htm

State Dept.

Main: www.state.gov
About the State Dept.: www.state.gov/aboutstate
News: www.state.gov/press
Secretary's Bio: www.state.gov/secretary
Employee Directory:
    www.foia.state.gov/mms/index.asp
List of Regional Offices:
    Passport Services: iafdb.travel.state.gov
Department Budget: www.state.gov/m/rm/rls

Transportation Dept.

Main: www.dot.gov
About the Transportation Dept.:
    www.dot.gov/about_dot.html
News: www.dot.gov/affairs/briefing.htm
Secretary's Bio: www.dot.gov/affairs/mineta.htm
List of Regional Offices:
    Federal Aviation Administration:
      www2.faa.gov/index.cfm/1040
    Federal Highway Administration:
      www.fhwa.dot.gov/field.html
    Federal Railroad Administration:
      www.fra.dot.gov/safety/regional/index.htm
    Federal Transit Administration:
      www.fta.dot.gov/office/regional
    Maritime Administration:
      www.marad.dot.gov/offices/index.html
    National Highway Traffic Safety Administration:
      www.nhtsa.dot.gov/nhtsa/whatis/regions
Department Budget:
    www.dot.gov/bib2004/bibindex.html

Treasury Dept.

Main: www.ustreas.gov
About the Treasury Dept.:
    www.ustreas.gov/topics/index.html
News: www.ustreas.gov/press
Secretary's Bio: www.ustreas.gov/press/officers
Directory of Treasury Officials:
    www.treas.gov/organization/officials.html
List of Regional Offices:
    Comptroller of the Currency:
      www.occ.treas.gov/district.htm
    Financial Management Service:
      www.fms.treas.gov/aboutfms/locations.html
    Internal Revenue Service:
      www.irs.treas.gov/localcontacts
    Office of Thrift Supervision:
      www.ots.treas.gov/regionals.html
Department Budget:
    www.ustreas.gov/budget/whatnew.htm

Veterans Affairs Dept.

Main: www.va.gov
About the Veterans Affairs Dept.:
    www.va.gov/about_va
News: www.va.gov/opa/pressrel/pressarchinternet.cfm
Secretary's Bio: www.va.gov/opa/bios
List of Regional Offices: www.vba.va.gov/ro_list.htm
Department Budget: www.va.gov/budget/summary

LEGISLATIVE BRANCH

Congress

U.S. Constitution: lcweb2.loc.gov/const/const.html
Legislative Process:
    www.house.gov/house/Legproc.html
How Laws Are Made:
    thomas.loc.gov/home/lawsmade.toc.html
Biographical Directory of the U.S. Congress:
    bioguide.congress.gov/biosearch/biosearch.asp
Election Statistics (1920–present):
    clerk.house.gov/members/election_information/
    elections.php

House

Main: www.house.gov
Annual Calendar:
    www.house.gov/house/2003_House_Calendar.htm
Daily Business:
    clerkweb.house.gov/floorsummary/floor.php3
Committees:
    www.house.gov/house/CommitteeWWW.html
Committee Hearing Schedules:
    thomas.loc.gov/home/hcomso.html
Pending Business:
    www.house.gov/house/floor/thisweek.htm
List of Roll Call Votes:
    clerk.house.gov/legisAct/votes.php
Leadership:
    www.house.gov/house/orgs_pub_ hse_ldr_www.html
Media Galleries:
    www.house.gov/house/mediagallery.html

Senate

Main: www.senate.gov
Annual Calendar: frist.senate.gov/calendar/2003
Daily Calendar:
    www.senate.gov/~nickles/legislative/today.cfm
Committees: www.senate.gov/committees/index.cfm
Committee Hearing Schedules: www.senate.gov/
    legislative/legis_legis_committees.html

List of Roll Call Votes:
www.senate.gov/legislative/legis_act_rollcall.html
Leadership: www.senate.gov/learning/
learn_leaders_leadership.html
Media Galleries: www.senate.gov/galleries
Executive Nominations:
judiciary.senate.gov/nominations.cfm

General Accounting Office

Main: www.gao.gov
About the General Accounting Office:
www.gao.gov/about.htm
Comptroller General's Bio:
www.gao.gov/cghome/dwbiog.html
GAO Reports: www.gao.gov/audit.htm

Government Printing Office

Main: www.access.gpo.gov
About the Government Printing Office:
www.access.gpo.gov/aboutgpo

Library of Congress

Main: www.loc.gov
Online Catalog: catalog.loc.gov
Thomas (Legislative Information on the Internet):
thomas.loc.gov
Copyright Office: www.loc.gov/copyright

JUDICIAL BRANCH

The Supreme Court

Main: www.supremecourtus.gov
About the Supreme Court:
www.supremecourtus.gov/about/about.html
News: www.supremecourtus.gov/publicinfo/press/
pressreleases.html
Biographies of the Justices:
www.supremecourtus.gov/about/
biographiescurrent.pdf
Supreme Court Docket:
www.supremecourtus.gov/docket/docket.html
Visiting the Supreme Court:
www.supremecourtus.gov/visiting/visiting.html

Federal Judicial Center

Main: www.fjc.gov

U.S. Federal Courts

Main: www.uscourts.gov
About the U.S. Federal Courts:
www.uscourts.gov/about.html
News: www.uscourts.gov/news.html
Publications: www.uscourts.gov/publications.html

GOVERNMENT OF THE UNITED STATES

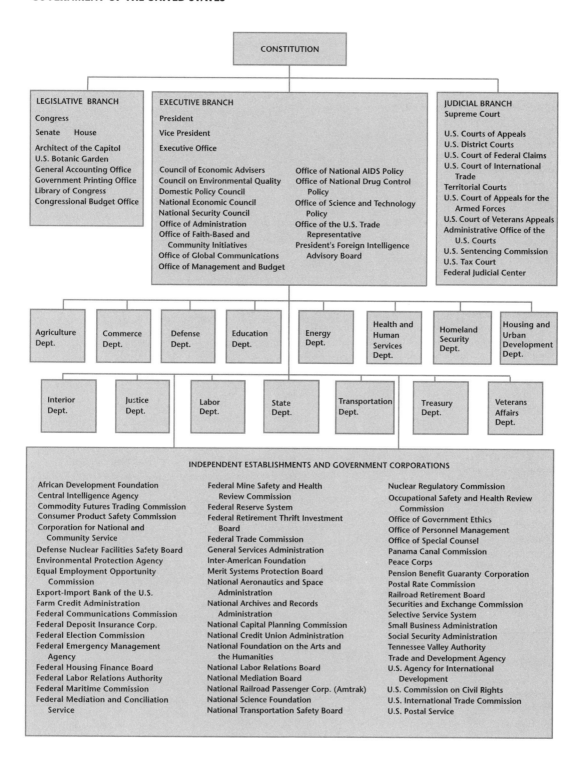

CONSTITUTION

LEGISLATIVE BRANCH

Congress

Senate   House

Architect of the Capitol
U.S. Botanic Garden
General Accounting Office
Government Printing Office
Library of Congress
Congressional Budget Office

EXECUTIVE BRANCH

President

Vice President

Executive Office

Council of Economic Advisers
Council on Environmental Quality
Domestic Policy Council
National Economic Council
National Security Council
Office of Administration
Office of Faith-Based and
    Community Initiatives
Office of Global Communications
Office of Management and Budget

Office of National AIDS Policy
Office of National Drug Control
    Policy
Office of Science and Technology
    Policy
Office of the U.S. Trade
    Representative
President's Foreign Intelligence
    Advisory Board

JUDICIAL BRANCH

Supreme Court

U.S. Courts of Appeals
U.S. District Courts
U.S. Court of Federal Claims
U.S. Court of International
    Trade
Territorial Courts
U.S. Court of Appeals for the
    Armed Forces
U.S. Court of Veterans Appeals
Administrative Office of the
    U.S. Courts
U.S. Sentencing Commission
U.S. Tax Court
Federal Judicial Center

Agriculture Dept.

Commerce Dept.

Defense Dept.

Education Dept.

Energy Dept.

Health and Human Services Dept.

Homeland Security Dept.

Housing and Urban Development Dept.

Interior Dept.

Justice Dept.

Labor Dept.

State Dept.

Transportation Dept.

Treasury Dept.

Veterans Affairs Dept.

INDEPENDENT ESTABLISHMENTS AND GOVERNMENT CORPORATIONS

African Development Foundation
Central Intelligence Agency
Commodity Futures Trading Commission
Consumer Product Safety Commission
Corporation for National and
    Community Service
Defense Nuclear Facilities Safety Board
Environmental Protection Agency
Equal Employment Opportunity
    Commission
Export-Import Bank of the U.S.
Farm Credit Administration
Federal Communications Commission
Federal Deposit Insurance Corp.
Federal Election Commission
Federal Emergency Management
    Agency
Federal Housing Finance Board
Federal Labor Relations Authority
Federal Maritime Commission
Federal Mediation and Conciliation
    Service

Federal Mine Safety and Health
    Review Commission
Federal Reserve System
Federal Retirement Thrift Investment
    Board
Federal Trade Commission
General Services Administration
Inter-American Foundation
Merit Systems Protection Board
National Aeronautics and Space
    Administration
National Archives and Records
    Administration
National Capital Planning Commission
National Credit Union Administration
National Foundation on the Arts and
    the Humanities
National Labor Relations Board
National Mediation Board
National Railroad Passenger Corp. (Amtrak)
National Science Foundation
National Transportation Safety Board

Nuclear Regulatory Commission
Occupational Safety and Health Review
    Commission
Office of Government Ethics
Office of Personnel Management
Office of Special Counsel
Panama Canal Commission
Peace Corps
Pension Benefit Guaranty Corporation
Postal Rate Commission
Railroad Retirement Board
Securities and Exchange Commission
Selective Service System
Small Business Administration
Social Security Administration
Tennessee Valley Authority
Trade and Development Agency
U.S. Agency for International
    Development
U.S. Commission on Civil Rights
U.S. International Trade Commission
U.S. Postal Service

Governors and Other State Officials

Political affiliations, when available, are indicated as follows: Democrat (D), Republican (R). For key officials of the District of Columbia and other Washington-area localities, see page 365.

Alabama   Web, www.alabama.gov

Gov. Bob Riley (R), State Capitol, 600 Dexter Ave., #N-104, Montgomery, 36130; Press: David Azbell, (334) 242-7100

Lt. Gov. Lucy Baxley (D), Alabama State House, 11 S. Union St., #725, Montgomery, 36130-6050, (334) 242-7900; fax, (334) 242-4661

Secy. of State Nancy Worley (D), State Capitol, 600 Dexter Ave., #S-105, Montgomery, 36130, (334) 242-7205; fax, (334) 242-4993

Atty. Gen. William Holcombe Pryor Jr. (R), Alabama State House, 11 S. Union St., 3rd Floor, Montgomery, 36130, (334) 242-7300; fax, (334) 242-7458

Treasurer Kay Ivey (R), State Capitol, 600 Dexter Ave., #S-106, Montgomery, 36130-2751, (334) 242-7500; fax, (334) 242-7592

Alaska   Web, www.state.ak.us

Gov. Frank Murkowski (R), State Capitol, P.O. Box 110001, Juneau, 99811-0001; Press: John Manly, (907) 465-3500

Lt. Gov. Loren Leman (R), State Capitol, P.O. Box 110015, Juneau, 99811-0015, (907) 465-3520; fax, (907) 465-5400

(No office of Secretary of State)

Atty. Gen. Gregg Renkes (R), P.O. Box 110300, Juneau, 99811, (907) 465-2133; fax, (907) 465-2075

Deputy Commissioner Tomas Boutin, P.O. Box 110405, Juneau, 99811-0405, (907) 465-2300; fax, (907) 465-2389

In Washington, D.C.: John Katz, Special Counsel, Office of State-Federal Relations, State of Alaska, 444 N. Capitol St. N.W., #336, 20001-1512, (202) 624-5858; fax, (202) 624-5857

Arizona   Web, www.az.gov

Gov. Janet Napolitano (D), State Capitol, 1700 W. Washington St., 9th Floor, Phoenix, 85007; Press: Kris Mayes, (602) 542-1342

(No office of Lieutenant Governor)

Secy. of State Jan Brewer (R), West Wing, State Capitol, 1700 W. Washington St., 7th Floor, Phoenix, 85007, (602) 542-4285; fax, (602) 542-1575

Atty. Gen. Terry Goddard (D), 1275 W. Washington St., Phoenix, 85007, (602) 542-5025; fax, (602) 542-1275

Treasurer David Petersen (R), 1700 W. Washington St., 1st Floor, Phoenix, 85007, (602) 542-5815; fax, (602) 542-7176

Arkansas   Web, www.accessArkansas.org

Gov. Mike Huckabee (R), State Capitol Bldg., #250, Little Rock, 72201; Press: Rex Nelson, (501) 682-2345

Lt. Gov. Winthrop P. Rockefeller (R), State Capitol Bldg., #270, Little Rock, 72201-1061, (501) 682-2144; fax, (501) 682-2894

Secy. of State Charlie Daniels (D), State Capitol Bldg., #256, Little Rock, 72201, (501) 682-1010; fax, (501) 682-3510

Atty. Gen. Mike Beebe (D), Tower Bldg., 323 Center St., #200, Little Rock, 72201-2610, (501) 682-2007; fax, (501) 682-8084

Treasurer Gus Wingfield (D), State Capitol Bldg., #220, Little Rock, 72201, (501) 682-5888; fax, (501) 682-3842

California   Web, www.state.ca.us

Gov. Gray Davis (D), State Capitol, Sacramento, 95814; Press: Steve Maviglio, (916) 445-2841

Lt. Gov. Cruz M. Bustamante (D), State Capitol, #1114, Sacramento, 95814, (916) 445-8994; fax, (916) 323-4998

Secy. of State Kevin Shelley (D), 1500 11th St., #600, Sacramento, 95814, (916) 653-6814; fax, (916) 653-4795

Atty. Gen. Bill Lockyer (D), P.O. Box 944255, Sacramento, 94244-2550, (916) 322-3360; fax, (916) 324-5205

Treasurer Philip Angelides (D), 915 Capitol Mall, #110, Sacramento, 95814, (916) 653-2995; fax, (916) 653-3125

In Washington, D.C.: **Paul Cunningham,** Director, Washington Office of the Governor, State of California, 444 N. Capitol St. N.W., #134, 20001, (202) 624-5270; fax, (202) 624-5280

Colorado   Web, www.colorado.gov

Gov. Bill Owens (R), State Capitol Bldg., #136, Denver, 80203-1792; Press: Dan Hopkins, (303) 866-2471

Lt. Gov. Jane Norton (R), State Capitol Bldg., #130, Denver, 80203, (303) 866-2087; fax, (303) 866-5469

Secy. of State Donetta Davidson (R), 1560 Broadway, #200, Denver, 80202, (303) 894-2200; fax, (303) 869-4860

Atty. Gen. Ken Salazar (D), 1525 Sherman St., 7th Floor, Denver, 80203, (303) 866-4500; fax, (303) 866-5691

Treasurer Mike Coffman (R), State Capitol Bldg., #140, Denver, 80203, (303) 866-2441; fax, (303) 866-2123

Connecticut   Web, www.state.ct.us

Gov. John G. Rowland (R), State Capitol, 210 Capitol Ave., #202, Hartford, 06106; Press: Chris Cooper, (860) 566-4840

Lt. Gov. M. Jodi Rell (R), State Capitol, 210 Capitol Ave., #304, Hartford, 06106, (860) 524-7384; fax, (860) 524-7304

Secy. of State Susan Bysiewicz (D), 30 Trinity St., Hartford, 06106, (860) 509-6200; fax, (860) 509-6209

Atty. Gen. Richard Blumenthal (D), 55 Elm St., Hartford, 06106, (860) 808-5318; fax, (860) 808-5387

Treasurer Denise L. Nappier (D), 55 Elm St., Hartford, 06106-1773, (860) 702-3000; fax, (860) 702-3043

In Washington, D.C.: Allan R. Guyut Jr., Director, Washington Office of the Governor, State of Connecticut, 444 N. Capitol St. N.W., #317, 20001, (202) 347-4535; fax, (202) 347-7151

Delaware   Web, delaware.gov

Gov. Ruth Ann Minner (D), Tatnall Bldg., William Penn St., Dover, 19901; Press: Gregory Patterson, (302) 744-4222

Lt. Gov. John C. Carney (D), Tatnall Bldg., 3rd Floor, 150 William Penn St., Dover, 19901, (302) 744-4333; fax, (302) 739-6965

Secy. of State Harriet Smith Windsor (D), 401 Federal St., #3, Dover, 19901, (302) 739-4111; fax, (302) 739-3811

Atty. Gen. M. Jane Brady (R), Carvel State Office Bldg., 820 N. French St., Wilmington, 19801, (302) 577-8500; fax, (302) 577-2610

Treasurer Jack Markell (D), Thomas Collins Bldg., 540 S. Dupont Hwy., #4, Dover, 19901-4516, (302) 744-1000; fax, (302) 739-5635

In Washington, D.C.: **Debbie Hamilton,** Director, Washington Office of the Governor, State of Delaware, 444 N. Capitol St. N.W., #230, 20001, (202) 624-7724; fax, (202) 624-5495

Florida   Web, www.state.fl.us

Gov. Jeb Bush (R), The Capitol, Tallahassee, 32399-0001; Press: Jill Bratina, (850) 488-5394

Lt. Gov. Toni Jennings (R), The Capitol, Pl-05, Tallahassee, 32399-0001, (850) 488-4711; fax, (850) 921-6114

Secy. of State Glenda Hood (R), The Capitol, Pl-02, Tallahassee, 32399-0250, (850) 245-6500; fax, (850) 414-5526

Atty. Gen. Charlie Crist (R), The Capitol, Tallahassee, 32399-1050, (850) 487-1963; fax, (850) 487-2564

Chief Financial Officer Tom Gallagher (R), 200 E. Gaines St., Tallahassee, 32399, (850) 413-3100; fax, (850) 488-6581

In Washington, D.C.: Nina Oviedo, Director, Washington Office of the Governor, State of Florida, 444 N. Capitol St. N.W., #349, 20001, (202) 624-5885; fax, (202) 624-5886

Georgia   Web, www.state.ga.us

Gov. Sonny Perdue (R), State Capitol, #203, Atlanta, 30334; Press: Kimberly King, (404) 656-1776

Lt. Gov. Mark Taylor (D), State Capitol, #240, Atlanta, 30334, (404) 656-5030; fax, (404) 656-6739

Secy. of State Cathy Cox (D), State Capitol, #214, Atlanta, 30334, (404) 656-2881; fax, (404) 656-0513

Atty. Gen. Thurbert E. Baker (D), 40 Capitol Square S.W., Atlanta, 30334-1300, (404) 656-3300; fax, (404) 657-8733

Treasurer Dan Ebersole, 200 Piedmont Ave., W. Tower, #1202, Atlanta, 30334, (404) 656-2168; fax, (404) 656-9048

Hawaii   Web, www.state.hi.us

Gov. Linda Lingle (R), State Capitol, Honolulu, 96813; Press: Lenny Klompus, (808) 586-0034

Lt. Gov. James "Duke" Aiona (R), State Capitol, 415 S. Beretania St., Honolulu, 96813, (808) 586-0255; fax, (808) 586-0231

(No office of Secretary of State)

Atty. Gen. Mark J. Bennett (R), 425 Queen St., Honolulu, 96813, (808) 586-1500; fax, (808) 586-1239

Treasurer Georgina Kawamura, 250 S. Hotel St., #305, Honolulu, 96813, (808) 586-1518; fax, (808) 586-1976

Idaho   Web, www.state.id.us

Gov. Dirk Kempthorne (R), State Capitol Bldg., West Wing, 700 W. Jefferson St., 2nd Floor, Boise, 83720-0034; Press: Mark Snider, (208) 334-2100

Lt. Gov. Jim Risch (R), State Capitol Bldg., 700 W. Jefferson St., #225, Boise, 83720-0057, (208) 334-2200; fax, (208) 334-3259

Secy. of State Ben Ysursa (R), State Capitol Bldg., 700 W. Jefferson St., #203, Boise, 83720-0080, (208) 334-2300; fax, (208) 334-2282

Atty. Gen. Lawrence Wasden (R), State Capitol Bldg., 700 W. Jefferson St., Boise, 83720-0010, (208) 334-2400; fax, (208) 334-2530

Treasurer Ron G. Crane (R), State Capitol Bldg., 700 W. Jefferson St., #102, Boise, 83720-0091, (208) 334-3200; fax, (208) 332-2960

In Washington, D.C.: Gary Smith, Deputy Chief of Staff, Washington Office of the Governor, State of Idaho, 444 N. Capitol St. N.W., #216, 20001, (202) 434-8045; fax, (202) 434-8047

Illinois   Web, www100.state.il.us

Gov. Rod Blagojevich (D), State House, #207, Springfield, 62706; Press: Cheryle Jackson, (217) 782-6830

Lt. Gov. Patrick Quinn (D), State House, #214, Springfield, 62706, (217) 782-7884; fax, (217) 524-6262

Secy. of State Jesse White (D), State House, #213, Springfield, 62706, (217) 782-2201; fax, (217) 785-0358

Atty. Gen. Lisa Madigan (D), James R. Thompson Ctr., 100 Randolph St., Chicago, 60601, (312) 814-3000

Treasurer Judy Baar Topinka (R), State House, #219, Springfield, 62706, (217) 782-2211; fax, (217) 785-2777

In Washington, D.C.: Sol Ross, Washington Representative, Washington Office of the Governor, State of Illinois, 444 N. Capitol St. N.W., #400, 20001, (202) 624-7760; fax, (202) 724-0689

Indiana   Web, www.state.in.us

Gov. Frank L. O'Bannon (D), State House, 200 W. Washington St., #206, Indianapolis, 46204; Press: Mary Dieter, (317) 232-4567

Lt. Gov. Joseph E. Kernan (D), State House, 200 W. Washington St., #333, Indianapolis, 46204-2790, (317) 232-4545; fax, (317) 232-4788

Secy. of State Todd Rokita (R), State House, 200 W. Washington St., #201, Indianapolis, 46204, (317) 232-6531; fax, (317) 233-3283

Atty. Gen. Steve Carter (R), Indiana Government Center South, 402 W. Washington St., 5th Floor, Indianapolis, 46204-2770, (317) 232-6201; fax, (317) 232-7979

Treasurer Tim Berry (R), State House, 200 W. Washington St., #242, Indianapolis, 46204, (317) 232-6386; fax, (317) 233-1928

In Washington, D.C.: Jeff Viohl, Director, Washington Office of the Governor, State of Indiana, 444 N. Capitol St. N.W., #428, 20001, (202) 624-1474; fax, (202) 624-1475

Iowa   Web, www.state.ia.us

Gov. Thomas J. Vilsack (D), State Capitol Bldg., Des Moines, 50319; Press: Matt Paul, (515) 281-5211

Lt. Gov. Sally Pederson (D), State Capitol Bldg., Des Moines, 50319, (515) 281-5211; fax, (515) 281-6611

Secy. of State Chester J. Culver (D), State Capitol, Hoover Bldg., #105, Des Moines, 50319, (515) 281-8993; fax, (515) 242-5953

Atty. Gen. Thomas J. Miller (D), Hoover Bldg., 2nd Floor, 1305 E. Walnut St., Des Moines, 50319, (515) 281-5164; fax, (515) 281-4209

Treasurer Michael L. Fitzgerald (D), State Capitol Bldg., Des Moines, 50319, (515) 281-5368; fax, (515) 281-7562

In Washington, D.C.: John Cacciatore, Director, Washington Office of the Governor, State of Iowa, 400 N. Capitol St. N.W., #359, 20001, (202) 624-5442; fax, (202) 624-8189

Kansas   Web, www.accesskansas.org

Gov. Kathleen Sebelius (D), State Capitol, #212-S, Topeka, 66612-1590; Press: Nicole Corcoran-Basso, (785) 296-3232

Lt. Gov. John E. Moore (D), State Capitol, #222-S, Topeka, 66612-1504, (785) 296-2213; fax, (785) 296-5669

Secy. of State Ron Thornburgh (R), Memorial Hall, 120 S.W. 10th St., 1st Floor, Topeka, 66612-1594, (785) 296-4564; fax, (785) 296-4570

Atty. Gen. Phill Kline (R), 120 S.W. 10th St., 2nd Floor, Topeka, 66612-1597, (785) 296-2215; fax, (785) 296-6296

Treasurer Lynn Jenkins (R), Landon State Office Bldg., 900 S.W. Jackson St., #201, Topeka, 66612-1235, (785) 296-3171; fax, (785) 296-7950

Kentucky   Web, www.kentucky.gov

Gov. Paul E. Patton (D), State Capitol, 700 Capitol Ave., #100, Frankfort, 40601; Press: Rusty Cheuvront, (502) 564-2611

Lt. Gov. Stephen L. Henry (D), State Capitol, 700 Capitol Ave., #100, Frankfort, 40601, (502) 564-2611; fax, (502) 564-2849

Secy. of State John Y. Brown III (D), State Capitol, 700 Capitol Ave., #152, Frankfort, 40601, (502) 564-3490; fax, (502) 564-5687

Atty. Gen. Albert B. Chandler III (D), State Capitol, 700 Capitol Ave., #118, Frankfort, 40601, (502) 696-5300; fax, (502) 564-2894

Treasurer Jonathan Miller (D), State Capitol Annex, West Wing, #183, Frankfort, 40601, (502) 564-4722; fax, (502) 564-6545

In Washington, D.C.: Kevin Goldsmith, Director, Washington Office of the Governor, State of Kentucky, 444 N. Capitol St. N.W., #224, 20001, (202) 220-1350; fax, (202) 220-1359

Louisiana   Web, www.state.la.us

Gov. Murphy J. "Mike" Foster Jr. (R), State Capitol, 900 3rd St., Baton Rouge, 70804-9004; Press: Marsanne Golsby, (225) 342-7015

Lt. Gov. Kathleen Babineaux Blanco (D), 900 N. 3rd St., Pentagon Barracks, Bldg. C, 2nd Floor, Baton Rouge, 70802, (225) 342-7009; fax, (225) 342-1949

Secy. of State Walter Fox McKeithen (R), Capitol Bldg., 800 N. 3rd St., 20th Floor, Baton Rouge, 70802, (225) 342-4479; fax, (225) 342-5577

Atty. Gen. Richard P. Ieyoub (D), State Capitol, 300 Capitol Dr., 22nd Floor, Baton Rouge, 70802, (225) 339-5191; fax, (225) 342-8703

Treasurer John Kennedy (D), State Capitol, 900 N. 3rd St., 3rd Floor, Baton Rouge, 70802, (225) 342-0010; fax, (225) 342-0046

Maine   Web, www.state.me.us

Gov. John Baldacci (D), 1 State House Station, Augusta, 04333-0001; Press: Doug Dunbar, (207) 287-3531

(No office of Lieutenant Governor)

Secy. of State Dan A. Gwadosky (D), Nash Bldg., 148 State House Station, Augusta, 04333-0148, (207) 626-8400; fax, (207) 287-8598

Atty. Gen. G. Steven Rowe (D), 6 State House Station, Augusta, 04333-0006. (207) 626-8800; fax, (207) 287-3145

Treasurer Dale McCormick (D), 39 State House Station, Augusta, 04333-0039, (207) 624-7477; fax, (207) 287-2367

Maryland   Web, www.state.md.us

Gov. Robert L. Ehrlich Jr. (R), State House, 100 State Circle, Annapolis, 21401; Press: Paul E. Schurick, (410) 974-3901

Lt. Gov. Michael Steele (R), State House, 100 State Circle, Annapolis, 21401, (410) 974-2804; fax, (410) 974-5882

Secy. of State Karl Aumann (R), State House, Annapolis, 21401, (410) 974-5521; fax, (410) 974-5190

Atty. Gen. J. Joseph Curran Jr. (D), 200 St. Paul Pl., Baltimore, 21202-2021, (410) 576-6300; fax, (410) 576-6404

Treasurer Nancy K. Kopp (D), Louis L. Goldstein Treasury Bldg., 80 Calvert St., #109, Annapolis, 21401, (410) 260-7533; fax, (410) 974-3530

In Washington, D.C.: Tom Hance, Director, Washington Office of the Governor, State of Maryland, 444 N. Capitol St. N.W., #311, 20001, (202) 624-1430; fax, (202) 783-3061

Massachusetts   Web, Mass.gov/portal/index.jsp

Gov. Mitt Romney (R), Executive Office, State House, #360, Boston, 02133; Press: Shawn Feddeman, (617) 727-6250

Lt. Gov. Kerry Healey (R), State House, #360, Boston, 02133, (617) 727-3600; fax, (617) 727-9725

Secy. of the Commonwealth William Francis Galvin (D), State House, #337, Boston, 02133, (617) 727-9180; fax, (617) 742-4722

Atty. Gen. Thomas F. Reilly (D), 1 Ashburton Pl., #2010, Boston, 02108-1698, (617) 727-2200; fax, (617) 727-5768

Treasurer Timothy P. Cahill (D), State House, #227, Boston, 02133, (617) 367-6900; fax, (617) 248-0372

In Washington, D.C.: Frank Micciche, Washington Representative, Washington Office of the Governor, Commonwealth of Massachusetts, 444 N. Capitol St. N.W., #208, 20001, (202) 624-7713; fax, (202) 624-7714

Michigan   Web, www.michigan.gov

Gov. Jennifer Granholm (D), George W. Romney Bldg., 111 S. Capitol, Lansing, 48933; Press: Elizabeth Boyd, (517) 373-3400

Lt. Gov. John D. Cherry Jr. (D), State Capitol Bldg., George W. Romney Bldg., #S-215, Lansing, 48909, (517) 373-6800; fax, (517) 241-3956

Secy. of State Terri Lynn Land (R), Treasury Bldg., 430 W. Allegan St., 1st Floor, Lansing, 48918-9900, (517) 373-2510; fax, (517) 373-0727

Atty. Gen. Mike Cox (R), 525 W. Ottawa, Lansing, 48909, (517) 373-1110; fax, (517) 373-3042

Treasurer Jay B. Rising, Treasury Bldg., 430 W. Allegan St., Lansing, 48922, (517) 373-3200; fax, (517) 373-4968

In Washington, D.C.: John Burchett, Washington Representative, Washington Office of the Governor, State of Michigan, 444 N. Capitol St. N.W., #411, 20001, (202) 624-5840; fax, (202) 624-5841

Minnesota   Web, www.state.mn.us

Gov. Tim Pawlenty (R), State Capitol, 75 Constitution Ave., #130, St. Paul, 55155; Press: Leslie Kupchella, (651) 296-3391

Lt. Gov. Carol Molnau (R), 130 State Capitol, #130, St. Paul, 55155, (651) 296-3391; fax, (651) 296-2089

Secy. of State Mary Kiffmeyer (R), State Office Bldg., 100 Constitution Ave., #180, St. Paul, 55155-1299, (651) 296-2079; fax, (651) 297-5844

Atty. Gen. Mike Hatch (D), 1400 NCL Tower, 445 Minnesota St., St. Paul, 55101, (651) 296-3353; fax, (651) 297-4193

Commissioner of Finance Dan McElroy (R), 658 Cedar St., #400, St. Paul, 55155, (651) 296-5900; fax, (651) 296-8685

In Washington, D.C.: Corey Weierke, Washington Representative, Washington Office of the Governor, State of Minnesota, 400 N. Capitol St. N.W., #365, 20001, (202) 624-5308; fax, (202) 624-5425

Mississippi   Web, www.ms.gov

Gov. Ronnie Musgrove (D), Walter Sillers Bldg., 550 High St., Jackson, 39201; Press: Lee Ann Mayo, (601) 359-3150

Lt. Gov. Amy Tuck (R), New Capitol Bldg., #315, 400 High St., Jackson, 39215, (601) 359-3200; fax, (601) 359-4054

Secy. of State Eric C. Clark (D), 401 Mississippi St., Jackson, 39205-0136, (601) 359-1350; fax, (601) 359-1499

Atty. Gen. Mike Moore (D), 450 High St., Jackson, 39201, (601) 359-3680; fax, (601) 359-3796

Treasurer Marshall G. Bennett (D), 1101 Woolfolk State Office Bldg. Ste. A, Jackson, 39205, (601) 359-3600; fax, (601) 359-2001

In Washington, D.C.: Fred Zeytoonjian, Director, Washington Office of the Governor, State of Mississippi, 444 N. Capitol St. N.W., #445, 20001, (202) 220-1330; fax, (202) 220-1333

Missouri   Web, www.state.mo.us

Gov. Bob Holden (D), State Capitol, #216, Jefferson City, 65101; Press: Mary Still, (573) 751-3222

Lt. Gov. Joe Maxwell (D), State Capitol, #121, Jefferson City, 65101, (573) 751-4727; fax, (573) 751-9422

Secy. of State Matt Blunt (R), State Capitol, #208, 600 W. Main St., Jefferson City, 65101, (573) 751-4936; fax, (573) 751-2490

Atty. Gen. Jeremiah W. "Jay" Nixon (D), Supreme Court Bldg., 207 W. High St., Jefferson City, 65102, (573) 751-3321; fax, (573) 751-0774

Treasurer Nancy Farmer (D), State Capitol, #229, Jefferson City, 65101, (573) 751-2411; fax, (573) 751-9443

In Washington, D.C.: Cristy Gallagher, Director, Washington Office of the Governor, State of Missouri, 400 N. Capitol St. N.W., #376, 20001, (202) 624-7720; (202) 624-5855

Montana   Web, www.discoveringmontana.com

Gov. Judy Martz (R), State Capitol, 1625 11th Ave., Helena, 59620; Press: Chuck Butler, (406) 444-3111

Lt. Gov. Karl Ohs (R), Capitol Station, 1625 11th Ave., Helena, 59620, (406) 444-5551; fax, (406) 444-4648

Secy. of State Bob Brown (R), State Capitol, #260, Helena, 59620-2801, (406) 444-2034; fax, (406) 444-3976

Atty. Gen. Mike McGrath (D), Justice Bldg., 215 N. Sanders St., Helena, 59601, (406) 444-2026; fax, (406) 444-3549

Dept. of Administration Director Scott Darkenwald, P.O. Box 201705, Helena, 59620, (406) 444-2032; (406) 444-2812

Nebraska   Web, www.state.ne.us

Gov. Mike Johanns (R), State Capitol, 1425 K St., Lincoln, 68509; Press: Chris Peterson, (402) 471-2244

Lt. Gov. David E. Heineman (R), State Capitol, #2315, Lincoln, 68509-4863, (402) 471-2256; fax, (402) 471-6031

Secy. of State John A. Gale (R), State Capitol, #2300, Lincoln, 68509-4608, (402) 471-2554; fax, (402) 471-3237

Atty. Gen. Jon Bruning (R), 2115 State Capitol, Lincoln, 68509, (402) 471-2682; fax, (402) 471-3297

Treasurer Lorelee Byrd (R), State Capitol, #2003, Lincoln, 68509-4788, (402) 471-2455; fax, (402) 471-4390, (402) 471-0816

Nevada   Web, www.silver.state.nv.us

Gov. Kenny Guinn (R), Capitol Bldg., 101 N. Carson St., Carson City, 89701; Press: Greg Bortolin, (775) 684-5670

Lt. Gov. Lorraine T. Hunt (R), Capitol Bldg., 101 N. Carson St., #2, Carson City, 89701, (775) 684-5637; fax, (775) 684-5782

Secy. of State Dean Heller (R), Capitol Bldg., 101 N. Carson St., #3, Carson City, 89701-4786, (775) 684-5708; fax, (775) 684-5725

Atty. Gen. Brian Sandoval (R), Capitol Complex, 100 N. Carson St., Carson City, 89701-4717, (775) 684-1100; fax, (775) 684-1108

Treasurer **Brian K. Krolicki (R)**, Capitol Bldg., 101 N. Carson St., #4, Carson City, 89701-4786, (775) 684-5600; fax, (775) 684-5623

In Washington, D.C.: **Michael Pieper**, Director, Washington Office of the Governor, State of Nevada, 444 N. Capitol St. N.W., #209, 20001, (202) 624-5405; fax, (202) 624-8181

New Hampshire   Web, www.state.nh.us

Gov. **Craig Benson (R)**, State House, 107 N. Main St., #208-214, Concord, 03301; Press: Demetrius Karoutsos, (603) 271-2121

(No office of Lieutenant Governor)

Secy. of State **William M. Gardner (D)**, State House, 107 N. Main St., #204, Concord, 03301, (603) 271-3242; fax, (603) 271-6316

Atty. Gen. **Peter W. Heed (R)**, 33 Capitol St., Concord, 03301-6397, (603) 271-3658; fax, (603) 271-2110

Treasurer **Michael A. Ablowich**, State House Annex, 25 Capitol St., #121, Concord, 03301, (603) 271-2621; fax, (603) 271-3922

New Jersey   Web, www.state.nj.us

Gov. **James E. McGreevey (D)**, State House, 125 W. State St., Trenton, 08625-0001; Press: Micah Rasmussen, (609) 292-6000

(No office of Lieutenant Governor)

Secy. of State **Regena L. Thomas (D)**, 125 W. State St., Trenton, 08625-0300, (609) 984-1900; fax, (609) 292-9897

Atty. Gen. **Peter C. Harvey (Acting)**, Justice Complex, West Wing, 8th Floor, Trenton, 08625, (609) 292-4925; fax, (609) 292-3508

Treasurer **John E. McCormac**, State House, 225 W. State St., Trenton, 08625, (609) 292-6748; fax, (609) 984-3888

In Washington, D.C.: **Tom Edwards**, Director, Washington Office of the Governor, State of New Jersey, 444 N. Capitol St. N.W., #201, 20001, (202) 638-0631; fax, (202) 638-2296

New Mexico   Web, www.state.nm.us

Gov. **Bill Richardson (D)**, State Capitol Bldg., #400, Santa Fe, 87300; Press: Billy Sparks, (505) 827-3000

Lt. Gov. **Diane Denish (D)**, State Capitol Bldg., #417, Santa Fe, 87503, (505) 827-3050; fax, (505) 827-3057

Secy. of State **Rebecca Vigil-Giron (D)**, 325 Don Gaspar, #300, Santa Fe, 87503, (505) 827-3600; fax, (505) 827-3634

Atty. Gen. **Patricia Madrid (D)**, Bataan Memorial, 407 Galisteo St., #260, Santa Fe, 85701, (505) 827-6000; fax, (505) 827-5826

Treasurer **Robert E. Vigil (D)**, State Treasurer's Office, 2019 Galisteo, Bldg. K, Santa Fe, 87505, (505) 955-1120; fax, (505) 955-1195

New York   Web, www.state.ny.us

Gov. **George E. Pataki (R)**, State Capitol, Albany, 12224; Press: Lisa Dewald Stoll, (518) 474-7516

Lt. Gov. **Mary O. Donohue (R)**, Executive Chamber, State Capitol, Albany, 12224, (518) 474-4623; fax, (518) 486-4170

Secy. of State **Randy A. Daniels (R)**, 41 State St., Albany, 12231, (518) 474-0050; fax, (518) 474-4765

Atty. Gen. **Eliot Spitzer (D)**, State Capitol, Albany, 12224-0341; (518) 474-7330

Treasurer **Aida Brewer**, Alfred E. Smith Office Bldg., 5th Floor, Albany, 12225, (518) 474-4250; fax, (518) 473-9163

In Washington, D.C.: **James Mazzarella**, Director, Washington Office of the Governor, State of New York, 444 N. Capitol St. N.W., #301, 20001, (202) 434-7100; fax, (202) 434-7110

North Carolina   Web, www.ncgov.com

Gov. **Michael F. Easley (D)**, Capitol Square, State Capitol Bldg., Raleigh, 27699-0301; Press: Fred Hartman, (919) 733-5811

Lt. Gov. **Beverly Perdue (D)**, State Capitol, Raleigh, 27699-0401, (919) 733-7350; fax, (919) 733-6595

Secy. of State **Elaine F. Marshall (D)**, P.O. Box 29622, Raleigh, 27626-0622, (919) 807-2005; fax, (919) 807-2010

Atty. Gen. **Roy Cooper (D)**, 114 W. Edenton St., Raleigh, 27602, (919) 716-6400; fax, (919) 716-6750

Treasurer **Richard Moore (D)**, 325 N. Salisbury St., Raleigh, 27603-1385, (919) 508-5176; fax, (919) 508-5167

In Washington, D.C.: **Jim McCleskey**, Director, Washington Office of the Governor, State of North Carolina, 444 N. Capitol St. N.W., #332, 20001, (202) 624-5830; fax, (202) 624-5836

North Dakota   Web, www.discovernd.com

Gov. **John Hoeven (R)**, State Capitol, 600 E. Boulevard Ave., Dept. 101, Bismarck, 58505-0001; Press: Kathy Ibach, (701) 328-2200

Lt. Gov. **Jack Dalrymple (R)**, State Capitol, 600 E. Boulevard Ave., Dept. 101, Bismarck, 58505-0001, (701) 328-4222; fax, (701) 328-2205

Secy. of State **Alvin A. Jaeger (R)**, State Capitol, Dept. 108, 600 E. Boulevard Ave., Bismarck, 58505-0500, (701) 328-2900; fax, (701) 328-2992

Atty. Gen. **Wayne Stenehjem (R)**, State Capitol, Dept. 125, 600 E. Boulevard Ave., 1st Floor, Bismarck, 58505-0040, (701) 328-2210; fax, (701) 328-2226

Treasurer Kathi Gilmore (D), State Capitol, Dept. 120, 600 E. Boulevard Ave., Bismarck, 58505-0600, (701) 328-2643; fax, (701) 328-3002

In Washington, D.C.: Craig Pattee, Director, Washington Office of the Governor, State of North Dakota, 444 N. Capitol St. N.W., #837, 20001-1512, (202) 624-6607; fax, (202) 544-5321

Ohio   Web, www.state.oh.us

Gov. Bob Taft II (R), Vern Riffe Center, 77 S. High St., 30th Floor, Columbus, 43215; Press: Ann Husted, (614) 466-3555

Lt. Gov. Jennette Bradley (R), Vern Riffe Center, 77 S. High St., 30th Floor, Columbus, 43215, (614) 466-3396; fax, (614) 644-0575

Secy. of State J. Kenneth Blackwell (R), 180 E. Broad St., 15th Floor, Columbus, 43215, (614) 466-2655; fax, (614) 644-0649

Atty. Gen. Jim Petro (R), 30 E. Broad St., 17th Floor, Columbus, 43215-3428, (614) 466-4320; fax, (614) 466-5087

Treasurer Joseph T. Deters (R), 30 E. Broad St., 9th Floor, Columbus, 43215, (614) 466-2160; fax, (614) 644-7313

In Washington, D.C.: Mike McGarey, Director, Washington Office of the Governor, State of Ohio, 444 N. Capitol St. N.W., #546, 20001, (202) 624-5844; fax, (202) 624-5847

Oklahoma   Web, www.state.ok.us

Gov. Brad Henry (D), State Capitol, 2300 N. Lincoln Blvd., #212, Oklahoma City, 73105; Press: Kym Koch, (405) 521-2342

Lt. Gov. Mary Fallin (R), State Capitol, 2300 N. Lincoln Blvd., #211, Oklahoma City, 73105, (405) 521-2161; fax, (405) 525-2702

Secy. of State Susan Savage (D), State Capitol, 2300 N. Lincoln Blvd., #101, Oklahoma City, 73105, (405) 521-3911; fax, (405) 521-3771

Atty. Gen. W. A. "Drew" Edmondson (D), State Capitol, 2300 N. Lincoln Blvd., #112, Oklahoma City, 73105, (405) 521-3921; fax, (405) 521-6246

Treasurer Robert A. Butkin (D), State Capitol, 2300 N. Lincoln Blvd., #217, Oklahoma City, 73105, (405) 521-3191; fax, (405) 521-4994

Oregon   Web, www.oregon.gov

Gov. Ted Kulongoski (D), State Capitol, #160, Salem, 97301-4047; Press: Mary Ellen Glynn, (503) 378-6496

(No office of Lieutenant Governor)

Secy. of State Bill Bradbury (D), State Capitol, #141, Salem, 97310, (503) 986-1523; fax, (503) 986-1616

Atty. Gen. Hardy Myers (D), Justice Bldg., 1162 Court St. N.E., Salem, 97310, (503) 378-4400; fax, (503) 378-4017

Treasurer Randall Edwards (D), 350 Winter St. N.E., #100, Salem, 97301-3896, (503) 378-4329; fax, (503) 373-7051

In Washington, D.C.: Rich Bechtel, Director, Washington Office of the Governor, State of Oregon, 400 N. Capitol St. N.W., #367, 20001, (202) 624-3535; fax, (202) 624-3537

Pennsylvania   Web, www.state.pa.us

Gov. Ed Rendell (D), Main Capitol Bldg., #225, Harrisburg, 17120; Press: Ramoa Oliver, (717) 787-2500

Lt. Gov. Catherine Baker Knoll (D), Main Capitol Bldg., #200, Harrisburg, 17120, (717) 787-3300; fax, (717) 783-0150

Secy. of the Commonwealth Pedro A. Cortés (Designee) (D), North Capitol Bldg., #302, Harrisburg, 17120, (717) 787-7630; fax, (717) 787-1734

Atty. Gen. D. Michael Fisher (R), Strawberry Square, 16th Floor, Harrisburg, 17120, (717) 787-3391; fax, (717) 787-8242

Treasurer Barbara Hafer (R), Finance Bldg., #129, Harrisburg, 17120, (717) 787-2991; fax, (717) 772-4234

In Washington, D.C.: Peter A. Peyser Jr., Director, Washington Office of the Governor, Commonwealth of Pennsylvania, 1001 G St. N.W., #400 East, 20001, (202) 638-3730; fax, (202) 638-3516

Rhode Island   Web, www.state.ri.us

Gov. Donald L. Carcieri (R), State House, Providence, 02903; Press: Jeffrey Neal, (401) 222-2080

Lt. Gov. Charles J. Fogarty (D), State House, #116, Providence, 02903, (401) 222-2371; fax, (401) 222-2012

Secy. of State Matt Brown (D), State House, #217, Providence, 02903-1105, (401) 222-2357; fax, (401) 222-1356

Atty. Gen. Patrick Lynch (D), 150 S. Main St., Providence, 02903-2856, (401) 274-4400; fax, (401) 222-1331

Treasurer Paul J. Tavares (D), State House, #102, Providence, 02903, (401) 222-2397; fax, (401) 222-6140

In Washington, D.C.: Tim Costa, Director, Washington Office of the Governor, State of Rhode Island, 444 N. Capitol St. N.W., #619, 20001, (202) 624-3605; fax, (202) 624-3607

South Carolina   Web, www.myscgov.com

Gov. Mark Sanford (R), State House, Columbia, 29211; Press: Will Folks, (803) 734-2100

Lt. Gov. R. Andre Bauer (R), 1100 Gerbais St., Columbia, 29202, (803) 734-2080; fax, (803) 734-2082

Secy. of State Mark Hammond (R), 1205 Pendleton St., #525, Columbia, 29201, (803) 734-2170; fax, (803) 734-1661

Atty. Gen. Henry McMaster (R), 1000 Assembly St., #519, Columbia, 29201, (803) 734-3970; fax, (803) 734-4323

Treasurer Grady L. Patterson Jr. (D), Wade Hampton Office Bldg., #118, Columbia, 29211, (803) 734-2101; fax, (803) 734-2039

In Washington, D.C.: Scott English, Director, Washington Office of the Governor, State of South Carolina, 444 N. Capitol St. N.W., #203, 20001, (202) 624-7784; fax, (202) 624-7800

South Dakota Web, www.state.sd.us

Gov. Michael Rounds (R), State Capitol, 500 E. Capitol Ave., Pierre, 57501-5070; Press: Mark Johnston, (605) 773-3212

Lt. Gov. Dennis Daugaard (R), State Capitol, 500 E. Capitol Ave., Pierre, 57501-5070, (605) 773-3212; fax, (605) 773-4711

Secy. of State Chris Nelson (R), State Capitol, 500 E. Capitol Ave., #204, Pierre, 57501-5070, (605) 773-3537; fax, (605) 773-6580

Atty. Gen. Larry Long (R), State Capitol, 500 E. Capitol Ave., Pierre, 57501-5070, (605) 773-3215; fax, (605) 773-4106

Treasurer Vernon L. Larson (R), State Capitol, 500 E. Capitol Ave., #212, Pierre, 57501-5070, (605) 773-3378; fax, (605) 773-3115

Tennessee Web, www.state.tn.us

Gov. Phil Bredesen (D), State Capitol, 1st Floor, Nashville, 37243-0001; Press: Lydia Lenker, (615) 741-2001

Lt. Gov. John S. Wilder (D), 1 Legislative Plaza, Nashville, 37219, (615) 741-2368; fax, (615) 741-9349

Secy. of State Riley C. Darnell (D), State Capitol, 1st Floor, Nashville, 37243-0305, (615) 741-2819; fax, (615) 741-5962

Atty. Gen. Paul G. Summers (D), 425 5th Ave. North, Cordell Hull Bldg., Nashville, 37243, (615) 741-3491; fax, (615) 741-2009

Treasurer Steve Adams (D), State Capitol, 1st Floor, Nashville, 37243-0225, (615) 741-2956; fax, (615) 253-1591

Texas Web, www.state.tx.us

Gov. Rick Perry (R), State Capitol, 1100 San Jacinto, Austin, 78701; Press: Phil Wilson, (512) 463-2000

Lt. Gov. David Dewhurst (R), State Capitol, Austin, 78711-2068, (512) 463-0001; fax, (512) 463-0039

Secy. of State Gwyn Shea (R), State Capitol, #1E.8, Austin, 78711, (512) 463-5770; fax, (512) 475-2761

Atty. Gen. Greg Abbott (R), Price Daniel Sr. Bldg., 8th Floor, Austin, 78711-2548, (512) 463-2100; fax, (512) 476-2653

Comptroller Carole Keeton Strayhorn (R), Lyndon B. Johnson State Office Bldg., 111 E. 17th St., Austin, 78774, (512) 463-4000; fax, (512) 475-0352

In Washington, D.C.: Ed Perez, Director, Office of State-Federal Relations, State of Texas, 122 C St. N.W., #200, 20001, (202) 638-3927; fax, (202) 628-1943

Utah Web, www.utah.gov

Gov. Michael O. Leavitt (R), State Capitol, #210, Salt Lake City, 84114; Press: Natalie Gochnour, (801) 538-1000

Lt. Gov. Olene S. Walker (R), State Capitol, #210, Salt Lake City, 84114, (801) 538-1520; fax, (801) 538-1557

(No office of Secretary of State)

Atty. Gen. Mark Shurtleff (R), State Capitol, #236, Salt Lake City, 84114-0810, (801) 366-0260; fax, (801) 538-1121

Treasurer Edward T. Alter (R), State Capitol, #215, Salt Lake City, 84114, (801) 538-1042; fax, (801) 538-1465

In Washington, D.C.: Joanne Snow Neumann, Director, Washington Office of the Governor, State of Utah, 400 N. Capitol St. N.W., #388, 20001, (202) 624-7704; fax, (202) 624-7707

Vermont Web, www.vermont.gov

Gov. Jim Douglas (R), Pavilion Office Bldg., 109 State St., 5th Floor, Montpelier, 05609; Press: Jason Gibbs, (802) 828-3333

Lt. Gov. Brian Dubie (R), State House, Montpelier, 05633, (802) 828-2226; fax, (802) 828-3198

Secy. of State Deborah L. Markowitz (D), Redstone Bldg., 26 Terrace St., Drawer 09, Montpelier, 05609-1101, (802) 828-2363; fax, (802) 828-2496

Atty. Gen. William H. Sorrell (D), Pavilion Office Bldg., 109 State St., Montpelier, 05609-1001, (802) 828-3171; fax, (802) 828-2154

Treasurer Jeb Spaulding (D), 133 State St., 2nd Floor, Montpelier, 05633-6200, (802) 828-2301; fax, (802) 828-2772

Virginia Web, www.state.va.us

Gov. Mark Warner (D), State Capitol, 3rd Floor, Richmond, 23219; Press: Ellen Qualls, (804) 786-2211

Lt. Gov. Tim Kaine (D), 900 E. Main St., #1400, Richmond, 23219-3523, (804) 786-2078; fax, (804) 786-7514

Secy. of the Commonwealth Anita A. Rimler (D), 1 Capitol Square, 830 E. Main St., 14th Floor, Richmond, 23219, (804) 786-2441; fax, (804) 371-0017

Atty. Gen. Jerry W. Kilgore (R), 900 E. Main St., Richmond, 23219, (804) 786-2071; fax, (804) 786-1991

Treasurer Jody M. Wagner (D), 101 N. 14th St., James Monroe Bldg., 3rd Floor, Richmond, 23218, (804) 225-2142; fax, (804) 225-3187

In Washington, D.C.: Jan Faircloth, Director, Washington Office of the Governor, Commonwealth of Virginia, 444 N. Capitol St. N.W., #214, 20001, (202) 783-1769; fax, (202) 783-7687

Washington   Web, www.access.wa.gov

Gov. Gary Locke (D), Legislative Bldg., 2nd Floor, Olympia, 98504-0002; Press: Roger Nyhus, (360) 902-4111

Lt. Gov. Bradley Scott Owen (D), Legislative Bldg., #304, Olympia, 98504-0482, (360) 786-7714; fax, (360) 786-7749

Secy. of State Sam Reed (R), 520 Union Ave. S.E., Olympia, 98504-0220, (360) 902-4151; fax, (360) 586-5629

Atty. Gen. Christine O. Gregoire (D), 1125 Washington St. S.E., Olympia, 98504-0100, (360) 753-6200; fax, (360) 664-0988

Treasurer Michael J. Murphy (D), Legislative Bldg., #240, Olympia, 98504-0200, (360) 902-9000; fax, (360) 902-9044

West Virginia   Web, www.state.wv.us

Gov. Bob Wise (D), State Capitol Bldg., 1900 Kanawha Blvd. East, Charleston, 25305; Press: Amy Shuler Goodwin, (304) 558-2000

Lt. Gov. Earl Ray Tomblin (D), Capitol Complex, Main Unit, #229, Charleston, 25305, (304) 357-7801; fax, (304) 357-7839

Secy. of State Joe Manchin III (D), 1900 Kanawha Blvd. East, #157-K, Bldg. #1, Charleston, 25305-0770, (304) 558-6000; fax, (304) 558-0900

Atty. Gen. Darrell V. McGraw Jr. (D), 1900 Kanawha Blvd. East, #26-E, Charleston, 25305-8924, (304) 558-8000; fax, (304) 558-0900

Treasurer John D. Perdue (D), State Capitol Bldg., #E-145, Charleston, 25305, (304) 558-5000; fax, (304) 558-4097

Wisconsin   Web, www.wisconsin.gov/state/home

Gov. Jim Doyle (D), State Capitol, #115-E, Madison, 53702-7863; Press: Dan Leistikow, (608) 266-1212

Lt. Gov. Barbara Lawton (D), State Capitol, #19-E, Madison, 53701, (608) 266-3516; fax, (608) 267-3571

Secy. of State Doug La Follette (D), 30 W. Mifflin St., 10th Floor, Madison, 53702, (608) 266-8888; fax, (608) 266-3159

Atty. Gen. Peg Lautenschlager (D), 123 W. Washington Ave., #117, Madison, 53707-7857, (608) 266-1221; fax, (608) 267-2779

Treasurer Jack Voight (R), 1 S. Pinckney, #550, Madison, 53707, (608) 266-1714; fax, (608) 266-2647

In Washington, D.C.: Sarah Neimeyer, Director, Washington Office of the Governor, State of Wisconsin, 444 N. Capitol St. N.W., #613 20001, (202) 624-5870; fax, (202) 624-5871

Wyoming   Web, www.state.wy.us

Gov. David Freudenthal (D), State Capitol, Cheyenne, 82002-0010; Press: Lara Azar, (307) 777-7434

(No office of Lieutenant Governor)

Secy. of State Joseph B. Meyer (R), State Capitol, Cheyenne, 82002, (307) 777-5333; fax, (307) 777-6217

Atty. Gen. Patrick J. Crank (D), 123 State Capitol, Cheyenne, 82002, (307) 777-7841; fax, (307) 777-6869

Treasurer Cynthia Lummis (R), 200 W. 24th St., Cheyenne, 82002, (307) 777-7408; fax, (307) 777-5411

Foreign Embassies, U.S. Ambassadors, and Country Desk Offices

The list that follows includes key foreign diplomats in the United States, U.S. ambassadors or ranking diplomatic officials abroad, and offices of the State Department that follow political, cultural, and economic developments in countries.

For information on investing or doing business abroad, contact the Commerce Department's Trade Information Center at (800) USTRADE (1-800-872-8723) or visit www.ita.doc.gov. For Eurasia, contact the Business Information Service for the Newly Independent States of the former Soviet Union (BISNIS) at (202) 482-4655 or subscribe to their listserv at www.bisnis.doc.gov/subscribe. For NAFTA countries, contact the NAFTA Office at (202) 482-0305 or (202) 482-0393 or visit www.mac.doc.gov/ftaa2005. The Office of the United States Trade Representative also offers trade information by region at www.ustr.gov/regions.

Afghanistan

Ambassador: Ishaq Shahryar.
Chancery: 2341 Wyoming Ave. N.W. 20008; (202) 483-6410; fax, (202) 483-6487.
U.S. Ambassador in Kabul: Robert Patrick John Finn.
State Dept. Country Office: (202) 647-9552.

Albania

Ambassador: Fatos Tarifa.
Chancery: 2100 S St. N.W. 20008; (202) 223-4942; fax, (202) 628-7342.
U.S. Ambassador in Tirana: James F. Jeffrey.
State Dept. Country Office: (202) 647-3747.

Algeria

Ambassador: Idriss Jazairy.
Chancery: 2137 Wyoming Ave. N.W. 20008; (202) 265-2800; fax, (202) 667-2174.
U.S. Ambassador in Algiers: Janet A. Sanderson.
State Dept. Country Office: (202) 647-4680.

Andorra

Chargé d'Affaires: Jelena Pia-Comella.
Chancery (U.N. Mission): 2 United Nations Plaza, 25th Floor, New York, NY 10017; (212) 750-8064; fax, (212) 750-6630.

Relations with Andorra are maintained by the U.S. Consulate in Madrid, Spain: George L. Argyros Sr., ambassador.
State Dept. Country Office: (202) 647-1412.

Angola

Ambassador: Josefina Perpétua Pitra Diakite.
Chancery: 2108 16th St. N.W. 20009; (202) 785-1156; fax, (202) 785-1258.
U.S. Ambassador in Luanda: Christopher W. Dell.
State Dept. Country Office: (202) 647-9858.

Antigua and Barbuda

Ambassador: Lionel A. Hurst.
Chancery: 3216 New Mexico Ave. N.W. 20016; (202) 362-5211; fax, (202) 362-5225.
U.S. Ambassador: Earl N. Phillips Jr. (resident in Bridgetown, Barbados).
State Dept. Country Office: (202) 647-4384.

Argentina

Ambassador: Eduardo P. Amadeo.
Chancery: 1600 New Hampshire Ave. N.W. 20009; (202) 238-6400; fax, (202) 332-3171.
U.S. Ambassador in Buenos Aires: Lino Gutierrez (nominee).
State Dept. Country Office: (202) 647-2401.

Armenia

Ambassador: Arman Kirakossian.
Chancery: 2225 R St. N.W. 20008; (202) 319-1976; fax, (202) 319-2982.
U.S. Ambassador in Yerevan: John Malcolm Ordway.
State Dept. Country Office: (202) 647-6758.

Australia

Ambassador: Michael Joseph Thawley.
Chancery: 1601 Massachusetts Ave. N.W. 20036; (202) 797-3000; fax, (202) 797-3168.
U.S. Ambassador in Canberra: J. Thomas Schieffer.
State Dept. Country Office: (202) 647-7828.

Austria

Ambassador: Peter Moser.
Chancery: 3524 International Court N.W. 20008; (202) 895-6700; fax, (202) 895-6750.
U.S. Ambassador in Vienna: Lyons Brown Jr.
State Dept. Country Office: (202) 647-2448.

Azerbaijan

Ambassador: Hafiz Mir Jalal Pashayev.
Chancery: 2741 34th St. N.W. 20008; (202) 337-3500; fax, (202) 337-5911.
U.S. Ambassador in Baku: Ross L. Wilson.
State Dept. Country Office: (202) 647-6048.

Bahamas

Ambassador: Joshua Sears.
Chancery: 2220 Massachusetts Ave. N.W. 20008; (202) 319-2660; fax, (202) 319-2668.
U.S. Ambassador in Nassau: J. Richard "Rick" Blankenship.
State Dept. Country Office: (202) 647-2621.

Bahrain

Ambassador: Shaikh Khalifa Bin Ali al-Khalifa.
Chancery: 3502 International Dr. N.W. 20008; (202) 342-1111; fax, (202) 362-2192.
U.S. Ambassador in Manama: Ronald E. Neumann.
State Dept. Country Office: (202) 647-6571.

Bangladesh

Ambassador: Syed Hasan Ahmad.
Chancery: 3510 International Dr. N.W. 20008; (202) 244-0183; fax, (202) 244-5366.
U.S. Ambassador in Dhaka: Mary Ann Peters.
State Dept. Country Office: (202) 647-9552.

Barbados

Ambassador: Michael King.
Chancery: 2144 Wyoming Ave. N.W. 20008; (202) 939-9200; fax, (202) 332-7467.
U.S. Ambassador in Bridgetown: Earl N. Phillips Jr.
State Dept. Country Office: (202) 647-2620.

Belarus

Chargé d'Affaires: Valentin Rybakov.
Chancery: 1619 New Hampshire Ave. N.W. 20009; (202) 986-1604; fax, (202) 986-1805.
U.S. Ambassador in Minsk: Michael G. Kozak.
State Dept. Country Office: (202) 736-4443.

Belgium

Ambassador: Franciskus Van Daele.
Chancery: 3330 Garfield St. N.W. 20008; (202) 333-6900; fax, (202) 333-3079.
U.S. Ambassador in Brussels: Stephen F. Brauer.
State Dept. Country Office: (202) 647-6592.

Belize

Ambassador: Lisa M. Shoman.
Chancery: 2535 Massachusetts Ave. N.W. 20008; (202) 332-9636; fax, (202) 332-6888.
U.S. Ambassador in Belize City: Russell F. Freeman.
State Dept. Country Office: (202) 647-3727.

Benin

Ambassador: Cyrille S. Oguin.
Chancery: 2124 Kalorama Rd. N.W. 20008; (202) 232-6656; fax, (202) 265-1996.
U.S. Ambassador in Cotonou: Pamela E. Bridgewater.
State Dept. Country Office: (202) 647-1596.

Bhutan

State Dept. Country Office: (202) 647-2141.

Bolivia

Chargé d'Affaires: Jaime Aparicio Otero.
Chancery: 3014 Massachusetts Ave. N.W. 20008; (202) 483-4410; fax, (202) 328-3712.
U.S. Ambassador in La Paz: V. Manuel Rocha.
State Dept. Country Office: (202) 647-3076.

Bosnia-Herzegovina

Ambassador: Igor Davidovic.
Chancery: 2109 E St. N.W. 20037; (202) 337-1500; fax, (202) 337-1502.

U.S. Ambassador in Sarajevo: Clifford G. Bond.
State Dept. Country Office: (202) 647-4195.

Botswana

Ambassador: Lapologang Caesar Lekoa.
Chancery: 1531-1533 New Hampshire Ave. N.W. 20036; (202) 244-4990; fax, (202) 244-4164.
U.S. Ambassador in Gaborone: Joseph Huggins.
State Dept. Country Office: (202) 647-9856.

Brazil

Ambassador: Rubens Barbosa.
Chancery: 3006 Massachusetts Ave. N.W. 20008; (202) 238-2700; fax, (202) 238-2827.
U.S. Ambassador in Brasilia: Donna J. Hrinak.
State Dept. Country Office: (202) 647-2407.

Brunei

Ambassador: Pengiran Anak Dato Puteh.
Chancery: 3520 International Court N.W. 20008; (202) 237-1838; fax, (202) 885-0560.
U.S. Ambassador in Bandar Seri Begawan: Gene B. Christy.
State Dept. Country Office: (202) 647-3276.

Bulgaria

Ambassador: Elena Poptodorova.
Chancery: 1621 22nd St. N.W. 20008; (202) 387-7969; fax, (202) 234-7973.
U.S. Ambassador in Sofia: James Pardew.
State Dept. Country Office: (202) 647-4850.

Burkina Faso

Ambassador: Tertius Zongo.
Chancery: 2340 Massachusetts Ave. N.W. 20008; (202) 332-5577; fax, (202) 667-1882.
U.S. Ambassador in Ouagadougou: J. Anthony Holmes.
State Dept. Country Office: (202) 647-1658.

Burma (See Myanmar)

Burundi

Ambassador: Antoine Ntamobwa.
Chancery: 2233 Wisconsin Ave. N.W., #212, 20007; (202) 342-2574; fax, (202) 342-2578.
U.S. Ambassador in Bujumbura: James Yellin.
State Dept. Country Office: (202) 647-4966.

Cambodia

Ambassador: Roland Eng.
Chancery: 4530 16th St. N.W. 20011; (202) 726-7742; fax, (202) 726-8381.
U.S. Ambassador in Phnom Penh: Charles Ray.
State Dept. Country Office: (202) 647-3095.

Cameroon

Ambassador: Jerome Mendouga.
Chancery: 2349 Massachusetts Ave. N.W. 20008; (202) 265-8790; fax, (202) 387-3826.
U.S. Ambassador in Yaounde: George M. Staples.
State Dept. Country Office: (202) 647-3138.

Canada

Ambassador: Michael Kergin.
Chancery: 501 Pennsylvania Ave. N.W. 20001; (202) 682-1740; fax, (202) 682-7701.
U.S. Ambassador in Ottawa: A. Paul Cellucci.
State Dept. Country Office: (202) 647-2170.

Cape Verde

Ambassador: Jose Brito.
Chancery: 3415 Massachusetts Ave. N.W. 20007; (202) 965-6820; fax, (202) 965-1207.
U.S. Ambassador in Praia: Donald C. Johnson.
State Dept. Country Office: (202) 647-0252.

Central African Republic

Ambassador: Emmanuel Touaboy.
Chancery: 1618 22nd St. N.W. 20008; (202) 483-7800; fax, (202) 332-9893.
U.S. Ambassador in Bangui: Mattie R. Sharpless.
State Dept. Country Office: (202) 647-2973.

Chad

Ambassador: Hassaballah Ahmat Soubiane.
Chancery: 2002 R St. N.W. 20009; (202) 462-4009; fax, (202) 265-1937.
U.S. Ambassador in N'Djamena: Christopher E. Goldthwait.
State Dept. Country Office: (202) 647-2973.

Chile

Ambassador: Andres Bianchi.
Chancery: 1732 Massachusetts Ave. N.W. 20036; (202) 785-1746; fax, (202) 887-5579.
U.S. Ambassador in Santiago: William R. Brownfield.
State Dept. Country Office: (202) 647-2296.

China

Ambassador: Yang Jiechi.
Chancery: 2300 Connecticut Ave. N.W. 20008; (202) 328-2500; fax, (202) 588-0032.
U.S. Ambassador in Beijing: Clark T. Randt Jr.
State Dept. Country Office: (202) 647-6803.

Colombia

Ambassador: Luis Alberto Moreno.
Chancery: 2118 Leroy Pl. N.W. 20008; (202) 387-8338; fax, (202) 232-8643.
U.S. Ambassador in Bogota: Anne W. Patterson.
State Dept. Country Office: (202) 647-3023.

Comoros

Ambassador: Vacant.
Chancery (U.N. Mission): 420 E. 50th St., New York, NY 10022; (212) 972-8010; fax, (212) 983-4712.
U.S. Ambassador: John Price.
State Dept. Country Office: (202) 736-4644.

Congo, Democratic Republic of the (Zaire)

Ambassador: Faida Mitifu.
Chancery: 1800 New Hampshire Ave. N.W. 20009; (202) 234-7690; fax, (202) 234-2609.
U.S. Ambassador in Kinshasa: Aubrey Hooks.
State Dept. Country Office: (202) 647-2216.

Congo, Republic of the

Ambassador: Serge Mombouli.
Chancery: 4891 Colorado Ave. N.W. 20011; (202) 726-5500; fax, (202) 726-1860.
U.S. Ambassador in Brazzaville: David H. Kaeuper.
State Dept. Country Office: (202) 647-1637.

Costa Rica

Ambassador: Jaime Daremblum.
Chancery: 2114 S St. N.W. 20008; (202) 234-2945; fax, (202) 265-4795.
U.S. Ambassador in San Jose: John Danilovich.
State Dept. Country Office: (202) 647-3518.

Côte d'Ivoire

Ambassador: Dago Pascal Kokora.
Chancery: 3421 Massachusetts Ave. N.W. 20007; (202) 797-0300; fax, (202) 462-9444.
U.S. Ambassador in Abidjan: Arlene Render.
State Dept. Country Office: (202) 647-1540.

Croatia

Ambassador: Ivan Grdesic.
Chancery: 2343 Massachusetts Ave. N.W. 20008; (202) 588-5899; fax, (202) 588-8936.
U.S. Ambassador in Zagreb: Lawrence G. Rossin.
State Dept. Country Office: (202) 647-1739.

Cuba

The United States severed diplomatic relations with Cuba in January 1961. Cuba's interests in the United States are represented by the Swiss embassy.
Cuban Interests Section: 2630 16th St. N.W. 20009; (202) 797-8518; fax, (202) 986-7283.
U.S. interests in Cuba are represented by the Swiss embassy: James C. Cason, U.S. principal officer in Havana.
State Dept. Country Office: (202) 647-9272.

Cyprus

Ambassador: Erato Kozakou Marcoullis.
Chancery: 2211 R St. N.W. 20008; (202) 462-5772; fax, (202) 483-6710.
U.S. Ambassador in Nicosia: Michael Klosson.
State Dept. Country Office: (202) 647-6112.

Czech Republic

Ambassador: Martin Palous.
Chancery: 3900 Spring of Freedom St. N.W. 20008; (202) 274-9100; fax, (202) 966-8540.
U.S. Ambassador in Prague: Craig R. Stapleton.
State Dept. Country Office: (202) 647-1457.

Denmark

Ambassador: Ulrik Federspiel.
Chancery: 3200 Whitehaven St. N.W. 20008; (202) 234-4300; fax, (202) 328-1470.
U.S. Ambassador in Copenhagen: Stuart A. Bernstein.
State Dept. Country Office: (202) 647-6582.

Djibouti

Ambassador: Roble Olhaye.
Chancery: 1156 15th St. N.W., #515, 20005; (202) 331-0270; fax, (202) 331-0302.
U.S. Ambassador in Djibouti: Donald Yamamoto.
State Dept. Country Office: (202) 647-8913.

Dominica

Ambassador: Vacant.

Chancery: 3216 New Mexico Ave. N.W. 20016; (202) 364-6781; fax, (202) 364-6791.

U.S. Ambassador: Earl N. Phillips Jr. (resident in Bridgetown, Barbados).

State Dept. Country Office: (202) 647-4384.

Dominican Republic

Ambassador: Hugo Guilliani Cury.

Chancery: 1715 22nd St. N.W. 20008; (202) 332-6280; fax, (202) 265-8057.

U.S. Ambassador in Santo Domingo: Hans Hertell.

State Dept. Country Office: (202) 736-4322.

Ecuador

Chargé d'Affaires: Carlos A. Jativa.

Chancery: 2535 15th St. N.W. 20009; (202) 234-7200; fax, (202) 667-3482.

U.S. Ambassador in Quito: Kristie A. Kenney.

State Dept. Country Office: (202) 647-3338.

Egypt

Ambassador: M. Nabil Fahmy.

Chancery: 3521 International Court N.W. 20008; (202) 895-5440; fax, (202) 244-4319.

U.S. Ambassador in Cairo: C. David Welch.

State Dept. Country Office: (202) 647-4259.

El Salvador

Ambassador: Rene A. León Rodriguez .

Chancery: 2308 California St. N.W. 20008; (202) 265-9671; fax, (202) 234-3834.

U.S. Ambassador in San Salvador: Rose M. Likins.

State Dept. Country Office: (202) 647-3505.

Equatorial Guinea

Ambassador: Teodoro Biyogo Nsue.

Chancery: 2020 16th St. N.W., #405, 20009; (202) 518-5700; fax, (202) 518-5252.

U.S. interests in Equitorial Guinea are represented by the U.S. embassy in Yaounde, Cameroon.

State Dept. Country Office: (202) 647-3138.

Eritrea

Ambassador: Girma Asmerom.

Chancery: 1708 New Hampshire Ave. N.W. 20009; (202) 319-1991; fax, (202) 319-1304.

U.S. Ambassador in Asmara: Donald J. McConnell.

State Dept. Country Office: (202) 736-4644.

Estonia

Ambassador: Sven Jürgenson.

Chancery: 1730 M St. N.W., #503, 20036; (202) 588-0101; fax, (202) 588-0108.

U.S. Ambassador in Tallinn: Joseph M. DeThomas.

State Dept. Country Office: (202) 647-8908.

Ethiopia

Ambassador: Ayele Kassahun.

Chancery: 3506 International Dr. N.W. 20008; (202) 364-1200; fax, (202) 686-9551.

U.S. Ambassador in Addis Ababa: Aurelia B. Brazeal.

State Dept. Country Office: (202) 736-4679.

Fiji

Ambassador: Anare Jale.

Chancery: 2233 Wisconsin Ave. N.W., #240, 20007; (202) 337-8320; fax, (202) 337-1996.

U.S. Ambassador in Suva: David Lyon.

State Dept. Country Office: (202) 736-4683.

Finland

Ambassador: Jukka Valtasaari.

Chancery: 3301 Massachusetts Ave. N.W. 20008; (202) 298-5800; fax, (202) 298-6030.

U.S. Ambassador in Helsinki: Bonnie McElveen-Hunter.

State Dept. Country Office: (202) 647-8431.

France

Ambassador: Jean-David Levitte.

Chancery: 4101 Reservoir Rd. N.W. 20007; (202) 944-6000; fax, (202) 944-6166.

U.S. Ambassador in Paris: Howard H. Leach.

State Dept. Country Office: (202) 647-3072.

Gabon

Ambassador: Jules-Marius Ogouebandja.

Chancery: 2034 20th St. N.W., #200, 20009; (202) 797-1000; fax, (202) 332-0668.

U.S. Ambassador in Libreville: Kenneth P. Moorefield.

State Dept. Country Office: (202) 647-1637.

Gambia, The

Ambassador: Essa Bokarr Sey.

Chancery: 1155 15th St. N.W., #1000, 20005; (202) 785-1399; fax, (202) 785-1430.

U.S. Ambassador in Banjul: Jackson C. McDonald.

State Dept. Country Office: (202) 647-3407.

Georgia

Ambassador: Levan Mikeladze.
Chancery: 1615 New Hampshire Ave. N.W., #300, 20009; (202) 387-2390; fax, (202) 393-4537.
U.S. Ambassador in Tbilisi: Richard M. Miles.
State Dept. Country Office: (202) 647-6795.

Germany

Ambassador: Wolfgang Ischinger.
Chancery: 4645 Reservoir Rd. N.W. 20007; (202) 298-4000; fax, (202) 298-4249.
U.S. Ambassador in Berlin: Daniel R. Coats.
State Dept. Country Office: (202) 647-2005.

Ghana

Ambassador: Alan Kyerematen.
Chancery: 3512 International Dr. N.W. 20008; (202) 686-4520; fax, (202) 686-4527.
U.S. Ambassador in Accra: Vacant.
State Dept. Country Office: (202) 647-1569.

Greece

Ambassador: George Savvaides.
Chancery: 2221 Massachusetts Ave. N.W. 20008; (202) 939-1300; fax, (202) 939-1324.
U.S. Ambassador in Athens: Thomas J. Miller.
State Dept. Country Office: (202) 647-6113.

Grenada

Ambassador: Denis G. Antoine.
Chancery: 1701 New Hampshire Ave. N.W. 20009; (202) 265-2561; fax, (202) 265-2468.
U.S. Ambassador: Earl N. Phillips Jr. (resident in Bridgetown, Barbados).
State Dept. Country Office: (202) 647-2621.

Guatemala

Ambassador: Antonio Arenales Forno.
Chancery: 2220 R St. N.W. 20008; (202) 745-4952; fax, (202) 745-1908.
U.S. Ambassador in Guatemala City: John R. Hamilton.
State Dept. Country Office: (202) 647-3559.

Guinea

Ambassador: Alpha Oumar Rafiou Barry.
Chancery: 2112 Leroy Pl. N.W. 20008; (202) 483-9420; fax, (202) 483-8688.
U.S. Ambassador in Conakry: R. Barrie Walkley.
State Dept. Country Office: (202) 647-1658.

Guinea-Bissau

Chargé d'Affaires: Henrique Adriano Da Silva.
Chancery: P.O. Box 33813, Rockville, MD 20033; (301) 947-3958; fax, (301) 947-3958.
The U.S. embassy in Bissau suspended operations in June 1998.
State Dept. Country Office: (202) 647-1540.

Guyana

Ambassador: Mohammed Ali Odeen Ishmael.
Chancery: 2490 Tracy Pl. N.W. 20008; (202) 265-6900; fax, (202) 232-1297.
U.S. Ambassador in Georgetown: Ronald Godard.
State Dept. Country Office: (202) 647-2621.

Haiti

Chargé d'Affaires: Harry Frantz Léo.
Chancery: 2311 Massachusetts Ave. N.W. 20008; (202) 332-4090; fax, (202) 745-7215.
U.S. Ambassador in Port-au-Prince: Brian Dean Curran.
State Dept. Country Office: (202) 736-4707.

The Holy See

Ambassador: The Most Reverend Gabriele Montalvo, apostolic nuncio.
Office: 3339 Massachusetts Ave. N.W. 20008; (202) 333-7121; fax, (202) 337-4036.
U.S. Ambassador in Vatican City: Jim Nicholson.
State Dept. Country Office: (202) 647-3072.

Honduras

Ambassador: Mario M. Canahuati.
Chancery: 3007 Tilden St. N.W., #4-M, 20008; (202) 966-7702; fax, (202) 966-9751.
U.S. Ambassador in Tegucigalpa: Larry L. Palmer.
State Dept. Country Office: (202) 647-0087.

Hungary

Ambassador: Andras Simonyi.
Chancery: 3910 Shoemaker St. N.W. 20008; (202) 362-6730; fax, (202) 966-8135.
U.S. Ambassador in Budapest: Nancy Goodman Brinker.
State Dept. Country Office: (202) 647-3238.

Iceland

Ambassador: Helgi Agustsson.
Chancery: 1156 15th St. N.W., #1200, 20005; (202) 265-6653; fax, (202) 265-6656.

U.S. Ambassador in Reykjavik: James I. Gadsden.
State Dept. Country Office: (202) 647-8378.

India

Ambassador: Lalit Mansingh.
Chancery: 2107 Massachusetts Ave. N.W. 20008; (202) 939-7000; fax, (202) 483-3972.
U.S. Ambassador in New Delhi: Robert D. Blackwill.
State Dept. Country Office: (202) 647-2141.

Indonesia

Ambassador: Soemadi D. M. Brotodiningrat.
Chancery: 2020 Massachusetts Ave. N.W. 20036; (202) 775-5200; fax, (202) 775-5365.
U.S. Ambassador in Jakarta: Ralph Boyce.
State Dept. Country Office: (202) 647-1221.

Iran

The United States severed diplomatic relations with Iran in April 1980. Iran's interests in the United States are represented by the Pakistani embassy.
Iranian Interests Section: 2209 Wisconsin Ave. N.W. 20007; (202) 965-4990; fax, (202) 965-1073.
U.S. interests in Iran are represented by the Swiss embassy in Tehran.
State Dept. Country Office: (202) 647-6111.

Iraq

The United States severed diplomatic relations with Iraq in February 1991. Iraq's interests in the United States are represented by the Algerian embassy.
Iraqi Interests Section: 1801 P St. N.W. 20036; (202) 483-7500; fax, (202) 462-5066.
The U.S. embassy in Baghdad is temporarily closed.
State Dept. Country Office: (202) 647-5692.

Ireland

Ambassador: Noel Fahey.
Chancery: 2234 Massachusetts Ave. N.W. 20008; (202) 462-3939; fax, (202) 232-5993.
U.S. Ambassador in Dublin: Richard J. Egan.
State Dept. Country Office: (202) 647-8027.

Israel

Ambassador: Daniel Ayalon.
Chancery: 3514 International Dr. N.W. 20008; (202) 364-5500; fax, (202) 364-5607.
U.S. Ambassador in Tel Aviv: Daniel C. Kurtzer.
State Dept. Country Office: (202) 647-3672.

Italy

Ambassador: Ferdinando Salleo.
Chancery: 3000 Whitehaven St. N.W. 20008; (202) 612-4400; fax, (202) 518-2151.
U.S. Ambassador in Rome: Melvin F. Sembler.
State Dept. Country Office: (202) 647-3746.

Jamaica

Ambassador: Seymour Mullings.
Chancery: 1520 New Hampshire Ave. N.W. 20036; (202) 452-0660; fax, (202) 452-0081.
U.S. Ambassador in Kingston: Sue M. Cobb.
State Dept. Country Office: (202) 647-2620.

Japan

Ambassador: Ryozo Kato.
Chancery: 2520 Massachusetts Ave. N.W. 20008; (202) 238-6700; fax, (202) 328-2187.
U.S. Ambassador in Tokyo: Howard H. Baker Jr.
State Dept. Country Office: (202) 647-3152.

Jordan

Ambassador: Karim Kawar.
Chancery: 3504 International Dr. N.W. 20008; (202) 966-2664; fax, (202) 966-3110.
U.S. Ambassador in Amman: Edward W. Gnehm Jr.
State Dept. Country Office: (202) 647-1022.

Kazakhstan

Ambassador: Kanat Saudabayev.
Chancery: 1401 16th St. N.W. 20036; (202) 232-5488; fax, (202) 232-5845.
U.S. Ambassador in Almaty: Larry C. Napper.
State Dept. Country Office: (202) 647-6859.

Kenya

Ambassador: Yusuf Abdulrahman Nzibo.
Chancery: 2249 R St. N.W. 20008; (202) 387-6101; fax, (202) 462-3829.
U.S. Ambassador in Nairobi: Johnnie Carson.
State Dept. Country Office: (202) 647-6473.

Kiribati

U.S. Ambassador in Majuro: Michael J. Senko.
State Dept. Country Office: (202) 736-4712.

Korea, Democratic People's Republic of (North)

Ambassador: LI Hyong Chol.

U.N. Mission: 820 E. 2nd Ave., 13th Floor, New York, NY 10017; (212) 972-3105; fax, (212) 972-3154.
State Dept. Country Office: (202) 647-7717.

Korea, Republic of (South)

Ambassador: Hang Sung Joo.
Chancery: 2450 Massachusetts Ave. N.W. 20008; (202) 939-5600; fax, (202) 797-0595.
U.S. Ambassador in Seoul: Thomas C. Hubbard.
State Dept. Country Office: (202) 647-7717.

Kuwait

Ambassador: Sheik Salem Abdullah Al-Jaber Al-Sabah.
Chancery: 2940 Tilden St. N.W. 20008; (202) 966-0702; fax, (202) 966-0517.
U.S. Ambassador in Kuwait City: Richard H. Jones.
State Dept. Country Office: (202) 647-6571.

Kyrgyzstan

Ambassador: Baktybek Abdrissaev.
Chancery: 1732 Wisconsin Ave. N.W. 20007; (202) 338-5141; fax, (202) 338-5139.
U.S. Ambassador in Bishkek: Stephen Young.
State Dept. Country Office: (202) 647-6740.

Laos

Ambassador: Phanthong Phommahaxay.
Chancery: 2222 S St. N.W. 20008; (202) 332-6416; fax, (202) 332-4923.
U.S. Ambassador in Vientiane: Douglas A. Hartwick.
State Dept. Country Office: (202) 647-2036.

Latvia

Ambassador: Aivis Ronis.
Chancery: 4325 17th St. N.W. 20011; (202) 726-8213; fax, (202) 726-6785.
U.S. Ambassador in Riga: Brian E. Carlson.
State Dept. Country Office: (202) 647-8908.

Lebanon

Ambassador: Farid Abboud.
Chancery: 2560 28th St. N.W. 20008; (202) 939-6320; fax, (202) 939-6324.
U.S. Ambassador in Beirut: Vincent M. Battle.
State Dept. Country Office: (202) 647-1030.

Lesotho

Ambassador: Molelekeng Rapolaki.
Chancery: 2511 Massachusetts Ave. N.W. 20008; (202) 797-5533; fax, (202) 234-6815.

U.S. Ambassador in Maseru: Robert G. Loftis.
State Dept. Country Office: (202) 647-9855.

Liberia

Chargé d'Affaires: Aaron B. Kollie.
Chancery: 5201 16th St. N.W. 20011; (202) 723-0437; fax, (202) 723-0436.
U.S. Ambassador in Monrovia: John W. Blaney.
State Dept. Country Office: (202) 647-0252.

Libya

The United States severed diplomatic relations with Libya in May 1980. Libya's interests in the United States are represented by the embassy of the United Arab Emirates.
Libyan Interests Section: 500 New Hampshire Ave. N.W. 20037; (202) 338-6500; fax, (202) 337-7029.
State Dept. Country Office: (202) 647-4674.

Liechtenstein

Ambassador: Claudia Fritsche.
Chancery: 1300 Eye St. N.W., #550W, 20005; (202) 216-0460; fax, (202) 216-0459.
U.S. Ambassador: Mercer Reynolds (resident in Bern, Switzerland).
State Dept. Country Office: (202) 647-0425.

Lithuania

Ambassador: Vygaudas Usackas.
Chancery: 2622 16th St. N.W. 20009; (202) 234-5860; fax, (202) 328-0466.
U.S. Ambassador in Vilnius: John F. Tefft.
State Dept. Country Office: (202) 647-8378.

Luxembourg

Ambassador: Arlette Conzemius.
Chancery: 2200 Massachusetts Ave. N.W. 20008; (202) 265-4171; fax, (202) 328-8270.
U.S. Ambassador in Luxembourg: Peter Terpeluk Jr.
State Dept. Country Office: (202) 647-6557.

Macedonia, Former Yugoslav Republic of

Ambassador: Nikola Dimitrov.
Chancery: 1101 30th St. N.W., #302, 20007; (202) 337-3063; fax, (202) 337-3093.
U.S. Ambassador in Skopje: Lawrence E. Butler.
State Dept. Country Office: (202) 647-2452.

Madagascar

Ambassador: Narisoa Rajaonarivony.
Chancery: 2374 Massachusetts Ave. N.W. 20008; (202) 265-5525; fax, (202) 265-3034.
U.S. Ambassador in Antananarivo: Wanda L. Nesbitt.
State Dept. Country Office: (202) 647-6453.

Malawi

Ambassador: Tony Kandiero.
Chancery: 2408 Massachusetts Ave. N.W. 20008; (202) 797-1007; fax, (202) 265-0976.
U.S. Ambassador in Lilongwe: Steven Browning (nominee).
State Dept. Country Office: (202) 647-9838.

Malaysia

Ambassador: Dato Sheikh Abdul Khalid Ghazzali.
Chancery: 3516 International Court N.W. 20008; (202) 572-9700; fax, (202) 572-9882.
U.S. Ambassador in Kuala Lumpur: Marie T. Huhtala.
State Dept. Country Office: (202) 647-3276.

Maldives

Ambassador: Hussain Shihab.
Chancery (U.N. Mission): 800 2nd Ave., #400E, New York, NY 10017; (212) 599-6195; fax, (212) 661-6405.
U.S. Ambassador: Jeffrey Lunstead (nominee; will reside in Colombo, Sri Lanka).
State Dept. Country Office: (202) 647-2351.

Mali

Chargé d'Affaires: Mahamane E. Bania Toure.
Chancery: 2130 R St. N.W. 20008; (202) 332-2249; fax, (202) 332-6603.
U.S. Ambassador in Bamako: Vicki Huddleston.
State Dept. Country Office: (202) 647-1658.

Malta

Ambassador: John Lowell.
Chancery: 2017 Connecticut Ave. N.W. 20008; (202) 462-3611; fax, (202) 387-5470.
U.S. Ambassador in Valletta: Anthony H. Gioia.
State Dept. Country Office: (202) 647-3746.

Marshall Islands

Ambassador: Banny De Brum.
Chancery: 2433 Massachusetts Ave. N.W. 20008; (202) 234-5414; fax, (202) 232-3236.
U.S. Ambassador: Michael J. Senko (resident in Majuro, Kiribati).
State Dept. Country Office: (202) 736-4712.

Mauritania

Ambassador: Mohamedou Ould Michel.
Chancery: 2129 Leroy Pl. N.W. 20008; (202) 232-5700; fax, (202) 319-2623.
U.S. Ambassador in Nouakchott: John W. Limbert.
State Dept. Country Office: (202) 647-3407.

Mauritius

Ambassador: Usha Jeetah.
Chancery: 4301 Connecticut Ave. N.W., #441, 20008; (202) 244-1491; fax, (202) 966-0983.
U.S. Ambassador in Port Louis: John Price.
State Dept. Country Office: (202) 736-4644.

Mexico

Ambassador: Juan Jose Bremer-Martino.
Chancery: 1911 Pennsylvania Ave. N.W. 20006; (202) 728-1600; fax, (202) 728-1698.
U.S. Ambassador in Mexico City: Antonio O. Garza Jr.
State Dept. Country Office: (202) 647-9894.

Micronesia

Ambassador: Jesse B. Marehalau.
Chancery: 1725 N St. N.W. 20036; (202) 223-4383; fax, (202) 223-4391.
U.S. Ambassador in Kolonia: Larry Miles Dinger.
State Dept. Country Office: (202) 736-4712.

Moldova

Ambassador: Mihail Manoli.
Chancery: 2101 S St. N.W. 20008; (202) 667-1130; fax, (202) 667-1204.
U.S. Ambassador in Chisinau: Pamela Hyde Smith.
State Dept. Country Office: (202) 647-6733.

Monaco

Consul: Maguy Maccario-Doyle.
Chancery (consulate): 565 5th Ave., 23rd Floor, New York, NY 10017; (212) 286-0500; fax, (212) 286-1574.
Relations with Monaco are maintained by the U.S. embassy in Paris, France: Howard H. Leach, U.S. ambassador in Paris.
State Dept. Country Office: (202) 647-3072.

Mongolia

Ambassador: Bold Ravdan.
Chancery: 2833 M St. N.W. 20007; (202) 333-7117; fax, (202) 298-9227.
U.S. Ambassador in Ulaanbaatar: John Dinger.
State Dept. Country Office: (202) 647-6803.

Morocco

Ambassador: Aziz Mekouar.
Chancery: 1601 21st St. N.W. 20009; (202) 462-7979; fax, (202) 265-0161.
U.S. Ambassador in Rabat: Margaret Tutwiler.
State Dept. Country Office: (202) 647-1724.

Mozambique

Ambassador: Armando Alexandre Panguene.
Chancery: 1990 M St. N.W., #570, 20036; (202) 293-7146; fax, (202) 835-0245.
U.S. Ambassador in Maputo: Sharon Wilkinson.
State Dept. Country Office: (202) 647-9857.

Myanmar (Burma)

Ambassador: U. Linn Myaing.
Chancery: 2300 S St. N.W. 20008; (202) 332-9044; fax, (202) 332-9046.
U.S. Chargé d'Affaires in Rangoon: Carmen M. Martinez.
State Dept. Country Office: (202) 647-3132.

Namibia

Ambassador: Leonard Nangolo Lipumbu.
Chancery: 1605 New Hampshire Ave. N.W. 20009; (202) 986-0540; fax, (202) 986-0443.
U.S. Ambassador in Windhoek: Kevin Joseph McGuire.
State Dept. Country Office: (202) 647-9855.

Nauru

U.S. Ambassador: David Lyon (resident in Suva, Fiji).
State Dept. Country Office: (202) 736-4683.

Nepal

Ambassador: Jai P. Rana.
Chancery: 2131 Leroy Pl. N.W. 20008; (202) 667-4550; fax, (202) 667-5534.
U.S. Ambassador in Kathmandu: Michael E. Malinowski.
State Dept. Country Office: (202) 647-1450.

Netherlands

Ambassador: Boudewijn Van Eenennaam.
Chancery: 4200 Linnean Ave. N.W. 20008; (202) 244-5300; fax, (202) 362-3430.
U.S. Ambassador at The Hague: Clifford M. Sobel.
State Dept. Country Office: (202) 647-2620.

New Zealand

Ambassador: John Wood.
Chancery: 37 Observatory Circle N.W. 20008; (202) 328-4800; fax, (202) 667-5227.
U.S. Ambassador in Wellington: Charles J. Swindells.
State Dept. Country Office: (202) 736-4745.

Nicaragua

Ambassador: Carlos J. Ulvert Sanchez.
Chancery: 1627 New Hampshire Ave. N.W. 20009; (202) 939-6570; fax, (202) 939-6545.
U.S. Ambassador in Managua: Barbara C. Moore.
State Dept. Country Office: (202) 647-1510.

Niger

Ambassador: Joseph Diatta.
Chancery: 2204 R St. N.W. 20008; (202) 483-4224; fax, (202) 483-3169.
U.S. Ambassador in Niamey: Dennise Mathieu.
State Dept. Country Office: (202) 647-1596.

Nigeria

Ambassador: Jibril Muhammad Aminu.
Chancery: 1333 16th St. N.W. 20036; (202) 986-8400; (202) 775-1385.
U.S. Ambassador in Abuja: Howard Jeter.
State Dept. Country Office: (202) 647-3469.

Norway

Ambassador: Knut Vollebaek.
Chancery: 2720 34th St. N.W. 20008; (202) 333-6000; fax, (202) 337-0870.
U.S. Ambassador in Oslo: John Doyle Ong.
State Dept. Country Office: (202) 647-6582.

Oman

Ambassador: Mohamed Ali Al-Khusaiby.
Chancery: 2535 Belmont Rd. N.W. 20008; (202) 387-1980; fax, (202) 745-4933.
U.S. Ambassador in Muscat: Richard L. Baltimore III.
State Dept. Country Office: (202) 647-6558.

Pakistan

Ambassador: Ashraf Jehangir Qazi.
Chancery: 2315 Massachusetts Ave. N.W. 20008; (202) 939-6200; fax, (202) 387-0484.
U.S. Ambassador in Islamabad: Nancy J. Powell.
State Dept. Country Office: (202) 647-9823.

Palau

Ambassador: Hersey Kyota.
Chancery: 1150 18th St. N.W., #750, 20036; (202) 452-6814; fax, (202) 452-6281.
U.S. Ambassador in Koror: Francis J. Ricciardone Jr.
State Dept. Country Office: (202) 647-5239.

Panama

Ambassador: Roberto Alfaro.
Chancery: 2862 McGill Terrace N.W. 20008; (202) 483-1407; fax, (202) 483-8416.
U.S. Ambassador in Panama City: Linda Ellen Watt.
State Dept. Country Office: (202) 647-4161.

Papua New Guinea

Chargé d'Affaires: Graham Michael.
Chancery: 1779 Massachusetts Ave. N.W., #805, 20036; (202) 745-3680; fax, (202) 745-3679.
U.S. Ambassador in Port Moresby: Susan S. Jacobs.
State Dept. Country Office: (202) 647-5239.

Paraguay

Ambassador: Leila Teresa Rachid Cowles.
Chancery: 2400 Massachusetts Ave. N.W. 20008; (202) 483-6960; fax, (202) 234-4508.
U.S. Ambassador in Asunción: John Keane.
State Dept. Country Office: (202) 647-2296.

Peru

Ambassador: Robert Danino.
Chancery: 1700 Massachusetts Ave. N.W. 20036; (202) 833-9860; fax, (202) 659-8124.
U.S. Ambassador in Lima: John R. Dawson.
State Dept. Country Office: (202) 647-4177.

Philippines

Ambassador: Albert F. Del Rosario.
Chancery: 1600 Massachusetts Ave. N.W. 20036; (202) 467-9300; fax, (202) 467-9417.
U.S. Ambassador in Manila: Francis J. Ricciardone.
State Dept. Country Office: (202) 647-3276.

Poland

Ambassador: Przemyslaw Grudzinski.
Chancery: 2640 16th St. N.W. 20009; (202) 234-3800; fax, (202) 328-6271.
U.S. Ambassador in Warsaw: Christopher R. Hill.
State Dept. Country Office: (202) 647-4139.

Portugal

Ambassador: Pedro Catarino.
Chancery: 2125 Kalorama Rd. N.W. 20008; (202) 328-8610; fax, (202) 462-3726.
U.S. Ambassador in Lisbon: John N. Palmer.
State Dept. Country Office: (202) 647-3746.

Qatar

Ambassador: Bader Omar Al-Dafa.
Chancery: 4200 Wisconsin Ave. N.W. 20016; (202) 274-1600; fax, (202) 237-0061.
U.S. Ambassador in Doha: Maureen Quinn.
State Dept. Country Office: (202) 647-6572.

Romania

Ambassador: Sorin Ducaru.
Chancery: 1607 23rd St. N.W. 20008; (202) 332-4846; fax, (202) 232-4748.
U.S. Ambassador in Bucharest: Michael E. Guest.
State Dept. Country Office: (202) 647-4272.

Russia

Ambassador: Yury Viktorovich Ushakov.
Chancery: 2650 Wisconsin Ave. N.W. 20007; (202) 298-5700; fax, (202) 298-5735.
U.S. Ambassador in Moscow: Alexander Vershbow.
State Dept. Country Office: (202) 647-9806.

Rwanda

Ambassador: Richard Sezibera.
Chancery: 1714 New Hampshire Ave. N.W. 20009; (202) 232-2882; fax, (202) 232-4544.
U.S. Ambassador in Kigali: Margaret K. McMillion.
State Dept. Country Office: (202) 647-2973.

Saint Kitts and Nevis

Ambassador: Izben Cordinal Williams.
Chancery: 3216 New Mexico Ave. N.W. 20016; (202) 686-2636; fax, (202) 686-5740.
U.S. Ambassador: Earl N. Phillips Jr. (resident in Bridgetown, Barbados).
State Dept. Country Office: (202) 647-2130.

Saint Lucia

Ambassador: Sonia Merlyn Johnny.
Chancery: 3216 New Mexico Ave. N.W. 20016; (202) 364-6792; fax, (202) 364-6728.
U.S. Ambassador: Earl N. Phillips Jr. (resident in Bridgetown, Barbados).
State Dept. Country Office: (202) 647-2130.

Saint Vincent and the Grenadines

Ambassador: Ellsworth I. A. John.
Chancery: 3216 New Mexico Ave. N.W. 20016; (202) 364-6730; fax, (202) 364-6736.
U.S. Ambassador: Earl N. Phillips Jr. (resident in Bridgetown, Barbados).
State Dept. Country Office: (202) 647-2130.

Samoa

Ambassador: Tuiloma Neroni Slade.
Chancery (U.N. Mission): 800 2nd Ave., #400D, New York, NY 10017; (212) 599-6196; fax, (212) 599-0797.
U.S. Ambassador: Charles J. Swindells (resident in Wellington, New Zealand).
State Dept. Country Office: (202) 736-4745.

San Marino

Consul: Sheila Rabb Weidenfeld, 1899 L St. N.W., #1160, 20036; (202) 223-3517.
Relations with San Marino are maintained by the U.S. consulate in Florence, Italy: Daria De Pierre-Hollowell, U.S. consul general.
State Dept. Country Office: (202) 647-3072.

São Tomé and Principe

Chargé d'Affaires: Domingos Ferreira.
Chancery (U.N. Mission): 122 E. 42nd St., #1604, New York, NY 10168; (212) 697-4211; fax, (212) 687-8389.
U.S. Ambassador in Libreville: Kenneth P. Moorefield.
State Dept. Country Office: (202) 647-1637.

Saudi Arabia

Ambassador: Prince Bandar Bin Sultan Bin Abdul Aziz.
Chancery: 601 New Hampshire Ave. N.W. 20037; (202) 342-3800; fax, (202) 944-3113.
U.S. Ambassador in Riyadh: Robert W. Jordan.
State Dept. Country Office: (202) 647-7550.

Senegal

Ambassador: Amadou Lamine Ba.
Chancery: 2112 Wyoming Ave. N.W. 20008; (202) 234-0540; fax, (202) 332-6315.
U.S. Ambassador in Dakar: Richard Allan Roth.
State Dept. Country Office: (202) 647-1540.

Serbia-Montenegro (See Yugoslavia)

Seychelles

Ambassador: Claude Morel.
Chancery (U.N. Mission): 800 2nd Ave., #400C, New York, NY 10017; (212) 972-1785; fax, (212) 972-1786.
U.S. Ambassador: John Price (resident in Port Louis, Mauritius).
State Dept. Country Office: (202) 736-4644.

Sierra Leone

Chargé d'Affaires: Hassan Mohamed Conteh.
Chancery: 1701 19th St. N.W. 20009; (202) 939-9261; fax, (202) 483-1793.
U.S. Ambassador in Freetown: Pete R. Chaveas.
State Dept. Country Office: (202) 647-2214.

Singapore

Ambassador: Chan Heng Chee.
Chancery: 3501 International Pl. N.W. 20008; (202) 537-3100; fax, (202) 537-0876.
U.S. Ambassador in Singapore: Franklin L. Lavin.
State Dept. Country Office: (202) 647-3276.

Slovak Republic

Ambassador: Martin Butora.
Chancery: 3523 International Court N.W., 20008; (202) 237-1054; fax, (202) 237-6438.
U.S. Ambassador in Bratislava: Ronald Weiser.
State Dept. Country Office: (202) 647-3191.

Slovenia

Ambassador: Davorin Kracun.
Chancery: 1525 New Hampshire Ave. N.W. 20036; (202) 667-5363; fax, (202) 667-4563.
U.S. Ambassador in Ljubljana: Johnny Young.
State Dept. Country Office: (202) 736-7152.

Solomon Islands

Chargé d'Affaires: Jeremiah Manele.

Chancery (U.N. Mission): 800 2nd Ave., #400L, New York, NY 10017; (212) 599-6192; fax, (212) 661-8925.
U.S. Ambassador: Susan S. Jacobs (resident in Port Moresby, Papua New Guinea).
State Dept. Country Office: (202) 736-4745.

Somalia

Washington embassy ceased operations May 1991. The U.S. embassy in Mogadishu is unstaffed.
State Dept. Country Office: (202) 647-8913.

South Africa

Chargé d'Affaires: Ronald Thandabantu G. Nhlapo.
Chancery: 3051 Massachusetts Ave. N.W. 20008; (202) 232-4400; fax, (202) 265-1607.
U.S. Ambassador in Pretoria: Cameron R. Hume.
State Dept. Country Office: (202) 647-9862.

Spain

Ambassador: Francisco Javier Ruperez-Rubio.
Chancery: 2375 Pennsylvania Ave. N.W. 20037; (202) 452-0100; fax, (202) 833-5670.
U.S. Ambassador in Madrid: George L. Argyros Sr.
State Dept. Country Office: (202) 647-3746.

Sri Lanka

Ambassador: Devinda Rohan Subasinghe.
Chancery: 2148 Wyoming Ave. N.W. 20008; (202) 483-4025; fax, (202) 232-7181.
U.S. Ambassador in Colombo: Jeffrey Lunstead (nominee).
State Dept. Country Office: (202) 647-2351.

Sudan

Chargé d'Affaires: Khidir Haroun Ahmed.
Chancery: 2210 Massachusetts Ave. N.W. 20008; (202) 338-8565; fax, (202) 667-2406.
U.S. Chargé d'Affaires in Khartoum: Jeffrey Millington.
State Dept. Country Office: (202) 647-4084.

Suriname

Ambassador: Henry Lothar Illes.
Chancery: 4301 Connecticut Ave. N.W., #460, 20008; (202) 244-7488; fax, (202) 244-5878.
U.S. Ambassador in Paramaribo: Daniel Johnson.
State Dept. Country Office: (202) 647-2620.

Swaziland

Ambassador: Mary M. Kanya.

Chancery: 1712 New Hampshire Ave. N.W. 20009; (202) 234-5002; fax, (202) 234-8254.
U.S. Ambassador in Mbabane: James D. McGee.
State Dept. Country Office: (202) 647-8434.

Sweden

Ambassador: Jan Eliasson.
Chancery: 1501 M St. N.W. 20005-1702; (202) 467-2600; fax, (202) 467-2699.
U.S. Ambassador in Stockholm: Charles A. Heimbold Jr.
State Dept. Country Office: (202) 647-8431.

Switzerland

Ambassador: Christian Blickenstorfer.
Chancery: 2900 Cathedral Ave. N.W. 20008; (202) 745-7900; fax, (202) 387-2564.
U.S. Ambassador in Bern: Mercer Reynolds.
State Dept. Country Office: (202) 647-0425.

Syria

Ambassador: Rostom Al-Zoubi.
Chancery: 2215 Wyoming Ave. N.W. 20008; (202) 232-6313; fax, (202) 234-9548.
U.S. Ambassador in Damascus: Theodore H. Kattouf.
State Dept. Country Office: (202) 647-1131.

Taiwan

Representation is maintained by the Taipei Economic and Cultural Representatives Office in the United States: 4201 Wisconsin Ave. N.W. 20016; (202) 895-1800.
The United States maintains unofficial relations with Taiwan through the American Institute in Taiwan: 1700 N. Moore St., Arlington, VA 22209-1996; (703) 525-8474; Therese Shaheen, Managing Director.
State Dept. Country Office: (202) 647-7711.

Tajikistan

Ambassador: Rashid Alimov.
U.S. Ambassador: Franklin P. Huddle (resident in Almaty, Kazakhstan).
State Dept. Country Office: (202) 647-6757.

Tanzania

Ambassador: Andrew Mhando Daraja.
Chancery: 2139 R St. N.W. 20008; (202) 939-6125; fax, (202) 797-7408.
U.S. Ambassador in Dar es Salaam: Robert V. Royall.
State Dept. Country Office: (202) 647-8284.

Thailand

Ambassador: Sakthip Krairiksh.
Chancery: 1024 Wisconsin Ave. N.W. 20007; (202) 944-3600; fax, (202) 944-3611.
U.S. Ambassador in Bangkok: Darryl N. Johnson.
State Dept. Country Office: (202) 647-3132.

Togo

Ambassador: Akoussoulelou Bodjona.
Chancery: 2208 Massachusetts Ave. N.W. 20008; (202) 234-4212; fax, (202) 232-3190.
U.S. Ambassador in Lomé: Karl W. Hofman.
State Dept. Country Office: (202) 647-2214.

Tonga

Ambassador: Akosita Fineanganofo (resident in London, England; Tonga does not have an embassy in the United States).
U.S. Ambassador: David Lyon (resident in Suva, Fiji).
State Dept. Country Office: (202) 736-4683.

Trinidad and Tobago

Ambassador: Marina Annette Valere.
Chancery: 1708 Massachusetts Ave. N.W. 20036; (202) 467-6490; fax, (202) 785-3130.
U.S. Ambassador in Port-of-Spain: Roy L. Austin.
State Dept. Country Office: (202) 647-2621.

Tunisia

Ambassador: Hatem Atallah.
Chancery: 1515 Massachusetts Ave. N.W. 20005; (202) 862-1850; fax, (202) 862-1858.
U.S. Ambassador in Tunis: Ronald Schlicher (nominee).
State Dept. Country Office: (202) 647-4371.

Turkey

Ambassador: O. Faruk Logoglu.
Chancery: 2525 Massachusetts Ave. N.W. 20008; (202) 612-6700; fax, (202) 612-6744.
U.S. Ambassador in Ankara: W. Robert Pearson.
State Dept. Country Office: (202) 647-6113.

Turkmenistan

Ambassador: Meret Bairamovich Orazov.
Chancery: 2207 Massachusetts Ave. N.W. 20008; (202) 588-1500; fax, (202) 588-0697.
U.S. Ambassador in Ashgabat: Laura E. Kennedy.
State Dept. Country Office: (202) 647-6859.

Tuvalu

Ambassador: David Lyon (resident in Suva, Fiji).
State Dept. Country Office: (202) 736-4683.

Uganda

Ambassador: Edith G. Ssempala.
Chancery: 5911 16th St. N.W. 20011; (202) 726-7100; fax, (202) 726-1727.
U.S. Ambassador in Kampala: Jimmy Kolker.
State Dept. Country Office: (202) 647-6453.

Ukraine

Ambassador: Kostyantyn Gryshchenko.
Chancery: 3350 M St. N.W. 20007; (202) 333-0606; fax, (202) 333-0817.
U.S. Ambassador in Kiev: Carlos Pascual.
State Dept. Country Office: (202) 647-8671.

United Arab Emirates

Ambassador: Al Asri Saeed Al Dhahri.
Chancery: 1255 22nd St. N.W., #700, 20037; (202) 243-2400; fax, (202) 243-2432.
U.S. Ambassador in Abu Dhabi: Marcelle M. Wahba.
State Dept. Country Office: (202) 647-6572.

United Kingdom

Chargé d'Affaires: Anthony Brenton.
Chancery: 3100 Massachusetts Ave. N.W. 20008; (202) 588-6500; fax, (202) 588-7870.
U.S. Ambassador in London: William S. Farish.
State Dept. Country Office: (202) 647-8027.

Uruguay

Ambassador: Hugo Fernandez Faingold.
Chancery: 2715 M St. N.W. 20007; (202) 331-1313; fax, (202) 331-8142.
U.S. Ambassador in Montevideo: Martin J. Silverstein.
State Dept. Country Office: (202) 647-2407.

Uzbekistan

Ambassador: Shavkat Shodiyevich Khamrakulov.
Chancery: 1746 Massachusetts Ave. N.W. 20036; (202) 887-5300; fax, (202) 293-6804.
U.S. Ambassador in Tashkent: John Edward Herbst.
State Dept. Country Office: (202) 647-6765.

Vanuatu

U.S. Ambassador: Arma Jean Karaer (resident in Port Moresby, Papua New Guinea).
State Dept. Country Office: (202) 647-5239.

Venezuela

Ambassador: Bernardo Alvarez-Herrera.
Chancery: 1099 30th St. N.W. 20007; (202) 342-2214; fax, (202) 342-6820.
U.S. Ambassador in Caracas: Charles S. Shapiro.
State Dept. Country Office: (202) 647-3338.

Vietnam

Ambassador: Nguyen Tam Chien.
Chancery: 1233 20th St. N.W., #400, 20036; (202) 861-0737; fax, (202) 861-0917.
U.S. Ambassador in Hanoi: Raymond F. Burghardt.
State Dept. Country Office: (202) 647-3132.

Western Samoa (See Samoa)

Yemen

Ambassador: Abdulwahab A. Al-Hajjri.
Chancery: 2600 Virginia Ave. N.W., #705, 20037; (202) 965-4760; fax, (202) 337-2017.
U.S. Ambassador in Sanaa: Edmund J. Hull.
State Dept. Country Office: (202) 647-6558.

Yugoslavia, Federal Republic of

Ambassador: Ivan Vujacic.
Chancery: 2134 Kalorama Road N.W. 20008; (202) 332-0333; fax, (202) 332-3933.
U.S. Ambassador in Belgrade: William D. Montgomery.
State Dept. Country Office: (202) 647-0608.

Zaire (See Congo, Democratic Republic of the)

Zambia

Ambassador: Inonge Mbikusita-Lewanika.
Chancery: 2419 Massachusetts Ave. N.W. 20008; (202) 265-9717; fax, (202) 332-0826.
U.S. Ambassador in Lusaka: Martin G. Brennan.
State Dept. Country Office: (202) 647-9857.

Zimbabwe

Ambassador: Simbi Veke Mubako.
Chancery: 1608 New Hampshire Ave. N.W. 20009; (202) 332-7100; fax, (202) 483-9326.
U.S. Ambassador in Harare: Joseph G. Sullivan.
State Dept. Country Office: (202) 647-9857.

Freedom of Information Act

Public access to government information remains a key issue in Washington. In 1966 Congress passed legislation to broaden access: the Freedom of Information Act, or FOIA (PL 89–487; codified in 1967 by PL 90–23). Amendments to expand access even further were passed into law over President Gerald Ford's veto in 1974 (PL 93–502).

Several organizations in Washington specialize in access to government information. See the "Freedom of Information" section in the Communications and the Media chapter for details (page 133).

1966 Act

The 1966 act requires executive branch agencies and independent commissions of the federal government to make records, reports, policy statements, and staff manuals available to citizens who request them, unless the materials fall into one of nine exempted categories:

• secret national security or foreign policy information
• internal personnel practices
• information exempted by law (e.g., income tax returns)
• trade secrets, other confidential commercial or financial information
• inter-agency or intra-agency memos
• personal information, personnel, or medical files
• law enforcement investigatory information
• information related to reports on financial institutions
• geological and geophysical information

1974 Amendments

Further clarification of the rights of citizens to gain access to government information came in late 1974, when Congress enacted legislation to remove some of the obstacles that the bureaucracy had erected since 1966. Included in the amendments are provisions that:

• Require federal agencies to publish their indexes of final opinions on settlements of internal cases, policy statements, and administrative staff manuals. If, under special circumstances, the indexes are not published, they are to be furnished to any person requesting them for the cost of duplication. The 1966 law simply required agencies to make such indexes available for public inspection and copying.

• Require agencies to release unlisted documents to someone requesting them with a reasonable description (a change designed to ensure that an agency could not refuse to provide material simply because the applicant could not give its precise title).

• Direct each agency to publish a uniform set of fees for providing documents at the cost of finding and copying them. The amendment allows waiver or reduction of those fees when in the public interest.

• Set time limits for agency responses to requests: ten working days for an initial request; twenty working days for an appeal from an initial refusal to produce documents; a possible ten-working-day extension that can be granted only once in a single case.

• Set a thirty-day time limit for an agency response to a complaint filed in court under the act; provide that the courts give such cases priority attention at the appeal, as well as the trial, level.

• Empower federal district courts to order agencies to produce withheld documents and to examine the contested materials privately *(in camera)* to determine if they are properly exempted.

• Require annual agency reports to Congress, including a list of all agency decisions to withhold information requested under the act; the reasons; the appeals; the results; all relevant rules; the fee schedule; and the names of officials responsible for each denial of information.

• Allow courts to order the government to pay attorneys' fees and court costs for persons winning suits against them under the act.

• Authorize a court to find that an agency employee has acted capriciously or arbitrarily in withholding information; stipulate that disciplinary action is determined by Civil Service Commission proceedings.

• Amend and clarify the wording of the national defense and national security exemption to make clear that it applies only to *properly* classified information.

• Amend the wording of the law enforcement exemption to allow withholding of information that, if disclosed, would interfere with enforcement proceedings, deprive someone of a fair trial or hearing, invade personal privacy in an unwarranted way, disclose the identity of a confidential source, disclose investigative techniques, or endanger law enforcement personnel; protect from disclosure all information from a confidential source obtained by a criminal law enforcement agency or a lawful national security investigation.

• Provide that separable non-exempt portions of requested material be released after deletion of the exempt portions.

• Require an annual report from the attorney general to Congress.

1984 Amendments

In 1984 Congress enacted legislation that clarified the requirements of the Central Intelligence Agency (CIA) to respond to citizen requests for information. Included in the amendments are provisions that:

• Authorize the CIA to close from FOIA review certain operational files that contain information on the identities of sources and methods. The measure removed the requirement that officials search the files for material that might be subject to disclosure.

• Reverse a ruling by the Justice Dept. and the Office of Management and Budget that invoked the Privacy Act to deny individuals FOIA access to information about themselves in CIA records. HR 5164 required the CIA to search files in response to FOIA requests by individuals for information about themselves.

• Require the CIA to respond to FOIA requests for information regarding covert actions or suspected CIA improprieties.

All agencies of the executive branch have issued regulations to implement the Freedom of Information Act.

To locate a specific agency's regulations, consult the general index of the *Code of Federal Regulations* under "Information availability."

Electronic Freedom of Information Act of 1996

In 1996 Congress enacted legislation that clarified that electronic documents are subject to the same FOIA disclosure rules as are printed documents. The 1996 law also requires federal agencies to make records available to the public in various electronic formats, such as e-mail, compact disc, and files accessible via the Internet. An additional measure seeks to improve the government's response time on FOIA requests by requiring agencies to report annually on the number of pending requests and how long it will take to respond.

Homeland Security Act of 2002

In 2002 Congress passed legislation that established the Homeland Security Department and exempted from FOIA disclosure rules certain information about national defense systems. Included in the act are provisions that:

• Grant broad exemption from FOIA requirements to information that private companies share with the government about vulnerabilities in the nation's critical infrastructure.

• Exempt from FOIA rules and other federal and state disclosure requirements any information about the critical infrastructure that is submitted voluntarily to a covered federal agency to ensure the security of this infrastructure and protected systems; require accompanying statement that such information is being submitted voluntarily in expectation of nondisclosure protection.

• Require the secretary of homeland security to establish procedures for federal agencies to follow in receiving, caring for, and storing critical infrastructure information that has been submitted voluntarily; provide criminal penalties for the unauthorized disclosure of such information.

Privacy Legislation

Privacy Act

To protect citizens from invasions of privacy by the federal government, Congress passed the Privacy Act of 1974 (PL 93–579). The act permitted individuals for the first time to inspect information about themselves contained in federal agency files and to challenge, correct, or amend the material. The major provisions of the act:

• Permit an individual to have access to personal information in federal agency files and to correct or amend that information.

• Prevent an agency maintaining a file on an individual from making it available to another agency without the individual's consent.

• Require federal agencies to keep records that are necessary, lawful, accurate, and current, and to disclose the existence of all data banks and files containing information on individuals.

• Bar the transfer of personal information to other federal agencies for non-routine use without the individual's prior consent or written request.

• Require agencies to keep accurate accountings of transfers of records and make them available to the individual.

• Prohibit agencies from keeping records on an individual's exercise of First Amendment rights unless the records are authorized by statute, approved by the individual, or within the scope of an official law enforcement activity.

• Permit an individual to seek injunctive relief to correct or amend a record maintained by an agency and permit the individual to recover actual damages when an agency acts in a negligent manner that is "willful or intentional."

• Exempt from disclosure: records maintained by the Central Intelligence Agency; records maintained by law enforcement agencies; Secret Service records; statistical information; names of persons providing material used for determining the qualification of an individual for federal government service; federal testing material; and National Archives historical records.

• Provide that an officer or employee of an agency who violates provisions of the act be fined no more than $5,000.

• Prohibit an agency from selling or renting an individual's name or address for mailing list use.

• Require agencies to submit to Congress and to the Office of Management and Budget any plan to establish or alter records.

Virtually all agencies of the executive branch have issued regulations to implement the Privacy Act. To locate a specific agency's regulations, consult the general index of the *Code of Federal Regulations* under "Privacy Act."

USA PATRIOT Act and Homeland Security Act of 2002

Following the terrorist attacks of September 11, 2001, Congress passed two laws that affected privacy issues: the USA PATRIOT Act (Uniting and Strengthening America by Providing Appropriate Tools Required to Intercept and Obstruct Terrorism; PL 107–56) and the Homeland Security Act of 2002 (PL 107–296).

Included in the USA PATRIOT Act are provisions that:

• Amend the federal criminal code to authorize the interception of wire, oral, and electronic communications to produce evidence of chemical weapons, terrorism, and computer fraud and abuse.

• Amend the Foreign Intelligence Surveillance Act of 1978 (FISA) to require an application for an electronic surveillance order or search warrant certifying that a significant purpose (formerly, the sole or main purpose) of the surveillance is to obtain foreign intelligence information. The administration of President George W. Bush has aggressively defended its use of wiretaps approved by the Foreign Intelligence Surveillance Court, which handles intelligence requests involving suspected spies, terrorists, and foreign agents. Established under FISA, this court operates secretly within the Justice Dept.

The Homeland Security Act of 2002 contains provisions that:

• Establish the Homeland Security Department.

• Exempt from criminal penalties any disclosure made by an electronic communication service to a federal, state, or local government. In making the disclosure, the service must believe that an emergency involving risk of death or serious physical injury requires disclosure without delay. Any government receiving such disclosure must report it to the attorney general.

• Direct the secretary of homeland security to appoint a senior department official to take primary responsibility for information privacy policy.

Name Index

Buggage, Cynthia, 826
Buhler, Donald A., 320, 458, 714
Buis, Thomas P., 41
Bulger, Margaret, 173
Bulger, Roger J., 377
Buline, Pam, 886
Bull, Stephen, 178
Bullman, W. Ray, 384
Bultman, Roger C., 555, 567
Bumps, Randy, 873
Bumpus, Jeanne, 16, 79, 326, 620, 640, 656, 706, 711, 720, 725, 861
Bunce, Harold, 431
Bunce, Marjorie, 879
Bundschuh, James, 200
Bunn, Sheila, 837
Bunning, Jim, R-Ky., 454, 780, 860–863, 867, 871
Bunton, David S., 454
Burbano, Fernando, 129
Burch, Kathleen, 398
Burchett, John, 896
Burdette, Victor, 563
Burgan, Mary, 199
Burgess, Jay, 504
Burgess, Jim, 275
Burgess, Ken, 874
Burgess, Michael C., R-Texas, 809
Burgess, Paulette, 823
Burgess, Philip M., 361
Burgess, Thomas R., 56
Burghardt, Günter, 267, 464, 491, 505
Burghardt, Raymond F., 916
Burke, Gordon, 581
Burke, Jane C., 558
Burke, John, 313
Burke, Kevin M., 103
Burke, Sheila, 161
Burke, William M., 189
Burkes, Wayne O., 528, 708, 719, 734, 736
Burks, Elizabeth Hurley, 851
Burks, Stacy, 871
Burleson, Carl E., 307, 709
Burner, Gary H., 84
Burnett, Jefferson G., 209
Burnett, Ruth, 885
Burney, David G., 303, 482
Burnham, Christopher B., 340
Burnham, Nealton J., 487
Burns, Conrad, R-Mont., 120, 138, 152, 213, 260, 293, 516, 640, 750, 781, 858, 861–862, 867, 872
Burns, Max, R-Ga., 809
Burns, William J., Jr., 510
Burr, Richard M., R-N.C., 809
Burris, James F., 582
Burroughs, Harry, 292, 302, 304, 315, 326, 482, 656
Burrows, Bob, 835
Burrus, William, 357
Burton, Alan, 632
Burton, Cynthia, 814
Burton, Dan, R-Ind., 531, 751, 780, 791–792, 809

Burton, LaVarne A., 384
Burton, Mack, 568
Burton, Rejean, 323
Burwell, Dollie, 804
Busch, Jeri B., 563
Busching, Mark, 803
Bush, Andrew, 680
Bush, George W., 333, 335, 338, 919
Bush, Jeb, 894
Bush, Laura, 335
Bushweller, Brian, 872
Bustamante, Cruz M., 893
Bustillo, Inés, 508
Butkin, Robert A., 899
Butler, Chuck, 897
Butler, Lawrence E., 909
Butler, Linda, 512
Butler, Malcolm, 509
Butler, Michelle, 844
Butler, Stephanie, 826
Butler, Susan, 840
Butler, Sydney J., 652
Butler, T. Wendell, 673
Butler, Tim, 829
Butora, Martin, 913
Butterfield, Jeanne, 477
Butters, Timothy, 615
Buyer, Steve, R-Ind., 778, 809
Buzby, Barry, 102
Buzzerd, Harry W., Jr., 103
Bybee, Jay S., 530
Byers, Jay, 808
Byers, Michael W., 573
Byers, Monte L., 765
Byington, Janet, 821
Byler, J. Daryl, 35
Bynum, Nadab O., 432
Byrd, Lorelee, 897
Byrd, Marylee, 134
Byrd, Ricardo C., 438
Byrd, Robert C., D-W.Va., 872
Byrd-Johnson, Linda, 212
Byrne, Michael F., 614
Byron, James E., 767
Bysiewicz, Susan, 894

Cabaniss, V. Dale, 351
Cabral, Sam, 548
Cacciatore, John, 895
Caddigan, Timothy, 127, 620
Cade, Dayna, 99, 491, 498, 605
Caden, Judith A., 581
Cady, John R., 45, 66, 302
Cafritz, Calvin, 29
Cahall, Nan, 841
Cahill, Laura, 880
Cahill, Mary Beth, 879
Cahill, Timothy P., 896
Cain, Angie, 832
Cain, William, 563
Calderwood, Jane, 885
Caldwell, Charles, 341
Caldwell, George L., 846
Caldwell, Nicki, 833
Calhoun, Cathy, 873

Calhoun, John A., 539
Caliendo, Madeline, 241
Caligiuri, Tony, 820
Calkin, Kelly, 822
Calkins, Barbara J., 387
Callahan, Debra J., 295
Callahan, Kateri, 726
Callaway, Robbie, 683
Callicott, Scott, 825
Callis, Dianne, 227
Calman, Donald, 147
Calmes, Alan, 168
Calnan, Jacqueline, 300
Calvert, Ken, R-Calif., 260, 269, 284, 330, 656, 779, 787, 794–795, 801, 809
Cambone, Stephen A., 624
Camp, Dave, R-Mich., 602, 620, 706, 711, 781, 796, 800–801, 809
Campanelli, Richard M., 2, 418, 530
Campbell, Ben Nighthorse, R-Colo., 7, 195, 213, 325, 396, 478, 482, 595, 748–749, 753, 779, 859, 862, 865, 867, 872
Campbell, Colin, 805
Campbell, Elizabeth E., 274
Campbell, Melanie L., 747
Campbell, Nancy Duff, 10, 215, 242
Campbell, Pauline, 241
Campbell, Stephen C., 732
Campbell, Stuart P., 678
Campbell, Terry, 886
Campbell, Vivian, 815
Campbell, William H., 340
Campbell-Dereef, Pam, 834
Campen, Tim, 334
Campos, Patricia, 103, 730
Canahuati, Mario M., 907
Canby, Anne P., 708
Cancienne, Martin, 850
Cannon, Bonnie, 813
Cannon, Carl, 144, 740
Cannon, Christopher B., R-Utah, 30, 529, 535, 810
Cannon, Michael, 771
Cano, Richard V., 60
Canova, Diane M., 416
Canova, Karen L., 402
Cantor, Eric, R-Va., 810
Cantrell, F. Daniel, 814
Cantwell, Maria, D-Wash., 872
Cantwell, Mike, 811
Capel, James, 842
Capito, Shelley Moore, R-W.Va., 751, 783, 790, 797–798, 801, 810
Capon, Ross B., 735, 737
Cappitelli, Susan B., 380
Capps, Lois, D-Calif., 810
Cappuccilli, Edmund, 266
Caprara, David, 25, 217, 675
Capuano, Michael E., D-Mass., 751, 778, 781, 790, 799, 802, 810
Carbonell, Ana M., 815
Carbonell, Josefina, 7, 686
Carcieri, Donald L., 899
Card, Andrew H., Jr., 335, 338

Flynn, Vickie, 816
Flyzik, Jim, 129
Foarde, John, 482
Foer, Albert A., 528
Fogarty, Charles J., 899
Fogash, Kenneth, 13, 129
Fogleman, Guy, 648
Foley, Jim, 870
Foley, Mark, R-Fla., 819
Foley, T. W., 573
Folks, Will, 899
Folsom, George, 467
Fones, Roger W., 527
Fong, Phyllis K., 343
Fontaine, Monita, 721
Foote, Steve L., 423
Forbeck, Helen, 804
Forbes, J. Randy, R-Va., 819
Forcash, Jeanette, 853
Ford, Carl W., Jr., 461, 609, 626
Ford, Chandra, 849
Ford, Delorice, 114
Ford, Harold E., Jr., D-Tenn., 819
Ford, Larry, 850
Ford-Roegner, Pat, 422
Fordham, Kirk, 819
Fording, Edmund, 661
Fore, Henrietta Holsman, 84, 99
Fore, Karmen, 815
Foreman, Anthony, 851
Foreman, Dave, 814
Forest, Mark, 815
Forman, Ira, 771
Fornataro, James, 354
Forno, Antonio Arenales, 907
Fornos, Werner, 414
Fortunat, Donna, 354
Foscarinis, Maria, 699
Fossella, Vito J., R-N.Y., 751, 778, 781,
   789–790, 819
Foster, Bob, 15, 77, 84, 93, 99, 106, 429,
   432, 449, 453, 457, 498, 528, 560, 613,
   790
Foster, Murphy J. "Mike," Jr., 896
Foster, Nancy, 53
Foster, Rebecca, 165
Foster, Serrin M., 533
Foster, Sonny, 882
Foster, William, 285
Foster-Bey, John, 25
Fotis, James J., 548
Fournier, Jim, 813
Fourquet, Jose, 492, 508
Fowler, Andrea, 134
Fowler, John M., 167
Fowler, Raymond D., 424, 666
Fox, Christopher, 388
Fox, Lynn, 132
Fox, Nancy, 819
Frace, Sheila E., 314
Fradkin, Hillel, 34, 193, 532, 592
Fradkin, Judith E., 412
Fragos-Townsend, Frances, 627
Frame, Robert T., 582
France, Roger, 850

Francis, David, 570
Francis, Les, 202
Francis, Nichole A., 819
Franco, Adolfo, 506
Franco, Barbara, 175
Franco, Omar, 816
Frank, Abe L., 178
Frank, Barney, D-Mass., 819
Frank, Martin, 406
Frank, Ralph, 469
Frankel, Mark S., 640
Frankel, Robert, 125, 151, 156, 160, 166
Franken, Mark, 473, 477
Frankland, Walter L., Jr., 100
Franklin, Joe T., 104
Franklin, Pat, 313
Franklin, Peter C., 606
Franklin, Rick, 819
Franks, Myrtis, 881
Franks, Trent, R-Ariz., 819
Fransen, James W., 758, 761
Frantum, Rachel, 174
Frantz, Bob, 465
Frantz, Brenda, 805
Franz, Marian, 595
Fraser, Loran G., 328
Frasier, Beecher, 814
Frazer, Gary D., 301, 304
Frazier, Johnnie, 343
Frazier, Raymond, 880
Frazier, Susan, 172
Freda, Sherry, 358
Fredrickson, Caroline, 872
Freeman, Anthony G., 228
Freeman, Beth, 878
Freeman, Carl H., 597
Freeman, Charles W., Jr., 513
Freeman, Peter, 137, 662
Freeman, Robert, 720, 725, 734
Freeman, Russell F., 903
Freeman, T. C., 871
Freemyer, Winsor, 841
Frei, Mark W., 282–284
Freling, Robert A., 286
Frelinghuysen, Rodney, R-N.J., 366, 778,
   781, 785, 819
French, Dwight K., 263
French, Ed, 881
French, Robert, 241
Freudenthal, David, 901
Fried, David, 832
Frieden, Lex, 689
Friedman, Bonnie, 251
Friedman, David, 10
Friedman, Eric, 809
Friedman, Gregory H., 343
Friedman, Jerry, 677
Friedman, Lawrence A., 529
Friedman, Stephen, 75
Friefeld, Wendy, 854
Friel, Candace, 821
Friend, Patricia A., 713
Frierson, Mel, 812
Frisby, Russell, 126

Frist, Bill, R-Tenn., 174, 748, 755, 782,
   863, 865–867, 877
Fritsche, Claudia, 909
Fritter, Carl, 169, 740
Fritts, Edward O., 122, 125, 146
Frohboese, Robin, 241
From, Alvin, 773
Fronzi, Anita, 854
Frost, Alberta, 59, 681
Frost, Martin, D-Texas, 819
Frost, Robert, 354
Frost, Whitney D., 847
Frumin, Alan S., 753
Fry, Edward D., II, 848
Fry, Tom A., 276, 286, 326, 660
Fuentes, Jennice, 822
Fugate, Jessica, 505
Fuller, Craig L., 383
Fuller, Kathryn S., 298, 306, 329
Fuller, Tim, 8
Funches, Jesse L., 341
Funderburk, John, 878
Funke, Lawrence A., 661
Furey, Jessica L., 289
Furlong, Catherine H., 87
Furuno, Alan, 803
Futrell, J. William, 294

Gaddis, Evan, 104, 276
Gaddy, C. Welton, 34, 771
Gadsden, James I., 908
Gaffney, Frank J., Jr., 591
Gaffney, Paul G., 566
Gaffney, Susan, 363
Gage, Larry S., 378
Gager, William C., 729
Gainer, Terrance W., 748
Gaines, Tim, 878
Gale, John A., 897
Galko, Vince, 883
Gallagher, Ace, 874
Gallagher, Brian, 29
Gallagher, Cristy, 897
Gallagher, James J., 506
Gallagher, Patricia, 168, 437
Gallagher, Peter A., 683
Gallagher, Tom, 894
Gallant, Lewis E., 64, 422, 542
Gallegly, Elton, R-Calif., 469, 483, 598,
   604, 627, 778, 779, 792–794, 797, 820
Gallegos, Jerry, 145
Gallin, John I., 405
Gallogly, Stephen J., 266, 323
Galvin, John M., 230
Galvin, William Francis, 896
Gambatesa, Linda, 335
Gambone, Ralph M., 574
Gambrell, Donna J., 12, 18
Gamse, David N., 687
Gandy, Kim, 6, 9, 532, 771
Gangloff, Deborah, 319
Gangloff, Eric J., 501
Gannon, John C., 490, 590, 602
Gans, Curtis, 746
Gans, John A., 382

Purtill, Patrick D., 685
Puryear, Michele A., 414
Puteh, Pengiran Anak Dato, 904
Putnam, Adam H., R-Fla., 345, 615, 620, 671, 780, 784, 787, 791, 801, 841, 856
Putney, John, 869
Pyke, Thomas, 129
Pyle, Margaret, 804

Qadir, Syed, 310, 612, 617, 722
Qazi, Ashraf Jehangir, 912
Quaadman, Tom, 819
Quaid, Andrea, 835
Quainton, Anthony C. E., 82, 494
Qualls, Ellen, 900
Qualters, Janet, 357
Quartey, Patricia, 134
Queen, Beverly, 225
Quigley, Lisa, 816
Quimby, Sandra, 170
Quinn, Gail, 534
Quinn, Jack, R-N.Y., 734, 782, 798–799, 842
Quinn, Maureen, 912
Quinn, Patrick, 895
Quinn, Warren, 442
Quirk, Daniel A., 688
Quist, Edward E., 340

Raber, Roger, 82
Rabern, Susan J., 340
Rabinovitz, Jeremy, 810
Rabkin, Norm, 519, 595
Raby, Julian, 159
Racicot, Marc, 775
Radanovich, George P., R-Calif., 168, 319, 321, 328, 778, 779, 789, 794, 842
Radke, John W., 564
Raduege, Harry D., Jr., 624
Radzely, Howard M., 524
Rafey, Joy, 202
Ragen, Timothy J., 303
Ragland, Barbara, 821
Rahall, Nick J., II, D-W.Va., 842
Railton, W. Scott, 251
Raines, Franklin D., 456
Rainey, Justen, 852
Rains, Alan T., Jr., 217
Rajaonarivony, Narisoa, 910
Raley, Bennett W., 323
Ralls, Stephen, 388
Ramaley, Judith A., 219
Ramey, Dave, 809
Raminger, Scott, 110
Ramirez, Saul, 430, 459
Ramonas, Denise Greenlaw, 759
Ramos, Frank, 116
Ramsey, Lisa, 884
Ramsey-Lucas, Curtis, 32
Ramstad, Jim, R-Minn., 752, 781, 800, 842
Rana, Jai P., 911
Rand, Ronald T., 132
Randle, Patricia A., 251, 759
Randt, Clark T., Jr., 905

Rangel, Charles B., D-N.Y., 750, 781, 800, 802, 842, 857
Rangel, Robert S., 589, 598, 786
Ransom, Alma, 7
Raphael, Molly, 740
Rapolaki, Molelekeng, 909
Rapoza, Robert A., 450
Rasco, Carol, 208, 219
Rasmussen, Micah, 898
Rassam, Gus, 302
Rathbun, Dennis K., 759
Rathbun, James P., Jr., 564
Ratkiewicz, Frank, 824
Ratliff, Frederick, 752
Ratzlaff, Jace, 836
Raub, William, 368
Rausch, P. Diane, 671
Ravdan, Bold, 911
Raven, Peter H., 641
Ravnitzky, Gail, 845
Rawson, Randall, 104, 261
Ray, Charles, 904
Ray, Charles G., 426
Ray, Judy, 820
Rayburn, Dorothy, 758
Rayman, Russell B., 717
Raymond, David, 653
Raymond, Pat, 40, 61, 371
Rayner, Marcus, 818
Raynes, Jeffry, 101
Read, Cathy, 354
Readdy, William, 671
Readinger, Thomas A., 326
Ream, Roger R., 189
Reardon, Susan, 244, 469
Redburn, F. Stevens, 428
Reddick, Eunice, 502
Redding, Jody, 882
Redding, Rebecca, 812
Reddington, John, 71
Reddy, Leo, 102
Reed, Bruce, 773
Reed, Carol Ann, 134
Reed, Craig R., 258
Reed, Jack, D-R.I., 752, 782, 856, 860, 865, 868, 883
Reed, Linda, 813
Reed, Sam, 901
Reed, William H., 594, 634
Reeker, Phil, 132
Reeves, Greg, 3, 348
Regalia, Martin A., 83, 227
Regelbrugge, Craig, 46, 652
Reger, Larry, 169
Reger, Mark, 340
Regula, Ralph, R-Ohio, 119, 182, 225, 252, 371, 597, 676, 702, 752, 778, 782, 785, 801, 842
Rehberg, Denny, R-Mont., 778, 842
Rehnquist, William H., 145, 521, 527, 531
Rehr, David K., 65
Reich, Allen A., 693
Reich, John, 90
Reichard, Dorothy M., 819

Reichenberg, Neil, 361
Reid, Bernice, 153
Reid, Harry, D-Nev., 755, 781, 859, 862, 865, 866, 867, 868, 883
Reid, James Paul, 498
Reid, Robert J., 430, 449
Reifschneider, Donna, 53, 70
Reifschneider, Francisco Jose Becker, 44
Reilly, Barbara, 494, 709
Reilly, Edward F., Jr., 545
Reilly, Robert, 841
Reilly, Thomas F., 896
Reilly-Hudock, Trish, 824
Reinecke, Peter, 878
Reinhart, Vincent R., 87
Reinsch, William A., 494
Reis, Robert, Jr., 495
Reischauer, Robert D., 680, 773
Reisenweber, John, 810
Reiter, Stuart, 129
Relerford, Barbara, 229
Rell, M. Jodi, 894
Rendeiro, John, 630
Rendell, Ed, 899
Render, Arlene, 905
Rendon, Florencio, 838
Rendon, Martin S., 471
Renick, Mary, 820
Renkes, Gregg, 893
Renninger, Karen, 132, 464
Rensberger, Judith, 381
Rényi, Judith, 192
Renzi, Rick, R-Ariz., 842
Resavage, Roy, 713
Reser, Lesley, 881
Ressel, Teresa, 340
Reut, Katrina, 229, 243, 247, 250
Reuther, Alan, 246, 730
Rey, Mark, 289
Reyes, Norma, 843
Reyes, Silvestre, D-Texas, 778, 842
Reyna, Benigno G., 547
Reyna, Michael M., 57
Reynolds, Bernie, 66
Reynolds, Dennis, 380
Reynolds, Emily, 759–760
Reynolds, Gerald, 212, 530
Reynolds, Margaret W., 158
Reynolds, Mercer, 909, 914
Reynolds, Thomas M., R-N.Y., 774, 782, 792, 795, 801, 843
Reynoldson, Jerry, 883
Reynoso, Cruz, 2, 530
Rhode, Patrick, 133
Ribbentrop, Richard, Sr., 98
Ricciardone, Francis J., 912
Rice, Edmund B., 493
Rich, Dorothy, 207
Rich, Laurie M., 11, 182
Richard, Joel C., 718
Richard, John, 30, 147, 522
Richard, Mark, 211, 695
Richard, William G., 838
Richards, Claude, 517
Richards, Cory L., 400, 413

Subject Index

Entries in **BOLD CAPS** are the names of chapters and appendices; entries in **bold** indicate major subjects in the chapters.

Africare, 501
AFT Healthcare, 385, 389–390
Aged persons. *See* Elderly
Agence France-Presse, 142
Agency for Health Care Research and Quality, 368
Agency for International Development (USAID)
    Africa Bureau, 500
    Asia and Near East Bureau, 501, 510
    Center for Environment, 265
    congressional liaison, 758
    Democracy, Conflict, and Humanitarian Assistance, 470
    Economic Growth, Agriculture, and Trade, 495
    Education, 495
    Europe and Eurasia Bureau, 503, 514
    Financial Officer, 340
    freedom of information contact, 134
    General Counsel, 524
    Global Health Bureau, 470
    Global Trade and Technology Network, 485
    Inspector General, 343
    Latin America and the Caribbean Bureau, 506
    library, 197
    Population and Reproductive Health, 413
    public affairs contact, 132
    small and disadvantaged business contact, 116
    Small and Disadvantaged Business Utilization/Minority Resource Center, 113
    U.S. Foreign Disaster Assistance, 470
Agency for Toxic Substances and Disease Registry, 308–309
Agribusiness Council, 50
Agricultural Cooperative Development International (ACDI/VOCA), 69, 495–496
Agricultural Marketing Service (AMS), 39
    Cotton, 51
    Dairy Programs, 51
    Fruit and Vegetable Program, 52
    Information, 39
    Livestock and Seed, 53, 70
    Poultry Programs, 70
    Science and Technology, 58
    Seed Regulatory and Testing, 48
    Tobacco, 56
    Transportation and Marketing, 48
Agricultural research and education, 41–44
Agricultural Research Service, 41, 59
    National Plant Germplasm and Genomes System, 48
AGRICULTURE AND NUTRITION (chap. 2), 38–71
    commodities and farm produce, 48–56
    cotton, 51
    dairy products and eggs, 51–52
    farm loans, insurance, and subsidies, 57–58
    fertilizer and pesticides, 44–46
    food and nutrition, 58–70
    fruits and vegetables, 52–53
    general policy, 39–48
    grains and oilseeds, 53–55
    horticulture and gardening, 46–47
    livestock and poultry, 70–71
    migrant and seasonal farmworkers, 235–236
    research and education, 41–44
    soil and watershed conservation, 47–48
    sugar, 55–56
    tobacco and peanuts, 56
    world food assistance, 67–70
Agriculture Dept. (USDA), 39

Agricultural Marketing Service. *See that heading*
Agricultural Research Service, 41, 48, 59
Animal and Plant Health Inspection Service. *See that heading*
Board of Contract Appeals, 39
Chief Economist, 39
Chief Information Officer, 129
Commodity Credit Corporation, 48, 57
Communications and Governmental Affairs, 11
congressional liaison, 758
consumer and emergency hotlines, 14
consumer contact, 11
Cooperative State Research, Education, and Extension Service. *See that heading*
Economic Research Service, 42, 53, 55, 56, 87, 256
Employment Compliance and Technical Assistance, 41
equal employment contact, 241
Executive Leadership Program for Mid-Level Employers, 240
Farm Service Agency. *See that heading*
Financial Officer, 340
Food and Nutrition Service. *See that heading*
Food, Nutrition, and Consumer Services, 39, 59
Food Safety and Inspection Service, 21, 60, 70, 217
Foreign Agricultural Service, 49, 67–68, 495
Forest Service. *See that heading*
fraud, waste, and abuse hotline, 14
freedom of information contact, 134
General Counsel, 524
Graduate School, 200, 221
    International Institute, 473
Grain Inspection, Packers, and Stockyards Administration, 53, 70
information, 39
Inspector General, 343
library, 197
Marketing and Regulatory Programs, 48
meat and poultry safety inquiries, 14
National Agricultural Library, 42, 60, 206
National Agricultural Statistics Service, 42, 87
National Agricultural Statistics Service Census and Survey, 41
National Arboretum, 46, 160, 651
Natural Resources and Environment, 289
Natural Resources Conservation Service, 47, 321
    Pest Management, 44
organizational chart, 43
Personnel Office, 350
Procurement Officer, 354
public affairs contact, 132
Publications Office, 130
Research, Education, and Economics, 42, 216–217
Risk Management Agency, 57
Rural Business-Cooperative Service, 43, 49, 285, 435
Rural Development, 57, 435, 451
Rural Housing Service, 435, 449
Rural Utilities Service, 270, 330, 435
Secretary, 338
small and disadvantaged business contact, 116
Web site, 136
World Agricultural Outlook Board, 68
Agri-Energy Roundtable, 50
AID. *See* Agency for International Development
AIDS Action, 408
AIDS Alliance for Children, Youth, and Families, 408–409

American Academy of Optometry, 393
American Academy of Otolaryngology-Head and Neck Surgery, 390–391
American Academy of Pediatrics, 23, 401
American Academy of Physician Assistants (AAPA), 390
American Advertising Federation, 112
American AIDS PAC, 766
American Alliance for Health, Physical Education, Recreation, and Dance, 176
American Anthropological Assn., 666
American Antitrust Institute (AAI), 528
American Apparel and Footwear Assn. (AAFA), 103
American-Arab Anti-Discrimination Committee, 10
American Arbitration Assn., 244, 479, 525
American Architectural Foundation, 187
American Art Museum, 161
American Arts Alliance, 153
American Assn. for Adult and Continuing Education, 222
American Assn. for Clinical Chemistry, 389, 661
American Assn. for Health Education, 385
American Assn. for Higher Education, 199
American Assn. for Homecare, 380
American Assn. for Laboratory Accreditation, 640
American Assn. for Marriage and Family Therapy, 682–683
American Assn. for Respiratory Care (AARC), Government Affairs, 418
American Assn. for the Advancement of Science (AAAS), 640
    Education and Human Resources Programs, 220
    International Programs, 645–646
    Scientific Freedom, Responsibility, and Law Program, 640–641
American Assn. of Advertising Agencies, 112
American Assn. of Airport Executives, 715
American Assn. of Blacks in Energy, 261
American Assn. of Blood Banks, 410
American Assn. of Children's Residential Centers, 401
American Assn. of Colleges for Teacher Education, 190
American Assn. of Colleges of Nursing, 390
American Assn. of Colleges of Osteopathic Medicine, 391
American Assn. of Colleges of Pharmacy, 199, 382, 385–386
American Assn. of Collegiate Registrars and Admissions Officers, 199
American Assn. of Community Colleges, 199
American Assn. of Engineering Societies, 653
American Assn. of Family and Consumer Sciences, 217
American Assn. of Health Plans, 375
American Assn. of Homes and Services for the Aging, Policy and Governmental Affairs, 398, 451
American Assn. of Immunologists, 389
American Assn. of Motor Vehicle Administrators (AAMVA), 725
American Assn. of Museums, 162
    Museum Assessment Program, 160
American Assn. of Pastoral Counselors, 32, 424
American Assn. of People with Disabilities, 690
American Assn. of Pharmaceutical Scientists, 382
American Assn. of Physics Teachers, 220
American Assn. of Political Consultants, 744
American Assn. of Port Authorities, 723–724
American Assn. of School Administrators, 190
American Assn. of State Colleges and Universities, 199
American Assn. of State Highway and Transportation Officials, 728
American Assn. of Suicidology, 424
American Assn. of University Professors (AAUP), 199

American Assn. of University Women (AAUW), 213
    Educational Foundation, 187
American Assn. on Mental Retardation (AAMR), 697
American Astronautical Society, 672
American Astronomical Society, 673
American Automobile Assn. (AAA), 725–726, 731
American Automotive Leasing Assn., 728–729
American Bakers Assn. (ABA), 65
American Bankers Assn. (ABA), 93
    BankPAC, 767
    Communications, 19
American Bankruptcy Institute, 529
American Baptist Churches U.S.A., Government Relations, 32
American Bar Assn. (ABA), 522
    Center on Children and the Law, 540, 683
    Central European and Eurasian Law Initiative, 505, 515
    Commission on Mental and Physical Disability Law, 30, 424, 690
    Criminal Justice, 538, 546
    Dispute Resolution, 525
    Intellectual Property Law, 109
    International Law and Practice, 479, 549
    International Legal Exchange Program, 474
    Standing Committee on Election Law, 744
    Standing Committee on Environmental Law, 293
    Taxation Section, 530
American Battle Monuments Commission, 572
American Benefits Council, 249
American Beverage Licensees, 64
American Blind Lawyers Assn., 549, 695
American Board of Opticianry and National Contact Lens Examiners Board, 393
American Boiler Manufacturers Assn., 104, 261
American Bus Assn., 726, 737
American Business Conference, 80
American Butter Institute, 52
American Cancer Society, National Government Relations, 411
American Canoe Assn., 176
American Center for International Labor Solidarity, 229
American Chamber of Commerce Executives, 80
American Chemical Society, 661
    Chemical Sector ISAC, 615
    Petroleum Research Fund, 661
    Project Bookshare, 196
American Chemistry Council, 661
American Chiropractic Assn., 388
American Civil Liberties Union (ACLU), 135, 532, 593–594
    internships, 188
    National Capital Area, 225–226
American Civil Liberties Union Foundation, National Prison Project, 546
American Clinical Laboratory Assn., 372
American Cocoa Research Institute, 55
American Coke and Coal Chemicals Institute, 273–274
American College of Cardiology, 391
American College of Dentists, 388
American College of Emergency Physicians, Government Affairs, 391
American College of Health Care Administrators, 381, 386
American College of Nurse-Midwives, 390, 401
American College of Obstetricians and Gynecologists, 391, 401
American College of Osteopathic Surgeons, 391
American College of Preventive Medicine, 391
American College of Radiology, 391
American College of Surgeons, 391

American College Testing (ACT), 199
American Conference of Academic Deans, 199
American Congress on Surveying and Mapping, 668
American Conservative Union (ACU), 590, 769
    congressional ratings, 766
American Corporate Counsel Assn., 529
American Correctional Assn. (ACA), 546
American Cotton Shippers Assn., 51
American Council for an Energy-Efficient Economy (ACEEE), 264
American Council for Capital Formation (ACCF), 80
American Council of Engineering Consultants, 653
    Research and Management Foundation, 653
American Council of Independent Laboratories (ACIL), 641
American Council of Life Insurers, 106
American Council of State Savings Supervisors, 93–94
American Council of Teachers of Russian, 157, 515
American Council of the Blind (ACB), 695
American Council of Trustees and Alumni, 199–200
American Council of Young Political Leaders, 474
American Council on Education (ACE), 200–201
American Councils for International Education, 157, 515
American Counseling Assn., Rehabilitation, 690–691
American Defense Institute (ADI), Pride in America, 563, 590
American Dental Assn. (ADA)
    Government Relations, 388
    Political Action Committee, 767
American Dental Education Assn., 388
American Dental Trade Assn., 388
American Diabetes Assn. (ADA), 412
American Dietetic Assn. (ADA), 62
American Educational Research Assn., 193
American Electronics Assn., 662
American Enterprise Institute for Public Policy Research (AEI)
    Economic Policy Studies, 80, 226
    Fiscal Policy Studies, 89
    Foreign and Defense Policy Studies, 465, 590–591
    internships, 188
    Social and Individual Responsibility Project, 677
American Ethical Union (AEU), Washington Ethical Action, 32
American Farm Bureau Federation (AFBF), 40
    congressional ratings, 766
American Farmland Trust (AFT), 47
American Federation of Government Employees (AFGE), 347–348
American Federation of Musicians, 244
American Federation of Police, 548
American Federation of School Administrators, 190
American Federation of State, County, and Municipal Employees (AFSCME), 765
American Federation of Teachers (AFT), 190
    Committee on Political Education, 765
American Feed Industry Assn. (AFIA), 53
American Fiber Manufacturers Assn., 103
American Film Institute (AFI) Silver Theater and Cultural Center, 155
American Financial Services Assn. (AFSA), 19
American Fisheries Society (AFS), 302
American Folklife Center, 173, 195
American Foreign Service Assn. (AFSA), 244–245, 469
American Forest and Paper Assn., Regulatory Affairs, 319, 444–445
American Forests, 319
American Foundation for AIDS Research (AmfAR), Public Policy, 409

American Foundation for the Blind, Governmental Relations, 695
American Friends Service Committee (AFSC), 32
American Frozen Food Institute, 65
American Gaming Assn., 176
American Gas Assn., 275
    Statistics, 268
American Gastroenterological Assn., 412
American Gear Manufacturers Assn., 104
American Geological Institute, 322, 658
American Geophysical Union, 656, 673
American Gold Star Mothers Inc., 584
American Hardwood Export Council, 319
American Health Care Assn., 381
    Political Action Committee (AHC-PAC), 767–768
American Health Lawyers Assn., 386, 549
American Health Quality Assn., 391
American Heart Assn., 416
American Helicopter Society, 712
American Hellenic Institute, 505
American Herbal Products Assn., 62, 299–300
American Highway Users Alliance, 731
American Hiking Society, 176, 328
American Historical Assn., 169
American history
    genealogy, 172–173
    military history, 570–574
    postal history, 359
    Washington area, 174–175
American Homeowners Foundation, 454
American Horse Protection Assn., 300
American Horticultural Society, 46
American Hospital Assn., 377
American Hotel and Lodging Assn., 179–180
American Humane Assn., Public Policy, 300, 683
American Immigration Lawyers Assn., 477
American Indian Heritage Foundation, 173
American Indians. *See* Native Americans
American Industrial Hygiene Assn., 252–253
American Inns of Court Foundation, 549
American Institute for Cancer Research, 411
American Institute for Conservation of Historic and Artistic Works, 169
American Institute for International Steel, 104
American Institute in Taiwan, 502
American Institute of Aeronautics and Astronautics (AIAA), 672, 712
American Institute of Architects, 167, 441–442
    American Architectural Foundation, 187
American Institute of Biological Sciences, 649
American Institute of Certified Public Accountants, 94
American Institute of Chemical Engineers, 661
American Institute of Physics, 664
American Institute of Ultrasound in Medicine, 380
American Institutes for Research, 666
American Insurance Assn., 106, 254
American Intellectual Property Law Assn., 109
American International Automobile Dealers Assn., 729
American Iron and Steel Institute, 324
American Israel Public Affairs Committee, 511
American Jewish Committee, Government and International Affairs, 32
American Jewish Congress, 32–33, 511, 535
American Kidney Fund, 417
American Kurdish Information Network (AKIN), 511–512

American Labor Education Center, 233
American Land Title Assn., 454
American League of Financial Institutions, 94, 457
American League of Lobbyists, 765
American Legion National Headquarters, 578
American Legion National Organization
    Operations and Training, 580
    Review and Correction Boards Unit, 580
American Legislative Exchange Council, 362
American Library Assn., 196
    Information Technology Policy, 138
American Logistics Assn., 632
American Lung Assn., 418
American Machine Tool Distributors Assn., 104
American Management Assn. International, 80
American Maritime Congress, 721
American Meat Institute, 65, 70
American Medical Assn. (AMA)
    Political Action Committee, 768
    Public and Private Sector Advocacy, 375, 392
American Medical Athletic Assn., 176
American Medical Group Assn., 386
American Medical Informatics Assn., 380
American Medical Rehabilitation Providers Assn., 691
American Medical Women's Assn., 392, 422–423
American Mental Health Counselors Assn., 424
American Mobile Telecommunications Assn., 127
American Moving and Storage Assn., 708
American Music Therapy Assn., 164
American Muslim Council, 10, 33
American National Standards Institute, Conformity
  Assessment, 101, 647
American Near East Refugee Aid, 512
American Network of Community Options and Resources, 691
American News Women's Club, 141
American Nursery and Landscape Assn., 46, 442
American Nurses Assn., 390
American Occupational Therapy Assn., 390, 691
American Optometric Assn., 393
American Orthotic and Prosthetic Assn., 380, 691
American Osteopathic Assn., 392
American Peanut Council, 56
American Petroleum Institute, 275
    Energy Sector ISAC, 615–616
    Policy Analysis and Statistics, 268
    Taxation, 275
American Pharmaceutical Assn., 382
American Physical Society, Public Information, 279, 665
American Physical Therapy Assn., 390, 691
American Physiological Society, 406
American Planning Assn., 433
American Plastics Council, 313
American Podiatric Medical Assn., 392
American Poetry and Literacy Project, 157, 218
American Political Science Assn. (APSA), 190
    Congressional Fellowship Program, 188
American Postal Workers Union (APWU), 357
    Committee on Political Action, 765
American Press Institute (API), 147
American Prosecutors Research Institute, 538
American Psychiatric Assn., 392, 424
American Psychological Assn., 424, 666
American Psychosomatic Society, 424–425
American Public Gas Assn., 275–276
American Public Health Assn., 372

American Public Human Services Assn., 677
American Public Power Assn., 270–271
American Public Transportation Assn. (APTA), 737
American Public Works Assn., 439–440, 706–707
American Recreation Coalition, 176, 328
American Red Cross, 69
    Armed Forces Emergency Services, 559, 578
    Disaster Services, 613, 622
    Emergency Communications, 559
    National Headquarters, 409, 410, 471–472
American Resort Development Assn., 177, 322, 433, 454
American Rivers, 331
American Road and Transportation Builders Assn., 728
American Roentgen Ray Society, 380
American Running Assn., 177
American Samoa's Delegate to Congress, 516
American Savings Education Council, 94
American School Food Service Assn., 206
American Security Council, 591
American Seed Trade Assn., 50
American Sheep Industry Assn., 70–71
American Short Line and Regional Railroad Assn., 734
American Society for Biochemistry and Molecular Biology, 649
American Society for Cell Biology, 649
American Society for Clinical Laboratory Science, 389
American Society for Clinical Nutrition, 62
American Society for Clinical Pathology, 389
American Society for Engineering Education, 220, 653
American Society for Horticultural Science, 46, 652
American Society for Industrial Security, 22, 629
American Society for Information Science and Technology,
  138, 196
American Society for Microbiology, 649
American Society for Nutritional Sciences, 62
American Society for Parenteral and Enteral Nutrition, 62
American Society for Pharmacology and Experimental
  Therapeutics, 382
American Society for Public Administration, 360
American Society for Therapeutic Radiology and Oncology,
  411
American Society for Training and Development (ASTD), 218,
  233
American Society of Access Professionals, 135, 594
American Society of Addiction Medicine, 392, 422
American Society of Appraisers, 454
American Society of Association Executives (ASAE), 80
American Society of Civil Engineers, 444, 653–654
American Society of Clinical Oncology, 411
American Society of Consultant Pharmacists, 386
American Society of Health-System Pharmacists, 382
American Society of Heating, Refrigerating, and Air
  Conditioning Engineers, 444
American Society of Interior Designers, 442
American Society of International Law, 479
American Society of Landscape Architects, 442
American Society of Mechanical Engineers, Public Affairs, 654
American Society of Naval Engineers, 609
American Society of Newspaper Editors, 147
American Society of Nuclear Cardiology, 392
American Society of Pension Actuaries, 106–107, 249
American Society of Plant Biologists, 652
American Society of Travel Agents, 180
American Sociological Assn., 666
American Soybean Assn., 54

Army Corps of Engineers, 329, 431, 632, 717
  Civil Emergency Management, 610
  Civil Works, 723
  Research and Development, 605
Army Dept., 586
  Acquisition, Logistics, and Technology, 605
  Arlington National Cemetery, Interment Services, 572
  Army Career and Alumni Programs, 563–564
  Army Clemency and Parole Board, 569
  Army Field Band, 573
  Army Housing, 633
  Army Reserve, 574
  Army Review Boards Agency, 567
  Board for the Correction of Military Records, 569
  Casualty Operations, 558, 584
  Ceremonies and Special Events, 573
  Chief Information Officer, 129, 617
  Chief of Chaplains, 555
  Chief of Staff, 586
  Civilian Personnel Policy, 556
  Collective Training Division, 565
  Community and Family Support Center, 558
  congressional liaison, 758
  Counterintelligence, Foreign Disclosure, and Security, 629
  Education, 565
  Enlisted Accessions, 564
  equal employment contact, 241
  Equal Employment Opportunity Agency, 556, 557
  espionage hotline, 14
  Financial Officer, 340
  freedom of information contact, 134
  G-1, 553
  General Counsel, 524
  Human Resources Directorate, 553, 567–568
  Individual Readiness Policy, 561
  Installations and Housing, 630, 633
  Institute of Heraldry, 570
  Intelligence, 623
  Judge Advocate General, 569
  Manpower and Reserve Affairs, 553
  Military Compensation and Entitlements, 563
  Military Personnel Management, 565
  Operations Research, 634
  organizational chart, 607
  Policy and Program Development, 631
  Procurement, 634
  public affairs contact, 132
  Publications Office, 130
  Repatriation and Family Affairs, POWs and MIAs, 562
  Research and Technology, 605
  Reserve Affairs, Mobilization, Readiness, and Training, 574
  Retirement Services, 564
  Security Force Protection and Law Enforcement, 570
  small and disadvantaged business contact, 116
  Surgeon General, 561
  U.S. Army Band, 573
  U.S. Center of Military History, 570
  Web site, 136
Army Distaff Foundation, 559, 564, 584
Army National Guard, 574–575
  Chaplain Service, 556, 575
Art in Embassies, 167
Art Services International, 162
Arthritis, 409
Arthur M. Sackler Gallery, 159, 160

Arts and Humanities, 151–167
  education, 154–155
  film, photography, and broadcasting, 155–157
  language and literature, 157–159
  museums, 159–164
  music, 164–165
  theater and dance, 165–166
  visual arts, 166–167
Asbestos Information Assn./North America, 308, 445
Asbestos ombudsman, 15
ASFE, 654
Ashoka: Innovators for the Public, 496
Asia, foreign affairs, 501–503, 510–514
Asia Foundation, 502, 512
Asia Society, 502, 512
AskERIC, 185
Aspen Institute, Policy Programs, 153
Asphalt Roofing Manufacturers Assn., 445
Aspira Assn., 214
Assassination Archives and Research Center, 172
Assessment, Evaluation, and Research Clearinghouse (ERIC), 185
Assisted Living Federation of America, 381
Associated Builders and Contractors, 440
Associated General Contractors of America, 440
Associated Landscape Contractors of America, 440
Associated Press, 142, 741
Assn. for Advanced Life Underwriting, 107
Assn. for Career and Technical Education, 222
Assn. for Childhood Education International, 207
Assn. for Commuter Transportation, 737
Assn. for Competitive Technology, 138
Assn. for Conflict Resolution, 525–526
Assn. for Education and Rehabilitation of the Blind and
  Visually Impaired, 211, 695
Assn. for Financial Professionals, 94–95
Assn. for Healthcare Philanthropy, 386
Assn. for Information and Image Management, 196
Assn. for Local Telecommunications Services, 126
Assn. for Manufacturing Technology, 101
Assn. for Maximum Service Television, 125
Assn. for Postal Commerce, 359
Assn. for Preservation of Historic Congressional Cemetery, 175
Assn. for Research in Vision and Ophthalmology, 393
Assn. for Supervision and Curriculum Development, 201, 207
Assn. for Suppliers of Printing and Publishing Technologies,
  Communications, 148
Assn. for Transportation Law, Logistics, and Policy, 707
Assn. for Women in Science, 9, 641
Assn. of Academic Health Centers, 377
Assn. of American Colleges and Universities (AACU), 201, 214
Assn. of American Geographers, 668
Assn. of American Law Schools, 201, 550
Assn. of American Medical Colleges, 392
Assn. of American Publishers, Copyright and New Technology,
  109–110, 147
Assn. of American Railroads, 735
Assn. of American Universities, 201
Assn. of American Veterinary Medical Colleges, 300
Assn. of Bituminous Contractors, 274
Assn. of Black Psychologists, 425
Assn. of Catholic Colleges and Universities, 201
Assn. of Civilian Technicians, 575
Assn. of Collegiate Schools of Architecture, 442
Assn. of Community Cancer Centers, 411

Cabinet departments. *See also specific department names*
    list of, 338
Cable News Network (CNN), 142
Cable services, 123
California Democratic Congressional Delegation, 749
Campaign for America's Future, 226, 769
Campaigns and Elections, 742–747
    election statistics and apportionment, 745
    political advocacy, 764–773
    voting, political participation, 745–747
Canada, foreign affairs, 506–510
Cancer, 410–412
    information hotline, 14
Candlelighters Childhood Cancer Foundation, 411
Capcon Library Network, 138
Capital Children's Museum, 162, 184
    education program, 160
Capital Research Center, 27
Capitol. *See* U.S. Capitol
Capitol Guide Service, 749
Capitol Police, 748
    Protective Services, 749
Cardiovascular disease, 416
CARE, 69, 496
Career College Assn., 202, 222
Cargo Airline Assn., 713
Caribbean affairs, 506–510
Caribbean/Latin American Action, 508
Caring Institute, 27
Carnegie Endowment for International Peace, 465–466
Carnegie Institution of Washington, 650, 660
Carpenters' Legislative Improvement Committee, 765
Catholic Charities USA, 33, 677
Catholic Foreign Mission Society of America (Maryknoll
  Fathers and Brothers), 35
Catholic Health Assn. of the U.S., 397
Catholic Information Center, 33
Catholic University, 200
Catholic War Veterans U.S.A., 578
Catholics for a Free Choice, 533
Cato Institute, 188, 769
Catoctin Mountain Park, 174
Caucuses, 749–753
CBS News, 142
Cellular Telecommunications and Internet Assn., 127
Cellular telephones, 126–128
Cemeteries and memorials, military, 572–573
Census Bureau, 344
    Customer Services Center, 745
    Decennial Census, 344
    Demographic Surveys Division, 231, 344
    Economic Programs, 73, 86
    Fertility and Family Statistics, 413
    Foreign Trade Statistics, 265, 485
    Geography, 667
    Governments Division, 86, 361, 430
    Housing and Household Economic Statistics, 344, 430–431
    information, 344
    library, 344
    Manufacturing and Construction, 86, 100, 431, 439
      Construction and Minerals, 99
    Population, 344, 745
    Publications Office, 130
    Redistricting Data Center, 745
    Service Sector Statistics Division, 86, 110

Vehicle Inventory and Use Survey, 704
Census, Population Data, 344–346
Center for a New American Dream, 27
Center for Applied Linguistics, 157–158
    National Clearinghouse for ESL Literacy Education, 218
Center for Auto Safety, 16, 308, 444, 731
Center for Biologics Evaluation and Research, 407
Center for Civic Education, Government Relations, 746
Center for Clean Air Policy, 308
Center for Community Change, 433, 451–452, 677–678
Center for Contemporary Arab Studies, 512
Center for Defense Information, 188, 591, 599
Center for Democracy, 466
Center for Democracy and Technology, 22, 138, 594
Center for Devices and Radiological Health, 312, 379
Center for Digital Democracy, 139
Center for Dispute Settlement, 526
Center for Drug Evaluation and Research, 381–382, 407–408,
    541
Center for Economic Organizing, 249
Center for Education Reform, 184
Center for Energy and Economic Development, 270
Center for Equal Opportunity, 239
Center for Food Safety and Applied Nutrition, 20, 59
Center for Global Development, 493
Center for Health, Environment, and Justice, 310–311
Center for Housing Policy, 430, 449
Center for Human Rights, 484
Center for Human Rights and Humanitarian Law, 483
Center for Immigration Studies, 477
Center for Individual Rights, 532
Center for Intercultural Education and Development, 474, 496
Center for International Policy, 508–509
Center for International Private Enterprise, 493
Center for Law and Education, 30, 184
Center for Law and Social Policy, 30, 678
Center for Media and Public Affairs, 121
Center for Media Education, 121
Center for Middle East Peace and Economic Cooperation, 512
Center for National Policy, 769
Center for National Security Studies, 135, 481, 594, 629
Center for Naval Analyses, 591
Center for Patient Advocacy, 373, 406
Center for Policy Alternatives (CPA), 188, 363
Center for Public Integrity, 342
Center for Public Service, 337
Center for Responsive Politics, 744
Center for Science in the Public Interest, 62, 64, 188
Center for Security Policy, 591
Center for Sickle Cell Disease, 415
Center for Strategic and Budgetary Assessments, 595
Center for Strategic and International Studies, 188, 466
Center for Study of Responsive Law, 30, 188, 522
Center for the Study of Digital Property, 110, 141
Center for the Study of Public Choice, 81
Center for the Study of Social Policy, 678
Center for the Study of the Presidency, 188, 337–338
Center for Veterinary Medicine, 299
Center for Voting and Democracy, 746
Center for Women Policy Studies, 9
Center for Women Veterans, 576
Center of Concern, 466
Center on Budget and Policy Priorities, 678
Center on Conscience & War, 554, 568, 623
Center on Disability and Health, 397, 692

recruitment, 563–564
retirement, 564
Defense policy. *See* National and Homeland Security
Defense Security Cooperation Agency, 596
Defense Security Service, 630
Defense Technical Information Center, 606–607, 646
Defense Threat Reduction Agency, 598
Defense Trade and Technology, 603–610
research and development, 605–610
Deloitte and Touche LLP Federal PAC, 767
Delphi International of World Learning, 474
Democracy International, 466
Democracy 21, 746
Democratic Congressional Campaign Committee, 773, 801
Democratic Governors' Assn., 773
Democratic Leadership Council, 773
Democratic National Committee (DNC), 773
Assn. of State Democratic Chairs, 773–774
Campaign Division, 746
Communications, 774
Finance, 774
internships, 188
Research, 774
Democratic Party, 773–774
Democratic Republican Independent Voter Education
Committee (DRIVE), 765
Democratic Senatorial Campaign Committee, 774
Democratic Technology and Communications Committee, 752
Dental care, 388–389
Departments, executive. *See specific department names*
Design and architecture, 441–442
Design arts, 125, 151, 155–156, 159–160, 166
Development assistance, 495–497
Development Group for Alternative Policies, 496
Diabetes, 412–413
Digestive diseases, 412–413
Digital Futures Coalition, 110
Dignity USA, 5
Diplomats and foreign agents, 468–470
Direct Marketing Assn., Ethics and Consumer Affairs
Government Affairs, 22, 112–113, 359
Disabilities, 688–698
blind and visually impaired, 694–695
deaf and hearing impaired, 695–697
education, 210–212
employment and training, 236–237
mental disabilities, 697–698
Disabilities and Gifted Education Clearinghouse
(ERIC), 185
Disability Resource Center, 692
Disability Rights Education and Defense Fund, Governmental
Affairs, 31, 692
Disabled American Veterans, 578–579, 692
Disabled Sports USA, 177, 692
Disarmament, 597–601
Discovery Theater, 166
Discrimination. *See* Civil Rights; Equal Employment
Opportunity
Dislocated workers, 235
Dismissals and disputes, 348–349
Dispute resolution, 524–526
Distance Education and Training Council, 222
Distilled Spirits Council of the U.S., 64
Distribution and LTL Carriers Assn., 708
Distributive Education Clubs of America, 184–185

District of Columbia
colleges and universities (list), 200
Executive Office of the Mayor, 365
history and culture, 174–175
local government, 365, 366
Metropolitan Police Dept., 144
DMA Nonprofit Federation, 359
Do No Harm: The Coalition of Americans for Research Ethics,
648
Doctors, 390–393
Document Management Industries Assn., 147
Documents. *See also* Libraries and Educational Media
Antitrust Division (DOJ), 527
General Accounting Office, 131, 644
Government Printing Office, 739
Senate Document Room, 739
DOD. *See* Defense Dept.
DOE. *See* Energy Dept.
DOI. *See* Interior Dept.
DOJ. *See* Justice Dept.
DOL. *See* Labor Dept.
Domestic Policy Council, 334
Domestic violence, 539–540
Door and Hardware Institute, 445
DOT. *See* Transportation Dept.
Drinking water, 314, 315, 331
hotline, 15
Drug control, 338, 421, 540–542
Drug Enforcement Administration (DEA), 484, 541
library, 197
Web site, 136
Drug industry, 381–384
Drug Policy Alliance, 383, 541–542
Drugs and drug abuse, 420–422
criminal law enforcement, 540–542
education and health programs, 205–206, 420–421
narcotics trafficking, 484–485
Ducks Unlimited, Governmental Affairs, 305
Dumbarton Oaks, 160, 162

Eagle Forum, 770
Earth sciences, 657–658
Earth Share, 27, 294
East Asia and Pacific affairs, 501–503
East Coast Migrant Head Start Project, 214
East-West Center, 502
Ecological Society of America, 650
Economic Development Administration, 428
Trade Adjustment and Technical Assistance, 100, 486
Economic Policy Institute, 82
Economic Research Service (USDA), 42, 53, 55, 56, 87, 256
Economic Strategy Institute, 493
Economics. *See* Business and Economics
Economics and Statistics Administration, 73, 100
Edison Electric Institute, 271, 294
Statistics, 268
EDUCATION (chap. 6), 181–223
adult, 221–223
agriculture, 41–44
arts and humanities, 154–155
bilingual and multicultural, 215–216
citizenship education, 216
congressional pages, 763
consumer education, 216–217
GED hotline, 15

Epilepsy Foundation, 419, 692
Episcopal Church, Government Relations, 34
Equal Employment Advisory Council, 239
Equal employment contacts at federal agencies (box), 241
Equal Employment Opportunity, 238–242
    departmental and agency contacts (box), 241
    military programs, 557
    minorities, 239–240
    unfair employment hotline, 14
    women, 240, 242
Equal Employment Opportunity Commission (EEOC), 2, 238
    Americans with Disabilities Act Policy Division, 689
    congressional liaison, 758
    equal employment contact, 241
    Field Programs, 238
    Financial Officer, 340
    freedom of information contact, 134
    General Counsel, 524
    information, 238
    Interagency Committee on Employees with Disabilities, 236–237
    library, 197
    Personnel Office, 350
    public affairs contact, 132
    Publications Office, 130
Equipment Leasing Assn. of America, 111
ERIC (Educational Resources Information Center), 182
    clearinghouses, 185
ERISA Advisory Council, 246–247
ERISA Industry Committee, 107, 249
Ernst and Young PAC, 767
Espionage, 14, 625
Essential Information, 147
Ethics
    congressional conduct standards, 760–761
    in government, 339–342
    inspectors general for federal agencies (box), 343
    Kennedy Institute of Ethics, 415–416, 651
    religion and ethics, 32–37
    in research, 648
Ethics and Public Policy Center, 193, 532
    Foreign Policy Program, 592
    Religion and Society Program, 34
Ethics Resource Center, 82, 185
Eugene and Agnes E. Meyer Foundation, 27
Eugene B. Casey Foundation, 28
Eurasia Foundation, 515
European affairs, 503–506
European-American Business Council, 505
European Commission, Press and Public Affairs, 267, 464, 491, 505
European Institute, 506
European Space Agency (ESA), 671–672
Evangelical Council for Financial Accountability, 28
Evangelical Lutheran Church in America, Governmental Affairs, 34
Even Start, 205
Every Child Matters, 684
EWA Information and Infrastructure Technologies, Inc., Surface Transportation ISAC, 616
Exceptional children, education programs for, 210, 211–212
Exchange programs, international, 473–475
Executive Council on Diplomacy, 470
Executive departments. *See specific department names*
Executive Dept. Cabinet Members (list), 338

Executive Office for Immigration Review, 476
Executive Office for U.S. Attorneys, 519
Executive Office for U.S. Trustees, 529
Executive Office of the President. *See also* White House
    Advisory Committee for Trade Policy and Negotiations, 485
    Council of Economic Advisers, 73
    Council on Environmental Quality, 289
    Domestic Policy Council, 334
    Intergovernmental Affairs, 361
    National Economic Council, 75
    National Science and Technology Council, 42–43, 290, 638
    National Security Council. *See that heading*
    Office of Administration, 334
    Office of Faith-Based and Community Initiatives, 676
    Office of Global Communications, 131, 461
    Office of National AIDS Policy, 408
    Office of National Drug Control Policy, 338, 421, 541
    Office of Science and Technology Policy. *See that heading*
    OMB. *See* Office of Management and Budget
    President's Foreign Intelligence Advisory Board, 461, 626
    Proliferation Strategy, Counterproliferation, and Homeland Defense, 598
    Public Liaison, 2
    U.S. Trade Representative, 267, 338, 490
Executive reorganization, 342, 344
Export Administration Review Board, 603
Export and import policies. *See* International Trade and Development
Export-Import Bank of the U.S., 486
    congressional liaison, 758
    equal employment contact, 241
    export finance hotline, 15
    Financial Officer, 340
    freedom of information contact, 134
    General Counsel, 524
    library, 197
    Personnel Office, 350
    Procurement Officer, 354
    public affairs contact, 132
    Web site, 136
EX-POSE, Ex-partners of Servicemembers for Equality, 559, 584
Extension Service (USDA). *See* Cooperative State Research, Education, and Extension Service
Extradition, 481
Eye Bank Assn. of America, 394

FAA. *See* Federal Aviation Administration
Fair housing, 450–452
Fair Labor Assn. (FLA), 230, 253
Fair Labor Standards Act, 229
Fairfax County, Virginia, 365
Falls Church, Virginia, city of, 365
Families. *See* Children and Families
Families Against Mandatory Minimums, 546
Families USA, 687
Family and Home Network, 684
Family, Career, and Community Leaders of America, 217
Family History Center, Church of Jesus Christ of Latter-day Saints, 172
Family planning, 413–414
Family Research Council, 770
Fannie Mae, 456
FARM (Farm Animal Reform Movement), 67, 71

food industries, 65–67
    meat and poultry safety inquiries, 14
    vegetarianism, 67
    world food assistance, 67–70
Food and Nutrition Information Center, 60, 206
Food and Nutrition Service, 59, 675
    Analysis, Nutrition, and Evaluation, 59, 681
    Child Nutrition, 59–60, 681
    Food Distribution, 60, 675–676
    Food Stamp Program, 60, 676
    Supplemental Food Programs, 60, 681
Food industries, 65–67
Food Industry ISAC, 616
Food Marketing Institute, 65
    Food Industry ISAC, 616
Food Processing Machinery and Supplies Assn., 65–66
Food Research and Action Center (FRAC), 63, 678
Food Safety and Inspection Service, 21, 60, 70, 217
Food Stamp Program, 60, 676
Foodservice and Packaging Institute (FPI), 313
Footwear Distributors and Retailers of America, 103
Ford's Theatre National Historic Site, 165, 174
Foreign agents, 468–470
Foreign Agricultural Service (FAS), 49, 495
    Commodity and Marketing Programs, 49
    Export Credits, 67
    International Cooperation and Development, 67–68
Foreign aid
    development assistance, 495–497
    humanitarian aid, 470–473
    world food assistance, 67–70
Foreign Claims Settlement Commission of the U.S., 480
Foreign policy. See International Affairs
Foreign Press Center, 144
Foreign Service Institute, School of Professional and Area
    Studies, 468
Foreign trade. See International Trade and Development
Foreign Trade Zones Board, 487
Forest Resources Assn., 320
Forest Service, 317
    Fire and Aviation Management, 19
    Fish, Wildlife, Rare Plants, Air, and Watershed, 303
    International Programs, 317
    National Forest System, 317
    Recreation Heritage and Wilderness Resources, 327
    Research and Development, 317–318
    State and Private Forestry, 318
    Youth Conservation Corps, 237, 318
Forests and rangelands, 317–320
Fort Washington Park, 174
Forum for State Health Policy Leadership, 373
Fossil Energy (DOE), 272
    Coal and Power Import and Export, 266
    Coal Fuels and Industrial Systems, 273
    Natural Gas and Petroleum Technology, 275
    Naval Petroleum and Oil Shale Reserves, 275, 623
Fossil Fuels, 272–278
    coal, 273–274
    oil and natural gas, 274–277
    pipelines, 277–278
Foster Grandparent Program, 25, 686–687
Foundation Center, 28, 189
Foundation for Exceptional Children, 210, 211–212
Foundation for Middle East Peace, 512
Foundation for Public Affairs, 770

Foundation for the Advancement of Chiropractic Tenets and
    Science, 419
Foundation for the Defense of Democracies, 629
Foundation for the National Institutes of Health, 406
Fox News, 142
Franking Commission, 742, 760
Freddie Mac, 456
Frederick Douglass National Historic Site, 159, 174
Free Congress Research and Education Foundation (FCF), 515,
    770
Freedom Forum, 142
Freedom Forum Newseum, 162–163
Freedom of information, 133–135
    contacts at federal agencies (box), 134
Freedom of Information Act, 917–918
Freedom of the press, 144, 146–147
Freer Gallery of Art, 159, 160
Freight and intermodalism, 708–709
French-American Chamber of Commerce, 506
Friends Committee on National Legislation (FCNL), 34, 466,
    599
Friends of Art and Preservation in Embassies, 167
Friends of the Earth (FOE), 264, 295, 651
Friends of the Jessup, 550
Friends of the National Zoo, 160
Frontiers of Freedom, 770–771
Fruits and vegetables, 52–53
FTC. See Federal Trade Commission
Fuels. See Energy
Fuels, alternative, 284–287
Fund for American Studies, 189
Fund for Animals, 300
Fund for Constitutional Government (FCG), 342
Fund for Investigative Journalism, 143
Fund for New American Plays, 165–166
Fund for the Feminist Majority, 188
Fundraising, 15, 22, 26
Future Fisherman Foundation, 177
Futures Industry Assn., 97

G7 Council, 494
Gadsby's Tavern Museum, 160
Gallaudet University, 196, 200, 211, 696
GAMA International, 107
Gannett News Service, 142
GAO. See General Accounting Office
Gardening and horticulture, 46–47
Gas and oil, 274–277
Gas Appliance Manufacturers Assn., 104, 276
Gas Technology Institute, Policy and Regulatory Affairs, 276
Gay and Lesbian Activists Alliance (GLAA), 5
Gay and Lesbian Victory Fund, 5
Gays and lesbians, civil rights, 5–6
GED Hotline on Adult Education, 15
Genealogy, 172–173
General Accounting Office (GAO), 76, 336, 519, 761
    Agriculture Issues, 39
    Applied Research and Methods, 137
    Chief Information Officer, 129
    Defense Capabilities and Management, 595, 596–597, 635
    Document Distribution Center, 131, 644
    Education, Workforce, and Income Security, 26, 182, 225,
        248, 362, 371, 576, 676, 700, 702
    Financial Office, 341
    Homeland Security and Justice, 595

Homeland Security Dept. (DHS), 587, 625
Border and Transportation Security Directorate, 602
budget, 594–595
Bureau of Citizenship and Immigration Services (BCIS), 179, 476, 601
Bureau of Customs and Border Protection. *See that heading*
Bureau of Immigration and Customs Enforcement, 601–602
Chief Financial Officer, 594
Chief Information Officer, 129
Chief Privacy Officer, 593
congressional liaison, 758
Critical Infrastructure Assurance Office, 619
Emergency Preparedness and Response Directorate, 612
Federal Computer Incident Response Center, 619
Federal Emergency Management Agency. *See that heading*
Federal Law Enforcement Training Center, 547, 602
Federal Protective Service, 339, 619
Financial Officer, 340
General Counsel, 524
Information Analysis and Infrastructure Protection Directorate, 614, 619
Inspector General, 343
Management Directorate, 595
National Communications System, 617
National Response Center, 310, 612, 617, 722
Office for Domestic Preparedness, 614
Office of the Secretary, 614
organizational chart, 588
Personnel Office, 350
Procurement Officer, 354
public affairs contact, 132
Science and Technology Directorate, 587–588
Secretary, 338
State and Local Coordination, 615
Terrorist Threat Integration Center, 625
Transportation Security Administration, 350, 619–620, 717
U.S. Coast Guard. *See that heading*
U.S. Secret Service, 127, 544, 620
Web site, 136
Homelessness, 698–699
Homosexuals, civil rights of, 5–6
Horatio Alger Assn. of Distinguished Americans, 216
Horticulture and gardening, 46–47
Hospice Foundation of America, 381
Hospices, 380–381
Hospitals, 377–378
Hostelling International—American Youth Hostels, 180
Hotel Employees and Restaurant Employees International, 66, 180
House Administration Comm., 792
access to congressional information, 739
campaigns and elections, 742
Capitol, 748
congress
pay and perquisites, 760
staff, 763
culture and recreation, 152
government information, 131
libraries, 194, 762
science and technology, 639
House Agriculture Comm., 784
agricultural research, education, 43
agriculture and nutrition, 39–40
animals and plants, 299

commodities, farm produce, 49
farm loans, insurance, and subsidies, 57–58
fertilizer and pesticides, 45
food and nutrition, 60, 61
forests and rangelands, 319
livestock and poultry, 70
rural areas, 435
social services and disabilities, 676
soil and watershed conservation, 47
sugar, 55
tobacco and peanuts, 56
water resources, 330
world food assistance, 68
House Appropriations Comm., 785
agriculture and nutrition, 40
air transportation, 711
arts and humanities, 152
banking, 93
borders, customs, and immigration, 602
business and economics, 76–77
campaigns and elections, 742
Capitol, 748
census, population data, 345
civil service, 347
communications and the media, 119
consumer protection, 13–14
defense trade and technology, 589, 609
disabilities, 690
District of Columbia, 366
education, 182
minorities and women, 213
emergency preparedness and response, 613
employment and labor, 225
energy, 259
environment and natural resources, 292
ethics in government, 341
food and nutrition, 61
government operations, 336
health, 371
housing and development, 428
intelligence and counterterrorism, 627
international affairs, 462–463
trade and development, 490
law and justice, 519
libraries and educational media, 194
maritime transportation, 719
military
aid and peacekeeping, 597
cemeteries and memorials, 572
construction, 633
motor vehicles, 724–725
national and homeland security, 589
nuclear weapons and power, 600–601
philanthropy, public service, and voluntarism, 26
postal service, 356
public health and environment, 621
rail transportation, 734
science and technology, 639
selective service, 622
social security, 702
social services and disabilities, 676
space sciences, 671
transit systems, 736
transportation, 706
U.S. territories and associated states, 516

social services, 677
tax violations, 530
unemployment benefits, 232
Housing, 448–453
fair housing, special groups, 450–452
military housing, 632–634
public and subsidized housing, 452–453
HOUSING AND DEVELOPMENT (chap. 12), 427–459
community and regional development, 431–439
construction, 439–448
fair housing, special groups, 450–452
general policy, 428–431
housing, 448–453
housing discrimination complaints, 14
military housing, 632–634
mortgages and finance, 456–458
property management, 458–459
public and subsidized housing, 452–453
real estate, 453–459
rural areas, 435–436
statistics, 430–431
Housing and Development Law Institute, 430
Housing and Urban Development Dept. (HUD), 428
Affordable Housing Programs, 437, 453
Affordable Housing Research and Technology, 443
Block Grant Assistance, 432
Chief Information Officer, 129
Community Planning and Development, 432, 698
Community Viability, 263, 289, 432
congressional liaison, 758
consumer and emergency hotline, 14
Economic Affairs, 431
Economic Development, 437–438
Entitlement Communities, 448–449
equal employment contact, 241
Fair Housing and Equal Opportunity, 450
Federal Housing Administration. *See that heading*
Federal Housing Enterprise Oversight, 456
FHIP/FHAP Support, 450–451
Field Management, 432
Financial Officer, 340
freedom of information contact, 134
General Counsel, 524
Healthy Homes and Lead Hazard Control, 309, 443
Housing, 449, 456–457
housing discrimination hotline, 14
HUD USER, 428
Inspector General, 343
Interstate Land Sales/RESPA (Real Estate Settlement
Procedure Act), 453
library, 197
Native American Programs, 451
organizational chart, 429
Personnel Office, 350
Policy Development and Research, 361–362, 428
Procurement Officer, 354
Program Evaluation, 428
public affairs contact, 132
Public and Indian Housing, 452
Public Housing and Voucher Program, 452
Public Housing Investments, 452
Publications Office, 130
Secretary, 338
small and disadvantaged business contact, 116
Special Needs Assistance Programs, 698–699

State and Small Cities, 432
Technical Assistance and Management, 432
Web site, 136
Housing Assistance Council, 435–436, 450, 699
Howard Hughes Medical Institute, 406
Howard University, 200
Center for Sickle Cell Disease, 415
Moorland-Spingarn Research Center, 172
HUD. *See* Housing and Urban Development Dept.
Hudson Institute, National Security Studies, 592, 679
Human Resources Research Organization, 666
Human rights, 482–484
Human Rights Campaign (HRC), 5–6, 409, 557
congressional ratings, 766
Political Action Committee, 768
Human Rights Watch, 483
Humane Society of the U.S., 300, 305
Animal Research Issues, 648
Humanitarian aid, 470–473
Humanities. *See* Arts and Humanities
Hurston/Wright Foundation, 158

Idea Alliance, 139, 147
IMF. *See* International Monetary Fund
Immigration and Naturalization, 179, 476–477, 601–603
aliens, employment and training, 235
regulations hotline, 14
Immigration and Refugees Services of America, 477
Import and export policies. *See* International Trade and
Development
Independent Community Bankers of America, 95
Independent Insurance Agents of America
Government Relations, Industry and State Relations, 107
Political Action Committee (INSURPAC), 768
Independent Liquid Terminals Assn., 276
Independent Lubricant Manufacturers Assn., 101
Independent Office Products and Furniture Dealers Assn., 101
Independent Petroleum Assn. of America, 276
Independent Sector, 28
Independent Women's Forum (IWF), 9
Indian Arts and Crafts Board, 173
Indian Health Service, 395, 418–419
Industrial and military planning and mobilization, 618
Industrial College of the Armed Forces, 565
Industrial Designers Society of America, 101, 442
Industrial Production, Manufacturing, 100–106
clothing and textiles, 102–104
electronics and appliances, 104
emergency preparedness, 618
steel, metalworking, machinery, 104–106
Industrial Research Institute, 101
Industrial Telecommunications Assn., 127
Industry Advisory Council, 663
Infectious diseases, 416–417
Information and exchange programs, international, 473–475
Information and Technology Clearinghouse (ERIC), 185
Information officers for federal agencies (box), 129
Information science, 137, 138, 139, 194, 196, 662. *See also*
Libraries and Educational Media
Information Sciences Institute, 139
Information Sharing and Analysis Centers, 615–616
Information Technology Assn. of America, 139, 663
Information Technology Industry Council, 140, 663
Infrastructure protection, 618–621
Initiative for Social Action and Renewal in Eurasia, 515